1997
IEEE/ACM International Conference on Computer-Aided Design

1997
IEEE/ACM International Conference on Computer-Aided Design

November 9 – 13, 1997 San Jose, California

Digest of Technical Papers

IEEE COMPUTER SOCIETY

Los Alamitos, California

Washington • Brussels • Tokyo

IEEE Computer Society Order Number PR08200
IEEE Order Plan Catalog Number 97CB36142
ACM Order Number 477973
ISBN 0-8186-8200-0
ISBN 0-8186-8201-9 (case)
ISBN 0-8186-8202-7 (microfiche)
ISSN 1092-3152

Additional copies may be ordered from:

IEEE Computer Society
Customer Service Center
10662 Los Vaqueros Circle
P.O. Box 3014
Los Alamitos, CA 90720-1314
Tel: + 1-714-821-8380
Fax: + 1-714-821-4641
E-mail: cs.books@computer.org

IEEE Service Center
445 Hoes Lane
P.O. Box 1331
Piscataway, NJ 08855-1331
Tel: + 1-908-981-1393
Fax: + 1-908-981-9667
mis.custserv@computer.org

IEEE Computer Society
13, Avenue de l'Aquilon
B-1200 Brussels
BELGIUM
Tel: + 32-2-770-2198
Fax: + 32-2-770-8505
euro.ofc@computer.org

IEEE Computer Society
Ooshima Building
2-19-1 Minami-Aoyama
Minato-ku, Tokyo 107
JAPAN
Tel: + 81-3-3408-3118
Fax: + 81-3-3408-3553
tokyo.ofc@computer.org

ACM Order Department
P.O. Box 12114, Church Street Station, New York, NY 10257
Tel: I-800-342-6626 (USA and Canada),
Tel: 1-212-626-0500 (All other countries),
Fax: 1-212-944-1318, Email: orders@acm.org

ACM European Service Center
Avenue Marcel Thiry 204, 1200 Brussles, Belgium
Tel: +44-1865-382-338
Fax: +44-1865-381-338
Email: europe@acm.org

Editorial production by Penny Storms

Cover art production by MP Associates

Printed in the United States of America by Technical Communication Services

IEEE
COMPUTER
SOCIETY

IEEE

Table of Contents

* *Paper not available at time of publication*

FOREWORD

On behalf of the organizing committees I would like to welcome you to the International Conference on Computer-Aided Design, being held once more in San Jose, in the same location as in recent years, but now under the name of the DoubleTree Hotel. This location, just off Highway 101, and with two international airports at less than half an hour's distance, is easily reachable, and the accomodations for the technical presentations, panels and tutorials are conveniently together in the north wing so that you may easily compose your personal daily program. Costs for attendance and hotels have been held down to the minimum.

The core of the conference is, of course, the technical program. A program committee of over sixty experts from industry and academia around the world was organized under the direction of Hiroto Yasuura. To do full justice to each submitted paper, the subcommittees were put together on the basis of the topic distribution of incoming manuscripts. After evaluating the papers individually, the committee members were confronted with the opinions of the other subcommittee members, enabling the preparation of a thorough review when all committee members met for a full day to establish the final selection and session division. In all, less than thirty percent of the submitted papers were accepted for inclusion in the final, high quality program.

At last year's ICCAD, the embedded tutorials were extremely well received and attended. Hence, the Executive Committee members again directed their efforts to carefully select a pair of ninety-minute presentations for the end of each conference day. The purpose of these tutorials is to make the community of tool developers aware of what is going on in the CAD world and what is urgently needed by today's designers. Two of the tutorials will be devoted to areas that will keep gaining importance in this century and are still lacking adequate CAD support: simulation of circuits working at radio frequencies and microelectromechanical systems. Richard Newton will help you identify the challenges in research and development of distributed design systems, a new approach to collaboration in designing complex electronic systems. Parallel to these, three areas, already recognized as of eminent importance for today's design of high performance circuits, get their present forefront outlined: verification, interconnect design, and tuning for performance.

Ellen Sentovich has invited John Ousterhout to offer ICCAD attendees a special treat: a plenary Monday evening event where its pioneer presents the status in scripting as a programming style quite different from what is predominantly used in CAD today and shares his views on what to expect in the next century.

Of course, ICCAD-97 will close with a day of tutorials once more organized by Rob Aitken, in which complete introductions to state-of-the-art CAD topics will be given by today's expert developers and educators. One tutorial targets timing analysis and optimization, which are already an integral part of the design process, but which become increasingly critical with the coming of deep-submicron. Given rapid advances in our ability to integrate components on one chip, we offer a second tutorial that concentrates on design at higher levels of abstraction, and a third tutorial that focuses on complete systems on a chip. The final tutorial overviews custom in-house wireless design systems, complete with the available tools and techniques for their hardware and software.

From the above you can see that we really are making efforts to make ICCAD the place where designers can get an update with the latest results in design automation, developers can learn what designers need most these days, and where the two groups can meet to exchange ideas, questions and answers. Thank you for joining us at ICCAD-97.

Ralph H. J. M. Otten
Conference Chair

Hiroto Yasuura
Technical Program Chair

CONFERENCE COMMITTEE

CONFERENCE CHAIR
Ralph H.J.M. Otten
Delft Univ. of Technology
Lab. for Circuits & Systems, Dept. EE
Mekelweg 4, 2628 CD Delft
The Netherlands
(31) 215-781600
otten@et.tudelft.nl

PROGRAM CHAIR
Hiroto Yasuura
Kyushu Univ.
Dept. of CS & CE, Info Sci. Grad School
Kasuga Koen, 6-1
Kasuga, 816 Japan
(81) 92-583-7620
yasuura@c.csce.kyushu-u.ac.jp

FINANCE/PUBLICATIONS CHAIR
David Ku
Escalade Corp.
2475 Augustine Dr.
Santa Clara, CA 95054
(408) 654-1617
ku@escalade.com

PAST CHAIR
Rob A. Rutenbar
Carnegie Mellon Univ.
Dept. of ECE
5000 Forbes Ave., Bldg. HH3107
Pittsburgh, PA 15213
(412) 268-5087
rutenbar@taurus.ece.cmu.edu

TUTORIAL CHAIR
Robert C. Aitken
Hewlett-Packard Co.
Design Tech. Ctr.
1501 Page Mill Rd.
Palo Alto, CA 94304-1126
(415) 857-2146
aitken@dtc.hp.com

PANEL CHAIR
Jacob White
Massachusetts Inst. of Technology
Dept. of EECS, Rm. 36-880
50 Vassar St.
Cambridge, MA 02139
(617) 253-2543
white@rle-vlsi.mit.edu

PUBLICITY & AV CHAIR
Ellen M. Sentovich
Cadence Berkeley Labs.
2001 Addison St., 3rd Fl.
Berkeley, CA 94704-1103
(510) 647-2807
ellens@cadence.com

EUROPEAN REPRESENTATIVE
Bernard Courtois
TIMA Lab.
46 Ave. Felix Viallet
Grenoble Cedex 38031, France
(33) 76-57-4615
bernard.courtois@imag.fr

ASIAN REPRESENTATIVE
Shuji Tsukiyama
Chuo Univ.
Dept. of Elect. & Elect. Engr.
1-13-27 Kasuga, Bunkyo-ku
Tokyo, 112 Japan
(81) 3-3817-1871
tsuki@elect.chuo-u.ac.jp

SIGDA REPRESENTATIVE
Robert A. Walker
Kent State Univ.
Dept. of Math & CS
Kent, OH 44242
(330) 672-4004
walker@mcs.kent.edu

IEEE CS/DATC REPRESENTATIVE
Charles W. Rosenthal
CWR-Engineering Consultants
3080 SW Fairmount Blvd.
Portland, OR 97201-1439
(503) 245-8398
c.rosenthal@ieee.org

CONFERENCE MANAGER
Kevin Lepine
MP Associates, Inc.
5305 Spine Rd., Ste. A
Boulder, CO 80301
(303) 530-4562
kevin@mpa-net.com

ICCAD-97 TECHNICAL PROGRAM COMMITTEE

Robert Aitken
Hewlett-Packard Co.
Palo Alto, CA
aitken@dtc.hp.com

Pranav Ashar
C&C Res. Labs., NEC USA, Inc.
Princeton, NJ
ashar@ccrl.nj.nec.com

Ronald D. Blanton
Carnegie Mellon Univ.
Pittsburgh, PA
blanton@ece.cmu.edu

Ivo Bolsens
IMEC
Leuven, Belgium
bolsens@imec.be

Eric Bracken
Ansoft Corp.
Pittsburgh, PA
bracken@ansoft.com

Daniel Brand
IBM Corp.
Yorktown Heights, NY
brand@watson.ibm.com

Forrest D. Brewer
Univ. of California
Santa Barbara, CA
forrest@ece.ucsb.edu

Jerry R. Burch
Cadence Berkeley Labs.
Berkeley, CA
jrb@cadence.com

Gianpiero Cabodi
Politecnico di Torino
Torino, Italy
cabodi@polito.it

Kuang-Chien Chen
Fujitsu Labs. of America, Inc.
Santa Clara, CA
kchen@fla.fujitsu.com

Chung-Kuan Cheng
Univ. of California at San Diego
La Jolla, CA
kuan@cs.ucsd.edu

Jue-Hsien Chern
Technology Modeling Assoc., Inc.
Sunnyvale, CA
chern@tmai.com

John M. Cohn
IBM Corp.
Richmond, VT
cohn@vnet.ibm.com

Jordi Cortadella
Univ. Politecnica de Catalunya
Barcelona, Spain
jordi@ac.upc.es

Bernard Courtois
TIMA Lab.
Grenoble, France
bernard.courtois@imag.fr

Wayne W.-M. Dai
Univ. of California
Santa Cruz, CA
dai@cse.ucsc.edu

Masato Edahiro
C&C Res. Labs., NEC Corp.
Kawasaki, Japan
eda@sbl.cl.nec.co.jp

Ibrahim M. Elfadel
IBM Corp.
Yorktown Heights, NY
elfadel@watson.ibm.com

Rolf Ernst
Tech. Univ. Braunschweig
Braunschweig, Germany
ernst@ida.ing.tu-bs.de

Robert J. Francis
Xilinx, Inc.
Toronto, ON, Canada
rjf@xilinx.com

Georges Gielen
Katholieke Univ. Leuven
Leuven, Belgium
gielen@esat.kuleuven.ac.be

Rajesh K. Gupta
Univ. of California
Irvine, CA
rgupta@ics.uiuc.edu

Sandeep K. Gupta
Univ. of Southern California
Los Angeles, CA
sandeep@boole.usc.edu

Dwight D. Hill
Synopsys, Inc.
Mountain View, CA
hill@synopsys.com

Sasan Iman
Escalade Corp.
Santa Clara, CA
iman@escalade.com

Masaki Ito
Hitachi Ltd.
Kanagawa-ken, Japan
itoh@kanagawa.hitachi.co.jp

Jawahar Jain
Fujitsu Labs. of America, Inc.
Santa Clara, CA
jawahar@fla.fujitsu.com

Rajeev Jayaraman
Xilinx, Inc.
San Jose, CA
rajeev@xilinx.com

Ahmed A. Jerraya
TIMA-CMP Lab.
Grenoble, France
jerraya@verdon.imag.fr

Niraj K. Jha
Princeton Univ.
Princeton, NJ
jha@ee.princeton.edu

David Ku
Escalade Corp.
Santa Clara, CA
ku@escalade.com

David D. Ling
IBM Corp.
Yorktown Heights, NY
dling@watson.ibm.com

Malgorzata Marek-Sadowska
Univ. of California
Santa Barbara, CA
mms@guitar.ece.ucsb.edu

ICCAD-97 TECHNICAL PROGRAM COMMITTEE

ICCAD-97 REVIEWERS

Magdy Abadir
Rajat Aggarwal
Robert Aitken
Enamul Amyeen
James Anderson
Fabio Angelillis
Peter Arato
Guido Araujo
Hideki Asai
Pranav Ashar
Toru Awashima
Iris Bahar
Felice Balarin
Jeffrey Bell
Vaughn Betz
Ronald DeShawn Blanton
Ivo Bolsens
Vamsi Boppana
Eric Bracken
Daniel Brand
Forrest D. Brewer
Oliver Bringmann
Premal Buch
Jerry R. Burch
Gianpiero Cabodi
Juan Antonio Carbalo
Jordi Carrabina
Robert Carragher
Francky Catthoor
V. Chandramouli
Douglas Chang
Shih-Chieh Chang
Tsin-Yuan Chang
Yaowen Chang
Kai-Yuan Chao
Chung-Ping Chen
De-Sheng Chen
Jwu-E Chen
Kuang-Chien Chen
Yung-Yuan Chen
Zhanping Chen
Chung-Kuan Cheng
Wei-Kai Cheng
Jue-Hsien Chern
Chenhuan Chiang
Eli Chiprout
Mike Chou
Amit Chowdhary
Kevin Chung
Min-Feng Chung
Johan Cockx
John M. Cohn
Jordi Cortadella
Bernard Courtois
Walter Daems
Wayne W.-M. Dai
Giovanni De Micheli
Bart De Smedt
Stefan Donnay
Masato Edahiro
Aiman El-Maleh
Ibrahim M. Elfadel
Shinya Emoto
Rolf Ernst
Robert J. Francis
Hisanori Fujisawa
Masahiro Fujita
Tomoyuki Fujita
Kunihiro Fujiyoshi
Youxin Gao
Edelweis Garcez
Ricard Gavalda
Joachim Gerlach
Georges Gielen
Manish Goel
Eugene Goldberg
Arny Goldfein
Wilsin Gosti
Pei-Ning Guo
Aarti Gupta
Rajesh K. Gupta
Sandeep K. Gupta
Subodh Gupta
Gary D. Hachtel
Ibrahim Hajj
Jonathan Halter
Cordula Hansen
Ikuo Harada
Abu Hassan
Toshihiro Hattori
Gunter Haug
Lei He
Hans Hegt
Gerald Heim
Keerthi Heragu
Andre Hergenhan
Dwight D. Hill
Yuzo Hirai
Inki Hong
Michael Hsiao
Frank Hsu
Ing-Jer Huang
Mike Hutton
Jim Hwang
Tin-Tin Hwang
TingTing Hwang
Yean-You Hwang
Sasan Iman
Yasuaki Inoue
Shinya Ishihara
Nagisa Ishiura

ICCAD-97 REVIEWERS

Tsuyoshi Isshiki
Tetsuro Itakura
Kazuhito Ito
Masaki Ito
Tomonori Izumi
Jawahar Jain
Rajeev Jayaraman
Ahmed A. Jerraya
Niraj K. Jha
Mark Johnson
Wen-Ben Jone
Jing-Yang Jou
Shyh-Jye Jou
Yoji Kajitani
Mineo Kaneko
Deyu Kao
William Kao
Tanay Karnik
Masaru Katayama
Hideyuki Kawakita
Omar Kebichi
Sunil Khatri
Kei-Yong Khoo
Hyungwon Kim
Shinji Kimura
Tomohisa Kimura
Darko Kirovski
Michael Kishinevsky
Susumu Kobayashi
Gernot Koch
Alex Kondratyev
Raymond Kong
Joseph Kozhaya
Dilip Krishnaswamy
David Ku
Shun-ichi Kubo
Thommy Kuhn
Yuji Kukimoto
Arno Kunzmann
Mototaka Kuribayashi
Walter Lange
David Lapotin
Chung-Len Lee
Chunho Lee
Kenny Lee
Kuen-Jong Lee
Kyung T. Lee
Domine Leenaerts
Yau-Tsun Steven Li
Jiing-Yuan Lin
Poyang Lin
Youn-Long Lin
David D. Ling
Joe Linoff
Frank Liu
Per B. Ljung
Paulo Maciel
Malgorzata Marek-Sadowska
Hans-Georg Martin
Akira Matsugawa
Osamu Matsumoto
Robert L. Maziasz
Dinesh Mehta
Noel Menezes
Shin-ichi Minato
Sujoy Mitra
Hideki Mitsubayashi
Hiroshi Miyashita
Akihiko Miyazaki
Toshiaki Miyazaki
Yuichi Miyazawa
Sundararajarao Mohan
Takashi Morie
Dinos Moundanos
Rajarshi Mukherjee
Rajeev Murgai
Enric Musoll
Sudip Nag
Akira Nagao
Farid N. Najm
Koji Nakajima
Shigetoshi Nakatake
Amit Narayan
Francisco Nascimento
Sani R. Nassif
Mahadevamurty Nemani
Jeff Newquist
Tuyen Nguyen
Tetsuo Nishi
Shinya Nishikawa
Masahiro Numa
Emil Ochotta
Kimihiro Ogawa
Takuji Ogihara
Takumi Okamoto
Ryosuke Okuda
Makiko Okumura
Kunle Olukotun
Hidetoshi Onodera
Shoji Otaka
Steve Otto
Andras Pahi
David Z. Pan
Christos Papachristou
Marios C. Papaefthymiou
SeungJoon Park
Enric Pastor
Janak H. Patel
Massoud Pedram
Kris Pister
Carl P. Pixley

ICCAD-97 REVIEWERS

Miodrag M. Potkonjak
Gang Qu
Janusz Rajski
Rajeev Ranjan
Subodh Reddy
Marta Rencz
June-Kyung Rho
Lluis Ribas
Michael Riepe
Jordi Riera
Jing Roddy
Wolfgang Rosenstiel
Charles Rosenthal
Don Ross
Kaushik Roy
Dan Saab
Kazuyuki Saijo
Toshiyuki Saito
Takayasu Sakurai
William Salefski
N. Sankarayya
Andisheh Sarabi
Hisashi Sasaki
Mamoru Sasaki
Toshinori Sato
Gurjeet Saund
Hirosi Sawada
Prashant Sawkar
Ellen M. Sentovich
Maria J. Serna
Lu Sha
Debendra Das Sharma
Wen-Zen Shen
Naveed Sherwani
Yuji Shigehiro
Takeshi Shima
Jyuo-Min Shyu
L. Miguel Silveira
Jens Ulrik Skakkebaek
Rajan Sree
Bill Stiehl
Chauchin Su
Ming Su
P.A. Subrahmanyam
Ashok Sudarsanam
Yasuhiro Sugimoto
Vladimir Szekely
Shigetaka Takagi
Atsushi Takahara
Atsushi Takahashi
Wataru Takahashi
Hajime Takakubo
Yasuhiro Takashima
Hideki Takeuchi
Kazuo Taki
Seiichiro Tani
Hiroshi Tanimoto
Alexandre Taubin
Peter Thole
Rob Thompson
Jerzy Tyszer
Taku Uchino
Hiroshi Uno
Akio Ushida
Wim van Bokhoven
David Van Campenhout
Geert Van der Plas
Lieven VandenBerg
Jan Vandenbussche
Jan Vandersteen
Srikanth Venkatraman
Steven Vercauteren
Wim Verhaegen
Diederik Verkest
Frederik Vermeulen
Chandu Visweswariah
Ted Vucurevich
Shinichi Wakabayashi
Duncan M. Walker
Hank Walker
Chuanyu Wang
Li-Chung Wang
Sying-Jyan Wang
Takahiro Watanabe
Christoph Weiler
Karlheinz Weiss
Jacob K. White
Jesse Whittemore
Ralph Wittig
D.F. Wong
Allen C.-H. Wu
Chang Wu
Cheng-Wen Wu
Tsung-Yi Wu
Mary Xin
Jin Xu
Songjie Xu
Alexandre Yakovlev
Hakan Yalcin
Masaaki Yamada
Toshinori Yamada
Kiyotaka Yamamura
Shigeru Yamashita
Hannah Yang
Yibin Ye
Toshihiko Yokomaru
Goichi Yokomizo
Michio Yotsuyanagi
Jian-Kun Zhao
Kai Zhu

TUTORIAL 1

TIMING ANALYSIS AND OPTIMIZATION: FROM DEVICES TO SYSTEMS

Speakers:

Anirudh Devgan, IBM Austin Research Lab., Austin, TX

Leon Stok, IBM Thomas J. Watson Research Ctr., Yorktown Heights, NY

Sandip Kundu, Intel Corp., Santa Clara, CA

Background: This tutorial is intended for researchers and practitioners of timing analysis and optimization in both ASIC and custom design environments. Basic knowledge of timing analysis and circuit theory would be useful.

Description: Timing analysis is an integral part of the design process at all levels of abstraction. Deep sub-micron design, including both custom design and ASIC design, rely heavily on timing analysis and optimization to achieve required performance. This tutorial presents a comprehensive description of timing analysis and optimization techniques. The tutorial is divided into three broad areas, with the first one covering transistor and interconnect level analysis and optimization. Logic level analysis and optimization and links to logic synthesis are described in the second part. Dependency of timing analysis on logic functionality and vice versa is presented in the last part.

Higher operating frequencies, newer process technologies and advanced circuit families require timing analysis and optimization to be done at the device level. The first part of the tutorial will present device and interconnect level techniques, including device and interconnect modeling, transistor level static timing, dynamic timing simulation, interconnect model reduction, buffer insertion and sizing.

Static timing analysis has been an integral part of performance driven logic synthesis. In logic synthesis environment, static timing analysis needs to have incremental update capability. Description of logic level static timing and optimization will include delay calculator language, logic restructuring, repowering and retiming.

Timing and functionality are interdependent. A topologically long path may not propagate a changing signal, in which case it is called a false path. For the purpose of accurate timing analysis all such paths must be excluded from consideration. In the last part of the tutorial, the false path analysis problem is described with discussion of two basic analysis techniques, one based on enumeration and examination of paths and the other based on threshold approach.

TUTORIAL 2

DESIGN TECHNOLOGY FOR BUILDING WIRELESS SYSTEMS

Speakers:

Rajesh K. Gupta, Univ. of California, Irvine, CA

Mani B. Srivastava, Univ. of California, Los Angeles, CA

Background: This tutorial is targeted for practicing engineers interested in system and IC design techniques for building wireless systems. CAD developers and researchers will develop an appreciation of the design tool requirements for wireless networked computing systems.

Description: The progress in IC technology is making chips that incorporate all the elements of a complete wireless radio system on a chip a real possibility. Such an "antenna-to-network" chip would incorporate an RF front end, baseband digital signal processing, link layer coding functions for error, compression, and encryption, and medium access control and other network protocols. This requires integration of analog circuits, high performance custom signal processing datapaths and cores, customized logic, embedded processor, and complex software environments on the same chip. The design, simulation, implementation, and testing techniques required for such chips are complex, as are the metrics to evaluate the performance. The current effort in standardization of pre-designed macromodules, often referred to as "core cells", is expected to play a major role in making it possible for designers to build complete and customized wireless systems on a chip. However, the diversity of macromodules required in such wireless systems on a chip represents a special challenge in almost all aspects of IC/System design. In this tutorial we present the state of the art in designing such systems, focusing on both the CAD problems that arise from such chips as well as on the tools and design techniques. The presentation is roughly divided into three parts: basics of wireless systems; VLSI design issues for wireless systems; design tools and techniques for hardware and software for wireless systems.

Rajesh Gupta is an assistant professor in Information and Computer Science at UC Irvine. His interests are in system-level design and CAD for embedded systems. Prior to his current position, he worked on CMOS, BiCMOS, ECL and high-speed GaAs chips while at Intel Corp.

Mani Srivastava is on the EE faculty at UCLA. His research activities include wireless and mobile ATM, low power wireless systems, adaptive wireless multimedia computing nodes, low power software programmable systems, and transformation-based DSP synthesis.

TUTORIAL 3

MODELING AND SYNTHESIS OF BEHAVIOR, CONTROL AND DATAFLOW

Speakers:

Raul Camposano, Synopsys, Inc., Mountain View, CA

Andrew Seawright, Synopsys, Inc., Mountain View, CA

Joseph Buck, Synopsys, Inc., Mountain View, CA

Background: This tutorial is for digital circuit designers, EDA professionals and researchers interested in the use of higher levels of abstraction in the design of digital systems. It covers a broad range of topics giving an overview of the techniques used in current "system level" tools.

Description: To tackle the exponential growth in the complexity of digital circuits, designers are moving to higher levels of abstraction in the design process. This tutorial aims to be an introduction to the state of the art in modeling and synthesis above the RTL level. The tutorial will focus in three areas: 1) the design and synthesis of digital systems using behavioral synthesis techniques, 2) the modeling and synthesis of complex controllers at using abstractions higher than FSMs and 3) the design and analysis of DSP/Dataflow systems using various data flow models and methods.

Raul Camposano will introduce the concepts of behavioral synthesis applied to the implementation of algorithms. Principles of scheduling, allocation, and advanced arithmetic optimization techniques will be covered. The section ends with some typical applications and results for behavioral synthesis.

Andrew Seawright will present an overview of techniques for describing control at higher levels of abstraction. The focus will be on methods for describing the "what" and not the "how" of the control problem while maintaining a cycle accurate representation. Methods for the synthesis of the underlying FSMs will be covered using classical FSM synthesis techniques and more recent implicit techniques.

Joseph Buck will present an overview of the DSP design process and introduce several models of data flow computation and their properties including Dynamic Data Flow, Synchronous Data Flow, and Boolean Data Flow models. System design flow, codesign, and the modeling of heterogenous systems will be covered.

Raul Camposano is Vice President and General Manager of the Synopsys Design Tools Group. Prior to his current position, he held different engineering positions, including Vice President of Engineering of the Synopsys Design Tools Group.

Andrew Seawright is an R&D staff member of the Synopsys Design Tools Group. He is a principal architect of the Dali environment for the design of structured control logic for telecommunications and related application domains.

Joseph Buck is a member of the Synopsys Advanced Technology Group working in the areas of DSP and Dataflow design technology. Prior to joining Synopsys he was a principal architect of the Ptolemy system.

TUTORIAL 4

CRITICAL TECHNOLOGIES AND METHODOLOGIES FOR SYSTEMS-ON-CHIPS

Speakers:

Wayne Dai, Univ. of California, Santa Cruz, CA

Howard Kalter, IBM Corp., Essex Junction, VT

Rob Roy, Intel Corp., Hillsboro, OR

Wayne Wolf, Princeton Univ., Princeton, NJ

Background: This tutorial is intended for designers, CAD tool developers, and researchers interested in systems-on-chips. It will examine the relationships between different design challenges to give the attendee a holistic view of the entire design process.

Description: This tutorial will present a survey of design challenges awaiting the industry in the systems-on-chips era. Systems-on-chips present new design challenges at every level of abstraction, ranging from the need to drive 500 MHz clocks across 100 million transistor chips to the problem of designing a complex chip to meet an ever-shortening product window. This tutorial will present problems in four areas critical for successfully designing systems-on-chips: Embedded RAM: various memory types; manufacturability, testability, diagnosability of embedded DRAM memory; technology and software tool requirements; chips that have used embedded memory; and a method of approach to the design problems. Low-power design, including circuit and system-level techniques. Low-power design is important not only for portable systems but also for any system where cooling and power supply costs are important. High-speed interconnect, which will be the dominant component of delay in many large systems-on-chips. Interconnection problems include modeling of deep submicron interconnect and placement and routing algorithms which take into account both delay and crosstalk. Hardware/software co-design, which is one of the few ways in which large, high-functionality chips can be designed in the short intervals required by today's markets. Co-design allows custom multiprocessors to be designed which efficiently implement application-specific systems. Problems include scheduling, allocation, processing element selection, and memory/communication synthesis.

Wayne Dai is an Associate Professor in the Computer Science and Engineering Department at UC Santa Cruz. He received his Ph.D. from UC Berkeley. He has extensively studied placement and routing for VLSI and MCM systems.

Howard L. Kalter is with IBM Corporation in Essex Junction, Vermont. He has worked on memory chip design on both static and dynamic memory, memory systems, and alterable logic and memory devices.

Rob Roy manages a low-power design group at Intel Corporation in Hillsboro, Oregon. Before joining Intel, he was with the NEC C&C Research Lab. Roy has conducted research in low-power design and core-based system design among other topics.

Wayne Wolf is an Associate Professor in the Department of Electrical Engineering at Princeton University. Before joining Princeton, he was with AT&T Bell Laboratories in Murray Hill, New Jersey. He has studied hardware/software co-design as well as many other areas of VLSI CAD.

KEYNOTE ADDRESS

John K. Ousterhout
Distinguished Engineer
Sun Microsystems, Inc.

Scripting languages such as Perl and Tcl represent a very different style of programming than system programming languages such as C or Java. In this talk I will explain why scripting languages provide more rapid application development than system programming languages and why scripting languages are becoming more and more important for applications of the future. I will also give a short history of Tcl (it was motivated by my work in ECAD in the early 1980's), describe its current status, and speculate about where Tcl is headed for the future, such as integration with Java.

John K. Ousterhout is a Distinguished Engineer at Sun Microsystems, Inc. His interests include scripting languages, user interfaces, operating systems, and distributed systems. He is the creator of the Tcl scripting language and the Tk toolkit. In the past, he led the development of the Sprite network operating system and several widely-used programs for computer-aided design, including Magic and Crystal. Ousterhout is a Fellow of the ACM and has received many awards, including the ACM Grace Murray Hopper Award, the National Science Foundation Presidential Young Investigator Award, and the UCB Distinguished Teaching Award. He received a B.S. degree in Physics from Yale University in 1975 and a Ph.D. in Computer Science from Carnegie Mellon University in 1980. From 1980 to 1994 he was a Professor in the Department of Electrical Engineering and Computer Sciences at the University of California at Berkeley.

SESSION 1A

DECISION DIAGRAM APPLICATIONS

Moderators:

Shin-ichi Minato, Stanford University, Stanford, CA

Jawahar Jain, Fujitsu Labs. of America, Inc.,

Santa Clara, CA

*PHDD: An Efficient Graph Representation for Floating Point Circuit Verification †

Yirng-An Chen
yachen@cs.cmu.edu

Randal E. Bryant
Randy.Bryant@cs.cmu.edu

Carnegie Mellon University, Pittsburgh, PA 15213

Abstract

*Data structures such as *BMDs, HDDs, and K*BMDs provide compact representations for functions which map Boolean vectors into integer values, but not floating point values. In this paper, we propose a new data structure, called Multiplicative Power Hybrid Decision Diagrams (*PHDDs), to provide a compact representation for functions that map Boolean vectors into integer or floating point values. The size of the graph to represent the IEEE floating point encoding is linear with the word size. The complexity of floating point multiplication grows linearly with the word size. The complexity of floating point addition grows exponentially with the size of the exponent part, but linearly with the size of the mantissa part. We applied *PHDDs to verify integer multipliers and floating point multipliers before the rounding stage, based on a hierarchical verification approach. For integer multipliers, our results are at least 6 times faster than *BMDs. Previous attempts at verifying floating point multipliers required manual intervention. We verified floating point multipliers before the rounding stage automatically.*

1 Introduction

Binary Moment Diagrams (BMDs) [3] have proved successful for representing and manipulating functions mapping Boolean vectors to integer values symbolically. They have been used in the verification of arithmetic circuits [4]. Clarke, *et al.* [7] extended BMDs to a form they call Hybrid Decision Diagrams (HDDs), where a function may be decomposed with respect to each variable in one of six ways, but without edge weights. Drechsler, *et al.* [10] extended Multiplicative BMDs (*BMDs) to a form called K*BMDs, where a function may be decomposed with respect to each variable in one of three ways, and with both additive and multiplicative edge weights. None of these diagrams can represent functions which map Boolean vectors to floating point values, unless rational numbers are introduced into the representation [2]. But using rational numbers in the representation requires more space to store the numerator and denominator separately, and more computation to extract the rational numbers.

Verification of floating point arithmetic circuits using any of these three diagrams requires the circuits to be divided into several sub-circuits for which specifications can be expressed in terms of integer functions and their operations [4, 6, 8]. The correctness of the overall circuit must be proved by users from the specifications of the verified sub-circuits. For instance, the floating point multiplier was divided into the circuits for the mantissa multiplication, the exponent addition, and the rounding in [6]. The verification of these three sub-circuits was performed automatically by word-level SMV [8], but the correctness of the entire multiplier must be proved by users from the verified specifications of these three sub-circuits. To avoid partitioning floating point arithmetic circuits for verification, it is necessary to have decision diagrams that represent and manipulate floating point functions efficiently.

†This research is sponsored by the Defense Advanced Research Projects Agency (DARPA) under contract number DABT63-96-C-0071.

In this paper, we propose a new representation, called Multiplicative Power Hybrid Decision Diagrams (*PHDDs), which improves on previous diagrams in representing floating point functions. *PHDDs can represent functions having Boolean variables as arguments and floating point values as results. This structure is similar to that of HDDs [7], except that they are based on powers-of-2 edge weights and complement edges for negation. We show that the size of floating point multiplication grows linearly with the word size. For floating point addition, we show that the complexity grows linearly with the mantissa size, but exponentially with the exponent size. It is still practical for formats up to IEEE double precision.

Based on a hierarchical verification methodology [3, 4], we have applied *PHDDs to verify different sizes and types of integer multipliers. Compared with *BMDs, *PHDDs are consistently six times faster and use less memory. We have also applied *PHDDs to verify different sizes and types of floating point multipliers before the rounding stage, which have never before been verified symbolically and automatically. Our results show that the verification of floating point multipliers requires minimal effort beyond integer multipliers. Our next step is to look into the rounding stage and entire floating point adders. Earlier results using HDDs [6] show that the rounding stage itself can be handled.

2 BMDs, *BMDs and HDDs

For expressing functions Boolean variables into integer values, BMDs[3] use the moment decomposition of a function:

$$
\begin{aligned}
f &= (1-x)\cdot f_{\overline{x}} + x\cdot f_x \\
&= f_{\overline{x}} + x\cdot(f_x - f_{\overline{x}}) \\
&= f_{\overline{x}} + x\cdot f_{\delta x} \qquad (1)
\end{aligned}
$$

where $\cdot$,$+$ and $-$ denote multiplication, addition and subtraction, respectively. Term f_x ($f_{\overline{x}}$) denotes the positive (negative) cofactor of f with respect to variable x, i.e., the function resulting when constant 1 (0) is substituted for x. By rearranging the terms, we obtained the third line of Equation 1. Here, $f_{\delta x} = f_x - f_{\overline{x}}$ is called the linear moment of f with respect to x. This terminology arises by viewing f as being a linear function with respect to its variables, and thus $f_{\delta x}$ is the partial derivative of f with respect to x. The negative cofactor $f_{\overline{x}}$ will be termed the constant moment, i.e., it denotes the portion of function f that remains constant with respect to x. This decomposition is also called positive Davio in K*BMDs [10]. Each vertex of a BMD describes a function in terms of its moment decomposition with respect to the variable labeling the vertex. The two outgoing arcs denote the constant and linear moments of the function with respect to the variable.

Clarke, *et al.* [7] extended BMDs to a form they call Hybrid Decision Diagrams (HDDs), where a function may be decomposed with respect to each variable in one of six decomposition types. In our experience with HDDs, we found that three of their six decomposition types are useful in the verification of arithmetic circuits. These

1092-3152/97 $10.00 © 1997 IEEE

three decomposition types are Shannon, Positive Davio, and Negative Davio. Therefore, Equation 1 is generalized to the following three equations according the variable's decomposition type:

$$f = \begin{cases} (1-x)\cdot f_{\overline{x}} + x\cdot f_x & (Shannon) \\ f_{\overline{x}} + x\cdot f_{\delta x} & (Positive\ Davio) \\ f_x + (1-x)\cdot f_{\delta\overline{x}} & (Negative\ Davio) \end{cases} \quad (2)$$

Here, $f_{\delta\overline{x}} = f_{\overline{x}} - f_x$ is the partial derivative of f with respect to $\overline{x}$. The BMD representation is a subset of HDDs. In other word, the HDD graph is the same as the BMD graph, if all of the variables use positive Davio decomposition.

x	y	f
0	0	1
0	1	2
1	0	4
1	1	8

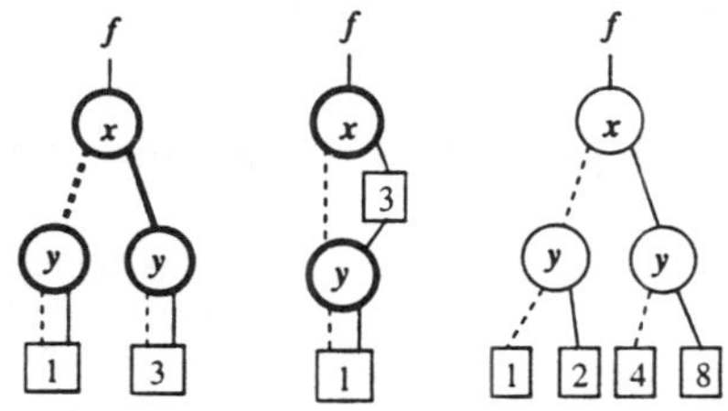

(a) (b) (c) (d)

Figure 1: **An integer function with Boolean variables, $f = 1 + y + 3x + 3xy$, is represented by (a) Truth table, (b) BMDs, (c) *BMDs, (d) HDDs with Shannon decompositions.** The dashed-edges are 0-branches and the solid-edges are the 1-branches. The variables with Shannon and positive Davio decomposition types are drawn in vertices with thin and thick lines, respectively.

As an example, Figure 1 show an integer function f with Boolean variables x and y represented by a truth table, BMDs, *BMDs, and HDDs with Shannon decompositions (also called MTBDD [9]). In our drawing, the variables with Shannon and positive Davio decomposition types are drawn in vertices with thin and thick lines, respectively. The dashed (solid) line from a vertex with variable x points to the vertex represented function $f_{\overline{x}}$, $f_{\overline{x}}$, and f_x (f_x, $f_{\delta x}$ and $f_{\delta\overline{x}}$) for Shannon, positive Davio and negative Davio decompositions, respectively. Figure 1.b shows the BMD representation. To construct this graph, we apply Equation 1 to function f recursively. First, with respect to variable x, we can get $f_{\overline{x}} = 1 + y$, represented as the graph of the dashed-edge of vertex x, and $f_{\delta x} = 3 + 3y$, represented by the solid branch of vertex x. Observe that $f_{\delta x}$ can be expressed by $3 \times f_{\overline{x}}$. By extracting the factor 3 from $f_{\delta x}$, the graph became Figure 1.c. This graph is called a Multiplicative BMD (*BMD) which extracts the greatest common divisor (GCD) from both branches. The edge weights combine multiplicatively. The HDD with Shannon decompositions can be constructed from the truth table. The dashed branch of vertex x is constructed from the first two entries of the table, and the solid branch of vertex x is constructed from the last two entries of the table.

Observe that if variables x and y are viewed as bits forming 2-bit binary number, X=y+$2x$, then the function f can be rewritten as $f = 2^{(y+2x)} = 2^X$. Observe that HDDs with Shannon decompositions and BMDs grow exponentially for this type of functions. *BMDs can represent them efficiently, due to the edge weights. However, *BMDs and HDDs cannot represent the functions as $f = 2^{X-B}$, where B is a constant, because they can only represent integer functions.

3 The *PHDD Data Structure

In this section, we introduce a new data structure, Multiplicative Power Hybrid Decision Diagrams (*PHDDs), to represent functions that map Boolean vectors to integer or floating point values. This structure is similar to that of HDDs, except that they use power-of-2 edge weights and negation edges. The power-of-2 edge weights allow us to represent and manipulate functions mapping Boolean vectors to floating point values. Negation edges can further reduce graph size by as much as a factor of 2 We assume that there is a total ordering of the variables such that the variables are tested according to this ordering along any path from the root to a leaf. Each variable is associated with its own decomposition type and all nodes of that variable use the corresponding decomposition.

3.1 Edge Weights

*PHDDs use three of HDD's six decompositions as expressed in Equation 2. Similar to *BMDs, we adapt the concept of edge weights to *PHDDs. Unlike *BMD edge weights, we restrict our edge weights to be powers of a constant c. Thus, Equation 2 is rewritten as:

$$\langle w, f\rangle = \begin{cases} c^w\cdot(((1-x)\cdot f_{\overline{x}} + x\cdot f_x) & (Shannon) \\ c^w\cdot(f_{\overline{x}} + x\cdot f_{\delta x}) & (Positive\ Davio) \\ c^w\cdot(f_x + (1-x)\cdot f_{\delta\overline{x}}) & (Negative\ Davio) \end{cases}$$

where $\langle w, f\rangle$ denotes $c^w \times f$. In general, the constant c can be any positive integer. Since the base value of the exponent part of the IEEE floating point format is 2, we will consider only c = 2 for the remainder of the paper. Observe that w can be negative, i.e., we can represent rational numbers. The power edge weights enable us to represent functions mapping Boolean variables to floating point values without using rational numbers in our representation.

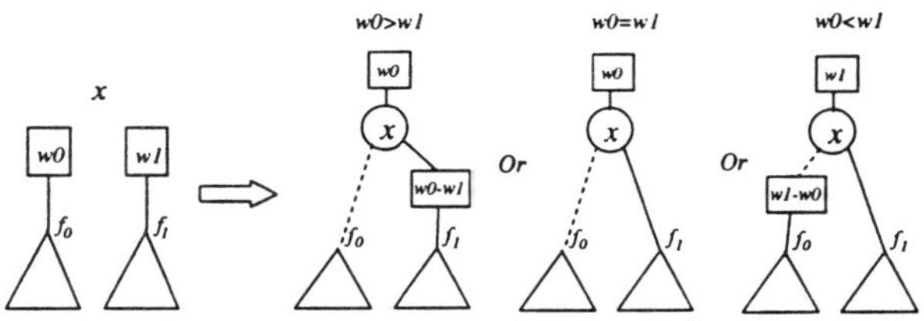

Figure 2: **Normalizing the edge weights.**

In addition to the HDD reduction rules [7], we apply several edge weight manipulating rules to maintain the canonical form of the resulting graph. Let $w0$ and $w1$ denote the weights at branch 0 and 1 respectively, and f_0 and f_1 denotes the functions represented by branch 0 and 1. To normalize the edge weights, we chose to extract the minimum of the edge weight $w0$ and $w1$. This is a much simpler computation than the GCD of integer *BMDs or the reciprocal of rational *BMDs [2]. Figure 2 illustrates the manipulation of edge weights to maintain a canonical form. The first step is to extract the minimum of $w0$ and $w1$. Then, the new edge weights are adjusted by subtracting the minimum from $w0$ and $w1$ respectively. A node is created with the index of the variable, the new edge weights, and pointers to f_0 and f_1. Base on the relation of $w0$ and $w1$, the resulting graph is one of three graphs in Figure 2. Note that at least one branch has zero weight. In addition, the manipulation rule of the edge weight is the same for all of the three decomposition types. In other words, the representation is normalized if and only if the following holds:

- The leaf nodes can only have odd integers or 0.
- At most one branch has non-zero weight.
- The edge weights are greater than or equal to 0, except the top one.

3.2 Negation Edge

Negation edges are commonly used in BDDs [1] and KFDDs [11], but not in *BMDs, HDDs and K*BMDs. Since our edge weights extract powers-of-2 which are always positive, negation edges are added to *PHDDs to increase sharing among the diagrams. In *PHDDs, the negation edge of function f represents the negation of f. Note that $-f$ is different from $\overline{f}$ for Boolean functions.

Negation edges allow greater sharing and make negation a constant computation. In *PHDD data structure, we use the low order bit the pointers to denote negation, as is done with the complement edge of BDDs. To maintain a canonical form, we must constrain the use of negation edges. Unlike KFDDs [11], where Shannon decompositions use a different method from positive and negative Davio decompositions, *PHDDs use the same method for manipulating the negation edge for all three decomposition types. *PHDDs must follow these rules: the zero edge of every node must be a regular edge, the negation of leaf 0 is still leaf 0, and leaves must be nonnegative. These guarantee the canonical form for *PHDDs.

4 Representation of Numeric Functions

*PHDDs can effectively represent numeric functions that map Boolean vectors into integer or floating point values. We first show that *PHDDs can represent integer functions with comparable sizes to *BMDs. Then, we show the *PHDD representation for floating point numbers.

4.1 Representation of Integers

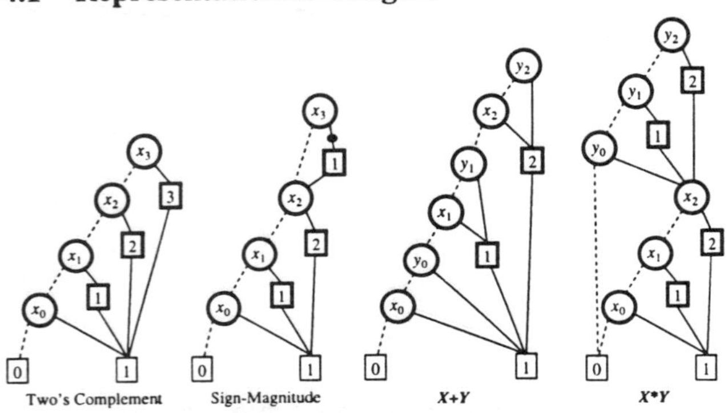

Figure 3: ***PHDD Representations of Integers and Integer operations.** Each variable uses positive Davio decomposition. The graphs grow linearly with word size.

*PHDDs, similar to *BMDs, can provide a concise representation of functions which map Boolean vectors to integer values. Let $\vec{x}$ represent a vector of Boolean variables: $x_{n-1}, \ldots, x_1, x_0$. These variables can be considered to represent an integer X according to some encoding, e.g., unsigned binary or two's complement. Figure 3 illustrates the *PHDD representations of several common encodings for integers. In our drawing of *PHDDs, we indicate the edge weight and leaf node in square boxes with thick and thin lines, respectively. Edge weight i represents 2^i and Unlabeled edges have weight 0 (2^0). An unsigned number is encoded as a sum of weighted bits. The *PHDD representation has a simple linear structure where the leaf values are formed by the corresponding edge weight and leaf 1 or 0. For representing signed numbers, we assume x_{n-1} is the sign bit. The two's complement encoding has a *PHDD representation similar to that of unsigned integers, but with bit x_{n-1} having weight -2^{n-1} represented by the edge weight $n-1$ and the negation edge. Sign-magnitude integers also have *PHDD representations of linear complexity, but with the constant moment with respect to x_{n-1} scaling the remaining unsigned number by 1, and the linear moment scaling the number by -2 represented by edge weight 1 and the negation edge. In evaluating the function for $x_{n-1} = 1$, we would add these two moments, effectively scaling the number by -1. Note that it is more logical to use Shannon decomposition for the sign bit.

Figure 3 also illustrates the *PHDD representations of several common arithmetic operations on integer data. Observe that the sizes of the graphs grow only linearly with the word size n. Integer addition can be viewed as summing a set of weighted bits, where bits x_i and y_i both have weight 2^i represented by edge weight i. Integer multiplication can be viewed as summing a set of partial products of the form $x_i 2^i Y$. In summary, while representing the integer functions, *PHDDs with positive Davio decompositions usually will get the most compact representation among these three decompositions.

4.2 Representation of Floating Point Numbers

Let us consider the representation of floating point numbers by IEEE standard 754. For example, the double-precision numbers are stored in 64 bits: 1 bit for the sign (S_x), 11 bits for the exponent (EX), and 52 bits for the mantissa (X). The exponent is a signed number represented with a bias (B) 1023. The mantissa represents a number less than 1. Based on the value of the exponent, the IEEE floating point format can be divided into four cases:

$$\begin{cases} (-1)^{S_x} \times 1.X \times 2^{EX-B} & If\ 0 < EX < All\ 1\ (normal) \\ (-1)^{S_x} \times 0.X \times 2^{1-B} & If\ EX = 0\ (denormal) \\ NaN & If\ EX = All\ 1\ \&\ X \neq 0 \\ (-1)^{S_x} \times \infty & If\ EX = All\ 1\ \&\ X = 0 \end{cases}$$

Currently, *PHDDs cannot handle infinity and NaN (not a number) cases in the floating point representation. Instead, assume they are normal numbers.

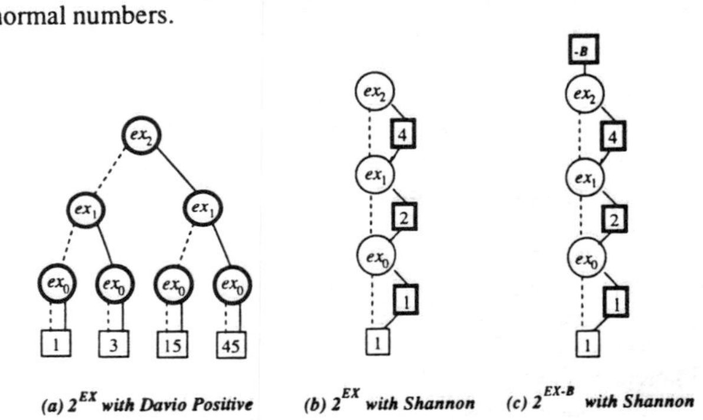

Figure 4: ***PHDD Representations of 2^{EX} and 2^{EX-B}.** The graph grows linearly in the word size with Shannon, but grows exponentially with positive Davio.

Figure 4 shows *PHDD representations for 2^{EX} and 2^{EX-B} using different decompositions. To represent function c^{EX} (in this case $c = 2$), *PHDDs express the function as a product of factors of the form $c^{2^i ex_i} = (c^{2^i})^{ex_i}$. In the graph with Shannon decompositions, a vertex labeled by variable ex_i has outgoing edges with weights 0 and c^{2^i} both leading to a common vertex denoting the product of the remaining factors. But in the graph with positive Davio decompositions, there is no sharing except for the vertices on the layer just above the leaf nodes. Observe that the size of *PHDDs with positive Davio decomposition grows exponentially in the word size while the size of *PHDDs with Shannon grows linearly. Interestingly, *BMDs have a linear growth for this type of function, while *PHDDs with positive Davio decompositions grow exponentially. To represent floating point functions symbolically, it is necessary to represent 2^{EX-B} efficiently, where B is a constant. *PHDD can represent this type of functions, but *BMDs, HDDs and K*BMDs cannot represent them without using rational numbers.

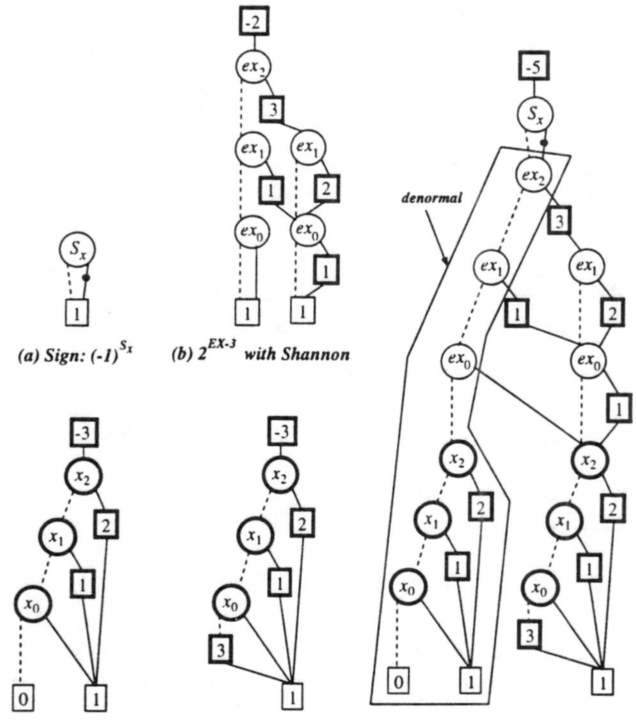

(a) Sign: $(-1)^{S_x}$ (b) 2^{EX-3} with Shannon

(c) Mantissa: 0.X (d) Mantissa: 1.X (e) Floating Point Encoding

Figure 5: **Representations of floating point encodings.**

Figure 5 shows the *PHDD representations for the floating point encoding, where EX has 3 bits, X has 4 bits and the bias B is 3. The sign S_x and $\vec{ex}$ variables use Shannon decomposition, while variables $\vec{x}$ use positive Davio. Figure 5.a shows the *PHDD representation for the sign bit $(-1)^{S_x}$. When S_x is 0, the value is 1; otherwise, the value is -1 represented by the negation edge and leaf node 1. Figure 5.b shows the *PHDD representation for the exponent part 2^{EX-3}. The graph is more complicated than Figure 4.c, because, in the floating point encoding, when $EX = 0$, the value of the exponent is $1 - B$, instead of $-B$. Observe that each exponent variable, except the top variable ex_2, has two nodes: one to represent the denormal number case and another to represent normal number case. Figure 5.c shows the representation for the mantissa part $0.X$ obtained by dividing X by 2^{-3}. Again, the division by powers of 2 is just adding the edge weight on top of the original graph. Figure 5.d shows the representation for the mantissa part $1.X$ which is the sum of $0.X$ and 1. The weight (2^{-3}) of the least significant bit is extracted to the top and the leading bit 1 is represented by the path with all variables set to 0. Finally, Figure 5.e shows the *PHDD representation for the complete floating point encoding. Observe that negation edges reduce the graph size by half. The outlined region in the figure denotes the representation for denormal numbers. The rest of the graph represents normal numbers. Assume the exponent is n bits and the mantissa is m bits. Note that the edge weights are encoded into the node structure in our implementation, but the top edge weight requires an extra node. It can be shown that the total number of *PHDD nodes for the floating point encoding is $2(n + m) + 3$. Therefore, the size of the graph grows linearly with word size. In our experience, it is best to use Shannon decompositions for the sign and exponent bits, and positive Davio decompositions for the mantissa bits.

4.3 Floating Point Multiplication and Addition

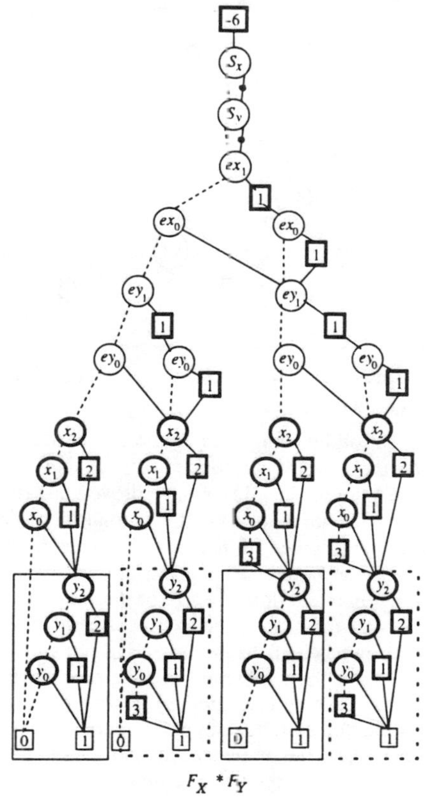

Figure 6: **Representation of floating point multiplication.**

This section presents floating point multiplication and addition based on *PHDDs. Here, we show the representations of these operations before rounding. In other words, the resulting *PHDDs represent the precise results of the floating point operations. For floating point multiplication, the size of the resulting graph grows linearly with the word size. For floating point addition, the size of the resulting graph grows exponentially with the size of the exponent part.

Let $F_X = (-1)^{S_x} \times v_x.X \times 2^{EX-B}$ and $F_Y = (-1)^{S_y} \times v_y.X \times 2^{EY-B}$, where v_x (v_y) is 0 if EX (EY) = 0, otherwise, v_x (v_y) is 1. EX and EY are n bits, and X and Y are m bits. Let the variable ordering be the sign variables, followed by the exponent variables and then the mantissa variables. Based on the values of EX and EY, $F_X \times F_Y$ can be written as: $(-1)^{S_x \oplus S_y} \times 2^{-2B} \times$

$$\begin{cases} 2^1 \times 2^1 \times (0.X \times 0.Y) & Case\ 0: EX = 0\ EY = 0 \\ 2^1 \times 2^{EY} \times (0.X \times 1.Y) & Case\ 1: EX = 0\ EY \neq 0 \\ 2^{EX} \times 2^1 \times (1.X \times 0.Y) & Case\ 2: EX \neq 0\ EY = 0 \\ 2^{EX} \times 2^{EY} \times (1.X \times 1.Y) & Case\ 3: EX \neq 0\ EY \neq 0 \end{cases}$$

Figure 6 illustrates the *PHDD representation for floating point multiplication. Observe that two negation edges reduce the graph size to one half of the original size. When $EX = 0$, the subgraph represents the function $0.X \times v_y.Y \times 2^{EY}$. When $EX \neq 0$, the subgraph represents the function $1.X \times v_y.Y \times 2^{EY}$. The size of exponent nodes grows linearly with the word size of the exponent part. The lower part of the resulting graph shows four mantissa products(from left to right): $X \times Y$, $X \times (2^3 + Y)$, $(2^3 + X) \times Y$, $(2^3 + X) \times (2^3 + Y)$. The first and third mantissa products share the common sub-function

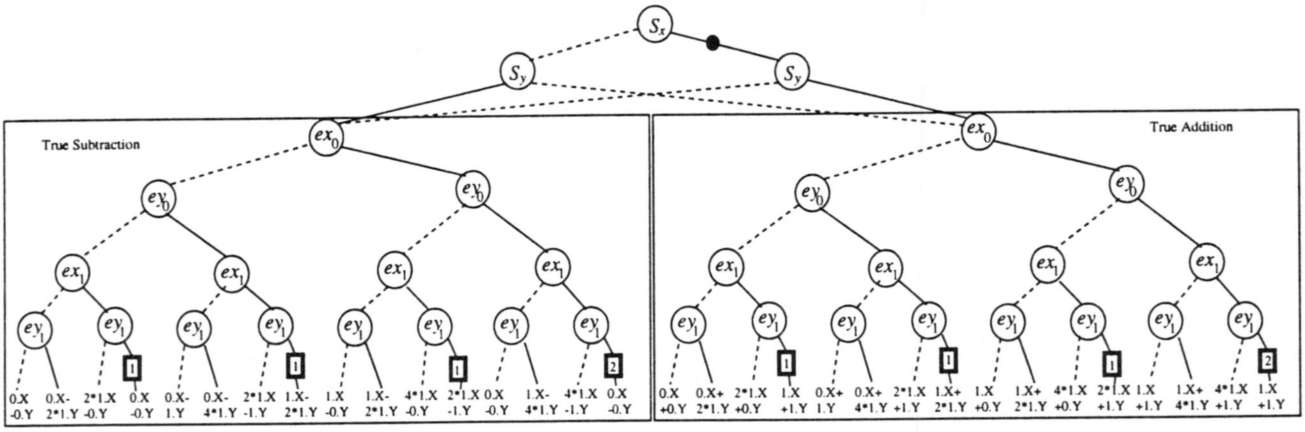

Figure 7: **Representation of floating point addition.** For simplicity, the graph only shows sign bits, exponent bits and the possible combinations of mantissa sums.

Y shown by the solid rectangles in Figure 6. The second and fourth products share the common sub-function $2^3 + Y$ shown by the dashed rectangles in Figure 6. In [5], we have proved that the size of the resulting graph of floating point multiplication is $6(n+m)+3$ with the variable ordering given in in Figure 6, where n and m are the number of bits in the exponent and mantissa parts.

For floating point addition, the size of the resulting graph grows exponentially with the size of the exponent part. In [5], we have proved that the number of distinct mantissa sums of $F_X + F_Y$ is $2^{n+3} - 10$, where n is the number of bits in the exponent part. Figure 7 illustrates the *PHDD representation of floating point addition with two exponent bits for each floating point operand. Observe that the negation edge reduces the graph size by half. According to the sign bits of two words, the graphs can be divided into two sub-graphs: true addition and true subtraction which represent the addition and subtraction of two words, respectively. There is no sharing among the sub-graphs for true addition and true subtraction. In true subtraction, $1.X - 1.Y$ has the same representation as $0.X - 0.Y$. Therefore, all $1.X - 1.Y$ entries are replaced by $0.X - 0.Y$. Since the number of distinct mantissa sums grows exponentially with the number of exponent bits, it can be shown that the total number of nodes grows exponentially with the size of exponent bits and grows linearly with the size of the mantissa part. Readers can refer to [5] for a detailed discussion of floating point addition. Floating point subtraction can be performed by the negation and addition operations. Therefore, it has the same complexity as addition.

In our experience, the sizes of the resulting graphs for multiplication and addition are hardly sensitive to the variables ordering of the exponent variables. They exhibit a linear growth for multiplication and exponential growth for addition for almost all possible ordering of the exponent variables. It is more logical to put the variables with Shannon decompositions on the top of the variables with the other decompositions.

5 Experimental Results

We have implemented *PHDD with basic BDD functions and applied it to verify arithmetic circuits. Integer multiplier circuits and *BMD package can be obtained from Yirng-An Chen's WWW page[1]. The circuit structure for four different types of multipliers are manually encoded in a C program which calls the BDD and *BMD operations. We also integrated our *PHDD package with the C program. Our measurements are obtained on Sun Sparc 10 with 256 MB memory.

5.1 Integer Multipliers

Circuits		CPU Time (Sec.)			Memory(MB)		
		16	64	256	16	64	256
Add-Step	*BMD	1.40	15.38	354.38	0.67	0.77	1.12
	*PHDD	0.20	2.24	39.96	0.11	0.18	0.64
	Ratio	7.0	6.8	8.9	6.0	4.3	1.8
CSA	*BMD	1.61	26.91	591.70	0.67	0.80	2.09
	*PHDD	0.25	3.45	50.72	0.14	0.30	0.88
	Ratio	6.4	7.8	11.7	4.8	2.7	2.4
Booth	*BMD	2.05	34.09	782.20	0.70	0.86	1.84
	*PHDD	0.21	2.97	62.56	0.14	0.30	1.26
	Ratio	9.7	11.5	12.5	5.0	2.9	1.5
Bit-Pair	*BMD	1.21	17.35	378.64	0.70	0.86	2.34
	*PHDD	0.20	2.17	36.10	0.15	0.33	1.33
	Ratio	6.0	8.0	10.5	4.7	2.6	1.8

Table 1: **Performance comparison between *BMD and *PHDD for different integer multipliers.** Results are shown for three different words. The ratio is obtained by dividing the result of *BMD by that of *PHDD.

Table 1 shows the performance comparison between *BMD and *PHDD for different integer multipliers with different word sizes. For the CPU time, the complexity of *PHDDs for the multipliers still grows quadratically with the word size. Compared with *BMDs, *PHDDs are at least 6 times faster, since the edge weight manipulation of *PHDDs only requires integer addition and subtraction, but *BMDs require a multiple precision representation for integers and perform costly multiple precision multiplication, division, and GCD operations. While increasing the word size, the *PHDD's speedup is increasing, because *BMDs requires more time to perform multiple precision multiplication and division operations. Interestingly, *PHDDs also use less memory than *BMDs, since the edge weights in *BMDs are explicitly represented by extra nodes, while *PHDDs embed edge weights into the node structure. The node sizes for both packages are 20 bytes.

5.2 Floating Point Multipliers

To perform floating point multiplication operations before the rounding stage, we introduced an adder to perform the exponent addition and logic to perform the sign operation in the C program. Table 2 shows CPU times and memory requirements for verifying floating point multipliers with fixed exponent size 11. Observe that

[1] http://www.cs.cmu.edu/~yachen/home.html.

Circuits	CPU Time (Sec.)			Memory(MB)		
	16	64	256	16	64	256
Add-Step	0.24	2.29	39.77	0.13	0.18	0.65
CSA	0.29	3.08	53.98	0.14	0.30	0.88
Booth	0.25	3.85	67.38	0.16	0.30	1.26
Bit-Pair	0.21	2.10	38.54	0.15	0.33	1.33

Table 2: **Performance for different floating point multipliers.** Results are shown for three different mantissa word size with fixed exponent size 11.

the complexity of verifying the floating point multiplier before rounding still grows quadratically. In addition, the computation time is very close to the time of verifying integer multipliers, since the verification time of an 11-bit adder and the composition and verification times of a floating point multiplier from integer mantissa multiplier and exponent adder are negligible. The memory requirement is also similar to that of the integer multiplier.

5.3 Floating Point Addition

Exponent Bits	No. of Nodes		CPU Time (Sec.)		Memory(MB)	
	23	52	23	52	23	52
4	4961	10877	0.2	0.7	0.4	0.7
5	10449	22861	0.7	1.3	0.7	1.1
6	21441	46845	1.1	3.5	1.1	2.0
7	43441	94829	2.7	6.9	1.9	3.8
8	**87457**	190813	**7.2**	16.8	**3.6**	7.5
9	175505	382797	15.0	41.3	7.2	14.8
10	351617	766781	33.4	103.2	14.3	29.5
11	703857	**1534765**	72.8	**262.4**	26.5	**54.9**
12	1408353	3070749	163.2	573.7	54.1	110.9
13	2817361	6142733	398.3	1303.8	112.5	226.0

Table 3: **Performance for floating point additions.** Results are shown for three different exponent word size with fixed mantissa size 23 and 52 bits.

Table 3 shows the performance measurements of precise floating point addition operations with different exponent bits and fixed mantissa sizes of 23 and 52 bits, respectively. Both the number of nodes and the required memory double, while increasing one extra exponent bit. For the same number of exponent bits, the measurements for the 52-bit mantissa are approximately twice the corresponding measurements for the 23-bit mantissa. In other words, the complexity grows linearly with the mantissa's word size. Due to the cache behavior, the CPU time is not doubling (sometimes, around triple), while increasing one extra exponent bit. For the double precision of IEEE standard 754 (the numbers of exponent and mantissa bits are 11 and 52 respectively), it only requires 54.9MB and 262.4 seconds. These values indicate the possibility of the verification of an entire floating point adder for IEEE double precision. For IEEE extended precision, floating point addition will require at least $226.4 \times 8 = 1811.2$MB memory. In order to verify IEEE extended precision addition, it is necessary to avoid the exponential growth of floating point addition.

6 Future Work

To verify circuit designs automatically, we would like to integrate the *PHDD package into word-level SMV [8] and extend word-level SMV, if needed, to handle the floating point arithmetic circuits. Then, we will look into the rounding stage and entire floating-point adders. Earlier results [6] show that the rounding stage itself can be handled with HDDs and therefore with *PHDDs. To verify entire floating point adders, we need to develop some techniques to avoid the exponential growth. Our representation for floating point addition represents the precise values of all possible combinations, but in the actual circuit design, there are only about 200 interesting mantissa sums. Based on this knowledge, we will develop a technique to avoid the exponential growth of floating point addition. As mentioned in previous sections, we will further pursue handling infinite and NaN cases. We need to develop some techniques or introduce special symbols to handle these cases.

Acknowledgement

We thank Xudong Zhao for valuable discussions on HDDs and verification of arithmetic circuits. We also thank Manish Pandey, Alok Jain, Shipra Panda and Bwolen Yang for proofreading this paper.

References

[1] BRACE, K., RUDELL, R., AND BRYANT, R. E. Efficient implementation of a BDD package. In *Proceedings of the 27th ACM/IEEE Design Automation Conference* (June 1990), pp. 40–45.

[2] BRYANT, R. E., AND CHEN, Y.-A. Verification of arithmetic functions with binary moment diagrams. Tech. Rep. CMU-CS-94-160, School of Computer Science, Carnegie Mellon University, 1994.

[3] BRYANT, R. E., AND CHEN, Y.-A. Verification of arithmetic circuits with binary moment diagrams. In *Proceedings of the 32nd ACM/IEEE Design Automation Conference* (1995), pp. 535–541.

[4] CHEN, Y.-A., AND BRYANT, R. E. ACV: An arithmetic circuit verifier. In *Proceedings of the International Conference on Computer-Aided Design* (November 1996), pp. 361–365.

[5] CHEN, Y.-A., AND BRYANT, R. E. *PBHD: An efficient graph representation for floating point circuit verification. Tech. Rep. CMU-CS-97-134, School of Computer Science, Carnegie Mellon University, 1997.

[6] CHEN, Y.-A., CLARKE, E. M., HO, P.-H., HOSKOTE, Y., KAM, T., KHAIRA, M., O'LEARY, J., AND ZHAO, X. Verification of all circuits in a floating-point unit using word-level model checking. In *Proceedings of the Formal Methods on Computer-Aided Design* (November 1996), pp. 19–33.

[7] CLARKE, E. M., FUJITA, M., AND ZHAO, X. Hybrid decision diagrams overcoming the limitations of MTBDDs and BMDs. In *Proceedings of the International Conference on Computer-Aided Design* (November 1995), pp. 159–163.

[8] CLARKE, E. M., KHAIRA, M., AND ZHAO, X. Word level model checking – Avoiding the Pentium FDIV error. In *Proceedings of the 33rd ACM/IEEE Design Automation Conference* (June 1996), pp. 645–648.

[9] CLARKE, E. M., MCMILLAN, K., ZHAO, X., FUJITA, M., AND YANG, J. Spectral transforms for large boolean functions with applications to technology mapping. In *Proceedings of the 30th ACM/IEEE Design Automation Conference* (June 1993), pp. 54–60.

[10] DRECHSLER, R., BECKER, B., AND RUPPERTZ, S. K*BMDs: a new data struction for verification. In *Proceedings of European Design and Test Conference* (March 1996), pp. 2–8.

[11] DRECHSLER, R., SARABI, A., THEOBALD, M., BECKER, B., AND PERKOWSKI, M. A. Efficient representation and manipulation of switching functions based on ordered Kronecker functional decision diagrams. In *Proceedings of the 31st ACM/IEEE Design Automation Conference* (June 1994), pp. 415–419.

Functional Simulation using Binary Decision Diagrams

Christoph Scholl   Rolf Drechsler   Bernd Becker

Institute of Computer Science, Albert-Ludwigs-University
79110 Freiburg im Breisgau, Germany
email: {scholl,drechsle,becker}@informatik.uni-freiburg.de

Abstract

In many verification techniques fast functional evaluation of a Boolean network is needed. We investigate the idea of using Binary Decision Diagrams (BDDs) for functional simulation. The area-time trade-off that results from different minimization techniques of the BDD is discussed. We propose new minimization methods based on dynamic reordering that allow smaller representations with (nearly) no runtime penalty.

1 Introduction

One of the most important tasks during the construction and design of *Integrated Circuits* (ICs) is the proof of correctness, i.e. the check whether a design fulfills its specification. Simulation is a basic task of many verification tools. Recently, methods based on decision diagrams have been proposed [1, 5] to speed up cycle based functional simulation. Decision diagrams are used to reduce the runtime, which is proportional to the number of logic gates in traditional approaches (like event driven simulation or levelized compiled code simulation), to runtimes which are proportional to the sum of the number of inputs and the number of outputs of the circuit. In [1] a BDD is translated into a *C* program. The number of operations to evaluate an input vector in the resulting program is very small, but the program has the drawback of being large in size. In practice, for such large programs memory bandwidth becomes a problem. An access to memory can take many clock cycles if the requested item resides in a level of the memory hierarchy which is very slow [6, 5]. Therefore in our approach to functional simulation a central problem is to minimize the amount of memory needed and to optimize memory traffic.

In this paper we investigate how the drawback of large simulation programs can be avoided, if we allow that the number of operations of the simulator to evaluate an input vector slightly increases. We apply (restricted) dynamic reordering techniques and study the effect on the trade-off between the average number of operations to evaluate an input vector and the size of the resulting simulator.

2 Preliminaries

In this section we introduce basic notations and definitions that are needed for the understanding of the paper.

2.1 Ordered Binary Decision Diagrams

Each Boolean function $f : \mathbf{B}^n \rightarrow \mathbf{B}$ can be represented by a *Binary Decision Diagram* (BDD) [2], i.e. a directed acyclic graph where a Shannon decomposition is carried out in each node.

A BDD is called *ordered* if each variable is encountered at most once on each path from the root to a terminal and if the variables are encountered in the same order on all such paths. A BDD is called *reduced* if it does not contain vertices either with isomorphic sub-graphs or with both edges pointing to the same node.

For functions represented by reduced, ordered BDDs efficient manipulations and evaluations are possible [2]. In the following only reduced, ordered BDDs are considered and for briefness these graphs are called BDDs.

An example from [2] shows the importance of the variable ordering for BDDs:

Example 1 *Let* $f_n = x_1x_2 + \ldots + x_{2n-1}x_{2n}$. *If the variable ordering is given by* $(x_1, x_2, \ldots, x_{2n})$ *the size of the resulting BDD is* $2n + 2$. *On the other hand if the variable ordering is chosen as* $(x_1, x_3, \ldots, x_{2n-1}, x_2, x_4, \ldots, x_{2n})$ *the size of the BDD is* 2^{n+1}. *Thus the number of nodes in the graph varies from linear to exponential depending on the variable ordering. In Fig. 1 the BDDs of the function* $f_3 = x_1x_2 + x_3x_4 + x_5x_6$ *with variable orderings* $(x_1, x_2, x_3, x_4, x_5, x_6)$ *and* $(x_1, x_3, x_5, x_2, x_4, x_6)$ *are illustrated. The left (right) outgoing edge of each node* x_i *denotes the cofactor* $f_{x_i=1}$ $(f_{x_i=0})$. *The example proves that the choice of the variable ordering largely influences the size of the BDDs.*

2.2 Boolean Relations

Each Boolean function $f : \mathbf{B}^n \rightarrow \mathbf{B}^m$ can be viewed as a Boolean relation which can be represented by its characteristic function:

1092-3152/97 $10.00 © 1997 IEEE

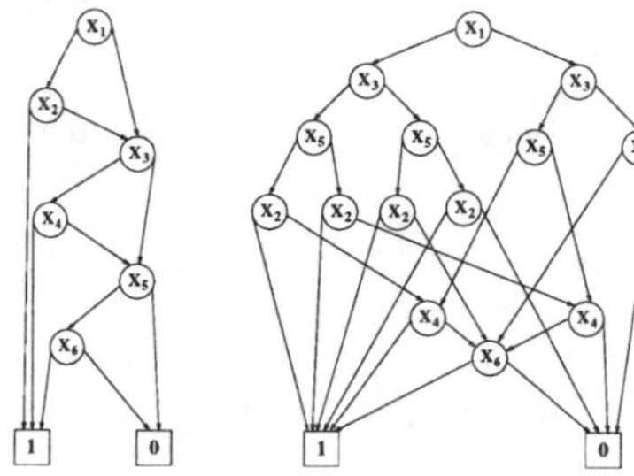

Figure 1: BDDs for function $f_3 = x_1x_2 + x_3x_4 + x_5x_6$

Definition 1 *A relation* $F \subseteq \{0,1\}^n \times \{0,1\}^m$ *is called* Boolean relation *with n inputs and m outputs. Each Boolean function* $f : \{0,1\}^n \to \{0,1\}^m$ *can be viewed as a Boolean relation* $R(f)$ *with*

$$(\epsilon, \delta) \in R(f) \iff f(\epsilon) = \delta\, (\forall \epsilon \in \{0,1\}^n, \delta \in \{0,1\}^m).$$

A Boolean relation F can be represented by its characteristic function, i.e. a Boolean function χ_F with $\chi_F(\epsilon, \delta) = 1$ iff $(\epsilon, \delta) \in F$.

If f has input variables $i_1, \ldots, i_n$ and we introduce additional output variables $o_1, \ldots, o_m$ (for $f_1, \ldots, f_m$ respectively), $\chi_{R(f)}$ can be computed by the following formula [3]:

$$\chi_{R(f)}(i_1, \ldots, i_n, o_1, \ldots, o_m) = \bigwedge_{i=1}^{m} (o_i \equiv f_i(i_1, \ldots, i_n)) \quad (1)$$

3 Functional Simulation

We briefly review previous work and then describe our approach.

3.1 Previous Work

3.1.1 Single-Output Circuits

If we transform a circuit into an (ordered) BDD, we can evaluate the corresponding function for a given input vector in time $\mathcal{O}(\#I)$, if $\#I$ is the number of inputs of the circuit. Since in typical circuits the number of gates $\#G$ is much larger than the number of inputs, this method is (at least asymptotically) much faster than traditional approaches, like event driven simulation or levelized compiled code simulation.

3.1.2 Multi-Output Circuits

If a multi-rooted BDD, i.e. a BDD representing a function f with $\#O$ outputs, is evaluated, the straightforward method would require time $\mathcal{O}(\#I \cdot \#O)$. If we represent the functional behavior by using the characteristic function of the relation $R(f)$ of f, the evaluation time can be reduced to $\mathcal{O}(\#I + \#O)$ as follows [1]:

- Compute a BDD representation for the characteristic function of the relation $R(f)$ of f. The characteristic function can be represented by a BDD with $\#I$ 'input variables' and $\#O$ 'output variables'. The BDD is constructed with the restriction that all the input variables occur in the ordering before the output variables.

- If we want to evaluate the characteristic function, we have the problem that we do not know the output vector, rather we need to determine it. But since all input variables occur in the ordering before the output variables, we can make use of the fact that each input vector produces a unique output vector: The evaluation can simply be done by starting from the single root of the BDD for the characteristic function and evaluating this BDD according to the values of the input variables. A unique path to the terminal 1 determines the values of the outputs. It is easy to find this path, because each node which is labeled by an output variable has exactly one outgoing edge to the terminal 0 and one edge to another node.

The major drawback of this method is that the number of nodes at the cut line between the input and the output variables is equal to the number of different combinations that can occur at the outputs. Since this number often is exponential in the number of outputs the restriction can be infeasible for practical applications. For this reason Ashar and Malik [1] proposed two methods.

One is based on an interleaving of input and output variables. An output variable is located in the ordering directly after the last input variable on which this output depends. To determine an ordering of the input and output variables under this restriction Ashar and Malik [1] use a heuristic from [9]. Since there is no output variable before any input variable it depends on, nodes labeled with output variables still have the property that there is exactly one outgoing edge to the terminal 0 and one edge to another node. Therefore it is still possible to evaluate the multi-output function in time $\mathcal{O}(\#I + \#O)$.

The second method to reduce the number of nodes of BDD representations uses a partition of the circuit. Then the method from [1] is applied only to the subcircuits of this partition. To evaluate the overall circuit for some input vector BDDs for several subcircuits have to be evaluated. Obviously, the partitioning method may increase the runtime, because the same input values are read more than once and/or intermediate variables are introduced.

McGeer et al. [5] also use a variable order with all input variables before the output variables they depend on. To optimize memory traffic they translate the decision diagram into an array, and a special-purpose program is automatically generated to traverse the array. In addition they use MDDs (*multi-*

valued decision diagrams) [8] instead of BDDs, where several BDD variables are combined into one MDD variable, such that the number of variables, which have to be evaluated, is reduced.

3.2 Optimization by Reordering

Reordering the variables of a BDD may have a large influence on the size of the representation (see e.g. Example 1).

We now study the effect of using dynamic variable ordering methods [4], like sifting [7], to reduce the size of the BDD representing the characteristic function. Here, we make no longer use of the restriction that the input and output variables should not be mixed.

If BDD sizes for these unrestricted reordering methods are smaller, we can choose larger subcircuits of the original circuit to be represented by BDDs for their characteristic functions, such that the number of evaluations of subcircuits is reduced.

However, in general, by dropping the ordering restriction above we can not further guarantee the time of $\mathcal{O}(\#I + \#O)$ to evaluate a multi-output function f which is represented by a BDD for $\chi_{R(f)}$.

3.3 Changed Evaluation Procedure

If we evaluate the BDD for the characteristic function, it is now possible to reach a node labeled by an output variable before all input variables are read, which this output depends on. Therefore we are not able to decide at this point which outgoing edge we have to follow. Both successors of this node can be different from the terminal 0. If we have reached such a node, we have to choose an arbitrary edge which we will follow. Thus, it is possible that we have to backtrack when it turns out that the decision at this output node was wrong. This is the case if we follow an edge starting from a node labeled by an input variable and reach terminal 0. Figure 2 shows the changed evaluation procedure.

Given: Boolean function $f : \{0,1\}^n \to \{0,1\}^m$,
BDD with node set V and root v_{root} for characteristic function $\chi_{R(f)}$
input variables $i_1, \ldots, i_n$, output variables $o_1, \ldots, o_m$,
label function $l : V \to \{i_1, \ldots, i_n, o_1, \ldots, o_m\} \cup \{0, 1\}$
input vector $(\epsilon_1, \ldots, \epsilon_n)$

Find: Output vector $(\delta_1, \ldots, \delta_m) = f(\epsilon_1, \ldots, \epsilon_n)$

Algorithm:

```
/* Let v^0 be the 0-son of a node v, v^1 the 1-son */
var stack outstack /* Stack with maximum depth m
          for nodes labeled with output variables */
v := v_root;
while (l(v) ≠ 1) do
    if (l(v) input variable)
      then
          /* Let l(v) be i_j */
          v := v^{ε_j};
          if (l(v) = 0)
            then
                v := pop(outstack);
                /* Let l(v) be o_k */
                δ_k := 0; v := v^0;
          fi
      else
          /* l(v) output variable, let l(v) be o_k */
          if (l(v^1) = 0)
            then
                δ_k := 0; v := v^0;
            else
                if (l(v^0) ≠ 0)
                  then
                      push(outstack, v);
                fi
                /* guess f_k(ε_1, ..., ε_n) = 1 */
                δ_k := 1; v := v^1;
          fi
    fi
od
```

Figure 2: Evaluation procedure.

3.4 Evaluation Sifting

As explained in the previous section the number of steps in the evaluation can be increased if we drop the ordering restriction that all output variables should appear after the input variables they depend on. On the other hand, experimental results (see Section 4) show that the BDD sizes are reduced to a large extent if we apply sifting without this ordering restriction. For this, it would be desirable to combine the two advantages of small BDDs and a few evaluation steps.

To estimate the cost to evaluate an arbitrary input vector we determine for a BDD the average number of read accesses to BDD nodes in the evaluation procedure of Figure 2, which are needed to evaluate a random input vector. Read accesses to BDD nodes constitute critical operations when the BDDs are large and memory management effects (e.g. page faults and cache misses) are of importance. The expected value for this number of read accesses to BDD nodes (for a random input vector) is denoted by E_{r_a} in the following.

Now we have two optimization goals in the computation of a variable order for the BDD of $\chi_{R(f)}$: First we would like to minimize the number of BDD nodes to represent $\chi_{R(f)}$ and secondly we would like to minimize the expected value E_{r_a}.

To take account of these two goals we change the cost function of sifting: Until now the cost function is only the size of the resulting BDD. To determine the optimal position of a variable in the variable order it is sifted to all possible positions and then, the position, where the resulting BDD size is minimized, is selected. Now the cost function is changed to some combination of BDD size and the expected value E_{r_a}. For each position of the variable we determine the new size $size^{new}$ of the resulting BDD and the new expected value $E^{new}_{r\_a}$. Then we choose the position for the variable where the expression

$$\alpha \cdot \frac{size^{new}}{size^{old}} + (1-\alpha) \cdot \frac{E^{new}_{r\_a}}{E^{old}_{r\_a}} \quad (2)$$

is minimized. ($size^{old}$ and $E^{old}_{r\_a}$, respectively, mean the BDD size and expected value before moving the variable, α is a number between 0 and 1 to influence the trade off between BDD sizes and read accesses in the evaluation.)

The resulting procedure is called *evaluation sifting* in the following.

3.4.1 Estimation of E_{r_a}

To estimate E_{r_a} we tried out two alternatives:

- If we assume that for a node v the probability to leave the subtree with root v^0 by a backtracking step of the evaluation procedure is independent from the probability to leave the subtree with root v^1, we can compute E_{r_a} bottom up in the BDD. However, since this assumption is only true for some special cases (e.g. when all output variables occur after the input variables), this will give only an estimation of E_{r_a}.
- To reduce the runtime for larger BDD sizes we also use another method for the estimation: We simulate $c \cdot n$ input vectors (for some small constant c) and count the average number of read accesses to the BDD in this way. (n is the number of variables in the BDD.)

4 Experimental Results

We performed experiments to compare sifting and evaluation sifting to the ordering strategy from [9, 1], where the input variables are located before the output variables they depend on.

Apart from BDD sizes for the different strategies, we determined for 500,000 random input patterns the average number of read accesses to BDD nodes in the evaluation procedure of Figure 2, which were needed to evaluate the input vectors, and finally we determined runtimes for the evaluation of the 500,000 random input vectors.

In columns TSLBS-ord of Table 1 we give results for the variable ordering strategy from [9, 1], in columns orig_sift results for the original sifting algorithm [7] and in columns eval_sift for evaluation sifting (we chose $\alpha = 0.5$ in formula (2) and used simulation to estimate E_{r_a}).

The sizes of the resulting BDDs are given counted in numbers of nodes in Table 1 (columns 'node'), the average numbers of read accesses are given in columns 'r.a.' and the simulation times in CPU seconds for 500,000 random input patterns measured on a SUN *Sparc 20* workstation (256 MB physical memory) in columns 'time'.

As easily can be seen there are some examples where the partitioning techniques proposed in [1] and [5] are needed for their method, since the BDDs for the characteristic function of the relation can not be constructed[1] for the variable ordering method from [9, 1].

In contrast, sifting can build the BDDs in all considered cases. Beside the cases where the other methods fail for some examples the size results of unrestricted sifting are up to a factor of 9 better than the results of the ordering heuristic from [9, 1].

For this reason we can expect that we will need substantially less subcircuits in the partition for larger circuits when we apply sifting (and this will lead to reduced evaluation times as explained in Section 3.1).

We now study the effect of the size reduction with respect to evaluation time for the circuits which could be represented in one partition. On a first view we can observe the "surprising" result that the average number of read accesses to BDD nodes increases for the original sifting algorithm in the worst case only by a factor of 1.5 compared to the variable ordering from [9, 1]. On the other hand, already for original sifting there are examples where the number of read accesses is reduced.

If we compare original sifting and evaluation sifting, we can see that it is possible to achieve a considerable reduction of read accesses and runtimes with only a small overhead in terms of node counts. There are circuits (e.g. c1908, rd73, rd84), for which the numbers of read accesses for evaluation sifting are reduced by about one half. Surprisingly, even the numbers for the ordering from [9, 1] (where no backtracking steps in the evaluation procedure can occur) are improved in most cases (while keeping the advantage of much smaller BDD sizes).

These unexpected results can be explained by the following observation:
In an optimized BDD it often occurs that less variables are tested until a terminal node is reached (see e.g. function from Example 1.) This effect leads to the fact that the additional read accesses due to 'wrong decisions' (see Section 3.3) of the evaluation procedure are more than compensated.

5 Conclusions and Future Work

We discussed the use of dynamic variable ordering for functional simulation. It turned out that the use of dynamic reordering has a large potential in this area.

We developed a modified version of the sifting algorithm (called evaluation sifting), which is able to combine advantages of sifting and variable orders with the restriction that all output variables are located after the input variables they depend on [9, 1]. The small BDD sizes of sifting are almost maintained, whereas

[1] We aborted the construction of the BDD for the relation, when more than 2,000,000 nodes were needed.

circuit	TSLBS-ord			orig_sift			eval_sift		
	nodes	r.a.	time	nodes	r.a.	time	nodes	r.a.	time
5xp1	93	22.50	2.94	71	25.49	3.81	74	23.77	3.54
alu2	289	18.68	2.67	279	19.09	2.52	295	13.49	1.99
apex7	4,665	86.65	12.70	2,323	107.67	15.25	2,479	84.44	11.96
b9	1,582	53.29	8.07	663	74.99	10.28	735	53.94	7.22
c432	9,530	28.64	7.99	1,584	30.06	4.49	1,730	26.26	4.03
c499	>2,000,000	-	-	14,235	259.44	71.00	17,017	225.06	51.55
c880	467,346	86.11	20.08	367,863	85.00	34.75	393,633	70.41	29.37
c1355	>2,000,000	-	-	15,957	274.50	67.19	16,926	242.76	53.20
c1908	>2,000,000	-	-	109,042	323.81	137.55	117,231	159.90	71.73
clip	171	16.50	2.25	103	17.84	2.52	102	16.98	2.61
count	145	30.75	4.82	142	29.75	4.57	184	15.73	3.03
e64	258	131.00	12.27	258	131.00	12.20	258	131.00	12.21
f51m	75	20.00	2.85	63	17.71	2.76	65	17.55	2.73
misex1	66	15.89	1.98	58	16.77	2.16	59	15.64	1.95
misex2	333	39.98	4.07	221	46.21	4.95	230	40.43	4.30
rd73	42	11.50	1.61	36	12.87	1.85	42	4.98	1.16
rd84	55	14.40	1.95	49	15.64	2.16	52	8.99	1.36
sao2	106	13.59	1.70	85	10.18	1.23	86	10.18	1.26
term1	5,541	30.01	3.99	578	31.18	4.02	612	30.13	3.94
vg2	171	22.98	3.05	140	21.63	2.60	140	21.54	2.58
z4ml	30	13.00	1.82	29	13.25	1.86	30	12.01	1.98

Table 1: Node counts, average number of read accesses and evaluation times for 500,000 random patterns

evaluation times in comparison to the variable order from [9, 1] are even improved.

Since the numbers of BDD nodes in our approach are much smaller we can expect that we will need substantially less subcircuits in the partition for larger circuits (and this will lead to reduced evaluation times as explained in Section 3.1).

At the moment we are integrating the concept of [5] to reduce the number of evaluations by combining several BDD variables into one MDD variable. Note that we thereby adjust evaluation sifting by changing the computation of E_{r_a} from Section 3.4 to estimate the number of operations in the evaluation procedure from [5] immediately on the basis of the BDD representing the characteristic function $\chi_{R(f)}$.

References

[1] P. Ashar and S. Malik. Fast functional simulation using branching programs. In *Int'l Conf. on CAD*, pages 408–412, 1995.

[2] R.E. Bryant. Graph - based algorithms for Boolean function manipulation. *IEEE Trans. on Comp.*, 35(8):677–691, 1986.

[3] E. Cerny and M.A. Marin. An approach to unified methodology of combinational switching circuits. *IEEE Trans. on Comp.*, 26:745–756, 1977.

[4] M. Fujita, Y. Matsunaga, and T. Kakuda. On variable ordering of binary decision diagrams for the application of multi-level synthesis. In *European Conf. on Design Automation*, pages 50–54, 1991.

[5] P.C. McGeer, K.L. McMillan, A. Saldanha, A.L. Sangiovanni-Vincentelli, and P. Scaglia. Fast discrete function evaluation using decision diagrams. In *Int'l Conf. on CAD*, pages 402–407, 1995.

[6] D.A. Patterson and J.L. Hennessy. *Computer Organization and Design. The Hardware/Software Interface.* Morgan Kaufman Publishers - CA, 1994.

[7] R. Rudell. Dynamic variable ordering for ordered binary decision diagrams. In *Int'l Conf. on CAD*, pages 42–47, 1993.

[8] A. Srinivasan, T. Kam, S. Malik, and R.E. Brayton. Algorithms for discrete function manipulation. In *Int'l Conf. on CAD*, pages 92–95, 1990.

[9] H. Touati, H. Savoj, B. Lin, R.K. Brayton, and A.L. Sangiovanni-Vincentelli. Implicit enumeration of finite state machines using BDDs. In *Int'l Conf. on CAD*, pages 130–133, 1990.

Generalized matching from theory to application *

Patrick Vuillod† Luca Benini Giovanni De Micheli

Stanford University
Computer Systems Laboratory
Stanford, CA 94305

Abstract

This paper presents a novel approach for post-mapping optimization. We exploit the concept of generalized matching, a technique that finds symbolically all possible matching assignments of library cells to a multi-output network specified by a Boolean relation. Several objectives are targeted: area minimization under delay constraints, power minimization under delay constraints and unconstrained delay minimization.

We describe the theory of generalized matching and the algorithmic optimization required for its efficient and robust implementation. A tool based on generalized matching has been implemented and tested on large examples of the MCNC'91 benchmark suite. We obtain sizable improvements in: (i) speed (6% in average, up to 20.7%); (ii) area under speed constraints (13.7% in average, up to 29.5%) and (iii) power under speed constraints (22.3% in average, up to 38.1%).

1 Introduction

Multiple-output technology-independent logic optimization based on Boolean relations (BRs) is potentially more powerful than traditional single-output optimization[1]. Unfortunately, BR-based techniques are more computationally expensive than traditional approaches such as algebraic [2] or *don't care*-based [6, 3] techniques and for this reason they have not yet succeeded as practical optimization engines. In [4] we introduced the concept of *generalized matching* (GM), a multiple-output Boolean matching technique which allows concurrent matching of two or more single-output library cells (or of one multiple-output cell) with a multi-output Boolean function. Generalized matching extends the Boolean relation-based approach to the technology dependent part of the synthesis flow.

Generalized matching, as formulated in [4], has the same drawback of its technology-independent counterpart, namely the high computational complexity. Hence, the formulation presented in [4] is very computationally demanding. In this work we introduce a new theoretical framework and algorithmic refinements that enable the application of GM to large circuits. We move from the observation that speed is usually the primary concern in synthesis. The timing budget for combinational logic is obtained from architectural specification. The first objective of synthesis is to produce an implementation that meets the timing constraints, and then to optimize secondary cost functions such as power or area.

When speed is the primary objective, two logic optimization problems have practical relevance: *unconstrained timing optimization* and *optimization of a secondary objective function* (area/power) *under tight timing constraints.* The solution to the first problem is useful for the designer to test the feasibility of the constraints. If the timing budget is exceeded after unconstrained timing optimization, the designer must re-design or re-partition the specification. The second problem is probably the most frequent in practice: the designer wants to obtain the minimum-area or minimum-power implementation that satisfies the timing constraint.

We apply GM in the last stages of the synthesis process, namely we target the incremental optimization of a *mapped netlist.* Post-mapping optimization is also known as *re-mapping.* Our starting point is a netlist that has already been optimized by traditional synthesis techniques [5] for maximum speed with area recovery. Re-mapping is applied to either increase speed, or reduce area/power without decreasing speed.

The main theoretical contribution of this paper is the formulation of an algorithm for the solution of the minimum-cost (area or power) timing-constrained generalized matching problem. Additionally, we have made several efforts to achieve efficiency and robustness, obtaining satisfactory results. We demonstrate the robustness of our approach by reporting results for all largest multi-level benchmarks in the MCNC'91 [15] suite. We obtain sizable improvements in speed, area under speed constraints and power under speed constraints. Moreover, re-mapping is most effective on larger netlists.

The paper is organized as follows. We first describe the rationale and high-level flow of our re-mapping approach (Section 2). In Section 3 we describe in detail the timing-constrained area minimization problem. In Section 4 we present experimental results. Constrained power minimization [16] and unconstrained speed optimization are not described in this paper (although we do provide experimental results) for space reasons.

2 The *re-mapping* approach

State-of-the art synthesis tools adopt a three-phase approach to logic optimization. First *technology-independent optimizations* are applied; then the network is mapped to the technology library of choice (*library binding*); finally the mapped netlist is further optimized by iterative algorithms that perform local transformations. We call *re-mapping* the last step [7, 8, 9]. Some re-mapping approaches [10] focus on changing the connectivity of the netlist in such a way that some gates either become redundant (and can be removed) or become sub-optimal (and can be replaced). Re-mapping transformations based on changes of the network connectivity are often called *re-wiring.*

We adopt a re-mapping approach. Starting from an optimized and mapped netlist, we apply our optimization engine to specific regions of the mapped netlist where local improvements are more likely. Once a target region is selected, it is optimized and, if optimization is successful, one or more cells are replaced with lower cost alternatives. Moreover, local wiring can be changed: the new cells may have different inputs. Hence, local re-wiring is performed as well.

Given a mapped network, the high level flow diagram of the re-mapping procedure is shown in Figure 1. Static timing analysis is performed and required times, arrival times and slacks

*Work partially supported by NSF contract MIP-9421129

†The author is now with Synopsys-Europe

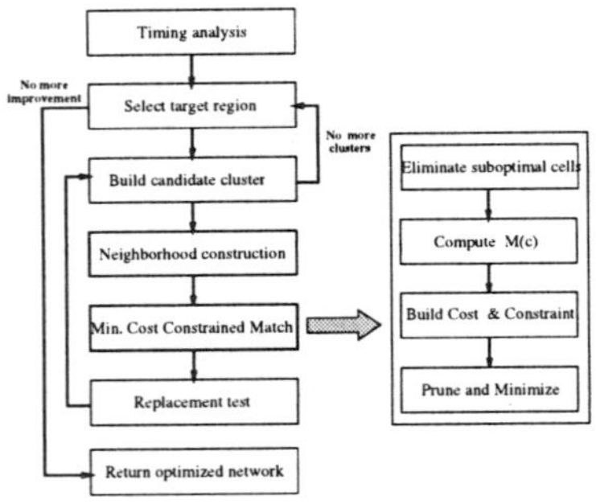

Figure 1: High-level flow of the re-mapping procedure

are computed for all nodes in the network. Then a breadth-first iteration on *target regions* of the network is started. From each target region, *candidate multi-output clusters* are generated and their neighborhood is analyzed to construct a Boolean relation representing the degrees of freedom available for the remapping of the cluster. Matching starts by eliminating library cells that are certainly sub-optimal, then the GM problem is solved by constructing a *matching function* M whose ON-set implicitly represents all possible replacements for cells in the candidate cluster.

The symbolic representation of timing constraint and area (or power) cost are built and the ON-set of M is first pruned by eliminating replacements that violate the constraints, then the minimum-cost replacements are selected from the pruned matching function. Replacement is performed if there is improvement with respect to the initial mapping. The breadth-first iteration is repeated until no further improvements are achieved.

A good choice of the target regions in the mapped netlist is paramount for the success of the re-mapping strategy. Different choice criteria are applied depending on the nature of the cost function that we want to optimize. Power and area are *extensive* cost functions, i.e. they depend on the entire circuit, while speed is an *intensive* cost function, i.e. it is determined only by a critical portion of the circuit (the slowest paths). When we optimize an extensive cost measure, we want to distribute the optimization effort on the entire netlist, while the optimization of an intensive cost function can be better achieved by focusing only on the critical portion.

For extensive cost functions (area and power), the target regions are the *multiple fanout points* (MFPs) of the network. There are two main reasons for this choice. First, traditional library binding algorithms follow a *cone-based* paradigm [11]. A very efficient search of the optimum mapping is performed on fanout-free regions of the circuit, but the search stops when MFPs are reached. As a result, the final implementation consists of highly optimized fanout-free regions connected by multiple fanout points. Roughly speaking, we target the loss of optimality caused by the interruption of the cone-based search when a MFP is reached. Second, since our optimization strategy is based on the computation of a Boolean relation expressing the degrees of freedom for the implementation of a multiple-output subnetwork, it is more likely to find degrees of freedom when the output functions of the subnetwork share some support variables. This is generally true when two or more gates driven by a MFP are considered as candidates for optimization.

Given a MFP, candidate clusters are generating by selecting sets of gates whose inputs or outputs are directly connected to the MFP. Although arbitrarily large clusters could be selected, the run time and memory requirements rapidly increases with the number of inputs and outputs in the cluster. For the sake of robustness and to keep run time under control we conservatively set the cluster size to two for all experiments reported in the paper. The selection of which cells to include in the clusters is decided by a *sliding window* algorithms (omitted for space reasons).

3 Min-cost Constrained Matching

In this section we focus on constrained minimization. Speed is the constraint and area is the optimization target. The clustering algorithm constructs candidate clusters starting from MFPs. Given the cluster we: i) build the Boolean relation that represents the degrees of freedom for matching created by the cluster's neighborhood; ii) perform minimum-area matching and guarantee that timing constraints are not violated. In the next subsections we describe how the two tasks are carried out. First we focus on the construction of the Boolean relation. Second, we provide the theoretical formulation of the generalized matching problem and we show how it can be solved efficiently. Third, we extend GM to take into account a cost function (area) and constraints (on timing) and we show how area can be minimized within timing constraints in computationally efficient fashion. In the following treatment we assume that the reader is familiar with Boolean algebra, BDD and ADD manipulation [6, 13].

3.1 Building the Boolean Relation

Let us consider a multi-output cluster function $\mathbf{f}$ embedded in a logic network as shown in Figure 2.

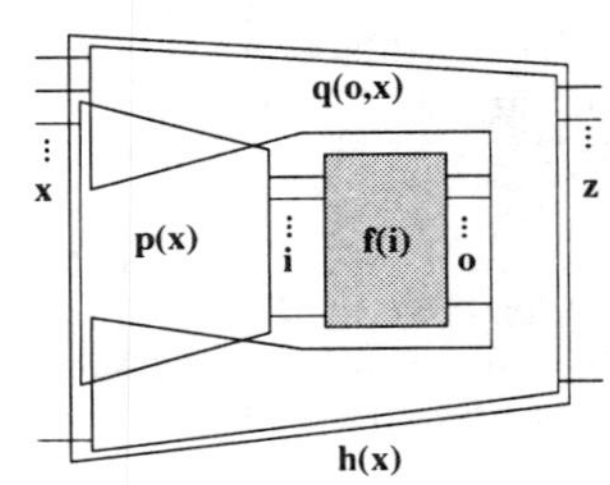

Figure 2: A multi-output cluster function embedded in its neighborhood

We adopt a formalism similar to that used by Watanabe et al. in [12]. We call $\mathbf{x}$ and $\mathbf{z}$ the vectors of Boolean variables at the inputs and the outputs of the network that embeds the cluster function $\mathbf{f}$. The functionality of such network is represented by the Boolean function $\mathbf{h}(\mathbf{x})$. We call it the *neighborhood* of $\mathbf{f}$. The inputs of the cluster function can be seen as a function $\mathbf{p}(\mathbf{x})$ of the inputs $\mathbf{x}$. The function $\mathbf{q}(\mathbf{o}, \mathbf{x})$ describes the behavior of the outputs $\mathbf{z}$ when the outputs of the cluster functions are seen as additional primary inputs.

From $\mathbf{h}$, $\mathbf{p}$ and $\mathbf{q}$ we obtain three characteristic functions: $H = \prod_j h_j(\mathbf{x})\overline{\oplus}z_j$, $P = \prod_j p_j(\mathbf{x})\overline{\oplus}i_j$ and $Q = \prod_j q_j(\mathbf{o}, \mathbf{x})\overline{\oplus}z_j$. The characteristic functions fully describe the neighborhood around the multi-output function $\mathbf{f}$. In particular, they enable the computation of a Boolean relation representing the maximum set of *compatible functions* of $\mathbf{f}$, i.e. functions that can implement $\mathbf{f}$ without changing the input-output behavior of $\mathbf{h}$. Watanabe et al. showed that the characteristic function $\mathcal{F}$ of the Boolean relation can be obtained with the following formula [12]:

$$\mathcal{F}(\mathbf{i},\mathbf{o}) = \forall_{\mathbf{x},\mathbf{z}}[(P(\mathbf{x},\mathbf{i}) \cdot Q(\mathbf{o},\mathbf{x},\mathbf{z})) \Rightarrow H(\mathbf{z},\mathbf{x})] \quad (1)$$

In words, $\mathcal{F}$ represents the set of values of $\mathbf{i}$ and $\mathbf{o}$ such that if Q is true and P is true, then H is true for all possible values of $\mathbf{x}$ and $\mathbf{z}$. Formula (1) allows us to find all functions $\mathbf{f}$ that, when composed with $\mathbf{p}$ and $\mathbf{q}$, produce exactly function $\mathbf{h}$. There are generally many functions with this property. These functions are represented by a Boolean relation, and $\mathcal{F}$ is the characteristic function of such relation.

Having shown how $\mathcal{F}$ can be computed when the neighborhood $\mathbf{h}$ is given, we need to clarify how $\mathbf{h}$ is selected. Ideally, we would like to compute $\mathcal{F}$ by considering as $\mathbf{h}$ the entire logic network, from primary inputs to primary outputs. This choice would give us the maximum degrees of freedom for the implementation of the cluster function [12]. Unfortunately this is computationally infeasible but for the smallest networks. Thus, the neighborhood has to be a small subset of the logic network, a "bubble" around the cluster function.

Notice that GM relies on finding a Boolean relation that gives the most degrees of freedom to the chosen cluster. Intuitively, we want to establish a relation between the outputs of $\mathbf{f}$ that gives more degrees of freedom than computing separately their *don't cares*.

Consider a two-output cluster function. To obtain an advantageous Boolean relation, we need to find nodes in the fanout cone and fanin cone of both outputs of $\mathbf{f}$. Intuitively, a common fanout node within the neighborhood is an indication that functionality at the neighborhood outputs is controlled by the interaction of both outputs. Similarly, a common fanin node implies that there is some sharing of information among the inputs of $\mathbf{f}$. If fanin and fanout cones of the components of $\mathbf{f}$ are disjoint, $\mathcal{F}$ represents the same degrees of freedom that can be expressed by *don't cares*. Since we consider clusters starting from MFPs, at least one common fanin exists. To build the neighborhood, we explore the transitive fanout and fanin of the cluster. We control complexity by limiting the search to a given depth.

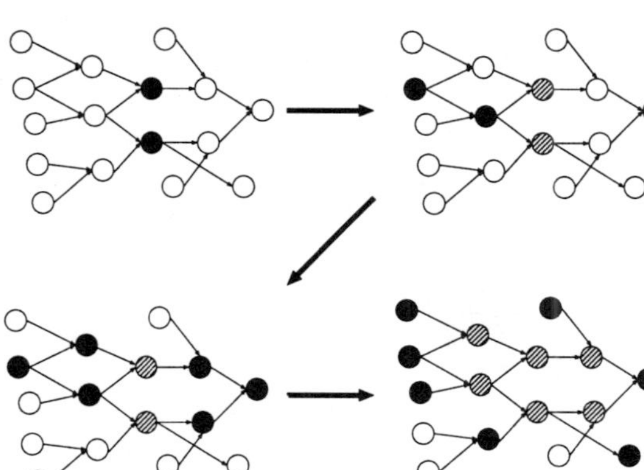

Figure 3: Building the neighborhood of a cluster.

Example 1 We show on Figure 3 how the neighborhood construction algorithm works. The picture represents a portion of a logic network, the vertices being logic gates and the arrows the connections between them. We start from a two-node cluster, marked in black in the top left part of the Figure 3. The parameter depth is set to 2. To build the neighborhood, we first select the reconvergent nodes in the transitive fanout and fanin of the clusters (with depth 2) from the cluster. These nodes are marked in black on the top right. The nodes on paths connecting the cluster with reconvergent nodes are marked in black on the bottom left. Finally, we take the "envelope" of these nodes to get the neighborhood. The neighborhood is the set of nodes marked in black in the bottom right part of Figure 3.

Given the neighborhood, the Boolean relation $\mathcal{F}$ is obtained by Equation 1. We build the BDDs of the Boolean relations P, H, and Q by traversing the neighborhood. $\mathcal{F}$ is then computed using Equation 1. The overall complexity depends on the computation of the relation H. Our neighborhood construction algorithm has been designed to minimize the complexity of the computation of H, while at the same time to obtain a final $\mathcal{F}$ expressing useful degrees of freedom.

3.2 Generalized Matching

The GM problem consists of finding all possible sets of n library cells that can implement one of the functions represented by $\mathcal{F}$ [4]. To accomplish this task we define the concept of *quotient function* $L(\mathbf{i},\mathbf{c})$ for our technology library. The pictorial representation of the quotient function is shown in Figure 4 for a simple library with $N_{lib} = 3$ cells, g_1, g_2 and g_3.

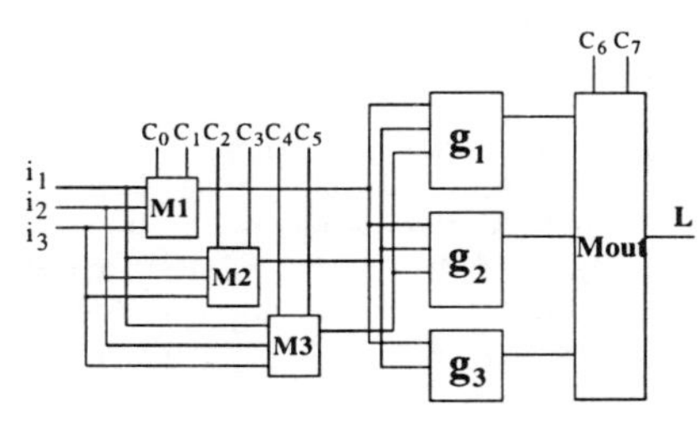

Figure 4: Quotient function of the target library.

In the figure, the blocks $M1$, $M2$, $M3$ and $Mout$ represent multiplexers, with control inputs $\mathbf{c} = [c_0, c_1, ..., c_7]^T$. The first three multiplexers control the input pin assignments. By changing the control inputs we can control how the external inputs are connected to the pins of the cells. Multiplexer $Mout$ controls cell selection: it selects which cell is connected to the output. For the sake of simplicity, we assume single-output library cells (as in Figure 4) in the following treatment. GM is applicable to multi-output cells as well [4].

In order to perform generalized matching, we need to check if a two-output cluster function $\mathbf{f}(\mathbf{i})$ can be replaced by two library cells. Remember that the cluster function and its degrees of freedom are represented by a Boolean relation $\mathcal{F}(\mathbf{i},\mathbf{o})$. We can express GM with a Boolean formula in L and $\mathcal{F}$ [4]:

$$M(\mathbf{c}) = \forall_{\mathbf{i}} \exists_{\mathbf{o}} \left(\mathcal{F}(\mathbf{i},\mathbf{o}) \cdot (L(\mathbf{i},\mathbf{c}_1) \overline{\oplus}\, o_1)(L(\mathbf{i},\mathbf{c}_2) \overline{\oplus}\, o_2)\right) \quad (2)$$

Where $\mathcal{F}$ is the Boolean relation for the cluster, L is the quotient function. Notice that for each output, we have distinct sets of control variables, hence $\mathbf{c} = [\mathbf{c}_1, \mathbf{c}_2]$. This is because each output of $\mathbf{f}$ can be matched by a different cell with different input assignments. $M(\mathbf{c})$ is called *matching function* and can in principle be computed by simply implementing Equation 2 with standard BDD operators.

The ON-set of $M(\mathbf{c})$ denotes all possible assignments of the cluster to two library cells with the property that the new implementation of the cluster function can replace the old one without changing the behavior observed at the neighborhood boundary. In other words, Equation 2 allows us to compute *all* cell selections and input assignments compatible with $\mathcal{F}$. If we replace the pre-existing implementation of **f** with any implementation in the ON-set of M, we are guaranteed that the input-output behavior of **h** is unchanged (more details on this can be found in [4]). Each minterm of $M(\mathbf{c})$ represents a solution. The assignments are easy to analyze, because they correspond to multiplexer selections.

The main practical problem in the computation of $M(\mathbf{c})$ is that, although the BDD representation of $M(\mathbf{c})$ is generally very compact, the same is not true for the intermediate results of the computation in Equation 2. Experimentally, we observed that BDD blowup was very common while computing the conjunction of $\mathcal{F}$ with the quotient functions and while computing the quantifications. We can express the final result, but there's a peak BDD size to overcome. To avoid going up to this peak, we partition the problem. We compute the matching function for each output separately, and use the partitioned solutions to reduce the size of the BDDs in Equation 2 before universal quantification. Notice that the procedure *does not* compromise the global optimality of the final solution. This claim will be clarified in the following discussion.

Again, we discuss the case of two outputs for the sake of simplicity. The matching function of output o_1 can be computed by the following formula:

$$M_1(\mathbf{c}_1) = \forall_{\mathbf{i}} \exists_{\mathbf{o}} \left(\mathcal{F}(\mathbf{i},\mathbf{o}) \cdot (\mathrm{L}(\mathbf{i},\mathbf{c}_1)\overline{\oplus} o_1)\right) \tag{3}$$

The same formula holds for output o_2 (after a change of indices from 1 to 2). Computing M_1 and M_2 separately can be much easier than computing M, because the BDDs have fewer support variables, and only one conjunction has to be computed before quantification. This observation is confirmed in practice. The computation of M_1 and M_2 requires much less memory than the computation of M.

It is easy to see that $M_1(\mathbf{c})$ and $M_2(\mathbf{c})$ are less constrained than $M(\mathbf{c})$: $M_1 \geq M$ and $M_2 \geq M$. $M_1(\mathbf{c})$ expresses all possible matches for output o_1, assuming that o_2 can be implemented by an arbitrary function of the inputs. In general the ON-set of M_1 (M_2) contains solutions that are not valid. All matches of f_1 (f_2) that are admissible only when f_2 (f_1) is a function that cannot be implemented by any cell in the library are in the ON-set of M_1 (M_2) but are *not* in the ON-set of M. A match can be in the ON-set of M only if it is valid for *both* outputs, while a match is in the ON-set of M_1 (M_2) simply if it is valid for f_1 (f_2), no matter what happens to f_2 (f_2). We can use the M_1 and M_2 as conservative bounds for pruning the search space of $M(\mathbf{c})$ because we know that if a value $\mathbf{c}^*$ is not in the ON-set of *both* M_1 *and* M_2, it will be in the OFF-set of M, and we do not need to take it into account when matching M.

The simplest way to exploit this property is to compute the *restriction* of $L(\mathbf{i},\mathbf{c}_1)$ and $L(\mathbf{i},\mathbf{c}_2)$ with respect to $M_1(\mathbf{c}_1)$ and $M_2(\mathbf{c}_2)$, respectively, and then compute M with Equation 2. In other words we can replace $L(\mathbf{i},\mathbf{c}_1)$ in Equation 2 with $L_{res}(\mathbf{i},\mathbf{c}_1)$ defined as follows (the same can be done for $L(\mathbf{i},\mathbf{c}_2)$):

$$L_{res}(\mathbf{i},\mathbf{c}_1) = \begin{cases} L(\mathbf{i},\mathbf{c}_1) & \text{if } M_1(c_1) = 1 \\ \textit{don't care} & \text{otherwise} \end{cases} \tag{4}$$

By computing M_1 and M_2 we prune the search space, and the computation of $M(\mathbf{c})$ is much faster. Notice that we do not make any approximation here. Our bound is conservative, and the matching function is computed exactly: $M(\mathbf{c})$ still gives us all possible assignments for the cluster. This method can be used for more than two input clusters. ,

3.3 Cost Function and Constraints

Until now, we have proposed a solution to the basic GM problem. Now we focus on its useful extension by considering cost functions and constraints. We assume that *area* is the cost function and *timing* is the constraint. Although we have a way to compute all possible legal replacements for **f** , we want get the minimum-area matchings satisfying the timing constraints. Hence, we need to apply a cost function to $M(\mathbf{c})$ and find at least one assignment $\mathbf{c}^*$ minimizing it. Moreover, we need to enforce the satisfaction of the constraints.

Our minimum-cost constrained matching algorithm merges GM with cost minimization and constraint enforcement. We exploit the existence of a previous implementation (since we are re-mapping) and of constraints to obtain *bounds* on the cost function and tight constraints. In this way we drastically prune the search space and further increase computational efficiency, without giving up optimality. We will first describe how bounding can improve the performance of our algorithm, then we will show how to find all minimum area matches, finally we describe how to prune solutions that violate the timing constraints.

It is not necessary to include in the quotient function cells and assignments for which we are certain that the global costs will be higher than that of the original implementation. Additionally, it is useless to express assignments that would violate the timing constraints. These assignments can be suppressed when building the quotient function. When computing $L(\mathbf{i},\mathbf{c}_1)$ and $L(\mathbf{i},\mathbf{c}_2)$, some library cells are not even included, because their area is too large. The area of a cell included in the quotient function must be $A < A_{old} - A_{MIN}$, where A_{old} is the area of the current implementation of **f** and A_{MIN} is the smallest area of any cell in the library.

After M_1 and M_2 have been computed, we can use both area and timing to further reduce the solution space that has to be explored by Equation 2. Consider area first. We call $A_{MIN,1}$ the minimum area of any match in M_1. All matches in M_2 such that area $A_2 \geq A_{old} - A_{MIN,1}$ can be pruned, because the total area of a solution involving them is certainly larger than A_{old}. The same reasoning can be done for M_1, A_1 and $A_{MIN,2}$.

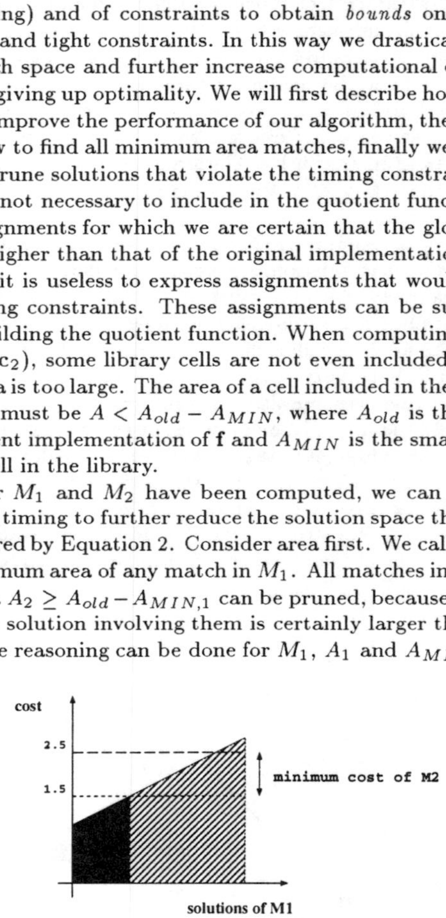

Figure 5: Bound on the partial solutions.

Example 2 Consider the example in Figure 5. The graph shows the cost of all solutions in M_1. The x-axis corresponds to the solutions, and the y-axis to the area cost. The cost 2.5 is the original cost of the cluster (for both outputs) before re-mapping. We assume that the minimum cost for M_2 (not shown) is 1. We can prune all solutions in M_1 that have a higher cost than $2.5 - 1 = 1.5$ without loss of optimality, because these solutions will lead to a higher cost than the original implementation of the cluster. The gray area corresponds to the solutions that we can discard. We keep only the solutions of M_1 in the black area.

For timing, the line of reasoning is similar, but more involved. Although we will discuss timing computation in greater detail, we just observe for now that delays depend on input loads, therefore, when we concurrently match two or more cells, we need to take into account the load that the cells cause on the fanin gates. We call $D_{Bound,2}$ the delay for a match in M_2 (i.e. a cell implementing f_2), assuming that the load caused by the cell implementing f_1 is the minimum among all matches in M_1. If $D_{Bound,2}$ exceeds the timing constraint, the match can be pruned. The same reasoning holds for M_1 and $D_{Bound,1}$.

Notice that both timing and area bounds are conservative and do not prune any match that can improve the current mapping of the cluster. Roughly speaking, we use area and timing to prune solutions in M_1 (M_2) that could not be optimal even if they were coupled to the best possible match in M_2 (M_1). The bounds are very useful in further decreasing the number of candidate matches for M and the efficiency of the computation of Equation 2.

Once $M(\mathbf{c})$ has been computed, we want to find the minimum-area assignment that satisfies the timing constraints. One solution would be to enumerate all the minterms of $M(\mathbf{c})$ and evaluate them for area and timing. This is not acceptable because the number of minterms of M can be large and an enumerative solution would be unacceptably slow.

A more efficient solution is to use ADDs [13] to build symbolically the cost function and the constraints. ADDs are appropriate because they represent in a compact way discrete functions, and they interface seamlessly with BDDs (they have the same structure, the only difference being that leaves can have any value).

To compute minimum-area matching, we build the ADD for the cost function with the same support variables as the BDD for $M(\mathbf{c})$. A path in the ADD leads to a leaf containing the area of the cell identified by the values of control variables encountered on the path. Once the ADD $A(\mathbf{c})$ of the cost function is build, we can compute the *product* with the BDD of the matching function and select the minterm pointing to the minimum value of it (product and minimum selection are standard ADD operators). Since the area of a cell is not affected by input assignment, the support of $A(\mathbf{c})$ contains only variables controlling the cell selection in the quotient function.

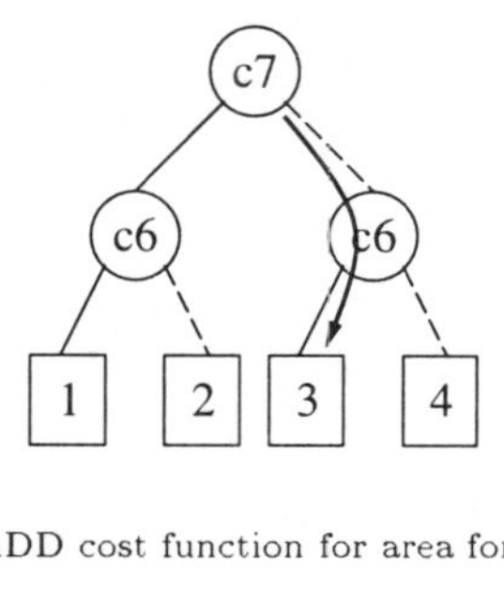

Figure 6: ADD cost function for area for 4 variables

Example 3 Consider a library $L = \{NAND2, AND2, NAND3, AND3\}$ with area costs respectively $\{1, 2, 3, 4\}$. The ADD $A(\mathbf{c})$ of the area cost function for this library is represented in Figure 6. The control variables for cell selection are c_7 and c_6. For instance, $c_6\bar{c_7}$ selects the NAND3 gate. In the ADD of the cost function, we see how the path with c_6 and $\bar{c_7}$ leads to the cost of the NAND3, i.e. 3. Assume that the matching function is $M(\mathbf{c}) = c_0c_1c_2c_3'c_4'c_5c_7$. Taking the minimum of the product $A(\mathbf{c}) \cdot M(\mathbf{c})$ we obtain the value 3, and the value $\mathbf{c}^*$ of the control variables for which $A(\mathbf{c}) \cdot M(\mathbf{c})$ is minimized is $\mathbf{c}^* = c_0c_1c_2c_3'c_4'c_5c_6c_7$.

The cost function for area can be computed once for all. Its number of nodes is very small, it's bounded by $2 \times |N_{lib}|$. All ADD operators involved in the construction of the symbolic representation of the cost function and its minimization over the ON-set of M have complexity $O(|M(\mathbf{c})| \cdot |A(\mathbf{c})|)$. $|M(\mathbf{c})|$ is the number of nodes in the BDD of the matching function, $|A(\mathbf{c})|$ is the number of nodes in the ADD of the cost function. Since usually both $|M(\mathbf{c})|$ and $|A(\mathbf{c})|$ are small (at most in the order of 100 BDD nodes for $|M(\mathbf{c})|$), the computation of the area cost is very fast compared to an enumeration of the minterms of M.

After finding the minimum area matches, the last step of the algorithm is to enforce the timing constraints. Constraints can be manipulated in a symbolic fashion as well. Before describing their ADD-based representation, we describe how timing constraints are computed. For each cluster output, arrival time and required time are computed. We can replace a cluster by an alternative implementation if the new arrival times at *all* cluster outputs do not exceed the required times. For timing constraints, we use the critical path of the circuit as the maximum delay that can exist from the primary inputs to the primary outputs. From this constraint, we compute the arrival and required times for all nodes.

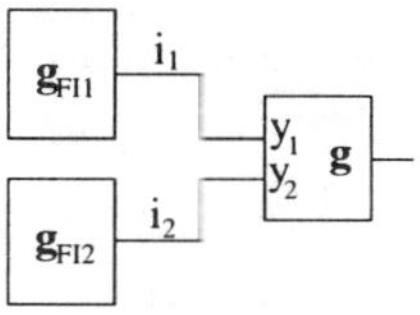

Figure 7: Delay computation for a gate

We use the *real delay model* as in SIS [5]. Consider a gate g with input pins $\mathbf{y} = [y_1, y_2, ..., y_n]^T$ shown in Figure 7. The pins are connected with inputs $\mathbf{i} = [i_1, i_2, ..., i_n]^T$. We assume that pin y_i is connected to input i_i. The arrival time at the output of the gate is:

$$t_{arr} = \max_{i=1,2,...,n} (t_{arr_i} + \alpha \times C_L + \beta_i) \quad (5)$$

α is the effective output resistance of the gate, C_L is the effective load capacitance at the output, and β_i is the pin-dependent intrinsic delay of the gate. Finally, t_{arr_i} is the arrival time at input i_i. It is a function of both i_i and y_i because it depends on the pin of gate g and the fanin gate g_{FIi} driving input i_i:

$$t_{arr_i} = K_i + \eta_i(C_{other_i} + C_{in_i}) \quad (6)$$

η_i is the effective output resistance of the fanin gate g_{FIi}, K_i is the part of t_{arr_i} depending on previous stages (and the intrinsic delay of the fanin gate), C_{other_i} is the load capacitance of the fanin gate that does not depend on g and C_{in_i} is the input load capacitance of pin y_i.

Observe that the arrival time at the output of a gate t_{arr} depends on the input assignment, if we change the assignment of pins to inputs, the arrival time may change for two reasons:

- the arrival time at the inputs t_{arr_i} changes,
- the intrinsic delay β_i changes because it is pin-dependent as well

In the quotient function $L(\mathbf{i}, \mathbf{c})$, input assignments are set by the control variables. The quotient function represents a set of cells and input assignments. Each one of such assignments is characterized by an arrival time to the output of the gate it represents. Hence, t_{arr} for a quotient function is a function of the control variables. In other words, for a cluster output that we want to match we can build the ADD $T_{arr}(\mathbf{c})$ of the arrival time: it represents the arrival time at the output for any input and cell assignment. A value $\mathbf{c}^*$ of the control variables selects a path in $T_{arr}(\mathbf{c})$ that leads to a leaf containing the value of the arrival time at the output when the cell and input assignment corresponding to $\mathbf{c}^*$ are chosen.

The computation of T_{arr} is complicated by the fact that we are concurrently matching a multi-output cluster function using multiple quotient functions. The complication arises when we compute the arrival time t_{arr_i} at the inputs i_i of the cluster. Remember that t_{arr_i} depends on the output resistance and the load capacitance. The gates in the fanin of the cluster are loaded with a capacitance that depends on how the pins of gates in the cluster are connected to them. In symbols: $T_{arr_i}(\mathbf{c}) = K_i + R_i(C_{other,i} + C_i(\mathbf{c}))$, where K_i, R_i and $C_{other,i}$ are constants, while $C_i(\mathbf{c})$ is an ADD representing how the load capacitance on input i changes with the input assignments of the cells in the quotient functions.

It is important to notice that T_{arr_i} depends on the entire $\mathbf{c}$. If we are matching a two-output cluster, T_{arr_i} is an ADD whose support includes both $\mathbf{c}_1$ and $\mathbf{c}_2$ (the control variables of quotient functions L_1 and L_2 in Equation 2). The computation of the arrival time at each output of the cluster is done with the following symbolic formula.

$$T_{arr}(\mathbf{c}) = \max_i(T_{arr_i}(\mathbf{c}) + \alpha(\mathbf{c}) \times C_L + \beta(\mathbf{c})) \quad (7)$$

Where T_{arr_i}, α and β are ADDs in the control variables, and all operators involved in the computation are standard ADD operators. The leaves of T_{arr} contain all possible arrival times for the output.

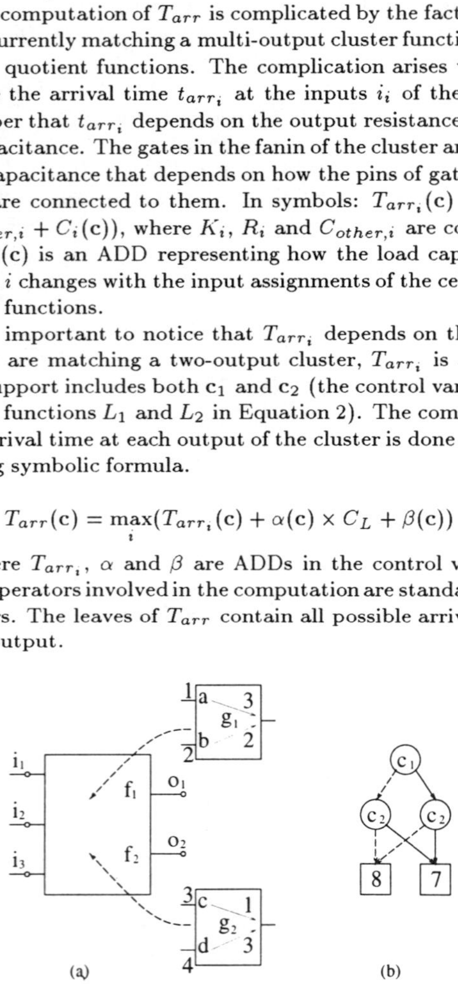

Figure 8: Symbolic representation of timing constraints

Example 4 Consider the situation shown in Figure 8: we want to compute the ADDs $T_{arr}(\mathbf{c})$ for the two outputs of the cluster of Figure 8 (a). We make several simplifying assumption for the sake of clarity. First, we assume that $K_i = 0$ and $C_{other_i} = 0$ for all inputs. The driving resistances have the same value for all inputs $\eta_i = 1$ and the load on o_1 and o_2 is null. Second, we assume that f_1 can be matched only by cell g_1 and f_2 can be matched only by cell g_2. The input loads and intrinsic propagation delays for the cells are shown in Figure 8 (a). Moreover, we assume that g_2 can be connected only to inputs i_2 and i_3, while we can connect the input pins of g_1 to i_1 and i_2. The connection of both pins of a cell to the same input is not allowed.

With these simplifying assumptions, we just need two control variables to express the degrees of freedom in the input assignments. Control variable c_1 controls the connection of g_1: $c_1 = 0$ means that pin a is connected with input i_1 and pin b is connected with input i_2. The opposite connection is chosen when $c_1 = 1$. Similarly, when $c_2 = 0$, pin c is connected with input i_2 and pin d is connected with input i_3.

Assume for example $c_1 = 0$, $c_2 = 0$. The arrival times at the inputs are $T_{arr_1}(0,0) = C_{in_1}(0,0) = 1$, $T_{arr_2}(0,0) = C_{in_2}(0,0) = 2 + 3 = 5$, $T_{arr_3}(0,0) = C_{in_3}(0,0) = 4$. For output o_1 the arrival time is $T_{arr}(0,0) = max\{(3+1),(2+5)\} = 7$ this is one leaf of the ADD $T_{arr}(c_1, c_2)$ representing the arrival time at o_1 for every combination of control variables. The complete ADD is shown in Figure 8 (b).

The algorithm for the computation of the constraint ADD is quite involved and it is not described for space reasons. The ADD of timing constraints is used to prune the matching function. This is done three times during GM. The first two times the timing constraint ADDs for M_1 and M_2 are computed and used for bounding, as discussed at the beginning of this subsection. The last time, after M has been computed, with the purpose of eliminating infeasible solutions.

3.4 The Complete Matching Algorithm

Having described all sub-tasks involved in performing minimum-cost constrained matching, we conclude our analysis by describing the complete matching algorithm. The pseudo-code of the algorithm for minimum-area matching under timing constraints is shown in Figure 9.

```
ComputeBRelOptimize(clusterF, Network)
  neighborhood = ComputeNeighborhood(clusterF, Network)
  bdd_rel = make boolean relation (neighborhood, clusterF)
  c = compute control variables according size of clusterF
  bdd_quot = compute_quotient_function_with_area_bounds( c )
  /* pass of matching output per output */
  foreach (o ∈ outputs (clusterF))
     bdd_m_only[o] = matching_func (o, bdd_quot);
  /* bounding with area and timing constraints */
  foreach (o ∈ outputs (clusterF))
     bdd_m_only[o] = bound_with_area (clusterF, bdd_m_only[]);
     bdd_m_only[o] = bound_with_timing_constraint (clusterF, bdd_m_only)
     if (bdd_m_only[o] == NIL)
       return (NIL);
     bdd_red_quot[o] = compress_quotient_function (bdd_quot, bdd_m_only[o])
  }
  bdd_m = matching_func (clusterF, bdd_red_quot[])
  bdd_m = timing_constr (bdd_m)
  bdd_best = get_best_area (bdd_m, add_area)
  /* In the case of one the three function fails:
  no match, or violation of the timing, or no best area
  than the current implementation */
  if (bdd_best == NIL)
     return (NIL);
  /* Puts the bdd_best in "readable" form, i.e. returns in best_match
  the cell number and the pin connections rather than a bdd */
  best_match = analyze_best_minterm (bdd_best)
  return (best_match);
```

Figure 9: Algorithm of the matching step

The algorithms first finds the neighborhood of the cluster function, and computes the Boolean relation `bdd_rel`, as seen in Subsection 3.1. Then the quotient functions are constructed disregarding the library cells whose area cannot improve the current solution, as seen in Subsection 3.3. The single-output matching functions are then computed by `matching_func`, and pruned using area bounds and timing constraints, as discussed in the second part of Subsection 3.3. The quotient functions are then compressed using the conservative bounds and the new smaller `bdd_red_quot` are used for performing full generalized matching on the reduced search space.

The resulting matching function is then pruned using timing constraints: in function `timing_constr` all solutions violating the constraint are eliminated. Finally, the cost function is applied and the subset of the ON-set of $M(\mathbf{c})$ containing minimum-cost solutions is obtained. The matching algorithm then "decodes" one of the minimum solutions and returns the cells and the input assignments for replacement. NIL is returned if there are no solutions improving the current mapping of the cluster.

Several performance-enhancing features complicate the algorithm. What is shown in Figure 9 is a simplified version. For example, caching of previous ADD and BDD computations is heavily exploited (not only the simple caching mechanisms provided by BDD packages), an advanced algorithm has been implemented for the compression of $M(\mathbf{c})$ after bounding and several corner conditions are flagged to speedup the computation of trivial cases.

4 Results

We have implemented a post-mapping optimization tool based on generalized matching. The tool reads a mapped circuit described in `blif` (or `slif`) and a library file, and runs the optimization. Several user-controlled parameters can be specified. The depth of the neighborhood can range from 0 to infinity. Specifying a depth of 0 reduces the neighborhood to the cluster, while depth of infinity means that the entire logic network is taken as neighborhood. The latter choice is of course only conceivable for small circuits.

The number of outputs of a cluster can be also controlled. We made experiments with up to four outputs. The number of inputs $\mathbf{i}$ of a cluster can be controlled as well. Usually they are assumed to be the inputs of the cells implementing the cluster in the original mapped netlist. However, additional input can be added taken from nodes in the neighborhood. With this simple modification, we can exploit the power of generalized matching to perform local re-wiring.

We can also change the cluster selection algorithm to select arbitrary sets of nodes as clusters. Experimentally, we observed that this is much less effective than starting from multiple fanout points, mainly because traditional logic optimization is already effective on fanout-free cones.

A generic cost function has to be a function returning an ADD which support are the control variables and leaves are the cost values. Of course, a new bounding function may be integrated with the new cost function. All the experimental statements in this paper rely on the fact that we can easily tune cost functions and bounds.

Memory optimization is the primary concern in the implementation. The tools uses the `Cudd` BDD package [14] which provides a rich set of operators on BDDs and ADDs and powerful memory management and caching features. We set up a memory limit of 1,000,000 BDD and ADD nodes. When this limit is reached, the matching function exits with the value `NIL` and the traversal continues. When the BDDs exceed the memory limit the program simply frees the memory and moves on.

Extensive tests demonstrated that bounding is necessary and effective. Without any bounding, the memory threshold is often reached when the number of inputs of the cluster is greater than 8. With bounding, we are below the threshold for up to 12 inputs. The compression of the matching functions using single-output matching as a conservative bound is probably the most useful algorithmic optimization. The size of the uncompressed quotient functions makes very difficult even to match two-output clusters, but the algorithm using separate matching and compression greatly increases the percentage of matchings that can be successfully carried out.

By using the aforementioned optimization, two-output matching can always be carried out, whereas three-output and four-output matching succeed in 60% and 40% of the cases respectively. For clusters with four or more outputs, memory blowup is too frequent to be acceptable. In order to improve the chances of success for for three or four outputs, we implemented tighter bounds that allow further compression of the quotient functions, but imply the loss of some potentially advantageous matches. We do not describe the implementation of such aggressive bounds for space limitations.

The BDD variable ordering has been set after extensive experimentation. We use a fixed variable order that minimizes the BDD peak size, regardless the intermediate results size. The order is the following. The control variables of the input multiplexers in the quotient function pin are at the bottom, preceded by the input variables, the output variables and the library selection variables. Different orders lead to BDD blowup with high probability. For this reason automatic reordering is not a good solution, because it can destroy the good ordering to reduce the size of intermediate results and it often cannot recover it when the peak is reached.

We have experimented our tool with a set of combinational MCNC benchmarks [15] including all larger ones. The benchmarks were first optimized with SIS [5] for minimum delay with area recovery, with script `script.delay` followed by the mapping command `map -n 1 -AFG`.

Our tool was run with the same parameter settings on all benchmarks, in an effort to demonstrate robustness and generality. We ran the matching algorithm on clusters of two outputs, with the neighborhood search limited to a depth of 3. We used a library based on an industrial technology file, with 75 cells, with up to five inputs. The number of inputs of the cluster was limited to 10.

We show in Table 1 the results on all the MCNC benchmarks for speed, area and power optimization. The starting point was the same for all optimizations, namely, the circuits mapped by SIS. The table gives for each benchmark the number of instances, the percentage gain and the run time in minutes (on SPARC20 with 256 Mb of memory) for each kind of optimization. The last line gives the average gain for each optimization. In the average, the gain is weighted by the size of the circuit.

We observe an average gain of 6% in speed, 13.7% in area and more than 22.3% in power. For area and power optimization, the critical path of the circuit has been constrained to remain the same as the original circuit: no trade off has been allowed between the delay constraint and the (area/power) cost function.

When looking at the results on a benchmark-by-benchmark basis, we observe that the quality of the optimization achieved is consistent when the cost function is changed. This phenomenon can be explained by the fact that some benchmarks have many MFPs and reconvergent fanout cones. Both these characteristics increase the effectiveness of our optimization tool. Notice also that very good improvements are obtained for the larger benchmarks. We conjecture that the global optimization of SIS is less efficient for large benchmarks, and re-mapping can recover a big fraction of the optimality loss.

The run times of the re-mapping tool are shorter (but of the same order) than those spent by SIS in technology independent and technology dependent optimization. Most of the time is spent in building the matching function and in universal quantification of the variables. The average time of a single match is in the order of the tenth of a second with this machine configuration. The percentage of successful matches, i.e., matches that find a better solution, range from 5% to 10%.

Table 2 provides detailed information on the trade-off involved in the optimization process. The first column contains the benchmark name. The second and the third columns give the percentage change (positive if gain, negative if loss) in area and power respectively when doing unconstrained delay optimization. The fourth column gives the percentage change in power for area optimization (no change is allowed in speed). The last column gives the change in area doing power optimization (again, speed is the constraint and no tradeoff are allowed with it).

We observe that delay optimization leaves area and power almost unchanged. This result is intuitive, since delay optimization focuses only on the critical path, which is a usually a small fraction of the entire circuits. Only few benchmarks have an increase in area or power, and for these two benchmarks the delay is only marginally reduced. We observe also that, in general area in not traded off for power and vice versa. In general area decreases when doing power optimization, and power decreases when doing area optimization. This is expected, since power is in first approximation the product between area and switching activity, hence it is related to area.

Bench	gates	speed		area		power	
		%	CPU	%	CPU	%	CPU
z4ml	48	1.97	2	4.35	1	13.24	1
b9	110	7.04	5	6.95	7	15.50	5
term1	179	0.47	12	8.42	27	14.12	26
C432	181	2.69	11	6.60	14	13.35	27
9symml	204	3.72	17	9.18	18	21.80	12
alu2	347	4.15	31	11.68	29	18.96	87
x4	364	1.36	5	4.29	10	15.98	10
C499	365	20.76	31	25.96	69	32.04	10
C880	377	6.34	45	6.59	29	12.42	64
C1908	508	5.48	46	14.68	88	15.88	54
C1355	524	6.48	89	16.97	15	15.77	53
too_large	573	1.22	21	5.31	37	16.03	27
x3	639	1.04	11	5.39	20	12.53	23
rot	671	2.18	30	7.81	31	14.22	22
apex6	691	3.84	33	4.19	24	13.63	30
alu4	697	6.66	72	8.58	45	16.15	149
frg2	774	5.78	24	8.47	25	21.53	29
vda	781	10.59	41	21.25	104	34.78	108
t481	863	4.39	40	10.42	64	22.75	51
C2670	943	1.39	46	10.85	111	14.69	40
dalu	966	1.96	24	7.30	76	20.28	75
k2	1212	4.88	45	6.04	117	10.33	142
C3540	1344	5.54	92	11.15	142	19.20	156
pair	1480	3.70	64	5.88	96	18.48	74
C5315	2039	9.61	218	8.74	271	13.43	187
des	3621	5.06	241	5.05	289	12.54	495
C7552	3716	9.45	306	29.55	417	38.14	268
C6288	4373	9.23	341	24.79	557	31.85	279
Total		6.05		13.71		22.39	

Table 1: Results on MCNC benchmarks.

5 Conclusions

In this paper we proposed a re-mapping approach that exploits the power of Boolean relations to optimize a mapped netlist under tight constraints. Our main objective is to build a powerful, robust and efficient optimization tool that can be applied to large circuits. We have presented the theoretical foundation of our approach and several algorithmic improvements that are needed to achieve the targeted robustness and speed. We tested the effectiveness of our approach on a large set of benchmarks. The results show that our optimization tool can reduce the area by more than 13.7% in average or reduce power by more than 22.3% without any speed penalty. Unconstrained speed optimization is effective as well (more than 6% average speed improvement is achieved). The optimization is performed starting from mapped circuits that have been optimized using traditional technology-independent and technology-dependent techniques. Hence, our tool has general applicability.

Bench	timing opt		area opt	power opt
	power	area	power	area
z4ml	2.22	3.30	11.50	0.40
b9	3.28	4.57	5.38	4.01
term1	0.14	0.51	5.28	2.08
C432	0.71	-0.48	-5.46	2.89
9symml	-0.84	0.40	10.48	5.04
alu2	1.35	2.69	9.63	6.27
x4	-0.09	0.00	11.66	2.27
C499	5.85	13.59	12.81	12.68
C880	0.60	1.06	-7.25	2.74
C1908	0.54	3.57	-5.67	3.34
C1355	4.06	5.06	12.14	10.78
too_large	0.18	0.41	3.91	1.03
x3	0.07	0.07	0.34	1.14
rot	0.27	0.35	1.72	3.90
apex6	0.35	0.17	1.68	0.62
alu4	1.36	2.39	6.29	4.74
frg2	0.87	1.28	17.18	4.41
vda	0.65	2.15	25.39	12.22
t481	0.76	2.40	10.15	5.03
C2670	0.39	0.36	-1.82	3.76
dalu	0.14	0.12	9.22	2.36
k2	0.40	1.55	-1.95	-2.00
C3540	1.50	2.38	6.35	4.54
pair	0.30	0.84	2.32	1.22
C5315	0.37	0.69	-9.80	0.92
des	0.29	1.02	4.98	2.20
C7552	0.69	0.94	27.67	20.19
C6288	6.70	7.27	17.53	14.73
Total	1.60	2.32	9.70	7.05

Table 2: Trade offs in optimizations.

References

[1] F. Somenzi et al., "Minimization of Boolean relations," in *ISCAS*, pp. 738–473, 1989.

[2] R. Brayton et al., "Multilevel logic synthesis," *IEEE Proceedings*, vol. 78, pp. 264–300, 1990.

[3] H. Savoj et al., "Extracting local don't cares for network optimization," in *ICCAD*, pp. 514–517, 1991.

[4] L. Benini et al., 'A survey of Boolean matching techniques for library binding," *TODAES*, vol. 2, n. 3, 1997.

[5] E. Sentovich et al., "Sequential Circuits Design Using Synthesis and Optimization," in *ICCD*, pp. 328-333, 1992.

[6] G. De Micheli. *Synthesis and optimization of digital circuits.* McGraw-Hill, 1994.

[7] K. Cheng et al., "Multi-level logic optimization by redundancy addition and removal," in *Euro-DAC*, pp. 373–377, 1993.

[8] W. Kunz et al., "Multi-level logic optimization by implication analysis," in *ICCAD*, pp. 6–13, 1994.

[9] B. Rohfleisch et al., "Logic clause analysis for delay optimization," in *DAC*, pp. 668–672, 1995.

[10] S. Chang et al., "Fast Boolean optimization by rewiring," in *ICCAD*, pp. 262–269, 1996.

[11] K. Keutzer, "DAGON: technology binding and local optimization by DAG matching," in *DAC*, pp. 341–347, 1987.

[12] Y. Watanabe et al., "Permissible functions for multioutput components in combinational logic optimization," *IEEE TCAD ICAS*, vol. 15, no. 7, pp. 734–744, 1996.

[13] R. Bahar et al., "Algebraic Decision Diagrams and their Applications," in *ICCAD*, pp. 188-191, 1993.

[14] F. Somenzi. *The CUDD package User's guide. Version 1.0.5* 1995.

[15] S. Yang, "Logic Synthesis and Optimization Benchmarks User Guide Version 3.0," *Tech. Rep. MCNC*, 1991.

[16] P. Vuillod et al., "Re-mapping for low power under tight timing constraints," *ISLPED*, 1997.

SESSION 1B

OPTIMIZATION AND SYNTHESIS FOR REACTIVE SYSTEMS

Moderators:

Rolf Ernst, Technical University Braunschweig,

Braunschweig, Germany

Charles Rosenthal, CWR-Engineering Consultants,

Portland, OR

Decomposition of Timed Decision Tables and its Use in Presynthesis Optimizations

Jian Li
Department of Computer Science
University of Illinois, Urbana-Champaign
Urbana, Illinois 61801

Rajesh K. Gupta
Information & Computer Science
University of California, Irvine
Irvine, California 92697

Abstract – *Presynthesis optimizations transform a behavioral HDL description into an optimized HDL description that results in improved synthesis results. In this paper we introduce the decomposition of Timed Decision Tables (TDT), a tabular model of system behavior. The TDT decomposition is based on the kernel extraction algorithm. By experimenting using named benchmarks, we demonstrate how TDT decomposition can be used in presynthesis optimizations.*

1 Introduction

Presynthesis optimizations have been introduced in [1] as source-level transformations that produce "better" HDL descriptions. For instance, these transformations are used to reduce control-flow redundancies and make synthesis result relatively insensitive to the HDL coding-style. They are also used to reduce resource requirements in the synthesized circuits by increasing component sharing at the behavior-level [2].

The TDT representation consists of a main table holding a set of rules (similar to the specification in a FSMD [3]), an auxiliary table which specifies concurrencies, data dependencies, and serialization relations among data-path computations, or *actions*, and a delay table which specifies the execution delay of each action.

The rule section of the model is based on the notions of *condition* and *action*. A condition may be the presence of an input, or the outcome of a test condition. A conjunction of several conditions defines a *rule*. A decision table is a collection of rules that map condition conjunctions into sets of actions. Actions include logic, arithmetic, input-output(IO), and message-passing operations. We associate an execution delay with each action. Actions are grouped into action sets, or compound actions. With each action set, we associate a concurrency type of *serial*, *parallel*, or *data-parallel* [4]. The structure of the rule section can be found in [1]

In additional to the set of rules specified in a main table (the rule section), the TDT representation includes two auxiliary tables to hold additional information about the execution delay of each action, serialization, data dependency, and concurrency type between each pair of actions.

Example 1.1. Consider the following TDT:

c_1	Y	Y	N	
c_2	Y	N	X	**delay**
$a_{1,1}$	1	0	0	1
$a_{1,2}$	1	0	0	3
$a_{2,1}$	0	1	0	4
$a_{2,2}$	0	1	0	2
$a_{3,1}$	0	0	1	6
$a_{3,2}$	0	0	1	1

	$a_{1,1}$	$a_{1,2}$	$a_{2,1}$	$a_{2,2}$	$a_{3,1}$	$a_{3,2}$
$a_{1,1}$		s				
$a_{1,2}$						
$a_{2,1}$				d		
$a_{2,2}$						
$a_{3,1}$						p
$a_{3,2}$						

An 'X' in the condition column indicates a Don't Care associated with the particular condition. When c_1 = 'Y' and c_2 = 'Y', actions $a_{1,1}$ and $a_{1,2}$ are selected for execution. Since action $a_{1,2}$ is specified as a successor of $a_{1,1}$, action $a_{1,1}$ is executed with a one cycle delay followed by the execution of $a_{1,2}$. Symbols 'd' and 'p' indicate actions that are data-parallel and parallel actions respectively. □

The execution of a TDT consists of two steps: (1) select a rule to apply, (2) execute the action sets that the selected rule maps to. More than two action sets may be selected for execution. The order in which to execute those action sets are determined by the concurrency types, serialization relations, and data dependencies specified among those action sets [4], indicated by 's', 'd', and 'p' in the table above. An action in a TDT may be another TDT. This is referred to as a *call* to the TDT contained as an action in the calling TDT.

Example 1.2. Consider the following calling hierarchy:

TDT_1

c_1	Y	N
a_1	1	0
TDT_2	0	1

TDT_2

c_2	Y	N
a_2	1	0
a_3	0	1

1092-3152/97 $10.00 © 1997 IEEE

When c_1 = 'N' the action needs to be invoked is the call to TDT_2, forces evaluation of condition c_2 resulting in actions a_2 or a_3 being executed. No additional information such as concurrency types needs to be specified between action a_1 and TDT_2 since they lie on different control paths. □

Procedure/function calling hierarchy in input HDL descriptions results in a corresponding TDT hierarchy. TDTs in a calling hierarchy are typically merged to increase the scope of presynthesis optimizations. Merging flattens the calling hierarchy specified in original HDL descriptions. In this paper we present TDT decomposition which is the reverse of the merging process. By first flattening the calling hierarchy and then extracting the commonalities, we may find a more efficient behavior representation which leads to improved synthesis results. This allows us to restructure HDL code. In this paper, we introduce HDL code-restructuring using TDT merging and decomposition transformations. This optimization belongs to a group of presynthesis optimizations such as column/row reduction and action sharing that have been presented earlier [1, 4, 2].

This paper is organized as follows. The next section introduces the notion of TDT decomposition and relates it to the problem of kernel extraction in an algebraic representation of TDTs. Section 3 presents an algorithm for TDT decomposition based on kernel extraction. Section 4 shows the implementation details of the algorithm and presents the experimental results. Finally, Section 5 concludes and presents our future plan.

2 TDT Decomposition

TDT decomposition is the process of replacing a flattened TDT with a hierarchical TDT that represents an equivalent behavior. As we mentioned earlier, decomposition is the reverse process of merging and together with merging, it allows us to produce HDL descriptions that are optimized for subsequent synthesis tasks and are relatively insensitive to coding styles. Since this decomposition uses procedure calling abstraction, arbitrary partitions of the table (condition/action) matrices are not useful.

Example 2.1. Consider the following TDT.

c_1	Y	Y	Y	Y	Y	Y	Y	Y	N	N	N	N
c_2	Y	Y	Y	N	N	N	N	N				
c_3				Y	Y	Y	Y	N				
c_4	Y	N	N									
c_5		Y	N									
c_6				Y	Y	N	N		Y	Y	N	N
c_7				Y	N	Y	N		Y	N	Y	N
a_1	1	1	1					1	1	1	1	1
a_2	1	1	1	1	1	1	1		1	1	1	1
a_3	1		1									
a_4	1											
a_5	1	1										
a_6				1		1			1		1	
a_7				1	1	1			1	1	1	
a_8				1	1		1		1	1		1
a_9								1				

Notice the common patterns in condition rows in c_6 and c_7, and action rows in a_6, a_7, and a_8. □

Above in Example 2.1 is a flattened TDT. The first three columns have identical condition entries in c_1 and c_2, and identical action entries in a_1 and a_2. These columns differ in rows corresponding to conditions $\{c_4, c_5\}$ and actions $\{a_3, a_4, a_5\}$, which appear only in the first three columns. This may result, for example, from merging a sub-TDT consisting of only conditions $\{c_4, c_5\}$ and actions $\{a_3, a_4, a_5\}$.

Figure 1 shows a hierarchy of TDTs which specify the same behavior as Example 2.1. The equivalence can be verified by merging the hierarchy of TDTs [4]. Note that the conditions and actions are partitioned among these TDTs.

TDT_1:

c_1	Y	Y	Y	N
c_2	Y	N	N	
c_3		Y	N	
a_1	1		1	1
a_2	1	1		1
TDT_2	1			
TDT_3		1		1
a_9			1	

TDT_2:

c_4	Y	N	N
c_5		Y	N
a_3	1		1
a_4	1		
a_5	1	1	

TDT_3:

c_6	Y	Y	N	N
c_7	Y	N	Y	N
a_6	1		1	
a_7	1	1	1	
a_8	1	1		1

Figure 1: One possible decomposition of the TDT in Example 2.1.

The commonality in the flattened TDT may not result from multiple calls to a procedure as indicated by TDT_3 in Figure 1. It could also be a result of commonality in the input HDL specification. If this is the case, extraction will lead to a size reduction in the synthesized circuit.

It is not always possible to decompose a given TDT into a hierarchical TDT as shown in Figure 1 above. Neither is it always valid to merge the TDT hierarchy into flattened TDT [4]. These two transformations are valid only when the specified concurrency types, data dependencies, and serializations are preserved. In this particular example, we assume that the order of execution of all actions follows the order in which they appear in the condition stub. For the transformations to be valid, in this particular example, we also note that the actions a_1 and a_2 do not modify conditions in called TDTs namely c_4 through c_7.

The structural requirements for TDT decomposition can be efficiently captured by a two-level algebraic representation of TDTs [2]. This representation only captures the control dependencies in action sets and hence is strictly a sub set of TDT information. We also restrict the TDT model to only limited-entry forms, one where actions matrix is a Boolean matrix. The utility of this form has been demonstrated earlier with respect to modeling of exception conditions [4]. For each condition variable c, we define a positive condition literal, denoted as l_c, which corresponds to an 'Y' value in a condition entry. We also define a negative condition literal, denoted as $l_{\bar{c}}$, which corresponds to an 'N' value in a condition entry.

We define a '·' operator between two action literals and two conditions literals which represents a conjunction operation. This operation is both commutative and associative [4].

A TDT is a set of rules, each of which consists of a condition part which determines when the rule is selected, and an action part which lists the actions to be executed once a rule is selected for execution. The condition part of a rule is represented as

$$\prod_{ce(i)\neq 'X';\ i=1,ncond} \kappa_i \tag{1}$$

$$\kappa_i = \begin{cases} l_{c_i}, \text{when } ce(i) = \text{'Y'} \\ l_{\bar{c}_i}, \text{when } ce(i) = \text{'N'} \end{cases}$$

where $ncond$ is the number of conditions in the TDT and $ce(i)$ is the condition entry value at the ith condition row for this rule. The action part of a rule is represented as

$$\prod_{ae(i)\neq '0';\ i=1,nact} l_{a_i} \tag{2}$$

where $nact$ is the number of actions in the TDT and $ae(i)$ is the action entry value at the ith action row for this rule. A rule is a tuple, denoted by

$$(\mathcal{K} : \alpha)$$

As will become clear later, for the purpose of TDT decomposition a rule can be expressed as a product of corresponding action and condition literals. We call such a product a *cube*. For a given TDT, T, we define an algebraic expression, E_T, that consists of disjunction of cubes corresponding to rules in T.

For simplicity, we can drop the '·' operator and ':' denotation and use 'c' or 'a' instead of l_c and l_a in the algebraic expressions of TDTs. These symbols follow only algebraic laws for symbolic computation. For treatment of this algebra, the reader is referred to [4].

Example 2.2. Here is the algebraic expression for the TDT in Example 2.1.

$$\begin{aligned} & E_{TDT\ 2.1} \\ = \quad & c_1c_2c_4a_1a_2a_3a_4a_5 + c_1c_2\bar{c}_4c_5a_1a_2a_5 \\ + \quad & c_1c_2\bar{c}_4\bar{c}_5a_1a_2a_3 + c_1\bar{c}_2c_3c_6c_7a_2a_6a_7a_8 \\ + \quad & c_1\bar{c}_2c_3c_6\bar{c}_7a_2a_7a_8 + c_1\bar{c}_2c_3\bar{c}_6c_7a_2a_6a_7 \\ + \quad & c_1\bar{c}_2c_3\bar{c}_6\bar{c}_7a_2a_8 + c_1\bar{c}_2\bar{c}_3a_1a_9 \\ + \quad & \bar{c}_1c_6c_7a_1a_2a_6a_7a_8 + \bar{c}_1c_6\bar{c}_7a_1a_2a_7a_8 \\ + \quad & \bar{c}_1\bar{c}_6c_7a_1a_2a_6a_7 + \bar{c}_1\bar{c}_6\bar{c}_7a_1a_2a_8 \end{aligned}$$

Note that there is no specification on delay, concurrency type, serialization relation, and data dependency. Also notice that 'c', '$\bar{c}$', and 'a' are short-hand notations for 'l_c', '$l_{\bar{c}}$', 'l_a' respectively. □

2.1 Kernel Extraction

During TDT decomposition, it is important to keep an action literal or condition literal within one sub-TDT, that is, the decomposed TDTs must partition the condition and action literals. To capture this, we introduce the notion of *TDT support*.

Definition 2.1 The **TDT-support** of an expression E_T is the set of action literals in E_T and positive condition literals corresponding to condition literals that appear in E_T.

Example 2.3. Expression $c_1\bar{c}_2c_3\bar{c}_6\bar{c}_7a_2a_8$ is a cube. Its TDT support is $\{c_1, c_2, c_3, c_6, c_7, a_1, a_8\}$. □

We consider here TDT decompositions into sub-TDTs that have disjoint TDT-supports. TDT decomposition uses algebraic division of TDT-expressions to identify sub TDTs. We define the algebraic division as follows:

Definition 2.2 Let $\{f_{dvnd}, f_{dvsr}, f_{quot}, f_{rem}\}$ be algebraic expressions. We say that f_{dvsr} is an **algebraic divisor** of f_{dvsr} when we have $f_{dvnd} = f_{dvsr} \cdot f_{quot} + f_{rem}$, the TDT-support of f_{dvsr} and the TDT-support of f_{quot} are disjoint, and $f_{dvsr} \cdot f_{quot}$ is non-empty.

An algebraic divisor is called a *factor* when the remainder is void. An expression is said to be *cube free* when it cannot be factored by a cube.

Definition 2.3 A **kernel** of an expression is a cube-free quotient of the expression divided by a cube, which is called the **co-kernel** of the expression.

Example 2.4. Rewrite the algebraic form of $TDT_{Example\ 2.1}$ as follows.

$$\begin{aligned} & E_{TDT2.1} \\ = \quad & c_1c_2a_1a_2(c_4a_3a_4a_5 + \bar{c}_4c_5a_5 + \bar{c}_4\bar{c}_5a_3) \\ + \quad & c_1\bar{c}_2c_3a_2(c_6c_7a_6a_7a_8 + c_6\bar{c}_7a_7a_8 + \bar{c}_6c_7a_6a_7 + \bar{c}_6\bar{c}_7a_8) \\ + \quad & c_1\bar{c}_2\bar{c}_3a_1a_9 \\ + \quad & \bar{c}_1a_1a_2(c_6c_7a_6a_7a_8 + c_6\bar{c}_7a_7a_8 + \bar{c}_6c_7a_6a_7 + \bar{c}_6\bar{c}_7a_8) \end{aligned}$$

The expression $c_4a_3a_4a_5 + \bar{c}_4c_5a_5 + \bar{c}_4\bar{c}_5a_3$ is a kernel of $TDT_{Example\ 2.1}$ with a corresponding co-kernel $c_1c_2a_1a_2$. Similarly, $c_6c_7a_6a_7a_8 + c_6\bar{c}_7a_7a_8 + \bar{c}_6c_7a_6a_7 + \bar{c}_6\bar{c}_7a_8$ is also a kernel of $TDT_{Example\ 2.1}$, with two corresponding co-kernels: $c_1\bar{c}_2c_3a_2$ and $\bar{c}_1a_1a_2$. □

3 Algorithm for TDT Decomposition

This section presents an algorithm for TDT decomposition. The core of the algorithm is similar to the techniques used in multi-level logic optimization. Therefore we first discuss how to compute algebraic kernels from TDT-expressions before we show the complete algorithm which calls the kernel computing core and addresses some important issues such as preserving data-dependencies between actions through TDT decomposition.

3.1 Algorithms for Kernel Extraction

A naive way to compute the kernels of an expression is to divide it by the cubes corresponding to the power set of its support set. The quotients that are not cube free are weeded out, and the others are saved in the kernel set [5]. This procedure can be improved in two ways: (1) by introducing a recursive procedure that exploits the property that a kernel of a kernel of an expression is also the kernel of this expression, (2) by reducing the search by exploiting the commutativity of the '$\cdot$' operator. Algorithm 3.1 shows a method adapted from a kernel extraction algorithm due to Brayton and McMullen [6], which takes into account the above two properties to reduce computational complexity.

Algorithm 3.1 A Recursive Procedure Used in Kernel Extraction

INPUT: a TDT expression e, a recursion index j;
OUTPUT: the set of kernels of TDT expression e;
extractKernelR(e, j) {
  $K = 0$;
  for $i = j$ to n **do**
    if ($|$ getCubeSet$(e, l_i)| \geq 2$) **then**
      C = largest cube set containing l_i s.t.
        getCubeSet(e, C) = getCubeSet(e, l_i);
      if ($l_k \notin C \ \forall k < i$) **then**
        $K = K \cup extractKernelR(e/e^C, i+1)$
  endfor
  $K = K \cup e$;
  return(K);
}

In the above algorithm, *getCubeSet*(e, C) returns the set of cubes of e whose support includes C. We order the literals so that condition literals appear before action literals. We use n as the index of the last condition literal since a co-kernel containing only action literals does not correspond a valid TDT decomposition. Notice that l_c and $l_{\bar{c}}$ are two different literals as we explained earlier. The algorithm is applicable to cube-free expressions. Thus, either the function e is cube-free or it is made so by dividing it by its largest cube factor, determined by the intersection of the support sets of all its cubes.

Example 3.1. After running Algorithm 3.1 on the algebraic expression of $TDT_{2.1}$ we get the following kernels:

$$
\begin{aligned}
k_1 &= E_{TDT\ 2.1};\\
k_2 &= c_2a_1a_2c_4a_3a_4a_5 + c_2a_1a_2\bar{c}_4c_5a_5 + c_2a_1a_2\bar{c}_4\bar{c}_5a_3\\
&+ \bar{c}_2c_3a_2c_6c_7a_6a_7a_8 + \bar{c}_2c_3a_2c_6\bar{c}_7a_7a_8 + \bar{c}_2c_3a_2\bar{c}_6c_7a_6a_7\\
&+ \bar{c}_2c_3a_2\bar{c}_6\bar{c}_7a_8;\\
k_3 &= c_4a_3a_4a_5 + \bar{c}_4c_5a_5 + \bar{c}_4\bar{c}_5a_3;\\
k_4 &= c_6c_7a_6a_7a_8 + c_6\bar{c}_7a_7a_8 + \bar{c}_6c_7a_6a_7 + \bar{c}_6\bar{c}_7a_8;\\
k_5 &= c_5a_5 + \bar{c}_5a_3;\\
k_6 &= c_7a_6 + \bar{c}_7;\\
k_7 &= c_7a_6a_7 + \bar{c}_7a_8;
\end{aligned}
$$

Note that k_6 has a cube with no action literals. This represents a TDT rule with no action selected for execution. □

3.2 TDT Decomposition

Our TDT decomposition scheme works as follows. First, the algebraic expression of a TDT is constructed. Then a set of kernels are extracted from the algebraic expression. The kernels are eventually used to reconstruct a TDT representation in hierarchical form. Not all the algebraic kernels may be useful in TDT decomposition since the algebraic expression carries only a subset of the TDT information. We use a set of filtering procedures to delete from the kernel sets kernels which corresponds to invalid TDT transformations or transformations producing models that results in inferior synthesis results.

Algorithm 3.2 TDT Decomposition

INPUT: a flattened TDT *tdt*;
OUTPUT: a hierarchical TDT with root *tdt'*;
decomposeTDT(*tdt*)
{
  sop ←constructAlgebraicExpression(*tdt*);
  K ←extractKernel(*sop*);
  trimKernel1(K, *sop*);
  trimKernel2(K, *sop*, *td*);
  trimSelf(k, *sop*);
  trimKernel3(k, *sop*);
  tdt' ←reconstruct_TDT_with_Kernels(*tdt*, K);
  return *tdt'*
}

The procedure *constructAlgebraicExpression*() builds the algebraic expression of *tdt* following Algorithm 3.3. The function *expression*() builds an expression out of a set of sets according to the data structure we choose for the two-level algebraic expression for TDTs. The complexity of the algorithm is $O(AR + CR)$ where A is the number of action in *tdt*, R is the number of rules in *tdt*, and C is the number of conditions in *tdt*.

Algorithm 3.3 Constructing Algebraic Expressions of TDTs

constructAlgebraicExpression(tdt) {
  for i = 1, C **do**
    construct a positive condition literal l_{c_i};
    construct a negative condition literal $l_{\bar{c}_i}$;
  endfor
  for i = 1, A **do**
    construct an action literal l_{a_i}
  endfor
  $R \leftarrow \phi$; // empty set
  for i = 1, R **do**
    $r \leftarrow \phi$;
    for j = 1, C **do**
      if $(ce(i, j)$ == 'Y') **then**

```
          r ←r ∪ {l_{c_i}};
        if (ce(i, j) == 'N') then
          r ←r ∪ {l_{c̄_i}};
      endfor;
      R ←R ∪ r;
    endfor
    return expression(R);
}
```

Procedure *extractKernel(sop)* calls the recursive procedure *extractKernelR(sop,* 1) to get a set of kernels of *sop*, the algebraic expression of *tdt*.

Some kernels appear only once in the algebraic expression of a TDT. These kernels would not help in reducing the resource requirement and therefore they are trimmed from K using procedure *trimKernel*1(). The number of co-kernels corresponds to the number of times sub-TDT that corresponds to a certain kernel is called in the hierarchy of TDTs.

Since information such as data dependency are not captured in algebraic form of TDTs, the kernels in K may not corresponds to a decomposition which preserves data-dependencies specified in the original TDT. These kernels are trimmed using procedure *trimKernel*2().

Algorithm 3.4 Removing Kernels Which Corresponds to an Invalid TDT Transformations

```
trimKernel2(K, e, tdt) {
  foreach k ∈ K do
    flag ←0;
    foreach q ∈ co − Kernels(k, e) do
      foreach action literal l_a of q do
        if a modifies any condition of k then
          foreach action literal l_α in k do
            if (l_a appears before l_α) then
              flag ←1;
          endforeach
      endforeach
    endforeach
    if (flag == 0) then
      K ←K − {k};
  endforeach
}
```

The worst case complexity of this algorithm is $O(AR + CR)$ since the program checks no more than once on each condition/action literal corresponding to a condition entry or action entry of *tdt*.

Example 3.2. Now we look at kernel $k_4 = c_6c_7a_6a_7a_8 + c_6\bar{c}_7a_7a_8 + \bar{c}_6c_7a_6a_7 + \bar{c}_6\bar{c}_7a_8$. Suppose it corresponds to TDT_3. Also suppose in Example 2.1, a_2 modifies c_6 and the result of a_2 is also used in a_6. Because a_2 modifies c_6, in the hierarchical TDT we need to specify that a_2 comes after TDT_3 to preserve the behavior. However, this violates the data dependency specification between a_2 and a_6. Therefore, under this condition given above, k_4 will be eliminated by *trimKernel*2(). □

An expression may be a kernel of itself with a co-kernel of '1' if it is kernel free. However this kernel is not useful for TDT decomposition. We use a procedure *trimSelf*() to delete an expression from its own kernel set for TDT decomposition. Also, as we mentioned earlier, a kernel of an expression's kernel is itself a kernel of this expression. However, in this paper, we consider TDT decomposition involving only two levels of calling hierarchies at a time. For this reason, we use *trimKernel*3() delete "smaller" kernels which are also kernels of other kernels of an expression.

Finally, we reconstruct a hierarchical TDT representation using the remaining algebraic kernels of the TDT expression. The algorithm is outlined below. It consists two procedures: *reconstruct_TDT_with_Kernel*(), and *constructTDT*() which is called by the other procedure to build a TDT out of an algebraic expression. Again, the worse case complexity of the algorithm is $O(CR + AR)$.

Algorithm 3.5 Construct a Hierarchical TDT Using Kernels

```
INPUT: a flattened TDT tdt, its algebraic expression
  exp, a set of kernels K of exp;
OUTPUT: a new hierarchical TDT;
re_Construct_TDT_with_Kernels(tdt, K, exp) {
  foreach k ∈ K do
    t ←constructTDT(tdt, k)
    generate a new action literal l_t for t;
    compute q and r s.t. exp = k · q + r;
    e ←l_t · q + r;
  endforeach
  return constructTDT(tdt, e);
}
```

Example 3.3. Assume expression $c_6c_7a_6a_7a_8 + c_6\bar{c}_7a_7a_8 + \bar{c}_6c_7a_6a_7 + \bar{c}_6\bar{c}_7a_8$ is the only kernel left after trimming procedures performed on the kernel set of the algebraic expression of $TDT_{Example\ 2.1}$. The following hierarchical TDT will be constructed.

TDT_1:

c_1	Y	Y	Y	Y	Y	N
c_2	Y	Y	Y	N	N	
c_3				Y	N	
c_4	Y	N	N			
c_5		Y	N			
a_1	1	1	1		1	1
a_2	1	1	1	1		1
a_3	1		1			
a_4	1					
a_5	1	1				
TDT_3				1		1
a_9					1	

TDT_3:

c_6	Y	Y	N	N
c_7	Y	N	Y	N
a_6	1		1	
a_7	1	1	1	
a_8	1	1		1

□

4 Implementation and Experimental Results

To show the effect of using TDT decomposition in presynthesis optimizations, we have incorporated our decomposition algorithm in PUMPKIN, the TDT-based presynthesis optimization tool [4]. Figure 2 shows the flow diagram of the process of presynthesis optimizations. The ellipse titled "kernel extraction" in Figure 2 shows where the TDT decomposition algorithm fits in the global picture of presynthesis optimizations using TDT.

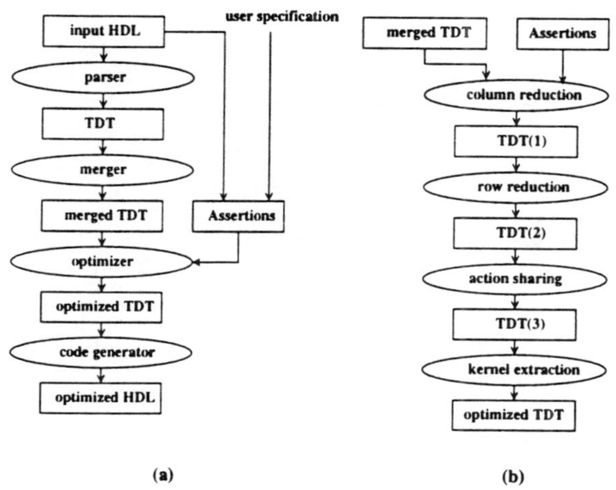

Figure 2: Flow diagram for presynthesis optimizations: (a) the whole picture, (b) details of the optimizer.

Our experimental methodology is as follows. The HDL description is compiled into TDT models, run through the optimizations, and finally output as a HardwareC description. This output is provided to the Olympus High-Level Synthesis System [7] for hardware synthesis under minimum area objectives. We use Olympus synthesis results to compare the effect of optimizations on hardware size. Hardware synthesis was performed for the target technology of LSI Logic 10K library of gates. Results are compared for final circuits sizes, in terms of number of cells. To evaluate the effectiveness of this step, we have turned off other optimizations and run PUMPKIN with several high-level synthesis benchmark designs.

Table 1 shows the results of TDT decomposition on examples designs. The design 'daio' refers to the HardwareC design of a Digital Audio Input-Output chip (DAIO) [8]. The design 'comm' refers to the HardwareC design of an Ethernet controller [9]. The design 'cruiser' refers to the HardwareC design of a vehicle controller. The description 'State' is the vehicle speed regulation module. All designs can be found in the high-level synthesis benchmark suite [7]. The percentage of circuit size reduction is computed for each description and listed in the last column of Table 1. Note that this improvement depends on the amount of commonality existing in the input behavioral descriptions.

Table 1: Synthesis Results: cell counts before and after TDT decomposition is carried out.

design	module	circuit size (cells)		Δ%
		before	after	
daio	phase_decoder	1252	1232	2
	receiver	440	355	19
comm	DMA_xmit	992	770	22
	exec_unit	864	587	32
cruiser	State	356	308	14

5 Conclusion and Future Work

In this paper, we have introduced TDT decomposition as a complementary procedure to TDT merging. We have presented a TDT decomposition algorithm based on kernel extraction on an algebraic form of TDTs. Combining TDT decomposition and merging, we can restructure HDL descriptions to obtain descriptions that lead to either improved synthesis results or more efficient compiled code. Our experiment on named benchmarks shows a size reduction in the synthesized circuits after code restructuring.

As a future work, we are exploring HDL optimization strategies based various presynthesis optimization techniques that lead to best synthesis results.

Acknowledgment. This research is supported in part by NSF CAREER Award MIP 95-01615 and an FMC Education Fund Fellowship.

References

[1] J. Li and R. K. Gupta, "HDL Optimization Using Timed Decision Tables," in *Proceedings of the* 33rd *Design Automation Conference*, pp. 51–54, June 1996.

[2] J. Li and R. K. Gupta, "Limited exception modeling and its use in presynthesis optimizations," in *Proceedings of the* 34th *Design Automation Conference*, June 1997.

[3] D. D. Gajski, F. Vahid, S. Narayan, and J. Gong, *Specification and Design of Embedded Systems.* Prentice Hall, 1994.

[4] J. Li and R. K. Gupta, "System modeling and presynthesis using timed decision tables," Tech. Rep. UCI ICS-TR-97-12, University of California, March 1997.

[5] G. D. Micheli, *Synthesis and Optimization of Digital Circuits.* McGraw-Hill, 1994.

[6] R. Brayton and C. McMullen, "The decomposition and factorization of boolean expressions," in *Proceedings of the IEEE International Symposium on Circuits and Systems*, 1982.

[7] G. D. Micheli, D. C. Ku, F. Mailhot, and T. Truong, "The Olympus Synthesis System for Digital Design," *IEEE Design and Test Magazine*, pp. 37–53, Oct. 1990.

[8] M. M. Ligthard, A. Bechtolsheim, G. D. Micheli, and A. E. Gamal, "Design of a digital input output chip," in *Custom IC Conference*, May 1989.

[9] D. Ku and G. D. Micheli, *High-level Synthesis of ASICs under Timing and Synchronization Constraints.* Kluwer Academic Publishers 1992.

A Predictive System Shutdown Method for Energy Saving of Event-Driven Computation

Chi-Hong Hwang and Allen C.-H. Wu
Department of Computer Science, Tsing Hua University
Hsinchu, Taiwan, 300, Republic of China
{chunghaw@cs.nthu.edu.tw}

Abstract

This paper presents a system-level power management technique for power saving of event-driven applications. We present a new predictive system-shutdown method to exploit sleep mode operations for power saving. We use an exponential-average approach to predict the upcoming idle period. We introduce two mechanisms, prediction-miss correction and pre-wakeup, to improve the hit ratio and to reduce the delay overhead. Experiments on four different event-driven applications show that our proposed method achieves high hit ratios in a wide range of delay overheads, which results in a high degree of power saving with low delay penalties.

1 Introduction

With the advent of portable computing and high density VLSI circuits, power dissipation has emerged as a principle design consideration in VLSI designs. In the past few years, a handful of power estimation and minimization methods have been reported for achieving low power designs at circuit, layout, logic, behavioral, and architectural levels. Several excellent reviews of power estimation and minimization techniques are given by Pedram [1], Devadas and Malik [2], and Najm [3, 4].

Low power VLSI designs can be achieved at various design levels. In this study, we focus on utilizing a predictive system-shutdown technique for power saving of event-driven applications. Power management techniques have been extensively applied to PC systems. For instance, the design of the PowerPC603 [5] applied two types of power management schemes: static and dynamic. In static power management, the system defines several sleep modes with various levels of power saving and delay overhead which can be controlled externally by software. In dynamic power management, the system will automatically detect the idle periods and disable the clocks on portions of the CPU. Apple's Mac PowerBooks [6] use a different approach which enters rest mode after 2 seconds of idle time. During rest mode, the processor is powered down but the I/O devices remain on. Typically, conventional shutdown approaches are carried out based on the rule of *go to sleep after the system has been idle for a predefined period of time*. However, this approach poses an obvious drawback - the system continues to consume power in that interval of idle time.

†This work was supported in part by the National Science Council of R.O.C. under Grant NSC 85-2221-E-007-034 and NSC 86-2221-E-007-021.

In a recent study, Srivastava et al. [7] conducted an extensive analysis on different system-shutdown approaches. Their sample traces on an X-server, an event-driven application, showed that it spends over 90% of its time in the blocked state and the average time visiting the blocked state is less than one second. As a result, the conventional approach will fail to effectively achieve power reduction on this type of application. They have proposed a predictive system-shutdown technique for energy saving of event-driven applications. They first collected sample traces of on-off activity on an X-server. Then, they proposed two predictive formulas based on the analysis of the sample traces. The first formula was obtained by using a general regression-analysis technique to correlate the length of the upcoming off period to the lengths of the previous on and off periods. The second formula was obtained by the observation of the on-off activity behavior. They observed that "the idle period following a long running period tends to be short". Based on this observation, they derived a formula which filters out the idle period fulfilling the above condition and the system enters the sleep state otherwise. Based on the two formulas, they conducted a series of experiments on an X client application. The results demonstrated that predictive shutdown techniques can reduce the power consumption by a large factor compared to the conventional method. However, one drawback of this approach is that the predictive formula is directly derived from the sample traces of a specific application. For different applications, different predictive formulas are needed in order to make accurate predictions.

In this paper, we present a new predictive system-shutdown method for event-driven applications. We use a well-known exponential-average approach to predict the upcoming idle period. We introduce two mechanisms, prediction-miss correction and pre-wakeup, to improve the hit ratio and to reduce the delay overhead. Experiments on four different event-driven applications are reported to demonstrate the effectiveness of our proposed method.

2 The proposed method

2.1 Energy saving using a system-shutdown technique

Figure 1 depicts a simple shutdown approach for event-driven applications. When the system detects an idle period, it will determine whether it should stay in the running state or enter the sleep state. If the system

1092-3152/97 $10.00 © 1997 IEEE

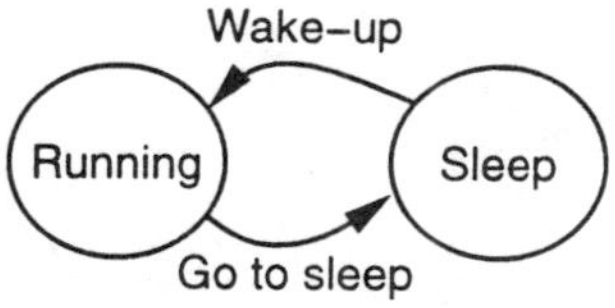

Figure 1: A simple shutdown approach.

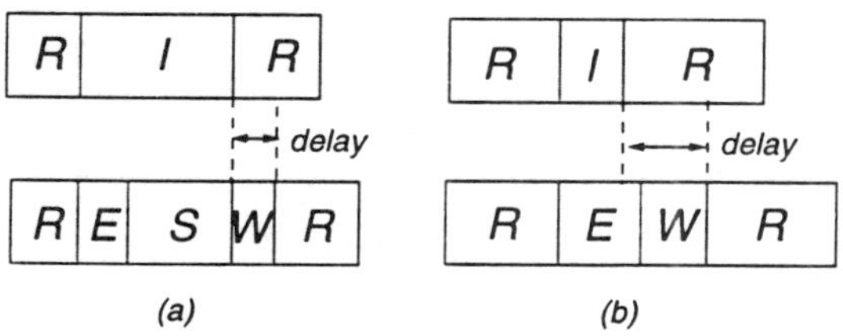

Figure 2: Two possible scenarios when applying a simple system-shutdown scheme:(a) $I \geq E$,(b) $I \leq E$.

decides to enter the sleep state, the system first performs a number of housekeeping procedures, such as backing-up data and system status. The system then stays in the energy-saving sleep state until an external wakeup signal occurs. When a wakeup signal occurs, the system will perform recovery procedures, such as data restoring, and then resume the running state. If the decision is not to enter the sleep state, the system stays in the running state as busy waiting. One of the crucial issues of this approach is *"whether or not to shutdown the system, and if so when?"* so that power dissipation of the system can be reduced. This issue will be discussed as follows.

Let I be the idle time period, E the delay overhead of entering the sleep state from the running state, S the sleeping time period, and W the delay overhead for resuming the running state from the sleep state (the wake up process). P_R and P_S are the power consumption values of the system in the running and sleep states, respectively. P_{EW} is the average power-dissipation overhead of entering the sleep state from the running state and resuming the running state from the sleep state. Typically, $P_R \geq P_{EW} \geq P_S$. Finally, EG denotes the energy gain of the system.

Assume that the system will enter the sleep state whenever it detects an idle period. Figure 2(a) shows the first scenario in which the idle period is longer than the delay overhead of entering the sleep state from the running state (i.e., $I \geq E$). Since $I \geq E$, the system will successfully enter the sleep state and resume the running state when a wake-up signal occurs. Under this condition, the energy gain EG is $P_R \cdot I - (E+W) \cdot P_{EW} - P_S \cdot S$ while the delay penalty is W. Figure 2(b) shows the second scenario in which the idle period is shorter than the delay overhead of entering the sleep state from the running state (i.e., $I \leq E$). In this case, the system will never enter the sleep state and will suffer a long delay penalty ($delay = W + (E - I)$) and a negative energy gain ($EG = I \cdot P_R - (E + W) \cdot P_{EW}$). Hence, in order to achieve energy saving, the idle period must be longer than the delay overhead for entering the sleep state from the running state (i.e., $I \geq E$).

Let us further analyze the minimum required idle period for achieving a positive energy gain as follows.

$$I \geq E, \tag{1}$$

$$\begin{aligned} EG &= I \cdot P_R - (E+W) \cdot P_{EW} - P_S \cdot S; && (2)\\ &= I \cdot P_R - (E+W) \cdot P_{EW} - P_S \cdot (I - E); && (3)\\ &= I \cdot (P_R - P_S) - E \cdot (P_{EW} - P_S) - W \cdot P_{EW}; && (4)\\ &> 0, && (5)\\ => \quad I &> \frac{E \cdot (P_{EW} - P_S) + W \cdot P_{EW}}{(P_R - P_S)}, && (6)\\ => \quad S_{th} &= \frac{E \cdot (P_{EW} - P_S) + W \cdot P_{EW}}{(P_R - P_S)}. && (7) \end{aligned}$$

The above derivations indicate that Eqns. 1 and 7 are the necessary conditions under which the idle period will achieve energy savings. We define S_{th} as the threshold idle period that results in energy saving of the system.

2.2 Prediction of idle periods

The analysis in the previous section indicates that predicting the idle period I is vital for an effective power management mechanism. However, the distribution and variation of I may be strongly dependent on the user behavior, target applications, working frequency, and operating system.

In our approach, we adapt the *exponential-average* approach [8] used in the CPU scheduling problem for the prediction of the idle period. In the CPU scheduling problem, operating systems need to predict the length of the next CPU burst in order to make appropriate process scheduling. In general, the next CPU burst is predicted as an accumulative average of the measured lengths of previous CPU bursts. Similarly, we can predict the next idle period by the accumulative average of the previous idle periods. The recursive prediction formula is shown below.

$$I_{n+1} = a \cdot i_n + (1 - a) \cdot I_n, \tag{8}$$

where I_{n+1} is the new predicted value, I_n is the last predicted value, i_n is the latest idle period, and a is a constant attenuation factor in the range between 0 to 1. In this formula, I_n is the inertia and i_n is the force to push the predicted idle period toward the actual idle period. We can use Eqn. 8 to predict the upcoming idle period, which is a function of the latest idle period and the previous predicted value. The parameter a controls the relative weight of recent and past history in the prediction. If $a = 0$, then $I_{n+1} = I_n$. In other words, the recent history has no effect. On the other hand, if $a = 1$, then $I_{n+1} = i_n$. In this case, the prediction only takes into account the most recent idle period but ignores the previous predictions. In our implementation, a is set to be 1/2 so that the recent history and past history are equally weighted. We can expand Eqn. 8 as below.

$$I_{n+1} = a \cdot i_n + a(1-a)i_{n-1} + \cdots + a(1-a)^n i_0 + (1-a)^{n+1} I_0. \tag{9}$$

Eqn. 9 indicates that the predicted idle period is the weighted average of previous idle periods. Early idle periods have less weight as specified by the exponential attenuation factors.

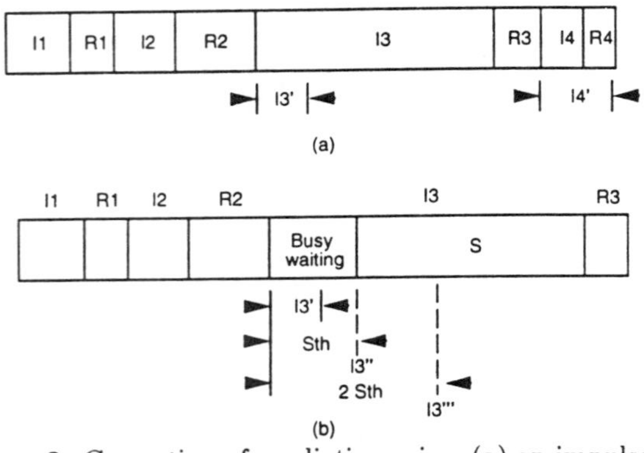

Figure 3: Correction of prediction miss: (a) an impulse-like idle period, (b) correction using a watchdog scheme.

2.3 Correction of prediction misses

The proposed prediction formula (Eqn. 8) can effectively predict idle periods in most cases except the occurrence of impulse-like idle periods - a sudden, very long idle period $I3$ occurs after continuous, nearly uniform idle periods - during the prediction process, as shown in Figure 3(a). For example, the user works on the system for a while and then goes to answer a telephone resulting in the system idling for a long period of time. When such an impulse-like idle period occurs, the prediction of the upcoming idle period $I3$ and the following one $I4$ will not be accurate. The reasons are discussed as follows. Recall that our proposed prediction formula (Eqn. 8) predicts the upcoming idle period by the accumulative average of the previous idle periods. When a very long idle period occurs after continuous, nearly uniform idle periods, the predicted value of this long idle period is often much lower than the actual idle period ($I3 > I3'$). This underestimation is undesirable for energy saving, especially when the predicted value is lower than S_{th}. In this case, the system will stay in the running state instead of entering the sleep state which results in a large amount of unnecessary power consumption. On the other hand, when predicting the idle period $I4$ which is followed a long idle period, our proposed formula tends to overestimate the duration of the idle period ($I4 < I4'$). It is also undesirable because the system may falsely enter the sleep state and suffers unnecessary power consumption and delays.

To alleviate the first problem, we use a watchdog scheme to periodically monitor the current idle period. When an idle period occurs, the system predicts the duration of the idle period. If the predicted value is lower than S_{th}, the system stays in the busy waiting state and starts up a timer to trace the actual idle period. The system then performs a new prediction every S_{th} time to determine whether the system should enter the sleep state. For example, in Figure 3(b), by the end of running state of $R2$, a long idle period $I3$ occurs at the end of a running state T. If the predicted idle period $I3'$ is lower than S_{th}, the system stays in the busy waiting state. After an S_{th} time period, the system performs the prediction again, resulting in $I3''$. If the predicted value is larger than S_{th}, then it enters the sleep state. Otherwise, it will perform idle period prediction after another S_{th} time.

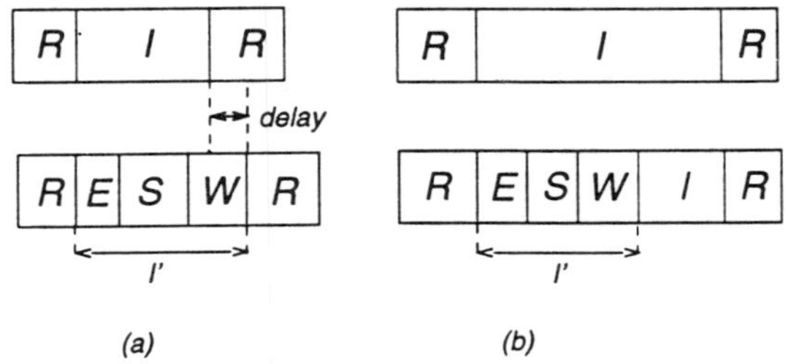

Figure 4: Examples of pre-wakeup model:(a) $I' > I$ *and* $D \leq W$, (b) $I' < I$.

To resolve the second problem, we add a saturation condition to Eqn. 8 as below.

$$if\ (ai_n + (1-a)I_n > cI_n)$$
$$I_{n+1} = cI_n, \tag{10}$$

where c is a constant. Under the saturation condition, the growing rate of I is limited to c times per update.

2.4 Pre-wakeup

As described in the previous section, when the system resumes the running state from the sleep state (i.e., system wake-up), the system needs to perform some recovery procedures. In other words, the system suffers a delay penalty of W by restoring the system status. This delay penalty may have a great impact on system responsiveness in some cases, especially when W is too long to be neglected. One way to resolve this problem is to pre-wakeup the system before the arrival of the next wakeup signal. This can be accomplished by predicting the occurrence of the next wakeup signal.

Let I be the actual idle period, I' the predicted idle period, and $D = |I' - I|$ the error of the prediction. Figure 4 depicts two possible scenarios when applying the pre-wakeup scheme. In the first scenario, we overestimate the predicted idle period by D (i.e., $I' > I$) and $D \leq W$. In this case, the system will wake up $W - D$ time ahead of the next wakeup signal, as shown in Figure 4(a). Thus, the delay penalty is D which is shorter than the original delay penalty W. In addition, the energy gain is $EG = I \cdot (P_R - P_S) - (E + W) \cdot (P_{EW} - P_S) - D \cdot P_S$. On the other hand, if $I' > I$ and $D \geq W$, the system will be woken up by the original wakeup signal. In this case, the pre-wakeup has no effect on the reduction of the delay penalty. Figure 4(b) shows the second scenario in which $I' < I$. In this case, the delay penalty is zero but the energy gain is reduced to $EG = (I - D) \cdot (P_R - P_S) - (E + W) \cdot (P_{EW} - P_S)$. In other words, when the predicted idle period is less than the actual idle period, there will be no responsiveness delay. However, the energy saving will not be as effective as the original one.

2.5 Control mechanism of the proposed method

Figure 5 shows the finite state machine of the proposed method which consists of three states: *running*, *correct*, and *sleep*. Initially, the system is in the running state. When an idle period occurs, the system predicts the duration I' of the upcoming idle period. If the predicted value is lower than the threshold value S_{th}, then the system resets the timer c and stays in the running

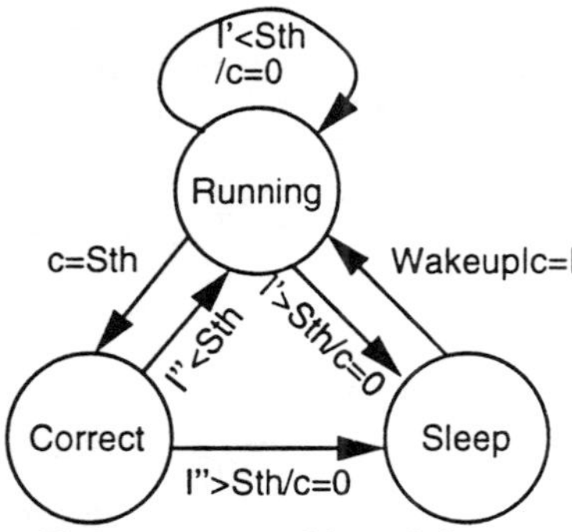

Figure 5: Finite state machine of the proposed method.

state as busy waiting. Otherwise, the system enters the sleep state. During the busy waiting, the system monitors the timer and enters the correct state every S_{th} of time. In the correct state, the system re-predicts the duration of the idle period. If the predicted value I'' is lower than S_{th}, then the system resumes the running state as busy waiting. Otherwise, it enters the sleep state. In the sleep state, the system will return to the running state when a wakeup signal arrives. If the pre-wakeup scheme is applied to the system, then the system will return to the running state either when a wakeup signal arrives or the system has been shutdown for a predicted idle period ($c = I'$).

3 Experiments

We have conducted experiments on four event-driven applications: (1) X-server, (2) Netscape, (3) telnet, and (4) tin. The experiments were conducted on a SPARC 10 workstation running the SunOS 4.1.3 operating system.

In our implementation, we set the constants $a = 0.5$ (Eqn. 8) and $c = 2$ (Eqn. 10). We assume $E = W = \frac{1}{2}T_{cost}$, where T_{cost} is the delay overhead. First, we determine the threshold idle period S_{th} (Eqn. 7). Recall that

$$S_{th} \geq \frac{E \cdot (P_{EW} - P_S) + W \cdot P_{EW}}{(P_R - P_S)}. \quad (11)$$

We assume that the average power dissipation of entering and resuming from the sleep state P_{EW} is same as the power consumed in the running state; i.e., $P_{EW} = P_R$. In addition, according to the data sheet of the PowerPC [5], we define the power dissipation in the sleep state to be approximately 5% of the power dissipation in the running state; i.e., $P_S = 0.05 \cdot P_R$. Hence,

$$S_{th} \approx \frac{1/2 \cdot T_{cost} \cdot (P_R - 0.05 \cdot P_R) + 1/2 \cdot T_{cost} \cdot P_R}{(P_R - 0.05 \cdot P_R)} \quad (12)$$

$$= \frac{0.5 * 1.95}{0.95} \cdot T_{cost} = 1.026 \cdot T_{cost}. \quad (13)$$

A reasonable value of S_{th} is larger than $1.026 \cdot T_{cost}$. In our implementation, we set $S_{th} = 1.5 \cdot T_{cost}$.

We also define two quality measures: Delay-Overhead (DO) and Energy-Saving (ES). Delay overhead is the ratio between the total elapsed time after applying the system-shutdown scheme (T_t') and the original elapsed time (T_t) as

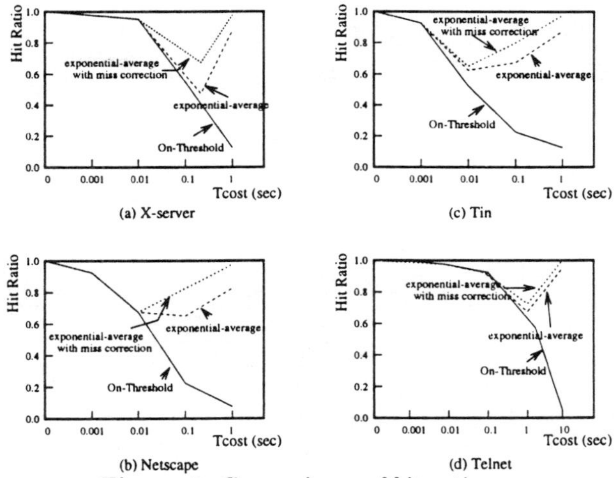

Figure 6: Comparisons of hit ratios.

$$DO = \frac{T_t' - T_t}{T_t} \times 100\%. \quad (14)$$

Let T_s be the elapsed time of the sleep state. The energy saving is the ratio between the total power dissipation before and after applying the system-shutdown scheme as

$$ES = \frac{P_R \cdot T_t}{P_R \cdot T_t' - T_s \cdot (P_R - P_S)}, \quad (15)$$

$$\approx \frac{P_R \cdot T_t}{P_R \cdot T_t' - T_s(P_R - 0.05 \cdot P_R)}, \quad (16)$$

$$= \frac{T_t}{T_t' - 0.95T_s}. \quad (17)$$

In the first experiment, we tested the hit ratio of our proposed method. We define a *hit* in two ways: (1) the system enters the sleep state and results in power saving or (2) the system does not enter the sleep state if it will not result in power saving. Figures 6(a), (b), (c), and (d) show the hit ratios of the four applications X-server, Netscape, Tin, and Telnet, respectively. T_{cost} is the delay penalty for shutting down the system. We have compared the hit ratios using three predictive methods: (1) $on-threshold(\infty)$ *based* [7], (2) our proposed method without miss correction, and (3) the proposed method with miss correction. The results show that when the T_{cost} is low (e.g.,0.001 second for Tin, 0.01 second for the X-server and Netscape, and 0.1 second for Telnet), both the $on-threshold(\infty)$ *based* and our method produced the same hit ratio. When the T_{cost} increases, the hit ratio of the $on-threshold(\infty)$ *based* method decreases rapidly. In contrast, our proposed method consistently gives high hit ratios. The results also show that the correction method improves the hit ratio by an average of 20% compared to that without applying the correction method.

In the second experiment, we compared the energy saving and delay overhead using five system-shutdown methods: (1) PM_{2sec}, (2) PM_{ThX}, (3) $PM_{Th\infty}$, (4) PM_I, and (5) PM_{II}. The first one is a method used in the Apple PC system [6] in which the system will enter

T_{cost}	PM_{2sec}	PM_{ThX}	PM_{ThInf}	PM_I	PM_{II}
X-server(Delay-Overhead(%)/Energy-Saving)					
0	0/3.75	0/16.8	0/18.73	0/18.70	0/18.70
1ms	0/3.75	.03/16.63	.03/18.53	.03/18.50	.03/17.99
10ms	.02/3.75	.3/15.29	.3/16.87	.03/16.80	.029/13.70
0.1s	.24/3.68	3.28/8.45	3.3/8.89	2.18/8.38	1.7/5.14
1s	2.58/3.18	17/1.14	48/1.53	8.3/3.29	1.8/1.92
Netscape(Delay-Overhead(%)/Energy-Saving)					
0	0/1.60	0/4.77	0/8.92	0/8.82	0/8.82
1ms	0/1.60	.11/4.72	.12/8.73	.12/8.63	.11/8.13
10ms	.07/1.60	1.33/4.29	1.38/7.34	1.14/7.18	.97/5.28
0.1s	.73/1.56	16.8/2.26	17.4/2.82	2.63/3.63	1.8/2.10
1s	8.11/1.30	13.34/0.88	321/0.39	10.44/1.37	.87/1.06
Tin(Delay-Overhead(%)/Energy-Saving)					
0	0/2.86	0/16.32	0/16.33	0/16.33	0/16.33
1ms	0/2.86	.06/16.02	.06/16.03	.06/16.02	.05/15.04
10ms	.03/2.85	.73/13.70	.73/13.71	.47/13.66	.38/9.92
0.1s	.35/2.80	9.48/5.59	9.5/5.58	1.71/7.43	1.32/3.74
1s	3.99/2.38	3.56/0.97	207/0.80	5.77/2.71	.92/1.54
Telnet(Delay-Overhead(%)/Energy-Saving)					
0	0/2.63	0/18.18	0/19.19	0/15.15	0/15.15
1ms	0/2.63	.01/18.08	.01/19.09	.01/15.08	.01/14.96
10ms	.05/2.62	.13/17.32	.13/18.23	.13/14.54	.13/13.49
0.1s	.57/2.55	1.43/12.16	1.43/12.60	1.42/10.72	1.34/7.11
1s	6.04/2.04	7.02/1.17	15.99/3.07	11.31/2.46	8.54/1.79

Table 1: Comparisons of various system shutdown methods.

the sleep state whenever a 2-second idle period is detected. The second and third methods were proposed by Srivastava et. al. [7]. To determine a reasonable threshold value for the second method, we first analyzed the relationship between on-off periods of the sample traces. The results show that we obtained the similar L-shaped on-off periods relationship as observed in [7] for the four applications. From the observations, we set the $T_{threshold}$ value to 50ms for T_{cost} in the range of 0-0.1 second and 2ms for T_{cost} of 1 second, 100ms for T_{cost} = 0-0.1 second and 1ms for $T_{cost} = 1$ second, 200ms for T_{cost} = 0-0.1 second and 1ms for $T_{cost} = 1$ second, and 40ms for T_{cost} = 0-0.1 second and 4ms for $T_{cost} = 1$ second, for the X-server, Netscape, Tin, and Telnet, respectively. The fourth method is our proposed method without applying the pre-wakeup scheme. The final method is our proposed method including the pre-wakeup scheme.

Table 1 shows the results. From the results, the following observations can be made. First, the PM_{2sec} method performs well when $T_{cost} = 1s$ but poorly when T_{cost} is in the range of 0 to 0.1 second. Second, when T_{cost} is in the range of 0 to 0.1 second, the $PM_{Th\infty}$ achieves the best power saving. However, when T_{cost} = 1, power saving drops sharply and delay overhead increases rapidly. For example, for the X-server application, it obtains 1.53 times power saving with 48% delay overhead. For the Netscape and Tin applications, it actually consumes more power (60% and 20% respectively) and the delay also increases by 2 to 3 times. This is due to the power and delay overhead caused by the large number of hit misses. Similarly, the PM_{Thx} method performs well when T_{cost} is in the range of 0 to 0.1 second but poorly when $T_{cost} = 1s$. On the other hand, our proposed method PM_I performs well in the entire range of T_{cost} = 0 to 1 second. Finally, when applying the pre-wakeup technique, the delay overhead can be reduced by sacrificing some power saving (PM_{II} v.s. PM_I). This is important for some timing critical applications. In our approach, we are able to tradeoff delay overhead and power saving by enabling and disabling the pre-wakeup function.

4 Conclusions

In this paper, we have presented a predictive shutdown method for event-driven computation. We have conducted experiments on four event-driven applications and compared our approach to two other system shutdown methods. The results have shown that when the shutdown overhead is high (e.g., $T_{cost} \geq 1$ second), the conventional method, such as that used by the Apple PowerPC, can achieve a reasonable power saving. However, this method does not achieve an effective power saving when the shutdown overhead is low (e.g., $T_{cost} <$ 1 second). On the other hand, when the shutdown overhead is low (e.g., $T_{cost} < 1$ second), a more aggressive predictive shutdown method [7] can achieve a higher degree of power saving compared to the conventional method. However, this method does not perform well when the shutdown overhead is high. In addition, because the predictive formula of this approach has to derived directly from the sample traces of the target application, we have to analyze the sample traces for each application in order to determine the threshold value. On the other hand, our proposed method depends solely on the history of the previous idle periods and the power dissipation of the target system (e.g., the average power consumption in the sleep and running states), which is independent of the target applications. Furthermore, the results have shown that our proposed method achieves high hit ratios for a wide range of shutdown overheads, which results in a high degree of power saving with low delay penalties.

Currently, our proposed method focuses on a single sleep mode. However, many processors provide a variety of sleep modes with different levels of power saving and shutdown overhead. Future work will extend our method to accomodate multi-level sleep modes.

References

[1] M. Pedram, "Power Minimization in IC Design: Principles and Applications," *ACM Trans. on Design Automation of Electronic Systems*, vol. 1, no. 1, pp.3-56, January, 1996.

[2] S. Devadas and S. Malik, "A Survey of Optimization Techniques Targeting Low Power VLSI Circuits," in *Proc. of the 32nd Design Automation Conf.*, pp. 242-247, 1995.

[3] F. N. Najm, "A Survey of Power Estimation Techniques in VLSI Circuits," *IEEE Trans. on VLSI Systems*, vol. 2, no. 4, pp.446-455, December 1994.

[4] F. N. Najm, "Power Estimation Techniques for Integrated Circuits," in *Proc. of the ICCAD*, pp. 492-499, 1995.

[5] S. Gary, "PowerPC: A Microprocessor for Portable Computers," *IEEE Design of Computers*, pp. 14-23, Winter 1994.

[6] Apple Computer Inc., "Power Manager IC and Reduced Power Modes," in *Technical Introduction to the Macintosh Family*, Reading, MA: Addison-Wesley, Oct. 1992.

[7] M. B. Srivastava, A. P. Chandrakasan, and R. W. Broderson, "Predictive System Shutdown and Other Architectural Techniques for Energy Efficient Programmable Computation," *IEEE Trans. on VLSI Systems*, pp. 42-54, vol. 4, no. 1, March 1996.

[8] J. L. Peterson and A. Silberschatz, *Operating System Concepts*, 2nd Ed., pp. 118-120, Addison-Wesley Publishing Co. Inc.

Micro-Preemption Synthesis: An Enabling Mechanism for Multi-Task VLSI Systems *

Kyosun Kim, Ramesh Karri
Department of ECE
University of Massachusetts
Amherst, MA 01002
{karri,kkim}@ecs.umass.edu

Miodrag Potkonjak
Department of Computer Science
University of California
Los Angeles, CA 90095
miodrag@cs.ucla.edu

Abstract - *Task preemption is a critical enabling mechanism in multi-task VLSI systems. On preemption, data in the register files must be preserved in order for the task to be resumed. This entails extra memory to save the context and additional clock cycles to restore the context. In this paper, we present techniques and algorithms to incorporate micro-preemption constraints during multi-task VLSI system synthesis. Specifically, we have developed: (i) algorithms to insert and refine preemption points in scheduled task graphs subject to preemption latency constraints, (ii) techniques to minimize the context switch overhead by considering the dedicated registers required to save the state of a task on preemption and the shared registers required to save the remaining values in the tasks, and (iii) a controller based scheme to preclude preemption related performance degradation.*

1 Introduction

1.1 Motivation

Task preemption is a critical enabling mechanism in a variety of application scenarios. Hard real-time computer systems have stringent timing requirements. In such systems, the deadlines for critical tasks are enforced by preempting less critical tasks. In soft real-time systems where infrequent deadline violations are tolerated, less important tasks are preempted to execute more important ones so as to meet some quality-of-service requirements. For example, in multimedia systems, video, voice, and data streams are scheduled and occasionally interrupted and resumed according to priority strategies to enforce soft end-to-end deadlines.

Along a different dimension, multi-task VLSI systems are becoming commonplace. For example, Motorola offers numerous DSP ASPPs [3]. An ASPP can be dynamically configured to one of the implemented tasks. Although the reconfiguration time of an ASPP may be very low (because reconfiguration entails moving from the final state of the current task to the start state of another task), it may not be acceptable for a critical task in a real-time system to wait until the current task is completed.

*This research was supported by an NSF CAREER grant MIP-9702676

On receiving a preemption request, the state of the active task must be saved, the context of the new task must be loaded and then executed. On completion of task execution, the state of the preempted task must be restored and the interrupted task resumed to completion. Important factors that should be considered while implementing task preemption include:

- **Preemption latency**: It is defined as the maximum time it takes from the instant a preemption request is received to the instant the task state is saved.
- **Context switch cost:** Hardware overhead incurred by the installation of a preemption handling scheme must be considered. A saved state should contain only enough information (and no more) so that the preempted task can be resumed at the precise point where it was interrupted. The task state should consist of the contents of the general purpose registers, the condition registers, and the relevant portion of background memory.
- **Performance degradation**: There are two main sources of performance degradation: (i) on a preemption request, some task states that have already been executed may be aborted. Retracing these aborted states adds to the finish time of the aborted task. (ii) Any scheme that saves the context of a preempted task in background memory may stall execution units.

In this paper we will present a systematic methodology for incorporating preemption constraints in multi-task VLSI systems. Specifically, we will show how **context switch cost** and **performance degradation** can be minimized while satisfying task specific throughput and **preemption latency** constraints.

1.2 A Motivating Example

Consider a system implementing two tasks A and B. Task A takes four clock cycles and task B takes six clock cycles for one iteration. Let A1, A2, A3, and A4 denote parts of task A that are executed in the first, second, third and fourth clock cycles respectively. Similarly, let B1, B2, B3, B4, B5 and B6 denote parts of task B that are executed in the first, second, third, fourth, fifth and sixth clock cycles respectively. The following assumptions were made while designing the micro-preemption controller.

1. A non-overlapping two-phase clock (CLK 1, CLK 2).
2. Activation of a new task (i.e. changing the SELECTED TASK signal) and transition of a task from one state to the next are synchronized with falling edge of CLK 2.
3. Setting and resetting of PREEMPT MASK is synchronized with falling edge of CLK 1.
4. A task preemption request is serviced when the PREEMPT MASK is low and SELECTED TASK is high and CLK 2 is falling.

A simulation snapshot of micro-preemption in the two-task VLSI system is shown in figure 1[1]. To minimize the controller and context switch overhead, we mandate that task A can be preempted in STATEs A1 and A3 alone. These are called **task preemption points**. Initially the system is in STATE A4. When the system goes to STATE A1, execution of a new task is requested by setting the SELECTED TASK to B and the data inputs to appropriate data values (these have not been shown here for simplicity). However, it is not a valid preemption request (since PREEMPT MASK is high). Even when a valid preemption request arrives in STATE A2 (i.e. all conditions in item 4 are satisfied) task A is not aborted immediately. Rather, the computation **rolls forward** to end of state A3 (the next preemption point) before the preemption request is serviced. Notice that it has taken two clock cycles from the time a valid preemption request arrived (beginning of STATE A2) to the time the new task (task B) became active (end of STATE A3). From the point of view of task B, this is its **preemption latency**. From the point of view of the multi-task VLSI system as a whole (and task A in particular) rolling forward of the computation has eliminated the performance degradation due to an immediate abort. In a nutshell, preemption points A1 and A3 have partitioned the execution of task A into two **critical sections** {A2, A3} and {A4, A1}. Similarly, **task preemption points** B2, B4 and B6 for task B partition it into three critical sections {B1, B2}, {B3, B4}, and {B5, B6}.

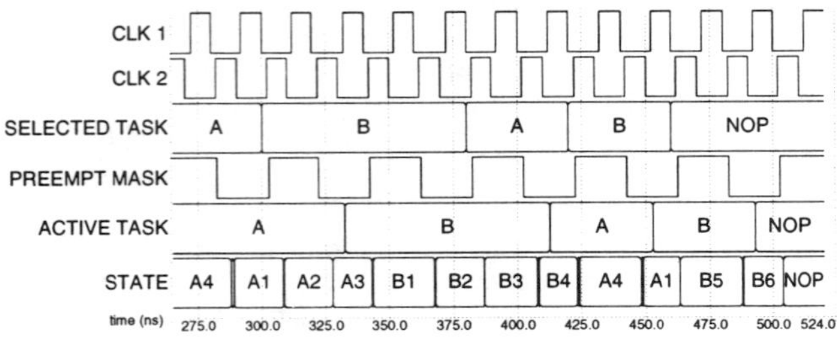

Figure 1: Simulation snapshot showing preemption request and servicing mechanism in a two-task VLSI system

[1] the controller has been implemented using 1μ SCMOS standard cell library and simulated using IRSIM.

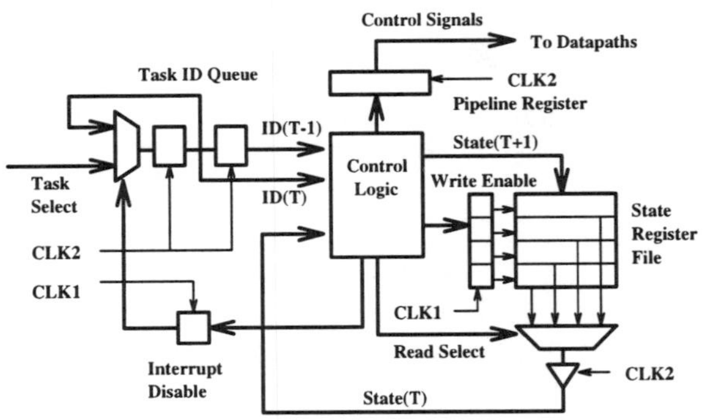

Figure 2: Controller for a multi-task VLSI system supporting micro-preemption

The controller is shown in figure 2. It is a collection of finite state machines (one for each implemented task) and has a state register file that holds the identification of the currently active task. At every clock cycle, a different task can be initiated or a preempted task resumed by the task select signal. The controller signals are pipelined so that the controller delay does not affect the critical path.

The rest of the paper is organized in the following way. We first briefly survey the related work along several dimensions. Next, we will discuss the computational and hardware models. In sections 3 and 4, we introduce our approach, formulate the micro-preemption synthesis problems, and describe the proposed algorithms for micro-preemption synthesis. Experimental results are presented in section 5. In section 6, we conclude by summarizing the results.

1.3 Related Research

Reconfigurable computing platforms are attracting a lot of attention recently. A fast growing billion dollar Field Programmable Gate Array (FPGA) industry is supported by a number of commercial and research tools [12]. A number of special purpose reconfigurable computers have been built. Early work in this direction includes the systems realized at University of Texas, Austin (TRAC) [5]. The Splash system enables reconfigurability to more than 100 different configurations which are well suited for several computational tasks in molecular biology [7]. Several generations of data path reconfigurable video-processors with accompanying compilation support have been developed at University of California, Berkeley [13]. Recently, Application Specific Programmable Processors (ASPPs) [16] have been introduced as an excellent candidate for multifunctional datapaths with frequent context switching. Though their functionalities must be determined in the design phase, a single ASPP implementing multiple functions obtains significant area savings when compared with the dedicated ASIC implementations of the functions.

Research in implementing interrupts is outlined next. The IBM 360/91 supports precise and imprecise interrupt handling [1]. Hwu and Patt [2] proposed a checkpointing approach to handling interrupts. The checkpoints (which incur some penalty in processor

performance) are used to divide the sequential instruction stream into smaller units to reduce the cost of resumption. Sohi [9] integrated the functions of reservation stations and reorder buffers into the register update unit to realize precise interrupts. In addition, Smith and Pleszkun [6] presented architectural solutions such as saving the intermediate state of vector instructions and saving a sequence of instructions that must be executed before saving the program counter. Mosberger et. al. [15] presented a software-only solution to the synchronization problem in uniprocessors. Their idea was to execute atomic sequences without any hardware protection, and to roll the sequence forward to the end, thereby preserving atomicity.
Behavioral synthesis has been active research area for more than two decades [8], and numerous outstanding systems have been built targeting both data path oriented and control oriented applications [8]. Synthesis systems that optimize power, testability and fault-tolerance [14] have been developed.

2 Computational/Hardware Models

Our computational model for a single task is homogeneous synchronous data flow [4]. Within this model, a task is represented as a hierarchical Control Data Flow Graph $G(N, E, T)$ (or CDFG), with nodes N representing the flow graph operations, and the edges E and T respectively the data and timing dependences between the operations.
In modern designs a variety of register file models have been used [10]. From among them we have selected the dedicated register file hardware model. This model clusters all registers in register files and each file is then connected only to the inputs of the corresponding execution units. An important benefit of the chosen hardware model is that it reduces the interconnect at the expense of additional registers.

3 Issues and Our Approach

On preemption, the data in the register files must be preserved somewhere in order for a task to resume. In general purpose microprocessors, these values are transferred to background memory before an interrupt is serviced. This technique is not acceptable in multi-task VLSI systems due to the attendant performance penalty. Alternately, a register windowing technique is used in the Sparc architecture [11]. In this scheme, data is saved in registers within the processor even when a new computation environment is required. However, it entails non-negligible area overheads for duplicated registers. In contrast, we propose an intuitively simple technique by classifying the edges in the CDFG and the registers hold them into two groups:

- **Dedicated registers**[2] (R_d^t) store the values of edges of a task that straddle preemption points. These edges that straddle a preemption point are called the **red** edges, and represent intermediate values essential to resume the task if preempted.
- **Shared registers** (R_s^t) are shared by the values associated with the remaining edges (of all tasks) in the system. These edges that do not straddle a preemption point are called the **green** edges. The dedicated registers of a task can also be used to store the values associated with the green edges in the task. However, the shared registers cannot be assigned to red edges.

Since dedicated registers cannot be shared between tasks, the associated context switch overhead is the sum of the dedicated registers over all tasks. On the other hand, the context switch overhead due to shared registers is the maximum value across all tasks. Overall, the context switch cost of a multi-task VLSI system with task set T is:

$$| R |= \sum_{t \in T} | R_d^t | + \max_{t \in T} | R_s^t | \quad (1)$$

Performance degradation resulting from aborting a task is eliminated by (i) partitioning the task states into **critical sections**, (ii) executing critical sections and (iii) preserving atomicity of a critical section by **rolling forward** to the end of a critical section on preemption. This is analogous to the classical approach to **precise interrupts**.
Next, we present algorithms for (i) preemption point insertion and (ii) preemption context synthesis that minimizes the context switch overhead during multi-task VLSI system synthesis. The optimization problem can be defined as follows:
Given an underlying hardware model and N scheduled tasks, each with its own time bound (λ) and maximum preemption latency (τ), insert preemption points, and bind edges to registers, so that the context switch overhead is minimized.
Initially, all tasks are scheduled in an integrated fashion by considering their word length, precision, hardware and topological similarities. Using the number of edges straddling a clock cycle as an estimate of the context switch overhead, preemption points are inserted. The resulting preemption point set for each task will have more than the minimum number of preemption points. In the next step these preemption point sets are refined. Finally, the preemption context is synthesized by binding edges to registers subject to preemption constraints. The output is then passed through hardware mapping and layout generation tools to synthesize a multi-task VLSI system.

3.1 Preemption Point Insertion

Towards investigating preemption point insertion, consider a task with five edges ($e_1, ..., e_5$), an application latency of eight clock cycles and an edge-to-register binding shown in figure 3. The register file has one input port and one output port which are accessed at the first half cycle and the last half cycle, respectively.
The register overhead of a preemption point can be estimated as the number of edges straddling it. For instance, assuming a preemption latency of three yields

[2] **coefficient registers** (R_c^t) that hold the constants used by the task are not targeted during the context switch optimization. This is because, generally these constants differ from one task to another and cannot share registers.

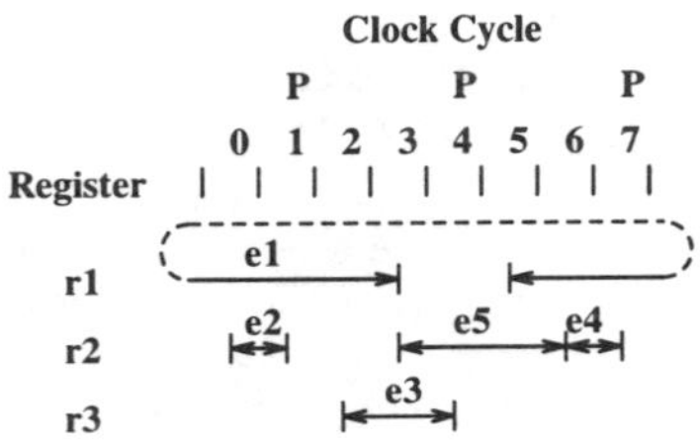

Figure 3: Preemption point insertion and register binding. The dotted line shows a cyclic dependency.

clock cycles 1, 4, and 7 as preemption points as shown in figure 3. The preemption points are marked by 'P'. On preemption point insertion, e_1 and e_5 become red edges and are assigned to two dedicated registers r_1 and r_2. e_3 becomes a green edge and is assigned to shared register r_3. e_2 and e_4 become green edges but are assigned to dedicated register r_2. Initially, preemption points are inserted one task at a time using a polynomial heuristic time algorithm **InsertPreemptionPoints()**. It incrementally inserts preemption points (into each task) such that the number of edges straddling the preemption points is minimized until the preemption latency constraint is satisfied.

3.2 Preemption Point Refinement

Minimizing dedicated registers alone does not reduce the context switch overhead. Instead, it may increase the number of shared registers and hence the total context switch overhead. For example, assume preemption points are inserted at clock cycles 0 and 5. Consider the following scenarios:

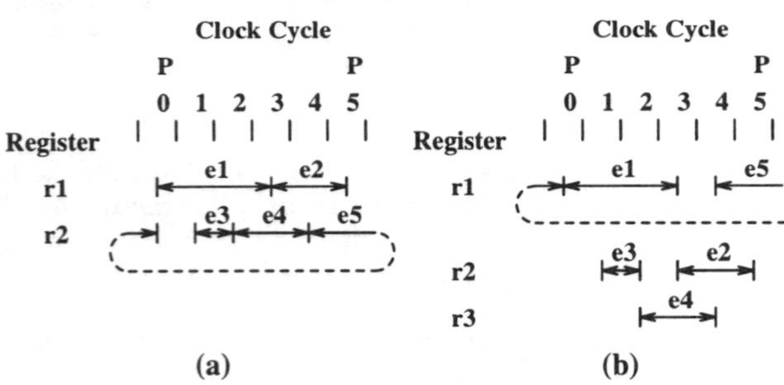

Figure 4: Shared register overhead

- **scenario 1 (figure 4 (a))** : Red edges e_1 and e_5 are assigned to dedicated registers r_1 and r_2, respectively. This results in two dedicated registers and zero shared registers for the task with a context switch overhead of two registers.
- **scenario 2 (figure 4 (b))**: Red edges e_1 and e_5 are bound to dedicated register r_1. The green edges e_2, e_3 and e_4 are bound to shared registers r_2 and r_3. This results in one dedicated register and two shared registers with a context switch overhead of three registers.

Scenario 1 is superior to **scenario 2** if all other tasks in the system do not require shared registers. **Scenario 2** is superior to **scenario 1** if at least one of the remaining tasks uses more than two shared registers.

Based on these observation it is clear that both the shared and dedicated registers must be considered in an integrated manner to optimize the context switch overhead.

```
    RefinePreemptionPoints (T, P) {
1:  for each t_i ∈ T {
2:    for (j ← 0; j <| P |; j++) {
3:      R[i][j] ← PreemptionContextSynthesis(E_i, P);
4:      p ← p_k s.t. NumberOfEdges(p_k) is
          max_{p_l ∈ P} NumberOfEdges(p_l) and
          MaxPreemptionLatency(P − {p_k}) ≤ τ_i;
5:      if (p = φ) break;
6:      P ← P − {p}; /* Prune a preemption point */
      }
    }
7:  PCCost_best ← infinite;
8:  while ((C ← GenerateConfiguration()) ≠ φ) {
9:    PCCost ← PreemptionContextCost(R, C);
10:   if (PCCost < PCCost_best)
        PCCost_best ← PCCost;
    }
  }
```

Figure 5: Algorithm for preemption point refinement - For each task t_i in task set T, E_i is the set of edges, λ_i is the input latency, and τ_i is the preemption latency.

For each task, we start from the preemption point sets generated by the insertion step. We then generate a list of candidate preemption point sets by pruning preemption points with large context switch overhead (steps 2-6 in **RefinePreemptionPoints()** in figure 5). Both dedicated and shared registers are used to compute the context switch overhead. Since the peak usage of shared registers cannot be known a priori, edges are bound to registers (using **PreemptionContextSynthesis()**) to evaluate the context switch overhead, exactly. This pruning technique is possible because for each task, preemption point insertion usually inserts more preemption points than are necessary. Finally, the best preemption point set one for each of the tasks is obtained by using the context switch cost function given by equation 1. This is summarized in steps 7-10.

Consider a multi-task VLSI system implementing three tasks, t_1, t_2, t_3 shown in figure 6. Following the preceding steps, task t_1 has two candidate preemption point sets (PPS) with context switch overheads (CSO) (3, 4) and (2, 5). Similarly, tasks t_2 and t_3 have four and three preemption point sets, respectively. The context switch overhead for each preemption point set is given as the two-tuple, (# of dedicated registers, # of shared registers). Selecting preemption point set 2 for t_1, preemption point set 4 for t_2 and preemption point set 3 for t_3 will result in a context switch cost of $(2 + 2 + 1) + \max(5, 7, 5) = 12$. The context switch cost of selecting preemption point set 2 for t_1, preemption point set 3 for t_2 and preemption point set 2 for t_3 is $(2 + 3 + 1) + \max(5, 5, 5) = 11$. From among the $2 \times 4 \times 3 = 24$ configurations, this has the lowest context switch overhead.

t_1	
PPS	CSO
1	(3, 4)
2	(2, 5)

t_2	
PPS	CSO
1	(5, 4)
2	(4, 5)
3	(3, 5)
4	(2, 7)

t_3	
PPS	CSO
1	(2, 4)
2	(1, 5)
3	(1, 5)

Figure 6: Candidate preemption point sets for tasks t_1, t_2 and t_3

3.3 Preemption Context Synthesis

The optimization problem associated with preemption context binding can be defined as:
Given a scheduled task and a set of preemption points, bind the edges to the registers so that (i) the red edges are bound to dedicated registers, and (ii) the total number of registers is minimized.

```
PreemptionContextSynthesis (E, P) {
  1. Classify edges into red and green
  2. Bind red edges to dedicated registers
  3. Bind green edges to dedicated or shared registers
}
                              (a)
Classify (E, P) {
  Red ← φ; Green ← E;
  foreach e ∈ E
    foreach p ∈ P
      if (lifetime of e overlaps p) {
        Green ← Green − {e}; Red ← Red ∪ {e}; }
}
                              (b)
Bind (E) {
  repeat {
    e ← e_k s.t. | e_k.nbr | is max_{e_i∈E} | e_i.nbr |;
    e.reg ← min r s.t. r ≠ n.reg ∀n ∈ e.nbr;
  } until ((E ← E − {e}) ≠ φ);
}
                              (c)
```

Figure 7: Algorithms for preemption context synthesis

The algorithm, outlined in figure 7, minimizes the number of dedicated registers first and then minimizes the number of shared registers. Initially, the algorithm groups the edges into red and green edges using **Classify ()**. Then the red edges are bound to dedicated registers. Finally, the green edges are bound. The ordering is important since while green edges can be bound to either the dedicated or the shared registers, red edges can only be bound to dedicated registers. A graph coloring heuristic **Bind ()** (outlined in figure 7 (c)) is used for binding. The edge with the largest number of bound neighbors (*nbr*) is selected and bound to a register (*reg*) which is not bound to any of its neighbors.

4 Experimental Results

Micro-preemption synthesis techniques proposed in this paper were validated on a set of DSP, video, control and communication applications. The selected applications span a wide range of complexities in computational structures and include Arai's fast DCT algorithm (ARAI), decimate-by-four wave digital filter (DECBY4), four-state linear controller (FSLC), Winograd's DFT for N = 8 (FFT8), digital wavelet transform (WAVELET) and ninth degree bireciprocal WDF with Butterworth response (WDF9). Synthesis modules for hardware mapping and layout generation from HYPER high level synthesis system were used to complete the synthesis trajectory.

4.1 Register Overhead Evaluation

multi-task VLSI system	allocation			# of registers		
	+	-	*	0-p	1-p	all-p
{ARAI, FFT8, WAVELET}	2	2	1	64	65 2%	86 34%
{FIR20, VETT, VOLTERRA}	2	2	2	81	88 9%	105 30%
{DECBY4, FSLC, NC, WANG}	2	3	2	119	134 13%	170 43%
{WDF7, WDF9, WDFB}	2	4	2	62	80 29%	91 47%
{DIF, LDI_LP, WDF5}	2	2	1	40	54 35%	68 70%
{ADAPT, LEE, CASCADE}	2	2	2	57	79 39%	92 61%

Table 1: Register overhead associated with micro-preemption

The results of six multi-task VLSI systems are summarized in table 1. The first column shows the applications implemented in each system. The next three columns summarize the hardware allocation. The last three columns give the number of registers for the case when no preemption points are inserted (0-p), when one preemption point is inserted (1-p), and when preemption points are inserted at all clock cycles (all-p). Using the 0-p case as the base line, the register overhead for the 1-p case varies from 2% to 39%. At the other extreme, the register overhead for the all-p case varies from 30% to 70%.

multi-task VLSI system	area (mm^2)		over
	0-p	all-p	head
{ARAI, FFT8, WAVELET}	40.8	43.2	6%
{FIR20, VETT, VOLTERRA}	94.2	98.0	4%
{DECBY4, FSLC, NC, WANG}	84.6	90.6	7%
{WDF7, WDF9, WDFB}	90.9	96.1	6%
{DIF, LDI_LP, WDF5}	28.4	31.4	11%
{ADAPT, CASCADE, LEE}	50.3	54.4	8%

Table 2: Area overhead associated with micro-preemption

We completed the synthesis trajectory by passing these designs through the hardware mapping and layout synthesis phase. The area overhead for the six designs using actual layouts are summarized in table 2. The areas are reported for the 0-p case and the all-p case. Again using the 0-p case as the basis, the area overhead for the all-p case varies from 4% to 11% as shown in the last column.

When compared to the background memory based schemes, the proposed scheme does not need (i) additional ports of the register files which are used to save/restore data to/from the background memories without stalling currently running task, (ii) additional buses to interconnect the register files to the background memories, and (iii) additional control logic to compute memory addresses. Since the preemption requests can be serviced in parallel without stalling the execution of the tasks, there is no performance penalty.

As the preemption latency increases, the number of dedicated registers decreases, the number of shared registers increases, and the total number of registers decreases monotonously. Finally, the number of coefficient registers is invariant to the preemption latency.

4.2 Register Transfer Level Analysis

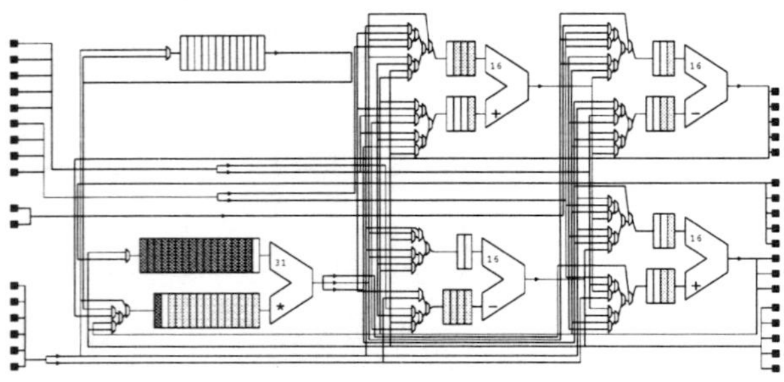

(a) preemption latency is 75% of the input latency.

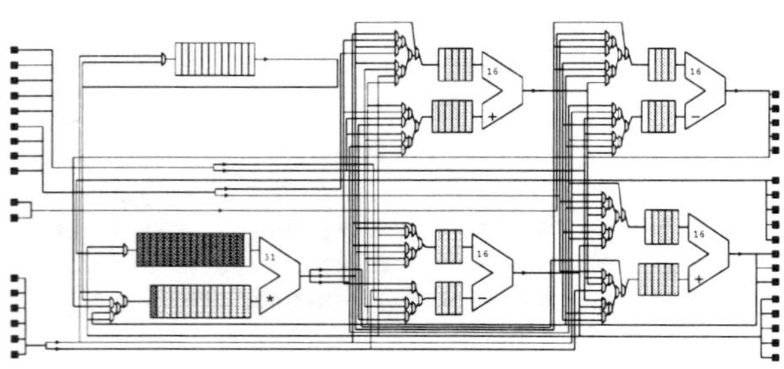

(b) preemption latency is 25% of the input latency.

Constant   Dedicated   Shared

Figure 8: Microarchitecture for the multi-task VLSI system implementing {ARAI, FFT8, WAVELET} for two preemption latencies.

The microarchitecture with preemption points for the multi-task VLSI system implementing {ARAI, FFT8, WAVELET} are shown in figure 8. Registers in the register files are classified as one of three types by using different gray levels as shown in the legend in figure 8. The number of registers increases by 15% (from 73 to 84) as the preemption latency decreases by 50%. However, since there is no interconnect overhead, the increase in the total chip area is very small.

5 Conclusions

We presented techniques and algorithms to incorporate micro-preemption constraints during multi-task VLSI system synthesis. The area overhead of the proposed scheme is under 12%. We have also implemented a controller based scheme to eliminate the performance degradation by (i) partitioning the task states into **critical sections**, (ii) executing critical sections and (iii) preserving atomicity by **rolling forward** to the end of the critical sections on preemption.

References

[1] D.W. Anderson, F.J. Sparacio, and F.M. Tomasulo, "The IBM System/360 Model 91: Machine philosophy and instruction-handling," IBM Journal, 11(1), pp. 8-24, 1967.

[2] W.W. Hwu and Y.N. Patt, "Checkpoint repair for high performance out-of-order execution machines," IEEE Trans Comp (36)12, pp. 1496-1514, 1987.

[3] G.D. Hillman, "DSP56200: An Algorithm-Specific Digital Signal Processor Peripheral", Proc IEEE, 75(9), pp. 1185-1191.

[4] E. A. Lee and D. C. Messerschmitt, "Static Scheduling of Synchronous Data flow Programs for Digital Signal Processing", IEEE Trans on Comp, 36(1), pp. 24-36, 1987

[5] G.J. Lipovsky, M. Malek, "Parallel Computing: Theory and Comparison", John Wiley.

[6] J.E. Smith and A.R. Pleszkun, "Implementing precise interrupts in pipelined processors," IEEE Trans ComP, 37(5), pp. 562-273, May 1988.

[7] M. Gokhale, et al., "SPLASH: A Reconfigurable Linear Logic Array", ICPP, 1990.

[8] M. C. McFarland and A. C. Parker and R. Camposano, "The high-level synthesis of digital systems", Proc IEEE, 78(2), pp. 301-318, 1990.

[9] G.S. Sohi, "Instruction issue logic for high-performance, interruptible, multiple functional unit, pipelined computers," IEEE Trans Comp, 39(3), pp. 349-359, 1990.

[10] J. Rabaey, et al., "Fast Prototyping of Data Path Intensive Architectures," IEEE Design & Test, 8(1), pp. 40-51, 1991

[11] R.J. Baron and L. Higbie, Computer Architecture Case Studies, Addison-Wesley, pp. 234-237, 1992.

[12] A. El Gamal, J. Rose, A. Sangiovanni-Vincentelli, "Synthesis Methods for Field Programmable Gate Arrays", Proc. of IEEE, 81(7), pp. 1013-1029, 1993.

[13] A.K. Yeung, J.M. Rabaey, "A 2.4 GOPS data-driven reconfigurable multiprocessor IC for DSP", ISSCC, pp. 108-109, 1995.

[14] K. Kim, R. Karri and M. Potkonjak, "Heterogeneous Built-In Resiliency of Application Specific Programmable Processors," Proc. of Intl Conf on CAD, pp. 406-411, Nov 1996.

[15] D. Mosberger, P. Druschel and L. Peterson, "Implementing Atomic Sequences on Uniprocessors Using Rollforward," Software-Practice and Experience, 26(1), pp. 1-23, Jan 1996.

[16] K. Kim, R. Karri and M. Potkonjak, "Synthesis of Application Specific Programmable Processors," Proc. of 34th DAC, pp. 353-358, Jun 1997.

SESSION 1C

ESTIMATION OF POWER BOUNDS

Moderators:

Farid N. Najm, University of Illinois, Urbana, IL

Wen-Zen Shen, National Chiao Tung University, Hsinchu, Taiwan

Power Sensitivity - A New Method to Estimate Power Dissipation Considering Uncertain Specifications of Primary Inputs *

Zhanping Chen
Electrical Engineering
Purdue University
W. Lafayette, IN 47907

Kaushik Roy
Electrical Engineering
Purdue University
W. Lafayette, IN 47907

Tan-Li Chou
Intel Corporation
Technology Department
Beaverton, OR 97006

Abstract

Power dissipation in CMOS circuits heavily depends on the signal properties of the primary inputs. Due to uncertainties in specification of such properties, the average power should be specified between a maximum and a minimum possible value. Due to the complex nature of the problem, it is practically impossible to use traditional power estimation techniques to determine such bounds. In this paper, we present a novel approach to accurately estimate the maximum and minimum bounds for average power using a technique which calculates the sensitivities of average power dissipation to primary input signal properties. The sensitivities are calculated using a novel statistical technique and can be obtained as a by-product of average power estimation using a Monte Carlo based approach. The signal properties are specified in terms of signal probability (probability of a signal being logic ONE) and signal activity (probability of signal switching). Results show that the maximum and minimum average power dissipation can vary widely if the primary input probabilities and activities are not specified accurately.

1 Introduction

The increasing use of portable computing and communication systems makes power dissipation a critical parameter to be minimized in circuit design. Therefore, power estimation tools are badly needed.

In order to accurately estimate power, traditional power estimation techniques [3, 4, 5, 6] require exact signal properties of primary inputs. However, accurate signal property values for primary inputs may not often be available. Since power dissipation strongly depends on the input signal properties, uncertainties in specifications of input signal properties make the estimation process difficult. In fact, average power dissipation of a circuit should be represented as a range given by $[Power_{min}, Power_{max}]$. Traditional power estimation techniques cannot deal with the complexity of the problem since it is practically impossible to try all ranges of signal properties to estimate the minimum and maximum average power dissipation, when the number of primary inputs is large. In this paper we present a novel approach to accurately estimate such bounds for average power dissipation using a technique which calculates the sensitivities of average power to primary input signal properties. The signal properties are specified in terms of signal probability and signal activity. The sensitivities are calculated using an efficient statistical technique and can be obtained as a by-product of average power estimation using a Monte Carlo based approach, the details of which are given in section 3.

*This research was supported in part by DARPA (F33615-95-C-1625), NSF CAREER award (9501869-MIP), IBM, AT&T, and Rockwell.

2 Preliminaries

2.1 Signal Probability and Activity

The primary inputs of a circuit are modeled to be *mutually independent strict-sense-stationary (SSS) mean-ergodic 1-0 processes* [5]. Under this assumption, the probability of the primary input node x_i, to assume logic ONE, $P(x_i(t))$, becomes constant and independent of time and is denoted by $P(x_i)$, the *equilibrium signal probability* of node x_i. $P(x_i)$ is the average fraction of clock cycles in which the equilibrium value of node x_i is logic ONE.

The *activity* $A(x_i)$ is defined as the average number of switching events per unit time. If we assume that all primary inputs to the circuits under consideration switch only at the leading edge of the clock and that the circuits are delay-free, we can define *normalized activity*, denoted by $a(x_i)$, as $A(x_i)/f$, where f is the clock frequency. Therefore, $a(x_i) = P(x_i(t-T)\bar{x}_i(t) + \bar{x}_i(t-T)x_i(t)) = P(x_i(t-T)\bar{x}_i(t)) + P(\bar{x}_i(t-T)x_i(t))$. Since x_i is *SSS*, $P(x_i(t-T)) = P(x_i(t)) = P(x_i)$. We also have $P(x_i(t)) = P(x_i(t-T)x_i(t)) + P(\bar{x}_i(t-T)x_i(t))$ and $P(x_i(t-T)) = P(x_i(t-T)x_i(t)) + P(x_i(t-T)\bar{x}_i(t))$. Therefore, we can derive

$$P(x_i(t-T)\bar{x}_i(t)) = P(\bar{x}_i(t-T)x_i(t)) = a(x_i)/2 \quad (1)$$

and

$$P(x_i(t-T)x_i(t)) = P(x_i) - a(x_i)/2 \quad (2)$$

$$P(\bar{x}_i(t-T)\bar{x}_i(t)) = 1 - P(x_i) - a(x_i)/2 \quad (3)$$

1092-3152/97 $10.00 © 1997 IEEE

2.2 Power Dissipation in CMOS Logic Circuits

Among the three sources of power dissipation – switching current, short-circuit current, and leakage current, the switching power is the most dominant in current day technology. Thus the average power for a CMOS circuit can be approximated by $Power_{avg} = \frac{1}{2}V_{dd}^2 \sum_{j \in all\ nodes} C_j\ A_j$, where V_{dd} is the supply voltage, C_j is the node capacitance, A_j is the activity at node j. Since A_j is proportional to the normalized activity a_j and C_j is approximately proportional to the fanout at node j, we can define the *normalized power dissipation measure* Φ as: $\Phi = \sum_{j \in all\ nodes} f_{anout}(j)\ a_j$, where $f_{anout}(j)$ is the fanout number at node j.

2.3 Power Sensitivity

To measure the effect of primary input uncertainties on power dissipation, we define *power sensitivity to primary input activity* $S_{a(x_i)}$ and *power sensitivity to primary input probability* $S_{P(x_i)}$ as follows:

$$S_{a(x_i)} = \lim_{\Delta a(x_i) \to 0} \frac{\Delta Power_{avg}}{\Delta a(x_i)} = \frac{\partial Power_{avg}}{\partial a(x_i)} \quad (4)$$

$$S_{P(x_i)} = \lim_{\Delta P(x_i) \to 0} \frac{\Delta Power_{avg}}{\Delta P(x_i)} = \frac{\partial Power_{avg}}{\partial P(x_i)} \quad (5)$$

where $a(x_i)$ and $P(x_i)$ are the activity and probability of primary input x_i, respectively.

$Power_{avg}$ is proportional to Φ. Therefore, we can define *normalized power sensitivity to primary input activity* $\zeta_{a(x_i)}$ and *normalized power sensitivity to primary input probability* $\zeta_{P(x_i)}$ in terms of Φ as follows:

$$\zeta_{a(x_i)} = \frac{\partial \Phi}{\partial a(x_i)} = \sum_{j \in allnodes} f_{anout}(j) \frac{\partial a_j}{\partial a(x_i)} \quad (6)$$

$$\zeta_{P(x_i)} = \frac{\partial \Phi}{\partial P(x_i)} = \sum_{j \in allnodes} f_{anout}(j) \frac{\partial a_j}{\partial P(x_i)} \quad (7)$$

where a_j is the activity of node j.

3 Efficient Statistical Technique to Estimate Power Sensitivity (*STEPS*)

A naive approach to estimate power sensitivity would be to simulate a circuit to obtain the average power dissipation based on nominal values of primary input signal probabilities and activities. Then assign a small variation to only one primary input and re-simulate the circuit. After all the primary inputs have been exhausted, power sensitivity can be obtained using $\Delta Power_i / \Delta\theta_i$, where θ_i can be $P(x_i)$ or $a(x_i)$. This naive method can be easily implemented. However, it involves $n+1$ times of power estimation. If the number of primary inputs is large, this method can be computationally expensive. Therefore, the naive simulation method is impractical for large circuits with large number of primary inputs. A practical symbolic method was proposed in [2]. However, this approach requires circuit partitioning for large circuits, which can introduce error. In this section we present an efficient technique (*STEPS*) to estimate power sensitivities as a by-product of statistical power estimation using a Monte Carlo based approach.

The basic idea of Monte-Carlo based statistical method to estimate power dissipation is to simulate a circuit with random patterns applied to primary inputs. Stopping criterion is used to determine when node activities have converged to its correct value [1]. Let us formulate how to estimate power sensitivity using Monte Carlo technique.

A logic circuit can be described by a set of completely specified Boolean functions. Each Boolean function maps primary input vector to an internal or primary output signal. The statistics of internal signals and primary output signals are completely determined by the logic transition at primary inputs. Therefore, the instantaneous power dissipation of a circuit is completely determined by two consecutive input vectors $\mathbf{V^0}$ and $\mathbf{V^T}$, where the superscripts denote time and T is the clock cycle. The expected value of average power can be expressed as follows:

$$E[Pwr] = \sum_{\mathbf{V^0},\mathbf{V^T}} Power(\mathbf{V^0}\ \mathbf{V^T}) P(\mathbf{V^0}\ \mathbf{V^T}) \quad (8)$$

where $\mathbf{V^0} = (I_1^0, I_2^0, \cdots, I_n^0)$ and $\mathbf{V^T} = (I_1^T, I_2^T, \cdots, I_n^T)$ are primary input vectors, and $I_i^0 = x_i^0$ or $\overline{x_i^0}$, and $I_i^T = x_i^T$ or $\overline{x_i^T}$. The power consumption in every clock cycle is a random variable and is denoted as Pwr. $Power(\mathbf{V^0}\ \mathbf{V^T})$ represents the power consumption due to the pair of input vectors $\mathbf{V^0}$ and $\mathbf{V^T}$. For a particular pair of consecutive vectors, $Power(\mathbf{V^0}\ \mathbf{V^T})$ is independent of the probability and activity values of primary inputs. The probability of having consecutive input vectors $\mathbf{V^0}$ followed by $\mathbf{V^T}$ is represented by $P(\mathbf{V^0}\ \mathbf{V^T})$. Therefore, power sensitivity can be expressed as follows:

$$\begin{aligned} \zeta_{\theta_i} &= \frac{\partial \Phi}{\partial \theta_i} \\ &= \frac{\partial E[Pwr]}{\partial \theta_i} \\ &= \sum_{\mathbf{V^0},\mathbf{V^T}} \left(Power(\mathbf{V^0}\ \mathbf{V^T}) \frac{\partial P(\mathbf{V^0}\ \mathbf{V^T})}{\partial \theta_i} \right) \end{aligned} \quad (9)$$

All the primary inputs are assumed to be spatially independent. Therefore, we have,

$$\frac{\partial P(\mathbf{V^0}\ \mathbf{V^T})}{\partial \theta_i} = P(I_1^0\ I_1^T) \cdots \frac{\partial P(I_i^0 I_i^T)}{\partial \theta_i} \cdots P(I_n^0\ I_n^T)$$

From basic calculus, we have

$$\frac{\partial P(I_i^0\ I_i^T)}{\partial \theta_i} = P(I_i^0\ I_i^T) \frac{\partial ln(P(I_i^0\ I_i^T))}{\partial \theta_i}$$

Substituting the above two equations into equation (9), we get,

$$\begin{aligned}\zeta_{\theta_i} &= \sum_{\mathbf{V^0},\mathbf{V^T}} \{Power(\mathbf{V^0V^T})P(\mathbf{V^0V^T}) \\ &\qquad \frac{\partial ln(P(I_i^0 I_i^T))}{\partial \theta_i}\} \\ &= E[Pwr\ \frac{\partial ln(P(I_i^0\ I_i^T))}{\partial \theta_i}] \qquad (10)\end{aligned}$$

Multiplying Pwr by a factor $\partial ln(P(I_i^0\ I_i^T))/\partial\theta_i$, we obtain a sample of power sensitivity. Therefore, power sensitivity can be estimated simultaneously with average power. The only expression left to be evaluated is $\partial ln(P(I_i^0\ I_i^T))/\partial\theta_i$. Since I_i^0 is either x_i^0 or $\overline{x_i^0}$ and I_i^T is either x_i^T or $\overline{x_i^T}$, we have four combinations for $P(I_i^0\ I_i^T)$: $P(x_i^0\ x_i^T)$, $P(\overline{x_i^0}\ \overline{x_i^T})$, $P(x_i^0\ \overline{x_i^T})$, and $P(\overline{x_i^0}\ x_i^T)$. Each of the expressions can be expressed in terms of probability and activity ($P(x_i)$ and $a(x_i)$) by equations (1), (2), and (3) (note that $x_i(t-T)$ and $x_i(t)$ are replaced by x_i^0 and x_i^T, respectively). Therefore, $\partial ln(P(I_i^0\ I_i^T))/\partial a(x_i)$ can be calculated as follows:

$$\begin{aligned}\frac{\partial ln(P(x_i^0\ x_i^T))}{\partial a(x_i)} &= \frac{\partial ln(P(x_i)-\frac{1}{2}a(x_i))}{\partial a(x_i)} \\ &= \frac{-\frac{1}{2}}{P(x_i)-\frac{1}{2}a(x_i)} \qquad (11)\\ \frac{\partial ln(P(\overline{x_i^0}\ \overline{x_i^T}))}{\partial a(x_i)} &= \frac{\partial ln(1-P(x_i)-\frac{1}{2}a(x_i))}{\partial a(x_i)} \\ &= \frac{-\frac{1}{2}}{1-P(x_i)-\frac{1}{2}a(x_i)} \qquad (12)\\ \frac{\partial ln(P(x_i^0\ \overline{x_i^T}))}{\partial a(x_i)} &= \frac{\partial ln(P(\overline{x_i^0}\ x_i^T))}{\partial a(x_i)} \\ &= \frac{\partial ln(\frac{1}{2}a(x_i))}{\partial a(x_i)} \\ &= \frac{1}{a(x_i)} \qquad (13)\end{aligned}$$

and $\partial ln(P(I_i^0\ I_i^T))/\partial P(x_i)$ has the following four combinations:

$$\begin{aligned}\frac{\partial ln(P(x_i^0\ x_i^T))}{\partial P(x_i)} &= \frac{\partial ln(P(x_i)-\frac{1}{2}a_i)}{\partial P(x_i)} \\ &= \frac{1}{P(x_i)-\frac{1}{2}a(x_i)} \qquad (14)\\ \frac{\partial ln(P(\overline{x_i^0}\ \overline{x_i^T}))}{\partial P(x_i)} &= \frac{\partial ln(1-P(x_i)-\frac{1}{2}a(x_i))}{\partial P(x_i)} \\ &= \frac{-1}{1-P(x_i)-\frac{1}{2}a(x_i)} \qquad (15)\\ \frac{\partial ln(P(x_i^0\ \overline{x_i^T}))}{\partial P(x_i)} &= \frac{\partial ln(P(\overline{x_i^0}\ x_i^T))}{\partial P(x_i)} \\ &= \frac{\partial ln(\frac{1}{2}a(x_i))}{\partial P(x_i)} = 0 \qquad (16)\end{aligned}$$

4 Power Sensitivity Method

Traditional power estimation techniques require exact specification of primary input signal distribution. However, in general, accurate primary input properties may not be available. Since power dissipation heavily depends on the input signal specifications, uncertain primary input specifications in turn result in uncertain average power dissipation. Therefore, average power should be represented by a range given by the maximum and minimum values of average power. However, traditional power estimation methods cannot handle the complexity of such estimation. It is practically impossible to exhaust all the 2^n (n is the primary input number) combinations of primary input specifications to obtain such bounds. Our method which calculates power sensitivities to primary input specifications, on the other hand, can deal with this complexity efficiently.

Section 3 shows that *STEPS* can estimate power sensitivity as a by-product of average power estimation with nominal values of signal probability and activity. Hence, the minimum and maximum average power of a circuit can easily be computed as follows:

$$\Phi_{min} = \Phi_{avg} - \sum_{i \in all\ PI's} \zeta_{a(x_i)} |\Delta a(x_i)| \qquad (17)$$

$$\Phi_{max} = \Phi_{avg} + \sum_{i \in all\ PI's} \zeta_{a(x_i)} |\Delta a(x_i)| \qquad (18)$$

Φ_{avg} is the average *normalized power dissipation measure.* It can be estimated during the average power estimation process using *STEPS* based on nominal values of primary input signal properties. $\zeta_{a(x_i)}$ is the power sensitivity to activity $a(x_i)$ of primary input x_i. $\Delta a(x_i)$ is the activity variation.

5 Experimental Results

We have implemented the power sensitivity method to estimate minimum and maximum average power dissipation considering uncertain primary input specifications. All the primary inputs are assumed to have probability and activity values (nominal) of 0.5 and 0.26, respectively.

The long run simulation method (naive technique described in section 4) is used as a figure of merit for *STEPS*. Sample number used in this experiment was 3000 while an activity variation of 0.05 was assumed for all the inputs. The comparison is shown in Table 1. The percentage difference is obtained using the expression $\sum|\zeta_{a(x_i)}(SIM) - \zeta_{a(x_i)}(STEPS)|/\sum\zeta_{a(x_i)}(SIM)$, where i varies from all primary inputs, $\zeta_{a(x_i)}(STEPS)$ is the power sensitivity obtained by *STEPS* and $\zeta_{a(x_i)}(SIM)$ is the power sensitivity obtained by simulation. The comparison is shown in Table 1. The CPU time is also shown for a SPARC 5 workstation. Since long run simulation method repeats the estimation procedure $n+1$ times (n is the number of primary inputs), execution time may be unacceptably

Table 1: **Comparison of two methods**

Circuit Chosen	PI's #	Gate #	CPU Time (s)		Diff %
			SIM	*STEPS*	
i1	25	33	519	19	2.1
i2	201	36	15502	78	1.4
i3	132	70	7896	57	1.2
i4	192	94	16960	95	0.2
i5	133	199	23326	223	2.0
i6	138	344	38877	328	1.8
i7	199	406	78514	422	0.3
i8	133	1183	119088	852	1.2
i9	88	353	33581	341	7.2
i10	257	2497	290744	1313	4.0
C432	36	160	8085	220	1.4
C499	41	202	11615	222	10.7
C880	60	357	5675	104	6.7
C1355	41	514	15791	426	6.8
C1908	33	880	19007	649	10.4
C2670	233	1161	160436	848	2.6
C3540	50	1667	48719	930	2.3
C5315	178	2290	-	1827	-
C6288	32	2416	46219	2110	11.9
C7552	207	3466	-	4093	-

long for large n. Let us consider circuit C7552. It takes approximately 4093 seconds of CPU time to complete one simulation run. The circuit has 207 primary inputs. It would take approximately 8.5×10^5 seconds (9.8 days) of CPU time to obtain power sensitivities. Circuits with prohibitively long execution time are identified by dashes in the "*SIM*" and "Diff %" columns of table 1. "Diff %" stands for percent difference between the results obtained by simulation and *STEPS*. *STEPS* can estimate power sensitivity simultaneously with average power, and hence, it is much faster than the naive simulation based approach.

Results for power sensitivities indicate that for some circuits power dissipation is much more sensitive to some primary inputs than others. A small activity variation of such highly sensitive primary inputs will result in a dramatic change of the average power. Consider circuit $i6$. The power sensitivities to activities of the 1st, 2nd, 60th, and 124th primary input (corresponding to primary input number 0, 1, 59, and 123 respectively in Figures 1 and 4) are 237, 276, 133, and 30 respectively. The power sensitivity to the activity of each of the other primary inputs is less than 4. If the activities of the 1st and 2nd primary input have a variation of ± 0.05, the power dissipation may change by 30%. Therefore, for power conscious designs, those sensitive primary inputs have to be accurately specified for accurate estimation of average power.

After obtaining power sensitivities, we use equations (17) and (18) to compute the minimum and maximum average power for each simulated circuit. For simplicity, all primary inputs are assumed to have the same activity variation of ± 0.05. However, our method is not limited to such assumption. Results of the minimum and maximum average power for ISCAS and MCNC benchmark circuits are shown in Figures 2 and 3. Results indicate that for some circuits minimum and maximum average power can vary widely if uncertain specifications of primary inputs exist. Consider circuit $i2$: maximum average power dissipation is 79 units, which is about 46% greater than minimum average power which is 53 units. It should be noted that we do not assume any delay models in deriving equation (10). Therefore, *STEPS* can handle different delay models for logic gates. Figures 5 and 6 give such bounds for average power based on unit delay model.

6 Conclusions

In this paper we have considered an accurate technique to estimate sensitivities of power dissipation to uncertainties in specification of signal properties of primary inputs. The sensitivities can be obtained as a by-product of the statistical power estimation technique, and hence, different delay models can be easily incorporated. Based on the sensitivity values, minimum and maximum average power can be easily estimated. Our results on ISCAS and MCNC benchmark circuits indicate that for some circuits power dissipation can be very sensitive to some primary inputs. A small activity variation of such sensitive inputs can cause power dissipation to change drastically. Results on minimum and maximum average power show that such bounds can vary widely if the primary input probabilities and activities are not specified accurately.

References

[1] R.Burch, F.Najm, P.Yang and T.Trick, "A Monte Carlo Approach for Power Estimation", *IEEE Trans. VLSI Systems*, Vol.1, No. 1, pp. 63-71, March, 1993.

[2] Z. Chen, K. Roy, and T.-L. Chou, "Sensitivity of Power Dissipation to Uncertainties in Primary Input Specification," *Custom Integrated Circuits Conference*, pp. 487-490, 1997.

[3] T.-L. Chou, K. Roy, and S. Prasad, "Estimation of Circuit Activity Considering Signal Correlations and Simultaneous Switching," *IEEE Intl. Conf. on Computer-Aided-Designed*, pp. 300-303, 1994.

[4] A. Ghosh, S. Devadas, K. Keutzer, and J. White, "Estimation of Average Switching Activity in Combinational and Sequential Circuits," *ACM IEEE Design Automation Conf.*, pp. 253-259, 1992.

[5] F.N.Najm, "Transition Density, A Stochastic Measure of Activity in Digital Circuits" *28th ACM IEEE Design Automation Conf.*, pp. 644-649, 1991.

[6] C.-Y. Tsui, M. Pedram, and A. M. Despain, "Exact and Approximate Methods for Calculating Signal and Transition Probabilities in FSMs," *Intl. Workshop on Low Power Design*, pp. 18-23, 1994.

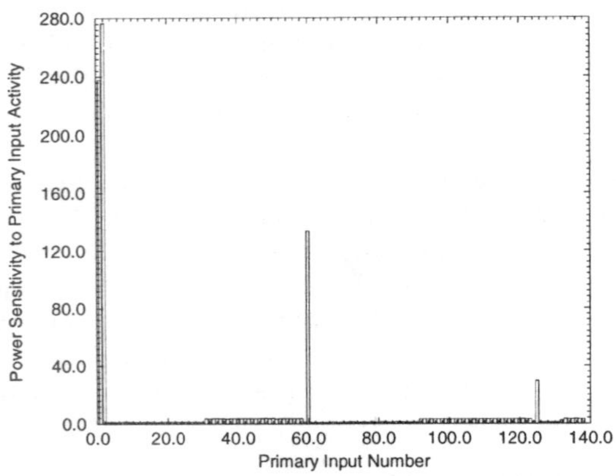

Figure 1: **Power sensitivity ζ_{a_i} obtained by simulation for circuit i6**

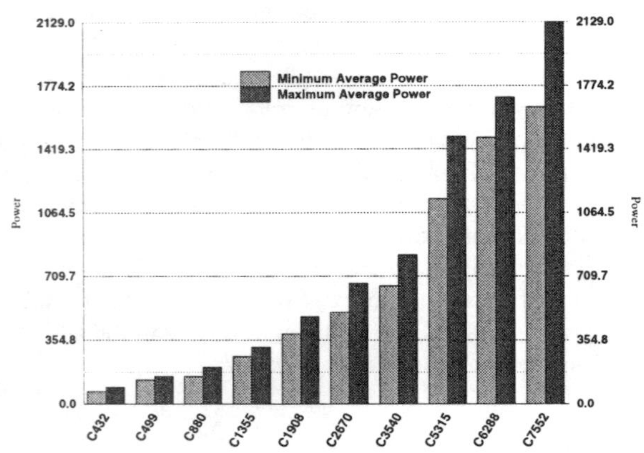

Figure 2: **Average power obtained using zero delay model for ISCAS benchmark circuits**

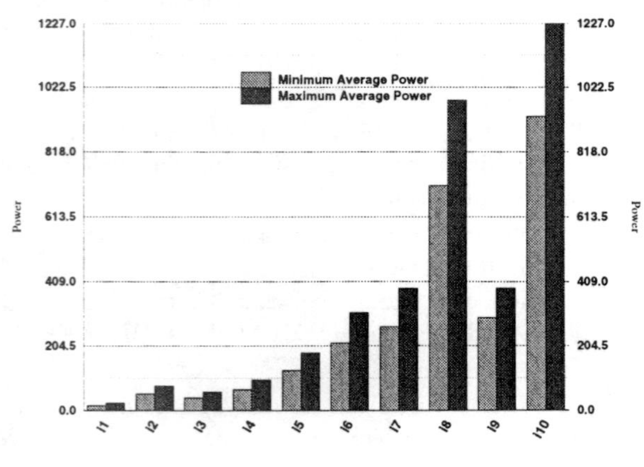

Figure 3: **Average power obtained using zero delay model for MCNC benchmark circuits**

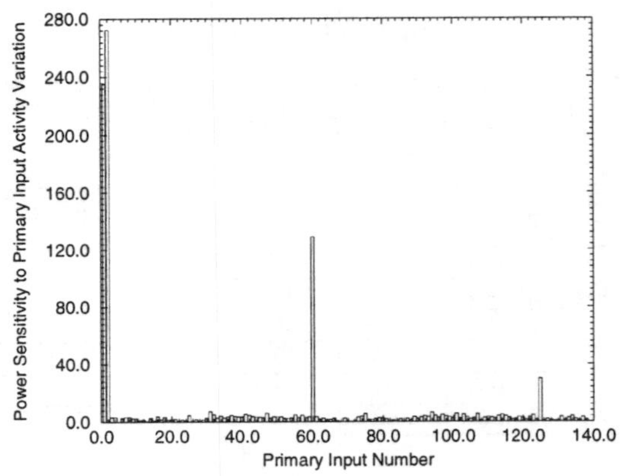

Figure 4: **Power sensitivity ζ_{a_i} obtained by *STEPS* for circuit i6**

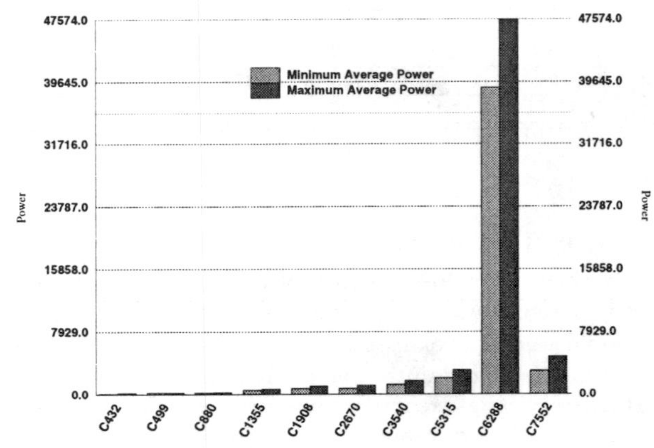

Figure 5: **Average power obtained using unit delay model for ISCAS benchmark circuits**

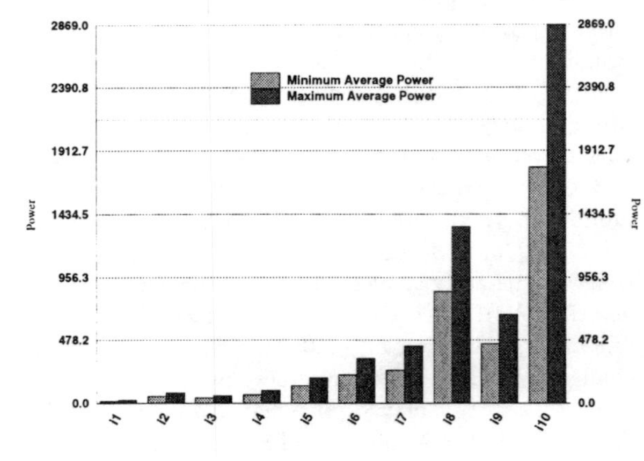

Figure 6: **Average power obtained using unit delay model for MCNC benchmark circuits**

Effects of Delay Models on Peak Power Estimation of VLSI Sequential Circuits

Michael S. Hsiao[†], Elizabeth M. Rudnick[††], and Janak H. Patel[††]

[†]Department of Electrical and Computer Engineering, Rutgers University, Piscataway, NJ

[††]Center for Reliable and High-Performance Computing, University of Illinois, Urbana, IL

Abstract

Previous work has shown that maximum switching density at a given node is extremely sensitive to a slight change in the delay at that node. However, when estimating the peak power for the entire circuit, the powers estimated must not be as sensitive to a slight variation or inaccuracy in the assumed gate delays because computing the exact gate delays for every gate in the circuit during simulation is expensive. Thus, we would like to use the simplest delay model possible to reduce the execution time for estimating power, while making sure that it provides an accurate estimate, i.e., that the peak powers estimated will not vary due to a variation in the gate delays. Results for four delay models are reported for the ISCAS85 combinational benchmark circuits, ISCAS89 sequential benchmark circuits, and several synthesized circuits.

1 Introduction

The continuing decrease in feature size and increase in chip density in recent years give rise to concerns about excessive power dissipation in VLSI chips. As pointed out in [1], large instantaneous power dissipation can cause overheating (local hot spots), and the failure rate for components roughly doubles for every $10°C$ increase in operating temperature. Knowledge of peak power dissipation can help to determine the thermal and electrical limits of a design.

The power dissipated in CMOS logic circuits is a complex function of the gate delays, clock frequency, process parameters, circuit topology and structure, and the input vectors applied. Once the processing and structural parameters have been fixed, the measure of power dissipation is dominated by the switching activity (toggle counts) of the circuit. It has been shown in [2] and [3] that, due to uneven circuit delay paths, multiple switching events at internal nodes can result, and power estimation can be extremely sensitive to different gate delays. Both [2] and [3] computed the *upper bound* of maximum transition (or switching) density of individual internal nodes of a combinational circuit via propagation of uncertainty waveforms across the circuit. However, these measures cannot be used to compute a tight upper bound of the overall power dissipation of the entire circuit.

Although maximum switching density of a given internal node can be extremely sensitive to the delay model used, it is unclear whether peak power dissipation of the entire circuit is also equally sensitive to the delay model. Since glitches and hazards are not taken into account in a zero-delay framework, the power dissipation measures from the zero-delay model may differ greatly from the actual powers. Will the peak power be vastly different among various non-zero delay models (where glitches and hazards are accounted for) in sequential circuits? Moreover, the delays used for internal gates in most simulators are mere estimates of the actual gate delays. Can we still have confidence in the peak power estimated using these delay measures considering that the actual delays for the gates in the circuit may be different? Since computing the exact gate delays for every gate in the circuit during simulation is expensive, does there exist a simple delay model such that the execution time for estimating power is reduced and an accurate peak power estimate can be obtained (i.e., the peak powers estimated will not vary due to a variation in the gate delays)?

Several approaches to measuring maximum power in CMOS VLSI circuits have been reported [4-10]. Unlike *average* power estimations [11-17], where signal switching probabilities are sufficient to compute the average power, *peak* power is associated with a specific starting circuit state S and a specific sequence of vectors Seq that produce the power. Two issues are addressed in this paper. First, given a (S_i, Seq_i) tuple that generates peak power under delay model DM_i, is it possible to obtain another tuple (S_j, Seq_j) that generates equal or higher dissipation under a different delay model DM_j? Second, will the (S_i, Seq_i) tuple generated for peak power under delay model DM_i also produce near peak power under a different delay model DM_j?

Four different delay models are studied in this work: **zero delay**, **unit delay**, **type-1 variable delay**, and **type-2 variable delay**. The three delay models used in [9] are the same as the first three delay models of this work. Measures of peak power dissipation are estimated for all four delay models over various time periods. Genetic algorithms (GA's) are chosen as the optimization tool for this problem as in [10]. GA's are used to find the vector sequences which most accurately estimate the peak power under various delay models as well as over various time durations. The estimates obtained for each delay model are compared with the estimates from randomly-generated sequences, and the results for combinational circuits are compared with the automatic test generation (ATG) based technique [9] as well. The GA-based estimates will be shown to achieve much higher peak power dissipation in short execution times when compared with the random simulation.

The remainder of the paper is organized as follows. Section 2 explains the delay models, and Section 3 discusses the peak power measures over various time periods. The GA framework for power estimation is described in Section 4. Experimental results on the effects of various delay models are discussed in Section 5, and Section 6 concludes the paper.

*This research was conducted at the University of Illinois and was supported in part by the Semiconductor Research Corporation under contract SRC 96-DP-109, in part by DARPA under contract DABT63-95-C-0069, and by Hewlett-Packard under an equipment grant.

2 Delay Models

Zero delay, unit delay, and two types of variable delay models are studied here. The zero delay model assumes that no delay is associated with any gate; no glitches or hazards will occur under this model. The unit delay model assigns identical delays to every gate in the circuit independent of gate size and numbers of fanins and fanouts. The type-1 variable delay model assigns the delay of a given gate to be proportional to the number of fanouts at the output of the gate. This model is more accurate than the unit delay model; however, fanouts that feed bigger gates are not taken into account, and inaccuracies may result. The fourth model is a different variable delay model which is based on the number of fanouts as well as the sizes of successor gates. The gate delay data for various types and sizes of gates are obtained from a VLSI library. The difference between the type-1 and type-2 variable delay models for a typical gate is illustrated in Figure 1. From the figure, the output capacitance of gate

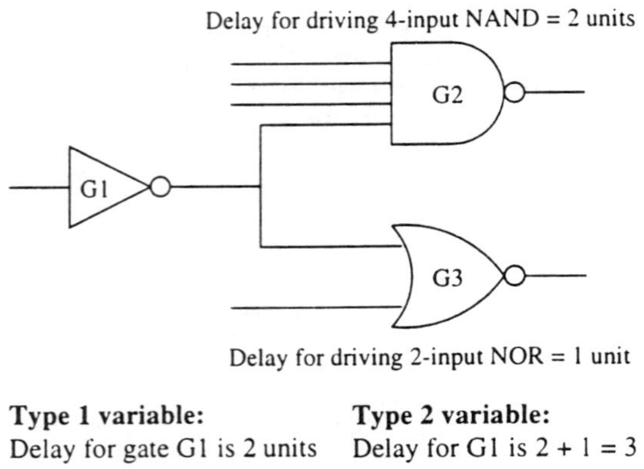

Figure 1: Variable Delay Models.

G1 is estimated to be 2 (the number of fanouts) in the type-1 variable delay model, while the delay calculated using the type-2 variable delay model is proportional to the delay associated with driving the successor gates **G2** and **G3**, or simply $2 + 1 = 3$. Since the type-1 variable delay model does not consider the size of the succeeding gates, the delay calculations may be less accurate.

3 Peak Power Measures

Three types of peak power are used in the context of sequential circuits for comparing the effects of delay models. An automatic procedure was implemented for various delay models that obtains these measures and generates the actual input vectors that attain them, as described in [10]. They are *Peak Single-Cycle Power*, *Peak n-Cycle Power*, and *Peak Sustainable Power*, covering time durations of one clock cycle, several consecutive clock cycles, and an infinite number of cycles, respectively. The unit of power used throughout the paper is energy per clock cycle and will simply be referred to as power. In a typical sequential circuit, the switching activity is largely controlled by the state vectors and less influenced by input vectors, because the number of flip-flops far outweighs the number of primary inputs. In all three cases, the power dissipated in the combinational portion of the sequential circuit can be computed as

$$P = \frac{V_{dd}^2}{2 \times clock\ period} \times \sum_{for\ all\ gates\ g} [toggles(g) \times C(g)],$$

where the summation is performed over all gates g, and $toggles(g)$ is the number of times gate g has switched from 0 to 1 or vice versa within a given clock cycle; $C(g)$ represents the output capacitance of gate g. In this work, we made the assumption that the output capacitance for each gate is proportional to the number of fanouts for all four delay models; however, assigned gate output capacitances can be handled by our optimization technique as well.

Peak single-cycle switching activity generally occurs when the greatest number of capacitive nodes are toggled between two consecutive vectors. For combinational circuits, the task is to search for a pair of vectors (V_1, V_2) that generates the most gate transitions. For sequential circuits, on the other hand, the activity depends on the initial state as well as the primary input vectors. The estimate for peak power dissipation can be used as a lower-bound for worst-case power dissipation in the circuit in any given time frame. Our goal in this work is to find and compare such bounds for the peak power dissipation of a circuit under different delay assumptions.

Peak n-cycle switching activity is a measure of the peak average power dissipation over a contiguous sequence of n vectors. This measure serves as an upper-bound to *peak sustainable power*, which is a measure of the peak average power that can be sustained indefinitely. Both measures are considered only for sequential circuits. The n-cycle power dissipation varies with the sequence length n. When n is equal to 2, the power dissipation is the same as the peak single-cycle power dissipation, and as n increases, the average power is expected to decrease if the peak single-cycle power dissipation cannot be sustained over the n vectors in the sequence.

We computed peak sustainable power by finding the synchronizing sequence for the circuit that produces greatest power [10]. Unlike the approach proposed in [7], where symbolic transition counts based on binary decision diagrams (BDD's) were used to compute maximum power cycles, no state transition diagrams are needed in our approach. Basically, the method used in [7] was to find the maximal average length cycle in the state transition graph, where the edge weights in the STG indicate the power dissipation in the combinational portion of the circuit between two adjacent states. However, the huge sizes of STG's and BDD's in large circuits make the approach infeasible and impractical. Our approach restricts the search for peak power loops to be a synchronizing sequence, thereby limiting the search to a subset of all loops, and the resulting peak power may not be a very tight lower bound. However, our experiments have shown that this approach still yields peaks higher than extensive random search [10].

4 GA Framework for Power Estimation

The GA framework used in this work is similar to the simple GA described by Goldberg [18]. The GA contains a population of *strings*, also called *chromosomes* or *individuals*, in which each individual represents a sequence of vectors. Peak n-cycle power estimation requires a search for the $(n + 2)$-tuple (S_1, V_1, ..., V_{n+1}) that maximizes power dissipation. This $(n + 2)$-tuple is encoded as a single binary string, as illustrated in Figure 2. The population size used is a function of the string length, which depends on the number of primary inputs, the number of flip-flops, and the vector sequence length n. Larger populations are needed to accommodate longer vector sequences in order to maintain diversity.

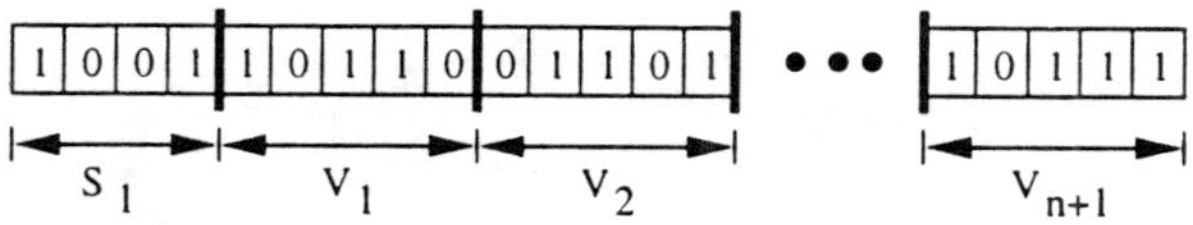

Figure 2: Encoding of an Individual.

The population size is set equal to $32 \times \sqrt{sequence\ length}$ when the number of primary inputs is less than 16 and $128 \times \sqrt{sequence\ length}$ when the number of primary inputs is greater than or equal to 16. Each individual in the population has an associated *fitness*, which measures the quality of the vector sequence in terms of switching activity, indicated by the total number of capacitive nodes toggled by the individual. The delay model and the amount of capacitive-node switching are taken into account during the evolutionary processes of the GA via the fitness function. The fitness function is a simple counting function that measures the power dissipated in terms of amount of capacitive-node switching in a given time period.

The population is first initialized with random strings. A variable-delay logic simulator is then used to compute the fitness of each individual. The evolutionary processes of *selection, crossover*, and *mutation* are used to generate an entirely new population from the existing population. This process continues for 32 generations, and the best individual in any generation is chosen as the solution. We use tournament selection without replacement and uniform crossover, and mutation is done by simply flipping a bit. In *tournament selection without replacement,* two individuals are randomly chosen and removed from the population, and the best is selected; the two individuals are not replaced into the original population until all other individuals have also been removed. Thus, it takes two passes through the parent population to completely fill the new population. In *uniform crossover,* bits from the two parents are swapped with probability 0.5 at each string position in generating the two offspring. A crossover probability of 1 is used; i.e., the two parents are always crossed in generating the two offspring. Since the majority of time spent by the GA is in the fitness evaluation, parallelism among the individuals can be exploited. Parallel-pattern simulation [19] is used to speed up the process in which 32 candidate sequences from the population are simulated simultaneously, with values bit-packed into 32-bit words.

5 Experimental Results

Peak powers for four different delay models were estimated for ISCAS85 combinational benchmark circuits, ISCAS89 sequential benchmark circuits [20], and several synthesized circuits, including **am2910**, a 12-bit microprogram sequencer [21]; **mult16**, a 16-bit two's complement shift-and-add multiplier; and **div16**, a 16-bit divider using repeated subtraction. Table 1 lists the total number of gates and capacitive nodes for all circuits. The total number of capacitive nodes in a circuit is computed as the total number of gate inputs. All computations were performed on an HP 9000 J200 with 256 MB RAM. Powers are expressed in terms of **peak switching frequency per node (PSF)**, which is the average frequency of peak switching activity of the nodes (ratio of the number of transitions on all nodes to the total number of capacitive nodes). Notice that for the non-zero delay models, PSF's greater than 1.0 are possible due to repeated switching on the internal nodes within one clock cycle.

Table 1: Numbers of Capacitive Nodes in Circuits

Circuit	Gates	Cap Nodes	Circuit	Gates	Cap Nodes
c432	204	343	s526	224	472
c499	276	440	s641	458	582
c880	470	755	s713	471	633
c1355	620	1096	s820	332	781
c1908	939	1523	s832	330	793
c2670	1567	2216	s1196	576	1041
c3540	1742	2961	s1238	555	1073
c5315	2609	4509	s1423	754	1243
c6288	2481	4832	s1488	687	1412
c7552	3828	6252	s1494	681	1418
s298	143	264	s5378	3043	4440
s344	196	295	s35932	18149	30317
s382	189	333	am2910	1055	1998
s400	195	349	mult16	755	1323
s444	212	379	div16	974	1760

We have previously shown that estimates made by our GA-based technique are indeed good estimates of peak power, and that if random-based methods were to achieve similar levels of peak power estimates, execution times are several orders of magnitude higher than for the GA-based technique [10]. Peak power estimation results will now be presented for the various delay models, and correlations between the delay models will be discussed.

5.1 Effects of the four delay models

For the ISCAS85 combinational circuits, Table 2 compares the GA-based results against the randomly-generated sequences as well as those reported in [9]. For each circuit, results for all four delay models are reported; the best among these is highlighted in **bold**. The estimates obtained from the best of randomly-generated vector-pairs, an ATG-based approach [9], and the GA-based technique are shown. The ATG-based approach used in [9] attempts to optimize the total number of nodes switching in the expanded combinational circuit; its results were compared against the best of only 10,000 random simulations. In our work, on the other hand, the number of random simulations depends on the GA population size, which is a function of the number of primary inputs in the circuit. Typically, the number of random simulations exceeds 64,000. The GA-based estimates are the highest for all of the circuits and for all delay models, except for one zero-delay estimate in c1355, where a 1.1% lower power was obtained. The average improvements made by the GA-based technique over the random simulations are 10.8%, 27.4% 38.5%, and 35.5%, for the four delay models, respectively. Since [9] estimated power on the expanded circuits, backtrace using zero-delay techniques was used. Consequently, only hazards were captured; zero-width pulses were not taken into account in the non-zero delay models. For this reason, our GA-based estimates are higher than all the estimates obtained in [9]. Furthermore, results from [9] suggested that peak power estimated from the unit-delay model consistently gave higher values than both zero-delay and type-1 variable-delay estimates. We do not see such consistency from our results in Table 2. The estimated powers from random simulations do not show such a trend either. Nevertheless, it is observed that peak powers for some circuits are very sensitive to the underlying delay model. For instance, in circuit c3540, the peak power estimates are 0.600, 2.684, 3.555, and 4.678 for zero, unit, type-1 variable, and type-2 variable delay models.

The results for sequential circuits using the four delay

Table 2: Peak Single-Cycle Power for ISCAS85 Combinational Circuits (expressed as PSF)

Circuit	Zero			Unit			Type-1 Variable			Type-2 Variable		
	Rnd	[9]	GA	Rnd	[9]	GA	Rnd	[9]	GA	Rnd	[9]	GA
c432	0.636	0.536	**0.805**	1.985	1.985	**2.362**	2.557	1.181	**3.399**	2.286	-	**2.522**
c499	0.648	0.480	**0.659**	**1.268**	0.950	**1.268**	**1.345**	0.575	**1.345**	1.345	-	**1.409**
c880	0.632	0.495	**0.809**	1.367	0.995	**1.689**	1.546	0.613	**1.710**	1.515	-	**1.951**
c1355	**0.539**	0.402	0.533	1.681	1.268	**3.260**	1.671	0.608	**2.707**	1.956	-	**2.676**
c1908	0.628	0.596	**0.638**	2.641	1.961	**3.446**	2.863	1.226	**4.000**	3.006	-	**4.182**
c2670	0.587	0.561	**0.623**	1.690	1.676	**2.251**	1.925	1.363	**2.750**	1.931	-	**2.825**
c3540	0.534	0.402	**0.600**	2.351	1.646	**2.684**	3.137	1.178	**3.555**	3.478	-	**4.678**
c5315	0.584	-	**0.631**	1.859	-	**2.733**	2.180	-	**3.205**	2.308	-	**3.263**
c6288	0.553	-	**0.660**	19.301	-	23.603	16.305	-	**24.245**	17.562	-	**25.179**
c7552	0.572	-	**0.602**	2.052	-	**2.821**	2.387	-	**2.833**	2.838	-	**3.238**
Impr			10.8%			27.4%			38.5%			35.5%

Impr: Average improvements over the best random estimates

Table 3: GA-Based Power Estimates for ISCAS89 Sequential Circuits (expressed as PSF)

Circuit	Single Cycle				N-Cycle				Sustainable			
	Z	U	V1	V2	Z	U	V1	V2	Z	U	V1	V2
s298	0.848	1.015	1.064	**1.095**	0.434	0.482	**0.505**	**0.505**	0.363	0.413	**0.416**	0.415
s344	0.797	**1.275**	1.017	1.057	0.537	0.698	0.723	**0.732**	0.502	**0.683**	0.637	0.677
s382	0.826	1.081	**1.129**	**1.129**	0.326	0.389	0.402	**0.405**	0.246	0.262	0.277	**0.280**
s400	0.822	1.106	**1.158**	**1.158**	0.320	0.390	**0.403**	0.399	0.220	0.252	0.271	**0.279**
s444	0.752	1.150	**1.198**	**1.198**	0.313	0.395	0.430	**0.439**	0.217	0.281	0.306	**0.309**
s526	0.790	**0.930**	0.905	0.905	0.305	0.335	0.335	**0.339**	0.217	0.241	0.235	**0.246**
s641	0.844	**2.869**	1.354	1.206	0.477	**1.252**	0.815	0.798	0.453	**0.902**	0.738	0.749
s713	0.823	**2.815**	1.932	1.308	0.494	**1.421**	0.881	0.840	0.443	**0.964**	0.779	0.824
s820	0.822	0.974	**1.047**	1.013	0.579	0.682	**0.695**	0.670	0.511	0.628	**0.645**	0.637
s832	0.823	0.984	**1.038**	1.016	0.565	**0.696**	0.675	0.687	0.553	0.647	**0.653**	0.645
s1196	0.605	1.027	1.003	**1.104**	0.558	0.743	0.774	**0.818**	0.536	0.775	**0.837**	0.796
s1238	0.622	**1.058**	1.042	1.042	0.529	0.742	0.809	**0.820**	0.507	0.796	**0.840**	0.811
s1423	0.854	**1.736**	1.455	1.438	0.557	**0.934**	0.898	0.852	0.411	0.604	0.640	**0.675**
s1488	0.674	**1.258**	1.069	1.074	0.593	0.778	**0.816**	0.776	0.490	0.663	**0.670**	0.646
s1494	0.673	**1.253**	1.072	1.078	0.586	0.790	**0.806**	0.804	0.486	**0.657**	0.649	0.648
s5378	0.753	1.114	1.351	**1.377**	0.550	0.727	0.760	**0.814**	0.337	**0.465**	0.432	0.464
s35932	0.641	1.543	**1.579**	1.521	0.522	**1.107**	1.027	0.955	0.522	**1.107**	1.093	1.097
am2910	0.509	3.128	4.945	**6.329**	0.366	1.662	2.231	**3.068**	0.381	1.295	2.012	**2.417**
mult16	0.881	2.543	2.688	**2.748**	0.441	0.872	**0.902**	0.857	0.347	**0.787**	0.753	0.759
div16	0.701	3.803	4.439	**8.103**	0.521	1.941	2.301	**3.249**	0.446	1.781	2.131	**2.829**
Impr	11.9%	12.3%	20.4%	22.3%	17.4%	32.5%	26.7%	32.0%	12.3%	23.8%	24.4%	30.2%

Z: Zero U: Unit **V1**: Type-1 Variable **V2**: Type-2 Variable

models are shown in Table 3. The length of the sequence in each case is set to 10 for N-cycle and sustainable power estimates. Results for best of the random simulations are not shown; however, the average improvements made by the GA-based estimates are shown at the bottom of the table. The number of random simulations is also the same as the number of simulations required in the GA-based technique. For the small circuits, the number of simulations is around 64,000. The GA-based estimates surpass the best random estimates for all circuits for all three peak power measures under all four delay models. The average improvements of the GA-based estimates for each delay model are shown in the bottom row of Table 3. Up to 32.5% improvement is obtained on the average for peak N-cycle powers.

Across the four delay models, estimates made from the zero-delay model consistently gave significantly lower power, since glitches and hazards were not accounted for. However, there is not a clear trend as to which of the other three delay models will consistently give peak or near peak power estimates. In circuits such as s641, s713, and am2910, the peak powers are very sensitive to the delay model. Over 100% increase in power dissipation can result when a different delay model is used. For some other circuits, such as s400, s444, s526, and s1238, the peak powers estimated are quite insensitive to the underlying delay model; less than 5% difference in the estimates is observed from the three delay models.

The execution times needed for the zero-delay estimates are typically smaller, since few events need to be evaluated, while execution times for the other three delay models are comparable. Table 4 shows the execution times for the GA optimization technique for the unit-delay model. The execution times are directly proportional to the number of events generated in the circuit during the course of estimation. For this reason, peak n-cycle power estimates do not take 10 times as much computation as peak single-cycle power for $n = 10$, since the amount of activity across the 10 cycles is not 10 times that of the peak single cycle. For circuits in which peak power estimates differ significantly among various delay models, the computation costs will also differ significantly according to the number of activated events. The

Table 4: Execution Times for the GA-Based Technique (seconds)

Circuit	Single cycle	N-cycle	Sustainable	Circuit	Single cycle	N-cycle	Sustainable	Circuit	Single cycle	N-cycle	Sustainable
s298	5.32	19.56	20.93	s713	50.17	237.0	293.8	s1494	78.96	355.2	470.5
s344	12.72	61.10	70.50	s820	28.11	145.0	217.2	s5378	563.4	2065	1920
s382	10.33	36.45	25.07	s832	29.34	144.4	212.9	s35932	23,200	84,449	66,411
s400	13.36	38.09	26.38	s1196	44.14	286.8	408.9	am2910	343.9	1695	1216
s444	12.67	40.79	27.15	s1238	53.99	301.8	421.7	mult16	155.8	365.2	338.2
s526	11.34	40.98	24.35	s1423	164.5	514.8	508.8	div16	542.1	2117	3450
s614	56.18	213.8	259.4	s1488	78.37	405.8	472.6				

Table 5: Effects of Various Delay Models for ISCAS85 Combinational Circuits

Circuit	Effects of Zero-Delay Vectors On...						Effects of Unit-Delay Vectors On...					
	Unit		Type-1 Var		Type-2 Var		Zero		Type-1 Var		Type-2 Var	
	Opt	Sim	Opt	Sim	Opt	Sim	Opt	Sim	Opt	Sim	Opt	Sim
c432	2.362	2.035	3.399	2.181	2.522	2.192	0.636	0.455	3.399	2.904	2.522	*3.032*
c499	1.268	1.043	1.345	1.070	1.409	1.052	0.659	0.532	1.345	1.268	1.409	1.268
c880	1.689	1.233	1.710	1.238	1.951	1.238	0.809	0.613	1.710	*1.779*	1.951	1.689
c1355	3.260	1.000	2.707	1.011	2.676	1.042	0.533	0.441	2.707	2.391	2.676	*3.143*
c1908	3.446	2.756	4.000	3.060	4.182	3.141	0.638	0.517	4.000	3.262	4.182	3.736
c2670	2.251	1.150	2.750	1.294	2.825	1.320	0.623	0.572	2.750	2.364	2.825	2.355
c3540	2.684	1.211	3.555	1.376	4.678	1.553	0.600	0.469	3.555	*3.570*	4.678	3.080
c5315	2.733	1.503	3.205	1.660	3.263	1.674	0.631	0.598	3.205	3.031	3.263	2.935
c6288	23.60	7.225	24.25	4.549	25.34	4.553	0.660	0.586	24.25	23.51	25.34	*25.39*
c7552	2.821	1.619	2.833	1.757	3.238	1.788	0.602	0.537	2.833	*3.089*	3.238	3.012
Dev		-75.5%		-61.4%		-61.7%		-18.9%		-5.2%		-2.8%

Circuit	Effects of Type-1 Var-Delay Vectors On...						Effects of Type-2 Var-Delay Vectors On...					
	Zero		Unit		Type-2 Var		Zero		Unit		Type-1 Var	
	Opt	Sim	Opt	Sim	Opt	Sim	Opt	Sim	Opt	Sim	Opt	Sim
c432	0.636	0.496	2.362	*2.373*	2.522	*3.399*	0.636	0.411	2.362	1.776	3.399	2.155
c499	0.659	0.557	1.268	1.252	1.409	1.270	0.659	0.495	1.268	1.227	1.345	*1.436*
c880	0.809	0.550	1.689	1.501	1.951	1.575	0.809	0.362	1.689	1.387	1.710	1.577
c1355	0.533	0.444	3.260	2.685	2.676	2.490	0.533	0.439	3.260	2.676	2.707	2.059
c1908	0.638	*0.642*	3.446	3.204	4.182	3.981	0.638	0.439	3.446	3.000	4.000	3.528
c2670	0.623	0.561	2.251	2.121	2.825	2.767	0.623	0.512	2.251	2.154	2.750	2.690
c3540	0.600	0.491	2.684	1.687	4.678	3.816	0.600	0.458	2.684	1.705	4.000	3.416
c5315	0.631	0.593	2.733	2.470	3.263	3.083	0.631	0.581	2.733	2.458	3.205	3.064
c6288	0.660	0.609	23.60	*23.94*	25.34	24.41	0.660	0.610	23.60	23.34	24.25	23.92
c7552	0.602	0.474	2.821	1.976	3.238	2.750	0.602	0.531	2.821	2.191	2.833	*3.138*
Dev		-17.4%		-6.3%		-3.0%		-26.2%		-9.1%		-7.0%

Dev: Average deviation of **Sim** from **Opt**

execution times required for the random simulations are very close to those of the GA-based technique since identical numbers of simulations are performed.

5.2 Cross-effects of delay models

Although peak powers are sensitive to the underlying delay model, it would be interesting to study if the vectors optimized under one delay model will produce peak or near-peak power under the other delay models. If we can find a delay model in which derived sequences consistently generate near peak powers under the other delay models, we can conclude that, although peak power estimation is sensitive to the underlying delay model, there exists a delay model by which optimized sequences generate high powers regardless of the delay model used.

Experiments were therefore carried out to study these cross-effects of delay models. Table 5 shows the results for the combinational circuits. For each circuit, the previously optimized peak power measures for various delay models (the same as those in Table 2) are shown in the **Opt** columns. The power produced from applying vectors optimized for a given delay model on the other three delay models are listed in the adjacent (**Sim**) columns. For example, in circuit c2670 under the zero-delay model (upper-left quadrant of the table), the original peak single-cycle switching frequency per node (PSF) for the unit-delay model was 2.251 (**Opt**); however, when vectors optimized for the zero-delay model are simulated using the unit-delay model, the measured PSF is 1.150 (**Sim**). The **Sim** measures that exceed the optimized (**Opt**) measures are *italicized*. At the bottom of the table, **Dev** shows the average amount that the *Sim* values deviated from the average *Opt* values. For instance, when the optimized vectors on the unit-delay model are simulated using the zero-delay assumption, an average deviation of 18.9% results from the GA-optimized zero-delay powers. On the average, the *Sim* peak powers deviated from the optimized values for all delay models as indicated by the *Dev* values. However, the vectors optimized for the zero-delay model produced significantly lower power when they were simulated in the non-zero delay environments; over 60% drops were observed from the GA-optimized powers, as indicated by the **Dev** metric. The vectors that were optimized on the remaining three delay models, on the other hand, deviated less significantly when simulated using other *non-zero* delay

Table 6: Effects of Optimized Zero-Delay Vectors on Other Delay Models (expressed as PSF)

Circuit	Effects On Unit Delay						Effects On Type-1 Variable Delay					
	Single-cycle		N-cycle		Sustainable		Single-cycle		N-cycle		Sustainable	
	Opt	Sim	Opt	Sim	Opt	Sim	Opt	Sim	Opt	Sim	Opt	Sim
s298	1.015	1.008	0.482	0.482	0.413	0.408	1.064	0.977	0.505	0.487	0.416	0.411
s344	1.275	0.932	0.698	0.637	0.683	0.627	1.017	0.939	0.723	0.647	0.637	0.538
s382	1.081	0.952	0.389	0.387	0.262	*0.288*	1.129	1.018	0.402	0.390	0.277	*0.294*
s400	1.106	0.977	0.390	0.380	0.252	0.239	1.158	1.029	0.403	0.386	0.271	0.242
s444	1.150	1.011	0.395	0.384	0.281	0.245	1.198	1.069	0.430	0.393	0.306	0.252
s526	0.930	0.917	0.335	*0.336*	0.241	0.238	0.905	0.900	0.335	*0.336*	0.235	*0.237*
s641	2.869	0.881	1.252	0.536	0.902	0.501	1.354	0.864	0.815	0.556	0.738	0.546
s713	2.815	0.953	1.421	0.594	0.964	0.512	1.932	1.028	0.881	0.650	0.779	0.567
s820	0.974	0.942	0.682	0.674	0.628	0.596	1.047	0.999	0.695	0.685	0.645	0.599
s832	0.984	0.952	0.696	0.659	0.647	0.646	1.038	1.000	0.675	*0.681*	0.653	*0.660*
s1196	1.027	0.886	0.743	*0.802*	0.775	0.731	1.003	0.947	0.774	*0.793*	0.837	0.767
s1238	1.058	0.894	0.742	*0.760*	0.796	0.707	1.042	0.981	0.809	0.789	0.840	0.724
s1423	1.736	1.152	0.934	0.790	0.604	0.512	1.455	1.043	0.898	0.766	0.640	0.551
s1488	1.258	1.191	0.778	0.758	0.663	0.650	1.069	1.022	0.816	0.783	0.670	0.642
s1494	1.253	1.193	0.790	0.752	0.657	0.622	1.072	1.028	0.806	0.776	0.649	0.632
s5378	1.114	1.008	0.727	0.658	0.465	*0.477*	1.351	1.038	0.760	0.668	0.432	*0.463*
s35932	1.543	1.543	1.107	0.778	1.107	0.664	1.579	1.399	0.929	0.761	1.093	0.733
am2910	3.128	1.175	1.662	0.886	1.295	0.803	4.945	1.409	2.231	1.806	2.012	1.051
mult16	2.543	1.056	0.872	0.565	0.787	0.782	2.688	1.045	0.902	0.531	0.753	0.747
div16	3.803	2.259	1.941	1.523	1.781	1.403	4.439	2.284	2.301	1.525	2.131	1.463
Dev		-34.2%		-22.5%		-16.8%		-33.0%		-16.3%		-18.3%

Dev: Average deviation of **Sim** from **Opt**

models, all less than 10% deviations.

For sequential circuits, we will first look at the vectors optimized under the zero-delay assumption. Table 6 shows the results. The **Opt** and **Sim** values are defined the same way as before. For example, in circuit s382, the peak single-cycle switching frequency per node (PSF) under unit delay was 1.081; however, when the vector sequence optimized for the zero-delay model is simulated using the unit-delay model, the measured PSF is 0.952. A similar format is used for the n-cycle and sustainable powers. Average deviation values **Dev** are also displayed at the bottom of the table. On average, the *Sim* powers deviated significantly from the powers optimized by the GA for both unit and type-1 variable delay models, as indicated in the **Dev** row. When examining the results for each circuit individually, none of the single-cycle vectors derived under the zero-delay model exceed the previously optimized peak powers for unit and type-1 variable delay models. However, on a few occasions, slightly higher peak n-cycle and sustainable powers have been obtained by the zero-delay-optimized vectors because of the difficulty in finding the optimum in the huge search space for the (n+2)-tuple needed for the peak n-cycle and sustainable powers. For the small circuits s298 to s526, the results show that the zero-delay-optimized vectors produced peak or near-peak powers for the unit and type-1 variable delay models as well. One plausible explanation for this phenomenon is that the peak switching frequencies (PSF's) for these circuits are small, typically less than 1.2, indicating that most nodes in the circuit do not toggle multiple times in a single clock cycle. For the other circuits, especially for circuits where high PSF's are obtained, the vectors obtained which generated high peak powers under zero-delay assumptions do *not* provide peak powers under non-zero delay assumptions. The last three synthesized circuits, am2910, mult16, and div16, show widened gaps. The effects on type-2 variable delay are similar to those on type-1 variable delay.

Similarly, vectors optimized under the non-zero-delay models were simulated using other delay models, and the results are shown in Table 7 for type-2 variable delay. The trends for the unit-delay and type-1 variable delay models are similar to those seen for the type-2 variable delay model. The results are not compared with the zero-delay model here, since their trends are similar to those for the combinational circuits, where large deviations exist. When the PSF's are greater than 2, a greater deviation is observed. Such cases can be seen in circuits s641, s713, am2910, and div16. For instance, the optimized peak single-cycle unit-delay power for s713 is 2.815, but the power produced by applying the vectors optimized for the type-2 variable delay model is only 1.273. On the contrary, less significant deviation is observed in circuits for which smaller PSF's are obtained. For the n-cycle and sustainable powers, although deviations still exist when compared with the GA-optimized vectors (shown in **Dev**), they are small deviations. Furthermore, deviations between type-1 and type-2 delay models are smaller when compared with the unit-delay model, suggesting that the two variable delay models are more correlated.

6 Conclusions

When estimating peak power under one delay model, it is crucial to have confidence that the estimate will not vary significantly when the actual delays in the circuit differ from the delay model assumed. Peak power estimation under four different delay models for single-cycle, n-cycle, and sustainable power dissipation has been presented. For most circuits, vector sequences optimized under the zero-delay assumption do not produce peak or near-peak powers when they are simulated under a non-zero delay model. Similarly, the vectors optimized under non-zero delay models do not produce peak or near-peak zero-delay powers. However, vector sequences optimized under non-zero delay models provide good measures for other non-zero delay models, with only a slight deviation, for most combinational circuits. For sequential circuits, small deviations are observed when the optimized

Table 7: Effects of Optimized Type-2 Variable-Delay Vectors on Other Delay Models

Circuit	Effects On Unit Delay						Effects On Type-1 Variable Delay					
	Single-cycle		N-cycle		Sustainable		Single-cycle		N-cycle		Sustainable	
	Opt	Sim	Opt	Sim	Opt	Sim	Opt	Sim	Opt	Sim	Opt	Sim
s298	1.015	0.936	0.482	*0.500*	0.413	0.411	1.064	*1.110*	0.505	0.505	0.416	0.416
s344	1.275	0.966	0.698	0.689	0.683	0.660	1.017	*1.020*	0.723	0.713	0.637	*0.663*
s382	1.081	1.063	0.389	0.371	0.262	0.253	1.129	1.129	0.402	0.405	0.277	0.277
s400	1.106	1.077	0.390	0.357	0.252	0.251	1.158	1.158	0.403	0.398	0.271	*0.276*
s444	1.150	1.150	0.395	0.362	0.281	0.270	1.198	1.198	0.430	*0.433*	0.306	0.306
s526	0.930	0.930	0.335	0.334	0.241	*0.244*	0.905	0.905	0.335	*0.339*	0.235	*0.245*
s641	2.869	0.574	1.252	0.607	0.902	0.530	1.354	1.055	0.815	0.796	0.738	*0.749*
s713	2.815	1.273	1.421	0.575	0.964	0.545	1.932	1.308	0.881	0.840	0.779	*0.824*
s820	0.974	0.964	0.682	0.657	0.628	*0.634*	1.047	1.031	0.695	0.671	0.645	0.640
s832	0.984	0.961	0.696	0.676	0.647	0.634	1.038	1.037	0.675	*0.690*	0.653	0.647
s1196	1.027	0.946	0.743	*0.765*	0.775	0.751	1.003	*1.108*	0.774	*0.793*	0.837	0.783
s1238	1.058	0.964	0.742	*0.757*	0.796	0.746	1.042	1.023	0.809	0.797	0.840	0.768
s1423	1.736	1.358	0.934	0.719	0.604	0.586	1.455	1.433	0.898	0.851	0.640	*0.677*
s1488	1.258	1.206	0.778	0.762	0.663	0.651	1.069	1.069	0.816	0.780	0.670	0.645
s1494	1.253	1.207	0.790	0.786	0.657	0.651	1.072	1.072	0.806	0.806	0.649	0.648
s5378	1.114	1.095	0.727	*0.775*	0.465	*0.493*	1.351	1.245	0.760	*0.785*	0.432	*0.480*
s35932	1.543	1.116	1.107	1.099	1.107	1.079	1.579	1.170	0.929	*1.027*	1.093	*1.097*
am2910	3.128	1.127	1.662	1.235	1.295	*1.435*	4.945	3.180	2.231	*2.420*	2.012	*2.103*
mult16	2.543	2.512	0.872	0.853	0.787	0.786	2.688	2.680	0.902	0.851	0.753	0.752
div16	3.803	2.502	1.941	1.650	1.781	1.273	4.439	*4.468*	2.301	*2.386*	2.131	2.002
Dev		-27.5%		-15.1%		-9.6%		-10.3%		+1.0%		-0.3%

Dev: Average deviation of **Sim** from **Opt**

peak powers are small, but when the optimized peak powers are large, i.e., nodes switch multiple times in a single cycle on the average, the estimated peak powers will be sensitive to the underlying delay model.

References

[1] C. Small, "Shrinking devices put the squeeze on system packaging," *EDN.*, pp. 41–46, February 1994.

[2] F. N. Najm and M. Y. Zhang, "Extreme delay sensitivity and the worst-case switching activity in VLSI circuits," *Proc. Design Automation Conf.*, pp. 623–627, 1995.

[3] C. Teng, A. M. Hill, and S. Kang, "Estimation of maximum transition counts at internal nodes in CMOS VLSI circuits," *Proc. Int. Conf. Computer-Aided Design*, pp. 366–370, 1995.

[4] S. Devadas, K. Keutzer, J. White, "Estimation of power dissipation in CMOS combinational circuits using boolean function manipulation," *IEEE Trans. Computer-Aided Design*, pp. 373–383, March 1992.

[5] H. Kriplani, "Worst case voltage drops in power and ground busses of CMOS VLSI circuits," *Ph. D. Thesis, Univ. of Illinois*, November 1993.

[6] H. Kriplani, F. Najm, P. Yang, and I. Hajj, "Resolving signal correlations for estimating maximum currents in CMOS combinational circuits," *Proc. Design Automation Conf.*, pp. 384–388, 1993.

[7] S. Manne, A. Pardo, R. I. Bahar, G. D. Hachtel, F. Somenzi, E. Macii, and M. Poncino, "Computing the maximum power cycles of a sequential circuit," *Proc. Design Automation Conf.*, pp. 23–28, 1995.

[8] C. Wang, K. Roy, and T. Chou, "Maximum power estimation for sequential circuits using a test generation based technique," *Proc. Custom Integrated Circuits Conf.*, 1996.

[9] S. Manich and J. Figueras, "Maximizing the weighted switching activity in combinational CMOS circuits under the variable delay model," *Proc. European Design & Test Conf.*, pp. 597–602, 1997.

[10] M. S. Hsiao, E. M. Rudnick, and J. H. Patel, "K2: An estimator for peak sustainable power of VLSI circuits," *Proc. Intl Symp. Low Power Electronics and Design*, 1997.

[11] A. Ghosh, S. Devadas, K. Keutzer, and J. White, "Estimation of average switching activity in combinational and sequential circuits," *Proc. Design Automation Conf.*, pp. 253–259, 1992.

[12] F. N. Najm, "A survey of power estimation techniques in VLSI circuits," *IEEE Trans. VLSI Systems*, vol. 2, no. 4, pp. 446–455, December 1994.

[13] T. Chou and K. Roy, "Statistical estimation of sequential circuit activity," *Proc. Int. Conf. Computer-Aided Design*, pp. 34–37, 1995.

[14] T. Chou and K. Roy, "Accurate power estimation of CMOS sequential circuits," *IEEE Trans. VLSI Systems*, vol. 4, no. 3, pp. 369–380, September 1996.

[15] T. Uchino, F. Minami, T. Mitsuhashi, and N. Goto, "Switching activity analysis using boolean approximation method," *Proc. Int. Conf. Computer-Aided Design*, pp. 20–25, 1995.

[16] C. Tsui, J. Monteiro, M. Pedram, A. Despain, and B. Lin, "Power estimation methods for sequential logic circuits," *IEEE Trans. VLSI Systems*, vol. 3, no. 3, pp. 404–416, September 1995.

[17] F. N. Najm, S. Goel, and I. N. Hajj, "Power estimation in sequential circuits," *Proc. Design Automation Conf.*, pp. 635–640, 1995.

[18] D. E. Goldberg, *Genetic Algorithms in Search, Optimization, and Machine Learning,* Reading, MA: Addison-Wesley, 1989.

[19] M. Abramovici, M. A. Breuer, and A. D. Friedman, *Digital Systems Testing and Testable Design.* New York, NY: Computer Science Press, 1990.

[20] F. Brglez, D. Bryan, and K. Kozminski, "Combinational profiles of sequential benchmark circuits," *Int. Symp. Circuits and Systems*, pp. 1929–1934, 1989.

[21] Advanced Micro Devices, "The AM2910, a complete 12-bit microprogram sequence controller," in *AMD Data Book*, AMD Inc., Sunnyvale, CA, 1978.

COSMOS: A Continuous Optimization Approach for Maximum Power Estimation of CMOS Circuits *

Chuan-Yu Wang and *Kaushik Roy*, ECE, Purdue University, West Lafayette, IN 47907-1285

Abstract

Maximum instantaneous power in VLSI circuits has a great impact on circuit's reliability and the design of power and ground lines. To synthesize highly reliable systems, accurate estimates of maximum power must be obtained in various design phases. Unfortunately, determining the input patterns to induce the maximum current (power) is essentially a combinatorial optimization problem. Even for circuits with small number of primary inputs (PI's), it is CPU time intensive to conduct exhaustive search in the input vector space. The only feasible way is to find good upper and lower bounds of the maximum power, and to make the gap between these two bounds as narrow as possible. In this paper, we present a continuous optimization approach to efficiently generate tight lower bounds of the maximum instantaneous power for CMOS circuits. In our approach, each primary input (PI) of the circuit is allowed to assume any real number between 0 and 1. Maximum power estimation for CMOS circuits is then transformed into a continuous optimization problem, in which a smooth function is maximized over a unit hypercube in the Euclidean space. The continuous problem can be solved efficiently to generate good lower bounds of the maximum power. Our experiments with ISCAS and MCNC benchmark circuits demonstrate the superiority of this approach. For all the circuits tested, the mean value of the ratio "CPU time of the continuous optimization approach divided by CPU time of the simulation-based technique" is equal to 0.41. For 60% of the circuits tested, our approach gives a better estimate (1.16 times larger, on an average) than the simulation-based technique does. Compared to the ATPG-based technique [3], the continuous optimization approach generates a tighter lower bound (1.19 times larger, on an average) of maximum power for 60% of all the circuits tested.

1 Introduction

Maximum power estimation in CMOS circuits is essential to determine the IR drop on supply lines and to optimize the power and ground routing. The estimation involves searching for two consecutive binary input vectors, which maximize the switching activity in the circuits. In the worst case, this problem has complexity exponential to the number of PI's (Primary Inputs) of the circuit. Hence, for large-scaled circuits, the only feasible approach is to generate tight upper and lower bounds of the maximum instantaneous power within reasonable amount of CPU time so that the gap between the bounds is as narrow as possible.

In the past, several approaches have been proposed to cope with maximum power estimation for CMOS circuits. In [5, 6], Kriplani et. al. propagated signal uncertainty through circuits to obtain a loose upper bound of the maximum power. The bound is then successively made tighter by partially enumerating the primary inputs (PI's). The progress of improving the upper bound is expected to be slow when the circuit has a large number of PI's. Moreover, without a good lower bound, the estimate of maximum power cannot be obtained with the upper bound alone. In [4], Devadas et. al. formulated power consumption of CMOS circuits as a *Boolean* function in terms of two consecutive primary input vectors. The function is then exactly maximized by a branch-and-bound technique. The process to obtain the expression of the *Boolean* function and to maximize it are both CPU time intensive. Hence, the application of this technique is limited to small circuits. In [3], Wang and Roy proposed an Automatic Test Pattern Generation (ATPG) based technique to efficiently generate good lower bounds of maximum power for large-scaled circuits. The application of this technique currently has its limitations. Some characteristics of logic gates (e.g. inertial delay) cannot be easily captured at the logic level via this technique.

In this paper, we present an approach which can efficiently generate tight lower bounds of maximum power for large-scaled circuits under arbitrary delay model. Traditional techniques estimate the maximum power of a circuit based on the operation of binary numbers (0 and 1). In our approach, the output of a logic gate is allowed to assume any real number between 0 and 1. A smooth function denoting power can be derived over a unit hypercube in the Euclidean space. Maximum power estimation is then transformed into a continuous optimization problem, which can be solved efficiently. Compared to the traditional estimation techniques based on random simulation, our approach can generate tighter lower bounds within much shorter CPU time. On the other hand, compared to the ATPG based technique, this approach can easily capture more characteristics of logic gates.

The paper is organized as follows. Section 2 describes and formulates the problem of maximum power estimation. Section 3 transforms the problem into a continuous optimization problem. In Section 4, we discuss some issues in solving the continuous problem. Experimental results are presented in Section 5. Finally, the conclusions are given in Section 6.

2 Formulation of the Problem

In this section, we first discuss how to calculate the transition count at the output of logic gates within a clock cycle. Based on such discussion, we then formulate the problem of maximum power estimation.

For synchronous circuits, let us assume that the switchings of PI's are synchronized at the leading edge of each clock cycle. However, spurious transitions may occur at internal gates due to different propagation delays through different paths. The output of a gate may have transient pulses (spurious transitions) before it is finally stabilized. Such spurious transitions consume power and hence, such phenomenon should be considered in the maximum power estimation.

In a CMOS circuit, the total energy dissipated due to two consecutive input vectors can be described as: $E = \frac{1}{2}V_{dd}^2 \sum_{\forall gate} C_{load}(g) * T(g)$, where $T(g)$ denotes the transition count at the output of gate g during the clock cycle, and $C_{load}(g)$ represents the capacitive load of g. Hence, the average value of the instantaneous power over the clock cycle is: $p_{ave} = \frac{E}{|T|}$, where $|T|$ denotes the length of a clock cycle. Under the assumptions that (i) instantaneous power is a continuous function of time, and (ii) $|T|$ is sufficiently small, it is reasonable to view p_{ave} as the instantaneous power during the clock cycle. $C_{load}(*)$ can be approximated by the fanout $(F(*))$ of logic gates. Therefore, instantaneous power is proportional to:

$$P(V_1, V_2) = \sum_{\forall gate} F(g) * T(g) \qquad (1)$$

where V_1 and V_2 denote the two consecutive input binary vectors applied to the circuit.

*This research was supported in part by DARPA (under contract F33615-95-C-1625), by NSF CAREER award (9501869-MIP), IBM Corporation, AT&T/Lucent, and Rockwell Corporation

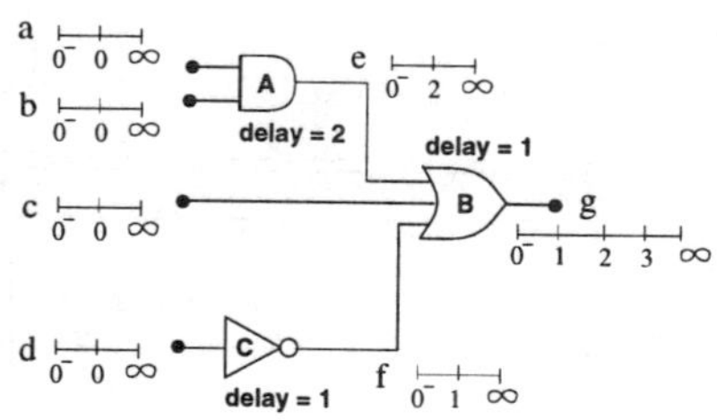

Figure 1: building time-sequences for a circuit

To calculate the transition count ($T(*)$) of a gate in a clock cycle, we associate with each gate a certain data structure to record the gate's output pattern. We call each such structure a *time-sequence* (a sequence of time instants at which the gate might switch). We implement the time-sequence of a gate as a linked list, in which each node represents a time instant at which the gate might switch. To avoid confusion, we refer to the nodes in time-sequences as *elements*. Each element in a time-sequence is associated with:

1. A start time, which denotes the corresponding switching time of the gate.
2. A logic value (0 or 1) which denotes the value at the output of the gate during a time interval beginning at the starting time of the element, and ending at the starting time of the next element.

The use of these structures will be described below.

Based on *static timing analysis* [10, 9], we have developed a procedure with linear complexity (in terms of the number of gates in the circuit) to create the time-sequences for a given circuit. By propagating the possible switching events level by level from PI's to PO's, the procedure can decide all the possible switching events at each node in the circuit, and equip the node with appropriate structure of time-sequence. Let us use the circuit in Figure 1 as an example. In Figure 1, each primary input (a, b, c, or d) is associated with two elements (with starting time 0^- and 0). Since the propagation delay of gate A is assumed to be 2, the time-sequence of node e is comprised of two elements with starting time 0^- and 2. Similarly, the time-sequence of node f can be built from that of primary input d. Finally, the time-sequence at the fanout of gate B is built by merging the time-sequences of node e, c, and f.

Based on the time-sequences, $T(g)$ in Equation 1 can be formulated as: $T(g) = \sum_{i=1}^{n(g)-1}(f_g(i) \oplus f_g(i+1))$. Here we use $n(g)$ to denote the number of elements in the time-sequence of gate g, and $f_g(i)$ to denote the logic value associated with the ith element of the time-sequence of gate g. Hence, we can define our problem as follows:

> *Maximize* $P(V_1, V_2) = \sum_{\forall gate} F(g) * \sum_{i=1}^{n(g)-1}(f_g(i) \oplus f_g(i+1))$
>
> *Subject to* $\mathcal{C} \equiv$ {**spatial correlation between logic gates**}

Note that $f_g(j)$ (denoting the value of the jth element of gate g) is decided by the value of the corresponding elements of the fanins of gate g. If we expand $f_g(j)$ from gate g toward primary inputs gate by gate, $f_g(j)$ can be represented as a Boolean function in terms of the entries of input vectors V_1 and V_2. $\mathcal{C}$ represents the structure of the logic circuit, and is the constraint set in this combinatorial optimization problem.

The above model describes the problem of maximum power estimation in circuits implemented with static CMOS gates. In the following section, we will discuss how to transform $P(V_1, V_2)$ into a function which is defined over the Euclidean space.

3 Transformation to Continuous Domain

We describe below a transformation which turns Boolean operators into arithmetic ones. After such transformation, $P(V_1, V_2)$ is well defined even if the entries in V_1 and V_2 are real numbers.

Any Boolean function can be transformed into an arithmetic function by repeatedly applying the following fundamental rules:

1. $a \vee b = a + b - ab$
2. $a \wedge b = a.b$ (a multiplied by b)
3. $\sim a = 1 - a$

where $\vee$, $\wedge$ and $\sim$ on the left-hand side are Boolean operators, while "+","-" and "." on the right-hand side are arithmetic operators. Any function transformed from some Boolean function according to these three rules preserves its original values at all vertices of $[0,1]^M$, where M is the number of dimensions of the function.

In the following discussion, we relax the entries in input vectors V_1 and V_2 from the discrete set $\{0,1\}$ to a continuous range [0,1]. To avoid ambiguity, let us use $\tilde{P}(V_1, V_2)$ to denote the function $P(V_1, V_2)$ after the relaxation. It can be noted that $\tilde{P}(*)$ is *continuous* and *differentiable* everywhere in $[0,1]^{2n}$, where n is the number of primary inputs of the circuit. Hence, the *gradient* of $\tilde{P}(*)$ (i.e. $\nabla\tilde{P}$) is defined everywhere in $[0,1]^{2n}$. This justifies our application of continuous optimization technique to $\tilde{P}(*)$.

Due to the smoothness and continuity of $\tilde{P}(*)$, we reach the following conclusion:

- Within the hypercube $[0,1]^{2n}$, if point a is sufficiently close to point b, the value of $\tilde{P}(a)$ and $\tilde{P}(b)$ tend to be the same. In other words, $||\tilde{P}(a) - \tilde{P}(b)|| \to 0$ if $||a - b|| \to 0$.

Suppose a relative maximum point v of $\tilde{P}(*)$ is sufficiently close to some vertex $\dot{v}$ of the hypercube $[0,1]^{2n}$. The vertex $\dot{v}$ tends to be a good choice to maximize the original combinatorial function $P(*)$ if v is sufficiently good for maximizing $\tilde{P}(*)$. This argument directly follows the above conclusion. Note that the maximum value of $\tilde{P}(*)$ over $[0,1]^{2n}$ is an upper bound of the maximum value of $P(*)$ over $\{0,1\}^{2n}$.

Since we are only interested in the discrete solutions, it is desired that the distance between the maxima (of $\tilde{P}(*)$) and vertices of the hypercube is as small as possible. Obviously there is no guarantee this is always the case. Hence, $\tilde{P}(*)$ is modified to favor this requirement. Some non-biasing term $T(*)$ is subtracted from the function $\tilde{P}(*)$ to make the maxima of $\tilde{P}(*)$ move toward the vertices of the hypercube $[0,1]^{2n}$. We call the term "non-biasing" because the term should vanish at the vertices. In all our experiments, we determine the non-biasing term as a summation of $2n$ concave functions: $T(X) = \sum_{i=1}^{2n} x_i(1-x_i)$. Here n is the number of primary inputs and x_i is the ith entry of vector X. It can be noted that $T(*)$ reaches its maximum value at $X = [0.5, 0.5, 0.5, ..., 0.5]$, and is also symmetric to this point. The resultant function $\widehat{P}(X) = \tilde{P}(X) - wT(X) = \tilde{P}(X) - w\sum_{i=1}^{2n} x_i(1-x_i)$ will be our objective function to be maximized. Here w is some positive real number used to adjust the shape of $\widehat{P}(*)$. For convenience, the notation $\widehat{P}(X) = \tilde{P}(X) - w\sum_{i=1}^{2n} x_i(1-x_i)$ will be used in the rest of this paper.

Let X denote the concatenation of the two input vectors V_1 and V_2. From above discussions, the corresponding continuous problem for maximum power estimation can be defined as follows:

> *Maximize* $\widehat{P}(X) = \sum_{\forall gate} F(g) * \sum_{i=1}^{n(g)-1}(\tilde{f}_g(i) + \tilde{f}_g(i+1) - 2\tilde{f}_g(i)\tilde{f}_g(i+1)) - w\sum_{i=1}^{2n} x_i(1-x_i)$
>
> *Subject to* $\mathcal{C} \equiv$ {**spatial correlation between signals**} $\cup \{x_i \in [0,1], i = 1(1)2n\}$

where n is the number of primary inputs of the circuit. We solve this constrained optimization problem based on the gradient method, which will be discussed next.

4 Optimization

We use the *steepest descent* strategy to find the maxima of the above constrained optimization problem. Starting from the neu-

Table 1: Results of ISCAS and MCNC benchmarks under unit-delay model

Benchmark Circuit	Number of gates	Number of of levels	Maximum Power			CPU Time (sec)		
			COSMOS	ATG	SIM	COSMOS	ATG	SIM
i1	33	25	99	86	92	1.62	0.12	18.3
i2	36	201	257	280	260	32.5	2.22	62.7
i3	70	132	182	202	274	6.32	0.37	52.7
i4	94	192	352	346	299	21.1	0.54	67.2
i5	199	133	1063	666	723	39.2	1.04	134.5
i6	344	138	1408	1268	1257	56.9	3.06	217.1
i7	406	199	1615	1457	1445	110.6	3.91	248.8
i8	1183	133	5281	5796	5689	372.2	27.0	758.1
i9	353	88	2711	2589	2605	151.3	8.16	361.7
i10	2497	257	12340	11082	10033	2230.5	118.7	2147.9
C432	160	17	717	945	761	38.4	1.34	119.7
C499	202	11	312	674	476	13.3	2.03	81.4
C880	357	24	1706	1403	1027	137.5	5.13	195.2
C1355	514	24	1922	1543	1939	288.2	27.1	322.7
C1908	880	40	4365	3337	4356	459.9	56.4	783.2
C2670	1161	32	5310	4170	4123	423.2	14.7	903.2
C3540	1667	47	7232	5451	6865	1130.8	38.7	1404.6
C5315	2290	49	9685	10736	10160	1317.5	38.6	2488.8
C6288	2416	124	106392	102975	95406	4362.1	178.7	22578.2
C7552	3466	43	15563	14971	14344	1605.2	74.1	4627.4

tral point (i.e. [0.5,0.5,0.5,...,0.5]) of $[0,1]^{2n}$, the following procedure will be performed iteratively until one of the stopping criteria is met:

1. Calculate $\nabla\widehat{P}$ (gradient of $\widehat{P}(*)$) at the point.
2. From the point, move along the direction of $\nabla\widehat{P}$ as far as possible until $\widehat{P}(*)$ starts to decrease. Goto 1.

The above iteration stops under any of the following conditions:

1. The search reaches some relative maximum point at which $\nabla\widehat{P} \to 0$.
2. The search is stuck at some point on the boundary of the hypercube $[0,1]^{2n}$, where the gradient of $\widehat{P}(*)$ is normal to the boundary.

During the search, the curve gradually moves toward the boundary of $[0,1]^{2n}$. We keep on measuring the distance between the search curve and the vertices of $[0,1]^{2n}$. The following expression is used in our experiments to represent the distance: $d(P) = \sum_{i=1}^{2n} 0.5 - ||0.5 - p_i||$. Here P is a point on the curve, p_i denotes the ith entry of P, and n is the number of primary inputs. $d(P) \to 0^+$ denotes that P is sufficiently close to some vertex of $[0,1]^{2n}$. Under such a condition, the vertex will be reported as a satisfactory solution for maximizing the original combinatorial function $P(*)$ (i.e. the instantaneous power).

At each iteration of the gradient method, the gradient at a point X is calculated as: $\nabla\widehat{P}(X) = (\partial\widehat{P}/\partial x_1,\ \partial\widehat{P}/\partial x_2,\ \partial\widehat{P}/\partial x_3,\ ...,\ \partial\widehat{P}/\partial x_{2n})$, where $\partial\widehat{P}/\partial x_i = (\widehat{P}(x_1, x_2, .., x_{i-1}, x_i + \Delta x, x_{i+1}, ..., x_{2n}) - \widehat{P}(x_1, x_2, .., x_{i-1}, x_i, x_{i+1}, ..., x_{2n}))/\ \Delta x$, $\Delta x \to 0^+$. Determining the exact expression for $\widehat{P}(*)$ (in terms of primary inputs) is CPU time intensive especially for large-scaled circuits. However, it is not necessary to obtain the expression for $\widehat{P}(*)$ to calculate the gradient. Instead, the value of $\widehat{P}(X)$ at a point X is obtained by simulating the circuit with the input vector $V_1 = (x_1, x_2, ..., x_n)$ followed by $V_2 = (x_{n+1}, x_{n+2}, ..., x_{2n})$. Here x_i is the ith entry of X, and is a real number between 0 and 1.

During the steepest descent process, it is possible that the search is stuck at some local maximum which is far away from the vertices of $[0,1]^{2n}$. In this case, no conclusion can be drawn about which vertex is most likely to maximize the instantaneous power. Two approaches can be used to cope with this situation:

- Choose a different starting point (instead of using the neutral point) to start the steepest descent process. A different starting point may result in a local maximum which is close to some vertex of $[0,1]^{2n}$.
- Increase w (weight of the non-biasing term) to adjust the shape of the objective function. Using a larger w will reduce the distance between the local maxima of $\widehat{P}(*)$ and the vertices of $[0,1]^{2n}$.

The second approach is adopted in our experiments. In the 40 circuits tested, we need to use a different setting (larger) of w for 2 circuits to make the search converge. In the future work, we will investigate the possibility of making w adaptive to the structure of the circuit, as well as the delay model.

5 Experimental Results

The proposed continuous optimization approach (*COSMOS*), together with the ATPG-based estimation (*ATG*) [3] and the random simulation approach (*SIM*), has been implemented in *C* under the Berkeley *SIS* environment.

We assume all the benchmark circuits are implemented with static logic gates. In *SIM*, PI's (primary inputs) to a circuit are modeled as stochastic processes each associated with a *signal probability* (the probability of taking the logic value of ONE) and *activity* (average number of transitions per unit time). To stress the circuits, PI's are specified to have signal probability and activity of 0.5 and 0.9 respectively, in order to ensure high switching activity at the inputs. We assume that the high switching activity at the inputs also produces high switching activity at the internal nodes of the circuit [1]. Without loss of generality, *unit* and *fanout* delay models are adopted in our experiments. In the *unit* delay model, each gate is associated with unit delay. In the *fanout* delay model, propagation delay of a gate is assumed to be the gate's fanout. Delay of a gate is roughly proportional to the gate's capacitive load, which is in turn proportional to the fanout of the gate. It should be mentioned that our technique can handle any delay model.

Table 1 shows the experimental results on ISCAS85 and MCNC benchmark circuits under the *unit* delay model. The results for the same set of benchmark circuits under the *fanout* delay model are shown in Table 2. For benchmark circuits $C6288$

Table 2: Results of ISCAS and MCNC benchmarks under fanout-delay model

Benchmark Circuit	Number of gates	Number of of levels	Maximum Power			CPU Time (sec)		
			COSMOS	ATG	SIM	COSMOS	ATG	SIM
i1	33	25	101	87	91	1.84	0.14	23.5
i2	36	201	260	270	250	35.5	2.06	78.0
i3	70	132	182	202	170	6.47	0.37	67.69
i4	94	192	352	346	288	12.8	0.56	88.2
i5	199	133	1063	666	642	20.9	1.02	168.6
i6	344	138	1408	1346	1248	25.6	3.34	240.2
i7	406	199	1615	1549	1481	60.0	4.10	284.7
i8	1183	133	7165	7516	6864	315.9	56.1	866.5
i9	353	88	4306	3106	5061	218.5	32.0	451.5
i10	2497	257	8847	15096	14692	5835.2	1616.4	2531.13
C432	160	36	828	944	831	91.6	32.2	140.1
C499	202	41	355	740	511	18.8	3.41	82.5
C880	357	60	1447	1238	1211	252.8	3.67	203.1
C1355	514	41	2424	1404	2251	129.3	47.0	336.7
C1908	880	33	4945	4235	5577	309.8	56.0	1091.5
C2670	1161	233	5129	5382	4768	597.5	34.2	1232.6
C3540	1667	50	7922	9002	10537	662.4	107.83	2102.0
C5315	2290	178	10945	13739	12290	689.7	61.8	3416.7
C6288	2416	32	105172	97023	118555	3658.4	386.7	32859.1
C7552	3466	207	15947	18279	17178	2381.9	191.4	6129.9

and $i10$ under the fanout delay model, we use a different setting of w to make the steepest descent process converge. This will take extra CPU time in the actual estimation process. The CPU time for these two circuits listed in Table 2 does not include this extra time.

In Tables 1 and 2, the instantaneous power of a circuit is calculated based on Equation 1: $P(V_1, V_2) = \sum_{\forall gate} F(g) * T(g)$. Here (V_1, V_2) is the input vector pair applied to the circuit; $F(g)$ is the fanout (denoting the capacitive load) of gate g, and $T(g)$ is the transition count at the output of gate g caused by V_1 and V_2. In *COSMOS*, the optimal choice(s) of (V_1, V_2) is obtained by searching the maxima of the function $\widehat{P}(V_1, V_2)$ over a unit hypercube in the Euclidean space. In the ATPG-based estimation, *ATG* maximizes the instantaneous power in the circuit by greedily assigning switchings to the outputs of the gates with large capacitive load. The switchings assigned are then justified by the ATPG technique [3]. In the estimation technique based on random simulation, *SIM* generates the optimal pair of (V_1, V_2) for stressing a circuit based on $10,000$ input patterns conforming to the signal probability of 0.5 and activity of 0.9 at PI's [3]. The CPU time is measured on a Sun *Sparc* 5 workstation.

From Tables 1 and 2, we can conclude the following significances of this continuous optimization approach (*COSMOS*):

1. Compared to the traditional simulation-based technique (*SIM*), this approach is superior in both speed and performance. In 24 out of the 40 circuits tested, this approach generates a tighter lower bound (1.16 times larger, on an average). For the 40 circuits, the mean value of the ratio "CPU time of the continuous optimization approach divided by CPU time of the simulation-based technique" is equal to 0.41.

2. Although *COSMOS* converges not as fast as the ATPG-based technique does, our approach is favored under the following conditions:

   - To estimate the power of a circuit under certain complicated delay model that the ATPG-based technique cannot be easily applied.

   - In 24 out of the 40 circuits tested, this approach generates a better estimate of maximum power (1.19 times larger, average speaking) than the ATPG-based technique does. A lower bound of high quality can be decided by these two approaches together.

6 Conclusions

In this paper, we have developed a continuous optimization approach for the maximum power estimation of CMOS circuits. Experimental results show that this approach is superior to the traditional simulation-based technique in both speed and performance. For 24 out of the 40 circuits tested, our approach gives a better estimate than the simulation-based technique does. For the 40 circuits, the mean value of the ratio "CPU time of the continuous optimization approach divided by CPU time of the simulation-based technique" is equal to 0.41. In maximum power estimation, this approach is an alternative to the ATPG-based technique.

References

[1] C.Su, C.Tsui, and Alvin M. Despain, "Saving Power in the Control Path of Embedded Processors," *IEEE Design and Test of Computers*, Vol. 11, No. 4, pp.32-41, winter,1994.

[2] S.Manne, A.Pardo, R.Bahar, G.Hachtel, F.Somenzi, E.Macii and M.Poncino "Computing the Maximum Power Cycles of a Sequential Circuit," in Proc. of *DAC*, 1995.

[3] C.-Y.Wang, K.Roy, and T.-L.Chou, "Maximum Power Estimation for Sequential Circuits Using a Test Generation Approach," *Custom Integrated Circuits Conference*, 1996.

[4] S.Devadas, K.Keutzer and J.White, "Estimation of Power Dissipation in CMOS Combinational Circuits," *IEEE Custom Integrated Circuits Conf.*, 1990.

[5] H.Kriplani, F.Najm, and I.Hajj, "Maximum Current Estimation in CMOS Circuits," in Proc. of *DAC*, 1992.

[6] H.Kriplani, F.Najm, P.Yang and I.Hajj, "Resolving Signal Correlations for Estimating Maximum Currents in CMOS Combinational Circuits," in Proc. of *DAC*, 1993.

[7] R.Burch, F.Najm, P.Yang and T.Trick, "A Monte Carlo Approach for Power Estimation," *IEEE Trans. VLSI Systems*, Vol.1, No. 1, pp.63-71, March 1993.

[8] M.Xakellis, F.Najm, "Statistical Estimation of the Switching Activity in Digital Circuits," in Proc. of *DAC*, 1994.

[9] J.K.Ousterhout, "A Switch-Level Timing Verifier for Digital MOS VLSI ," *IEEE Trans. Computer-Aided Design*, Vol. CAD-4, pp.336-348, June 1985.

[10] R.B.Hitchcock, "Timing Verification and Timing Analysis Program," in Proc. of *DAC*, 1982.

SESSION 1D

BLOCK KRYLOV METHODS FOR INTERCONNECT MODELING

Moderators:

Peter Feldmann, Bell Labs., Lucent Technologies.,

Murray Hill, NJ

Jacob K. White, Massachusetts Institute of Technology,

Cambridge, MA

PRIMA: Passive Reduced-order Interconnect Macromodeling Algorithm*

Altan Odabasioglu, Mustafa Celik+, and Lawrence T. Pileggi
Department of Electrical and Computer Engineering
Carnegie Mellon University
Pittsburgh, PA 15213

Abstract

This paper describes PRIMA, an algorithm for generating provably passive reduced order N-port models for RLC interconnect circuits. It is demonstrated that, in addition to requiring macromodel stability, macromodel passivity is needed to guarantee the overall circuit stability once the active and passive driver/load models are connected. PRIMA extends the block Arnoldi technique to include guaranteed passivity. Moreover, it is empirically observed that the accuracy is superior to existing block Arnoldi methods. While the same passivity extension is not possible for MPVL, we observed comparable accuracy in the frequency domain for all examples considered. Additionally, a path tracing algorithm is used to calculate the reduced order macromodel with the utmost efficiency for generalized RLC interconnects.

1. Introduction

As integrated circuits and systems are designed with smaller feature sizes and for faster operation, RLC interconnect effects have a more dominant impact on signal propagation than ever before. In addition, parasitic coupling effects and reduced power supply voltage levels make interconnect modeling increasingly important. Since these interconnect models can contain thousands of tightly coupled R-L-C components, reduced order macromodels are imperative [1][2][3][4]. Ideally, a simulator would isolate the large linear portions of the circuit from the nonlinear elements (e.g., transistor models) and preprocess them into reduced order multiport macromodels.

It is well known that an N-port can be fully represented by its admittance parameters in the Laplace domain, however, the objective is to apply model order reduction to produce low order rational approximations for each entry in **Y**(s) (see Fig.1). To find **Y**(s), voltage sources are connected to the ports and the currents into the ports are measured. The voltage sources are the inputs to the system and the port currents are the outputs. A single-input single-output (SISO) N-port model approach would perform model order reduction on each term Y_{ij} individually. Both Asymptotic Waveform Evaluation (AWE) [1] and Padé via Lanczos (PVL) [2], which are Padé approximations, can perform SISO reduction by matching 2q moments for a qth order approximation of each Y_{ij} term. The Arnoldi Algorithm [4] can also be used to obtain SISO approximations, however it matches only q moments for a qth order approximation. MPVL (Matrix Padé via Lanczos) [5] and Block Arnoldi [6] are multi-input multi-output (MIMO) versions of PVL and Arnoldi respectively. In the block techniques, the system Modified Nodal Analysis (MNA) matrices are directly reduced by matrix transformations.

Regardless of the reduction method used in all of the approaches cited above, the reduced order model of an RLC circuit can have unstable poles. It is always possible to obtain an asymptotically stable model by simply discarding the unstable poles, however, passivity is not guaranteed. In addition, discarding unstable poles requires re-adjustment of the residues to improve the quality of the approximation. Passivity uncertainty is problematic since even the test for N-port passivity can be very costly for a large number of ports [7]. The coordinate transformed Arnoldi Algorithm [8] was introduced as a remedy for the instability problem, but it does not guarantee passivity. The passivity extension of this stable Arnoldi algorithm was recently developed in [9], however its applicability is limited to RC circuits only. The PACT algorithm [3] proposed a new direction for passive reduced-order model for RC circuits based on congruence transformations. The same authors proposed Split Congruence Transformations [10] for passive reductions of RLC circuits, producing equivalent circuit realizations. In [10], however, the extra steps required to split the transformation matrix can result in a decrease in accuracy and efficiency. Moreover, the passivity proof is somewhat controversial, and we will consider a more complete proof in this paper.

$$\begin{bmatrix} I_1(s) \\ \vdots \\ I_N(s) \end{bmatrix} = \underbrace{\begin{bmatrix} Y_{11}(s) & \dots & Y_{1N}(s) \\ \vdots & & \vdots \\ Y_{N1}(s) & \dots & Y_{NN}(s) \end{bmatrix}}_{\mathbf{Y}(s)} \begin{bmatrix} V_1(s) \\ \vdots \\ V_N(s) \end{bmatrix}$$

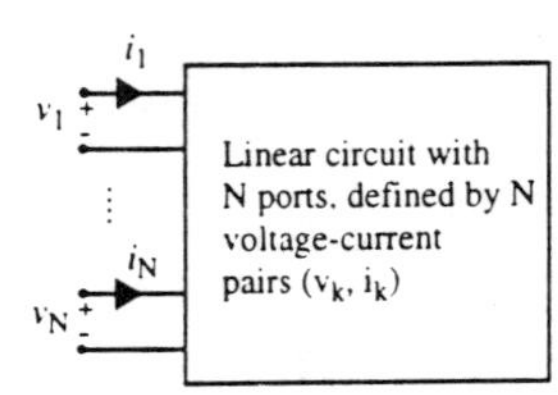

FIGURE 1: The multiport representation of a linear circuit.

+He is now with Motorola, Austin, TX 78721.

*This work was supported in part by the Defense Advanced Research Projects Agency, sponsored by the Air Force Office of Scientific Research under grant number F49620-96-1-0069, and by grants from Intel Corporation and SGS-Thomson Microelectronics.

A passive system denotes a system that is incapable of generating energy, and hence one that can only absorb energy from the sources used to excite it [11]. As we will show in Section 2.2., passivity is an important property to satisfy because stable, but not passive macromodels can produce unstable systems when connected to other stable, even passive, loads. A property in classical circuit theory states that: interconnections of stable systems may not necessarily be stable; but (strictly) passive circuits are (asymptotically) stable; and arbitrary interconnections of (strictly) passive circuits are (strictly) passive, and, therefore, (asymptotically) stable [12].

In this paper, we propose a Passive Reduced-order Interconnect Macromodeling Algorithm, PRIMA, based on the Block Arnoldi Algorithm but with congruence transformations that produce provably passive reduced order macromodels for arbitrary RLC circuits. PRIMA has accuracy comparable to MPVL and superior to Block Arnoldi. Furthermore, the block Arnoldi vectors are generated with the utmost efficiency following the algorithms in RICE [13] that are used to calculate moments. This includes efficient handling of interconnect trees and meshes, as in RICE, but with renewed focus on efficient handling of large problems with a huge number of mutual inductances.

2. Background

To obtain the admittance matrix of a multiport, voltage sources are connected to the ports. The multiport, along with these sources, constitutes the Modified Nodal Analysis (MNA) equations:

$$\begin{aligned} \mathbf{C}\,\dot{\mathbf{x}}_n &= -\mathbf{G}\,\mathbf{x}_n + \mathbf{B}\,\mathbf{u}_p \\ \mathbf{i}_p &= \mathbf{L}^T\,\mathbf{x}_n \end{aligned} \tag{1}$$

The $\mathbf{i}_p$ and $\mathbf{u}_p$ vectors denote the port currents and voltages respectively and

$$\mathbf{G} \equiv \begin{bmatrix} \mathbf{N} & \mathbf{E} \\ -\mathbf{E}^T & \mathbf{0} \end{bmatrix} \qquad \mathbf{C} \equiv \begin{bmatrix} \mathbf{Q} & \mathbf{0} \\ \mathbf{0} & \mathbf{H} \end{bmatrix} \qquad \mathbf{x}_n \equiv \begin{bmatrix} \mathbf{v} \\ \mathbf{i} \end{bmatrix} \tag{2}$$

where **v** and **i** are the MNA variables corresponding to the node voltages, inductor and voltage source currents respectively. The $n \times n$ matrices **G** and **C** represent the conductance and susceptance matrices (except that the rows corresponding to the current variables are negated as in [7]). **N**, **Q** and **H** are the matrices containing the stamps for resistors, capacitors and inductors respectively. **E** consists of ones, minus ones and zeros, which represent the current variables in KCL equations. Provided that the original N-port is composed of passive linear elements only, **Q**, **H** and **N** are symmetric nonnegative definite matrices. This implies **C** is also symmetric and nonnegative definite. Since this is an N-port formulation, whereby the only sources are the voltage sources at the N port nodes, **B=L**. But we maintain the separate **B** and **L** notation for generality of the equations.

Returning to equation (1), following the notation in [2] we define

$$\mathbf{A} \equiv -\mathbf{G}^{-1}\mathbf{C} \text{ and } \mathbf{R} \equiv \mathbf{G}^{-1}\mathbf{B}\,. \tag{3}$$

With unit voltages at the ports, taking the Laplace transformation of (1) and solving for the port current variables, the y-parameter matrix is given as

$$\mathbf{Y}(s) = \mathbf{L}^T(\mathbf{I}_n - s\mathbf{A})^{-1}\mathbf{R} \tag{4}$$

where $\mathbf{I}_n$ is the $n \times n$ identity matrix. It is apparent from (4) that the eigenvalues of **A** represent the inverses of the poles of **Y**(s).

Using any of the aforementioned model-order reduction techniques, we can find reduced order rational approximations to $Y_{jk}(s)$ terms, for all j, k ≤ N. The reduced-order **Y**(s) can then be simulated along with other nonlinear and linear portions of the complete circuit using a simulator that employs either recursive convolution [14] or state-space realization [7], both of which have linear complexity. If the reduction is block, the reduced order multi-input multi-output circuit can also be realized using linear circuit elements.

2.1.Block Arnoldi Algorithm

The Block Arnoldi algorithm reduces the system matrix **A** in (3) to a small block upper Hessenberg matrix $\mathbf{H}_q$. To do so requires an orthonormal basis, **X**, for the corresponding Krylov space which satisfies the following:*

$$\begin{aligned} colsp(\mathbf{X}) &= Kr\left(\mathbf{A}, \mathbf{R}, \left\lfloor \frac{q}{N} \right\rfloor\right) \\ \mathbf{X}^T\,\mathbf{A}\,\mathbf{X} &= \mathbf{H}_q \\ \mathbf{X}^T\,\mathbf{X} &= \mathbf{I}_q \end{aligned} \tag{5}$$

where N is the number of ports and $\mathbf{I}_q$ is a $q \times q$ identity matrix. The Krylov space is defined as

$$Kr(\mathbf{A}, \mathbf{R}, k) \equiv colsp[\mathbf{R}, \mathbf{A}\mathbf{R}, \mathbf{A}^2\mathbf{R}, \ldots, \mathbf{A}^k\mathbf{R}]\,. \tag{6}$$

Finding the reduced order admittance matrix can be explained by a change of variable,

$$\mathbf{x}_n = \mathbf{X}_{\{n x q\}}\,\mathbf{z}_q\,. \tag{7}$$

where $\mathbf{z}_q$ is now the reduced order system variable, which reduces the number of unknowns in the system (q is generally much smaller than n). Substituting (7) into (1), then multiplying the first equation by $\mathbf{X}^T\mathbf{G}^{-1}$ yields

$$\begin{aligned} \mathbf{H}_q\dot{\mathbf{z}}_q &= \mathbf{z}_q - \mathbf{X}^T\,\mathbf{R}\,\mathbf{u}_p \\ \mathbf{i}_p &= \mathbf{L}^T\mathbf{X}\,\mathbf{z}_q \end{aligned} \tag{8}$$

Therefore, in the Laplace domain,

$$\hat{\mathbf{Y}}(s) = \mathbf{L}^T\mathbf{X}(\mathbf{I}_q - s\mathbf{H}_q)^{-1}\mathbf{X}^T\,\mathbf{R} \tag{9}$$

where $\mathbf{I}_q$ is a $q \times q$ identity matrix.

The reduced order system equations and admittance matrix are given by (8) and (9) respectively. The poles of

*The $\lfloor \cdot \rfloor$ operator is the truncation to the nearest integer towards zero.

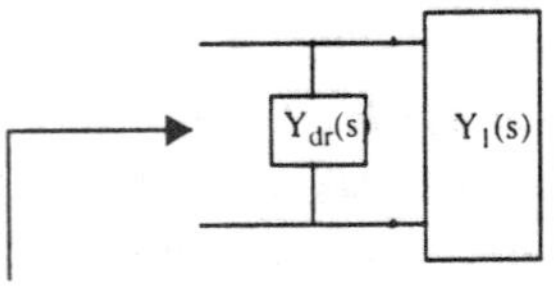

$$Y_1(s) = \frac{s+4}{s^2+2s+5}$$
$$Y_{dr}(s) = 0.06 + 0.056s$$

$$Z_c(s) = \frac{s^2+2s+5}{0.056s^3+0.172s^2+1.4s+4.3} \Rightarrow \text{Poles at: } -3.074,\ \pm 5j$$

FIGURE 2: A non-passive system example demonstrating potential instability.

the reduced order system are the reciprocal eigenvalues of $\mathbf{H}_q$. A complete pole/residue decomposition can be obtained by eigendecomposing $\mathbf{H}_q$. Using the information in [6], it can be shown that the first $\left\lfloor \frac{q}{N} \right\rfloor$ moments of $\hat{\mathbf{Y}}(s)$ in (9) match those of $\mathbf{Y}(s)$ in (4).

2.2.Importance of Passivity

It is always possible to come up with stable reduced order macromodels by utilizing a number of heuristics, however, none of these tricks can be used to obtain provably passive approximations. Moreover, in [7] it was shown that the test for passivity of an AWE-reduced N-port macromodel is prohibitive in terms of CPU run time cost. Fig.2 is a numerical example generated in [7] that demonstrates the passivity problem. $Y_1(s)$ in this figure represents a reduced order transfer function which has all poles and zeros in the left half plane. $Y_{dr}(s)$ represents a capacitor and resistor in parallel. If we drive this circuit with a current source, it will oscillate at $2.5/\pi$ Hz. To show that it is also a practical problem, we took a simple interconnect and connected the load and the nonlinear driver as shown in the examples section in Fig.5. The interconnect is represented by a fifth order approximation obtained by PVL [2]. The figure clearly shows the growing oscillations at the output (instability) although all of the poles obtained from PVL were stable. A Thevenin equivalent linear driver with a resistance of 2 ohms generates a similar instability for this 2-port example.

3. PRIMA: Passive Reduced-order Interconnect Macromodeling Algorithm

The Block Arnoldi Algorithm is employed in PRIMA to generate the orthonormal basis for a congruence transformation matrix. After $\left\lfloor \frac{q}{N} \right\rfloor + 1$ (the extra step is not necessary when $\frac{q}{N}$ is an integer) iterations of PRIMA, the $n \times q$ matrix $\mathbf{X}$ is found such that:

$$colsp(\mathbf{X}) = Kr\left(\mathbf{A}, \mathbf{R}, \left\lfloor \frac{q}{N} \right\rfloor\right)$$
$$\mathbf{X}^T\mathbf{X} = \mathbf{I}_q \tag{10}$$

FIGURE 3: The Passive Reduction Algorithm

- Connect voltage sources to the multiport & obtain the MNA matrices as in (2).
- Set $[\,\mathbf{b}_1 \mid \mathbf{b}_2 \mid \ldots \mid \mathbf{b}_p\,] = \mathbf{B}$ and $[\,\mathbf{l}_1 \mid \mathbf{l}_2 \mid \ldots \mid \mathbf{l}_p\,] = \mathbf{L}$
- Solve $\mathbf{GR} = \mathbf{B}$ for $\mathbf{R}$
- $(\mathbf{X}_0, \mathbf{K}) = qr(\mathbf{R})$; qr factorization of $\mathbf{R}$
- Set $n = int\left(\frac{q}{N}\right) + 1$
- For $k=1, 2, \ldots, n$
  - Set $\mathbf{V} = \mathbf{C}\mathbf{X}_{k-1}$
  - Solve $\mathbf{G}\,\mathbf{X}_k^{(0)} = \mathbf{V}$ for $\mathbf{X}_k^{(0)}$
  - For $j=1, \ldots, k$
    - $\mathbf{H} = \mathbf{X}_{k-j}^T\mathbf{X}_k^{(j-1)}$
    - $\mathbf{X}_k^{(j)} = \mathbf{X}_k^{(j-1)} - \mathbf{X}_{k-j}\mathbf{H}$
  - $(\mathbf{X}_k, \mathbf{K}) = qr(\mathbf{X}_k^{(k)})$; qr factorization of $\mathbf{X}_k^{(k)}$
- Set $\mathbf{X} = [\mathbf{X}_0\ \mathbf{X}_1\ \ldots\ \mathbf{X}_{k-1}]$ and truncate $\mathbf{X}$ so that it has q columns only.
- Compute $\tilde{\mathbf{C}} = \mathbf{X}^T\mathbf{C}\,\mathbf{X}$, $\tilde{\mathbf{G}} = \mathbf{X}^T\mathbf{G}\,\mathbf{X}$
- Find eigendecomposition of $\tilde{\mathbf{G}}^{-1}\tilde{\mathbf{C}}$: $\tilde{\mathbf{G}}^{-1}\tilde{\mathbf{C}} = \mathbf{S}\Lambda\mathbf{S}^{-1}$ *
  $\Lambda = diag(\lambda_1, \lambda_2, \ldots, \lambda_q)$
- To find poles and residues for $\hat{Y}_{i,j}(s)$:
  - Solve $\tilde{\mathbf{G}}\mathbf{w} = \mathbf{X}^T\mathbf{b}_j$ for $\mathbf{w}$*
  - Set $\mu = \mathbf{S}^T\mathbf{X}^T\mathbf{l}_i$ and $\nu = \mathbf{S}^{-1}\mathbf{w}$
  - $\hat{Y}_{i,j}(s) = \sum_{n=1}^{q} \frac{\mu_n \nu_n}{1 + s\lambda_n}$
- Set $\hat{\mathbf{Y}}(s) = \begin{bmatrix} \hat{Y}_{1,1} & \ldots & \hat{Y}_{1,p} \\ \vdots & & \vdots \\ \hat{Y}_{p,1} & \ldots & \hat{Y}_{p,p} \end{bmatrix}$

*Inversion of $\tilde{\mathbf{G}}$ can be avoided.

In the classical Arnoldi approach [4], the reduced order $\mathbf{Y}(s)$ is calculated using the qxq upper Hessenberg matrix in (5) as shown in (9):

$$\hat{\mathbf{Y}}(s) = \mathbf{L}^T\mathbf{X}(\mathbf{I} - s\mathbf{H})^{-1}\mathbf{X}^T\mathbf{R} \tag{11}$$

In our variation, the conductance and susceptance matrices are directly reduced so that passivity is preserved during reduction. Applying the change of variable $\mathbf{x}_n = \mathbf{X}_{\{nxq\}}\tilde{\mathbf{x}}_q$ in (1), and multiplying the first row by $\mathbf{X}^T$ from (10) yields

$$(\mathbf{X}^T\mathbf{C}\,\mathbf{X})\dot{\tilde{\mathbf{x}}}_q = -(\mathbf{X}^T\mathbf{G}\,\mathbf{X})\tilde{\mathbf{x}}_q + (\mathbf{X}^T\mathbf{B})\mathbf{u}_p$$
$$\mathbf{i}_p = (\mathbf{L}^T\mathbf{X})\,\tilde{\mathbf{x}}_q \tag{12}$$

The reduced order MNA matrices are, therefore,

$$\tilde{\mathbf{C}} = \mathbf{X}^T\mathbf{C}\,\mathbf{X} \qquad \tilde{\mathbf{G}} = \mathbf{X}^T\mathbf{G}\,\mathbf{X}$$
$$\tilde{\mathbf{B}} = \mathbf{X}^T\mathbf{B} \qquad \tilde{\mathbf{L}} = \mathbf{X}^T\mathbf{L} \tag{13}$$

These types of transformations are known as congruence transformations. Congruence transformations were first introduced by [3] for order reduction of circuits. From (12) and (13), the reduced Y(s), namely $\hat{Y}(s)$, is now

$$\hat{Y}(s) = \tilde{L}^T(\tilde{G} + s\tilde{C})^{-1}\tilde{B} \tag{14}$$

Since the size of $\tilde{G}$ and $\tilde{C}$ is typically very small, it is easy to find the poles and zeros of $\hat{Y}(s)$ by eigendecomposition. The complete algorithm is given in Fig.3. It employs the Block Arnoldi Algorithm using modified Gram-Schmidt orthogonalization [6], which is mathematically equivalent to ordinary Gram-Schmidt process, but behaves better numerically [15]. In addition, it is possible to avoid the inversion of $\tilde{G}$ to find the poles and residues by using a generalized eigendecomposition. In this case, the computation of $\tilde{G}^{-1}\tilde{B}$ can be avoided by using (31) and replacing it by X^TR. It is observed that this scheme is numerically much better.

The complexity of the algorithm to produce q poles for an N-port is slightly less than AWE, PVL and MPVL. It requires 1 LU factorization (or path tracing equivalent as explained in Section 4.) of the **G** (MNA conductance) matrix, which dominates all the other computational costs and is common in all reduction techniques. However, to find q poles, only q backward-forward substitutions are needed, whereas in MPVL, PVL and AWE, twice as many are required. As in MPVL, there will be only one eigendecomposition to find the poles and residues, whereas PVL requires N^2 eigendecompositions, since for each $Y_{ij}(s)$, there will be a different T_q. AWE will solve the N^2 different Hankel matrices to get to the poles.

3.1.Preservation of Passivity

If the system described by (1) and (2) is reduced by the transformations in (13), it can be shown that the reduced system is always passive. In [16], necessary and sufficient conditions for the system admittance matrix $\hat{Y}(s)$ (eqn. (14)) to be passive are:

1. $\hat{Y}(s^*) = \hat{Y}^*(s)$ for all complex s, where * is the complex conjugate operator.

2. $\hat{Y}(s)$ is a positive matrix, that is $z^{*T}(\hat{Y}(s) + \hat{Y}^{*T}(s))z \geq 0$ for all complex values of s satisfying Re(s) > 0 and for any complex vector **z**.

The second condition also implies the analyticity of $\hat{Y}(s)$ for Re(s) > 0, since $\hat{Y}(s)$ is a rational function of s (details in [16]). Therefore, the test of analyticity is unnecessary.

Due to the fact that the reduced matrices, $\tilde{G}$, $\tilde{C}$, $\tilde{B}$ and $\tilde{L}$ are all real since the transformation matrix, **X**, is real, condition 1 is automatically satisfied. To show that condition 2 is satisfied, we first set $Y_h(s) = \hat{Y}(s) + \hat{Y}^T(s^*)$ and use the property $\tilde{B} = \tilde{L}$ (since **B**=**L** in our formulation when there are no sources inside the N-port, $X^TB = X^TL$) and some algebra to obtain,

$$z^{*T}Y_h(s)z = z^{*T}(\tilde{B}^T(\tilde{G} + s\tilde{C})^{-1}\tilde{B} + \tilde{B}^T(\tilde{G} + s^*\tilde{C})^{-T}\tilde{B})z \tag{15}$$
$$= z^{*T}\tilde{B}^T(\tilde{G} + s\tilde{C})^{-1}[(\tilde{G} + s\tilde{C}) + (\tilde{G} + s^*\tilde{C})^T](\tilde{G} + s^*\tilde{C})^{-T}\tilde{B}z$$

Setting $w = (\tilde{G} + s^*\tilde{C})^{-T}\tilde{B}z$ and $s = j\omega + \sigma$ yields,

$$z^{*T}Y_h(s)z = w^{*T}[(\tilde{G} + (\sigma + j\omega)\tilde{C}) + (\tilde{G} + (\sigma - j\omega)\tilde{C})^T]w$$
$$= w^{*T}[\tilde{G} + \tilde{G}^T + \sigma(\tilde{C} + \tilde{C}^T)]w \tag{16}$$
$$= w^{*T}X^T[G + G^T + \sigma(C + C^T)]Xw$$

Similarly, let $y = Xw$ to get

$$z^{*T}Y_h(s)z = y^{*T}[G + G^T + \sigma(C + C^T)]y \tag{17}$$

Since **C** is symmetric, $C^T + C = 2C$. **C** is known to be nonnegative definite (since we negate the rows corresponding to current variables as in (2)), so

$$y^{*T}\sigma(C^T + C)y = 2\sigma y^{*T}Cy \geq 0 \tag{18}$$

for any complex vector **y** and σ=Re(s) > 0. **N** (the resistor stamps) is a symmetric nonnegative definite matrix, therefore

$$y^{*T}(G^T + G)y = y^{*T}\left(\begin{bmatrix} N & E \\ -E^T & 0 \end{bmatrix}^T + \begin{bmatrix} N & E \\ -E^T & 0 \end{bmatrix}\right)y = y^{*T}\begin{bmatrix} 2N & 0 \\ 0 & 0 \end{bmatrix}y \geq 0 \tag{19}$$

is also nonnegative definite for any complex vector **y**. From (17), (18) and (19), it follows that the second passivity condition is satisfied.

3.2.Preservation of Moments

The transformation in (13) preserves $\left\lfloor \frac{q}{N} \right\rfloor$ moments of the original system, which is the same as the classical Block Arnoldi reduction and half of that in MPVL. The proof is as follows. The exact (block) moments, M_i, of the circuit are given as:

$$M_i = L^T A^i R \tag{20}$$

where $A \equiv -G^{-1}C$, $R \equiv G^{-1}B$ and **G**, **C**, **B**, **L** are the system matrices as defined in (1).

Likewise, the moments of the PRIMA reduced order system are given by

$$\hat{M}_i = \tilde{L}^T\tilde{A}^i\tilde{R} \tag{21}$$

where $\tilde{A} \equiv -\tilde{G}^{-1}\tilde{C}$, $\tilde{R} \equiv \tilde{G}^{-1}\tilde{B}$ and $\tilde{G}$, $\tilde{C}$, $\tilde{B}$, $\tilde{L}$ are as defined in (13). Substitution of (13) in (21) yields:

$$\hat{\mathbf{M}}_i = \mathbf{L}^T\mathbf{X}[-(\mathbf{X}^T\mathbf{G}\,\mathbf{X})^{-1}(\mathbf{X}^T\mathbf{C}\,\mathbf{X})]^i(\mathbf{X}^T\mathbf{G}\,\mathbf{X})^{-1}\mathbf{X}^T\mathbf{B} \quad (22)$$

It is shown in [6] that the Arnoldi algorithm yields

$$\mathbf{A}^i\mathbf{R} = \mathbf{X}\;\mathbf{H}_q^i\,\mathbf{X}^T\,\mathbf{R}, \qquad 0 \le i < \left\lfloor \frac{q}{N} \right\rfloor. \quad (23)$$

Rearranging the terms and using the definitions from (13):

$$\begin{aligned} \mathbf{A}\,\mathbf{A}^{i-1}\mathbf{R} &= \mathbf{X}\;\mathbf{H}_q^i\,\mathbf{X}^T\,\mathbf{R} \\ -\mathbf{G}^{-1}\mathbf{C}\,\mathbf{A}^{i-1}\mathbf{R} &= \mathbf{X}\;\mathbf{H}_q^i\,\mathbf{X}^T\,\mathbf{R} \\ -\mathbf{C}\,\mathbf{A}^{i-1}\mathbf{R} &= \mathbf{G}\,\mathbf{X}\;\mathbf{H}_q^i\,\mathbf{X}^T\,\mathbf{R} \\ -\mathbf{X}^T\mathbf{C}\,\mathbf{A}^{i-1}\mathbf{R} &= \mathbf{X}^T\mathbf{G}\,\mathbf{X}\;\mathbf{H}_q^i\,\mathbf{X}^T\,\mathbf{R} \end{aligned} \quad (24)$$

$$-\mathbf{X}\,(\mathbf{X}^T\mathbf{G}\,\mathbf{X}\,)^{-1}\mathbf{X}^T\mathbf{C}\,\mathbf{A}^{i-1}\mathbf{R} = \mathbf{X}\;\mathbf{H}_q^i\,\mathbf{X}^T\,\mathbf{R} \quad (25)$$

Inserting (23) in (25) results in:

$$\mathbf{K}\,\mathbf{A}^{i-1}\mathbf{R} = \mathbf{A}^i\mathbf{R}, \qquad 0 \le i < \left\lfloor \frac{q}{N} \right\rfloor \quad (26)$$

where

$$\mathbf{K} = -\mathbf{X}\,(\mathbf{X}^T\mathbf{G}\,\mathbf{X}\,)^{-1}\mathbf{X}^T\mathbf{C}\,. \quad (27)$$

From (26), it can be shown by recursion that

$$\mathbf{K}^i\mathbf{R} = \mathbf{A}^i\mathbf{R}, \qquad 0 \le i < \left\lfloor \frac{q}{N} \right\rfloor \quad (28)$$

Therefore, using (27) it follows that

$$\mathbf{X}[-(\mathbf{X}^T\mathbf{G}\,\mathbf{X})^{-1}(\mathbf{X}^T\mathbf{C}\,\mathbf{X})]^i = \mathbf{K}^i\,\mathbf{X} \quad (29)$$

Replacing $\mathbf{X}[-(\mathbf{X}^T\mathbf{G}\,\mathbf{X})^{-1}(\mathbf{X}^T\mathbf{C}\,\mathbf{X})]^i$ in (22) with $\mathbf{K}^i\,\mathbf{X}$ yields

$$\hat{\mathbf{M}}_i = \mathbf{L}^T\mathbf{K}^i\,\mathbf{X}(\mathbf{X}^T\mathbf{G}\,\mathbf{X})^{-1}\mathbf{X}^T\mathbf{B} \quad (30)$$

Evaluating (26) when i=0 gives

$$\mathbf{X}\,(\mathbf{X}^T\mathbf{G}\,\mathbf{X}\,)^{-1}\mathbf{X}^T\mathbf{B} = \mathbf{R} \quad (31)$$

Then from (30) and (31),

$$\hat{\mathbf{M}}_i = \mathbf{L}^T\mathbf{K}^i\,\mathbf{R}, \qquad 0 \le i < \left\lfloor \frac{q}{N} \right\rfloor. \quad (32)$$

Finally, combining (32) and (28) with (20), it follows that

$$\hat{\mathbf{M}}_i = \mathbf{M}_i, \qquad 0 \le i < \left\lfloor \frac{q}{N} \right\rfloor \quad (33)$$

Note that the number of poles in each entry of $\mathbf{Y}(s)$ is q, and we have matched the first $\left\lfloor \frac{q}{N} \right\rfloor$ moments at all N ports, yielding a total of q moments. The number of moments matched in PRIMA is, therefore, the same as that for the Block Arnoldi algorithm and half as many as matched by MPVL.

4. Integration of PRIMA within RICE

For all of the model order reduction schemes, the LU decomposition of the MNA conductance matrix ($\mathbf{G}$ in (2)) dominates the run time. In [13], RICE (Rapid Interconnect Circuit Evaluation) was described as a general path tracing algorithm to obtain moments with optimal efficiency for interconnect trees and mesh structures. Using RICE to calculate moments, the explicit construction and inversion of $\mathbf{G}$ is avoided, and the moments are more accurate than those obtained via matrix factorization.

The moments of the circuit can be obtained recursively from:

$$\begin{aligned} \mathbf{M}_0 &= \mathbf{G}^{-1}\mathbf{B} \\ \mathbf{M}_k &= \mathbf{G}^{-1}\mathbf{C}\mathbf{M}_{k-1} \qquad k > 0 \end{aligned} \quad (34)$$

where the matrices $\mathbf{G}$, $\mathbf{C}$ and $\mathbf{B}$ are as defined in (2). As shown in [1], this can be viewed as recursive dc circuit solutions, when capacitors and inductors are replaced by current and voltage sources respectively, with the values derived from the columns of $\mathbf{CM}_{k-1}$. The Krylov vectors, which can be viewed as well conditioned moments, can be obtained from a very similar recursive scheme:

1. Obtain zeroth moment and orthonormalize it:

$$\text{Solve } \mathbf{M}_0 \text{ from } \mathbf{G}\,\mathbf{M}_0 = \mathbf{B} \quad (35)$$

$$\mathbf{X}_0 = orth(\mathbf{M}_0) \quad (36)$$

2. Recursively obtain higher order Krylov vectors:

$$\text{Solve } \mathbf{M}_k \text{ from } \mathbf{G}\,\mathbf{M}_k = \mathbf{C}\mathbf{X}_{k-1} \quad (37)$$

$$\mathbf{X}_k^{\zeta} = \mathbf{M}_k - \mathbf{X}_{k-1}(\mathbf{X}_{k-1}^T\mathbf{M}_k) - \ldots - \mathbf{X}_0(\mathbf{X}_0^T\mathbf{M}_k) \quad (38)$$

$$\mathbf{X}_k = orth(\mathbf{X}_k^{\zeta}) \quad (39)$$

The "*orth*" operator can be implemented as a simple Gram-Schmidt orthonormalization procedure. The space spanned by the block Krylov terms $(\mathbf{X}_k, \mathbf{X}_{k-1}, \ldots, \mathbf{X}_0)$ is called the Krylov space. Therefore, the Krylov vectors can be obtained via a path tracing procedure using RICE-like routines to solve for equations (35) and (37).

The Krylov space constitutes the congruence transformation matrix, $\mathbf{X}$ in PRIMA. The reduced MNA matrices $\tilde{\mathbf{G}}$ and $\tilde{\mathbf{C}}$ are

$$\tilde{\mathbf{C}} = \mathbf{X}^T\mathbf{C}\,\mathbf{X} \qquad \tilde{\mathbf{G}} = \mathbf{X}^T\mathbf{G}\,\mathbf{X}. \quad (40)$$

Note, however, that the matrices $\mathbf{C}\,\mathbf{X}$ and $\mathbf{G}\,\mathbf{X}$ are obtained using RICE without explicitly constructing $\mathbf{G}$ and $\mathbf{C}$. The columns of $\mathbf{C}\,\mathbf{X}$ are the values of current and voltage sources that are used to replace capacitors and inductors at each moment computation stage. This information is easily obtained during a path trace [13]. The kth block of $\mathbf{G}\,\mathbf{X}$ (i.e. $\mathbf{GX}_k$) is a function of previous blocks of $\mathbf{G}\,\mathbf{X}$ and $\mathbf{CX}_{k-1}$ since from (38),

$$\mathbf{GX}_k^{\zeta} = \mathbf{GM}_k - \mathbf{GX}_{k-1}(\mathbf{X}_{k-1}^T\mathbf{M}_k) - \ldots - \mathbf{GX}_0(\mathbf{X}_0^T\mathbf{M}_k) \quad (41)$$

and using $\mathbf{G}\,\mathbf{M}_k = \mathbf{CX}_{k-1}$,

$$GX_k^{\zeta} = CX_{k-1} - GX_{k-1}(X_{k-1}^T M_k) - \ldots - GX_0(X_0^T M_k) \quad (42)$$

5. Time-domain simulation of the macromodels

For a complete circuit simulation, the nonlinear elements should be simulated along with the reduced order macromodels. There are two ways to include the PRIMA macromodels into circuit simulators such as SPICE [17]. One approach is in terms of the frequency domain y-parameters. Combining the nonlinear time domain analysis in SPICE with the frequency dependent y-parameters requires convolution of $O(T^2)$ complexity, where T is the number of simulation time-points. For this reason, recursive convolution [14] and time-domain y-parameter macromodels [7] were developed, where the complexity is linear with the number of time-points. The second method is the direct stamping (i.e. circuit model realization). Since the reduction method we use is block, the reduced matrices can be directly stamped into the SPICE MNA matrices. Noticing that the reduced order q-variable system has the equation shown in (12) and (13), and recognizing that it is possible to introduce $\tilde{x}_q$ as a circuit variable into the MNA matrix, the direct stamps for the macromodel can be generated as below:

$$\begin{bmatrix} \text{Stamps for } f(x_{NL}, u_p) & 0 & 0 & \\ & I_N & 0 & \\ 0 & 0 & I_N & -\tilde{L}^T \\ 0 & -\tilde{B} & 0 & \left(\tilde{G} + \tilde{C}\frac{d}{dt}\right) \end{bmatrix} \begin{bmatrix} x_{NL} \\ u_p \\ i_p \\ \tilde{x}_q \end{bmatrix} = \begin{bmatrix} v_{NL} \\ v_p \\ 0 \\ 0 \end{bmatrix} \quad (43)$$

In (43), x_{NL} denotes the other variables of the circuit (other node voltages and currents) u_p and i_p are port voltages and currents respectively, and $\tilde{x}_q$ denotes the extra variables that are introduced from the inclusion of realized macromodel into the circuit. Since $\tilde{C}$ is a symmetric and real matrix, it can be diagonalized using singular value decomposition. In this case, all the capacitance values will be real and positive, since they will be the singular values of $\tilde{C}$. Note that it is also possible to come up with a realization scheme similar to (43) starting from $\hat{Y}(s)$.

6. Results

In this section, PRIMA is demonstrated and compared with other approaches. All reductions are done using RICE v5.0, a program which integrates the PRIMA algorithm with the RICE moment calculation routines. For the frequency domain examples, the y-parameters are compared with the reduced order models from different reduction methods. Time domain results via recursive convolution are obtained using a modified version of SPICE3f4 [18]. For all the examples, the poles obtained via PRIMA were observed to be *stable*.

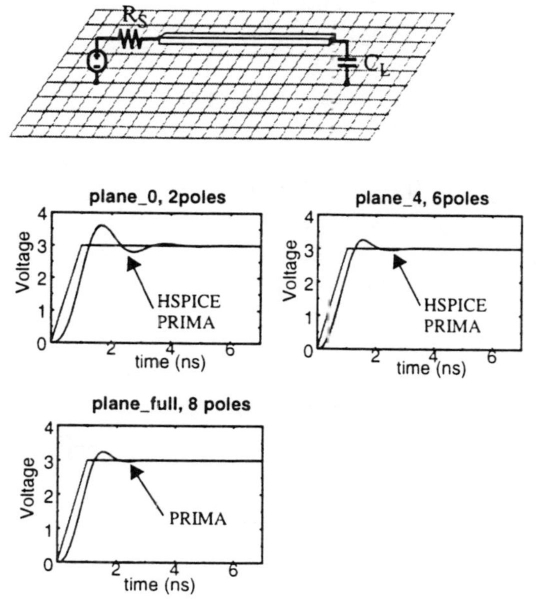

Circuit complexity

Circuit name	# of R	# of L	# of K
plane_0	859	858	0
plane_4	859	858	17,892
plane_full	859	858	183,693

Run time comparisons

Circuit name	HSPICE	PRIMA	RecConv
plane_0	39.97 secs	0.25 secs	0.03 secs
plane_4	17,343 secs	1.23 secs	0.05 secs
plane_full	can not run	11.73 secs	0.05 secs

FIGURE 4: Mesh ground plane example

6.1.Mesh ground plane

With the ability to calculate a large number of poles accurately, PRIMA can be applied to analysis problems which include complex, high frequency responses. One such application is the R-L mesh plane encountered in MCM and packaging problems. Since such a problem is strongly coupled, the L-matrix is dense and thereby destroys the matrix sparsity in a classical SPICE simulation. In this example, the ground plane is modeled by a 20x20 mesh, and each square is modeled as a resistor and an inductor. The coupling can be adjusted to make the inductance matrix sparse as described in [19]. There is an RL line over the ground plane that is terminated with a capacitor load, as shown in Fig.4. Also shown in the figure are time domain results from PRIMA and HSPICE for various levels of L-matrix sparsity. The full matrix response is also shown for PRIMA, but the HSPICE simulation would not complete its run due to memory and run-time limits.

This circuit is a worst-case interconnect topology for a path tracing algorithm [13] (all loops), however, RICE v5, our path tracing implementation of PRIMA, showed excellent speed-up over HSPICE, a commercial circuit simulation tool. The table in this figure also includes the time required for recursive convolution of the reduced-order model in SPICE3f, denoted by RecConv.

6.2.Nonlinear driver driving a transmission line

Fig.5 shows a lossy transmission line represented by 40 lumped RLC sections and reduced to 5 poles using both PVL and PRIMA. Although all of the poles from PVL were stable (i.e. negative real parts), the overall PVL response was clearly unstable as shown in Fig.5. The 5th order approximation from PRIMA is indistinguishable from the exact response, which was obtained by an HSPICE simulation for this example.

6.3.Coupled noise for a two-bit bus

Next consider the two-bit bus driven by CMOS inverters in Fig.6. One of the drivers is switching while the other is quiet. The interconnect, consisting of 40 coupled RLC sections, is modeled as a 4-port and reduced by PRIMA. Transient analysis is done using recursive convolution. The time domain waveforms at the load end are compared for various order of approximations. Since this is a 4-port, an 8 pole approximation corresponds to matching only m_0 and m_1 generated by four different sources. The plot shows that in the time domain, even the coupled noise can be accurately simulated using the 8 poles from PRIMA. Although the interconnect inductance was exaggerated in this example to make the approximation more difficult, it is observed that an 8th order approximation is sufficient to capture the coupled noise from the active driver to the quiet load end.

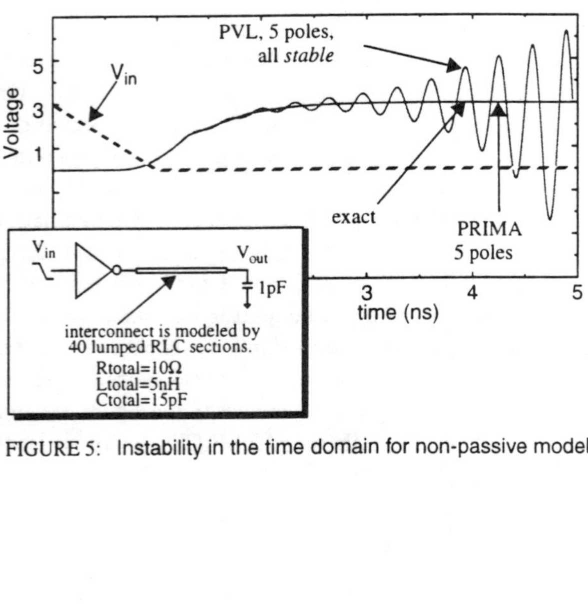

FIGURE 5: Instability in the time domain for non-passive model

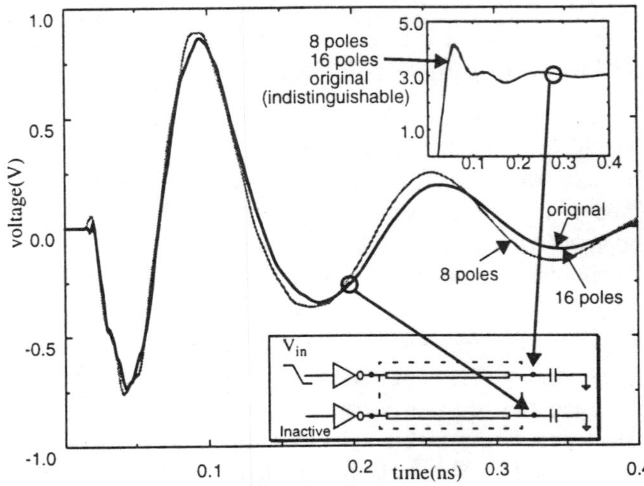

FIGURE 6: Waveform comparisons for a four port.

To compare the difference between direct realization and y-parameter based simulation (i.e. recursive convolution here), the reduced order circuit (via PRIMA) is simulated using both techniques. In the direct realization, $\tilde{C}$ is diagonalized to increase the speed. The run times are given in Table 1. Although the circuit is relatively small (i.e. **G** is only *300x300*), the gain in using a PRIMA reduced macromodel and y-parameter based simulation is about 50x over direct realization. For larger circuits such as the mesh plane example, this gain is expected to be much larger. Direct realization is inferior when the order of approximation gets bigger, mainly because the dense $\tilde{G}$ matrix gets larger.

TABLE 1: Run time comparisons

Exact	Reduced	
Full simulation	Simulated after Direct Realization	Simulated by Y-parameter based
17.78 sec	0.6 with 8 poles	0.18 s. with 8 poles
	3.98 s. with 16 poles	0.28 s. with 16 poles
	10.29 s. with 24 poles	0.32 s. with 24 poles

6.4.Six coupled transmission lines

The second example is a 12-port containing six coupled transmission lines modeled by 40 coupled RLC sections. The input admittance ($Y_{11}(s)$), reduced by Block Arnoldi, MPVL and PRIMA are compared with the exact input admittance in Fig.7 using 48th order approximations in all cases. Block Arnoldi captures the exact response up to 16 GHz, while MPVL and PRIMA match up to 28 GHz. When the order of approximation is increased to 72 poles, it is observed that the frequency spectrum is captured up to 60 GHz by MPVL and PRIMA.

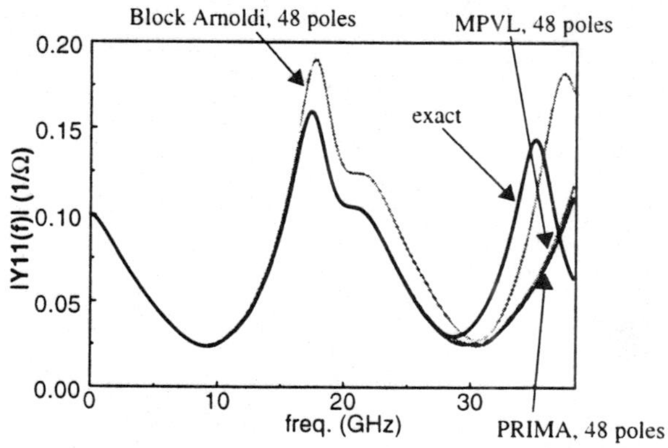

FIGURE 7: $Y_{11}(s)$ in frequency domain for six coupled TR. lines.

6.5.Large Coupled RLC Circuit

The third example in Fig.8 displays the responses for a 3-port composed of densely coupled RLC circuits. Approximations are done using 25 poles for the three methods. As can be observed from the figure, both PRIMA and MPVL capture the entire frequency spectrum.

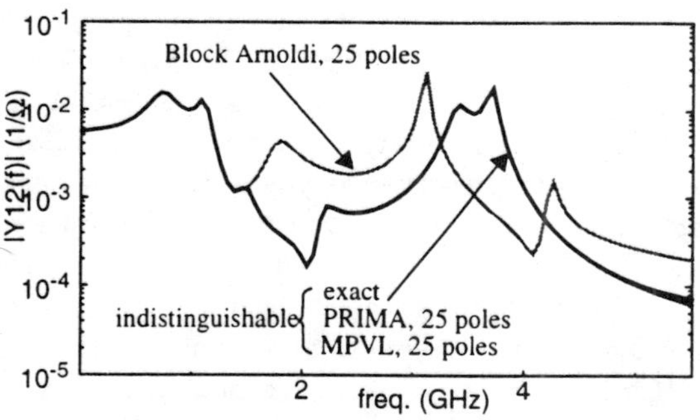

FIGURE 8: 3-Port consisting of a large lumped RLC circuit.

7. Conclusions

This paper presented a novel algorithm for producing provably passive macromodels for arbitrary RLC circuits. The method uses a Block Arnoldi algorithm to generate the vectors needed for applying a transformation to the macromodel MNA matrices. Empirical results show that PRIMA produces comparable or superior results in terms of accuracy with respect to all other known reduction techniques, but superior in that it guarantees the passivity that is critical for time domain analyses. The implementation of PRIMA with path tracing algorithms from RICE enables extremely accurate high frequency response approximations of enormous, complex, RLC circuits with excellent efficiency.

The PRIMA algorithm presented in this paper can be easily extended to implement a number of heuristics such as moment shifting [13] and frequency shifting [20]. However, these heuristics are unnecessary and merely increase the complexity.

BIBLIOGRAPHY

[1]L. T. Pillage and R. A. Rohrer, "Asymptotic waveform evaluation for timing analysis", *IEEE Trans. Computer-Aided Design*, vol. 9, no. 4, pp. 352-366, Apr. 1990.

[2]P. Feldmann and R. W. Freund, "Efficient linear circuit analysis by Padé approximation via the Lanczos process", *IEEE Trans. on CAD*, vol. CAD-14, pp. 639-649, May 1995

[3]K. J. Kerns, I. L. Wemple, and A. T. Yang, "Stable and efficient reduction of substrate model networks using congruence transforms" *IEEE/ACM Proc. ICCAD*, pp. 207-214, Nov. 1995

[4]L. M. Silveira, M. Kamon and J. White, "Efficient reduced-order modeling of frequency-dependent coupling inductances associated with 3-D interconnect structures", *IEEE/ACM Proc. DAC*, pp. 376-380, Jun. 1995

[5]P. Feldmann and R. W. Freund, "Reduced-order modeling of large linear subcircuits via a block Lanczos algorithm", *IEEE/ACM Proc. DAC*, pp. 474-479, Jun.. 1995

[6]D. L. Boley, "Krylov space methods on state-space control models", *Circuits Syst. Signal Process*. vol.13, no.6, pp. 733-758, 1994

[7]S. Y. Kim, N. Gopal and L. T. Pillage, "Time-Domain Macromodels for VLSI Interconnect Analysis", *IEEE Trans. on CAD*, vol 13, No. 10, pp. 1257-1270, Oct. 1994

[8]L. M. Silveira, M. Kamon, I. Elfadel and J. White, "A coordinate-transformed Arnoldi algorithm for generating guaranteed stable reduced-order models of arbitrary RLC circuits", *IEEE/ACM Proc. ICCAD*, pp. 288-294, Nov. 1996

[9]I. M. Elfadel and David D. Ling, "Zeros and passivity of Arnoldi-reduced-order models for interconnect networks", *IEEE/ACM Proc. DAC*, pp. 28-33, Jun. 1997

[10]K. J. Kerns and A. T. Yang, "Preservation of Passivity During RLC Network Reduction via Split Congruence Transformations", *IEEE/ACM Proc. DAC*, pp. 34-39, Jun. 1997

[11]B. D. Anderson and S. Vongpanitlerd, *Network analysis and synthesis*. Prentice-Hall, Inc., 1973

[12]R. A. Rohrer and H. Nosrati, "Passivity considerations in stability studies of numerical integration algorithms", *IEEE Trans. on Circuits and Systems*, vol. CAS-28, no. 9, pp. 857-866, Sep. 1981

[13]C. L. Ratzlaff and L. T. Pillage, "RICE: Rapid interconnect circuit evaluation using AWE", *IEEE Trans. CAD*, vol. 13, no. 6, pp. 763-776, Jun. 1994

[14]V. Raghavan, J. E. Bracken and R. A. Rohrer, "AWESpice: A general tool for the accurate and efficient simulation of interconnect problems", *IEEE/ACM Proc. DAC*, Jun. 1992

[15]G. H. Golub and C. F. Van Loan, *Matrix Computations*. John Hopkins Univ. Press, 2nd ed., 1989

[16]E. S. Kuh and R. A. Rohrer, *Theory of Linear Active Networks*. Holden-Day Inc., 1967

[17]L. W. Nagel, "SPICE2, a computer program to simulate semiconductor circuits", Technical Report ERL-M520, UC-Berkeley, May 1975

[18]T. L. Quarles, "The SPICE3 implementation guide", Tech. Rep. Memo ERL-M89/44, U. of California, Berkeley, 1989

[19]B. Krauter and L. T. Pileggi, "Generating sparse partial inductance matrices with guaranteed stability", *IEEE/ACM Proc. ICCAD*, pp. 45-52, Nov. 1995

[20]X. Huang, "Padé approximation of linear(ized) circuit responses", Ph.D. Thesis, Carnegie Mellon Univ., Nov. 1990

A Block Rational Arnoldi Algorithm for Multipoint Passive Model-Order Reduction of Multiport RLC Networks

I. M. Elfadel David D. Ling

IBM T. J. Watson Research Center
Yorktown Heights, NY 10598
{elfadel,dling}@watson.ibm.com

Abstract

Recent work in the area of model-order reduction for RLC interconnect networks has been focused on building reduced-order models that preserve the circuit-theoretic properties of the network, such as stability, passivity, and synthesizability [1, 2, 3, 4, 5]. Passivity is the one circuit-theoretic property that is vital for the successful simulation of a large circuit netlist containing reduced-order models of its interconnect networks. Non-passive reduced-order models may lead to instabilities even *if they are themselves stable. In this paper, we address the problem of guaranteeing the accuracy and passivity of reduced-order models of multiport RLC networks at any finite number of expansion points. The novel passivity-preserving model-order reduction scheme is a block version of the* rational *Arnoldi algorithm [6, 7]. The scheme reduces to that of [5] when applied to a single expansion point at zero frequency. Although the treatment of this paper is restricted to expansion points that are on the negative real axis, it is shown that the resulting passive reduced-order model is superior in accuracy to the one that would result from expanding the original model around a single point. Nyquist plots are used to illustrate both the passivity and the accuracy of the reduced-order models.*

1 Introduction

It is well known [8] that multiport RLC networks are passive, in the sense that they are energy dissipators. Passive networks are necessarily stable, but the converse is not true. Passivity and stability differ in the following fundamental way: while the connection of two stable networks is not necessarily stable, any multiport connection of passive networks is guaranteed to be passive.

This closure property is of paramount importance from a practical point of view for the following reason. The reduced-order model is intended to replace the original interconnect in the global netlist. It will have the same drivers and loads as the original model. The output impedances of the drivers and the input impedances of the loads are represented by passive elements. If the reduced-order model is only stable but not passive, there is no guarantee that the network composed of output impedances, reduced-order model, and input impedances is stable.[1] In the absence of such a guarantee the simulation and analysis of the circuit may become problematic. A *passive* reduced-order model eliminates this concern.

One of the first attempts at designing passivity-preserving model-order reduction algorithms for multiport RC interconnect networks is the PACT algorithm of [11] where matrix congruence transformations are used to preserve the positivity of the energy-storage and DC matrices, a fundamental requirement for passivity. As yet unpublished is the work described in [3, 10] which addresses the issues of passivity for both RC and RLC networks and proposes, for multiport RC networks, an algorithm based on the Choleski decomposition that makes the PVL algorithm [12] into a passivity-preserving one. Recently [4], the PACT algorithm has been extended to the RLC case using *split* congruence transformations. The splitting operation is designed to decouple the capacitive behavior of the RLC network from its inductive one, thus preserving the algebraic properties of the MNA matrices of the original network model. More recently [5], a reduction algorithm based on the Arnoldi iteration [13, 1] has been shown to guarantee the passivity of the reduced-order model without requiring a "splitting operation" for the congruence transformation matrix. It is worth noting, in this passivity context, that a symmetrized version of the PVL algorithm [2] was shown to preserve the passivity of one-port RC networks using the stronger requirement of RC Cauer-synthesizability.

One engineering concern in the use of model-order reduction algorithms is that the model be accurate not just at a single point in the frequency spectrum

[1] An example of such a situation is given in [9]. See also [3, 10] for interesting theoretical insights.

but over a whole range of frequencies. This situation typically arises when dealing with microwave circuits. Reduction algorithms that address this concern are the complex frequency hopping algorithm [14] and the multipoint rational Krylov algorithm [7].

The main contribution of this paper is to extend the recent passivity preserving Arnoldi algorithm to the multipoint expansion case. The vehicle of the extension is the use of the block *rational* Arnoldi algorithm [6], the classical Arnoldi iteration being a *polynomial algorithm*. It is rigorously shown that for any multiport RLC network, the block rational Arnoldi reduced-order model is passive and satisfies the required accuracy at all the expansion points. Nyquist plots are used to illustrate both the passivity and the accuracy of the resulting models. Recall that a Nyquist plot contains both the magnitude and phase information of the network driving-point impedance (admittance). Moreover, the Nyquist plot of a passive network is entirely contained in the right-half complex plane.

The next section of this paper introduces the basic circuit notation and the multipoint model-order reduction formulation. In Section 3, the block rational Arnoldi model-order reduction algorithm is described, its accuracy properties at the expansion points are proved, and the passivity of the rational-Arnoldi reduced-order model is rigorously shown. Numerical results along with their Nyquist plot illustrations are presented in Section 4.

2 Background

The modified nodal analysis (MNA) equations of a multiport, linear, time-invariant RLC network are given by

$$\begin{aligned} \mathcal{L}\,\dot{x} &= -\mathcal{G}\,x + P\,u \\ y &= P^T x + Du \end{aligned} \tag{1}$$

where, $x \in \mathbb{R}^n, u \in \mathbb{R}^p, y \in \mathbb{R}^p$ are, respectively, the state-space, input and output vectors of the p-port network, and $\mathcal{L}, \mathcal{G} \in \mathbb{R}^{n\times n}$ are, respectively, its energy-storage and DC matrices. [2] The $p \times p$ matrix D accounts for the direct gain from the input to the output. In terms of the circuit elements and variables, the above quantities are expressed as follows:

$$x \equiv \begin{bmatrix} v \\ i \end{bmatrix} \quad \mathcal{L} \equiv \begin{bmatrix} C & O \\ O & L \end{bmatrix} \quad \mathcal{G} \equiv \begin{bmatrix} G & B \\ -B^T & O \end{bmatrix} \tag{2}$$

[2]These matrices will be assumed nonsingular, which would exclude networks with resistive meshes, capacitive loops, or inductive cutsets.

with v and i being the capacitor node voltages and the inductor branch currents, respectively. The square matrices C, L, and G, are all symmetric, positive definite and denote, respectively, the nodal capacitance, inductance, and conductance matrices of the RLC circuit. It follows that the matrix $\mathcal{L}$ is symmetric, positive definite, and that the symmetric part of $\mathcal{G}$ is positive semidefinite. The matrix B is rectangular and denotes the incidence matrix of the inductor branches.

Assuming that p currents are injected at the input ports, the network driving-point impedance is the $p\times p$ transfer matrix given by

$$Z(s) = P^T(\mathcal{G} + s\mathcal{L})^{-1} P \tag{3}$$

In multipoint model-order reduction, we are given m distinct points $s_1, s_2, \ldots, s_m$ and m integers $n_1, n_2, \ldots, n_m$, and we are asked to find a reduced-order driving-point impedance $\tilde{Z}(s)$ such that

$$\frac{d^{k-1}\tilde{Z}}{ds^{k-1}}(s_i) = \frac{d^{k-1}Z}{ds^{k-1}}(s_i), \quad 1 \le k \le n_i, \quad 1 \le i \le m. \tag{4}$$

In other words, at each point s_i the original and the reduced-order model must have equal moments up to order n_i. Or, equivalently, both models must have the same Taylor series expansion up to order $(n_i - 1)$ at each point s_i. Matching at multiple points should intuitively result in a reduced-order model that has better accuracy over a wider region of the complex plane than what would be obtained with a single-point matching at, say, the DC point.

Assume that the quadruplet $[\tilde{\mathcal{G}}, \tilde{\mathcal{L}}, \tilde{P}, D]$ is a state-space realization of $\tilde{Z}$, then the matching conditions can be expressed by the matrix equalities

$$\begin{aligned} &\tilde{P}^T \left\{ \left(\tilde{\mathcal{G}} + s_i\tilde{\mathcal{L}}\right)^{-1} \tilde{\mathcal{L}} \right\}^{k-1} \left(\tilde{\mathcal{G}} + s_i\tilde{\mathcal{L}}\right)^{-1} \tilde{P} \\ &= P^T \left\{ (\mathcal{G} + s_i\mathcal{L})^{-1} \mathcal{L} \right\}^{k-1} (\mathcal{G} + s_i\mathcal{L})^{-1} P \end{aligned} \tag{5}$$

Note that the matrix D is the same for both models and therefore it does not appear in these equalities.

For each point s_i, there is a Krylov subspace $\mathcal{K}_{n_i}$ spanned by the columns of the matrices

$$span\left(N_i, M_iN_i, M_i^2N_i, \ldots, M_i^{n_i-1}N_i\right)$$

where $M_i \equiv (\mathcal{G} + s_i\mathcal{L})^{-1}\mathcal{L}$ and $N_i \equiv (\mathcal{G} + s_i\mathcal{L})^{-1} P$. Note that these subspaces arise naturally from the matrix moment matching formulas (5).

In the context of direct Padé approximation reduction methods like Asymptotic Waveform Evaluation (AWE) [15], the complex frequency hopping (CFH) algorithm [14] has been proposed to deal with multipoint expansions. In CFH, the expansion points lie on the imaginary axis of the complex plane, and a binary search strategy for choosing these points based on the required accuracy of the reduced-order model is used. The main objective in CFH is to improve the accuracy of the reduced-model *poles* compared to those obtained using AWE.

In the context of indirect, iterative Krylov subspace methods, an algorithm for multipoint model-order reduction using a rational Lanczos process was developed in [7]. A family of algorithms employing unions of Krylov subspaces to produce multipoint moment matching is proposed in [16].

In both the direct and indirect approaches to multipoint expansion, the problem of preserving the passivity of interconnect network models has not been addressed. The algorithm of the next section can be viewed as a synthesis of the rational Lanczos algorithm of [7] that preserves multipoint moments with the Arnoldi algorithm of [5] that preserves passivity. This synthesis results in a model-order reduction algorithm that preserves the passivity and the moments up to a given order for multiport RLC interconnect networks.

Algorithm **1 (Block Rational Arnoldi)**

```
arnoldi(input 𝒢, ℒ, P, σ1, σ2, ..., σN;
  output W, 𝒢̃, ℒ̃, P̃)
{
  Initialize:
    Solve :  (𝒢 + σ1ℒ)U0 = P
    W0 = orth(U0)
  for (i = 1; i <= N − 1; i++)
  {
    if σ(i+1) == σi,  Vi = ℒWi
    else Vi = P
    Solve (𝒢 + σ(i+1)ℒ)Ui = Vi
    for (j = 0; j <= i − 1; j++)
    {
      Hji = Wj^T Ui
      Ui = Ui − Wj Hji
    }
    Wi = orth(Ui)
  }
  W = [W0, W1, ···, W(n−1)]
  𝒢̃ = W^T 𝒢 W
  ℒ̃ = W^T ℒ W
  P̃ = W^T P
}
```

3 Block Rational Arnoldi

The block rational Arnoldi algorithm proposed in this paper is an adaptation of the rational Krylov algorithm introduced in [6] in the context of the nonsymmetric eigenvalue problem. In order to simplify the presentation, only real-valued expansion points are used in Algorithm 1.

To obtain the points $\sigma_1, \sigma_2, \ldots, \sigma_N$, (refer to Algorithm 1) from the points $s_1, s_2, \ldots, s_m$, each point s_i is repeated a number of times equal to n_i, the expansion order at the i-th point. In other words, $N = n_1 + n_2 + \ldots + n_m$.

Note that at each iteration $i \in [1, N-1]$, Algorithm 1generates p columns of the matrix $\boldsymbol{W}$, where p is the number of ports. Therefore, the order of the reduced-order model, which is equal to the number of columns of $\boldsymbol{W}$, is pN. A basic requirement is that pN must be much smaller than n, the number of energy-storage elements in the network.

The operator *orth* refers to the Gramm-Schmidt orthonormalization procedure. This operation is used to orthonormalize the vectors of each $n \times p$ matrix block $\boldsymbol{U}_i$, $0 \leq i \leq N-1$, resulting from running the block Arnoldi algorithm. Another way of ensuring that the columns of $\boldsymbol{W}_i$ are orthonormal is by setting $\boldsymbol{W}_i = \boldsymbol{U}_i \boldsymbol{Z}_i^{-1}$ where $\boldsymbol{Z}_i$ is the Choleski factor of the symmetric, positive definite matrix $\boldsymbol{U}_i^T \boldsymbol{U}_i$.

The innermost iteration of Algorithm 1, which runs over $j \in [0, i-1]$, is nothing but a classical *block* orthogonalization process that orthogonalizes the new matrix block $\boldsymbol{U}_i$ with respect to *all* the previous matrices $\boldsymbol{W}_0, \boldsymbol{W}_1, \ldots, \boldsymbol{W}_{i-1}$. The net result of the algorithm is an $n \times pN$ matrix $\boldsymbol{W}$ with orthonormal columns, i.e., $\boldsymbol{W}^T \boldsymbol{W} = \boldsymbol{I}_{pN}$, the identity matrix of order pN.

The (*if, else*) condition at the start of each major iteration controls when and how to pass from one expansion point to another. As long as $\sigma_{i+1} = \sigma_i$ (we are still at the same expansion point), the algorithm proceeds as in any Krylov subspace iteration, i.e., it generates the next block of Krylov vectors and orthogonalizes it with respect to *all* the previous blocks. When $\sigma_{i+1} \neq \sigma_i$, the algorithm restarts at the input matrix $\boldsymbol{P}$ so as to produce the Krylov iterates corresponding to the expansion point at σ_{i+1}. In other words, the occurrence of the condition $\sigma_{i+1} \neq \sigma_i$ signals that the Krylov subspace $\mathcal{K}_{\sigma_i}$ has been completely spanned and that the spanning of the Krylov subspace $\mathcal{K}_{\sigma_{i+1}}$ is about to start.

Note finally that the block Arnoldi algorithm of [5]

can be derived as a special case from Algorithm 1 by setting $\sigma_1 = \sigma_2 = \ldots = \sigma_N = 0$.

Based on this algorithm, the matrices of the reduced-order model are given by[3]

$$\tilde{\mathcal{G}} = \boldsymbol{W}^T \mathcal{G} \boldsymbol{W}, \quad \tilde{\mathcal{L}} = \boldsymbol{W}^T \mathcal{L} \boldsymbol{W}, \quad \tilde{\boldsymbol{P}} = \boldsymbol{W}^T \boldsymbol{P} \qquad (6)$$

The driving-point matrix impedance is then given by

$$\tilde{\boldsymbol{Z}}(s) = \tilde{\boldsymbol{P}}^T \left(\tilde{\mathcal{G}} + s\tilde{\mathcal{L}}\right)^{-1} \tilde{\boldsymbol{P}} \qquad (7)$$

In fact, due to the symmetry in the problem, the reduced-order model can be alternatively and more efficiently computed via a symmtric Lanczos method [16].

The moment-matching properties of Algorithm 1 hold due to the following two facts:

1. The full rank of $\boldsymbol{W}$ which is guaranteed by its column orthonormality.
2. The union of the Krylov subspaces generated at the different expansion points satisfies the inclusion formula:

$$\cup_{k=1}^{m} \mathcal{K}_{n_k} \subseteq span\{\boldsymbol{W}\}. \qquad (8)$$

The sufficiency of these conditions for multipoint moment matching is rigorously explored and proven in [16]. The seminal connections between Krylov subspaces and moment matching are presented in [17].

The extra computational cost to obtain the additional moment matching accuracy is a new LU factorization for each expansion point. Note that the number of expansion points can be traded off with the matching order at each point, thus resulting in (perhaps significantly) fewer Krylov iterations at each point. The total computational cost of the new algorithm to obtain a given level of accuracy may be less than that incurred by a single-point algorithm.

Passive networks are networks whose net electrical energy balance is nonpositive, i.e., the energy that is dissipated by the network is at least equal to the energy supplied by the sources. The fundamental theorem relating passivity to the network's linear response is the following [8]:

Theorem 1 *A one-port network is passive if and only if its driving-point impedance (admittance), denoted by $F(\sigma + j\omega)$, is positive real, i.e,*

$$(pr1) \qquad \forall \sigma \in \mathbb{R}, F(\sigma) \in \mathbb{R}$$
$$(pr2) \qquad \forall \sigma \geq 0, Re\{F(\sigma + j\omega)\} \geq 0$$

[3] We have dropped the matrix $\boldsymbol{D}$ as it is the same for both the original and the reduced-order models.

For a multiport network with driving-point matrix impedance, $\boldsymbol{G}(s)$, a sufficient condition for passivity [8] is that for any real vector $\boldsymbol{u} \in \mathbb{R}^p$, the transfer *function* $F(s) = \boldsymbol{u}^T \boldsymbol{G}(s) \boldsymbol{u}$ is positive real.

The main theoretical result of this paper is an extension to multipoint model reduction of the one obtained in [5] for the single-point case. It is stated as follows:

Theorem 2 *The multiport reduced-order model of driving-point impedance $\tilde{\boldsymbol{Z}}(s)$ is passive.*

Proof. Let $\boldsymbol{u} \in \mathbb{R}^p$, and let $z(s) \equiv \boldsymbol{u}^T \tilde{\boldsymbol{Z}}(s) \boldsymbol{u}$. First it is clear that $z(s)$ is real whenever its argument s is real. Next let $s \equiv \sigma + j\omega$ with $\sigma > 0$, $\boldsymbol{x} \equiv \tilde{\boldsymbol{P}}\boldsymbol{u}$, and

$$\boldsymbol{y} \equiv \left(\tilde{\mathcal{G}} + \bar{s}\tilde{\mathcal{L}}\right)^{-T} \boldsymbol{x},$$

where $\bar{s}$ is the complex conjugate of s. Then

$$\begin{aligned}
2Re\{z(s)\} &= z(s) + z(\bar{s}) \\
&= \boldsymbol{x}^T \left(\tilde{\mathcal{G}} + s\tilde{\mathcal{L}}\right)^{-1} \boldsymbol{x} + \boldsymbol{x}^T \left(\tilde{\mathcal{G}} + \bar{s}\tilde{\mathcal{L}}\right)^{-T} \boldsymbol{x} \\
&= \boldsymbol{x}^T \left(\tilde{\mathcal{G}} + s\tilde{\mathcal{L}}\right)^{-1} \left[\left(\tilde{\mathcal{G}} + s\tilde{\mathcal{L}}\right)\right. \\
&+ \left.\left(\tilde{\mathcal{G}} + \bar{s}\tilde{\mathcal{L}}\right)^T\right] \left(\tilde{\mathcal{G}} + \bar{s}\tilde{\mathcal{L}}\right)^{-T} \boldsymbol{x} \\
&= \boldsymbol{y}^* \left(\mathcal{G} + s\mathcal{L} + \mathcal{G}^T + \bar{s}\mathcal{L}^T\right) \boldsymbol{y} \\
&= \boldsymbol{y}^* \left(\mathcal{G} + \mathcal{G}^T + \sigma(\mathcal{L} + \mathcal{L}^T)\right) \boldsymbol{y}.
\end{aligned}$$

The conclusion that $Re\{F(s)\} \geq 0$, whenever $Re\{s\} \geq 0$ results from the fact that the symmetric matrices $\mathcal{G} + \mathcal{G}^T$ and $\mathcal{L} + \mathcal{L}^T$ are both positive semidefinite. □

4 Results

In this section, the Nyquist plot is used to illustrate, for some numerical examples, both the accuracy and the passivity of the reduced-order model obtained with a MATLAB implementation of the passive block rational Arnoldi Algorithm 1.

The circuit used in these examples is a 4-port RLC network with 2500 capacitors and 25 inductors. Two 8-pole reduced-order models are computed for this network. The first model is obtained using the PRIMA algorithm [5] by matching two moments at DC, while the second model is computed using the block rational Arnoldi algorithm of this paper by matching one moment at DC and another moment at the real shift $s = 10$. A set of magnitude Bode plots, step-response plots, and Nyquist plots are given.

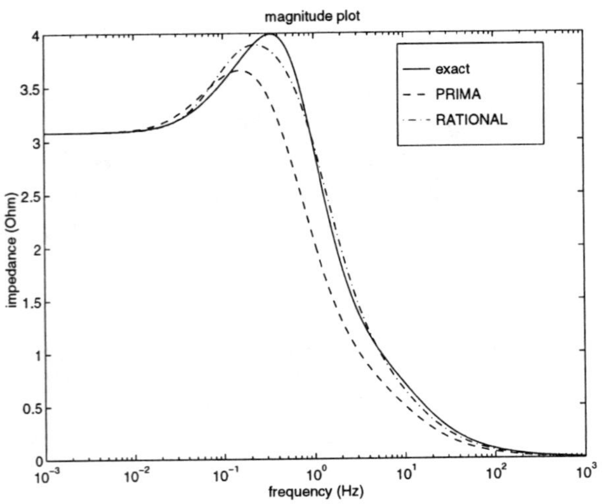

Figure 1: Driving-point impedance at port 1: Magnitude Bode plot

Figure 1 is the magnitude plot of the driving-point impedance of port 1. It clearly shows that the resonant peak of the network is more closely approximated with the multipoint algorithm than with the single-point algorithm. This increased accuracy is also reflected in the step response plot. Note that both the transient and the overshoot are approximated rather well with the block rational Arnoldi. This better approximation is essential when using the model in the context of timing analysis (transient) or noise analysis (overshoot).

It has been the tradition, in model-order reduction publications, to display only these two types of plots. In Figure 3, the Nyquist plot[4] of the driving-point impedance at port 1 is shown. This plot has the following two advantages. First, it contains both the magnitude and phase information about the network impedance. Second, it provides a graphical test of port passivity. Indeed, it is well known [8] that the Nyquist plots of positive real transfer functions lie entirely in the right half of the complex plane. The accuracy of the block rational Arnoldi algorithm vs. PRIMA is again illustrated in Figure 3. Moreover, both algorithms lead to driving-point impedances whose Nyquist plots lie entirely in the right-half plane.

The reader is invited to contrast the behavior of the Nyquist plot in the driving-point case (Figure 3) vs. the transfer function case (Figure 4). In the latter, the reduced-order models may cross into the left-half plane. Note that this is not a violation of passivity or of Theorem 2, as passivity is a driving-point concept, i.e., electrical quantities and their duals must be measured at the *same* ports.

[4]The Nyquist plot displays the imaginary part of the transfer function $Z(j\omega)$ computed on the $j\omega$ axis vs. its real part.

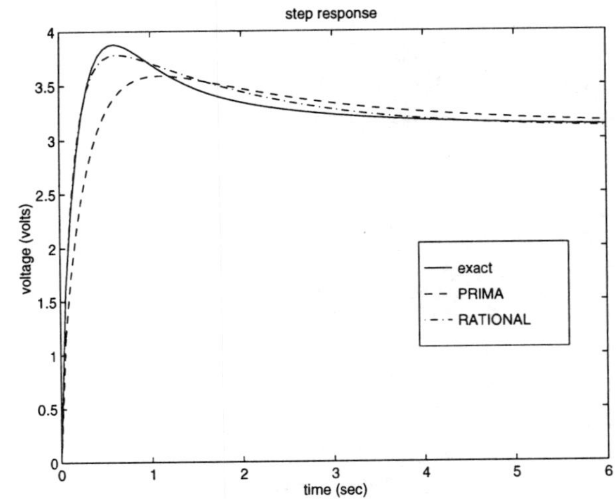

Figure 2: Driving-point impedance at port 1: Step response

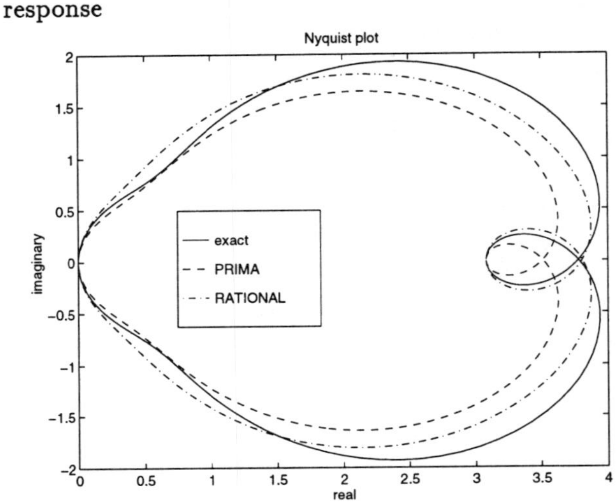

Figure 3: Driving-point impedance at port 1: Nyquist plot

5 Conclusions

In this paper, the passivity-preserving Arnoldi algorithm of [5] was extended to the case where the reduced-order model is required to satisfy accuracy requirements at more than one expansion point. The vehicle of this extension was a block version of the *rational* Arnoldi algorithm [6] adapted to the modeling context so as to satisfy predefined moment matching requirements. Those requirements are met via the Krylov subspace inclusion formula (8) [16]. Nyquist plots were used to illustrate the accuracy and the pas-

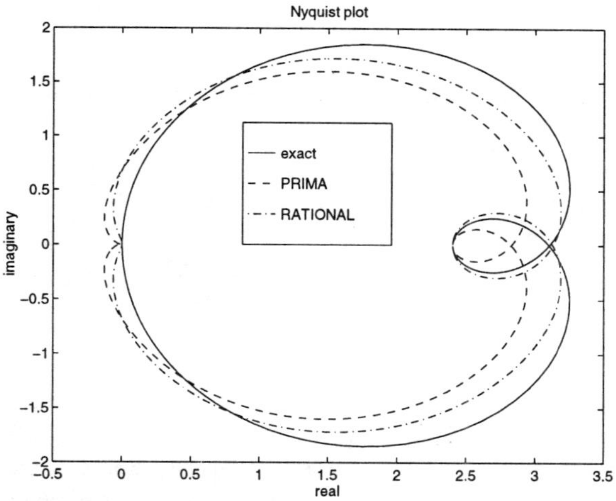

Figure 4: Transfer function from Port 1 to Port 2: Nyquist plot

sivity of the driving-point impedances of the reduced-order models.

Acknowledgments: A model-order reduction tool based on a multipoint block rational Arnoldi algorithm, using both real and complex expansion points and including procedures for the automatic generation of expansion points, has been implemented at the IBM Austin Research Laboratory [18]. Discussions with the members of the developement team have been instrumental in furthering our own understanding of rational Arnoldi algorithms and in helping to write this paper.

In particular, we would like to acknowledge Eric Grimme for many useful comments on an earlier draft of this paper and Eli Chiprout for many helpful discussions.

We would also like to thank Altan Odabasioglu for communicating [5], and Ken Shepard, L. Miguel Silveira and Jacob White for useful discussions.

References

[1] L. M. Silveira, M. Kamon, I. M. Elfadel, and J. White. Coordinate-transformed Arnoldi for generating guaranteed stable reduced-order models for RLC circuits. In *ICCAD'96*, pages 288 - 294, San Jose, CA, November 1996.

[2] R. W. Freund and P. Feldmann. Reduced-order modeling of large passive linear circuits by means of the SyPVL algorithm. In *ICCAD'96*, pages 280-287, San Jose, California, November 1996.

[3] J. Eric Bracken. Passive modeling of linear interconnect networks. Technical report, ECE, CMU, 1996. submitted for publication.

[4] K. J. Kerns, I. L. Wemple, and A. T. Yang. Preservation of passivity during RLC network reduction via split congruence transformations. In *34rd DAC*, Anaheim, CA, June 1997. To appear.

[5] A. Odabasioglu, M. Celik, and L. Pileggi. PRIMA: Passive reduced-order interconnect macromodeling algorithm. *Submitted to IEEE Trans. CAD*, 1997.

[6] A. Ruhe. The rational Krylov algorithm for nonsymmetric eigenvalue problems iii: complex shifts for real matrices. *BIT*, 34:165-176, 1994.

[7] K. Gallivan, E. Grimme, and P. Van Dooren. A rational Lanczos method for model reduction. *Numerical Algorithms*, 12:33-63, 1996.

[8] E. A. Guillemin. *Synthesis of Passive Networks*. John Wiley and Sons, 1957.

[9] S. Y. Kim, N. Gopal, and L. T. Pillage. Time-domain macromodels for vlsi interconnect analysis. *IEEE Trans. on CAD*, 13(10):1257-1270, October 1994.

[10] J. Eric Bracken. Algorithms for passive modeling of linear interconnect networks. Technical report, ECE, CMU, 1996. submitted for publication.

[11] K. J. Kerns, I. L. Wemple, and A. T. Yang. Stable and efficient reduction of large, multiport RC networks by pole analysis via congruence transformations. In *33rd DAC*, pages 280 - 285, Las Vegas, NV, May 1996.

[12] P. Feldmann and R. W. Freund. Efficient linear circuit analysis by Padé approximation via the Lanczos process. *IEEE Trans. CAD*, 14:639-649, May 1995.

[13] L. Miguel Silveira, Mattan Kamon, and Jacob K. White. Efficient reduced-order modeling of frequency-dependent coupling inductances associated with 3-d interconnect structures. In 32nd *DAC*, pages 376-380, San Francisco, CA, June 1995.

[14] E. Chiprout and M. S. Nakhla. Analysis of interconnect networks using complex frequency hopping (CFH). *IEEE Trans. CAD*, 14(2):186-200, February 1995.

[15] L. T. Pillage and R. A. Rohrer. Asymptotic Waveform Evaluation for Timing Analysis. *IEEE Trans. CAD*, 9(4):352-366, April 1990.

[16] E. Grimme. *Krylov Projection Methods for Model Reduction*. PhD thesis, Coordinated-Science Laboratory, University of Illinois at Urbana-Champaign, 1997.

[17] C. D. Villemagne and R. E. Skelton. Model reduction using a projection formulation. *Int. J. Control*, 46:2141 - 2169, 1987.

[18] Eli Chiprout. 1997. Private communication.

Multipoint Padé Approximation using a Rational Block Lanczos Algorithm

Tuyen V. Nguyen* and Jing Li**

*IBM Austin Research Laboratory, Austin, TX 78758, tuyenn@austin.ibm.com

**Advanced Design Technology, Motorola Inc., Austin, TX 78730, jingli@adttx.sps.mot.com

Abstract

This paper presents a general rational block Lanczos algorithm for computing multipoint matrix Padé approximation of linear multiport networks, which model many important circuits in digital, analog, or mixed signal designs. This algorithm generalizes a novel block Lanczos algorithm with a reliable adaptive scheme for breakdown treatment to address two drawbacks of the single frequency Padé approximation: poor approximation of the transfer function in the frequency domain far away from the expansion point and the instability of the reduced model when the original system is stable. In addition, due to smaller Krylov subspace corresponding to each frequency point, the rational algorithm also alleviates the possible breakdowns when computing high order approximations. The cost of full backward orthogonalization with respect to all previous Lanczos vectors in a rational Lanczos algorithm, as compared to a partial backward orthogonalization in a single point Lanczos algorithm, is offseted by more accurate and smaller order approximations.

1. Introduction

Iterative methods based on Krylov subspace for computing partial eigenvalues or solutions of large sparse linear systems have found widespread use in different branches of science and engineering. Recently, these methods have also found their way into circuit simulation for the reduced order modeling of large linear(ized) circuits. The application of model reduction techniques such as Padé approximation to general linear circuit analysis has been made popular by the well known Asymptotic Waveform Evaluation (AWE) method [3]. Recently, the Lanczos based methods [4][5][6] have been developed to address the inherent numerical stability problem in AWE and has promoted Krylov subspace methods as the method of choice for the reduced order modeling of large lumped linear circuits.

In order to address some of the issues related to the Lanczos method for single point Padé approximation, especially the poor approximation of the frequency response away from the Padé expansion frequency σ_0 and instability of the reduced model given a stable original system, rational Lanczos algorithm has been developed to compute multi-point Padé approximation [2]. This paper is a generalization of the work reported in [2] to the block case. It presents a general rational block Lanczos algorithm based on a novel adaptive block Lanczos technique with a reliable breakdown treatment [1]. The paper is organized as follows. Section 2 briefly presents the basic rational Lanczos algorithm. Section 3 presents multipoint Padé connection. Section 4 presents some results to demonstrate the soundness of the basic algorithm. Section 5 summarizes and concludes the paper.

2. Rational Block Lanczos Algorithm (MABLE)

This section provides a brief description of the rational block Lanczos algorithm MABLE, which is an extension of the single point block Lanczos algorithm ABLE [1] with a novel breakdown treatment scheme. Consider the general multiple input multiple output system

$$\begin{aligned} F\dot{x} &= Ax + Bu \\ y &= Cx \end{aligned} \tag{1}$$

where x is the state vector of size n, u and y are the input and output vectors of size p. F and A are $n x n$ square matrices. B and C^T are matrices of size $n x p$. The matrix transfer function of system (1) can be written as

$$\begin{aligned} H(s) &= C(sF - A)^{-1}B \\ &= -C[I - \sigma(A - \sigma_i F)^{-1}F]^{-1}(A - \sigma_i F)^{-1}B \end{aligned} \tag{2}$$

where $s = \sigma + \sigma_i$, with σ_i being the expansion frequency.

In order to simplify the discussion, the same number of moments is assumed at each expansion frequency. Let τ be the total number of expansion frequencies, η be the number of moments at each frequency, and ν be the total number of moments at all frequency points. Then $\nu = \tau\eta$. Also the frequency index is denoted by $1 \le i \le \tau$; the moment index at each frequency is denoted by $1 \le j \le \eta$; and the global moment index is denoted by k, where $k = (i-1)\eta + j$. The basic steps of the rational block Lanczos algorithm are given below:

<u>Algorithm 1</u>:

1. Get starting vectors $S_0 = (A - \sigma_1 F)^{-1}B$ *and* $R_0 = C^T$

2. Dualize $S_0 = Q_1 H_{10}$ *and* $R_0 = P_1 G_{10}$ *such that* $P_1^T Q_1 = I$

3. For $i = 1{:}\tau$

For $j = 1{:}\eta$

1. $k = (i-1)\eta + j$

2. /* Generating the next Lanczos vector */

(a) if $j < \eta$ *and* $i \le \tau$, $S_k = (A - \sigma_i F)^{-1} F Q_k$ *and* $R_k = F^T(A - \sigma_i F)^{-T} P_k$

(b) else if $j = \eta$ *and* $i < \tau$,

$S_k = (A - \sigma_{i+1} F)^{-1} B H_{10}^{-1}$ *and* $R_k = F^T(A - \sigma_{i+1} F)^{-T} C^T G_{10}^{-1}$

*(c) else /** $j = \eta$ *and* $i = \tau$ **/*

$S_k = (A - \sigma_1 F)^{-1} F Q_\eta$ *and* $R_k = F^T(A - \sigma_1 F)^{-T} P_\eta$

3. /* Back orthogonalization with respect to previous Lanczos vectors */

(a) $H_k = \mathbf{P}_k^T S_k$ *and* $G_k = \mathbf{Q}_k^T R_k$

where $\mathbf{P}_k = [P_1 \dots P_k]$ *and* $\mathbf{Q}_k = [Q_1 \dots Q_k]$

(b) $S_k := S_k - \mathbf{Q}_k H_k$ *and* $R_k := R_k - \mathbf{P}_k G_k$

4. /* Scaling and breakdown detection */

(a) QR factorizations: $S_k = Q_{k+1} H_{k+1,k}$ *and*
$R_k = P_{k+1} G_{k+1,k}$
(b) Singular Value Decomposition:
$P_{k+1}^T Q_{k+1} = U_k \Sigma_k V_k^H$
(c) $Q_{k+1} := Q_{k+1} V_k \Sigma_k^{-1/2}$, $P_{k+1} := P_{k+1} \overline{U_k} \Sigma_k^{-1/2}$
(d) $H_{k+1,k} := \Sigma_k^{1/2} V_k^H H_{k+1,k}$ *and*
$G_{k+1,k} := \Sigma_k^{1/2} U_k^T G_{k+1,k}$

end / j*/*

end / i */*

In the above algorithm, step (3.2) is to generate the new Lanczos vector. Note that the new starting vector for the next frequency is generated by step (3.2b). H_{10}^{-1} and G_{10}^{-1} are simply scaling matrices to simplify the derivation of the rational Lanczos subspace. Since the starting vector C^T does not generate any new information except at the initial expansion point, the iteration sequence is arranged to generate the next vector of the Lanczos iteration for the left Krylov subspace at the expansion point σ_{i+1}. Step (3.2a) is the normal Lanczos iteration at each expansion point, and step (3.2c) is to generate the last Lanczos vector for the left Krylov subspace at the first expansion point. Step (3.3) is to perform the back-orthogonalization with respect to the previous Lanczos vectors. Step (3.4) is to perform the scaling to ensure that $P_{k+1}^T Q_{k+1} = I$. The singular value decomposition is also used to detect breakdowns [1]. In the following derivation, the relationship between the original system and the reduced systems generated by Algorithm 1 will be developed. The subspaces generated by different steps of the algorithm will be mapped to a common subspace at an arbitrary reference frequency σ_s. First, consider the relationship for the right Krylov subspace $K_R = \{Q_1, Q_2, \ldots, Q_\nu\}$. For the case where $j < \eta$ and $i \le \tau$, combining steps (3.2a), (3.3b), and (3.4a) yields

$$Q_{k+1} H_{k+1,k} = (A - \sigma_i F)^{-1} F Q_k - \mathbf{Q}_k H_k \tag{3}$$

Equation (3) can be written as

$$\begin{bmatrix} \mathbf{Q}_k & Q_{k+1} \end{bmatrix} \begin{bmatrix} H_k \\ H_{k+1,k} \end{bmatrix} = (A - \sigma_i F)^{-1} F \mathbf{Q}_k E_k \tag{4}$$

where $Q_k = \mathbf{Q}_k E_k$ and E_i $(1 \le i \le k)$ is an $kp \times p$ tall thin matrix with an identity matrix of dimension p at the ith block and zeros elsewhere. Eq. (4) can be rewritten as

$$\begin{aligned} &(A - \sigma_s F)\mathbf{Q}_{\nu+1} \begin{bmatrix} H_k \\ H_{k+1,k} \\ 0 \end{bmatrix} \\ &= F\mathbf{Q}_{\nu+1} \left\{ (\sigma_i - \sigma_s) \begin{bmatrix} H_k \\ H_{k+1,k} \\ 0 \end{bmatrix} + \begin{bmatrix} E_k \\ 0 \\ 0 \end{bmatrix} \right\} \end{aligned} \tag{5}$$

In a similar fashion, the remaining two steps (3.2b) and (3.2c) will yield the following expressions

$$\begin{aligned} &(A - \sigma_s F)\mathbf{Q}_{\nu+1} \left\{ \begin{bmatrix} H_k \\ H_{k+1,k} \\ 0 \end{bmatrix} - \begin{bmatrix} E_1 \\ 0 \\ 0 \end{bmatrix} \right\} \\ &= F\mathbf{Q}_{\nu+1} \left\{ (\sigma_{i+1} - \sigma_s) \begin{bmatrix} H_k \\ H_{k+1,k} \\ 0 \end{bmatrix} - (\sigma_1 - \sigma_s) \begin{bmatrix} E_1 \\ 0 \\ 0 \end{bmatrix} \right\} \end{aligned} \tag{7}$$

$$\begin{aligned} &(A - \sigma_s F)\mathbf{Q}_{\nu+1} \begin{bmatrix} H_\nu \\ H_{\nu+1,\nu} \end{bmatrix} \\ &= F\mathbf{Q}_{\nu+1} \left\{ \begin{bmatrix} E_\eta \\ 0 \end{bmatrix} + (\sigma_1 - \sigma_s) \begin{bmatrix} H_\nu \\ H_{\nu+1,\nu} \end{bmatrix} \right\} \end{aligned} \tag{8}$$

Putting all the steps together, one can express equations (5), (7) and (8) in a common form as

$$(A - \sigma_1 F)\mathbf{Q}_{\nu+1} \mathbf{H}_{\nu+1,\nu} = F\mathbf{Q}_{\nu+1} \mathbf{L}_{\nu+1,\nu} \tag{9}$$

where the kth column block vectors of $\mathbf{H}_{\nu+1,\nu}$ and $\mathbf{L}_{\nu+1,\nu}$ are given by Eq. (5), (7), or (8), depending upon the values of i and j, for $1 \le k \le \nu$. Observe that if $\sigma_s = \sigma_1$, the last row block vector of $\mathbf{L}_{\nu+1,\nu}$ is always zero. From now on, assume that $\sigma_s = \sigma_1$. With $\mathbf{P}_\nu^T \mathbf{Q}_{\nu+1} = \begin{bmatrix} I_{\nu\nu} & 0 \end{bmatrix}$, Eq. (9) can be rewritten as

$$\mathbf{H}_{\nu\nu} = \mathbf{P}_\nu^T (A - \sigma_1 F)^{-1} F \mathbf{Q}_\nu \mathbf{L}_{\nu\nu} \tag{10}$$

A similar relationship for the left Krylov subspace $K_L = \{P_1, P_2, \ldots, P_\nu\}$ can be expressed in a common form as

$$\mathbf{P}_{\nu+1} \mathbf{G}_{\nu+1,\nu} = F^T (A - \sigma_1 F)^{-T} \mathbf{P}_{\nu+1} \mathbf{K}_{\nu+1,\nu} \tag{11}$$

with

$$\mathbf{G}_{\nu\nu}^T = \mathbf{K}_{\nu\nu}^T \mathbf{P}_\nu^T (A - \sigma_1 F)^{-1} F \mathbf{Q}_\nu \tag{12}$$

where $\mathbf{G}_{\nu+1,\nu}$ and $\mathbf{K}_{\nu+1,\nu}$ are the counterparts of $\mathbf{H}_{\nu+1,\nu}$ and $\mathbf{L}_{\nu+1,\nu}$.

Comparing equations (10) and (12), we obtain the following relationship between the right and left Krylov subspaces

$$\mathbf{K}_{\nu\nu}^T \mathbf{H}_{\nu\nu} = \mathbf{G}_{\nu\nu}^T \mathbf{L}_{\nu\nu} \tag{13}$$

3. Multipoint Padé Connection

It can be shown that the reduced systems in left and right Krylov subspaces match up to $2\nu + 1$ moments of the original system. This property is referred to as the multipoint Padé connection. First, the projection of the original system as defined in Eq. (1) onto the right Krylov subspace K_R can be accomplished by defining the transformation $x = \mathbf{Q}_\nu \mathbf{L}_{\nu\nu} x_R$, where x_R is the state variable in the reduced system. The reduced system can then be written as

$$\begin{aligned} F_R \dot{x}_R &= A_R x_R + B_R u \\ y &= C_R x_R \end{aligned} \tag{14}$$

where $F_R = \mathbf{H}_{\nu\nu}$, $A_R = \mathbf{L}_{\nu\nu} + \sigma_1 \mathbf{H}_{\nu\nu}$, $B_R = \mathbf{P}_\nu^T (A - \sigma_1 F)^{-1} B$, and $C_R = C\mathbf{Q}_\nu \mathbf{L}_{\nu\nu}$.

Similarly, the projection of the original system onto the left Krylov subspace K_L using the transformation $x = \mathbf{Q}_\nu x_L$ results in the following reduced system

$$\begin{aligned} F_L \dot{x}_L &= A_L x_L + B_L u \\ y &= C_L x_L \end{aligned} \tag{15}$$

where $F_L = \mathbf{G}_{\nu\nu}^T$, $A_L = \mathbf{K}_{\nu\nu}^T + \sigma_1 \mathbf{G}_{\nu\nu}$, $B_L = \mathbf{K}_{\nu\nu}^T \mathbf{P}_\nu^T (A - \sigma_1 F)^{-1} B$, and $C_L = C\mathbf{Q}_\nu$.

Next consider the oblique projector $\pi = \mathbf{Q}_\nu \mathbf{P}_\nu^T$. Due to the biorthogonality (i. e. duality) of $\mathbf{P}_\nu$ and $\mathbf{Q}_\nu$, $\pi Q = Q$ and $P^T \pi = P^T$ if $Q \in K_R$ and $P \in K_L$. In other words, if a (block) vector is already in the Krylov subspace, the application of the projector to this vector will produce the same vector. This is the key property in proving the multipoint Padé connection between the original system and the reduced systems as obtained by Algorithm 1. Define the lth moments of the original system and the reduced systems around the expansion frequency σ_i as

$$\begin{aligned} M_{il} &= C[(A - \sigma_i F)^{-1} F]^l (A - \sigma_i F)^{-1} B \\ \hat{M}_{il} &= C_R[(A_R - \sigma_i F_R)^{-1} F_R]^l (A_R - \sigma_i F_R)^{-1} B_R \\ \tilde{M}_{il} &= C_L[(A_L - \sigma_i F_L)^{-1} F_L]^l (A_L - \sigma_i F_L)^{-1} B_L \end{aligned} \tag{16}$$

Theorem 1: For $l \geq 0$, the moments of the two reduced systems as defined by Eq. (14) and Eq. (15) are exactly the same, i. e. $\hat{M}_{il} = \tilde{M}_{il}$.

Proof: See [8].

As a result of Theorem 1, only one of the two reduced systems needs to be considered since the moments of the two systems are identical.

Theorem 2: Let the lth moments of the original system and the reduced systems obtained by the rational Lanczos algorithm around the expansion frequency σ_i be defined by Eq. (16). Then the first $(2\nu + 1)$ moments of the original system and the reduced systems are identical, i. e. $M_{il} = \hat{M}_{il} = \tilde{M}_{il}$, for $1 \leq i \leq \tau$ and $0 \leq l \leq 2\eta - 1$.

Proof: See [8].

4. Examples

A 2x2 matrix representation of a simple lumped two port network is used to illustrate the rational block Lanczos algorithm as well as to highlight the advantage of multipoint Padé approximation. In other words, in this example the number of inputs and outputs for the system described by Eq. (1) is 2. The total number of states is 156, i. e. the size of the system matrix A is 156x156, the size of B is 156x2, and the size of C is 2x156. The comparison of the matrix transfer functions of the original system and the reduced systems obtained by the (single expansion point) adaptive block Lanczos algorithm ABLE [1] as well as the rational block Lanczos algorithm reported in this paper is given below. Fig. 1 shows the real and imaginary parts of a diagonal entry (H22) of the 2x2 transfer matrix. The size of the reduced system using ABLE for a single point approximation (about $s = 0$) is 74. The size of the reduced system using the rational block Lanczos algorithm or Multi-point ABLE (MABLE) is 18. Three expansion points at 1KHz, 1MHz, and 1GHz with a maximum order of 3 at each frequency are chosen by simple inspection. This example illustrates the superior accuracy of the MABLE results at a much lower order of approximation. In addition, the MABLE algorithm also alleviates the breakdown problem associated with single point Lanczos algorithm. For example, in computing a single point approximation of order 74, ABLE must perform two breakdown corrections: one at the reduced system size of 13 and the other at the reduced system size of 50. The MABLE algorithm encounters no breakdowns due to smaller Krylov subspaces at each frequency (6 in this case). As to efficiency, the MABLE algorithm requires full backward orthogonalization with respect to all previous Lanczos vectors while, in principle, a single point Lanczos algorithm only requires backward orthogonalization with respect to two immediate previous Lanczos vectors. However, in practice, a more elaborate partial orthogonalization is usually necessary to avoid the loss of biorthogonality or duality among the Lanczos vectors during the iteration [1]. As demonstrated by this example, the cost of full backward orthogonalization in the MABLE algorithm is more than offseted by the accuracy and compactness of the reduced model.

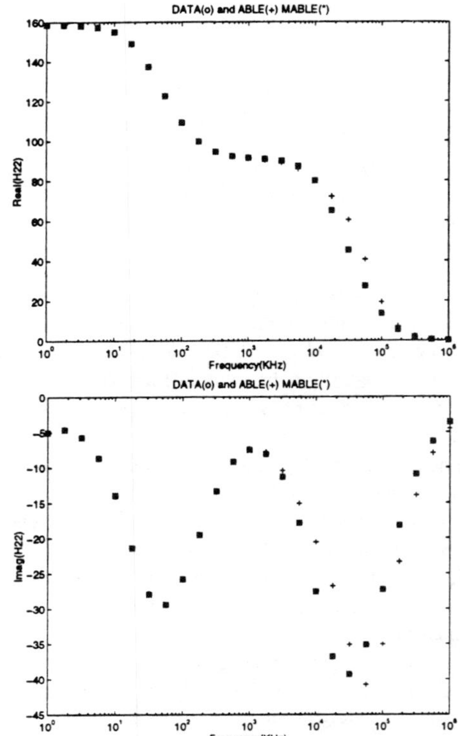

(a)

(b)

Fig. 1: *The real and imaginary parts of a diagonal entry (H22) of the matrix transfer function: data from original system (o), reduced system obtained by ABLE (+), and reduced system obtained by Multipoint-ABLE (*)*

The second example is adopted from [7]. The circuit schematic is shown in Fig. 2. The line length is 5cm and the line parameters are given by

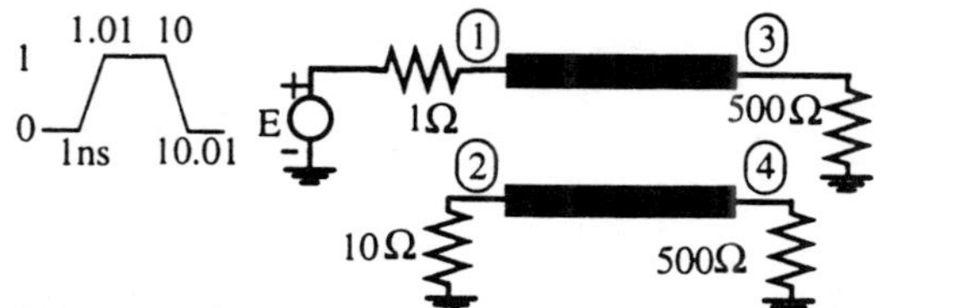

Fig. 2: *An example of an unsymmetrical two conductor transmission line with frequency dependent parameters.*

$$R = \begin{bmatrix} 0.8 & 0 \\ 0 & 0.5 \end{bmatrix} \frac{\Omega}{cm} \quad L = \begin{bmatrix} 9 & 3 \\ 3 & 7 \end{bmatrix} \frac{nH}{cm} \quad C = \begin{bmatrix} 1.2 & -0.6 \\ -0.6 & 1.4 \end{bmatrix} \frac{pF}{cm}$$

$$G = \begin{bmatrix} 5(10^{-5}) & 0 \\ 0 & 10^{-4} \end{bmatrix} \frac{1}{\Omega cm}, K = \begin{bmatrix} 2.8(10^{-4}) & 0 \\ 0 & 1.2(10^{-4}) \end{bmatrix} \frac{\Omega\sqrt{s}}{cm}$$

This example was chosen for easy computation of the exact solution using Fast Fourier Transform (FFT). The impedance matrix is given by $Z(s) = R + sL + K\sqrt{s}$ to simulate the skin effect. In this example, the table of data for the admittance and the propagation matrices are generated over a wide frequency range from 1KHz to 100GHz with 5 points per decade. Then each entry of these matrices is fitted individually using the approach described in [7]. The least square fitting procedure [7] produces an approximation of order 170 for the admittance matrix $Y_0(s)$, and an approximation of order 153 for the propagation matrix $E(s)$. Then the state space models for these matrices of rational function approximations are reduced to lower order systems using ABLE and MABLE for comparison. Note that in the original approximation each entry of the matrix has its own set of poles. In the reduced model, all the entries share the same set of poles. For MABLE, the expansion frequencies for the admittance matrix $Y_0(s)$ are 0.0001, 0.01, 1, and 10 GHz with a maximum order of 3 at each frequency. The total order of the reduced model for $Y_0(s)$ is 24. The expansion frequencies for the propagation matrix $E(s)$ are 0.01, 1, 10, and 100 GHz with a maximum order of 4 at each frequency. The total order of the reduced model for $E(s)$ is 32. The time domain waveforms at nodes 2 and 3 as obtained by using the exact distributed model of the line, the MABLE reduced models and the ABLE reduced models of $Y_0(s)$ and $E(s)$ are shown in Fig. 5. The orders of the ABLE reduced models are 40 for $Y_0(s)$ and 32 for $E(s)$ in computing the time domain waveforms. The exact waveforms as obtained by FFT and waveforms obtained by using the MABLE reduced models of order 24 for $Y_0(s)$ and 32 for $E(s)$ are indistinguishable.

5. Summary and Conclusions

This paper presents a rational block Lanczos algorithm for the computation of multipoint matrix Padé approximation of general multi-input multi-output (MIMO) systems. The method is based upon a general block Lanczos algorithm with a novel adaptive scheme to treat breakdowns. The method presented in this paper provides a reliable, accurate, and efficient algorithm to compute high order Padé approximations of large linear multiport circuits. A number of examples have been presented to demonstrate the superior accuracy and compactness of the reduced models generated by the rational multi-point block Lanczos algorithm as compared to the single point block Lanczos algorithm. Due to the scope of this paper,

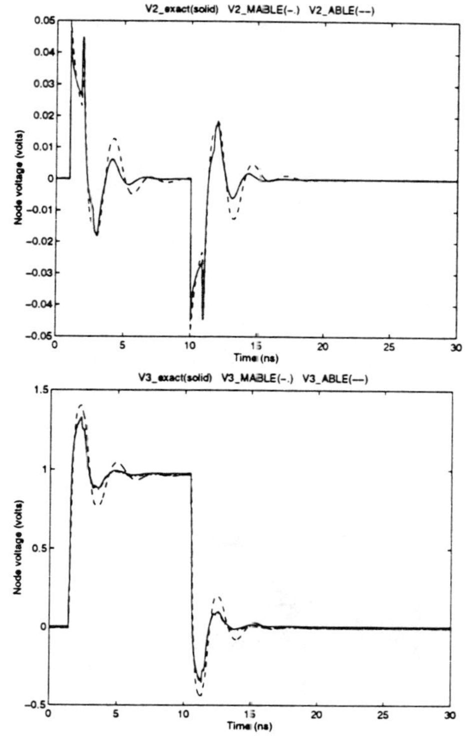

(a)

(b)

Fig. 3: *Voltage waveforms at nodes 2 and 3 of the circuit shown in Fig. 3 as obtained by using: exact distributed model of the line (solid), MABLE reduced models of line parameters (-.), and ABLE reduced models of line parameters (--).*

other important issues such as the convergence criteria of the Ritz values, the adaptation of the breakdown treatment to the multipoint case, and the modeling error estimation are not discussed. More formal approaches to the selection of the expansion frequencies will also be explored.

References

[1] Z. Bai, D. Day, and Q. Ye, "ABLE: an Adaptive Block Lanczos Method for Non-Hermitian Eigenvalue Problems," Research Report 95-04, Dept. of Mathematics, Univ. of Kentucky, May 1995.

[2] K. Gallivan, E. Grimme, and P. Van Dooren, "Padé Approximation of Large-Scale Dynamic Systems with Lanczos Methods", *Proc. IEEE Conf. on Decision and Control*, vol.1, pp. 443-448, 1994.

[3] L. T. Pillage and R. A. Rohrer, "Asymptotic Waveform Evaluation for Timing Analysis," *IEEE Trans. Computer-Aided Design*, vol. 9, pp. 352-366, Apr. 1990.

[4] P. Feldmann and R. W. Freund, "Efficient Linear Circuit Analysis by Padé Approximation via the Lanczos Process," *IEEE Trans. Computer-Aided Design*, vol. 14, pp. 639-649, May 1995.

[5] K. Gallivan, E. Grimme, and P. Van Dooren, "Asymptotic Waveform Evaluation via a Lanczos Method," *Appl. Math. Lett.*, vol. 7, No. 5, pp.75-80, 1994.

[6] P. Feldmann and R. W. Freund, "Reduced-Order Modeling of Large Linear Subcircuits via a Block Lanczos Algorithm," *Proc. ACM/IEEE DAC*, pp. 474-479, June 1995.

[7] T. V. Nguyen, J. Li, and Z. Bai, "Dispersive Coupled Transmission Line Simulation Using an Adaptive Block Lanczos Algorithm," *Proc. CICC*, pp. 457-460, May 1996.

[8] T. V. Nguyen and J. Li, "A Rational Adaptive Block Lanczos Algorithm for Reduced Order Modeling of Linear(ized) Circuits," Motorola Technical Report.

SESSION 2A

MULTI-LEVEL SYNTHESIS AND COVERING PROBLEM

Moderators:

Robert J. Francis, Xilinx, Inc., Toronto, Ontario, Canada

Olivier Courdert, Synopsys, Inc., Mountain View, CA

The Disjunctive Decomposition of Logic Functions

Valeria Bertacco
Computer Systems Lab.
Stanford University

Maurizio Damiani
Synopsys, Inc.
Mountain View, CA

Abstract

We present an algorithm for extracting a disjunctive decomposition from the BDD representation of F. The output of the algorithm is a multiple-level netlist exposing the hierarchical decomposition structure of the function. The algorithm has thoretical quadratic complexity in the size of the input BDD. Experimentally, we were able to decompose most synthesis benchmarks in less than one second of CPU time, and to report on the decomposability of several complex ISCAS combinational benchmarks. We found the final netlist to be often close to the output of more complex dedicated optimization tools.

1 Introduction

The decomposition of a logic function $F(x_1, \cdots, x_n)$ is the identification of a set of functions $A_i(x_i)$ with no variables in common , and a function L such that [1, 2, 3]:

$$F = L(A_0, \cdots, A_i, \cdots)$$

The decomposition of a function is desirable for several reasons. First, it is obviously one method for passing from a flat representation of F to a multiple-level one. It leads to a clustering of the inputs in simpler - and smaller - logic blocks, thereby reducing area and interconnect. This latter property is especially desirable in many implementation technologies, such as FPGAs or deep-submicron, where wiring resources are scarce or costly in terms of delay. Moreover, it exposes a parallelism in the computation of F, by evidencing the independence in the computation of the functions A_i. This parallelism can be exploited both in hardware, leading to faster realizations, as well as during simulation.

Because of its importance, decomposition is a classic subject of switching theory,still being researched [1, 2, 3, 4, 5, 6, 7, 8, 9, 10].

Known exact decomposition algorithms are based on the *decomposition chart* method of Ashenhust and Curtis [1]. The method is based on constructing *trial partitions* of the set of variables and then of verifying on the decomposition chart that F can indeed be decomposed using that clustering of its inputs. Unfortunately, because of the potentially exponential number of trial partitions, exact decomposition is usually confined to functions of few variables. It is worth noting, however, that simplified techniques, such as algebraic factorization [4], have been extremely successful in transforming large two-level covers in multiple-level representations, and have been extended in various ways to include other forms of decomposition.

This paper presents two contributions. First, we present a novel, efficient exact decomposition procedure. The procedure is BDD-based , and it determines the decomposition of function directly from that of its cofactors. Its complexity is bounded by $|F|^2 \times n_F$, where $|F|$ and n_F denote the number of BDD nodes and input variables of F, respectively. In practice, we found the procedure to be very fast, as we were able to determine the decomposition of most benchmark circuits in less than five seconds on a PC. We have also derived -we believe for the first time- the decompositions of several combinational ISCAS benchmarks.

The decomposition engine is the core of a logic optimization tool, LODE. LODE outputs a netlist for a function $F(x_1, \cdots, x_n)$ based on its decomposition. If F has no disjunctive decomposition, the output is constructed using the decomposition of the cofactors F_0, F_1 of F with respect to its first variable, x_1. Interestingly, since the decomposition of F is essentially unique [1], it could be shown that the netlist output by LODE is also canonical. Moreover, it is again generated in time proportional to $|F|^2$. Although LODE is currently missing many optimization opportunities, we found it in practice to produce netlists of comparable quality - sometimes better - to SIS, in a small fraction of the CPU time, for several synthesis benchmarks.

2 Terminology.

Hereafter, we assume the reader be familiar with BDDs [11, 12]. Let $\mathcal{B}$ denote the Boolean set $\{0, 1\}$. A logic function is a mapping $F : \mathcal{B}^n \rightarrow \mathcal{B}^m$. Hereafter, lower-case and upper-case letters will denote logic variables and functions, respectively. We will be mostly concerned with **scalar** functions $F : \mathcal{B}^n \rightarrow \mathcal{B}$. We use boldface to indicate vector-valued functions. The ith component of a vector function $\mathbf{F}$ is indicated by $\mathbf{F}_i$.

We say that a function F **depends** on a variable x_i if $\partial F / \partial x_i$ [13] is not the constant function 0. We call **support** of F the set S_F of variables F depends on. The **size** of S_F is the number of its elements, and it is indicated by $|S_F|$. Two functions F, G are termed **disjoint-support** if they share no support variables, *i.e.* $S_F \cap S_G = \phi$.

2.1 Disjunctive Decompositions.

The decomposition of a function F consists of finding other, simpler functions L and A_i such that

$$F(x_1, \cdots, x_n) = L(A_1(x_1, \cdots), A_2(x_1, \cdots), \cdots) \quad (1)$$

Definition 1. *A function $L(a_1, \cdots, a_k)$, $n > k \geq 2$ is said to* **reduce** *a function $F(x_1, \cdots, x_n)$ if there are k non-constant disjoint-support functions $A_1, \cdots, A_k$ that satisfy*

1092-3152/97 $10.00 © 1997 IEEE

Eq. (1). F is said to be **prime** *if it cannot be decomposed by* **any** *L.* □

The functions A_i will be termed **formal inputs** of the decomposition of F. The list of formal inputs to F will be indicated as F/L, and termed **decomposition list** of F. We call **disjunctive decomposition** of F any pair $(L, F/L)$ that satisfies Eq. (1).

If F is decomposable, it is possible to characterize its decomposition as follows:

- there is a **unique** prime function L decomposing it, up to permutations/complementations of its formal inputs.
- if L has support size $|S_L| > 2$, then also the functions in F/L are uniquely determined, up to complementation/permutation.
- if L has support size $|S_L| = 2$ then F is decomposable in **exactly one** of the following ways :
  - as the OR of disjoint-support functions; the functions of F/L are uniquely identified for the decomposition of finest granularity [14];
  - as the complement of a OR-decomposed function ; again, the functions of F/L are uniquely identified for the decomposition of finest granularity [14];
  - as the XOR/XNOR of disjoint-support functions; the functions in F/L are identified modulo complementation.

If a nontrivial function A belongs to F/L, we take the **cofactor** F_A (or $F(A = 1)$) to be the function $L(A = 1, \cdots)$. Notice that, because of the uniqueness of L and of the other elements in F/L, this function is unique and shares no variables with A.

2.2 Representing decompositions.

We represent the decomposition of the function F rooted at a BDD node N by annotating N with a decomposition type field `type`; and a sorted list `list` of BDD nodes, representing the decomposition list of F. The field `type` can take on the values `OR, NOR, XOR, XNOR, PRIME, UNDEF`, depending on the type of decomposition. Initially, `type` is `UNDEF`. After application of the decomposition procedure, `type` can only take one of the other values.

Each node of `list` points to a BDD node. This node is the root of one of the formal inputs A_i.

The ambiguity due to permutations and complementations is resolved by sorting the functions according to their supports, and by not allowing complement edges in `list`.

Example 1. Consider the function $F = MAJORITY(a \oplus b, c + d, ef)$. Its BDD is shown in Fig.(1), along with the annotation of the root node and of significant other decompositions. □

In order to resolve ambiguities in the representation, we adopt the following rules:

1. Lists are sorted by order of top variable, that is , a function A_i appears before A_j if the top variable of A_i is ranked higher than that of A_j.
2. pointers to BDDs in decomposition lists of type XOR, XNOR, or PRIME cannot be complemented.

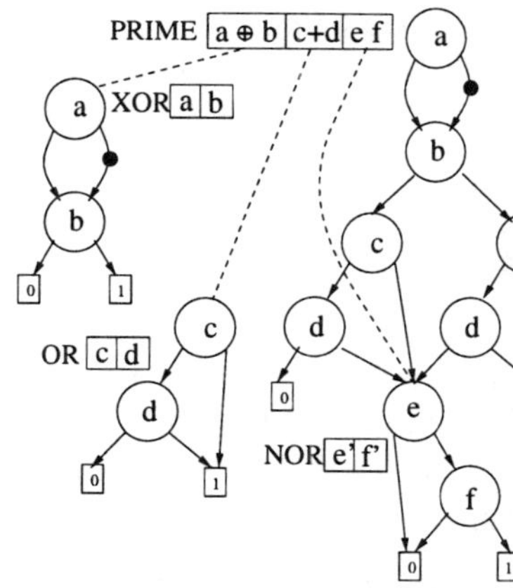

Figure 1. BDD and decomposition annotation for the function of Example (1).

As each function in the decomposition list F/L may be itself decomposable, the lists associated with the decomposition of F form a tree, hereafter called the **decomposition tree** of F.

3 Shannon- and disjunctive- decompositions.

A BDD node, with root variable z, represents a function $F(z, x_1, \cdots, x_n)$ as

$$z' F_0(x_1, \cdots, x_n) + z F_1(x_1, \cdots, x_n) \tag{2}$$

where $F_0 = F(z = 0)$; $F_1 = F(z = 1)$. Our goal is to infer a decomposition

$$F = L(A, B, \cdots) \tag{3}$$

from the decompositions of F_0, F_1. This inference mechanism is the basis of the decomposition algorithm of Section (4).

The link between the decomposition of F and that of its cofactors is conceptually simple. For example, if a function A belongs to the decomposition tree of both F_0 and F_1, then it must belong to the decomposition tree also of F. Unfortunately, several cases and sub-cases need be considered in practice. These are enumerated below.

We now describe in detail how the decomposition structure of F is reflected in that of its cofactors. Moreover, we show how the information on the decomposition of the two cofactors is sufficient to infer the decomposition of F.

The top variable z of F can appear in the decomposition of a function F in only one of the four following ways :

1 : F is the OR/NOR of z/z' with a function A, $z \notin S_A$;

2 : $F = z \oplus A$, $z \notin S_A$.

3 : Cases 1 and 2 do not hold, and z belongs to the support of one formal input of F (say, A), with $|S_A| \geq 2$;

4 : Cases 1 and 2 do not hold, and z is one of the formal inputs of F.

We now analyze the consequences of these cases on the decomposition of F_0, F_1.

Case 1.

In this case, one of $F(z = 0)$, $F(z = 1)$ is a constant. Viceversa, suppose that one cofactor is a constant (say,

$F_1 = 1$, the other cases being symmetric). In this case, trivially $F = F_0 + z$, hence `F.type = OR` and the decomposition list of F is that of F_0 plus z.

Case 2.

Clearly, in this case, $F_0 = F_1'$. Verifying $F_0 = F_1'$ is sufficient to infer the decomposition of F as $F = z \oplus F_0$.

Case 3.

Suppose z belongs to the support of a function (say, A) with nontrivial support $|S_A| \geq 2$. We need to distinguish two sub-cases :

3.a Neither cofactor of A ($A_{z=0}$, $A_{z=1}$) is a constant;

3.b Exactly one cofactor of A is a constant.

Notice that the case of both cofactors being constants rules out the possibility that $|S_A| \geq 2$.

Case 3.a

In this case, F_0, F_1 are :

$$F_0 = L(A(z=0), B, \cdots); \quad F_1 = L(A(z=1), B, \cdots) \quad (4)$$

In other words, F_0 and F_1 are decomposable by the same function L. Moreover, the decomposition *lists* of F_0 and F_1 will coincide, except for *at most* one element ($A(z=0)$ vs. $A(z=1)$).

Viceversa, suppose that F_0 and F_1 have decompositions containing functions A_0 and A_1, respectively, and such that

$$\begin{aligned} F_0(A_0 = 0) &= F_1(A_1 = 0) \quad \text{and} \\ F_0(A_0 = 1) &= F_1(A_1 = 1) \end{aligned} \quad (5)$$

it then follows that, by forming $A = z'A_0 + zA_1$, one can write

$$F = F_0(A, \cdots) = F_1(A, \cdots) \quad (6)$$

Example 2. Consider function $F = MAJORITY(\bar{a}b + ad, c+e, fg)$, and its cofactors $F_0 = F(a=0), F_1 = F(a=1)$. Both cofactors are annotated as `PRIME` functions, with decomposition lists $b, c+e, fg$ and $c+e, d, fg$, respectively. The two lists differ in exactly one element (b instead of d), and moreover, Eq. (5) holds for $A_0 = b, A_1 = d$. Hence the inference of the decomposition $\bar{a}b + ad, c+e, fg$ for F. □

Example 3. Consider the function $F = MAJORITY(a \oplus b, c+e, fg)$. In this case, F_0 and F_1 have identical decomposition lists $b, c+e, fg$. We infer the decomposition by observing that the only possibility is that in Eq. (5), $A_1 = A_0'$. We then test Eq. (5) using first $A_0 = b$, $A_1 = b'$. Since the test succeeds, we list $A = z'A_0 + zA_1 = z \oplus A_0$ in the decomposition list of F, along with $c+e, fg$. □

Case 3.b

We only consider the case where the cofactor $A(z=1) = 1$ (*i.e.* $A = z + A_0$), the other cases being symmetric.

Suppose that F has decomposition $F = L(A, B, C, \cdots)$. Then

$$F_0 = L(A_0, B, C, \cdots); \quad F_1 = L(1, B, C, \cdots). \quad (7)$$

In particular, the element A_0 is missing from the decomposition of F_1, and $F_0(A_0 = 1) = F_1$.

Viceversa, suppose that F_0 has a decomposition containing a function A_0, that $S_{A_0} \cap S_{F_1} = \phi$, and that $F_0(A_0 = 1) = F_1$. In this case, one can write

$$F = F_0(A_0 + z, \cdots). \quad (8)$$

Example 4. Consider the function $F = MAJORITY(a + b, c, d+e)$. Consider the cofactors $F_0 = F(a=0) = MAJORITY(b, c, d+e)$ and $F_1 = F(a=1) = c+d+e$. In this case, b is the only function of F_0 (just a variable, in this case) not in the support of F_1. The test $F_0(b=1) = F_1$ is satisfied; hence $A = a + b$ and the decomposition list of F is that of F_0 with A replacing b. □

Case 4.

F must be of type `PRIME`, and the function z belongs to its list of formal inputs. The decomposition tree - and hence the decomposition list - of F can be constructed from those of F_0, F_1 as follows:

1. If a function A belongs to the decomposition tree of F_0 and $S_A \cap S_{F_1} = \phi$, then A belongs to the decomposition tree of F, along with its descendants.
2. If a `PRIME` function A belongs to the decomposition tree of F_0, F_1, then it belongs to that of F, along with all its descendants.
3. If a OR/NOR function A belongs to the decomposition tree of F_0, and a OR/NOR function B belongs to the decomposition tree of G, then the OR of the functions common to the decomposition lists of A and B belongs to the tree of F;
4. If a XOR function A is in the tree of F_0, and a XOR function is in the tree of F_1, then the XOR of the common terms belongs to the tree of F.
5. The decomposition list of F contains all functions obtained by rules 1-4 that do not have ancestors.

Rule (3) above accounts for the fact that if a function $A = a+b+c$ decomposes F_0 and , say $B = a+b+d$ decomposes F_1, then $a+b$ certainly decomposes F. Similarly for rule (4).

Example 5. Consider the function $F = a'(b+c)(d+e+f) + a(b+c+d)(e+f+g)$. By rule (1), the function g belongs to the tree of F. By rule (3), the functions $b+c$ and $e+f$ belong to the decomposition of F. Eventually, the function d belongs to the decomposition of F by Rule (2). The decomposition list of F is then $a, b+c, d, e+f, g$. □

Rules 1-5 are sufficient to construct the decomposition tree/list of F:

Theorem 1. *If a function A belongs to the decomposition tree of F, then one of conditions $1-4$ above must hold true for A.* □

4 A BDD-based decomposition procedure.

In this section we present the algorithm for annotating the decomposition of a function F on its BDD representation. The annotation is accomplished in a single sweep of

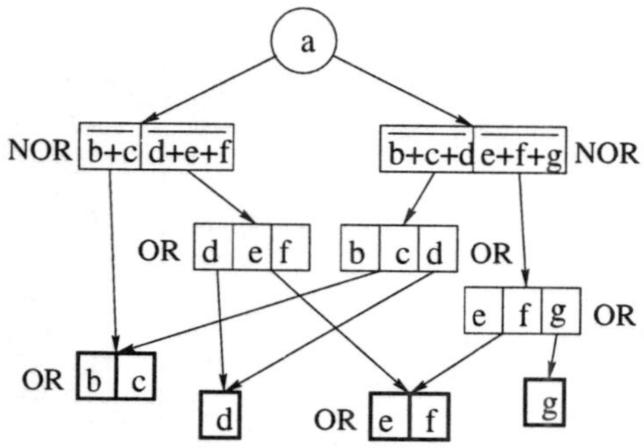

Figure 2. Construction of the decomposition tree for the Example (5).

the BDD nodes, sorted topologically in a linear array. During the sweep, each node is inspected, and the decomposition of the function rooted at that node is determined, from that of the children. The node is then labeled with a pointer to its decomposition list and annotated with its decomposition type.

The decomposition method is enumerative. We try to verify Cases 1 to 3b of Section (3), in order. If we fail, a node is annotated PRIME and its decomposition list constructed as in Case 4.

```
DEC decompose(BDD* node) {
    DEC left = node->left->decomposed;
    DEC right = node->right->decomposed;
    VAR var   = node->argument;

    // check if any cofactors are constant:
    res = decompose_ornor(var, left, right);
    if (res) return(res);

    // check if the cofactors
    // are each other's complements
    res = decompose_xor(var, left, right);
    if (res) return(res);

    // check if var belongs to a subfunction
    res = decompose_case3(var, left, right);
    if (res) return(res);

    // construct the new decomposition list
    res = decompose_prime(var, left, right);
    assert(res);
    return(res);
}
```

4.1 Synthesis.

LODE generates a netlist from a depth-first traversal of the decomposition of F as follows:

```
synthesis(F) {
  if (F.synthesized) return(F.synthesized);
  switch (F.type) {
    case PRIME :
      F_0 = disjoint_cof(F, F.dec.first');
      F_1 = disjoint_cof(F, F.dec.first);
      N0 = synthesis(F0);
      N1 = synthesis(F1);
      NC = synthesis(F.dec);
      return(MUX(NC, N0, N1));
    case OR, XOR, NOR :
      for F_0 in F.dec
          F[i] = synthesis(F_0); i++;
      return(OR/NOR/XOR(F[])); }
}
```

5 Experimental results.

The procedures of this paper have been implemented in C and tested on several combinational logic benchmarks. The CPU time was taken on a PC equipped with a 150 MHz Pentium and 96Mbyte of main memory.

Table (1) below reports results on the decomposability of some large combinational and sequential benchmarks. Column DEC reports the number of decomposable outputs, while CPU time is reported in seconds. The decompositions themselves are often of interest. For instance, in some sequential circuits, such as s1494, the next-state outputs are often ANDed with the same signal (v13_D_0C). Most of the outputs of C880 contain complex functions of the same formal input AND(72GAT[12], 68GAT[11], 13GAT[2], 73GAT[13]). The output is also often the OR of these complex functions with 255GAT[54], 259GAT[55], etc... Synthesis benchmarks are mostly decomposable. The decomposition of some circuits, such as DES, *pair*, etc ... also evidences regular designs, that we cannot describe here for reasons of space. For some ISCAS circuits, we have also been able to decompose some of the outputs corresponding to complex functions.

Table (2) below compares the literal counts obtained by LODE against those obtained by SIS running rugged_script. Finally, table (3) reports the CPU time employed by LODE for the decomposition.

For the largest benchmarks, the limited set of BDD transformations of LODE do not compensate for the exceptional growth of the BDD representation with respect to the original representation. We are currently working towards a partitioning strategy and enriching the transformation set.

6 Conclusions.

We have presented an algorithm for the disjunctive decomposition of logic functions, starting from a BDD representation. The algorithm has worst-case complexity quadratic in the BDD size. We found it very fast in practice, as we were able to obtain the decomposition of all benchmark functions in a few minutes in the worst case. We have been able to present results on the decomposability of complex benchmarks for the first time. Moreover, we have been able to generate a very compact, canonical multiple-level circuit directly from a BDD representation.

We are currently investigating some implications of the present work: First, the possibility of generating the decompositio form of this paper directly from a netlist. Second, we are exploring the applicability of this representation to rapid prototyping, technology mapping and reachability analysis.

References

[1] R. Ashenhurst. The decomposition of switching functions. In *Proceedings of the International Symposium on the Theory of Switching*, pages 74–116, April 1957.

[2] J. P. Roth and R. M. Karp. Minimization over boolean graphs. *IBM Journal*, pages 661–664, April 1962.

Circuit	Inputs	Outputs	DEC	CPU time
C1355	41	32	0	91.25s
C1908	33	25	7	7.58s
C3540	50	22	0	21.10s
C432	36	7	1	1.23s
C499	41	32	0	83.47s
C880	60	26	25	2.71s
CM42	4	10	10	0.15s
CM85	11	3	3	0.27s
alu4	14	8	4	0.37s
apex6	135	99	99	2.62s
apex7	49	37	36	1.03s
comp	32	3	3	0.71s
count	35	16	16	0.73s
frg2	143	139	126	2.86s
k2	45	45	35	1.04s
pair	173	137	125	4.02s
rot	135	107	77	22.62s
vda	17	39	20	0.40s
x3	135	99	99	2.69s
x4	94	71	65	1.90s
apex1	45	45	35	1.01s
apex2	38	3	3	1.14s
apex4	9	19	4	0.33s
apex5	114	88	82	2.34s
e64	65	65	64	1.31s
misex2	25	18	17	0.57s
seq	41	35	34	1.10s
s1196	32	32	14	0.71s
s1238	32	32	14	0.75s
s1423	91	79	71	12.48s
s1488	14	25	19	0.36s
s1494	14	25	19	0.34s
s420	35	18	18	0.75s
s444	24	27	21	0.54s
s641	54	42	35	1.12s
s953	45	52	22	20.97s

Table 1. Decomposability of some large benchmark circuits.

Circuit	IN	OUT	Original literals	LODE literals	SIS literals
9symml	9	1	277	76	223
CM150	21	1	77	47	51
PARITY	16	1	60	60	60
alu2	10	6	453	354	357
cmb	16	4	62	36	51
f51m	8	8	169	98	91
lal	26	19	221	134	105
mux	21	1	92	47	51
term1	34	10	624	165	197
ttt2	24	21	341	258	216
s1494	14	25	1393	793	661
s298	17	20	244	146	114
s526	24	27	445	257	191
s832	23	24	769	431	352

Table 2. Experimental result and comparisons against SIS.

Circuit	IN	OUT	LODE CPU time	SIS CPU time
9symml	9	1	0.26s	25.83s
CM150	21	1	0.51s	0.51
PARITY	16	1	0.38s	0.27
alu2	10	6	0.28s	106.56s
cmb	16	4	0.36s	0.31
f51m	8	8	0.26s	2.23
lal	26	19	0.55s	2.21
mux	21	1	0.48s	0.55
term1	34	10	0.75s	16.22s
ttt2	24	21	0.55s	5.10
s1494	14	25	0.34s	65.77s
s298	17	20	0.40s	1.83
s526	24	27	0.52s	5.62
s832	23	24	0.54s	27.66s

Table 3. CPU time for decomposition and comparisons against SIS.

[3] H. A. Curtis. *A New Approach to the Design of Switching Circuits.* Van Nostrand, Princeton, N.J., 1962.

[4] R.K. Brayton and C. McMullen. The decomposition and factorization of boolean expressions. In *ISCAS, Proceedings of the International Symposyium on Circuits and Systems*, pages 49–54, 1982.

[5] R. Murgai, Y. Nishizaki, N. Shenoy, R.K. Brayton, and A. Sangiovanni-Vincentelli. Logic synthesis fro programmable gate arrays. In *Proceedings 27th ACM/IEEE Design Automation Conference*, pages 620–625, June 1990.

[6] Kevin Karplus. Representing boolean functions with if-then-else dags. Technical Report UCSC-CRL-88-28, Baskin Center for ComputerEngineering & Information Sciences, 1988.

[7] Kevin Karplus. Using if-then-else dsgs for multi-level logic minimization. Technical Report UCSC-CRL-88-29, Baskin Center for ComputerEngineering & Information Sciences, 1988.

[8] Kevin Karplus. Using if-then-else dsgs to do technology mapping for field-programmable gate arrays. Technical Report UCSC-CRL-90-43, Baskin Center for ComputerEngineering & Information Sciences, 1990.

[9] K.-R. Pan Y.-T.Lai and M. Pedram. Obdd-based functional decomposition: algorithms and implementation. *IEEE Trans. on CAD/ICAS*, 15(8):977–990, August 1996.

[10] T. Sasao. Multiple-valued decomposition of generalized boolean functions and the complexity of programmable logic arrays. *IEEE Trans. on Computers*, C-30(9):635–643, September 1981.

[11] R. E. Bryant. Graph-based algorithms for boolean function manipulation. *IEEE Trans. on Computers*, 35(8):677–691, August 1986.

[12] K. S. Brace, R. L. Rudell, and R. E. Bryant. Efficient implementation of a BDD package. In *Proc. DAC*, pages 40–45, June 1990.

[13] Edward J. McCluskey. *Logic Design Principles With Emphasis on Testable Semicustom Circuits.* Prentice-Hall, 1986.

[14] V. Bertacco and M. Damiani. Boolean function representation based on disjoint-support decompositions. submitted to *ICCD 96*, to appear, October 1996.

[15] O. Coudert and J.C. Madre. A unified framework for the formal verification of sequential circuits. In *Proc. ICCAD*, pages 126–129, November 1990.

Speeding Up Technology-Independent Timing Optimization by Network Partitioning

Rajat Aggarwal*
Lattice Semiconductor Corporation,
Milpitas, CA
rajat@lscsjc.latticesemi.com

Rajeev Murgai, Masahiro Fujita
Fujitsu Laboratories of America, Inc.
Santa Clara, CA
{murgai,fujita}@fla.fujitsu.com

Abstract

Technology-independent timing optimization is an important problem in logic synthesis. Although many promising techniques have been proposed in the past, unfortunately they are quite slow and thus impractical for large networks. In this paper, we propose DEPART, a delay-based partitioner-cum-optimizer, which purports to solve this problem. Given a combinational logic network that is to be optimized for timing, DEPART divides it into sub-networks using timing information and a constraint on the maximum number of gates allowed in a single sub-network. These sub-networks are then dispatched, one by one, to a standard timing optimizer. The optimized sub-networks are re-glued, generating an optimized network. The challenge is how to partition the original network into sub-networks so that the final solution quality after partitioning and optimization is comparable to that from the timing optimizer. We propose a partitioning technique that is timing-driven and is simple yet effective. We compare DEPART with speed_up [21], a state-of-the-art timing optimization tool, and with various partitioning techniques such as min-cut based and region growing, on a suite of large industrial and ISCAS circuits. On more than half of the benchmarks, DEPART yields run-time improvements of 20 to 450 times over a normal invocation of speed_up (the overall average improvement being 8 times), without compromising the solution quality much. Min-cut and region growing partitioning schemes, not being timing-driven, perform poorly in terms of the final circuit delay.

1 Introduction

Timing optimization of a digital circuit is an important problem in logic synthesis. It can be performed at different stages of the design process. For instance, *technology-independent optimization* is done before the circuit is mapped on to a technology, whereas *technology-dependent optimization* is carried out during or after mapping. In this paper, we will deal only with technology-independent timing optimization, which addresses the following problem: *Given a Boolean network, the arrival times at the primary inputs, the required times at the primary outputs, and a delay model, obtain a logically equivalent network that meets the required time constraints under the given delay model.*

Many timing optimization techniques have been proposed in literature. They are mostly based on transformations that designers use to speed up circuits. Some of these techniques are *rule-based* such as LSS [8] and SOCRATES [4]. They use a pre-defined set of local transformations based on design style and the target technology to improve the delay. Others use *algorithms* to optimize the circuit. For instance, [9, 22] determine a set of nodes whose restructuring improves the overall circuit performance. The choice of these nodes is made so as to obtain the maximum delay improvement with a minimum area increase. Some algorithmic techniques reduce delay by using network don't cares and permissible functions to re-express node functions using early arriving signals [6]; some others use delay-driven clustering and subsequent collapsing and optimization [23], while others either eliminate long paths that cannot be sensitized by any input vector [5] or reduce the delay of the longest sensitizable path [19].

speed_up [21] is a state-of-the-art, topology-based performance optimizer that uses a variety of transformations to optimize the network. These include tree-height reduction [22, 9], timing-driven cofactoring [12], generalized bypass transform [15], timing-driven simplification, timing-driven decomposition, etc. These transformations are local in that they attempt to resynthesize a small part of the network. The best possible timing improvement of each node using these transformations is computed. Finally, a set of nodes on which the transformations should be applied is selected. The selection is based on obtaining maximum timing improvement with minimum area increase.

Although speed_up delivers very good-quality solutions (in terms of circuit delay), it turns out that its run-times are exorbitantly large, especially on large circuits and sometimes even on moderately large circuits. For instance, as shown in the column "*Run-time*: speed_up" of Table 3, speed_up takes 35387 cpu seconds – about 10 hours – to optimize a 1000-gate circuit Ind-1 and over 35 hours for the 1500-gate circuit *table3*. Although speed_up generates high-quality solutions, such run-times are simply not acceptable – timing optimization would slow down the entire design cycle.

We propose DEPART, a delay-based logic partitioner-cum-timing optimizer. DEPART assumes that a timing optimizer already exists and then aims to improve the run-time of this optimizer on large or moderately large networks, without modifying the optimizer and without sacrificing the solution quality. It achieves this goal by suitably partitioning the network into sub-networks and dispatching them to the optimizer one by one. The optimized sub-networks are re-glued, generating an optimized network. The challenge is how to partition the original network into sub-networks so that the final solution quality after partitioning and optimization is comparable to that from the timing optimizer. We propose a partitioning technique that is timing-driven and is simple yet effective. The paper is organized as follows. Related work on network partitioning is in Section 2. Section 3 presents our algorithm DEPART. The experimental results are presented in Section 4.

*This work was done when the first author was an intern at Fujitsu Labs of America in the summer of 1996.

1092-3152/97 $10.00 © 1997 IEEE

2 Related Work

Most of the research work in partitioning has targeted the objective of minimizing the number of nets crossing partition boundaries while balancing the sizes of the partitions [13, 2]. This objective is relevant during floorplanning and placement, where tightly-connected components are to be placed in close proximity so as to minimize the total routing length and congestion.

More relevant to us is the problem of partitioning for synthesis. One such work is BEAT_NP [7], a partitioning tool that enables the logic synthesis tool BOLD [3] to handle larger circuits during area optimization. CPU times were reduced by 1 to 3 orders, but were often accompanied by an optimization loss of about 30 to 50%. [10] proposes a network partitioning and resynthesis scheme based on reconvergent fanout regions of the network (*petals* and *corollas*). The goal once again is to resynthesize large networks for smaller layout areas. [17] also targets the same goal. It partitions the network into disjoint sub-networks and optimizes them for minimum area. Nodes in a sub-network are chosen on the basis of common transitive fanins.

Not much work has been done on partitioning aimed at timing optimization of large networks. However, we must mention the problem of *clustering for minimum delay* addressed in [14, 16, 18]: given that an edge crossing cluster boundaries incurs a fixed delay D and that each partition can accommodate no more than M gates, partition the network such that the delay through the network is minimized. This problem is different from the one we are targeting in two respects:

1. the delay D is not relevant to our problem.
2. we are interested in partitioning so that after timing-driven restructuring and optimization, the network delay is minimized. The *clustering for minimum delay* problem does not change the network structure - except possibly replicating some gates.

3 DEPART: DElay optimization using PARTitioning

The main idea of our algorithm DEPART - DElay optimization using PARTitioning - is shown in the flowchart of Figure 1. DEPART reads in an unoptimized network represented in terms of 2-input gates and returns a network optimized for timing, also in terms of 2-input gates. Optimization is achieved by first dividing the given network into sub-networks or partitions, each of which has no more than M (two-input) gates. However, some of our partitioning schemes may initially yield sub-networks with more gates, in which case some gates are temporarily deleted from the partitioned networks to make the networks amenable for further partitioning and size reduction. This further partitioning is achieved by recursively invoking the main algorithm DEPART on the smaller network. The deleted gates are added back to the optimized network returned by DEPART, thus restoring the original logic functionality. On the other hand, if a partitioned network has no more than M gates, the network is handed over to the timing optimizer directly, which attempts to improve the network timing and returns an optimized network. Finally, all the optimized partitioned networks are merged appropriately, generating the optimized network.

DEPART is oblivious to the algorithms employed within the timing optimizer. So, a designer can embed his or her favorite optimizer within DEPART and potentially speed it up. In the current implementation we chose **speed_up**, since it is a state-of-the-art program and generates high-quality solutions.

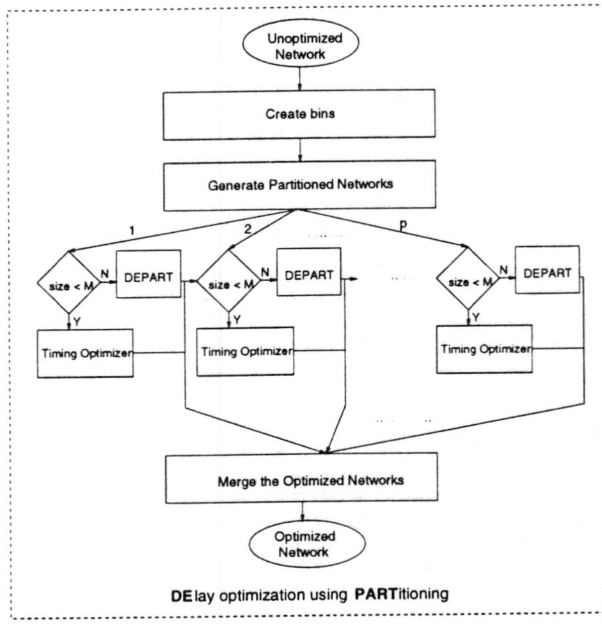

Figure 1: Flowchart of DEPART: DElay optimization using PARTitioning

To see why partitioning can potentially improve the run-time, assume that the worst case complexity of timing optimization is $f(N)$, where N is the number of gates in the unpartitioned network η. Let us also assume that the numbers of gates in the p partitioned networks generated by DEPART are $N_1, N_2, \ldots, N_p$. Ignoring the time taken for computing the partitions (which, as we will see, is negligible anyway), the worst-case complexity for partitioning-based delay optimization, such as DEPART, is $\sum_{i=1}^{p} f(N_i)$. The partitioning-based optimization will be faster if

$$f(N) = f(\sum_{i=1}^{p} N_i) > \sum_{i=1}^{p} f(N_i).$$

In the above, we assumed $N = \sum_{i=1}^{p} N_i$, i.e., the partitions are disjoint. The inequality holds if f is worse than linear. Since timing optimization is NP-hard, f is actually exponential. Then, partitioning-based optimization will definitely be much faster. Typically, practical timing optimization algorithms are not exact but are heuristic in nature. However, they perform tasks that have higher than linear complexities. For instance, **speed_up** [21] computes selection sets through the network and picks the best set by solving a covering problem, which is known to have exponential complexity in the worst-case. So, even for a heuristic optimizer, partitioning should improve the run-time.

With partitioning-based optimization the danger, however, is that we may lose out on optimization, because the optimizer sees only a part of the entire network at any time. The crucial issue, then, is *how to partition the network such that the final solution quality (primarily timing, but also area) after partitioning and optimization is comparable with that of a standard optimizer*, say **speed_up**. Partitioning algorithms in DEPART are timing-driven, i.e., they cluster network nodes with a view to rendering the forthcoming performance optimization effective - from the point of view of both circuit performance and CPU time. DEPART first creates bins; each bin contains a subset of primary outputs and their transitive fanin nodes. From the bins, partitioned networks (or sub-

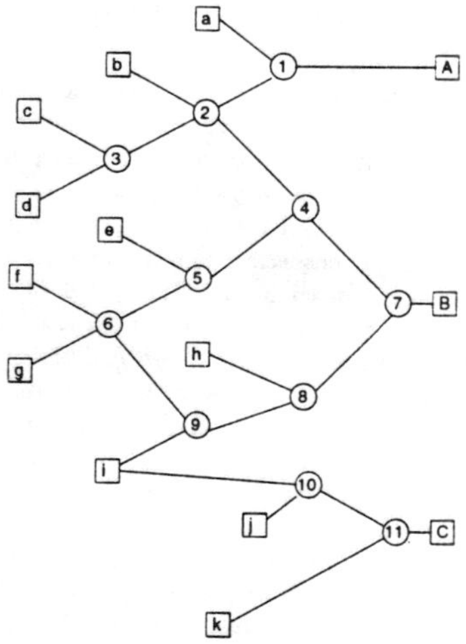

Figure 2: Example network consisting of three primary outputs A, B, and C, and primary inputs a through k.

networks) are generated and sent to the timing optimizer. The resulting optimized sub-networks are glued together yielding the optimized network. These steps are described in the next few subsections.

We will explain this algorithm with the help of a running example – the network η of Figure 2. η has eleven primary inputs (PIs) a through k, three primary outputs (POs) – A, B, C, and eleven internal nodes (or gates) 1 through 11. Although not shown, the signal flow is from left to right.

3.1 Creating Bins

We divide the network into bins, each containing some primary outputs and their transitive fanins (TFIs). The crucial point is to decide which outputs should be grouped together in a bin. We developed three strategies.

1. **Minimum bins**: In this strategy, the outputs are grouped based on the number of TFI nodes they share. Outputs that share many TFI nodes are placed in one bin. Recall that no partition (and hence bin) should have more than M gates. Our goal is to minimize the number of bins needed to accommodate all the primary outputs and their transitive fanins, without violating the constraint M. Since each bin would correspond to a partitioned network, minimizing bins minimizes the number of partitioned networks resulting in better optimization.

   The problem of grouping outputs in minimum bins subject to the size constraint M is similar to the **bin-packing problem** [11], in which items with weights are to be packed in minimum number of uniform bins each of capacity C such that the sum of the weights of the items in a bin is at most C. Apart from some minor technicalities, the correspondence between the two problems is quite straightforward. Each primary output o_i along with its transitive fanin is considered an item, whose weight $w(o_i)$ is the number of gates in the transitive fanin of the output. The capacity C of each bin is M, which means that no more than M gates can be accommodated in each bin. The goal is to use fewest bins to store all the items.

   On the outputs whose TFIs have at most M gates, we apply the standard best-fit decreasing heuristic [11]. Each of the remaining outputs is stored in a separate bin.

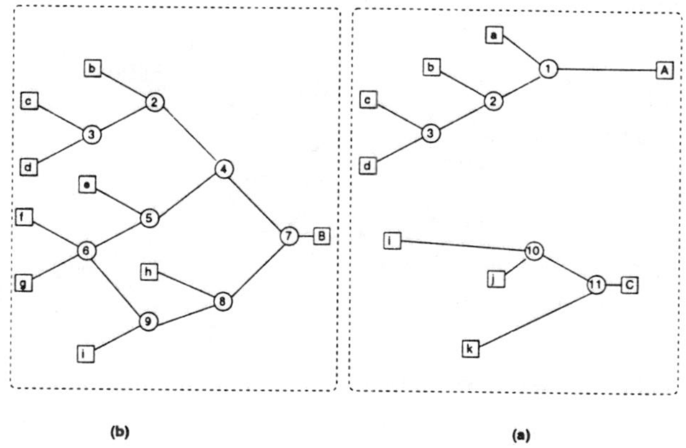

Figure 3: Bins created with $M = 5$ and `minimum bins`

   We illustrate bin creation on the example network of Figure 2. The transitive fanins of A, B, and C have 7, 16, and 5 nodes respectively, out of which 3, 8, and 2 are internal nodes (or gates). Let M be 5. First, we create special bins for outputs with weights more than 5. The only such output is B, and we obtain the bin (b) in Figure 3. We sort the remaining outputs, A and C, on the number of TFI gates. We obtain the sorted list $L = \{A, C\}$. A and its TFI are placed in a newly created bin, (a). It turns out that C can also fit in the same bin. Note that we are considering gates and not PI/POs while checking the fitting of items into bins. The bin (a) is now full to capacity.

2. **Criticality information**: The basic idea is to group critical primary outputs in fewest bins. A critical output is one that needs to be speeded up in order to improve the performance of the circuit (we will make the notion of criticality more precise shortly). Non-critical primary outputs are not sent for optimization, thus reducing the total run-time tremendously.

   First, a delay trace is carried out on the network to determine the arrival times, required times, and slacks at all the nodes of the network. The arrival times of the primary inputs can be set by the user, 0 being the default. If no required times are set at the outputs, they are set to be the maximum arrival time of an output. A primary output is critical if its slack is at most t% of the maximum arrival time of some network output, where t is a user-specified number. In case no required times are set at the outputs, we can alternatively define an output to be critical if its arrival time is at least $(100 - t)$% of the maximum arrival time. If t is 0, only the latest arriving outputs are critical. If it is 100, all the outputs are critical.

   After the delay trace, non-critical outputs are determined and ignored from consideration. The critical outputs are sorted into list L, the most critical output being first. Then, a bin-packing-like method is used to group the sorted critical outputs and their TFIs into bins. The first output from L is placed in a new bin. Thereafter, at any step, the next output is fetched from L and considered for placement in the same bin as the last output. Thus, an attempt is made to place critical outputs in fewest bins solely based on criticality information (and not on node sharing, which was the case in the `minimum bins` approach).

   Let us consider the example of Figure 2. Assume that each gate has a delay of 1 unit, and that all inputs arrive at time

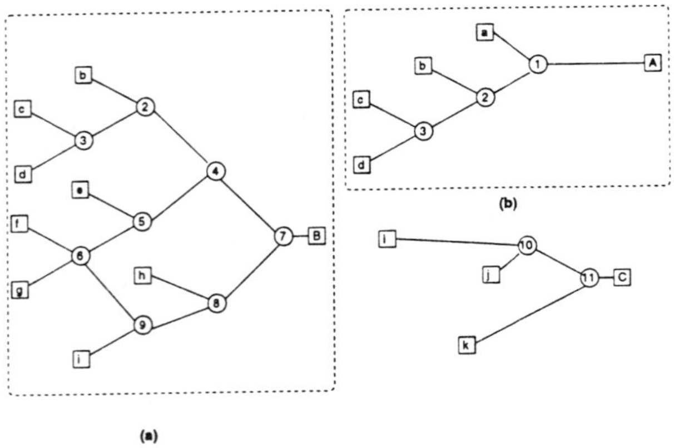

Figure 4: Bins created with $M = 5$ and `criticality`

0. After delay trace, we find that the arrival times of A, B, and C are 3, 4, and 2 respectively. If $t = 25$, any output with arrival time at least 75% of 4 (= 3) is critical. So A and B are critical and C is not. Two bins are created, one with B and the other with A. This is shown in Figure 4. C is ignored from consideration.

3. **Minimum Critical Bins**: This strategy is a cross between the last two. As in `criticality`, non-critical outputs are removed from consideration. Then critical outputs are placed in bins using the strategy employed in `minimum bins`. Note the difference between this strategy and `criticality`. In `criticality`, critical outputs are placed solely on the basis of criticality information, whereas in `minimum critical bins`, they are placed solely on the basis of TFI information.

   For our example, `minimum critical bins` creates the same bins as created by `criticality` in Figure 4. However, the order in which the bins will be processed will be different. We will explain this later.

Each bin generates a partitioned network that is sent to the timing optimizer. The next subsection describes how partitioned networks are generated from bins.

3.2 Generating Partitioned Networks From Bins

Bin-creation phase generates information about the primary outputs and nodes present in each bin. This information is used to derive partitioned networks. Bins, in general, share nodes. TFI of an output that belongs to bin A may share some nodes with TFI of an output belonging to bin B. While creating networks from bins, one has to decide whether these common nodes should be replicated in each network or just be present in one of them. We propose three ways to handle this:

1. **No-Overlap**: In this option, no overlap is allowed among partitioned networks, except for primary inputs. Assume that bins are traversed in some order (we will address the ordering issue soon). If bin X has an internal node (or gate) n that is present in bin Y earlier in the order, but not in any bin prior to Y, n will be included in the network for Y, but not in the network for X. Instead, a *dummy primary output* fed by n is introduced in the network corresponding to Y. Also, in the network corresponding to X, a *dummy primary input* is added. However, not every common node n is converted into dummy input and output; only the boundary nodes, as explained below.

   Figures 5(a) and 5(b) show the networks generated from the bins of Figure 3 using `no-overlap`. For the sake of the example, assume that the bins are processed in the order 3 (a), 3 (b). Creating the network from 3 (a) is straightforward – include all the nodes of bin 3 (a) in the partitioned network. Next, 3 (b) is processed. Primary inputs b, c, d, and nodes 2 & 3 are common to bins 3 (a) and 3 (b). However, none of the nodes b, c, d, and 3 fan out to a node that is in bin 3 (b) but not in bin 3 (a). So b, c, d, and 3 are not made primary inputs for the network 5 (b). However, node 2 fans out to node 4, which is in bin 3 (b) and not in 3 (a). So a dummy primary output $2A$ is introduced in network 5 (a). Similarly, dummy primary input $2a$ is added to network 5 (b). It is implicit that $2A$ and $2a$ are essentially the same signal. Adding $2A$ to the network 5 (a) ensures that during timing optimization of the network 5 (a), node 2 is retained, so that it can be later composed into the optimized network 5 (b) at the primary input $2a$.

   Although `no-overlap` does not carry any area penalty, it can break a critical path several times, potentially resulting in a loss of optimization. This fact motivated us to devise the bin creation heuristic `criticality` in its current form. By sorting the outputs by criticality and grouping the highly critical ones in the first few bins, the algorithm attempts to retain complete input to output (I/O) paths of more critical outputs in a single sub-network.

2. **Complete-Overlap**: This option lies on the other end of the spectrum. Nodes common to different bins are replicated in the corresponding networks. Each partitioned network thus retains all the nodes of the corresponding bin. Referring to the running example, the networks corresponding to the bins of Figure 3 are identical to those of Figure 3.

   This option allows maximum flexibility in terms of timing optimization (modulo the loading effects), since complete I/O paths are available to the optimizer. However, it typically results in a huge area penalty.

3. **Critical-Overlap**: Here only critical nodes are replicated. The intuition is that the timing optimizer can optimize better when complete critical paths are available. Also, by restricting replication to critical nodes, area penalty is reduced. As for the non-critical nodes, they are not duplicated, but are converted to *dummy primary inputs* and *dummy primary outputs* appropriately as described in `no-overlap`.

Processing Order for Bins: In order to generate networks from bins, bins have to be processed in some order. This order can have a great impact on the kinds of networks generated and hence the run-time and solution quality.

In `minimum bins` and `minimum critical bins` options, bins are traversed in the order of increasing sizes (i.e., used capacities). To understand why, consider our example. In `minimum bins`, we would first process bin (a) of Figure 3, since it has only 5 gates, as compared to the special, large bin (b), which has 8 gates. Next, we come to bin (b). With the `no-overlap` option, the gates common to the two bins are excluded from the network generated from bin (b). As shown in Figure 5 (b), this network has 6 gates. This ordering scheme then helps to reduce the sizes of the networks that would have been otherwise large.

In `criticality`, bins are traversed in the order they were created – the most critical first. For our example, `minimum critical bins` and `criticality` generate identical bins. However, in `minimum critical bins` the bin with output B, being larger, is processed after the bin with output A. This implies that with the

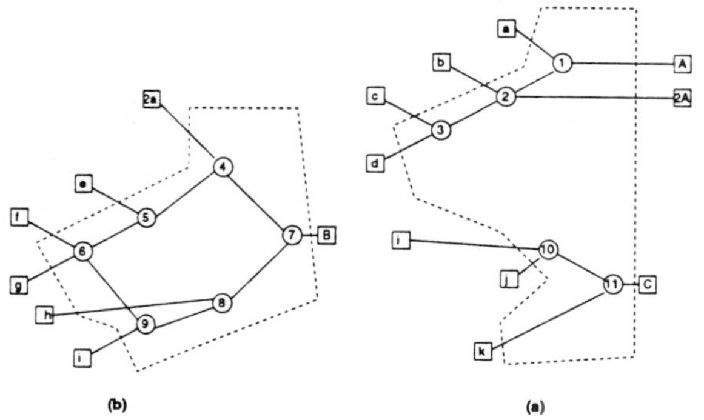

Figure 5: Partitioned networks generated with `no-overlap`

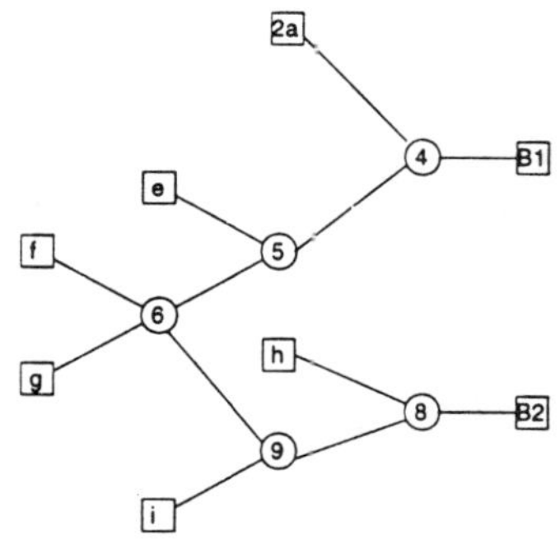

Figure 6: The network generated by the second level partitioner after deleting the primary output B.

`no-overlap` option, nodes 2 and 3 will be deleted from the network for B. With `criticality`, B will be processed first (since it is more critical), and nodes 2 and 3 will be deleted from the network of A.

3.3 Optimizing the Partitioned Networks

After partitioned networks have been created, they are sent for timing optimization. However, it may happen that some partitioned networks have more than M gates. For instance, the network of Figure 5 (b) has 6 nodes, and further partitioning is needed to reduce the size to no more than $M = 5$. We incorporate this by defining a recursive optimization-partitioner. When the number of internal nodes, S, of the partitioned network is no more than M, we enter the **base level** optimization: partitioned network is sent directly to the standard timing optimizer such as `speed_up`. However, when S is greater than M, the partitioned network is sent to a **second level partitioner-cum-optimizer**. This partitioner-cum-optimizer program appropriately selects a primary output P from the partitioned network,[1] deletes P, converts all its immediate fanins to primary outputs, and makes a recursive call to the main partitioning algorithm DEPART on the network thus obtained.

The intuition behind this strategy is the following. First recall that the network at this stage is in terms of 2-input gates and therefore the number of fanins of P is 2. After deleting P, these fanins are converted into primary outputs. If the sizes of the TFIs of each of these outputs are roughly the same ($\sim S/2$), and furthermore if $S/2 \leq M$, the outputs will satisfy the capacity constraint M during the first level of recursion itself. If $S/2 > M$, further recursion may be needed, but the process will quickly lead to partitions of sizes at most M.[2] An advantage of this method is that a path in the original network completely resides in the new network, except perhaps for the terminal node, if that happens to be P.

The partitioned network in Figure 5(a) has 5 nodes. Since $M = 5$, this sub-network is directly sent to the timing optimizer (the base case). However, the network in Figure 5(b) has 6 nodes, and is sent to the second level partitioner-cum-optimizer. The second level optimizer selects the primary output B, deletes it, and converts its immediate fanins 4 and 8 to primary outputs $B1$ and $B2$. Figure 6 shows the network thus generated. This network has 5 gates, and when sent recursively to DEPART, it is immediately sent to the timing optimizer. However, if M was 4, in the recursive call to DEPART, the network of Figure 6 would go through the steps of bin creation and network creation. Note that each of the two outputs $B1$ and $B2$ has 3 internal nodes. So two bins will be generated. Both corresponding networks will satisfy the M constraint and hence would be sent to the timing optimizer.

Now we explain how timing information is propagated between the partitioned networks during optimization. Assume that the original network η is partitioned into networks $\eta_1, \eta_2, \ldots, \eta_p$. Also assume that the partitioned networks are sent for optimization in the same order, i.e., η_1 first and η_p last. Say at some stage, η_i is sent for optimization. Then, after optimization, the arrival times of the primary outputs of η_i may change. If some primary output of η_i is a dummy output, it feeds dummy input(s) of other partitioned network(s), say η_j. The new arrival time is used to update arrival time of the corresponding dummy primary input(s), so that when η_j is optimized later (assuming $j > i$), the timing information used in optimization is the updated one. In fact, in DEPART, we make sure that if $i < j$, no dummy primary input of η_i is connected to a dummy primary output of η_j. Thus, the arrival time information of η_i depends only on the arrival times of the real primary inputs of η and possibly of the dummy primary outputs of networks $\eta_k, k < i$.

3.4 Combining the Optimized Partitioned Networks

After all the partitioned networks have been optimized, they are merged to form an optimized network having the same functionality as the original network. The optimized partitioned networks are merged by patching up the corresponding dummy primary outputs and dummy primary inputs. For instance, if (a) and (b) of Figure 5 are the optimized partitioned networks, after merging we obtain the optimized network shown in Figure 2. The only dummy primary input-output pair is $(2a, 2A)$. At the time of merging, the fanin of $2A$, node 2, is made to fan out to all the fanouts of $2a$, which, in this case, is the single node 4. Both $2a$ and $2A$ disappear after merging.

Thus we obtain a functionally-identical, timing-optimized circuit. Next, we report the experimental results on a set of industrial and ISCAS benchmarks.

4 Experimental Results

DEPART is implemented in the sis framework [20], the logic synthesis system from the University of California, Berkeley. In the

[1] P is the latest arriving output.

[2] It can happen that the sizes of the two TFIs are disparate for many consecutive recursion calls. In that case, we limit the maximum depth of recursion and then call the timing optimizer on the network at the final level.

Bench.	#I/P	#O/P	#Lev.	#Lit.
Ind-1	8	8	37	1074
Ind-2	8	8	23	435
C880	60	26	35	684
C6288	32	32	92	4962
C7552	207	108	35	3976
C3540	50	22	40	2222
seq	41	35	17	2937
apk2	1263	1218	33	22096
alu4	14	8	28	1745
apex5	114	85	24	1346
C5315	178	123	32	2911
C2670	233	139	20	1379
table3	14	14	55	1456
apex3	54	50	14	2750
des	256	245	22	5889
pair	173	137	28	2949

Table 1: Characteristics of the benchmarks used as test inputs

current implementation, DEPART invokes `speed_up` on each subnetwork. Since `speed_up` lets one specify the delay model to be used during optimization, so does DEPART. Currently, DEPART uses the *unit delay model*, which assigns a delay of one to each 2-input gate and thus estimates the circuit delay to be the number of levels.[3]

The benchmarks used in the experiments come from two sources: some are combinational ISCAS benchmarks and the rest (i.e., Ind-1, Ind-2, apk2) are industrial circuits. We first optimized the benchmarks for minimum area (i.e., factored form literals) using the standard sis optimization script, `script.rugged` [20], twice with a timeout option of 1 hour each time and then applied `eliminate -1; speed_up -i` to obtain networks that would be starting points for all the experiments. `eliminate -1` collapses all nodes that do not save any literals into their fanouts. `speed_up -i` performs a timing-driven decomposition on each network node and produces a network that has either inverters or two-input gates. Table 1 shows the numbers of primary inputs, primary outputs, levels, and literals in these networks. With the exceptions of Ind-2 and *C880*, the criterion for selecting a benchmark was that it should have at least 1000 two-input gates (roughly equal to the number of literals).

DEPART uses several control parameters that influence the final solution quality and run-time, such as the maximum size of a partitioned network M, the bin creation heuristic, degree of overlap between partitions, etc. We did extensive experimentation to determine the best values for them. The best values were found to be $M = 200$, bin creation – a combination of `criticality` and `minimum bins`, overlap among partitioned networks – `no overlap` [1].

4.1 Comparison with Other Schemes

In this section we compare and analyze results of DEPART with `speed_up` (invoked on the entire network), and two partitioning-based schemes:

1. hMETIS, a state-of-the-art min-cut-based partitioning algorithm [13], and
2. a region growing algorithm based on connectivity information.

None of these partitioning schemes are driven by timing considerations. A comparison with them would highlight the significance of a timing-driven partitioning scheme such as DEPART.

hMETIS is a multi-level min-cut partitioning algorithm. It is a very fast and accurate scheme that partitions a netlist into a pre-specified number of approximately equal-sized clusters and minimizes the total number of nets crossing the cluster boundaries. It produces k partitions using a bisection algorithm recursively. hMETIS first coarsens the netlist in multiple levels to get a smaller representative netlist. A partitioning solution is calculated on the smaller netlist which is then refined in the uncoarsening phase. These coarsening and uncoarsening phases allow hMETIS to obtain a global picture, resulting in a high-quality solution. These phases also help in reducing the run-time, since most of the computation is performed on the smaller netlist.

We implemented a region growing algorithm, using a recursive bisection technique. The bisection process starts from a randomly selected node and grows in a breadth-first fashion a region around it of nodes tightly connected to it [13] until half of the nodes of the netlist are in this region. The nodes belonging to the grown region are assigned to the first part and the rest to the second part. The process is repeated on the two parts until k partitions are obtained.

Timing optimizer (`speed_up`) is invoked on each cluster obtained by either partitioning algorithm (hMETIS or region growing algorithm). Timing information (such as arrival times) is updated and propagated to other clusters after each invocation. This is similar to the timing optimization step in DEPART. The difference between DEPART and these partitioning techniques is the target cost function. As described earlier, DEPART attempts to generate partitions with a view to maximizing the optimization potential of the timing optimizer. These techniques, however, do not pay any attention to timing. Instead, they either minimize the total number of nets crossing the cluster boundaries (hMETIS) or maximize the connectivity within each cluster (region growing).

`speed_up` is invoked with unit delay model (so it minimizes the number of levels) and depth of collapse of transitive fanin region equal to 4.

For hMETIS and region growing, we set the number of clusters to the number of nodes divided by M (=200).

Tables 2 and 3 show comparison of various techniques. For each benchmark, numbers of levels and literals (a measure of network area) before and after timing optimization (with and without partitioning) are reported. For each technique, run-times on Sun SPARCstations 20 are reported in seconds in Table 3.

From Table 2, we deduce that with respect to number of levels, on average, DEPART is about 6.6% worse than `speed_up`[4] and in terms of literals, it is marginally better. However, Table 3 shows that on average, it is more than 8 times faster than `speed_up`. It is interesting to note that `speed_up` takes about 10 hours on Ind-1, which has about 1000 2-input gates. DEPART, however, takes about 15 minutes (which is 40 times less) and generates same number of levels and fewer gates! On *table3*, DEPART is more than 450 times faster than `speed_up` (`speed_up` takes 35.5 hours and DEPART only 4.7 minutes) – with only 7% penalty in the number of levels. Run-time improvements by factors of 20 to 40 can be seen in many other examples, such as Ind-2, *C880*, *C3540*, *seq*, *alu4*,

[3] Singh concludes in [21] that optimized networks generated using unit delay model have post-map delays comparable with delays of networks generated using more sophisticated models, such as unit fanout model, library model, etc. We reached the same conclusion using a similar set-up and a 0.5-micron technology library [1].

[4] "% Change" in the table is with respect to the original network (the column "Org"). The figure 6.6%, although not in the table, is obtained from a pairwise comparison between `speed_up` and DEPART.

Bench.	Levels					Literals				
	Org	speed_up	m-c	r-g	DEPART	Org	speed_up	m-c	r-g	DEPART
Ind-1	37	30	34	37	30	1074	1383	1117	1074	1249
Ind-2	23	18	22	22	20	435	553	451	447	465
C880	35	18	21	35	21	684	1005	1007	684	913
C6288	92	70	78	92	75	4962	5582	6139	4962	6367
C7552	35	21	29	35	22	3976	4505	4566	3976	4577
C3540	40	31	33	40	33	2222	2414	2331	2222	2382
seq	17	14	15	17	15	2937	2964	2940	2937	3003
apk2	33	16*	32	33	16	22096	22094*	22375	22096	21666
alu4	28	25	28	28	26	1745	1937	1745	1745	1917
apex5	24	14	16	24	14	1346	1580	1954	1346	1580
C5315	32	21	27	32	25	2911	3387	3067	2911	3099
C2670	20	17	18	20	17	1379	1469	1405	1379	1482
table3	55	41	52	54	44	1456	2287	1493	1458	2750
apex3	14	12	13	14	12	2750	2790	2770	2750	2810
des	22	19	20	22	20	5889	6043	6508	5889	6223
pair	28	17	17	28	20	2949	3282	3950	2949	3158
% Change		-27.45	-14.81	-0.40	-22.87		16.36	12.49	0.17	15.78

Org original benchmark -- before optimization
m-c Min-cut approach of hMETIS
r-g Region Growing

Table 2: Comparing speed_up, min-cut based hMETIS, region growing and DEPART. *: the best network at the time of abortion, which was done after more than 2 days. % Change is with respect to "Org".

C5315, *C2670*, and *pair*. This improvement is achieved at the cost of a very small delay penalty, maximum penalty being about 15%. Three factors contribute towards such an advance:

1) the inherent run-time advantage of partitioning – this was discussed in Section 3,

2) Partitioning is timing-driven:

a. Partitions are formed with timing optimization in mind.

- Outputs are grouped in a bin, keeping in mind gate-sharing (to save area) and criticality (for timing).
- Complete I/O paths are handed to the optimizer (as much as possible).
- Non-critical outputs are ignored.

b. Updated timing information is propagated from an optimized partition to partitions yet to be optimized.

3) careful parameter-tuning in DEPART.

We also noted that the CPU time taken only by the partitioning algorithm (i.e., not including the time taken by speed_up for timing optimization) is negligible as compared to the time spent in calls to speed_up – it is about 4% of the total time.

Sometimes, though rarely, DEPART takes appreciable run-time. For our benchmark suite, it happens only on one example, *apex3*; DEPART takes about 16 hours. We believe this is due to speed_up (which is invoked from within DEPART many times) taking long time to choose selection-sets for applying the transformations. speed_up builds a binary decision diagram (BDD) to solve the selection-set problem and the size of the BDD cannot be predicted before-hand.

It is interesting to study the relative performance on the largest circuit in the benchmark suite: apk2. First of all, speed_up did not terminate in more than 2 days. So, for comparison, we decided to select the final network generated by speed_up at the time of abortion (speed_up is an iterative algorithm and at the end of each iteration one can save the best network generated so far). The run-time reported is the time taken to generate the final network when the program was aborted. DEPART and speed_up yield the same number of levels. DEPART has about 5% area penalty, but is about 15 times faster than speed_up. We also observed that speed_up was using more than 1000 MB of memory at the time of abortion. This was causing thrashing and a slow-down of the entire optimization process.

Note that DEPART makes run-time calls to speed_up, without using any information about the algorithms employed within it.

The overall performance of min-cut-based hMETIS is far from satisfactory. On average, it results in 19.8% more levels than speed_up and about 12.9% more levels than DEPART. For the benchmark apk2, DEPART reduced the number of levels from 33 to 16, whereas hMETIS reduced it only to 32! Thus there is a strong case for using a timing-driven partitioner. The quality of the resulting circuit can be quite bad with min-cut. Except for one example (C7552), hMETIS run-times are comparable to DEPART's.

The results of region growing algorithm are very poor. Except for two benchmarks, namely, Ind-2 and *table3*, there was no improvement on any of the other benchmarks. Even on Ind-2 and *table3*, the improvements were marginal. The reason behind this is that partitioning, not being timing-driven, was unsuccessful to give complete I/O paths to the timing optimizer.

We also compared DEPART with the *clustering for minimum delay* algorithm, which was mentioned in Section 2. The implementation of [16] is not very practical, since it results in about 30 to 70% gate-replication. We modified this algorithm to generate clusters without replication and redefined the meaning of the inter-cluster delay D to be more suitable for our application. It turns out that DEPART is twice as fast and generates faster and smaller circuits. Due to space limitations, we omit the details; they can be found in [1].

Finally, we mapped unoptimized and optimized circuits on to Fujitsu's 0.5-micron technology library. The technology mapper was run in delay-minimization mode. Although we do not report the mapped results due to space constraint, we found that on average, the delay through a mapped network generated by DEPART is about the same as through that generated by speed_up – about 1% more [1].

Bench.	Run-time			
	speed_up	m-c	r-g	DEPART
Ind-1	35387.0	173.1	3.3	941.4
Ind-2	3026.6	30.0	2.9	114.2
C880	13367.7	327.2	1.8	388.4
C6288	12728.3	1655.2	55.3	2151.5
C7552	2522.5	56572.0	38.1	459.6
C3540	22671.7	363.6	11.1	336.4
seq	18557.0	449.9	19.3	626.7
apk2	76922.2*	6931.3	2029.1	5001.5
alu4	7698.9	108.9	7.8	333.0
apex5	343.2	781.0	5.7	137.2
C5315	6377.5	570.0	20.0	175.7
C2670	3179.8	148.4	6.9	101.3
table3	128323.4	136.8	5.9	282.9
apex3	127026.9	817.9	16.6	57455.9
des	4490.1	4576.0	47.9	1879.2
pair	4087.5	834.8	20.8	186.1
% Change	209.07	-36.53	-98.80	-73.73

m-c Min-cut approach of hMETIS
r-g Region Growing

Table 3: Comparing run-times of **speed_up**, min-cut based hMETIS, region growing, and DEPART. The %Change is with respect to the average value of run-times of the four techniques. *: the best network at the time of abortion, which was done after more than 2 days.

Future work is in at least two directions:
1) The performance of DEPART is far from satisfactory on *apex3* – it takes more than 15 hours to finish. We need to investigate this further and come up with a better methodology.
2) DEPART is built on top of a timing optimizer. Further gains in run-times can be accrued if the underlying timing optimizer can be speeded up.

References

[1] R. Aggarwal, R. Murgai, and M. Fujita. Speeding Up Technology-Independent Timing Optimization. In *Fujitsu Labs of America Internal Memorandum*, September 1996.

[2] Charles J. Alpert and Andrew B. Kahng. Recent directions in netlist partitioning. *Integration, the VLSI Journal*, 19(1-2):1–81, 1995.

[3] K. Bartlett, D. Bostick, G. Hachtel, R. Jacoby, M. Lightner, M. Moceyunas, C. Morrison, and D. Ravenscroft. Bold: A multi-level logic optimization system. In *Proceedings of the International Conference on Computer-Aided Design*, 1987.

[4] K. Bartlett, W. Cohen, A. J. De Geus, and G. D. Hachtel. Synthesis of Multi-level Logic Under Timing Constraints. In *IEEE Transactions on Computer-Aided Design*, October 1986.

[5] H. Chen and D. Du. Circuit Enhancement by Eliminating Long Paths. In *Proceedings of the Design Automation Conference*, pages 249–252, 1992.

[6] K. C. Chen and S Muroga. Timing Optimization for Multi-Level Combinational Circuits. In *Proceedings of the Design Automation Conference*, pages 339–344, 1990.

[7] H. Cho, G. Hachtel, M. Nash, and L. Setiono. BEAT_NP: A Tool for Partitioning Boolean Networks. In *Proceedings of the International Conference on Computer-Aided Design*, pages 10–13, 1988.

[8] J. Darringer, D. Brand, J. Gerbi, W. Joyner, and L.Trevillyan. LSS: A system for Production Logic Synthesis. *IBM Journal of Research and Development*, 28(5):326–328, September 1984.

[9] G. De Micheli. Performance-Oriented Synthesis of Large-Scale Domino CMOS Circuits. *IEEE Transactions on Computer-Aided Design*, CAD-6(5):751–765, 1987.

[10] Sujit Dey, Franc Brglez, and Gershon Kedem. Corolla based Circuit Partitioning and Resynthesis. In *Proceedings of the Design Automation Conference*, pages 607–612, 1990.

[11] M. R. Garey and D. S. Johnson. *Computers and Intractability*. W. H. Freeman and Co., NY, 1979.

[12] P. Gutwin and P. C. McGeer. Delay predictor for technology-independent logic equations. In *Proceedings of the International Conference on Computer Design*, pages 468–471, 1992.

[13] G. Karypis, R. Aggarwal, V. Kumar, and S. Shekhar. Hypergraph Partitioning: Application in VLSI Domain. In *Proc. ACM/IEEE Design Automation Conference*, 1997.

[14] E. L. Lawler, K. N. Levitt, and J. Turner. Clustering to Minimize Delay in Digital Networks. In *IEEE Transactions on Computers*, pages 47–57, January 1969.

[15] P. C. McGeer, R. K. Brayton, A. L. Sangiovanni-Vincentelli, and S. K. Sahni. Performance Enhancement through the Generalized Bypass Transform. In *Proceedings of the International Conference on Computer-Aided Design*, pages 184–187. IEEE, 1991.

[16] R. Murgai, R. K Brayton, and A. Sangiovanni-Vincentelli. On Clustering for Minimum Delay/Area. In *Proceedings of the International Conference on Computer-Aided Design*, November 1991.

[17] Y. Nakamura and T. Yoshimura. A Partitioning-based Logic Optimization Method for Large Scale Circuits with Boolean Matrix. In *Proceedings of the Design Automation Conference*, pages 653–657, 1995.

[18] R. Rajaraman and D. F. Wong. Optimal Clustering for Delay Minimization. In *Proceedings of the Design Automation Conference*, pages 309–314, June 1993.

[19] A. Saldanha, H. Harkness, P. C. McGeer, R. K. Brayton, and A. Sangiovanni-Vincentelli. Performance Optimization Using Exact Sensitization. In *Proceedings of the Design Automation Conference*, pages 425–429, 1994.

[20] E. M. Sentovich, K. J. Singh, L. Lavagno, C. Moon, R. Murgai, A. Saldanha, H. Savoj, P. R. Stephan, R. K. Brayton, and A. Sangiovanni-Vincentelli. *SIS: A System for Sequential Circuit Synthesis*. Memorandum No. UCB/ERL M92/41, Electronics Research Laboratory, College of Engineering, University of California, Berkeley, CA 94720, May 1992.

[21] K. J. Singh. *Performance Optimization of Digital Circuits*. PhD thesis, UC Berkeley, December 1992.

[22] K. J. Singh, A. R. Wang, R. K. Brayton, and A. Sangiovanni-Vincentelli. Timing Optimization of Combinational Logic. In *Proceedings of the International Conference on Computer-Aided Design*, pages 282–285. IEEE, 1988.

[23] H. J. Touati, H. Savoj, and R. K. Brayton. Delay Optimization of Combinational Logic circuits by Clustering and Partial Collapsing. In *Proceedings of the International Conference on Computer-Aided Design*, pages 188–191. IEEE, November 1991.

Negative Thinking by Incremental Problem Solving: Application to Unate Covering

Evguenii I. Goldberg[†,‡] Luca P. Carloni[‡] Tiziano Villa[§] Robert K. Brayton[‡]

Alberto L. Sangiovanni-Vincentelli[‡]

[‡] Department of EECS, University of California at Berkeley, Berkeley, CA 94720

[†] Academy of Sciences of Belarus, Minsk

[§] PARADES, Via di S.Pantaleo, 66, 00186 Roma

Abstract

We introduce a new technique to solve exactly a discrete optimization problem, based on the paradigm of "negative" thinking. The motivation is that when searching the space of solutions, often a good solution is reached quickly and then improved only a few times before the optimum is found: hence most of the solution space is explored to certify optimality, but it does not yield any improvement of the cost function. So it is quite natural for an algorithm to be "skeptical" about the chance to improve the current best solution.

For illustration we have applied our approach to the unate covering problem. We designed a procedure, *raiser*, implementing a negative thinking search, which is incorporated into a common branch-and-bound procedure. *Raiser* is invoked at a node of the search tree which is deep enough to justify negative thinking.

Raiser tries to detect a hard core of the matrix corresponding to the node by augmenting an independent set of rows in order to increase incrementally the cost of the minimum solutions covering the matrix. Eventually either *raiser* prunes the subtree rooted at the node (having found a lower bound equal or greater than the current best solution) or returns a new solution that becomes the current best one.

Experiments show that our program, AURA, outperforms both ESPRESSO and our enhancement of ESPRESSO using Coudert's limit lower bound [3]. It is always faster and in the most difficult examples either has a running time better by up to two orders of magnitude, or the other programs fail to finish due to timeout or spaceout. The package SCHERZO is faster on some examples and loses on others, due to a less powerful pruning strategy of the search space, partially mitigated by a more effective computation of the maximal independent set.

1 Introduction

A common approach to find an exact solution to problems in combinatorial optimization is branch-and-bound (BAB), which improves over exhaustive enumeration, because it avoids the exploration of some regions of the solution space, when it can certify by means of lower bounds that they do not contain a solution better than the current best one.

To ground the exposition in a concrete domain, in this paper we consider BAB applied to the solution of the Unate Covering Problem (UCP), that is of great interest in logic synthesis and operations research [4]. For the sake of simplicity we consider the case of UCP where all columns have the same cost. Such version of UCP is defined as follows. *Given a Boolean matrix A (all entries are 0 or 1), find a minimum size subset of columns of A such that every row of A is covered by at least one column of the subset.* A row i is covered by a column j if $A_{ij} = 1$. We will denote an instance of UCP with matrix A as $UCP(A)$.

An exact solution of UCP is typically obtained by a branch-and-bound recursive algorithm, which has been implemented in successful computer programs [7, 6]. Branching is done by columns, i.e., subproblems are generated by considering whether a chosen branching column is or is not in the solution.

A run of the algorithm, call it *mincov*, can be described by its computation tree. The root of the computation tree is the input of the problem, an edge represents a call to *mincov*, an internal node is a reduced input. A leaf is reached when a complete solution is found or the search is bounded away. From the root to any internal node there is a unique path, which is the current path for that node. The path leading to the node gives a partial solution and a submatrix A_N obtained from A by removing some rows and columns. On the path some columns are included in the partial solution; we denote by $path(A_N)$ the set of columns included in the partial solution.

Suppose that we know that any minimal cover of A_N is greater or equal to a value $L(A_N)$. The value is called a lower bound of the solutions of $UCP(A_N)$. So the size of any solution of $UCP(A)$ including the columns in $path(A_N)$ is greater or equal to $L(A_N) + |path(A_N)|$. So if we found before a solution $best$ with the same or a smaller number of columns, i.e., $|best| \leq L(A_N) + path(A_N)$ we can stop the recursion and backtrack to the parent node of A_N.

Denote by $K(A_N)$ the value $|best| - L(A_N) - |path(A_N)|$. The condition to stop the recursion is given by $K(A_N) \leq 0$. On the other hand, if $K(A_N)$ has a large positive value, usually it means that $L(A_N)$ is far from the size of a minimal solution to $UCP(A_N)$ and so a lot of branching is expected from A_N before a leaf can be reached.

Suppose that there is no way of improving the solution $best$ in the search tree rooted at A_N, yet $K(A_N)$ is positive. Usually a branch-and-bound algorithm must continue branching. However, there is another way of making $K(A_N)$ negative or zero: it is to improve the lower bound $L(A_N)$.

The first way is "positive", in the sense that the algorithm tries to construct a better solution, and branching columns are chosen in the hope of improving the current best solution. The second way is "negative", in the sense that the algorithm tries to disprove that there is a better solution in the tree rooted at A_N.

To compare the role of "negative" and "positive" ways of search, notice that at the n-th level of the computation tree we can have up to 2^n nodes, i.e., subproblems. It is an experimental fact that usually in the first leaf a solution very close to the minimum one is found, so only few improvements are required to get a minimum solution. Therefore "positive" search will succeed and yield a new better solution only in a few of the 2^n subproblems. In the overwhelming majority of the subproblems "negative" search is more natural. The less frequently the best current solution is improved during the search, the more "negative" search is justified. In turn this is

1092-3152/97 $10.00 © 1997 IEEE

related to how much the solution space is "diversified", i.e., different solutions have different costs. Notice that BAB uses "negative thinking" in optimization problems by finding lower bounds, and in decision problems by checking the consistency of the partial solution with the current subproblem.

To exploit both "positive" and "negative" search, BAB is modified as follows. We start solving the initial problem with "positive thinking" in the ordinary column branching mode, called PT-mode. Then, when the number of subproblems generated in the column branching mode becomes large "enough", each subproblem is solved in the "negative thinking" mode, called NT-mode. In optimization problems modes are switched depending on the ratio of the expected number of improvements to the number of subproblems generated at this level of the search tree. The smaller the ratio, the more appropriate is to switch to the NT-mode.

Let P be a subproblem to be solved in NT-mode and suppose that if the cost of P is greater than a given $ubound$ then solving P cannot give a better solution (w.l.o.g., assume to solve a minimization problem). The aim of the algorithm in the NT-mode is to prove that there is no solution of P with cost less than $ubound$.

We propose a new way to implement "negative thinking": incremental problem solving (IPS). When solving a problem A incrementally, we start with a subproblem A' of A, such that the solutions of A' can be represented compactly. Then we modify gradually A' by making it more complex to come closer to the full problem A and we recompute the set of solutions of the modified problem. When applying "negative thinking", we try to find first the most difficult "obstacles" in the sequence from A' to A with the goal to prove that no solution of A' can overcome the obstacles and be extended to a solution of A.

More precisely, let P' be a subproblem of P such that its set of solutions $Sol(P')$ can be represented in a compact form. Each solution of P' from $Sol(P')$ can be considered as a seed from which one may grow some solutions of P. In the NT-mode, the algorithm tries to show that no solution of P with $cost(P) < ubound$ can grow from any solution $S \in Sol(P')$. A naive approach is to form a sequence of problems $P_1, \cdots, P_n$, where $P_1 = P'$ and $P_n = P$. At each step one recomputes $Sol(P_i)$ starting from $Sol(P_{i-1})$ and discards all solutions in $Sol(P_i)$ with a cost greater than $ubound$. If, after removing the solutions costing more or as $ubound$, $Sol(Pi) = \emptyset$, for some $P_i, i \leq n$, then there is no solution of P with cost less than $ubound$. A direct implementation of this approach has two drawbacks:

1. The size of the representation of $Sol(P_i)$ may grow exponentially.

2. There are different ways of approaching P from P'. Each specific seed solution $S \in Sol(P')$ is extended more quickly to a solution costing more or as $ubound$ by a specific sequence of augmentations, different from those appropriate for another solution $\hat{S} \in Sol(P')$.

As a remedy we propose the paradigm of clusterization of solutions. We group in a cluster the solutions that are similar, in the sense of having the same witnesses of the fact that they cannot produce solutions of P costing less than $ubound$.

In this paper we present an incremental UCP solver called *raiser*. Although we demonstrate our technique on UCP it can be applied to any discrete optimization problems with a monotone cost function, i.e., for which a minimum solution of a subproblem has a smaller cost than that of the initial problem.

The paper is organized as follows. Section 2 shows how an incremental solver is incorporated into the standard branch-and-bound procedure for UCP. The idea of incremental improvement of the lower bound is sketched in Section 3, while Section 4 describes how the solutions of UCP are represented and recomputed. The raising procedure is explained in detail in Section 5 and experimental results are discussed in Section 6. Conclusions are given in Section 7.

2 Incorporating an Incremental Solver into Branch-and-Bound

The flow of a UCP solver based on branch-and-bound is shown in Fig. 1. The parts of text in bold font refer to the incremental solver and will be explained below. For details the reader is referred to [4]. Given a matrix A, existing UCP solvers employ column branching to decompose the problem and use a maximal set of independent (non-intersecting) rows ($MSIR$) to compute a lower bound of $UCP(A)$ (since no column covers two rows from $MSIR$) [1].

```
branch_and_bound(A, Sol, n) {
    /* A = matrix of UCP, Sol = current (partial) solution */
    /* n = "range" of raiser, best = best current solution */
    if (A = ∅)
        return(Sol) /* new best solution */
    /* Column and row dominance */
    simplify(A)
    /* Lower bound evaluation */
    MSIR = find_msir(A)
    if ((lower_bound(A) + cost(Sol)) ≥ cost(best))
        return(∅)
    /* Is the current node within the range of raiser ? */
    if (((|MSIR| + cost(Sol) + n) ≥ cost(best)) {
    /* n' exact amount to raise */
        n' = cost(best) − (|MSIR| + cost(Sol))
        return(raiser(A, MSIR, n'))
    }
    /* select a branching column */
    j = select_column(A)
    /* Decomposition: A1(A2) for including (not including) j
    in solution */
    Sol1 = Sol ∪ {j}
    Sol2 = Sol
    for (i = 1; i ≤ 2; i + +)
        {New = branch_and_bound(Ai, Soli, n)
        if (cost(New) < cost(best)) {
            best = New
            if (cost(best) ≤ (cost(Sol) + |MSIR|)
                return(best)
        }
    }
    return(best)
}
```

Figure 1: Branch-and-Bound enhanced by incremental solver

A procedure n-raiser, performing "negative thinking", is invoked when $MSIR$ is a lower bound not sufficient to prune the subtree rooted at the current node, but increasing the lower bound by n would allow such pruning. The n-raiser starts from the subproblem $UCP(MSIR)$ whose solution space is very regular and then tries to extend it gradually to A. The n-raiser either returns a minimum cost solution of $UCP(A)$, if the lower bound cannot be raised by n, or returns the empty solution.

[1]A lower bounding technique based on linear programming relaxation, as commonly done in ILP, has been tested successfully for solving covering problems and reported in [5].

The parameter n is specified a-priori and is the same for all invocations of *raiser* in the column branching mode. The value of n is usually a small number in the range from 2 to 4 for two reasons:

1. if n is small then the node is deep enough to warrant the application of negative thinking,
2. if n is small then one can make use of the fact that $UCP(MSIR)$ has a regular solution space.

Note that improving the lower bound even by a small amount may lead to considerable runtime reductions. For example, in [1] it was reported a new technique for pruning the search tree called limit lower bound. Sometimes the technique allows to reduce the search tree size by ten times. It can be shown that the limit lower bound technique prunes no more branches of the search tree than *1-raiser*.

The detailed description of the raiser is given in Sections 3, 4 and 5.

3 Incremental Improvement of the Lower Bound

Given an optimization problem such that for any subproblem the cost of a minimum solution of the problem is greater than or equal to that of the subproblem, the size of a minimum solution of the subproblem gives a **lower bound** on the the size of a minimum solution of the problem (called **cost monotonicity assumption**). This fact is of practical interest if it is not difficult to find a minimum solution of the subproblem.

Denote by $min(UCP(A))$ the size of a minimum solution of $UCP(A)$ and let A' be a submatrix of matrix A, consisting of some rows of A, i.e., $Col(A) = Col(A')$ and $Row(A') \subseteq Row(A)$. Any $UCP(A')$ where A' is a submatrix of A satisfies the cost monotonicity assumption, since $min(UCP(A')) \leq min(UCP(A))$. We call **lower bound submatrix** a submatrix A' whose minimum solution is used for evaluating a lower bound for $UCP(A)$. If A' is a $MSIR$ then $min(UCP(A')) = |Row(A')|$. We are now going to describe the idea underlying the method for an incremental improvement of the lower bound.

Denote by $A' + A_r$ the submatrix of A obtained by adding to A' a row $A_r \in Row(A) \setminus Row(A')$. Let S be a solution of $UCP(A)$. A column $j \in S$ is called **redundant** if $S \setminus \{j\}$ is also a solution of $UCP(A)$. If a solution of $UCP(A)$ does not contain redundant columns then it is said to be **irredundant**. Denote by $Sol(A', m)$ the set of solutions of $UCP(A')$ which includes all the irredundant solutions consisting of m or fewer columns. So $Sol(A', m)$ contains all the irredundant solutions of size from $min(UCP(A'))$ to m columns. So if $m = min(UCP(A'))$ then $Sol(A', m)$ gives exactly the set of all minimum solutions of $UCP(A')$.

Suppose that for a lower bound submatrix A' of A we know a set of solutions $Sol(A', m)$. The lower bound given by A' is equal to $m = min(UCP(A'))$. Let us add a row A_p of A to A'. Obviously $Sol(A' + A_p, m) \subseteq Sol(A', m)$, since in general some solutions from $Sol(A', m)$ do not cover A_p and so are not contained in $Sol(A' + A_p, m)$. So after having added a set of rows $A_{i_1}, .., A_{i_k}$ of A to A', we can reach a stage when $Sol(A' + A_{i_1} + .. + A_{i_k}, m) = \emptyset$, meaning that we improved the lower bound for $UCP(A)$ by 1 taking as a lower bound the submatrix $A' + A_{i_1} + .. + A_{i_k}$. If $Sol(A' + A_{i_1} + .. + A_{i_k}, r) = \emptyset, r \geq m$ we improved the lower bound by $r - m + 1$.

So an attractive idea is to start from a submatrix A' which is an $MSIR$ (since the solutions of an $MSIR$ can be represented compactly) and then to add rows to the $MSIR$ with the goal to improve the initial lower bound given by $|MSIR|$. The proposal relies on the intuition that, knowing $Sol(A', m)$, it is not difficult to recalculate $Sol(A' + A_p, m)$ and, adding one row at a time, eventually we may reach the desired lower bound improvement. In Section 4.1 we discuss how to recalculate solutions. This "naive" way of raising the lower bound may require too much memory. In Sections 4.2 and 5 we introduce a technique to avoid the problem: clustering solutions in cubes and branching by clusters.

To motivate the theory that will be developed, we show by an example how to raise the lower bound incrementally. Consider the following matrix A_N that cannot be reduced by dominance.

	0	1	2	3	4	5	6	7	8	9
0	1	1	.	.	.	.	.	.	.	.
1	.	.	1	1	.	.	.	.	.	.
2	.	.	.	.	1	1	.	.	.	.
3	.	.	.	.	.	.	1	1	.	.
4	1	.	.	.	.	.	.	.	1	.
5	.	1	.	.	.	.	.	.	1	.
6	.	.	1	.	.	.	.	.	.	1
7	.	.	.	1	.	.	.	.	.	1
8	.	.	.	.	.	1	1	.	.	.
9	.	.	.	.	1	.	.	1	.	.

Suppose that A_N is the submatrix corresponding to the node N of a column branching search tree, such that the cost of the best solution found is 7 and the partial solution Sol contains 1 column.

An $MSIR$ is made by the 4 rows A_0, A_1, A_2 and A_3. Since $cost(best) - cost(Sol) - |MSIR| = 2$, potentially the lower bound could be raised by 2. The set of irredundant solutions of $UCP(MSIR)$ is equal to $C_0 = \{0, 1\} \times \{2, 3\} \times \{4, 5\} \times \{6, 7\}$. Select row A_4 from the rest of the matrix. The solutions of the matrix made by the rows A_0, A_1, A_2, A_3 and A_4 are represented by the union of the following two sets: $C_1 = \{0\} \times \{2, 3\} \times \{4, 5\} \times \{6, 7\}$ and $C_2 = \{1\} \times \{2, 3\} \times \{4, 5\} \times \{6, 7\} \times \{8\}$.

Consider independently the sets C_1 and C_2 starting with the solutions from C_1. Select row A_5 that is not covered by any solution in C_1. So each solution from C_1 must be augmented by a column covering A_5, which transforms C_1 into $C_1' = \{0\} \times \{2, 3\} \times \{4, 5\} \times \{6, 7\} \times \{1, 8\}$. Note that all solutions in C_1' consist of 5 columns. Now select row A_6. The solutions that have 5 columns, cover A_6, and can be obtained from the solutions in C_1' form the set $C_1'' = \{0\} \times \{2\} \times \{4, 5\} \times \{6, 7\} \times \{1, 8\}$. But no solution in C_1'' covers row A_7 and therefore each solution from the set must be augmented by a column to cover also A_7. It means that no solution from C_1 can be "extended" to a set of ≤ 5 columns covering all rows from A_N.

Consider solutions from C_2. If we select row A_6, then all the solutions that have 5 columns, cover A_6 and can be obtained from the solutions in C_2 form the set $C_2' = \{1\} \times \{2\} \times \{4, 5\} \times \{6, 7\} \times \{8\}$. But no solution in C_2' covers row A_7 and therefore each solution from the set must be augmented by a column to cover also A_7. It means that no solution from C_2 can be "extended" to a set of ≤ 5 columns covering all rows from A_N. So the lower bound is raised to 6 and the branch corresponding to A_N can be pruned.

4 Representation and Recomputation of the Solutions

In order to present the algorithm for raising the lower bound we must describe how the set of solutions of a matrix is represented and updated.

4.1 Recomputation of the Solutions

Let A' be a submatrix of A and A_p a row from $Row(A) \setminus Row(A')$. Let S be a solution of $UCP(A)$. Denote by $O(A_p)$ the set $\{j \mid A_{pj} = 1\}$, i.e., the set of all columns covering A_p and by

$Rec(A' + A_p, S)$ the set of solutions of $UCP(A' + A_p)$ obtained according to the following rules:

1. if S is a solution of $UCP(A'+A_p)$, then $Rec(A'+A_p, S) = \{S\}$;
2. if S is not a solution of $UCP(A' + A_p)$, i.e., no column of S covers A_p then $Rec(A'+A_p, S) = \{S \cup \{j\} \mid j \in O(A_p)\}$.

So $Rec(A' + A_p, S)$ gives the solutions of $UCP(A' + A_p)$ that can be obtained from the solution S of $UCP(A')$. According to 2., if S is not a solution of $UCP(A' + A_p)$, then we obtain $|O(A_p)|$ solutions of $UCP(A' + A_p)$ by adding to S the columns covering A_p.

Theorem 4.1 *For any irredundant solution $S^* \in UCP(A' + A_p)$ there is an irredundant solution $S \in UCP(A')$ such that S^* is an element of $Rec(A' + A_p, S)$.*

The proof of the theorem is omitted for lack of space. There are examples showing that $Rec(A' + A_p, S)$ may contain also redundant solutions.

Corollary 4.1 *Let Sol be a set containing all irredundant solutions of $UCP(A')$. Let $Sol^* = \bigcup_{S \in Sol} Rec(A' + Ap, S)$, then Sol^* contains every irredundant solution $S^* \in UCP(A' + Ap)$.*

Proof. It is a direct consequence of Theorem 4.1. □

4.2 Cubes of Solutions

In line of principle, given the operator *Rec*, one could add one row at a time to A' and build the set of irredundant solutions of $UCP(A)$ from the set of irredundant solutions of $UCP(A')$. This "naive" approach must be discarded because of two disadvantages:

1. The size of the set of irredundant solutions may grow exponentially in the number of added rows.
2. Suppose that we want to raise the lower bound of $MSIR$ by small n and that S is a solution of $UCP(MSIR)$. It may happen that in order to raise S by n we need to add only a small set of rows from $Row(A) \setminus Row(MSIR)$. Denote the set $R(S)$. Let S' be another solution of $UCP(MSIR)$ and suppose that to raise it by n we need to add a small set of rows $R(S')$. The problem is that $R(S)$ and $R(S')$ are usually different. In other words, when we add rows to $MSIR$ we want to add a minimal number of rows which raise all solutions of $MSIR$ by n. But, since these small sets $R(S)$ are usually different for different solutions S from $UCP(MSIR)$, we actually need to add almost all rows.

To solve the previous issues we propose to clusterize solutions that can be raised by the same rows from $Row(A) \setminus Row(MSIR)$. This is achieved by the introduction of *cubes of solutions*, a data structure inspired by multi-valued cubes. Applying the operator *Rec* to a cube of solutions one obtains a collection of cubes of solutions, thereby providing a clusterization of the recomputed solutions. This will support later the design of a raising algorithm based on branching in clusters of solutions, each cluster being one of the recomputed cubes of solutions.

Note however that cubes should not be considered as the only convenient way to clusterize solutions. We believe that studying clusterizations based on different data structures, e.g., binary decision diagrams, will yield interesting results.

As anticipated, we represent the solutions of $UCP(A)$ by sets with a structure of multi-valued cubes [8]. We define a **cube** to be the set $C = D_1 \times \cdots \times D_d$ where $D_i \cap D_j = \emptyset, i \neq j$ and $D_i \subset Col(A)$, $1 \leq i, j \leq d$. The subsets D_i are the **domains** of cube C. So cube C denotes a set of sets consisting of d columns. In contrast to standard cubes used for the representation of multi-valued functions here cubes may have different numbers of domains. For example, if $|Col(A)| = 10$, then sets $C_1 = \{1, 5\} \times \{2, 6, 7\} \times \{3, 4\}$ and $C_2 = \{1\} \times \{2, 4\} \times \{3, 7\} \times \{5, 6, 10\}$ are both cubes.

Let A' be a $MSIR$ of A. The set of all irredundant solutions (which are at the same time minimum) of $UCP(A')$ can be represented as the cube $O(A_{i_1}) \times \cdots \times O(A_{i_d})$, where $A_{i_1}, \cdots, A_{i_d}$ are the rows forming A'.

Let A' be a submatrix of A and A_p be a row from $Row(A) \setminus Row(A')$. Let $C = D_1 \times \cdots \times D_d$ be a cube of solutions of $UCP(A')$. From the definition of the *Rec* operator it follows that

$$Rec(A' + A_p, C) = part1(C) \cup part2(C) \times O(A_p) \quad (1)$$

where $part1(C)$ is the set of solutions contained in C which cover A_p and $part2(C)$ is the set of solutions contained in C which do not cover A_p.

There are three cases:

1. If $D_i \subseteq O(A_p)$ for some i, $1 \leq i \leq d$, then any solution from C covers the row A_p and so $Rec(A' + A_p, C) = C$.
2. If $O(A_p) \cap D_i = \emptyset$ for any i, $1 \leq i \leq d$, then no solution from C covers A_p and so $Rec(A'+A_p, C) = C \times O(A_p) = D_1 \times \cdots \times D_d \times O(A_p)$.
3. If 1. and 2. are not true, i.e., no D_i is a subset of $O(A_p)$ and $O(A_p)$ intersects at least one domain (without loss of generality, we assume that A_p intersects the first r domains, i.e., $D_1, \cdots, D_r$), then cube C can be partitioned into the following $r + 1$ pairwise not intersecting cubes:

$$C_1 = D_1 \cap O(A_p) \times D_2 \times \cdots \times D_d$$

$$C_2 = D_1 \setminus O(A_p) \times D_2 \cap O(A_p) \times D_3 \times \cdots \times D_d$$

$$C_3 = D_1 \setminus O(A_p) \times D_2 \setminus O(A_p) \times D_3 \cap O(A_p) \times \times D_4 \times \cdots \times D_d$$

$$\cdots \quad (2)$$

$$C_r = D_1 \setminus O(A_p) \times \cdots \times D_{r-1} \setminus O(A_p) \times \times D_r \cap O(A_p) \times D_{r+1} \times \cdots \times D_d$$

$$C_{r+1} = D_1 \setminus O(A_p) \times \cdots \times D_{r-1} \setminus O(A_p) \times D_r \setminus O(A_p) \times D_{r+1} \times \cdots \times D_d$$

It is not hard to check that the union $C_1 \cup \cdots \cup C_{r+1}$ gives the cube C and that for any pair $C_i, C_j, i \neq j, C_i \cap C_j = \emptyset$. Moreover, the first r cubes give the solutions of $UCP(A')$ from C which cover A_p and the cube C_{r+1} gives the solutions of $UCP(A')$ from C which do not cover A_p. Therefore

$$part1(C) = C_1 \cup \cdots \cup C_r, \quad part2(C) = C_{r+1}. \quad (3)$$

Equations 1–3 realize the *Rec* operator as defined in Section 4.1 and characterized by Theorem 4.1. Notice that here we force the *Rec* operator to generate non-intersecting cubes of solutions; this is not a consequence of the definition of *Rec*, but is an additional requirement introduced now to avoid considering the same partial solution in more than one branch.

We mentioned that in the computation of *Rec* some redundant solutions may be introduced. The following revised definition of *Rec* avoids the generation of obviously redundant solutions obtained from the application of formula (1). Namely, any solution S' of $UCP(A' + A_p)$ from $part2(C) \times O(A_p)$ that strictly contains a solution S'' of $UCP(A' + A_p)$ from $part1(C)$ is redundant since it contains more columns than S''.

Theorem 4.2 *If the computation of the Rec operator is modified as follows:*

$$Rec(A' + A_p, C) = part1(C) \cup part2(C) \times \times[O(A_p) \setminus (D_1 \cup \cdots \cup D_d)] \quad (4)$$

no irredundant solution of $A' + A_p$ is discarded.

The proof of the theorem is omitted for lack of space.

5 The Raising Procedure

5.1 Overview of the Raising Algorithm

As anticipated in Section 2, we propose an *n-raiser* procedure which is called in the column branching mode as described in Fig. 1. Let A be the covering matrix corresponding to the node where n-raiser is invoked and A' be an $MSIR$ of A. We start with the set of irredundant solutions of $UCP(A')$, represented by the cube $C = O(A_{i_1}) \times \cdots \times O(A_{i_d})$, in which $A_{i_1}, \cdots, A_{i_d}$ are the rows in the $MSIR$. Then choose a "good" row of A from those not in A', say row A_p. According to Equations (1–5), $Rec(MSIR(A) + A_p, C)$ can be represented by $r+1$ cubes where r is the number of rows of the $MSIR(A)$ intersecting A_p. Then perform recursively the process for each of the $r+1$ cubes, i.e., choose a new row from those not yet selected for each of the $r+1$ cubes of solutions and split each cube according to Equations (1–5).

The process can be described by a search tree, called **cube branching tree**. The initial cube of solutions C corresponds to the root node, to which we associate also a pair of matrices $MSIR(A)$ and $A - MSIR(A)$ (i.e., matrix A without the rows of $MSIR(A)$). In each node a choice of an unselected row from the second matrix of the node is made. The chosen row is removed from the second matrix of the pair and added to the first matrix of the pair. So the first matrix gives a "lower bound submatrix" for the node.

The number of branches leaving a node is equal to the number of cubes in which the cube corresponding to the node is partitioned by the *Rec* operation, and each child of a node gets one of the cubes obtained after splitting. So the cube corresponding to a node represents a set of solutions covering the first submatrix of the pair.

The flow of *n-raiser* is shown in Fig. 2. The recursion terminates if one of the two following conditions hold:

1. There is a node such that there are no rows left in the second matrix of the pair and the corresponding cube has k domains, where $k < |MSIR| + n$. This means that the lower bound $|MSIR|$ cannot be improved by n and any solution from $Cube$ consists of fewer columns than the current best one, since *n-raiser* is invoked if $|MSIR| + n + cost(Sol) = cost(best)$ where Sol is the partial solution found in the column branching mode before invoking the raiser. Then a solution from $Cube$ is selected as the current best and the range of raiser is reduced to $n - (cost(old\_best) - cost(best))$ since the gap between the current best solution and $MSIR$ is reduced.

2. From all branches, nodes are reached corresponding to cubes with a number of domains greater than $|MSIR| + n$. In this case the lower bound has been raised to $|MSIR| + n$, since no solution S of $UCP(A)$ exists such that $|S| \leq |MSIR| + n$.

If neither pruning condition holds the procedure *raise_or_trim* is invoked to address the following two cases, which let us modify the cube of solutions without branching:

1. If a row A_p exists such that no solution from $Cube$ covers A_p, then there is no splitting of the cube, since *Rec* yields only one cube $C \times O(A_p)$. Row A_p is removed from A'' and added to A'.

2. If there exists a row A_p intersecting only one domain D_i of $Cube$ and the number of domains in $Cube$ is equal to $|MSIR| + n - 1$ then only two cubes are generated after splitting. The first cube is from $part1(Cube)$ and is obtained by reducing domain D_i to $D_i \cap O(A_p)$. The second cube has one more domain and can be discarded since the total number of domains in the cube is $|MSIR| + n$. Row A_p is removed from A'' and added to A'.

The previous conditions are checked in $raise\_or\_trim$ by iterating through the rows of A'' until both conditions are false for any row from A''.

After all these special cases have been addressed, a new row A_p is selected by $select\_row$. The row A_p is removed from A and drives the splitting of $Cube$. The strategy to select the best row in order to split the current $Cube$, before calling recursively $raiser$, looks for the row of A which intersects the minimum number of domains of $Cube$. The reason is to reduce the number of branches from the node, i.e., the number of domains intersecting the row to be added plus 1. In case of ties between different rows, the row having the highest weight is chosen. The weight of a row A_p is defined as:

$$\prod_{k=1}^{m} \frac{|D'_{i_k}|}{|D_{i_k}|}$$

where m is the number of domains of $Cube$ intersecting A_p, D_{i_k} is a domain intersected by A_p and $D'_{i_k} = D_{i_k} \setminus O(A_p)$. So the weight of A_p is just the fraction of solutions from $Cube$ that do not cover A_p, which we want to maximize when selecting a new row. If $D'_{i_k} = \emptyset$, for some k, this means that A_p is covered by any solution from $Cube$. Such a row is simply removed from A'' and added to A'.

5.2 Correctness of n-raiser

The correctness of the n-raiser procedure, applied to matrix A with lower bound $|MSIR(A)|$, can be argued using the notions of *subsolution* or *partial solution* and of *complete set of solutions*, introduced as follows.

A set S' of columns of A is a **subsolution** or **partial solution** of $UCP(A)$ if it is a solution of a subproblem A', but is not a solution of $UCP(A)$.

Let C be the cube of subsolutions corresponding to $MSIR(A)$, then C has the property that for any solution S of $UCP(A)$ there is a subsolution from C which is contained in S. Indeed, since S covers all the rows of A, including those contained in $MSIR(A)$, then S contains $|MSIR(A)|$ columns covering the submatrix $MSIR(A)$ that form a subsolution from C. A set of subsolutions is **complete** if for any solution S of $UCP(A)$ there is a subsolution from the set which is contained in S. So the set of subsolutions contained in the cube C is complete.

Let S' be a solution of subproblem $UCP(A')$. Denote by $Gen(S')$ the set of irredundant solutions of $UCP(A)$ that contain S'. Similarly, if C is a set of partial solutions, denote by $Gen(C)$ the set of irredundant solutions of $UCP(A)$, each of which contains a solution from C.

Lemma 5.1 *Let S' be a solution of $UCP(A')$ and A_p be a row from $Row(A) \setminus Row(A')$. Then $Gen(S') \subseteq Gen(Rec(A' + A_p, S'))$ where Rec is the recalculation operation defined in Section 4.1.*

Proof. Let S be a solution of $UCP(A)$ containing S', i.e., $S \in Gen(S')$. If S' covers row A_p then $Rec(A' + A_p, S')$ is equal to $\{S'\}$ and so $Gen(Rec(A' + A_p, S'))$ contains S. If S' does not cover A_p, then $Rec(A' + A_p, S')$ contains every solution $S' \cup \{j\}$, $j \in O(A_p)$. Moreover, S contains S' and, since it covers A_p, it obviously contains a column $j \in O(A_p)$. So again

```
/* n-raiser returns an empty solution if lower bound of
UCP(A) can be raised to |MSIR| + n. If not, it returns
a current minimum solution of UCP(A) */

raiser(A', A'', Cube, n) {
    /* A' = MSIR, A'' = A - A', Cube = solutions of
    UCP(MSIR) */
    /* Cost of solutions from Cube exceeds lower bound by n */
    if (number_of_domains(Cube) > |MSIR| + n)
        return(∅)
    /* No rows to add ? */
    if (A'' = ∅) {
        /* Extract new best solution */
        best = extract(Cube)
        /* Recalculate range of raiser */
        n' = n - (cost(Old_best) - cost(best))
        n = n'
        return(best)
    }

    /* Process rows that do not split Cube */
    raise_or_trim(A', A'', Cube)
    /* Select a row to add */
    A_j = select_row(Cube, A'')
    A' = A' + A_j; A'' = A' - A_j
    /* split Cube. Note that Cube_{r+1} has one more domain */
    Cube = Cube_1 ∪ ··· ∪ Cube_r ∪ Cube_{r+1}
    /* Call raiser recursively */
    for (i = 1; i ≤ (r + 1); i + +) {
        New_sol = raiser(A', A'', Cube_i, n)
        if (cost(New_sol) < cost(best))
            best = New_sol
    }
    return(best)
}
```

Figure 2: *n-raiser* algorithm

$Gen(Rec(A' + A_p, S'))$ contains S. □

From Lemma 5.1 it follows that the *Rec* operation preserves the completness of a set of subsolutions.

Theorem 5.1 *The n-raiser procedure finds correctly a larger lower bound or a smaller upper bound.*

Proof. n-raiser starts with the set of solutions of $UCP(MSIR)$, which is a complete set of partial solutions of $UCP(A)$. Since the *Rec* operation preserves completness, the set of all "boundary" cubes, i.e., cubes corresponding to either leaf nodes of the search tree or to the nodes not yet split, is a complete set of partial solutions. When we apply an n-raiser to A we actually try to find a complete set of partial solutions containing at least $|MSIR(A)|+n$ columns. If such a set is found then no solution of $UCP(A)$ has less than $|MSIR(A)| + n$ columns, and so the procedure n-raiser succeeds in increasing the lower bound by n.

Suppose that there is no complete set of partial solutions consisting of at least $|MSIR(A)|+n$ columns. It means that n-raiser finds a leaf node with a cube containing solutions of $|MSIR(A)| + n'$ columns where $n' < n$. In that case we update the n-raiser into an n'-raiser and continue the search. If the n'-raiser succeeds we return a solution of $|MSIR(A)| + n'$ columns which is minimal.

If the n'-raiser fails then there is a solution of $UCP(A)$ consisting of $|MSIR(A)| + n''$ columns, where $n'' < n'$. Then we update the n'-raiser into an n''-raiser and continue the search. □

6 Experimental Results

We have implemented a program AURA to solve UCP and we have compared it with the routine *mincov* available in ESPRESSO, with MINCOV_LLB, that is our implementation of some features of SCHERZO and with the results of the real SCHERZO implemented by O. Coudert. The program SCHERZO is the most effective solver of UCP currently reported. Its main features have been described in the literature [3, 2, 1]; they include a better heuristic selection of the $MSIR$, logarithmic lower bound, left hand side lower bound, limit lower bound, and partition-based pruning. Of these features we have implemented in MINCOV_LLB, to the best of our understanding of the original description, the following two: better heuristic selection of the $MSIR$ and limit lower bound. The limit lower bound is a major novelty of SCHERZO, which accounts for strong savings in the number of nodes of the computation tree compared to the original *mincov* of ESPRESSO.

The benchmarks belong to three different classes: in Table 1 there are difficult cases from the collection of ESPRESSO (we start from the matrix obtained by ESPRESSO after removing the essential primes), in Table 2 there are random generated matrices with varying row/column ratios and densities, in Table 3 there are matrices encoding constraints satisfaction problems from [9]. The experiments have been performed with a 2GB 300Mhz Alpha with timeout set to 3 days of cputime.

The tables report two types of data for comparison: the number of nodes of the column branching computation tree and the running time. About the number of nodes we clarify that

1. AURA has two types of nodes: those of the column branching computation tree and those of the cube branching computation tree (called A-nodes in the tables). Indeed AURA follows a dual strategy, i.e., it builds the column branching computation tree, but when at a node the difference between the upper bound and the lower bound is less or equal to the raising parameter r (or $maxRaiser$), AURA calls the procedure $raiser$ which builds a cube branching computation tree, appended at the node where $raiser$ was called. So we need to report both numbers of nodes to measure a run of AURA.

2. Nodes of the cube branching computation tree usually take much less computing time than those of the column branching computation tree, even though it is not known a-priori a time ratio between the two types of nodes. The reason is that in each node of the column branching mode expensive procedures for finding dominance relations and the $MSIR$ are applied.

3. The raising parameter is an input to AURA. Currently we have experimented with some values and we report in the tables the value used in a specific run. The higher is the raising parameter, the fewer column branching nodes compared to cube branching nodes there will be. With a value high enough, there will be a single column node and the rest will be all row nodes.

We compared also with the real SCHERZO, whose author was kind enough to run for us the examples. There is a large gap in many cases between the results of SCHERZO and those of MINCOV_LLB, which is our implementation of a subset of SCHERZO. A major reason may be that our reimplementation of the better heuristic selection of the $MSIR$, even though it follows the hint given by Coudert, in practice does not mimic well enough the one in SCHERZO; moreover, as already said, SCHERZO features additional improvements that we did not implement. It is important to underline that:

1. both AURA and MINCOV_LLB exploit the same re-implementation of Coudert's better heuristic selection of the $MSIR$;

2. AURA could be improved noticeably by reproducing more successfully the better heuristic selection of the $MSIR$ or any other feature of SCHERZO. In other words, AURA demonstrates a dual search technique, which may benefit from other improvements to standard branch and bound.

3. in overall SCHERZO has been implemented more efficiently, as magnified also by the circumstance that it is comparatively faster on a slower machine.

The experiments show that AURA outperforms ESPRESSO and MINCOV_LLB. It is always faster and in the most difficult examples either it has a running time advantage up to two orders of magnitude or the other programs fail due to timeout (3 days) or spaceout (2G). Instead SCHERZO is a very tough competitor, which is faster on the examples from Table 1, but has a less effective pruning strategy in those of Tables 2 and 3, partially compensated by a better $MSIR$. The example *saucier.t* is an extreme case where the virtues of AURA prevail. Recently O. Coudert kindly provided us with a copy of SCHERZO, to let us analyze in depth the comparative features of the two programs. We will report on the study as soon as done. We expect to transfer to AURA the better computation of the $MSIR$ apparently implemented in SCHERZO.

We do not have a systematic comparison with the results by BCU, a recent ILP-based covering solver [5]. However, the intuition is that an algorithm based on linear programming is better suited for problems with a solution space diversified in the costs, i.e., for problems which are "closer" to numerical ones. To test the conjecture we asked the authors of [5] to run BCU on *saucier.t*, whose solution space is poorly diversified (a minimum solution has 6 columns, while most of the irredundant solutions cost in the range from 6 to 8). BCU ran out of memory after 20000 seconds of computations (the information was kindly provided by S.Liao), while AURA completed the example in less than 3 minutes.

7 Conclusions

We have introduced a new technique to solve exactly a discrete optimization problem, based on the paradigm of "negative" thinking. The motivation is that when searching the space of solutions often a good solution is reached quickly and then it is improved only a few times before the optimum is found; so most of the solution space is explored to certify optimality, but it does not yield any improvement in the cost function. This suggests that more powerful lower bounding would speed up the search dramatically, as shown by the introduction of the limit lower bound [3]. Our approach is more radical because when we are dealing with a subspace of solutions unlikely to improve the upper bound, we switch the search strategy to a different one geared to raise the lower bound. To design a search strategy which realizes negative thinking we introduced *cubes of solutions*, a data structure inspired by multi-valued cubes. Applying the operator *Rec* to a cube of solutions one obtains a collection of cubes of solution, thereby providing a natural clustering of the recomputed solutions. As argued in the paper, clustering is required to design a recursive algorithm based on branching in subsets of solutions and allows the lower bound to be raised independently starting from different subsets of solutions.

For illustration we applied our technique to the unate covering problem, usually solved exactly by a branch-and-bound procedure, where one lower bounds by means of an independent set of rows, and branches on columns. We have designed a dual search technique, called $raiser$, which is invoked when the difference between the upper bound and the lower bound is within a parameter $maxRaiser$, that we are free to set. The procedure $raiser$ tries to detect a hard core of the matrix to be solved (lower bound submatrix), augmenting an independent set of rows in order to increase incrementally the cardinality of the minimum solutions that cover it. Eventually either this incremental raising yields a lower bound that matches the current upper bound and so we are done, or we produce a better solution. $Raiser$ defines a computation tree whose nodes have associated a lower bound submatrix and a cube of solutions. The selection of a next row induces the recomputation of all the solutions of the lower bound submatrix augmented by the next row, as disjoint cubes of solutions. Each such cube together with the augmented matrix defines a new node; operationally $raiser$ calls itself recursively passing as parameters each such disjoint cube of solutions and the augmented lower bound submatrix. It would be interesting to explore a mixed approach where one accumulates some cubes of solutions at the same node and fewer recursive calls are made, trading off time vs. memory.

The reported experiments show that our program AURA, outperforms ESPRESSO and MINCOV_LLB, which is the algorithm in ESPRESSO enhanced by our implementation of Coudert's limit lower bound. The package SCHERZO is faster than AURA on the examples from Table 1, but it has a less effective pruning strategy in those of Tables 2 and 3, partially compensated by a better $MSIR$.

Future work includes a more careful study of some algorithmic design issues, like the selection of the next row, trading-off number of nodes vs. number of cubes stored in a node, and setting automatically and adaptively the raiser parameter.

A more basic line of research is the exploration of data structures different from cubes since the latter are just the simplest way of representing sets of partial solutions. We believe that studying various ways of representing implicitly sets of solutions is a promising direction of investigation to rescue branch-and-bound from its current limits. Another important direction of future research is to apply the negative thinking approach to other problems.

References

[1] O. Coudert. Two-level logic minimization: an overview. *Integration*, 17-2:97–140, October 1994.

[2] O. Coudert. On solving binate covering problems. In *The Proceedings of the Design Automation Conference*, pages 197–202, June 1996.

[3] O. Coudert and J.C. Madre. New ideas for solving covering problems. In *The Proceedings of the Design Automation Conference*, pages 641–646, June 1995.

[4] T. Kam, T. Villa, R. Brayton, and A. Sangiovanni-Vincentelli. *Synthesis of FSMs: functional optimization*. Kluwer Academic Publishers, 1996.

[5] S. Liao and S. Devadas. Solving covering problems using LPR-based lower bounds. In *The Proceedings of the Design Automation Conference*, June 1997.

[6] J.-K. Rho and F. Somenzi. Stamina. *Computer Program*, 1991.

[7] R. Rudell. Espresso. *Computer Program*, 1987.

[8] R. Rudell and A. Sangiovanni-Vincentelli. Multiple-valued minimization for PLA optimization. *IEEE Transactions on Computer-Aided Design*, CAD-6:727–750, September 1987.

[9] Tiziano Villa. *Encoding Problems in Logic Synthesis*. PhD thesis, University of California, Berkeley, Electronics Research Laboratory, May 1995. Memorandum No. UCB/ERL M95/41.

matrix	R × C (Sparsity)	Sol.	ESPRESSO		SCHERZO		MINCOV_LLB		AURA		
			nodes	time	nodes	time	nodes	time	nodes/A-nodes	time	r
exps	680 × 696 (1.2%)	76	13	0.0	na	na	13	0.0	13/0	0.0	3
fout	177 × 431 (2.4%)	38	161	1.3	na	na	49	0.7	18/44	0.2	2
max512	559 × 515 (1.3%)	113	111	1.4	na	na	25	0.4	19/25	0.4	3
addm4	832 × 1073 (0.6%)	165	121	3.6	na	na	29	1.1	17/11	0.6	2
mlp4	530 × 594 (0.99%)	109	2122	22.6	24	0.1	153	4.3	34/206	1.3	3
pdc	6904 × 19021 (0.34%)	94	195	62.7	44	6.1	88	58	41/132	52.9	3
lin.rom	1030 × 1076 (0.9%)	120	370	29.1	238	4.7	106	10.1	61/240	7.7	3
ex5	831 × 2428 (2%)	37	-	time	616091	2450.5	597644	214300	155/169245	1315.2	4
prom2	1924 × 2611 (0.31%)	278	-	time	25993	5149.2	-	time	1478/1097624	24071.4	3
max1024	1090 × 1264 (0.52%)	245	-	time	531618	9583.6	-	time	12402/3850628	36240	3

Table 1: Results from *Espresso Benchmarks*

matrix	R × C (Sparsity)	Sol.	ESPRESSO		SCHERZO		MINCOV_LLB		AURA		
			nodes	time	nodes	time	nodes	time	nodes/A-nodes	time	r
tc.90	50 × 100 (90%)	2	135	2.6	2	0.0	3	0.3	3/1	0.1	3
tc.70	50 × 100 (70%)	2	135	3.5	2	0.0	3	0.2	3/1	0.1	3
tc.50	50 × 100 (50%)	3	2569	13.9	107	0.6	107	2.3	5/32	0.1	3
tc.30	50 × 100 (30%)	4	12047	37.8	65	0.3	1061	7.1	11/203	0.2	3
tc.10	50 × 99 (10%)	8	843	3.3	90	0.1	131	0.7	17/166	0.1	3
tr.10	100 × 50 (20%)	8	12466	59.6	2077	4.1	2232	21.1	94/2529	2.9	3
tr.20	100 × 50 (40%)	5	16905	49	1823	3.9	2193	19.2	31/951	1.7	3
tr.30	100 × 50 (60%)	3	947	9.5	63	0.9	61	3.4	5/26	0.3	3
tr.40	100 × 50 (80%)	2	73	4.3	2	0.0	3	0.6	3/1	0.3	3
ts.90	100 × 100 (90%)	2	175	21.2	2	0.0	3	2.6	3/1	1	3
ts.70	100 × 100 (70%)	3	5083	47.0	167	5.3	163	15.8	5/112	0.7	3
ts.50	100 × 100 (50%)	4	66147	316.4	4011	20.2	3137	67.3	7/1030	1.6	3
ts.30	100 × 100 (30%)	5	116307	792.8	1752	8.5	8997	139.6	35/1108	2.5	3
ts.10	100 × 100 (10%)	12	-	time	95573	187.3	175255	1255.1	5043/201091	129.3	3

Table 2: Results from *Random Generated Matrices*

matrix	R × C (Sparsity)	Sol.	ESPRESSO		SCHERZO		MINCOV_LLB		AURA		
			nodes	time	nodes	time	nodes	time	nodes/A-nodes	time	r
bbara.t	45 × 26 (41%)	7	61	0.02	0	0.0	7	0	7/2	0	3
dk512x.t	91 × 59 (45%)	6	213	0.24	55	0.0	57	0.15	9/24	0.04	3
ex4inp.t	91 × 240 (46%)	5	5279	16.81	17	0.3	19	0.66	9/14	0.27	3
ex5inp.t	36 × 34 (48%)	4	64	0.05	4	0.0	6	0.01	6/2	0.01	3
ex6inp.t	28 × 96 (48%)	4	639	0.54	35	0.0	103	0.28	7/23	0.03	3
maincont.t	105 × 67 (35%)	7	504	0.69	68	0.0	101	0.4	11/12	0.06	3
opus.t	45 × 63 (45%)	5	121	0.1	7	0.0	5	0.01	5/2	0.01	3
ricks.t	78 × 363 (47%)	5	20	0.37	10	0.2	12	0.36	8/43	0.33	3
saucier.t	171 × 6207 (47%)	6	-	mem	186927	5441.0	-	mem	10/76	222.47	3

Table 3: Results from *Encoding Problem Matrices*

SESSION 2B

CODE GENERATION AND PROCESSOR DESIGN

Moderators:

P.A. Subrahmanyam, Stanford University, Stanford, CA

Rolf Ernst, Technical University Braunschweig, Braunschweig, Germany

DSP Address Optimization Using A Minimum Cost Circulation Technique

Catherine Gebotys
Department of Electrical and Computer Engineering,
University of Waterloo, Waterloo, Ont N2L 3G1 Canada

This paper presents a new approach to solving the DSP address assignment problem. A minimum cost circulation approach is used to efficiently generate high performance addressing code in polynomial time. Addressing code size improvements of up to 7 times are obtained, accounting for up to 1.6 times improvement in code size and performance of compiler-generated DSP code. Results also show that memory layout has a small effect on code size and performance when optimal addressing is used. This research is important for industry since this value-added technique can improve code size, power dissipation and performance, without increasing cost.

1. Introduction

As DSP applications are rapidly growing more complex, some designers are moving from full custom digital circuitry to programmable processors or in-house cores to obtain lower risk solutions. The DSP core is a DSP processor that can be reused and combined with program/data memory, dedicated logic, plus ASICs, and incorporated onto a large silicon chip, providing a cost efficient and flexible solution for many typical embedded applications requiring low power and high reliability. These systems demand small code size and high performance. Due to increasing complexities, high level compilation is a necessity. However the biggest drawback to both DSP processors or DSP core use is the code generation.

The use of conventional code generation techniques and even compilers specifically designed for commercial DSP processors produce very inefficient code [1,2]. There are many more limitations placed upon code generation for the DSP processor than for the general purpose processor. The difficulty arises from non-homogeneous register sets, small number of very specialized registers, very specialized functional units, restricted connectivity, limited addressing, and highly irregular datapaths[1].

Limited addressing modes and the use of address registers are also typical. For example many DSP processors assume auto-increment/decrement addressing modes for sequential accessing of data variables from memory will be used heavily. In particular there are a number of index registers which point to addresses in memory. The addresses in the index registers can be incremented or decremented at negligible cost. However adding or subtracting offsets (not equal to zero or one) to these index registers requires a specific instruction and therefore has a performance, code size, and energy dissipation cost associated with it. The auto-increment/decrement addressing subsumes address arithmetic instructions and requires shorter instructions[2] than other forms of addressing. Unfortunately it is assumed that efficient data memory layout has been performed to support this type of addressing. Given that these DSP processors must meet tight timing requirements using very small code space (all on chip ROM), the code generation problem is a very difficult one[2]. Typically DSP processors are difficult to use requiring long product development times (using a large number of assembler programmers) even though the program may be less than 1K program ROM. The need for decreasing time to market, development costs, and maintenance costs, demands the use of high level language compilation. All of these factors imply several challenges in writing efficient code generators for such DSP processors. This is even more difficult for in-house core instruction set architecture which requires retargetable compilation.

2. Problem Description and Related Work

The following problem, problem 1 given below, is an important part of the code optimization problem that will be studied in this paper. For simplicity let us assume that an algorithm to implement the application has already been assigned based upon accuracy required, low energy implementation, etc.. The algorithm is composed of basic blocks, which are given as a partially ordered list of code operations. For the problem definition below we assume that there is one target DSP processor or core defined with an instruction set architecture. The target processor supports indirect addressing, in particular there is one or more index registers which point to an address in memory and whose value can be incremented or decremented at negligible cost. Data layout is performed by using the approach described in [2] for single offset assignment layout or by a compiler or user.

Problem 1. Assume we are given initial code generated for the target processor and a memory layout (or sequence) of the data variables. Given the number of index registers in the target processor and the costs of loading an index register with a new value, and adding/subtracting a value to/from the index registers, the problem is to generate addressing code such that performance is maximized and the code size and estimated energy cost is minimum.

The performance and code size costs are exact measures of how many extra cycles or instructions will be required. By minimizing the number of instructions generated we are also minimizing energy dissipation. However the problem should also support instruction level power models[5]. Extensions to this problem also include supporting

1092-3152/97 $10.00 © 1997 IEEE

addressing with fixed offset whose value is stored in a index register in addition to the auto-increment/decrement addressing.

Although many researchers have studied code generation for DSP processors or ASIPs [1], fewer have studied address generation. Researchers in [2] defined the single (and general) offset assignment problem and used a modification of Kruskal's algorithm[7] within a recursive algorithm (later extended by [2]), to modify memory layout for reduced code size. Researchers in [4] introduced a C code transformation approach to make better use of address calculation units. Address generation has been shown to account for a large percent of energy dissipation in [3] and researchers have studied instruction-level power models[5].

In this manuscript a new approach is presented to solve problem 1, DSP address code generation. Unlike previous research, we study the problem of given a data layout in memory, generate optimal addressing code to minimize code size, or maximize performance. This is a valued added approach, that can be used to improve any compiler generated DSP code by returning the code optimized for addressing or it can be used in combination with a data memory layout technique such as [2,9] to further optimize code generation. It supports cases where the data memory layout may be predefined at an interface with another processor or external I/O in the system. A minimum cost circulation technique is used to obtain optimal solutions in polynomial time.

The following terminology will be used in this paper: $AR=\{AR1,..ARn\}$ the set of n index registers. $|AR|=$ the number of index registers (n) in the processor. v_t means that data variable v is accessed at time t. This access may be a read or write. $d(v)$ is the memory address for variable v. $G=(V,A)$ is a graph G composed of vertices V and arcs A. $x_{i\rightarrow j}$ is the flow from vertex i to vertex j, where $i,j\varepsilon V$ and $i\rightarrow j\varepsilon A$. $c_{i\rightarrow j}$ is the capacity on arc $i\rightarrow j$. $e_{i\rightarrow j}$ is the cost of flow on arc $i\rightarrow j$. The next section will provide an introduction to minimum cost circulation. The following sections, will show how the DSP addressing code generation is mapped into a circulation problem and provide examples to illustrate the technique. Finally examples will be presented to explore the impact of data layout on addressing code generation.

3. Introduction to Circulations

To introduce the circulation problem, we will first discuss network flow and it's extension to circulations. The network flow problem is defined on a directed acyclic graph, G, composed of vertices and arcs, $G=(V,A)$, where each arc has a capacity associated with it. The capacity is a real valued quantity where arc $i\rightarrow j$, $i,j\varepsilon V$, has an associated capacity $c_{i\rightarrow j}$. Let the variable, $x_{i\rightarrow j}$, represent the flow in arc $i\rightarrow j$. We will call this the flow variable. For any vertex in the graph the flow into the vertex is equal to the flow out of the vertex (known as the conservation of flow [7]). The flow along any arc (in the same direction as the arc) must be positive valued (and also may be greater than or equal to a positive lower bound placed on that arc) but less than or equal to the capacity of that arc. There are two special vertices in this graph called vertex S and vertex T. The flow out of vertex S is equal to the flow into vertex T. Arcs incident to S only leave vertex S and arcs incident to vertex T only are directed into vertex T. The maximum flow problem [7] is to find the maximum amount of flow from vertex S to vertex T through the network graph, such that the conservation of flow is maintained.

To study the minimum cost circulation problem[7] we add an arc from vertex T to vertex S (that circulates the flow in the graph). Each arc has a cost which is also a real valued quantity where arc $i\rightarrow j$ has associated cost $e_{i\rightarrow j}$. The problem is to find the flow through this graph with the minimum cost such that the sum over all arcs of the multiplication of the flow in each arc and the cost of each arc is minimum. The following equations represent the formulation of the minimum cost circulation problem as a mathematical programming problem.

$$\text{Minimize} \sum_{i\rightarrow j} e_{i\rightarrow j}x_{i\rightarrow j} \ \text{Subject to} \sum_{i|i\rightarrow j} x_{i\rightarrow j} - \sum_{k|j\rightarrow k} x_{j\rightarrow k} = 0,\ \forall j,j\varepsilon V.$$

$$0\leq l_{i\rightarrow j} \leq x_{i\rightarrow j} \leq c_{i\rightarrow j},\ \forall(i\rightarrow j)\varepsilon A, i,j\varepsilon V.$$

In the problem above, the capacities $c_{i\rightarrow j},\forall(i\rightarrow j)\varepsilon A$ and costs $e_{i\rightarrow j},\forall(i\rightarrow j)\varepsilon A$ are given. The problem is to solve for values of $x_{i\rightarrow j}$ that represent the flows in the network graph, $G=(V,A)$, such that the objective function is minimum. As long as the capacities and the lower bounds on flow ($l_{i\rightarrow j}$), are integer, we can be guaranteed of obtaining integer flows in the solution of this problem [7]. This problem can be solved in polynomial time using linear programming or more commonly by using faster and more efficient network algorithms[7].

4. Methodology and Modeling

This section will briefly describe the methodology for DSP address optimization, problem 1, and how the minimum cost circulation formulation is used to solve problem 1. First an algorithm or task flow graph is selected for the application based upon cost, performance and energy dissipation requirements and transformations are performed. Initial code generation is performed and a memory layout specified by the compiler or generated post process similar to the technique in [2,10] is performed. Finally the minimum cost circulation approach is applied to generate addressing code. The two sections below will describe in detail how the minimum cost network flow is used to solve problem 1.

To model problem 1 as a circulation problem, we first have to develop a graph, as shown in figure 1. The memory layout (used as x-axis in figure 1b)) along with the variable access sequence (the y-axis in figure 1b)) is used to form the graph. For example the x-axis in figure 1b) corresponds to storing data variables bi, br (shared with ci

), *ar* (shared with *cr*), and *ai* from left to right. The y-axis (from top to bottom) represents the access of data variables *ar*, *br*, *bi*, *ai*, *ar*, *cr*, *ai*, *br*, and *ci*, as defined in figure 1a) code. Each vertex in the graph (placed in the appropriate x-y coordinate in figure 1) represents a variable access in the initial code sequence (figure 1a)), $v_t \varepsilon V$, $t \varepsilon \{1,2,...x\}$. Vertices S and T are added to the graph representing times 0 and $x+1$ respectively. Arcs from the S vertex to all vertices in the graph (except vertex T) are added. Arcs from each vertex v_t to all other vertices accessed after time t (including vertex T) are also added. All of these arcs are not shown in figure 1b). Finally one more arc from vertex T to vertex S is added. Next, capacities and costs are assigned to each arc in the network flow graph and the minimum cost flow problem is solved. The capacity of all arcs is one except the arc from vertex T to S which has capacity equal to the maximum number of index registers in the target processor, $|AR|$.

The costs per arc can now be set up to reflect the actual costs of code size, performance, or energy dissipation. The path of each flow identifies a partition of accessed variables that will be assigned to one index register. As each unit of flow passes from T to S it accumulates a cost representing the instruction for loading of an initial value into the index register (*lark* in the C2x[6]). As each unit of flow passes through the vertices between S to T it accumulates any costs associated with adding or subtracting of offsets. For example if an offset is required, for example $|d(i)-d(j)|=$ *offset* >1 for arc $i \rightarrow j$, a cost of one would be required representing a separate instruction (for example *adrk* or *sbrk* in the C2x[6], see figure 1e)). In figure 1b), flows in the solution of the minimum cost circulation problem, providing optimal address generation for code in figure 1a), are shown. Only the arcs with non-zero flow in the solution appear for illustration purposes. The total flow from vertex S to T and vica versa is two, thus the solution requires two index registers in figure 1b) ($ar0$,$ar1$). Figure 1c) provides the actual code corresponding to the solution shown in the graph in figure 1b). There is always an additional cost of one for the C2x processor in any solution of the minimum cost circulation problem, representing the instruction *larp*0 which identifies the current index register[6].

The formulation of the address generation problem as a minimum cost circulation problem is shown below. For illustration purposes the costs for the auto-increment/decrement addressing problem will be formulated below using the TMS320C2x DSP processor[6] (C2x). However in general other auto-increment/decrement addressing modes used in other DSP processors can also be supported. The cost for using an offset whose value is greater than one is one instruction in the C2x instruction set $e_{v_t \rightarrow u_{t2}}=1$, $\forall t \leq t2$, $v_t, u_{t2} \varepsilon V$, $|d(v)-d(u)|>1$. The cost for using each index register is the cost to load each index register with an initial value which again is one instruction in the C2x instruction set ($e_{T \rightarrow S}=1$). Equation (1) represents the

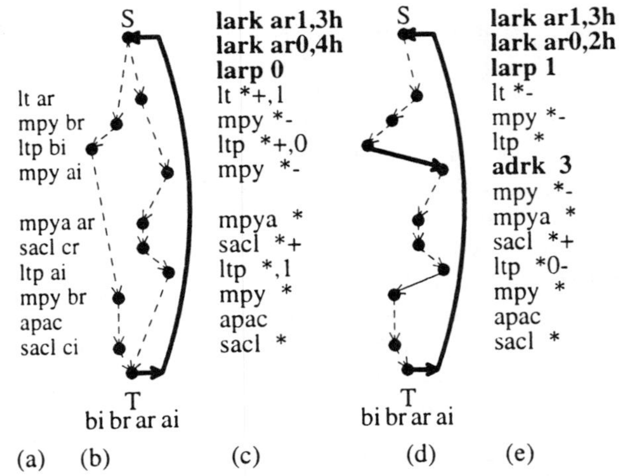

Figure 1. The code in a) is transformed into a flow graph with optimal min cost circulation in b) and C2x code in c). A circulation in d) with code in e) using offset register *ar*0 and *adrk*.

conservation of flow equation (including vertices S,T). Equation (2) ensure that the flow into and out of each data access variable, is equal to one. Finally equation (3) sets the arc capacities and lower bounds. Alternatively, equation (2) can be transformed into a pure circulation problem as presented in section 3. In this case each data access vertex in the graph is replaced by an arc whose lower bound is set to one (which has the same effect as equation (2)). This lower bound along with the conservation of flow inequality (1) is used along with inequality (3) to formulate the circulation problem.

$$\textit{Minimize} \sum_{i \rightarrow j} e_{i \rightarrow j} x_{i \rightarrow j}$$

$$\textit{Subject to} \sum_{i | i \rightarrow j} x_{i \rightarrow j} - \sum_{i | j \rightarrow i} x_{j \rightarrow i} = 0, \forall j \varepsilon V. \tag{1}$$

$$\sum_{i | i \rightarrow v_t} x_{i \rightarrow v_t} = 1, \sum_{j | v_t \rightarrow j} x_{v_t \rightarrow j} = 1, \forall v_t \neq S,T, v_t \varepsilon V. \tag{2}$$

$$1 \leq x_{T \rightarrow S} \leq |AR|, \; 0 \leq x_{i \rightarrow j} \leq 1, \forall (i \rightarrow j) \varepsilon A, (i \rightarrow j) \neq (T \rightarrow S). \tag{3}$$

This model can easily be extended to generate addressing code that additionally supports a fixed non-zero *offset* (*offset*>1) that is loaded into a index register and used to increment the address stored in any other index register by the *offset* amount (such as that capability provided in C2x processor with the $AR0$ register[6], ARi+=$AR0$, see figure 1e) *0+). In this case we extend the cost formulation as follows, for *offset*: $e_{v_t \rightarrow u_{t2}}=0$, $\forall t \leq t2$, $v_t, u_{t2} \varepsilon V$, $|d(v)-d(u)| \leq 1$, or $|d(v)-d(u)|=$*offset*. $e_{v_t \rightarrow u_{t2}}=1$, $\forall t \leq t2$, $v_t, u_{t2} \varepsilon V$, *otherwise*. Application to different types of data structures (arrays, pointers, etc) can also be supported. Although the extension of this circulation technique to loops and conditionals in general is NP-complete (ie. the multicommodity flow problem), an iterative application of the circulation techniques can be performed to handle these cases and achieve locally optimal solutions.

5. Experimental Results

Several DSP applications are used to illustrate this methodology. Code was generated using the Texas Instrument's (TI) C compiler[6] for the TMS320C2x and C3x DSP processors (which have very different addressing capabilities). The minimum cost circulation was solved on a Sun using a LP solver[8], although faster cpu times are possible using network solvers[7].

Table 1 illustrates the optimized results compared to the TI compiler generated addressing. Optimal addressing code (#instr) was generated for compiler generated DSP code using the same memory layout as the compiler. Results were compared with the initial code generated from TI compiler (CS, code size) which included the addressing code (#instr). Therefore the improvement (Impr) in performance and code size shown in table 1 is only due to optimal address generation. The cpu run times were all under 3 seconds. The last two rows in table 1 provided 1.5 times improvement in code size for the C3x processor where the optimized use of indirect addressing provided greater opportunity for implementation of parallel instructions.

Table 1. Optimized vs. Compiler-Generated Addressing Code

Ex	TI Compiler		Optimized		Impr
	CS	#instr	CS	#inst	
hp1	87	39	54	6	1.6
hp2	78	30	54	6	1.4
lms	79	36	49	6	1.6
fft	183	69	123	9	1.4
dct	210	72	149	11	1.4
fft/3x	93	34	60	10	1.5
dct/3x	69	34	46	15	1.5

Table 2. Different Memory layouts vs Address Generation

# of Index Regs	1	2	3	4
#instr for TI-mem	24	13	8	7
#instr for Krusk-mem	9	6	5	5

Table 2 presents the results of using different memory layouts (TI-generated, TI-mem, and as in [2], Krusk-mem) on the address generation problem for a variation of the least means square algorithm. For a fixed number of index registers, the optimal size of addressing code (#instr) is shown. To further analyze the impact of memory layout on optimal address code generation, the complement of the data access graph was used to obtain a poor memory layout. The optimal address generation technique was applied and the results for several examples (taken from table 1) were an additional cost of at most two instructions.

6. Discussions and Conclusions

In summary code size and performance savings from 1.3 to 1.6 (see table 1) were attained by optimizing the address generation code across several DSP examples. The technique presented in this paper performs optimal address code generation for a given memory layout. Since fewer instructions are used, a reduction in energy dissipated will also be obtained with this technique. Since there may be more than one solution which provides optimal performance and code size, the methodology would then solve for minimum energy using instruction-level models of estimated energy dissipation, as researched for general purpose processors in [5]. This problem can be solved in polynomial time using efficient network flow solvers. Since this address generation is dependent upon the memory layout, this could be used in conjunction with a search technique to find optimal memory layout and address generation. In combination with optimized code generation tools[10], larger savings in code size and improvements in performance are attainable.

In contrast to previous research[2,9,4] which examined the general offset assignment problem or other addressing techniques, we have presented a optimal polynomial technique which can work in conjunction with any data memory layout technique such as in[2] or with memory layout generated by a compiler. Results show that memory layout has a small effect on code size and performance when optimal addressing code is used. This may also be advantageous when memory layout is constrained by interfacing with external systems or when it is performed by an algorithm the user has selected and does not wish to change. It also allows a decomposition approach, or task by task approach to code generation since one can fix memory layout at the beginning of a task according to what was used in previous tasks in contrast to [2] which cannot support a fixed memory layout. This provides a value-added advantage where code can be quickly generated by a compiler and optimized for addressing without changing the memory layout. We have introduced a methodology for optimal address generation given memory layout that has provided significant improvements in performance and code size across several DSP applications. The author would like to thank Craig Ranta for his work. This research is supported in part by grants from NSERC and ITRC.

References

[1] P.Marwedel, G.Goossens Eds. **Code Generation for Embedded Processors**, Kluwer Acad Pub, 1995.

[2] S.Liao et al. "Storage Assignment to Decrease Code Size" ACM SIGPLAN Conf Prog. Lang Des and Impl, 1995.

[3] S.Wuytack et al. "Power Exploration for Data Dominated Video Applications", ISLPED, p359-364, 1996.

[4] C.Liem, P.Paulin, A.Jerraya "Address Calculation for Retargetable Compilation and Exploration of Instruction-Set Architectures" DAC, 1996.

[5] V.Tiwari, S.Malik,A.Wolfe, "Power Analysis of Embedded Software ;A First Step Towards Software Power Minimization, IEEE Trans on VLSI, Vol. 2, No. 4, Dec 1994, p437-445,

[6] **TMS320C2x User's Guide**, Texas Instruments Inc., 1993.

[7] E.Lawler **Combinatorial Optimization: Networks and Matroids** Holt, Rinehart and Winston, 1976.

[8] Brooke, Kendrick, Meeraus, "GAMS", Scientific Press, 1988.

[9] R.Leupers, P.Marwedel, "Algorithms for Address Assignment in DSP Code Generation", ICCAD 1996, 109-112.

[10] C.Gebotys, "An Efficient Model for DSP Code Generation: Performance, Code Size, Estimated Energy", Proc of Int'l Symp on Sys Synth, Sept 1997.

Application-Driven Synthesis of Core-Based Systems

Darko Kirovski*, Chunho Lee*, Miodrag Potkonjak*, and William Mangione-Smith°
* Computer Science Department, ° Electrical Engineering Department
University of California, Los Angeles, CA 90095-1596

Abstract

We developed a new hierarchical modular approach for synthesis of area-minimal core-based data-intensive systems. The optimization approach employs a novel global least-constraining most-constrained heuristic to minimize the instruction cache misses for a given application, instruction cache size and organization. Based on this performance optimization technique, we constructed a strategy to search for a minimal area processor core, and an instruction and data cache which satisfy the performance characteristics of a set of target applications. The synthesis platform integrates the existing modeling, profiling, and simulation tools with the developed system-level synthesis tools. The effectiveness of the approach is demonstrated on a variety of modern real-life multimedia and communication applications.

1 Introduction

A typical application-specific core-based system consists of a processor core, instruction and data cache cores, and number of hardware accelerators and control blocks. Numerous ASIC manuals and documents outline the fact that most of the IC area is dedicated to the processor core and associated caches. We present a novel hierarchical fully modular approach for synthesis of core-based data-intensive ASICs that focuses on minimizing area assigned to the processor core and the cache subsystem with respect to the performance requirements of a set of target applications. The system-level approach for design of core-based implementations uses as a performance optimization technique a global least-constraining most-constrained probabilistic heuristic as a compile-time strategy for basic block static relocation [Kir97]. The goal of the synthesis approach is to select an area-minimal processor core and cache configuration that satisfy the performance requirements of a set of target applications.

Trace-driven simulation is used to accurately evaluate performance of the cache subsystem and to obtain the application execution profile. The on-line Stanford Cache Design Tool (CDT [Fly96]) is used to estimate cache access latency and area based on properties such as cache total size, line size, feature size, replacement policy, and associativity. Data extrapolated from the available literature for commercial programmable cores is used as a simplified model to approximate processor core performance with respect to its area.

In order to bridge the gap between the profiling and modeling tools from the two traditionally independent synthesis domains (architecture and CAD), we developed a new synthesis and evaluation platform. The platform integrates the existing modeling (Stanford CDT), profiling (SHADE [Cme94]) and simulation (DINEROIII [Hill88]) tools with the developed system-level synthesis tools. Application profiles are acquired through the use of SHADE augmented with custom trace analyzer. The result of the trace analysis is an application control flow graph augmented with information on spatial and temporal correlation of branch executions. We evaluate cache subsystem performance by running the application execution on the DINEROIII cache simulator. The effectiveness of the approach and the constructed simulation and evaluation platform is demonstrated on a variety of modern real-life applications, such as JPEG and MPEG codecs, GSM speech encoders, and public key protocols.

2 Previous Work

The related work can be traced through two areas: application-specific system optimization and evaluation.

Systems on silicon are becoming an important focus area for both research and commercial developers [Bol94]. Shortened design cycles, due to market pressure, have encouraged the use of predesigned processor cores. At the same time, market pressure to reduce system cost for consumer products has spurred the development of system level synthesis techniques [Pot95, Chi96, Sub96]. As embedded applications have become more sophisticated and commercially relevant, system level synthesis has also become increasingly important [Gup93, Gaj94, Hen95, Lee96].

The increased interest in embedded system design with reusable core components has encouraged the development of high level architecture and ASIC evaluation models. For example, The Microprocessor Report presents a monthly summary of the area and performance of numerous commercial processors [MPR96]. Instruction and data caches, as the highest level of the memory hierarchy, have been thoroughly studied in [Hill88, Jou93].

We have developed a new unified framework for synthesis and optimization that ties together some of the existing methods for system modeling and optimization. To the best of our knowledge, this is the first synthesis to use software code mapping to enable hardware savings.

3 Preliminary Discussion

In this section we describe the hardware performance models for caches and processor cores. Three factors combine to influence system performance: cache miss rates, processor performance, and system clock speed. The approach that we use here is to leverage existing models to estimate the area and performance of both caches and processor cores. This approach allows the synthesis approach to be rapidly updated and applied to new environments with new technology.

The on-line Stanford CDT is used to evaluate the impact of cache design choices on area and latency. Caches typically found in current embedded systems range from 128B to 32KB. Since higher associativity can result in significantly higher access time, we consider only direct mapped, and 2-way set associative caches. We used a fixed cache line size of 32 bytes. This decision attempts to eliminate the well known cache penalty tradeoff problem. Large cache lines generally result in increased latency while fetching from main memory, while short cache lines increase access latency due to greater control hardware. We estimated the cache miss penalty based on the operating frequency and external bus width for each system investigated. This penalty ranges between 4 and 20 system clock cycles. Write-back was adopted instead of write-through due its superior performance in uniprocessor systems [Jou93], though at increased hardware cost. Each of the processors considered is constrained by the Flynn limit, and thus is able to issue at most a single instruction per clock period. The caches were designed to have a single access port. A sample overview of the estimated cache model is presented in Table 1. Cache access latency and area is computed for a number of organizations and sizes, all with implementation feature size fixed at 0.5 μm and 6 transistors per CMOS SRAM cell.

Cache	Property	1KB	2KB	4KB	8KB	96KB
Direct	Area(mm^2)	2.11	3.81	7.20	13.96	161.7
Mapped	Clk(ns)	3.79	3.97	4.16	4.5	6.79
2-way	Area(mm^2)	2.38	4.02	7.29	13.8	156.1
	Clk(ns)	5.67	5.75	5.94	6.23	8.54

Table 1: A sample of the cache area and latency model.

Microprocessor	MHz	MIPS	Tech.(μm)	mm^2
ARM 810	75	80	0.5	29
Motorola 403GC	33	41	0.5	30
ARM StrongArm	200	230	0.35	33
i486GXSF	33	18	0.8	18
MIPS4650	133	175	0.6	32
Hitachi SH7708	100	100	0.6	34
LSI Logic CW4001	60	53	0.5	3.5
LSI Logic TR4101	81	30	0.35	2

Table 2: A sample of the processor model.

Information on microprocessor performance and area was collected from datasheets as well as from the CPU Center Info web site [CPU]. A sample of the collected data is presented in Table 2. The range of microprocessor core area varies from 2 to 34 mm^2, while the clock frequencies range within 33-200MHz.

4 The New Synthesis Approach

Figure 1 illustrates the synthesis framework. In this section we describe the role of each module and how modules are combined into an integrated synthesis system.

The core module in the synthesis flow is a global least-constraining most-constrained heuristic that guides the algorithm for basic block relocation [Kir97]. Basic blocks are repositioned statically, in a way that frequently sequentially executed basic blocks are mapped into different cache lines. The temporal correlation of branch outcomes is used to further improve cache performance by putting additional constraints on the basic block mapping. Code repositioning is accomplished with negligible increase in the static program memory size. The modification required to the program involves basic block motion, branch target updating, and branch insertion.

The application driven search for a core and cache system with minimal area requires using trace-driven cache simulation for each promising point considered in the design space. We attack these problems by carefully searching the space using bounded divide-and-conquer search algorithms with conservative sharp bounds and by providing powerful performance estimation techniques.

The developed synthesis tools are augmented with the ability to synthesize a single-chip programmable ASIC system which satisfies the requirements of multiple applications. This system requirement represents a realistic design expectation for most modern non-preemptive multi-task application specific systems. The synthesis technique considers each microprocessor core and selects the instruction and data cache design with minimal area that satisfies the individual performance requirements of all applications. The configuration which has the minimum processor and cache total area is returned as the best solution.

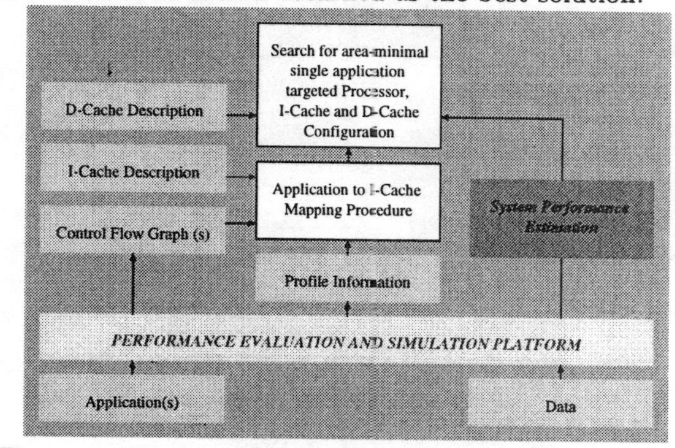

Figure 1: The hierarchical modular synthesis approach.

System performance is evaluated using a platform which integrates simulation, modeling, and profiling tools (see Figure 2). SHADE is a tracing tool which allows users to define custom trace analyzers and thus collect rich information on runtime events. SHADE currently profiles only SPARC binaries. The executable binary program is dynamically translated into host machine code. The tool provides to the translated code a stream of data directly executed to simulate and trace the original application code. A custom analyzer composed of approximately 2,000 lines of C code, is linked to SHADE to control and analyze the generated trace information. The analyzer sources relevant trace information from SHADE and builds a control flow graph (CFG) corresponding to the dynamically executed code. The analysis consists of two passes. The first pass determines the boundaries of basic blocks, while the second pass constructs a CFG by adding control flow information between basic blocks. We also collect the frequencies of control transfers through each basic block, and branch temporal correlation [Kir97]. Once the CFG is obtained, an algorithm is employed to reposition application basic blocks in such a way that instruction cache misses are minimized. Our experimentation uses a basic block relocation look up table to simulate the relocation of basic blocks in main memory. An entry in the basic block relocation table consists of two elements: the original and optimized starting address of the basic block. To simulate cache performance of a given application and data stream, we use a trace-driven cache simulator DINEROIII. System cache is described using a number of qualitative and quantitative parameters such as instruction and data cache size, replacement policy, associativity, etc.

The system optimization process is composed of a sequence of activations of each of these tools. The SHADE analyzer traces program and data memory references as well as the CFG. The CFG is used to drive the code reposition module which produces a new application mapping table. Stream of references are sent to a program that uses the basic block relocation look up table to map from the original into the optimized address space. The remapped trace of addresses, along with all unmodified data memory references, are sent to DINEROIII for cache simulation.

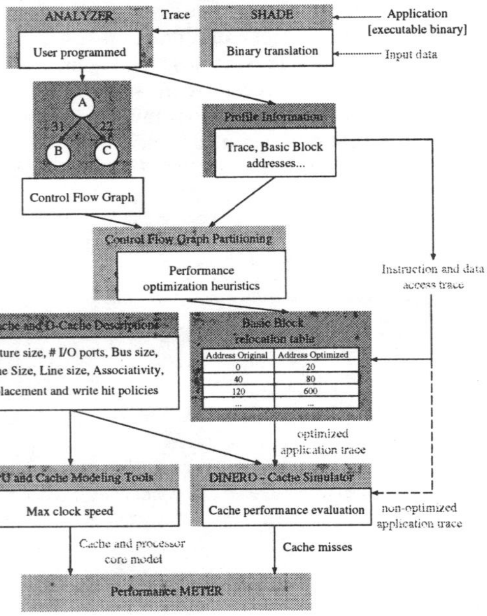

Figure 2: Synthesis flow of application-driven programmable core-based systems.

The final system performance was computed using the following formula: $CPI = \frac{SysClkFreq}{MIPS} + CacheMissRatio \cdot CacheMissPnlty$, where $CacheMissRatio$ was computed during the trace driven simulation of the cache subsystem. $CacheMissPnlty$, $SysClkFreq$, and $MIPS$ are system parameters introduced in Section 3.

5 Synthesis Optimization Algorithms

The problems encountered in the synthesis of systems on silicon and competitive optimization algorithms are described in this section. First, the algorithm for basic block relocation is discussed. Then, based on the obtained code repositioning table and therefore, improved cache performance, we assemble an area-efficient system configuration (core and cache structure) which satisfies application specific performance requirements. Finally, a case study is performed involving application-driven system resource allocation a set of non-preemptive target applications.

For each type of processor core
  For $I\_cache :: size = 128B..maxB, sets = 1..2$
    Selection: Perform Binary Search for
    D_cache of minimal size such that the
    configuration $(core, I\_cache, D\_cache)$
    satisfies the application performance requirements.
Return the overall configuration of minimal total area.

At any point during the algorithm, search is terminated along paths dominated by any other already pessimistically evaluated solution.

Figure 3: Pseudo code for the resource allocation procedure.

The proposed application-driven system-level synthesis technique employs basic block repositioning based upon profile information for optimization of the program execution performance. Block repositioning aims for application execution on fixed hardware resources with minimal number of cache misses. The optimization problems involved in the basic block relocation are defined, their computational complexity is established, and an efficient algorithm is proposed in [Kir97].

The second phase of the synthesis strategy conducts a search for a minimal-area system configuration which satisfies the performance requirements of the target application. The search algorithm is described using the pseudo-code shown in Figure 3.

For each microprocessor core type we perform a search for the smallest overall cache structure which satisfies the application's requirements. The search starts by selecting a set of instruction cache sizes among which it is reasonable to expect that the best solution is found. For each of the sample I-cache sizes, a search is performed in order to find the smallest D-cache size which results in cache miss ratio smaller than some value defined by the application's guaranteed timing constraints. Since the function that describes a cache miss ratio monotonically decreases with the increase of the cache size we employ binary search on the logarithmic scale of data cache sizes. The final solution is a configuration of a core, I-cache and D-cache which has the smallest total area. The search is terminated when the current solution is dominated by some existing minimal solution. Dominated solutions are found in one of the following two ways:

- For Fixed core A, the best cache subsystem so far recorded for A totals Q bytes. Fixed I-cache equals P bytes. We do not evaluate D-caches larger than $Q - P$ bytes.
- Best core-cache configuration totals R square millimeters. If we use core A of area X we terminate the search whenever the sum of the I-cache and D-cache exceeds $R - X$ square millimeters.

Since trace-driven simulation is performed every time a particular cache system is evaluated, we opt to use an approximation method in order to get faster but still accurate configuration performance measurements. In order to generate optimistic estimations we analyze the "quality" of application's CFG partitioning based on the profile information. The cost function used to evaluate the solution is:

$$Cost(TCFG, SetOfPart.) = \frac{\alpha \cdot \sum_{i,j \in SetOfPart.,i \neq j} w_{a \in i, b \in j} - \beta \cdot \sum_{i \in SetOfPart.} w_{a \in i, b \in i}}{\sum_{i,j \in SetOfPart.,i \neq j} 1}$$

This function is directly proportional to the sum of weights of edges that connect nodes between any two different cache line partitions and sum of weights of edges that connect nodes in the same cache line partition. The cost function is normalized with the cardinality of the set of edges which connect nodes in different cache line partitions. Parameters α and β were experimentally determined and validated using the meta-algorithmics methodology [Kir97]. The resulting performance estimation offset was within 5% of the simulated performance measurements.

The performance estimation function was used in our experiments in the following way. For a fixed I-cache size and a given microprocessor core we used a performance estimation technique to select the W most promising solutions ($W = 3$). Then, for those W solutions we used trace-driven simulation to find the D-cache size which results in the minimal number of overall cache misses.

Finally, previous algorithm is augmented with a capability of finding the minimal area-optimal core and cache configuration such that performance requirements of multiple non-preemptive applications are satisfied. Such synthesis task corresponds to the real-life case since many embedded communications and computing systems are composed of a set of non-preemptive real-time applications. In order to provide multiple application targeted resource allocation, the algorithm presented in Figure 3 needs only be augmented with an improved selection step. The modification includes considering a conjunction of application requirements, rather than fulfilling a single performance constraint (see Figure 4).

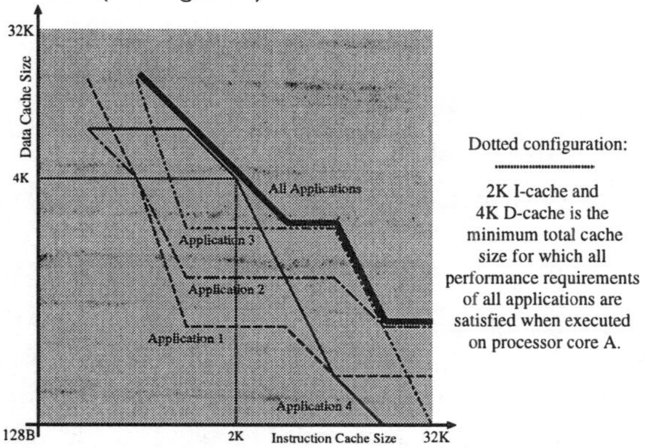

Figure 4: Best instruction cache setups for a single core, four applications with fixed performance requirements and a set of fixed data cache sizes.

6 Experimental Results

We used six applications to demonstrate the effectiveness of the approach: JPEG software (Independent JPEG Group), MPEG-1 and MPEG-2 software (MPEG Software Simulation Group), PGP software, and implementation of the GSM and G.721 wireless communication protocols. The developed application driven synthesis approach resulted in area-minimal system configurations as presented in Table 3. The first column contains the application description. The next three columns describe the allocated core and cache configuration followed by the total required area for the system. The obtained results acknowledge the domination of LSI Logic cores due to their exceptional performance vs. area ratio. The size of these cores points out to the fact that defining an area minimal cache subsystem for a particular application is a goal of major importance for the system designer. The diversity of selected cache structures implies that finding the area-minimal cache subsystem is an important task.

Appl.	Core	I-$	D-$	mm^2	$/Total
JPEG enc.	CW4001	1KB	1KB	7.7	43%
JPEG dec.	CW4001	1KB	2KB	9.4	63%
PGP encr.	TR4101	512B	1KB	5.0	60%
MPEG dec.	StrongArm	1KB	512B	36	8%
G.721 enc.	TR4101	1KB	128B	4.3	53%
GSM enc.	CW4001	512B	128B	4.7	25%

Table 3: Area-minimal system configurations for a given applications.

Appl.	Processor	I-$	D-$	mm^2	$/Total
G.721 enc. MPEG dec. JPEG dec. PGP encr.	StrongARM	1KB	1KB	37	9%
GSM enc. JPEG dec. JPEG enc. PGP encr.	CW4001	1KB	2KB	9.4	63%

Table 4: Area-minimal system configurations for two application mixes.

We assembled two application mixes and performed search for area minimal configurations that satisfy performance requirements of all applications in the mix. The results are presented in Table 4. The columns in Table 4 correspond to the columns in Table 3. The area-optimal cache configuration for each application mix is selected among cache subsystems with dominating performance. The percentage of the total IC's area dedicated to the cache subsystem, as well as strong diversity among selected minimal area cache subsystems for different applications and different timing constraints indicate the necessity of involving sophisticated system level synthesis approaches in order to minimize product's total area while still satisfying product's timing constraints.

7 Conclusion

We developed and evaluated a novel hierarchical approach for synthesis of programmable core-based applications. The approach synthesizes an area-optimal processor and cache system for the most common system environment, a set of non-preemptive target applications. The efficiency of the synthesis approach was tested on a set of modern multimedia and communication applications.

References

[Bol94] I. Bolsens, K. Rompaey, H. De Man, "User requirements for designing complex systems on silicon", VLSI Signal Processing VII, pp. 63-72, 1994.

[Chi96] M. Chiodo, et. al. "A case study in computer-aided co-design of embedded controllers", Design Automation for Embedded Systems, Vol.1, No.1-2, pp. 51-67, 1996.

[Cme94] B. Cmelik, D. Keppel, "Shade: a fast instruction-set simulator for execution profiling", SIGMETRICS Conference on Measurement and Modeling of Computer Systems, Vol.22, No.1, pp. 128-37, 1994.

[CPU] http://infopad.eecs.berkeley.edu/CIC/

[Fly96] M.J. Flynn, "Computer Architecture: Pipelined and Parallel Processor Design", Jones and Bartlett, Boston, MA, 1996. (http://umunhum.Stanford.EDU/tools/cachetools.html)

[Gaj94] D.D. Gajski, et al. "A System-Design Methodology: Executable Specification Refinement", Euro-DAC, pp. 458-463, 1994.

[Gar79] M.R. Garey, D.S. Johnson, "Computers and intractability : a guide to the theory of NP-completeness", W. H. Freeman, San Francisco, CA, 1979.

[Gup93] R.K. Gupta and G. De Micheli, "Hardware-software cosynthesis for digital systems", IEEE Design and Test of Computers, Vol.10, No.7, pp. 29-41, 1993.

[Hen95] J. Henkel, R. Ernst, "A path-based technique for estimating hardware runtime in HW/SW-cosynthesis", 8th International Symposium on System Synthesis, pp. 116-121, 1995.

[Hill88] M.D. Hill, "A case for direct-mapped cache", IEEE Computer, pp. 25-40, 1988.

[Jou93] N.P. Jouppi, "Cache write policies and performance", 20th Annual International Symposium on Computer Architecture, San Diego, CA, Vol.21, No.2, pp. 191-201, 1993.

[Kir97] D. Kirovski, et al., "Synthesis of core-based application-specific systems", Technical Report, CSD, UCLA, 1997.

[Lee96] T.-G. Lee, W.-J. Fang, A.C.-H. Wu, "The design and implementation of a cooperative design-view environment for interactive partitioning applications", Software - Practice and Experience, Vol.26, No.10, pp. 141-160, 1996.

[Lie96] C. Liem, P. Paulin, A. Jerraya, "Address calculation for retargetable compilation and exploration of instruction-set architectures", 33rd Design Automation Conference, 1996.

[MPR96] Microprocessor Report, all issues, 1996.

[Pot95] M. Potkonjak, W.H. Wolf, "Cost Optimization in ASIC implementation of Periodic Hard-Real Time Systems using Behavioral Synthesis Techniques", ICCAD, pp. 446-451, 1995.

[Sub96] P.A. Subrahmanyam, A. Sharma, "Issues in developing realtime multimedia applications for a multiprocessor system", 4th Intl. Workshop on Parallel and Distributed Real-Time Systems, pp. 147-155, 1996.

Power Optimization using Divide-and-Conquer Techniques for Minimization of the Number of Operations

Inki Hong, Miodrag Potkonjak and Ramesh Karri†
Computer Science Department, University of California, Los Angeles, CA 90095
†Dept. of Electrical and Computer Engineering, University of Massachusetts, Amherst, MA 01003

Abstract

We develop an approach to minimizing power consumption of portable wireless DSP applications using a set of compilation and architectural techniques. The key technical innovation is a novel divide-and-conquer compilation technique to minimize the number of operations for general DSP computations. Our technique optimizes not only a significantly wider set of computations than the previously published techniques, but also outperforms (or performs at least as well as other techniques) on all examples. Along the architectural dimension, we investigate coordinated impact of compilation techniques on the number of processors which provide optimal trade-off between cost and power. We demonstrate that proper compilation techniques can significantly reduce power with bounded hardware cost. The effectiveness of all techniques and algorithms is documented on numerous real-life designs.

1 Introduction

The applications of portable wireless market are defined by their intrinsic demand for portability, flexibility, cost sensitivity and by their high digital signal processing (DSP) content. Portability translates into the crucial importance of low power design, flexibility results in a need for programmable platforms implementation, and cost sensitivity narrows architectural alternatives to a uniprocessor or a few off-the-shelf standard processors. The key optimization degree for satisfying this set of requirements comes from properties of typical portable computations. The computations are mainly linear, but rarely 100% linear due to either need for adaptive algorithms or nonlinear quantization elements. Such computations are well suited for static compilation and quantitative optimization.

Our goal is to develop synthesis and compilation methods and tools for realization of typical DSP wireless applications on single and multiple programmable processors. Furthermore, we study achievable power-cost tradeoffs when parallelism is traded for power reduction.

The main technical innovation of the research is the first approach for minimizing the number of operations in *general* computations. The approach optimizes not only significantly wider set of computations than the other previously published techniques [11], but also outperforms or performs at least as well as other techniques on all examples. To the best of our knowledge this is the first optimization-intensive approach for minimizing the number of operations in *general* computations. The second technical highlight is the quantitative analysis of cost *vs* power trade-off on multiple programmable processors. We derive a condition under which the optimization of the cost-power product using parallelization is beneficial.

2 Preliminaries

We selected as a computational model synchronous data flow (SDF) [4]. The syntax of a targeted computation is defined as a hierarchical control-data flow graph (CDFG) [8]. The only relevant speed metric is throughput. We assume that all types of operations take one clock cycle for their execution, as it is the case in many modern DSP processors. In the case of a multi-processor, we make the following additional assumptions: (i) all processors are homogeneous, (ii) inter-processor communication does not cost any time and hardware, and (iii) effective switched capacitance increases linearly with the number of processors.

The power model used in this research is built on three established facts. First, the number of operations at the machine code-level is proportional to the number of operations at high-level language [2]. Secondly, the power consumption in programmable processors is directly proportional to the number of operations, regardless of what the mix of operations being executed is [13]. Finally, our model follows the power consumption and timing models in digital CMOS circuits presented in [1]. Based on these

[1]Ramesh Karri was supported by an NSF CAREER grant MIP-9702676. Inki Hong and Miodrag Potkonjak were partially supported by a MICRO 96-182 grant. Inki Hong was also supported by a DAC fellowship.

three facts, we conclude that if the targeted implementation platform is a single CMOS processor, reduction in the number of operations is the key to power minimization.

3 Related Work

Power minimization efforts across all levels of design abstraction process are surveyed in [10]. Parhi and Messerschmitt [6] presented optimal unfolding of linear DSP computations. Potkonjak and Rabaey [7] addressed the minimization of the number of multiplications and additions in linear computations in their maximally fast form so that the throughput is preserved. Sheliga and Sha [9] presented an approach to minimizing the number of operations in linear computations. Srivastava and Potkonjak [11] developed an approach to minimizing power for linear computations, based on the minimization of the number of operations. A variant of their technique is used in "conquer" phase of our approach. Our approach is different from theirs in two respects. First, their technique can handle only linear computations, while our approach can optimize *general* computations. Secondly, our approach outperforms their techniques for linear computations.

4 Single Programmable Processor

The power minimization of single processor is based on the the minimization of the number of operations. The core of the approach to minimizing the number of operations is presented in the pseudo-code of Figure 1.

```
Decompose a computation into strongly connected
components(SCCs);
Any adjacent trivial SCCs are merged into a sub part;
Use pipelining to isolate the sub parts;
For each sub part
  Minimize the number of delays using retiming;
  If (the sub part is linear)
    Apply optimal unfolding;
  Else
    Apply unfolding after isolating nonlinear operations;
Merge linear sub parts to further optimize;
Schedule merged sub parts to minimize memory usage;
```

Figure 1. Minimizing the number of operations for general DSP computations

The first step of the approach is to identify the computation's strongly connected components(SCCs), using the depth-first search-based algorithm [12]. For any pair of operations A and B within an SCC, there exist both a path from A to B and a path from B to A. The graph formed by all SCCs is acyclic. Thus, the SCCs can be isolated from each other using pipeline delays, which enables us to optimize each SCC separately. The inserted pipeline delays are treated as inputs or outputs to the SCC. As a result, every output and state in an SCC depend only on the inputs and states of the SCC. In this sense, the SCC is isolated from the rest of the computation and can be optimized separately. Note that this isolation is not affected by unfolding. For trivial SCCs with only one node, unfolding fails to reduce the number of operations. Thus, any adjacent trivial SCCs are merged together before the isolation step, to reduce the number of pipeline delays used.

The number of delays in each sub part is minimized using retiming by the Leiserson-Saxe algorithm [5]. Note that smaller number of delays will require smaller number of operations since both the next states and outputs depend on the previous states. SCCs are further classified as either linear or nonlinear. Minimization of the number of operations for linear computations is NP-complete [9]. We have adopted an approach of [11] for the optimization of linear sub parts, which uses unfolding and the maximally fast procedure [7]. We note that instead of maximally fast procedure, the ratio analysis by [9] can be used. [11] has provided the closed-form formula for the optimal unfolding factor with the assumption of dense linear computations, which means that every output and state are linear combinations of all inputs and states with no 0, 1, or -1 coefficients. For sparse linear computations, they have proposed a heuristic which continues to unfold until there is no improvement. We have made the simple heuristic more efficient with binary search, based on the unimodality property of the number of operations on unfolding factor [11].

When a sub part is classified as nonlinear, we apply unfolding after the isolation of nonlinear operations. All nonlinear operations are isolated from the sub part so that the remaining linear sub parts can be optimized. All arcs from nonlinear operations to the linear sub parts are considered as inputs to the linear sub parts, and all arcs from linear sub parts to the nonlinear operations are considered as outputs from the linear sub parts. If every output and state of the nonlinear sub part depend on nonlinear operations, then unfolding with the separation of nonlinear operations is ineffective in reducing the number of operations.

It is often beneficial to decompose a computation into larger sub parts than SCCs, especially when there are many intermediate outputs between SCCs. This observation leads us to an approach to merging sub parts for further reducing the number of operations. We consider merging of any adjacent arbitrary sub parts. Suppose we consider merging of sub parts i and j. The gain $GAIN(i,j)$ of merging sub parts i and j can be computed as follows: $GAIN(i,j) = COST(i) + COST(j) - COST(i,j)$, where $COST(i)$ is the optimized number of operations for sub part i and $COST(i, j)$ is the optimized number of operations for the merged sub part of i and j. To compute the gain, $COST(i, j)$ must be computed, which requires constant coefficient matrices $A, B, C,$ and D for the merged sub part of i and j. It is easy to construct the matrices using the depth-first search [12]. Sub part merging is performed by a greedy optimization approach. The algorithm is straightforward. Until there is no improvement, merge the pair of sub parts which produces the highest gain.

5 Multiple Programmable Processors

When multi-processors are used, potentially more savings in power can be obtained. Using k processors increases throughput k times when there is full parallelism in the computation, while effective switched capacitance increases k times as well. There exists full parallelism in all the real-life examples considered since the feedback loops can be computed in parallel and there exist more operations outside feedback loops than required.

One can reduce the voltage so that the clock frequency of all k processors is reduced by a factor of k. It is always beneficial to use more processors in terms of power with the following two limitations: (i) the amount of parallelism available limits the improvement in throughput and the critical path of the computation is the maximum achievable throughput and (ii) when supply voltage approaches close to threshold voltage, the improvement in power becomes so small that the cost of adding a processor can not be justified. We want to find the number of processors which minimizes power cost-effectively.

Design	Init. Ops	[11]	New Method	Reduction % From [11]	Reduction % From Init. Ops
dist	48	47.3	36.4	23.0	24.2
chemical	41	33	29.6	10.3	27.8
DAC	2098	2098	1327.83	36.7	36.7
modem	213	213	148.83	30.1	30.1
GE controller	180	180	105.26	41.5	41.5
APCM receiver	2238	N/A	1444.19	N/A	35.4
Audio Filter	228	N/A	92.0	N/A	59.7
Video Filter	398	N/A	184.5	N/A	53.7
VSTOL	1686	N/A	876	N/A	47.9

Table 1. Minimizing the number of operations for real-life examples; N/A - Not Applicable

We propose a PN product as a measure of cost effectiveness, where P is the power consumption normalized to that of optimized single processor solution and N is the number of processors used. The smaller the PN product is the more cost-effective the solution is. If PN is smaller than 1, using N processors has decreased the power consumption by a factor of more than N. It depends on the power requirement and the cost budget for the implementation how many processors the implementation should use. PN products monotonically increase with respect to the number of processors. From the values of PN in all the cases considered on the standard CMOS platforms, we observe that cost effective solutions usually use only a few processors.

Design	V_{init}	V_t	New Volt	Pow Red
dist	5.0	1.1	3.76	2.33
	3.3	0.7	2.70	1.96
	1.3	0.3	1.10	1.84
	0.5	0.1	0.42	1.88
	0.25	0.06	0.21	1.82
chemical	5.0	1.1	3.61	2.65
	3.3	0.7	2.61	2.21
	1.3	0.3	1.07	2.04
	0.5	0.1	0.41	2.10
	0.25	0.06	0.21	2.02
DAC	5.0	1.1	3.81	2.72
	3.3	0.7	2.50	2.75
	1.3	0.3	1.00	2.69
	0.5	0.1	0.38	2.80
	0.25	0.06	0.19	2.66
modem	5.0	1.1	4.02	2.21
	3.3	0.7	2.65	2.23
	1.3	0.3	1.05	2.19
	0.5	0.1	0.40	2.25
	0.25	0.06	0.20	2.17
GE controller	5.0	1.1	3.65	3.21
	3.3	0.7	2.39	3.25
	1.3	0.3	0.96	3.16
	0.5	0.1	0.36	3.31
	0.25	0.06	0.18	3.12

Table 2. Minimizing power consumption on single programmable processor for linear examples

Based on these observations, we have developed the strategy for the multiple processor implementation. First, power for single processor implementation is minimized using the technique in Section 4. Next, increase the number of processors until the PN product is below the given maximum value. The maximum value is determined based on the power requirement and the cost budget for the implementation. The strategy produces solutions with only a few processors, in many cases single processor.

6 Experimental Results

Our set of benchmark designs include all the examples used in [11] as well as the following typical portable DSP applications: DAC - 4 stage NEC digital to analog converter for audio signals; modem - 2 stage NEC modem; GE controller - 5-state GE linear controller; APCM receiver - Motorola's adaptive pulse code modulation receiver; Audio Filter - ADC followed by 18 order parallel filter; Video Filter - two ADCs followed by 12-order 2D IIR filter; and VSTOL - VSTOL robust observer structure aircraft speed controller. DAC, modem, and GE controller are linear and the rest are nonlinear. The examples from [11] are all linear, which include ellip, iir5, wdf5, iir6, iir10, iir12, steam, dist, and chemical.

Table 1 presents the results of our technique for minimizing the number of operations. The fifth and sixth columns of Table 1 provide the reduction percentage of our method from [11] and from the initial number of operations, respectively. Our method achieves the same number of operations as [11] for ellip, iir5, wdf5, iir6, iir10, iir12, and steam while it reduces the number of operations by 23 and 10.3% for dist and chemical, respectively. All the examples from [11] are small single-input single-output (SISO) linear computations, except dist and chemical which are two-inputs single-output linear computations, which results in no room for further improvement from [11]. Our method reduces the number of operations by an average 39.7% for the examples that previous techniques are either ineffective or inapplicable. Tables 2 and 3 present the results of our technique for minimizing power on single processor for various technologies. Our method results in power reduction by an average factor of 3.43.

Due to space limitation, the experimental results for multi-processors were omitted. For the results, we refer to [3]. Our method achieves cost-effective solutions with very low power penalty compared to the solutions which only optimize power without considering hardware cost.

Design	V_{init}	V_t	New Volt	Pow Red
APCM receiver	5.0	1.1	3.85	2.62
	3.3	0.7	2.53	2.64
	1.3	0.3	1.01	2.58
	0.5	0.1	0.38	2.68
	0.25	0.06	0.19	2.56
Audio Filter	5.0	1.1	3.03	6.76
	3.3	0.7	1.85	6.54
	1.3	0.3	0.8	6.58
	0.5	0.1	0.3	7.11
	0.25	0.06	0.16	6.44
Video Filter	5.0	1.1	3.24	5.15
	3.3	0.7	2.12	5.24
	1.3	0.3	0.85	5.04
	0.5	0.1	0.32	5.37
	0.25	0.06	0.17	4.94
VSTOL	5.0	1.1	3.43	4.10
	3.3	0.7	2.25	4.15
	1.3	0.3	0.90	4.02
	0.5	0.1	0.34	4.25
	0.25	0.06	0.17	3.96

Table 3. Minimizing power on single programmable processor for nonlinear examples

7 Conclusion

We introduced an approach to minimizing power using compilation and architectural techniques. The key technical innovation is a compilation technique for minimizing the number of operations which synergistically uses several transformations within a divide and conquer optimization framework. The approach not only deals with *general* computations, but also outperforms previous techniques for limited computation types. We also investigated the impact of compilation techniques on the number processors which provide optimal trade-off of cost and power. The experimental results on a number of real-life designs demonstrated the effectiveness of the proposed approach.

References

[1] A.P. Chandrakasan, S. Sheng, and R.W. Broderson. Low-power CMOS digital design. *IEEE J. of Solid-State Circuits*, 27(4):473–484, 1992.

[2] P.D. Hoang and J.M. Rabaey. Scheduling of DSP programs onto multiprocessors for maximum throughput. *IEEE Trans. on Signal Processing*, 41(6):2225–2235, 1993.

[3] I. Hong, M. Potkonjak, and R. Karri. Power optimization using divide-and-conquer techniques for minimization of the number of operations. Technical report, Computer Science Department, UCLA, 1997.

[4] E.A. Lee and D.G. Messerschmitt. Synchronous dataflow. *Proc. of the IEEE*, 75(9):1235–1245, 1987.

[5] C.E. Leiserson and J.B. Saxe. Retiming synchronous circuitry. *Algorithmica*, 6(1):5–35, 1991.

[6] K.K. Parhi and D.G. Messerschmitt. Static rate-optimal scheduling of iterative data-flow programs via optimum unfolding. *IEEE Trans. on Computers*, 40(2):178–195, 1991.

[7] M. Potkonjak and J. Rabaey. Maximally fast and arbitrarily fast implementation of linear computations. *ICCAD*, pages 304–308, 1992.

[8] J. Rabaey, C. Chu, P. Hoang, and M. Potkonjak. Fast prototyping of data path intensive architectures. *IEEE Design & Test of Computers*, 8(2):40–51, 1991.

[9] M. Sheliga and E.H.-M. Sha. Global node reduction of linear systems using ratio analysis. *International Symposium on High-Level Synthesis*, pages 140–145, 1994.

[10] D. Singh, J. Rabaey, M. Pedram, F. Catthoor, S. Rajgopal, N. Sehgal, and T. Mozdzen. Power conscious cad tools and methodologies: A perspective. *Proc. of the IEEE*, 83(4), 1995.

[11] M. Srivastava and M. Potkonjak. Power optimization in programmable processors and ASIC implementations of linear systems: Transformation-based approach. *Design Automation Conference*, pages 343–348, 1996.

[12] R.E. Tarjan. Depth first search and linear graph algorithms. *SIAM J. on Computing*, 1(2):146–160, 1972.

[13] V. Tiwari, S. Malik, and A. Wolfe. Power analysis of embedded software: a first step towards software power minimization. *IEEE Trans. on VLSI Systems*, 2(4):437–445, 1994.

SESSION 2C

HIGH-LEVEL POWER PREDICTION AND REDUCTION

Moderators:

Chandu Visweswariah, IBM Corp., Yorktown Heights, NY

Wen-Zen Shen, National Chiao Tung University, Hsinchu, Taiwan

High-Level Area and Power Estimation for VLSI Circuits†

Mahadevamurty Nemani and Farid N. Najm

ECE Dept. and Coordinated Science Lab.
University of Illinois at Urbana-Champaign
Urbana, Illinois 61801

Abstract

This paper addresses the problem of computing the area complexity of a multi-output combinational logic circuit, given only its functional description, i.e., Boolean equations, where area complexity is measured in terms of the number of gates required for an optimal multi-level implementation of the combinational logic. The proposed area model is based on transforming the given multi-output Boolean function description into an equivalent single-output function. The model is empirical, and results demonstrating its feasibility and utility are presented. Also, a methodology for converting the gate count estimates, obtained from the area model, into capacitance estimates is presented. High-level power estimates based on the total capacitance estimates and average activity estimates are also presented.

1. Introduction

Rapid increase in the design complexity and reduction in design time have resulted in a need for CAD tools that can help make important design decisions *early* in the design process. To do so, these tools must operate with a design description at a high level of abstraction. One design criterion that has received increased attention lately is power dissipation. This is due to the increasing demand for low power mobile and portable electronics. As a result, there is a need for *high level power estimation* and optimization. Specifically, it would be highly beneficial to have a power estimation capability, given only a *functional* view of the design, such as when a circuit is described only with Boolean equations. In this case, no structural information is known - the lower-level (gate-level or lower) description of this function is not available. Of course, a given Boolean function can be implemented in many ways, with varying power dissipation levels. We are interested in predicting the *nominal* power dissipation that a minimal area implementation of the function would have.

For a combinational circuit, since the only available information is its Boolean function, we consider that its power dissipation will be modeled as follows:

$$P_{avg} \propto \mathcal{D}_{avg}\mathcal{A}\mathcal{C}_{avg} \qquad (1)$$

where $\mathcal{D}_{avg}$ is an estimate of the average node switching activity that a gate-level implementation of this circuit would have, $\mathcal{A}$ is an estimate of the gate count (assuming some target gate library), and $\mathcal{C}_{avg}$ is an estimate of the average node capacitance (including drain capacitance and interconnect loading capacitance). The estimation of $\mathcal{D}_{avg}$ was covered in [1-3]. The problem of estimating $\mathcal{A}$ from a high-level description of the circuit corresponds to the problem of high-level area estimation. This problem is of independent interest, as the information it provides can be very useful, for instance, during floorplanning. The estimation of gate count (or simply, area) $\mathcal{A}$ of single-output Boolean functions was explored in [4, 5], where the problem was addressed using a notion of complexity of the on-set and the off-set of a Boolean function. In this paper the authors propose an area model to predict the area complexity of multi-output Boolean functions. This area model is based on a transformation, which transforms the given multi-output Boolean function into an equivalent single-output function. The transformation is such that it helps us infer the area complexity of the multi-output Boolean function from the area complexity of the single-output function, thus enabling the utilization of the complexity based area model of [5], developed for single-output functions.

However, the proposed area model, like its single-output counterparts [4, 5], is inherently limited to circuits which do not have large exclusive-or arrays in them. Circuits with large exclusive-or arrays are also the source of problems in other CAD areas, such as BDD construction for verification. One way around the problem of exclusive-or arrays is to require that the Boolean function specification explicitly list exclusive-or gates. In that case, these can be identified up-front and excluded from the analysis, so that the proposed method is applied only to the remaining circuitry. In any case, in the remainder of this paper we will not consider circuits composed of large exclusive-or arrays.

Before leaving this section, we should mention some previous work on layout area estimation from an RTL view. Wu et. al. [6] proposed a layout area model for datapath and control for two commonly used layout architectures based on the transistor count. For datapath units, the average transistor count was obtained by averaging the number of transistors over different implementations and, for control logic, they calculate the number of transistors from the sum of products (SOP) expression for the next state and control signals.

† This work was supported in part by Intel Corp., by Rockwell, and by an NSF CAREER Award (MIP-9623237).

1092-3152/97 $10.00 © 1997 IEEE

A similar model was proposed by Kurdahi et.al. [7]. Both these models consider the effect of interconnect on the overall area, while [7] considers the effect of cell placement on the overall area. Since the controller area, in [6, 7], is estimated based on the number of AND and OR gates required to implement the SOP expression, the optimal number of gates required to implement the function can be much smaller than the above sum. This is because it is frequently possible to apply logic optimization algorithms to give a much better implementation.

2. The Multi-Output Area Model

We aim to estimate the *minimum* number of gates ($\mathcal{A}$) required for a multi-level implementation the function, given only its high level description (Boolean equations) and a target technology library. The area model proposed for single-output Boolean functions [4, 5] is based on the notion of complexity of the on and off-sets of a Boolean function. One such complexity measure which will be used in this paper is the *linear measure*, defined in [5].

Our approach to solving the multi-output area estimation problem is inspired by the multi-valued logic approach to address the problem of two-level minimization of multi-output Boolean functions [8]. The approach is based on transforming a binary-valued, multi-output Boolean function into an equivalent multi-valued-input, single-output (binary-valued) Boolean function. The transformation is accomplished by adding an m-valued input to the Boolean function. Each value of the multi-valued input corresponds to one of the original m outputs. In our approach we perform a similar transformation, except that we use $\lceil \log_2(m) \rceil$ binary-valued inputs to implement an m-valued input. An equivalent way of representing the transformation is to think of the additional $\lceil \log_2(m) \rceil$ binary-valued inputs as control signals of a multiplexor, and that the value of the control word corresponds to the output being selected. This corresponds to multiplexing the m outputs of a m-output Boolean function, as shown if Fig. 1. The original n input m output function f is thus transformed to a $(n + \lceil \log_2 m \rceil)$ input, single-output Boolean function $\hat{f}$. Since $\hat{f}$ is a single-output function, its area can be computed by the application of the area model of [5]. It must be noted that since we are applying the area estimation technique to $\hat{f}$, which is made up of all the outputs, we are in effect dealing with all the outputs at the same time and thus automatically accounting for the effect of sharing.

A natural question to ask is, what is the relation between the (optimal) area of f and that of $\hat{f}$. To answer this question, consider the following two scenarios. In the first scenario, let all the outputs of the multi-output Boolean function be the same. In this case the area of the multi-output Boolean function is equal to the area of any of its outputs. Also note that the prime implicants of the on and off-sets of $\hat{f}$ are independent of the control inputs. Hence the complexity measure of $\hat{f}$ is equal to the complexity measure of any of the outputs of f. Also, as all the outputs of the function are the same, there is no need for the multiplexor. Thus the area contribution of the multiplexor to the overall area of a minimized $\hat{f}$ is zero. Now consider the second scenario. Here, assume that all the outputs of the multi-output Boolean function have disjoint support sets. It then follows that the optimal area of $\hat{f}$ is equal to the sum of the optimal area complexity of f and the area complexity of the multiplexor. Thus one has to subtract the area of the multiplexor from the area complexity of $\hat{f}$ in order to get the area complexity of f. Moreover every prime implicant in the on and off-sets of $\hat{f}$ contains all the control inputs.

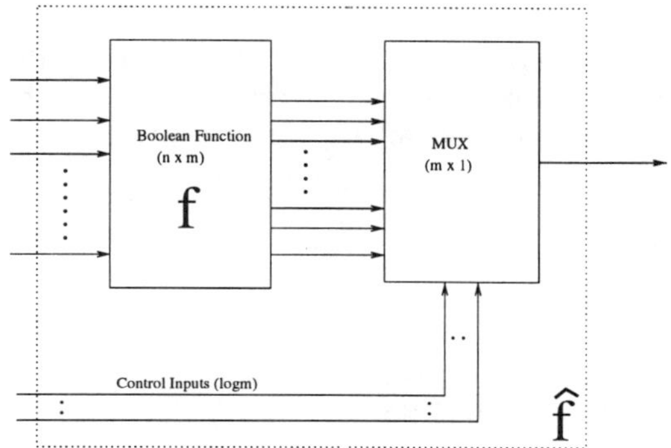

Figure 1. Transformation of a m output Boolean function into a single output Boolean function.

In the first scenario, when the contribution of the multiplexor to the area of $\hat{f}$ was zero, we saw that the control inputs were absent from all the prime implicants, while in the second scenario when the contribution of the multiplexor to the area of $\hat{f}$ is maximum, we saw that all the control inputs are present in every prime implicant of $\hat{f}$. Thus there seems to be a correlation between the influence of the multiplexor on the area of $\hat{f}$ and the number of control inputs in the prime implicants of $\hat{f}$.

The difference $\mathcal{A}(\hat{f}) - \mathcal{A}(f)$ represents the area contribution of the multiplexor to an optimal area implementation of $\hat{f}$. Note that after optimization it might so happen that certain control inputs become redundant for certain outputs. This manifests itself as some control inputs being absent in some prime implicants of on and off-sets of $\hat{f}$. Thus, we may think of $\mathcal{A}(\hat{f}) - \mathcal{A}(f)$ as representing the area of a *reduced* multiplexor resulting from the optimization. This reduced multiplexor area is related to the number of remaining control signals, which leads us to a method for estimating this area, as follows.

From the above considerations, we propose that an appropriate area model for a multi-output function f, in terms of the area of $\hat{f}$ and the area of a m to 1 multiplexor is given by

$$\mathcal{A}(f) = \mathcal{A}(\hat{f}) - \alpha \mathcal{A}_{mux} \quad (2)$$

where $\mathcal{A}_{mux}$ is the area complexity of an m to 1 multiplexor, and $0 \leq \alpha \leq 1$ is a coefficient that represents the contribution of the multiplexor to the area complexity of $\hat{f}$. In the following, we present an approach for estimating α.

Note that the complexity measure [5] of a m to 1 multiplexor is given by $\lceil \log_2 m \rceil + 1$, i.e., the complexity of a m to 1 multiplexor is proportional to the number of control inputs. This is true because every prime implicant of a m to 1 multiplexor has a size given by $\lceil \log_2 m \rceil + 1$. In [5] it was observed that the area complexity ($\mathcal{A}_{mux}$) is approximately exponential in the complexity measure. Hence it follows that:

$$\mathcal{A}_{mux} \propto 2^{\lceil \log_2 m \rceil} \quad (3)$$

Let C_i denote the number of control inputs in a prime implicant P_i. Then define C_{on} to be the average number of control inputs in a prime implicant belonging to the on-set of $\hat{f}$, so that:

$$C_{on} = \frac{\sum_{i=1}^{K_{on}} C_i}{K_{on}} \quad (4)$$

where K_{on} is the number of prime implicants in the on-set of $\hat{f}$. Similarly, one can define C_{off}. From the above discussion it follows that C_{on} and C_{off} can be used to measure the area contribution of the multiplexor to an optimal area implementation of $\hat{f}$. Notice that the optimal implementation of $\hat{f}$ will contain a (implicit) reduced multiplexor whose area depends on the smaller of C_{on} and C_{off}. Thus, we can model this area contribution, in a fashion analogous to equation (3), as:

$$\mathcal{A}(\hat{f}) - \mathcal{A}(f) \propto 2^{\min\{C_{on}, C_{off}\}} \quad (5)$$

It then follows from equations (3) and (5) that:

$$\alpha = 2^{\min\{C_{on}, C_{off}\} - \lceil \log_2 m \rceil} \quad (6)$$

It must be noted that α can be computed with minimal effort from the prime implicants of $\hat{f}$, and once α is available, $\mathcal{A}(f)$ can be computed using (2).

3. High-Level Area Estimation Flow

The transformation, as stated in the previous section, does not place any restriction on the number of outputs that can be dealt with at a time (m). However, we have observed that in practice there is a trade-off between run time of the area estimation procedure and m. As the value of m increases we observed that the time taken to generate the prime implicants usually increases. However, using too small a value of m can affect the accuracy by overestimating the area, as the sharing between all outputs is not captured. After experimenting with different values of m, it was found that a reasonable choice for the value of m was 16.

Typically, a multi-output Boolean function has outputs with varying support set sizes. Outputs whose support set size is very small, for instance 1, 2 or 3, consume very little area. For these outputs very little area optimization can be done. One can make a reliable area prediction for such outputs without having to resort to the above approach. In fact it was found that an area estimate of two gates for outputs whose support set size is two, and an estimate of three gates for outputs with support set size of three, works very well in practice. As far as outputs with support set size of one are concerned, their contribution to an optimal area implementation depends on whether or not they are realized by inversion of a primary input signal. Those which are realized by inversion are assumed to contribute an area of one gate while the rest are assumed not to contribute to the area. The above approach yields benefits in terms of both run time and accuracy, and has been adopted in our area estimation procedure. The flow diagram for the overall area estimation procedure is given in Fig. 2.

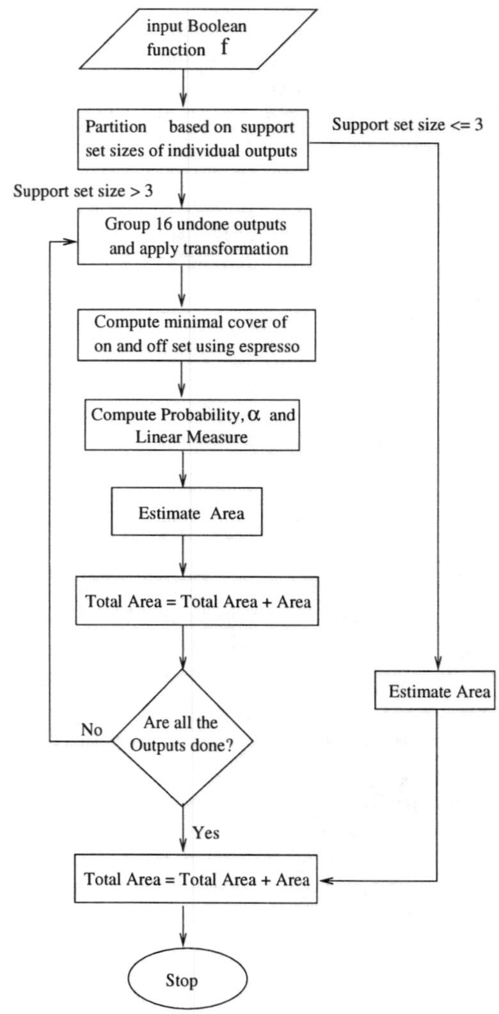

Figure 2. Flow of the Area estimation Procedure.

The area estimation tool reads an input description of f and partitions the function into two sub-functions. One sub-function (f_1) comprises of all outputs whose support set size is less than or equal to three, while the other (f_2), comprises of all outputs whose support set size is greater than three. The partitioning of the network into f_1 and f_2 can be performed by a breadth first search and is fairly inexpensive. We estimate the area of f_1 in the following fashion:

$$\mathcal{A}(f_1) = \beta|f_1^1| + 2|f_1^2| + 3|f_1^3| \tag{7}$$

Here, $|f_1^1|$ is the number of outputs in f_1 with support set size equal to 1, β is a fraction of these outputs which are realized by inversion of a primary input signal, $|f_1^2|$ is the number of outputs in f_1 with support set size equal to 2, and $|f_1^3|$ is the number of outputs in f_1 with support set size equal to 3. For estimating the area of f_2 we use the transformation based approach described above. Let the outputs of f_2 be grouped into I groups of size sixteen each. Let the Boolean function comprising of the ith group of outputs be g_i. We apply the multiplexor transformation to g_i, and compute α, probability and the *linear measure* of the resultant $\hat{g}_i$. We then compute the area complexity of g_i using (2) and (6). This procedure is repeated until all the outputs have been used up, and the area of f_2 is estimated as:

$$\mathcal{A}(f_2) = \sum_{i=1}^{I} \mathcal{A}(g_i) \tag{8}$$

Finally, the area of f is computed as:

$$\mathcal{A}(f) = \mathcal{A}(f_1) + \mathcal{A}(f_2) \tag{9}$$

It must be noted that the proposed area model does not account for area sharing across groups.

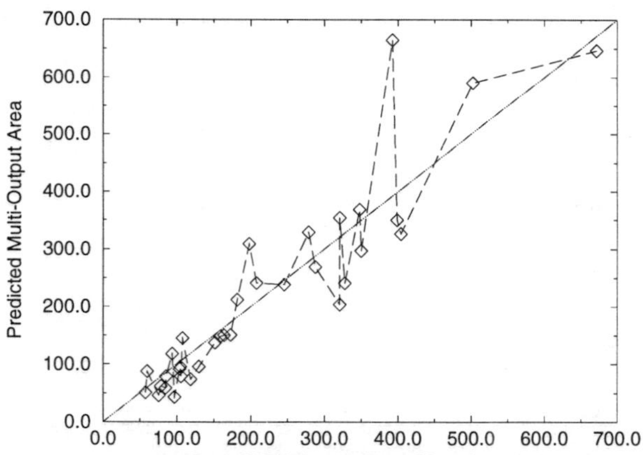

Figure 3. Actual Area versus Predicted Area.

3.1 Empirical Results

The above proposed area model for multi-output functions was tested on several ISCAS-89 and MCNC benchmark circuits. These circuits are listed in Table 1 which, in addition to primary input and output counts, shows the functionality of these benchmarks. These circuits were optimized in SIS using *rugged.script* for optimization, and mapped using the library *lib2.genlib*. The area predicted using the area model was compared with the SIS optimal area.

The performance of the model on all the benchmarks in Table 1, except *s*13207* and *s*35932, is shown in Fig. 3. Circuit *s*13207* is a modified version of *s*13207, obtained by deleting the primary outputs which contain exclusive-or arrays in them. The SIS-optimal area of *s*13207* was 1367. The estimated area for this circuit was 1045. The circuit *s*35932 could not be optimized in SIS in one piece. Hence the circuit was partitioned based on the support set sizes (in a fashion similar to the above discussion) and optimized separately in SIS. The resulting SIS-area that was obtained was 7252. The area estimated by the area estimation tool was 8761.

Table 1.
Characteristics and run-times for the benchmark function set

CIRCUIT Name	Circuit Function	Inputs	Outputs	CPU Time sec
b9	Logic	41	21	5.7
c8	Logic	28	18	4.9
example2	Logic	85	66	28
frg2	Logic	143	139	268
i7	Logic	199	67	23.1
i8	Logic	133	81	81.5
i6	Logic	138	67	17.5
cht	Logic	47	36	6.5
alu2	ALU	10	6	12.8
alu4	ALU	14	8	104
term1	Logic	34	10	17.4
ttt2	Logic	24	21	6.25
apex6	Logic	135	99	45.3
apex7	Logic	49	37	20.3
x1	Logic	51	35	12.8
x3	Logic	135	99	53
x4	Logic	94	71	28.6
vda	Logic	17	39	39.3
k2	Logic	45	45	170.1
s298	Controller	17	20	4.4
s386	Controller	13	13	4.2
s400	Controller	24	27	8.5
s444	Controller	24	27	8.5
s510	Controller	25	13	6.9
s526	Controller	24	27	10.4
s526n	Controller	24	27	10
s641	Controller	59	43	41.4
s713	Controller	58	42	42.3
s820	Controller	37	24	16.3
s832	Controller	37	24	16.5
s953	Controller	39	52	38.8
s1196	Logic	28	32	163
s1238	Logic	28	32	141
s1494	Controller	27	25	26.8
s1488	Controller	27	25	29.3
s13207	Logic	152	783	212.8
s35932	Logic	1763	1728	942.4

The execution time required by our area estimation tool is also given in Table 1, in cpu seconds on a SUN sparc5 with 24 MB RAM. We compared these run times, on the above benchmarks, with one run of SIS using *script.rugged* followed by SIS technology mapping. The speedup obtained is shown in Fig. 4. The figure shows a speedup between 2x and 24x. Notice that a speedup of 10x was obtained on large benchmarks like *s*35932 and *s*13207*. It must be kept in mind that the reported SIS time for *s*35932 was obtained after the circuit was partitioned. Strictly speaking the circuit was not completed in SIS. Hence we believe that on large benchmarks the speedups that can be obtained in practice can be significant.

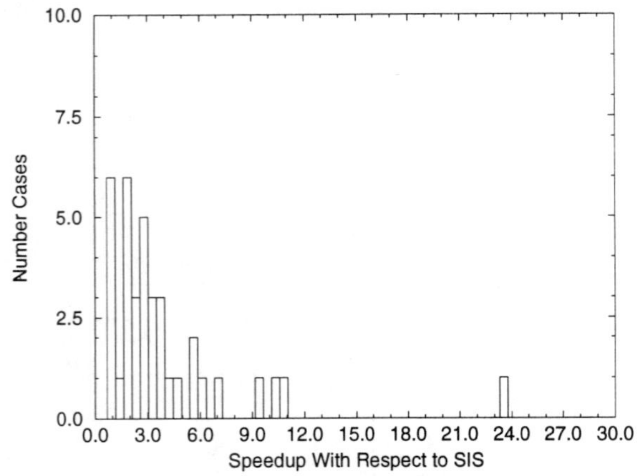

Figure 4. Speed up versus Number of Cases.

4. Estimation of $\mathcal{C}_{avg}$

In order to estimate the power, one needs to estimate not only the area complexity but also $\mathcal{C}_{avg}$, which is the average node capacitance (including interconnect) in a circuit. If $\mathcal{C}_{tot}$ is the total circuit capacitance of an optimal area implementation and $\mathcal{A}$ is the number of gates, then:

$$\mathcal{C}_{avg} = \frac{\mathcal{C}_{tot}}{\mathcal{A}} \tag{10}$$

This quantity depends on the target gate library and on the fan-out structure of the circuit. In order to estimate this, it is assumed that one has access to a few area optimal circuit implementations in the desired target library. This does not appear to be an unreasonable assumption. In this case, an estimate of $\mathcal{C}_{avg}$ can be obtained by performing an average of the $\mathcal{C}_{avg}$ estimates obtained from the area optimal circuit implementations.

In order to test the accuracy of this approach, only a few benchmarks from the benchmark set listed in Table 1 were used to obtain an estimate of $\mathcal{C}_{avg}$. These benchmarks were *s*13207*, *s*35932, *k*2 and *i*8. This estimated value of $\mathcal{C}_{avg}$ was used to compute $\mathcal{C}_{tot}$, assuming that the exact value of $\mathcal{A}$ was available. The estimated value of $\mathcal{C}_{tot}$ was compared with the true value of $\mathcal{C}_{tot}$, and the results are shown in Fig. 5, which validates the above estimation procedure for $\mathcal{C}_{avg}$.

The estimated value of $\mathcal{C}_{avg}$ was combined with the estimated area complexity of Boolean functions to obtain an estimate of the total capacitance of the Boolean function, $\mathcal{C}_{tot}$. The plot comparing the actual versus predicted values of $\mathcal{C}_{tot}$, when both $\mathcal{A}$ and $\mathcal{C}_{avg}$ are estimated, is shown in Fig. 6.

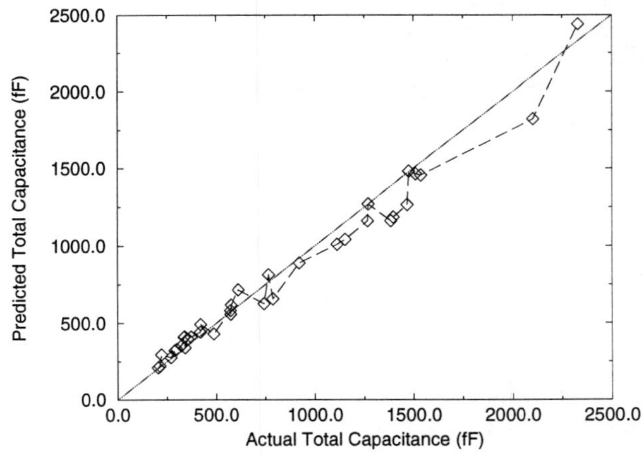

Figure 5. Error between actual and estimated values of $\mathcal{C}_{tot}$ assuming $\mathcal{A}$ is known.

5. High-Level Power Estimation

The area estimate can be used to estimate the power dissipated by a Boolean function, by combining it with average activity estimates [3] and the average node capacitance estimate. We will compare our power estimates to the power dissipated by a gate level optimal area implementation of the Boolean function under two different timing models, namely, the zero-delay model and the general-delay timing model [3]. In the case of the *general-delay* timing model the delays were obtained from a gate library and an event driven simulation was performed.

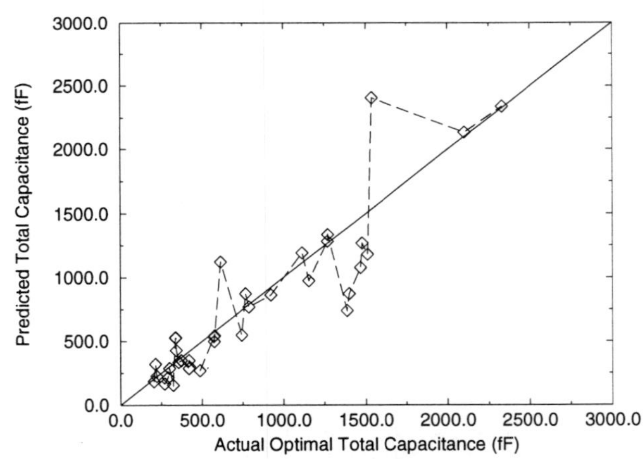

Figure 6. Actual versus Estimated values of $\mathcal{C}_{tot}$ versus Number of Cases.

It must be noted that the activity prediction model [3] does not account for the increase in switching activity due to glitches, as is probably to be expected from a high-level model. Hence it is important to check the accuracy of the high-level power model against the zero-delay simulation results. This is shown in Fig. 7. Since the activity prediction model [3] depends on the input switching statistics of the circuit, we varied the signal probabilities at the circuit inputs from 0.1 to 0.9. Thus, each benchmark circuit is represented by a number of data points in the figure.

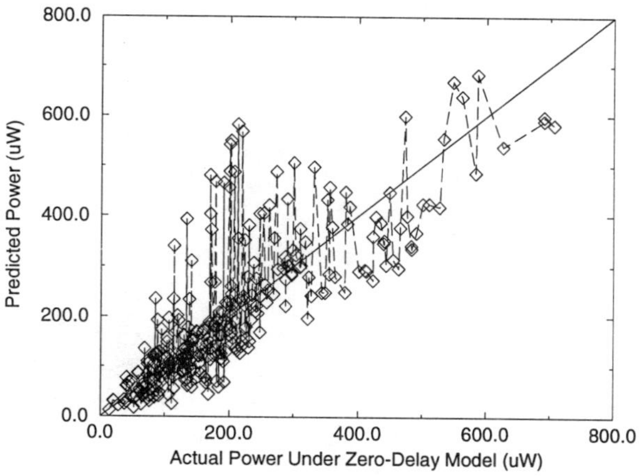

Figure 7. Comparison between actual zero-delay power and predicted power.

For the benchmarks *vda* and *k*2, the predicted power is significantly different from the actual zero-delay power inspite of the fact that the predicted total capacitance is very close to the true value of total capacitance. This is because of an over-estimation in the average activity of the circuit. The correlation plot between predicted and actual zero-delay power obtained after removal of the power estimates corresponding to these two circuits is shown in Fig. 8. The better agreement in this plot shows that indeed for all but two of the benchmarks considered, the method works rather well. These two circuits are responsible for most of the bad points in Fig. 7.

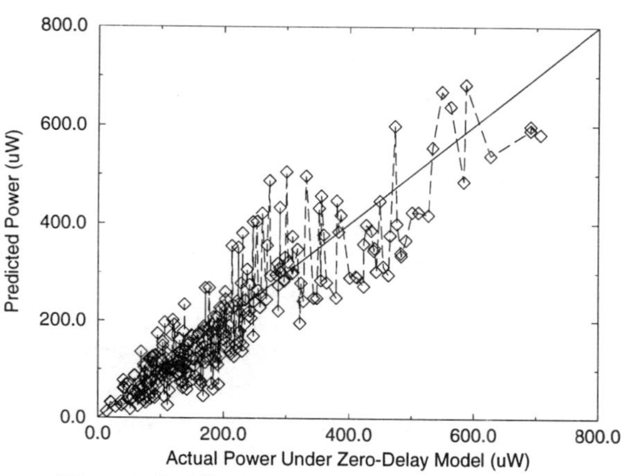

Figure 8. Comparison between actual zero-delay power and predicted power after deletion of points corresponding to *vda* and *k*2.

We also compared the predicted power against the general-delay simulation results. This is shown in Fig. 9. As is to be expected, the error in the prediction increases. This is due to the possible presence, in the general-delay case, of multiple transitions per cycle at a logic node, i.e., glitches.

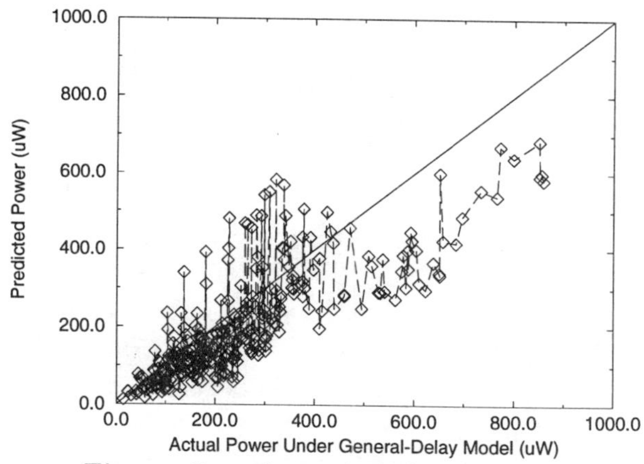

Figure 9. Comparison between actual general-delay power and predicted power.

6. Conclusions

In this paper we presented a new area model to predict the area complexity of multi-output Boolean functions. This was based on transforming the multi-output function at hand to an equivalent single-output function. The advantages of this model is that no additional characterization in necessary beyond that done for single-output functions. Moreover it offers a natural framework to account for sharing occurring in a multi-output function. The predicted capacitance was then combined with average activity estimates [3] to get high level power estimates.

References

[1] F. Najm, "Towards a High-Level Power Estimation Capability," *ACM/IEEE International Symposium on Low-Power Design*, pp. 87–92, 1995.

[2] D. Marculescu, R. Marculescu and M. Pedram, "Information theoretic measures of energy consumption at register transfer level," *International Symposium of Low Power Design*, pp. 81-86, 1995.

[3] M. Nemani and F. Najm, "Towards a high-level power estimation capability," *IEEE Trans. on Computer Aided Design*, vol. 15, no. 6, pp. 588-589, June 1996.

[4] M. Nemani and F. Najm, "High-level power estimation and the area complexity of Boolean functions," *International Symposium of Low Power Electronics and Design*, pp. 329-334, 1996.

[5] M. Nemani and F. Najm, "High-Level Area Prediction for Power Estimation," *Custom Integrated Circuits Conference*, 1997.

[6] A. C-H. Wu, V. Chaiyakul and D. D. Gajski, "Layout area models for high level synthesis," *International Conference on Computer Aided Design*, pp. 34-37, 1991.

[7] F. J. Kurdahi, D. D. Gajski, C. Ramachandran and V. Chaiyakul, "Linking register transfer and physical levels of design," *IEICE Transactions on Information and Systems*, September 1993.

[8] G. De Micheli, *Synthesis and Optimization of Digital Circuits*, New York, NY: McGraw-Hill Inc., 1994.

Optimizing Computations in a Transposed Direct Form Realization of Floating-Point LTI-FIR Systems *

N. Sankarayya and **K. Roy**
Purdue University
Dept. of Electrical & Computer Engineering
West Lafayette, IN 47907-1285
sankar, kaushik @ecn.purdue.edu

D. Bhattacharya
Texas Instruments Inc.
13510 N. Central Expressway
Dallas, TX 75243
bhattach@sunspot.hc.ti.com

Abstract

The inherent computational redundancy in discrete-time LTI-FIR system response computations in Digital Signal Processing have been exploited in a variety of ways to minimize the computational complexity. We present an improved algorithm-level computational optimization that uses sorted recursive differences between coefficients representing the system transfer function with a Floating-Point number representation to extract maximum benefits from this redundancy. It can be applied to any LTI-FIR system and there is no deterioration in accuracy compared to directly using the coefficients. The results for several practical FIR systems show that there is a significant reduction in the computational complexity, hence power consumed, using this technique.

1 Introduction

The recent proliferation of high-performance portable battery-powered electronic gadgets that make extensive use of Digital Signal Processing (DSP) like cellular phones, laptop computers, etc. has made power consumption in VLSI DSPs an increasingly important issue. This has made low-power-high-performance VLSI DSP an important research area. One of the most basic operations performed in DSP applications is the Finite Impulse Response (FIR) computation. As is well known, the output of a Linear Time-Invariant (LTI) system can be obtained by convolving in the time domain the input to the system and the transfer function of the system. For discrete-time LTI-FIR systems, this can be expressed mathematically as:

$$Y_j = \sum_{n=0}^{N-1} C_n.X_{j-n} \tag{1}$$

The notation A_r is used to denote the r-th term of the sequence A. X and Y are the discrete-time input and output signals, respectively, represented as sequences. The sequence C represents the transfer function of the system. For FIR filters, C also corresponds to the set of filter coefficients and the length of the sequence which is N, is called the number of taps or the length of the filter.

FIR system realizations can vary widely from one that uses dedicated hardware multipliers and adders to one that uses software executed by a general purpose processor and its ancillary units. A combination of hardware and software that allows sharing of multi-purpose hardware units (like adders and multipliers), without using a full-fledged processor can also be used. In all these implementations the basic FIR computation algorithm called the *multiply and accumulate* (MAC) sequence, remains the same: for any j, each *product term* $C_n.X_{j-n}$ in Eqn. (1) is computed, and they are added up to obtain Y_j. Therefore the large number of taps required for practical narrow-transition bandwidth FIR filters [4] means a large number of multiplications per filter output and hence more power dissipated in multiplications.

2 Low-Power FIR Filter Realization

There are three sources of power dissipation in CMOS circuits: switching power P_{sw}, short-circuit power P_{sc}, and leakage power $P_{leakage}$ [3]. P_{sw} is often the most significant source, therefore efforts to reduce the power consumed in FIR system realizations, focus on reducing P_{sw}.

Since multiplications represent the most complex task in FIR computations, a lot of research has been carried out on reducing the complexity of or totally eliminating multiplications in computing the product terms in Eqn. (1). Some of these also lead to a reduction in the net switching power consumed and hence low-power FIR system realizations. Some of these earlier efforts towards reducing the complexity of multiplications are : approximation by signed and unsigned powers-of-two coefficients (2PFIR) [6, 21], coefficient representation using redundant number systems

*This research was supported in part by DARPA (F33615-95-C-1625), NSF CAREER award (9501869-MIP), IBM, AT&T and Rockwell

including Canonical Signed Digits (CSD) encoding [17] and Residue Number Systems (RNS) [10], coefficient word-length reduction using sigma-delta modulation [15, 18] and linear predictive coding [22], filter realization as a prefilter-equalizer pair [7, 8] or as cascaded sub-filters [19] with an overall reduced multiplication complexity, the use of Distributed Arithmetic architectures for filter implementation [5], multiplier-less stored-product digital filters (SPDF) using ROMs [14], the frequency-response masking technique for design of filters [23], realization of filters using multi-stage interpolation and decimation units [9, 20, 16] and the extraction of common sub-expressions across coefficients for maximizing computational reusage [1, 2, 11, 12]. While significant reductions have been achieved using these techniques, quite a few rely on approximating the optimally designed coefficients to achieve their results.

3 Sorted Recursive Differences

We had earlier analyzed the usage of recursive differences between coefficients, called the Differential Coefficients Method (DCM) [13] for reducing the complexity of multiplications. One limitation of DCM was that it could be applied only to systems where the envelope generated by the coefficient sequence (and various orders of differences) is a smoothly varying continuous function, thus it was beneficial largely for low-pass FIR filters. We present an improved version of DCM, called the *Sorted Recursive Differences* (SRD) method, which uses recursive sorting of coefficients and various orders of differences to maximize the computational reduction. This recursive sorting is made possible by the Transposed Direct Form of FIR output computation. Thus there are no restrictions on the coefficient sequence to which it is applicable (or the sequences of various orders of differences). The effective word-length reduction using DCM was not the same for each coefficient. Instead of pessimistically using the worst case reduction as we did earlier we will now use a simple statistical estimate for the effective reduction in the number of ones in the coefficients. The earlier analysis was implicitly for a fixed-point implementation because it used the ratios of the dynamic ranges of various orders of differences to arrive at the effective word-length reduction. This paper presents the application of SRD to a Floating-Point (FP) number representation and it is shown that there are significant benefits in terms of computational reduction in doing this.

3.1 Differential Coefficients Method

We first present a brief recapitulation of DCM [13]. The *first-order differences* $\delta^1_{k-1/k}$ between consecutive terms C_k and C_{k-1} of the sequence C, was defined using the recurrence:

$$C_k = C_{k-1} + \delta^1_{k-1/k} \quad \text{for } k=1 \text{ to } (N-1) \tag{2}$$

Therefore a product term C_kX_j can be expressed recursively in terms of the previous product term $C_{k-1}X_j$ and the first-order partial product $\delta^1_{k-1/k}X_j$. Thus we can compute all product terms involving data X_j, excepting the first C_0X_j which has to be computed directly, by computing only the first-order partial products by actual multiplication and adding them to previous product terms. This was called the *first-order differences algorithm* for computing the filter output and it requires $N-1$ extra additions for computing all product terms.

We can also use greater orders of differences to recursively define coefficients. The *second-order differences* $\delta^2_{k-2/k}$, between consecutive first-order differences, was defined using the recurrence:

$$\delta^1_{k-1/k} = \delta^1_{k-2/k-1} + \delta^2_{k-2/k} \quad \text{for } k=2 \text{ to } (N-1) \tag{3}$$

From this definition and Eqn. (2), except C_0 and C_1, all other coefficients can be expressed as:

$$C_k = C_{k-1} + \delta^1_{k-2/k-1} + \delta^2_{k-2/k} \quad \text{for } k=2 \text{ to } (N-1) \tag{4}$$

Thus we can compute all first-order partial products involving data X_j, excepting the first one $\delta^1_{0/1}X_j$ which has to be computed directly, by computing only second-order partial products $\delta^2_{k-2/k}X_j$ by actual multiplication and adding them to previous first-order partial products. And all product terms, except the first, can be generated recursively if we have all the first-order partial products and the first product term. For example if we compute C_0X_j and $\delta^1_{0/1}X_j$ by direct multiplication, C_1X_j can be obtained as $C_0X_j + \delta^1_{0/1}X_j$ and C_2X_j can be obtained by computing $\delta^2_{0/2}X_j$ by multiplication and adding it to the sum of C_1X_j and $\delta^1_{0/1}X_j$. All remaining product terms can be obtained likewise by computing only one second-order partial product by multiplication and this was called the *second-order differences algorithm.*

The algorithm was generalized to use upto m-th order differences, with the m-th order difference defined as:

$$\delta^m_{k-m/k} = \delta^{m-1}_{k-m+1/k} - \delta^{m-1}_{k-m/k-1} \tag{5}$$
$$\text{for } k=m \text{ to } (N-1);\ m=2 \text{ to } (N-1)$$

The recurrence relation between coefficients using m-th order differences is as follows:

$$C_k = C_{k-1} + \sum_{i=1}^{m-1} \delta^i_{k-i-1/k-1} + \delta^m_{k-m/k} \tag{6}$$
$$k=m \text{ to } (N-1);\ m=2 \text{ to } (N-1)$$

We can again compute each product term incrementally as shown before for the second-order differences algorithm and each product term from C_mX_j upwards will require computation of only one m-th order partial product by multiplication. It can be seen that a total of : $1+2+\cdots+(m-1)+m(N-m) = \frac{m}{2}(2N-m-1)$, extra additions are needed.

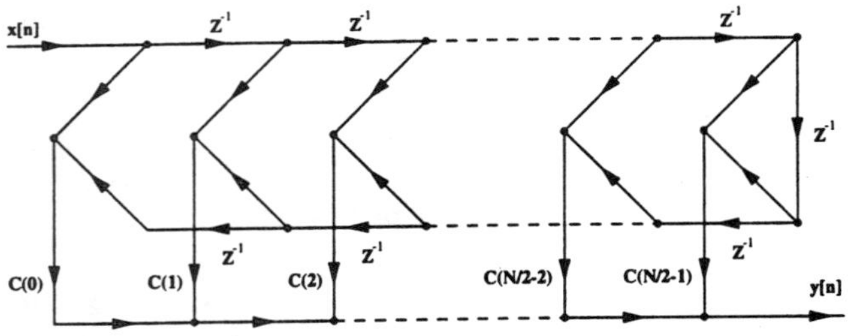

Figure 1: Signal flow graph for Direct Form realization of an even length FIR system.

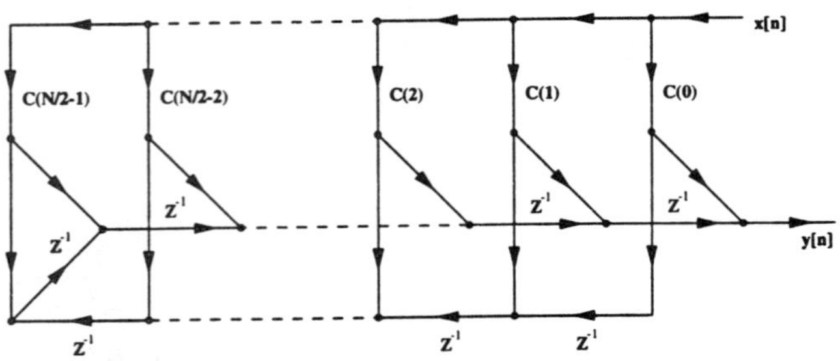

Figure 2: Signal flow graph for Transposed Direct Form realization of the same FIR system.

3.2 Transposed Direct Form Computation

In a Transposed Direct Form (TDF) FIR computation, all N product terms involving a particular data are computed before any product term with the next sequential data is computed. The product terms are accumulated in N different registers since they belong to N sequential outputs. The effective throughput remains the same as direct form computation. Signal flow graphs for direct form and TDF computation are shown in Figs. 1 and 2 respectively.

One advantage of using TDF lies in the fact that it does not matter in which order we compute the product terms involving a particular data so long as we accumulate them in the right registers. Therefore we can sort the coefficients in non-decreasing (or non-increasing) order before taking first order differences. It can be shown that this ordering minimizes the sum of the absolute value of first order differences. Sorting can also be applied to differences. Thus we can generate the second order differences from the sorted set of first order differences. This could be recursively done upto any order of differences. The various permutations of the sets of different orders of differences needed for a correct restoration could be hardwired in the control unit. This would enable it to accumulate partial products in appropriate locations so that the correct output is produced. Thus if DCM is applied in a TDF realization with recursive sorting we can eliminate the restrictions that were earlier imposed on the coefficients and various orders of differences for DCM to be viable.

3.3 Number Representation

Whereas sorting guarantees that differences of all orders will be non-negative, the coefficients can be positive or negative. When two consecutive coefficients in the sorted sequence are of opposite signs the magnitude of the algebraic difference between them is larger than the magnitude of either one. To decrease the range of the coefficients (hence smaller differences) we will use absolute values to compute differences and then manipulate the sign. As an example consider two consecutive coefficients C_r, C_{r+1}, with values +0.8 and -0.9. The first-order differences algorithm would compute $C_{r+1}X_j$ as: $C_rX_j + \delta^1_{r/r+1}X_j$. Let $\delta^1_{r/r+1}$ be generated as the difference between the absolute values of C_r and C_{r+1}, which in this case is +0.1. Then we can compute the partial product $+0.1X_j$, add it to C_rX_j and complement the sign-bit of the sum to obtain the correct value of $C_{r+1}X_j$. The sign-bit manipulation could be handled by the control unit and if the differences are known in advance the necessary sequence of sign-bit manipulations could be hardwired in the control unit. As another example suppose the two terms had values -0.7 and +0.6. In this case too we could compute $+0.1X_j$, add it to C_rX_j and complement the sign-bit of the sum to obtain the correct value of $C_{r+1}X_j$. Thus we see that a sign-magnitude number representation is very suitable for SRD and differences will be computed between absolute values of terms and it is assumed that necessary sign-bit changes are done by the control unit.

Towards further reducing the magnitudes of differences, we looked at the benefits of using a simplified Floating-Point (FP) number representation for the coefficients and data. Note that the mantissas of non-zero coefficients will always lie between 0.5 and 1 if they are normalized, thus allowing the same percentage precision for all coefficients. If differences are computed between mantissas, since only the mantissas are actually multiplied together in a FP multiplication, and if the $\lceil N/2 \rceil$ (symmetric filter) mantissas are uniformly distributed in the range 0.5 to 1, the average first-order difference can be expected to to be : $(1 - 0.5)/\lceil N/2 \rceil \approx 1/N$. For example if we have 50 taps, this amounts to a 5 to 6 bits drop in magnitude of the mantissas of first-order differences. Therefore compared to the mantissas of C the first 5 to 6 bits of these will be all zeroes. A larger N therefore leads to smaller magnitudes of first-order differences. This is also roughly true for higher orders of differences. However since the distribution is not really uniform and to prevent the accumulation of the spread (small and large magnitude differences representing the tail ends of a more realistic Gaussian distribution) we could normalize the mantissas each time we take differences without changing the accuracy. However the controller will have to track a set of exponents associated with each order of difference to shift the partial products when recursively restoring, by the amounts they were shifted when normalizing. In the following analysis, for the sake of simplicity, we will ignore the computations involving the exponents and the sign-bits.

4 Multiplication Complexity Analysis

Let the coefficients or the differences (as appropriate) be the multiplier and and the data be the multiplicand. Let the word-widths used for mantissas of coefficients and data be W_c and W_x bits, respectively. The word-width required for a product term is therefore $(W_c + W_x)$ bits.

To analyze the computational reduction using SRD we will express a multiplication as equivalent shifts and additions. A multiplication will be performed by repeatedly adding the multiplicand to the left end of a partial sum, with the MSB of the multiplicand aligned with the second MSB of the partial sum (to allow for a carry from the addition). The multiplicand will be added only if the multiplier bit is one. The partial sum will be arithmetically right shifted by one bit after each addition. At the beginning of the multiplication the partial sum will be initialized to zero or the multiplicand, depending on whether the LSB of the multiplier is zero or one. The word-width of the partial sum will be equal to the word-width of a product term.

Consider the application of this model to a W_x bit by W_c bit multiplication. Since additions are skipped where the multiplier bits are zero, the number of additions required for a W_c bits wide multiplier can range from $(W_c - 1)$ to zero and it can be considered a discrete random variable (RV) between these bounds. Assuming a uniform distribution it has an expected value of : $\mathcal{E}\{n_a\} = \frac{1}{2}(W_c - 1)$ (any other symmetrical density function, for example a truncated Gaussian distribution, will give the same result). The expected value of this RV will be used to obtain a statistical estimate of the number of additions. Each addition of the W_x bits wide multiplicand can be considered equivalent to $(W_x + 1)$ one bit full additions. Therefore we get the expected value of the total number of one bit full additions for the multiplication as:

$$n_A = (W_x + 1)\mathcal{E}\{n_a\} = \frac{1}{2}(W_x + 1)(W_c - 1) \qquad (7)$$

Similarly we can arrive at an expression for the total expected number of shifts. Since a partial sum needs a width of $(W_c + W_x)$ bits, right shifting it by one bit involves shifting a field $(W_c + W_x)$ bits wide and $(W_c - 1)$ such one bit shifts are needed for an W_x by W_c multiplication. This can be considered equivalent to a total of $(W_c + W_x)(W_c - 1)$ one bit shifts. Alternatively, if we assume that a multiple bit shifter (like array shifters, barrel shifters or logarithmic shifters) is used and that a run of zeroes in the multiplier is handled in a single shift operation, the number of shifts would be approximately the same as the number of adds, since each add must be preceded by a shift (of variable size). We get the expected value of the number of variable sized shifts for the multiplication as:

$$n_S \approx (W_c + W_x)\mathcal{E}\{n_a\} = \frac{1}{2}(W_c + W_x)(W_c - 1) \qquad (8)$$

For a symmetric (or antisymmetric) N tap FIR filter we have only $\lceil N/2 \rceil$ unique coefficients and the unique multipliers for SRD is the sequence : $C_0, \delta^1_{0/1}, \cdots, \delta^{m-1}_{0/m-1}, \delta^m_{0/m}, \delta^m_{1/m+1}, \cdots, \delta^m_{\lceil N/2 \rceil - m - 1/\lceil N/2 \rceil - 1}$. The notation $|\delta^m_{k-m/k}|$ will be used to denote the reduced word-width required for the mantissa of $\delta^m_{k-m/k}$. An expected value of the number of ones in each SRD multiplier is derived below. A reduction in the magnitudes of the mantissas by taking differences can be considered as effectively skewing the distribution of the total number of ones in its binary representation, since a string of MSBs will be all zero. Let n'_a be the discrete one dimensional RV for the number of adds required for each SRD multiplier. Assuming a symmetrical distribution (this was verified by simulations) over its domain and using the relationship derived earlier between the word sizes of the multiplicand and multiplier and the total expected number of adds required for our shift and add model, we obtain: $n'_A = (W_x + 1)\mathcal{E}\{n'_a\}$ for each SRD multiplier. For example for $\delta^m_{k-m/k}$ it is : $\frac{1}{2}(W_x + 1)(|\delta^m_{k-m/k}| - 1)$. Summing up, we get the net expected number of adds for all the SRD multipliers as:

$$\begin{aligned}\sum_{\forall \text{mults}} n'_A &= \sum (W_x + 1)\mathcal{E}\{n'_a\} \\ &= \frac{1}{2}(W_x + 1)\Big(\sum_{k=m}^{\lceil N/2 \rceil - 1} |\delta^m_{k-m/k}| + \sum_{k=1}^{m-1} |\delta^k_{0/k}| \\ &\quad + |C_0| - \lceil N/2 \rceil \Big) = N'_A \qquad (9)\end{aligned}$$

We can likewise obtain the net expected number of adds using the coefficients directly as:

$$\begin{aligned}\sum_{\forall \text{mults}} n_A &= \frac{1}{2}(W_x + 1)\Big(\sum_{k=0}^{\lceil N/2 \rceil - 1} |C_k| - \lceil N/2 \rceil \Big) \\ &= \frac{1}{2}(W_x + 1)(W_c - 1)\lceil N/2 \rceil = N_A \qquad (10)\end{aligned}$$

The expected value of the number of adds can be directly used to approximate the expected value of the number of shifts as mentioned before. Therefore from Eqns. (8) and (9) we get the net expected value of the shifts required for the SRD multipliers as:

$$\begin{aligned}\sum_{\forall \text{mults}} n'_S &= \sum (W_c + W_x)\mathcal{E}\{n'_a\} \\ &= \frac{(W_c + W_x)}{(W_x + 1)} N'_A = N'_S \qquad (11)\end{aligned}$$

Likewise for the direct form multipliers we get :

$$\sum_{\forall \text{mults}} n_S = \frac{(W_c + W_x)}{(W_x + 1)} N_A = N_S \qquad (12)$$

Table 1: Maximum Savings in adds using SRD

FIR Sys.	N	Simulated max S_{ADD}, opt m			
		8 bits	12 bits	16 bits	24 bits
Low Pass	51	37.9, 2	24.9, 3	23.8, 4	11.0, 1
	101	56.0, 2	44.3, 3	39.8, 4	30.7, 5
	201	63.5, 2	56.5, 4	52.5, 3	45.1, 5
Band Stop	51	46.0, 2	31.1, 3	23.5, 4	11.5, 6
	101	50.4, 2	44.7, 3	36.9, 4	30.2, 4
	201	62.2, 2	55.5, 2	50.1, 3	43.9, 5
Band Pass	51	43.5, 2	32.7, 3	23.9, 4	12.4, 3
	101	51.4, 2	43.8, 3	36.9, 3	30.3, 4
	201	62.9, 2	55.8, 3	50.2, 4	43.4, 5
High Pass	51	34.9, 2	21.5, 3	23.0, 4	12.4, 1
	101	53.9, 2	43.6, 3	39.6, 3	31.9, 5
	201	62.8, 2	56.2, 4	52.6, 3	45.5, 6

Table 2: Savings in shifts using SRD

FIR Sys.	N	Simulated S_{SHIFT} at opt m			
		8 bits	12 bits	16 bits	24 bits
Low Pass	51	87.10	82.27	82.81	19.35
	101	95.19	94.27	93.33	83.62
	201	98.64	99.29	94.35	93.51
Band Stop	51	89.13	84.83	81.22	74.14
	101	94.19	93.40	92.71	74.16
	201	98.51	89.62	92.86	93.13
Band Pass	51	88.17	85.42	81.63	46.71
	101	94.80	93.03	82.51	74.28
	201	98.52	97.99	97.48	92.78
High Pass	51	86.05	82.09	84.32	20.96
	101	95.56	94.85	84.60	85.15
	201	98.61	99.46	94.82	96.44

4.1 Overhead Additions for SRD

In Section 3.1 we had derived an expression for the extra additions using m-th order differences. These additions will be pessimistically taken to each be the width of a product term. Substituting $\lceil N/2 \rceil$ in place of N (symmetric case), the net number of equivalent one-bit overhead additions using SRD follows as:

$$N_A'' = \frac{m}{2}(2\lceil N/2 \rceil - m - 1)(W_c + W_x) \qquad (13)$$

The percentage savings in adds and shifts follows as:

$$S_{ADD} = [1 - (N_A' + N_A'')/N_A] * 100 \qquad (14)$$

$$S_{SHIFT} = [1 - N_S'/N_S] * 100 \qquad (15)$$

5 Simulation Results

The results of simulating four different kinds of linear-phase LTI-FIR systems of 51, 101 and 201 tap lengths is presented below. The simulator was developed in MATLAB and it was used to track the exact number of adds and shifts required for direct form and SRD computations. The metrics are for computation of all $\lceil N/2 \rceil$ product terms with a randomly generated data. The coefficients of these systems and the data were generated as floating point numbers with four different mantissa word-widths of 8, 12, 16 and 24 bits. Table 1 shows the maximum percentage savings in the net number of adds using SRD over DF computation as defined by Eqn. (14) and the order m at which the maximum savings was obtained. Though higher order differences reduce the multiplication complexity the overhead additions required by SRD increase with increasing orders of differences. Thus there is a point at which the

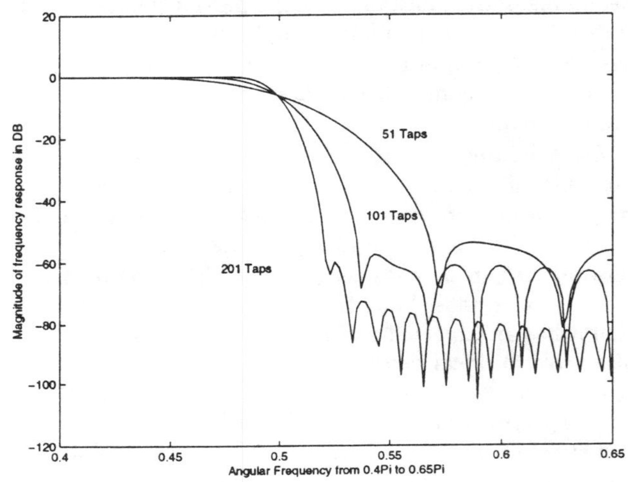

Figure 3: Detail of frequency response for the example low-pass filter in Tables 1 and 2 designed using a Hamming window.

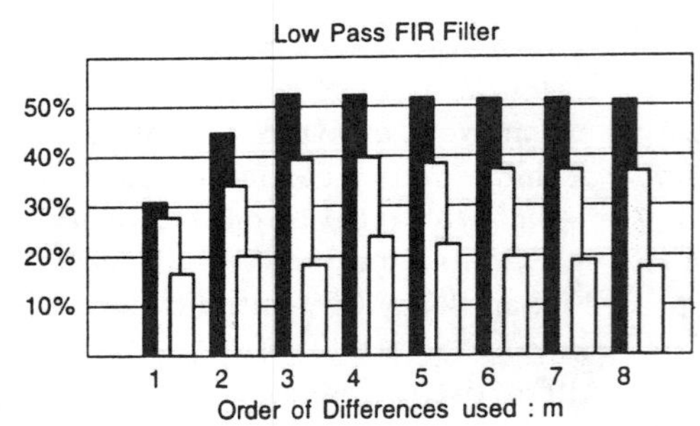

Figure 4: Savings in adds for the same low-pass filter, as a function of the order of differences using 16 bit mantissas. The black bars are for N = 201, the grey bars are for N = 101, the white bars are for N = 51.

overall number of adds is minimized. This is explicitly shown in Fig. 4 which plots the net savings in adds as a function of the order of differences used for our first example which is a low-pass FIR filter. It can be seen that there is a maxima at a different order for each of the three tap lengths. It can also be seen that the maximum savings increases with tap length as was explained in Section 3.3. Table 2 shows the percentage savings in the net number of shifts as defined by Eqn. (15) at the optimum order m at which the net adds is minimized. It is also possible to arrive at an optimum order based on the minimum weighted sum of net adds and shifts.

6 Conclusion

We have presented an improved version of the Differential Coefficients Method called the Sorted Recursive Differences Method. It has been shown that using the SRD method in a transposed direct form FIR structure with a Floating-Point number representation can result in a greatly reduced multiplication complexity as compared to direct form computation. The MATLAB simulation results presented for four practical FIR systems, confirm the theoretical predictions of reduced multiplication complexity. This computational reduction results in a net reduced switching and hence lower power consumption. The statistical analysis used to quantify the computational reduction can be applied to other multiplier models. For example, for an array multiplier a decrease in the number of ones in the multiplier words can be related to a decrease in switching activity within the multiplier and consequently to a lower power consumption.

References

[1] A. Chatterjee, R. K. Roy and M. A. d'Abreu, "Greedy hardware optimization for linear digital systems using number splitting and repeated factorization", *6th Intl Conf on VLSI Design*, Jan 1993, India, pp. 154-159.

[2] A. G. Dempster and M. D. Macleod, "Use of minimum-adder multiplier blocks in FIR digital filters", *IEEE Trans on Ckts & Sys II-Analog & Digital Signal Proc*, v 42, n 9, Sep. 1995, pp. 569-577.

[3] A. P. Chandrakashan and R. Brodersen, "Low power digital CMOS design", *Kluwer Academic Publishers*, 1996.

[4] D. M. Kodek and K. Steiglitz, "Filter-length word-length tradeoffs in FIR digital filter design", *IEEE Trans on Acoustics, Speech & Signal Proc*, v ASSP-28, n 6, Dec 1980, pp. 739-744.

[5] H. J. Shin et. al., "Custom design of CMOS low-power high-performance digital signal-processing macro for hard-disk-drive applications", *IBM Journal of Research & Development*, v 39, n 1-2, Jan-Mar 1995, pp 83-90.

[6] H. Samueli, "An improved search algorithm for the design of multiplierless FIR filters with powers-of-two coefficients", *IEEE Trans on Ckts & Sys*, v 36, n 7, July 1989, pp. 1044-1047.

[7] J. W. Adams and A. N. Willson Jr., "A new approach to FIR digital filters with fewer multipliers and reduced sensitivity", *IEEE Trans on Ckts & Sys*, v CAS-30, n 5, May 1983, pp. 277-283.

[8] J. W. Adams and A. N. Willson Jr., "Some efficient digital prefilter structures", *IEEE Trans on Ckts & Sys*, v CAS-31, n 3, Mar 1984, pp. 260-265.

[9] L. R. Rabiner and R. E. Crochiere, "A novel implementation for narrow-band FIR digital filters", *IEEE Trans on Acoustics, Speech & Signal Proc*, v ASSP-23, n 5, Oct 1975, pp. 457-464.

[10] M. A. Soderstrand and K. Al-Marayati, "VLSI implementation of very-high-order FIR filters", *IEEE Intl Symp on Ckts & Sys*, v 2, 1995, pp. 1436-1439.

[11] M. Mehendale, S.D. Sherlekar and G. Venkatesh, "Coefficient optimization for low power realization of FIR filters", *IEEE Workshop on VLSI Signal Processing*, Japan, 1995.

[12] M. Yagyu, A. Nishihara and N. Fujii, "Fast FIR digital filter structures using minimal number of adders and its application to filter design", *IEICE Trans Fundamentals*, v E79-A, n 8, Aug 1996, pp. 1120-1128.

[13] N. Sankarayya, K. Roy and D. Bhattacharya, "Algorithms for low-power and high speed FIR filter realization using differential coefficients", *IEEE Trans on Ckts & Sys II-Analog & Digital Signal Proc*, v 44, n 6, June 1997, pp. 488-497.

[14] O. Monkewich and W. Steenaart, "Stored product digital filtering with non-linear quantization", *IEEE Intl. Symp on Ckts & Sys*, 1976, pp. 157-160.

[15] P. W. Wong and R. M. Gray, "FIR filters with sigma-delta modulation encoding", *IEEE Trans on Acoustics, Speech & Signal Proc*, v 38, n 6, June 1990, pp. 979-989.

[16] P. P. Vaidyanathan, "Efficient and multiplierless design of FIR filters with very sharp cutoff via maximally flat building blocks", *IEEE Trans on Ckts & Sys*, v CAS-32, n 3, Mar 1985, pp. 236-244.

[17] R. Hartley, "Optimization of CSD multipliers for filter design", *IEEE Intl. Symp on Ckts & Sys*, v 4, 1991, pp. 1992-1995.

[18] S. R. Powell and P. M. Chau, "Efficient narrow-band FIR and IFIR filters based on powers-of-two sigma-delta coefficient truncation", *IEEE Trans on Ckts & Sys II-Analog & Digital Signal Proc*, v 41, n 8, Aug 1994, pp. 497-505.

[19] T. Saramaki, "Design of FIR filters as a tapped cascaded interconnection of identical subfilters", *IEEE Trans on Ckts & Sys*, v CAS-34, n 9, Sept 1987, pp. 1011-1029.

[20] T. Saramaki, Y. Neuvo and S. K. Mitra, "Design of computationally efficient interpolated FIR filters", *IEEE Trans on Ckts & Sys*, v 35, n 1, Jan 1988, pp. 70-87.

[21] Y. C. Lim and S. R. Parker, "FIR filter design over a discrete powers-of-two coefficient space", *IEEE Trans on Acoustics, Speech & Signal Proc*, v ASSP-31, n 3, June 1983, pp. 583-590.

[22] Y. C. Lim, "Predictive coding for FIR filter word-length reduction", *IEEE Trans on Ckts & Sys*, v CAS-32, n 4, Apr 1985, pp. 365-371.

[23] Y. C. Lim, "Frequency-response masking approach for the synthesis of sharp linear phase digital filters", *IEEE Trans on Ckts & Sys*, v CAS-33, n 4, Apr 1986, pp. 357-364.

Achievable Bounds On Signal Transition Activity*

Sumant Ramprasad, Naresh R. Shanbhag, and Ibrahim N. Hajj
Coordinated Science Laboratory
University of Illinois at Urbana-Champaign
Urbana, IL 61801

Abstract

Transitions on high capacitance busses in VLSI systems result in considerable system power dissipation. Therefore, various coding schemes have been proposed in the literature to encode the input signal in order to reduce the number of transitions. In this paper we derive achievable lower and upper bounds on the expected signal transition activity. These bounds are derived via an information-theoretic approach in which symbols generated by a source (possibly correlated) with entropy rate $\mathcal{H}$ *are coded with an average of* R *bits/symbol. These results are applied to, 1.) determine the activity reducing efficiency of different coding algorithms such as Entropy coding, Transition coding, and Bus-Invert coding, 2.) bound the error in entropy-based power estimation schemes, and 3.) determine the lower-bound on the power-delay product. Two examples are provided where transition activity within 4% and 8% of the lower bound is achieved when blocks of 8 and 13 symbols respectively are coded at a time.*

1 INTRODUCTION

The on-chip dynamic power dissipation of CMOS circuits at a node is given by, $P_D = \frac{1}{2}TC_LV_{dd}^2f$, where T is the transition activity at the node, C_L is the capacitance, V_{dd} is the supply voltage, and f is the frequency of operation. At the system level, off-chip busses have capacitances, C_L, that are orders of magnitude greater than those found on signal lines internal to a chip. Therefore, transitions on these busses result in considerable system power dissipation. To address this problem, various signal encoding techniques have been proposed in the literature to encode the data before transmitting it on a bus so as to reduce the expected and the peak number of transitions. Hence, the signal encoding approaches in literature achieve power reduction by reducing T while keeping C_L more or less unaltered. In this paper we derive achievable lower and upper bounds on the expected transition activity for any coding algorithm. These bounds are derived via an information-theoretic approach in which each symbol of a source (possibly correlated) with *entropy rate* $\mathcal{H}$ is coded with R bits on average. The concept of *entropy*, $\mathcal{H}$, from information theory was first employed for single-bit signals, albeit in an empirical manner, in the area of high-level power estimation [2,3]. In contrast, the work presented here is non-empirical, applicable to multi-bit signals, independent of the coding algorithm, and completely unravels the connection between the bounds on transition activity and entropy. This work is a continuation of our effort in developing an information-theoretic view of VLSI computation [5], whereby equivalence between computation and communication is being established.

In section II, we present the preliminaries necessary for the development in the rest of the paper. In section III, the main result is presented in the form of *Theorem 1*. In section IV, we employ Theorem 1 to, 1.) derive lower and upper bounds for different coding algorithms, 2.) bound the error in entropy-based power estimation schemes, and 3.) determine the lower-bound on the power-delay product. We also present two examples where transition activity within 4% and 8% of the lower bound is achieved.

2 PRELIMINARIES

Let X be a discrete random variable with alphabet $\mathcal{X}$ and probability mass function $p(x) = \Pr(X = x)$, $x \in \mathcal{X}$. A measure of the information content of X is given by its *entropy* $H(X)$, which is defined as [1], $H(X) = -\sum_{x\in\mathcal{X}} p(x)\log_2 p(x)$ bits. The *joint entropy* $H(X_1, X_2, \ldots, X_n)$ of a sequence of discrete random variables $(X_1, X_2, \ldots, X_n)$ with a joint distribution $p(x_1, x_2, \ldots, x_n)$ is defined as, $H(X_1, X_2, \ldots, X_n) = -\sum p(x_1, x_2, \ldots, x_n)\log_2 p(x_1, x_2, \ldots, x_n)$ bits. The *entropy rate* of a stochastic process $\{X_i\}$ is defined by, $\mathcal{H} = \lim_{n\to\infty} \frac{1}{n}H(X_1, X_2, \ldots, X_n)$ bits, when the limit exists. The function $H(x)$ is defined on the real interval [0,1] as, $H(x) = -x\log_2 x - (1-x)\log_2(1-x)$ bits. The function $H(x)$ maps the probability of a binary-valued, independent variable to its entropy. The inverse, $H^{-1}(y)$, of H, is defined on the real interval [0,1] as, $H^{-1}(y) = x$, if $y = H(x)$ and $x \in [0, \frac{1}{2}]$. The function $H^{-1}()$ maps the entropy of a binary-valued, independent variable to a probability value that lies between 0 and $\frac{1}{2}$. The *transition activity* of a bit-level signal, b_n, is defined as, $t = \Pr(b_n = 0 \text{ and } b_{n-1} = 1) + \Pr(b_n = 1 \text{ and } b_{n-1} = 0)$. We define a *level encoding* algorithm to be the case where the symbol '0' is coded with the bit '0' and the symbol '1' is coded with the bit '1'. In a *transition encoding* algorithm, the symbol '0' is coded by transmitting the previous transmitted bit and the symbol '1' is coded by trans-

*This work was supported by National Science Foundation CAREER award MIP-9623737 and Joint Services Electronics Program under contract #00014-96-1-0129.

1092-3152/97 $10.00 © 1997 IEEE

mitting the complement of the previous transmitted bit. Hence, a '1' is coded with a transition and a '0' with no transition. Table 1 shows an example of transition coding.

3 ACHIEVABLE BOUNDS

In order to derive bounds on transition activity, we will employ Lemmas 1 and 2 presented below. Lemma 1 bounds x given $y \leq H(x)$. Lemma 2 employs Lemma 1 to bound the expected number of 1's in a sequence of bits with a certain entropy rate $\mathcal{H}$. Theorem 1 employs Lemma 2 to bound the number of transitions/symbol of a source with a certain entropy rate $\mathcal{H}$ given that each symbol is coded employing an expected number of R bits. The proofs are presented in the Appendix.

Lemma 1 *For all (x, y) such that $x \in [0, 1]$ and $y \in [0, 1]$, if $y \leq H(x)$ then, $H^{-1}(y) \leq x \leq 1 - H^{-1}(y)$.*

Lemma 2 *If $\{B_i\}$ is a 0-1 valued stochastic process with entropy rate greater than or equal to $\mathcal{H}$ and if $p_b = \lim_{n\to\infty} \frac{1}{n}\sum_{i=1}^{n} B_i$ exists then, $H^{-1}(\mathcal{H}) \leq p_b \leq 1 - H^{-1}(\mathcal{H})$.*

Theorem 1 *Let,*

1. *$\mathcal{H}$ be the entropy rate of a stochastic source $\{X_i\}$,*
2. *the symbols be coded in a uniquely decodable manner into bits $\{B_i\}$ employing an expected number of $R(> \mathcal{H})$ bits/symbol,*
3. *the bits be transmitted in some arbitrary manner over a finite set of wires such that a receiver can uniquely decode the bits, and*
4. *T be the expected number of transitions in the bits on the wires per symbol (i.e. $\lim_{n\to\infty} \frac{1}{n}\sum_{i=1}^{n} B_i \bigoplus B_j$ exists, where B_j precedes B_i on the same wire and $\bigoplus$ is the exclusive-or operator) then, $H^{-1}(\frac{\mathcal{H}}{R})R \leq T \leq (1 - H^{-1}(\frac{\mathcal{H}}{R}))R$.*

The lower and upper bounds on transition activity computed by Theorem 1 for different values of R are shown in Figure 1. Any coding algorithm will need to reside in the region shown in Figure 1. The transition activity can be made arbitrarily close to 0 by increasing R. In practice, however, R will typically be less than approximately $10\mathcal{H}$ because most of the reduction in the lower bound is achieved by the time $R = 10\mathcal{H}$.

4 APPLICATIONS OF BOUNDS

In this section, we provide applications of Theorem 1. We first employ Theorem 1 and the value of R specified by a coding algorithm to derive bounds for that algorithm.

4.1 Entropy Coding

An entropy code is one for which the expected number of bits/symbol is equal to the entropy of the source.

Corollary 1 *For an entropy coder, $T = \frac{\mathcal{H}}{2}$.*

Proof: *From Theorem 1 and since $R = \mathcal{H}$ for an entropy coder we have, $H^{-1}(1)\mathcal{H} \leq T \leq (1 - H^{-1}(1))\mathcal{H}$. Substituting $H^{-1}(1) = \frac{1}{2}$, we get $T = \frac{\mathcal{H}}{2}$.* ¶

Therefore, as shown in Figure 1, the lower and upper bounds on T are identical for entropy coding.

4.2 Transition Coding

We will redefine transition coding slightly in this subsection as coding the less probable symbol ('0' or '1') with a transition and the other symbol with no transition.

Corollary 2 *Transition coding achieves the lower bound on the transition activity for an i.i.d. source with alphabet $\mathcal{X} = \{0, 1\}$ when $R = 1$ bit/symbol.*

Proof: *From Theorem 1 and since $R = 1$, we have $H^{-1}(\mathcal{H}) \leq T \leq 1 - H^{-1}(\mathcal{H})$. Since the source is i.i.d. with alphabet $\{0,1\}$, $H^{-1}(\mathcal{H})$ is also the probability of a '0' or the probability of a '1', whichever is less. Hence we can achieve the lower bound on the transition activity by coding the less probable symbol ('0' or '1') with a transition and the other symbol with a no transition.* ¶

The upper bound on transition activity of $1 - H^{-1}(\mathcal{H})$ is greater than or equal to the upper bound of $\frac{\mathcal{H}}{2}$ in [2]. This is because, in the proof of the upper bound in [2], the implicit assumption is made that the symbol '0' is coded with the bit '0' and the symbol '1' is coded with the bit '1', i.e., level coding is employed. It is possible to achieve the higher transition activity of $1 - H^{-1}(\mathcal{H})$ for the same entropy if the more probable symbol is coded with a transition.

4.3 Bounds For 1-bit Redundant Codes

In algorithms such as Bus-Invert coding [6], the transition activity on the bus is reduced by employing an additional bit. We now calculate the lower bound for any coding algorithm that uses 1 bit of redundancy. Thus $R = \mathcal{H} + 1$ and from Theorem 1, the expected transition activity is bounded by, $(\mathcal{H} + 1)H^{-1}(\frac{\mathcal{H}}{\mathcal{H}+1}) \leq T \leq (\mathcal{H} + 1)(1 - H^{-1}(\frac{\mathcal{H}}{\mathcal{H}+1}))$. The extra bit may be either an extra line on the bus, or an extra clock to transfer the data. If $\mathcal{H} = 8$ then the lower bound is 2.4506 transitions/symbol. For uniformly distributed, temporally independent data, Bus-Invert coding achieves a transition activity of 3.269 transitions/symbol which is 33.40% above the lower bound. The lower bound can be approached by coding larger and larger blocks of bits. Now, assume the source entropy, $\mathcal{H}$, is increased and $R = \mathcal{H} + 1$. The ratio $\frac{\mathcal{H}}{\mathcal{H}+1}$ approaches 1 and T approaches $\frac{\mathcal{H}}{2}$. Thus, as the entropy increases, the benefit of Bus-Invert coding or any 1-bit redundant code is reduced. The above analysis can be extended for a k-bit redundant code.

4.4 Error Bounds For Entropy-Based Power Estimation Schemes

The bounds on transition activity from Theorem 1 can be employed to calculate the maximum error in schemes that estimate power dissipation from entropy [2,3]. For given $\mathcal{H}$ and R, the error in estimating T, will be less than or equal to the maximum of the difference between the upper bound and the estimate of T, and the difference between the estimate of T and the lower bound. As an example, assume that a source with entropy $\mathcal{H} = 6$ bits is transmitted over an 8-bit bus. Since $R = 8$, the lower bound on transition activity at the bus can be calculated from Theorem 1 to be 1.716. The upper bound, assuming no glitching, is 6.284. Assuming an estimate, T_e, for transition activity, the error in the estimate is less than $\max(T_e - 1.716, 6.284 - T_e)$. If additional information beyond $\mathcal{H}$ and R is not available, then it is not possible to obtain tighter bounds on the error in estimating transition activity. This is because the bounds on transition activity are achievable.

4.5 Lower Bound On Power-Delay

If the capacitance C_L, the supply voltage V_{dd}, and the frequency of operation, f, are given, then the minimum average power dissipation is proportional to the lower bound on the transition activity. The delay (for instance, for transmitting the data on a bus) is proportional to R. Hence the lower bound on the power-delay product, $PowerDelay_{min}$, given $\mathcal{H}$ and R, is given by, $PowerDelay_{min} = KH^{-1}(\frac{\mathcal{H}}{R})R^2$, where K is a constant of proportionality. The graph of $PowerDelay_{min}$ versus R for a given value of $\mathcal{H}$ is shown in Figure 2. For given $\mathcal{H}$, we can find the R that minimizes $PowerDelay_{min}$ by equating its derivative with respect to R to 0. The value of R that minimizes $PowerDelay_{min}$ is found to be, $R_{min,power-delay} = 1.25392\,\mathcal{H}$. Thus, a source with entropy rate, $\mathcal{H}$, requires approximately an average of $1.25\mathcal{H}$ bits/symbol to encode for minimum power-delay product. If $R > 1.25\mathcal{H}$, then the delay increases resulting in a non-optimal power-delay product. Similarly, if $R < 1.25\mathcal{H}$ then the power component increases because less redundancy is being added.

4.6 Bounds For An i.i.d. Source

Consider an i.i.d. source with a 5 symbol alphabet $\mathcal{X} = \{A, B, C, D, E\}$ with probabilities $\frac{1}{2}$, $\frac{1}{4}$, $\frac{1}{8}$, $\frac{1}{16}$, and $\frac{1}{16}$ respectively. The entropy rate is equal to $\frac{15}{8}$ bits. If an average of $R = 3$ bits are employed to code a symbol then from Theorem 1, the bounds on transition activity are, $0.468426 \leq T \leq 2.531574$. We now calculate the actual transition activity that is achieved by various coding algorithms and compare them with the bounds. To simplify the calculation of transition activity, we assume transition coding is employed to transmit the bits, i.e., a '1' is transmitted with a transition and a '0' is transmitted with no transition. Thus, the number of transitions is equal to the number of 1's. We can make the assumption of transition coding in the examples because the purpose of the examples is to show the existence of coding algorithms that approach the lower bound.

Entropy Coding Followed By Spatial Redundancy Coding: In this algorithm, we initially employ an entropy coder to code the symbols employing the minimum expected number of bits/symbol. A code that achieves the entropy is A = 0, B = 10, C = 110, D = 1110, and E = 1111. At the output of the entropy coder we have an average of $\frac{15}{8}$ bits/symbol. Since $R = 3$ bits/symbol, if we code a block of 15 bits from the entropy coder with 24 bits, we can employ the redundancy to reduce the number of transitions. This is an extension of Bus-Invert coding and results in a code in which the expected number of transitions (or 1's) is 0.565499 transitions/symbol, which is within 18% of the lower bound.

Probability Based Coding: An alternative algorithm to reduce the number of transitions is by coding the most probable symbol A as 000 or no transitions, B = 001, C = 010, D = 100, and E = 011. The expected number of transitions/symbol is 0.5625, which is within 17% of the lower bound. We can further reduce the number of transitions by coding blocks of symbols. The transition activity/symbol for different block sizes is shown in Figure 3. Thus, we can achieve a transition activity within 4% of the lower bound by employing a block size of 8.

4.7 Bounds For A Markov Process

Consider the 3-state stationary Markov process U_1, U_2, ... having the transition matrix P_{ij} in Table 2 [1]. Thus the probability that S_1 follows S_3 is equal to zero. An algorithm to encode the process will consist of 3 codes C_1, C_2, and C_3 (one for each state S_1, S_2, and S_3), where C_i is a code mapping from elements of the set $\{S_1, S_2, S_3\}$ into a code-word in C_i (see Table 3 for an example). To encode the current symbol S_j, we note the previous symbol S_i and select code C_i. We send the code-word in C_i corresponding to S_j. This is repeated for the next symbol. The stationary distribution of this Markov chain is $\mu = \left[\frac{2}{9}, \frac{4}{9}, \frac{1}{3}\right]^T$. The entropy rate of the stationary Markov process is given by [1], $H(\mathcal{X}) = -\sum_{ij} \mu_i P_{ij} \log_2 P_{ij} = \frac{4}{3}$ bits. A code that achieves the entropy rate is shown in Table 3. If $R = 2$ bits/symbol, then from Theorem 1, $0.347904 \leq T \leq 1.652096$ transitions/symbol. The transitions/symbol for entropy coding followed by redundancy coding and probability based coding is shown in Figure 4 for different block sizes. We can achieve a transition activity within 8% of the lower bound with a block size of 13 symbols.

APPENDIX

We now present proofs of Lemma 2 and Theorem 1. The proof of Lemma 1 is omitted because of lack of space and because it can be verified from a plot of $H()$. The proofs of achievability of Lemma 2 and Theorem 1 [4] are also omitted due to lack of space.

Proof Of Lemma 2

From the definitions of entropy rate and $\mathcal{H}$ in the statement of Lemma 2, $\mathcal{H} \leq \lim_{n\to\infty} \frac{1}{n}H(B_1, B_2, \ldots, B_n) \Rightarrow \mathcal{H} \leq \lim_{n\to\infty} \frac{1}{n}\sum_{i=1}^{n} H(B_i)$ [Independence bound on entropy] $\Rightarrow \mathcal{H} \leq H(\lim_{n\to\infty} \frac{1}{n}\sum_{i=1}^{n} B_i)$ [Jensen's inequality and concavity of H] $\Rightarrow \mathcal{H} \leq H(p_b)$ [Since $p_b = \lim_{n\to\infty} \frac{1}{n}\sum_{i=1}^{n} B_i$]. Thus, we can substitute $\mathcal{H}$ for y and p_b for x in Lemma 1 to obtain Lemma 2. ¶

Proof Of Theorem 1

Let $(B_1, B_2, \ldots, B_n)$ be the n bits that encode a block of N symbols $(X_1, X_2, \ldots, X_N)$, where this mapping from the symbol sequence $(X_1, X_2, \ldots, X_N)$

to the bit sequence (B_1, B_2, ..., B_n) can only be either one-to-many or one-to-one (and not many-to-one or many-to-many) because the coded bitstream needs to be uniquely decodable. Since the symbols are coded employing an expected number of R bits/symbol, for large N, $n = NR$. The entropy rate, $\mathcal{H}_b$, of the code bits is given by, $\mathcal{H}_b = \lim_{n\to\infty} \frac{1}{n} H(B_1, B_2, \ldots, B_n)$ $\Rightarrow$ $\mathcal{H}_b$ $=$ $\lim_{n\to\infty} \frac{1}{n} \sum p(b_1, b_2, \ldots, b_n)$ $\log_2 p(b_1, b_2, \ldots, b_n)$ [From the definition of joint entropy] $\Rightarrow$ $\mathcal{H}_b \geq \lim_{N\to\infty} \frac{1}{NR} \sum p(x_1, x_2, \ldots, x_N)$ $\log_2 p(x_1, x_2, \ldots, x_N)$ [From $n = NR$ and the possibility of a 1-many mapping. The inequality will be an equality if the mapping from symbols to bits is one-to-one.] $\Rightarrow \mathcal{H}_b \geq \frac{\mathcal{H}}{R}$.

Define a function g on $(B_1, B_2, \ldots, B_n)$ as, $(C_1, C_2, \ldots, C_n) = g(B_1, B_2, \ldots, B_n)$, where, $C_i = B_i \bigoplus B_j$, and B_j and B_i are transmitted on the same wire and B_j immediately precedes B_i. If B_i is the first bit transmitted on the wire, then B_j is '0'. Bit C_i is transmitted on the same wire and in the same order as bit B_i. Clearly, we can compute B_i given C_i as, $B_i = C_i \bigoplus C_j$, where C_j and C_i are transmitted on the same wire and C_j immediately precedes C_i. If C_i is the first bit transmitted on the wire, then C_j is '0'. Since (B_1, B_2, ..., B_n) and (C_1, C_2, ..., C_n) are functions of each other and $\mathcal{H}_b \geq \frac{\mathcal{H}}{R}$ we have, $\lim_{n\to\infty} \frac{1}{n} H(C_1, C_2, \ldots, C_n) = \lim_{n\to\infty} \frac{1}{n} H(B_1, B_2, \ldots, B_n) = \mathcal{H}_b \geq \frac{\mathcal{H}}{R}$. Let $p_c = \lim_{n\to\infty} \frac{1}{n} \sum_{i=1}^{n} C_i$, where p_c is the probability of C_i being a '1'. The limit exists because of assumption (4) in Theorem 1. Since C_i is a binary random variable, $p_c n$ is the expected number of 1's in (C_1, C_2, ..., C_n) for large n. Substituting p_c for p_b and $\frac{\mathcal{H}}{R}$ for $\mathcal{H}$ in Lemma 2 we have, $H^{-1}(\frac{\mathcal{H}}{R}) \leq p_c \leq 1 - H^{-1}(\frac{\mathcal{H}}{R})$. Since there are on the average R bits/symbol and C_i is '1' iff there was a transition at B_i, $T = p_c R$. Multiplying the inequality $H^{-1}(\frac{\mathcal{H}}{R}) \leq p_c \leq 1 - H^{-1}(\frac{\mathcal{H}}{R})$ by R and substituting $p_c R$ with T we have Theorem 1. ¶

References

[1] T. M. Cover and J. A. Thomas, "Elements of Information Theory," John Wiley & Sons, 1991.

[2] D. Marculescu, R. Marculescu, and M. Pedram, "Information theoretic measures for power analysis," *IEEE Trans. CAD*, pp. 599–610, June 1996.

[3] M. Nemani and F. Najm, "Towards a High-Level Power Estimation Capability," *IEEE Trans. CAD*, pp. 588–598, June 1996.

[4] S. Ramprasad, N. R. Shanbhag, and I. N. Hajj, "Achievable bounds on signal transition activity," *submitted to IEEE Trans. VLSI.*

[5] N. R. Shanbhag, "A mathematical basis for power-reduction in digital VLSI systems," *IEEE Trans. CAS II* (to appear).

[6] M. R. Stan and W. P. Burleson, "Bus-Invert Coding for Low-Power I/O," *IEEE Trans. VLSI*, pp. 49–58, March 1995.

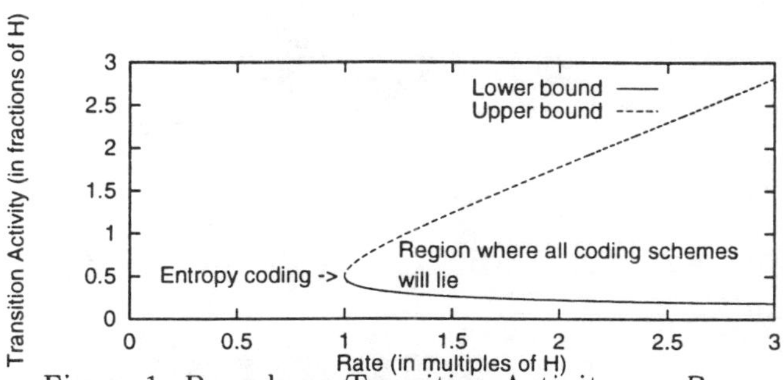

Figure 1: Bounds on Transition Activity vs. R

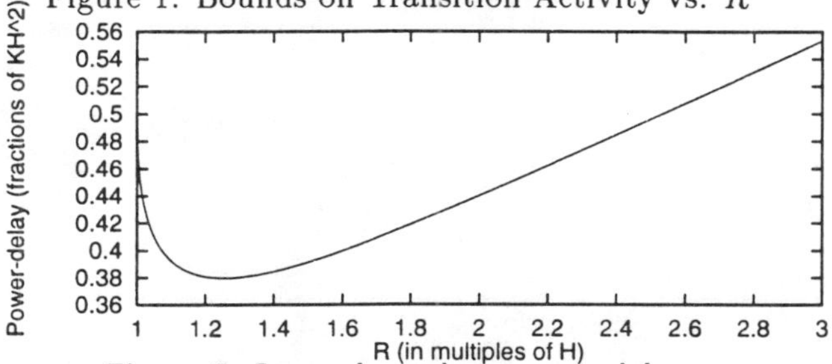

Figure 2: Lower bound on power-delay

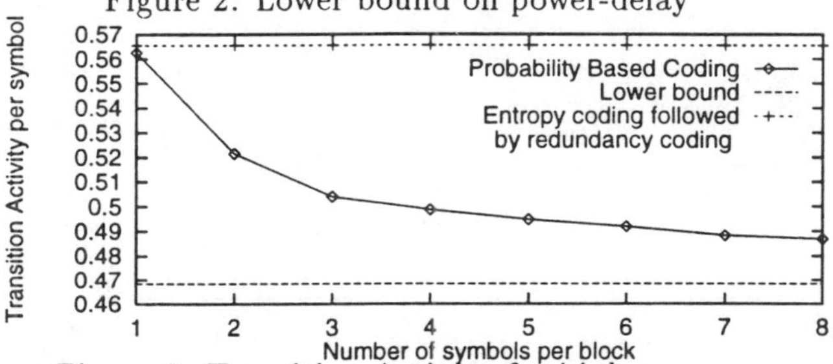

Figure 3: Transition Activity for i.i.d. source

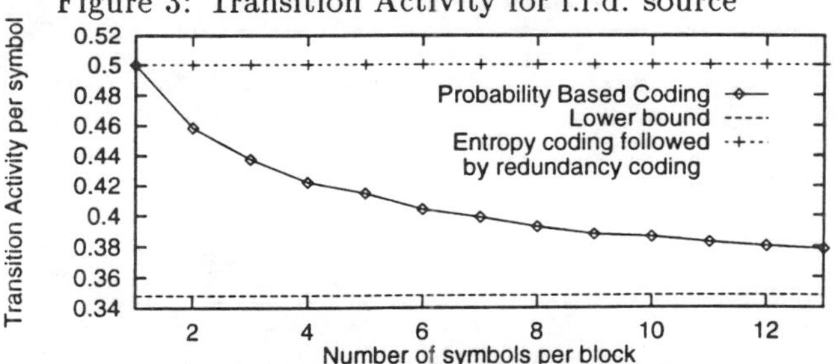

Figure 4: Transition Activity for Markov Process

Table 1: Transition Coding

Time	Level Code	Transition Code
0	000000	000000
1	000011	000011
2	000010	000001
3	010000	010001

Table 2: Transition Matrix

Previous state	S_1	S_2	S_3
S_1	$\frac{1}{2}$	$\frac{1}{4}$	$\frac{1}{4}$
S_2	$\frac{1}{4}$	$\frac{1}{2}$	$\frac{1}{4}$
S_3	0	$\frac{1}{2}$	$\frac{1}{2}$

Table 3: Entropy Code for Markov Process

	S_1	S_2	S_3
C_1	0	10	11
C_2	10	0	11
C_3	–	0	1

SESSION 2D

NOISE ANALYSIS AND MODELING

Moderators:

Lawrence T. Pileggi, Carnegie Mellon University, Pittsburgh, PA

Jue-Hsien Chern, Technology Modeling Associates, Inc., Sunnyvale, CA

Circuit noise evaluation by Padé approximation based model-reduction techniques

Peter Feldmann

Bell Laboratories
Murray Hill, NJ 07974

Roland W. Freund

Bell Laboratories
Murray Hill, NJ 07974

Abstract

This paper introduces a new circuit noise analysis and modeling method. The noise analysis method computes an analytic expression of frequency, in rational form, which represents the Padé approximation of the noise power spectral density. The approximation can be carried out efficiently, to the required accuracy, using a variant of the PVL [1] or MPVL [2] algorithms. The new method is significantly more efficient than traditional methods for noise computation at numerous frequency points. In addition, it allows for a compact and cascadable modeling of noise that can be used in system level simulations.

1 Introduction

Noise is a fundamental phenomenon in electronic circuits caused by the small fluctuations in currents and voltages that occur within the devices in the circuit. The fluctuations are due mainly to the discontinuous nature of electric charge. Determining the effects of noise is very important, as noise often represents the fundamental limit of circuit or system performance.

Noise analysis algorithms for circuits in DC steady-state have been available for a long time in programs such as SPICE [6]. The results of such programs is the noise power over a range of frequencies in tabulated form. Circuit or system designers, typically reduce the information contained in the noise spectrum to one single number such as the *noise figure* [3]. While such compact representations offer good insight, and are very convenient for back-of-the-envelope calculations, CAD tools at both the circuit and the system levels can take advantage of the more accurate and complete information available in the noise spectrum, and, in return, offer more accurate analysis.

In this paper we introduce an algorithm which computes the noise power spectral density as a closed form rational expression. More specifically, the algorithm computes the Padé approximation of the noise power spectral density using the numerically robust and efficient Lanczos [4] method. The spectrum is computed to the required accuracy over the frequency range of interest. This method is significantly more efficient than repeatedly evaluating the noise power over a fine frequency grid. However, the real advantage of the new approach consists in the compact noise models that get produced. These compact noise models with the spectral density specified as rational expressions can be accepted by the algorithm as input noise sources. In other words, the algorithm can consume its own output, thus lending itself to a hierarchical analysis methodology.

For example, the circuit designer, designs an amplifier, analyzes it, and produces a high-level model, say, of its transfer function and of its output noise spectrum. The system designer uses models for all the components to performs, using the same noise analysis algorithm, a system-level simulation. No information is lost due to a too narrow interface between circuit-level and system-level models.

The paper is organized as follows: In the next section we review the circuit noise analysis problem. In Section 3 we reformulate the noise spectral density expression in a form compatible with Padé via Lanczos, (PVL), model reduction. Section 4 discusses the application of the PVL algorithm to this particular problem. Finally, in Section 5, we illustrate the noise analysis problem with a few circuit examples and then present a few concluding remarks.

2 Review of circuit noise analysis

The principal mechanisms of noise in integrated circuits are [3]: thermal, shot, and flicker noise. Mathematically, device noise is modeled by stochastic processes [5]. Stochastic processes, represent ansambles of functions of time, $\mathbf{n}(t)$, and are characterized in terms of statistical averages, such as the mean and autocorrelation, in the time domain, or the power spectral density in the frequency domain.

Thermal noise, is caused by the thermal agitation of the electrons and occurs in almost all devices. Thermal noise is modeled by a parallel current source, the value of which is a zero mean stochastic process with a frequency independent (*white noise*) spectral density equal to

$$S_{\text{th}}(\omega) = 4kTG, \tag{1}$$

where k is Boltzman's constant, T the absolute temperature, and G the conductance.

Shot noise, is due to the fact that the current through a PN junction consists of discrete charge carriers randomly crossing a potential barrier. Shot noise in a junction is also modeled by a parallel, white noise current source. The spectral density of shot noise is

$$S_{\text{sh}}(\omega) = 2qI_d, \tag{2}$$

where q is the electron charge and I_d the average junction current.

Flicker (or $\frac{1}{f}$) noise, occurs in all active devices and even in some resistors due to mechanisms that are not well understood. Flicker noise is modeled by a stochastic process with a frequency dependent spectral density

$$S_{\text{fl}}(\omega) = K_1 \frac{I^a}{(2\pi\omega)^b}, \tag{3}$$

where I is the average direct current, K_1 is a technology dependent constant characterizing a particular device and process, a is a constant in the range $0.5 - 2.0$, and b is a constant of about one, (hence the name $\frac{1}{f}$ noise).

In this paper we only consider circuits with a constant excitation in steady-state (DC). The noise analysis methods presented below can also be applied to circuits with time varying bias conditions [7], but such an extension is beyond the scope of the present paper. Moreover, noise is assumed to represent a "small" perturbation to the circuit.

The circuit equations under these assumptions are

$$f(x(t), \frac{d}{dt}x(t), b_0, n(t)) = 0. \tag{4}$$

Here, $x(t)$ is the vector of circuit variables, typically currents and voltages, b_0 is the constant (DC) excitation, and $n(t)$ is a vector of "small" perturbations caused by the noise sources.

Moreover, we assume that the circuit is stable and therefore the solution of the noiseless circuit x_0, is constant in time and satisfies

$$f(x_0, 0, b_0, 0) = 0, \tag{5}$$

since, obviously, $\frac{d}{dt}x_0 = 0$.

The response of the circuit in the presence of the perturbation perturbation, $z(t)$, of the DC solution

$$f(x_0 + z(t), \frac{d}{dt}z(t), b_0, n(t)) = 0. \tag{6}$$

Assuming that the noise perturbation is "small", the first order Taylor expansion of the circuit equations (6) around the DC solution is sufficiently accurate

$$f(x_0, 0, b_0, 0) + Gz(t) + C\frac{d}{dt}z(t) - Bn(t) = 0 \tag{7}$$

where $G = \left.\frac{\partial f}{\partial x}\right|_{x_0,0,b_0,0}$, $C = \left.\frac{\partial f}{\partial \dot{x}}\right|_{x_0,0,b_0,0}$, and $B = -\left.\frac{\partial f}{\partial n}\right|_{x_0,0,b_0,0}$. Subtracting (5), we are left with just the linear, differential equations for the perturbation signals

$$Gz(t) + C\frac{d}{dt}z(t) = Bn(t). \tag{8}$$

The vector stochastic process $\mathbf{n}(t)$ is specified in terms of its frequency domain cross-spectral density matrix where $S_{xx}(\omega)$. The diagonal elements in $S_{xx}(\omega)$ represent the power spectral density of each noise source, and the off-diagonal elements describe statistical coupling of noise signals. In practical cases, S_{xx} will almost always be a diagonal matrix.

The noise analysis problem reduces to that of the propagation of a stochastic process through a linear system. The general expression of the noise power spectral density at the output of the linear system, S_{yy} is given by the well known formula [5]

$$S_{yy}(j\omega) = H(j\omega)S_{xx}(j\omega)H^{\text{H}}(j\omega) \tag{9}$$

When only one output is analyzed, $S_{yy}(j\omega)$ is just a scalar function of frequency. For more than one output, $S_{yy}(j\omega)$ is a full matrix, the dimension of which is the number of outputs The diagonal elements of $S_{yy}(j\omega)$ represent the power spectral density of the noise at each output and the off-diagonal elements represent the cross-spectral density.

The many-to-one vector transfer function of the linear system from the noise sources to an output port of interest is

$$H(j\omega) = l^{\text{T}}(G + j\omega C)^{-1}B \tag{10}$$

where l denotes the incidence vector that corresponds to the output port of interest. More generally, when more than one output is considered, we have a many-to-many matrix-transfer-function from noise sources to the outputs

$$H(j\omega) = L^{\mathrm{T}}(G + j\omega C)^{-1}B, \tag{11}$$

where L is the incidence matrix of the output ports.

From the formula (9), using (10), we obtain the following expression for the noise power spectral density at the output of the system

$$S_{yy}(j\omega) = l^{\mathrm{T}}(G + j\omega C)^{-1}BS_{xx}(j\omega)B^{\mathrm{T}}(G + j\omega C)^{-\mathrm{H}}l. \tag{12}$$

The noise analysis method implemented in SPICE [6], evaluates this expression efficiently, for a given ω, using the solution of the adjoint system

$$x_a(j\omega) = (G + j\omega C)^{-\mathrm{H}}l.$$

thus reducing (12) to

$$S_{yy}(j\omega) = x_a^{\mathrm{H}}(j\omega)BS_{xx}(j\omega)B^{\mathrm{T}}x_a(j\omega), \tag{13}$$

The SPICE noise computation algorithm computes the noise power only at a given frequency. When we are interested in the spectrum of the noise we must repeat the procedure for a large number of frequencies.

We now introduce a novel noise analysis method which computes a closed form rational expression for the noise power spectral density over a wide frequency range. This method is more efficient than the classical method, when noise needs to be computed over a frequency grid. Moreover, the closed form expression represents a compact model of the noise spectrum, and can be used hierarchically in system simulations.

3 Reformulated noise spectral density

For the following, it will be convenient to introduce the new variable $s := j\omega$. Note that, in order to be "physically" meaningful, the variable s has to be purely imaginary. For now, we thus assume that s is purely imaginary. Later on, we will drop this constraint and treat s as a general complex variable.

The new noise analysis and modeling algorithm relies on the computation of the Padé approximation to the noise power spectral density expression (12). The Padé approximation of a general transfer function expression of the form

$$F(s) = \tilde{l}^{\mathrm{T}}(\tilde{G} + s\tilde{C})^{-1}\tilde{r}, \tag{14}$$

where $\tilde{r}$ and $\tilde{l}$ are vectors of length $\tilde{N}$, and $\tilde{G}$ and $\tilde{C}$ are $\tilde{N} \times \tilde{N}$ matrices, can be computed efficiently with the PVL (Padé via Lanczos) algorithm [1]. At first glance, it appears that noise-type transfer functions (12) are very different from (14). However, we will show that there are vectors $\tilde{r}$, $\tilde{l}$ and matrices $\tilde{G}$, $\tilde{C}$ so that the functions (12) and (14) agree for all purely imaginary s, i.e., for all physically meaningful values of s.

First, consider the case when the noise sources are all white. Then S_{xx} is not a function of the frequency, and thus the function (12) reduces to

$$F(s) = l^{\mathrm{T}}(G + sC)^{-1}BS_{xx}B^{\mathrm{T}}(G + sC)^{-\mathrm{H}}l. \tag{15}$$

Here, we have used the new variable $s = j\omega$. We rewrite (15) by introducing two new vectors, u, and v

$$\begin{aligned} F(s) &= l^{\mathrm{T}}u, \\ v &= (G + sC)^{-\mathrm{H}}l, \\ u &= (G + sC)^{-1}BS_{xx}B^{\mathrm{T}}(G + sC)^{-\mathrm{H}}l \\ &= (G + sC)^{-1}BS_{xx}B^{\mathrm{T}}v \end{aligned} \tag{16}$$

The vectors u and v represent, therefore, the solution of a system of linear equations

$$\begin{bmatrix} 0 & (G + sC)^{\mathrm{H}} \\ G + sC & -BS_{xx}B^{\mathrm{T}} \end{bmatrix} \begin{bmatrix} u \\ v \end{bmatrix} = \begin{bmatrix} l \\ 0 \end{bmatrix} \tag{17}$$

From (16) and (17) we obtain

$$F(s) = \begin{bmatrix} l^{\mathrm{T}} & 0 \end{bmatrix} \left(\begin{bmatrix} 0 & G^{\mathrm{T}} \\ G & -BS_{xx}B^{\mathrm{T}} \end{bmatrix} + s \begin{bmatrix} 0 & -C^{\mathrm{T}} \\ C & 0 \end{bmatrix} \right)^{-1} \begin{bmatrix} l \\ 0 \end{bmatrix} \tag{18}$$

exactly of the form (14), amenable to PVL reduction.

Unfortunately, as shown in the previous section, not all noise sources are white. In order to be able to treat more general noise sources, we actually consider a more general class of noise-type transfer functions. More precisely, we study functions of the form

$$F(s) = l^{\mathrm{T}}(G + sC)^{-1}BP^{-1}(s)B^{\mathrm{T}}(G + sC)^{-\mathrm{H}}l. \tag{19}$$

Here, l is a real vector of length N, G and C are real $N \times N$ matrices, B is a real $N \times M$ matrix, and $P(s)$ is a *matrix polynomial*

$$P(s) = P_0 + P_1 s + P_2 s^2 + \cdots + P_L s^L, \tag{20}$$

whose coefficients P_i, $i = 0, 1, \ldots, L$, are $M \times M$ matrices. We assume that P_L is not a zero matrix, so that L is the *degree* of the matrix polynomial $P(s)$. The form (19) can express practically all interesting noise power spectral densities. The degree L itself can be arbitrary; however, the cases of low degree such as $L = 0, 1, 2$ are the most important ones. For example, for $L = 0$ and $P_0 = S_{xx}^{-1}$, the function (19) reduces to the case (15) of white noise. The flicker noise frequency dependent power spectral density (3) can also be well approximated by an expression of form (19) by expanding the denominator into a power series

$$S_{\text{fl}}(\omega) = K_1 I^a \left(c_0 + c_1 s + c_2 s^2 + \dots\right)^{-1} \quad (21)$$

Rewriting the noise-type transfer function $F(s)$ given by (19) in the form (14) then allows us to compute Padé-based reduced-order models for $F(s)$ by simply applying the PVL algorithm to the representation (14) of $F(s)$.

Next, we show how to transform (19) to form (14). Consider the linear system

$$\begin{bmatrix} 0 & (G+sC)^{\mathrm{H}} & 0 & 0 & \cdots & 0 \\ G+sC & 0 & B & 0 & \cdots & 0 \\ 0 & B^{\mathrm{T}} & P_0+sP_1 & sP_2 & \cdots & sP_L \\ 0 & 0 & sI & -I & \cdots & 0 \\ \vdots & \ddots & \ddots & \ddots & \ddots & \vdots \\ 0 & \cdots & \cdots & 0 & sI & -I \end{bmatrix} \begin{bmatrix} x \\ y \\ z_1 \\ z_2 \\ \vdots \\ z_L \end{bmatrix} = \begin{bmatrix} l \\ 0 \\ 0 \\ 0 \\ \vdots \\ 0 \end{bmatrix} \quad (22)$$

From the last $L-1$ blocks of equations in (22), it follows that

$$z_i = s z_{i-1} \quad \text{for all} \quad i = 2, 3, \dots, L, \quad (23)$$

and thus

$$z_i = s^{i-1} z_1 \quad \text{for all} \quad i = 2, 3, \dots, L. \quad (24)$$

Using the third block of equations in (22), together with (24) and (20), we get

$$\begin{aligned} B^{\mathrm{T}} y &= -(P_0 + sP_1) z_1 + sP_2 z_2 + \dots + sP_L z_L \\ &= -\left(P_0 + sP_1 + s^2 P_2 + \dots + s^L P_L\right) z_1 \\ &= -P(s) z_1. \end{aligned} \quad (25)$$

By the first two blocks of equations in (22), we have

$$\begin{aligned} y &= (G+sC)^{-\mathrm{H}} l, \\ x &= -(G+sC)^{-1} B z_1. \end{aligned} \quad (26)$$

Combining (25) and (26), we get

$$x = (G+sC)^{-1} B (P(s))^{-1} B^{\mathrm{T}} (G+sC)^{-\mathrm{H}} l. \quad (27)$$

Next, we observe that, for purely imaginary s, the linear system (22) can be rewritten in the form

$$\left(\tilde{G} + s\tilde{C}\right) \tilde{x} = \tilde{l}. \quad (28)$$

Here, $\tilde{x}$ and $\tilde{l}$ are vectors of length $\tilde{N}$ d defined by

$$\tilde{x} = \begin{bmatrix} x \\ y \\ z_1 \\ \vdots \\ z_L \end{bmatrix} \quad \text{and} \quad \tilde{l} = \begin{bmatrix} l \\ 0 \\ 0 \\ \vdots \\ 0 \end{bmatrix}, \quad (29)$$

and $\tilde{G}$ and $\tilde{C}$ are $\tilde{N} \times \tilde{N}$ matrices given by

$$\tilde{G} = \begin{bmatrix} 0 & G^{\mathrm{T}} & 0 & 0 & \cdots & 0 \\ G & 0 & B & 0 & \ddots & 0 \\ 0 & B^{\mathrm{T}} & P_{\mathrm{C}} & 0 & \ddots & \vdots \\ 0 & 0 & 0 & -I & \ddots & 0 \\ \vdots & \ddots & \ddots & \ddots & \ddots & 0 \\ 0 & \cdots & \cdots & 0 & 0 & -I \end{bmatrix} \quad (30)$$

and

$$\tilde{C} = \begin{bmatrix} 0 & -C^{\mathrm{T}} & 0 & 0 & \cdots & 0 \\ C & 0 & 0 & 0 & \ddots & 0 \\ 0 & 0 & P_1 & P_2 & \ddots & P_L \\ 0 & 0 & I & 0 & \ddots & 0 \\ \vdots & \ddots & \ddots & \ddots & \ddots & 0 \\ 0 & \cdots & \cdots & 0 & I & 0 \end{bmatrix} \quad (31)$$

Using (19), and (28) to (31), it follows that

$$\begin{aligned} F(s) &= l^{\mathrm{T}} (G+sC)^{-1} B (P(s))^{-1} B^{\mathrm{T}} (G+sC)^{-\mathrm{H}} l \\ &= l^{\mathrm{T}} x = \tilde{l}^{\mathrm{T}} \tilde{x} \\ &= \tilde{l}^{\mathrm{T}} \left(\tilde{G} + s\tilde{C}\right)^{-1} \tilde{l}. \end{aligned} \quad (32)$$

This shows that, for purely imaginary s, the noise-type transfer function (19) is indeed of the form (14) with $\tilde{l} = \tilde{r}$, $\tilde{G}$, and $\tilde{C}$ defined in (31).

Of particular interest are several special cases

- The case $L = 1$

  Here $\tilde{l}$, $\tilde{G}$, and $\tilde{C}$ reduce to

$$\tilde{l} = \begin{bmatrix} l & 0 & 0 \end{bmatrix}^{\mathrm{T}}, \quad \tilde{G} = \begin{bmatrix} 0 & G^{\mathrm{T}} & 0 \\ G & 0 & B \\ 0 & B^{\mathrm{T}} & P_0 \end{bmatrix}, \tilde{C} = \begin{bmatrix} 0 & -C^{\mathrm{T}} & 0 \\ C & 0 & 0 \\ 0 & 0 & P_1 \end{bmatrix}. \quad (33)$$

- The case $L = 0$

This is the case (15) that all noise sources are white. It is covered by (33) with $P_0 = S_{xx}^{-1}$ and $P_1 = 0$. However, in this case, we eliminate the third block rows and columns in (33) and obtain

$$\tilde{l} = \begin{bmatrix} l \\ 0 \end{bmatrix}, \tilde{G} = \begin{bmatrix} 0 & G^{\mathrm{T}} \\ G & -B^{\mathrm{T}} S_{xx}^{-1} B \end{bmatrix}, \tilde{C} = \begin{bmatrix} 0 & -C^{\mathrm{T}} \\ C & 0 \end{bmatrix} \tag{34}$$

This is exactly the form arrived at in (18).

4 Application of PVL

Now that we have shown how to reformulate noise-type transfer function $F(s)$ given by (19) in the "PVL" form (14), it is straightforward to employ PVL to generate reduced-order models. Recall that, in our case, $\tilde{l} = \tilde{r}$ in (14).

First, we choose a real expansion point s_0, and compute, $\mathcal{L}$ and $\mathcal{U}$ as the factorization

$$\tilde{G} + s_0 \tilde{C} = \mathcal{L} \cdot \mathcal{U}. \tag{35}$$

Then, setting $s = s_0 + \sigma$, we rewrite (14) as follows:

$$\begin{aligned} F(s_0 + \sigma) &= \tilde{l}^{\mathrm{T}} \left(\tilde{G} + s_0 \tilde{C} + \sigma \tilde{C} \right)^{-1} \tilde{l} \\ &= \left(\mathcal{U}^{-\mathrm{T}} \tilde{l} \right)^{\mathrm{T}} \left(I + \sigma \mathcal{L}^{-1} \tilde{C} \mathcal{U}^{-1} \right)^{-1} \left(\mathcal{L}^{-1} \tilde{l} \right). \end{aligned} \tag{36}$$

We then apply the Lanczos process to the matrix $A = \mathcal{L}^{-1} \tilde{C} \mathcal{U}^{-1}$, using $b = \mathcal{L}^{-1} \tilde{l}$ and $c = \mathcal{U}^{-\mathrm{T}} \tilde{l}$ as the right, respectively left, starting vector. After running the Lanczos process for n iterations, we obtain an $n \times n$ tridiagonal matrix, T_n, such that the function

$$F_n(s_0 + \sigma) = \left(c^{\mathrm{T}} b \right) \cdot e_1^{\mathrm{T}} \left(I + \sigma T_n \right)^{-1} e_1 \tag{37}$$

where e_1 represents the first unit vector of length n, is just an n-th *Padé approximant* to $F(s_0 + \sigma)$. More precisely, $F_n(s_0 + \sigma)$ is a rational function of σ with numerator polynomial of degree at most $n - 1$ and denominator polynomial of degree at most n such that

$$F_n(s_0 + \sigma) = F(s_0 + \sigma) + \mathcal{O}(n^{q(n)}), \tag{38}$$

where $q(n)$ is maximal. In the generic case, $q(n) = 2n$. Note that (38) just states that the Taylor expansions of F_n and F about the expansion point s_0 agree in as many leading Taylor coefficients as possible. We note that all quantities involved in the Lanczos process are real, as long as the coefficient matrices $P_0, P_1, \ldots, P_L$ of (20) are real, which is usually the case.

We observe that the reduced-order model for the noise spectral density of a circuit module will always have the form in (37), which results from the PVL algorithm. If the reduced order models of circuit modules are used in higher level simulations, expressions of the form in (37) appear in the $S_{xx}(s)$ noise source spectral density matrix of the system simulation. The resulting output noise spectral density of the system will have the form

$$F(s) = l^{\mathrm{T}} (G + sC)^{-1} B (P_0 + sP_1)^{-1} B^{\mathrm{T}} (G + sC)^{-\mathrm{H}} l, \tag{39}$$

therefore, compatible with PVL, as shown for the special case $L = 1$ in (33).

Finally, we must make some comments, regarding properties of the PVL algorithm specific to its application to "noise"-type problems. So far, we have made no assumptions on the matrix polynomial

$$P(s) = P_0 + P_1 s + P_2 s^2 + \cdots + P_L s^L. \tag{40}$$

If the function $F(s)$ describes the noise power spectral density of a circuit, then $P(s)$ needs to be such that

$$F(j\omega) > 0 \quad \text{for all} \quad \omega > 0. \tag{41}$$

Ideally, the PVL algorithm is stopped as soon as the Padé approximant F_n has converged to F in the frequency case of interest, i.e., if

$$|F(j\omega) - F_n(j\omega)| \leq \texttt{tol} \quad \text{for all} \quad \omega \in [\omega_{\min}, \omega_{\max}]. \tag{42}$$

Together with (41), this ensures that the Padé-based reduced-order model

$$F_n(s_0 + \sigma) = \left(c^{\mathrm{T}} b \right) \cdot e_1^{\mathrm{T}} \left(I + \sigma T_n \right)^{-1} e_1 \tag{43}$$

satisfies

$$F_n(j\omega) \gtrsim 0 \quad \text{for all} \quad \omega \in [\omega_{\min}, \omega_{\max}]. \tag{44}$$

This observation is important if we want to use the reduced-order model as noise sources in a high-level simulation.

As a final note, we remark that the discussion in this and previous sections can be generalized for the computation of the cross-spectral density matrix of multiple outputs. In the multiple output case the l and $\tilde{l}$ vectors become matrices and MPVL will be used instead of PVL.

5 Examples

We applied the noise computation algorithm on a number of circuits. The first example is the 741 operational amplifier. The size of the problem is 55 variables. Figure 1 shows the exact transfer function of the

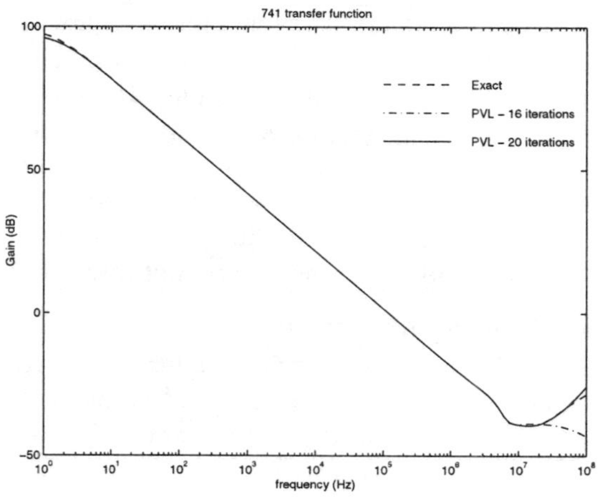

Figure 1: 741 gain

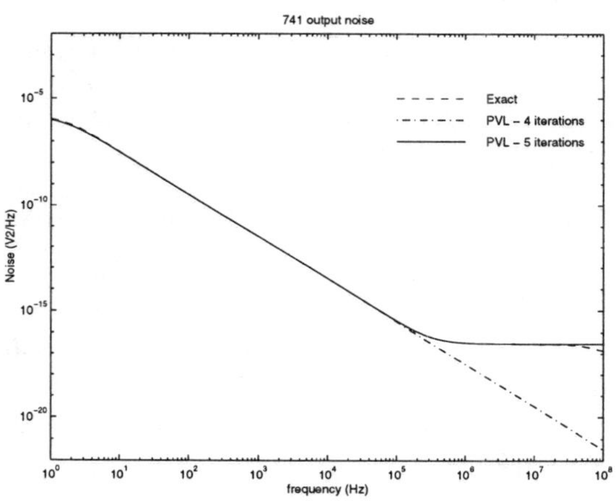

Figure 2: 741 noise

amplifier compared to the PVL reduced order models of orders 16 and 20. The order 20 approximation captures the behavior of the amplifier almost exactly. Figure 2 shows the amplifier output noise power spectral density over the same frequency range. Here, a Padé approximations of order 5 is already sufficient to capture the noise spectrum.

The next example is a 5-th order Cauer filter which uses ten 741 opamps as building blocks. The total size of the problem is 463 variables. Figures 3 and 4 show the transfer function and the output noise spectrum computed exactly, and with PVL. We observe that we need roughly the same number of iterations to obtain an almost perfect match of both the transfer function and the noise spectrum.

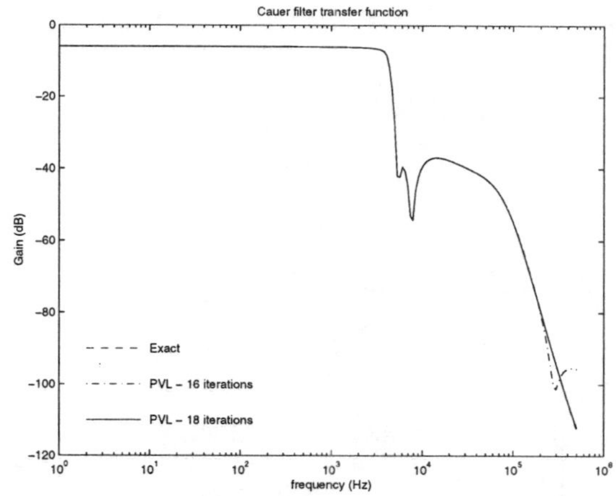

Figure 3: Cauer filter transfer characteristic

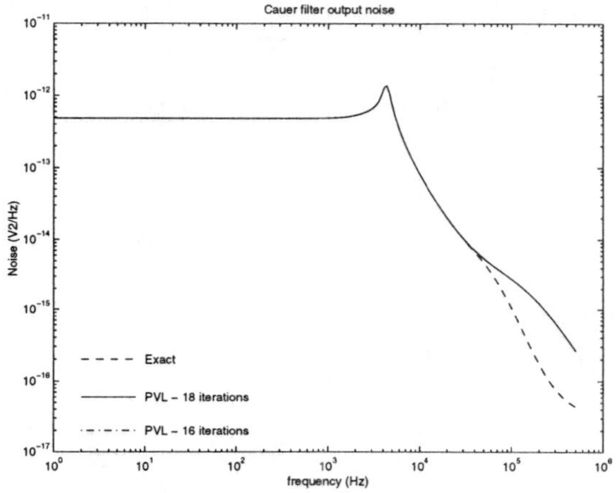

Figure 4: Cauer filter noise

The final example is a bandpass filter derived from a 3-rd order Chebyshev low-pass prototype, and implemented with single amplifier biquads. It also uses the 741 opamp as a building block. The problem size is 147. Figures 5 and 6 show the transfer function and the output noise spectrum computed exactly, and with PVL. We observe that we need 18 iterations to match the transfer function and only 14 to match the noise spectrum.

6 Conclusions

In this paper we have introduced a new noise analysis method which computes the noise power spectral density of a circuit node or the cross-spectral density of a number of nodes. The results are presented in the form of a closed form polynomial rational function of frequency which represents a Padé approximation of the true noise spectral density. This method is significantly more efficient than the classical noise analysis method for predicting noise over a range of frequencies. The main advantage of the method, however, is the fact that it produces a reduced-order model of the noise generated by the circuit under analysis. This model can then be employed, using the same algorithm in a system-level analysis. The noise analysis algorithm accepts the noise source power spectral density in a rational polynomial form. This form covers practically all possible noise sources of interest.

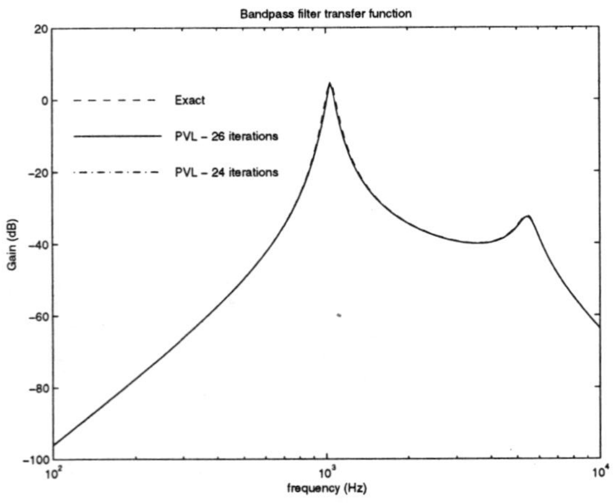

Figure 5: Bandpass filter transfer characteristic

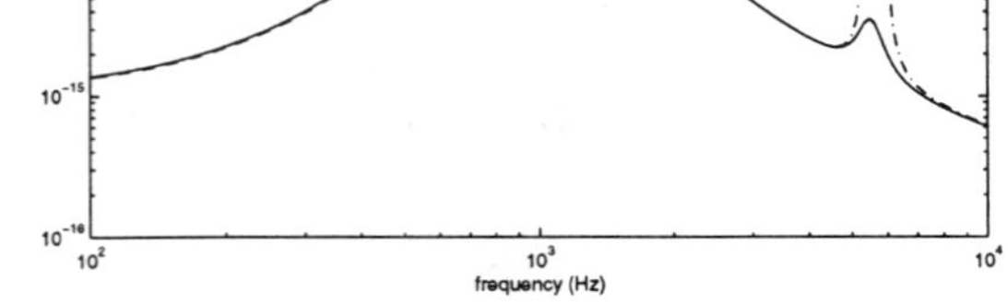

Figure 6: Bandpass filter noise

Acknowledgments

We wold like to thank our colleagues: Peter Kinget, David Lee, Jaijeet Roychwdhury, and Lászlo Tóth, for useful discussions and help with examples.

References

[1] P. Feldmann and R. W. Freund, *Efficient linear circuit analysis by Padé approximation via the Lanczos process*, IEEE Trans. Computer-Aided Design **14** (1995), 639–649.

[2] P. Feldmann and R. W. Freund, *Reduced-order modeling of large linear sub-circuits via a block Lanczos algorithm*, Proc. 32nd Design Automation Conference, ACM, New York, 1995, pp. 474–479.

[3] P.R. Gray and R.G. Meyer, *Analysis and Design of Analog Integrated Circuits* 3rd. edition, New York, N.Y.: John Wiley, 1993.

[4] C. Lanczos, *An iteration method for the solution of the eigenvalue problem of linear differential and integral operators*, J. Res. Nat. Bur. Standards **45** (1950), 255–282.

[5] A. Papoulis, *Probability, Random Variables, and Stochastic Processes*, 3rd. edition, New York, N.Y.: McGraw-Hill, 1991.

[6] Rohrer, R.A., Nagel L., Meyer, R. and Weber, L., *Computationally efficient electronic-circuit noise calculations*, IEEE J. Solid State Circuits, vol. SC-6, pp. 204-213, 1971.

[7] J. Roychowdhury and P. Feldmann. "A New Linear-Time Harmonic Balance Algorithm for Cyclostationary Noise Analysis in RF Circuits," Proc. Asia and South-Pacific Design Automation Conference, Jan 1997.

Global Harmony: Coupled Noise Analysis for Full-Chip RC Interconnect Networks

K. L. Shepard, V. Narayanan, P. C. Elmendorf[1], and Gutuan Zheng[1]
IBM T. J. Watson Research Center, Yorktown Heights, NY 10598
[1]IBM Microelectronics, Fishkill, NY

Abstract

Noise is becoming one of the most important metrics in the design of VLSI systems, certainly of comparable importance to area, timing, and power. In this paper, we describe Global Harmony, a methodology for the analysis of coupling noise in the global interconnect of large VLSI chips being developed for the design of high-performance microprocessors. The architecture of Global Harmony involves a careful combination of static noise analysis, static timing analysis, and reduced-order modelling techniques. We describe a reduced-order modelling approach that allows for passive multiport reduction of RC netlists as impedance macromodels while preserving the symmetry and sparsity of the state matrices for efficient storage. We describe how the macromodels are practically employed to perform coupling analysis and how timing constraints can be used to limit pessimism in the analysis.

1 Introduction

As CMOS technology scales into the deep submicron regime, noise immunity has become a metric for the analysis and design of VLSI systems of comparable importance to area, timing, and power. An essential component of the noise in VLSI chips comes from capacitive coupling between signal lines. The need to better understand and control coupling comes as scaling and performance requirements in general have created new demands for the analysis and design of interconnect networks.

Reduced-order modelling techniques have become an important method for analyzing linear interconnect networks. RLC analysis must be increasingly applied to analyzing clock trees, power buses, and off-chip interconnect to control clock skew and dI/dt noise. A more critical application for reduced-order modelling, however, remains the large RC netlists resulting from the global chip interconnect extraction. These extractions are typically on the scale of tens of thousands of nets. AWE-based modelling of RC networks has been an essential part of timing analysis for more than five years[1]. Reduced-order modelling techniques must now be extended to consider the effects of coupling on noise and delay. There are three questions that need to be answered by this analysis, all potentially in the presence of coupled switching activity on other nets:

- What is the effective loading on each driver?
- What is the delay and slew at the receivers?
- What noise will be coupled at the receiver of an otherwise static net due to switching on other nets?

We describe a methodology, Global Harmony, which addresses these three issues and is being applied to the design of complex microprocessors.

The architecture we describe is a careful marriage of static timing analysis and static noise analysis[2]. Global Harmony consists of several important components – a reduced-order modelling algorithm that guarantees passive macromodelling of RC networks, a representation of this macromodel that allows for efficient storage and access, a timing rule structure that uses this macromodel with timing information to perform delay and noise analysis, and a noise analysis engine that considers temporal correlation of switching signals.

2 Overview of Global Harmony

The noise and timing methodology employed in the design of complex microprocessors is shown in Figure 1[3]. The shaded region in the figure denotes those pieces described in this paper as part of the architecture of Global Harmony.

1092-3152/97 $10.00 © 1997 IEEE

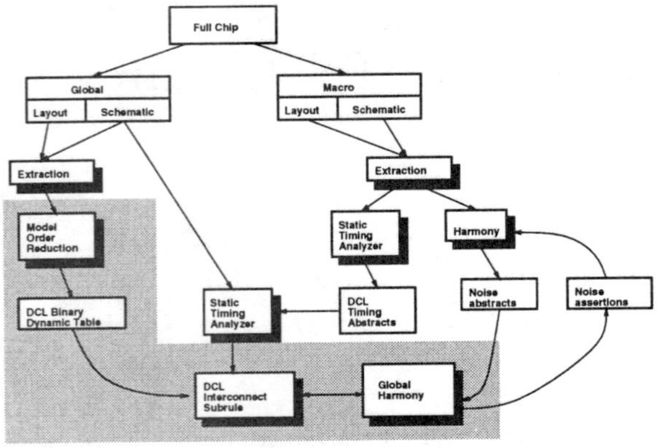

Figure 1: Global Harmony architecture

The timing and noise analysis methodology rely on a two-level hierarchical approach to practically manage the complexity of designs with tens of millions of transistors. This methodology involves identifying groups of 10,000 - 200,000 transistors as *macros*. Macros are individually laid out and floorplanned on the chip. They are timed using static timing analysis and abstracted in Delay Calculation Language (DCL)[4]. Similarly, static noise analysis (Harmony[2]) is performed on each macro and noise abstracts are generated for the global analysis. In some cases, noise assertions are returned back to Harmony analysis.

The global level consists of the interconnection network between the macros which contains all the long wire runs of the chip. The coupling capacitances between the macro and global levels are handled by treating them as worst-case hostile coupling sources in both the Harmony and Global Harmony analyses. The extraction of the global interconnect results in an RC networks that is reduced to a collection of multiport impedance macromodels, one for each net in the design, stored as a DCL binary dynamic table (BDT). The details of this reduction are described in Section 3. In Section 4, we describe how a DCL interconnect subrule model reads the BDT, folds in linearizations of the drivers and receivers and calculates the coupled noise. In Section 4, we describe the Global Harmony engine which computes the noise and flags violations, applying timing information obtained directly from the static timing environment. Section 5 describes in more detail the careful marriage of static timing and static noise analysis. In particular, we describe how timing information is used to reduce pessimism in coupled noise analysis and how the effects of noise on delay are considered in static timing analysis. Some results are briefly presented in Section 6.

3 Passive reduced-order modelling of coupled RC networks

The reduction part of Global Harmony begins with an extracted RC netlist for the global interconnect stored as a compressed binary file. The reduced-order modelling approach employed for Global Harmony guarantees passive, multiport macromodels with symmetry that allows for efficient storage of the results.

The first step in the reduction process is to identify a *net complex* for each net in the design. The *primary net* of the complex is the net on which we are trying to calculate the noise; that is, the net which should be statically quiet. The complex also includes *secondary nets* of significant coupling to the primary net. To determine which secondary nets to include in a complex, a coupling capacitance threshold ratio of total coupling to the secondary net in question to the self capacitance of the primary net, C_{coup}/C_{self} is used. Coupling capacitors with couplings below this threshold are treated as capacitors tied to ground. Couplings between the significant secondary nets and nets other than those already in the net complex are grounded. A representative net complex is shown in Figure 2(a).

We now describe the algorithm employed to reduce the state size of these RC net complexes. Modified nodal analysis (MNA) is used to stamp conductance and capacitance matrices according to the multi-input, multi-output, linear time-invariant differential equations:

$$\begin{aligned} C\dot{x} &= -Gx + Bi \\ v &= B^T x \end{aligned} \tag{1}$$

$x, v, i \in \mathbb{R}^n$ are the state, output voltage, and input current vectors, respectively. For a system with n nodes and r ports, $G, C \in \mathbb{R}^{n \times n}$ are the symmetric, positive semidefinite conductance and capacitance matrices, respectively. The state vector is ordered so that the first r elements represent the port voltages. With this choice of ordering, the r-by-r matrix formed by the top r rows of the input-output matrix $B \in \mathbb{R}^{n \times r}$ is the identity and the rest of the B matrix is zero. Moving into the Laplace domain, Equations 1 lead to an expression for the r-by-r multiport impedance matrix for the net complex.

$$v(s) = Z(s)i(s) \tag{2}$$

$$Z(s) = B^T(G + sC)^{-1}B \tag{3}$$

We choose impedance macromodelling over admittance macromodelling[5, 6, 7] because of the ease with which we can fold linearized driver and receiver models into the analysis. Because a net complex in general does not have a DC path to ground, the impedance matrix is singular at $s = 0$. Because of this, the conductance matrix $\boldsymbol{G}$ will in general be singular.

As a result, a nonzero expansion point s_o must be chosen for the moment matching. Using the change of variable $s = s_o + \tilde{s}$, Equation 3 becomes

$$Z(s_o + \tilde{s}) = \boldsymbol{B}^T(\mathcal{G} + \tilde{s}\boldsymbol{C})^{-1}\boldsymbol{B} \tag{4}$$

where $\mathcal{G} = \boldsymbol{G} + s_o\boldsymbol{C}$. $\mathcal{G}$ will be symmetric positive definite for a choice of real positive s_o. We then employ a multiport extension of the symmetric Lanczos process[8, 9] as shown in Algorithm 1 which is applicable to symmetric, positive-definite $\mathcal{G}$. The Cholesky factorizations can be performed because $\mathcal{G}$ is positive definite and $\boldsymbol{W}$ (after deflation) and $\boldsymbol{B}$ have full column rank[10].

Algorithm **1 (Symmetric Lanczos)**

lanczos(input $\boldsymbol{C}, \mathcal{G}, \boldsymbol{B}, q$; output $\tilde{\boldsymbol{H}}_p, \tilde{\boldsymbol{B}}_p$)
{
Initialize:
Set $\boldsymbol{V}_0 = 0, \boldsymbol{T}_0 = 0, \boldsymbol{\beta}_1 = \boldsymbol{I}$
Cholesky factor: $\boldsymbol{\rho}^T\boldsymbol{\rho} = \boldsymbol{B}^T\mathcal{G}^{-1}\boldsymbol{B}$
$\boldsymbol{T}_1 = \mathcal{G}^{-1}\boldsymbol{B}\boldsymbol{\rho}^{-1}, \boldsymbol{V}_1 = \boldsymbol{B}\boldsymbol{\rho}^{-1}$
for $(j = 1;\ j \leq q;\ j{+}{+})$ {
$\boldsymbol{H}_{j,j} = \boldsymbol{\alpha}_{j-1} = \boldsymbol{V}_j^T\mathcal{G}^{-1}\boldsymbol{C}\boldsymbol{T}_j$
$\boldsymbol{W} = \boldsymbol{C}\mathcal{G}^{-1}\boldsymbol{V}_j - \boldsymbol{V}_j\boldsymbol{\alpha}_{j-1} - \boldsymbol{V}_{j-1}\boldsymbol{\beta}_{j-1}^T$
Deflate $\boldsymbol{W}$ to $\boldsymbol{W}'$
Cholesky factor:
$\boldsymbol{R}^T\boldsymbol{R} = \boldsymbol{W}'^T\mathcal{G}^{-1}\boldsymbol{W}'$
$\boldsymbol{V}_{j+1} = \boldsymbol{W}'\boldsymbol{R}^{-1}$
$\boldsymbol{T}_{j+1} = \mathcal{G}^{-1}\boldsymbol{W}'\boldsymbol{R}^{-1}$
$\boldsymbol{H}_{j,j+1} = \boldsymbol{H}_{j+1,j}^T = \boldsymbol{\beta}_{j+1} = \boldsymbol{V}_{j+1}^T\mathcal{G}\boldsymbol{W}$
}
$\tilde{\boldsymbol{V}}_p = [\boldsymbol{V}_1\boldsymbol{V}_2\cdots\boldsymbol{V}_q]$
$\tilde{\boldsymbol{B}}_p = [\boldsymbol{\rho}; \boldsymbol{0}]$
$\tilde{\boldsymbol{H}}_p = (\boldsymbol{H}_{i,j}),\ i, j = 1, \cdots, q$
}

Algorithm 1 results in a reduced-order model of order p:

$$\boldsymbol{Z}_p(s_o + \tilde{s}) = \tilde{\boldsymbol{B}}_p^T\left(\boldsymbol{I} + \tilde{s}\tilde{\boldsymbol{H}}_p\right)^{-1}\tilde{\boldsymbol{B}}_p \tag{5}$$

where $\boldsymbol{Z}_p \in \mathbb{R}^{r\times r}$ and $p = p_1 + p_2 + \cdots + p_q$ where p_j is the rank of $\boldsymbol{V}_j$. $\boldsymbol{Z}_p(s)$ matches the first $2q$ coefficients of $\boldsymbol{Z}(s)$[11]. $\tilde{\boldsymbol{H}}_p \in \mathbb{R}^{p\times p}$ is a block tridiagonal matrix such that:

$$\tilde{\boldsymbol{H}}_p = \tilde{\boldsymbol{V}}_p^T\mathcal{G}^{-1}\boldsymbol{C}\mathcal{G}^{-1}\tilde{\boldsymbol{V}}_p \tag{6}$$

The deflation of $\boldsymbol{W}$ performed as part of Algorithm 1 deserves additional comment. As the Lanczos iteration approaches convergence, the matrix $\boldsymbol{W}$ will lose column rank[12]. This can happen easily for those net complexes in which it is not true that the number of nodes n is much greater than the number of ports r ($n \gg r$). In the Golub-Underwood block Lanczos procedure[13], the linearly independent columns of the $\boldsymbol{W}$ matrix are replaced with randomly generated vectors orthogonalized to all the preceeding columns of $\boldsymbol{V}_j$. We instead employ a deflation procedure similar to Cullum and Donath[14]. This means that the block size on successive iterations will decrease as the $\boldsymbol{W}$ matrix loses rank.

The computational cost of Algorithm 1 is dominated by the factorization of the symmetric positive definite $\mathcal{G}$ matrix. To perform this factorization efficiently, we make use of a modified version of the multifrontal algorithm[15] for sparse Cholesky factorization embodied in the Watson Symmetric Sparse Matrix Package (WSSMP)[16].

We choose an expansion frequency s_o for the reduction which is associated with a typical net Elmore delay. We generally use the same expansion frequency for all nets. We then monitor the convergence of the Frobenius norm of the matrix:

$$\tilde{\boldsymbol{B}}_p^T\left(\boldsymbol{I} + \tilde{\boldsymbol{B}}_p\boldsymbol{C}_{port}\tilde{\boldsymbol{B}}_p^T - s_o\tilde{\boldsymbol{H}}_p\right)^{-1}\tilde{\boldsymbol{B}}_p\boldsymbol{G}_{port} \tag{7}$$

to determine the order of the reduction to be used. $\boldsymbol{G}_{port}$ is a diagonal conductance matrix with diagonal elements chosen to be a large default conductance. This equation follows directly from the results of Section 4. This is in lieu of other schemes that monitor the convergence of the eigenvalues[17] or the magnitude of the residue[18].

Passivity is the property that the network always dissipates energy and has been of considerable current interest[19]. It is a well-known result of network theory that the combination of two passive networks is guaranteed to be passive, while the combination of two asymptotically stable networks is not guaranteed to be asymptotically stable. Therefore, ensuring passivity of the macromodel is essential for ensuring the stability[20] of the final system used for noise analysis, which comes from combining the interconnect with the driver and receiver models. In fact, the driving point impedance $\boldsymbol{Z}_p$ in Equation 5 is already passive. To prove this, we need to develop a few results. The first is a test for passivity:

Theorem 1 *A multiport linear interconnect network is passive if and only if the impedance matrix $Z(s)$ satisfies:*

1. $Z(s^*) = Z^*(s)$, $\forall s \in \mathbb{C}$
2. *$Z(s)$ is* positive; *that is,* $z^{*T}(Z(s) + Z^T(s^*))z \geq 0$, $\forall z \in \mathbb{C}^p$ *and* $\forall s \in \mathbb{C}$ *with* $Re(s) > 0$.

The proof of Theorem 1 can be found in several reference on linear network theory[21, 22, 23]. In addition, to prove passivity, we will need the following result:

Theorem 2 *The matrix $\tilde{H}_q$ generated by the symmetric Lanczos process is symmetric, positive semidefinite.*

Proof. Let x be an arbitrary non-zero vector in $\mathbb{R}^p$. Then

$$\begin{aligned} x^T \tilde{H}_q x &= x^T \tilde{V}_q^T \mathcal{G}^{-1} C \mathcal{G}^{-1} \tilde{V}_q x \\ &= (\mathcal{G}^{-1} \tilde{V}_q x)^T C (\mathcal{G}^{-1} \tilde{V}_q x) \\ &= (\tilde{T}_q x)^T C (\tilde{T}_q x) \\ &\geq 0 \end{aligned}$$

The inequality results from the fact that C is positive semidefinite. □

We are now finally in the position to claim the following.

Theorem 3 *The reduced-order impedance macromodel Z_p produced by the symmetric Lanczos process for RC circuits is passive.*

Proof. To prove this, it is necessary to prove the two conditions in Theorem 1. The first follows from the fact that $\tilde{B}_p$ and $\tilde{H}_p$ are all real. To prove the second condition of Theorem 1, it is necessary to show that:

$$z^{*T}(Z_p(s) + Z_p(s^*))z \geq 0 \quad \forall z \in \mathbb{C}^p$$

for any s such that $Re(s) \geq 0$. From Equation 5 and taking $\tilde{s} = \sigma + i\omega$,

$$\begin{aligned} z^{*T}(Z_p(s) + Z_p(s^*))z &= z^{*T} \tilde{B}_p^T \left[(I + \tilde{s}\tilde{H}_p) + (I \right. \\ &\qquad \left. + \tilde{s}^* \tilde{H}_p)^T \right] \tilde{B}_p z \\ &= 2w^{*T}(I + \sigma \tilde{H}_p) w \\ &\geq 0 \end{aligned}$$

where $w = (I + \tilde{s}^* \tilde{H}_p)^{-T} \tilde{B}_p z$ Because the matrix $\tilde{H}_p$ is positive semidefinite by Theorem 2, $I + \sigma \tilde{H}_p$ is symmetric, positive definite for all $\sigma \geq 0$. □

These interconnect macromodels are stored as DCL binary dynamic tables (BDT) which are subsequently utilized by a DCL interconnect subrule for noise analysis. We take advantage of the sparsity in storing the $\tilde{H}_p$ and $\tilde{B}_p$ matrices. The $\tilde{H}_p$ matrix is symmetric and block tridiagonal. The $\tilde{B}_p$ matrix is zero except for the top r-by-r which is upper triangular.

4 Interconnect modelling for noise

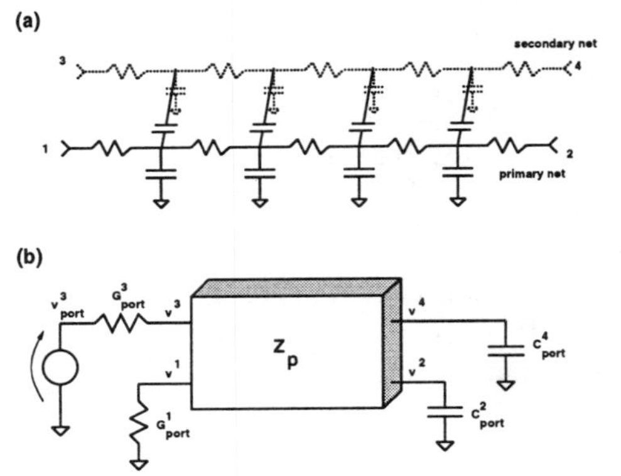

Figure 2: Multiport modelling of global interconnect. (a) A typical net complex consisting of a primary net coupled (in this case) to a single secondary net. (b) The driver resistances are receiver capacitances are folded into the multiport impedance macromodel.

Following reference [2], we classify noise by type. Noise that reduces the node voltage below the supply level is denoted V_H, while noise that increases a node voltage above the ground level is denoted V_L. Noise may also be bootstrapping if it increases a node voltage above the supply level (V_H^*) or below the ground level(V_L^*). As part of the macro-level static noise analysis, noise abstracts are generated for macro blocks. These noise abstracts contain linearized capacitances for each primary input and pull-up and pull-down driver resistances for each primary output. Drive resistances are determined by the linear region of the FET $I_D - V_{DS}$ characteristic. As part of the static noise analysis of the macro, the maximum amount of noise for each output that can be propagated for each of V_L and V_H noise types is calculated. For each input or output that is sensitive to noise, a *noise tolerance* is stored in the abstract by noise type. This is calculated using a sensitivity analysis at the first restoring logic gate from the pin in the macro-level static noise analysis[2].

The noise abstracts are then used along with the interconnect macromodels to check the noise on global interconnect. A DCL interconnect subrule performs the noise calculation from the macromodels loaded with the BDT. We first fold the driver resistance and receiver capacitances into the multiport impedance as shown in Figure 2(b). The $\boldsymbol{Z_p}$ macromodel is given by:

$$\boldsymbol{v} = \tilde{\boldsymbol{B}}_p^T(\boldsymbol{I} + \tilde{s}\tilde{\boldsymbol{H}}_p)^{-1}\tilde{\boldsymbol{B}}_p\boldsymbol{i} \qquad (8)$$

where $\tilde{s} = s - s_o$. If we let $\boldsymbol{x}$ denote the new state variable set, then the equations become:

$$\begin{aligned} \boldsymbol{x} &= \tilde{\boldsymbol{B}}_p\boldsymbol{i} - \tilde{s}\tilde{\boldsymbol{H}}_p\boldsymbol{x} \\ \boldsymbol{v} &= \tilde{\boldsymbol{B}}_p^T\boldsymbol{x} \end{aligned}$$

When receiver capacitances are added at the ports then the port currents become:

$$\boldsymbol{i} \rightarrow \boldsymbol{i} - s\boldsymbol{C}_{port}\tilde{\boldsymbol{B}}_p^T\boldsymbol{x}$$

We now apply voltage sources $\boldsymbol{v}_{port}$ at the ports through a diagonal port conductance matrix $\boldsymbol{G}_{port}$.

$$\boldsymbol{i} = \boldsymbol{G}_{port}(\boldsymbol{v}_{port} - \tilde{\boldsymbol{B}}_p^T\boldsymbol{x})$$

The conductance of the primary net driver is obtained from the drive resistance stored in the noise abstract. Diagonal conductance elements associated with capacitive receivers are zero, while the conductance associated with the secondary net drivers are set to a large default value. Using these expressions, one finds that the transfer function between the voltage sources and the ports of the interconnect are given by:

$$\boldsymbol{v} = \tilde{\boldsymbol{B}}_p^T(\boldsymbol{I}+s\boldsymbol{A})^{-1}(\boldsymbol{I}+\tilde{\boldsymbol{B}}_p\boldsymbol{G}_{port}\tilde{\boldsymbol{B}}_p^T-s_o\boldsymbol{H})^{-1}\tilde{\boldsymbol{B}}_p\boldsymbol{G}_{port}\boldsymbol{v}_{port} \qquad (9)$$

where

$$\boldsymbol{A} = \left(\boldsymbol{I} + \tilde{\boldsymbol{B}}_p\boldsymbol{G}_{port}\tilde{\boldsymbol{B}}_p^T - s_o\boldsymbol{H}\right)^{-1}\left(\tilde{\boldsymbol{B}}_p\boldsymbol{C}_{port}\tilde{\boldsymbol{B}}_p^T + \boldsymbol{H}\right).$$

$\boldsymbol{A}$ is diagonalized as $\boldsymbol{S}\boldsymbol{\Lambda}\boldsymbol{S}^{-1}$, resulting in

$$\begin{aligned} \boldsymbol{v} &= \tilde{\boldsymbol{B}}_p^T\boldsymbol{S}(\boldsymbol{I}+s\boldsymbol{\Lambda})^{-1}\boldsymbol{S}^{-1}\left(\boldsymbol{I}+\tilde{\boldsymbol{B}}_p\boldsymbol{G}_{port}\tilde{\boldsymbol{B}}_p^T - s_o\boldsymbol{H}\right)^{-1} \\ &\quad \times\tilde{\boldsymbol{B}}\boldsymbol{G}_{port}\boldsymbol{v}_{port} \end{aligned} \qquad (10)$$

Let $\boldsymbol{\mu}_i$ denote the ith column of $\tilde{\boldsymbol{B}}_p^T\boldsymbol{S}$ and $\boldsymbol{\nu}_i$ the ith row of

$$\boldsymbol{S}^{-1}\left(\boldsymbol{I}+\tilde{\boldsymbol{B}}_p\boldsymbol{G}_{port}\tilde{\boldsymbol{B}}_p^T - s_o\boldsymbol{H}\right)^{-1}\tilde{\boldsymbol{B}}\boldsymbol{G}_{port}\boldsymbol{v}_{port}.$$

Then

$$\boldsymbol{v} = \sum_i \frac{\boldsymbol{\mu}_i\boldsymbol{\nu}_i}{1+s\lambda_i}\boldsymbol{v}_{port} \qquad (11)$$

where $\boldsymbol{\mu}_i\boldsymbol{\nu}_i \in \mathbb{R}^{r\times r}$ and the λ_i are the diagonal elements of $\boldsymbol{\Lambda}$. The sum is over all the eigenvalues of $\boldsymbol{A}$. For a particular transfer function, one of the residues k_i is chosen from each $\boldsymbol{\mu}_i\boldsymbol{\nu}_i$ matrix. The time-domain response to a saturate ramp waveform of slew t_r such as that assumed to be at each switching secondary net driver, is given by:

$$v(t) = \begin{cases} m\sum_i\left[k_i\lambda_i\left(e^{-t/\lambda_i}-1\right)-k_it\right] \\ \quad \text{for } 0 \le t \le t_r \\ \sum_i\left[mk_i\lambda_i\left(e^{-t/\lambda_i}-e^{-(t-t_r)/\lambda_i}\right)-k_i\right] \\ \quad \text{for } t \ge t_r \end{cases} \qquad (12)$$

where $m = V_{dd}/t_r$, the slope of the switching secondary net. Because of the *driver linearization* approximation, superposition applies.

5 The interaction of static timing and static noise analysis

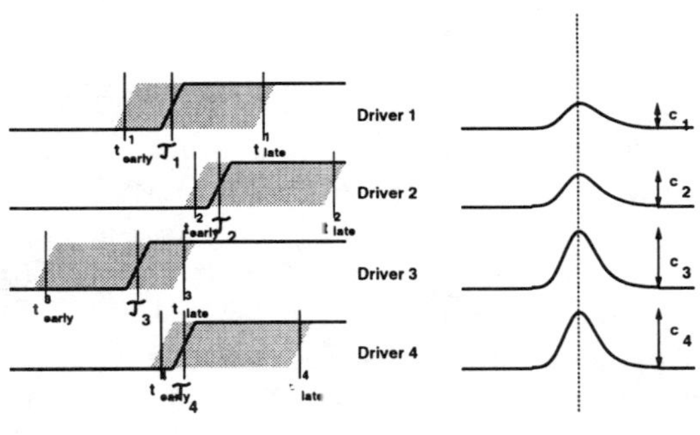

Figure 3: Timing orthogonality. The switching times τ_i are chosen so that the peak noises align.

The Global Harmony architecture shown in Figure 1 includes a tight coupling with the static timing analysis of the same design. This enables timing information to be used in the calculation of noise and noise information to be used in the calculation of timing. For the former case, we obtain secondary net driver slews from the timer model. Timing windows, as defined by the earliest and latest possible arrival time, are determined for each secondary net driver. This allows us to calculate the worst possible noise in the presence of arrival time constraints, reducing pessimism in the analysis. The problem can be formally stated as follows. Let c_i be the peak noise on a given primary receiver associated with driver i. Let t^i_{early} be the earliest arrival time associated with secondary driver i and let t^i_{late} be the latest arrival time associated with secondary driver i. In addition, let τ_i be the switching time associated with secondary net driver i, such that all the noise peaks align for the primary receiver in question. Let x_i be the binary variable indicating whether the given secondary net driver is switching, and let n be the number of secondary nets. The problem is then to maximize:

$$\sum_{i=1}^{n} c_i x_i \tag{13}$$

such that the following $2n$ constraints can be satisfied for all i:

$$(t^i_{late} - \tau_i - t_{ref})x_i \geq 0 \tag{14}$$

$$(\tau_i + t_{ref} - t^i_{early})x_i \geq 0 \tag{15}$$

where t_{ref} is a continuous variable determining the absolute time reference for the τ_i. In this form, the problem takes the form of a mixed integer programming problem. Alternately, the constraints can be reformulated to remove t_{ref} and consider only relative times. For all $i \neq j$,

$$(t^i_{late} - t^j_{early} - \tau_i + \tau_j)x_i x_j \leq 0 \tag{16}$$

$$(t^j_{late} - t^i_{early} + \tau_i - \tau_j)x_i x_j \leq 0 \tag{17}$$

We refer to these constraints as *timing orthogonality*. Because t^i_{early} and t^i_{late} result from early and late path propagation in static timing analysis, the timing windows incorporate the switching of the secondary-net drivers due to hazards.

This formulation assumes a certain "sharpness" to the noise peaks, since when the peak falls outside the windows, its contribution is taken as zero. We utilize a branch-and-bound algorithm[24, 25] to solve this problem since the noise on each subtree can be easily bounded by the assumption that each node in that subtree is contributing. The maximum noise of Equation 13 is added to the propagate noise from the noise abstracts for each receiver and compared against the noise margins also contained in the noise abstracts. A noise "slack" report results. These slacks are based on pessimistic dc noise margins at the macro inputs. To eliminate this pessimism, one can perform a Harmony run on the macro using assertions of the actual input noise generated from Global Harmony.

Even when the entire design satisfies the condition of *noise stability*[2] as verified by static noise analysis, coupled noise in the interconnect can still have a significant effect on timing. The coupled noise calculation is generally performed only after a converged timing solution is calculated. The algorithm employed in Global Harmony to handle the effects of noise on delay is essentially an iterative one:

1. Perform an initial timing with all secondary nets grounded.

2. Freeze the arrival time windows and slews at each driver.

3. Reset the timing model and recalculate all delays including the effects of coupling in the interconnect analysis. The *frozen* secondary net driver information is used for this analysis.

4. Go to step 2 and repeat until convergence.

We now consider the calculations performed as part of step 3. Following the usual practice in static timing analysis, we first find the waveform at the driver, abstract it as a saturate ramp, and propagate it forward to each of the net receivers. To find the driver waveform, we calculate:

$$\begin{aligned} i_{port} &= G_{port}\Big[I - \tilde{B}_p^T(I + sA)^{-1}(I + \tilde{B}_p G_{port}\tilde{B}_p^T \\ &\quad -s_0 H_q)^{-1}\tilde{B}_p G_{port}\Big] v_{source} \end{aligned}$$

G_{port} in this case differs from that used in Equation 9 in that a very small primary driver resistance is used to effectively attach the driver output voltage waveform directly to the multiport. Diagonalizing A as in Equations 10 and 11 yields the following expression for the driver current:

$$\begin{aligned} i_{driver}(t) &= \textstyle\sum_n \sum_i m_n \Big[-k_i^n \lambda_i (e^{-(t-t_i)/\lambda_i} - 1)u(t - t_i) \\ &\quad +k_i^n \lambda_i (e^{-(t-t_i')/\lambda_i} - 1)u(t - t_i')\Big] \end{aligned}$$

where the outer sum is over the primary and secondary drivers and the inner sum is over the eigenvalues of A. The waveforms at the primary and secondary drivers are assumed to be saturate ramps with slopes m_i which begin at time t_i and end at time t_i' (i. e. $t_i' - t_i = |V_{dd}/m_i|$). k_i^n is the residue due to the ith pole with the nth driver contributing. Opposite direction switching (negative m_i) produces the worst-case load, while same-direction switching (positive m_i) produces the best-case load. The driver waveform is first calculated for the case of grounded secondary nets. Secondary net arrival times (i. e. the t_i) are chosen so that the peak noise at the primary driver, as determined by the techniques of Section 4 arrives at the 50% response point of this driver waveform. This heuristic seems to work well in determining the worst (or best) response. We then use an effective-C[26] iteration to find the driver waveform, because of the use of driver delay characterizations based on lumped capacitance. In the presence of a more general nonlinear driver model, recursive convolution techniques[5, 27] can be used.

Calculating the delay and slew follows similarly. In this case, each receiver waveform is calculated for the case of grounded secondary nets and then the secondary net arrival times are chosen so that the peak noise arrives at the 50% response point of this receiver waveform.

6 Results

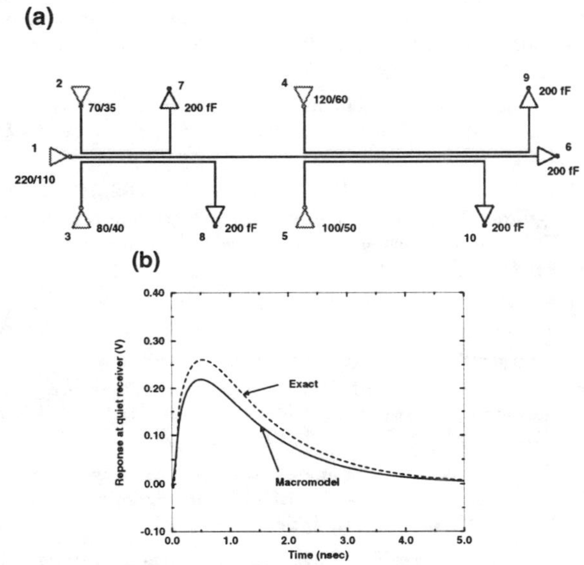

Figure 4: Test interconnect structure (a) The net complex consisting of a primary net and four secondary nets. (b) The response on the primary net receiver 6 due to the switching of driver 4. Both the exact and macromodel responses are shown.

Figure 4(a) shows one of the test structure used to verify our interconnect analysis. This is a net complex consisting of four secondary nets. The interconnect is $0.8\mu m$-thick aluminum of $0.45\mu m$ width and $0.45\mu m$ spacing. The primary net is $5mm$ long. Driver sizes (as widths in microns) and loads are also indicated in the figure. There are 129 state variables in the original network. The Z_p macromodel used in this design has $p = 10$ and $s_o = 10^8 sec^{-1}$. Figure 4(b) shows the exact and approximate noise waveshapes at the primary net driver due to a switching driver 4 with a 100-psec slew.

In Figure 5, we shows typical "noise slack" results in histogram form for a Global Harmony run on a section of a high-performance CMOS microprocessor with 7714 receivers. The noise tolerance at each input is set to zero for this run so that the full spectrum of the coupling noise can be observed. The supply voltage is 1.7 V.

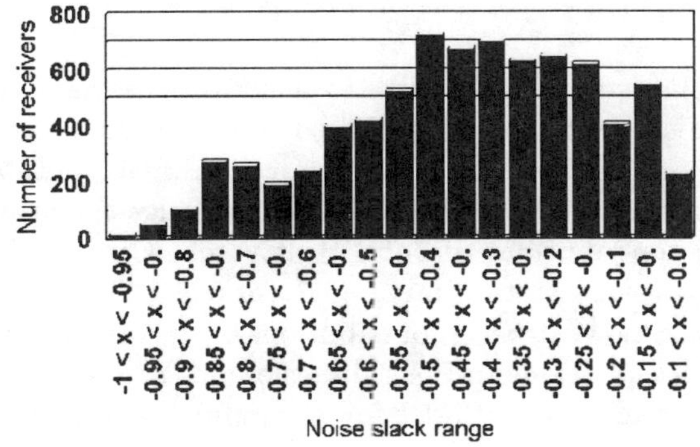

Figure 5: Noise slack histogram for a section of a high-performance CMOS microprocessor. Noise slacks are in volts. The supply voltage is 1.7 V.

Figure 6 shows a noise-on-delay calculation for a reasonably typical point-to-point global net, 1.3 mm long, coupled to eleven secondary nets. With worst-case simultaneous switching of the secondary nets, the effective capacitance increases from 170 fF to 250 fF. The net delay increases from about 130 ps to 200 ps.

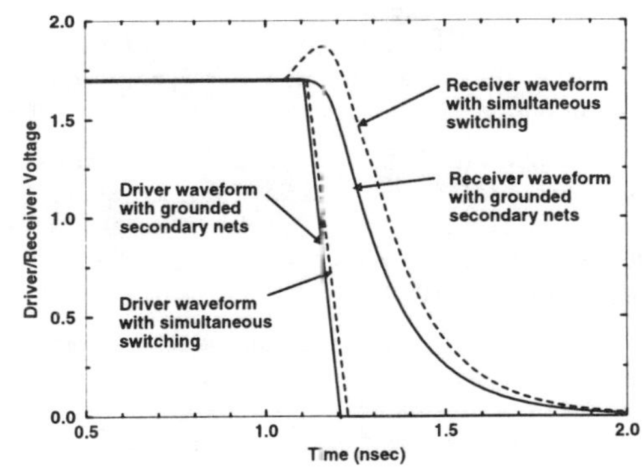

Figure 6: Effect of coupling on interconnect response of typical global net

7 Conclusions

In this paper, we have described a methodology for performing global noise analysis as part of a static noise analysis methodology. This incorporates a unique combination of timing and noise analysis and employs a reduced-order modelling algorithm that allows for passive interconnect macromodelling and efficient storage of the macromodel result.

8 Acknowledgements

The authors would like to acknowledge many useful discussion with Abe Elfadel, Eli Chiprout, Anshul Gupta, Chandu Visweswariah, Joe Rahmeh, and Paul Villarrubia. The authors also acknowledge the invaluable contributions of John Beatty to DCL and Alex Suess to the static timing environment. The authors also acknowledge the contributions of the microprocessor design teams in Poughkeepsie and Yorktown. We also thank Abe Elfadel for a careful reading of the manuscript.

References

[1] L. T. Pillage and R. A. Rohrer. Asymptotic Waveform Evaluation for Timing Analysis. *IEEE Trans. CAD*, 9(4):352–366, April 1990.

[2] K. L. Shepard and V. Narayanan. Noise in deep submicron digital design. In *Proceedings of the IEEE/ACM International Conference on Computer-Aided Design*, pages 524–531, San Jose, CA, November 1996.

[3] K. L. Shepard, S. Carey, E. Cho, B. Curran, R. Hatch, D. Hoffman, S. McCabe, G. Northrop, and R. Seigler. Design Methodology for the G4 S/390 Microprocessors. *IBM Journal of Research and Development*, 1997. To be published.

[4] Delay Calculation Language (DCL) and Procedural Interface (PI). Technical report, CAD Framework Initiative. Version 1.0.1.

[5] Vivek Raghavan, J. Eric Bracken, and Ronald A. Rohrer. AWESpice: A General Tool for the Accurate and Efficient Simulation of Interconnect Problems. In 29th *ACM/IEEE Design Automation Conference*, pages 87–92, Anaheim, California, June 1992.

[6] Seok Yoon Kim, Nanda Gopal, and Lawrence T. Pillage. AWE Macromodels of VLSI Interconnect for Circuit Simulation. In *Proceedings of the IEEE/ACM International Conference on Computer Aided-Design*, pages 64–70, Santa Clara, California, November 1992.

[7] Seok-Yoon Kim, Nanda Gopal, and Lawrence T. Pillage. Time-domain macromodels for VLSI interconnect analysis. *IEEE Trans. CAD*, 13:1257 – 1270, 1994.

[8] R. W. Freund and P. Feldmann. Reduced-order modeling of large passive linear circuits by means of the SyPVL algorithm. In *ICCAD'96*, pages 280–287, San Jose, California, November 1996.

[9] Roland W. Freund and Noël M. Nachtigal. Software for simplified Lanczos and QMR algorithms. *Applied Numerical Mathematics*, 19:319–341, 1995.

[10] G. H. Golub and C. F. Van Loan. *Matrix Computation.* The Johns Hopkins University Press, third edition, 1996.

[11] Peter Feldmann and Roland W. Freund. Reduced-order modeling of large linear subcircuits via a block lanczos algorithm. In 32nd *ACM/IEEE Design Automation Conference*, pages 474–479, San Francisco, California, June 1995.

[12] Jane K. Cullum and Ralph A. Willoughby. *Lanczos Algorithms for Large Symmetric Eigenvalue Computations, Volume I: Theory.* Birkhaeuser, 1985.

[13] G. H. Golub and R. Underwood. The block lanczos method for computing eigenvalues. In J. R. Rice, editor, *Mathmatical Software III*, pages 361–377. Academic Press, New York, 1977.

[14] J. Cullum and W. E. Donath. A block lanczos algorithm for computing the q algebraically largest eigenvalues and a corresponding eigenspace for large, sparse symmetric matrices. In *Proceeding of the IEEE Conference on Decision and Control*, pages 505–509, 1974.

[15] Joseph W. H. Liu. The multifrontal method for sparse matrix solution: Theory and practice. *SIAM Review*, 34:82–109, 1992.

[16] Anshul Gupta and Fred Gustavson. WSSMP: Watson symmetric sparse matrix package. Technical report, IBM T.J. Watson Research Center, 1997. Research Report RC 20645.

[17] P. Feldmann and R. W. Freund. Efficient linear circuit analysis by Padé approximation via the Lanczos process. *IEEE Trans. CAD*, 14:639–649, May 1995.

[18] I. J. Jaimoukha and E. M. Kasenally. Oblique projection methods for large scale model reduction. *SIAM J. Matrix Anal. Appl.*, 16:602 – 627, 1995.

[19] I. Elfadel and D. D. Ling. Zeros and passivity of arnoldi-reduced-order transfer functions for interconnect networks. In *34th DAC*, 1997. to appear.

[20] L. Miguel Silveira, Mattan Kamon, Ibrahim Elfadel, and Jacob White. A Coordinate-Transformed Arnoldi Algorithm for Generating Guaranteed Stable Reduced-Order Models of RLC Circuits. In *IEEE/ACM International Conference on Computer-Aided Design*, pages 288 – 294, San Jose, CA, November 1996.

[21] E. S. Kuh and R. A Rohrer. *Theory of Linear Active Networks.* Holden-Day, 1967.

[22] E. A. Guillemin. *Synthesis of Passive Networks.* John Wiley and Sons, 1957.

[23] K. S. Narendra and J. H. Taylor. *Frequency Domain Criterion for Absolute Stability.* Academic Press, 1973.

[24] G. Nemhauser and L. Wolsey. *Integer and Combinatorial Optimization.* Wiley, 1988.

[25] C. Papadimitriou and K. Steiglitz. *Combinatorial Optimization.* Prentice-Hall, 1982.

[26] Curtis L. Ratzlaff, Satyamurthy Pullela, and Lawrence T. Pillage. Modelling the RC-interconnect effects in a hierarchical timing analyzer. In *Custom Integrated Circuits Conference*, pages 15.6.1 – 15.6.4, 1992.

[27] J. E. Bracken, V. Raghavan, and R. A. Rohrer. Interconnect Simulation with Asymptotic Waveform Evaluation. *IEEE Trans. Circuits Syst.*, 39(11):869–878, November 1992.

Efficient Coupled Noise Estimation for On-Chip Interconnects

Anirudh Devgan
Austin Research Laboratory
IBM Research Division, Austin TX 78758
devgan@austin.ibm.com

Abstract

Noise analysis and avoidance is an increasingly critical step in deep submicron design. Ever increasing requirements on performance have led to widespread use of dynamic logic circuit families and its other derivatives. These aggressive circuit families trade off noise margin for timing performance making them more susceptible to noise failure and increasing the need for noise analysis. Currently, noise analysis is performed either through circuit or timing simulation or through model order reduction. These techniques in use are still inefficient for analyzing massive amount of interconnect data found in present day integrated circuits. This paper presents efficient techniques for estimation of coupled noise in on-chip interconnects. This noise estimation metric is an upper bound for RC circuits, being similar in spirit to Elmore delay in timing analysis. Such an efficient noise metric is especially useful for noise criticality pruning and physical design based noise avoidance techniques.

1. Introduction

Timing and power analysis have always been critical in the design process. With increasing operating frequencies, noise analysis and avoidance is becoming equally important, or in some cases, more important than timing and power analysis. Advances in process technology allow shrinking of the minimum distance between adjacent wires. This has led to increase in the coupling capacitance from a net to its neighbors. Furthermore, the distance between two wires can be reduced more than the height of the wire itself. The thickness of the wire is typically greater than its width, causing an increase in ratio of coupling capacitance to the total capacitance. For present day processes, the ratio of coupling capacitor to the grounded capacitor can be as high as 35%. Due to the increase in the coupling capacitance, a switching net can electrical affect its neighboring nets. If the neighboring net is quiet, this capacitive coupling induces a noise pulse which can have a detrimental effect on the circuit response.

The criticality of the noise analysis problem is also dependent on the type of logic circuits used in the design. Some logic circuits are more susceptible to noise than others. Over the last several years, dynamic logic circuit families and its derivatives have gained wide spread acceptance. Dynamic circuits use a clock signal or clock-like signal to precharge the output voltage. The circuit is then evaluated by a N-tree structure. The advantage of dynamic logic is that the capacitive load on the previous stage is reduced. The previous stage has to drive the capacitance of only the NMOS transistor, as compared to the capacitance of both the NMOS and PMOS transistors in CMOS logic. However, the switching point of dynamic logic gates is the threshold voltage of the NMOS transistor, rather than typically half of the supply voltage for CMOS. Hence, dynamic logic circuits trade noise margin to reduce the circuit delay. This reduced noise margin and increased noise susceptibility mandates greater use of noise analysis. The problem of noise failure can be more severe than the problem of timing failure. For most circuits, timing failure can be recovered by increasing the clock speed and thus allowing more time for signal propagation. However, noise is caused by, among other things, capacitive coupling and input slope, which are much more difficult to control from the chip terminals. For example, changing the capacitive coupling normally requires rewiring the chip. If the noise problem goes undetected to fabrication, correcting it may cause an expensive second fabrication run.

Various transient analysis techniques can be used to estimate noise. Circuit or timing simulation techniques, like SPICE[3], can be used. In cases when the problem can be modeled as a linear circuit (which it can be for most coupled noise problems), specialized linear model reduction techniques [4][5] are typically used[2]. Model reduction helps in reducing the computational cost, but in several cases, the cost is still unacceptable given the enormous complexity of interconnects. Using modern moment matching methods, it may still require more than a day to compute the noise in a modern microprocessor. The constrains on efficiency are even greater if noise analysis is to be used within a physical design system. Most of the current physical design systems use a geometric model for noise (e.g based on geometric distance between wires, etc.). However, these simple formulae do not have an electrical and circuit theoretic formulation and are hence inaccurate. And use of accurate moment matching or simulation techniques is often inefficient, both for noise verification and noise avoidance. Hence, a more efficient electric metric for noise analysis is needed to address these requirements.

This paper presents an electrical metric for efficiently estimating the coupled noise for on-chip interconnects. It determines the maximum noise induced on a net (or a set of nets) by a switching net (or set of switching nets). Nets with any circuit topology can be analyzed by this metric. The metric can be computed by inspection for most typical interconnects. It determines an upper bound on the coupled noise for RC and overdamped RLC interconnects. The paper is organized as follows. Section 2 presents the noise estimation technique, followed in Section 3 by techniques for efficient computation. Results are presented in Section 4 followed by conclusions.

2. Noise Estimation

Coupled noise in interconnect networks is caused by capacitive coupling between an active (or aggressor) net and a passive (or victim) net. Consider the circuit shown in Figure 1. For noise coupling, the aggressor net is the net that switches state, where as the victim net is quiet or maintains its present state. Figure 2 represents the general circuit model of the coupled noise problem, where the aggressor and victim nets can have any topologies. The victim net, the aggressor net and the coupling between them is represented by a linear circuit description.

1092-3152/97 $10.00 © 1997 IEEE

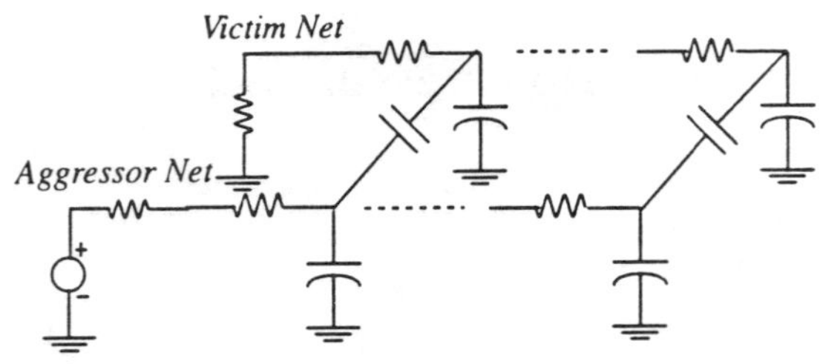

Figure 1 *Circuit schematic with aggressor and victim net for coupled noise.*

In general, the number of victim nets and number of aggressor nets may be more than one. Initially, the case with one victim and one aggressor is analyzed. This can be easily extended to the case with multiple victim and aggressor nets.

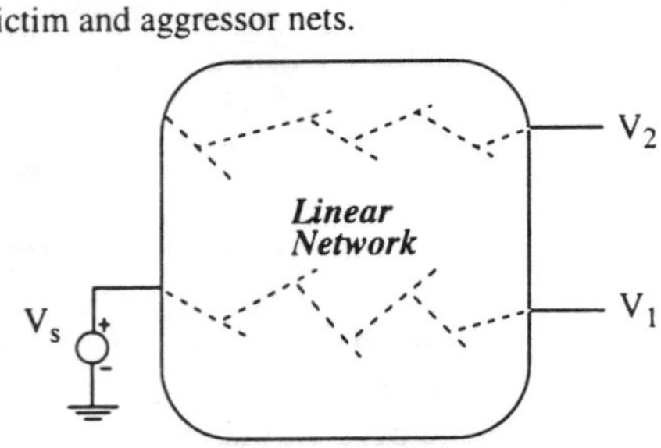

Figure 2 *General circuit representation for coupled noise.*

The circuit equations for circuit shown in Figure 2 can be written as

$$\begin{bmatrix} C_1 & C_c \\ C_c & C_2 \end{bmatrix} \begin{bmatrix} \dot{v}_1 \\ \dot{v}_2 \end{bmatrix} = \begin{bmatrix} A_{11} & A_{12} \\ A_{21} & A_{22} \end{bmatrix} \begin{bmatrix} v_1 \\ v_2 \end{bmatrix} + \begin{bmatrix} B_1 \\ B_2 \end{bmatrix} v_s \qquad (1)$$

where v_1 is a vector of node voltages in the aggressor net, v_2 is a vector of node voltages in the victim net, and v_s is the input to the aggressor net. Or, in the Laplace Domain,

$$sC_1V_1 + sC_cV_2 = A_{11}V_1 + A_{12}V_2 + B_1V_s \qquad (2)$$

The first state equation in Equation (1) can be rewritten as,

$$V_1 = (sC_1 - A_{11})^{-1}[(A_{12} - sC_c)V_2 + B_1V_s] \qquad (3)$$

For the coupled noise waveform V_2,

$$sC_cV_1 + sC_2V_2 = A_{21}V_1 + A_{22}V_2 + B_2V_s \qquad (4)$$

Or, (5)

$$(sC_2 - A_{22})V_2 = (A_{21} - sC_c)(sC_1 - A_{11})^{-1}[(A_{12} - sC_c)V_2 + B_1V_s] + B_2V_s \qquad (6)$$

Alternatively,

$$[(sC_2 - A_{22}) - (A_{21} - sC_c)(sC_1 - A_{11})^{-1}(A_{12} - sC_c)]V_2 = (A_{21} - sC_c)(sC_1 - A_{11})^{-1}B_1V_s + B_2V_s \qquad (7)$$

However, the interconnect networks that cause coupled noise have special characteristics, which can be identified as follows.

[1]. $A_{12} = 0$

Non zero value of A_{12} would indicate a resistive or DC path from the aggressor net to victim net. It would mean that both the aggressor and victim net are electrically the same net or signal, which is not the case. Hence, A_{12} is zero for all coupled noise problems.

[2]. $A_{21} = 0$

Non zero value of A_{21} would indicate a resistive or DC path from the victim net to the aggressor net. It would mean that both the aggressor and victim net are electrically the same net or signal, which is not the case. Hence, A_{21} is zero for all coupled noise problems.

[3]. $B_2 = 0$

Non zero value of B_2 would indicate a resistive or DC path from the source, V_s, to the victim net as well as the aggressor net. It would mean that a source is directly exciting the victim net and notion of coupled noise is meaningless. Hence, B_2 is zero for all coupled noise problems.

Hence the circuit description of the coupled noise circuit, shown in Figure 2, can be rewritten as,

$$\begin{bmatrix} C_1 & C_c \\ C_c & C_2 \end{bmatrix} \begin{bmatrix} \dot{v}_1 \\ \dot{v}_2 \end{bmatrix} = \begin{bmatrix} A_{11} & 0 \\ 0 & A_{22} \end{bmatrix} \begin{bmatrix} v_1 \\ v_2 \end{bmatrix} + \begin{bmatrix} B_1 \\ 0 \end{bmatrix} v_s \qquad (8)$$

Hence Equation (6) can be simplified to,

$$[(sC_2 - A_{22}) - sC_c(sC_1 - A_{11})^{-1}sC_c]V_2 = -sC_c(sC_1 - A_{11})^{-1}B_1V_s \qquad (9)$$

Let,

$$H(s) = \frac{V_2(s)}{V_s(s)} \qquad (10)$$

As seen from Equation (9), $H(s)$ has a zero at $s = 0$. This is true for all networks that exhibit coupled noise. The zero at $s = 0$ is due to the fact that the coupling between the aggressor and victim net is purely capacitive.

The fact that $H(s)$ has a zero at $s = 0$ allows us to compute the maximum possible noise that can ever be induced on the victim net V_2. If the input to the circuit, V_s, is an infinite ramp, output of the aggressor net V_1 is also an infinite ramp, but it is delayed by the signal delay in the aggressor net. However, all nodes in the victim net exponentially chargeup to their respective finite maximum steady state value. If input to the circuit, V_s, is a finite ramp (which it typically is) or if the input is an infinite ramp, the derivative of coupled noise, $\dot{V}_2$, is zero at $t = \infty$ and the coupled noise V_2 has a finite maximum value.

The value of this finite maximum value can be computed from Equation (10) through use of the final value theorem.

Final value of $V_2(s)$ at $t = \infty$ is given by

$$V_{2,max} = \lim_{s \to 0} sV_2(s) \quad (11)$$

Or

$$V_{2,max} = \lim_{s \to 0} sH(s)u(s) = \lim_{s \to 0} sH(s)\frac{\dot{u}}{s^2} = \lim_{s \to 0} H(s)\frac{\dot{u}}{s} \quad (12)$$

Applying the final value theorem and combining it with Equation (9) yields,

$$V_{2,max} = -A_{22}^{-1}C_cA_{11}^{-1}B_1\dot{u} \quad (13)$$

Equation (13) gives the maximum amount of coupled noise that can be induced on the victim net V_2, for the given linear circuit, i.e. A_{11}, A_{22}, C_1, C_c and C_2, and the input slope, $\dot{u}$. Equation (13) yields an upper bound because the monotonicityy of the RC circuit response[7][8]. In the presence of the inductors, if the circuit is over-damped or critically damped, the monotonicity is still maintained.

3. Circuit Interpretation and Computation

The maximum coupled noise given by Equation (13) is relatively easy to evaluate. We will now present steps and necessary circuit conditions to further simplify the computation.

Equation (13) can be rewritten as,

$$V_{2,max} = A_{22}^{-1}C_c\dot{V}_{1,ss} \quad (14)$$

Where,

$$\dot{V}_{1,ss} = -A_{11}^{-1}B_1\dot{u} \quad (15)$$

Equation (14) can be rewritten as,

$$V_{2,max} = A_{22}^{-1}I_c \quad (16)$$

Where,

$$I_c = C_c\dot{V}_{1,ss}. \quad (17)$$

The computation of maximum coupled noise can be decomposed into the following three steps:

- Computation of $\dot{V}_{1,ss} = -A_{11}^{-1}B_1\dot{u}$. This requires circuit analysis of the Aggressor net.
- Computation of $I_c = C_c\dot{V}_{1,ss}$. This requires a multiplication step.
- Computation of $V_{2,max} = A_{22}^{-1}I_c$. This requires circuit analysis of the Victim net.

Step1: Computation of $\dot{V}_{1,ss}$

The computation of the steady state ramp derivative on the aggressor net is illustrated in Equation Figure 3. The input source is replaced by a voltage source of value equal to the input derivative, $\dot{V}_s$. All the capacitors in the aggressor net are replaced by open circuits and all coupling capacitors to the victim net are not considered in the this circuit. The solution of the circuit so obtained gives the steady state ramp derivative, $\dot{V}_{1,ss}$, at each corresponding node. The solution of this circuit involves the matrix factorization of the aggressor net's dissipative matrix. However, for typical interconnects, this solution is trivial as shown in the next subsection.

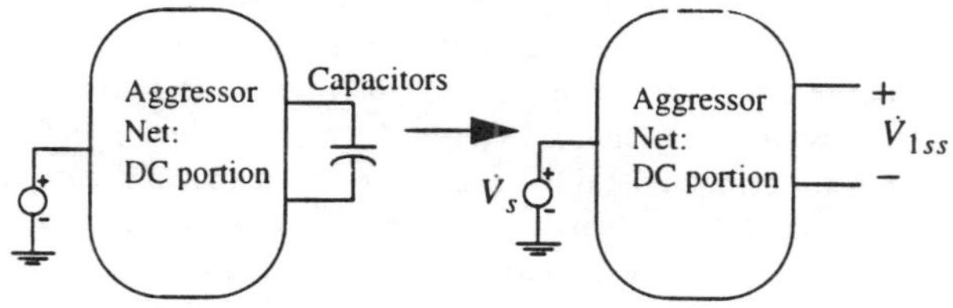

Figure 3 *Circuit Transformation to compute* $\dot{V}_{1,ss}$.

Step1: Typical Interconnects:

Figure 4 shows the computation of the steady state derivative for the aggressor net for typical interconnects. For on chip interconnects, the nets do not have a dissipative (or DC) path to ground. A dissipative path to ground in the interconnection would mean DC loss of signal, which typical is not the case for on chip interconnects.

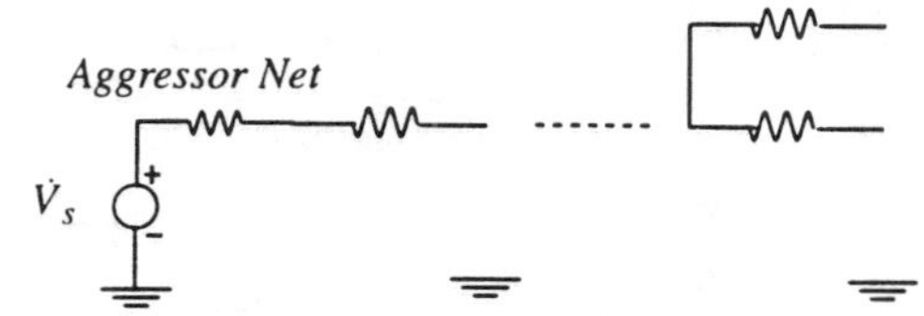

Figure 4 *Computation of* $\dot{V}_{1,ss}$ *for typical interconnects.*

In the typical case of no dissipative path to ground, computation of $\dot{V}_{1,ss}$ is trivial. In such a case, there is no current flow in the circuit shown in Figure 4, and $\dot{V}_{1,ss} = \dot{V}_s$.

In summary, $\dot{V}_{1,ss} = \dot{V}_s$, in case of no resistive path to ground in the aggressor net

Step2: Computation of I_c

This step involves a simple multiplication step that converts the steady state derivative of the aggressor net to a current on the victim net using the coupling capacitor matrix, C_c. For a node i in the victim net

$$I_i = \sum_{\forall j} C_{c,ij}\dot{V}_{1j,ss} \quad (18)$$

where $C_{c,ij}$ is the coupling capacitor between node i on the victim net(s) to node j on the aggressor net. $\forall j$ indicates the summation of all nodes in the aggressor net (or set of aggressor nets) capacitively coupled to node i on the victim net.

Step3: Computation of N_{max} or $V_{2,max}$

Figure 5 shows the computation of the maximum induced noise on the victim net. The capacitors on the victim net are replaced by the coupling currents, I_c, from the computation in step 2. Note that I_c is a vector of currents. Each capacitive node in the victim net is replaced by a current source of value corresponding to its index in the I_c vector. The voltage on a node in this circuit gives the maximum noise than can be coupled at that node. That is, the voltage of each node, say voltage $V_{2,i}$ at node i, gives the maximum noise that can be induced at the node i. The computation of the maximum induced noise requires a DC solution of the victim net. The cost of this DC solution is a single matrix factorization.

Step3: Typical Interconnects

Figure 6 shows the computation of the victim net for typical interconnects. As mentioned in the previous section, the solution of the maximum induced noise requires a DC solution of the victim net. This cost is in addition to the cost of DC solution of the aggressor net in order to determine the steady state derivative and coupling currents. However, as mentioned earlier, for typical interconnects, the solution of aggressor net is trivial and does not require any computation cost. Similarly, for typical interconnects, the solution of the victim net is also greatly simplified and requires only a linear time evaluation which can be carried out by inspection.

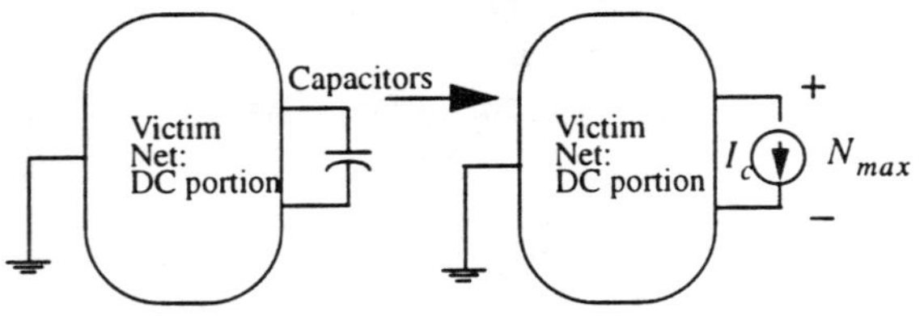

Figure 5 *Circuit transformation for computation of maximum noise* N_{max}.

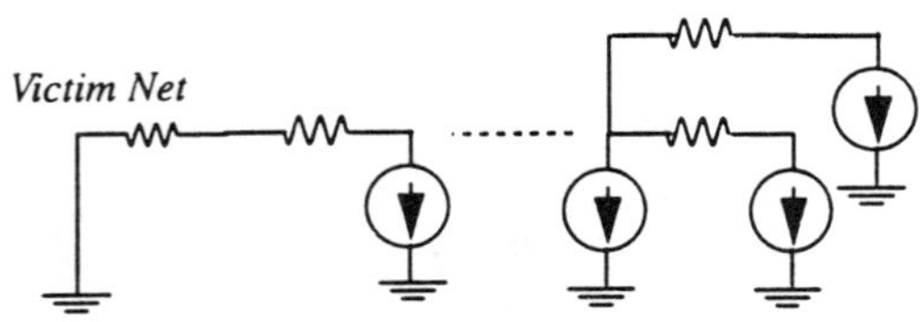

Figure 6 *Computation of* N_{max} *for typical interconnects.*

Consider the sample 3RC circuit in Figure 7 to illustrate the computation of N_{max} by inspection for typical interconnects.

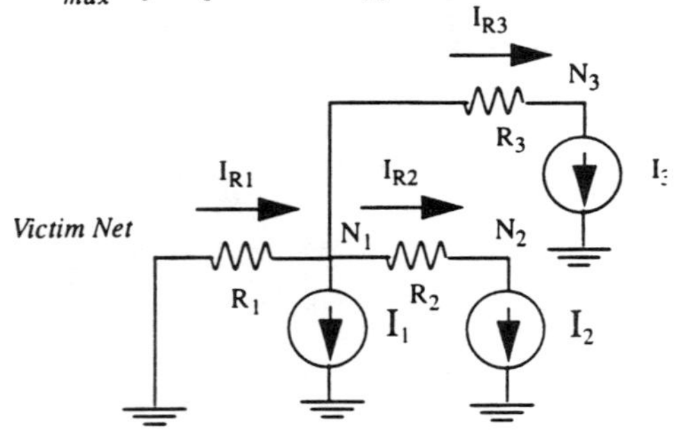

Figure 7 *Illustration of solution by inspection for maximum induced noise for typical interconnects.*

The maximum induced noise at each node can be written by inspection as,

$$N_{max,1} = V_{2.1} = -R_1(I_1 + I_2 + I_3) \tag{19}$$

$$N_{max,2} = V_{2.2} = -R_1(I_1 + I_2 + I_3) - R_2 I_2 \tag{20}$$

$$N_{max,3} = V_{2.3} = -R_1(I_1 + I_2 + I_3) - R_3 I_3 \tag{21}$$

The maximum coupled noise can also be written as,

$$N_{max,1} = -R_1(C_{c1} + C_{c2} + C_{c3})\dot{u} \tag{22}$$

$$N_{max,2} = -R_1(C_{c1} + C_{c2} + C_{c3})\dot{u} - R_2 C_{c2}\dot{u} \tag{23}$$

$$N_{max,3} = -R_1(C_{c1} + C_{c2} + C_{c3})\dot{u} - R_3 C_{c3}\dot{u} \tag{24}$$

In general, for a tree structure, the maximum induced noise, $N_{max,i}$, at node i can be computed as,

$$N_{max,i} = R_i \sum_{\forall L} I_j + N_{max,i-1} \tag{25}$$

Where $\forall L$ denotes the summation of all coupling currents at nodes which are in the load (i.e. in direction of the victim sink) of that particular node in the victim net. And $N_{max,i-1}$ denotes the noise at the previous node (towards the root of the tree).

Since the metric is an closed form expression, it can also be used to computed the maximum allowable coupling capacitance given the noise budget. This value of the coupling capacitance can then be used to compute the distance between the nets.

So the cost of computing the maximum coupled noise is the multiplication to computed the coupling currents and multiplications shown in Equation (25) to computed the coupled voltage. The complexity of this computation is significantly lower than either transient analysis through numerical integration or moment matching methods.

In the case of multiple aggressor nets, linear superposition is used. I_c in Equation (25) is computed for each aggressor net by multiplying its respective capacitive coupling by the respective input slope of each aggressor net. I_c's from each aggressor net are added together to compute the total current which can then be used to compute the maximum noise. In case of timing orthogonality, the summation of currents from the aggressor nets has to be performed differently. Timing orthogonality, in this case, implies that the arrival time windows on the different aggressor nets are different. In such a case only the aggressor nets with overlapping arrival time windows have to be considered in computing the maximum noise on the victim net(s).

4. Results

The techniques described in the previous sections have been implemented in a noise computation tool. This section presents noise accuracy and computation speed results on various interconnect structures.

The peak coupled noise on the victim net for a typical small RC interconnect structure with a rise time of 200ps and power supply voltage of 1.8v is computed by circuit simulation and proposed metric. Table 1: summarizes the results for ten nodes in the circuit. As seen for the table, the proposed metric and the simulation results show an excellent match. Table 2: summarizes the peak coupled noise for the same circuit but with a faster rise time of 100ps and power supply of 1.8v. In this case, the metric is more conservative, over estimation the peak noise by 14.11% in the worst case. The accuracy of the metric degrades with reduction in rise times of the signal of the aggressor net. However, note that the peak noise predicted is always more than the actual obtained by simulation. If the rise time is small, like in the second example, the smaller rise time does not allow the circuit to reach the ramp steady state noise (which the metric predicts). Hence, the metric predicts a value of the peak noise which is greater than the actual peak noise.

The loading of the interconnect normally does not allow for very small rise times. The accuracy of the metric should normally be acceptable for several noise verification, noise pruning and physical design applications.

Node	Circuit Simulation	Proposed Metric
1	0.0084	0.0084
2	0.0160	0.0160
3	0.0227	0.0227
4	0.0286	0.0286
5	0.0336	0.0336
6	0.0378	0.0379
7	0.0412	0.0412
8	0.0437	0.0438
9	0.0454	0.0454
10	0.0462	0.0463

Table 1: Comparison of Noise as computed by circuit simulation and the proposed metric. Units of noise are volts.

Node	Circuit Simulation	Proposed Metric	% Error
1	0.0147	0.0168	7.73%
2	0.0277	0.0319	13.1%
3	0.0392	0.0454	13.65%
4	0.0492	0.0572	13.98%
5	0.0578	0.0673	14.11%
6	0.0651	0.0757	14.00%
7	0.0709	0.0824	13.95%
8	0.0752	0.0875	14.05%
9	0.0782	0.0908	13.87%
10	0.0797	0.0925	13.83%

Table 2: Comparison of Noise as computed by circuit simulation and the proposed metric with rise time of 100ps. Units of noise are volts.

Table 3: shows the run time comparison of the proposed metric with an Krylov subspace based Arnoldi model reduction package for several RC circuits. These circuits are RC trees, with capacitive coupling between aggressor and victim net, and with no DC path to ground in the interconnect. The drivers are modeled by linear resistance and a voltage source, where as the victim net is modeled by a linear resistance. The computation of the metric is performed both through matrix factorization(Equation (13)) and by inspection(Equation (25)). The Arnoldi-based model reduction engine uses matrix solution to compute the circuit response. Hence, the comparison of the Arnold-based model reduction to the proposed metric (matrix factorization) is more appropriate. It should be noted that path tracing techniques can also be used in Arnoldi-based model reduction.

As seen from the table, for the matrix based comparison the metric shows significant computational advantage over the model reduction technique. The model reduction requires repeated matrix factorizations, solution for eigenvalues for the reduced system and time exponential evaluations. It should be noted however, that the model reduction technique can be used to obtain the complete transient response of the noise waveform. But, if only peak noise is of interest, which it is for several applications, the proposed metric is more efficient.

Circuit	Number of Elements	Arnoldi Model Reduction	Proposed Metric (Matrix Method)	Proposed Metric (By Inspection)
ckt1	500	.2s	.00s	.00s
ckt2	5,000	5.86s	.07s	.01s
ckt3	50,000	145s	3.44s	.05s
ckt4	500,000	-	360.55s	.35s

Table 3: Comparison of runtime for the proposed metric with model reduction techniques.

5. Conclusions

This paper has presented an efficient metric for computing the maximum coupled noise for on-chip interconnects. The noise metric can be used to compute noise in nets of any circuit topology. For typical interconnects, the noise can be computed in linear time. The computations can be performed by inspection instead of sparse matrix construction and factorization. The metric is an upper bound, with the error in estimation increasing with decrease in rise time. The techniques presented in this paper for noise computation are significantly more efficient than previous techniques, such as, moment matching methods or numerical integration.

6. References

[1]. R.R Tummala and E.J. Ryamszewski,"Microelectronics Packaging Handbook" Van Nostrand Reinhold, 1989.

[2]. K. Shephard and V. Narayan, "*Noise in Submicron Digital Design*", IEEE/ACM International Conference on Computer Aided Design, Nov 1996.

[3]. L.W. Nagel. *SPICE2, A Computer Program to Simulate Semiconductor Circuits.* Technical Report ERL-M520, UC-Berkeley, May, 1975.

[4]. L. T. Pillage and R. A. Rohrer. Asymptotic Waveform Evaluation for Timing Analysis. *IEEE Trans. Computer-Aided Design.* 9(4):352-366, April, 1990.

[5]. P. Feldmann and R.W. Fruend, "Reduced-order modeling of large linear subcircuits via a block Lanczos algorithm", *In Proceedings of ACM/IEEE Design Automation Conference*, pp. 474-479, 1995.

[6]. W.C.Elmore,"The Transient Response of Damped Linear Networks with particular regard to Broadband Amplifiers", *J. Applied Physics* 19,pp. 55-63, 1948.

[7]. P. Penfield and J. Rubinstein, "Signal delay in RC tree networks", *In Proceedings of ACM/IEEE Design Automation Conference*, pp. 613-617, 1981.

[8]. R. Gupta, B. Tutuianu and L.T.Pileggi, "The Elmore Delay as a Bound for RC Trees with Generalized Input Signals, *IEEE Transactions on Computer Aided Design*, Vol 16 No 1, pp. 95-104, Jan 1997.

SESSION 3A

HIGH LEVEL VALIDATION

Moderators:

Christos Papachristou, Case Western Reserve University, Cleveland, OH

Joachim Kunkel, Synopsys, Inc., Mountain View, CA

Efficient Circuit Partitioning to Extend Cycle Simulation Beyond Synchronous Circuits

Charles J. DeVane*
Viewlogic Systems, Inc.
Marlboro, MA 01752-4615

Abstract

Cycle simulation techniques, such as levelized compiled code, can ordinarily be applied only to synchronous designs. They usually cannot be applied to designs containing circuit features like combinational paths, multiple clock domains, generated clocks, asynchronous resets, and transparent latches. This paper presents a novel partitioning algorithm that partitions a non-cycle-simulatable circuit containing these features into sub-circuits that can be cycle simulated. Cycle simulation techniques can be applied to the individual sub-circuits, and the whole collection of sub-circuits can be simulated together using conventional co-simulation techniques. Empirical results demonstrate that this approach brings the benefits of cycle simulation to circuits that were previously impossible to cycle simulate. The partitioning algorithm requires time and space linear in the size of the circuit, and in practice is very fast. We also discuss how the key ideas presented here can be applied to accelerate HDL simulation.

1 Introduction

The rapidly expanding size and complexity of digital systems has caused simulation to become a major bottleneck in the design flow. To overcome this bottleneck, designers are increasingly willing to abandon traditional event-driven timing simulation and adopt a combination of static timing analysis and functional simulation. Static timing analysis relieves the simulator from the burden of verifying timing, so that only the circuit's logical function needs to be simulated. The circuit can be simulated at a level of abstraction higher than event-driven timing simulation using faster algorithms.

In contexts where simulation of timing is not needed, levelized compiled code (*LCC*) has been used very successfully on large, purely synchronous designs. This technique consumes very little memory and is usually very fast, but it generally supports only a zero delay model of logic and is appropriate only for synchronous circuits. This model of simulation is sometimes called *cycle simulation*, because it focuses on computing circuit values only on clock cycle boundaries.

Unfortunately, most designs are not purely synchronous but include features like combinational paths, asynchronous resets, transparent latches, multiple clock domains, and generated clocks which are not readily supported by the cycle simulation abstraction. It can be feasible to cycle simulate these features in a test environment where the stimulus is a predetermined set of test vectors. However, it is increasingly important to verify circuits in context inside a complete system. Problems arise as soon as a circuit with any of these features is embedded in a system simulation where external feedback may cause the circuit input to be a dynamic function of the circuit outputs.

How can we exploit cycle-simulation algorithms like LCC to simulate circuits with these features within a complete system simulation? If circuits that cannot be cycle-simulated can be automatically and efficiently partitioned into subcircuits that can be cycle-simulated then the benefits of cycle simulation algorithms can be extended to a broader class of circuits. Using conventional co-simulation techniques, a hybrid simulation environment can apply cycle simulation to the subcircuits that allow it, and conventional event-driven simulation to the rest of the circuit (see Figure 1). Hybrid environments similar to this are already widely used to support requirements like mixed-signal simulation, third-party models, mixed-language HDL simulation, etc. The key problem, then, is how to partition circuits into cycle-simulatable sub-circuits.

In this paper we present an algorithm to partition circuits into cycle-simulatable sub-circuits. The algorithm is efficient, generally being linear in both time and space, and very fast in practice. We first establish a notion of cycle simulation as a level of abstraction, and then review prior work in this light. Next we define a class of circuits that can be cycle-simulated. Then we discuss several common circuit features which preclude cycle simulation: combinational paths, multiple

*The author's current address is: The MathWorks, Inc., Natick, MA 01760; cdevane@mathworks.com.

1092-3152/97 $10.00

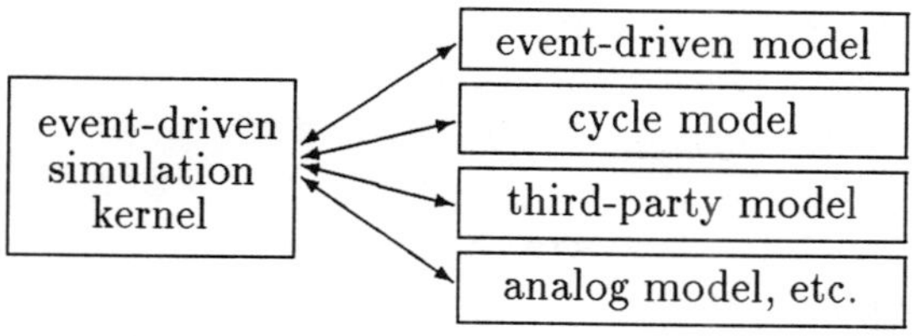

Figure 1: Hybrid simulation environment supporting event models and cycle models as well as other forms of simulation.

clock domains, generated clocks, asynchronous resets, and transparent latches. For each case it is shown how to partition the circuit for efficient simulation. An efficient algorithm is presented that performs the desired circuit partitioning, along with a brief sketch of the proof of correctness and analysis of complexity. Experimental results of applying this partitioning to actual industrial designs are then presented to demonstrate the efficiency and effectiveness of the algorithm. The paper closes with an application of these structural ideas to accelerating HDL simulation.

2 Background

2.1 The Cycle Simulation Abstraction

A hierarchy of abstraction for circuit simulation is illustrated in Figure 2. At higher levels of abstraction less information is computed, which leads to faster algorithms. However, these faster algorithms are only applicable to circuits for which the abstraction is appropriate. Conversely, at lower levels of abstraction more information is computed, leading to algorithms that are slower but more broadly applicable. For example, SPICE2[7] is much slower than event-driven logic simulation, but can be applied to analog circuits for which event-driven logic simulation is inappropriate.

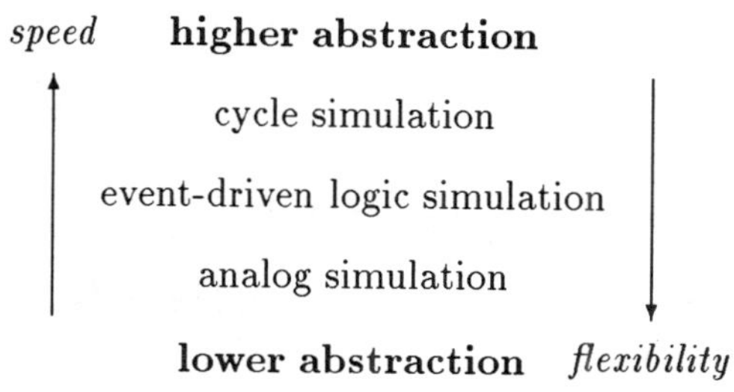

Figure 2: A hierarchy of abstraction for circuit simulation.

The term *cycle simulation* is sometimes equated with LCC simulators [2] [4] [9]. However, this paper uses the term more generally to describe any simulation algorithm that focuses on computing and storing only the values of circuit outputs and storage elements at most once per clock cycle. By this definition cycle simulation operates at a higher level of abstraction than event-driven logic simulation. Because they compute and store fewer values at fewer time points, algorithms that exploit the cycle simulation abstraction can be expected to have an inherent performance advantage for appropriate circuits.

It is important to distinguish between the level of abstraction supported (or exploited) by a simulator and the algorithms used to implement the simulator, because multiple algorithms may be used to support a given level of abstraction. For example, instead of using LCC a cycle simulator can use techniques such as branching code [1] [6] or threaded code [5]. Likewise, an event-driven simulator need not have a run-time event queue [3].

2.2 Previous Work

HSS/3[2], Terse[4], and SSIM[9] all demonstrate the performance potential of software LCC simulators. Terse can also perform static timing analysis during model compilation. However, all these systems were restricted to synchronous designs.

Research continues to improve the performance of event-driven simulation. However, due to the difference in levels of abstraction, the performance of event-driven simulation still has not approached that of cycle simulation. For example, VeriSUIF[3] used compiler optimization techniques to eliminate the run-time event queue while maintaining the event-driven abstraction. It achieved impressive performance for an event-driven simulator, but still falls short of cycle simulation. Although VeriSUIF is a compiled simulator and incorporates a form of levelization, it does not use what is conventionally known as LCC as in [2][4][9]. By comparison, VeriSUIF's levelization optimization is limited in its ability to suppress multiple evaluations. Because VeriSUIF supports the event-driven abstraction, computing intermediate values at intermediate time points, its performance potential is necessarily limited compared to cycle simulation. Another potential performance problem may be compilation time.

Another relevant approach to improving simulation performance is *demand-driven* simulation, as illustrated by BACKSIM[8]. BACKSIM did not support timing analysis and was used essentially as a cycle simulator. During simulation, BACKSIM uses a depth-first search to recursively walk backward through the circuit, collecting only the information required to compute the desired output values. BACKSIM can be viewed as using *dynamic levelization* at run-time instead of the compile-time *static levelization* used by LCC simulators. The general concept of demand driven evaluation can be seen behind our notion of *fanin* gates (Section 3.2).

Several event-driven simulators have sought higher

performance by exploiting techniques like LCC at a relatively fine granularity. These simulators could be considered as hybrids between the event-driven abstraction and the cycle abstraction. For example, HSS/4[2] implemented event-driven scheduling of fanout-free trees of gates, where the trees are evaluated obliviously. Similarly, LECSIM[10] reduces scheduling overhead by employing two partitioning strategies. First, it groups each strongly connected component into a single block which is evaluated by LCC inside a small loop that iteratively evaluates the block until it stabilizes. This scheme is much cheaper than using the main scheduling mechanism. Second, LECSIM can group fanout-free trees into single blocks for scheduling. Our approach can be viewed as an extension of this hybridization, where we use a different partitioning that typically results in a far coarser level of granularity.

3 Extending Cycle Simulation

This section first defines a class of circuits which can be cycle-simulated. Several common circuit features that preclude cycle simulation are discussed as well as how each feature affects partitioning for efficient simulation.

3.1 Assumptions

For simplicity, assume that all circuit primitives are either combinational gates or registers (storage elements). Initially registers are assumed to be only edge-triggered flip flops but in Section 3.7 registers are extended to include transparent latches. All primitives have some connected inputs and some connected outputs. All signals have uni-directional signal flow; i.e., any bi-directional signals have been converted to uni-directional signals using bus resolution primitives. The circuit contains no combinational feedback (asynchronous state machines).[1] Only zero-delay simulation semantics are of interest.

Throughout this paper the term *gate* designates an arbitrary combinational logic function of any complexity and bit width, assuming only that it contains no state. For example, a gate may be as simple as a 1-bit 2-input AND, or as complex as a 64-bit carry-lookahead adder.

3.2 Circuits Which Can Be Cycle-Simulated

The key idea behind cycle simulation is to compute circuit values only at clock edges. Furthermore, cycle simulation is usually only concerned with the values of registers and circuit outputs.

[1] Combinational cycles can be handled by extracting them into a separate partition which is co-simulated along with the other partitions, similar to LECSIM's handling of strongly connected components [10].

This, however, implies that cycle simulation only makes sense for circuits that are controlled by a clock – synchronous state machines. Other circuits, such as purely combinational logic or asynchronous state machines don't make sense for cycle simulation because they may require evaluation at times other than clock edges.

To define more precisely a class of circuits that can be cycle-simulated begin by considering a single edge-triggered register. Clearly this can be correctly simulated by only evaluating it on the active edge of the clock. Now consider Figure 3. Zero-delay simulation semantics only require evaluating this circuit at the active clock edge to get correct results. This is because the input of the combinational gate will change only in response to the active clock edge. This reasoning can be extended to any number of gates as long as their transitive fanin is derived strictly from the outputs of registers sharing the same clock.

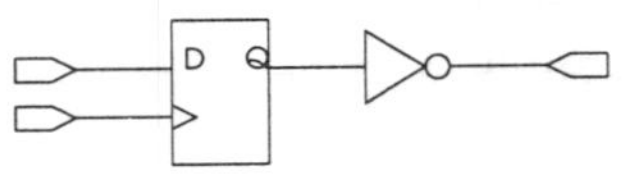

Figure 3: A register with a fanout gate.

Next consider Figure 4. Conventional event-driven techniques will evaluate the combinational gate any time its inputs change, which could be many times per clock cycle. However, its output is used only on the active clock edge. Since only the values of registers and outputs need to be computed, the gate only needs to be evaluated on the active clock edge. As before, this reasoning can be extended to any number of gates as long as their transitive fanout ultimately goes strictly to the inputs of registers sharing the same clock.

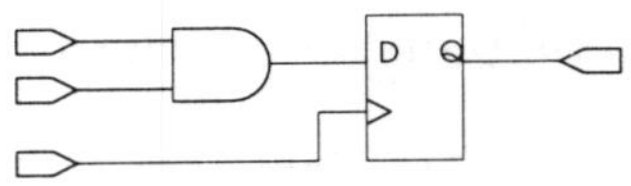

Figure 4: A register with a fanin gate.

A circuit which can be cycle-simulated is defined as a collection of edge-triggered registers sharing the same clock plus all the combinational gates which meet either or both of the following conditions:

1. the gate's entire transitive fanin comes from the registers, or

2. the gate's entire transitive fanout goes to the registers.

Gates meeting condition 1 are called *fanout* gates, because they are the fanout of the registers of the circuit.

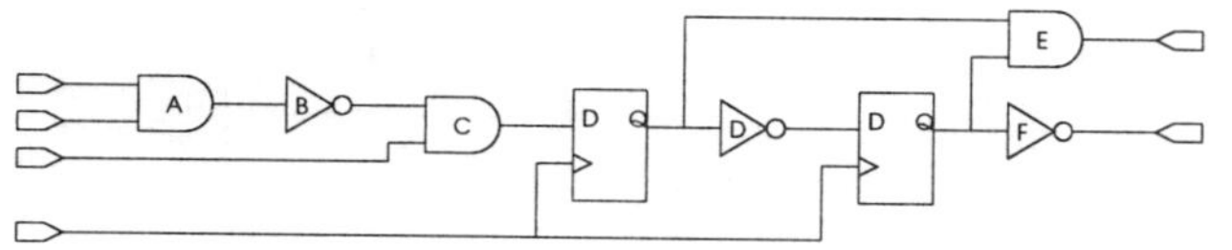

Figure 5: Examples of fanin and fanout gates.

Gates meeting condition 2 are called *fanin* gates, because they are the fanin of the registers of the circuit.

Figure 5 shows an instructive example. Both registers share the same clock. Gates A, B, and C meet condition 1. Gates E, and F, meet condition 2. Gate D meets both conditions.

3.3 Combinational Paths

What about gates that meet neither condition? Assume for the moment that all registers in the circuit share the same clock. If a gate does not meet condition 1 then its transitive combinational fanin must include the circuit's input. Similarly, if the gate does not meet condition 2 then its transitive combinational fanout must include the circuit's output. So there must be some combinational path from a circuit input through the gate and on to a circuit output. Figure 6 illustrates this situation. Gate G is neither a fanin nor a fanout gate. The combinational path through gate G is shown in bold.

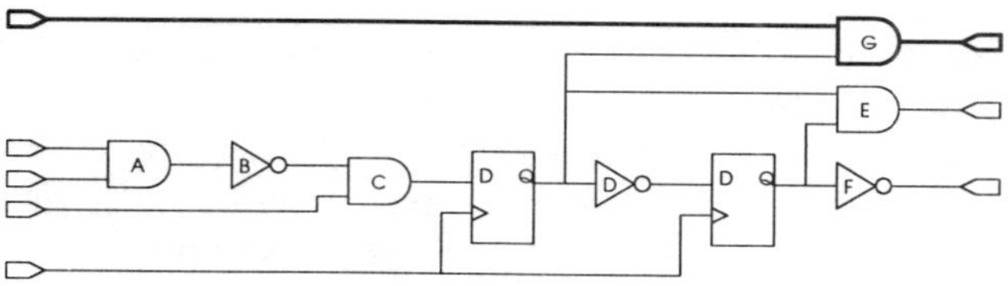

Figure 6: Gate G cannot be cycle-simulated due to a combinational path.

How should these gates be simulated? If the simulation environment simply exercises the circuit with vectors in a relatively synchronous fashion, it may be acceptable to evaluate these gates once per clock cycle (or once per vector). However, an event-driven simulation environment has no *a priori* knowledge of when the gate's inputs change, or when its output is needed. Hence, for correctness, the gate should be evaluated whenever its inputs change. These gates are called *input-triggered* gates.

If all the registers in the circuit share a clock, the circuit can be subdivided into two partitions: a *clock-triggered partition* containing all the registers plus all the fanin and fanout gates and an *input-triggered partition* containing all the remaining gates. The clock-triggered partition need be evaluated only once per clock cycle, while the input-triggered partition must be evaluated whenever its inputs change. Figure 7 illustrates the partitioning of Figure 6.

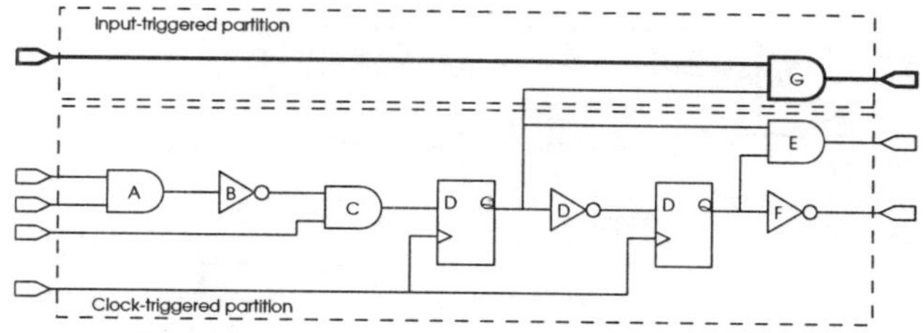

Figure 7: Partitioning into *clock-triggered* and *input-triggered* partitions.

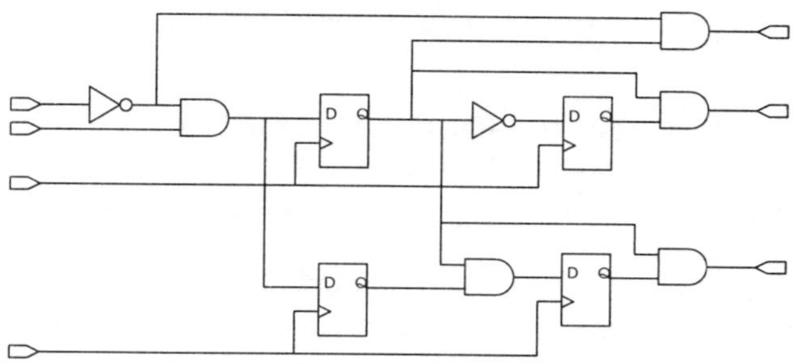

Figure 8: A circuit with multiple clock domains.

Nothing has been said about how the two partitions should be evaluated. Any evaluation technique can be used for either partition, including LCC, threaded code [5], branching code [1] [6], etc.

3.4 Multiple Clock Domains

Introducing registers with different clocks (i.e., multiple clock domains), as illustrated in Figure 8, requires strengthening the definition of fanin and fanout gates.

It is not enough simply to restrict the transitive combinational fanout of fanin gates only to registers: all the registers must share the same clock. Clearly, such a fanin gate can be associated with the registers in its fanout and evaluated only when those registers are clocked. Similarly the transitive combinational fanin of fanout gates must be restricted to registers sharing the same clock. Such a fanout gate should be associated with the registers in its fanin and only evaluated when those registers are clocked.

This introduces an ambiguity in the partitioning. Some gates can be both a fanout gate of one clock domain, and a fanin gate of a different clock domain. The choice of which domain the gate is associated with is arbitrary, and may be made according to other expedients. For example, the choice could be made to minimize signals that cross domains.

Some gates may fail to be fanin or fanout gates of any partition. It is no longer the case that such gates must

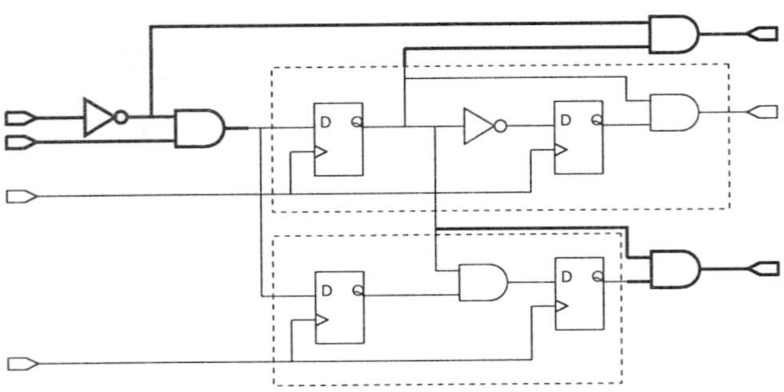

Figure 9: Partitioning of the circuit from Figure 8.

lie on a combinational path from circuit input to circuit output. A gate that fails to be a fanout gate must have transitive combinational fanin either from two or more clock domains, or from a circuit input plus one or more clock domains. Likewise, a gate that fails to be a fanin gate must have transitive combinational fanout either to two or more clock domains, or to a circuit output plus one or more clock domains.

To simulate these circuits we extend the previous partitioning strategy to construct one clock-triggered partition for each clock, and one input-triggered partition. All the registers that share a clock are placed into that clock's clock-triggered partition together with the associated fanin and fanout gates. All the gates that are neither fanin nor fanout gates are placed into the input triggered partition. Figure 9 shows the result of partitioning on the circuit of Figure 8. The gates in the input-triggered partition are shown in bold.

3.5 Generated Clocks

So far the discussion has assumed that all the clock signals are inputs to the circuit. What if some clocks are generated within the circuit? Consider Figure 10. Gate A is a fanin gate since it only drives the data input of the register. But gate B, which drives a register's clock input, is different. If gate B is made a fanin gate associated with the register and evaluated only when the register is clocked, neither it nor the register will ever be evaluated. Rather, the partition must be evaluated whenever gate B's inputs change. But this may increase the number of inputs the partition is sensitive to and complicate the partition evaluation code by forcing it to detect the rising edge of the internal signal.

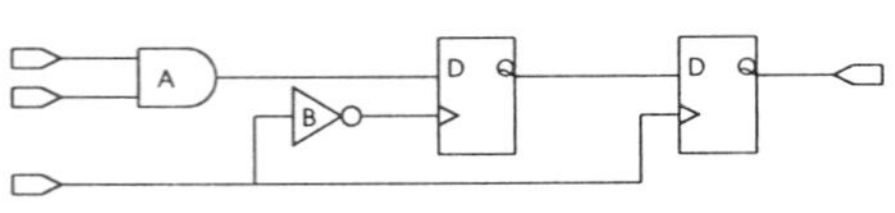

Figure 10: A circuit with a generated clock.

A simpler approach, illustrated in Figure 11, makes the register's clock input an input to the register's partition. This forces B into another partition as either a fanout gate or an input-triggered gate, as determined by the rest of B's context. The simulation environment can provide the necessary clock edge detection, as it must be doing anyway to support co-simulation of multiple circuit partitions. The desired partitioning is achieved by treating the clock inputs of registers exactly as if they were circuit outputs. This will prevent the driving gate from being a fanin gate, thus forcing it to be a fanout gate or an input-triggered gate and forcing the clock signal to be an input to the register's partition.

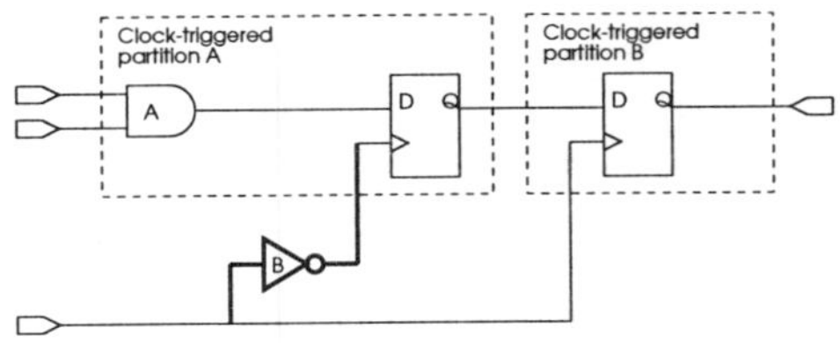

Figure 11: Partitioning of the circuit from Figure 10.

3.6 Asynchronous Resets

So far all partitions have been sensitive only to a single input, the clock, or else sensitive to all inputs. Asynchronously reset registers present an issue because they must be evaluated not only on the active clock edge but also when the reset is asserted. This is readily handled by extending the notion of clock domains into *trigger domains*. A *trigger* is any $<signal, event>$ tuple which causes a register to require evaluation. A *trigger domain* is all the logic that is sensitive to a set of triggers. For example, all the registers that are clocked by $<risingedge, CLK>$ and reset by $<fallingedge, \overline{RESET}>$ together with their fanin and fanout gates form a single trigger domain.

3.7 Transparent Latches

So far all storage primitives have been edge-triggered flip flops, which need to be evaluated only on the asserting edge of the clock (or reset). Transparent latches present a problem because they must be evaluated not only on clock edges, but also on data edges when the clock is asserted. Their behavior is essentially combinational during the active clock phase.

For the purposes of cycle simulation, some design methodologies can model transparent latches as edge-triggered flip flops. For example, this is frequently the case for multi-phase clock methodologies that use transparent latches as the primary storage element. In these cases latches can be converted into edge-triggered flip flops. The flip flops can be clocked on the opening or closing edge of the clock, whichever is most appropriate for the individual design.

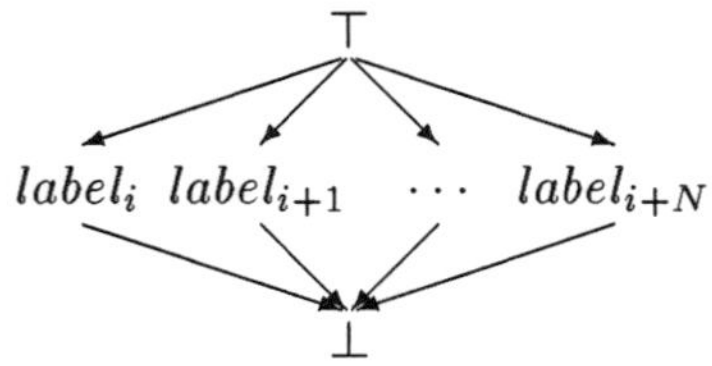

Figure 12: Lattice of values for representing fanin and fanout information.

However, some designs will not simulate correctly without genuinely transparent latch behavior. This case can be handled by treating both the clock and data inputs to the latch as sensitive inputs. The latch must be evaluated on the opening edge of the latch clock, and whenever the data changes.

4 The Partitioning Algorithm

The input to our partitioning algorithm is a network of registers and combinational gates connected by unidirectional signals.

Recall that *gate* refers to an arbitrary combinational logic function of any complexity or width, and *register* refers to either edge-triggered flip flops or level-sensitive latches. Gates and registers are collectively referred to as *primitives*. For convenience, the network also contains primitives representing the circuit inputs and outputs.

The circuit must contain no cycles of combinational gates; i.e., any cycles in the network must be broken by registers.

The output is the same network with all primitives labeled according to their assigned partition; i.e., all primitives with the same label are in the same partition.

For computing transitive combinational fanin and transitive combinational fanout and labeling primitives we use a lattice of values as in Figure 12. The lattice includes a label for each partition. Registers are labeled according to their trigger sets. Gate are initially labeled with $\top$ to indicate that no fanin (fanout) information is known about the gate. If fanin from (fanout to) only one partition i is discovered the gate will be relabeled $label_i$. If fanin from (fanout to) multiple partitions is discovered the gate will be relabeled $\bot$.

Each gate has the following fields:

gate.fanin the lattice value for the gate's transitive fanin;

gate.fanout the lattice value for the gate's transitive fanout;

gate.partition the final partition assignment for the gate.

Each register has a field `reg.partition` to hold the register's label. All of these fields are initialized to $\top$.

Conceptually, the algorithm has four phases. First, the registers are partitioned according to trigger sets such that all the registers that share a given set of triggers are contained in their own partition. These partitions are the kernels of the clock-triggered partitions. The final circuit partitioning will have these partitions plus the (possibly empty) input-triggered partition. Each partition (including the input-triggered partition) is assigned a unique label from the lattice. Each register is labeled with its partition's label.

Second, fanin information is propagated forward from register outputs and circuit inputs to the gates, leaving each gate labeled according to its transitive combinational fanin. This is accomplished using a depth-first search which first recursively visits all of a gate's fanin before labeling the gate. The recursive search stops at registers, which have already been labeled, and circuit inputs, which are treated as if labeled with the input-triggered partition's label. If all the gate's fanin are labeled identically then the gate receives that label; otherwise the gate is labeled with $\bot$. This label is stored in `gate.fanin`.

Third, fanout information is propagated backward from register inputs and circuit outputs to the gates, leaving each gate labeled according to its transitive combinational fanout. This is accomplished using a depth-first search which first recursively visits all of the gate's fanout before labeling the gate. The recursive search stops at registers, which have already been labeled, and circuit outputs, which are treated as if labeled with the input-triggered partition's label. As a special case, sensitive register inputs (e.g., clock, asynchronous reset, or latch data inputs) are handled as if they were circuit outputs. If all the gate's fanouts are labeled identically then the gate receives that label; otherwise the gate is labeled with $\bot$. This label is stored in `gate.fanout`.

Finally each gate is classified as fanin, fanout or input-triggered and assigned its final label. If `gate.fanout` is neither $\bot$ nor the input-triggered partition's label then the gate is a fanin gate and `gate.fanout` is assigned to `gate.partition`. Otherwise, if `gate.fanin` is neither $\bot$ nor the input-triggered partition's label then the gate is a fanout gate and `gate.fanin` is assigned to `gate.partition`. If the gate can be neither a fanin gate nor a fanout gate, the gate belongs in the input-triggered partition and that partition's label is assigned to `gate.partition`.

Once a gate is classified, `gate.fanin` is no longer needed, so in practice it may share the same storage with `gate.partition`.

5 Proof and Analysis

The proof of correctness is straightforward and the details are omitted for brevity. Correct propagation of fanin and fanout information can be proven by induction on the length of combinational paths. The gate classification and labeling is constructed from the definitions of fanin and fanout gates.

Analysis of space and time complexity is also straightforward. The space and effort of collecting trigger sets is proportional to the number of registers multiplied by the number of sensitive inputs per register, which is ordinarily a small constant (usually at most 3). This is clearly bounded by the size of the network. Propagation of fanin and fanout information are each performed by depth-first searches, which require time and space proportional to the size of the network. Thus the complete algorithm requires space and time linearly proportional to the size of the network.

6 Empirical Results

6.1 Implementation

The partitioning algorithm has been incorporated in a VHDL hybrid event-driven/cycle simulator based on a commercially available VHDL simulator. The portion of a design that conforms to a synthesizable subset of VHDL (for example, an ASIC design) can be simulated as a cycle model or in normal event-driven mode. The non-synthesizable portion (typically a testbench requiring file I/O) is simulated in event-driven mode.

The cycle models are constructed by first synthesizing and optimizing a network of RTL-level primitives, such as wide logic gates, adders, multipliers, encoded multiplexers, etc. Note that each RTL primitive is the equivalent of many conventional gates. The model compiler's circuit optimizations can selectively transform transparent latches into edge-triggered flip-flops triggered on either the opening or closing edge of the clock (Section 3.7), and can also transform asynchronously reset registers into synchronously reset registers. The circuit is then partitioned and a 2-state or 4-state LCC model, using native code, is generated for each partition. The partition models are combined with a highly efficient "microkernel" to form a single model which interfaces to the host VHDL simulator through its C language interface. The microkernel manages all interaction amongst the partitions, and between the partitions and the host simulator.

6.2 Measurements

To demonstrate the utility of this approach, Table 1 gives empirical measurements taken on three "industrial strength" test cases. The first of these, case M, is a model of the MIPS R3000 microprocessor executing an instruction diagnostic. The other two cases are ASIC designs from industry. Each design includes a testbench running in event-driven mode.

RTL primitives is the primitive count for each design after optimizations. *Total partitions* is the number of partitions produced for each design, followed by a breakdown of partition types. *Clock-triggered (1 signal)* is the number of partitions that were sensitive to only a single signal; *clock-triggered (2 signals)* is the number of partitions sensitive to two signals. *input-triggered* indicates whether an input-triggered partition was generated. *Partitioning time* is the approximate time in seconds which the cycle model compiler spent in the partitioning algorithm running on a Sun Sparc 20 with 256MB of memory. *Partitioning memory* is the approximate memory required by the partitioning algorithm in addition to the basic network data structures. Due to a refinement in the implementation only 4 bytes per primitive are required.

A detailed discussion of the simulator's architecture and performance is beyond the scope of this paper, but some performance numbers are given to compare the hybrid simulation to the same design simulated purely in the event-driven simulator. *Hybrid acceleration* is the directly measured overall speedup gained by using hybrid simulation versus purely event-driven simulation. *Cycle fraction* is a conservative estimate of how much of the design was accelerated using cycle simulation, measured as a fraction of the purely event-driven simulation time. *Cycle acceleration* is a conservative estimate of how much the cycle fraction was accelerated. *Event density* is an estimate of the fraction of signals that changed value during a cycle model evaluation.

test case	M	S	N
RTL primitives	2,051	42,949	96,063
total partitions	1	4	11
clock-triggered (1 signal)	1	1	5
clock-triggered (2 signals)	0	2	5
input-triggered	no	yes	yes
partitioning time (secs)	.18	2.3	6.5
partitioning memory (KB)	8	168	375
hybrid acceleration	6.8x	9.9x	1.8x
cycle fraction	88%	91%	75%
cycle acceleration	34x	55x	3.8x
event density	17%	16%	1%

Table 1: Partitioning and simulation performance for three large designs.

6.3 Discussion

The partitioning algorithm runs very fast and consumes very little memory. In fact, in all cases the time spent on partitioning was less than 1% of the total model compilation time. Memory consumption was a similarly negligible fraction.

Case M is the archetypical purely synchronous cycle-simulatable circuit. The entire model falls into one partition, and is accelerated substantially.

Case S is more typical of real designs. It contains one clock domain that is entirely asynchronously reset. It contains another clock domain which is partly asynchronously reset, so the reset portion goes in one partition and the remainder in another partition. It also includes a substantial amount of logic in combinational paths.

Case N is a very large and very complex design. Its relatively poor acceleration is accounted for by the low event density. Using threaded compiled code might have produced better performance than LCC for this design. It would not be difficult for a simulator to incorporate both algorithms, offering the user a choice, or even dynamically switching between them during simulation by periodically measuring the event density.

The most important point about this data is that real industrial designs containing multiple clock domains, asynchronous resets, generated clocks, combinational paths, etc. were simulated *correctly* using a cycle simulation algorithm within a system simulation context.

7 Accelerating HDL designs

The ideas beneath the notions of fanin and fanout gates can be generalized into an "optimizing" transformation to accelerate conventional HDL simulation.

Suppose an HDL program contains *clocked processes* which are sensitive to only a few signals (e.g., CLK and $RESET$), and *combinational processes* which are sensitive to all their inputs. If the values computed by a combinational process are used only by a clocked process, then the combinational process can be merged into the clocked process. This is analogous to grouping fanin gates with their registers. Similarly, if all the input values used by a combinational process come from a clocked process, then the combinational process can be merged into the clocked process. This is analogous to grouping fanout gates with their registers.

Merging processes in this fashion has two benefits. First, reducing the sensitivity list of the combinational processes may reduce the frequency of evaluation. Second, reducing the interprocess data flow reduces the number of queued events, which are expensive.

8 Conclusions

We have presented a novel circuit partitioning algorithm that extends the benefits of cycle simulation to circuits that were previously not cycle-simulatable. The algorithm is efficient, and fast in practice. Results showed that this approach does indeed yield substantial performance improvements for very large industrial designs. We also showed how the key ideas underlying this structural algorithm can be applied to accelerating HDL simulations as well.

Acknowledgements

Thanks to Rick Sullivan and Mark Coiley for introducing me to this problem, for the numerous ideas they contributed, and especially for many lively and enjoyable debates. Thanks also to John Bond and Tim McBrayer for their proofreading and very helpful suggestions.

References

[1] Pranav Ashar and Sharad Malik. Fast functional simulation using branching programs. In *Proceedings of the IEEE International Conference on Computer-Aided Design*, November 1995.

[2] Zeev Barzilai, J. Lawrence Carter, Barry K. Rosen, and Joseph D. Rutledge. Hss–a high speed simulator. *IEEE Transactions on Computer-Aided Design*, pages 601–617, July 1987.

[3] Robert M. French, Monica S. Lam, Jeremy R. Levitt, and Kunle Olukotun. A general method for compiling event-driven simulations. In *Proceedings of the Design Automation Conference*, pages 151–156, 1995.

[4] Craig Hansen. Hardware logic simulation by compilation. In *Proceedings of the Design Automation Conference*, pages 712–715, 1987.

[5] David M. Lewis. Hierarchical compiled event-driven logic simulation. In *Proceedings of the IEEE International Conference on Computer-Aided Design*, November 1989.

[6] Patrick C. McGeer, Kenneth L. McMillan, Alexander Saldanha, Alberto L. Sangiovanni-Vincentelli, and Patrick Scaglia. Fast discrete function evaluation using decision diagrams. In *Proceedings of the IEEE International Conference on Computer-Aided Design*, November 1995.

[7] L. W. Nagel. Spice2: A comuter program to simulate semiconductor circuits. Technical Report Rep. No ERL-M520, Electronics Research Laboratory, University of California, Berkeley, CA, May 1975.

[8] Steven P. Smith, M. Ray Mercer, and Bishop Brock. Demand driven simulation: Backsim. In *Proceedings of the Design Automation Conference*, pages 181–187, 1987.

[9] Laung-Terng Wang, Nathan E. Hoover, Edwin H. Porter, and John J. Zasio. Ssim: A software levelized compiled-code simulator. In *Proceedings of the Design Automation Conference*, 1987.

[10] Z. Wang and P. M. Maurer. Lecsim: A levelized event driven compiled logic simulator. In *Proceedings of the Design Automation Conference*, pages 491–496, 1990.

Verifying Correct Pipeline Implementation for Microprocessors

Jeremy Levitt and Kunle Olukotun
Computer Systems Laboratory, Stanford, CA 94305

Abstract

We introduce a general, automatic verification technique for pipelined designs. The technique is based on a scalable, formal methodology for analysing pipelines. The key advantages to our technique are: it specifically targets pipeline control, making it more efficient; it requires no explicit specification, since it compares hardware against itself; it can be used within the broader framework of hierarchical verification; and, it can be easily extended to handle certain "complex" pipelined structures.

1 Introduction

Even with improved verification techniques, formal verification of entire systems such as a microprocessor design is likely to remain an intractable problem. However, by taking advantage of a design's hierarchical structure and by partitioning the design into functional units, the correctness of many important design components can be formally verified. And, at a certain level of abstraction, designers can verify that these components interact correctly with one another.

The application of formal verification techniques can greatly increase a designer's confidence in their design. Formal verification techniques explore the state space of a design very efficiently, allowing them to provide a level of coverage that is much greater than that practically achievable through either simulation or emulation. Formal verification techniques can also be applied early on in the design cycle, enabling them to expose bugs earlier which will reduce design costs and time-to-market.

To be capable of verifying a particular component in the design hierarchy, formal verification techniques must be able to abstract both the component's interactions with other components and the behaviour of the component's sub-components.

Formal verification techniques must also address the difficulty in determining correctness criteria for design components. To verify that a component is correctly implemented, some specification of the component's correct behaviour is required. However, while the correct behaviour may be specified for an aggregate system, it is often not specified for arbitrary design components. The components in a design are, after all, the result of designers attempting to meet overall system specifications. They are part of the implementation; they are not part of the original specifications.

In this paper we present a formal verification technique based on the methodology introduced in [5] for verifying the correctness of microprocessor pipelines. We extend this methodology, called *unpipelining*, making it more general, more automatic and easier to use. The key benefits of unpipelining are: it verifies a design against itself, thus removing the need for an external specification; it can be used within the framework of hierarchical verification; and it is scalable to longer, more complex pipelines.

Unpipelining builds on previous work [7] [3] by using equality checking with interpreted and uninterpreted functions to abstract hardware at lower levels of the hierarchy and to abstract the interface with other design components.

2 General Approach

Unpipelining differs from other techniques for verifying pipelined designs [1][2][4][10] in that it uses domain specific knowledge about pipeline implementation techniques to analyze the pipeline structure of a design. Using the results of this analysis, unpipelining automatically reverse engineers a pipeline through a series of transformations called *pipeline deconstruction*. Each application of pipeline deconstruction shortens the pipeline by merging its last two stages into one single stage.

To verify that a given pipeline has been correctly implemented, we prove that the behaviour of the pipeline is preserved after each deconstruction transformation. Any bugs in the pipeline's implementation will be exposed, since they will cause the proof to fail for some iteration of pipeline deconstruction. If all the deconstruction transformations are successful, then not only is the pipeline verified, but it has been transformed into an functionally equivalent unpipelined design. This equivalent design can then be used at a higher level of the verification hierarchy as a simple abstraction for the pipelined component.

The proof requirements are automatically constructed using knowledge of the pipeline and of the deconstruction transformation most recently applied. An automatic decision procedure for determining the validity of expressions containing interpreted and uninterpreted functions with

1092-3152/97 $10.00 © 1997 IEEE

equality [7] [3] determines whether or not the proof requirements are satisfied. The use of a decision procedure for uninterpreted functions allows for lower levels of the design hierarchy that are not relevant to the proof to be easily abstracted. The ability of the decision procedure to handle interpreted functions allows for the use of an abstract interface to other components in the system that interact with the pipelined component.

The rest of this paper is organized as follows. Section 3 introduces standard pipeline implementation techniques and defines what it means for a pipeline to be correctly implemented. Section 4 discusses pipeline analysis and the associated notion of a pipeline template. Section 5 explains the process of pipeline deconstruction. Section 6 goes through the proof processes. Section 7 presents experimental results; Section 8 details the limitations of the unpipelining method; and Section 9 presents conclusions.

3 Pipeline Model

Pipelining is an implementation technique that increases instruction execution rate. A pipeline divides the execution of an instruction into a number of steps. Each step is known as a pipeline stage. The number of stages in the pipeline is called the pipeline *depth*.

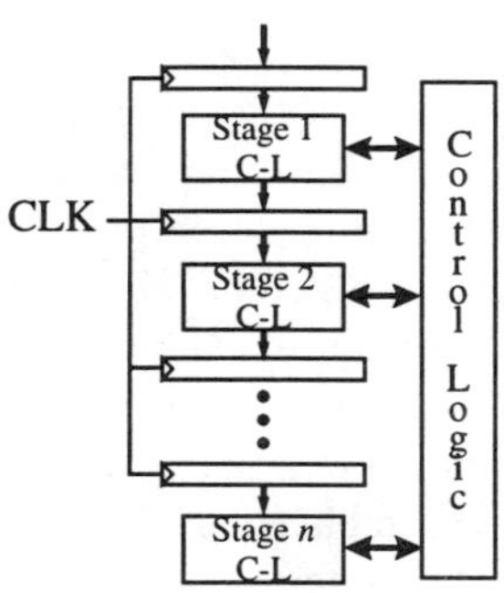

Figure 1. A Pipelined Circuit

We model a pipeline as a set of next-state equations. Non-control logic, particularly the datapath component, is abstracted using uninterpreted functions. The contents of memory elements such as caches and register files are accessed and modified explicitly using interpreted read and write functions. This abstraction separates verification of the pipeline from verification of the memory subsystems.

State-elements in the support set for the next-state equations fall into one of two categories: external-state and pipeline-state. External-state includes programmer visible state such as register files and the program counter, and it includes state supplied by units separate from the pipeline such as cached values and interrupts signals. Pipeline-state is made up of the state held in the latches between pipeline stages.

The program counter (PC) is a specific element of external-state that designates the start of the pipeline. The first stage in executing an instruction to determine its PC; the next-state equation for the PC belongs in the first pipeline stage. Based on the number of cycles it takes a for a change in the PC to propagate to the left hand side of a next-state equation, the remaining next-state equations are partitioned into pipeline stages.

(EQ 1) is an example of a next-state equation for a PC, where *ex* is asserted when an exception is raised and *br* is asserted when a branch is to be taken. Variables with subscript *n* are next-state variables and those with subscript *c* are current-state variables.

$$pc_n = MUX2\,(ex_n, ex\text{-}pc_n, MUX2\,(br_n, br\text{-}pc_n, pc_c + 4)) \quad \text{(EQ 1)}$$

In a correctly functioning pipeline, instructions appear to execute atomically and independently. Inserting NOPs should not change the results produced by a program. This is similar to the concept of flushing a pipeline [2] [4], since by inserting enough NOPs instructions will pass through the pipeline one-at-a-time. This definition allows for the verification of a pipeline implementation without having to know the ISA it executes.

Definition 1: *A pipeline implementation is correct if adding NOPs into a program does not change the results produced by the program.*

Pipeline hazards arise when an instruction executing in an earlier pipeline stage requires a result from an instruction executing in a later pipeline stage. This is due to either a control dependency or a data dependency between the two instructions. There are three basic techniques for coping with pipeline hazards: bypassing, squashing and stalling [5][6].

The pipeline control logic is comprised of logic to implement bypassing, squashing and stalling. This logic is built from the logic blocks shown in Figure 2. The actions of individual logic blocks are coordinated through a common bypassing/squashing/stalling control input, forming an aggregate control block. The particular function implemented by an aggregate block can be determined from its circuit topology.

All the pipeline control logic is assumed to match one of the topologies in Figure 2.

Property 1: *There is no control logic which does not match the any of the topologies in Figure 2.*

Pipelines implemented using standard techniques [6] will satisfy Property 1, and a couple of other properties listed below. These properties, which are easily checked, will be used later.

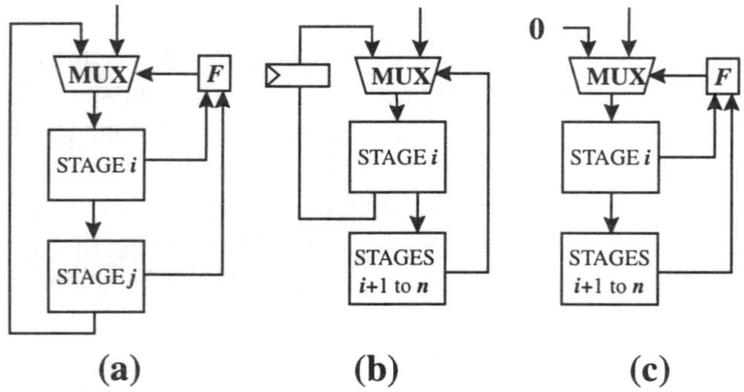

Figure 2. Logic blocks used to build pipeline control

Property 2: *A pipeline stage containing a nullified (or squashed) instruction will not activate any pipeline control logic or modify any external-state.*

Property 2 states that nullified instructions should not have any effect on other instructions in the pipeline, nor should they change the results produced by previous instructions.

Property 3: *If* i *and* j *are the deepest stages supporting squash or stall control lines* c_i *and* c_j *respectively and* $i<j$, *then* c_j *dominates* c_i.

Property 3 states that control dependencies are resolved in program order. If both control lines affect the same stage, then either c_i logically cannot be asserted when c_j is, or c_i is a don't care value when c_j is asserted.

Figure 3 shows an example of a pipeline in execution where instruction i_4 squashes the instructions behind it in the pipeline due to a mispredicted taken-branch, and sets the program counter to fetch the target instruction. Pipeline stages two through six have been labeled IF, ID, EX, MEM and WB respectively, corresponding to the five stages of instruction execution presented in [6]. Dividing the pipeline slightly differently than [6], we also have an initial PC stage which contains the next-state equation for the program counter. Notice that although instructions i_5 and i_6 start execution in the PC stage, they do not complete execution in the WB stage.

	Cycle	0	1	2	3	4	5	6	7
Stages	PC	i_5	i_6	i_7	i_8	i_9	i_{10}	i_{11}	i_{12}
	IF	i_4	i_5	X	i_7	i_8	i_9	i_{10}	i_{11}
	ID	i_3	i_4	X	X	i_7	i_8	i_9	i_{10}
	EX	i_2	i_3	i_4	X	X	i_7	i_8	i_9
	MEM	i_1	i_2	i_3	i_4	X	X	i_7	i_8
	WB	i_0	i_1	i_2	i_3	i_4	X	X	i_7

Figure 3. Instruction i_4 is a taken branch

4 Pipeline Templates

Analysis of a pipelined design requires more than identifying and classifying all the control logic into the blocks in Figure 2. Blocks that share the same multiplexer control line act in unison. Unpipelining analysis involves understanding how these blocks work together to control the flow of instructions through the pipeline.

A pipeline interlock, for example, is implemented using one logic block to squash the instruction in stage i and introduce a bubble into the pipeline, while other logic blocks stall all instructions executing in stages above stage i. The blocks all share the same control line that is asserted to trigger the interlock. In the case of an exception, multiple blocks of logic will squash instructions executing in different stages. Again, all the blocks share the same control line that is asserted when an exception occurs; the control line is also used to select the exception program counter.

Both the pipeline deconstruction and the verification steps need to know the function of each control line in the pipeline. Pipeline deconstruction must know how to transform the aggregate logic associated with a control line. Pipeline verification must understand what effect transforming the logic has on the flow of instructions through the pipe.

To match aggregate logic, identified by a shared control line, with a particular function and the knowledge required for pipeline deconstruction and verification, we use a *pipeline template*. A pipeline template is akin to a regular expression for matching logic networks and embodies the design intent of a certain circuit topology. An example of the template for matching the logic to squash instructions on a mispredicted branch as in Figure 3 is shown in Figure 4. Templates are parameterized; for instance, a single template matches the control logic implementing a pipeline interlock at any stage in a pipeline of arbitrary depth.

Each aggregation of control logic in a pipeline must match against a template. Once an aggregation of control logic is associated with a template, the information required for pipeline deconstruction and verification can be requested from the template.

The use of templates makes it easy to extend the verification system. If an exotic pipeline uses an aggregation of control logic not recognized by our system, the required template can be added. Creating such a template should not be difficult for the designers, since it simply reflects an understanding of how they designed the pipeline. However, our system already contains templates that match many of the standard control mechanisms for coping with pipeline hazards. Assuming an appropriate template exists, matching against it is done automatically.

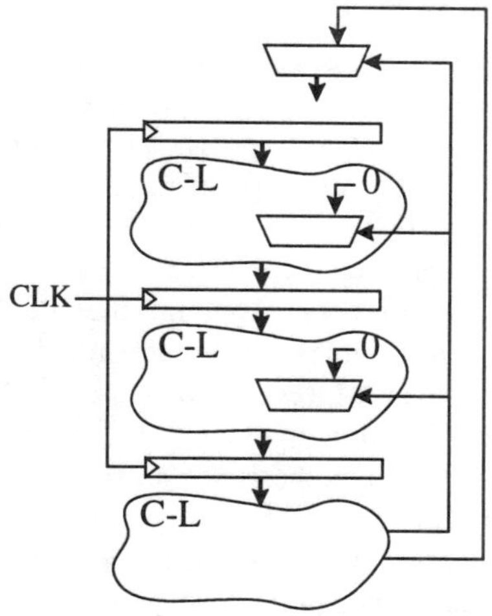

Figure 4. Template for squashing instructions on a mispredicted branch

5 Deconstruction

Pipeline deconstruction transforms a pipeline of depth n to one of depth $n\text{-}1$ by merging stages n and $n\text{-}1$. If it were not for pipeline hazards, this would be a very simple transformation that just removes the latch between stages n and $n\text{-}1$. However, the feedback required by the pipeline control logic to cope with hazards complicates things. In order to merge stages n and $n\text{-}1$, any control logic that uses values from stage n to deal with a hazard may need to be modified to ensure that it still deals with the hazard correctly.

Pipeline deconstruction is guided by knowledge of how pipeline control has been implemented; the first step in pipeline deconstruction is to look up the templates that correspond to each aggregation of control logic using a value from stage n. The template for each aggregate indicates how the control inputs should be modified. Control logic can be either left unchanged, removed, or adjusted (replace control input) as shown in Figure 5.

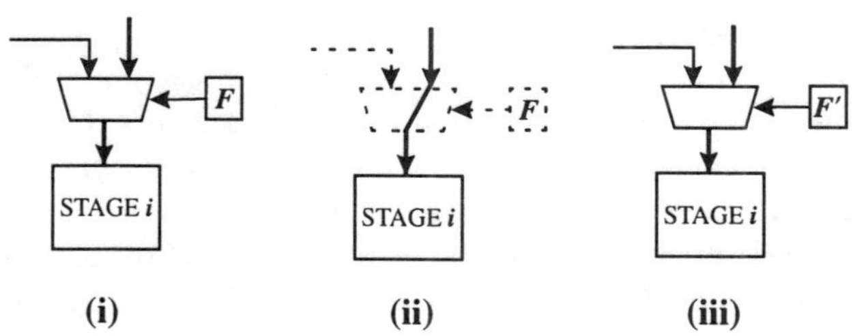

Figure 5. (i) unchanged, (ii) removed, (iii) adjusted

Once the control logic has been modified, the latch between stages n and $n\text{-}1$ can be removed. For next-state equations, this corresponds to replacing all instances of current-state variables in the next-state equations for stage n with their next-state version. In the next-state equations for stage $n\text{-}1$, any next-state variables representing external-state are replaced with current-state versions to avoid creating unclocked feedback.

Figure 6 and Figure 7 shows the six-stage pipeline introduced in Section 3 after two and three iterations of unpipelining. Figure 6 merges the EX/MEM/WB stage of Figure 7 with the ID stage. Notice that the squash happens a cycle earlier and affects one less instruction. A pipeline hazard has been removed.

	Cycle	0	1	2	3	4	5	6	7
Stages	PC	i_5	i_6	i_7	i_8	i_9	i_{10}	i_{11}	i_{12}
	IF	i_4	i_5	X	i_7	i_8	i_9	i_{10}	i_{11}
	ID	i_3	i_4	X	X	i_7	i_8	i_9	i_{10}
	EX/ MEM/ WB	i_2	i_3	i_4	X	X	i_7	i_8	i_9

Figure 6. DLX pipeline after two iterations of deconstruction.

	Cycle	0	1	2	3	4	5	6	7
Stages	PC	i_5	i_7	i_8	i_9	i_{10}	i_{11}	i_{12}	i_{13}
	IF	i_4	X	i_7	i_8	i_9	i_{10}	i_{11}	i_{10}
	ID/ EX/ MEM/ WB	i_3	i_4	X	i_7	i_8	i_9	i_{10}	i_{11}
		i_3	i_4	X	i_7	i_8	i_9	i_{10}	i_{11}

Figure 7. DLX pipeline after three iterations of deconstruction.

Conceptually, pipeline deconstruction removes control logic that deals with pipeline hazards present only in the n state pipeline, and leaves intact control logic that deal with hazards common to both pipelines.

Pipeline deconstruction is a mechanical process. For a correctly implemented pipeline, each iteration of pipeline deconstruction will produce an equivalent pipeline that is one stage shorter. Pipeline deconstruction is repeated until either a bug is found in the pipeline, or until all the pipeline control logic has been eliminated and the pipeline contains only two stages: one stage containing the next-stage equation for the program counter, and one stage containing all the other next-stage equations.

6 Verification

A two-stage pipeline (one of the stages being the PC stage) trivially meets Definition 1 for a correctly implemented pipeline. Since such a pipeline executes only one instruction at a time, inserting NOPs into a program will not change the results produced. NOPs do not modify any program state, and thus there exists no mechanism for them to change the results produced by any other instructions.

Definition 2: *Two pipelines are equivalent if they produce the same results for every program.*

The verification task is to prove that an initial n-stage pipeline is equivalent to the two-stage variant produced by pipeline deconstruction. We break this down into n-2 subtasks; after each application of a pipeline deconstruction transformation we prove that the transformed pipeline is still equivalent. If there is a bug in the pipeline implementation, some iteration of pipeline deconstruction will not produce an equivalent pipeline. Otherwise, if each iteration of pipeline deconstruction produces an equivalent pipeline, then the pipeline is bug free.

Let pipeline P' be the result of applying a single pipeline deconstruction transformation to pipeline P. To prove that P' is equivalent to P we use an inductive argument on the number of execution cycles. We assume that all programs that run for i cycles on P' where $i < k$ produce the same results when run on pipeline P, and then prove that if this is the case, then all programs that run for k cycles on P' must also produce the same results on P.

The results produced by a program are contained in the external-state variables. $v@i$ denotes the value of variable v after i cycles of execution; primed variables belong to P' and unprimed variables belong to P. For each external-state variable in P', we form an induction hypothesis of the form $v'@k = v@\hat{k}$ that relates values in P' to those in P. The base cases are true by construction of P'. To prove the inductive cases, we use the next-state equations for P' to expand $v'@k$ so that it uses only values from cycles $i < k$. The induction hypothesis are then substituted in, eliminating all the primed variables. With $v'@k$ expressed only in terms of variables in P, we prove that $v'@k$ and $v@\hat{k}$ are equivalent. The proof is performed by an automatic decision procedure.

There are three main questions to address in the proof. First, which variables require induction hypotheses? The next-state equations for external-state variables refer to pipeline-state, and these equations are essential to the proof. In order to use them we also need induction hypotheses for some pipeline-state variables.

Second, how are the induction hypothesis formed? As seen from the DLX example in the previous section, it is not obvious. The execution of instructions on pipelines P and P' do not match cycle for cycle.

Third, how are the induction hypotheses proven? They must be expanded and bundled with all the necessary information to create formulas suitable for the automatic decision procedure. We address each of these questions in the following sections.

6.1 Selecting Induction Hypotheses

The next-state equations express a value in cycle i in terms of values in cycle $i-1$. Using the next-state equations, $v'@k$ can be replaced with an expression containing only values in cycles $i < k$. For example, if the next-state equation for v' is: $v'_n = f(w'_c, \ldots, z'_c)$, where f is some combination logic function, then, $f(w'@k-1, \ldots, z'@k-1)$ can be substituted in place of $v'@k$. Applying the induction hypotheses, unprimed variables can be substituted for primed variables, to derive an expression for $v'@k$ that is entirely in terms of variables from pipeline P.

In addition to induction hypothesis for all the external-state variables, we also need induction hypothesis for some pipeline-state variables. While the next-state equations can be used to substitute pipeline-state variables, feedback in the pipeline guarantees that some pipeline-state variables will always be present no matter how many substitutions are performed. For the substitution process to terminate, certain additional key induction hypothesis are required. Determining these hypotheses is equivalent to determining where to break the feedback paths in the pipeline.

For each of the logic blocks in Figure 2, we break the feedback where it connects to the multiplexor as shown in Figure 8. At each point where the feedback is broken, a new variable and its associated next-state equation is added to the set of next-state equations. The new variable is included in the list of variables for which an induction hypothesis is required. This process breaks all the feedback in the model.

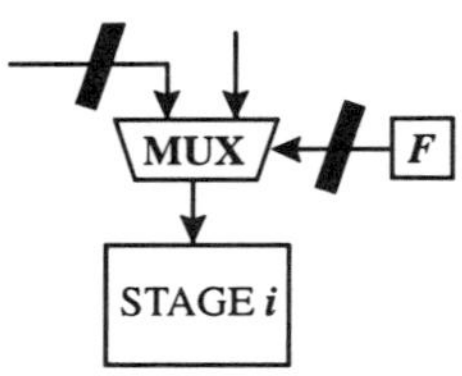

Figure 8. Breaking feedback in pipeline control

However, to ensure that valid induction hypotheses are generated for the new variables, preprocessing of the initial pipeline description is required. The transformations occurs only once, before any pipeline deconstruction transformations are applied. Preprocessing is necessary because in cycles where the output of the control block's multiplexer is a don't-care value, the pipeline will operate correctly even if different feedback values are present in P and P'. Although there is nothing wrong with the original pipeline, induction hypothesis generated from the description would not be satisfied. For example, if the instruction in the pipeline state is a NOP, then the control logic can do whatever it wants since the value it selects will not be used.

We transform the logic so that the output of the multiplexer is selected only if we care about its value. If we don't care about its value, we bypass the control logic. Figure 8 shows the modifications. With these modifications, we will automatically generate the correct induction hypothesis for the variables introduced by cuts in the feedback. Currently, this transformation is manually performed; although, it would not be hard to automate.

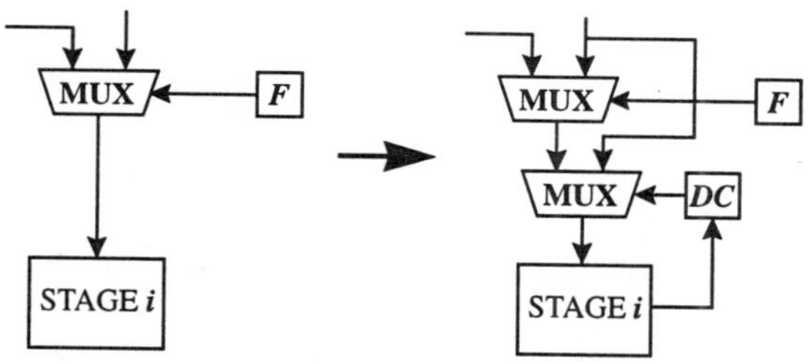

Figure 9. Preprocessing Pipeline Control

6.2 Formulating Induction Hypotheses

The shorter pipeline P' is guaranteed to execute programs in fewer cycles than P. Results produced in stage *n* of P will be at least a cycle latter than those produced by P'. And, since P' does not have to deal with some of the pipeline hazards in P, the execution rate for P' may be higher. For instance, P' may disrupt the flow of instructions less by resolving branches sooner or by eliminating pipeline interlocks.

First, consider the case where P' has the *same* execution rate as P. Pipeline deconstruction will have only removed latches between stages *n* and *n-1*, and perhaps some bypassing logic. The effect of this is to cause any variables updated in stage *n* of P to be updated a cycle earlier in P'. Let $T(v)$ return the stage containing the next-state equation for v. (EQ 2) expresses this variables-in-stage-*n*-are-one-cycle-early relationship

$$v'@i = \begin{cases} v@i & ;T(v) < n \\ v@(i+1) & ;T(v) \equiv n \end{cases} \qquad \text{(EQ 2)}$$

Unfortunately, these hypotheses are too simple to apply in the case where the aggregate control logic for stalling or squashing has been changed by an iteration of the unpipelining transformation. Such modifications reflect a pipeline hazard that exits in P, but does not exist in P'. For every cycle pipeline P loses stalling or squashing because of this hazard, P' will end up another cycle further ahead in execution. The exact number of cycles P falls behind P' cannot be predicted in general; it depends on the particular program being executed.

We introduce induction variables to compensate for the difference in execution rates between P and P'. An induction variable s_i^c is associated with each aggregate control block that has been modified by the current iteration of pipeline deconstruction, where c is the control line that defines the aggregate. Each induction variable counts up how many cycles pipelines P and P' are out of synchronization due to differences in the aggregate control blocks defined by their respective c and c'. The two pipelines are re-synchronized by summing up the induction variables that define all the aggregate control blocks modified by pipeline deconstruction.

Let C be the set of all control signals defining such aggregate control blocks. The induction variables are defined as follows. All s_0^c where $c \in C$ are initialized to zero (EQ 3). Whenever an aggregate control block disrupts the pipeline flow, allowing P' to get one cycle ahead of P, the counter for that block is incremented (EQ 4). Otherwise, the counter remains the same (EQ 5).

$$s_0^c \equiv 0 \qquad \text{(EQ 3)}$$

$$c@\left(i + 1 + \sum_{e \in C} s_i^e\right) \Rightarrow \left(s_{i+1}^c \equiv s_i^c + 1\right) \qquad \text{(EQ 4)}$$

$$\neg c@\left(i + 1 + \sum_{e \in C} s_i^e\right) \Rightarrow \left(s_{i+1}^c \equiv s_i^c\right) \qquad \text{(EQ 5)}$$

For a concrete example of how the induction variables are used to synchronize P and P', consider the 4-stage pipeline, P, of Figure 6 and the 3-stage pipeline, P', of Figure 7. For all instruction/stage pairs in P', a corresponding instruction/stage pair can be found in P. Although after enough cycles, all pairs in P' eventually end up a cycle ahead of their match in P, the advancement does not occur for all stages simultaneously. The PC has already gained a cycle in cycle one, whereas values in the EX/MEM/WB stage don't gain an extra cycle until cycle three. From (EQ 4), if $s_1 = 0$, then $s_2 = 1$. An offset is used to match the change in the value of the induction variable s_i to the advancement of the values in a stage of P' versus P. The PC is offset +1, meaning that $PC'@i = PC@i + s_{i+1}$.

The offset for each stage comes from the template for the aggregate control logic associated with the induction variable. Let $\lambda(c, k)$ return the offset for a control signal c. The inductive hypotheses are:

$$v'@i = \begin{cases} v@\left(i + \sum_{e \in C} s^e_{i+\lambda(e, T(v))}\right) & ;T(v) < n \\ v@\left(i + 1 + \sum_{e \in C} s^e_{i+\lambda(e, n)}\right) & ;T(v) \equiv n \end{cases} \qquad \text{(EQ 6)}$$

For the template in Figure 4, the offsets are shown below:

$T(v)$	1	2	3	4
$\lambda(c, T(v))$	1	1	0	0

Figure 10. Offsets for template in Figure 4

The induction hypotheses relate variables in every cycle of P' to variables in P.

6.3 Proving Induction Hypothesis

The final step is to prove that all the induction hypotheses hold. An automatic decision procedure for a subset of first-order logic expressions [3] automates the proof process. The decision procedure checks if expressions are valid. (An expression p is valid if $\neg p$ is *not* satisfiable.) Thus, an induction hypothesis $v'@k = v@\hat{k}$ must be combined with the information contained in the next-state equations for P and the invariants which define the induction variables to create a first-order logic formula that is suitable for the decision procedure.

The left-hand-side expression $v'@k$, as described above, is converted into an expression containing only values defined in cycles $i < k$, and the induction hypotheses are applied to replace the primed variables with unprimed variables. Paralleling the expansion of $v'@k$ by substitution of next-state equations for P', is the expansion of $v@\hat{k}$ by next-state equations for P. This results in $v'@k = v@\hat{k}$ being converted to an expression where the left-hand-side and the right-hand-side are pretty similar.

The expression, however, may not be valid as is, since the next-state equations for P' may not be exactly the same as those for P, depending on the control logic removed by pipeline deconstruction. In order to deduce that the left and right-hand sides are equivalent, additional invariants are required. These invariants include (EQ 4) and (EQ 5) for specific values of i, the next-state equations for certain variables in P at specific values of i, and information about the consequences of asserting control signals $c \in C$.

As the pipeline is deconstructed, the differences between P and P', and the extra invariants required to prove each induction hypothesis are recorded. The removal of bypassing logic requires the inclusion of the next-state equation for the 0-input to the multiplexer. The removal of stalling logic requires the inclusion of the next-state equation for the 1-input to the multiplexer.

Invariants concerning the consequences of asserting control signals allow for the resolution of different synchronization variables that appear on the left and right-hand sides. The necessary information is contained in the template for the aggregate control logic, and the appropriate assertions are automatically constructed for each aggregate control block affected by pipeline deconstruction.

For example, say a control signal br indicating a mispredicted branch is asserted in cycle i and this results in the squashing of instructions in stages n-1 to 2. Then for the next n-2 cycles, a squashed instruction will occupy stage n. Since br is produced in stage n, br will not be asserted during those cycles. In fact, no control signal will be asserted from any stage that is occupied by a squashed instruction. (EQ 7) shows the invariant generated for the br signal.

$$br@\left(i+1+\sum_{e \in C} s_i^e\right) \Rightarrow$$
$$\neg br@\left(i+2+\sum_{e \in C} s_i^e\right) \wedge \ldots \wedge \neg br@\left(i+n-1+\sum_{e \in C} s_i^e\right) \quad \text{(EQ 7)}$$

These invariants are all conjoined. A formula in which the induction hypothesis is implied by the conjunction is built and fed through the automatic decision procedure. If the formulas (proof requirements) for all the induction hypothesis are valid, then the pipelines are equivalent.

7 Experimental Results

The deepest pipeline we have experimented with is a 12-stage pipeline that implements a RISC-style ISA with six operation classes: ALU immediates, 3-register ALUs, branches, jumps, loads and stores. The 12-stage pipeline uses a predict-not-taken strategy to speculatively execute instructions. The branch penalty is five cycles and jumps have a penalty of three cycles. The pipeline has a load-interlock between the load/store stages and the execute stages.

With the exception of the preprocessing as discussed in Section 6.1 the proof was automatic. Pipeline deconstruction and generation of the proof requirements took 8.79s on an SGI Indy with a 200MHz R4400. As is expected, the proof was the most time intensive step. Figure 11 shows the verification time required per iteration of pipeline deconstruction, and the number of induction hypothesis generated. As the pipeline is deepened, the number of induction hypothesis increases. However, the time required to verify each iteration of pipeline deconstruction is not related to the depth of the pipeline; it is related to the complexity of the control logic removed in a given iteration.

The proofs were performed by SVC [3], an automatic tool developed at Stanford University for deciding the validity of expressions in a subset of first-order logic. The decision procedure in SVC was augmented with heuristics to cache successful case splits (case splits defined in [3]). This helped SVC find more optimal orderings for case splits, significantly improving its performance and extending the complexity of the pipelines we could handle.

Stages Merged	Execution Time	# Ind. Hypotheses
11 & 12	46.9s	26
10 & 11	11.4s	22
9 & 10	4.8s	21
8 & 9	3.9s	20
7 & 8	6.0s	19
6 & 7	6.1s	7
5 & 6	4.4s	7
4 & 5	2.4s	6
3 & 4	1.5s	6
2 & 3	1.6s	6

Figure 11. Execution time to verify 12-stage pipeline

8 Limitations

Although more automatic and scalable than other methods, unpipelining is less general in its applicability. It is not suitable for verifying pipelines that implement instruction set architectures (ISAs) which expose pipeline artifacts such as delayed loads and branches; though, for such cases it can still be helpful when applied in conjunction with other methods. While techniques such as [1][2][4] are most effective on pipelines that *do* expose pipeline artifacts and are much less effective on pipelines that do not, unpipelining is best suited for pipelines that *do not* expose pipeline artifacts.

Unpipelining relies on the use of a standard design style in order to deconstruct a pipeline. Other methods place no restrictions on the design style; however, they require designers to manually construct certain non-trivial specifications and mapping functions [1][2][4]. There is a clear trade-off between design freedom on one hand and ease of verification on the other. The ability of unpipelining to understand how a pipeline has been implemented is key to its superior scalability.

Currently, the don't care conditions for bypass control logic must be determined manually. This step could be automated. And, as with other proposed methods, unpipelining requires the manual abstraction of datapath an other unimportant (for the purpose of verifying a pipeline implementation) components.

9 Conclusions

We have described an automatic technique based on unpipelining for verifying microprocessor pipelines. This technique extends unpipelining by making it more general and more automatic. We have implemented our technique using an automatic decision procedure and demonstrated that the technique can be used to prove the correctness of deep, complex pipelines.

The primary advantages of our technique are that it requires no specification, that it is scalable to deeper pipelines, and that it handles the pipeline control logic for squashing and stalling instructions naturally. We have demonstrated that our technique can verify a class of pipelines that are deeper and more complex than can be verified using other methods. This technique gains its advantage from understanding pipeline implementation techniques, and is thus more restrictive than other methods in that certain standard design practices need to be adhered to. Although it is not directly applicable to pipelines that implement ISA's with artifacts such as delayed loads or delayed branches, these artifacts have been removed in the most modern RISC ISA's such as the DEC Alpha AXP architecture.

References

[1] V. Bhagwati and S. Devadas, "Automatic Verification of Pipelined Microprocessors," in *Proceedings of 31st Design Automation Conference*, San Diego CA, June 1994.

[2] J. R. Burch and D. L. Dill, "Automatic Verification of Pipelined Microprocessor Control," in *Conference on Computer-Aided Verification,* Lecture Notes in Computer Science, vol 18, pp 68–80, Springer-Verlag, 1994.

[3] C. Barrett, D. L. Dill and J. Levitt, "Validity Checking for Combinations of Theories with Equality" in Proceedings of *The International Conference on Formal Methods in Computer-Aided Design*, Palo Alto, CA, November 1996.

[4] J. R. Burch, "Techniques for Verifying Superscalar Microprocessors" in Proceedings of *The 33nd ACM/IEEE Design Automation Conference*, Las Vegas NV, June 1996.

[5] J. Levitt and K. Olukotun, "A Scalable Formal Verification Methodology for Pipelined Microprocessors" in Proceedings of *The 33nd ACM/IEEE Design Automation Conference*, Las Vegas NV, June 1996.

[6] J. Hennessy and D. Paterson, *Computer Architecture: A Quantitative Approach, 2nd ed.* Morgan Kaufman, 1996.

[7] R. B. Jones, D. L. Dill, J. R. Burch, "Efficient Validity Checking for Processor Verification," in *Proceedings of The International Conference on Computer Aided Design*, San Jose CA, Nov, 1995.

[8] M. C. McFarland, "Formal Verification of Sequential Hardware: A Tutorial," *IEEE Transactions on computer-Aided Design of Integrated Circuits and Systems*, vol. 12, no. 5, May 1993.

[9] K. McMillan, "Fitting Formal Methods into the Design Cycle," in *Proceedings of 31st Design Automation Conference*, San Diego CA, June, 1994.

[10]M. Srivas and M. Bickford, "Formal Verification of a Pipelined Microprocessor" *IEEE Software*, vol. 7, no. 5), pp. 52–64, Sept. 1990

A Quantitative Approach to Functional Debugging

Darko Kirovski and Miodrag Potkonjak
Computer Science Department, University of California, Los Angeles, CA 90095-1596

Abstract

We introduce a novel cut-based debugging paradigm. It coordinates design emulation and simulation and enables fast transition from one to another. Emulation or functional implementation is used for fast application execution; simulation provides complete design observability and controllability. The implementation of the new debugging approach poses several CAD tasks. We formulate the optimization tasks and develop constraint-based heuristics to solve them. Effectiveness of the approach is demonstrated on a set of designs.

1 Introduction

Functional debugging dominates both development time and cost of modern design process [12]. The existing, widely employed, approaches for functional debugging are design simulation and chip emulation or fabrication. Design simulation results in complete observability and controllability of the simulated architecture. Unfortunately, simulation is extremely computation intensive process. Emulated or fabricated designs on the other hand provide full execution speed, but limited observability and controllability of the design internal structure.

We propose a new paradigm for debugging of integrated circuits. The paradigm integrates design emulation and simulation in a way that the advantages of the two are combined, while the disadvantages are eliminated. The debugging method is fully transparent; it can be used in conjunction with any existing or future synthesis system or manual design approach as a postprocessing step. To develop and explain the proposed debugging process we introduce the notion of a *complete cut* of a computation. A *complete cut* is a set of variables generated within one computation iteration which bisects all possible paths in the computation. Such set of variables fully determines the state of the machine.

The functional debugging process, includes four steps: test input generation, error detection, error diagnosis, and error correction. The test input vectors generated in the first phase are used to drive the design emulation. While primary inputs, cuts and outputs are stored in the permanent storage of the supervising workstation, error detection techniques are deployed to signal to the workstation whether the emulation should be terminated. Upon error detection, the error has to be localized and characterized. This is done by running the design simulation on a workstation starting from a designer selected breakpoint. The computation is continued from the selected breakpoint due to the recorded cuts and their primary inputs and outputs. Error is diagnosed using a symbiosis of the design simulation and emulation. Design simulation is used for accurate system function test, while the emulation is used for fast execution of the test input vectors. The exchange of information between the simulation and emulation domain is accomplished by observing breakpoints' complete cuts of both test domains. Upon error diagnosis the emulator is updated or built-in fault tolerance mechanisms are activated. The ability to read/write breakpoint cuts from/to the emulated design is enabled by the design for debugging postprocessing step. It inserts hardware resources into the initial design specification.

The diagnosis approach and accompanying optimization issues are illustrated using 4th order continued fraction infinite impulse response (CF IIR) filter [3]. Figure 1 shows the computation before and after scheduing.

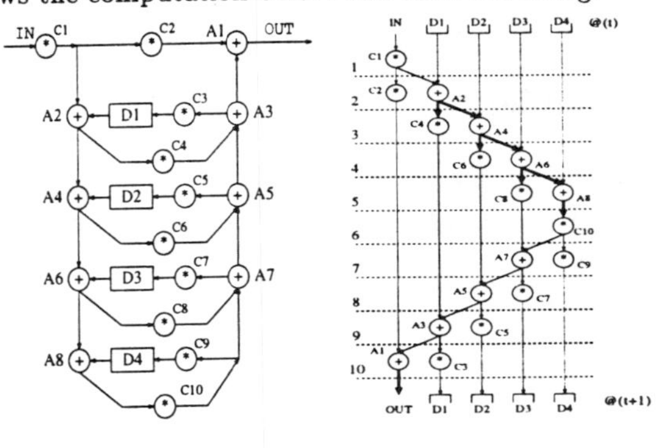

(a) Computation CDFG. (b) Scheduled CDFG.

Figure 1: Optimal cut example for 4th order CF IIR filter.

The design for debugging aims for allocating minimal hardware resources to enable design observability and controllability. One possible solution is to select variables $D1$, $D2$, $D3$, and $D4$ as a complete cut. Since these variables are concurrently alive, they have to be stored in four different registers. In order to provide design controllability and observability, the designer has to have the ability to read/write into those registers from the designated I/O pins. Since four registers are in the cut, four register-to-I/O connections have to be allocated. If the cut is defined among the output variables of adders $A2$, $A4$, $A6$, and $A8$ (bold lines), only one register is required to hold the values of the cut variables, since they are not alive simultaneously during the computation. Now, only one instance of the selection hardware is dedicated to the register which holds the cut. Cut dispensing is performed in four consecutive control steps (cycles 2, 3, 4, and 5). Note that in both cases the variable included in the cut but not mentioned is the actual output of the chip.

2 Related Work

The most comprehensive treatment of debugging has been conducted in the software compiler domain. Several debuggers, such as GDB [10] and Purify [1], have been widely used. The majority of efforts related to debugging in the compiler domain have been dedicated to symbolic level debugging on uniprocessors.

Numerous processors are supported by in-circuit emulators which enable efficient debugging [7], [11]. An in-

1092-3152/97 $10.00 © 1997 IEEE

circuit emulator of a processor is a system that can imitate the behavior of the microprocessor. The major drawback of in-circuit emulation is high cost. An FPGA-based emulation is sometimes used during development of new microprocessors (e.g. Quickturn, MentorGraphics). Potkonjak et al. [8] propose a design for debugging technique. Their technique focuses only on the error diagnosis phase. It assumes that the designer specifies the debugging variables at design time and only provides controllability and observability of the specified variables.

3 Preliminaries

We outline all relevant debugging and design for debugging background material. For the sake of conceptual simplicity all our examples follow a synchronous computation data flow model [6]. Such restriction on the computation model imposed by the proposed debugging technique is very mild. We assume deterministic hardware behavior and continuous semi-infinite operation mode (not necessarily periodic). We do not impose any register-transfer level restrictions on the interconnection scheme of the hardware model. The four key debugging assumptions are:

- The design is fully specified and its functionality and realization is not disturbed by the debugging process with the exception of enabling the user to write into specific controllable variables.
- In order to support debugging, we allocate additional debugging hardware to satisfy all debugging requirements. The goal is to add as little as possible hardware and in particular, I/O pins.
- For proper debugging support, all variables in the optimal cut should be controllable and observable in the same iteration of the computation.
- Required controllable and observable variables are not known at compile or synthesis time. The goal is to enable simultaneous complete controllability and observability of all user defined variables.

4 The New Debugging Approach

The essence of the new approach is the establishment of the concept of a complete cut. It provides information exchange between the two execution domains with small hardware overhead. *A complete cut is subset of variables which contains sufficient information required to correctly continue the computation.* A complete cut corresponds to a subset of variables in the computation which bisects all paths between states that delimit successive computation iterations. If one has complete controllability and observability over the values for all variables in the complete cut for a specific breakpoint, the computation can be continued functionwise correctly from that breakpoint. The cut-based debugging approach is conducted using the following two phases of the design and debugging process:

- Design postprocessing - We define the cut from the initial design specification at the functional level and augment the design specification with cut statements.
- Error diagnosis - Simultaneous and coordinated execution of the emulator and appropriate simulator.

In the first phase, the computation iteration at the behavioral level of specification is logically partitioned into two or more components such that the cut between the partitions is complete. The synthesis support for exchange of information between simulation and emulation has the following three degrees of design freedom:

- The determination of variables which form the cut;
- The determination of the exact control step when a particular variable is read from its register or replaced by a user specified value.
- The assignment of specific sets of I/O pins used to transfer variables to or from the chip.

The optimization procedure has a unique goal: to add minimum hardware resources into the initial design, while obtaining its full controllability and observability.

The debugging environment consists of a workstation and interfaced fabricated integrated circuit or emulator. The designer starts the debugging process by preparing a set of test inputs intuitively or using a software tool which searches the test input generation database. Once the test vectors are determined, functional testing starts at the emulation testbed. While test inputs are forwarded to the chip, the workstation stores the debugging information in permanent storage. For each iteration of the computation, its primary inputs, complete cut and resulting outputs are stored into a workstation supervised cut-database.

If error is detected, the next step in the debugging flow is to provide the designer with a set of tools to diagnose, i.e. locate and characterize the error. At this point the cut-database is searched for cuts which might point and clear out the error. The designer, guided by a debugging guidance tool, selects the most suspicious cut and runs a cycle-accurate chip simulation on the workstation. If the simulator provides sufficient information, the error can be discovered at that point. Otherwise, the designer continues the investigation by intuitively modifying internal registers likely to discover the error. The modification is followed by the simulation of the next iteration's cut. Once the cut is retrieved from the cycle-accurate simulator, all variables in the cut-set are injected into the design emulator while tempering the appropriate input vector. The generated outputs in the next few iterations are likely to uncover the error.

5 Synthesis for Debugging

The determination and integration of the inserted debugging resources is performed by a number of fully modular tasks. The goal is to select a set of variables which represent a control data flow graph (CDFG) cut such that all variables in the set are stored in minimal number of registers. The computation graph and timing bounds have to allow all variables in the cut-set to be output from the chip through a designated set of I/O pads within a single computation iteration. The synthesis flow resumes searching for an optimal output scheduling of the cut-set variables. The schedule has to be determined so that the number of connections between the output pins and registers containing the cut-set variables is minimal. After cut-set variables are assigned and scheduled, the initial specification is updated with the set of resources which enable cut output.

The design flow points out to three fundamental problems which enable optimal integration of debugging resources with the initial design specification. Each of these problems is proven to be NP-complete in [5]. In the first phase of the design for debugging flow we consider two fundamental problems: cut selection and checking whether the cut-set can be scheduled out from the chip. In the second phase, when the optimal cut-set is defined, the problem that arises is how to schedule the cut-set variables to specific I/O pins in such a way that minimal number of register-to-port connections are inserted into the initial design specification.

Cut Selection. The goal is to find a cut-set of variables S which partitions the control data flow graph into two subgraphs such that there exists no path in the initial CDFG which connects the two partitions and does not require computation of at least one variable in the set. In addition to that, the variable set has to be of minimal cardinality of registers that store the cut variables. In order to explain this problem and describe the developed heuristics, we introduce a set of definitions.

A scheduled CDFG is given for each variable V_i: the control step C_i^{start} when it is created and steps C_i^{first}, C_i^{last} when V_i is used for the first and last time. An assigned CDFG has all its variables assigned to distinct registers. The read life-time of variable V stored in register R begins at the control step when variable V is computed until the control step when variable V is overwritten by another variable W or it is recomputed. In the latter case the read life-time of a variable spans across the iteration. *Write life-time of variable V stored in register R starts at the control step when variable V is computed and ends at the step when V is used for the first time. An input sensitive graph - ISG - is a directed graph with multiple input nodes and single output node. Arbitrary number of edges is connected to a single input or single output. At most one edge connects an output to an input. A port is a set of K I/O pins. When variable V is assigned to port P, then V is output or input in its entirety through port P in one control step.*

Algorithms that support controllability are identical with the exception that write life-times are used instead of read life-times. The problem formulation is stated using the standard Garey-Johnson format [4].

PROBLEM: Optimal Cut-Set for Debugging.

INSTANCE: *Control data flow graph G with read life-times of its variables, variable-to-register assignments, P ports, and a set S of control steps when each port is busy.*

QUESTION: *Is there a subset of variables V such that each path in the control data flow graph G contains at least one variable $V_i \in V$, the cardinality of the set of registers that contains each variable $V_j \in V$ equals K, and there exists such schedule that each variable $V_j \in V$ can be output through P ports at control steps not included in S?*

ISG = $Construct\_ISG(CDFG)$.
ISG = $Input\_Sens\_Trans\_Closure(ISG, CDFG)$.
Search in the solution space for the optimal
input-sensitive dominating set D in the ISG. Optimality of
the set is described as minimal number of registers storing
all variables in D. There has to exist a schedule such that
all variables in D can be output through a given set of ports.

Figure 2: Pseudo-code for the optimal cut search.

For each pair of edges $E_{M_a^o, M_{b,m}}, E_{M_b^o, M_{c,m}} \in ISG$
such that $E_{M_a^o, M_{b,m}}$ connects M_a^o to M_b and
$E_{M_b^o, M_{c,m}}$ connects M_b^o to M_c
If the difference in control steps between the starts of read
life-times of nodes (variables) A and C is less or equal
than the total number of control steps in one iteration
Insert edge $E_{M_a^o, M_{c,m}}$ connecting M_a^o and $M_{c,m}$.

Figure 3: $Input\_Sens\_Trans\_Closure(ISG, CDFG)$.

We developed a new least-constraining most-constrained global heuristic which constructs its solution based on the analysis of the ISG presentation of the initial CDFG. The pseudo-code of the heuristic is given in Figure 2. The ISG is built from the CDFG according to the pseudo-code in Figure 4. An important step in the algorithm is the input-sensitive transitive closure operation performed on the ISG. This operation is described using the pseudo-code in Figure 3. Using the definition of scheduled and assigned input sensitive graph, the initial problem can be reformulated as:

P: Input Dominating Set of an ISG.

I: *Input sensitive graph G with read life-times of its variables, variable-to-register assignments. P ports and a set S of control steps when each port is busy.*

Q: *Is there an input dominating set of variables V such that each input is covered with at least one variable in V, the cardinality of the set of registers that contains all variables from V equals K, and there exists a schedule such that all variables in V can be output through P ports at control steps not included in S?*

For each node $N_i \in CDFG$
Create a node $M_i \in ISG$.
For each edge E_{N_i, N_j} directed from N_i to N_j
Create an input port $M_{i,m}$ for M_i,
where m is the index of the input port.
For each edge E_{N_i, N_j} directed from N_i to N_j
Create an edge $E_{M_i^o, M_{j,m}}$ which connects M_i^o and $M_{j,m}$,
where M_i^o is the output port of M_i,
and $M_{j,m}$ is the mth input of M_j.

Figure 4: $Construct\_ISG(CDFG)$.

The pseudo-code of the proposed heuristic is shown in Figure 5. The objective function that evaluates the proposed cut-sets is run-time dependent. Initially, the algorithm favors solutions with as few as possible storing registers. As the search progresses, the cost's dominating factor becomes the equilibrium of read life-time periods of the selected variables.

Preprocessing: Set of primary output variables
$V_i^{output} \in ISG$ is static part of the cut. Variables
read-alive during the iteration are static part of a cut.

1. Select a random subset of nodes $CS \in ISG$, such that
CS covers all node inputs in ISG. Best solution $CS* = CS$.
If there does not exist a schedule such that CS can be
output through P ports at steps not included in S go to 1.
Repeat $GLOBAL$ times
Update random subset of nodes $\in CS$ such that at least
one node input is uncovered. Randomly select a subset of
nodes $subCS$ from (ISG - CS) that covers the uncovered
set of inputs. Merge $subCS$ and CS.
If Cost(CS) < Cost($CS*$ and there exists schedule
such that CS can be output through P ports: $CS* = CS$.
Repeat $LOCAL$ times
$CS+ = CS*$. Update random subset of nodes $\in CS+$
such that at least one node input is uncovered. Randomly
select a subset of nodes $subCS$ from (ISG - $CS+$) which
covers the uncovered set of inputs. Merge $subCS$ and $CS+$.
If Cost($CS+$) < Cost($CS*$) and there exists schedule
such that CS can be output through P ports: $CS* = CS+$.

Return: $CS*$ as the optimal input dominating set.

Figure 5: Search for the optimal input dominating set.

Cut-Set Output Scheduling. The design has to be able to output all variables in the cut-set through a limited number of I/O ports within a single iteration. We propose a most-constrained least-constraining heuristic technique to solve this problem.

P: Scheduling of a Set of Variables in a CDFG.

I: *Set of variables V, each with its read life-time. P ports and a set S of steps when each port is busy.*

Q: *Is there a schedule such that all variables in V can be output through P ports at control steps not in S?*

The heuristic developed for this problem assigns variables to ports in a greedy fashion (pseudo-code shown in Figure 6). First, the constraint of each control step C_i in the scheduled and assigned CDFG is calculated as the number C_i^{var} of variables being read-alive during that step. For each variable V_i, its constraint is computed as a sum of C_j^{var}, where j is in the set of control steps when V_i is read-alive. Consequently, the most constrained variable is assigned to the least constraining step. Constraints are computed and variables are scheduled to control steps until all variables in the cut-set are not output scheduled.

Variable-to-Port Scheduling. The second phase of the synthesis for debugging process has as an input the selected cut-set from the first phase and the information about the read life-times of each variable as well as its storing register. The number of output ports is also available. The key design question is to assign each cut-set variable to a specific output port in a way that the number of connections between registers and I/O ports is minimal.

Repeat until all variables are not scheduled
  For each variable V_i
    If V_i can be scheduled only in one control step C_j,
    schedule V_i to C_j and any port P_x available at C_j.
  For each control step C_i
    Set C_i^{var} as number of all variables read-alive at C_i.
  Schedule variable V_i with $max(Cost(V_i)) =$
  $max(\frac{\sum_{j=AllControlSteps}(C_j^{var} \cdot ReadAlive(V_i,C_j)}{ReadLifeTime(V_i)-1})$
  to control step C_k which has $min(C_k^{var})$
  and any port P_x still available at C_k.

$ReadAlive(V_i, C_j)$ returns 1 if V_i is read-alive at C_j. Otherwise, it returns zero. $ReadLifeTime(V_i)$ returns the number of control steps for which V_i is read-alive.

Figure 6: Pseudo-code for the cut-set output scheduling.

P: Optimal Output Scheduling of a Set of Variables in a CDFG for Debugging.

I: *Set of variables V, each with its read life-time and designated register. P ports and associated set S of control steps when each port is busy.*

Q: *Is there a schedule such that all variables can be output through P ports at control steps not included in S, and the cardinality of register-port connections is K?*

We first partition the problem into two fully modular optimization subproblems. Initially, register to port assignment is performed such that optimization requirements are met and variables of the proposed cut-set can be output through all designated ports. In the second phase, for each port, all variables that are assigned to it are scheduled for output. For the assignment problem we develop a global most-constrained least-constraining heuristic described using the pseudo-code in Figure 7. The heuristic iteratively assigns most-constrained variables (registers) to least-constraining ports. Objective function that quantifies the constraint of variable V_i is:

$$Cost(V_i) = \sum_{j=AllControlSteps} \frac{C_j^{var}}{ReadLifeTime(V_i)-1}$$

where $ReadLifeTime(V_i)$ returns the number of control steps for which V_i is read-alive. Similarly, the objective function that quantifies the constraint of port P_x is:

$$Cost(P_x) = \sum_{j=AllVariables} \frac{ReadLifeTime(V_j) \cdot Assigned(V_j,P_x)}{1+NumberOfRegistersAlreadyAssignedToP_x}$$

where $Assigned(V_j, P_x)$ returns 1 if V_j is already assigned to P_x. Otherwise, it returns 0.

For each control step C_i set C_i^{var} as number
of variables read-alive during C_i.
Repeat until all variables are assigned to ports
  Assign variable V_i with $max(Cost(V_i)) =$
  $max(\sum_{j=AllCtrlSteps} \frac{C_j^{var}}{ReadLifeTime(V_i)-1})$
  to port P_x which has $min(Cost(P_x)) =$
  $min(\sum_{j=AllVars} \frac{ReadLifeTime(V_j) \cdot Assigned(V_j,P_x)}{1+NumberofregsalreadyassignedtoP_x})$.

Figure 7: Pseudo-code for variable-to-port matching.

In our experimentations we used a probabilistic version of the heuristic which iteratively generated randomized solutions. The problem of assigning a set of variables with their read life-times to a single port is equivalent to the problem of **maximum bipartite matching** (pp. 601, [2]) which can be efficiently solved in polynomial time.

6 Experimental Results

We applied the new design for debugging approach on several real-life designs [11]. Table 1 shows the experimental results. The first column indicates the name of the evaluated design. Next five columns describe the behavioral structure of the design: the number of available steps, the length of the critical path, the number of computation variables, the number of used registers and the number of states. The performed design for debugging analysis generated complete cuts displayed in column seven. First, the number of variables included in the cut is presented and then the number of register-to-port connections required to schedule the injection and dispensing of the selected cut. In all cases only one I/O port was sufficient to support full observability and controllability.

Design	Structure					Cut
Descr.	Ctrl steps	Crtcl path	Variables	Registers	States	Vars/ Regs
Linear GE controller1	12 24	12 12	43 43	19 23	5 5	8/3 13/1
Wavelet filter	16 32	16 16	31 31	20 20	15 15	15/1 15/1
D/C conv.	132 132	132 264	354 354	167 171	74 74	76/3 77/2
8th order CF IIR	18 36	18 18	35 35	19 19	8 8	8/1 8/1
Long echo canceller	2566 5132	2566 2566	1082 1082	1056 1061	1024 1024	1027/5 1027/4

Table 1: Experimental results: low hardware overhead.

7 Conclusion

We introduced a cut-based debugging paradigm which integrates design emulation and simulation in a way that advantages of both domains are fully utilized. We identified the associated optimization synthesis tasks and developed global heuristics to solve them. The experimental results clearly indicate the power of the new approach.

References

[1] G. Brooks, et al. "A new approach to debugging optimized code", SIGPLAN Notices, Vol.27, No.7, pp.1-11, 1992.

[2] T.H. Cormen, C.E. Leisserson, R.L. Rivest, "Introduction to Algorithms", The MIT Press, Cambridge, MA, 1990.

[3] R.E. Crochiere, A.V. Oppenheim, "Analysis of Linear Networks", Proc. of IEEE, Vol.63, No.4, pp. 581-595, 1975.

[4] M.R. Garey, D.S. Johnson, "Computers and intractability: a guide to the theory of NP-completeness", W. H. Freeman, San Francisco, CA, 1979.

[5] D. Kirovski, M. Potkonjak, "A Quantitaive Approach to Functional Debugging", Technical Report, CSD, UCLA, 1997.

[6] E.A. Lee and D.G. Messerschmitt, "Static Scheduling of Synchronous Data Flow Programs for Digital Signal Processing", IEEE Trans. on Computers, Vol. 36, No. 1, pp. 24-35, 1987.

[7] D. Phillips, "Advanced in-circuit emulation design", Mini/Micro Southwest, pp. 8/2/1-4, 1984.

[8] M. Potkonjak, S. Dey, K. Wakabayashi, "Design for Debugging of Application Specific Designs", ICCAD, pp. 295-301, 1995.

[9] J. Rabaey, et al., "Fast Prototyping of Datapath-Intensive Architectures", Design and Test of Computers, Vol.8, No.2, pp. 40-51, 1991.

[10] R.M. Stallman, et al. "A guide to the GNU source-level debugger", Free Software Foundation, Cambridge, MA, 1991.

[11] P. Wynn, "In-circuit emulation for ASIC-based designs", VLSI Systems Design, Vol.7, No.10, pp. 38-45, 1986.

[12] L. Yang, et al. "System design methodology of UltraSPARC-I", Design Automation Conference, pp. 7-12, 1995.

SESSION 3B

TIMING ANALYSIS

Moderators:

Chandu Visweswariah, IBM Corp., Yorktown Heights, NY

Wen-Zen Shen, National Chiao Tung University, Hsinchu, Taiwan

Approximate Timing Analysis of Combinational Circuits under the XBD0 Model[1]

Yuji Kukimoto† Wilsin Gosti† Alexander Saldanha‡ Robert K. Brayton†

Department of Electrical Engineering and Computer Sciences
University of California, Berkeley, CA 94720†
Cadence Berkeley Laboratories, Berkeley, CA 94704‡

{kukimoto,wilsin,brayton}@eecs.berkeley.edu saldanha@cadence.com

Abstract

This paper is concerned with approximate delay computation algorithms for combinational circuits. As a result of intensive research in the early 90's [3, 8] efficient tools exist which can analyze circuits of thousands of gates in a few minutes or even in seconds for many cases. However, the computation time of these tools is not so predictable since the internal engine of the analysis is either a SAT solver [8] or a modified ATPG algorithm [3], both of which are just heuristic algorithms for an NP-complete problem. Although they are highly tuned for CAD applications, there exists a class of problem instances which exhibits the worst-case exponential CPU time behavior. In the context of timing analysis, circuits with a high amount of reconvergence, e.g. C6288 of the ISCAS benchmark suite, are known to be difficult to analyze under sophisticated delay models even with state-of-the-art techniques. For example [8] could not complete the analysis of C6288 under the mapped delay model. To make timing analysis of such corner case circuits feasible we propose an approximate computation scheme to the timing analysis problem as an extension to the exact analysis method proposed in [8]. Sensitization conditions are conservatively approximated in a selective fashion so that the size of SAT problems solved during analysis is controlled. Experimental results show that the approximation technique is effective in reducing the total analysis time without losing accuracy for the case where the exact approach takes much time or cannot complete.

1 Introduction

During late 80's and early 90's significant progress [2, 8] was made in the theory of exact gate-level timing analysis. In this, false paths are correctly identified so that exact delays can be computed. As the theory progressed, the efficiency and size limitation of actual implementations of timing analysis tools were dramatically improved [3, 8]. Although state-of-the-art implementations can handle circuits composed of thousands of gates under mapped delay models, it is evident that the current size limitation is far from satisfactory for analyzing industrial-strength circuits. Furthermore, even if they can handle large circuits, the computation time is often prohibitively large especially when delay models are elaborate.

To alleviate this problem several researchers have proposed approximate timing analysis algorithms. The goal is to compute a conservative yet accurate enough approximation of true delays in less computation time to make analysis of large circuits tractable.

Huang *et al.* [4, 6] proposed, as part of optimization techniques used in exact analysis, a simple approximation heuristic, in which a complex timed Boolean calculus expression at an internal node is simplified to a new independent variable arriving at the latest time referred to in the original expression. This simplification is applied only when the number of terms in the Boolean calculus expression exceeds a certain limit, to control the computational complexity. Accuracy loss comes from the fact that the original functional relationship is completely lost by the substitution. They also investigated a more powerful approximation technique in [5], in which each timed Boolean calculus formula is under- and over-approximated by sum of literals and products of literals respectively so that each sensitizability check, which is a satisfiability problem in the exact analysis, can be performed conservatively in polynomial time. Since this approximation is fairly aggressive to guarantee the polynomial time complexity, estimated delays do not seem accurate enough to be useful. Unfortunately their results, shown in [5], are not clear about the accuracy of approximate delays. They merely showed ratios of internal nodes whose delays match the exact delays at the nodes. No result was shown on the accuracy of circuit delays.

More recently Yalcin *et al.* [11] proposed an approximation technique, which utilizes user's knowledge about primary inputs. They categorize each primary input either as data or control and label all the internal nodes either data or control using a certain rule. The sensitization condition at each node is then simplified conservatively so that it becomes independent of the data variables. The intuition behind this is that the delay of a circuit is most likely determined by control signals while data signals have only minor effects in the final delay. [11] shows experimentally that a dramatic speed-up is possible without losing much accuracy for unit-delay timing analysis based on static sensitization. Unfortunately this sensitization criterion is known to underapproximate true delays, i.e. it is not a safe criterion, which defeats the whole purpose of timing analysis. More recently they confirmed that a similar speed-up and accuracy can be achieved for a correct sensitization criterion (the floating mode) under the unit-delay model [9]. Although an application of the same technique to more sophisticated delay models is theoretically possible, it is not clear whether their algorithm can handle large circuits under those delay models. Moreover, their CPU times for exact analysis are much worse than state-of-the-art implementations available, which cancels some of the speed-up since their speed-up is reported relative to this slower algorithm[1].

In this paper we apply their idea of using data/control separation to a state-of-the-art timing analysis technique [8] to design an approximate algorithm. The sensitization criterion here is the XBD0 model [8], which is one of the well-accepted delay models shown to be correct and accurate. In addition a novel technique to control the complexity of the analysis is proposed. The combination of these two ideas leads to a new approximation scheme, which for

[1]This work was supported by SRC-97-DC-324.

[1]One of the reasons why their exact algorithm is slower is that they try to represent in BDD all the input minterms that activate the longest sensitizable delay while most of the state-of-the-art techniques determine the delay without representing those input minterms explicitly.

1092-3152/97 $10.00 © 1997 IEEE

some extreme cases shows a speed-up of 70x, while maintaining accuracy within the noise range.

This paper is organized as follows. Section 2 summarizes false path analysis, which forms a basis of this work. We specially focus on the technique proposed in [8]. Section 3 proposes two approximation schemes and discusses how they can be selectively applied to trade off accuracy and speed-up. Experimental results are given in Section 4. Section 5 concludes the paper.

2 Preliminaries

In this section, we review sensitization theory for the false path problem. Specifically, the theory developed in [8] is detailed below since the analysis following this section is heavily based on this particular theory.

2.1 Functional Delay Analysis

Functional delay analysis, or *false path analysis*, seeks to determine when all the primary output signals of a Boolean network become stable at their final values given maximum delays of each gate and arrival times at the primary inputs. Since some paths may never be sensitized, the stable time computed by functional delay analysis can be earlier than the time computed by topological delay analysis, thereby capturing the timing characteristic of the network more accurately. Those paths along which signals never propagate are called *false paths*.

The extended bounded delay-0 model [8], the XBD0 model, is the delay model most commonly used in false path analysis. It is the underlying model for the floating mode analysis [1] and viability analysis [7]. Under the XBD0 model, each gate in a network has a maximum positive delay and a minimum delay which is zero. Sensitization analysis is done under the assumption that each gate can take any delay between its maximum value and zero.

The core idea of [8] is to characterize recursively the set of all input vectors that make the signal value of a primary output stable to a constant by a given required time. Once these sets are identified both for constants 0 and 1, one can compare these against the on-set and the off-set of the primary output respectively to see if the output is indeed stable for all input vectors by the required time. The overall scenario of computing true delay is to start by setting the required time to the longest topological delay minus $\delta > 0$ and gradually decrease it until some input vector cannot make the output stable by the required time. The next to the last required time gives an approximation to the true arrival time at the output. This process of guessing the next required time can be sped up and refined by making use of a binary search.

Let us illustrate how we can compute these sets. Let n and d_n be a node (gate) in a Boolean network $\mathcal{N}$ and the maximum delay of the node n respectively[2]. Let $\chi^t_{n,v}$ be the characteristic function of the set of input minterms under which the output of the node n becomes stable to a constant $v \in \{0,1\}$ by time t. Let f_n be the local functionality of the node n in terms of immediate fanins $m_1, \ldots, m_k$ of n. For ease of explanation, let $f_n = m_1 m_2$, i.e., n is a two-input AND gate. It is clear from the functionality of the AND gate that to set n to a constant 1 by time t, both of the fanins of n, m_1 and m_2, are required to be stable at 1 by time $t - d_n$. This is equivalent to

$$\chi^t_{n,1} = \chi^{t-d_n}_{m_1,1} \cdot \chi^{t-d_n}_{m_2,1}.$$

Note that the two χ functions for the fanins are AND'ed to take the intersection of the two sets. Similarly, to set n to a constant 0 by time t, at least one of the fanins must be stabilized to 0 by time $t - d_n$.

$$\chi^t_{n,0} = \chi^{t-d_n}_{m_1,0} + \chi^{t-d_n}_{m_2,0}$$

Here the two χ functions are OR'ed to take the union of the two conditions. It is easy to see that the above computations can be generalized to the case where the local functionality of n is given as an arbitrary function in terms of its fanins as follows.

$$\chi^t_{n,v} = \sum_{p \in P^v_n} [\prod_{m_i \in p} \chi^{t-d_n}_{m_i,1} \cdot \prod_{\overline{m_i} \in p} \chi^{t-d_n}_{m_i,0}]$$

where P^1_n and P^0_n are the sets of all primes of f_n and $\overline{f_n}$ respectively. One can easily verify that the recursive formulations for the AND gate shown above are captured in this general formulation by noticing $P^1_n = \{m_1 m_2\}, P^0_n = \{\overline{m_1}, \overline{m_2}\}$ for $f_n = m_1 m_2$. The terminal cases are given when the node n is a primary input x.

$$\begin{aligned} \chi^t_{x,1} &= x && \text{if } t \geq arr(x) \\ &= 0 && \text{otherwise} \\ \chi^t_{x,0} &= \overline{x} && \text{if } t \geq arr(x) \\ &= 0 && \text{otherwise} \end{aligned}$$

where $arr(x)$ denotes the arrival time of x. The above formulas simply say that a primary input is stable only after its given arrival time. The key observation of this formulation is that characteristic functions can be computed *recursively*.

Once characteristic functions for constants 0 and 1 are computed at a primary output, two comparisons are made: one for the characteristic function for 1 against the on-set of the output, and the other for the characteristic function for 0 against the off-set of the output. Each comparison is done by creating a Boolean network which computes the difference between two functions and using a SAT solver to check whether the output of the network is satisfiable. The Boolean network is called a χ-network.

2.2 Optimal Construction of χ-Networks

To argue the approximation algorithms presented in this paper, further details on the construction of χ-networks need to be understood. We have mentioned that a χ-network is constructed recursively from a primary output. In [8] further optimization to reduce the size of χ-networks is discussed.

Given a required time at a primary output, assume that a backward required-time propagation of $\mathcal{N}$ is done to primary inputs so that the list of all required times at each internal node is computed. The propagation is done so that all the potential required times are computed at each node instead of the earliest required time. If the χ-network is constructed naively, for each internal node in $\mathcal{N}$, a distinct node is to be created for each required time in the list. This, however, is not necessary since it is possible that different required times exhibit the same stability behavior, in which case having a single node in the χ-network for the required times is enough. To detect such a case a forward arrival-time propagation from primary inputs to primary outputs is performed to compute the list of all potential arrival times at each node. Note that each potential arrival time corresponds to the topological delay of a path from a primary input to the internal node. Therefore the stability of the node can only change at those times. In other words between two adjacent potential arrival times, one cannot see any change in the stability.

Consider an internal node $n \in \mathcal{N}$. Let $R = (r_1, \ldots, r_p)$ and $A = (a_1, \ldots, a_q)$ denote the sorted list of required times and that of arrival times respectively at node n. Consider χ function $\chi^{r_i}_{n,v} (v = 0, 1)$. Let $a_j \in A$ be the maximum arrival time such that $a_j \leq r_i$. Since there is no event happening between time a_j and r_i, $\chi^{r_i}_{n,v} = \chi^{a_j}_{n,v}$. Matchings from required times to arrival times are

[2] It is possible to differentiate rise delays from fall delays. In this paper, however, we do not distinguish between them to simplify exposition.

performed in this fashion to identify the subset of A that is required to compute the final χ function. This optimization avoids creating redundant nodes in the χ network thereby reducing the size of the χ network without losing any accuracy in analysis. Only those arrival times which have a match with required times yield nodes in the χ network.

Another type of optimization suggested in [8] is to generate the list of arrival times more carefully. For each potential arrival time, equivalence between the corresponding χ function and the on-set or the off-set (whichever suitable) is checked by a satisfiability call and a new node is created in χ network only if the two functions are different. Otherwise, the original function or its complement is used as it is. Although this requires additional CPU time spent on satisfiability calls, it is experimentally confirmed that the size reduction of the final χ network is so significant that the the total run-time decreases in most cases.

3 Approximation Algorithms

3.1 Limitation of the Exact Algorithm

Although the exact algorithm proposed in [8] can handle many circuits of thousands of gates, it still has a size limitation. If a large network is given and timing analysis is requested under a detailed delay model like the technology mapped delay model, it is likely that the algorithm runs practically forever[3]. Even if timing analysis is tractable, the computation time can be too large to be practical.

As seen in the previous section, the exact timing analysis consists of repeated SAT solver calls. More precisely, for each time tested at a primary output, a χ-network is constructed such that the network computes the difference between the on-set (off-set) of the primary output and the set of input vectors which make the primary output stable to value 1 (0) by the given time. If the output never becomes 1 for any input assignment, i.e. it is not satisfiable, we know that the output becomes stable completely by the time tested. To test whether this condition holds, a SAT formula which is satisfiable only if the output is satisfiable is created directly from the χ network, and a SAT solver is called on it. The size of the SAT formula is roughly proportional to the size of the χ network. The main difficulty in the analysis of large networks is that due to a potentially large size of the χ networks, the size of SAT formulas generated can be too large for a SAT solver to solve even after the optimization discussed in the previous section has been applied[4]. In the following we discuss how to control the size of χ networks without losing much accuracy.

3.2 Reducing the Size of χ Networks for Effective Approximation

The main reason why χ networks become large in the exact approach is that χ functions at many distinct arrival times must be computed for internal nodes. This size increase occurs when there are many distinct path delays to internal nodes due to the reconvergence of the circuit. Therefore our goal is to control the number of distinct arrival times considered at each internal node. More specifically we only create a small number of χ functions at each internal node. This strategy avoids the creation of huge χ networks thereby controlling the size of SAT formulas generated.

Although this idea certainly helps reduce the size of χ networks, it must be done carefully so that the correctness of the analysis is guaranteed. We must never underapproximate true delays since otherwise the timing analysis could miss timing violations when used in the context of timing verification. Overapproximation is acceptable as long as reasonable accuracy is maintained. We guarantee this property by selectively underapproximating stability of signals. This underapproximation in turn overapproximates instability of signals thereby guaranteeing that estimated delays are never underapproximated.

The key idea on approximation is to modify the mapping from required times to arrival times discussed in Section 2.2 so that only a small set of arrival times forms the image of the mapping. Given the sorted set of required times $R = (r_1, \ldots, r_p)$ and the sorted set of arrival times $A = (a_1, \ldots, a_q)$ at an internal node n, the mapping $f : R \mapsto A$ used in the exact analysis is defined as

$$f(r) = \begin{cases} \max a_i \in A \text{ such that } a_i \leq r & \text{if } r \geq a_1 \\ -\infty & \text{otherwise} \end{cases}$$

Since the stability of the signal at the node increases monotonically as time elapses by the definition of χ functions, it is safe to change the mapping so that it maps a required time to a time earlier than the time defined in the above. This corresponds to underapproximation of the signal stability. Thus, by modifying the mapping under this constraint so that only a small set of arrival times is required, one can control the number of nodes to be introduced in the χ network without violating the correctness of the analysis. Depending on how the original mapping in the exact analysis is changed several conservative approximation schemes can be devised. Two such approximation schemes are described next.

3.2.1 Topological Approximation

The most aggressive approximation, which we call *topological approximation*, is to map required times either to the topological arrival time (a_q[5]) or to $-\infty$. More formally, the mapping f^T is defined as follows.

$$f^T(r) = \begin{cases} a_q & \text{if } r \geq a_q \\ -\infty & \text{otherwise} \end{cases}$$

It is easy to see that f^T is a conservative approximation of f. Since $\chi_{n,1}^{a_q} = n$ and $\chi_{n,0}^{a_q} = \overline{n}$, there is no need to create a new node for the χ function in the χ network[6]. Instead the node function or its complement of the original network can be used for the χ function. For the other arrival time $-\infty$, $\chi_{n,v}^{-\infty} = 0$ for $\forall v \in \{0,1\}$. Therefore it is sufficient to have a constant zero node in the χ network and use it for all the cases where the zero function is needed. Since neither of the arrival times needs any additional node in the χ network, this approximation never increases the size of the χ network. If this reduction is applied at all nodes, the analysis simply becomes pure topological analysis. Therefore, this approximation makes sense only if it is selectively invoked on some subset of nodes. A selection strategy is described later.

3.2.2 Semi-Topological Approximation

The second approximation scheme, called *semi-topological approximation*, is slightly milder than the first in terms of the power of simplifying χ networks. In this, required times are mapped to two arrival times again, but the times chosen are different. The times to be picked are 1) the arrival time, say a_e, matched with r_1 in the exact mapping f and 2) the topological arrival time a_q, which is the same as in the first approximation. The first approximation and this one are different only if $a_e \neq -\infty$, in which case the second one

[3]The algorithm is CPU intensive rather than memory intensive since the core part of the algorithm is SAT.

[4]Theoretically it is not necessarily true that a smaller SAT formula is easier to solve. However we have observed that the size of SAT formulas is well correlated with the time the solver takes.

[5]To be precise, a_q can be earlier than the topological arrival time if an intermediate satisfiability call has already verified that by time a_q the signal is stabilized completely.

[6]Notice that the χ network always includes the original circuit.

gives a more accurate approximation. To be precise, the definition of the new mapping function f^S is as follows.

$$f^S(r) = \begin{cases} a_e & \text{if } r < a_q \\ a_q & \text{otherwise} \end{cases}$$

If $a_e \neq -\infty$, the χ function for time a_e is now computed explicitly, and the corresponding node is added to the χ network. Similar extensions which give tighter approximations are possible by allowing more arrival times to remain after the mapping. A set of various approximations gives a tradeoff between compactness of χ networks and accuracy of analysis.

3.3 Control/Data Dichotomy in Approximation Strategies

In [11] Yalcin *et al.* proposed to use designer's knowledge on control-data separation of primary inputs for effective approximate timing analysis. They applied this idea to speed up their timing analysis technique using conditional delays [10] by simplifying signal propagation conditions of data variables. We adapt their idea, of using this knowledge, to the XBD0 analysis to develop a selection strategy of various approximation schemes.

3.3.1 Labeling Data/Control Types

Given data/control types of all primary inputs, each internal node is labeled data or control based on the following procedure. All the nodes in the network are visited from primary inputs to primary outputs in a topological order. At each node the types of its fanins are examined. If all of them are data, the node is labeled data; otherwise it is labeled control. Hence nodes labeled data are *pure* data variables with no dependency on control variables, while those labeled control are all the other variables with some dependency on control variables. This labeling policy is different from the one used in [11], where a node is labeled data if at least one of its fanins is labeled data. In their labeling, nodes labeled data are variables with some dependency on data whereas nodes labeled control are pure control variables. The difference between the two labelings is whether pure data variables or pure control variables are distinguished. Our labeling will lead to tighter approximations.

3.3.2 Applying Different Approximations based on Data/Control Types

Once all the nodes are labeled, different approximation schemes are applied at nodes based on their types. The strategy is as follows.

If a node is a control variable, the semi-topological approximation f^S is applied while if a node is a data variable, the topological approximation f^T is applied. The intuition is to use a tighter approximation for control variables to preserve accuracy while performing maximum simplification for data variables assuming they have less impact on delays than control variables.

3.3.3 Extracting Control Circuitry for Further Approximation

If the approximation so far is not powerful enough to make analysis tractable, further approximation is possible by extracting only the control-intensive portion of the circuit and performing timing analysis on the subcircuit. The extraction of the control portion is done by stripping off all pure data nodes from the original network under analysis. Note that any circuit can be decomposed into a cascade circuit where the nodes in the driving circuit are labeled as data and those in the driven circuit control by the definition of data variables. Therefore, the primary inputs of the subcircuit are the boundary variables which separate the subcircuit from the pure data portion. We assume conservatively that delays of the pure data portion of the circuit are the same as topological delays, which gives arrival times at the primary inputs of the extracted circuit. Analysis is then performed on this subcircuit as if it were the circuit given. Notice that this has a similar flavor to the approximation proposed in [4].

The difference between this approximation and the previous method is that the subcircuit has a new set of primary inputs, which are assumed independent. However, it is possible that in the original circuit only a certain subset of signal combinations appears at the boundary variables. Since this approximation assumes that all signal combinations can show up, the analysis becomes pessimistic[7]. For example, if a signal combination which does not appear on the cut makes a long path sensitizable, it can make delay estimation unnecessarily pessimistic. Although this method is more conservative than the one without subcircuit extraction, it reduces the size of a circuit to be analyzed much more significantly than the other one.

4 Experimental Results

We implemented the new approximation scheme on top of the implementation of [8] under SIS environment. To evaluate the effectiveness of the approximation, we focused on timing analysis of mapped ISCAS combinational circuits, which is generally much more time-consuming than analysis based on simpler delay models. In Table 1[8] the results on three circuits whose exact analysis takes more than 20 seconds on a DEC Alpha Server 7000/610 are shown[9]. Each circuit is technology-mapped first with the option specified in the second column using the `lib2.genlib` library. The delay of the circuit is then analyzed using three techniques. The first one (exact) is the exact method presented in [8]. The remaining two are approximate methods; the second, called approx(1), is the technique in Section 3.3.2 and the third, called approx(2), is the one in Section 3.3.3 which involves subcircuit extraction. Control/Data specification for the primary inputs of these circuits are the same as those in [11][10]. For each of the three analyses, estimated delay and CPU time are shown in the last two columns. One can observe that accuracy is preserved in the three examples in both of the approximation methods while CPU time is reduced significantly.

Table 2 summarizes a similar experiment for C6288, an integer multiplier, which is known to be difficult for exact timing analysis due to a huge amount of reconvergence. Since all the primary inputs are data variables, the approximate techniques proposed are degenerated into topological analysis. To avoid this inaccuracy all the primary inputs were set to control. Note that this sets all intermediate nodes to control. We then applied the first approximate method under this labeling. Although the approximation is not so powerful as the original algorithms, this at least enables us to reduce the size of χ networks without giving up accuracy completely. Since there is no data variable in the network, only approx(1) was tried. Significant time saving was achieved with only a slight overapproximation in terms of analysis quality. The exact analysis is not only more CPU-time intensive but also much more memory-intensive than the approximate analysis. In fact we could not complete any of the three exact analyses within 150MB of memory. They ran out of memory in a couple of minutes. These exact analyses were possible after

[7]If the set of all possible signal combinations at the boundary variables can be represented compactly, one can safely avoid this pessimism by multiplying the additional constraint to the SAT formula generated.

[8]Timing analysis was done in the linear search mode [8] where the decrement time step is 0.1 and the error tolerance is 0.01.

[9]If exact analysis is already efficient, approximation cannot make significant improvement in CPU time; in fact the overall performance can be degraded due to additional tasks involved in approximation.

[10]More precisely, C1908(1) and C3540(1) in [11] were used.

circuit	tech.map	#gates	topological delay	type of approx.	estimated delay	CPU time
C1908	`-m 1`	536	39.25	exact	34.77	29.1
				approx(1)	34.77	8.9
				approx(2)	34.77	5.4
C1908	`-m 0`	602	40.76	exact	35.76	41.2
				approx(1)	35.76	12.0
				approx(2)	35.76	5.2
C3540	`-n 1 -AFG`	1113	35.88	exact	35.66	727.0
				approx(1)	35.66	559.5
				approx(2)	35.66	502.9

Table 1: Exact analysis vs. Approximate analysis (CPU time in seconds on DEC AlphaServer 7000/610)

circuit	tech.map	#gates	topological delay	type of approx.	estimated delay	CPU times
C6288	`-m 1`	2429	127.23	exact	123.87	7850.2
				approx(1)	123.94	169.2
	`-m 0`	2371	123.51	exact	119.16	18956.2
				approx(1)	119.21	257.1
	`-n 1 -AFG`	2911	114.62	exact	112.92	15610.5
				approx(1)	112.86	1690.9

Table 2: Exact analysis vs. Approximate analysis on C6288 (CPU time in seconds on DEC AlphaServer 7000/610)

the memory limit was expanded to 1GB. The last example needs an additional explanation. In this example the estimated delay by the approximate algorithm is smaller than that by the exact algorithm although in Section 3 we claimed that the approximation algorithm never underapproximates exact delay. The reason for this is that the SAT solver is not perfect. Given a very hard SAT problem, the solver may not be able to determine the result under a given resource, in which case the solver simply returns Unknown. This is conservatively interpreted as being satisfiable in the timing analysis. In this particular example the SAT solver returned Unknown during the exact timing analysis, which resulted in an overapproximation of the estimated delay, while in the approximate analysis the SAT solver never aborted because of the simplification of χ networks and gave a better overapproximation. This example shows that the approximate analysis gives not only computational efficiency but also better accuracy in some cases.

To compare the exact and the approximate methods further, we examined the total CPU time of the exact analysis to see how it can be broken down. For the first example of C6288 the exact analysis took 714.7 seconds to conclude that any path of length 123.93 is false, which is about four times longer for the approximate analysis to conclude that the delay of the circuit is 123.94. The situation is much worse in the second example, where the exact analysis took 18390.8 seconds to conclude that any path of length 119.21 is false while the approximate method took only about 1.4% of this time to finish off the entire analysis.

5 Conclusions

We have proposed new approximation algorithms as an extension to the XBD0 timing analysis [8]. The core idea of the algorithms is to control the size of sensitization networks to prevent the size of SAT formulas to be solved from getting large. The use of knowledge on data/control separation of primary inputs originally proposed in [11] was adapted to choose an appropriate approximation at each node. We showed experimentally that the technique helps simplify the analysis while maintaining accuracy well within the accuracy of the delay model.

Acknowledgments

Hakan Yalcin kindly offered detailed data on ISCAS benchmark circuits.

References

[1] H.-C. Chen and D. H.-C. Du. Path sensitization in critical path problem. *IEEE Transactions on Computer-Aided Design*, 12(2):196–207, February 1993.

[2] S. Devadas, K. Keutzer, and S. Malik. Computation of floating mode delay in combinational circuits: Theory and algorithms. *IEEE Transactions on Computer-Aided Design*, 12(12):1913–1923, December 1993.

[3] S. Devadas, K. Keutzer, S. Malik, and A. Wang. Computation of floating mode delay in combinational circuits: Practice and implementation. *IEEE Transactions on Computer-Aided Design*, 12(12):1924–1936, December 1993.

[4] S.-T. Huang, T.-M. Parng, and J.-M. Shyu. A new approach to solving false path problem in timing analysis. In *Proceedings of IEEE International Conference on Computer-Aided Design*, pages 216–219, November 1991.

[5] S.-T. Huang, T.-M. Parng, and J.-M. Shyu. A polynomial-time heuristic approach to approximate a solution to the false path problem. In *Proceedings of 30th ACM/IEEE Design Automation Conference*, pages 118–122, June 1993.

[6] S.-T. Huang, T.-M. Parng, and J.-M. Shyu. Timed boolean calculus and its applications in timing analysis. *IEEE Transactions on Computer-Aided Design*, 13(3):318–337, March 1994.

[7] P. C. McGeer and R. K. Brayton. *Integrating Functional and Temporal Domains in Logic Design*. Kluwer Academic Publishers, 1991.

[8] P. C. McGeer, A. Saldanha, R. K. Brayton, and A. Sangiovanni-Vincentelli. Delay models and exact timing

analysis. In T. Sasao, editor, *Logic Synthesis and Optimization*, pages 167–189. Kluwer Academic Publishers, 1993.

[9] H. Yalcin. Private communication, March 1997.

[10] H. Yalcin and J. P. Hayes. Hierarchical timing analysis using conditional delays. In *Proceedings of IEEE/ACM International Conference on Computer-Aided Design*, pages 371–377, November 1995.

[11] H. Yalcin, J. P. Hayes, and K. A. Sakallah. An approximate timing analysis method for datapath circuits. In *Proceedings of IEEE/ACM International Conference on Computer-Aided Design*, pages 114–118, November 1996.

Timing Analysis Based on Primitive Path Delay Fault Identification

Mukund Sivaraman* and Andrzej J. Strojwas
Carnegie Mellon University, Pittsburgh, PA 15213

Abstract

We present a novel timing analysis mechanism which is based on identifying primitive path delay faults (primitive PDFs) in a circuit. We show that this approach gives the exact maximum delay of the circuit under the floating mode of operation assumption. Our timing analysis approach provides a framework where component delay correlations and signal correlations arising from fabrication process, signal propagation, and signal interaction effects can be handled very accurately. Under these effects, timing analysis using previously reported floating mode timing analyzers, e.g., viability, TrueD-F etc., is very pessimistic. Our timing analysis approach based on primitive PDF identification is also more efficient than conventional floating mode path sensitization analysis mechanisms in situations where critical paths need to be re-identified due to component delay speedup (e.g., post-layout delay optimization). We demonstrate the applicability of our timing analysis approach for a variety of benchmark circuits, and demonstrate the pessimism of conventional floating mode timing analysis approaches in accounting for signal propagation effects.

1. Introduction

Over the past ten years, the problem of determining the maximum delay of a combinational circuit accounting for path sensitization has been the focus of intense research. In this context, it has been proved in [6] that the maximum delay of a family of circuits (i.e., a given circuit netlist whose component delays vary within specified ranges) is bounded by the maximum delay, determined under a floating mode of operation assumption, of that circuit instance whose component delay values are set to their individual maximum values. Based on this, numerous floating mode timing analyzers have been reported [3][5] which assume component delays to be fixed at their individual maximum values and perform the path sensitization under a floating mode of operation assumption. However, the implicit assumption here is that all component delays can simultaneously be set to their individual maximum values. This may not be the case due to component delay correlations and signal correlations arising from fabrication process fluctuations, signal propagation effects (gate output transition time affects delay of not just immediate fanout gates, but also of succeeding downstream logic), and signal interaction effects (capacitive coupling, multiple gate input transitions). The assumption that all component delays can simultaneously be at their individual maximum values is a very pessimistic way of accounting for these effects, therefore these previously reported floating mode timing analyzers are very conservative in their delay estimates. Moreover, their sensitization mechanisms offer no way of accounting for these effects in a more realistic manner.

This research was supported by the Semiconductor Research Corporation under grant No. DC068-95.

* Presently with the Design Technology Center, Hewlett-Packard Co., Palo Alto, CA.

The floating mode timing analysis mechanism proposed in this paper forms a framework that can handle these fabrication process, signal propagation, and signal interaction effects very accurately. Our timing analysis mechanism is based on identifying primitive path delay faults (primitive PDFs [12]). It can be derived from the work in [12] that primitive PDFs are the path sets which determine circuit stabilization time. Our ***Primitive PDF Identification based Timing Analysis (PITA)*** mechanism can find the *realizable* maximum circuit delay under the floating mode of operation accurately. Moreover, it finds a set of paths, called *primitive anchor paths*, the maximum of whose delays gives the maximum circuit delay. The primitive anchor path set is a subset of all paths in the circuit which satisfy the $SENV_{loose}$ criterion [6], consequently there are fewer primitive anchor paths in a circuit than viable paths [3].

The primitive PDFs in a circuit do not depend on component delays. So if all 'long' primitive PDFs (i.e., those with delay greater than some lower bound value) are identified, they need not be re-identified if one or more components are speeded up. Thus, in a delay optimization scenario, our sensitization analysis needs to be done only once. In contrast, using previously reported floating mode sensitization analyses in this scenario would require iteratively identifying and speeding up critical paths, necessitating re-evaluation of the sensitizability of at least a

1092-3152/97 $10.00 © 1997 IEEE

subset of the paths at every iteration.

In the next section, we explain primitive PDFs and introduce necessary terminology. In Section 3, we establish the relationship between primitive PDFs and the maximum delay of a circuit. Section 4 discusses our timing analysis mechanism. Section 5 compares our method to previously reported ones. Results for benchmark circuits are presented in Section 6. We present our conclusions in Section 7.

2. Background

2.1. Primitive path delay faults

Under the *path delay fault model* [8], a *path is said to have a delay fault* if its delay is greater than a given timing constraint. A single path delay fault (SPDF) corresponds to a delay fault on a single path. A non-robust SPDF corresponds to a path that is singly non-robustly testable [9][10]. The side-input conditions along the gates of such a path are the same as that for a statically sensitizable path [2], so such a path may also be called a *singly statically sensitizable path.* A multi path delay fault (MPDF) corresponds to the simultaneous presence of delay faults on more than one path. A non-robust MPDF corresponds to a jointly non-robustly testable (jointly statically sensitizable) path set. For a path set $\Pi = \{\pi_1, \pi_2, ...\}$ to be jointly statically sensitizable, only those gate side-inputs along each path π_i which do not lie on any other path $\in \Pi$ need to satisfy the static sensitization conditions.

In the example shown in Figure 1 [11], the path set

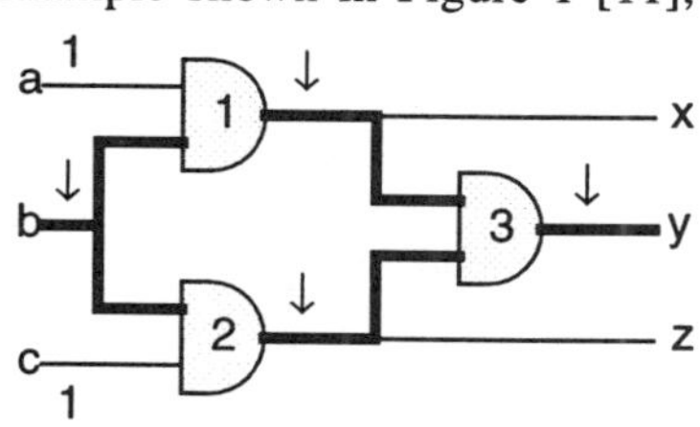

Figure 1. Illustration of an MPDF.

{↓*b-g1-g3-y*, ↓*b-g2-g3-y*} is jointly statically sensitizable. Moreover, for the test shown, the circuit output *y* is faulty only if the delays of both paths ↓*b-g1-g3-y* and ↓*b-g2-g3-y* are greater than the timing constraint T, since they both present final controlling values to gate *g3*. In other words, the delay of the jointly statically sensitized path set {↓*b-g1-g3-y*, ↓*b-g2-g3-y*} is determined by the shorter of the two paths.

In general, given a set of paths Π ($\Pi = \{\pi_1, \pi_2, ...\}$), a path delay fault (PDF) Π corresponds to the simultaneous presence of delay faults on all the paths $\in \Pi$. A jointly non-robust PDF corresponds to a jointly non-robustly testable (*jointly statically sensitizable*) path set. All occurrences of the word 'jointly' in this document should be interpreted to mean 'singly' when the cardinality of the path set is equal to 1. Also, we will use the terms 'PDF' and 'path set' interchangeably, and the terms 'non-robustly testable' and 'statically sensitizable' interchangeably in the remainder of the text. Note that the delay of a jointly statically sensitizable path set Π is determined by the shortest path $\in \Pi$. This can be easily inferred from the argument presented above in the context of Figure 1. More precisely, under a non-robust test for Π, along each of the paths $\in \Pi$, any side-input with a controlling final value has to belong to another path $\in \Pi$ (because Π is *jointly* statically sensitized), and so the shortest path $\in \Pi$ will present the earliest controlling value at each such gate.

Primitive PDFs have been formally defined in [12]. Informally, singly statically sensitizable paths belong to the set of primitive PDFs. Also, sets of paths Π, which are jointly statically sensitizable and *minimal* (i.e., no subset of Π is jointly statically sensitizable), belong to the set of primitive PDFs. Also note that since the single/joint static sensitization criterion (gate side-inputs must eventually settle to non-controlling values) is delay independent, the set of primitive PDFs in a circuit remains the same even if component delays change (i.e., the set of primitive PDFs is delay invariant).

Furthermore, the authors of [12] have stated and proved a theorem which we restate as follows:

Theorem 1: *The circuit will exhibit fault free timing behavior for all input vectors and for all timing constraints larger than some given value (say, T) if and only if it can be guaranteed that all the primitive path sets are free of delay faults for T.*

Note that a primitive path set is delay fault free if even one of its constituent paths has delay less or equal to the given timing constraint. This follows directly from the fact that the delay of a jointly statically sensitizable path set is determined by the shortest path belonging to the path set.

2.2. Terminology

A *family of circuits* corresponds to a given logic-level circuit netlist with associated component delay models. The delay of a component depends on many factors: input transition time, output loading, signal activity on neighboring components, internal component state (i.e., floating node voltage in MOS gates), fabrication process fluctuations, supply voltage and operating temperature. A circuit instance is normally defined as a circuit obtained by setting the fabrication process parameters to fixed values. For our purposes however, we define a *circuit instance* to be a circuit obtained by setting its component delays to fixed values within their respective component delay models. In the remainder of the text, we will use the term *circuit* to imply a family of circuits, unless noted otherwise.

The *maximum circuit instance delay* under a given mode of operation assumption is the maximum delay of the circuit instance over all possible inputs under this mode of operation, accounting for path sensitization. The *maximum circuit delay* under a given mode of operation assumption and a given component delay model is the maximum delay of the circuit over all possible inputs under the given mode of operation and over all circuit instances possible under the given component delay model, again accounting for path sensitization. The circuit instance at which this maximum occurs is termed the *worst-case circuit instance*. The *maximum path delay* is the maximum delay a path can attain for a given component delay model.

3. Relating primitive PDFs to timing analysis

3.1. Maximum circuit instance delay

Say a given circuit has a set of primitive path sets $\mathcal{P} = \{\Pi_{p1}, \Pi_{p2}, ..., \Pi_{pN}\}$. Let us denote the circuit instance by the variable $\underline{x}$, which represents all the parameters that determine the delay of each component in the circuit. From Theorem 1, we can bound the maximum delay of the circuit instance as the maximum of the primitive path set delays at that instance, i.e.:

$$\text{maxdelay}_{\underline{x}}(\text{ckt}) = \max\{\text{delay}_{\underline{x}}(\Pi_{p1}), ..., \text{delay}_{\underline{x}}(\Pi_{pN})\} \quad \text{(EQ1)}$$

We call this the *PITA maximum circuit instance delay.* Recall that the delay of a primitive path set (for that matter, any jointly statically sensitizable path set) Π, $\Pi = \{\pi_1, \pi_2, ..., \pi_n\}$, is determined by the shortest path $\in \Pi$, i.e.,

$$\text{delay}_{\underline{x}}(\Pi) = \min\{\text{delay}_{\underline{x}}(\pi_1), ..., \text{delay}_{\underline{x}}(\pi_n)\} \quad \text{(EQ2)}$$

The shortest path $\pi_{pi,j}$, which determines the delay of the primitive path set Π_{pi} at circuit instance $\underline{x}$, is called the *primitive anchor path* of Π_{pi}. Correspondingly, given an arbitrary jointly statically sensitizable path set $\Pi = \{\pi_1, \pi_2, ..., \pi_n\}$, the shortest path π_j, which determines the delay of Π at circuit instance $\underline{x}$, is called the *anchor path* of Π.

Theorem 2: *The PITA maximum circuit instance delay is exactly equal to the maximum circuit instance delay under the floating mode of operation.*

Proof: Since every non-primitive path set (i.e., a jointly statically sensitizable path set that is not minimal) in the circuit is a superset of some primitive path set, every non-primitive path set's delay is upper bounded by some primitive path set's delay. Therefore, the PITA maximum circuit instance delay, which is the maximum of all the primitive path set delays (i.e., the maximum of all the primitive anchor path delays), is also equal to the maximum of the delays of all jointly statically sensitizable path sets (i.e., the maximum of all anchor path delays). The set of all anchor paths in a circuit are exactly those paths in the circuit that satisfy the $SENV_{loose}$ criterion. This follows directly from the gate side-input conditions along a path that satisfies the $SENV_{loose}$ criterion (at each gate along the path, the on-path input is the earliest arriving controlling value, otherwise all inputs to the gate settle to non-controlling values). Therefore, the PITA maximum circuit instance delay is exactly equal to the maximum delay of the circuit instance found using the $SENV_{loose}$ criterion, which is equal to the maximum circuit instance delay under the floating mode of operation assumption. ■

In proving Theorem 2, we notice that the set of all anchor paths in a circuit are exactly those paths in the circuit that satisfy the $SENV_{loose}$ criterion. We also know that the set of all primitive anchor paths is a subset of the set of all anchor paths. We therefore infer the following:

Corollary 2: *The number of primitive anchor paths in a circuit is less than the number of paths in the circuit that satisfy the $SENV_{loose}$ criterion, and consequently also less than the number of viable paths in the circuit.*

3.2. Maximum circuit delay

The maximum circuit delay is given as the maximum of the maximum circuit instance delay (Equation EQ1) over all possible circuit instances:

$$\begin{aligned}\text{maxdelay}(\text{ckt}) &= \max_{\forall \underline{x}} \text{maxdelay}_{\underline{x}}(\text{ckt}) \\ &= \max_{\forall \underline{x}} [\max\{\text{delay}_{\underline{x}}(\Pi_{p1}), ..., \text{delay}_{\underline{x}}(\Pi_{pN})\}] \\ &= \max\left\{\max_{\forall \underline{x}} \text{delay}_{\underline{x}}(\Pi_{p1}), ..., \max_{\forall \underline{x}} \text{delay}_{\underline{x}}(\Pi_{pN})\right\} \\ &= \max\{\text{maxdelay}(\Pi_{p1}), ..., \text{maxdelay}(\Pi_{pN})\}\end{aligned} \quad \text{(EQ3)}$$

We call this the *PITA maximum circuit delay.* The maximum delay of a primitive path set (in fact, any jointly statically sensitizable path set) Π, $\Pi = \{\pi_1, \pi_2, ..., \pi_n\}$, can be derived from Equation EQ2:

$$\begin{aligned}\text{maxdelay}(\Pi) &= \max_{\forall \underline{x}} \text{delay}_{\underline{x}}(\Pi) \\ &= \max_{\forall \underline{x}} \min\{\text{delay}_{\underline{x}}(\pi_1), ..., \text{delay}_{\underline{x}}(\pi_n)\}\end{aligned} \quad \text{(EQ4)}$$

When the component delays are completely uncorrelated, the above expression can be rewritten as:

$$\text{maxdelay}(\Pi) = \min\left\{\max_{\forall \underline{x}} \text{delay}_{\underline{x}}(\pi_1), ..., \max_{\forall \underline{x}} \text{delay}_{\underline{x}}(\pi_n)\right\} \quad \text{(EQ5)}$$

i.e.:

$$\mathrm{maxdelay}(\Pi) = \min\{\mathrm{maxdelay}(\pi_1), \ldots, \mathrm{maxdelay}(\pi_n)\} \quad \text{(EQ6)}$$

This implies that under the assumption that the delay of each component varies independently of the others within the given bounds, the maximum delay of a jointly statically sensitizable path set is given by the minimum of the maximum delay of each path belonging to this set. Note that since the component delays vary mutually independently, the maximum delay of each path π_i in Equation EQ6 can be found by adding up the maximum possible delay values of the components along π_i. Under independently varying component delays, the PITA maximum circuit delay is given by Equation EQ3 and Equation EQ6.

Theorem 3: *When the component delays are assumed to vary independently of each other, the PITA maximum circuit delay is exactly equal to the maximum circuit delay under the floating mode of operation.*

Proof: It has been proved in [6] that assuming independently varying component delays and under the floating mode of operation assumption, the maximum circuit delay is equal to the maximum circuit instance delay of that circuit instance whose component delay values are set to their individual maximum values. For this worst-case circuit instance, we can infer from Theorem 2 that the PITA maximum circuit instance delay is exactly equal to the maximum circuit instance delay under the floating mode of operation. Hence proved.

■

If component delays are correlated (to a large or a small extent), it may not be possible to set the delay of all components simultaneously to their individual maximum values (i.e., the circuit instance corresponding to all component delays set simultaneously to their individual maximum values may be unrealizable). Therefore, previously reported floating mode timing analyzers which perform the sensitization analysis under a floating mode of operation with all component delays set to their individual maximum values will yield a pessimistic estimate of the realizable maximum circuit delay. By using Equation EQ3 and Equation EQ4 to find the maximum circuit delay under a general component delay model, the PITA maximum circuit delay will not be pessimistic in this regard.

Theorem 4: *For any component delay model, the PITA maximum circuit delay is exactly equal to the realizable maximum circuit delay under the floating mode of operation.*

Proof: We can infer from Theorem 2 that the PITA maximum circuit instance delay is exactly equal to the maximum circuit instance delay under the floating mode of operation, i.e, equations Equation EQ1 and Equation EQ2 determine exactly the maximum delay of a circuit instance. Maximizing these equations over all possible (i.e., realizable) circuit instances give equations Equation EQ3 and Equation EQ4, which is precisely the PITA maximum circuit delay for any given component delay model. Hence proved.

■

4. Primitive PDF identification based timing analysis - PITA

The PITA approach is shown in Figure 2. It takes as

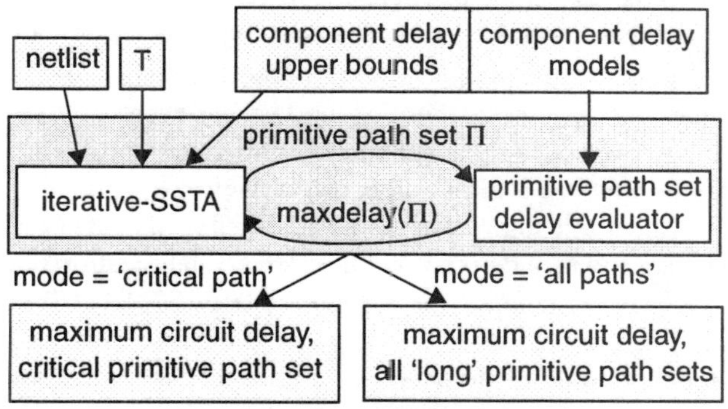

Figure 2. The PITA approach.

input the gate-level netlist, a lower bound value T on the circuit delay, the component delay models and their respective upper bound (maximum) delay values. PITA operates in two modes. In the 'critical path' mode, it outputs the maximum circuit delay and the associated critical primitive path set (i.e., the primitive path set whose primitive anchor path determines this delay). In the 'all paths' mode, it identifies all 'long' primitive path sets, i.e., those primitive path sets whose maximum delays are greater than the input lower bound threshold value T.

The core of the PITA methodology is based on the *iterative-SSTA* (*iterative* Signal Stabilization Time Analysis) algorithm, which is used to identify primitive path sets whose delay upper bounds are greater than some lower bound threshold value. The iterative-SSTA procedure uses only the upper bounds on the component delays to identify these primitive path sets. Every time such a primitive path set is identified, the *primitive path set delay evaluator* is invoked which computes the maximum delay of the primitive path set using the user-input component delay models.

In the 'all paths' mode, the lower bound T value remains constant at the input value, so primitive path sets whose delay upper bounds are greater than the input T value are identified and reported as 'long' primitive path sets. In the 'critical path' mode however, as primitive path sets with delay upper bounds greater than T are identified, T is updated to the maximum of the maximum primitive path set delay found so far. The updated T value is then used as the new lower bound threshold for further identifying primitive path sets, and this process continues until no further primitive path sets are found. The resulting T value is the PITA maximum circuit delay.

4.1. Iterative-SSTA

We have previously reported our primitive path set identification procedure [13] which is based on the iterative-SSTA algorithm. We only give a brief overview of the procedure here.

Consider a 4-valued logic system {S0, S1, U0, U1}, which represents the possible signal values under a 2-vector delay test $\bar{v} = <v_1, v_2>$. The symbols S0, S1, U0, and U1 represent the stable logic 0 value, the stable logic 1 value, possible transitions for the test but eventually settling to a logic 0 value, and possible transitions but eventually settling to a logic 1 value, respectively.

Under this logic system, for a 2-input AND gate (with inputs *a* and *b*, and output *x*), there are 16 stabilization scenarios since each gate input can be one of S0, S1, U0, or U1. Each stabilization scenario can be derived from the excitation table of the AND gate enhanced with the new logic system and delay constraints, shown in Figure 3. We

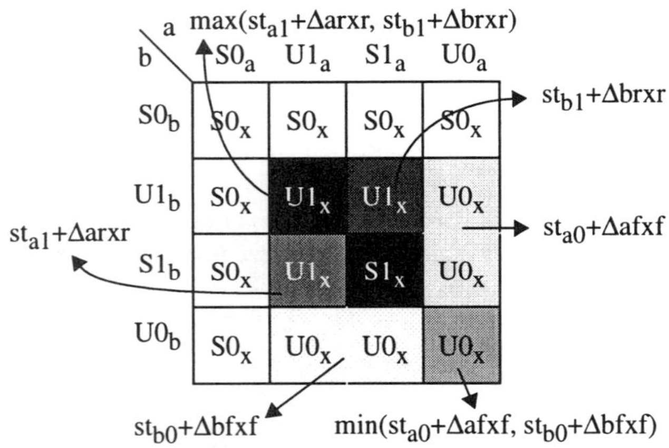

Figure 3. Stabilization table for an AND gate.

call this the *stabilization table* for the AND gate. Here, $U0_a$ means (a = U0), st_{x0} represents the time at which node *x* stabilizes to a logic 0 value, Δafxf represents the *a-to-x* gate delay for a falling input (and consequently a falling output), and so on. For instance, the bottom rightmost scenario is interpreted as follows: if both *a* and *b* can have transitions but eventually settle to a logic 0 value, then the gate output *x* stabilizes with possible hazards to a logic 0 value, and it is guaranteed to stabilize to its final logic value within the time $\min(st_{a0}+\Delta afxf, st_{b0}+\Delta bfxf)$.

From the stabilization table for a gate type, we can write out the SOP (Sum of Products) expression corresponding to all the stabilization scenarios. We call this the *stabilizing time expression propagation rule* (or, *ST-expression propagation rule*) for the gate type. The ST-expression propagation rule for the 2-input AND gate is:

$$
\begin{aligned}
st_{x0} > T_x \quad \Rightarrow \quad & U0_a \wedge (S1_b \vee U1_b) \wedge \quad (st_{a0}+\Delta afxf > T_x) \\
\vee \; & (S1_a \vee U1_a) \wedge U0_b \wedge \quad (st_{b0}+\Delta bfxf > T_x) \\
\vee \; & U0_a \wedge U0_b \quad \wedge \quad (st_{a0}+\Delta afxf > T_x) \wedge (st_{b0}+\Delta bfxf > T_x) \\
st_{x1} > T_x \quad \Rightarrow \quad & U1_a \wedge (S1_b \vee U1_b) \wedge \quad (st_{a1}+\Delta arxr > T_x) \\
\vee \; & (S1_a \vee U1_a) \wedge U1_b \wedge \quad (st_{b1}+\Delta brxr > T_x)
\end{aligned}
$$

Note here that $(S1_b \vee U1_b)$ and $(S1_a \vee U1_a)$ in the product terms can be interpreted as the appropriate side-input settling to a final non-controlling logic value under the floating mode of operation, while $U0_a$, $U0_b$, $U1_a$, and $U1_b$ in the product terms can be interpreted as the on-path input settling to a final 0/1 logic value under the floating mode of operation.

Starting from the primary inputs, we build *stabilizing time expressions* (*ST-expressions*) at each node in a levelized fashion by combining the ST-expressions at the gate inputs according to the ST-expression propagation rule at that gate. For a primary input *a*, the ST-expression is:

$$st_{a0} > T_a \;\Rightarrow\; a(0-) \wedge \overline{a(0+)}, \quad st_{a1} > T_a \;\Rightarrow\; \overline{a(0-)} \wedge a(0+)$$

where a(0-) is the value of *a* for the first vector of the test and a(0+) is the value of *a* for the second vector of the test vector pair. The general form for the ST-expression at a node *n* is:

$$
\begin{aligned}
st_{n0} > T_n \quad \Rightarrow \quad & Bcond_{n0}^{1} \wedge \{Cexpr_{n0}^{1} > T_n\} \\
\vee \; & \ldots \wedge \{\ldots\} \\
\vee \; & Bcond_{n0}^{N0} \wedge \{Cexpr_{n0}^{N0} > T_n\} \\
st_{n1} > T_n \quad \Rightarrow \quad & Bcond_{n1}^{1} \wedge \{Cexpr_{n1}^{1} > T_n\} \\
\vee \; & \ldots \wedge \{\ldots\} \\
\vee \; & Bcond_{n1}^{N1} \wedge \{Cexpr_{n1}^{N1} > T_n\}
\end{aligned}
$$

where $Bcond_{n0}^{k}$ $(1 \le k \le N0)$, $Bcond_{n1}^{k}$ $(1 \le k \le N1)$ represent the Boolean conditions in terms of the primary input variables a(0-), a(0+), ..., such that node *n* may have transitions but stabilizes ultimately to a logic 0 and a logic 1 value respectively. $\{Cexpr_{n0}^{k} > T_n\}$ $(1 \le k \le N0)$, $\{Cexpr_{n1}^{k} > T_n\}$ $(1 \le k \le N1)$ are and-expressions of symbolic constraints on partial paths upto node *n*, and are of the form $\{(delay[path_i] > T_n) \wedge (delay[path_j] > T_n) \wedge \ldots\}$. It can be inferred that each Cexpr corresponds to a PDF (SPDF/MPDF) consisting of partial paths from the primary inputs to node *n*, and the corresponding Bcond represents its single/joint non-robust testability conditions (single/joint static sensitizability conditions).

While combining the ST-expressions at the gate inputs according to the ST-expression propagation rule at that gate, the terms corresponding to those symbolic partial path delay constraints which cannot be satisfied for the given component delay upper bound values are pruned away. Thus, the ST-expression at a node represents in SOP form the 'long' non-robust partial PDFs and their respective non-robust tests.

By propagating the ST-expressions through the levels of logic in a circuit, we can obtain all non-robust PDFs (i.e., jointly statically sensitizable path sets) at each circuit output. However, given a path set of cardinality m, there may be many path sets of cardinality n (> m) which are supersets of this path set, and hence are not primitive. Computation of these non-primitive path sets adds to the memory overhead, and therefore is not computationally efficient. To overcome this problem, we do not compute the complete ST-expression at each node in one shot. Instead, we do this iteratively, where in each iteration i, we compute the ST-expression at each node only for a range $[l_i, u_i]$ of path set cardinalities. At the end of the ith iteration, we identify the primitive path sets in the range of cardinalities $[l_i, u_i]$. This information is then stored on the edges of the circuit, and is used for pruning path sets of higher cardinalities during the ST-expression propagation in succeeding iterations.

4.2. Primitive path set delay evaluation

The delay evaluator is invoked every time the iterative-SSTA algorithm finds a primitive path set whose delay upper bound (i.e., maximum delay using component delay upper bounds) is greater than T. The delay evaluator finds the maximum delay of the primitive path set for the given component delay model. The delay evaluator is specific to the component delay model. For component delay models that are mutually independent (fixed, monotone speedup [3], and bounded delay models [7]), Equation EQ6 is used to evaluate this delay. If component delays are correlated, then Equation EQ4 must be used.

5. Comparisons

The basis for our primitive path set identification procedure is the stabilization tables for individual gate types (e.g., refer to Figure 3 for the stabilization table of a 2-input AND gate). These stabilization tables correspond to the SENV sensitization criterion, which is the set of necessary and sufficient conditions for a path to be sensitizable under the floating mode of operation assumption. The sensitization criterion proposed in [4] also corresponds to the SENV criterion. However, the manner in which the sensitization criterion is applied for timing analysis is different between the two. In [5] (which is a companion paper of [4]), an approach has been presented to answer the question "Is there a true path of delay ≥ T?". This is based on simultaneously determining the sensitizability of all paths whose delays are greater than or equal to T, and it works by finding a test for a single stuck-fault at the circuit output using a timed D-calculus that is derived from the SENV criterion. To find the maximum circuit instance delay, the algorithm may need to be run multiple times for different T values. In PITA, only gate functionality is used to identify primitive paths sets. The component delay upper bounds are used only to prune jointly statically sensitized partial path sets whose delay upper bounds are less than some threshold value, and are not used to determine which gate input signal dominates the gate output at each gate. In other words, instead of performing a delay-dependent resolution at each gate, the partial path delay constraints are stored symbolically in the ST-expression at the gate. The component delay model itself is used only by the delay evaluator to compute the maximum delay of the primitive path sets. The advantage of doing so is in the ability to handle fabrication process effects, signal propagation effects, and signal interaction effects.

5.1. General component delays

The significance of the PITA approach is underscored in dealing with fabrication process, signal propagation, and signal interaction effects. Under these effects, not all components along a path may exhibit their maximum delay values simultaneously, so adding up component delay maxima (or upper bounds) along paths will result in a very pessimistic upper bound of the realizable maximum path delay. It may be argued that using a conventional floating mode timing analyzer, the maximum circuit delay accounting for these effects may be found as a two step process: firstly, determine the critical path using the floating mode timing analyzer with the component delays set at their individual upper bounds, and then find the maximum delay of the critical path accounting for these effects. This analysis is incorrect since, for the component delay value combination where the delay of the critical path is maximized under these effects, the path may be false. Moreover, a path whose delay upper bound is less than that of this critical path may in fact have a larger maximum delay. Essentially, without creating symbolic partial path delay expressions during the path sensitization analysis, the best the previously reported floating mode timing analyzers can do is to report as maximum circuit delay, the delay found by performing path sensitization analysis with all component delays simultaneously set to their maximum values.

In PITA, the iterative-SSTA algorithm uses the component delay upper bounds (i.e., component delay maxima) to identify primitive path sets whose delay upper bounds exceed the current lower bound threshold value, and the delay evaluator uses Equation EQ4 to determine the maximum primitive path set delay using component delay models that account for these fabrication process, signal propagation, and signal interaction effects. This procedure will result in the realizable maximum circuit delay. Note that the maximum primitive path set delay evaluation may not be a trivial task: a non-linear numerical optimization may need to be performed if the component delays are expressed as functions of fabrication process fluctuations, and a signal hazard analysis may need to be performed to determine the worst-case scenario in the case of signal interaction effects.

5.2. Post-layout delay optimization

In the post-layout delay optimization scenario, given a circuit layout which has sensitizable paths whose delays exceed some given timing constraint, the objective is to speed up the circuit such that all sensitizable paths have delay less than the timing constraint. In this scenario, it follows from Theorem 1 that it is necessary and sufficient to speed up all the 'long' primitive anchor paths (i.e., those primitive anchor paths whose maximum delay is greater than the given timing constraint). PITA can be executed in 'all paths' mode to identify all 'long' primitive path sets, which can then be speeded up using transistor resizing, wire resizing, interconnect re-routing, buffer insertion etc. Here, the sensitization analysis to identify primitive path sets needs to be done only once.

If a conventional floating mode timing analyzer were to be used in this scenario, the path sensitization analysis may have to be performed multiple times. We justify this in the following argument. In the post-layout delay optimization scenario, say all the 'long' sensitizable paths (i.e., those whose delays exceed the given timing constraint) have been identified using some floating mode timing analyzer. It can be shown that it is neither necessary, nor sufficient to speed up all these 'long' sensitizable paths. Essentially, when a 'long' sensitizable path is speeded up, it may result in other 'long' sensitizable paths becoming false and also result in some 'long' false paths becoming sensitizable. Therefore, the path sensitizabilities would have to be re-evaluated every time a 'long' sensitizable path is speeded up, resulting in a situation where critical paths are identified and speeded up one at a time in an iterative manner. This is very inefficient compared to the manner in which PITA needs to be used just once.

6. Results

Results obtained from using PITA to determine the maximum circuit delay of some large ISCAS'85, ISCAS'89 and Logic synthesis'91 benchmark circuits are shown in Table 1 for two component delay models: the *unit component delay model* where every component (gate, wire) in the circuits is assumed to have unit delay, and a *k-factor delay model* [14] where gate delays are

Table 1: PITA results.

Circuit	No. gates	No. paths	Unit delay		K-factor delays		
			PERT	PITA	PERT	PITA (no correl)	PITA (correl)
c880	402	17284	100	100	100	100	93.08
c432	251	583652	100	100	100	97.65	94.19*
c499	502	795776	100	100	100	100	99.47
c1355	598	8.34 e6	100	100	100	-	-
c1908	664	1.46 e6	100	93.10	100	97.19	95.32
c3540	1366	5.74 e7	100	-	100	95.61	94.69
c5315	2328	2.68 e6	100	98.10	100	98.38	96.51
dalu	2061	121636	100	100	100	94.44	81.02*
k2	2748	20808	100	100	100	100	76.87
i10	3194	1.38 e7	100	96.26	100	93.57	83.20*
i8	3590	105242	100	94.29	100	93.37	90.06
s13207.1	8592	2.69 e6	100	-	100	99.67	99.12
s1423	674	89452	100	100	100	99.18	94.09
s15850.1	10197	3.29 e8	100	-	100	96.17	94.92
s38584.1	21308	2.16 e6	100	100	100	100	97.87
s5378	3208	27046	100	100	100	100	99.30
s713	452	43624	100	92.45	100	93.67	90.64
s9234.1	5944	489708	100	100	100	99.55	95.02

expressed as empirically obtained functions of input transition time and output load capacitance.

In the results for each circuit in the unit component delay model, the PITA maximum circuit delay is shown normalized relative to the maximum topological delay (PERT delay [1]). Fairly large circuits (~21K gates, ~14 million paths) were handled by PITA for the unit delay model. However, the program ran out of memory for c3540, s13207.1 and s15850.1 before giving any result.

Results for the k-factor delay model are shown in the last three columns of the result table. The k-factor delay models for the gate library were obtained from SGS-Thomson Microelectronics, Agrate, Italy. Since we did not use circuit layouts, the load capacitance at each gate was assumed to be proportional to its fanout and the interconnect delays were assumed to be zero. Under the k-factor delay model, the upper bounds on the delay from a gate input to the gate output were calculated by evaluating the appropriate k-factor function under the maximum possible input transition time that can be seen by that gate input. The PERT delay shown is found by using these component delay upper bounds. Also, the transition time at a gate input affects the delay of the gate and also the transition time of the gate output, which in turn affects the delay of the fanout gates. Hence, component delays are correlated under the k-factor delay model due to signal propagation effects. Previously reported floating mode timing analyzers cannot account for these correlations since they use partial path delay upper bounds (derived by adding component delay maxima) during the path sensitization analysis to determine which signal dominates at a gate input. Results obtained by ignoring these correlations are shown in the 'PITA (no correl)' column, which is the delay that would be reported by these floating mode timing analyzers, while the PITA *realizable* maximum circuit delay determined by incorporating these correlations is shown in the final column. Once again, the circuit delay numbers are shown normalized with respect to the corresponding PERT delay. It is observed for many circuits that not accounting for component delay correlations during the path sensitization analysis is as pessimistic as (or in some cases, even more pessimistic than) not accounting for path sensitization. For e.g., for circuit k2, path sensitization analysis without accounting for component delay correlation does not decrease the maximum circuit delay estimate at all, while PITA path sensitization analysis accounting for component delay correlation tightens the maximum circuit delay estimate by 23.13% (=100– 76.87).

For circuits c432, dalu and i10, the program ran out of memory while calculating primitive path sets of high cardinalities. Nevertheless, the PITA implementation successfully identified 'long' primitive path sets of lower cardinalities, therefore, the numbers shown (marked with an asterisk) are lower bounds on the maximum circuit delay. Also note that the program ran out of memory for c1355 without giving any result. It is interesting to observe that the benchmark circuits for which the program ran out of memory for the two component delay models (i.e., the unit component delay model and the k-factor delay model) are different. This is because the effectiveness of ST-expression pruning in the iterative-SSTA algorithm depends on the component delay upper bounds, which are different for the two models.

For both component delay models, most circuits took only a few seconds of CPU time on an IBM/RS6000 58H PowerPC computer with 256 Mbytes of real memory. Some of the larger ones took a few minutes of CPU time, but note that the CPU time is very dependent on the choice of the user-input lower bound T value, and hence has not been reported here.

7. Conclusions

We have developed a new method for timing analysis (PITA) based on identifying primitive path sets in a circuit using component delay upper bounds and evaluating their maximum delay for user-input component delay models. We have defined the PITA maximum circuit instance delay as the maximum of the delays of the primitive path sets in the circuit, and proved that it is exactly equal to the maximum circuit instance delay under the floating mode of operation. Furthermore, the PITA maximum circuit delay is also shown to determine exactly the maximum circuit delay under the floating mode of operation. Previously published floating mode timing analyzers are capable of determining the maximum circuit delay accurately only for independently varying component delays, and are pessimistic in the presence of fabrication process, signal propagation, and signal interaction effects. The PITA approach provides a framework where these effects can be taken into account very accurately since the iterative-SSTA algorithm outputs symbolic primitive path set information rather than performing a delay-dependent resolution at each gate. We have demonstrated this for benchmark circuits for a k-factor delay model. It is also argued that post-layout delay optimization can be more efficiently performed with PITA than with conventional floating mode timing analyzers because the set of primitive path sets is invariant with respect to delay.

References

[1] T. Kirkpatrick and N. Clark, "PERT as an aid to logic design," IBM Tech. Rep., 1966.

[2] J. Benkoski, E. Vanden Meersch, L. J. M. Claesen, H. De Man, "Timing verification using statically sensitizable paths," *IEEE Trans. Computer-Aided Design*, vol. 9, Oct. 1990, pp. 1073-1084.

[3] P. McGeer and R. Brayton, "Efficient algorithms for computing the longest viable path in a combinational network," *Proc. 26th Design Automation Conf.*, 1989, pp. 561-567.

[4] S. Devadas, K. Keutzer, and S. Malik, "Computation of floating mode delay in combinational logic circuits: Theory and algorithms," *IEEE Trans. Computer-Aided Design*, vol. 12, Dec. 1993, pp. 1913-1922.

[5] S. Devadas, K. Keutzer, S. Malik, and A. Wang, "Computation of floating mode delay in combinational logic circuits: Practice and implementation," *IEEE Trans. Computer-Aided Design*, vol. 12, Dec. 1993, pp. 1923-1936.

[6] H. Chen and D. Du, "Path sensitization in critical path problem," *Proc. TAU'90*, ACM-SIGDA, 1990.

[7] S. Devadas, K. Keutzer, S. Malik, and A. Wang, "Certified timing verification and the transition delay of a logic circuit," *IEEE Trans. VLSI Systems*, vol. 2, Sept. 1994, pp. 333-342.

[8] G. L. Smith, "Model for delay faults based upon paths," *Proc. Int'l Test Conference*, Nov. 1985, pp. 324-349.

[9] C. J. Lin and S. M. Reddy, "On delay fault testing in logic circuits," *IEEE Trans. Computer-Aided Design*, vol. 6-5, Sept. 1987, pp. 694-703.

[10] E. S. Park and M. R. Mercer, "Robust and nonrobust tests for path delay faults in a combinational circuit," *Proc. Int'l Test Conf.*, 1987, pp. 1027-1034.

[11] S. M. Reddy, "Delay faults: Modeling, fault simulation, and test generation," *Int'l Test Conf.*, 1995, Tutorial 8.

[12] W. Ke and P. R. Menon, "Synthesis of delay-verifiable combinational circuits," *IEEE Trans. Computers*, vol. 44-2, Feb. 1995, pp. 213-222.

[13] M. Sivaraman and A. J. Strojwas, "Primitive path delay fault identification," *Proc. 10th Int'l Conf. on VLSI Design*, 1997, pp. 95-100.

[14] N. H. E. Weste and K. Eshraghian, "Principles of CMOS VLSI design," *2nd edition, Addison-Wesley Publishing Company*, 1993.

Approximate Algorithms for Time Separation of Events *

Supratik Chakraborty David L. Dill
Computer Systems Laboratory, Stanford University, Stanford, CA 94305

Abstract

We describe a polynomial-time approximate algorithm for computing minimum and maximum time separations between all pairs of events in systems specified by acyclic timing constraint graphs. Even for acyclic graphs, the problem is NP-complete. We propose finding an approximate solution by first approximating the non-convex feasible space with a suitable convex "envelope", and then solving the problem efficiently in the approximate convex space. Unlike previous works, our algorithm can handle both min and max type timing constraints in the same system, and has a computational complexity that is polynomial in the number of events. Although the computed separations are conservative in the worst-case, experiments indicate that our results are highly accurate in practice.

1. Introduction

Finding bounds on the time separation between events has emerged as a central problem in analysis of hardware designs. The results of such an analysis can be used for interface timing verification [7]; for design optimization of timed asynchronous circuits [8]; for determining delay padding for eliminating hazards in asynchronous circuits [6]; for obtaining optimal clock schedules in synchronous circuits [9]; or for performance analysis of concurrent systems.

In this paper, we propose a new *polynomial-time approximate algorithm* for finding the minimum and maximum time separations between *all pairs* of events in a concurrent system, given bounded propagation delays between events, and the type of timing constraint (min or max) associated with each event. Unlike several previous works [1, 7, 10, 2, 5], our algorithm has a worst-case time complexity that is *polynomial* in the number of events, *and* can handle *both* min and max type constraints in the same system. A limitation of our current approach is that it applies only to systems representable by *acyclic* timing constraint graphs. However, this still encompasses a large and important class of applications.

It has been shown by previous researchers [7] that the general form of the problem is NP-complete. The computational difficulty stems from the non-convex shape of the feasible space of a system of constraints involving min and max functions. We, therefore, propose to first approximate the non-convex feasible space with a convex "envelope". Since every point in the feasible space is contained in the approximate convex space, maximizing the separation between two events in the approximate space yields an upper bound on the maximum achievable separation in the original feasible space. Ideally, we would like to find the smallest convex space (convex hull) that contains the feasible space. Unfortunately, finding a convex hull in n dimensions is itself intractable. So, we propose a new approximation methodology for obtaining a small convex envelope of the non-convex feasible space.

Our method proceeds by representing each min (or max) constraint with an *equivalent* combination of linear inequalities among the variables. We then successively derive other linear inequalities from this equivalent combination, ensuring that at each step, the feasible space of the derived system of inequalities contains the feasible space of the set of inequalities from which it is derived. The resulting system of linear inequalities, with a feasible space that is necessarily convex, then constitutes an approximation to the original min (or max) constraint. We then use a polynomial-time algorithm to find bounds on the separation between every pair of events in the approximate convex space. Although our computed bounds represent conservative approximations to the true bounds in the worst-case scenario, experiments on several large systems have shown that our results are highly accurate in practice.

1.1. Related work

Previous work in this area comes from a wide spectrum of contexts. McMillan and Dill [7] proposed a cubic-time algorithm for the acyclic max-only constraint problem. A branch-and-bound algorithm for systems with both min and max constraints was also proposed in [7]. However, this has a worst-case exponential time complexity. Vanbekbergen et al. proposed an algorithm for systems with both min and max constraints in [10]. Unfortunately, their algorithm is incorrect. The work of [8] computes loose bounds on the time separation of events in cyclic graphs containing only max type events. Burks and Sakallah formulated the problem as a *min-max linear program* (mmLP) and proposed two exact algorithms in [2]. Unfortunately, both algorithms have worst-case exponential time complexity. The work of Hulgaard et al. [5] proposed an interesting algorithm for computing the exact maximum separation between two *specific*

*This work was supported by a grant from the Semiconductor Research Corporation (Contract No. 96-DJ-389) and a gift from Sun Microsystems

events in a cyclic process graph with max type events. Their algorithm, however, has a worst-case exponential time complexity. Extensions of this algorithm to deal with extended free choice and unique choice have been proposed in [4]. Lavagno and Sangiovanni-Vincentelli used a variant of the present problem to find optimum delay paddings to eliminate hazards in asynchronous circuits [6]. Several other timing analyzers have been developed that either cater to specific applications [1] or deal with fixed delays between events [3].

2. The timing analysis problem

The setup for our timing analysis problem is as follows: We have a concurrent system where event i occurs at time t_i, and $\delta_{i,j}$ represents the delay in the propagation of event i to event j. The delays $\delta_{i,j}$ are constrained to lie within fixed upper and lower bounds $d_{i,j}$ and $D_{i,j}$. Each event i is also associated with a min or max operator that determines how its time of occurrence relates to those of other events.

Such a system of constraints can be represented by a timing constraint graph where nodes represent events and directed edges represent dependencies between the occurrence times of events. A directed edge from event i to event j is labeled $[d_{i,j}, D_{i,j}]$, representing the delay $\delta_{i,j}$. If an event f is associated with a max (min) operator, the node corresponding to f is labeled max (min). As an example, Figure 1 shows the timing constraint graph for the following system of timing constraints:

$$\begin{array}{lcl} t_a & = & t_a + \delta_{s,a}; \\ t_b & = & \min(t_s + \delta_{s,b},\ t_a + \delta_{a,b}); \\ t_c & = & \max(t_a + \delta_{a,c},\ t_b + \delta_{b,c}) \\ t_d & = & \min(t_a + \delta_{a,d},\ t_b + \delta_{b,d}) \\ 0 & \leq & \delta_{s,a},\ \delta_{a,b},\ \delta_{a,c},\ \delta_{b,c},\ \delta_{a,d},\ \delta_{b,d} \ \leq \ 1 \\ 1 & \leq & \delta_{s,b} \leq 3 \end{array}$$

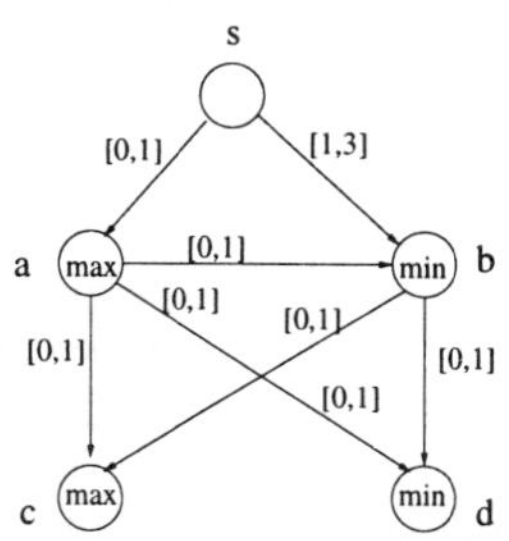

Figure 1. Example of a timing constraint graph

Given such a timing constraint graph, our goal is to determine bounds on the minimum and maximum achievable values of $(t_i - t_j)$ for every pair of events i and j. Since $\min(t_i - t_j) = -\max(t_j - t_i)$, it suffices to determine the maximum value of $(t_i - t_j)$ for every *ordered pair* of events (i, j). We restrict our analysis to acyclic timing constraint graphs, which can, however, have multiple *source* events (events with no incoming edges), provided bounds on the separations between the source events are given.

2.1. An approximation strategy

The feasible space of a system of constraints involving min and max functions is non-convex. This renders standard convex optimization techniques inapplicable. In this section, we describe a method to compute a convex envelope of the non-convex feasible space.

Mathematically, each non-linear equation of the form:

$$t_f \ = \ \max(t_i + \delta_{i,f},\ \ldots\ t_k + \delta_{k,f}) \qquad (1)$$

can be represented using the following *equivalent* system of linear inequalities:

$$\begin{array}{cc} (t_f \geq t_i + d_{i,f}) & \wedge \\ \vdots & \wedge \\ (t_f \geq t_k + d_{k,f}) & \wedge \\ \left(\begin{array}{cc} (t_f \leq t_i + D_{i,f}) & \vee \\ \vdots & \vee \\ (t_f \leq t_k + D_{k,f}) & \end{array} \right) & \end{array} \qquad (2)$$

where $\wedge$ represents conjunction and $\vee$ represents disjunction of the truth or falsity of each linear inequality.

Now, let s be an arbitrary event in the system, and let $\Delta_{s,i}$ represent an upper bound (achievable or not) of the separation $(t_i - t_s)$. It follows that $t_i \leq t_s + \Delta_{s,i}$. Combining this with $t_f \leq t_i + D_{i,f}$ (see inequalities (2)), we obtain $t_f \leq t_s + \Delta_{s,i} + D_{i,f}$.

Reasoning analogously, we can relate t_s to the occurrence times of the other predecessors of f. This gives us the following system of linear inequalities derived from (2):

$$\begin{array}{cc} (t_f \geq t_i + d_{i,f}) & \wedge \\ \vdots & \wedge \\ (t_f \geq t_k + d_{k,f}) & \wedge \\ \left(\begin{array}{cc} (t_f \leq t_s + \Delta_{s,i} + D_{i,f}) & \vee \\ \vdots & \vee \\ (t_f \leq t_s + \Delta_{s,k} + D_{k,f}), & \end{array} \right) & \end{array} \qquad (3)$$

The disjunction of inequalities in (3) can be further approximated to give:

$$t_f \ \leq \ t_s + \max_{l \in preds(f)} (\Delta_{s,l} + D_{l,f}), \qquad (4)$$

where we have used the notation $preds(f)$ to denote the set of events l that have a directed edge to f in the timing constraint graph. Since the event s was arbitrarily chosen, inequality (4) holds for *all* events in the system. However, choosing s to be the same as f does not yield any useful information, since t_f appears on both sides of inequality (4). Therefore, applying inequality (4) to all events other than f, we get the following system of linear inequalities as an approximation to the non-linear equation (1).

$$\begin{array}{c} (\wedge_{i \in preds(f)}\ (t_f \ \geq \ t_i + d_{i,f})) \quad \bigwedge \\ (\wedge_{all\ s \neq f}\ (t_f \ \leq \ t_s + \max_{l \in preds(f)} (\Delta_{s,l} + D_{l,f}))). \end{array} \qquad (5)$$

This leads to the following important observation.

Observation 1 : *$-d_{i,f}$ is an upper bound of $\Delta_{f,i}$, for all $i \in preds(f)$. Similarly, $\max_{l \in preds(f)} (\Delta_{s,l} + D_{l,f})$ is an upper bound of $\Delta_{s,f}$, for all $s \neq f$.*

A min constraint $t_f = \min(t_i + \delta_{i,f}, \ldots t_k + \delta_{k,f})$ can be similarly approximated, leading to the following observation:

Observation 2 : *$D_{i,f}$ is an upper bound of $\Delta_{i,f}$ for all $i \in preds(f)$. Similarly, $\max_{l \in preds(f)}(\Delta_{l,s} - d_{l,f})$ is an upper bound of $\Delta_{f,s}$ for all events $s \neq f$.*

Note that any solution of the original non-linear equation (e.g., equation (1)) is also a solution of the corresponding approximate system of linear inequalities (e.g., inequalities (5)). Since the feasible space of the latter is necessarily convex, we have effectively determined a convex envelope of the non-convex feasible space of the non-linear equation. For example, consider the following system of of timing constraints:

$$\begin{array}{lcl} t_3 & = & \max(t_1 + \delta_{1,3},\ t_2 + \delta_{2,3}) \\ 1 & \leq & \delta_{1,3}, \delta_{2,3}\ \leq\ 3 \\ \Delta_{1,2} & = & \Delta_{2,1}\ =\ 1 \end{array}$$

Figure 2(a) shows the feasible space of this system. The volume contained within the solid V-shaped entity and extending infinitely in both directions along the turning-corner of the V represents points where this system of constraints is satisfied. Our approximation gives the following system of linear inequalities for this system:

$$\begin{array}{lll} t_3 \geq t_1 + 1; & t_3 \leq t_1 + 4; & t_3 \geq t_2 + 1; \\ t_3 \leq t_2 + 4; & -1 \leq t_2 - t_1 \leq 1 & \end{array}$$

The feasible space of this system of inequalities is shown in Figure 2(b). Clearly this includes the non-convex space of Figure 2(a).

2.2. A polynomial-time approximate algorithm

In this section, we use observations 1 and 2 of Section 2.1 to design a polynomial-time algorithm for computing bounds on the separation between every pair of events. Our algorithm accepts as inputs a finite, acyclic timing constraint graph with n events, and bounds on the separation between the source events. The events are topologically sorted with event 0 being a source event. The output of our algorithm is an $n \times n$ matrix Δ, where $\Delta_{i,j}$ contains an upper bound on $(t_j - t_i)$, i.e., $t_j - t_i \leq \Delta_{i,j}$.

The Δ matrix is computed in an incremental fashion as follows: We start off with $\Delta_{0,0}$ which trivially has the value 0. We then compute $\Delta_{1,0}, \Delta_{1,1}$ and $\Delta_{0,1}$ (see Figure 3). Next, we compute $\Delta_{2,0}, \Delta_{2,1}, \Delta_{2,2}, \Delta_{0,2}$ and $\Delta_{1,2}$ (see Figure 3). This process is repeated for increasing values of the topological index, effectively constructing the Δ matrix "layer-by-layer" as shown in Figure 3. The ith such "layer"

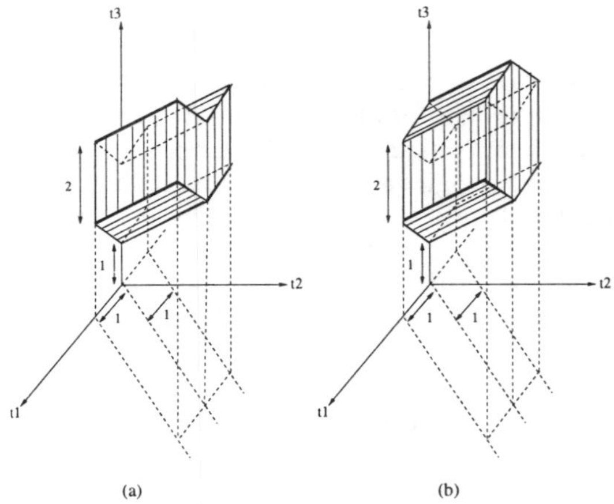

Figure 2. Illustrating the inclusion of the original feasible space in the approximate convex space.

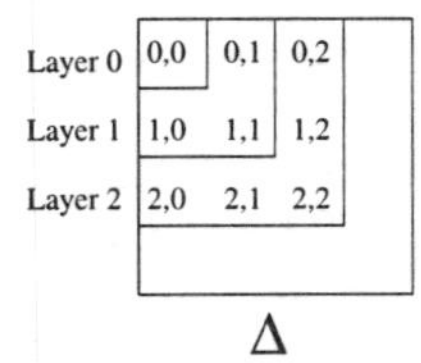

Figure 3. Layer wise construction of the Δ matrix

of the Δ matrix is comprised of the entries $\Delta_{j,i}$ and $\Delta_{i,j}$, where $0 \leq j \leq i$.

The rationale behind this layer-wise construction is as follows: All events in $preds(i)$ have topological indices less than i. It therefore follows from observations 1 and 2 in Section 2.1 that initial estimates of $\Delta_{s,i}$ and $\Delta_{i,s}$, for all $s \in \{0, \ldots, i-1\}$, can be computed using the entries in the $(i \times i)$ sub-matrix of Δ comprised of rows 0 through $(i-1)$ and columns 0 through $(i-1)$. Moreover, since the timing constraint graph is acyclic, the timing of event i cannot affect the maximum separation between events with indices less than i. Consequently, the entries in the $(i \times i)$ sub-matrix mentioned above are not affected by the timing of event i. This suggests that we first compute the entries in the $(i \times i)$ sub-matrix comprised of rows 0 through $(i-1)$ and columns 0 through $(i-1)$, and then use the computed entries in this sub-matrix to compute the ith layer of the Δ matrix. Applying this method for increasing values of i from 1 through $(n-1)$ yields the Δ matrix layer-by-layer.

Figure 4 shows the steps of our timing analysis algorithm. We initialize the Δ matrix and then compute upper bounds on the maximum separation times a layer at a time. For each layer i, we first compute initial estimates of as many entries as possible using observation 1 or 2 of Section 2.1 (depending on the type of operator associated with event i). Thereafter, we use these estimates and previously computed entries in layers $\leq i$ to compute the other entries in layer i. This computation is similar to finding the shortest path to (from) event i from (to) other events $< i$. If, during this computation, we find that the value of an entry can be further refined using observation 1 or 2 of Section 2.1, we perform this refinement in the steps marked (*) in Figure 4.

Initialization:

```
for each i in 0 to (n − 1)
  for each j in 0 to (n − 1)
    if (i == j)   Δ_{i,i} = 0;
    else if (i, j are source events)
      Δ_{i,j} = given value;
    else   Δ_{i,j} = +∞;
```

Main Algorithm:

```
for each i in 1 to (n − 1)
  1. Compute_Initial_Estimates(i);
  2. if (i is max type)
       for each j in 0 to (i − 1)
         Δ_{i,j} = min_{k ∈ preds(i)}(Δ_{k,j} − d_{k,i});
         if (j is max type)
(*)        Δ_{i,j} = min(Δ_{i,j}, max_{k ∈ preds(j)}(Δ_{i,k} + D_{k,j});
     else if (i is min type)
       for each j in 0 to (i − 1)
         Δ_{j,i} = min_{k ∈ preds(i)}(Δ_{j,k} + D_{k,i});
         if (j is min type)
(*)        Δ_{j,i} = min(Δ_{j,i}, max_{k ∈ preds(j)}(Δ_{k,i} − d_{k,j});
```

Compute_Initial_Estimates(i: index)

```
if (i is max type)
  for each j in preds(i)   Δ_{i,j} = −d_{j,i};
  for each j in 0 to (i − 1)
    Δ_{j,i} = max_{k ∈ preds(i)}(Δ_{j,k} + D_{k,i})
else
  for each j in preds(i)   Δ_{j,i} = D_{j,i};
  for each j in 0 to (i − 1)
    Δ_{i,j} = max_{k ∈ preds(i)}(Δ_{k,j} − d_{k,i})
```

Figure 4. Time separation of events algorithm

The complexity of our algorithm is $O(n^2.p)$, where $p = \max_{all\ events\ i} |preds(i)|$. In practice, p is usually bounded by a small constant. Therefore, our algorithm has $O(n^2)$ complexity for all practical purposes.

2.3. An example

We now apply our algorithm to the timing constraint graph of Figure 1. The Δ matrix generated is shown in Table 1. It may be verified that all our computed bounds are exact.

	s	a	b	c	d
s	0	1	2	3	2
a	0	0	1	2	1
b	0	0	0	1	1
c	0	0	0	0	1
d	0	0	1	2	0

Table 1. Δ matrix for our example.

In Section 2.1, we saw that each min or max constraint can be equivalently represented by the conjunction and disjunction of simple linear inequalities (see inequalities (2)). As a simple approximation, one may choose to disregard the disjunctive constraints, since taking these into account turns the feasible space non-convex. Applying this simple approximation to the system represented in Figure 1 gives:

$$t_a \geq t_s + 0; \quad t_a \leq t_s + 1; \quad t_b \leq t_a + 1; \quad t_b \leq t_s + 3;$$
$$t_c \geq t_a + 0; \quad t_c \geq t_b + 0; \quad t_d \leq t_a + 1; \quad t_d \leq t_b + 1.$$

This system admits the solution: $t_s = t_a = t_b = t_c =$ any large positive number, and $t_d = 0$. Therefore, an upper bound on $(t_b - t_d)$ subject to this system of constraints is $+\infty$. In reality, however, the achievable upper bound of $(t_b - t_d)$ in Figure 1 is 1.

To understand what went amiss, observe that $t_d = min(t_a + [0,1],\ t_b + [0,1])$ yields the system of inequalities: $(t_d \leq t_a + 1) \wedge (t_d \leq t_b + 1) \wedge ((t_d \geq t_b + 0) \vee (t_d \geq t_b + 0))$. With $t_d = 0$ and $t_b = t_a =$ a large positive number, both the disjunctive clauses are violated. Therefore, this cannot be a solution to the system. This shows that it is important not to disregard the disjunctive constraints in inequations (2). Our algorithm takes these into account by means of the approximations described in Section 2.1.

3. Experimental results

We have implemented our timing analysis algorithm and applied it to several concurrent system specifications. Our benchmarks include cyclic constraint graphs from [5] and [8] unfolded to varying degrees. These are named "hr-n" and "mr-n" in Table 2, where different values of r indicate different cyclic graphs, and n denotes the degree of unfolding. The benchmark"mcmill" was obtained from [7], while "diffeq" was obtained from an analysis of an asynchronous differential equation solver chip [11]. The other benchmarks were obtained as systems of timing constraints during timing simulation of ISCAS85 circuits. Table 2 shows some of our analysis results. For each benchmark, we report the number of events (n), and the number of non-trivial min/max constraints (with ≥ 2 arguments) in the system. This gives us a basis for comparing our run times with those of [2].

In order to quantify the accuracy of our results, we define the accuracy of our algorithm by computing the fraction of all time separations that we are able to compute exactly. For problems involving only max constraints, we obtain the exact separations using the algorithm of [7]. Comparing these with the bounds computed by our algorithm shows that our algorithm produces exact results for all benchmarks involving only max constraints. Unfortunately, we currently don't have an implementation of an exact algorithm for solving systems with both min and max functions. Consequently, we are unable to report the accuracy of our results for benchmarks involving both min and max functions (an exception is "mcmill", which was small enough to allow manual checking). However, we believe that our results are highly accurate in these cases as well, since our algorithm does not treat max-only systems in any special way.

Table 2 also shows the time taken by our algorithm to analyze each benchmark. These times are on a MIPS R5000 150 MHz processor with 128 MBytes of main memory, and do not include the time to read in the timing constraint graph and topologically sort the events. We find that for the max-only problem, our algorithm is approximately 3 times faster than the algorithm of [7]. For systems with both min and max functions, our run times may be compared with those of [2]. Table 3 lists the run times for some of the largest systems analyzed in [2]. Since the computing platforms are not the same, a direct comparison would be unfair. Nevertheless, an inspection of the CPU times in Tables 2 and 3 indicates that for systems of comparable sizes, our algorithm computes **all $\mathbf{n^2}$** separations in much less time than that required by the algorithm of [2] to compute the maximum value of **only one objective function**. Unfortunately, the exact benchmarks used in [2] were not available for analysis.

Bench-mark Name	Evts. (n)	Min/max fns.	t_1 (s)	t_2 (s)	Accuracy
h1-64	321	316	0.49	1.48	1.0
h1-256	1281	1276	8.65	26.31	1.0
h1-512	2561	2556	36.69	113.77	1.0
h2-64	385	379	0.75	2.21	1.0
h2-256	1537	1531	13.17	40.31	1.0
h2-512	3073	3067	55.63	171.86	1.0
m1-64	641	255	1.55	4.97	1.0
m1-256	2561	1023	27.87	92.05	1.0
m1-512	5121	2047	120.69	417.89	1.0
mcmill	13	5	0.00	N/A	1.0
diffeq	258	48	0.21	N/A	N/A
c1355	948	537	2.78	N/A	N/A
c7552	5258	2343	133.14	N/A	N/A
c6288	4189	3356	65.38	N/A	N/A

Evts. (n) : # events,
Min/max fns. : # min/max functions with ≥ 2 arguments,
t_1 : Time for $\mathbf{n^2}$ separations by our method on R5000,
t_2 : Time for $\mathbf{n^2}$ separations by [7] on R5000

Table 2. Computing all pairs of separations

Benchmark Name	Min/max functions	Time (s) for **one objective function** on DEC5000 ([2])
s444	30	0.574
s1423	74	15.5
s9234	227	105.9
s38584	1452	1965.7

Table 3. Optimizing one linear function

In summary, our experiments indicate that our algorithm produces results with a high degree of accuracy while remaining efficient. The power of our approach lies in the ability to achieve high degrees of accuracy and efficiency even when analyzing large systems containing *both* min and max type timing constraints.

4. Conclusion

We have proposed a new polynomial-time approximate algorithm for finding minimum and maximum separations between events in concurrent systems. Unlike several previous approaches, our algorithm handles *both* min and max type constraints in the same system and has a complexity that is polynomial in the number of events. While the separations computed by our algorithm are conservative in the worst-case, experiments show that our results achieve a high degree of accuracy. The results of such an analysis can be used in the analysis, optimization and verification of concurrent and asynchronous systems.

5. Acknowledgments

We are thankful to Kenneth Y. Yun and Julio Arceo of the University of California, San Diego for providing us with the details of the "diffeq" benchmark.

References

[1] T. Amon and G. Borriello. An approach to symbolic timing verification. In *Proceedings of the 29th DAC*, June 1992.
[2] T. M. Burks and K. A. Sakallah. Min-max linear programming and the timing analysis of digital circuits. In *Proceedings of the ICCAD*, Nov. 1993.
[3] S. M. Burns. *Performance Analysis and Optimization of Asynchronous Circuits*. PhD thesis, California Institute of Technology, 1991.
[4] H. Hulgaard and S. M. Burns. Bounded delay timing analysis of a class of CSP programs with choice. In *Proceedings of the 1st ASYNC*, Nov. 1994.
[5] H. Hulgaard, S. M. Burns, T. Amon, and G. Borriello. An algorithm for exact bounds on time separation of events in concurrent systems. Technical report, Department of Computer Science and Engineering, University of Washington, Feb. 1994. Tech. Report No. UW-CSE-94-02-02.
[6] L. Lavagno and A. Sangiovanni-Vincentelli. Linear programming for optimum hazard elimination in asynchronous circuits. *Journal of VLSI Signal Processing*, 7(1):137–60, Feb. 1994.
[7] K. L. McMillan and D. L. Dill. Algorithms for Interface Timing Verification. In *Proceedings of the ICCD*, Oct. 1992.
[8] C. J. Myers and T. H.-Y. Meng. Synthesis of timed asynchronous circuits. *IEEE Transactions on VLSI Systems*, 1(2):106–119, June 1993.
[9] K. A. Sakallah, T. N. Mudge, and O. A. Olukotun. checkTc and minTc: Timing verification and optimal clocking of digital circuits. In *Proceedings of the ICCAD*, Nov. 1990.
[10] P. Vanbekbergen, G. Goossens, and H. D. Man. Specification and analysis of timing constraints in signal transition graphs. In *Proceedings of the European DAC*, Mar. 1992.
[11] K. Y. Yun, P. A. Beerel, V. Vakilotojar, A. E. Dooply, and J. Arceo. The design and verification of a high-performance low-control-overhead asynchronous differential equation solver. In *Proceedings of the 3rd ASYNC*, April 1997.

SESSION 4A

EMBEDDED TUTORIAL: MICROELECTROMECHANICAL SYSTEMS

Moderator:

Bernard Courtois, TIMA Lab., Grenoble, France

SESSION 4B

EMBEDDED TUTORIAL: OPTIMIZATION TECHNIQUES FOR HIGH-PERFORMANCE DIGITAL CIRCUITS

Moderator:

Rob A. Rutenbar, Carnegie Mellon University,

Pittsburgh, PA

Optimization Techniques for High-Performance Digital Circuits

Chandu Visweswariah
IBM Thomas J. Watson Research Center
Yorktown Heights, NY 10598, U.S.A.
chandu@watson.ibm.com

Abstract

The relentless push for high performance in custom digital circuits has led to renewed emphasis on circuit optimization or tuning. The parameters of the optimization are typically transistor and interconnect sizes. The design metrics are not just delay, transition times, power and area, but also signal integrity and manufacturability. This tutorial paper discusses some of the recently proposed methods of circuit optimization, with an emphasis on practical application and methodology impact.

Circuit optimization techniques fall into three broad categories. The first is dynamic tuning, based on time-domain simulation of the underlying circuit, typically combined with adjoint sensitivity computation. These methods are accurate but require the specification of input signals, and are best applied to small data-flow circuits and "cross-sections" of larger circuits. Efficient sensitivity computation renders feasible the tuning of circuits with a few thousand transistors. Second, static tuners employ static timing analysis to evaluate the performance of the circuit. All paths through the logic are simultaneously tuned, and no input vectors are required. Large control macros are best tuned by these methods. However, in the context of deep submicron custom design, the inaccuracy of the delay models employed by these methods often limits their utility. Aggressive dynamic or static tuning can push a circuit into a precipitous corner of the manufacturing process space, which is a problem addressed by the third class of circuit optimization tools, statistical tuners. Statistical techniques are used to enhance manufacturability or maximize yield.

In addition to surveying the above techniques, topics such as the use of state-of-the-art nonlinear optimization methods and special considerations for interconnect sizing, clock tree optimization and noise-aware tuning will be briefly considered.

1 Introduction

Automatic circuit optimization is an essential part of rapidly, repeatably and robustly designing high-performance circuits. The relentless push for ever higher performance in digital circuits, the need to design circuits of greater complexity, the emphasis on custom design and shrinking product cycles have led to an increased interest in optimization techniques.

Given a logically correct circuit schematic, the circuit tuning problem can be stated as that of optimally assigning sizes to transistors and/or wires. The *performance metrics* are (some subset of) delay, transition time, area, power dissipation, signal integrity, additional timing constraints, layout constraints and manufacturability. Most of these metrics are nonlinear functions of the tunable parameters. Each metric can be presented as either an *objective function* or a *constraint*. The *parameters* of the problem are transistor and wire sizes, and these parameters are usually required to lie within *simple bounds*. Many circuit tuning problems are best stated as *minimax* problems in which the optimizer is required to minimize the maximum of a set of functions. For example, the problem may be stated as minimizing the worst delay across several paths through the logic.

This tutorial paper will address various methods that are used to solve circuit optimization problems. Only continuous optimization problems will be considered in this paper, as opposed to discrete problems (such as choice of gates from a discrete library, reordering of input pins and buffer insertion).

Circuit optimization techniques fall into three broad categories: dynamic tuning (discussed in Section 2), static tuning (Section 3) and statistical tuning (Section 4). Application of state-of-the-art nonlinear optimization methods to circuit tuning is a vast subject in its own right. Section 5 is devoted to some practical considerations in the choice and application of optimization packages. Special topics such as interconnect tuning, optimization of clock distribution networks and noise-aware tuning are briefly mentioned in Section 6. Finally, some promising avenues of future research are enumerated in Section 7.

2 Dynamic tuning

Dynamic tuning[1, 2, 3, 4, 5, 6, 7] implies circuit optimization based on dynamic time-domain simulation of the underlying circuit. The typical flow of a dynamic tuner is shown in Fig. 1. Under the control of the nonlinear optimizer, tunable parameters are set to their initial values and a simulation is performed. The measurements of interest, and the gradients of each measurement with respect to all tunable parameters are fed back to the optimizer. Based on this information, the nonlinear optimization package suggests a new *solution vector*, which is a new assignment of parameter values that is expected to improve the circuit. The iterative process is carried to convergence, or until a user-specified maximum number of iterations is reached. Convergence is typically judged by *sufficient stationarity* combined with *sufficient feasibility*, or a determination of infeasibility. Stationarity implies smallness of the *projected gradient* in the sub-

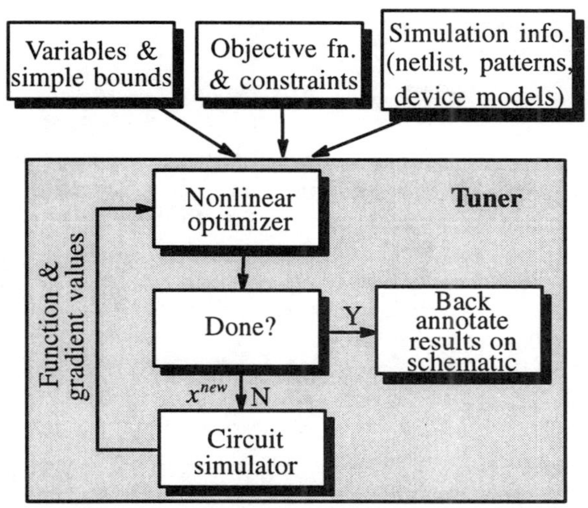

Figure 1: Typical flow of a dynamic tuner.

space of variables that are not at their bounds and feasibility implies that all constraints are satisfied.

The *parameters* in dynamic tuning usually include transistor and wire sizes and they must conform to simple bounds. *Ratio-ing* of transistor widths to one another must be permitted. Further, *grouping* of similar structures is useful to ensure that corresponding transistors of the structures are maintained at the same size during the tuning procedure. For example, a 64-bit multiplexor may have to be tuned so that the corresponding transistors of each group have the same final sizes, thus permitting a regular layout. The *measurements* in dynamic tuning usually include area (often modeled by the sum of the tunable transistor widths), delay and transition time or slew. The objective function and constraints are expressed in terms of these measurements. *Minimax optimization* is a useful feature whereby the worst of a set of measurements is minimized. For example, the problem may be stated as minimizing the worst delay of m paths through the circuit, as shown below.

$$\underset{x \in \Re^n}{\text{minimize}} \quad \underset{i \in \{1, 2, \cdots, m\}}{\text{maximum}} \quad c_i(x). \tag{1}$$

Note that the optimizer has no *a priori* knowledge of which of these paths exhibits the worst delay. Further, different paths may be critical during different iterations of the optimization.

The main advantage of dynamic tuning is its accuracy. The tuning is realistic since it is based on full-blown transient simulation. Likewise, *false paths* are avoided in contrast to static tuning methods. If the transistor sizing at any iteration causes failure of a measured signal to switch correctly, the transient simulation is able to detect this situation. In such a case, a *non-working circuit* has been obtained, usually because of the optimizer taking too aggressive a step. Recovery from this situation is implemented by requiring the optimizer to cut back on its step size and trying again.

However, dynamic tuning suffers from a number of disadvantages. The main disadvantage of dynamic tuning is that it is specific to the input pattern sensitizations and measurements specified. Unlike static tuning, it is not possible to tune any but the smallest circuit for all possible input patterns and all possible paths through the logic. The initial parameter assignments should reflect a working and simulatable circuit in which the logical transitions of interest occur.

As with the use of any optimizer, the solution obtained is only as good as the problem specification. Dynamic tuning is particularly vulnerable to designers omitting tacit requirements and then encountering unexpected results. For example, if the input stage of a circuit is tunable, the optimizer may blow up its size, taking advantage of the fact that in the simulation, this gate is driven by a voltage source! Making the input stage non-tunable or constraining the input capacitance seen by the previous stage will lead to more realistic results. Another insidious problem is that transistors that do not switch during the simulation are shrunk to their minimum size in order to satisfy an area constraint, or to reduce the loading on other transistors that do switch. Yet another example is that the target delay on a net may be met by the optimizer but the transition time may be unacceptable. A disciplined approach to accurately expressing all aspects of the problem at hand is essential to making good use of any optimization program!

Dynamic tuning is most often applied to small dataflow circuits in which the critical paths are well known and the input patterns to sensitize these paths are easy to come by. The relative computational inefficiency of these tools also limits the size of circuit that can be tuned.

2.1 Gradient computation

The bottleneck in dynamic tuning is often the computation of time-domain gradients. Gradients are typically computed by the circuit simulator. There are two well known methods of computing the gradients, the *direct method*[8] and the *adjoint method*[9]. The reader is referred to [10] for a tutorial description of the theory behind these two methods. This section will present a quick overview of these two methods and their applicability to the circuit optimization problem.

The direct method is based on direct differentiation of the branch constitutive relations (BCRs) that govern the electrical behavior of the elements of the circuit. The relations thus derived represent a *sensitivity circuit* of the same topology as the original circuit but with different circuit elements. The solution of this related circuit yields the sensitivity of all measurements with respect to a single parameter. Fortunately, the system matrix of the original and sensitivity circuits are the same at each time instant, and hence the cost of LU factorization can be amortized during the analysis of the sensitivity circuit. Note that the sensitivity circuit must be solved as many times as the number of parameters, which is expensive for large numbers of tunable parameters.

The adjoint method is the method of choice for computing gradients of large circuits. In the circuit context, the adjoint method is best understood as an application of Tellegen's theorem[11]. As in the direct method, an associated circuit called the *adjoint circuit* is formed. The adjoint circuit has the same topology as the nominal circuit, but different electrical elements. Like the direct method, the LU factors of the nominal circuit can be re-used during the adjoint analysis, modulo some time point mismatch issues, as discussed below. Control is reversed and time run backwards during the adjoint analysis. Finally, the waveforms of the original and adjoint circuits are convolved to yield the required sensitivities.

The main advantage of the adjoint method is that it yields the gradients of one function with respect to *all* the parameters in a single adjoint analysis. However, because time is run backwards, the nominal and adjoint analyses cannot be carried out simultaneously. Further, it is not easy to make the time points of the two analyses coincide, leading to a clumsy time point mismatch problem. The convolution of waveforms is an additional source of computational and memory overhead in the adjoint method.

The single function which forms the sensitivity function in the adjoint method can be any scalar differentiable function of any number of circuit measurements[6]. Nonlinear optimizers often build *merit functions* which are internal functions that are iteratively minimized to solve the problem at hand. For example, LANCELOT[12] builds the following merit function Φ.

$$\Phi = f(x) + \sum_{i=1}^{n} \lambda_i c_i(x) + \frac{1}{2\mu} \sum_{i=1}^{n} c_i^2(x), \qquad (2)$$

where $f(x)$ is the objective function, $c(x)$ are n equality constraints, λ are the Lagrange multipliers or dual variables and μ is a penalty parameter that controls the weight of the quadratic augmentation of the Lagrangian.

The gradient of such merit functions can be found in the course of a single adjoint analysis. If the optimizer needs only the gradients of the merit function and not the gradients of individual constraints or objective functions, these gradients can be computed extremely efficiently. Even if individual gradients are desired, to the extent that objective functions and constraints are expressed as differentiable functions of multiple measurements, the adjoint method can be applied to compute the gradients of these individual functions as "adjoint groups."

With either method of computing gradients, *chain ruling and combining* of gradients is essential. When the width of a transistor varies, the associated intrinsic parasitic capacitances as well as the diffusion capacitances on the source and drain vary. The sensitivity of each measurement with respect to these parasitics has to be computed, and then chain ruled and combined to obtain the composite sensitivity with respect to all ramifications of the variation of the parameter of interest.

2.2 Practical implementation

Most dynamic tuners are limited to a few 10s of transistors. DELIGHT.SPICE[1] was one of the early practical implementations of a dynamic circuit optimization capability. The ability to handle *semi-infinite constraints* was implemented in that package (see Section 5.2 for a discussion of semi-infinite constraints). Further, the need for a good user interface was stressed.

It has been shown that gradient computation of large circuits is practical provided a fast circuit simulator[13, 10] with device modeling simplifications is used. In this context, gradient computation can be extremely efficient[14, 15, 16, 10, 5, 6]. Depending on the modeling simplifications used, the associated sensitivity or adjoint circuit can be trivial to solve. In the case of SPECS[13], the associated circuit consists of disconnected capacitors, with impulses of charge transferred between the capacitors at times corresponding to event times in the nominal transient solution. Further, the piecewise nature of the waveforms reduces the cost of otherwise costly convolutions. Expressions can be telescoped to create convolution routines that are significantly faster than general-purpose convolution codes.

Recently, a SPECS-based tuner called JiffyTune[5, 6, 7] was reported to tune a circuit with 6,900 transistors in about 2 hours of CPU time (the circuit had 4,128 tunable transistors, 41 delay constraints, an area objective function and involved 125 cycles of simulation). An intuitive graphical user interface was part of JiffyTune, allowing users to specify the tuning problem by pointing and clicking in a schematic environment. Results of tuning were graphically back-annotated onto the schematic. All details of the tuning problem were stored as attributes of the schematic. So if the circuit had to be re-tuned in any situation (change of technology, change in requirements, re-mapping), the re-tuning could be accomplished at the push of a button. Thus the tuning environment encouraged and facilitated design re-use.

Some remarks about how dynamic tuning fits into the overall design methodology are in order. If dynamic tuning is used on small, full-custom circuits, then the specification of the problem and the layout of the resulting schematic can be performed manually. However, in order to apply dynamic tuning to larger circuits, the difficulty in coming up with input patterns and the concomitant post-tuning layout problem must be addressed. For example, the critical paths as identified at the end of a static tuning (or even a static timing analysis) can be carved out, sensitized and automatically fed to a dynamic tuner. Dynamic tuning is most effective at the schematic level before layout. On an extracted schematic, the correspondence between transistor sizes and associated diffusion capacitances is often lost, making it impossible to obtain electrically accurate gradients. An extractor that produces netlists in which parasitics are parameterized by the size of associated devices would fill this methodology gap which currently prevents post-layout tuning.

3 Static tuning

Static tuning implies circuit optimization based on *static timing analysis*[17]. One of the earliest static tuners was TILOS[18]. In these approaches[19], transistors are usually modeled by equivalent RC circuits. The actual values of the resistances and capacitances are computed during a pre-characterization procedure. The delay of each channel-connected set of transistors is computed using the *Elmore delay model*[20, 21]. Alternatively, delay macromodels are used in [22]. Conventional static timing analysis is used to determine the critical path. The delay of the critical path can then be expressed as a function of the widths of transistors. This expression is a *posynomial function* (a particular algebraic form, see [23]) of transistor widths. The observation is then made that by a simple variable substitution, the posynomial function can be converted to a *convex function*. Thus any local minimum is guaranteed to be a global minimum.

The procedure in TILOS and derivative tools is to start all transistors at their minimum widths, and iteratively bump up the width of the transistor to which the critical path is most sensitive at each step of the algorithm. The procedure is repeated until the lowest critical path delay through the circuit is found. More recently, power optimization has also been proposed in this general framework[24, 25].

The main advantages of static timing analysis are its pattern independence and its speed. Very large circuits can be tuned relatively quickly. All paths are implicitly taken into account because of the underlying static timing basis. The designer is freed of the onus of coming up with input patterns or identifying critical paths. Since many industrial designs are verified by static timing analysis, there are obvious advantages to carrying out static tuning in that same general framework. Further, interconnect delay can easily be modeled and accommodated into this framework.

Unfortunately, static timing analysis has a number of drawbacks. The most serious one is accuracy. Elmore delays do not provide reasonable accuracy in the context of high-performance sub-micron circuits. Thus a gain of 20% or more in performance based on Elmore delay models may not have improved the circuit in reality! Other modeling techniques like "collapsing" each logic gate into an equivalent inverter significantly degrade the accuracy. Unfortunately, the mathematical elegance of mapping the problem into a convex one and the intuitive satisfaction of finding a global minimum are rendered void by the crudeness of the delay approximation. Improving the accuracy of the delay model by, for example, taking into account input waveform shapes, can destroy the posynomial nature of the formulation.

The second major drawback of static tuning is the false path problem. The optimizer may be hard at work tuning false paths through the circuit, and therefore unable to achieve any performance gains in the paths that really matter. But this problem is no more or less serious than the false path problem in static timing analysis, and if the circuit "sign-off" is based on static timing analysis, this activity may be a legitimate one. The third problem with static tuning is the lack of delay models that are functions of transistor sizes. Often, analytic delay models are built up for gates in a library as a function of input slope and output load. These models are quite accurate provided one stays within the "sweet spot," or a reasonable range of input slopes and output loads in which the models are valid. Unfortunately, such models are built by an exhaustive and time-consuming SPICE-based characterization process. These models generally do not exist as a function of transistor widths, thus making them unusable during tuning of transistor sizes. Finally, starting with all transistors set to their minimum size could lead to circuits that may not even have the correct logical transitions. Dynamic tuners, since they are based on a realistic simulation of the circuit, have the advantage of being able to detect such "non-working" circuits and attempting to recover from them.

Static timing analysis in the context of custom circuits is successful only when each *channel-connected component* (or "DC-connected component" or "strongly connected component") is timed using a dynamic simulator of reasonable accuracy under the covers. For tuning purposes, the fast gradient computation methods of Section 2.1 can then be exploited. Unfortunately, there are no credible, gradient-based static tuners built with such timers used for the underlying analysis.

4 Statistical tuning

Yield loss on a fabrication line can be attributed to *catastrophic* and *parametric* (or *circuit-limited*) yield loss. Catastrophic yield loss is due, for example, to dust particles that cause opens or shorts on metal lines. Parametric yield loss, which is discussed in this section, occurs due to inherent manufacturing variations, leading to chips that do not have the required performance characteristics. In *sorted designs* like microprocessor chips, this degradation can mean that insufficient chips end up in the high-performance, high-profit bin. In non-sorted designs (for example, a bus controller chip) circuits below a performance threshold must be thrown away. Across the chip linewidth variations (ACLVs) constitute the single dominant set of parameters that lead to variations in the performance of the circuit. Statistical tuning is the process of changing design parameters to minimize the circuit-limited yield loss.

Aggressive tuning of a circuit often drives it into a corner of the process space, thus causing its yield to suffer. This problem has been studied extensively in the literature and [26] is a good tutorial introduction to the subject. In addition, the books [27, 28] provide a survey of the state-of-the-art and provide extensive pointers to further reading, while [29] is a useful reference on the topic of creating and building statistical models.

The approaches to various aspects of statistical tuning are listed below.

- In *Monte Carlo* analysis, the parametric space is sampled and the design simulated at each sample point. Of course, this method assumes that distributions of the parameters are known. Further, by various *principal component* and *correlation* analyses, the number of independent parameters is reduced so as to limit the dimensionality of the space being sampled and therefore the number of simulations required. The results of the simulation runs can be used to determine both the distribution and worst-case behavior of the circuit.

  Designs are often simulated at multiple *process corners*, which is a simple form of Monte Carlo analysis. It is possible in the context of a dynamic tuner to replicate the nominal objective function(s) and constraints across all process corners, and simultaneously tune at all process corners[6]. Nominal objective functions are transformed into minimax functions across the process corners.

- *Extreme case analysis* is aimed at finding the worst-case behavior of the circuit given a statistical model of the parameter variations. The goal is not to predict the statistical distribution of the performance, but to predict the worst-case. A simple statement of the problem would be, for example, to maximize the delay of a circuit by optimally assigning transistor lengths from a pre-characterized distribution.

- *Yield prediction and optimization* seek to explicitly model the yield characteristics of a circuit as a response surface. Once this is done, the actual parametric yield of a circuit in the face of manufacturing variations can be predicted. Further, based on the yield model, the circuit can be modified to maximize the yield.

- *Design centering* methods do not explicitly compute or model yields. Instead, they take the approach that pushing the circuit deeper into the interior of the feasible region in the space of parameter variations will result in a more robust circuit and therefore higher yields. While design centering methods operate on such a geometric model of the feasible region, method-of-moments-based techniques implicitly attempt to move designs away from regions of low yield to regions of high yield without seeking to explicitly compute the feasible region[30].

Despite much research on the topic of statistical tuning, Monte Carlo and extreme case analyses are the most popular approaches; industrial practice consists predominantly of these two methods. The advantages of these methods that are not shared by the other techniques are that they are easy to understand and in a form that is easily accessible to the design engineer.

5 Optimization methods

5.1 Choice of optimization method

The choice of the optimization method for circuit tuning is crucial. Some introductory comments on this topic are in order. Circuit tuning is a nonlinear problem that cannot be solved by a linear optimizer; no amount of familiarity with linear optimization on the part of the developer can overcome this limitation! From the point of view of mathematical optimization, geometric programming[31] is an old technique whose development predates the considerable advances in the field. Because of its inherent inflexibility it is rarely the most appropriate method and is essentially abandoned by researchers in nonlinear optimization. Our desire to preserve flexibility and solve large tuning problems logically drives us towards the choice of large-scale, general-purpose nonlinear optimization packages.

Circuit tuning is best approached by *gradient-based nonlinear optimization.* In the absence of gradients, large problems cannot be solved and one is typically limited to problems in a few 10s of variables. Worse, there is often no guarantee of convergence or optimality in such "gradient-free" techniques. The efficient computation of gradients and even Hessians (matrix of second partial derivatives) is key to effective optimization of large circuits. Note that gradient-based optimizers attempt to converge to a local feasible and stationary point; there is no guarantee of global optimality.

When tuning is applied to real-life situations, one finds that there is a need for flexibility in the statement of the problem. For combinational logic, we might want to minimize area subject to a delay constraint. For custom, high-performance circuitry, we may want to minimize delay at any cost. For dynamic logic, we may have numerous timing constraints. To handle multiple paths through the logic, minimax optimization is indispensable. Therefore, tuning tools should allow the user to choose the objective function and the constraints depending on the situation at hand. Thus an optimizer that can accommodate general constraints must be chosen.

The good news is that there has been tremendous progress in general-purpose nonlinear optimization methods during the last two decades (see the book [32] for a good introduction to optimization methods; [33, 34, 35] for more advanced discussions and [36] for a practical guide on optimization software; also see the pair of articles [37, 38] for a discussion of unconstrained and constrained optimization methods, respectively; and finally [39, 40] for surveys of the state-of-the-art). Many pioneering attempts at circuit optimization during the late '60s and '70s are now being revisited since we have the optimization methods and computing horsepower to make those approaches practical for the first time.

The two best known large-scale optimizers that fit the bill are MINOS[41] and LANCELOT[12]. Further, by taking advantage of some features of the CUTE testing environment[42], a user can easily benchmark many different nonlinear optimizers by expressing the optimization problem in the SIF language[12]. SIF allows the user to exploit *group partial separability*[12] in the statement of the tuning problem[22], which is particularly advantageous in static tuning. LANCELOT is best at solving highly nonlinear large-scale problems with nonlinear constraints. MINOS is advantageous when the constraints are linear or near-linear and the number of degrees of freedom at the solution is small.

5.2 Application of optimization methods

Nonlinear optimization packages are sophisticated software programs with a wealth of options. One can often reap rich awards by utilizing the available options wisely and by customization of the optimization code to the problem at hand. Hence, these packages must be applied not as black boxes but with care and if possible, with the help of a knowledgeable optimization person.

The circuit analysis carried out at each iteration of the tuning is more CPU intensive than the nonlinear optimization algorithm. Hence, every effort must be made during the optimization procedure to reduce the number of iterations, even at the cost of expensive computations. This situation leads to an interesting and unusual proposition for nonlinear optimization packages, which are usually tailored to analytic problems in which function and gradient evaluations are relatively inexpensive. Analytic problems do not exhibit noise in the data, whereas any simulation-based data is inherently noisy. Most nonlinear optimizers are not tailored to handle noise in the data and must be customized to some extent. The customization may consist of choices of settings or tolerances, or even modification of the algorithms. Great care must be taken in the choice of stopping criteria, tolerances for bound checks, tolerances on step sizes, initial choice of trust-region radius, etc.,[5].

Minimax optimization can be approached in a number of ways. The simplest is to remap the problem from

$$\begin{array}{lll} \text{minimize} & \text{maximum} & c_i(x) \\ x \in \Re^n & i \in \{1, 2, \cdots, m\} & \end{array} \qquad (3)$$

to

$$\begin{array}{ll} \text{minimize} & z \\ x \in \Re^n, z & \\ \text{subject to} & z \geq c_i(x), \quad i \in \{1, 2, \cdots, m\}. \end{array} \qquad (4)$$

The linear variable z is minimized, subject to the constraint that it is larger than each of the constituent $c_i(x)$ constraints; therefore, at optimality, z is as small as possible but larger than all the $c_i(x)$ values. Two "tricks" can be used to make the minimax optimization more effective. The first is to initialize z to the largest of the $c_i(x)$ values after the first function evaluation, thus starting off the problem in a feasible state. The second is to initialize the Lagrange multipliers corresponding to the constraints in (4) above to $1/m$, since the first-order Kuhn-Tucker conditions[34] dictate that the Lagrange multipliers must sum to unity at optimality.

In addition to providing gradients, if at all possible, Hessian (second partial derivative) information must be provided to the optimizer. In the absence of such information, the optimizer usually applies qausi-Newton low rank updates[35] on an initial guess (e.g., scaled unity matrix) of the Hessian, requiring a large number of iterations to build up good curvature information. Providing Hessian data to the optimizer dramatically reduces the number of iterations required to solve optimization problems.

The observation has been made that the optimizer usually introduces variables of its own to remap the problem when necessary. For example, slack variables are commonly introduced to convert inequalities to equality constraints. Further, new linear variables are added to accommodate minimax functions as in (4). These variables are independent of the problem variables, and hence any change in the sub-space of these variables does not require a re-evaluation of the circuit. One can thus consider *two-step updates*[43] or *spacer steps*[44] in this sub-space. Since these slack and pseudo-variables often occur in a known and simple functional form in the merit function of the optimizer, the merit function can be additionally optimized in the sub-space of these variables at each iteration of the optimization, without having to pay any additional circuit analysis cost. This "second step" has been found to improve the overall effectiveness of the optimization.

Two other types of optimization deserve mention. It has been argued that circuit tuning is a *multi-criterion optimization problem*[45] and what the designer really wants is the entire set of *Pareto optimal points*[46]. In practice, however, either repeated "goal-based" single-criterion optimization runs or repeated optimization runs with different weights on the various objective functions suffice to understand the inherent trade-offs involved. Second, the accommodation of *semi-infinite constraints* is a useful feature of any circuit tuner[1]. The statement of a semi-infinite problem is

$$\begin{array}{ll} \text{minimize} & f(x) \\ x \in \Re^n & \\ \text{subject to} & g(x,p) \leq 0 \quad \text{for all} \quad p^u \leq p \leq p^l. \end{array} \qquad (5)$$

For example, the user may want to minimize area (f in (5) above), subject to the delay through the circuit (g) being less than a certain target, for *any* power supply value (the semi-infinite parameter p) in a certain range. Unfortunately, methods for multi-criteria optimization and accommodation of semi-infinite constraints (especially when multi-dimensional) make a tuner less efficient and much more complicated. These enhancements are not used in practice.

6 Special topics

6.1 Interconnect tuning

Performance optimization of interconnect is the subject of a separate paper by J. Cong et al in these proceedings, and so will be mentioned only briefly here. A survey of interconnect optimization methods can be found in [47]. With finer metal lines, a higher fraction of the total delay is due to on-chip interconnect, and hence more attention needs to be paid to this part of the design. Simultaneous tuning of gates and interconnect[48, 49, 6] has been shown to yield superior results to tuning just the interconnect or just the drivers. Further, reduced order modeling of interconnect[50, 51, 52] has allowed the analysis of large interconnect networks in a computationally efficient manner. The availability of sensitivities[53] makes these macromodels attractive from a tuning perspective.

In practice, local nets and short global nets are usually sized to have the minimum allowed width. Long global nets are either made wider, or the delay improved by the manual insertion of buffers or repeaters. Interconnect tuners work best when they are tightly coupled to the floorplanner and layout data. Recently, many approaches to wire sizing, buffer placement and topology changes have appeared in the literature[47]. The challenge for the future is a holistic solution that combines all three approaches. Special considerations are in order for the design of power distribution[54] and clock distribution networks. In the case of clock distribution networks, the design is usually carried out in two phases[55]. First the topology of the clock network is determined. Then the buffers are placed and wires sized so as to both minimize the skew to the target points and reduce sensitivity to process variations. Transmission line effects may be important during this procedure[56].

6.2 Noise-aware tuning

Signal integrity and noise analysis are increasingly important and challenging aspects of high-speed digital design. Noise checking is usually carried out on a static basis in the same framework as static timing analysis[57]. However, noise-aware tuning can be applied to both static and dynamic methods. In the simplest case, additional noise constraints can be added to the tuner. These constraints can be derived from rules of thumb related to noise considerations, or from detailed analysis. The rules of thumb may take a simple form such as ratio-ing of device sizes. More formally, stability criteria[57] can be added to the tuning procedure as additional constraints.

There is usually a direct trade-off between noise immunity and performance. For example, the half-latch in a dynamic gate can be sized for aggressive performance, but there is a concomitant loss in noise margin. In digital circuits, channel lengths are usually not tuned; they are left at their minimum allowed size. However, in the context of the tradeoff between noise and performance, one could consider tuning device lengths. Tuning of device lengths can therefore play a significant role in noise-aware tuning (and, in fact, in statistical tuning since length variations are the primary cause of circuit-limited yield).

7 Avenues of future research

Tuning of circuits on a static-timing basis is one of the most challenging problems faced today. Maintaining sufficient timing accuracy while tuning large problems in the presence of arbitrary timing constraints is a difficult problem. Noise-aware tuning will gain prominence as more formal noise analysis methods are developed. Computation of Hessians of circuits will go a long way in making tuning more efficient. Further into the future, the solution of mixed continuous/integer problems will enable designers to optimize continuous variables simultaneously with discrete ones. Design centering and yield optimization require further work before they can enter the mainstream IC design process. For the brave, multi-criteria optimization and accommodation of semi-infinite constraints pose a long series of challenges.

8 Acknowledgments

The author owes a debt of gratitude to Andy Conn for generously sharing his deep knowledge of and long experience with nonlinear optimization. Ruud Haring was a partner in the author's circuit tuning efforts from the beginning and ensured that the tools developed were in line with designers' needs. Special appreciation is due to Sani Nassif for help with the "Statistical tuning" section, to Phillip Restle for his assistance on clock and interconnect tuning, and to Ken Shepard for help with the "Noise-aware tuning" section. The author would like to thank Prabhakar Kudva and Phillip Restle for suggestions on the manuscript. Finally, the author is grateful to the members of the JiffyTune and EinsTuner projects: Phil Strenski, Chai Wah Wu, Bill Wright, Nam Nguyen, Abe Elfadel, David Ling, Paula Coulman, Greg Morrill, Indraneel Das, Katya Scheinberg, Peter O'Brien, Jeff Soreff and Walt Molzen.

References

[1] W. Nye, D. C. Riley, A. Sangiovanni-Vincentelli, and A. L. Tits. DELIGHT.SPICE: An optimization-based system for the design of integrated circuits. *IEEE Transactions on Computer-Aided Design of ICs and Systems*, CAD-7(4):501–519, April 1988.

[2] R. K. Brayton and R. Spence. *Sensitivity and optimization*, volume 2 of *CAD of Electronic Circuits*. Elsevier Scientific Publishing Co., Amsterdam, The Netherlands, 1980.

[3] R. K. Brayton, G. D. Hachtel, and A. L. Sangiovanni-Vincentelli. A survey of optimization techniques for integrated-circuit design. *Proceedings of the IEEE*, 69(10):1334–1362, October 1981.

[4] J.-M. Shyu and A. Sangiovanni-Vincentelli. ECSTASY: a new environment for IC design optimization. *IEEE International Conference on Computer-Aided Design*, pages 484–487, November 1988.

[5] A. R. Conn, P. K. Coulman, R. A. Haring, G. L. Morrill, and C. Visweswariah. Optimization of custom MOS circuits by transistor sizing. *IEEE International Conference on Computer-Aided Design*, pages 174–180, November 1996.

[6] A. R. Conn, R. A. Haring, C. Visweswariah, and C. W. Wu. Circuit optimization via adjoint lagrangians. *IEEE International Conference on Computer-Aided Design*, November 1997.

[7] A. R. Conn, P. K. Coulman, R. A. Haring, G. L. Morrill, C. Visweswariah, and C. W. Wu. Jiffytune: circuit optimization using time-domain sensitivities. *IEEE Transactions on Computer-Aided Design of ICs and Systems*, 1997. Submitted for publication.

[8] D. A. Hocevar, P. Yang, T. N. Trick, and B. D. Epler. Transient sensitivity computation for MOSFET circuits. *IEEE Transactions on Computer-Aided Design of ICs and Systems*, CAD-4(4):609–620, October 1985.

[9] S. W. Director and R. A. Rohrer. The generalized adjoint network and network sensitivities. *IEEE Transactions on Circuit Theory*, CT-16(3):318–323, August 1969.

[10] L. T. Pillage, R. A. Rohrer, and C. Visweswariah. *Electronic circuit and system simulation methods*. McGraw-Hill, 1995.

[11] B. D. H. Tellegen. A general network theorem, with applications. *Philips Research Reports*, 7:259–269, 1952.

[12] A. R. Conn, N. I. M. Gould, and Ph. L. Toint. *LANCELOT: A Fortran Package for Large-Scale Nonlinear Optimization (Release A)*. Springer Verlag, 1992.

[13] C. Visweswariah and R. A. Rohrer. Piecewise approximate circuit simulation. *IEEE Transactions on Computer-Aided Design of ICs and Systems*, 10(7):861–870, July 1991.

[14] P. Feldmann, T. V. Nguyen, S. W. Director, and R. A. Rohrer. Sensitivity computation in piecewise approximate circuit simulation. *IEEE Transactions on Computer-Aided Design of ICs and Systems*, 10(2):171–183, February 1991.

[15] T. V. Nguyen, P. Feldmann, S. W. Director, and R. A. Rohrer. SPECS simulation validation with efficient transient sensitivity computation. *IEEE International Conference on Computer-Aided Design*, pages 252–255, November 1989.

[16] T. V. Nguyen. Transient sensitivity computation and applications. Technical Report CMUCAD-91-40, Carnegie Mellon University, Pittsburgh, PA, 1991.

[17] R. B. Hitchcock, Sr., G. L. Smith, and D. D. Cheng. Timing analysis of computer hardware. *IBM Journal of Research and Development*, pages 100–105, January 1982.

[18] J. P. Fishburn and A. E. Dunlop. TILOS: A posynomial programming approach to transistor sizing. *IEEE International Conference on Computer-Aided Design*, pages 326–328, November 1985.

[19] S. S. Sapatnekar, V. B. Rao, P. M. Vaidya, and S. M. Kang. An exact solution to the transistor sizing problem for cmos circuits using convex optimization. *IEEE Transactions on Computer-Aided Design of ICs and Systems*, CAD-12(11):1621–1634, November 1993.

[20] W. C. Elmore. The transient analysis of damped linear networks with particular regard to wideband amplifiers. *Journal of Applied Physics*, 19(1):55–63, 1948.

[21] P. Penfield and J. Rubinstein. Signal delay in rc tree networks. In *Proceedings of the 2nd Caltech VLSI Conference*, pages 269–283, March 1981.

[22] M. D. Matson and L. A. Glasser. Macromodeling and optimization of digital MOS VLSI circuits. *IEEE Transactions on Computer-Aided Design of ICs and Systems*, CAD-5(4):659–678, October 1986.

[23] R. J. Duffin, E. L. Peterson, and C. Zener. *Geometric programming - theory and applications*. John Wiley and Sons, New York, 1967.

[24] S. S. Sapatnekar and W. Chuang. Power vs. delay in gate sizing: conflicting objectives? *IEEE International Conference on Computer-Aided Design*, pages 463–466, November 1995.

[25] P. K. Sancheti and S. S. Sapatnekar. Optimal design of macrocells for low power and high speed. *IEEE Transactions on Computer-Aided Design of ICs and Systems*, CAD-15(9):1160–1166, September 1996.

[26] R. Spence and R. S. Soin. *Tolerance design of electronic circuits*. Addison-Wesley Publishing Company, 1988.

[27] J. C. Zhang and M. A. Styblinski. *Yield variablity optimization of integrated circuits*. Kluwer Academic Publishers, 1995.

[28] S. W. Director and W. Maly, editors. *Statistical approach to VLSI*, volume 8 of *Advances in CAD for VLSI*. North-Holland, 1994.

[29] C. Michael and M. Ismail. *Statistical modeling for computer-aided design of MOS VLSI circuits*. Kluwer Academic Publishers, 1993.

[30] G. Kjellstrom and L. Taxen. Stochastic optimization in system design. *IEEE Transactions on Circuits and Systems*, July 1981.

[31] J. G. Ecker. Geometric programming: methods, computations and applications. *SIAM review*, 22(3):338–362, July 1980.

[32] S. G. Nash and A. Sofer. *Linear and nonlinear programming*. McGraw-Hill, 1996.

[33] J. E. Dennis, Jr. and R. B. Schnabel. *Numerical methods for unconstrained optimization and nonlinear equations*. Society for Industrial and Applied Mathematics, Philadelphia, 1996.

[34] R. Fletcher. *Practical methods of optimization*. John Wiley and Sons, Chichester, second edition, 1987.

[35] P. E. Gill, W. Murray, and M. H. Wright. *Practical optimization*. Academic Press, London and New York, 1981.

[36] J. J. Moré and S. J. Wright. *Optimization software guide*. Society for Industrial and Applied Mathematics, Philadelphia, 1993.

[37] J. E. Dennis, Jr. and R. B. Schnabel. Unconstrained optimization. In G. L. Nemhauser, A. H. G. Rinnooy Kan, and M. J. Todd, editors, *Optimization*, volume 1 of *Handbooks in operations research and management science*, pages 73–170. North-Holland, Amsterdam, The Netherlands, 1989.

[38] P. E. Gill and W. Murray. Constrained optimization. In G. L. Nemhauser, A. H. G. Rinnooy Kan, and M. J. Todd, editors, *Optimization*, volume 1 of *Handbooks in operations research and management science*, pages 73–170. North-Holland, Amsterdam, The Netherlands, 1989.

[39] A. R. Conn, Nick Gould, and Ph. L. Toint. Algorithms for large-scale constrained nonlinear optimization: a current survey. In E. Spedicato, editor, *Algorithms for continuous optimization: the state of the art*, pages 287–332, Dordrecht, The Netherlands, 1994. Kluwer Academic Publishers. Volume 434 of *NATO ASI Series C: Mathematical and Physical Sciences*.

[40] A. R. Conn, N. I. M. Gould, and Ph. L. Toint. Methods for nonlinear constraints in optimization calculations. In I. S. Duff and G. A. Watson, editors, *The state of the art in numerical analysis*, pages 363–390. Oxford University Press, 1997.

[41] B. A. Murtagh and M.A. Saunders. MINOS 5.1 user's guide. Technical Report SOL 83-20R, Stanford University, Stanford, CA, December 1983. revised January 1987.

[42] I. Bongartz, A. R. Conn, N. I. M. Gould, and Ph. L. Toint. CUTE: constrained and unconstrained testing environment. *ACM Transactions on Mathematical Software*, 21(1):123–160, March 1995.

[43] A. R. Conn, L. N. Vicente, and C. Visweswariah. Two-step algorithms for nonlinear optimization with structured applications. Research Report (in preparation), IBM T. J. Watson Research Center, Yorktown Heights, NY 10598, USA, 1997.

[44] D. P. Bertsekas. *Constrained Optimization and Lagrange Multipliers Methods*. Academic Press, London, 1982.

[45] M. R. Lightner and S. W. Director. Multiple criterion optimization for the design of electronic circuits. *IEEE Transactions on Circuits and Systems*, CAS-28(2):169–179, March 1981.

[46] P. L. Yu. Multiple criteria decision making: five basic concepts. In G. L. Nemhauser, A. H. G. Rinnooy Kan, and M. J. Todd, editors, *Optimization*, volume 1 of *Handbooks in operations research and management science*, pages 663–699. North-Holland, Amsterdam, The Netherlands, 1989.

[47] J. Cong, L. He, C-K. Koh, and P. H. Madden. Performance optimization of VLSI interconnect layout. *Integration*, 21:1–94, January 1996.

[48] J. J. Cong and C.-K. Koh. Simultaneous driver and wire sizing for performance and power optimization. *IEEE Transactions on VLSI Systems*, 2(4):408–425, December 1994.

[49] N. Menezes, R. Baldick, and L. T. Pileggi. A sequential quadratic programming approach to concurrent gate and wire sizing. *IEEE International Conference on Computer-Aided Design*, pages 144–151, November 1995.

[50] L. T. Pillage and R. A. Rohrer. Asymptotic waveform evaluation for timing analysis. *IEEE Transactions on Computer-Aided Design of ICs and Systems*, 9:352–366, April 1990.

[51] P. Feldmann and R. W. Freund. Efficient linear circuit analysis by Padé approximation via the Lanczos process. *IEEE Transactions on Computer-Aided Design of ICs and Systems*, 14(5):639–649, May 1995.

[52] L. M. Silveira, M. Kamon, I. Elfadel, and J. White. A coordinate-transformed Arnoldi algorithm for generating guaranteed stable reduced-order models of RLC circuits. *IEEE International Conference on Computer-Aided Design*, pages 288–294, November 1996.

[53] R. W. Freund and P. Feldmann. Efficient small-signal circuit analysis and sensitivity computations with the PVL algorithm. *IEEE International Conference on Computer-Aided Design*, pages 404–411, November 1994.

[54] H. H. Chen and D. D. Ling. Power supply noise analysis methodology for deep-submicron VLSI chip design. *Proc. 1997 Design Automation Conference*, pages 638–643, June 1997.

[55] E. G. Friedman (Editor). *Clock distribution networks in VLSI circuits and systems*. IEEE Press, 1995.

[56] P. J. Restle, K. A. Jenkins, A. Deutsch, and P. W. Cook. Measurement and analysis of on-chip transmission line effects in a 400mhz microprocessor. *IEEE Journal of Solid State Circuits*, 1997. To be published.

[57] K. L. Shepard and V. Narayanan. Noise in deep submicron digital design. *IEEE International Conference on Computer-Aided Design*, pages 524–531, November 1996.

SESSION 5A

SEQUENTIAL CIRCUIT OPTIMIZATION

Moderators:

Marios Papaefthymiou, University of Michigan,

Ann Arbor, MI

Narendra V. Shenoy, Synopsys, Inc.,

Mountain View, CA

Sequential Optimisation without State Space Exploration

A Mehrotra* S Qadeer* V Singhal† R K Brayton* A Aziz‡ A L Sangiovanni-Vincentelli*

Abstract

We propose an algorithm for area optimisation of sequential circuits through redundancy removal. The algorithm finds *compatible* redundancies by implying values over nets in the circuit. The potentially exponential cost of state space traversal is avoided and the redundancies found can all be removed at once. The optimised circuit is a safe delayed replacement of the original circuit. The algorithm computes a set of compatible sequential redundancies and simplifies the circuit by propagating them through the circuit. We demonstrate the efficacy of the algorithm even for large circuits through experimental results on benchmark circuits.

1 Introduction

Sequential optimisation seeks to replace a given sequential circuit with another one optimised with respect to some criterion – area, performance or power, in a way such that the environment of the circuit cannot detect the replacement. In this work, we deal with the problem of optimising sequential circuits for area. We present an algorithm which computes sequential redundancies in the circuit by propagating implications over its nets. The redundancies we compute are compatible in the sense that they form a set that can be removed simultaneously. Our algorithm works for large circuits and scales better than those algorithms that depend on state space exploration.

The starting point of our work is [1], in which a method was described to identify sequential redundancies without exploring the state space. The basic algorithm is that for any net, two cases are considered: the net value is 0 and the net value is 1. For each case, constants as well as unobservability conditions are learnt on other nets. If some other net is either set to the same constant for both cases, or to a constant in one case and is unobservable in the other, it is identified as redundant. For example, consider the trivial circuit shown in Figure 1. For the value $n1 = 0$ the net $n2$ is unobservable and for the value $n1 = 1$, the net $n2$ is 1. Thus net $n2$ is stuck-at-1 redundant. However, the redundancies found by the method in [1] are not compatible in the sense that they remain redundant even in the

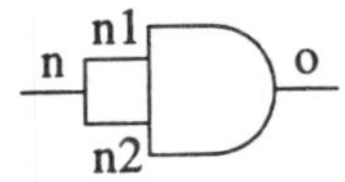

Figure 1: Example of incompatible redundancies

presence of each other. For instance, the redundancy identification algorithm will declare both the inputs n_1 and n_2 as stuck-at-1 redundant. However, for logic optimisation, it is incorrect to replace *both* the nets by a constant 1.

The straightforward application of Iyer's method to redundancy removal is to identify one redundancy by their implication procedure, remove the redundancy and iterate until convergence. Our goal is to learn all *compatible* implications in the circuit in one step and use the compatibility of these implications to remove all the redundancies simultaneously (in this sense our method for finding compatible unobservabilities is related to the work in [2, 3] for computing compatible ODC's (observability don't cares)). This is our first contribution. Secondly, we generalise the implication procedure by combining it with recursive learning [4] to enhance the capability of the redundancy identification procedure. Recursive learning lets us perform case split on unjustified gates so that it is possible to learn more implications at the expense of computation time. Consider the circuit in Figure 2. Setting net a to 0 implies that net f is 0. If we set a to 1, $a1$ becomes 1, but the AND-gate connected to $a1$ remains unjustified. If we perform recursive learning for the two justifications: $d = 0$ and $d = 1$, then for the former case, net f becomes 0, and for the latter case, f becomes unobservable because e is 1. Thus, for all the possible cases, either f is 0 or it is unobservable. Hence f is declared stuck-at-0 redundant. Recursive learning helps identify these kinds of new redundancies. We present data which shows that we are able to gain significant optimisations on large benchmark circuits using these two new improvements. In fact, for some circuits, we find that recursive learning not only gives us more optimisation, it is even faster since a previous recursive learning step makes the circuit simpler for a later stage.

We do not assume designated initial states for circuits. For sequential optimisation, we use the notion of c-delay replacement [1, 5]. This notion guarantees that every possible input-output behaviour that can be observed in the new circuit after it has been clocked for c cycles after power-up, must have been present in the old circuit. In contrast to the work in [5, 6], the synthesis method presented here does not require state space

*University of California at Berkeley, Berkeley, CA 94720
†Cadence Berkeley Labs, Berkeley, CA 94704
‡University of Texas at Austin, Austin, TX 78712

1092-3152/97 $10.00 © 1997 IEEE

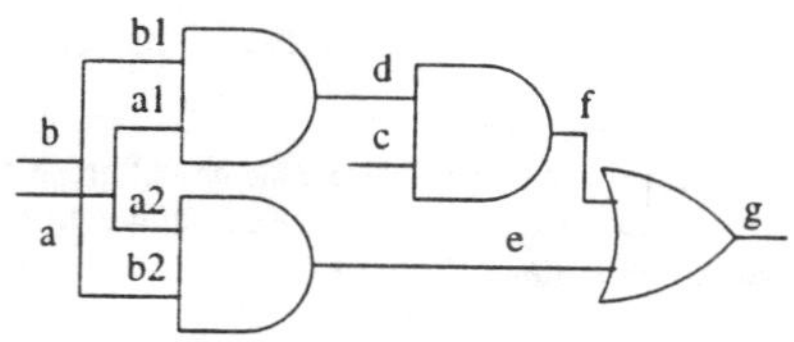

Figure 2: Example of recursive learning

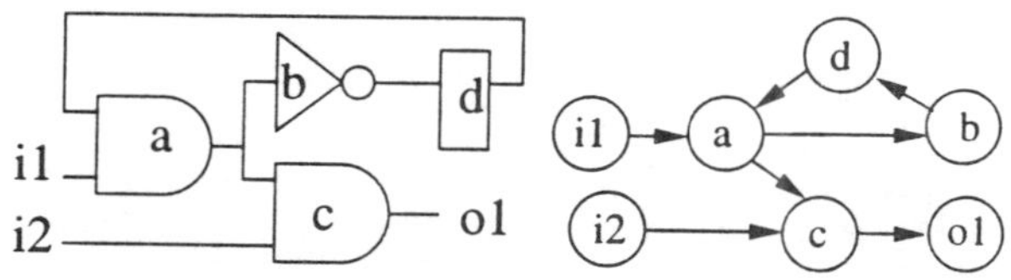

Figure 3: A circuit and its graph

traversal, and can therefore be applied to large sequential circuits. Recursive learning has been used earlier for optimisation, as described in [7], but their method is applied only to combinational circuits and they do not use unobservability conditions. Another procedure to do redundancy removal is described in [8], but as [9] shows, their notion of replacement is not compositional and may also identify redundancies which destroy the initialisability of the circuit. We have therefore chosen to use the notion of safe delayed replacement which preserves responses to all initialising sequences. We are interested in compositionality because we would like a notion of replacement that is valid without making any assumptions about the environment of the circuit. This is why our replacement notion is safer than that used in [10] which identifies sequential redundancies by preserving weak synchronising sequences. Their work implicitly assumes that the environment of the circuit has total control so that it can supply the arbitrary sequence that the redundancy identification tool has in mind. Our approach does not pose any such restrictions.

The rest of the paper is organised as follows. In Section 2, we present our algorithm to compute compatible redundancies on combinational and sequential circuits. In Section 3, we present experimental results on some large circuits from the ISCAS benchmark set. In Section 4, we conclude with some directions for future work.

2 Redundancy Removal

We present an algorithm for sequential circuits that have been mapped using edge-triggered latches, inverters and 2-input gates; note that any combinational implementation can be mapped to a circuit containing only inverters and 2-input gates. We use the notion of circuit graph for explaining our algorithm. A *circuit graph* is a labelled directed graph whose vertices correspond to primary inputs, primary outputs, logic gates and latches, and edges correspond to wires between the elements of the circuit. The label of a vertex identifies the type of element it represents (e.g. two-input gates, inverters or latches). We refer to an edge in the circuit graph as a *net*. Figure 3 shows an example of a circuit graph.

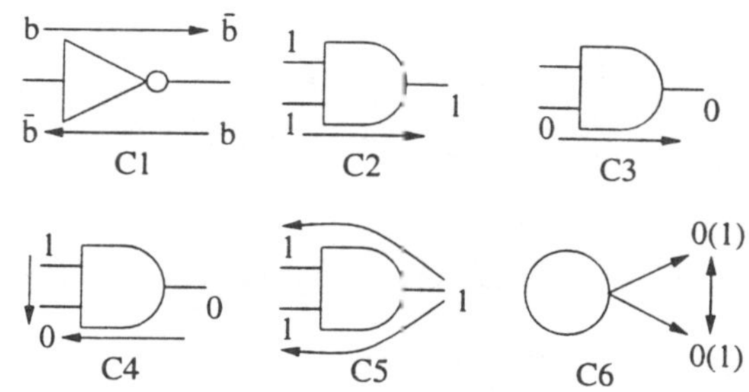

Figure 4: Rules for implying constants

2.1 Combinational redundancies

We explain our algorithm and prove its correctness for combinational circuits and later extend it to sequential circuits. Consider a circuit graph $\mathcal{G} = (V,E)$ of a circuit, where V is the set of vertices and E is the set of nets. An *assumption* A on the subset $P \subseteq E$ is a labelling of the nets in P by values from the set $\{0,1\}$. Let $n \in P$ be a net. We write $A : n \mapsto v$ if A labels the net n with the value v. An assumption is denoted by an ordered tuple. The set of all possible assumptions on the set P of nets is denoted by $\mathcal{A}_P$. Consider the set $P = \{m,n\}$. The assumption labelling m with 0 and n with 1 is denoted by $\langle m \mapsto 0, n \mapsto 1\rangle$ and $\mathcal{A}_P = \{\langle m \mapsto 0, n \mapsto 0\rangle, \langle m \mapsto 0, n \mapsto 1\rangle, \langle m \mapsto 1, n \mapsto 0\rangle, \langle m \mapsto 1, n \mapsto 1\rangle\}$. An assumption $A \in \mathcal{A}_P$ is *inconsistent* if it is not satisfiable for any assignments to the primary inputs of the circuits. For instance, an assumption of 0 at the input and 1 at the output of an AND gate is inconsistent.

In the algorithm, values are implied at nets in $E \setminus P$ from an assumption on P. We imply either constants or *unobservability* indicators at nets. We indicate unobservability at a net by implying a symbolic value $\otimes$ at it. Let $R = \{0,1,\otimes\}$ be the set of all possible value that can be implied at any net. An *implication* is a label $(n_i = r)$ where n_i is a net and $r \in R$. Figure 4 illustrates the rules for implying constants. Rules C1, C2, C3 and C5 are self-explanatory. Rule C4 states that for an AND gate, 0 at the output and 1 at an input implies 0 at the other input. Rule C6 states that a constant at some fanout net of a gate implies the same constant at all other fanout nets. Figure 5 illustrates the rules for implying $\otimes$'s. Rule O1 states that 0 at an input of an AND gate implies a $\otimes$ at the other input. Rule O2 states that a $\otimes$ at every fanout net of a gate implies a $\otimes$ at every fanin net of that gate. Note that constants can be implied in both directions across a gate while $\otimes$ propagates only backwards. We have shown rules only for inverters and AND gates but similar rules can be easily formulated for other gates as well. We use these rules to label the edges of the circuit graph. A constant (0 or 1) label on a net indicates that

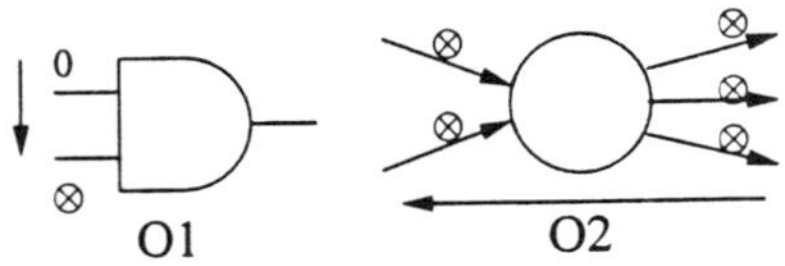

Figure 5: Rules for implying unobservability

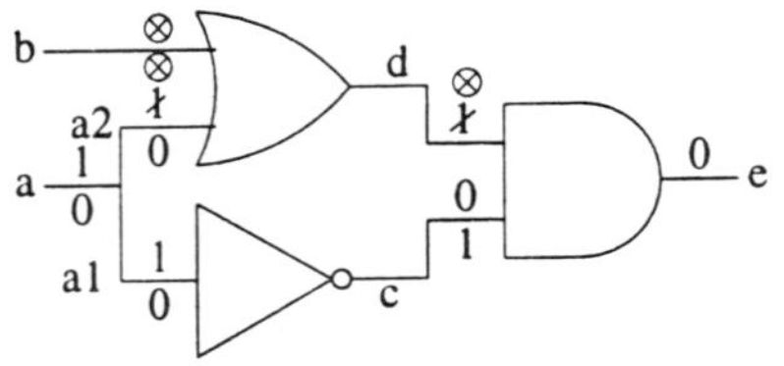

Figure 6: Overwriting constants with unobservability indicators

the net assumes the respective constant value under the current assumption. A ⊗ label indicates that the net is not observable at any primary output. Hence, it can be freely assigned to either 0 or 1 under the current assumption. Suppose for every assumption in $\mathcal{A}_P$, some net n is labelled either with constant v or with ⊗, then we can safely replace n with constant v. This is because we have shown that under every possible assumption, either the net takes the value v or its value does not affect the output. We can therefore conclude that net n is *stuck-at-v* redundant.

We are concerned about the compatibility of all labellings because otherwise we run the danger of marking nets with labels so that all labels are not consistent. For example, consider the circuit in Figure 1. For the purpose of identifying redundancies, [1] would infer the implications $(n1 = 1)$ and $(n2 = 1)$ from the assumption $\langle n \mapsto 1\rangle$. Additionally, the assumption $\langle n \mapsto 0\rangle$ implies that $(n1 = 0)$ and $(n2 = *)$; similarly $\langle n \mapsto 0\rangle$ implies that $(n2 = 0)$ and $(n1 = *)$ (notice that [1] use the symbol $*$ to denote unobservability while we use ⊗ to denote *compatible* unobservability). So, [1] would rightly claim that both $n1$ and $n2$ are *stuck-at-1* redundant in isolation; however, for redundancy removal it is easy to see that we cannot set both $n1$ and $n2$ to 1 simultaneously. This is why we want to make all labellings compatible.

A sufficient condition for the redundancies to be compatible is to ensure that the procedure for computing implications from an assumption returns *compatible* implications, i.e., every implication is valid in the presence of all other implications. It is easy to see that if the labelling of edges in the circuit graph is done by invoking the rules described above and no label is ever overwritten, then the set of learnt implications will be compatible. For instance, in the circuit of Figure 1, once $n1$ is labelled with ⊗, a ⊗ cannot be inferred at $n2$ because $(n1 = \otimes)$ cannot be overwritten with $(n1 = 0)$. But this approach is conservative and will miss some redundancies. In Figure 6, we show an example where overwriting a constant with a ⊗ yields a redundancy which could not have been found otherwise. We

```
redundancy_remove (G = (V,E))
/* find and remove redundancies from the circuit graph */
while (there is an unvisited net n in the circuit graph) {
   S := learn_implications (G, ⟨n ↦ 1⟩)
   T := {(l = v) | (l = v) ∈ S ∨ (l = ⊗) ∈ S}
   S̄ := learn_implications (G, ⟨n ↦ 0⟩)
   T̄ := {(l = v) | (l = v) ∈ S̄ ∨ (l = ⊗) ∈ S̄}
   R := T ∧ T̄
   for every implication (n = v) ∈ R set net n to constant v
   propagate constants and simplify
}

learn_implications (G = (V,E),A)
/* propagate implications on the circuit graph given an assignment */
{
   forall n such that A : n ↦ v {
      label n ← v
   }
   while (some rule can be invoked) {
      let (n = b) be the new implication
      if (b = ⊗)
         label n ← b
      if ((n = b) conflicts with a current label)
         return {l = * | l ∈ E}
      else
         label n ← b
   }
   return set of all current labels
}
```

Figure 7: Combinational redundancy removal algorithm

propagate implications from assumptions on the net a. The implications from $\langle a \mapsto 0\rangle$ are written below and those from $\langle a \mapsto 1\rangle$ are written above the wires. Note that while propagating implications from $\langle a \mapsto 1\rangle$, $a2$ and d are initially labelled with 1 but after labelling c with 0, the labels at d and $a2$ are successively overwritten with ⊗'s. Hence, $a2$ is found to be *stuck-at-0* redundant. As a result, the OR gate can be removed. We prove later in this section that this overwriting does not make previously learnt implications invalid, i.e., compatibility of implications is maintained, if the only overwriting that is allowed is that of constants with unobservability indicators.

Our algorithm for removing combinational redundancies is given in Figure 7. The function *learn_implications* takes as input an assumption A on an arbitrary subset of nets and labels nets with values from $\{0, 1, \otimes\}$ learnt through implications. Initially all nets n such that $A : n \mapsto v$ is an assumption, are labelled. Then we derive new labels by invoking the rules C1-C6 and O1-O2 and similar rules for other kinds of two input gates. Note that at all times each net has a unique label and constants can be overwritten with ⊗'s but not vice-versa. It returns the set of all final labels. The function *redundancy_remove* takes as input a circuit graph $\mathcal{G}$ and calls *learn_implications* successively with assumptions $\langle n_i \mapsto 0\rangle$ and $\langle n_i \mapsto 1\rangle$ on the singleton subset $\{n_i\}$. The two sets of labels are used to compute all pairs n and v such that n is *stuck-at-v* redundant. We later show that our labelling procedure for learning implica-

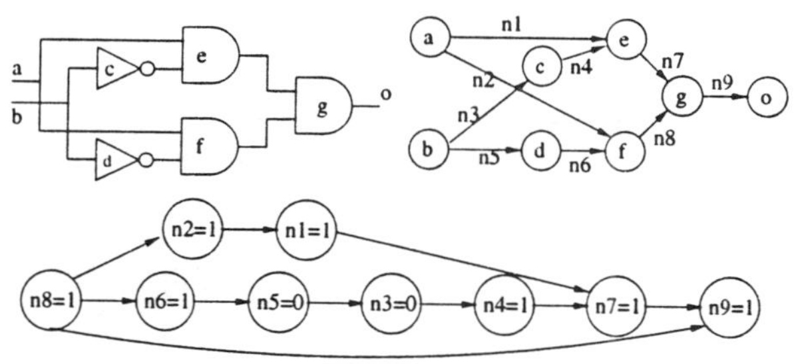

Figure 8: An implication graph

tions guarantees that all such redundancies can be removed simultaneously. These redundancies are used to simplify the network. The process is repeated until all nets have been considered. Note that the function *redundancy_remove* considers assumptions on only a single net but in general any number of nets could be used to generate assumptions. We later show results for the case when we considered assumptions on two nets, the second one corresponding to the unjustified node closest to n_i. This is an instance of recursive learning.

We now formalise the notion of a valid label as one for which an *implication graph* exists. We will use the notion of implication graph for proving the compatibility of the set of labels generated by the algorithm. Let A be an assumption on a set P of nets. An *implication graph* for the label $(n = r)$ from assumption A is a directed acyclic graph $G_I = (V_I, E_I, L_I)$, where L_I is a set of labels of the form $(m = a)$ for some net m and some $a \in \{0, 1, \otimes\}$ labelling every vertex $v \in V_I$, such that

- Every root [1] vertex is labelled with $(m = a)$ where $A : m \mapsto a$
- There is exactly one leaf [2] vertex $v \in V_I$ which is labelled $(n = r)$
- For any vertex $v \in V_I$, if v is not a root node the implication labelling it can be obtained from the implications labelling its parents by invoking an inference rule.

An example of an implication graph for the label $(n9 = 1)$ from the assumption $\langle n8 \mapsto 1 \rangle$ is shown in Figure 8. A set of labels C derived from an assumption A is *compatible* if for every label $C \in C$ there exists an implication graph $G_C = (V_C, E_C, L_C)$ of C from A such that $L_C \subseteq C$.

We now prove the compatibility of implications returned by our labelling procedure. At each step, the labelling procedure either labels a node for the first time or overwrites a constant with a $\otimes$. We prove the invariant that at any time, the current set of implications C is compatible. We must prove that if a label is overwritten with a new label, every other label must have an implication graph which does not depend on the overwritten label. This claim is proved in the following lemma and is needed for all current labels to be simultaneously valid. Note that overwriting a 0 with a 1 (or vice-versa) implies an inconsistent assumption and the procedure exits.

[1] A vertex with no incoming edges

[2] A vertex with no outgoing edges

Lemma 2.1 *Let A be a consistent assumption. If a label $(m = a)$ is overwritten by the label $(m = \otimes)$ in the current set of labels, then for all labels $(n_j = b_j)$, there is an implication graph such that $(m = a)$ is not a label of any vertex in the graph.*

Proof: We call net m a parent of net n if there is a node v of the circuit graph such that m is an incoming arc and n an outgoing arc of v. We also say that n is a child of m. We say m is a sibling of n if there is a node v such that both m and n are outgoing edges of v.

We prove the claim by contradiction. Suppose it is false. Let the replacement of $(m = a)$ by $(m = \otimes)$ be the first instance that makes it false. Therefore, there was an implication graph for each current implication before this happened. Let $(n_j = b_j)$ be an implication that does not have a valid implication graph now. Consider any path in the old implication graph for a net n_j, $(n_1 = b_1) \to \cdots \to (n_j = b_j)$, such that $(m = a)$ is the ith implication on the path. We consider the case where b_j is a constant. Hence, all b_k's in the path are constants since a $\otimes$ at a net can only imply a $\otimes$ at another. The case in which $b_k = \otimes$ is considered later. We show that if the assumption A is consistent then it is possible to replace $n_i = b_i$ in the implication graph for n_j. There are three cases on the relation between n_{i-1} and n_i.

Case 1: The circuit edge n_{i-1} is a child of n_i. $\otimes$ can be inferred at n_i only if either $n_{i-1} = \otimes$ is a current implication or $n_{i'} = 0$ is a current implication and $n_{i'}$ and n_i are inputs to an AND gate. In the first case, the fact that an implication graph existed in which n_{i-1} was labelled with a constant is contradicted. In the second case, n_{i-1} is the output of an AND gate, whose two inputs are n_i and $n_{i'}$. Since $(n_{i-1} = b_{i-1}) \to (n_i = b_i)$ is a valid inference, either $n_{i-1} = 1$ (to imply $n_i = 1$ and $n_{i'} = 1$) or $n_{i-1} = 0$ and $n_{i'} = 1$ (to imply $n_i = 0$). In either case $n_{i'} = 1$ which contradicts $n_{i'} = 0$.

Case 2: n_{i-1} and n_i are siblings and $(n_{i-1} = b_{i-1}) \to (n_i = b_i)$ is an application of Rule C6. If n_{i+1} is either the parent or a sibling of n_i then $n_i = b_i$ can be removed from the implication graph for $n_j = b_j$, i.e., $(n_{i-1} = b_{i-1}) \to (n_{i+1} = b_{i+1})$ is a valid implication. If n_{i+1} is a child of n_i, then $\otimes$ can be inferred at n_i only if either $n_{i+1} = \otimes$ is a current implication or $n_{i'} = 0$ is a current implication and $n_{i'}$ and n_i are inputs to an AND gate. In the first case, the fact that an implication graph existed in which n_{i+1} was labelled with a constant is contradicted. In the second case, clearly n_{i+1} is labelled with 0, i.e., $b_{i+1} = 0$ otherwise the assumption A is inconsistent, and the path $(n_i = b_i) \to (n_{i+1} = b_{i+1})$ can be replaced by the path $(n_{i'} = 0) \to (n_{i+1} = 0)$. Note that to get a new implication graph for $n_j = b_j$, we need the implication graph for $n_{i'} = 0$ but that exists and is not affected by the overwriting of the previous label of

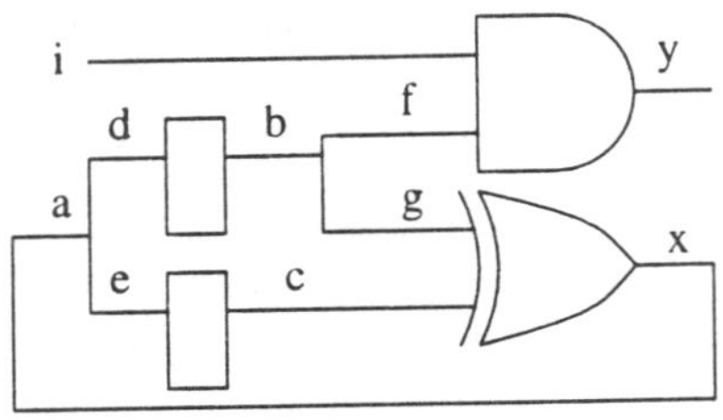

Figure 9: Sequential circuit C

n_i with $\otimes$.

Case 3: n_{i-1} is a parent of n_i. The reasoning is same as in Case 2.

Thus we have shown that if the assumption was consistent, each vertex labelled with $(n_i = b_i)$ in the implication graph of a current implication $(n_j = b_j)$ can be replaced with some other current implication. This shows that the replacement of $n_i = b_i$ by $n_i = \otimes$ does not falsify the claim which is a contradiction.

Now we consider the case in which $b_j = \otimes$. Then, there is a greatest k such that b_k is a constant, b_l is constant for all $1 \leq l \leq k$, and $b_l = \otimes$ for all $k < l \leq j$. From the proof before, we know there exists an implication graph for $n_k = b_k$ in which $n_i = b_i$ is not used. This yields an implication graph for $n_j = b_j$ in which $n_i = b_i$ is not used. ■

Lemma 2.2 *Let A be a consistent assumption. Then the set of labels returned by the algorithm is compatible.*

Proof: At each step in the algorithm, either a value is implied at a net for the first time or a constant is overwritten by a $\otimes$. The proof of this lemma follows by induction on the number of steps of the algorithm and by using Lemma 2.1 to prove the induction step. ■

Theorem 2.1 *Let n_i stuck-at-v_i redundant, for all $1 \leq i \leq n$, be the set of redundant faults reported by the algorithm. Then the circuit obtained by setting $n_i = v_i$ for all $1 \leq i \leq n$ is combinationally equivalent to the original.*

2.2 Sequential redundancies

Now we extend the algorithm for combinational circuits described in the previous section to find sequential redundancies by propagating implications across latches. The implications may not be valid on the first clock cycle since the latches power-up nondeterministically and have a random boolean value initially. Nevertheless, we can use the notion of k-delayed replacement which requires that the modified circuit produce the same behaviour as the original only after k clock cycles have elapsed. Thus, for example, if implying constant v at a latch output from constant v at its input yields a redundancy, a 1-delay replacement [3] is guaranteed on the removal of that redundancy.

[3] If we have latches where a reset value is guaranteed on the first cycle of operation, it is sufficient to ensure that the constant v is equal to the reset value; in this case the replacement is a 0-delay replacement.

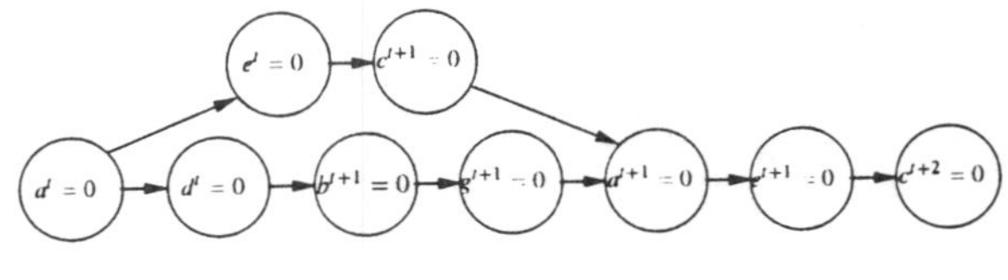

Figure 10: A sequential implication graph from assumption $a^t = 0$ for the circuit C

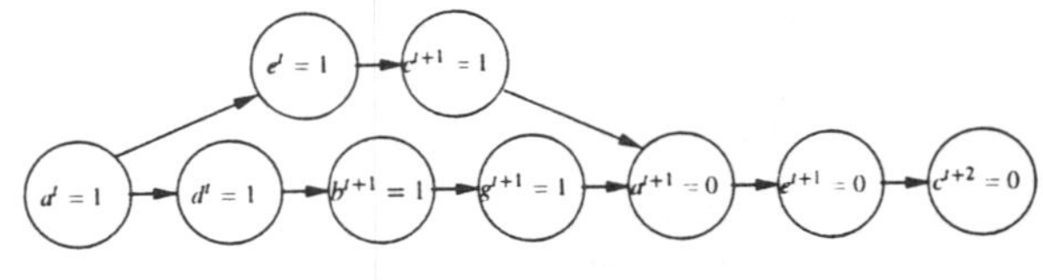

Figure 11: An incorrect sequential implication graph from assumption $a^t = 1$ for the circuit C

The notion of a label in the implication graph is modified so that it also contains an integer time offset with respect to a global symbolic time step t. The rules for learning implications are exactly the same as before with the addition of a new rule which allows us to propagate implications across latches: when we go across a latch we modify the time offset accordingly, e.g. if the output of a latch is labelled with 1 and offset -2, the input of the latch can be labelled with 1 and offset -3. An example of an implication graph for the circuit C in Figure 9 is shown in Figure 10.

This example also shows a potential problem with learning sequential implications. Consider the circuit C in Figure 9. For the two assumptions $\langle a^t \mapsto 0\rangle$ (a is 0 at t and t denotes the global symbolic time) and $\langle a^t \mapsto 1\rangle$ we get two implication graphs (in Figures 10 and 11) which both imply $(c^{t+2} = 0)$. This might lead us to believe that the $c = 0$ is a (2-cycle) redundancy. However, the new circuit obtained by replacing c with 0, if it powers up in state 11 (each latch at 1), remains forever in 11 with the circuit output $x = 1$. However, the original circuit produces $x = 0$ for all time $t \geq 1$, no matter which state it powers up in. Thus we do not have a k-delay replacement for any k. The reason for this incorrect redundancy identification is that in order to infer $(c^{t+2} = 0)$ from the assumption $\langle a^t \mapsto 1\rangle$, we needed $(c^{t+1} = 1)$. However, if we replace net c with 0 (i.e., for all times), c could not have been 1 at $t+1$.

One way of solving the above problem is to ensure that no net is labelled with different labels for different times. We will label a net with at most one label, and if a net is labelled we will associate a list of integers with this label which denotes the time offset when this label is valid. Thus, for the above example, during the implication propagation phase for the assumption $\langle a^t \mapsto 1\rangle$ we will never infer $(a^{t+1} = 0)$ and we will not get the second implication graph in Figure 10. Labeling one net with at most one label also obviates the need for the validation step described in [1].

The algorithm replaces a net n with the constant v if for some time offset t', it is either labelled with v or is unobservable for all assumptions. With each such replacement, we associate a time k as follows [1]. To validate a redundancy n *stuck-at-v* at time t', we have a set of implication graphs, one for each assumption, that imply either $n^{t'} = v$ or $n^{t'} = \otimes$. Let t'' be the least time offset on any label in these implication graphs such that for some net m, $m^{t''}$ is labelled with a constant. Then $k = 0$ if $t'' > t'$ otherwise $k = t' - t''$. We say that n is k-cycle *stuck-at-v* redundant. We use the following theorem to claim that the circuit obtained by replacing net n with constant v is a k-delayed safe replacement.

Lemma 2.3 ([1]) *Let a net n be k-cycle stuck-at-v redundant. Then the circuit obtained by setting net $n = v$ results in a k-delayed safe replacement of the original circuit.*

As in the combinational case, we allow overwriting of constants with unobservability indicators. We make sure that the label at net n at time $t + a$ is overwritten only if the new label is $\otimes$ and net n is not labelled at any other time offset (this is to prevent the problem shown in Figure 11). This may make our algorithm dependent on the order of application of rules, but we have not explored the various options. The proof of the following two lemmas follows by easy extensions of Lemmas 2.1 and 2.2.

Lemma 2.4 *Let A be a consistent assumption. If a label $m^t = a$ is replaced with $m^t = \otimes$ in the current set of labels, then for all labels $m_j^{t'_j} = b_j$, there is an implication graph such that $m^t = a$ is not a label in the graph.*

Lemma 2.5 *Let A be a consistent assumption. Then the set of labels returned by the algorithm is compatible.*

Hence, the redundancies reported by the algorithm are compatible with each other and all redundancies can be removed simultaneously to get a delayed safe replacement.

Theorem 2.2 *Let n_i k_i-cycle stuck-at-v_i redundant, for all $1 \leq i \leq n$, be the set of redundant faults reported by the algorithm. Let $K = \Sigma_{1 \leq i \leq n} k_i$. Then, the circuit obtained by setting net $n_i = v_i$ forall $1 \leq i \leq n$, is a K-delay safe replacement of the original.*

Proof: From Lemma 2.5, we know from that for all $1 \leq i \leq n$, n_i is k_i-cycle stuck-at-v_i redundant in the circuit obtained by setting $n_j = v_j$ for all $j \neq i$. It has been shown in [5] that for any circuits C, D and E, if C is an a-delay replacement for D and D is a b-delay replacement for E then C is $(a + b)$-delay replacement for E. The desired result follows easily by induction on n from this property of delay replacements. ■

Circuit Name	Redundancy Removal				With Recursive Learning			
	red	LR	A1	%	red	LR	A2	%
s349	0	0	345	0	0	0	345	0
s382	0	0	437	0	0	0	437	0
s386	0	0	251	0	0	0	251	0
s499	0	0	605	0	0	0	605	0
s526	1	0	472	0.4	1	0	472	0.4
s820	0	0	499	0	1	0	492	1.4
s832	0	0	456	0	1	0	443	2.8
s953	0	0	920	0	2	0	717	22.6
s1238	0	0	998	0	3	0	890	5.4
s1269	0	0	1140	0	20	0	1100	3.5
s1488	0	0	1034	0	0	0	1034	0
s1512	0	0	1337	0	0	0	1337	0
s3271	0	0	2828	0	0	0	2828	0
s3384	0	0	3775	0	1	0	3767	0.2
s4863	0	0	3368	0	0	0	3368	0
s5378	29	3	3538	2.1	30	4	3504	3.0
s9234	0	0	2854	0	2	0	2795	2.1
s13207	11	3	7590	0.4	22	5	7509	1.4
s15850	103	0	10571	1.3	113	0	10495	2.0
s35932	64	0	32006	0.3	64	0	32006	0.3
s38417	183	2	32746	0.9	219	41	31917	3.4
s38584	144	0	29069	0.5	124	0	28167	3.6
cordic	80	0	10636	0.5	81	0	16360	0.5

For legend see Table 2.

Table 1: Experimental results for combinational redundancies

3 Experimental Results

We present some experimental results for this algorithm. We demonstrate that our approach of identifying sequential redundancies yields significant reduction in area and is better than the approach which removes only combinational redundancies. We also show that for most examples, recursive learning gives better results then the simple implication propagation scheme. In fact for many circuits, recursive learning could identify redundancies where the simple implication propagation scheme is unable to find any.

This algorithm was implemented in SIS [11]. The circuit was first optimised using `script.rugged` which performs combinational optimisation on the network. The optimised circuit was mapped with a library consisting of 2-input gates and inverters. The sequential redundancy removal algorithm was run on the mapped circuit. The propagation of implications was allowed to propagate 15 time steps forward and 15 time-steps backward from the global symbolic time. Table 2 shows the mapped (to MCNC91 library) area of the circuits obtained by running `script.rugged` and that obtained by starting from that result and applying redundancy removal algorithm. For very large circuits (s15850 and larger), BDD operations during the `full_simplify` step in `script.rugged` were not performed. We report results for those circuits on which our algorithm was able to find redundancies.

As mentioned earlier, our algorithm starts with an assumption on the nets and implies values on other nets of the circuit. We implemented two flavors of selection of assumptions. In

Circuit	Attributes				Redundancy Removal						With Recursive Learning					
Name	PI	PO	L	A	red	C	LR	A1	%	time	red	C	LR	A2	%	time
s349	9	11	15	345	0	0	0	345	0	0.5	9	105	0	330	4.3	1.0
s382	3	6	21	436	0	0	0	437	0	0.9	2	5	0	434	0.7	2.1
s386	7	7	6	251	1	1	0	245	2.5	0.5	1	2	0	245	2.5	0.9
s499	1	22	22	605	19	32	0	583	3.6	5.1	16	30	0	581	4.0	9.9
s526	3	6	21	480	1	1	0	472	0.4	0.8	1	0	0	472	0.4	2.3
s820	18	19	5	499	0	0	0	499	0	1.7	1	0	0	492	1.4	2.9
s832	18	19	5	456	0	0	0	456	0	1.6	2	0	0	431	5.5	2.6
s953	16	23	29	920	0	0	0	920	0	3.7	3	0	10	632	31.3	6.3
s1238	14	14	18	998	0	0	0	998	0	3.5	3	0	0	890	10.1	5.4
s1269	18	10	37	1140	0	0	0	1140	0	2.9	21	8	0	1094	4	3.8
s1488	8	19	6	1034	0	0	0	1034	0	5.0	154	149	0	863	16.5	8.7
s1512	29	21	57	1337	2	2	0	1333	0.3	3.3	147	146	9	1092	18.3	5.6
s3271	26	14	116	2828	0	0	0	2828	0	12.9	6	5	0	2801	1.0	25.5
s3384	43	26	183	3775	0	0	0	3775	0	15.8	4	1	1	3745	0.8	18.7
s4863	49	16	83	3386	80	160	0	3319	1.9	23.1	82	164	0	3313	2.2	33.4
s5378	35	49	163	3616	574	1995	25	2959	19.6	22.0	1145	6992	58	2261	37.5	19.9
s9234	19	22	138	2854	102	1414	0	2752	3.8	22.8	102	1414	0	2752	3.8	22.4
s13207	31	121	453	7681	49	518	28	7035	8.4	66.9	92	733	70	6317	17.8	32.1
s15850*	14	87	540	10704	199	1841	6	10415	2.7	272.4	163	1650	43	9380	10.0	493.7
s35932*	35	320	1728	32092	64	0	0	32006	0.3	1339.4	64	0	0	32006	0.3	5010.3
s38417*	28	106	1464	33055	591	887	42	31943	3.4	1139.4	1129	9245	97	29718	10.1	1763.7
s38584*	12	278	1285	29252	102	168	0	29016	0.8	1193.5	114	400	5	28656	2.9	2157.4
cordic*	35	9	271	10688	81	73	0	10636	0.5	251.8	66	56	8	8939	16	242.6

* `full_simplify` not run.

All times reported on an Alpha 21164 300MHz dual processor with 2G of memory.

PI	number of primary inputs	PO	number of primary outputs
L	number of latches	A	Mapped area after `script.rugged`
A1	Mapped area after redundancy removal	A2	Mapped area after redundancy removal with recursive learning
red	number of redundancies removed	LR	Number of latches removed
C	Upper bound on c, where the new circuit is a c-delay replacement	time	CPU time
%	Percentage area reduction		

Table 2: Experimental results for sequential redundancies

the first case a conflicting assignment was assumed on one net and values were implied on other nets. The second case was similar to the first except that once the implications could not propagate for an assumption on a net, we performed a naïve version of case splitting only on the net which was closest to the original net from which the implications were propagated and implications common in the two cases were also added in the set of implications learnt for the original net.[4] This enabled us to propagate implications over a larger set of nets in the network and hence to discover more redundancies at the expense of CPU time. Table 2 indicates the area reduction obtained both by simple propagation and by performing this recursive learning. We find that even for this naïve recursive learning we get reduction in area in most of the circuits over that obtained without case split. For instance, for S5378 we were able to obtain 37.5% area reduction with recursive learning as against 19.6% without it. For most of the medium sized circuits we were not able to obtain any reduction in area without recursive learning. For large circuits also we were able to obtain approximately 5-10% area reduction. S35952 was an exception where we did not obtain any more reduction in area. Except for this circuit the CPU time for recursive learning was less than twice the CPU time for redundancy removal without it. This suggests that more sophisticated recursive learning based techniques could yield larger area reduction without prohibitive overhead in terms of CPU time.

Since our algorithm also identified combinational redundancies, we wanted to quantify how many of the redundancies were purely combinational. To verify this we ran our algorithm on the circuits for combinational redundancy removal only. Table 1 shows the area reduction due to combinational redundancies only with and without recursive learning. In most cases, the number of redundancies identified in Table 2 is significantly larger than the set of combinational redundancies identified by our algorithm. Only for S35952 and S953 did the combinational redundancy removal result in approximately the same area reduction as the sequential redundancy case.

For the example circuits presented here we were able to achieve 0-37% area reduction. In a number of cases the algorithm was able to remove a significant number of latches. In all cases, the new circuit is a C-delay safe replacement of the original circuit. The C reported in Table 2 is actually an upper bound. For most of the delay replaced circuits $C < 10000$. However most practical circuits operate at speeds exceeding 100 MHz in present technology. $C < 10000$ for a circuit would

[4] If a node is unjustified during forward propagation of implications then case-split is performed by setting the output net to 0 and 1. If the node is unjustified during backward propagation case split is achieved by setting one of the two inputs to the input controlling value (0 for (N)AND gate and 1 for (N)OR gate) at a time and propagating the implications backward.

require the user to wait for at most 100 μs before useful operation can begin. This is not a severe restriction.

We are unable to compare sequential redundancy removal results with the previous work of Entrena and Cheng [8] because as we noted earlier, their notion of sequential replacement, which is based on the conservative 0,1,X-valued simulation, is not compositional (unlike the notion of delay replacement that we use).

4 Future Work

Our redundancy removal algorithm does not find the complete set of redundancies. We can extend this scheme in several ways to identify larger sets. For instance, instead of analyzing two assumptions due to a case split on a single net we could case split on multiple nets and intersect the implications learnt on this larger set of assumptions. One such method is to incrementally select those which are at the frontier where the first phase of implications died out. Additionally, if we split on multiple nets it is possible to detect pairs of nets such that if one is replaced with another the circuit functionality does not change. With our current approach, because we split on a single net, one of the nets in this pair is always a 1 or a 0, which means that we are only identifying stuck-at-constant redundancies.

For this algorithm we map a given circuit using a library of two input gates and inverters. A different approach would be to use the original circuit and propagate the implications forward and backward by building the BDD's for the node function in terms of it's immediate fanins. We intend to compare the running times and area reduction numbers of our approach with such a BDD based approach. In addition, BDD based approaches may allow us to do redundancy removal for multi-valued logic circuits as well in a relatively inexpensive way. We can extend the notion of redundancy for multi-valued circuits to identify cases where a net can take only a subset of its allowed values. Then latches of this kind can be encoded using fewer bits.

5 Acknowledgements

We had useful discussions with Mahesh Iyer during the course of this work. Miron Abramovici gave us the example of Figure 1. The comments by the referees also helped to improved the paper.

References

[1] M. A. Iyer, D. E. Long, and M. Abramovici, "Identifying Sequential Redundancies Without Search," in *Proc. of the Design Automation Conf.*, (Las Vegas, NV), pp. 457–462, June 1996.

[2] S. Muroga, Y. Kambayashi, H. C. Lai, and J. N. Culliney, "The Transduction Method - Design of Logic Networks Based on Permissible Functions," in *IEEE Trans. Computers*, Oct. 1989.

[3] H. Savoj, *Don't Cares in Multi-Level Network Optimization.* PhD thesis, University of California Berkeley, Electronics Research Laboratory, College of Engineering, University of California, Berkeley, CA 94720, May 1992.

[4] W. Kunz and D. K. Pradhan, "Recursive Learning: A New Implication Technique for Efficient Solution to CAD Problems - Test, Verification and Optimization," *IEEE Trans. Computer-Aided Design*, Sept. 1994.

[5] V. Singhal, C. Pixley, A. Aziz, and R. K. Brayton, "Exploiting Power-up Delay for Sequential Optimization," in *Proc. European Design Automation Conf.*, (Brighton, Great Britain), pp. 54–59, Sept. 1995.

[6] S. Qadeer, V. Singhal, R. K. Brayton, and C. Pixley, "Latch Redundancy Removal without Global Reset," in *Proc. Intl. Conf. on Computer Design*, (Austin, TX), pp. 432–439, Oct. 1996.

[7] M. Chatterjee, D. K. Pradhan, and W. Kunz, "LOT: Logic Optimization with Testability - New Transformations using Recursive Learning," in *Proc. Intl. Conf. on Computer-Aided Design*, (San Jose, CA), pp. 318–325, Nov. 1995.

[8] L. Entrena and K.-T. Cheng, "Sequential Logic Optimization by Redundancy Addition and Removal," in *Proc. Intl. Conf. on Computer-Aided Design*, (Santa Clara, CA), pp. 310–315, Nov. 1993.

[9] M. A. Iyer, *On Redundancy and Untestability in Sequential Circuits.* PhD thesis, Illinois Institute on Technology, 1995.

[10] I. Pomeranz and S. M. Reddy, "On Removing Redundancies from Synchronous Sequential Circuits with Synchronizing Sequences," *IEEE Trans. Computers*, vol. 45, pp. 20–32, Jan. 1996.

[11] E. M. Sentovich, K. J. Singh, L. Lavagno, C. Moon, R. Murgai, A. Saldanha, H. Savoj, P. R. Stephan, R. K. Brayton, and A. L. Sangiovanni-Vincentelli, "SIS: A System for Sequential Circuit Synthesis," Tech. Rep. UCB/ERL M92/41, Electronics Research Lab, Univ. of California, Berkeley, CA 94720, May 1992.

Minimum Area Retiming with Equivalent Initial States [1]

Naresh Maheshwari
Department of Electrical & Computer Engineering
Iowa State University, Ames IA 50011, USA
naresh@iastate.edu

Sachin S. Sapatnekar
Department of Electrical & Computer Engineering
University of Minnesota, Minneapolis, MN 55455, USA
sachin@ece.umn.edu

Abstract

Traditional minimum area retiming algorithms attempt to achieve their prescribed objective with no regard to maintaining the initial state of the system. This issue is important for circuits such as controllers, and our work addresses this problem. The procedure described generates bounds on the retiming variables that guarantee an equivalent initial state after retiming. A number of possible sets of bounds can be derived, and each set is used to solve a minimum area retiming problem that is set up as a 0/1 mixed integer linear program, using a new technique that models the maximal sharing of flip-flops at latch outputs. The best solution is found through enumeration of these sets, terminated on achievement of a calculated lower bound. Experimental results show that after a small number of enumerations, optimal or near-optimal results are achievable.

1 Introduction

Retiming [1] is a technique for optimizing sequential circuits by relocating memory elements. Two common variations of this problem are: *minperiod* retiming in which the clock period is minimized without regard to the number of flip-flops (FF's) in the final circuit, and (constrained) *minarea* retiming in which the number of FF's is minimized subject to a target clock period. Retiming has also been applied to level-clocked circuits e.g. in [2, 3].

One problem associated with the application of retiming is preserving the initial state of the circuit, which is determined by the initial values of the registers in the circuits. Whenever the initial state of the circuit is an integral part of its behavior (for example, in controllers), it is necessary to find an equivalent initial state for the retimed circuit. An initial state in the retimed circuit is equivalent to the initial state in the original circuit if for any input sequence applied to both the circuits (original circuit started in the initial state and the retimed circuit started in the equivalent initial state) the same sequence of outputs is produced [4].

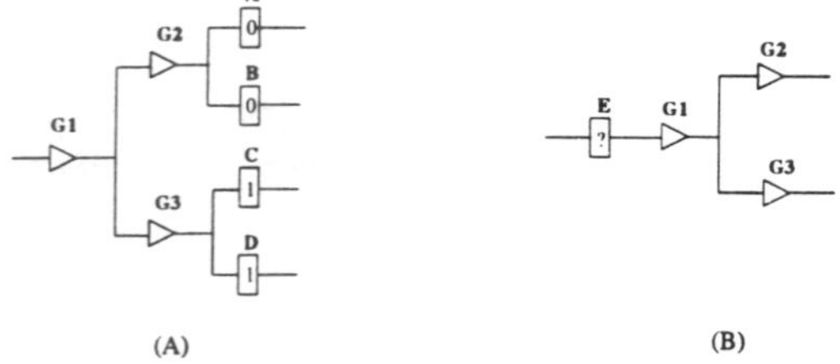

Figure 1: (A) Original circuit. (B) Retimed circuit

It is not always possible to find an equivalent initial state for the retimed circuit. For example in Figure 1(a), if the initial value of FF's {A,B,C,D} are {0,0,1,1} respectively, then the retimed circuit in Figure 1(b) cannot be initialized to have the same behavior as the original circuit. This is because an equivalent initial value of FF E in the retimed circuit cannot be found. On the other hand, an equivalent initial state can always be found for forward motion of FF's (i.e., in the direction of signal flow). This concept was used in [5] to compute initial states of retimed circuits by using only forward moves. FF's could be removed from all primary outputs and inserted at all primary inputs, and the problem was reduced to determining the initial values for the inserted FF's; their values could be obtained from the state machine description of the circuit. However, this approach may require modifications in the combinational logic which may increase the clock period.

Since a retiming for a given clock period is not unique, another possible retiming may exist, for which an equivalent initial state can be found without any circuit modifications. Reverse retiming [4] finds this retiming by disallowing FF moves across the primary outputs and by minimizing backward (against the signal flow) motion.

For digital circuit design, the useful objective function is that of constrained minimum area retiming. However, none of the above methods considers the area penalty during retiming since they perform minperiod retiming rather than minarea retiming. In this work we solve the problem of minarea retiming with equivalent initial states and call it *minarea initial state retiming*. We use bounds on the retiming variables to allow backward motion of FF's only if an equivalent initial value exits. Therefore any retiming thus obtained is guaranteed to have an equivalent initial state. Retiming across the host vertex is not allowed since it may require modifications to the original circuit. We also provide a new formulation that takes into account the initial value of the FF's while modeling the maximal sharing of FF's at the outputs of multiple fanout gates.

2 Background

As in [1] a sequential circuit can be represented by a directed graph $G(V, E)$, where each vertex v corresponds to a gate, and a directed edge e_{uv} represents a connection from the output of gate u to the input of gate v, through zero or more FF's. Each edge has a weight $w(e_{uv})$, which is the number of FF's between the output of gate u and the input of gate v. Each vertex has a constant delay $d(v)$. A special vertex, the host vertex, is introduced in the graph, with edges from to all primary inputs of the circuit, and edges from all primary outputs. A retiming is a labeling of the vertices $r : V \rightarrow Z$, where Z is the set of integers. The retiming label $r(v)$ for a vertex v represents the number of FF's moved from its output to its inputs.

The minarea retiming problem (without regard to initial states) was formulated as a linear program (LP) in [1]. Let $FI(v)$ $[FO(v)]$ be the fanin [fanout] sets of gate v respectively. The objective function in the LP represents the number of FF's added by retiming, and the constraints ensure a valid retimed circuit that satisfies the target clock period. This LP is a dual of a network mincost flow problem and hence can be solved efficiently. Minaret [6] reduces the size of this LP by adding lower and upper bounds on the variables; the details are omitted here. The reduced LP has the form:

$$\begin{array}{lll} \text{minimize} & \sum_{v \in V} [(|FI(v)| - |FO(v)|) \cdot r(v)] & (1) \\ \text{subject to} & r(u) - r(v) \leq c_{uv} & \forall \text{ constraints } \in C \\ & L_u \leq r(u) \leq U_u & \forall u \in V \end{array}$$

where C is the reduced constraint set [6].

[1] This work was supported in part by the National Science Foundation under award MIP-9502556 and a Lucent Technologies DAC Graduate Scholarship.

1092-3152/97 $10.00 © 1997 IEEE

3 Ensuring Equivalent Initial States

The requirement of initial state equivalence imposes restrictions in addition to those in traditional minarea retiming. Thus the number of FF's obtained in minarea retiming is, by definition, a lower bound on the number of FF's obtainable by a minarea equivalent state retiming. We call this lower bound Γ.

However it is not always possible to achieve this lower bound. As an example, consider the circuit with unit delay gates shown in Figure 1. The minarea retiming for a clock period of 2 units, and without regard to initial state requires only 1 FF. However, if the initial values of FF's {A,B,C,D} are {0,0,1,1}, any minarea initial state retiming will require 2 FF's. Furthermore, the optimal number of FF's depends on the initial state of the original circuit. If the initial values for FF's {A,B,C,D} are {0,1,1,1}, then any minarea initial state retiming will have 3 FF's.

Even in cases where the lower bound Γ is achievable with equivalent initial states, there would, in general, be multiple retimings with optimal number of FF's. Some of these retimings may not have equivalent initial states, and hence we must restrict our solution space to exclude such solutions. One way to do this is to disallow backward motion of FF's across a gate if the FF's at its output do not have compatible values. The presence of FF's with incompatible logic values at the output of a gate is called a *conflict*. A conflict at the output of a gate prevents it from being retimed in the backward direction. Therefore to ensure that any retiming obtained has an equivalent initial state we update the upper bound U_v on gate v in the LP of Equation (1), so that no backward retiming is allowed across a gate with a conflict at its outputs. This new upper bound $J_v \leq U_v$ ensures a valid equivalent state. Notice that we do not update the lower bounds since the forward motion of FF's always results in an equivalent initial state.

In the remainder of this section, we will describe techniques to obtain these new upper bounds. Minaret [6] obtains the upper bounds by moving FF's backwards until they are about to violate a period constraint; the number of the FF's moved across any gate gives its upper bound. Unlike Minaret which does not associate any logic values with the FF's, we associate a three valued (1,0,X) logic value with every FF, where X is a don't care which can be assigned to either 0 or 1. A logic value of 0 [1] is compatible with both 0 and X [1 and X], but logic values 0 and 1 are not compatible with each other.

A gate can only be retimed backwards if it has FF's at all of its fanouts and all of these FF's have compatible logic values. The procedure maintains a list of gates that can be retimed. In each step, a gate is plucked from the list and retimed, and the list is updated. Whenever FF's are moved from the outputs of a gate to its inputs, we must assign logic values to the new FF's added at the inputs. These logic values must be equivalent to the original value at the gate output in order to maintain state equivalence. This assignment may be unique or non-unique and is similar to justification in ATPG [7].

Unique justification at a gate occurs if the gate has a single input, or the logic value at the output is X (all inputs are assigned to logic X). A logic value of 1 at the output of AND/NOR gates or logic 0 at the output of OR/NAND gates also results in unique justifications. If there are multiple possible mappings for the logic value at the output to the logic values at the inputs, then we have to make a choice (or decision) and we have *non-unique justification* at the gate. A logic value of 1 at the output of an OR (NAND) gate is an example of non-unique justification and we can assign any input to logic value 1(0) and the rest to X.

Let us define a justification set as a backward propagation of logic values until the primary inputs, or until a conflict is reached. Note that non-unique justifications at gates permit a number of such justification sets; we denote one such possible justification set as Δ^i. Then each such Δ^i will give us Λ^i, a set (one for each gate) of justification upper bounds. For each Δ^i we solve the minarea LP with the upper bounds Λ^i. If the number of FF's so obtained is not equal to the minarea lower bound Γ, we backtrack and obtain another justification set Δ^j to give us a different Λ^j. This process can be repeated until the minarea lower bound Γ is achieved or until all justification sets have been enumerated.

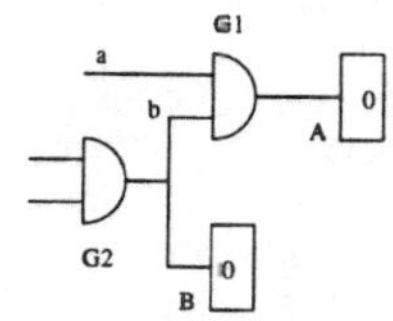

Figure 2: An example of pruning technique

The number of justification sets to be explored is exponential in the worst case; however, this number can be pruned by removing suboptimal Λ^i's from consideration. As an example, consider the circuit in Figure 2 with the logic values of FF A and FF B equal to 0. Since the output of the AND gate G1 is at logic 0, there are two possible mappings for the equivalent values at a and b. However the choice of setting input a to X and input b to 0 is better than the choice of $a = 0$ and $b =$ X, since the presence of FF B with logic 0 will force the X on line b to 0. Thus we make the choice of $a = 0$ and $b = 0$, which is suboptimal to the choice of $a =$ X and $b = 0$, since X on input a could potentially move further in the backward direction than a 0. For another pruning strategy, consider two sets of justification upper bounds Λ^i and Λ^j. If we have $J_v^i \leq J_v^j \ \ \forall \ v \in V$, then the feasible region of Λ^j includes the feasible region of Λ^i, and hence there is no need to solve the LP corresponding to Λ^i.

4 FF Sharing

The LP in Equation (1) assumes that the FF's at the fanouts of a gate are not shared amongst the different fanouts. However, to accurately model the minimum number of FF's in a circuit, we must take maximal FF sharing into account. In [1] a mirror vertex is added for every gate with more than one fanout to model this maximal sharing. This model preserves the LP's duality to a mincost flow problem, and can be solved efficiently. Unfortunately, this model assumes that an FF can be combined with any other FF, and hence is not applicable to minarea initial state retiming where FF's have logic values associated with them, and an FF with logic 1 can not be shared with one with logic value 0. The situation is complicated by the fact that two FF's can be shared only if the FF's at their fanins (if any) are also shared. We present a new 0/1-MILP formulation to model the sharing when FF's have logic values 1 or 0. This modeling is used for all gates with a conflict at their output. For all other gates the simpler model of [1] is used. We will first present the model and then illustrate it through an example.

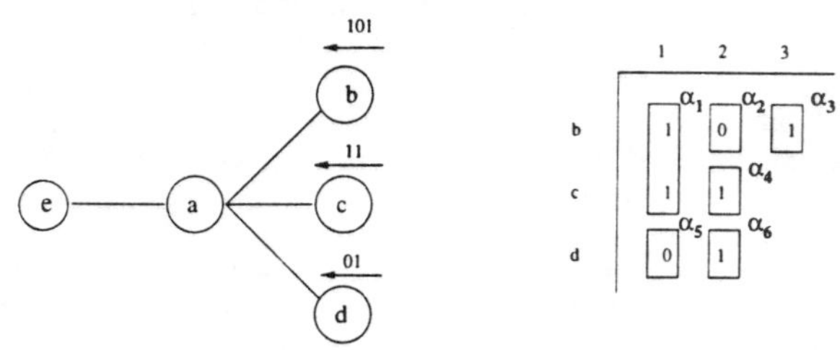

Figure 3: An example for FF sharing

The justification process of Section 3 determines the logic values of all FF's that can possibly arrive at a gate's fanouts. Notice that there is a sequence of these "possible" FF's at every output of every gate, and the final retiming may contain only a prefix of this sequence. The logic values of these possible FF's at the fanouts of a gate u are represented by a table T_u with $|FO(u)|$ rows as shown in Figure 3, where $FO(u)$ is the fanout set of gate u. Each row, $v \in FO(u)$ has $J_v + w(e_{uv})$ entries, each of which is either a 0 or a 1. Since a maximum of J_v FF's can be moved across gate v to its input, and $w(e_{uv})$ FF's already exist between gate u and gate v, the maximum number of FF's between gate u and gate v that may require conditional sharing is $J_v + w(e_{uv})$. FF's moved forward across gate u to its output can be shared unconditionally and will be handled later. The value in the vth row and k^{th} column of the table is denoted by $T_u(v,k)$. We define a sharing class S_i to contain a set of values that can be shared, and represent the set of sharing classes for the fanouts of gate u by N_u. Two values (p,q) and (r,s) in T_u can be shared (i.e., belong to the same sharing class) only if $q = s$ and $T_u(p,i) = T_u(r,i)$ for $i = 0, \cdots, s-1$. A function $class(T_u(v,k))$ gives the index of the sharing class for entry (v,k) in table T_u, e.g., $S_{class(T_u(v,k))}$ is the sharing class containing the kth FF between gate u and its fanout v (counting from u). All the FF's in a sharing class can be shared with each other, and hence require only one physical FF. Each sharing class S_i is represented in the MILP by a variable $\alpha_i \in \{0,1\}$. If $\alpha_i = 1$ in the optimal solution of the MILP, then the FF's of sharing class S_i share a physical FF and the sharing class S_i is said to be active.

The minarea LP in Equation (1) is modified to model the conditional sharing represented by the sharing classes. For every gate u with a conflict at its outputs, the corresponding objective function term is given by Equation (2); for all other gates it is as in [1].

$$(|FI'(u)| - 1) \cdot r(u) - \beta_u + \sum_{\forall\, i \in N_u} \alpha_i \qquad (2)$$

Here $FI'(u)$ is the set of fanins that have only a single output, i.e., $FI'(u) = \{v | v \in FI(u)\ AND\ |FO(v)| = 1\}$. The first term $(|FI'(u)|-1) \cdot r(u)$ in Equation (2) models the increase in the number of FF's when gate u is retimed by one unit, and is similar to the model in [1]. It assumes a shared cost of one at the fanouts of gate u for any set of FF's retimed across gate u, in either direction. Since a gate can be retimed backwards only if all FF's at its output have same logic values, the shared cost at the outputs before retiming is indeed one, as modeled by this term. Notice that since $r(u) \leq J_u$, no set of FF's with shared cost greater than one, can ever be retimed backwards across gate u. In forward retiming, all FF's inserted at the outputs of a gate have the same logic values, and so the shared cost at fanouts of gate u in forward retiming is also one. The second term $\beta_u \geq 0$ is a correction factor applied to correctly model the situation in which a set of FF's moves forward across gate u and all its fanouts. It is active only during forward retiming steps, and models the number of FF's removed from the fanout junction of gate u by forward retiming. $\beta_u \geq 0$ ensures that unconditionally shared FF's are not added to the fanouts of gate u by backward retiming, since conditional sharing under backward retiming is to be modeled by the α_i's.

As mentioned earlier $\alpha_i = 1$ implies that the sharing class S_i is active, therefore $\sum_{\forall\, i \in N_u} \alpha_i$ denotes the number of active sharing classes at the fanouts of gate u. Since each active sharing class requires one FF, the number of active sharing classes is also the number of physical FF's required at the fanouts of gate u. The minimization of the objective function will force the maximal sharing at the outputs of gate u.

In order to correctly model the cost, all the FF's at the fanout of a gate u must have their costs accounted for in the objective function. To achieve this we add the following constraint for $\forall\ v \in FO(u)$.

$$w(e_{uv}) + r(v) \leq -\beta_u + \sum_{k=1}^{J_v + w(e_{uv})} \alpha_{class(T_u(v,k))} \qquad (3)$$

The left hand side of Equation (3), minus $r(u)$, is the number of FF's between gate u and v after retiming. $\sum_{k=1}^{J_v + w(e_{uv})} \alpha_{class(T_u(v,k))}$ represents the total number of active sharing classes between gate u and v, β_u is the number of FF's removed from the fanout of gate u by forward retiming (0 in case of backward retiming), while $r(u)$ is the number of FF's removed from the fanout of gate u. Hence the right hand side of Equation (3), minus $r(u)$, represents the number of available shared FF's between gate u and v. Thus Equation (3) ensures that the number of FF's between any two gates is less than or equal to the number of shared FF's between them. Notice that the number of shared FF's is the number of available FF's , all of which do not have to be utilized by a particular fanout.

To ensure that the kth FF retimed across gate v activates its own sharing class variable $\alpha_{class(T_u(v,k))}$, we ensure that $\forall v \in FO(u)$

$$\left\{\alpha_{class(T_u(v,k))} \geq \alpha_{class(T_u(v,k+1))}\right\}\ k = 1 \ldots J_v + w(e_{uv}) - 1$$

By requiring that the variable $\alpha_{class(T_u(v,k))}$ be active before the variable $\alpha_{class(T_u(v,k+1))}$, this constraint ensures that the kth FF retimed across gate v does not activate $\alpha_{class(T_u(v,k+1))}$. The kth FF retimed across gate v can not activate $\alpha_{class(T_u(v,k-1))}$, since before the kth FF can be retimed across gate v, the $k-1^{th}$ FF must have already been retimed and its class variable $\alpha_{class(T_u(v,k-1))}$ would already be active. The constraint in Equation (3) will ensure that the number of active sharing classes on a fanout is greater or equal to the number of FF's on that fanout. Thus the kth FF retimed across gate v will activate its own sharing class. The first FF in a sharing class S_i that arrives at the fanout junction activates the sharing class variable α_i, incurring a cost of one in the objective function. The remaining FF's in that sharing class can then arrive without incurring any extra cost in the objective function.

Example: Consider the circuit in Figure 3 shown with the sharing classes in its table of logic values. The LP for this circuit is

$$Minimize : -r(b) - r(c) - r(d) + \alpha_1 + \alpha_2 + \alpha_3 + \alpha_4 + \alpha_5 + \alpha_6 - \beta_a$$

$$\text{subject to} \quad r(b) + \beta_a \leq \alpha_1 + \alpha_2 + \alpha_3$$
$$r(c) + \beta_a \leq \alpha_1 + \alpha_4$$
$$r(d) + \beta_a \leq \alpha_5 + \alpha_6$$
$$\alpha_1 \geq \alpha_2 \geq \alpha_3$$
$$\alpha_1 \geq \alpha_4\ ;\ \alpha_5 \geq \alpha_6$$
$$\beta_u \geq 0\ ;\ \alpha_i \in \{0,1\}\ \forall i$$

Positive Retiming: Suppose we want to model the sharing for $r(a) = 0$, $r(b) = 3$, $r(c) = 1$ and $r(d) = 2$. Then the optimal objective function value of the above LP is -1, which gives the correct increase in the number of FF's from the original circuit in Figure 4(a) to the retimed circuit in Figure 4(b).

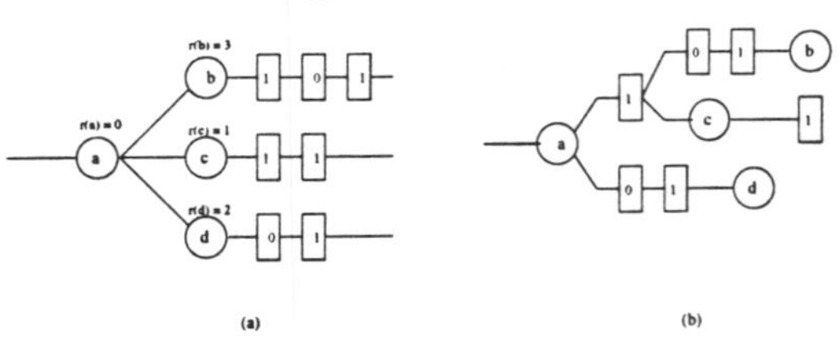

Figure 4: Example of positive retiming

Negative retiming: Now suppose we want to model the sharing for $r(a) = -2$, $r(b) = -2$, $r(c) = -1$ and $r(d) = -1$. Then the optimal objective function value is 3, which is the increase in the number of FF's from the original circuit in Figure 5(a) to the retimed circuit in Figure 5(b). As can be seen one FF is shared for the edges e_{ac} and e_{ad} even though they where not in the same sharing class. This is possible because the FF's moved forward to the outputs of gate a hence they all have same logic value without regard to the sharing

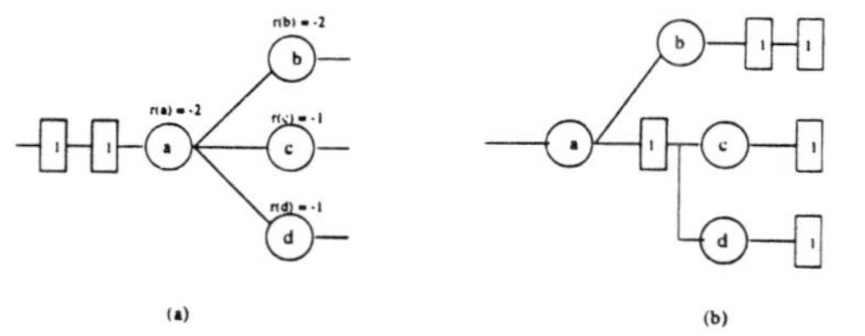

Figure 5: Example of negative retiming

class which are defined for backward movements. Thus these FF's can be shared and our formulation correctly models the cost.

The actual problem of FF sharing is to find the optimal sharing between logic values 0, 1 and X. Logic X can be shared with either 0 or 1 but not both, and is hard to model. To avoid this problem we have converted all X's to either 0 or 1 before formulating the MILP.

5 Experimental Results

We have implemented an initial state minarea retiming based on the presentation in this work. Our justification algorithm makes random choices in case of a non-unique justification and generates an LP for each of the Λ_i's. If the lower bound Γ is not achieved, then we perform a justification based on another random decision. This is continued until the lower bound is reached or a user specified number of iterations have been completed, and the best solution is reported. Although it may seem arbitrary to use random decisions, our experimental results show that the algorithm gives us good engineering solutions that are close to the (possibly unachievable) lower bound. As in [4] we assume the initial state of all FF's to be zero.

Table 1: Minarea Initial State Retiming

Circuit	$\|G\|$	P	Γ	# FF's	T_{exec}
s27	11	6.0	3	3	0.01s
s208.1	105	10.0	8	8	0.02s
s298	120	6.0	22	22	0.40s
s382	159	7.0	23	23	2.59s
s386	169	11.0	6	6	0.04s
s344	161	14.0	19	19	1.77s
s349	162	14.0	19	19	1.62s
s526n	195	6.0	30	30	0.95s
s510	212	11.0	7	7	0.12s
s420.1	219	12.0	17	17	0.07s
s641	380	74.0	19	19	0.11s
s713	394	74	19	19	0.18s
s967	395	12.0	35	35	28.52s
s938	447	16.0	33	33	1.45s
s1196	530	24.0	18	18	0.08s
s1238	5.09	22.0	18	18	0.08s
s1269	570	19.0	84	84	0.26s
s1423	658	53.0	76	76	8.77s
s1488	654	16.0	7	7	0.11s
s1494	648	16.0	7	7	0.13s
s3330	1790	14.0	110	110	0.58s
s5378	2780	21.0	173	173	3m 18s
s9234.1	3271	38.0	134	134	21m 18s
s635	287	66.0	35	42	22.6s
s953	396	13.0	27	32	32m 02s
s1512	781	23.0	70	71	1h 51m 19s
s3271	1573	15.0	168	169	16m 46s
prolog	1602	13.0	122	124	16m 40s
s3384	1686	27.0	167	168	55m 42s
s15850.1	9618	63.0	525	544	3h 9m 56s

If for a given justification set Δ_i there are no gates with conflicts, the mincost flow problem is solved using a network simplex algorithm; else we use *lp_solve* [9] to solve the MILP.

Table 1 shows the number of gates $|G|$, the target clock period P, and the lower bound on the number of FF's Γ for ISCAS89 circuits. We also show the minimum number of FF's obtained with equivalent initial state retiming and the execution time T_{exec} on a HP 9000/777 C110 workstation with 128 megabytes of RAM. Notice that the run times here can be much higher then those in [6] since here we may solve multiple MILP's, rather than a single mincost flow problem. As can be seen from the results, for many circuits the lower bound is achieved very fast; in almost all of these cases, the lower bound Γ is achieved in the first iteration. For some circuits, the lower bound was not reached, and in this case we report the best solution obtained in 50 iterations (5 iterations for s15850.1)[2]. In these circuits, the solution reported by our algorithm is very close to Γ and corresponds to a good engineering solution. We found that the percentage of gates with conflicts is very small ($< 1\%$ for most circuits), and this enables the MILP to be solved in reasonable time.

6 Conclusion

We have presented a method for obtaining minarea retiming subject to maintaining a given clock period and an equivalent initial state. A new scheme based on justification is used to derive bounds on the retiming variables. A new model for maximal FF sharing has been presented as the idea of mirror vertices used by Leiserson and Saxe in [1] cannot be applied to the initial state retiming problem.

We are currently working on modeling the FF sharing for all logic values including X's and on techniques to prune the number of justification sets required to get the optimal solution. In [10] a technique is presented which allows backward retiming of gates with conflicts by adding extra logic to the circuit. We are investigating means to incorporate this approach in our model. This will enable us to retime gates with conflicts at their outputs, potentially achieving better area optimization.

REFERENCES

[1] C. E. Leiserson and J. B. Saxe, "Retiming synchronous circuitry," *Algorithmica*, vol. 6, pp. 5–35, 1991.

[2] M. C. Papaefthymiou and K. H. Randall, "TIM: A timing package for two-phase, level-clocked circuitry," *Proc. DAC* , pp. 497–502, 1993.

[3] N. Maheshwari and S. S. Sapatnekar, "A practical algorithm for retiming level-clocked circuits," in *Proc. ICCD*, pp. 440–445, 1996.

[4] G. Even, I. Y. Spillinger, and L. Stok, "Retiming revisited and reversed," *IEEE Transactions on Computer-Aided Design*, vol. 15, pp. 348–357, Mar. 1996.

[5] H. J. Touati and R. K. Brayton, "Computing the initial states of retimed circuits," *IEEE Transactions on Computer-Aided Design*, vol. 12, pp. 157–162, Jan. 1993.

[6] N. Maheshwari and S. S. Sapatnekar, "An improved algorithm for minimum-area retiming," in *Proc. DAC*, pp. 2–7, 1997.

[7] M. Abramovici, M. A. Breuer, and A. D. Friedman, *Digital Systems Testing and Testable Design*. New York, NY: W. H. Freeman and Company, 1990.

[8] S. Kundu *et al.*, "A small test generator for large designs," in *Proc. ITC*, pp. 30–40, 1992.

[9] M. Berkelaar, *LP_SOLVE USER'S MANUAL*, 1992.

[10] V. Singhal, S. Malik, and R. K. Brayton, "The case for retiming with explicit reset circuitry," in *Proc. ICCAD*, pp. 618–625, 1996.

[2]The reader is reminded from our previous discussion that the lower bound is not guaranteed to be achievable.

Decomposition and Technology Mapping of Speed-Independent Circuits Using Boolean Relations*

Jordi Cortadella, Univ. Politècnica de Catalunya, Barcelona, Spain
Michael Kishinevsky, Alex Kondratyev, The University of Aizu, Japan
Luciano Lavagno, Politecnico di Torino, Italy
Enric Pastor, Univ. Politècnica de Catalunya, Barcelona, Spain
Alex Yakovlev, University of Newcastle upon Tyne, United Kingdom

Abstract

This paper presents a new technique for decomposition and technology mapping of speed-independent circuits. An initial circuit implementation is obtained in the form of a netlist of complex gates, *which may not be available in the design library. The proposed method iteratively performs* Boolean decomposition *of each such gate F into a two-input combinational or sequential gate G available in the library and two gates H_1 and H_2 simpler than F, while preserving the original behavior and speed-independence of the circuit. To extract functions for H_1 and H_2 the method uses* Boolean relations, *as opposed to the less powerful algebraic factorization approach used in previous methods. After logic decomposition, the overall library matching and optimization is carried out. Logic resynthesis, performed after speed-independent signal insertion for H_1 and H_2, allows for sharing of decomposed logic. Overall, this method is more general than the existing techniques based on restricted decomposition architectures, and thereby leads to better results in technology mapping.*

1 Introduction

Speed-independent circuits are *hazard-free under the unbounded gate delay model.* [4, 9, 6] provide general conditions for logic implementability of specifications into *complex gates*. The latter are allowed to have an arbitrary fanin.

To achieve greater practicality more recent work has been focused on the development of logic decomposition techniques. It falls into two categories. One of them attempts to achieve logic decomposition through the use of *standard architectures*. The other group comprises work targeting the decomposition of complex gates directly, by finding a behavior-preserving interconnection of simpler gates. In both cases, the major functional issue, in addition to logic simplification, is that the decomposed logic must not violate the original *speed-independent specification*.

Two examples of the first category are [1, 8]. The basic circuit architecture includes *C* elements (acting as latches) and combinational logic. This logic is assumed to consist of *AND* gates with potentially unbounded fain and unlimited input inversions and bounded fanin *OR* gates. *Monotonic Cover* (MC) requirements ensure implementability of a specification in this "standard-C" architecture and have an intuitive objective of making the first level (AND) gates work in a *one-hot* fashion with acknowledgment through one of the C-elements. Following this approach, methods for speed-independent decomposition into *implementable* libraries have been developed. E.g., the method of [13] decomposes (if possible) existing gates (e.g., a 3-input *AND* into two 2-input *AND*s), without any further search of the implementation space, and the method of [7] extends the decomposition to more complex (algebraic) divisors, but does not tackle the limitation of the initial MC architecture.

*This work has been funded by ESPRIT ACiD-WG Nr. 214949, CICYT TIC 95-0419, EPSRC grants GR/L24038 and GR/K70175, and MURST (project "VLSI Architectures").

The best representative of the second category appears to be the work of S. Burns [3]. It provides general conditions for speed-independent decomposition of complex (sequential) elements into two sequential elements (or a sequential and a combinational element). Notably, these conditions are analyzed using the original (unexpanded) behavioral model, thus improving the efficiency of the method. This work is, in our opinion, a big step in the right direction, but addresses mainly correctness issues. It does not describe how to use the efficient correctness checks in an optimization loop, and does not allow the sharing of a decomposed gate by different signal networks.

In [14, 12] methods for technology mapping of fundamental mode and speed-independent circuits using complex gates were presented. These methods however only identify when a set of simple logic gates can be implemented as a complex gate, but cannot perform a speed-independent decomposition of a signal function in case it does not fit into a single gate. A BDD-based implementation of [12] is used after decomposition as a post-optimization step in this work.

In our present work we are considering a more general framework which allows use of *arbitrary gates and latches* available in the library to decompose a complex gate function, as shown in Figure 1. In that respect, we are effectively making progress towards the more flexible second approach. The basic idea of this new method is as follows.

An initial complex gate is characterized by its function F. The result of decomposition is a library component designated by G and a set of (possibly still complex) gates labeled $H_1, H_2, \ldots H_n$. The latter are decomposed recursively until all elements are found in the library and optimized to achieve the lowest possible cost. We thus by and large put no restrictions on the implementation architecture in this work. However, as will be seen further, for the sake of practical efficiency, our implemented procedure deals only with the 2-input gates and/or latches to act as G-elements in the decomposition. The second important change of this work compared to [7] is that the new method is based on a full scale Boolean decomposition rather than just on algebraic factorization. This allows us to widen the scope of implementable solutions and improve on area cost (future work will tackle performance-oriented decomposition).

Our second goal in generalizing the C-element based decomposition has been to allow the designer to use more *conventional types of latches*, e.g. D-latches and SR-latches, instead of C-elements that may not exist in conventional standard-cell libraries. Furthermore, as our experimental results show (see Section 6), in many cases the use of standard latches instead of C-elements helps improving the circuit implementations considerably.

The power of this new method can be appreciated by looking at the example `hazard.g`.The original STG specification and its state graph are shown in Figure 2,a and b. The initial implementation using the "standard C-architecture" and its decomposition using two input gates by the method described in [7] are shown in Figure 2,c and d. Our new method produces a much cheaper

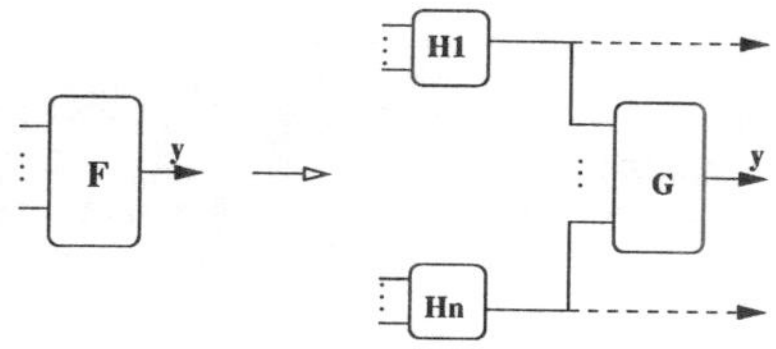

Figure 1: Framework for speed-independent decomposition

solution with just two D-latches, shown in Figure 2,e. Despite the apparent triviality (for an experienced human designer!) of this solution, none of the previously existing automated tools has been able to obtain it. Also note that the D-latches are used in a *speed-independent* fashion, and are thus free from meta-stability and hazard problems.

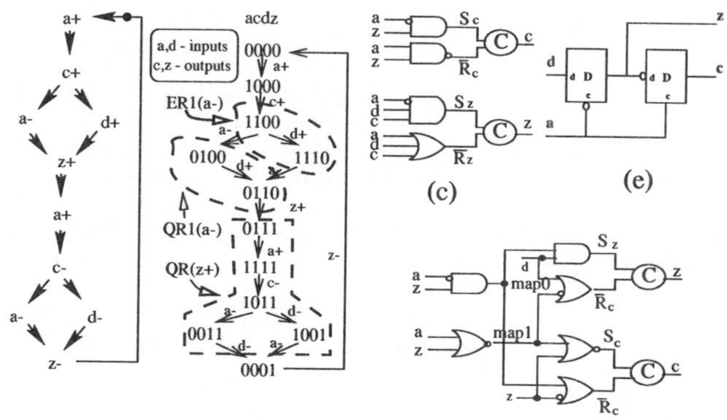

(a) (b) (c) (d) (e)

Figure 2: An example of Signal Transition Graph (a), State Graph (b) and their implementation (c)(d)(e) (benchmark `hazard.g`)

The paper is organized as follows. Section 2 introduces the main theoretical concepts. Section 3 presents an overview of the method. Section 4 describes the Boolean relation-based decomposition technique in more detail. Section 5 briefly describes its algorithmic implementation. Experimental results are presented in Section 6.

2 Background

2.1 State Graphs and Logic Implementability

A *State Graph* (SG) is a labeled directed graph whose nodes are called *states*. Each arc of an SG is labeled with an *event*, that is a rising ($a+$) or falling ($a-$) transition of a signal a in the specified circuit. We also allow notation $a*$ if we are not specific about the direction of the signal transition. Each state is labeled with a vector of signal values. An SG is *consistent* if its state labeling $v : S \rightarrow \{0,1\}^n$ is such that: in every transition sequence from the initial state, rising and falling transitions alternate for each signal. Figure 2,b shows the SG for the Signal Transition Graph in Figure 2,a, which is consistent. We write $s \xrightarrow{a}$ ($s \xrightarrow{a} s'$) if there is an arc from state s (to state s') labeled with a.

The set of all signals whose transitions label SG arcs are partitioned into a (possibly empty) set of inputs, which come from the environment, and a set of outputs or state signals that must be implemented. In addition to consistency, the following two properties of an SG are needed for their implementability in a speed-independent logic circuit.

The first property is *speed-independence*. It consists of three parts: determinism, commutativity and output-persistence. An SG is called *deterministic* if for each state s and each label a there can be at most one state s' such that $s \xrightarrow{a} s'$. An SG is called *commutative* if whenever two transitions can be executed from some state in any order, then their execution always leads to the same state, regardless of the order. An event a^* is called persistent in state s if it is enabled at s and remains enabled in any other state reachable from s by firing another event b^*. An SG is called *output-persistent* if its output signal events are persistent in all states and no output signal event can disable input events. Any transformation (e.g., insertion of new signals for decomposition), if performed at the SG level, may affect all three properties.

The second requirement, *Complete State Coding* (CSC), becomes necessary and sufficient for the existence of a logic circuit implementation. A consistent SG satisfies the CSC property if for every pair of states s, s' such that $v(s) = v(s')$, the set of output events enabled in both states is the same. (The SG in Figure 2,b is *output-persistent* and has CSC.) CSC does not however restrict the type of logic function implementing each signal. It requires that each signal is cast into a *single atomic* gate. The complexity of such a gate can however go beyond that provided in a concrete library or technology.

The concepts of excitation regions and quiescent regions are essential for transformation of SGs. A set of states is called an *excitation region* (ER) for event a^* (denoted by $ER(a^*)$) iff $s \in ER(a^*) \Leftrightarrow s \xrightarrow{a^*}$. The *quiescent region* (QR) (denoted by $QR(a^*)$) of a transition a^*, with excitation region $ER(a^*)$, is the set of states in which a is stable and keeps the same value. Examples of ER and QR are shown in Figure 2,b.

2.2 Property-preserving event insertion

Event insertion is an operation on an SG which selects a subset of states, splits each of them into two states and creates, on the basis of these new states, an excitation region for a new event. Figure 3 shows the chosen insertion scheme, analogous to that used by most authors in the area [15]. We say that an inserted signal *a is acknowledged* by a signal b, if b is one of the signals delayed by the insertion of a, (the same terminology will be used for the corresponding transitions). For example, d acknowledges x in Figure 3.

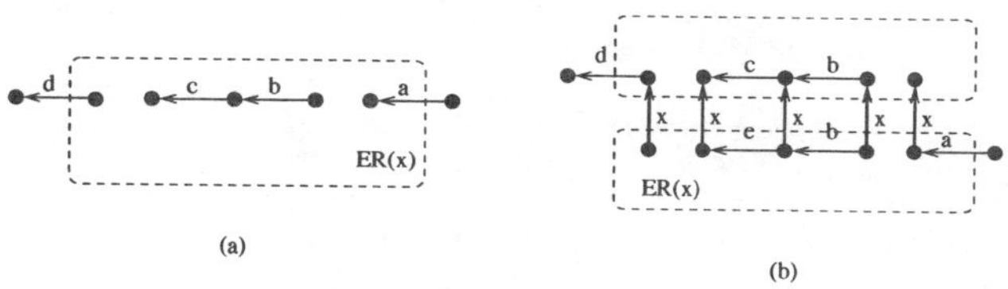

Figure 3: Event insertion: (a) before, (b) after insertion

State signal insertion must preserve the *speed-independence* of the original specification. The events corresponding to an inserted signal x are denoted $x*$, $x+$, $x-$, or, if no confusion occurs, simply by x. Let A be a deterministic, commutative SG and let A' be the SG obtained from A by inserting event x. We say that an insertion state set $ER(x)$ in A is a *speed-independence preserving set (SIP-set)* iff: (1) for each event a in A, if a is persistent in A, then it remains persistent in A', and (2) A' is deterministic and commutative. The formal conditions for the set of states r to be a SIP-set can be given in terms of intersections of r with the so-called state diamonds of SG [5].

A new signal is inserted using an *I-partition* of a set of states S into four blocks: $\{ER(x+), QR(x+), ER(x-), QR(x-)\}$ (similar to [15]). $QR(x-)(QR(x+))$ defines the states in which x will have the stable value 0 (1). $ER(x+)$ ($ER(x-)$) defines the excitation region of x in the new SG A'. To distinguish between the sets of states for the excitation (quiescent) regions of the inserted signal x in an original SG A and the new SG A' we will refer to them as $ER_A(x*)$ and $ER_{A'}(x*)$ ($QR_A(x*)$ and $QR_{A'}(x*)$), respectively. If the insertion of x preserves consistency and persistency, then the only transitions crossing boundaries of the blocks are the following: $QR(x-) \to ER_A(x+) \to QR(x+) \to ER_A(x-) \to QR(x-)$.

Example 2.1 *Figure 4 shows three different cases of the insertion of a new signal x into the SG for the* `hazard.g` *example. The insertion using $ER_A(x+)$ and $ER_A(x-)$ of Figure 4,a does not preserve speed-independence as the SIP set conditions are violated for $ER_A(x+)$ since transition $d+$, enabled in state 1100, will be delayed in state 0100 after inserting x.*

When signal x is inserted by the excitation regions in Figure 4,b then its positive switching is acknowledged by transitions $a-$, $d+$, while its negative switching by transition $z-$. The corresponding excitation regions satisfy the SIP conditions and the new SG A', obtained after insertion of signal x, is shown in Figure 4,b. Note that the acknowledgment of $x+$ by transitions $a-$, $d+$ results in delaying some input signal *transitions in A' until $x+$ fires. This changes the original I/O interface for SG A, because it requires the environment to look at the new signal before it can change a and d. This is generally undesirable and hence this insertion is rejected.*

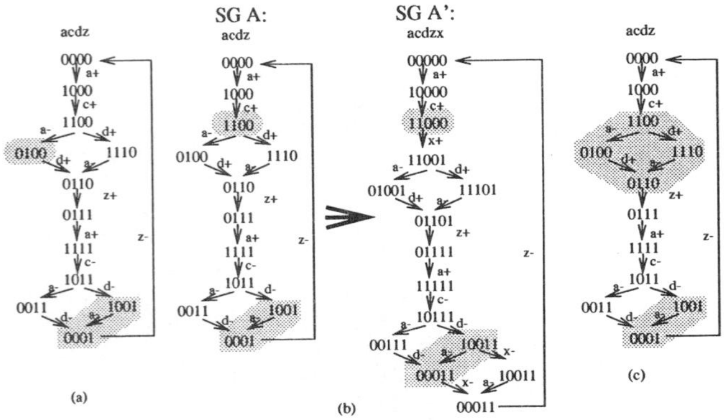

Figure 4: Different cases of signal insertion for benchmark `hazard.g`: violating the SIP-condition (a), changing the I/O interface (b), correct insertion (c)

The excitation regions $ER_A(x+)$ and $ER_A(x-)$ shown in Figure 4,c are SIP sets. They comply with the original I/O interface because positive and negative transitions of signal x are acknowledged only by output signal z. This insertion scheme is valid.

2.3 Basic definitions about Boolean Functions and Relations

An incompletely specified (scalar) Boolean function is a mapping $F: B^n \to \{0, 1, -\}$, where $B = \{0, 1\}$ and '$-$' is a *don't care* value. The subsets of domain B^n in which F holds the 0, 1 and don't care value are respectively called the *OFF-set*, *ON-set* and *DC-set*. F is *completely specified* if its DC-set is empty. We shall further always assume that F is a completely specified Boolean function unless said otherwise specifically.

A variable $x \in X$ is *essential* for function F (or F is dependent on x) if there exist at least two minterms $v1, v2$ different only in the value of x, such that $F(v1) \neq F(v2)$. The set of essential variables for a Boolean function F is called the *true support* of F and is denoted by $sup(F)$. It is clear that for an arbitrary Boolean function its support may not be the same as the true support. E.g., for a support $X = \{a, b, c\}$ and a function $F(X) = \overline{b} + c$ the true support of $F(X)$ is $sup(F) = \{b, c\}$, i.e. only a subset of X.

The *cofactor* of $F(X)$ with respect to x_i ($\overline{x_i}$) is defined as $F_{x_i} = F(x_1, \ldots, x_i = 1, \ldots, x_n)$ ($F_{\overline{x_i}} = F(x_1, \ldots, x_i = 0, \ldots, x_n)$, respectively). The Shannon expansion of a Boolean function $F(X)$ is based on its cofactors: $F(X) = x_i F_{x_i} + \overline{x_i} F_{\overline{x_i}}$. The *Boolean difference*, or *Boolean derivative*, of $F(X)$ with respect to $x_i \in X$ is defined as $\delta F / \delta x = F_{x_i} \oplus F_{\overline{x_i}}$

```
do
    foreach non-input signal x do
        solutions(x):=∅;
        foreach gate G ∈ {latches, and2, or2} do
            solutions(x):=solutions(x) ∪ decompositions(x,G);
        endfor
        best_H(x) := Best SIP candidate from solutions(x);
    endfor
    if foreach x, best_H(x) is implementable
    or foreach x, best_H(x) is empty then exit loop;
    Let H be the most complex best_H(x);
    Insert signal z implementing H, derive new SG;
forever
Library matching;
```

Figure 5: Algorithm for logic decomposition and technology mapping.

A function $F(x_1, \ldots, x_i, \ldots, x_n)$ is *unate in variable x_i* if either $F_{\overline{x_i}} \leq F_{x_i}$ or $F_{x_i} \leq F_{\overline{x_i}}$ under ordering $0 \leq - \leq 1$. In the former case ($F_{\overline{x_i}} \leq F_{x_i}$) it is called *positive unate in x_i*, in the latter case *negative unate in x_i*. A function that is not unate in x_i is called *binate* in x_i. A function is (positive/negative) *unate* if it is (positive/negative) *unate* in all support variables. Otherwise it is binate. For example, the function $F = a + b + \overline{c}$ is positive unate in variable a because $F_a = 1 \geq F_{\overline{a}} = b + \overline{c}$.

For an incompletely specified function $F(X)$ with a DC-set, let us define the DC function $F_{DC}: B^n \to B$ such that $ON(F_{DC}) = DC(F)$. We will say that a function $\widetilde{F}$ is an *implementation of* F if $F \cdot \overline{F_{DC}} \leq \widetilde{F} \leq F + F_{DC}$.

A *Boolean relation*, R, is a generalization of a Boolean function, where a point in the domain B^n can be associated with several points in the codomain, i.e. $R \subseteq B^n \times \{0, 1\}^m$ [2, 11]. Sometimes, we use the "$-$" symbol as a shorthand in denoting elements in the codomain vector, e.g. -0 for 10 and 00. Boolean relations play an important role in multi-level logic synthesis [11], and we shall use them in our decomposition method.

Consider a set of Boolean functions $\mathcal{H} = \{H_1, H_2, \ldots, H_m\}$ with the same domain. Let $R \subseteq B^n \times \{0, 1\}^m$ be a Boolean relation with the same domain as functions from $\mathcal{H}$. We will say that $\mathcal{H}$ is *compatible* with R if for every point v in the domain of R the vector of values $(v, H_1(v), H_2(v), \ldots, H_m(v))$ is an element of R.

3 Overview of the method

Our proposed method for sequential decomposition of speed-independent circuits aimed at technology mapping consists of three main steps:

1. Synthesis via decomposition based on Boolean relations;
2. Signal insertion and generation of a new SG;
3. Library matching

The first two steps are iterated until all functions are decomposed into implementable gates or no further progress can be made. Each time a new signal is inserted (step 2), resynthesis is performed for all output signals (step 1). Finally, step 3 collapses decomposed gates and matches them with library gates. The pseudo-code for the technology mapping algorithm is given in Figure 5.

By using a speed-independent initial SG specification, a complex gate implementation for each SG signal is guaranteed to be speed-independent. Unfortunately this gate may be too large to be implemented in a library. The goal of the proposed method is to break this gate *starting from its output* by using *sequential* (if its function is self-dependent, i.e. it has internal feedback) or *combinational* gates.

Given a vector X of SG signals and given one non-input signal $y \in X$ we try to decompose the function $F(X)$ into (line 2 of algorithm in Figure 5):

- a combinational or sequential gate with function $G(Z, y)$, where Z is a vector of newly introduced signals,
- a vector of combinational[1] functions $\mathcal{H}(X)$ for signals Z,

so that $G(\mathcal{H}(X))$ implements $F(X)$. Moreover, we require the newly introduced signals to be speed-independent (line 3).

The problem of representing the flexibility in the choice of the $\mathcal{H}$ functions has been explored, in the context of combinational logic minimization, by [18] among others. Here we extend its formulation to cover also *sequential* gates (in Sections 4.1 and 4.3). This is essential in order to overcome the limitations of previous methods for speed-independent circuit synthesis that were based on a specific architecture. Now we are able to use a broad range of sequential elements, like set and reset dominant SR latches, transparent D latches, and so on. We believe that overcoming this limitation of previous methods (that could only use C elements and dual-rail SR-latches) is one of the major strengths of this work. Apart from dramatically improving some experimental results, it allows one to use a "generic" standard-cell library (that generally includes SR and D latches, but not C elements).

The algorithm proceeds as follows. We start from an SG and derive a logic function for all its non-input signals (line 1). We then perform an implementability check for each such function as a library gate. The largest non-implementable function is selected for decomposition. In order to limit the search space, we currently try as candidates for G (line 2):

- all the sequential elements in the library (assumed to have two inputs at most, again in order to limit the search space),
- two-input *AND, OR* gates with all possible input inversions.

The set of function pairs (H_1, H_2) compatible with the Boolean relation is then checked for speed-independence (line 3), as described in Section 2.2. If both are not speed-independent, the pair is immediately rejected.

Then, both H_1 and H_2 are checked for approximate (as discussed above) implementability in the library, in increasing order of estimated cost. We have two cases:

1. both are speed-independent and implementable: in this case the decomposition is accepted,
2. otherwise, the most complex implementable H_i is selected, and the other one is merged with G.

The latter is a heuristic technique aimed at keeping the decomposition balanced. Note that at this stage we can also implement H_1 or H_2 as a *sequential gate* if the *sufficient* conditions described in Section 4.3 are met.

The procedure is iterated as long as there is progress or until everything has been decomposed (line 4). Each time a new function H_i is selected to be implemented as a new signal, it is inserted into the SG (line 6) and resynthesis is performed in the next iteration.

The incompleteness of the method is essentially due to the greedy heuristic search that accepts the smallest implementable or non-implementable but speed-independent solution. We believe that an exhaustive enumeration with backtracking would be complete even for non-autonomous circuits, by a relatively straightforward extension of the results in [16].

At the end, we perform a Boolean matching step ([10]) to recover area and delay (line 7). This step can merge together the simple 2-input combinational gates that we have (conservatively) used in the decomposition into a larger library gate. It is guaranteed not to introduce any hazards if the matched gates are atomic.

[1] The restriction that $\mathcal{H}(X)$ be combinational will be partially lifted in Section 4.3.

4 Logic decomposition using Boolean relations

4.1 Specifying permissible decompositions with BRs

In this paper we apply BRs to the following problem.

Given an incompletely specified Boolean function $F(X)$ for signal $y, y \in X$, decompose it into two-levels $y = G(Z, y)$; $Z = \mathcal{H}(X)$ such that $G(\mathcal{H}(X), y)$ implements $F(X)$ and functions G and $\mathcal{H}$ have a simpler implementation than F (any such $\mathcal{H}$ will be called permissible).

The first-level function $\mathcal{H}(X) = \{H_1(X), \ldots, H_n(X)\}$ is a multi-output logic function, specifying the behavior of internal nodes of the decomposition, $Z = \{z_1, \ldots, z_n\}$ [2].

At each step of decomposition a small mappable piece (function G) is cut from the potentially complex and unmappable function F. For a selected G all permissible implementations of function $\mathcal{H}$ are specified with a BR and then via minimization of BRs a few best compatible functions are obtained. All of them are verified for speed-independence by checking SIP-sets. The one which is speed-independent and has the best estimated cost is selected.

Since the true support of function F can include the output variable y, it can specify sequential behavior. In the most general case we perform two-level *sequential* decomposition such that both function G and function $\mathcal{H}$ can be sequential, i.e., contain their own output variables in the true supports. The second level of the decomposition is made sequential by selecting a latch from the library as a candidate gate, G. The technique for deriving a sequential solution for the first level $\mathcal{H}$ is described in Section 4.3.

We next show by example how all permissible implementations of decomposition can be expressed with BRs.

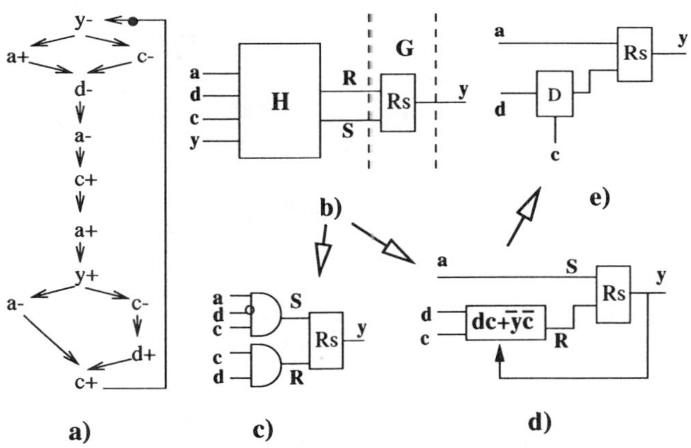

Figure 6: Sequential decomposition for $y = ac\overline{d} + y(\overline{c} + \overline{d})$

Example 4.1 *Consider the STG in Figure 6,a, whose SG appears in Figure 7,a. Signals a, c and d are inputs and y is an output. A possible implementation of the logic function for y is $F(a, c, d, y) = ac\overline{d} + y(\overline{c} + \overline{d})$. Let us decompose this function using as G a reset-dominant Rs-latch represented by the equation $y = G(R, S, y) = \overline{R}(S + y)$ (see Figure 6,b). At the first step we specify the permissible implementations for the first level functions $R = H_1$ and $S = H_2$ by using the BR specified in Figure 7,b. Consider, for example, vector $a, c, d, y = 0000$. It is easy to check that $F(0,0,0,0) = 0$. Hence, for vector 0000 the table specifies that $(R, S) = \{11, 10, 00\} = \{1-, -0\}$, i.e. any implementation of R and S must keep for this input vector* either 1 *at*

[2] For simplicity we consider the decomposition problem for a single-output binary function F, although generalization for the multi-output and multi-valued functions is straightforward.

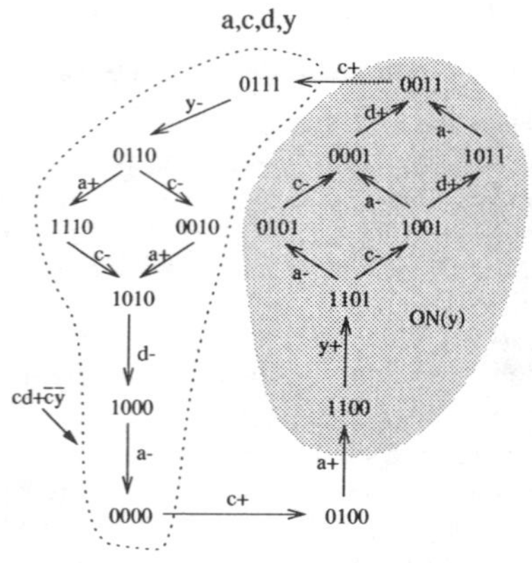

(a)

$acdy$	F	RS
0000	0	1–,–0
0001	1	0–
0010	0	1–,–0
0011	1	0–
0100	0	1–,–0
0101	1	0–
0110	0	1–,–0
0111	0	1–
1000	0	1–,–0
1001	1	0–
1010	0	1–,–0
1011	1	0–
1100	1	01
1101	1	0–
1110	0	1–,–0
1111	–	–

(b)

Figure 7: (a) State graph, (b) Decomposition of y by an Rs latch

Region	D-latch C, D	Rs R, S	AND H_1, H_2	OR H_1, H_2
$ER(y+)$	11	01	11	$\{1-, -1\}$
$QR(y+)$	$\{0-, -1\}$	0–	11	$\{1-, -1\}$
$ER(y-)$	10	1–	$\{0-, -0\}$	00
$QR(y-)$	$\{0-, -0\}$	$\{1-, -0\}$	$\{0-, -0\}$	00
unreachable	– –	– –	– –	– –

Table 1: Boolean relations for different gates

R or 0 at S. On the other hand, only one solution $R = 0,\ S = 1$ is possible for the input vector 1100 which corresponds to setting the output of the Rs-latch to 1. The Boolean relation solver will find, among others, the two solutions illustrated in Figure 6,c,d: (1) $R = cd$; $S = ac\overline{d}$ and (2) $R = cd + \overline{y}\,\overline{c}$; $S = a$. Any of these solutions can be chosen depending on the cost function.

Table 1 specifies compatible values of BRs for different types of gates: a D-latch, a reset-dominant Rs-latch, a two input AND gate and a two input OR gate. All states of an SG are partitioned into four subsets, $ER(y+)$, $QR(y+)$, $ER(y-)$, and $QR(y-)$, with respect to signal y with function $F(X)$ for which decomposition is performed. All states that are not reachable in the SG form a DC-set for the BR. E.g., for each state, s, from $ER(y+)$ only one compatible solution, 11, is allowed for input functions H_1, H_2 of a D-latch. This is because the output of a D-latch in all states, $s \in ER(y+)$ is at 0 and $F(s) = 1$. Under these conditions the combination 11 (clock and data inputs are both high) is the only possible input combination that implies 1 at the output of a D-latch. On the other hand, for each state $s \in QR(y+)$, the output $y = 1$ and $F(s) = 1$, hence it is enough to require either data input to be in 1 or clock input to be in 0 to keep the output of a latch in 1. This is expressed by values $\{0-, -1\}$ in the second line of the table.

4.2 Functional representation of Boolean relations

Given an SG satisfying CSC requirement, each output signal $y \in X$ is associated with a unique *incompletely* specified function $F(X)$, whose DC-set represents the set of unreachable states. $F(X)$ can be represented by three *completely* specified functions, denoted $ON(y)(X)$, $OFF(y)(X)$ and $DC(y)(X)$ representing the ON-, OFF-, and DC-set of $F(X)$, such that they are pairwise disjoint and their union is a tautology.

Let a generic n-input gate be represented by a Boolean equation $q = G(Z, q)$, where $Z = \{z_1, \ldots, z_n\}$ are the inputs of the gate, and q is its output. The gate is sequential if q belongs to the true support of $G(Z, q)$.

We now give the characteristic function of the Boolean relation for the implementation of $F(X)$ with gate G. It represents *all* permissible implementations of $z_1 = H_1(X), \ldots, z_n = H_n(X)$ that allow F to be decomposed by G.

$$BR(y)(X, Z) = ON(y)(X) \cdot G(Z, y) + OFF(y)(X) \cdot \overline{G(Z, y)} + DC(y)(X) \quad (1)$$

Given characteristic function (1), the corresponding table describing Boolean relation can be derived using cofactors. For each minterm m with support in X, the cofactor $BR(y)_m$ gives the characteristic function of all compatible values for $z_1, \ldots, z_n$ (see example below).

Finding a decomposition of F with gate G is reduced to finding a set of n functions $\mathcal{H}(X) = (H_1(X), \ldots, H_n(X))$ such that

$$BR(y)(X, \mathcal{H}(X)) = 1 \quad (2)$$

Example 4.2 (Example 4.1 continued.) *The SG shown in Figure 7.a corresponds to the STG in Figure 6. Let us consider how the implementation of signal y with a reset-dominant Rs latch can be expressed using the characteristic function of BR. Recall that the table shown in Figure 7.b represents the function $F(a, c, d, y) = ac\overline{d} + y(\overline{c} + \overline{d})$ and the permissible values for the inputs R and S of the Rs latch. The ON-, OFF-, and DC-sets of function $F(a, c, d, y)$ are defined by:*

$$\begin{aligned} ON(y) &= y(\overline{c} + \overline{d}) + ac\overline{d} \\ OFF(y) &= \overline{y}(\overline{a} + \overline{c} + d) + \overline{a}cd \\ DC(y) &= acdy \end{aligned}$$

The set of permissible implementations for R and S is characterized by the following characteristic function of the BR specified in the table. It can be obtained using equation 1 by substituting expressions for $ON(y)$, $OFF(y)$, $DC(y)$, and the function of an Rs-latch, $\overline{R}(S + y)$:

$$BR(y)(a, c, d, y, R, S) = \overline{R}Sac\overline{d} + \overline{R}y(\overline{c} + \overline{d}) + (R + \overline{S})\overline{y}(\overline{a} + \overline{c} + d) + \overline{a}cd(R + \overline{S}\overline{y}) + acdy$$

This function has value 1 for all combinations represented in the table and value 0 for all combinations that are not in the table (e.g., for $(a, c, d, y, R, S) = 000001$). For example, the set of compatible values for $acdy = 0110$ is given by the cofactor $BR(y)_{\overline{a}cd\overline{y}} = R + \overline{S}$ which correspond to the terms 1– and –0 given for the Boolean relation for that minterm.

Two possible solutions for $BR(y)(a, c, d, y, R, S) = 1$ corresponding to Figure 6,c,d are:

(1) $R = cd$; $S = ac\overline{d}$ (2) $R = cd + \overline{y}\,\overline{c}$; $S = a$

4.3 Two-level sequential decomposition

Accurate estimation of the cost of each solution produced by the Boolean relation minimizer is essential in order to ensure the quality of the final result. The minimizer itself can only handle combinational logic, but often (as shown below) the best solution can be obtained by replacing a combinational gate with a sequential one. This section discusses some heuristic techniques that can be used to identify when such a replacement is possible without altering the asynchronous circuit behavior, and without undergoing the cost of a full-blown sequential optimization step. Let us consider our example again.

Example 4.3 (Example 4.1 continued.) *Let us assume that the library contains three-input AND, OR gates and Rs-, Sr- and D-latches. Implementation (1) of signal y by an Rs-latch with inputs R=cd and S=$ac\overline{d}$ matches the library and requires two AND gates* *(one with two and one with three inputs) and one Rs-latch. The implementation (2) of y by an Rs-latch with inputs R=$cd+\overline{y}\,\overline{c}$ and S=a would be rejected, as it requires a complex AND-OR gate which is not in the library. However, when input $\overline{y}$ in the function $cd + \overline{y}\,\overline{c}$ is replaced by signal R, the output behavior of R will not change, i.e. function R=$cd + \overline{y}\,\overline{c}$ can be safely replaced by R=$cd + R\overline{c}$. The latter equation corresponds to the function of a D-latch and gives the valid implementation shown in Figure 6,e.*

Our technique to improve the accuracy of the cost estimation step, by partially considering sequential gates, is as follows:

1. Produce permissible functions $z_1 = H_1(X)$ and $z_2 = H_2(X)$ via the minimization of Boolean relations (z_1 and z_2 are always combinational as $z_1, z_2 \notin X$).
2. Estimate the complexity of H_1 and H_2:
   if H_i matches the library **then** *Complexity* = cost of the gate
   else *Complexity* = literal count
3. Estimate the possible simplification of H_1 and H_2 due to adding signals z_1 and z_2 to their supports, i.e. estimate the complexity of the new pair $\{H_1', H_2'\}$ of permissible functions $z_1 = H_1'(X, z_1, z_2)$, $z_2 = H_2'(X, z_1, z_2)$.
4. Choose the best complexity between H_1 (H_2) and H_1' (H_2').

Let us consider the task of determining H_1' and H_2' as in step 3. Let A be an SG encoded by variables from set V and let $z = H(X, y)$, such that $X \subseteq V, y \in V$, be an equation for the new variable $z \notin V$ which is to be inserted in A. The resulting SG is denoted A'=$Ins(A, z$=$H(X, y))$ (or A'=$Ins(A, z_1, \ldots, z_k)$ when more than one signal is inserted).

A solution for Step 3 of the above procedure can be obtained by minimizing functions for signals z_1 and z_2 in an SG $A' = Ins(A, z_1, z_2)$. However this is rather inefficient because the creation of SG A' is computationally expensive. Hence instead of looking for an exact estimation of complexity for signals z_1 and z_2 we will rely on a heuristic solution, following the ideas on input resubstitution presented in Example 4.3. For computational efficiency, the formal conditions on input resubstitution should be formulated in terms of an original SG A rather than in terms of the SG A' obtained after the insertion of new signals[3].

Lemma 4.1 *Let Boolean function $H(X, y)$ implement the inserted signal z.Function H can be represented as $H(X, y) = Fy + G\overline{y} + R$, where F, G and R are Boolean functions not depending on y. Let $H'(X, z) = z(F + G) + R$, then SGs A'=$Ins(A, z$=$H(X, y))$ and A''=$Ins(A, z$=$H'(X, z))$ are isomorphic iff the following conditions are satisfied:*

$$\delta H(X, y)/\delta y \cdot S^* \equiv 0 \quad (1) \qquad F * G * \overline{R} \cap S^+ \equiv 0 \quad (2),$$

where S^* and S^+ are characteristic Boolean functions describing sets of states $ER_A(z+) \cup ER_A(z-)$ and $ER_A(z+)$ in A, respectively.

Informally Lemma 4.1 states that resubstitution of input y by z is permissible if in all states where the value of function $H(X, y)$ depends on y, the inserted signal z has a stable value. The conditions of Lemma 4.1 can be efficiently checked within our BDD-based framework. They require to check two tautologies involving functions defined over the states of the original SG A.

Example 4.4 (Example 4.1 continued.) *Let input R of the RS-latch be implemented as $cd + \overline{y}\,\overline{c}$ (see Figure 6,d). The ON-set of function H=cd+$\overline{y}\,\overline{c}$ is shown by the dashed line in Figure 7,a. The input border of H (denoted by $IB(H)$) is the set of states by which its ON-set is entered in the original SG A, i.e. $IB(H) = \{0111\}$. By similar consideration we have that $IB(\overline{H}) = \{0100\}$. These input borders satisfy the SIP conditions and hence $IB(H)$ can be taken as $ER_A(R+)$, while $ER_A(R-)$ must be expanded beyond $IB(\overline{H})$ by state 1100 for not to delay the input transition $a+$ ($ER_A(R-) = \{0100, 1100\}$).*

H is negative unate in y and hence Condition 2 of Lemma 4.1 is always satisfied. The set of states where the value of function H essentially depends on signal y is given by the function $\delta H(X, y)/\delta y = a\overline{c}$. Cube $a\overline{c}$ has no intersection with $ER_A(R+) \cup ER_A(R-)$ and Condition 1 of Lemma 4.1 is also satisfied. Therefore literal $\overline{y}$ can be replaced by literal R, thus producing a new permissible function R=$cd + R\overline{c}$.

[3]Note that this heuristic estimation covers only the cases when one of the input signals for a combinational permissible function H_i is replaced by the feedback z_i from the output of H_i itself. Other cases can also be investigated, but checking them would be too complex.

5 Implementation aspects

The method for logic decomposition presented in the previous section has been implemented in a synthesis tool for speed-independent circuits. The main purpose of such implementation was to evaluate the potential improvements that could be obtained in the synthesis of speed-independent circuits by using a Boolean-relation-based decomposition approach. Efficiency of the current implementation was considered to be a secondary goal at this stage of the research.

5.1 Solving Boolean relations

In the overall approach, it is required to solve BRs for each output signal and for each gate and latch used for decomposition. Furthermore, for each signal and for each gate, several solutions are desirable in order to increase the chances to find SIP functions.

Previous approaches to solve BRs [2, 17] do not satisfy the needs of our synthesis method, since (1) they minimize the number of terms of a multiple-output function and (2) they deliver (without significant modifications to the algorithms and their implementation) only one solution for each BR. In our case we need to obtain *several compatible solutions* with the primary goal of *minimizing the complexity of each function individually.* Term sharing is not significant because two-level decomposition of a function is not speed-independent in general, and hence each minimized function must be treated as an *atomic* object. Sharing can be exploited, on the other hand, when re-synthesizing the circuit after insertion of each new signal. For this reason we devised a heuristic approach to solve BRs. We next briefly sketch it.

Given a BR $BR(y)(X, Z)$, each function H_i for z_i is individually minimized by assuming that all other functions H_j ($i \neq j$) will be defined in such a way that $\mathcal{H}(X)$ will be a compatible solution for BR. In general, an incompatible solution may be generated when combining all H_i's. Taking the example of Figure 7, an individual minimization of R and S could generate the solution $R = cd$ and $S = 1$.

Next, a minterm with *incompatible* values is selected, e.g. $\overline{a}\overline{c}\overline{d}\overline{y}$ for which $RS = 01$ but only the compatible values $1-$ or -0 are acceptable. New BRs are derived by freezing different compatible values for the selected minterm. In this case, two new BRs will be produced with the values $1-$ and -0, respectively for the minterm $\overline{a}\overline{c}\overline{d}\overline{y}$. Next, each BR is again minimized individually for each output function and new minterms are frozen until a compatible solution is obtained.

This approach generates a tree of BRs to be solved. This provides a way of obtaining several compatible solutions for the same BR. However, the exploration may become prohibitively expensive if the search tree is not pruned. In our implementation, a branch-and-bound-like pruning strategy has been incorporated for such purpose. Still, the time required by the BR solver dominates the computational cost of the overall method in our current implementation. Ongoing research on solving BRs for our framework is being carried out. We believe that the fact that we pursue to minimize functions individually, i.e. without caring about term sharing among different output functions, and that we only deal with 2-output decompositions, may be crucial to derive algorithms much more efficient than the existing approaches.

5.2 Selection of the best decomposition

Once a set of compatible solutions has been generated for each output signal, the best candidate is selected according to the following criteria (in priority order):

1. At least one of the decomposed functions must be speed-independent.
2. The acknowledgment of the decomposed functions must not increase the complexity of the implementation of other signals (see section 5.3).
3. Solutions in which all decomposable functions are implementable in the library are preferred.
4. Solutions in which the complexity of the largest non-implementable function is minimized are preferred. This criterion helps to balance the complexity of the decomposed functions and derive balanced tree-like structures rather than linear ones[4].
5. The estimated savings obtained by sharing a function for the implementation of several output signals is also considered as a second order priority criterion.

Among the best candidate solutions for all output signals, the function with the largest complexity, i.e. the farthest from implementability, is selected to be implemented as a new output signal of the SG.

The complexity of a function is calculated as the number of literals in factored form. In case it is a sequential function and it matches some of the latches of the gate library, the implementation cost is directly obtained from the information provided by the library.

5.3 Signal acknowledgment and insertion

For each function delivered by the BR solver, an efficient SIP insertion must be found. This reduces to finding a partition $\{ER_A(x+), QR_A(x+), ER_A(x-), QR_A(x-)\}$ of the SG A such that $ER_A(x+)$ and $ER_A(x-)$ are restricted to be SIP-sets (Section 2.2). In general, each function may have several $ER_A(x+)$ and $ER_A(x-)$ sets acceptable as ERs. Each one corresponds to a signal insertion with different acknowledging outputs signals for its transitions. In our approach, we perform a heuristic exploration seeking for different $ER_A(x+)$ and $ER_A(x-)$ sets for each function. We finally select one according to the following criteria:

- Sets that are only acknowledged by the signal that is being decomposed (i.e. local acknowledgment) are preferred.
- If no set with local acknowledgment is found, the one with least acknowledgment cost is selected. The cost is calculated by incrementally deriving the new SG after signal insertion.

As an example consider the SG of Figure 4,c and the insertion of a new signal x for the function $x = c + d$. A valid SIP set for $ER_A(x+)$ would be the set of states $\{1100, 0100, 1110, 0110\}$, where the state $\{1100\}$ is the input border for the inserted function. A valid SIP set for $ER_A(x-)$ would be the set of states $\{1001, 0001\}$. With such insertion, $ER_A(x+)$ will be acknowledged by the transition $z+$ and $ER_A(x-)$ by $z-$. However, this insertion is not unique. For the sake of simplicity, let us assume that a and d are also output signals. Then an insertion with $ER_A(x+) = \{1100\}$ would be also valid. In that case, the transition $x+$ would be acknowledged by the transitions $a-$ and $d+$.

[4]Different criteria, of course, may be used when we also consider the delay of the resulting implementation, since then keeping late arriving signals close to the output is generally useful and can require unbalanced trees.

Circuit	literals/latches		CPU	Area	Area SI	
	old	new	(secs)	non-SI	2i	3i
alloc-outbound	14/4	12/2	8	264	256	264
chu133	12/1	12/1	4	208	210	200
chu150	14/2	8/3	8	144	144	160
converta	12/3	8/3	9	312	232	224
dff	12/2	0/2	1	128	80	80
ebergen	20/3	6/2	3	176	136	136
half	2/2	2/3	1	176	138	130
hazard	12/2	0/2	1	112	96	96
master-read	30/9	26/13	112	688	668	634
mp-forward-pkt	12/3	14/1	5	232	224	232
mr1	36/9	26/10	253	592	762	846
nak-pa	20/4	18/1	12	248	304	328
nowick	16/1	16/1	6	232	232	304
ram-read-sbuf	20/4	22/3	23	360	378	344
rcv-setup	10/1	8/1	1	120	128	128
rpdft	22/1	22/0	12	176	200	216
sbuf-ram-write	22/6	20/3	79	288	378	338
sbuf-send-ctl	22/5	22/2	16	280	262	250
sbuf-send-pkt2	32/5	30/5	113	296	530	304
seq-mix	30/6	30/7	64	592	586	664
seq4	18/7	18/5	131	400	582	450
trimos-send	36/8	12/9	101	480	600	644
vbe5b	10/2	8/4	2	216	204	226
vbe5c	4/3	2/3	2	216	168	168
vbe6a	16/7	32/10	16	600	456	456
vbe10b	28/7	26/11	35	608	552	584
wrdatab	48/7	30/9	290	608	708	714
Total	530/114	430/116		8752	9214	9129

Table 2: Experimental results.

5.4 Library mapping

The logic decomposition of the non-input signals is completed by a technology mapping step aimed at recovering area and delay based on a technology-dependent library of gates. These reductions are achieved by collapsing small fanin gates into complex gates, provided that the gates are available in the library. The collapsing process is based on the Boolean matching techniques proposed by Mailhot et al. [10], adapted to the existence of asynchronous memory elements and combinational feedback in speed-independent circuits. The overall technology mapping process has been efficiently implemented using BDDs.

6 Experimental results

6.1 Results in decomposition and technology mapping

The method for logic decomposition presented in the previous sections has been implemented and combined with the algebraic method presented in [7]. The results obtained from a set of benchmarks are shown in Table 2. The benchmarks correspond to those presented in [7] that were completely decomposed into 2-input gates.

The columns "literals/latches" report the complexity of the circuits derived after logic decomposition into 2-input gates. The results obtained by the method presented in this paper ("new") are significantly better than those obtained by the method presented in [7] ("old"). Note that the library used for the "new" experiments was deliberately restricted to D, Sr and Rs latches (i.e. without C-elements, since they are generally not part of standard cell libraries). This improvement is mainly achieved because of two reasons:

- The superiority of Boolean methods versus algebraic methods for logic decomposition.
- The intensive use of different types of latches to implement sequential functions compared to the C-element-based implementation in [7].

However, the improved results obtained by using boolean methods are paid in terms of a significant increase in terms of CPU time. This is the reason why the boolean method has been combined with the algebraic method (instead of substituting it), in such a way that boolean relations are only solved to find solutions that improve the cost of the solutions previously obtained by using algebraic methods.

6.2 The cost of speed independence

The second part of Table 2 is an attempt to evaluate the cost of implementing an asynchronous specification as a speed-independent circuit. The experiments have been done as follows. For each benchmark, the following script has been run in SIS, using the library `asynch.genlib`: `astg_to_f; source script.rugged; map`. The resulting netlists reported in column `area non-SI` could be considered a lower bound on the area of the circuit regardless of its hazardous behavior (i.e. the circuit only implements the correct function for each output signal, without regard to hazards). `script.rugged` is the best known general-purpose optimization script for combinational logic.

The columns labeled `area SI` report the results obtained by the method proposed in this paper. We report results on two strategies for decomposition before mapping the circuit onto a library:

- Decompose all gates into 2-input gates (`2i`).
- Decompose all gates into 3-input gates (`3i`).

Experiments have also been run for 4-input gates, with no tangible improvements. In both cases, decomposition and mapping preserve speed independence, since we do not use gates (such as MUXes) that may have a hazardous behavior when the select input changes. There is no clear evidence that performing an aggressive decomposition into 2-input gates is always the best approach for technology mapping. The insertion of multiple-fanout signals offers opportunities to share logic in the circuit, but also precludes the mapper from taking advantage of the flexibility of mapping tree-like structures. This trade-off must be better explored in forthcoming work.

Looking at the best results for non-SI/SI implementations, we can conclude that preserving speed independence does not involve a significant overhead. In our experiments we have shown that the reported area is similar[5]. Some benchmarks were even more efficiently implemented by using the SI-preserving decomposition. We impute these improvements to the efficient mapping of functions into latches by using Boolean relations.

7 Conclusions and future work

In this paper we have shown a new solution to the problem of multi-level logic synthesis and technology mapping for asynchronous speed-independent circuits. The method consists of three major parts. Part 1 uses Boolean relations to compute a set of candidates for logic decomposition of the initial complex gate circuit implementation. Thus each complex gate F is iteratively split into a two-input combinational or sequential gate G available in the library and two gates H_1 and H_2 that are simpler than F, while preserving the original behavior and speed-independence of the circuit. The best candidates for H_1 and H_2 are selected for the next step, providing the lowest cost in terms of implementability and new signal insertion overhead. Part 2 of the method performs the actual insertion of new signals for H_1 and/or H_2 into the state graph specification, and re-synthesizes logic from the latter. Thus parts 1 and 2 are applied to each complex gate that cannot be mapped into the library. Finally, Part 3 does library matching to recover area and delay.

This method improves significantly over previously known techniques [1, 8, 7]. This is due to the significantly larger optimization space exploited by using (1) Boolean relations for decomposition and (2) a broader class of latches[6]. Furthermore, the ability to implement sequential functions with SR and D latches significantly improves the practicality of the method.

In the future we are planning to improve the Boolean relation solution algorithm, aimed at finding a set of optimal functions compatible with a Boolean relation. This is essential in order to improve the CPU times and synthesize successfully more complex specifications.

References

[1] P. A. Beerel and T. H-Y. Meng. Automatic gate-level synthesis of speed-independent circuits. In *Proceedings of the International Conference on Computer-Aided Design*, November 1992.

[2] R. K. Brayton and F. Somenzi. An exact minimizer for boolean relations. In *Proceedings of the International Conference on Computer-Aided Design*, pages 316–319, November 1989.

[3] S. Burns. General conditions for the decomposition of state holding elements. In *International Symposium on Advanced Research in Asynchronous Circuits and Systems, Aizu, Japan*, March 1996.

[4] T.-A. Chu. *Synthesis of Self-timed VLSI Circuits from Graph-theoretic Specifications*. PhD thesis, MIT, June 1987.

[5] J. Cortadella, M. Kishinevsky, A. Kondratyev, L. Lavagno, and A. Yakovlev. Complete state encoding based on the theory of regions. In *International Symposium on Advanced Research in Asynchronous Circuits and Systems, Aizu, Japan*, March 1996.

[6] M. A. Kishinevsky, A. Y. Kondratyev, A. R. Taubin, and V. I. Varshavsky. *Concurrent Hardware. The Theory and Practice of Self-Timed Design*. John Wiley and Sons Ltd., 1993.

[7] A. Kondratyev, J. Cortadella, M. Kishinevsky, L. Lavagno, and A. Yakovlev. Technology mapping for speed-independent circuits: decomposition and resynthesis. In *Third International Symposium on Advanced Research in Asynchronous Circuits and Systems, Eindhoven*, April 1997.

[8] A. Kondratyev, M. Kishinevsky, B. Lin, P. Vanbekbergen, and A. Yakovlev. Basic gate implementation of speed-independent circuits. In *Proceedings of the Design Automation Conference*, 1994.

[9] L. Lavagno and A. Sangiovanni-Vincentelli. *Algorithms for synthesis and testing of asynchronous circuits*. Kluwer Academic Publishers, 1993.

[10] F. Mailhot and G. De Micheli. Algorithms for technology mapping based on binary decision diagrams and on boolean operations. *IEEE Transactions on Computer-Aided Design*, 12(5):599–620, May 1993.

[11] G. De Micheli. *Synthesis and Optimization of Digital Circuits*. McGraw-Hill, Inc., 1994.

[12] Enric Pastor, Jordi Cortadella, Alex Kondratyev, and Oriol Roig. Structural methods for the synthesis of speed-independent circuits. In *Proc. of European Design and Test Conference*, pages 340 – 347, Paris(France), March 1996.

[13] P. Siegel and G. De Micheli. Decomposition methods for library binding of speed-independent asynchronous designs. In *Proceedings of the International Conference on Computer-Aided Design*, pages 558–565, November 1994.

[14] P. Siegel, G. De Micheli, and D. Dill. Automatic technology mapping for generalized fundamental mode asynchronous designs. In *Proceedings of the Design Automation Conference*, June 1993.

[15] P. Vanbekbergen, B. Lin, G. Goossens, and H. De Man. A generalized state assignment theory for transformations on Signal Transition Graphs. In *Proceedings of the International Conference on Computer-Aided Design*, pages 112–117, November 1992.

[16] V. I. Varshavsky, M. A. Kishinevsky, V. B. Marakhovsky, V. A. Peschansky, L. Y. Rosenblum, A. R. Taubin, and B. S. Tzirlin. *Self-timed Control of Concurrent Processes*. Kluwer Academic Publisher, 1990. (Russian edition: 1986).

[17] Y.Watanabe and R.K. Brayton. Heuristic minimization of multiple-valued relations. *IEEE Transactions on Computer-Aided Design*, 12(10):1458–1472, October 1993.

[18] Y.Watanabe, L.M.Guerra, and R.K. Brayton. Permissible functions for multioutput components in combinational logic optimization. *IEEE Transactions on Computer-Aided Design*, 15(7):732–744, July 1996.

[5] Taking the best results from `2i` and `3i` the total is 8582

[6] In fact, any sequential gate could be used, including, e.g., asymmetric C elements, the only limit being the size of the space to be explored.

SESSION 5B

ADVANCED SCHEDULING TECHNIQUES

Moderators:

Miodrag M. Potkonjak, University of California,

Los Angeles, CA

David Ku, Escalade Corp.,

Santa Clara, CA

Scheduling and Binding Bounds for RT-Level Symbolic Execution*

Chuck Monahan Forrest Brewer

Department of Electrical and Computer Engineering
University of California, Santa Barbara, U.S.A.
chuck@bears.ece.ucsb.edu, forrest@ece.ucsb.edu

Abstract

This paper generalizes ALAP bounds for the exact scheduling problem on a pre-defined data path. Conventional bounds are inapplicable because of the possible requirement of re-computing operands for minimal schedule length. Efficient techniques are presented for constructing the new bounds which are sensitive to point-to-point delays via transitive memory units. An efficient operand mapping bound is also described. Based on these two bounds, time improvement factors of 50 have demonstrated in exact scheduling results.

1. Introduction

HLS techniques are typically aimed at relatively unconstrained synthesis tasks such as RT synthesis of a new design. However, the large cost of verification and the gaining popularity of data-path cores creates the need for constrained synthesis for a given (pre-defined) data-path. Miyazaki[4] proposed the first system for this task, however, that system used heuristic techniques which missed much of the inherent design freedom. In a similar vein, retargetable microcode compilers make limited use of the total possible connectivity of a data-path by restricting the communications to a small set of pre-defined μOps. Scheduling for these constraints can be managed by ASAP[4] or by tree matching[2,3]. By contrast, we proposed using RT-level symbolic data path execution to perform exact scheduling of DFG's (data-flow graphs) on a preexisting data path.[5] This technique utilizes reachable state analysis on an automata representing both the data path and operand constraints to perform a systematic analysis of the design freedom. The price of this increased design exploration is its substantial computational complexity since at each step, every feasible automata state that represents possible generation of operands is implicitly constructed. This process implicitly constructs every feasible schedule and is exact, however, it is potentially costly. In this paper, we describe novel scheduling bounds which allow exact results for the data-path constrained scheduling problem, but which substantially decrease the run time by removing states which can lead only to suboptimal schedules.

Reachable state analysis had been previously utilized for scheduling in the work of Yang [8] and of Coehlo [1], but these techniques were addressing scheduling without communication constraints. Scheduling for a pre-defined data path, however, presents new challenges. Fundamentally, the system cannot guarantee that an operand will be created only once in an optimal schedule. This is true even for optimal schedules. An operand may require recomputation when insufficient storage or switching logic exists, as occurs in the example shown in Fig. 1. In this figure, while executing the DFG, o_1 must be overwritten when o_2 is computed in order

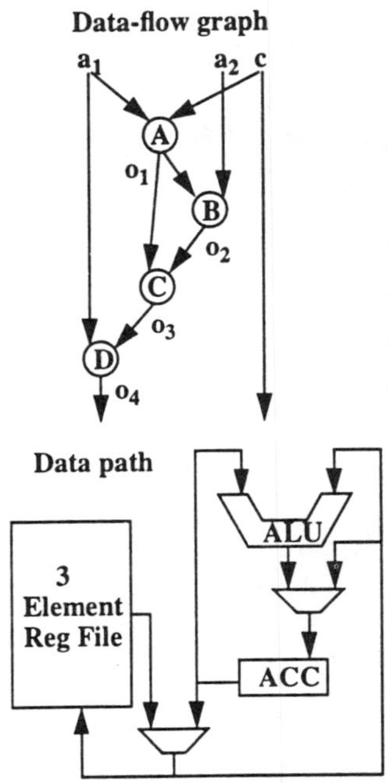

Schedule

Cycle	ALU	ACC	Reg
C0			$\{a_1, a_2, c\}$
C1		a_1	$\{a_1, a_2, c\}$
C2	A	o_1	$\{a_1, a_2, c\}$
C3	B	o_2	$\{a_1, c\}$
C4		o_2	$\{a_1, o_2, c\}$
C5		a_1	$\{a_1, o_2, c\}$
C6	A	o_1	$\{a_1, o_2, c\}$
C7	C	o_3	$\{a_1, c\}$
C8	D	o_4	$\{c\}$
C9			$\{o_4, c\}$

Figure 1. Scheduling example.

to maintain the required set of operands. This potential for rescheduling operations means that no operation can be excluded solely on the merit that it has been previously scheduled. It is this exclusion of operations and their associated parent operands which permits conventional bounds to maintain a manageable size for the reachable state analysis.

Clearly, an operation need not be considered for (re)scheduling if it could not have a measurable effect in the remaining execution cycles. These constraints on the scheduling of an operation are commonly referred to as ALAP (as late as possible) bounds. The use of ALAP bounds has been shown to be extremely effective for scheduling problems which lacked communication constraints.[7] The construction techniques for ALAP bounds must address two additional issues to make them applicable for scheduling on a pre-defined data path. First, due to the possible recomputation of operands, the ALAP bound of an operand must be based on the ALAP bounds of every child operation since we cannot guarantee that the first instance of an operation will satisfy all dependencies. The example in Fig. 1 demonstrates this requirement, where the o_1's ALAP bound is derived from the ALAP bound of o_3 instead of o_2. Secondly, the bounds must be extended to account for the limitations of the switching network, memory units and function units, instead of solely the number of function units as is conventionally done. The first issue is applicable to the problem, while the second

* This work has been generously supported by UC MICRO 96-142 and Mentor Graphics Corp.

TABLE 1. Behavioral Constraints

Behavior	Restrictions
Latch	$\lvert\Phi_i\rvert = 1$, $\lvert\Theta_i\rvert = 1$, and $\Sigma_i = \varnothing$
Register file	$\lvert\Sigma_i\rvert = \lvert\Theta_i\rvert$
Multiplexer	$\lvert\Phi_i\rvert > 0$, $\lvert\Theta_i\rvert = 1$, and $\lvert\Sigma_i\rvert \geq \log_2(\lvert\Phi_i\rvert)$
Function unit	$\lvert\Theta_i\rvert > 0$

issue makes the bound useful.

This paper presents a technique for constructing ALAP bounds based on operand routing constraints instead of function unit availability. This same technique is subsequently extended to further restrict the reachable state analysis by providing bounds on storage locations. Both of these topics are presented after a brief review of symbolic data path execution. This review consists of a description of the input requirements (Section 2) in which the flexibility of the representation is highlighted, an overview to the automata representation and reachable state analysis (Section 3.1), and an introduction into the incorporation of operand lifetime bounds (Section 3.2).

2. Input Formats

In this section, the format for specifying the data path and DFG are presented. The formats were selected to permit the specification of a wide variety of designs. The input format does include a few restrictions which are designed to clarify behavior that would be otherwise ambiguous.

2.1. Data path

The data path is modeled as a tuple (C, W). Each element, c_i, of C is a data path component defined by $(\Sigma_i, \Phi_i, \Theta_i)$. The set Σ_i defines the set of control lines which connect to component c_i. The set Φ_i defines an ordered set of unidirectional input ports for c_i. The final set, Θ_i, defines for c_i an unordered set of unidirectional output ports.[1] While two components may share common control lines, they must always have disjoint input and output port sets. The function $C(\theta)$ will be used to identify the associated component from an output port specification.

A number of useful data path attributes may be gathered from these definitions. The set Σ describes the complete set of control lines, $\{\sigma_1, \sigma_2, \ldots, \sigma_n\}$, as defined by $\Sigma = \bigcup_i \Sigma_i$. The set Θ describes the complete set of output ports, $\{\theta_1, \theta_2, \ldots, \theta_m\}$, as defined by $\Theta = \bigcup_i \Theta_i$.

Operands are transported between output and input ports over the data path's set of wires, W. We impose the constraint that each wire, w_i, emanates from only one output port but may fanout to drive many input ports.[2] Therefore, each w_i is defined by an output port, θ_i, and a set of input ports. Additionally, each input port, ϕ, may only be driven by a single wire, which permits the function $W(\phi)$ to uniquely identify the wire connected to a specified input port.

Each data path component is assigned one of the four behavior types. Memory elements are represented by either latches or register files. Switching logic, used to conditionally transfer existing operands to different wires, is distinguished from combinational logic which creates new operands. In general, all switching components are modeled as multiplexers, and combinational logic blocks are referred to as function units. While modeling of external input and output ports pose no additional challenges for the proposed techniques, they are omitted for the sake of clarity.[5] The arrangement of these components and their connecting wires must ensure that each loop described by a consistent set of directional ports contains at least one memory device to prevent feedback races. All additional constraints are based upon the component's behavioral type and are summarized in Table 1. The behavior of many conventional data path components will not directly correspond to one of these base behaviors. Such components need to be either manually or automatically partitioned into the various functional components connected by wires as in the example in Fig. 2.

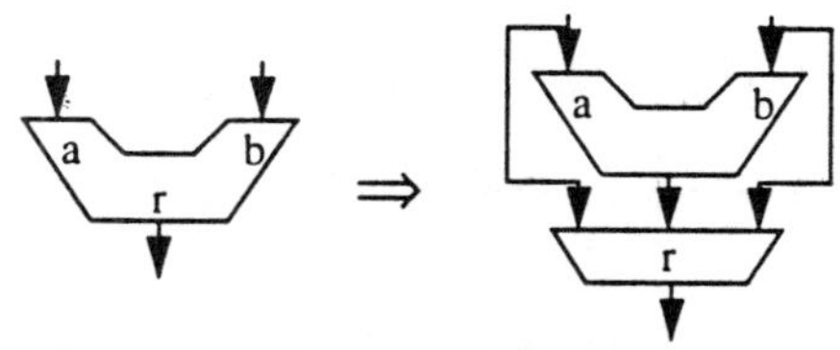

Figure 2. Expressing a function unit's feed-through capacity.

2.2. Data-Flow Graph

Data-flow graphs specify the dependencies between operands and operations. For our system, these graphs form directed, acyclic hypergraphs. A DFG is a tuple (P, E) where P is a set of operands and E is a set of operations. Each operation is defined as the four-tuple $e(\theta, \vec{\sigma}, \Pi, p)$ where θ is an output port which will produce the result, $\vec{\sigma}$ is the control vector for the component, $C(\theta)$, Π is an ordered set of input operands, $(\pi_1, \pi_2, \ldots, \pi_n)$, where $\pi_i \in P$, and p is the resulting operand. The following restrictions are placed on operation specifications: 1) $C(\theta)$ must identify a function unit and 2) $\lvert\Pi\rvert$ must equal the number of input ports for the specified function unit. This second restriction permits a direct assignment of input operands to input ports; a "null" operand is used as a place holder for input ports with no associated input operand in a given operation. An operand p_1 is said to be a parent of operand p_2 and p_2 is said to be the child of p_1 iff $\exists e_i \in E \mid p_1 \in \Pi_i \cap p_2 = p_i$.

There are some non-traditional elements of our DFG model. 1) There are no restrictions on the number of operations which may generate any operand p_k as expressed in EQ. 1. In the presence of multiple operations, each operation provides a unique, alternative method to generate the operand.

$$\lvert \exists e_i \in E \mid p_i = p_k \rvert \geq 0 \quad (1)$$

2) The operation mapping explicitly lists a function unit's output port. Traditionally, this association is made by an operation map. But, the large disparity in function unit descriptions combined with the potential for highly tailored operations made such an operation table impractical. The enumeration of the associative and commutative operands as well as equivalent function unit listings, which are traditionally handled by the operation map, is accommodated through the use of alternative operations. 3) No two operands may be equivalent, where equivalency between two operands p_1 and p_2 is defined by EQ. 2. When equivalent operands are detected, they should be merged into a single operand; this can be done either automatically or manually.

$$\exists e_i, e_{j \neq i} \in E \mid (\Pi_i = \Pi_j, p_i = p_1, p_j = p_2, \theta_i = \theta_j, \vec{\sigma}_i \cap \vec{\sigma}_j \neq \varnothing) \quad (2)$$

3. Representing Data paths

This section will introduce our automata-based data-path model, discuss applications which may utilize it, and finally discuss a variety of optimizations and performance improvements.

1. Bidirectional ports are modeled by combinations of unidirectional ports, switching elements, and switching control restrictions.
2. Designs which drive a line from multiple sources typically utilize coordinated switching elements. Such designs are accommodated by merging these switching elements into a single functional component with a single source.

3.1. Automata model

A symbolic automata is used to represent the storage of operands in memory components, the motion of operands on the switching network, and the creation of operands in function units. In its most general form, this automata is defined by the five-tuple $(V, \Sigma, N, S_0(V), S_f(V'))$.

V represents a finite set of states. Each state represents the contents of each of the data path's memory components. This set may be partitioned into the various disjoint components $V = V_1 \times V_2 \times \ldots \times V_n$ where V_i is the contents of a single memory device. In general, $V_i \subseteq P_i$, where $P_i = P$. We define the set of variables V as the present state variables and create a second set of variables V′ for the next state variables.

The automata inputs are defined as the set of control lines, Σ, introduced in Section 2.1. State relations are defined by the transform relation N: $V \rightarrow V'$. This relation maps the set of feasible next states, given the set of present states and all possible control line settings. This relation is symbolically represented as N(V, V′). While N(V, V′) describes the transform relation for the entire automata, separate transform relations may be defined for each portion of the state space denoted by N_i for $\Sigma \times V \rightarrow V'_i$. The use of the control lines permits the complete transform relation to be expressed as:

$$N(V, V') = \exists_{\sigma \in \Sigma} [\bigcap_i N_i(\Sigma, V, V'_i)].$$

Such relations are well defined for a given state and control vector because of the restrictions placed upon the input format. First, the restriction that each bus has a single source means that any control vector describes a set of distinct paths through the switching network. Restricting latches to single operands and the use of control lines to select operands from register files means that only distinct operands may appear at any path source emanating from a memory device. Restricting the DFG to contain only unique operations means that only distinct operands may be produced by function units given a set of distinct operands at the inputs and a control vector. In the absence of a direct mapping between a given state/control-vector pair and the operation for a given device, the operand produced by that device is a special "null" operand. The absence of cyclical paths ensures that each path destination will have a distinct operand associated with the path's source.

$S_0(V)$ and $S_f(V')$ represent a set of initial and final states for the automata. The ability to specify sets of initial and final states gives the designer greater flexibility in determining both the proper initial and final state for the model. Schedules which link a state in $S_0(V)$ with a state from $S_f(V')$ may be found using symbolic reachable state analysis from $S_0(V)$. Towards this end we compute $S_j(V)$, the set of reachable states on the jth iteration of the clock. In general, this set is generated by computing:

$$S_j(V') = \exists_{v \in V} [S_{j-1}(V) \cap N(V, V')].$$

The complexity of each $N_i(\Sigma, V, V'_i)$ may be reduced significantly by using the set of present states, making the following computation more feasible:

$$S_j(V') = \exists_{v \in V} \left[\exists_{\sigma \in \Sigma} [\bigcap_i [S_{j-1}(V) \cap N_i(\Sigma, V, V'_i)]] \right].$$

A *bounded minimum-cycle scheduler* is defined as a system which identifies the set of state transitions satisfying $S_j(V') \cap S_f(V') \neq \varnothing$ where j is minimized and below a specified upper bound. Upon j reaching this upper bound, the scheduler reports the infeasibility of the scheduling problem. The resulting schedules are extracted through a backwards-reachable-state analysis of the relation set generated by the reachable state analysis.

3.2. Lifetime optimizations

On a given iteration, each individual relation, N_i, need only represent the set of states reachable from $S_j(V)$. It is sufficient if the relation is defined over any $S''_j(V)$ where $S_j(V) \subseteq S''_j(V)$. Therefore, the set of relations $N^\circ_{i,j}(\Sigma, V, V'_i)$ is utilized instead of $N_i(\Sigma, V, V'_i)$ to represent the state relation $\Sigma \times S''_j(V) \rightarrow V'_i$. This new set of relations are generated dynamically for each iteration of the reachable state analysis.

The dynamic construction of transform relations is performed as follows. On each clock cycle, the set of operands, P, may be partitioned into a set of dead and a set of potentially active operands. We define an optimal set of dead operands, D_j, to include operands whose storage in some memory element at clock cycle k does not affect the reachable state analysis. The set of active states, A_j, is defined as $A_j \equiv P - D_j$. Given this partition, the individual transform relations may be constructed from the conditions under which operand p_k is present in device c_i, represented as $N'_{i,k}(\Sigma, V)$. The specification of $N^\circ_{i,j}(\Sigma, V, V'_i)$ is constrained by the set of active operands, as in:

$$\left[\bigcap_{p_k \in (A_j \cap P_i)} N^\circ_{i,j,k}(\Sigma, V, V'_i) \right], \text{ where } N^\circ_{i,j,k}(\Sigma, V, V'_i) = \quad (3)$$

$$[v'_{i,k} \cap N'_{i,k}(\Sigma, V)] \cup [\bar{v}'_{i,k} \cap ((\Sigma \times S_j(V)) - N'_{i,k}(\Sigma, V))].$$

While this representation is much smaller than the general transform, it requires a set of ordered operands for the set D_j. The following observations can be made about constructing such a set: If D_j is defined as the optimal set of dead operands, a suboptimal set D_j' may be constructed where $D'_j \subseteq D_j$. Such a set is suboptimal since $N^\circ_{i,j}(\Sigma, V, V'_i)$ will be more complicated than strictly required but it is still exact.

To construct the set D_j', we define an operand's lifetime as the first cycle on which it may be scheduled (birth) and the last cycle on which one of its children may be scheduled (death). Such a lifetime constitutes the cycles during which an operand must be present in the set of active operands. Operand p_k should remain in the set of dead operands until the following test is passed.

$$\bigcup_i (N'_{i,k}(\Sigma, V) \cap S_j(V)) \neq \varnothing$$

Unfortunately, no such simple test exists to determine when p_k should return to the dead list.

3.3. ALAP bound generation

While lifetimes can not be determined exactly, they may be bounded relative to the minimal cycle bound provided to the scheduler. From such a limit, ALAP bounds can be derived for the operation set based on the routing restrictions imposed by the data path. From these ALAP bounds, an upper bound on the death of an operand may be determined. Since an operand is no longer required after all of its children have been produced, the operand p_k is effectively dead once the cycle equals:

$$\max_{e_i \in E | p_k \in \Pi_i} [\text{ALAP}(e_i)].$$

Towards this end, we note that the DFG as well as the set of final states create requirements on an operand's possible storage in the data path. For example, each operation specifies an operand and input port pair which must be satisfied in addition to the resulting operand and output port pair. Each final state encoding specifies where an operand must be stored from which a set of input ports can be determined. To meet the requirements of the final states or the operations, an operand must traverse the data path to get from where it was created by an operation to the proper input port.

The data path provides many obstacles to the movement of operands. The switching network will often support only a limited amount of connectivity. While operands do traverse memory devices, they will suffer the delay of at least one cycle. These limitations combined with the constraints derived from the simultaneous transfer of multiple operands account for a majority of the cycles in a schedule. By formalizing the minimal delay of a single operand traversing from specific locations, useful scheduling bounds may be derived.

We define the function $\tau(\theta_i, w_j)$ to represent the minimal number of memory devices which lay on a path between output port θ_i and wire w_j. To compute this function, we construct a series of sets, $\tau_{j,x}$, where each set indicates the output ports which can be connected to wire w_j by traversing no function units, x memory devices, and as many multiplexers as required. The definition of $\tau_{j,x}$ depends upon the component, c_k, which drives the wire as in:

$$\tau_{j,x} = \begin{cases} \bigcup_{\phi \in \Phi_k} \tau_{W(\phi),x} & c_k = \text{multiplexer} \\ \theta_i \cup \bigcup_{\phi \in \Phi_k} \tau_{W(\phi),x-1} & \text{where } c_k = \text{latch or reg. file} \\ \theta_j & \text{otherwise} \end{cases}$$

The output port, θ_i, of a memory device could be dropped, but they are included for use in Section 3.4. Additionally, we note that $\tau_{j,x}$ only needs to be defined for values of x from 0 to the number of memory devices. Given this series of sets, $\tau(\theta_i, w_j)$ returns the lowest value x, where $\theta_i \in \tau_{j,x}$.

Each operation is assigned an ALAP bound based on the time it takes to route the resulting operand to its specified position. These bounds start with the set of operations which produce operands which explicitly appear in the final state specification are evaluated. The bound for these operations is computed from the delay required to store the resulting operand, p_k, into the memory devices specified in the final state set. Since the user can specify multiple, alternative final states, each state is evaluated separately to determine which provides the smallest delay, as in:

$$\text{last cylce} - \left\{ \min_{S_j \in S_f(V)} \left[\max_{v_{i,k} \in S_j} \left(\min_{\phi \in \Phi_i} \tau(W(\phi), \theta) \right) \right] \right\}$$

The evaluation of each final state must ensure that the operand is sent to all of that state's specified memory devices, but the operand is allowed to utilize the input port which provides quickest route to that memory device. The ALAP bound for the remaining set of operations is defined by EQ. 4. This bound determines that last cycle on which the operation result could be used as an input operand. The notation, ϕ_{e_2, p_k}, used in EQ. 4 identifies the input port of c_j (where $c_j = C(\theta)$) associated with operand p_k.

$$\text{ALAP}(e_1) = \max_{e_2 \in E \mid p_k \in \Pi_2} [\text{ALAP}(e_2) - \tau(W(\phi_{e_2, p_k}), \theta)] \quad (4)$$

These ALAP bounds differ dramatically from the computation of traditional ALAP bounds. One difference is the fact that this proposed method utilizes resource constraints in terms of routing restrictions instead the number functional unit types. However, the central difference stems from the accommodation of operand recomputation. Because of this capacity, EQ. 4 must use the maximum ALAP bound instead of the minimal bound. Use of the minimal bound indicates the last cycle on which an operation could fulfill the timing requirements of all of the subsequent operations. Since we have no guarantee that this operation result will be used for all of the subsequent operations, we determine the last cycle on which the result can fulfill the requirements for one of the subsequent operations. This policy means that input operands may have an ALAP bound which is later than the resulting operand as shown

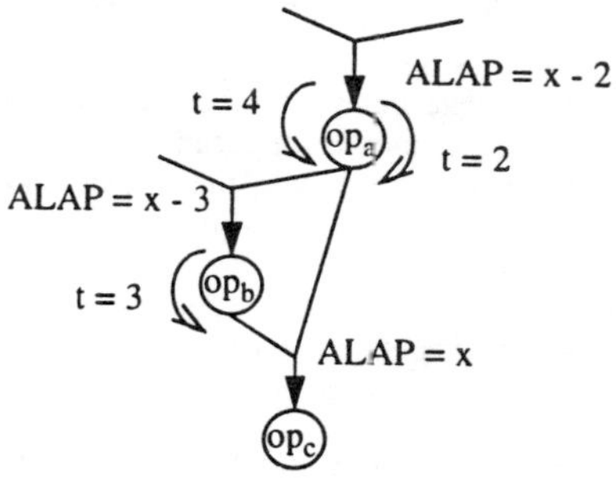

Figure 3. Fluctuating ALAP bounds due to operand fanout.

in Fig. 3. Fortunately, this policy accommodates the fact that not every operation must be executed since any operation may have an alternative.

3.4. Memory coloring

The advantage of the reachable state analysis which we have described is its exhaustive evaluation of the data path freedom. This can also be a disadvantage when the exhaustive nature evaluates the storage of operands in inappropriate memory devices. When this occurs, many states which are unproductive or inferior will be analyzed alongside productive and superior states thereby needlessly raising the complexity of the analysis. To limit this complexity, we shall identify which operands should never be stored in a particular memory device.

The DFG's association of operations and function units may be used to further constrain the construction of each $N'_{i,k}(\Sigma, V)$. The first observation is that the behavior of each function unit is limited to the set of associated operands. This notion of restrictions can be generalized to restrictions on the use of memory devices for storage of particular operands. For example, Fig. 4 depicts a component arrangement where operands in latch 1 must feed directly into the multiplier. Since use of the multiplier is only defined for a specific subset of operations, only those operands which would be defined as an input operand for such an operation need be stored in that latch. This underscores the basic principle that while a memory device may store any operand, there is an identifiable subset of operands which it need never store. We therefore redefine the set of operands, P_i, used by a memory device, c_i, to contain only these essential operands. Since $P_i \subseteq P$ instead of $P_i = P$, the complexity of each $N_i(\Sigma, V, V'_i)$ as well as the set of unique feasible states are reduced. Furthermore, the quality of the results of the reachable state analysis is maintained since these excluded operands can not effect that data path's ability to create operands.

To identify the set of memory devices which should store an operand, we make the following observations. First, the data flow graph indicates the set of function unit input ports at which an operand can appear. Second, the final state requirements specify the set of memory unit input ports at which an operand can appear. Third, operands must travel to these input ports by a combination of wires, memory device, and multiplexers. Therefore, we define a collection of output ports for each wire, w_i, represented by

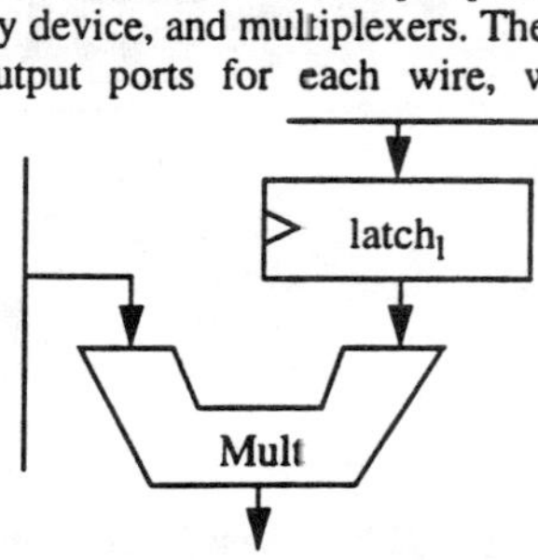

Figure 4. Dedicated latch

$\tau'_i = \bigcup_x \tau_{i,x}$, which can reach w_i without any bound on the number of cycles. Finally, given the list of wires connected to these input ports, we can determine all of the output ports which can route the operand p_k to any of the locations it may need to reach. Since we defined $\tau_{i,x}$ to include the output ports of memory devices, this list of output ports will exclude ports for memory devices whose outputs are not important for the use of operand p_k.

We define $\Omega(p_k)$ as the set of relevant output ports to operand p_k. Each port set is defined by both the final state specification and set of operations which use p_k, as in:

$$\Omega(p_k) = \{ \bigcup_{v_{i,k} \in S_f(V)} [\Theta'_i \cup \bigcup_{\phi \in \Phi_i} (\tau'_{w(\phi)})] \} \cup \{ \bigcup_{e_l | p_k \in \Pi_l} [\tau'_{w(\phi_{e_l, p_k})}] \}$$

where ϕ_{e, p_k} identifies the input port associated with operand p_k. When considering the requirements placed on the final state, it is important to include the output ports of memory device specified in the final state as well as the ports which can reach this device. From this, a new operand list, $P_i = \bigcup_{p_k \in P'} p_k | \Theta_i \subseteq \Omega(p_k)$, is generated for each memory device with which to simplify EQ. 3.

4. Results

A series of tools were developed to demonstrate the feasibility of these techniques. Each tool utilized an in-house BDD package and was run on a 141MHz SPARC Ultra with 416MB of memory.

4.1. Data paths

Our benchmarks utilize five different example data paths each of which exhibits different requirements. Four of these data paths are variations of the high level description of Texas Instruments' TMS32010 DSP processor. While the first design mirrors the TMS32010's data-path portion, the second design incorporates a second global bus to investigate the effect of added connectivity. The third and fourth designs mirror the first two except that a two-cycle pipelined multiplier is substituted for the single cycle multiplier. Each of these four designs were coded utilizing the base component behavior types introduced in Section 2.1 and are depicted as a composite in Fig. 5. The dashed lines represent a second bus which was added for the two-bus examples. The addition of the second bus permitted the A multiplexer and the t latch to be replaced by a single multiplexer, B. For those design with the pipeline multiplier, a latch and second pipeline stage are inserted between the multiplier and multiplexer C.

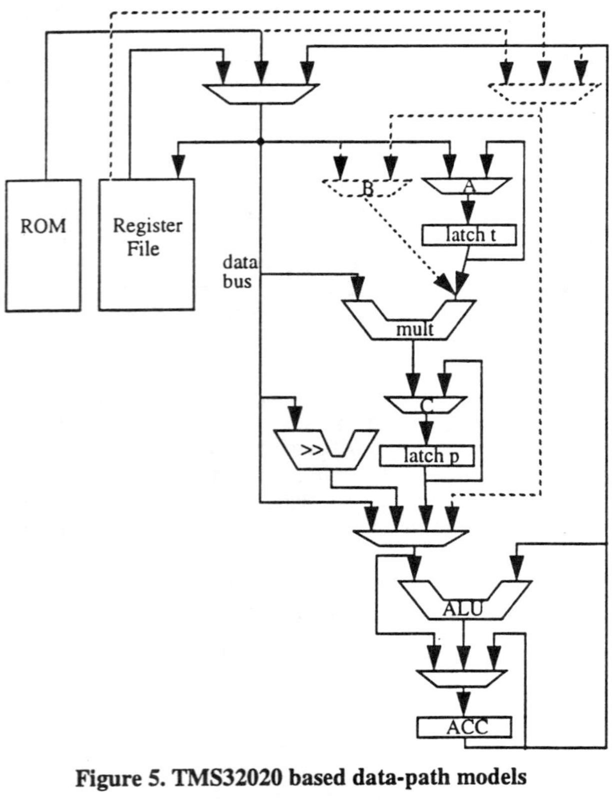

Figure 5. TMS32020 based data-path models

For the fifth benchmark, we wanted to demonstrate our ability to accommodate dedicated register files in the data path. While such architectures are accommodated by a variety of compiler techniques, there are few such benchmarks in the literature. Therefore, we introduce a "Dual Register" data path which is used as our fifth benchmark and is depicted in Fig. 6.

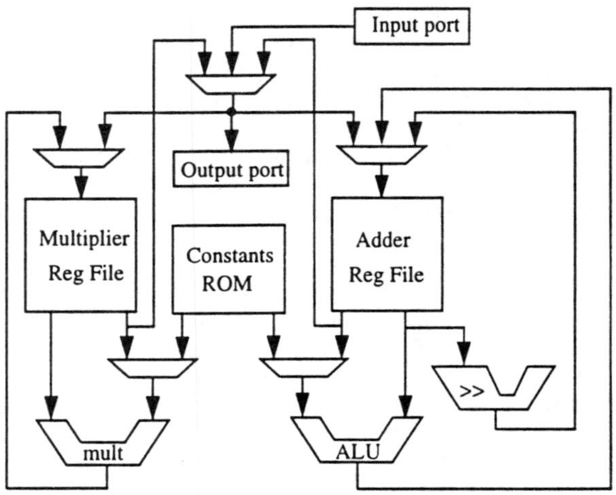

Figure 6. Dual register data path

4.2. Data flows

The scheduling benchmarks utilized three DFG's: differential equation(diff_eq), 3x3 determinant (3x3_det), and differential heat release computation (dhrc). The determinant benchmark that we introduce is specified in Fig. 7a. Additionally, the dhrc benchmark contained many operations specific to memory index operations which were inappropriate for our model. Therefore, the modified dhrc benchmark shown in Fig. 7b was utilized. Each of these data flows specify commutativity for each operand pair under the assumption that the ALU supports both forms of subtraction. Finally, each of these DFG's were checked for redundant operations (as defined by EQ. 2) and automatically merged such operands during each of the executions.

4.3. Relative performance

Table 2 lists the run times for the bounded minimum-cycle scheduler. The benchmarks are organized by their DFG, listing the data path, the number of cycles associated with the minimum schedule length, and the execution times. The quality of the scheduling results are not modified by the proposed techniques since no heuristic pruning is involved, but the complexity of the reachable state analysis and the resulting run times are very dependent upon the pruning techniques employed.

The first column, "neither" lists the run times resulting from executing the reachable state analysis utilizing every previously published pruning techniques. The "color" column lists the run times when memory coloring is utilized. Substantial benefits are visible in data paths which contained memory devices dedicated to a function unit input such as the "t latch" in the single bus

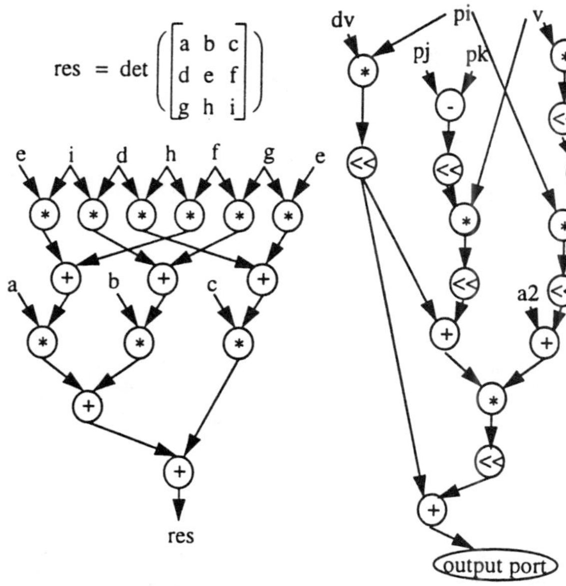

a) 3x3 determinate b) modified dhrc

Figure 7. Example data-flow graphs.

tms32010 designs. The benefit for each of these single bus benchmarks is relatively uniform for each DFG. This result is expected since the reduction to the state space is dependent upon theDFG's operation set. The occasional increase in execution times associated with the other benchmarks reflects the overhead due to the computation of the τ sets.

The results for our proposed ALAP bounds are compared against two sets of run times. In addition, to the run times listed under "neither", a set of run times are listed corresponding to bounding the reachable state analysis with ALAP derived solely from the function unit resources, "FALAP". The results from using this traditional bound are mixed. Examples containing the dual-register file data path or the diff_eq DFG show only slight improvements in run times, if any. By contrast, the ALAP bounds derived from the complete set of data path resources, "DALAP", demonstrate a consistent set of improvements.

Fig. 8 demonstrates how these benefits are realized for a particular example. Here we see the constant growth in the set of

TABLE 2. Exact scheduling results

Data Flow	Data Path			# Cyc	Run Time (sec) neither	color	FALAP	DALAP	both
diff eq	tms 320 10	1-cyc mult.	1 bus	17	250	125	240	195	97
			2 bus	12	23	23	23	19	19
		pipe mult	1 bus	17	565	350	539	301	191
			2 bus	13	109	109	97	51	37
	dual register file			12	15	15	16	16	16
3x3 det	tms 320 10	1-cyc mult.	1 bus	20	4,744	1,486	3,627	2,098	686
			2 bus	13	266	278	188	92	94
		pipe mult	1 bus	20	11,214	5,412	8,109	2,625	1,395
			2 bus	13	798	812	474	77	78
	dual register file			22	414	419	411	382	398
dhrc	tms 320 10	1-cyc mult.	1 bus	22	2,507	486	2,258	790	168
			2 bus	19	1,050	1,052	664	333	277
		pipe mult	1 bus	23	16,045	2,353	13,242	1,180	273
			2 bus	21	1,533	1,560	1,031	325	326
	dual register file			19	102	105	106	37	37

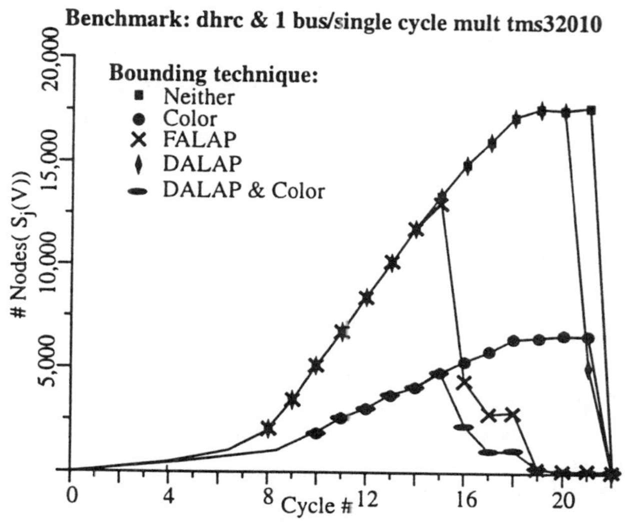

Figure 8. Cycle by cycle performance comparison.

reachable states, until the set is intersected with the set of final states. By employing the ALAP bounds, the size of the reachable state set is reduced as the analysis approaches the anticipated final clock cycle as elements are removed which have no impact on the solution set. Finally, when these techniques are combined with the memory coloring (corresponding run times are in listed in column "both") the size over all cycles is limited by reducing the set of states from which the reachable state analysis must consider.

5. Conclusion

This paper has shown that ALAP bounds can be posed for the pre-existing data path scheduling problem and that they are a powerful means of reducing the scheduling complexity. The primary constraint of a data path is its ability to route operands between various required points. This constraint was utilized to pose superior ALAP bounds. Additionally, the analysis of the movement freedom proves useful in pruning memory bindings which are inappropriate for specific operands. Although the operands may be stored at these locations, their presence can not effect the solution set and only complicates the state representation. These bounds have possible application in generalizations of this problem such as floorplanning constraint scheduling.

6. References

[1] C. N. Coelho Jr, G. De Micheli, "Dynamic Scheduling and Synchronization Synthesis of Concurrent Digital Systems under System-Level Constraints", *Proc. IEEE Int. Conf. Computer-Aided Design*, 1994

[2] R Leupers, P. Marwedel, "Retargetable Generation of Code Selectors from HDL Processor Models" in *Proceedings of European Design & Test Conference (ED & TC)*, Paris/France, 1997

[3] P. Marwedel, G. Goosens (eds.), *Code Generation for Embedded Processors*, Kluwer Academic Publishers, 1995.

[4] T. Miyazaki and M. Ikeda, "High Level Synthesis Using Given Datapath Information", *IEECE Trans. Fundamentals*, Oct 1993

[5] C. Monahan, F. Brewer, "Symbolic Modeling and Evaluation of Data Paths", *32nd Design Automation Conference Proceedings*, San Francisco, 1995.Conference Proceedings, San Francisco, 1995.

[6] C. Monahan, *Symbolic Data Path Modeling*, Ph.D. Thesis University of California, Santa Barbara, 1997

[7] A. Timmer, *From Design Space Exploration to Code Generati on*, Ph.D. Thesis Eindhoven University of Technology, 1996

[8] J. C.-Y. Yang, G. De Micheli, and M. Damiani, "Scheduling and Control Generation with Environmental Constraints based on Automata Representations", *IEEE Trans. CAD/ICAS*, Feb. 1996.

High-level Scheduling Model and Control Synthesis for a Broad Range of Design Applications

Chih-Tung Chen and Kayhan Küçükçakar
Unified Design System Laboratory
Motorola, Inc.
E-mail: {chen,kayhan}@adtaz.sps.mot.com

Abstract

This paper presents a versatile scheduling model and an efficient control synthesis methodology which enables architectural (high-level) design/synthesis systems to seamlessly support a broad range of architectural design applications from datapath-dominated digital signal processing (DSP) to micro-processors/controllers and control-dominated peripherals, utilizing multi-phase clocking schemes, multiple threading, data-dependent delays, pipelining, and combinations of the above. The work presented in this paper is an enabling technology for high-level synthesis to go beyond traditional datapath-dominated DSP applications and to start becoming a viable and cost-effective design methodology for commodity ICs such as micro-processors/controllers and control-dominated peripherals.

1. Introduction

High-level synthesis (HLS) offers a methodology which promises a significant productivity increase by raising the abstraction level of digital design. A tutorial on HLS methodology and past research can be found in [1] and [2]. After close to two decades of research, commercial HLS tools have been introduced recently [3] and have seen some production use. But, it is not yet known how soon HLS will become a mainstream technology for production designs.

In a cost and benefit study of the HLS methodology conducted in Motorola, several challenges to HLS tools were found such as offering significantly better cycle-time and defect reduction than RTL/logic synthesis while incurring no deterioration of design quality, providing interactive and incremental design process for better user control, and most importantly supporting a broad range of architecture design applications including datapath-dominated designs like DSP, processor-type designs like micro/DSP/co-processors, and control-dominated designs like peripherals.

The demand of supporting a broad range of design applications is due to the fact that adopting the HLS methodology is a drastic design paradigm shift for designers as well as design organizations. It requires considerable investment from them in training and time to incorporate HLS into the existing design flows and to become mature enough for production design, verification, and optimization throughout the new design flows. Hence, without supporting a broad range of design applications, the return of the investment on a domain-specific HLS methodology becomes sporadic and often unjustified.

To accelerate the industrial adoption of HLS, we have developed *Matisse* [4], a versatile architectural design tool, which answer many challenges described earlier. It is beyond the scope of this paper to describe the differences of Matisse from traditional HLS. This paper addresses two of the important issues; namely, the *scheduling model* and *control synthesis.* Our contribution is that the proposed approaches are versatile and capable of uniformly specifying and implementing static, dynamic, and pipeline scheduling with considerations of clocking and synchronization, which are essential for the successful application of HLS to a broad range of designs in the commodity ICs. Additionally, several unique techniques utilized in our control synthesis are presented, including clocking-driven coarse-grain control partitioning, FSM optimization, and control signal merging via default values. These techniques improve the efficiency of the synthesized controllers and are found to be crucial for commodity IC applications.

In the remainder of this paper, we begin with the related work in Section 2. Our scheduling model and the supported clocking scheme are illustrated in Section 3. Section 4 describes the control synthesis and its unique techniques in detail. In Section 5, we present results obtained from industrial designs including a case study on the effectiveness of FSM optimization and a power-consumption trade-off study of single-clock versus multi-phase clock designs. Finally, we conclude this paper with some future directions in Section 6.

2. Related Work

Static non-pipeline scheduling model and the associated control synthesis have been the subjects of intensive high-level synthesis research in last two decades. Park reported a pipeline scheduling method for synthesis of pipelines from behavioral specifications [5]. The generation of the control path for Park's pipeline scheduling model was subsequently addressed by Weng [6]. Girczyc applied the concept of functional pipelining similar to Park's to pipeline individual loops (loop winding) [7]. Prabhu described a pipeline synthesis system which utilizes a pipelined controller in junction with functional pipelining in the data path for improving the design throughput [8].

In the area of dynamic scheduling, relative scheduling was introduced by Ku to address scheduling with unbounded-delay operations [9]. Additionally, they used a relative control synthesis approach to generate an interconnection of interacting FSMs.

Papachristou et. al proposed a multi-phase clocking architecture model and technique for synthesis of low power RTL implementations [10]. However, the associated control synthesis was not addressed.

To our best knowledge, no prior scheduling model and control synthesis were found to address the issues of static, dynamic, and

1092-3152/97 $10.00 © 1997 IEEE

pipeline scheduling along with single or multi-phase clocking scheme uniformly.

3. Unified Scheduling Model

The scheduling model in this context is regarded as the specification method and representation of the scheduling information and **not** the scheduling algorithms.

In a study of various industrial designs with designers, we created a list of HLS design modeling techniques required to support the majority of designs for datapath-dominated, control-dominated and processor-type applications. As listed in Table 1, they are (1) conditional branching and looping, (2) operation chaining, (3) multi-cycle delays, (4) data-dependent delays, (5) multi-thread execution, (6) pipelining, and (7) multi-phase clocking.

Table 1: Frequent HLS modeling techniques.

Category	1	2	3	4	5	6	7
datapath dominated	X	X	X			X	
control dominated	X	X	X	X	X		X
processor type	X	X	X	X		X	X

In this section, we will present a hierarchical scheduling model for uniformly specifying all the above styles of execution and sequencing. The novelty of our scheduling model is that the specification of clocking and synchronization is no longer global. They are specified locally at each schedulable entity (operation or statement) along with typical attributes like offset and delay.

3.1. Clocking schemes

The supported clocking scheme can include a single clock (master clock), multiple phase clocks, and a mixture of a master clock and one or more phase clocks. As shown in Figure 1, when phase clocks are used, they are required to be synchronous and have the same period called the primary cycle. The primary cycle is further divided into a number of pickets. Each phase clock is restricted to have one active pulse per primary cycle. The duration and active level (high or low) of the active pulse are specified at the picket level. If a master clock is used together with phase clocks, the primary cycle is a multiple of master cycles for the purpose of synchronization.

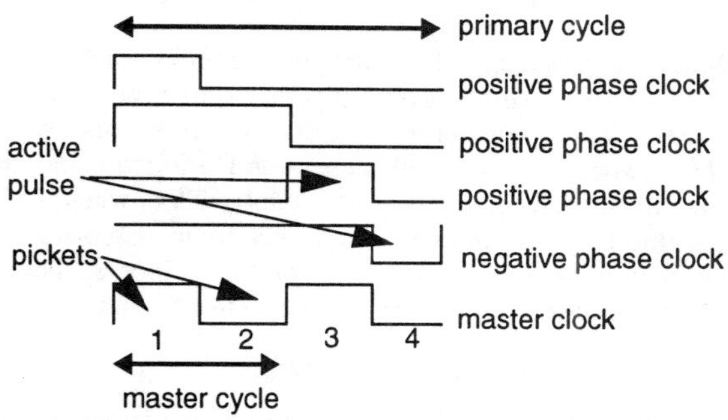

Figure 1. Supported clocking schemes

3.2. Hierarchical scheduling

The procedural HDL description can contain control-flow constructs such as branching and iteration. The control flow specification is modeled through the hierarchy of our scheduling model. The hierarchy is defined by the compound statements such

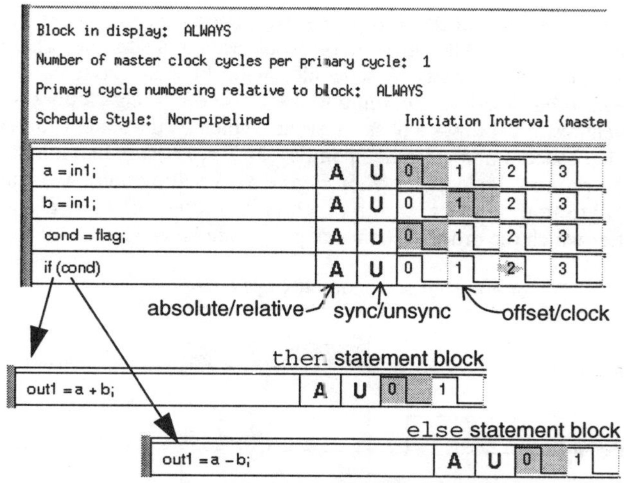

Figure 2. Example of hierarchical scheduling

as `if`, `case` and `while`. The generic entity in the hierarchy is called a *statement block* which comprises of a list of statements to be scheduled together according to their data flow and user (serialization) dependencies. Each compound statement in a statement block creates another level of the hierarchy with one or more statement blocks corresponding to the branching bodies or the loop body. Figure 2 shows an example of a behavioral description in Verilog HDL where the branching statement `if (cond)` further links to the two statement blocks of its `then` and `else` bodies at the next level. Note that the offsets of the `then` and `else` blocks shown in Figure 2 are relative to their parent `if` statement.

The semantics of the hierarchical scheduling model is recursively defined as follows. When a statement block is activated, the statements in that statement block execute according their scheduling specifications. The execution of a compound statement involves activating zero or more of the associated statement blocks and is complete when all the activated statement blocks are complete. An activated statement block is complete when the execution of all its statements are complete.

3.3. Intra-block scheduling

Let S be a statement block which comprises of a list of statements. The intra-block scheduling model defines the execution of each statement s_i in S by a tuple of attributes (p_i, y_i, o_i, c_i, d_i); namely reference point p_i, phase synchronization mode y_i, offset o_i, clock waveform c_i, and delay d_i.

Reference point. The p_i attribute defines the reference time $T(p_i)$ to which s_i is scheduled relatively, and is a subset of S such that $\forall s_j \in p_i$, s_i has a dependency on s_j and s_j is a compound statement with a non-deterministic or unbounded delay $D(s_j)$. Formally, $T(p_i)$ can be expressed as:

$$T(p_i) = max(T(S), T(s_j) + D(s_j)|_{s_j \in p_i})$$

where $T(S)$ is the activation time of statement block S, $T(s_j)$ is the start time of s_j, and $D(s_j)$ is the duration of s_j.

If s_i doesn't depend on any compound statement within statement block S, i.e. p_i is an empty set, $T(p_i)$ is equal to $T(S)$; in other words, s_i is scheduled with respect to the beginning of S. The latter case is called absolute scheduling in Matisse, whereas the opposite is relative scheduling.

Synchronization mode. The y_i attribute is a boolean flag indicating whether or not to use phase synchronization and is only applicable to multi-phase clock scheduling. When y_i is true, the reference time to which s_i is scheduled is deferred to $T'(p_i)$ which is the beginning of the next primary cycle after the original reference time $T(p_i)$. This attribute is mostly used to a situation where the statements (events) E scheduled with different phase clocks need to be executed according to the phase order; e.g., a phase-2 event always follows a phase-1 event. Typically, the statements in E have a common reference point p_E. If $T(p_E)$ occurs in a middle of a primary cycle as shown in Figure 3, by setting both $y(s_i)$ and $y(s_j)$ to true, s_i and s_j have a synchronized reference time $T'(p_E)$ after which the order of the clock phases are known statically.

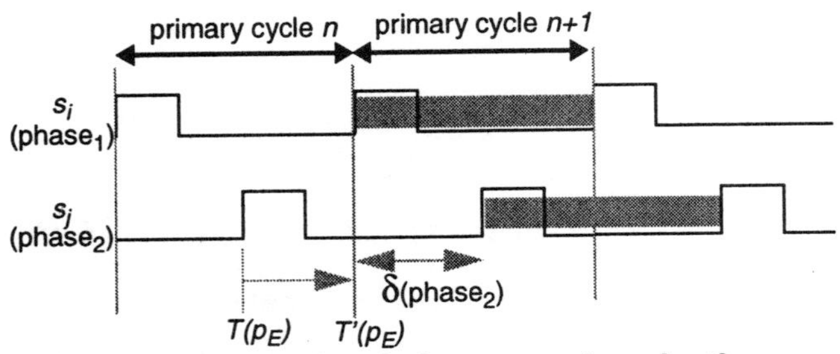

Figure 3. Example of phase synchronization

Offset, clock and delay. The o_i attribute is an integer value $\in Z^{0,+}$ for specifying the offset in cycles of the selected clock c_i after the reference time $T(p_i)$ or $T'(p_i)$. By giving the c_i (clock) attribute locally to each statement (operation), multi-phase clock scheduling and synchronization are enabled in our model. Finally, the d_i (delay) attribute is also an integer value and used for specifying multi-cycle operations

Start time calculation. Table 2 expresses the start time $T(s_i)$ under three scenarios; namely, phase unsynchronized with a zero offset, phase unsynchronized with a non-zero offset, and phase synchronized.

Table 2: Statement start times

y_i	o_i	$T(s_i)$
0	0	$T(p_i)$
0	>0	$T(p_i) - \delta(p_i) + o_i{*}period(c_i)$
1	X	$T'(p_i) + \delta(c_i) + o_i{*}period(c_i)$

The first two rows express $T(s_i)$ without phase synchronization (y_i=0). In such case, s_i should start ASAP after the reference point $T(p_i)$. When offset o_i is 0, $T(s_i)$ is same as $T(p_i)$ as shown in the 1st row. The 2nd row expresses $T(s_i)$ when o_i is not 0. In such case, s_i will be started at the beginning of the cycle o_i after $T(p_i)$. In this equation, $period(c_i)$ is the cycle length of c_i and $\delta(p_i)$ is called the reference point lapse time. The reference point lapse time $\delta(p_i)$ is defined as the delay from the beginning of the first cycle to the reference time $T(p_i)$. It is used due to the cases where $T(p_i)$ is not inline with the clock edges of c_i (especially in multi-phase clocking designs) as shown in Figure 4. Typically, $\delta(p_i)$ is 0; in other words, the entire first cycle is available. A non-zero reference point lapse time occurs when statement s_i depends on events which are not synchronized with the clock c_i.

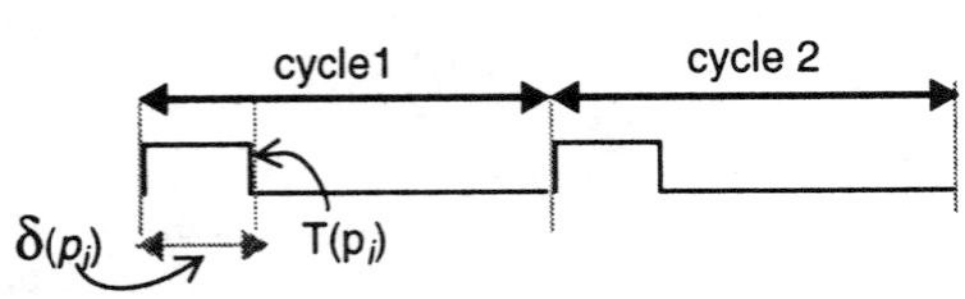

Figure 4. Example of a reference point lapse time

Finally, the 3rd row expresses the start time $T(s_i)$ when phase synchronization is used (y_i=1). In such as, $T(s_i)$ becomes the beginning of cycle o_i after $T'(p_i)$, the deferred reference time as shown in Figure 3. Since the clock edges of c_i may not be in line with the primary cycles, a phase lapse time $\delta(c_i)$ is defined as the delay from the beginning of a primary cycle to the beginning of the subsequent clock cycle of c_i, also illustrated in Figure 3.

3.4. Pipeline scheduling

Our scheduling model supports functional and loop pipelining. Functional pipelining [5] is regarded as a form of scheduling under a global *initiation interval.* The initiation interval represents the time interval between two consecutive executions of a scheduled design behavior. Loop pipelining (also called loop folding or winding) is a localized functional pipelining of a loop. The local initiation interval defines the time interval between two consecutive executions of a scheduled loop body. In our model, these two forms of pipelining are modeled the same way since the functional pipelining can be regarded as the loop body of the design process.

In our hierarchical scheduling model, pipeline scheduling can be specified at the top level or to an individual loop. The pipeline execution is implicitly applied to the statement blocks within the scheduling sub-hierarchy derived from the top-level statement block or the loop statement. The following restrictions are also assumed. All the statements within the scheduling sub-hierarchy must use the same clock and absolute scheduling. Additionally, nested loops are not supported in a pipeline.

Pipeline scheduling changes the delay definition of a pipelined loop. Let s_i be a loop statement with n_i iterations and with a loop body LB_i whose latency is $D(LB_i)$. If s_i is not pipelined, $D(s_i)$ is equal to n_ix$D(LB_i)$. However, if s_i is pipelined with an initiation interval I_i, $D(s_i)$ becomes $(n_i\text{-}1)$xI_i + $D(LB_i)$ as shown in Figure 5 where $(n_i\text{-}1)$xI_i is the time it takes to initiate the last iteration.

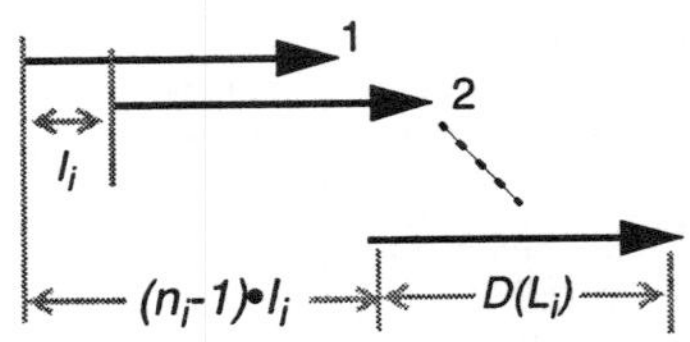

Figure 5. Loop pipelining

Within the pipelined scheduling sub-hierarchy, each statement is associated with an additional pipeline start time. Let s_j be a statement in LB_i, the pipeline start time $T^p(s_j)$ is equal to $(T(s_j)\text{-}T(s_i))$ % I_i where % is a modulus operator. During pipeline execution, s_j will be executed periodically at mxI_i+$T^p(s_j)$ where $m \in Z^{0,+}$ until s_i (the loop) is complete. Note that some statement in LB_i may execute more than n_i times in a pipelined loop s_i. The extra executions occur during pipeline filling and/or flushing.

4. Unified Control Synthesis

Control synthesis for HLS is a process of generating a control unit which will drive the data path as required by the schedule and using the values derived from the resource/interconnect allocation. A tutorial on control synthesis for HLS can be found in [11].

As stated earlier, control synthesis in Matisse is required to support static/dynamic scheduling, single/multi-phase clocking, multi-thread executions, and loop pipelining seamlessly and uniformly. Additional critical requirements are that no extra cycles are introduced for nested branching and loop entry/exit unless explicitly specified and that conditional blocks or while loops can be skipped with combinational delay (zero cycle skip). To achieve this aggressive goal, we developed a template-driven hierarchical control synthesis with an additional optimization step.

4.1. Hierarchical control model

The multitude of scheduling styles to be supported, compounded with multi-phase clocking schemes, makes the traditional flat and single-FSM control model ineffective. We chose to utilize a hierarchical control model which somewhat resembles to our hierarchical scheduling model. Figure 6 shows that the hierarchical control model is an interconnection of hierarchical control blocks, each of which is responsible for controlling a statement block in our scheduling model. Each control block CB_i has a pair of hand-shaking signals $\texttt{start}_\texttt{i}$ and $\texttt{done}_\texttt{i}$ for transferring control flow to and from its parent control block.

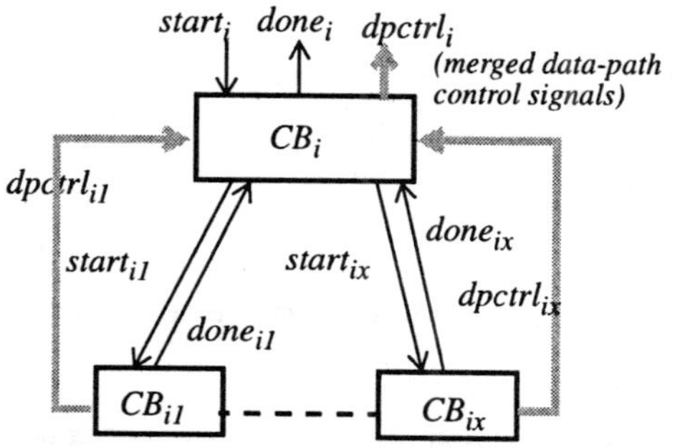

Figure 6. Example of hierarchical control model

4.2. Control block

As shown in Figure 7, a control block CB_i further comprises an interconnection of one or more control elements $\{CE_{i,1}, \ldots, CE_{i,n}\}$ and three types of peripheral circuits: *B*, *D*, and *M*.

***Coarse-grain FSM partitioning*.** The responsibility for executing the statements in the statement block of CB_i according to the specified schedule are divided among control elements $\{CE_{i,1}, \ldots, CE_{i,n}\}$, where the core of each control element $CE_{i,j}$ is an FSM. A coarse-grain partitioning is performed to divide the statements into groups $\{G_{i,1}, \ldots, G_{i,n}\}$ such that each group of statements $G_{i,j}$ has a common reference point $p_{i,j}$, the same phase synchronization mode $y_{i,j}$, and most importantly the same clock $clk_{i,j}$. As a result, the execution of the statements in each group $G_{i,j}$ only have different offsets with respect to $T(p_{i,j})$ or $T'(p_{i,j})$. Furthermore, the different offsets share the same discrete unit, the clock cycle of $clk_{i,j}$. Therefore, it can be seen easily that a single FSM in control element $CE_{i,j}$ is sufficient to control the execution of statements $G_{i,j}$. The structure of a control element will be discussed later in Section 4.3.

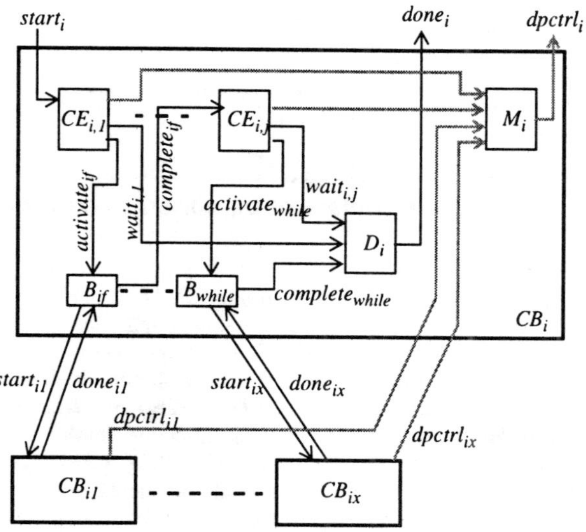

Figure 7. Template of control block

Within control block CB_i, each control element $CE_{i,j}$ receives a list of input signals $P_{i,j}$ required by its reference point $p_{i,j}$. $P_{i,j}$ is either $\{\texttt{start}_\texttt{i}\}$ if $p_{i,j}$ is empty (absolute scheduling) or $\{\texttt{complete}_\texttt{s} \mid s \in p_{i,j}\}$. The signal $\texttt{complete}_\texttt{s}$ is driven by one of the *B* circuit for signalling the completion of the compound statement *s*. $CE_{i,j}$ begins its execution when each signal in $P_{i,j}$ is raised and subsequently raises its $\texttt{wait}_\texttt{i,j}$ signal when its execution is finished. The data-path control signals driven by $CE_{i,j}$ are sent to an *M*-type peripheral circuit for merging.

***Flow control*.** *B* circuits are used to implement the control flow of compound statements such as `if`, `case`, and `while`. They are responsible for the `start/done` signals between CB_i and its child control blocks and raise the `complete` signals when the execution of the compound statements are finished. For example, let B_c be the *B* circuit for a conditional statement *c* with *K* branches $\{br_1, \ldots, br_K\}$. The input signal of B_c is $\texttt{activate}_\texttt{c}$ from a control element $CE_{i,j}$ where $c \in G_{i,j}$. $CE_{i,j}$ raises $\texttt{activate}_\texttt{c}$ during the cycle that *c* begins executing. The function of B_c can be expressed as the following logic equations.

$$start_{br_k} = activate_c \cdot cond_{br_k}$$

$$complete_c = \sum_{k=1}^{K} done_{br_k} + activate_c \cdot \prod_{k=1}^{K} \overline{cond_{br_k}}$$

where $\texttt{cond}_\texttt{br}$ denotes the branching condition of *br*. The first equation implements the branching control by raising the `start` signal of a branch whose condition is true and when *c* begins its execution ($\texttt{activate}_\texttt{c}$=1). The second equation raises $\texttt{complete}_\texttt{c}$ when the selected branch is done or there is no branch to be taken. For a loop statement *l*, the $\texttt{start}_\texttt{lb}$ signal driven by B_l becomes the iteration control of the loop body *lb*. For example, let *l* be a `while` loop. One way to implement B_l is as follows:

$$start_{lb} = (activate_l + done_{lb}) \cdot cond_l$$

$$complete_l = done_{lb} \cdot \overline{cond_l}$$

***Done detection*.** The *D* circuit D_i in Figure 7 is responsible for raising the `done` signal when the execution of the control block CB_i is finished. Recall from Section 3.2, the completion of CB_i requires the completion of all the statements in its statement block, which is the time that all the control elements $\{CE_{i,1}, \ldots, CE_{i,n}\}$ have raised their `wait` signals and all the *B* circuits in CB_i have raised their `complete` signals.

In general, it's not necessary for D_i to depend on all the `wait` and `complete` signals because there often exist some precedence relationships among these signals. A simple static timing analysis on the schedule of CB_i's statement block can be performed to eliminate those `wait` and `complete` signals that have precedence of other signals. Consequently, the remaining `wait` and `complete` signals are the ones whose assertions can only be determined dynamically. Often, there is only one remaining signal for D_i to depend on. In such cases, D_i becomes a wire connecting the signal directly to $\texttt{done}_\texttt{i}$. However, if there are two or more remaining signals, their assertions may not be simultaneous, D_i may need to memorize some input assertions using latches or flip-flops.

Control signal merging. Since we utilize a distributed multi-FSM control model, the data-path control signals with more than one driver need to be merged before connecting to data-path components. As shown in Figure 7, the control signals from the control elements and the child control blocks are merged hierarchically through an *M* circuit. A typical approach for signal merging is to use data selectors such as multiplexers, which requires generating additional data selection logic.

By exploiting the fact that the HLS designs should be free of resource conflicts and by making use of default control values, we have developed an efficient technique to merge control signals via simple logic; hence, improving area and performance. The basic idea is as follows. If all the sources (FSMs) of a data-path control signal send a pre-defined default value whenever there is no specific (active) control value required to performed the scheduled statements, then the data-path control signal will not be asserted by two or more different active control values at any given time. Otherwise, the design is not free of resource conflicts because the associated data-path component will be asked to perform different functions at the same time. Formally, let *cs* be a 1-bit control signal with multiple sources $\{cs_1, \ldots, cs_M\}$ and a default control value $dval_{cs}$. The merging function can be expressed as follows:

$$cs = \sum_{i=1}^{M} cs_i \qquad \text{if } \mathrm{dval}_{cs} = 0$$

$$cs = \prod_{i=1}^{M} cs_i \qquad \text{if } \mathrm{dval}_{cs} = 1$$

If *cs* is a multi-bit signal, the merging can be done by bit-wise *OR*ing or *AND*ing the source signals depending on the default value of each individual bits. Alternatively, if an *n*-bit control signal does not utilize all the possible 2^n values, one can encode the used values first to reduce the number of bits for merging. The encoded control signal can then be decoded just once after the final merging.

4.3. Control element

As discussed in the previous section, each control element $CE_{i,j}$ controls a group of statements $G_{i,j}$ which have a common reference point $p_{i,j}$, the same phase synchronization mode $y_{i,j}$, and most importantly the same clock $clk_{i,j}$. Figure 8 shows that $CE_{i,j}$ consists of a finite-state machine $FSM_{i,j}$, a *R*-type peripheral circuit $R_{i,j}$, and an optional phase synchronization flip flop.

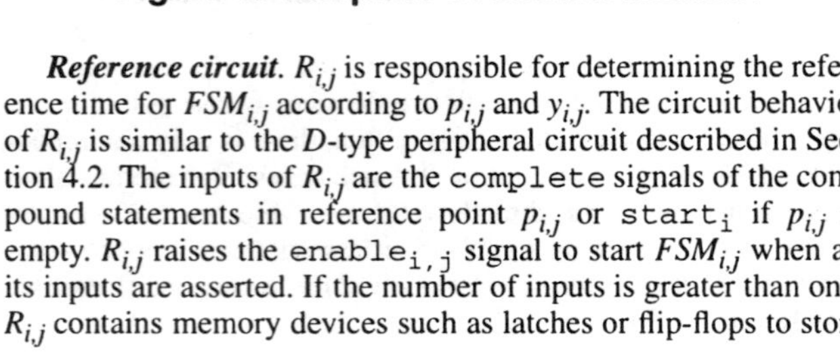

Figure 8. Template of control element

Reference circuit. $R_{i,j}$ is responsible for determining the reference time for $FSM_{i,j}$ according to $p_{i,j}$ and $y_{i,j}$. The circuit behavior of $R_{i,j}$ is similar to the *D*-type peripheral circuit described in Section 4.2. The inputs of $R_{i,j}$ are the `complete` signals of the compound statements in reference point $p_{i,j}$ or `start`$_i$ if $p_{i,j}$ is empty. $R_{i,j}$ raises the `enable`$_{i,j}$ signal to start $FSM_{i,j}$ when all its inputs are asserted. If the number of inputs is greater than one, $R_{i,j}$ contains memory devices such as latches or flip-flops to store their assertions. If $y_{i,j}$ (phase synchronization mode) is true, an additional flip-flop clocked by a `sync` signal as shown in Figure 8 is inserted at the output of $R_{i,j}$ to generate a phase synchronized `enable'`$_{i,j}$. The `sync` signal is typically one of the phase clocks which defines the boundaries of primary cycles; e.g., the phase-1 clock.

Control FSM. $FSM_{i,j}$ is the core of $CE_{i,j}$ which asserts the associated data-path control signals or the `activate` signal of each compound statement in $G_{i,j}$ at the specified offset. $FSM_{i,j}$ is an *L*-state FSM with circular state transitions and clocked with $clk_{i,j}$. *L* is the latency of $G_{i,j}$'s schedule excluding the delays of the compound statements. Figure 9 shows the basic circular state transitions of $FSM_{i,j}$, where the assertions of the data-path control signals or the `activate` signal for each statement *x* in $G_{i,j}$ are assigned to state o_x.

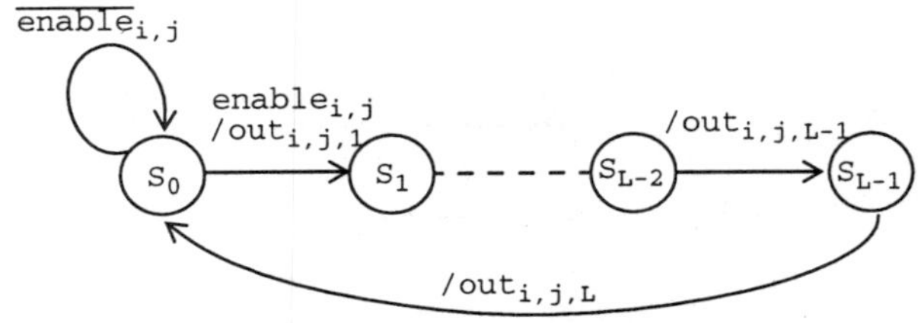

Figure 9. Basic state-transition graph of $FSM_{i,j}$

4.4. Pipeline control block

In our control synthesis, loop pipelining is done in a special pipeline control block which controls the entire loop body. As shown in Figure 10, the external interface of a pipeline control block remains the same as non-pipeline control blocks. Hence, it can co-exist with other control blocks seamlessly. Within a pipeline control block, there are one pipeline control element $CE^P{}_i$, one pipeline *D*-type peripheral circuit $D^P{}_i$, and zero or more shift registers for storing conditional values.

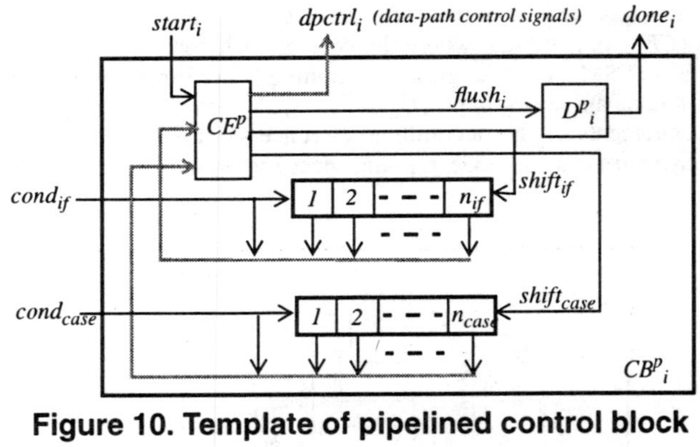

Figure 10. Template of pipelined control block

Pipeline control element. $CE^P{}_i$ is an FSM with $I^c{}_i$ states, where $I^c{}_i$ is the discrete initiation interval. The assertions of each statement *s* within the pipeline scheduling sub-hierarchy is assigned to state $\lfloor T^P(s)/period(clk_i) \rfloor$ where $T^P(s)$ is the pipeline start time as defined in Section 3.4. As with non-pipeline control elements, the state transitions of $CE^P{}_i$ are also circular.

Conditional assertions. The assertions are conditional if the statement *s* within the pipeline scheduling sub-hierarchy is enclosed by one or more conditional statements. The condition for the assertions is the conjuction of all the branching conditions of the enclosing conditional statements. Due to the nature of pipeline execution, if the latency of a conditional statement is longer than initiation interval, multiple instances of a conditional statement will be executed concurrently. However, throughout the execution of each instance, the conditional value for conditional assertions should always be the one at the time the instance is initiated. Hence, we utilize shift registers to store the history of the conditional values.

Let $sreg_c$ be the shift register for a conditional statement c with latency $D(c)$. The number of c instances, n_c, executing concurrently is $\lceil D(c)/I \rceil$. The length of $sreg_c$ is also n_c. $CE^p{}_i$ raises signal `shift`$_c$ at the cycle $\lfloor T^p(c)/period(clk_i) \rfloor$ in which a new c instance is initiated. Raising `shift`$_c$ cause $sreg_c$ to shift once and store a new value of $cond_c$. For each statement s within c, the source of $cond_c$ which s should use for its conditional assertions depends on *it's* offset with respect to the beginning of c. For example, Figure 11 shows the execution of three instances and each of which is divided into three stages of length I. At the beginning of c_1, a new $cond_{c,1}$ is stored in $sreg_c[1]$ and used during its 1st stage execution. By the time c_2 is initiated, c_1 is executing the 2nd stage and $cond_{c,1}$ is now shifted to $sreg_c[2]$. Hence, $sreg_c[2]$ is the source of $cond_c$ used by the 2nd stage execution. Formally, the source of $cond_c$ for each statement s within a conditional statement c can be expressed as $sreg_c[\lceil (T(s)-T(c))/I \rceil]$.

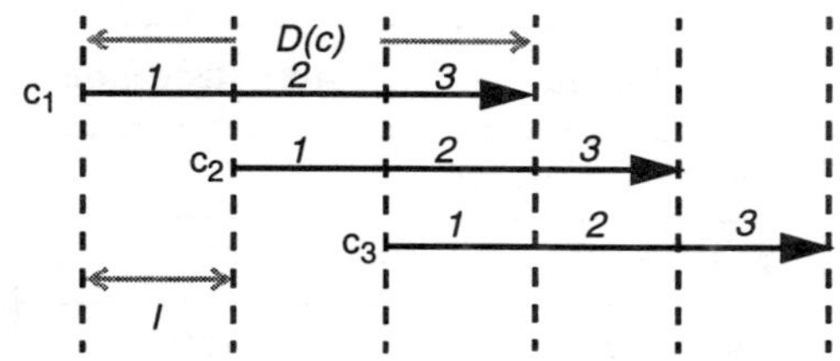

Figure 11. Pipeline instances

Pipeline done. The `done`$_i$ signal driven by the $D^p{}_i$ circuit also becomes more involved than the non-pipeline counterparts. Recall that the fundamental part of our pipeline execution (loop pipelining) is to initiate a new iteration of loop body every initiation interval (see Figure 5) until the loop exit condition is met. However, the pipeline execution is not yet complete at that moment due to the fact that there are still $(\lceil D(L_i))/I \rceil - 1)$ iterations yet to be finished. The process of completing the remaining active iterations is typically called pipeline flushing. In our pipeline control model, $CE^p{}_i$ raises signal `flush`$_i$ at the first pipeline state when `start`$_i$ is dropped and continues the execution of the remaining iterations. $D^p{}_i$ is a delay circuit, such as a counter, which raises `done`$_i$ after a pre-determined number of cycles for the remaining execution, which is $\lceil (D(L_i)-I)/period(clk_i) \rceil$ cycles.

4.5. Optimization

Although our hierarchical control model with multiple distributed FSMs is extremely flexible and capable of supporting all the its objectives uniformly, we also found that there is room for optimization; in particular, the portions of the design which use static scheduling and a single clock. We developed two types of optimization techniques; namely, logic collapsing and FSM collapsing. The primary goal of both techniques is to collapse a sub-hierarchy of control blocks if possible into a single entity. Thus, both the state registers and the logic of merging data-path control signals can be reduced.

Logic collapsing is a bottom-up technique which recursively collapses stateless control elements, control blocks, and *B*-type circuits (see Section 4.2). Recall from Section 4.3 that each control element $CE_{i,j}$ contains an L-state FSM. $CE_{i,j}$ becomes stateless when L is 1, meaning that the FSM degenerates into a combinational circuit. A logic collapsible entity denotes an entity whose behavior degenerates into logic functions. Two logic collapsible entities are mutually collapsible if they have the same starting cycle and clocking. Figure 12 shows an example of logic collapsing an `if` statement where both `then` and `else` parts are mutually collapsible.

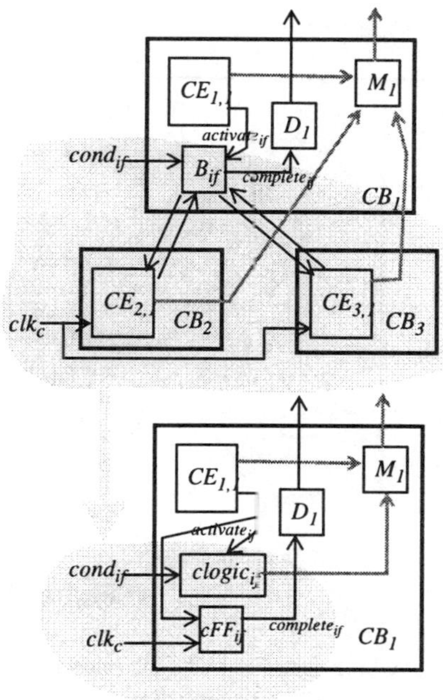

Figure 12. Example of logic collapsing

FSM collapsing is also a bottom-up technique which recursively collapses control elements, control blocks, and B-type circuits which are FSM collapsible. A FSM collapsible entity denotes an entity whose behavior can be implemented by a single-thread FSM. Therefore, control elements, by default, are FSM collapsible. Two FSM collapsible entities are mutually collapsible if they share the same clocking and there exists a common reference point among them. By sharing the same clocking and a common reference point, the execution of two single-thread FSMs are in lock steps; hence, they can be statically merged into one. There are two common ways of merging single-thread FSMs; namely, state sharing and state connecting. State sharing is applicable to two or more single-thread FSMs whose executions can share common starting and ending points. An example of state sharing is shown in Figure 13(a). The result of state sharing is a new single-thread FSM whose state number is equal to the one with more states and the outputs become conditional by the respective FSM `enable` signals. State connecting, on the other hand, is suitable for two or more *mutually exclusive* single-thread FSMs whose executions can share common starting and ending points. Figure 13(b) shows an example of two mutually exclusive single-thread FSMs. State connecting creates two new starting and ending states $S_{c,0}$ and $S_{c,1}$ to replace the ones used by original FSMs. The original mutually exclusive execution is achieved through two conditional state transitions emitting from $S_{c,0}$.

5. Experiments

In this section, we first report the range of design applications that the work described in this paper was used. Following that, a case study of FSM optimization is presented. Finally, the support

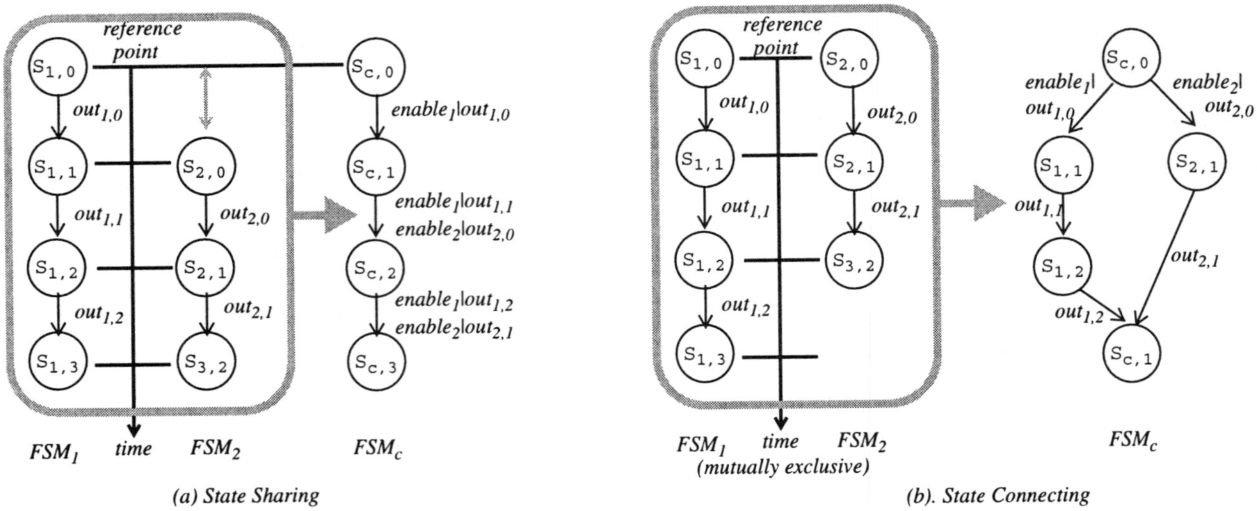

Figure 13. Example of FSM collapsing

of multi-phase clocking schemes is demonstrated with an experiment of single vs. multi-phase clocking on power consumption.

5.1. Coverage of design applications

The scheduling model and control synthesis presented in this paper are implemented in an industrial HLS system, *Matisse,* and has been successfully used in a broad range of industrial designs for evaluation or production. The designs included hard-wired DSPs, an encryption/decryption engine, a bus-to-bus interface, a control-dominated peripheral, and a microcontroller. Table 3 lists some notable designs and their underlying HLS modeling techniques (refer to Table 1 for numbering scheme). So far in all of these projects, the area and performance of the automatically generated controllers were found or estimated by the designers to be comparable to traditional RTL design techniques.

Table 3: Designs and modeling coverage

Design	1	2	3	4	5	6	7
ADPCM predictor	X	X	X			X	
Encryption/decryption	X	X			X		
Bus-to-bus interface	X	X		X	X		X
Vector I/O buffer	X	X		X	X		
FIR filter	X	X	X			X	
8-bit microcontroller	X	X	X	X			

5.2. A case study of FSM optimization

To study the effectiveness of our logic and FSM collapsing techniques, we conducted a case study on 3 designs in Table 3. For each design, we generated a full hierarchical controller and an optimized controller using both logic and FSM collapsing. The generated controllers were synthesized using Synopsys Design Compiler using the same set up, including the library and the performance constraints.

It can be seen from Table 4 that an optimized controller can achieve up to 48% area reduction over an unoptimized one. We also found that the amount of area improvement is design-specific and proportional to the room allowed for optimization.

Table 4: Results of FSM Optimization

Design	Area Reduction
8-bit microcontroller	48%
FIR Filter	37%
ADPCM predictor	18%

5.3. Effects of clocking on power

Since multi-phase clocking schemes are supported in Matisse and Matisse also provides an environment for architectural power optimization [12], we set out to experiment a power saving technique using multi-phase non-overlapping clocks proposed by Papachristou et al [10]. The basic idea is as following. Given a schedule, instead of using traditional resource and interconnect allocation using a single clock with a frequency f, their technique utilizes n non-overlapping clocks with frequency f/n and a datapath architecture with n disjoint modules, each running on a distinct clock. Additionally, two special allocation methods were proposed to map each node in the data-flow graph (DFG) into a specific module according to the operation's time step in a modulus fashion. For example, nodes scheduled at time step t are mapped to a module running on CLK_k where k is $t \bmod n$. The authors argued that their approach can achieve lower power consumption than traditional HLS designs due to a "capacitance reduction" effect and the reduced frequency. Power savings up to 50% were reported in their paper.

We implemented various designs of the example described in their paper. Due to the limited space of this paper, please refer to [10] for the detailed description of the example and design schematics. Each design, including the controller, synthesized into gates using Synopsys Design Compiler and power was estimated by an accurate gate-level power estimation tool [13]. Table 5 summarizes the experimental results

Circuit1 is a single-clock design with two add/subtract ALUs and used by the authors for comparison with *circuit2* which is a two-clock design. With a set of random input test vectors, *circuit2* indeed was found to achieve 39% power reduction over *circuit1*. Since circuit1 and circuit2 have different resource allocations and clocking schemes, it was not apparent what the individual effects were on power savings. We found that all architectures generated by the multi-phase clock technique can still be clocked by a single clock with clock gating at registers. Hence, we implemented *circuit3* which has the same architecture as *circuit2* but uses a single clock. As shown in Table 5, by comparing *circuit2* and *circuit3*, the power savings by the multi-phase clock technique alone becomes 23%. Finally, we implemented another two-clock design, *circuit4*, which was given by the authors using their integrated allocation method (Figure 7 in [10]). It was also found to consume less power than single-clock designs, but not better than *circuit2*. Note that the controllers synthesized by our tool for *circuit2* and *circuit4* consist of two FSMs driven by two specified non-overlapping clocks respectively.

Table 5: Effects of clocking on power

Design	Clocking/Arch.	Power	Area	Func. Units
Circuit1	1 clock	1.00	1000	2(+/-)
Circuit2	2 clocks	0.61	1111	2(+), 1(-)
Circuit3	1 clock, same architecture as circuit2	0.77	1115	2(+), 1(-)
Circuit4	2 clocks, integrated allocation version	0.68	1388	2(+), 1(-)

6. Conclusion

We have presented a novel scheduling model and an efficient control synthesis which seamlessly and uniformly support static/dynamic scheduling, single/multi-phase clocking, multi-thread execution, and loop pipelining. Our contribution is an enabling technology for HLS to go beyond traditional datapath-dominated DSP applications and to start becoming a viable and cost-effective design methodology for commodity ICs such as micro-processors/controllers and control-dominated peripherals.

The presented scheduling model and control synthesis have been implemented in an industrial HLS system and used to successfully design many industrial designs for evaluation or production, including digital filters, an encryption/decryption engine, a bus-to-bus interface, a high-speed vector I/O buffer, and a micro-controller. We also showed the effectiveness of our optimization techniques which make our hierarchical control synthesis as efficient as traditional single flat FSM control synthesis for static scheduling while capable of supporting dynamic scheduling and multi-phase clocking schemes. Finally, we conducted a study on a power-saving technique using multi-phase clocking as proposed in [10].

We believe that there are still other opportunities for further optimizing our hierarchical control model. Furthermore, micro-coded controllers along with hardwired FSMs should be supported due to the increasing need of architecture reuse and programmable designs.

7. Acknowledgments

We would like to thank Thomas E. Tkacik and Rajesh Gupta for their stimulating discussions during the development of this work and Jie Gong for her extensive review of the paper.

8. References

[1] M. C. McFarland, A. C. Parker and R. Camposano, "The High-Level Synthesis of Digital Systems", *In Proceedings of IEEE*, 78(2):301-318, February 1990.

[2] R. A. Walker and R. Camposano, *A Survey of High-Level Synthesis Systems*, Kluwer Academic Publishers, 1991.

[3] *Behavioral Compiler*, Synopsys, Inc.

[4] *Matisse User Manual*, Motorola, Inc., 1995.

[5] N. Park. and A. C. Parker, "Sehwa: A Software Package for Synthesis of Pipelines from Behavioral Specifications", *IEEE Transaction on Computer-Aided Design*. 7(3): 356-370, March 1988.

[6] J.-P. Weng and A. C. Parker, "CSG: control path synthesis in the ADAM system", *In Proc. 6th International Workshop on High-Level Synthesis*, pp. 52-64, 1992.

[7] E. Girczyc, "Loop Winding - A Data Flow Approach to Functional Pipelining", *In Proceedings of International Symposium on Circuits and Systems*, pp. 382-385, 1987.

[8] U. Prabhu and B. M. Pangrle, "Superpipelined control and data path synthesis", *In Proceedings of Design Automation Conference*, pp. 638-43, June, 1992.

[9] D. Ku and G. De Micheli, *High-Level Synthesis of ASICs under Timing and Synchronization Constraints*, Kluwer Academic Publishers, 1992.

[10] C. Papachristou, M. Spinning, and M. Nourani, "An effective power management scheme for RTL design based on multiple clocks", *In Proceedings of Design Automation Conference*, pp. 337-342, June, 1996.

[11] G. De Micheli, *Synthesis And Optimization of Digital Circuits*, pp. 166-178, McGraw-Hill, 1994.

[12] C.-T. Chen and K. Kucukcakar, "An Architectural Power Optimization Case Study using High-level Synthesis", To appear in *Proceedings of International Conference on Computer Design*, October, 1997.

[13] B. George, G. Yeap, M. G. Wloka, S. C. Tyler, and D. Gossain, "Power Analysis for Semi-Custom Design", *In Proceedings of IEEE Custom Integrated Circuits Conference*, pp. 249--252, May, 1994.

Wavesched: A Novel Scheduling Technique For Control-flow Intensive Behavioral Descriptions

Ganesh Lakshminarayana, Kamal S. Khouri, and Niraj K. Jha
Department of Electrical Engineering,
Princeton University, Princeton, NJ 08544

Abstract

In this paper, we present a novel scheduling algorithm targeted towards minimizing the average execution time of control-flow intensive behavioral descriptions. Our algorithm uses a control-data flow graph (CDFG) model, which preserves the parallelism inherent in the application. It explores previously unexplored regions of the solution space through its ability to overlap the schedules of independent iterative constructs, whose bodies share resources. It also incorporates well-known optimization techniques like loop unrolling in a natural fashion. This is made possible by a general loop-handling technique, which we have devised. Application of the algorithm to several common benchmarks demonstrates up to 4.8-fold improvement in expected schedule length over existing scheduling algorithms, without paying a price in terms of the best- and worst-case schedule lengths required to execute the behavioral description (in fact, frequently, the best/worst-case schedule lengths are also better for our algorithm).

1 Introduction

The scheduling problem arises in many different forms in divergent fields of study. Scheduling of operations on functional units and variables on registers in high-level synthesis, instructions on a processor during compilation, packets on communication links in networks, and tasks on processing elements in distributed computing are a few typical examples.

In high-level synthesis, there are three different kinds of behavioral descriptions: data-dominated, control-flow intensive (CFI), and control-dominated. Data-dominated descriptions are characterized by a predominance of arithmetic operations and the absence of control-flow constructs. CFI descriptions reflect a mix of arithmetic and logical operations, and control flow structures like loops and conditional operations. Control-dominated applications are characterized predominantly by control-flow operations. Problems in the digital signal and image processing domains, such as filtering, convolution, and discrete cosine transform, translate into data-dominated descriptions. Applications related to network protocol handling, and many other network-centric applications are characterized by CFI descriptions. Sequencers, which generate sequences of signals to control events in a process, are control-dominated. The scheduling problem for each of these domains has its own unique flavor, and distinct classes of algorithms are used to handle the problems in each domain. A survey of scheduling techniques for data-dominated applications can be found in [1]. Scheduling for control-dominated applications was considered in [2] and [3].

In this paper, we deal with the scheduling problem for high-level synthesis of CFI behavioral descriptions. The algorithm accepts as input, a CDFG, a target clock period, and an allocation constraint (restrictions on the number and type of different library elements allowed) and produces a scheduled CDFG which is optimized for average execution time. It is assumed that the type of library element executing each operation is known.

Past research in scheduling of CFI behaviors has modeled the input description as a *control flow graph* (CFG), which is basically a graphical description of a sequential program based implementation of the functionality. Scheduling techniques based on this model were presented in [4]-[7]. While the CFG model is well suited to capture execution of instructions on a general-purpose uniprocessor, it has been shown to be inadequate in exploiting the parallelism inherent in typical CFI applications. CDFG models, equipped to handle control and data dependencies, without sequentializing independent operations, and algorithms for scheduling CDFGs, were presented in [8]-[10]. While these algorithms exploit parallelism within loop structures, they are incapable of optimizing across loop boundaries, and do not support loop unrolling. Methods such as those presented in [11,12] are capable of exploiting loop unrolling and pipelining to enhance performance, but are not capable of performing concurrent optimization of independent loops. A survey of various techniques targeted towards achieving better schedules for very large instruction word processors, which is closely related to the problem of scheduling for high-level synthesis, can be found in [13].

Our scheduler, called *Wavesched* for its wave-like scheduling ability, uses a CDFG model of the input behavioral description. It can parallelize the execution of independent loops whose bodies share resources. The scheduler is also capable of transcending loop boundaries in its quest for a globally optimal solution, *i.e.* it subsumes several well-known optimization techniques such as loop unrolling and functional pipelining. This is made possible by a general technique we have developed to handle inter-iteration dependencies that arise as a result of loop unrolling. Our algorithm can support multi-cycled and pipelined functional units and perform chaining to enhance cycle time utilization. A synergy of the above techniques results in schedules which are optimized for average execution time and have same or better best- and worst-case execution time characteristics as those produced by conventional schedulers.

2 Background

In this section, we discuss the basic concepts used in our work. First, we describe our CDFG model with an example. Next, we describe state transition graphs (STGs), which help to describe schedules. This is followed by an introduction to the concept of concurrent loop optimization and an example illustrating the power of this technique. We then present a general technique for keeping track of inter- and intra-loop dependencies, which allows a unified treatment of loops and other conditional operations.

2.1 Preliminaries

High-level synthesis starts with the compilation of the input behavioral description, usually written in a high-level hardware description language like VHDL or Hardware C, into a CDFG. A CDFG is a directed graph, whose nodes represent operations, and edges represent dependencies between operations. In CFI descriptions, the dependencies are of two types: data and control. An edge represents a data dependency if the source node of the edge produces data that the sink node consumes. Existence of a control dependency between nodes implies that the execution of the

1092-3152/97 $10.00

sink node depends on the outcome of the execution of the source node. Figures 1 and 2 show a behavioral description written in a

```
int TEST1 ( int k1, int k2, int a, int b){
   int x1, x2, var1, var2, var3, var4, var5;
   x1 = 10;
   x2 = 0;
   for (int count = 0; count ≤ k1; count++) {
   // <= 1 and ++1
      if (x1 < 100) { // <1
         var1 = a + x1; // +1
         var2 = 5 + var1; // +2
         x1 = var2 × 3; // *1
      } else {
         var3 = a + x1; // +3
         x1 = var3 × 7; //*2
      }
   }
   for (int count1 = 0; count1 ≤ k2; count1++) {
   // <= 2 and ++2
      var5 = b + x2; // +4
      x2 = 6 × var5; // *3
   }
   return (x1 + x2); // +5
}
```

Figure 1: A fragment of code, TEST1, written in a high-level language

high-level language and the CDFG corresponding to the description, respectively. The comment at the end of each statement indicates the operation in the CDFG it corresponds to. Variable declarations and initializations do not correspond to operations in the CDFG. Data dependencies in the CDFG are indicated by continuous arcs, and control dependencies, by broken arcs. The **then** and **else** branches of an **if** statement are represented by placing + and − symbols, respectively, adjacent to operations executed in these cases. For example, operation +1, which is in the **then** branch of the **if** statement <1, has an incoming control dependency marked by a +, and operation +3, which is in the **else** branch of the same **if** statement, is fed by a control dependency marked by a − symbol. Note that the value that gets assigned to *x1* depends upon whether operation <1 evaluates to *true* or *false*. This is expressed by means of a *select* operation, which assigns to its output, either of two values, at its *l* and *r* input ports, depending on the value at *s*. Though, in general, an operation can execute only if all its data dependencies are known, a select operation can execute if the value at port *s* is known, and data are available at the selected input port. For the CDFG shown in Figure 2, variable *x1* is the output of select operation **Sel1** whose input ports *l*, *r*, and *s* are fed by ∗1, ∗2, and <1, respectively. An edge is also annotated with the initial value of the variable it corresponds to. Edges in a CDFG are of two types: reverse and forward edges. Reverse edges are those that represent data and control dependencies between operations belonging to different iterations of the same loop body, and forward edges represent dependencies within an iteration of a loop. Conditional edges in the CDFG are annotated with their probability of occurrence. For example, operation <1 evaluates to *true* with a probability of 0.5, and operation <=1 evaluates to *true* with a probability of 0.98.

Variables *x1* and *x2* in the CDFG do not directly feed operation +5, but feed operations := 1 and := 2 instead. These intermediate operations are control-dependent on operations <= 1 and <= 2, respectively. They ensure that operation +5 can only execute when both loops have finished execution. In general, when an operation outside a loop body (sink) is dependent on the result of

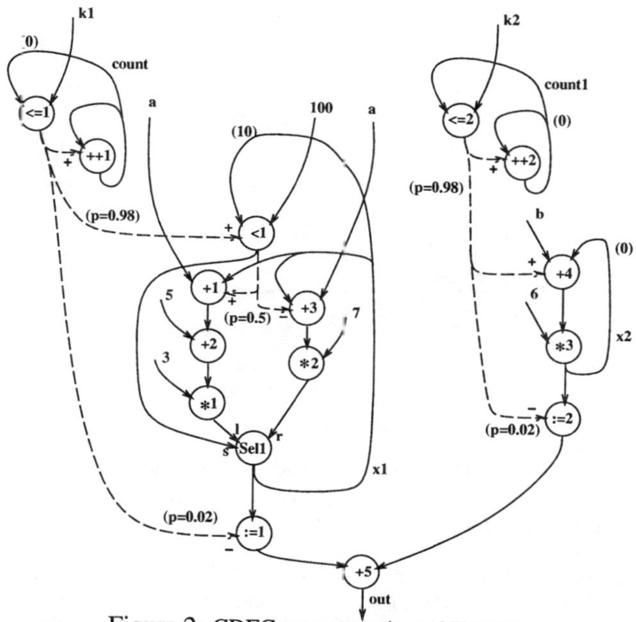

Figure 2: CDFG representation of TEST1

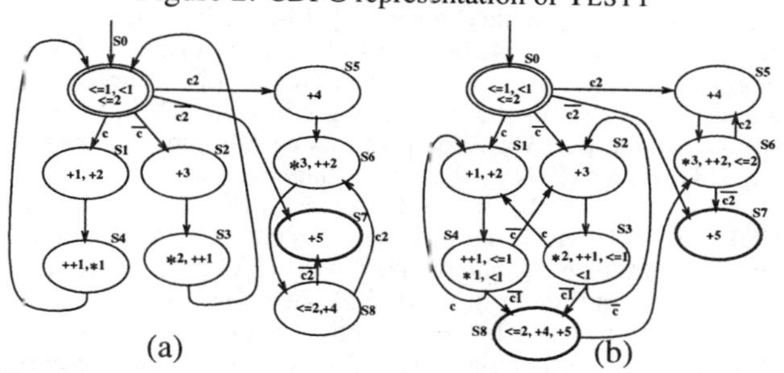

Figure 3: (a) A schedule produced by PBS, and (b) a schedule produced by LDS

an operation inside the loop (source), the result of the source operation feeds an intermediate operation which is control-dependent on the operation that performs the loop test. The sink operation is sourced by the intermediate operation. These intermediate operations are referred to as *endloop* operations. These operations do not have a physical implementation, and are incorporated into the CDFG for ease of representation and handling.

On completion, the scheduler outputs an STG describing the schedule. The STG is a directed graph whose nodes represent states and edges represent transitions between states. Nodes in the STG have information about the operations executed in the corresponding state, and edges capture the conditions under which a state transition takes place.

2.2 Concurrent loop optimization

In this subsection, we describe concurrent loop optimization, a technique which helps overlap the schedules of the independent loop bodies which share resources. To motivate this technique, we present schedules derived using some existing algorithms, without the benefit of this technique and contrast them with the schedule produced by our scheduler *Wavesched*. We consider the scheduling of the CDFG shown in Figure 2 under the following allocation constraints: a multiplier of type *mult1*, two adders of type *add1*, three comparators of type *comp1*, and two incrementers. Each of these functional units is assumed to take one cycle. Suppose that the following chains of operations can be performed in one cycle: (a) two additions, (b) a multiplication followed by a comparison, (c) a comparison followed by an increment, (d) a comparison followed by an addition, (e) an addition followed by a comparison, (f)

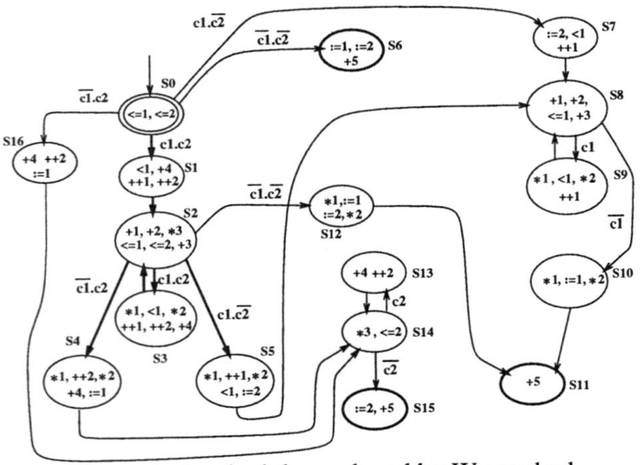

Figure 4: A schedule produced by Wavesched

two comparisons, (g) a comparison followed by a multiplication, and (h) an increment followed by a comparison.

Figures 3(a), 3(b) and 4 represent the STGs obtained by path-based scheduling (PBS) [4], loop-directed scheduling (LDS) [5] and *Wavesched*, respectively, under the above constraints. Start states are represented by double ellipses, and terminal states, by bold ellipses. The method given in [5] for deriving the expected number of cycles for schedules, which is applicable to CFGs, was modified to make it applicable to CDFGs [14]. The expected number of cycles for the schedules produced by PBS, LDS, and *Wavesched*, respectively, computed using this modified method, are 248 *cycles*, 199.94 *cycles*, and 120.09 *cycles*.

The reason for the above difference is that the two loops in CDFG TEST1, which are actually independent, and can be executed in parallel, are sequentialized in the CFG. As a result, for the STGs shown in Figures 3(a) and 3(b), the execution of the second loop can begin only after the execution of the first is terminated. However, in the schedule produced by our algorithm, the execution of these parallel loops is overlapped in time. With both loops executing in parallel, our schedule would complete one iteration of each loop in two cycles by appropriately skewing the execution of the operations in the loops to ensure that resource constraints are satisfied. The bold edges in Figure 4 represent transitions between states where both loops execute concurrently. The schedules produced by PBS and LDS, however, cannot take advantage of this effect. Therefore, one iteration of each loop still takes two clock cycles, but these iterations are sequential as opposed to parallel, resulting in a 1.7-fold slowdown in performance for LDS, relative to our method.

The above example illustrates that the performance of schedulers based on the CFG model is heavily dependent on the structure of the CFG. If a CFG, which parallelized the execution of loops, were used as input to the LDS or PBS algorithms, the schedule produced would have been similar to the one produced by our algorithm. However, we are not aware of any algorithm that derives the "best" CFG for a given behavioral description, under a given set of allocation constraints. Therefore, a scheduling technique that can effectively use the flexibility afforded by the CDFG representation is essential in exploiting parallelism in the input description. Details of our scheduling algorithm, which satisfies the above criterion, can be found in Section 3. Note that, in this case, the algorithm described in [6], while partially addressing the limitations of CFG-based scheduling, would not significantly improve the performance of the schedule over that of LDS because it is restricted to reordering of operations within basic blocks.

At this stage, we would like to point out that some synthesis systems do not allow control-dependency chaining, *i.e.* an operation cannot be scheduled in the same state that generates the condition necessary for its execution. If specified, our scheduling algorithm can either enforce this restriction, or benefit from the flexibility that results from its absence. For the ease of exposition, this restriction is assumed to be in effect for schedules produced by *Wavesched*. However, this restriction is not enforced for the schedules shown in Figures 3(a) and (b).

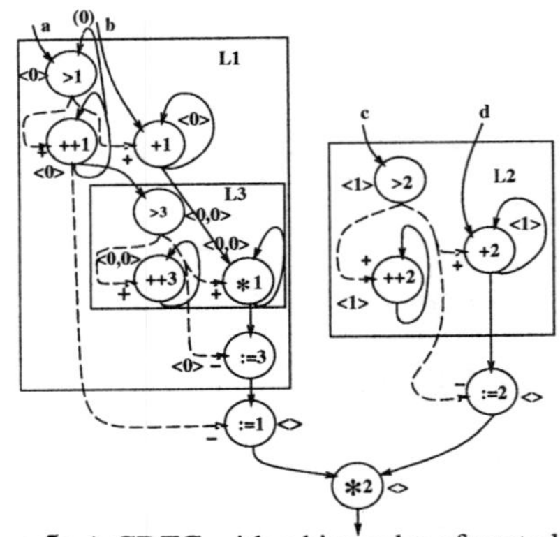

Figure 5: A CDFG with a hierarchy of nested loops

Our algorithm supports *implicit unrolling* of loops. The user can specify a bound on the number of times, U, a loop can be unrolled. This implies that the scheduler has the option of unrolling the loop up to U times during the course of its execution. If the CDFG contains nested loops, different loops in the nest can be unrolled as deemed appropriate. A state could, therefore, potentially contain operations belonging to several different loops and to different iterations of the same loop body. Hence, we need a mechanism to keep track of the position of an operation in the loop hierarchy and handle inter-iteration dependencies induced by loop unrolling. Section 2.3 presents a technique we have devised for this purpose.

2.3 Handling loop-induced dependencies

From the example presented in the previous section, it is clear that the ability to perform inter- and intra-loop optimizations is a desirable feature for a CFI scheduler. Incorporating these techniques into a scheduling algorithm requires a general technique to keep track of loop-induced dependencies. The techniques presented here are geared towards simplifying loop handling by making loops appear "just like" other conditional dependencies.

In this subsection, we present (a) a numbering convention to keep track of different iterations of an operation (presented in Section 2.3.1), and (b) a means of deriving fanin-fanout relationships between operations augmented with the derived loop iteration numbers (presented in Section 2.3.2).

To motivate the analysis in this subsection, we consider the following problem, which is common to most scheduling algorithms: that of identifying the schedulable successors of an operation which has just been scheduled. If loop unrolling is not allowed, this procedure can be carried out through structural analysis of the CDFG. First, we derive the set, *Succ_set*, of fanouts of the scheduled operation. If all fanins of an operation, *succ* $\in$ *Succ_set*, have been scheduled, *succ* is considered schedulable. If loop unrolling is allowed, structural analysis of the CDFG is not sufficient to perform this task. This is because different iterations of the same operation can co-exist, and in order to schedule a specific iteration of an operation, we need to ensure that the correct iterations of its fanins have been scheduled. For example, for the CDFG shown in Figure 5, operation $*1$, which occurs in the third iteration of the outer loop and the second iteration of the inner loop is schedulable only if the third iteration of operation $+1$, and the second inner loop iteration of the third outer loop iteration of operation > 3 have been scheduled.

2.3.1 Keeping track of loop iterations

Loops can be viewed as inducing a hierarchical structure on the CDFG. Operations which are not part of any loop have a hierarchical level of 0, operations which are embedded in exactly one loop have a hierarchical level of 1, and so on. This hierarchical structure can be represented as a tree.

Definition 1 *The* loop number *of an operation is defined as an ordered set consisting of the numbers assigned to different loops that this operation is a part of. The set is ordered by increasing hierarchical level.*

For instance, the loop number of operation $++3$ in Figure 5, which is a part of loop $L3$, numbered 0, at hierarchical level 1, and loop $L1$, numbered 0, at hierarchical level 0, is $< 0,0 >$. The number of elements in an operation's loop number is the same as its hierarchical level. Every operation in Figure 5 is annotated with its loop number.

The hierarchical level of an endloop operation is one less than that of the loop it helps terminate. For example, operation $:= 3$, which serves to transfer the result of operation $*1$ outside loop $L3$, takes on loop number $< 0 >$. This represents a hierarchical level of 0, while operations in the body of loop $L3$ have a hierarchical level of 1.

Each loop that contains an operation, can be unrolled an arbitrary number of times (bounded by a user-specified constant). Operations in different iterations of the same loop are distinguished by their *loop counts.*

Definition 2 *If an operation embedded in n loops, numbered a_1, a_2, ..., a_n in increasing hierarchical order, represents the b_ith iteration of the loop numbered a_i, its loop count is given by* $< b_1, b_2, \ldots, b_n >$.

2.3.2 Identifying operation fanin-fanout relationships

Section 2.3.1 introduced a means of representing different iterations of the same operation. In this subsection, we seek to infer inter- and intra-iteration dependencies among operations. The most natural way to represent such relationships is through a directed graph, called the *composite CDFG*, whose nodes are referred to as *composite operations.* A composite operation possesses information about the operation it represents, its loop number, and its loop count. It is represented as $\{op, ln, lc\}$ where op identifies the operation, and ln and lc its loop number and loop count, respectively. Function $OP(C_{op})$ returns the operation that composite operation C_{op} corresponds to.

We now present a method to construct the edges of the composite graph. First, we formally state the problem we wish to solve. We then relate the loop number of a composite operation to that of its fanins. This result is utilized to establish a relationship between the loop count of a composite operation and that of its fanins.

Problem statement: Given composite operations C_{op1} and C_{op2}, find the conditions under which C_{op1} is a fanin of C_{op2}, given that $OP(C_{op1})$ is a fanin of $OP(C_{op2})$.

Lemma 1 *If* $C_{op1} = \{op1, ln1, lc1\}$ *sources* $C_{op2} = \{op2, ln2, lc2\}$, *then either (a) ln1 is a prefix* [1] *of ln2, or (b) ln2 is a prefix of ln1 and C_{op2} has a hierarchical level one less than C_{op1}.*

Lemma 2 *If C_{op1} sources C_{op2} and the hierarchical level of C_{op1} is n, then (a) the first $n-1$ elements of the loop counts of C_{op1} and C_{op2} are identical, and (b) the nth element of the loop count of C_{op2} exceeds by one (is equal to) the nth element of the loop count of C_{op1}, if the edge connecting $OP(C_{op1})$ to $OP(C_{op2})$ is a reverse (forward) edge.*

Proofs of these lemmas are available in [14].

Table 1 gives the loop count of a fanout operation Y of operation X. X is assumed to have a loop number of $< a_1, a_2, \ldots, a_n >$ and a loop count of $< b_1, b_2, \ldots, b_n >$. *N.I.* stands for next iteration, and a *yes (no)* in this column indicates that Y is connected to X by means of a reverse (forward) edge. In rows 1 and 2 of the table, X and Y belong to the same loops and, therefore, have the same loop numbers. The loop count of Y is either the same as the loop count of X (row 1) or exceeds the loop count of X by one in the nth position (row 2), where n is the hierarchical level of X, depending upon whether X and Y belong to the same loop iteration, or are one iteration apart. Rows 3 and 4 correspond to a case where the loop number of X is a prefix of the loop number of Y, *i.e.* Y belongs to every loop that X is a part of, but the converse is not true. In this case, the last $m-n$ elements of the loop count of Y cannot be inferred from the loop count of X and the nth element of the loop count of Y either equals or is one greater than the nth element of the loop count of X, depending upon whether or not X and Y belong to the same iteration of the deepest loop to which both belong. In the last row, Y represents an endloop operation of the deepest loop X belongs to. By Lemma 2, the first $n-1$ elements of the loop counts of X and Y are equal, thus completely specifying the loop count of Y.

Table 1: Table of successors

	loop number(Y)	*N.I.*	*loop count(Y)*
1	$< a_1, a_2, \ldots, a_n >$	*no*	$< b_1, b_2, \ldots, b_n >$
2	$< a_1, a_2, \ldots, a_n >$	*yes*	$< b_1, b_2, \ldots, b_n + 1 >$
3	$< a_1, a_2, \ldots, a_m >$ *where* $(m > n)$	*yes*	$< b_1, b_2, \ldots, b_{n-1}, b_n + 1, b'_{n+1}, \ldots, b'_m >$
4	$< a_1, a_2, \ldots, a_m >$ *where* $(m > n)$	*no*	$< b_1, b_2, \ldots, b_{n-1}, b_n, b'_{n+1}, \ldots, b'_m >$
5	$< a_1, a_2, \ldots, a_{n-1} >$	*n/a*	$< b_1, b_2, \ldots, b_{n-1} >$

3 The Algorithm

In this section, we describe our scheduling algorithm in detail. We first outline the algorithm and illustrate its application to a CDFG. We then describe its constituent parts.

3.1 Outline

Figure 6 shows our scheduling algorithm. The algorithm accepts as input, a CDFG, an allocation constraint, a clock cycle time, and a bound on the number of times a loop can be unrolled. Control dependency edges in the CDFG are annotated with their probabilities of occurrence. The allocation constraint specifies the numbers and types of functional units available to the scheduler. Module selection (assignment of a functional unit type to each operation in the CDFG) is assumed to have been performed prior to scheduling. The scheduler returns an STG which represents the schedule.

We illustrate the scheduling process using the CDFG shown in Figure 2. The allocation, clock cycle, and chaining constraints are the same as those used for the example in Section 2.2. We assume for this example that a loop can be unrolled no more than once.

Definition 3 *The frontier of a state is the set of all composite operations which are immediately schedulable upon leaving the state.*

Our basic approach is constructive: we construct an STG from a CDFG by packing operations from the CDFG into states in the STG, beginning with the first level of operations in the CDFG. A state receives a set of operations to schedule; these operations constitute a subset of any one of its immediate predecessor's frontier. The frontier grows as operations are scheduled in the state (statements **11** to **16** in the pseudocode), because the scheduling of operations renders more operations schedulable. When a state is fully packed, the operations in its frontier are stored in the array *Unscheduled_immediate_successors*, which is indexed by state. States whose immediate successors have not been identified are stored in a queue, *State_q*. Statement **3** illustrates the formation of the queue. States are successively dequeued **(24)**. When a state, s, is dequeued, the operations on its frontier are packed

[1] ln_i is a prefix of ln_j if the hierarchical level of $ln_i \leq$ hierarchical level of ln_j and the first p elements of ln_i are identical to the first p elements of ln_j, where p is the hierarchical level of ln_i.

into states which represent the immediate successors of s. If the fully grown state is not identical to any known state, then it is enqueued (**22**) and the composite operations on its frontier are stored in the array *Unscheduled_immediate_successors* (**21**). This state will be dequeued in turn. When the queue is empty (**23**), we have a complete STG which describes the schedule.

The first step, during scheduling, is the identification of the set of operations, *initial*, that can be scheduled initially. The elements of this set are operations whose first iteration depends only upon primary inputs. In our example (see Figure 2), operations $<= 1$ and $<= 2$ fall into this category. Keeping track of the iteration number of every operation embedded in a loop is accomplished by working with composite operations (defined in Section 2.3.2). Statement **5** handles the conversion of the operations in *initial* into composite operations. Since we are dealing with the first iteration of operation $<= 1 (<= 2)$, whose loop number is $< 0 >$ $(< 1 >)$, the corresponding loop count is $< 0 > (< 0 >)$.

At this stage, we capture the conditions under which different subsets of *initial_composite* execute, and create states which are responsible for scheduling the corresponding subsets. This is done by first identifying the control dependency edges feeding the composite operations in *initial_composite* (**7**). Each of these control edges can evaluate either to *true* or *false*. Different combinations of truth values on the control dependency edges result in activation of different subsets of *initial_composite*. Statement **8** identifies different combinations of truth values on the control dependency edges and statement **9** extracts the subset of *initial_composite* that is activated on this combination of truth values. Suppose that, in this case, when *condition_inputs* is an empty set, the statement "**foreach** combination of conditions (*condition*, *condition_inputs*)" allows exactly one iteration through the following loop. Then *S_condition* evaluates to *initial_composite* because no composite operation in *initial_composite* has any incoming control dependency edges. Once a subset of composite operations has been identified, we form a state, *new_st*, which shares with its successors, the responsibility of scheduling the composite operations in *S_condition* (**10**). The state grows with the scheduling of composite operations present in *S_condition* and their successors. This expansion continues until no more composite operations can be added to a state. The expansion of a state (statements **11** through **16**) can be halted by allocation, clock cycle, and loop unrolling constraints. A three-stage process controls the scheduling of composite operations to a state:

1. Selection of a composite operation, *new_C*, from *S_condition*: the selection process should identify the "best" composite operation whose inclusion in *new_st* respects allocation, clock cycle, and loop unrolling constraints (**12**). In our example, composite operation $s0 = \{<= 1, < 0 >, < 0 >\}$ is selected.
2. Addition of the schedulable successors of *new_C* to *S_condition*: when an operation is scheduled, immediate successors of this operation, whose predecessors have been scheduled, become eligible for scheduling. In our example, completion of the composite operation $\{<= 1, < 0 >, < 0 >\}$ implies that its immediate successors, $s1 = \{++1, < 0 >, < 0 >\}$, $s2 = \{:=1, <>, <>\}$, and $s3 = \{<1, < 0 >, < 0 >\}$, can be scheduled. *S_condition* is augmented by the addition of *s1*, *s2*, and *s3* (**15**). Therefore, *S_condition* constitutes a frontier of composite operations which sweeps over the surface of the CDFG as scheduling progresses.
3. Removal of *new_C* from *S_condition* (**16**).

One more iteration through the innermost loop schedules composite operation $\{<= 2, < 0 >, < 0 >\}$ in *new_st* and adds $\{++2, < 0 >, < 0 >\}$, $\{+4, < 1 >, < 0 >\}$, and $\{:= 2, <>, <>\}$ to *S_condition*. At this point, no additional composite operations

```
Wavesched (CDFG G, ALLOCATION_CONSTRAINT C,
        CLOCK_PERIOD clk, UNROLL_BOUND U, STG S){
0  SET<OPERATION> initial = get_level_1_operations(G);
   //level 1 operations are defined as those operations which,
   //when all loop edges (reverse edges) in G are removed,
   //depend only on primary inputs
1  STATE S0; //create a start state
2  STATE parent_state = S0;
3  QUEUE<STATE> State_q; //create a queue of states
4  ARRAY<SET<COMPOSITE_OPERATION>> Unscheduled_-
   immediate_successors;//An array, indexed by state, which
   // stores the composite operations which are immediately
   // schedulable upon leaving the state
5  SET<COMPOSITE_OPERATION> initial_composite = Make_-
   composite(initial);//construct composite operations from
   //the operations in initial with loop counts initialized to 0.
6  loop_forever() {
7    SET<COMPOSITE_OPERATION> condition_inputs =
     composite operations whose outputs are control
     dependency edges feeding operations in initial_composite;
8    foreach combination of conditions (condition,
     condition_inputs) {//condition corresponds to the
       //assignment of a specific set of truth values to the
       //results of the composite operations in condition_inputs
9      SET<COMPOSITE_OPERATION> S_condition =
         under_condition(condition, initial_composite);
       //Extracts all operations in initial_condition that will
       //execute under condition
10     STATE new_st;
11     loop_forever() {
12       COMPOSITE_OPERATION new_C =
           Select_composite_operation(S_condition, C, clk, U);
13       if (new_C == NULL) break; //no more operations
         can be scheduled in this state
         else{
14         add_composite_operation_to_state(new_C, new_st);
15         add_schedulable_successors(new_C, S_condition);
16         remove_composite_operation(S_condition, new_C);
       }}
17     S_successors = S_condition;
18     if (new_st is identical to an existing state, P)
19       add an arc in S, labeled condition,
         from parent_state to P;
       else {
20       add an arc in S, labeled condition,
         from parent_state to new_st;
21       Unscheduled_immediate_successors[new_st]
           = S_condition;
22       append(new_st, State_q);
     }}
23 if (is_empty(State_q) == 1) break;//STG complete, exit
24 STATE s = dequeue_top(State_q);
25 Initial_composite = Unscheduled_immediate_successors[s];
}}
```

Figure 6: Our scheduling algorithm

can be scheduled in *new_st* because of the assumption related to control-dependency chaining. Therefore, the **break** statement at line **13** is executed, transferring flow of control outside to loop. We check to see if *new_st* is identical to any existing state (**18**). The process of inferring equality between states is described in [14]. Since this is not the case, we add an arc from the parent state, *S0*, to *new_st*, labeled 1, which implies that there is an unconditional transition from *S0* to *new_st* (**20**). The immediate successors of *new_st* are invested with the responsibility of scheduling the composite operations remaining in *S_condition*. *new_st* is then appended to *State_q* and immediately dequeued. Its frontier constitutes *initial_composite* which is handled in the manner described above.

3.2 Selecting the best composite operation

Since the process of selecting the "best" composite operation can be computationally intensive, we use a heuristic. Our method is based on the fact that operations in the CDFG which feed primary outputs through long paths are more critical (*i.e.* less mobile) than operations which feed primary outputs through short paths and, therefore, the former need to be scheduled earlier. The length of a path is measured as the sum of the delays of its constituent operations.

In data-dominated descriptions, with no loops and conditional operations, the longest path between any pair of operations is fixed. In CFI descriptions, some paths could be input-dependent. Therefore, the longest path between a pair of operations must be defined with respect to a given input. For example, the longest path between operations <1 and $+5$ in Figure 2 depends on the number of iterations of the loop containing <1, which depends on the value of $k1$. Since our scheduling algorithm is geared towards minimizing the average execution time, we use the expected length of the longest path from a composite operation to a primary output as a metric to rank different composite operations. We next outline a procedure to compute the expected length of the longest path and illustrate its application to a CDFG.

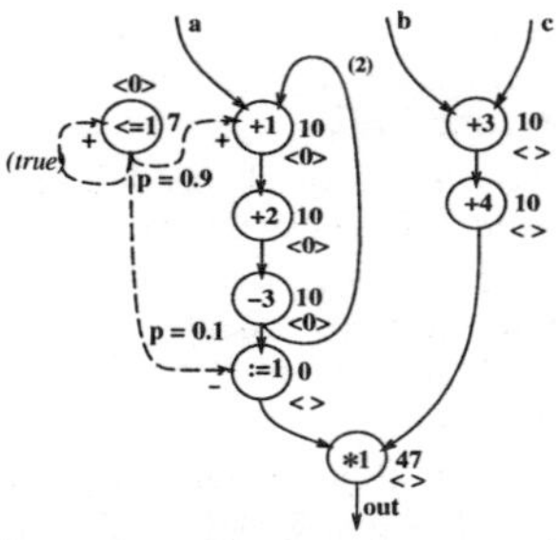

Figure 7: Illustration of composite operation selection

Example 1: Consider the CDFG shown in Figure 7. Control dependency edges are annotated with their probabilities of occurrence, and operations with the corresponding functional unit delays and loop numbers. For example, operation $+1$ is assigned to an adder type which takes $10ns$ to execute and has a loop number $< 0 >$. Suppose we are faced with the question of selecting a composite operation from the set $\{\{+1, < 0 >, < 3 >\}, \{+3, <>, <>\}\}$. We first evaluate the expected length of the longest path assuming that no loop unrolling is performed and then incorporate the effect of unrolling. Assuming that no unrolling is performed:

$$\begin{aligned} E(\lambda(+1, out)) &= 10 + E(\lambda(+2, out)) \\ &= 20 + E(\lambda(-3, out)) \\ &= 30 + 0.9 \times E(\lambda(+1, out)) + 0.1 \times 47 \\ \Rightarrow E(\lambda(+1, out)) &= 347ns \end{aligned} \qquad (1)$$

where $E(\lambda(op1, op2))$ is the expected length of the longest path connecting operations *op1* and *op2*. Note that this delay corresponds to the length of the longest path connecting the *zero*th iteration of operation $+1$ to *out*. Since we are dealing with the third iteration of operation $+1$, we need to subtract, from our estimate, the time taken to perform three iterations of the loop, which turns out to be $30 \times 3 = 90ns$. This yields an expected maximum path length of $257ns$ for the composite operation $\{+1, < 0 >, < 3 >\}$. Adopting a similar procedure for operation $\{+3, <>, <>\}$ results in an expected longest path length of $57ns$. Therefore, operation $\{+1, < 0 >, < 3 >\}$ is chosen to be scheduled in the state under consideration. We can see that this would be a good choice because operation $+1$ is on the critical path while operation $+3$ is not. ∎

3.3 Synthesizing compact STGs

The techniques presented in this section help keep the size of the STG small, without significantly compromising the average execution time of the schedule. These techniques are based on identifying probable and improbable threads of execution and optimizing the probable threads for speed and the improbable threads for STG compactness.

Consider statement **8** in Figure 6. This statement extracts all possible assignments of truth values for the composite operations that feed the operations of *initial_composite* through control dependency edges. Statement **9** packs all operations which are activated under a given combination of conditions into *S_condition*, which is passed on to a newly created state for scheduling. Not all combinations of conditions are equi-probable. We identify all combinations of conditions whose probability falls below a certain user-specified threshold, t_p. The subsets of *initial_composite* which are activated under any one of these combinations are fused into a single set *S_improbable*, which is considered for scheduling. The state created for scheduling these composite operations is tagged as a *compact state*. Note that, in doing so, we have traded the option of separately optimizing the threads of execution represented by the combinations of conditions represented in *S_improbable* for STG compactness. The children of a compact state are tagged compact. For the frontiers of compact states, the algorithm presented in Figure 6 is modified by replacing statements **7** and **8** by the corresponding statements in Figure 8. The techniques presented in this example can reduce the size of the controller by a significant amount without much compromise in the average schedule length of the design. For the example TEST1 presented in Section 2, the STG shown in Figure 4 is synthesized assuming $t_p = 1$, which represents a schedule optimized for compactness. The number of states in the schedule is 17, eight less than the number of states that would be obtained if the CDFG were synthesized with $t_p = 0$. In this case, both schedules have the same average length; in general, however, a large value of t_p would result in a longer schedule.

```
7   SET<COMPOSITE_OPERATION> loop_tests = loop test of
      operations whose outputs feed operations of
      initial_composite through control dependency edges
8   foreach combination of conditions (condition, loop_tests) {
      //condition corresponds to the assignment of a specific
      //set of truth values to the results of the composite
      //operations in loop_tests
```

Figure 8: Optimizing for compactness

4 Experimental results

The techniques described in this paper were implemented in a program called *Wavesched*, written in C++. We evaluated this program by using it to produce schedules for several commonly available benchmarks. These schedules were compared against those produced by LDS [5] and PBS [4], with respect to the following metrics: (a) expected number of cycles, (b) number of states in the STG produced, and (c) the smallest and largest number of cycles taken to execute the behavioral description. In general, finding the largest number of cycles taken to execute a behavioral description is a hard problem. However, for the examples considered in this paper, static analysis of the description was sufficient to find the number. For *Wavesched*, a value of 0.2 was used for t_p (defined in Section 3.3).

Table 2 summarizes the results obtained. The columns labeled *E.N.C.*, *#states*, *best-case*, and *worst-case* represent, respectively,

Table 2: Expected number of cycles, number of states, best- and worst-case number of cycles results

CDFG	*Clk*	*E.N.C.*			*#states*			*best-case*			*worst-case*		
		ws	LDS	PBS	*ws*	LDS	PBS	*ws*	LDS	PBS	*ws*	LDS	PBS
GCD	13	13.9	14.4	18.2	6	5	5	1	1	1	386	386	513
Maha	13	3.3	6.0	6.0	12	10	10	3	5	5	4	7	7
Cordic	13	41.0	60.0	79.0	9	8	8	3	3	3	515	771	1026
Test1	13	178.6	301.7	349.8	24	12	12	1	1	1	766	1538	1791
Saxpy	13	104.0	501.0	501.0	8	6	6	104	501	501	104	501	501
Paulin	13	7.0	11.0	11.0	7	11	11	7	11	11	7	11	11

the expected number of cycles, number of states in the STG produced, smallest number of cycles, and largest number of cycles taken to execute the STG. Minor columns *ws*, LDS, and PBS represent schedules produced by *Wavesched*, LDS, and PBS, respectively. We used a library of functional units (their delays given in brackets) which consists of (a) an adder *ad1* (10*ns*), (b) a subtractor *sb1* (10*ns*), (c) a multiplier *mlt1* (23*ns*), (d) a less-than comparator *cmp1* (10*ns*), (e) an equality comparator *eq1* (5*ns*), (f) an incrementer *inc1* (5*ns*), (g) a multi-bit OR gate *or1* (3*ns*), and (h) a shifter *s1* (10*ns*). We allowed all schedulers to take advantage of multicycling and data chaining, and allowed control chaining. The following chains of operations were assumed to execute in one cycle: (a) two additions, (b) two subtractions, (c) a comparison followed by either an increment or an addition or a subtraction or a shift, and (d) two comparisons. The following chains of operations were assumed to execute in two cycles: (a) a comparison followed by a multiplication, and (b) a multiplication followed by a comparison. The cycle time was fixed at 13 *ns* for all examples. Note that the chain of two operations frequently executes in much less time than the addition of their execution times. The allocation constraints for an example can be found by looking up the entries in Table 3. For example, the allocation constraint for *GCD* is one subtractor, one less-than comparator, three equality comparators, and one multi-bit OR gate.

The results obtained indicate that *Wavesched* produced an average expected schedule length speedup of 2.1 over schedules obtained using LDS, and 2.2 over schedules obtained using PBS. The average price paid in terms of the number of states was a 26% increase for *Wavesched* compared to LDS and PBS. Note that an increase in the number of states need not be reflected in a similar increase in circuit area. We believe that the improvement in performance will be worth paying the small price in area, if any. For the example *Test1*, the schedule produced by *Wavesched*, upon synthesis with an in-house system, resulted in a controller-datapath circuit whose layout area was only 1.7% more than that produced using *LDS*, though *Wavesched* incurred a 100% overhead in the number of states in the schedule. We also note that, for *Wavesched*, the number of cycles in the shortest and longest paths is smaller than or equal to the corresponding numbers for LDS and PBS. The CPU times, measured on an SGI Indy workstation, with a MIPS R4400 CPU running at 175 *MHz*, were under 30 seconds for all the examples.

Table 3: Allocation constraints for the examples in Table 2

Circuit	*ad1*	*sb1*	*mlt1*	*cmp1*	*eq1*	*inc1*	*or1*	*s1*
GCD	-	1	-	1	3	-	1	-
Maha	2	2	-	2	-	-	-	-
Cordic	2	2	1	1	1	2	-	2
Test1	2	-	2	3	-	2	-	-
Saxpy	2	-	2	-	2	2	-	-
Paulin	2	2	2	-	-	-	-	-

5 Conclusions

In this paper, we presented a novel scheduling technique which is geared towards minimizing the expected execution time for CFI behavioral descriptions. It uses a CDFG model which preserves the parallelism inherent in the application. It can perform optimizations within and across loop boundaries and implicitly unroll loops to improve the average schedule length. This is made possible through a general loop representation technique which we have devised. It also performs concurrent loop optimzation. Experiments performed on several benchmarks show expected schedule length speedups of upto 4.8 over schedules produced by existing schedulers.

References

[1] D. D. Gajski, N. Dutt, A. Wu, and S. Lin, *High-Level Synthesis: Introduction to Chip and System Design.* Kluwer Academic Publishers, Boston, 1992.

[2] W. Wolf, A. Takach, C. Huang, and R. Mano, "The Princeton university behavioral synthesis system," in *Proc. Design Automation Conf.*, pp. 182–187, June 1992.

[3] D. Ku and G. D. Micheli, "Relative scheduling under timing constraints," *IEEE Trans. Computer-Aided Design*, vol. 11, pp. 696–718, June 1992.

[4] R. Camposano, "Path-based scheduling for synthesis," *IEEE Trans. Computer-Aided Design*, vol. 10, pp. 85–93, Jan. 1991.

[5] S. Bhattacharya, S. Dey, and F. Brglez, "Performance analysis and optimization of schedules for conditional and loop-intensive specifications," in *Proc. Design Automation Conf.*, pp. 491–496, June 1994.

[6] R. Bergamaschi, S. Raje, I. Nair, and L. Trevillyan, "Control-flow versus data-flow scheduling: Combining both approaches in an adaptive scheduling system," *IEEE Trans. VLSI Systems*, vol. 5, pp. 82–100, Mar. 1997.

[7] Y. Fann, M. Rim, and R. Jain, "Global scheduling for high-level synthesis applications," in *Proc. Design Automation Conf.*, pp. 542–546, June 1994.

[8] S. Amellal and B. Kaminska, "Functional synthesis of digital systems with TASS," *IEEE Trans. Computer-Aided Design*, vol. 13, pp. 537–552, May 1994.

[9] T. Kim, N. Yonezawa, J. W. S. Liu, and C. L. Liu, "A scheduling algorithm for conditional resource sharing- a hierarchical reduction approach," *IEEE Trans. Computer-Aided Design*, vol. 13, pp. 425–438, Apr. 1994.

[10] K. Wakabayashi and T. Yoshimura, "A resource sharing and control synthesis method for conditional branches," in *Proc. Int. Conf. Computer-Aided Design*, pp. 62–65, Nov. 1989.

[11] A. Aiken, A. Nikolau, and S. Novack, "Resource-constrained software pipelining," *IEEE Trans. Parallel and Distributed Systems*, vol. 6, pp. 1248–1269, Dec. 1995.

[12] D. M. Lavery and W. W. Hwu, "Modulo scheduling of loops in control-flow intensive non-numeric programs," in *Proc. Int. Symp. Microarchitecture*, pp. 126–137, Dec. 1996.

[13] B. R. Rau and J. A. Fisher, "Instruction-level parallel processing: History, overview, and perspective," *J. Supercomputing*, vol. 7, pp. 9–50, July 1993.

[14] G. Lakshminarayana, K. S. Khouri, and N. K. Jha, "Wavesched: A novel scheduling technique for control-flow intensive behavioral descriptions," Tech. Rep CE-J97-001, EE Dept., Princeton Univ.

SESSION 5C

CLOCK DESIGN AND OPTIMIZATION

Moderators:

Masato Edahiro, C&C Research Labs., NEC Corp.,

Kawasaki, Japan

Jason Cong, University of California,

Los Angeles, CA

Optimal Wire and Transistor Sizing for Circuits with Non-Tree Topology

Lieven Vandenberghe*
Electrical Engineering Dept.
University of California
Los Angeles, CA 90095-1594
vandenbe@ee.ucla.edu

Stephen Boyd*
Information Systems Laboratory
Electrical Engineering Dept.
Stanford University
Stanford, CA 94305-9510
boyd@isl.stanford.edu

Abbas El Gamal
Information Systems Laboratory
Electrical Engineering Dept.
Stanford University
Stanford, CA 94305-9510
abbas@isl.stanford.edu

Abstract

Conventional methods for optimal sizing of wires and transistors use linear RC circuit models and the Elmore delay as a measure of signal delay. If the RC circuit has a tree topology the sizing problem reduces to a convex optimization problem which can be solved using geometric programming. The tree topology restriction precludes the use of these methods in several sizing problems of significant importance to high-performance deep submicron design including, for example, circuits with loops of resistors, *e.g.*, clock distribution meshes, and circuits with coupling capacitors, *e.g.*, buses with crosstalk between the lines. The paper proposes a new optimization method which can be used to address these problems. The method uses the dominant time constant as a measure of signal propagation delay in an RC circuit, instead of Elmore delay. Using this measure, sizing of any RC circuit can be cast as a convex optimization problem which can be solved using the recently developed efficient interior-point methods for semidefinite programming. The method is applied to two important sizing problems — sizing of clock meshes, and sizing of buses in the presence of crosstalk.

1 Introduction

The classical approach to optimal sizing of wires and transistors assumes a linear RC circuit model and uses *Elmore delay* as a measure of signal propagation delay. This approach finds its origins in [8, 13, 9]. In particular, Fishburn and Dunlop [9] were first to observe that if the resistors form a tree with the input voltage source at its root and all capacitors are grounded, the Elmore delay of an RC circuit is a *posynomial function* of the conductances and capacitances. This observation has the important consequence that convex programming, specifically geometric programming, can be used to optimize Elmore delay under area and power constraints. Geometric programming forms the basis of the TILOS program and of several extensions and related programs developed since then. We refer to [6] for a comprehensive recent survey.

The tree topology restriction, however, precludes the use of these Elmore delay methods in several sizing problems of significant importance to high performance deep submicron design including circuits with capacitive coupling between the nodes, *e.g.*, buses with crosstalk, and circuits with loops of resistors, *e.g.*, clock meshes.

In this paper we present a new optimal sizing method which can be used to address these problems. The method uses the *dominant time constant* as a measure of signal delay, instead of Elmore delay. The motivation for this choice is that the dominant time constant of a general RC circuit is a quasiconvex function of the conductances and capacitances. In particular we show that it can be optimized using semidefinite programming for which efficient methods have recently been developed. The Elmore delay, on the other hand, has no useful convexity properties except when the RC circuit has a tree topology. Moreover practical experience suggests that the numerical values of the dominant time constant are quite close to threshold delay (and to the Elmore delay).

We apply our method to two important sizing problems. The first is the problem of sizing a clock mesh (§4). The results illustrate that, to a certain extent, our method can be used to design the interconnect *topology* (in addition to sizing). The second problem is the simultaneous sizing of bus line widths and spacings taking into account coupling capacitances between neighboring bus lines (§5). This problem is important in deep submicron design where the cou-

*Research supported in part by AFOSR (under F49620-95-1-0318) and NSF (under ECS-9222391 and EEC-9420565)

pling capacitance can be significantly higher than the plate capacitance. The results illustrate that optimizing dominant time constant allows us to control not only the signal propagation delay, but also indirectly the crosstalk between the lines. Since the circuit has nongrounded capacitors, this is not possible using Elmore delay.

The outline of the paper is as follows. In §2 we describe the RC circuit model considered in the paper, and define the dominant time constant. In §3 we show that sizing problems using the dominant time constant as a measure of delay lead to semidefinite programming problems, for which efficient methods have recently been developed. In §4 and §5 we describe the application of our method to sizing of clock meshes and buses with crosstalk. Additional theoretical background, and more examples, are presented in [20].

2 The dominant time constant

We consider linear resistor-capacitor (RC) circuits that can be described by the differential equation

$$C\frac{dv}{dt} = -G(v(t) - u(t)), \tag{1}$$

where $v(t) \in \mathbf{R}^n$ is the vector of node voltages, $u(t) \in \mathbf{R}^n$ is the vector of independent voltage sources, $C \in \mathbf{R}^{n\times n}$ is the capacitance matrix, and $G \in \mathbf{R}^{n\times n}$ is the conductance matrix. We assume that C and G are symmetric and positive definite. We are interested in design problems in which C and G depend on some design parameters $x \in \mathbf{R}^m$. Specifically we assume that the matrices C and G are *affine* functions of x, *i.e.*,

$$\begin{aligned} C(x) &= C_0 + x_1C_1 + \cdots + x_mC_m, \\ G(x) &= G_0 + x_1G_1 + \cdots + x_mG_m, \end{aligned} \tag{2}$$

where C_i and G_i are symmetric matrices.

Linear RC models of the form (1) are often used as approximate models for transistors and interconnect wires. When the design parameters are the physical widths of conductors or transistors, the conductance and capacitance matrices are affine in these parameters, *i.e.*, they have the form (2).

We are interested in how fast a change in the input u propagates to the different nodes of the circuit, and in how this propagation delay varies as a function of the variables x. To simplify notation, we will consider the autonomous equation $Cdv/dt = -Gv$. We assume the circuit starts at initial condition $v(0)$ and will study the rate at which the voltages

$$v(t) = e^{-C^{-1}Gt}v(0) \tag{3}$$

become small. We distinguish three possible measures for the circuit propagation delay.

- *The threshold delay* at node k is the first time after which v_k stays below some given threshold level $\alpha > 0$, *i.e.*,

  $$T_k^{\mathrm{thres}} = \inf\{\, T \mid |v_k(t)| \leq \alpha \text{ for } t \geq T \,\}.$$

  We call the maximum threshold delay to any node the *critical threshold delay* of the circuit.

- The *Elmore delay* at node k is defined as

  $$T_k^{\mathrm{elm}} = \int_0^\infty v_k(t)\, dt.$$

  While T_k^{elm} is always defined, it can be interpreted as a measure of delay only when $v_k(t) \geq 0$ for all $t \geq 0$, *i.e.*, when the node voltage is nonnegative (which is the case in RC circuits with grounded capacitors if $v(0) \geq 0$). We can express the Elmore delay in terms of G, C, and $v(0)$ as

  $$T_k^{\mathrm{elm}} = e_k^T G^{-1} C v(0)$$

  where e_k is the kth unit vector. We define the *critical Elmore delay* as the largest Elmore delay at any node, *i.e.*, $T^{\mathrm{elm}} = \max_k T_k^{\mathrm{elm}}$.

- The *dominant time constant* is defined as

  $$T^{\mathrm{dom}} = -1/\lambda_1 \tag{4}$$

  where $\lambda_1, \ldots, \lambda_n$ denote the poles of the circuit, *i.e.*, the eigenvalues of $-C^{-1}G$, sorted in decreasing order, *i.e.*, $0 > \lambda_1 \geq \cdots \geq \lambda_n$. The dominant time constant is a meaningful measure of delay since each voltage can be expressed as a sum of decaying exponentials

  $$v_k(t) = \sum_{i=1}^{n} \alpha_{ik} e^{\lambda_i t},$$

  and the dominant time constant gives the time constant of the slowest of these exponentials.

The threshold delay is the most natural of these three measures, but it is difficult to handle mathematically. It depends on the design parameters x in a very complicated way. Methods for direct optimization of T^{thres} require simulating the circuit to obtain the value of T^{thres} and its derivatives (sensitivity with respect to variations in x). Such methods are necessarily local, *i.e.*, not guaranteed to find a globally optimal design, and limited to small circuits.

The Elmore delay is widely used for optimal circuit sizing (see, *e.g.*, [9, 15, 3, 16, 14, 11]). However, as pointed out in the introduction, it can be efficiently optimized only in circuits with a tree topology.

The dominant time constant T^{dom} is a complicated function of G and C (it is the negative inverse of the largest zero of the polynomial $\det(sC+G)$). However it can be expressed in a form that will be very useful to us:

$$T^{\text{dom}} = \min\{\, T \mid TG - C \geq 0 \,\},$$

where the inequality means that $TG - C$ is positive semidefinite. In particular,

$$T^{\text{dom}}(x) \leq T_{\max} \iff T_{\max}G(x) - C(x) \geq 0. \quad (5)$$

In other words, an upper bound on the dominant time constant is equivalent to a *linear matrix inequality* (LMI), *i.e.*, a *convex* constraint in x, regardless of the topology of the circuit. This also means that T^{dom} is a *quasiconvex* function of x, *i.e.*, its sublevel sets $\{x \mid T^{\text{dom}}(x) \leq T_{\max}\}$ are convex sets for all $T_{\max}$.

3 Semidefinite programming

In this section we show that sizing problems based on dominant time constant can be cast in terms of two standard optimization problems with LMI constraints.

The most common problem is the *semidefinite programming* (SDP) problem, in which we minimize a linear function subject to an LMI:

$$\begin{array}{ll} \text{minimize} & c^T x \\ \text{subject to} & A(x) \geq 0, \end{array} \quad (6)$$

where $A(x) = A_0 + x_1 A_1 + \cdots + x_m A_m$, $A_i = A_i^T \in \mathbf{R}^{n \times n}$. Semidefinite programs are convex optimization problems, and can be solved very efficiently using recent interior-point methods (see, *e.g.*, [12, 19]).

As an example, suppose the area of the circuit described by (2) is a linear function of the variables x_i. This occurs when the variables represent the widths of transistors or conductors (with lengths fixed as l_i), in which case the circuit area has the form

$$a_0 + x_1 l_1 + \cdots + x_m l_m$$

where a_0 is the area of the fixed part of the circuit. We can minimize the area subject to a bound on the dominant time constant $T^{\text{dom}} \leq T_{\max}$, and subject to upper and lower bounds on the widths by solving the SDP

$$\begin{array}{ll} \text{minimize} & \sum_{i=1}^{m} l_i x_i \\ \text{subject to} & T_{\max}G(x) - C(x) \geq 0 \\ & x_{\min} \leq x_i \leq x_{\max}, \quad i = 1, \ldots, m. \end{array} \quad (7)$$

The optimal solutions of (7) are on the tradeoff curve, *i.e.*, they are *Pareto optimal* for area and dominant time constant. By solving this SDP for a sequence of values of $T_{\max}$, we can compute the exact optimal tradeoff between area and dominant time constant.

A second common optimization problem with LMI constraints has the form

$$\begin{array}{ll} \text{minimize} & \lambda \\ \text{subject to} & \lambda B(x) - A(x) \geq 0 \\ & B(x) > 0, \quad C(x) \geq 0, \end{array} \quad (8)$$

where A, B, and C are symmetric matrices that are affine functions of x, and the variables are x and $\lambda \in \mathbf{R}$. This problem is called the *generalized eigenvalue minimization problem* (GEVP). GEVPs are quasiconvex and can also be solved efficiently using interior-point methods [1, 12].

For example, the problem of minimizing the dominant time constant, subject to an upper bound on the area and upper and lower bounds on the variables, can be cast as a GEVP

$$\begin{array}{ll} \text{minimize} & T \\ \text{subject to} & TG(x) - C(x) \geq 0 \\ & \sum_{i=1}^{m} l_i x_i \leq A_{\max} \\ & x_{\min} \leq x_i \leq x_{\max}, \quad i = 1, \ldots, m. \end{array}$$

with variables T and x.

4 Sizing of clock meshes

The possibility of optimizing RC circuits with loops of resistors is of importance to high-performance microprocessor design where the clock signal is distributed using a mesh instead of a tree. In [7], Desai, Cvijetic, and Jensen describe the design of the clock distribution network on a DEC-alpha processor, and note, "there is a need for algorithms for sizing large non-tree networks." Minimizing the dominant time constant instead of Elmore delay is a promising technique to achieve exactly that goal.

Figure 1 shows the example that we consider in this paragraph. The circuit consists of a mesh of interconnect wire. The number of segments per row or column is N (and the number of nodes in the circuit is equal to $n = (N+1)^2$). We model each interconnect segment (the rectangular elements in Figure 1) as a π-segment, as in Figure 2. The optimization variables are the N^2 segment widths x_i (with constraints $0 \leq x_i \leq w_{\max}$).

Each node of the mesh has a capacitive load C_i. The network is driven by voltage sources with output conductance G_0. The sources switch between zero and

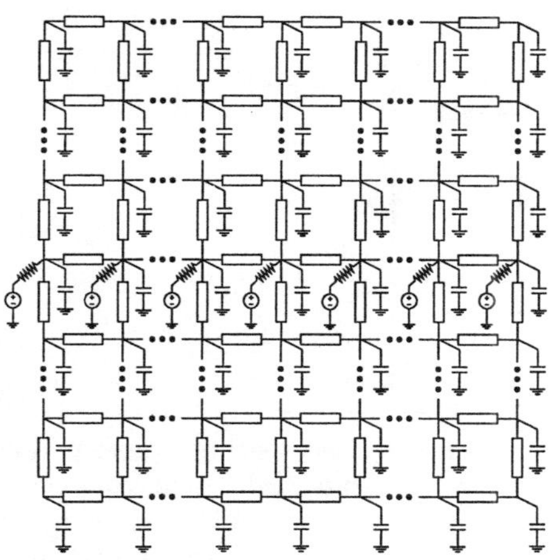

Figure 1: Clock distribution network modeled as an RC mesh. Each rectangular element represents a wire, which we model as a single π-segment as in Figure 2. The drivers switch simultaneously. We are interested in the tradeoff between delay (dominant time constant) and total dissipated power. The variables are the widths of the N^2 segments, where N is the number of segments in each column and row.

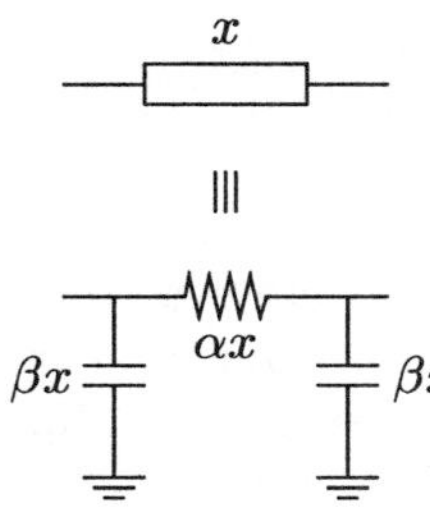

Figure 2: A segment of an interconnect wire with width x is modeled as a conductance αx and two capacitances to the ground βx.

one simultaneously and at a fixed frequency. Therefore the energy dissipated in once cycle is equal to

$$\mathbf{1}^T C(x)\mathbf{1} = \sum_{i=1}^{n} C_i + 2\beta \sum_{i=1}^{N^2} x_i,$$

which is a linear function of the variables x ($\mathbf{1}$ is the n-vector with all components equal to one). This means we can minimize the dissipated power subject to a bound on the dominant time constant by solving the SDP

$$\begin{array}{ll} \text{minimize} & \mathbf{1}^T C(x)\mathbf{1} \\ \text{subject to} & T_{\max} G(x) - C(x) \geq 0 \\ & 0 \leq x_i \leq w_{\max}, \quad i = 1, \ldots, N^2. \end{array} \tag{9}$$

By solving the SDP (9) for different values of $T_{\max}$, we can trace the exact tradeoff curve between dissipated power and dominant time constant. This is shown in Figure 4 for the numerical values

$$N = 4, \quad G_0 = 1, \quad \alpha = 1, \quad \beta = 0.5, \quad w_{\max} = 1,$$

and for load capacitances as indicated in Figure 3.

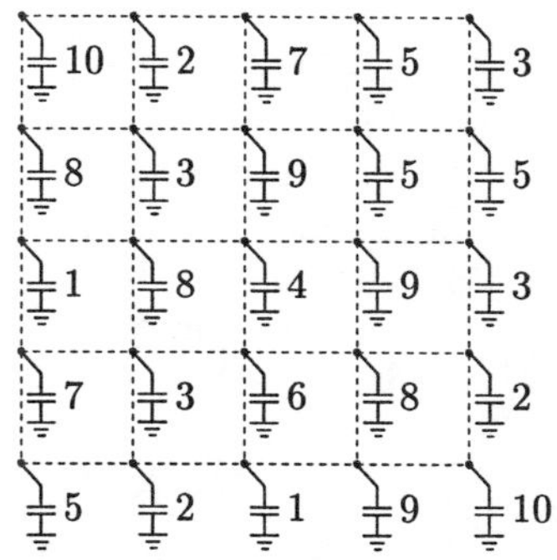

Figure 3: RC mesh example with 4×4 segments, and the numerical values of the load capacitances used in the calculation.

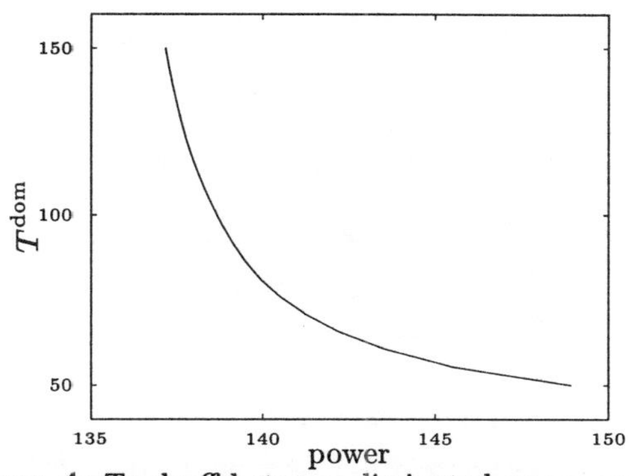

Figure 4: Tradeoff between dissipated power and dominant time constant.

Figure 5 shows the solution for two different points on the tradeoff curve ($T^{\text{dom}} = 55$ and $T^{\text{dom}} = 100$).

We note that the topology is different in the two cases. More segments are used in the circuit on the left, which has a small dominant time constant and large power consumption (large total capacitance). In the solution on the right, fewer segments are used and they are smaller, which reduces the power dissipation but increases the dominant time constant.

Figure 6 shows the fastest and the slowest step responses in both circuits, when a step input is applied simultaneously to the five voltage sources in the middle row. Note in particular that the values of the three delay measures are very close (and in fact, the dominant time constant approximates the 50%-threshold delay better than the Elmore delay). This observation is confirmed by many other examples (see [20]).

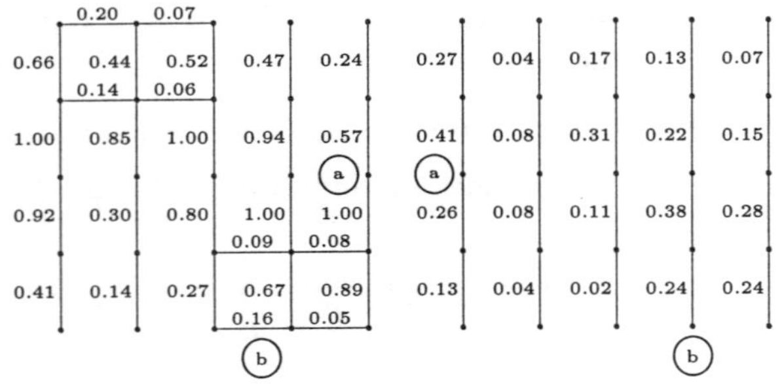

Figure 5: Optimal solution for two points on the tradeoff curve: $T^{\rm dom} = 50$ (left) and $T^{\rm dom} = 100$ (right). The numbers indicate the optimal widths x_i of the segments; the segments with width $x_i = 0$ are not shown.

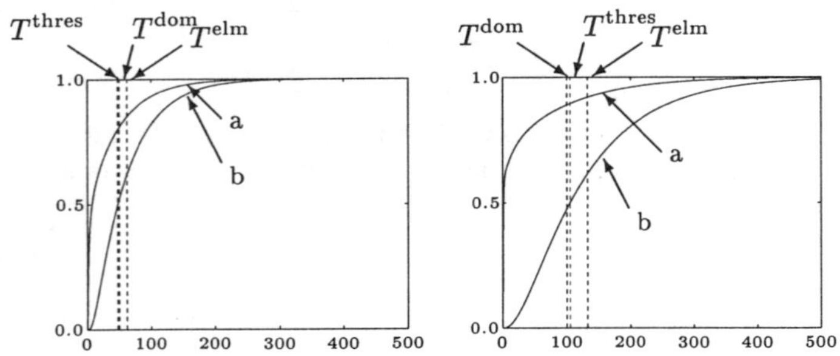

Figure 6: Step responses for the two solutions in Figure 5. The plots show the responses at the fastest (a) and the slowest (b) node in Figure 5. We also show the critical 50%-threshold delay, the critical Elmore delay, and the dominant time constant.

5 Sizing of buses with crosstalk

The second application demonstrates another important advantage of using dominant time constant instead of Elmore delay: the ability to take into account non-grounded capacitors.

The problem is to determine the optimal line widths *and* spacings for a bus taking into account the coupling capacitances between the lines. We consider an example with three wires, each consisting of five segments, as shown in Figure 7. The optimization variables are the widths w_{ij}, and the distances s_1 and s_2 between the wires.

The RC model of the three wires is shown in Figure 8. The wires are connected to a voltage source with output conductance G at one end, and to capacitive loads at the other end. As in the previous example, each segment is modeled as a π-segment, with conductance and capacitance proportional to the segment width w_{ij}. We include a parasitic capacitance between the wires. We assume that there is a capacitance between the jth segments of wires 1 and 2, and between the jth segments of wires 2 and 3, with total

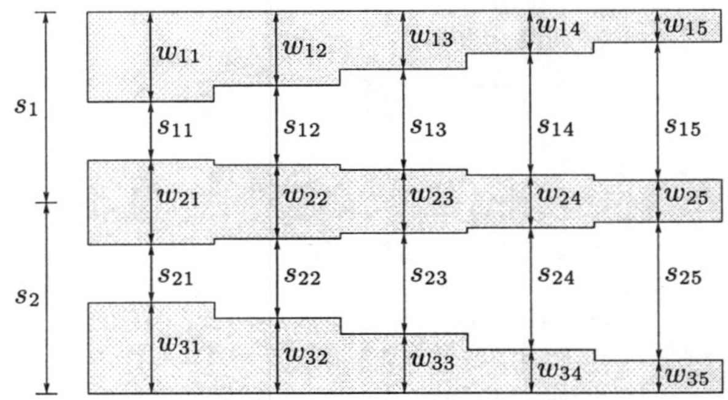

Figure 7: Wire sizing and spacing. Three parallel wires consisting of five segments each. The conductance and capacitance of the jth segment of wire i is proportional to w_{ij}. There is a capacitive coupling between the ith segments of wires 1 and 2, and between the ith segments of wires 2 and 3, and the value of this parasitic capacitance is inversely proportional to s_{1i}, and s_{2i}, respectively. The optimization variables are the 15 segment widths w_{ij} and the distances s_1 and s_2.

values inversely proportional to the distances s_{1j} and s_{2j}, respectively. To obtain a lumped model, we split this distributed capacitance over two capacitors: the capacitance between segments j of wires 1 and 2 is lumped in two capacitors with value γ/s_{1j}; the total capacitance between segments j of wires 2 and 3 is lumped in two capacitors with value γ/s_{2j}. This leads to the RC circuit in Figure 8.

We also impose the constraints that the distances s_{ij} between the wires must exceed a value $s_{\min}$, and that wire widths are less than $w_{\max}$. We can minimize the total width $s_1 + s_2$ of the three wires subject to a bound on the dominant time constant of the circuit, by solving the optimization problem

$$\begin{array}{ll} \text{minimize} & s_1 + s_2 \\ \text{subject to} & T_{\max} G(w) - C(w,s) \geq 0 \\ & s_{1j} = s_1 - w_{1j} - 0.5 w_{2j}, \;\; j = 1,\ldots,5 \\ & s_{2j} = s_2 - w_{3j} - 0.5 w_{2j}, \;\; j = 1,\ldots,5 \\ & s_{ij} \geq s_{\min}, \;\; i = 1,2, \;\; j = 1,\ldots,5 \\ & w_{ij} \leq w_{\max}, \;\; i = 1,2,3, \;\; j = 1,\ldots,5, \end{array} \qquad (10)$$

in the variables s_1, s_2, w_{ij}, s_{ij}. Note that the capacitance matrix contains terms that are inversely proportional to the variables s_{ij}, and therefore problem (10) is *not* an SDP. However, it is shown in [20] that by a change of variables $t_{ij} = 1/s_{ij}$, problem (10) can be

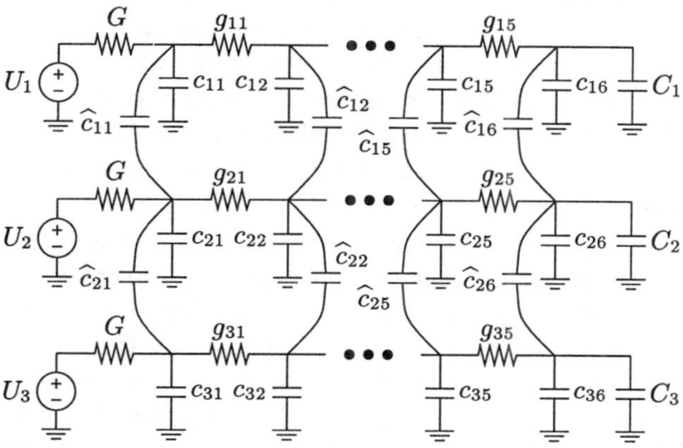

Figure 8: RC model of the three wires shown in Figure 7. The wires are connected to voltage sources with output conductance G at one end, and to load capacitors C_i at the other end. The conductances g_{ij} and capacitances c_{ij} are part of the π-models of the wire segments. The capacitances $\widehat{c}_{ij}$ model the capacitive coupling. The conductances and capacitances depend on the geometry of Figure 7 in the following way: $g_{ij} = \alpha w_{ij}$, $c_{i1} = \beta w_{i1}$, $c_{ij} = \beta(w_{ij} + w_{i(j-1)})$ $(1 < j < 6)$, $c_{i6} = \beta w_{i5}$, $\widehat{c}_{i1} = \gamma / s_{i1}$, $\widehat{c}_{ij} = \gamma/s_{ij} + \gamma/s_{i(j-1)}$ $(1 < j < 6)$, $\widehat{c}_{i6} = \gamma/s_{i5}$.

reformulated as a convex optimization problem

$$\begin{array}{ll} \text{mimimize} & s_1 + s_2 \\ \text{subject to} & T_{\max} G(w) - C(w,t) \geq 0 \\ & 1/t_{1j} \leq s_1 - w_{1j} - 0.5 w_{2j}, \;\; j = 1, \ldots, 5 \\ & 1/t_{2j} \leq s_2 - w_{3j} - 0.5 w_{2j}, \;\; j = 1, \ldots, 5 \\ & 0 \leq t_{ij} \leq 1/s_{\min}, \; i = 1, 2, \;\; j = 1, \ldots, 5 \\ & w_{ij} \leq w_{\max}, \; i = 1, 2, 3, \; j = 1, \ldots, 5, \end{array} \tag{11}$$

with variables s_1, s_2, t_{ij}, and w_{ij}. Problem (11) can be readily cast as an SDP (see [20]).

Figures 9 through 12 illustrate the solution of (10) for two values of $T_{\max}$, assuming the parameter values

$$\begin{array}{lllll} G = 100, & C_1 = 10, & C_2 = 20, & C_3 = 30, & \\ \alpha = 1, & \beta = 0.5, & \gamma = 2, & s_{\min} = 1, & w_{\max} = 2. \end{array}$$

Figures 9 and 10 illustrate a solution for $T_{\max} = 130$. The widest wire is number three, since it drives the largest load, the narrowest wire is number one, which drives the smallest load. We also see that the smallest distance between the wires is equal to its minimum allowed value of 1.0, which means that the cross-coupling did not affect the optimal spacing between the wires. Figure 10 shows the output voltages for steps applied to one of the wires, while the two other input voltages remains zero.

Figures 11 and 12 illustrate a solution for $T_{\max} = 90$. Note that here the distance between the second

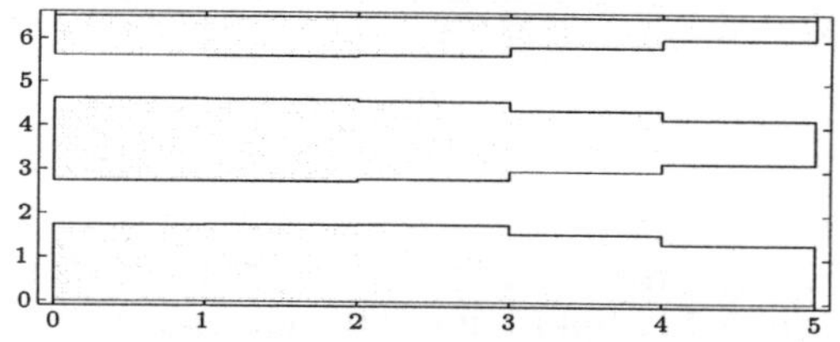

Figure 9: Solution of (10) for $T_{\max} = 130$. Note that the distance between the wires is equal to its minimal allowed value of 1.0

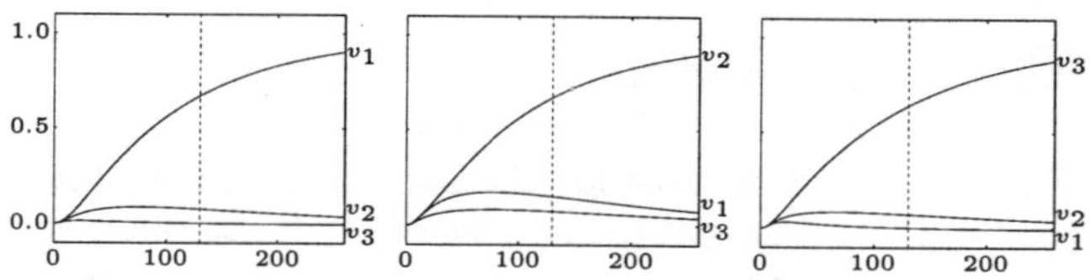

Figure 10: Responses for solution of Figure 9. The voltages at the output nodes due to a step applied to the first wire (left figure), second wire (center), or third wire (right). The dashed line marks the dominant time constant.

and third wires is larger than the minimum allowed value of 1.0. The other figures show the output voltages for the same situations as above.

Note that we cannot guarantee that the peak due to crosstalk stays under a certain level. This would be a specification in practice, but it is difficult to incorporate into the optimization problem. However we influence the level indirectly: minimizing the dominant time constant makes the crosstalk peak shorter in time (since the dominant time constant determines how fast all voltages settle around their steady-state value). Indirectly, this also tends to make the magnitude of the peak smaller (as can be seen by comparing the crosstalk levels for the two solutions in the examples).

A practical heuristic based on the dominant time constant minimization that would guarantee a given peak level is as follows. We first solve problem (10) for a given value of $T_{\max}$. Then we simulate to see if crosstalk level is acceptable. If not, we increase the spacing of the wires until it is. Then we determine the optimal wire sizes again, keeping the wires at least at this minimum distance. This iteration is continued until it converges. The dominant time constant of the final result will be at least as good as the first solution and the crosstalk level will not exceed the maximum level.

6 Conclusions

We presented a new method for wire and transistor sizing. The method uses the dominant time con-

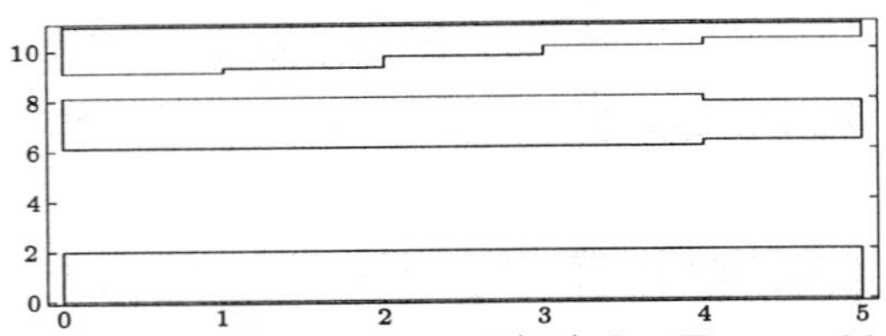

Figure 11: Solution of (10) for $T_{\max} = 90$.

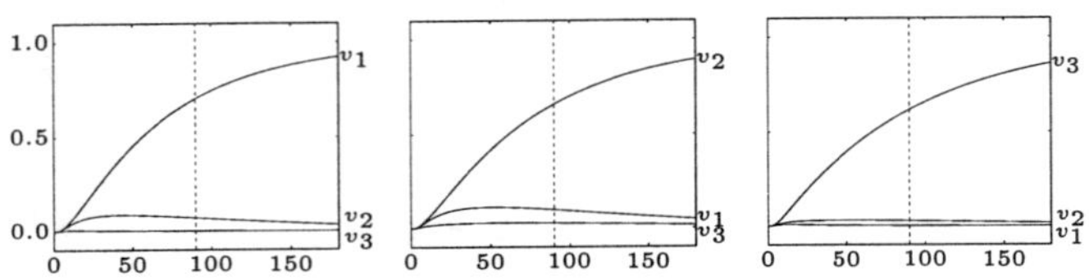

Figure 12: Responses for the solution shown in Figure 11. The voltages at the output nodes, due to to a step applied to the first wire (left figure), second wire (center), or third wire (right). The dashed line marks the dominant time constant.

stant as a measure of signal delay in RC circuits. The main advantage of using this measure is that RC circuits with general non-tree topologies can be optimally sized using convex optimization. This is in contrast to the Elmore delay sizing methods which only work for RC trees. We demonstrated the power of this method by applying it to two important examples of significant practical importance: sizing of clock meshes, and sizing of buses in the presence of crosstalk.

The method we described uses the recently developed interior-point methods for semidefinite programming (see, *e.g.*, [12, 19]). Since real world sizing problems are likely to be very large we briefly discuss the complexity of the SDP methods. Two factors determine the overall complexity of these methods: the total number of iterations and the complexity of an iteration. It can be shown that the number of iterations to solve an SDP to a given accuracy ϵ grows at most as $O(\sqrt{n}\log(1/\epsilon))$, where n is the size of the matrix $A(x)$ in (6) [12]. In practice the performance is even better than suggested by this worst-case bound. The number of iterations usually lies between 5 and 50, almost independently of problem size. For practical purposes it is therefore fair to consider the total number of iterations as constant, and to regard the complexity of an iteration as dominating the overall complexity.

Each iteration involves solving a large system of linear equations to compute search directions. Little can be said about the complexity of this computation since it largely depends on the degree to which the structure of the problem can be exploited. If the problem has no structure, *i.e.*, if the matrices A_i in (6) are completely dense, then the complexity of one iteration is $O(mn^3 + m^2n^2)$. This is the case for the general-purpose SDP solvers SP and SDPSOL [17, 21], that were used in the examples discussed in this paper. These solvers can handle problems with up to several hundred variables without difficulty, but become impractical for larger problems.

In most applications, however, there is a great deal of structure that can be exploited, and specialized solvers can be orders of magnitude more efficient than general-purpose solvers (see for a few examples, [18, 2]). In particular the SDP problems arising in dominant time constant minimization exhibit two forms of sparsity that can be exploited in a specialized solver. First, the capacitance and conductance matrices C and G are usually sparse matrices (indeed C is often diagonal). Second, each variable x_i affects only a very small number of elements of C and G (*i.e.*, the different matrices C_i and G_i in (2) are extremely sparse).

We conclude by discussing the differences between Elmore delay and the dominant time constant. The most important difference is that the dominant time constant *always* leads to tractable convex or quasiconvex optimization problems, with no restrictions on circuit topology. This follows from (5) which holds regardless of the circuit topology. Specifically, we note the following advantages.

- Elmore delay optimization applies only to circuits with one input source. The dominant time constant can be applied to circuits with multiple sources, a problem that has only recently received attention [4, 5].

- The Elmore delay in an RC tree is a posynomial function if the conductances depend on one variable only. For dominant time constant optimization the conductance and capacitances can be general affine functions of the variables.

- The circuits may contain loops of resistors, *e.g.*, clock meshes. Although for grounded capacitor RC circuits with loops of resistors, the Elmore delay is still a meaningful approximation of signal delay [10, 22, 23], it does not have the simple posynomial form as it does for RC trees, and convex optimization cannot be used to minimize it.

- The possibility of handling non-tree topologies allows us to design the topology of the interconnection itself. For example in the optimization of a clock mesh we start with a full grid of possible wire segments. After optimal wire sizes are computed, some (and often, many) of the wires have zero widths, which means they are not needed in the circuit (see also [4] for problems of designing interconnection topology).

- Dominant time constant minimization handles circuits with capacitive coupling between the nodes (see §5).

The Elmore time constant, in addition to being quite useful as a measure of delay when sizing RC trees, is sometimes more appropriate to use than the dominant time constant. We give here two examples where this is the case.

- Consider a path consisting of several stages of buffered wire segments. The total Elmore delay of the path is the sum of the Elmore delays of the segments, and is still a posynomial function that can be efficiently minimized by geometric programming. In contrast it is not possible to efficiently minimize the sum of the dominant time constants, since in general the sum of quasiconvex functions is not quasiconvex.

- The dominant time constant is useful as an alternative to the critical Elmore delay, *i.e.*, the Elmore delay to the node with the slowest response. It is not a good measure for the delay to the other nodes.

References

[1] S. Boyd and L. El Ghaoui. Method of centers for minimizing generalized eigenvalues. *Linear Algebra and Applications, special issue on Numerical Linear Algebra Methods in Control, Signals and Systems*, 188:63–111, July 1993.

[2] S. Boyd, L. Vandenberghe, and M. Grant. Efficient convex optimization for engineering design. In *Proceedings IFAC Symposium on Robust Control Design*, pages 14–23, September 1994.

[3] W. Chuang, S. S. Sapatnekar, and I. N. Hajj. Timing and area optimization for standard-cell VLSI circuit design. *IEEE Transactions on Computer-Aided Design*, 14(3):308–320, 1995.

[4] J. Cong and L. He. Optimal wiresizing for interconnects with multiple sources. In *Proceedings of the IEEE International Conference on Computer-Aided Design*, pages 568–574, 1995.

[5] J. Cong and L. He. Optimal wiresizing for interconnects with multiple sources. *ACM Transaction on Design Automation of Electronic Systems*, 1, 1996.

[6] J. Cong, L. He, C.-K. Koh, and P. H. Madden. Performance optimization of VLSI interconnect layout. *Integration, the VLSI journal*, 21:1–94, 1996.

[7] M. P. Desai, R. Cvijetic, and J. Jensen. Sizing of clock distribution networks for high performance CPU chips. In *Proceedings of the 33rd ACM/IEEE Design Automation Conference*, pages 389–394, 1996.

[8] W. C. Elmore. The transient response of damped linear systems with particular regard to wideband amplifiers. *Journal of Applied Physics*, 19:55–63, 1948.

[9] J. P. Fishburn and A. E. Dunlop. TILOS: a posynomial programming approach to transistor sizing. In *Proceedings ICCAD'85*, pages 326–328, 1985.

[10] T.-M. Lin and C. A. Mead. Signal delay in general *RC* networks. *IEEE Transactions on Computer-Aided Design*, 3(4):321–349, 1984.

[11] N. Menezes, R. Baldick, and L. T. Pileggi. A sequential quadratic programming approach to concurrent gate and wiring sizing. In *Proceedings of the IEEE International Conference on Computer-Aided Design*, pages 144–151, 1995.

[12] Yu. Nesterov and A. Nemirovsky. *Interior-point polynomial methods in convex programming*, volume 13 of *Studies in Applied Mathematics*. SIAM, Philadelphia, PA, 1994.

[13] J. Rubinstein, P. Penfield, and M. A. Horowitz. Signal delay in *RC* tree networks. *IEEE Transactions on Computer-Aided Design*, 2(2):202–211, 1983.

[14] S. Sapatnekar, V. B. Rao, P. Vaidya, and S.-M. Kang. An exact solution to the transistor sizing problem for CMOS circuits using convex optimization. *IEEE Transactions on Computer-Aided Design*, 12:1621–1634, 1993.

[15] S. S. Sapatnekar. Wire sizing as a convex optimization problem: exploring the area-delay tradeoff. *IEEE Transactions on Computer-Aided Design*, 15(8):1001–1011, 1996.

[16] J.-M. Shyu, A. Sangiovanni-Vincentelli, J. P. Fishburn, and A. E. Dunlop. Optimization-based transistor sizing. *IEEE Journal of Solid-State Circuits*, 23(2):400–409, 1988.

[17] L. Vandenberghe and S. Boyd. SP*: Software for Semidefinite Programming. User's Guide, Beta Version.* Stanford University, October 1994. Available at `http://www-isl.stanford.edu/people/boyd`.

[18] L. Vandenberghe and S. Boyd. A primal-dual potential reduction method for problems involving matrix inequalities. *Mathematical Programming*, 69(1):205–236, July 1995.

[19] L. Vandenberghe and S. Boyd. Semidefinite programming. *SIAM Review*, 38(1):49–95, March 1996.

[20] L. Vandenberghe, S. Boyd and A. El Gamal. Optimizing dominant time constant in RC circuits. Technical report, Information Systems Laboratory, Stanford University, November 1996.

[21] S.-P. Wu and S. Boyd. SDPSOL: *A Parser/Solver for Semidefinite Programming and Determinant Maximization Problems with Matrix Structure. User's Guide, Version Beta.* Stanford University, June 1996.

[22] J. L. Wyatt. Signal delay in *RC* mesh networks. *IEEE Transactions on Circuits and Systems*, 32:507–510, 1985.

[23] J. L. Wyatt. Signal propagation delay in *RC* models for interconnect. In A. E. Ruehli, editor, *Circuit Analysis, Simulation and Design*, volume 3, pages 254–291. Elsevier, 1987.

Clock-Tree Routing Realizing a Clock-Schedule for Semi-Synchronous Circuits*

Atsushi TAKAHASHI, Kazunori INOUE[†‡] and Yoji KAJITANI

Dept. of Electrical and Electronic Engineering
Tokyo Institute of Technology
Tokyo 152, Japan

[†]Hitachi ULSI Engineering
3-1-1 Higashi-Koigakubo, Kokubunji
Tokyo 185, Japan

Abstract

It is known that the clock-period can be shorter than the maximum of signal-delays between registers if the clock arrival time to each register is properly scheduled. The algorithm to design an optimal clock-schedule was given. In this paper, we propose a clock-tree routing algorithm that realizes a given clock-schedule using the Elmore-delay model. Following the deferred-merge-embedding (DME) framework, the algorithm generates a topology of the clock-tree and determines the locations and sizes of intermediate buffers simultaneously. The experimental results show that this method constructs clock-trees with moderate wire length compared with that of zero-skew clock-trees.

1 Introduction

In layout synthesis, the distribution of the clock is critical to the performance of sequential circuits. In the *complete-synchronous* system, the clock is assumed to be distributed periodically and simultaneously to every register. Therefore, the *clock-skew*, the maximum difference of delays to the clock pins on registers from the clock source is a negative effect against speeding up a sequential circuit. Thus efforts have been towards its elimination. Surveys are found in [13, 5].

While, in the *semi-synchronous* system, the clock is assumed to be distributed periodically to every register, but not necessarily simultaneously. A *clock-timing* of a register is the difference between clock-delays to the register and to a reference register. A *clock-schedule* is a set of clock-timings of registers. Given signal-delays between registers, a clock-schedule that realizes the minimum clock-period is called an *optimum clock-schedule*. An optimum clock-schedule in a semi-synchronous system is determined by a graph theoretical algorithm [21]. It is known that the clock-period of an optimum clock-schedule is usually shorter than the maximum signal-delay between registers. The minimum clock-period is also obtained by a linear programming [12], or by using the decision version of the problem with binary search strategy [8]. Similar discussions are found in multi-phase clock-schedule [19, 15, 20].

The crucial problem in semi-synchronous system design is the layout realization of the clock-schedule. We call a clock-tree that realizes the given clock-schedule a *schedule-clock-tree*. In this paper, we propose a schedule-clock-tree routing algorithm.

Neves and Friedman [16, 17, 18] proposed the methods that construct a topology of a schedule-clock-tree and determine the specification of delay at each edge of the clock-tree. However no specific routing algorithm to embed the topology in the Manhattan plane is given. The main target of their works is for hierarchical data path design.

Zero-skew clock-tree routing is a kind of schedule-clock-tree designs. Tsay [22] mentioned that there is an algorithm for zero-skew clock-tree routing that can be extended to general schedule-clock-tree design by adding a fictitious delay element on each clock pin. The deferred-merge embedding (DME) algorithm was introduced for zero-skew clock-tree routing independently by Edahiro [9, 11], Chao et al. [2, 3], and Boese and Kahng [1, 3]. There are many related researches using the DME framework [4, 6, 7, 14, 23, 24, 25]. Surveys concerned with the DME framework and clock synthesis are found in [13, 5].

The DME algorithms consist of two phases, the bottom-up phase of topology generation and the top-down phase of embedding the topology on the Manhattan plane. The most successful DME algorithm, called the clustering-based DME algorithm [10], constructs a topology of clock-tree by merging a pair of nearest-neighbors in bottom-up phase. The connection between two subtrees seldom makes a detour since any two subtrees are usually balanced. Thus the small total connection length is achieved. However, in schedule-clock-tree routing, the required connection length often differs significantly from the Manhattan distance between roots of two subtrees because two subtrees may be unbalanced due to the clock-timing assigned to each register.

A schedule-clock-tree routing algorithm proposed in this paper follows the clustering-based DME algorithm in [10]. However, the proposing algorithm selects a merging pair such that the required connection length is small in the way as used in [3]. Moreover, the buffer insertion and sizing are considered in bottom-up topology generation phase in the way as used in [23, 4]. In the top-down phase of embedding, each internal vertex of the clock-tree is embedded in the Manhattan plane so that the connection length from the parent vertex is minimized.

*This work was supported in part by CAD21 and in part by Grant-in-Aid for Scientific Research of the Ministry of Education, Science and Culture of Japan.

‡This work was performed while the author was at TIT.

1092-3152/97 $10.00 © 1997 IEEE

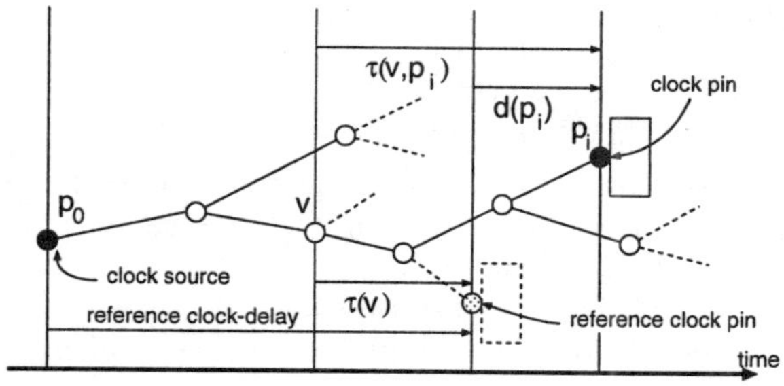

Figure 1: Delays in a schedule-clock-tree.

The experimental results showed that this method constructs a schedule-clock-tree with the moderate wire length compared with that of a zero-skew clock-tree. For randomly generated pin locations and clock-schedule, the total connection length was about 1.8 times larger than that of a zero-skew clock-tree.

The rest of the paper is organized as follows. In Section 2, we give basic definitions and the overview of the problem. The generation of merging-segment is discussed in Sections 3. The definition of the merging-cost of a merging-segment is given in Section 4. The outline of the proposed algorithm SCT-Routing is given in Section 5. In Section 6, we describe the buffer insertion and sizing procedure. The experimental results are presented in Section 7. Section 8 is the conclusion.

2 Preliminaries

Assume that locations of the clock source pin p_0 and clock pins on registers $P = \{p_1, p_2, \ldots, p_n\}$ on the Manhattan plane, and a clock-schedule S of registers are given. We construct a clock-tree T that realizes S using the Elmore-delay model.

A clock from p_0 arrives at each clock pin p_i with some delay which is called the *clock-delay* of p_i. To describe the clock-schedule we take an arbitrary (maybe an imaginary) register as the reference register such that it is ticked by a clock with the *reference clock-delay.* Then pin p_i is ticked $d(p_i)$ time after the reference clock pin is ticked. $d(p_i)$ is called the *clock-timing* of p_i. In this paper, we choose the reference register so that the clock-timing $d(p_i)$ of each register is non-negative. If the reference clock pin is ticked on time $(\ldots, -t, 0, t, 2t, \ldots)$ where t is the clock-period of the circuit concerned, then p_i is ticked on time $(\ldots, -t + d(p_i), d(p_i), t + d(p_i), 2t + d(p_i), \ldots)$.

A clock-tree T is a rooted binary tree whose root corresponds to p_0 and n leaves correspond to pins in P. For a given schedule S, T is called a *schedule-clock-tree* of S if S is realized by T. A subtree T_v is defined as the subtree of T rooted by a vertex v in T. Let $\tau(v)$ be the difference of the reference clock-delay from the clock-delay to v in T, and $\tau(v, p_i)$ be the propagation delay from v to a pin p_i in T_v. In a schedule-clock-tree, $\tau(v) = \tau(v, p_i) - d(p_i)$ for any pin p_i in T_v. See Fig. 1.

The delay model is analyzed in the following. Let r and c denote the resistance and capacitance per unit length of wire, respectively. Let v_1 and v_2 be the children of v on T, and l_1 and l_2 be the wire length from v to v_1 and v_2, respectively.

Let $C(v)$ be the total load capacitance of v including wire capacitance as well as gate capacitance. Then $C(v)$ is calculated by

$$C(v) = \begin{cases} c_i & \text{if } v = p_i, \\ c_{buf} & \text{if a buffer is inserted into } v, \\ C^*(v) & \text{otherwise,} \end{cases}$$

where $C^*(v) = C(v_1) + C(v_2) + c(l_1 + l_2)$, and c_i and c_{buf} are the load capacitance of pin p_i and the input capacitance of the inserted buffer, respectively. Similarly, $\tau(v)$ is calculated by

$$\tau(v) = \begin{cases} -d(p_i) & \text{if } v = p_i, \\ \tau^*(v) + \tau_{buf} & \text{if a buffer is inserted into } v, \\ \tau^*(v) & \text{otherwise,} \end{cases}$$

where $\tau^*(v) = rl_1\left(\frac{cl_1}{2} + C(v_1)\right) + \tau(v_1)$ and τ_{buf} is the internal delay of the inserted buffer.

Here, similar to the zero-skew routing [22], the following equation derived from π-model is assumed to be satisfied in a schedule-clock-tree:

$$\tau^*(v) = rl_2\left(\frac{cl_2}{2} + C(v_2)\right) + \tau(v_2). \quad (1)$$

A location of v is called a *delay-balance-point* of two subtrees if Eq. (1) is satisfied when the wire length connecting to the root of each subtree is equal to the Manhattan distance.

In our algorithm, we list, if exist, delay-balance-points of two subtrees such that the required connection length is equal to the Manhattan distance between the roots of two subtrees as the candidates of the parent vertex locations of two subtrees. If there is no such point, we list the candidate location of either child such that the distance between two children is minimal as the (candidate) parent vertex location. We call such a set of candidate locations of the parent vertex v a *merging-segment* of two subtrees, and denoted by $ms(v)$. For the clock pin p_i, the merging-segment $ms(p_i)$ is defined as the location of p_i.

3 Generating Merging-Segment

Let l denote the Manhattan distance between merging-segments $ms(v_1)$ and $ms(v_2)$. By Eq. (1) assuming $l_1 + l_2 = l$, we have that

$$l_1 = \frac{\tau(v_2) - \tau(v_1) + rl(C(v_2) + cl/2)}{r(cl + C(v_1) + C(v_2))}.$$

If $0 \le l_1 \le l$ then no detour is requested to connect two subtrees and there are delay-balance-points of two subtrees T_{v_1} and T_{v_2} with the minimum connection length which form $ms(v)$ of Manhattan arc with ± 1 slope. In case that $l_1 < 0$ or $l_1 > l$, we conclude that the two subtrees are too much out of balance. If $l_1 < 0$ then we place v on the root v_1 expecting to minimize the total connection length. The connection between v and v_2 makes a detour. The required connection length l_2' is

$$l_2' = \frac{\sqrt{(rC(v_2))^2 + 2rc(\tau(v_1) - \tau(v_2))} - rC(v_2)}{rc}.$$

If $l_1 > l$ then we place v on the v_2, and the length l_1' of the connection between v and v_1 is

$$l_1' = \frac{\sqrt{(rC(v_1))^2 + 2rc(\tau(v_2) - \tau(v_1))} - rC(v_1)}{rc}.$$

In either case, the merging-segment $ms(v)$ of two subtrees consists of a single location which is contained in either $ms(v_1)$ or $ms(v_2)$.

4 Merging-Cost of Merging-Segment

The *merging-cost* of two merging-segments consists of the required wire length connecting two merging-segments and the buffer insertion penalty.

The required wire length connecting two subtrees T_{v_1} and T_{v_2} tends to be large as the difference between $\tau(v_1)$ and $\tau(v_2)$ is large although v_1 is near v_2. In zero-skew routing by nearest-neighbors strategy as in [10], the connection seldom makes a detour since the difference between $\tau(v_1)$ and $\tau(v_2)$ is relatively small. However, in schedule-clock-tree routing, we should take the detour into account. Thus we take the required connection length rather than the distance as the part of the merging-cost.

The clock-tree without any intermediate buffers is impractical since the load capacitance of the clock source is too large. Intermediate buffers are inserted into the clock-tree for the purpose to separate capacitances, to reduce clock-delays and total power dissipation, and to improve the reliability against process variations. Moreover, it is possible to reduce the total connection length by buffer insertion.

We insert one buffer into a vertex if the load capacitance of the vertex exceeds the predefined value c_{lim}. Otherwise, we determine whether to insert a buffer or not according to a cost since excessive buffer insertion may cause negative effects such as area or power dissipation by the buffers. We introduce the buffer insertion penalty $P(v)$ of subtree T_v

$$P(v) = \begin{cases} \log \frac{c_{lim}}{2C^*(v)} & \text{if a buffer is inserted into } v \\ & \text{and } 2C^*(v) < c_{lim}, \\ 0 & \text{otherwise.} \end{cases}$$

$P(v)$ controls the buffer insertion when the load capacitance is small. The cost depends on this penalty, but also depends on the required connection length.

For a pair of two subtrees, there are four situations with respect to the buffer insertion into the roots of two subtrees. We select one situation for the pair by the procedure mentioned in Section 6.1. The insertion depends on the combination of two subtrees. Note that the buffer is inserted into the root of a subtree or not is fixed when the subtree is merged to the other subtree.

Moreover, we assume that the inserting buffer can be selected from various sizes of buffers $\{b_1, b_2, \ldots, b_m\}$. The input capacitance of each buffer is c_{buf}. The internal delay of each buffer depends on its load capacitance. However, we assume that for any buffers b_i and b_j $(i < j)$, the internal delays τ_{buf_i} and τ_{buf_j} satisfy $\tau_{buf_i} > \tau_{buf_j}$ for the same load capacitance. The detailed sizing procedure for two subtrees are described in Section 6.2.

The *merging-cost* $mc(v)$ of two subtrees T_{v_1} and T_{v_2} is defined following the situation selected by the procedure in Section 6,

$$mc(v) = l + \beta(P(v_1) + P(v_2))$$

where l and β denote the required connection length and the constant coefficient, respectively. Note that either $P(v_1)$ or $P(v_2)$ is 0 since we insert buffers into both roots of two subtrees only if the total load capacitance of each subtree exceeds c_{lim}.

```
Algorithm Topology Generation:
K := {ms(p_i) | 1 ≤ i ≤ n};
While (|K| > 1){
    G(V,E) := GRAPH(K);
    Repeat MID(1, |K|/k, |K| − 1) times {
        Find e(v_1, v_2) from G(V,E) such that the
        weight is minimum;
        If ({ms(v_1), ms(v_2)} ⊆ K) {
            Compete ms(v) from ms(v_1) and ms(v_2);
            K := (K − {ms(v_1), ms(v_2)}) ∪ {ms(v)};
        }
        Delete e(v_1, v_2) from G(V,E);
    }
}
```

Figure 2: The bottom-up phase of SCT-Routing.

5 Schedule-Clock-Tree Routing

The proposing schedule-clock-tree routing algorithm SCT-Routing follows the DME framework.

In the bottom-up phase of topology generation, the tree of merging-segments are constructed which represent possible locations (merging-segment) of vertices in a schedule-clock-tree.

Let K denote a set of merging-segments which initially consists of all the clock pin locations, that is, $K = \{ms(p_i)\}$. The algorithm iteratively finds the pair in K, that is, $ms(v_1)$ and $ms(v_2)$, such that the weight of edge $e(v_1, v_2)$ is minimal in the merging-cost graph whose vertices correspond to K and weight of the edge represents the *merging-cost* of two merging-segments. The edge set of the merging-cost graph consists of the edges $e(v_i, v_j)$ such that the merging-cost of $ms(v_i)$ and $ms(v_j)$ is minimal over all $ms(v_j)$ or minimal over all $ms(v_i)$ $(i \neq j)$. A new merging-segment $ms(v)$ is computed for vertex v from delay-balance-points of two subtrees T_{v_1} and T_{v_2}. K is updated by adding $ms(v)$ and deleting both $ms(v_1)$ and $ms(v_2)$. After $n-1$ operations, K consists of the merging-segment for the root of the topology.

The bottom-up phase is shown in Fig. 2. In the algorithm, $GRAPH(K)$ represents a merging-cost graph generation and $MID(a, b, c)$ is a function that returns the middle value of a, b and c. The merging-cost graph is updated after several mergings for speed-up.

In the top-down phase of embedding, the exact locations of vertices are determined in the reverse order of the bottom-up phase. First, the location of the root v of the tree of merging-segments is determined on the merging-segment $ms(v)$ so as to minimize the Manhattan distance from the clock source pin. Once the location of a vertex is determined, the locations of its children on merging-segments are easily determined so as to minimize the Manhattan distance from the parent vertex location. The top-down phase is shown in Fig. 3.

6 Buffer Insertion and Sizing

6.1 Buffer Insertion

For each pair of two subtrees, there are four situations with respect to the buffer insertion into the roots v_1

Algorithm Topology Embedding:

1. Choose the location of the root v of the tree of merging-segments from $ms(v)$ such that the Manhattan distance from the clock source pin is minimal. Connect the clock source pin and v.
2. Local-Embedding(v);

Procedure Local-Embedding (v):

1. **If** (v has children) {
2. Choose the locations of children v_1 and v_2 from $ms(v_1)$ and $ms(v_2)$, respectively, such that the Manhattan distance from v is minimal. Connect v and v_1. Connect v and v_2;
3. Local-Embedding(v_1);
4. Local-Embedding(v_2);

}

Figure 3: The top-down phase of SCT-Routing.

and v_2 of two subtrees. However, we consider at most two situations for each pair. In the following, we show the procedure that determines the situation for each pair depending on whether $C^*(v_1)$ and $C^*(v_2)$ exceed c_{lim} or not.

In case that neither $C^*(v_1)$ nor $C^*(v_2)$ exceeds c_{lim}, the cost without buffer insertion is first calculated, which is the required connection length. If no detour is requested, the procedure adopts this situation, that is, a buffer is inserted into neither root of the subtree. Otherwise, the connection to either v_1 or v_2 makes a detour. Without loss of generality, we assume that the connection to v_1 makes a detour. Then the cost when the buffer is inserted into v_1 is calculated, which is $l' + \beta P(v_1)$ where l' is the required connection length. Then, the procedure selects the lower cost situation.

In case that $C^*(v_1)$ exceeds c_{lim}, but $C^*(v_2)$ does not, the cost when a buffer is inserted into v_1 is first calculated, which is the required connection length. If no detour is requested, the procedure adopts this situation. Otherwise, we calculate the cost when the buffer is inserted into both v_1 and v_2, which is $l' + \beta P(v_2)$ where l' is the required connection length. Then the procedure selects the lower cost situation. The procedure similarly selects the situation when $C^*(v_2)$ exceeds c_{lim}, but $C^*(v_1)$ does not.

In case that both $C^*(v_1)$ and $C^*(v_2)$ exceed c_{lim}, the procedure selects the situation that buffers are inserted into both v_1 and v_2. The cost is the required wire length.

6.2 Buffer Sizing

First, we consider the case that a buffer is inserted into v_1, but not into v_2. By Eq. (1) assuming $l_1 + l_2 = l$, we have that

$$l_1 = \frac{\tau(v_2) - (\tau^*(v_1) + \tau_{buf}) + rl(C(v_2) + cl/2)}{r(cl + c_{buf} + C(v_2))}$$

where τ_{buf} is the internal delay of the inserted buffer. If $\tau_{buf} \leq \tau(v_2) - \tau^*(v_1) + rl(C(v_2) + cl/2)$ then $l_1 \geq 0$, that is, no detour is requested to connect v and v_2. Similarly if $\tau_{buf} \geq \tau(v_2) - \tau^*(v_1) - rl(c_{buf} + cl/2)$ then if $l_1 \leq l$, that is, no detour is requested to connect v and v_1.

Table 1: Statistics of the tested examples.

data	# of pins	width [μm]	height [μm]
r1	267	6998	7000
r2	598	9401	9313
r3	862	9700	9850
r4	1903	12697	12698
r5	3101	14292	14522

The internal delay of a buffer is related to the size of the buffer. The size and power dissipation of a buffer is small when the internal delay is large. To minimize the detour and the size and power of a inserted buffer, we insert a buffer such that the internal delay is maximal unless the connection from v to v_2 makes a detour. Similarly, we select a buffer inserting into v_2 when no buffer is inserted into v_1.

Next we consider the case that buffers are inserted into both v_1 and v_2. The required connection length from v to v_1 (v_2) depends on both inserted buffers. If $C^*(v_1)$ or $C^*(v_2)$ does not exceed c_{lim}, then we first select the buffer of the root whose load capacitance exceeds c_{lim} by the above procedure assuming no buffer is inserted into the other. And then, we select the buffer of the other root by the above procedure. Otherwise, we test the inserted buffers pair into v_1 and v_2 from the maximum delay buffer to the minimum delay buffer for v_1, and from the minimum delay buffer to the maximum delay buffer for v_2. We select the first pair such that the connection from v to v_2 makes no detour.

7 Experimental Results

The proposed schedule-clock-tree routing algorithm SCT-Routing is implemented in C++. We test it on five different examples used in [22], though the location and load capacitance of each pin are randomly generated. The statistics of the examples are shown in Table 1. The load capacitance c_i of pin p_i is ranged from 30 to 80 fF. The buffer size is chosen from 20 varieties and the maximum load capacitance of buffers c_{lim} is 2 pF. The process parameters are set to $r = 60$ mΩ and $c = 0.04$ fF. We use the algorithm parameters $\beta = 1000$, $k = 2$.

7.1 Schedule-Clock-Tree Algorithms

Our SCT-Routing and the clustering-based DME algorithm (developed for zero-skew routing) in [10], called ZS-Routing here, are applied to schedule-clock-tree routing. The results are shown in Table 2.

In Table 2, ZS and ZS+S correspond to ZS-Routing. SCT and SCT\B correspond to SCT-Routing, but no intermediate buffers are inserted in SCT\B. The clock-timing of each register is set to 0 ns in ZS, while either 0.0 ns, 0.5 ns, 1.0 ns, 1.5 ns, or 2.0 ns is assigned to registers in the other cases. The total connection length, the total connection length over that in ZS, the clock-delay from the clock source pin to a reference clock pin, and the numbers of inserted intermediate buffers are shown in columns "len", "ratio", "d", and "buf", respectively.

The results show that the simple nearest-neighbors strategy, adopted in [10], is not well applicable for schedule-clock-tree generation. The resultant total

Table 2: The results of ZS-Routing and SCT-Routing.

	ZS		ZS+S			SCT\B			SCT			
algorithm	ZS-Routing					SCT-Routing						
buffer	no intermediate buffers								with intermediate buffers			
clock-timing	0 [ns]		from 0 to 2 [ns] by 0.5 [ns] step									
data	len [μm]	d [ns]	len [μm]	ratio	d [ns]	len [μm]	ratio	d [ns]	len [μm]	ratio	d [ns]	buf
r1	147,392	1.82	3,947,102	26.78	13.02	310,379	2.11	4.13	266,514	1.81	4.78	62
r2	294,797	6.07	9,034,421	30.65	51.08	636,612	2.16	7.44	543,183	1.84	6.35	129
r3	366,265	5.85	13,139,596	35.87	83.45	815,826	2.23	7.38	679,889	1.86	6.93	177
r4	727,893	21.75	28,361,307	38.96	198.30	1,514,973	2.08	21.75	1,310,030	1.80	9.17	350
r5	1,063,507	38.52	45,920,134	43.18	327.47	2,195,560	2.06	50.56	1,886,817	1.77	5.16	515

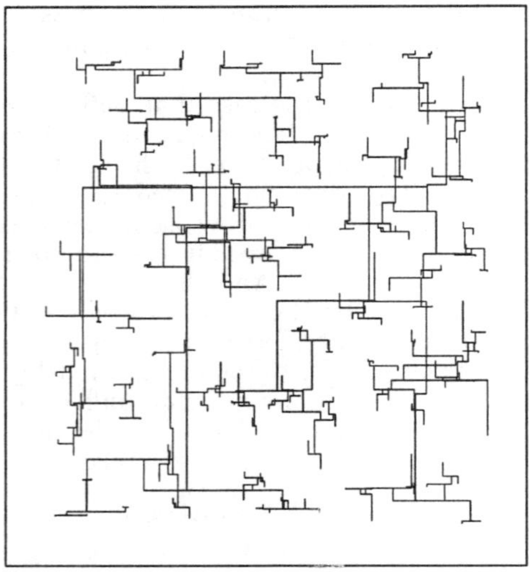

Figure 4: A zero-skew clock-tree layout of the example r1 by ZS-Routing.

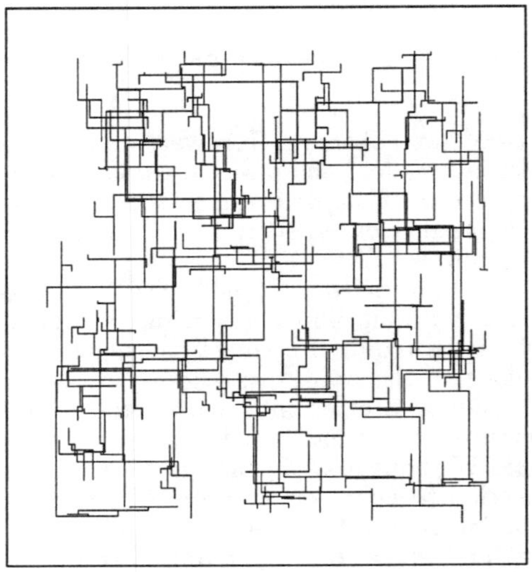

Figure 5: A schedule-clock-tree layout of the example r1 by SCT-Routing.

connection length of the schedule-clock-tree is more than 25 times larger than that of the zero-skew clock-tree. A zero-skew clock-tree layout of the example r1 by ZS-Routing is shown in Fig. 4 for a reference.

The total connection lengths of both SCT\B and SCT are far smaller than that of ZS-Routing for the same input data. Inserted intermediate buffers reduce both the total wire lengths and clock-delays. The clock-delay reductions are significant for large clock-tree. The total connection length by SCT-Routing is about 1.8 times larger than that of the zero-skew clock-tree. A schedule-clock-tree layout result of the example r1 by SCT-Routing is shown in Fig. 5.

7.2 Clock-Schedule Dependence

When the variation of clock-timings assigned to each register is large, the total connection length of SCT-Routing is large. In Table 3 the results when either clock-timing from 0 to 2 ns by 1 ps step is assigned to each register are shown. The average wire length ratio is 2.63 with respect to ZS-Routing for zero-skew routing. Although the numbers of inserted buffers are increased, the clock-delays are almost same compared with the results in Table 2.

The maximum difference of clock-timings also affects the total connection length and clock-delay. In Table 3 the results when either clock-timing from 0 to 10 ns by 2.5 ns step is assigned to each register are also shown. The wire length ratios increase compared with the results in Table 2, especially for small size data. The clock-delays also increase although the number of inserted buffers are small.

7.3 Schedule-Clock-Tree Consisting of Zero-Skew Trees

If the set of pins is classified such that the clock-timing of each class is same, it is possible to construct a schedule-clock-tree as the sum of zero-skew clock-trees each designed for each class.

In Table 4, the results for the same data used in Table 2 are shown when we construct five zero-skew clock-trees for the registers each assigned to the same clock-timing by SCT-Routing. Although the numbers of inserted buffers are relatively small, the total connection length is larger than that of the original SCT-Routing.

8 Conclusions

In this paper, we show that we can construct a schedule-clock-tree for semi-synchronous circuit design

Table 3: The results of SCT-Routing for different clock-timings.

clock-timing	from 0 to 2 ns by 1 ps step				from 0 to 10 ns by 2.5 ns step			
data	len [μm]	ratio	d [ns]	buf	len [μm]	ratio	d [ns]	buf
r1	343,853	2.33	4.09	227	411,754	2.79	28.05	22
r2	793,969	2.69	5.59	500	674,988	2.29	13.24	45
r3	995,917	2.72	7.67	704	849,932	2.32	13.79	59
r4	1,967,399	2.70	6.18	1556	1,593,813	2.00	15.03	133
r5	2,914,751	2.74	6.11	2502	2,299,953	2.16	21.28	198

Table 4: Schedule-clock-tree using zero-skew clock-trees (clock-timings are from 0 to 2 ns by 0.5 ns step).

data	len [μm]	ratio	buf
r1	308,366	2.09	10
r2	674,844	2.29	34
r3	863,385	2.36	52
r4	1,673,431	2.30	101
r5	2,422,248	2.28	162

with moderate wire length compared with that of a zero-skew clock-tree.

It seems that the reliability of a general schedule-clock-tree against the temperature or process variation is inferior to that of a zero-skew clock-tree, since a constructed clock-tree is unbalanced due to the clock-timing difference. We should analyze the sensitivity of the constructed schedule-clock-trees and improve our algorithm to increase the reliability.

The generation of feasible buffer placement in our algorithm is also the future work.

The performance of a constructed schedule-clock-tree highly depends on a given clock-schedule. It is possible to adopt techniques such as mentioned in Section 7.3 depending on the given clock-schedule. Another way is to restrict the variety of the clock-schedules. It is apparent that there exists a clock-schedule whose required wire length of clock-tree is far smaller than that of a zero-skew clock-tree. We believe that high-performance circuits with less wire length of the clock-tree, can not be constructed without following the concept of the semi-synchronous framework. This paper includes a basic consideration for the semi-synchronous system design.

References

[1] K. D. Boese and A. B. Kahng, "Zero-skew clock routing trees with minimum wirelength," in *Proc. IEEE 5th ASIC Conf.*, pp. 1.1.1–1.1.5, 1992.

[2] T. H. Chao, Y. C. Hsu, and J. M. Ho, "Zero skew clock net routing," in *Proc. 29th DAC*, pp. 518–523, 1992.

[3] T. H. Chao, Y. C. Hsu, J. M. Ho, K. D. Boese, and A. B. Kahgn, "Zero skew clock routing with minimum wirelength," *IEEE Trans. on Circuits and Systems*, vol. 39, no. 11, pp. 799–814, 1992.

[4] Y. P. Chen and D. F. Wong, "An algorithm for zero-skew clock tree routing with buffer insertion," in *Proc. European Design and Test Conf.*, pp. 66–71, 1996.

[5] J. Cong, L. He, C. K. Koh, and P. H. Madden, "Performance optimization of VLSI interconnect layout," *INTEGRATION, the VLSI journal*, vol. 21, pp. 1–94, 1996.

[6] J. Cong, A. B. Kahng, C. K. Koh, and C. W. A. Tsao, "Bounded-skew clock and Steiner routing under Elmore delay," in *Proc. 1995 ICCAD*, pp. 66–71, 1995.

[7] J. Cong and C. K. Koh, "Minimum-cost bounded-skew clock routing," in *Proc. ISCAS 95*, vol. 1, pp. 215–218, 1995.

[8] R. B. Deokar and S. S. Sapatnekar, "A graph-theoretic approach to clock skew optimization," in *Proc. ISCAS '94*, vol. 1, pp. 407–410, 1994.

[9] M. Edahiro, "Minimum skew and minimum path length routing," *NEC Research & Development*, vol. 32, no. 4, pp. 569–575, 1991.

[10] M. Edahiro, "A clustering-based optimization algorithm in zero-skew routings," in *Proc. 30th DAC*, pp. 612–616, 1993.

[11] M. Edahiro and T. Yoshimura, "Minimum path-length equidistant routing," in *Proc. APCCAS 92*, pp. 41–46, 1992.

[12] J. P. Fishburn, "Clock skew optimization," *IEEE Trans. on Computers*, vol. 39, no. 7, pp. 945–951, 1990.

[13] E. G. Friedman, ed., *Clock Distribution Networks in VLSI Circuits and Systems: A Selected Reprint Volume*. IEEE Press, 1995.

[14] D. J. H. Huang, A. B. Kahng, and C. W. A. Tsao, "On the bounded-skew routing tree problem," in *Proc. 32nd DAC*, pp. 508–513, 1995.

[15] D. A. Joy and M. J. Ciesielski, "Placement for clock period minimization with multiple wave propagation," in *Proc. 28th DAC*, pp. 640–643, 1991.

[16] J. L. Neves and E. G. Friedman, "Topological design of clock distribution networks based on non-zero clock skew specifications," in *Proc. 36th Midwest Symp. on Circuits and Systems*, pp. 468–471, 1993.

[17] J. L. Neves and E. G. Friedman, "Circuit synthesis of clock distribution networks based on non-zero clock skew," in *Proc. ISCAS '94*, vol. 4, pp. 175–178, 1994.

[18] J. L. Neves and E. G. Friedman, "Minimizing power dissipation in non-zero skew-based clock distribution networks," in *Proc. ISCAS '95*, vol. 3, pp. 1577–1579, 1995.

[19] K. A. Sakallah, T. N. Mudge, and O. A. Olukotun, "Analysis and design of latch-controlled synchronous digital circuits," in *Proc. 27th DAC*, pp. 111–117, 1990.

[20] T. G. Szymanski, "Computing optimal clock schedules," in *Proc. 29th DAC*, pp. 399–404, 1992.

[21] A. Takahashi and Y. Kajitani, "Performance and reliability driven clock scheduling of sequential logic circuits," in *Proc. ASP-DAC '97*, pp. 37–42, 1997.

[22] R. S. Tsay, "Exact zero skew," in *Proc. 1991 ICCAD*, pp. 336–339, 1991.

[23] A. Vittal and M. Marek-Sadowska, "Power optimal buffered clock tree design," in *Proc. 32nd DAC*, pp. 497–502, 1995.

[24] J. G. Xi and W. W. M. Dai, "Jitter-tolerant clock routing in two-phase synchronous systems," in *Proc. 1996 ICCAD*, pp. 316–320, 1996.

[25] J. G. Xi and W. W. M. Dai, "Useful-skew clock routing with gate sizing for low power design," in *Proc. 33rd DAC*, pp. 383–388, 1996.

A Hierarchical Decomposition Methodology for Multistage Clock Circuits

Gary Ellis

IBM Microelectronics,
IBM, Austin, TX 78758

Lawrence T. Pileggi and Rob A. Rutenbar

Department of Electrical and Computer Engineering,
Carnegie Mellon University, Pittsburgh, PA 15213

Abstract†

This paper describes a novel methodology to automate the design of the interconnect distribution for multistage clock circuits. We introduce two key ideas. First, a hierarchical decomposition of the layout divides the problem into a set of local Steiner-wired latch clusters (to minimize and balance local capacitance) fed globally by a balanced binary tree (to maximize performance). Second, we recast the global clock distribution problem as a simultaneous optimization of clock topology, clock segment routing, wiresizing, and buffering. The hierarchical decomposition reduces the problem complexity and allows use of more aggressive optimization techniques. Integration of the geometric and electrical optimizations likewise allows more aggressive performance goals. Experiments with an industrial design comprising over 16,000 latches demonstrate the efficiency of the approach: a complete clock distribution solution met a 200MHz cycle time specification with only 310ps of skew, met strict current density constraints, exhibited good delay matching across uniform wire width and device variations, and was completed in under 10 CPU hours.

1 Introduction

It has been shown that clock skew can reduce system performance by as much as 10% in high speed VLSI designs [1]. Further, the delay dominance of the interconnects for modern technologies has put more control of this skew problem into the hands of the physical designer. As such, the convergence upon a good clock circuit layout requires tight interaction between the clock circuit synthesis, placement, and timing analysis steps. Currently, the automation process of multistage clock circuit design is divided into two steps; circuit topology selection with routing [2][4][6,9], followed by a buffer insertion and wiresizing step [5][10][11][12]. The first step produces a clock circuit topology with a wire or delay-balanced routing. The second step inserts repowering buffers into this large net and sizes the devices and individual wire segments to satisfy performance constraints. Although the buffer insertion steps consider delay sensitivities for manufacturability concerns, the routing algorithms which provide their input circuits do not consider this. As a result, arbitrary topology and routing decisions are made which are blind to the needs of the buffering and sizing steps and may seriously impact the quality of the results. Further, other manufacturability concerns, such as electromigration, have been left unaddressed. Finally, all of the algorithms for these two-step approaches deal with the circuit in a flat manner.

In this paper, a more complete framework has been developed which combines the steps of topology selection, routing, wiresizing, and buffer insertion. By combining all of these steps together, topologies can be selected which respect the requirements of the repowering buffers during the optimization. This permits the investigation of physical design solutions which balance the driven loads using the interconnect network alone, removing the need for additional *dummy* loading to equalize delays [15][16]. Further, a new wiresizing scheme is introduced to address the concerns of electromigration. Finally, the complexity problems associated with a flat treatment of the circuit have been avoided by the use of a hierarchical decomposition approach; we extend here the ideas of [20] from the simpler case of single-stage unbuffered clocks to the more general multistage problem. This paper presents an overview of the algorithms and implementation details that support this methodology; additional details may be found in [19].

This paper is organized as follows. The hierarchical decomposition is introduced in Section 2. The overall optimization strategies for the global and local portions of this decomposition are outlined in Sections 3 and 4. The details of the buffer modeling and wiresizing used in this strategy are given in Sections 5 and 6. The experimental results of Section 7 clearly show the merits of this approach, while Section 8 gives our concluding remarks and some suggestions for future work.

2 Hierarchical Decomposition

Since the best single stage routing methods require extensive topology search algorithms [8][9], designs larger than a few thousand latches remain intractable. Fortunately, the performance of the network is dominated by the large delays near the root of the tree, and this allows for a tremendous savings in effort by using a convenient partitioning of the circuit. It is apparent that the size of the problem could be reduced considerably by largely ignoring the details of the leaf wiring and concentrating on the longer upper wires of the tree during optimization. This observation has motivated a hierarchical decomposition of the problem: a collection of Steiner-wired latch clusters connected by a balanced wire tree. This decomposition of the circuit and how it fits in the design flow is illustrated in Figure 1.

Figure 1. Flow of clock optimization methodology.

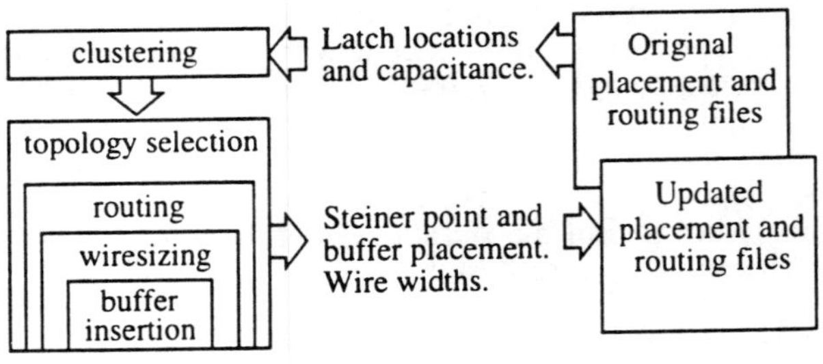

First, the latch locations and latch pin capacitances are taken from the placement and routing files of the pre-placed ASIC. The latches are then clustered into small groups for the local clock signal distribution. These clusters are passed to the global distribution optimizer which uses a tightly integrated set of algorithms to construct the global clock tree. These algorithms include topology selection, routing (Steiner point placement), wiresizing, and buffer insertion. The placement of the clock objects and the wire width specifications are then passed along as constraints which augment the placement and routing files of the design.

3 Global Distribution Optimization

For the optimization of the global distributions, we have adopted a simulated annealing method similar to [9]. All simulated annealing

†. This work was supported by the Semiconductor Research Corporation under contract 96-DC-068.

problem formulations may be described in four basic parts: 1) the state representation, 2) the move set, 3) the cost function, and 4) the cooling schedule. The annealer vigorously explores complete alternative tree topologies, and invokes deterministic Steiner point placement techniques to render a complete routing for each visited topology. Each complete tree is then sized and buffered, as we shall describe later in this section, for each annealing perturbation. The central idea is to search aggressively for an optimal clock layout, and to evaluate each layout after a fast, heuristic sizing and buffering calculation. For the global distribution, the state is represented by a *binary tree* as shown in Figure 2. The actual Steiner point locations are found by the *Deferred Merge Embedding* (DME) technique of [7]. Also, *snake wire* is not included in the routing as its effect is small and it is unlikely to be used in practice.

Figure 2. Binary tree representation of the state.

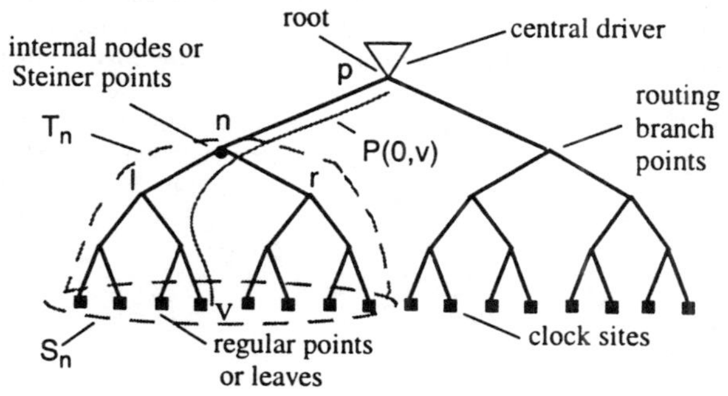

Each node, n, has both a left, l, and a right, r, child as well as a parent node, p. The other notation adopted here is defined concretely below:

$P(u, v)$ = set of segments on the path from node u to v

n = a segment on path $P(u, v)$

l_n = Manhattan length of segment n $= |x_n - x_p| + |y_n - y_p|$

T_n = subtree driven by segment n

S_n = set of clock sites of subtree n

$$Cd_n = \sum_{j \in T_n} c_j + \sum_{j \in S_n} C_j = \text{downstream capacitance} \quad (1)$$

$$td_n = \frac{t_l + td_l + t_r + td_r}{2}$$

$= 0$ for clock sites

$$t_n = r_n\left(\frac{c_n}{2} + Cd_n\right) = \text{delay of wire segment n}$$

The delays are computed in a bottom-up manner and td_n at any node is the *average* node-to-site path delay from n to any of its sites, $s \in S_n$. Since we are interested in zero-skew trees, these path delays are often (but not always) all the same.

To this point, current methodologies have held buffer insertion and wiresizing as strictly postprocessing steps. As it was pointed out in [12], the power-delay product of a clock distribution network can be reduced significantly with the insertion of repowering buffers. However, there did not seem to be a great difference between various buffer insertion-point and sizing configurations (although this may change for deep submicron technologies). In short, finding the best of these buffer insertion configurations for a given design may be too expensive with too little performance improvement to justify merging this optimization step with the others. On the other hand, it would be a mistake to simply optimize a single stage without any knowledge of the buffering to be added later. In this work, we choose a compromise: optimize a multistage tree with a fixed buffer and size configuration, *i.e.* fixed levels of the tree at which the Steiner branch points will be driven by buffers. We refer to this as a *constant* buffer insertion heuristic. The intention is to find a layout that satisfies this configuration well with only minor postprocessing modifications. It should be noted that the problem of selecting the buffer sizes and insertion points is not addressed in this paper. One possible approach is to use the algorithm presented in [12] on a MMM [2] or zero-skew [4, 9] clock tree to estimate the buffer sizes and locations, and then use this configuration with the optimization described here. It is assumed that such decisions will be made by the designer in a clock planning step. Finally, it should be noted that the constant buffer insertion heuristic used here is not an integral part of the optimization strategy and is adopted in the interest of computational time only.

This constant buffer insertion configuration method is illustrated in Figure 3. First, all tree topology manipulations are made without any knowledge of the buffering. This allows a full exploration of the geometric design space without being inhibited by the levelization that buffering inherently introduces. This is actually accomplished by *erasing* all of the buffers in the tree before changing the topology and then *inserting* buffers into the new tree according to the given constant buffer configuration. The tree is then routed from the bottom-up, now accounting for the delay effects of the buffers. Wire sizes are then selected for the segments to reduce current densities and interconnect delays without impacting skew.

Figure 3. Buffer insertion steps.

a) Manipulations performed on single stage tree. b) Buffer insertion step. c) Multistage tree is routed and wiresized.

For the move set, the fundamental state manipulator is the reconnection of a single subtree within the state. This is accomplished by removing the parent node from the tree graph and reconnecting it to form a different topology. The global optimization cost function is a weighted sum of figures of merit which include the *average delay*, a *skew* term, and the *total wire length* of the global route. These terms are defined concretely below:

$$\text{delay} = RoCd_0 + \frac{1}{|S_0|}\sum_{p \in P}\sum_{i \in p} \rho l_i\left(\frac{\varepsilon l_i}{2} + Cd_i\right)$$

$$\text{skew sum} = \sum_{i \in T_0} |td_l + t_l - td_r - t_r| \quad (2)$$

$$\text{wirelength} = \sum_{i \in T_0} l_i$$

Here, P is the set of all root-to-site paths in the network and the root is commonly denoted as node 0. In the skew sum term, td_l and td_r represent the subtree delays of the left and right children respectively. The delays t_l and t_r represent the interconnect delays of the wires connecting the left and right subtrees to node i. Ideally, these delays should balance, and their difference should be zero for all nodes in the design. In cases where the layout is poorly balanced, this sum can effectively capture the skew introduced by any and all nodes in the circuit.

A modified version of the Lam-Delosme cooling schedule [17] is used to control the progression of the state to a good globally optimized solution, and the number of moves performed at each temperature is proportional to the number of objects in the state. Although much care has been taken to *tune* the schedule to this problem, the parameters found for one design do not vary much for the other benchmarks. The specific values for the temperatures or weights are not presented here, but it should be noted that the most emphasis was placed on the wirelength term, and the least emphasis was on the average delay.

4 Local Distribution Optimization

The latch clustering ideas from [20] are used for the local distribution of the clock, which are reviewed here briefly for clarity. To find the topology and routing of the local distribution, the Delaunay triangulation is used. The interest in this construction is simply with the *near neighbor* information that it conveys about objects in a 2D space. The intention is to use a Delaunay triangulation to produce a graph of nearby clock sites to identify which clock sites are close to one another and can possibly be wired together. The connecting edges will also supply us with a means of estimating the cluster route lengths. An example of this is shown in Figure 4 below where a Delaunay triangulation has been constructed from the clock sites of the Tsay r1 benchmark (a) and the resulting latch clustering is shown in (b).

Figure 4. The Delaunay triangulation and latch clustering.

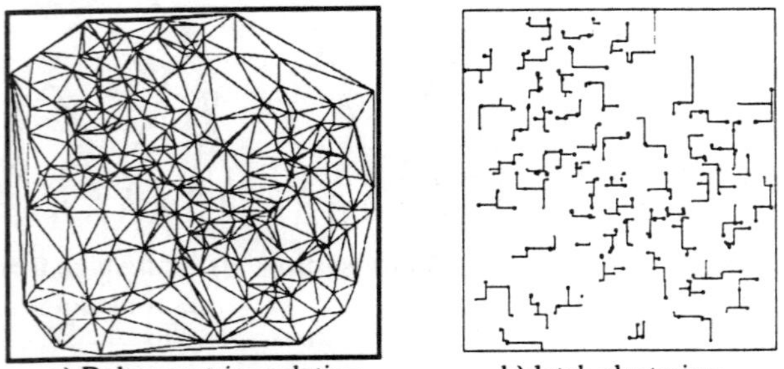

a) Delaunay triangulation b) latch clustering

As with the global route optimization, simulated annealing is used to find an optimal local clustering. The state of the local distribution is given in Figure 5. We will consider the vertices, v, as clock sites (latches) and the edges, e, as possible wire connections. If two sites are to be connected together, the edge connecting their corresponding vertices is deemed to be *on*. A cluster can therefore be represented by a subgraph, $Gc(Vc,Ec)$, whose sites correspond to vertices, $v \in V_c$, and connecting wires correspond to *on* edges, $e \in E_c$. For the sake of minimizing wire, the restriction that cluster subgraphs will not contain any cycles is imposed. The Steiner wire estimates, shown in Figure 5b, are found by using a greedy version of the L-flipping algorithm given in [14]. We have found through experimentation that this algorithm finds routes which are typically 30% shorter than a zero-skew route connecting the same points.

All of the fundamental moves employed to manipulate the state exchange a single latch between any two clusters. Whenever a latch is exchanged, the Steiner wire estimate algorithm is re-run on the source and target clusters to assess any change in total wire use and capacitive loading. In addition, cluster splitting moves have been implemented so that the total number of clusters need not remain constant. The local optimization cost function is a weighted sum of the following terms:

$$
\begin{aligned}
\text{load penalty} &= \sum_{k \in K} \left| C_k - C_{fan} \right| \\
\text{skew penalty} &= \sum_{k \in K} (S_k - S_{limit})\, u(S_k - S_{limit}) \\
\text{total wirelength} &= \sum_{k \in K} \sum_{e \in E_k} |e| + \gamma D(\sqrt{|K|} - 1)
\end{aligned}
\qquad (3)
$$

where, $u(x)$ is the usual Heaviside step function ($u(x) = 1$ if $x > 0$, and $= 0$ otherwise). K is the set of all clusters and E_k is the set of *on* edges in cluster k ($|e|$ is the wire length of the connecting edge, as computed by the greedy L-flipping algorithm). The first term biases the clustering toward a solution where the average capacitive loading is near some specified fanout target, C_{fan}. The second term limits the size of each cluster so that the intra-cluster skew will remain low for each local route. It is important to note that the global optimization step will select the tap point to each cluster when the global tree is constructed and, consequently, the skew can only be estimated during the clustering step. The tap points are constrained to the latch locations themselves so the term, S_k, is a *worst-case* intra-cluster skew estimate:

$$
S_k = \rho \sum_{e \in E_k} |e| \left(\frac{\varepsilon \sum_{e \in E_k} |e|}{2} + \sum_{v \in V_k} C_v \right) \qquad (4)
$$

Equation (4) is the delay found by driving all of the latches in a cluster through a single segment whose length is equal to the wire used by this local route. It is usually very pessimistic in practice, but provides us with a strict upper-bound. The final term in (3) is simply the total wirelength of all of the local routes plus an *estimate* of the global route length. The global estimator part is an empirically derived equation. Here, D is the chip diameter and γ is a constant selected to be about 1.2.

Figure 5. The state representation of the latch clustering.

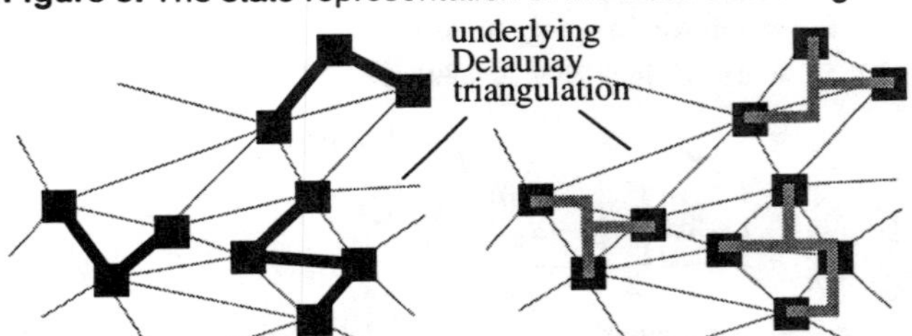

a) three clusters with *on* edges b) with routing estimates

5 Buffer Modeling

In this section, the modeling for the repowering buffers is described. The design of the repowering buffer is a pair of series connected inverters. The first inverter acts as an input stage and cleans up the risetime of the input signal for the second inverter. Without the first inverter, there would be a potential for signal degradation if the previous stage is heavily loaded. The second stage has been sized (30X minimum transistor width) to drive a typical interconnect network on a 1cm chip in a 0.35um process.

In this work, we use a linear circuit approximation, similar to that of [18], to model this buffer design: a time-dependent time-delayed ramp voltage source with a fixed output impedance. The time delay and risetime of the ramp voltage source are controlled only by the input signal to the buffer input. The driven interconnects are modeled by the admittance approximation technique of O'Brien and Savarino [13]. In our application, a reduced order circuit (pi-model) is computed which approximates the response of the complete interconnect network with the driven loads. To compute the buffer delays, an equation for the transient response of the linearized buffer model when driving an arbitrary pi-model has been derived. This parameterized equation is solved by using the Newton-Raphson technique for each buffer in the design.

The accuracy of such linear buffer models and interconnect driving-point model has been demonstrated in [18] and [13] respectively, and we have observed similar results in this work. In Section 7, we will investigate how the accumulation of these errors over several levels of buffering impacts the final design. In the next section, the wiresizing technique used with this buffer modeling is discussed.

6 Wiresizing a Multistage Design

Recall that our goal is to wiresize the routed clock layout we create after each perturbation of the clock topology proposed by the annealer. Hence, the constraints are not only to handle sizing for performance and reliability, but also to complete this operation very quickly. It has been demonstrated in [12] that *reducing* the delay sensitivity of a multistage design is often more desirable than *minimizing* it in the interest of wire area (and power). Further, we will show here that such a minimization of sensitivity (and delay) may not be possible for some multistage designs. In this section, a new fast wiresizing technique useful with multistage clock circuits is discussed.

For the single stage designs of [5][10][11], the delay can be minimized as the driver output impedance, *Ro*, is usually small for large drivers (~10 Ohms) and the loading, *Cd*, is very large for root wires. This results in very wide root wires (10X to 20X w_{min}) which have little sensitivity to width variations. For multistage designs, however, the repowering buffers are much smaller and, therefore, have larger output impedances (100 to 500 Ohms). Coupled with driving smaller loads, such delay minimization algorithms can produce very narrow interconnect wires, with the optimal wire width near or below w_{min} in many cases. Although these widths are optimal and the design has low delay sensitivity at the nominal point, the design is still susceptible to wire width variations. This is illustrated in Figure 6.

Figure 6. Effect of width variations on an optimal sizing.

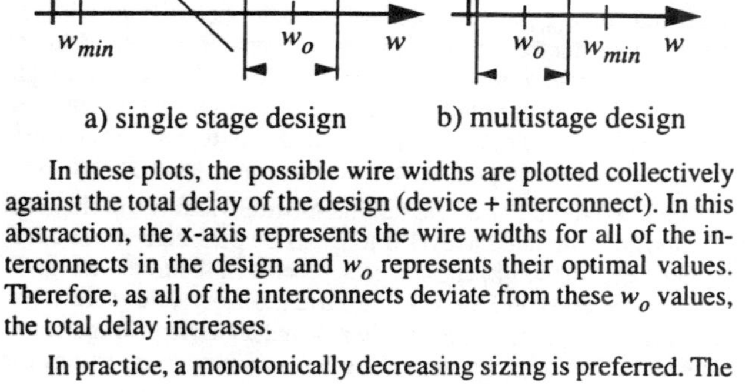

In these plots, the possible wire widths are plotted collectively against the total delay of the design (device + interconnect). In this abstraction, the x-axis represents the wire widths for all of the interconnects in the design and w_o represents their optimal values. Therefore, as all of the interconnects deviate from these w_o values, the total delay increases.

In practice, a monotonically decreasing sizing is preferred. The high current carrying wires near the root are widened to reduce current densities while, at the leaves, the currents are low so they are set to w_{min} to reduce loading and save power. In this work, a special *balanced wiresizing scheme* is adopted which follows this idea. In this scheme, a fixed maximum wire width is selected for the segments that are directly driven by the buffer. Then, where each wire splits (Steiner point) as the route progresses to the leaves, the wire segment width is reduced by half. This sizing progression continues to the sink pins of the subtree or until the minimum wire width is reached.

The motivation for this sizing is an attempt to equalize the current densities across the design. As a first order approximation, the peak current, i_n, through any wire segment, *n*, is a function of the capacitive load driven by the segment, Cd_n, and the risetime of the driving signal (Figure 7). In this diagram, r_n and c_n are the wire resistance and capacitance of the segment computed from the width, w_n, the length, l_n, and the height, *h* (assumed to be a constant for all interconnects), of *n* and the bulk resistivity, ρ, and capacitance per unit area, ε, of the interconnect layer. dV_n/dt is the fastest rate of change of the voltage at node *n*. It may be approximated by $Vdd/2tr$ (where *tr* is the 10% to 50% risetime). The maximum current density is this peak current divided by the cross-sectional area of the segment, $w_n h$.

The loads, *Cd*, in a clock net are wire capacitance dominated and are typically very large in comparison to the individual segment capacitances, *c*. As any path is traversed in such a binary tree from a driver to any pin, the driver load is cut roughly in half at each branch (or Steiner) point, splitting the driving current equally. With each child segment carrying half of the parent's current, only half the wire width is needed to achieve the same current density as the parent segment. In short, this sizing scheme tries to achieve the same current density for all of the segments along any driver-to-pin path. Although this sizing scheme is intended for the equalization of current densities, it is still possible to seek minimum delay sensitivity. To see this, consider the average root-to-latch delay:

$$\begin{aligned}\overline{td} &= \frac{1}{N}\sum_{s \in S_0}\left(\sum_{i \in B(root,s)} tbuff_i + \sum_{i \in P(root,s)} tint_i\right) \\ &= \frac{1}{N}\sum_{s \in S_0}\left(\sum_{i \in B(root,s)} Ro_i Cd_i + \sum_{i \in P(root,s)} 2^i \rho \frac{l_i}{w}\left(\frac{\varepsilon l_i w}{2^{i+1}} + Cd_i\right)\right)\end{aligned} \tag{5}$$

which includes both buffer and interconnect delays ($tbuff_i$ and $tint_i$). The notation used here is the same as above with the addition of $B(u,v)$ which is the set of buffers on the path from node *u* to *v*. Here, the buffer delays are modeled by constant output impedances, Ro_i, and the interconnect delays are in the usual Elmore [3] form. This is a lower order approximation when compared to the modeling of the previous section, but it does capture the dominant behavior of the circuit. All paths from the *root* node to each of the *N* latches in the design, $s \in S_0$, are considered in this sum. The wire width, *w*, corresponds to the maximum wire width of the route at the driving point of each buffer and the wire segments decrease in width as the paths trace out to their targets. From the derivative of this delay with respect to *w*, the optimal width is

$$w_o = \sqrt{\frac{\sum_{s \in S_0}\sum_{i \in P(root,s)} 2^i \rho l_i \sum_{j \in S_i} C_j}{\sum_{s \in S_0}\sum_{i \in B(root,s)} Ro_i \varepsilon \sum_{j \in T_i} \frac{l_j}{2^j}}} \tag{6}$$

When such an optimal initial width is realizable the design will have minimum sensitivity, otherwise a larger width must be selected and the sizing scheme can only produce a roughly equal distribution current densities along any path. In the next section, the experimental results will demonstrate the utility of this sizing scheme and the buffer modeling in this optimization framework.

Figure 7. Estimating the current through an interconnect.

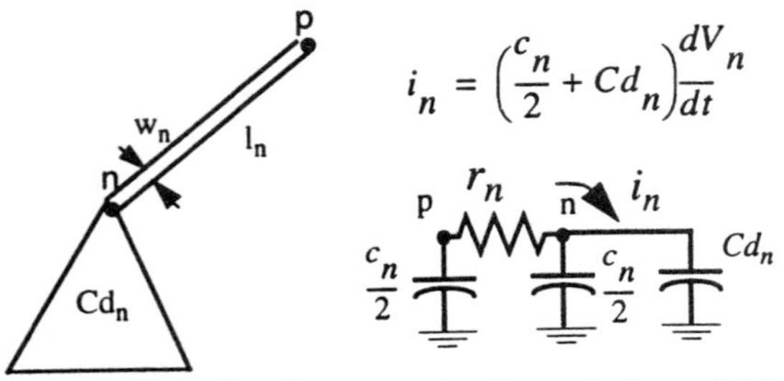

a) abstraction of a wire segment and subtree   b) circuit equivalent of (a)

7 Experimental Results

To investigate the validity of this methodology, the clock optimization framework and supporting algorithms given above have been implemented in C and were run on several test cases. In Section 7.1, the results from [20] are revisited to demonstrate the advantages of the hierarchical decomposition. Then, the merits of our new simultaneous application of the topology search, routing, and wiresizing are demonstrated in Section 7.2. Section 7.3 gives a detailed look at the new balanced wiresizing scheme and Section 7.4 demonstrates the complete framework on a large multistage ASIC design.

7.1 Hierarchical Decomposition

To investigate the validity of the hierarchical decomposition the standard set of Tsay benchmarks [4] have been used. Our intention here is to compare the solutions obtained by splitting the problem to those obtained from a *flat* circuit approach. The optimizer was first run on the benchmark set to produce flat single stage designs. The same benchmarks were then broken into local and global problems and solved in tandem by our algorithms. All routes use minimum wire widths, although wiresizing will be considered in the next section. Table 1 shows the difference in wireability and performance between the flat solutions and the split versions.

Table 1. Comparison of flat and split solutions.

benchmark		flat			hierarchical decomp.		
	sites	wire (Kum)	delay (ns)	skew (ps)	wire (Kum)	delay (ns)	skew (ps)
r1	267	124	1.13	2	115	0.42	28
r2	598	242	3.28	17	231	1.10	41
r3	862	310	3.78	27	294	1.24	46
r4	1903	625	14.4	38	596	4.53	34
r5	3101	952	26.5	4	891	8.40	47

First, we note that even our flat solutions compare favorably with the best previously disclosed solutions in [8][9], *e.g.*, the average wirelength improvement is about 2%. But, the shortest-path wiring used at cluster level in our hierarhical solution saves an average of 6% over the our best flat solutions. This reduction of leaf wire use also reduces the downstream loading capacitance and improves the performance of the network by more than 3X in most cases. Such a reduction in delay can reduce the process induced skew. Finally, the sacrifice to the timing is minimal as the skew (worst-case intra-cluster skew + global skew) is less than 50ps for all designs. In all of these cases, the designs have been optimized without the use of *snake wire*. The small amount of skew introduced by omitting this extra wire shows that such detour paths are unnecessary.

7.2 Tandem vs. Simultaneous Routing and Sizing

To demonstrate the merits of our new simultaneous application of the topology search, routing, and wiresizing, the circuits from the above hierarchical decomposition results have been wiresized using a single-pass delay optimizer, similar to the one described in [5]. This wiresizing algorithm is not the same as the one presented in Section 6, but simply finds a minimum delay wiresizing, without the electromigration constraints. The same circuits were then re-optimized with this single-pass wiresizing delay optimizer in the inner-loop of the annealing. A comparison of the results is given below.

Table 2. Comparison of sized solutions.

benchmark		tandem			simultaneous		
	sites	wire (Kum)	wire area (Kum^2)	delay (ns)	wire (Kum)	wire area (Kum^2)	delay (ns)
r1	267	115	153	0.13	117	148	0.12
r2	598	231	268	0.75	231	292	0.26
r3	862	294	409	0.27	297	380	0.29
r4	1903	596	788	0.77	608	765	0.73
r5	3101	891	1124	1.36	905	1121	1.21

In these results, wire area has been included as it is a good figure of merit when comparing different wiresizing solutions. The skew results have been omitted as they remain below 50ps in all cases. First, notice that the wirelength, wire area, and delay results are very similar for both the tandem and the simultaneous solution strategies. In one case (r2), however, the performance of the tandem solution is nearly three times that of its simultaneously solved counterpart. Upon further inspection, we have found the problem to lie with the selected topology for this circuit. This suggests that performing simultaneous topology, routing, *and* sizing will avoid poor topology choices which can occur if the steps are kept separate.

7.3 Balanced Wiresizing Scheme

The next experiment will demonstrate the new wiresizing scheme of Section 6 and validate equation (6). Here, the r2 benchmark of Tsay [4] has been selected from the optimized flat circuits of Table 1 as an example of a large single stage clock circuit. When applied to this circuit, equation (6) produced an optimal width of 10.5um for the widest wire segment. Here, the driver impedance is $Ro = 10$ Ohms. The tree was then sized with no lower bound restriction on the wire widths. Although unrealistic without such a width restriction, this sizing produces the theoretical *minimum delay sensitivity* circuit. The wires were then resized with a minimum wire width limit of w_{min} = 1um imposed, which is consistent with the technology of this benchmark. Figure 8 compares the total delay of each circuit (driver + interconnect) as all wire widths are varied from 50% to 150% of their nominal values. This plot shows that equation (6) does indeed predict the optimal width for minimum delay sensitivity as well as the impact of the minimum wire width restriction.

The sized circuit with the minimum wire width restriction was extracted and simulated with HSPICE and the peak currents and current densities of the upper 14 wire segments in the tree were measured and are given in Figure 9 (the current density values are in parentheses). All current values are in mA and all current densities are in mA/um^2. The original unsized circuit (minimum wire widths for all segments) has been included for comparison. These figures clearly show how this sizing scheme equalizes current densities across the interconnect network.

Figure 8. Delay sensitivity minimization.

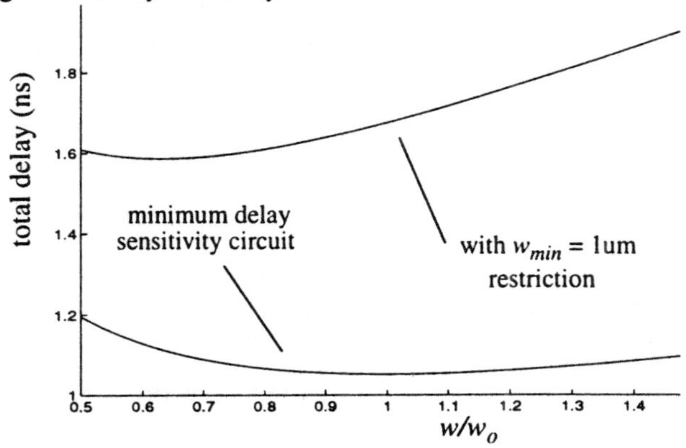

Figure 9. Peak segment currents and current densities.

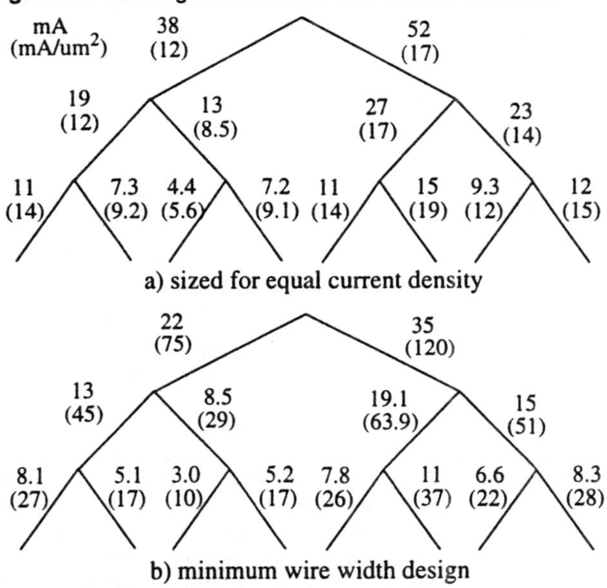

7.4 Large ASIC design

A 16,818 latch ASIC design on a 1.2cm X 1.2cm chip has been obtained from the IBM ASIC foundry of Burlington, VT, and was processed by these techniques. Many of the detailed specifications of this circuit are regarded as confidential and could not be released. As a result, the circuit has been cast in a 0.35um technology, giving each latch an input capacitance between 1fF and 5fF (ρ = 42 mOhm um, ε = 0.35 fF/um^2, h = 0.15 um). Realistic circuit performance specifications were selected for this design and are summarized as follows:

Table 3. Performance specs for ASIC design.

	design target
performance	200MHz (T = 5ns)
skew tolerance	500ps

The skew tolerance here stems from the rule of thumb that the skew should not be permitted to impact the design by more than 10% of the cycle time.The circuit was clustered with these fan-out and skew limitations: C_{target} = 500fF, S_{limit} = 50ps. All of the clusters are routed with wires of minimum width (0.35um) for wireability and power concerns. The output impedance of the repowering buffers used gives an optimal maximum wire width of 0.04um for this design, which is too small to be realized. We know that by selecting any larger wire width, the delay will only increase and the sensitivity will be roughly constant across the design space (see Figure 6). As a result, the maximum wire width for the global interconnects has been set to 1.4um (4X that of w_{min}) to meet the delay target of 5ns.

The resulting layouts of the local and global distribution are given in Figure 11 and the physical details are summarized in Table 4. Note that the chip layout is very detailed with 16,818 latches, so only the lower 1mm X 1mm portion of the latch clustering is shown. The solve time for this circuit was 1.1 hours for the local distribution and 8.0 hours for the global distribution on an IBM PowerPC 850 running AIX 4.1. This circuit was then extracted and simulated using HSPICE. Both the estimated and simulated performance of the circuit are given in Table 5.

Table 4. Summary of 16K latch circuit physical design.

tree wirelength (Kum)	521	no. of clusters	1032
tree wire area (Kum^2)	345	avg. latches/cluster	16
cluster wirelength (Kum)	1,465	no. of buffer levels	5
total wirelength (Kum)	1,986	no. of buffers	87

Table 5. Summary of 16K latch circuit performance.

	predicted	HSPICE
delay (ns)	5.32	4.76
skew (ps)	224	310

Although the actual average root-to-latch delay (measured from the input of the central driver to the input of the latches) was below the performance target (5ns), both the actual skew and average rise-time were higher than expected. Nonetheless, the optimization does a good job of balancing the buffer loading and delays, resulting in low predicted and actual skew. Further, the accuracy of the modeling is sufficiently good and does not accumulate significant error over the many stages of this large design.

As a final experiment into the quality of the circuit generated, we investigate the effect of uniform process variations on the interconnect design. If the interconnect distribution has been well designed and balanced, then we should expect that only a small amount of skew will be introduced when the design is exposed to uniform over- and under-etching. To clarify this, consider the illustration of load and delay matching in Figure 10.

Figure 10. Delay mismatch due to wire width variation.

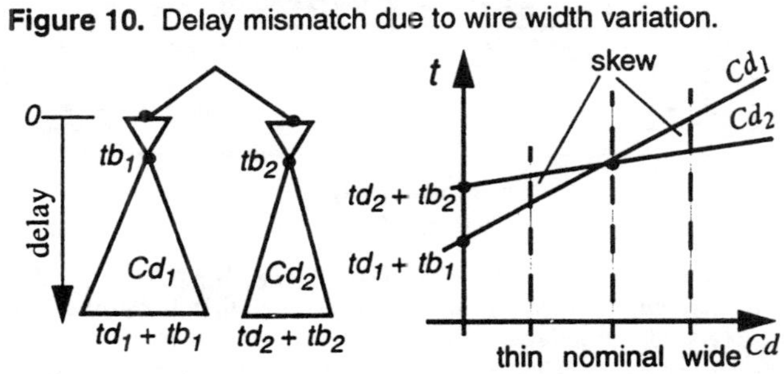

a) matching two buffers b) load line of (a)

In this vertical delay diagram, two identical buffers with different subtree loads (Cd_1 and Cd_2) are being matched. In this example, subtree 1 is larger (in wirelength and wire area) than subtree 2 but they are both routed in such a way as to equalize their total interconnect and buffer delays (*i.e* $td_1 + tb_1 = td_2 + tb_2$). As a result, any wire width variations will cause a greater change in the path delay of buffer and subtree 1 ($td_1 + tb_1$) then in buffer and subtree 2 ($td_2 + tb_2$), as illustrated in Figure 10b. A similar argument can be made for device variations (where the output impedance varies instead of the capacitive load), so the minimization of this type of effect is desirable.

Figure 11. ASIC latch clustering and multistage tree layout.

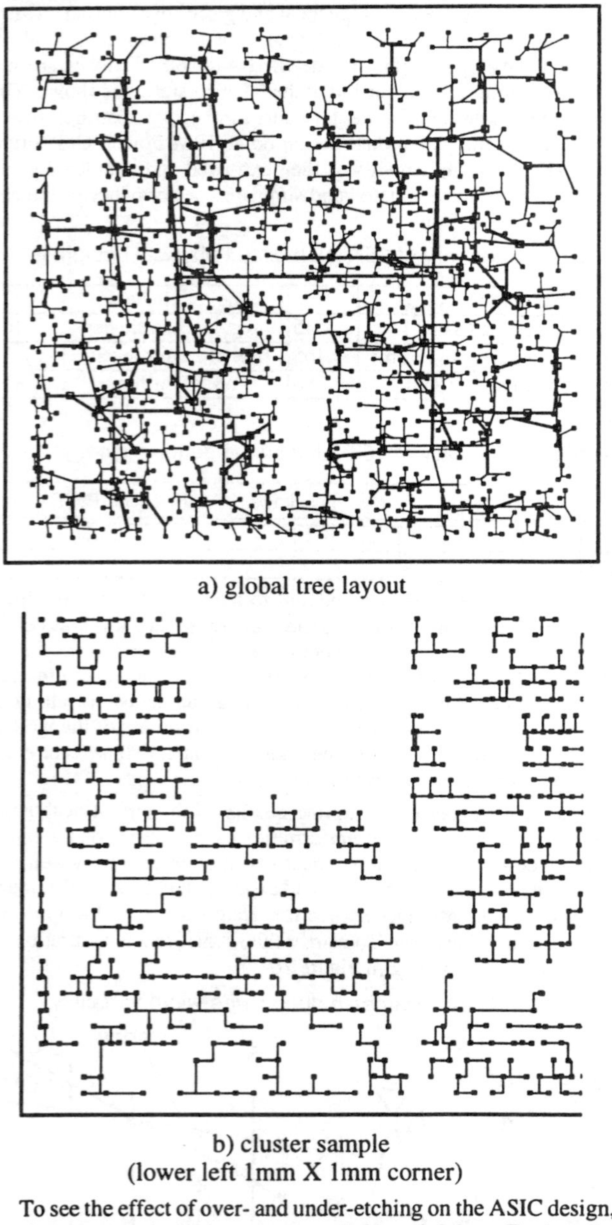

a) global tree layout

b) cluster sample
(lower left 1mm X 1mm corner)

To see the effect of over- and under-etching on the ASIC design, each interconnect in the layout was varied by +/- 0.1um. Further, the circuit was also simulated at the extreme process corners (fast N and P devices and slow N and P devices) to observe the effect of uniform device variations on the performance. The results are shown in Table 6.

Table 6. Effect of uniform process variations.

	nominal	over-etched (-0.1um)	under-etched (+0.1um)	fast N and P	slow N and P
delay (ns)	4.76	4.51	4.99	3.91	6.58
std dev. (ps)	58	64	55	63	54
skew (ps)	310	323	305	327	285

For this design, the devices cause more delay variation than the interconnects. The interconnect-caused delay variations are within +/- 250ps while the device-caused variation is about an order of magnitude larger. Nonetheless, the standard deviation and skew numbers indicate that the distribution of delays does not change much as the various loads tend to increase or decrease together. This is a result of both the optimization and wiresizing scheme. The optimizer balances delays by finding similar subtrees for all of the buffers at each stage. This creates interconnect subtrees which are of similar size across any given buffer level. Further, the wiresizing scheme tends to create similar segment delays across any level of the tree by enforcing the same wire width on segments which are of roughly the same length. Taken together, these properties tend to make the clock circuit look similar, both geometrically and electrically, along any root-to-latch path. These results demonstrate this and show the benefits of such a design approach in the face of uniform process variations.

8 Conclusions

We have presented a comprehensive clock circuit optimization framework for ASICs. This approach has been motivated by the shortcomings of the current multistep design methodology, which are exhibited when faced with the aggressive performance and manufacturability concerns of modern submicron ASIC technology. This methodology allows for the simultaneous application of topology selection, routing, wiresizing, and buffer insertion algorithms for the optimization of multistage clock circuits. A hierarchical decomposition of the circuit has been used to reduce the complexity of these large multistage ASIC designs. This methodology has been applied to a realistic ASIC design of 16,818 latches in a 0.35um process and has produced a clock distribution with a performance level over 200MHz and a skew of less than 400ps. Further, these skew results remain tight under both interconnect and device process variations. These results were obtained in less than 10hours of CPU time on an IBM PowerPC 850 and have been verified by HSPICE. In future work, we will explore methods for optimization with respect to cross-chip non-uniform variations. Further, improving the accuracy of the linearized device models used seems limited. Therefore, an investigation into either delay look-up tables or an accurate wire and device sizing postprocessing step is prudent.

Acknowledgment

We are grateful to David Hathaway of IBM for his many insightful discussions about clock circuit design methodologies and to Dr. Micheal Trick of IBM for providing the ASIC design. We would also like to thank John Shewchuk of the Computer Science Department at Carnegie Mellon University for providing his tool, *Triangle,* which produced the Delaunay triangulations used in this work. Finally, we would like to acknowledge Dr. Ren-Song Tsay of Avant!, Inc. for providing the benchmark latch placements.

References

[1] H. Bakoglu, *Circuits, Interconnections, and Packaging for VLSI.* Reading, MA: Addison-Wesley, 1990.

[2] M. Jackson, A. Srinivasan, and E. Kuh, "Clock routing for high performance ICs," *Proc. of ACM/IEEE DAC*, pp. 573-579, June 1990.

[3] W. C. Elmore, "The transient response of damped linear networks with particular regard to wideband amplifies," *Journal of Applied Physics*, Volume 19, pp. 55-63, January 1948.

[4] R.-S. Tsay, "An exact zero-skew clock routing algorithm," *IEEE Trans. on CAD*, Vol. CAD-12, No. 2, pp. 242-249, February 1993.

[5] M. Edahiro, "Delay minimization for zero-skew routings," *Proc. of IEEE ICCAD*, pp. 563-566, November 1993.

[6] T.-H. Chao, J.-M. Ho, Y.-C. Hsu, K. Boese, and A. Kahng, "Zero-skew clock routing with wirelength minimization," *IEEE Trans. on Circuits and Systems*, vol. 39, pp. 799-814, November 1992.

[7] K. D. Boese and A. B. Kahng, "Zero-skew clock routing trees with minimum wirelength," *Proc. of IEEE International Conference on ASICs*, pp. 17-21, September 1992.

[8] M. Edahiro, "A clustering-based optimization algorithm in zero-skew routings," *Proc. of ACM/IEEE DAC*, pp. 612-616, June 1993.

[9] N.-C. Chou and C.-K. Cheng, "Wire length and delay minimization in general clock net routings," *Proc. of IEEE ICCAD*, pp. 552-555, November 1993.

[10] S. Pullela, N. Menezes, and L. T. Pillage, "Reliable non-zero skew clock trees using wire width optimization," *Proc. of ACM/IEEE DAC*, pp. 165-170, June 1993.

[11] N. Menezes, A. Balivada, S. Pullela, and L. T. Pillage, "Skew reduction in clock trees using wire width optimization," *Proc. of IEEE CICC*, pp. 9.6.1-9.6.4, May 1993.

[12] S. Pullela, N. Menezes, J. Omar, and L. T. Pillage, "Skew and delay optimization for reliable buffered clock trees," *Proc. of the IEEE ICCAD*, pp. 556-562, November 1993.

[13] P. O'Brien and T. Savarino, "Modeling the driving-point characteristic of resistive interconnects for accurate delay estimation", *Proc. of the IEEE ICCAD*, pp. 512-515, November 1989.

[14] J.-M. Ho, G. Vijayan, C. Wong, "New algorithms for the rectilinear steiner tree problem," *IEEE Trans. on CAD*, Vol. 9, No. 2, pp. 185-193, February 1990.

[15] S. Ganguly and S. Hojat, "Clock distribution design and verification for PowerPC microprocessors," *Proc. of the IEEE ICCAD*, pp. 58-61, November 1995.

[16] A. Rincon, M. Trick, T. Guzowski, "A proven methodology for designing one-million-gate ASICs," *Proc. of the IEEE CICC*, pp. 4.1.1-4.1.8, May 1996.

[17] J. Lam and J. M. Delosme, "Performance of a new annealing schedule", *Proc. of ACM/IEEE DAC*, pp. 306-311. June 1988.

[18] N. Menezes, R. Baldick, L. Pileggi, "A sequential quadratic programming approach to concurrent gate and wire sizing", *Proc. of the IEEE ICCAD*, November 1995.

[19] G. Ellis, *The Physical Design of Clock Circuits*, Ph.D thesis, Department of Electrical and Computer Engineering, Carnegie Mellon University, 1997.

[20] G. Ellis, L. T. Pileggi, R. A. Rutenbar, "A hierarchical decomposition methodology for single-stage clock circuits", *Proc. of the IEEE CICC*, pp. 7.1.1-7.1.4, May 1997.

SESSION 5D

CIRCUIT SIMULATION AND OPTIMIZATION

Moderators:

Ibrahim M. Elfadel, IBM Corp.,

Yorktown Heights, NY

Wim van Bokhoven, Eindhoven University of Technology,

Eindhoven, The Netherlands

A New High-Order Absolutely-Stable Explicit Numerical Integration Algorithm for the Time-Domain Simulation of Nonlinear Circuits

R. Griffith and M. Nakhla
Department of Electrical Engineering
Carleton University
Ottawa, Ontario. Canada. K1S 5B6

Abstract

A new numerical integration method for the time domain simulation of nonlinear circuits is presented. The new method does not belong to the traditional class of linear multistep methods. Consequently it is free from Dahlquist's barriers in terms of stability and order. The new method is shown to be both A-stable and at the same time of arbitrarily high order. In addition, the method is explicit in nature and does not require matrix inversion at each time step. Examples of linear and nonlinear circuit simulation are included.

The proposed method significantly speeds up the time domain simulation of nonlinear circuits as it combines the efficiency of an explicit method with the accuracy and large step size possible with high order.

1 Introduction

The tendency towards ever larger circuits with ever more complex devices is stretching the limits of current simulation methods. Time domain simulation of large nonlinear circuits poses a particular problem as most commonly used simulators are based on implicit linear multistep numerical integration methods which have a computational cost that is an increasingly steep nonlinear function of the circuit size. At the same time decreasing circuit feature sizes and faster signal speeds are creating devices with more complex models. It is clear that some way must be found to increase computational efficiency without sacrificing any accuracy in the analysis if current simulation practices are to continue to be followed.

Explicit numerical integration methods are intrinsically faster than commonly used implicit methods. Explicit methods directly calculate the solution at each step. Implicit integration methods solve a system of equations for each solution step often requiring iterative solution methods [1, 2] to satisfy nonlinear algebraic equations. Solution of the equations is the main computational cost in the analysis of large networks. Implicit methods are commonly used in circuit simulation because of their stability. Lack of stability causes the normally efficient explicit methods to be unsuitable for circuit simulation.

Traditional linear multistep(LMS) numerical integration methods, both explicit and implicit, are based on polynomial approximations in the time domain [1, 2, 3]. In this paper a new explicit method based on rational function approximation in the time domain is proposed. When certain conditions are placed on the coeffients of the rational function the method is stable over the entire left half plane and the problems faced by previous explicit methods are avoided. In addition it will be shown the method can be of high order without sacrificing any stability properties. This allows larger step sizes to be taken than with previously available methods.

2 Numerical Integration Using Rational Function Approximations

Dahlquist [4] has shown that

1. An explicit LMS method cannot be A-stable (Dahlquist's barrier #1),
2. A LMS algorithm that is A-Stable cannot exceed order 2 (Dahlquist's barrier #2),
3. The trapezoidal rule is the most accurate A-stable LMS method of order 2,
4. A-stable methods of order higher than 2 exist but not in LMS form.

The first three points are commonly known and are applied in the form of step size control for LMS methods. The last point serves as the basis for the new method presented in this section which does not fall into the category of LMS methods and thus is not constrained by Dahlquist's barriers.

1092-3152/97 $10.00

Consider the initial-value problem

$$\dot{\mathbf{x}} = \mathbf{f}(\mathbf{x}, t)\ , \quad \mathbf{x}(t=0) = \mathbf{x}_0 \tag{1}$$

where $\mathbf{f}() : \Re^{N+1} \mapsto \Re^{N}$ is a vector valued function from the $(N+1)$ dimensional $(\mathbf{x}, t)$ Euclidean space R^{N+1} into the N dimensional $\mathbf{x}$ space R^N. The proposed method provides solution to (1) using a sequence of local approximation functions $\mathbf{x}_i(t), t_{i-1} \leq t \leq t_i$, $i = 1, 2, 3, \cdots$. For each component $x^{(k)}$ of the vector $\mathbf{x}$ a rational function approximation is developed at the point t_{i-1} as

$$x_i^{(k)}(t) = \phi_{m/n}^{(k,i)}(h) = \frac{\sum_{j=0}^{m} a_j h^j}{\sum_{j=0}^{n} b_j h^j}, \qquad h = t - t_{i-1} > 0 \tag{2}$$

where $a_j, b_j \in \Re$ are parameters of the approximation with $b_0 = 1$. The method is stepped in time by evaluating $x_i^{(k)}(t_i)$ and using this as the initial condition for the next approximation $\mathbf{x}_{i+1}(t)$. A new set of approximations $\phi_{m/n}^{(k,i)}(h)$ is calculated for each interval as the method is stepped.

To test the stability properties of the method consider the test equation introduced by Dahlquist [4]

$$\frac{d\,x}{d\,t} = qx\ , \quad x(t=0) = x_0 \tag{3}$$

and applying (2) successively for M intervals yields the solution

$$x_M = x_0[\phi(h)]^M \tag{4}$$

where $\phi(t)$ is a rational function approximation to $\exp(qt)$. For the numerical method to be stable the solution x_M should approach zero. As $M \to \infty$ this will be the case if the approximation ϕ meets the definition of A-acceptability so that $|\phi(h)| < 1$.

Detailed study of rational approximations and maximal approximants [5, 6, 7, 8, 9] has shown that

First Ehle Conjecture [7]:

The A-acceptable maximal approximants $\phi_{m/n} \in \Pi_{m/n}$ *to* $\exp(z)$ *are exactly those approximants for which* $0 \leq m \leq n \leq m+2$.

That $m \leq n$ to assure A-acceptability is reasonably obvious as the asymptotic behavior of (2) as $z \to \infty$ is $a_m z^m / b_n z^n$. Proof of the whole conjecture was first provided in [8].

Thus the rational function $\phi(h)$ will be A-acceptable if it is a maximal approximant to $exp(z)$ and the conditions on m and n are observed. Restricting the rational function to be an A-acceptable maximal approximate, maximizes its accuracy, and results in the function being a Padé approximate by definition [10]. Other choices of form for the rational function might meet the A-acceptable criteria, but they would not be maximal approximate.

3 Computation of the Rational Function Approximation

Methods for the construction of the required approximant are well known [10] and are based on expanding $x(t)$ in a Taylor series as

$$x(t) = \sum_{j=0} c_j t^j \tag{5}$$

where c_j, $j = 0, 1, 2, \cdots$ are the time domain moments of x. Given the Taylor series of order p, a rational approximation is constructed such that

$$\phi_{m/n}(t) = \sum_{j=0}^{p} c_j t^j + \mathcal{O}(p+1) \tag{6}$$

where $\phi_{m/n}(t)$ is given by (2) and the first $p = m+n+1$ moments are matched by the rational approximation. Calculation of the coeffients a_j, b_j of the rational function approximation in terms of the moments c_j is straight forward [10] and will not be described here.

Without loss of generality, calculation of the time-domain moments required for approximating $x_i(t)$ will be described using $t_{i-1} = 0, x(0) = x_0$ as the point of reference. At t_{i-1}, x is replaced with its Taylor series representation in (1) giving

$$\sum_{j=1} c_j j t^{j-1} = f(t, \sum_{j=0} c_j t^j), \quad c_0 = x_0 \tag{7}$$

$$= \sum_{j=0} d_j t^j \tag{8}$$

Equating powers of t in (8) gives

$$c_{j+1}(j+1) = d_j \tag{9}$$

as a recursive formula for calculating c_j.

Expansions for common functions have been derived [11] such that an implementation for generalized equations can be done by storing equations in graph form. When the ith moment is required at the root of the graph a depth first traversal is done calculating the ith moment of each branch and applying the appropriate functional relationship at each node to calculate the required moment. The moments are calculated sequentially and the algorithm was implemented using local storage at nodes where the ith moment depends on moments $j, j < i$ to minimize recursion.

4 Application to Circuit Equations

Consider a nonlinear network described by the modified nodal analysis [2] formulation

$$\mathbf{C}\frac{d\mathbf{v}}{dt} + \mathbf{G}\,\mathbf{v} + \mathbf{F}(\mathbf{v}) = \mathbf{b}(t) \tag{10}$$

where $\mathbf{C}$, $\mathbf{G}$ are matrices that represent the linear lumped elements in the circuit as well as additional structural entries required by the MNA formulation, $\mathbf{F}(\mathbf{v})$ represents the nonlinear lumped elements and $\mathbf{b}(t)$ represents the input waveforms.

Using (7)-(10) we get

$$\mathbf{G}\mathbf{v}_0 + \mathbf{F}_0(\mathbf{v}_0) = \mathbf{b}_0 \quad (11)$$

$$\mathbf{C}\mathbf{v}_j \times j + \mathbf{G}\mathbf{v}_{j-1} + \mathbf{F}_{j-1} = \mathbf{b}_{j-1}, \quad j > 0 (12)$$

where $\mathbf{F}_j$ and $\mathbf{b}_j$ are the time domain moments of $\mathbf{F}(\mathbf{v}(t))$ and $\mathbf{b}(t)$ respectively.

Equation (12) represents an explicit recursive relationship for evaluation of the time-domain moments.

It should be noted that even when simulating nonlinear networks, no iterations or LU decompositions of the circuit matrices are required during the transient solution. In addition the method is multirate and of variable order in the sense that it is not constrained to have the same order of approximation or the same step size for all of the components of the solution. It is possible to identify slow changing signals and avoid recalculating the associated rational functions [11]. In addition error criteria can be formulated as a function of order and step size.

5 Examples

5.1 Linear System

Consider the linear system

$$\dot{\mathbf{x}} = \begin{bmatrix} -1 & 8 \\ -1 & -10 \end{bmatrix} \mathbf{x}, \ \mathbf{x}(0) = \begin{bmatrix} 1 \\ 1 \end{bmatrix} \quad (13)$$

with the response for $x^{(1)}$ as plotted in Figure 1. The rational function approximation $\phi_{3/4}$ for $x^{(1)}$ in the interval starting at $t = 0$ is

$$x_1^{(1)}(t) = \frac{1 + 12.986t + 9.4001t^2 - 6.9813t^3}{1 + 5.9860t + 14.998t^2 - 19.202t^3 + 11.096t^4} \quad (14)$$

Figure 1 shows $x^{(1)}$ as calculated using $\phi_{3/4}$ and steps of $h = .75$. Equation (14) was used for the interval $(0, .75)$ in Figure 1, then the method was stepped, and a new approximation was used for the next interval. It should be noted that (14) could have been used for the entire interval $(0, 3)$ or even $(0, \infty)$ as a good approximation to the exact solution. Figure 2 shows (14) plotted against the exact solution for the interval $(0, 10)$, essentially solving this entire interval in one step. The rational functions used in this method are smooth and intermediate points can be calculated by direct evaluation of the function.

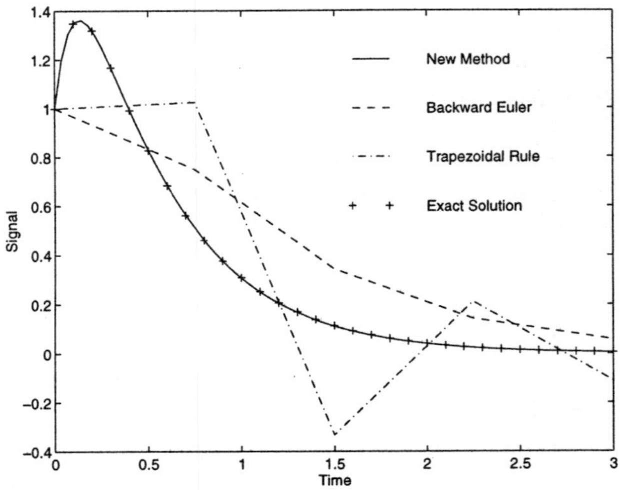

Figure 1: Solution of the simple linear system of (13) using different methods with a step size of $h = 0.75$.

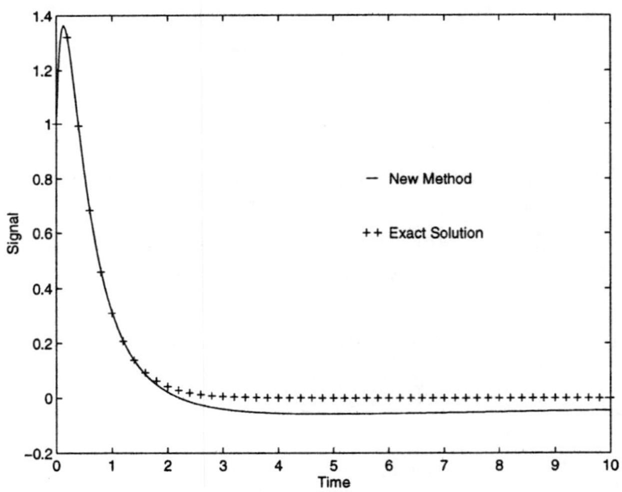

Figure 2: A single step solution to (13) using the function of Equation (14).

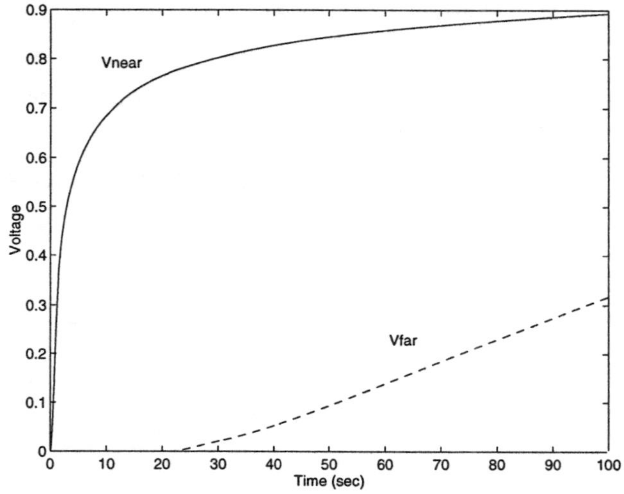

Figure 3: Response of a stiff system.

5.2 A Stiff Circuit

An RC circuit was constructed with 19 resistors and 19 capacitors and the component values chosen so that the eigenvalues of the state space formulation ranged from -4.236 to -0.00617 a ratio of almost 700. The response near the source and far end of this stiff system is shown in Figure 3 as calculated using a step size of 10 seconds. $\phi_{8/8}$ functions were used for all of the waveforms. The step size used is much larger than the $2/4.236 = .47$ second limit beyond which the forward Euler method is unstable.

The results are practically identical to those calculated using HSPICE which required 108 iterations to cover the time period. Including the step of the 1 second rise time of the input the new method used 11 steps to solve the same interval. The new method did not require the inversion of the circuit matrix at any time point whereas implicit methods such as those used in HSPICE require at least one LU decomposition of the circuit equations at each time point.

5.3 Transistor Circuit

Figure 4 shows the response of a simple, one transistor, common emitter, inverter circuit. An Ebers-Moll model was used for the transistor.

Eleven time steps with $\phi_{4/4}$ rational functions were used for the simulation. Again no inversions of circuit matrices were required during any of these steps. HSPICE required 302 iterations to solve the same example. Each Newton's iteration in HSPICE involved one LU decomposition of the circuit matrix.

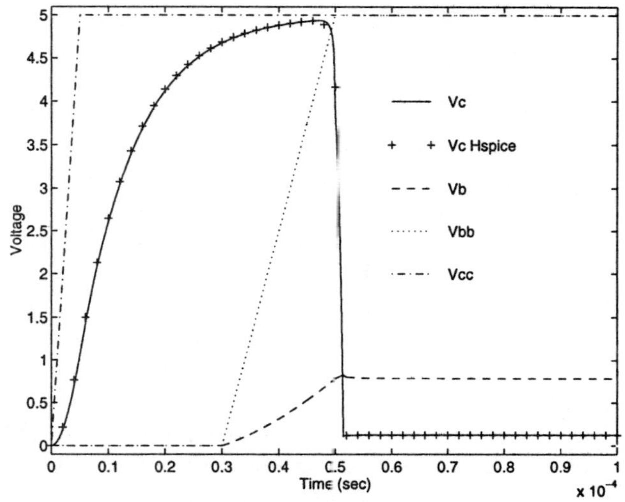

Figure 4: Response of a simple one transistor inverter circuit.

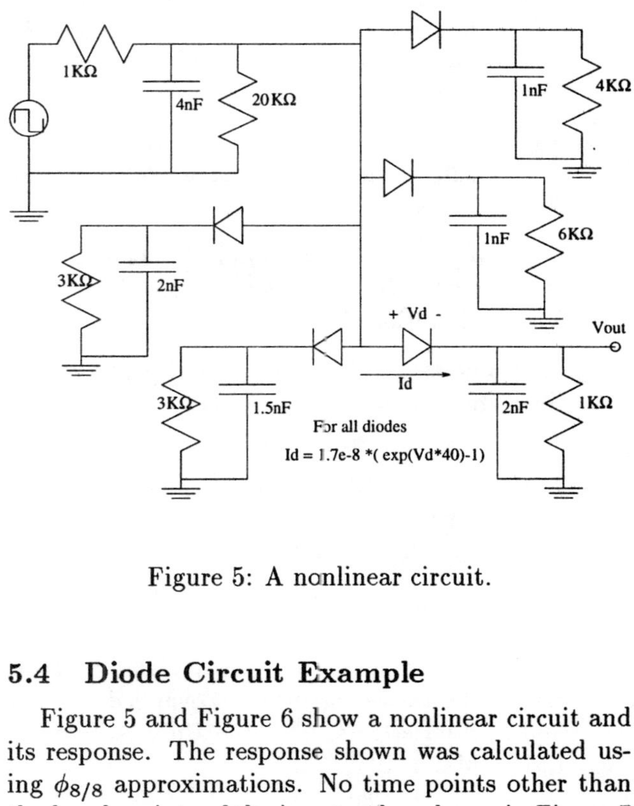

Figure 5: A nonlinear circuit.

5.4 Diode Circuit Example

Figure 5 and Figure 6 show a nonlinear circuit and its response. The response shown was calculated using $\phi_{8/8}$ approximations. No time points other than the break points of the input pulse, shown in Figure 7 were required (shown in the figure by vertical dashed lines). Again the results agreed with HSPICE and the proposed method required no inversion of the circuit matrices during the transient solution. HSPICE required 307 iterations to solve this circuit.

6 Conclusion

A new explicit numerical integration technique for the time-domain simulation of nonlinear networks has been presented. The method was shown to be of arbitrarily high-order while preserving A-stability.

The new method can perform nonlinear time domain circuit simulation without inverting circuit matrices or doing Newton's iterations. Avoiding these traditionally CPU intensive operations gives the method speed advantages over previously used techniques. In addition the method is of high-order allowing large step sizes and can be used with multirate techniques to further increase its efficiency.

The new method is not a linear multistep method and is a departure from techniques that have become entrenched in popular simulators such as SPICE. The techniques associated with the presented method offer new opportunities in the development of circuit simulators.

References

[1] Leon O. Chua and Pen-Min Lin, *Computer Aided Analyis of Electric Circuits: Algorithms and Computational Techniques*, Prentice-Hall, 1975.

[2] Jiri Vlach and Kishor Singhal, *Computer Methods for Circuit Analysis and Design*, Van Nostrand Reinhold, 1983.

[3] E. Hairer, S. P. Nørsett, and G. Wanner, *Solving Ordinary Differential Equations I*, Springer-Verlag, 2 edition, 1993.

[4] G. Dahlquist, "A special stability problem for linear multistep methods," *BIT*, vol. 3, pp. 27–43, 1963.

[5] Byron L. Ehle, "High order a-stable methods for the numerical solution of systems of D.E.'s," *BIT*, vol. 8, pp. 276–278, 1968.

[6] Byron L. Ehle, *On Padé Approximations to the Exponential Function and A-Stable Methods for the Numerical Solution of Initial Value Problems*, Ph.D. thesis, Department of Applied Analysis and Computer Science at the University of Waterloo, March 1969.

[7] B. L. Ehle, "A-stable methods and padé approximations to the exponential," *SIAM Journal on Mathematical Analysis*, vol. 4, pp. 671–680, 1973.

[8] G. Wanner, E. Hairer, and S.P. Nørsett, "Order stars and stability theorems," *BIT*, vol. 18, pp. 475–489, 1978.

[9] A. Iserles and S. P. Nørsett, *Order Stars*, Chapman & Hall, 1991.

[10] G. A. Baker, *Essentials of Padé Approximants*, Academic Press, New York, 1975.

[11] R. Griffith and M. Nakhla, "Explicit nonlinear time-domain circuit simulation," *To be submitted.*

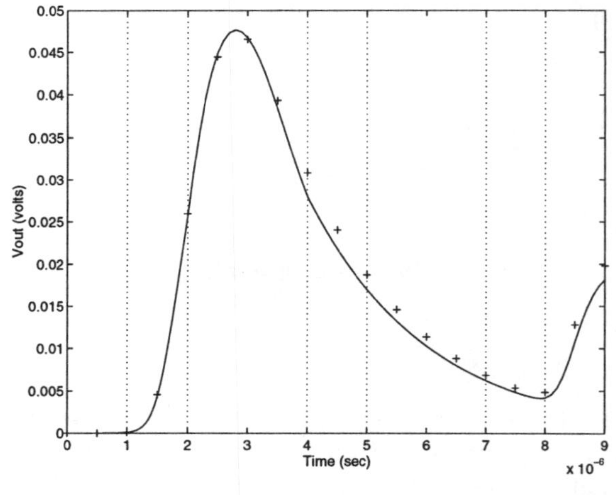

Figure 6: Response of the circuit of Figure 5.

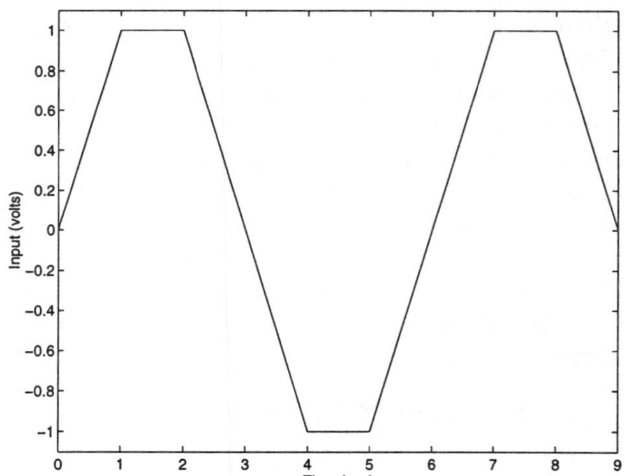

Figure 7: The input used for the circuit of Figure 5.

Circuit Optimization via Adjoint Lagrangians

Andrew R. Conn, Ruud A. Haring, Chandu Visweswariah, Chai Wah Wu
IBM T. J. Watson Research Center, Yorktown Heights, NY 10598

Abstract

The circuit tuning problem is best approached by means of gradient-based nonlinear optimization algorithms. For large circuits, gradient computation can be the bottleneck in the optimization procedure. Traditionally, when the number of measurements is large relative to the number of tunable parameters, the direct method[2] is used to repeatedly solve the associated sensitivity circuit to obtain all the necessary gradients. Likewise, when the parameters outnumber the measurements, the adjoint method[1] is employed to solve the adjoint circuit repeatedly for each measurement to compute the sensitivities. In this paper, we propose the adjoint Lagrangian method, which computes all the gradients necessary for augmented-Lagrangian-based optimization in a single adjoint analysis. After the nominal simulation of the circuit has been carried out, the gradients of the merit function are expressed as the gradients of a weighted sum of circuit measurements. The weights are dependent on the nominal solution and on optimizer quantities such as Lagrange multipliers. By suitably choosing the excitations of the adjoint circuit, the gradients of the merit function are computed via a single adjoint analysis, irrespective of the number of measurements and the number of parameters of the optimization. This procedure requires close integration between the nonlinear optimization software and the circuit simulation program.

The adjoint Lagrangian formulation has been implemented in the JiffyTune tool [12]which optimizes delay, area, slew (transition time) and power measurements by adjusting transistor widths and wire sizes. Speedups of over 35x have been realized in the gradient computation procedure by using the adjoint Lagrangian formulation, leading to speedups of up to 2.5x in the overall optimization procedure. Perhaps more importantly, these speedups have rendered feasible the tuning of large circuits. A circuit with 6,900 transistors was optimized in under two hours of CPU time.

1.0 Introduction and motivation

The push towards high-performance, low-power, custom digital integrated circuits has led to a renewed emphasis on circuit optimization (tuning). This problem is best approached by means of gradient-based nonlinear optimization. In the case of dynamic tuning[10,16], function and gradient values are determined by means of a dynamic (time-domain) analysis of the underlying circuit. In the case of static optimization[11,15,17,18,19], a static timing analysis[23] is relied upon to analyze new iterates produced during the optimization process. If circuit blocks are modeled by analytic delay equations, these equations can be differentiated symbolically to determine gradients. Unfortunately, this procedure is not applicable to custom circuits because of the lack of availability of delay models for arbitrary transistor-level circuits. This problem is overcome by running dynamic simulations of each block of the design on the fly. In either type of tuning, gradient computation is often the bottleneck in the optimization procedure. Gradients are generally computed by the direct[2] or adjoint[1,3] method. The direct method requires as many simulations of the associated sensitivity circuit as the number of tunable parameters. In the adjoint method, the simulation of the adjoint circuit is repeated as many times as the number of measurements.

In this paper, we present a method by which the gradients of a circuit for the purposes of augmented-Lagrangian-based optimization can be obtained by means of a single measurement-at-a-time adjoint analysis, irrespective of the number of measurements and the number of tunable parameters. Thus the gradient computation bottleneck is ameliorated. This method of gradient computation has been applied in the context of a dynamic circuit optimization tool called JiffyTune[12]. The enhanced gradient computation allows additional constraints at a relatively low incremental cost, which is particularly significant for tuning dynamic circuits.

JiffyTune adjusts transistor widths and wire sizes to optimize power, area, delay and slews. Any combination of objective function, equality and inequality constraints is accommodated. JiffyTune uses SPECS[6,9] for fast simulation and sensitivity analysis[4,5,14]. SPECS employs piecewise approximate device models and event-driven simulation to gain an average speedup of 70x over AS/X[7,8] with a relative inaccuracy of 5%. Hence JiffyTune can tune at best to within 5% accuracy. However, simulation with AS/X before and after tuning has been used to corroborate the circuit improvements predicted by JiffyTune[12]. The function and gradient values are fed to LANCELOT, a general-purpose, large-scale nonlinear optimization package[13,21,22] which employs an augmented Lagrangian formulation and a trust-region approach.

2.0 Demonstration by means of an example

The concept of the adjoint Lagrangian formulation is first demonstrated using a simple example. Referring to Figure 1(a), let us assume that the circuit of interest has just one input, one output v, tunable parameters $x_1, x_2, \ldots, x_n$ and that the optimization problem is to minimize d_1, subject to $d_2 = T$, where d_1 is the 50% crossing point of the falling transition at the output, d_2 is the 50% crossing point of the rising transition and T is a constant target value. The output waveform is shown in Figure 1(a). Let us assume that the nonlinear optimizer builds an augmented Lagrangian[31,32]

1092-3152/97 $10.00 © 1997 IEEE

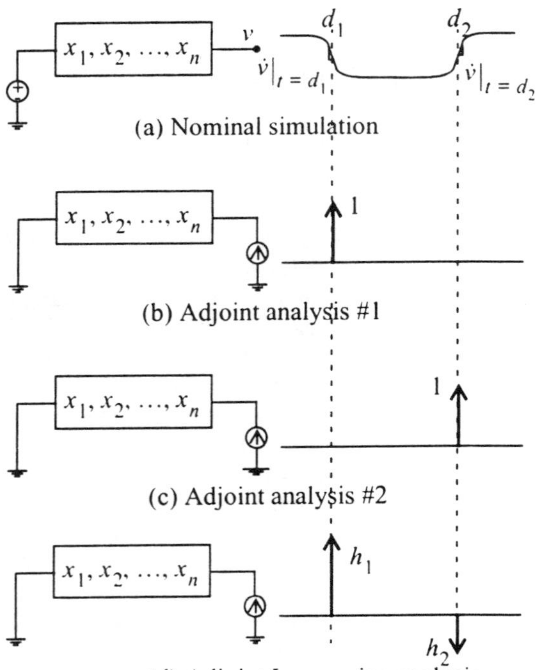

Figure 1. Demonstration of the adjoint Lagrangian formulation by means of an example.

merit function of the following form: $\Phi = d_1 + \lambda\left(d_2 - T\right) + \frac{1}{2\mu}\left(d_2 - T\right)^2$, where λ is the Lagrange multiplier corresponding to the constraint, and μ is a penalty parameter used to weight the quadratic augmentation of the Lagrangian. At each iteration, the simulator is required to compute d_1, d_2, $\partial d_1/\partial x_i$ and $\partial d_2/\partial x_i$ for all i. The quantities d_1 and d_2 are computed by a nominal transient analysis (Figure 1(a)). We will first describe how the "measurement-at-a-time" adjoint analysis method is used to determine the sensitivities. First, an adjoint circuit is formed and configured as shown in Figure 1(b). The adjoint circuit is excited by a current source with a unit Dirac impulse at time d_1, i.e., $\delta(t - d_1)$ [34]. Time and control are reversed during the analysis of the adjoint circuit and the nominal waveforms are convolved with the adjoint waveforms to yield $\left.\frac{\partial v}{\partial x_i}\right|_{t = d_1} = \mathrm{conv}(x_i)$, for all i, where v is the output and $\mathrm{conv}(x_i)$ represents the convolution between the appropriate nominal and adjoint waveforms for each problem variable x_i. The required gradients $\partial d_1/\partial x_i$ are then computed using

$$\frac{\partial d_1}{\partial x_i} = -\left.\frac{\frac{\partial v}{\partial x_i}}{\frac{\partial v}{\partial t}}\right|_{t = d_1} = -\frac{\left.\frac{\partial v}{\partial x_i}\right|_{t = d_1}}{\left.\dot{v}\right|_{t = d_1}} = -\frac{\mathrm{conv}\ (x_i)}{\left.\dot{v}\right|_{t = d_1}}, \quad (1)$$

where $\left.\dot{v}\right|_{t = d_1}$ is the slope of the nominal voltage waveform v at time d_1. Next, the adjoint analysis is repeated as shown in Figure 1(c) to similarly determine the gradients $\partial d_2/\partial x_i$ for all i. Finally, the gradients are assembled by the optimizer as follows: $\frac{\partial \Phi}{\partial x_i} = \frac{\partial d_1}{\partial x_i} + \left[\lambda + \frac{(d_2 - T)}{\mu}\right]\frac{\partial d_2}{\partial x_i}$. The method described above requires two adjoint analyses and two sets of convolution integrals. Instead, the adjoint Lagrangian method recognizes that the gradients of the merit function are the gradients of a linear combination of circuit measurements, i.e., $\frac{\partial \Phi}{\partial x_i} = \frac{\partial}{\partial x_i}\left(h_1 d_1 + h_2 d_2\right)$ where the coefficients h_1 and h_2 are known and can be treated as constants once the nominal simulation has been completed. Hence, a single adjoint analysis is enough to determine the gradients of Φ with respect to all the variables of the problem, as shown in Figure 1(c). Thus two impulses of heights $h_1 = \frac{-1}{\left.\dot{v}\right|_{t = d_1}}$ and $h_2 = \frac{-1}{\left.\dot{v}\right|_{t = d_2}}\left[\lambda + \frac{(d_2 - T)}{\mu}\right]$ are applied during a single adjoint analysis. Note that the heights of the impulses are functions of the nominal simulation results ($\left.\dot{v}\right|_{t = d_1}$, $\left.\dot{v}\right|_{t = d_2}$ and d_2) and the optimizer variables λ and μ. The analysis and convolution integrals are carried out as before to obtain $\frac{\partial \Phi}{\partial x_i} = \mathrm{conv}(x_i)$, for all i. Thus two adjoint analyses have been replaced by one. Although the gradients of the composite merit function can be computed by this method (see also [33,34]), the gradients of the individual measurements are not computed and cannot be recovered. In general, if an optimization problem involves m measurements, the adjoint Lagrangian method will obtain a speedup of $O(m)$ over regular (one-measurement-at-a-time) adjoint analysis. The next section will describe how the gradients of any differentiable scalar merit function of any number of circuit measurements can be computed with respect to any number of parameters by means of a single adjoint analysis.

3.0 Theory

This section will describe how the gradients of any merit function can be computed via a single adjoint analysis. Suppose the merit function of interest is $\Phi = g(f_1, f_2, \ldots, f_F, c_1, c_2, \ldots, c_C)$ where g is any differentiable function, the f_j are objective functions and the c_j are constraints. Further, let these objective functions and constraints be defined as differentiable functions

$$\begin{aligned} f_j &= f_j(m_1, m_2, \ldots, m_M), j = 1, 2, \ldots, F \\ c_j &= c_j(m_1, m_2, \ldots, m_M), j = 1, 2, \ldots, C \end{aligned} \quad (2)$$

of the circuit measurements m_k. Thus Φ can be expressed as a scalar differentiable function of the circuit measurements. We are required to find the gradient of Φ with respect to all the x_i, $i = 1, 2, \ldots, n$ parameters of the optimization. Now

$$\frac{\partial \Phi}{\partial x_i} = \sum_{j=1}^{F} \frac{\partial g}{\partial f_j}\frac{\partial f_j}{\partial x_i} + \sum_{j=1}^{C} \frac{\partial g}{\partial c_j}\frac{\partial c_j}{\partial x_i}, \forall i$$
$$= \sum_{j=1}^{F}\left(\frac{\partial g}{\partial f_j}\sum_{k=1}^{M}\frac{\partial f_j}{\partial m_k}\frac{\partial m_k}{\partial x_i}\right) + \sum_{j=1}^{C}\left(\frac{\partial g}{\partial c_j}\sum_{k=1}^{M}\frac{\partial c_j}{\partial m_k}\frac{\partial m_k}{\partial x_i}\right), \forall i. \quad (3)$$

Rearranging the summations,

$$\frac{\partial \Phi}{\partial x_i} = \sum_{k=1}^{M}\frac{\partial m_k}{\partial x_i}\left[\sum_{j=1}^{F}\frac{\partial g}{\partial f_j}\frac{\partial f_j}{\partial m_k} + \sum_{j=1}^{C}\frac{\partial g}{\partial c_j}\frac{\partial c_j}{\partial m_k}\right], \forall i. \quad (4)$$

All the terms inside of the square brackets of the right hand side of (4) are known once the nominal simulation has been completed, since the analytic forms of g, f_j and c_j and the nominal values of the measurements m_k, are known. The terms within the square brackets can depend on the nominal simulation results, as well as optimization parameters such as slack variables, Lagrange multipliers, penalty parameters, etc... Equation (4) can be written as $\frac{\partial \Phi}{\partial x_i} = \sum_{k=1}^{M} h_k \frac{\partial m_k}{\partial x_i} = \frac{\partial}{\partial x_i}\left[\sum_{k=1}^{M} h_k m_k\right]$, for all i since the h_k can be treated as constants after the nominal simulation. So far, all we have done is to write the gradients of the merit function as the gradients of a linear combination of measurements, which is always possible provided g, f_j and c_j are differentiable. Following the derivation of adjoint sensitivities in[1], we will demonstrate how to pick adjoint circuit excitations so that the gradient of the merit function can be efficiently computed.

Let each measurement be expressible as a time-domain convolution integral of the form $m_k = \int_{t_0}^{t_f} \{v_I, i_V\} p_k(\tau)\, d\tau$ where v_I are voltages of independent current sources, i_V are the currents of independent voltage sources, t_0 is the start time of the transient simulation, t_f the end time, $\{v_I, i_V\}$ denotes one of v_I and i_V and p_k is a time-domain function that will be used as the excitation in the adjoint circuit at the measurement point. Without loss of generality, all measurements can be written in terms of the voltages of independent current sources and currents of independent voltage sources, since a zero-valued current (voltage) source can always be added in parallel (series) with the voltage (current) to be measured. For example, a measurement which is a voltage value at any time t is expressed as $m_k = \int_{t_0}^{t_f} v_{Ik}(\tau)\,\delta(\tau - t)\, d\tau$ so that p_k is a unit Dirac impulse at time corresponding to t. A measurement which is a crossing time requires $p_k(\tau) = \frac{-\delta(\tau - t_{cross})}{\dot{v}|_{t = t_{cross}}}$. A power measurement which integrates the current through a voltage source from time t_{start} to t_{end} can be written as $p_k(\tau) = u(\tau - t_{start}) - u(\tau - t_{end})$, where $u(t)$ is the unit step function. The Elmore delay of a signal[24] can also be expressed as an integral. Expression of the measurements as convolution integrals is essential to the computation of sensitivities by the adjoint method.

Following[1], Tellegen's theorem[28] is invoked on the nominal circuit and an adjoint circuit with the same topology, but arbitrary elements. Then Tellegen's theorem is again invoked on the perturbed circuit and the adjoint circuit. The difference between the two sets of resulting equations is integrated over the time period of simulation. Time is run backwards and appropriate choices of branch constitutive relations (BCRs) are made in the adjoint circuit to yield the expression

$$\sum_I \int_{t_0}^{t_f}\left(-\delta v_I \hat{i}_I\right)dt + \sum_V \int_{t_0}^{t_f}(\delta i_V \hat{v}_V)\, dt = \sum_R \delta R \int_{t_0}^{t_f} i_R \hat{i}_R dt$$
$$+ \sum_C \left[C\hat{v}_C(t_0)\,\delta v_C(t_0) - \delta C \int_{t_0}^{t_f} \hat{v}_C \dot{v}_C dt\right] + \sum_{\substack{\text{other}\\ \text{elements}}} \ldots \quad (5)$$

In writing (5), adjoint circuit quantities are represented with a carat (ˆ) symbol and δ is used to represent perturbations in circuit values (not to be confused with the use of δ for time-domain Dirac functions). The terms on the right hand side have been shown only for the linear resistors and capacitors in the circuit, but the equation is valid only when summed over all the elements of the circuit. Note that $\hat{i}_I$, the current of independent current sources in the adjoint circuit and $\hat{v}_V$, the voltage of independent voltage sources in the adjoint circuit are the adjoint excitations that must be chosen in order to express the sensitivity function of interest.

In general, (5) can be summarized as

$$\sum_{Is} \int_{t_0}^{t_f}\left(-\delta v_I \hat{i}_I\right)dt + \sum_{Vs} \int_{t_0}^{t_f}\left(\delta i_V \hat{v}_V\right)dt = \sum_l \beta_l \delta x_l \quad (6)$$

by proper choice of adjoint circuit elements, where δx_l and β_l represents the variation in the sensitivity parameters and the corresponding convolutions respectively. We manipulate the left hand side of (6) to the form $\sum_{k=1}^{M} h_k \delta m_k$ by choosing $\hat{v}_V$ and $\hat{i}_I$ to be $\hat{v}_V(\tau) = u(\tau - t_{start}) - u(\tau - t_{end})$, $\hat{i}_I(\tau) = -\delta(\tau - t_{cross})$ and $\hat{i}_I(\tau) = \frac{\delta(\tau - t_{cross})}{\dot{v}_I|_{t = t_{cross}}}$ for a power, voltage, and crossing time measurement respectively. All other sources are set to zero. These are the current and voltage excitations that would be applied *one at a time* if we were interested in finding the sensitivities of the individual measurements. Instead, we weight each these waveforms by the corresponding h_k. Substituting them into (6), we obtain $\delta\Phi = \sum_{k=1}^{M} h_k \delta m_k = \sum_l \beta_l \delta x_l$. As $\delta x_l \to 0$, the required sensitivities can be picked off as $\frac{\partial\Phi}{\partial x_l} = \beta_l$ in the course of a single adjoint analysis. Note that this result cannot be derived from simple superposition, since the adjoint circuit is a time-varying circuit.

4.0 Practical considerations

4.1 Features of JiffyTune

The adjoint Lagrangian formulation was implemented in the dynamic circuit optimization tool JiffyTune. Some features of JiffyTune are mentioned here. See [12] for more details.

- JiffyTune permits area, delay (crossing time) and power measurements. The objective function and weighted constraints are expressed in terms of these measurements. For example, a slew function is written as the difference between the 10% and 90% crossing times. If multiple objective functions are defined, a weighted sum of these functions is minimized. Both equality and inequality constraints are permitted. Inequalities are internally converted to equality constraints in LANCELOT by the addition of slack variables.
- Transistor widths can have simple bounds and can be ratioed to one another. Similar structures can be grouped so that in all instances of the structure, corresponding transistors have the same width, thus permitting a regular layout. Sensitivities are computed with respect to all tunable transistors and wires and then combined by chain-ruling to obtain the composite sensitivities with respect to the independent variables.
- Minimax optimization (e.g., minimizing the worst of n path delays, without *a priori* knowledge of which delay is the worst) is supported by converting $\min_x \left[\max_i \{f_i(x)\} \right]$ to $\min_{x,z} z$ subj. to $z \geq f_i(x), \forall i$, where z is a new variable of the problem. The variable z is initialized to $\max_i \left[f_i\left(x^0\right) \right]$ after the first function evaluation, and the Lagrange multipliers corresponding to the inequalities that include z are initialized to $1/n$ where n is the number of minimax constraints, since the first order Kuhn-Tucker conditions[26] require that these multipliers sum up to unity at optimality.
- Each iteration of JiffyTune is expensive since it involves one SPECS simulation and, if the step is accepted, one gradient computation. To reduce the number of iterations, the optimizer takes aggressive steps wherever possible. Occasionally, such steps lead to circuit failures, wherein a signal transition of interest does not occur. Such situations are automatically detected and the trust-region radius of LANCELOT is reduced before making another attempt. If a certain number (5 is the default) of consecutive failures is detected, the optimization is abandoned. In practice, automatic recovery is almost always successful. The best results encountered during the course of the optimization are saved in all cases.
- If a circuit is tuned for optimal nominal performance, its manufacturability[20] may have been adversely affected. Therefore, two manufacturability modes are provided in JiffyTune. In the first mode, the final tuned circuit is simulated at each of the specified process corners so that the designer can obtain a quick idea of the performance spread. In the second mode, the circuit is *simultaneously* tuned at multiple process corners. Constraints are replicated at each specified process corner. An objective function for the nominal problem is converted to a corresponding minimax problem across the process corners. Similarly, a nominal minimax problem is mapped to a new minimax problem wherein the constraints of the nominal minimax problem are replicated at each process corner of interest. Thus, in all cases, the nominal problem is remapped into a new problem in a standard nonlinear optimization form, which ensures that tuning is carried out simultaneously at all the process corners.
- JiffyTune includes an easy-to-use graphical user interface in the Cadence schematic framework[29]. Designers can specify the optimization problem in a familiar "point-and-click" CAD tool environment. The system guides the designer through the specification procedure, suggesting, for example, that slew constraints be added each time an output delay measurement is added. The final tuned transistor widths as well as corresponding circuit delays can be back-annotated onto the schematic. All the tuning criteria are stored as attributes of the schematic, so that in the event of a technology re-map, new device models, new loading information or new timing requirements, the circuit can be re-tuned at the push of a button, facilitating design re-use.

4.2 Implementation

Some special considerations that were taken into account during the implementation of the adjoint Lagrangian formulation are listed in this section.

Sorting of pulses and impulses. Once the nominal simulation has been completed, the values of the measurements are known. Then the excitations for the adjoint circuit are created. The pulses and impulses of the adjoint circuit are appropriately scaled and sorted in reverse time order to be applied to the adjoint circuit in an event-driven manner. Event-driven techniques are used both to analyze the adjoint circuit and to carry out the necessary convolutions. In SPECS, the convolutions are typically between piecewise linear and piecewise constant waveforms[4,5,14]. To speed up the adjoint analysis, the time origin is shifted to the time of the first externally applied excitation to the adjoint circuit. Once all the excitations of the adjoint circuit have been applied, a faster convolution algorithm is employed since all waveforms are piecewise constant from that time onwards.

Multiple adjoint Lagrangian groups. SPECS allows multiple "adjoint Lagrangian groups," each of which contains a weighted sum of measurements as the sensitivity function of interest. The adjoint circuit is analyzed as many times as the number of groups, and one set of gradients is reported for each group. Multiple groups are necessary for Hessian computation (see below).

Scaling of the adjoint circuit excitations. Once the transient simulation has been completed in a new optimization iteration, the measurement values from SPECS are fed to JiffyTune. LANCELOT uses the measurement values to update its merit function and decides whether to accept the proposed step. If the step is rejected, gradient computation is skipped. If the step is accepted, LANCELOT provides to JiffyTune the values of the slack variables, Lagrange multipliers, penalty parameter and scale factors. It is important that these values be provided *after* any initializations, spacer steps[30] or two-step updates[27] in the optimizer, since these updates can change the optimizer variables which contribute to the merit function whose gradients are desired. JiffyTune uses these values to determine the scale factor h_k to be applied for each measurement which is in the form $h_k = l_k + \sum_{i=1}^{M} n_{ki} m_i$ where l_k and n_{ki} are elements of a vector and sparse matrix that are created as a result of all the chain ruling described in Section 3.0.

Hybrid scheme for the computation of the Hessian. LANCELOT builds a quadratic model of the merit function at each iteration. The Hessian matrix is built up by low-rank quasi-Newton update methods such as the SR1 or BFGS[25] method. For a quadratic function $f(x)$ we have, for any direction d, $\nabla^2 f(x) d = \nabla f(x+d) - \nabla f(x)$. Analogously, the quasi-Newton condition maintains an approximate Hessian B satisfying $Bd = \gamma$, where γ is the appropriate gradient difference. The idea of a low rank update is to modify B with new gradient difference information at moderate cost, while maintaining the quasi-Newton condition.

In "minor iterations" of LANCELOT, only the problem variables and slacks change. In "major" iterations terminated by sufficient stationarity, either the penalty parameter μ or the Lagrange multipliers λ change, depending on whether sufficient feasibility has been achieved on the inner unconstrained problem. The merit function that LANCELOT builds is $\Phi = f(x) + \sum_i \lambda_i c_i(x) + \frac{1}{2\mu} \sum_i c_i^2(x)$, where f is the objective function and c_i are the constraints. Hence the Hessian is given by

$$\nabla^2 \Phi = \nabla^2 f + \sum_i \lambda_i \nabla^2 c_i + \frac{1}{\mu} \sum_i \left(c_i \nabla^2 c_i + \nabla c_i \nabla c_i^T \right). \quad (7)$$

At each minor iteration and at the start of each major iteration where λ s are changed, low-rank quasi-Newton updates are used on the approximation of $\nabla^2 \Phi$. However, whenever a major iteration begins for which μ is changed, $B_{k+1} = B_k + \left(\frac{1}{\mu_{new}} - \frac{1}{\mu_{old}} \right) \sum_i \left(\nabla c_i \nabla c_i^T \right)$ is used to incrementally update the Hessian approximation. Hence, in this situation, the gradients of each constraint are required. Since each constraint may in turn depend on multiple measurements, multiple "adjoint Lagrangian groups" are used in SPECS. Thus a *hybrid scheme* is employed wherein adjoint Lagrangian gradient computation is used with just one group at every minor iteration and at the start of every major iteration where λ s are changed, but an adjoint analysis with as many groups as the number of constraints is used at the start of each major iteration when μ has changed. Although the latter is more expensive, the reduction in iterations due to starting such major iterations with a better Hessian approximation makes up for the added computational cost. As an initial approximation at the first iteration, $\nabla^2 f$ and $\nabla^2 c_i$ are taken to be zero, and $\nabla c_i \nabla c_i^T$ is computed explicitly from the gradients of the constraints.

Hessian updates with respect to slack variables. By taking advantage of the form in which slack variables occur in the augmented Lagrangian, the Hessian entries with respect to slack variables can be explicitly computed. However, using explicitly computed values violates the quasi-Newton condition[25] when standard Hessian update formulas are used. Hence, we have developed modified update formulas which satisfy both the quasi-Newton condition and allow us to assign explicitly computed Hessian entries. For example, consider a problem with one inequality constraint c and objective function f. The augmented Lagrangian function Φ is given by $\Phi = f(x) + \lambda(c(x) + s) + \frac{1}{2\mu}(c(x) + s)^2$, where s is the slack variable. Clearly $\nabla_s^2 \Phi = \frac{1}{\mu}$. If this is applied after the regular Hessian updates, the quasi-Newton condition will be violated. Instead, in general, we use the rank-two update

$$B_{k+1} = B_k + \frac{1}{v_k^T E s_k} \left[(y_k - B_k s_k) v_k^T E + E v_k (y_k - B_k s_k)^T \right] - \frac{(y_k - B_k s_k)^T s_k}{\left(v_k^T E s_k \right)^2} E v_k (E v_k)^T, \quad (8)$$

where at the ith iteration, B_i is the Hessian approximation, y_i is the change in $\nabla \Phi$, s_i is the step and E is a diagonal matrix with a zero on the diagonal corresponding to each slack variable and one otherwise. This update formula preserves the quasi-Newton condition[25]. If the entries of the Hessian approximation with respect to the slack variables are correctly set in B_0, then the update formula (8) guarantees that they remain correctly set after each update. By choosing v_k as one of $(y_k - B_k s_k)$, s_k and y_k, we obtain modified SR1 (Symmetric rank-1), PSB (Powell-symmetric-Broyden) and DFP (Davidon-Fletcher-Powell) Hessian updates, respectively. By adding the term $-\left(s_k^T E B_k s_k\right) w_k w_k^T$ to the modified DFP update where $w_k = E\left(\frac{1}{y_k^T E s_k} y_k - \frac{1}{s_k^T E B_k s_k} B_k s_k\right)$, we obtain the modified BFGS (Broyden-Fletcher-Goldfarb-Shanno) update[25]. Since the minimax auxiliary variables z also appear quadratically in the augmented Lagrangian, a similar Hessian update can be derived to include them.

5.0 Results

JiffyTune has been used to tune a number of high-performance circuits, as reported in[12]. First, results on gradient computation are presented, followed by circuit optimization results using the new method of gradient computation.

5.1 Gradient computation

The adjoint Lagrangian formulation was first tested on a

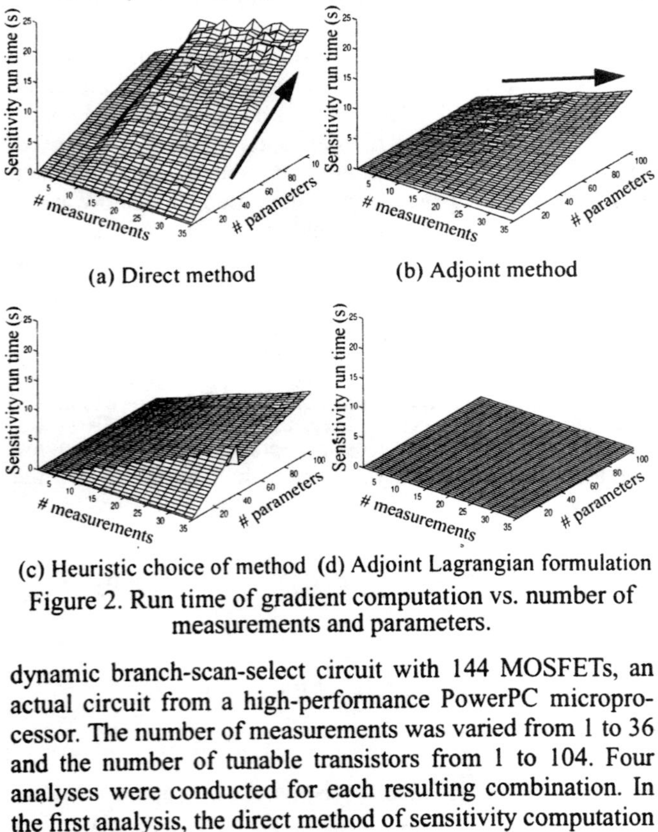

(a) Direct method (b) Adjoint method

(c) Heuristic choice of method (d) Adjoint Lagrangian formulation

Figure 2. Run time of gradient computation vs. number of measurements and parameters.

dynamic branch-scan-select circuit with 144 MOSFETs, an actual circuit from a high-performance PowerPC microprocessor. The number of measurements was varied from 1 to 36 and the number of tunable transistors from 1 to 104. Four analyses were conducted for each resulting combination. In the first analysis, the direct method of sensitivity computation was used. The run time of sensitivity computation as a function of the number of measurements and parameters is shown in Figure 2(a). The incremental cost of each additional sensitivity parameter is quite high (see the arrow in Figure 2(a)), as predicted by the theory. Figure 2(b) shows the run time using the adjoint method, computing the gradients of individual measurements. Again, as indicated by the arrow, the growth of run time with each additional measurement is quite high. In Figure 2(c), the run time of our previous production version is shown, in which a heuristic is used to pick the sensitivity analysis method. If the number of parameters is more than three times the number of measurements, the adjoint method is chosen. The figure shows a ridge where the program switched from the direct to the adjoint method. Finally, Figure 2(d) shows the run time of the adjoint Lagrangian formulation wherein a single adjoint analysis was used to compute the gradients of the merit function with respect to all parameters. Figure 2 clearly demonstrates not only the speedup obtained by the adjoint Lagrangian method, but also *the relatively slow growth of run time with respect to the number of parameters and number of measurements.*

The adjoint Lagrangian formulation was tested on a set of 16 benchmark circuits, whose characteristics are shown in Table 1. An adjoint sensitivity analysis was performed on each circuit to compute the individual gradients of measurements. Then the sensitivity analysis was repeated with an adjoint Lagrangian formulation, using a set of weights to form a linear combination of the measurements, as shown earlier. The gradients of the former analysis were combined in a post-processing step using the same weights, to compose the gradients of the composite merit function. The two sets of gradients were then compared. Across all the circuits, a total of 707,081 gradients were compared with the worst inaccuracy among all these gradients between regular adjoint analysis and adjoint Lagrangian analysis being 5.8e-12 (in units of either ns/μ or mW/μ), showing that the adjoint Lagrangian formulation does indeed produce the same results.

TABLE 1. Characteristics of benchmark circuits.

Name	# MOS	# Ind. par.	# Dep. par.	# Meas.	#Constraints	Obj. func. ?	Minimax ?
lau	24	4	16	3	1	Y	N
morrill	8	3	3	2	1	N	N
davies	235	15	87	2	1	Y	N
durham	204	11	2	4	2	N	N
Novpow	17	4	0	3	1	Y	N
fleischer	228	104	80	5	5	Y	Y
clkgen	28	17	10	6	5	N	N
Nov01	17	4	0	6	4	N	N
nor_xor	15	9	2	16	8	Y	Y
delay	70	16	48	33	17	N	N
hot	70	16	48	33	17	N	N
cold	70	16	48	33	17	N	N
delay_minmx	70	16	48	33	17	Y	Y
hot_minmx	70	16	48	33	17	Y	Y
cold_minmx	70	16	48	33	17	Y	Y
IOmux	6,900	60	4,068	82	41	Y	Y

The run times and speedups for gradient computation alone and for simulation combined with gradient computation per iteration are shown in Table 2 and graphically in Figure 3. All CPU times in this paper are on an IBM RISC System/6000 model 590 workstation. Unlike in Table 1, the number of measurements in Table 2 and Figure 3 excluded delay measurements on primary inputs whose gradients are known to be 0. A speedup of up to 36x is observed on circuits with a large number of measurements, which then leads to a speedup of up to 4.2x per iteration of JiffyTune. Figure 3 shows the speedup of simulation combined with gradient computation, speedup of just the gradient computation and the number of non-trivial measurements in each benchmark. From the discussion of Section 3.0, the number of measurements is an upper bound on the practically achievable speedup. On some of the smaller examples, a speedup higher than the theoretically predicted speedup is due to the granularity of CPU time measurements.

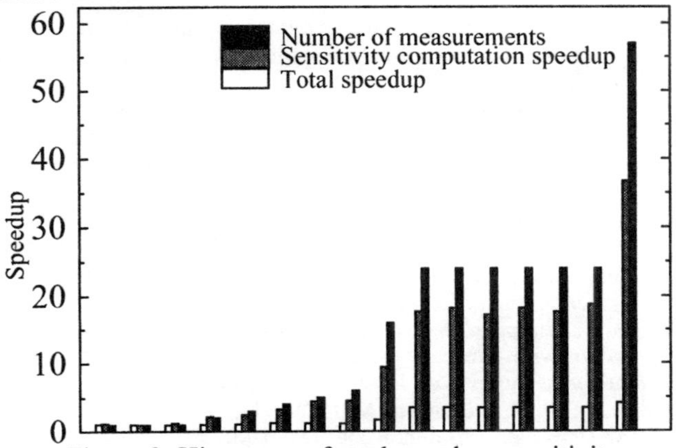

Figure 3. Histogram of total speedup, sensitivity

5.2 Circuit optimization

The benchmark circuits of Table 1 were optimized using the adjoint Lagrangian formulation and the new method of Hessian updates. As indicated in Section 4.2, a hybrid scheme was employed. The speedups shown in the last column of Table 2 are eroded during the optimization procedure due to an increased number of iterations and to various overheads and tasks that are common to the old and new implementations. Furthermore, because of the hybrid scheme, a "group" adjoint Lagrangian formulation is used for some major iterations. However, some gains in CPU time were observed with little loss in the quality of results. The real benefit of the adjoint Lagrangian formulation is seen in large problems, particularly problems with a large number of measurements. The results of optimizing the IOmux circuit of Tables 1 and 2 are presented in more detail below.

The IOmux circuit tuning problem was formulated as an area minimization with 41 timing constraints and a high weight on the area objective function. The area (approximated by the sum of the transistor widths) began at 31, 128 μm. The measurement-at-a-time adjoint method reduced the area to 14, 065 μm in the course of 30 optimization iterations. The total CPU time required was 270.7 minutes, consisting of 83.4 minutes of transient simulation and 187.3 CPU minutes of gradient evaluation time. With the adjoint Lagrangian formulation, after 30 iterations, the area was 15, 188 μm and the sum of the constraint violations is reduced by 20%. The run time is reduced to a total of 108.3 minutes, consisting of 83.2 minutes of transient simulation CPU time and 25.1 minutes of gradient evaluation time. Thus, the overall speedup in the optimization was 2.5x, while the speedup in the total gradient computation portion is 7.5x. Thus the gradient computation bottleneck has been effectively addressed, leaving the transient simulation as the dominant portion of the total run time!

TABLE 2. Sensitivity computation and total speedups.

Name	# MOS	# Meas.	#Pa-rs.	Sens.CPU time(s) Adj-oint	Adj. Lag.	Sens. speed-up	TotalCPU time (s) Adj-oint	Adj. Lag.	Total speed-up
lau	24	1	20	0.12	0.1	1.2	1.42	1.3	1.1
morrill	8	1	6	0.01	0.01	1.0	0.27	0.26	1.0
davies	235	1	102	0.58	0.48	1.2	12.4	12.8	0.97
durham	204	2	13	0.46	0.21	2.2	5.86	5.63	1.0
Novpow	17	3	4	0.05	0.02	2.5	0.47	0.43	1.1
fleischer	228	4	184	1.91	0.58	3.3	5.98	4.77	1.3
clkgen	28	5	27	0.31	0.07	4.4	1.3	1.05	1.2
Nov01	17	6	4	0.09	0.02	4.5	0.51	0.44	1.2
nor_xor	15	16	11	0.66	0.07	9.4	1.83	1.07	1.7
delay	70	24	64	6.2	0.35	17.7	8.15	2.32	3.5
hot	70	24	64	6.2	0.34	18.2	8.14	2.32	3.5
cold	70	24	64	6.19	0.36	17.2	8.12	2.32	3.5
delay _minmx	70	24	64	6.2	0.34	18.2	8.14	2.33	3.5
hot _minmx	70	24	64	6.19	0.35	17.7	8.12	2.34	3.5
cold _minmx	70	24	64	6.19	0.33	18.8	8.13	2.33	3.5
IOmux	6,900	57	4,128	690	18.8	36.7	882	210	4.2

In the above example, the adjoint Lagrangian formulation reduced the CPU time of the circuit optimization from more than $4\frac{1}{2}$ hours to under 2 hours. This speedup is expected to improve further as the method is applied to larger circuits, thus rendering such optimizations feasible. Further, the adjoint Lagrangian formulation allows additional constraints at a relatively low incremental cost. This feature has a significant methodology impact, particularly for self-timed and dynamic circuits in which the number of timing "checks" that have to be satisfied during tuning can be very large.

6.0 Conclusions

An adjoint Lagrangian formulation for the computation of circuit gradients was proposed. For the purposes of optimization, the gradients of an augmented Lagrangian merit function can be computed in a single adjoint analysis, irrespective of the number of parameters or measurements.

Speedups of over 30x were demonstrated in the gradient computation procedure, thus addressing the bottleneck in circuit optimization programs. This gradient computation scheme has been used in JiffyTune, a dynamic circuit optimization tool, and circuits with up to 6,900 transistors have been tuned in under two hours of CPU time. The low incremental cost of additional constraints makes the optimizer amenable to tuning dynamic circuits, which typically have a large number of timing constraints. Improved methods for performing Hessian updates and better stopping criteria are currently being investigated to enhance the efficiency of the circuit optimization.

7.0 Acknowledgments

The authors would like to thank Ali Sadigh, Abe Elfadel and the reviewers for their suggestions on this manuscript.

8.0 Bibliography

[1] S. W. Director and R. A. Rohrer, "The generalized adjoint network and network sensitivities," *IEEE Trans. on Circuit Theory*, Vol. CT-16, No. 3, August 1969, pp. 318-323.

[2] D. A. Hocevar, P. Yang, T. N. Trick and B. D. Epler, "Transient sensitivity computation for MOSFET circuits," *IEEE Trans. on CAD of ICs and Systems*, Vol. CAD-4, No. 4, October 1985, pp. 609-620.

[3] R. K. Brayton and R. Spence, *Sensitivity and optimization*, Elsevier Scientific Publishing Co., Amsterdam, The Netherlands, CAD of Electronic Circuits, Vol. 21980.

[4] T. V. Nguyen, P. Feldmann, S. W. Director and R. A. Rohrer, "SPECS simulation validation with efficient transient sensitivity computation," *IEEE Int. Conf. on CAD*, November 1989, pp. 252-255.

[5] P. Feldmann, T. V. Nguyen, S. W. Director and R. A. Rohrer, "Sensitivity computation in piecewise approximate circuit simulation," *IEEE Trans. on CAD of ICs and Systems*, Vol. 10, No. 2, February 1991, pp. 171-183.

[6] C. Visweswariah and R. A. Rohrer, "Piecewise approximate circuit simulation," *IEEE Trans. on CAD of ICs and Systems*, Vol. 10, No. 7, July 1991, pp. 861-870.

[7] R. D. Kimmel, "AS/X user's guide," Tech. report, IBM GTD, Hopewell Junction, NY, August 1989.

[8] W. T. Weeks, "AS/X theory manual," Tech. report, IBM GTD, Hopewell Junction, NY, September 1989.

[9] C. Visweswariah and J. A. Wehbeh, "Incremental event-driven simulation of digital FET circuits," *Proc. 1993 Design Automation Conference*, June 1993, pp. 737-741.

[10] W. Nye, D. C. Riley, A. Sangiovanni-Vincentelli and A. L. Tits, "DELIGHT.SPICE: An optimization-based system for the design of integrated circuits," *IEEE Trans. on CAD of ICs and Systems*, Vol. CAD-7, No. 4, April 1988, pp. 501-519.

[11] J. P. Fishburn and A. E. Dunlop, "TILOS: A posynomial programming approach to transistor sizing," *IEEE Int. Conf. on CAD*, November 1985, pp. 326-328.

[12] A. R. Conn, P. K. Coulman, R. A. Haring, G. L. Morrill and C. Visweswariah, "Optimization of custom MOS circuits by transistor sizing," *IEEE Int. Conf. on CAD*, November 1996, pp. 174-180.

[13] A. R. Conn, N. I. M. Gould and Ph. L. Toint, *LANCELOT: A Fortran Package for Large-Scale Nonlinear Optimization (Release A)*, Springer Verlag, 1992.

[14] T. V. Nguyen, "Transient sensitivity computation and applications," Tech. report CMUCAD-91-40, Carnegie Mellon University, 1991.

[15] N. Menezes, R. Baldick and L. T. Pileggi, "A sequential quadratic programming approach to concurrent gate and wire sizing," *IEEE Int. Conf. on CAD*, November 1995, pp. 144-151.

[16] J.-M. Shyu and A. Sangiovanni-Vincentelli, "ECSTASY: a new environment for IC design optimization," *IEEE Int. Conf. on CAD*, November 1988, pp. 484-487.

[17] S. S. Sapatnekar and W. Chuang, "Power vs. delay in gate sizing: conflicting objectives?," *IEEE Int. Conf. on CAD*, November 1995, pp. 463-466.

[18] M. D. Matson and L. A. Glasser, "Macromodeling and optimization of digital MOS VLSI circuits," *IEEE Trans. on CAD of ICs and Systems*, Vol. CAD-5, No. 4, October 1986, pp. 659-678.

[19] P. K. Sancheti and S. S. Sapatnekar, "Optimal design of macrocells for low power and high speed," *IEEE Trans. on CAD of ICs and Systems*, Vol. CAD-15, No. 9, September 1996, pp. 1160-1166.

[20] R. K. Brayton, G. D. Hachtel and A. L. Sangiovanni-Vincentelli, "A survey of optimization techniques for integrated-circuit design," *Proc. of the IEEE*, Vol. 69, No. 10, October 1981, pp. 1334-1362.

[21] A. R. Conn, N. I. M. Gould and Ph. L. Toint, "Global convergence of a class of trust region algorithms for optimization with simple bounds," *SIAM J. on Numerical Analysis*, Vol. 25, 1988, pp. 433-460, See also same J., pp. 764-767, volume 26, 1989.

[22] A. R. Conn, N. I. M. Gould and Ph. L. Toint, "A globally convergent augmented Lagrangian algorithm for optimization with general constraints and simple bounds," *SIAM J. on Numerical Analysis*, Vol. 28, No. 2, 1991, pp. 545-572.

[23] R. B. Hitchcock, Sr., G. L. Smith and D. D. Cheng, "Timing analysis of computer hardware," *IBM J. of Research and Development*, January 1982, pp. 100-105.

[24] W. C. Elmore, "The transient analysis of damped linear networks with particular regard to wideband amplifiers," *J. of Applied Physics*, Vol. 19, No. 1, 1948, pp. 55-63.

[25] P. E. Gill, W. Murray and M. H. Wright, *Practical optimization*, Academic Press, London and New York, 1981.

[26] R. Fletcher, *Practical methods of optimization*, John Wiley and Sons, Chichester, 1987.

[27] A. R. Conn, L. N. Vicente and C. Visweswariah, "Two-step algorithms for nonlinear optimization with structured applications," Res. report, IBM T.J. Watson Res. Ctr., Yorktown Heights, NY, 1997 (in preparation).

[28] B. D. H. Tellegen, "A general network theorem, with applications," *Philips Research Reports*, Vol. 7, 1952, pp. 259-269.

[29] Cadence Design Systems Inc., "Design Entry: Composer Users' Guide 4.3," 1994.

[30] D. P. Bertsekas, *Constrained Optimization and Lagrange Multipliers Methods*, Academic Press, London, 1982.

[31] M. R. Hestenes, "Multiplier and gradient methods," *J. of Optimization Theory and Applications*, Vol. 4, 1969, pp. 303-320.

[32] M. J. D. Powell, "A method for nonlinear constraints in minimization problems," in *Optimization*, R. Fletcher, ed., Academic Press, London and New York, 1969.

[33] G. D. Hachtel, R. K. Brayton, and F. G. Gustavson, "The sparse tableau approach to network analysis and design," *IEEE Trans. on Circuit Theory*, Vol. CT-18, No. 1, January 1971, pp. 101-113.

[34] R. K. Brayton and S. W. Director, "Computation of delay time sensitivities for use in time domain optimization," *IEEE Trans. on Circuits and Systems*, Vol. CAS-22, No. 12, December 1975, pp. 910-920.

State Transformation in Event Driven Explicit Simulation

Tuyen V. Nguyen and Anirudh Devgan
IBM Austin Research Laboratory
Austin, TX 78758
tuyenn;devgan@austin.ibm.com

Abstract

This paper presents a general method for incorporating state transformation in event driven explicit simulation. One inherent assumption in this type of simulation algorithm is the state independence which allows the algorithm to process the states independently in an event driven manner at the transistor level. Numerical problems arise when an inappropriate state representation of the circuit, in which the states are not truly independent, is chosen. In principle, any similarity transformation of the state equation can be employed to transform the circuit into a more convenient state space for numerical solution. This paper develops a systematic scheme to derive an appropriate state transformation, and to incorporate the state transformation in such a way to maintain the efficiency of event driven explicit simulation algorithms.

1. Introduction

With design trends continuously moving towards higher clock speed, higher density, and higher levels of integration on chip, the need for fast circuit simulation of large and complex integrated circuits is well known. There have been two major approaches in improving the efficiency of (circuit) transient simulation. Common to all approaches is the use of circuit partitioning and event driven simulation to exploit the spatial sparsity and the temporal latency of large circuits. One approach is to simplify circuit topology to a set of primitives, especially for MOS circuits, in addition to employing simplified device models, such as piecewise quadratic models, to derive the analytical solutions of the node voltages. This approach is embodied in the simulator ILLIADS [3]. The other major approach employs simplified device models to speed up the computation of the numerical solutions during a transient analysis. Piecewise constant (PWC) device models are employed in SPECS [4] and ADAPTS [5]. More general PWL models have been used in various timing analyzers and simulators [1][6]. The Adaptively Controlled Explicit Simulation (ACES) algorithm [2], has been developed to exploit the efficiency of explicit integration algorithm while ensuring the numerical stability of the integration at an incremental cost instead of the full cost of an implicit algorithm. The basic idea is to incrementally approach the steady state while ensuring the stability and efficiency of the integration algorithm.

In event driven simulation, an implicit assumption is that the states are independent so that they can be processed separately. If some of the states are strongly coupled or dependent, these states have to be processed as a group. In other words, the choice of the state variables for a state representation of a given circuit is not appropriate in the sense that the chosen states are not truly independent. This situation arises quite often in extracted circuits, which contain numerous parasitic resistors of small values. For example, given a resistor as shown in Fig. 1, the two capacitors at the two

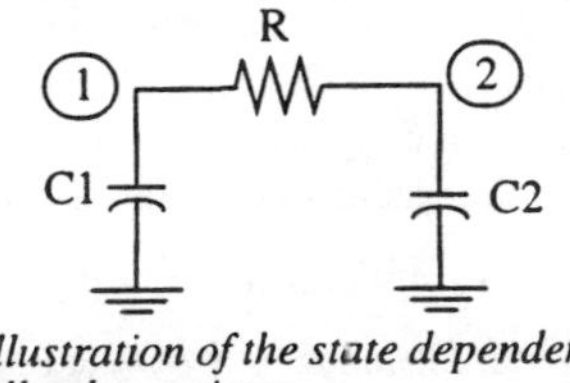

Fig. 1: *A simple illustration of the state dependency problem associated with a small value resistor*

nodes of the resistor are usually chosen to be the state variables in a typical circuit formulation such as Modified Nodal Analysis (MNA). In the degenerate case of a zero valued resistor or voltage source, the two states are actually the same. Even if the value of the resistance is very small, i.e. the two nodes close to being shorted, then the two chosen state variables are not truly independent. In the following, a number of numerical problems associated with the case of small resistors mentioned above are discussed.

Matrix ill-conditioning

The first one is the numerical ill conditioning problem due to the resistor being stamped into the MNA circuit matrix equation as a conductance term with $G = 1/R$ in the admittance form

$$i_R = Gv_R = G(v_1 - v_2).$$

The reason that resistors are stamped as conductors is to avoid introducing extra unknowns into the MNA matrix equation, in which the capacitor voltages and inductor currents are chosen as state variables. However, if R is small, then G is large and it may degrade the numerical conditioning of the matrix equation. One way to avoid this problem is to stamp the resistor in its impedance form as

$$v_R - Ri_R = v_1 - v_2 - Ri_R = 0$$

Note that this impedance form introduces the extra unknown current variable i_R into the matrix equation. Note further that this stamping does not address the state dependency problem though it may alleviate the numerical conditioning problem.

State Dependency in Explicit Simulation

The state dependency problem is evident in explicit integration algorithm such as Forward Euler (FE). Given the Branch Constitutive Relation (BCR) of a capacitor as $i_C = C\dot{v}_C$, the FE stamp of the capacitor at each time t is given by

$$v_C(t) = v_C(t - \Delta t) + \frac{\Delta t}{C} i_C(t - \Delta t)$$

where $t - \Delta t$ is the previous time point and Δt is the time step. The above equation represents the BCR of a voltage source, and the

1092-3152/97 $10.00 © 1997 IEEE

equivalent circuit of the simple structure shown in Fig. 1 using FE integration is shown in Fig. 2 below. As illustrated by Fig. 2, if R is

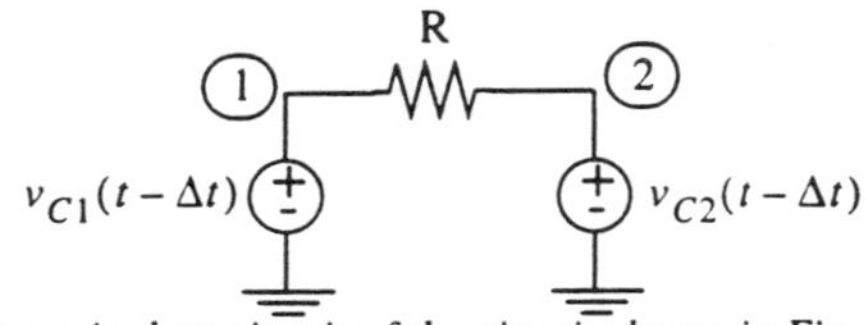

Fig. 2:*The equivalent circuit of the circuit shown in Fig. 1 at time t using an explicit (Forward Euler) integration for the capacitors.*

small or zero in the degenerate case, the equivalent circuit includes an illegal loop of voltage sources. This state dependency problem will affect any explicit integration algorithm that simply update the capacitor voltages at a given time using only values at previous time points.

State Dependency in Implicit Simulation

The problem of state dependency is handled automatically in an implicit integration scheme because all the states are "implicitly" processed together at the same time. For example, using Backward Euler (BE) as the implicit integration scheme, the stencil of a capacitor in the MNA matrix equation at each time t can be written as

$$v_C(t) = \frac{\Delta t}{C} i_C(t) + v_C(t - \Delta t) = G_{eq} i_C(t) + V_{eq}$$

In circuit theoretic terms, this equation represents an equivalent circuit consisting of a resistor with conductance $G_{eq} = (\Delta t)/C$ in series with a voltage source $V_{eq} = v_C(t - \Delta t)$. Using these equivalent circuits for the two capacitors, the circuit shown in Fig. 1 can be redrawn as shown in Fig. 3 below. In this case, even if $R = 0$, the

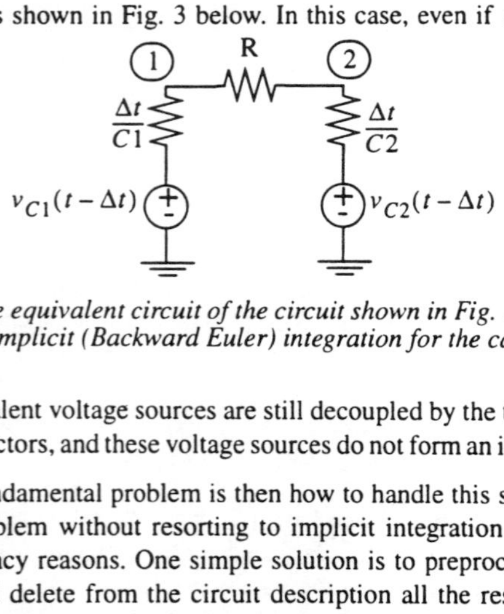

Fig. 3:*The equivalent circuit of the circuit shown in Fig. 1 at time t using an implicit (Backward Euler) integration for the capacitors*

two equivalent voltage sources are still decoupled by the two equivalent conductors, and these voltage sources do not form an illegal loop.

The fundamental problem is then how to handle this state dependency problem without resorting to implicit integration algorithms for efficiency reasons. One simple solution is to preprocess a given circuit and delete from the circuit description all the resistors with small values below a specified tolerance. However, this approach may require setting different tolerances for different circuit configurations. Moreover, in some cases, it may be necessary to retain these small resistors in the circuit description. For example, given a long RC interconnect with many taps along the interconnect, it is necessary to retain the small resistors in each RC section of the interconnect to get the total resistance loading of the line. This problem obviates the need to develop an algorithmic approach, other than circuit pruning, to handle this problem. It is the goal of this paper to present such an approach using the event driven Adaptively Controlled Explicit Simulation (ACES) algorithm as an implementation vehicle. This paper is organized as follows. In section 2 of the paper, a simple example is presented to review the basic ACES algorithm as an implementation vehicle and illustrate the numerical problems due to state dependency. The main results of the paper are presented in section 3. This section discusses a general and systematic method to incorporate state transformation into event driven explicit simulation, especially its implementation in ACES. Section 4 presents some additional examples and simulation results on real circuits using state transformation. Section 5 summarizes the paper.

2. State Dependency in Event Driven Explicit Simulation

Consider a simple 2RC circuit as shown in Fig. 4 This simple exam-

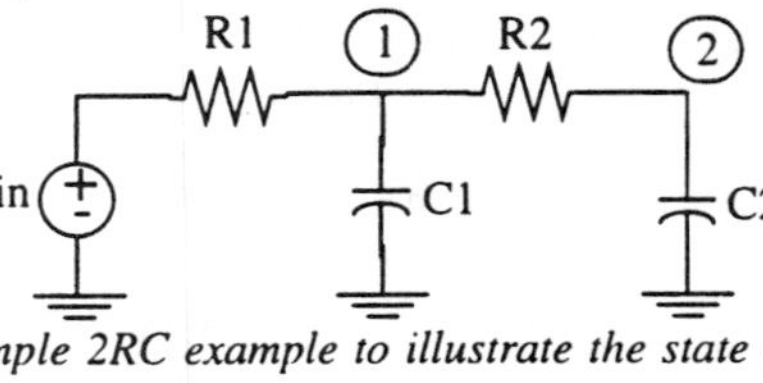

Fig. 4: *A simple 2RC example to illustrate the state dependency problem*

ple is used to review the basic ACES algorithm and to illustrate the problem of state dependence. The state equation of the circuit can be written as

$$\begin{bmatrix} C_1 & 0 \\ 0 & C_2 \end{bmatrix} \begin{bmatrix} \dot{v}_1 \\ \dot{v}_2 \end{bmatrix} = \begin{bmatrix} -\left(\frac{1}{R_1} + \frac{1}{R_2}\right) & \frac{1}{R_2} \\ \frac{1}{R_2} & -\frac{1}{R_2} \end{bmatrix} \begin{bmatrix} v_1 \\ v_2 \end{bmatrix} + \begin{bmatrix} 1 \\ 0 \end{bmatrix} V_{in} \quad (1)$$

where the capacitor voltages have been chosen to be the state variables. Let V_{in} be a unit step function, $C_1 = C_2 = 1F$, $R_1 = 1\Omega$, and $R_2 = 10^{-6}\Omega$. Then the state equation can be written as

$$\begin{bmatrix} \dot{v}_1 \\ \dot{v}_2 \end{bmatrix} = \begin{bmatrix} -(1 + 10^6) & 10^6 \\ 10^6 & -10^6 \end{bmatrix} \begin{bmatrix} v_1 \\ v_2 \end{bmatrix} + \begin{bmatrix} 1 \\ 0 \end{bmatrix} V_{in} \quad (2)$$

Assume that the circuit is initially at rest, i.e $v_1 = v_2 = 0$ at $t = 0$. Also assume a unit step input, i. e. $V_{in} = 1$ and $\dot{V}_{in} = 0$ at $t = 0^+$. Then, applying the ACES algorithm to compute the time to quiescence [2] for the two states yields $\Delta t_1 = -(\dot{v}_1(0))/(\ddot{v}_1(0)) \approx 10^{-6}$ and $\Delta t_2 = 0$, which implies that the input excitation has not reached the second node at this time point. In other words, one is interested only in non-zero time step at each time point. Hence, $\Delta t = \Delta t_1 = 10^{-6}$.

Continue the ACES algorithm to the next time point, $t_1 = t_0 + \Delta t = 10^{-6}$. Note that v_1 is now in quiescence and it should not dictate the computation of the next time step. Hence the time to quiescence for v_2 is given by

$$\hat{\Delta t} = -(\dot{v}_2(t_1))/(\ddot{v}_2(t_1)) = 1 + 10^{-6}.$$

Then, at the next time point, $t_2 = t_1 + \hat{\Delta t}$, both states will be quiescence and the simulation is completed. The result of this simple simulation for v_2 is shown in Fig. 5 together with the result obtained by AS/X, the IBM internal circuit simulator. Fig. 5 shows the result obtained by ACES with a voltage error tolerance $\varepsilon_v = 0.001$, where

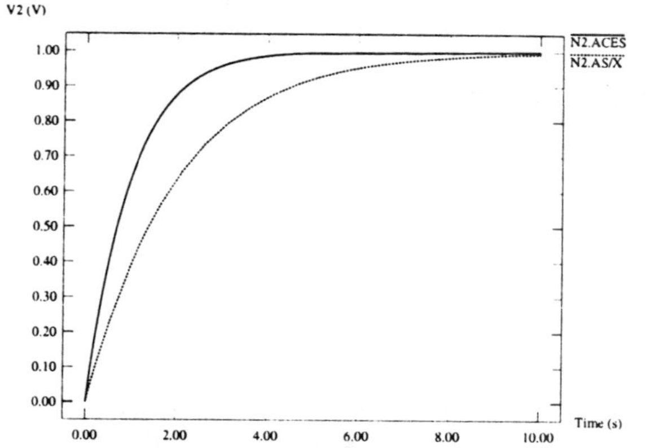

Fig. 5: *ACES simulation result (without state transformation) as compared to AS/X for the simple 2RC circuit shown in Fig. 4 with an error tolerance of 0.001.*

$\varepsilon_v = \frac{1}{2}\ddot{v}(\Delta t)^2$. Even with this fairly tight tolerance, the ACES result shows significant discrepancy as compared to the AS/X result. This problem is due to the fact that the two states are treated as independent and processed one at a time.

From the circuit point of view, when v_1 enters quiescence, ACES replaces C_1 by a zero valued current source, i. e. C_1 becomes an open circuit and the time constant of this new circuit is given by $\tau = (R_1 + R_2)C_2 = 1 + 10^{-6}$. This is exactly the time to quiescence or the time to steady state for this new circuit, assuming a first order approximation for v_2. However, this is not the correct time constant for the original circuit. Ignoring the effect of the small resistor R_2, the correct time constant is given by $\tau = R_1(C_1 + C_2) = 2$. This discrepancy illustrates the problem in assuming the independence of strongly coupled state variables.

In order to resolve this problem, an appropriate state space representation of the circuit must be chosen in such a way that the states of this space are truly independent. One obvious choice is the eigenspace of the circuit. Compute the eigen-decomposition of the system matrix as

$$A = \begin{bmatrix} -\left(\frac{1}{R_1} + \frac{1}{R_2}\right) & \frac{1}{R_2} \\ \frac{1}{R_2} & -\frac{1}{R_2} \end{bmatrix} = \begin{bmatrix} -(1 + 10^6) & 10^6 \\ 10^6 & -10^6 \end{bmatrix} \approx T\Lambda T^{-1} \quad (3)$$

where

$$T = \begin{bmatrix} \frac{1}{\sqrt{2}} & \frac{1}{\sqrt{2}} \\ -\frac{1}{\sqrt{2}} & \frac{1}{\sqrt{2}} \end{bmatrix}, T^{-1} = \begin{bmatrix} \frac{1}{\sqrt{2}} & -\frac{1}{\sqrt{2}} \\ \frac{1}{\sqrt{2}} & \frac{1}{\sqrt{2}} \end{bmatrix}, \text{and } \Lambda = \begin{bmatrix} -2(10^6) & 0 \\ 0 & -0.5 \end{bmatrix} \quad (4)$$

Define the transformed state variables as $\begin{bmatrix} y_1 & y_2 \end{bmatrix}^T = T^{-1}\begin{bmatrix} v_1 & v_2 \end{bmatrix}^T$. The transformed state equation can then be written as

$$\begin{bmatrix} \dot{y}_1 \\ \dot{y}_2 \end{bmatrix} = \Lambda \begin{bmatrix} y_1 \\ y_2 \end{bmatrix} + T\begin{bmatrix} 1 \\ 0 \end{bmatrix} V_{in} = \Lambda \begin{bmatrix} y_1 \\ y_2 \end{bmatrix} + \begin{bmatrix} 1/\sqrt{2} \\ 1/\sqrt{2} \end{bmatrix} V_{in} \quad (5)$$

Now apply the ACES algorithm to this system. At $t = 0$, $y_1 = y_2 = 0$. From the state equations, it can be seen that $\dot{y}_1 \neq 0$, $\dot{y}_2 \neq 0$, $\ddot{y}_1 \neq 0$, and $\ddot{y}_2 \neq 0$. Hence the time step can be computed as

$$\Delta t = min(\Delta t_1, \Delta t_2) = min\left(-\frac{\dot{y}_1}{\ddot{y}_1}, -\frac{\dot{y}_2}{\ddot{y}_2}\right) = \frac{1}{2}(10^{-6})$$

At the next time point $t_1 = \Delta t = 0.5(10^{-6})$, $\dot{y}_1 = \ddot{y}_2 = 0$. Hence y_1 will stay in quiescence and the time to quiescence for y_2 can be computed as

$$\hat{\Delta t} = -\frac{\dot{y}_2}{\ddot{y}_2} = 0.5$$

In this case, the ACES algorithm captures the correct time constant of the original circuit. This simple example has clearly illustrated the need to select an appropriate state space in which the state variables are truly independent so that an event driven explicit algorithm such as ACES can be applied to provide accurate simulation results.

3. State Transformation for Event Driven Explicit Simulation

The eigen-space representation is an ideal space for event driven explicit simulation because the modes of the circuit are decoupled and can be processed sequentially. However, this approach is clearly impractical due to a number of reasons. First the computation of the eigen-decomposition is expensive. Moreover, once the eigen-decomposition is known, the solution can be computed directly without resorting to numerical integration. Avoiding the eigen-decomposition is exactly the goal of numerical integration algorithm. So the question is how to determine an appropriate state transformation. One possible approach is to perform an approximate or inexact eigen-computation. This alleviates the cost of a full eigen-computation. However, for non-linear circuits, an eigen-computation needs to be performed for every new linearization of the nonlinear equations. Another approach is to perform a partial eigen-computation. This is a basically a model reduction problem, especially for large linear circuits. This approach is a standard technique for reduced order modeling of large linear circuits in general nonlinear simulation of circuits with large linear subcircuits. The advantage of this approach is that it can prune out the non dominant eigen-states, such as the state due to the large eigenvalue $(2(10^6))$ in the 2RC example above. However, this approach is not practical for nonlinear circuits.

In general, there is a need to have a simple transformation matrix in order not to degrade the efficiency of event driven explicit simulation technique such as ACES. Note again that one key assumption of circuit level (not logic level or macromodel or block level) event driven simulation is that the states are independent or DC decoupled so that the excitation can be propagated from the input source to the various nodes in the circuit in an event driven manner. For example, the unit step excitation from the input source of the above 2RC circuit will propagate first to node 1, and then to node 2. However, when the two nodes are strongly DC coupled, the algorithm will yield erroneous results as discussed in the previous section. The key idea is to process the two states simultaneously. Note that the eigen-transformation described in the previous section transforms the input matrix

$\begin{bmatrix}1 & 0\end{bmatrix}^T$ to $\begin{bmatrix}1/\sqrt{2} & 1/\sqrt{2}\end{bmatrix}^T$. In the original state space, the input directly affects only v_1. In the transformed state space, the input directly affects both y_1 and y_2 simultaneously. Hence the key idea in constructing a simple transformation matrix is to make sure that all the transformed states will be dependent on all the original states. In this way, any input that affects at least one state in the original space will affect all the states in the transformed space. In this way, the set of coupled transformed states can be processed simultaneously during the "electrical" event propagation. For the 2RC circuit example, one such simple transformation matrix is given as

$$T = \begin{bmatrix}1 & -1 \\ 1 & 1\end{bmatrix} \quad (6)$$

This matrix looks like a simple scaling of the transformation matrix T^{-1} (the inverse eigenvector matrix) discussed in the previous section. In general, this is not the case. The transformation matrix in Eq. (6) is simply to make every transformed states dependent upon all the original state variables. In order to bring out the effect of the capacitor values, let 's choose $C_1 = 0.5$ and $C_2 = 2$. Also select the capacitor charges, denoted by q_1 and q_2 as the state variables in the original space, i. e. $\begin{bmatrix}q_1 & q_2\end{bmatrix}^T = \begin{bmatrix}C_1v_1 & C_2v_2\end{bmatrix}^T$. And the transformed state variables are defined as

$$\begin{bmatrix}y_1 \\ y_2\end{bmatrix} = T\begin{bmatrix}q_1 \\ q_2\end{bmatrix} = \begin{bmatrix}1 & -1 \\ 1 & 1\end{bmatrix}\begin{bmatrix}q_1 \\ q_2\end{bmatrix}$$

An ACES simulation is then performed for this circuit. Note that the times to quiescence (an "electrical" event in ACES) are computed for the transformed state variables. The local truncation error control is performed for the original state variables (the node voltages) in this case. The waveform at node 2 as obtained by the ACES simulation with state transformation is shown in Fig. 6 together with the AS/X simulation result. Note that the state transformation helps ensure the accuracy of ACES simulation.

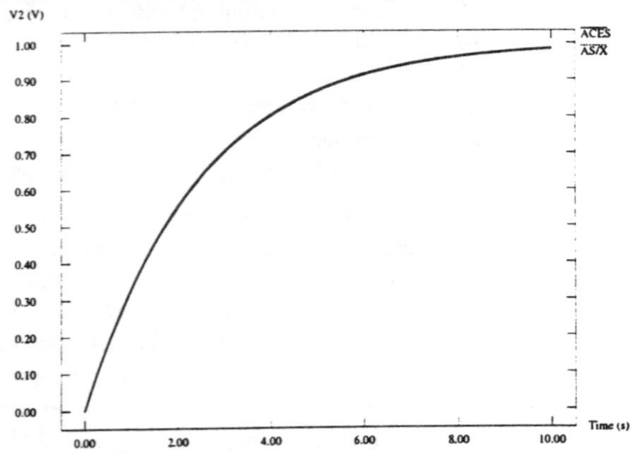

Fig. 6: *ACES simulation result (with state transformation) as compared to AS/X for the simple 2RC circuit shown in Fig. 4*

In general, if there are no coupling among the states, then the transformation matrix is simply an identity matrix. Suppose there are n coupled states, then the submatrix corresponding to these n states will be of the form

$$T_{nxn} = \begin{bmatrix}+1 & -1 & -1 & \dots & -1 \\ +1 & +1 & -1 & \dots & -1 \\ +1 & +1 & +1 & \dots & -1 \\ & & & \dots & \\ +1 & +1 & +1 & \dots & +1\end{bmatrix}$$

For example, given a circuit with 7 states among which there are two sets of coupled states: {2,3,4} and {6,7}, then the transformation matrix for this circuit can be written as

$$T = \begin{bmatrix}1 & 0 & 0 & 0 & 0 & 0 & 0 \\ 0 & 1 & -1 & -1 & 0 & 0 & 0 \\ 0 & 1 & 1 & -1 & 0 & 0 & 0 \\ 0 & 1 & 1 & 1 & 0 & 0 & 0 \\ 0 & 0 & 0 & 0 & 1 & 0 & 0 \\ 0 & 0 & 0 & 0 & 0 & 1 & -1 \\ 0 & 0 & 0 & 0 & 0 & 1 & 1\end{bmatrix}$$

This simple structure allows the transformation matrix to be constructed in a systematic manner during the processing of the circuit. For example, a simple two phase procedure to construct this type of transformation matrix can be described as follows. First initialize the transformation matrix T to be an identity matrix. Then in the first phase of processing the circuit, check if the terminals (which are assumed to be states for simplicity) or nodes of a given resistive element (or device) are coupled. If the nodes are coupled, then enter the appropriate nonzero entries, which corresponds to the indices of the nodes in the state vector, in the transformation matrix. The purpose of this phase is to record the coupling information in the matrix. In the second phase, the transformation matrix will be processed row by row to determine different groups of coupled states. Then the submatrices of the type described above for these groups of coupled states will be recorded in the transformation matrix.

The next question is how to incorporate state transformation into ACES. A straightforward approach is simply transform the original state equation into a new state equation and perform the analysis in the transformed space. However, it should be noted that the transformed space is used to compute the time to quiescence for the transformed states while the local truncation error is still performed in the original space. Therefore, it is simpler to impose the constitution relation or the quiescence condition for the transformed states in terms of the original states to solve for the necessary variables in the original space. Then the variables in the transformed space can be computed by applying the transformation matrix to the original states. These ideas will be illustrated below using a simple Modified Nodal Analysis (MNA) circuit formulation in the derivative space [2].

In order to simplify the presentation and to bring out the difference between the basic ACES algorithm and the modified algorithm to handle state transformation, assume that there are no inductors, current sources, floating capacitors, and floating voltage sources. These circuit elements can be incorporated into the formulation in a straightforward manner once the basic algorithm has been established. Under these assumptions, during a quiescence period [2], the MNA formulation of the circuit in the derivative space can be written as

$$\begin{bmatrix} G_{cc} & G_{cv} & E_{cc} & 0 \\ G_{vc} & G_{vv} & 0 & E_v \\ K_c & 0 & E_{qc} & 0 \\ 0 & U_v & 0 & 0 \end{bmatrix} \begin{bmatrix} \dot{v}_c \\ \dot{v}_v \\ \ddot{q}_c \\ \ddot{q}_v \end{bmatrix} = \begin{bmatrix} 0 \\ 0 \\ h_c \\ \dot{v}_v \end{bmatrix} \tag{7}$$

where G_{cc}, G_{cv}, G_{vc}, and G_{vv} are submatrices of the conductance matrix formed by resistive elements; E_{cc}, E_{qc}, E_v, and U_v are submatrices of 1's and 0's to pick out the appropriate capacitor/source voltages or currents; K_c and h_c represent the changeable portion of the MNA equation during the simulation depending upon whether the states are in quiescence or not. In general, the first two rows of Eq. (7) represents Kirchoff Current Law (KCL) equations at all voltage and capacitance nodes. The third row represents the Branch Constitutive Relations (BCR) and/or the quiescence conditions for the capacitors. The fourth row represents the BCRs for the voltage sources.

Now define the state transformation $y_c = Tq_c$. Initially when all the states are non-quiescent, the BCRs for the transformed states can be written as $\dot{y}_c = TC\dot{v}_c$. In circuit theoretic terms, the transformed states can be considered as voltage controlled current sources. In this case, the stamps in the MNA matrix of Eq.(7) can be set as follows: $K_c = TC$, $E_{qc} = 0$, and $h_c = \dot{y}_c$. Suppose at time t, the jth (transformed) state enters quiescence. Then $\ddot{y}_{cj}(t) = t_j^T\ddot{q}_c(t) = 0$ and the stamps in the MNA matrix can be modified as $k_{cj}^T = 0$, $e_{qc,j}^T = t_j^T$, and $h_{cj} = 0$, where t_j^T is the jth row of T, k_{cj}^T is the jth row of K_c, and $e_{qc,j}^T$ is the jth row of E_{qc}. In this case, the transformed state in quiescence can be treated as a zero valued current controlled current source. In this case, partition the vector of transformed states as

$$y_c = \begin{bmatrix} y_{cn} \\ y_{cs} \end{bmatrix} = \begin{bmatrix} T_n \\ T_s \end{bmatrix} q_c \tag{8}$$

where y_{cn} denotes the subvector of transformed states that are not in quiescence, and y_{cs} denotes the subvector of transformed states that are in quiescence; T_n and T_s are appropriate partitions of the transformation matrix T. Then the MNA equation as shown in Eq.(7) can be rewritten as

$$\begin{bmatrix} G_{cc} & G_{cv} & E_{cc} & 0 \\ G_{vc} & G_{vv} & 0 & E_v \\ T_nC & 0 & 0 & 0 \\ 0 & 0 & T_s & 0 \\ 0 & U_v & 0 & 0 \end{bmatrix} \begin{bmatrix} \dot{v}_c \\ \dot{v}_v \\ \ddot{q}_c \\ \ddot{q}_v \end{bmatrix} = \begin{bmatrix} 0 \\ 0 \\ \dot{y}_c \\ 0 \\ \dot{v}_v \end{bmatrix} \tag{9}$$

where the third row of Eq.(9) describes the non-quiescent transformed states, and the fourth row describes the quiescent transformed states. The modified ACES algorithm with state transformation is summarized in the pseudocode below.

Algorithm with state transformation:

1. Update sources

2. Update original state variables (for all states):
$\dot{q}_c(t-) = \dot{q}_c(t-\Delta t) + \ddot{q}_c(t-\Delta t)\Delta t$ *and*
$v_c(t-) = v_c(t-\Delta t) + \dot{v}_c(t-\Delta t)\Delta t$

2b. Update the transformed states:
$\dot{y}_c(t-) = T\dot{q}_c(t-)$ for quiescent states, and $\dot{y}_c(t-) = 0$ for quiescent states

3. Check quiescence conditions for y_c

4. Setup the MNA matrix and solve for $\dot{v}_c(t+)$, $\ddot{q}_c(t)$, *and* $\ddot{q}_v(t)$.

5. Compute $\dot{q}_c(t+) = C\dot{v}_c(t+)$ *and* $\ddot{v}_c(t) = C^{-1}\ddot{q}_c(t)$ *for all states*

5b. Compute $\dot{y}_c(t+) = T\dot{q}_c(t+)$ *and* $\ddot{y}_c(t) = T\ddot{q}_c(t)$ *for non-quiescent states*

6. Compute time to quiescence for non-quiescent states, $t_{qs} = -[\dot{y}_c(t)/(\ddot{y}_c(t))]$

7. Set $\Delta t = min(t_{qs})$

In the above algorithm, the quiescence conditions are checked for the transformed states, not the original states. The advantage of this algorithm is that there is no need to explicitly construct the transformed space. The solution procedure is still performed in the original space with minimal modification of the matrix equation to impose the BCRs and/or the quiescence conditions for the transformed states. In the next section, some examples will be presented to assess the overhead of the modified ACES algorithm and its accuracy as compared with the basic ACES algorithm.

4. Examples

The first example is a simple nonlinear circuit consisting of a driver driving four buffers. Each connection between the driver and a given buffer is an 8 RC interconnect model. The schematic of the circuit is shown in Fig. 7. This example is to illustrate the complication due to circuit partitioning which may couple a port to an internal state of a given partition. This situation arises when parasitic resistances are added to the terminals of a MOSFET model. For example, there are five partitions P1 to P5 in the circuit shown in Fig. 7. Ports numbered 1 to 3 will be coupled to the internal states of partition P1 if the resistor at the end of the lines T1 to T3 are shorted. In a standard ACES algorithm, a partition is processed only if a port attached to the partition has an event. A port event is initiated when the volt-

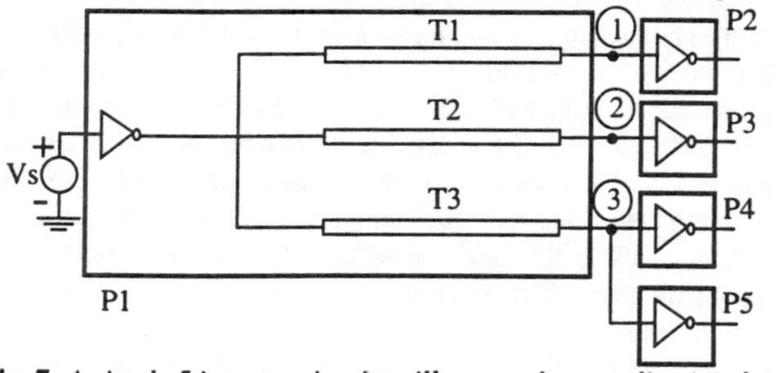

Fig. 7: *A simple 5 inverter circuit to illustrate the complication due to circuit partitioning when using state transformation*

age slope at the port has an appreciable change. Otherwise, the partition is not processed even if the port information is updated when another partition connected to the same port has an event. For example, assume partition P2 has an event at a given time point. In processing partition P2, the voltage and the slope at port 1 will be updated. If the slope has a significant change (above a given tolerance), then partition P1 will be processed at the same event time. Otherwise, P1 will not be processed. However, in the case port 1 is coupled to an internal state of P1, P1 will have to be processed regardless of whether P1 has a significant change in voltage slope or not. This processing is necessary to take the coupling into account when computing all the necessary information for the next event. A sample run is performed for this circuit with the first, last, and two middle resistors of the lines are shorted to produce different modes of coupling among the internal states and the ports of P1. In this case, the ACES simulation without state transformation requires 309718 events and 34.36 CPU seconds. The ACES simulation with state transformation requires only 3822 events and 2.77 CPU seconds. The ACES simulation results are compared with AS/X simulations and shown in Fig. 8 at the output of partition P2.

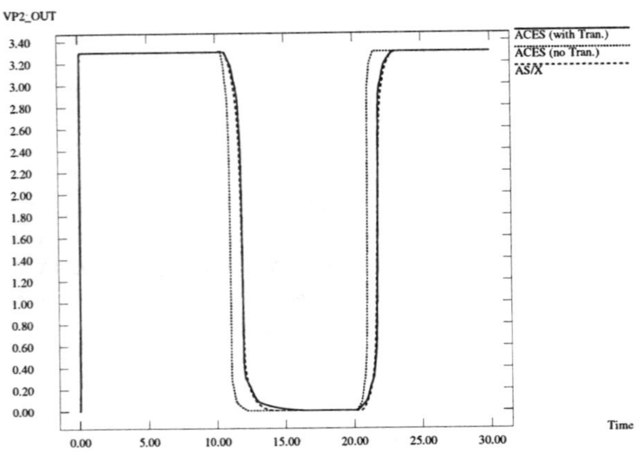

Fig. 8: *ACES simulation results (with and without state transformation) as compared to AS/X at the output of partition P2 as shown in Fig. 7.*

The last example is an industrial design of a 4 bit ALU. The circuit consists of 282 MOSFETs and 156 nodes. Without parasitic resistances added to the MOSFET models, the ACES simulation requires only 7298 events and 1.17 CPU seconds while the AS/X simulation requires 50 CPU seconds. With a number of parasitic resistances added to the circuit, the AS/X simulation requires about the same 50 CPU seconds. In this case, the ACES simulation with state transformation requires 17640 events and 5.73 CPU seconds. The waveforms at an output node of the circuit as obtained by ACES simulation with and without parasitic resistances and by AS/X are shown in Fig. 9. Note that the difference between the ACES waveforms is due to the state transformation. In the case of no parasitic resistances (and no transformation), the time to quiescence is computed for the original state. In the case of state transformation, the time to quiescence is computed for the transformed states.

5.Summary

This paper has identified the dependency of the states in the state space description of a given circuit as the cause for some numerical

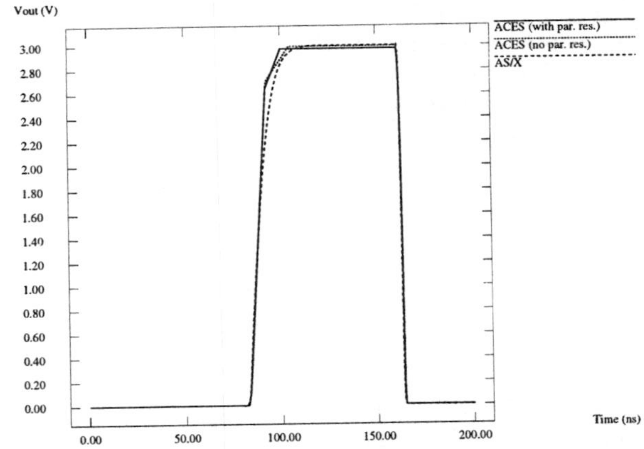

Fig. 9: *ACES simulation results (with and without parasitic resistances) as compared to AS/X at the output of an industrial 4 bit ALU circuit.*

problems in event driven explicit simulation algorithms such as ACES. State transformation has also been proposed to address this problem. A novel algorithm has been developed to derive systematically a simple state transformation and to include such a transformation in an efficient manner. A number of examples have been included to illustrate the concept and the complication in using state transformation as well as to demonstrate its effectiveness.

References

[1] J. T. J. Van Eijndhoven, A Piecewise Linear Simulator for Large Scale Integrated Circuits, Ph.D Thesis, Eindhoven Institute of Technology, 1984.

[2] A. Devgan and R. A. Rohrer, "Adaptively Controlled Explicit Simulation," *IEEE Trans. Computer-Aided Design*, vol. 13, pp.746-762, June 1994.

[3] Y.H. Shih and S. M. Kang, "ILLIADS: A Fast Timing and Reliability Simulator for Digital MOS Circuits," *IEEE Trans. Computer-Aided Design*, pp. 1387-1402, Sept. 1993.

[4] C. Visweswariah and R. A. Rohrer, "Piecewise Approximate Circuit Simulation," *IEEE Trans. Computer-Aided Design*, pp. 861-870, July 1991.

[5] A. D. Stein, T. V. Nguyen, B. George, and R. A. Rohrer, "ADAPTS: A Digital Transient Simulation Strategy for Integrated Circuits," *Proc. DAC*, June 1991.

[6] S. Lin, M. M. Sadowska, and E. S. Kuh, "Stepwise Equivalent Circuit Simulation Technique," *IEEE Trans. Computer-Aided Design*, pp. 672-683, May 1993.

[7] R. Kao and M. Horowitz, "Timing Analysis using Piecewise Linear RSIM," *IEEE Trans. Computer-Aided Design*, pp. 1498-1512, Dec. 1994.

SESSION 6A

NEW IDEAS IN ENCODING

Moderators:

Ellen M. Sentovich, Cadence Berkeley Labs.,

Berkeley, CA

Pranav Ashar, C&C Research Labs., NEC USA, Inc.,

Princeton, NJ

A Fast and Robust Exact Algorithm for Face Embedding

Evguenii I. Goldberg[†,‡] Tiziano Villa[§] Robert K. Brayton[‡]

Alberto L. Sangiovanni-V incentelli[‡]

‡ Department of EECS
University of California at
Berkeley,Berkeley, CA 94720

† Academy of Sciences of
Belarus, Minsk

§ PARADES,
Via di S.Pantaleo,
66, 00186 Roma

Abstract

We present a new matrix formulation of the face hypercube embedding problem that motivates the design of an efficient search strategy to find an encoding that satisfies all faces of minimum length. Increasing dimensions of the Boolean space are explored; for a given dimension constraints are satisfied one at a time. The following features help to reduce the nodes of the solution space that must be explored: candidate cubes instead of candidate codes are generated, cubes yielding symmetric solutions are not generated, a smaller sufficient set of solutions (producing basic sections) is explored, necessary conditions help discard unsuitable candidate cubes, early detection that a partial solution cannot be extended to be a global solution prunes infeasible portions of the search tree.

We have implemented a prototype package MINSK based on the previous ideas and run experiments to evaluate it. The experiments show that MINSK is faster and solves more problems than any available algorithm. Moreover, MINSK is a robust algorithm, while most of the proposed alternatives are not. Besides most problems of the complete MCNC benchmark suite, other solved examples include an important set of decoder PLAs coming from the design of microprocessor instruction sets.

1 Introduction

Consider a set of symbols S and an **encoding** function $e : S \rightarrow B^k$, for a given k, that assigns to each symbol $s \in S$ a code $e(s)$, i.e., a binary vector of length k. Usually the only requirement is that e is injective, i.e., that different symbols are mapped to different binary vectors. In various applications it is important to satisfy other encoding constraints, in order to obtain a code that is correct or desirable to meet a certain objective. Either the encoding length k is part of the problem instance or it is an unknown to be found (usually minimized) by the procedure that satisfies the given encoding constraints [15].

Given a set of symbols S, a **face constraint** c_f is a subset $S' \subseteq S$ specifying that the symbols in S' are to be assigned to one *face* (or subcube) of a binary k-dimensional cube, without any other symbol sharing the same face. Face constraints are generated by multiple-valued (input) literals in two-level and multi-level multi-valued minimization [15]. As an example, given symbols a, b, c, d, e, an input constraint involving symbols a, b, c is denoted by (a, b, c). An encoding satisfying (a, b, c) is given by $a = 111$, $b = 011$, $c = 001$, $d = 000$ and $e = 100$ and the face spanned by (a, b, c) is $--1$. Notice that the vertex 101 is not and should not be assigned to any other symbol.

Given a set of face constraints $\mathcal{C}_f$, it is always possible to find an encoding that satisfies it, as long as one is free to choose a suitable code length. It is a well-known fact that for $k = \mid S \mid$ any set $\mathcal{C}_f$ is satisfied by choosing as e the *1-hot* encoding function (which assigns to a state s_i the binary vector that is always 0 except for a position to 1, the latter denoting state s_i). It is an important combinatorial optimization problem, sometimes called [16] **face hypercube embedding**, to find the minimum k and a related $e : S \rightarrow B^k$ such that $\mathcal{C}_f$ is satisfied. The decision version of this problem is NP-complete [11].

An exact solution based on a branch-and-bound strategy to search the partially ordered set of faces of hypercubes was described first in [16], but it is not computationally practical. An exact solution by reduction to the problem of satisfaction of encoding dichotomies [1] was proposed in [17]. It uses a reduction by J. Tracey [14] of the exact satisfaction of encoding dichotomies to a unate covering problem. This approach was made more efficient in [11], by improving the step of generating maximal compatibles of encoding dichotomies. Recently the problem of satisfaction of encoding dichotomies has been revisited in [3], adapting techniques to find primes and solving unate covering with binary decision diagrams that have been so successful in two level logic minimization [2]. From the experimental point-of-view none of the previous algorithms has performed up to expectations, being unable to solve exactly various instances of moderate size and practical interest. Moreover, algorithms reducing encoding dichotomies to unate covering have a dismal behavior when the problem instance consists mostly of uniqueness encoding dichotomies (i.e., encoding dichotomies with only one state in each block), because they generate most of the encoding columns, which are 2^k for $k = \mid S \mid$.

Heuristic solutions to the face embedding problem have been reported in many papers [10, 4, 12, 5, 17, 13]. A heuristic solution satisfies all face constraints, but does not guarantee that the code-length is minimum. A related problem, that is not of interest in this paper, is the one of fixing the code-length and maximizing a gain function of the constraints that can be satisfied in the given code-length. We refer to [15] for background material on satisfaction of encoding constraints and their sources in logic synthesis.

In this paper we present a new matrix formulation of the face hypercube embedding problem that inspires the design of an efficient exact search strategy. This algorithm satisfies the constraints one by one by assigning to them intersecting cubes in the encoding Boolean space. The problem of finding a set of cubes with a minimum number of coordinates satisfying a given intersection matrix was first formulated in [18] without any relation to encoding problems. No algorithm to solve the problem was described. The relation between the face embedding problem and the construction of intersecting cubes was employed in an heuristic algorithm described in [12, 5]. The first formulation of a simple criterion of when a set of cubes satisfies a set of constraints was given in [6]. We use some theoretical notions, e.g., basic sections, introduced

[1] An encoding dichotomy on S is a bipartition (S_1, S_2) such that $S_1 \cup S_2 \subseteq S$.

1092-3152/97 $10.00 © 1997 IEEE

first in [7, 8]. The following features speed up the search of our algorithm: candidate cubes instead of candidate codes are generated, symmetric cubes are not generated, a smaller sufficient set of solutions (producing basic sections) is explored, necessary conditions help discard unsuitable candidate cubes, early detection that a partial solution cannot be extended to be a global solution prunes infeasible portions of the search tree. The experiments with a prototype implementation in a package called MINSK show that our algorithm is faster, solves more problems than any available alternative and is robust. All problems of the MCNC benchmark suite were solved successfully, except four of them unsolved or untried by any other tool. Other collections of examples were solved or reported for the first time, including an important set of decoder PLAs coming from the design of microprocessor instruction sets.

In Section 2 we present a theoretical formulation based on matrix notation. How to avoid the generation of symmetrical solutions is explained in Section 3. In Section 4 we describe a new algorithm to satisfy face constraints. Experimental results are provided in Section 5. Section 6 concludes the paper with remarks on what has been achieved and future work.

2 Matrix Formulation of the Face Embedding Problem

Given a matrix M, denote by $Row(M)$ its rows and $Col(M)$ its columns. $M_{i.}$ denotes the i-th row of M and $M_{.j}$ denotes the j-th column of M. The **multiplicity** of a column $C_{.j}$ of M, $mult(j)$ is the number of times that $C_{.j}$ occurs in M. We use the term vector to indicate a one dimensional matrix, when there is no need to specify whether it is regarded as a row or a column. Vectors are called **binary** or **two-valued** if their entries are 0 or 1 and **3-valued** if their entries are 0 or 1 or $-$. A **singleton** vector has a unique 1.

Given two 2-valued vectors v_1 and v_2 of the same length, their **disjunction** $v_1 \cup v_2$ is the vector v whose i-th entry is the disjunction of the i-th entries of v_1 and v_2. Similar definition holds for the **conjunction** of v_1 and v_2. A vector v_1 **covers** a vector v_2 if, whenever the i-th entry of v_2 is 1, the i-th entry of v_1 is 1. A vector v_1 **intersects** a vector v_2 if for at least an index i, the i-th entry of v_1 and v_2 is 1.

2.1 Constraint and Solution Matrices

Given a set of symbols S and a set of face constraints C_f on S, the **constraint matrix** is a matrix with as many rows as constraints and columns as symbols. Entry (i, j) is 1 iff the i-th constraint contains symbol j, otherwise it is 0. For don't care face constraints, the don't care states have a $-$ in the corresponding position of the constraint matrix.

Consider the set of constraints $C_f = \{(s_3s_4s_6s_9), (s_3s_5), (s_1s_4s_7), (s_2s_3s_6), (s_7s_8), (s_{11}s_{12})\}$. Then the related constraint matrix is:

Example 2.1

$$C = \left[\begin{array}{cccccccccccc} s_1 & s_2 & s_3 & s_4 & s_5 & s_6 & s_7 & s_8 & s_9 & s_{10} & s_{11} & s_{12} \\ \hline 0 & 0 & 1 & 1 & 0 & 1 & 0 & 0 & 1 & 0 & 0 & 0 \\ 0 & 0 & 1 & 0 & 1 & 0 & 0 & 0 & 0 & 0 & 0 & 0 \\ 1 & 0 & 0 & 1 & 0 & 0 & 1 & 0 & 0 & 0 & 0 & 0 \\ 0 & 1 & 1 & 0 & 0 & 1 & 0 & 0 & 0 & 0 & 0 & 0 \\ 0 & 0 & 0 & 0 & 0 & 0 & 1 & 1 & 0 & 0 & 0 & 0 \\ 0 & 0 & 0 & 0 & 0 & 0 & 0 & 0 & 0 & 1 & 1 & 0 \end{array}\right]$$

In the sequel we will refer usually to a set of face constraints C_f by its encoding matrix C and we will not distinguish the two. Notice that there is no need to add singleton constraints, because we guarantee that different codes are assigned to different states, including the states whose columns in C_f are equal.

Given an encoding e that satisfies a constraint matrix C, e defines a face for each constraint of C, i.e., the minimum subcube that contains the codes of the states in the constraint.

For a given constraint matrix C and integer n, consider a **face matrix** S with $Row(C)$ rows (**faces** or **cubes**) and n columns (**sections**), whose entries may be 0 or 1 or $-$. Each row may be regarded as a subcube in the n-dimensional Boolean space. If there exists an encoding e such that, for each $i \in Row(S)$, the i-th row of S is the face that e defines for the i-constraint of C, then we say that S is a **solution face matrix** of C or that S **satisfies** C and that the i-th row of S is a **solution cube** of the i-th constraint.

One verifies that S is a solution face matrix of C, by constructing an **intersection matrix** T_S whose rows are the cubes of S and whose columns are the minterms of B^n, where entry (i, j) is 1 iff minterm j is in cube i. Then S satisfies C if for any column $C_{.j}$, the matrix T_S contains no less than $mult(C_{.j})$ columns equal to $C_{.j}$. In other words, we require that each minterm (code of a state) belongs only to those faces to which it is restricted by the constraints; moreover, if there are equal columns in the constraint matrix, for each of them there must be a different minterm. In this way, there is at least one injective function $f_{C \to T_S}$ that associates to each column of C one column of T_S.

Given a matrix S satisfying C, an encoding e_S that satisfies C can be extracted with the following rule: select an injective function $f_{C \to T_S}$, whose existence is guaranteed because S satisfies C, then encode state i (i.e., column i of C) with the minterm of the column $f_{C \to T_S}(i)$ in T_S. Such an encoding satisfies C because each code lies only in the faces corresponding to the constraints to which the state belongs.

Example 2.2 *Given the previous C and $n = 4$, consider*

$$S = \left[\begin{array}{cccc} - & 0 & 1 & - \\ 1 & 0 & - & 0 \\ 1 & - & - & 1 \\ - & - & 1 & 0 \\ - & 1 & 0 & 1 \\ 0 & - & 0 & 0 \end{array}\right]$$

S satisfies C as it is shown by building the matrix

$$T_S = \left[\begin{array}{cccccccccccccccc} 1001 & 0110 & 1010 & 1011 & 1000 & 0010 & 1101 & 0101 & 0011 & 0100 & 0000 & 0111 & 0001 & 1100 & 1111 & 1110 \\ \hline 0 & 0 & 1 & 1 & 0 & 1 & 0 & 0 & 1 & 0 & 0 & 0 & 0 & 0 & 0 & 0 \\ 0 & 0 & 1 & 0 & 1 & 0 & 0 & 0 & 0 & 0 & 0 & 0 & 0 & 0 & 0 & 0 \\ 1 & 0 & 0 & 1 & 0 & 0 & 1 & 0 & 0 & 0 & 0 & 0 & 0 & 0 & 1 & 0 \\ 0 & 1 & 1 & 0 & 0 & 1 & 0 & 0 & 0 & 0 & 0 & 0 & 0 & 0 & 0 & 1 \\ 0 & 0 & 0 & 0 & 0 & 0 & 1 & 1 & 0 & 0 & 0 & 0 & 0 & 0 & 0 & 0 \\ 0 & 0 & 0 & 0 & 0 & 0 & 0 & 0 & 0 & 1 & 1 & 0 & 0 & 0 & 0 & 0 \end{array}\right]$$

An encoding e_S that satisfies C can be extracted from S, with the following injection from columns of C to columns of T_S: $e(s_1) = 1001$, $e(s_2) = 0110$, $e(s_3) = 1010$, $e(s_4) = 1011$, $e(s_5) = 1000$, $e(s_6) = 0010$, $e(s_7) = 1101$, $e(s_8) = 0101$, $e(s_9) = 0011$, $e(s_{10}) = 0100$, $e(s_{11}) = 0000$, $e(s_{12}) = 0111$.

Notice that columns of T_S corresponding to the following groups of codes $\{0100, 0000\}$, $\{0111, 0001, 1100\}$, $\{1001, 1111\}$, $\{0110, 1110\}$ *are equal, which gives freedom in selecting an encoding satisfying C. For example, if we permute codes 0100 and 0000 in the previous encoding e_S or assign to $e(s_{12})$ code 0001 instead of 0111 we still get an encoding satisfying C. So many different encodings satisfying C specify the same set of faces.*

2.2 Basic Sections

Given a constraint matrix C and an encoding e, the set of the minimal cubes such that each of them contains the codes of the symbols in a corresponding constraint of C defines the rows of a face matrix S. If e satisfies C then S is a solution face matrix of C. The operation of a finding the minimal cube that contains the codes of the states that appear in a given constraint is captured exactly by the notion of basic section that we are going to define next. Informally, given a constraint matrix C, the columns of a face matrix S such that there is an encoding e (that may or may not satisfy C) for which the rows of S are the minimal cubes containing the codes of the constraints of C are basic sections.

Consider a vector d (whose elements are 0 or 1) with $|Col(C)|$ entries. We can regard d as an **encoding column**, i.e., an assignment of 0 or 1 to each symbol. An encoding function $e : S \to B^k$ defines a set of k encoding columns $e_1, \cdots, e_k$ (i.e., the columns of e), where the i-th entry of e_j is 1 (is 0) if and only if the j-th coordinate of $e(s_i)$ is 1 (is 0).

Let us compare the set of columns that have a 1 in $C_{i.}$ (i-th row of C) with the set of columns that have a 1 in d. There are the following cases:

1. d covers $C_{i.}$, i.e., all columns that have a 1 in $C_{i.}$ have a 1 in d. Say that the comparison returns a 1.
2. d does not intersect $C_{i.}$, i.e., no column that has a 1 in $C_{i.}$ has a 1 in d. Say that the comparison returns a 0.
3. d intersects but does not cover $C_{i.}$, i.e., a proper subset of the columns that have a 1 in $C_{i.}$ have a 1 in d. Say that the comparison returns a $-$.

So given a d, let us denote by $bs(d)$ a column vector with $|Row(C)|$ entries of value 1, 0, or -, where the i-th entry is 1, 0 or $-$, according to whether the previous comparison of d and $C_{i.}$ returns a 1, 0 or $-$.

Definition 2.1 *A 3-valued column B is called a* **basic section** *for C if there is a vector d such that $B = bs(d)$.*

Example 2.3 *Consider*

$$C = \begin{bmatrix} 1 & 1 & 0 & 0 & 0 \\ 0 & 1 & 1 & 0 & 0 \\ 0 & 0 & 1 & 1 & 0 \\ 0 & 0 & 0 & 1 & 1 \end{bmatrix}$$

The encoding $e(s_1) = 000$, $e(s_2) = 100$, $e(s_3) = 110$, $e(s_4) = 111$, $e(s_5) = 101$ satisfies C. The minimal cubes containing the codes assigned by e to the symbols in each constraint of C define a face matrix S:

$$S = \begin{bmatrix} - & 0 & 0 \\ 1 & - & 0 \\ 1 & 1 & - \\ 1 & - & 1 \end{bmatrix}$$

which satisfies C as seen by building the intersection matrix

$T_S =$

	000	001	010	011	100	101	110	111
−00	1	0	0	0	1	0	0	0
1−0	0	0	0	0	1	0	1	0
11−	0	0	0	0	0	0	1	1
1−1	0	0	0	0	0	1	0	1

The encoding columns of the encoding are $e_1 = 01111$, $e_2 = 00110$, $e_3 = 00011$, and they yield the basic sections $bs(e_1) = -111$, $bs(e_2) = 0-1-$, $bs(e_3) = 00-1$. The rows of the matrix of the basic sections are the minimal cubes spanned by the codes of the states in the constraints of C.

Theorem 2.1 *Given a constraint matrix C and an encoding e with encoding columns $e_1, \ldots, e_k$, the basic sections $bs(e_1), \ldots, bs(e_k)$ define the set of minimal cubes such that each of them contains the codes of the symbols in a corresponding constraint of C (even if e does not satisfy C). Moreover, if e satisfies C the basic sections $bs(e_1), \ldots, bs(e_k)$ define a face matrix that satisfies C.*

It is worthwhile to clarify that a matrix S that satisfies a constraint matrix does not consist necessarily (only) of basic sections. A trivial case comes from "redundant" solutions, obtained by adding to a solution matrix S an arbitrary column (so not necessarily a basic section). A more interesting case comes from a solution matrix S whose faces are not minimal subcubes yielded by a corresponding encoding e. However, the following theorem shows that it is sufficient to consider only basic sections to find a minimum solution to face hypercube embedding.

Theorem 2.2 *Given a solution face matrix S' of the constraint matrix C there is always a solution face matrix S of C with the same number of columns that consists only of basic sections.*

Proofs of the theorems are omitted for lack of space.

3 Characterization of Symmetric Solutions

A crucial feature of an efficient algorithm to solve face embedding constraints is the ability to avoid the consideration of symmetric solutions, i.e., solutions that differ only by permutations and inversions of variables of the encoding space. We will refer to permutations and inversions of variables as symmetric transformations or symmetries.

If a matrix S is a solution of C then any matrix S' obtained from S by permutations and (bit-wise) inversions of columns is a solution of C. So if for example, in matrix S there are no columns that are equal or equal after inversion then there exist $n!\ 2^n$ ($n!$ for permutations and 2^n for inversions) different solutions obtained by symmetries of S. For example for $n = 6$ ($n = 7$) $n!\ 2^n$ is equal to 46080 (645120). Generation of such solutions is useless because they all have the same cost as S. All solutions produced by symmetries of S form an equivalence class of which it suffices to consider a representative to solve the problem.

In Section 4 we will present a procedure *search_boolean_space* that finds a solution face matrix S in an n-dimensional boolean space, if such a solution exists. Let us write $S^{(i)}$ for a solution face matrix satisfying the matrix $C^{(i)}$, which stands for the matrix C restricted to the first i rows.

The procedure builds incrementally a matrix S by finding first a solution $S^{(1)}$ for the first constraint C_1, then augmenting it to a solution $S^{(2)}$ for constraints C_1,C_2 and so on, until all constraints are considered. More precisely, when handling the i-th constraint, one generates the set $Sat(C_i)$ of all cubes satisfying it and selects a cube $F \in Sat(C_i)$. Then one verifies whether $S^{(i)}$ formed by appending cube F to $S^{(i-1)}$ satisfies $C^{(i)}$. If not, another cube of $Sat(C_i)$ is tried and, if none works, one backtracks further to a different choice of a cube $F' \in Sat(C_{i-1})$ such that $C^{(i-1)}$ is satisfied by $S^{(i-2)}$ augmented by F'.

Now we show how to avoid the generation of symmetrical solutions. Let $S^{(i-1)}$ be a face matrix satisfying $C^{(i-1)}$. Let A be a set of column numbers and suppose that all columns of $S^{(i-1)}$ from A are equal. Let F',F'' be n-component cubes which differ only in the columns from A. Denote by $S'^{(i)}$ and $S''^{(i)}$ the solutions obtained by augmenting $S^{(i-1)}$ by cubes F' and F'' respectively. If there is a permutation of columns from A transforming F' to F'' then the same permutation transforms $S'^{(i)}$ into $S''^{(i)}$, i.e., solutions $S'^{(i)}$ and $S''^{(i)}$ are symmetrical. It is not hard to show that cube F' can be transformed into cube F'' by a permutation of columns from A if and only if both cubes have the same numbers of 0 and 1 entries in the columns from A.

Assume that the columns of $C^{(i-1)}$ from A are not only equal, but also they do not contain 0 and 1 entries. Suppose that there is a permutation and inversion of columns from A transforming F' into F''. Then the same permutation and inversion transform $S'^{(i)}$ into

$S''^{(i)}$. It is not hard to show that cube F' can be transformed to F'' by a permutation and inversion of columns from A if and only if both cubes have the same number of - entries in the columns from A.

Example 3.1 *Consider C given in Example 2.1 for $n = 4$. When generating the solutions of $C^{(1)}$, i.e., cubes satisfying C_1 we need to generate only cubes having different number of - entries since matrix $C^{(0)}$ is empty, which can be interpreted as the case of all columns of $C^{(0)}$ equal and not containing 0 and 1 entries. So the candidate cubes to satisfy the first constraint are: $----$ (4 dashes), $1---$ (3 dashes), $11--$ (2 dashes), $111-$ (1 dash), 1111 (0 dashes). None of them can be obtained by a symmetric transformation of another and any other cube of 4 components can be obtained from one of the cubes above by a permutation and inversion of components . Note that there is freedom in selecting cubes representing an equivalence class. So instead of $11--$ we could select any cube having two dashes, for example $0--1$.*

Suppose that we have already chosen cube $11--$ to solve $C^{(1)}$, i.e., to satisfy the first constraint. So $S^{(1)}$ consisting of cube $11--$ has two groups of equal columns: $\{1,2\}$ and $\{3,4\}$. Note that the columns of the second group do not contain 0 and 1 entries. Generating cubes satisfying C_2 we want to avoid considering symmetrical solutions $S^{(2)}$. To do so we must skip the generation of cubes that have the same number of 0 and 1 entries in the columns of the first group and the same number of - in the columns of the second group. There are six patterns of two components having different number of 0 and 1 entries : $--$ (0 zeroes, 0 ones), $1-$ (0 zeroes, 1 ones), $0-$ (1 zeroes, 0 ones), 11 (0 zeroes, 2 ones), 00 (2 zeroes, 0 ones), 01 (1 zeroes, 1 ones). These patterns give 6 possible combinations of the values of the first and second components of candidate cubes. There are 3 patterns of two components having different number of dashes: $--$ (2 dashes) , $1-$ (1 dash), 11 (0 dashes). These patterns give 3 possible combinations of the values of the third and fourth components of candidate cubes.

All together we obtain $6 \times 3 = 18$ combinations: $----$, $--1-$, $--11$, $1---$, $1-1-$, $1-11$, $11--$, $111-$, 1111, $0---$, $0-1-$, $0-11$, $01--$, $011-$, 0111, $00--$, $001-$, 0011. Augmenting $S^{(1)}$ by a cube from the previous set we obtain 18 different matrices none of which can be obtained by symmetrical transformation from another.

4 An Exact Algorithm to Find a Minimum Solution

In Fig. 1 we present the flow of an algorithm *find_solution* that finds a minimum solution of a constraint matrix C. It starts with the minimum dimension (log of the number of constraints) and it increases it until a solution is found. It is guaranteed to terminate because every constraint matrix can be satisfied by an encoding of length k, if k is the number of symbols; more precisely by an 1-hot encoding. Usually a much shorter encoding length suffices.

4.1 The Search Strategy

The key feature of the proposed algorithm is that it searches sets of cubes, instead of sets of codes. Since a set of cubes may correspond to many sets of codes (see Example 2.1), the algorithm explores simultaneously many encodings. Once a satisfactory set of cubes is found, it is straighforward to extract from it a satisfying encoding.

For a given dimension, the search of a satisfying encoding is carried through by the routine *search_space*, that returns a solution face matrix S that satisfies C. Once S is known, it is easy, as shown in Example 2.2, to find an encoding of the symbols that satisfies C.

Before calling *search_space* the constraints are ordered as mentioned in Section 4.5 and then processed in that order. Each call of *search_space* processes a new constraint. *Seach_space* keeps a current partial solution $Curr\_Sol$ that satisfies all the constraints from the first to the last constraint that has been processed. It satisfies a constraint by generating a cube that encodes the constraint (a row of S). A constraint is satisfied if there is a cube such that, by adding it to the current solution, we satisfy the constraint matrix restricted to the constraints from the first to the one currently processed.

Once the current constraint has been satisfied the current solution is updated and *search_space* calls itself recursively with a new constraint. If the current solution cannot be extended to satisfy the current constraint, *search_space* backtracks and tries a different cube for the last constraint that was satisfied by $Curr\_Sol$ and it continues to backtrack until it finds a partial solution $Curr\_Sol$ which can be extended to satisfy the constraint currently processed. The procedure *found_solution* tests whether a face matrix is a solution of a set of constraints, by constructing the intersection matrix T_S as shown in Section 2.1.

The following enhancements reduce the nodes of the search tree that *search_space* has to explore to find a minimum solution:

1. Candidate cubes are generated by a procedure *generate_cand_cubes* that avoids the generation of symmetric solutions, based on the theory presented in Section 3.

2. The procedure *generate_cand_cubes* eliminates also the cubes that would yield a matrix S with sections which are not basic, as allowed by Theorem 2.2 and explained in Section 4.2.

3. Cubes that do not satisfy the necessary conditions of Section 4.3 to be valid extensions of the current solution are discarded by a procedure *discard_cand_cubes*.

4. When trying to extend the current solution, the procedure *unsat_constr* checks first whether any of the constraints not yet processed is unsatisfiable by an extension of the current solution; if so, *search_space* backtracks to modify the current solution. See Section 4.4 for more discussion.

4.2 Restriction to Basic Sections

In Section 2 we highlighted the fact that not all solution face matrices S consist entirely of basic sections, but we argued in Theorem 2.2 that basic sections are sufficient to find a minimum solution. Therefore when generating cubes that are candidate solutions of face constraints it is profitable to reject those that would produce an S with some sections which are not basic. The rejection is performed in the following way.

Suppose that the algorithm is processing constraint C_i. At this time a solution $S^{(i-1)}$ satisfying $C^{(i-1)}$ is known. Suppose that all 3-valued columns of $S^{(i-1)}$ are basic sections. Adding to $S^{(i-1)}$ a cube F we extend each column of $S^{(i-1)}$ by one entry. The j-th column of $S^{(i-1)}$ can be extended in three ways according to the j-th component of F being equal to 0,1 or -. E.g., suppose that if the j-th component of F is equal to 0 then the j-th column of $S^{(i)}$ is not a basic section. Then when constructing cubes satisfying C_i we need to avoid the generation of those that have 0 in the j-th component.

So to guarantee that all produced solutions $S^{(i)}$ consist only of basic sections we need to generate cubes which correspond to "correct" extensions of columns of $S^{(i-1)}$. According to Definition 2.1, a 3-valued column is a basic section if there is a boolean vector d such that $bs(d)$ is equal to the column. We use a branch-and-bound algorithm that, given a column, checks whether the column is a basic section. We do not report here the details of the algorithm.

```
find_solution(C) {
    /* order the constraints */
    C = sort_constraints(C)
    for (cube_size = lg⌈| C |⌉; TRUE ; cube_size + +) {
    cur_constr = 1  /* cur_constr is the index of the current constraint to satisfy */
    Sol = search_space(C, cube_size, ∅, cur_constr, {(1, ..., cube_size))}
    if Sol = ∅
        continue
    else
        return Sol
    }
}

search_space(C, cube_size, Curr_Sol, cur_constr, Classes) {
    /* Curr_Sol satisfies all constraints */
    if cur_const >| C |
        return Curr_Sol
    /* early detection of unsatisfiable constraints given Curr_Sol */
    if unsat_constr(C, Curr_Sol, cur_constr)
        return ∅
    /* generate candidate cubes CCubes excluding symmetric solutions
    and enforcing that all solutions consist only of basic sections */
    CCubes = generate_cand_cubes(C, cube_size, cur_constr, Curr_sol, Classes)
    /* sort candidate cubes in order of increasing size */
    CCubes = sort_cand_cubes(CCubes)
    /* eliminate candidate cubes that cannot satisfy constraints */
    CCubes = discard_cand_cubes(C, cur_constr, Curr_sol, CCubes)
    /* find a cube extending Curr_Sol to satisfy also current constraint */
    for (cur_cube = 1; i <| CCubes | ; cur_cube + +) {
        New_Curr_Sol = Curr_Sol ∪ cur_cube
        /* test if New_Curr_Sol satisfies constraints from 1 to cur_constr */
        if not found_solution(C, cur_constr, New_Curr_Sol)
            continue  /* not a solution: try another cube */
        /* solution found: recompute equivalence relation on columns */
        /* try to extend current solution to satisfy also next constraint */
        Sol = search_space(C, cube_size, New_Curr_Sol, cur_constr + 1, New_Classes)
        if Sol ≠ ∅
            return Sol
    }
    return ∅  /* current solution cannot be extended to satisfy also current constraint */
}
```

Figure 1: Algorithm to find a minimum solution.

4.3 Removal of Unsuitable Cubes

Let $S^{(i-1)}$ be a partial solution and $Cand(C_i)$ be a set of candidate cubes for satisfying C_i that do not contain symmetric cubes nor cubes leading to sections that are not basic. Before checking if $S^{(i-1)}$ together with a cube $F \in Cand(C_i)$ is a solution of $C^{(i)}$, it is worthy to test whether F satisfies some necessary conditions. Precisely we discard a cube $F \in Cand(C_i)$ it at least one of three conditions holds:

1. The number of 1s in C_i is greater than 2^n where n is the number of $-$s in F.
2. There is a k such that cube F covers the cube specified by the k-th row of $S^{(i-1)}$, i.e., F satisfies C_k, but row $C_{i.}$ does not cover (dominate) row $C_{k.}$. In this case there is a column $C_{.m}$ of C such that $C_{im} = 0$ and $C_{km} = 1$, that does not appear in the intersection matrix of the set of cubes obtained by adding cube F to $S^{(i-1)}$.
3. There is a k such that $C_{k.}$ intersects $C_{i.}$, but the number of 1s in their intersection is greater than 2^n where n is the number of $-$s in the cube obtained by the intersection of F and the cube specified by the k-th row of $S^{(i-1)}$.

4.4 Early Detection of Unsatisfied Constraints

Constraints are processed one by one in a predefined order. Suppose that on the path leading to the current node of the search tree we have already chosen 4 cubes satisfying the first 4 constraints and that now we are trying to satisfy the 5-th constraint. Suppose also that all constraints from the 5-th to the 19-th are satisfiable, but that the 20-th is unsatisfiable, given the current choice of the first 4 cubes. So checking the satisfiability of one constraint at a time, we would discover that the 20-th constraint is unsatisfiable only after having processed all constraints up to the 19-th one; then we would start backtracking to another cube satisfying the 19-th constraint and we would try again to satisfy the 20-th one, and so on for all the cubes that satisfy the 19-th constraint. We would repeat this time-consuming process for all constraints from to the 19-th to the 5-th one, before discovering that we must modify the solution to the first 4 constraints, in order to extend it to a solution that satisfies the constraints up to the 20-th one.

To prevent such unrobust behaviour and lessen the dependency on how the constraints are sorted initially, we employ early detection of unsatisfied constraints. At each node of the search tree with i satisfied constraints, the algorithm checks first that any of the remaining unprocessed constraints is satisfiable, given the current choice of cubes which satisfy the first i constraints. Although this checks requires some extra calculations at each node of the search tree, it is fully justified by the drastic reduction of the search tree size.

4.5 Sorting of Constraints

Constraints are sorted with the goal to prune branches of the search tree at the earliest possible stages. We have two sorting criteria. The first one selects as next constraint the one that intersects the highest number of already selected constraints. Ties are broken selecting the constraint with the highest number of 1s. The second criterion selects according to the highest number of 1s and breaks ties with the highest number of intersected rows.

5 Results

We implemented the algorithm described in Section 4 in a prototype package in C called MINSK (Minimum INput Satisfaction Kernel) and we applied it to a set of benchmarks available in the literature. The benchmarks are partitioned into three sets: FSMs from the MCNC collection, reported in Table 2; FSMs collected from various other sources, reported in the upper part of Table 4; decode PLAs of the VLSI-BAM project, provided by Bruce Holmer [9], reported in the lower part of Table 4. In all cases, face constraints were generated with ESPRESSO [1]. In the tables we report: the name of the example, the number of symbols to encode ("#states"), the logarithm of the number of symbols ("min. len.") together with the minimum code length to satisfy all input constraints known so far ("best known"), and the minimum code length to satisfy all input constraints found by MINSK ("min. sol."). Besides, the tables show the number of calls of the routine *found_solution* ("#checks"), the number of recursive calls of the routine *search_space* ("#calls"), and the CPU time for a 300 Mhz DEC ALPHA workstation. We did not report data on examples where the constraints were few and MINSK found a solution in no time. We found an exact solution for all the examples, except the FSMs *tbk, s1488, s1494, s298* none of which has been solved before. For some examples, like *donfile, scf, dk16* exact solutions were never found automatically before; for others, like *ex2* an exact solution was found automatically by NOVA [16] with the option *-e ie*, but at the cost of an unreasonable CPU time (60172.6 s. on 60Mhz DEC RISC workstation) [2].

Up to now four exact algorithms have been tried to solve face hypercube embedding. The first is available as an option in NOVA *-e ie*, the second is based on a reduction to satisfaction of encoding dichotomies by means of unate covering [17, 11], the third is an implicit implementation with ZBDDs of the latter [3], and the last is a simplification of the third, where instead of prime dichotomies one uses all possible encoding dichotomies [3]. In Table 3 we compare the performance of MINSK with the last three previous algorithms, based on the data recently reported in [3]. We are aware that the experiments presented in [3] were run with a 75 Mhz SuperSparc workstation with 96 MB memory and a timeout of 2 hours. The purpose of the comparison is to evaluate the behaviors of the various algorithms, not to discuss specific running times. We included in Table 3 all the interesting examples, leaving out "easy" cases where all algorithms behaved similarly.

The experiments warrant the following practical conclusions:

- MINSK is a robust algorithm, that solves in no time problems with few constraints and requires more time when the set of constraints is larger and more difficult.
- MINSK is also superior in running times to the other programs in the more difficult cases, showing that the key ingredients of its search strategy, such as generating cubes and not codes, avoiding symmetric solutions and sections which are not basic, prune away large suboptimal portions of the search space. The exact option of NOVA instead is hopelessly slow in the more difficult cases, because it enumerates codes and not cubes and does not avoid the generation of symmetric encodings.
- The implicit algorithms of [3] rely on a very sophisticated unate covering package that represents the table with ZBDDs. MINSK instead is a simple-minded implementation, whose strength lies only in the underlying theory. The running times of MINSK can be improved a lot by making more efficient some critical routines such as *found_solution*.

6 Conclusions

We have presented a new matrix formulation of the face hypercube embedding problem that motivates the design of an efficient search strategy to find an encoding that satisfies all faces of minimum length. Increasing dimensions of the Boolean space are explored; for a given dimension constraints are satisfied one at a time. The following features help to reduce the nodes of the solution space that must be explored: candidate cubes instead of candidate codes are generated, symmetric solutions are not generated, a smaller sufficient set of solutions (producing basic sections) is explored, necessary conditions help discard unsuitable candidate cubes, early detection that a partial solution cannot be extended to be a global solution prunes infeasible portions of the search tree.

We have implemented a prototype package MINSK based on the previous ideas and run experiments to evaluate it. The experiments show that MINSK is faster and solves more problems than any available algorithm. Moreover, MINSK is a robust algorithm, while most of the proposed alternatives are not. All problems of the MCNC benchmark suite were solved successfully, except four of them unsolved or untried by any other tool. Other collections of examples were solved or reported for the first time, including an important set of decoder PLAs coming from the design of microprocessor instruction sets.

We know that the current implementation of MINSK is simple-minded and leaves room for improvements to speed-up more the program. For instance, the satisfaction check with the intersection matrix T_S is expensive and currently not optimized. Other areas of improvement to cope with difficult examples lie in the computation of a lower bound on the Boolean space dimension tighter than $\ln\ states$; and in a dynamic choice of the next cube and its size, based on a tighter analysis of the cube occupancy requirements of the existing constraints.

Moreover, we want to generalize the existing theory and algorithm in the following directions:

1. Solving face constraints with don't cares, that is an important practical problem.
2. Solving mixed problems that include constraints in the form of encoding dichotomies.

[2] An solution of 7 was erroneously reported as exact in [16] for *dk16*, whereas the minimum solution has 6 bits.

Name	#states	#cons.	min. len. / best known	min. sol.	#checks	#calls	time (secs)
bbsse	16	5	4 / 6	6	127	9	0.02
beecount	7	6	3 / 4	4	75	9	0.01
cse	16	9	4 / 5	5	219	11	0.03
dk14	7	9	3 / 4	4	137	16	0.02
dk15	4	6	2 / 4	4	66	12	0.01
dk16	27	24	5 / $\leq$ 8	6	622653	8686	161.45
dk17	8	7	3 / 4	4	162	9	0.01
dk27	7	4	3 / 3	3	42	5	0.00
dk512	15	9	4 / 5	5	569	12	0.06
donfile	24	24	5 / $\leq$ 6	6	245476	1722	48.14
ex1	20	8	5 / 7	7	1522	15	0.47
ex2	19	8	5 / 6	6	666	13	0.13
ex3	10	6	4 / 5	5	195	11	0.02
ex5	9	7	4 / 5	5	99	13	0.01
ex6	8	9	3 / 4	4	87	11	0.01
ex7	10	6	4 / 5	5	71	12	0.01
keyb	19	18	5 / 7	7	3676	184	1.62
kirkman	16	6	4 / $\leq$ 6	6	52	10	0.01
lion9	9	10	4 / 4	4	194	11	0.02
mark1	15	4	4 / 5	5	72	8	0.01
planet	48	10	6 / 6	6	2044	11	0.40
pma	24	13	5 / na	7	37339	687	14.42
s1	20	5	5 / 5	5	334	6	0.03
s1488	48	24	6 / na	-	-	-	timeout
s1494	48	24	6 / na	-	-	-	timeout
s208	18	5	5 / na	6	162	8	0.02
s27	6	6	3 / na	4	80	9	0.01
s298	218	47	9 / na				timeout
s386	13	5	4 / na	6	124	9	0.02
s420	18	5	5 / na	6	162	8	0.02
s820	25	10	5 / na	6	1832	13	0.38
s832	25	10	5 / na	6	1848	13	0.35
sand	32	5	5 / 6	6	131	7	0.02
scf	121	14	7 / $\leq$ 8	7	6239	17	2.82
sse	16	5	4 / 6	6	127	9	0.02
styr	30	16	5 / 6	6	973	18	0.29
tbk	32	73	5 / $\leq$ 18	-	-	-	timeout
tma	20	9	5 / na	6	2086	71	0.43
train11	11	11	4 / 5	5	8534	256	1.06

Figure 2: Experiments with FSMs from MCNC Benchmark Set.

From some preliminary analysis, both extensions are amenable to the current frame, with some appropriate modifications to the test when a candidate matrix is a solution and the introduction of the equivalent of a face for an encoding dichotomy.

Notice that the reduction of face hypercube embedding to satisfaction of encoding dichotomies [11, 3] has shown experimentally that face hypercube embedding in a sense contains the hardest instances of the problem to satisfy encoding dichotomies. This fact justifies our strategy to solve the former first and extend it later to the latter.

References

[1] R. Brayton, G. Hachtel, C. McMullen, and A. Sangiovanni-Vincentelli. *Logic Minimization Algorithms for VLSI Synthesis*. Kluwer Academic Publishers, 1984.

[2] O. Coudert. Two-level logic minimization: an overview. *Integration*, 17-2:97–140, October 1994.

[3] O. Coudert and C.-J. Shi. Ze-Dicho: an exact solver for dichotomy-based constrained encoding. In *The Proceedings of the International Conference on Computer Design*, pages 426–431, 1996.

[4] S. Devadas, A. Wang, R. Newton, and A. Sangiovanni-Vincentelli. Boolean decomposition in multilevel logic optimization. *IEEE Journal of solid-state circuits*, pages 399–408, April 1989.

[5] C. Duff. Codage d'automates et theorie des cubes intersectants. *Thèse, Institut National Polytechnique de Grenoble*, March 1991.

[6] E.I. Goldberg. Metody bulevogo kodirovaniya znachenij argumentov predicatov (methods of boolean encoding of predicate arguments values). *Preprint No. 3, Institute of Engineering Cybernetics, Academy of Sciences of Belarus*, 1991. (In Russian).

[7] E.I. Goldberg. Matrix formulation of constrained encoding problems in optimal PLA synthesis. *Preprint No. 19, Institute*

Name	ImpDicho time(s.)	ZeDicho time(s.)	Dicho time(s.)	MINSK time(s.)
dk16	spaceout	timeout	spaceout	161.45
dk512	timeout	timeout	238.72	0.06
donfile	timeout	timeout	spaceout	48.14
ex1	433.85	128.63	spaceout	0.47
ex2	timeout	timeout	spaceout	0.13
ex4	timeout	timeout	timeout	0.00
keyb	timeout	14.43	125.2	1.62
planet	spaceout	timeout	spaceout	0.40
s1	timeout	timeout	timeout	0.03
sand	spaceout	timeout	spaceout	0.02
scf	spaceout	timeout	spaceout	2.82
styr	spaceout	timeout	timeout	0.29
tbk	spaceout	timeout	spaceout	timeout

Figure 3: Comparison with Other Approaches.

Name	#states	#cons.	min. len.	min. sol.	#checks	#calls	time (secs)
apla	29	10	5	7	1267	14	0.45
lange	6	7	3	4	128	15	0.01
papa	7	9	3	4	162	19	0.02
scud	8	17	3	6	1102	77	0.28
tlc34stg	35	19	6	6	3635	20	1.22
viterbi	68	6	7	7	4510	7	1.07
vmecont	32	41	5	9	25958139	22354	95424.37
ir1a	128	2	7	8	22	4	0.01
ir1b	128	4	7	8	549	7	0.21
ir1c	128	5	7	8	1224	7	0.62
ir1d	128	11	7	9	402694	2299	512.10
ir2	128	8	7	8	10374	35	6.00
ir2m	128	11	7	8	31468	13	20.43
ir3	128	11	7	8	18075	13	13.89
ir4m	128	5	7	8	733	7	0.32

Figure 4: Experiments with FSMs from Other Sources (upper part of the table) and Decode PLAs of the VLSI-BAM (lower part).

of Engineering Cybernetics, Academy of Sciences of Belarus, 1993.

[8] E.I. Goldberg. Face embedding by componentwise construction of intersecting cubes. *Preprint No. 1, Institute of Engineering Cybernetics, Academy of Sciences of Belarus*, 1995.

[9] B. Holmer. A tool for processor instruction set design. In *The Proceedings of the European Design Automation Conference*, pages 150–155, September 1994.

[10] G. De Micheli, R. Brayton, and A. Sangiovanni-Vincentelli. Optimal state assignment for finite state machines. *IEEE Transactions on Computer-Aided Design*, pages 269–285, July 1985.

[11] A. Saldanha, T. Villa, R. Brayton, and A. Sangiovanni-Vincentelli. Satisfaction of input and output encoding constraints. *IEEE Transactions on Computer-Aided Design*, 13(5):589–602, May 1994.

[12] G. Saucier, C. Duff, and F. Poirot. State assignment using a new embedding method based on an intersecting cube theory. In *The Proceedings of the Design Automation Conference*, pages 321–326, June 1989.

[13] C.-J. Shi and J. Brzozowski. An efficient algorithm for constrained encoding and its applications. *IEEE Transactions on Computer-Aided Design*, pages 1813–1826, December 1993.

[14] J. Tracey. Internal state assignment for asynchronous sequential machines. *IRE Transactions on Electronic Computers*, pages 551–560, August 1966.

[15] T. Villa, T. Kam, R. Brayton, and A. Sangiovanni-Vincentelli. *Synthesis of FSMs: logic optimization*. Kluwer Academic Publishers, 1997.

[16] T. Villa and A. Sangiovanni-Vincentelli. NOVA: State assignment for optimal two-level logic implementations. *IEEE Transactions on Computer-Aided Design*, 9(9):905–924, September 1990.

[17] S. Yang and M. Ciesielski. Optimum and suboptimum algorithms for input encoding and its relationship to logic minimization. *IEEE Transactions on Computer-Aided Design*, 10(1):4–12, January 1991.

[18] A.D. Zakrevskii. *Logicheskii sintez kaskadnykh skhem (Logic synthesis of cascaded circuits)*. Nauka, 1981. (in Russian).

An Output Encoding Problem and a Solution Technique

Subhasish Mitra, LaNae J. Avra and Edward J. McCluskey

Center for Reliable Computing
Departments of Electrical Engineering and Computer Science
Stanford University, Stanford, California 94305

Abstract

We present a new output encoding problem as follows: Given a specification table, such as a truth table or a finite state machine state table, where some of the outputs are specified in terms of 1's, 0's and don't cares, and others are specified symbolically, and assuming that the minimum number of bits are used to encode the symbolic outputs ($\lceil log_2 n \rceil$ bits for n symbolic outputs), determine a binary code for each symbol of the symbolically specified output column such that the total number of output functions to be implemented after encoding the symbolic outputs and compacting the columns is minimum. There are several applications of this output encoding problem, one of which is to reduce the area overhead while implementing scan or pseudo-random BIST in a circuit with one-hot signals. We develop an exact algorithm to solve the above problem and present experimental data to validate the claim that our encoding strategy helps to reduce the area of a synthesized circuit.

1. INTRODUCTION

Column compaction plays a major role in the synthesis of digital systems [1]. In *column compaction*, the number of output functions for a given specification is reduced by merging outputs which are logically equivalent, or can be made equivalent through assignment of *don't cares*. Two examples of output column compaction are shown in Fig. 1. Given a set of output columns, the problem of finding the smallest set that can be obtained by compacting the given set is related to the *maximum clique partitioning problem*, which is an NP-Complete problem [2]. This smallest set of compacted outputs is called the *minimum cardinality output column cover*. Column compaction can greatly reduce circuit area; this is not only true for the PLA implementation of the circuit [3] but also for multi-level logic circuits.

0 0		0	0 -		0
1 1	→	1	- 1	→	1
1 1		1	1 1		1
0 0		0	0 -		0

Figure 1. Examples of column compaction.

The different types of encoding problems, studied in the past, are the *finite state machine (FSM) state encoding* problem and the *input* and the *output* encoding problem. Techniques for FSM state encoding have been discussed in [4, 5, 6, 7, 8, 9, 10]. The input encoding problem has been reported in [11, 12]. One version of the output encoding problem, with a goal to reduce the number of product terms of a logic function, has been discussed in [13]. Another version of the output encoding problem is discussed in [14]. A heuristic solution to the output encoding problem which uses column compaction to reduce the number of outputs after the symbols are encoded is given in [15]. However, this algorithm does not consider any existing non-symbolic (binary) outputs when determining the encoding for the symbols of the symbolic output column.

In this paper, we present an output encoding problem whose objective is different from those mentioned above. The input to our problem is a specification table of a combinational (or sequential) circuit in terms of a truth table (or state table) such that some of the outputs are specified in terms of 0's, 1's and *don't cares* while the other outputs are symbolically specified. The problem is to encode the symbols in the symbolic output column, using $\lceil log_2 n \rceil$ bits for n symbolic outputs, so that after encoding, the cardinality of the output column cover computed using column compaction is minimum. Section 2 explains the motivation behind studying this type of an output encoding problem. Section 3 presents our output encoding algorithm for the case in which the specification table does not contain any *don't cares* in its output part. In Sec. 4, we extend the algorithm of Sec. 3 to handle *don't cares* in the outputs of the specification. Experimental results are reported in Sec. 5 followed by conclusion in Sec. 6.

2. MOTIVATION

Consider the specification shown in Table 1. Output columns c_1, c_2, c_3 and c_4 of Table 1 are specified in terms of 1's, 0's and don't cares — they constitute the *B-set*, the bound set. The last output column of Table 1 is symbolic — it is referred to as the *S-column*, the symbolic column. In this paper, we will consider specification tables containing a single symbolic output column (S-column) for simplicity. We can handle cases with multiple symbolic output columns by choosing an appropriate ordering of the symbolic outputs and repeatedly applying the algorithm reported in this paper.

For Table 1, since we have seven distinct symbols in the S-column, we need 3 bits to encode them. Table 2(a) shows one possible encoding of the symbols in the S-column and Table 2(b) shows the truth table for the corresponding function to be realized after column compaction. In Table 2(b), c_5, c_6 and c_7 represent the symbolic outputs.

1092-3152/97 $10.00 © 1997 IEEE

Table 1. Truth table with symbolic output.

Input	Encoded Output $c_1\ c_2\ c_3\ c_4$	Symbolic output
10101	1 0 1 0	X_1
01100	0 0 1 0	X_2
10001	1 0 0 1	X_3
01111	- 1 - 0	X_2
11110	0 - 0 -	X_4
01010	1 1 - 0	X_5
11111	1 0 - 0	X_1
1110-	0 - 1 1	X_6
11011	1 0 1 1	X_7
01001	0 1 0 1	X_4

Table 2(a). Encoding.

Signals	Encoding
X_1	100
X_2	111
X_3	101
X_4	011
X_5	010
X_6	110
X_7	001

Table 2(b). Compacted Truth Table.

Input	Outputs $c_1\ c_2\ c_3\ c_4$	$c_5\ c_6\ c_7$
10101	1 0 1 0	1 0 0
01100	0 0 1 0	1 1 1
10001	1 0 0 1	1 0 1
01111	- 1 - 0	1 1 1
11110	0 - 0 -	0 1 1
01010	1 1 - 0	0 1 0
11111	1 0 - 0	1 0 0
1110-	0 - 1 1	1 1 0
11011	1 0 1 1	0 0 1
01001	0 1 0 1	0 1 1

Table 3(a). Encoding.

Signals	Encoding
X_1	110
X_2	010
X_3	101
X_4	001
X_5	100
X_6	011
X_7	111

3(b). Compacted Truth Table.

Input	Output $\underline{c_1}\ \underline{c_2}\ c_3\ \underline{c_4}$
10101	1 0 1 0
01100	0 0 1 0
10001	1 0 0 1
01111	0 1 1 0
11110	0 - 0 1
01010	1 1 0 0
11111	1 0 1 0
1110-	0 - 1 1
11011	1 0 1 1
01001	0 1 0 1

It is possible to reduce the number of output columns after column compaction if we encode the symbols of Table 1 as shown in Table 3(a). The column compacted truth table is shown in Table 3(b). In Table 3(b), columns c_1, c_2 and c_4 represent the symbolic outputs.

This output encoding problem has many applications. Digital systems are often specified in terms of a combination of binary valued and symbolic signals. This problem is applicable to reduce the area of scan-based [16] designs containing one-out-of-n (one-hot) signals, as described in [17]. This algorithm can serve as a pre-processing step for FSM state encoding.

3. ENCODING ALGORITHM FOR FULLY SPECIFIED OUTPUTS

In this section, we present our output encoding algorithm with the assumption that the output columns belonging to the B-set are fully specified with 1's and 0's for simplicity. We consider the example of Table 4 for illustration. We describe the three basic steps of our algorithm as follows:

Step 1: Find Inconsistent Columns: Find all pairs of rows, p and q, in Table 4 for which the S-column has the same value and $c_i \in$ B-set has different values. Then c_i is said to be *inconsistent*. For this example, the B-set is $\{c_1, c_2, c_3, c_4, c_5, c_6\}$. Here, c_1 has a 1 in the second row and a 0 in the 4th row; but the S-column has X_2 in both of these rows. Hence, c_1 is inconsistent. Column c_3 is also inconsistent for symbolic output X_3.

Step 2: Create reduced consistent output table: Remove inconsistent columns from the specification table to obtain the *consistent output table* (COT). Merge equal rows of COT to obtain *reduced consistent output table* (RCOT). Table 5 is the RCOT for Table 4. Since there are 6 symbolic outputs, we use $m = 3$ bits to encode them.

Step 3: *i*-column counting check: Any set of i columns of the RCOT ($i \le m$) having any of the 2^i possible binary values of length i appearing more than 2^{m-i} times in the rows of the RCOT cannot reduce the size of the output column cover after encoding the symbols. All sets of i columns that satisfy this i-column counting check form elements of *column-count-set-i* (CCS-i). For Table 5, CCS-1 = $\{\{c_2\}, \{c_5\}, \{c_6\}\}$, CCS-2 = $\{\{c_2, c_5\}, \{c_5, c_6\}, \{c_2, c_6\}\}$, CCS-3 = NULL. $\{c_4\}$ is not included in CCS-1 because the number of 1's in the c_4 column is 5 (greater than 4). We terminate this step when either a CCS set is NULL or CCS-m has been generated.

Table 4. Specification Table.

c_1	c_2	c_3	c_4	c_5	c_6	Symbol
0	0	1	1	1	0	X_1
1	0	0	1	0	1	$\mathbf{X_2}$
1	0	**0**	1	1	1	$\mathbf{X_3}$
0	0	0	1	0	1	$\mathbf{X_2}$
0	1	1	1	0	0	X_4
0	1	0	1	1	0	X_5
1	0	1	1	1	1	X_3
1	1	0	0	0	0	X_6
1	0	**1**	1	1	1	$\mathbf{X_3}$
1	0	0	1	0	1	X_2

Table 5. The RCOT.

c_2	c_4	c_5	c_6	Symbol
0	1	1	0	X_1
0	1	0	1	X_2
0	1	1	1	X_3
1	1	0	0	X_4
1	1	1	0	X_5
1	0	0	0	X_6

For Table 4, we can encode the symbols using three bits in such a way that two of the three columns, representing the symbolic outputs, can be merged with the existing output columns by column compaction. We choose any member of CCS-2, say, $\{c_2, c_5\}$. The first two bits in the encoding of a particular symbol will have the same pattern as the one present under the columns c_2 and c_5 in the row corresponding to that symbol in the RCOT. We determine the third bit such that the codes assigned to the symbols are distinct. Thus, referring to Table 4, X_1 can be encoded as 010, X_2 as 000, X_3 as 011, X_4 as 100, X_5 as 110 and X_6 as 101. It is straightforward to prove the optimality of our solution [18]. It should be noted that if we allowed 4 bits to encode the symbolic outputs of Table 4, then all output columns corresponding to the four encoding bits could be merged with c_2, c_4, c_5 and c_6. In that case, we can iterate step 3 incrementing the number of encoding bits until all the encoding bit outputs can be merged with the existing outputs or we reach a point where we have tried to encode n symbolic outputs using n bits.

4. ENCODING ALGORITHM FOR INCOMPLETELY SPECIFIED OUTPUTS

The basic steps of the algorithm described in Sec. 3 can be extended to handle don't cares in the B-set.

Table 6. Specification Table.

c_1 c_2 c_3 c_4 c_5 c_6	Symbolic
0 - 1 0 - 0	X_1
1 0 - - - -	X_2
1 - - - 1 -	X_3
0 - - - - 1	X_2
0 1 0 0 0 0	X_4
0 1 1 0 - -	X_5
- - 1 1 - -	X_3
1 1 1 0 0 0	X_6
- - - 1 1 -	X_3
- - 1 0 - -	X_2

Table 7. The RCOT.

c_2 c_3 c_4 c_5 c_6	Symbolic
- 1 0 - 0	X_1
0 1 0 - 1	X_2
- 1 1 1 -	X_3
0 1 0 0 0	X_4
1 1 0 - -	X_5
1 1 0 0 0	X_6

Consider the specification shown in Table 6. The RCOT is shown in Table 7. The CCS-1 set is $\{\{c_2\}, \{c_5\}, \{c_6\}\}$. For calculating CCS-2 and CCS-3 we must ensure that the count of the *fully specified* binary strings (binary strings containing no don't cares) only need to satisfy the bounds discussed in step 3 of the algorithm in Sec. 3. Thus, CCS-2 is $\{\{c_2, c_5\}, \{c_2, c_6\}$ and $\{c_5, c_6\}\}$. CCS-3 is a null set and we choose $\{c_2, c_5\}$, a member of CCS-2, for providing the first two bits in the encoding of the symbols using 3 bits. Next, we solve the problem of assigning 0's and 1's to the *don't cares* in columns c_2 and c_5 so that the output columns representing the symbolic outputs can be merged with c_2 and c_5. We formulate the problem as a bipartite graph matching problem [2]. We form a weighted bipartite graph as follows: Set V_1 contains vertices corresponding to each symbolic output with a label equal to the string formed by the entries in the row corresponding to that symbolic output under columns c_2 and c_5 of Table 7. Set V_2 contains 4 vertices each having a label that is a distinct binary pattern of length 2. For each $u \in V_1$ and $v \in V_2$ we have an edge (u, v) of weight 1 if and only if the label of v contains 1(0) in all positions in which the label of u contains 1(0). We add two more vertices to the graph — the *source* and the *sink*. There is an edge of weight 1 from the source vertex to each member of V_1. There is an edge of weight $2^{3-2} = 2$ from each member of V_2 to the sink.

The graph along with the source and the sink nodes and the edge weights is shown in Fig. 2. We solve the maximum network flow problem on the graph using the Ford-Fulkerson method [19]. The solid edges show the final mapping. The first two bits in the encoding of X_1, X_2, X_3, X_4, X_5 and X_6 are 00, 01, 01, 10, 11 and 10, respectively. Hence, one encoding of X_1, X_2, X_3, X_4, X_5 and X_6 is 001, 010, 011, 100, 111 and 101, respectively. Note that there may be multiple solutions to this bipartite graph matching problem. Hence, our algorithm can be further refined by selecting a mapping of members of V_1 to the members of V_2 based on some heuristic following the observations developed in [13] and [14].

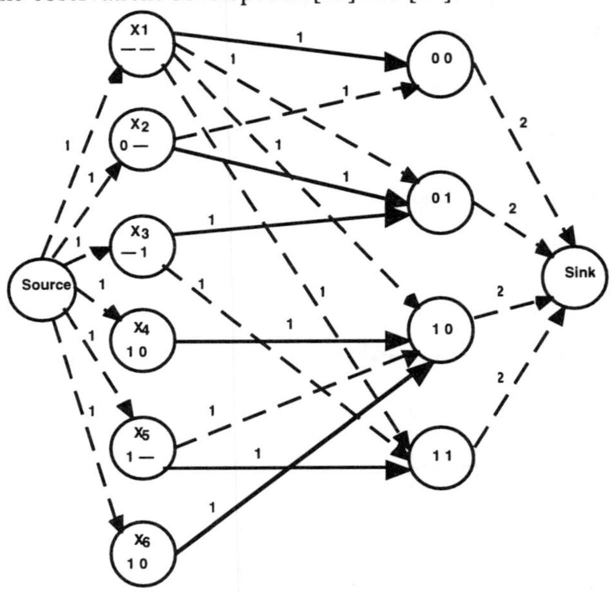

Figure 2. The Graph for the Maximum Flow Problem.

5. EXPERIMENTAL RESULTS

In this section, we present experimental results. We added a symbolic output column to the MCNC FSM benchmarks and varied the number of symbols in the symbolic output column; depending on the symbol count, the number of encoding bits required were either 3 or 4.

Table 8. Area results for our output encoding algorithm (best case) and the worst case which never merges any output column.

FSM Name	3 bits for encoding		4 bits for encoding	
	Our algo.	Worst Case	Our algo.	Worst Case
bbara	*205	225	*285	346
bbsse	316	364	316	378
bbtas	*98	99	*103	147
dk14	223	266	223	294
dk15	206	208	206	257
dk17	*182	191	*231	304
ex1	721	750	721	781
ex6	254	312	254	405
mc	93	96	93	96
opus	235	260	235	356
tav	73	143	73	188
tma	444	543	444	548

*: These are the cases where all the output columns could not be merged by our algorithm because the cardinality of the B-set is less than the number of bits needed to encode the symbols.

We entered symbolic values in the S-column to ensure that there exists an output encoding, for which all the columns generated due to the encoding of the symbols could be merged with the existing outputs (members of the B-set), assuming that the number of encoding bits did not exceed the number of existing non-symbolic (binary) output columns. We applied our output encoding algorithm to encode the symbolic output columns, then compacted the outputs using column compaction. We then optimized these specifications using *sis* [20]. For comparison purposes, we then encoded the symbolic outputs such that none of the outputs corresponding to the encoding bits could be merged by column compaction with the pre-existent outputs (members of the B-set). This is the worst-case encoding. The results are shown in Table 8. Although our scheme works for both combinational and sequential logic specifications, we used FSM benchmarks because we are investigating FSM synthesis techniques for one-hot signals, as mentioned in Sec. 2 [17]. For both cases, we used NOVA [10] to encode the FSM states and used the recommended *rugged* script to perform multi-level logic optimization. Finally, we used the LSI Logic g10p library [21] for technology mapping. Table 8 shows the area values (in terms of LSI Logic g10p cell units) obtained using our output encoding algorithm and the worst-case output encoding where none of the encoding bits could be merged with the already existent non-symbolic output columns by compaction.

6. CONCLUSION

In this paper, we have presented a new output encoding algorithm whose objective is to encode the symbols in the symbolic output column of the specification table using $\lceil \log_2 n \rceil$ bits for n symbolic outputs in such a way that the number of output functions, after performing the encoding and subsequent output column compaction, is minimum. An application of this algorithm is to generate a low-area circuit that always maintains a one-hot encoding on certain signals, even during scan or BIST operations as discussed in [17]. This algorithm can also be used as a pre-processing step for FSM state encoding. Although the algorithm produces a minimum solution and the worst case running time is exponential in the number of bits used to encode the symbolic outputs, our algorithm achieves significant speedup through iterative refinement by removing from consideration inconsistent output columns or sets of output columns. As the experimental results show, the circuits generated using our output encoding algorithm have significantly less area (0.9 % to 49 % for 3 bits, 8 % to 61 % for 4 bits) than worst-case circuits generated without considering output column compaction during the encoding of the symbols. In this paper, we have considered specifications with a single symbolic output column. In case of multiple symbolic output columns, we can integrate our technique with the output encoding algorithm reported in [15] to achieve a minimum number of output columns in the final table.

7. ACKNOWLEDGMENT

This work was supported by the Advanced Research Projects Agency under prime contract No. DABT63-94-C-0045. Thanks to Robert B. Norwood and Jonathan T. Y. Chang of Center for Reliable Computing, Stanford University, for their comments regarding this work.

8. REFERENCES

[1] Wei, R. and C Tseng, "Column Compaction and Its Application to The Control Path Synthesis," *Proc. ICCAD-87*, pp. 320-323, 1987.

[2] Cormen, T. H., et. al., *Introduction to Algorithms*, The MIT Press and McGraw-Hill, 1989.

[3] Brayton, R. K., et. al., *Logic Minimization Algorithms for VLSI Synthesis*, Kluwer Publishers, 1984.

[4] Ashar, P., S. Devadas and A. R. Newton, *Sequential Logic Synthesis*, Kluwer Academic Publishers, 1991.

[5] Dolotta, T. A., and E. J. McCluskey, "The Coding of Internal States of Sequential Circuits," *IEEE Trans. Comput.*, EC-13, pp. 549-562, Oct. 1964.

[6] De Micheli, G., et. al., "Optimal State Assignment for Finite State Machines," *IEEE Trans. on CAD.*, CAD 4(3), 269-285, July 1985.

[7] Du, X., et. al. "MUSE: A MUltilevel Symbolic Encoding Algorithm for State Assignment," *IEEE Trans. on CAD*, 10(1), pp. 28-38, Jan. 1991.

[8] Lin, B. and A. R. Newton, "Synthesis of Multiple Level Logic from Symbolic High-Level Description Languages," *VLSI 89*, pp. 187-196, Elsevier, 1990.

[9] Tumbush, G. L. and J. E. Brandeberry, "A State Assignment Technique for Sequential Machines using J-K Flip-Flops," *IEEE Trans. Comput.*, pp. 85-86, Jan. 1974.

[10] Villa, T. and A. Sangiovanni-Vincentelli, "NOVA: State Assignment of Finite State Machines for Optimal Two-Level Logic Implementation", *IEEE Trans. on CAD*, 9(9), pp. 905-924, Sept. 1990.

[11] Buijs, F., et. al., "Synthesis of Multi-Level Logic with one symbolic input," *EDAC-91*, pp. 60-64, 1991.

[12] Yang, S., et. al., "Optimum and Sub-optimum Algorithms for Input Encoding and Its Relation to Logic Minimization," *IEEE Trans. on CAD*, 10(1), pp. 4-12, Jan. 1991.

[13] Devadas, S. and A. R. Newton, "Exact Algorithms for Output Encoding, State Assignment and Four Level boolean Minimization," *IEEE Trans. on CAD*, 10(1), pp. 13-27, Jan. 1991.

[14] Saldanha, A. and R. H. Katz, "PLA Optimization Using Output Encoding," *ICCAD*, pp. 478-481, 1988.

[15] Binger, D. and D. W. Knapp, "Encoding Multiple Outputs for Improved Column Compaction," *Proc. ICCAD-91*, pp. 230-233, 1991.

[16] McCluskey, E. J., *Logic Design Principles with Emphasis on Testable Semicustom circuits*, Prentice-Hall, Eaglewood Cliffs, NJ, USA, 1986.

[17] Mitra, S., L. J. Avra and E. J. McCluskey, "Scan Synthesis for One-hot Signals", *Proc. ITC*, Nov. 1997.

[18] Mitra, S., L. J. Avra and E. J. McCluskey, "An Output Encoding Problem and a Solution Technique", *Technical Report, Center for Reliable Computing, Stanford University*, CRC TR 97-1, 1997.

[19] Ford, L. R. and D. R. Fulkerson, *Flows in Networks*, Princeton University Press, 1962.

[20] Sentovich, E., *et. al.*, "SIS: A System for Sequential Circuit Synthesis", *ERL Memo. No. UCB/ERL M92/41*, Department of EECS, UC Berkeley, CA 94720.

[21] *G10-p Cell-Based ASIC Products Databook*, LSI Logic, May 1996.

OPTIMIST: State Minimization for Optimal 2-Level Logic Implementation

Robert M. Fuhrer   Steven M. Nowick*
Department of Computer Science
Columbia University
New York, NY 10027

Abstract

We present a novel method for state minimization of incompletely-specified finite state machines. Where classic methods simply minimize the number of states, ours directly addresses the implementation's logic complexity, and produces an exactly optimal implementation under input encoding. The method incorporates optimal "state mapping", i.e., the process of reducing the symbolic next-state relation which results from state splitting to an optimal conforming symbolic function. Further, it offers a number of convenient sites for applying heuristics to reduce time and space complexity, and is amenable to implementation based on implicit representations. Although our method currently makes use of an input encoding model, we believe it can be extended smoothly to encompass output encoding as well.

1 Introduction

State minimization is the problem of finding a machine realizing the input/output behaviour of a given FSM, with fewer internal states [11, 17, 12]. This is an important step in sequential synthesis: implementing unminimized FSM's often leads to considerably larger and/or slower implementations. However, it is well known that the classic formulation for state minimization expresses a *heuristic* – reducing the number of states only *tends* to decrease logic complexity. Early on, Hartmanis observed [9] that this heuristic sometimes fails; realizations having more states may be simpler to implement. Moreover, there may be many minimum-state realizations of a given FSM, and their logic complexity can vary significantly [18, 16]. Hence, simply targeting any minimum-state solution is insufficient.

The major contribution of this paper is a state minimization method which, in contrast to existing ones, directly targets logic complexity. In particular, we define and solve the *optimal state minimization problem*, that of finding for a given FSM a realization having minimum 2-level logic complexity over all realizations.

Classic sequential synthesis comprises several steps: state minimization, state encoding, 2-level logic minimization, multi-level optimization and technology mapping. Each step has traditionally been treated as an isolated problem, which limits early steps most severely. In [7], a key insight into optimal state encoding was presented: *symbolic* logic minimization can be performed *concurrently* with state encoding. More recent methods for optimal encoding have been developed [20, 8] based on the same insight, but yielding even better results.

We borrow this insight, and take it one step further: symbolic logic minimization is performed concurrently with *both* state minimization and state encoding. Our method is cast as a unique form of generalized prime implicant minimization [8]. Specifically, symbolic prime implicants are generated, and a binate covering problem is formed and solved, yielding a reduced machine and logic cover.

Our paper offers a novel theoretical framework for formulating and solving the optimal state minimization problem. We demonstrate that our method identifies optimal solutions which are inaccessible to existing tools, due to their focus on minimum cardinality state covers. In addition, we provide initial results of a CAD tool implementation.

The structure of the paper is as follows. Section 2, provides background on state minimization, state assignment and related work. Section 3 then gives a general overview of our method, with a focus on the major issues. Sections 4, 5 and 6, provide greater detail on the three major components of our method: symbolic prime generation, binate constraint generation, and symbolic instantiation, respectively. Two examples in Section 7 demonstrate the procedure and show results unattainable by existing methods. Finally, Section 8 provides some experimental results, and Section 9 presents conclusions and future work.

2 Background and Related Work

A *completely-specified* Finite State Machine (FSM) $\mathcal{M}$ is defined [16, 6] by the tuple $\langle \mathcal{I}, \mathcal{O}, \mathcal{S}, \mathcal{S}_0, \mathcal{T}, \mathcal{F} \rangle$, where $\mathcal{I}$ is the input alphabet, $\mathcal{O}$ is the output alphabet, $\mathcal{S}$ is the set of states, $\mathcal{S}_0 \subset \mathcal{S}$ is the (set of) initial state(s), $\mathcal{T} = \mathcal{T}(i, s) \in \mathcal{S}, i \in \mathcal{I}, s \in \mathcal{S}$ is the transition function, and $\mathcal{F} = \mathcal{F}(i, s) \in \mathcal{O}, i \in \mathcal{I}, s \in \mathcal{S}$ is the output function.

An *incompletely-specified* FSM (ISFSM) is defined similarly, except that $\mathcal{T} \subset \mathcal{I} \times \mathcal{S} \times \mathcal{S}$ and $\mathcal{F} \subset \mathcal{I} \times \mathcal{S} \times \mathcal{O}$ are relations, rather than functions.[1]

*This research was funded in part by NSF CAREER Award MIP-9501880 and by an Alfred P. Sloan Research Fellowship.

[1] Where clear, a functional notation will be used for ISFSM's.

For the unreduced machine, we restrict attention to the common subclass of ISFSM's where, $\forall i \in \mathcal{I}, \forall s \in \mathcal{S}$, the next-state $\mathcal{T}(i,s)$ is either a singleton state or else is completely unspecified (denoted $\mathcal{T}(i,s) = \mathcal{S}$). Likewise, it is assumed that output $\mathcal{O}(i,s)$ is either a single value or unspecified.

2.1 State Minimization

We now review basic definitions given in [11].

A pair of states (s_a, s_b) *implies* states (s_c, s_d) *under input* $\mathcal{I}_k$ iff $\{\mathcal{T}(\mathcal{I}_k, s_a), \mathcal{T}(\mathcal{I}_k, s_b)\} = \{s_c, s_d\}$.

A pair of states is *output-compatible* iff corresponding output values agree wherever both are specified.

A pair of states is *compatible* iff they are output-compatible and imply no incompatible pair of states.

A set of states is a *compatible* iff it consists of pairwise-compatible states.

Compatible c_a *implies* compatible c_b *under input* I_k iff $\{\mathcal{T}(\mathcal{I}_k, s), \forall s \in c_a\} = c_b$.

Compatible c is a *maximal compatible* iff it is a proper subset of no other compatible.

The *implied set* $P(c)$ of a compatible c is the set of compatibles implied by c over all inputs, excluding singleton states, subsets of c, and proper subsets of compatibles in $P(c)$.

Compatible c_a *excludes* c_b iff $c_b \subset c_a$ and $P(c_a) \subseteq P(c_b)$.

Compatible c is a *prime compatible* iff it is excluded by no other compatible.

A set C of compatibles is *closed* iff every element of the implied set of each compatible $c \in C$ is contained by some compatible in C.

A set C of compatibles is a *cover* for $\mathcal{M}$ iff for every state $s \in \mathcal{S}$ there exists a compatible $c \in C$ such that $s \in c$.

The classic state minimization problem can now be defined as finding a minimum cardinality closed cover of prime compatibles of $\mathcal{M}$. In the sequel, we designate the resulting reduced machine as $\mathcal{M}'$.

2.2 The State Mapping Problem

Given an incompletely-specified FSM, a state reduction often defines a *set* of compatible realizations [17, 11]. In this case, the next-state behaviour of the resulting ISFSM forms a *relation*, so that different next-state bindings are possible. This flexibility gives rise to the *state-mapping problem* [15], in which the symbolic relation is reduced to a conforming symbolic function. The function is obtained by choosing a specific next-state wherever a choice exists. This choice has a direct impact on logic quality, and is a pivotal issue for optimal state minimization.

$\mathcal{M}$	0	1
s_0	s_0,0	s_2,0
s_1	s_1,0	s_1,-
s_2	s_1,-	s_0,1

$\mathcal{M}'$	0	1
$s'_0 = \{s_0, s_1\}$	s'_0,0	s'_1,0
$s'_1 = \{s_1, s_2\}$	$\{s_1\}$,0	s'_0,1

Figure 1: State table before and after minimization

The state mapping problem is illustrated in Figure 1, taken from [15]. A choice of next-state in $\mathcal{M}'$ at total state $\langle\, 0\ s'_1 \,\rangle$ exists; it can be assigned to either s'_0 or s'_1. The best cover achievable[2] when state mapping s_1 to s'_1 in that total state has 4 terms. In contrast, state mapping to s'_0 yields a 3-term cover.

2.3 Optimal State Assignment as Input Encoding

As our strategy for optimal state minimization is the *concurrent* reduction and assignment of states, we now review basic concepts in optimal state assignment.

The problem of *optimal state assignment* is that of finding an assignment of N-bit binary values to the internal states of an (IS)FSM so as to minimize the logic complexity of the resulting realization. One useful approximation to this problem is known as *input encoding*. As we use an input encoding formulation in our approach to optimal state minimization, we briefly give an overview. For further details, see [7], or, for recent extensions for hazard-free encoding of asynchronous machines, see [10].

Input encoding, like several approaches to optimal encoding, has two steps:

1. *Symbolic 2-level logic minimization*
2. *Constrained encoding*

In input encoding, symbolic logic minimization is performed by temporarily "1-hot encoding" the states. The present state is then treated as a multi-valued input [19], while each next state is treated as a *disjoint* binary output function. Multi-valued minimization [19] produces the desired 2-level symbolic cover. The structure of this symbolic cover reflects that of the target realization.

Using this cover, encoding constraints are generated. The constraints are then solved, yielding an encoding with which the symbolic cover can be "instantiated" to produce a correct binary implementation. The resulting 2-level realization has *identical* cardinality to the original symbolic cover.[3]

2.4 Previous Work

The topic of state minimization has been researched extensively over several decades. Hartmanis observed in [9] that the minimum cardinality solution does not always yield the best implementation. The problem was later approximated as a search for a closed cover *of minimum cardinality* and solved exactly in [11]. In [13], the relationship of state reduction to implementation complexity was explored via an elegant theoretical framework, which unfortunately did not provide a solution to the problem.

Several recent methods have been focused on producing minimum cardinality covers. Efficient algorithms have been produced for solving the problem exactly ([12], [14]), and heuristics ([12]) have been developed for inexact solutions. These two fronts have seen considerable progress.

Only a few recent attempts have been made to address the more general problem of *optimal* state minimization. In STAMINA [12], some attention is paid

[2] assuming an input-encoded implementation

[3] Modulo the well-known "all-0 code" issue; see [6].

to implementation complexity, but no attempt at direct nor exact solutions was made. A somewhat more direct approach was taken by Avedillo et al. [1], but results were less than encouraging (they were not even compared with a state reduction tool, but rather with NOVA, a state assignment tool, which did better on already-minimized FSM's), and no theoretical results are given. Finally, Calazans [3] offers a framework within which both optimal encoding and state minimization can be expressed. In it, state reduction is modeled as the assignment of two or more states to the same code. This insight constitutes one of the cornerstones of our method. Unfortunately, the only solution method given is a simple, greedy method which fares relatively poorly. Worse, it is not evident how to express a high-quality solution method within that formulation.

Two recently developed CAD optimization techniques are also relevant to our work, though created for other purposes. First, Devadas and Newton [8] address the problem of exact state encoding via *GPI minimization*. In this method, *generalized* symbolic primes (*GPI's*) are formed, and a constrained binate covering problem is then solved which both selects a set of GPI's and produces a compatible state encoding. The basic flow – symbolic prime generation followed by constrained covering – is used in our present method, but with considerably different symbolic primes and constraints.

Second, Lin and Somenzi [15] introduce a technique for the exact minimization of symbolic relations. Of particular interest is its application to exact state encoding, incorporating an elegant method for state mapping. The symbolic relation they minimize, however, is the *result* of state minimization; state minimization itself is not addressed.

3 Optimal State Minimization: Overview

This section provides a general overview of our optimal state minimization method.

Optimal state minimization is defined as finding, for a machine $\mathcal{M}$, a reduced machine $\mathcal{M}'$ with compatible behaviour and minimum logic complexity. Our method is cast as a form of symbolic GPI (generalized prime implicant) minimization which encapsulates both state encoding *and* state minimization. The method has 5 steps:

1. Generate state compatibles
2. Generate symbolic primes
3. Generate binate constraints
4. Solve constraints
5. Instantiate symbolic cover

First, state compatibles are formed by any of various standard methods (e.g., STAMINA [12]). Next, a novel form of symbolic prime called *RGPI's*, based on GPI's [8], is generated. A set of binate constraints which identify the valid realizations is then formed. These constraints are solved so as to minimize logic cardinality using a binate solver (e.g., Scherzo [5]). The solution is a set of selected compatibles and a set of selected RGPI's. These are trivially combined during cover instantiation, to produce the reduced machine $\mathcal{M}'$ and its symbolic realization. From there, input encoding constraints can be immediately generated and solved to produce an optimal encoding.

We now give an overview of the 3 steps unique to our method: symbolic prime generation, binate constraint generation, and cover instantiation. Further details are provided in Sections 4 through 6.

3.1 Symbolic Primes

A *symbolic product* is a product of literals over an mvi domain [6]. Each value taken by a symbolic output is called a *symbolic part*. A *symbolic implicant* is a symbolic product which satisfies the following two properties: (i) it contains no OFF-set minterm of any *binary output* to which it contributes; (ii) for each *symbolic output* to which it contributes, it asserts all symbolic parts specified in the minterms which it contains. A symbolic implicant of an FSM is expressed as a 4-tuple $p : \langle \texttt{in ps ns out} \rangle$, denoting the input, present-state, next-state and output fields.

Our procedure forms a set of symbolic implicants on the unreduced machine, which can be used to cover portions of various reduced machines, after a suitable transformation. These implicants are maximal over $\mathcal{M}$ in an intuitive sense. Specifically, we define a novel type of symbolic prime implicant, called a *restricted generalized (prime) implicant*, or *RG(P)I*, a variant of a GPI, formed on the unreduced machine.

GPI's were introduced in [8] as a kind of symbolic prime implicant, each "tagged with" (i.e., having a field comprising) a *set* of next-states. The tag contains *all* next-states which are specified in all total states the GPI contains. For example, in Figure 1, the symbolic implicant $g_a : \langle - \ s_0 \ s_0, s_2 \ 0 \rangle$ is a GPI, where $\texttt{ns}= \{s_0, s_2\}$.

We now formally define RGI's, and an easily-calculated subset of RGPI's called *RGPI seeds.*

Definition 3.1 *An* **RGI** *is a symbolic implicant whose next-state field consists of compatible states.*

Intuitively, the selection of an RGI corresponds to a state-mapping choice. Note that the next-state field of an RGI (if non-empty) is a set of states, i.e. a *compatible*, in the unreduced machine. This compatible, if selected, will appear as a *single state* in the reduced machine. Therefore, the RGI will be bound to (at most) one symbolic next-state in the reduced machine, as required by the input encoding formulation.

Definition 3.2 *An RGI p_1* **contains** *RGI p_2 iff each field of p_1 contains the corresponding field of p_2.*

Definition 3.3 *An* **RGPI seed** *is an RGI which is contained* only *by RGI's with unequal next-state fields.*

Example: Figure 1 has the following RGPI seeds:

$p_0 : \langle 0 \ s_0 \ s_0 \ 0 \rangle$ $\quad p_1 : \langle 0 \ s_0, s_1, s_2 \ s_0, s_1 \ 0 \rangle$
$p_2 : \langle 0 \ s_1, s_2 \ s_1 \ 0 \rangle$ $\quad p_3 : \langle 0 \ s_2 \ s_1 \ 1 \rangle$
$p_4 : \langle 1 \ s_0 \ s_2 \ 0 \rangle$ $\quad p_5 : \langle 1 \ s_1 \ s_1 \ 1 \rangle$
$p_6 : \langle - \ s_1 \ s_1 \ 0 \rangle$ $\quad p_7 : \langle 1 \ s_0, s_1 \ s_1, s_2 \ 0 \rangle$

$p_8 : \langle 1 \; s_1, s_2 \; s_0, s_1 \; 1 \rangle$ $\quad$ $p_9 : \langle 0 \; s_1, s_2 \; s_1, s_2 \; 0 \rangle$
$p_{10} : \langle - \; s_1, s_2 \; s_0, s_1 \; 0 \rangle$ $\quad$ $p_{11} : \langle - \; s_2 \; s_0, s_1 \; 1 \rangle$

Note that $\{s_0, s_1\}$ is a compatible, but $\{s_0, s_2\}$ is not. Therefore, p_1 is an RGI, but GPI $g_a : \langle - \; s_0 \; s_0, s_2 \; 0 \rangle$ is not. Furthermore, $p_b : \langle 0 \; s_0, s_1 \; s_0, s_1 \; 0 \rangle$ is an RGI, but is not an RGPI, since p_1 contains p_b and has the same next-state field. On the other hand, although p_1 contains p_0, its next-state field is different, and so p_0 is a distinct RGPI. □

We generate RGPI seeds by a slightly modified version of a GPI generation algorithm [8], which will be described in Section 4.

While RGPI seeds are the basic covering objects which will be used, it will be shown in Section 4 that a more general class, RGPI's, is in fact needed.[4]

Definition 3.4 *An* **RGPI** *is an RGI which is contained* only *by RGI's with unequal input or next-state fields.*

The class of RGPI's includes RGPI seeds, as well as smaller RGPI's which result from reducing seeds in the input dimension, to allow finer-grained covering.

3.2 Constraint Generation

Once RGPI's are generated, constraints are formulated to insure a valid and optimal implementation. The solution is a set of selected compatibles and RGPI's. There are 3 main objectives. First, reduced machine $\mathcal{M}'$ must be a realization of $\mathcal{M}$. Second, the selected set of RGPI's must constitute a cover for $\mathcal{M}'$. Third, the resulting cover must have minimum cardinality. We now outline the constraints; details are provided in Section 5.

The first objective is ensured by two sets of constraints. Each corresponds to a classic state minimization constraint: that the state compatibles form a cover, and that the cover be closed. State covering constraints are precisely as described in [11].

The second objective, covering $\mathcal{M}'$, is met by a novel set of constraints. Each selected compatible identifies a unique state in the reduced machine. Our constraints ensure that each ON-set minterm of this reduced state is covered by some (instantiated) RGPI.

The third objective, minimum logic cardinality, is met by the binate solver, which finds a minimum-cost solution. To make cost a straightforward calculation, we introduce one extra column variable per RGPI. Only these column variables have non-zero cost.

3.3 Symbolic Instantiation

Symbolic instantiation is the process by which selected RGPI's are transformed one-for-one into a symbolic realization of $\mathcal{M}'$. To describe the process, we consider each of the 4 fields of an RGPI.

Formally, for $p = \langle I, \; PS, \; NS, \; O \rangle$ we define

$$p' = \text{Instantiate}(p) = \langle I, \; PS', \; NS', \; O \rangle$$

[4]Note that RGPI seeds are GPI's, while RGPI's in general are not.

The *input* and *output* fields of p are unchanged by instantiation.

The *next-state* field of p is a *compatible* of $\mathcal{M}$. Note that this compatible corresponds to a *single row* in the reduced machine. Hence, an RGPI's next-state field identifies a unique state of $\mathcal{M}'$, and is mapped trivially:

$$NS' = \text{ the unique state of } \mathcal{M}' \text{ corresponding to } NS$$

The role of the RGPI in the reduced machine is thus to contribute to (at most) a *single* symbolic next-state. This role reflects our use of an input encoding formulation, where each next-state in the reduced machine is treated as a distinct function. Therefore, each RGPI embodies a *uniform state mapping* over some cube of $\mathcal{M}'$ to a *specific* reduced state of $\mathcal{M}'$.

Finally, the *present-state* field of an RGPI contains one or more symbolic states. To a first approximation, an RGPI will be mapped so as to cover *all selected* compatibles c which contain the present state field of that RGPI. That is, the RGPI is regarded as covering the class of compatibles which are contained within its present state field.

Example: RGPI $p_8 : \langle 1 \; s_1, s_2 \; s_0, s_1 \; 1 \rangle$ in Figure 1 contributes to (compatible) next-states $\{s_0, s_1\}$ of $\mathcal{M}$, and has present states $\{s_1, s_2\}$. Therefore, in the reduced table $\mathcal{M}'$, p_8 maps to the product $p'_8 : \langle 1 \; s'_1 \; s'_0 \; 1 \rangle$. The resulting present state field contains $s'_1 = \{s_1, s_2\}$; the next-state field consists of the single reduced next-state s'_0 (which corresponds to the original compatible set $\{s_0, s_1\}$). □

As indicated, for the present state, we can include in PS' all selected compatibles contained by PS. This scheme works in some cases, but fails to capture the full flexibility of state mapping in others. In Section 6, we define the precise mapping for PS which circumvents this problem.

Example: One solution to the constrained covering problem, for Figure 1, consists of (i) compatibles $s'_0 \equiv \{s_0, s_1\}$ and $s'_1 \equiv \{s_1, s_2\}$, and (ii) RGPI's $\{p_1, p_7, p_8\}$ shown below.

$p_1 : \langle 0 \; s_0, s_1, s_2 \; s_0, s_1 \; 0 \rangle$ $\quad$ $p'_1 : \langle 0 \; s'_0, s'_1 \; s'_0 \; 0 \rangle$
$p_7 : \langle 1 \; s_0, s_1 \; s_1, s_2 \; 0 \rangle$ $\quad$ $p'_7 : \langle 1 \; s'_0 \; s'_1 \; 0 \rangle$
$p_8 : \langle 1 \; s_1, s_2 \; s_0, s_1 \; 1 \rangle$ $\quad$ $p'_8 : \langle 1 \; s'_1 \; s'_0 \; 1 \rangle$

The selected RGPI's, $\{p_1, p_7, p_8\}$, can be instantiated as symbolic implicants $\{p'_1, p'_7, p'_8\}$ of reduced machine $\mathcal{M}'$. It is easy to verify that the result is a cover for $\mathcal{M}'$. Observe that the input and output fields are unchanged; only the present-state and next-state fields are transformed. Further, each mapped implicant contributes to at most 1 state. Note that the state mapping choice at $\langle 0 \; s'_1 \rangle$ is resolved to s'_0 by the binding effected by p'_1. □

4 Symbolic Primes: RGPI's

The structure of this section is as follows. First, we present an RGPI seed generation algorithm. Next, we highlight the problem arising from restricting solutions to RGPI seeds. Finally, we describe the solution to this problem – use of a larger set of symbolic primes, the complete set of RGPI's.

4.1 Generating RGPI Seeds

RGPI seeds are generated by a modified version of an existing "k-cube" algorithm [8]. First, "0-cubes" are generated, which essentially record the next-state and output in each total state. Then, an iterative "merge-and-dominate" step is performed. The algorithm produces seeds with "tight-fitting" next-state fields, which exactly equal the set of next-states specified within each cube. Finally, a simple post-processing step (not shown) expands the next-state fields to larger compatibles, yielding the remaining seeds.

```
merge(s_a, s_b) :=
      s_a ∪ s_b  if compatible(s_a, s_b) and neither = φ,
      s_a        if s_b = DC,
      s_b        if s_a = DC,
      φ          otherwise
generate-0-cubes() {
   cubes_0 := φ;
   foreach total state τ = ⟨IN PS⟩ do
      OUT := {o_i | output i ≠ 0 in τ };
      NS := {s} iff T(IN, PS) = s, else DC;
      cubes_0 := cubes_0 ∪ { ⟨IN PS OUT NS⟩ };   }
generate-k-cubes() {
   generate-0-cubes();
   for k := 1 to kMax do
      cubes_k := φ;
      for each pair p_i, p_j in cubes_{k-1} do
         if distance(p_i, p_j) = 1 then
            IN' := IN_i ∪ IN_j;
            PS' := PS_i ∪ PS_j;
            NS' := merge(NS_i, NS_j);
            OUT' := OUT_i ∩ OUT_j;
            if (¬empty(NS') ∧ ¬empty(OUT')) then
               cubes_k := cubes_k ∪ {⟨IN', PS', NS', OUT'⟩};
               if (OUT' = OUT_i) ∧ (NS' = NS_i)
                  mark p_i dominated;
               if (OUT' = OUT_j) ∧ (NS' = NS_j)
                  mark p_j dominated;   }
```

4.2 Non-Seed RGPI's

It is not always possible to construct an optimal solution using only RGPI seeds. The reason is the incompatibility of RGPI's which intersect and implement next-state, but disagree. Their incompatibility results from their commitment to bind the next-state entries of contained total states to *conflicting* states. Lacking finer-grained cubes, this interference results in cases where only sub-optimal solutions are produced, or where no cover exists.

Example: The following table, when reduced using compatibles $\{s_1, s_2\}$ and $\{s_2, s_3\}$, cannot be covered by RGPI seeds alone:

$\mathcal{M}$	00	01	11	10
s_0	s_1,-	s_2,-	s_3,-	s_4,1
s_1	s_1,1	s_1,1	s_4,-	s_4,-
s_2	s_2,1	s_2,-	s_4,0	s_4,0
s_3	s_2,-	s_3,0	s_4,0	s_4,0
s_4	s_4,0	s_4,1	s_4,1	s_4,1

Consider the RGPI seeds $p_1 : \langle 0{-} \;\; s_0, s_1, s_2 \;\; s_1, s_2 \;\; 1 \rangle$ and $p_2 : \langle -1 \;\; s_0 \;\; s_2, s_3 \;\; 1 \rangle$. These seeds are incompatible: they intersect in total state $\langle 01\, s_0 \rangle$, but have different next-state fields ($\{s_1, s_2\}$ vs. $\{s_2, s_3\}$), representing conflicting state mappings. Yet, p_1 and p_2 are both essential for covering minterms at $\langle 00\, s_0 \rangle$ and $\langle 11\, s_0 \rangle$, respectively. Hence no solution exists, using only RGPI seeds. □

Clearly, RGPI seeds are not fine-grained enough to express the full flexibility of state mapping. In some cases, no solution consisting solely of RGPI seeds exists; in others, no optimum solution exists. In general, an optimum solution requires a combination of RGPI seeds and finer-grained symbolic cubes. To see the kind of cubes that are needed, consider following reduction of the above machine.

Example:

$\mathcal{M}'$	00	01	11	10
$s'_0 = \{s_0\}$	s'_1,-	$\{s_2\}$,-	s'_2,-	s'_3,1
$s'_1 = \{s_1, s_2\}$	s'_1,1	s'_1,1	s'_3,0	s'_3,0
$s'_2 = \{s_2, s_3\}$	$\{s_2\}$,1	s'_2,0	s'_3,0	s'_3,0
$s'_3 = \{s_4\}$	s'_3,0	s'_3,1	s'_3,1	s'_3,1

There are two state mapping choices in $\langle 01\, s'_0 \rangle$: s'_1 and s'_2. If we choose mapping s'_1, we require an implicant which covers the isolated s'_2 minterm at $\langle 11\, s'_0 \rangle$; however, no RGPI seed maps onto such an implicant. If we choose s'_2, two distinct implicants are required to cover the minterms s'_1 at $\langle 00\, s'_0 \rangle$ and $\langle 01\, s'_1 \rangle$; no RGPI seed maps onto either implicant. □

We need smaller RGPI's to gain finer control over state-mapping. Specifically, we require a set of implicants with smaller input and/or present-state fields.

Example: An optimal cover can be constructed, if the set of RGPI seeds is augmented with the following RGPI's: $p_{1a} : \langle 00 \;\; s_0, s_1, s_2 \;\; s_1, s_2 \;\; 1 \rangle$, $p_{1b} : \langle 0{-} \;\; s_1, s_2 \;\; s_1, s_2 \;\; 1 \rangle$, and $p_{2a} : \langle 11 \;\; s_0 \;\; s_2, s_3 \;\; 1 \rangle$. □

We now show how such non-seed cubes as p_{1a}, p_{1b}, and p_{2a} above can be derived from RGPI seeds by restricting their input and/or present-state fields. Two distinct approaches are used. For cubes restricted in the present-state field, we introduce decision variables into constrained covering which determine the selected subset of reduced states. For cubes restricted in the input field, we simply refine RGPI seeds in the input dimension. In the following sections, we describe both approaches.

4.3 Present State Field

Non-seed RGPI's which span fewer reduced states are obtained, by associating a set of Boolean decision variables $\{\gamma_{p,c}\}$ with each RGPI p. Each $\gamma_{p,c}$ is set to true iff RGPI p is to be mapped so as to span the reduced state corresponding to c. Thus, the present-state mapping of p is incorporated into the constrained covering step. The $\gamma_{p,c}$ assignments chosen during covering are later used in symbolic instantiation.

$\gamma_{p,c}$ is well-defined only for compatibles c which are contained in $PS(p)$, since including any other c would not result in an implicant of $\mathcal{M}'$. Therefore, we define $\Gamma_p = \{c \mid c \subseteq PS(p), c \in C\}$, and reserve a $\gamma_{p,c}$ for each c in Γ_p.

4.4 Input Field

Non-seed RGPI's which are smaller in the input dimension are obtained, by simply "refining" RGPI seeds, reducing them in all possible inputs, and adding the resulting sub-cubes to the RGPI set.

5 Constraint Generation

Once RGPI generation is completed, constraints must be generated. There are five distinct sets of constraints, each addressing a specific requirement on valid realizations. Two (sets 1 and 3 below) correspond directly to classic state minimization constraints, which ensure a closed cover of state compatibles. One set (set 2) ensures that the ON-set of the reduced machine is covered by the selected RGPI's. An additional set (set 4) ensures that the machine is state-mapped consistently by the selected RGPI's. The final set of constraints (set 5) provides the solver with a trivial means of determining the cover's cost.

The covering problem can be expressed as a constraint matrix, where each row is a constraint and each column is a decision variable. The covering matrix contains three kinds of columns: state compatibles, RGPI's, and "γ" variables, which modulate RGPI instantiation. Note that many constraints are binate, as in state reduction [11] and relation minimization [15, 2].

5.1 Constraints

The columns in the covering matrix are:

c_i	–	include compatible c_i in state cover
p_i	–	include RGPI p_i in symbolic cover
γ_{p_i,c_i}	–	make RGPI p_i span c_i in $\mathcal{M}'$

The constraint clauses, which correspond to covering matrix rows, are shown below, grouped in five sections according to purpose. Each section consists of a set of similar clauses, all of which must be satisfied. The final Boolean expression is a conjunction of all rows/clauses in all five sections.

1. *State Covering*
   Each unreduced state must be covered by some state compatible (reduced state).
   $\forall$ states s of $\mathcal{M}$
   $$c_{i_1} + c_{i_2} + \cdots + c_{i_N}$$
   where $s \in c_{i_k}$.
2. *Compatible Selection $\Rightarrow$ RGPI Selection* ("Functional Covering")
   Each ON-set minterm of each output and next-state of $\mathcal{M}'$ must be covered. Since selecting a compatible corresponds to adding a row in the reduced table, this constraint ensures that every ON-set minterm in the reduced row is covered.

   $\forall$ compatibles c_k
   $$\prod_{\forall m' \in c_k} \{\overline{c_k} + \gamma_{p_1,c_k} + \gamma_{p_2,c_k} + \cdots + \gamma_{p_N,c_k}\}$$
   Here, m' refers to the ON-set minterms lying in c_k, corresponding to either an output or the next-state in the *reduced* machine $\mathcal{M}'$. Each clause ensures that some RGPI p_i will be mapped over c_k (i.e. γ_{p_i,c_k} will be true), and hence will cover m' in $\mathcal{M}'$.

   Although the minterms m' in row c_k of the reduced machine are not yet explicitly available, they can easily be derived. Let $i \in \mathcal{I}$ be any input value. The corresponding minterm m' is an ON-set minterm of a binary *output function* f_j in reduced machine $\mathcal{M}'$ iff, for some unreduced state $s \in c_k$, $f_j(s,i) = 1$. Minterm m' is considered an ON-set minterm of the *symbolic next-state* of the reduced machine $\mathcal{M}'$ iff for some unreduced state $s \in c_k$, $\mathcal{T}(s,i) = \tilde{s}$, for some singleton state $\tilde{s}$; that is, the next-state is specified in s. In this case, the next-state in m' will also be specified.

   For each ON-set minterm, m', those γ_{p_i,c_k} are included in the above constraints where (i) p_i contributes to the corresponding output or next-state, and (ii) also contains the minterm (i.e. intersects input column i).
3. *RGPI Selection $\Rightarrow$ Compatible Selection*
   If an RGPI which implements next-state is selected, the corresponding state compatible must also be selected.
   $\forall$ RGPI's $p_i \mid NS(p_i) \neq \phi$
   $$\overline{p_i} + c_k$$
   where compatible $c_k = NS(p_i)$.

   This constraint corresponds to a classic closure constraint [11]. An RGPI which implements next-state identifies a unique reduced state to which the next-state of all contained total states is uniformly state mapped. Hence, RGPI selection implies a commitment to select the compatible corresponding to its next-state field. Note that an RGPI implementing only outputs has no such constraint.
4. *Implicant Incompatibility*
   Two RGPI's are incompatible if they intersect in some selected compatible, but disagree on next-state.
   $\forall$ RGPI's $p_i, p_j \mid i \neq j,\ IN(p_i) \cap IN(p_j) \neq \phi,$
   $NS(p_i) \neq \phi, NS(p_j) \neq \phi, NS(p_i) \neq NS(p_j),$
   $\forall$ compatibles $c_k \subseteq PS(p_i) \cap PS(p_j)$
   and $\mathcal{T}(IN(p_i) \cap IN(p_j), c_k) \neq \mathcal{S}$
   $$\overline{c_k} + \overline{\gamma_{p_i,c_k}} + \overline{\gamma_{p_j,c_k}}$$
   If two RGPI's implement next-state and disagree, and intersect in some compatible c_k, they can both be mapped over c_k only if the next-state is unspecified ($\mathcal{T}(\mathcal{I}_a, s) = \mathcal{S}$) throughout the region of intersection. Otherwise, there is a conflict: a total state would be simultaneously mapped in two

ways. We must either not select c_k, or not map one of the RGPI's onto reduced state c_k.

5. *Implicant Cost*
   Mapping an RGPI over a reduced state implies selecting that RGPI.

   $\forall$ RGPI's p_i, $\forall$ compatibles $c_k \in \Gamma_{p_i}$

   $$\overline{\gamma_{p_i,c_k}} + p_i$$

   This is a bookkeeping device to make it easier for the solver to determine the solution cost (logic cover cardinality). The variable p_i is true when p_i is mapped over *at least one* reduced state.

5.2 Flow of Constraint Solution

The implications interconnecting the various constraints can be envisioned in a "flow" from, e.g., state covering (set 1) to functional covering (set 2) to state implication (set 3), and so on. To better illustrate the relationships, we offer the following solution scenario[5]:

1. We start by selecting a compatible c_i to cover some state, say, s_0. This satisfies the corresponding clause from set 1.
2. The selection of compatible c_i implies covering conditions on the ON-set minterms m' of $\mathcal{M}'$ lying in c_i (set 2). We choose one such minterm, and map an eligible RGPI p over c_i to cover it, by setting γ_{p,c_i} to true.
3. This now requires adding p to the cover (set 5).
4. Selecting p implies selecting the compatible c_j associated with p's next-state field, if any (set 3). If c_j was not previously selected, new covering constraints must be satisfied, and we recur on step 2.
5. If there are uncovered minterms in c_i, continue at step 2.
6. If there are uncovered states, continue at step 1.

At any point, the currently selected RGPI's may be incompatible (set 4) with RGPI's mentioned in covering clauses (set 2) for a specific compatible. If so, the latter RGPI's cannot be mapped over that compatible, and the corresponding γ's are removed from consideration in this sub-tree. There may then be no RGPI eligible to cover some minterm in step 2. If so, the sub-problem has no solution, and backtracking occurs.

6 Symbolic Instantiation

We now define symbolic instantiation precisely, taking into account the γ variables associated with each RGPI. These were introduced in section 4 to gain finer control over the shape of instantiated implicants.

Symbolic instantiation is defined with respect to a selected set of compatibles (and hence a reduced machine $\mathcal{M}'$), along with the set of γ variable assignments identifying specific reduced states to span. Specifically,

$$p' = \text{Instantiate}_{\gamma_p}(p)$$

[5] which can be regarded as a crude recursive-descent algorithm

where γ_p is a set of Boolean variables associated with p. Each member of γ_p is associated with a compatible contained in $PS(p)$. We thus let

$$p' = \text{Instantiate}_{\gamma_p}(p) = \langle I,\ PS',\ NS',\ O \rangle$$

with NS' as before, but, for the present state field:

$$PS' = \{ \text{ reduced states } s' \mid \begin{array}{l} \gamma_{p,c} = 1 \text{ and} \\ s' \text{ corresponds to } c \end{array} \}$$

7 Examples

We now present two examples. The first illustrates our procedure by giving partial results of each step for the simple example in Figure 1. We show both the optimal cover, corresponding to the optimal state mapping, and a sub-optimal cover, resulting from sub-optimal mapping. The second example demonstrates results not obtainable by other existing methods.

Example: (from Figure 1)

$\mathcal{M}$	0	1
s_0	s_0,0	s_2,0
s_1	s_1,0	s_1,-
s_2	s_1,-	s_0,1

Maximal compatibles:
$MC = \{\{s_0, s_1\}, \{s_1, s_2\}\}$.
Prime compatibles:
$PC = \{c_0, \ldots, c_4\} \equiv \{\{s_0\}, \{s_1\}, \{s_2\}\} \cup MC$.

The RGPI seeds were given in section 3.1. There are no non-seed RGPI's. A subset of the constraints follows, in POS form, and grouped by section:

State Covering (all shown):

$$(c_0 + c_3)(c_1 + c_3 + c_4)(c_2 + c_4)$$

Functional Covering (shown for c_0, c_3, c_4):

The first clause ensures that the minterm for s_0 in $\langle\, 0\ s_0 \,\rangle$ is covered. p_0 satisfies the clause when γ_{p_0,c_0} is set to true, which maps p_0 over c_0.

$$(\overline{c_0} + \gamma_{p_0,c_0} + \gamma_{p_1,c_0})(\overline{c_0} + \gamma_{p_4,c_0} + \gamma_{p_7,c_0})$$
$$(\overline{c_3} + \gamma_{p_1,c_3})(\overline{c_3} + \gamma_{p_7,c_1})$$
$$(\overline{c_4} + \gamma_{p_1,c_4} + \gamma_{p_2,c_4} + \gamma_{p_{10},c_4})(\overline{c_4} + \gamma_{p_8,c_4} + \gamma_{p_{10},c_4})$$
$$(\overline{c_4} + \gamma_{p_8,c_4}) \cdots$$

Compatible Implication (shown for $p_0, \ldots, p_3$):

$$(\overline{p_0} + c_0)(\overline{p_1} + c_3)(\overline{p_2} + c_1)(\overline{p_3} + c_1) \cdots$$

Implicant Incompatibility (shown for p_0, p_1):

$$(\overline{c_0} + \overline{\gamma_{p_0,c_0}} + \overline{\gamma_{p_1,c_0}})(\overline{c_1} + \overline{\gamma_{p_1,c_1}} + \overline{\gamma_{p_2,c_1}})$$
$$(\overline{c_2} + \overline{\gamma_{p_1,c_2}} + \overline{\gamma_{p_2,c_2}})(\overline{c_4} + \overline{\gamma_{p_1,c_4}} + \overline{\gamma_{p_2,c_4}})$$
$$(\overline{c_2} + \overline{\gamma_{p_1,c_2}} + \overline{\gamma_{p_3,c_2}})(\overline{c_1} + \overline{\gamma_{p_1,c_1}} + \overline{\gamma_{p_6,c_1}}) \cdots$$

Implicant Cost (shown for p_0, p_1):

$$(\overline{\gamma_{p_0,c_0}} + p_0)(\overline{\gamma_{p_1,c_0}} + p_1)(\overline{\gamma_{p_1,c_1}} + p_1)(\overline{\gamma_{p_1,c_2}} + p_1)$$
$$(\overline{\gamma_{p_1,c_3}} + p_1)(\overline{\gamma_{p_1,c_4}} + p_1) \cdots$$

Selecting compatibles $\{s_0, s_1\}$ and $\{s_1, s_2\}$ gives two state-mapping choices in $\langle\, 00\ s_1' \,\rangle$, as observed earlier. The sub-optimal 4-RGPI cover $\{p_1, p_7, p_9, p_{11}\}$ corresponds to choosing s_1'. Our method instead finds the minimum cover $\{p_1, p_7, p_{11}\}$, with 3 RGPI's, which corresponds to the optimal state-mapping of s_0'. □

Example: The following example demonstrates that our method, which examines *non-minimum* cardinality state covers, forms the optimal solution which other methods cannot find. In contrast, $\mathcal{M}$, when fully reduced (as other methods would do), results in a sub-optimal logic cover.

$\mathcal{M}$	00	01	11	10
s_0	s_2,1	s_1,0	s_1,-	s_0,0
s_1	s_2,0	s_1,-	s_1,-	-,-
s_2	s_2,-	s_1,1	s_1,1	s_0,1

Prime compatibles: $\{s_0\}$ and $\{s_1, s_2\}$.

$\mathcal{M}'$	00	01	11	10
s_0'	s_1',1	s_1',0	s_1',-	s_0',0
s_1'	s_1',0	s_1',1	s_1',1	s_0',1

$\mathcal{M}$, reduced via $\{s_0\}$ and $\{s_1, s_2\}$.

The minimum logic covers for these two machines are shown below, for $\mathcal{M}$ on the left (RGPI's), and for $\mathcal{M}'$ on the right (instantiated RGPI's):

$p_1 : \langle 00 \; s_0, s_2 \; s_2 \; 1 \rangle$ $\quad$ $p_1' : \langle 0- \; s_0', s_1' \; s_1' \; 0 \rangle$
$p_2 : \langle -1 \; s_0, s_1, s_2 \; s_1 \; 0 \rangle$ $\quad$ $p_2' : \langle 00 \; s_0' \; s_1' \; 1 \rangle$
$p_3 : \langle 10 \; s_0, s_1, s_2 \; s_0 \; 0 \rangle$ $\quad$ $p_3' : \langle -1 \; s_1' \; s_1' \; 1 \rangle$
$p_4 : \langle 00 \; s_0, s_1, s_2 \; s_2 \; 0 \rangle$ $\quad$ $p_4' : \langle 10 \; s_0', s_1' \; s_0' \; 0 \rangle$
$p_5 : \langle -- \; s_2 \; - \; 1 \rangle$ $\quad$ $p_5' : \langle 11 \; s_0', s_1' \; s_1' \; 1 \rangle$
$p_6' : \langle 10 \; s_1' \; s_0' \; 1 \rangle$

It is not hard to show that these two state and logic covers are two different solutions to our constraints.

Our method produces the optimal (unreduced) implementation $\mathcal{M}$, with cover $p_1, \ldots, p_5$ and 3 states. Consider p_5, which is selected in our cover. Its use enables a minimum cover, since it covers all the ON-set minterms of the output in s_2. In contrast, p_5 cannot be used in machine $\mathcal{M}'$, since it cannot be mapped over s_1'. As a result, in $\mathcal{M}'$, 2 RGPI's are needed to cover the output's ON-set minterms in s_2. Our method therefore finds the minimum cover based on the selection of compatible $\{s_2\}$, and discards the sub-optimal solution based on $\{s_1, s_2\}$.

It is important to observe that the minimum logic cover was only achievable by using *non-prime* compatibles ($\{s_1\}$ and $\{s_2\}$), which in turn necessitated a non-minimum cardinality state cover. Thus, our method finds the optimal solution, while existing tools, which only consider minimum-cardinality state covers of prime compatibles, cannot guarantee minimum logic complexity. □

8 Experimental Results

The algorithm was implemented in C++ and run under MkLinux for PowerPC. Results appear below for a small set of examples, using only RGPI seeds. For comparison, STAMINA [12] was run on the same tables. For each, the number of compatibles, seeds, covering constraints, run-time and products is given. Entries marked with a † used *all* compatibles; others used only prime compatibles.

FSM						#products[a]	
	i/o/s	c	seeds	constr	time	OPT	Stam
lisom	1/2/3	5†	16	142	0.3	3	3
minst	2/1/3	4†	20	226	0.4	5	6
lion9	2/1/9	5	42	219	1006	8	8

[a] Symbolic products after mvi minimization.

Figure 2: Experimental Results

9 Conclusions and Future Work

We have presented the first method for optimal state minimization which directly and accurately targets logic complexity, achieving a provably exactly optimal result under input encoding. The method is computationally expensive, however, and would benefit greatly from heuristic and inexact variations. Unlike some methods, ours provides several opportunities to reduce complexity, e.g. using prime or maximal compatibles, RGPI seeds only, or heuristic binate solvers, while retaining a strong minimization framework. For more efficient exact solution, recent innovations in implicit methods [4, 14] hold particular promise. With all of these choices, we believe our method offers a framework encompassing a spectrum of solutions.

A limitation to the current work is the large size of the RGPI set. Initial investigation suggests cases where the set can be pruned, while still guaranteeing an optimum solution. This is an important area for further research.

Although we have only provided limited benchmarks, we expect that future experimentation will prove our method competitive with existing methods (e.g. STAMINA, SMAS). Finally, we anticipate that an extension to output encoding will yield a definitive solution to this problem.

Acknowledgments. We greatly thank Dr. Olivier Coudert (Synopsys) for early access to Scherzo, and Dr. Ruchir Puri (IBM) for insightful discussions.

References

[1] M.J. Avedillo, J.M. Quintana, and J.L. Huertas. Smas: A program for the concurrent state reduction and state assignment of finite state machines. In *ISCAS*, pages 1781–1784, 1991.

[2] R.K. Brayton and F. Somenzi. An exact minimizer for boolean relations. In *ICCAD-1989*, pages 316–319.

[3] N.L.V. Calazans. Boolean constrained encoding: A new formulation and a case study. In *ICCAD-1994*, pages 702–706.

[4] O. Coudert and J. Madre. Implicit and incremental computation of primes and essential primes of boolean functions. In *DAC-1992*, pages 36–44.

[5] O. Coudert and J.C. Madre. New ideas for solving covering problems. In *DAC-1995*, pages 641–646.

[6] G. De Micheli. *Synthesis and Optimization of Digital Circuits*. McGraw-Hill, 1994.

[7] G. De Micheli, R.K. Brayton, and A. Sangiovanni-Vincentelli. Optimal state assignment for finite state machines. *IEEE Trans. on CAD*, CAD-4(3):269–285, July 1985.

[8] S. Devadas and A.R. Newton. Exact algorithms for output encoding, state assignment, and four- level boolean minimization. *IEEE Trans. on CAD*, CAD-10(1):13–27, January 1991.

[9] J. Hartmanis et al. Some dangers in state reduction of sequential machines. *Information and Control*, pages 252–260, September 1962.

[10] R.M. Fuhrer, B. Lin, and S.M. Nowick. Symbolic hazard-free minimization and encoding of asynchronous finite state machines. In *ICCAD-1995*, 1995.

[11] A. Grasselli and F. Luccio. A method for minimizing the number of internal states in incompletely specified sequential networks. *IEEE TEC*, EC-14:350–359, June 1965.

[12] G. Hachtel, J.K. Rho, F. Somenzi, and R. Jacoby. Exact and heuristic algorithms for the minimization of incompletely specified state machines. *IEEE Trans. on CAD*, CAD-13(2):167–177, February 1994.

[13] J. Hartmanis and R.E. Stearns. *Algebraic Structure Theory of Sequential Machines*. Prentice-Hall, 1966.

[14] T. Kam, T. Villa, R.K. Brayton, and A. Sangiovanni-Vincentelli. A fully implicit algorithm for exact state minimization. In *DAC-1994*.

[15] B. Lin and F. Somenzi. Minimization of symbolic relations. In *ICCAD-1990*, pages 88–91.

[16] E.J. McCluskey. *Logic Design Principles*. Prentice-Hall, 1986.

[17] M. Paull and S. Unger. Minimizing the number of states in incompletely specified sequential switching functions. *IRE Trans. on Elec. Comp.*, EC-8:356–367, Sept. 1959.

[18] R. Puri, 1995. Private communication.

[19] R. Rudell and A. Sangiovanni-Vincentelli. Multiple valued minimization for PLA optimization. *IEEE Trans. on CAD*, CAD-6(5):727–750, Sept. 1987.

[20] T. Villa and A. Sangiovanni-Vincentelli. NOVA: state assignment of finite state machines for optimal two-level logic implementation. *IEEE Trans. on CAD*, 9(9):905–924, Sept. 1990.

SESSION 6B

SYNTHESIS WITH COMPLEX COMPONENTS

Moderators:

Forrest D. Brewer, University of California,

Santa Barbara, CA

Kunle Olukotun, Stanford University,

Stanford, CA

Resource Sharing in Hierarchical Synthesis*

Oliver Bringmann and Wolfgang Rosenstiel

Forschungszentrum Informatik an der Universität Karlsruhe (FZI)
Haid-und-Neu-Str. 10-14, 76131 Karlsruhe, Germany
and Universität Tübingen, Sand 13, 72076 Tübingen, Germany

Abstract

This paper presents a new approach to hierarchical high-level synthesis with respect to internal register-transfer structures of complex components. Entire subdesigns can efficiently be used as complex components at a higher hierarchical level of the design. After synthesis, the calculated schedule of each subdesign is added to its register-transfer component model. This enables the sharing of unused subcomponents across different hierarchical levels of the design. Especially, subcomponents of autonomous components, with a separate controller, can also be shared. As a result, the presented methodology offers a high degree of optimization to hierarchically specified designs.

1 Introduction

In modern system design, the specification of complex systems, which can be hierarchically composed of several subsystems is becoming increasingly important. In this context, the complexity of the subsystems, also called components, is increasing as well. Examples for such subsystems are microprocessor cores, application specific functional units (e.g. DCT, FFT), and interface controllers. However, state-of-the-art high-level synthesis systems produce insufficient results in terms of quality of the result and execution time when considering large applications [1].

This paper addresses the problem of optimized integration of already synthesized system specifications as complex register-transfer components, in the further high-level synthesis flow. For this, it is important that the behavioral specification, the synthesized register-transfer structure, and the already determined schedule of the used components are known during further high-level synthesis steps. Among others, the essential features of such components are the visible, hierarchical composed component structure, the usage of a separate controller, and the data-dependent timing. Hence, such components can be autonomous in the entire system. Finally, components should have the capability to share subcomponents with other components across different hierarchical levels, with respect to their visible structures. If necessary, the used components may be modified during synthesis of the enclosing system. This allows an efficient specification of less area consuming hierarchical designs while synthesis time can be reduced.

1.1 Related Work

A closer investigation of existing approaches shows, that the terms *hierarchical synthesis* and *complex components* are not used uniformly at algorithmic level. We can identify three different methodologies, which use the term hierarchical synthesis:

1. Data-flow graph clustering or partitioning methods followed by the synthesis of the clusters and partly of the clustered data-flow graph.
2. Using already synthesized systems as components, but without regard to internal component structures ("*black-box reuse*").
3. Using already synthesized systems as components with the possibility of sharing subcomponents with regard to internal component structures ("*white-box reuse*").

One of the first clustering methods involves collecting all operations with a high similarity measure into one cluster [2]. The allocation and assignment of functional units, registers, and multiplexers are determined separately for each cluster. The scheduling algorithm considers the whole data-flow graph and takes specific cluster restrictions into account. An extension to this approach can be found in APARTY (System Architect's Workbench) [3], in which the user can choose a partitioning strategy like control, data, procedure-call, procedure-data and operation clustering. Another clustering approach extracts regular structures from the data-flow graph in order to create an additional level of hierarchy [4]. Then, the same scheduling algorithm is used to synthesize each cluster, and subsequently the clustered data-flow graph. The CATHEDRAL-III system [5] uses another clustering approach for synthesis. In addition to the other approaches, clusters with similar functional units are

* This work is partially supported by the DFG.

1092-3152/97 $10.00 © 1997 IEEE

merged after the clustering step in order to build complex data-path elements and to increase the cluster size [6]. A larger cluster size allows an enlarged design space exploration as opposed to the local decisions of other clustering techniques. A further data-flow graph partitioning technique proceeds scheduling in a bottom-up traversal of the loop/subroutine hierarchy. One modern example is the *Synopsys Behavioral Compiler* [7].

The first methodology perform scheduling in a bottom-up traversal of the cluster or the given loop/subroutine hierarchy. The second mentioned approach for hierarchical synthesis allows the usage of already synthesized components for further high-level synthesis tasks without regarding specific component structures. The register-transfer library used in the Hebe system [8], which is integrated in the Olympus synthesis system, can contain any component that is specified in HardwareC. A similar approach is integrated in AMICAL [9], with the difference that a proprietary component intermediate format is used for synthesis. However, all previous mentioned approaches perform component reuse and resource sharing just at one hierarchical level of the design, without respect to its component structures ("black-box reuse").

Our approach presented in this paper offers a technique of hierarchical synthesis according to the methodology under 3 and supports "white-box reuse". Figure 1 illustrates the proposed hierarchical synthesis technique. The entire system is synthesized in a bottom-up traversal of the hierarchy. Each symbol represents a subdesign which is saved in the component library after synthesis. The component model of the library includes the VHDL behavioral description, the RT structure, and the calculated schedule. The enhanced component model is a prerequisite to perform subcomponent sharing of autonomous components. Both VHDL models are the basis for supporting the simulation of the entire system at algorithmic level as well as RT level.

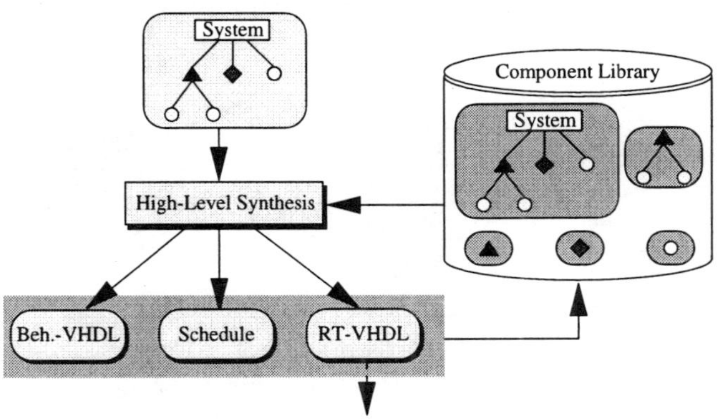

Figure 1. Hierarchical Synthesis with Component Model

Another requirement for hierarchical synthesis is a visible and changeable structure of complex components, which can be composed hierarchically from subcomponents. Furthermore, a behavioral simulation of the entire system, including the chosen register-transfer components, should be supported.

A closer investigation of the existing approaches shows that specific libraries developed for the respective high-level synthesis systems and technology-oriented libraries can be distinguished. Specific libraries are used in the high-level synthesis tools System Architect's Workbench (SAW) [3], Synopsys Behavioral Compiler [7], Hebe [8], and NEAT [10]. The libraries differ in the complexity of their components, but neither consideration of specific component structures nor behavioral simulation at algorithmic level, including the used register-transfer components, are supported. Only some recently introduced approaches consider an enhanced component model. OSCAR [11] and ISE [12] represent complex component as behavior templates in order to match multiple operations by a single component. Additionally, in [12] components may contain multiple functional outputs. In contrast to the other systems mentioned, CATHEDRAL-III [5] uses a constructive approach. Complex data-path elements are constructed from primitive operators, which are mapped to primitive library components, or to hardware building blocks of a module generator. Reusing complex components as primitive operators or complex data-path elements is not possible. A similar technique is used in the pre-synthesis system ACE [13]. Their component models are more abstract, but the system only provides some architectural transformations, like component merging, in order to increase the potential of resource sharing within components.

GENUS [14] is a generic, technology oriented register-transfer library used by the high-level synthesis system BdA, formerly VSS. GENUS automatically generates a component for an operation from elementary function units. But it is not possible to hierarchically combine elementary components to build complex components. Hence, several operations of a given behavioral specification can not be assigned to such complex components. Simulation models in VHDL can be generated for functional simulation as well as timing simulation.

Hierarchical synthesis in terms of reusing complete designs as components at a higher hierarchical level is either performed without regarding specific component structures or infeasible due to the lack of flexible component features. Therefore, the component concept must be extended and the synthesis must be enhanced, in order to handle complex components. Components should especially be able to be reconfigured or partially re-synthesized so that their subcomponents can be shared with other components. In contrast to black-box reuse with direct assignment to the corresponding DFG operation, the degree of optimization is increased.

This paper is organized as follows: Section 2 describes

the basic concepts of hierarchical synthesis. Section 3 addresses the hierarchical resource sharing problem of autonomous, parallel working components. Some examples, including experimental results, are presented in section 4. Finally, this paper concludes with a summary in section 5.

2 A Concept for Hierarchical Synthesis

In this section, we explain in more detail our hierarchical synthesis concept. First, the identification of complex components is described. Then, the most important task in hierarchical synthesis, the sharing of subcomponents across different levels of hierarchy, is outlined.

2.1 Identification of Complex Components

The first task that has to be solved during hierarchical synthesis is the identification of complex components in the control-data flow graph, distinguishing *direct component instantiation* and *component matching*. Direct component instantiation denotes a user specified component instantiation in the algorithmic specification. In this case, the user may preset the allocation of a complex component by invoking the corresponding procedure in the specification. The term component matching denotes the matching of component and system data-flow subgraphs, in order to identify suitable optimized complex components for the design. The basis of component matching is the component behavioral specification, which can easily be transferred into a control-data flow graph. Thus, the matching problem needs to be solved for both the data-flow subgraphs and the control-flow subgraphs of the specification.

Figure 2 illustrates both mentioned possibilities of complex component identification with three levels of hierarchy. In the first step, the mult-add subcomponent has been identified as a part of component f_3. Component f_3 has been instantiated directly by node f_3 of the overall system and can also be identified as a part of the overall system.

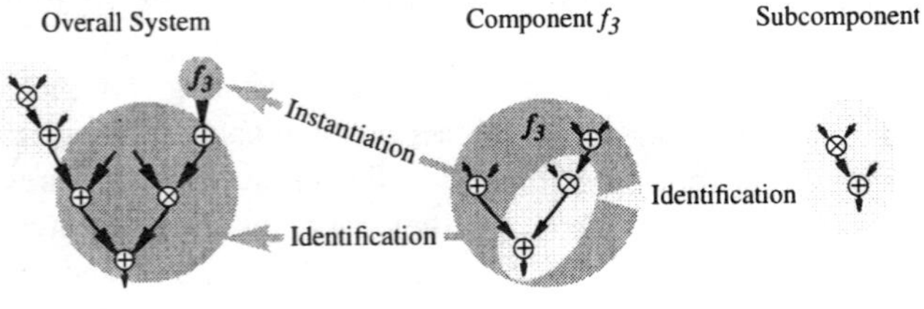

Figure 2. Identification of Complex Components

For the sake of clarity, this example illustrates only the data-flow graph matchings. The task of component identification is to be integrated in allocation as well as scheduling. Thereby, the synthesis system has to decide automatically whether specialized and optimized complex components or several primitive components are allocated. After scheduling, all DFG operations covered by one component are folded into a single complex operation node. Hence, no enhancements are needed in the further synthesis steps. Due to space limitations, this task is beyond the scope of this paper.

2.2 Hierarchical Resource Sharing

The most important task during hierarchical synthesis is the sharing of subcomponents across different hierarchical levels of the design. This aims at reusing an already synthesized design as a complex component at a higher hierarchical level with respect to the internal component structure and the already determined component schedule. The component schedule lists all used subcomponents per clock step. In the case of sharing subcomponents, the component structure is needed in order to estimate the additional required area and to extract the set of allocated subcomponents. All unused subcomponents at one clock step can now be added to the set of allocated and unused components of the overall system.

Figure 3 clarifies the sharing of subcomponents of the example given in figure 2, simplified to components without separate controllers. The starting point is the data-flow graph of the overall system and the schedule of the already synthesized component f_3. Assuming that component f_3 is used for the second part of the system data-flow graph (see figure 2), just one complex component f_3, is needed to cover the overall system. This is true, due to sharing the mult-add subcomponent of component f_3 with the remaining multiply and add operations of the overall system. Note that the allocation of one complex component f_3 implies the allocation of one mult-add and one add component, due to the visible structure of component f_3. The allocation of one mult-add component does not cause a resource conflict at clock step 3 of the system schedule because a pipelined component with an initiation interval of one clock step is assumed.

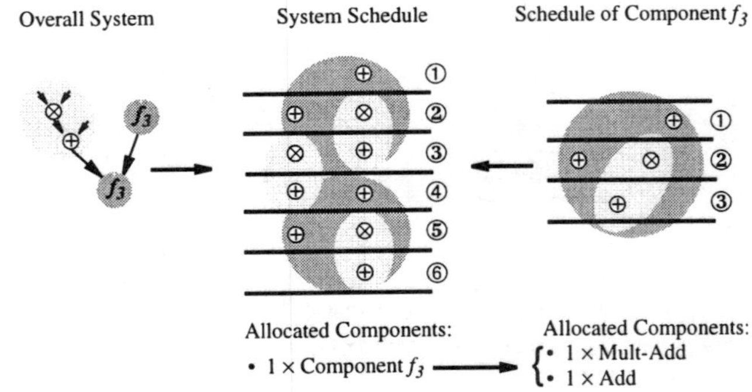

Figure 3. Hierarchical Resource Sharing

In the following, we want to extend the hierarchical resource sharing to autonomous, parallel working components with separate controllers.

3 Hierarchical Resource Sharing of Autonomous Components

Here we will concentrate on hierarchical resource sharing, applicable to autonomous, parallel working components. Especially, the additional needed calculations to perform subcomponent sharing of autonomous components are presented in this section.

3.1 Component Model

The underlying component model is not restricted to specific synthesis limitations. It consists of a flowgraph, representing the functional specification, a hierarchical schedule, the generated RT structure, and the physical component attributes.

Definition 1. A *component* of a design is denoted by the tuple $C := \langle FG, \mathcal{HS}, FSMD, P\rangle$, where FG is an intermediate flowgraph format, compiled from an algorithmic specification, for instance written in VHDL, $\mathcal{HS}$ denotes the component schedule, which will be defined next, $FSMD$ represents the synthesized RT structure as a finite state machine with datapath, and P describes the common physical component attributes, e.g. timing, area, and power consumption.

This data structure can be used for specifying both system under synthesis and instantiated components. In contrast to conventional component models, our model is much more detailed, in order to provide all necessary component information for hierarchical resource sharing. Next, the formal definition of a hierarchical schedule is given.

Definition 2. A *hierarchical schedule* of a component C is denoted by the tuple $\mathcal{HS}(C) := \langle V, E, t, OP, IC, C\rangle$, where

- V is a set of nodes representing clock steps, conditional branches, or nested loops, respectively.
- $E \subset L \times V$ is a set of edges with $L := \{v_l \in V : t(v_l) = loop \vee t(v_l) = branch\}$, where
- the function $t(v_l) \in \{operation, loop, branch\}$ denotes the type of a node $v_l \in V$.
- The relation $OP(v_{op})$, $\forall\ (v_{op} \in V : t(v_{op}) = operation)$ refers to the scheduled operations of the clock step v_{op}.
- The function $IC(v_l)$, $\forall\ (v_l \in V : t(v_l) = loop)$ returns the minimal iteration count ic_{min} and the maximal iteration count ic_{max}, where *iteration count* denotes the number of iterations of a loop, which may depends on outer loop iterators.
- The function $C(op)$, $\forall\ op \in OP(v_{op})$ refers to the instantiated component or component type of an operation op.

The hierarchical schedule $\mathcal{HS}(C)$ of a component represents a tree, with the property that only nodes of type *loop* or *branch* can have descendants. The children of one node represent the schedule of this loop, or branch path, respectively. The root node represents the entire process and has an infinite iteration count ($ic_{max} = \infty$). An unbounded iteration count, which can not be statically determined, is denoted by $ic_{max} = u$. In case of a statically determined iteration count, the formulas ic_{min} and ic_{max} are equal. In order to be more general and to avoid the distinction between system and components, the term module is used as a genus.

3.2 Sharing Interval

Resource sharing among different modules is only possible, if the state of the concerning modules can be determined statically. On the condition that some modules may be autonomous in the entire system and using a separate controller, the module state is determined, once the module under synthesis communicates with the other modules. The state of a module in which such a data transfer is initiated, is called *synchronization point* ($v_{sp} \in V$). The reset state is a priori a synchronization point. During list scheduling, a module state can be determined, as soon as the corresponding synchronization point is reached. Resource sharing is now possible until a loop, with an unbounded iteration count ($ic_{max} = u$) is reached and then only during the first ic_{min} iteration of this loop, such a state is called *desynchronization point*. Once the next synchronization point is reached, resource sharing is possible again. Note that one module can have multiple sharing intervals.

Definition 3. The *sharing interval* of a module M regarding state v_t is given by the set $SI(M, v_t)$ and denotes the set of states between a synchronization point and a desynchronization point, such that $v_t \in SI(M, v_t)$ holds.

The size of a sharing interval depends on the underlying module model. Modules without a separate controller (type $\mathcal{MT}1$) are always statically determined (see figure 3). Hence, all further calculation in this section are not needed for this module type. Modules with a separate controller and data-independent timing (type $\mathcal{MT}2$) permit the static calculation of their state. Only modules with a separate controller and unbounded data-dependent delay (type $\mathcal{MT}3$) have a restricted sharing interval, which can be calculated as mentioned above. Figure 4 illustrates sharing intervals for the different module types. For the sake of clarity, the hierarchical schedule of modules with a separate controller is represented as a state transition graph of a FSM, and its datapath is not shown. In this case a sharing interval ending at the first transition of the FSM representation with unbounded iteration count. The states R and W represent read and write communication to other modules and are the synchronization points of the examples. Therefore, module type $\mathcal{MT}3$ of figure 4 contains two sharing intervals, the first beginning at state R, and the second beginning at state W.

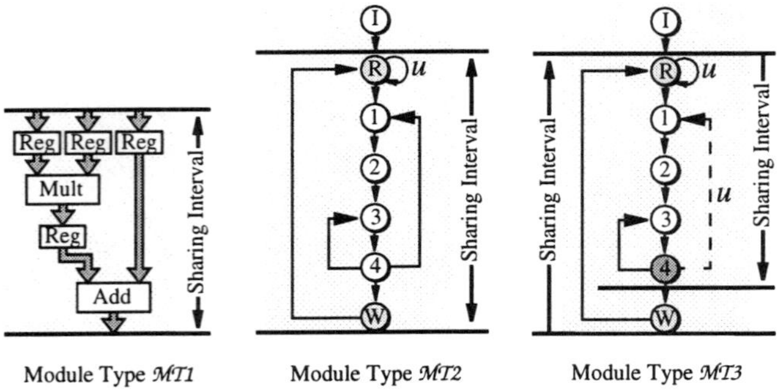

Figure 4. Sharing Intervals of Different Examples

3.3 Clock Cycle Space of a State

In the case of modules with separate controllers, all clock cycles of a module state, depending on their iteration space, have to be calculated, where the *iteration space* of a module is defined by the iteration counts of all loops. Note that loops with loop increment or loop decrement greater than one can be handled similarly, because only the iteration count has to be taken into account. Now, we will define the clock cycle space of a module state.

Definition 4. The *clock cycle space* $CCS(v_t)$ denotes the set of all clock cycles in which the considered module M is in the given state v_t, within the previous calculated sharing interval $SI(M, v_t)$.

The clock cycle space depends directly on its loop nesting. A single loop with ten iterations, for instance, implies that all states of the loop body are reached ten times.

Before the calculation of the clock cycle space is given, three helpful functions are defined. First, the number of clock cycles of a loop body v_l is given by $csteps_{LB}(v_l) = |\{v_c : v_c \in children(v_l) \wedge t(v_c) = operation\}|$, where $children(v_l)$ denotes the set of direct succesors of v_l. Secondly, the set of all subloops of a loop v_l is defined by $subloops(v_l) = \{v_s : v_s \in children(v_l) \wedge t(v_s) = loop\}$. Thirdly, the set $loopH(v_{sp}, v_t) = \{v_s : v_s \in descendant(v_{sp}) \wedge v_s \in ancestor(v_t) \wedge t(v_s) = loop\}$ specifies all subloops of the loop hierarchy $\langle v_{sp}, v_t \rangle$, where the sets $descendant(v_t)$ and $ancestor(v_t)$ represent the transitive closure to the direct successors or predecessors of v_t, respectively. Next, we calculate the *clock cycle space* of a given state v_t:

$$CCS(v_t) = csteps_{LB}(v_t) + \sum_{v_l \in loopH(v_{sp}, v_t)} csteps_{LH}(v_l) \cdot x_{v_l},$$

subject to $\quad 0 \le x_{v_l} < ic_{max}(v_l), \ \forall\, v_l \in loopH(v_{sp}, v_t),$

where

$$csteps_{LH}(v_l) = csteps_{LB}(v_l) + \sum_{v_s \in subloops(v_l)} ic_{max}(v_s) \cdot csteps_{LH}(v_s).$$

The function $csteps_{LH}(v_l)$ denotes the number of clock cycles of a given loop hierarchy v_l. Figure 5 illustrates the calculation of the clock cycle space with a simple example. The edge labels denote the iteration count of the corresponding loop. The outermost loop represents the entire process. Note that the innermost loop is specified with an iteration count of three. The clock cycle space is shown for the states 1, 2, 3, 4, and 5.

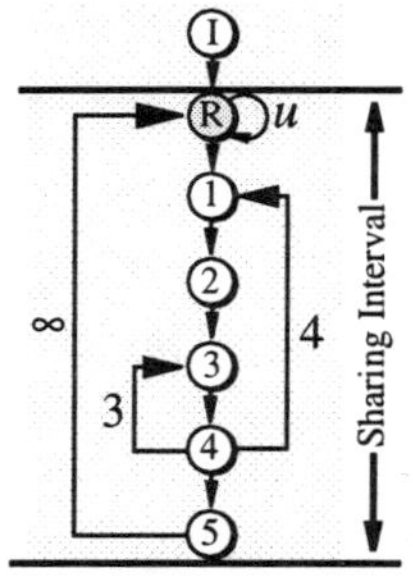

$CCS(\{1,2\}) := 8 \cdot x_1 + \{1,2\}$; where $0 \le x_1 < 4$

$CCS(\{3,4\}) := 8 \cdot x_1 + 2 \cdot x_2 + \{3,4\}$; where $0 \le x_1 < 4,\ 0 \le x_2 < 3$

$CCS(1) := \{1, 9, 17, 25\}$

$CCS(2) := \{2, 10, 18, 26\}$

$CCS(3) := \{3, 5, 7, 11, 13, 15, 19, 21, 23, 27, 29, 31\}$

$CCS(4) := \{4, 6, 8, 12, 14, 16, 20, 22, 24, 28, 30, 32\}$

$CCS(5) := \{33\}$

Figure 5. Clock Cycle Space $CCS(R, v_t)$ of an Example

3.4 Collision Set

The clock cycles spaces of all modules containing shareable submodules have to be calculated and examined, in order to determine whether submodules can be shared of two or more modules.

Definition 5. Assuming that module M_1 is in state v_t and a submodule s_2 contained in module M_2 should also be used *in* M_1, then the *collision set* $COL(M_1, v_t, M_2, s_2)$ is given by

$$CCS_{M_1}(v_t) \cap \left(\bigcup_{\substack{v_l \in SI(M_2, v_t) \cap \\ used(M_2, s_2)}} CCS_{M_2}(v_l) \right), \text{ where}$$

$used(M_2, s_2)$ denotes all states of module M_2, in which submodule s_2 is in use, within the given sharing interval $SI(M_2, v_t)$, so that $SI(M_1, v_t) \subseteq SI(M_2, v_t)$ holds.

The collision set describes, whether resource conflicts arises by applying resource sharing across different levels of hierarchy of autonomous modules.

Definition 6. A collision set $COL(M_1, v_t, M_2, s_2)$ is called *collision-free*, if and only if $COL(M_1, v_t, M_2, s_2) = \varnothing$ holds.

Generally, a submodule s_j of module M_j can be used in state v_t of module M_i, or can be shared with module M_i, if $COL(M_i, v_t, M_j, s_j)$ is collision-free. In this case, the clock cycle space of M_i covers the clock cycle spaces of M_j in which the submodule s_j is not being used. This is the complementary set of the above defined union of used submodules. It should be noted, that checking, whether a module contains submodules which are able to perform a chosen operation $op \in OP(v_t)$ should be done before calculating the collision set. This is the remaining step of conventional resource sharing techniques.

Figure 6 shows the collision set of state 3 of the module M_1 with an assumed demand of one adder. The module M_2

contains one allocated add component, which is used in the state set {2, 4, 5}. Because the determined collision set is collision-free, the module M_1 may use the add submodule of the module M_2.

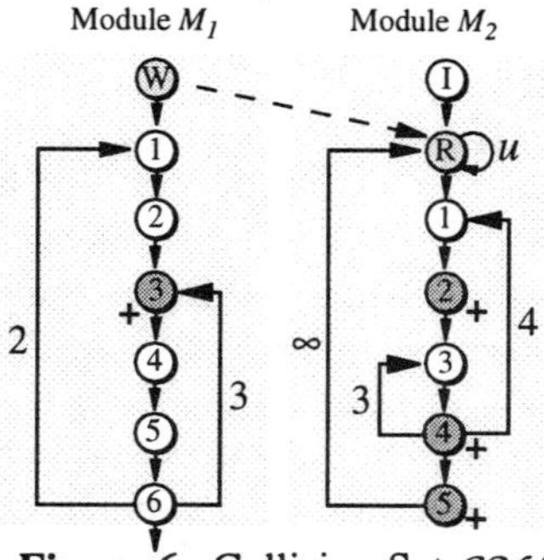

$$CCS_{M_1}(W,3) := 14 \cdot x_1 + 4 \cdot x_2 + 3; \text{ where } 0 \le x_1 < 2, 0 \le x_2 < 3$$
$$CCS_{M_1}(W,3) := \{3, 7, 11, 17, 21, 25\}$$
$$used(C,+) := \{2, 4, 5\}$$
$$CCS_{M_2}(R,2) := \{2, 10, 18, 26\}$$
$$CCS_{M_2}(R,4) := \{4, 6, 8, 12, 14, 16, 20, 22, 24, 28, 30, 32\}$$
$$CCS_{M_2}(R,5) := \{33\}$$
$$COL := CCS_{M_1}(W,3) \cap (CCS_{M_2}(R,2) \cup CCS_{M_2}(R,4) \cup CCS_{M_2}(R,5))$$
$$COL = \varnothing \Rightarrow \textbf{collision-free}$$

Figure 6. Collision Set $COL(M_1, 3, M_2, +)$ of an Example

3.5 Collision Set Intersection Problem

For the case of loops with a small iteration count, the collision set can be determined by simple set operations. However, this results in an exhaustive enumeration, with an intractable complexity. For example, if two nested loops have been specified, both with an iteration count of 1000, the corresponding clock cycle space consists of one million members. Therefore, we will use the following integer problem solving technique.

The collision set $COL(M_i, v_t, M_j, s_j)$ can be decomposed into $|SI(M_j, v_t) \cap used(M_j, s_j)|$ subproblems which can be solved independently as follows:

$$CCS_{M_i}(v_t) \cap CCS_{M_j}(v_j),\ \forall\ v_j \in SI(M_j, v_t) \cap used(M_j, s_j).$$

Now we are able to formulate the *collision set intersection problem.*

Definition 7. The *collision set intersection problem* is defined by $CCS_{M_i}(v_t) - CCS_{M_j}(v_j) = 0,\ \forall\ v_j \in SI(M_j, v_t) \cap used(M_j, s_j)$, subject to $0 \le x_{v_l} < ic_{max}(v_l), \forall\ v_l \in loopH(v_{sp}, v_t)$. Due to the linearity of CCS, the equation has the structure:

$$(A_{M_i} - A_{M_j}) \cdot x = b_{M_i} - b_{M_j},$$

subject to $x < ic_{max}(v_l),\ x \in \mathbb{N}^d,\ with\ d = |loopH(v_{sp}, v_t)|$.

Now, we are interested in the question, whether an integer solution of the equation exists, which satisfies the constraints $0 \le x < ic_{max}(v_l)$. This problem can be solved in four steps. First, an unimodular matrix U and an echelon matrix D are to be found, such that $A \cdot U = D$ holds [16], where $A = A_{M_i} - A_{M_j}$. The matrix U describes the matrix transformations being applied to generate integer solutions. Second, the existence of an integer solution of the unrestricted equation can be determined by applying the gcd test to $D \cdot s = b$, where $b = b_{M_i} - b_{M_j}$ [16]. Thirdly, if the gcd test is successful, the equation $x = U \cdot s$ describes all integer solutions and can be inserted in the constraint system: $0 \le U \cdot s < ic_{max}(v_l)$, $x \in \mathbb{N}^d$. Finally, the existence of a feasible integer solution in the remaining polyhedron can be tested by applying the extended integer Fourier-Motzkin projection [15], [17], which is recommendable due to the simple constraint system. Consequently, if no integer solution is found, the collision set CCS is collision-free and thus, resource sharing is possible.

In general, the extended Fourier-Motzkin projection has an exponential worst-case complexity depending on the number of variables. Nevertheless, the computation time for synthesis can be kept low, because the number of variables is limited by the maximum levels of nested loops. For real problems, the nesting loop level is smaller than five. Furthermore, the algorithm can stop once a collision is detected. Most of the collisions can already be detected by the very efficient gcd test. Due to the very simple constraint system, the average complexity of the algorithm can be further reduced. Their influence on the entire synthesis time is less than one percent in all tested cases.

3.6 Conditional Branches

If the specification contains conditional branches ($\exists\ v_l \in V : t(v_l) = branch$), occurring when using *if* or *case* constructs, the calculation of the collision set must be extended. In this context, two cases have to be distinguished. First, if the branch condition depends on outer loops and can be predicted, then disjunctive clock cycle spaces has to be calculated independently for each alternative path. Accordingly, the collision set intersection problem has to be solved for all disjunctive clock cycle spaces. Second, in case of data dependent unbounded conditions, a submodule may be shared in a given state, only if the submodule are unused in all alternative paths. Hence, the set of used submodules, needed to determine the collision set COL, is calculated by the union of the *used* sets of all alternative paths.

4 Implementation into CADDY-II

This section outlines the integration of hierarchical resource sharing into the high-level synthesis system CADDY-II. The underlying synthesis algorithms are only summarized here. A more detailed description can be found in [18], [19], [20] and [21]. The main synthesis steps performed in the CADDY-II system are *data-flow analysis, allocation, scheduling, binding, data-path generation* and *controller generation.* During allocation a suitable component set is selected. Tasks of scheduling are the assignment of operations to clock steps and to component types under resource constraints. The mapping of operations to component instances and the allocation of registers are the tasks of the binding. The presented hierarchical resource sharing approach has been integrated within scheduling and binding.

List-scheduling is used as scheduling algorithm, driven

by a global estimation function, which is based on the probabilities of scheduling DFG operations to control steps. In each step of the list-scheduling algorithm, all ready operations are mapped to unused components, which are able to execute the corresponding operation. If an already allocated autonomous module contains a subcomponent, which can perform an operation out of the ready set, the collision set with respect to the currently scheduled state is calculated. Since the current loop is not necessarily completely scheduled, the remaining delay is expressed by additional parameters, therefore the collision set has to be calculated with respect to this parameters. The determined parametric solutions are used as scheduling constraints of the outer loops. During scheduling of the outer loops the algorithm decides, whether the constraints for sharing subcomponents of autonomous modules can be fulfilled, suitably. During binding, the collision set is calculated again, but with fully determined variables in order to perform the mapping of an operation to a specific component or subcomponent instance.

5 Experimental Results

Experimental results of our approach on several designs, including some benchmark circuits, are given in this section. First, just for reasons of comparability the results for the fifth order elliptic wave filter benchmark are given. This benchmark demonstrates two essential features of our hierarchical synthesis approach: First, recognition of complex component structures in the system data-flow graph, and second, the possibility of sharing subcomponents. Table 1 shows some results for different allocations with and without subcomponent sharing, and compares this with the traditional component model. In this table, a component with a data initiation interval of one clock cycle and an execution time of two clock cycles is specified by the notation '1 : 2', for instance.

Table 1. 5th Order Elliptical Wave Filter

with complex components						without complex components			
resources			clock steps (cs)			resources			clock steps (cs)
+	MAC	MAC	with sharing	without sharing	gain	+	*	*	
1 : 1	1 : 2	1 : 3				1 : 1	1 : 1	1 : 2	
1	1	0	16	20	4	2	1	0	16
2	1	0	15	15	1	3	1	0	15
1	2	0	14	19	5	3	2	0	14
1	0	1	18	21	3	2	0	1	19
1	0	2	17	21	4	3	0	2	17

As a result, we get the performance improvements listed in column entitled "gain". In this example the, speed-up of the design is up to 5 clock cycles with equal hardware costs. This is because the multiply-accumulate component may share the internal adder, if an additional adder is needed. In contrast, if subcomponent sharing is not supported, a resource conflict can only be solved by adding a further clock step. The CPU time for the filter on a Sun SPARC 20 was less than 2 seconds for a fixed set of allocated components and less than 12 seconds for an enlarged design space exploration by synthesizing different sets of automatically allocated components.

Second, we will present the results of the FDCT benchmark, shown in table 2. The given component costs are taken from [11] and amount 10 units for using an adder, 20 units for using an multiplier, and 25 units for using a multiply-accumulate unit. The column entitled "costs" is filled with the area-time product as cost function. Applying subcomponent sharing, a speedup of up to 8 clock cycles can be achieved. In comparison to non-encapsulated components, the performance results of the synthesized circuits are equal in most of the determined cases, while the area costs can be reduced. Particularly, the optimal circuit in relation to the area delay ratio is synthesized using two multiply-accumulate units and two adders. The CPU time for the FDCT benchmark was less than 4 seconds for a fixed set of allocated components and less than 16 seconds for an enlarged design space exploration.

Table 2. Fast Discrete Cosine Transformation

with complex components							without complex components			
resources				clock steps (cs)			resources			clock steps (cs)
+ / −	*	MAC		with sharing	without sharing	gain	+ / −	*		
10	20	25	costs				10	20	costs	
1	0	3	765	9	14	5	4	3	900	9
1	0	2	720	12	18	6	3	2	770	11
1	1	2	990	11	19	8	3	3	810	9
2	0	2	700	11	16	5	4	2	880	11
2	1	2	900	10	13	3	4	3	900	9
2	0	3	855	9	13	4	5	3	990	9
2	0	1	810	18	20	2	3	1	900	18
1	1	1	715	13	21	8	2	2	780	13
2	2	1	850	10	13	3	3	3	810	9
2	1	1	715	11	13	2	3	2	770	11

Finally, the results of the simulated annealing processor taken from [22] are presented. At first, the needed floating-point components and then the overall simulated annealing algorithm have been specified. The high-level synthesis system CADDY-II maps all floating-point operations to the previous designed components and synthesizes the entire system hierarchically with respect to the used floating-point components. All instantiated subcomponents of the floating-point components are now ready to be used as shared components within the entire simulated annealing design. The floating-point multiplier for instance, consists of an integer multiplier, an integer adder, and a barrel shifter. These components can be used additionally for other integer arithmetic operations of the whole design. As a result, all specified arithmetic operations could be covered by the subcomponents of the floating-point units. Table 3 lists the synthesized results for a hierarchical and a inline-expanded description. By using encapsulated components, the controller size of the simulated annealing processor could be reduced to 46% of the controller size of the inline-expanded description by an equal performance. The CLB count is related to the Xilinx XC4000 family and is given to get more detailed information. The CPU time could be reduced from 20 to 7 seconds when using the hierarchical description.

Table 3. Simulated Annealing Processor

Components		Hierarchical Description	Inline-Expanded Description	Area Reduction
Datapath:	Multiplier	1	1	0 %
	Add/Sub	2	2	0 %
	Barrelshifter	1	1	0 %
	Leading_Zero	1	1	0 %
	Comparator	2	3	33 %
	Multiplexer	19	27	30 %
	Register	11	12	8 %
Controller:	Gate Equivalents	158	307	49 %
	CLBs	56	104	46 %
	States	11	26	58 %

In summary, the presented results show several advantages of the hierarchical synthesis method regarding complex component structures. When using subcomponent sharing, the synthesized circuits need less clock cycles under resource constraints, and are less area consuming under timing constraints. Furthermore, the run-time of the synthesis algorithm could be decreased compared to non-hierarchical approaches.

6 Summary and Conclusion

This paper presented a new approach for hierarchical high-level synthesis regarding complex component structures. The presented experimental results encourage further investigations in this area. The advantages of the presented approach are:

- The concept of complex components offers the basis for a hierarchical synthesis methodology with respect to specific component structures, in order to increase the degree of optimization.
- Resource sharing can be performed across different levels of hierarchy of parallel working components, with a separate controller.
- The modification of the components can be done after binding, such that the synthesis time can be kept low.
- Each synthesized submodule can be reused in the same design as a complex register-transfer component.
- Multiple instances of one component have to be synthesized only once.

7 References

[1] R. Bergamaschi: *Productivity Issues in High-Level Design: Are Tools Solving the Real Problems?*. Proceedings of DAC, 1995.

[2] M. McFarland, T. Kowalski: *Incorporating Bottom-Up Design into Hardware Synthesis*. IEEE Transactions on CAD, vol. 9, pp. 938-950, 1990.

[3] D. E. Thomas, E. D. Lagnese, R. A. Walker, J. A. Nestor, J. V. Rajan, R. L. Blackburn: *Algorithmic and Register-Transfer Synthesis: The System Architect's Workbench*. Kluwer, 1990.

[4] D. Sreenivasa Rao, F. Kurdahi: *Hierarchical Design Space Exploration for a Class of Digital Systems*. IEEE Transactions on CAD, vol. 1, pp. 282-295, 1993.

[5] W. Geurts, F. Catthoor, H. De Man: *Quadratic Zero-One Programming-Based Synthesis of Application-Specific Data Paths*. IEEE Transactions on CAD, vol. 14, pp. 1-11, 1995.

[6] W. Geurts, F. Catthoor, H. De Man: *Time Constrained Allocation and Assignment Techniques for High Throughput Signal Processing*. Proceedings of DAC, 1992.

[7] T. Ly, D. Knapp, R. Miller, D. MacMillen: *Scheduling using Behavioral Templates*. Proceedings of DAC, 1995.

[8] D. C. Ku, G. De Micheli: *High-Level Synthesis of ASICs Under Timing and Synchronization Constraints*. Kluwer, 1992.

[9] P. Kission, H. Ding, A. Jerraya: *VHDL Based Design Methodology for Hierarchy and Component Re-Use*. Proceedings of EURO-VHDL, 1995.

[10] A. Timmer, M. Heijligers, L. Stok, J. Jess: *Module Selection and Scheduling using Unrestricted Libraries*. Proceedings of EDAC, 1993.

[11] B. Landwehr, P. Marwedel, R. Dömer: *OSCAR: Optimum Simultaneous Scheduling, Allocation and Resource Binding Based on Integer Programming*, Proceedings of EURO-VHDL, 1994.

[12] R. Ang: *Library Insertion and Reuse of Datapath Components in High-Level Synthesis*. PhD Thesis, University of California, Irvine, 1996.

[13] B. G. Hald, J. Madsen: *A Flexible Representation for High-Level Synthesis*. Proceedings of 2nd Asian Pacific Conference on Hardware Description Languages, 1994.

[14] P. Jha, N. Dutt: *Design Reuse through High-Level Library Mapping*. Proceedings of European Design & Test Conference, 1995.

[15] M. Wolfe: *High Performance Compilers for Parallel Computing*. Addison-Wesley, 1996.

[16] U. Banerjee: *Loop Transformations for Restructuring Compilers: The Foundations*. Kluwer, 1993.

[17] William Pugh: *The Omega Test: a fast and practical integer programming algorithm for dependence analysis*. Proceedings of Supercomputing, 1991.

[18] W. Rosenstiel, H. Krämer: *Scheduling and Assignment in High-Level Synthesis*. In R. Camposano, W. Wolf: High-Level VLSI Synthesis, Kluwer, 1991.

[19] P. Gutberlet, J. Müller, H. Krämer, W. Rosenstiel: *Automatic Module Allocation in High-Level Synthesis*. Proceedings of EURO-DAC, 1992.

[20] P. Gutberlet, H. Krämer, W. Rosenstiel: *CASCH - a Scheduling Algorithm for High-Level Synthesis*. Proceedings of EDAC, 1991.

[21] P. Gutberlet, W. Rosenstiel: *Timing Preserving Interface Transformations for the Synthesis of Behavioral VHDL*. Proceedings of EURO-VHDL, 1994.

[22] B. Eschermann, O. Haberl, O. Bringmann, O. Seitz: COSIMA: *A Self-Testable Simulated Annealing Processor for Universal Cost Functions*. Proceedings of EuroASIC, 1992.

Generalized Resource Sharing

S. Raje R. A. Bergamaschi

IBM T. J. Watson Research Center, NY, USA

Abstract

Resource sharing is one of the main tasks in high-level synthesis, and although many algorithms have addressed the problem there are still several limitations which restrict the generality and applicability of current algorithms. Most clique-partitioning-based algorithms use local and inaccurate cost-functions which result in inefficient results. This paper presents algorithms for the resource sharing problem on registers and functional units, and shows how they overcome the limitations of existing algorithms.

The main characteristics of this work are: interleaved register and functional unit merging in a global clique partitioning based framework, accurate merging cost estimation, accurate interconnect cost estimation, relative control cost taken into account, and efficient false loop elimination. The results obtained show significant improvements in the delay of designs, while also minimizing area, specially for large designs with many sharing possibilities.

1 Introduction

Resource sharing is one of the main problems in high-level and register-transfer-level synthesis. The problem consists in minimizing the number of registers and functional units used in a design with the primary goal of minimizing area. Extra cost metrics such as delay and power have also been considered.

Several algorithms have been proposed for sharing registers and functional units. These algorithms can be broadly classified into *constructive* or *global* algorithms. Constructive algorithms, such as EMUCS [1], build the data-path one element at a time. Global algorithms [2], are usually based on *clique partitioning* techniques. The registers or functional units to be merged are mapped onto a *Compatibility Graph*, which is partitioned into cliques. The advantages of this approach are that it allows for more global solutions than the (greedy) constructive approaches, and tend to produce better results. Although clique partitioning techniques for resource sharing have been widely adopted by several systems, strong limitations which have not yet been addressed still remain. This paper presents a generalized formulation and algorithms for global clique-partitioning-based resource sharing which overcome many of the limitations of current algorithms. It also detects and eliminates false loops, possibly introduced by sharing, more efficiently than previously published. The following paragraphs explain these limitations and introduce the algorithms in this paper which overcome them.

Sharing order: In all algorithms to date, sharing of registers is done separately from sharing of functional units, that is, either register sharing is done first followed by functional unit sharing (as in Facet [2]), or vice-versa. This is inefficient because it directly impacts the accuracy of the cost computation. The algorithm presented in this paper shares both registers and functional units in the same clique partitioning formulation.

Cost computation: In most systems, the cost associated with merging resources is a purely local metric, which can severely impact the advantage of a global clique partitioning approach, and produce poor results.

In this paper, the primary cost metric is based on a projected area savings that would result if the whole clique were actually formed. That is, instead of measuring the cost of a single merging, the algorithm computes the final cost as if the whole clique is merged. Moreover, this cost takes into account actual technology-dependent values and accurate interconnection costs (using multiplexer-based point-to-point interconnections).

Interconnect costs: When sharing two elements, one can compute the resulting interconnection costs based on the inputs and outputs of the two elements at that stage. However, future mergings involving elements connected to the inputs or outputs of the merged nodes may change the interconnection cost, invalidating the original computation.

In this paper, the cost function also considers whether the inputs and outputs of the two elements being merged are compatible. If so, they may be merged in the future, which will reduce the interconnection cost of the current merging. This *compatibility look-ahead* mechanism is called *Future_Connectivity*.

Another source of inaccuracy is the handling of commutative inputs to functional units. The approach presented in this paper allows all elements to swap all inputs every time a new element is added to a clique.

False loop elimination: The algorithm in [3] identifies a number of potential loop-forming mergings and removes the corresponding compatibility edges from the compatibility graph. This algorithm can be very inefficient because it removes far more compatibility edges than really needed, which in turn prevents possible cost-effective mergings.

The algorithm in [4] uses zero-one quadratic programing to do resource sharing. It eliminates false

1092-3152/97 $10.00 © 1997 IEEE

loops by imposing additional constraints to their mathematical program. Additional constraints costs run-time, which is already high for algorithms that use quadratic programing.

The false loop elimination algorithm described in this paper is more efficient because it is embedded within the clique partitioning algorithm. Once a compatibility edge is selected for merging, the algorithm checks whether that merging will definitely cause a false loop by doing a topological analysis of the resulting network, and if so, the merging is not carried out and the edge is deleted. In this way, only a minimal number of edges is removed from the compatibility graph, thus allowing for more mergings to be considered.

Control logic effects: Resource sharing is usually done with little or no knowledge of the effects on control area. In general, control area is difficult to estimate because of the logic optimizations of the controller during the logic synthesis step.

The resource sharing algorithm presented in this paper looks at the control equations associated with each data-path element and uses that as a secondary decision metric when selecting elements to be merged.

2 Framework

The starting point for this resource sharing algorithm is an initial data-path and controller generated from a scheduled control and data flow graph [5]. Based on this initial data-path and controller, and the scheduled control/data flow graph, the complete *compatibility graph* (CG) is derived. This graph is the union of the compatibility graphs for registers and functional units.

Figure 1 shows a simple VHDL description and the corresponding scheduled control/data flow graph. This example uses "*wait until not clock'stable and clock='1'*" statements to represent either the scheduled states (as given by a scheduling algorithm) or states explicitly declared by the designer, resulting in a finite-state machine controller with five states. The initial data-path and controller and compatibility graph for this example are given in Figure 2, where *o1* to *o5* are operations and *a*, *b*, *c*, *d* are registers. Among the control signals generated by the controller there are some which are needed in the initial data-path (e.g., *ld_a*, represented by solid arrows) and some which are *potential* control signals (represented by dashed arrows), that are not needed in the initial data-path but may be needed if elements are shared. For example, signal *o1_sel* associated with adder *o1* is not yet needed because *o1* is a single function operator. However, if *o1* is merged with *o5* then both controls *o1_sel* and *o5_sel* will be needed to select the different functions in the resulting ALU. This resource sharing algorithm looks at both types of controls for determining control costs as well as detecting false loops due to sharing.

3 Cost Computation

The heuristic for forming cliques is fully based on costs. These costs are not necessarily proportional to

```
-- in1, in2, in3 are inputs
-- out1, out2, out3 are outputs
process
 begin
  wait until not clk'stable and clk='1';
  if (c1) then
    a:=in1+in2;                 -------- (o1)
    wait until not clk'stable and clk='1';
    out1<=a;
  else
    b:=in1+in2;                 -------- (o2)
    wait until not clk'stable and clk='1';
    if (c2) then
      c:=in2+in3;               -------- (o3)
      d:=in1+in3;               -------- (o4)
    else
      c:=in3;
      wait until not clk'stable and clk='1';
      out2<= b;
    endif;
    wait until not clk'stable and clk='1';
    out3<=c-d;                  -------- (o5)
  endif;
  wait until not clk'stable and clk='1';
end process;
```

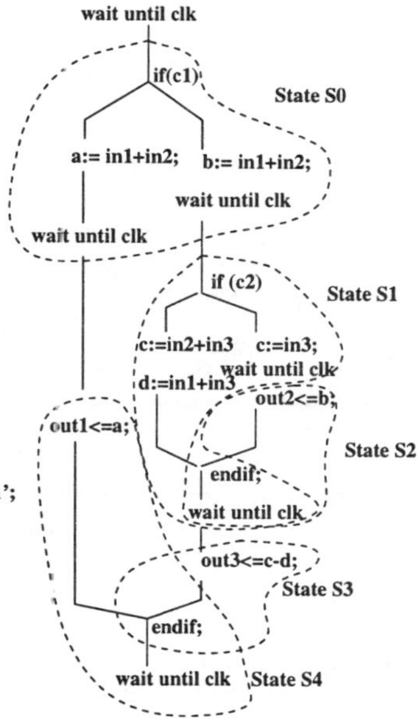

Figure 1: Behavioral Description and corresponding scheduled Control/Data-flow graph

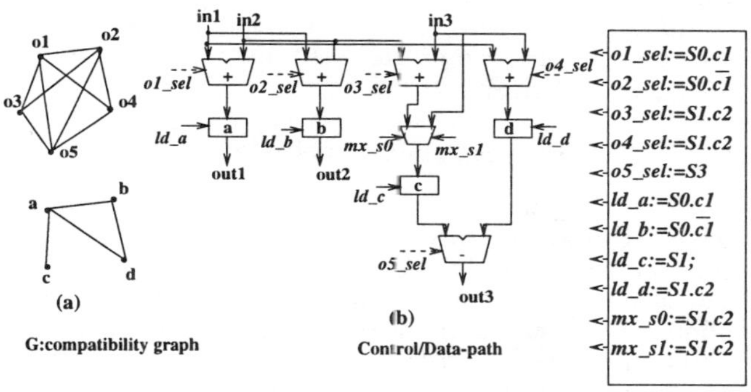

Figure 2: (a) Compatibility graph (b) Initial data-path and controller.

the size of the cliques or to the minimum number of cliques. The partitioning algorithm selects compatibility edges for merging based on the costs of all edges at any time. As a result, several cliques may be formed concurrently, instead of the traditional clique heuristic which forms cliques one-by-one with the goal of minimizing the cost of the clique being formed and the total number of cliques. The goal of this algorithm is to minimize the cost of all cliques together, which may or may not result in the minimum number of cliques. The primary cost is measured as area, but by accurately estimating interconnection costs, the interconnections are minimized, which has a direct effect on delay.

This algorithm uses a single compatibility graph which is a union of the functional unit compatibility graph and the register compatibility graph. Edges connecting registers or functional units may be selected at any time and merged in different cliques, effectively interleaving register and functional unit merging. This allows for more accurate estimation of the interconnection costs and makes the algorithm less dependent on the order in which registers and functional units are shared.

The partitioning algorithm works iteratively by selecting a compatibility edge based on the cost function and merging the nodes connected by the edge.

The cost function is actually not a single number but a decision tree based on different metrics. The decision tree for selecting an edge works as follows:

Step 1: Compute the *Projected_Area_Savings* of all compatibility edges. Select the subset of edges whose *Projected_Area_Savings* fall within $N\%$ of the top savings value. The value for N was empirically chosen to be around 80%. These initial set of edges then go to the secondary selection criteria.

Step 2: Compute the *Future_Connectivity* of all edges selected in Step 1. Select the subset of edges with *Future_Connectivity* within 80% (empirically chosen) of the best value. Pass this subset of edges to the tertiary selection criteria.

Step 3. If more than one edge is left in Step 2, compute the *Control_Similarity* of those edges and select the edge that has the highest *Control_Similarity*. Remaining ties are broken by using the highest *Projected_Area_Savings* followed by the highest *Future_Connectivity*.

3.1 Projected Area Savings

The *Projected_Area_Savings* for a compatibility edge estimates the area savings resulting from merging, not only the two nodes (connected by the edge) but also any other node that could end up in the same clique. In other words, it estimates the cost of the full clique, if formed. This helps overcome the locality effect of computing the cost based on the two end nodes alone.

This saving is the product of the total area savings (active area and interconnection area saved) when merging the two end-nodes of an edge and the number of common neighbours to the two nodes being merged, as described in the formula:

$$\begin{aligned} &Projected\_Area\_Savings(e) = \\ &(Active\_Area\_Savings(e) + Connectivity\_Savings(e)) \\ &\qquad * (Commonality(e) + 1) \end{aligned}$$

Algorithms for computing Active_Area_Savings(e) and Connectivity_Savings(e) are given in the following sections. Commonality(e) is the number of common neighbours to both end nodes of edge e. Although there is no guarantee that the whole clique will be formed, this projected area is a more global cost than the edge cost alone.

3.1.1 Active Area Savings

Active_Area_Savings is defined as the difference between the sum of the areas for the two end-nodes and the area of the shared resource that would implement the operations in the two nodes if the edge were to merge. In the formula below, edge e connects nodes v_i and v_j:

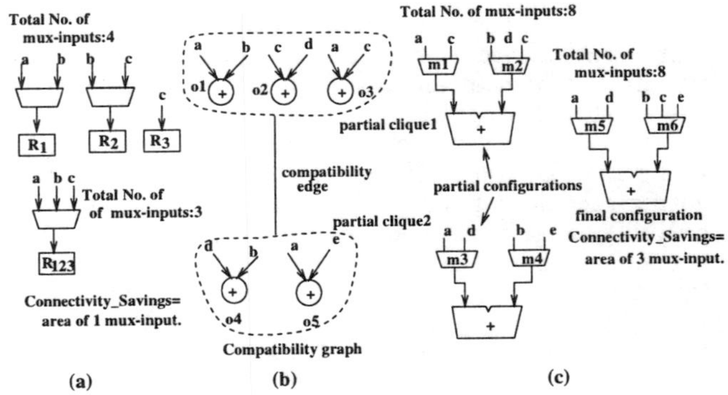

Figure 3: (a) Computing Connectivity_Savings for registers (b) Compatibility graph for operations and initial multiplexer configurations for the partial cliques. (c) Multiplexer configuration for the final clique and computation of Connectivity_Savings for operations.

$$\begin{aligned} Active\_Area\_Savings(e) &= area(v_i) + area(v_j) \\ &\quad - area(v_i, v_j) \end{aligned}$$

The area values are computed based on a technology library using the estimation algorithms described in [6].

3.1.2 Connectivity Savings

When two nodes are shared, the inputs have to be reconnected to the merged node possibly causing the creation of multiplexers. Connectivity_Savings is defined as the difference between the sum of the interconnections to the two elements and the final interconnections to the merged element, where interconnections are implemented as point to point multiplexers. The unit used is not number of inputs but the actual area of the multiplexers needed.

$$\begin{aligned} Connectivity\_Savings(e) &= mux\_area(v_i) \\ &\quad + mux\_area(v_j) - mux\_area(v_i, v_j) \end{aligned}$$

Calculation of Connectivity_Savings for edges with register end nodes is straightforward and is derived from the current data path. Special care is taken to consider the actual inputs independently of any existing multiplexer. In Figure 3a for example, the algorithm looks at the multiplexer inputs connected to R_1 and R_2 and at the final multiplexer connected to the merged node R_{123}. Trees of muxes in the initial data-path are collapsed into single-level muxes, so that the input count reaching the registers or operations is accurate.

Calculation of Connectivity_Savings for operations is a more involved procedure. It is critical to the accuracy of this computation to be able to permute inputs to commutative operations, as this affects directly the required number of inputs to the multiplexers.

Most algorithms use a purely greedy permutation each time a new element is added to a clique. Suppose that operations *o1* to *o5* in Figure 4 are gradually combined into a clique one by one. Using a greedy permutation of the new element inputs leads to suboptimal results as indicated in the top part of Figure 4.

The algorithm used in this paper permutes all the inputs each time a new element is added to the clique

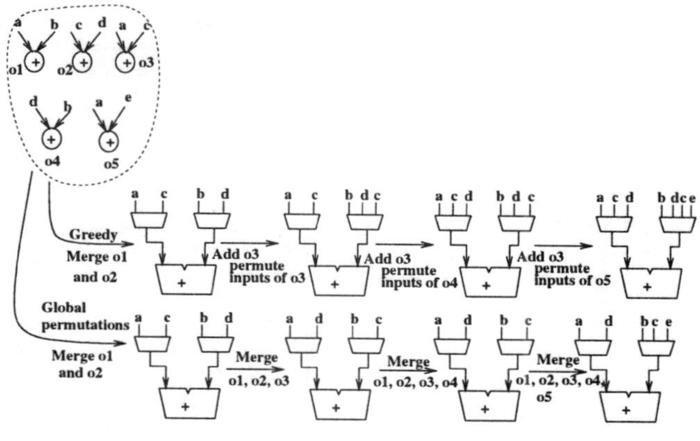

Figure 4: Comparing greedy and global input permutations on commutative operations.

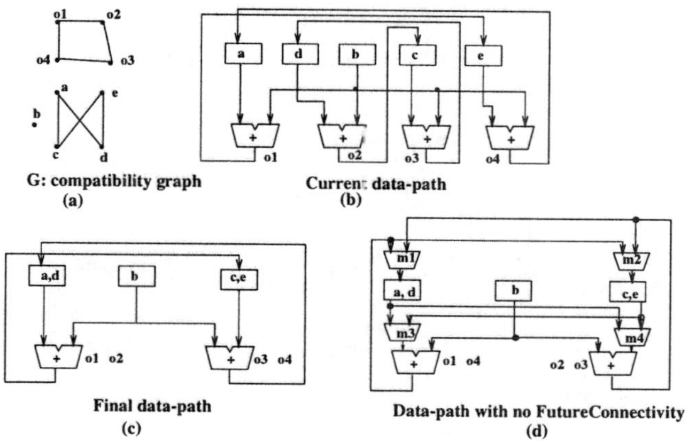

Figure 5: (a) Compatibility graph (b) Initial data-path (c) Final data-path using Future_Connectivity as a criteria (d) Data-path using only Connectivity as the criteria

and is able to find the optimal permutation resulting in the minimum number of multiplexer inputs, as indicated in the bottom part of Figure 4. For a full detailed description of the algorithm , see [7].

As an example of Connectivity_Savings for operations, consider the compatibility graph in Figure 3b, in which two partial cliques have already been formed and the algorithm needs to compute interconnection costs involved in merging them. The Connectivity_Savings is the difference in the areas of input multiplexers to both partial cliques and the areas of the input multiplexers in the final merged clique. Permuting the inputs of all operations using the algorithm above results in the multiplexers shown in Figure 3b (for the partial cliques) and Figure 3c (for the merged clique). The Connectivity_Savings equals the area of three fewer multiplexer inputs.

3.2 Future Connectivity

Future_Connectivity is a measure of savings in interconnections due to future mergings involving inputs and outputs of the current nodes being merged. Distinct inputs and outputs of two nodes may eventually be merged into a single resource; this is not reflected in the Connectivity_Savings number for an edge but is captured in the Future_Connectivity.

Figure 5 shows an initial data-path and the associated compatibility graph, where a, b, c, d, e are registers and $o1$, $o2$, $o3$, $o4$ are operations, all of which have a common input b.

The Connectivity_Savings for each of the compatibility edges $(o1, o2)$, $(o1, o4)$, $(o2, o3)$, $(o3, o4)$ is -2 multiplexer inputs, as a 2-input multiplexer will be required for any of these mergings (and there were no multiplexers in the initial data-path). Connectivity_Saving therefore cannot decide on which edge is better for merging (note that the Projected_Area_Savings are also the same for all edges).

Future_Connectivity looks at the registers connected to the inputs of the operations and checks if they are compatible. Register a and d are compatible and could eventually be merged, whereas register a and e are not compatible and could not share the same register. It follows that preference should be given to merging operations $o1$ and $o2$ instead of operations $o1$ and $o4$ because the inputs to $o1$ and $o2$ are likely to be merged in the future resulting in fewer interconnections (when compared to merging $o1$ and $o4$). Similar arguments can be made about merging $o1$ and $o2$ over $o2$ and $o3$. Future_Connectivity is a measure of the above preference.

Future_Connectivity for an edge is measured as the number of compatible edges among the nodes that form the left input set plus the number of compatible edges among nodes that form the right input set plus the number of compatible edges among outputs of the nodes being merged. For operations, this measure takes place after a "good" permutation of inputs is found, (see [7]).

In Figure 5, edge $(o1, o2)$ has Future_Connectivity of 1 (since a is compatible with d), whereas edge $(o1, o4)$ has Future_Connectivity of 0. Using Future_Connectivity as a criteria to merge edges the algorithm results in a final data-path as shown in Figure 5(c). Figure 5(d) shows a possible outcome for the data-path when Future_Connectivity is not considered as one of the merging criteria.

3.3 Control Similarity

Control_Similarity measures the amount of commonality between the control conditions associated with the execution of the two end operation nodes of an edge or the load-enable conditions of the two end register nodes. This commonality is measured as the number of common support variables in the control conditions for the two nodes. The support variables are extracted from the BDDs representing the control conditions. These conditions can either be *active* conditions already present in the initial data-path or *potential* conditions activated only when nodes are merged.

Merging of functional units or registers may result in extra control logic to be created. In the case of registers, this extra control logic is represented by the load_enable of the merged register (which should be

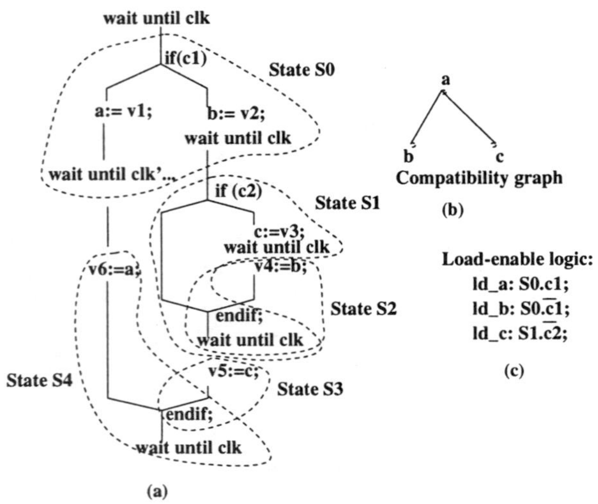

Figure 6: (a) Control/data-flow graph (b) Compatibility graph for the registers (c) Control Equations for the load-enable signals for registers

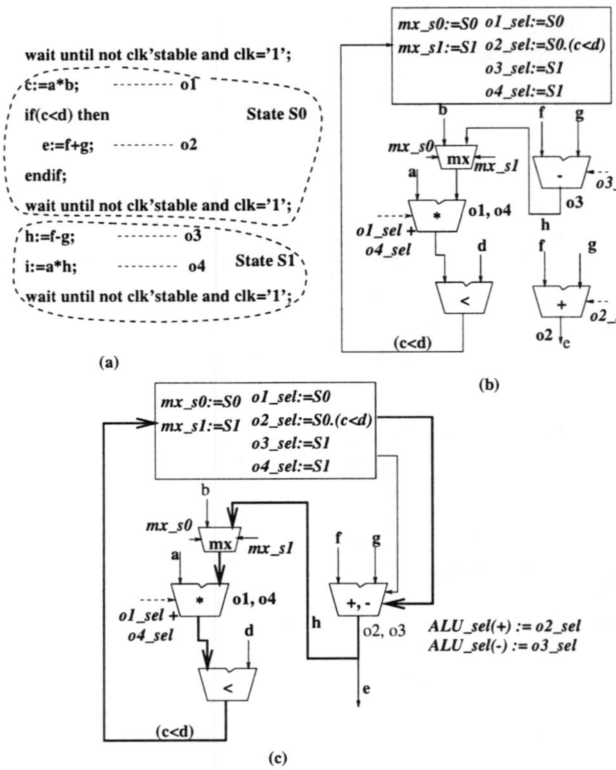

Figure 7: (a) Behavioral description, (b) Data-path and controller, (c) Data-path and controller if operations $o2$ and $o3$ are merged.

the OR of the original load-enable's) and by the select signals on input multiplexers. In the case of functional units, the extra control logic is represented by the select signals on the resulting ALU (if different functions are merged) and by the select signals on input multiplexers. The higher the number of common support variables in the *OR'ed* controls, the higher the probability that the resulting control can be optimized.

Figure 6a shows a fragment of a scheduled control/data flow graph. This example has 5 states, $S0$ through $S4$. The compatibility graph for registers a, b, and c is given in Figure 6b and the load-enable conditions, shown in Figure 6c, are a combination of the state value and the conditions on the branches of the control/data flow graph.

In this case the Projected_Area_Savings and Future_Connectivity are the same for both edges, (a, b) and (a, c). However, if a and b share a single register the resulting load-enable control of this register $R_{a,b}$ will be $S0.c1 + S0.\overline{c1} = S0$, whereas if a is shared with c the load-enable control of register $R_{a,c}$ will be $S0.c1 + S1.\overline{c2}$ which requires more gates to be implemented. The edge (a, b) should therefore be preferred over the edge (a, c) for merging. The Control_Similarity metric represents such preference.

In Figure 6, the Control_Similarity for edge (a, b) is 1 ($c1$ is a common support variable) and the Control_Similarity for edge (a, c) is 0. Note that since the state value is encoded in a state register which is common to all control signals, the state variable is not counted.

4 False Loop Elimination

The elimination of false loops is embedded within the sharing algorithm. No preprocessing is done to remove edges that could potentially lead to false loops as in [3]. When an edge is finally selected for merging (based on the cost criteria presented earlier), the algorithm checks if merging the two nodes will cause a false loop in the design. If it does, then the edge is discarded and removed from the compatibility graph. The algorithm to detect false loops in the design essentially traverses the data-path graph and the controller (both *active* and *potential* controls). A *depth-first search* is performed starting from the output of one of the nodes, and follows the combinational data and control paths. If the traversal reaches the other node then a false loop exists, in which case the edge is discarded.

Figure 7 shows a fragment of a behavioral description and the corresponding data-path and controller, and suppose that $o1$ and $o4$ have already been merged. Operations $o2$ and $o3$ have the same inputs and can also be shared. Based on the Active_Area_Savings and Connectivity_Savings these two operations are good candidates for merging. The false loop detection algorithm starts the depth-first traversal on the output of $o3$, which leads to multiplexer mx, to multiplier $o1, o4$, to the comparator and into the controller. As the output of the comparator is in the support of control signal $o2\_sel$, the traversal follows $o2\_sel$ reaching adder $o2$. Operation $o2$ is therefore reachable from operation $o3$ and merging the two would lead to a false loop in the design.

The above false loop elimination approach removes far fewer compatible edges than the one described in [3]. An edge is removed only once it is selected for merging and it is known for certain that merging the nodes leads to a false loop in the design. This technique allows for more cost effective mergings.

5 Generalized Resource Sharing: Complete Algorithm

Each step in the algorithm has already been explained in the previous sections. The pseudo-code below gives the overall sequence of steps involved in the complete algorithm.

```
Generalized_Resource_Sharing
(Compatibility graph CG,
 Initial data-path DPG,
 Initial Controller CTR) {
  while (edge_in_CG) {
    e = Select_Edge_to_Merge(CG, DPG, CTR);
    if (e == NULL) break;
    if (False_Loop_Detection(e, DPG, CTR))
      remove_edge (e, CG);
    else {
      merge_nodes(e);
      update_compatibility_graph(G);
      update_data_path_controller(DPG, CTR);
    }
  }
}
```

Procedure **Select_Edge_to_Merge** computes all the area, interconnections, future connectivity and control costs in all edges and selects one based on the selection criteria described in section 3. Then procedure **False_Loop_Detection** is called to check if merging the selected edge causes a false loop; in which case the edge is removed from CG. Otherwise the two end nodes of the edge are merged and the compatibility graph, the data-path graph and the controller are updated. This is repeated until no further edges are found in CG or no more edges can be found worthy of merging.

This algorithm does not require all edges in CG to be merged. If merging an edge is considered at some point in the algorithm to increase the cost permanently, then it is never selected. This is called a *stopping criteria*. If an edge has negative Projected_Area_Savings and has no common neighbours, it is highly unlikely that it will improve the cost of the design and thus it is not selected (Select_Edge_to_Merge returns null if all remaining edges in CG fall in this case).

6 Results

The generalized resource sharing algorithm has been implemented and tested with benchmarks and industrial examples. The results were compared against results produced by a coloring-based resource sharing algorithm [8] which aims primarily at producing minimum number of cliques, thus trying to minimize the number of functional units and registers. The algorithm in [8] does not attempt to eliminate false loops.

All examples were synthesized using both algorithms and the numbers of registers, functional units and multiplexers are compared. In addition, the results were submitted to logic synthesis for optimization and mapping and the final values of area and delay are compared.

For initial reference, Table 1 gives the total number of register bits, the number and type of functional units and the number of multiplexer bits present in the initial data path prior to resource sharing. Note that chaining is allowed, so operations can be connected to other operations or registers directly or through multiplexers.

Benchmarks	Initial Data Path		
	Reg bits	FUs	MUX bits
DIFFEQ	176	1(<), 2(+), 6(*), 2(-)	0
ELLIPTF	384	26(+), 4(*)	0
FRISC	96	12(+), 12(-), 3(=), 1(>)	1134
KALMANM	64	5(+), 10(-), 10(=), 1(<=), 5(*)	440
M6502	593	14(+), 6(-), 11(=), 2(>), 2(>=)	1484
MAHA	36	5(=), 8(+), 8(-)	64
RCV8251	19	2(-), 4(=)	53
Example 1	0	20(+), 24(=), 8(<), 8(>)	5192
Example 2	0	55(+), 22(-), 31(=), 2(<), 24(<=), 3(>), 24(>=)	3402
Example 3	0	16(-), 30(=), 4(/ =)	3104
Example 4	0	8(+), 4(=)	3998

Table 1: Initial data path: registers bits, functional units and input multiplexer bits. Each functional unit is a multi-bit operator.

All results were obtained by directing the two algorithms to merge only operations of the same kind, that is, adders with adders, subtracters with subtracters, etc. The algorithm can also handle merging of different operations in a multi-function unit.

Table 2 shows the number of register bits, the number and type of functional units, the number of multiplexer bits, and the area and delay values obtained after logic synthesis for the two resource sharing algorithms. Area and delay values are given in normalized area units (au) and delay units (du) respectively. Percentage improvements in area (%A) and delay (%D) are also given. From this table it can be seen that the algorithm in this paper produced better results in almost all cases, with several being significantly better in both area and delay.

The coloring algorithm [8] produced data-path with false loops in Elliptf, M6502 and Maha, so the delay values for these examples could not be computed reliably by static timing analysis. The generalized algorithm did marginally worse in Elliptf and Maha and better in M6502 despite removing some of the compatibility edges. The area results for Kalman show a significant increase because of an extra multiplier created by the generalized algorithm, which resulted from the elimination of an edge between two multiplication operations to avoid a false loop. The coloring algorithm did not create a false loop in Kalman due to a different merging order among edges which, by chance, did not produce a false loop.

Table 3 compares the number of edges removed by the generalized resource sharing algorithm to eliminate false loops against the number of edges removed by the algorithm in [3]. It can be seen that the gen-

Benchmarks	Coloring [8]					New Generalized Sharing Algorithm					% Improvements	
	Reg bits	FUs	MUX bits	Area	Delay	Reg bits	FUs	MUX bits	Area	Delay	%A	%D
Diffeq	80	1(<), 1(-) 1(+), 2(*)	336	4294	26.10	80	1(<), 1(-) 1(+), 2(*)	224	3942	24.33	8.2	6.8
Elliptf	160	2(+), 1(*)	720	5572	-	160	6(+), 1(*)	720	5998	25.02	-7.6	-
Frisc	96	2(+), 1(-) 3(=), 1(>)	990	5011	15.87	96	2(+), 1(-) 3(=), 1(>)	910	4786	15.36	4.5	3.2
Kalman	40	2(+), 2(-) 3(=), 2(*) 1(<=)	668	6677	31.47	24	3(+), 3(-) 5(=), 3(*) 1(<=)	496	8089	24.05	-21.1	23.6
M6502	119	4(+), 1(-) 4(=), 2(>) 1(>=)	1911	11373	-	110	5(+), 2(-) 5(=), 2(>) 1(>=)	1273	9484	17.28	16.6	-
Maha	12	5(=), 1(+) 1(-)	100	777	-	12	5(=), 2(+) 2(-)	112	801	11.83	-3.1	-
Rcv8251	11	1(-), 2(=)	76	1551	7.96	12	1(-), 3(=)	50	1366	6.17	11.9	22.5
Example 1	0	4(+), 24(=) 2(<), 2(>)	2292	17735	24.84	0	4(+), 24(=) 2(<), 2(>)	1940	16525	19.23	6.8	22.6
Example 2	0	15(+), 11(-) 1(<), 16(<=) 2(>), 16(>=) 31(=)	2682	50966	25.15	0	15(+), 11(-) 1(<), 16(<=) 2(>), 16(>=) 31(=)	2490	49099	20.29	3.7	19.3
Example 3	0	6(-), 29(=) 3(/ =)	1424	3862	15.91	0	6(-), 30(=) 3(/ =)	1360	3493	11.18	9.6	29.7
Example 4	0	4(+), 2(=)	1729	6252	9.45	0	4(+), 2(=)	1565	4686	5.17	25.0	45.3

Table 2: Resource sharing results for high-level synthesis benchmarks and industrial examples.

eralized resource sharing algorithm removes far fewer edges than the algorithm in [3].

The execution time for the generalized resource sharing algorithm ranged from 0.1 to 7.8 seconds for the example with the largest compatibility graph. The largest compatibility graph had over 2000 edges. Examples with several thousand edges have been synthesized in proportional run times. CPU times were measured on a IBM RS/6000 133 MHz workstation.

Benchmarks	Total No. of Compatibility Edges	No. of Edges Removed by [3]	No. of Edges Removed by the Generalized Sharing Alg.
Frisc	322	63	0
Kalman	376	178	4
M6502	526	157	2
Maha	111	42	5
Rcv8251	13	1	0

Table 3: Number of edges removed to avoid false loops.

7 Conclusions

This paper presented an efficient algorithm for resource sharing in high-level and RT-level synthesis. Algorithms were given for the most important problems in resource sharing, namely area and interconnection costs, control cost and false loop elimination.

Among the new concepts presented in this paper are: interleaved register and functional unit merging; accurate computation of interconnection cost, including global permutation of inputs; future connectivity costs based on the compatibility of inputs and outputs of the nodes being merged; control similarity costs; and efficient false loop elimination.

These algorithms were integrated into a generalized resource sharing system which produces results with comparable or better area and significantly better delay when compared to traditional resource sharing algorithms (targetted to minimizing the number of cliques).

References

[1] C. Hitchcock III and D. Thomas, "A method of automated data path synthesis," in *Proceedings of the 20th ACM/IEEE Design Automation Conference*, pp. 484–489, ACM/IEEE, June 1983.

[2] C. J. Tseng and D. P. Siewiorek, "Automated synthesis of data paths in digital systems," *IEEE Transactions on Computer-Aided Design*, vol. CAD-5, pp. 379–395, July 1986.

[3] L. Stok, "False loops through resource sharing," in *Proceedings of the IEEE International Conference on Computer-Aided Design*, pp. 345–348, IEEE, November 1992.

[4] W. Geurts, F. Catthoor, and H. De Man, "Quadratic zero-one programming-based synthesis of application-specific data paths," *IEEE Transactions on Computer-Aided Design*, vol. CAD-14, pp. 1–11, January 1995.

[5] R. Bergamaschi, R. O'Connor, L. Stok, M. Moricz, S. Prakash, A. Kuehlmann, and D. S. Rao, "High-level synthesis in an industrial environment," *IBM Journal of Research and Development*, vol. 39, pp. 131–148, January/March 1995.

[6] R. Camposano and R. A. Bergamaschi, "Redesign using state splitting," in *Proceedings of The European Design Automation Conference*, (Glasgow, Scotland), pp. 157–161, IEEE, March 1990.

[7] R. A. Bergamaschi, *The Development of a High-Level Synthesis System for Concurrent VLSI Systems*. PhD thesis, University of Southampton, Southampton, England, February 1989.

[8] R. A. Bergamaschi, R. Camposano, and M. Payer, "Allocation algorithms based on path analysis," *INTEGRATION, the VLSI Journal*, vol. 13, pp. 283–299, September 1992.

Exploiting Off-Chip Memory Access Modes in High-Level Synthesis *

Preeti Ranjan Panda   Nikil D. Dutt   Alexandru Nicolau

Department of Information and Computer Science
University of California, Irvine, CA 92697-3425, USA

Abstract

Memory-intensive behaviors often contain large arrays that are synthesized into off-chip memories. With the increasing gap between on-chip and off-chip memory access delays, it is imperative to exploit the efficient access mode features of modern-day memories (e.g., page-mode DRAMs) in order to alleviate the memory bandwidth bottleneck. Our work addresses this issue by: (a) modeling realistic off-chip memory access modes for High-Level Synthesis (HLS), (b) presenting algorithms to infer applicability of HLS with these memory access modes, and (c) transforming input behavior to provide further memory access optimizations during HLS. We demonstrate the utility of our approach using a suite of memory-intensive benchmarks with a realistic DRAM library module. Experimental results show a significant performance improvement (more than 40%) as a result of our optimization techniques.

1 Introduction

As library modules used in ASIC designs increase in complexity, existing high-level synthesis strategies will need to be modified to accommodate various aspects of complex interface protocols. One such complex module that has universal use in a wide variety of applications, is memory. Arrays in behavioral specifications are typically assigned to memories during synthesis. If these arrays are small enough, they may be mapped into on-chip RAMs. However, many applications involve large arrays, which need to be stored in off-chip memories, such as DRAM. Consequently, it is essential to employ a reasonably accurate model for memory operations during synthesis. Modern memories have efficient access modes (such as *page mode* and *read-modify-write*), that are known to improve the access bandwidth[6]. Since the newer generation of memories (Extended Data Out DRAMs, Synchronous DRAMs, etc.) all incorporate these access modes, it is important to develop a methodology for incorporating realistic memory library interface protocols into high-level synthesis, so that scheduling, allocation and binding algorithms can exploit these features to generate faster and more efficient designs.

Several memory-related issues, such as memory *allocation*[2, 12], *packing*[9, 8], *estimation*[3], and *selection*[1] have been addressed in previous research on high-level synthesis. Most of them target register files (also referred in literature as *foreground memory*) and on-chip RAMs and ROMs (sometimes called *background memory*) that share space on the same chip as an ASIC. The problem of clustering of behavioral variables into single- and multi-ported register files has been addressed in [17, 10, 16].

In [11], a scheduling algorithm using *behavioral templates* is described. A behavioral template represents a complex operation in a Control Data Flow Graph (CDFG) by enclosing several individual CDFG nodes, and fixing their relative schedule. Templates allow a better representation of memory access operations than single multicycled CDFG nodes, and lead to better schedules. However, since different memory operations are treated independently, typical features of realistic memory modules (e.g., page mode for DRAM) cannot be exploited, because the scheduler has to assume the worst-case delay for every memory operation, resulting in relatively longer schedules.

In this paper, we make the following contributions towards incorporation of off-chip memory accesses in high-level synthesis:

1. We present models for the well-known operation modes of off-chip memories (e.g., various DRAMs), which can be effectively incorporated into HLS tools.
2. We present algorithms for inferring the applicability of the memory access modes to memory references in the input behavior.
3. We outline techniques for transforming the Control-Data Flow Graph (CDFG) for the input behavior to incorporate the memory access modes, so as to obtain an efficient schedule.

*This work was partially supported by grants from ARPA (MDA904-96-C-1472), NSF (MIP-9708067) and ONR (N00014-93-1-1348).

2 Memory Access Optimizations in DRAMs

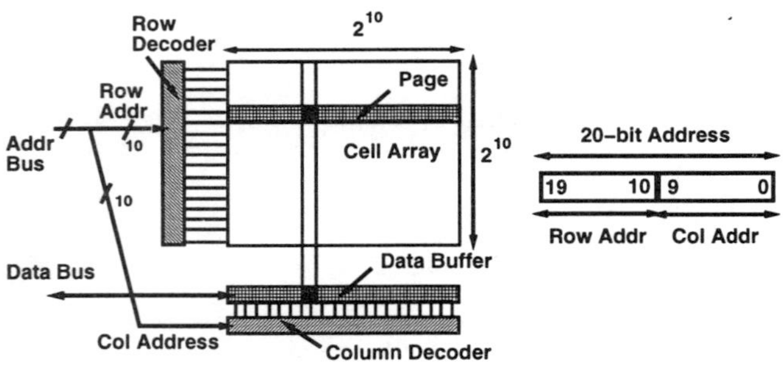

Figure 1. Typical DRAM Organization

Figure 1 shows a simplified view of the typical organization of a DRAM with 2^{20} words (= 1 M words), with the core storage array consisting of a $2^{10} \times 2^{10}$ square. A 20-bit logical address for accessing a data word in the DRAM is split into a 10-bit *Row Address* – consisting of the most significant 10-bits (bits 19 . . . 10); and a 10-bit *Column Address* – consisting of the least significant 10 bits (bits 9 . . . 0). The Row Decoder selects one of 2^{10} rows (or DRAM *pages*) using the row address, and the *Column Decoder* uses the column address to select the addressed word from the selected page. Since the row and column addresses are used over disjoint time intervals, the address bus is time-multiplexed between row and column addresses in order to save pin count. The following feature, called *page mode access*, is an important organizational attribute that results in significant access time reduction: *The row-decoding step physically copies an entire page into a data buffer (Figure 1), anticipating spatial locality, i.e., expecting future references to be from the same page. If the next memory access is to a word in the same page, the row-decoding phase can be omitted, and the data fetched directly from the data buffer, leading to a significant performance gain.*

Modern DRAMs commonly utilize the following six memory access modes:

Read Mode – single word read, involving both row-decode and column-decode.

Write Mode – single word write, involving both row-decode and column-decode.

Read-Modify-Write (R-M-W) Mode – single word update, involving read from an address, followed by write *to the same address*. This mode involves one row-decode and column-decode stages each, and is faster than two separate Read and Write accesses.

Page Mode Read – successive reads to multiple words in the same page.

Page Mode Write – successive writes to multiple words in the same page.

Page Mode Read-Modify-Write – successive R-M-W updates to multiple words in the same page.

In order to motivate the need for explicitly modeling and exploiting these modes, we demonstrate the effect on design performance in HLS between scheduling with normal read operation, versus scheduling that exploits the page mode read of a DRAM. The sample library memory module used in this paper is the IBM11T1645LP Extended Data Out (EDO) DRAM, and the input behavior is the *FindAverage* routine in Figure 3(a), where the scalar variable *av* is mapped to an on-chip register, and the array $b[0 \ldots 3]$ is stored in off-chip memory.

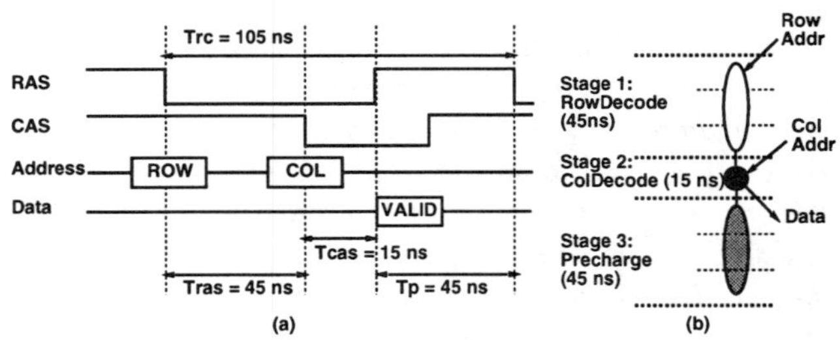

Figure 2. (a) Timing diagram for Memory Read cycle (b) Model for Memory Read operation

Figure 2(a) shows a simplified timing diagram of the *read cycle* of the $1M \times 64$-bit EDO DRAM. The Memory Read cycle is initiated by the falling edge of the RAS (Row Address Strobe) signal, at which time the row address is latched from the address bus. The column address is latched at the falling edge of CAS (Column Address Strobe) signal, which should occur at least T_{ras} = 45 ns later. Following this, the data is available on the data bus after T_{cas} = 15 ns. Finally, the RAS signal is held high for at least T_p = 45 ns to allow for *bit-line precharge*, which is necessary before the next memory cycle can be initiated.

From the above timing characteristics, we can derive a CDFG node cluster for the memory read operation, which consists of 3 stages (Figure 2(b)): (1) row decode; (2) column decode; and (3) precharge. The row and column addresses are available at the first and second stages respectively, and the output data is available at the beginning of the third stage. Techniques for formally deriving the node clusters from interface timing diagrams have been studied in the interface synthesis works such as [4], and can be applied in this context.

Assuming a clock cycle of 15 ns, and a 1-cycle delay for the addition and shift operations, we derive the schedule shown in Figure 3(b) for the code in Figure 3(a), using the memory read model in Figure 2(b). Since the four accesses to array b are treated as four independent memory reads, each of these incurs the entire read cycle delay of $T_{rc} = 105$ ns, i.e., 7 cycles, requiring a total of $7 \times 4 = 28$ cycles.

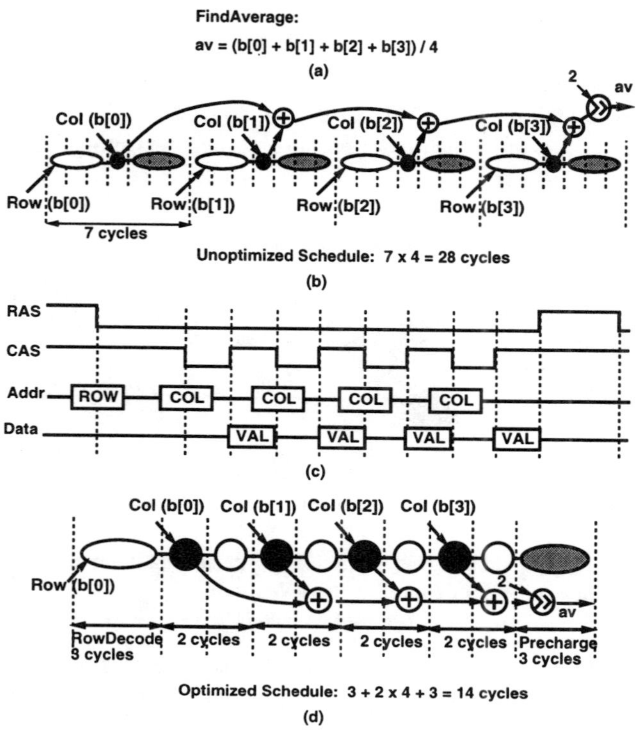

Figure 3. (a) Code for *FindAverage* (b) Treating the memory accesses as independent Reads (c) Timing diagram of *page mode read* cycle (d) Treating the memory accesses as one page mode read cycle

However, DRAM features such as page mode read can be efficiently exploited to generate a much tighter schedule for behaviors such as the *FindAverage* example, which access data in the same page, in succession. Figure 3(c) shows the timing diagram for the *page mode read* cycle, and Figure 3(d) shows the schedule for the *FindAverage* routine using the page mode read feature. Note that the page mode does not incur the long row decode and precharge times between successive accesses, thereby eliminating a significant amount of delay from the schedule. In this case, the column decode time is followed by a *minimum pulse width* duration for the CAS signal, which is also 15 ns in our example. Thus, the effective cycle time between successive memory accesses has been greatly reduced, resulting in an overall reduction of 50% in the total schedule length.

The key feature in the dramatic reduction of the schedule length in the example above is the recognition that the input behavior is characterized by memory access patterns that are amenable to the page mode feature, and the incorporation of this observation in the scheduling phase. In the following sections, we first provide synthesis models for the various access modes available in modern off-chip memories, and then describe a technique that incorporates the models into HLS by transforming the input behavior accordingly.

3 Representing Memory Accesses for HLS

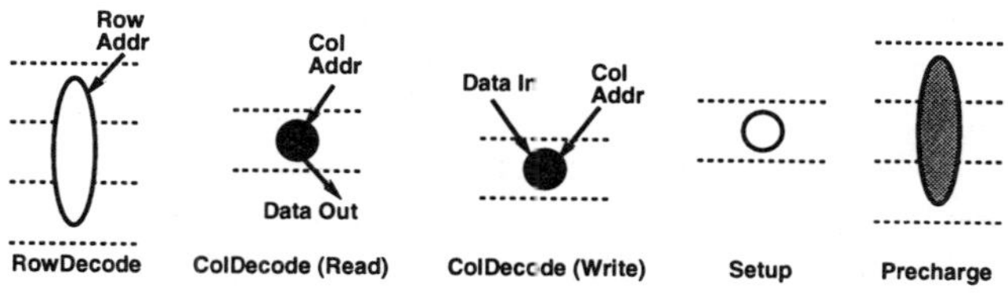

Figure 4. CDFG nodes used for memory operations

Instead of a single memory access node in the CDFG, we model memory operations corresponding to the different access modes using finer-grained memory access nodes (Figure 4). The **RowDecode** node is a multicycle operator that marks the beginning of any memory operation. The node has one input – the row address of the location, which should be ready before this node is scheduled. The **ColDecode (Read)** and **ColDecode (Write)** nodes form the second stage of the memory read and write operations. The **ColDecode (Read)** node has one input – the column address, and one output – the data read. The **ColDecode (Write)** node has two inputs – the column address, and the data to be written. The **Setup** node serves as a "delay" node in order to implement minimum delay constraints between successive stages of a memory operation. The **Precharge** node is a multicycle node that marks the last stage of a memory cycle. Physically, it signifies the restoration of the memory bit-lines to the initial state, so that the next operation can be initiated after the completion of this stage.

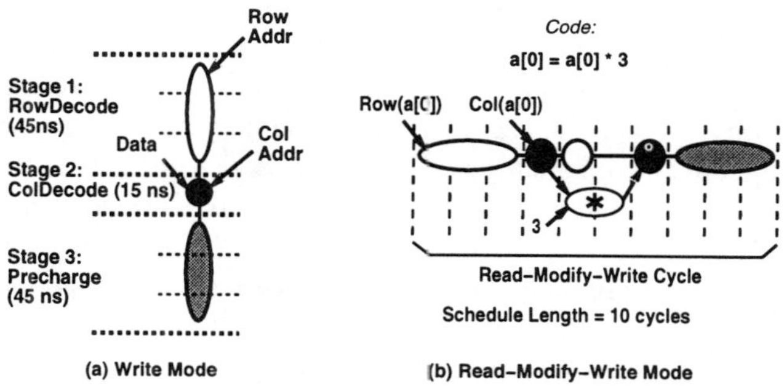

Figure 5. CDFG models of memory operations

For each memory access mode, we build composite memory access nodes in the CDFG, based on the access protocol for that mode.

Read Mode: This mode was described in Section 2.

Write Mode: The memory write operation has similar timing characteristics to the read operation. The CDFG node cluster for the write cycle is shown in Figure 5(a). The ColDecode node used in the second stage is the **ColDecode (Write)** node identified in Figure 4.

Read-Modify-Write Mode: The Read-Modify-Write (R-M-W) mode is illustrated in Figure 5(b) with a simple behavioral statement: $a[0] = a[0] * 3$, which involves the reading and writing of memory address for $a[0]$. The schedule requires 10 cycles. Note that, an extra control step is introduced between the *setup* and *write* stages, because the '$*$'-operation requires 2 cycles. If the operation were to be modeled as separate read and write cycles, we would require: $2 \times 7 = 14$ cycles.

Page Mode Read: This mode was described in Section 2. The **Page Mode Write** and **Page Mode R-M-W** modes are constructed similarly.

4 Incorporation of Memory Models in HLS

The memory operations described in Section 3 were designed to exploit typical behavioral memory access patterns. This requires analysis of the CDFG to identify behavioral patterns that can be optimized by the various efficient memory access modes, and transformation of the CDFG to incorporate the optimizations. The actions that need to be performed include: (1) *clustering* of scalar variables; (2) *reordering* of memory accesses in the CDFG; (3) *hoisting* conditional memory operations; and (4) *loop transformations*.

4.1 Clustering of Scalars

Scalar variables are normally assigned to on-chip registers. However, if the number of such variables is large, it might be necessary to store these variables in memory. A related optimization problem that arises in this address assignment is that, consecutive accesses to two different scalar variables can be implemented as a single page mode operation if both are located in the same memory page. Suppose the off-chip memory has a page size of P words. The following problem needs to be solved: *Group the scalar variables into clusters of size P (to reside in the same memory page), such that the number of consecutive accesses to the same memory page is maximized.* The technique we use is similar to the solution of an analogous problem in the context of cache memory, where scalar variables are grouped into clusters of size L (where L is the size of a *cache line*), so as to minimize the number of cache misses[14].

At the end of this step, all variables are assigned a memory address. We assume, for convenience, that the first element of all arrays are aligned to a memory page boundary. Similarly, each row of a multi-dimensional array is padded so that all rows begin at a page boundary, unless the array is small enough to be accommodated in one page.

4.2 Reordering of Memory Accesses

The correct ordering of memory accesses is critical for exploiting efficient memory access modes such as R-M-W. For example, in the code: "$a[i] = b[i] + a[i]$", the sequence of accesses: *"Read $b[i]$ → Read $a[i]$ → Write $a[i]$"* allows the utilization of the R-M-W mode for the address $a[i]$, while the sequence *"Read $a[i]$ → Read $b[i]$ → Write $a[i]$"* does not allow the mode, because of the intervening *"Read $b[i]$"* operation.

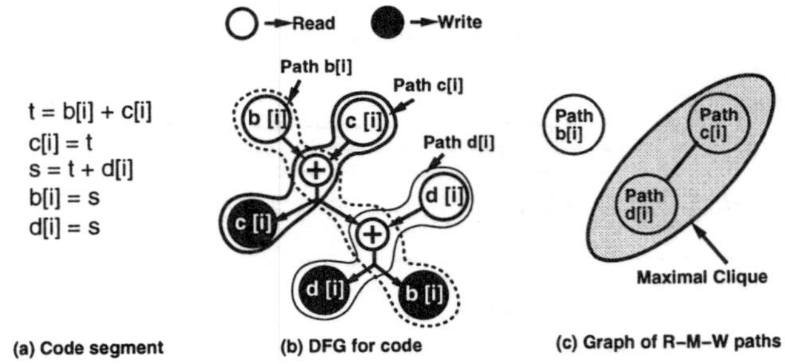

Figure 6. Ordering of memory operations determines possibility of exploiting R-M-W mode

Figure 6(a) shows an example basic block of code for which the corresponding DFG is shown in Figure 6(b). Figure 6(b) also shows three possible R-M-W paths, for addresses $b[i]$, $c[i]$, and $d[i]$. Note that it is not possible to implement the memory accesses to all the three locations as R-M-W operations. For example, if we implement the $c[i]$ path as an R-M-W operation, then the $b[i]$ path can no longer be implemented as R-M-W, because *"Read $b[i]$"* has to occur before *"Write $c[i]$"*, thus forcing the $b[i]$ path to be split into separate *"Read $b[i]$"* and *"Write $b[i]$"* operations.

In general, only one of a pair of intersecting paths can be implemented as R-M-W. In order to minimize the schedule length for a DFG, we need to maximize the number of R-M-W paths. The problem can be shown to be NP-complete by building a graph G, in which the nodes represent the DFG paths, and an edge exists between two nodes if the corresponding paths are non-intersecting (Figure 6(c)). Determining the maximal number of R-M-W paths in the DFG is now the problem of finding the *maximal clique* in G, which is known to be NP-complete. The greedy heuristic described in [15] can be used to solve this problem. However, since the number of such paths are very small in typical behaviors, an exhaustive solution can also be used.

4.3 Hoisting

Due to the time-multiplexing of the memory address bus between row and column addresses, a scheduling optimization is possible when two addresses in the same memory page are accessed from different paths of a conditional

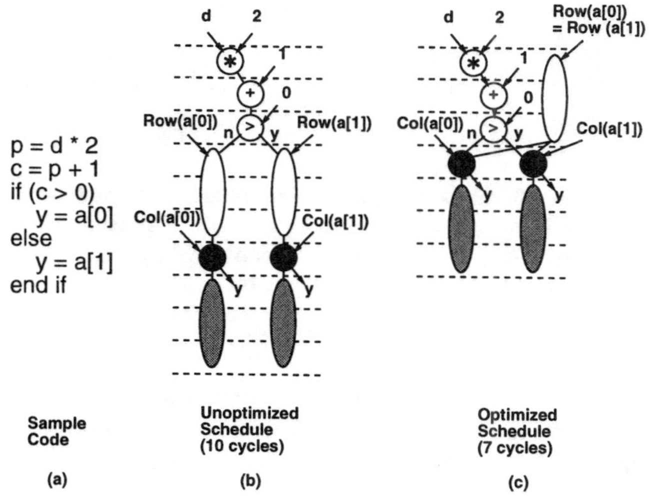

Figure 7. Hoisting Optimization

branch. Consider the behavior shown in Figure 7(a). Assume that variables p, c, d, and y are stored in on-chip registers, whereas array a is stored in off-chip memory. Either $a[0]$ or $a[1]$ is fetched from memory, depending on the result of the conditional evaluation ($c > 0$). A simple schedule, using the 3-stage read cycle model of Figure 2(b), and the assumption that $+, *$, and $>$ operations require 1 cycle, results in a schedule of length 10 cycles (Figure 7(b)). However, the knowledge that $a[0]$ and $a[1]$ reside in the same memory page (memory address assignments are statically computed) allows us to infer that both have the same row address, and hence, the read cycle could be initiated before the comparison operation. The schedule resulting from this optimization results in a length of only 7 cycles (Figure 7(c)). Output y is available after 7 cycles in the unoptimized schedule, but after only 4 cycles in the optimized schedule. We call this optimization – *hoisting* of the RowDecode stage. The *hoisting* optimization is also applicable for two elements x and y in the same page, accessed in different conditional paths C_1 and C_2 in the following cases: (1) x is written in C_1 and y is written in C_2; (2) x is read in C_1 and y is written in C_2; and (3) x is read or written in C_1, and there is no memory access in C_2[15].

4.4 Loop Transformations

In order to utilize the page mode operations, the CDFG for the behavior has to be transformed to reflect the page mode operation. Since most of the computation occurs in the innermost loops of nested loop structures, we concentrate on the memory accesses in the innermost loops.

Loops accessing single page per iteration

If a loop accesses locations from only a single memory page per iteration, e.g., there is only one read operation (*Read* $a[i]$) per iteration, the page mode operations can be applied directly by restructuring the loop so that it iterates over the array in blocks of P iterations (where P is the page size, in words), so that we have one page mode read for every P iterations. Figure 8(a) shows a section of the CDFG of an example loop with a single memory access ($a[i]$) in one iteration. We introduce an inner loop in which upto P elements from the same page are accessed. The transformed CDFG is shown in Figure 8(b). Note that the RowDecode and Precharge nodes enclose the inner CDFG loop, forming one complete page mode operation.

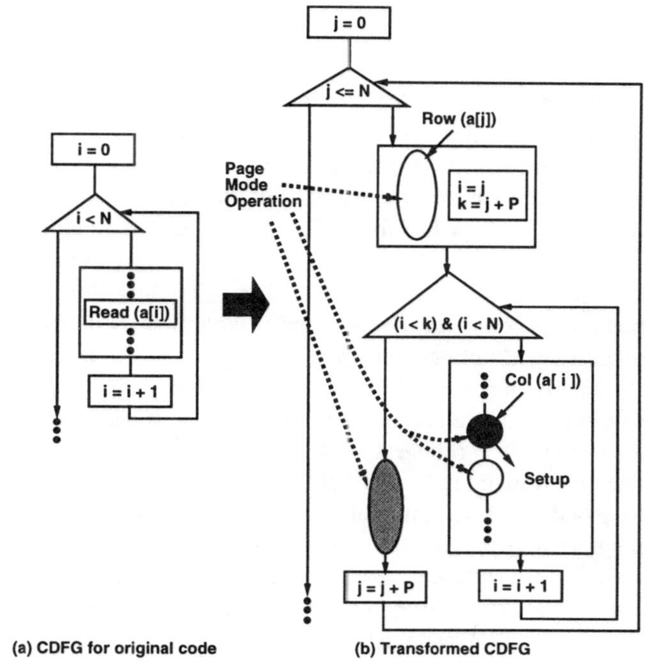

Figure 8. CDFG Transformation for page mode operation

Loops accessing multiple pages per iteration

If more than one array is accessed in one loop iteration, the transformation shown in Figure 8 cannot be directly applied, because different arrays usually lie in different memory pages. In such cases, we can use a well known transformation, *loop unrolling*[7], to create the opportunity for utilizing page mode operations. Figure 9(a) shows an example loop in which three different arrays, a, b, and c are accessed in an iteration. If the loop is unrolled once (Figure 9(b)), elements of the same array can be accessed in succession, leading to performance improvement resulting from page mode operation. In Figure 9, $r1, s1, t1$, etc. are registers into which memory elements are read in a *Read* operation, and from which memory elements are written in a *Write* operation.

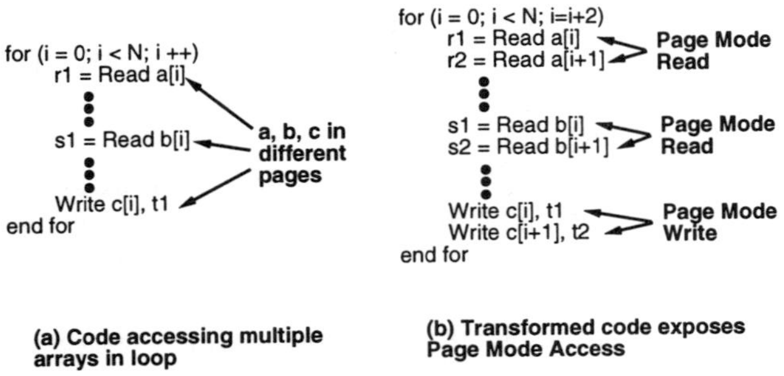

Figure 9. Loop unrolling helps exploit page mode operations

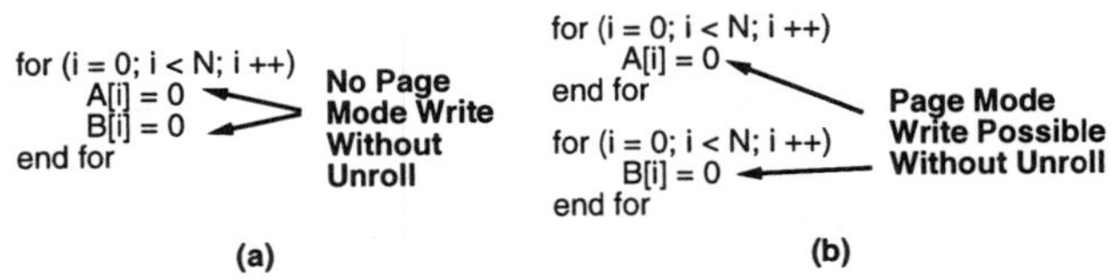

Figure 10. (a) Loop with disjoint subgraphs in body – there is no data dependence between the 2 statements (b) Split loop – page mode write can now be applied to the individual loops

Note that the unrolled loop in Figure 9(b) has a higher register requirement. Thus, the unrolling factor is constrained by the maximum number of on-chip registers available. Suppose we are given a register file of R registers. We first do an initial scheduling of the loop body (basic block) using *list scheduling*[7], to determine the number of registers, r, required for one iteration. Let m be the number of memory accesses in the loop body. Note that all memory accesses will not necessarily result in page mode accesses after unrolling. Let m' be the number of accesses that result in page mode accesses. If the loop is unrolled i times, we need $(m' \cdot i)$ registers to store the $(m' \cdot i)$ values. However, the remaining $(r - m')$ registers, which are used in the loop body to store temporary variables and non-page mode memory accesses, need not be duplicated, since they can be reused in the different iterations that constitute the unrolled loop. Thus, if the total number of registers allowed in the register file is R, we must have:

$$m' \cdot i + (r - m') \leq R \tag{1}$$

i.e., the loop unrolling factor, i, is given by:

$$i \leq \frac{R - r + m'}{m'} \tag{2}$$

or

$$i = \left\lfloor \frac{R - r + m'}{m'} \right\rfloor \tag{3}$$

Loops with disjoint subgraphs in body

A loop body is said to consist of disjoint subgraphs if the DFG representing the body (basic block) can be divided into more than one subgraph with no data dependence across their memory operations (i.e., no data dependence edges from one subgraph to the other). In such a case, each subgraph with at least one memory access in it, can be split into a different loop in order to better utilize page mode memory operation.

An example loop with disjoint subgraphs in its body is shown in Figure 10(a). The two statements in the loop body have no data dependence. We can split the loop into two loops, as shown in Figure 10(b), so that page mode write can now be applied to the individual loops without unrolling. Page mode operations without loop unrolling are preferable because unrolling increases the register requirements, and also limits the number of memory accesses in one page mode cycle, due to register file size constraints.

5 The CDFG Transformation Algorithm

Algorithm *TransformCDFG* in Figure 11 outlines the sequence of steps for transforming the CDFG of the behavior into an optimized form, so that a scheduling algorithm, such as list scheduling, can be invoked on the transformed CDFG. After performing the scalar variable clustering step, we perform the Reordering, Hoisting and Loop Splitting transformations in sequence, followed by restructuring of the resulting loops, if applicable. The complexity of the algorithm is that of the dominant loop restructuring (with multiple pages per iteration) step — $O(Bn^2)$, where n is the number of CDFG nodes and B is the number of loop nests in the behavior.

6 Experiments

We tested our proposed optimizations for utilizing efficient memory access features, on benchmark examples from the digital signal processing and scientific computing domains, all of which share the common characteristic that they process large data arrays. We present a summary of our experimental results in this section.

Column 1 of Table 1 shows the list of benchmark examples (taken from [13]) on which we performed our experiments. *Beam* (Beamformer) is a DSP application involving temporal alignment and summation of digitized signals from an N-element radar antenna array. *Dequant* is the de-quantization routine in the MPEG decoder application. *DHRC* (Differential Heat Release Computation) is an algorithm modeling the heat release in a combustion engine. *IDCT* (Inverse Discrete Cosine Transform), *LeafComp*, and *LeafPlus* are modules from the MPEG decoder application.

Algorithm *TransformCDFG*
Input: G – CDFG; R – Max. allowed Register File Size; P – Memory Page Size
Output: Transformed CDFG

1. Cluster scalar variables into groups of size P and assign memory addresses.
2. **for** each basic block B in G do
   Reorder to exploit R-M-W and page mode in B.
3. **for** each conditional node in G
   Perform *Hoist* transformation, if applicable.
4. **for** each innermost loop L in G
   Perform *Loop Splitting* transformation, if applicable.
5. **for** each loop L' in updated G
   if single page accessed in one iteration
     Perform *Loop Restructuring* for page mode
   else
     Perform *Loop Unroll* and *restructuring*

Figure 11. Algorithm for incorporating memory optimization transformations into the CDFG for scheduling

Madd and *MMult* are matrix addition and multiplication routines respectively. *Lowpass* is an image processing application that applies a low-pass filter to an image. *SOR* (Successive Over-Relaxation) is an algorithm used in evaluating partial differentiation equations. Column 2 shows the number of basic blocks in each benchmark.

Benchmark	B	Memory Modes				Optimizations			
		rmw	pr	pw	prmw	C	R	H	L
Beam	10	Y	Y	Y	N	N	Y	N	Y
Dequant	5	N	Y	Y	N	N	N	Y	Y
Dhrc	2	N	Y	N	N	N	N	N	N
Idct	13	N	Y	Y	N	N	N	N	Y
LeafComp	7	N	Y	Y	N	N	N	Y	Y
LeafPlus	5	N	Y	Y	N	N	N	Y	Y
Lowpass	4	Y	Y	N	N	N	Y	N	N
Madd	4	N	Y	Y	N	N	N	N	Y
MMult	6	N	Y	N	Y	N	N	N	Y
SOR	4	Y	Y	N	N	N	Y	N	N

Table 1. Memory optimizations applied to benchmarks

Table 1 shows the memory modes utilized by the memory accesses in the various benchmark examples, and the applicable optimizations. Columns 3, 4, 5, and 6 show (with letter 'Y') which examples had memory access patterns for which the Read-Modify-Write (rmw) mode, page mode read (pr), page mode write (pw), and page mode read-modify-write (prmw) respectively, were applied. Columns 7, 8, 9, and 10 show the CDFG transformation techniques – *Clustering*(C), *Reordering*(R), *Hoisting*(H), and *Loop Transformations*(L) – that were applied to each example. Note that the scalar clustering technique could not be applied to any of the examples, as the number of scalars in the example was too small, and could be stored in the register file we used.

We compared the execution time due the schedules generated by 3 techniques: (1) **Coarse-grain** – the traditional HLS approach, where memory access operation is treated as a multicycled operation; (2) **Fine-grain** – a more refined memory access model (e.g., the template strategy of [11]), with each memory access operation being treated as an independent 3-stage operation; and (3) **Optimized** – our proposed CDFG transformation-based approach, followed by the application of list scheduling.

We used the approximate timing characteristics of the IBM11T1645LP EDO DRAM memory chip, with a 15ns clock. We used the following operator delays: ALU – 1 cycle; multiplier – 2 cycles; divider – 4 cycles; RowDecode and Precharge operators – 3 cycles; and ColDecode and Setup operators – 1 cycle. We used a memory page size of 256 words and register file size of 16 words. We assumed that the number of ALUs, multipliers, and dividers is 1 each; and the register file has 2 read ports and 1 write port.

Benchmark	Cycle Count (Coarse-Grain)
Beamformer	1,251,844
Dequant	4,226
Dhrc	6,784
Idct	63,521,284
LeafComp	2,562
LeafPlus	3,074
LowPass	1,159,202
Madd	360,706
MMult	46,285,058
SOR	690,860

(a)

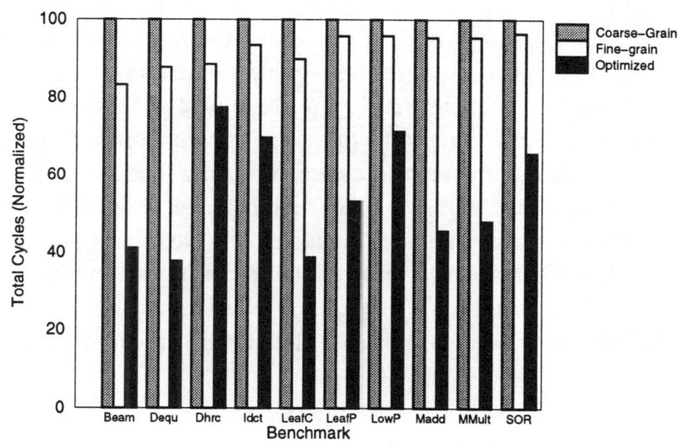

(b)

Figure 12. (a) Cycle count for Coarse-Grain (b) Summary of Results

Figure 12 summarizes the experimental results for the benchmark examples on which we tested our technique. Figure 12(a) shows the number of clock cycles required by the coarse-grain technique for each benchmark. On the x-axis of Figure 12(b), we show the benchmark examples, and on the y-axis, we show the total execution times for the schedules generated by the three techniques: Coarse-grain, Fine-grain, and Optimized, normalized to the cycle count of Coarse-grain, which is taken as 100.

The Optimized technique results in the fastest schedules, as seen from Figure 12(b). On an average, Optimized achieves a performance improvement of 45.2% over Coarse-grain, and an improvement of 40.8% over the Fine-grain technique. The performance improvement in the case of Optimized is the consequence of efficient utilization of the memory features such as read-modify-write and page mode.

The performance improvement for the Optimized technique above could be at the expense of a slight increase in controller area due to increased number of control states as compared to the controllers required for the Coarse-grain and Fine-grain schedules when the page mode operation is used. We used the *misII* synthesis package[5] to optimize the control logic for each case, and studied the control overhead for our optimization technique. We observed that the controllers generated from the Optimized schedules have an average area only 14.9% larger than those generated from Coarse-grain, and 10.3% larger than those generated from Fine-grain, for the benchmark examples[15]. Given the significant improvement in performance with our optimizations, we believe the control overhead is justifiable.

An important property of dynamic RAM is that the internal data bits need to be refreshed at regular intervals, since each bit is implemented as a capacitor. The refresh intervals of typical DRAMs are fairly large — the IBM11T1645LP has a refresh interval of 128 ms. The time taken to perform a single *Refresh cycle* (which results in one whole DRAM page being refreshed) is comparable to the duration of any other access, such as *Read cycle*. As a post-processing step, the schedule generated from the input behavior is adjusted to incorporate the refresh cycles, ensuring that they do not overlap in time with any other memory operation, since the DRAM is unavailable for Reads and Writes during the refresh. This is not an overhead due to our approach because the refresh circuitry is needed for DRAMs, no matter what synthesis technique is used. The details are described in [15].

7 Conclusions

Off-chip memories, such as DRAMs, have several well-known features that permit efficient data access. Present-day synthesis tools and algorithms targeting on-chip memory storage treat different behavioral memory accesses independent of each other, thereby ignoring several optimization possibilities in memory accesses that arise in the context of off-chip memories. We presented synthesis models for various off-chip memory access modes, as well as a technique for analyzing a behavior to determine memory accesses that can be optimized by exploiting the available memory features. We transform the CDFG of the given behavior into an optimized form, incorporating the efficient memory access features. Our experiments, based on the timing characteristics of a commercial DRAM chip, have indicated an average performance improvement of more than 40%, as a result of our optimization techniques.

Our technique for incorporating the synthesis models for memories into HLS is independent of the actual HLS tasks of scheduling, etc., and can be easily incorporated as a preprocessing step into existing HLS design flows. The technique could also be utilized to optimize the interface with other types of modules with complex interfaces and timing characteristics, such as LAN controllers. Future research includes extending the optimization techniques to work in the presence of more complex array index expressions.

References

[1] S. Bakshi and D. Gajski, "A Memory Selection Algorithm for High-Performance Pipelines," Proceedings of EuroDAC, 1995.

[2] F. Balasa, et al., "Dataflow-driven Memory Allocation for Multidimensional Signal Processing Systems," Proc. ICCAD, 1994.

[3] F. Balasa, F. Catthoor, and H. D. Man, "Background Memory Area Estimation for Multidimensional Signal Processing Systems," IEEE Trans. on VLSI Systems, Vol. 3, No. 2, June 1995.

[4] P. Chou, R. Ortega, and G. Borriello, "Interface Co-Synthesis Techniques for Embedded Systems", Proc. ICCAD, Nov. 1995.

[5] R. K. Brayton, et al., "MIS: A multiple level logic optimization system," IEEE Trans. on CAD, vol. CAD-6, no. 6, Nov 1987.

[6] M. J. Flynn, "Computer architecture – pipelined and parallel processor design," Jones & Bartlett publishers, 1995.

[7] D. Gajski, et al., "High Level Synthesis: Introduction to Chip and System Design," Kluwer Academic Publishers, 1992.

[8] P. K. Jha and N. Dutt, "Library mapping for memories," European Design and Test Conference, March 1997.

[9] D. Karchmer and J. Rose, "Definition and Solution of the Memory Packing Problem for Field-Programmable Systems," IEEE International Conference on Computer Aided Design, November, 1994.

[10] T. Kim and C. L. Liu, "Utilization of Multiport Memories in Data Path Synthesis," Design Automation Conference, 1993.

[11] T. Ly, et al., "Scheduling using Behavioral Templates," 32nd ACM/IEEE Design Automation Conference, June, 1995.

[12] P. E. R. Lippens, et al., "Allocation of Multiport Memories for Hierarchical Data Streams," Proc. ICCAD, November, 1993.

[13] P. R. Panda and N. D. Dutt, "1995 High Level Synthesis Design Repository," Intl. Symp. on System Synthesis, September 1995. (ftp://ftp.ics.uci.edu/pub/HLSynth95)

[14] P. R. Panda, et al., "Memory Data Organization for Improved Cache Performance in Embedded Processor Applications," ACM Transactions on DAES, Vol. 2, No. 4, October 1997.

[15] P. R. Panda, et al., "Exploiting Off-Chip Memory Access Modes in High-Level Synthesis," Tech. Rep. #97-32, U.C. Irvine, 1997.

[16] L. Ramachandran, D. Gajski, and V. Chaiyakul, "An algorithm for array variable clustering," Proc. ED&TC, 1994.

[17] L. Stok and J. A. G. Jess, "Foreground memory management in data path synthesis," International Journal of Circuit Theory and Applications, vol.20, no.3, pp. 235-55, 1992.

SESSION 6C

PARTITIONING PART I

Moderators:

Naveed Sherwani, Intel Corp.,

Hillsboro, OR

Chung-Kuan Cheng, University of California at San Diego,

La Jolla, CA

Replication for Logic Bipartitioning

Morgan Enos, Scott Hauck, Majid Sarrafzadeh
Department of Electrical and Computer Engineering, Northwestern University, Evanston, IL 60208
{morgan, hauck, majid}@ece.nwu.edu

Abstract

Logic replication, the duplication of logic in order to limit communication between partitions, is an effective part of a complete partitioning solution. In this paper we seek a better understanding of the important issues in logic replication. By developing new optimizations to existing algorithms we are able to significantly improve the quality of these techniques, achieving up to 12.5% better results than the best existing replication techniques. When integrated into our already state-of-the-art partitioner, we improve overall cutsizes by 37.8%, while requiring the duplication of at most 7% of the logic.

1 Introduction

Logic partitioning is one of the critical issues in CAD for digital logic. For most applications the goal is to minimize the communication between partitions while ensuring that each partition is no larger than the capacity of the target device. While it is possible to solve the case of unbounded partition sizes exactly [3], the case of balanced partition sizes is NP-complete [9]. As a result, numerous heuristic algorithms have been proposed [1].

We have already demonstrated that a careful integration of existing bipartitioning techniques, along with some new approaches and optimizations, can yield a bipartitioning algorithm significantly better than the current state-of-the-art [12]. Our algorithm achieved a 8% improvement over PROP [5], 16% improvement over FBB [19], 22% improvement over Paraboli [18] and MELO [2], 50% improvement over Fiduccia-Mattheyses [7], and a 58% improvement over EIG1 [10] [2], some of the best current bipartitioning algorithms.

In this paper, we seek to understand the critical issues in logic replication, the selective duplication of logic to reduce the resulting cutset. We examine most of the current logic replication literature, integrating it into our already extremely efficient partitioning system. We also develop techniques to significantly improve the quality of their results, yielding much smaller cutsets. This will lead to a complete logic bipartitioning algorithm with replication which delivers superior results.

1.1 Optimized FM

Most of the algorithms for replication use the Fiduccia-Mattheyses (FM) algorithm [7]. FM is a widely used algorithm, and as such a number of ideas have emerged which improve upon the basic design. By a judicious combination of these ideas, improvements in performance can be realized. This is the premise behind Strawman [11] [12], for this partitioner actually consists of many techniques which achieve a synergistic reduction in cut size. As far as we know, this partitioner delivers the best standard bipartitioning results in the literature today. Because of these strong results we have chosen to use this system as a base for our replication work.

Although a complete description of the Strawman partitioner is beyond the scope of this paper, it will be important to understand three of its optimizations.

- **Random initial partition creation.** The partitioner randomly creates an initial partition, and multiple runs of the partitioner use different initial partitions.
- **Hierarchical clustering and iterative unclustering.** The algorithm clusters the circuit recursively, building a hierarchy of clusters. Then it first partitions at the top level of the hierarchy. Once it can find no improvement, the highest level of clustering is removed, and the partitioning resumed. This continues until all clusterings are removed.
- **Higher-level gains.** We use higher-level gains as proposed by Krishnamurthy [15]. This is a tie-breaking mechanism for nodes with identical gains which adds some foresight to the algorithm. A net contributes an nth level gain of +1 to a node *S* on the net if there are n-1 other nodes on the net in the same partition as *S* which are unlocked, and zero which are locked. A net contributes a -1 nth level gain to a node *S* on the net if there are n-1 unlocked nodes on the net in the partition opposite to *S*, and zero locked.

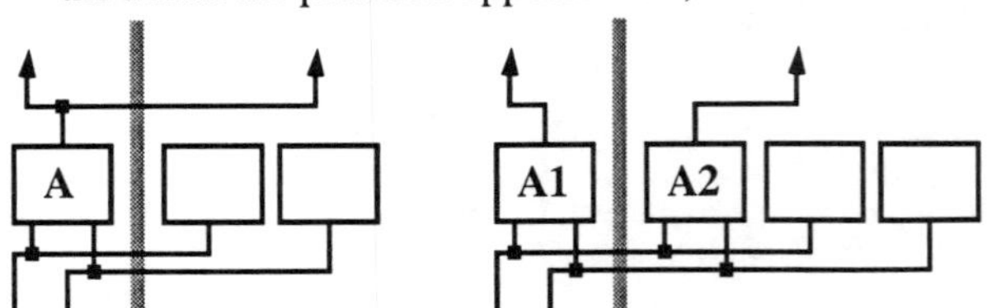

Figure 1. An example of node replication. Node **A** is replicated into **A1** and **A2**, yielding a gain of 1.

1.2 Methodology

Replication for cut minimization seeks out cells that when replicated reduce the number of nets in the cut set. Replication reduces the number of cut nets in a partition by creating redundancy in signal pathways.

As Figure 1 illustrates, the output net of a replicated cell need no longer span partitions since each partition has

1092-3152/97 $10.00 © 1997 IEEE

its own copy of the cell to generate the signal. However, to ensure that the correct signal is generated, every input net of the original cell must also input the replicated cell. Hence, the gain of cell replication is:

(Eqn. 1) | cut outputs | - | uncut, *unreplicated* inputs |

By *unreplicated* input net we refer to input nets of the cell that have a replicated source. Since such nets can never be cut, they are excluded from the gain calculation.

To determine the effectiveness of the replication algorithms, we run each thirty times on a SPARC5 on the benchmarks in Table 1. Partitions are allowed to grow to at most 53.6% of the circuit size (Strawman normally allows a partition to grow to 51% of total circuit size, and by allowing 5% of the logic to be replicated we reach an upper limit of $.51*1.05 \cong 0.536$). When using Strawman to produce partitions for comparison against the various replication algorithms, we allow each partition to grow to 53.6% of the original circuit size. We also require that if a circuit input is replicated, a net must be added to the cutset to carry the input between partitions [6].

The 11 benchmarks used in this paper are given in Table 1. Although this is a subset of the circuits typically used in partitioning research, these were the only circuits available to us that contained information on what node generates a given net, which is necessary for replication.

benchmark	# cells	# nets	# iopads	# pins
s5378	3225	3176	88	8241
s9234	6098	6076	45	15026
s13207	9445	9324	156	23442
s15850	11071	10984	105	27209
C6388	1956	1924	64	7046
biomed	6494	6442	77	24537
prim2	3035	3028	128	11294
struct	1952	1920	64	5535
s35932	19880	19560	359	55420
s38584	22451	22173	294	61309
s38417	25589	25483	138	64299

Table 1. Characteristics of benchmark circuits.

In this paper we investigate most of the replication algorithms from the literature, as well as some novel extensions. Throughout this paper, algorithms directly from the literature will be referred to as "Basic".

2 Kring/Newton Replication

The algorithm proposed by Kring and Newton (KN) is a fairly straight-forward adaptation of FM to support cell replication [14]. In the FM algorithm, a node can exist in one of two states dependent upon which partition it is currently located. Kring and Newton introduce a third state – replication, in which a node exists in both partitions simultaneously. Also, nodes now have two potential moves: unreplicated nodes can either be replicated or moved to the other partition, and replicated nodes can be unreplicated into either of the two partitions.

The Kring/Newton algorithm always requires that unreplication move with a positive gain be taken before any normal moves, and disallows replication moves with a gain of less than 1. Our experiments indicate that allowing replication moves with a gain of 0 are useful, and our version of Kring/Newton allows such moves.

2.1 Basic Kring/Newton

The simplest way to integrated KN replication into Strawman is to replace Strawman's final FM run on the unclustered circuit with the KN algorithm. Essentially, this is the KN algorithm performed on an optimized initial partition – a modification proposed by Kring and Newton which was found to be useful for larger benchmarks.

2.2 Higher-Level Gains

In general, if we have two moves that have the same impact on the cutsize, but one is a normal move and the other is a replication move, we should choose the normal move in order to limit the amount of replication. To do this we set all higher-level gains of replication moves to $-\infty$. This achieves a slight improvement over KN with a normal gain function (Table 2), and thus all future KN variants will be performed with higher-level gains.

Bench.	Straw	Basic KN	KN HLG	KN Clust.	KN Grad.
s5378	60	41	39	48	43
s9234	45	30	32	33	32
s13207	67	53	48	49	43
s15850	52	43	43	39	41
C6288	50	33	33	34	33
biomed	161	136	137	126	130
prim2	133	114	114	110	114
struct	33	33	33	33	33
s35932	46	39	39	28	23
s38584	50	35	35	46	32
s38417	55	51	49	47	49
Mean	60.8	48.2	47.7	47.6	44.7
Time	17.4	17.3	17.6	17.1	19.7
Rep %	0.0%	4.2%	4.5%	6.2%	3.5%

Table 2. Comparison of different optimizations to KN replication. "HLG" is higher-level gains. Each algorithm is executed thirty times, and the best cutsize is kept. "Time" is the geometric mean total CPU minutes for all 30 runs for a given benchmark. "Rep %" is the average percentage of the logic that is replicated to achieve the best cut for each benchmark.

2.3 Extension to Clustering

It was hoped that by earlier application of KN, better results might be achieved via increased opportunity for replication. So rather than perform KN style replication only after complete unclustering, KN replication was performed at each clustering level in place of the Strawman FM algorithm. To facilitate replication at each level of the clustering hierarchy, the total allowed circuit expansion was evenly distributed among all levels, and so if there were seven clustering levels, and we allowed up to seven percent circuit expansion via replication, then KN would be allowed to expand the circuit by one percent at each clustering level. Such expansion is cumulative.

2.4 Gradient Method

As the FM algorithm progresses the partitions get steadily better. Early in the algorithm there may be many high gain moves, and the partitioner radically changes the current partitioning. However, in later iterations the current partitioning is close to the final result, and the partitioner makes relatively minor alterations to the partitioning. When we add replication to this process, it can create a significant amount of duplication early in the partitioning process, limiting the partitioner's ability to change the current partitioning. Thus, replicating too early can degrade the final results. To deal with this, in Gradient KN we only attempt further replication when the cut sizes between successive inner-loop iterations of the Strawman FM algorithm change by less than ten percent. The circuit is expanded as in the previous section.

2.5 Kring/Newton Results

The results for the various optimizations to the KN algorithm are given in Table 2. As can be seen, basic KN produces results 20.7% better than the non-replicating algorithm. Higher-level gains improve this by an additional 0.8%, hierarchical partitioning yields an additional 0.2%, and the Gradient approach yields an additional 4.8%. This produces an overall 26.5% improvement over the basic Strawman algorithm.

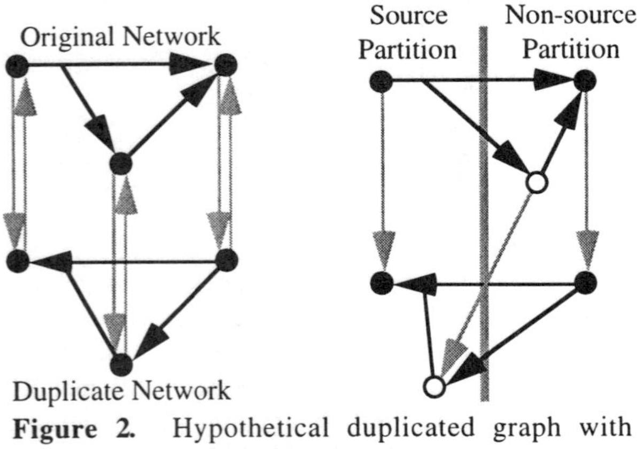

Figure 2. Hypothetical duplicated graph with infinite edges in both directions between original and duplicated nodes (left). Gray arrows are infinite weight edges. The replication graph has infinite edges only from original to duplicate (right). A duplicate node in the source partition with it's original in the non-source partition is considered duplicated (such as the node shown in white).

3 DFRG

Another move based approach is the Directed Fiduccia-Mattheyses on a Replication Graph, or DFRG [17]. DFRG uses a directed version of FM, where one partition is designated the "source" partition, and a net is considered cut only if one of its sources is in the source partition, and one of its sinks is in the other partition.

Imagine that we duplicate the circuit graph , and in the duplicate we reverse the signal flow direction (sources become sinks, sinks become sources). We connect each node to its duplicate with two infinite weight edges (edges that should never be cut), one directed from original to duplicate, another from duplicate to original (see Figure 2 left). This means that a node and its duplicate will always been in the same partition. Assuming a partitioning does not cut an infinite weight edge, it can be shown that the directed cutsize of this graph is the same as the undirected cutsize of the nets in the original graph. Thus, a directed partitioning of this graph is equivalent to an undirected partitioning of the original graph.

In DFRG partitioning we use the same graph, but remove the infinite weight edges from duplicate to original (the other edge remains). In this graph we can now have an original node in the non-source partition and its duplicate in the source partition (Figure 2 right). All such nodes will be replicated, and the directed cutsize of this graph accurately reflects this. Specifically, it can be shown that all input nets to a replicated node will be in the directed cutset unless their source is replicated, and the outputs of a replicated node are never in the directed cutset. Thus, performing directed partitioning of this replication graph allows partitioning and replication of the original graph to be performed simultaneously.

For basic DFRG we obtain an initial partition via Strawman and use DFRG as a post-processor. This is essentially DFRG performed upon a good initial partition.

Bench.	Straw	Basic DFRG	DFRG HLG	DFRG Clust.
s5378	60	40	41	41
s9234	45	34	34	32
s13207	67	54	47	63
s15850	52	45	44	45
C6288	50	33	33	33
biomed	161	136	136	107
prim2	133	114	116	121
struct	33	33	33	33
s35932	46	39	39	24
s38584	50	37	35	29
s38417	55	48	48	45
Mean	60.8	48.9	48.2	44.9
Time	17.4	27.8	31.6	48.2
Rep %	0.0%	3.5%	3.5%	5.1%

Table 3. Comparison of DFRG optimizations.

3.1 Higher-Level Gains

A net can be uncut either by moving all sources to the "non-source" partition, or by moving all sinks to the "source" partition. By moving a source, one does not lose any opportunities for uncutting a net via sink movements, and by moving a sink, one does not lose any opportunities for uncutting the net via source movements. Since source and sink motion operates independently in determining the state of a net, we use the following higher-level gains formulation: a cut net contributes +1 to the nth level gain of a source node S if S is in the "source" partition, and there are n-1 other unlocked sources of the net, and no locked sources, in the "source" partition; a cut net contributes a -1 to the nth level gain of a source node S if S is in the "non-source" partition, and there are n-1 unlocked sources, and no locked sources, in the source partition; Higher-level gains for sink nodes are defined similarly. For ease of implementation, only cut nets contribute to the higher level gains of a node.

3.2 Extension to Clustering

Because DFRG more than doubles the size of the network, we thought that it would benefit from reducing the problem size via clustering. Thus, we perform DFRG at each clustering level in place of the Strawman FM, and gradually expand the maximum circuit size as in the KN extension to clustering. The clustering is performed upon the original graph, and the replication graph is created from the clustered graph at each clustering level.

3.3 DFRG Results

The results for the various optimizations to the DFRG algorithm are given in Table 3. As can be seen, basic DFRG produces results 19.6% better than the non-replicating algorithm. Higher-level gains improve this by an additional 1.1% and DFRG hierarchical partitioning yields an additional 5.5%. Combined together, these techniques produce an overall 26.2% improvement over the basic Strawman algorithm.

4 Flow Based Techniques

The final algorithms are significantly different from the preceding in that they are flow based rather than move based. The flow based algorithms strive to capitalize on a flow network formulation which derives an optimal minimum-cut replication set (without size bounds) when provided with an initial partition. To develop this technique, we require the following definitions [4] [8]:

A *flow network*, G = (V,E), is a directed graph in which each edge, (u,v) ∈ E, has a non-negative capacity, and there exists two special nodes S, T ∈ V designated as a source and sink respectively.

A *flow* in G is a function f: V x V → $\Re$ (where "$\Re$" is the set of reals) such that

(1) $f(u,v) \le c(u,v), \quad u,v \in V,$
where c(u,v) is the capacity of the edge (u,v) ∈ E

(2) $f(u,v) = -f(v,u), \quad u,v \in V$

(3) $\sum_{v \in V} f(u,v) = 0, \quad u \in V - \{S,T\}$

Ford-Fulkerson max-flow/min-cut theorem [8]:

For any network the maximal flow value from S to T is the size of a minimum cut in G.

4.1 The Optimal Algorithm for Unconstrained Replication Size [13, 20]

Given an initial partitioning of the vertices we select a source partition arbitrarily. We form a flow network by creating a node S, which will be the source of the network, and clustering with S nodes in the source partition which we would like to act as a sources of flow in the network (see Figure 3 left). We also create a node T, which will be the sink of the network, and cluster with T all nodes which are in the non-source (sink) partition, and are attached to edges which have their source in the source partition. All edges which have their source in the sink partition are removed from the network, and all remaining edges are given a capacity of one.

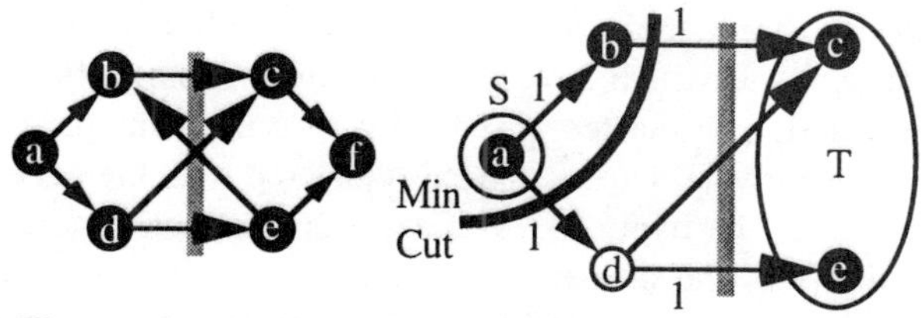

Figure 3. A directed graph (left) is turned into a flow graph. Once a maximum flow is found, which induces a minimum cut, nodes between the min cut and the original partitioning are replicated (right). The replicated node is shown in white.

We push as much flow from S to T as we can, and thus by the Ford-Fulkerson Theorem we produce a minimum cut. We find the minimum cut closest to T by a breadth-first search from T, and every node in partition X on the sink side of the minimum cut is replicated. By replicating these nodes we place all edges in the minimum cut into the cut set, and guarantee that any other edge which has its source in the source partition is not in the cut set. The original graph is then reestablished; we select the opposite partition as the source partition, and we repeat the above. By finding the replication subset which minimizes the cut edges which have their source in each partition we find the replication set which minimizes the number of cut edges for this partitioning.

The above algorithm has two limitations: it applies only to directed graphs (not hypergraphs), and it assumes unbounded partition size. By extending this algorithm to incorporate directed hyper-edges or size constraints we lose optimality, and therefore must resort to heuristics.

4.2 Hyper-MAMC (Min-Area Min-Cut) [20]

To use the network flow formulation we must reduce hyperedges to edges. This is done as shown in Figure 4. For each hyperedge we create a hypernode with an edge of weight 1 from the source to the hypernode, and an edge of infinite weight from the hypernode to each sink. In this way, we restrict each hyperedge to unit flow, and ensure that the hyperedge can only be cut in the edge from the source to the hypernode. This guarantees that each hyperedge contributes at most once to the minimum cut derived from the maximum flow.

Figure 4. Reduction of hyper-edges to normal edges. White node is the hyper-node.

Hyper-MAMC proceeds similarly to the optimal algorithm, pushing flow through the network and finding nodes to be replicated. However, before replicating these nodes it first checks if this replication would exceed the partition size limits. If so, we determine all hyperedges which have their source clustered with the network source, and which have positive flow. A sink of such a hyperedge is selected, provided it is in the same partition as the network source, and it is clustered with the network source. The hyper-MAMC algorithm is then rerun. By doing this the chosen sink cannot be replicated, and it now acts as a source of flow. This can increase the flow, and reduce the size of the replication set (see Figure 5). This process of incrementing the flow is repeated until the the replication set size is acceptable. Once we have a sufficiently small set for replication, we dismantle the flow network, select the opposite partition, and repeat.

A peculiarity of this algorithm is that we may exceed partition size limits, yet there may be no node available to cluster with the source. This is caused by large numbers of nodes in the active partition which are unreachable from the network source. However, this is a fairly rare event, and when it occurs we default to a directed-FM (see MC-Rep below) on the modified network graph.

4.2.1 Node Choice for Source Clustering

When creating the flow network we must choose nodes to cluster together to create the network source. The most obvious candidates for source clustering are circuit inputs (IBUFs). These nodes tend to be liberally scattered about both partitions, and presumably every node in the graph is reachable through some IBUF. However, it appears that a random node selection tends to produce better results. This is likely due to the variability in node selection which it introduces, providing the algorithm with an opportunity to get "lucky" with its source choice when iterated multiple times.

Bench.	Hyper-MAMC					
	IBUF	RANDOM				
		2.0	1.0	0.5	0.25	0.125
s5378	46	44	42	41	39	40
s9234	31	32	29	29	28	29
s13207	45	46	48	47	46	45
s15850	40	39	39	38	37	37
C6288	34	34	33	33	33	33
biomed	70	92	79	75	73	83
prim2	115	120	112	109	110	110
struct	34	33	33	33	33	33
s35932	39	39	39	39	39	39
s38584	26	28	26	25	25	25
s38417	40	40	37	37	37	38
Mean	43.2	44.5	42.5	41.8	41.2	42.0
Time	24.7	21.7	22.5	23.4	24.3	21.9

Table 4. Effect of source choice on cut size for Hyper-MAMC. Initial partitions are generated by Strawman with a maximum partition size of 51%.

When choosing nodes randomly to cluster with the source, we select the number of nodes as a function of initial directed cut size. The initial directed cut size is the number of hyperedges which have their source in the chosen partition, and one or more sinks in the opposite partition. Table 4 details the various source selection strategies. The IBUF column uses all IBUFs in the source partition as flow sources. The other columns randomly select a number of sources equal to X * directed_cut_size,

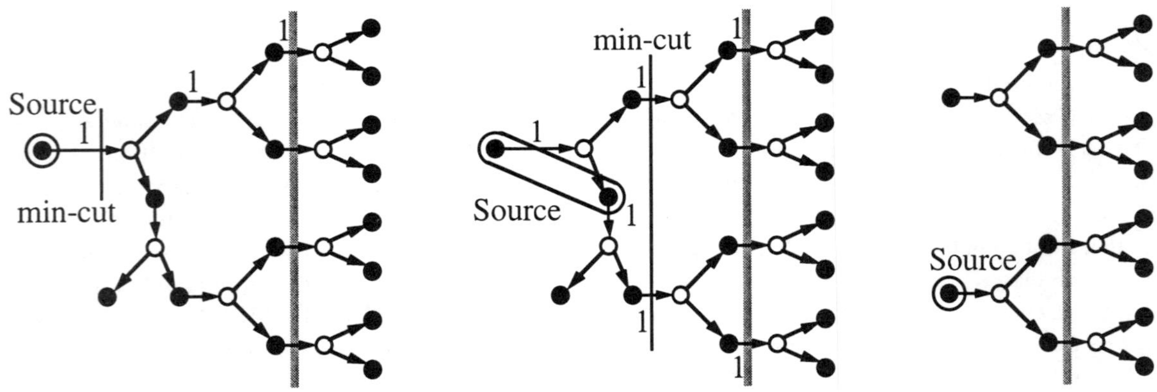

Figure 5. Given an initial flow network that replicates too much logic (left), incrementing the flow reduces the replication set and increases the cut size (center). However, nodes which cannot be reached from the source, such as those at the top of the figure at right, will always be replicated.

where X is the number listed in the column heading. Randomly selecting a number of sources equal to one-quarter the directed cut size produces the best cuts. Therefore all future hyper-MAMC variants in this paper will incorporate this strategy of source selection.

Bench.	Straw	Initial Partition size limit		
		49%/51%	48%/52%	47%/53%
s5378	60	39	40	41
s9234	45	28	31	35
s13207	67	46	44	47
s15850	52	37	38	39
C6288	50	33	33	33
biomed	161	73	61	84
prim2	133	110	113	107
struct	33	33	33	33
s35932	46	39	23	39
s38584	50	25	25	25
s38417	55	37	36	38
Mean	60.8	41.2	39.1	43.1
Time	17.4	24.3	24.3	21.8

Table 5. Effect of initial partition size limit on Hyper-MAMC.

4.2.2 Initial Partition Variation

In move-based algorithms, size limits were expressed as maximum partition sizes, limiting both partition size imbalance and replication. Thus, with a limit of 53.6% of the logic, one partition could contain 53.6% of the logic an have no replication, or both partitions could contain 46.4% unreplicated logic and 7.2% replicated logic. This ability to trade size imbalance with replication yields an added optimization opportunity. Hyper-MAMC is a post-processing algorithm, where the partitioning of the circuit, and thus the partition size imbalance, must be fixed before replication begins. In Table 5 we explore how the limits applied to partition size imbalance affect the final results. The results indicate that improving initial partition quality does indeed improve the cuts created by hyper-MAMC, but we must leave the algorithm some room to operate. All hyper-MAMC variants in this paper will use an initial partition size limit of 52%/48% circuit size.

4.2.3 Node Choice for Incrementing Flow

When faced with an large replication set, the hyper-MAMC algorithm will increment the flow by clustering a node with the network source. We can attempt to find the best node by testing each node, and determining which produces the best result. Unfortunately this exhaustive search is too time consuming, and therefore the hyper-MAMC algorithm includes a threshold parameter for use with node choice [19]. When incrementing the flow, and choosing from among a threshold number of nodes or less, we determine the effects of incrementing the flow to each node, and use that node which produced the best results (least increase in max-flow, with ties broken by the largest decrease in total size of nodes replicated). If we have more than a threshold number of nodes to choose from we choose arbitrarily.

As shown in Table 6, small threshold values have little impact on partition quality. Apparently there are few occasions where the node choice falls below the threshold value on these benchmarks. Unfortunately, a higher threshold value tends to greatly slow the algorithm. To avoid this performance penalty, we decided to select the initial partition (produced by Strawman) which produced the best final cut size after performing hyper-MAMC with a zero size threshold, and then run a high threshold hyper-MAMC on only this initial partition. This amortizes the time cost of a high threshold hyper-MAMC run over all thirty iterations of hyper-MAMC.

Bench.	Straw	Threshold		Amortized			Random	MC-Rep
		0	25	50	100	200	5	
s5378	60	40	40	40	40	40	39	44
s9234	45	31	31	31	28	28	28	37
s13207	67	44	44	44	44	44	42	61
s15850	52	38	38	38	38	38	38	50
C6288	50	33	33	33	33	33	33	33
biomed	161	61	61	61	58	58	58	127
prim2	133	113	113	113	108	108	106	121
struct	33	33	33	33	33	33	33	33
s35932	46	23	23	23	23	23	23	23
s38584	50	25	25	25	25	25	25	25
s38417	55	36	36	36	36	36	34	44
Mean	60.8	39.1	39.1	39.1	38.4	38.4	37.8	46.3
Time	17.4	21.9	37.6	26.3	28.1	32.0	59.7	21.7

Table 6. Effect of node choice for incrementing flow on partition quality. Threshold columns try all node choices when the number of choices is less than the threshold, and otherwise randomly pick a single node. Amortized columns run threshold 0, pick the best of 30 runs, and then uses the listed threshold on just that best partitioning. Random 5 always randomly tries 5 nodes each time the flow must be incremented. MC-Rep results are also included.

Replication Algorithm	Cutsize	Improvement over Straw	Improvement over Basic Alg.	Time (minutes, 30 runs)
Strawman	60.8	—	—	17.4
KN	48.2	20.7%	—	17.3
higher-level gains	47.7	21.5%	1.0%	17.6
clustering	47.6	21.7%	1.2%	17.1
gradient	44.7	26.5%	7.3%	19.7
DFRG	48.9	19.6%	—	27.8
higher-level gains	48.2	20.7%	1.4%	31.6
clustering	44.9	26.2%	8.2%	48.2
Hyper-MAMC	43.2	28.9%	—	24.7
flow source node choice	41.2	32.2%	4.6%	24.3
partition variation	39.1	35.7%	9.5%	24.3
flow incr. node choice	37.8	37.8%	12.5%	59.7
MC-Rep	46.3	23.8%	—	21.7

Table 7. Summary of optimizations. Basic algorithms are shown in bold, followed by the new optimizations in this paper. "Improvement over Strawman" represents how much each replication technique improves over a non-replicated bipartitioning. "Improvement over Basic Algorithm" is how much better the optimized version does as compared to the unoptimized replication technique (i.e. the version taken directly from the literature). All algorithms are allowed to generate partitions containing at most 53.6% of the logic through both bipartitioning imbalance and replication.

An alternative to a threshold function is to instead always randomly choose a small number of nodes to test whenever we must increment the flow. In this way we always make a (somewhat) informed decision about what node to add to the source set. Although this greatly increases the processing time, we reduce this time by also amortizing the cost, only optimizing the best of the 30 runs as determined by threshold 0 runs. This techniques is used in the "Random 5" column of Table 6.

4.2.4 Hyper-MAMC Replication Results

The results for the various optimizations to the Hyper-MAMC algorithm are given in Table 4 - Table 6. As can be seen, the choice of flow sources can make a significant difference, with randomly picking 1/4 as many sources as the cutsize of the initial partitioning producing a 4.6% improvement over using the circuit's IBUFs. Balancing the amount of flexibility given to the partitioner verses the amount of replication allowed is also an issue, providing up to a 9.3% difference. Finally, always evaluating five random nodes to add to the source when incrementing the flow is important, providing a 3.3% improvement over just randomly adding nodes. However, this does almost triple the runtime, even though this technique is only applied to the most promising of the 30 partitioning attempts. Combining these approaches produces cutsizes 37.8% smaller than the unreplicated version, significantly better than any other technique.

4.3 MC-Rep [13]

MC-Rep is a simpler version of Hyper-MAMC. Just as in Hyper-MAMC it uses the minimum cut in a flow network to form the replication set. However, unlike Hyper-MAMC, if the the replication set is too large we re-establish the original hypergraph. All nodes which were not in the selected partition are permanently locked, and a directed FM is performed upon the hypergraph. We only allow replication and unreplication moves , and only by nodes which were in the selected partition. In this way, a replication set is derived that meets the size limit. We then select the opposite partition and repeat.

We apply the lessons learned from hyper-MAMC and randomly cluster a number of nodes equal to twenty-five percent of the directed cut size to create the network source. We also use Strawman to generate an initial partition with 48%/52% size limits. As shown in Table 6, MC-Rep performs significantly worse than Hyper-MAMC, which is able to stay closer to the basic network flow formulation for unbounded size replication.

6 Conclusion

We have investigated replication, seeking to develop the best possible bipartitioning results. In the process we were able to reduce cutsizes by 37.8% over Strawman's already impressive results. Also, these improvements are obtained with relatively little logic duplication, with most techniques replicating less than 5% of the logic.

The replication techniques in the literature are not so much partitioning algorithms in their own right, but are optimizations to be added into an existing partitioner. In order to perform a comparison we have implemented most of the replication algorithms from the literature within our Strawman system. Thus, we can directly compare all of the algorithms on the same benchmarks, with the same size constraints, using the same partitioner. The only difference is the replication techniques. This comparison is shown in Table 7, which includes all of the algorithms discussed in this paper. Results are included for comparing the optimized replication techniques against non-replicating Strawman, as well as the new optimized replication techniques proposed in this paper against the basic versions from the literature. As can be seen, our optimized algorithms achieve a 12.5% to 13.5% improvement over the existing techniques even factoring out the benefits of our Strawman bipartitioner.

Achieving these high-quality results has required innovative optimizations to the individual algorithms. To improve the KN algorithm we extended it to take advantage of higher-level gains and recursive clustering. We also developed the Gradient method to delay replication until the latter stages of partitioning, avoiding ignorant replication moves. Combined together, this improves the results by 7.3%. To improve the DFRG algorithm we developed a directed graph partitioning formulation for higher-level gains and extended the algorithm to work under recursive clustering. This achieved a 8.2% improvement over the basic DFRG algorithm. Finally, we improved the Hyper-MAMC algorithm by carefully considering which nodes should be used as flow network sources, by varying the amount of size imbalance allowed for bipartitioning verses replication, and by developing methods for deciding which nodes to add as flow sources, and thus reduce the replication set. This provides a 12.5% improvement over the basic Hyper-MAMC algorithm, and generates the best results for any single replication technique.

Our investigations of Functional Replication [16] do not appear here because of space limitations. It produces only a 6% improvement over Strawman, making it less interesting than the other approaches.

As has been demonstrated in this paper, achieving the greatest possible partitioning quality requires the careful consideration not only of individual techniques, but also how these techniques fit together. Optimizations such as higher-level gains, multiple random initializations, and recursive clustering may be key to achieving the best standard bipartitioning results, but integrating replication techniques into such a system can cause significant added concerns. Also, subtle issues such as node choice for flow sources and incrementing flows can easily be overlooked, yet can provide significant quality improvements. Thus we believe that as we continue to add to the repertoire of replication techniques, we must also consider how these techniques can be added to what is already known to produce the best overall algorithm.

References

[1] C. J. Alpert, A. B. Kahng, "Recent Directions in Netlist Partitioning: A Survey", *Integration: the VLSI Journal*, Vol. 19, No. 1-2, pp. 1-81, 1995.

[2] C. J. Alpert, S.-Z. Yao, "Spectral Partitioning: The More Eigenvectors, The Better", *Design Automation Conference*, pp. 195-200, 1995.

[3] C. K. Cheng, T. C. Hu, "Maximum Concurrent Flow and Minimum Ratio-cut", *Technical Report CS88-141*, University of California, San Diego, December, 1988.

[4] T. H. Cormen, C.E. Leiserson, R.L. Rivest, *Introduction to Algorithms*, MIT Press/McGraw-Hill, Cambridge, MA, 1990.

[5] S. Dutt, W. Deng, "A Probability-Based Approach to VLSI Circuit Partitioning", *Design Automation Conference*, pp. 100-105, 1996.

[6] M. Enos, M.S., "Replication for Logic Bipartitioning", Master's Thesis, Northwestern University, Department of ECE, 1996.

[7] C. M. Fiduccia, R. M. Mattheyses, "A Linear-Time Heuristic for Improved Network Partitions", *Design Automation Conference*, pp. 241-247, 1982.

[8] L.R. Ford, D.R. Fulkerson, *Flows in Networks*, Princeton Univ. Press, Princeton, NJ, 1962.

[9] M. Garey, D. S. Johnson, *Computers and Intractability: A Guide to the Theory of NP-Completeness*, San Francisco, CA: Freeman, 1979.

[10] L. Hagen, A. B. Kahng, "New Spectral Methods for Ratio Cut Partitioning and Clustering", *IEEE Transactions on Computer-Aided Design*, Vol. 11, No. 9, pp. 1074-1085, Sept. 1992.

[11] S. A. Hauck, *Multi-FPGA Systems*, Ph.D. dissertation, University of Washington, Dept. of CSE., pp. 131-168, 1995.

[12] S. Hauck, G. Borriello, "An Evaluation of Bipartitioning Techniques", *Chapel Hill Conference on Advanced Research in VLSI*, pp. 383-402, March, 1995.

[13] L. J. Hwang, A. El Gamal, "Min-Cut Replication in Partitioned Networks", *IEEE Transactions on Computer-Aided Design*, Vol. 14, No. 1, pp. 96-106, Jan 1995.

[14] C. Kring, A. R. Newton, "A Cell-Replicating Approach to Mincut-Based Circuit Partitioning", *International Conference on Computer-Aided Design*, pp. 2-5, 1991.

[15] B. Krishnamurthy, "An Improved Min-Cut Algorithm for Partitioning VLSI Networks", *IEEE Transactions on Computers*, Vol. C-33, No. 5, pp. 438-446, May 1984.

[16] R. Kuznar, F. Brglez, B. Zajc, "Multi-way Netlist Partitioning into Heterogeneous FPGAs and Minimization of Total Device Cost and Interconnect", *Design Automation Conference*, pp. 238-243, 1994.

[17] L. Liu, M. Kuo, C. K. Cheng, T. C. Hu, "A Replication Cut for Two-Way Partitioning", *IEEE Transactions on Computed-Aided Design*, Vol. 14, No. 5, May 1995, pp. 623-632.

[18] G. M. Riess, K. Doll, F. M. Johannes, "Partitioning Very Large Circuits Using Analytical Placement Techniques", *Design Automation Conference*, pp. 646-651, 1994.

[19] H. H. Yang, D. F. Wong, "Efficient Network Flow Based Min-Cut Balanced Partitioning", *International Conference on Computer-Aided Design*, pp. 50-55, 1994.

[20] H. H. Yang, D. F. Wong, "New Algorithms for Min-Cut Replication in Partitioned Circuits", *International Conference on Computer-Aided Design*, pp. 216-222, 1995.

Partitioning Around Roadblocks: Tackling Constraints with Intermediate Relaxations

Shantanu Dutt
dutt@eecs.uic.edu
Dept. of Electrical Eng. and Comp. Science
Univ. of Illinois at Chicago
Chicago, IL 60607, USA

Halim Theny
theny@ee.umn.edu
Dept. of Electrical and Comp. Eng.
Univ. of Minnesota
Minneapolis, MN 55455, USA

Abstract

Constraint satisfaction during partitioning and placement of VLSI circuits is an important problem, and effective techniques to address it lead to high-quality physical design solutions. This problem has, however, been cursorily treated in previous partitioning and placement research. Our work presented here addresses the balance-ratio constraint, and is a crucial first step to an effective solution to the general constraint-satisfaction problem. In current iterative-improvement mincut partitioners, the balance-ratio constraint is tackled by disallowing moves that violate it. These methods can lead to sub-optimal solutions since the process is biased against the movement of large cells and clusters of cells. We present techniques for an informed relaxation process that attempts to estimate whether relaxing the constraint temporarily will ultimately benefit the mincut objective. If so, then a violating move is allowed, otherwise it is disallowed. The violations are corrected in future moves so that the final solution satisfies the given constraint. On a set of ACM/SIGDA PROUD benchmark circuits with actual cell sizes, we obtained up to 38% and an average of 14.5% better cutsizes with as little as 13% time overhead using our techniques compared to the standard method of not allowing any relaxation.

1. Introduction

Motivation

The partitioning problem for any given objective is inherently a constraint-driven one. The most common constraint is the balance-ratio of total sizes that the two subsets of a partition must satisfy. Other frequently encountered partitioning constraints include limits on the sizes, pins and prices in multiple-FPGA partitioning [7], [8], balance ratios for multiple cell types (this occurs in FPGA placement and in pin assignment), upper bound on the deterioration of an objective, say, wire-area minimization, of an initial placement when the circuit is hierarchically re-partitioned for another objective, say, timing minimization (this arises in multiple-objective placement), and even distributions of external nets and internal pins among the subcircuits of a partition (to avoid congestion [10]). Constraint satisfaction during partitioning and placement of VLSI circuits is an important problem, and effective techniques to address it lead to high-quality physical design solutions. This problem has, however, been cursorily treated in previous partitioning and placement research. For example, a widely used practice for constraint-satisfaction is to disallow cell moves that violate a constraint, which over-constrains the partitioner leading to sub-optimal results. Our work presented here addresses the balance-ratio constraint, and is a crucial first step to an effective solution to the general constraint-satisfaction problem. During the hierarchical partitioning of a circuit in partition-driven placement tools [11], the pre-specified balance-ratios are very important constraints that lead to an area-minimal balanced layout of the circuit (see Fig. 1).

This balance-constrained partitioning problem can be stated as follows. Given a netlist G which describes cell connectivities and cell sizes in a circuit, construct k sub-circuits of G with a balance-ratio of $r_1 : r_2 : ... : r_k$, and an acceptable tolerance of $\pm t$ such that some objective functions are optimized. In an attempt to satisfy the balance-ratio, however, movement of larger cells and clusters can be restricted thus leading to sub-optimal results. Figures 2 illustrates these problems in which restricted movements of large cells and clusters lead to larger cutsizes.

PastWork

All the general iterative-improvement partitioning techniques such as FM [3], LA [4], PROP [1], GFM [5], GMetis [6], and hMETIS [12] do not allow any type of relaxation. They assume unit-size cells, which do not work well for general/macro-cell circuits. Wei and Cheng proposed a ratio-cut method and applied it to general-cell circuits with certain pre-specified balance-ratios [9]. Their results, however, became much worse as the balance-ratio went closer to 1:1. Until recently, partitioning techniques with minor relaxations were employed in multiple-FPGA partitioning which generally has many constraints [7] [8]. Kuznar, Brglez and Kozminski [7] used the cost function to levy large penalties on violating moves. This causes the partitioner to accept very few violating moves, which most likely produces results identical to not allowing any relaxation—there are no results in [7] comparing relaxed and non-relaxed formulations. Woo and Kim [8] relaxed constraints by reducing the originally specified constraints (e.g., doubling the numbers of pins required in each FPGA) for some pre-specified passes. The partition process may terminate with violations if the number of pre-specified passes is greater than or equal to the total number of passes, in which case the process has to start over with a different initial partition. These two relaxed partitioning techniques provided ad hoc solutions to tackling constraints, that were specific to the particular problem. In contrast, our approach provides a general framework for partitioning in the presence of constraints and uses informed intermediate relaxation techniques for this purpose.

New Approaches

We propose branch-and-bound approaches to constraint-driven partitioning that allows intermediate constraint relaxation during cell moves in order to ensure better results. The new methods can be generally stated as follows. In the first approach, on every cell move which results in constraint violation, the cost and benefit of allowing the violating move is estimated. The accepted moves are those which potentially give better results (compared to disallowing the moves) taking into consideration that a valid cut-point cannot be established until the violation is corrected in future "reverse"

1092-3152/97 $10.00 © 1997 IEEE

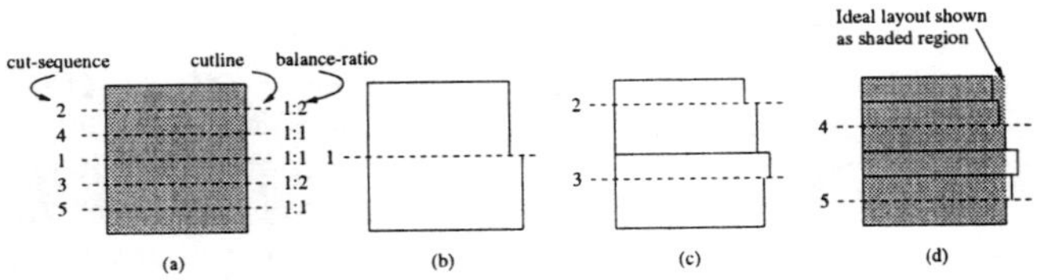

Figure 1: Uneven rows in standard cell layout due to errors in the balance-ratio. (a) The "ideal" layout with zero balance-ratio errors. (b)-(d) Uneven rows leading to some unused spaces in the final layout, and thus a larger layout area.

moves. In the second, lower time-complexity technique based on statistical studies, a "benefit factor" and "acceptance threshold" are computed for a violating move. Depending on the stage of the partitioning process and the location and status of the violating cell and its neighbors, the move is accepted if the benefit factor is greater than the acceptance threshold. In order to keep the computation complexity reasonable, we do not backtrack in the move process using either of the above approaches; hence it becomes very critical for our benefit estimator to be accurate.

The rest of the paper is organized as follows. In Sec. 2. we formally state the balance-constraint based partitioning problem, and recap the relevant gain formulation of PROP [1]. Section 3. shows examples of the advantage of intermediate relaxations of the balance constraint, and then discusses general approaches to relaxed constraint-satisfaction. Section 4. presents the particular techniques for tackling the balance-ratio constraint in the context of the PROP partitioning method. In Sec. 5. we present experimental results, and conclude in Sec. 6.

2. The Bi-partitioning Problem with Balance Constraints

The balance-constrained mincut bi-partitioning problem can be formally stated as follows. A circuit is represented by a hypergraph $G = (V, E)$, where $V = \{v_1, v_2, ..., v_n\}$ is the set of vertices that represent *cells* or *modules* in the circuit, and $E = \{n_1, n_2, ..., n_e\}$ is the set of hyperedges which represent *nets* in the circuit; hence, n and e are the total numbers of cells and nets in G, respectively. Each net n_i will be represented as a subset of the cells that it connects. The *area* of each cell is denoted as $a(v_i)$, where $1 \leq i \leq n$. In a bi-partitioning problem, V is partitioned into two subsets, V_1 and V_2, such that each v_i belongs to either V_1 or V_2. We denote the set of nets crossing V_1 and V_2 by E_{cut}, and the total size of V_1, V_2 by $|V_1|$, $|V_2|$ respectively. Therefore, $|V_j| = \sum_{v_i \in V_j} a(v_i)$ for j = 1 and 2.

There are one or more objectives and constraints that any partitioner must achieve and comply with, respectively. One of the most common objective is to minimize the cutsize of the cutset which is defined as $cutsize = \sum_{n_i \in E_{cut}} w(n_i)$, where $w(n_i)$ is the *weight* or *cost* of net associated with n_i. Based on this objective, every cell u in the circuit is assigned a gain $gain(u)$. This gain is defined differently for different partitioners like FM, LA, and PROP, and have different degrees of sophistication in terms of futuristic non-local information they capture; PROP uses the most advanced gain formulation [1] while FM uses the simplest. We have thus incorporated our relaxation techniques into PROP.

PROP defines a probabilistic gain for every cell u and its adjacent nets based on the cells' initially estimated approximate probabilities. A cell u's probability $p(u)$ is then computed from its gain using a monotonically increasing function $f(g(u))$ (usually a linear function). The probabilistic gain of cell u (assume $u \in V_1$) is given by $gain(u) = \sum_{n_i \in E(u)} w(n_i) g_{n_i}(u)$, where each gain component $g_{n_i}(u)$ for net n_i is computed as

$$g_{n_i}(u) = \Big(\prod_{u_x \in n_{i,1}} p(u_x)\Big)/p(u) - \prod_{u_y \in n_{i,2}} p(u_y) \qquad (1)$$

where $E(u)$ is the set of all nets connected to cell u, and $n_{i,j} = n_i \cap V_j$, for $j = 1, 2$.

As in other iterative-improvement methods, to begin the partition process, PROP refines the cells' probabilistic gains and probabilities with one or two iterations of gain calculation and probability assignment. Then, the cell with the best gain in either subset is chosen as the *base* cell to move if the move does not violate any constraint. This cell is moved to the other side and locked. At this point, gains of all neighboring cells are updated, and the *immediate gain* (i.e., immediate decrease of increase in the cutset) is recorded. These steps continue until all the cells are moved and hence locked (this process is called a *pass*). At the end of each pass, actual moves are made to that point which gives the maximum prefixsum of immediate gains. Note that since no violations are allowed, all constraints are met at every move. A number of passes are performed until there is no further improvement in a pass.

One of the fundamental constraints in bi-partitioning is the required balance in the sizes of V_1 and V_2. Assuming $|V_1| \leq |V_2|$, the constraint can be stated as $r - t \leq \frac{|V_1|}{|V_1|+|V_2|} \leq r + t$.

There could be other objectives and constraints as well in the partitioning framework as mentioned earlier. The most common approach used in previous partitioning techniques for tackling constraints has been to strictly comply with them in every step of the process. This leaves significant room for obtaining better quality solutions (in terms of the given objective(s)) by allowing intermediate constraint relaxation.

3. Tackling Constraints with Intermediate Relaxation

3.1. The Need for Relaxation

Most partitioning methods that do not relax size-balance constraints work reasonably for circuits such as gate arrays that have uniform cell sizes. However, when they are applied to circuits with general-cells or macro-cells that have varying sizes, these algorithms suffer from a propensity to freeze the movement of large cells that would immediately violate the balance constraint. To illustrate this problem, consider the example shown in Fig. 2. Let A be the total area of the circuit. Cells labeled from 1 to 4 have areas of $A/8$ each, and cells labeled from 5 to 12 have areas of $A/16$ each. The balance ratio r is 0.5 (50%-50%) with a tolerance t of 0.1 (10%). Without any relaxation, cells 1 to 4 will be "stuck" in their initial subsets due to their large sizes, while cells 5 to 12 have more freedom to move around as shown in Fig. 2(b). However, if we allow a relaxation of at least $A/8$ ($relax = 1/8$), cells 1 to 4 can move freely as dictated by their gains, and this results in the optimum solution shown in Fig. 2(c) that satisfies the $r = 0.5$ constraint.

Freeing up the movement of large cells is not the only advantage of a "relaxed" partitioner. Relaxed partitioning also helps in removing natural clusters that straddle the cutline by blocks of uni-directional moves that temporary violate the balance constraint; in a non-relaxed partitioner, these clusters can get locked in the cutset due to alternating moves in the two directions.

The idea behind our relaxation approach is illustrated in Fig. 3. Figure 3(a) shows a portion of a plot of the cutsize versus cell moves that are all non-violating; therefore, each point along the curve is a valid prefix point, with M being the mincut point. The best moves following M are violating moves that would actually continue to reduce the cutsize, but are rejected in a non-relaxed

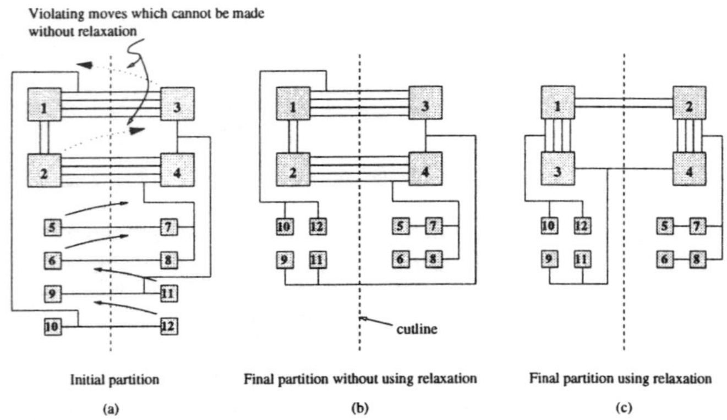

Figure 2: An example showing the advantage of allowing relaxations. (a) The initial partition along with moves needed to achieve a minimum cutsize. Final partition of an algorithm that (b) does not allow intermediate relaxations, and (c) allows intermediate relaxations.

partitioner. In contrast, with relaxed partitioner (Fig. 3(b)), these violating moves are allowed if it is estimated that the next fewest reverse moves will correct the violations with a minimum deterioration in the cutsize such that there is an overall improvement after the correction. The relaxed moves shown with a solid line in Fig. 3(b) result in a smaller mincut (indicated as point M'). Our methods estimate right after point M (and in general, at every violating move) the benefit of making violating moves followed by reverse moves, without backtracking the move process.

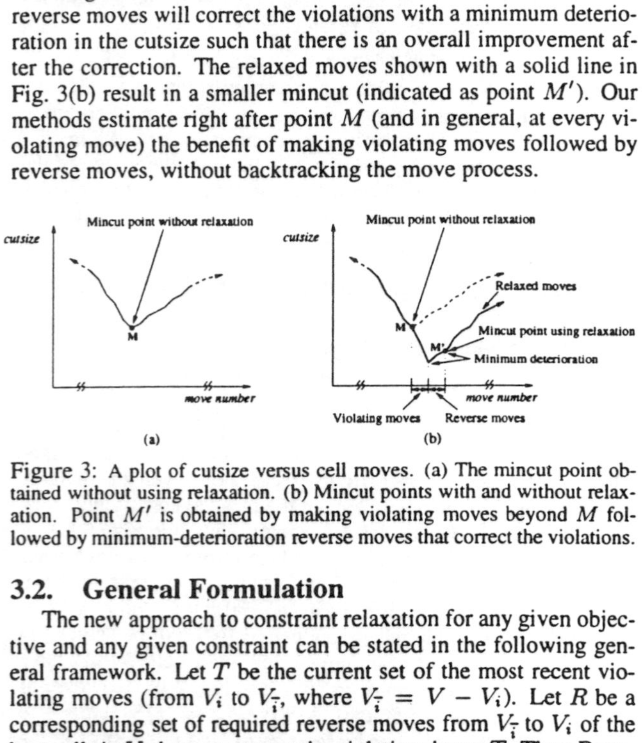

Figure 3: A plot of cutsize versus cell moves. (a) The mincut point obtained without using relaxation. (b) Mincut points with and without relaxation. Point M' is obtained by making violating moves beyond M followed by minimum-deterioration reverse moves that correct the violations.

3.2. General Formulation

The new approach to constraint relaxation for any given objective and any given constraint can be stated in the following general framework. Let T be the current set of the most recent violating moves (from V_i to $V_{\bar{i}}$, where $V_{\bar{i}} = V - V_i$). Let R be a corresponding set of required reverse moves from $V_{\bar{i}}$ to V_i of the best cells in $V_{\bar{i}}$ that can correct the violation due to T. Thus R represents moves that can correct the violations due to T, and in the process will cause the minimum deterioration of the optimization objective (see Fig. 3). Initially, before any violating moves have been made, $T = R = \emptyset$. Let v be the best move to make at the current point in the move process. If v does not add to the accumulated violation due to T, then we move v. Otherwise, we search for a set of cells $rev(v)$, $rev(v) \cap R = \emptyset$, that can be reverse-moved in order to compensate for v's violation such that

$$adv(v) + adv(R \cup rev(v) \mid v) > adv(R) \qquad (2)$$

where $adv(y)$ (read "advantage of y") is the estimated improvement in the optimization objective due to the movement of cell y ($adv(y)$ can be negative), and for a set S of cells, $adv(S) = \sum_{y \in S} adv(y)$. Further, $adv(y \mid x)$ is the estimated improvement obtained by moving cell y after cell x has been moved—$adv(y)$ can be positively or negatively affected by cell x's move, and this is generally negative if x and y on opposite sides of the partition. Further, $adv(S \mid x) = \sum_{y \in S} adv(y \mid x)$. The LHS (left-hand side) of Ineq. 2 is the estimated objective improvement on pursuing the path of moving v followed by $R \cup rev(v)$ to correct the total violation, while the RHS is the estimated objective improvement obtained by only moving cells in R to correct the current violation; note that a legal partition point can only be taken when there are no violations. Cell v would then be moved if $rev(v)$ exists, otherwise the best cell from R is moved.

3.3. Application to Balance Constraints

Our current approaches apply to constraints in the size ratio between V_i and $V_{\bar{i}}$, and the objective is the minimum cutsize between the two subsets. They use the fundamental idea given by Ineq. 2

Let $(u_1, u_2, ..., u_m)$ be the ordering of the unlocked cells in $V_{\bar{i}}$ by decreasing gains. If T is the most recent set of violating moves from V_i to $V_{\bar{i}}$ and $z = \sum_{v_i \in T} a(v_i)$ is the total size of the violations, then $R = \bigcup_{j=1}^{r} u_i$, where $|\bigcup_{j=1}^{r} u_i| \geq z$, and $|\bigcup_{j=1}^{r-1} u_i| < z$. $adv(y) = g(y)$ is the probabilistic gain of cell y. If v is the current best node of size $a(v)$ whose move adds to the violation, then $rev(v) = \bigcup_{r+1}^{t} u_i$, where $|\bigcup_{i=r+1}^{t} u_i| \geq a(v)$ and $|\bigcup_{i=r+1}^{t+1} u_i| < a(v)$. The move of v is accepted if (following the general condition of Ineq. 2)

$$(1-\alpha)g(rev(v)) + g(v) - \alpha g(R) > 0 \qquad (3)$$

The negative term in Ineq 3 corresponds to the average-case decrease in gains of cells $y \in R$ due to an average of α connections between v and y.

Further, in order to obtain a fair number of points at which legal mincuts can be considered, reverse moves (with minimum deterioration of the mincut) will have to periodically occur to correct the violations. Hence, violations are allowed to occur until a relaxation limit $relax$ is reached, and reverse moves are made after this point.

4. Incorporating Relaxations in PROP

4.1. Estimation Method

We present here an accurate version of the estimator in the LHS of Ineq. 2. There are two sources of this accuracy: (i) a look-ahead technique that incorporates the decrease in the gain of future reverse-moves R' (moves beyond $R \cup rev(v)$) due to the current violating move v, and (ii) an exact calculation of the decrease in gain in $R \cup rev(v) \cup R'$ due to u's move.

Due to the presence of clusters straddling the cutline, a violating move from side V_i will most likely be followed by further violating moves from V_i. In order to accurately estimate the effect of moving v on all reverse moves that will potentially need to be made after the current block of violating moves end, we associate a set of potential future reverse-move cells R' in $V_{\bar{i}}$ $(R' \cap (R \cup rev(v)) = \emptyset)$ corresponding to future violating moves. In this manner, the estimator can "look-ahead" further, and hence predict more accurately the expected improvement in the cutsize after the current block of violating moves and the reverse correcting moves are completed. Specifically, R' is the highest-order subset of $V_{\bar{i}} - (R \cup rev(v))$ ordered by decreasing gains. The size of R' depends on the relaxation limit ($relax$), and incrementally changes as the violating moves occur; $|R \cup rev(v) \cup R'| \leq \beta |relax|$ where $0 \leq \beta \leq 1$, is the lookahead parameter, and $|relax| = relax|V|$, is the size of the total relaxation allowed.

We next describe a precise calculation of the decrease in the gains of cells in $R \cup rev(v) \cup R'$ due to the move of cell v. Recall again that since v is a violating move, its effect on the gains of all future reverse-move cells need to be considered, since a valid cut point can only be taken for the maximum prefix computation after all these reverse-moves have been made. If $rev(v)$ corresponding to the current violating move of $v \in V_i$ can be found in $V_{\bar{i}}$, then $g(rev(v)) = \sum_{y \in rev(v)} g(y)$, where $g(y)$ is the probabilistic gain of cell y. Assuming $y \in V_2$, each component $g_{n_i}(y)$ of $g(y)$ can be reformulated as

$$g_{n_i}(y) = g^+_{n_i}(y) - g^-_{n_i}(y) \quad (4)$$

where from Eqn. 1, $g^+_{n_i}(y) = (\prod_{y_{x'} \in n_{i,2}} p(y_{x'}))/p(y)$ and $g^-_{n_i}(y) = \prod_{y_{y'} \in n_{i,1}} p(y_{y'})$.

The "conditional" gain $g(y \mid v)$ of a cell y in $R \cup rev(v) \cup R'$ can be accurately computed as

$$g(y \mid v) = g(y) - \sum_{n_i \in E(y) \cap E(v)} g^+_{n_i}(y) \quad (5)$$

The rationale behind this computation is that, if there is a currently positive gain component $g^+_{n_i}(y)$ of some $y \in R \cup rev(v) \cup R'$ on a common net n_i between y and v, then $g^+_{n_i}(y)$ will become 0 when v is moved to $V_{\bar{i}}$ and locked. Thus the estimating condition becomes

$$g(v) + g(rev(v)) - \sum_{y \in R \cup rev(v) \cup R'} \sum_{n_i \in E(y) \cap E(v)} g^+_{n_i}(y) > 0 \quad (6)$$

On every violating move attempt, the benefit is estimated based on Ineq. 6. A violation is rejected and reverse moves started if either Ineq. 6 is not satisfied, or $z + a(v) > |relax|$ where z is the total size of most recent violating moves (T), and $a(v)$ is the size of the current violating cell v. No violations are permitted during the reverse process in order to guarantee the availability of a fair numbers of legal positions at which the maximum prefix can be computed. The relaxation resumes once violations are corrected. If the estimation is accurate enough, the cost of the cutsize after moving the current block of violating moves followed by the required reverse-moves, will be lower than disallowing any or fewer violating moves.

A high-level description of the estimation algorithm on a violating move is given in Fig. 4. The timing complexity of GainEstim(v) is $O(|rev(v)| + \sum_{v \in n_i} |n_i|)$. On the average, $|rev(v)|$ will be a constant, and assuming a constant fraction of the n moves attempted are violations, the additional complexity of PROP-REX$_{est}$ (PROP with relaxation using GainEstim) will be at most $\frac{1}{2} \sum_{n_i \in E} \rho^2_{n_i} = O(n \rho^{cell}_{max} \rho^{net}_{max})$ where ρ_{n_i} is the number of pins on net n_i, ρ^{cell}_{max} is the maximum number of pins on any cell in G, and ρ^{net}_{max} is the maximum number of pins on any net in G.

4.2. Weighted Benefit Method

In an attempt to reduce the timing complexity of PROP-REX$_{est}$, we investigated a weighted benefit method that captures heuristic information on the benefit of making a violating move. We denote $B(v)$, $0 \le B(v) \le 1$, as the total weighted "benefit" of moving a violating cell v with size $a(v)$ from V_i to $V_{\bar{i}}$. $B(v)$ is defined as $B(v) = \sum_{i=1}^{c} w_i b_i$, where c is the total number of factors considered, w_i, $0 \le w_i \le 1$, is the weight on benefit b_i, $0 \le b_i \le 1$, and $\sum_{i=1}^{c} w_i = 1$. We considered three benefit factors. The first factor is the normalized gain difference between the highest-gain cells $v \in V_i$ and $u \in V_{\bar{i}}$. The second factor is the ratio of the total "available" violation (which is $|relax| - z - a(v)$,

Procedure GainEstim(v)
Begin
/* The violating move being attempted is of cell v with size $a(v)$ from V_1 to V_2 */
If size of $T + a(v)$ exceeds relaxation limit $|relax|$ **then**
Reject violation;
return
Determine $rev(v)$ and R' in V_2 such that:
(1) $|rev(v)| \ge a(v)$;
(2) $|R \cup rev(v) \cup R'| \le \beta |relax|$; /* $0 \le \beta \le 1$ */
(3) $rev(v)$ immediately follows R and R' immediately follows $rev(v)$ in the ordered set of unlocked cells in V_2 with decreasing gains.
If $rev(v)$ does not exist **then**
Reject violation; **return**
$R = R \cup rev(v)$; $penalty(v) = 0$;
For every net n_i adjacent to v and unlocked in V_2 **do**
For every $y \in n_i$ **do**
If $y \in R \cup rev(v) \cup R'$ **then**
$penalty(v) = penalty(v) + g^+_{n_i}(y)$;
End
End
If $g(v) + g(rev(v)) - penalty(v) \le 0$ **then**
/* This is identical to Ineq. 6 */
Reject violation; **return**
else
Accept violation; **return**
End

Figure 4: The benefit estimation algorithm for a violating move.

where z is the total violation so far and $a(v)$ is the size of the violating cell v) and the maximum allowable violation $|relax|$. The third factor is the ratio of the total size of free cells in $V_{\bar{i}}$ that will result after correcting all violations and $|F_{V_{\bar{i}}}|$, the current total free cell size in $V_{\bar{i}}$. Hence $B(v)$ is given by

$$B(v) = w_1(\phi(g(v) - g(u))) + w_2\left(1 - \frac{z + a(v)}{|relax|}\right) + w_3\left(1 - \frac{z + a(v)}{|F_{V_{\bar{i}}}|}\right) \quad (7)$$

where $\phi()$ is a linear function that normalizes the gain difference to a number between 0 and 1. Based on our experiments, the best values for each weight has been determined to be $w_1 = 0.5$, $w_2 = 0.25$ and $w_3 = 0.25$. Essentially $B(v)$ captures the notion that a violating cell should have a high probability of being allowed to move, if the gain difference between v and u is high, if the current violations are far from the relaxation limit, and the move process

Test Case	Cells	Nets	IO	Avg	Stdv	Max	Min
avq_large	25178	25384	64	1845.4	1075.8	4176	16
avq_small	21918	22124	64	1914.9	1140.2	4176	16
biomed	6514	5742	97	2006.1	1102.0	4176	16
industry2	12637	13419	495	32935	18220	116480	1
industry3a	15406	21924	374	93494	36463	237568	64
primary1	859	904	107	14004	11175	30000	25
primary2	3039	3028	132	11254	6526.7	30000	25
s13207*	8772	8651	152	884.7	115.4	900	16
s15850*	10470	10383	101	891.5	86.4	900	16
s35932*	18148	17828	335	882.7	122.4	900	16
s38417*	23949	23843	134	895.1	65.9	900	16
s38584*	20995	20717	290	887.8	103.2	900	16
s9234*	5866	5844	41	893.8	73.7	900	16
sioo	664	408	62	2862.3	1125.0	3551	1
struct	1952	1920	64	1460.7	518.8	2320	16

Table 1: Benchmark circuit characteristics. Circuits with a * suffix are gate-array circuits for which there are only two distinct sizes (gates and pads). **Cells** is the total number of cells (including I/O pads), **Nets** is the total number of nets, **IO** is the number of I/O pads, **Avg** is the average cell size, **Stdv** is standard deviation of cell sizes, and **Max/Min** are the maximum/minimum cell sizes in the circuit.

Test Case	Cutsize & Time											
	FM-20 No-Relaxation			**FM-60** No-Relaxation			**PROP-20** No-Relaxation			**PROP-20** Blind Relaxation		
	Min	Avg	Time	Min	Avg	Time	Min	Avg	Time	Min	Avg	Time
avq_large	692	875.2	19.03	536	840.1	18.62	381	511.9	40.09	323	504.4	46.82
avq_small	472	693.5	15.67	384	688.8	15.78	363	487.8	39.10	366	493.9	39.35
biomed	117	192.8	3.77	108	185.2	3.92	92	142.5	11.54	101	157.4	12.34
industry2	331	843.1	10.27	331	835.0	10.37	267	381.2	38.45	278	421.7	45.88
industry3a	330	714.1	11.71	276	679.5	11.56	324	504.6	49.37	292	445.8	44.97
primary1	63	81.3	0.20	51	80.6	0.19	52	65.0	0.75	49	66.2	0.70
primary2	229	286.6	1.53	229	304.2	1.35	154	200.4	6.70	166	220.4	6.00
s13207*	86	137.8	4.43	86	137.0	4.48	78	110.9	9.49	81	119.8	10.18
s15850*	115	173.5	5.51	108	180.3	5.58	84	116.8	13.93	92	122.2	15.33
s35932*	162	246.6	11.53	148	243.3	11.64	74	96.0	28.49	73	91.3	28.61
s38417*	374	505.8	15.75	373	522.4	15.17	97	137.8	46.52	98	161.6	40.71
s38584*	113	346.8	17.36	113	336.5	17.72	83	127.4	52.89	76	134.3	52.50
s9234*	62	98.9	3.01	58	106.1	2.89	56	94.5	6.28	53	101.5	6.85
sioo	37	53.8	0.12	35	53.5	0.13	29	29.0	0.30	28	28.0	0.33
struct	46	62.6	0.46	45	61.8	0.46	38	51.8	1.54	43	56.8	1.74
Total	3229	5312.4	120.35 $\times 20 =$ 2407.0	2881	5254.3	119.86 $\times 60 =$ 7191.6	2172	3057.6	345.44 $\times 20 =$ 6908.8	2119	3125.3	352.31 $\times 20 =$ 7046.2
% Improvement Over FM-20 no-relaxation	-	-	-	10.78	1.09	-198.78	32.73	42.44	-187.03	34.38	41.17	-192.74
% Improvement Over FM-60 no-relaxation	-12.08	-1.1	66.53	-	-	-	24.61	41.81	3.93	26.45	40.52	2.02

Table 2: Comparisons of cutsizes for $r = 0.5$ (50%-50% balance constraint) with $t = 0.005$ (0.5% tolerance) produced by FM for 20 and 60 runs without relaxation, PROP with 20 runs without relaxation, and PROP with 20 runs with blind relaxation (i.e., without using our new benefit estimation techniques). The **Min** column is the best result from all the runs, the **Avg** column shows the average cutsize over those runs, and the **Time** column is the CPU time (in seconds) per run.

is far from the point at which all cells are locked.

A violating move with benefit $B(v)$ will be accepted if it is above a certain threshold $T(v)$ that depends on the difference Δcut between the current cutsize cut_c and the minimum cutsize cut_{min} found so far. This is best modeled by a $tanh$ function given by

$$T(v) = f(\Delta cut) = 1 - \frac{1}{2}(tanh(\frac{\Delta cut}{f_h} - f_v) + 1) \quad (8)$$

where f_h and f_v are control variables which reshape the function curve as shown in Fig. 5(a).

The weighted benefit method is applied selectively along certain portions of the cutsize curve. The main aim is to reduce the time overhead of using `GainEstim` at every violating move, without sacrificing the cutsize significantly. The critical junctures to perform accurate benefit estimations for violating moves are when the current cutsize cut_c is decreasing, and is either near the minimum cutsize cut_{min} found so far, or it has just decreased below cut_{min} (see Fig. 5(b)). These portions are critical since new mincut points will be occurring in these regions, and it is desirable to have valid prefix points here. Thus if the possibility of violating moves present themselves in these portions of the cutsize curve, then it is important to evaluate their benefits accurately by applying `GainEstim` in these sections.

In the regions where cut_c is increasing beyond cut_{min} or is decreasing but still far away from cut_{min} (see Fig. 5(b)), it is not necessary to have valid prefix points. Thus the less accurate, though still informed, weighted benefit method can be used. At the same time, it is beneficial to allow more violations in portions where Δcut is increasing, or is decreasing but large, in an effort to decrease cut_c below cut_{min}. Also, so that valid prefix points can be found soon after cut_c decreases below cut_{min}, it is essential to make fewer violating moves when Δcut is small and cut_c is decreasing toward cut_{min}. All these desirable characteristics are facilitated by the $tanh()$ based threshold function as shown in Fig. 5(a).

The timing complexity per violating move of the weighted benefit method is a constant. Thus the timing complexity of PROP-REX$_{comb}$ (PROP with relaxation, using both `GainEstim` and weighted benefit methods) is reduced to $O(n\rho^{cell}_{max}\rho^{net}_{max}\gamma)$ where γ is the fraction of violating moves occurring at $cut_c \leq cut_{min}$. Empirical results show γ to be around 1/3.

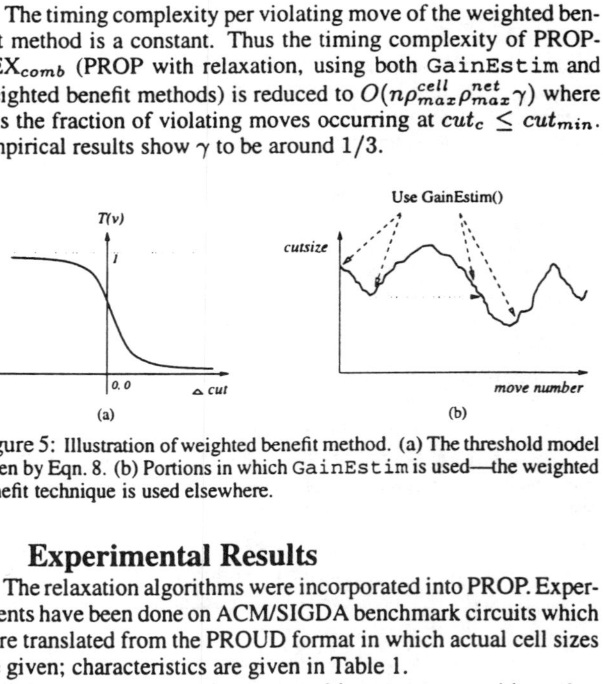

(a) (b)

Figure 5: Illustration of weighted benefit method. (a) The threshold model given by Eqn. 8. (b) Portions in which `GainEstim` is used—the weighted benefit technique is used elsewhere.

5. Experimental Results

The relaxation algorithms were incorporated into PROP. Experiments have been done on ACM/SIGDA benchmark circuits which were translated from the PROUD format in which actual cell sizes are given; characteristics are given in Table 1.

All experimental results presented here were run with a tolerance (t) of 0.005 (0.5%) for a balance ratio (r) of 0.5 (50%-50%), 0.45, 0.4 and varying relaxation limits ($relax$ = 0.01 to 0.05), on a SPARCStation 20. The first set of results given in Table 2 compare FM (20 and 60 runs–60 runs make its speed comparable to PROP with 20 runs), PROP (both without relaxations), and PROP with a "blind" relaxation, where all violating moves are just "blindly" accepted and reversed once the relaxation limit is reached (0.05 for the results shown), both with 20 runs. PROP without relaxation is better than FM-20 by about 33% in mincut and 42.5% in average-cut, and is better than FM-60 by about 25%

Test Case	Cutsize & Time of PROP-REX$_{est}$ for $r = 0.5$						Cutsize & Time of PROP-REX$_{comb}$ for $r = 0.5$					
	$relax = 0.01$			$relax = 0.03$			$relax = 0.01$			$relax = 0.03$		
	Min	Avg	Time	Min	Avg	Time	Min	Avg	Time	Min	Avg	Time
avq_large	334	494.8	58.44	295	482.2	79.68	294	483.2	46.70	278	481.6	48.99
avq_small	274	452.0	50.49	249	462.1	68.72	274	471.9	43.61	274	452.1	47.27
biomed	93	134.4	13.48	88	137.9	14.92	91	132.7	12.74	94	147.5	12.72
industry2	206	351.9	45.67	230	359.4	48.59	239	372.8	50.05	234	375.1	43.44
industry3a	274	385.4	48.55	274	413.3	52.32	275	439.6	43.97	275	429.6	44.07
primary1	47	58.5	0.89	47	64.7	0.90	47	56.7	0.96	48	62.9	0.87
primary2	154	194.8	5.80	161	204.8	5.85	146	197.8	6.84	152	205.7	7.38
s13207*	74	106.4	11.27	85	116.1	14.16	79	109.5	11.83	89	113.5	11.69
s15850*	80	108.0	18.50	72	112.5	19.65	85	111.2	16.22	88	115.5	15.48
s35932*	73	88.0	31.14	73	91.3	44.08	73	90.7	26.81	73	81.9	29.61
s38417*	72	136.8	51.27	97	147.5	67.09	86	148.6	52.27	72	139.7	54.27
s38584*	70	124.7	58.43	68	126.8	67.21	62	129.8	65.30	66	111.5	63.89
s9234*	55	83.8	6.90	52	89.1	8.23	53	77.0	6.55	48	81.6	6.69
sioo	28	28.6	0.38	28	28.9	0.34	28	28.2	0.34	28	28.6	0.36
struct	41	48.1	1.69	37	48.2	1.83	37	50.4	1.91	38	52.9	2.16
Total	1875	2796.2	402.90	1856	2884.8	493.57	1869	2900.1	386.10	1857	2879.7	388.89
% Improvement. Over PROP-20 no-relaxation	13.67	8.55	-16.63	14.55	5.65	-42.88	13.95	5.15	-11.77	14.50	5.82	-12.58

Table 3: Cutsizes and improvements on benchmark circuits achieved by PROP-REX$_{est}$ (left half) and PROP-REX$_{comb}$ (right half) for $r = 0.5$ and $t = 0.005$.

in mincut and 42% in average cut. This establishes that PROP is indeed a very good partitioning algorithm for circuits with varying cell sizes ([1] established this fact for circuits with unit cell sizes), and is thus a good candidate for trying to improve further using our new relaxation techniques. PROP with blind relaxation is only 2% better in mincut than PROP without relaxation, but is slightly worse in the average cut. This underscores the need to have good benefit estimation techniques for violating moves—only allowing relaxation in the move process is not enough. Table 3 shows that the new benefit estimation methods perform well in predicting and allowing only "good" violating moves.

Table 3 compares the results of PROP without relaxation to PROP-REX$_{est}$ and PROP-REX$_{comb}$ for a look-ahead factor (β) of 0.5 for 20 random runs. From Table 3, PROP-REX$_{est}$ achieves significant improvements on large general-cell circuits such as avq_large, avq_small, industry2, and industry3a by as much as 37%. Overall, there are improvements of 14.55% and 16.25% in mincut over all circuits for $relax = 0.03$ and $relax = 0.05$, respectively. This indicates that the estimator does work well in predicting "good" violating moves. PROP-REX$_{est}$ is about 1.43 times slower than PROP (for $relax = 0.03$).

From Table 3, PROP-REX$_{comb}$ achieves significant improvements for general-cell circuits; for circuit avq_large, there is an improvement of 38% in mincut for $relax = 0.05$. Over all circuits, PROP-REX$_{comb}$ achieves an improvement of 14.5% in mincut for $relax = 0.03$. These improvements are comparable to those of PROP-REX$_{est}$, though PROP-REX$_{comb}$ is only about 1.13 times slower than PROP (for $relax = 0.03$). We have also obtained experimental results for $r = 0.45$ and $r = 0.4$, that show that PROP-REX$_{comb}$ achieves an overall improvement of 10% for both balance ratios.

6. Conclusions

We proposed a new general non-backtracking branch-and-bound approach to the important problem of constraint-driven partitioning, and then presented specific techniques for tackling one of the most important and commonly applied constraints, a prespecified balance-ratio on the sizes of the subcircuits of a partition. Effective constraint satisfaction was either overlooked in past partitioning work (e.g., [1], [3], [4], [5] and [6]), or was treated cursorily in others ([7], [8]). Our new techniques estimate the "goodness" of accepting violations compared to disallowing them, based on probabilistic cell gains, look-aheads for future violations, and weighted benefits. Incorporating the new methods within the state-of-the-art partitioner PROP yields improvements of up to 38% on general-cell circuits, and 18% on gate-array circuits with an average improvement of 14.5%, and a timing overhead of only around 13%.

The work presented in this paper represents a crucial first step towards formulating effective relaxation techniques for a variety of constraints that occur naturally in the physical design of VLSI circuits. In future work, relaxation methods will be developed for other important constraints, such as those mentioned in Sec. 1., and a precise general formulation will be developed that can be effectively applied to most constraints.

References

[1] S. Dutt and W. Deng, "A probability-based approach to VLSI circuit partitioning", *Proc. Design Automation Conf.*, June 1996, pp. 100-105.

[2] S. Dutt and W. Deng, "VLSI Circuit Partitioning by Cluster-Removal Using Iterative Improvement Techniques", *Proc. IEEE/ACM Int'l Conf. on Computer-Aided Design*, April 1996, pp. 92-99.

[3] C.M. Fidducia and R.M. Mattheyses, "A linear-time heuristic for improving network partitions", *Proc. Nineteenth Design Automation Conf.*, 1982, pp. 175-181.

[4] B. Krishnamurthy, "An improved mincut algorithm for partitioning VLSI networks", *IEEE Trans. on Computers*, vol. C-33, no. 5, May 1984, pp. 438-446.

[5] J. Li, J. Lillis and C-K. Cheng, "Linear decomposition algorithm for VLSI design applications", *Proc. IEEE/ACM Int'l Conf. on Computer-Aided Design*, 1995, pp. 223-228.

[6] C.J. Alpert and A.B. Kahng, "A hybrid multilevel/genetic approach for circuit partitioning", *Physical Design Workshop*, 1996, pp. 100-105.

[7] R. Kuznar, F. Brglez and K. Kozminski, "Cost minimization of partitions into multiple devices", *Proc. ACM/IEEE Design Automation Conf.*, 1993, pp. 315-320.

[8] N.-S. Woo and J. Kim, "An efficient method of partitioning circuits for multiple-FPGA implementation" *Proc. ACM/IEEE Design Automation Conf.*, 1993, pp. 202-207.

[9] Y.C. Wei and C.K. Cheng, "An Improved Two-Way Partitioning Algorithm with Stable Performance", *IEEE Trans. on Computer-Aided Design*, vol. 10, no. 12, December 1991, pp. 1502-1511.

[10] Y. Sun, R. Gupta, and C.L. Liu, "Congestion-Balanced Placement for FPGAs", *Physical Design Workshop* 1996, pp. 163-168.

[11] P.R. Suaris and G Kedem, "A Quadrisection-Based Combined Place and Route Scheme for Standard Cells", *IEEE Trans. on Computer-Aided Design*, vol. 8, no. 3, March 1989, pp. 234-24[illegible].

[12] George Karypis, Rajat Aggarwal, Vipin Kumar and Shashi Shekhar, "Multi-level Hypergraph Partitioning: Application in VLSI Domain", *Proc. Design Automation Conf.*, June 1997.

Adaptive Methods for Netlist Partitioning

Wray L. Buntine, Lixin Su, A. Richard Newton and Andrew Mayer
Dept. of Electrical Engineering and Computer Sciences
Room 520 Cory Hall, Univ. of Cal., Berkeley, CA, 94720-1770

Abstract

An algorithm that remains in use at the core of many partitioning systems is the Kernighan-Lin algorithm and a variant the Fidducia-Matheysses (FM) algorithm. To understand the FM algorithm we applied principles of data engineering where visualization and statistical analysis are used to analyze the run-time behavior. We identified two improvements to the algorithm which, without clustering or an improved heuristic function, bring the performance of the algorithm near that of more sophisticated algorithms. One improvement is based on the observation, explored empirically, that the full passes in the FM algorithm appear comparable to a stochastic local restart in the search. We motivate this observation with a discussion of recent improvements in Monte Carlo Markov Chain methods in statistics. The other improvement is based on the observation that when an FM-like algorithm is run 20 times and the best run chosen, the performance trace of the algorithm on earlier runs is useful data for learning when to abort a later run. These improvements, implemented with a simple adaptive scheme, are orthogonal to techniques used in state-of-the-art implementations, and therefore should be applicable to other VLSI optimization algorithms.

1 Introduction

In discrete optimization, there are several broad classes of techniques for developing an algorithm. In *local search* [1] a neighborhood space is created and algorithms update a current solution by local moves around that space. Some variations of this are gradient descent which makes the most locally promising move at each step, simulated annealing [16] which makes a move in a stochastic direction based on the theory of Gibbs sampling [8], and tabu search which enforces restrictions on the ordering in which variables can be updated [10]. Another approach, *problem decomposition* breaks the problem down into smaller components, which are then solved separately, and their solutions spliced back together to offer a solution to the original problem.

Netlist partitioning [3] is one approach to the general idea of problem decomposition. In the two-way min-cut netlist partition problem, one is given a hypergraph whose nodes are referred to as cells, and whose hyper-edges are referred to as nets. The cells are to be split into two partitions such that the minimum number of nets have cells in both partitions. These cut nets are referred to as the *cut-set*. This is the hypergraph version of the graph partitioning problem. Typically, a balance constraint is also enforced whereby the area of each partition must lie in a given interval.

Hypergraph partitioning is generally useful in constraint satisfaction problems for the following reason. For an arbitrary constraint satisfaction problem, (V,C), where there are variables V and constraints C, suppose the variables are split into two partitions V_1 and V_2 and constraints C_1 and C_2 are wholly contained within the partitions V_1 and V_2 respectively, and constraints C_{1+2} are cut (so $V_1 \cup V_2 = V$ and $C_1 \cup C_2 \cup C_{1+2} = C$). Then under reasonable conditions on the nature of the constraints, one can first solve the problem of (V_1,C_1), express the solutions for V_1 as partial evaluations of the cut constraints C_{1+2} taking values V_{1+2}, and finally solve the remaining induced problem $\left(V_2+V_{1+2}, C_2+C'_{1+2}\right)$. If the cutset size $|C_{1+2}|$ is small then one solves two smaller problems instead of one large problem. While we restrict ourselves here to a two-way partitioning, in general a good k-way partitioning can be similarly invaluable for simplifying a problem. Related graphical constructions are used to decompose probability distributions, linear equations, and constraints in design [15].

Common local search techniques for netlist partitioning are the Kernighan-Lin (KL) algorithm and the Fidducia-Matheysses (FM) algorithm [3]. While these have some similarities with their cousin, the Lin-Kernighan (LK) algorithm for the traveling salesman problem [12], the algorithms are in fact very different. The LK algorithm is frequently within 2% of optimal on large problems, whereas the FM must be run repeatedly, perhaps 50 times, before a solution would be found that is near optimal, and on large problems (10,000 or more nodes), many times more might be needed. Of course, by current theory and algorithms one rarely knows what is truly optimal. One run of the FM algorithm really corresponds to the inner loop of the LK algorithm. Recent state of the art algorithms for partitioning

1092-3152/97 $10.00 © 1997 IEEE

such as PROP [5], PANZA [13], and STRAWMAN [11] apply more clever heuristics for choosing the next node, techniques for finding an initial partition, or they preprocess the problem via clustering. However, two out of three of these algorithms still retain the FM or KL algorithm at their core, and usually run it repeatedly.

We apply principles of *data engineering* where visualization and statistical analysis are used to analyze data gathered from a process, in this case the run-time performance of the algorithm. Whereas Hauck and Borriello [11] systematically explored a number of variations around the standard FM algorithm, in this research, we sought to understand and thereby improve specific details of the existing algorithms. We have identified two statistically motivated improvements to the algorithm. Interestingly enough, these two improvements lead us to develop a new algorithm which is comparable to PROP in performance on some standard test problems. We see the general maxim "speed over smarts" apply because our approach merely places an adaptive wrapper around the simple "local search with tabu list" core of FM without requiring sophisticated approximation techniques or clustering.

For background on the netlist partitioning problem the KL and FM algorithms, and many other algorithms of interest, we refer the reader to the excellent review article by Alpert and Kahng [3]. In our Section 3, experiment details and protocol are discussed. Comparison of algorithms is fraught with difficulty, so we take some care in this section to outline the precautions we took. In the following sections we introduce the analyses we did that motivated our work. We gathered some data on the runs, and performed a number of basic statistical tests, from which we formulated two hypotheses about how the algorithms were really operating. These are also explained in Section 4 and later in Section 6. From the understanding we gleaned from the experiments, we devised a modified control for a FM-style algorithm which is introduced in Section 7.

2 Basic Algorithm

The basic KL algorithm is outlined below, and for more detail we refer the reader to [3] or many of the textbooks in VLSI design. Some initial partition is used, in our case a random partition. The algorithm uses a data structure (usually buckets, linked lists or heaps) that gives for each cell the immediate "gain" (measured in terms of reduction of cutset size) obtained if that cell were to be moved to the other partition. The data structure handles operations such as "fetch the cell with the best gain," "remove the cell from the available list," "update the cell's gain," etc. The choice of this structure and its method for tie-breaking (LIFO, FIFO) can impact the performance significantly. More advanced algorithms might have more advanced move heuristics such as 2-step look-ahead. The algorithm proceeds in *passes*. In each pass, all cells are initially *unlocked* and available to be moved. The unlocked cell with the highest gain is drawn from the data structure, moved to the other partition, and all other cell's gains are updated (in the simplest case this just involves looking at the neighbors). Then this drawn cell is locked (or placed on a tabu list) until the end of the pass. This proceeds until all cells are locked, and no more moves are possible. So all cells are swapped, and we now have a mirror of the partition we started with (in the binary case). The algorithm has just finished one pass through all the cells, and the least cutset-size partition in the pass is taken as the starting partition for the next pass. The KL algorithm typically has 5-10 passes for the smaller circuits, and 10-30 for the larger circuits. The algorithm terminates when no improvement in cutset size is obtained for a pass. A good summary of modifications to the basic algorithm, and further pointers to literature can be found at [11, 3].

In our implementation in C, netlist partitions are constrained to contain between 45% and 55% of the area (the 45-55% balance criteria), and each cell and pin is assumed to have unit area for this purpose. The algorithms are run from random initial placements, and cells are stored in a bucket structure, an array of doubly-linked lists indexed by the gain from making a swap. Tie breaking (accessing the doubly-linked list) is done in a LIFO fashion [11, 3].

3 Experimental details

All experiments are run on a DEC Alpha 5000/400MHz with 128Mb of memory. The larger data sets used for experimentation were obtained from Alpert's website (`http://vlsicad.cs.ucla.edu/~cheese/`) which in turn are netlist versions of some standards from TU Munich from their copy of the ACM/SIGDA Layout Benchmark Suite from MCNC. Some smaller test problems were from the Berkeley OCTTOOLS environment. The details are listed in Table 1. Notice in some cases the pins are 0 due to the earlier processing of the netlist (in our experiments pins and cells are treated identically). Trials were also run with Dutt and Deng's recently released C++ code for FM partitioning, lookahead, and their PROP algorithm [5]. Use of Dutt and Deng's code is discussed in the appendix. We have compared our FM implementation in both timing and resultant cutset size to Dutt and Deng's C++ code, with the timing differences explainable by our use of C.

Finally, in comparing results from algorithms with unequal times, we use the *best-of-X wrapper*. This wrapper runs the faster algorithm multiple times so that the algorithms being compared have approximately equal run time (ignoring discretization effects). Results are then reported for the best of the X ran. For instance if comparing PROP against FM, typically a best-of-5 wrapper would be used.

Dataset	Nets	Cells	Pads
C1355	245	73	204
C1908	282	249	58
C2670	529	348	296
C3540	811	761	72
C5315	907	729	296
C6288	1925	1893	64
biomed	5742	6514	0
struct	1920	1952	0
industry2	13419	12637	0
industry3	21923	15406	0
avq-small	22124	21853	65
avq-large	25384	25113	65
s9234	5844	5866	0
s13207	8651	8772	0
s15850	10383	10470	0
s35932	17828	18148	0
s38417	23843	23949	0
s38584	20717	20995	0
golem	144949	103048	0

Table 1: Summary of the Data sets

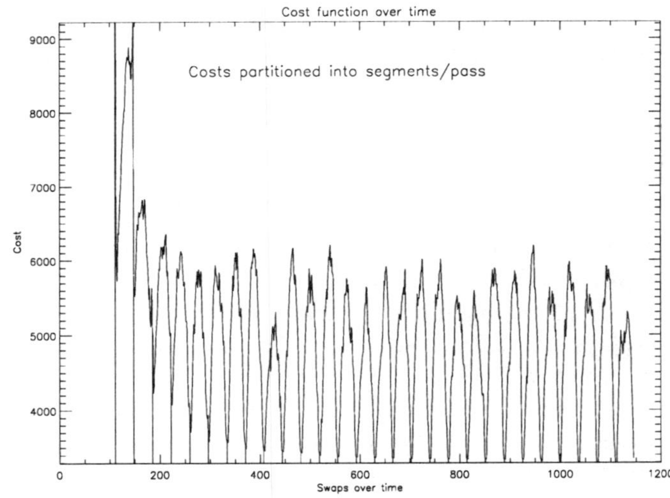

Figure 1: Typical behavior of cost

Our full algorithm corresponds to about 40-60 FM runs, depending on the data set, so for each data set X is chosen accordingly to make a time-equalized comparison.

4 Why full passes in the FM algorithm?

The basis of our research is the following observation. Shown in Figure 1 is the microscopic behavior of the cost function during a typical run of the algorithm. The X-axis corresponds to swaps, and the Y-axis is the evaluated cost function. The lines drawn vertically from the cost curve down to the X-axis indicate the start/end of a pass. Note that the first three passes have not been included in the figure since these would dwarf the above curves as the algorithm is mostly performing rapid gradient descent initially.

What is most interesting about the figure is the inverted "U" shape of the costs during each later pass. The first pass or two (not shown) are "U" shaped as the algorithm does rapid gradient descent. Note that the end point of each pass is identical in cost to the starting point, due to the symmetry of swapping every cell. The inverted "U" shape means that the algorithm invariably chooses the best partition from near the beginning or the end of the pass. This makes sense if one considers that the algorithm is merely making local changes towards the end of a run, and the local changes therefore lie near the beginning or end of the pass. This raises the question, what does the effort for the middle 95% of the pass achieve? We refer to a *full pass* as one that eventually locks every node during its course. In view of this we made the following hypothesis:

Hypothesis 1: The use of full passes in the later passes of the FM algorithm is serving the purpose of performing a local restart for the algorithm, and this goal can also be achieved by stochastic local moves.

To test out the hypothesis, we designed and ran a number of experiments. We modified FM so that no pass would run for more than half way through. We call this *Half-pass FM*. Second, we implemented a stochastic variation of FM. The stochastic variation has two complementary aspects: we would like to introduce shorter passes, but with shorter passes alone, the performance of the algorithm is poorer (results of an experiment not reported here). Therefore, the introduction of a means of escaping local minima is also introduced using stochasticity. Components of this stochastic FM (SFM) are as follows:

Initial FM passes: Full passes are done for the first 4 passes, and thereafter, passes are stopped short, and occasional stochastic passes are used to escape local minima. The initial passes in FM are mostly running down-hill, with the cutset size decreasing. The full passes initially seemed to be important to settle the search in a good local region, perhaps due to the nature of tabu search used in FM. Significant stochasticity is injected into the algorithm by the starting point for search so there seemed no benefit in introducing additional stochasticity.

Short Passes: These passes are constrained to be less than 15% in size of a full pass, and as the algorithm converges, the pass length is decreased yet more using a simple adaptive scheme. The current pass length is set to 200% of the length of the successful prefix of the previous pass, but is constrained to not go below 2% of a full pass. We refer to these passes as *short passes*. Note we view this implementation of a short pass is being a straw-man for the purposes of our experimentation, and we make no claim about the parameters (15%,200%,2%) being carefully tuned, or theoretically justified. The justification for this scheme is as follows: passes cannot be too short (hence, 2%) or no neighborhood search is done; once a reasonable state is found (in the initial 4 FM passes) passes do not need to be long on the basis of evidence shown in Figure 1 (hence, 15%); finally, shortening passes on the basis of the length of previous passes seems to be an inherently dangerous practice (hence 200% of the previous pass).

Stochastic Passes: the second kind of pass we use is to escape local minima. The stochastic pass does not choose the top or best cell to move (according to gain), but instead draws the "next best cell" repeatedly from the gain bucket structure and then rejects it with probability δ, where δ is set so that the probability of drawing a down-hill (favorable) move if one exists is 0.8. That is, prefer swaps at the top of the gain bucket array, and with probability about 0.8, move down-hill. Moreover, the stochastic pass will move ρ percent of a full pass where $\rho \in [0.02, 0.10]$ and is selected uniformly. Again, we make no claim about the parameters $(0.8, 0.02, 0.10)$ being carefully tuned, or theoretically justified. On one particular problem the stochastic pass performed poorly in comparison with the full pass, and in this case we played with the parameter ρ with some success. The justification for this choice is as follows: the stochastic pass is implemented to generally go down-hill at each move, and the stochastic pass is allowed variable length. We found the length of the stochastic pass is a determiner of the algorithm's performance, but in simple studies we could not find a way to judge an appropriate length so randomization of the length seemed a fair middle ground. Clearly, the stochastic pass could not be too long or too short. A long stochastic pass is no different to a full restart of the algorithm.

Stochastic FM: Our stochastic FM goes as follows: When the algorithm reaches a local optimum (the most recent pass chose its first state as the best new state), it then runs one stochastic pass to attempt to escape followed by a sequence of regular short passes until another local optimum is reached. If the new local optimum is superior, then this becomes the current state, otherwise the algorithm restarts from the previous local optimum. In this way, the algorithm repeatedly does gradient descent, and on reaching a local minimum attempts to jump out with a stochastic pass. As it stands this algorithm never terminates, so we terminate if no improvement is gained after 100 passes, or if a time-bound is exceeded. We call this *stochastic FM*, as given in Figure 2. Depending on the problem used and the time bound, stochastic FM may do 2 to 20 times as many passes as regular FM. While this approach might remind one of simulated annealing, the algorithm is quite different, as discussed in Section 5.

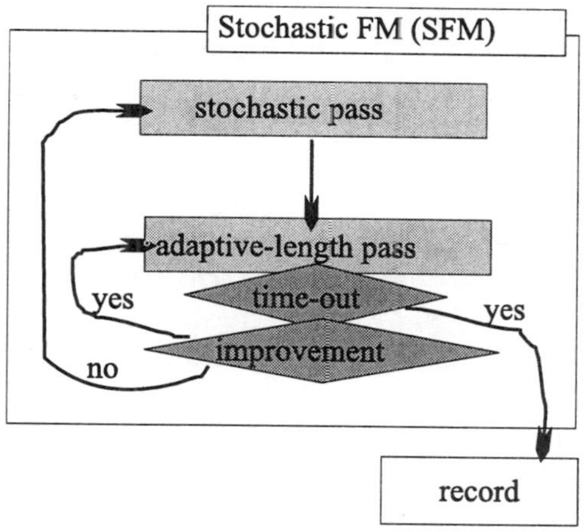

Figure 2: Stochastic FM

These two FM variations, half-pass and stochastic, are compared empirically against standard FM in Table 2. Stochastic FM labelled SFM is run for about the same time as regular FM by setting the time-bound appropriately. Half-pass FM is labelled 1/2-FM. It is clear that the half-pass FM is a terrible algorithm. It seems the full passes, de-

Dataset	FM	SFM	1/2-FM
C1355	22.6± 4.1	21.4± 3.2	28.5± 6.9
C1908	38.7± 3.3	36.6± 2.6	43.5± 6.9
C2670	38.2± 6.8	35.5± 4.4	40.7± 6.1
C3540	84.1± 14.6	80.7± 11.7	105± 21.1
C5315	47.2± 10.4	48.7± 3.6	68.3± 13.7
C6288	86.9± 24.3	94.3± 15.7	121± 24.6
biomed	214± 39.5	240± 18.8	256± 31.4
struct	55.1± 10.5	48.3± 5.5	92.8± 10.8
industry2	769± 193	923± 103	1269± 175
industry3	568± 185	516± 223	999± 347
avq-small	609± 132	698± 95.5	1196± 154
avq-large	774± 175	795± 78.8	1332± 185
s9234	93.4± 27.3	113± 24.4	201± 35.3
s13207	131± 22.7	144± 14.8	187± 25.1
s15850	186± 37.3	200± 36.7	301± 36.0
s35932	191± 47.4	305± 57.4	531± 75.1
s38417	521± 70.8	484± 38.6	560± 89.9
s38584	289± 105	481± 134	887± 139
golem	3156± 318	2990± 201	6228± 836

Table 2: Results for FM vs. Stochastic (SFM) vs. Half-pass (1/2-FM)

spite all their overhead, are necessary for the performance of the FM algorithm[1]. Note we believe this is an artifact of the property that for binary partitioning, the state at the end of a pass is a mirror of the state at the start of the pass, and we expect this would not hold for other related algorithms. Stochastic FM is a reasonable algorithm. In some larger problems it is inferior, however. Given that we have done little to tune the performance of the stochastic component of the algorithm, we believe there is considerable room for improvement. Playing with the parameters on some hard problems (for instance the *s38584* problem) showed we could get considerably better performance. While it appears that one of our more efficient stochastic passes is not comparable to one full pass in terms of contribution to the final result, this is not in contradiction with our hypothesis, and the stochastic FM algorithm is yielding reasonable performance all up. We concluded that Hypothesis 1 has good evidence in its favor.

One obvious question that arises from all this is: What happens if the stochastic FM is allowed to run for longer? We conducted a variety of experiments to explore this question. It seems that in general, the longer the stochastic algorithm is run, the better the performance over time equalized best-of-X FM, yet more support for our hypothesis. The longer stochastic FM algorithm routinely yields improvements of up to 25% over time-equalized best-of-X FM. The shorter (middle) version of stochastic FM in these experiments runs for about 6 regular FM runs. The longer version runs for the equivalent of 50 regular FM runs but usually terminates far shorter since we have the algorithm terminate if there is no improvement of cost after 100 passes. Surprisingly we found that best-of-X shorter SFM was comparable with longer SFM in minimum cutset size after being time-equalized, so there seemed little reason to distinguish between restarting the algorithm or letting it run for longer.

5 Notes on Stochastic Search Algorithms

The stochastic technique we have introduced in the previous section could be compared with simulated annealing, for instance reviewed in [16]. We note that by most accounts, standard simulated annealing is not competitive with best-of-X FM so we did not implement it. There are several differences between our stochastic FM and standard implementations of simulated annealing. First, stochastic passes are only introduced into our SFM algorithm at the point of a local minima. All other times, standard gradient descent via a variation of FM is used. Thus our approach is sampling the space of local minima stochastically, not the full search space. This would seem to be a more appropriate technique for optimization. Second, our approach has a very different stochastic component. The FM core maintains a list of all possible moves at each point, and the stochastic element samples efficiently from that, with a high probability of an upward move. In contrast, standard simulated annealing only samples one move at a time, so is not able to sample high quality moves as efficiently as our variation.

Simulated annealing in its popular form is based on the theory of Gibbs sampling. While Gibbs samplers are seeing a resurgence in statistics, it is well known that they are inefficient. Some basic problems are discussed in [14], and a simple explanation is as follows: Gibbs samplers generally take $O(N^2)$ to move N steps, more or less because of the fact that the standard deviation of a sample is $O(1/\sqrt{N})$, and hence the sum of the sample is $O(\sqrt{N})$ away from the mean. One might argue that the use of tabu lists in local search could be justified on the same grounds—the full space is more slowly traversed if moves are allowed to be entirely local instead of enforcing some discrete analogue to line-search.

More recent methods for Monte Carlo Markov Chain sampling use better proposal distributions or more sophisticated methods for taking multiple steps. To use stochastic methods in search, one clearly needs these more efficient samplers. We view our approach as an *ad hoc* technique for introducing stochasticity in search without having to suffer the known inefficiencies of the Gibbs samplers inside standard simulated annealing.

6 Making multiple runs more efficient

One can see from Figure 1 that the last half of the run is mostly just polishing the final solution. Moreover, the standard deviations in the final cutset size for multiple FM runs are quite large in comparison with the improvements made in the last half or two-thirds of the run. We gathered data over many runs of many different problems, and determined that the correlation coefficient between the intermediate and final cutset sizes approaches 1.0 towards the end of the run, and is already quite high half-way through the run.

Perhaps one could estimate part way through a run that the current run could not, with high probability, improve sufficiently fast to produce a new lower cost winner. The plot of different costs in Figure 3 shows the progress of the cutset size after each pass for 20 different runs on the "avq-large" dataset. Lines are shaded grey depending on the size of the final cutset. From the plot, the potential of cutting-off runs at about pass 7 is clear. A good time to perform the corresponding test on the "golem" dataset is at pass 13. Since we cannot determine "7" or "13" ahead of time for different datasets, we need to do so adaptively as the algorithm gains empirical experience on the particular

[1] This is a fact we are sure many researchers and Kernighan and Lin are aware of.

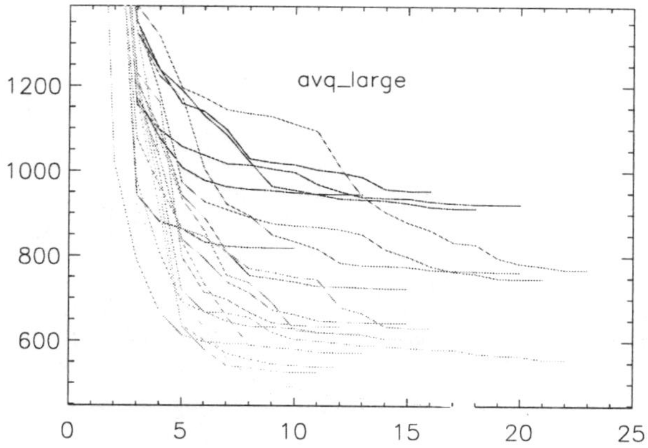

Figure 3: Multiple FM runs from the avq-large domain

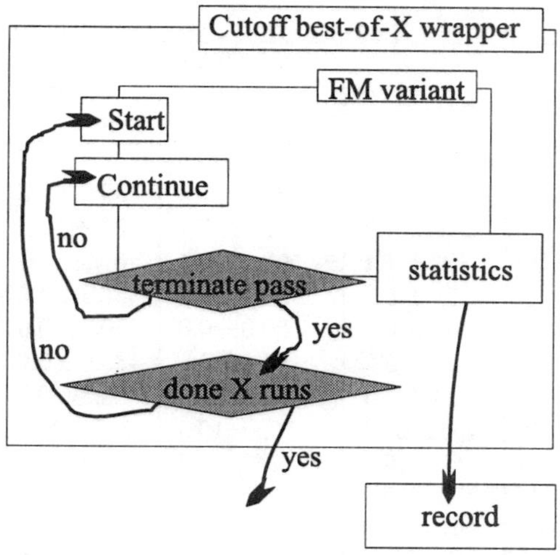

Figure 4: Cutoff best-of-X wrapper

dataset. Such a strategy could be considered to be a serial, on-line version of the "go with the winners" algorithm for tree search suggested by Aldous [2].

We have implemented this algorithm in the following simple way, shown in Figure 4. We place a "cutoff best-of X" wrapper around the FM variant we are running. It records data about runs and passes during operation. After each pass, it performs a simple quality test to see if this run is converging fast enough. The quality test is an adaptive component of the algorithm that improves in rigor as the algorithm proceeds. It passes the first 5 runs without trouble, and thereafter checks to see if the current pass has cutset size as good as the same numbered pass in previous runs that were in the lower 20-th percentile of final cutset size. The lower 20-th percentile of N runs is estimated conservatively: take the run with the $Max(4,N/5)$-th smallest final cutset size. The wrapper runs X runs in all. Again, this quality test is a simple, *ad hoc* adaptive scheme we have used as a straw-man for the purposes of testing out the basic concept.

We applied this wrapper to standard FM. This makes the best-of-X algorithm run about 20% faster, and appears to have little detrimental effect on performance. When running best-of-X FM and cutoff b-of-20 FM for the same amount of time, cutset size reductions where 0-15%, for instance on golem mean cutset size went from 2618 down to 2435 when using cutoff runs. We believe there is considerable room for improvement in our implementation. For instance, we could reduce running time further with a smarter adaptive core.

7 A proposed new algorithm: ASFM

We have combined the above two affects—stochastic passes to escape local minima, and cutoff runs to abort potentially poor runs—in the one algorithm we call *ASFM*, where the "AS" stands for "adaptive stochastic". Since the code for these two modifications discussed in Sections 4 and 6 do not interact, to implement this we merely set both sets of switches in our implementation. We explored two variations of this basic implementation, where the stochastic element was allowed to run for a shorter or longer period of time, corresponding in time to roughly 6 or 10-15 times a full FM run. As before, all results are time equalized using the best-of-X wrapper. The results for these experiments are given in Table 3.

The longer stochastic version appeared superior so we chose that as our winning algorithm. This is our final ASFM. As a comparison, we compare our algorithm with Dutt and Deng's PROP in Tables 4 and 5. Table 4 gives the average performance for each algorithm over 10 repeated trials. For the trials reported in Table 4, X for PROP is about 5-7 runs, and X for FM is about 25-40. Because of the differences in implementation, these comparisons should be taken with a grain of salt. The problem where key differences arise between ASFM and PROP is *s38417*, and indicates the clear superiority of the heuristic rules in PROP. However, with some tuning of our stochastic parameters, we were able to get closer to the performance of PROP.

Results in Table 4 are the average of 10 runs. The best results from these runs are given in Table 5, giving the best performance achieved, and the total time taken to achieve that for both ASFM (for ten trials) and best-of-X PROP (which has its real times given), and the value X used for PROP. For instance, for one run of *38584*, ASFM takes approximately 2 minutes, and 30 seconds on *biomed.* When compared with the results of Hauck and Borriello [11] run on a much slower machine, the results in Table 4 are comparable, not the best results in Table 5. This difference between ASFM and the quality of solutions in [11] can be largely attributed to the effects of clustering. The final col-

Dataset	b-of-X FM	b-of-X cutoff b-of-20 short SFM	cutoff b-of-20 long SFM
C1355	17.6± 0.5	17.3± 0.5	17.3± 0.5
C1908	32.7± 1.6	30.9± 1.6	30.3± 2.2
C2670	25.4± 1.2	19.3± 1.7	21.9± 2.9
C3540	63.1± 1.1	60.2± 0.4	61.3± 1.3
C5315	36.8± 6.9	32.2± 3.2	32.3± 3.2
C6288	50.3± 0.7	50.0± 0.0	50.2± 0.6
biomed	135± 5.2	94.2± 4.1	83.0± 0.0
struct	42.0± 1.4	39.6± 1.7	38.8± 0.7
industry2	403± 64.4	293± 10.3	285± 27.9
industry3	262± 19.7	248± 6.7	247± 7.7
avq-small	300± 30.7	244± 25.9	252± 31.0
avq-large	391± 30.5	339± 37.2	304± 33.8
s9234	52.0± 2.3	47.5± 1.4	46.2± 1.9
s13207	87.9± 9.4	82.9± 5.6	78.1± 5.3
s15850	113± 12.8	85.9± 8.0	77.0± 7.9
s35932	117± 10.6	87.6± 13.8	83.5± 19.1
s38417	372± 22.6	310± 33.5	282± 28.7
s38584	136± 8.7	114± 12.9	84.1± 12.0
golem	2403± 119	2123± 137	1834± 247

Table 3: Results for best-of-X FM vs. short and long ASFM

Dataset	b-of-X FM	b-of-X PROP	ASFM
C1355	17.6± 0.5	18.1± 1.0	17.3± 0.5
C1908	32.7± 1.6	30.8± 1.6	30.3± 2.2
C2670	25.4± 1.2	18.1± 0.9	21.9± 2.9
C3540	63.1± 1.1	64.3± 2.5	61.3± 1.3
C5315	36.8± 6.9	30.1± 2.3	32.3± 3.2
C6288	50.3± 0.7	51.0± 2.7	50.2± 0.6
biomed	135± 5.2	88.4± 6.0	83.0± 0.0
struct	42.0± 1.4	37.5± 3.3	38.8± 0.7
industry2	403± 64.4	246± 35.4	285± 27.9
industry3	261± 19.7	292± 33.0	247± 7.7
avq-small	300± 30.7	307± 53.6	252± 31.0
avq-large	391± 30.5	na	304± 33.8
s9234	52.0± 2.3	50.9± 5.5	46.2± 1.9
s13207	87.9± 9.4	88.6± 13.2	78.1± 5.3
s15850	112± 12.8	83.5± 12.0	77.0± 7.9
s35932	117± 10.6	72.2± 3.7	83.5± 19.1
s38417	372± 22.6	97.2± 18.0	282± 28.7
s38584	136± 8.7	70.2± 10.3	84.1± 12.0
golem	2403± 119	1785± 190	1834± 247

Table 4: Results for FM, PROP and ASFM

Dataset	bof-10 ASFM	time in secs.	bof-X PROP	time in secs.	X	best publ.
C1355	17	4.8	17	6.8	73	*
C1908	29	5.05	29	7.25	58	*
C2670	18	10.20	17	14.84	73	*
C3540	60	19.71	61	28.35	47	*
C5315	29	24.5	28	35.3	62	*
C6288	50	55.6	50	81.3	33	*
biomed	83	312.1	84	451.3	51	83
struct	37	49.4	35	70.8	61	33
industry2	240	698.7	199	1007	38	174
industry3	241	811.1	243	1171	50	241
avq-small	204	1229	214	1762	77	129
avq-large	241	1583	na	na	79	127
s9234	42	185.0	45	266	71	40
s13207	71	257.8	73	374	59	57
s15850	66	313.5	54	454	50	44
s35932	61	727.0	73	1052	60	42
s38417	231	995.3	57	1436	51	49
s38584	65	1102	56	1582	56	47
golem	1429	13197	1625	18952	113	*

Table 5: Best results for PROP and ASFM

umn in Table 5 lists the best known result from [11, 6, 13].

8 Discussion

First, we believe the interpretation of full passes we give in Section 4 is a significant insight into FM and KL-style algorithms. For instance, this explains why k-way partitioning with FM and KL-style algorithms does not perform well. For k-way partitioning with k greater than 2, the final state in the pass is not a mirror of the initial state, so as the pass proceeds, the states just drift away from the initial state and a second local move is not created at the end of the pass. The subsequent comparison between our modified stochastic search algorithm and simulated annealing (discussed in Section 5) also indicates there is considerable potential for improved stochastic search algorithms of a very different flavor to standard simulated annealing. Our methods and results throws additional light on the role of stochasticity in search, and alternatives was of introducing it; compare with the empirical investigations by Gent and Walsh on satisfiability [9].

The results of the experiments in Section 7, when compared with results from state-of-the-art algorithms recorded in the literature such as PROP [5] STRAWMAN [11] and PANZA [13] are competitive. Since PROP is itself an iterated algorithm with full passes, and STRAWMAN uses FM as its basis, it is realistic that our approach can also be used to speed up these algorithms even more. We do not advocate the use of our approach to replace sophisticated algorithms such as these others, but rather for fine-tuning of these approaches, or as a rapid prototyping approach for other optimization problems where one cannot afford the research effort required to devise more sophisticated techniques.

Because the stochastic and adaptive approach we use has not undergone much fine tuning, we believe there is considerable room for our ASFM algorithm to improve. For instance, the stochastic pass in SFM could be further explored, and the means of adapting the cutoff in ASFM could be put on a more solid statistical foundation. Local stochastic perturbation (similar to our stochastic pass) has been explored, for instance, in satisfiability [9], and it appears that well-motivated perturbations are superior to random ones. Moreover, our algorithm has an embedded adaptive component that illustrates, albiet in a simple context, the use of learning within constraint satisfaction. Simple adaptive schemes are beginning to see more use in search [7], as authors attempt to fine-tune key algorithm parameters dynamically.

Acknowledgments

Many thanks to John Lillis and Jeremy Frank for their guidance. This work was supported in part by the Semiconductor Research Corporation under Contract 1997-DC324 and by the Digital Equipment Corporation.

References

[1] E.H.L. Aarts and J.K. Lenstra, editors. *Local Search in Combinatorial Optimization*. John Wiley and Sons, 1995.

[2] D. Aldous and U. Vazirani. "Go with the winners" algorithms. In *Proc. 35th Symp. Foundations of Computer Sci.*, pages 492–501, 1994.

[3] C. J. Alpert and A. B. Kahng. Recent developments in netlist partitioning: A survey. *Integration: the VLSI Journal*, 19(1–2):1–81, 1995.

[4] G.L. Bilbro, W.E. Snyder, and R.C. Mann. Mean-field approximation minimizes relative entropy. *Jnl. Opt. Soc. of America A*, 8(2):290–295, 1991.

[5] S. Dutt and W. Deng. A probability-based approach to VLSI circuit partitioning. In *Proc. Design Automation Conference*, 1996.

[6] S. Dutt and W. Deng. VLSI circuit partitioning by cluster-removal using iterative improvement techniques. In *IEEE/ACM Int. Conf. on CAD*, pages 194–200, 1996.

[7] J. Frank. Learning short term weights for GSAT. In *IJCAI-97*, Nagoya, Japan, 1997.

[8] S. Geman and D. Geman. Stochastic relaxation, Gibbs distributions, and the Bayesian relation of images. *IEEE Trans. on PAMI*, 6:721–741, 1984.

[9] I.P. Gent and T. Walsh. Towards an Understanding of Hill-climbing for Procedures for SAT. In *11th Nat. Conf. on AI*, MIT Press, 1935.

[10] F. Glover. Tabu search – part I. *ORSA Journal on Computing*, 1989.

[11] S. Hauck and G. Borriello. An evaluation of bipartitioning techniques. 1996. Submitted.

[12] D.S. Johnson and L.A. McGeoch. The travelling salesman problem: A case study in local optimization. In E.H.L. Aarts and J.K. Lenstra, editors, *Local Search in Combinatorial Optimization*. John Wiley and Sons, 1995.

[13] J. Li, J. Lillis, and C.-K. Cheng. Linear decomposition algorithm for VLSI design applications. In *IEEE Int. Conf. on CAD*, pages 223–228, 1995.

[14] R.M. Neal. Probabilistic inference using Markov chain Monte Carlo methods. TR CRG-TR-93-1, Dept. of Computer Science, University of Toronto, 1993.

[15] S.Y. Reddy, K.W. Fertig, and D.E. Smith. Constraint management methodology for conceptual design tradeoff studies. In *ASME Design Eng. Tech. Conf. and Computers in Eng. Conf.*, Irvine, California, 1996.

[16] P.J.M. van Laarhoven and E.H.L. Aarts. *Simulated Annealing: Theory and Applications*. D. Reidel, Dordrecht, 1987.

Appendix: Compilation and parameter details

Unfortunately our compiler (g++ version 2.7.2) would not optimize Dutt and Deng's code without producing memory errors so we ran their code unoptimized. To be fair, we therefore shrank their times by a factor of 0.7 when making timing comparisons. Our own code is written in C and was optimized with "gcc -O2". PROP was run with the following parameters: algorithm=0 iter=1 ratio=0.45 initProb=0.98 upper=1.75 lower=-1.75 min=0.4, recommended by Dutt.

SESSION 6C

ANALOG MODELING AND TESTING

Moderators:

Wim van Bokhoven, Eindhoven University of Technology,

Eindhoven, The Netherlands

Georges Gielen, Katholieke University Leuven,

Leuven, Belgium

Symbolic Analysis of Large Analog Circuits with Determinant Decision Diagrams*

C.-J. Richard Shi Xiangdong Tan
Department of Electrical and Computer Engineering
University of Iowa, Iowa City, Iowa 52242

Abstract

Symbolic analog-circuit analysis has many applications, and is especially useful for analog synthesis and testability analysis. In this paper, we present a new approach to exact and canonical symbolic analysis by exploiting the **sparsity** *and* **sharing** *of product terms. It consists of representing the symbolic determinant of a circuit matrix by a graph—called determinant decision diagram (DDD)—and performing symbolic analysis by graph manipulations. We showed that DDD construction and DDD-based symbolic analysis can be performed in time complexity proportional to the number of DDD vertices. We described a vertex ordering heuristic, and showed that the number of DDD vertices can be quite small—usually orders-of-magnitude less than the number of product terms. The algorithm has been implemented. An order-of-magnitude improvement in both CPU time and memory usages over existing symbolic analyzers ISAAC and Maple-V has been observed for large analog circuits.*

1. Introduction

Symbolic analysis is to calculate the behavior or the characteristic of a circuit in terms of symbolic parameters. It offers many advantages than numerical simulation in many applications such as optimum topology selection, design space exploration, behavioral model generation, and fault detection [8]. However, symbolic analysis has not been widely used by analog designers, and was once judged as completely inefficient [13]. The root of the difficulty is that: the number of product terms in a symbolic expression may increase exponentially with the size of a circuit. For example, for a BiCMOS amplifier that has about 15 nodes and 25 devices (transistors, diodes, resistors and capacitors), the determinant of the circuit matrix contains more than 10^{11} product terms [19]. Any manipulation and evaluation of symbolic expressions will require CPU time at best linear in the number of terms, and therefore have both the time and space complexities exponential in the size of a circuit.

To cope with large analog circuits, modern symbolic analyzers [6] rely on two techniques—hierarchical decomposition and symbolic simplification—developed in the past decade. Hierarchical decomposition is to generate symbolic expressions in the nested instead of the expanded form [9, 16]. Symbolic simplification is to discard those insignificant terms based on the relative magnitudes of symbolic parameters and the frequency defined at some nominal design points or over some ranges. It can be performed before/during the generation of symbolic terms [3, 10, 15, 21] or after the generation [5, 7, 19]. Exploitation of these techniques has enabled the use of symbolic simulators in several university research projects [2, 6, 7, 20]. However, both techniques have some major deficiencies. Manipulation (other than evaluation) of a nested expression usually requires complicated and time-consuming procedures; e.g., sensitivity calculation in [12] and lazy approximation in [15]. On the other hand, simplified expressions only have a sufficient accuracy at some points or frequency ranges. Even worse, simplification often losses certain information, such as sensitivity with respect to parasitics, which is crucial for circuit optimization and testability analysis.

In this paper, we present a new approach to exact symbolic analysis, which is capable of analyzing analog integrated circuits substantially larger than those previously handled. It is based on the two observations on symbolic analysis of large analog circuits: (a) the circuit matrix is sparse and (b) a symbolic expression often shares many sub-expressions. Under the assumption that all the matrix elements are distinct, each product term involves a subset of all the symbolic parameters. Therefore, we adapt Zero-suppressed Binary Decision Diagrams (ZBDDs)—introduced originally for representing sparse subset systems [14]—to represent a symbolic determinant. This leads to a new

*This work is sponsored by U.S. Defense Advanced Research Projects Agency (DARPA) under grant number F33615-96-1-5601 from USAF, Wright Laboratory, Manufacturing Technology Directorate, and by Rockwell Semiconductor Systems.

1092-3152/97 $10.00 © 1997 IEEE

interpreted graph, called Determinant Decision Diagram (DDD). The DDD representation has several advantages over both the expanded and arbitrarily nested forms of a symbolic expression. First, similar to the nested form, the DDD representation is compact for a large class of analog circuits. A ladder-structured network can be represented by graphs where the number of vertices (called the DDD size) grows linearly in the number of symbolic parameters. Second, similar to the expanded form, our representation is canonical, i.e., every determinant has a unique representation. Finally, evaluation and manipulation of symbolic determinants (such as sensitivity calculation and approximation) have time complexity proportional to the DDD size.

This paper is organized as follows: Section 2 introduces the background and basic notation for the rest of the paper. Section 3 presents the notion of determinant decision diagrams as an application of ZBDD to represent symbolic determinants. Section 4 describes an effective heuristic for ordering DDD vertices so that the resulting DDD has a smallest or near-smallest size. DDD-based algorithms for symbolic analysis and applications are described in Section 5. Experimental results are presented in Section 6. Section 7 concludes the paper.

2. Notations and Problem Statement

In this section, we introduce some basic notations and concepts that will be used in the rest of the paper.

2.1. Subset Systems and Zero-Suppressed Binary Decision Diagrams

Let V be a *set* of elements. The number of elements in V is called the *cardinality* of V, denoted by $|V|$. The set of all *subsets* of V is called the *power set* of V, denoted by 2^V. A subset X of the power set, written as $X \subseteq 2^V$, is called a *subset system* of V.

A subset system X of V can be decomposed with respect to an element v in V into two unique subset systems, X_v and $X_{\overline{v}}$, where X_v is the set of subsets of V belonging to X that contain v, from which v has been removed, and $X_{\overline{v}}$ is the set of subsets of V belonging to X that do not contain v. For instance, let $X = \{\{v_1, v_2\}, \{v_1, v_3, v_5\}, \{v_3, v_4, v_5\}\}$. Then we have $X_{v_1} = \{\{v_2\}, \{v_3, v_5\}\}$, and $X_{\overline{v}_1} = \{\{v_3, v_4, v_5\}\}$. This decomposition can be represented graphically by a decision *vertex*. It is labeled by v_1, and represents the subset system X. As illustrated in Fig. 1(a), the vertex has two outgoing edges: one points to X_{v_1} (called *1-edge*), and the other to $X_{\overline{v}_1}$ (called *0-edge*). We say that the edges are *originated* from the vertex. If X is recursively decomposed with respect to all the elements of V, one obtains a binary decision tree whose leaves are $\{\{\}\}$ and $\{\}$, respectively. For convenience, we denote leaf $\{\{\}\}$ by the 1-terminal, and $\{\}$ by the 0-terminal.

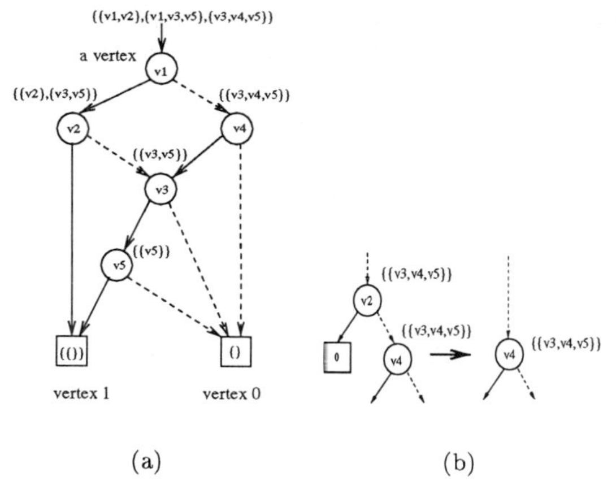

Figure 1: A ZBDD example.

When a subset system X is decomposed with respect to an element that does not appear in X, then its 1-edge points to the 0-terminal. This is illustrated in Fig. 1(b) for decomposing $X = \{\{v_3, v_4, v_5\}\}$ with respect to v_2. To make the diagram compact, Minato suggested the following *zero-suppression* rule for representing sets of *sparse* subsets: eliminate all the vertices whose 1-edges point to the 0-terminal vertex and use the subgraphs of the 0-edges, as shown in Fig. 1(b) [14]. A Zero-suppressed Binary Decision Diagram (ZBDD) is such a zero-suppressed graph with the following two rules due to Bryant [1]: *ordered*—all the elements of V, if one appears, will appear in a fixed order in all the paths of the graph, and *shared*—all equivalent subgraphs are shared. ZBDD is a canonical representation of a subset system, i.e., every subset system has a unique ZBDD representation under a given vertex ordering. For example, Fig. 1(a) is a unique ZBDD representation for the subset system $\{\{v_1, v_2\}, \{v_1, v_3, v_5\}, \{v_3, v_4, v_5\}\}$ with respect to ordering v_1, v_2, v_4, v_3 and v_5. For convenience, every non-terminal vertex is indexed by an integer number greater than those of its descendant vertices [14]. How all the non-terminal vertices are indexed is called *vertex ordering*.

A path from a non-terminal vertex to the 1-terminal is called *1-path*. It defines a subset of V. The subset consists of all the elements of V from which the 1-edges in the 1-path originate. The number of vertices in a ZBDD is called its *size*.

2.2. Matrices, Determinants & Cofactors

Let $e = \{1, ..., n\}$ be a set of integers. Let A denote a set of m elements, called *symbolic parameters* or simply *symbols*, $\{a_1, ..., a_m\}$, where $1 \le m \le n^2$ and each symbol is labeled by a unique pair (r, c), where $r \in e$ and $c \in e$. Often, we write A as an $n \times n$ (square) *matrix*, denoted by $\mathbf{A}$, and use $a_{r,c}$ to denote the element of matrix $\mathbf{A}$ at row r and column c. We sometimes use $r(a)$ and $c(a)$ to denote, respectively, the row and column indices of element a.

$$\mathbf{A} = \begin{pmatrix} a_{1,1} & a_{1,2} & ... & a_{1,n} \\ a_{2,1} & a_{2,2} & ... & a_{2,n} \\ ... & ... & ... & ... \\ a_{n,1} & a_{n,2} & ... & a_{n,n} \end{pmatrix}.$$

If $m = n^2$ the matrix is said to be *full*, otherwise *sparse*. The *determinant* of $\mathbf{A}$, denoted by $det(\mathbf{A})$, is defined by

$$\begin{vmatrix} a_{1,1} & a_{1,2} & ... & a_{1,n} \\ a_{2,1} & a_{2,2} & ... & a_{2,n} \\ ... & ... & ... & ... \\ a_{n,1} & a_{n,2} & ... & a_{n,n} \end{vmatrix} = \sum_{j_1 \neq ... \neq j_n} (-1)^p \cdot a_{1,j_1} ... a_{n,j_n}. \tag{1}$$

Here $(j_1, j_2, ..., j_n)$ is a permutation of e, and p is the number of permutations needed to make the sequence $(j_1, j_2, ..., j_n)$ monotonically increasing. The right hand side of Eq. (1) is a symbolic expression of $det(\mathbf{A})$ in the *expanded* form, more precisely, the *sum-of-product* form, where each *term* is an algebraic product of n symbolic parameters. We note that each symbol can be assigned a real or complex value for analog circuit simulation.

Let p, $p \subseteq e$, and q, $q \subseteq e$ such that $|p| = |q|$. The square matrix obtained from the matrix $\mathbf{A}$ by deleting those rows not in p and columns not in q forms a *submatrix* of $\mathbf{A}$, and is represented by $\mathbf{A}(p, q)$. It has dimension $|p|$ by $|q|$.

Let $a_{r,c}$ be the element of $\mathbf{A}$ at row r and column c. Let $\mathbf{A}_{a_{r,c}}$ be the $(n-1) \times (n-1)$-matrix obtained from the matrix $\mathbf{A}$ by deleting row r and column c, and let $\mathbf{A}_{\overline{a}_{r,c}}$ be the $n \times n$-matrix obtained from $\mathbf{A}$ by setting $a_{r,c} = 0$. Then, the determinant of matrix $\mathbf{A}$ can be *expanded* as below in a way similar to Shannon expansion for Boolean functions:

$$det(\mathbf{A}) = a_{r,c}(-1)^{r+c} det(\mathbf{A}_{a_{r,c}}) + det(\mathbf{A}_{\overline{a}_{r,c}}), \tag{2}$$

where $(-1)^{r+c} det(\mathbf{A}_{a_{r,c}})$ is referred to as the *cofactor* of $det(\mathbf{A})$ with respect to $a_{r,c}$, and $det(\mathbf{A}_{\overline{a}_{r,c}})$ as the *reminder* of $det(\mathbf{A})$ with respect to $a_{r,c}$. The determinant $det(\mathbf{A}_{a_{r,c}})$ is called the *minor* of $det(\mathbf{A})$ with respect to $a_{r,c}$.

2.3. Symbolic Analysis Problem

Consider a linear(ized) time-invariant analog circuit. Its system equation can be formulated by, for example, the modified nodal analysis (MNA) approach in the following general form [17]:

$$\mathbf{Tx} = \mathbf{w}. \tag{3}$$

The *circuit unknown vector* $\mathbf{x}$ may be composed of node voltages and branch currents, and the *circuit matrix* $\mathbf{T}$ is usually large and sparse.

Symbolic analysis of analog circuits can be stated as the problem of solving the symbolic equation (3), i.e., to find a symbolic expression of any circuit unknown in terms of symbolic parameters in $\mathbf{T}$ and symbolic excitations expressed by $\mathbf{w}$. According to Cramer's rule, the kth component x_k of the unknown vector $\mathbf{x}$ is obtained as follows:

$$x_k = \frac{\sum_{i=1}^{n} w_i \, (-1)^{i+k} \, det(\mathbf{T}_{t_{i,k}})}{det(\mathbf{T})}. \tag{4}$$

Most symbolic simulators are targeted at finding various network functions, each being defined as the ratio of an output unknown from $\mathbf{x}$ to an input from $\mathbf{w}$. These are special cases of (4) or the ratios of the two expressions in the form of (4).

Note that $(-1)^{i+k} det(\mathbf{T}_{t_{i,k}})$ in (4) is the cofactor of $det(\mathbf{T})$ with respect to element $t_{i,k}$ of matrix $\mathbf{T}$ at row i and column k. Therefore, the core issue in analog symbolic analysis is how to find symbolic expressions of $det(\mathbf{T})$ and the cofactors of $det(\mathbf{T})$. In the rest of the paper, we focus on how to represent a symbolic determinant (Sections 3 and 4), and how to compute, manipulate, and evaluate a symbolic determinant (Section 5). For the simplicity, we assume that all the entries in $\mathbf{T}$ are distinct. This assumption has been used in previous symbolic analysis approaches; methods have been proposed to formulate the symbolic equations to meet (or closely meet) this assumption [7, 17].

3. Representation of Symbolic Matrix Determinants

In this section, we apply the notation of zero-suppressed binary decision diagram (ZBDD) to represent a symbolic matrix determinant. A key observation is that the circuit matrix is sparse, and many times, a symbolic expression may share many sub-expressions. For example, consider the following determinant

$$det(\mathbf{M}) = \begin{vmatrix} a & b & 0 & 0 \\ c & d & e & 0 \\ 0 & f & g & h \\ 0 & 0 & i & j \end{vmatrix} = adgj - adhi - aefj - bcgj + bchi$$

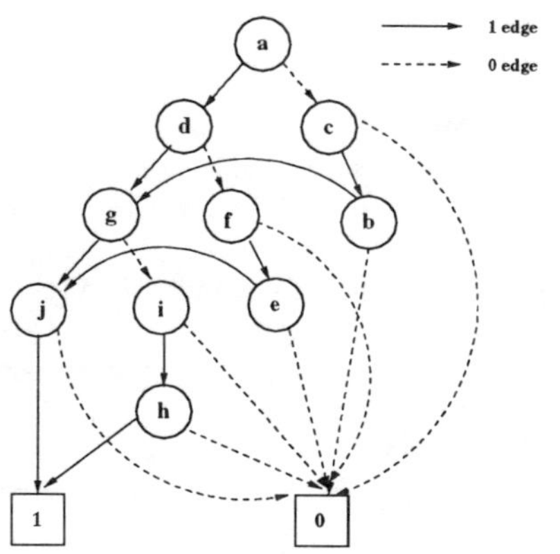

Figure 2: A ZBDD representing $\{adgi, adhi, afej, cbgj, cbhi\}$.

We note that subterms ad, gj, and hi appear in several product terms, and each product term involves a subset (four) out of ten symbolic parameters. Therefore, we view each symbolic product term as a subset, and use a ZBDD to represent the subset system composed of all the subsets each corresponding to a product term. Figure 2 illustrates the corresponding ZBDD representing all the subsets involved in $det(\mathbf{M})$ under ordering $a > c > b > d > f > e > g > i > h > j$. It can be seen that subterms ad, gj, and ih have been shared in the ZBDD representation.

We can view the resulting ZBDD as a graphical representation of recursive application of determinant expansion formula (2) in Section 2.2 with the expansion order $a, c, b, d, f, e, g, i, h, j$. Each vertex is labeled with the matrix entry with respect to which the determinant is expanded, and it represents all the subsets contained in the corresponding submatrix determinant. The 1-edge points to the vertex representing all the subsets contained in the cofactor of the current expansion, and 0-edge points to the vertex representing all the subsets contained in the reminder.

To embed the signs of the product terms of a symbolic determinant into its corresponding ZBDD, we consider one step of matrix expansion with respect to $a_{r,c}$ as defined by (2). The sign is $(-1)^{r+c}$. Note that r and c are, respectively, the row and column indices of the element $a_{r,c}$ in the submatrix, say $\mathbf{A}'$, before this step of expansion. Let the *absolute* row and column indices of the element $a_{r,c}$ in the original matrix $\mathbf{A}$ before any expansion be $r(a_{r,c})$ and $c(a_{r,c})$, respectively. Then, we observe that $r+c$ is equal to the number of rows in $\mathbf{A}'$ with absolute indices less than $r(a_{r,c})$ plus the number of columns in $\mathbf{A}'$ with absolute indices less than $c(a_{r,c})$. We also note that all the rows and columns in $\mathbf{A}'$ except that of $a_{r,c}$ are represented in the subgraph rooted at the vertex pointed to by the 1-edge of vertex $a_{r,c}$ Therefore, the sign of a non-terminal vertex v, denoted by $s(v)$, can be defined recursively as follows:

1. Let $P(v)$ be the set of ZBDD vertices that originate the 1-edges in any 1-path rooted at v. Then
$$s(v) = \prod_{x \in P(v)} sign(r(x) - r(v))\ sign(c(x) - c(v)), \tag{5}$$
where $r(x)$ and $c(x)$ refer to the absolute row and column indices of vertex x in the original matrix, and u is an integer so that
$$sign(u) = \begin{cases} 1 & \text{if } u > 0, \\ -1 & \text{if } u < 0. \end{cases}$$
2. If v has an edge pointing to the 1-terminal vertex, then $s(v) = +1$.

This is called the *sign rule*. For example, in Fig. 3, vertices c, f, and i are assigned a negative sign $(-)$ by using the sign rule.

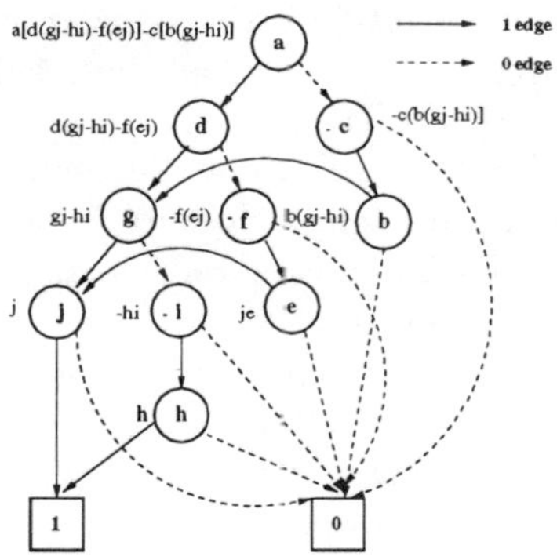

Figure 3: A determinant decision diagram for $\mathbf{M}$.

It can be verified that all 1-paths originating from the same vertex yield the same sign, and the product of all the signs in a path is exactly the sign of the corresponding product term. For example, consider the 1-path $acbgih$ in Fig. 3. The vertices that originate all the 1-edges are c, b, i, h, their corresponding signs are $-$, $+$, $-$ and $+$, respectively. Their product is $+$. This is the sign of the symbolic product term $cbih$.

Formally, let $\mathbf{A}$ be an $n \times n$ sparse matrix with a set of distinct m symbolic parameters $\{a_1, ..., a_m\}$, where $1 \leq m \leq n^2$. Each symbolic parameter a_i is associated with a unique pair $r(a_i)$ and $c(a_i)$, which denote, respectively, the row index and column index of a_i. A *determinant decision diagram* is a signed rooted directed acyclic graph with two terminal vertices, namely the 0-terminal vertex and the 1-terminal vertex. Each non-terminal vertex a_i is associated with a sign, $s(a_i)$, determined by the sign rule defined by (5). It has two outgoing edges, called 1-edge and 0-edge, pointing respectively to D_{a_i} and $D_{\overline{a}_i}$. A determinant decision graph having root vertex a_i denotes a matrix determinant D defined recursively as

1. If a_i is the 1-terminal vertex, then $D = 1$.
2. If a_i is the 0-terminal vertex, then $D = 0$.
3. If a_i is a non-terminal vertex, then $D = a_i\ s(a_i)\ D_{a_i} + D_{\overline{a}_i}$.

Here $s(a_i)D_{a_i}$ is the *cofactor* of D with respect to a_i, D_{a_i} is the *minor* of D with respect to a_i, $D_{\overline{a}_i}$ is the *reminder* of D with respect to a_i, and operations are algebraic multiplications and additions.

4. Vertex Ordering

A key problem in many decision diagram applications is how to select a vertex ordering, since the size of the resulting decision diagram strongly depends on the chosen ordering. In this section, we describe an efficient heuristic for selecting a good vertex ordering.

Suppose that $\mathbf{A}$ is an $n \times n$ matrix with m non-zero elements (entries, or symbols). The vertex ordering problem is how to *label* all the nonzero elements in $\mathbf{A}$ using integers 1 to m so that the resulting DDD constructed with the chosen order has a small size. As stated in Section 2.1, those elements labeled by smaller integers will appear close to the leaves, or the bottom, of the DDD, and the root is labeled by m.

We propose a vertex ordering heuristic, based on the refinement of a well-known strategy for Laplace expansion of a sparse matrix [7]. The basic idea is to label those columns or rows with fewer nonzero elements with larger indices. Elements in those dense rows and columns will be labeled using small indices. Intuitively, this strategy increases the possibility of DDD subgraph sharing. Figure 4 describes the proposed heuristic MATRIX_LABELING($\mathbf{A}(p,q)$) for labeling all the elements in $\mathbf{A}(p,q)$. In the algorithm, $\mathbf{A}(p-\{i\}, q-\{j\})$ denotes the matrix obtained from $\mathbf{A}(p,q)$ by removing row i and column j. We keep a global counter k. Initially k is set to 1, and $p = q = e$.

We have shown that the heuristic is optimal for a class of circuit matrices, called *band matrices.* Band matrices are matrices that have only non-zero elements at positions (i,i), $(i-1,i)$ and $(i+1,i)$. The MNA matrices for ladder networks—an important class of structures in analog design—are band matrices. For an n-by-n band matrix, the number of DDD vertices is equal to the number of non-zero elements in the matrix, that is $3n-2$, whereas the number of expanded product terms is $F(n+1)$, an $(i+1)$-th Fibonacci number. Each product term involves n symbols. To store all the product terms without considering sharing, the memory requirement is proportional to $nF(n+1)$. In Fig. 5, the number of DDD vertices is plotted against the number of product terms. Note that any symbolic manipulation using the expended form would have time complexity at best proportional to $nF(n+1)$.

```
MATRIX_LABELING(A(p,q))
select column j (row i) that has least non-zeros
s ← all the rows i (columns j) so that a_{i,j} ≠ 0
for all row i (column j) in s from the one
      with least non-zeros
   if exist unlabeled elements in A(p − {i}, q − {j})
      MATRIX_LABELING(A(p − {i}, q − {j}))
for all row i (column j) in s from the one
      with most non-zeros
   if a_{i,j} has not been labeled
      label a_{i,j} by k and then increment k
```

Figure 4: A DDD vertex ordering heuristic.

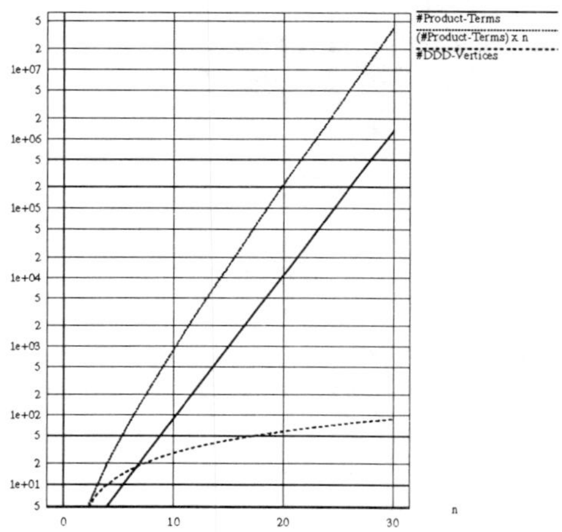

Figure 5: Band-matrix DDD sizes vs numbers of terms.

5. Construction and Manipulation of Determinant Decision Diagrams

In this section, we show that, using determinant decision diagrams, algorithms needed for symbolic analysis and its applications can be performed with the time complexity proportional to the size of the diagrams being manipulated, *not the number of 1-paths in the diagrams, i.e., product terms in the symbolic expressions.* Hence, as long as the determinants of interest can be represented by reasonably small graphs, our algorithms are quite efficient.

Table 1: Summary of Basic Operations.

Operation	Result
VERTEXONE()	return 1
VERTEXZERO()	return 0
COFACTOR(D,s)	return the cofactor of D wrt s
REMINDER(D,s)	return the reminder of D wrt s
MULTIPLY(D,s)	return $s \times D$
DDD_OF_MATRIX(**A**)	construct DDD for matrix **A**
EVALUATE(D)	return the value of D

```
COFACTOR(D, s)
if (D.top < s) return 0
if (D.top = s) return D1
if (D.top > s) return GETVERTEX(D.top,
        COFACTOR(D1, s), COFACTOR(D0, s))
```

```
REMINDER(D, s)
if (D.top < s) return D
if (D.top = s) return D0
if (D.top > s) return GETVERTEX(D.top,
        REMINDER(D1, s), REMINDER(D0, s))
```

```
MULTIPLY(D, s)
if (D.top < s) return GETVERTEX(s, D, 0)
if (D.top = s) return GETVERTEX(s, D1, D0)
if (D.top > s) return GETVERTEX(D.top,
        MULTIPLY(D1, s), MULTIPLY(D0, s))
```

```
DDD_OF_MATRIX(A(p, q))
1  if (A = 0) return VertexZero()
2  if (A = 1) return VertexOne()
3  let s be a non-zero element at row i and column j
4      return GETVERTEX(s,
           DDD_OF_MATRIX(A(p − {i}, q − {j})),
           DDD_OF_MATRIX(A|s=0))
```

```
EVALUATE(D)
if (D = 0) return 0
if (D = 1) return 1
return EVALUATE(D0) +
       s(D) * D.top * EVALUATE(D1)
```

A basic set of operations on matrix determinants and their implementations are summarized in Table 1. Most operations are simple extensions of subset operations introduced by Minato on ZBDDs [14]. For the clarity of the description, the steps for computing the signs associated with DDD vertices, using the sign rule defined in Section 3, are not shown. In the implementation, GETVERTEX($D.top$, D_1, D_0) is to generate (or copy) a vertex for a symbol $D.top$ and two subgraphs D_1 and D_0. A hash table is used to keep each vertex unique, and vertex elimination and sharing are managed mainly by GETVERTEX. A cache is used to memorize the results of recent operations, and it is referred to by every recursive call. This avoids duplicate executions for equivalent subgraphs.

Evaluation: Given a determinant decision diagram pointed to by D and a set of numerical values for all the symbolic parameters, EVALUATE(D) computes the numerical value of the corresponding matrix determinant. EVALUATE(D) naturally exploits subexpression sharing in a symbolic expression, and has time complexity *linear* in the size of the diagram.

Construction: Let $\mathbf{A}(e, e)$ be an n-by-n symbolic matrix, where e is a set of integers from 1 to n. DDD_OF_MATRIX($\mathbf{A}(p, q)$) constructs a determinant decision diagram of a submatrix of $\mathbf{A}$ with row set $p \subseteq e$ and column set $q \subseteq e$ such that $|p| = |q|$ for a given ordering of symbolic parameters. It can be viewed as a generalized Laplace expansion procedure of matrix determinants. In line 3 of the procedure DDD_OF_MATRIX, a non-zero element s is picked up, and the matrix is expanded. Due to the canonical property of DDD, s can be any non-zero matrix element, and the resulting DDD is always the same. However, the most efficient construction is to use the element with the largest integer label in line 3.

Cofactor and Sensitivity: COFACTOR(D, s) is to compute the cofactor of a symbolic determinant D represented by a DDD with respect to symbolic parameter s. It is perhaps the most important operation in symbolic analysis of analog circuits. For example, the sensitivity of D with respect to s is exactly its cofactor with respect to s. The network functions can be obtained by first computing some cofactors, and then combining these cofactors using Cramer's rule.

6. Experimental Results

We have tested the proposed algorithms on a set of circuits varying from RLC filters to bipolar and MOS integrated circuits, which includes

- *filter*, a cascade bandpass active filter [8],
- *miller*, a two-stage miller compensated MOS opamp [7],
- $\mu A741$, a bipolar opamp containing 26 transistors and 11 resistors, with the schematic in Fig. 6,
- *cascode*, a CMOS cascode opamp containing 22 transistors with the schematic in Fig. 7,
- *ladder7, ladder10, ladder21*, 7, 10 and 21 section cascade resistive ladder networks,
- some RLC filters, named *butter*, *rlctest*, *vcstest*, *ccstest* and *big*.

For nonlinear integrated circuits, DC analyses are performed using SPICE, and the resulting small signal models are used for symbolic analysis.

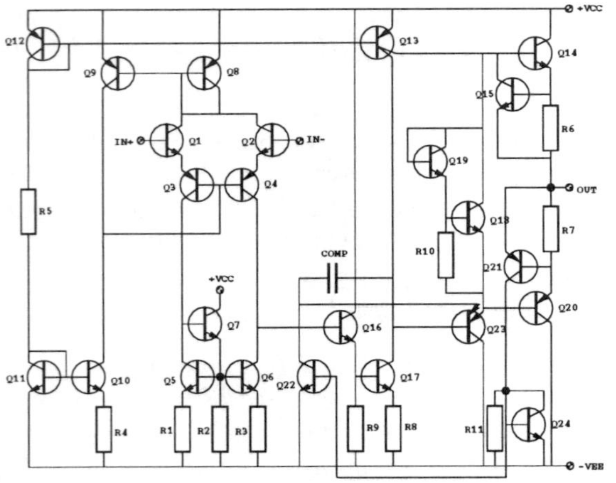

Figure 6: Circuit schematic of bipolar $\mu A741$.

Table 2 describes the statistics of all the test circuits and the resulting DDD sizes. Columns 2 to 6 describe respectively the number of nodes in each circuit, the number of non-zero elements in each circuit matrix, the number of product terms in each symbolic determinant, and the number of vertices in the resulting DDD representation without and with the use of the ordering heuristic described in Fig. 4. For each circuit, the number of DDD vertices without ordering is the average of that of ten randomly generated orderings.

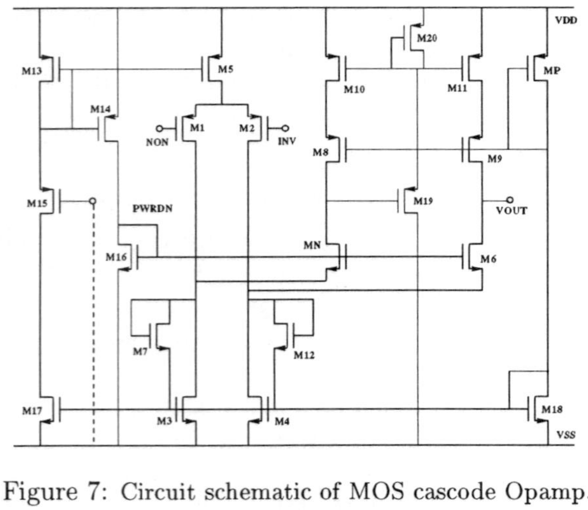

Figure 7: Circuit schematic of MOS cascode Opamp.

From Table 2, we can make several observations:

1. Ordering leads to DDDs significantly smaller than that of non-ordering. For ladder networks *ladder7*, *ladder10*, *ladder21*, the numbers of DDD vertices are exactly the numbers of non-zero matrix elements.

Table 2: DDD sizes with/without vertex ordering.

ckt name	#nod	#ele	#term	#vertex (no-order)	#vertex (order)
miller	7	23	37	109	55
butter	8	19	21	102	19
ladder7	9	22	34	135	22
rlctest	10	37	352	877	130
ccstest	10	35	260	746	109
ladder10	11	31	144	637	31
vcstest	11	37	402	1024	104
cascode	15	77	232363	372579	2110
filter	20	46	82	939	52
ladder21	23	64	28657	92783	64
$\mu A741$	24	89	374884	-*	7431
big	33	101	7.31×10^6	-	905

-*: out of memory.

2. For a small circuit, the number of DDD vertices may be greater than the number of product terms. This is not surprising, since the number of DDD vertices without exploiting sharing would be the number of product terms times the number of symbolic parameters in each product term.
3. For a large circuit, the number of DDD vertices can be several orders of magnitude smaller than the number of product terms.
4. Further, the difference becomes more dramatic with the increase of the circuit size.

We compare our program with *ISAAC* [7] and *Maple-V* [4]. *ISAAC* is a well-known special-purpose symbolic analyzer designed for analog integrated circuits. *Maple-V* is a general-purpose mathematic package capable of solving linear equations symbolically. To use *Maple-V*, we use our program to set up the circuit equations and then feed the circuit matrices to *Maple*. All data are obtained using a SUNsparc 20 with 32M memory. The results are described in Table 3. We can observe that our program runs significantly faster than both *ISAAC* and *Maple-V*, and uses much less memory. For slightly large circuits, both *ISAAC* and *Maple-V* ran out of memory.

Table 3: The DDD algorithm vs ISAAC and Maple-V.

ckt	ISAAC		Maple-V		DDD	
	CPU(s)	Mem	CPU(s)	Mem	CPU(s)	Mem
butter	0.61	493k	0.03	10.9k	0.033	8.1K
ladder7	1.05	980k	0.63	250k	0.033	8.1k
miller	0.49	640k	0.6	250k	0.066	24.5k
rlctest	–*	–	17.3	15.2M	0.10	49.1k
vcstest	–	–	99.9	20.1M	0.10	73.1k
ladder21	–	–	–	–	0.066	32.7k
cascode	–	–	–	–	7.62	4.9M
$\mu A741$	–	–	–	–	9.13	5.2M
big	–	–	–	–	4.01	2.8M

–*: out of memory.

To verify the correctness of our symbolic analysis algorithms, we have implemented a frequency-domain circuit simulator based on DDD evaluation. For all the test circuits, our simulator produced the exactly same results as SPICE did.

7. Conclusions

In this paper, a graph representation, called determinant decision diagrams (DDDs), for symbolic matrix determinants is proposed and symbolic analysis algorithms for analog circuits are presented. Unlike previous approaches based on either the expanded form or the nested form representations of symbolic expressions, DDD-based symbolic analysis exploits the sparsity and sharing in a canonical manner. With an efficient vertex ordering heuristic, we showed that the number of vertices in a DDD is quite small—usually several orders of magnitude smaller than the number of product terms in the expanded form. This enables the exact analysis of such large analog circuits as $\mu A741$ for the first time. In contrast to the nested form, our representation is unique. Symbolic analysis algorithms such as determinant evaluation, driving cofactor computation, network function construction, and sensitivity calculation can be performed in time complexity proportional to the number of DDD vertices.

References

[1] R. E. Bryant, "Graph-based algorithms for Boolean function manipulation", *IEEE Trans. Computer*, pp. 677–691, 1986.

[2] R. Carmassi, M. Catelani, G. Iuculano, A. Liberatore, S. Manetti, and Marini, "Analog network testability measurement: a symbolic formulation approach", *IEEE Trans. Instrumentation and Measurement*, vol. 40, pp. 930–935, Dec. 1991.

[3] S.-M. Chang, J.-F. MacKey, and G. M. Wierzba, "Matrix reduction and numerical approximation during computation techniques for symbolic analog circuit analysis", pp. 1153–1156 in *Proc. IEEE Int. Symp. Circuits and Systems*, 1992.

[4] B. W. Char, *et. al.*, *Maple V: Language Reference Manual*, Springer-Verlag, 1991.

[5] F. V. Fernández, J.D. Martín, A. Rodríguez-Vázquez and J. L. Huertas, "On simplification techniques for symbolic analysis of analog integrated circuits", pp. 1149–1152 in *Proc. IEEE Int. Symp. Circuits and Systems*, 1992.

[6] F. V. Fernández and A. Rodríguez-Vázquez, "Symbolic analysis tools—the state of the art", pp. 798–801 in *Proc. IEEE Int. Symposium on Circuits and System*, 1996.

[7] G. Gielen and W. Sansen, *Symbolic Analysis for Automated Design of Analog Integrated Circuits*, Kluwer Academic Publishers, 1991.

[8] G. Gielen, P. Wambacq and W. Sansen, "Symbolic analysis methods and applications for analog circuits: A tutorial overview", *Proc. IEEE*, vol. 82, no. 2, pp. 287–304, Feb. 1994.

[9] M. M. Hassoun and P. M. Lin, "A hierarchical network approach to symbolic analysis of large scale networks", *IEEE Trans. Circuits and Systems*, vol. 42, no. 4, pp. 201–211, April 1995.

[10] Jer-Jaw Hsu and Carl Sechen, "DC small signal symbolic analysis of large analog integrated circuits", *IEEE Trans. Circuits and Systems*, vol. 41, no. 12, pp. 817–828, Dec. 1994.

[11] P. M. Lin, *Symbolic Network Analysis*, Elsevier Science Publishers B.V., 1991.

[12] P. M. Lin, "Sensitivity analysis of large linear networks using symbolic program", pp. 1145–1148 in *Proc. IEEE Int. Symp. Circuits and Systems*, 1992.

[13] W. J. McCalla and D. O. Pederson, "Elements of computer-aided analysis", *IEEE Trans. Circuit Theory*, vol. 18, pp. 14–26, 1971.

[14] S. Minato, "Zero-suppressed BDDs for set manipulation in combinatorial problems", pp. 272–277 in *Proc. 30th IEEE/ACM Design Automation Conference*, Dallas, TX, June 1993.

[15] S. J. Seda, M. G. R. Degrauwe and W. Fichtner, "Lazy-expansion symbolic expression approximation in SYNAP", pp. 310–317 in *Proc. IEEE Int. Conf. Computer Aided Design (ICCAD)*, 1992.

[16] J. A. Starzky and A. Konczykowska, "Flowgraph analysis of large electronic networks", *IEEE Trans. Circuits and Systems*, vol. 33, no. 3, pp. 302–315, March 1986.

[17] J. Vlach and K. Singhal, *Computer Methods for Circuit Analysis and Design*, Van Nostrand Reinhold, New York, 1994.

[18] P. Wambacq, G. Gielen and W. Sansen, "A cancellation-free algorithm for the symbolic simulation of large analog circuits", pp. 1157–1160 in *Proc. IEEE Int. Symp. Circuits and Systems*, 1992.

[19] P. Wambacq, G. Gielen and W. Sansen, "A new reliable approximation method for expanded symbolic network functions", pp. 584–587 in *Proc. IEEE Int. Symp. Circuits and Systems*, 1996.

[20] Z. You, E. Sánchez-Sinencio, and J. P. de Gyvez, "Analog system-level fault diagnosis based on a symbolic method in the frequency domain", *IEEE Trans. Instrumentation and Measurement*, vol. 44, no. 1, pp. 28–35, Jan. 1995.

[21] Q. Yu and C. Sechen, "A unified approach to the approximate symbolic analysis of large analog integrated circuits", *IEEE Trans. Circuits and Systems*, vol. 43, no. 8, pp. 656–669, August 1996.

A Behavioral Signal Path Modeling Methodology for Qualitative Insight in and Efficient Sizing of CMOS Opamps

Francky Leyn, Walter Daems*, Georges Gielen*, Willy Sansen
Katholieke Universiteit Leuven, Belgium

Abstract

This paper describes a new modeling methodology that allows to derive systematically behavioral signal path models of operational amplifiers. Combined with symbolic simulation, these models provide high qualitative insight in the small-signal functioning of a circuit. The behavioral signal path model provides compact interpretable expressions for the poles and zeros that constitute the signal path. These expressions show which design parameters have dominant influence on the position of a pole/zero and thus enable a designer to control a manual interactive sizing process. The methodology consists of the application of a sequence of abstractions, so that one gradually progresses from a full device to a full behavior circuit representation. During this translation, qualitative insight and design requirements are obtained. The methodology is implemented in an open tool called EF2ef. *The behavioral signal path model is also used for optimization based sizing in order to achieve pole placement in an efficient way. For optimization based sizing, a new strategy for hierarchical penalty function composition is proposed, which allows sequential pruning of the design space. Combined with an operating point driven DC formulation and local minimax optimization, a fast sizing method is obtained which can be used for interactive design space exploration. Experimental results of both modeling and sizing are shown.*

I. Introduction

Modeling an analog circuit is an important step in analog circuit design. Modeling provides insight in the operation of the circuit. This insight can be used to size or synthesize a new circuit and is a prerequisite in order to design successfully, be it manually, be it with an optimizer.

Modeling a circuit in many cases is time consuming. Therefore, reuse of the circuit knowledge is interesting. In order to be reusable, the knowledge must be formalized. Formalization of knowledge in a certain language not only documents the derived model, but also allows one to use the model in a sizing environment. After formalization the model can be interchanged between different designers. This is useful for redesigns and technology migrations.

Different small-signal modeling methodologies exist. The methodologies can be distinguished depending on their accuracy, generation of qualitative insight and time to deduce the model. Traditional techniques like modified nodal analysis (*MNA*) [1] model a circuit exactly but generate no physical insight. Symbolic simulation [2] gives an approximate transfer function and provides additional qualitative insight. In this paper a *behavioral signal path modeling* methodology for analog integrated circuits is presented with as strongest point the generation of qualitative insight.

We are looking for an automated sizing method which is fast enough to allow *interactive design space exploration*. This way the designer is able to explore the different trade-offs present in the design space. In order to achieve this, we need a computationally efficient sizing method. This is achieved using an operating point driven DC formulation, a behavioral signal path model which is also used for pole placement, *sequential design space pruning* and local minimax optimization.

In section 2 the merits of behavioral signal path modeling are discussed. In section 3 the modeling methodology is described. In section 4 the modeling tool EF2ef is presented. In section 5 the use of the behavioral signal path models for optimization based sizing is shown. In section 6 some examples are shown and conclusions are given in section 7.

II. Behavioral signal path modeling

Modified nodal analysis and symbolic simulation both look at the total transfer function of the complete circuit. The different effects that constitute the small-signal behavior are combined together in the total transfer function. From a certain circuit size on, this makes it hard to isolate the different contributions individually. In order to gain real qualitative insight [3] into a circuit and also to perform an efficient sizing (e.g. through pole placement), the different effects should be available separately. One has to work *locally* instead of globally, much like expert designers do. Therefore, knowledge of the location of poles and zeros that constitute the transfer function is the key to good design.

A behavioral signal path model, as depicted in Fig. 1, shows the signal flow with its different poles and zeros. This is a powerful representation for multiple reasons. It shows all the different conversions from current to voltage and vice versa. It shows

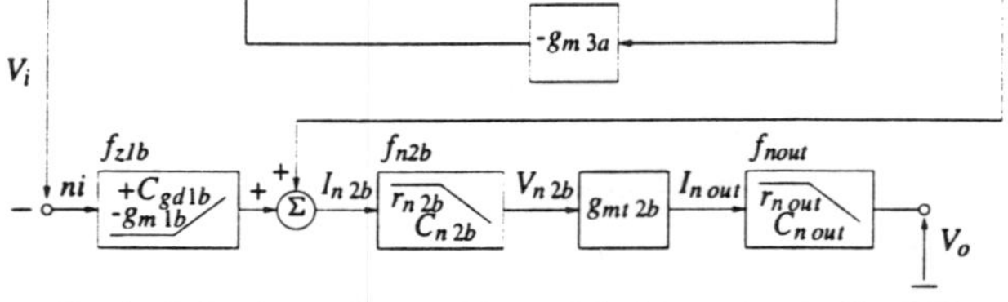

Fig. 1. Behavioral signal path model of a current buffer OTA.

* Walter Daems and Georges Gielen are respectively research assistant and research associate of the Belgian Fund of Scientific Research

1092-3152/97 $10.00 © 1997 IEEE

the different encountered poles/zeros that cause a de-/increase in transfer along the signal path. A behavioral signal path model provides qualitative insight: regardless of the actual numerical values, the effect on the total transfer function of a shift of a pole or zero can be predicted. The different poles are a function of the small-signal parameters of the different devices and are modeled with compact symbolic equations, which makes them interpretable. The equations can be used for pole placement in both a manual interactive and optimization based sizing scheme. Pole placement is used in order to achieve first order behavior for frequencies up to the gain-bandwidth of the circuit.

In a manual interactive sizing scheme with SPICE or a constraint based sizing scheme with DONALD [4], one has to determine which design parameters must be changed in order to fulfill certain design requirements or specifications. Because the explicit equations of the poles and zeros of the behavioral signal path model are compact, they are fully comprehensible. This enables the designer to control the sizing process. Because he knows which parameters have dominant influence on the position of a pole, he can push the design in a certain direction by placing a pole or zero. The dominant impact of the different design parameters on the various performance parameters is known.

In the case of optimization based sizing, these models allow pole placement by adding penalty terms to the goal function if the poles and zeros occur before the *GBW* of the amplifier. They can be used by equation compilers like DONALD [4] or ASTRX [5]. Since the expressions are compact and explicit, they are more efficient than numerical techniques like *AWE* [6] which typically has a CPU cost of one DC analysis [7] or the QZ-algorithm [8], which is only applicable for circuits of moderate size [9].

Behavioral signal path models allow the derivation of design requirements. If a circuit contains feedback loops (like in Fig. 1), stability requirements must be fulfilled in order to obtain a stable circuit. Unlike other modeling methodologies, behavioral signal path modeling allows one to derive expressions for these design requirements.

III. Incremental modeling methodology

Analog circuit modeling evolves around three orthogonal axes. Modeling thus involves three independent choices:

- circuit representation (device - behavior)
- solution method (*MNA*/symbolic simulation with possible hierarchical extensions)
- formalization language ↔ target engine (SPICE, VHDL-AMS, DONALD, ASTRX)

Incremental modeling is a methodology that allows one to gradually move on the circuit representation axis from a full device to a full behavior representation. The basic step in incremental modeling is an *abstraction*. An abstraction is a transformation of the circuit, mostly topological, which allows one to simplify the circuit. During such a step, one makes abstraction of certain circuit functionality. An abstraction chain is depicted in Fig. 2. One starts with the reference topology T_R composed out of its devices. If one understands the function of certain parts of it, one makes an abstraction or transformation τ for those parts. The circuit representation becomes mixed device-

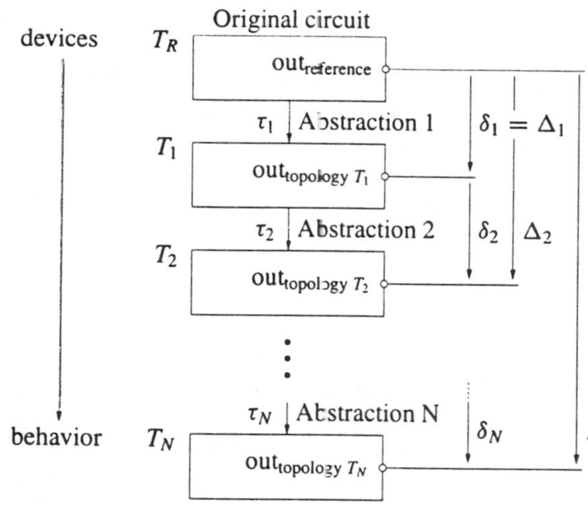

Fig. 2. Incremental modeling as a chain of abstractions.

behavior. While making subsequent abstractions τ_i, one gradually progresses from devices to behavior. If one fully understands the circuit, one is thus able to replace the complete circuit by a behavioral equivalent T_N:

$$T_N = (\tau_N \circ \ldots \circ \tau_2 \circ \tau_1) T_R = \left(\mathop{\circ}_{j=1}^{N} \tau_j \right) T_R$$

We are interested in a small-signal variable S like the magnitude or phase of the transfer along the signal path. This variable $S(T, Q, f)$ is function of the topology T, the operating point Q and frequency f. Each abstraction provides additional qualitative insight. The price paid for this is loss of accuracy. Two error measures can be considered. The *incremental error* δ_i gives the error introduced by the considered abstraction τ_i. It is the error between topology T_i and the previous topology T_{i-1}:

$$\delta_i S(Q, f) = S(T_i, Q, f) - S(T_{i-1}, Q, f)$$

The *total error* Δ_i is the error between topology T_i and the original reference circuit T_R. It is the error introduced by all previous abstractions together; the accumulation of the incremental errors:

$$\Delta_i S(Q, f) = S(T_i, Q, f) - S(T_R, Q, f)$$

These errors are determined over a considered frequency range $[f_l, f_u]$ and for a certain (set of) operating point(s) $V_Q = \{Q_j | j\}$. Good models have a small deviation in multiple operating points. Good models are *global models* that track the operating point. For optimization based sizing one needs global models since the optimizer will propose operating points spread over the complete design space. Behavioral signal path modeling generates such models, since each significant effect in the signal path is modeled. The goal of behavioral signal path modeling is thus to gain as much qualitative understanding without losing too much accuracy.

Some examples of abstractions:

- Replace a floating admittance by its Y-parameter equivalent as depicted in Fig. 3. Although the number of components increases, the state-space representation remains unchanged. Each component of the Y-parameter equivalent corresponds to a single entry of the *MNA*-stamp because they are connected to ground, which is the *MNA* datum node. This abstraction is powerfull because it allows one to isolate the effects between different nodes by explicit components. This way, it is always possible to obtain a signal flow diagram of a circuit. In many cases, the admittances of the Y-parameter equivalent can be lumped together with other circuit elements.

- Replace a floating transconductance by components that represent the entries of the *MNA*-stamp.
- Remove components of a Y-parameter equivalent. This is equivalent to removing *MNA* entries in the state-space representation. The Sherman-Morrison criterion allows efficient reduction of the state-space matrix [10].
- Replace parts of a signal path by a behavioral pole/zero equivalent. For poles this is mostly a topology where a RC-tank is isolated between a node and ground and where a transconductance pumps current onto that node. For zeros this is mostly the lumping of a transconductance g_m and a transcapacitance c_m. The two forms are depicted in Fig. 4. The expressions for the corner frequency of these building blocks are compact and highlight the dominant impact of certain design parameters.
- Replace a coupling capacitor C by its Y-parameter equivalent. The floating admittance $Y = sC$ is replaced by two grounded capacitances C and two grounded transcapacitances $c_m = C$. The transcapacitances mostly occur in parallel with a transconductance which allows one to replace them by a behavioral zero stage.
- Replace a generic one-stage amplifier as depicted in Fig. 5 by a behavioral second-order system and a positive zero. By replacing the coupling capacitor C_c by its Y-parameter equivalent and replacing the RC-tanks and transconductance-transcapacitance pair by their behavioral equivalent, the behavioral signal path model depicted in Fig. 5 is obtained. In the case of Miller compensation, coupling between in- and output is required. A transfer as depicted in Fig. 5, where the inverse of the feedback $|1/H|$ intersects the forward transfer $|G|$, resulting in pole splitting, is required. The design requirement $1/(2\pi f_{d\,ol} C_c) < |A_{R0}|$ and explicit expressions for the closed loop poles $f_{d\,cl}$ and $f_{nd\,cl}$ are

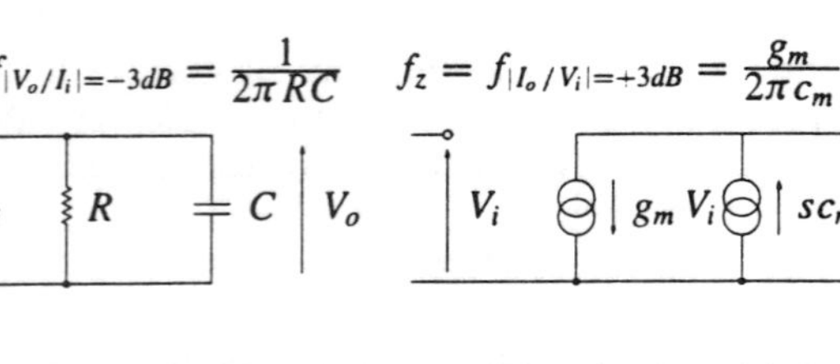

Fig. 3. ***Y*-parameter equivalent of a floating admittance.**

$$f_p = f_{|V_o/I_i|=-3dB} = \frac{1}{2\pi RC} \qquad f_z = f_{|I_o/V_i|=+3dB} = \frac{g_m}{2\pi c_m}$$

Fig. 4. Topologies that allow easy determination of behavioral poles/zeros.

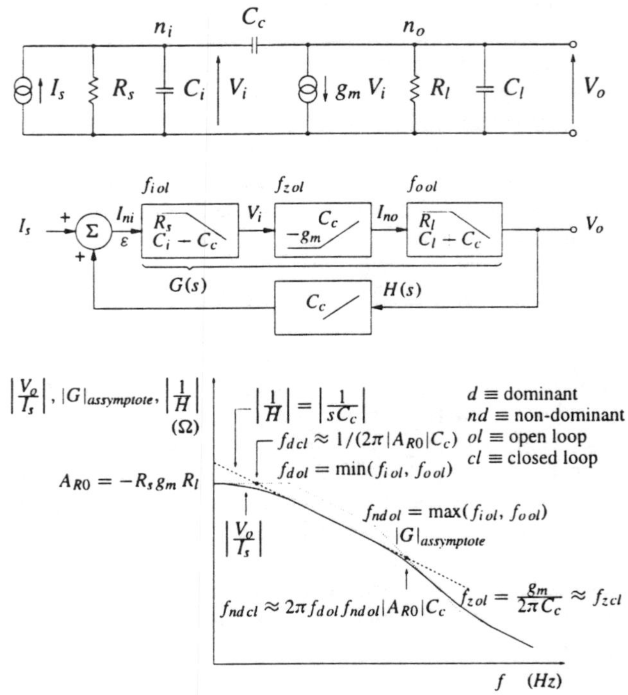

Fig. 5. Schematic of a generic one-stage amplifier, its behavioral signal path equivalent and the transfer function in the case of Miller-effect.

obtained.

- Substitute an input transistor with a transconductance amplifier with an associated positive zero.
- Replace dynamic cascode loads with a behavioral equivalent output impedance. This abstraction introduces hierarchy into the model. The equivalent output impedance can be determined exactly or approximately. For a MOS cascode stage consisting out of a bias transistor M_b and a cascode transistor M_c, an approximate but accurate equivalent impedance is given by $r_{eq} = r^*_{ob} + r_{oc}(1 + g_{mc} r^*_{ob}) + r_{Dc}$ with $r^*_{ob} = (r_{Sb} \parallel r_{BSb} + r_{ob}) \parallel r_{BDc} + r_{Db} + r_{Sc}$ in parallel with $c_{eq} = C_{GDc} + C_{BDc}$.
- Short a branch between two nodes and delete the elements between these nodes. This abstraction is mostly applied for series resistors like r_S, r_D, r_B, r_C and r_E. This abstraction reduces the number of nodes. The size of the *MNA*-matrix is reduced, which results in shorter execution times.
- Remove certain elements with negligible influence on the transfer function. This is mostly done for parasitics like C_μ and r_μ. Parasitics like C_{GB}, r_{BD} and r_{BS} mostly can be lumped with other components, which makes their removal unnecessary.
- Reconnect small-signal components.
- Ground biasing nodes and remove biasing transistors. This abstraction assumes that the biasing nets are perfectly decoupled.
- Ground the tail node of a differential pair. This is in fact a sequence of three abstractions. In the first abstraction, one replaces the current source by its equivalent output impedance. In the second abstraction, this impedance is assumed to be infinite. In the third abstraction, the branch impedance seen from the tail node is assumed to be equal for both branches. In that case the tail node is virtually grounded for differential signals.

• Replace a current mirror by a behavioral signal path equivalent.

In the context of symbolic simulation, the different abstractions can be seen as *simplification before generation* [11] steps: the topology is simplified before the coefficients of the closed form transfer function $TF(s) = \sum_i a_i s^i / \sum_j b_j s^j$ are generated. The obtained expressions are more compact, which improves the interpretability. By combining both behavioral signal path modeling and symbolic simulation, high qualitative insight is obtained.

The introduction of an abstraction is mostly driven by recognition of well known building blocks or specific interconnection patterns. This allows one to build an expert system based on the logic programming paradigm that suggests the designer which abstractions could be used for which parts of the circuit. The expert system contains rules for *building block recognition* [12]. These rules also allow to determine the nodes of the signal path. This information can then be used to associate an abstraction with a certain building block. A PROLOG example that detects the abstraction for a cascode bias stage is given below. The cascode bias abstraction results in the removal of the current source transistors and the grounding of the tail node of the differential pair.

```
diff_pair(X,Y,N) :- source(X,N), source(Y,N),
  gate(X,G1),  gate(X,G2),  G1 \== G2,
  drain(X,D1), drain(X,D2), D1 \== D2.
cascode_bias(X,Y,N) :- drain(X,Nc), source(Y,Nc)
  gate(X,Gx), bias(Gx), gate(Y,Gy), bias(Gy),
  source(X,Sx), power(Sx),
  drain(Y,Dy), diff_pair(K,L,Dy).
abstraction(cascode_bias, [X,Y,N]) :-
  cascode_bias(X,Y,N).
```

Incremental modeling can be automated with algorithm 1. As input we take a set of operating points $V_Q = \{Q_j | j\}$ in order to check the generality of the model. In step 1, the functionality of the circuit components is determined. In step 2 and 3, ideal biasing is assumed. In step 6 the series resistors are removed. Although these floating elements could be replaced by their Y-parameter equivalent, this gives rise to highly interconnected signal flow diagrams, which are rarely interpretable. This step is justified because the error introduced by removing these elements is low. In the cases where these elements have significant influence on the transfer (e.g. output stages), they mostly can be incorporated into the equivalent output impedance of that stage (step 4). In step 7, each entry of the *MNA* stamp of a floating circuit element is replaced by an equivalent circuit element which always has one grounded node. In step 8, lumping is performed, resulting in a reduction of the number of circuit elements. In step 9, the parasitics are removed one after another, with as criterion the introduced total error if they were removed.

If a behavioral signal path model is not required, the algorithm can be used as a model reduction technique (simplification before generation in the context of symbolic simulation). In step 2 and 3 the bias circuitry is then replaced by its small-signal equivalent. Step 6 can be postponed and transfered to step 9.

Incremental modeling allows one to transform small-signal modeling into control theory modeling. This gives the modeling methodology a strong foundation. Incremental modeling is a suitable methodology to go from full device to full behavior.

Algorithm 1: Automated incremental modeling

```
    input : maximal total error Δ_max S for frequency range [f_l, f_u]
            set of operating points V_Q = {Q_j | j}
            reference topology T_R with transistor instantiations
1   building block recognition and signal path detection
2   ground tail nodes and remove current source transistors
3   ground biasing nets and remove biasing transistors
4   replace cascode loads with an equivalent output impedance
5   small-signal expansion of transistor models
6   removal of series resistors
7   replace floating elements by their MNA circuit equivalent
8   lump resistors, capacitors and transconductances
9   do forever
      begin
10      Determine for all remaining non-lumped parasitics P_i
            Δ*_i S = max_{Q∈V_Q} max_{f∈[f_l, f_u]} |Δ_i S(Q, f)|
11      Determine Δ*S = min_i Δ*_i S
12      if Δ*S ≤ Δ_max S
            then remove all parasitics P_i for which Δ*_i S = Δ*S
            else exit
      end
```

For textbook designs, going from full device to full behavior in one step still may be feasible. However, from a certain circuit complexity on, this step is too big and must be split up. Incremental modeling is a systematic modeling method in the sense that it guides the efforts to go from full device to full behavior. One knows the error introduced by each abstraction, which allows one to detect erroneous abstractions, introduced by reasoning faults.

IV. Open modeling tool EF2ef

The modeling methodology described above is implemented in an open tool called EF2ef (Electronic Format t(w)o Electronic Format). It has a *pipelined architecture with a generic backbone*. Its software architecture is depicted in Fig. 6. Starting point is a netlist in a certain hardware description language. With a markup processor dedicated for that hardware language, the netlist information is converted to the generic EF2ef internal tool format, which is a structured text format. On the internal tool format, all kind of abstractions can be performed. Each abstraction is implemented as a text filter and changes the pipeline text stream. At the end of the pipeline, the state-space representation of the circuit is solved with modified nodal analysis [1] or symbolic simulation [2]. Both are implemented as filters. The formalization of the resulting analytical model is done with a back end dedicated for the desired formalization language.

The software architecture of EF2ef is non-monolithic. It consists of a library of filters. The user can reconfigure the

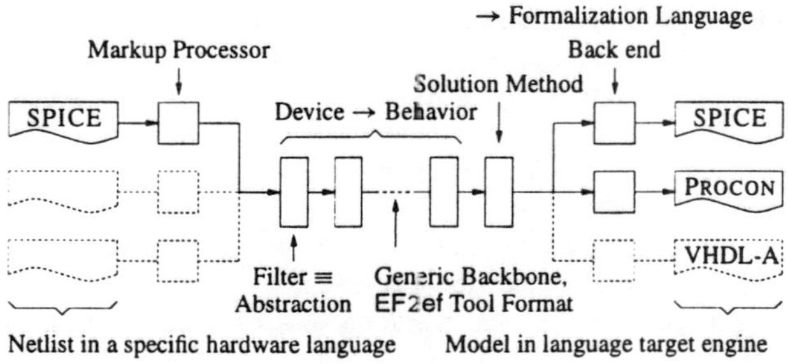

Fig. 6. Software architecture of EF2ef.

pipeline to his own needs if necessary. This way, the flexibility required for analog circuit modeling is obtained. Although we feel the EF2ef library is quite complete, the situation may occur where an user wants to add a new abstraction. Addition of new filters is simplified because the programming language to implement a filter can be choosen freely and because the used data structure is text which is easy accesible. The system is thus extendible, which makes it an open system.

V. Optimization based sizing

OTA's and opamps must have first order behavior up to the gain-bandwidth. In order to obtain this, the different nondominant poles and positive zeros in the signal path must occur at frequencies beyond the gain-bandwidth. Imposing these design requirements is called *pole placement.*

A quantity expressing the first order behavior is the phase margin. Out of the phase margin, one can determine if nondominant poles occur before the unity gain frequency f_u. The phase margin *PM* could thus be used for pole placement. However, a pole or zero only has an influence on the phase in a region of one decade before and after its corner frequency (corresponding to one decade I_{DS} and/or V_{GS}-V_T). This implies that if a pole or zero falls outside the region between one decade before and one decade after the unity gain frequency f_u, its influence on the phase margin *PM* is negligible. This makes that a local optimizer, guided by the decrease in goal function, has insufficient notion about what direction to move, because the phase sensitivity is too low. Only a computationally expensive global optimization algorithm is able to find the "hole" in the design space where the nondominant poles and zeros are placed correctly.

So, how can we achieve pole placement using an efficient local optimizer? One can determine the poles and zeros of the total transfer function. This can be done in several ways. One can use polynomial interpolation [8] in order to determine the coefficients of the closed form transfer function $TF(s) = \sum_i a_i s^i / \sum_j b_j s^j$. Out of the numerator and denominator polynomials, the zeros respectively poles can be determined using an iterative root solving algorithm. Another method is to apply the iterative QZ-algorithm [8] on the system matrix equation, generating the system poles and zeros in a direct way. Both methods are iterative, CPU intensive, provide weak guarantee concerning convergence and are only applicable for circuits of moderate size [9]. Another method is asymptotic waveform evaluation *AWE* [6]. This method delivers a reduced complexity model with AC circuit response below a specifiable limit. However, the algorithm requires the iterative solving of a set of simultaneous nonlinear equations, or a more direct iterative root solving [6], which both introduce weak convergence guarantee and moreover typically have a CPU cost of one DC analysis [7]. Since all the previous mentioned techniques are numerical of nature, they provide no qualitative insight in the small-signal functioning of a circuit.

The poles and zeros in the behavioral signal path model are local and determine the global poles and zeros of the total transfer function. If the local nondominant poles and zeros occur beyond the gain-bandwith *GBW* of the circuit, the global poles and zeros of the total transfer function will also do so. Given the algorithm for automated incremental modeling, one is able to derive *explicit, compact, iteration free* equations for the poles and zeros that constitute the transfer function. These numerical efficient expressions allow pole placement in a very efficient way. They allow to generate penalty functions which are able to guide a local optimizer, even if the local poles and zeros occur decades beyond or below the unity gain frequency f_u. If a global optimizer is used, increased optimization speed can be expected.

By using an *operating point driven DC formulation* [13], one obtains a robust design plan, that is always DC consistent and has minimal dimension. Possible convergence problems as in the case of simulation based sizing are lacking since one only has to compute a set of one-dimensional root solving problems. The DC problem is solved in the design plan itself, instead of transfering it to the optimizer as is done in a relaxed DC formulation [14]. This way, the optimization problem has minimal dimensionality and the obtained optimum is guaranteed to be DC consistent. The solvability space Ω_S of the design plan is identical to the theoretical solvability space $\{W_E, L_E, I_{DS}, V_{DS}, V_{GS} - V_T \in \mathbb{R}_0^+\}$. The starting point is obtained directly by specifying the operating point.

The solvability space Ω_S can be subdivided into other spaces as depicted in Fig. 7. The manufacturability space Ω_M is the set of circuits that can be produced with a given technology. The operationality space Ω_O contains all circuits that have proper DC biasing. The transistors of a current source or current mirror must be biased in saturation regime in order to operate properly. Transistors used as resistors for common mode feedback must be biased in the linear region. The functionality space Ω_F contains all designs that provide the functionality they are intended for. For an OTA this is first order behavior up to the gain-bandwith. In order to achieve this, design requirements must be fulfilled. The applicability space Ω_A contains designs that fulfill the given specifications. If all specifications are fulfilled, there is still room left to make a trade-off between different performance parameters. These designs are typically situated at the edge of the different subspaces of the manufacturability space. They contain minimal length devices and transistors biased near the edge of the saturation/linear operation region. The design requirements are just fulfilled and some specifications are just met.

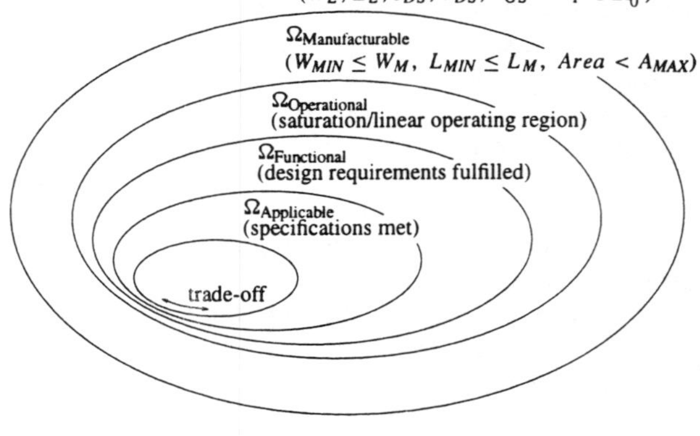

Fig. 7. Spaces encountered in optimization based sizing of analog circuits.

With each of these spaces, one can associate inequality functions. These on their turn can be used to generate penalty functions. The subdivision of the manufacturability is now used in a *hierarchical penalty function composition strategy*. The trade-off function gets the reference weight W_R. The penalties of the enclosing applicability space Ω_A get weights of $10W_R$. The weights of the other enclosing spaces are 10^2W_R for Ω_F, 10^3W_R for Ω_O and 10^4W_R for Ω_M. This way, the different design problems are tackled only when it makes sense to do so. The same divide and conquer strategy is used by designers when designing manually. First, one ensures that the circuit has a proper operating point. It makes no sense to fulfill the design requirements if a circuit is badly biased. Once the design requirements are fulfilled, one tries to achieve the specifications. During an optimization one thus sequentially prunes the design space.

The trade-off function $\zeta(X)$ which is function of the independent optimization variables X, allows one to interchange different performance parameters $p_i(X)$ against one another using steering factors β_i:

$$\zeta(X) = W_R \sum_i \beta_i p_i(X)$$

An inequality function has negative or zero value if the corresponding condition is fulfilled and positive if it isn't. The inequality $f_i < ub$ is converted into the inequality function $h_i = W(f_i - ub)$ where W represents the weighting factor. The inequality $lb < f_i$ corresponds to the inequality function $h_i = W(lb - f_i)$. The trade-off function $\zeta(X)$ is now combined with the inequality functions h_j:

$$\varphi(X) = \max_j \theta_j(X) \; with \; \begin{cases} \theta_0 = \zeta(X) & \text{trade-off in } \Omega_{Applicable} \\ \theta_j = \zeta(X) + W_j h_j(X), & j \neq 0 \end{cases}$$

The optimal design solution is found at the minimum of this function. An optimal design therefore fulfills the following *minimax* condition:

$$\varphi^* = \min_X \varphi(X) = \min_X \max_j \theta_j(X) = \varphi(X^*)$$

where X^* represents the optimal vector of independent design variables which result in an optimal design in Ω_A.

In each point X only one function $\theta_j(X)$ determines the maximum function. This has the advantage that only one function determines the convexity and/or presence of local optima. The more functions are summed, the more correlation is introduced and thus the more risk that convexity is absent and the higher the chance for local optima. For the minimax optimization, the algorithm of Dem'yanov and Malozemov [15] is used.

Scaling of the independent input variables, performance variables and inequality functions is essential in order to obtain good conditioned optimization problems. The purpose of *scaling* is to linearize strongly nonlinear functions to a maximum extent, in order to ease and accelerate the optimization process. Almost all encountered equations in analog circuit design have logarithmic behavior. For the device equations, $\log I_{DS}$ depends in an asymptotically linear way on $\log V_{GS}$ and $\log V_{DS}$. The same is valid for the small-signal parameters. The expressions for poles also have a logarithmic nature (bode/pole-zero plot). Logarithmic transformations are therefore mostly the appropriate scaling method.

VI. Examples

The modeling methodology described above has been tested on three circuits: a pMOS Miller OTA, a current buffer OTA [16] and a class-AB amplifier [17]. The current buffer OTA is depicted in Fig. 8. The first abstraction is the grounding of the biasing nets *cmrpp*, *cmrp* and *cmrn*. Next the tail node *n1* is grounded and the bias transistors M6 and M7 are removed. Then the cascode loads M4a-M5a and M4b-M5b are replaced by their equivalent impedance $r_{eq} = r_{o4} + r_{o5}(1 + g_{m5}r_{o4}) \parallel c_{eq} = C_{GD} + C_{BD}$. The capacitors C_{GD1a}, C_{GD1b}, C_{GD3a} and C_{GD3b} are replaced by their Y-parameter equivalent. The transconductance $g_{mt2a} = g_{m2a} + g_{mb2a}$ is replaced by a transconductance between *n3* and ground and an equivalent resistor $r = 1/g_{mt2a}$ is placed between *n2a* and ground. The same procedure is followed for g_{mt2b}. Next, r_{o2a} is removed and replaced by a resistor between *n3* and ground with value $r_{o1a3a} + r_{o2a}(1 + g_{mt2a}r_{o1a3a})$ with $r_{o1a3a} = r_{o1a} \parallel r_{o3a}$. The same is done for r_{o2b}. Next, the transcapacitance $c_{mn2b \to n3}$ pumping current on node *n3* and controlled by V_{n2b} is removed. After a lumping step the circuit is now reduced to a form where RC-tanks are isolated between a node and ground, which allows one to replace them by a behavioral equivalent. The transconductance-transcapacitance pairs are also replaced by their behavioral equivalent. Now we can make abstractions at the behavioral level. The zeros of the positive signal path become active decades later than the cut-off frequency of the positive signal path, regardless of the operating point Q. This allows one to remove them. Finally, the behavioral signal path model depicted in Fig. 1 is obtained. During the modeling, the number of circuit elements is reduced from 75 to 17.

The loop I_{n2a}-V_{n2a}-I_{n3}-V_{n3}-I_{n2a} (Fig. 1) forms a second order system with damping ratio $\zeta = (f_{n2a} + f_{n3})/(2f_n)$ and natural frequency $f_n = \sqrt{f_{n2a}f_{n3}(1 + r_{n2a}g_{mt2a}r_{n3}g_{n3a})}$. In order to avoid ringing on node *n3*, the design requirement $3GBW_{2a} = 3r_{n2a}g_{mt2a}r_{n3}g_{m3a}f_{n3} < f_{n2a}$ must be fulfilled.

The computationally efficient behavioral signal path model of Fig. 1 was derived with EF2ef. Together with an efficient operating point driven DC formulation [13] and some manually derived equations for offset, slew rate and output range, the goal function was defined using the hierarchical penalty func-

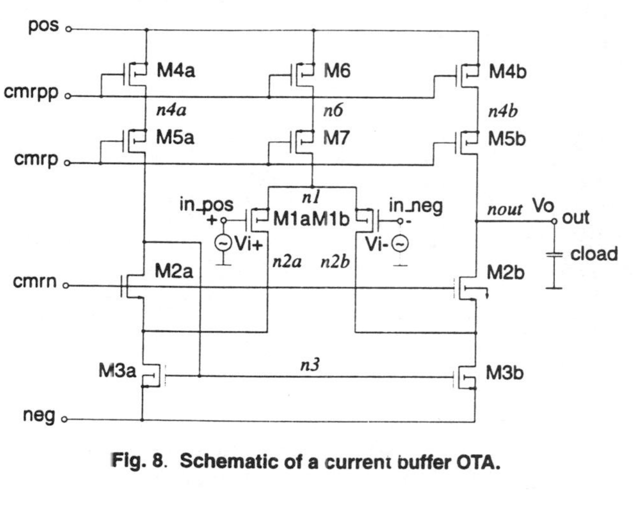

Fig. 8. Schematic of a current buffer OTA.

tion composition method described above. Combined with local minimax optimization, a very efficient optimization based sizing method is obtained. All these models were formalized into PROCON, the language used by the contraint programming tool DONALD [18]. The DONALD tool was used to generate a minimal cost computational path [18], which was then dumped to C. This code was then loaded by the local minimax optimization engine MINIMAN [13][15]. The optimum is obtained typically after 100 iterations.

In Table I, a set of specifications is given. Also given are the obtained performances and frequencies of the poles and zeros along the signal path when the design requirement $3GBW_{2a} < f_{n2a}$ is taken into account. The technology used is MIETEC CMOS 0μ7. The cut-off frequency GBW_{2a}=458MHz of the positive signal path determines the second pole of the total transfer function. The transfer function gets an additional decay of 20dB up to twice that frequency (916MHz), where a negative zero occurs. From that zero on, the output signal is halved and only the negative signal path determines the output signal. At the frequency f_{n2b}=1.38GHz, the decay in the negative signal path is reflected in another total transfer function pole. The positive zero f_{z1b} =3.42GHz also occurs in the total transfer function. Since the presence of a pole or zero is felt even a decade earlier, the phase margin PM =60°at the unity gain frequency f_u =251MHz is thus determined by the GBW_{2a}, f_{n2b}, the negative zero at $2GBW_{2a}$ and the positive zero f_{z1b}. The pole f_{n2a} of the internal loop is pushed against the $3GBW_{2a}$ border, resulting in a critically damped feedback loop. In Fig. 9, the incremental error on $|V_o/V_i|$ in function of the frequency is shown for the different abstractions. The errors are relatively small. Morever, the error peaks occur at frequencies beyond the unity gain frequency of 251MHz.

If the stability requirement is disregarded, the optimizer returns a design for which the design requirement $3GBW_{2a}$ = $8.78GHz \not< f_{n2a}$ = $1.09GHz$ is violated. The second order system has complex conjugated poles with a natural frequency f_n=1.38GHz and a damping ratio ζ = 0.396. At the frequency f_n=1.38GHz, the total transfer gets an additional decay of 40dB/dec. At $\sqrt{2}f_n$=1.96GHz, the signal is halved and two negative zeros occur. An additional pole and positive zero in the total transfer occur at respectively f_{n2b}=1.09GHz and f_{z1b} =2.93MHz. All these poles and zeros determine the phase margin PM =60°at f_u =333MHz.

spec	value	required
I_{tot}	3mA	$\leq$ 3mA
PM	60°	$\geq$ 60°
A_{v0}	90.9dB	$\geq$ 60dB
V_{off}	2.58mV	$\leq$ 5mV
SR	162V/μs	$\geq$ 150$V/\mu s$
OR	1.5V	$\geq \pm$1.5V
f_u	251MHz	max
$Area$	0.122mm^2	

$3GBW_{2a}$	$\leq f_{n2a}$	$\not\leq f_{n2a}$
f_u	251MHz	333MHz
GBW	271MHz	349MHz
$3GBW$	814MHz	1.05GHz
f_{z1b}	3.42GHz	2.93GHz
$f_{n2a,2b}$	1.38GHz	1.09GHz
GBW_{2a}	458MHz	1.74GHz
$3GBW_{2a}$	1.38GHz	8.78GHz
f_{n3}	30.0kHz	67.6kHz
f_{nout}	7.77kHz	9.61kHz

TABLE I

Specifications and obtained performance if the design requirement $3GBW_{n2} \leq f_{n2a}$ is fulfilled. Frequencies for a design where the internal stability requirement is fulfilled, respectively not fulfilled.

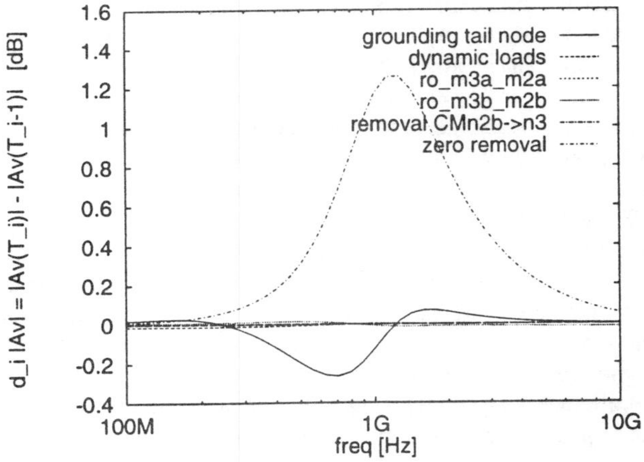

Fig. 9. Incremental error in function of the frequency for the different abstractions.

Modeling a class-AB opamp like the Hogervorst opamp [17] depicted in Fig. 11 is complicated by the presence of source and sink currents during large signal operation. The first abstraction therefore is to model transient behavior in the time domain. We assume quasi-stationary operation for all capacitors, except for the load capacitance $C_{n\,out}$. We consider the negative zero transition, where the sink current is maximal. This is modeled by adding a current source at the ouput node in the DC schematic. Due to the sink current, class-AB operation occurs, which results in the cut-off of M_{11b}. The transistors M_{8b}, M_{9b} and M_{10b} form a double cascode. The behavioral signal path model for this situation is depicted in Fig. 10. During the modeling, the number of circuit elements is reduced from 135 to 36.

VII. Conclusions

An incremental modeling methodology for the generation of behavioral signal path models has been presented. It offers the following advantages:

- High qualitative insight in a circuit is obtained that can be used for manual interactive sizing with SPICE, constraint based sizing with DONALD or optimization based sizing.
- Qualitative insight is generated locally, not at the global circuit level; the different effects are available individually.
- Qualitative understanding is generated by going from devices to behavior. By also applying symbolic simulation, additional qualitative insight is obtained.
- The poles and zeros that compose the transfer function are derived, not the poles and zeros of the total transfer function. These poles are directly available for pole placement.
- The three orthogonal axes encountered in analog circuit modeling are covered by the open modeling tool EF2ef.

For optimization based sizing, a strategy for hierarchical penalty function composition that allows sequential pruning of the design space was proposed. Together with an operating point driven DC formulation and local minimax optimization, an efficient sizing method is obtained, which allows interactive design space exploration.

Acknowledgment

Support from Robert Bosch GmbH is acknowledged.

References

[1] Chung-Wen Ho, Albert. E. Ruehli, and Pierce A. Brennan. The modified nodal approach to network analysis. *IEEE Transactions on Circuits and Systems*, 22(6):504–509, June 1975.

[2] Georges Gielen, Piet Wambacq, and Willy M. C. Sansen. Symbolic analysis methods and applications for analog circuits: a tutorial overview. *Proceedings of the IEEE*, 82(2):287–304, February 1990.

[3] Brian C. Williams and Johan de Kleer. Qualitative reasoning about physical systems: a return to roots. *Artificial Intelligence*, 51(1-3):1–9, October 1991.

[4] K. Swings and W. Sansen. Donald: a workbench for interactive design space exploration and sizing of analog circuits. In *Proceedings EDAC*, pages 475–479. IEEE, February 1991.

[5] E. Ochotta, L. Carley, and R. Rutenbar. ASTRX/OBLX: tools for rapid synthesis of high-performance analog circuits. In *Proceedings ACM/IEEE DAC*, pages 24–30. IEEE, 1994.

[6] Lawrence T. Pillage and Ronald A. Rohrer. Asymptotic waveform evaluation for timing analysis. *IEEE Transactions on Computer-Aided Design*, 9(4):352–366, April 1990.

[7] Eli Chiprout and Michel S. Nakhla. *Asymptotic waveform evaluation and moment matching for interconnect analysis*. Kluwer Academic Publishers, Massachusetts, 1994.

[8] Jiri Vlach and Kishore Singhal. *Computer methods for circuit analysis and design*. Van Nostrand Reinhold, New York, 1983.

[9] X. Huang. *Padé approximation of linear(ized) circuit responses*. PhD thesis, Carnegie Mellon University, November 1990.

[10] Ralf Sommer, Eckhard Hennig, Guido Dröge, and Ernest-Helmut Horneber. Equation-based symbolic approximation by matrix reduction with quantitative error prediction. *Alta Frequenza - Rivista di elettronica*, 5(6):317–325, November 1993.

[11] Q. Yu and C. Sechen. Approximate symbolic analysis of large analog integrated circuits. In *Proceedings IEEE/ACM ICCAD*, pages 664–671. IEEE/ACM, 1994.

[12] Leon Sterling and Ehud Shapiro. *The art of Prolog: advanced programming techniques*. The MIT Press, Massachusetts, 1994.

[13] Francky Leyn, Walter Daems, Georges Gielen, and Willy Sansen. Analog circuit sizing with constraint programming modeling and minimax optimization. In *Proceedings ISCAS*. IEEE, 1997.

[14] P. C. Maulik and L. R. Carley. Automating analog circuit design using constrained optimization techniques. In *Proceedings ICCAD*. IEEE, November 1993.

[15] V. F. Dem'yanov and V. N. Malozemov. *Introduction to minimax*. John Wiley & Sons Ltd., New York, 1974.

[16] John A. Fisher and Rudolf Koch. A highly linear CMOS buffer amplifier. *IEEE Journal of Solid-State Circuits*, 22(3):330–334, June 1987.

[17] Ron Hogervorst, John P. Tero, Ruud G. H. Eschauzier, and Johan H. Huijsing. A compact power-efficient 3V CMOS rail-to-rail input/output operational amplifier for VLSI cell libraries. *IEEE Journal of Solid-State Circuits*, 29(12):1505–1513, December 1994.

[18] Koen Swings. *Analog circuit design using constraint programming*. PhD thesis, Katholieke Universiteit Leuven, May 1995.

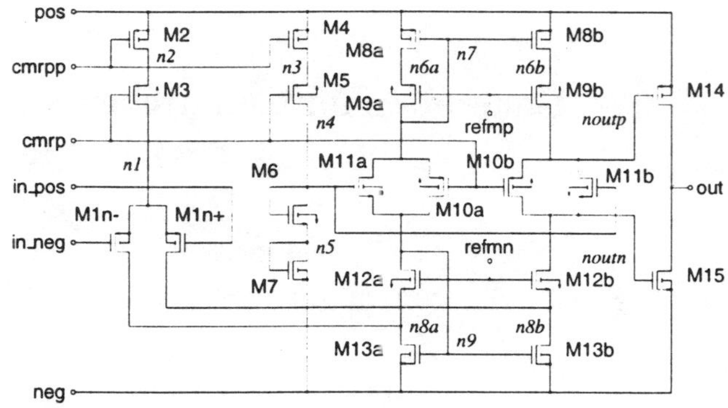

Fig. 11. Schematic of the Hogervorst class-AB opamp.

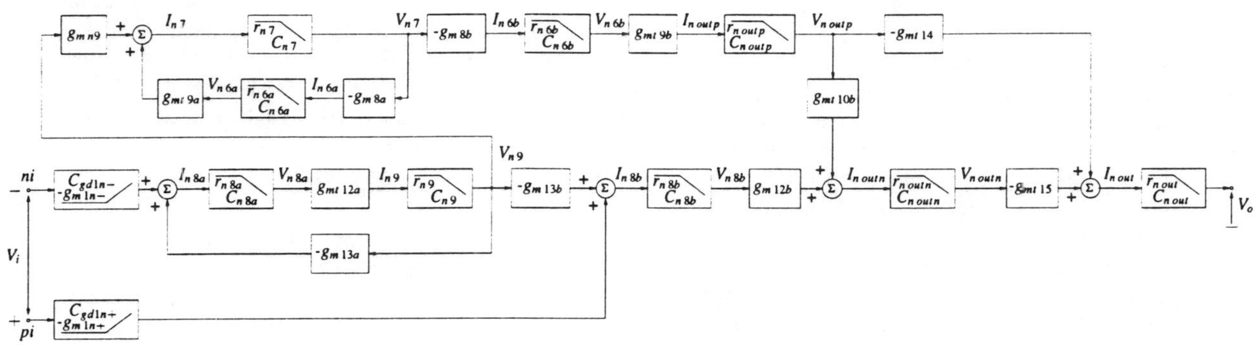

Fig. 10. Behavioral signal path model of the Hogervorst class-AB opamp.

Test Generation for Comprehensive Testing of Linear Analog Circuits Using Transient Response Sampling

Pramodchandran N. Variyam and Abhijit Chatterjee
School of Electrical Engineering, Georgia Institute of Technology, Atlanta, Georgia 30332.

Abstract

The problem of testing analog components continues to be the bottleneck in reducing the time-to-market of mixed-signal ICs. In this paper, we present a test generation algorithm for implicit functional testing of linear analog circuits using transient response sampling. Each specification of the circuit under test (CUT) imposes bounds on individual parametric deviations under the single fault assumption. These bounds are mapped on to "acceptable" ranges of measurements of the transient response of the CUT at various sample points using time domain sensitivity calculations. Any circuit that "passes" the applied test is also guaranteed to meet its specifications. The simplicity of the test waveform, reduced test generation time and test time show that this testing method is a good alternative to existing testing schemes.

1. Introduction

With recent advancements in DSP and wireless communication, mixed-signal ICs are being used aggressively in industry. Nevertheless, testing continues to be the bottleneck in reducing time-to-market of mixed-signal ICs. The current practice in industry is to measure the circuit specifications and pass or fail the CUT based on the results of the tests. This test process is inherently expensive. In this paper we present an implicit test generation algorithm assisted by fast sensitivity computation which ensures that if the CUT "passes" the generated tests, then it implicitly satisfies all its specifications. Thereby, a large reduction in test cost is achieved.

In [1] the authors discuss an algorithm for efficient *functional testing* of analog ICs. In [2-4], it has been shown that many catastrophic faults can be detected by DC testing. Sinusoidal testing has been addressed by many researchers [5-7] and involves evaluating the steady state response of the CUT for fault detection. The transient testing schemes presented in [8-11] are more efficient in comparison to sinusoidal testing schemes. In [12], a set of DC and low frequency sinusoids are used for *implicit functional* testing. Pan and Cheng in [13], propose an innovative testing scheme for linear analog circuits using transient response measurements. However, their algorithm needs to be trained on large sets of failure data requiring many circuit simulation steps. The implicit functional testing scheme we present in this paper uses sensitivities to derive efficient transient tests. The test generator is assisted by a fast fault simulator, FLYER [14] which further speeds up the test generation process. Moreover, the proposed testing scheme is easily amenable to low-cost BIST [15]. In the following, we first give an overview of the test generator and then present details of the proposed algorithm.

2. Overview of the test generator

We first state the problem to be solved. Given the netlist of the circuit and its specifications, we desire to compute the optimal test stimulus and the times at which the transient response of the CUT is to be sampled for highest fault detectability and yield. This has to be done in such a way so as to ensure, as best as possible, that if the CUT "passes" the tests, then all its specifications are also implicitly met and vice versa. We also want to minimize the test time and the number of times the output is sampled. Figure 1 shows an overview of the proposed test generator. First, the circuit specifications are related to the maximum allowed deviations of circuit parameters under fault using the MIST PROFIT [16] software. The circuit netlist is preprocessed to form the adjoint circuit [17, 18]. In order to simulate the CUT and its adjoint using FLYER [14], we extract the state matrix of the circuit from its netlist. Methods for computing the state matrices from tree link [19] analysis and nodal analysis techniques [20,21] have been investigated in the past. In this work we use a simple method based on element stamps to construct the state matrices from the nodal admittance matrix. Stated concisely, specific row elimination operations are applied to a modified nodal admittance matrix of the CUT, to obtain its state variable representation. Using the respective state matrices, FLYER can simulate the CUT and its adjoint very fast and compute the time domain sensitivities of the parameters to the circuit output using the adjoint method [18]. The optimizer in the test generation program uses the sensitivities to determine the optimum test stimulus waveform and sample points for transient testing. The test generation algorithm is described in detail in the next section.

3. Test generation algorithm

For mapping the specifications to the worst case deviations (see Figure 1) in the circuit parameters, consider a circuit with q specifications, $P = [p_1, p_2, ..., p_q]$. Assume that the acceptable values of specifications p_k, $1 \le k \le q$, lie in the range $p_k - \Delta p_k$ and $p_k + \Delta p_k$. The vector $\boldsymbol{\Delta P} = [\Delta p_1 \ \Delta p_2 ..... \Delta p_q]$ is specified by the circuit designer or design customer. If the measured

This research was supported by Air Force Material Command and Advanced Research Project Agency, Contract Number F30602-95-C-0266

value of p_k is outside the above range, then p_k is said to be *violated*.

Now consider the l circuit parameters, $C = [c_1, c_2, ..., c_l]$. We want to compute the smallest deviation Δc_j in the value of the parameter c_j, $1 \le j \le l$, that is always guaranteed to violate at least one of the specifications p_k, $1 \le k \le q$. However, while performing this calculation, one must take into account the fact that due to manufacturing process variations, the value of c_j is not exact and can only be predicted to lie in the range $(c_j - \delta c_j, c_j + \delta c_j)$. δc_j is said to be the *tolerance* in the value of c_j. Let $S_{c_j}^{p_k}$, $1 \le k \le q$, $1 \le j \le l$, be the first order sensitivity of the specification p_k to the parameter c_j. Let ε_{jk} be the deviation in the value of parameter c_j from the nominal that is guaranteed to violate specification p_k in the presence of tolerances in other parameters. This is computed using Equation 1. In order to compute Δc_j we need to calculate the minimum of the allowed deviations (ε_{jk}) over all specifications. This is computed using Equation 2.

$$|\varepsilon_{jk}| = \frac{\sum_{\substack{i=1 \\ i \ne j}}^{l} \left|\delta c_i \cdot S_{c_i}^{p_k}\right| + |\Delta p_k|}{\left|S_{c_j}^{p_k}\right|} \quad (1)$$

$$|\Delta c_j| = minimum(|\varepsilon_{j1}|, \ldots, |\varepsilon_{jq}|) \quad (2)$$

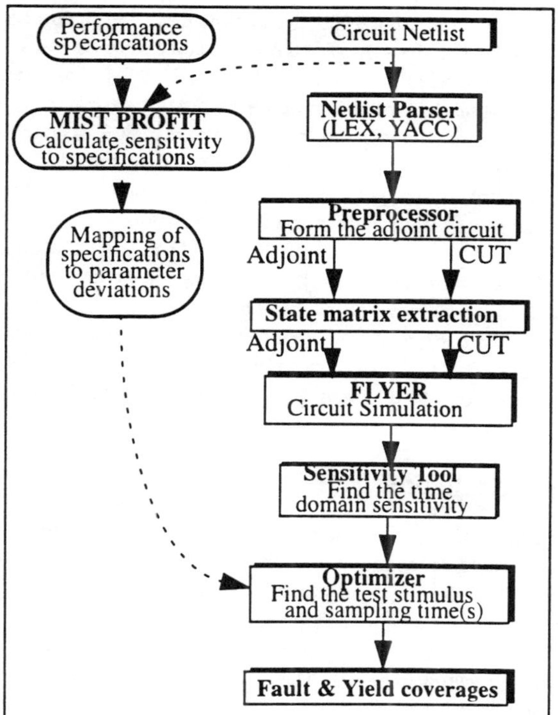

FIGURE 1. Software components of the test generator

3.1 Formulation of cost function for optimization

Assume that a test stimulus is given and our goal is to evaluate how good the supplied stimulus performs as a test for the CUT. We will use the following analysis to formulate a cost function for test generation and then later show how this cost function is used to drive the search for the optimal test stimulus and sample times (see optimizer in Figure 1).

Let the measurement of the transient response of the CUT at time t_k for the nominal value of c_j be given by M_{jk} (note that M_{jk} can be a voltage or current value). In the presence of tolerances in all the components c_i, $i \ne j$, $1 \le i \le l$, and in the presence of the deviation Δc_j in the value of component c_j that is guaranteed to violate at least one specification of the CUT, we desire to compute $|\Delta M_{jk}|$, the largest possible change in the measurement M_{jk}. Equation 3 describes how $|\Delta M_{jk}|$ is computed. The range of "acceptable" measurements $(M_{jk} - |\gamma_k|, M_{jk} + |\gamma_k|)$ is determined by $|\gamma_k|$ which is computed as given in Equation 4.

$$|\Delta M_{jk}| = \sum_{\substack{i=1 \\ i \ne j}}^{l} \left|S_{c_i}^{M_{jk}} \cdot \delta c_i\right| + \left|S_{c_j}^{M_{jk}} \cdot \Delta c_j\right| \quad (3)$$

$$|\gamma_k| = maximum(|\Delta M_{1k}|, \ldots, |\Delta M_{lk}|) \quad (4)$$

Note that the nominal values of the measurement M_{jk} for all $1 \le j \le l$, are identical and correspond to the fault-free measurement value defined as Mff_k. Let the measured value of the response at time t_k during test be given by $Mtest_k$. If $Mtest_k < Mff_k - |\gamma_k|$ or $Mtest_k > Mff_k + |\gamma_k|$, then under the single fault assumption, it is implicitly guaranteed that there exists a faulty parameter value c_1 or c_2 or.... or c_l that causes a circuit specification to be violated. Let the value of c_j under fault be given by c_j'. With every sample time t_k and every parameter c_j, $1 \le j \le l$, we associate a deviation $|\Delta ctest_{jk}|$ such that whenever

$$c_j' < c_j - |\Delta ctest_{jk}| \text{ or } c_j' > (c_j + |\Delta ctest_{jk}|),$$
$$Mtest_k < Mff_k - |\gamma_k| \text{ or } Mtest_k > (Mff_k + |\gamma_k|).$$

Simply stated, any deviation of c_j larger than $|\Delta ctest_{jk}|$ is *guaranteed* to cause $Mtest_k$ to "fail". Note that this must hold in the presence of tolerances in all the components c_i, $1 \le i \le l, i \ne j$. Such a value of $|\Delta ctest_{jk}|$ is computed using Equation 5. Suppose we have r sample points. Then the smallest $|\Delta ctest_{jk}|$ that will cause one of the r measurements $Mtest_k$, $1 \le k \le r$ to fail ($|\Delta ctest_j|$) is given by Equation 6. The test waveform and sampling points need to be selected in such a way so as to minimize the difference between the detectable worst case deviation in components due to the derived test set and those derived from the specifications. For generating the test we define a normalized cost function as given in Equation 7. The test waveform parameters (pulse width for a rectangular pulse, rise time for a ramp input etc.) can be optimized using the cost function in (7). The test generation procedure is illustrated with pulse input waveforms.

$$|\Delta ctest_{jk}| = \frac{\sum_{\substack{i=1 \\ i \neq j}}^{l} \left|\delta c_i \cdot s_{c_i}^{Mff_k}\right| + |\gamma_k|}{\left|s_{c_j}^{Mff_k}\right|} \quad (5)$$

$$|\Delta ctest_j| = minimum(|\Delta ctest_{j1}|, \ldots, |\Delta ctest_{jr}|) \quad (6)$$

$$Cost = \sum_{j=1}^{l} \frac{(c_j)^2}{(|\Delta c_j| - |\Delta c_{testj}|)^2} \quad (7)$$

Figure 2 shows the pulse waveform. The test generation algorithm selects an optimum pulse width PW_i and a sampling time t_i through exhaustive search over the range $0 \le PW_i \le Tmax_1$, $0 \le t_i \le Tmax_2$ where $Tmax_1$ and $Tmax_2$ are the limits imposed by the simulator FLYER [14]. The algorithm for test generation is given in Algorithm *FindOptimumTest* shown below. The two inner *while* loops find the optimum PW_i and t_i. The outer *while* loop adds the pulse and sampling time to the generated test set.

Input: Maximum test time
Procedure *FindOptimumTest*
total test time = 0, cost = 0, Set of pulses and sample times={Φ}
while *((total test time < Maximum test time) or (no significant improvement in cost)*
    while *(PW_i < $Tmax_1$)*
        while *(SampleTime < $Tmax_2$)*
            Calculate Cost using Equation 7
            if *(there is significant improvement in cost)*
                Store PW_i and t_i
            end if
        end while
    end while
    Add PW_i and t_i to the set of pulses and sample times
end while
Print test waveform, Sample time points, thresholds.

Algorithm FindOptimumTest

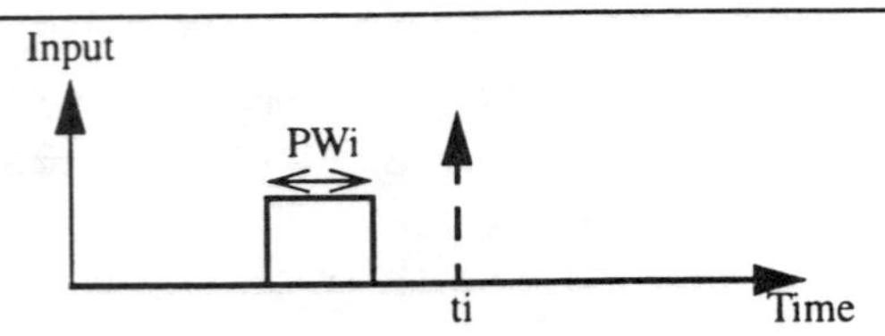

FIGURE 2. Test waveform

3.2 How good is the generated test?

The quality of the generated test is measured by fault and yield coverages. Yield coverage is defined as the ratio of the number of good circuits that pass the test to the actual number of good circuits. In our approach we are testing for worst case parameter deviations, hence we will never be rejecting a good circuit. Thus we always get 100% yield coverage. Fault coverage is defined as the ratio of the number of faulty circuits detected by the test to the total number of faulty circuits. In order to estimate the fault coverage of the generated test, we divide the faults into two categories. 1) catastrophic faults 2) parametric faults. As we detect all the faults which cause a deviation of more than $|\Delta ctest_j|$, we have 100% fault coverage of catastrophic faults. The fault coverage of parametric faults is computed by injecting a large number of random parameter variations (assuming independent normal distribution of the parameters) into the CUT and checking whether the test detects the fault.

4. Test generation results

We discuss the results of test generation on a biquadratic low pass filter (Figure 3). Tolerances of the components were taken as 1%. The nominal values of a set of specifications of the filter and their allowed deviations from the nominal are shown in Table 1. Maximum allowed deviations of the circuit components imposed by the specifications are shown in Table 2. The generated test stimulus and the CUT response for the biquadratic filter are shown in Figure 4. The sampling points, nominal output of the fault free circuit and the maximum allowed deviations of the output for passing/failing the CUT are shown in Table 3. The values of $|\Delta ctest_j|$ for various parameters are listed along with that of $|\Delta c_j|$ in Table 2. All the faults which cause R1 to deviate more than 17.3% from its nominal value are detected by the test. However, if R1 deviates more than 11.05%, the circuit is faulty. Since the test generation algorithm is driven by the worst case situation we loose fault coverage for the deviation in R1 in the range [11.05%, 17.3%].

The parametric fault coverage of the derived test was estimated by simulating 1000 circuit instances (described in Section 3.2). The 3σ value for the parameters were taken as 1%. The estimated fault coverage was around 80% for parametric faults. Thus the overall fault coverage with catastrophic faults also taken into consideration, is greater than 80%. The overall test time for the sinusoidal testing scheme presented in [5] is approximately 60ms while our approach samples the output 4 times over a total test time of 5.29ms to achieve an overall coverage (yield + fault coverage) of 1.8. The impulse sampling technique presented in [13], takes 30 samples over a test time of 25ms to achieve an overall coverage of 1.9. The analysis presented here results in a reduced cpu time for test generation of around 200s compared to the method presented in [13] which takes 1400s of cpu time just for the Monte Carlo simulations alone.

5. Conclusion

We have presented a comprehensive test generation algorithm which derives the faults from the specifications and design tolerances of the CUT and generates very efficient tests. The simplified analysis approach presented reduces the overall test generation time as well as the testing time considerably over existing testing schemes. The next steps will involve incorporation of more realistic multiple fault models and extension of the test generation algorithm to handle practical non linear circuits as well.

Specifications	Nominal Value (P_j)	Allowed deviation (ΔP_j)
Bandwidth (Hz)	202.4	20.2
Maximum Gain	1.154	0.12
DC gain	1.0	0.1
Gain @ 150Hz	1.05	0.1
Fall Time (ms)	0.15	0.01

TABLE 1. Specifications of the filter

Parameter	$\lvert\Delta ctest\rvert_j$ (%)	$\lvert\Delta c_j\rvert$(%)	Parameter	$\lvert\Delta ctest\rvert_j$ (%)	$\lvert\Delta c_j\rvert$(%)
R1	17.3	11.05	R5	20.1	14
R2	36.5	14.4	R6	20.1	11
R3	20.7	14.0	C1	31	20.2
R4	20.1	14.0	C2	20.7	14

TABLE 2. Allowed deviations of the parameters

Test ID	Sampling Time (ms)	Nominal Output (mV)	$\lvert\gamma_k\rvert$ (mV)	Cost
1	0.82	-131.6	22.35	695
2	2.69	-551.15	79.51	913
3	4.13	-600.92	105.60	1353
4	5.29	-663.79	114.57	1470

TABLE 3. Test for biquadratic filter

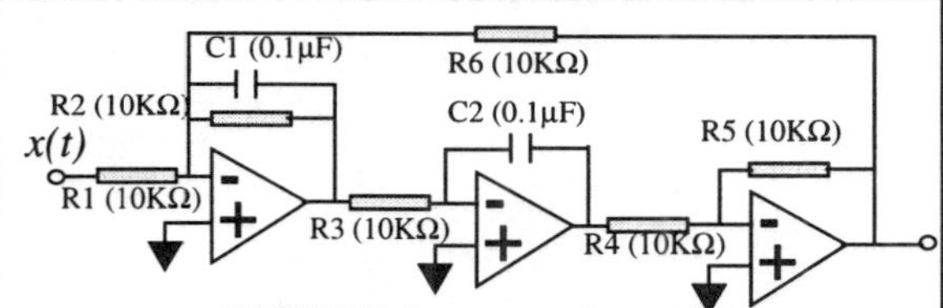

FIGURE 3. Biquadratic filter

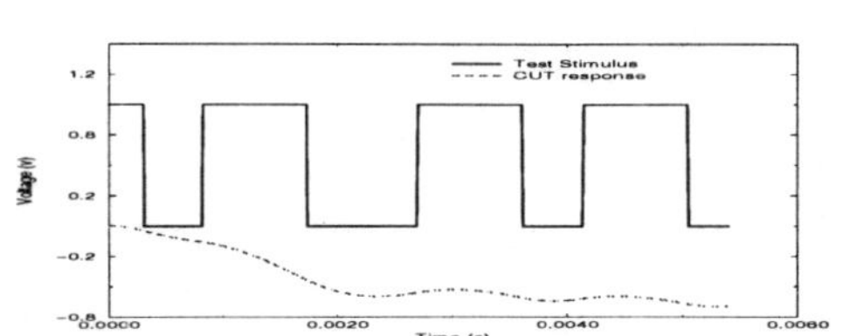

FIGURE 4. Test for biquadratic filter

References

[1] Linda Milor and A. S. Vincentelli, "Minimizing production test time to detect faults in analog integrated circuits," *IEEE Transactions on Computer-Aided Design,* Vol. 13, No. 6, pp. 796-813

[2] L. Milor and V. Viswanathan. "Detection of catastrophic faults in analog integrated circuits," *IEEE Transactions on Computer-Aided Design.* pp. 114-130, 1989.

[3] M. J. Marlett and J. A. Abraham. "DC-IATP: An iterative analog circuit test generation program for generating DC single pattern tests," *Proceedings, IEEE International Test Conference.* pp. 839-845, 1988.

[4] G. Devarayanadurg and M. Soma. "Analytical fault modeling and static test generation for analog ICs," *Proceedings, IEEE International Conference on Computer-Aided Design,* Nov. 1994.

[5] N. Nagi, A. Chatterjee, A. Balivada and J. A. Abraham. "Fault-based automatic test generator for linear analog devices," *Proceedings, International Conference on Computer Aided Design,* pp. 88-91, 1993.

[6] A. Abderrahman, E. Cerny and B. Kaminska, "CLP-Based Multifrequency test generation for analog circuits," *VLSI Test Symposium,* 1997, pp. 158 - 165.

[7] Weiwei Mao et. al. "Test generation for linear analog circuits," *Proceedings, IEEE Custom Integrated circuits Conference,* pp. 521-524, 1995.

[8] Sheng-Jen Tsai, "Test vector generation for linear analog devices," *Proceedings, IEEE International Test Conference,* pp. 592-597, 1991.

[9] G. Devarayanadurg and M. Soma, Dynamic test signal design for analog ICs," *International Conference for Computer Aided Design,* 1995. pp. 627-629.

[10] H. H. Zheng, A. Balivada and J. A. Abraham, "A novel test generation approach for parametric faults in linear analog circuits," *VLSI Test Symposium,* 1996. pp. 470-475

[11] Ashok Balivada, Jin Chen and J. A. Abraham. "Analog testing with time response parameters," *IEEE Design and Test of Computers,* pp. 18-25, Vol 13, 1996.

[12] W. M. Lindermeir, H. E. Graeb and K. J. Antreich, "Design based analog testing by characteristic observation inference," *International Conference on Computer Aided Design,* 1995. pp. 620-626.

[13] C. Y. Pan and K. T Cheng, "Test generation for linear Time Invariant Analog circuits," *International Mixed-Signal Testing Workshop,* 1997, pp. 93-100.

[14] Pramodchandran N. Variyam and Abhijit Chatterjee, "FLYER: Fast fault simulation of linear analog circuits using polynomial waveform and perturbed state representation," *Proceedings, International Conference on VLSI Design,* pp 408-412, 1997.

[15] Pramodchandran N. Variyam, Abhijit Chatterjee and Naveena Nagi, "Low-Cost and Efficient Digital-Compatible BIST for Analog Circuits Using Pulse Response Sampling," *Proceedings, VLSI Test Symposium,* 1997, pp. 261-266.

[16] R. Voorakaranam et. al. "Hierarchical specification-driven analog fault modeling for efficient fault simulation and diagnosis," *Proceedings, International Test Conference,* 1997. (to appear)

[17] UNIX Programmers reference manual.

[18] L. T. Pillage, R. A. Rohrer and C. Visweswariah, *Electronic Circuits and Systems Simulation Methods,* McGraw-Hill, Inc.

[19] E. S. Kuh and R. A. Rohrer. "The state-variable approach to network analysis," *Proceedings of the IEEE,* pp. 672-685, 1965.

[20] Yi Kang, "Systematic method for obtaining state-space representation of nonlinear dynamic circuits using MNA," *IEEE Electronic letters,* pp 2028-2030, Vol 28, 1992.

[21] S. Natarajan, "A systematic method for obtaining state equations using MNA," *IEE Proceedings-G,* pp. 341-346, Vol 138, 1991.

SESSION 7A

SEQUENTIAL CIRCUIT VERIFICATION

Moderators:

Carl P. Pixley, Motorola, Inc., Austin, TX

Gianpiero Cabodi, Politecnico di Torino, Torino, Italy

Reachability Analysis Using Partitioned-ROBDDs

Amit Narayan Adrian J. Isles Jawahar Jain[1] Robert K. Brayton
Alberto L. Sangiovanni-Vincentelli

Department of Electrical Engineering and Computer Sciences,
University of California, Berkeley, CA 94720

Abstract

In this paper, we address the problem of finite state machine (FSM) traversal, a key step in most sequential verification and synthesis algorithms. We propose the use of partitioned-ROBDDs to reduce the memory explosion problem associated with symbolic state space exploration techniques.

In our technique, the reachable state set is represented as a partitioned-ROBDD [26]. Different partitions of the Boolean space are allowed to have different variable orderings and only one partition needs to be in memory at any given time.

We show the effectiveness of our approach on a set of ISCAS89 benchmark circuits. Our techniques result in a significant reduction in total memory utilization. For a given memory limit, partitioned-ROBDD based method can complete traversal for many circuits for which monolithic ROBDDs fail. For circuits where both partitioned-ROBDDs as well as monolithic-ROBDDs cannot complete traversal, partitioned-ROBDDs can reach a significantly larger set of states.

1 Introduction

A large number of problems in VLSI-CAD including verification and synthesis of sequential circuits require efficient techniques to perform state enumeration of finite state machines (FSMs). For a given sequential circuit, the number of reachable states can be exponential in the number of state elements present in the circuit. A popular approach to deal with this 'state explosion problem' consists of implicitly representing the set of reachable states and the transition relation of an FSM as Reduced Ordered Binary Decision Diagrams (ROBDDs) [5, 7, 12, 27, 32]. In many cases, ROBDDs can represent a large number of states very compactly, thus allowing automatic verification and synthesis of systems having large state spaces. However, in many other cases, the ROBDD representation is not compact. In fact, the size of an ROBDD representing the set of reachable states of a circuit can be exponential in the number of state holding elements present in the circuit. Unfortunately, circuits which exhibit this worst case complexity do frequently arise in practice. This problem, commonly known as the ROBDD 'memory explosion problem', places a limit on the complexity of circuits that can be processed using ROBDDs.

Many researchers have addressed this problem of ROBDD memory explosion and have proposed alternative representations for Boolean functions which are more compact than ROBDDs (sometimes exponentially so) on certain classes of functions. Some of these are Free BDDs [1, 14, 30], Functional Decision Diagrams (FDDs) [22], ZBDDs [25], OKFDD [13], k-OBDDs [2], IBDDs [19], partitioned-ROBDDs [20, 26], $\oplus$-OBDDs [33], TBDDs [1], Canonical TBDDs [15] etc.

In spite of the theoretical advances made in the area of Boolean function representation, ROBDDs still remain the most popular representation for many problems arising in sequential circuit verification and synthesis. One important reason behind this is that the effectiveness of these alternative representations has not been adequately demonstrated on practical problems. In particular, nobody (to the best of our knowledge) has shown an application of these representations in the context of sequential circuits.

[1] Fujitsu Laboratories of America, Santa Clara, CA 95054

Recently, Narayan, Jain, Fujita and Sangiovanni-Vincentelli [26] discussed a representation for Boolean functions, called partitioned-ROBDDs. Partitioned-ROBDDs, besides being canonical and efficiently manipulable, can be exponentially more compact than monolithic ROBDDs in representing certain classes of Boolean functions. Experimental results on a set of hard combinational circuits showed a significant improvement in memory requirement.

In this paper, we show how partitioned-ROBDDs can be applied for performing reachability analysis on sequential circuits. Reachability analysis constitutes the core computation of many sequential synthesis and verification algorithms. We present an algorithm to create the partitioned-ROBDD representation for the set of reachable states starting from a sequential netlist. The algorithm is built on top of a conventional reachability algorithm and can fully leverage other advances made in the BDD technology and reachability analysis. In this sense, it is backward compatible with other approaches. We have implemented our algorithm in the VIS [16] environment using the CUDD package from University of Colorado [31]. Experimental results on a set of ISCAS89 and ISCAS89-addendum93 circuits show up to 2 orders of magnitude reduction in space required to represent the set of reachable states. For a given memory limit, the partitioned-ROBDD based reachability algorithm can complete traversal for many circuits on which monolithic-ROBDDs fail. For hard circuits where both monolithic-ROBDDs and partitioned-ROBDDs are unable to complete traversal, partitioned-ROBDDs are able to reach a significantly larger number of states than monolithic ROBDDs.

The rest of the paper is organized as follows. In Section 2, we briefly review partitioned-ROBDDs and show an example of a sequential circuit where partitioned-ROBDDs can be exponentially more compact than monolithic ROBDDs in representing the set of reachable states. In section 3, we briefly review the monolithic ROBDD based FSM traversal algorithm and some previous approaches to deal with the memory explosion problem. In Section 4, we present our algorithm of partitioned-ROBDD based FSM traversal and discuss some implementation issues. Experimental results are presented in Section 5.

2 Partitioned-ROBDDs

The idea of partitioning was used to discuss a function representation scheme called partitioned-ROBDDs in [18, 20] which was then extensively developed in [26]. In this section, we first briefly review the definition of partitioned-ROBDDs and then show an example of sequential circuit verification where the set of reachable states has an exponential ROBDD representation but can be efficiently represented by partitioned-ROBDDs using only polynomial space.

2.1 Partitioned-ROBDDs: Definition

Assume that we are given a Boolean function $f : B^n \to B$, defined over n inputs $X_n = \{x_1, \ldots, x_n\}$. The partitioned-ROBDD representation, χ_f, of f is defined as follows [20, 26]:

Definition 1 *Given a Boolean function $f : B^n \to B$ defined over X_n, a partitioned-ROBDD representation χ_f of f is a set of k function pairs, $\chi_f = \{(w_1, f_1), \ldots, (w_k, f_k)\}$ where, $w_i : B^n \to B$ and $f_i : B^n \to B$, are also defined over X_n and satisfy the following conditions:*

1092-3152/97 $10.00 © 1997 IEEE

- *1.* w_i *and* f_i *are represented as ROBDDs with the variable ordering* π_i*, for* $1 \le i \le k$.
- *2.* $w_1 + w_2 + \ldots + w_k = 1$
- *3.* $w_i \wedge w_j = 0$*, for* $i \ne j$
- *4.* $f_i = w_i \wedge f$*, for* $1 \le i \le k$

Here, $+$ and $\wedge$ represent Boolean OR and AND respectively. The set $\{w_1, \ldots, w_k\}$ is denoted by W. Each w_i is called a *window function* and represents a part of the Boolean space over which f is defined. Intuitively speaking, in partitioned-ROBDDs the Boolean space is divided into k partitions (using the window functions $w_i \in W$). The functionality of f is represented over each partition as a separate ROBDD f_i. ROBDDs for different partitions can have different variable orders.

Partitioned-ROBDDs are canonical and various Boolean operations can be efficiently performed on them just like ROBDDs. In addition, they can be exponentially more compact than ROBDDs for certain classes of functions. The practical utility of this representation was demonstrated by constructing ROBDDs for the outputs of combinational circuits. Recently, it was proved by Bollig and Wegener [4] that the class of partitioned-ROBDDs form a strict hierarchy i.e. for any given k, there are functions which have a polynomial $(k+1)$-partitioned-ROBDD representation but no polynomial k-partitioned-ROBDD representation. Therefore, by increasing the number of partitions, we can increase the class of functions that become tractable. An excellent comparison of the computational power of various BDD based representations and partitioned-ROBDDs can be found in [3].

2.2 Partitioned-ROBDD: An Example

The examples used in [26] to prove that partitioned-ROBDDs can be exponentially more compact than monolithic ROBDDs are somewhat artificial in the sense that one is unlikely to encounter these functions in real-life circuits. Here we present a more realistic example of sequential circuit verification where partitioned-ROBDD representation of the set of reachable states is exponentially more compact than the monolithic representation. This example is taken from [24] and consists of verifying whether two hardware implementations of a bounded queue are equivalent (Figure 1). The first implementation is a *shift register* in which the most recent item is always stored in location 0, and all items shift over when a new item is inserted. The second implementation is a *ring buffer*, where a "head pointer" points to the oldest item, and the items themselves remain fixed. The two circuits can be verified by constructing the product machine and checking that the outputs of the two circuits are always equal [12]. To check this, we need to construct the set of reachable states. To get a small ROBDD representation

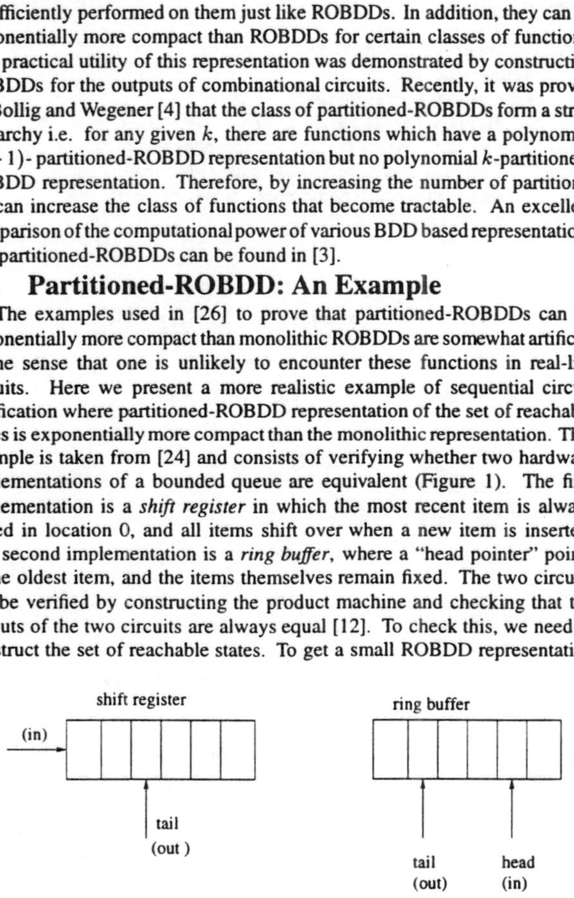

Figure 1: *Two implementation of FIFO queue*

for the reachable states, we need to put the related state variables together in the variable order of the ROBDD representing the set of reachable states. However, since the location of the head pointer is not fixed, we cannot fix an order which keeps the related variables together. Notice that although there is no order which is good for ROBDDs, if we fix the position of the head pointer then there is a one-to-one correspondence between the locations of the two queues. Therefore for a given location of the head pointer, we can find an ordering which leads to a small ROBDD for the reachable state set. Since ROBDDs are restricted to have only one order, any variable ordering leads to an exponentially sized ROBDD. Partitioned-ROBDDs, on the other hand can employ different orders for different partitions. Therefore, if we select the different locations of the head pointer as our window functions, then for each window function there is a one-to-one correspondence between the state variables of the two implementations. For each window function we can select the variable ordering which keeps these related state variables together, resulting in a small partitioned-ROBDD representation.

Notice that a free-BDD representation of the above example is also polynomial. However, using free-BDDs in sequential verification is difficult because of the inherent difficulties associated in performing existential quantification on them.

3 Reachability Analysis: Monolithic ROBDDs

In this section, we discuss the standard monolithic algorithm for reachability analysis and some improvements that have been proposed for it. The partitioned-ROBDD based traversal algorithm uses the monolithic ROBDD based algorithm in its inner loop (to perform fixed point on individual partitions). Therefore, it is able to take advantage of all of these improvements.

3.1 Standard Algorithm

The standard reachability algorithm is based on a breadth-first traversal of finite-state machines [12, 23, 32]. The algorithm takes as inputs the set of initial states, $I(s)$, expressed in terms of the present state variables, s, and a transition relation, $T(s, s', i)$, which represents the valid state transitions in the FSM. Given a set of states, $R(s)$, that the system can reach, the set of next states, $N(s')$, is calculated by taking the image of $R(s)$ under $T(s, s', i)$ (referred to as $IMAGE(R(s), T(s, s', i))$ in the algorithms). Figure 2 shows the outline of this algorithm.

```
FSM_TRAVERSAL(I(s), T(s,s',i) ) {
    R(s) = F(s) = I(s)
    while (F(s) ≠ 0) {
        N(s') = IMAGE[F(s), T(s,s',i)]
        F(s) = N(s' ← s) ∧ R̄(s)
        R(s) = R(s) + F(s)
    }
}
```

Figure 2: *Standard Reachability Algorithm*

3.2 Enhancements to the Standard Algorithm

The FSM traversal algorithm presented in Figure 2 needs the ROBDD representations of $T(s, s', i)$ and $R(s)$. The algorithm will not be able to terminate if either of the two ROBDDs become very large. Many techniques have been proposed which can substantially reduce the memory required to represent $T(s, s', i)$ and $R(s)$ as ROBDDs.

3.2.1 Partitioned Transition Relation

To control the size of transition relations, Burch, Clarke and Long [6] propose the use of partitioned transition relations. In this method, instead of using a monolithic ROBDD representation of the transition relation, the transition relations of different latches are kept as separate ROBDDs (or clustered into small groups of latches [28]). Since ROBDDs representing the individual latch transition relations are typically much smaller than when they are combined, this method can result in substantial memory savings. In addition, it allows for early quantification of variables which are not present in the support of other transition relations [17, 8, 32]. This technique can also result in substantial savings in memory during image computation. Notice though, that the term 'partitioning' is being used here in a totally different context; in the partitioned-transition relation approach, the set of latches are being partitioned into different groups while in partitioned-ROBDDs, it is the Boolean space which is being partitioned. In fact, the two approaches are orthogonal and partitioned-transition relations are used in the inner loop of our approach.

For large circuits, even the ROBDDs of the individual latches can become very large. In these cases [9, 21] suggest the use of intermediate variables to control the size of transition relations . These intermediate variables can be quantified out along with the present state variables during the image computation step.

3.2.2 Reducing Intermediate Memory Requirements

Most of the techniques for controlling the size of the ROBDD representation of $R(s)$ are based on the observation that the set of reachable states usually has a much smaller representation at the fixed-point as compared to the peak size observed during the intermediate stages of computation. These techniques [29, 10, 11] try to reduce the intermediate peak memory requirement by changing the order in which the states are visited during traversal. Of these, [10, 11] is the most closely related to our approach. We will do a more detailed comparison with their work in section 6.

4 Reachability Analysis: Partitioned-ROBDDs

In this section, we describe our partitioned-ROBDD based reachability analysis algorithms in detail. This algorithms is built on top of the standard BFS algorithm and thus benefits from the improvements discussed in the previous section.

Before describing the algorithm in detail, let us first take a look at image computation step for partitioned-ROBDDs. Suppose we are given the partitioned-ROBDD representation, χ_R, of $R(s)$ where, $\chi_R = \{(w_j(s), R_j) | 1 \leq j \leq k\}$ satisfying conditions 1-4 in Definition 1. We want to get the partitioned-ROBDD representation, χ_N, of the set of next states. Suppose we take the image of R_j under $T(s,s',i)$ to obtain N_j for $1 \leq j \leq k$. These N_j's obtained under the image of $T(s,s',i)$ are not disjoint and hence cannot be used in the partitioned-ROBDD representation of $N(s)$ (Definition 1). There are two simple solutions to this problem. One is that we re-partition these N_j's according to the window function W and assign the min-terms in $w_i \wedge N_j$ to partition i. However, since we want to maintain different orders for different partitions, this computation can be expensive if performed at every step of image computation. Another solution is that we continue with the reachability analysis on the N_j's obtained for a few more steps and then re-partition to obtain a partitioned-ROBDD representation. The problem with this approach is that in the intermediate stages of computation, the same stages can be visited multiple times making it hard to detect when a fixed point is reached and leading to unnecessary extra computation.

We propose an alternative solution to the above based on the following observation. Let us assume that we are given a partitioned-ROBDD representation $\chi_R = \{(w_j(s), R_j) | 1 \leq j \leq k\}$. If we take the image of R_j under $T_{jj}(s,s',i)$, where $T_{jj}(s,s',i) = w_j(s)w_j(s')T(s,s',i)$, we get,

$$N_j(s') = \exists_{s,i}[w_j(s)w_j(s')T(s,s',i)R_j(s)] \qquad (1)$$

Since $w_j(s')$ is independent of the variables to be quantified, it can be taken out of existential quantification, giving us the following equation:

$$N_j(s') = w_j(s')[\exists_{s,i}[w_j(s)T(s,s',i)R_j(s)]] \qquad (2)$$

Equation 2 shows that the image of R_j under $T_{jj}(s,s',i)$ lies completely within the partition j. Similarly, the image, N_l of R_j under $T_{jl}(s,s',i)$ where $T_{jl}(s,s',i) = w_j(s)w_l(s')T(s,s',i)$, will lie completely within the partition l. This simple observation forms the basis of our algorithm. We perform multiple steps of image computation on each R_j under T_{jj}. Since these steps of image computation add states only within the same partition, and since different partitions are disjoint, we are guaranteed that the same state is not being visited multiple times within different partitions. Once a fixed-point is reached within a partition j, transition relations $T_{jl}(s,s',i)$ are used to communicate the new set of states to the partition l for $1 \leq l \leq k$ and $l \neq j$. The overall flow of the partitioned-ROBDD based algorithm is outlined in Figure 3.

The POBDD_REACH algorithm takes BDDs representing the transition relation $T(s,s',i)$, the set of initial states $I(s)$ of an FSM M and an integer k. The result of the algorithm is the set of reachable states of M represented as POBDD: $\chi_R = \{(w_j(s), R_j) | 1 \leq j \leq k\}$. Associated with each partition, j, is a $bddMgr_j$. Each BDD manager is free to choose a unique ordering that minimizes the number of nodes in its partition. In addition to $R_j(s)$, each partition utilizes k transition relations. These transition relations are computed for each j using $T_{jl}(s,s',i) = w_j(s)w_l(s')T(s,s',i)$ $(1 \leq l \leq k)$. Intuitively, T_{jl} represents the transitions from states in window j to states in window l. POBDD_REACH attempts to minimize memory usage by only keeping the reachable state set and transition relations associated with one partition in memory at a given time. The reachable state sets for partitions not being processed are saved on disk. The transition relations for partitions not being processed are freed and recomputed when needed.

```
POBDD_REACH( I(s), T(s,s',i), k ) {

    {w_j(s)} = COMPUTE_WINDOWS( T(s,s',i) )
    {bddMgr_j} = CREATE_BDD_MANAGERS( k )
    eventQueue = INITIALIZE_QUEUE( {w_j(s), I(s), T(s,s',i)} )
    {C_j(s) = φ}

    while(|eventQueue| ≠ 0 ) {
      newQueue = φ
      foreach (j ∈ eventQueue) {
        R_j(s) = LOAD_FROM_DISK( bddMgr_j, j)) + C_j(s)
        FREE( C_j(s) )
        {T_jl(s,s',i)} = MAKE_TRs( bddMgr_j, j )
        N_j(s) =FSM_TRAVERSAL( R_j(s), T_jj(s,s',i) )
        F_j(s) = R̄_j(s) ∧ N_j(s)
        R_j(s) = R_j(s) + F_j(s)
        if(F_j(s) ≠ 0 ) {
          foreach ( l s.t. ( (1 ≤ l ≤ k) & (l ≠ j))) {
            N_l(s' ← s) =IMAGE(R_j, T_jl(s,s',i) )
            C_l(s) = MGR_COMM( N_l(s),
                          bddMgr_j, bddMgr_l, φ) + C_l(s)
            if(|C_l(s)| ≠ 0)  l → newQueue
          }
        }
        SAVE_TO_DISK( bddMgr_j, R_j(s) )
        FREE( R_j(s) )
        FREE( {T_jl(s,s',i)} )
      }
      eventQueue = newQueue
    }
}
```

Figure 3: *POBDD_REACH Algorithm*

Given $I(s)$, $T(s,s',i)$ and k, function COMPUTE_WINDOWS returns a set of window functions $\{w_j(s)\}$. The heuristic used to determine these window functions is discussed in Section 4.1.

The algorithm maintains an array, $eventQueue$, which keeps track of the partitions on which reachability has to be performed. This array is initialized using the function INITIALIZE_QUEUE, which computes the set of initial states for each partition. Each $I_l(s)$ is computed by taking the image of $I(s)$ under $T_{jl}(s,s',i)$ for $1 \leq j \leq k$ and adding it to $w_l(s) \wedge I(s)$. Note that taking this image is necessary in the present form of the algorithm in order to account for cases where $T_{jj} \wedge w_j(s) \wedge I(s) = \phi$. Partition l is inserted into $eventQueue$ only if $I_l(s)$ is non empty. INITIALIZE_QUEUE initially saves all partitions to disk.

Once the initial states of each partition are computed, the algorithm proceeds by loading $R_j(s)$ from disk and then performing a fixed point computation using T_{jj}. Next, $k-1$ image computations are performed under T_{jl} (for $l \neq j$) to communicate the information about the new states, $F_j(s)$, added in partition j. For this communication between managers, we keep a communication cache, C_l, which is a BDD in memory that keeps the states that can be reached from the new states $F_j(s)$ of other partitions j, $j \neq l$ under the image of $T_{jl}(s,s',i)$. Note that since C_l is defined in $bddMgr_l$,

MGR_COMM must be called using $bddMgr_j$ and $bddMgr_l$ as arguments. Each C_l is saved in memory and added to the set of reachable states in l the next time it is loaded from disk. The sets Partition l is added to the $newQueue$ if C_l is non-empty. The algorithm continues until no new partitions need to be processed.

The function MGR_COMM (Figure 4) takes a BDD f that is defined in the BDD manager $srcMgr$, and returns a BDD g that is functionally equivalent to f but defined in the BDD manager $destMgr$. The function also takes the table $computedTable$ as an argument which maps BDD nodes in the $srcMgr$ to equivalent nodes in the $destMgr$ that have been previously computed by the function. Initially, the $computedTable$ is empty. Note that MGR_COMM does not require $srcMgr$ and $destMgr$ to have the same variable orderings. Although this computation can be expensive in the worst case, we have not found this to be a bottleneck in the examples that we have run.

```
MGR_COMM(f, srcMgr, destMgr, computedTable ){
    if( f == 0 ) return bdd_zero(destMgr)
    if( f == 1 ) return bdd_one(destMgr)
    if( g = computedTable(f) ) return g
    t = MGR_COMM( bdd_then(srcMgr, f),
                  srcMgr, destMgr, computedTable )
    e = MGR_COMM( bdd_else(srcMgr, f),
                  srcMgr, destMgr, computedTable )
    g = ite(topVar(f), t, e)
    (f, g) -> computedTable
    (f̄, ḡ) -> computedTable
    return g
}
```

Figure 4: *Algorithm to convert between BDD managers*

4.1 Partitioning Heuristic

Currently we use a static algorithm to obtain the window functions in which the number of partitions is specified a priori. Window functions, $w(s)$'s, are cubes on the present state variables. The algorithm assigns a cost to each variable and selects the best $log_2 k$ variables (for k partitions) for partitioning. From these $log_2 k$ variables k partitions are created which correspond to all the binary assignments of these variables. Our goal is to create small and balanced partitions. For this we define the cost of partitioning a transition relation $T(s, s', i)$ on variable s as

$$cost_s(T) = \alpha[p_s(T)] + \beta[r_s(T)] \tag{3}$$

where $p_s(T)$ represents the partitioning factor and is given by,

$$p_s(T) = max(|T_s|, |T_{\overline{s}}|) \tag{4}$$

and $r_s(T)$ represents the redundancy factor and is given by,

$$r_s(T) = |T_s| + |T_{\overline{s}}| \tag{5}$$

Here, T_s and $T_{\overline{s}}$ represent the positive and the negative cofactors of T with respect to s respectively. Notice that a lower partitioning factor is good as it implies that the worst of the two partitions is small and similarly a lower redundancy factor is good since it implies that the total work involved in creating the two partitions is less.

If $T(s, s', i) = \prod_{k=1}^{m} T_k(s, s', i)$ is a 'partitioned-Transition Relation' (see Section 3.2.1), then the cost of partitioning for a variable s is defined as:

$$cost_s(T) = \sum_{k=1}^{m} \frac{cost_s(T_k)}{T_k} \tag{6}$$

Notice that although our current heuristic for window function selection only gives window functions which are cubes on the present state variables, in the algorithm or implementation there is nothing which restricts us from using more general window functions (which can be arbitrary functions of s). Also, our current heuristic for window function selection is based on only the transition relation. We are currently implementing another heuristic which dynamically increases the number of partitions if the partitions become very large.

4.2 Use of $\overline{w}_j$ as Don't Cares

In our algorithm, the part of the Boolean space covered by $\overline{w}_j(s)$ is used as don't cares while performing traversal in partition j. Since we use only T_{jj} while traversing partition j, it ensures that no extra states are added to this partition if we use the space $\overline{w}_j(s)$ as don't cares. This don't care set, $\overline{w}_j(s)$, is used to minimize the BDDs of $R(s)$,$N(s)$ and $F(s)$ inside the FSM_TRAVERSAL routine. A good heuristic to minimize BDDs f in the presence of don't cares $\overline{w}_j(s)$, is to take the cofactor of f with respect to $w_j(s)$. Since, in the present implementation $w_j(s)$ is a cube, taking the cofactor of f with respect to it is *guaranteed* to reduce the size of the BDDs in the intermediate steps. Before communicating the new states to other partitions under $T_{jl}(s, s', i)$, we take the conjunction of R_j returned by the FSM_TRAVERSAL algorithm (which uses don't cares) with $w_j(s)$ to ensure that no extra states are added to partition l.

4.3 Use of Size and Depth Thresholds

The POBDD_REACH algorithm presented in Figure 3 provides us with considerable flexibility in terms of changing the order in which the state space is traversed. This can be done by choosing different schedules for processing the $eventQueue$, imposing a 'size' threshold such that BDDs of any one partition do not become very large or placing a depth threshold for the number of steps of reachability that are performed for each partition.

5 Experimental Results

We have implemented our algorithm of Section 4 in the VIS [16] environment using the BDD package from the University of Colorado at Boulder [31] which incorporates state-of-the-art algorithms for dynamic reordering. All results are reported using DEC Alpha architecture with 250MHz clock. The data-size limit was set to 128Mb (except for s1423 in Table 2 for which we used a DEC Alpha with 300MHz clock and a data-size limit of 256Mb was set).

In Table 1 and Table 2 we compare the results of reachability using monolithic ROBDDs and partitioned-ROBDDs. We use the algorithm proposed by Ranjan, Aziz, Brayton, Plessier and Pixley [28] as the reference algorithm for monolithic ROBDDs. We use the same algorithm with exactly the same parameter settings in the inner-loop of partitioned-ROBDDs to perform fixed-point computation on each partition. We present two sets of result with different values of the parameter image_cluster_size [28] to test the robustness of our results. The image_cluster_size represents the maximum number of BDD nodes allowed in each cluster of the partitioned transition relation (see Section 3.2.1). Dynamic reordering was enabled at all times with the default settings of the parameters. Column 3 (labeled ROBDD) reports the memory and time resource used in generating the monolithic ROBDD representation. Column 4 (labeled Partitioned-ROBDD) reports the results for the partitioned-ROBDD based reachability analysis algorithm. The columns labeled |S| represent the number of states that could be reached using the respective approach before the memory limit was exceeded and the columns labeled Size report the memory required in representing the state set and is measured in terms of the number of nodes in the BDD representation. For partitioned-ROBDDs, the size refers to the size of the largest partition since only one partition needs to be active in the memory at a given time. The column labeled 'k' represents the number of partitions constructed for partitioned-ROBDDs. The column labeled 'Time' reports the total time taken for cases where traversal could be completed.

As the tables clearly indicate, partitioned-ROBDD based traversal is always able to reach more states and the representation in terms of BDDs is always smaller than monolithic ROBDDs. Given the memory-limit of 128Mb, partitioned-ROBDDs are able to complete traversal for s1269, s1512 and s3330 while monolithic ROBDDs are able to complete traversal only for one of these circuits, namely s1512. Even in this case, partitioned-ROBDDs are able to finish traversal in significantly less time. The gains in memory are even more impressive. Partitioned-ROBDDs are almost always an order of magnitude more compact than monolithic ROBDDs (even while representing a larger state space). In particular, for s3330, monolithic ROBDD based representation requires more than 400000 nodes to represent 1.17×10^{17} states (for image_cluster_size = 100) while partitioned-ROBDDs can complete traversal and represent all 7.2778×10^{17} states in about 4000 nodes; a factor of 100 reduction. This is surprising because the reduction was achieved by creating only 4 partitions.

We have plotted the BDD size profile, as a function of the number of states reached for s3330 to check whether the intermediate memory requirement of partitioned-ROBDDs is also small or not. Again, partitioned-ROBDDs have a much better behavior compared to monolithic ROBDDs as shown in Figure 5. Similar results were obtained for other circuits. In particular, for s1423 we observed that by making only 4 partitions, the partitioned-ROBDD algorithm was able to reach a significantly more number of states. In fact, the partitioned-ROBDD based algorithm was able to reach more states (8.0554×10^{10}) than monolithic ROBDD based algorithm in just a few seconds and needed only 14151 nodes to represent them. Once again over a factor of 100 improvement in representing a state set of comparable size.

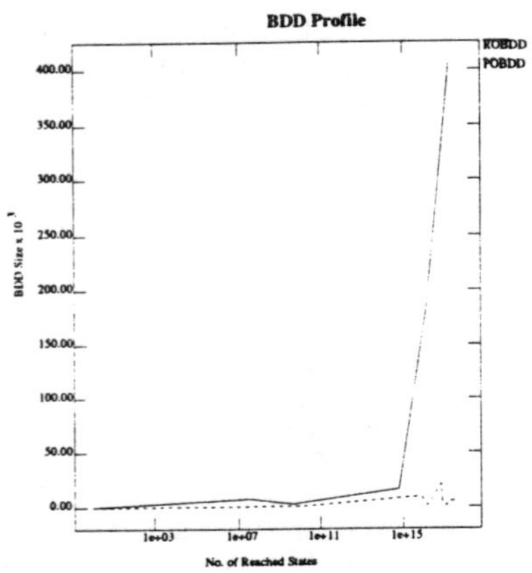

Figure 5: *BDD Profile of s3330*

6 Comment on Related Work

Cabodi, Camurati and Quer [10, 11] also use a notion of partitioning to represent the set of reachable states. At the first glance, their approach appears to be somewhat similar to ours. However, there are significant differences between the two works. In their approach, when the set of reached states becomes larger than a certain threshold, it is split into two or more partitions. Reachability is then performed on these partitions separately after which the sets are combined to obtain a monolithic representation of the reachable state set. The goal here is to reduce the intermediate memory requirement instead of creating a partitioned-ROBDD representation. Since, reachability is performed on the different partitions using $T(s, s', i)$ (unlike our approach where we use $T_{jj}(s, s', i)$ for the jth partition), it suffers from the same problems as were discussed in the beginning of section 4. Further, since the partitions have to be combined later on, their approach is not able to use (at least in the present form) different orders for different partitions. As most of the gains in cube based partitioning come from the fact that different partitions can have different orders, this poses a serious restriction on the effectiveness of their approach. It can be proved, in fact, that for input variable based partitioning, without allowing different partitions to have different variable orderings, partitioning can achieve only linear reduction in space as opposed to partitioned-ROBDDs where the gains can be exponential. An example of such a case is the buffer-queue verification example of section 2. In addition to these, differences exist in the details of the algorithms and their implementations. These include our use of an event queue, a different partitioning heuristic, our use of don't cares, communication between managers with different orderings and control on the scheduling of the partitions. Unfortunately, a direct comparison of results could not be made since we did not have a copy of their package.

7 Conclusions

In this paper, the use of partitioned-ROBDDs for performing reachability analysis on sequential circuits has been proposed. We have shown, by means of an example, that compared to monolithic ROBDDs, partitioned-ROBDDs can represent the reachable state set of some circuits in exponentially less space. In addition, we have presented an algorithm to construct the partitioned-ROBDD representation of the set of reachable states starting from the set of initial states and the transition relation of a system. Our algorithm allows different partitions to have different variable orderings and only one partition needs to be present in memory at any given time. Further, multiple steps of reachability can be performed independently before any communication between partitions is needed.

Experimental results have been very encouraging. Our algorithm has been implemented in the VIS environment and we have observed up to two orders of magnitude reduction in memory usage. For a given memory limit, the partitioned-ROBDD based algorithm was able to complete traversal for many circuits on which monolithic ROBDDs failed. For circuits where both monolithic ROBDDs and partitioned-ROBDDs could not complete traversal, partitioned-ROBDDs were able to cover a significantly larger state space.

Future research is directed towards improving the efficiency of our algorithm. In particular, we are experimenting with different partitioning heuristics. We are currently implementing a dynamic partitioning algorithm, which increases the number of partitions whenever the size of a particular partition crosses a certain threshold. Finally, since reachability can be performed on each partition separately, with only minimal communication between partitions, we feel that our algorithm is particularly suitable for parallel implementation.

8 Acknowledgements

The authors would like to thank Dr. M. Fujita for his help in the earlier stages of this project, and Amit Mehrotra and Ravi Gunturi for their critical review of the draft. This work was supported in part by Semiconductor Research Corporation contract #97-DC-324.

References

[1] J. Bern, C. Meinel, and A. Slobodova. Efficient OBDD-Based Boolean Manipulation in CAD Beyond Current Limits. In *DAC*, pages 408–413, June 1995.

[2] B. Bollig, M. Sauerhoff, D. Sieling, and I. Wegener. Hierarchy Theorems for kOBDDs and kIBDDs. *Accepted for publication in Theoretical Computer Science*, 1997.

[3] B. Bollig and I. Wegener. Partitioned-BDDs vs. Other BDD Models. In *To be published in IWLS 97*, Tahoe City, CA, May 1997.

[4] B. Bollig and Ingo Wegener. manuscript, Personal communication, 1997.

[5] R. E. Bryant. Graph-based Algorithms for Boolean Function Manipulation. *IEEE Transactions on Computers*, C-35:677–691, August 1986.

[6] J. R. Burch, E. M. Clarke, and D. E. Long. Symbolic Model Checking with Partitioned Transition Relations. In *DAC*, pages 403–407, June 1991.

[7] J. R. Burch, E. M. Clarke, K. L. McMillan, and D. L. Dill. Symbolic Model Checking: 10^{20} States and Beyond. *Information and Computation*, 98(2):142–170, 1992.

[8] G. Cabodi and P. Camurati. Symbolic FSM Traversals Based on the Transition Relation. *Manuscript Submitted to Transaction on Computer-Aided Design*, 1994.

[9] G. Cabodi, P. Camurati, and S. Quer. Auxillary variables for extending symbolic traversal techniques to data paths. *31st Design Automation Conference*, pages 289–293, 1994.

[10] G. Cabodi, P. Camurati, and S. Quer. Improved reachability analysis of large finite state machines. *ICCAD*, pages 354–360, 1996.

Ckt	#FF	ROBDD			Partitioned-ROBDD			
		$\|S\|$	Size	Time	$\|S\|$	Size	Time	k
s1269	37	1.3077×10^7	20862	N/A	1.1313×10^9	550	906	2
s1512	57	1.6574×10^{12}	687	7226.5	1.6574×10^{12}	649	3238.5	2
s3271	116	4.1292×10^{22}	193593	N/A	9.3374×10^{24}	85677	N/A	4
s3330	132	5.9573×10^{14}	125600	N/A	7.2778×10^{17}	6411	1031.6	8
s4863	104	3.9746×10^{15}	13270	N/A	3.1460×10^{17}	2156	N/A	8
s1423	74	7.99116×10^9	469271	N/A	1.4787×10^{15}	394136	N/A	4

Table 1: *ISCAS-89 Circuits: Image_Cluster_Size = 5000*

Ckt	#FF	ROBDD			Partitioned-ROBDD			
		$\|S\|$	Size	Time	$\|S\|$	Size	Time	k
s1269	37	1.3077×10^7	15886	N/A	7.300×10^8	499	N/A	4
s1512	57	1.6574×10^{12}	687	2066	1.6574×10^{12}	581	1426	4
s3271	116	3.5143×10^{23}	159146	N/A	1.0096×10^{28}	39381	N/A	4
s3330	132	1.1728×10^{17}	404213	N/A	7.2778×10^{17}	4202	672.3	4
s4863	104	3.9746×10^{15}	14273	N/A	3.1460×10^{17}	2156	N/A	8

Table 2: *ISCAS-89 Circuits: Image_Cluster_Size = 100*

[11] G. Cabodi, P. Camurati, and S. Quer. Disjunctive partitioning and partial iterative squaring: An effective approach for symbolic traversal of large circuits. *DAC*, 1997.

[12] O. Coudert, C. Berthet, and J. C. Madre. Verification of Sequential Machines Based on Symbolic Execution. In *Proc. of the Workshop on Automatic Verification Methods for Finite State Systems*, Grenoble, France, 1989.

[13] R. Drechsler *et. al.* Efficient representation and manipulation of switching functions based on Ordered Kronecker Functional Decision Diagrams. In *DAC*, pages 415–419, 1994.

[14] J Gergov and Ch. Meinel. Efficient Boolean Manipulation With OBDD's can be Extended to FBDD's. *IEEE Transaction on Computers*, 43(10):1197–1209, 1994.

[15] E. Goldberg, Y. Kukimoto, and R. K. Brayton. Canonical TBDD's - A New Data Structure for Boolean Functions. In *Proc. of the Intl. Workshop on Logic Synthesis*, May 1997.

[16] The VIS Group. VIS: A System for Verification and Synthesis. In *CAV*, volume 1102 of *LNCS*, pages 428–432. Springer-Verlag, 1996.

[17] R. Hojati, S.C. Krishnan, and R. K. Brayton. Heuristic Algorithms for Early Quantification and Partial Product Minimization. Technical Report UCB/ERL M93/58, Electronics Research Lab, Univ. of California, Berkeley, CA 94720, July 1993.

[18] J. Jain. On Analysis of Boolean Functions. *Ph.D Dissertation, Dept. of Electrical and Computer Engineering, The University of Texas at Austin*, 1993.

[19] J. Jain, J. Bitner, M. Abadir, J. A. Abraham, and D. S. Fussell. Indexed BDDs: Algorithmic advances in techniques to represent and verify Boolean functions. *IEEE Transactions on Computers (to appear)*.

[20] J. Jain, J. Bitner, D. S. Fussell, and J. A. Abraham. Functional partitioning for verification and related problems. *Brown/MIT VLSI Conference*, March 1992.

[21] J. Jain, A. Narayan, C. Coelho, S. Khatri, A. Sangiovanni-Vincentelli, R. Brayton, and M. Fujita. Decomposition Techniques for Efficient ROBDD Construction. In *Formal Methods in CAD 96*, LNCS. Springer-Verlag, 1996.

[22] U. Kebschull *et. al.* Multilevel logic synthesis based on Functional Decision Diagrams. *European DAC*, pages 43–47, 1992.

[23] K. L. McMillan. *Symbolic Model Checking*. Kluwer Academic Publishers, 1993.

[24] K. L. McMillan. A conjunctively decomposed boolean representation for symbolic model checking. In *Computer-Aided Verification*, pages 13–25, 1996.

[25] S. Minato. Zero-suppressed BDDs for set manipulation in combinatorial problems. In *DAC*, June 1993.

[26] A. Narayan, J. Jain, M. Fujita, and A. L. Sangiovanni-Vincentelli. Partitioned-ROBDDs - A Compact, Canonical and Efficiently Manipulable Representation for Boolean Functions. *ICCAD*, November 1996.

[27] C. Pixley. A Computational Theory and Implementation of Sequential Hardware Equivalence. pages 293–320, June 1990.

[28] R. K. Ranjan, A. Aziz, R. K. Brayton, B. Plessier, and C. Pixley. Efficient BDD Algorithms for FSM Synthesis and Verification. In *Proc. of the Intl. Workshop on Logic Synthesis*, Tahoe City, NV, May 1995.

[29] K. Ravi and F. Somenzi. High-density reachability analysis. *ICCAD*, 1995.

[30] D. Sieling and I. Wegener. Graph-driven OBDDs - a new data structure for Boolean functions. *Theoretical Computer Science*, 1995.

[31] F. Somenzi. CUDD: CU Decision Diagram Package, Release 2.1.1. *Department of Electrical and Computer Engineering, University of Colorado at Boulder*, February 1997.

[32] H. J. Touati, H. Savoj, B. Lin, R. K. Brayton, and A. L. Sangiovanni-Vincentelli. Implicit State Enumeration of Finite State Machines using BDD's. In *ICCAD*, pages 130–133, November 1990.

[33] S. Waack. On the descriptive and algorithmic power of Parity Ordered Binary Decision Diagrams. In *Proc. of STACS*, LNCS. Springer-Verlag, 1997.

Record & Play: A Structural Fixed Point Iteration for Sequential Circuit Verification*

Dominik Stoffel *Wolfgang Kunz*
Institute of Computer Science III
University of Potsdam
14415 Potsdam, Germany

Abstract

This paper proposes a technique for sequential logic equivalence checking by a structural fixed point iteration. Verification is performed by expanding the circuit into an iterative circuit array and by proving equivalence of each time frame by well-known combinational verification techniques. These exploit structural similarity between designs by local circuit transformations. Starting from the initial state, for each time frame the performed circuit transformations are stored ("recorded") in an instruction queue. In subsequent time frames the instruction queue is re-used ("played") and updated when necessary. At some point the instruction queue does not need to be modified any more and is valid in all subsequent time frames. Thus, a fixed point is reached and machine equivalence is proved by induction. Experimental results show the great promise of this approach to verify circuits after re-synthesis and retiming.

1 Introduction

This paper addresses the problem of logic equivalence checking for synchronous sequential circuits. Only completely specified machines are considered. Equivalence of two finite state machines with known initial state can be established by proving the equivalence of the initial state: let *A* and *B* denote two completely specified finite state machines with initial states $S_{0,A}$ and $S_{0,B}$, respectively. The finite state machines *A* and *B* are called equivalent if and only if for every possible input sequence the same output sequence is produced if both machines are in their respective initial state. In this paper we assume that either the initial state (or a set of initial states) is known for each machine, or an initializing sequence is given to bring the circuit into a well-defined state after power-up. We do not consider the problem of *safe replaceability* as raised by [14].

Conventionally the problem of logic equivalence checking for sequential circuits has been approached by a fixed point iteration based on BDD-based image computations [5]. This is referred to as "symbolic" FSM traversal and has been developped further, e.g., in [3, 4, 6, 15, 16]. In particular, van Eijk [6] describes a BDD-based method exploiting functional dependencies between state variables which is related to the method presented here.

Since BDD-based FSM traversal often suffers from state explosion for large designs, Huang et al. [8, 9] explored structural techniques based on sequential ATPG. Their approach to equivalence checking is based on the assumption that practical designs under comparison often contain a lot of equivalent state variables. The procedure in [8, 9] starts with a set of candidate pairs for equivalent state variables and performs an induction-based filtering process to eliminate the wrong candidates. It is assumed that simple relationships exist between state variables that can be obtained by simulation. This is promising for circuits with very similar encodings but may fail in other cases. Therefore, we take a different approach. Our work is based on the observation that a fixed point iteration for FSM traversal can also be formulated based on structural concepts. This results in a "structural" FSM traversal that leads to a natural way of exploiting similarities between designs but does not rely on the equivalence of state variables.

2 General Idea

Our approach is based on modelling the finite state machine (FSM) by an iterative circuit array. Each combinational block implements the transition function $\delta(\underline{s}, \underline{x})$ and output function $\lambda(\underline{s}, \underline{x})$ of the FSM. The vector $\underline{s}$ denotes the present state variables and $\underline{x}$ denotes the primary inputs of the circuit. The next state variables are denoted $\underline{z}$. Each block in the circuit array describes the behaviour of the machine for a certain time interval [*t*, *t*+1] and is simply referred to as *time frame*.

Most techniques for sequential equivalence checking consider a specific product machine [7]. This product machine is obtained by connecting the corresponding inputs to a common fanout stem and attaching an XOR gate to the outputs. If the machines are equivalent the product machine produces a sequence of zeros for all valid input sequences. In our approach we consider the iterative circuit array of the product machine shown in Figure 1. The XOR tree for the outputs is like in a combinational *miter* [1] and is omitted in Figure 1.

In order to anchor the combinational comparison on a common basis for both circuits without making any assumptions on the equivalence of state variables as in [8, 9], we start our procedure at the initial state that we assume is known for both circuits.

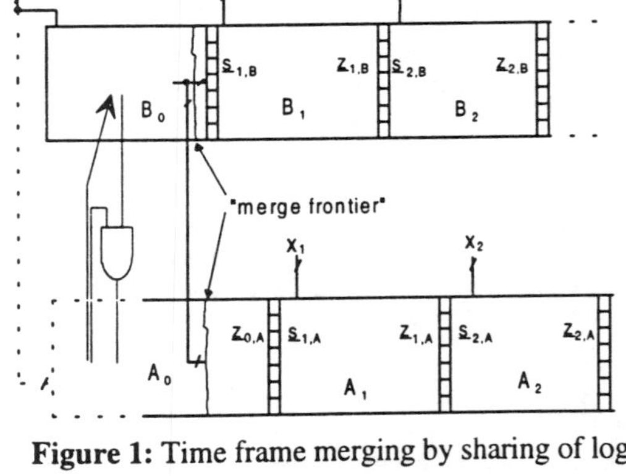

Figure 1: Time frame merging by sharing of logic

Consider Figure 1. The verification procedure is based on performing logic transformations identified by implications as described in [10, 11]. As we proceed time frame by time frame, the combinational logic of one machine is "merged" with the combinational logic of the other machine. We speak of the "merge frontier" denoting a set of gates that identifies a border line between the circuitry that is shared between the two machines and the separate circuitry for each machine. This is schematically shown in Figure 1.

Note that the iterative circuit array is a concatenation of identical combinational blocks. Therefore, many transformations that allow us to merge the logic of some time frame of

*Part of this research was performed while both authors were on sabbatical at the Mentor Graphics Boston Research Laboratories

1092-3152/97 $10.00 © 1997 IEEE

machine A with the logic of some time frame of machine B remain valid also in the next time frame. The only reason why some transformation at time t might no longer be valid at time $t+1$ is that certain *controllability don't care conditions* [7] have been used at time t that are not valid at time $t+1$. However, similarly as the image computations of the conventional verification approach [5] identify all reachable states after a finite number of iterations, all different don't care sets at the nodes in the circuit array have been examined after a finite number of time frames.

Therefore, it is our goal to identify a set of circuit transformations between the nodes of machine A and machine B that is valid in all time frames. The basic instrument to find such a set is an *instruction queue* Q_t that contains a set of instructions for circuit transformations at some time t. The instruction queue is processed in a *first-in-first-out* manner. Circuit transformations at time t are stored in Q_t in the order in which they have been performed. This is operation is called "*record*". In the next time frame at $t+1$, we try to make maximum use of the instructions recorded previously and for each recorded circuit transformation we check whether or not it is still valid at time $t+1$. Only if it is invalid it is removed from the instruction queue, otherwise the transformation is performed also at $t+1$. This process of re-using the stored instructions is referred to as "*play*". If the circuit transformations in the instruction queue are not sufficient to establish the equivalence of the output signals at time $t+1$ additional transformations are identified and recorded.

By *recording* and *playing* the instruction queue is improved in each time frame. Finally, an instruction queue is created that remains valid also in the next time frame and which completes the task of proving the equivalence for the circuit outputs. Now it remains to be shown that this instruction queue is also valid in all future time frames. To permit this induction a *cutting* procedure is applied to the circuit array. The cut must be selected such that the don't care conditions needed for the validity of the circuit transformations are still present in the selected part of the circuit array. Most don't care conditions that allow us to merge logic between the two machines by local transformations are induced by the previous merging steps. Therefore, it is usually sufficient to keep only a few levels of logic in front of the merge frontier and to cut off all circuitry starting from the beginning of the circuit array up to a few levels before the merge frontier. If an instruction queue can be played a sufficient number of times, it is guaranteed that the combinational structure in the circuit array repeats periodically. Then we say that our procedure has reached a "structural fixed point". This is a simplified summary of the proposed method. It is described in more detail in the following section.

3 The *record & play* procedure

Figure 2 shows the proposed algorithm for FSM equivalence checking. Routine *record&play()* is given in Table 1. The different steps of the algorithm are illustrated by means of an example depicted in Figure 3 to Figure 9.

The variables *stub_levels* and *p_max* must be defined by the user as will be discussed later. At the beginning of each iteration a new time frame is attached to the current circuit array. Initially, the circuit array is empty. Whenever a new time frame is attached we assign constant values of the state variables to the corresponding nodes in the circuit array and simplify the logic accordingly. Initially, the constant values are given by the initial state. Note that these constant values may propagate to the next state variables. Consider the example in Figure 3. For both machines we are given an initial state of 0 for all registers. This leads to the situation shown in the left part of Figure 4. A constant value of 0 has propagated to the next state vector and it is $j_1 = 0$. This value will be propagated further when the next time frame is attached.

After the time frame has been attached the algorithm optimizes the logic to facilitate equivalence checking at the outputs in this and subsequent time frames. This optimization is performed in a controlled way by an instruction queue in order to detect a fixed point. For each time frame we store a set of instructions Q_t that keeps exact records of all transformations performed in that time frame. Routine *record&play()* has the task to select one of the previous instruction queues and to determine for the selected queue whether or not the recorded circuit transformations are still valid in the current time frame. If this is not the case another instruction queue is tried. Trying a large number of instruction queues can be time consuming, therefore the user-defined parameter *p_max* is used to restrict the search to the last *p_max* instruction queues. If no instruction queue is found that can be played successfully, new circuit transformations are identified and stored in the instruction queue. In our example, no previous instruction queue exists. The circuit is optimized as shown in the right part of Figure 4 and the performed transformations are stored in Q_0. For reasons of simplicity, in our example, node substitutions are considered as the only possible type of circuit transformations.

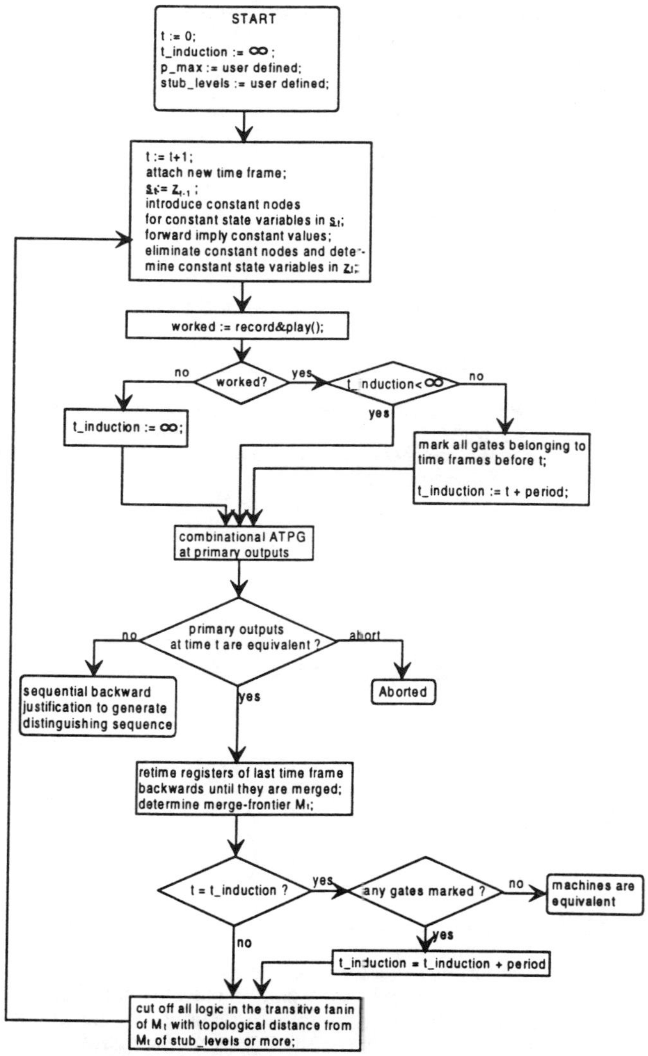

Figure 2: sequential equivalence checking algorithm

Next, it is checked whether the primary outputs in the current time frame are equivalent. If this is not the case, the circuits are not equivalent and a backward justification process like in conventional sequential ATPG tools is invoked to calculate a distinguishing sequence.

```
/* routine operates on a global data structure for the current miter array
   with present state variables s and next state variables z and has t,
   t_induction, period and p_max of Figure 2 as global variables */

record&play()
{
  if (t_induction < ∞) /* trying induction */
       PLAY := {Q_t-period};
  else /* check old queues to find fixed point */
       PLAY := { Q_i | i ∈ {t-1, t-2, ..., t-p_max} and s_i = s_t};

  worked := NO;
  for (each Q_i ∈ PLAY)
  {   worked := YES;
      Q_t := ∅;
      for (each instruction α_j ∈ Q_i)
      {   verify whether or not circuit transformation α_j is valid
          in current time frame;
          if (valid)
          {   execute α_j (perform circuit transformation);
              Q_t := Q_t ∪ {α_j}; /* put in queue */
          }
          else worked := NO;
      }
      if (worked = YES)
      {   period := t - i;
          break;
      }
      else reverse all transformations made for Q_i;
  }
  if (worked = NO)
  {   Q_t := ∅;
      for (each node in circuit array)
      {   identify implication based circuit transformation, α;
          if (α reduces literal count of circuit array)
          {   perform transformation α;
              Q_t := Q_t ∪ {α}; /* put in queue */
          }
      }
  }
  return (worked);
}
```

Table 1: Routine *record&play()*

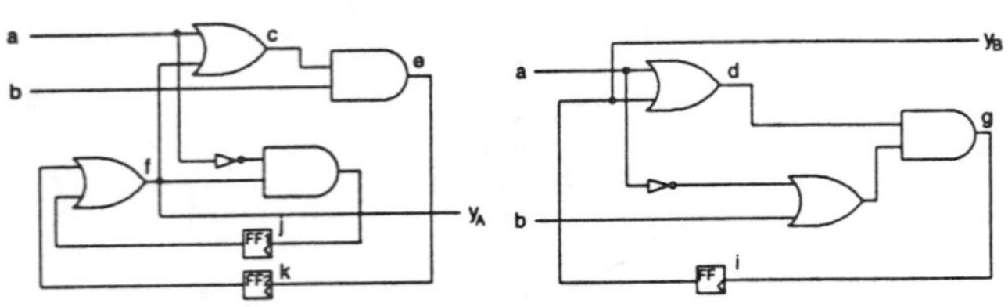

Figure 3: Circuit examples with initial states $S_{0,A} = S_{0,B} = \underline{0}$

The algorithm now determines whether previously processed portions of the circuit array can be cut off. Note that our algorithm only performs local transformations in the circuit array. For this reason it does usually not affect the quality of the performed circuit transformations if we cut off previously processed circuitry in a sufficiently large distance from the currently active area. A heuristic procedure based on *retiming* [12] determines the "merge frontier". This is accomplished by moving the registers at the end of the last time frame backwards until they are located in fanout branches such that different branches of the same fanout stem feed registers of different machines. The corresponding fanout stems represent the nodes of the merge frontier. The detailed description of this procedure must be omitted here for reasons of brevity. The cut through the circuit array is located in the transitive fanin of the merge frontier. In principle, *false negatives* can occur as a result of this cutting process. However, in practice we can always avoid false negatives by leaving a sufficient number of logic levels in front of the merge frontier. This number of logic levels is called *stub_levels* in Figure 2 and is a user-defined parameter. Typical values are between 0 and 5.

Consider again the right portion of Figure 4. We only consider the registers that are not assigned a constant value and are still physically present in the circuit array. These are the registers at k_1 and i_1. Note that k_1 stems from machine A and i_1 from machine B. They are located in fanout branches of the same fanout stem, hence e_0 belongs to the merge frontier, which here does not have any other nodes. In the example, we assume *stub_levels* = 0. Hence the circuit array can be cut at signal e_0 and a new time frame is attached. The result is shown in the left portion of Figure 5. The newly introduced variable at the cut line is called s.

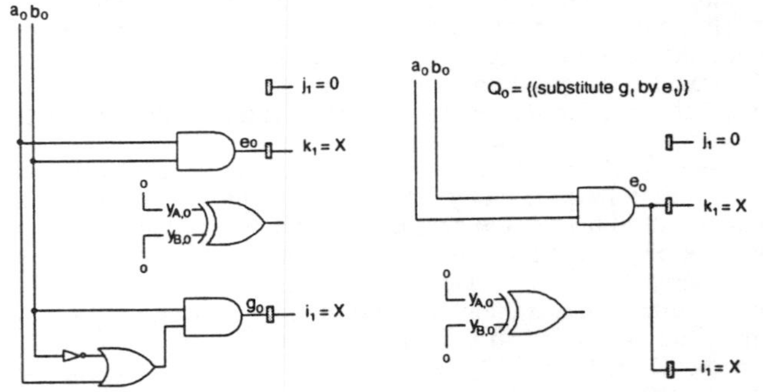

Figure 4: Circuit array in first iteration

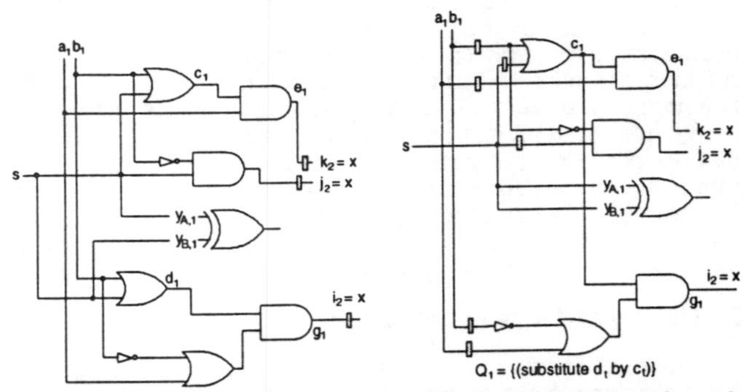

Figure 5: Circuit array in second iteration before (left) and after (right) merging

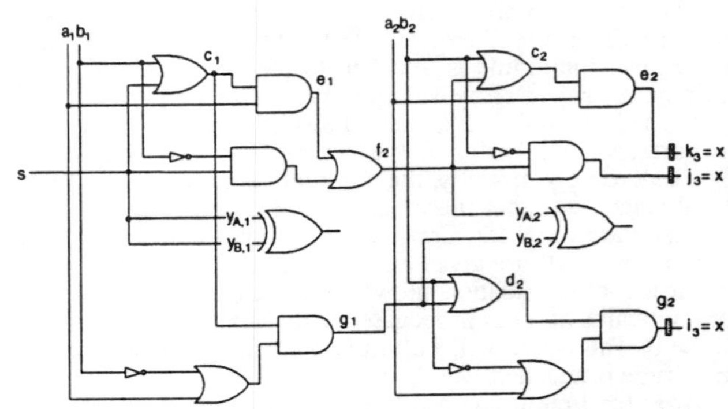

Figure 6: Circuit array in third iteration before merging

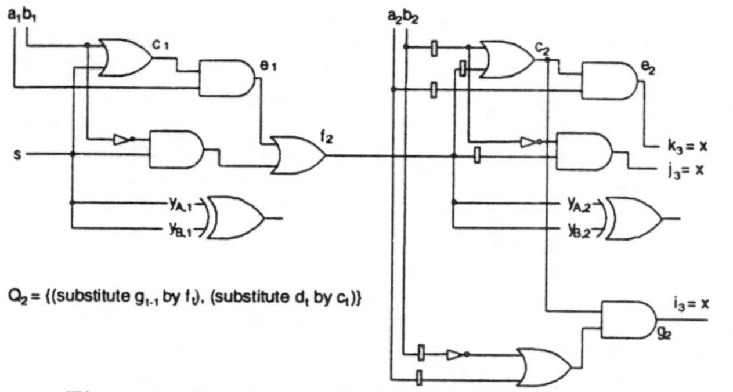

Figure 7: Circuit array in third iteration after merging

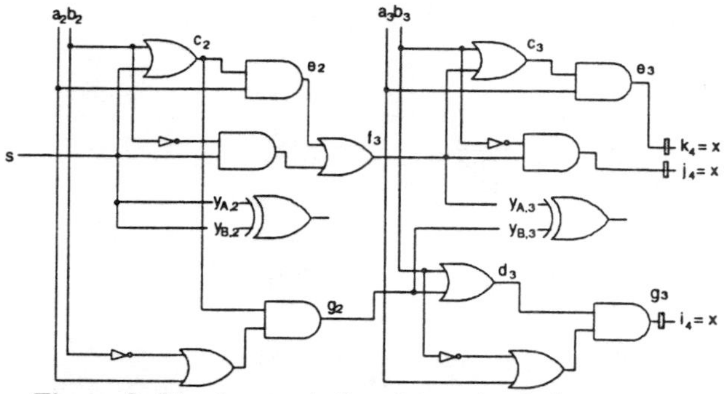

Figure 8: Circuit array in fourth iteration before merging

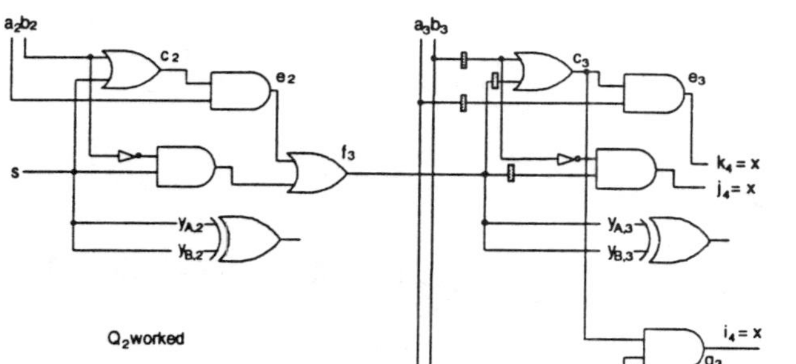

Figure 9: Circuit array in fourth iteration after merging

After a new time frame has been appended it is always checked whether a previous instruction queue can be played. As given by the definition of set *PLAY* in routine *record&play()* an instruction queue can only be played if it was recorded with the same constant values at the state variables as are given in the current time frame. In our example, no instruction queue can be played. New transformations are recorded in Q_1 as shown in the right portion of Figure 5. As a result of the optimization it is trivial to determine the equivalence of the primary outputs. Next, a merge frontier is determined as shown in the right portion of Figure 5. Assuming *stub_levels* = 0 we can cut the circuit array at the stems of these fanout systems. Here, this does not result in any removal of logic.

A new time frame is attached as shown in Figure 6 and a new instruction queue must be recorded. The transformations lead to the circuit array shown in Figure 7. We determine a new merge frontier suggesting a cut at signal f_2. The next iteration leads to the circuit array of Figure 8. Just like in the previous time frame no constant values exist at the state variables and it is determined in *record&play()* that the instruction queue Q_2 can be played. Actually, all recorded transformations turn out to be valid in the current time frame so that the circuit of Figure 9 results.

If an instruction queue has been played successfully the algorithm enters the induction mode. This is done by setting variable *t_induction* to t + *period* where *period* is the number of cycles since the successful instruction queue has been recorded. In most practical cases, this is the most recently recorded instruction queue so that *period* = 1. Furthermore, to ensure the correctness of the induction all gates belonging to time frames prior to the current time frame are marked. The algorithm continues the iteration and in each new time frame the instruction queue recorded at time t - *period* is played. This is done until all queues of a period have been played. Remember that we have marked all gates of previous time frames when we started the induction mode. We continue to play the instruction queues until all marked gates have disappeared as a result of the cutting procedure. At this point, it is guaranteed that the combinational structures generated in the circuit array will repeat periodically and hence, a *structural fixed point* of the iteration is reached.

Note that our method is not restricted to a unique initial state. If a set of initial states is used additional circuitry must be attached in front of the first time frame that encodes the given set of initial states. This is similar to the notion of the *stub circuit* to be described in the next section. If an initializing sequence is given the above iteration has to be slightly modified. Instead of assigning an initial state at the state variables, the values of the initializing sequence are assigned to the primary inputs for each iteration. During the application of the initializing sequence the equivalence check at the outputs is switched off unless the designer wants to check the equivalence of the machines also during the initializing process [14].

4 Discussion of Theoretical Issues

For a better understanding of the *record&play* procedure we now consider a more general formulation of a structural fixed point iteration. We consider a FSM $M = (I, S, \delta, S_0, O, \lambda)$ where I is the input alphabet, S is the set of states, $\delta: S \times I \rightarrow S$ is the next-state function, S_0 is the initial state, O is the output alphabet and $\lambda: S \times I \rightarrow O$ is the output function. For simplicity we restrict our discussion to a single initial state, however, a set of initial states can be treated in a similar way. To examine the nature of the proposed fixed point iteration we can ignore the output behavior of the machine, i.e., we only consider the corresponding *finite state transition structure* FST $H = (I, S, \delta, S_0)$.

We consider the iterative circuit array of the FST expanded from time 0 to time t. At time 0 the circuit array is initialized, i.e., the initial state is assigned to the state variables. The upper part of Figure 10 shows the time frame for time t. The transition function $\delta(\underline{s}, \underline{x})$ is implemented by combinational circuitry denoted A.

Let $S(t)$ denote the set of states reachable at state variables $\underline{s}_t$ and let $S(t+1)$ denote the set of states reachable at the next state variables $\underline{z}_t$. Figure 10 shows a decomposition of δ into functions δ'_t and σ_t. The combinational circuitry A' with output vector $\underline{c}_t$ of length k implements function $\delta'_t(\underline{s}, \underline{x})$. The circuit labelled $STUB_t$ implements function $\sigma_t(\underline{c}_t)$ and is called *stub circuit*. The *stub function* σ_t is defined to be a function that maps the set of all combinations of value assignments at the variables $\underline{c}_t$ to exactly those combinations of value assignments at $\underline{z}_t$ that correspond to the reachable states $S(t+1)$, i.e., we define $\sigma_t : \{0, 1\}^k \rightarrow S(t+1)$. Furthermore, for a valid decomposition it must hold that $\sigma_t(\delta_t'(\underline{s}, \underline{x})) = \delta(\underline{s}, \underline{x})$.

This decomposition has an important property: if we cut through the circuit array at the variables $\underline{c}_t$ and only maintain the circuit array starting from $STUB_t$, the set of reachable states at the variables $\underline{z}_t$ or at any state variables of later times does not change. By the above decomposition in combination with cutting off all logic in front of the stub circuit we loose functional information telling us under what conditions at the inputs in previous time frames we can reach certain states at time t+1. However, by definition of this decomposition we do not loose the information what states are reachable at time t+1 or later. Therefore, this decomposition and cut can be considered as structural analogy to the *existential abstraction* operation used in the image computations for the conventional BDD-based fixed point iteration.

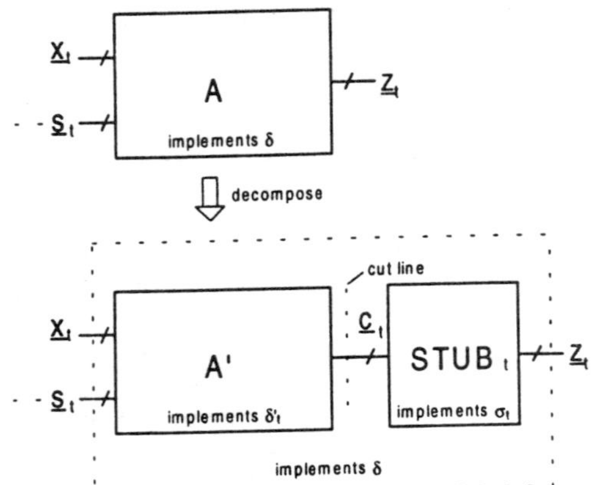

Figure 10: Existential abstraction - in a structural way

The question arises how this decomposition can be computed. One possibility is to choose $\delta' = \delta$. In this case the stub function σ_t has to be determined such that all combinations of values that can occur in the circuit array at $\underline{c}_t$ are mapped to identical values at $\underline{z}_t$, and the combinations of value assignments that can not occur at $\underline{c}_t$ are mapped to values at $\underline{z}_t$ that can occur in the circuit array. A synthesis procedure for the a stub circuit can be formulated based on the AND/OR reasoning graphs of [10, 17]. Assume that the unreachable states at a time t are represented by a list of cubes. As an example for such a cube, assume that (z_1 = 1, z_2 = 1, z_3 = 0, z_4 = X) denotes some unreachable states for the next state variables at time t. Also assume that the cube list is prime. Therefore, if value assignments $z_1 = 1$ and $z_2 = 1$ are made it can be *implied* that z_3 must be 1 to obtain a reachable state. Hence, in the given circuit array, z_1z_2 must be an implicant for z_3. Implicants that consist of literals belonging to arbitrary nodes in a Boolean network can be calculated using the method described in [10, 17]. Therefore, the stub circuit can be constructed as follows. For each next state variable at time t calculate all prime implicants that exist in terms of the other next state variables at time t and add them to the cover of the current next state variable. This introduces redundancy in the circuit but does not change its function. In fact, the combinational circuit implementing the added implicants represents a stub circuit according to the above definitions. We can now cut off all other logic without affecting the number of reachable states at $\underline{z}_t$.

In practice, approximate solutions must be considered. Instead of only calculating implicants for the state variables we perform implication-based transformations at *all* nodes in the network. Our heuristic to "merge" as much logic as possible between the different parts of the product machine is the attempt to compress all information about the reachability of states (and internal don't cares) into a relatively small area of the circuit array near the next state variable of the last time frame. If we did not put any restrictions on the recursion depth and computed all implicants at the next state variables we would always succeed in finding a decomposition with the above properties.

Based on this combinational decomposition we can formulate the fixed point iteration shown in Figure 11. In each iteration the above described decomposition is performed to create the stub circuit. Then all logic in front of the stub circuit is cut off. As explained, this does not affect the set of reachable states at the state variables of all future time frames. Note an important difference to the conventional FSM traversal. In each iteration we only take into account the number of states reachable exactly at time t but not the set of all states reachable at any time 0, 1, ...t. This must be considered when detecting the fixed point. The fixed point is reached when there is a sequence $S(t)$, $S(t+1)$, ... $S(t+p)$ of sets of states reachable at time t, t + 1, ... $t+p$ that repeats with a period of length p. This is detected by determining that the decomposition steps to produce the stub circuit are the same as the steps performed p time frames earlier. In our practical implementation an instruction queue is used for this purpose. Since we are dealing with a *finite* state machine the sets of states reachable at a given time must repeat with a finite period and it follows that the fixed point iteration of Figure 11 reaches a fixed point for any completely specified, deterministic FST after a finite number of steps.

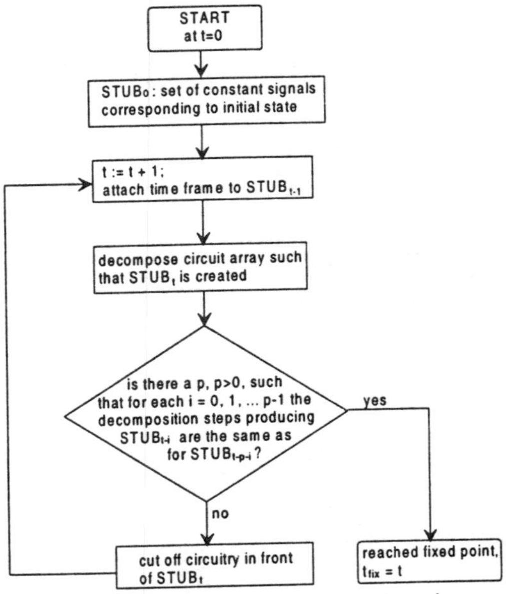

Figure 11: Structural fixed point iteration

Fortunately, p is very small for most practical circuits. This is confirmed by our experimental results as well as a theoretical analysis. This analysis must be omitted for reasons of brevity but can be summarized as follows: suppose we are given a machine M that is strongly connected [7]. We consider all q cycles in the state transition graph of M. Let $P = \{p_1, p_2, ...p_q\}$ be a set of integer numbers such that each number corresponds to the length of a cycle in the state transition graph of M. Then, the period p in our procedure is given by the *greatest common divisor* for all numbers in P. This explains why a period of 1 is sufficient for most practical cases. If the machine is not strongly connected the same result applies for the *strongly connected component* (SCC) of the machine.

Since the *record&play* procedure of the previous section only calculates an approximate solution to the above decomposition problem the resulting stub circuit represents a superset of $S(t)$, i.e., we may consider more states than are actually reachable. As discussed earlier, this can lead to false negatives. However, since a complete symbolic state traversal is impossible for most large designs usually the same information about unreachable states and local don't cares that has been used by the synthesis tool can also be compressed into the stub circuit using local transformations.

On the other hand, the fact that we may consider more states than are actually reachable can have a very beneficial effect.

With an approximate decomposition we may reach a fixed point much faster than with the exact solution.

Note that the methods [8, 9] can be useful as a preprocessing phase to our approach. If equivalent state variables can be determined then the corresponding substitutions can be added to the instruction queue for *every* time frame so that a fixed point is reached much faster.

5 Experimental Results

A prototype of the described approach has been incorporated into the HANNIBAL [10] package. We evaluated the techniques by verifying circuits of the ISCAS89 benchmark set against the optimized and retimed circuits. The circuits were optimized by kerneling (using *fx* in SIS). After optimization retiming is performed (using *retime* in SIS). The resulting circuits were verified against the original ones. For the original circuits we assumed an initial state of 0 for all registers.

Circuit		***record&play*** (HANNIBAL)		***verify_fsm*** (SIS)
Name	# registers	# iterations til fixed point	CPU-time (h:min:sec)	CPU-time (h:min:sec)
s208	8	15	0: 00: 08	0: 00: 03
s298	14	10	0: 00: 09	0: 00: 03
s344	15	9	0: 00: 11	0: 00 06
s349	15	9	0: 00: 11	0: 00: 06
s382	21	16	0: 00: 17	0: 00: 38
s386	6	9	0: 00: 48	0: 00: 01
s420	16	27	0: 00: 43	0: 27: 19
s444	21	16	0: 00: 18	0: 00: 28
s510	6	12	0: 00: 35	0: 00: 02
s526	21	21	0: 00: 35	0: 00: 12
s635	32	37	0: 01: 32	unable
s641	19	9	0: 00: 12	0: 00: 08
s713	19	9	0: 00: 12	0: 00: 09
s820	5	17	0: 36: 50	0: 00: 04
s832	5	16	0: 26: 37	0: 00: 04
s838	32	51	0: 08: 13	unable
s953	29	11	0: 01: 09	0: 00: 12
s1196	18	6	0: 00: 40	0: 00: 08
s1238	18	6	0: 00: 46	0: 00: 08
s1423	74	14	0: 03: 31	unable
s1512	57	16	0: 04: 09	> 30 h
s3271	116	19	0: 21: 17	unable
s3330	132	9	0: 11: 33	unable
s3384	183	17	0: 31: 24	unable
s4863	104	8	0: 36: 52	unable
s5378	179	36	0: 55: 23	unable
s6669	239	11	0: 47: 15	unable

Table 2: Verification of optimized and retimed circuits

A difficulty in our experimental evaluation comes from the fact that for larger circuits SIS cannot compute the initial state after retiming, because it uses symbolic FSM traversal for this task. Therefore, we developped a simple retiming algorithm that moves all registers as far as possible into forward direction. The new initial state can simply be calculated by forward implication of the old initial state. We applied our own retiming method to those circuits where SIS did not move any registers. In this way, we ensured that the encoding for all optimized circuits differs drastically from the encoding of the unoptimized original circuits and no simple relationships exist between state variables.

Table 2 shows our experimental results for a SUN Ultra I workstation. In [8, 9] a different notion of equivalence is used and no results are shown for circuits that are both optimized and retimed. Therefore we compare our techniques only with the conventional verification approach by symbolic FSM traversal. The results for *verify_fsm* in SIS are shown in the left column of Table 2. The results show the feasibility and great potential of this approach to verify circuits after synthesis and retiming. With our technique the verification could be completed within acceptable CPU-time for several cases where the conventional approach fails. In all cases the fixed point was reached with $p\_max = 1$.

Conclusion

Based on a combinational decomposition procedure we have introduced a method for structural FSM traversal. Our approach is promising in applications where the designs under comparison have been modified by a sequence of local transformations. This is the case after most industrial synthesis procedures and retiming. Future work will examine whether the proposed fixed point iteration is useful to verify typical engineering changes at the RTL level, like modifying the pipelining of the circuit.

References

[1] Brand D.: "Verification of Large Synthesized Designs", *Proc. Int. Conf. on Computer-Aided Circuit Design* (ICCAD), Santa Clara, pp. 534-537, Nov. 1993.

[2] Bryant R.: "Graph-based algorithms for Boolean function manipulation", *IEEE Transactions on Computers*, vol. 35, pp. 677-691, August 1986.

[3] Cabodi G., Camurati P., Quer S.: "Improved Reachability Analysis of Large Finite State Machines", *Proc. Int. Conf. on Computer-Aided Design* (ICCAD), pp. 354-360, 1996.

[4] Cho H. et al.: "A Structural Approach for State Space Decomposition for Approximate Reachability Analysis", *Proc. IEEE Int. Conf. on Computer Design*, pp. 236-239, 1994.

[5] Coudert O., Berthet C., and Madre J.Ch.: "Verification of Synchronous Sequential Machines Based on Symbolic Execution", in *Lecture Notes in Computer Science*, vol. 407, (Automatic Verification Methods for Finite State Systems, International Workshop, Grenoble, France), Springer-Verlag, June 1989.

[6] van Eijk C.A.J., and Jess J.A.G.: "Exploiting Functional Dependencies in Finite State Machine Verification", *Proc. European Design & Test Conf.*, pp. 9-14, 1996.

[7] Hachtel G., and Somenzi F.: *Logic Synthesis and Verification Algorithms*, Kluwer Academic Publishers, Boston 1996.

[8] Huang S.Y., Cheng K.T., Chen K.C., and Gläser U.: "An ATPG-based Framework for Verifying Sequential Equivalence" *Proc. Int. Test Conference*, 1996.

[9] Huang S.Y., Cheng K.T., Chen K.C., and Gläser U.: "On Verifying the Correctness of Retimed Circuits" *Proc. Great Lakes Symposium on VLSI*, 1996.

[10] Kunz W., and Stoffel D.: "Reasoning in Boolean Networks - Logic Synthesis and Verification Using Testing Techniques" *Kluwer Academic Publishers*, Boston 1997.

[11] Kunz W., Stoffel D., and Menon P.: "Multi-Level Logic Optimization and Equivalence Checking by Implication Analysis", *IEEE Transaction on Computer-Aided Design*, Vol.16, no.3, pp. 266-281, March 1997.

[12] Leiserson C.E., and Saxe J.B.: "Retiming Synchronous Circuitry", *Algorithmica*, vol. 6., pp. 5-35, 1991.

[13] McMillan K.L.: "Symbolic Model Checking", *Kluwer Academic Publishers*, 1993.

[14] Pixley C., Singhal V., Aziz A., and Brayton R.K.: "Multi-level Synthesis for Replaceability", *Proc. Int. Conf. on Computer-Aided Design* (ICCAD), pp. 442-449, 1994.

[15] Quer S. et al.: "Incremental Re-encoding for Symbolic Traversal of Product Machines", *Proc. European Design Automation Conf.*, 1996.

[16] Ravi K., and Somenzi F.: "High Density Reachability Analysis", *Proc. Int. Conf. on Computer-Aided Design* (ICCAD), pp. 154-158, 1995.

[17] Stoffel D., and Kunz W.: "AND/OR Reasoning Graphs for Determining Prime Implicants in Multi-Level Combinational Networks", *Proc. Asia and South Pacific Design Automation Conference* (ASP-DAC), pp. 529 - 538, Japan, 1997.

Forward Model Checking Techniques Oriented to Buggy Designs

Hiroaki Iwashita and Tsuneo Nakata
Fujitsu Laboratories Ltd.
1-1 Kamikodanaka 4-chome, Nakahara-ku, Kawasaki 211-88, Japan
hiroaki@flab.fujitsu.co.jp

Abstract

Forward model checking is an efficient symbolic model checking method for verifying realistic properties of sequential circuits and protocols. In this paper, we present the techniques that modify the order of state traversal on forward model checking, and that dramatically improve average CPU time for finding design errors. A failing property has to be checked again and again to analyze the bug until it is corrected. The techniques, therefore, can have significant impacts on actual verification tasks. We use a modified regular/ω-regular expression to represent a set of illegal state transition sequences of an FSM. It makes the problem clear and gives us a sense of depth-first traversal, not on the state space, but on the property.

1 Introduction

Model checking is now attracting a great deal of industrial attention. It is beginning to be applied to commercial designs of digital circuits. Since many bugs are found in an early stage of design, model checking and correction must be repeated at this stage. A quick response from the model checker is desired, especially when design errors still remain. Ordinary model checkers, however, spend huge CPU time for checking a large design no matter whether it has a bug or not. It is the purpose of this paper to present efficient techniques for checking buggy designs.

Symbolic model checking is a successful technique in verifying sequential circuits and protocols, which uses binary decision diagrams (BDDs) [1] for symbolic representations of state sets and transition relations [3, 4, 5]. Forward model checking is an efficient variant of symbolic model checking, which replaces backward state traversal in ordinary symbolic model checking with forward state traversal. It have been shown that CTL model checking [2, 6, 7] can be done mainly based on symbolic forward state traversal [10]. We often observe that the forward model checking algorithm works much better than the ordinary backward algorithm.

We present practical aspects of forward model checking in this paper. We redefine forward model checking as a problem of finding an error trace of a finite state machine (FSM) using symbolic forward state traversal. It makes the problem clear and gives us a sense of depth-first traversal not on the state space but on the property. By introducing a mixture manner of breadth-first and depth-first traversals on the property, we can expect a model checker to find an error trace rapidly. The techniques keep advantages of symbolic model checking, and are very different from logic simulation. They still guarantee the perfect coverage and can find complicated error traces including cycles.

In Section 2, we rearrange the model checking problems. Section 3 describes basic forward model checking operations. Improved state traversal techniques are presented in Section 4. Experimental results and conclusions are given in Section 5 and Section 6, respectively.

2 Backward and forward model checking

2.1 Path set expressions

We define a class of modified regular/ω-regular expressions, called *path set expressions* (*PSEs*) in this paper, to represent a set of possible error traces (illegal state transition sequences). A propositional formula represents a set of states at which the formula holds. We make no distinction between such a formula and a set of states in this paper. Let p and q be propositional formulas, α a PSE representing finite sequences, and β, γ arbitrary PSEs, then:

- $[p]$ matches every one-step sequence (s_1) such that s_1 satisfies p. We use '$\bullet$' as an abbreviation of '$[true]$'.
- $[p]^*[q]$ matches every finite sequence $(s_1, \ldots, s_n)$ for $n \geq 1$, such that $s_1, \ldots, s_{n-1}$ satisfy p if $n \geq 2$, and s_n satisfies q.
- $[p]^\omega$ matches every infinite sequence $(s_1, s_2, \ldots)$ such that s_k satisfies p for all $k \geq 1$.
- $\alpha\ \beta$ matches every sequence $(s_1, \ldots, s_n, s_{n+1}, \ldots)$ such that the finite sequence $(s_1, \ldots, s_n)$ matches α and the sequence $(s_{n+1}, \ldots)$ matches β.
- $\alpha : \beta$ matches every sequence $(s_1, \ldots, s_n, \ldots)$ such that the finite sequence $(s_1, \ldots, s_n)$ matches α and the sequence $(s_n, \ldots)$ matches β.

1092-3152/97 $10.00 © 1997 IEEE

- $\beta + \gamma$ represents the union of β and γ.

Note that we introduced an extended operator ':', which means concatenation of two expressions with one-step overlap. PSEs do not match a null sequence. Repeat operators '$*$' and 'ω' are only applicable to expressions representing one-step sequences. An 'ω' operator appears only at the end of concatenation.

For example, where i represents the set of initial states, a set of error traces "Illegal condition c is satisfied" is written as "$[i] : \bullet^*[c]$", and a set of error traces "A request have been made (r) but is not acknowledged ($\neg a$) forever" is written as "$[i] : \bullet^*[r] : [\neg a]^\omega$".

2.2 Path set expression model checking

When a set of possible error traces on FSM M is given by PSE α, model checking is done by finding a state transition sequence on M matched by α, or by proving that no sequence on M matches α. It is similar to a problem of language containment between two finite ω-automata [8, 9], except that the PSE represents the complement of the property automaton. The language containment algorithm checks the product automaton of M and the property automaton. For model checking on a PSE, however, no product machine is constructed and the original machine M is traversed along the PSE.

We define two functions $bw(\alpha)$ and $fw(\alpha)$ to carry out model checking. They are functions from a PSE to a formula representing a set of states. $bw(\alpha)$ represents the set of start states of sequences matched by α. $fw(\alpha)$ represents the union of the set of final states of finite sequences matched by α and the set of states visited infinitely often along infinite sequences matched by α. Intuitively, $bw(\alpha)$ evaluation means backward traversal along α and $fw(\alpha)$ evaluation means forward traversal along α. Each result is not a constant false value representing an empty set if and only if one or more sequence on M is matched by α. Checking $bw(\alpha) = \mathit{false}$ is called *backward model checking* on α, and checking $fw(\alpha) = \mathit{false}$ is called *forward model checking* on α. Moreover, when α is in the form of $\alpha_1 : \alpha_2$, we can also check it by evaluating α from both sides: $fw(\alpha_1) \wedge bw(\alpha_2) = \mathit{false}$.

2.3 Backward evaluation procedure

Backward PSE evaluation is based on traditional CTL model checking techniques [2, 6, 7]. The following equations show the procedure to convert a PSE into a CTL formula using operators **EX**, **EU**, and **EG** (assuming that p and q represent sets of states and α and β are sub-expressions of a PSE):

$$
\begin{aligned}
bw([p]) &= p \\
bw([p]^*[q]) &= \mathbf{E}\,(p\,\mathbf{U}\,q) \\
bw([p]^\omega) &= \mathbf{EG}\,p \\
bw([p]\;\alpha) &= p \wedge \mathbf{EX}\,bw(\alpha) \\
bw([p]^*[q]\;\alpha) &= bw([p]^*[bw([q]\;\alpha)]) \\
bw([p] : \alpha) &= p \wedge bw(\alpha) \\
bw([p]^*[q] : \alpha) &= bw([p]^*[bw([q] : \alpha)]) \\
bw(\alpha + \beta) &= bw(\alpha) \vee bw(\beta).
\end{aligned}
$$

2.4 Forward evaluation procedure

We regard $fw([p]\;[q])$, $fw([p] : [q]^*[r])$, and $fw([p] : [q]^\omega)$ as basic operations of forward evaluation. Their details are shown later in Section 3. Using them, forward evaluation of a PSE is given as follows (assuming that p and q represent sets of states and α and β are sub-expressions of a PSE):

$$
\begin{aligned}
fw([p]) &= p \\
fw([p]^*[q]) &= q \\
fw([p]^\omega) &= fw([p] : [p]^\omega) \\
fw(\alpha\;[p]) &= fw([fw(\alpha)]\;[p]) \\
fw(\alpha\;[p]^*[q]) &= fw([fw(\alpha\bullet)] : [p]^*[q]) \\
fw(\alpha\;[p]^\omega) &= fw([fw(\alpha\bullet)] : [p]^\omega) \\
fw(\alpha : [p]) &= fw(\alpha) \wedge p \\
fw(\alpha : [p]^*[q]) &= fw([fw(\alpha)] : [p]^*[q]) \\
fw(\alpha : [p]^\omega) &= fw([fw(\alpha)] : [p]^\omega) \\
fw(\alpha + \beta) &= fw(\alpha) \vee fw(\beta).
\end{aligned}
$$

2.5 Backward versus forward model checking

In general, backward model checking may be better than forward model checking for some examples, and vice versa. In most actual examples of PSE model checking, however, we observe that forward model checking is more efficient than backward model checking. It is remarkable for PSEs ending with an ω operator, which are in common use. Let us consider model checking on $[p] : [q]^\omega$ as an example. The backward method first looks for all cycles in the entire space of q and then checks their reachability from p through q, while the forward method looks for cycles only in the restricted space of q that are reachable from p through q. It makes forward model checking more efficient than backward model checking, on the assumption that the size of search space affects the computational cost. Although this assumption is not always true for symbolic state traversal, it is practically true because the computation is usually simplified with don't-care information of the search space.

3 Basic forward operations

3.1 Forward transition evaluation

The first basic forward operation is $fw([p]\;[q])$, which represents the set of states that satisfy q and that are reachable with just one transition from some state satisfying p. We can easily translate this definition into the following rule using the image computation operator *Img* as shown in [10]:

$$fw([p]\,[q]) \;=\; Img(p) \wedge q. \tag{1}$$

3.2 Forward reachability evaluation

The second operation is $fw([p]:[q]^*[r])$, which represents the set of states that satisfy r and that are reachable from some state satisfying p with zero or more transitions only through states satisfying q. The following procedure is essentially the same as $FwdUntil(p,q) \wedge r$ proposed in [10]. It is computed by forward state traversal procedure starting from p:

$$Q_i \;=\; \begin{cases} p & (i=0), \\ Img(Q_{i-1} \wedge q) \wedge \neg \bigvee_{j=0}^{i-1} Q_j & (i \geq 1). \end{cases} \tag{2}$$

The image computation is repeated until $Q_i = false$. Assuming $Q_n = false$, the result of the operation is given as follows:

$$\begin{aligned} fw([p]:[q]^*[r]) \;&=\; r_0 \vee \cdots \vee r_{n-1}, \\ r_i \;&=\; Q_i \wedge r. \end{aligned} \tag{3}$$

When we are checking $fw([p]:[q]^*[r]) = false$ rather than exactly evaluating $fw([p]:[q]^*[r])$, we do not always need to repeat the image computation n times. The procedure can be terminated as soon as we find some $r_i \neq false$.

3.3 Forward cycle evaluation

The final basic operation is $fw([p]:[q]^\omega)$, which represents the set of states visited infinitely often along infinite sequences matched by $[p]:[q]^\omega$. Actually, we do not need exact computation of $fw([p]:[q]^\omega)$ and only need to check $fw([p]:[q]^\omega) = false$ (there is no infinite sequence matched by $[p]:[q]^\omega$) in forward model checking, because an 'ω' operator appears only at the end of concatenation.

Procedure $FwdGlobal(p,q)$ proposed in [10] can be used to check $fw([p]:[q]^\omega) = false$. Here is an alternative procedure, which is more efficient than $FwdGlobal(p,q)$. We compute $Q_0, Q_1, \ldots$ as follows:

$$Q_i \;=\; \begin{cases} p \wedge q & (i=0), \\ Img(Q_{i-1}) \wedge q & (i \geq 1). \end{cases} \tag{4}$$

The image computation is repeated until we find either cases listed below:

$$\textbf{Case 1:}\ \exists n \geq 0,\ \ Q_n = false. \tag{5}$$

$$\textbf{Case 2:}\ \begin{cases} \exists m \geq 0,\ \exists n \geq m+1,\ \ Q_m \neq false, \\ Q_m \wedge \neg \bigvee_{k=m+1}^{n} Q_k = false. \end{cases} \tag{6}$$

$fw([p]:[q]^\omega) = false$ in the first case and $fw([p]:[q]^\omega) \neq false$ in the second case. Assuming the first case, every path from $p \wedge q$ through q has finite length that is n state transitions or less. Thus, there is no sequence matched by $[p]:[q]^\omega$. Assuming the second case, every state in Q_m is also included in one of $Q_{m+1}, \ldots, Q_n$. It means that every state in Q_m has a backward path to some state in Q_m. We can repeat retracing such paths and visit Q_m infinitely often. Since the state space is finite, we eventually visit some state s in Q_m twice. Thus, there is a cycle from s to s along which q keeps holding, and some infinite sequence including the cycle is matched by $[p]:[q]^\omega$.

4 Modifying the order of state traversal

4.1 Partitioned state traversal

Forward model checking is basically achieved by a series of image computations, which means breadth-first state traversal. When the set of start states in a PSE is partitioned into subsets, we can use a mixture manner of breadth-first and depth-first traversals.

Let β be the PSE that includes α as a prefix. Assuming that $fw(\alpha) = a_1 \vee \cdots \vee a_n$, $fw(\beta)$ can be evaluated with n state traversals starting from $a_1, \ldots, a_n$. When $\alpha = [p]:[q]^*[r]$, equation (3) gives a reasonable partitioning of $fw(\alpha)$ since it represents grouping under similarities based on distance from p. We can use it for evaluating the PSE that includes $[p]:[q]^*[r]$ as a prefix. For example:

$$\begin{aligned} fw([p]:[q]^*[r]\,[s]) \;&=\; fw([r_0 \vee \cdots \vee r_{n-1}]\,[s]) \\ &=\; fw([r_0]\,[s]) \vee \cdots \vee fw([r_{n-1}]\,[s]). \end{aligned}$$

We generalize it for each basic forward operations. Assuming that $p = p_1 \vee \cdots \vee p_n$, $fw([p]\,[q])$ is divided simply as follows:

$$fw([p]\,[q]) \;=\; \bigvee_{i=1}^{n} fw([p_i]\,[q]). \tag{7}$$

For $fw([p]:[q]^*[r])$ and $fw([p]:[q]^\omega)$, the first subsets are given by $fw([p_1]:[q]^*[r])$ and $fw([p_1]:[q]^\omega)$ respectively. Subsequently, we do not need to traverse the paths that have been traversed once in the previous computations:

$$fw([p]:[q]^*[r]) \;=\; \bigvee_{i=1}^{n} fw([p_i]:[q \wedge \neg t_{i-1}]^*[r]). \tag{8}$$

$$fw([p]:[q]^\omega) \;=\; \bigvee_{i=1}^{n} fw([p_i]:[q \wedge \neg t_{i-1}]^\omega). \tag{9}$$

t_i represents the subset of q composed of the states that have already been visited on and before the i-th sub-computation:

$$t_i \;=\; \begin{cases} false & (i=0), \\ t_{i-1} \vee fw([p_i]:[q \wedge \neg t_{i-1}]^*[q]) & (i \geq 1). \end{cases} \tag{10}$$

Model	#FFs	#States	Depth	Description	Property
atm_sw	54	2.0×10^5	126	ATM-switch [11]	$[i]:\bullet^*[r]:\bullet^*[\neg c]=\emptyset$, fail
dh_1	46	4.0×10^3	21	BUS protocol	$[i]:\bullet^*[r]:[\neg a]^\omega=\emptyset$, fail
dh_2	66	7.9×10^6	17	Cache coherence	$[i]:\bullet^*[r_1]\,[\neg a_1]^*[r_2]:[\neg a_1]^*[a_1]:[\neg a_2]^\omega=\emptyset$, fail
					$[i]:\bullet^*[r]:[\neg a]^\omega=\emptyset$, pass
dh_3	96	3.7×10^8	40	Cache coherence	$[i]:\bullet^*[r]:[\neg a]^\omega=\emptyset$, fail
vpp	101	2.4×10^{11}	18	VLIW pipeline	$[i]:\bullet^*[r]:[\neg a]^\omega=\emptyset$, fail
pipe_s1	35	4.4×10^7	11	Superscalar pipeline	$[i]:\bullet^*[r]:[\neg a]^\omega=\emptyset$, fail
pipe_s2	35	4.5×10^7	11	Superscalar pipeline	$[i]:\bullet^*[r]:[\neg a]^\omega=\emptyset$, pass
pipe_d1	73	5.7×10^{17}	11	Superscalar pipeline	$[i]:\bullet^*[r]:[\neg a]^\omega=\emptyset$, fail
pipe_d2	73	5.7×10^{17}	11	Superscalar pipeline	$[i]:\bullet^*[r]:[\neg a]^\omega=\emptyset$, pass

Table 1: Benchmark examples

Computation of t_i is not a large overhead since we can reuse the i-th intermediate result of (8) or (9).

4.2 Layered state traversal

Let β be the PSE that includes α as a prefix and $fw(\alpha)=a_1\vee\cdots\vee a_n$. We get a subset of $fw(\beta)$ as a result of the state traversal from each a_i, which is possibly partitioned as $b_i=b_{(i,1)}\vee\cdots\vee b_{(i,m_i)}$. The order of partitioned state traversal is written as follows:

$$a_1,\ldots,a_n,(b_{(1,1)},\ldots,b_{(1,m_1)}),\ldots,(b_{(n,1)},\ldots,b_{(n,m_n)}).$$

If we are checking $fw(\beta)=false$, the computation can be terminated as soon as some $b_{(i,j)}\neq false$ is found. Thus, we optimize the order of state traversal to get $b_{(i,j)}$ earlier, by interleaving $fw(\alpha)$ and $fw(\beta)$ evaluations:

$$a_1,(b_{(1,1)},\ldots,b_{(1,m_1)}),\ldots,a_n,(b_{(n,1)},\ldots,b_{(n,m_n)})\;.$$

We also modify the order of state traversal recursively on every prefix. As a result, model checking is achieved in layered manner, which is mixture of breadth-first and depth-first traversal over the PSE.

We use $r_0,\ldots,r_{n-1}$ in equation (3) to make partitions. The first subset r_0 can be computed in small CPU time compared with that for computing all subsets. We can dramatically reduce CPU time for completing the first several partial evaluations over the PSE, which gives us a chance to notice a design error quickly.

5 Experimental results

Table 1 summarizes benchmark examples. They are based on industrial circuits and have been used for verification of the circuits. We checked one actual property for each model except dh_2. For dh_2, we checked one failing property and one passing property. pipe_s2 (pipe_d2) is a revised version of pipe_s1 (pipe_d1). We used the same property for each version. The property passes on the later version, while it fails on the earlier version.

	VIS1.2	BINGO1.4		
Model	CTL	CTL	FW	FW+L
atm_sw	4420 sec	191 img 763 sec 42.0 MB	126 img 342 sec 31.5 MB	51 img 22 sec 2.6 MB
dh_1	8 sec	35 img 13 sec 0.9 MB	29 img 4 sec 0.7 MB	20 img 2 sec 0.5 MB
dh_2	>500 MB	96 img 2919 sec 42.3 MB	78 img 618 sec 22.4 MB	31 img 19 sec 5.4 MB
dh_3	>500 MB	>500 MB	77 img 20052 sec 265.6 MB	53 img 812 sec 28.6 MB
vpp	>500 MB	29 img 331 sec 22.6 MB	26 img 53 sec 6.7 MB	21 img 27 sec 5.2 MB
pipe_s1	10 sec	27 img 27 sec 4.1 MB	26 img 11 sec 4.1 MB	20 img 3 sec 3.0 MB
pipe_d1	>500 MB	>500 MB	25 img 2455 sec 144.0 MB	14 img 157 sec 45.3 MB

Table 2: Results for failing properties

	VIS1.2	BINGO1.4		
Model	CTL	CTL	FW	FW+L
dh_2	67296 sec	64 img 2174 sec 39.1 MB	63 img 360 sec 20.4 MB	178 img 551 sec 21.9 MB
pipe_s2	6 sec	32 img 33 sec 4.5 MB	30 img 9 sec 3.7 MB	58 img 12 sec 3.6 MB
pipe_d2	38439 sec	>500 MB	25 img 939 sec 66.3 MB	58 img 1252 sec 66.5 MB

Table 3: Results for passing properties

The results are shown in Table 2 and Table 3. Standard CTL model checking (labeled 'CTL'), standard forward model checking (labeled 'FW'), and forward model checking with layered state traversal algorithm (labeled 'FW+L') were tested on BINGO [10]. Rows in each box show the total number of image computations (including pre-image computations in 'CTL'), CPU time, and memory usage. We also experimented with VIS [12] version 1.2 for reference. Execution parameters for VIS were set based on one of its standard script, '`script_model_check.robust`'. We provided a good initial BDD variable order for each benchmark, and turned off dynamic variable reordering of BINGO and VIS to measure basic performance of the algorithms. All benchmarks were run on a 167MHz Sun Ultra 1 workstation under a memory limit of 500 megabytes.

Table 2 indicates that layered traversal is very efficient in average for failing properties. We obtained one-figure improvements in CPU time and memory usage for large examples. Although the efficiency of layered traversal should depend on the design error, actual design errors have been found effectively in our all examples. Table 3 indicates that layered traversal is not far inferior to the ordinary breadth-first state traversal for passing properties. CPU time was somewhat increased; however, memory usage was comparable. It means that we can safely use the layered traversal even if we cannot expect whether the property fails.

It is generally recognized that design errors sometimes lead the model to random behavior and make symbolic state traversal expensive. The 'FW' results of `pipe_d1` and `pipe_d2` show such a situation. `pipe_d1` has a design error and it is more expensive to check than `pipe_d2`. The problem was avoided in 'FW+L' because the error was found without searching the entire space.

6 Conclusions

We have presented model checking techniques for early design stages at which design errors make many properties fail. They are based on symbolic forward state traversal along path set expressions in a layered manner. Although the techniques do not bring about speedups for finding all theoretical bugs, they dramatically improve average CPU time for finding actual bugs. The failing property has to be checked again and again to analyze the bug until it is corrected. The techniques, therefore, can have significant impacts on actual verification cycles. Since they do not increase memory usage even if the property passes, we can always use them safely. We have a chance to find design error without searching the entire space. It sometimes avoids a memory explosion problem on model checking of a buggy design.

While the expressive power of path set expressions is now limited to keep consistency with CTL model checking, syntactic extension would be possible in future. Layered state traversal algorithm repeats partial state traversal over a path set expression incrementally. It would be also interesting to consider layered state traversal algorithm in the context of incremental refinement or automatic abstraction.

Acknowledgments

We would like to thank Randal E. Bryant, Edmund M. Clarke, and Fumiyasu Hirose for valuable discussions.

References

[1] R. E. Bryant, "Graph Based Algorithm for Boolean Function Manipulation," in *IEEE Transactions on Computers*, C-35(8), pp. 677–691, 1986.

[2] E. M. Clarke, E. A. Emerson, and A. P. Sistla, "Automatic Verification of Finite-State Concurrent Systems Using Temporal Logic Specifications," in *ACM Transitions on Programming Languages and Systems*, 8(2), pp. 244–263, 1986.

[3] J. R. Burch, E. M. Clarke, K. L. McMillan, and D. L. Dill, "Sequential Circuit Verification Using Symbolic Model Checking," *Proc. 27th DAC*, pp. 46–51, 1990.

[4] J. R. Burch, E. M. Clarke, K. L. McMillan, D. L. Dill, and L. J. Hwang, "Symbolic Model Checking: 10^{20} States and Beyond," in *Information and Computation*, 98(2), pp. 142–170, 1992.

[5] O. Coudert and J. C. Madre, "A Unified Framework for the Formal Verification of Sequential Circuits," in *Proc. ICCAD-90*, pp. 126–129, 1990.

[6] K. L. McMillan, *Symbolic Model Checking*, Kluwer Academic Publishers, 1993.

[7] E. M. Clarke, O. Grumberg, K. L. McMillan, and X. Zhao, "Efficient Generation of Counterexamples and Witness in Symbolic Model Checking," in *Proc. 32nd DAC*, pp. 427–432, 1995.

[8] Z. Har'El and R. P. Kurshan, "Software for Analytical Development of Communications Protocols," in *AT&T Technical Journal*, 69(1), pp. 45–59, 1990.

[9] H. J. Touati, R. K. Brayton, and R. P. Kurshan, "Testing Language Containment for ω-automata Using BDD's," in *Proc. 1991 International Workshop on Formal Methods in VLSI Design*, 1991.

[10] H. Iwashita, T. Nakata, and F. Hirose, "CTL Model Checking Based on Forward State Traversal," in *Proc. ICCAD-96*, pp. 82–87, 1996.

[11] B. Chen, M. Yamazaki, and M. Fujita, "Bug Identification of a Real Chip Design by Symbolic Model Checking," in *Proc. European Design and Test Conference*, pp. 132–136, 1994.

[12] The VIS Group, "VIS: A System for Verification and Synthesis," in *Proc. 8th Conference on Computer Aided Verification*, pp. 428–432, 1996.

SESSION 7B

BIST

Moderators:

Janusz Rajski, Mentor Graphics Corp.,
Wilsonville, OR
Ronald D. Blanton, Carnegie Mellon University,
Pittsburgh, PA

BIST TPG for Faults in System Backplanes *

Chen-Huan Chiang and Sandeep K. Gupta
Electrical Engineering – Systems
University of Southern California, Los Angeles, CA 90089-2562

Abstract

A built-in self-test (BIST) methodology to test system backplanes by using BIST functionality in each of its constituent boards is presented. Since the configurations of systems changes frequently, at the system level, the proposed methodology employs a simple test schedule *which can be easily changed whenever the system configuration is changed. Since the boards used in such systems are designed for use in a wide variety of systems, the proposed methodology defines the* test objectives *to be achieved by a board's BIST circuit in terms of the board's edge pin connections, independent of the configurations of the systems in which the board may be used. It is shown that the combination of the proposed test schedule and the availability, on each board in the system, of any BIST circuit that satisfies the proposed test objectives, guarantees safe testing of faults in backplanes.*

A programmable test architecture *and an algorithm to program the architecture to obtain BIST that satisfies the test objectives is also presented. Finally, the applicability and effectiveness of the methodology is demonstrated via its application to multiple configurations of an example system that uses a VME backplane.*

1. Introduction

Large industrial systems are typically implemented using sub-systems, which are implemented on separate boards and integrated using a backplane. By providing standardized interconnects between boards, backplanes make it possible to build systems that can be constantly updated and/or grown using a wide variety of off-the-shelf boards. Since the backplane is the main communication link of such systems, its error free operation is crucial to the system's operability. Besides the faults caused over time by the hostile environments in which many such systems operate, faults can be introduced whenever a board is removed, replaced, or added. Such faults can be caused due to reasons such as loose or improper connections, or bent connector pins. Hence, built-in self-test (BIST) circuitry for backplane testing will find frequent use.

The objective of *backplane testing* is to test the interconnect structure of the *system bus* which resides in the backplane and the interconnect structure of the *edge pin connectors* which connect each board to the system bus. During backplane testing, all the *local nets* on each board are assumed to be well tested. Similar to how the IEEE 1149.1 boundary scan architecture (BSA) [12] test access port (TAP) port helps interconnect testing between chips at board level, we assume and exploit the presence of a *test bus* which is either a part of system bus or comprises of a few extra lines added to help the interconnect testing at the backplane level. This test bus can be either 1149.1 multi-drop extension [14, 26, 27] or IEEE 1149.5 module test and maintenance (MTM) bus [13].

Despite bearing significant similarities with testing of inter-chip interconnects via boundary scan at board level, backplane testing poses several new and unique requirements. Firstly, while at the board level, during BIST, all the boundary scan cells (BSCs) can be configured as a single scan chain under a single controller, at the backplane level, the cells in each board must form a separate chain, where each chain is controlled by a distinct on-board controller. Typically, the on-board controllers are controlled by a single master controller via the test bus. The presence of multiple chains and two-level hierarchical control necessitates coordination between the on-board controllers, altering the manner in which multi-driver conflicts are avoided and high fault coverage is obtained. More importantly, unlike the configuration of a board, which remains relatively fixed, the configuration of backplane interconnect changes continually as boards are removed, replaced, or added. Furthermore, the BIST circuitry in each board should be assumed to be designed by a different designer, without any a-priori knowledge of the exact system configuration. A new framework is required to develop BIST for backplanes that can take into account all these differences.

Most previous work in testing interconnects focused on the development of deterministic tests for interconnect between chips at the board level [7, 9, 15, 17, 22, 25, 28]. As pointed out above, the extension of these board level methods to backplane testing is non-trivial. In the interconnect test phase of [8], only board level interconnects are tested. Once the global knowledge of the system configuration and net lists of each constituent board are available, test methods used at board level are extended to test system level interconnect in [1, 2], where a dominant short fault model is

*This research was funded by Lucent Technologies and NSF CAREER Award no. MIP-9502300

1092-3152/97 $10.00 © 1997 IEEE

also defined to address shorts between outputs of components employing different technologies. The walking enable algorithm [18] uses disable and enable vectors that enable one board at a time to make backplane testing independent of changes in system configuration. The decentralized BIST [23] addresses interconnect testing at both board and backplane levels. Even though the BIST circuitry is decentralized, the BIST circuitry on each board is required to be an exact copy of their BIST architecture. This limits the applicability of the method in scenarios where off-the-shelf boards from different manufactures are used.

In this paper, we propose a framework to design BIST that uses the walking enable approach [18] in its backplane level *test schedule*, in which one board is activated at a time, but employs a more compact set of patterns to test the faults in the activated board's *edge pin connector nets*, i.e. the interconnection between the edge pin connector boundary scan cells (PCCs) and each pin of the board. By identifying the required test information and defining test objectives for BIST on each board in the system, the proposed methodology achieves near independence from system configuration and complete independence from how the BIST circuitry in each board achieves the specified test objectives, and guarantees the achievement of complete fault coverage in short test time and the avoidance of any multi-driver conflicts during backplane testing.

A BIST architecture that satisfies the requirements of the proposed methodology is presented. A test pattern generator (TPG) design procedure, based on the generalized input reduction techniques [5] where the notions of *incompatibility* [4] and *conditional incompatibility* [5] are used to describe the test objectives that a TPG must satisfy, can be used to program the test architecture to achieve safe testing and complete fault coverage in short time and low area overhead. Finally, all the features of the proposed backplane test methodology, along with its ability to easily adapt to changes in a system's configuration, are demonstrated via its application to test the backplanes of three versions of a system that uses a VME backplane.

2. Background

2.1. Backplane Nets

According to the characteristics of the drivers, backplane nets can be classified as 3-state nets, bidirectional nets, simple nets, wired-AND nets and wired-OR nets. A 3-state net is driven by one or more 3-state drivers, each of which has a data cell and a corresponding control cell. A 3-state driver is said to be *enabled (disabled)* when the enable (disable) value is assigned to the corresponding control cell. A bidirectional net is driven by at least one bidirectional driver which acts like a receiver when disabled (by the assignment of its disable value to the corresponding control cell) and becomes a 3-state driver with a receiver when enabled. It can be shown that, for our problem, bidirectional nets and 3-state nets are equivalent. Hence, in the following, we only consider 3-state nets, but our methodology can be applied to backplanes with bidirectional nets. A simple net is driven by a single 2-state driver, while a wired-AND(OR) net is driven by multiple drivers of a suitable design.

A 3-state net is said to be *disabled* when all its drivers are simultaneously disabled. To simplify the discussion, we assume that a disabled 3-state net holds a logic-1 value; however, our results can also be applied to nets that hold a logic-0. We also assume that the driving strength of an enabled 3-state driver is significantly higher than that of a disabled one. We say that a simple net is *disabled*, when a logic-1 value is assigned to its driver, so that it holds the same value as that of a disabled 3-state net. A driver of a wired-AND(OR) net is said to be *disabled* when a logic-1(0) is assigned. A wired-AND(OR) net is said to be *disabled* when all of its drivers are disabled simultaneously. Note that the resulting value of a wired-AND(OR) net is the same as that obtained by the evaluation of a logic AND(OR) gate whose inputs are the drivers of the wire net.

In the following, we consider the faults associated with the *edge pin connector nets* (i.e. the connections between the PCCs of a board and the pins of its edge pin connectors), *edge pin connectors*, and the *backplane nets* (i.e. the interconnections in the backplane chassis). We assume that any two driver pins in the edge pin connector of a board always constitute distinct backplane nets.

2.2. Conflict-Avoidance Constraints

If boundary scan is used to test faults in backplane nets, then the application of a test pattern that enables multiple drivers driving opposite values on a given net can cause circuit damage by causing excessive current flow. While the application of such patterns can be avoided easily if deterministically generated test patterns are applied under external control, BIST TPG must be carefully designed to ensure that the test sequence generated is constrained in such a manner that it does not apply any illegal patterns. These constraints are referred to as *conflict-avoidance constraints* (referred to as essential constraints in [5]).

2.3. Fault Model

A *stuck-at* fault affects the entire net while an *open* may only affect a part of the net. The behavior of an open depends on the technology of the receivers of the net. In the following, we assume, for all types of nets, except wired-OR, that a logic-1 value is captured by a receiver when one or more opens disconnect it from the drivers. For wired-OR nets, when disconnected due to opens, the receivers are assumed to capture a logic-0.

The technology and driving strengths of the output drivers involved in a short affect the behavior of a short fault [2, 16, 10]. The behavior can be either deterministic or non-deterministic. The deterministic behaviors due to shorts between two backplane nets can be further characterized as 0(1)-dominant and net-dominant faults [2], where 0(1)-dominant faults are generalizations of the traditional AND(OR) short faults and a net-dominant fault is equivalent to the traditional strong driver short.

In the following, the dominant short fault model captures shorts in backplane interconnects, while the open and stuck-at fault models cover most of the other defects that are usually seen at backplane level, such as bent connector pins and loose connection. Only *pairwise shorts* are considered because multiple net shorts are automatically detected if pairwise shorts are detected.

2.4. Test Conditions

Test conditions for a fault characterize all possible tests that can detect the fault. They are used by our BIST design methodology to reduce the TPG size and/or test length while ensuring complete fault coverage.

Since a stuck-at fault on a net affects the whole net, it is necessary and sufficient to drive the net with a logic-0(1) value to detect the stuck-at-1(0) fault on the net.

Any set of test patterns that detects opens at pins of each driver of a backplane net also guarantees the detection of all other *detectable open faults* (defined in [20]) in the net. To detect such an open on a backplane net, a test must: (i) enable one of its drivers and disable all its other drivers; (ii) apply a logic-0 (logic-1 for wired-OR nets) to the enabled driver; (iii) check the response captured at *all* its receivers.

Test conditions for pairwise shorts between two backplane nets a and b, where either a or b is a 3-state or wired-AND(OR) net, are either (i) disable one net, say a, and enable the other net, say b, and apply a value that is opposite to the value of the disabled net a, or (ii) enable both nets and drive both possible sets of opposite values on them, i.e. '0' on net a and '1' on net b **and** vice versa, to detect the dominant shorts. If nets a and b are both simple nets, test condition (ii) above must be satisfied.

3. Methodology for Backplane Testing

The first characteristic of the proposed BIST methodology is its ability to easily adapt to changes in the system configuration, without requiring large amounts of information about the constituent boards and their BIST features. This is accomplished by the use of a simple *test schedule* that relies on the availability of multi-mode BIST circuitry on each board. Secondly, the requirements of the multi-mode BIST in each board is specified in terms of the information that is normally available during board design. Thirdly, the methodology does not require any specific BIST implementation; any BIST circuitry that satisfies the requirements is acceptable. This is especially attractive, since typically systems use boards from multiple vendors; in such a context, the availability of desired BIST functionality is significantly more realistic to assume than the availability of a specific BIST circuitry.

3.1. Test Scheduling

We assume that the test bus and system bus architectures belong to multi-drop architecture where a master controls several slaves in the system. Further, we assume that we can incorporate the test bus master into the same board as the system master. The main task of the test bus master is to execute a *test schedule* comprised of multiple *test sessions*. In each test session, the master is responsible for appropriately configuring the BIST circuitry of each board in the system, allowing the BIST circuits to perform self-test, and finally collecting and checking the signatures. At the beginning of each session, the master also communicates the expected value of the signature to each slave.

The BIST circuitry in each board can be configured in two main modes: active and inactive (described in detail in the following). In the active mode, a board's BIST circuitry applies a sequence of tests to, and captures test responses from, its PCCs; in the inactive mode, it applies a fixed pattern but captures response as in the active mode. Since the boundary scan chain length may be different for each board in the system, each session begins with the master determining the number of shift clocks required to apply tests in that session. This number is used for *test synchronization*— the BIST circuit in board that is activated during the session uses this number to apply test patterns and the BIST circuits in both the active and inactive boards during the session use this number to determine when they should capture responses.

The walking enable strategy [18] is used as the overall test schedule, i.e. in each session the BIST circuitry of one board in the system is configured in the active mode while those of all other boards in the system are configured in the inactive mode. The overall test schedule is comprised of sessions in which each board is activated in turn, and requires only the knowledge of the number of boards in the system and their locations (i.e. the backplane slot to which they are connected). The simplicity of the strategy allows easy update of the backplane self-test after each system update.

3.2. Specifications of Multi-mode BIST

The requirements of the BIST circuitry on each board will now be specified in such a way that any BIST circuitry that satisfies them, when used along with the above schedule, will cover all faults in and among the nets in any given backplane and guarantee the avoidance of multi-driver conflicts.

Though the proposed framework makes use of BIST circuitry in all boards, it relies heavily on the BIST circuitry in the master board. The reliance on the master is justified due to several reasons. Firstly, the master is always present in the system, even in a system with minimal configuration. Secondly, since, functionally, the system design is intricately related to the design of the master board, it can be assumed that the system designer has significant say in the design of the master board (at least greater say than in the design of off-the-shelf boards used as slaves). Finally, since a system contains a single master but multiple slaves, it is more economical to design more complicated BIST circuitry in the master, especially if that helps simplify the design of BIST in all the slave boards. Clearly, a methodology that imposes simpler requirements on the BISTs of slave boards will gain wider acceptance among the manufacturers of off-the-shelf slave boards.

Due to above reasons, in its active mode, the BIST in the master board is required to test all the faults that it can. For most backplane bus standards, such as VME, since most backplane nets are connected to the master, most faults can be tested by the master. Under some conditions, this can simplify the design of BIST circuitry in each slave board to the point that it requires only the inactive mode — greatly decreasing its complexity. Also, the BIST in master board functions as the master test controller that controls the modes of the BIST circuitry in slave boards and implements the overall test schedule. Next, we describe the requirements that need to be satisfied by the BIST circuitry in various boards in their active and inactive modes.

3.3. Inactive Mode

In the inactive mode, the drivers of all 3-state, simple and wired-AND(OR) backplane nets on the board are disabled. Hence, in this mode, the board applies a single fixed pattern to its edge pin connector nets. In addition, all its local nets are disabled. The BIST is required to capture the response at all the receiver PCCs, at specified intervals, and to compress the response.

3.4. Active Mode

During the active mode, the BIST TPG of a board must generate patterns that achieve the test objectives of the board. In addition, it should capture response at the receiver PCCs and hold each board level local net in its disabled state.

As discussed above, the test objectives are defined more aggressively for the master board. For this purpose, in addition to the backplane net classification given in Section 2.1, the backplane nets are further classified according to the location of their drivers as: (i) *type-m nets*, at least one of whose drivers is on the master board, and (ii) *type-s nets*, none of whose drivers is on the master board. (Note that each type-m net is, by definition, connected to at least one driver PCC of the master board.) Next, the test objectives for the master and each slave are defined in terms of the faults in their edge pin connector nets that they must cover.

3.4.1. Active Mode of the Master Board

The set of tests generated during the active mode by the BIST in the master board must guarantee the detection of (i) stuck-at faults in each type-m backplane net, (ii) open faults at the output pins of all driver PCCs on the board, and (iii) pairwise shorts between all pairs of type-m backplane nets. In addition, each test must ensure the avoidance of all multi-driver conflicts in the board's edge pin connector nets. Since the overall test schedule ensures that only a single board BIST is activated during any given session, this condition only imposes requirements on the board's driver PCCs that drive a given net.

3.4.2. Active Mode of a Slave Board

The test objectives of the slave board can be simplified by eliminating the faults that have been detected during the active mode of the master board. Hence, during the active mode of a slave board it should generate a set of patterns that guarantees the detection of (i) stuck-at faults in each type-s backplane net that is driven by one or more of its PCCs, (ii) open faults at the output pins of all driver PCCs on the board, and (iii) pairwise shorts between all pairs of type-s backplane nets that have at least one driver on the board. In addition, each pattern must ensure the avoidance of multi-driver conflicts on the board's edge pin connector nets.

Note that all the above requirements are defined in terms of the information about the board's own PCCs and the knowledge of which of its PCCs belong to certain type-m nets. The former is also required for functional design of the board and hence available; the latter is also known a-priori for most nets in typical backplane standards. If a backplane net driven by one or more of a board's PCCs cannot be definitely classified as a type-m net, it can be treated as type-s. This will still guarantee safe and complete testing; however, the test length would be higher.

3.5. Completeness of the Proposed Strategy

In this section, we will first show how the BIST methodology proposed above is guaranteed to detect all faults in any given backplane.

The system backplane interconnect faults to be considered include: (a) stuck-at faults at edge pin connector nets on each board; (b) open faults at edge pin connector nets on each board; (c) pairwise shorts between edge pin connector nets on each board; (d) stuck-at faults in backplane nets; (e) open faults in backplane nets, and (f) pairwise shorts between backplane nets. Since a stuck-at fault is assumed to affect the faulty net completely, faults in the category (a) are equivalent to those in (d). Faults in the category (c) are equivalent to those in (f); therefore, no pairwise shorts between an edge pin connector net and a backplane net need to be considered. Pairwise shorts between backplane nets (category (f)) can be further classified into: (f-1) pairwise shorts between two backplane nets which are driven by drivers on the same board, and (f-2) those between two backplane nets which are driven by drivers on the different boards. The test objectives for each board explicitly require coverage of faults in categories (d) and (f-1). The faults in category (f-2) are implicitly tested during the test schedule because it is guaranteed that, sometime during testing, one net involved in such a pairwise short will be on an active board, while both logic-1 and logic-0 values will be applied to test stuck-at faults, and the other will be on an inactive board holding a steady disabled value.

As mentioned in the test conditions for opens, once the open faults at pins of all the drivers of a net are detected, all detectable opens at the net are detected. Therefore faults in category (e) dominate those in category (b) which are explicitly covered by the test objectives of each board. Hence, in the test schedule, the combination of the test objectives of the master board and those of all the slave boards in the system covers all the interconnect faults in the system backplane. Therefore the complete fault coverage can be guaranteed by the proposed methodology.

Up to this point we have shown how the proposed backplane test methodology is independent from system configuration and that it guarantees complete coverage of system backplane interconnect faults. We now address how the proposed methodology avoids multi-driver conflicts on both local nets and backplane nets. Since the local nets of each board are assumed to be well tested and remain disabled at all times during backplane testing, the avoidance of multi-driver conflicts on local nets is guaranteed. For backplane nets, the test schedule guarantees that, during any session, drivers on all but the active board are disabled. Furthermore, it is assumed that any two driver pins on a board always constitute distinct nets in the backplane. Hence, the multi-driver conflicts can be avoided by merely satisfying the conflict-avoidance constraints described as a part of the test objectives of each board.

The above test objectives can be used by the TPG design procedure described in Section 5 to program the test architecture described next.

4. Proposed BIST Architecture

In this section, a system interconnect test architecture which can be used to implement the proposed system backplane test methodology is proposed. The proposed test architecture consists of: (i) a *Master BIST* on the master board, and (ii) a *Slave BIST* on each slave board in the system. The architecture of both the Master BIST and Slave BIST is as shown in Figure 1. Typically each Slave BIST can be further simplified as the test objectives are reduced due to the absence of certain types of drivers on the slave board. The active and inactive modes are provided, and the independence from system configuration, test synchronization, and the avoidance of multi-driver conflicts on local nets can be

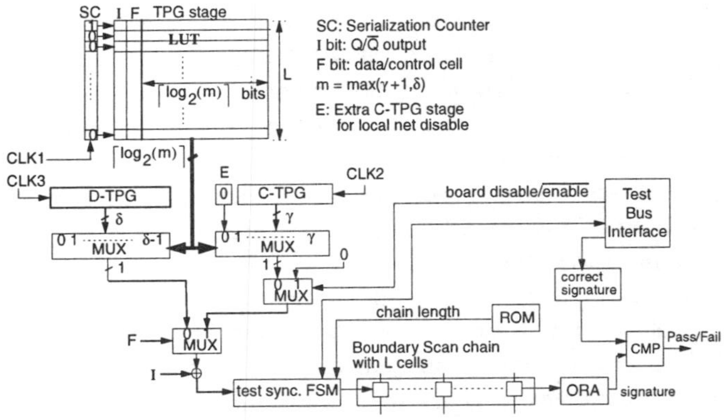

Figure 1. Master (Slave) BIST architecture.

achieved by the use of hardware features in the proposed system test architecture.

As shown in Figure 1, the proposed BIST architecture contains a look-up table (LUT), two test pattern generators (a C-TPG that generates tests for the control cells in the boundary scan chain and a D-TPG that generates tests for the data cells), a read-only memory (ROM), a test synchronization finite state machine (TS-FSM), an output response analyzer (ORA) and a test bus interface.

4.1. Data Encapsulation

The board level information required for backplane testing is stored in the LUT. The number of entries in the LUT is equal to the length of the board's boundary scan chain (L). Each entry of this table corresponds to a specific BSC in the board's scan chain and has a total of ($\lceil \log_2 m \rceil + 2$) bits (where γ is the C-TPG size, δ is the D-TPG size, and $m = max(\gamma, \delta)$) and contains the following information: (i) the bit F specifies whether the cell is a control or data cell and is used to obtain the data to be scanned either from C-TPG or D-TPG, (ii) the next $\lceil \log_2 m \rceil$ bits are then used to select the appropriate stage of the selected TPG, and (iii) the bit I is used to scan into BSC either the content of the selected TPG stage or its complement. For each control cell entry, the I-bit represents the enable value of corresponding control cell. The I-bit of a data cell and the $\lceil \log_2 m \rceil$ bits for C-TPG/D-TPG stage are programmed in different manner for the following two types of BSCs:

1. PCC: These cells are connected to the backplane nets. For PCCs, the I bit of each data cell entry represents the polarity (Q or $\overline{Q}$) of the output of the appropriate D-TPG stage, while each control cell scans in the positive (negative) output of the appropriate C-TPG stage if it is enable high (low). The assignment to the appropriate TPG stage is determined by the TPG design procedure described later in Section 5.
2. Non-PCC: These cells are connected to the local nets on the board. Each non-PCC entry of the LUT is designed in such a manner that all local nets are disabled to avoid conflicts by their assignment to an extra stage

of the C-TPG that always outputs a '0' value which generates the disable value for each non-PCC control cell, by using the bit I of the LUT.

4.2. BIST Operation

The signature register, the ORA and two TPGs form the core of the BIST architecture. The signature register contains the correct signature of the expected output response for ORA, which is obtained from the master at the beginning of each test session. The C-TPG is a γ-stage one-hot counter while the D-TPG can be a δ-stage linear feedback shift register (LFSR), a δ-stage one-hot counter, or a counting sequence generator that generates $\lceil \log_2(2\delta + 2) \rceil$ patterns.

When the board is activated by the system test controller via the test bus interface, the BIST architecture generates appropriate test patterns and synchronizes with other boards. The test patterns are then scanned into the boundary scan chain and applied to the backplane nets (while avoiding conflicts on local nets); after test application, the response is captured. Finally, the BIST circuit compresses the output response into a signature.

Since the boundary scan chain length may be different for each board in a system, test synchronization is achieved by using appropriate circuitry in the system test controller on the master board and the TS-FSM on each board. Based on the boundary scan chain length (L) stored in each on-board ROM, which is sent to the master board by each on-board TS-FSM, the longest boundary scan chain length, L_{max}, is selected by the system test controller and sent back to the TS-FSM on each slave board. TS-FSM then appends additional PAUSE states (defined in the BSA TAP controller) after the desired test patterns are shifted into the scan chain. This helps synchronize the application of a pattern by the active board and the capture of the responses by all boards.

The application of a single pattern begins by clocking of the C-TPG and/or D-TPG to generate a new test pattern. In the following, we assume that the D-TPG is clocked once for each pattern while the C-TPG is clocked after the application of each set of |D-TPG| patterns, where |D-TPG| denotes the length of the sequence generated by the D-TPG. Once a new pattern is generated, the contents of both TPGs are held constant while the serialization counter is clocked L times and held constant for $(L_{max} - L)$ for test synchronization. In the first L clocks during this period, the LUT entry corresponding to the BSC whose content is being shifted in is accessed and used to select appropriate stage of either the C-TPG or D-TPG and its content inverted, if so specified by the table entry, and shifted into the BSC.

When the master (slave) board is in-activated, Master (Slave) BIST disables all the PCCs control cells but still collects responses from the backplane nets and computes a signature.

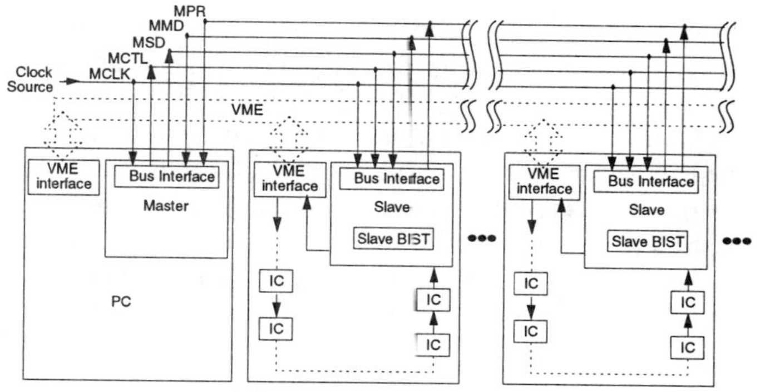

Figure 2. 1149.5 MTM/1149.1 Ext. in a VME backplane.

5. BIST TPG Design Procedure

The key objective of the TPG design is to assign all BSCs to corresponding TPGs with minimum number of stages, subject to conflict-avoidance constraints and constraints which ensure that the test objectives specified by the methodology are achieved. That is, the BIST TPG design procedure is used to program the LUT of the proposed system backplane test architecture. The constraints can be written using the notions of *incompatibility* [4] and *conditional incompatibility* [5]. Therefore, the TPG design procedure can be written as follows:

$$\begin{cases} \text{Minimize } |\text{C-TPG}| \times |\text{D-TPG}|, \\ \text{subject to (i) conflict-avoidance constraints;} \\ \qquad \text{(ii) constraints for achieving test objectives,} \end{cases} \quad (1)$$

where |TPG| denotes the length of the sequence generated by a TPG. The branch-and-bound algorithm proposed in [5] can also be used to solve the problem specified by (1) to obtain a TPG design.

If the objective of TPG design is the minimization of the LUT size, the above formulation can be modified to minimize max(|C-TPG|, |D-TPG|), instead of minimizing their product.

6. Case Study — VME Backplane

VME is a popular open standard system for industrial applications such as telecommunication, real-time systems, and multi-processing. It includes definitions for VME boards, backplanes and protocols. It is so well defined that some other standards, such as VIX (mostly seen in automatic test and data acquisition systems) and CompactPCI (a rugged version of PCI), are also based on it. With increasing demand for system testing, 1149.5 MTM bus is being proposed to be a part of the new VME64 Extensions [24].

Either the 1149.5 MTM bus or 1149.1 Extension can be used as the test bus for backplane testing as shown in Figure 2. In the MTM test bus environment, a system test controller (which itself can be controlled by a PC) is assumed to be at the master board; a test bus slave interface [8, 11, 21] which can communicate with the BSA on each board, is also assumed to be present on each slave board. In the 1149.1 Extension environment, a BSM [3] controlled by a PC resides in the master board and TI ASP [14, 26, 26] can be used as the test bus slave interface [19]. Our BIST architecture can communicate with both test bus environments, provided that there exists an appropriate interface which can decode the instructions sent by the master, and is otherwise independent of the test bus architecture.

In the following case study, each VME board in the system is assumed to be equipped with a VME interface (such as Tundra's Universe Chip [6]). The VME interface chip connects to the VME backplane bus which consists of 104 signals: one input signal, one output signal, 5 pairs of daisy chain input/output signals (4 pairs for bus grant signals and one pair for interrupt acknowledge signal) and 92 bidirectional signals. These signals form 92 type-m bidirectional nets, 5 daisy chain connections (5 type-m 3-state nets on the master board and 5 type-s 3-state nets on each slave board) in the backplane and two untestable nets (the input-only and the output-only signals), which are ignored during testing. The maximum number of data BSCs that a control cell controls in the 92 type-m bidirectional nets is 32 and this number decides the minimum D-TPG size. Except for a few buffer chips between the VME interface chip and the VME backplane, none of the other chips on the board connect to the backplane; therefore, each backplane net is driven by only one output or bidirectional BSC per board.

In a VME backplane, there are at most 21 slots. Let us consider three different system configurations: (a) the master board and one slave board; (b) the master board and 9 slave boards; and (c) the maximum configuration, the master board with 20 slave boards. In the proposed system interconnect BIST methodology, the Master BIST and the Slave BISTs are independent from the system configuration. Hence they are identical for the all three system configurations. However, because of the different test objectives, the Master BIST is required to cover faults on and between (92+5 = 97) type-m nets, while each Slave BIST is required to cover faults on its 5 type-s nets as described in the test objectives of the proposed methodology. The BIST TPG design procedure then generates Master BIST designs consisting of either (a) a 1-stage C-TPG and a 49-stage one-hot D-TPG (minimum test time), or (b) a 4-stage C-TPG and a 16-stage one-hot D-TPG (minimum LUT area overhead). It generates a Slave BIST design consisting of a 1-stage C-TPG and a 3-stage one-hot D-TPG that provides the minimum test time as well as LUT area overhead. As we further investigate this case, the result of using the one-hot counter D-TPG and input reduction can be improved by the generalized input reduction TPG design procedure to design a counting sequence D-TPG [5]. For the Master BIST, a counting sequence D-TPG with only 6 stages can replace the 49-stage one-hot D-TPG for minimum test time while a 5-stage counting sequence D-TPG can replace the 16-stage one-hot D-TPG for the minimum LUT area overhead. No further improvement can be obtained for Slave BISTs by using counting sequence.

The only major difference between these three system configurations in the proposed system interconnect BIST architecture is the total test time. Let us consider one of the BIST architectures above, which has minimum test time for the Master (Slave) BIST using a 1(1)-stage C-TPG and a 6(3)-stage counting sequence D-TPG, which generates $1 \times 6(1 \times 3)$ test vectors. If the longest boundary scan chain lengths in the system are l_a, l_b and l_c for configurations (a), (b) and (c), respectively, then the total test time in each configuration in terms of number of test clocks (considering number of clocks for scan shifts, one more clock for applying the test vector and capturing the response simultaneously, and one additional cycle to shift out the final response) are $(6(l_a+1)+3(l_a+1)+l_a \approx 10l_a)$, $(6(l_b+1)+3(l_b+1)\times 9+l_b \approx 34l_b)$, and $(6(l_c+1)+3(l_c+1)\times 20+l_c \approx 67l_c)$.

The decentralized BIST approach in [23] as well as the walking enable algorithm [18] (try to) enable only one backplane net at a time to avoid conflicts. Therefore, if the decentralized BIST approach or walking enable algorithm (the intra-board counting version) is used for the above three configurations, at least, $(7(l_a+1)\times 2+l_a \approx 15l_a)$, $(7(l_b+1)\times 10+l_b \approx 71l_b)$, and $(7(l_c+1)\times 21+l_c \approx 148l_c)$ (where $7 = \lceil log_2(97+2)\rceil$) test clocks are needed. The proposed TPG achieves the same objectives at a lower test length because it can avoid conflicts while enabling multiple backplane nets. Furthermore, faults detected during the active mode of the master board are eliminated from the test objectives of the slaves to simplify Slave BIST circuitry and further decrease the test time.

The walking enable algorithm [18] was developed for deterministic test generation and did not consider the test issues for BIST. While our test methodology adopts its walking approach as the test schedule at the higher level, it achieves test parallelism at the board level and replaces complicated external test equipments. In the decentralized BIST approach, output response analysis is handled in the master module while in our proposed test architecture, this is done in a distributed fashion in each slave board. Finally, the proposed BIST architecture is truly independent of the system size. As has been discussed earlier, the need to replicate identical BIST TPGs compromises the applicability of the decentralized BIST approach [23] in a multi-vendor context.

7. Conclusion

In this paper, we have presented a new BIST methodology for testing faults in and between the nets in system backplane, pins of the board's edge pin connectors, and edge pin connector boundary scan nets on the boards.

The proposed test methodology assumes that each board in the system contains BIST circuitry that can be configured in *active* or *inactive* mode. In the active mode, the BIST circuitry on a board applies a set of test patterns to the board's driver PCCs that achieve specified test objectives. It also captures and compresses the response to each test. In the inactive mode, a specified fixed value is applied to each driver PCC on the board and the response is collected and compressed. To ensure that the BIST circuitry is useful in any system in which the board is used, the test objectives are specified in terms of the board's PCC nets, independent of the configurations of the systems in which the board will be used.

To simplify the test objectives (and hence the BIST circuitry) for the large number of slave boards used in a system, the BIST in the (single) master board in the system, in its active mode, is required to generate tests to detect all faults in the backplane which can be detected by the master alone.

At the system level, to ensure that BIST can be easily adapted to changes in system configuration, a simple *test schedule* is adopted. The test schedule comprises of a set of sessions, where in each session, the BIST circuitry of one board is configured in its active mode while those of all other boards are in-activated. While this test schedule can be viewed as a generalization of the enable strategy proposed in [18], the proposed methodology achieves faster testing by using a more efficient test set in the enable mode.

It has been shown that the combination of this test schedule and the availability, in each board, of *any BIST circuitry that satisfies the above test objectives* guarantees safe testing of all faults in the backplane and edge pin connector nets. Note that, unlike the decentralized BIST proposed in [23], the proposed methodology does not require the BIST circuitry on each board to be identical. We believe that this makes the proposed methodology significantly easier to apply to practical systems, which employ boards designed by a number of different vendors.

A programmable test architecture and procedures to program this test architecture to obtain BIST circuitry for the master as well as slave boards are also presented. The applicability and efficiency of the proposed methodology is demonstrated via its application to test the VME backplane in three configurations of an example system.

The proposed architecture can be recursively applied throughout the test hierarchy of the system. Also, the TPG design procedure is flexible and, whenever necessary, changes in test quality and diagnostic resolution can be easily accommodated by adding/removing constraints.

Research is currently being conducted on testing simultaneously the board and backplane level interconnects, and on testing backplanes of systems that contain some boards which do not have the BIST capability required by the above methodology.

References

[1] F. W. Angelotti. Modeling for Structured System Interconnect Test. In *Proceedings IEEE International Test Conference*, pages 127–133, 1994.

[2] F. W. Angelotti, W. A. Britson, K. T. Kaliszewski, and S. M. Douskey. System Level Interconnect Test In A Tristate Environment. In *Proceedings IEEE International Test Conference*, pages 45–53, 1993.

[3] AT&T. *AT&T Boundary-Scan Master Manual*. AT&T, 1993.

[4] C.-A. Chen. *Test Generation and Embedding for Built-In Self-Test*. PhD thesis, Department of Electrical Engineering-Systems, University of Southern California, Los Angeles, 1995.

[5] C.-H. Chiang and S. K. Gupta. BIST TPGs for Faults in Board Level Interconnect via Boundary Scan. In *IEEE VLSI Test Symposium*, pages 376–382, 1997.

[6] T. S. Corporation. Tundra Universe User Manual.

[7] P. Goel and M. T. McMahon. Electronic Chip-In-Place Test. In *Proceedings IEEE International Test Conference*, pages 83–90, 1982.

[8] O. F. Haberl and T. Kropf. Self Testable Boards with Standard IEEE 1149.5 Module Test and Maintenance (MTM) Bus Interface. In *Proceedings European Design and Test Conference*, pages 220–225, 1994.

[9] A. Hassan, V. K. Agarwal, B. Nadeau-Dostie, and J. Rajski. BIST of PCB Interconnects Using Boundary-Scan Architecture. *IEEE Transactions on CAD*, 11(10):1278–1288, Oct. 1992.

[10] W.-C. Her, L.-M. Jin, and Y. El-Ziq. An ATPG Driver Selection Algorithm for Interconnect Test with Boundary-Scan. In *Proceedings IEEE International Test Conference*, pages 382–388, 1992.

[11] J.-H. Hong, C.-H. Tsai, and C.-W. Wu. Hierarchical testing Using the IEEE Std 1149.5 Module Test and Maintenance Slave Interface Module. In *Proceedings Asian Test Conference*, pages 50–55, 1996.

[12] IEEE. *IEEE Standard Test Access Port and Boundary-Scan Architecture*. IEEE, 1993.

[13] IEEE. *IEEE Standard Module Test and Maintenance (MTM) Bus Protocol*. IEEE, 1995.

[14] T. I. Inc. SN74ABT8996, Addressable Scan Ports, Multidrop-addressable IEEE STD 1149.1 TAP Transceivers, Aug 1994. TI Web Site, SCBS489.

[15] N. Jarwala and C. W. Yau. A New Framework for Analyzing Test Generation and Diagnosis Algorithms for Wiring Interconnects. In *Proceedings IEEE International Test Conference*, pages 63–70, 1989.

[16] F. D. Jong, J. S. Matos, and J. M. Ferreira. Boundary Scan Test, Test Methodology, and Fault Modeling. *Journal of Electronic Testing: Theory and Applications*, 2:77–88, Mar. 1991.

[17] W. H. Kautz. Testing for Faults in Wiring Networks. *IEEE Transactions on Computers*, c-23(4):358–363, Apr. 1974.

[18] W. Ke. Backplane Interconnect Test In A Boundary-Scan Environment. In *Proceedings IEEE International Test Conference*, pages 717–724, 1996.

[19] W. Ke, D. Le, and N. Jarwala. A Secure Data Transmission Scheme for 1149.1 Backplane Test Bus. In *Proceedings IEEE International Test Conference*, pages 789–796, 1995.

[20] J.-C. Lien and M. A. Breuer. Maximal Diagnosis For Wiring Networks. In *Proceedings IEEE International Test Conference*, pages 96–105, 1991.

[21] C. Poirier. IEEE 1149.5 To 1149.1 Data and Protocol Conversion. In *Proceedings IEEE International Test Conference*, pages 527–535, 1993.

[22] W. Shi and W. K. Fuchs. Optimal Interconnect Diagnosis of Wiring Networks. *IEEE Transactions on VLSI Systems*, 3(3):430–436, Sept. 1995.

[23] C. Su, S.-J. Jou, and Y.-T. Ting. Decentralized BIST for 1149.1 and 1149.5 Based Interconnects. In *Proceedings European Design and Test Conference*, 1996.

[24] VITA. *VME64 Extension Draft Standard*. VITA, 1996.

[25] P. T. Wagner. Interconnect Testing with Boundary Scan. In *Proceedings IEEE International Test Conference*, pages 52–57, 1987.

[26] L. Whetsel. A Proposed Method of Accessing 1149.1 in a Backplane Environment. In *Proceedings IEEE International Test Conference*, pages 206–216, 1992.

[27] L. Whetsel. Hierarchically Accessing 1149.1 Applications in a System Environment. In *Proceedings IEEE International Test Conference*, pages 517–526, 1993.

[28] C. W. Yau and N. Jarwala. A Unified Theory for Designing Optimal Test Generation and Diagnosis Algorithms for Board Interconnects. In *Proceedings IEEE International Test Conference*, pages 318–324, 1989.

A Test Synthesis Technique Using Redundant Register Transfers†

Chris Papachristou

Computer Engineering Department
Case Western Reserve University
Cleveland, Ohio 44106

Mikhail Baklashov

Synopsys, Inc.
310 N. Mary Ave.
Sunnyvale, CA 94086

Abstract

This paper presents a test synthesis technique for behavioral descriptions. The technique is guided by two testability metrics which quantify the controllability and observability of behavioral variables and structural signals. The method is based on utilizing redundant register transfers in the datapath to produce a test behavior with better controllability and observability properties. This approach allows to avoid unnecessary insertions of test structures in the data path. A test scheme for conditional statements has been developed involving minimal changes in the controller. Our experimental results show improvements in fault coverage at modest hardware overhead.

1. Introduction

The need for fast time-to-market and increased productivity have motivated research towards high-level design and test (behavioral and register-transfer level (RTL)) [WagDey96]. Design for Test (DFT) techniques have been developed from ad hoc insertion of control or observe points to test structures such as scan chains and built-in self-test (BIST). Some EDA vendors have already automated DFT analysis and insertion for these test structures in their tools. The area of Test Synthesis has emerged dealing with the integration of DFT structures in a design.

Test synthesis at the behavioral and RTL has been the subject of considerable recent research with the aim to improve the testability of behavioral and RTL designs. Several researches addressed the issue of synthesizing testable datapaths with low area overhead. [ChPap91] presented a technique to synthesize testable datapaths starting from a behavioral description. [PaGuBr95] described a datapath allocation algorithm optimizing test registers to be used for BIST. In [RaDePo94] a high level synthesis system based on partial scan selection was reported. The authors presented several techniques to improve testability of synthesized circuits including transformations, scheduling and assignment. [RaTy] presented a comprehensive test schme for datapaths based on the Arithmetic BIST concept. [PenKu94] presented a testability analysis method at RTL using partial scan insertion along with VHDL behavioral modifications. Another approach on modifying behavioral descriptions was given in [ChKS94]. Based on this analysis, test statements which are executed only in test mode, are added to improve the controllability and observability of all the variables in the description. [PapCa95] proposed a general BIST scheme by adding test behavior, executed only in the test mode. A test behavior is obtained by inserting test points in the original behavior to enhance the testability of required internal signals. However, the test points need extra primary I/O implemented by TPGRs (Test Pattern Generator Registers) and MISRs (Multiple Input Signature Registers).

Depending on the area overhead and fault coverage constraints, the synthesized circuit may need post-RTL-synthesis testability analysis. For example, unnecessary extra TPGRs or MISRs in the datapath can be avoided by changing the test behavior. Such testability enhancements, if found, need to be accommodated in the controller behavior as well. Note that the hardware overhead related to such accomodations, if carefully chosen, will impact only the controller. This is the essential point in our approach as we will discuss it later, i.e. to effect post-RTL synthesis modifications without changing the datapath, possibly exploiting false control paths in test mode. In computation-intensive applications, such as digital signal processing (DSP), telecommunications and image processing the controller constitutes a small part of the total circuit and hence the controller hardware overhead for required testability modifications should be low.

In Section 2, we will review the background and fundamentals of our methodology. In section 3, we discuss testability analysis and metrics that we use. Sections 4 and 5 discuss our test synthesis approach whereas Section 6 highlights our test scheme for conditions. Section 7 provides experimental results, and Section 8 the conclusion.

†This work was partially supported by the Semiconductor Research Corporation (SRC) under Contract No. DJ-527.

2. Test Synthesis Approach

2.1 Behavioral Test Scheme

We consider the testability problem of RTL designs consisting of a pair of datapath-controller. The datapath is provided by a netlist of RTL components, i.e. functional blocks (FU) or ALUs and MUXes, and the controller is provided by a control flow FSM. These descriptions of datapath-controller are sometimes referred to as "functional RTL" and are usually modeled in VHDL or Verilog. A functional RTL design can be captured from a high level synthesis system or can be directly provided using a hardware design language e.g. VHDL. The behavior of the RTL design is embedded in the control flow FSM. We target computation-intensive applications such as DSP for which the controller implementation is relatively simple in comparison to the datapath.

Our approach to testing functional RTL designs is based on the notion of *minimal behavioral BIST* [PapCa95], [NouPap97]; for this scheme, all input/output variables and signals of the RTL are mapped into BIST input/output registers of the RTL circuit (TPGRs and MISRs). The scheme is *minimal* in the sense that no insertion is done within the RTL datapath; no internal variables are made BIST or test points. This means that the datapath is tested as a whole by placing a TPGR across all the primary inputs to the datapath, and an MISR across all the primary outputs. During testing, as the TPGR generates test patterns, the datapath is exercised according to its test mode behavior. Thus for the RTL design we have a *design behavior* performed on the datapath during normal operation along with a *test behavior* which is executed during testing. We distinguish accordingly the design behavior and the test behavior modes. A switch function between these two modes is incorporated in the controller.

Ideally, a test behavior should be the same as the design behavior; this would simplify the testing problem to testing the circuit according to its behavior for which it was synthesized. In reality, however, the RTL design is not synthesized with apriori testability considerations at the high level. Thus there are may be some testability problems in terms of signal controllability/observability at the RTL. Our aim is to modify the design behavior producing a test behavior so that the datapath will be successfully tested, in terms of fault coverage. Both the design and test behaviors are mapped into sequences of register-transfer paths at the RTL. However, the test behavior can utilize true as well as *false* register transfer paths, with the objective to improve testability. The identification of hard-to-test areas is based on the testability evaluation of VHDL behavioral descriptions. In our previous research, we have developed two testability metrics, randomness and transparency, which quantify controllability and observability of signals and variables are used. These metrics are reviewed later in this section after discussing the overall system.

2.2 System Overview

Shown in Fig. 1 are the main tools of our test analysis and synthesis technique. There are four major tools that we have implemented:
a) the VHDL compiler, b) the CDFG (control data flow) simulator, c) the register-transfer generator, c) the test behavior generator. The fifth tool, the high-level synthesizer, is an independent tool which can be provided by other sources, commercial or not. The common interface format for all these tools is the VHDL language. The general flow follows. The VHDL descriptions are compiled into internal design by the VHDL compiler representation producing a CDFG graph. Our Graph Simulator performs testability analysis of the CDFG using probabilistic simulation. Several algorithms have been developed to compute the metrics employing the Monte Carlo Simulation; their description is beyond the scope of this paper. The High Level synthesizer transforms the CDFG into a functional RTL design, meaning an RTL datapath together with a control flow FSM (design behavior). The register transfer generator captures the register transfer set (true and false) from the synthesizer. Finally, the Test Behavior generator based on inputs from the Graph Simulator and the Register Transfer generator, produces a test behavior for the RTL circuit.

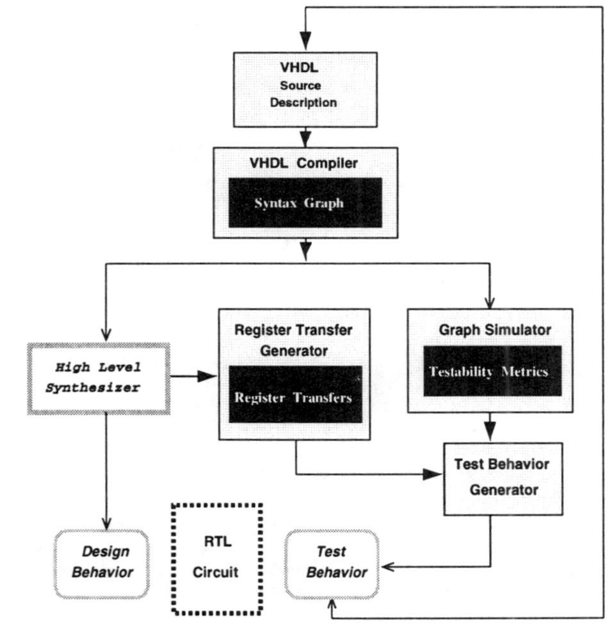

Figure 1: Testability Analysis and Synthesis Tool

We have implemented the algorithms as well as a VHDL compiler in our tools. These tools are shown in Fig. 1 with gray color filled rectangular boxes.

2.3 Testability Metrics

Several testability metrics for RTL modules based on the notion of entropy have been introduced by researchers [ThAb89], [ChPap91]. These metrics are used to evaluate testability at an early design stage [ChLP92], [ChKS94], [Flo97]. These metrics quantify how the quality of pseudorandom values deteriorates

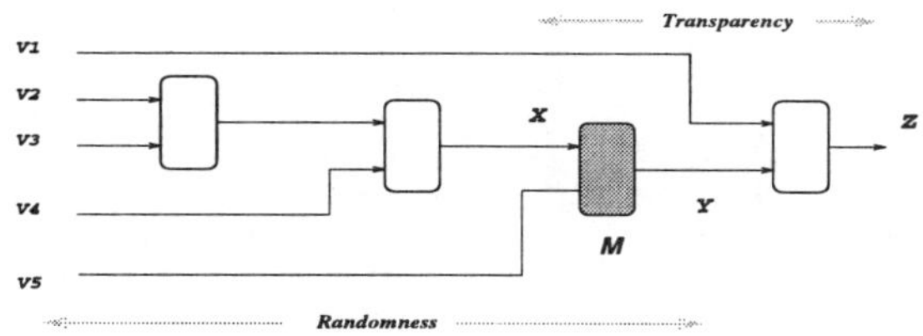

Figure 2: Randomness and Transparency.

as they propagate through the RTL circuit and how easily an erroneous value is propagated to an observable point.

In [ChPap91] the definitions for transparency and randomness were given only for a single FU. We extended those definitions to both the behavioral level and the RTL using a graph G representing either CDFG (behavior) or a netlist of RTL modules (datapath). Fig.2 shows a graph G for these two metrics.

The **transparency** metric, $TG(e, v, G)$, of the input signal, e, regarding node v in graph G is defined as the probability of observing the one-bit data variations on signal e through the graph outputs.
The **randomness** metric, $RG(v, G)$, of given node v in graph G is defined as the ratio of the node computed entropy and the node maximum entropy.

3. Testability Analysis Issues

3.1 Computation of Behavioral Metrics

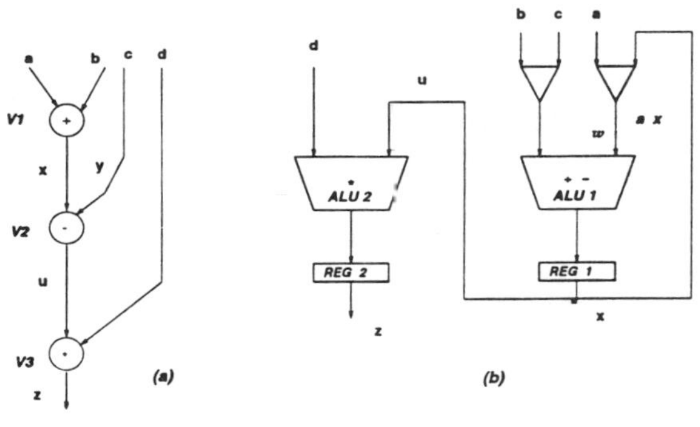

Figure 3: Behavioral-Structural Testability Scheme

During behavioral design capture phase the VHDL compiler verifies the syntax of the original VHDL description and produces a syntax graph. The syntax graph is a mapping of the language statements to nodes and edges according to the VHDL behavior. Since the syntax graph itself does not contain any information about data dependencies occurring in the graph we build the CDFG to allow for testability analysis.

The CDFG nodes represent input and output signal variables declared in the interface part of a design entity, process internal, and compiler generated intermediate variables. The randomness/transparency metrics of CDFG are computed for each edge/vertex in the behavior. The testability analysis proceeds to obtain the same values for the data path.

Monte Carlo simulation techniques have been proposed to simulate non-embedded modules and create comprehensive libraries of metrics to analyze the entire behaviors. The complexity of generating these libraries is very high. Unlike previous works, we perform computations of behavioral testability metrics over the entire VHDL behavior and completely rely on the whole CDFG Monte Carlo simulation techniques to compute the metrics. We calculate simulation-based controllability and observability metrics for VHDL behaviors represented in terms of CDFG and develop algorithms for metric computation. Our behavioral testability model [BMi97] prescribes for each node of the CDFG three attributes, one for controllability, and two for observability, transparency. The randomness computation algorithm is pretty straightforward and based on Monte Carlo Simulation of the whole graph. The transparency computations for the whole graph dictates many different considerations that must be taken into account. Development and implementation of the corresponding algorithm required a much more challenging effort as compared to randomness computation.

3.2 Relation of Behavioral and Structural Metrics

Structural testability metrics at the RTL can be computed by the same Monte Carlo simulation process as with the behavioral metrics. However, the data path netlist is more complex than the CDFG for the computation because the allocation generates loops and Mux conditions due to resource binding. We propose another technique to compute structural RTL metrics from the behavioral that takes into consideration the resource allocation binds the CDFG operations into ALUs of a data path. Let us consider a behavioral description of the circuit shown by the flow graph of Fig. 3 (a), where every edge of the graph is assigned a behavioral variable such as a and x. Fig. 3 (b) shows an RTL implementation of the behavior where resource allocation binds the operations into two FUs. The interconnects of the RTL, e.g. w, are produced by binding CDFG edges, e.g. a and x. In our test scheme when following the behavior, in every cycle through the behavior each CDFG edge is traversed by one pattern. However, in the RTL implementation of the behavior, the interconnects may be traversed by several patterns during the behavioral cycle, as many as the bound variables. Thus "blending" of the a and x patterns appears on the net w and these patterns are employed for testing FU_1. The testability metrics of the interconnect variables w in the RTL are computed by analyzing the probability distributions of the blended or bound variables. We exploit the special nature of binding or pattern blending to pre-compute the RTL testability metrics from the behavioral metrics.

Let R_a and R_x denote the randomness of a and x, respectively, in the behavior of Fig. 3 (a). Let R_w denote the randomness of the interconnect w in the RTL structure of Fig. 3 (b). Further, let M_a denote the "moment" of variable a, defined as follows.
$M_a = \sum p_a^2$ and $M_x = \sum p_x^2$ where $\{p_a\}$ and $\{p_x\}$ are the probability distributions of variables a and x assuming that we apply a pseudorandom set of input patterns at the inputs of the behavior. Similarly $M_w = \sum p_w^2$ where $\{p_w\}$ is the probability distribution of the variable w. Then

$$R_w \approx C_1(R_a + R_x)/2 + C_2(M_a + M_x)/2 + C_3 \quad (3.1)$$

This formula has been obtained using a simple analysis model and some approximation. The precise details are omitted here. As a result of this analysis, the randomness of the bound variable R_w can be expressed as a linear combination of the average of the randomness and the average of the moments of the behavioral variables that are bound into w. The coefficients C_1, C_2 and C_3 depend on the behavior bit-length n. Furthermore, for the transparency metric T_a, T_x and T_w we have found a simpler relationship based only on averages;

$$T_w = (T_a + T_x)/2 \quad (3.2)$$

The details of the above derivation is in [BMi97].

4. Test Synthesis Overview

After register allocation is done behavioral variables are binded or *renamed* by their corresponding registers. We identify all datapath transfers containing one destination register and two source registers connected to a functional unit (FU). However, only a few transfers are utilized in the behavioral path whereas a larger number of transfers are not used in the normal behavior. We distinguish respectively *active* and *passive* transfers. Passive transfers are non-active transfers by the design behavior but could be activated in a test mode; when that happens a passive transfer is also called a *test transfer*. Active transfers themselves are also largely used in test mode. However, the basic idea of this paper is to utilize some passive transfers during the test synthesis process with better testability properties.

The randomness of the destination register defines the randomness of that particular transfer. Fig. 4 shows a transfer in the behavioral path, active transfer A, with low randomness, and two transfers, B_1 and B_2, with high randomness which are in the test paths (passive transfers). The test patterns appearing at $Reg2$ of A have low controllability to test successfully the adjacent path including multiplexer, FU and register. Since these transfers have higher controllability properties they may be considered as suppliers of test patterns for $Reg2$ instead of the design transfer. However, test transfers may increase the number of test sessions and prolong the test application time. It will be shown later that, at most, only one additional test session is needed. Two test sessions can be then scheduled in parallel.

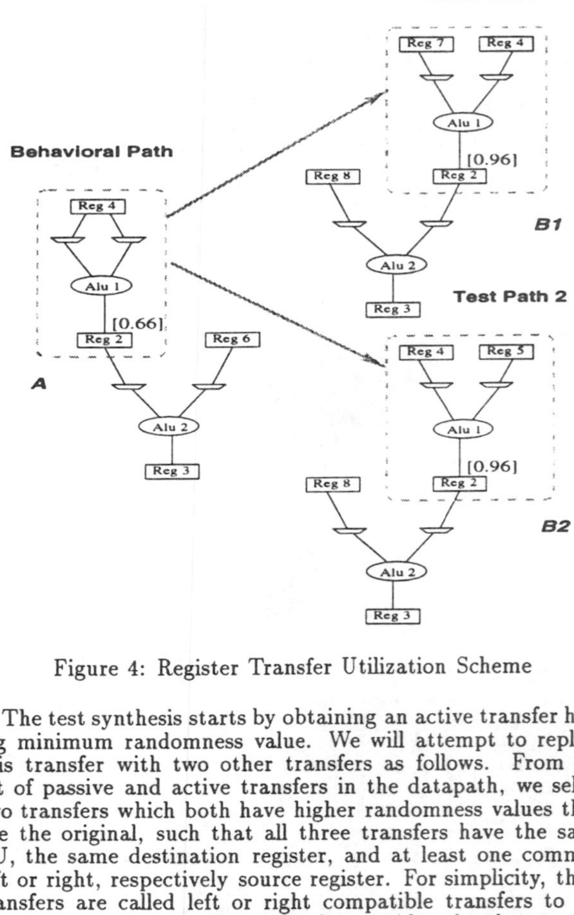

Figure 4: Register Transfer Utilization Scheme

The test synthesis starts by obtaining an active transfer having minimum randomness value. We will attempt to replace this transfer with two other transfers as follows. From the set of passive and active transfers in the datapath, we select two transfers which both have higher randomness values than the the original, such that all three transfers have the same FU, the same destination register, and at least one common left or right, respectively source register. For simplicity, these transfers are called left or right compatible transfers to the original, respectively. For example, consider the three transfers in Fig. 4. Transfer A in the behavioral path, has low randomness. Suppose, that the first transfer B_1 in the test path replaces the design transfer. Transfer B_1 is right compatible to A because A and B_1 have the same destination register $Reg2$ and common one of the source registers $Reg4$ – right source of B_1. Such a replacement increases the randomness of $Reg2$ from 0.66 to 0.96. We require one of the source registers in the transfer to be the same because we want to keep exercising one path segment of the transfer from $Reg4$ to $Alu1$. For exercising the other path segment from $Reg4$ to $Alu1$ transfer B_2, Fig. 4, in the second test path is needed, and B_2 is left compatible to A. Both compatible test transfers B_1 and B_2 need further scheduling to synthesize the complete test session. For example, if the first test transfer B_1 has primary input registers it can replace the design transfer without further scheduling. The second transfer will need to be scheduled and an additional test session will be created.

Let us assume that we found the first test transfer B_1 in Fig. 4 to be used as a replacement of the design transfer. Note B_1 is passive - not used by the design behavior. Then, consider the second test transfer B_2 which is active. We can omit the second transfer from the test behavior because we do not need to reexercise the same paths. We call such a register transfer B_2 equivalent to A transfer. Thus, when two transfers have the same source registers and share the same FU regardless of their destination registers they are said to be equivalent. Since equivalent transfers exercise the same paths, finding such equivalent transfers will allow to avoid additional test sessions. This will be shown in the next section.

Following is an overview of the major functions, steps S1 through S7, of our test synthesis approach.

S1. *Rand_Compute(v,G)* - Compute randomness and transparency in the CDFG graph.

S2. *Bind_Compute(n,D)* - Compute randomness and transparency in the datapath.

S3. *Rtl_Generate(D)* - Generate register transfer set S for the datapath.

S4. *Rename(v,r,G)* - Rename variables by their register names based on binding.

S5. *Find_Min(v,t,G,D)* - Find a node corresponding to a minimal randomness transfer.

S6. *Pool_Rtl(t,S)* - From set S select the transfers with high randomness.

S7. *Schedule(t,D)* - Schedule an additional test session if needed.

The application of the functions will be demonstrated in the next section. Let us assume that during allocation one behavioral variable x with low randomness and another variable a with high randomness are mapped into the same register $R(x,a)$. The randomness of $R(x,a)$ increases because of combining the test patterns of each of the variables. There may also be a case when another two variables y and z, with low enough randomness (but higher than the one of x), get mapped to a different register $R(y,z)$ such that the randomness of $R(y,z)$ remains low. The question that can be raised here is what variable to consider for potential testability problems. It is easily seen that variable with *low* randomness is of interest in this particular case rather than the variable x with the lowest randomness. Using this observation, we suggest to analyze the datapath randomness values to find the variable with relatively low randomness. If we start the analysis with the CDFG it may lead to obtaining wrong variables.

Once the datapath is synthesized all register transfers are extracted by analyzing the datapath netlist. When the minimum randomness value corresponding to a datapath register is found, we check the behavioral variables bound to that register. From the set of such variables we search for the variable with the lowest randomness. The variable with relative minimum randomness value is defined as

$$v_{min} = \min(S_r, r, D)$$

where S_r is a set of variables bound to register r of datapath D. We will now use a formal notation for a register transfer. A register transfer, $d_r \stackrel{v_d}{\Leftarrow} r_i \cdot r_j \cdot alu$, is an RTL transfer where d_r is a destination register, r_i and r_j are left and right source registers connected to arithmetic logic unit alu, and v_d is the low randomness variable bound to d_r.

5. First Case Example

The first case example is a third degree polynomial equation expressed by the formula $y = (a * x + b) * x^2 + c * x + d$. After parsing its VHDL description we generate a sequence of three address statements as follows:

$$V0 := x * a; V1 := V0 + b; V2 := x * x; V3 := V1 * V2; V4 := c * x; V5 := V4 + d; y := V3 + V5$$

The intermediate variables on the statement left hand sides are compiler generated. We used the high-level synthesis system SYNTEST [HarPa92] to obtain the scheduled data-flow graph and datapath.

After the scheduling and resource allocation phases each variable gets allocated into a register. Such variable-register pairs are shown for each node of the graph in Fig. 5. As seen,

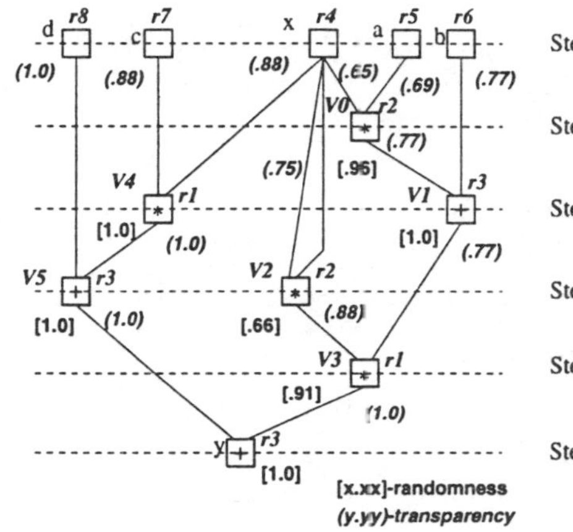

Figure 5: DFG after register renaming of variables

variable $V2$ has the minimum randomness value, .66, and it gets binded into register $r2$ when the datapath gets synthesized. The transfer corresponding to this randomness deterioration is $r2 \stackrel{V2}{\Leftarrow} r4 \cdot r4 \cdot alu1$. In Fig. 6, the randomness and transparency values are shown for each wire of the datapath. The register transfer segment having the minimum randomness value turns out to be the wire connecting the output of $Reg2$ and the middle input of $Mux2$. Binding specifications give us the only variable bound to this wire is $V2$ and thus in this example it is the same variable for both, the graph and the datapath, that causes the randomness deterioration. As we go along we define a notation to be used in describing our technique. Let S^T be the set of all transfers found in the datapath. Let S^A be the set of active transfers used by the design behavior after register binding of variables is done; let S^P be the set of passive transfers in the datapath such that $S^P \cap S^A = \emptyset$. Then $S^T = S^A \cup S^P$. For this example

$$S^A = \{r2 \stackrel{V0}{\Leftarrow} r5 \cdot r4 \cdot alu1, r3 \stackrel{V1}{\Leftarrow} r6 \cdot r2 \cdot alu2, r2 \stackrel{V2}{\Leftarrow} r4 \cdot r4 \cdot alu1, r1 \stackrel{V3}{\Leftarrow} r3 \cdot r2 \cdot alu1, r1 \stackrel{V4}{\Leftarrow} r4 \cdot r7 \cdot alu1, r3 \stackrel{V5}{\Leftarrow} r1 \cdot r8 \cdot alu2, r3 \stackrel{y}{\Leftarrow} r1 \cdot r3 \cdot alu2\}$$

$$S^P = \{r1 \Leftarrow r4 \cdot r4 \cdot alu1, r2 \Leftarrow r4 \cdot r7 \cdot alu1, r1 \Leftarrow r5 \cdot r4 \cdot alu1, r2 \Leftarrow r2 \cdot r3 \cdot alu1, r1 \Leftarrow r2 \cdot r4 \cdot alu1, r2 \Leftarrow r2 \cdot r4 \cdot alu1,$$

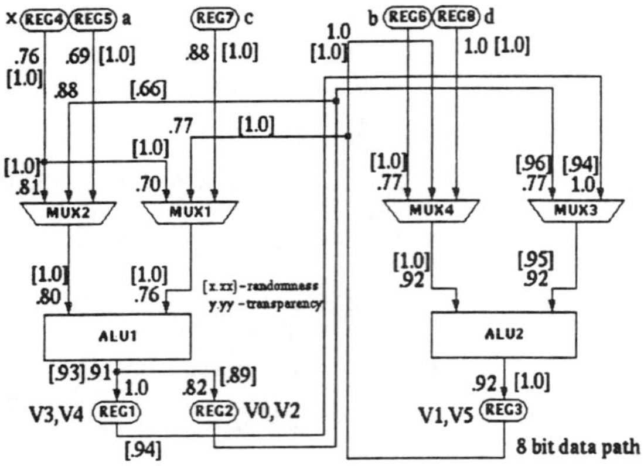

Figure 6: Behavioral Test Scheme for Polynom1

$$r1 \Leftarrow r2 \cdot r7 \cdot alu1, r2 \Leftarrow r2 \cdot r7 \cdot alu1, r1 \Leftarrow r4 \cdot r3 \cdot alu1,$$
$$r2 \Leftarrow r4 \cdot r3 \cdot alu1, r1 \Leftarrow r5 \cdot r3 \cdot alu1, r2 \Leftarrow r5 \cdot r3 \cdot alu1,$$
$$r3 \Leftarrow r6 \cdot r1 \cdot alu2, r3 \Leftarrow r3 \cdot r2 \cdot alu2, r3 \Leftarrow r8 \cdot r2 \cdot alu2,$$
$$r1 \Leftarrow r5 \cdot r7 \cdot alu1, r2 \Leftarrow r5 \cdot r7 \cdot alu1\}$$

We obtain $| S^T | = | S^A | + | S^P | = 7 + 17 = 24$. This means we come up with twice larger space of the passive transfers for the datapath configuration as compared to the active transfers. By definition, The randomness of the active transfer depends on the randomness of variables bound to its destination register. The placement of source registers is also of importance, because the transfer is a non commutative instance as opposed to some commutative operations it might perform. Each transfer carries control signal information that comprises multiplexer select and register load signals.

In this example, there are only three distinguished destination registers for 24 transfers, which are $r1$, $r2$, $r3$. Therefore, if any transfer happens to have low randomness there may well be another compatible transfer (having the same destination register and one common source register) with higher randomness. To find higher randomness compatible transfers we check for two transfer sets, for left and right source register compatibility, respectively. For the transfer $d_r \overset{v_d}{\Leftarrow} r_i \cdot r_j \cdot alu$, the sets are

$$K = \{k : \{d_r \Leftarrow r_k \cdot r_j \cdot alu\} \qquad r_k \neq r_i$$

$$M = \{m : \{d_r \Leftarrow r_i \cdot r_m \cdot alu\} \qquad r_m \neq r_j$$

We do not consider the case when at least one of two sets is empty because the test behavior cannot be found according to our test technique. Note that in this case an insertion of extra test point in the datapath is needed. The case when two sets are nonempty is of primary interest, since two compatible transfers for the test mode may be found to replace the one with low randomness. In this example, the transfer having the lowest randomness is A: $r2 \overset{V2}{\Leftarrow} r4 \cdot r4 \cdot alu1$ In the following we list the set S of all possible transfers and particularly the sets K and M of transfers that are left and right compatible to A. Again we need two transfers to replace A because we need maintain exercising the datapath elements corresponding to transfer A. A preference is being given for transfers that have a primary input register as one of the source registers.

$$r2 \Leftarrow r2 \cdot r4 \cdot alu1 \in K(passive, \in S^P) \tag{5.1}$$

$$r2 \overset{V0}{\Leftarrow} r5 \cdot r4 \cdot alu1 \in K(active, \in S^A) \tag{5.2}$$

$$r2 \Leftarrow r4 \cdot r3 \cdot alu1 \in M(passive, \in S^P) \tag{5.3}$$

$$r2 \Leftarrow r4 \cdot r7 \cdot alu1 \in M(passive, \in S^P) \tag{5.4}$$

We now evaluate each of the above transfers. Transfer (5.1) has register $r2$ as a destination register. This transfer could be activated with variable $V0$ having higher randomness and having been scheduled two time steps prior to $V2$. However, transfer (5.2) has a primary input register $r5$ with the highest randomness. Transfers (5.3) and (5.4) also have the highest randomness but the preference is being given to the last one, (4). Thus, the second (5.2) and fourth (5.4) transfers have to be selected in test mode.

In the next step, before the test behavior is generated, we check for existing equivalent transfers in set S. This allows us to remove redundancy in test behavior and hence prevent the datapath elements from multiple exercising. The idea is to swap one of the compatible transfers by an equivalent transfer which is active and hence it can remain the same in test mode. Fortunately, the previously selected transfers (5.2) and (5.4) have their equivalent transfers in S^T. They are:

$$r1 \Leftarrow r5 \cdot r4 \cdot alu1 \in S^P(passive)$$
$$r1 \Leftarrow r4 \cdot r7 \cdot alu1 \in S^A(active)$$

We cannot tell apart these transfers as to their randomness quality because they all have primary input registers as source registers. This shows there exist two choices to synthesize the test behavior. Note for test behavior synthesis the life times of variables mapped to the destination registers of two active transfers should not to be overlapped. Let us consider the first choice, when using the second (2) transfer. Suppose, that after scheduling and allocation variable $V0$ mapped to the register,$r2$, of the second transfer is being read before the variable $V2$ gets written into the same register. Therefore, the variable life times do not overlap and, in test mode, variable $V2$ can be used in the transfer instead of variable $V0$. The fourth (4) transfer can be eliminated due to the presence of its equivalent transfer. Now, we consider the second choice, when using the fourth (4) transfer. Note that we do not do the variable life time analysis because this transfer is passive. In the test mode, it becomes active with variable $V2$ mapped to its destination register. The second (2) transfer is not needed because of existing its equivalent transfer in the design behavior. Finally,the results are two test behaviors shown in Fig. 7.

```
entity Poly_Test is
port ( a,b,c,d,x :
            in BIT_VECTOR(7 downto 0);
       test : in BIT;
       y : out BIT_VECTOR(7 downto 0) );
end Poly_Test;

architecture Test of Poly_Test is
begin
  process
    variable V0,V1,V2,V3,V4,V5 : BIT;
  begin
      V0 := x * a ;
      V1 := V0 + b;
      if test = '1'
      then
        V2 := a * x ; -- test mode
      else
        V2 := x * x ; -- design mode
      V3 := V1 * V2 ;
      V4 := c * x;
      V5 := V4 + d;
      y <= V3 + V5;
  end process;
end Test;
```

```
entity Poly_Test is
port ( a,b,c,d,x :
            in BIT_VECTOR(7 downto 0);
       test : in BIT;
       y : out BIT_VECTOR(7 downto 0) );
end Poly_Test;

architecture Test of Poly_Test is
begin
  process
    variable V0,V1,V2,V3,V4,V5 : BIT;
  begin
      V0 := x * a ;
      V1 := V0 + b;
      if test = '1'
      then
        V2 := x * c ; -- test mode
      else
        V2 := x * x ; -- design mode
      V3 := V1 * V2 ;
      V4 := c * x;
      V5 := V4 + d;
      y <= V3 + V5;
  end process;
end Test;
```

Figure 7: Modified Test Behaviors for Polynom1

In analyzing the first test behavior we see that in the test mode the operation, $V2 := x * x$ is not used. It was replaced by the operation, $V2 := a * x$, which is now mapped to the second (2) transfer. As seen in Fig. 8 the randomness values get considerably improved. The critical connection from the output of *Reg2* to the middle input of *Mux2* gets a randomness increase of .3. The only noticed decrease of .05 in the observability value at the left input of *Mux1* can be treated as an acceptable one.

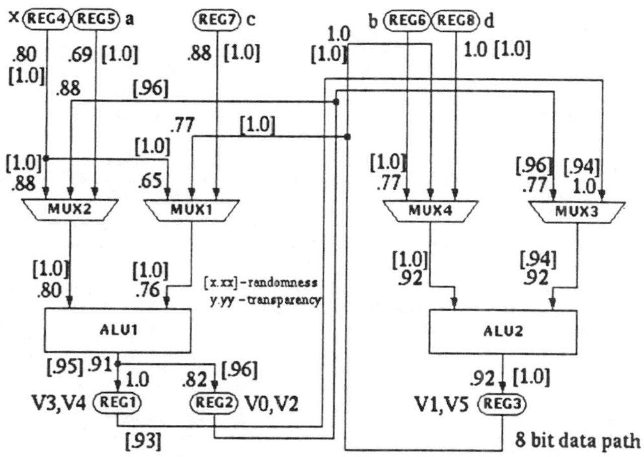

Figure 8: Modified Test Scheme for Polynom1

6. Test Scheme for Conditionals

Our test synthesis approach based on test behavior cannot be directly applied to CDFGs with conditions. Conditional variables in the CDFG are not always explicitly defined relative to the internal variables of the algorithm. Disregarding conditions in many cases may lead to very low fault coverage results for synthesized implementations. We decided to cover the following two types of conditional structures. One which does not have a conditional variable in its branch basic blocks, and the other one which has a conditional variable in its branch basic blocks. The second type of conditional structure is of importance because of possible degradation in randomness and transparency of other variables in conditional branches. In the following we will describe briefly a specific technique to our test scheme for conditions.

There are two aspects of our technique for conditions: a) test controller implementation and b) compiler transformations. We want all conditions in test mode to be equally likely executed. This will provide the same probability of appearance of the test patterns in any conditional basic block and make possible to employ the randomness and transparency computations. If we try to randomize the status signals from the datapath we will allow for equally likely executing the conditional branches in test mode. Such randomizing can be treated as masking the results of conditional expressions during testing and does not depend on the number of conditions, or how conditions might be nested. A test logic comprising two logical gates that perform such randomizing has been designed. Its schematic is in Fig. 9 and can be considered as an insertion in the controller circuitry. Hardware overhead is negligible and includes two additional gates and a 1 bit TPGR. The next-state register is represented as a microprogram counter with CNT (count) and LD (load). N condition selection bits select one of 2^N possible status signals. The selected signal is inverted, if needed, with condition inversion input and the appropriate conditional branch is executed.

In test mode the test signal is asserted allowing randomly to execute both branches. The condition test logic determines whether to assert CNT or LD based on the conditions that occured in the behavioral mode. In the test condition mode asserting the signals CNT and LD would happen equally likely.

For the second aspect, we perform transformations on VHDL behavioral descriptions for IF-THEN-ELSE and CASE statements and insert additional statements which are executed only in test mode. Fig. 10 shows three transformations for THEN, ELSE and CASE branches.

When doing these transformations we assume that the high-level synthesizer will allocate the same statements in IF-THEN-ELSE or CASE conditional branches into one FU. In this case we avoid any hardware overhead related to introducing additional FUs.

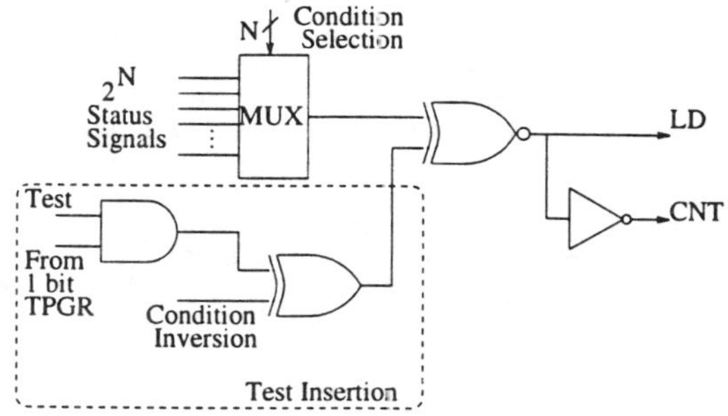

Figure 9: Condition Test Logic

```
for (All Expressions) do {
  If Then-Branch has Exp &
     Else-Branch does not have Exp
  then
     Copy Exp from Then-Branch into Else-Branch
  end if
 }
end for
```

(a)

```
for (All Expressions) do {
  If Else-Branch has Exp &
     Then-Branch does not have Exp
  then
     Copy Exp from Else-Branch into Then-Branch
  end if
 }
end for
```

(b)

```
for (All When-Branches) do {
  for (All Expressions in Branch(k)) do {   /* k is a Branch index */
    if Exp(k) is not in SetOfExp(Branch(l))  /* l is a Branch index other than k */
     then Copy Exp(k) into all other Branches
     end if ;
  }
  end for
}
end for
```

(c)

Figure 10: Transformations for Conditions

Some other references for test control conditionals are in [HsRP96] [LeJW93] and [Gu97].

6.1 Second Case Example

We demonstrate the test scheme for conditional statements on the following benchmark example. It performs a Fast Fourier Transform (FFT) algorithm and uses two conditional IF-THEN-ELSE branches. Testability analysis for randomness and transparency has been performed based on the assumption of equally likely each branch executions. Additional test statements along with expressions were inserted inside two conditional branches in VHDL description, producing two conditional test enhancements. It is worth noticing low transparency values appears only for constants and cannot be improved by making them observable outputs. One of the solutions on increasing constant transparencies might involve combining constants in a coefficient memory. This approach is sometimes used in practical DSP applications.

7. Experimental Results

The results of our test synthesis technique employing behavioral and structural testability metrics are in Table I. The randomness and transparency computations for both, the behavioral control-data flow graphs and the structural datapaths have been done using our testability tools. All examples are 8-bit and have been synthesized using the high level synthesis tool, SYNTEST, and implemented with the computer-aided design tool, COMPASS. For fault simulation we used the AT&T's fault simulator, GENTEST. Random test patterns have been obtained by simulating TPGR in COMPASS. TPGRs, MISRs have been synthesized in the datapaths to compare their hardware overhead with that of the normal registers. For controller testing we wire the outputs of state flip-flops (FFs), which are load register and select multiplexer lines, to the primary outputs of the datapaths through specially designed multiplexers controlled by a 1-bit test signal. The table summarizes the complete hardware overhead for TPGRs and MISRs in the data paths, controller hardware overhead for handling the test statements, condition logic and additional multiplexers.

For the first two examples test behaviors have been found to get high enough fault coverage with insertion TPGRs and MISRs in the datapath and modifying the controller description. The hardware overhead related to wiring control signals from FFs we counted as controller hardware overhead.

The results for Fft feature our test synthesis technique applied to conditions. As it was described in the previous section, we found a specific test scheme along with the controller circuitry and obtained considerable improvement in fault coverage (18%) with hardware overhead 11%. The hardware overhead for the test condition logic is 0.4% and can be well neglected. For the last three benchmark examples the randomness and transparency values turned out to be very high and no test synthesis in terms of behavioral modifications has been performed. We applied only behavioral test scheme to test these three circuits and achieved high fault coverage with insertion only TPGRs and MISRs.

8. Conclusions

We have developed and tested a quantitative approach for behavioral and structural test synthesis using BIST. We proposed a testability technique to test the datapaths synthesized from behavioral descriptions with conditions. The basic idea behind the proposed methodology is to take advantage of redundancies inherent in the structure to change the test behavior. In analyzing redundant register transfers we found that by modifying the design behavior some of them might be used in test mode with improving the testability of the datapath. The behavioral modifications for conditional descriptions were developed along with the conditional logic for the controller. All this required a change in the datapath controller. We accommodated such changes in controller descriptions and computed the hardware overhead. The advantages of our scheme are avoiding redundant hardware when possible and test controller simplicity. The experimental results showed improvement in fault coverage.

Although testability of the controller has not been dealt with specifically in this paper, our earlier approach on controller testability discussed in [PapCa95] could directly apply here as well. That approach uses structural analysis and insertion to enhance the testability of the controller and the interface between the datapath and the controller. Again, for DSP oriented applications, the overhead of the controller testability insertion, and the controller itself for that matter, in comparison to the datapath is relatively small.

References

[ChKS94] C. Chen, T. Karnic and D. Saab, Structural and Behavioral Synthesis for Testability Techniques, IEEE Trans. on CAD, pp. 777-785, June 1994.

[ChMen89] C.H.Chen and P.R.Menon, An Approach to Functional Level Testability Analysis, International Test Conference, pp. 373-379, 1989.

[ChPap91] S. Chiu and C. Papachristou, A Design for Testability Scheme with Applications to Data Path Synthesis, Design Automation Conference, June 1991.

[HarPa92] H. Harmanani, C. Papachristou, S. Chiu and M. Nourani, SYN-TEST: An Environment for System Level Design for Test, Proc. EURO-DAC'92, Sept. 1992.

[NouPap97] M. Nourani, C. Papachristou, Structural BIST Insertion Using Behavioral Test Analysis, European Design and Test Conf. (ED&TC-97), pp. 64-68, March 1997.

[ThAb89] K. Thearling and J. Abraham, An Easily Computed Functional Level Testability Measure, 1989 International Test Conference, pp. 381-390, 1989.

[RaTy93] J. Rajski and J. Tyszer, Test Responses Compaction in Accumulators with Rotate Carry Adders, IEEE Trans. on CAD, Vol. 12, N. 4, pp. 531-539, April 1993.

[KuPen89] K. Kuchcinski and Z. Peng, Testability Analysis in a VLSI High-Level Synthesis System, Microprocessing and Microprogramming, 28, pp. 295-300, 1989.

[Gu97] X. Gu, E. Larsson, K. Kuchinski, Z. Peng, A Controller Testability Analysis and Enhancement Technique, European Design and Test Conf. (ED&TC-97), pp. 153-157, March 1997.

[PapCa95] C.A. Papachristou and J.E. Carletta, Test Synthesis in the Behavioral Domain, Proc. Int'l Test Conf., pp. 698-702.

[PaGuBr95] I. Parulkar, S. Gupta and M. Breuer, Data Path Allocation for Synthesizing RTL Designs with Low BIST Area Overhead, 32nd Design Automation Conference, pp. 395-401, 1995.

[PenKu94] Z. Peng and K. Kuchcinski, Automated Transformation of Algorithms into RTL Implementations, IEEE Trans. CAD, pp. 150-165, Feb. 1994.

[RaDePo94] R.K. Roy, S. Dey and M. Potkonjak Test Synthesis Using High-Level Design Information, International Test Conference, pp. 1-6, 1994.

[WagDey96] K.D. Wagner and S. Dey, High-Level Synthesis for Testability: A Survey and Perspective, 33rd Design Automation Conference, pp. 131-136, 1996.

[BMi97] M. Baklashov, C. Papachristou, Behavioral-Structural Testability Modeling and Synthesis for BIST with Applications to High-Level Synthesis, SRC Report T97122 , June 1997.

[LeJW93] T.-C. Lee, N.K. Jha, and W.H. Wolf, A Conditional Resource Sharing Method for Behavioral Synthesis of Highly Testable Data Paths' Intern. Test Conf. (ITC-93), pp. 744-753, Oct. 1993.

[HsRP96] F.F. Hsu, E.M. Rudnick, and J.H. Patel, Enhancing High-Level Control-Flow for Improved Testability, Intern. Conf. Comp.-Aided Design (ICCAD-96), pp. 322-328, Nov. 1996.

[Flo97] M. L. Flottes, R. Pires, B. Rouzeyre, Analyzing Testability from Behavioral to RT Level, European Design and Test Conf. (ED&TC-97), pp. 158-165, March 1997.

Table 1: Complete Test Results

Circuit Name	Trans.Count (DP+Contr)	Fault Cover. Before Insertion	Fault Cover. After Insertion	Test Time (cycles)	TPGR+MISR (8-bit)	Load,Sel FFs	Hardware Overhead (DP+Contr)
Polynom1	4934+1497	94.2%	96.3%	350	5+1	19	12.61%
Polynom2	983+134	87.7%	98.0%	800	3+1	11	6.32%
Fft	8631+2915	76.9%	94.9%	300	4+2	41	10.76%
Diff	6468+1597	92.4%	98.2%	250	4+3	22	8.37%
Elliptic	14847+4931	89.6%	97.8%	350	16+6	56	14.42%
Wave	9762+2387	92.9%	99.1%	400	12+3	47	13.27%

Built-In Test Generation for Synchronous Sequential Circuits

Irith Pomeranz and Sudhakar M. Reddy +
Electrical and Computer Engineering Department
University of Iowa
Iowa City, IA 52242

Abstract

We consider the problem of built-in test generation for synchronous sequential circuits. The proposed scheme leaves the circuit flip-flops unmodified, and thus allows at-speed test application. We introduce a uniform, parametrized structure for test pattern generation. By matching the parameters of the test pattern generator to the circuit-under-test, high fault coverage is achieved. In many cases, the fault coverage is equal to the fault coverage that can be achieved by deterministic test sequences. We also investigate a method to minimize the size of the test pattern generator, and study its effectiveness alone and in conjunction with the insertion of test-points.

1. Introduction

A large number of techniques for built-in self-test (*BIST*) were developed for combinational circuits and fully-scanned sequential circuits [1], [2]. *BIST* for synchronous sequential circuits has received limited attention [3]-[5]. The need to develop *BIST* techniques for synchronous sequential circuits is motivated by the fact that if the combinational logic of the circuit is not tested separately, then there is no need to configure the circuit flip-flops into a test pattern generator during test mode, and the circuit flip-flops can be left unmodified. This allows at-speed testing of the circuit under its normal operation conditions.

Built-in test generation methods for synchronous sequential circuits that modify some of the circuit flip-flops were described in [3] and [4]. In [3], a subset of the flip-flops are incorporated into a partial scan or *BIST* register and the resulting sequential circuit is tested using weighted random patterns. In [4], a hold mode is added to selected flip-flops. While a flip-flop is in the hold mode, its value does not change. This mode is used in order to apply to the combinational logic of the circuit an appropriately biased set of random patterns. For example, if a state variable y assumes the value 1 only rarely, then by holding a state that assigns the value 1 to y, the average frequency with which a 1 is obtained on y can be increased. A similar method was used in [6], except that in [6] all the flip-flops are controlled together, whereas in [4] the hold mode of every modified flip-flop is controlled independently. The methods of [3] and [4] modify the circuit flip-flops to increase the set of reachable states, thus increasing the fault coverage that can be obtained. In this work, we are interested in maximizing the fault coverage by selecting a built-in test pattern generator for primary input sequences without modifying the circuit flip-flops. Techniques that modify the sequential behavior of the circuit can be used to further increase the fault coverage if necessary.

+ Research supported in part by NSF Grant No. MIP-9220549, and in part by NSF Grant No. MIP-9357581

A method to generate input sequences to test a synchronous sequential circuit using built-in test pattern generators without modifying the circuit flip-flops was proposed in [5]. In [5], a sequence of pseudo-random primary input patterns produced by an *LFSR* is modified by holding selected input values fixed for several time units. Experimental results for benchmark circuits are reported in [5], showing fault coverages which are close to the fault coverages achieved by deterministic test sequences. Although the fault coverages reported in [5] are very high, they are not complete. In this work, we propose a test generation scheme suitable for *BIST* that allows higher fault coverages to be obtained. In many cases, the fault coverage is as high as that achieved by deterministic test generation. Under the proposed scheme, a test pattern is applied to the circuit every clock cycle, and allows at-speed testing of the circuit.

An effective test pattern generator (*TPG*) for *BIST* must be a circuit having an area efficient implementation, capable of generating test sequences that achieve high fault coverages. To satisfy these goals we use a preselected parametrized *TPG* structure. We determine the parameters based on circuit properties so as to maximize the fault coverage achieved; however, the overall structure of the *TPG* remains the same. We use in this work a randomized search for the appropriate parameters. We expect that a deterministic search using appropriate heuristics or a directed search such as genetic optimization would allow even higher fault coverages to be obtained at lower area overheads.

The basic structure of the *TPG* is as follows. A k-bit counter is allowed to cycle through its 2^k states a number of times denoted by the parameter R. The state of the counter at time unit u is equal to the binary representation of u, and it is denoted by $Q[u]$. The sequence of counter states is denoted by Q. We have $Q = (0\ 1 \cdots 2^k - 1\ 0\ 1 \cdots 2^k - 1 \cdots)$. Input i of the circuit-under-test (*CUT*) is determined by a decoding logic driven by the counter and characterized by two parameters L_i and U_i such that $0 \le L_i \le U_i \le 2^k - 1$. Input i is set to 1 when $L_i \le Q[u] \le U_i$; otherwise, input i is set to 0. Thus, the sequence assigned to input i consists of L_i 0s followed by $U_i - L_i + 1$ 1s and $2^k - 1 - U_i$ 0s. This sequence is repeated R times. For example, for $k = 3$, $L_i = 2$ and $U_i = 6$, the sequence (00111110), repeated R times, is applied to input i of the *CUT*. The logic block used for producing the sequence on input i has an implementation called a *comparison unit* in [7].

The paper is organized as follows. The *TPG* structure is described in Section 2. The selection of the *TPG* parameters is described in Section 3, including the bounds $\{L_i, U_i\}$ that determine the sequences of 1s on the *CUT* inputs. We describe a basic scheme where the values of the bounds $\{L_i, U_i\}$ are unrestricted, and then introduce a scheme with restricted bound values. The latter *TPG*s have lower hardware overheads. Experi-

1092-3152/97 $10.00 © 1997 IEEE

mental results are presented in Section 4, including results of the basic scheme, results of the extended scheme with restricted bound values, and results of the latter scheme in conjunction with test-point insertion. Section 5 concludes the paper.

2. The *TPG* structure

The overall structure of the *TPG* for an n-input circuit is shown in Figure 1. The boxes containing L_i, U_i for $1 \le i \le n$ are comparison units whose structure is described below. A k-bit counter is used to drive the comparison units. At time unit u, the ith comparison unit accepts the k-bit state $Q[u]$ of the counter, and produces the value 1 if and only if $Q[u]$ satisfies $L_i \le Q[u] \le U_i$.

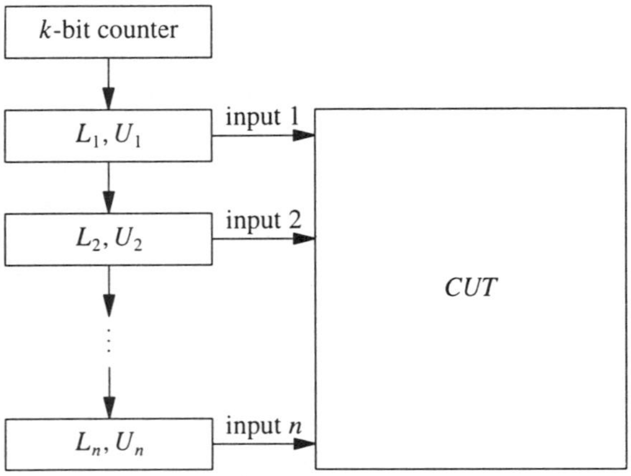

Figure 1: The *TPG* structure

The structure of a comparison unit [7] is shown in Figure 2. The $\ge L$ block produces the value 1 if and only if the input vector represents a binary number whose value is L or more; and the $\le U$ block produces the value 1 if and only if the input vector represents a binary number whose value is U or less. The comparison block inputs are denoted $x_1, x_2, \cdots, x_k$. The counter outputs are denoted $q_1, q_2, \cdots, q_k$ where q_1 is the most significant counter bit and q_k is the least significant counter bit. In Figure 1, we connect x_i to q_i for $1 \le i \le k$. The implementation of a $\ge L$ or $\le U$ block with k inputs requires at most $k - 1$ gates [7].

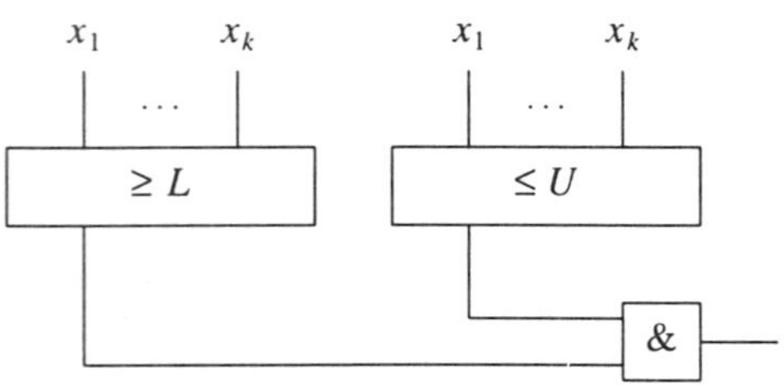

Figure 2: A comparison unit

To minimize the number of comparison blocks needed to implement a given *TPG*, we observe that a $\le U$ block can be implemented using the complemented output of a $\ge L$ block, where $L = U + 1$. This is because the function $\le U$ is the complement of the function $> U$, or $\ge U + 1$. In the implementation of the *TPG*, each bound (original lower bound L or one obtained through complementation of an upper bound U) needs to be implemented only once. For example, if a three input circuit has $L_1 = U_2 + 1 = L_3$, and $U_1 + 1 = U_3 + 1$, then the implementation of Figure 3 can be used. Note that only $\ge L$ blocks are used in this implementation, and their outputs are complemented when they replace $\le U$ blocks.

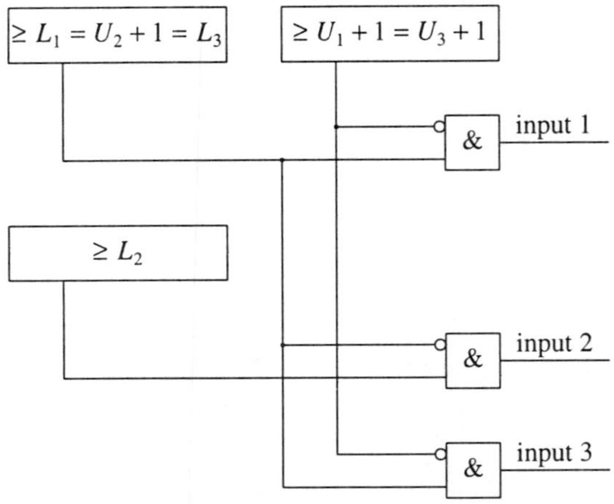

Figure 3: An example of a *TPG*

In some cases, a single *TPG* may not be sufficient to achieve the desired fault coverage for the circuit. In this case, multiple *TPG*s may be used. If more than one *TPG* is needed to achieve the desired fault coverage for a circuit, a multiplexer is required on each input of the *CUT* to select the logic corresponding to the appropriate *TPG*. The control input of the multiplexers can be driven from a counter whose frequency is $R2^k$ lower than the frequency of the counter that drives the comparison units. This will allow each *TPG* to apply a sequence of length $R2^k$ before it is replaced by the next *TPG*. As in the case of a single *TPG*, if multiple *TPG*s use the same bound, then the bound need only be implemented once.

In the discussion above, we ordered the inputs to the comparison units in the same way as the counter outputs. Thus, for a comparison unit with inputs $x_1, x_2, \cdots, x_k$, x_i was connected to the counter output q_i for $1 \le i \le k$. With this configuration, we obtain a single run of 1s on every input of the *CUT* every time the counter goes through a complete cycle. For example, consider a 2-input circuit driven by a 3-bit counter. Suppose that $L_1 = 2$, $U_1 = 4$, $L_2 = 4$ and $U_2 = 5$. Then the sequence shown in Table 1(a) is applied to the *CUT* every time the counter goes through a complete cycle. The 1s on each *CUT* input appear consecutively in this case. It is possible to achieve more varied test sequences by permuting the inputs of the comparison units compared to the counter outputs. For example, let the inputs of the first comparison unit in the example above be x_{11}, x_{12}, x_{13}. Suppose that x_{11} is connected to q_2, x_{12} is connected to q_3, and x_{13} is connected to q_1. Let us use the same bounds as above, $L_1 = 2$ and $U_1 = 4$. The sequence applied to the first *CUT* input is determined as follows.

$(q_1q_2q_3) = (000)$ implies $(x_{11}x_{12}x_{13}) = (000)$. 0 is not within the bounds $L_1 = 2$ and $U_1 = 4$. The *CUT* input is 0.

$(q_1q_2q_3) = (001)$ implies $(x_{11}x_{12}x_{13}) = (010)$. 2 is within the bounds $L_1 = 2$ and $U_1 = 4$. The *CUT* input is 1.

The complete sequence on the first *CUT* input is shown in Table 1(b) under column *CUT input 1*. We also show the values of x_{11}, x_{12}, x_{13} for every counter state. For the second comparison unit with bounds $L_2 = 4$ and $U_2 = 5$, we connect its inputs such that $(x_{21}x_{22}x_{23}) = (q_3q_1q_2)$. The complete sequence on the second *CUT* input is also shown in Table 1(b).

By permuting the inputs of the comparison units as illustrated above, we add another degree of freedom in determining

Table 1: An example of input permutations
(a) Unpermuted inputs

q_1	q_2	q_3	CUT input 1	CUT input 2
0	0	0	0	0
0	0	1	0	0
0	1	0	1	0
0	1	1	1	0
1	0	0	1	1
1	0	1	0	1
1	1	0	0	0
1	1	1	0	0

(b) Permuted inputs

			x_{11}	x_{12}	x_{13}	CUT	x_{21}	x_{22}	x_{23}	CUT
q_1	q_2	q_3	q_2	q_3	q_1	input 1	q_3	q_1	q_2	input 2
0	0	0	0	0	0	0	0	0	0	0
0	0	1	0	1	0	1	1	0	0	1
0	1	0	1	0	0	1	0	0	1	0
0	1	1	1	1	0	0	1	0	1	1
1	0	0	0	0	1	0	0	1	0	0
1	0	1	0	1	1	1	1	1	0	0
1	1	0	1	0	1	0	0	1	1	0
1	1	1	1	1	1	0	1	1	1	0

the *TPG* output sequences (or the *CUT* test sequences), and a higher fault coverage may potentially be obtained by the resulting test sequence.

3. Selecting the *TPG* parameters

Our approach to determining the *TPG* parameters is based on simulation of randomly selected *TPG*s. We first describe the basic *TPG* selection procedure, and then extend it to reduce the total number of bounds required.

3.1 Basic procedure

The procedure used for selecting a single *TPG* is given below as Procedure 1. The procedure is described for a given counter length k and a given number of repetitions of the counter sequence R_1. The procedure selects the *TPG* out of a set of N_{try} randomly determined *TPG*s, as follows. The parameters L_i and U_i ($1 \le i \le n$) for each *TPG* and its input permutation are randomly selected in Step 2 of Procedure 1. The output sequence T produced by each *TPG* is computed in Step 3, and the circuit is simulated under T in Step 4. The length of the sequence T is $2^k R_1$. The number of faults detected by the j-th *TPG* is recorded in variable N^j_{det}. This process is repeated for N_{try} *TPG*s (cf. Steps 1-5 of Procedure 1). The *TPG* that results in the highest fault coverage is selected in Step 6. This *TPG* is allowed to generate a sequence of length $2^k R_2$ ($R_2 > R_1$) in Steps 7 and 8.

Procedure 1: Selecting *TPG* parameters

(1) Set $j = 1$.

(2) For every *CUT* input i:

  (a) Select a pair of numbers (L^j_i, U^j_i) such that $0 \le L^j_i \le 2^k - 1$, $0 \le U^j_i \le 2^k - 1$ and $L^j_i \le U^j_i$.

  (b) Select a permutation of the counter outputs $< q^j_{i1}, q^j_{i2}, \cdots, q^j_{ik} >$.

(3) Generate the test sequence T produced during R_1 cycles of the counter by the *TPG* where (a) *CUT* input i is characterized by bounds L^j_i and U^j_i for $1 \le i \le n$, and (b) input x^j_{im} of the i-th comparison unit is connected to output q^j_{im} of the counter for $1 \le m \le k$ and $1 \le i \le n$.

(4) Fault simulate the circuit under the sequence T produced in Step 3. Let N^j_{det} faults be detected.

(5) Set $j = j + 1$. If $j \le N_{try}$, where N_{try} is a preselected number, go to Step 2.

(6) Select the *TPG*, j_0, for which $N^{j_0}_{det}$ is maximum.

(7) Generate the test sequence T produced by *TPG* j_0 during R_2 cycles.

(8) Fault simulate the circuit under the test sequence T produced in Step 7.

(9) Stop: The faults detected are the ones that will be detected by the selected *TPG*.

To increaes the fault coverage obtained by the *TPG* selected by Procedure 1, we describe next two extensions.

Let a *TPG* selected by Procedure 1 produce a test sequence T. Simple modifications of the *TPG* allow modified versions of T to be applied to the *CUT*. These modified versions of T may detect faults that are not detected by T, thus increasing the fault coverage. We consider the following modifications of T and their combination. First, by adding multiplexers and inverters on the *TPG* outputs (or the *CUT* inputs) and allowing complemented values to be applied to the *CUT*, the sequence T' which is the complement of T can be applied to the *CUT*. Second, by using an up/down counter instead of a counter that can only count up, the sequence T_r which is the reverse of T can be applied to the *CUT*. In addition, by using both the down count and the complemented *TPG* outputs, it is possible to apply to the *CUT* the sequence T'_r which is the complemented sequence T' applied in reverse order. An example of the four versions of T for a three-input circuit is shown in Table 2. Procedure 1E given below is the same as Procedure 1 except that the modified sequences described above are used as well.

Table 2: An example of a modified sequence

T			T'			T_r			T'_r		
0	0	0	1	1	1	1	0	1	0	1	0
0	1	1	1	0	0	1	0	0	0	1	1
1	0	0	0	1	1	0	1	1	1	0	0
1	0	1	0	1	0	0	0	0	1	1	1

Procedure 1E: Selecting *TPG* parameters (extended)

(1) Set $j = 1$.

(2) For every *CUT* input i:

  (a) Select a pair of numbers (L^j_i, U^j_i) such that $0 \le L^j_i \le 2^k - 1$, $0 \le U^j_i \le 2^k - 1$ and $L^j_i \le U^j_i$.

  (b) Select a permutation of the counter outputs $< q^j_{i1}, q^j_{i2}, \cdots, q^j_{ik} >$.

(3) Generate the test sequence T produced during R_1 cycles of the counter by the *TPG* where *CUT* input i is characterized by bounds L^j_i and U^j_i for $1 \le i \le n$, and input x^j_{im} of the ith comparison unit is connected to output q^j_{im} of the counter for $1 \le m \le k$ and $1 \le i \le n$.

(4) Fault simulate the circuit under the test sequence T produced in Step 3 (fault simulation with fault dropping starts from the complete set of target faults). Let $N^j_{det,1}$ faults be detected.

(5) Complement T and fault simulate the *CUT* under the complemented sequence T' (fault simulation with fault dropping is used starting from the set of faults left undetected in Step 4). Let $N^j_{det,2}$ faults be detected.

(6) Reverse the order of the vectors in T' and fault simulate the CUT under the reverse test sequence T'_r. Let the number of detected faults be $N^j_{det,3}$.

(7) Complement T'_r and fault simulate the CUT under the resulting sequence T_r. Let the number of detected faults be $N^j_{det,4}$.

(8) Let $N^j_{det} = N^j_{det,1} + N^j_{det,2} + N^j_{det,3} + N^j_{det,4}$.

(9) Set $j = j + 1$. If $j \le N_{try}$, where N_{try} is a preselected number, go to Step 2.

(10) Select the TPG, j_0, for which $N^{j_0}_{det}$ is maximum.

(11) Generate the sequence T produced by TPG j_0 during R_2 cycles. Fault simulate the circuit under T (start from the complete set of target faults).

(12) Complement the test sequence T and fault simulate the circuit under the complemented test sequence T'.

(13) Reverse the test sequence T' and fault simulate the circuit under the reverse test sequence T'_r.

(14) Complement the test sequence T'_r and fault simulate the circuit under the reverse test sequence T_r.

(15) Stop: The faults detected in Steps 11-14 are the ones that will be detected by the selected TPG.

If the TPG selected by Procedure 1 or Procedure 1E is not sufficient to detect all the faults in the CUT, we repeat Procedure 1 or Procedure 1E with the faults left undetected to select additional TPGs, until the accumulated fault coverage reaches the desired level or no improvement in fault coverage is possible. This procedure is summarized as Procedure 2 next. Procedure 2E is similar to Procedure 2, except that Procedure 1E is used in Step 2 instead of Procedure 1.

Procedure 2 (2E): Selecting multiple *TPG*s

(1) Let F be the set of target faults.

(2) Apply Procedure 1 (1E) to select a TPG that detects the maximum number of faults out of F. Let F_{det} be the set of faults detected by the selected TPG.

(3) If $F_{det} = \phi$, stop: No additional TPGs are selected.

(4) Set $F = F - F_{det}$. If $F = \phi$, stop: All the target faults are detected by the selected TPGs.

(5) Go to Step 2.

In our implementation, Procedure 2 (or Procedure 2E) is applied with counter lengths $k = 10, 11, 12, 13$, and the best result is selected. Theoretically, any TPG that can be produced using a counter of length k_1 can also be produced using a counter of length $k_2 > k_1$ by ignoring the most significant bits of the counter or by permuting them such that they drive the least significant bits of the comparison units and selecting appropriate bounds. However, in practice, Procedures 1 and 1E explore only a limited number of TPGs, and therefore, may not yield increasingly better TPGs as k is increased.

The area of the TPG selected for a circuit depends on the number of *different* bounds used. Two bounds are said to be the same if they are computed using the same input permutation, and their values are the same. For a circuit with n inputs, m TPGs and a counter of length k, the number of different bounds is not larger than $\min\{2mn, k!2^k\}$. The term $2mn$ results from the fact that each circuit input needs two bounds for each TPG. The term $k!2^k$ results from the fact that there are 2^k different bound values for a counter of length k, and there are $k!$ permutations of the comparison unit inputs, each resulting in a different set of bound values. Each bound is implemented using at most $k - 1$ 2-input gates. In addition, at most one 2-input gate is required to *AND* the two bounds of each comparison unit. The total number of 2-input gates is thus $\le (k-1) \cdot \min\{2mn, k!2^k\} + n$. In most practical cases, $2mn < k!2^k$, and the number of 2-input gates is at most $(2(k-1)m + 1)n$. This area can be reduced by incorporating techniques such as test-point insertion to allow a smaller number of TPGs to be used. They may also make the approach described in the following section more effective.

3.2 *TPG*s with limited sets of bounds

Our goal in this subsection is to replace the term $k!2^k$ in the expression determining the worst-case number of bounds by a smaller value. The new value is a constant, typically smaller than the term $2mn$, thus potentially reducing the number of different bounds. We achieve this goal by imposing two restrictions on the bound values. First, we limit the number of permutations allowed for the comparison unit inputs. In our experiments, we use only the permutation of the comparison unit inputs where $x_i = q_i$ for $1 \le i \le k$. Thus, the term $k!$ is removed. In addition, we only allow bounds taken out of a preselected set B containing a preselected number of bounds N_B. For a given number of bounds N_B, we define $L_r = 2^k / N_B$. We allow only bounds that are multiples of L_r, i.e., $B = \{0, L_r, 2L_r, 3L_r, \cdots, (N_B - 1)L_r\}$. For example, for $k = 8$ and $N_B = 4$, we obtain $L_r = 256/4 = 64$ and $B = \{0, 64, 128, 192\}$. In Step 2 of Procedure 1 (or Procedure 1E), bounds are randomly selected out of the set B.

As a result of the restrictions above, the number of different bounds required to implement a set of m TPGs for an n-input circuit using a counter of length k is bounded by $\min\{2mn, N_B\}$. In our experiments we used $N_B = 4$, ensuring that at most four bounds would have to be implemented (in fact, a bound of 0 does not need to be implemented, since every counter state is larger than or equal to 0; therefore, the number of bounds is at most $\min\{2mn, N_B - 1\}$). With $N_B = 4$, the number of 2-input gates required to realize the TPG is $\le 3(k-1) + n$.

4. Experimental results

In this section, we describe the results obtained by applying Procedure 2 and Procedure 2E to ISCAS-89 benchmark circuits. For comparison purposes, we include in Table 3 the fault coverage reported in [5] using the hold method proposed there. We also report in Table 3 the highest fault coverage reported for several deterministic test generation procedures. Finally, we include in the last column of Table 3 the fault coverage obtained by applying 100,000 random patterns.

Table 3: Comparison

circuit	hold	determ	rand
s208	NA	63.72	43.72
s298	NA	86.04	84.74
s344	NA	96.20	96.20
s382	86.0	90.73	13.28
s386	NA	81.77	71.35
s420	NA	41.63	33.72
s444	80.4	87.76	12.66
s526	NA	80.00	9.37
s641	NA	86.51	86.51
s820	57.8	95.76	49.29
s1196	NA	99.76	98.79
s1423	86.3	90.89	62.97
s1488	NA	97.17	71.27
s5378	74.4	78.47	66.54

The following parameters were used in the implementation of Procedures 2 and 2E. The numbers of repetitions of the counter sequence are $R_1 = 1$ and $R_2 = 2$. The counter lengths considered are $k =$ 10, 11, 12 and 13. We report only the shortest counter length that resulted in the best fault coverage using the smallest number of *TPG*s. The number of *TPG*s tried in Procedure 1 and 1E is $N_{try} = 5$.

When a *TPG* is allowed to produce $R2^k$ test patterns which are then simulated on the *CUT*, we capture the last pattern u_{eff} effective in detecting any new fault. We refer to the length of the test sequence up to u_{eff} as the *effective test length.* If multiple *TPG*s are used, the total effective test length is the sum of the effective test lengths for all the *TPG*s used.

In the following subsections we describe the results obtained with unlimited bound values, and when the bound values are restricted. We also present results of the latter scheme in conjunction with test-point insertion.

4.1 Unlimited bounds

The results obtained for several benchmark circuits by applying Procedure 2 using the parameters above are given in Table 4. After circuit name we show the counter length k, the number of *TPG*s used, the total effective length for all the *TPG*s, and the fault coverage achieved. Following the fault coverage we show how the fault coverage compares to the maximum fault coverage reported for deterministic test generation, and to the fault coverage reported in [5]. We enter <, > or = to indicate that the fault coverage achieved by the proposed method is smaller than, larger than or equal to the fault coverage it is compared to. We also enter a ? when the corresponding fault coverage is not known. It can be seen that the fault coverage is higher than that reported in [5] in all the cases considered; however, the fault coverage is lower in many cases than that achievable by deterministic test generation. Increasing the values of R_1, R_2 and N_{try}, or allowing Procedure 2 to go through additional iterations, did not have significant effects on the results of Table 4.

Table 4: Results of Procedure 2

circuit	k	e.len	*TPG*s	f.c	targ	[5]
s208	11	2428	4	63.26	<	?
s298	11	721	2	86.04	=	?
s344	12	3908	4	96.20	=	?
s382	10	3066	5	88.97	<	>
s386	12	10714	4	79.95	<	?
s420	13	4264	2	41.16	<	?
s444	11	5208	3	87.76	=	>
s526	13	19819	3	78.92	<	?
s641	11	8739	6	86.51	=	?

The results of Procedure 2E for the same benchmark circuits and for additional ones are shown in Table 5. The same parameters used to obtain Table 4 are used in this case. The effective length for Procedure 2E is computed as follows. For each *TPG*, we compute the maximum effective length of its output sequence T, its complement T', its reverse T_r and its complemented reverse T'_r. We then add up all the maximum effective lengths. It can be seen by comparing Tables 4 and 5 that Procedure 2E achieves higher fault coverages than Procedure 2 using fewer *TPG*s. Procedure 2E reaches the target fault coverage set by deterministic test sequences more often than Procedure 2.

The number of different bounds obtained for the *TPG*s in Tables 4 and 5 is typically equal to the worst-case of $\min\{2mn, k!2^k\}$. In the following subsection we report the results obtained by restricting the possible bounds to a subset B of size N_B, as described in Section 3.2

Table 5: Results of Procedure 2E

circuit	k	e.len	*TPG*s	f.c	targ	[5]
s208	11	2599	3	63.26	<	?
s298	10	899	1	86.04	=	?
s344	12	3407	1	96.20	=	?
s382	12	4694	2	89.47	<	>
s386	12	4840	2	81.77	=	?
s420	12	15670	5	41.63	=	?
s444	12	4603	2	87.76	=	>
s526	13	19864	4	79.28	<	?
s641	13	6352	1	86.51	=	?
s820	13	46973	8	82.82	<	>
s1196	13	43574	8	99.11	<	?
s1423	11	17629	8	90.89	=	>
s1488	12	12194	3	97.17	=	?
s5378	12	39141	12	75.34	<	>

4.2 Restricted bounds

In the experiments reported in this section we use Procedure 2E with the value of k used in Table 5. We restrict the number of different bounds to $N_B = 4$. The results are reported in Table 6. The results of Table 5 are repeated in column $N_B = unl$ for ease of comparison. It can be seen that the fault coverage for restricted bounds is lower than the fault coverage when the bounds are unrestricted. However, even this lower fault coverage is higher than that of [5] for most of the circuits where a comparison is possible. In addition, the loss of fault coverage may be justified by the reduced number of bounds and thus the reduced hardware complexity of the *TPG*s. Techniques such as test point insertion may be used to compensate for this effect.

Table 6: Results using restricted bounds

	N_B=4		$N_B = unl$	
circuit	TPGs	f.c	TPGs	f.c
s208/11	3	61.40	3	63.26
s298/10	4	85.06	1	86.04
s344/12	4	92.98	1	96.20
s382/12	2	87.72	2	89.47
s386/12	8	73.44	2	81.77
s420/12	3	40.23	5	41.63
s444/12	1	86.08	2	87.76
s526/13	1	78.38	4	79.28
s641/13	10	83.51	1	86.51
s1423/11	19	77.49	8	90.89

4.3 Restricted bounds with test-point insertion

In this subsection, we consider the *TPG*s selected in Table 6 for $N_B = 4$. These *TPG*s have the lowest area overhead of all the *TPG*s considered in the previous subsections; however, they usually result in the lowest fault coverage. To increase the fault coverage, we consider two schemes for test point insertion as described next.

We describe the test point insertion schemes for a *TPG* made of m *TPG*s, $TPG_1, TPG_2, \cdots, TPG_m$, designed for a circuit with a set of faults F. In both schemes, we simulate the sequences produced by the *TPG*s in the order $TPG_1, TPG_2, \cdots, TPG_m$, and drop all the faults detected by each *TPG* before the next one is considered. In the first scheme, test-points are inserted after every *TPG* is considered. As a result, when TPG_{j_1} is considered, test-points may be inserted to detect faults that are also detected by TPG_{j_2} where $j_2 > j_1$. In the second scheme, we first drop all the faults detected by all the *TPG*s, and then reconsider each *TPG* for test-point insertion. In the first scheme, it may be possible to omit a *TPG*, say TPG_j, if all the faults it detects are already detected by $TPG_1, \cdots, TPG_{j-1}$, simulated earlier. In the second scheme, all the *TPG*s will remain necessary. However, the first scheme may require more test-points, since test-points are inserted even for faults that may be detected by a *TPG* simulated later. The two schemes are described in more detail next. For simplicity of presentation, we refer to the sequences T, T', T_r and T'_r produced by a *TPG* as the *TPG* output sequence $\tilde{T}$.

The first test-point insertion scheme proceeds as follows. For TPG_1, we generate the *TPG* output sequence $\tilde{T}_1$, and simulate the set of target faults F under $\tilde{T}_1$. Let $\tilde{T}_1$ detect a subset of faults F_1. We simulate every fault $f \in F - F_1$ under the test sequence $\tilde{T}_1$ again, this time capturing every line v to which 0/1 or 1/0 values are propagated in the presence of f. Each such line, if selected as a test-point, will ensure that f can be detected by $\tilde{T}_1$. We use a covering procedure to select a minimal number of test-points to cover all the faults in $F - F_1$ that are detectable through test-points. Let the set of faults detected through test-points be F'_1. We drop from F all the faults in $F_1 \cup F'_1$. Next, we consider TPG_2. We generate the *TPG* output sequence $\tilde{T}_2$, and simulate F under $\tilde{T}_2$. Let $\tilde{T}_2$ detect a subset of faults F_2. We simulate every fault $f \in F - F_2$, and capture potential test-point locations for the fault. We then check whether the fault is detected by any one of the test-points already selected for TPG_1. For the remaining faults in $F - F_2$, we select additional test-point locations using a covering procedure. We denote the set of faults detected by TPG_2 through test-points by F'_2. We drop from F all the faults in $F_2 \cup F'_2$. The same process is repeated for all the *TPG*s. If $F_j \cup F'_j = \phi$ for *TPG* j, then *TPG* j can be omitted without reducing the fault coverage.

The second test-point insertion scheme proceeds as follows. We first generate the *TPG* sequence $\tilde{T}_j$ for every TPG_j, and drop the faults detected from F. We then reconsider each *TPG* separately. When TPG_j is considered, we simulate every fault $f \in F$ under the test sequence $\tilde{T}_j$ again, this time capturing every line v to which 0/1 or 1/0 values are propagated in the presence of f. Every fault detectable through an already selected test-point is dropped from F. We then use a covering procedure to select a minimal number of test-points to cover all the faults in F that are detectable through test-points when $\tilde{T}_j$ is applied. The same process is repeated for all the *TPG*s.

The results of test-point insertion using the *TPG*s produced for $N_B = 4$ in Table 6 are shown in Table 7. For each scheme, we show the number of *TPG*s that were useful for detecting any new faults (for Scheme 2, this number is equal to the number of *TPG*s in Table 6). We then show the total number of test-points inserted, and the final fault coverage obtained. Under column *targ* we mark whether the fault coverage is lower than or equal to the fault coverage achievable by deterministic test generation. For this comparison to be meaningful, we only consider faults that can be detected by deterministic test generation without test-points. It can be seen that Scheme 1 places more test-points, but requires fewer *TPG*s. Scheme 2 places fewer test-points but uses all the *TPG*s of Table 6. Compared to Table 6, the fault coverage is always increased. The fault coverage is not always equal to the target fault coverage achievable by deterministic test generation procedures. This is due to the fact that some detectable faults are never activated by the selected *TPG*s. The fault coverage can be increased by performing test-point insertion together with *TPG* selection. We did not implement this option. We point out that the area overhead for comparison units in this case includes the implementation of at most three bounds, requiring at most $(3(k-1)+n)$ 2-input gates.

Table 7: Results using restricted bounds and test-points

	scheme 1				scheme 2			
circuit	TPGs	t.p	f.c	targ	TPGs	t.p	f.c	targ
s208/11	2	10	63.72	=	3	5	63.72	=
s298/10	2	9	86.04	=	4	2	86.04	=
s344/12	4	21	95.61	<	4	8	95.61	<
s382/12	1	8	89.47	<	2	7	89.47	<
s386/12	4	65	81.51	<	8	22	81.51	<
s420/12	2	12	41.63	=	3	5	41.63	=
s444/12	1	8	87.76	=	1	8	87.76	=
s526/13	1	9	80.00	=	1	8	87.76	=
s641/13	4	64	86.30	<	10	13	86.30	<

5. Concluding remarks

We proposed a structure for a built-in test pattern generator for synchronous sequential circuits. The motivation for considering built-in test of synchronous sequential circuits is that the circuit flip-flops may be left unmodified, and test application may be done at-speed. The proposed test pattern generator had a uniform, parametrized structure. By matching the parameters of the test pattern generator to the circuit-under-test, high fault coverage was achieved for benchmark circuits. In many cases, the fault coverage was equal to the fault coverage that can be achieved by deterministic test sequences. Reduced area overheads were achieved by restricting the parameter values and inserting test-points to compensate for the lower fault coverage that may result.

Several extensions of the proposed approach may be useful in reducing the hardware overhead and increasing the fault coverage. More careful selection of *TPG* parameters may yield improved results at lower hardware overheads. Incorporation of test-points during the *TPG* selection process may allow fewer *TPG*s and fewer bounds to be used.

References

[1] V. D. Agrawal, C. R. Kime and K. K. Saluja, "A Tutorial on Built-In Self-Test Part 1: Principles", IEEE Design and Test of Computers, March 1993, pp. 73-82.

[2] V. D. Agrawal, C. R. Kime and K. K. Saluja, "A Tutorial on Built-In Self-Test Part 2: Applications", IEEE Design and Test of Computers, June 1993, pp. 69-77.

[3] H. Wunderlich, "The Design of Random-Testable Sequential Circuits", in Proc. 19th Fault-Tolerant Computing Symp., June 1989, pp. 110-117.

[4] F. Muradali, T. Nishida and T. Shimizu, "A Structure and Technique for Pseudorandom-Based Testing of Sequential Circuits", Journal of Electronic Testing: Theory and Applications, 1995, pp. 107-115.

[5] L. Nachman, K. K. Saluja, S. Upadhyaya and R. Reuse, "Random Pattern Testing for Sequential Circuits Revisited", in Proc. 26th Fault-Tolerant Computing Symp., June 1996, pp. 44-52.

[6] M. Abramovici, K. Rajan and D. Miller, "FREEZE: A New Approach for Testing Sequential Circuits", in Proc. 29th Design Autom. Conf., June 1992, pp. 22-25.

[7] I. Pomeranz and S. M. Reddy, "On Synthesis-for-Testability of Combinational Logic Circuits", in Proc. 32nd Design Automation Conf., June 1995, pp. 126-132.

SESSION 7C

PARTITIONING PART II

Moderators:

Charles J. Alpert, IBM Austin Research Lab., Austin, TX

Atsushi Takahashi, Tokyo Institute of Technology, Tokyo, Japan

Hierarchical Partitioning for Field-Programmable Systems†

Vi Chi Chan* and David Lewis
Department of Electrical and Computer Engineering, University of Toronto
billy@lsil.com, lewis@eecg.toronto.edu

Abstract

This paper presents a new recursive bipartitioning algorithms targeted for a hierarchical field-programmable system. It draws new insights into relating the quality of bipartitioning algorithm to circuit structures by the use of the partitioning tree [11]. The final algorithm proposed not only forms the basis for the partitioning solution of a 1-million gate Field Programmable System [1] but can also be applied to general VLSI or multiple-FPGA partitioning problems.

1.0 Introduction

The reprogrammability of FPGAs has made possible a number of systems for rapid prototyping and emulation. These multiple-FPGA designs, primarily aimed at ASIC applications, tend to be severely pin limited. Since the pin constraints of the FPGA are hard limits, and low in terms of the number of pins per device, high quality partitioning is necessary to achieve acceptable utilization of the FPGA. Most common methods, based on Fiduccia-Mattheyses (FM) [2] cannot achieve reasonable utilization.

This paper addresses hierarchical partitioning for Field Programmable (FP) systems, with particular regard to the Transmogrifier-2 (TM-2) [1]. This paper focuses on bipartitioning with special attention to the quality of overall partitioning result across all levels of recursive bi-partitioning, rather than a single bi-partitioning. The algorithm devised is also a high quality bi-partitioner in its own right. The specific techniques introduced in this paper are:

(1) A new adaptive FM iterative partitioning procedure.

(2) The use of spectral partitioning methods to prune the network to exploit circuit structure and remove nets that would otherwise distort the partitioning.

(3) The use of the partitioning tree to explain the effectiveness of FM, KL-FM [3] in terms of circuit structure.

† This work was supported by Micronet, Canada.

* Now with the Toronto Design Centre, LSI Logic Corp. of Canada.

Our implementation of this algorithm is 10-50% more effective than previously published bipartitioners.

Section 3 of this paper discusses background information of this research. Section 4, 5 and 6 present the above mentioned research while Section 7 presents the experimental results. Section 8 concludes with summary and suggestion for future work.

2.0 Previous Work

Traditional partitioning schemes can be divided into two major categories: iterative or analytical.

The most commonly used iterative method is Fiduccia-Mattheyses (FM) [2] partitioning. This method consists of multiple *passes*. In each pass, random partitions are improved iteratively by cell movements from one partition to the other until no further improvement in cutset size is observed.

Many passes (each begin with a unique random starting point) are usually needed to produce good results, especially when circuits are large (as random partition assignment cannot sufficiently cover the solution space). Out of the many passes, only the best pass results are saved. Information captured by all the other passes is lost.

Many modifications/improvements of the FM method are available. Krishnamurthy [3] suggested the use of gain vectors instead of single gain values to reduce ambiguity when choosing cells to move; Hagen et. al [4] introduced locality in cell selection by using LIFO queue as data structure instead of simple linked list. Although each has its own benefit, neither of them improves partitioning result significantly, largely because they do not introduce any means for the algorithm to climb over steep hills of valleys where local minima reside.

Another partitioning algorithm suggested by Kernighan and Lin [5] is more successful in improving the results of FM[R]. The KLFM algorithm divides the partitions $\{A, B\}$ generated by FM into 4 sub-partitions

1092-3152/97 $10.00

$\{A_0, A_1, B_0, B_1\}$ by applying FM partitioning to A and B. These 4 sub-partitions are swapped an merged to form new initial partitions $\{C, D\}$ for another pass of FM, i.e. $C = A_0 \cup B_0$, $D = A_1 \cup B_1$ or $C = A_0 \cup B_1$, $D = A_1 \cup B_0$. This procedure of sub-dividing, swapping and re-partitioning is continued until no further improvement on the cutset is observed.

This method produces much better results per iteration because it explores different combinations of sub-partitions to form initial partitions, instead of just a single trial of random partition assignment. By doing so, this method is effectively exploring different way to construct the partitioning tree at the top level (as can be seen later in this paper).

The other major partitioning technique is analytical partitioning. Among different methods in this area, the spectral method (eigenvector embedding [6]) has received much attention recently. In this method, the circuit is represented in an hypergraph from which a symmetric non-negative definite matrix (the Laplacian $Q = D - A$) is derived (after transforming multi-point nets into cliques). The eigenvalue of Q can be expressed as $\lambda = \frac{x'Qx}{|x|^2}$, where x is the corresponding eigenvector. If we consider x as a one-dimensional mapping of the cells in the circuits, the quantity $x'Qx$ is equivalent to $\sum_{(v_i, v_j) \in E_H} (x_i - x_j)^2$, the sum of the quadratic distances between connected cells. For a normalized eigenvector x, $\lambda = x'Qx$. Therefore, the smaller the λ, the smaller the sum of the quadratic distances between connected cells. In a connected graph, this quantity can be used as a heuristic measure of placement or partitioning quality, i.e. by minimizing this sum of quadratic distances, the distances between heavily connected cells should also be minimized, yielding a natural clustering of cells from which good quality partitions can be determined. Since Q has 0 as its smallest eigenvalue, the first non-trivial solution to this minimization problem is thus the second smallest eigenvalue of Q and its corresponding eigenvector.

Although popular, the spectral method has been shown [10][12] to be sensitive to changes in circuit structures. This result, however, also implies that if only we can choose the information processed by the analytical method (selecting certain connections between cells and mask out others), we can target specific area of a circuit for partitioning.

Our interest in partitioning is motivated in particular by a field-programmable rapid-prototyping called the Transmogrifier-2 (TM-2)[1]. This system contains a number of FPGAs, up to 32 in a full sized system, and a collection of partial crossbars providing interconnected between the FPGAs. At a conceptual level, there are up to 5 levels of crossbar, where level i provides interconnect between a collection of 2^i FPGAs. An overview of the architecture is given in Fig. 2.1, and for full details consult ref. [1].

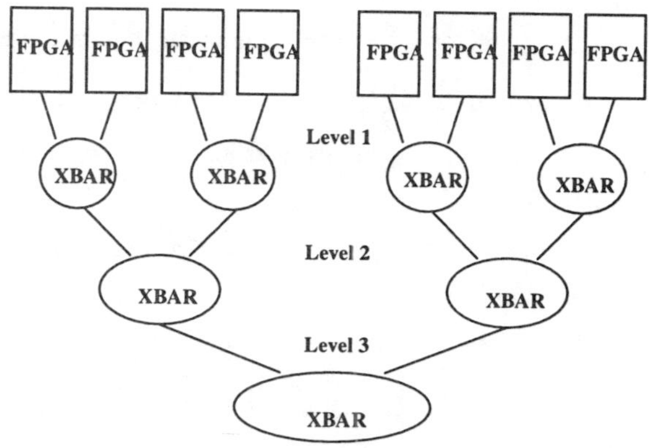

Figure 2.1 Hierarchical model of the TM-2 routing architecture

3.0 Algorithms

This section of the paper describes our algorithm development. There are three main features of our algorithm.

3.1 Adaptive FM

In the traditional FM procedure a large number of passes is usually required to obtain a good result; several hundred passes can be required for large circuits.

To avoid this disadvantage, a new method of retaining information from each of the partitions generated by FM is proposed. This method adaptively produces new initial partitions using previous good partitioning results. For each pass, an initial placement vector is constructed, using a weighted placement value that depends on all previous partitioning results. Each gate is initially assigned to the left or right side depending on the weighted average of its final position at the end of previous passes. The weighting factor is based on the quality of the final result in each previous pass, so that good results are weighted higher than poor results. The result of each pass is only used if the cutset size is within 20% of the best cutset size seen so far. A minor complication occurs in that left and right are arbitrary partitions (i.e. the partition with each gate swapped from left to right is identical in cost, but appears to be the exact opposite partition.) The algorithm must optionally swap the partitioning to determine the orientation that is most similar to the previous partition. This is done by comparing the number of cells that have the same orientation as in the result of the best pass so far. If this is less than half, the left and right partitions are swapped before they are used to calculate their contribution to the initial weighting of the next pass.

(1) Generate initial partitions $\{A_0, B_0\}$ by a random procedure followed by FM, with cutset size c_0 and scaling factor $s_0 = 1/c_0$. Generate the orientation vector $P_0 = \{p_0, p_1, \ldots, p_n\}$ where $p_i = -1$ iff $v_i \in A_0$, and $p_i = 1$ iff $v_i \in B_0$. From P_0 and s_0, derive a weighted placement vector: $X = \{x_0, x_1, \ldots, x_n\}$, where $x_i = p_i \times s_0$. Record the best cutset and the best orientation vector (partition assignments) as c_{best} and P_{best}.

(2) Set $k = 1$. Generate a new partition $\{A_k, B_k\}$ as in (1).

(3) If $0.8 \le \frac{c_k}{c_{best}} \le 1.2$, goto step (4) else (5).

(4) Compare the orientation vector P_k with P_{best}. If the majority of partition assignments disagree between P_k and P_{best} (i.e. the sum of $xor(P_k, P_{best}) > n/2$) then flip the orientation of P_k. Update the placement vector X: $x_i = x_i + (s_1 \times p_i)$, where p_i is the i-th element of the adjusted P_k. If $c_k < c_{best}$, update $P_{best} = P_k$ and $c_{best} = c_k$, goto step (6).

(5) $k = k + 1$, if $k > k_{max}$, goto (7); else produce new partition $\{A_k, B_k\}$ as in (1), goto step (3).

(6) Sort the placement vector X to produce a one-dimensional embedding of cells. The optimal cut point is determined within the cutratio constrain, forming partitions $\{A_{k+1}, B_{k+1}\}$. FM is then applied to give $\{A_{k+1}, B_{k+1}\}$, Set $k = k + 1$. if $k > k_{max}$, goto step (7), else goto step (3).

(7) The best partition result P_{best} is restored as the output. End.

This algorithm is graphically represented in Figure 3.1.

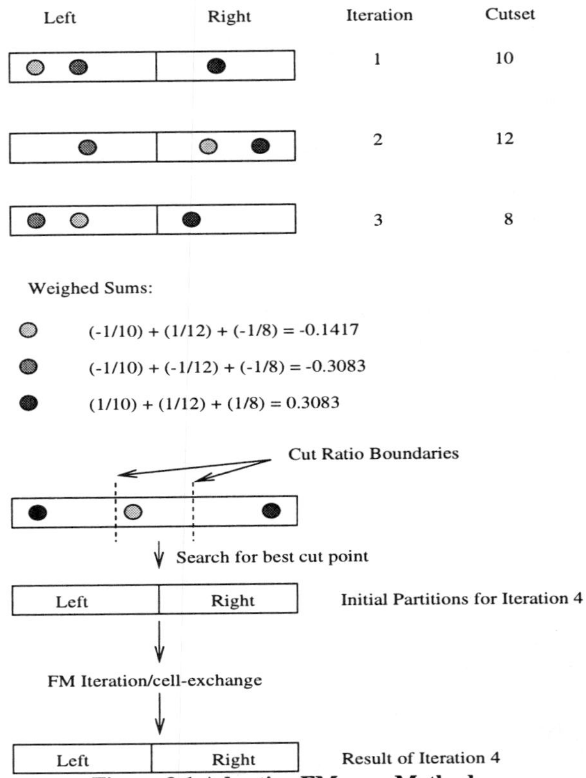

Figure 3.1 Adaptive FM pass Method

Experiments were carried out to compare this new method with that of traditional random initial placement scheme. These experiments estimated the number of passes required to achieve an acceptable result, defined as within 5% of the best that can be achieved. Since the best possible is not known, we used FM for 200 passes and adopted this as an estimate of the best possible. The first acceptable pass is define as the first pass of FM that comes within 5% of the final result. On average, it takes 83 passes of FM to come within 5% the 200 pass result. The adaptive method achieves cut counts 23% smaller, and takes only 35 passes on average. The reduction in CPU time is much more dramatic because later FM passes converge much more quickly to their final result. CPU time is reduced 92%. The results are summarized in Table 1.

3.2 Partitioning Tree Based Placement

The adaptive FM method shows that partitioning results can be significantly improved if more information about the circuit is gathered. In fact, as circuits grow larger and more complex, circuit structure information will be more important to the success of partitioning of the circuit.

The partitioning tree (Figure 3.2) is a graphical repre-

Table 3.1 Adaptive FM vs. Conventional FM

Test Circuits	Size - # of Logic Gates	Conventional FM			Adaptive FM			% Improvement on Cutset Size
		First Acceptable Pass	Best Cutset Size	CPU Time (sec.)	First Acceptable Pass	Best Cutset Size	CPU Time (sec.)	
balu	801	183	84	19.33	183	84	19.45	0.00%
primary1	833	24	58	2.87	24	58	3.90	0.00%
bm1	882	166	60	31.63	9	76	0.97	-26.67%
test4	1515	18	132	5.80	98	140	29.63	-6.06%
test3	1607	22	109	10.23	60	115	27.64	-5.50%
test2	1663	66	186	23.02	40	183	13.28	1.61%
test6	1752	150	108	65.51	150	108	61.53	0.00%
struct	1952	18	162	8.85	10	46	3.73	71.60%
test5	2595	38	273	31.82	9	251	7.97	8.06%
19ks	2844	78	244	145.79	6	160	9.42	34.43%
primary2	3024	66	314	162.11	9	173	10.42	44.90%
s9234	5866	36	312	213.29	7	212	34.58	32.05%
biomed	6514	179	364	1303.78	6	182	32.40	50.00%
s13207	8772	79	311	1069.42	8	163	121.06	47.59%
s15850	10470	30	481	526.38	7	316	111.63	34.30%
industry2	12637	177	609	7415.62	8	224	169.56	63.22%
s35932	18148	7	1103	669.27	4	871	239.64	21.03%
s38584	20995	100	1751	8812.52	30	1327	1841.39	24.21%
s38417	23949	147	1082	23493.47	8	524	899.39	51.57%
avg.		83	7743	2316.35	35	5213	191.45	23.49%

sentation of circuit structure as affected by recursive bipartitioning process. It has been used in placement algorithm or the estimation of circuit parameters [11], but seldom has it been used to motivate the partitioning algorithm before.

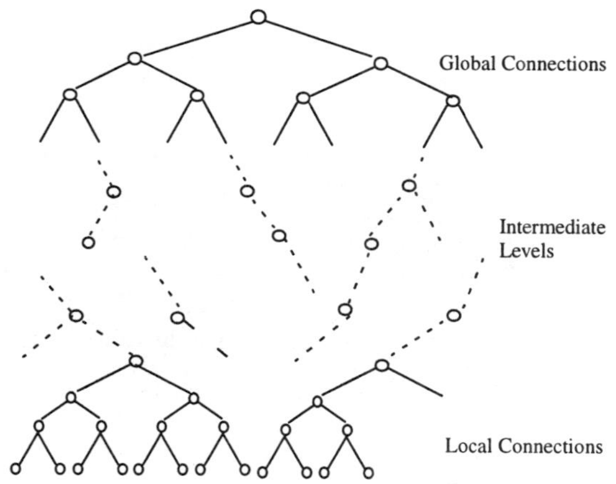

Figure 3.2 Partitioning Tree

When considering partitioning algorithms, especially algorithms which involve exchanging cells or groups of cells, the partitioning tree can be used to demonstrate the effectiveness in exploring circuit structure by such algorithms, e.g.:

(1) KL-partition exchange scheme exchanges sub-partitions at the top of the tree. Branches at the top 2 levels are affected the most.

(2) FM cell exchanges swap cells individually. The effect of cell exchanges propagate up from the leaves of the tree.

The GORDIANL [9] based bipartitioning algorithm PARABOLI [8] recursively bipartitions down to single cell, effectively traversing the entire partitioning tree and building it from bottom up to find the best bipartition point for the circuit.

The traditional partitioning scheme of KLFM (KL-partition exchange followed by FM passes) attempts to explore different combination of the upper level branches while allow the cell movement at the bottom to refine the results. For small circuits, such an approach can sufficiently cover the entire partitioning tree structure. For large circuits, a considerable subset of the middle portion of the circuits is not explored (since the effect of FM cell movement weaken as it propagates upward, affecting fewer upper level branches).

3.3 New Bipartitioning Algorithm

From the above section, it is clear that a good partitioning algorithm must be able to extract information from the entire partitioning tree to be effective. However, little is known about how the middle portion of the partitioning tree can be explored.

Considering the spectral method, we realize that since the entire circuit is transformed into the Laplacian matrix Q, any connectivity information must also be stored in the matrix and partitions generated by the spectral method will have information related to the middle portion of the partitioning tree too. Therefore, our first attempt is to combine the KLFM algorithm with the spectral method, forming a new algorithm called KLEFM.

The KLEFM algorithm uses the spectral method to produce an initial partition (by determining cut point in the one-dimensional embedding generated by the eigenvector) which is then processed by one pass of KLFM. The results are encouraging (Table 3.2): on average, it is 55% better than 20 passes of FM and 40% better than EIG1 [6].

Table 3.2 Comparison of Adaptive FM to Eigenvalue and KLFM

	Cut Count		
Circuit	20 Adaptive FM Passes	EIG1	KLEFM
19ks	251	179	141
bm1	64	75	61
primary1	59	75	52
primary2	314	254	161
test02	186	196	109
test03	109	85	60
test04	132	207	57
test05	279	167	107
test06	134	295	67
balu	89	110	39
struct	162	49	54
biomed	394	286	153
s13207	311	110	89
s15850	481	125	72
industry2	700	525	384
Total	**3665**	**2738**	**1655**

However, straight-forward application of the spectral method is not desirable because of it is sensitive to circuit structure. In another experiment [12], a small number (< 5%) of nets were removed from test circuits. The spectral method shows large variance in the partition results over small changes in circuit structure. Because we are only interested in using the spectral method to extract the information related to medium connectivities, feeding the spectral method with the entire circuit seem unnecessary. In light of the fact that spectral method is sensitive to changes in circuit structure, it is also possible that by giving the spectral method the entire netlist, some connectivity information at the global or local levels would interfere with our objective. If we can select connectivities related only to the middle portion of the partitioning tree, we can use the spectral technique to produce partition that only reflects the circuit information in that area of the partitioning tree.

The middle portion of the partitioning tree represents cells that are connected in medium connectivities (i.e. not too locally nor globally connected). The spectral technique produces a linear embedding of cells related to the quadratic distances between connected cells. It is a heuristic measure of how the cells should be placed to minimize the sum of the quadratic distances between connected cells. Thus, it is reasonable to assume that cells that are placed close together have local connectivities and that cells placed far apart have global connectivities.

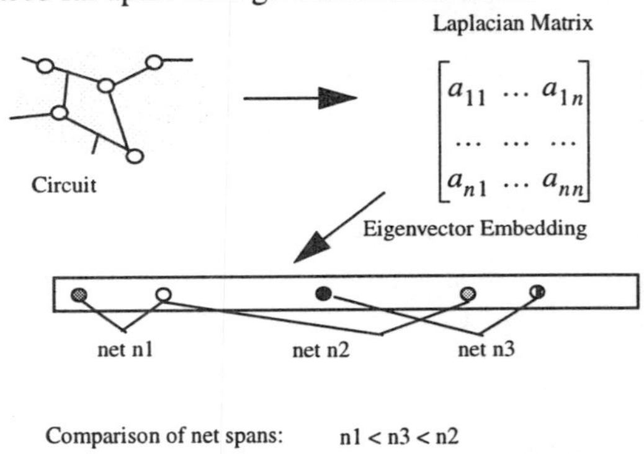

Figure 3.3 Eigenvector Embedding and Net Spans

We define the *span* of a net to be the distance (in the 1-dimensional embedding) between the farthest cells connected by the net. The assumption made earlier allows us to remove nets with extremely large or extremely small spans, in order to extract nets with medium connectivities. By reconstructing a new graph with only those nets and partition it with the spectral method, we screen out the global and local portions of the nets from the circuit, allowing the spectral method to just focus on the medium connectivity information. The algorithm is thus as follows:

(1) Transform circuit into graph $G(V, E)$ using a clique model.

(2) Generate the Laplacian matrix Q and extract the 2nd smallest eigenvalue/vector pair (λ, x).

(3) For each net n_i, calculate the span $s_i = max(x_{i0}, \ldots, x_{ik}) - min(x_{i0}, \ldots, x_{ik})$, where $x_{i0}, \ldots, x_{ik}$ are coordinates of cells connected to n_i.

(4) Sort vector $S = \{s_o, \ldots, s_N\}$.

(5) Remove the top 5% and bottom 5% of the sorted list, which represent the global and local connections of the original circuit.

(6) Construct a new graph $G'(V', E')$ with the remaining nets. Repeat step (2) for this new graph.

(7) Partition the eigenvector embedding as in the spectral method.

(8) The partition is then processed by KLFM.

(9) 20 passes of Adaptive FM is the followed to refine the result.

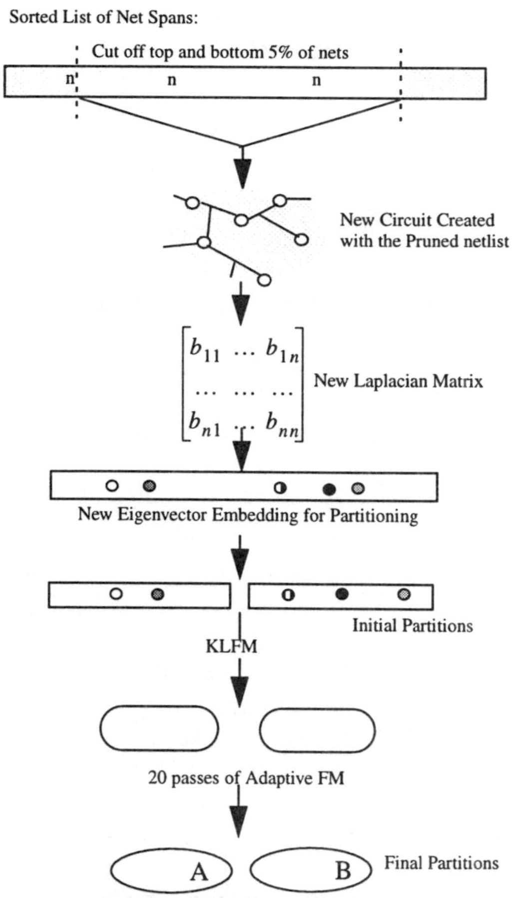

Figure 3.4 Hierarchical Partitioning Algorithm

Figure 3.4 shows the algorithm flow while Table 3.3 presents the experimental results. On average, the proposed algorithm out-performs EIG1, PARABOLI [8] and MELO [7] by 50%, 17% and 10% respectively.

4.0 TM-2 specific algorithms

Several other changes were also implemented to tailor the proposed algorithm to the TM-2 routing structure:

(1) The original FM cost function (simple cutset), was replaced by a pin usage cost function. In multiple FPGA systems, a wire between 2 FPGAs introduces two pins (one for each FPGA) while a primary IO introduces one pin. When nets divided at the top level of the hierarchy is further divided in the lower level, more and more pins are introduced. At the lower level, the simple cutset cost function no longer reflects the wire resources usage accurately. To accurately model the FPGA pin cost, a pin usage gain function was developed for the FM procedure, outlined as follows. An appropriate gain update function is also necessary, and is described in [12].

Pinuage Gain Calculation:
Given: c - any given cell in the circuit

$N = \{n_0, \ldots, n_k\}$ - nets connected to c

$P = \{p_0, \ldots, p_m\}$, I/O pins connected to c

A - partition contains c, B - the opposite partition

U_A and U_B are number of pins in A and B

$\wp_{max}$ - set of partitions that have the highest pin usage

Output: g - the gain of cell c

```
begin
  g ← 0
  Use original FM gain calculation to calculate g
  for all p_i in P, begin
    group cells connected to p_i into {℘_A, ℘_B}, where ℘_A
    contains cells in A, ℘_B is defined similarly.
    if ( |℘_A| = 1 and A ∈ ℘_max ) then
      if ( |℘_B| > 0 or ( |℘_B| = 0 and U_A > U_B + 1)) then
        g ← g + 1
      end if
    end if
    if ( |℘_B| = 0 and B ∈ ℘_max ) then
      g ← g − 1
    end if
  end for
end
```

Table 3.3 Comparison between EIG1, PARABOLI, MELO and the Proposed Algorithm

Circuit	Cut Count				% Improvement Compare to:		
	EIG1	PAR	MELO	Our Algo.	EIG1	PAR	MELO
19ks	179	-	119	129	27.93%	-	-8.40%
bm1	75	-	48	47	37.33%	-	2.08%
prim1	75	53	64	49	34.67%	7.50%	23.44%
prim2	254	146	169	160	37.01%	-9.50%	5.33%
test02	196	-	106	100	48.98%	-	5.67%
test03	85	-	60	66	22.35%	-	-10.00%
test04	207	-	61	69	66.67%	-	-13.11%
test05	167	-	102	90	46.11%	-	11.76%
test06	295	-	90	66	77.63%	-	26.67%
balu	110	41	28	27	75.46%	34.15%	3.57%
struct	49	40	38	36	26.53%	10.00%	5.26%
biomed	286	135	115	83	70.98%	38.52%	27.83%
s9234	166	74	79	49	70.48%	33.78%	37.97%
s13207	110	91	104	75	31.82%	17.59%	27.88%
s15850	125	91	52	55	56.00%	39.56%	-5.77%
ind2	525	193	319	224	57.33%	-16.06%	29.78%
TOTAL	**2904**		**1554**	**1324**	**avg. 49.30%**	**avg. 17.28%**	**avg. 10.62%**

(2) A post-processing stage was also introduced to route the crossbar structure to remove congestion in any overly crowded crossbars (see [12]). Because of the implementation of the TM-2 [1], higher level crossbars can be used to route lower level connections, but not vice versa.

(3) A balancing scheme was devised to determine the appropriate cut-ratios at each level of bi-partition. This scheme dynamically determines the cut-ratio to use at each level by considering the cutset produced and the number of levels below the hierarchy, trying to avoid congestion at the lower level induced by unbalanced top level partitions. The detail of this scheme can also be obtained from ref. [12].

5.0 Experimental Results

The new hierarchical partitioning algorithm was applied to all the large (>1500 4-LUTs) circuits in the MCNC LGSynth93 benchmark. Since there are multiple levels of wiring resources, the results have been graphed and compared on each of the levels. Figure 4.1 shows a comparison of the routing resources required the top level of an 8-FPGA system. It compares recursive FM to our algorithm since no direct comparison could be made with other published results. Because it is difficult to find circuits of sufficient size to fill a significant proportion of the TM-2, we used a scaled version for the experiments. This defines a boundary of feasible systems based on hypothetical FPGAs with pin counts that scale as $\sqrt{n}$, where n is the number of gates per FPGA. The partitioner is also capable of using the capacity of the FPGAs to determine the utilization necessary at each stage in partitioning. As the required utilization of the FPGAs decreases, the imbalance of partition sizes increases, causing lower wire counts, but requiring larger FPGAs. Each curve in the plot shows the cut count as the utilization of the FPGAs is varied from 80% down to 20%. The solid lines show results for our algorithms and the dashed for recursive FM. The solid curve at the lower portion of the graph shows the TM-2 feasible boundary (the $\sqrt{n}$ curve). As FPGA sizes increases, the partitioner has more freedom to perform better partitioning, thus the solid lines drop down below the feasible boundary, indicating that the design is implementable with the TM-2 structure. From this graph, we can see clearly that FM fails to produce partitions that are feasible under the TM-2 architecture. 10 out of the 11 test circuits could be mapped into a scaled 8-FPGA TM-2 system with utilization ranging from 20 to 80%. If recursive FM is used, only 2 out of the 11 circuits could fit into the scaled system. Comparisons are also made in 4, 16 and 32-FPGA system and the results are presented in [12].

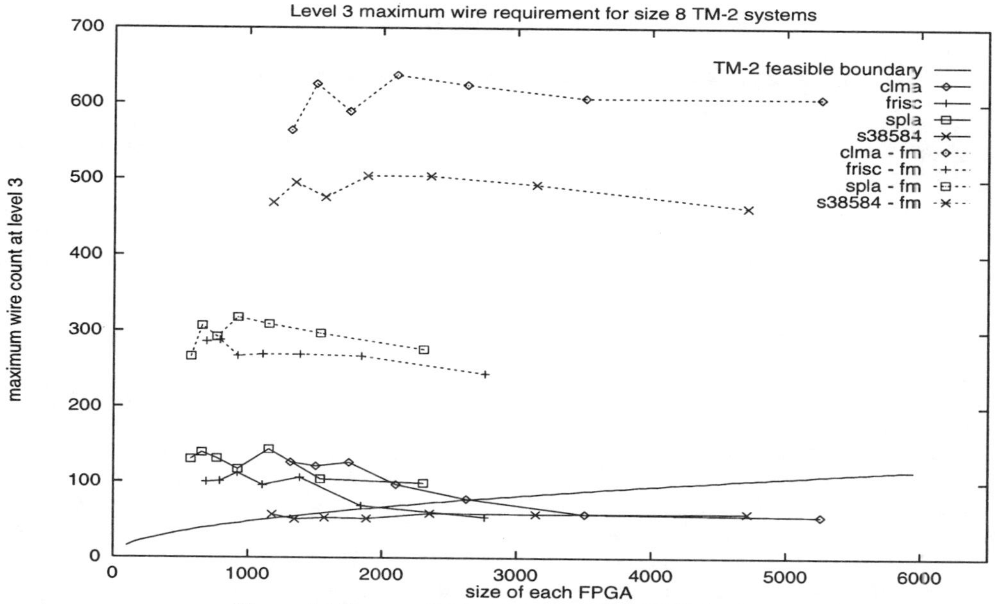

Figure 4.1 Proposed Algorithm vs. FM (8-FPGA System)

6.0 Conclusions

This paper presents a top-to-bottom partitioning scheme for a hierarchical FPGA system. The bi-partitioning procedure, when applied alone, produces results that are 10-50% better than previously published bi-partitioning methods. The effective use and combination of the spectral method and KLFM allows us to explore circuit information at different level of the partitioning tree. When applied to hierarchical system, the proposed algorithm produces more fits (10 vs. 2) than recursive FM procedure, allowing logic utilization to increase while maintaining a feasible wiring requirement.

As circuit designs become more complex and highly integrated, circuit partitioning must look for ways to improve the partition result for placement and routing. This research along with other recent partitioning research [13] show that one of the way to improve circuit partitioning is by extracting information from circuit structure, be it through clustering or through heuristic approach of the partitioning tree. This research also provides insights into partitioning problem relating to circuit structure and hierarchical partitioning.

7.0 References

[1] D.M. Lewis, D.R. Galloway, M. van Ierrsel, J. Rose and P. Chow, " The Transmogrifier-2: A 1-Million Gate Rapid Prototyping System", FPGA 97.

[2] C.M. Fiduccia and R.M. Mattheyses, "A Linear-time Heuristic for Improving Network Partitioning", 19th Design Automation Conference, 1982, pp. 175-181.

[3] B. Krishnamurthy "An Improved Min-Cut Algorithm For Partitioning VLSI Networks", IEEE Transactions On Computers, Vol. C-33, No. 5., 1984, pp 438-446.

[4] L. Hagen, D. Huang and A. Kahng, "On Implementation Choices for Iterative Improvement Partitioning Algorithms", 1995.

[5] B.W. Kernighan and S. Lin, "An Efficient Heuristic Procedure for Partitioning Graphs", Bell System Technical Journal, Vol. 49, No. 2, 1970, pp. 291-307.

[6] L.Hagen and A. Kahng "Fast Spectral Methods for Ratio Cut Partitioning and Clustering", ICCAD, 1991, pp. 10-13.

[7] C.J. Alpert and S. Yao "Spectral Partitioning: The More Eigenvectors, The Better", 32nd Design Automation Conference, 1995, pp. 195-200.

[8] B.M. Riess, K. Doll and F.M. Johannes "Partitioning Very Large Circuits Using Analytical Placement Techniques", 31st Design Automation Conference, 1994, pp 646-651.

[9] G. Sigl, K. Doll, F.M. Johannes "Analytical Placement: A Linear or a Quadratic Objective Function?", 28th Design Automation Conference, 1991, pp. 427-431.

[10] S. Guattery and G. Miller, "On The Performance of Spectral Graph Partitioning Methods", 6th Annual ACM/SIAM Symposium on Discrete Algorithms 1995.

[11] L. Hagen, A. Kahng, F. Kurdahi and C. Ramachandran, "On the Intrinsic Rent Parameter and Spectral-based Partitioning Methodologies", IEEE Transactions on Computer-Aided Design of Integrated Circuits and Systems, Vol. 13. No. 1. 1994, pp. 27-37

[12] Vi Chi Chan, "M.A.Sc. Thesis: A Partitioning Algorithm for the Transmogrifier-2", University of Toronto, 1997.

[13] S. Dutt and W. Deng, "VLSI Circuit Partitioning by Cluster-Removal Using Iterative Improvement Techniques", ICCAD, 1996, pp. 194-200.

Hybrid Spectral/Iterative Partitioning

Jason Y. Zien

IBM Almaden Research Center
650 Harry Road, San Jose, CA 95120

Pak K. Chan, Martine Schlag

Computer Engineering, UCSC
Santa Cruz, CA 95064

Abstract

We develop a new multi-way, hybrid spectral/iterative hypergraph partitioning algorithm that combines the strengths of spectral partitioners and iterative improvement algorithms to create a new class of partitioners. We use spectral information (the eigenvectors of a graph) to generate initial partitions, influence the selection of iterative improvement moves, and break out of local minima. Our 3-way and 4-way partitioning results exhibit significant improvement over current published results, demonstrating the effectiveness of our new method. Our hybrid algorithm produces an improvement of 25% over GFM for 3-way partitions, 41% improvement over GFM for 4-way partitions, and 58% improvement over ML_F for 4-way partitions.

1 Introduction

This paper describes a new multi-way, hybrid spectral/iterative, hypergraph partitioning algorithm, which consolidates iterative and spectral information in a multi-level partitioning framework. Previously, researchers combined the two approaches by finding a solution using a spectral algorithm and then performing iterative improvement on it [1, 2, 3]. The simultaneous use of spectral and traditional gain costs is found in the single-pass constructive heuristic presented in [4]; but it is not used for iterative improvement. In contrast, our work provides a tightly coupled integration of spectral and iterative improvement methods. Our contributions include the use of circular orderings to generate multiple initial partitions, using spectral information within a Kernighan-Lin/Fiduccia-Mattheyses iterative improvement algorithm [5] to break ties in gain, and using spectral information to break out of local minima which may trap standard iterative improvement algorithms. Our partitioner produces significant improvements over [6] and [7].

1.1 Spectral Partitioning and Maximum Sum Vector Partitioning

Given a graph with n vertices, we wish to find k partitions of this graph. An $n \times n$ adjacency matrix, A, has entries a_{ij} that represent the weight of an edge between vertices v_i and v_j. The $n \times n$ diagonal degree matrix, D, has entries d_{ii} equal to the sum of the weights of all edges on vertex v_i. M is the $n \times n$ diagonal matrix whose m_{ii} entry is the size of vertex i. The Laplacian matrix is $Q = D - A$. Spectral partitioning uses the eigenvectors associated with the smallest eigenvalues of Q. The eigenvectors are the solution to a relaxed version of the partitioning problem known as the quadratic placement problem. A generalization of the spectral partitioning problem which takes vertex sizes m_{ii} into account was solved by [3]. Different numbers of eigenvectors can be used in creating partitions. For instance, the authors of [8] use the 2nd eigenvector to form partitions; multiple eigenvectors are used in [1, 4, 9]. To be general, let us assume we are using d eigenvectors. Let X_d be the $n \times d$ matrix composed of the first d eigenvectors of Q. Let Λ_d be the $d \times d$ diagonal matrix composed of the first d eigenvalues (λ_1, ..., λ_d) of Q. H_d is a diagonal matrix whose entries are all γ, with $\gamma \geq \lambda_d$. In maximum sum vector partitioning (MSVP), the scaled matrix of eigenvectors is represented by $V_d = MX_d\sqrt{H_d - \Lambda_d}$ where X_d and Λ_d satisfy $QX_d = MX_d\Lambda_d$ [10], with $\gamma = |\lambda_2| + |\lambda_d|$. This is an extension of the methods of [9, 11]. An experimental verification of this embedding choice is given in [10].

Let the vector ν_i be the ith row of V_d. In MSVP we wish to divide the vectors ν_i into k distinct sets of vectors, corresponding to the k partitions. Let $T_h = \sum_{\nu_i \in P_h} \nu_i$ be sum of each of those sets of vectors with $1 \leq h \leq k$. The goal of MSVP is to maximize $\sum_{h=1}^{k} ||T_h||^2$. When $d = n$, it has been shown that maximum sum vector partitioning is equivalent to minimizing the sum of the edges cut in graph partitioning [9]. More eigenvectors provides a closer approximation to the graph partitioning problem. However, there is a dilemma as a partitioner uses more eigenvectors: the multi-dimensional embedding becomes increasingly difficult to take advantage of. Note that when $d = n$, the eigenvector computation can be omitted and the maximum sum partitioning methods can be applied to the graph matrix.

2 Hybrid Spectral/Iterative Partitioning

The classic Kernighan-Lin and Fiduccia-Mattheyses (KLFM) algorithm is the basis for most modern iterative partitioning algorithms. Because KLFM algorithms are so sensitive to initial starting points, a large number of random starts is required to obtain good solutions. Researchers have sought ways to create more stable performance by using clustering

1092-3152/97 $10.00 © 1997 IEEE

and multiple levels of hierarchy.

The primary advantage of spectral algorithms is that they are able to find a globally optimal solution to a relaxed version of the partitioning problem. They have been found to perform well on partitioning problems using the ratio-cut cost function [8], although the relaxed continuous-space solution may not be close to the optimal discrete partitioning solution. However, spectral partitioning methods have their weaknesses. For example, constraints such as partition size, partition topology, and pin limits are difficult to incorporate, although there are some exceptions [4]. Further more, due to the conversion from a hypergraph into a graph, optimal solutions for the resulting graph do not necessarily correspond to optimal solutions for the original hypergraph, although they are close. Since only one deterministic solution is available, there are no alternatives if the solution is poor. With all of the above difficulties, it is no wonder that spectral algorithms have been found to be worse than some iterative partitioning algorithms [12]. Researchers have also tried to combine spectral and iterative methods by using a spectral partitioner to obtain the initial partition for an iterative method, but the results were inferior to using random starts [2]. What if we consolidate spectral information with iterative improvement algorithms to obtain one unified method which combines the advantages of both methods? We can utilize the global information from a spectral algorithm within an iterative partitioning framework and gain the benefits of both methods.

2.1 Overview

Figure 1 illustrates our multi-level partitioner. Spectral information can be used in the contraction algorithms, initial partitioning, and in the iterative improvement process. The eigenvectors and eigenvalues of a graph are computed during the initial partitioning. We can optionally recompute the eigenvectors in the *expand* phase if desired. In our benchmarks, we recompute eigenvectors during expansion, unless otherwise noted.

Our iterative improvement algorithm is a KLFM style algorithm. We have extended it to support k-way partitions by iteratively working on one partition at a time. Each partition is used in turn as the target partition. The only moves considered are those in which vertices move from one of the $k-1$ other partitions into the target partition, or out of the target partition and into one of the $k-1$ other partitions. We use spectral information in the updating of the neighbor gains to break ties and influence the move sequence. Our implementation uses heaps to store vertex gains rather than buckets, in order to support the non-integer gains in our hybrid spectral/iterative algorithm.

2.2 Using Spectral Information

There are 3 key areas in iterative improvement algorithms that can be augmented using spectral information: 1. initial partition generation, 2. breaking ties when choosing the next move to make, and 3. jumping out of local minima.

```
ALGORITHM: MLH
INPUT: hypergraph, target number of partitions,k,
        maximum contracted size
OUTPUT: k-way partitioning solution
METHOD:
Read hypergraph
While (graph > maximum contracted size) {
    Contract graph
}
for i=1 to max_iterations {
    Create Initial k-way Partitioning
    Rotary KLFM or Flow Iterative Improvement
    While (graph not fully expanded) {
        Expand graph, map solution
        Rotary KLFM or Flow Iterative Improvement
    }
}
```

Figure 1: The multi-level partitioning algorithm.

2.2.1 Generating Initial Partition

We focus on solving the k-way partitioning problem for small values of k, such as 2,3 or 4. Higher dimensional techniques are discussed in [13, 14]. We use the 2nd and 3rd *scaled* eigenvectors to obtain a two-dimensional embedding. Henceforth, we refer to *scaled eigenvectors*, V_d, simply as *eigenvectors*. We limit ourselves to planar embeddings for practical reasons: it is easy to generate orderings of vertices, the computation of the first 3 eigenvectors is fast, and we can visually examine and understand our results.

As discussed earlier, the partitioning result based on the eigenvectors is remote from the original problem. Figure 2 illustrates the "loose" correspondence between the initial and final solution costs for our SWEEPB algorithm on 100 initial starting points. Because iterative improvement itself is sensitive to the starting solution, we generate many initial partitions.

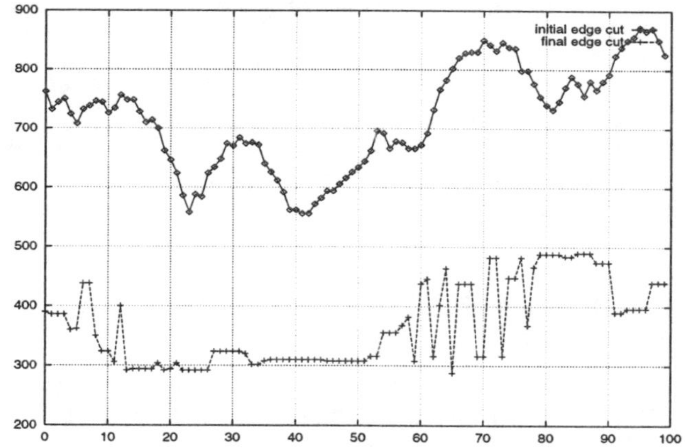

Figure 2: Initial (top) and final (bottom) hyperedge cuts for circuit p2_ga.

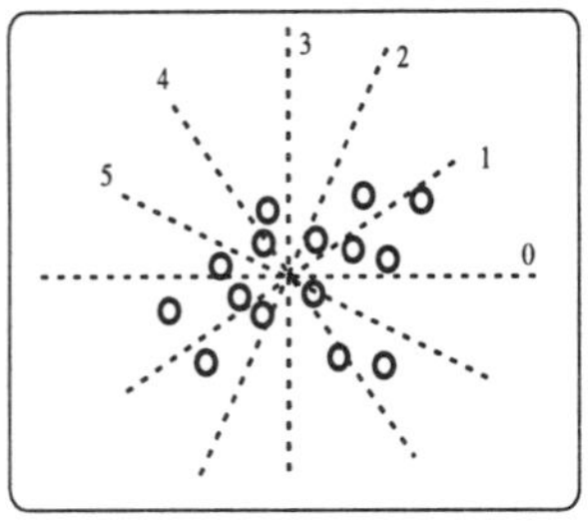

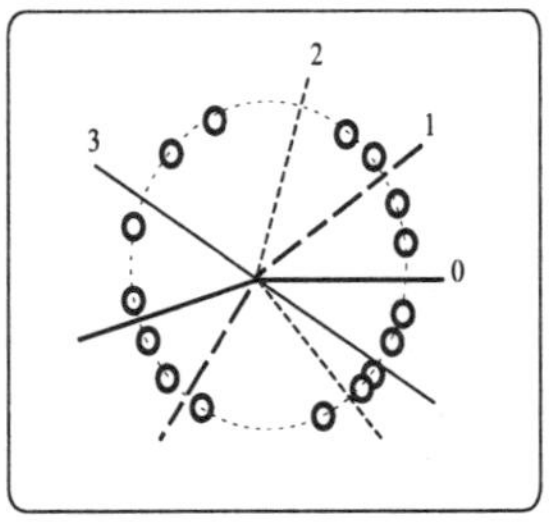

Figure 3: The SWEEPA (left) and SWEEPB (right) algorithms.

An obvious method for generating initial partitions is to divide the plane with k evenly-spaced cutting lines emanating from the origin, (the SWEEPA algorithm in Figure 3). The lines are rotated by $\frac{\pi}{k\rho}$ to form another initial partition and this process is repeated to obtain ρ initial starting points, each of which is improved upon by iterative refinement, which also enforces partition balance constraints.

When the planar embedding has large areas of empty space, the SWEEPA algorithm often generates the same initial partitioning. In addition, balance constraints may initially be violated. The SWEEPB algorithm overcomes these problems by creating a circular ordering of the vertices by the *angle* of their vectors with respect to the (1,0) vector. The vertices are divided into k nearly even sized partitions. The next initial solution is obtained by starting $\frac{n}{k\rho}$ nodes away from the previous one. For example, in the SWEEPB diagram in Figure 3, where we have $\rho = 4$.

2.2.2 Balance

We use soft constraints to enforce balance in partitions. The balance parameter *bal* limits the minimum and maximum partition sizes as follows: $(1 - bal)||P_t|| \leq ||P_h|| \leq (1 + bal)||P_t||$. Here, P_h is an arbitrary partition, h, and $||P_t||$ is the target partition size, which is the sum of the sizes of all vertices divided by k, the number of partitions desired. By default, $bal = 0.1$.

After every iterative improvement vertex move is made, we evaluate the cost of a solution. Typically, this cost is just the desired cost function, such as the ratio-cut cost, or the number of hyperedges cut. We add an auxiliary cost to that number to discourage imbalanced partitions. This auxiliary cost is equal to 10 times the amount of imbalance of every partition.

2.2.3 Breaking Ties and Avoiding Local Minima

Iterative improvement methods are very sensitive to tie-breaking strategies when vertices are selected for movement. We break ties by using spectral information. The "gain" of a vertex is a weighted sum of the standard cut gain and our spectral gain:

$$gain = \alpha \cdot cut\_gain + \beta \cdot spectral\_gain. \quad (1)$$

After each vertex move in iterative improvement, the neighbors of the moved vertex must have their gains updated. The *cut_gain* is the weight of the hyperedges that become uncut by a move.

The *spectral gain* comes from a 2-dimensional placement of vertices in the plane. Recall that each vector in the plane represents a vertex. Let T_h be the sum of all the vectors in partition P_h. The spectral gain of a vector ν_i with respect to a destination partition P_h is calculated as $||\nu_i + T_h||^2$. The vector sums, T_h, of each of the k target partitions are calculated at the beginning of each pass, and are not dynamically updated as moves are made. The spectral gain is negated when the target destination is not the same partition as the last moved vertex. This encourages groups of vertices to move to the same target destination in connected groups, as in the FM-CLIP algorithm [12].

When $\alpha = 1$, and $\beta = 0$, our algorithm behaves as the standard KLFM algorithm. When $\beta > 0$, the spectral gain information is used to influence the selection of the vertices. We have two methods of incorporating spectral information. Our first method, HYBRID, is a simple tie-breaking strategy where we set $\alpha = 1.0$ and $\beta = 0.1$. The spectral information contributes only a small portion to the gain so that in effect, it is mainly used to break ties in gain.

Our second method, HYBRID_ALT, focuses on breaking out of local minima. The KLFM improvement algorithm makes greedy moves based on the cut gain. If we are able to make moves using some other objective cost function, then we can break out of local minima. In the HYBRID_ALT method, we alternately run our KLFM improvement algorithm using $\alpha = 1.0$, $\beta = 0.0$ and $\alpha = 0.0$, $\beta = 1.0$.

3 Multi-level Spectral Partitioning

In this section, we consider a number of implementation choices that would have a significant effect on the final partitioning result.

Hypergraph to graph conversion: We use the star graph model to convert hypergraphs into graphs, as in [4]. By following the method of [11] we chose the edge weights of the star graph to be $\frac{\sqrt{8}}{\sqrt{d}}$ to minimize the discrepancy between the best and worst case quadratic placement of nodes on a unit span ([10] gives details).

Contraction algorithm: We use the heavy edge matching cost function due to [15]. This cost function contracts the edges with the highest weights, which would be the most undesirable to cut. We convert the hypergraph into a graph, sort the edges based on the edge weight, and match any unmatched pairs of vertices as edges are picked in order of decreasing cost.

Levels of hierarchy: One of the contributing parameters of contraction is the clustering or matching method, which has been studied extensively. Less attention has been paid to the levels of contraction. As the number of levels of hierarchy increases, the initial problem solution becomes more remote from the original problem. The best solutions may be precluded due to the contraction algorithm. This is offset by the fact that more levels of iterative improvement can be run when there are more hierarchical levels.

Many researchers have used a fixed number of levels of contraction. Other researchers have chosen to contract the graph until the number of nodes reaches a target size, such as 35 [7], or 100 nodes [15]. We ran some benchmark circuits for the unit-size vertex tests, and evaluated the results for different numbers of *max nodes*, and also an unlimited number of nodes (which corresponds to no levels of contraction). Our evaluation suggested that we should use a 200-node maximum contracted graph size for 2-way partitioning, and 400 nodes for three- and 4-way partitioning.

Disconnected graphs: Disconnected graphs lead to extremely unbalanced partitions (partitions where each connected component is in its own partition). We handle this problem by introducing dummy edges to connect the graph. These edges are introduced immediately before the eigensolver is invoked, and are then removed immediately after, so that they do not affect any edge cut costs. For star graphs, we introduce a hyperedge which is connected to an arbitrary vertex in each of the components. Others have used higher-order eigenvectors to handle disconnected graphs [9]. Shau [16] used different pairs of lower-order eigenvectors. Since we did not observe unusually poor performance for graphs using our "dummy-edge" method, we did not resort to higher order eigenvectors.

4 Results on MCNC Benchmarks

We compared our hybrid algorithms against existing published results. Our partitioner was implemented in C++. We replaced the traditional KLFM bucket implementation with heaps in order to support non-integer gains due to our hybrid cost function, Equation (1). We contracted graphs until there were at most 400 nodes, and generated 20 initial partitions ($\rho = 20$) using the SWEEPB initial partitioning method. We examined both the HYBRID tie-breaking algorithm as well as the HYBRID_ALT algorithm that alternates between spectral and iterative gain costs.

Our partitioner performs well on 2-way partitioning, but is not superior to the best 2-way partitioners. The detailed benchmark results are in [10]. The strength of our partitioner lies in combining global spectral information with iterative improvement. Global information becomes even more important in 3-way and 4-way partitioning, which is perhaps why our 3-way and 4-way results, are substantially better than other partitioners.

4.1 Comparison against GFM and PD

We compared the number of hyperedges cut by our hybrid algorithms to the GFM [6] and Primal-Dual (PD) algorithm [17], using the actual vertex sizes. We omitted graph `t5` because in 4-way partitioning, the largest node in `t5` is larger than that allowed by balance constraints. Each partition was allowed a balance factor of $bal = 0.5$.

Tables 1 and 2 show the results of our hybrid partitioner compared with the previously published results of [6]. The last row, Gmean, is the geometric mean over all of the circuits. In the three-way partitioning,

Circuit	PD	GFM	KFMC	HybridA	Hybrid
p1_ga	56	74	66	66	68
p1_sc	77	76	74	74	69
p2_ga	377	259	179	184	179
p2_sc	370	261	198	180	186
t2	81	81	81	81	81
t3	108	101	81	77	73
t5	80	85	88	89	83
t6	157	104	66	58	50
Gmean	126.62	113.48	94.93	92.17	88.70

Table 1: Comparison of hyperedges cut of our Hybrid and HybridA 3-way partitioning against the GFM and PD partitioner using actual vertex sizes.

Circuit	PD	GFM	KFMC	HybridA	Hybrid
p1_ga	102	107	98	87	91
p1_sc	107	110	90	86	99
p2_ga	459	335	229	215	228
p2_sc	426	354	234	236	226
t2	217	182	131	132	124
t3	170	162	104	101	105
t5	213	208	144	153	139
t6	189	145	103	67	68
Gmean	205.41	182.70	132.59	122.85	124.34

Table 2: Comparison of hyperedges cut of our Hybrid and HybridA 4-way partitioning against the GFM and PD partitioner using actual vertex sizes.

our HYBRID_ALT method gives a 19% improvement, and HYBRID gives a 25% improvement over GFM. In four-way partitioning, HYBRID_ALT is 41% better than GFM and HYBRID is 38% better than GFM.

As a control experiment, we also show the results 20 iterations of our implementation of a multi-level, k-way FM-CLIP algorithm to determine whether the hybrid algorithm was really the source of improvement, rather than other factors, such as contraction method, levels of contraction, or our multi-way improvement method. We found that our best hybrid method was 7% better than FM-CLIP in 3-way partitioning, and 19% better in 4-way partitionings. As the number of desired partitions increases, use of global spectral information becomes more important. Although multi-level contraction substantially improves upon the standard KLFM cut gain, by incorporating spectral costs as well, even further improvements can be made.

4.2 Comparison against ML_F and GORDIAN

We compared our hybrid algorithm to the ML_F [7] and GORDIAN algorithms [18]. We also report our multi-level implementation of the FM-CLIP algorithm. These tests use unit vertex sizes with a balance factor of $bal = 0.1$. Table 3 shows that our HYBRID partitioner is 12.1% better than our implementation of the multi-level FM-CLIP algorithm, 58.4% better than the ML_F algorithm, and 175.1% better than GORDIAN in terms of the number of hyperedges cut. Our hybrid method is able to effectively use the global spectral information to substantially improve upon other partitioning methods.

The execution time of our partitioner is slower than

Circuit	Hybrid	HybridA	KFMC	ML_F	Gordian
biomed	239	210	280	311	479
industry2	337	386	458	398	1179
industry3	763	752	784	830	1965
p1_ga	94	96	112	126	157
p2_ga	265	275	293	346	502
s13207	136	113	164	472	590
s15850	122	109	147	347	678
Gmean	220.57	212.89	259.64	356.62	619.42

Table 3: Comparison of hyperedges cut of our Hybrid and HybridA 4-way partitioning against ML_F and GORDIAN using unit-size vertices.

that of other partitioners due to the use of heap data structures. Heaps are necessary in order to support non-integer gains in iterative improvement for our hybrid algorithm. Three-way partitioning execution time results vary from 80 seconds to 1100 seconds on a Sun Ultra 170.

5 Conclusion

We have developed a new hybrid spectral/iterative partitioning algorithm and have demonstrated that it performs better than the best known 3 and 4-way partitioners. Our hybrid algorithm is only the first step in developing newer, more sophisticated iterative improvement algorithms. The key ideas that need further research includes the use of new gain cost functions to influence move selection and new objective functions that allow iterative improvement algorithms to break out of local minima. Future research includes using higher dimensions (more eigenvectors) to generate the initital partitions, and investigating methods for speeding up hybrid partitioning.

Acknowledgments

The authors acknowledge the support from the National Science Foundation under Grant number MIP-9223740.

References

[1] E. R. Barnes, "Partitioning the nodes of a graph," *Proc. of Graph Theory with Applications to Algorithms and Computer Science*, pp. 57–72, 1985.

[2] S. Hauck and G. Borriello, "An evaluation of bipartitioning techniques," in *Chapel Hill Conference on Advanced Research in VLSI*, pp. 383–402, 1995.

[3] J. Y. Zien, M. Schlag, and P. K. Chan, "Multilevel spectral hypergraph partitioning with arbitrary vertex sizes," in *ICCAD*, pp. 201–204, 1996.

[4] P. K. Chan, M. Schlag, and J. Y. Zien, "Spectral-based multiway FPGA partitioning," *IEEE Trans. on CAD*, vol. 15, pp. 554–560, May 1996.

[5] C. M. Fiduccia and R. M. Mattheyses, "A linear-time heuristic for improving network partitions," in *Proc. of 19th DAC*, pp. 175–181, 1982.

[6] L.-T. Liu, M.-T. Kuo, S.-C. Huang, and C.-K. Cheng, "A gradient method on the initial partition of FM algorithm," in *ICCAD*, 1995.

[7] C. J. Alpert, J.-H. Huang, and A. B. Kahng, "Multilevel circuit partitioning," in *34th DAC*, vol. 34, 1997.

[8] A. Pothen, H. D. Simon, and K.-P. Lious, "Partitioning sparse matrices with eigenvectors of graphs," *SIAM Journal Matrix Analysis Appl.*, vol. 11, pp. 430–452, July 1990.

[9] C. J. Alpert and S.-Z. Yao, "Spectral partitioning: The more eigenvectors, the better," in *Proc. of the 32nd DAC*, pp. 195–200, June 1995.

[10] J. Y. Zien, P. K. Chan, and M. Schlag, "Hybrid spectral/iterative partitioning," Tech. Rep. UCSC-CRL-97-09, Uni. of CA, Santa Cruz, 1997.

[11] J. Frankle and R. M. Karp, "Circuit placements and cost bounds by eigenvector decomposition," in *ICCAD*, pp. 414–417, November 1986.

[12] S. Dutt and W. Deng, "VLSI circuit partitioning by cluster-removal using iterative improvement techniques," in *ICCAD*, pp. 194–200, 1996.

[13] P. K. Chan, M. Schlag, and J. Y. Zien, "Spectral k-way ratio-cut partitioning and clustering," *IEEE Trans. on CAD*, vol. 13, pp. 1088–1096, Sept. 1994.

[14] C. J. Alpert and A. B. Kahng, "Multiway partitioning via geometric embeddings, orderings, and dynamic programming," *IEEE Trans. on CAD*, vol. 14, pp. 1342–1358, Nov. 1995.

[15] G. Karypis and V. Kumar, "Analysis of multilevel graph partitioning," Tech. Rep. 95-037, Univ. of Minnesota, Computer Science, Aug. 95.

[16] J. Shau, "Spectral partitioning with diagonal perturbations," UC Santa Cruz, June 97. M.S. Thesis.

[17] C. W. Yeh, C. K. Cheng, and T. T. Lin, "A general purpose multiple-way partitioning algorithm," *IEEE Trans. on CAD*, pp. 1480–1488, 1994.

[18] J. M. Kleinhans, G. Sigl, F. M. Johannes, and K. J. Antreich, "Gordian: VLSI placement by quadratic programming and slicing optimization," *IEEE Trans. on CAD*, vol. 10, no. 3, pp. 356–365, 1991.

Large Scale Circuit Partitioning With Loose/Stable Net Removal And Signal Flow Based Clustering [1]

Jason Cong, Honching Peter Li, Sung Kyu Lim, Toshiyuki Shibuya* and Dongmin Xu
UCLA Department of Computer Science, Los Angeles, CA 90095
*Fujitsu Laboratories LTD., Kawasaki, Japan

In this paper, we present an efficient Iterative Improvement based Partitioning (IIP) algorithm called LSR/MFFS, that combines signal flow based Maximum Fanout Free Subgraph (MFFS) clustering algorithm with Loose and Stable net Removal (LSR) partitioning algorithm. The MFFS algorithm generalizes existing MFFC decomposition method from combinational circuits to general sequential circuits in order to handle cycles naturally. We also study the properties of the nets that straddle the cutline carefully, and introduce the concepts of the *loose* and *stable* nets as well as effective ways to remove them out of the cutset. The LSR/MFFS algorithm first applies LSR algorithm to clustered netlist generated by MFFS algorithm for global-level cutsize optimization and then declusters netlist for further cutsize refinement.

As a result, the LSR/MFFS algorithm has achieved the best cutsize result among all the bipartitioning algorithms published in the literatures with very promising runtime performance. In particular, it outperforms the recent state-of-the-art IIP algorithms LA3-CDIP, CLIP-PROP$_f$ [8], Strawman [12], hMetis-FM [13], and MLc [1] by 17.4%, 12.1%, 5.9%, 3.1%, and 1.9%, respectively. It also outperforms the state-of-the-art non-IIP algorithms Paraboli [17], FBB [19], and PANZA [16] by 32.0%, 21.4%, and 1.4%, respectively.

1 Introduction

Circuit partitioning divides a given circuit into a collection of smaller subcircuits to minimize the number of connections among the subcircuits, subject to the area balance constraint. The circuit partitioning problem becomes more important as VLSI technology reaches submicron device dimensions; a single VLSI chip can contain over 10 million gates for the 0.25 micron technology and beyond. As a result, the hierarchical layout strategy using the divide-and-conquer technique is indispensable in order to make the VLSI layout problem tractable.

The existing circuit partitioning algorithms in the literature can be roughly classified into two classes; constructive methods, such as the spectral-based methods [11, 3] and the network flow-based method [19], and iterative improvement methods (also referred as group migration or move based methods). In practice, iterative improvement based partitioning (IIP) algorithms have been used extensively due to the following advantages over the other approaches; (i) area balance constraint, pre-assignment of cells, and non-uniformity in cell sizes can be easily accommodated, (ii) one can easily control the runtime vs cutsize trade-off by controlling the number of iterations. Some of the best known methods include the Kernighan & Lin (KL) algorithm [14], the Fiduccia & Mattheyses (FM) algorithm [9], and Krishnamurthy's lookahead scheme [15]. To reduce the computational complexity for partitioning large-scale circuits, clustering methods have been introduced. In this case, clusters are first identified and collapsed, and the resulting clustered circuit is partitioned using existing partitioning methods. Among many promising studies on circuit clustering methods, we focus on the extension of signal flow based Maximum Fanout Free Cone (MFFC) approach [4, 6, 7]. A comprehensive survey of various techniques in circuit partitioning and clustering can be found in [2].

In this paper, we present a large-scale IIP algorithm named LSR/MFFS. It integrates three individual algorithms to accomplish both global and local-level cutsize optimization; Loose net Removal (LR), existing Stable Net Transition [18] (SNT), and Maximum Fanout Free Subgraph (MFFS) algorithm. The LR and SNT algorithms focus on nets instead of cells to reduce the cutsize by attempting to remove two special kinds of nets; *loose* and *stable* net (to be defined in the subsequent sections). Our study shows that LR is effective in dynamically identifying clusters during cell movements, while SNT enables the partitioning algorithm to jump out of local minima efficiently. The intergration of these two net removal schemes results in a very powerful IIP algorithm named Loose and Stable net Removal (LSR).

In order to reduce the runtime and prune non-optimal soltions from the solution space, we developed signal flow based MFFS clustering algorithm that promotes simultanoeus movement of logically dependent cells during the cell moves. Our LSR/MFFS algorithm first clusters the circuit using the MFFS clustering algorithm, then applies the LSR algorithm to the clustered circuit, and finally declusters the circuit and applies LSR algorithm again for further cutsize refinement. Our experiments indicate that LSR/MFFS partitioning algorithm has achieved the best cutsize results with very promising runtime performance among all the partitioning algorithms reported in the recent literature.

The remainder of the paper is organized as follows. Section 2 presents the LSR based partitioning algorithm. Section 3 presents signal flow based MFFS clustering algorithm. Section 4 provides experimental results. Section 5 concludes the paper with our ongoing research.

[1] This work was partially supported by DARPA/ITO under Contract J-FBI-93-112, NSF Young Investigator Award MIP-9357582, and Fujitsu Laboratories at America under the 1995 and 1996 California MICRO Programs. Many thanks are due to the authors of hMetis [13] for their helpful discussions on runtime performance.

1092-3152/97 $10.00 © 1997 IEEE

2 LSR based Partitioning Algorithm

2.1 Review of IIP Algorithms

An *iterative improvement* partitioning (IIP) algorithm such as FM [9] uses the notion of *cell gain* to represent the reduction in the cutsize if the cell is moved to another block. Starting from a random initial *partition* and precomputed gain of entire cell, IIP algorithm selects the maximum gain cell c that satisfies the size constraint to move. A cell is labeled *free* if it has not been moved so far and *locked* otherwise. The *neighbors* of c are the free cells of the nets that are incident to c. After c is moved and locked, gain of its neighbors is updated for the next move. This cell move continues until all the free cells that do not violate the area constraint are moved, and we backtrack the move sequence to retrieve the one that produces the minimum cutsize. This entire process is called a *pass*, and a new pass is attempted until there is no further improvement in terms of cutsize. In this case, these multiple passes constitute a *run*.

IIP algorithm usually adopts a special data structure called *bucket* that supports fast update and retrieval of cell gains. Recently, the LIFO bucket [10] scheme is proposed to ensure that the cells with the most recently updated gain to be chosen first among other cells with the same gain, providing different perspective in breaking ties. This scheme is designed to promote the *locality* of cell moves where all the neighbors of the currently moved cell are chosen to move subsequently. However, locality can easily be disrupted by the update of other cells with higher gain values under this scheme. Dutt and Deng [8] proposed a more efficient way of promoting the locality. They viewed the cell gain as the sum of *initial* and *updated* gain, where the former refers to the cell gain computed before any move, and the latter refers to the sum of dynamically updated gain values from the cell move afterwards. Their strategy is based on the observation that relying only on the updated part of the gain in choosing the next cell encourages the neighboring cells to move subsequently and thus establishes the locality. They also noted that this locality promotes closely connected components in the circuit (= clusters) that straddle the cutline to be removed out of the cutset and thus establishes *cluster removal*. As a result, their algorithm CLIP/CDIP achieved the best cutsize result among all the published IIP algorithms prior to their work. However, their strategy is not free from the frequent tie-breaking situation, still relying on LIFO bucket and lookahead capability such as LA3 [15].

2.2 LSR Partitioning Algorithm

We present in this section stronger yet simpler form of cluster removal strategy by gradually increasing the cell gains of the neighbors connected to the currently chosen cell via *loose* nets until all of them are moved to one block. This strategy encourages the neighboring cells to be chosen subsequently and thus maintains the locality. It also reduces the frequency of tie-breaking situation significantly since the rank of cells in the bucket is determined according to the increased gain values. We shall first present the concept of loose nets and its relation to cluster removal, then present a modified cell gain computation of Loose-net Removal (LR) algorithm and its enhancement with Stable Net Transition (SNT) [18]. The following discussion focuses on bipartitioning case, but LSR can be easily extended to handle multiway partitioning.

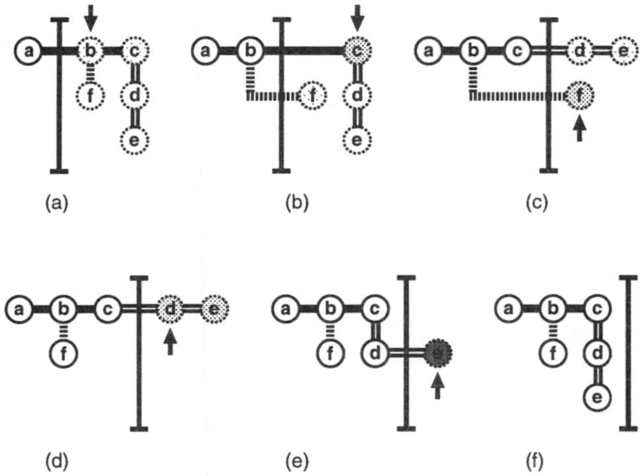

Figure 1: Removing 3 nets $\{a, b, c\}$, $\{b, f\}$, and $\{c, d, e\}$ with LR. Arrow points to cells chosen to move, and dotted and solid circle denote free and locked cell, respectively. Shade indicates cells with LR's cell gain increase, which darkens as the increase accumulates.

2.2.1 Loose Net Removal

During each pass of IIP algorithm, *free* net contains only free cells, and a *locked* net has locked cells in two blocks. A net is defined to be *loose* if it has locked cells in exactly one block and at least one free cell in the other block. The *anchor* block of a loose net n is defined as the block that contains the locked cells of n, and the other block that has one or more free cells of n is called *tail* block. Once a free cell c of a free net n is moved and locked into a block B, net n immediately becomes loose with B being its anchor. For example, in Figure 1-a, net $\{a, b, c\}$ is a loose net with the left block being its anchor. But if any of the free cells of the loose net in its tail block, say b or c, is moved and locked at a non-anchor block, the net will remain locked into the cutset thereafter during the entire pass. In other words, every net in the final cutset follows the *free* → *loose* → *locked* state transition, so our primary goal is to prevent as many loose nets from becoming locked as possible.

The basic idea of Loose net Removal (LR) algorithm is to focus on the free cells of a loose net in the tail block while they remain free. It intentionally increases the cell gains associated with moving those cells to its anchor block so that they are more likely to be selected during the subsequent moves. That is, our primary goal is to prevent the corresponding loose net from becoming locked into the cutset. A natural question arises on what to do with the free cells of a loose net located *inside* the anchor. We do not restrict the movement of these cells to non-anchor block since they can participate in removal of other loose nets. In case these cell moves fail to overcome the local minima and degrade the solution quality, conventional FM-type backtrack can always reverse these moves. After each cell move, LR considers free cells of all loose nets that are incident to the currently moved cell, promoting these cells to move to their anchor blocks by increasing their gains. Therefore, LR is effective in maintaining the locality of cell movement and thus establishing the cluster removal effect.

2.2.2 Cell Gain Increase Function

Removal of the given initial loose net causes additional loose nets to form subsequently, necessitating rules to set priority in removing these nets. The magnitude of cell gain increase due to a given loose net n is then computed as follows;

$$incr(n) = \left\lfloor \frac{max\_net\_size}{size(n)} \cdot \frac{\sum_{c \in L_n} deg(c)}{\sum_{c \in F_n} deg(c)} \right\rfloor$$

where max_net_size denotes the size of the largest net in the given netlist, $size(n)$ denotes the number of cells of n, and $deg(c)$ denotes the number of nets incident to cell c. L_n denotes the set of all locked cells of n in the anchor, and F_n denotes the set of all free cells of n in the tail. The above equation favors small nets, dense connectivity at the anchor, and sparse connectivity at the tail to encourage the algorithm to focus on relatively easy-to-remove loose nets.

```
LR()
while (there exists free cell)
   c = pick cell with maximum gain;
   move and lock cell c;
   for (each net n incident to cell c)
      update gain of cells in net n;
      if (n is loose net)
         for (each free cell f of net n not in anchor)
            if (f.gain + incr(n) < T)
               f.gain = f.gain + incr(n);
endwhile
```

Figure 2: Loose Net Removal Algorithm (single pass)

The LR algorithm based on the modified gain computation is described in Figure 2. Some important points to note in regards to cell gain increase of LR are as follows; First, the same amount of increase is added uniformly to all free cells of loose nets, and the increases are accumulated until the loose net is completely removed to a single block or possibly locked into the cutset. Second, a threshold value T limits the total accumulated value of cell gain, which enables us to adopt conventional array-based bucket structure [9]. Note that the only reason for the gain increase is to ensure that the target cells are chosen to move prior to other cells. Our study shows that a fairly small threshold value 100 can accomplish this goal without a major performance degradation. Third, the conventional cell gain update is still applied to the neighbors before the increase. This is necessary while choosing the next good initial seed for LR after completing removal of the current cluster. Lastly, the increase eliminates the necessity of special tie-breaking strategy due to the expanded cell gain range. The conventional cell gain ranges from $-p$ to p, where p represents the maximum number of nets incident to a single cell. Since the entire cells are distributed into this short range, most other IIP algorithms require special tie-breaking strategies such as LIFO bucket [10] or lookahead capability [15]. However, LR reduces the frequency of tie-breaking situation significantly since the rank of cells in the bucket is determined according to the increased gain values.

Our experiments show that this simple strategy works surprisingly well; LR alone ourperforms LIFO-FM, LIFO-LA3, LIFO-LA3-CLIP, and LIFO-LA3-CDIP by 8.2% to 54.4% improvement in terms of minimum cutsize of 20 runs with less CPU time (interested reader is referred to [5] for details). This convinces us that our simple cluster removal scheme focusing on the free cells of loose nets is very effective without any kind of tie-breaking enhancement. Figure 1 shows an example of removing three nets $n_1 = \{a, b, c\}$, $n_2 = \{b, f\}$, and $n_3 = \{c, d, e\}$ from the cutset with LR. First of all, LR increases the gain of b and c since n_1 is a loose net (1-a). Since LR favors shorter nets, n_2 will be chosen first to be removed by moving b (1-b). Then, LR first finishes removing n_1 (1-c) prior to n_2 (1-d). Finally, n_3 is removed (1-f). This example shows only a single direction of LR, but the similar process can be performed in the other direction, enabling us to balance the cut.

2.3 Loose and Stable Net Removal

A net is defined to be ***stable*** if it has remained cut throughout the entire run. Shibuya et al [18] observed that more than 80% of the nets in the final cutset are stable, and these nets trap FM algorithm into local minima and limit the solution quality. From this observation, they proposed an hill-climbing method called Stable Net Transition (SNT) that enables FM algorithm to systematically explore more local minima yet still with a reasonable CPU time.

After a run of FM algorithm terminates, the initial and the final cutsets are compared to detect stable nets. Then a stable net is randomly picked and all of its cells are moved into the smallest block, causing the stable net to be removed from the cutset. If a cell is moved once during this process, it cannot be moved to other blocks during a handling of another stable net. This process is repreated until a predetermined percentage of the stable nets are processed or no more move is possible. Then, another run of FM is performed using the outcome of the stable net removal as its initial partition. Usually the cutsize increases right after removing the stable net, but such hill-climbing is not so costly because SNT promotes higher rate of convergence and shorter duration of runs due to the fact that moving the stable nets only would result in a minor perturbation of the current configuration compared to an entirely new random initial configuration.

The idea of stable net removal can be combined naturally with loose net removal. LR dynamically removes nets in the cutset during the cell moves, whereas SNT statically removes nets from the cutset at the end of cell moves. Integrating these two net removal schemes results in a powerful partitioner named Loose and Stable net Removal (LSR).

3 MFFS Based Clustering Algorithm

Efficient clustering algorithms are important to improve the quality of the partitioning results and to speed up partitioning algorithms by reducing the number of nodes to be partitioned. In this section, we present a signal flow and logic dependency based clustering algorithm MFFS, which generalizes existing MFFC decomposition method [4] from combinational circuits to general sequential circuits.

The MFFC based clustering algorithm has been reported to provide natural clustering solution for combinational circuits [4, 6]. A modified MFFC algorithm for sequential circuits has been presented in [7], but the capability of this algorithm to detect directed cycles is limited. In general, the MFFC algorithm is mainly applied to combinational circuits. In the following section, we introduce a clustering method based on the Maximum Fanout Free Subgraph (MFFS), which can overcome the restriction of MFFC clustering.

3.1 Definition of MFFS

We first rewrite the definition of FFC and MFFC as follows. One can verify that our new definition is equivalent to that in [4].

Definition 1 (FFC & MFFC) *For a given node v in a combinational circuit,*

$$\begin{aligned} FFC_v &= \{u \mid \textit{every path from } u \textit{ to some PO} \\ &\qquad \textit{passes through } v \textit{ in the circuit}\} \\ MFFC_v &= \{u \mid \textit{for all } FFC_v, u \in FFC_v\} \end{aligned}$$

Now, it is natural for us to extend FFC and MFFC to Fanout Free Subgraphs (FFS) and Maximum Fanout Free Subgraphs (MFFS) for the clustering of general sequential circuits.

Definition 2 (FFS & MFFS) *For a given node v in a sequential circuit,*

$$\begin{aligned} FFS_v &= \{u \mid \textit{every path from } u \textit{ to some PO} \\ &\qquad \textit{passes through node } v \textit{ in the circuit}\} \\ MFFS_v &= \{u \mid \textit{for all } FFS_v, u \in FFS_v\} \end{aligned}$$

3.2 MFFS Construction Algorithm

For a given netlist NL and a node v, the MFFS cluster rooted at v can be obtained by using the following procedure:

1. Convert the given netlist to a directed graph, $G(N, E)$, where N is a set of nodes which correspond to the cells in the netlist, and E is a set of directed edges. A directed edge (i, j) exists if node j is a fanin of node i.
2. Cut all the fanout edges of the root node v; search all other nodes in graph $G(N, E)$ starting from the primary outputs (POs) of the netlist. The nodes in $G(N, E)$ that are not traversed belong to the $MFFS_v$.

This algorithm is named as the MFFS construction algorithm.

Theorem 1 *The time complexity of the MFFS construction algorithm is $O(|N| + |E|)$, where $|N|$ is the number of nodes and $|E|$ is the number of edges in $G(N, E)$.*

3.3 MFFS Clustering Algorithm

The MFFS construction algorithm tells us how to obtain one MFFS cluster. If we want to cluster the entire netlist, we need to apply MFFS construction algorithm repeatedly. Our MFFS clustering algorithm works as follows:

For a given netlist NL, let *roots* = {all POs of NL}. Then, we take out a node $v \in$ *roots* and use the MFFS construction algorithm to construct $MFFS_v$. This process is repeated until *roots* is empty. Then we remove all the currently constructed MFFS clusters from NL, and obtain a reduced netlist NL' whose POs are the input nodes to the removed MFFS clusters. We repeat the same procedure for the new netlist NL' recursively until all cells in netlist NL are grouped into MFFS clusters. One can refer to [5] for an example, illustrating how the algorithm works.

Theorem 2 *The time complexity of the MFFS clustering algorithm is $O(|N| \times (|N| + |E|))$ in the worst case, where $|N|$ is the number of nodes and $|E|$ is the number of edges in the directed graph, $G(N, E)$.*

3.4 Speedup of MFFS Algorithm

Although our MFFS clustering algorithm can find good clusters, its runtime can be long for large cicuits due to the fact that each MFFS construction requires the search of the entire netlist. Since in practice we usually have a maximum size limit to each cluster, we have developed a heuristic version of MFFS clustering algorithm that only searches a subset of the circuit every time. We call this algorithm MFFSd(h), where h indicates the depth of the circuit to be searched. Given a node v, this algorithm constructs an approximate of $MFFS_v$ as follows:

1. Perform breadth-first search from node v of depth h in $G(N,E)$ and put all encountered nodes in set SC_v.
2. For every node in SC_v, if its fanout nodes are not in SC_v, put them into set PPO_v (called pseudo POs).
3. Apply the MFFS Construction Algorithm, described in Section 3.2, on the subcircuit formed by SC_v and PPO_v with all nodes. in PPO_v being considered as POs. We can then obtain a cluster rooted at node v.
4. repeat (1) until all nodes has been clustered.

Since only a small number of cells need to be searched to find a cluster in step (3) when h is set to be small, we can consider that this step takes constant time. Therefore, the resulting MFFSd(h) clustering algorithm requires only $O(|N| + |E|)$ time.

4 Experimental Result

We have implemented our LSR/MFFS and MFFSd(h) algorithm, compiled with gcc v2.4, and tested them on SUN SPARC5-85. Table 1 lists some characteristics of benchmark circuits used in our experiments. Selection of test circuits is limited to those with signal direction, but most of them are used in common among other published papers. The bipartitioning results are obtained using the minimum cutsize of 20 runs under 45-55% area balance criterion and real cell sizes. The runtime is measured in seconds.

4.1 Cutsize Reduction Trend

The experimental result summerized in Table 1 shows the cutsize reduction trend starting from the basic FM to our most enhanced LSR/MFFS. We tested FM, SNT, LR, and LSR with and without MFFS clustering/declustering. The following observations are made from this set of experiment regarding various enhancements developed in this paper; (i) Signal flow based MFFS clustering indeed helps to reduce the cutsize and runtime. This is evident from the comparison between FM vs FM/MFFS, SNT vs SNT/MFFS, etc. (ii) LR is the most effective contributor in terms of cutsize reduction. This is revealed from the comparison between FM vs LR and FM/MFFS vs LR/MFFS. (iii) SNT provides good initial partition and improves both cutsize and runtime, when combined with LR. This is apparent from the comparison between FM vs SNT, LR vs LSR, FM/MFFS vs SNT/MFFS and LR/MFFS vs LSR/MFFS.

Benchmark Circuits					No Clustering Based				MFFS Clustering Based			
name	# cell	AVR	CT1	CT2	FM	SNT	LR	LSR	FM	SNT	LR	LSR
s1423	619	1.0	0.9	1.9	12	14	13	13	12	12	12	12
sioo	664	4.6	2.3	2.6	25	25	25	25	25	25	25	25
s1488	686	1.0	0.9	1.4	48	45	44	42	42	42	43	43
balu	801	12.9	2.0	3.8	27	27	27	27	27	27	27	27
prim1	833	6.7	3.2	5.9	43	42	42	42	43	42	42	43
struct	1952	2.5	17.9	12.1	42	45	33	33	39	52	33	33
prim2	3014	6.7	34.8	22.1	174	167	121	122	133	122	131	119
s9234	5866	1.0	36.7	9.7	49	54	41	43	42	43	41	40
biomed	6514	4.5	87.8	30.5	83	83	83	83	100	84	84	84
s13207	8772	1.0	73.9	14.1	90	74	75	70	91	65	73	61
s15850	10470	1.0	84.9	17.6	113	73	73	65	72	70	44	43
s35932	18148	1.0	420.8	32.1	100	128	45	44	48	76	45	44
s38584	20995	1.0	565.1	44.5	52	52	49	47	52	52	47	47
avq.sm	21918	4.5	1287.3	116.1	321	378	135	139	273	172	127	127
s38417	23949	1.0	452.2	45.1	176	112	53	55	119	147	51	50
avq.lg	25178	4.5	1473.2	90.2	491	380	145	131	251	168	127	127
Total	-	-	4543.9	449.7	1846	1699	1004	981	1369	1261	952	925
Time	-	-	-	-	214.6	100.9	326.0	279.0	139.1	102.1	206.5	162.6

Table 1: Characterization of the benchmark circuits and cutsize reduction from various enhancements. AVR stands for Area Variation Ratio (= max cell area/min cell area). Clustering time using MFFS and MFFSd(h) algorithms are reported under CT1 and CT2 column, respectively. The total CPU time of single run of each partitioning algorithm is listed under Time row.

4.2 Comparison to Published Results

Table 2 summerizes the comparisons of LSR/MFFS with other recently published state-of-the-art partitioning algorithms in terms of cutsize and runtime. We reported the sum of total elapsed CPU time for 10 runs of partitioning (and clustering, if applicable) 13 circuits under IIP algorithms.

IIP algorithms in comparison include LA3-CDIP, CLIP-PROP$_f$ [8], Strawman [12], hMetis-FM$_{20}$ [13], and MLc-100 [1]. The experiment shows that LSR/MFFS consistently outperforms non-clustering based algorithms LA3-CDIP and CLIP-PROPf by 17.4% and 12.1%, respectively, in terms of cutsize. In addition, LSR/MFFS outperforms multi-level clustering based Strawman, hMetis-FM$_{20}$ and MLc-100 by 5.9%, 3.1%, and 1.9%, respectively. The comparison of runtimes to other IIP algorithms except hMetis also reveals the performance superiority of LSR/MFFS.

Non-IIP algorithms in comparison include PANZA [16], Paraboli [17], and FBB [19]. LSR/MFFS again consistently outperforms these algorithms by 1.4%, 32.0%, and 21.4%, respectively. PANZA omitted runtime in their report, and the average runtime for each run of FBB tested on SPARC10 sums to 921.3 sec for 7 circuits tested, whereas LSR/MFFS spends only 79.8 sec. In overall, LSR/MFFS has achieved the best cutsize result among all the partitioning algorithms published in the literature with very promising runtime.

5 Conclusion & Ongoing Work

In this paper, we introduced the notion of loose net and presented the LR (Loose net Removal) algorithm. LR was then enhanced with existing SNT (Stable Net Transition) scheme [18] for eliminating hard-to-remove nets from the cutset. We also generalized the existing MFFC decomposition method to come up with signal flow based MFFS (Maximum Fanout Free Subgraph) clustering algorithm. The LSR/MFFS algorithm first applies LSR algorithm to clustered netlist generated by MFFS algorithm for global-level cutsize optimization and then declusters netlist for further cutsize refinement. As a result, LSR/MFFS partitioning algorithm has achieved the best cutsize results among all the partitioning algorithms reported in the recent literature.

Our ongoing research includes (i) extension of MFFS algorithm to support multi-level cluster hierarchy as well as various runtime improvement schemes, (ii) extension of LR to handle multiway partitioning efficiently, and (iii) development of a mincut-based placement algorithm exploiting the promising performance of LSR/MFFS.

REFERENCES

[1] C. J. Alpert, D. Huang, and A. B. Kahng. "Multilevel circuit partitioning". In *Proc. ACM/IEEE Design Automation Conf.*, pages 530–533, 1997.

[2] C. J. Alpert and A. B. Kahng. "Recent directions in netlist partitioning: a survey". *Integration, the VLSI Journal*, pages 1–81, 1995.

[3] C. J. Alpert and S. Z. Yao. "Spectral partitioning: The more eigenvectors, the better". In *Proc. ACM/IEEE Design Automation Conf.*, pages 195–200, 1995.

[4] J. Cong and Y. Ding. "On area/depth trade-off in LUT-based FPGA technology mapping". In *Proc. 30th ACM/IEEE Design Automation Conf.*, pages 213–218, 1993.

[5] J. Cong, P. Li, S. K. Lim, T. Shibuya, and D. Xu. "Large scale circuit partitioning with loose/stable net removal and signal flow based hierarchical clustering". Technical Report 970005, CS Dept. of UCLA, 1997.

	IIP Algorithms						Non-IIP Algorithms		
	CDIP	$PROP_f$	Straw	hMetis	MLc	**LSR/MFFS**	PANZA	Paraboli	FBB
circuit	[8]	[8]	[12]	[13]	[1]	-	[16]	[17]	[19]
s1423	-	-	-	-	-	**12**	15	16	13
sioo	-	-	-	-	-	**25**	25	45	-
s1488	-	-	-	-	-	**43**	44	50	-
balu	27	27	27	27	27	**27**	27	41	-
prim1	52	51	49	50	47	**43**	-	-	-
struct	36	33	33	33	33	**33**	33	40	-
prim2	152	152	143	145	139	**119**	-	-	-
s9234	44	42	42	40	40	**40**	40	74	70
biomed	83	84	83	83	83	**84**	83	135	-
s13207	70	71	57	55	55	**61**	66	91	74
s15850	67	56	44	42	44	**43**	44	91	67
s35932	73	42	47	42	41	**44**	43	62	49
s38584	47	51	49	47	47	**47**	47	55	47
avq.sm	148	144	131	130	128	**127**	-	-	-
s38417	79	65	53	51	49	**50**	49	49	58
avq.lg	145	143	140	127	128	**127**	-	-	-
Total1	1023	961	898	872	861	**845**	-	-	-
Total2	-	-	-	-	-	**509**	516	749	-
% Imp	17.4	12.1	5.9	3.1	1.9	-	1.4	32.0	21.4
Time	5817	5611	12577	***[1]	3455	**2054**	-	24619	-

Table 2: Comparison of LSR/MFFS to other published algorithms. Total1 is based on 13 common test circuits under IIP algorithms, whereas Total2 is based on 12 common test circuits under non-IIP algorithms. Our runtime includes MFFSd(h) clustering time from Table 1.

[6] J. Cong, Z. Li, and R. Bagrodia. "Acyclic multi-way partitioning of boolean networks". In *Proc. ACM/IEEE 31st Design Automation Conf.*, pages 670–675, 1994.

[7] J. Cong and D. Xu. "Exploiting signal flow and logic dependency in standard cell placement". In *Proc. Asia and South Pacific Design Automation Conf.*, pages 399–404, 1995.

[8] S. Dutt and W. Deng. "VLSI circuit partitioning by cluster-removal using iterative improvement techniques". In *Proc. Int'l Conf. on Computer-Aided Design*, pages 194–200, 1996.

[9] C. Fiduccia and R. Mattheyses. "A linear time heuristic for improving network partitions". In *Proc. ACM/IEEE Design Automation Conf.*, pages 175–181, 1982.

[10] L. Hagen, D. Huang, and A. B. Kahng. "On implementation choices for iterative improvement partitioning algorithms". In *Proc. ACM/IEEE European Design Automation Conf.*, 1995.

[11] L. Hagen and A. B. Kahng. "A new approach to effective circuit clustering". In *Proc. Int'l Conf. on Computer-Aided Design*, pages 422–427, 1992.

[12] S. Hauck and G. Borriello. "An evaluation of bipartitioning techniques". *submitted to IEEE Trans. on Computer-Aided Design*, 1996.

[13] G. Karypis and V. Kumar. "Multilevel hypergraph partitioning : Application in VLSI domain". In *Proc. ACM/IEEE Design Automation Conf.*, pages 526–529, 1997.

[14] B. Kernighan and S. Lin. "An efficient heuristic procedure for partitioning of electrical circuits". *Bell System Technical Journal*, 1970.

[15] B. Krishnamurthy. "An improved min-cut algorithm for partitioning VLSI networks". *IEEE Trans. on Computers*, pages 438–446, 1984.

[16] J. Li, J. Lillis, and C. K. Cheng. "Linear decomposition algorithm for VLSI design applications". In *Proc. ACM/IEEE Design Automation Conf.*, pages 223–228, 1995.

[17] B. M. Riess, K. Doll, and F. M. Johannes. "Partitioning very large circuits using analytical placement techniques". In *Proc. ACM/IEEE 31st Design Automation Conf.*, pages 646–651, 1994.

[18] T. Shibuya, I. Nitta, and K. Kawamura. "SMINCUT: VLSI placement tool using min-cut". *Fujitsu Scientific & Technical Journal*, pages 197–207, 1995.

[19] H. Yang and D. F. Wong. "Efficient network flow based min-cut balanced partitioning". In *Proc. IEEE Int. Conf. on Computer-Aided Design*, pages 50–55, 1994.

[1] A direct comparison between hMetis and LSR/MFFS is not possible since hMetis used SGI R10000 200MHz for collecting runtime. However, private communication between the authors indicates that hMetis is about 1.4 times faster.

SESSION 7D

EFFICIENT TECHNIQUES FOR PARASITICS EXTRACTION

Moderators:

David D. Ling, IBM Corp., Yorktown Heights, NY

Sani R. Nassif, IBM Corp., Austin, TX

IES^3: A Fast Integral Equation Solver for Efficient 3-Dimensional Extraction

Sharad Kapur David E. Long
Bell Laboratories, Lucent Technologies
Murray Hill, NJ 07974

Abstract

Integral equation techniques are often used to extract models of integrated circuit structures. This extraction involves solving a dense system of linear equations, and using direct solution methods is prohibitive for large problems. In this paper, we present IES^3 (pronounced "ice cube"), a fast Integral Equation Solver for three-dimensional problems with arbitrary kernels. Extraction methods based on IES^3 are substantially more efficient than existing multipole-based approaches.

1 Introduction

Parasitic extraction of IC packages and interconnect is now critical because of increases in operating frequencies and reductions in operating voltages. Extraction procedures based on integral equations [10, 13] are robust and have many advantages over finite-difference or finite-element schemes, including good conditioning, reduction in dimensionality, and the ability to treat arbitrary regions. However, they have one overriding disadvantage: the high cost of working with large dense matrices. In this paper, we present IES^3 ("ice cube"), an Integral Equation Solver for three-dimensional problems involving *arbitrary* kernels, and show that this new solver has significant performance advantages compared to competing approaches.

The fast multipole method (FMM) [3], while originally developed for particle simulation problems, can be combined with iterative techniques to solve the dense integral equation matrices that arise from the Laplace equation. Parameter extraction programs such as FastCap [7] and FastHenry [5] use the FMM for accelerating the dense matrix-vector products required by an iterative solver. Because the FMM is tailored to the $1/||x - x'||$ kernel, dealing with common situations such as layered dielectrics is difficult. For example, in FastCap this requires discretizing the dielectric boundaries and introducing extra unknowns for the polarization charge [8, 10]. This can result in a large increase in problem size. An extractor based on IES^3 has no such difficulty: it simply incorporates the variation in dielectrics into the Green's function.

Surprisingly, even for extraction problems that only involve the Laplace kernel, IES^3 is faster and more memory-efficient than FastCap, as we show in Section 4. This is because IES^3 provides greater compression than the FMM, though at the cost of a more expensive preprocessing phase. In extraction problems, the number of matrix-vector multiplies is typically large; hence the added compression provided by IES^3 more than makes up for the FMM's smaller startup cost. In contrast, in a particle simulation environment where the geometry (and hence the matrix) changes after each multiply, the FMM has a definite advantage [3].

We did not have access to the Precorrected-FFT version of FastCap [9], but based on the relative performance of both approaches to the FMM version of FastCap, we believe that our approach still has performance advantages. Also note that there have been recent advances in the FMM algorithms [2], but they have not yet been incorporated into extraction programs such as FastCap.

IES^3 uses the fact that large parts of the integral operator matrix are numerically *low rank*. The singular value decomposition (SVD) is an extremely effective tool for the compression of rank-deficient matrices [12]. Based on this observation, Kapur and Zhao [6] describe a scheme for recursively partitioning and compressing the matrix. This compressed representation is then used to compute matrix-vector products during an iterative solve. While these products are fast ($O(N \log N)$ time), the method suffers from an $O(N^2)$ preprocessing phase. This justifies its use only in situations where there are a large number of multiplies. The main result of this paper is a new interpolation-based construction procedure that reduces the preprocessing time to $O(N \log N)$. As a result, IES^3 is dramatically faster than the earlier method while still retaining the same degree of compression.

2 Formulation of the problem

We consider integral equations such as

$$\phi(x) = \int_{R'} G(x, x')\sigma(x')\, dR' \tag{1}$$

where ϕ is the known "right-hand side" (for historical reasons, written on the left), σ is the unknown to be solved for, R is the region of integration and G is the kernel (or Green's function). For example, in the standard problem of capacitance extraction in three dimensions, ϕ is the potential, σ is the surface charge density, R ranges over the surfaces of conductors, and G is the free-space Green's function $1/(4\pi\epsilon_0\|x - x'\|)$. To solve such a problem numerically, we must first discretize the region and reduce (1) to a matrix equation. In engineering applications, first-order collocation schemes are adequate. The domain R is subdivided into regions $\{R_1, R_2, \ldots, R_N\}$, a collocation point x_j is chosen in each region R_j, and σ is assumed to be piecewise constant over each region. Then (1) reduces to the following set of equations:

$$\phi(x_i) = \sum_{j=1}^{N} \left(\int_{R'_j} G(x_i, x')\, dR'_j \right) \sigma(x_j) \qquad 1 \le i \le N. \tag{2}$$

If we define the dense matrix $A = \{a_{ij}\}$ by

$$a_{ij} = \int_{R'_j} G(x_i, x')\, dR'_j, \qquad 1 \le i, j \le N. \tag{3}$$

then the system (2) is equivalent to the matrix equation $\phi = A\sigma$. While our algorithm does not assume any particular method of discretization and does not depend on the Green's function, we do assume that the problem has been reduced to matrix form. For the remainder of this paper, A will denote the $N \times N$ matrix (3) associated with the integral equation. For notational convenience, we assume that N is a power of 2.

3 Rapid matrix solution

Direct solution of the linear system $A\sigma = \phi$ via Gaussian Elimination requires $O(N^2)$ storage and $O(N^3)$ time and is impractical for large problems. Fortunately, typical systems arising from integral equations almost always have an asymptotically bounded condition number and can be solved by Krylov-subspace iterative schemes such as Conjugate Gradient [12] or GMRES [11]. Iterative solvers require application of the matrix A to a sequence of recursively generated vectors. The dominant costs become the $O(N^2)$ time and space required for constructing and storing the matrix and the $O(N^2)$ time required for each matrix-vector product. In this section, we describe IES[3], a kernel-independent algorithm that reduces each of these costs to $O(N \log N)$ for typical problems.

3.1 A simple example

The idea behind our algorithm (and other fast algorithms such as the FMM) is to exploit the fact that typical Green's functions vary smoothly with distance. Consider the situation depicted in Figure 1. Suppose that $X = \{x_1, x_2, \ldots, x_n\}$ and $Y = \{y_1, y_2, \ldots, y_n\}$ are two sets of points in R^3 separated by a distance d. Let $H(x, y)$ be the function giving the interaction between the points. Then the influence of Y on X is can be computed by multiplication of the $n \times n$ matrix $B = \{b_{ij}\} = \{H(x_i, y_j)\}$ with a vector. Direct evaluation of this product would require n^2 operations. However, if d is relatively large, and the function H is smooth, then the numerical rank of the matrix B is small compared to n. Intuitively the influence due to a point y_j is very similar to the influence of its neighbors. As a result, the columns of B are nearly linearly dependent.

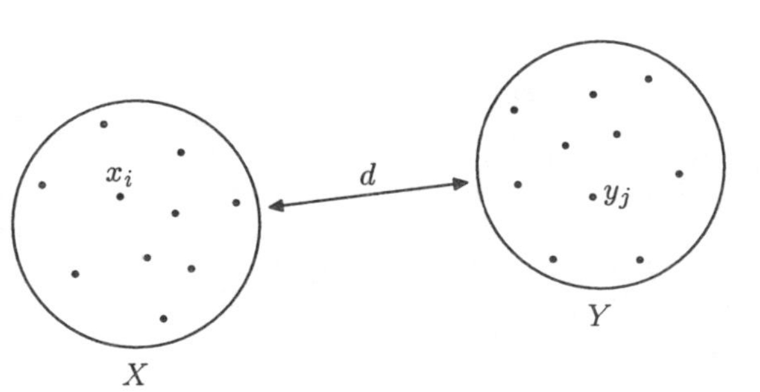

Figure 1: Well-separated regions

We take advantage of this fact using the Singular Value Decomposition (SVD) [12]. The SVD of B is given by

$$B = USW$$

where

$$UU^* = W^*W = I,$$

and $S = \mathrm{diag}(s_1, \ldots, s_n)$ with $s_1 \ge s_2 \ge \cdots \ge s_n \ge 0$. The numerical rank of a matrix to a precision ϵ is the integer r such that $s_r/s_1 < \epsilon$. Clearly, if B is of rank r then it can be approximated as[1]

$$\tilde{B} = U(:, 1{:}r)S(1{:}r, 1{:}r)W(1{:}r, :)$$

with

$$\|B - \tilde{B}\| < \epsilon.$$

Given the SVD of the matrix B of rank r, a matrix-vector product can be computed in $(2n + 1)r$ operations by multiplying the vector in turn by $W(1{:}r, :)$, $S(1{:}r, 1{:}r)$, and $U(:, 1{:}r)$. When $r \ll n$ it is much more efficient to multiply with B in this manner.

Use of the SVD to represent B requires no prior knowledge of the function H, in contrast to the multipole approach which is based on a Taylor series approximation of H. This added flexibility does not reduce the compression that is achieved. In fact, as our numerical experiments in Section 4 show, we obtain *substantially greater compression* than the multipole schemes.

Even though we use the SVD for the theoretical development of our algorithm, it is sufficient to use the Gram-Schmidt process [12]. Given an $n \times n$ matrix B and a user specified tolerance ϵ, the Gram-Schmidt process computes the numerical rank r of B and an $n \times r$ orthogonal matrix U which spans the column space of B. B can be approximated as UV where $V = U^*B$. Decomposing B in this way is faster than computing the SVD of B.

[1] We use Matlab notation for submatrices. $U(:, 1{:}r)$ denotes the submatrix consisting of columns 1 through r of U. Similarly, $W(1{:}r, :)$ denotes the submatrix consisting of the first r rows of W.

3.2 Ordering

To compress the integral operator matrix A in (3), which represents both *near and far* interactions, we need to identify large submatrices that correspond to interactions between well-separated regions. (As we saw in the previous subsection, such submatrices can be compactly represented as low-rank UV products.) In some situations, this is easily achieved. For example, in a one-dimensional problem, the natural ordering of points by their position in space is a good one, yielding a matrix whose *rank map* is shown in Figure 2. (This example is drawn from Section 3-2 of [4]. The problem is to solve for the surface current induced on a conducting cylinder by an impressed electric field, and the Green's function G is the Helmholtz kernel $H_0^2(k\|x - x'\|)$.) The rank map shows the partitioning of the matrix A into submatrices and the rank of each submatrix. The structure of this rank map is typical in problems where the storage requirements drop from $O(N^2)$ to $O(N \log N)$.

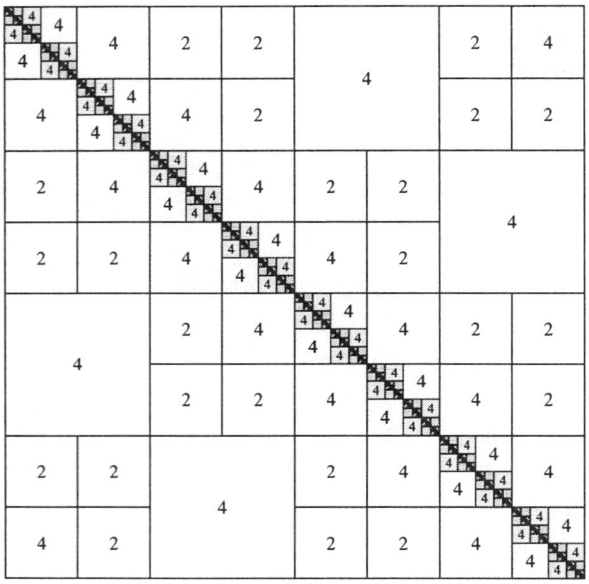

Figure 2: Rank map for a one-dimensional Helmholtz kernel ($N = 2048$)

In general, our goal is to find a permutation matrix P such that $\tilde{A} = P^{-1}AP$ is highly compressible. Ideally, all strong interactions should be close to the diagonal in $\tilde{A}$, as in Figure 2. For two- and three-dimensional problems there is generally no permutation P that can completely accomplish this. Nevertheless, the following heuristic based on recursive subdivision yields excellent results and requires only $O(N \log N)$ time. We assume that there is a spatial coordinate associated with each element in the discretization. Under this assumption, the problem reduces to one of ordering a set of points such that points that are close in space are also close in the ordering. For notational simplicity, we present the algorithm for the two dimensional case.

1. If the current set of points S is the singleton $\{(x, y)\}$ then return the sequence $\langle(x, y)\rangle$.

2. Otherwise compute the bounding box for the points in S. We assume without loss of generality that the longest dimension corresponds to the x-axis. Equally divide S into two disjoint sets S_1 and S_2 such that $x_1 \leq x_2$ for all points $(x_1, y_1) \in S_1$ and $(x_2, y_2) \in S_2$. Recursively order S_1 and S_2 and concatenate the results to obtain the ordering for S.

The rank map for a three-dimensional problem after ordering with this technique is shown in Figure 4. This problem corresponds to capacitance extraction for structure of Figure 3 [8]. Although there are some strong interactions off the diagonal, the rank map is similar to the one in Figure 2. For the remainder of the paper, we will assume that all matrices have been ordered in this fashion.

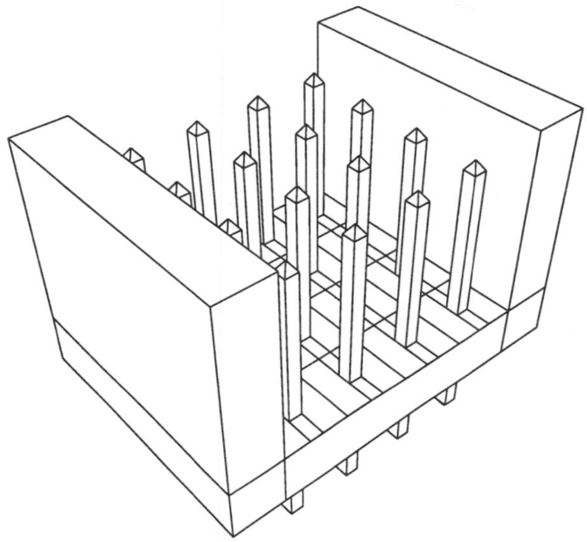

Figure 3: The backplane connector example from [8]

3.3 Compression in $O(N^2)$ time

In this subsection, we briefly describe the algorithm of [6] for the recursive UV decomposition of A. The main difference between the algorithm of [6] and IES[3] is in the construction of the compressed representation of the matrix. However, the basic structure of the two algorithms is the same: both partition the matrix by a recursive subdivision scheme. In [6], the construction proceeds as follows.

1. If the dimension n of the current submatrix B is less than b, where b is a small fixed number, then:

   (a) Use the Gram-Schmidt procedure to obtain an orthonormal column basis to a user specified precision ϵ. If the size of the basis r is greater than $n/2$ then B is simply stored as a dense matrix.

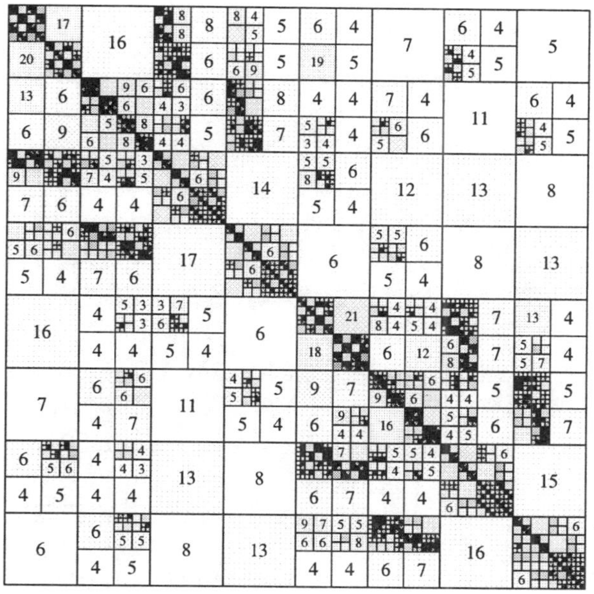

Figure 4: The rank map for the backplane connector example (discretized into $N = 10672$ panels)

(b) Otherwise let U be the $n \times r$ matrix whose columns are the basis. Compute $V = U^*B$.

2. If n is at least b, then construct the representation of the four submatrices $B(1{:}n/2, 1{:}n/2)$, $B(1{:}n/2, n/2+1{:}n)$, $B(n/2+1{:}n, 1{:}n/2)$, and $B(n/2+1{:}n, n/2+1{:}n)$. If these child submatrices are all low rank, i.e., are represented as UV decompositions, then

   (a) Construct a decomposition UV for B by merging (as described below).

   (b) If the size of this decomposition is smaller than the sum of the sizes of the child submatrix representations then represent B by U and V. Otherwise represent B by the child submatrices.

3. If some submatrix is not low rank, then represent B by its four children.

The merging process constructs a decomposition $U_{12}V_{12}$ for the matrix

$$\begin{bmatrix} U_1V_1 \\ U_2V_2 \end{bmatrix}$$

where U_1, V_1, U_2, and V_2 have dimensions $n \times r_1$, $r_1 \times n$, $n \times r_2$, and $r_2 \times n$ respectively, and where U_1 and U_2 are both orthogonal. We run the Gram-Schmidt procedure on the rows of V_1 and V_2 to obtain a row basis of size r. V_{12} is the $r \times n$ matrix whose rows are this basis. The $2n \times r$ matrix U_{12} is given by

$$\begin{bmatrix} U_1V_1V^* \\ U_2V_2V^* \end{bmatrix}.$$

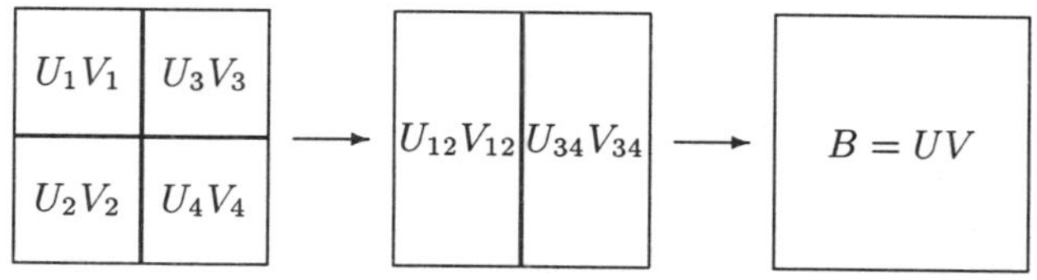

Figure 5: The merging process.

Note that the matrix V_{12} generated by this procedure is orthogonal. Three merges (two vertical and one horizontal) yield the UV representation of B in Step 2a above. As a result of the final horizontal merge, U is orthogonal. The process is illustrated in Figure 5. Note that directly using the Gram-Schmidt process to construct the UV decomposition of B would require $O(n^2r)$ operations. In contrast, merging requires only $O(nr^2)$ steps. For rank deficient matrices ($r \ll n$) merging is much more efficient.

Computing a matrix-vector product with the final compressed representation of is done with the following recursive algorithm.

1. Let B of size $n \times n$ be the current submatrix, x be the current input vector, and y be the current output vector. If B is represented densely, then compute $y = Bx$ directly.

2. If B is represented as UV, then compute $y = U(Vx)$.

3. If B is represented as a combination of four submatrices
$$\begin{bmatrix} B_1 & B_3 \\ B_2 & B_4 \end{bmatrix},$$
then $y(1{:}n/2) = B_1x(1{:}n/2) + B_3x(n/2+1{:}n)$ and $y(n/2+1{:}n) = B_2x(1{:}n/2) + B_4x(n/2+1{:}n)$.

This summarizes the algorithm described in [6] for compression of A and the computation of matrix-vector products. Empirically, the compression obtained is much higher than that achieved by the multipole algorithms. This leads to a faster matrix-vector multiply. However, the construction of the UV decompositions requires at least $O(N^2)$ operations while constructing the multipole representation requires only $O(N \log N)$ steps. In situations where the construction cost can be amortized over a large number of solves (as is the case in [6]), the UV representation is more efficient. But when there are few solves, the multipole approach is faster overall. In the following subsection we present an improved construction procedure that requires subquadratic time. This makes our method substantially faster than the multipole algorithms in most cases.

3.4 Compression in subquadratic time

The key idea behind IES[3] is to exploit smoothness in the entries of the interaction matrix. By using interpolation, we can build the UV decomposition without examining all n^2 entries.

Consider constructing a UV decomposition of the interaction matrix B for the situation shown in Figure 6. Let S_X and S_Y be sets of p sampling points in X and Y respectively. The idea for reconstructing B is to use the influence of S_Y on X to construct a column basis for B. Then the influence of Y on S_X is used to express each column of B in terms of this basis. The columns of B that have not been completely sampled (which correspond to points in $Y - S_Y$) are interpolated based on the sampling S_X of rows. More specifically, the influence due to any point in Y on X is approximated by a linear combination of the influences of the sampling points S_Y. Hence if C is the $n \times p$ matrix of columns of B corresponding to points in S_Y, then a column basis for C should also span the columns of B (the validity of this is discussed below). Define U to be the $n \times r$ matrix obtained by running the Gram-Schmidt process on the columns of C. To get the coefficients of the columns of B in the basis represented by U, we use the sampling points S_X. Let R be the $p \times n$ matrix of rows of B corresponding to points in S_X and let $\tilde{U}$ be the $p \times r$ matrix of rows of U corresponding to these same points. Finally, define V to be the solution (in the least squares sense) to $\tilde{U}V = R$. Then B is approximated by UV.

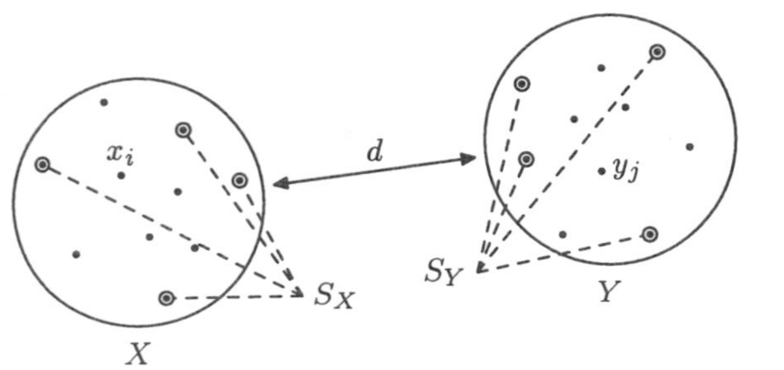

Figure 6: Well-separated regions with sampling points

In the old algorithm, U was the result of running the Gram-Schmidt process on all the columns of B. Clearly, obtaining U from C instead of B is only justified when there are sufficient sampling points to reconstruct the interaction. The issue is akin to interpolation of an unknown function. When the function is smooth (in the sense that the derivatives over the interval have a known bound), the accuracy of the interpolation can be rigorously controlled by the number and location of sampling points [12]. However, when designing a general-purpose algorithm, requiring bounds on the derivatives of the function is usually very conservative. Empirically, given the assumptions that the function is smooth, the sets are well separated, and the sampling is reasonably uniform, the interpolation can be made arbitrarily accurate. Hence, instead of derivative information, our algorithm uses a statically-determined map which indicates the low-rank regions of the matrix A and information about appropriate sampling points within each such region. We provide default methods that compute this information based purely on the spatial coordinates of elements. For typical kernels these default routines suffice. As an example, a static map of the interactions for the backplane connector mentioned in Subsection 3.2 is shown in Figure 7. Figure 4 shows the rank map for the same example; note the close correspondence between the two. Also note that the static map is conservative, in that many of the small submatrices shown on the static map have merged into larger low-rank matrices in Figure 4.

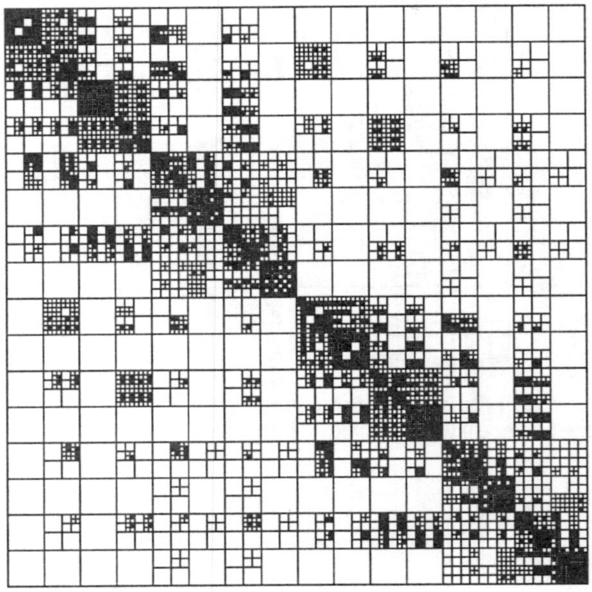

Figure 7: The static sampling map for the backplane connector example

The new algorithm is exactly the same as the one in Subsection 3.3, except for the addition of a new base case:

> If the statically determined map indicates that B should be low rank, then sample B and construct the UV decomposition as discussed at the start of this subsection.

For a (statically-identified low-rank) submatrix B of size $n \times n$ and rank r, the algorithm takes only $O(r^2 n)$ operations to construct U and V. As a result, this simple change dramatically reduces the construction time for the compressed representation of A. For general problems it is difficult to give a bound for the complexity, but for the simple case of a one-dimensional problem (where we assume that the rank of each of the submatrices is r), the time is $O(r^2 N \log N)$.

4 Experimental results

In this section, we present experimental results for IES^3. All tests were run on an SGI machine (200 MHz R10000 CPU).

4.1 Comparison to FastCap

We begin by comparing IES^3 to the FMM-based FastCap program (version 2) [7, 8]. To make a fair comparison, we modified FastCap to use our algorithm within FastCap's iterative solver. The discretization, matrix formulation, and preconditioning were unchanged. The relative tolerance was set to give the same accuracy as FastCap's default two-term multipole expansions. Results for a number of the standard examples supplied with FastCap are presented in Table 1. For FastCap we computed the memory requirements by subtracting the preconditioner memory and the "miscellaneous" memory from the total memory use reported. Error is determined by running the same examples at a much higher accuracy and computing $||C - \tilde{C}||/||C||$ where C and $\tilde{C}$ are the high- and low-accuracy capacitance matrices, respectively. For the RAM cell example, the default tolerances only yielded one digit of accuracy for both methods. The example was run with tighter tolerances for both.

The first two examples in the table involve conductors in free space, while the last two also include dielectric interfaces. For examples with dielectrics, FastCap uses a finite-difference approximation to compute normal components of the electric field at the dielectric interfaces. This computation is done after the potential is evaluated, since incorporating it directly would require substantial alterations to the multipole algorithm (as discussed in the appendix of [8]). Because IES^3 is not restricted to any specific kernel, we chose to incorporate the same finite-difference computation directly into the matrix. We could as easily have analytically differentiated the potential to avoid the inaccuracies inherent in finite-differencing.

The memory required by IES^3 can be as little as one-fifth that required by FastCap. As a consequence, IES^3 is much faster than FastCap for larger problems and those involving many conductors. Our startup overhead is still substantial for small examples such as the via structure. For medium-sized examples such as the backplane connector, IES^3 is almost two and one-half times faster.

4.2 Simulation of an RF test socket

As an example of a problem involving a non-classical kernel, we consider capacitance extraction for an RF IC test socket. Figure 8 shows a cross-sectional view of one side of the socket. The socket is mounted on a single-layer board with a ground plane. In the figure, $\epsilon_1 = 3.08$ is the effective dielectric for the socket and $\epsilon_2 = 9.8$ is the dielectric constant of the circuit board. Figure 9 is a three-dimensional mesh of the socket, computed using a surface mesh generator[2]. The picture also shows the solution for the charge distribution on the socket when a potential difference of one volt is applied to the first pin. To decrease the size of the problem, we use an adaptive mesh, with finer discretization at corners and edges. This reflects the expected rapid variation in charge density in these regions. Due to the large separation between the two sides of the socket, it was sufficient to model only one side.

[2]Triangle: A Two-Dimensional Quality Mesh Generator and Delaunay Triangulator, by Jonathan Shewchuk

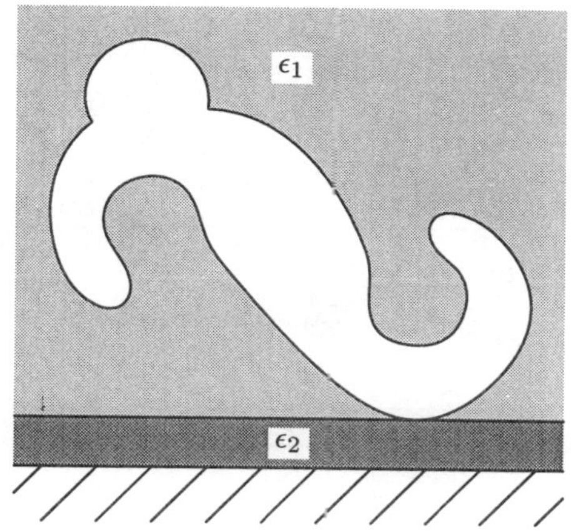

Figure 8: Cross section of one side an RF IC socket, showing dielectric layers and ground plane

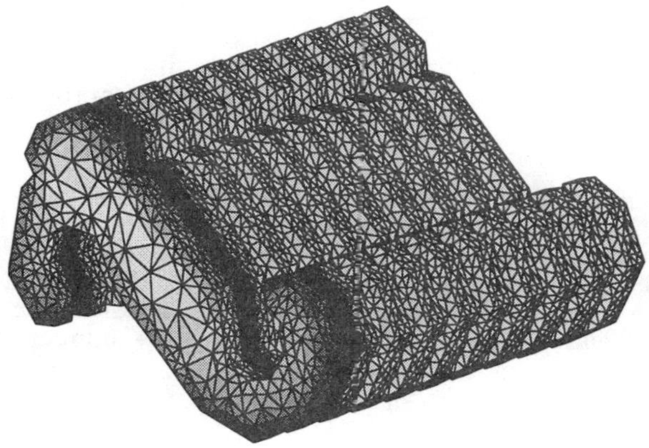

Figure 9: Discretization and charge distribution of the socket with one volt applied to pin one

A standard first-order collocation scheme of the type discussed in Section 2 was used together with a modified Green's function incorporating the layered dielectrics and ground plane [13]. This Green's function takes the form of an infinite series. Fortunately, for dielectric constants that are relatively close, the series is rapidly convergent and can be numerically approximated with ten to fifteen terms.

For the construction of the matrix A, we use analytic integration for the singular integrals when the collocation point lies in the triangular panel and low-order Gaussian integration when the point does not.

Experimental results for the capacitance extraction are given in Table 2 and Figure 10. For lower levels of discretization, we compare three methods: standard Gaussian Elimination (G.E. in the table), GMRES using a direct matrix multiply, and our algorithm. For direct GMRES and IES^3, a tolerance of 10^{-2} was used. The memory and time required to construct the matrix (for both Gaussian Elimination and GMRES) is shown in the second and third columns. Memory is in MB and time is in CPU seconds. The "Error"

Example	Panels	FastCap Time (sec)	FastCap Mem. (MB)	FastCap Error	IES^3 Time	IES^3 Mem.	IES^3 Error
5x5 bus crossing	7360	185	66	3e-3	105	26	6e-3
via structure	6126	45	37	1e-3	60	22	4e-3
backplane connector	10672	675	165	4e-3	280	45	3e-3
RAM cell	6129	480	135	1e-2	195	26	1e-2

Table 1: Comparison of IES^3 to the FMM-based scheme in FastCap

	Direct Methods					IES^3					
			G.E.	GMRES							
Panels	Mem.	Cons.	Solve	Solve	Error	Mem.	Cons.	Solve	Error	C_{11}	C_{12}
1320	13	40	10	20	1e-3	2	20	10	3e-3	905	-474
2500	48	140	70	90	1e-3	5	65	25	4e-3	906	-484
4440	150	435	385	290	1e-3	11	150	50	5e-3	898	-477
8500	(550)	(1650)	(2700)	(1050)	—	24	375	90	—	892	-469
15690	(1870)	(5425)	(17000)	(3600)	—	54	865	230	—	891	-467

Table 2: Comparison of IES^3 to direct methods

columns give relative errors in the capacitance matrices, as compared to Gaussian Elimination. The "Solve" columns show CPU times for doing ten solves (one per pin). The construction time for IES^3 includes the time to compress the matrix. The capacitance matrix entries C_{11} and C_{12} are in fF. The numbers in parenthesis are extrapolated values.

The capacitance matrix entries have converged to two digits of accuracy at a discretization of $N = 15690$. At this level of discretization, memory requirements made the direct methods impractical. Even if memory were available, IES^3 would be twenty times faster than Gaussian Elimination and eight times faster than GMRES. Note that both the time and memory required by IES^3 are growing almost linearly with problem size. The total time required for the largest problem is less than twenty minutes.

The extracted capacitance values were used for building an equivalent circuit model for the socket. The coupling between pins was measured using a network analyzer. Figure 11 shows predicted crosstalk with our model, as compared to measurements. The two agree to about 3 dB.

As an aside, it is interesting that a carefully-engineered and machine-optimized Gaussian Elimination code [1] is extremely competitive with iterative techniques for medium-sized problems. This is because modern machines tend to be memory bound rather than CPU bound. In such an environment, we feel that the primary benefit of codes such as IES^3 is the dramatic memory reduction that they offer.

5 Conclusions

In this paper we presented IES^3, a fast general-purpose integral equation solver. The algorithm uses a combination of SVD-based compression and an iterative solver. The compressed representation of the integral operator matrix is constructed in $O(N \log N)$ time by combining a recursive partitioning strategy with interpolation of the function that defines the matrix entries. Unlike the kernel-specific multipole algorithms, IES^3 does not depend on the particular form of the Green's function. Further, our scheme gives higher compression even for those kernels for which the multipole methods were developed. We demonstrated IES^3 on three-dimensional capacitance extraction problems. On large problems with Laplace kernels, our method uses half the time of FastCap and only about one-fifth the memory. Because IES^3 is not kernel-specific, we solve examples involving multiple dielectric layers using a modified Green's function, thereby restricting the discretization only to conductor surfaces. On one such example, an RF test socket, IES^3 required an order of magnitude less time and thirty five times less memory than direct GMRES. While we have discussed IES^3 only in the context of extraction problems, it should also be useful for other purposes, such as full wave problems involving Helmholtz kernels.

Acknowledgements

Prashant Singh provided the description and measurements for the socket example. We thank Jacob White and his group at MIT for making the FastCap program and the associated examples available for benchmarking purposes.

References

[1] E. Anderson et al. *LAPACK User's Guide, Release 2.0.* SIAM Publications, Philadelphia, 2nd edition, 1995.

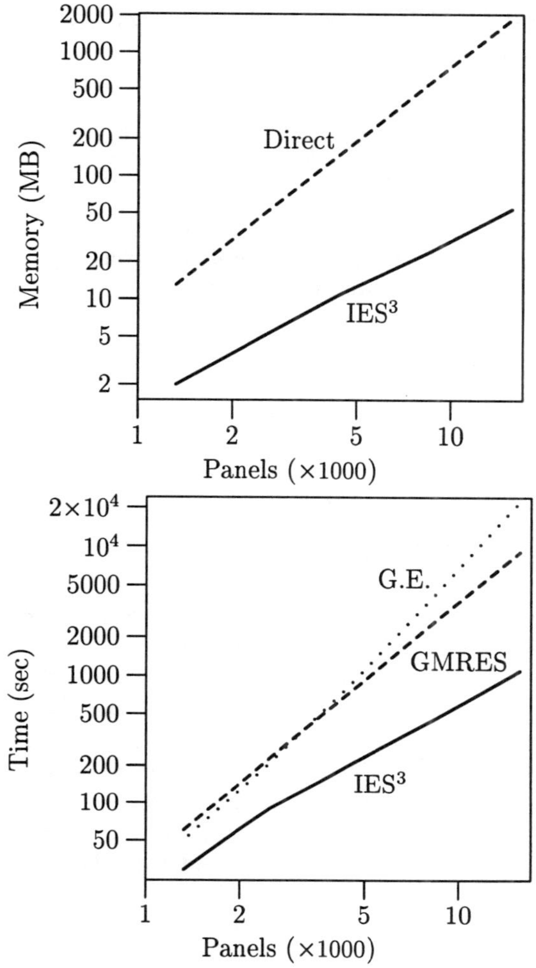

Figure 10: Time and memory requirements for the RF test socket example at various levels of discretization

[2] L. Greengard and V. Rohklin. A new version of the fast multipole method for the Laplace equation in three dimensions. Technical Report YALEU/DCS/RR-1115, Yale University Department of Computer Science, September 1996.

[3] L. Greengard and V. Rokhlin. A fast algorithm for particle simulations. *Journal of Computational Physics*, 73(2):325–348, December 1987.

[4] R. F. Harrington. *Field Computation by Moment Methods.* IEEE Press, New York, 1991.

[5] M. Kamon, M. J. Tsuk, and J.White. FASTHENRY: A multipole-accelerated 3-d inductance extraction program. *IEEE Transactions on Microwave Theory and Techniques*, 42(9):1750–1758, September 1994.

[6] S. Kapur and J. Zhao. A fast method of moments solver for efficient parameter extraction of MCMs. In *34th Design Automation Conference*, pages 141–146, June 1997.

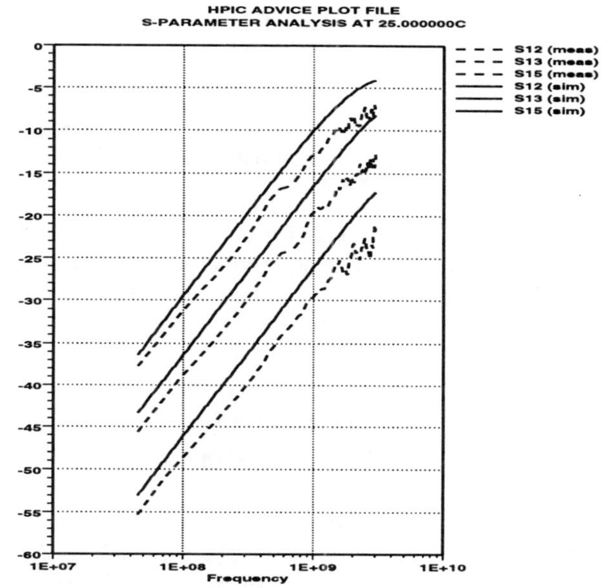

Figure 11: Comparison of simulated S parameters versus measurements

[7] K. Nabors and J. White. Fastcap: A multipole-accelerated 3-d capacitance extraction program. *IEEE Transactions on Computer-Aided Design*, 10(10):1447–1459, November 1991.

[8] K. Nabors and J. White. Multipole-accelerated capacitance extraction for 3-d structures with multiple dielectrics. *IEEE Transactions on Circuits and Systems*, 39(11):946–954, November 1992.

[9] J. R. Philips and J. White. A precorrected-FFT method for capacitance extraction of complicated 3-d structures. In *International Conference on Computer-Aided Design*, November 1994.

[10] S. M. Rao, T. K. Sarkar, and R. F. Harrington. The electrostatic field of conducting bodies in multiple dielectric media. *IEEE Transactions on Microwave Theory and Techniques*, 32(11):1441–1448, November 1984.

[11] Y. Saad and M. H. Shultz. GMRES: A generalized minimal residual algorithm for solving nonsymmetric linear systems. *SIAM Journal on Scientific and Statistical Computing*, 7(3):856–869, July 1986.

[12] J. Stoer and R. Bulirsch. *Introduction to Numerical Analysis.* Springer-Verlag, New York, 1979.

[13] W. T. Weeks. Calculation of coefficients of capacitance of multiconductor transmission lines in the presence of a dielectric interface. *IEEE Transactions on Microwave Theory and Techniques*, 18(1):35–43, January 1970.

FastPep: A Fast Parasitic Extraction Program for Complex Three-Dimensional Geometries

Mattan Kamon* Nuno Marques+ Jacob White*

* Research Laboratory of Electronics
Dept. of Electrical Engineering and Computer Science
Massachusetts Institute of Technology
Cambridge, MA, 02139.

\+ INESC/Cadence European Labs.
Dept. of Electrical and Computer Engineering
Instituto Superior Técnico
Lisboa, 1000 Portugal

Abstract

In this paper we describe a computationally efficient approach to generating reduced-order models from PEEC-based three-dimensional electromagnetic analysis programs. It is shown that a recycled multipole-accelerated approach applied to recent model order reduction techniques requires nearly two orders of magnitude fewer floating point operations than direct techniques thus allowing the analysis of larger, more complex three-dimensional geometries.

1 Introduction

A well known approach to modeling coupled inductive and capacitive effects is the Partial Element Equivalent Circuit (PEEC) approach [1]. However, for complex three dimensional structures, the number of densely coupled circuit elements can be in the tens of thousands obviating the PEEC circuit's use in circuit simulators. Recent model order reduction approaches could be applied, but even computing the reduced model may be too computationally expensive. In this paper we describe a computationally efficient approach to generating low order models from these large circuit models. The approach is also ripe for acceleration techniques such as the Fast Multipole Method [2, 3] or the Precorrected-FFT [4] approach allowing the analysis of larger, more complex three-dimensional geometries.

In Section 2 we discuss the PEEC discretization from which we derive the large dense linear system describing the interconnect. In Section 3 we describe using recent model order reduction techniques to generate models for efficient coupled circuit-interconnect simulation, and describe methods of accelerating the computation. Finally in Section 4, we present results of this interconnect modeling tool called FASTPEP.

This work was supported by the Semiconductor Research Corporation, an AFOSR MURI Contract, and grants from Harris Semiconductor, Cadence Design Systems and the Portuguese JNICT programs PRAXIS XXI.

2 Formulation

In the area of interconnect analysis, perhaps the best known integral equation approach is the Partial Element Equivalent Circuit (PEEC) method [1]. To model current flow in the PEEC method, the interior of conductors is divided into a grid of volume *filaments*, each of which carries a constant current density along its length, as shown in Figure 1-a. To model charge accumulation, the surface of each conductor is covered with *panels*, each of which holds a constant charge density.

The interconnection of the filaments and panels, plus sources, $\boldsymbol{V}_t$, at the terminal pairs, generates a "circuit" whose solution gives the desired admittance parameters. Each filament is a branch of the circuit, as well as each panel as shown in Figure 1-b for a transmission line structure. For illustration, Figure 1-b coarsely models a two conductor line with terminating load Z_L. The length of the line is broken into three sections where each section consists of a bundle of three filaments. Two panels are connected at the nodes in between the sections. Each section of the line is broken into a bundle of filaments in order to model skin and proximity effects as shown in Figure 1-a.

The constitutive relations for the elements can be written as a single matrix in $\mathbb{C}^{b\times b}$, $b = f + p$, where f is the number of filaments and p the number of panels, by noting that the charge on the panels is related to current via $\boldsymbol{I}_b^p = \frac{d}{dt}\boldsymbol{q}_p$, and by viewing the node voltage at the panels as a branch voltage relative to ground, $\boldsymbol{V}_b^p = \boldsymbol{V}_n - 0$:

$$\boldsymbol{V}_b = \begin{bmatrix} \boldsymbol{V}_b^f \\ \boldsymbol{V}_b^p \end{bmatrix} = \begin{bmatrix} \boldsymbol{Z}_L & 0 \\ 0 & \boldsymbol{P}/s \end{bmatrix} \begin{bmatrix} \boldsymbol{I}_b^f \\ \boldsymbol{I}_b^p \end{bmatrix} = \boldsymbol{Z}\boldsymbol{I}_b, \quad (1)$$

where $s = j\omega$, $\boldsymbol{Z}_L\boldsymbol{I}_b^f \equiv (\boldsymbol{R} + s\boldsymbol{L})\boldsymbol{I}_b^f = \boldsymbol{V}_b^f$ with $\boldsymbol{L}$ as

1092-3152/97 $10.00 © 1997 IEEE

the dense filament partial inductance matrix, $\boldsymbol{R}$, the diagonal resistance matrix, and $\boldsymbol{V}_n = \boldsymbol{P}\boldsymbol{q}_p$ where $\boldsymbol{P}$ is the dense panel potential coefficient matrix.

To generate a system of equations, the circuit solution technique known as Mesh Analysis can be used whose solution gives the terminal admittance, $\boldsymbol{Y}_t$. The mesh approach has been used in the context of interconnect analysis in [5] and [6].

Kirchoff's voltage law, which implies that the sum of branch voltages around each mesh in the network must be zero, is represented by

$$\boldsymbol{M}\boldsymbol{V}_b = \begin{bmatrix} \boldsymbol{M}_f & \boldsymbol{M}_p \end{bmatrix} \begin{bmatrix} \boldsymbol{V}_b^f \\ \boldsymbol{V}_b^p \end{bmatrix} = \boldsymbol{V}_s \tag{2}$$

where $\boldsymbol{V}_s$ is the mostly zero vector of source voltages, $\boldsymbol{M}_f$ sums filament voltages, and $\boldsymbol{M}_p$ sums panel voltages. The mesh currents, $\boldsymbol{I}_m$, are related to the branch currents, $\boldsymbol{I}_b$ via $\boldsymbol{M}^t\boldsymbol{I}_m = \boldsymbol{I}_b$.

To write the system in a state space form, the mesh currents and panel voltages are assigned states similar to the nodal voltages and inductor currents in Modified Nodal Analysis. Combining Eqns. (1), and (2) yields a first order system in state space form,

$$\begin{aligned} s\mathcal{L}\,\boldsymbol{x} &= -\mathcal{R}\,\boldsymbol{x} + \boldsymbol{B}\,\boldsymbol{V}_t \\ \boldsymbol{I}_t &= \boldsymbol{B}^T\boldsymbol{x}. \end{aligned} \tag{3}$$

where

$$\boldsymbol{x} = \begin{bmatrix} \boldsymbol{I}_m \\ \boldsymbol{V}_b^p \end{bmatrix}, \boldsymbol{V}_t = \begin{bmatrix} \boldsymbol{V}_s \\ 0 \end{bmatrix}, \mathcal{L} = \begin{bmatrix} \boldsymbol{M}_f\boldsymbol{L}\boldsymbol{M}_f^t & 0 \\ 0 & \boldsymbol{P}^{-1} \end{bmatrix},$$

$$\mathcal{R} = \begin{bmatrix} \boldsymbol{M}_f\boldsymbol{R}\boldsymbol{M}_f^t & \boldsymbol{M}_p \\ -\boldsymbol{M}_p^t & 0 \end{bmatrix}, \boldsymbol{B} = \begin{bmatrix} \boldsymbol{I} \\ 0 \end{bmatrix}.$$

Since $\boldsymbol{R}$ is a diagonal matrix, and $\boldsymbol{M}_f$ and $\boldsymbol{M}_p$ are sparse, then $\mathcal{R}$ is sparse. However, to form the first block of $\mathcal{L}$ requires $O(f^2)$ operations and memory since $\boldsymbol{L} \in \mathbb{R}^{f\times f}$ is dense. Similarly, the second block, $\boldsymbol{P}^{-1}$, requires $O(p^2)$ operations and memory to form, and then $O(p^3)$ operations to invert. For complex geometries with tens of thousands of filaments and panels, such growth rates are severely limiting. In the next section we discuss a more efficient technique for generating reduced order models from (3).

3 Coupled Circuit-Interconnect Simulation and Passive Model Order Reduction

To design with the admittance information available from (3), it is necessary to perform coupled simulation with nonlinear devices, such as CMOS drivers and receivers. Nonlinear devices require time domain simulation, and thus the admittance information is necessary from DC conditions up to the highest frequency of interest in the circuit.

One approach to coupling the PEEC-based package models with circuits is to include (3) in a circuit simulator instead of solving for the terminal behavior [1]. This approach has the drawback that the size of the system in (3) can easily be very large if high-accuracy is desired. Another possibility is to construct and solve (3) for various values of ω and then use some rational fitting algorithm to compute a model for the package [7, 8]. However, a more computationally efficient approach is to apply model order reduction techniques to (3) to derive a smaller approximation for direct insertion into a circuit simulator.

3.1 Model Order Reduction

The idea of model order reduction is to reduce (3), which can be on the order of tens of thousands, to a much smaller system which still captures the dominant behavior of the original system. For moment matching techniques, one wishes to derive a rational function whose moments, or terms in the Taylor series expansion, match that of the original admittance function, $\boldsymbol{Y}_t(s)$, up to some order. From (3), the admittance function can be expanded about $s = 0$ as

$$\boldsymbol{Y}_t(s) = \boldsymbol{B}^T\left(\mathcal{R} + s\mathcal{L}\right)^{-1}\boldsymbol{B} = \sum_{k=0}^{\infty} \boldsymbol{m}_k s^k, \tag{4}$$

where the moments can be easily obtained from

$$\boldsymbol{m}_k = -\boldsymbol{B}^T(\mathcal{R}^{-1}\mathcal{L})^k\mathcal{R}^{-1}\boldsymbol{B}.$$

Thus we seek an approximation, $\tilde{\boldsymbol{Y}}_t(s) = \sum_{k=0}^{\infty} \tilde{\boldsymbol{m}}_k s^k$, such that $\tilde{\boldsymbol{m}}_k = \boldsymbol{m}_k, k = 1, \ldots, q$. Since $\boldsymbol{Y}_t(s)$ represents a passive circuit, we require $\tilde{\boldsymbol{Y}}_t(s)$ also be passive, which can be guaranteed via the numerically stable Arnoldi-based PRIMA model order reduction algorithm [9]. In order to apply PRIMA about $s = 0$, both $\mathcal{L}$ and $\mathcal{R}$ must be positive-semidefinite. The condition on $\mathcal{L}$ follows since $\boldsymbol{P}$ and $\boldsymbol{L}$ are positive definite. Also, since every filament is modeled as resistor in series with an inductor, $\mathcal{R}$ is both positive semidefinite and nonsingular.

3.2 Recycled iterative solver

Application of any moment matching scheme about $s = 0$ requires the computation of repeated matrix-vector products with the matrix $(\mathcal{R}^{-1}\mathcal{L})$ in order to obtain a reduced-order model. For instance, an

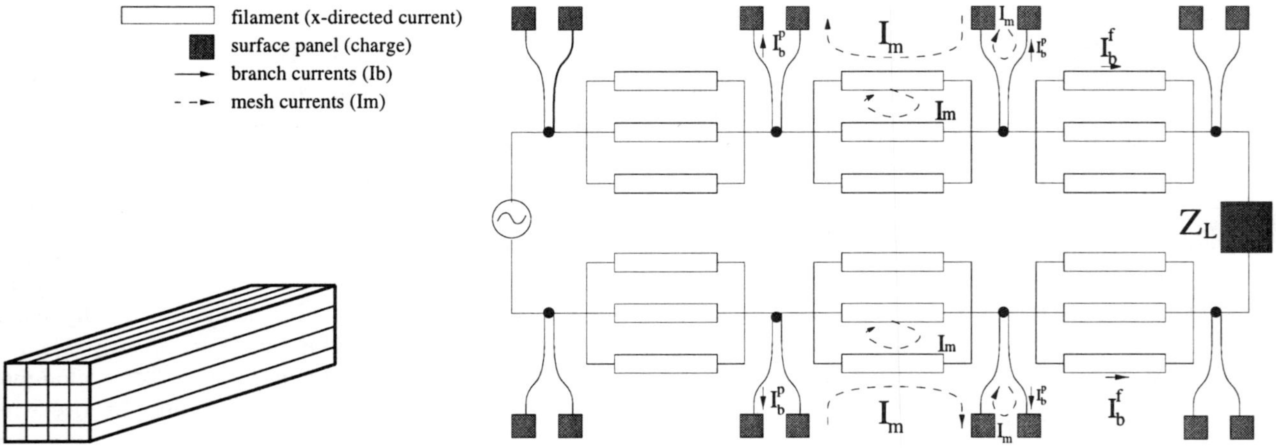

(a) (b)

Figure 1: a) A section of conductor and its bundle of volume filaments; b) A circuit describing the mesh quantities for two parallel conductors divided into 3 sections each.

Arnoldi type algorithm requires $q-1$ such products to produce an order q model. However, because the partial inductance matrix $\boldsymbol{L}$ and potential coefficient matrix, $\boldsymbol{P}^{-1}$, which appear in $\boldsymbol{\mathcal{L}}$, are both large and dense, many multiplications by $\boldsymbol{\mathcal{L}}$ can be prohibitively expensive. In particular, if done directly, multiplication by $\boldsymbol{P}^{-1}$, would require an initial dense matrix factorization which is $O(p^3)$ operations. For modern packaging structures, for which p exceeds ten thousand, such a factorization is prohibitive.

The expensive factorization can be avoided by noting that the computation $\boldsymbol{q} = \boldsymbol{P}^{-1}\boldsymbol{v}$ is equivalent to solving for the panel charges, $\boldsymbol{q}$, given a set of voltages, $\boldsymbol{v}$. It is thus possible to use a preconditioned, Krylov-subspace iterative method to solve $\boldsymbol{P}\boldsymbol{q} = \boldsymbol{v}$ as outlined in Algorithm 1 [10]. Note that the dominant cost of each iteration is the $O(p^2)$ computation of a dense matrix-vector product, $\boldsymbol{P}\boldsymbol{w}$, to acquire the next vector in the subspace.

In the standard approach, for every product $\boldsymbol{\mathcal{L}}\boldsymbol{x}$, the iterative algorithm would be called to solve $\boldsymbol{P}^{-1}\boldsymbol{v}$, generating a new subspace $span\{\boldsymbol{w}, \boldsymbol{P}\boldsymbol{w}, \boldsymbol{P}^2\boldsymbol{w}, \ldots\}$, and a new set of search direction, $\boldsymbol{w}_k$. If the number of $\boldsymbol{\mathcal{L}}\boldsymbol{x}$ products is large, the advantage of an iterative method would be degraded by the large number of total $\boldsymbol{P}\boldsymbol{w}$ products necessary. One is thus lead to consider reusing the search directions from the previous solves [11, 12]. While the recycled vectors are not optimal for the next $\boldsymbol{v}$, the cost of computing the solution along those directions is negligible compared to a single $\boldsymbol{P}\boldsymbol{w}$ product.

The $O(p^2)$ operations of the iterative algorithm can be reduced further by using a multipole-accelerated iterative algorithm [3] whose cost and memory has been shown to grow only as $O(p)$. Similarly, the computation of the product $\boldsymbol{M}_f\boldsymbol{L}\boldsymbol{M}_f^t$ can be performed in $O(f)$ operations also via the multipole-algorithm [5].

Algorithm **1 (Iterative Scheme for $\boldsymbol{P}\boldsymbol{q} = \boldsymbol{v}$)**

guess $\boldsymbol{q}^0$
Initialize the search direction
  $\boldsymbol{w}^0 = \boldsymbol{v} - \boldsymbol{P}\boldsymbol{q}^0$
for $k = 1, \ldots$ {
  Select $\boldsymbol{w}^k \in span\{\boldsymbol{w}^0, \boldsymbol{P}\boldsymbol{w}^0, \ldots, \boldsymbol{P}^{k-1}\boldsymbol{w}^0\}$
    such that the new solution
      $\boldsymbol{q}^k = \boldsymbol{q}^{k-1} + \boldsymbol{w}^k$
    minimizes $||\boldsymbol{r}^k|| = ||\boldsymbol{v} - \boldsymbol{P}\boldsymbol{q}^k||$
  if $||\boldsymbol{r}^k|| < tolerance$, return solution $\boldsymbol{q}^k$
}

4 Results

In this section we present results from the mesh formulated parasitic extraction program, FASTPEP. To verify that the formulation is correct, consider modeling a long two conductor transmission line with this 3D tool. The characteristic impedance of the line was computed as $Z_0 = 97.43\Omega$. By using a matched termination, $Z_L = Z_0$, the input impedance is constant, $Z(f) = Z_0$, for all frequencies f. To verify that the FASTPEP formulation is correct, the two conductors were taken to be $1cm$ long and discretized into 558 filaments, and 768 panels. Such a discretization leads to a 2033 state system. As seen from Figure 2, the full system matches closely to the exact solution. Notice

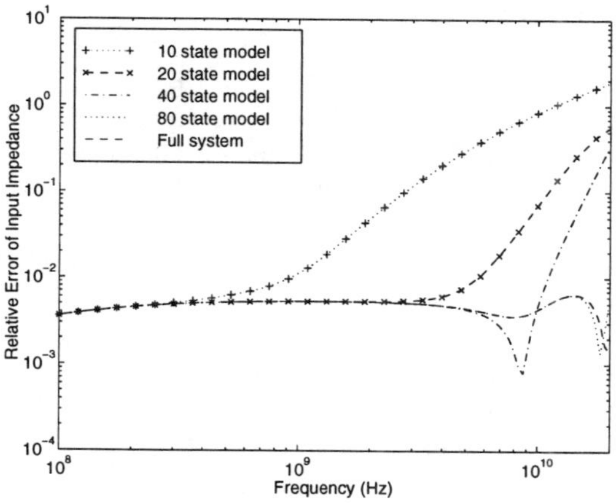

Figure 2: Relative error for models for matched transmission line

also that for a reduced order model with 1% error, a 20th order model is valid up to 6 GHz, a 40th order model up to 12 GHz, and an 80th order model past 20GHz (to about 26GHz).

Next, to demonstrate the efficiency of the recycled iterative scheme, consider refining the discretization of the transmission line of the previous example and extracting a 50th order model. Figure 3 shows the number of floating point operations (flops) required for direct factorization with back substitution, a non-recycled Krylov-subspace method, a recycled Krylov method, and multipole-accelerated recycled Krylov method, for various levels of discretization. Our implementation of FASTPEP uses direct matrix-vector products and thus the multipole-accelerated times are projected based on flop counts from multipole-accelerated capacitance and inductance codes [3, 5]. The error tolerance of the iterative algorithm was chosen such that the difference between models produced by the iterative scheme versus direct factorization differed by less than 1% up to 100 GHz. As can be seen from the figure for an original 15409 state system, the recycled scheme performs an order of magnitude faster than direct factorization, and similarly, the multipole algorithm would provide another order of magnitude speed up. Note that the CPU time comparison would be similar to the flop count comparison for the direct factorization and direct recycled iterative scheme, however the overhead in arranging the multipole computation would shift its curve slightly upward.

To demonstrate FASTPEP's utility as a 3D solver, consider analyzing a printed circuit board connector from Teradyne, Inc, as shown in Figure 4. The connector has four outer conductors and one middle ground conductor which widens in the center to provide shielding. Here the number of states in the original discretized system is 3018 which was generated from 845 filaments and 1182 panels. The results of generating models with 80 and 250 states are compared to the exact response in Figure 5. Note the strong improvement from 80 to 250 states.

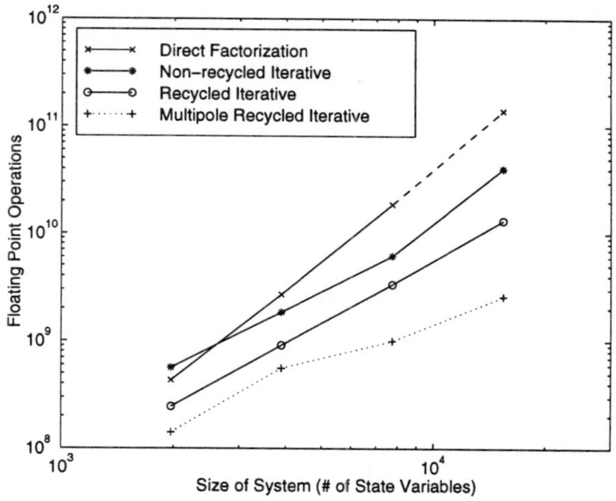

Figure 3: Flop count for different methods of computing $\boldsymbol{P}^{-1}\boldsymbol{x}$.

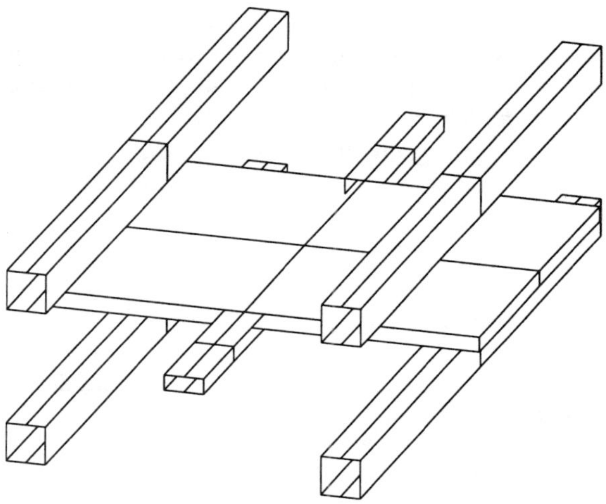

Figure 4: A 3D connector

5 Conclusions

In this paper we showed that combining a recycled Krylov-subspace iterative algorithm and multipole-acceleration with the PEEC method with Mesh Analysis can be used to efficiently generate low order models of three-dimensional interconnect structures.

As can be seen from Figure 5, a 250th order model

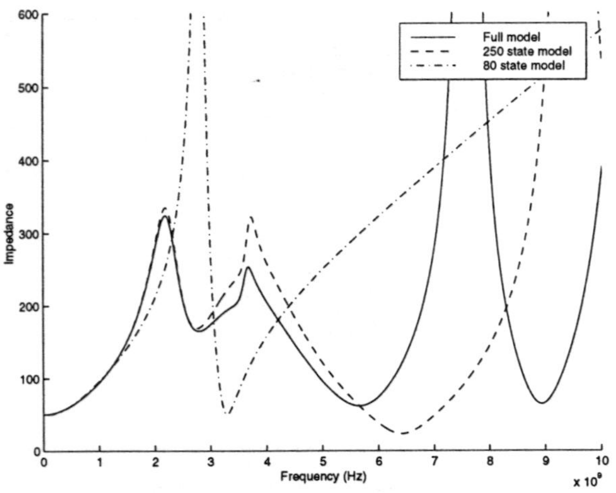

Figure 5: Various reduced order models for the connector

was needed to capture the response up to 3 GHz. Future work involves fast methods for generating models about expansion points other than $s = 0$ for more compact models.

The authors would like to thank Mark Gailus for the valuable discussions and the motivational example.

References

[1] Albert E. Ruehli. Equivalent Circuit Models for Three-Dimensional Multiconductor Systems. *IEEE Transactions on Microwave Theory and Techniques*, MTT-22(3):216–221, March 1974.

[2] L. Greengard and V. Rokhlin. A fast algorithm for particle simulations. *Journal of Computational Physics*, 73(2):325–348, December 1987.

[3] K. Nabors and J. White. Fast capacitance extraction of general three-dimensional structures. *IEEE Trans. on Microwave Theory and Techniques*, June 1992.

[4] J. R. Phillips. Error and complexity analysis for a collocation-grid-projection plus precorrected-FFT algorithm for solving potential integral equations with Laplace or Helmholtz kernels. In *Proceedings of the 1995 Copper Mountain Conference on Multigrid Methods*, April 1995.

[5] M. Kamon, M. J. Tsuk, and J. White. Fasthenry: A multipole-accelerated 3-d inductance extraction program. *IEEE Transactions on Microwave Theory and Techniques*, 42(9):1750–1758, September 1994.

[6] J. Garrett, A. Ruehli, and C. Paul. Efficient frequency domain solutions for sPEEC EFIE for modeling 3d geometries. In *Proceedings of the Zurich Symposium on Electromagnetic Compatibility*, pages 179–184, Zurich, Switzerland, March 1995.

[7] L. Miguel Silveira, Ibrahim M. Elfadel, Jacob K. White, Monirama Chilukura, and Kenneth S. Kundert. Efficient Frequency-Domain Modeling and Circuit Simulation of Transmission Lines. *IEEE Transactions on Components, Packaging, and Manufacturing Technology - Part B: Advanced Packaging*, 17(4):505–513, November 1994.

[8] Tuyen V. Nguyen, Jing Li, and Zhaojun Bai. Dispersive coupled transmission line simulation using an adaptive block lanczos algorithm. In *International Custom Integrated Circuits Conference*, pages 457–460, 1996.

[9] Altan Odabasioglu, Mustafa Celik, and Lawrence Pileggi. Prima: Passive reduced-order interconnect macromodeling algorithm. *CMU Report*, 1997.

[10] Yousef Saad. *Iterative Methods for Sparse Linear Systems.* PWS Publishing Company, 1995.

[11] R. Telichevesky, K. Kundert, and J White. Efficient AC and noise analysis of two-tone RF circuits. In *Proceedings 33rd Design Automation Conference*, Las Vegas, Nevada, June 1996.

[12] J. R. Phillips, E. Chiprout, and D. D. Ling. Efficient full-wave electromagnetic analysis via model-order reduction of fast integral transforms. In *Proceedings 33rd Design Automation Conference*, Las Vegas, Nevada, June 1996.

Transform Domain Techniques for Efficient Extraction of Substrate Parasitics

Ranjit Gharpurey and Srinath Hosur
DSPSR&D Center, Texas Instruments Inc., Dallas, TX 75243

Abstract

A semi-analytical technique for computation of the frequency-behavior of silicon substrates is demonstrated. The technique uses a boundary element approach, that utilizes the complex substrate Green Function and the two-dimensional Fast Fourier Transform. The resultant dense system matrix is sparsified by application of orthogonal transform operators on the matrix representing the system. Three transform operators are evaluated for this purpose - the Discrete Cosine Transform (DCT), the Discrete Wavelet Transform (DWT) and the Discrete Hadamard Transform (DHT). The application of any one of these operators provides a rigorous sparsification technique, which significantly reduces the computation time.

The Green Function is computed in the two layers at the top of the substrate. This is done so that contacts in the oxide layer can be included in the substrate model, along with contacts in the silicon substrate. Hence, substrate loss terms in metal interconnect lines and in line-to-line interaction models, can be evaluated using this technique. Extraction of a simple circuit-simulator compatible model from frequency-domain data is discussed.

1: Introduction

Increasing frequencies of operation of silicon circuits have exacerbated the problem of isolation in integrated circuits. An accurate determination of circuit parasitics, including finite substrate impedance, is essential for meaningful circuit simulation. Silicon substrates have been treated as purely resistive in the past [1], [2], [3]. The resistive approximation is valid only when the dielectric relaxation times of the layers composing the substrate cause an insignificant reactance at the highest frequencies of interest. This may not be the case in general, especially above a GHz, where silicon circuits are finding increasing application. Harmonics generated by circuit non-linearities can also exist in the frequency range in which reactive effects are of importance. Modeling of bond-pad losses, substrate losses of metal interconnect lines and substrate losses in line-to-line coupling are also important, especially in RF circuit design. Numerical techniques for frequency-dependent substrate modeling have been presented in the past [4], [5]. However the requirement for fine meshes makes these techniques slow for medium and large size problems.

The substrate is modeled as a layered lossy dielectric (Fig. 1), in the technique presented here, with each dielectric layer characterized by a complex dielectric constant.

$$\varepsilon = \varepsilon_r - j\varepsilon_i \tag{1}$$

The loss term equals the conductivity of the layer divided by the frequency of operation. The boundary conditions assumed on each surface are shown in Fig. 1.

The theory underlying the method is outlined in the next section. Extensive reference is made here to the technique presented in [1], which was also based on a boundary element formulation. In [1], substrates were considered purely resistive. Contacts were restricted to the top-most layer (Fig. 1) of the substrate, and were of zero-thickness. In the work presented here, the top-most layer is assumed to be oxide dielectric. Hence substrate contacts are in the second layer from the surface. The finite thickness of the contacts is also modeled, as discussed in the next section.

One of the problems with the application of the Boundary Element Technique is that the method yields a dense system of equations. Inversion of the resultant matrices is an $O(N^3)$ process, for NxN matrices. Thus, treating large problems becomes progressively difficult with increasing N. Heuristics have been presented in [1], [2] and [3] for solving this system, where contacts at a sufficient distance from a particular contact are lumped together. However, a more rigorous approach is to solve the system of equation in a transform domain, where some of the off-diagonal matrix-elements are made negligibly small by application of the transform operator. Application of such techniques in image processing for compression are well known [6]. The operators considered in our work include the DCT, the DWT and the DHT. These techniques are discussed in Section 3.

Contacts are treated as equipotential regions. The contact-to-contact complex impedance is extracted at certain discrete frequencies and appropriate passive element models are computed from the complex data, as shown in Section 4. These passive element models can be included in circuit simulators.

2: Theory: The Substrate Green Function and Coefficients of Potential

The technique uses the Green function of the medium which provides the potential at point $\mathbf{r}_1$ due to a point charge at $\mathbf{r}_2$. An arbitrary point $\mathbf{r}$ is defined by its coordinates in the cartesian system, i.e. (x,y,z). The lateral extent of the coordinates is given by the range [0,a] and [0,b], in the X and Y directions respectively. The vertical extent of $\mathbf{r}$ is limited to any location in the top two layers of the substrate.

Following the methodology of [1], in order to compute the contact-to-contact impedance matrix, a coefficient-of-potential matrix is generated at first, using the substrate Green function in a convolution integral. The matrix is then inverted to obtain a coefficient of induction matrix. As in [1], the coefficient of potential matrix is denoted by $[P]$, where each element p_{ij} represents the average potential induced on contact-i due to a unit charge on contact-j. In the remainder of this section, the computation and properties of the complex ratio p_{ij} will be discussed.

Three formulations are described for p_{ij}. The case when both contacts are in silicon or one contact is in silicon and the other contact is in oxide is described in section 2.1. The case when both contacts are in oxide is similar to the case described in [1] and is discussed in section 2.2.

2.1: Contacts defined in Silicon

Consider two contacts i and j with corner XY coordinates given by $(a_1,b_1):(a_2,b_2)$ and $(a_3,b_3):(a_4,b_4)$ respectively. Also assume that contact-i is at a depth of z_1 from the surface and contact-j is at a depth of z_2 from the sur

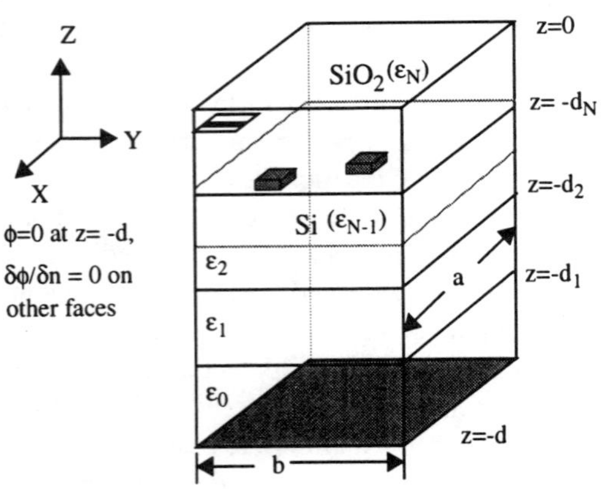

FIGURE 1: Cross-Section of Substrate

face. It can be shown, using a method similar to [2], that the coefficient p_{ij} defined above is given by a two-dimensional series

$$p_{ij} = p_{ij}^{00} + \sum_{m=0}^{\infty}\sum_{n=0}^{\infty} C_{mn} \cdot k_{mn}^{N1}(z_1,z_2)(\eta_i \cdot \eta_j) \quad (2)$$

where $N1= N\text{-}1$ and $C_{mn} = 4$ for $(m,n)>0$, $C_{mn} = 2$ for $(m=0$ or $n=0)$ and $C_{mn} = 0$ for $(m=n=0)$. The term for $m=n=0$, i.e. p_{ij}^{00} is given by

$$p_{ij}^{00} = (\beta_{N1}^{00} \cdot z_l + \Gamma_{N1}^{00})/(ab\beta_{N1}^{00}\varepsilon_{N1}) \quad (3)$$

β_{N1}^{00} and Γ_{N1}^{00} are computed iteratively as shown below for k=N1.

$$\begin{bmatrix}\beta_k\\ \Gamma_k\end{bmatrix} = \begin{bmatrix}\dfrac{\varepsilon_{k-1}}{\varepsilon_k} & 0\\ \left(\dfrac{\varepsilon_{k-1}}{\varepsilon_k}-1\right)d_k & 1\end{bmatrix}\begin{bmatrix}\beta_{k-1}\\ \Gamma_{k-1}\end{bmatrix} \quad (4)$$

where $\beta_0 = 1.0$, $\Gamma_0 = d$ and $k \in [1, N]$. The other terms in (2) are defined below.

$$\eta_i = ab\frac{(\sin(\delta a_2) - \sin(\delta a_1))(\sin(\zeta b_2) - \sin(\zeta b_1))}{(a_2 - a_1)(b_2 - b_1) \cdot mn\pi^2}$$

$$\eta_j = ab\frac{(\sin(\delta a_4) - \sin(\delta a_3))(\sin(\zeta b_4) - \sin(\zeta b_3))}{(a_4 - a_3)(b_4 - b_3) \cdot mn\pi^2}$$

where $\delta = m\pi/a, \zeta = n\pi/b$.

$$k_{mn}^{N1}(z_l,z_u) = \frac{g_{mn}^{N1}\cosh(\gamma(z_l + d_N)) + \sinh(\gamma(z_l + d_N))}{(ab\gamma\varepsilon_{N1})\left(1 + g_{mn}^{N1}\left(\dfrac{\varepsilon_N}{\varepsilon_{N1}}\right)\tanh(\gamma d_N)\right)} \times$$

$$\left(\cosh(\gamma\overline{z_u + d_N}) - \left(\frac{\varepsilon_N}{\varepsilon_{N1}}\right)\sinh(\gamma\overline{z_u + d_N})\tanh(\gamma d_N)\right) \quad (5)$$

where $\gamma = \sqrt{\delta^2 + \zeta^2}$, $z_u = max(z_1,z_2)$ and $z_l = min(z_1,z_2)$, and

$$g_{mn}^{N1} = \left(\frac{\beta_{N1}\tan h(\gamma(d - d_N)) + \Gamma_{N1}}{\beta_{N1} + \Gamma_{N1}\tan h(\gamma(d - d_N))}\right) \quad (6)$$

β_{N1} and Γ_{N1} are derived as shown below, for k=N1.

$$\begin{bmatrix}\beta_k\\ \Gamma_k\end{bmatrix} = \begin{bmatrix}\left(\dfrac{\varepsilon_{k-1}}{\varepsilon_k}\right) - \theta_k^2 & \left(\dfrac{\varepsilon_{k-1}}{\varepsilon_k} - 1\right)\theta_k\\ \left(1 - \dfrac{\varepsilon_{k-1}}{\varepsilon_k}\right)\theta_k & 1 - \dfrac{\varepsilon_{k-1}}{\varepsilon_k}\theta_k^2\end{bmatrix}\begin{bmatrix}\beta_{k-1}\\ \Gamma_{k-1}\end{bmatrix} \quad (7)$$

where $\theta_k = \tan h(\gamma_{mn} \times (d - d_k))$, $\beta_0 = 1.0$, $\Gamma_0 = 0$

Equation (2) is computed by using the Discrete Cosine Transform as discussed in [1]. The DCT has complex coefficients in the case discussed here.

The form for p_{ij} discussed here is used when all contacts are in silicon, and the finite thickness of the contacts is to be taken into account. This form is useful in a majority of the cases, when the substrate parasitic is required for devices. Using the finite-contact thickness is important, especially for contacts that are in close proximity.

When one contact is in silicon and the other in oxide, the continuity in potential at the silicon-oxide interface provides us with a convenient way to compute the coefficients k_{mn}. If we assume that z_l is in silicon and z_u is in the oxide, then we have

$$k_{mn}(z_l, z_u) = k_{mn}(z_l, -d_N)\left(\frac{\cosh(\gamma z_u)}{\cosh(\gamma d_N)}\right) \quad (8)$$

where $k_{mn}(z_l, -d_N)$ is computed from (5). Eq. (8) assumes that the unit charge is placed on the contact in silicon and the potential is observed in oxide. The converse case is identical owing to the symmetry of p_{ij} under exchange of i and j. The expression for p_{ij}^{∞} is identical to (3).

2.2: Contacts in Oxide

When both the contacts considered are located in the oxide layer, the expression for p_{ij} is similar to (2). The expression for p_{ij}^{00} in this case is given by (3) with the subscript $N1$ being replaced by N, indicating computation in the surface layer. The coefficients k_{mn} are given by

$$k_{mn}(z_1, z_2) = \frac{g_{mn}^{N}\cosh(\gamma z_l) + \sinh(\gamma z_l)}{(ab\gamma\varepsilon_N)} \times \cosh(\gamma z_u) \quad (9)$$

g^N_{mn} is given by (6) with $N1$ replaced by N and $\gamma(d-d_N)$ replaced by (γd).

2.3: Modeling of Finite Contact-Thickness

To model contact thickness, the upper and lower surfaces of contacts are treated independently as contacts of zero thickness and extracted as such. After extraction, the resultant matrix is reduced by combining together the top and the bottom plates of the contacts. This is electrically equivalent to shorting the top and the bottom plates together. This procedure is justified when the lateral size of the contacts is much larger than the distance between the top and the bottom plates, since the lateral field in the region between the plates will be negligible in this case.

For computational reasons, the contact bottom plates are modeled at any one of M discrete depth levels which is the closest to the real depth of the contact. This is done because modeling M levels requires computation of M(M+1)/2 DCT coefficients. Thus using a continuum of depths is not desirable.

While M(M+1)/2 DCTs need to be computed, all the DCT coefficients do not have to be stored. This is because optimization of layout for minimizing substrate coupling does not require modeling the finite depth of junctions. Layout optimization can be performed assuming zero-depth contacts. Once the coordinates of the contacts are fixed, an accurate extraction is performed. However in this case, only those DCT coefficients that are applicable to the given layout are stored [2].

Contacts are usually sub-divided into finer contacts for higher accuracy. With each contact modeled by its top-plate and bottom-plate the number of sub-contacts in the problem can become very large. This can be avoided by using a much smaller number of sub-contacts on one of the plates.

3: Matrix Sparsification

As remarked earlier, the system of equations resulting from the earlier section ([P][Q]=[V], see [1]), is dense. As such, as the size of [P] (NxN) increases, computation time goes up as N^3. Direct inversion of [P] should therefore be avoided for large values of N. In [1], [2] and [3], heuristics for reducing the size of the matrix have been demonstrated, by using a multipole-like approach to the problem. It is difficult to estimate in these methods, a priori, the size of the bounding box beyond which the panels may be approximated.

In solving the above system of equations, minimal computations are required if the matrix [P] is diagonal. Thus, if [P] can be reduced to a near diagonal matrix or a matrix with a sparse structure by some transformation, we could take advantage of this sparsity to reduce computational time and storage. For a general [P], the eigen-decomposition results in a diagonal matrix. However, this requires $O(N^3)$ computations. If [P] is a circulant matrix its Fourier transform is diagonal. This observation motivates us to try and use different orthonormal transformations to obtain a sparse structure for a general [P] in the transform domain.

In this work, we solve the system of equations in a transform domain, by first applying the transformation operator to the matrix [P], and [V], and then solving the resultant system of equations given by

$$[A]^T[P][A][Q]' = [A]^T[V] \quad (10)$$

$$[Q] = [A][Q]' \quad (11)$$

where [A] is the matrix representation of the transformation operator. The operator [A] is unitary and orthonormal. The operators are chosen such that the energy is concentrated in a few elements in the transform domain, and most elements can be neglected, because their relative magnitude is small. Doing so makes the matrix sparse. The relative error in the solution vector [Q] is bounded by $\kappa\|\delta(A^TPA)\|/\|A^TPA\|$, where κ is the condition number of [P]. The quantity $\delta(A^TPA)$ is made small by appropriate choice of $[A]$ in order to minimize the error in the approximation. It should be observed that the matrix $[P]$ representing a boundary value problem is generally ill-conditioned, implying a large value of κ. Thus it is important to choose the appropriate $[A]$. Also, different choices of $[A]$ leads to different sparsity structures depending on the structure of $[P]$. For example, if $[P]$ is circulant, a Fourier transform diagonalizes $[P]$, therefore for this case it is the best choice. In this paper, three operators were evaluated and compared. These are the DCT, the DWT and the DHT.

The Discrete Cosine Transform (DCT)

The DCT is used extensively for compressing speech and video information. We therefore use it in the analogous application suggested here. Any of the several forms of DCT documented in literature can be used [6].

As an example, in this paper, we consider the following matrix representation for the DCT.

$$a_{ij} = \sqrt{\frac{2}{N}}k_i \cos\left(\pi i\left(j + \frac{1}{2}\right)/N\right) \quad (12)$$

where $k_i=1/2^{0.5}$ for $i = 0$ or N, else $k_i=1$.

The Discrete Wavelet Transform (DWT)

The DWT, unlike the DCT or the Fourier transform uses basis functions which have a finite support. This implies that when a DWT is applied on a step, the discontinuity is localized to a few transform coefficients. In contrast, when a DCT is applied on a step, the effect discontinuity is spread over all DCT coefficients. This property of the DWT makes it an obvious choice for our application. The DWT matrix $[\Psi]$ can be written as the product

$$[\Psi] = [\Psi_{\log_2(N)}][\Psi_{\log_2(N)-1}]\ldots[\Psi_2][\Psi_1], \quad (13)$$

where each matrix $[\Psi_k]$ can be written as

$$[\Psi_k] = \begin{bmatrix} \begin{bmatrix} I_{N-2^{\log_2 N-k+1}} \end{bmatrix} & [0] \\ [0] & [D_k] \end{bmatrix}, \quad (14)$$

where $[I_l]$ is an lxl identity matrix and [0] denotes a null matrix. For a dyadic DWT, the $(N/2^{k-1})$x$(N/2^{k-1})$ matrix $[D_k]$ is composed of two $(N/2^k)$x$(N/2^{k-1})$ sub-matrices which are obtained as follows: the first row of the first $(N/2^k)$x$(N/2^{k-1})$ sub-matrix is the wavelet filter coefficient vector $[c]$, padded appropriately by zeros. Each of the remaining rows is then obtained by a circular shift of the immediate previous row by two elements. The second $(N/2^k)$x$(N/2^{k-1})$ portion of $[D_k]$ is obtained similarly, but with its first row as $[d]$ padded appropriately by zeros. The elements of $[d]$ are given as

$$d_l = (-1)^l c_{M-l-1}, 0 \le l \le M-1, \quad (15)$$

where M is the length of the vector $[c]$. While $[c]$ can be chosen to correspond to any of the several different known wavelets, in our work, we use the $[c]$ corresponding to Haar wavelet due to its computational simplicity.

The Discrete Hadamard Transform (DHT)

The DHT operator matrix of order 2^N is generated by the following algorithm

$$[H_N] = \frac{1}{\sqrt{N}}\begin{bmatrix} H_{N-1} & H_{N-1}^T \\ H_{N-1}^T & -H_{N-1} \end{bmatrix}, \quad (16)$$

where $H_1 = 1$. The DHT is of interest because of its computational simplicity.

It should be noted that each of the above transforms is of size 2^N, where N is an integer. Thus, the size of the matrix $[P]$ is restricted to 2^N.

Simulation experiments show that the DWT and the DHT have the highest efficiency in terms of the number of elements that are below a threshold, post-transformation. This is shown in the fill-in maps of a sample matrix [P], for a five node problem, where the size of the matrix is 512x512 (Fig. 2a-d) and the threshold is 1e-3.

Application of the DHT operator to the matrix $[P]$ is more computationally efficient because it involves mere additions and subtractions. Generation of the DHT operator can be done as shown in (16) above, or from an FFT butterfly operation, with the butterfly coefficients set to 1, which makes the computation trivial. Also, it was seen that if each of the contacts is divided into powers of two number of panels, the DHT offers significant sparsification (Fig.2d). Combined with its low computational complexity, the DHT therefore offers significant promise.

Z(Ω)	DCT	DWT	DHT	Full Inv
Z_{12}	1152-i 1.9	2837-i 17	2883-i 12.3	2895-i 11
Z_{13}	494-i 2	568-i 1.8	591-i 1.8	586-i 1.76
Z_{14}	2424+i 24	2712-i 17	2695- i 10	2822-i 10.9
Z_{15}	964-i 3.1	942-i 2.4	986-i 3.6	995-i 3.64

TABLE 1. Impedance values (powers-of-2 contact divisions)

Z(Ω)	DCT	DWT	DHT	Full Inv
Z_{12}	694-i 11.9	3177-i 14	2520-i 79	2847-i 11
Z_{13}	1171-i 58	575-i 1.9	591-i 0.6	577-i 1.76
Z_{14}	1369+i 37	2442-i 27	1739- i 49	2761-i 10.5
Z_{15}	953-i 10.9	954-i 3.7	953-i 18	1003-i 3.67

TABLE 2. Impedance values (non-powers-of-2 contact divisions)

The sparse matrices generated above using the DWT can be used directly in a Cholesky decomposition [7]. Those generated by the other transforms do not in general have a form suitable for LU decomposition. The Cuthill-McKee algorithm [8] has been used to permute the rows and columns, so as to reduce the bandwidth of the matrix. Finally, a brief comparison is shown in Tables 1 & 2 for the resistance and reactance of a five-node problem, with 512x512 divisions is shown, for all three transforms, with an error threshold of 1e-3 compared to the maximum value of the matrix. The resistance and reactance at 1GHz, connecting the first node to the other four nodes, are shown in the tables. Table 1 shows the impedance values when the contacts are divided in powers of two. Table 2 shows the impedance values when the number of divisions are not powers of 2. The substrate is two layered silicon with surface layer resistivity of 0.1Ω–cm and bulk resistivity of 1Ω–cm, with a dielectric permittivity of 11.

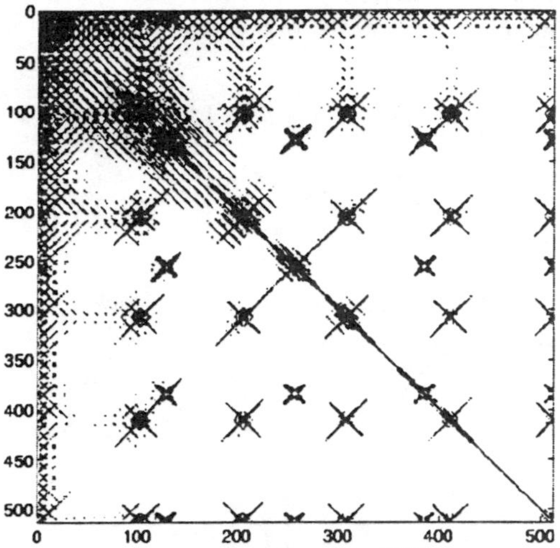

FIGURE 2a. Fill In Pattern with DCT

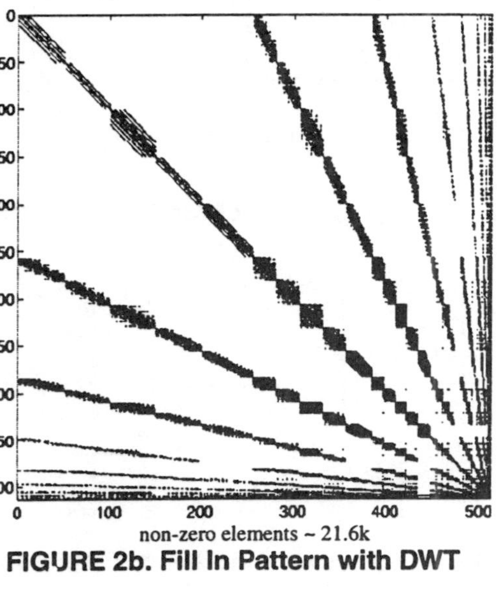

FIGURE 2b. Fill In Pattern with DWT

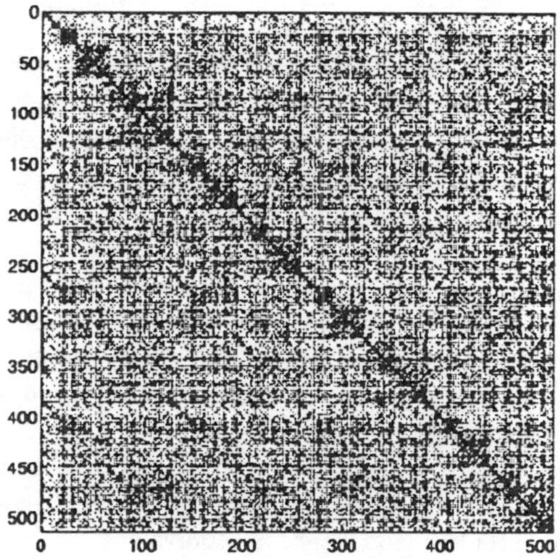

FIGURE 2c. Fill In Pattern with DHT (non-powers-of-two divisions)

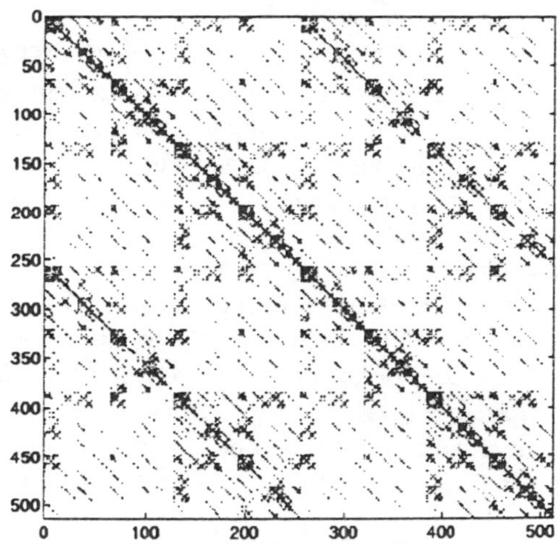

FIGURE 2d: Fill in Pattern with DHT (powers-of-two divisions)

It can be observed from the above tables that for a threshold of 1e-3, the DWT offers a very good match in both cases. The DHT is accurate for the case shown in Table 1. It can be seen from Fig. 2d that the fill-in for this case is the minimum. The DCT does not provide good results for either case[1], although the results are comparatively better for powers-of-two sub-divisions.

4: Extraction of Simulator-Compatible Models

The boundary element technique shown here is a frequency domain method. The impedances in the substrate

1. The DCT gave good results (to within 5%) with a threshold of 1e-4.

problem are evaluated at discrete frequencies. In order to include the substrate-model in a circuit simulator such as SPICE, it is necessary to model the contact-to-contact impedance by equivalent passive elements.

The substrate impedance at the surface consists of an infinite number of poles and zeroes, because of the distributed nature of the problem. A simple scheme to model the impedance is to extract the impedance at several frequencies, and fit it with the numerator and denominator polynomials, in ω, of an approximate rational function. The number of frequencies computed will determine the number of poles and zeroes included in the approximate model. Increasing the order of the approximation will, in general, result in a closer match to the correct solution. This procedure fits a reduced order polynomial to an infinite-pole problem and hence is equivalent to the Pade approximation [9]. A passive element (RCLM) model can be generated from the polynomials described above, provided that the representation of the impedance is a Positive Real Function as discussed in [10].

This technique results in good fits, but the substrate mesh size increases as $O(M^2)$, where M is the number of substrate contacts, which is usually undesirable. Additionally the DCT of the substrate Green Function has to be computed at K frequency points, where K is the sum of the number of poles and zeroes in the impedance function, which also increases the computation time.

We therefore restrict the polynomial orders to a maximum of two poles. Typically a one pole (RC) match is developed, by considering the low-frequency impedance and the impedance near its 3dB roll-off point.

This approximation yields good results as can be seen from the example below in Fig. 3. The figure shows the impedance elements Z_{12}, Z_{10} and Z_{20} for two square contacts, 100μm to a side spaced at 50μm separation, where 0 signifies the backplane. The exact model is extracted by sweeping the frequency from 0.1GHz to 20GHz in steps of 0.1GHz. The substrate is a low-resistivity type [1], with a 10μm thick p-layer (10 Ωcm) and a 5μm thick oxide. The bulk layer is 100μm thick (0.1 Ωcm).

It was observed in our work, that at very high frequencies (> ~20GHz), in epi substrates (e.g. p on p+), the real part of the impedance Z_{12}, became negative (Fig. 3). This behavior of the impedance is not unphysical, within the electrostatic approximation. At sufficiently high frequencies, the impedance in the epi-layer appears primarily capacitive, while the impedance in the bulk region remains resistive. Thus the substrate impedance can be represented by the intuitive model shown in Fig. 4. A Y-Δ transform of the model shows that the real part of Z_{12} is indeed negative. Since the substrate extractor generates a Δ model of the substrate, the negative real part is expected. At low frequencies, the epi-layer does not look capacitive, and therefore the real part of Z_{12} is positive.

The above behavior of Z_{12}, cannot be modeled by a passive RCLM single-port impedance. This is so because the positive real condition mentioned earlier is violated. The simple model shown in Fig. 3 cannot model this behavior. This problem will be addressed later. It should be observed, however, that this issue arises at frequencies in the region of 20GHz for practical substrates. Behavior up to this frequency is well modeled by the simple model shown below. This behavior is not observed in p- on p substrates described in [1].

5: Conclusions

A technique for extraction of substrate models at high frequencies has been presented. The technique can be applied to problems of very large size, with reasonable computational cost, by use of the operator-based matrix sparsification techniques. The DWT and DHT operators were found to be very effective. Frequency domain models

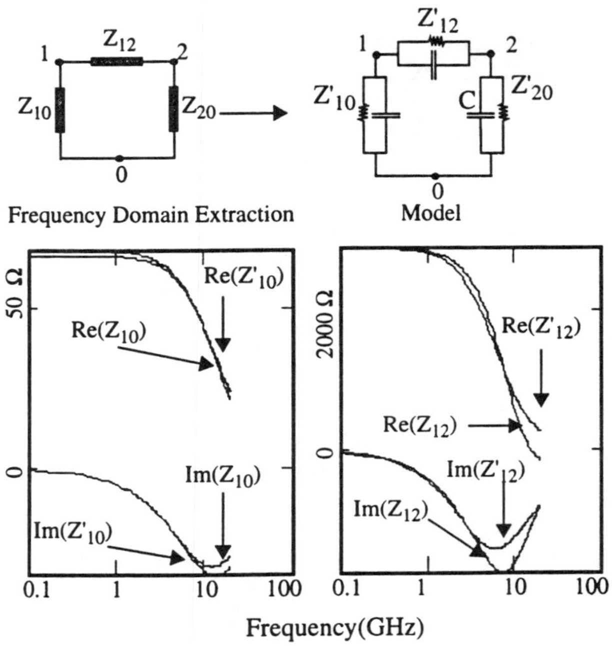

FIGURE 3: Comparison of Model and Frequency Data

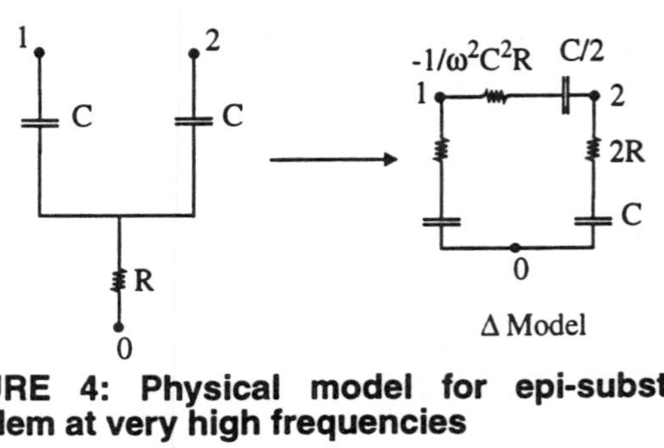

FIGURE 4: Physical model for epi-substrate problem at very high frequencies

consisting of passive elements were extracted. Low-order approximations are employed to avoid unnecessary increase in computation complexity in the circuit simulation, while preserving the essentials of the frequency response of the substrate. High order models can however be synthesized with an appropriate choice of test frequencies, to generate positive real impedance transfer functions.

6: Acknowledgments

Helpful comments and discussions with Kannan Krishna of TI-DSPRDC are gratefully acknowledged. Thanks are also due to Ali Niknejad of UC Berkeley for useful discussions.

7: References

[1]"*Modeling and Analysis of Substrate Coupling in Integrated Circuits*", R. Gharpurey and R. G. Meyer, IEEE Journal of Solid State Circuits, March 96, Vol. 31.

[2]"*Modeling and Analysis of Substrate Coupling in Integrated Circuits*", R. Gharpurey, ERL-U.C.Berkeley, ERL #M95/47.

[3]"*Verification Techniques for Substrate Coupling and their Application to Mixed-Signal IC Design*", N. K. Verghese, D. A. Allstot and M. A. Wolfe, IEEE Journal of Solid State Circuits, March 96, Vol. 31.

[4]"*A Unified Approach to Simulating Electrical and Thermal Substrate Coupling Interactions in ICs*", N. K. Verghese, S. S. Lee and D. J. Allstot, ICCAD Digest of Technical Papers, Santa Clara, USA, Nov. 7-11, 1993.

[5]"*Modeling Substrate Effects in the Design of High-Speed Bipolar ICs*", M. Pfost, H. Rein and T. Holzwarth, IEEE-Journal of Solid State Circuits, Oct. 96, Vol. 31.

[6]"*Discrete Cosine Transform, Algorithms, Applications, Advantages*", K. R. Rao and P. Yip, Boston, Academic Press, 1990.

[7]"*Fast Positive Definite Linear System Solvers*", A.H. Tewfik and M. Kim, IEEE Trans. Signal Processing, vol. 42, no. 3, pp. 572-585, March 1994.

[8]"*Sparse Matrices*", R. P. Tewarson, New York: Academic Press, 1973.

[9]"*Essentials of Pade Approximants*", G. A. Baker, Academic Press, 1975.

[10]"*Introduction to Circuit Synthesis and Design*", Gabor C. Temes and Jack W. LaPatra, McGraw Hill Inc., 1977.

SESSION 8A

EMBEDDED TUTORIAL: EDA AND THE NETWORK

Moderator:

David Ku, Escalade Corp., Santa Clara, CA

EDA and the Network

Mark D. Spiller and A. Richard Newton
Department of Electrical Engineering and Computer Sciences
University of California at Berkeley

Abstract

Digital computer networks are playing an increasingly important role in the evaluation, distribution, integration, and management of EDA systems. Tools, libraries, design data, and a variety of both design and manufacturing services are accessible today via networks. Networks are also playing a central role in the integration of system design teams, teams that involve a variety of both business and technical disciplines as well as widely distributed geographical locations. Throughout the history of EDA, the architectures used to integrate and distribute computation and interaction have played a central role in the overall design methodology and so have had a major, indirect impact on the choice of the most effective tools, algorithms, and data structures. In this paper, a number of the factors involved in the choice of a suitable architecture for EDA integration are reviewed and a number of ongoing developments and challenges are presented.

1. Introduction

From the very earliest days of Electronic Design Automation (EDA) more than thirty years ago, the particular *computing infrastructure* available to chip designers, EDA tool developers, and EDA system integrators has played a key role in determining overall chip design methodology. In so doing, it has also played a major role in establishing the resulting tool architectures and algorithms used to implement design systems.

By computing infrastructure we mean all of the general-purpose facilities, both hardware and software, used by EDA professionals and designers to do their job. Today, these include operating systems, storage systems, programming languages and development environments, user interaction technologies in both hardware and software, and, of course, computer networks.

Over the past three decades, there have been a number of significant changes in computer infrastructure and every change has brought with it a significant change in research emphasis as well as to the EDA industry. Computer-Aided Design (CAD) programs were originally designed for batch-input, line printer output (e.g. Spice[1]), and formed the basis of the CAD tool industry. With the advent of multitasking operating systems and direct inter-program communication (e.g. Multics[2], Unix[3]), along with "personal minicomputers" (i.e. workstations), the concept of the *software tool* was introduced to electronic system design and the EDA industry was established in the early 1980s. We have seen the impact of similar changes in user interaction technologies. For example, symbolic layout entry moved from character-based CRT approaches[4], to stick diagrams on vector displays[5], to today's raster fill abstractions (e.g. [6,7]). In each case, the layout methodology that could be expressed by the display hardware and associated software ultimately determined the layout data structure and most suitable compaction algorithm.

This infrastructure is always evolving and at certain times the changes are so profound that they have an almost revolutionary impact on EDA. We believe that the explosive growth in the development of wide-area network infrastructure over the past few years and into the next century, especially the Internet, along with significant developments in user interaction hardware and software (e.g. high-performance video and 3D graphics technologies) can fuel another revolution in the way EDA systems are organized and so how the industry itself is structured. We say "can" rather than "will" because history has demonstrated that the ultimate outcome of such a change is also a function of where industry and government choose to spend their research and development dollars. The way in which the EDA, semiconductor, and chip design industries are organized and relate to one another *will* find another "fixed-point" in the future--the changes are already apparent. However, the particular form of that structure and its overall technical as well as business efficiency will be a very strong product of the attention the industry pays to the rapid changes in infrastructure occurring around it and

1092-3152/97 $10.00 © 1997 IEEE

how it chooses to invest in taking advantage of these developments.

We envisage the *entire EDA community organized as a single, integrated, distributed environment that is continually evolving and adapting*, much as the basic Internet infrastructure is organized today. Groups may choose to publish or protect particular aspects of their work but *the overall community is fully integrated at the service layer*, facilitating a tight coupling among EDA vendors, their customers, and research communities throughout the world. With appropriate investments in basic engineering and EDA software services, EDA users should be able to *construct their own* "virtual" EDA systems that couple tools, libraries, design and validation services, as well as manufacturing, component acquisition, and product distribution, from internal developments, other companies, universities, and individuals throughout the world. Globally-distributed product creation teams consisting of hundreds or perhaps thousands of professionals, from many different organizations and disciplines, from engineering to marketing and sales, should be able to collaborate closely on complex design tasks and bring new products to market quickly and reliably.

One way of organizing the major aspects of network and visualization technologies are shown in Figure 1.

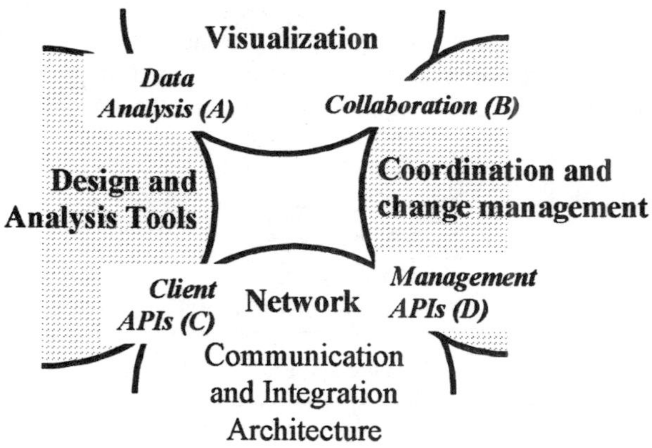

Fig. 1: Major Aspects of an Integration Architecture

New visualization hardware, including both input as well as output technologies, and associated software support can deliver significant advances in our ability to visualize complex data sets and their evolution (A) as well as aid in the management of collaborative work distributed over geographic space as well as time (B). However, it is the network and communication architecture that will play the most fundamental role in determining the overall organization of the electronics industry and so we have chosen this aspect as the emphasis of this paper. It is the most fundamental building-block upon which the design, analysis, and service tools are layered, as well as the necessary design coordination and work-flow management systems.

Innovation in the application of the network in EDA, for commercial as well as university research and instruction, is occurring at a very high pace today. For that reason, we have not attempted to record all of the ongoing activities in the area but rather focus on a number of specific architectural issues central to sustaining broad development and growth in the community. Where appropriate, we reference representative work in an area but are not able to refer to all of the excellent ongoing activities, especially on the client side, due to space limitations.

In Section 2, the main requirements of a distributed service infrastructure are defined and a number of architectural approaches to meeting these requirements are reviewed in Section 3. Selected examples of services that are under development today and would benefit from such an infrastructure are presented in Section 4.

2. Network Services

As mentioned earlier, many of the basic ideas behind the transformation of a traditional operating system to an *infrastructure of computing services* were introduced in the Multics project[2], an inspiration for the later Unix developments at Bell laboratories. Unfortunately, that project was hampered significantly by the lack of a reliable high-speed networking infrastructure. As is already apparent in EDA, network-based applications are becoming significantly more popular than their stand-alone desktop counterparts as they are a lot easier to maintain (e.g. for version management, service, use tracking for planning purposes, and platform management). In addition, queuing theory demonstrates that centralized (virtual) serving of application cycles is more efficient in both cost and utilization than a collection of smaller servers, where desktop systems represent the degenerate case of one "server" per user. These arguments are part of the thrust for the adoption of Network Computers[8].

Unfortunately, network-based services remain very difficult to deploy and maintain. Network services can experience a wide range of loads, with very high burst requirements at times, and there are a number of very challenging system design issues that must be overcome in order to maintain a high response time, constant availability, and meet capacity requirements. Such services must be able to adapt well to an ever-evolving environment, with an increasingly varied client population (in terms of software, hardware, and network connectivity). Because of the potentially slow connectivity to clients and lengthy delivery times, coupled with the potentially long transaction times encountered in EDA applications, such services must be able to handle hundreds of outstanding tasks simultaneously.

If our vision of a single, integrated EDA community is to be achieved, the following challenges must be met:

- **Scalability:** Network services must support exponential growth in the number of users (service providers as well as designers) and servers (tool, information, data storage, etc.)
- **Availability:** Access must be uninterrupted and any service degradation due to catastrophic failure in the infrastructure should be "graceful" and its impact limited in scope.
- **Adaptability:** Users, services, and servers will be added and removed incrementally. The infrastructure must be able to adapt automatically to such continuous changes without the need to maintain a consistent global state for all users.
- **Robustness:** Any failure which may result in loss of data or other aspects of design state must be recoverable efficiently and incrementally. No failure should be able to compromise the security of information stored in the network or in transit.
- **Cost effectiveness:** All of the above attributes must be achieved cost effectively and such that any economies of scale in the network can be exploited efficiently.

In the early part of this decade, EDA systems were built upon a framework model that could be characterized as shown in Figure 2[34].

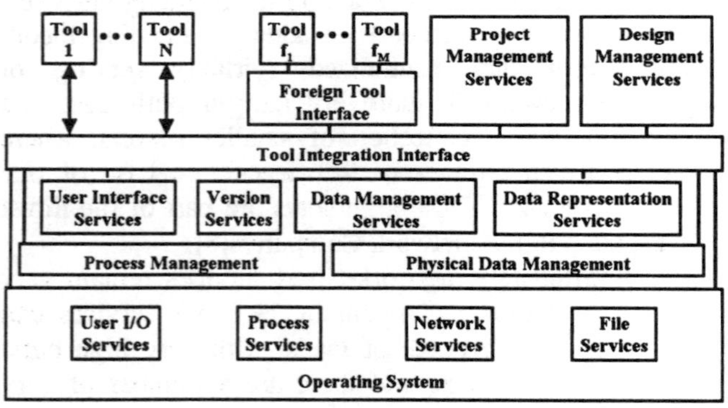

Fig. 2: EDA Framework Model[34]

Operating system services were abstracted as supporting *user interaction, process services, local storage*, or *network services.* These facilities were then grouped into those that supported *process management* and those that supported *physical data management*, including distributed data management on a network. This underlying classification of services is well-suited to a multitasking process/communication model as presented by traditional Unix systems, for example, and as used extensively for EDA systems integration today. Other services, usually specialized in some way for the peculiarities of the EDA problem, are shown at the next layer. These include the services related to advanced user interface, design versioning and configuration management, and EDA data representation semantics. *Applications*, whether design tools, project management applications, or users themselves, can apply these facilities to implement their particular task.

When the network is viewed as the central aspect of an overall EDA integration architecture, the major change to this diagram is that the local distinction between process, network, and secondary storage services is eliminated. All of these services can be considered simply as different aspects of the abstraction of services provided via the network.

The two basic components of such a modern distributed architecture are then the *computational nodes*, often referred to today as *clients, servers*, or *peers*, depending on their respective responsibilities in the overall system, and the *interconnection network.* For the purposes of this analysis, we define the *service layer* as representing all the facilities used to link these two worlds, as illustrated in Figure 3. For simplicity, we will use the term *client* here to represent any user of the network: human, tool, and information or manufacturing service and assume that most of the more EDA-specific *other services* referred to above are provided as part of a client Applications Programming Interface (API).

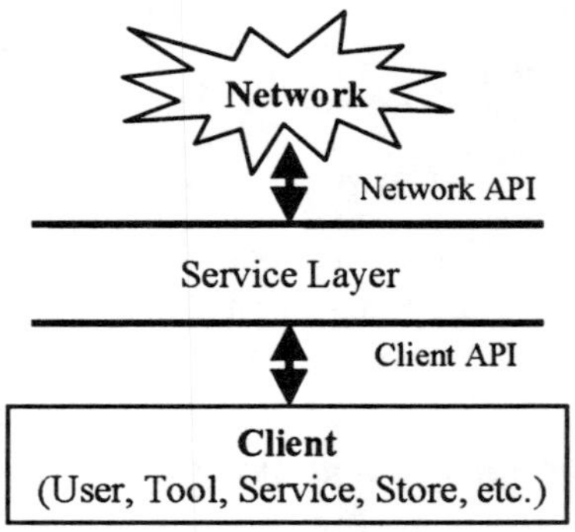

Fig. 3: The Service Layer

The different architectural approaches under development for implementing the infrastructure needed to meet the requirements outlined above can be seen as different approaches to the implementation of this service layer.

2.1 Design Transaction Management

The traditional transactional database world is primarily concerned with the ACID properties (atomicity, consistency, isolation, and durability)[9], essentially providing strong semantics but at very high cost and implementation complexity. As pointed out in [10], ACID makes no guarantee regarding availability and an ACID service would rather be unavailable than relax the ACID constraints.

In the EDA world, there are almost always a very complex set of dependencies to manage: among a design and its sub-components, different views of the design, analysis and synthesis tools, design services, and human collaborators in the design and manufacturing process.

On the other hand, at a number of points in the design process, it is more important to maintain high availability and low latency access to information than to ensure strong consistency or durability of the data. Approximate answers, based on stale information[11] or incomplete soft state[12], that are delivered quickly may be more valuable than precise data delivered more slowly or requiring some form of transitive closure across the entire design state. The semantics resulting from these requirements have been referred to as BASE[10]--Basically Available, Soft State, Eventual Consistency, and we will use this definition here. There is a strong analogy between the application-level needs of BASE systems and the traditional requirements of implementing high-performance software on "bad" multiprocessors (i.e. processors where remote memory access latencies are significantly longer--often orders of magnitude longer--than cache miss latencies on a uniprocessor.)[13]

In the presence of a potentially unreliable and unpredictable network fabric like that of the Internet, any successful EDA service layer will require both ACID and BASE component services. As distinct from the traditional Web-based services of today, where the balance is very much in the direction of BASE requirements, the implementation of distributed design and manufacturing will require a more intimate relationship between these two worlds, both of which are undergoing significant research and development (e.g. [14-21]).

In a Client-Service-Network (CSN) approach, illustrated in Figure 2, the particular characteristics of the service layer in its implementation of both ACID and BASE modes of operation is likely to be application dependent (task domain dependent). Therefore, the design challenge is finding an architecture that can address as broad a range of EDA requirements as possible. The service layer can be thought of as providing a client APIs for the delivery of abstract datatypes (of all types, from video services to software programs and data components) to and from the client. A key requirement of such a standard API is that the abstract datatype handlers implemented in the service layer not change very rapidly over time since such changes are likely to affect many clients. There are generally two approaches in use today to deal with the evolution of such datatypes--either provide *plug-in* datatype support to facilitate evolution of the interface or try to be sure the datatypes served are as application-independent as possible. For example, selecting standard MPEG2 for all video services, no matter what the particular application, would be such an approach. In either case, there is no ideal solution and the mechanisms used to implement the interfaces must be selected with evolution in mind.

3. A Proxy-Based Approach

If the service layer is viewed as the interface between clients and the network as mentioned above, it can also be seen as the client's *agent*, or *proxy*, in negotiations among the various players involved in the EDA virtual network. As such, it plays the important role of orthogonalizing the local needs of the client (user, service, tool, information store, etc.) from the network infrastructure. Such an approach is illustrated schematically in Figure 4.

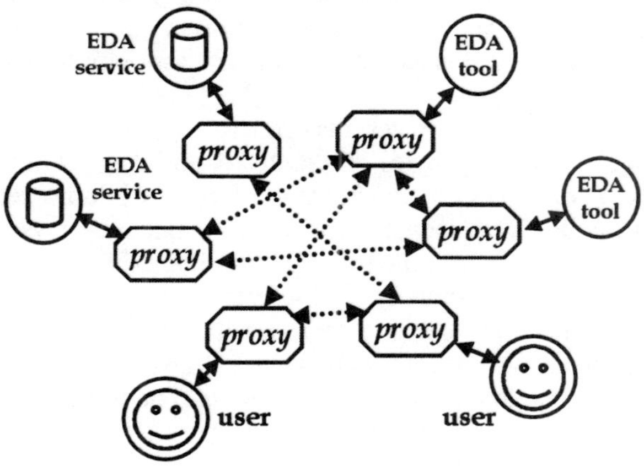

Fig. 4: A Proxy-Based Distributed Architecture

Proxies can implement many roles on the client side in such an architecture. They can play the role of the conventional legacy tool "wrapper"[34] by hiding a custom interface for a particular tool or class of tools on the client side, presenting instead the generic system interface. They can also be used for data distillation[18] or datatype transcoding to provide a better match between the needs of a particular client (a user on a low-speed mobile link, for example) and the virtual server infrastructure the client is using. Finally, proxies can of course play their most common role in use today, that of data hiding and security management.

On the network side, each proxy shares the same view of the world. The negotiations for services and service quality among proxies must demonstrate high availability, security, and reasonable performance for both ACID as well as BASE operations. It is via the network interface that the system must meet its goals of scalability, availability, robustness, and adaptability. This is also an area under active research and one which lends itself to many modern innovations. For example, in the WELD project[42], we are exploring the use of probabilistic learning, based on Bayesian reasoning[40] as an approach to managing aspects of the adaptability and robustness concerns. The implementation of an efficient BASE technology would suggest the use of caching techniques to improve overall system performance. However, significant issues remain in the implementation of effective ACID behavior when distributed caches are implemented in the face of a potentially unreliable physical network link layer. This is a topic of active research as well.

Some approaches that have been suggested for maintaining consistency in the distributed data network include the use of separate "control" and "data" distribution. In one approach, the use of a broadcast mechanism, such as the MBONE[45] has been suggested for control-state management (e.g. "who has the master copy of a dataset?") while data-sets or programs themselves are shipped around via unicast point-to-point mechanisms[43].

Modern VLSI designs consist of working sets approaching 4 gigabytes of data today and designs in the future will require considerably larger working sets, unless the EDA industry finds truly effective ways of implementing partitioned design (via the exploitation of regularity or hierarchy). However, no matter what approach is used, working-set size will remain large if the performance of modern computers and computer clusters is to be exploited effectively. Network performance is increasing significantly in most organizations but there is likely to remain the need to move the tool to the data at times rather than move the data to the tool. One of the clients envisioned in the distributed network described above can be seen as a data repository, requesting service from tools as they migrate around the network. While not yet capable of handling practical EDA tasks, much of the architecture and technology needed to implement such a model has been developed(e.g. [24]).

One interesting architectural approach to these issues is the use of clusters of commodity workstations interconnected by a very high-speed local network[10]. In this approach, service-independent software architectures for managing partial failures and administering large clusters of machines remains a challenge.

A simplified view of the major components of a proxy that might be used in this architecture is shown in Figure 5.

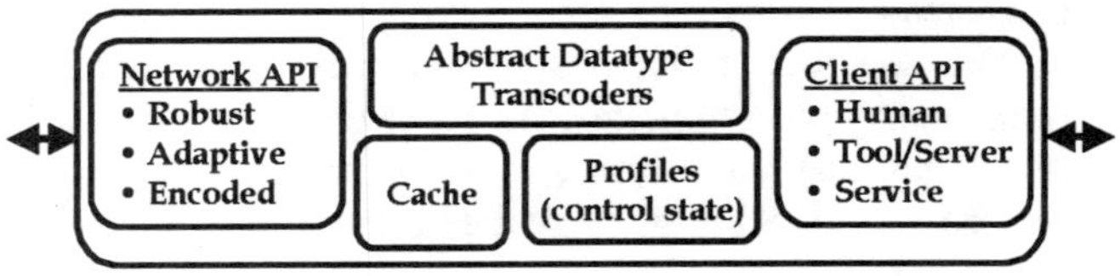

Fig. 5: Schematic Diagram of an EDA Proxy

In this approach, all proxies in the EDA network would be relatively simple and architecturally identical. On the client side, different API's are used to extend the interface for human, tool, data/processor cluster, or service use. On the network side, the API's implement the various criteria associated with network reliability, availability, and security outlined earlier. The proxy would be provided with a number of abstract datatype handlers as plug-ins, would store client-specific information locally in a profile, and would implement a cache. Some experimental systems have been implemented which register the client for interaction with other clients in the network and which implement a "heartbeat" scheme for periodically checking the reliability of communication links[25]. These schemes could be extended to provide an adaptable network fabric that adjusts automatically to problems with computer or network reliability issues.

4. Other Services

As mentioned earlier, it would be impossible to do justice here to all of the ongoing research and development in data visualization, collaboration, and work flow management that involve the network and that have a relationship to EDA. Rather, in the space available we reference a number of the key resources and highlight some important directions for the future.

Once a network infrastructure has been selected, a variety of approaches can be taken to implement client-oriented services, such as data manipulation and querying (e.g.[14-17]), visualization for design and collaboration (e.g.[31-32]), work flow management (e.g.[22,25-27,36]), and library and part management (e.g.[28-30]).

Much of the distributed tool flow and collaboration work to date has been implemented under the X-Windows architecture or, more recently, using Tcl/Tk[37]. An excellent review of these projects and extensive references can be found in [22]. More recent developments utilize the Java programming environment and JavaBeans[44] and a number of efforts are investigating the application of CORBA[46] as well.

From an EDA on the network perspective, the REUBEN system[22] features *user-defined and reconfigurable execution sequences* by creating dependency edges between program nodes (application icons) and file nodes (data icons), *data-dependent execution sequences* by dynamic scheduling of path as well as loop executions, and *host-transparency* as to the location of applications and data (both can reside on any host with a unique IP address). The system is presently written in Tcl and makes use of popular protocols such as telnet and ftp. . There are a number of commercial systems available that already tackle specific aspects of the distributed workflow management task for EDA (e.g.[27-30]).

CREW, The Collaboratory for Research on Electronic Work at the University of Michigan[31], focuses on the design of new organizations and the technologies of voice, data, and video communication that make them possible. The site contains an comprehensive set of on-line references to work on collaboration at many different levels.

Another major project that involves the application of visualization technologies to collaboration is DARPA's Intelligent Collaboration & Visualization (IC&V) program[32] is chartered to enable teams, consisting of individuals with specific roles, and teams of teams to collaborate more effectively through distributed information systems that encode relevant knowledge, expertise, and semantics and that permit multiple, shareable views of common collaborative information spaces. Their Web site contains a number of efforts that could eventually be very useful in the EDA world.

5. Summary

Computing infrastructure will continue to play a much larger role in determining overall EDA tool integration strategies, approaches to data visualization and collaboration, and even the most effective choice of algorithms for tools, than most EDA professionals realize.

With the appropriate investments in research and development over the next few years, we can expect to see significant developments in the *service layer*, as described here. These developments will enable transparent distributed EDA systems that are reliable and secure and that enable distributed collaborative design. Associated developments in visualization technologies, both for data and to support collaboration, are likely to make such environments both efficient and effective for the design and transfer to manufacturing of electronic systems.

Eventually, the operating system as we know it will cease to exist as many of the facilities we describe here migrate closer to the underlying hardware. Recent advances in operating systems and networking both demonstrate this trend and provide the technical underpinnings for another step forward. In particular, work in distributed file systems (e.g. [39]) has succeeded in providing efficient location-transparent access to data. For a glimpse into one possible future here, see [33,38].

No matter what direction we head, it is clear that electronic system design is poised to benefit early from these revolutionary developments in the use of distributed computing infrastructure. The EDA systems in use a decade from now will bear virtually no resemblance to the systems in use today.

6. Acknowledgements

Our work in Web-based electronic design is supported in part by DARP under Contract DABT63-95-C-0074 and by the Digital Equipment Corp., Hughes Research, Hewlett Packard, and Synopsys. Their support is gratefully acknowledged. We would also like to thank Wray Buntine, Francis Chan, Andrew Mayer, Michael Shilman and the members of the WELD team for their contributions to this work.

7. References

[1] L. W. Nagel and D. O. Pederson, "Simulation Program with Integrated Circuit Emphasis," *Proc. 16th Midwest Symp. Circ. Theory*, Waterloo, Canada, April 1973.

[2] F. J. Corbato and V. A. Vyssotsky, "Introduction and Overview of the Multics System," *AFIPS Conference Proceedings*, No. 27, pp.185-195, Fall Joint Computer Conf., 1965. (At http://www.lilli.com/fjcc1.html.)

[3] The *Bell System Technical Journal, Special Issue on UNIX*, Vol.57, No.6, Jul-Aug., 1978, contains a collection of papers describing UNIX.

[4] D. Gibson and S. Nance, "SLIC - Symbolic Layout of Integrated Circuits," *Proc. 13th ACM/IEEE Design Automation Conference*, pp.434-440, June 1976.

[5] J. D. Williams, "STICKS - A Graphical Compiler for High-Level LSI Design," *AFIPS Conference Proceedings*, Vol.47, pp.289-295, June 1978.

[6] N. Weste, "Virtual Grid Symbolic Layout" *Proc. 18th ACM/IEEE Design Automation Conf.*, pp.225-233, 1981.

[7] J. Ousterhout, et al., "Magic: A VLSI Layout System," *Proc. 21st ACM/IEEE Design Automation Conf.*, pp.152-159, June 1984.

[8] T. R. Halfhill, Inside the Web PC, *Byte Magazine*, pp. 22-36, March 1996

[9] J. Gray, "The Transaction Concept: Virtues and Limitations, " *Proc. VLDB*, pp.144-154, Cannes, France, Sept. 1981

[10] A. Fox, et al., "Extensible Cluster-Based Scalable Network Services," *Proc. 16th ACM Symposium on Operating Systems Principles (SOSP-16)*, St. Malo, France, Oct. 1997.

[11] A. Demers, et al., "The Bayou Architecture: Support for Data Sharing Among Mobile Users," available at www.parc.xerox.com/csl/projects/bayou/pubs/ba-mcw-94/www/MobileWorkshop_1.html

[12] D. Clark, "Policy Routing in Internet protocols," *Internet Request for Comments No.1102*, May 1989.

[13] A. D. Birrell, et al., "Grapevine: An Exercise in Distributed Computing," *Comm. of the ACM*, 25(4), Feb. 1984

[14] See *Infoscape*, at http://www.infoscape.com

[15] See *NetDynamics*, at http://www.netdynamics.com

[16] See *ObjectStore*, at http://www.odi.com.

[17] See *Objectivity Version 5* at http://www.objectivity.com.

[18] A. Fox, et al., "Adapting to Network and Client Variability via On-Demand Dynamic Distillation," *Proc. ACM 7th International Conf. on Architectural support for Programming Languages and Operating Systems*, Cambridge, MA, Oct. 1-5, 1996.

[19] *The Distributed Clients Project*, can be found at http://www.osf.org/www/dist_client.

[20] A. D. Joseph, et al., "Rover: A Toolkit for Mobile Information Access," *Proc. 15th ACM Symposium on Operating Systems Principles*, Copper Mountain, CO., Dec. 1995

[21] M. Abrams, et al., "Caching Proxies: Limitations and Potentials," *Proc. 4th International World Wide Web Conf.*, Boston, MA, Dec. 1995

[22] H.Lavana, et al., "Executable Workflows, "A Paradigm for Collaborative Design on the Internet," *Proc. 34th ACM/IEEE Design Automation Conference*, June 1997. Also available at http://www.cbl.ncsu.edu/publications/

[23] Javaworld online magazine contains many useful Java references at http://www.javaworld.com

[24] See *Marimba, Inc.* at http://www.marimba.com

[25] M. Spiller, "Architecture and Infrastructure for a Distributed Design Environment--A Server Perspective", MS Report, University of California at Berkeley, August 1997

[26] F. Chan, "Architecture and Infrastructure for a Distributed Design Environment--A Client Perspective," MS Report, University of California at Berkeley, May, 1997

[27] See *Runtime Design Automation*, at http://www.rtda.com

[28] See *Synchronicity* at http://www.syncinc.com

[29] See *Electronic Design and Technology Network* (EDTN) at http://www.edtn.com

[30] See *Aspect Development, Inc.*, at http://www.aspectonline.com

[31] See *CREW, The Collaboratory for Research on Electronic Work* at www.crew.umich.edu,

[32] See *DARPA's Intelligent Collaboration & Visualization program (IC&V)* at http://www.ito.darpa.mil/ResearchAreas96/IntellCollabVisual.html

[33] William J. Bolosky, et al., "Operating System Directions for the Next Millennium," *Position Paper*, available at http://www.research.microsoft.com/research/os/Millennium/mgoals.html

[34] D. S. Harrison, et al., "Electronic CAD Frameworks,". *Proceedings of the IEEE*, Vol.78, No.2, pp.1062-1081, Feb. 1990.

[35] J.Daniell and S.W. Director, "An Object Oriented Approach to CAD Tool Control Within a Design Framework," *IEEE Transactions on Computer-Aided Design*, Vol.10, No.6, pp.98-713, Jun. 1991.

[36] A. Casotto and A. L. Sangiovanni-Vincentelli, "Automated Design Management Using Traces," *IEEE Trans on Computer-Aided Design*, Vol.12, No.8, pp.1077-1095, Aug. 1993.

[37] J. K. Ousterhout. *Tcl and the Tk Toolkit*, Addison-Wesley, 1994.

[38] Amin Vahdat, et al. "Turning the Web Into a Computer," available at http://now.cs.berkeley.edu/WebOS/webos.ps, 1996.

[39] Kistler & Satya 92] J. J. Kistler and M. Satyanarayanan. "Disconnected Operation in the Coda File System." *ACM Trans. on Computer Systems*, Vol. 10, No.1, pp.3–25, Feb. 1992.

[40] Special Issue on Bayesian Networks: *Comm. of the ACM.*, vol. 38, no. 3,.March, 1995,

[41] P. van der Wolf, *CAD Frameworks: Principles and Architecture*, Kluwer Academic Publishers, Boston, 1994

[42] *WELD: Web Based Electronic Design* can be found under www-cad.eecs.Berkeley.edu/Respep/Research/weld, March, 1996.

[43] E. Brewer, University of California at Berkeley, Private Communication.

[44] A number of excellent references for JavaBeans can be found at http://splash.javasoft.com/beans/.

[45] An excellent introduction to the MBONE, "MBONE (Multicast Backbone)" by Jean Bunn, Geneva University, is available at http://www.unige.ch/seinf/mbone.html

[46] See "The Object Management Group's Common Object Request Broker Architecture (OMG/CORBA)" at http://www.acl.lanl.gov/CORBA/ for more details and an extensive list of references.

SESSION 8B

EMBEDDED TUTORIAL: INTERCONNECT DESIGN FOR DEEP SUBMICRON ICS

Moderator:

Shuji Tsukiyama, Chuo University, Tokyo, Japan

Interconnect Design for Deep Submicron ICs

Jason Cong*, Zhigang Pan, Lei He, Cheng-Kok Koh and Kei-Yong Khoo
Computer Science Department
University of California, Los Angeles, CA 90095 †

Abstract

Interconnect has become the dominating factor in determining circuit performance and reliability in deep submicron designs. In this embedded tutorial, we first discuss the trends and challenges of interconnect design as the technology feature size rapidly decreases towards below 0.1 micron. Then, we present commonly used interconnect models and a set of interconnect design and optimization techniques for improving interconnect performance and reliability. Finally, we present comparisons of different optimization techniques in terms of their efficiency and optimization results, and show the impact of these optimization techniques on interconnect performance in each technology generation from the 0.35μm to 0.07μm projected in the National Technology Roadmap for Semiconductors.

I. Interconnect Trends and Challenges

The driving force behind the impressive advancement of the VLSI circuit technology has been the rapid scaling of the feature size, i.e., the minimum dimension of the transistor. It decreased from 2 μm in 1985 to 0.35 μm in 1996. According to the National Technology Roadmap for Semiconductors (NTRS) [1], it will further decrease at the rate of 0.7× per generation (consistent with Moore's Law) to reach 0.07 μm by 2010. Table I lists the main characteristics of each technology generation in the NTRS. Such rapid scaling has two profound impacts. First, it enables much higher degree of on-chip integration. The number of transistors per chip will increase by more than 2× per generation to reach 800 millions in the 0.07 μm technology. Second, it implies that the circuit performance will be increasingly determined by the interconnect performance. The interconnect design will play the most critical role in achieving the projected clock frequencies in the NTRS. This paper presents the trends and challenges of interconnect design in current and future technologies and discusses the available solutions.

In order to better understand the significance of interconnect design in the future technology generations, we performed a number of experiments based on the interconnect parameters provided in the NTRS as shown in the bold face in Table II. Since the NTRS parameters are for the first metal (M1) layer only, which is usually not suitable for global interconnects, we also derived the interconnect parameters for the M4 layer,[1] which are also shown in Table II. Furthermore, we derived a set of device parameters as shown in Table III based on the data on processes and device in the NTRS. Using these sets of parameters, we carried out extensive simulations using HSPICE to quantitatively measure the interconnect performance and reliability in future technology generations and obtained the following results:

(1) Interconnect delay is clearly the dominating factor in determin-

Tech. (μm)	0.35	0.25	0.18	0.13	0.10	0.07
Year	1995	1998	2001	2004	2007	2010
# transistors	12M	28M	64M	150M	350M	800M
Clock (MHz)	300	450	600	800	1000	1100
Area (mm^2)	250	300	360	430	520	620
Wiring levels	4-5	5	5-6	6	6-7	7-8

TABLE I Summary of NTRS [1]

Tech.	0.35	0.25	0.18	0.13	0.10	0.07
Metal 1 Interconnect						
W	**0.40**	**0.30**	**0.22**	**0.15**	**0.11**	**0.08**
S	**0.60**	**0.45**	**0.33**	**0.25**	**0.16**	**0.12**
R	**0.15**	**0.19**	**0.29**	**0.82**	**1.34**	**1.34**
C	**0.17**	**0.19**	**0.21**	**0.24**	**0.27**	**0.27**
AR_M	**1.5:1**	**2:1**	**2.5:1**	**3:1**	**3.5:1**	**4:1**
AR_V	**2.5:1**	**3:1**	**3.5:1**	**4.2:1**	**5.2:1**	**6.2:1**
Metal 4 Interconnect						
W	1.00	0.76	0.56	0.38	0.28	0.20
S	1.50	1.125	0.825	0.625	0.40	0.30
R	0.04	0.050	0.076	0.22	0.35	0.36
Metal 4 with min. spacing and width						
C_a	0.031	0.025	0.021	0.018	0.018	0.017
C_f	0.046	0.042	0.040	0.040	0.042	0.037
C_x	0.056	0.072	0.086	0.090	0.107	0.119
Metal 4 with 2× min. spacing and 2× min. width						
C_a	0.061	0.051	0.044	0.038	0.041	0.035
C_f	0.066	0.060	0.055	0.054	0.054	0.051
C_x	0.020	0.031	0.041	0.045	0.056	0.063

TABLE II Interconnect parameters. W and S are the minimum width and spacing in μm, respectively. R and C are the unit-length resistance and total capacitance in $\Omega/\mu m$ and $fF/\mu m$, respectively. AR_M and AR_V are the aspect ratios of the metal and via, respectively. C_a, C_f and C_x are the area, fringe and coupling capacitances per unit length in fF/μm, respectively.

Tech.	0.35	0.25	0.18	0.13	0.10	0.07
C_g	0.225	0.158	0.097	0.050	0.031	0.016
R_d	18.7	22.8	23.8	29.4	31.1	28.3
T_x	0.113	0.084	0.057	0.031	0.020	0.011

TABLE III Device parameters. C_g and R_d are the input capacitance in fF and output resistance in kΩ of an unit-sized gate, respectively. T_x is the intrinsic delay of a gate in ns.

*Email: cong@cs.ucla.edu

†This work is partially supported by the NSF Young Investigator Award MIP-9357582 and a grant from Intel under the California MICRO Program.

[1] We assume that the minimum width and spacing of M4 is 2.5 times those of M1. The aspect ratios AR_M and AR_V are used to determine the metal thickness and the dielectric thickness for all layers. For M1, we assume that the substrate and M2 are the ground planes; and for M4, we assume that M3 and M5 are the ground planes. The total capacitance, including the area capacitance, fringing capacitance, and coupling capacitance components, are obtained using the 3D field solver FastCap [2]. Based on these assumptions, our capacitance values for M1 closely match those given in the NTRS.

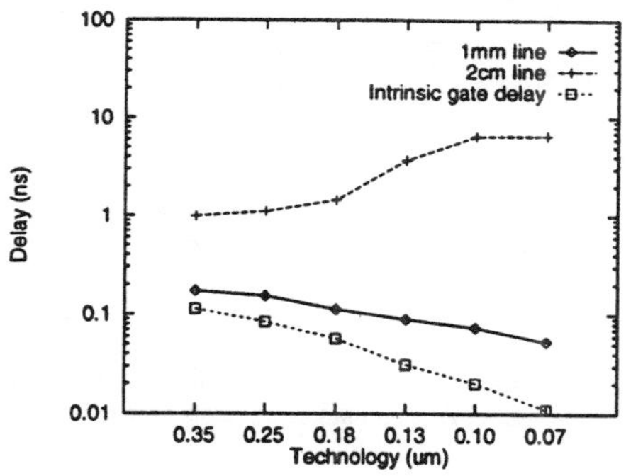

Fig. 1 Global and local interconnect delays versus gate delays.

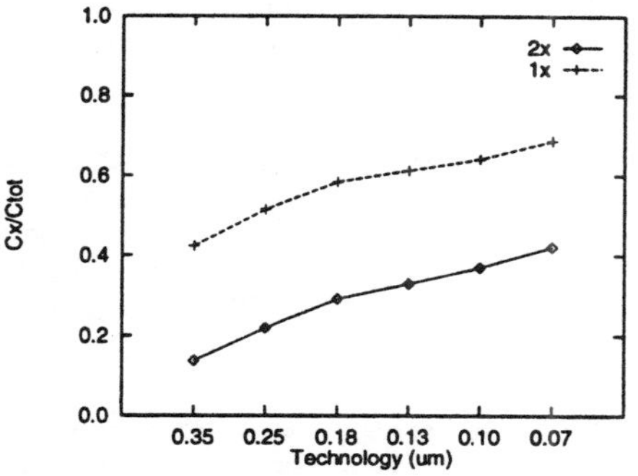

Fig. 2. Ratio of coupling capacitance to total capacitance of M4 interconnect with the minimum width and spacing (1×) and two times the minimum width and spacing (2×).

ing the circuit performance. As shown in Fig. 1, as we advance from the 0.35 μm technology to the 0.07 μm technology, the intrinsic gate delay decreases from over 100 ps to around 10 ps, the delay of a local interconnect (1 mm) decreases from over 150 ps to around 50 ps, while the delay of a global interconnect (2 cm) increases from around 1 ns to over 6 ns[2]. Clearly, aggressive interconnect optimization is needed in order to achieve the clock frequencies projected in Table I. In Section IV, we shall show how various existing interconnect optimization techniques will limit the growth of interconnect delays.

(2) The coupling capacitance between adjacent lines will be a major component in the total capacitance due to the increase of wire aspect ratio and the decrease of the line spacing. But its value is very sensitive to spacing. As shown in Fig. 2, the ratio of the coupling capacitance to the total capacitance for a wire on M4 with the minimum spacing to its two neighbors increases from around 40% to around 70% when the technology progresses from 0.35 μm to 0.07 μm. When we increase the spacing to two times the minimum, the same ratio becomes from around 15% to around 40% for different technology generations. Therefore, proper spacing is very important in deep submicron interconnect designs.

(3) The coupling noise between adjacent wires will become a important factor in deep submicron designs due to the increase of coupling capacitance. Our experimental results in Fig. 3 shows that if we restrict the peak noise value to be $15\% Vdd$, the maximum allowable length on M4 using the minimum spacing decreases from over 4000 μm to almost 500 μm when the technology progresses from 0.35 μm to 0.07 μm. The same figure also shows the wire length

[2]Both sets of interconnect delays are based on the assumption of the minimum wire width and two times minimum spacing on M4 with optimal driver sizing.

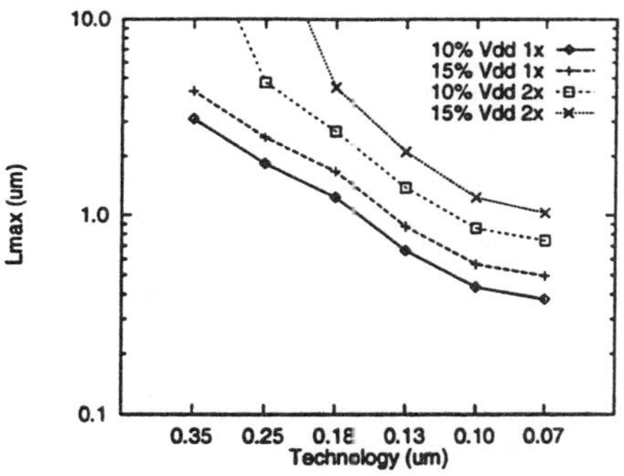

Fig. 3. Maximum allowable length (in log scale) for parallel M4 lines with the minimum width and spacing (1×) and two times the minimum width and spacing (2×) when the peak coupled noise is limited to 10% and 15% of the supply voltage.

limits under two times the minimum spacing and with $10\% Vdd$ peak noise tolerance.

Since most existing works have been on interconnect performance optimization, this tutorial covers only the modeling and optimization techniques for interconnect delay minimization. The remainder of this paper is organized as follows: Section II discusses commonly used interconnect and gate delay models for layout optimization. Sections III presents the techniques for interconnect layout design and optimization. Section IV compares a number of interconnect optimization techniques in terms of their efficiency and solution quality and shows their impact on interconnect delay reduction in each technology generation projected in the NTRS. Due to the page limitation, the authors are able to present only a small subset of results on the topics covered in this paper. A more comprehensive survey and bibliography is available in [3].

II. Delay Modeling

A. Interconnect Modeling

In order to consider both wire resistance and capacitance and model the distributive nature of the interconnects, a routing tree is usually modeled as an RC tree by dividing each long wire into a sequence of wire segments and modeling each wire segment as an L-type or π-type of RC circuit. The number of R, C elements can be large when the length of each segment is chosen to be small for a better approximation of the distributed nature of the interconnects or a greater degree of flexibility in wiresizing optimization. Therefore, a reduced-order RC model is often computed to approximate the large RC tree using the moment matching technique.

Let $h(t)$ be the impulse response at a node of a RC tree. The transfer function $H(s)$ of the circuit, which is the Laplace transform of $h(t)$, can be represented as

$$H(s) = \int_0^\infty h(t)e^{-st}dt = \sum_{i=0}^{\infty} \frac{(-1)^i}{i!} s^i \int_0^\infty t^i h(t)dt. \quad (1)$$

The i-moment of the transfer function m_i is defined to be the unsigned coefficient of the i-th power of s in Eqn. (1)

$$m_i = \frac{1}{i!}\int_0^\infty t^i h(t)dt. \quad (2)$$

Moments of an RC tree can be computed efficiently using recursive methods (see [3] for details).

The first moment $m_1 = \int_0^\infty t \cdot h(t)dt$, also called the *Elmore delay model* [4], is most commonly used for delay estimation in an RC tree. In essence, the Elmore delay model uses the mean of the impulse response $h(t)$ to approximate the 50% delay of the step response (under the step input), which corresponds to the median of the impulse response. It was shown that the Elmore delay from source s_0 to node i in an RC tree can be computed by the following simple equation [5]:

$$t(s_0, i) = \sum_{k \in Path(s_0, i)} R_k \cdot Cap(k), \tag{3}$$

where $Path(s_0, i)$ is the unique path from source s_0 to node i in an RC tree, R_k is the resistance at node k, and $Cap(k)$ is the total capacitance of the subtree rooted at node k. In general, the Elmore delay of a sink in an RC tree gives an upper bound on the actual 50% delay of the sink under the step input [6].

The Elmore delay allows us to explicitly express the signal delay as a simple algebraic function of the geometric parameters of the interconnect (the lengths and widths of wires), so that it can be easily used for interconnect optimization. It was shown that the Elmore delay model offers reasonably good *fidelity* for interconnect layout optimization, i.e., an optimal or near-optimal solution obtained under the Elmore delay model is also close to optimal according to actual (SPICE-computed) delays (see [3] for details). But the absolute value of Elmore delay may not be very accurate. So, it is not suitable to be used directly for accurate circuit timing analysis.

Higher order moments can be used for more accurate reduced-order RC models. The *Asymptotic Waveform Evaluation* (AWE) method [7] based on Padé approximation uses higher order moments to constructs a q-pole transfer function $\hat{H}(s)$, called the reduced-order *q-pole model*,

$$\hat{H}(s) = \sum_{i=1}^{q} \frac{k_i}{s - p_i}, \tag{4}$$

to approximate the actual transfer function $H(s)$, where p_i are poles and k_i are residues, all of which can be determined uniquely by matching the initial boundary conditions and the first $2q - 1$ moments of $H(s)$ to those of $\hat{H}(s)$ [7]. The response waveform in the time domain under the step input is given by

$$\hat{h}(t) = \sum_{i=1}^{q} k_i e^{p_i t}. \tag{5}$$

The choice of order q depends on the accuracy required but is usually much less than the order of the circuit. In practice, $q \leq 5$ is often used. It is difficult, however, to represent the poles and residues in $\hat{H}(s)$ explicitly in terms of design parameters of the interconnect in a closed-form expression, which makes the moment-matching method difficult to use for interconnect optimization directly[3]. Some delay metrics based on higher order moments, such as the central moments and the explicit RC delay using the first three moments, are summarized in [3]. Note that except for the Elmore delay model, which is defined for a monotonic response only, the techniques presented above still holds when interconnects are modeled as RLC trees.

Recent progresses on reduced-order models include the use of the PVL (Padé Via Lanczos) method for Padé approximation without direct moment computation [8, 9], the congruence transformations to create reduced RC networks which are guaranteed to be stable and passive [10], and the coordinate-transformed Arnoldi algorithm that can be applied to general RLC network [11]. The objective of these algorithms is to overcome the numerical instability of the AWE method.

[3]Sensitivity-based methods have been proposed to use higher order moments for fast timing analysis to greedily guide the optimization process to a local optima.

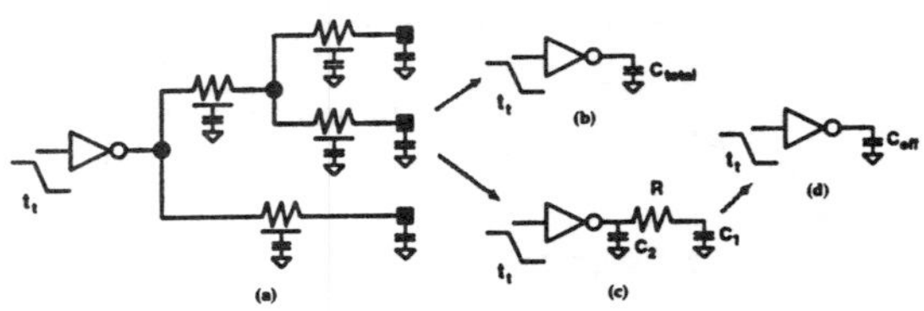

Fig. 4. (a) An inverter driving an RC interconnect. (b) The same inverter driving the total capacitance of the net in (a). (c) A π-model of the driving point admittance for the net in (a). (d) The same inverter driving the effective capacitance of the net in (a). The input signal has a transition time of t_t.

B. Driver Modeling

In this subsection, we collectively refer to gates, buffers, or transistors as drivers. We present two commonly used approaches to model the drivers for delay computation with interconnects. The first approach is a switch-resistor model comprised of an effective linear resistor driven by a voltage source (usually assuming a step input or ramped input). The effective resistance of a driver usually depends on the transition time of the input signal, the loading capacitance, and the size of the driver. For example, one can use a resistor of fixed value R_{eff} to model a driver by selecting an appropriate capacitance load C and matching the 50% delay of the driver driving the load with that of the equivalent RC circuit $(0.7R_{eff}C)$ under the step-input. A more accurate model, called the *slope model*, uses a one-dimensional table to compute the effective driver resistance based on the concept of rise-time ratio [12]. It first uses the output load and transistor size to compute the *intrinsic rise-time* of the driver, which is the rise-time at the output under the step input. The input rise-time of the driver is then divided by the intrinsic rise-time of the driver to produce the *rise-time ratio* of the driver. The effective resistance is represented as a piece-wise linear function of the rise-time ratio and stored in a one-dimensional table. Given a driver, one first computes its rise-time ratio and then calculates its effective resistance R_{eff} by interpolation according to its rise-time ratio from the one-dimensional table. Multi-dimensional tables can also be used for computing and storing the effective driver resistance as a function of the input slope, output load, etc. The switch-resistor model has the advantage that the coupling with the interconnect can be easily modeled by including the effective driver resistance in the interconnect RC tree for delay and/or waveform computation. But it may be difficult to model the non-linear behavior of the driver.

The second approach for driver modeling characterizes the behavior of a driver (such as the driver delay and the output transition time) using all relevant parameters of the input signal(s) and the output load. This allows for very accurate modeling, but the gate delay and the interconnect delay must be computed separately. For example, one can pre-characterize, the delay (t_d) and output transition times (t_f and t_r) of a driver in terms of the input transition time t_t and the total load capacitance C_L using accurate circuit simulation such as SPICE. The characterized results can then be stored in a *look-up table* where each entry is in the form: $\{t_t, C_L, (t_d, t_f, t_r)\}$. Such a model can be very accurate if one can afford the time and space to generate a detailed multi-dimensional table for each gate. Alternatively, one can store the characterization data much more compactly in the form of *k-factor equations* [13, 14], such as:

$$t_d = (k_1 + k_2 \cdot C_L) \cdot t_t + k_3 \cdot C_L^3 + k_4 \cdot C_L + k_5 \tag{6}$$

$$t_f = (k_1' + k_2' \cdot C_L) \cdot t_t + k_3' \cdot C_L^2 + k_4' \cdot C_L + k_5' \tag{7}$$

where $k_{1\ldots5}$ and $k'_{1\ldots5}$ are determined based on linear regression or least square fits on the characterization data.

C. Delay Computation

In general, we are interested to compute the total delay from the input of a driver to one of the sinks (an input to a gate in the next stage) in its output net, called the *stage delay*. When the interconnect is modeled as a lump capacitance (Fig. 4(b)) with no interconnect resistance, the computation of the stage delay is straightforward. Using the switched-resistor driver model, the stage delay is simply $R_d \cdot (C_L + C_I)$ (for a step voltage source) where C_L and C_I are the load capacitance and interconnect capacitance, respectively. Using a pre-characterized driver model, the stage delay can be obtained by table look-up and interpolation or computed from the k-factor equations directly.

When a distributed RC interconnect model is used in junction with a switch-resistor driver model, the stage delay can be easily computed by first constructing a new RC network that combines the interconnect model with the driver's effective resistance and then compute the delay through an RC network using the methods discussed in Section II.A. This shows the advantage of the switch-resistor driver model where the interaction between the driver and the interconnect can be easily modeled.

When a distributed RC interconnect model is used in junction with a pre-characterized driver model, the driver delay and the interconnect delay need to be computed separately and added up together to obtain the stage delay. Moreover, the interaction between the driver and the interconnect model should be considered during the driver pre-characterization. Since a distributed RC interconnect has many parameters, the information usually need to be "compressed" for driver pre-characterization. For example, the *π-model* [15] was proposed to approximate the driving point (i.e, the output of the driver) admittance as shown in Fig. 4(c). The values of C_1, C_2 and R in a π-model (see Fig. 4(c)) can be computed by

$$C_1 = y_2^2/y_3, \quad C_2 = y_1 - (y_2^2/y_3), \quad R = -(y_3^2/y_2^3). \tag{8}$$

where y_1, y_2 and y_3 are the first three moments of the driving point admittance, which can be computed recursively in a bottom-up fashion, starting from the sinks of the interconnect tree. In this case, the driver can be characterized using C_1, C_2 and R in addition to the input transition time, etc. for driver delay computation.

Since a very large look-up table or complex k-factor equations and very extensive simulations are needed to account for all possible combinations of C_1, C_2 and R in a π-model, the *effective capacitance model* [14] was proposed to allow drivers to be still pre-characterized in terms of a single load capacitance, even when used to drive distributed RC interconnects. The effective capacitance model first computes a π-model to approximate the driving point admittance, and then compute iteratively an "effective capacitance," denoted C_{eff} as in Fig. 4(d), using the following expression:

$$\begin{aligned} C_{eff} \;=\; & C_2 + C_1 \cdot \Bigg[1 - \frac{R \cdot C_1}{t_D - t_x/2} + \\ & \frac{(R \cdot C_1)^2}{t_x (t_D - t_x/2)} \cdot e^{\frac{-(t_D - t_x)}{R \cdot C_1}} \cdot (1 - e^{\frac{-t_x}{R \cdot C_1}}) \Bigg] \end{aligned} \tag{9}$$

where $t_D = t_d + t_t/2$ and $t_x = t_D - t_f/2$, and t_d and t_f are obtained from the k-factor equations in terms of the effective capacitance and the input transition t_t. The iteration starts with using the total interconnect and sink capacitance as the loading capacitance C_L to get an estimate of t_D and t_x through the k-factor equations. A new value of the effective capacitance is computed using Eqn. (9) and it is used as the loading capacitance for the next iteration of computation. The process stops when the value of C_{eff} does not change in two successive iterations. At the end of the iterative process, we also obtain t_d and t_f at the gate output. The effective capacitance, which is smaller than C_{total} in Fig. 4(b), captures the fact that not all the capacitance of the routing tree and the sinks is seen by the driver due to the effect of interconnect *resistance shielding*, especially in deep submicron design with fast logic gates of lower driver resistance. A so-called resistance model (*R-model*) was also proposed in [14] to better approximate the slow decaying tail portion of the response waveform when the driver is behaving like a resistance to ground. The model can be used to further account for the interaction between the RC interconnect and the driver when computing the interconnect delay [16]. These methods illustrate the complication of the interaction between the driver model and the interconnect model in the deep submicron design.

III. INTERCONNECT LAYOUT OPTIMIZATION

Given the growing importance of interconnects, interconnect optimization needs to be considered in every step of the layout design process. We propose a performance-driven layout design flow as shown in Fig. 5, in which planning and optimization for global interconnects are carried out during the floorplan stage and further interconnect optimization is performed during global routing. In this section, we discuss various optimization techniques that can be applied in this flow for interconnect delay minimization, including wirelength minimization, device sizing, interconnect topology optimization, buffer insertion, optimal wiresizing, and simultaneous device and interconnect optimization.

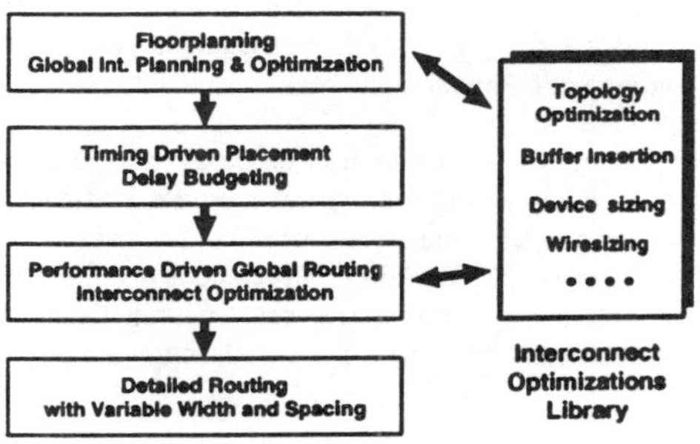

Fig. 5 Layout design flow for deep submicron ICs.

A. Wirelength Minimization

A very effective way to reduce the interconnect delay is to minimize the wirelength of timing-critical nets, so that their total capacitances are reduced. Placement has the biggest impact on the wirelength. Timing-driven placement methods can be classified into the *net-based approaches* and *path-based approaches*. For net-based approaches, a delay budgeting algorithm is first applied on the netlist to compute the timing slack for each net (or two-terminal subnet) (e.g. [17]). These slacks are then translated into wirelength upper bound constraints (e.g. [18]) or the net weights in the optimization objective function used by the placement engine. Path-based approaches usually use mathematical programming techniques and consider the path-based timing constraints directly in the problem formulation (e.g. [19]). In both cases, the estimated wirelengths of the timing critical nets (often measured in terms of the half perimeter of the net bounding box) are minimized during the placement, possibly at the expense of the wirelengths of non-timing critical nets.

Wirelength minimization can also be carried out during global routing by constructing an optimal (or near-optimal) Steiner tree (OST) for each timing-critical net. The commonly used methods include iterative addition of Steiner points, optimal merging of edges of a minimum spanning tree (MST), or iterative refinement of an MST. These methods are surveyed in [3]. However, when the interconnect resistance needs to be considered as well, wirelength minimization alone during global routing may not lead to the minimum interconnect delay. Interconnect topology optimization needs to be considered.

B. Interconnect Topology Optimization

It was shown in [20] that when the *resistance ratio*, defined to be the driver effective resistance over the unit wire resistance, is small enough, both the total wirelength (i.e. the total interconnect capacitance) and interconnect topology will impact the interconnect delay. The first step in interconnect topology optimization is to minimize or control the path-lengths from the driver to the timing-critical sinks to reduce the interconnect RC delays. A number of algorithms have been developed to minimize both the path-lengths and the total wire-length in a routing tree. For example, the *bounded-radius bounded-cost* (BRBC) algorithm [21] bounds the radius (i.e. the maximum path-length between the driver and a sink) in the routing tree while minimizing its total wire-length. It first constructs an MST, then eliminates the long paths by adding 'short-cuts' into the MST and computing a shortest path tree of the resulting graph. Other algorithms in this class include the AHHK tree construction and the 'performance oriented spanning tree' construction, which are discussed in [22] and [3]. In particular, it was shown in [20] that a minimal length shortest path tree in the Manhattan plane (called the *A-tree*) can be constructed very efficiently using a bottom-up merging heuristic with sizable delay reduction yet only a small wire-length overhead compared to the OST. The A-tree construction method has been extended to signal nets with multiple drivers (as in signal busses) [23].

Further optimization of interconnect topology involves using more accurate delay models during routing tree topology construction. For example, the Elmore delay model was used in [24] and the 2-pole delay model was used in [25] to evaluate which node or edge to be added to the routing tree during iterative tree construction. Other methods, such as the alphabetical tree and P-tree construction are also summarized in [3].

C. Device Sizing

When we have a good estimate of the interconnect capacitive load of a net, the size of its driving gate can be optimized for delay minimization. For a heavy capacitive load, a chain of cascaded drivers is usually used. The *driver sizing* problem is to determine both the number of driver stages and the size for each driver. Using the simple switch-resistor RC model and ignoring the capacitance of the driver output and the wire connecting to consecutive drivers, one can show that if the loading capacitance is C_L and the stage number is N, the ratio of two consecutive drivers (called the stage ratio) should be a constant $(\frac{C_L}{C_0})^{1/N}$ in order to achieve the minimum delay. When N is not fixed, the optimal stage ratio $f = e$ and the stage number is $N = ln(\frac{C_L}{C_g})$. When the more accurate driver delay model is used with consideration of the driver input transition time and output capacitance, the result in [26] shows that the optimal stage ratio f satisfies $f = e^{(\alpha+f)/f}$ where α is the ratio between the intrinsic output capacitance and the input gate capacitance of the inverter. For the technology used in [26], α is about 1.35 and the optimal stage ratio is in the range of 3–5 instead of e.

In general, *transistor sizing* can be used to determine the optimal width for each transistor to optimize the overall circuit performance. This technique is often used in cell generation and full-custom layout. It is usually assumed that the transistor can be assigned a continuous width. The early work TILOS [27] used the simple switch-resistor model for transistors, formulated the transistor sizing problem as a posynomial program, and applied a greedy sensitivity based method. The sensitivity of a transistor is defined to be the delay reduction due to a unit increment of its size. The algorithm starts with a minimum-sized solution, and timing analysis is applied. The transistor with the largest sensitivity is increased by a user defined factor and then timing analysis is applied again. This procedure terminates when the timing specification is satisfied or all sensitivities are zero or negative. Recent advances in transistor sizing include the use of more accurate transistor delay model with consideration of the input waveform slope, and the use of linear programming, convex programming, or other non-linear programming techniques for computing a global optimal solution. Similar techniques have also been used for *discrete gate sizing* (also called *cell sizing*) in ASIC designs, which assumes that each gate has a discrete set of pre-designed implementations (cells) from a given cell library. The gate sizing algorithm chooses an appropriate cell for each gate for performance optimization. These techniques are summarized in [3].

D. Buffer Insertion

Buffer insertion (also called *repeater insertion*) is another common and effective technique to use active device areas to trade for reduction of interconnect delays. Since the Elmore delay of a long wire grows quadratically in terms of the wirelength, buffer insertion can reduce interconnect delay significantly.

A polynomial-time dynamic programming algorithm was presented in [28] to find the optimal buffer placement and sizing for RC trees under the Elmore delay model. The formulation assumes that the possible buffer positions (called legal positions), possible buffer sizes, and the required arrival times at sinks are given, and maximizes the required arrival time at the source. The algorithm includes both bottom-up synthesis of possible buffer assignment solutions at each node and top-down selection of the optimal solution. In the bottom-up synthesis procedure, for each legal position i for buffer insertion, a set of possible buffer assignments, called *options*, in the subtree T_i rooted at i is computed. For a node k which is the parent of two subtrees T_i and T_j, the list of options for T_k is generated from the option lists of T_i and T_j based on a merging rule and a pruning rule, so that the number of options for T_k is no more than the sum of the numbers of options for T_i and T_j plus the number of possible buffer assignments in the edge coming to k. As a result, if the total number of legal positions is N and there is one type of buffer, the total number of options at the root of the entire routing tree is no larger than $N + 1$ even though the number of possible buffer assignments is 2^N. After the bottom-up synthesis procedure, the optimal option which maximizes the required arrival time at the source is selected. Then, a top-down back-tracing procedure is carried out to select the buffer assignment solution that led to the optimal option at the source.

E. Wiresizing Optimization

It was first shown in [20, 29] that when wire resistance becomes significant, as in the deep submicron design, proper wire-sizing can effectively reduce the interconnect delay. Assuming each wire has a set of discrete wire widths, their work presented an optimal wire-sizing algorithm for a single-source RC interconnect tree to minimize the sum of weighted delays from the source to timing-critical sinks under the Elmore delay model. They showed that an optimal wiresizing solution satisfies the monotone property, the separability, and the dominance property. Based on the dominance property, the lower (or upper) bounds of the optimal wire widths can be computed efficiently by iterative local refinement, starting from a minimum-width solution (or maximum-width solution for computing upper bounds). Each local refinement operation refines the width of an edge in the routing tree assuming all other edge widths are fixed. The lower and upper bounds usually meet, which leads to an optimal wiresizing solution. Otherwise, a dynamic programming based method is used to compute the optimal solution within the lower and upper bounds. This method is very efficient, capable of handling large interconnect structures, and leads to substantial delay reduction. It has been extended to optimize the routing trees with multiple drivers, routing trees without a priori segmentation of long wires, and to meet the target delays using Lagrangian relaxation. The reader may refer to [3] for more details.

An alternative approach to wiresizing optimization computes an optimal wiresizing solution using bottom-up merging and top-down selection [30] in a very similar way as the buffer insertion algorithm presented in the preceding subsection. At each node v, a set of irredundant wiresizing solutions of the subtree rooted at v is generated by merging and pruning the irredundant wiresizing solutions of the subtrees rooted at the children nodes of v. Eventually, a set of irredundant wiresizing solutions is formed at the driver for the entire routing tree, and an optimal wiresizing solution is chosen by a top-down selection process. The approach has the advantages that the optimization is targeted at meeting the required signal arrival times at sinks directly, and it can be easily extended to be combined with routing tree construction and buffer insertion as shown in the next section.

Further studies on wiresizing optimization include using more accurate delay models, such as higher-order RC delay models [31] and lossy transmission line models [32], and understanding the optimal wire shape under the assumption that non-uniform continuous wiresizing is allowed to each wire segment [33]. These results are discussed in more details in [3]. All these algorithms, however, optimize the wire widths of a single net and ignore the coupling capacitance between adjacent nets, which can be significant in deep submicron designs. Recently, an efficient algorithm named GISS (global interconnect sizing and spacing) was developed to optimize the widths and spacings for multiple nets simultaneously with consideration coupling capacitance for delay minimization [34]. It reported substantial further delay reduction compared to the single net wire sizing algorithms.

F. Simultaneous Device and Interconnect Optimization

The most effective approach to performance optimization is to consider the interaction between devices and interconnects, and optimize both of them at the same time. Two approaches are discussed in this subsection.

F.1. Simultaneous Device and Wire Sizing

The simultaneous driver and wire sizing (SDWS) problem was studied in [35] and later generalized to simultaneous buffer and wire sizing (SBWS) in a buffered routing tree [36]. In both cases, the switch-resistor model is used for the driver and the Elmore delay model is used for the interconnects modeled as RC trees. The objective function is to minimize the sum of weighted delays from the first stage of the cascaded drivers through the buffered routing tree to timing-critical sinks. It was shown that the dominance property still holds for SDWS and SBWS problems and the local refinement operation, as used for wiresizing, can be used iteratively to compute tight lower and upper bounds of the optimal widths of the driver, buffers, and wires efficiently, which often leads to an optimal solution. Dynamic programming or bounded enumeration can be used to compute the optimal solution within the lower and upper bounds when they do not meet. This approach has been shown to be very effective for optimizing very large buffered trees, yielding substantial reduction on both delay and power dissipation compared to manual designs.

In fact, it was recently shown in [37] that the dominance property holds for a large class of objective functions called *general CH-posynomials*. Based on this general result, the work in [37] is able

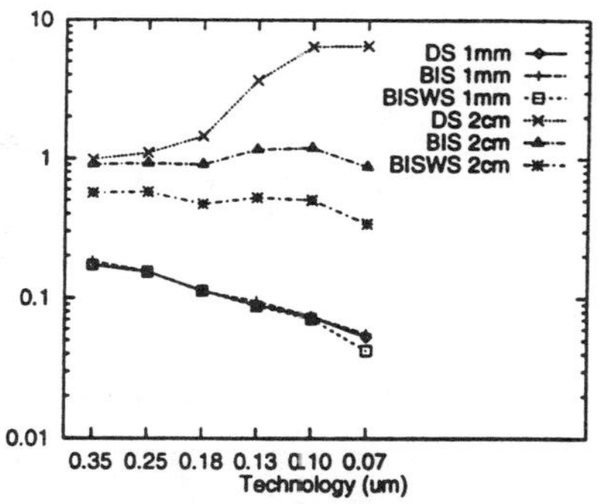

Fig. 6. Delays of 1 mm and 2 cm M4 lines under driver sizing only (DS), buffer insertion and sizing (BIS) and buffer insertion and sizing and wiresizing (BISWS).

to perform simultaneous transistor and wire sizing efficiently given a general netlist (not limited to buffered trees). A significant advantage of the CH-posynomial formulation is that it can handle more accurate transistor models, including both simple analytical models or more accurate table-lookup based models obtained from detailed simulation to consider the effect of the waveform slope, which leads to better optimization results. Other studies on simultaneous device and wire sizing include using higher order RC delay models for the interconnect by either matching to the target moments or using a q-pole transfer function for sensitivity analysis. The reader may refer to [3] for more details.

F.2. Simultaneous Topology Construction with Buffer and Wire Sizing

The *wiresized buffered A-tree (WBA-tree)* algorithm was proposed [38] for simultaneous routing tree topology construction, buffer insertion and wiresizing. It naturally combines the A-tree construction algorithm [20] and the simultaneous buffer insertion and wiresizing algorithm [30], as both use bottom-up construction techniques. The WBA algorithm includes a bottom-up synthesis procedure and a top-down selection procedure. During the bottom-up synthesis procedure, it selects two subtrees for merging with consideration of both minimization of wirelength and maximization of the estimated arrival time at the source. As a result, it is able to achieve both *critical path isolation* and a *balanced load decomposition*, as often used for fanout optimization in logic synthesis. The WBA algorithm has been extended recently to explore multiple interconnect topologies at each subtree and use high-order RLC delay models based on efficient incremental moment computation in partially constructed routing trees [39].

Other methods have also been proposed for simultaneous topology construction and wire sizing, including a greedy dynamic wire sizing during iterative routing tree construction and use of link insertion with dynamic wire sizing to create non-tree topologies. These algorithms are summarized in [3].

IV. Optimization Results and Comparative Studies

A. Impact of Interconnect Optimization on Future Technology Generations

We applied three interconnect optimization techniques for interconnect delay minimization of a 2 cm global interconnect and a 1 mm local interconnect for each technology generation in NTRS. The three optimization algorithms include (i) optimal driver sizing (DS), (ii) optimal buffer insertion and sizing (BIS), and (iii) optimal buffer insertion, sizing and wiresizing (BISWS). The delays of the optimized interconnect structures in each technology generation are shown in Fig. 6, and detailed description of the optimization results by BISWS

	Tech.	0.35	0.25	0.18	0.13	0.10	0.07
2 cm line	t_d (ns)	0.57	0.57	0.47	0.53	0.50	0.34
	$\#B$	2	3	3	6	9	11
	ABS	565	992	1370	2237	3094	4535
	AWS (μm)	6.00	5.83	6.03	6.10	5.72	5.25
	$\%WS$	91.4	96.2	97.6	99.3	99.6	99.8
1 mm line	t_d (ns)	0.17	0.15	0.11	0.09	0.07	0.04
	$\#B$	1	1	1	1	1	2
	ABS	71	91	111	161	231	711
	AWS (μm)	1.00	0.76	0.61	0.68	0.73	1.45
	$\%WS$	0	0	17	72	84	96

TABLE IV Results of Buffer Insertion and Sizing and Wiresizing. $\#B$ is the number of buffers inserted. ABS is the average buffer size normalized to minimum feature size. AWS is the average wire size. $\%WS$ is the percentage of wire segments with sizing larger than minimum width.

are shown in Table IV. We have several observations from this set of results.

1. The impact of buffer insertion and buffer/wire sizing for local interconnects is minimal after proper driver sizing, even for the technologies below 0.1 μm.
2. Buffer insertion/sizing and wire sizing have very significant impact for global interconnects, especially as the technology progresses to very deep submicron designs. In the 0.07 μm technology, BIS reduces the interconnect delay by almost a factor of 10. When wiresizing is allowed, BISWS further reduces the interconnect delay by 40% to 50%.
3. Interconnect design will be highly complex in deep submicron technologies. For example, the optimization result of the 2 cm global interconnect by BISWS contains 11 buffers with 99.8% wires being sized above the minimum width. Clearly, a global interconnect is no longer a simple metal line. It becomes a complex circuitry with optimized devices and wires in deep submicron designs! Considering the fact that there will be over 800 million transistors and 7-8 routing layers, with an estimated total wire length over 10 kilometers per chip in the 0.07 μm technology, we need highly efficient and scalable layout systems to support the various interconnect optimization techniques discussed in this paper.
4. Although the best interconnect optimization technique (BISWS) is able to reduce the global interconnect delay by up to 20× compared with the un-optimized designs in the same technology generation, if we compare the delays of best optimized global interconnects in different technology generations, it only decreases slightly by about 40% from 0.35 μm to 0.07 μm. This clearly indicates that such optimization alone will not achieve over 3× performance increase from the 0.35 μm to 0.07 μm technologies as expected in Table I. Therefore, innovations in system architectures, interconnect architectures, and interconnect technologies are needed to achieve the predicted performance targets in NTRS.

B. Comparisons of Various Interconnect Optimization Algorithms

In this subsection, we provide a comparative study of a number of interconnect optimization algorithms presented in Section III in terms of their efficiency and optimality, so that one can make proper choices for his or her optimization needs in practice. We use the interconnect optimization package developed in our group at UCLA in the past five years, named TRIO (Tree, Repeater, and Interconnect Optimization) for this set of experiments. The TRIO package includes many interconnect optimization algorithms presented in Section III and also offers the capability to combine them in different ways to provide a wide spectrum of interconnect optimization solutions. In particular, we shall compare the following four optimization strategies:

- **T+B+W**: A-tree construction (Section III.F.2), followed by optimal buffer insertion and sizing (Section III.F.1) with B=10 buffer sizes, then followed by optimal wiresizing using bundled local refinement [40] based on the dominance property (Section III.E) with W=18 wire widths.
- **TB+SBWS**: simultaneous topology and buffer optimization (Section III.F.2) with B=3 followed by simultaneous buffer and wiresizing (Section III.F.1) with B=40 and W=18.
- **Tbw+SBWS**: simultaneous topology, buffer insertion and sizing, and wiresize optimization (Section III.F.2) with very limited choices of buffer sizes and wire widths (B=3 and W=3), followed by simultaneous buffer and wire sizing (SBWS in Section III.F.1) with B=40 and W=18.
- **TBW**: simultaneous topology construction, buffer insertion and sizing, and wiresize optimization (Section III.F.2) with B=10 and W=8.

These algorithms are applied to three sets of randomly generated multi-terminal nets of 5, 10 and 20 pins, respectively, with pins uniformly distributed within a 10 mm by 10 mm area. Each set contains three instances. The optimization results are shown in Table V based on the 0.18 μm technology. We have several observations:

1. Simultaneous device and interconnect optimization by TBW usually produces the better results compared to other separate optimizations, with up to 20% additional delay reduction compared to T+B+W.
2. The bottom-up dynamic programming technique used in TBW can be very timing consuming (even run in polynomial time) with large number of choices of buffer sizes and wire widths (up to 6 minutes on the average for 20-pin nets).
3. For buffer or/and wire sizing, local refinement based optimization (SBWS) using the dominance property is much more efficient than the bottom-up dynamic programming technique used in TBW. SBWS can handle a large number of buffer sizes and wire widths in a fraction of a second. Therefore, proper combination of TBW and SBWS provides a good trade-off of efficiency and optimality. Our results show that Tbw+SBWS has less than 1% difference compared to TBW in terms of solution quality, but runs more than 10 times faster. Therefore, Tbw+SBWS is our recommended solution for most interconnect optimization applications.

The UCLA TRIO package also includes a number of other interconnect optimization routines, such simultaneous transistor and wire sizing (STIS), global interconnect sizing and spacing (GISS), etc. whose results are not able to be included here due to the space limitation. The TRIO package can accommodate a number of layout constraints, such as the upper and lower bounds of each wire segments, allowed buffer locations, etc. It also interfaces with a 2.5D capacitance extractor and can produce the optimization results directly into the HSPICE netlist format for detailed timing simulation. All the delay results reported in this paper are obtained by HSPICE simulations.

V. Conclusions

In this tutorial, we have shown the trends and challenges of interconnect design as the technology feature size decreases to below 0.1 μm based on the data in NTRS. We presented a set of commonly

		Algorithms			
		T+B+W	TB+SBWS	Tbw+SBWS	TBW
5 pins		0.40	0.39	0.35	0.34
	t_d	0.47	0.48	0.38	0.38
	(ns)	0.42	0.41	0.36	0.35
	CPU (s)	0.1	0.1	1.4	15
10 pins		0.42	0.37	0.34	0.33
	t_d	0.56	0.56	0.44	0.44
	(ns)	0.47	0.45	0.38	0.38
	CPU (s)	0.8	1.0	6.4	76
20 pins		0.45	0.43	0.38	0.39
	t_d	0.54	0.48	0.42	0.41
	(ns)	0.46	0.43	0.38	0.38
	CPU (s)	1.6	4.0	27.6	350

TABLE V Comparison of Algorithms. t_d is the average delay time for each net (each row is one net) and CPU is the average running time on a Sun Ultra2 workstation with 256 Mbytes of memory.

used interconnect and driver models and presented a set of interconnect design and optimization techniques which have proven to be very effective for improving interconnect performance and reliability. Our experimental results show that these optimization techniques have a very significant impact on the performance of the global interconnects, with different degree of efficiency and optimality.

The research on interconnect modeling and optimization have been focused mainly on interconnect delay minimization in the past several years. Given the growing importance of coupling noise as discussed in Section 1 and other concerns on signal reliability, we expect to see much more research on modeling and optimization on signal reliability of interconnects in the near future.

REFERENCES

[1] Semiconductor Industry Association, *National Technology Roadmap for Semiconductors*, 1994.

[2] K. Nabors and J. White, "Fastcap: A multipole accelerated 3-D capacitance extraction program," *IEEE Trans. on Computer-Aided Design of Integrated Circuits and Systems*, vol. 10, pp. 1447–1459, Nov. 1991.

[3] J. Cong, L. He, C.-K. Koh, and P. H. Madden, "Performance optimization of VLSI interconnect layout," *Integration, the VLSI Journal*, vol. 21, pp. 1–94, 1996.

[4] W. C. Elmore, "The transient response of damped linear networks with particular regard to wide-band amplifiers," *Journal of Applied Physics*, vol. 19, pp. 55–63, Jan. 1948.

[5] J. Rubinstein, P. Penfield, Jr., and M. A. Horowitz, "Signal delay in RC tree networks," *IEEE Trans. on Computer-Aided Design of Integrated Circuits and Systems*, vol. CAD-2, pp. 202–211, July 1983.

[6] R. Gupta, B. Tutuianu, B. Krauter, and L. T. Pillage, "The Elmore delay as a bound for RC trees with generalized input signals," in *Proc. Design Automation Conf*, pp. 364–369, June 1995.

[7] L. T. Pillage and R. A. Rohrer, "Asymptotic waveform evaluation for timing analysis," *IEEE Trans. on Computer-Aided Design of Integrated Circuits and Systems*, vol. 9, pp. 352–366, Apr. 1990.

[8] P. Feldmann and R. W. Freund, "Efficient linear circuit analysis by Padé approximation via the Lanczos process," in *Proc. European Design Automation Conf.*, 1994.

[9] P. Feldmann and R. W. Freund, "Reduced-order modeling of large linear subcircuits via a block Lanczos algorithm," in *Proc. Design Automation Conf*, pp. 474–479, 1995.

[10] K. J. Kerns, I. L. Wemple, and A. T. Yang, "Stable and efficient reduction of substrate model networks using congruence transforms," in *Proc. Int. Conf. on Computer Aided Design*, pp. 207–214, 1995.

[11] L. M. Silveira, M. Kamon, I. Elfadel, and J. White, "A coordinate-transformed Arnoldi algorithm for generating guaranteed stable reduced-order models for RLC circuits," in *Proc. Int. Conf. on Computer Aided Design*, pp. 288–294, 1996.

[12] J. K. Ousterhout, "Switch-level delay models for digital MOS VLSI," in *Proc. Design Automation Conf*, pp. 542–548, 1984.

[13] N. H. E. Weste and K. Eshraghian, *Principles of CMOS VLSI Design: a Systems Perspective*. Addison-Wesley, second ed., 1993.

[14] J. Qian, S. Pullela, and L. T. Pileggi, "Modeling the "effective capacitance" for the RC interconnect of CMOS gates," *IEEE Trans. on Computer-Aided Design of Integrated Circuits and Systems*, vol. 13, pp. 1526–1535, Dec. 1994.

[15] P. R. O'Brien and T. L. Savarino, "Modeling the driving-point characteristic of resistive interconnect for accurate delay estimation," in *Proc. Design Automation Conf*, pp. 512–515, Nov. 1989.

[16] N. Menezes, S. Pullela, and L. T. Pileggi, "Simultaneous gate and interconnect sizing for circuit-level delay optimization," in *Proc. Design Automation Conf*, pp. 690–695, June 1995.

[17] P. S. Hauge, R. Nair, and E. J. Yoffa, "Circuit placement for predictable performance," in *Proc. Int. Conf. on Computer Aided Design*, pp. 88–91, 1987.

[18] W. Swartz and C. Sechen, "Timing driven placement for large standard cell circuits," in *Proc. Design Automation Conf*, pp. 211–215, 1995.

[19] A. Srinivasan, K. Chaudhary, and E. S. Kuh, "RITUAL: Performance driven placement algorithm for small cell ics," in *Proc. Int. Conf. on Computer Aided Design*, pp. 48–51, 1991.

[20] J. Cong, K. S. Leung, and D. Zhou, "Performance-driven interconnect design based on distributed RC delay model," in *Proc. Design Automation Conf*, pp. 606–611, 1993.

[21] J. Cong, A. B. Kahng, G. Robins, M. Sarrafzadeh, and C. K. Wong, "Provably good performance-driven global routing," *IEEE Trans. on Computer-Aided Design of Integrated Circuits and Systems*, vol. 11, pp. 739–752, June 1992.

[22] A. B. Kahng and G. Robins, *On Optimal Interconnections for VLSI*. Kluwer Academic Publishers, 1994.

[23] J. Cong and P. H. Madden, "Performance driven routing with multiple sources," in *Proc. IEEE Int. Symp. on Circuits and Systems*, pp. 1.203–1.206, 1995.

[24] K. D. Boese, A. B. Kahng, and G. Robins, "High-performance routing trees with identified critical sinks," in *Proc. Design Automation Conf*, pp. 182–187, 1993.

[25] D. Zhou, F. Tsui, and D. S. Gao, "High performance multichip interconnection design," in *Proc. 4th ACM/SIGDA Physical Design Workshop*, pp. 32–43, Apr. 1993.

[26] N. Hedenstierna and K. O. Jeppson, "CMOS circuit speed and buffer optimization," *IEEE Trans. on Computer-Aided Design of Integrated Circuits and Systems*, vol. CAD-6, pp. 270–281, Mar. 1987.

[27] J. P. Fishburn and A. E. Dunlop, "TILOS: A posynomial programming approach to transistor sizing," in *Proc. Int. Conf. on Computer Aided Design*, pp. 326–328, 1985.

[28] L. P. P. P. van Ginneken, "Buffer placement in distributed RC-tree networks for minimal Elmore delay," in *Proc. IEEE Int. Symp. on Circuits and Systems*, pp. 865–868, 1990.

[29] J. Cong and K. S. Leung, "Optimal wiresizing under the distributed Elmore delay model," in *Proc. Int. Conf. on Computer Aided Design*, pp. 634–639, 1993.

[30] J. Lillis, C. K. Cheng, and T. T. Y. Lin, "Optimal wire sizing and buffer insertion for low power and a generalized delay model," in *Proc. Int. Conf. on Computer Aided Design*, pp. 138–143, Nov. 1995.

[31] N. Menezes, S. Pullela, F. Dartu, and L. T. Pillage, "RC interconnect synthesis—a moment fitting appraoch," in *Proc. Int. Conf. on Computer Aided Design*, pp. 418–425, 1994.

[32] T. Xue, E. S. Kuh, and Q. Yu, "A sensitivity-based wiresizing approach to interconnect optimization of lossy transmission line topologies," in *Proc. IEEE Multi-Chip Module Conf.*, pp. 117–121, 1996.

[33] C.-P. Chen, H. Zhou, and D. F. Wong, "Optimal non-uniform wire-sizing under the Elmore delay model," in *Proc. Int. Conf. on Computer Aided Design*, pp. 38–43, 1996.

[34] J. Cong, L. He, C.-K. Koh, and Z. Pan, "Global interconnect sizing and spacing with consideration of coupling capacitance," in *Proc. Int. Conf. on Computer Aided Design*, 1997.

[35] J. Cong and C.-K. Koh, "Simultaneous driver and wire sizing for performance and power optimization," *IEEE Trans. on Very Large Scale Integration (VLSI) Systems*, vol. 2, pp. 408–423, Dec. 1994.

[36] J. Cong, C.-K. Koh, and K.-S. Leung, "Simultaneous buffer and wire sizing for performance and power optimization," in *Proc. Int. Symp. on Low Power Electronics and Design*, pp. 271–276, Aug. 1996.

[37] J. Cong and L. He, "An efficient approach to simultaneous transistor and interconnect sizing," in *Proc. Int. Conf. on Computer Aided Design*, pp. 181–186, Nov. 1996.

[38] T. Okamoto and J. Cong, "Buffered Steiner tree construction with wire sizing for interconnect layout optimization," in *Proc. Int. Conf. on Computer Aided Design*, pp. 44–49, Nov. 1996.

[39] J. Cong and C.-K. Koh, "Interconnect layout optimization under higher-order RLC model," in *Proc. Int. Conf. on Computer Aided Design*, 1997.

[40] J. Cong and L. He, "Optimal wiresizing for interconnects with multiple sources," *ACM Trans. on Design Automation of Electronics Systems*, vol. 1, pp. 478–511, Oct. 1996.

SESSION 9A

POWER ESTIMATION AND MODELING

Moderators:

Kaushik Roy, Purdue University, West Lafayette, IN

Chandu Visweswariah, IBM Corp., Yorktown Heights, NY

Accurate Power Estimation for Large Sequential Circuits†

Joseph N. Kozhaya and Farid N. Najm

ECE Dept. and Coordinated Science Lab.
University of Illinois at Urbana-Champaign
Urbana, Illinois 61801

Abstract

A power estimation approach is presented in which blocks of consecutive vectors are selected at random from a user-supplied realistic input vector set and the circuit is simulated for each block starting from an unknown state. This leads to two (upper and lower) bounds on the desired power value which can be quite tight (under 10% difference between the two in many cases). As a result, the power dissipation is obtained by simulating only a fraction of the potentially very large vector set.

1. Introduction

Power dissipation of VLSI circuits is a major concern of the semiconductor industry. Excessive power dissipation in integrated circuits causes overheating, which can lead to soft errors or permanent damage. It also limits battery life in portable equipment. Thus, there is a need to accurately estimate the power dissipation of an IC during the design phase.

Several approaches have been proposed for power estimation [1], especially for estimation at the gate-level. However, even at the gate-level, the problem is not yet completely solved. At least two open problems remain: 1. *Accurate* and *fast* estimation of the average power dissipated by individual gates, typically inside an optimization loop, and 2. *Accurate* and *fast* estimation of the total average power dissipation in *large* sequential circuits. The words "accurate" and "fast" are emphasized in both cases to indicate that existing techniques are either inaccurate and fast or accurate and slow. The fact that the first problem is not yet solved has recently been clearly illustrated in [2]. In this paper, we will argue and demonstrate that the second problem is also still open, and we offer a new method which provides accurate and fast estimation of the total average power of large sequential circuits.

Since the power is pattern-dependent, the average power dissipation of a circuit is not well-defined until a specific vector set is chosen. For combinational circuits, this may not be very critical, because different vector sets may dissipate approximately the same power, provided they have approximately equal values of *switching activity*. Thus, using a set of randomly generated vectors (with the right statistics) may be appropriate for these circuits. However, this does not hold for sequential circuits, because a real vector set (as opposed to a randomly generated, artificial vector set) may contain specific vector sequences that put the circuit in specific operational modes or sub-spaces of its large state space and, in different operational modes, the circuit may dissipate quite different values of power. All one has to do is think of all the many different operational modes of a large micro-processor. Thus, for sequential circuits, the power may be *critically* dependent on the specific vector sequences that occur during typical operation.

Most existing techniques of power estimation consider simply the average switching activity and signal probability of the input signals and use either static probability propagation methods [3–6] or dynamic Monte Carlo simulation using randomly generated vectors [7, 8]. In either case, one runs the risk of taking the circuit into parts of its state space where it does not belong, i.e., into modes of operation that are unrealistic and may never be exercised in practice. When this happens, there is no guarantee that the estimated power has any relation to what the circuit will actually dissipate under typical operation.

To illustrate this problem, we have considered a number of sequential circuits and constructed two sets of input vectors for each. Both sets of vectors have the same switching activity and signal probability for each input node. However, in one vector set, the input signals were generated at random, without any correlation between them, and in the other non-zero correlations were considered, both in space (between pairs of bits in the same vector) and in time (between pairs of consecutive vectors). The intention is that these correlations would mimic to some degree the relationships that typically exist between signals, such as signals resulting from decoded instructions or general control signals. Note that these correlations are only the simplest kinds of correlation relations, because they do not model the temporal correlations that can exist in vector streams over *several* clock cycles. We emphasize this point to indicate that proposed approaches that use correlation coefficients [9] may be able to handle pairwise correlations between bits in a vector or between consecutive vectors, but cannot handle the variety of other input signal relations that can exist in sequential circuits. Even with just these

† This work was supported in part by the Semiconductor Research Corporation (SRC-DP-96-109), by Rockwell, and by an NSF CAREER Award (MIP-9623237).

simple correlations applied, big differences are possible in the resulting power values, as shown in Table I where Pwr(uc) refers to power dissipated under the uncorrelated vector set and Pwr(co) is the power due to the correlated vector set. The error (Err) is measured as the difference between the two power values, divided by the power due to the correlated set. Note that the power in both cases (uncorrelated and correlated inputs) was measured using the same simulator, so that the errors are due only to the presence of the additional correlations in one vector set but not in the other.

Table I.
DIFFERENCE IN POWER VALUES (in mW) DUE TO PRESENCE OF CORRELATION IN THE VECTOR SET.

Ckt	#input	#latch	#gate	Pwr(uc)	Pwr(co)	Err(%)
s298	3	14	119	0.3152	0.2615	20.54
s349	9	15	161	0.3924	0.3181	23.36
s386	7	6	159	0.4122	0.3591	14.80
s444	3	21	181	0.2085	0.1692	23.25
s526n	3	21	194	0.3375	0.2545	32.58
s641	35	19	379	0.3232	0.2982	8.38
s820	18	5	289	0.4912	0.3998	22.86
s1196	14	18	529	1.4719	1.7009	-13.46
s1488	8	6	653	0.3729	0.1796	107.63
s35932	35	1728	16065	13.8721	12.2942	12.83

It would seem, therefore, that the only truly accurate power estimation method for sequential circuits is to simulate the circuit for a specific *realistic* and *typical* vector set. We refer to such a vector set as the *power vector set.* If one has a power vector set which is short enough to simulate in its entirety, then this would certainly be the method of choice. However, in practice it is very hard (almost impossible) to specify a power vector set which is both short-enough for simulation and long-enough to cover all the interesting operational modes of a large sequential circuit. Microprocessor designers will usually agree that millions of vectors may be needed in order to satisfactorily exercise their large designs.

To solve this problem, we propose a method of power estimation that takes a (potentially very long) power vector set and provides an estimate of the total power by simulating only a fraction of the vector set. The vectors to be simulated are selected by repeatedly choosing blocks of consecutive vectors at random, until certain accuracy criteria are met. We call this a *block-sampling* approach. From the repeated simulations of the blocks, we collect statistics on the *mean upper bound* and *mean lower bound* for the power per block. Using standard Monte-Carlo mean estimation techniques, the two means can be estimated with user-specified accuracy and confidence without having to simulate all blocks. The net effect is that only a fraction of the total vector set is simulated and accurate tight bounds on the total power are estimated, yielding a viable accurate power measure.

2. Problem formulation

Let $u_1, u_2, \ldots, u_m$ be the primary input nodes of a sequential logic circuit and let $x_1, x_2, \ldots, x_n$ be the *present state* lines. For simplicity of presentation, we have assumed that the circuit contains a single clock that drives a bank of edge-triggered flip-flops. On the falling edge of the clock, the flip-flops transfer the values at their inputs to their outputs. The inputs $u_i(k)$ and the *present state* values $x_i(k)$ determine the *next state* values $x_i(k+1)$ and the circuit outputs, where k denotes the clock cycle, so that the circuit implements a *finite state machine* (FSM).

Suppose a power vector set is provided which consists of the input vectors $U(1), U(2), \ldots, U(M)$, where $U(k) = [u_1(k)\ u_2(k)\ \ldots\ u_m(k)]$ is the input vector applied during cycle k, and M is the total number of vectors. We assume that the initial state vector $X(1)$ is well-defined, so that there exists a well-defined resulting sequence of state vectors $X(1), X(2), \ldots, X(M)$, where $X(k) = [x_1(k)\ x_2(k)\ \ldots\ x_n(k)]$. The initial state need not be known, it only needs to be well-defined, i.e., not arbitrary or variable, in order for the power (due to this vector set) to be well-defined.

The total energy dissipated in the circuit in the kth cycle, denoted $e(k)$, is a function of $X(k-1)$, $X(k)$, $U(k-1)$, and $U(k)$. For $e(1)$, since $X(0)$ and $U(0)$ are not defined, we arbitrarily define $e(1) = 0$. Over a block of K consecutive input vectors, starting at cycle i, the average power dissipated is (where K is a constant, the same for any i):

$$P_K(i) = \frac{1}{KT} \sum_{k=i}^{i+K-1} e(k) \qquad (1)$$

where T is the clock period, and the desired total power dissipation P (over the whole vector set) is given by:

$$P = \frac{1}{MT} \sum_{k=1}^{M} e(k) = \frac{1}{M} \sum_{i=-K+2}^{M} P_K(i) \qquad (2)$$

Notice that for the last $K-1$ blocks, for which $i + K - 1 > M$, one should use $e(k) = 0$ in (1) for all $k = M+1, \ldots, M+K-1$. The same applies to the first $K-1$ blocks, $e(k) = 0$ for $k = -K+2, \ldots, 0$. This is required in order for the average power per block to be equal to the average power per cycle, leading to (2). If we now consider a probability experiment in which a block of vectors is chosen at random from the power vector set so that all blocks are equi-probable, then the average power per block becomes a random variable, denoted $\mathbf{P_K}$, which takes values in the set $\{P_K(-K+2), P_K(1), P_K(2), \ldots, P_K(M)\}$. We will use bold font to denote random quantities. From (2), it becomes clear that the total power is the following *mean* or *expected value*:

$$P = E[\mathbf{P_K}] \qquad (3)$$

where $E[\cdot]$ denotes the expected value operator. If $P_K^u(i)$ and $P_K^l(i)$ are upper and lower bounds on $P_K(i)$, respectively, then we can also talk about the random variables $\mathbf{P_K^u}$ (random upper bound value) and $\mathbf{P_K^l}$ (random lower bound value), and it also becomes clear that:

$$E[\mathbf{P_K^l}] \leq P \leq E[\mathbf{P_K^u}] \tag{4}$$

In the next section, we propose a practical method for estimating the two bounds in (4).

3. Proposed approach

If it were possible to obtain sample values of $P_K(i)$ for a sufficient number of values i, it would then be possible to estimate P based on (3) to any desired accuracy (with some specified confidence) using traditional statistical methods of mean-estimation. However, since the FSM state at the start of a block is unknown, this cannot be done. Instead, our approach is based on equation (4) and involves using mean estimation techniques to find two bounds on the unknown power value.

Briefly stated, we make N random choices for the block start index i (let these constitute a set of indices I) from which we compute by simulation N sample values of each of the random variables $\mathbf{P_K^u}$ and $\mathbf{P_K^l}$. We then compute the two means:

$$E[\mathbf{P_K^u}] \approx \frac{1}{N}\sum_{i\in I} P_K^u(i) \quad \text{and} \quad E[\mathbf{P_K^l}] \approx \frac{1}{N}\sum_{i\in I} P_K^l(i) \tag{5}$$

which we can use as bounds on the desired power value P, based on (4). It remains to describe how to perform the simulation in order to obtain $P_K^u(i)$ and $P_K^l(i)$, and how to choose values for K and N. These topics are covered below.

3.1 Block simulation

The simulation of a block of vectors is complicated by the fact that the state of the FSM at the beginning of that block is not known. Therefore, we set the FSM to an all-X state (all state bits are in the unknown state) and perform 3-valued gate-level simulation, with the values (0, 1, X). During the simulation of the block, we compute two bounds on the power due to that block. The upper (lower) bound is found by assuming that every signal transition containing an X value actually occurs with the X replaced by either a 0 or a 1, whichever leads to the larger (smaller) power dissipation for that transition. For instance, if the output of a gate makes a X $\rightarrow$ 1 transition, then it is assumed to be a 0 $\rightarrow$ 1 transition for purposes of computing the upper bound and a 1 $\rightarrow$ 1 transition for purposes of computing the lower bound. For purposes of continuing the simulation, the transition is kept as X $\rightarrow$ 1. Other cases are treated similarly. In this way, the true (unknown) signals in the circuit are guaranteed to be sub-sets of the simulated signals, and the true power for that block is guaranteed to be between the two resulting bounds $P_K^u(i)$ and $P_K^l(i)$.

The reason that this method can be useful in practice is that in many cases, many of the X values become definite 0 or 1 values during three-valued simulation (more on this in section 4). In fact, we have found that sufficiently many X values become known that the two bounds resulting from the simulation of one vector block can be very close, close enough to constitute a viable measure of power.

Note that any kind of simulator may be used - the measured power will be as accurate as the simulation model. Since we are computing the total power of the circuit (and not the powers of individual gates), we find that a logic simulator with a good timing model is sufficient. In our implementation, every gate has a scalable delay value, depending on the output loading capacitance due to its drain capacitance and the MOSFET gate capacitance of the logic gates on the fanout branches. Our simulator is event-driven, so that the estimated power includes the power due to glitches (i.e., hazards). Let $n_k^l(i)$ and $n_k^u(i)$ be lower and upper bounds on the number of logic transitions made by node i in clock cycle k, respectively. These are computed during the simulation by simply considering that signal transitions involving an X value can be interpreted in multiple ways as explained above, including one way representing the most power per transition and another way representing the least. Thus, for example, upon observing a $0 \rightarrow X$ transition at node i, we would increment $n_k^u(i)$ (due to the $0 \rightarrow 1$ possibility) and not increment $n_k^l(i)$ (due to the $0 \rightarrow 0$ possibility). From this, the total energy dissipated in clock k is bounded by $e^l(k) \leq e(k) \leq e^u(k)$, where the energy bounds are computed as follows:

$$e^l(k) = \frac{1}{2}\sum_i V_{dd}^2 C_i n_k^l(i) \tag{6}$$

$$e^u(k) = \frac{1}{2}\sum_i V_{dd}^2 C_i n_k^u(i) \tag{7}$$

respectively, where C_i is the node capacitance and the summations are taken over all gate/latch output nodes in the circuit. The reason for the $1/2$ coefficient is that, on average, half the transitions will be low-to-high and the other half will be high-to-low. From this, the block upper/lower bound values $P_K^u(i)$ and $P_K^l(i)$ are computed in a way similar to equation (1), as follows:

$$P_K^l(i) = \frac{1}{KT}\sum_{k=i}^{i+K-1} e^l(k) \tag{8}$$

$$P_K^u(i) = \frac{1}{KT}\sum_{k=i}^{i+K-1} e^u(k) \tag{9}$$

3.2 Choice of block size

The choice of block size, K, can affect the tightness of the bounds in (4). This is because the larger the block is, the more probable it can be that more X values will be converted to definite 0 or 1 values during the simulation. On the other hand, K should not be too large because beyond some point there will typically be very little or no reduction in the number of X values. In the development leading to equation (2), it was made clear that K should be a constant (the same for all blocks). However, during the simulation of a block of vectors, if it is found that $P_K(i)$ has already been estimated with sufficient accuracy before all K vectors have been simulated, there would clearly be no reason to continue the simulation of that block. Therefore, we use a dynamic scheme in which we may simulate only $K' < K$ vectors from a block, with K being the *hard limit* on the number of simulation vectors per block. In our implementation, this hard limit was chosen empirically, by looking at a large number of simulations, and we found that a value of $K = 500$ is appropriate. Typical plots are shown in Figs. 1 and 2. In practice, say for a micro-processor design, the value of K would probably have to depend on the instruction set and on the number of instructions that may be required to constitute meaningful processing tasks.

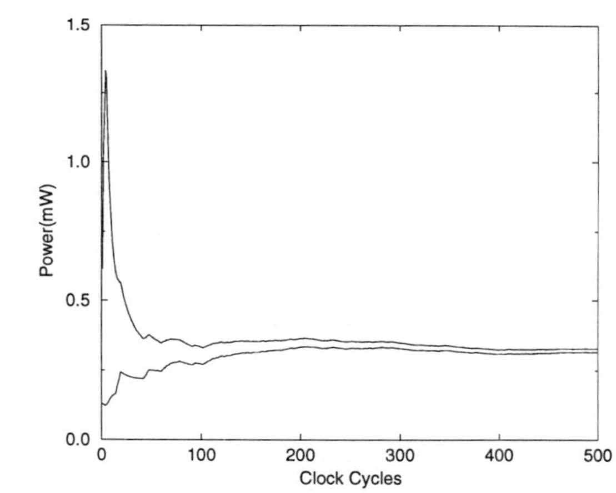

Figure 1. Upper and lower power bounds under a correlated vector set for circuit s1423 (74 latches and 657 gates).

As for the choice of K', we use the following heuristic approach to determine when to stop the simulation within a block. For every simulation cycle, we compute the latest value of the slope of the power waveform - this is a waveform which is obtained by taking the average at every time point of the two power bound waveforms. When this slope becomes small (relative to a built-in threshold), then we check the *tightness* of the bounds. The tightness is defined as the difference between the two block power bounds divided by their average. It can be shown that if the bounds on the power of every block satisfy a given tightness specification, then the two bounds on the total power in equation (4) also satisfy the same tightness. If the tightness is less than a user-specified value, then we stop the simulation of that block. Otherwise, if the tightness is not small enough but does not change for a number (in our implementation, 10) of consecutive clock cycles, then we also stop.

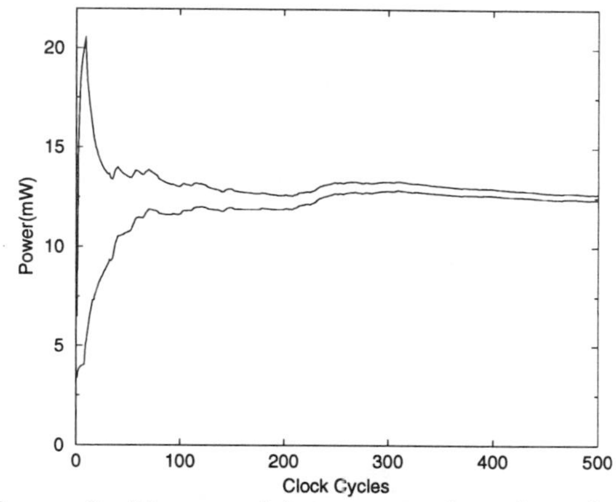

Figure 2. Upper and lower power bounds under a correlated vector set for circuit s35932 (1728 latches and 16,065 gates).

3.3 Choice of sample size

The choice of sample size, N, affects the quality of the approximations in (5). It should be clear that the larger N is, the better the approximation; but how much should N be for a certain desired error-tolerance? This is the classical problem of mean-estimation in statistics. We will briefly review the mean-estimation procedure with reference to an arbitrary random variable $\mathbf{x}$ whose mean $E[\mathbf{x}]$ is to be estimated from N sample values $x_1, \ldots, x_N$, using:

$$E[\mathbf{x}] \approx \mu_N = \frac{x_1 + \cdots + x_N}{N} \tag{10}$$

which is what is done in (5).

In order for the results below to be true, the values $x_1, \ldots, x_n$ should be observed values of *independent, identically distributed* random variables. To guarantee this, in our work, the start of a block is chosen completely at random every time, independently of all prior block positions, using a uniform random number generator that gives a value between $-K+2$ and M. With this, the value μ_N is a sample of a random variable, called the *sample mean* [10], whose mean is equal to $E[\mathbf{x}]$ and whose variance is equal to σ^2/N, where σ^2 is the variance of $\mathbf{x}$. Furthermore, based on the *Central Limit Theorem* [10], the distribution of the sample mean approaches the *normal distribution* for large N. The minimum number of samples, N, to satisfy near-normality is typically about 30 [11]. With $(1-\alpha)$ confidence, it then follows that [11]:

$$-z_{\alpha/2} \leq \frac{\mu_N - E[\mathbf{x}]}{\sigma/\sqrt{N}} \leq z_{\alpha/2} \tag{11}$$

where $0 < \alpha < 1$ and where $z_{\alpha/2}$ is defined so that the area to its right under the standard normal distribution curve is equal to $\alpha/2$. The value of $z_{\alpha/2}$ for a given

α can be easily found using standard statistical tables. It is also known [11] that for such large sample sizes (N larger than about 30), one may use an approximation by which $s_N/\sqrt{N}$ is used as a replacement to $\sigma/\sqrt{N}$, where s_N is the standard deviation of the observed N data values $x_1, \ldots, x_N$, measured as follows:

$$s_N^2 = \frac{1}{N-1}\sum_{i=1}^{N}(x_i - \mu_N)^2 \tag{12}$$

Therefore, with confidence $(1-\alpha)$, we have:

$$\frac{|\mu_N - E[\mathbf{x}]|}{\mu_N} \leq \frac{z_{\alpha/2}s_N}{\mu_N\sqrt{N}} \tag{13}$$

If ϵ_1 is a small positive number, and if N is large enough to achieve:

$$\frac{s_N}{\mu_N\sqrt{N}} \leq \frac{\epsilon_1}{z_{\alpha/2}} \tag{14}$$

then ϵ_1 places an upper bound on the relative error of the sample, with $(1-\alpha)$ confidence:

$$\frac{|\mu_N - E[\mathbf{x}]|}{\mu_N} \leq \frac{z_{\alpha/2}s_N}{\mu_N\sqrt{N}} \leq \epsilon_1 \tag{15}$$

This may also be expressed as the relative deviation from the mean $E[\mathbf{x}]$:

$$\frac{|\mu_N - E[\mathbf{x}]|}{E[\mathbf{x}]} \leq \frac{\epsilon_1}{1-\epsilon_1} = \epsilon \tag{16}$$

Here, $\epsilon > 0$ is defined as the user-specified *error tolerance*, and α (or $1-\alpha$) is the user-specified *confidence*. Thus equation (14) provides a stopping criterion that determines when to stop sampling in order to yield the accuracy specified in (16) with confidence $(1-\alpha)$. Notice that the required number of samples N is not known a priori, but is determined only when (14) is first met. In our work, in computing (5), we impose a minimum sample size of 30, for the reasons explained above, so that we start checking if (14) is satisfied only after N is larger than or equal to 30.

The above discussion is applicable for estimating both the mean upper and lower bounds on the power dissipation, $E[\mathbf{P_K^u}]$ and $E[\mathbf{P_K^l}]$. Since the number of iterations required to estimate $E[\mathbf{P_K^u}]$ may be different from that required for $E[\mathbf{P_K^l}]$, we continue the sampling until condition (14) has been met for both means.

4. Experimental results

The technique proposed above has been implemented and tested on a number of ISCAS-89 sequential benchmark circuits [12], after mapping them to a gate library with delay and capacitance values typical of 0.5μ CMOS technology. According to [13], *almost all* circuits that are functionally initializable are also logically initializable (with 3-valued logic simulation). Since practical circuits will always be functionally initializable, we have restricted our results to the subset of the ISCAS-89 circuits that are known to be logically initializable. Other than this, no special considerations were used in picking the circuits below. Only two circuits were shown in [13] to be functionally but not logically initializable and, on these two circuits, our method does not work very well. While more circuits may need to be tested, this may mean that the method is best suited to circuits that are known to be logically initializable.

Since no input vector sets are available for these benchmarks, we have tried to mimic the correlations that exist in real vector sets by generating a long correlated vector set consisting of 100,000 vectors. The correlation coefficients were changed arbitrarily every 100 vectors. Thus, the statistical properties of the vectors vary widely depending on where they are in the 100,000 vector stream. For each circuit, we first estimated the power due to the whole 100,000 vectors by simulation, and then used our block sampling approach to estimate the power, with 5% error-tolerance ($\epsilon = 0.05$) and 95% confidence ($\alpha = 0.05$).

Table II.
PERFORMANCE UNDER CORRELATED INPUT VECTORS. EXECUTION TIME WAS MEASURED ON A SUN SPARC 5.

Ckt	LB	UB	Power	Tight(%)	#cycle	Time(s)
s298	0.2928	0.3120	0.3024	6.3517	3685	18.90
s349	0.2949	0.3109	0.3029	5.2906	5540	34.67
s386	0.2883	0.3030	0.2957	4.9689	2492	24.22
s444	0.1867	0.2026	0.1946	8.1650	6178	42.10
s526n	0.2820	0.2977	0.2898	5.4316	3779	29.38
s641	0.2827	0.2972	0.2899	4.9803	2824	58.86
s820	0.3013	0.3203	0.3108	6.1218	4799	98.85
s1196	1.1151	1.1635	1.1393	4.2502	118	4.90
s1488	0.3772	0.4056	0.3914	7.2549	13085	438.95
s35932	12.3395	12.9631	12.6513	4.9293	2726	3728.69

Table II shows the tightness of the power bounds and the speed of convergence. For some details of these circuits (gate count, etc.), the reader is referred to Table I. The table lists the power upper (UB) and lower (LB) bounds in mW, and the average of the two under the "Power" column (also in mW). The tightness of the bounds was measured as the difference between them divided by their average, expressed as a percentage. The values illustrate that the bounds can be quite tight in most cases. The table also lists the total number of cycles (i.e., vectors) that were required for convergence and the CPU time required.

The power estimated by our block sampling approach (average of the two bounds) was compared to that computed by simulation of the whole 100,000 vector set, and the results are shown in Table III. It is clear that the errors are very small and that all are below the specified 5% error tolerance. Table III also includes a column named "Compaction." This is the ratio of the number of vectors simulated by the block sampling method, to the total number of vectors (100,000) in the power vector set. In many cases, it turns out to be enough to simulate only around 5% of the total vector set. In some cases, this ratio is larger, up to 13% in one case. Thus, the net effect is that the power is estimated by simulating only a small fraction of the total vector set. This feature is essential for simulation of large sequential circuits. Effectively, an *implicit compaction* of the vector set has been achieved. The adjective "implicit" denotes the fact that this was done on the fly, during the simulation, rather than up-front. We feel that this is the correct way of performing compaction, mainly because, as seen in Tables II and III, the number of vectors required for convergence depends very much on the special characteristics of the circuit and is not determined simply by signal statistics or by circuit size. Sometimes smaller circuits require more cycles to converge.

Table III.
SHOWS THE ERROR BETWEEN SIMULATION OF ALL 100,000 CORRELATED VECTORS AND USING THE BLOCK SAMPLING (BS) SCHEME.

Ckt	Power(AV)	Power(BS)	err(%)	Compaction
s298	0.298088	0.302420	-1.4	0.03685
s349	0.296436	0.302960	-2.2	0.0554
s386	0.293828	0.295707	-0.6	0.02492
s444	0.188459	0.194680	-3.3	0.06178
s526n	0.285039	0.289894	-1.77	0.03779
s641	0.288030	0.289987	-4.1	0.02824
s820	0.304192	0.310878	-2.2	0.04799
s1196	1.151242	1.139382	1.0	0.00118
s1488	0.387748	0.391459	-3.5	0.13085
s35932	12.454792	12.651351	-1.6	0.02726

5. Conclusion

We have proposed a simulation-based method for estimating the power dissipation of sequential circuits. The method works by sampling blocks of consecutive vectors from a user-supplied (potentially very long) power vector set. Since the state of the circuit at the beginning of each block is unknown, we put the circuit in an all-X state and simulate it for one block using three-valued logic simulation. The simulator includes delay information, so that it does capture glitching activity. During the simulation of each block, we compute an upper bound and a lower bound on the power due to that block, which we found can be very tight. The blocks are selected at random from anywhere in the power vector set, and the process is repeated until, using statistical methods of mean estimation, the upper and lower bounds on the power have been determined with sufficient (user-specified) accuracy and confidence.

A major advantage of the method is that the state of the sequential circuit is always guaranteed to be valid - the FSM never goes outside its valid state space. Thus, the estimated power corresponds to realistic typical circuit operation. Another advantage of the method is that only a fraction of the vectors in the (potentially huge) power vector set need to be simulated. For the 100,000 vector sets that we considered, this fraction varied between 0.1% and 13%.

References

[1] F. Najm, "A survey of power estimation techniques in VLSI circuits," *IEEE Trans. on VLSI Systems*, vol. 2, no. 4, pp. 446–455, Dec. 1994.

[2] D. Brand and C. Visweswariah, "Inaccuracies in power estimation during logic synthesis," *Int'l Conf. on Computer-Aided Design*, pp. 388–394, 1996.

[3] A. A. Ismaeel and M. A. Breuer, "The probability of error detection in sequential circuits using random test vectors," *Journal of Electronic Testing*, vol. 1, pp. 245–256, January 1991.

[4] G. D. Hachtel, E. Macii, A. Pardo, and F. Somenzi, "Probabilistic analysis of large finite state machines," *Design Automation Conf.*, pp. 270–275, June 1994.

[5] J. Monteiro and S. Devadas, "A methodology for efficient estimation of switching activity in sequential logic circuits," *Design Automation Conf.*, pp. 12–17, June 6–10, 1994.

[6] C-Y Tsui, M. Pedram, and A. M. Despain, "Exact and approximate methods for calculating signal and transition probabilities in FSMs," *Design Automation Conf.*, pp. 18–23, June 6–10, 1994.

[7] F. Najm, S. Goel, and I. Hajj, "Power Estimation in Sequential Circuits," *Design Automation Conf.*, pp. 635–640, 1995.

[8] T-L. Chou and K. Roy, "Statistical estimation of sequential circuit activity," *Int'l Conf. on Computer-Aided Design*, pp. 34–37, 1995.

[9] R. Marculescu, D. Marculescu, and M. Pedram, "Efficient power estimation for highly correlated input streams," *Design Automation Conf.*, pp. 628–634, June 12–16, 1995.

[10] M. H. DeGroot, *Probability and Statistics*, 2nd Edition. Reading, MA: Addison-Wesley, 1986.

[11] I. R. Miller, J. E. Freund, and R. Johnson, *Probability and Statistics for Engineers*, 4th Edition. Englewood Cliffs, NJ: Prentice-Hall Inc., 1990, pp. 210–211.

[12] F. Brglez, D. Bryan, and K. Koźmiński, "Combinational profiles of sequential benchmark circuits," *IEEE International Symposium on Circuits and Systems*, pp. 1929–1934, 1989.

[13] J. Wehbeh, D. G. Saab, "On the Initialization of Sequential Circuits," *IEEE Int'l Test Conf.*, Altoon, PA, pp. 233–239, 1994.

Fast Power Estimation for Deterministic Input Streams *

Luca Benini # Giovanni De Micheli # Enrico Macii ‡ Massimo Poncino ‡ Riccardo Scarsi ‡

Stanford University
Computer Systems Laboratory
Stanford, CA 94305

‡ Politecnico di Torino
Dip. di Automatica e Informatica
Torino, ITALY 10129

Abstract

The power dissipated by digital systems under realistic input stimuli is not accurately described by a single average value, but by a waveform that shows how power consumption varies over time as the system responds to the inputs. In this paper, we face the problem of obtaining accurate power waveforms for combinational and sequential circuits under typical usage patterns. We propose a multi-level simulation engine that achieves high accuracy in estimating the average power as well as the time-domain power waveform with high computational efficiency.

1 Introduction

Power estimation for validation and sign-off is a critical step in the design process. In this phase, accuracy is a key requirement, but there are hard constraints on the time that can be dedicated to power estimation. Moreover, it is important to estimate the power dissipated by the system while running typical applications, i.e., streams of validation patterns are usually available or can be produced with a relatively low effort by the designer. Unfortunately, such pattern sets are usually extremely large; hence, performing accurate (and slow) power estimation on the complete sets is simply computationally infeasible.

Recent research [1, 2, 3] has addressed the problem of selecting small subsets of large pattern sets so as to guarantee that the estimate of the average power obtained on the subset is as close as possible to the actual average power dissipation of the circuit when simulated with the complete pattern set.

In this paper, we tackle the problem of input pattern selection from a novel point of view. Based on the observation of real-life systems, we claim that the average power does not fully characterize the power dissipation of a circuit, and that a *time-domain power waveform* can provide a much more complete source of information. We move from the experimental evidence that typical, deterministic input streams are such that the average power dissipated by the circuit can vary widely when distinct subsets of consecutive patterns are simulated. We thus propose a technique, leveraging multi-level simulation, that can be used to quickly, yet accurately extract the average power, as well as the power waveform for deterministic input streams for which the *running average*, taken over a fixed number input patterns, of the circuit power dissipation follows an "up-down staircase" curve.

From the user point of view, a fast cycle-based simulation is performed on the complete input stream. During the simulation, the monitoring of an *indicator function* provides information on the variations of the input stream and power dissipation. Accurate power simulation is automatically dispatched when needed for tracking the changes in the "local" mean value of the input stream. The tool automatically constructs the time-domain power waveform and optionally computes its average.

*This work is partially supported by NSF under contract MIP-9421129

The indicator function may not depend on the primary inputs only. As long as the internal state of the system is available during cycle-based simulation, its value can be taken into account as well. The same holds for the system outputs. In general, any information available during cycle-based simulation can be exploited for constructing an indicator function. Obviously, there is a trade-off between the accuracy of such function and the overhead it imposes on cycle-based simulation. Our method is practical only if it guarantees that the time spent on fast cycle-based simulation (T_c), plus the overhead for the computation of the indicator function (T_{ind}), plus the time required to perform accurate power simulation on the the sample (T_{sample}) is much smaller than the time required to perform accurate power simulation on the entire input stream (T_{pow}).

We have benchmarked the capabilities of our tool on large subsets of the ISCAS'85 [4] and the ISCAS'89 [5] circuit suites. In particular, given a circuit and an input stream, we have compared the average power value calculated using our technique to that obtained by switch-level simulation [6] of the entire input stream. Results are highly satisfactory, since the average error is between 4.5% and 6.1% for the combinational examples, and between 2.2% and 6.4% for the sequential circuits, depending on the type of indicator function used. Moreover, the estimated power waveforms match closely the actual ones.

2 Related Work

There are two techniques in the literature which are somehow related to ours. The power ratio method [7] is based on multi-level simulation. It postulates that the power estimate, P_{est}, provided by high-level, fast power simulation is proportional to the power, P_{acc}, estimated with accurate simulation. In symbols: $P_{acc} = P_{est} \cdot K$. The unknown proportionality constant, K, is simply obtained by first computing both P_{acc} and P_{est} for a small subset of the complete input stream, and then by taking their ratio. Unfortunately, for deterministic, designer-supplied streams, K is usually far from being constant; in these cases, the method may lead to inaccurate estimates.

Stratified random sampling [8], though developed as an alternative to Monte Carlo methods, has some similarities to the technique we propose here. In fact, it generally requires only a small number of accurate simulations to achieve power estimates which are acceptable and, as for our method, it exploits a high-level power estimator to direct the choice of the patterns that will be simulated with high accuracy. In the form it has been presented, however, it targets the estimation of average power of input streams for which some statistical constraints, such as error and confidence level, are given; in addition, its effectiveness has been demonstrated only for combinational circuits. On the contrary, our approach works for purely deterministic input streams, it can provide the user with information on the average power values, as well as the changes of power dissipation over time, and it properly and accurately handles sequential circuits.

3 Tracking Staircase Behavior

Consider a measurable property $P(T)$ of a circuit that changes over time (in our case, power is the property of interest). We assume discretized time. A time quantum is called *cycle*. The property has an *up-down staircase average* behavior, *staircase* for brevity, over time when its running (or sliding) average taken over a window of N cycles, $P_N(T)$, changes in a non-monotonic fashion, with long plateaus where $P_N(T)$ is approximately constant mixed with regions where it changes rapidly. Figure 1 (a) shows the diagram of a time-varying property $P(T)$ with staircase behavior, and Figure 1 (b) shows the diagram of $P_N(T)$. The value of N (the averaging length) is shown as well. Notice that $P_N(T)$ is not defined for the first N time points.

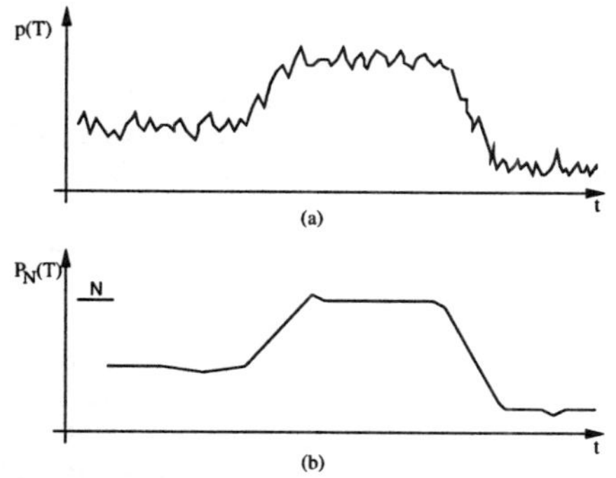

Figure 1: Waveforms for $P(T)$ (a) and $P_N(T)$ (b).

The power dissipated by many real-life circuits, such as microprocessors running realistic work-loads, has staircase behavior [9]. The key observation is that such behavior appears to be induced by the input streams which are processed by the circuits in typical operating conditions. Extensive experimentation [10, 11] has shown that, when the input streams are randomly generated, composed by uniformly distributed, uncorrelated patterns, the power dissipation does not have a staircase behavior. On the contrary, $P_N(T)$ is a roughly constant function, as long as N is sufficiently large to smooth out cycle-by-cycle variations due to the strong pattern dependency of power. Obviously, we would like to accurately estimate the power dissipation induced in a circuit by realistic input streams which are not uniformly distributed, nor uncorrelated. Most of the pattern sets usually provided by the designers for typical hardware modules (e.g., RT-level macros, cores, microcontrollers) tend to induce a staircase behavior on the power dissipation.

Our target is a challenging one, because it requires a difficult trade-off choice. The number of samples, N, taken to compute the running average is the key parameter for achieving the desired accuracy. If we choose an excessively large N, we loose accuracy in the estimation of the average power waveform $P_N(T)$. The larger N, the more $P_N(T)$ resembles to a constant. On the other hand, if N is too short, the noise in the estimation of the average power will be too large (because of the effect of pattern dependency) and accuracy will be compromised as well.

Power estimation in the staircase situation is further complicated by computational issues. As explained in the introduction, we cannot afford to simulate entire input streams with an accurate power simulator. Therefore, we exploit information available during fast high-level simulation (hereafter called *Level 1* for brevity) to reduce the number of slow, accurate low-level simulations (hereafter called *Level 2*) needed to estimate the power. Differently from the existing techniques, this information is used to estimate how power changes over time when the given input stream is applied at the circuit inputs.

3.1 The Indicator Function

We call *indicator function* the Level 1 information exploited to track the variations in switching activity of the input stream. The basic requirement for the indicator function is that it must change over time, and its changes should be related to the variations of the power dissipation. Notice that this is a much milder requirement than simple proportionality (as requested by the power ratio method).

We propose a set of alternative indicator functions based on sampling the (zero-delay) switching activity and the value of the nodes in Level 1 simulation. Tuning the number and choice of the sampling points allows us to:

- Trade off accuracy for computational overhead (increasing the number of sampling points increases the overhead in Level 1 simulation);
- Exploit designer knowledge, if possible, to select specific nodes that should be sampled to increase the accuracy of the indicator.

We focus on indicator functions that do not require any designer intervention in the choice of the sampling points. Our target is to build a fully automated procedure for power estimation that can be applied successfully even without complete understanding of the design functionality and hardware architecture. In [12], it was observed that there exists strong correlation between power dissipation in a combinational logic circuit and the switching activity at its inputs and outputs. A similar conclusion was reached in [13, 14]; in these works, the power dissipated by a combinational design, possibly described at the functional-level, was approximated by a combination of the circuit input and output *entropy*, two quantities which are strictly related to the input and output switching activities.

The basic claim in [12] is that power dissipation can be predicted with reasonable accuracy by computing a function of input-output switching. In symbols:

$$P^{n+1} = f(i_1^n \oplus i_1^{n+1}, \ldots, i_{n_i}^n \oplus i_{n_i}^{n+1}, o_1^n \oplus o_1^{n+1}, \ldots, o_{n_o}^n \oplus i_{n_o}^{n+1} \quad (1)$$

where P^{n+1} is the power dissipated during the $n+1$-st simulation cycle, i_k^n and i_k^{n+1} are respectively the value of input k at the beginning of cycles n and $n+1$, o_k^n and o_k^{n+1} are respectively the output values at the end of cycles n and $n+1$. The function f is a general (possibly non-linear) mapping $f : B^{n_i+n_o} \rightarrow \mathcal{R}$. The choice of the sampling points for our indicator functions is based on a similar assumption. We propose the following criteria, sorted by increasing accuracy and computational overhead:

- Sampling only the primary inputs. The main limitation of this criterion is that it does not consider any information on how input switching propagates through the logic. Moreover, for sequential circuits, the effect of internal state on power dissipation is not taken into account. On the other hand, this criterion has minimum overhead. Indeed, Level 1 simulation is not even needed, and analysis of the input stream is sufficient to extract the required information.
- Sampling primary inputs and outputs. This criterion increases the information on internal switching, since the end effect of the input propagation is sampled. Again, this criterion is targeted towards combinational circuits, since it does not account for internal state. Compared to the previous one, this choice of sampling points has higher overhead: The number of sampling points increases and, more importantly, Level 1 simulation must be executed for computing the correct output values.

- Sampling primary inputs and outputs, as well as the inputs and outputs of the flip-flops. This is the full cycle boundary information that is usually available in Level 1 simulation (which is cycle accurate). This criterion has considerably higher overhead than the first two (the number of sampling points is greatly increased), but it is well-suited for dealing with sequential circuits, because the internal state is exposed.
- Estimating the full zero-delay activity (as in the power ratio method and in stratified random sampling), including internal nodes in the combinational logic. This criterion has very high overhead, because it prevents fast compiled cycle-based simulation (at Level 1) to "compile away" internal nodes. Moreover, it is not possible to perform Level 1 simulation at a different level of abstraction, because the values of the internal nodes cannot be sampled (they do not exist at higher abstraction). Although zero-delay simulation is still much faster than full-delay event-driven simulation (or switch-level simulation), it may be more than one order of magnitude slower than compiled, cycle-based simulation.

The sampling criteria listed above span the trade-off between completeness of the monitored information and computational overhead. It should be noted that the overhead strongly depends on the available Level 1 simulation. State-of-the-art fast cycle-based simulators have the capability of collapsing internal nodes or using compact data representations to accelerate the computation. The overhead can be estimated based on how much of this acceleration capability must be given up.

The computation of the indicator function requires not only the choice of the sampling points, but also the specification of how the sampled information should be used to compute a measure that tracks the temporal variations of the average power. The main problem is that power is strongly pattern dependent: Its value can change widely in successive clock cycles. For this reason, our indicator function must include a short-term time averaging operation. The simplest one is then the number of switching events averaged over a short number of cycles, N_c:

$$I(T) = \frac{\sum_{t=T-N_c}^{T} \sum_{i \in S} \rho_i^t}{N_c} \tag{2}$$

where S is the set of sampling points, ρ_i^t are Boolean variables that have value 1 when the sampling point i switches between cycle $t-1$ and t ($\rho_i^t = i^{t-1} \oplus i^t$). The choice of N_c in Equation 2 is critical. It should be long enough to smooth out fluctuations due to single-pattern dependence, but it should be short enough to capture the staircase behavior. The issue of how to select N_c will be discussed in Section 4.

Notice that Equation 2 defines the indicator as a function of time. The short-term average can be seen as a *sliding window*: At time T, we consider N_c sets of values of the sampling points, one for each simulation cycle from time $T - N_c$ to T. The sliding window average is well-suited to estimate variations over time, because it evolves in parallel with the advancement of the global simulation time. This is in sharp contrast with stratified random sampling, where samples can be selected and averaged together in any order, without any constraint on temporal adjacency.

The simple time-averaged sum of switching events can be replaced by more complex indicator functions. The one we have adopted computes the weighted sum of switching events averaged over N_c:

$$I(T) = \frac{\sum_{t=T-N_c}^{T} \sum_{i \in S} w_i \rho_i^t}{N_c} \tag{3}$$

In this case, ρ_i^t of Equation 3 is replaced by $w_i \rho_i^t$. The weights w_i represent the relative influence of the switching of sampling point i. Several algorithms can be devised for the computation of w_i (notice that such algorithms must be run only once at the beginning of the estimation process). Possible choices of w_i are:

1. Expected capacitance (based on node fanout) for internal nodes when the most expensive choice of sampling points is used;
2. For primary outputs and flip flop inputs: Estimate of the complexity (i.e., number of gate equivalent) in the fanin cone;
3. For primary inputs and flip-flop outputs: Estimate of the complexity (i.e., number of gate equivalent) in the fanout cone.

A generic, user-specified non-linear (weighted) combination of values and transitions averaged over N_c might also be adopted. However, this indicator function is not investigated here, since we target a fully automated power estimation process.

Concluding the section, we want to stress that the fundamental use of any indicator function $I(T)$ is *not* to provide an estimate of the power consumption at Level 1 (such estimates have limited accuracy and may be interesting only during design exploration). Instead, we use $I(T)$ to extract information on the variations over time of the average power dissipation. How this can be done and how such information is fruitfully exploited to determine accurate power estimates is the subject of the next section.

4 Multi-Level Power Simulation

Our multi-level simulation engine is conceptually simple. Given a long stream of N_{tot} input patterns, a high-level and a low-level description of the circuit under analysis, the Level 1 simulation is started. Level 1 simulation runs three additional tasks:

1. Monitoring the sampling points required for the computation of the indicator function;
2. Computing the indicator function $I(T)$;
3. Performing the *staircase test* on $I(T)$.

The choice of the sampling points and the computation of $I(T)$ have been discussed in Section 3. The purpose of the staircase test is to decide, based on the changes over time of $I(T)$, when to fire the Level 2 simulation. Whenever the staircase test triggers, the inputs and state values are extracted from Level 1 information and used to set the initial state for Level 2 simulation. After that, the multi-level simulation can proceed in lock-step.

Level 2 simulation continues until a *stopping criterion* is satisfied. Such criterion decides when sufficient accurate power data have been collected to obtain a reliable short-term average power estimate $P_{avg}(T)$ (notice that P_{avg} is a function of time). The value $P_{avg}(T)$ is a point in the average power waveform. T is conventionally set to the value assumed in the last cycle of Level 2 simulation.

At the end of the simulation, all N_{tot} patterns have been simulated at Level 1, but only N_{sample} patterns have been simulated at Level 2. Typically, $N_{sample} << N_{tot}$. The end results is a set of values $\mathcal{P} = \{P_{avg}(T_1), ..., P_{avg}(T_s)\}$, where $T_1 < ... < T_s$. The power values $P_{avg}(T_i)$ and the times T_i are a set of samples of the *power waveform* of the circuit.

The performance of our multi-level scheme is measured by the speed-up achieved with respect to accurate simulation of the entire input stream, because this is the only known way to extract complete power information on systems with staircase behavior.

The speed-up is defined by the following equation:

$$SP = \frac{T_{pow}}{T_c + T_{ind} + T_{sample}} \quad (4)$$

where T_{pow} is the time needed to simulate the circuit for N_{tot} cycles at Level 2, T_c is the time for simulating N_{tot} cycles at Level 1, T_{ind} is the time overhead caused by the calculation of both the indicator function and the staircase tests, and T_{sample} is the time required to simulate N_{sample} cycles at Level 2 during multi-level simulation.

The accuracy of the multi-level scheme can be measured by comparing the average power, P_{avg}, obtained by simulating the complete input stream at Level 2 with the estimate, P_{avg}^{est}, obtained by averaging the power samples $P_{avg}(T_i)$. Clearly, the latter must be weighted with the *duration* of the samples: $P_{avg}^{est} = \sum_{i=1}^{s} \tau_i P_{avg}(T_i)$. The duration τ_i of $P_{avg}(T_i)$ is defined as:

$$\tau_i = \frac{T_i - T_{i+1}}{N_{tot} T_{clk}} \quad (5)$$

where T_{clk} is the clock period of the system. The weighted average is needed because our technique extracts new power samples only when the staircase behavior is detected, i.e., when we are moving from one plateau to another. If the average power remains on a plateau for a long time, only one power sample is extracted, but it represents the average power dissipation of a very long time interval.

The definition of our multi-level estimation strategy is completed by addressing the following three open issues:

- How to choose N_c, i.e., the length of the short-term, sliding window average needed for computing $I(T)$.
- How to use the value of $I(T)$ to decide when firing accurate simulation to track the staircase behavior (i.e., providing the definition of the staircase test).
- How long to run accurate power simulation every time it is started by the staircase test on $I(T)$ (i.e., providing the definition of the stopping criterion).

4.1 Choosing N_c

The choice of the parameter N_c, that is, the length of the sliding window for the running average, is a key point for the success of the entire strategy. If N_c is too small, the value of $I(T)$ will be noisy: The pattern-dependent fluctuations of the indicator function may change the value of $I(T)$ too much and too rapidly. As a result, it may become impossible to discern slow variations of $I(T)$ due to staircase behavior from fast variations due to pattern dependence. The consequence of this problem is that the staircase test is triggered too often and too many Level 2 simulations are executed, causing a marked slow-down of the multi-level simulation engine.

On the other hand, if N_c is too large, $I(T)$ may have excessive *inertia* and change too slowly. In this case, the variations of $I(T)$ over time may be smoothed down to a constant average value that does not represent the variation of the average value over time. As a consequence, the staircase test is almost never satisfied. The multi-level simulation becomes really fast (a minimum number of Level 2 simulations is executed), but accuracy in tracking the power waveform is lost.

To avoid both pitfalls, the choice of N_c must be a compromise between good tracking capability and noisiness. Our procedure for choosing N_c is based on a calibration process. We move from the observation that, when uniformly distributed, uncorrelated patterns are fed to the system, the average power does not have a staircase behavior and tends to converge to a constant value. We conjecture that the same holds for the indicator functions.

Before starting the multi-level simulation on the input stream, we perform a calibration Level 1 simulation with independent, uncorrelated input patterns. The simulation is run until convergence is reached on the average value of I. Assume that the calibration simulation converges in N_{M_I} cycles. N_{M_I} is the number of simulation cycles needed for convergence on a stable average value of I when the input patterns are independent and uncorrelated. This value is significant for our purposes, because it gives us information on the number of cycles needed to smooth out only the power variations due to strong pattern dependence. The calibration simulation allows us to separate the effects. During calibration, the power does not have a staircase behavior, but it is still strongly pattern dependent.

The number of cycles for short-term average, N_c, is chosen to be $N_c = kN_{M_I}$, $0 < k \leq 1$. When $k = 1$, we have a *high inertia* $I(T)$. When $k < 1$, we may be able to track fast step-wise variations, but we may sometimes take a simple fluctuation due to strong pattern dependency at the beginning (the end) of a step. The choice depends on the target of the power estimation process. If we are mainly interested in obtaining a single average power value with maximum efficiency, k should be chosen close to one (or even larger, if we suspect extremely long plateaus and we have huge N_{tot}). On the contrary, if we need great accuracy on the estimate of the average power value, or we want to finely sample the power waveform, k should be close to 0.5. The price paid for the increase in accuracy is a longer runtime (a larger number of Level 2 simulations are required). Values of $k < 0.5$ are not advisable for performance reasons.

4.2 Staircase Test

During Level 1 simulation, $I(T)$ is computed on every simulation cycle. Although $I(T)$ is defined at every clock cycle, it is meaningless formulating a staircase test that involves decisions taken on time intervals shorter than N_c, being this the maximum resolution. The test is based on an upper bound on variations of $I(T)$; the procedure for its application is the following:

- Level 2 simulation is first started to obtain the first power sample. Concurrently, $I(T)$ is computed. When Level 2 simulation is stopped (through the criterion described later), the value of $I(T_0)$ at the stopping time T_0 is stored.
- Level 1 simulation and the computation of the indicator function are carried on to $T > T_0$. The staircase test is not applied until $T = T + \beta T_{clock} N_c$, where $\beta \geq 1$. As mentioned above, the rationale for this choice is to provide a lower bound on the granularity at which the staircase behavior is tested. The interval during which the test is disabled is called *recovery interval*.
- After the recovery interval, the test is applied at every clock cycle T. A staircase behavior is detected when:

  $$\Delta|I(T)| > \gamma \Delta_{max}|I| \quad (6)$$

  where $\Delta|I(T)| = |I(T_0) - I(T)|$, γ is a coefficient smaller than one, and $\Delta_{max}|I|$ is an upper bound to variations of $|I|$. In the case of the simple indicator function of Equation 2, $\Delta_{max} = N_c|S|$, where $|S|$ is the cardinality of the set of nodes in the circuit whose switching activity is sampled by the indicator function.
- If the test is satisfied, the power is estimated through Level 2 simulation. Upon stopping of the latter (at time T_2), $I(T_2)$ is stored and the process is restarted.

Parameter γ controls the sensitivity of the test; its typical range is $0.1 < \gamma < 0.5$. The choice of γ is again dictated by a trade-off between sensitivity and accuracy in the estimation.

4.3 Stopping Criterion

The last decision to be taken is when to stop the Level 2 simulation after it is started by the staircase test. The simplest choice is to execute Level 2 simulation for a fixed number of clock cycles. Unfortunately, no simple criterion is available for the choice of such number.

We adopt an adaptive strategy, where the number of Level 2 simulations is variable and depends on the operating conditions. More specifically, the stopping criterion is based on a convergence test on the average power value. Although this choice is intuitively attractive, it is heuristic and relies on the assumption that on the short term, the average power dissipation appears non-staircase, hence it converges rather rapidly to a constant average value.

Clearly, this assumption is not true in general. More in detail, two problems may arise. The first is premature convergence: The Level 2 simulation is stopped because convergence on the average is reached too rapidly (for example, if, by chance, the power dissipated at the first two or three cycles of Level 2 simulation is almost constant). The second, and more serious, is lack of convergence. In this case, Level 2 simulation never stops. To mitigate both problems, we provide the following lower bound on the number of vectors that must be simulated in Level 2: $\eta_L N_c$, with $\eta_L < 1$, typically between 0.5 and 1. Similarly, the upper bound is $\eta_U N_c$, with $\eta_U > 1$, typically between 2 and 3. The rationale of these bounds is based on the observation that the convergence of power estimation is related to convergence on the indicator function, although it is expected to be slower.

Concluding this section, we would like to emphasize that, although no strong convergence results or accuracy bounds are available for our technique, this limitation is shared by all other methods presented in the literature when applied to realistic power estimation problems (i.e., estimation of the power dissipation for sequential systems with user-provided input streams). Experimental evidence, detailed in Section 5, confirms the robustness and flexibility of our approach, which appears to be a viable, albeit heuristic, power estimation strategy for the realistic staircase situation. More work is needed to gain a complete theoretical understanding of the mathematical models for power dissipation in this general setting.

5 Experimental Results

In order to investigate the applicability and the accuracy of our methodology, we have performed three sets of power estimation experiments, and we have checked the so computed results against the ones we have obtained through exhaustive transistor-level simulation using Irsim [6]. In the following sections we report on our findings.

The algorithm has shown remarkable robustness for what concerns the values of the user-defined tuning parameters that control the performance and accuracy. To select such values we have ran a set of experiments on a small combinational circuit (a few tens of gates) and we have chosen the values that have given the minimum error (on average power estimation) for an overall 100X speed-up. The parameter values are the following: $k = 0.5$, $\beta = 1$, $\gamma = 0.2$, $\eta_L = 0.5$ and $\eta_U = 2$. The same values have been used for all experiments described in the following three sections.

In spite of the satisfactory results we have obtained, we conjecture that even more accurate (or faster) estimates could be obtained by tuning the parameters for each example. However, this would greatly increase the time required to obtain the power estimates (parameter tuning should be taken into account when measuring the speed-up).

5.1 Combinational Circuits

In a first set of experiments, we have considered all the ISCAS'85 examples [4]. The circuits were first optimized for area, and then mapped for area using SIS [15] onto a gate-library consisting of 2-input NAND and NOR gates, inverters, and buffers.

Table 1 reports the data for the ten considered benchmarks. Columns *Circ*, *I*, *O*, and *G* give the number of circuit inputs, outputs, and gates. Column *Estimated Power* shows the average power values obtained with the technique of this paper, while column *Actual Power* provides the values obtained through complete transistor-level simulation of the input stream. Column *Estimated Power* is further split in three sets of columns, one for each of the three sampling points selection criteria we have considered, namely, input (column *In*), input/output (column *In-Out*), and global activity (column *Intern*). Each column reports the average power (*Pow*), the absolute value of the relative error, with respect to the actual power ($|E|$), the number of Level 2 simulations triggered (*L2*), and the time required to complete the estimation (*T*), measured in seconds on a DEC AXP 1000/400 with 256 MB of RAM. Finally, column N_c tells the size of the sliding window N_c, specific for each circuit, that we have used in the indicator function. All power values in this, and in the following tables, are expressed in mW.

Since the benchmark circuits do not come with typical input patterns, we built input streams trying to emulate real-life usage sequences. The generated input streams have very high temporal correlation (i.e., correlation between successive patterns), very high spatial correlation (i.e., correlation between input variables) and, more importantly, are highly non-stationary. The average input switching activity is changed abruptly and wide variations are imposed several times in the stream. Between variations, the average input switching activity is roughly constant, although the vectors are correlated. The complete streams consisted of 50,000 patterns.

The error between the power values provided by our tool and the ones obtained through complete transistor-level simulation of the input stream are very limited, namely, 6.1%, 5.9%, and 4.5%, depending on the selected sampling criterion. On the other hand, the simulation time reduction is substantial (between one and two orders of magnitude).

As expected, the choice of a more accurate criterion for sample points selection yields increasingly accurate estimates. However, it should be observed that the difference in accuracy is quite small. This is of great interest when the Level 1 simulation is carried out at a high level of abstraction, e.g., behavioral simulation. In this case, the knowledge of the internal switchings is not available, and the designer can rely only on I/O information.

Figure 2 shows, in the case of benchmark c432, how the three sampling criteria (the top three plots, from left to right), behave in tracking the power waveform obtained by simulation of the given input stream. The piecewise-constant approximation of the power waveform, obtained with the indicator function based on I/O sampling, is the bottom left plot. The actual power waveform is the bottom right plot. Obviously, the scales for the ordinates of the top three plots are different from those of the bottom two, since the indicator function provide numbers of weighted switching events, as opposed to actual power values. Comparing the two bottom plots, it can be observed that the indicator function based on I/O activity provides sufficient information to track the staircase behavior of the power for combinational circuits. Notice, however, that we approximate the power with a piecewise-constant waveform, hence the cycle-by-cycle accuracy is limited. More refined interpolation schemes can be used to improve cycle-by-cycle accuracy [16].

Circ	I	O	G	Estimated Power													Actual Power	
				In				In-Out				Intern				N_c	Pow	T
				Pow	$\|E\|$	L2	T	Pow	$\|E\|$	L2	T	Pow	$\|E\|$	L2	T			
c432	37	6	265	0.72	7.5	15	9	0.72	7.5	15	9	0.71	6.4	15	9	158	0.67	2125
c499	41	32	525	1.33	6.4	13	10	1.36	8.8	11	8	1.30	4.0	15	11	110	1.25	2281
c880	60	26	431	1.42	9.2	16	11	1.42	9.2	15	11	1.41	8.4	13	9	91	1.30	2160
c1355	41	32	525	1.38	2.2	9	6	1.38	2.2	9	6	1.38	2.2	8	5	220	1.35	4813
c1908	33	25	529	1.78	2.3	13	21	1.75	1.1	16	30	1.74	0.9	13	24	197	1.73	7804
c2670	233	140	808	2.69	0.4	13	21	2.69	0.4	13	21	2.69	0.4	13	21	112	2.68	9483
c3540	50	22	1289	5.43	4.4	12	252	5.31	2.1	15	301	5.14	1.1	12	246	311	5.20	12102
c5315	178	123	1759	6.50	1.7	12	170	6.52	2.0	13	171	6.50	1.7	19	311	303	6.39	10209
c6288	32	32	3240	9.79	8.1	9	3237	9.81	7.9	9	3316	9.96	6.5	8	3675	307	10.66	32663
c7552	207	108	2314	10.14	18.9	8	1432	10.19	18.5	16	1560	10.82	13.6	15	1470	425	12.51	10812
Average					6.1				5.9				4.5					

Table 1: Power Estimation Results for Combinational Circuits.

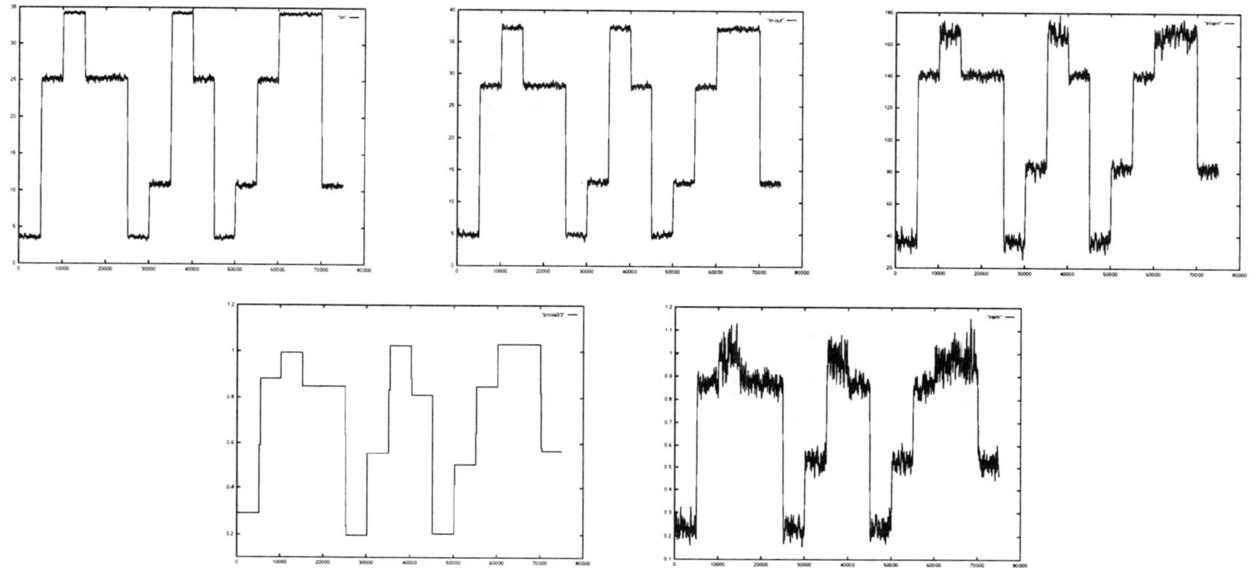

Figure 2: Indicator Functions, Piecewise-Constant Approximation, and Actual Power Profile for Benchmark c432.

5.2 Sequential Circuits

The second set of experiments concerns sequential circuits. We have selected a subset of the ISCAS'89 benchmarks [5], so as to create a representative sample, in terms of functionality, size, and topological structure (sequential depth, number of inputs, outputs, and flip-flops), of the existing examples.

Table 2 shows the results obtained for these circuits (column *FF* indicates the number of flip-flops). Notice that for these experiments the indicator functions we have used are the following: i) primary input and primary output activity (column *In-Out*); ii) primary input, primary output, and state (i.e. flip-flop inputs and outputs) activity (column *In-Out-State*); iii) complete internal activity (column *Intern*).

As for the combinational examples, our method yields accurate estimates, the average errors being 6.4%, 3.5%, and 2.2%, depending on the sampling points selection approach. Execution times are still much smaller (about one order of magnitude) than those required by exhaustive simulation.

For some sequential circuit topologies, the temporal behavior of the indicator function based solely on input-output switching is not necessarily informative enough on the actual power. This is because, for sequential circuits having far more latches than primary inputs, the degree of switching at the primary inputs has a limited correlation to the overall activity (and thus power); rather, this is mainly driven by the switching at the present state lines, which induces most of the switching inside the combinational logic.

Figure 3 shows a graphical view of this fact. The plots at the top of the figure refer to circuit s298. This circuit clearly falls into the class of circuits just described, since it has 3 inputs and 14 latches. Although the input stream for the circuit has an average switching activity with staircase behavior, the power dissipation (the top right plot) has very weak correlation with the input switching activity (the staircase behavior is heavily smoothed out). Nevertheless, our tool tracks the behavior of the power dissipation very well, because the indicator function observes the switching activity of the state variables as well. The piecewise-constant approximation of the power dissipation is shown in the top left plot. The plots at the bottom of the figure, on the other hand, refer to circuit s344; in this case, waveforms seem to exhibit a "combinational" behavior, in the sense that the input activity has a considerable control over the internal degree of switching (and, consequently, power dissipation). Power has a staircase behavior that is easily tracked by our tool.

In general, we expect realistic sequential circuits to have a behavior similar to s298. In other words, sampling state information is key for achieving good accuracy. This conjecture is confirmed even by our average power dissipation estimates. The accuracy of the estimate based on input, output and state activity is much better than that based on just input and output activity. Obviously, the most accurate estimate is obtained if we use the complete internal switching activity information (but, in this case, the computation of $I(T)$ may be computationally expensive, because it requires gate-level zero-delay simulation).

Circ	I	O	FF	G	Estimated Power													Actual Power	
					In-Out				In-Out-State				Intern				N_c	Pow	T
					Pow	$\|E\|$	L2	T	Pow	$\|E\|$	L2	T	Pow	$\|E\|$	L2	T			
s298	3	6	14	136	0.045	9.6	20	30	0.048	2.8	24	31	0.048	2.6	31	34	115	0.050	293
s344	9	11	15	151	0.080	2.2	10	21	0.080	2.2	10	21	0.081	1.9	14	28	122	0.082	454
s420	18	1	16	168	0.035	12.7	12	20	0.038	6.1	14	20	0.039	4.4	15	23	125	0.040	272
s444	3	6	21	181	0.038	16.5	10	14	0.042	5.1	12	29	0.046	0.8	23	26	123	0.046	136
s510	19	7	6	268	0.095	8.2	15	43	0.091	4.6	17	41	0.098	3.5	27	33	131	0.095	225
s713	35	23	17	189	0.061	3.9	13	25	0.061	4.4	14	27	0.060	2.2	16	29	142	0.058	422
s1196	14	14	18	647	0.189	5.0	12	67	0.188	4.4	12	66	0.185	2.7	13	80	115	0.180	956
s1423	17	5	74	757	0.250	1.5	12	83	0.250	1.4	24	172	0.253	0.3	13	179	180	0.254	825
s5378	35	49	164	1585	0.444	0.7	14	198	0.444	0.7	13	154	0.444	0.7	15	208	154	0.447	1513
s13207	31	121	669	2693	0.515	4.3	12	85	0.510	3.4	12	89	0.510	3.2	12	90	163	0.493	1770
Average						6.4				3.5				2.2					

Table 2: Power Estimation Results for Sequential Circuits.

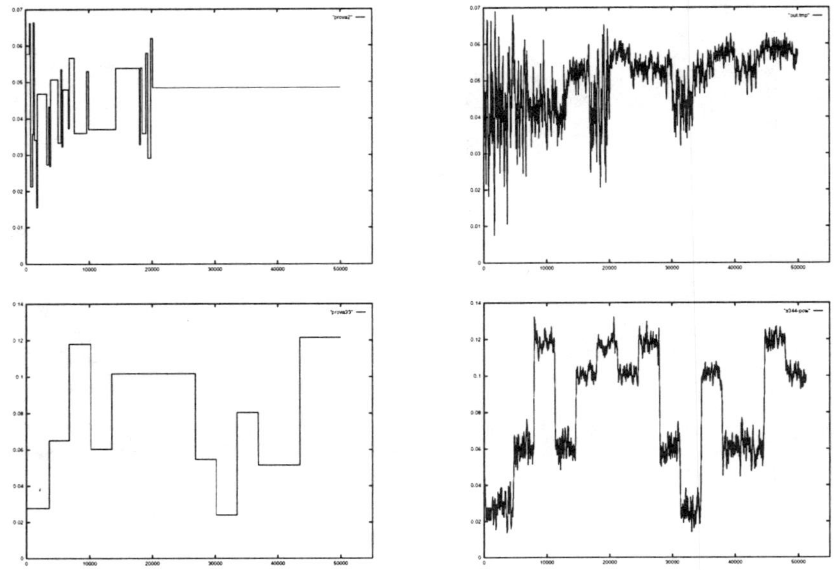

Figure 3: Different Behavior of Two Sequential Benchmarks.

It is worth observing that the accuracy of the average power estimates for sequential circuits is not deteriorated with respect to the combinational ones. Average errors are indeed inferior, although this is probably due to the nature of the benchmarks. In the general case, we expect similar accuracy when an Input-Output-based $I(T)$ is used for combinational circuits and an Input-Output-State-based $I(T)$ is used for sequential circuits.

5.3 Case Study

The effectiveness of the power estimation methodology of this paper is best illustrated by analyzing its application to a real-life system. We designed a fully-functional programmable digital filter. Starting from a behavioral description in Verilog, we synthesized a gate-level implementation using Synopsys Design Compiler, then we obtained the transistor-level implementation in a $2\mu m$ CMOS technology. The design contained 2190 gates (approximately 4000 transistors).

The flow graph of the filter is shown in Figure 4 (a). All coefficients are programmable, hence any transfer function with three forward and two backward coefficients can be implemented. The input, output, and coefficients are 8 bit wide. The high-level architecture of the design is shown in Figure 4 (b). The inputs are: IN (the input bus, 8 bit wide), CADDR (the address bus, 3-bit wide, used for programming the coefficients), LD (the load signal, used for programming the coefficients) and RESET. The only output is OUT (the output bus, 8 bit wide).

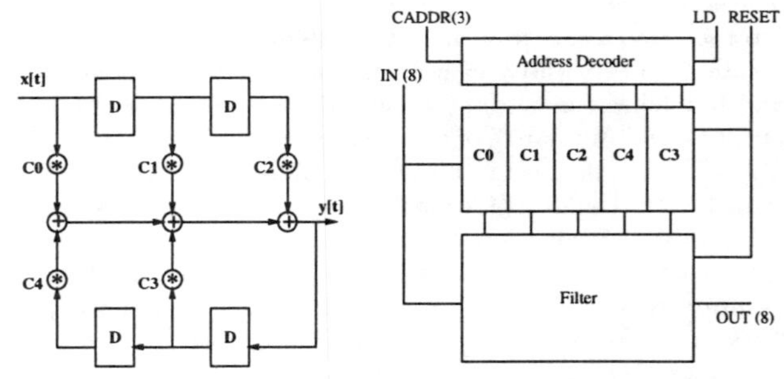

(a) (b)

Figure 4: Flow Graph (a) and Architecture (b) of the Filter.

During normal operation, the LD and RESET signals are low, the input data streams are provided on IN, one new datum per clock cycle, and the output contains the filtered data, one per clock cycle. The filter coefficients can be re-programmed by: i) Setting LD; ii) Selecting the coefficient with CADDR; iii) Providing the coefficient value on IN. One new coefficient can be programmed per clock cycle. During programming, the output does not contain valid data. The coefficients and the internal registers are reset (to 0) by rising the RESET signal. Reset takes one clock cycle.

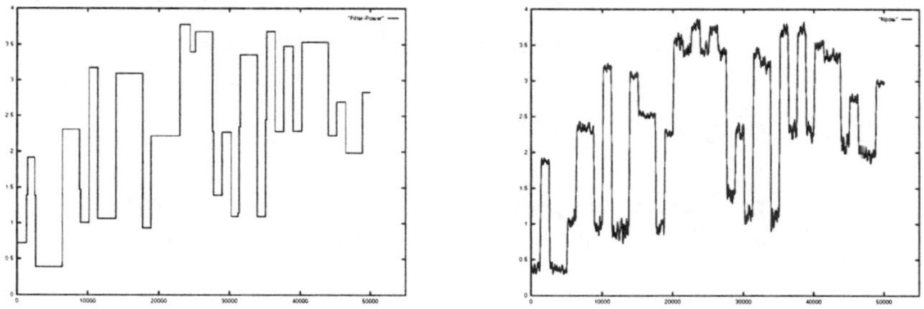

Figure 5: Piecewise-Constant Approximation (Left) and Actual Power Profile (Right) for the Simulated Input Stream.

Although this is a simple design, the programmable filter is complex enough to show the usefulness of our power estimation methodology. First, notice that even during normal operation, successive inputs IN can be strongly correlated, and have widely varying switching activity over time (consider, for example, speech signals, with bursts of sounds and pauses). Moreover, by re-programming the coefficients, we can completely change the type of filtering performed, and the switching activity. Since re-programming is expected to be a rather rare occurrence, it is important to detect when it happens, because power dissipation after re-programming can change widely.

In our experiments, we created a (long) typical usage stream, including reset and re-programming phases. Then, we tracked the power dissipation of the filter over time using our power estimation tool. One important characteristics of the design is that it is has internal state, and its behavior is determined by the coefficient values, that change very rarely (and require a maximum of 5 consecutive clock cycles to be modified).

The filter has been simulated under an input stream consisting of the repeated and interleaved application of a set of patterns to program the coefficients and a burst of input data. Obviously, depending on the type of data to be processed, not all five coefficients need to be re-programmed. The total length of the stream was 50,000 patterns. Figure 5 compares the estimated power waveform of the input stream to the actual power waveform calculated by exhaustive simulation. For this experiment, N_c was equal to 147, all other tuning parameters have the same values used for both the combinational and the sequential benchmarks. Table 3 shows the power values obtained from the application of the input patterns of Figure 5 to the filter.

Estimated Power					Actual Power	
I(T)	Pow	$\|E\|$	L2	T	Pow	T
In-Out	2.362	4.4	24	513	2.262	5020
In-Out-State	2.351	3.9	23	442		
Intern	2.334	3.1	20	382		

Table 3: Power Estimation Results for the Programmable Filter.

6 Conclusions and Future Work

In this work we demonstrated how a multi-level simulation engine can be exploited to achieve accurate power estimation in a small fraction of the time that would be needed to perform an accurate simulation on the entire pattern stream. Under realistic input stimuli, the average power dissipation of digital systems is often better described by an up-down staircase function than by a single value. Our multi-level simulation approach achieves high accuracy in tracking how average power varies over time.

A fast simulation of the entire, user provided, input stream is performed. During high-level simulation an indicator function is computed that provides information on when and how often the short-term average power dissipation is expected to change. Low-level accurate simulation is dispatched on small portions of the input stream whenever it is needed for quantitatively tracking how power dissipation is changing over time. When the entire input stream has been simulated, only a small fraction has been simulated with the slow and accurate power simulator, but the power waveform and the average power are estimated typically within a few percents from the actual ones.

Although we provided extensive experimental evidence of the efficiency and accuracy of our approach (on both standard benchmarks and a realistic case study), more work needs to be done in two directions. First, we plan to apply our tool to much larger systems such as microprocessors and DSP chips, where typical input streams are actual user applications and software benchmarks. Second, we want to investigate the theoretical properties and the domain of applicability of our method.

References

[1] D. Marculescu, R. Marculescu, M. Pedram, "Stochastic Sequential Machine Synthesis Targeting Constrained Sequence Generation," DAC-33, pp. 696-701, Las Vegas, NV, June 1996.

[2] R. Marculescu, D. Marculescu, M. Pedram, "Adaptive Models for Input Data Compaction for Power Simulators," ASPDAC-2, pp. 391-396, Chiba, Japan, January 1997.

[3] R. Marculescu, D. Marculescu, M. Pedram, "Hierarchical Sequence Compaction for Power Estimation," DAC-34, pp. 570-575, Anaheim, CA, June 1997.

[4] F. Brglez, H. Fujiwara, "A Neutral Netlist of 10 Combinational Benchmark Circuits and a Target Translator in Fortran," ISCAS-85, Kyoto, Japan, June 1985.

[5] F. Brglez, D. Bryan, K. Koźmiński, "Combinational Profiles of Sequential Benchmark Circuits," ISCAS-89, pp. 1929-1934, Portland, OR, May 1989.

[6] A. Salz, M. Horowitz, "IRSIM: An Incremental MOS Switch-Level Simulator," DAC-26, pp. 173-178, Las Vegas, NV, June 1989.

[7] S-Y. Huang, K-T. Cheng, K-C. Chen M. T-C. Lee, "A Novel Methodology for Transistor-Level Power Estimation," ISLPED-96, pp. 67-72, Monterey, CA, August 1996.

[8] C-S. Ding, C-T. Hsieh, Q. Wu, M. Pedram, "Stratified Random Sampling for Power Estimation," ICCAD-96 San Jose, CA, pp. 577-582, November 1996.

[9] D. Singh, "Prospects for Low Power Microprocessor Design," IWLPD-94, Keynote Address, pp. 1, Napa Valley, CA, April 1994.

[10] F. Najm, S. Goel, I. Hajj, "Power Estimation in Sequential Circuits," DAC-32, pp. 635-640, San Francisco, CA, June 1995.

[11] V. Saxena, F. Najm, I. Hajj, "Monte-Carlo Approach for Power Estimation in Sequential Circuits," EDTC-97, pp. 416-420, Paris, France, March 1997.

[12] L. Benini, A. Bogliolo, M. Favalli, G. De Micheli, "Regression Models for Behavioral Power Estimation," PATMOS-96, pp. 179-187, Bologna, Italy, September 1996.

[13] M. Nemani, F. Najm, "Towards a High-Level Power Estimation Capability," IEEE Trans. on CAD, Vol. 15, No. 6, pp. 588-598, June 1996.

[14] D. Marculescu, R. Marculescu, M. Pedram, "Information Theoretic Measures For Power Analysis," IEEE Trans. on CAD, Vol. 15, No. 6, pp. 599-609, June 1996.

[15] E. M. Sentovich, K. J. Singh, C. W. Moon, H. Savoj, R. K. Brayton, A. Sangiovanni-Vincentelli, "Sequential Circuits Design Using Synthesis and Optimization," ICCD-92, pp. 328-333, Cambridge, MA, October 1992.

[16] L. Benini, G. De Micheli, E. Macii, M. Poncino, R. Scarsi, "Quick Generation of Temporal Power Waveforms for RT-Level Hard Macros," ISIS-97, Austin, TX, October 1997, To Appear.

A Power Modeling and Characterization Method for Macrocells Using Structure Information

Jiing-Yuan Lin, Wen-Zen Shen, Jing-Yang Jou

Dept. of Electronics Engineering and Institute of Electronics
National Chiao Tung University, Hsinchu 30050, Taiwan R.O.C.

Abstract

To characterize a macrocell, a general method is to store the power consumption of all possible transition events at primary inputs in the lookup tables. Though this approach is very accurate, the lookup tables could be huge for the macrocells with many inputs. In this paper, we present a new power modeling method which takes advantage of the structure information of macrocells and selects minimum number of primary inputs or internal nodes in a macrocell as state variables to build a state transition graph (STG). Those state variables can completely model the transitions of all internal nodes and the primary outputs. By carefully deleting some state variables, we further introduce an incomplete power modeling technique which can simplify the STG without losing much accuracy. In addition, we exploit the property of the compatible patterns of a macrocell to further reduce the number of edges in the corresponding STG. Experimental results show that our modeling techniques can provide SPICE-like accuracy and can reduce the size of the lookup table significantly comparing to the general approach.

1. Introduction

Recently, several behavior level power estimators [1-4] considered the modeling and characterization of datapaths based on input statistics. However, as stated in [5], input statistics is highly dependent on the application the circuit is running on and the context of the usage of the circuit. Therefore, the energy models of macrocells which are derived from specific input statistics may not match that of the operating environment.

To overcome the drawbacks of the input statistics modeling, a simple modeling method is proposed in [6] to characterize the power consumption caused by all possible transition events at primary inputs. We refer to this technique as the **primary input oriented (PI-oriented)** power modeling technique. During the logic simulation, the power estimator monitors the power events occurring at the primary inputs of each macrocell and computes the total power consumption as the sum of the power consumption of each event. This technique can provide accurate estimation results; however, for a macrocell with n inputs, it needs a lookup table with size of 2^{2n} to record the characterization data. Moreover, the complexity is too high for this exhaustive characterization. To reduce the size of lookup table, Mehta et. al. [5] presented a clustering algorithm to characterize the energy dissipation of macrocells. They first simulate the characterized circuit with m random vectors ($m << 2^{2n}$) by a switch-level simulator. Then, according to the simulated switching capacitances, they group closely related energy patterns to obtain clusters which will be used to characterize the circuit. Because $m << 2^{2n}$, e.g., m=500 for n=11 in their experiments, the number of clusters obtained would be far less than 2^{2n}. So, this approach can achieve a significant reduction on the size of lookup table. However, the accuracy would be sacrificed because the energy value of each input transition vector which is not simulated is undefined and is used as don't-care during clustering.

For a macrocell, there could be two or more input patterns which generate the same states of all internal nodes in the macrocell. In this paper, we refer to these patterns as **compatible patterns**. A **compatible pattern set** is the collection of all compatible patterns. Input sequence formed by compatible patterns will not cause any signal transitions at any internal nodes. As an example, Fig. 1(a) shows a schematic diagram of a 2-to-1 multiplexer and Fig. 1(b) shows its extended truth table in terms of the internal nodes and the output node. In the truth table, we find that input patterns 000 and 010 have the same values of internal nodes and the output node and thus are compatible patterns. Similarly, patterns 001 and 101, 011 and 111, 100 and 110 are all compatible patterns. Thus, there are four compatible pattern sets in this example. Although the sequences formed by these compatible patterns do not make signal transitions in the macrocell, they are used for characterization in the PI-oriented power modeling technique. This would waste memory space for storing data and CPU time of power characterization process.

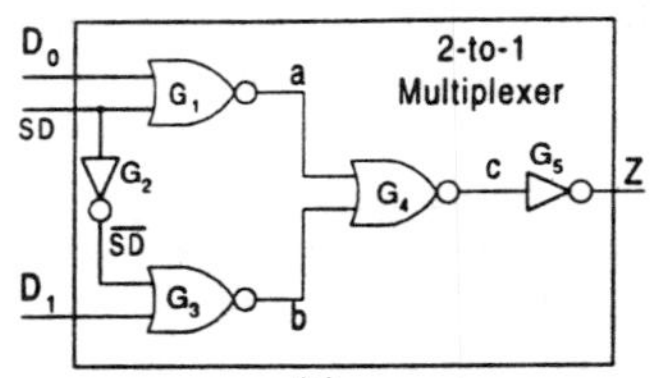

(a)

D_0	D_1	SD	a	b	c	Z	$\overline{SD}$
0	0	0	1	0	0	1	1
0	0	1	0	1	0	1	0
0	1	0	1	0	0	1	1
0	1	1	0	0	1	0	0
1	0	0	0	0	1	0	1
1	0	1	0	1	0	1	0
1	1	0	0	0	1	0	1
1	1	1	0	0	1	0	0

(b)

Fig. 1. A 2-to-1 multiplexer and its extended truth table.

In this paper, we propose a structure-oriented power modeling technique for macrocells. In our approach, in addition to PIs, all internal nodes in a cell are also considered as potential state variables for building a state transition graph (STG) where the state variables can be used to completely model the signal transitions of all internal nodes and POs. Based on the model, we will consider the compatible patterns for reducing the characterization vectors while retaining the accuracy as that provided by the PI-oriented technique. For some macrocells, the constructed STG may still be very complicated. To further reduce the complexity of STG, we introduce an incomplete power modeling technique which can effectively simplify the STG without losing much accuracy.

1092-3152/97 $10.00

2. A Complete Power Modeling Technique

For a macrocell, if we can model all the possible transition events at the internal nodes, we can get an accurate estimation of its power consumption. In this paper, if a power model can model all the signal transitions of internal nodes in a macrocell, then it is called a **complete power modeling technique**. As mentioned before, PI-oriented power modeling is a complete power modeling technique. For a circuit with n inputs, it performs power characterization with $2^n \times 2^n$ sequences. We can model these sequences by using a state transition graph (STG) where the graph has 2^n states to represent the 2^n possible input combinations at time n-1 and each state has 2^n outgoing edges to represent the 2^n possible input combinations at time n. We refer to such STG which is built for the complete power modeling as a **complete modeling STG**. Though PI-oriented power modeling technique can provide accurate results, the sizes 2^{2n} would be easily exploded.

In this section, we try to find a complete power modeling technique using STG with smaller number of edges as compared to that of the PI-oriented power modeling technique. Fortunately, the property of compatible patterns in a circuit can be used to achieve this goal. For a circuit, after running exhaustive logic simulation, we can build an extended truth table in terms of all internal nodes and POs as shown in Fig. 1(b). From the truth table, we can find all the compatible pattern sets which are equal to the number of states in STG. For a 2-to-1 multiplexer shown in Fig. 1, there are four compatible pattern sets and thus the corresponding STG shown in Fig. 2 has only four states, where a, b, c, Z, $\overline{SD}$ are taken as state variables and D_0, D_1, SD are the input variables.

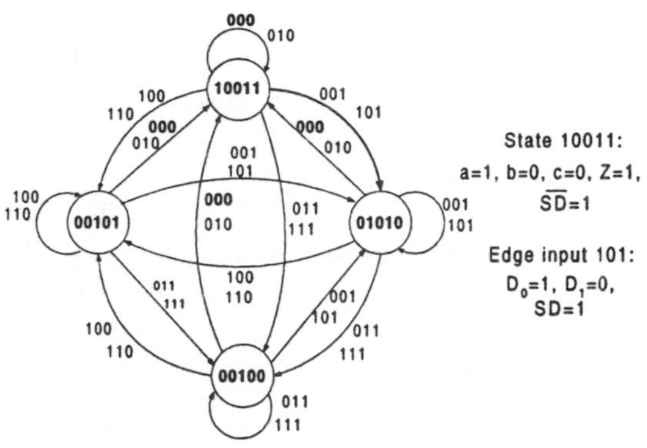

Fig. 2 The complete modeling STG of a 2-to-1 multiplexer.

This graph can model all possible transitions of internal nodes; therefore, it is a complete modeling STG. In addition, the number of states is four which is only half of that needed for PI-oriented power modeling STG. In this power modeling technique, the number of states is always less than or equal to that of PI-oriented power modeling technique. The worst case is when all internal nodes have different values for each input pattern. In summary, the STG constructed by this power modeling technique has $N \times 2^n$ edges where N is the number of states and $N \leq 2^n$.

The difference on power consumed by the compatible patterns is only due to the feedthrough current and the charging/discharging current of parasitic capacitances inside the gates which are driven directly by primary inputs. In general, this power is much smaller than the power of the whole macrocell. If we neglect this power, then the outgoing edges corresponding to the compatible patterns can be merged into a single edge for each state. Fig. 3 shows the STG after merging the compatible patterns. In this simplified STG, the total number of edges is $N \times N$ where N is the number of states. The number of edges is independent of the number of primary inputs. This STG is referred to as the **complete modeling STG with merged edges**.

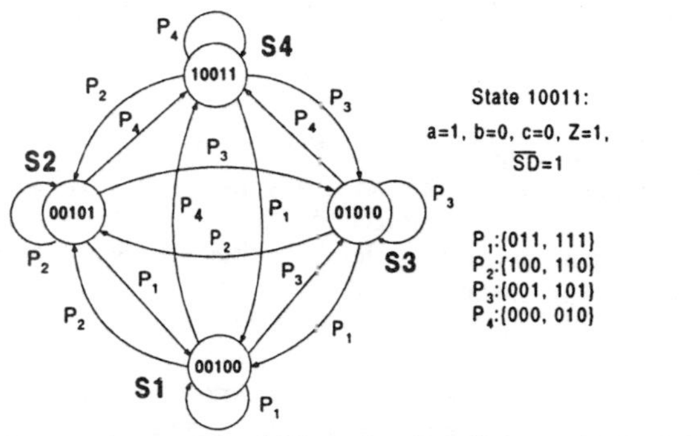

Fig. 3 The complete modeling STG of a 2-to-1 multiplexer with merged edges.

3. An Incomplete Power Modeling Technique

In Fig. 2, we use all internal nodes as state variables for modeling the signal transitions in the circuit. In fact, if we utilize the logic relationship among internal nodes, it is possible to use only part of those nodes as state variables to model the entire circuit. Finding a minimum set of nodes which can completely model all the transitions serves two purposes. First, we only need to check those nodes in the truth table when we evaluate the circuit for finding the compatible patterns. Second, we can possibly remove part of those nodes from the complete modeling STG to form a simpler STG while losing little accuracy. In this paper, if a power modeling technique can not completely model all the nodes in a macrocell, we call it an **incomplete power modeling technique**. The STG constructed for an incomplete power modeling technique is referred to as an **incomplete modeling STG**.

In this section, we first propose an algorithm for selecting a minimum set of internal nodes and primary inputs as state variables for the complete modeling STG. Then, we present an algorithm to remove some state variables of the complete modeling STG to form an incomplete modeling STG.

Let's define some notations first. In Fig. 1, node Z incurs signal transitions whenever node c makes transition, and vice-versa. Node Z and node c are referred to as **transition compatible nodes** in this paper. For transition compatible nodes, we only need to select one of them as state variable when we construct the STG. Because the output value of a logic gate is determined by its input values, if the state transition graph already uses all the inputs of the gate as state variables, the output of the gate does not need to be selected as a state variable. In Fig. 1, the signal transitions of node c can be modeled by the transitions of nodes a and b. Nodes a and b are referred to as the **transition dominating nodes** of node c. On the contrary, node c is the **transition dominated node** of nodes a and b. Therefore, our goal is to find a minimum set of transition dominating nodes which can completely model all the transitions in the macrocell and to use those nodes as state variables for constructing STG.

For a macrocell, if the inside of it has no feedback loop, we call this cell **combinational cell.** A combinational cell has an important property that the logic value of a node is only dependent on the logic states of its transitive fan-in nodes. Given a circuit, we can levelize the netlist starting from primary inputs with level 0 and label the level of each node i with l_i. If a logic gate has m inputs with levels $l_1, l_2, .., l_m$, we define the level of its output as

$$\min(l_1, l_2, .., l_m) + 1.$$

Based on this definition, the nodes with at least one primary input as its inputs would be in level 1. Any node with level higher than 1 is driven directly or indirectly by the nodes in level 1. Thus, if we choose all the nodes in level 1 as state variables and collect them in a **state variable set (SVS)**, the STG can completely model the transition behavior of all nodes in the circuit. In addition to the nodes in level 1, some additional primary inputs can also be selected as state variables to form a simpler complete modeling STG where some state variables in the original SVS can possibly be replaced.

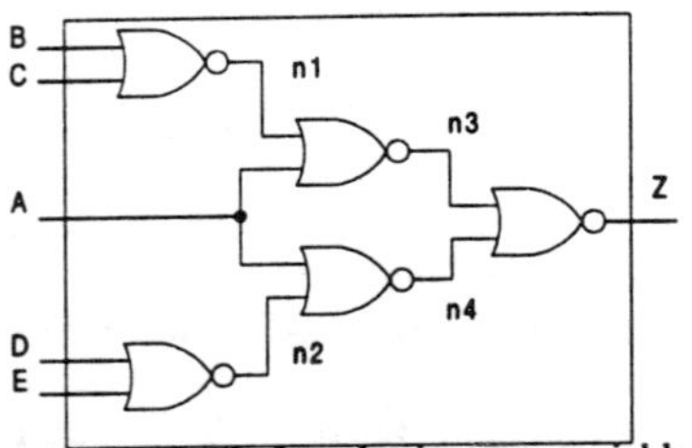

Fig. 4 An example for selecting state variables.

As an example shown in Fig. 4, the nodes $n1$, $n2$, $n3$, and $n4$ constitute the state variable set for a complete power modeling technique first. Thus, SVS={$n1$, $n2$, $n3$, $n4$}. After removing the invalid states such as 1010 ($n1$=1, $n2$=0, $n3$=1, $n4$=0), the corresponding STG would have 9 states and 81 edges. However, if we choose nodes $n1$, $n2$, and input A as state variables, (SVS={$n1$, $n2$, A}), we can reduce the number of states to 8 (2^3) and the number of edges to 64. Thus, the basic idea of our algorithm is to find a minimum set of the nodes with level 0 or level 1 such that the corresponding complete modeling STG has the fewest states. Algorithm 1 shows the pseudo-code of our algorithm.

Algorithm 1
Input: the netlist of a macrocell
Output: state variable set
State_Variable_Selection_for_Complete_Modeling()
{
levelize the netlist;
select the nodes in level 1 as state variables and put them into SVS_{orig};
$SVS_{final} \leftarrow SVS_{orig}$;
for each state variable combination C_i in SVS_{orig} {
backtrace the circuit from the nodes in C_i to PI and collect their transition dominating nodes in a set TGN;
forward traverse the circuit from the primary inputs in TGN to the nodes in level 1 and find the state variables SV which can be modeled by those inputs;
$SVS_{new} \leftarrow SVS_{orig} + TGN - SV$;
if STG(SVS_{new}) is simpler than STG(SVS_{final})
$SVS_{final} \leftarrow SVS_{new}$;
/* STG(SVS_{new}) is the STG built by SVS_{new}. */
}
return (SVS_{final});
}

If the CPU time is limited, we can perform heuristic enumeration instead of exhaustive enumeration for the state variable combinations to obtain a near-optimal solution. After applying above algorithm on the 2-to-1 multiplexer, $\overline{SD}$, a, and b are selected as the state variables. Fig. 5(a) and (b) show the truth table for the state variables and the corresponding state transition graph, respectively.

D_0	D_1	SD	a	b	$\overline{SD}$
0	0	0	1	0	1
0	0	1	0	1	0
0	1	0	1	0	1
0	1	1	0	0	0
1	0	0	0	0	1
1	0	1	0	1	0
1	1	0	0	0	1
1	1	1	0	0	0

(a)

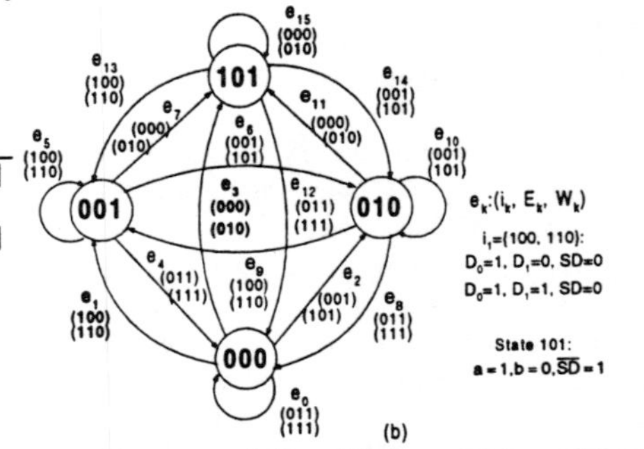

(b)

Fig. 5 (a) The truth table of the state variables, (b) the complete modeling STG of a 2-to-1 multiplexer.

This state transition graph is similar to the graphs proposed in [7] and [8]. In Fig. 5(b), each edge e_k:(i_k, E_k, W_k) models the power consumption of the state transition from one state to another state. i_k is the input patterns. E_k is the edge activity number, which denotes the number of traverse times of the edge when a set of sequential patterns are applied. W_k is the total energy consumed when the edge is traversed each time. Thus, if all the E_ks and the W_ks of each edge k are known, the total energy consumption can be obtained by summing up the $E_k \times W_k$. The patterns inside the parenthesis under the label of each edge are the compatible patterns which trigger the state transition.

Although the number of edges is less than that of PI-oriented power modeling technique, the complete modeling STGs can still be very complicated and have a large number of edges for some macrocells. Therefore, if we can remove some state variables and edges from the STGs without losing much accuracy, the power characterization process would become more efficient. As mentioned before, we only select the nodes in level 0 and level 1 as state variables in SVS. Any node n_i with level higher than 1 ($l_i \geqq 2$) can be completely modeled by those state variables. However, if a node n_i and its fanout nodes are all in the SVS, the nodes which are modeled by node n_i can also be modeled by its fanout nodes collectively. Therefore, node n_i can be potentially deleted from SVS without changing the modeling capability for the nodes with $l_i \geqq 2$. The only loss in accuracy is that the power consumption of node n_i can not be estimated accurately by any single edge in the incomplete modeling STG and is distributed in some edges instead.

In addition to the above consideration, we should also consider the amount of power consumed by node n_i before deleting it from SVS. If node n_i contributes most power of the whole macrocell, deleting it from SVS would result in significant loss in accuracy. In general, the node that has larger capacitive loading than others would potentially dissipate more power. Therefore, in our approach, if the ratio of the capacitive loading of node n_i over the total capacitive loading of the whole macrocell is larger than a specified threshold value, we will retain the state variable in SVS. Otherwise, the state variable would be deleted. In this paper, the ratio is referred to as **loading ratio**.

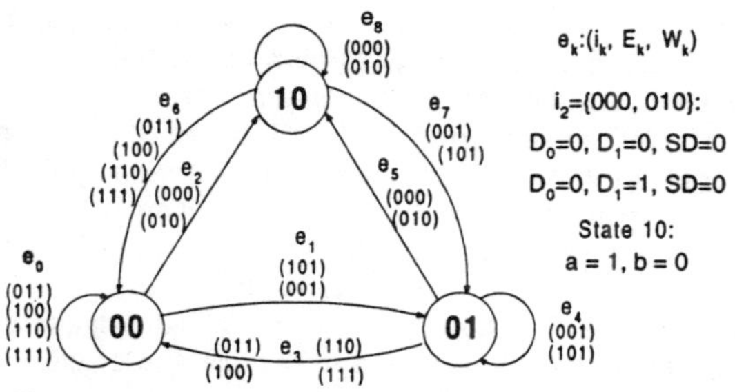

Fig. 6 The incomplete modeling STG of a 2-to-1 multiplexer.

As the example of 2-to-1 multiplexer, both node $\overline{SD}$ and its fanout node b are in the SVS of the complete modeling STG. If we delete $\overline{SD}$ from the SVS, the signal transitions at nodes a, b, c, and Z all can be modeled by the state variables a and b. Fig. 6 shows the new STG after removing state variable $\overline{SD}$.

The algorithm of selecting the state variables of incomplete modeling STG is shown as follows.

Algorithm 2
Input: the netlist of a macrocell, the state variable set (*SVS*) of complete power modeling, the threshold value (*THV*)
Output: the SVS of incomplete power modeling

```
State_Variable_Selection_for_Incomplete_Modeling()
{
    for each state variable SV in SVS {
        collect the fanout nodes of SV in FON;
        if (SVS ∩ FON = FON and LR(SV) < THV)
            SVS = SVS - SV;
        /* LR(SV) is the loading ratio of SV */
    }
    return(SVS);
}
```

After applying the above algorithm on a complete modeling STG with N states, the resulting incomplete modeling STG may have M states and M×M edges where M ≦ N.

4. Power Characterization and Calculation of Edge Activity Number

4.1. Power Characterization

Once the STG is built, we need to characterize the energy consumption (W_k) associated with each edge. In our approach, we use SPICE simulation to do this work. We have built an automatic procedure for power characterization which accounts for the effect of input slop and output loading. To characterize the W_k of each edge in STG, we need a set of input sequences which can traverse each edge. The sequences can be derived from the behavior of STG. As the example shown in Fig. 5(b), to characterize the state transition from state 000 to state 001, we need to set the state to *000* at time *n-1*, apply input *100* or *110* at time *n*, and calculate the difference of the energies measured at time *n* and *n-1*. Because we use SPICE simulation for power characterization, the power consumption of each characterized edge includes not only the dynamic power due to state transitions but also the short-circuit power and the leakage power.

4.2. Calculation of Edge Activity Number

To estimate the energy consumption of a macrocell, we also need to calculate the edge activities (E_k) of each edge in the corresponding STG. Here we use a state enumeration method which is simple and accurate. The transition waveforms of the inputs of macrocells are monitored when we perform logic simulation. We then enumerate the corresponding STG using those transition waveforms. As the logic simulation is over, we can obtain the activity numbers of each edge of the STG. This approach is very simple but it can accurately capture the signal correlation of inputs during the logic simulation.

5. Experimental Results

The power characterization and estimation algorithms have been implemented in C language on a SUN SPARCstation 20 with 256 Mbytes of memory. To evaluate the quality of our approach, several macrocells and several circuits constructed by bit-slice cells are tested. The transistor models used are the level 3 model of 0.8um SPDM CMOS technology provided by CIC (Chip Implementation Center in Taiwan). The signal probabilities and transition densities of the primary inputs are assigned to be 0.5 for all macrocells and the bit-slice circuits. Based on the input characteristics, a random pattern generator generates 1000 patterns with 10ns clock cycle time for running both SPICE and Verilog simulations.

In Table 1, the size of lookup table needed for the PI-oriented power modeling technique is shown in the fifth column. The subsequent columns show the table sizes and the characterization time for the complete and incomplete power modeling techniques respectively. In these macrocells, the threshold value of the loading ratio is specified as 0.15 for constructing the incomplete modeling STGs. The characterization time shown is the total CPU run-time for characterizing all edges of the STG with one fixed output loading and one fixed input slop. The time units labeled *s* represents seconds and *hr* represents hours. In general, a macrocell would be characterized several times with different output loadings and input slops. Therefore, the whole characterization time would be several times of that shown in the table. The characterization is done only once even though the characterization time is long for some macrocells. In this table we find that the lookup table size of 4-bit Fast Adder can not be further reduced after applying the incomplete power modeling technique. This is because the nodes in level 1 are all symmetrical and thus no any state variables in the complete modeling STG can be removed. The CPU time of constructing the complete and incomplete modeling STGs are within 8 seconds for most macrocells except the circuits of 2-bit ALU and 4-bit Fast Adder which, however, are also within 100 seconds.

In Table 2, the second to seventh columns show the average power consumption and CPU time of the exact SPICE simulation and the estimations using the complete and incomplete power modeling techniques respectively. The percentage shown in the parenthesis under the estimated data denotes the estimation error as compared to the SPICE estimation. The experimental results show that most of the power estimations based on the two proposed power modeling techniques are very close to those estimated by the exact SPICE simulation except the incomplete modeling of the circuit Mux81. This is because the internal nodes of Mux81 are all in level 1 and most of them are deleted from the SVS based on the specified threshold value of loading ratio. If we set a lower threshold value, the estimation error would be reduced at the expense of increasing the size of lookup table.

Table 3 shows the estimation results of an 8-bit ripple carry adder, an 8-bit arithmetic logic unit, and an 8-bit by 8-bit array multiplier. These circuits are constituted with the bit-slice cell. For each circuit, we estimate the power of each bit-slice cell individually by using the complete modeling STG with merged edges and then obtain the total power by summing up the estimated powers of them. The experimental results show that our modeling technique provides within 7% error of SPICE simulation on average while the CPU consumes more than 3 orders of magnitude less CPU time.

Table 1: Lookup table sizes needed for some macrocells.
(n: no. of inputs, m: no. of internal and output nodes, k: no. of transistors)

Macrocell	n	m	k	Lookup table sizes			Characterization time	
				PI-oriented ($2^n \times 2^n$)	Our approach complete (N×N)	Our approach incomplete (M×M)	Our approach complete (N×N)	Our approach incomplete (M×M)
1-bit Half Adder	2	4	16	16	9	9	4.6s	4.6s
1-bit Full Adder	3	4	28	64	16	16	11.5s	11.5s
Mux21	3	5	16	64	16	16	8.8s	8.8s
Mux41	6	8	22	4096	256	256	210s	210s
Mux81	11	10	62	4194304	16384	576	10.9hr	0.3hr
4-bit Parity Checker	4	7	32	256	81	16	51.3s	10.8s
XOR	2	2	10	16	9	4	4.8s	3.2s
1-bit ALU	8	18	72	65536	484	256	968s	504s
2-bit ALU	10	33	214	1048576	15376	625	22.2hr	1.16hr
4-bit Fast Adder	9	31	212	262144	26244	26244	29.3hr	29.3hr

Table 2: Estimation results for some macrocells.

Macrocell	Average Power (uw)			CPU time (sec.)		
	SPICE	Our approach complete (N×N)	Our approach incomplete (M×M)	SPICE	Our approach complete (N×N)	Our approach incomplete (M×M)
1-bit Half Adder	267.11	253.39 (-5.13%)	253.39 (-5.13%)	310.6	1.78	1.78
1-bit Full Adder	465.58	483.97 (3.95%)	483.97 (3.95%)	582	1.93	1.93
Mux21	264.22	257.68 (-2.47%)	257.68 (-2.47%)	365	1.45	1.45
Mux41	355.81	348.12 (-2.16%)	348.12 (-2.16%)	607	2.99	2.99
Mux81	1033	980.21 (-5.11%)	854.83 (-17.24%)	2043	11.18	12.92
4-bit Parity Checker	521.09	533.66 (2.41%)	524.13 (0.58%)	977.5	2.81	2.12
XOR	140.4	134.45 (-4.24%)	133.73 (-4.75%)	278.9	1.53	1.25
1-bit ALU	1157.9	1084.1 (-6.37%)	1078.64 (-6.85%)	2410	2.85	3.54
2-bit ALU	2715.8	2644.37 (-2.63%)	2622.22 (-3.45%)	4785	11.45	6.91
4-bit Fast Adder	3060.4	2997.26 (-2.06%)	2997.26 (-2.06%)	4932	12.1	12.1

Table 3: The experimental results of bit-slice circuits.

Circuit	No. of inputs	No. of internal nodes	No. of transistors	Average Power (uw)		CPU Time (secs.)	
				SPICE	our approach	SPICE	our approach
8-bit ripple carry adder	17	32	224	5136	5330.8 (3.79%)	9694	10.1
8-bit ALU	22	144	576	10759	9884.3 (-8.13%)	37760	26.5
8-bit by 8-bit Multiplier	16	352	1856	39270	36050 (-8.2%)	176273	41.84

6. Conclusion and Future Works

For a macrocell with many inputs, PI-oriented power modeling technique is no longer applicable. In this paper, we present a structure-oriented power modeling technique to solve this problem. Based on the structure information of macrocells, we propose a STG to completely model all the signal transitions of the internal nodes of the macrocells. To further simplify the STG, we also present an incomplete power modeling technique. In addition, we exploit the compatible patterns of a macrocell to further reduce the number of edges of the corresponding STG. Experimental results show that our modeling techniques can provide SPICE-like accuracy and reduce the size of the lookup table significantly.

In the incomplete power modeling technique, all the state variables in the final SVS are in level 0 or level 1. If we are allowed to loose more accuracy to obtain a simpler STG, we can consider to include the nodes whose levels are higher than 1 in the final SVS. This possibly can further reduce the lookup table size of the circuit 4-bit Fast Adder. We will investigate this possibility in the future. Moreover, the characterization complexity is too high to characterize some macrocells using the SPICE simulation. We can use switch-level power estimator or PowerMill instead of SPICE to characterize the macrocells when the requirements on the accuracy are not strict as in high-level or RT-level power estimation. This could reduce the characterization time dramatically.

Reference

[1] Pual E. Landman and Jan M. Rabaey, "Architecture Power Analysis: The Dual Bit Type Method," *IEEE Trans. on VLSI Systems*, pp. 173-187, June 1995.

[2] Pual E. Landman and Jan M. Rabaey, "Activity-Sensitive Architecture Power Analysis," *IEEE Trans. on CAD*, pp. 571-587, June 1996.

[3] Renu Mehra and Jan M. Rabaey, "Behavioral Level Power Estimation and Exploration," *Proc. International Workshop on Low Power Design*, pp.197-202, April 1994.

[4] A. Raghunathan, S. Dey and N. K. Jha, "Register-Transfer Level Estimation Techniques for Switching Activity and Power Consumption," *Proc. IEEE/ACM International Conference on Computer-Aided Design*, pp. 158-165, Nov. 1996.

[5] Huzefa Mehta, Robert M. Owens, Mary J. Irwin, "Energy Characterization based on Clustering," Proc. *33rd ACM/IEEE Design Automation Conference*, pp. 702-707, June 1996.

[6] Huzefa Mehta, Robert M. Owens, Mary J. Irwin, "Instruction-level Power Profiling," *Proc. International Conference on Acoustics, Speech and Signal Processing*, May 1996.

[7] Jiing-Yuan Lin, Tai-Chien Liu, and Wen-Zen Shen, "A Cell-Based Power Estimation in CMOS Combinational Circuits," *Proc. IEEE/ACM International Conference on Computer-Aided Design*, pp. 304-309, Nov. 1994.

[8] J. H. Satyanarayana and K. K. Parhi, "HEAT: Hierarchical Energy Analysis Tool," *Proc. 33rd ACM/IEEE Design Automation Conference*, pp. 9-14, June 1996.

SESSION 9B

PARTITIONING FOR HW/SW CODESIGN

Moderators:

Allen C.-H. Wu, Tsing Hua University, Hsinchu, Taiwan

Frank N. Vahid, University of California, Riverside, CA

Transformational Partitioning for Co-Design of Multiprocessor Systems

Gilberto Fernandes Marchioro
Jean-Marc Daveau
Ahmed Amine Jerraya

System-Level Synthesis Group
TIMA/INPG - Grenoble, France

Abstract

This paper presents the underlying methodology of Cosmos, an interactive approach for hardware/software co-design capable of handling multiprocessor systems and distributed architectures. The approach covers the co-design process through a set of user guided transformations allowing semi-automatic partitioning. The transformations are based on a powerful set of primitives for functional partitioning, structural reorganization and communication transformation. It leads to a fast transformation of a system-level specification into an architecture with a short design time and fast exploration of design space. The application of this approach is illustrated using a design example starting from a system-level specification given in SDL to a distributed hardware/software architecture described in C/VHDL. We show that the use of transformational approach allows:

1. *Application of the expertise of the designer during partitioning;*
2. *the user to understand the results of the co-design process;*
3. *the process to take into account partial existing solutions;*
4. *large design space exploration;*
5. *the designer to start from a very high-level specification language of the system to be designed.*

1 Introduction

Partitioning is becoming a bottleneck in the process of designing complex electronic systems under short time-to-market and low cost constraints. In this paper the word system means a multiprocessor distributed real time system composed of programmable processors executing software and dedicated hardware processors communicating through a complex network. Such a system may be implemented as a single chip, a board or a geographically distributed system.

In a traditional design methodology, designers make the hardware/software partitioning at an early stage during the development cycle. The different parts of the system are designed by different groups. The integration of these different parts leads generally to a late detection of errors meaning higher cost and longer delay needed for the integration step. Besides, this early partitioning restrains the ability to investigate a better partitioning trade-off and the different parts of the system are generally oversized in order to reduce last-minute risks.

1.1 Motivation and Objectives

A new generation of methods is emerging and maturing, these methods are able to handle mixed hardware/software systems at the behavioral-level. They are called co-design tools ([4], [6], [11], [12], [24], [28]). Co-design may provide a drastic increase in productivity by making easier concurrent design of different parts of a distributed system and by automating the partitioning and the integration steps. However, co-design issues several challenges ([25]):

1. The development of modern co-design methods has created an exaggerated hope for having general purpose automatic partitioning tools that would start from a functional specification and produce an optimal solution reducing design time and cost. Indeed, several successful automatic partitioning approaches have been reported in the literature ([3], [17], [19], [27]). However, most of these works restrict the problem to a single application domain or make use of simple estimation methods. These restrictions limit the applicability of these partitioning methods to complex systems including several hardware and software processors.

   What makes automatic partitioning difficult is the non availability of a universal estimation method that can be used during partitioning for selecting the right solution.

   The evaluation of a distributed architecture is a complex process depending on a large number of criteria such as: efficiency, reliability, maintainability, portability, usability. Some of these criteria can entail a long list of sub-criteria. For example, efficiency may involve speed, cost, power consumption, volume or area. For each criterion a metric value has to be associated. In addition, the weights of these criteria may be different according to the application domain as well as the technology used. For instance, reliability will be the major criterion when dealing with systems concerning human life security. For other systems, such as portable multi-media systems, cost and power consumption will be the major criteria. It is then clear that it is quite hard to define a realistic evaluation procedure even for a specific application domain.

A realistic issue, for dealing with the partitioning, seems to be semi-automatic methods allowing the designer to mix manual and automatic design.

2. The designer needs to understand the results of automatic partitioning in order to be able to analyze it. This means that co-design tools should provide facilities that show correspondence between the initial specification and the resulting architecture.

3. It is often the case that the designer has a good solution in mind when he/she starts the co-design process. This may be a partial solution like fixing a communication model or fixing the number of processors of the resulting architecture. This means that co-design tools should take into account partial solutions and allow the designer to control the co-design process.

4. The design of complex system is generally an iterative process where several solutions need to be explored before finding the 'right' one. This means that co-design should allow easy design space exploration based on the specific criteria selected by the designer.

As long as these challenges are not solved, co-design will remain restricted to specialists for specific applications.

1.2 Previous Work

Most current research in co-design fall in one of the three categories:

1. ASIP (Application Specific Integrated Processor) co-design: In this case, the designer starts with an application, builds a specific programmable processor and translates the application into software code executable by the specific processor ([20], [22]). In this scheme the hardware/software partitioning includes the instruction set design. The cost function is generally related to area, execution speed and/or power.

2. Hardware / Software synchronous system co-design: In this case, the target architecture of co-design is a software processor acting as a master controller, and a set of hardware accelerators acting as co-processors. Within this scheme two kinds of partitioning have been developed: software oriented partitioning ([11]) and hardware oriented partitioning ([14]). Most of the published work in co-design falls in this scheme. They generally use a simple cost function related to area, to processor cost for software and to speed for hardware. Vulcan ([14]), Codes ([5]), Tosca ([7]), and Cosyma ([11]) are typical co-design tools for synchronous systems.

3. Hardware/Software for distributed systems: In this case, co-design is the mapping of a set of communicating processes (task graph) onto a set of interconnected processors (processor graphs). This co-design scheme includes behavioral decomposition, processor allocation and communication transformation ([12], [27]). Most of the existing partitioning methods restrict the cost function to parameters such as real time constraints ([8], [27]) or cost ([13]).

In this paper we will restrict our discussion to co-design tools of the third category.

Coware ([10]) handles very well multiprocessor co-design during the latest design phases. However, it starts from a C/VHDL where partitioning is already done. Specsyn ([12]) is a precursor for the co-design of multiprocessors. It allows automatic partitioning and design space exploration. However, SpecSyn doesn't help the designer to understand the produced architecture and it doesn't allow a co-design with partial solution. Siera ([24]) provides a powerful scheme for co-design of multiprocessor systems based on the re-use of components. It allows co-design with partial solutions. However it doesn't provide automatic partitioning. Ptolemy provides a powerful environment for co-design of multiprocessors ([22]). However its partitioning ([17]) is restricted to DSP applications and doesn't allow partial solutions.

1.3 Contribution

The main contribution of this paper is to present a user guided transformational approach for co-design. We present the underlying design methodology and show the efficiency of our refinement based approach for hardware/software co-design. The intention of this approach is to solve the four challenges mentioned in the section I.A. It covers the design process through a set of user guided transformations that allows semi-automatic partitioning synthesis with predictable results. The lack of realistic estimation methods is compensated by the expertise of the designer. A large design space exploration is available through multiple trials and a fast feedback as an implementation of the initial specification can be quickly obtained.

Several aspects of the Cosmos approach have already been presented in the literature. This paper focuses on the methodological aspect from the designer's point of view and not on the algorithms and techniques used in Cosmos. Most of the details of the intermediate model Solar and the behavioral transformation primitives are detailed in [4], the communication synthesis methods are explained in [9] and the code generation (C/VHDL) techniques can be found in [26]. However for a improved clarity of the paper we will introduce the models and techniques used when needed.

The rest of this paper details this partitioning scheme and illustrates its efficiency through an example. Section II deals with transformational partitioning. The design representation models used during the co-design are described in section III. Section IV explains three types of refinement actions: behavioral transformation, structural decomposition and communication transformation primitives. Section V illustrates the user guided transformational partitioning through an example. Finally sections VI and VII present our conclusions and show the results and the strength of our methodology.

2 User Guided Transformational Partitioning

The user guided transformational methodology assumes that the designer starts with an initial specification and an architectural solution in mind. System design from specification to implementation is performed through a set of primitives allowing the designer to transform the system, following an incremental refinement scheme, in a distributed model that matches the architectural solution. All the refinement transformations are performed automatically. The decisions are made by the designer who uses his knowledge and experience to achieve the desired solution.

Each step reduces the gap between specification and realization by fixing some implementation details (communication protocol, generating software or hardware code) or by preparing future implementation steps (merging and scheduling several processes to execute them in a single processor). The transformations must satisfy the designer's imposed constraints without changing the functionality of the system.

In the case of Cosmos, the user guided transformational approach makes use of three specification formats as shown in Figure 1. The initial specification is given in the system-level specification language SDL. The user controls the refinement process through a set of transformation primitives. All the refinement process is based on an intermediate form called Solar. The output is a virtual prototype of the architecture given in a distributed C/VHDL model.

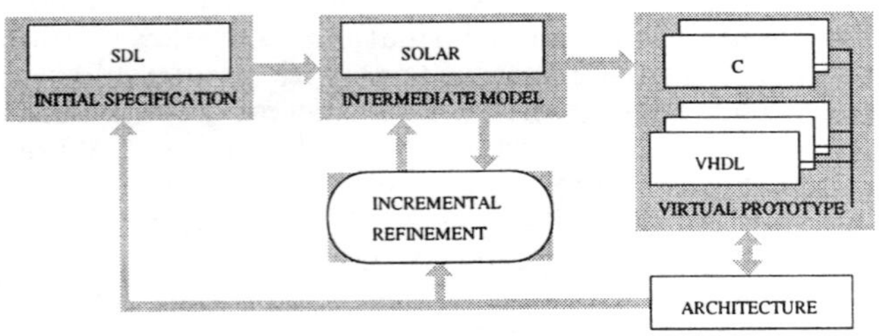

Figure 1: Specification models.

Within Cosmos, the partitioning steps are implemented through a set of primitives that performs basic transformations such as split, merge, move, flat and map. The system provides three sets of primitives working on the system structure, behavior and communication. The designer guides the interaction process and chooses the transformations needed in order to obtain the desired solution. A new implementation can be obtained by changing the primitives sequence activation.

The organization of partitioning into several small steps reduces the complexity of the problem. The designer controls the partitioning history within an interactive environment, through fine grain control of the synthesis process. This methodology can be seen as a human guided compilation where the designer spends additional effort to produce an efficient implementation ([18]). The designer has good design process control. To facilitate the user's interaction for incremental transformations, a graphical interface has been developed.

3 Internal Design Representations

This section introduces a design model, called Solar, used for transformational partitioning ([16]). The different refinement steps use Solar as an intermediate representation. Each step makes transformations on a Solar model.

Solar supports high-level communication concepts including channels and global variables shared over concurrent processes. It is possible to model most system-level communication schemes such as message passing, shared resources and other more complex protocols. Solar models system-level constructions in a synthesis-oriented manner. The underlying model combines two powerful system-level concepts: extended finite state machine (EFSM) for behavioral description and, remote procedure call (RPC) for the specification of high-level communication (Figure 2).

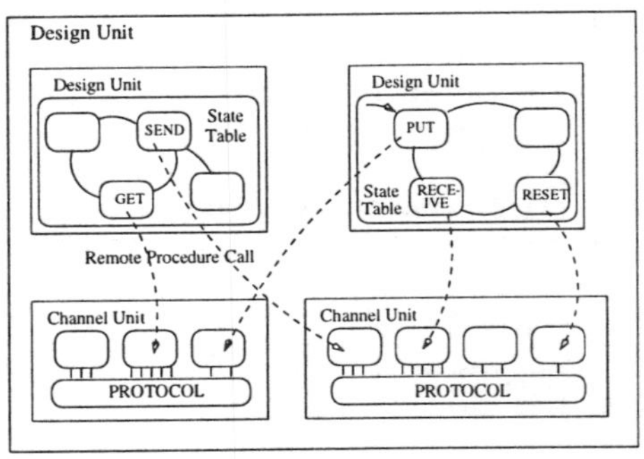

Figure 2: EFSMs using RPC communication.

The basic concepts are: State Tables, Design Units and Channel Units.

- The State Table is the basic constructor for behavior descriptions. A state table is an EFSM composed of an unlimited combination of states and state tables (behavioral hierarchy). All of these states can be executed sequentially, concurrently, or both. A state table has attributes to handle exceptions, global variables, reset and default states. Transitions between states are not level restricted. In other words, transitions may traverse hierarchical boundaries (global transitions).

- The Design Unit construct allows the structuring of a system description into a set of interacting subsystems (processes). These subsystems interact with the environment using a well defined boundary. A design unit can be specified as a set of communicating design units (structural hierarchy) or as a set of interacting state tables. The communication between design units can be performed in two different ways, first by means of classic port concept where single wires send data in one or two directions or by means of communication channels with a well defined protocol.

- The Channel Unit performs the communication between any number of design units. The model mixes the principles of monitors and message passing, also known as remote procedure call ([2]). The use of a RPC to invoke channel services allows a flexible representation, with a clear semantic. These communication schemes can be described separately from the rest of the system, allowing modular design and specification. A channel unit consists of many individual connections and it acts not only as a transport mechanism for the communicated data, it also provides a handshaking interface to ensure both the synchronization and the avoidance of access conflicts. The channel is composed of a controller, a set of methods and a set of interconnected signals. The controller stores the resource's current state. The access to the channel is governed by a fixed set of methods (services) that are the visible part of the channel. The utilization of an extensible library of protocols permits the reuse of existing components. If a communication unit that implements the protocol, services and average rate required is not found in the library, the designer can adapt an existing communication unit (increase the bus width or buffer size for example) rather than building from scratch.

4 Transformation Primitives

The partitioning process is composed of three types of transformations, these are: functional decomposition, structural reorganization and communication transformation. Functional decomposition acts on the state tables to allow refined behavioral descriptions. Structural reorganization acts on design units to allow refined structure of the system. Communication transformation acts on channel units to allow refined communication protocols. All these refinements make use of a set of five primitives called split, merge, move, flat and map to decompose, compose and transform Solar objects. Figure 3 summarizes these partitioning primitives.

For each transformation an applicability condition is associated. It defines constraints on the application of the transformations. Before the application of any transformation requested by the designer, the system checks the applicability conditions. The designer can apply the primitives in any order as long as the application conditions of these primitives are fulfilled.

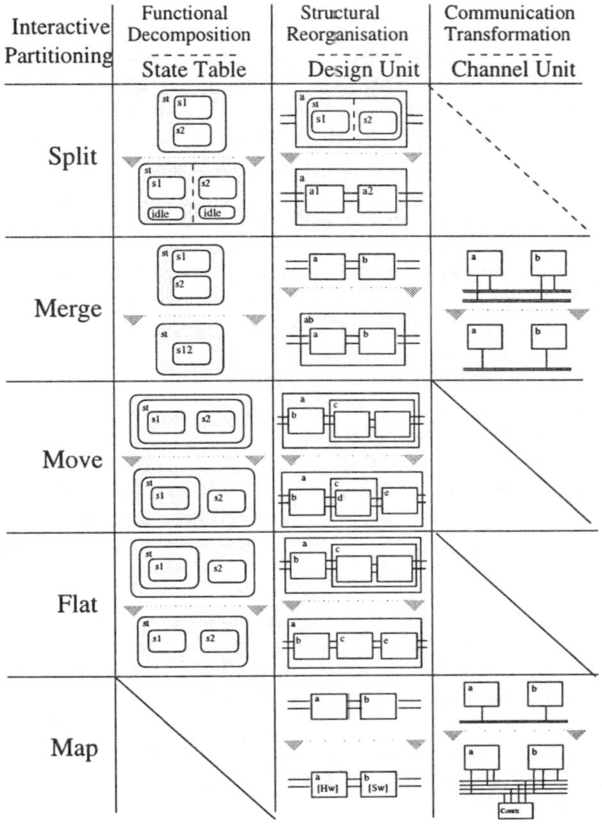

Figure 3: Decomposition, reorganization and communication primitives

5 Functional Decomposition

The functional decomposition primitives are used to transform behaviors i.e. state tables. A brief description follows (the term machine is used to represent a state or a state table):

- Split: decompose a sequential machine into a set of sub-machines. Each resulting machine can be placed in a different partition. Control signals and wait states are added to each machine to represent the revised process control.

- Merge: groups a set sequential machines into a unique machine to permit the sharing of resources (registers and functional units).

- Move: transforms the hierarchy of a given machine. It can be used to move a code from a software realization to a hardware realization and vice-versa.

- Flat: flatten a machine's hierarchy.

5.1 Structural Reorganization

The structural refinement goal is to distribute the behavior into a set of design units that correspond to the final processors. In this case, the application of these primitives transforms the structure hierarchy. Each primitive may be applied several times during structural reorganization. These primitives realize also an automatic reorganization of the interconnection between modules. Hereby follows a description of the structural reorganization primitives:

- Split: works on the behavior of parallel processes (state tables) in order to split then into a set of independent modules (design units). Each module will communicate with the others by means of I/O signals and channels. The data shared between the split machines (global variables) are converted to abstract channels in the new representation. These abstract channels are usually mapped to a shared variable communication protocol. In each generated module, global variable accesses are replaced by calls to remote services offered by a channel. Basically a channel's read and write services are used to access these variables.

- Merge: groups a set of modules into a new design unit. This operation is generally used to cluster the modules that will be assigned to the same processor into a single design unit.

- Move: moves a design unit in the hierarchy. This primitive is usually used to prepare a merge operation.

- Map: permits the identification of hardware and software realization options for each process.

- Flat: performs a structural flattening operation on the hierarchy.

5.2 Communication Transformation

This step transforms a system composed of processes that communicate via high-level primitives (through abstract channels) into interconnected processes that communicate via signals. Cosmos makes use of a channel library composed of basic protocol templates. Two primitives are available for the communication transformation:

- Map: assign a physical communication unit to each high-level communication channel and generate the interfaces between the interconnected units.

- Merge: allows replacement of two or more abstract channels by another abstract channel. In several cases this leads to a cost reduction. The application of this transformation is restricted, the resulting channel needs to have an implementation in the library.

6 Applications

This section details the application of the transformational approach to a co-design example, a Robot Arm Controller. In this example we will illustrate the overall design flow of Cosmos, from a system-level specification given in SDL to a distributed hardware/software architecture described in C/VHDL. The use of SDL allows for fivefold reduction of the size of system specification when compared to distributed C/VHDL models. All the transformations applied in this section are fast enough to look instantaneous during an interactive session. None of the primitives require more than 5 seconds CPU time on a Sparc 20 workstation.

6.1 Robot Arm Controller example

The Robot Arm Controller is a system that adjust the position and speed parameters of eighteen motors belonging to a robot arm with three fingers. This computation is intended to avoid discontinuous motor operation problems. The change in a motor's speed should follow a smooth curve for acceleration and deceleration for mechanical reasons. This application requires that the system react in less than 6 ms.

The basic block diagrams of this system, in SDL, is shown in Figure 4. Figure 4.a shows the overall process and blocks hierarchy of the SDL description. Figure 4.b shows a graphical representation of the top level of hierarchy of the SDL model. The system is made of three blocks that interacts through channels. Figure 4.c details the organization of the *AdaptativeSpeedControl* block into three processes communicating through "signalroute". These figures are made using a commercial SDL environment called ObjectGeode ([21]).

In a brief functional description, the *AdaptativeSpeedControl* block receives positions from the *HostMachine* block. The *AdaptativeSpeedControl* calculates the speed required for each motor in order to make all the motors reaching the desired position at the same time. The motor with the longest distance to go runs at the maximal speed and the speed of the other motors are adapted to this one. The output speed desired for each motor is send in the form of speed control pulses to the *MotorSender* block. This block converts the pulses into control signals to each motor.

The main blocks of this specification are:

- *HostMachine* process is the interface between the user and the system, it takes care of segment storage and motors' constants calculation.

- *DistanceCalculation* stores up to date information about the distance to go for every motor according to the current position.

- *DistributionControl* process identifies the motor that must run at maximal speed and sends scaled commands to the other controllers.

- *SpeedControl* process converts the input steps into a curve that respects the worst case maximum load acceleration and deceleration curves of the motors.

- *MotorSender* is the interface to the stepper motors that converts the speed into frequency pulses.

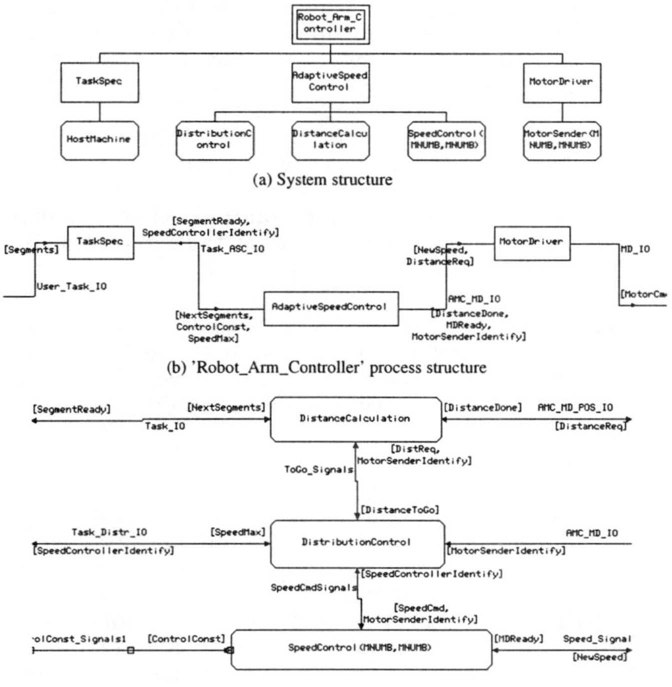

(a) System structure

(b) 'Robot_Arm_Controller' process structure

(c) 'AdaptativeSpeedControl' block structure

Figure 4: Input SDL representation.

The constraints for this design are: the time needed to complete the total movement must be minimal, the change in velocity must be as smooth as possible and the overshoot at the end position must be minimal.

The *SpeedControl* block is responsible for computing the number of speed control pulses with a specified final position and a current state of a motor. This block contains a digital filter based on a Fuzzy Logic algorithm to generate the smooth acceleration curve. During partitioning the *SpeedControl* and the *MotorSender* blocks were assigned to hardware and the other blocks to software. In this architecture implementation, the processes with extensive computation were assigned to have a hardware implementation to respect the system time constraints. Figure 5 shows the use of refinement primitives on the Solar representation.

The results of the refinement steps is shown in Solar graphical representation. Figure 5.a-b shows the structure of the initial SDL model when translated into Solar. In this model, boxes represent design units, lines represent wires and bold lines represent channels. Figure 5.c shows the result of a set of transformations, including flat and merge operations on the initial structure and, merge and map on the channels. The abstract channels were mapped on protocols from the library. In Figure 5.d-e we can see a graphical representation of the finite state machines resulting after the application of the structural merge operations.

In Solar, the behavior is represented by state tables and shown as a hierarchy of nested boxes where each box represent a state or a state table.

The *SpeedControl* and *MotorSender* blocks are allocated eighteen times. An instance for each motor was

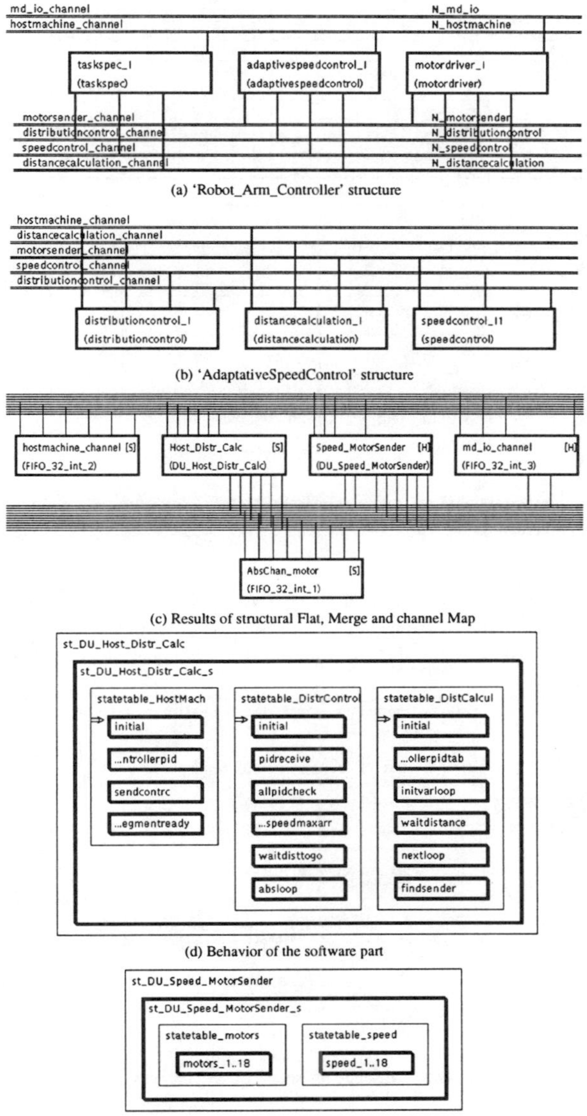

(a) 'Robot_Arm_Controller' structure

(b) 'AdaptativeSpeedControl' structure

(c) Results of structural Flat, Merge and channel Map

(d) Behavior of the software part

(e) Behavior of the hardware part

Figure 5: Refinement steps.

necessary to arrive at the desired throughput. In Figure 6 we can see the final system structure and parts of the generated C/VHDL code.

In this example, the descriptions size in number of lines were: 717 lines for the SDL initial input, 2848 lines for the resulting C file resulted and, 853 lines in VHDL for each motor instance.

7 Evaluation

This work is related to design methodology for mixed hardware/software system. Our objective has been to bridge the link between the system-level specification and hardware/software architecture design, providing a short design time and fast exploration of the design space. In order to achieve this goal we employ a user guided transformational approach.

The co-design methodology described for incremen-

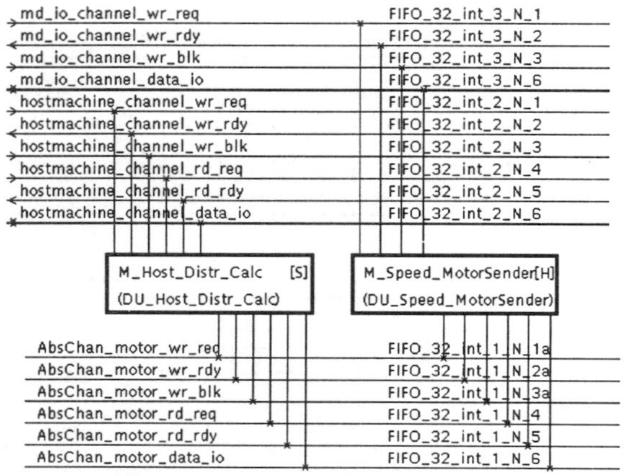

(a) 'Robot_Arm_Controller' final structure

```
int distancecalculation()
{
  ........

  switch(statetable_distancecalculationNextState)
   {
     case initialState :
     {
       hostmachine_channel_putsdl_signalProc(&(segmentready));
       updated= FALSE;
       motornr=  0 ;
       statetable_distancecalculationNextState= initloopState;
     } break;
     case waitdistanceState :
     {
       distancecalculation_channel_getsdl_signalProc(&(received_signal));
       if ((received_signal)==( 1 ))
       {
         distributioncontrol_channel_putsdl_marrProc(&(distancetogo),&(togo))
         statetable_distancecalculationNextState= waitdistanceState;
         break;
       }
```

(b) Partial C-code of 'distancecalculation' process

```
architecture speedcontrol1_behaviour of speedcontrol1 is
 begin
   process
.....
   begin
     StateTable_statetable_speedcontrol1: loop
       case statetable_speedcontrol1_NextState is
         when(initial) =>
             vin_1:= 0;
             motorsender1_channel_putsdl_integer( sdl_signal=> 3, param_1=> 0);
             statetable_speedcontrol1_NextState:= waitk;
             exit StateTable_statetable_speedcontrol1;
         when(waitk) =>
             speedcontrol1_channel_getsdl_signal( sdl_signal=> received_signal)
             if (received_signal = 1) then
                speedcontrol1_channel_getsdl_integer( param_1=> ctrlconst);
                statetable_speedcontrol1_NextState:= waitspeed;
                exit StateTable_statetable_speedcontrol1;
             end if;
```

(c) Partial VHDL-code of 'speedcontrol' process

Figure 6: Virtual prototype.

tal refinement satisfies the challenges outlined in Section I.A, we have:

1. Semi-automatic approach to partition a functional specification: The designer's interaction is though needed because realistic estimation methods are not available. It is possible to manipulate complex systems in a wide range of application domains.

2. Predictability of partitioning results: The user selects the elements that will be transformed by each operation. The result is immediately obtained and a graphical viewer permits a quick design examination and control over the operation flow.

3. Use of designer expertise: If the designer has a solution in mind he/she can force it through the use of the appropriate sequence of transformations. The initial solutions obtained by the system can be used by the designer in order to explore new solutions.

4. Design exploration of implementation options: The user guided transformational approach allows the user to force the co-design process in order to obtain a given solution. The Cosmos system is fast enough to allow the exploration of several solutions.

The main limitation of the present version is the lack of good and reliable estimation functions. In present version the user needs to produce a C/VHDL model in order to have a realistic estimation of his solution.

8 Conclusion

We presented a realistic semi-automatic methodology for co-design capable to handle multiprocessor distributed systems. This methodology is based on a powerful set of primitives for functional partitioning, structural reorganization and communication transformation. The co-design starts with a system-level specification given in SDL. This initial model is refined through a user guided compilation process in order to produce a distributed hardware/software architecture described in C/VHDL.

The use of this approach was illustrated through an example. In contrast with other co-design approaches, the transformational approach provides an elegant solution for the main challenges imposed by co-design of distributed systems, i.e.

1. using the expertise of the designer for partitioning;

2. allowing the user to understand the details of the co-design process;

3. taking into account partial solutions;

4. fast exploration of the co-design space.

Acknowledgments

This work was supported by: France Telecom/CNET under Grant 941B113; SGS-Thomson; Esprit program under project COMITY (23015) and project CODAC (OMI 24129) and; MEDEA program under project SMT AT403.

References

[1] M. Abid, A. Changuel, A. A. Jerraya, Exploration of Hardware/Software Design Space Through a Codesign of Robot Arm Controller, In Proceedings European Design Automation Conference with EURO-VHDL'96, Geneva, Switzerland, pp. 42-47, September 1996.

[2] Andrews, Concurrent Programming, Principles and Practice, Benjamin/Cummings (eds), Redwood City, Calif., pp. 484-494, 1991.

[3] E. Barros, W. Rosentiel, X. Xiong, A Method for Partitioning UNITY Language in Hardware and Software, Proceedings of European Design Automation Conference (Euro-DAC), 1994.

[4] T. Ben-Ismail, K. O'Brien, A. A. Jerraya, PARTIF: Interactive System-level Partitioning, VLSI Design Vol. 3 no 3-4, pp. 333-345, 1995.

[5] K. Buchenrieder, A Prototyping Environment for Control-Oriented HW/SW Systems using State-Charts, Activity-Charts and FPGA's, Proceedings of European Design Automation Conference with Euro-VHDL, Grenoble, France, pp. 60-65, September 1994.

[6] J. Buck, S. Ha, E. Lee, Ptolemy: A framework for simulating and prototyping heterogeneous systems, International Journal of Computer Simulation, January 1994.

[7] P. Camurati, F. Corno, P. Prinetto, C. Bayol, B. Soulas, System-Level Modeling and Verification: A Comprehensive Design Methodology, Proceedings European Design & Test Conference (EDAC-ETC-EuroASIC), Paris, France, February 1994.

[8] M. Chiodo, D. Engels, A. Vincentelli, A case Study in Computer Aided Codesign of Embedded Controllers, Design Automation for Embedded Systems, Vol. 1, No. 1-2, pp. 51-67, January 1996.

[9] J. M. Daveau, T. Ben-Ismail, G. F. Marchioro, A. A. Jerraya, Protocol Selection and Interface Generation for HW-SW Codesign, IEEE Transactions on VLSI Systems, Special issue on Design Automation of complex integrated systems, September 1996.

[10] DeMan, I. Bolsens, B. Lin, K. Van-Rompaey, S. Vercauteren, D. Verkest, Co-design for DSP systems, NATO ASI Hardware/Software Codesign, Tremezzo, June 1995.

[11] R. Ernst, J. Henkel, Th. Benner, M. Trawny, The COSYMA Environment for Hardware/Software Cosynthesis, Journal of Microprocessors and Microsystems, Butterworth-Heinemann, 1995.

[12] D. Gajski, F. Vahid, S. Narayan, J. Gong, Specification and Design of Embedded Systems, Prentice-Hall, Inc. Englewood Cliffs, New Jersey, 1994.

[13] J. Gong, D. Gajski, S. Narayan, Software Estimation from Executable Specifications, Proceedings European Design & Automation Conference (EuroDAC), IEEE CS Press, Grenoble, France, September 1994.

[14] R. Gupta, G. DeMicheli, Hardware-Software Cosynthesis using Reprogrammable Components, IEEE Design & Test of Computers, vol. 10, n. 3, pp. 29-41, September 1993.

[15] D. Harel, Statecharts: a Visual Formalism for Complex Systems, Science of Computer Programming, n. 8, North-Holland, pp. 231-274, 1987.

[16] A. A. Jerraya, K. O'Brien, Solar: An Intermediate Format for System-Level Modeling and Synthesis, in "Computer Aided Software/Hardware Engineering", J. Rozenblit, K. Buchenrieder (eds), IEEE Press, Piscataway, N. J. , pp. 147-175, 1994.

[17] A. Kalavade, E. A. Lee, The Extended Partitioning Problem: Hardware/Software Mapping, Scheduling, and Implementation-bin Selection, Proceedings of Sixth Workshop on Rapid Systems Prototyping, pp. 12-18, June 1995.

[18] C. W. Krueger, Software Reuse, ACM Computing Surveys, vol. 24, no. 2, pp. 131-183, June 1992.

[19] E. D. Lagnese, D. E. Thomas, Architectural partitioning of system-level synthesis of integrated circuits, IEEE Trans. CAD/ICAS, vol. 10, no. 7, pp. 847-860, July 1991.

[20] P. Marwedel, G. Goessens, Code Generation for Embedded Processors (DSP), Kluwer Academic Publishers, 1995.

[21] ObjectGeode, http://www.verilogusa.com/og/og.html.

[22] P. Paulin, C. Liem, T. May, S. Sutarwala, DSP Design Tool Requirements for Embedded Systems: A Telecommunication Industrial Perspective, in Journal of VLSI Signal Processing (special issue on synthesis for real-time DSP), Kluwer Academic Publishers, 1994.

[23] R. Saracco, P. A. Tilanus, CCITT SDL: an Overview of the Language and its Applications' Computer Networks and ISDN Systems, Special issue on CCITT SDL, vol. 13 No 2, pp. 65-74, 1987.

[24] M. Srivastava, R. Brodersen, SIERA: A unified framework for rapid-prototyping of system-level hardware and software, IEEE Transactions on Computer-Aided Design of Integrated Circuits and Systems, pp. 676-693, June 1995.

[25] P. A. Subrahmanyam, W. Wolf, Hardware-Software Codesign for Embedded Systems, in ASP-DAC'95, Makuhari Messe, Chiba, Japan. pp. 1-72, 1995.

[26] C. A. Valderrama, A unified model for co-simulation and co-synthesis of mixed hardware/software systems, ED&TC'95, Paris France, 6-9 March 1995.

[27] W. Wolf, Hardware-Software Co-Design of Embedded Systems, PROCEEDINGS OF THE IEEE, vol. 82, no. 7, pp. 967-989, July 1994.

[28] W. Wolf, Object-Oriented Co-Synthesis of Distributed Embedded Systems, in Proceedings CHDL'95, IFIP, 1995.

Hardware / Software Partitioning for Multi-function Systems

Asawaree Kalavade
DSP and VLSI Systems Research Dept.,
Bell Labs, Holmdel, NJ 07733.
kalavade@bell-labs.com

P. A. Subrahmanyam
DSP and VLSI Systems Research Dept.,
Bell Labs, Holmdel, NJ 07733.
subra@bell-labs.com

Abstract

We are interested in optimizing the design of multi-function embedded systems that run a pre-specified set of applications, such as multi-standard audio/video codecs and multi-system phones. Such systems usually have stringent performance constraints and tend to have mixed hardware-software implementations. The current state of the art in the hardware/software codesign of such systems is to design for each application separately. This often leads to application-specific sub-optimal decisions and inconsistent mappings of common nodes in different applications.

We use these as the guiding principles to formulate, as a codesign problem, the design and synthesis of an efficient hardware-software implementation for a multi-function embedded system. Our solution methodology is to first identify nodes that represent similar functionality across different applications. Such "common" nodes are characterized by several metrics. These metrics are quantified and used by a hardware/software partitioning tool to map common nodes to the same resource as far as possible. We demonstrate how this is achieved by modifying a traditional partitioning algorithm (GCLP) used to partition single applications. The overall result of the system-level partitioning process is (1) a hardware or software mapping and (2) a schedule for execution for each node within the application set. On an example set consisting of three video applications, we show that the solution obtained by the use of our method is 38% smaller than that obtained when each application is considered independently.

1. Introduction

Many of the recent research efforts in hardware-software codesign for embedded systems focus on the design of embedded systems optimized for a *particular* application. However, there is a growing class of embedded systems that needs to execute a *set of applications* rather than just a single application. Such systems fall into two broad categories. The first consists of systems that execute multiple applications concurrently, e.g., set-top boxes with concurrent applications like audio, video, and web browsing. The second category includes multi-function systems that support multiple functions or applications of which only one is executed at any instant, depending on external factors. Such multi-function systems offer alternatives between various functionalities — the specific alternative is typically selected at run time. Consider, for example, an audio decoding system that decodes several audio algorithms such as AC3, MPEG2, ADPCM, LPC, etc. Any one of these decoding algorithms may be active at a particular time, based on the service quality requirements and the network bandwidth availability. Another example is a video encoding system that runs MPEG2, H.261, JPEG, etc. Depending on whether the user is watching a movie or conducting a video conference, one of these applications would run at a given time. In this paper we focus on the design of multi-function systems. Note that we use terms "function" and "application" interchangeably.

Due to time-to-market pressures as well as the inherent suitability of some parts of the applications to either hardware or software, it is quite common for such embedded systems to have mixed hardware-software implementations. The current state of the art in the *codesign* of these systems is to separately design for each application. Using this methodology, the resulting solution consists of separate implementations for each such application, possibly on the same chip or board. Although designing for each application independently reduces the design time, the resulting solution might have a larger system area. This is because optimizing the implementation for each application independently often leads to application-specific implementation decisions that do not necessarily yield the best overall cost-performance results. For example, focussing on individual applications might lead to a decision to use specialized (but not very reusable) hardware modules, whereas investing the same or comparable area in a programmable processor core might have yielded a module with a much higher degree of reuse across different applications. Further, since the applications in the mix are often related, there are often several commonalities *between* the applications. For example, a discrete cosine transform (DCT) function may occur in several video applications. When applications are considered independently, a hardware implementation may be selected for the DCT in one application, while a software implementation might be selected in the other application. However, from the viewpoint of optimizing the system as a whole, it might be beneficial to maintain consistency in mapping common nodes. For these reasons, we believe that, when designing for a multi-application set, it is important to consider all the applications in the set simultaneously, rather than designing for individual applications.

We use these as the guiding principles to formulate, as a codesign problem, the design and synthesis of an efficient hardware-software implementation for a multi-function embedded system. In Section 2, we define the multi-application codesign problem. In Section 3, we discuss some related work. In Section 4, we describe two methods to solve the problem. In Section 5, we demonstrate the use of the proposed methods with the help of an example application set consisting of three video applications. We compare the system area obtained when each application is considered independently, to the system area obtained by applying the two methods. The resultant solution is 8% smaller when the first method is used and 38% smaller with the second method.

2. Problem Definition

We begin by assuming that we are given a set $AP = \{A_1,$

1092-3152/97 $10.00 © 1997 IEEE

$A_2, \ldots, A_k\}$ of k applications, only one of which is active at a given time. In particular, we consider applications that have a periodic repetitive behavior. One iteration through the application A_j is assumed to be specified as a directed acyclic graph (DAG, $G = (N, A)$), where nodes N specify computations of "large" level of granularity (e.g. DCT, FIR, etc.) and arcs A specify data and control precedences between nodes. Each application A_j has a timing constraint that specifies the maximum allowable time D_j for executing one iteration of the application.

The system architecture model assumed in this paper consists of three types of resources: (1) one or more programmable processor cores that execute the software component of the nodes mapped to software, (2) a set of hardware accelerators that implement the functionality of the nodes mapped to hardware, and (3) coprocessors, attached to the programmable processors, that accelerate the execution of certain nodes. We assume a template-based architecture, where the interface between the hardware and software components is selected by the designer from among a set of pre-defined mechanisms. The costs associated with these communication modules are abstracted. The actual number of processor cores and the types and numbers of hardware units used in the final implementation is determined by the system-level design process, as described in Section 4.

The multi-application codesign problem is formally defined as follows: Given a set AP = {$A_1, A_2, \ldots A_k$} of applications, where each application A_j has a timing constraint D_j, design an implementation that can support all the applications from the given set. Any one application may be active at run-time and its timing constraints should be met. The design objective is to minimize the overall hardware area.

Given an architecture template and a set *AP* of applications, the codesign task consists of determining (1) the mapping of nodes, in all the applications, to either hardware or software, and (2) the schedule for the execution of the nodes within each application. The mapping is used to construct the overall system architecture. The schedule is used to generate the software for each application. When a particular application runs on the final system, it follows its particular execution schedule.

3. Related Work

While we not aware of any work that directly addresses the problem as we have defined it above, there have been several efforts in the related area of ASIP (Application Specific Instruction Processor) synthesis [1][2][3][4][5]. The ASIP design problem is to design a domain-specific processor by selecting the optimal "instruction set" for a class of applications. Typically, the class of applications is analyzed to find the most commonly used instructions and a datapath and controller for that instruction set is designed. The problem we are interested in here is *to design a system-level hardware-software architecture optimized for a class of applications.* We focus on finding commonalities between applications at a higher level of granularity than is typically considered when designing ASIPs. We do not address the design of the programmable processor itself, but focus on the optimal mapping of components of the applications to the processor or custom hardware accelerators.

Potkonjak *et al.* [6] address the problem of combining several concurrent tasks onto a single ASIC instead of designing a separate ASIC for each task. They discuss an iterative algorithm that combines tasks onto a single ASIC, based on their bitwidth requirements, register counts, source and destination locations, etc. We are concerned with a different problem here, that of selecting the best hardware or software implementation for each node in each application such that the overall system cost is minimized. Also, we are concerned with nodes at a higher level of granularity.

4. Solution Methodology

The proposed solution methodology for the multi-application codesign problem is shown in Figure 1. The set of specified applications is first analyzed to extract commonality measures across applications. In Section 4.1, we identify some measures, such as repetitions and performance-area trade-off, which can be used to characterize nodes across all the applications. We also present simple methods to quantify these measures and provide an intuitive explanation of how they can be used in the partitioning process. The hardware-software partitioning tool is then applied to each application. The partitioning algorithm uses the commonality measures to bias the mappings of nodes that are common across applications. In Section 4.3, we describe two methods to partition the nodes in the applications into hardware and software. These methods are based on a previously developed algorithm, called GCLP [7], used to partition a single application. The GCLP algorithm is summarized in Section 4.2.

4.1. Commonality Measures

The general approach for computing the commonality measures is as follows. First, the "common" nodes, i.e., nodes that represent similar functionality across different applications, are identified. A simple approach to identify common nodes is to have the user tag all nodes in all applications with a *rootname* and *parameters*. Rootnames are matched across all applications. Parameters are used to detect exact or partial matches. An example of a partial match is that between the two nodes <DCT, 1 block> and <DCT, 8 blocks>. Each node is then tagged with a node type; nodes that match have the same node type. In the above example, both nodes can run on the same resource with minor changes to the control logic and are said to have the same node type. Alternatively, more sophisticated techniques such as template matching [8] can be used to detect matches. The set of common nodes consists of nodes that repeat over applications in the set.

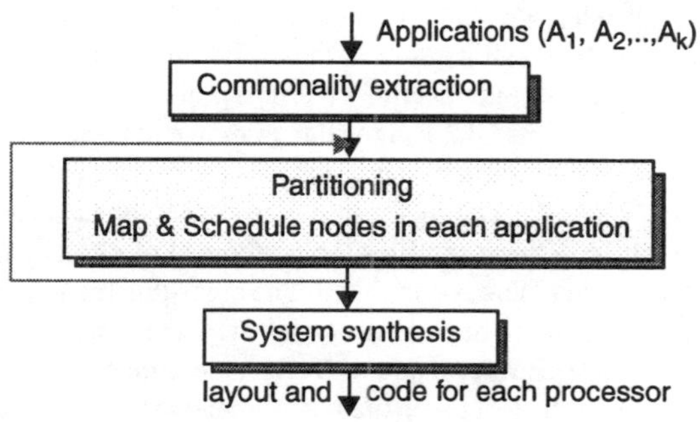

Figure 1 Solution methodology.

Next, each node is analyzed to compute measures that characterize the node. We have identified some properties and propose simple techniques to quantify them. In Section 4.3, we describe the use of these metrics in the partitioning tool.

1. (*R*) Repetitions of a node: The repetitions (R_i) of a node i is computed as the number of occurrences, across all the applications, of nodes of the same type as the type of node i. The repetitions measure can be used in two ways. A node that appears more frequently (high R value) can be given a priority for a custom hardware implementation. In other words, if a node occurs many times in different applications, implementing it in custom hardware makes sense since it gets reused over many applications. Alternatively, the repetitions measure can be used to maintain consistency in mapping; when mapping nodes with a high R value all its instances can be mapped to either hardware or software.
2. (*PA*) Performance-area ratio of a node: The performance-area ratio (PA_i) of a node i is measured as the ratio of the performance gain (speedup achieved by implementing node i in hardware) to the area penalty to be paid for the hardware implementation. Nodes with a higher PA ratio indicate a higher benefit in being mapped to a hardware implementation.
3. (*U*) Urgency of a node: The urgency (U_i) of a node i is computed as the number of times a node of the same type as that of node i appears on the critical paths for the different applications. A node that appears on the critical path in a larger number of applications is more "urgent" and can be given preference for a faster implementation.
4. (*C*) Concurrency of a node: The concurrency C_i of a node i is the number of "concurrent" instances of the node. C_i can influence the number of instances of node i when it is implemented in hardware. For example, if the concurrency for node i is 2, it indicates that, on an average, two instances of node type i are active at any time and hence we can include two hardware accelerators for node type i.

A commonality vector $<R_i, PA_i, U_i, C_i>$ is computed for each node. Nodes with the same type have the same commonality vectors. For each property, the values are normalized across all the nodes. The cumulative effect of the properties can be incorporated by combining different measures. In Section 4.3 we show how some of these measures are used in the partitioning process.

4.2. Partitioning Single Independent Applications

In this section we briefly summarize the original GCLP algorithm [7], which is used to partition a single application *independent* of other applications. In Section 4.3.1 and Section 4.3.2 we describe two modifications to the GCLP algorithm that can be applied to the multi-application codesign problem.

The flow of the GCLP algorithm is shown in Figure 2. N represents the set of nodes in the graph. N_U is the set of unmapped nodes at the current step. N_U is initialized to N. For each node i, a local attribute δ_i that quantifies the preference of i to a hardware or a software mapping is computed. The algorithm then maps one node per step. At the beginning of each step, the global time criticality measure GC is computed. GC is a measure of how critical time is at that step, i.e., given the nodes already mapped so far and the required finish time of the application, GC is indicative of the

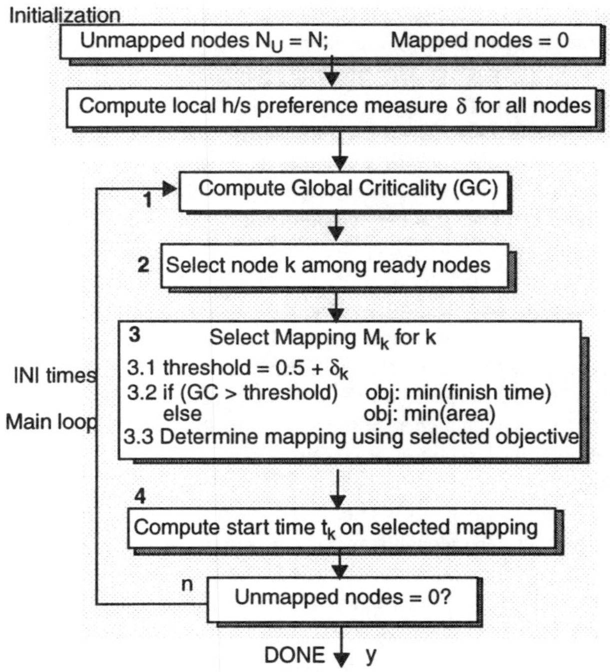

Figure 2 Flow of GCLP Algorithm

slack available at that instant. Unmapped nodes whose predecessors have already been mapped and scheduled are called *ready* nodes. A node is selected for mapping from the set of ready nodes using an urgency criterion. GC and δ_i of the selected node i are then used to select the mapping objective as shown. Using this objective, the selected node is assigned a mapping (M_i). The mapping is also used to determine the start time for the execution of node (t_i). This set of start times defines the schedule for the system. The process is repeated $|N|$ times over all nodes.

4.3. Partitioning Multiple Applications

We now describe two methods for partitioning multiple applications. These methods modify the GCLP algorithm.

4.3.1 Method A

In this method, the partitioning algorithm is modified to incorporate two basic factors that influence the mapping of a node when multiple applications are considered:

1. If a node is repeated in several applications (high R measure), it might be beneficial to bias its mapping toward hardware. By sharing a hardware implementation for repeated nodes, other less frequently appearing nodes may get mapped to software, leading to a overall reduction in hardware area.
2. If a node takes a small area when implemented in hardware, relative to all nodes in all applications, and if the difference in software and hardware execution times is high (high PA measure), it might be beneficial to bias the mapping of the node toward hardware. This may free up the software resource for nodes that might otherwise be expensive in hardware.

These two factors can be put to use when considering the mapping of multiple applications. We define for each node i, a commonality measure $CM_i = \rho R_i + \pi PA_i$, where R_i is the repetitions measure, PA_i is the performance-area trade-off measure, and ρ and π are user-defined weights. CM_i is normalized over all the nodes in the application. As shown in procedure A below, the CM_i measure is used to bias the threshold in the GCLP algorithm.

Procedure A

1. Identify "common" nodes and count the number of instances of each common node over all the applications. The value of the repetitions measure R_i is obtained by normalizing the number of instances with respect to the largest number thus obtained; this yields a value for R_i between 0 and 1.
2. Compute the performance-area trade-off measure for each node i as $PA_i = (ts_i - th_i) / ah_i$, where ts_i and th_i are the execution times of node i in software and hardware respectively and ah_i is the hardware area for node i. Normalize PA_i over all the nodes to a value between 0 and 1.
3. Compute for each node i, the commonality measure $CM_i = \rho R_i + \pi PA_i$ using user-specified weights ρ and π. Normalize CM_i to a value between 0 and 0.5.
4. For each application A_a, run $GCLP\text{-}A(A_a)$.

Algorithm GCLP-A

This is a variant of the GCLP algorithm described in Figure 2, where step 3 in GCLP is replaced as follows:

3. Determine mapping M_i for i
   3.1 $threshold = 0.5 - CM_i$.
   3.2 if($GC > threshold$) M_i=hardware, else M_i=software

The interpretation of step 4 is as follows. For nodes with a non-zero CM_i value, the threshold is reduced to below its default value of 0.5. The *GC* at that step of the algorithm is compared to this modified threshold. If the *GC* is above the threshold, a hardware mapping is selected. By lowering the threshold with the commonality measure, a hardware bias is introduced. If *GC* is below the threshold, a software mapping is used. The mapping decision for common nodes is thus made by considering the combination of application-specific requirements (dictated by *GC*) as well as inter-application demands (modeled by CM_i). Nodes that are not common get mapped such that feasibility is met, while still attempting to minimize the total area.

4.3.2 Method B

This method attempts to maintain a "consistency" in the way common nodes are mapped. The key idea is to map the applications in a particular order and to propagate information about the mapping decisions made. The propagation allows information about mapping decisions within an application to be *shared* between applications. The procedure for method B is summarized below.

Procedure B

1. Compute commonality measures *R* and *PA* for all nodes, as described earlier.
2. Compute application criticality (*AC*) for all the applications in the set. AC_j is computed as $(\Sigma\, ts_i)/D_j$, where ts_i is the execution time of node i when implemented in software, and D_j is the required finish time for application A_j. The smaller the ratio, the fewer the hardware resources required to implement A_j and the lower the criticality of the application.
3. Order the applications by *AC* such that the most critical application (largest *AC*) is considered first.
4. For each A_a in this order, run $GCLP\text{-}B(A_a, shared\_mapping)$

Algorithm GCLP-B

This is a variant of the GCLP algorithm described in Figure 2, where step 3 in GCLP is replaced as follows.

```
3. Determine mapping M_i for i:
   3.1 if (computed_shared_mapping(i) ==1)    {
          /* node type mapped before*/
          if (shared_mapping(i) == hardware)
                threshold = 0.5 - R_i /* lower threshold */
          else if (shared_mapping(i) == software)
                threshold = 0.5 + R_i /* raise threshold */
       } else    /* no earlier shared mapping */
                threshold = 0.5 - PA_i.
   3.2 if(GC > threshold) M_i = hardware, else M_i =software
   3.3 Update shared mapping
```

The interpretation of step 4 is as follows. Let i be the node being considered at a particular step. If a node of the same type as node i has been mapped by a previously considered application, the goal is to try to preserve that mapping for node i. This is accomplished by biasing the threshold in the direction of the previous selection. Thus, if the earlier mapping was hardware, the threshold is lowered by the repetitions measure R_i, favoring a hardware implementation for this node. Similarly, if a node of the same type as node i has been previously mapped to software, the threshold is raised by the repetitions measure R_i, thus favoring a software implementation. Note that the mapping of node i is not *hardcoded* to the mapping selected previously; instead, it is "biased" toward that mapping. By lowering the threshold for a node that has a previous mapping in hardware, its chances of getting mapping to hardware are increased (see 3.2). However, the state of the current application, as reflected by *GC*, is also considered. A hardware mapping is selected only if *GC* is greater than the modified threshold. Thus the mapping of common nodes is biased towards a mapping that maintains consistency across all applications, while making sure the application-specific constraints are also taken into consideration. If no node of the type of node i has been mapped before, the *PA* measure is used to select its mapping. In this case, this tries to select the best possible mapping for the node, considering the effect of the current application only.

The order in which applications are selected is important in this method. One possible approach is to select the most critical application first and map its nodes in a way that best meets the timing constraints. Other nodes then follow the mapping decisions made by the more critical applications, unless their local preference strongly dictates otherwise. We are also experimenting with other orderings of applications.

5. Numerical Results

In this section we report the results obtained for designing an implementation for a system running a set of video applications. In Section 5.2, we present the solution obtained when each application is considered independently. The solutions obtained by using methods A and B are discussed in Section 5.3 and Section 5.4 respectively. The solutions obtained by using the methods proposed in this paper are found to be superior (have smaller area) to the solution obtained when each application is considered independently. We have implemented the GCLP algorithm and its proposed variants. Each run through the partitioning algorithm takes less than a second of CPU time on a Sparc20.

5.1. Application set and system architecture

We consider the application set consisting of: (1) MPEG2 video encode (M2E), (2) H.261 decode and encode (H), and (3) MPEG2 video decode (M2D). Such a mix is representative of the different functions running on an add-on card in a laptop PC, where the user may be watching a movie (MPEG2 video decode), or conducting a video conference (H.261 encode/decode), or transmitting video data (MPEG2 video encode). Table 1 summarizes the details of the applications in the application mix and their timing constraints. Several nodes are repeated over the different applications (e.g.: the node Inverse Quantizer appears 4 times, the node Motion Estimator appears 2 times).

App.	frame size	frame rate	latency (cycles)	# nodes	application criticality
M2E	CCIR601	12 fps	6110	11	3.27
M2D	CCIR601	15 fps	8888	7	1.23
H	CIF	15 fps	16666	24	1.68

Table 1: Applications (MPEG2 encode:M2E, MPEG2 decode:M2D, H.261 encode/decode:H).

We assume a system architecture as shown in Figure 3, consisting of a single programmable processor (PP) and multiple coprocessors (CP) and hardware accelerators {HW}; the actual number of coprocessors and the number and types of hardware accelerators are determined by the partitioning algorithm. The programmable processor can implement all the nodes, representing the software implementation. The coprocessor can implement some of the nodes. We assume a SIMD vector coprocessor that can implement the following functions: dct/idct, quantizer/iquantizer, Frame Add/Sub, Motion compensation, and Loop Filter. The hardware accelerators implement specific functionality. We assume hardware accelerators for nodes such as a motion estimator, and a variable length encoder. Table 2 summarizes the different resource types available The software execution times for the nodes are measured by a detailed simulation on a media processor. The hardware execution times and areas for the nodes are abstracted from an actual implementation of a video conferencing system developed in our lab. Different system implementations are quantified by a "system cost", which is the total hardware area required over and above the programmable processor.

Type of Resource		Type of Resource	
Programmable Processor	PP	Error Decoder	HW6
SIMD Coprocessor	CP	Error Encoder	HW7
Motion Estimator	HW1	Encode Src Processor	HW8
Variable Length Encoder	HW2	Encode Sink Processor	HW9
Variable Length Decoder	HW3	Decode Src Processor	HW10
H.261 Source Processing	HW4	Decode Sink Processor	HW11
H.261 Sink Processing	HW5		

Table 2: Resource types in the system architecture

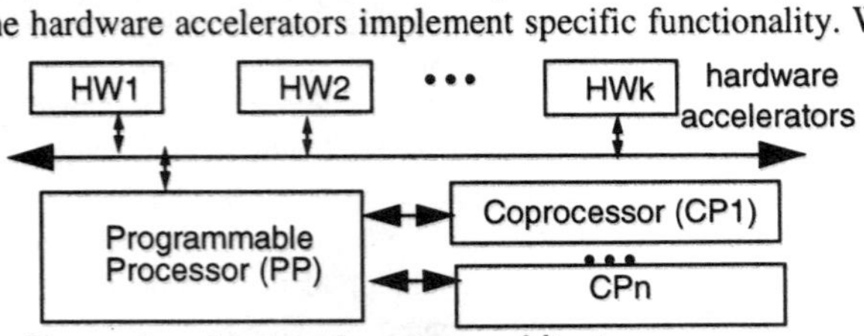

Figure 3 Assumed system architecture

5.2. Experiment 1: Independent Mapping

We first run each application independently through the original GCLP algorithm. Table 3 summarizes the resultant hardware resources used for each application and the total system area. The total area for the application set is computed by summing the areas of the union of the hardware resources used in the three applications. Note that H requires two instances of CP.

Application	Hardware Resources Used	System Cost
M2E	HW1, HW2, HW8	103
M2D	HW3, HW10	25
H	CP, CP, HW1, HW2, HW4, HW5, HW8, HW11	199
Set	CP, CP, HW1, HW2, HW3, HW4, HW5, HW8, HW10, HW11	224

Table 3: Results of Experiment 1

5.3. Experiment 2: Method A

Recall that in method A, *threshold* = 0.5 - CM_i, where $CM_i = \rho R_i + \pi PA_i$. We present three sets of results with (ρ, π) taking

Case	App.	Hardware Resources Used	System Cost
	M2E	CP, HW1, HW2, HW8	103
	M2D	HW3, HW10	25
	H	CP, CP, HW1, HW3, HW4, HW8	193
(2A) CM = R	Set	CP, CP, HW1, HW2, HW3, HW4, HW8, HW10	206
	M2E	CP, HW1, HW2, HW8	103
	M2D	HW3, HW10	25
	H	CP, CP, HW1, HW2, HW4, HW5, HW8, HW11	199
(2B) CM = PA	Set	CP, CP, HW1, HW2, HW3, HW4, HW5, HW8, HW10, HW11	224
	M2E	CP, HW1, HW2, HW8	103
	M2D	HW3, HW10	25
	H	CP, CP, HW1, HW2, HW4, HW8	181
(2C) CM=R+PA	Set	CP, CP, HW1, HW2, HW3, HW4, HW8, HW10	206

Table 4: Results of Experiment 2

values (1,0), (0,1), and (1,1). Table 4 summarizes the results. Recall that the goal of this method is to map nodes with high repetitions to hardware.

In case 2A, nodes idct, mc, sub, and dct are mapped to hardware (since they have higher repetitions), as against software in experiment 1. This is achieved by changing the threshold values when mapping these nodes. As a consequence, nodes with lower repetitions such as vld and sink3 get mapped to software. This results in a 8% lower system area. In case 2B, the *PA* measures do not help improve the solution over experiment 1, since PA measures alone have the same effect as δ in the original GCLP. In case 2C, the combined effect of *PA* and *R* is the same as the effect of *R* alone.Thus, the use of repetitions measure in method A seems to reduce the system area by 8% in this example

5.4. Experiment 3: Method B

Recall that in this method, applications are considered in a specific order and mapping state is maintained between applications. The goal is to maintain consistency when mapping nodes of the same type. The applications are considered in the order of application criticality (sequence M2E-H-M2D). Table 5 summarizes the results.

Application	Hardware Resources Used	System Cost
M2E	CP, HW1, HW2, HW8	103
H	CP, HW1, HW2, HW4, HW5, HW8, HW9, HW11	139
M2D	CP	65
Set	CP, HW1, HW2, HW4, HW5, HW8, HW9, HW11	139

Table 5: Results of Experiment 3

Method B gives a much better solution than that obtained in either of the first two experiments. In particular, the solution is 38% smaller than that obtained when applications are considered independently. This may be attributed to the fact that method B incorporates some of the design principles in method A and also takes the consistency into consideration. *Note that the solution for M2D by itself is worse than in experiment 1.* The advantage is a reduced overall system cost since the same coprocessor is used in all applications, instead of special hardware accelerators that were used for this application when considered independently.

6. Conclusion

We have formulated, as a codesign problem, the design and synthesis of an efficient hardware-software implementation for an embedded system that runs a pre-specified set of applications. The goal is to design an implementation that can support all the applications from the given set. Any one application may be active at run-time and its timing constraints should be met. The design objective is to minimize the overall area of the system.

Although this problem can be viewed as one that involves an ASIP (application specific instruction processor) design, we have intentionally formulated the problem in a manner that avoids automatic processor design. Instead, we assume that the architecture is selected from among a set of given templates and that the processor core is available. Further, the applications are assumed to be specified at a "coarse" level of granularity. These assumptions have been made with a view to reducing the complexity of the problem, while still allowing for solutions that are useful in practice.

The key idea of our approach is to analyze the set of applications to extract commonalities across nodes in different applications. We identified several measures that characterize the nodes and defined ways to quantify them. These measures are used in the partitioning process to bias the mapping of a node. In general, the mapping decision for common nodes is made by considering the combination of application-specific requirements (dictated by the global criticality within the application) as well as inter-application demands (modeled by the commonality measures). Nodes that are not common across applications get mapped in a way such that feasibility is met, while still attempting to minimize the total area. In particular, we presented two methods to partition such application sets. In the first method, nodes that are repeated more often across different applications are biased towards hardware, so as to improve the utilization of the specialized hardware accelerators. In the second method, applications are considered in a specific order for partitioning, dictated by the relative criticality of applications. Mapping decisions made in one application are shared with other applications in an attempt to maintain consistency of mapping common nodes. When mapping a node type for the first time, its *PA* measure is used to select its mapping. In this way, the best possible mapping is selected for the node, considering the effect of the current application only. Based on the experiments carried out so far, this method appears to be superior to the first method (the resultant solution is 38% smaller). This is attributed to the fact that method B incorporates some of the design principles in method A and also takes the consistency into consideration.

7. References

[1] J. Sato, *et al.* "PEAS-I: A Hardware/Software Codesign System for ASIP Development", *IEICE Transactions on Fundamentals of Electronics, Communications and Computer Sciences,* March 1994, vol.E77-A, (no.3):483-91.

[2] N. Ngoc et al. "A Hardware/Software Partitioning Algorithm for Designing Pipelined ASIPs with least gate counts", *Proc. 33rd DAC,* June 1996, pp. 527-32.

[3] H. Ing-Jer, A. M. Despain, "Generating Instruction Sets and Microarchitectures from Applications", *Proc. of ICCAD* 94, p. 391-6.

[4] P. Paulin, C. Liem, T. May, S. Sutarwala, "DSP Design Tool Requirements for Embedded Systems: A Telecommunications Industrial Perspective", *Journal of VLSI Signal Processing,* Special issue on synthesis for real-time DSP, 9(1/2): 23-47, January 1995.

[5] W. Zhao, C. A. Papachristou, "Synthesis of Reusable DSP cores based on Multiple Behaviors", *Proc. of ICCAD 96,* pp. 103-109.

[6] M. Potkonjak, W, Wolf, "Cost Optimization in ASIC Implementation of Periodic Hard-real time systems using behavioral synthesis techniques", *Proc. ICCAD 95,* pp. 446-51.

[7] A. Kalavade, "The Extended Partitioning Problem: Hardware/Software Mapping, Scheduling, and Implementation-bin Selection", Journal of Design Automation of Embedded Systems, vol.2, no. 2., Mar 1997, pp. 226-163. http://www.bell-labs.com/user/kalavade.

[8] D. Rao, F. Kurdahi, "Partitioning by Regularity Extraction", *Proc. 29th DAC,* pp. 235-238, 1992.

MOGAC: A Multiobjective Genetic Algorithm for the Co-Synthesis of Hardware-Software Embedded Systems

Robert P. Dick and Niraj K. Jha

Department of Electrical Engineering
Princeton University
Princeton, New Jersey 08544

Abstract

In this paper, we present a hardware-software co-synthesis system, called MOGAC, that partitions and schedules embedded system specifications consisting of multiple periodic task graphs. MOGAC synthesizes real-time heterogeneous distributed architectures using an adaptive multiobjective genetic algorithm that can escape local minima. Price and power consumption are optimized while hard real-time constraints are met. MOGAC places no limit on the number of hardware or software processing elements in the architectures it synthesizes. Our general model for bus and point-to-point communication links allows a number of link types to be used in an architecture. Application-specific integrated circuits consisting of multiple processing elements are modeled. Heuristics are used to tackle multi-rate systems, as well as systems containing task graphs whose hyperperiods are large relative to their periods. The application of a multiobjective optimization strategy allows a single co-synthesis run to produce multiple designs which trade off different architectural features. Experimental results indicate that MOGAC has advantages over previous work in terms of solution quality and running time.

1 Introduction

Hardware-software co-design is the process of concurrently defining the software and hardware portions of an embedded system while considering dependencies between the two [1]. Designers rely on their experience with past systems when estimating the resource requirements of a new system. Since *ad hoc* design exploration is time-consuming, an engineer typically selects a conservative architecture after little experimentation, resulting in an unnecessarily expensive system. Most research in the area of hardware-software co-design has focused on easing the process of design exploration. Automating this process falls within the more specialized realm of co-synthesis. Given an embedded system specification, a co-synthesis system determines the hardware and software processing elements (PEs) needed as well as the communication links to be used. In addition, the system assigns each task to a PE and determines the PEs to which each link is connected. Finally, a schedule is provided for each PE and communication link such that all real-time constraints are met [2]. Co-synthesis systems generate feasible, low-cost architecture descriptions without designer intervention.

There are four tasks which must be carried out by a co-synthesis system:

- **Allocation:** Determine the quantity of each type of PE and communication link to use.
- **Assignment:** Select a PE to execute each task upon. Choose a link to use for each communication event.
- **Scheduling:** Determine the time at which each task and communication event occurs.
- **Performance evaluation:** Compute the price, speed, and power consumption of the solution.

Related work often limits the co-synthesis solution space to architectures consisting of one CPU and one application-specific integrated circuit (ASIC). Most real-life embedded systems are composed of multiple general-purpose processors and ASICs, *i.e.*, they are distributed heterogeneous architectures [1]. We will consider the general problem in which the numbers and types of PEs and links in an architecture are not bounded.

Optimal co-synthesis is an intractable problem. Allocation/assignment and scheduling are each known to be NP-complete for distributed systems [3]. It is, therefore, not surprising that all co-synthesis systems which rely on optimal mixed integer linear programming [4] and exhaustive exploration [5] can only be applied to small instances of the co-synthesis problem. Heuristics have seen some success with larger instances of the distributed system co-synthesis problem. The constructive algorithm used in [6] was the first to target low power. However, like iterative improvement algorithms [2],[7], conventional constructive algorithms may become trapped in local minima. A genetic algorithm was previously applied to the hardware-software partitioning problem [8]. However, in this work only one general-purpose processor was allowed, there were no provisions for synthesizing systems with multi-rate periodic task graphs, and a limited communication link model was used. In addition, run-times were not given and the genetic algorithm only optimized one variable: price.

MOGAC synthesizes distributed heterogeneous embedded systems. Price and power consumption are optimized under a number of hard constraints. MOGAC uses a communication model that is capable of synthesizing systems with multiple busses and point-to-point communication links. ASICs consisting of multiple PEs are modeled. MOGAC applies heuristics which allow multi-rate systems to be scheduled in reasonable time even when the least common multiple (LCM) scheduling method [9] would otherwise require a large number of task graph copies to be made. MOGAC's use of a multiobjective genetic algorithm allows it to provide a designer with multiple solutions which trade off different system costs.

This work was supported in part by an NSF Graduate Fellowship and in part by NSF under Grant No. MIP-9423574.

1092-3152/97 $10.00 © 1997 IEEE

2 Preliminaries

In this section, we present preliminary concepts used in co-synthesis algorithms and genetic algorithms.

2.1 Embedded System Model

In this subsection, we provide high-level descriptions of the data types MOGAC operates on. Information about the computations carried out upon them can be found in Section 3.

Cost: A cost is a variable that a co-synthesis system attempts to minimize. Price, power consumption, and schedule length are examples of costs.

Task graph: A task graph is a directed acyclic graph in which each node is associated with a task and each edge is associated with a scalar describing the amount of data that must be transferred between the two connected tasks. The *period* of a task graph is the amount of time between the earliest start times of its consecutive executions. A node with no outgoing edges is called a *sink* node. A *deadline*, the time by which the task associated with the node must complete its execution, exists for every sink node. However, other nodes may also have deadlines associated with them. The deadline of a task graph is the maximum of all the deadlines specified in it.

Processing element: A PE executes tasks. Two types of PEs are modeled: *grouped PEs* and *independent PEs*. Independent PEs represent general-purpose processors which can only execute one task at a time. However, multiple grouped PEs may be located on the same integrated circuit (IC), upon which multiple tasks may execute simultaneously. This provides a model for ASICs which are capable of carrying out different tasks at the same time. The following information establishes the relationships between tasks and independent PEs:

- A two-dimensional array indicating the worst-case execution time of each task on each independent PE.
- A two-dimensional array indicating the average power consumption of each task on each independent PE.

In addition to these arrays, independent PEs have price and idle power consumption values. The following information establishes the relationship between tasks and grouped PEs:

- A two-dimensional array indicating the relative worst-case execution time of each task on each grouped PE.
- A two-dimensional array indicating the relative average power consumption of each task on each grouped PE.
- A two-dimensional array indicating the peak power consumption of each task on each grouped PE.

Grouped PEs do not have an inherent price. However, each grouped PE is assigned to an IC which does have a price. The following variables are associated with ICs: price, pin count, device count, idle power consumption, peak power dissipation, speed, and power efficiency. Each grouped PE places device count and pin count requirements on the IC to which it is assigned. For an architecture to be valid, each IC must meet the pin count and device count requirements of the grouped PEs assigned to it. In addition, each IC must meet the peak power dissipation requirements of the tasks assigned to the grouped PEs implemented on it.

The worst-case execution time for a task assigned to a grouped PE is equivalent to its relative worst-case execution time divided by the speed of the IC on which the grouped PE is implemented. The task's average power consumption is its relative average power consumption divided by the power efficiency of the IC on which the task's grouped PE is implemented.

Communication link: Communication links have the following attributes: packet size, average power consumption per packet, worst-case communication time per packet, price, number of contacts, and idle power consumption.

Each task graph edge must be assigned to a communication link. The worst-case communication time and average power consumption of an edge are linearly dependent on the number of packets of data transferred through its link. The number of contacts a link supports is the number of ICs it can connect, *i.e.*, a link with two contacts is a point-to-point link. A link with more than two contacts is a bus. In previous distributed computing work, it is commonly assumed that communication between tasks which are assigned to the same IC consumes an insignificant amount of time and power. We also make this assumption.

Constraints: If one of the system's costs is higher than its *hard constraint*, the system is invalid. For example, the schedule length of a task graph cannot exceed its hard real-time constraint. Valid systems may have costs which are higher than their *soft constraints*, although it is desirable to reduce a cost until it is lower than its soft constraint.

Strings: The *PE allocation string* is an array of integers. Each integer represents the number of instances of a PE type present in a solution. For a genetic algorithm to function properly, it is important for its strings to preserve locality, *i.e.*, similar entries must be located closer to each other in the strings than dissimilar entries [10]. As mentioned earlier, the relationship between tasks and PEs is defined by a collection of two-dimensional arrays. For the purpose of characterizing a PE type, the one-dimensional arrays corresponding to that PE type are selected from these two-dimensional arrays. Thus, each PE can be characterized by a collection of one-dimensional arrays and some scalars. The first step in ordering the PE allocation string is to collapse each PE type's arrays into scalars. This conversion is done by taking a sum of each array's entries and weighting each entry with the number of tasks, of the type corresponding to that entry's position, which exist in the embedded system specification. After this step, the PE is described by a collection of scalars, *i.e.*, a vector. A locality-preserving heuristic is then used to impose an order on these vectors. The *link allocation string* and *IC allocation string* are similar to the PE allocation string and they are ordered using similar algorithms.

The *task assignment string* is an ordered string of PE instance references specifying the PE to which each task is assigned. This string is ordered by conducting a depth-first traversal of all the task graphs in the system specification. The *grouped PE assignment string* is an ordered string of IC instance references specifying the IC to which each grouped PE is assigned.

The *link connectivity string* is an ordered string of independent PE and IC instance references specifying the independent PEs and ICs to which each communication link is connected. The order of link types in this string is based on their order in the link allocation string.

2.2 Genetic Algorithms

Genetic algorithms maintain a pool of solutions which evolve in parallel over time. Genetic operators are applied to the solutions in the current pool to obtain a new generation of solutions. The lowest quality solutions are then removed from the pool [10]. Genetic algorithms excel at simultaneously optimizing multiple conflicting costs. They have the ability to escape local minima and communicate information between solutions.

Next, we define some basic terms used to discuss genetic algorithms. In a conventional genetic algorithm, every solution is represented by a *string* of values (usually Boolean). Although we discuss the genetic algorithm used by MOGAC in conventional terms, no primitive Boolean string is ever computed. As discussed in Section 2.1, strings in MOGAC are more intricate than those used in conventional genetic algorithms. Genetic operators are applied directly to the complex data structures which represent a solution. Such algorithms are sometimes called evolutionary algorithms.

In conventional genetic algorithms, all changes to strings are brought about by three operators. *Reproduction* makes a copy of a solution. *Mutation* randomly changes part of a solution's description. Conventionally, a bit in the solution's string is inverted. *Cross-over* combines parts of different solutions. This is the operator that gives genetic algorithms their strength; it allows different solutions to share information with each other. Conventionally, two strings are cut at the same offset from their starting points and the portions following the cut are swapped. The operators used by MOGAC are analogous to, but more complicated than, conventional genetic operators.

2.3 Multiobjective Optimization

The co-synthesis problem is inherently one of multiobjective optimization. There are numerous costs and improving one cost of a system often results in the degradation of another. Most past co-synthesis systems have dealt with this optimization problem by using a linear weighted sum to collapse all of the system costs into one variable and optimizing this variable. For this method to be successful, the weighting array used must be appropriate for the problem instance as well as the designer's desired solution. Unfortunately, the co-synthesis problem is too complicated for an instance's best weighting array to be known without first exploring that instance's Pareto-optimal set of solutions, *i.e.*, those solutions which can only be improved in one area by being degraded in another. It is impossible, however, to explore the Pareto-optimal set of solutions if an arbitrary weighting array has been used to collapse all costs into a single value.

Multiobjective genetic algorithms avoid the problems associated with collapsing multiple costs into one value. In such algorithms, solutions are ranked relative to each other, *i.e.*, a solution's rank is the number of other solutions to which it is not in some way inferior. The use of a multiobjective genetic algorithm allows MOGAC to explore the Pareto-optimal solution set instead of relying on an arbitrary weighting array to guide its search.

3 Algorithm Description

In this section, we give a description of the algorithms used in MOGAC.

3.1 Overview of the Algorithm

In this subsection, we present a high-level description of MOGAC's hierarchical genetic algorithm for co-synthesis. Initially, there are approximately 400 members in MOGAC's solution pool. As shown in Figure 1, the pool is broken into clusters of solutions. Every solution within a cluster has the same allocation strings. However, each solution's assignment and link connectivity strings may differ from those of other solutions within the cluster. Allocation string cross-over only occurs between clusters of solutions. Assignment string cross-over and link connectivity string cross-over only occur between solutions in the same cluster.

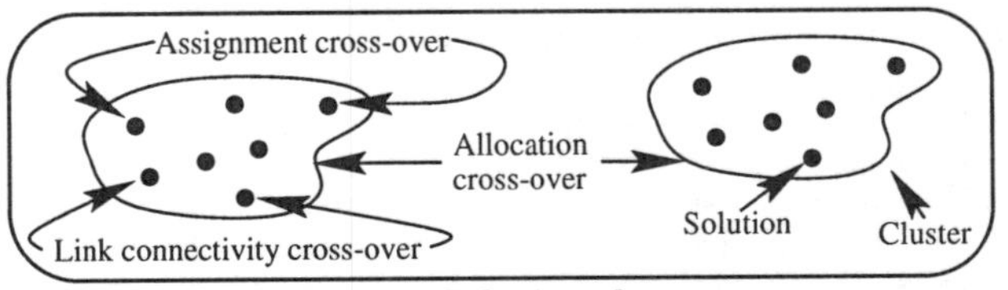

Figure 1: Solution clusters

Each solution's allocation string is initialized with a heuristic constructive algorithm; PEs are randomly selected until there exists at least one PE upon which each task can execute. Despite the simplicity of this heuristic, it frequently produces high-quality allocations. From this starting point, the genetic algorithm searches for higher-quality allocations. During the first generation or two, many of the solutions are invalid because there are not sufficient resources available to carry out tasks rapidly enough to meet the system's real-time deadlines. As the allocation strings mutate, more PEs and links become available and are incorporated into solutions through assignment string mutation and connectivity string mutation.

At this point, the evolve-evaluate cycle starts to supply feedback to the genetic algorithm. Solutions, which have adequate resources to meet their real-time constraints, consume little power, and make the best use of these resources, dominate other solutions. Non-inferior solutions, those which are not dominated by any other solutions, reproduce more often than dominated solutions but occasionally dominated solutions reproduce as well. Infrequently, allocation cross-over occurs, changing an entire cluster of solutions simultaneously.

MOGAC treats all non-inferior solutions equally even if they violate hard constraints. After each generation, MOGAC displays the costs of the members of its non-inferior solution set. At any time, the designer may halt the system and examine an individual solution in detail. If the designer chooses not to interfere with the co-synthesis run, MOGAC automatically adapts its parameters based upon its solution pool's rate of improvement. At the end of a run, the system presents its user with all of the valid non-inferior solutions it found.

3.2 Parameter Adaptation

In this subsection, we discuss the manner in which MOGAC adapts its own parameters. In general, each parameter has a starting value and an adaptation rate. At the end of each generation in which the quality of the solution pool did not improve, the relevant parameters are adjusted by their adaptation rates. When an improvement occurs, the relevant parameters are reset to their initial values. If a pre-specified number of generations pass without improvement, the co-synthesis run halts.

MOGAC has a number of static parameters. Although these parameters can be changed from run to run, they do not adapt during a run. There are a fixed number of clusters in the solution pool and each cluster contains a fixed number of solutions. In addition, the ratio of real to total task graph copies is constant throughout a run (see Section 3.3).

Most parameters are dynamic; they adapt based upon the rate at which the quality of the solution pool is improving. The frequency with which each genetic operator is applied is parametric and adaptable. There are a number of parameters which control the aggressiveness of MOGAC's genetic operators. Other parameters control the probability of a superior solution being replaced by an inferior one. If desired, these values can be set to monotonically decrease during a co-synthesis run, allowing MOGAC to approximate a simulated annealing algorithm.

3.3 Multi-Rate Systems

As mentioned in Section 1, co-synthesis systems which use the results in [9] to guarantee valid schedules for multi-rate systems have difficulty synthesizing architectures in which the hyperperiod, *i.e.*, the LCM of the periods of all task graphs, is much larger than the periods of individual task graphs. For such systems, it is necessary to assign and schedule the tasks and communication events in numerous copies of some task graphs. The number of copies of a task graph is the system's hyperperiod divided by the graph's period. Past work has dealt with this problem by forcing corresponding tasks in different copies of the same task graph to be assigned to the same PE instance [2]. Although this does reduce the complexity of assignment and scheduling, it decreases the flexibility of a co-synthesis system. To derive the most efficient architecture for a given system specification, it may be necessary to assign corresponding tasks in two copies of a task graph to different PEs. MOGAC uses two heuristics to tackle system specifications with large hyperperiods. The first of these is an extension of a method used in real-time computing [11].

Hyperperiod contraction: The problems caused by large hyperperiods can be reduced by tightening the periods of some task graphs. Consider a system consisting of two periodic task graphs, where the first has a period of 12, and the second has a period of 13. The hyperperiod is, therefore, 156. If we tighten the period of the second task graph to 12, however, the system's hyperperiod reduces to 12.

The designer has full control over the aggressiveness with which the hyperperiod contraction heuristic is applied. MOGAC allows the designer to specify the maximum and minimum acceptable periods for each task graph in the system. Subject to these constraints, a period for each task graph is calculated such that the number of task graph copies needed for LCM scheduling is minimized.

Scalable implicit task graph copies: We have developed a method in which some of the task graph copies in the hyperperiod are *implicit* and some are *real* (see Figure 2). Each implicit copy has a real *parent*. Implicit copies are not entered in a solution's task assignment string; they share the assignment string of their parent. Although it is still necessary to schedule implicit task graph copies, there is no need to prioritize the nodes of these copies; the implicit task graph node priorities are equivalent to the parent task graph node priorities (see Section 3.6). Additionally, the absence of implicit copies from a solution's task assignment string reduces the size of the genetic algorithm's solution space, thus speeding optimization. Selecting a ratio of the number of real task graph copies to the total number of task graph copies involves making a trade-off between potential solution quality and MOGAC's run-time. This decision is left to the designer.

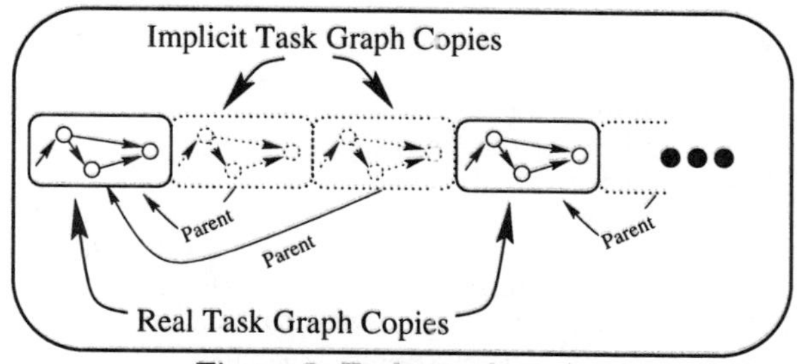

Figure 2: Task graph copies

3.4 Ranking and Reproduction

In this subsection, we explain the manner in which solutions and clusters are selected for reproduction.

Solution ranking and reproduction: Solutions within a cluster are ranked using the method presented in Section 2.3. In each generation, a pre-specified number of solutions within each cluster are eliminated to make space for the reproduction of other solutions. Solutions are selected for reproduction by indexing inward from the highest-ranking solution with a Gaussian random variable. The inverse of the variance of this variable is defined as *elitism*. MOGAC's elitism is specified by the user. A designer can choose to protect the highest-ranked solutions in the solution pool from mutation and cross-over or to allow the modification of any solution.

Cluster ranking and reproduction: Ranking clusters is more complicated than ranking solutions. Each solution has one set of costs. Thus, determining whether it dominates another solution is straightforward. Clusters, however, contain numerous solutions; each cluster is associated with a number of sets of costs. We extend the concept of domination to take partial domination into account. Cluster domination is represented by a scalar instead of a Boolean value. The definition of rank must also be adjusted when it is applied to clusters. Let x and y be clusters. $nis\,(x)$ is the set of non-inferior solutions in x. $dom\,(a, b)$ is 1 if a is not dominated by b and 0 otherwise. Then,

$$clust\_dom\,(x, y) = \max_{a \in nis(x)} \sum_{b \in nis(y)} dom\,(a, b)$$

and,

$$rank[x] = \sum_{y \in \text{set of clusters} \wedge y \neq x} clust\_dom\,(x, y)$$

Once cluster ranks have been determined, cluster reproduction is analogous to solution reproduction.

3.5 Evolution

In this subsection, we give an overview of mechanisms through which the solution pool evolves. Evolution in MOGAC is hierarchical. The cluster-level genetic operators simultaneously affect every solution in a cluster, while solution-level operators only affect individual solutions within a cluster. Solution-level operators are typically applied more frequently than cluster-level operators.

Cluster-level operators: PE allocation mutation causes a PE to be added or removed from a cluster's allocation. PE allocation cross-over selects two PE type cut-points at random and two clusters at random. The PE counts of the PE types between the cut-points are swapped between the selected clusters. The link allocation and IC allocation operators are analogous to the PE allocation operators.

Solution-level operators: Task assignment mutation causes a randomly selected task to assign itself to a different PE instance. Task assignment cross-over selects two task cut-points at random and two solutions at random. The PE assignments of the tasks between the cut-points are swapped between the selected solutions.

Grouped PE assignment mutation causes a randomly selected grouped PE to assign itself to a different IC instance. Grouped PE assignment cross-over selects two grouped PE assignment cut-points at random and two solutions at random. The IC assignments of the grouped PEs between the cut-points are swapped between the selected solutions.

Link connectivity mutation causes a link instance to randomly reconnect itself to independent PE and IC instances. Link connectivity cross-over selects two link cut-points at random and two solutions at random. For each link between the cut-points, the list of independent PE and IC instances to which the link is connected is swapped between the selected solutions.

3.6 Scheduling

Scheduling occurs in MOGAC's inner loop. Since the use of a sophisticated, but slow, algorithm would reduce the design space that can be explored in a given amount of time, we use a heuristic list scheduling algorithm that, in the theoretical worst case, runs in time $\mathcal{O}\left(edges^2 + nodes^2\right)$. However, the typical run-time is $\mathcal{O}\left(edges + nodes\right)$. The scheduling algorithm is tailored to periodic systems and can even handle the case when task graphs have periods less than their deadlines.

Prioritization: The priority of every task in each of the system's real task graph copies is calculated. Each task graph copy has an earliest start time (EST) which is determined by multiplying its position in the hyperperiod by its period. The EST of every task is determined by conducting a topological sort beginning at the start node of each real task graph copy and propagating the execution times of the tasks along each path forward. The latest start time (LST) of every node is determined similarly, by propagating the execution times of tasks backward from the nodes which have deadlines.

A node's *slack* is the difference between its LST and EST. A node's *cumulative slack* is the sum of the slacks of the nodes along the highest-slack path from that node to the graph's start node. A topological sort of the graph, beginning at the start node, allows each node's cumulative slack to be calculated. At re-converging paths, the maximum of the cumulative slacks of the parents is propagated forward. Nodes with low cumulative slacks have higher priorities than nodes with high cumulative slack. This prioritization method was selected because of its speed ($\mathcal{O}\left(nodes + edges\right)$) and the ease with which it can be applied to multi-rate systems. Cumulative slack provides reasonable relative priorities for nodes in different task graphs. Additionally, this prioritization method is compatible with the scalable implicit task graph copy heuristic described in Section 3.3.

Once node priorities have been determined, the nodes from the first copy of each task graph are introduced into a priority-ordered list. When a graph copy's start time is reached, the next real or implicit copy of that graph is introduced into the priority list. An offset is added to the cumulative slack of the nodes of all of the subsequent copies of each graph. This offset is a weighted sum of the task graph's highest cumulative slack and its period, multiplied by the index of the task graph copy, *i.e.*,

$$offset = (k_1 \cdot max\_cum\_slack + k_2 \cdot period) \cdot graph\_index$$

where k_1 and k_2 are constants.

Edge scheduling: Before a node is scheduled, all of its incoming edges are scheduled. For each incoming edge, the earliest possible finish time for the associated communication event is noted. For each link that may be used to carry out communication along a given edge, communication time is computed in the following manner,

$$commun\_time = time\_per\_packet \cdot \left\lceil \frac{data\_quantity}{packet\_size} \right\rceil$$

The communication event finish time is found by locating the earliest unused time slot in the link's schedule with a size equal to or larger than the $commun\_time$ which starts after the parent task finishes executing. As a result of this step, the total time required to schedule edges is actually

$$\mathcal{O}\left(\begin{matrix} max\_links \\ on\_edge \end{matrix} \times \begin{matrix} number \\ of\_edges \end{matrix} \times \begin{matrix} max\_events \\ on\_link \end{matrix}\right)$$

Fortunately, $max\_links\_on\_edge$ is rarely greater than 3 and $max\_events\_on\_link$ is usually significantly less than $number\_of\_edges$.

Once the earliest finish time for each edge has been computed, the communication events are scheduled in order of decreasing earliest finish time. Scheduling an edge may affect the earliest finish times of the remaining edges. Therefore, the earliest finish time of each edge is recomputed immediately before it is scheduled. However, the edges are not re-prioritized after each scheduling event because this would significantly slow down the scheduling algorithm.

Node scheduling: The PE instance to which each node is assigned is determined by the genetic algorithm. After all of a node's incoming edges have been scheduled, the node's task is scheduled to its PE in the earliest time slot which is large enough to allow it to execute and starts after the latest incoming communication event has completed.

3.7 Performance Evaluation

Performance evaluation consists of calculating a solution's costs and determining how severely they violate the soft and hard constraints imposed by the designer. In this subsection, we will explain how MOGAC does performance estimation and then describe the process by which raw performance metrics are converted into system costs.

Cost calculation: System price, task graph completion time, and system power consumption are computed during cost calculation. System price is determined by taking the sum of the prices of all ICs, independent PEs, and links in the allocation strings. The completion time of each node in a task graph is recorded during scheduling (see Section 3.6). Therefore, the completion times of all nodes with deadlines are available for inspection. System power consumption is computed by stepping through

Table 1: Hou's examples

Example	Hou		COSYN		MOGAC		
	Price	CPU Time (s)	Price	CPU Time (s)	Price	CPU Time (s)	Tuned CPU Time (s)
Hou 1 & 2 (unclustered)	170	10,205	N. A.	N. A.	170	5.7	2.8
Hou 3 & 4 (unclustered)	210	11,550	N. A.	N. A.	170	8.0	1.6
Hou 1 & 2 (clustered)	170	16.0	170	6.9	170	5.1	0.7
Hou 3 & 4 (clustered)	170	3.3	N. A.	N. A.	170	2.2	0.6

each PE and link's hyperperiod schedule, obtaining the system energy required (this includes the idle PE/link energy), and dividing the energy by the hyperperiod [6].

Constraint violation: A system's constraint violations are derived from its costs and the constraints imposed by the designer. Solutions have a number of hard constraints. Although solutions in which one or more hard constraints have been violated are invalid, MOGAC treats them no differently than other solutions during its run. Solutions which violate their hard constraints are removed only at the end of a co-synthesis run.

Each system specification has price and average power consumption soft constraints. Typically, the desired price is set to 0. Thus,

$$price\_violation = \max(0,\ price - desired\_price)$$

A system's average power violation is calculated in a similar manner.

Every task graph has one or more nodes with specified deadlines. A system's hard real-time constraint violation is the sum of the time constraint violations of all such nodes in all of the real and implicit task graph copies in the system. For every IC, the peak power dissipation, pin count, and device count requirements of all the grouped PEs assigned to that IC are summed. When an IC is not capable of meeting the requirements of the grouped PEs assigned to it, the appropriate hard constraint violations in the solution are increased.

4 Experimental Results

MOGAC is a prototype consisting of approximately 18,000 lines of C++ and Bison code. Our results were obtained on a 200 MHz Pentium Pro system with 96 MB of main memory running the Linux operating system. We compare our results with those of Yen [2], Hou [7], and COSYN [6], which were obtained on a SPARCstation 20, as well as those of Prakash and Parker [4], which were obtained on a Solbourne Series5e/900 (similar to a SPARC 4/490). The CPU times are given in seconds.

MOGAC's input consists of two ASCII files. The first file specifies the attributes of each PE, IC, and link type which may be used to implement an architecture. In addition, this file specifies the relationships between PEs and tasks, *i.e.*, for each PE it contains arrays specifying the worst-case execution times, average power consumptions, and peak power consumptions of each task on that PE. The second file specifies the topologies, periods, deadlines, tasks, and communication flows associated with all of the task graphs comprising the system specification. MOGAC outputs one or more solutions. Each solution is a system architecture consisting of a price, power consumption, PE allocation, IC allocation, link allocation, grouped PE assignments, task assignments, link connectivities, task schedules for each PE, and communication event schedules for each link.

4.1 Price Optimization

MOGAC has a slew of parameters which can be modified to tune its performance. Although every problem has its own optimal parameter settings, it would be inappropriate to only report the CPU time necessary to achieve a given solution if significantly more time was spent finding a good set of parameters. We, therefore, use the same set of parameters for all of the examples presented in this subsection. In addition, the same value is used to seed MOGAC's random number generator for every result presented in this paper.

It was necessary to trade off run-time against solution quality when selecting a general parameter set for the examples in this subsection. Using a smaller solution pool and cluster pool would have allowed MOGAC to more rapidly come to low-cost solutions for simpler examples. However, the solution quality for more complex examples would have been decreased. For illustrative purposes, run-times achieved by tuning MOGAC's parameters to an individual problem's complexity, as well as run-times achieved when using the general parameter set, are shown in the following tables.

Table 1 compares MOGAC's performance with that of COSYN [6] and Hou's system when each is run on the clustered and unclustered versions of Hou's task graphs [7]. Task clustering is the process of using a prepass to collapse multiple tasks into a cluster of tasks. This cluster is treated like a single task during assignment and scheduling, *i.e.*, all the tasks in a cluster are executed on the same PE. Clustering reduces the complexity of the co-synthesis problem by decreasing the number of tasks which must be assigned. It is important, however, that tasks which communicate a large amount of data with each other be placed in the same cluster. This is due to the fact that communication between tasks which are assigned to the same PE is less expensive than communication between tasks which are assigned to different PEs. Hou used a task clustering algorithm which takes communication quantity and task execution efficiency into account. We use the same clusters as Hou when comparing our results with those of his system's, and those of COSYN.

It is interesting to observe the impact of increased problem complexity upon MOGAC and Hou's system. MOGAC's CPU time increases slightly when it solves the unclustered versions of Hou's examples instead of the clustered versions. In contrast, Hou's system takes approximately 1,000 times as long to produce solutions. Despite consuming significantly less CPU time, in one case MOGAC produces a lower-price architecture than Hou's system.

The hyperperiod contraction heuristic described in Section 3.3 was applied to the clustered and unclustered versions of the task graphs called Hou 3 & 4. The period of one of the task graphs in these examples was contracted by 5%.

Table 2: Prakash & Parker's examples

Example ⟨Performance⟩	Prakash & Parker		COSYN		MOGAC		
	Price	CPU Time (s)	Price	CPU Time (s)	Price	CPU Time (s)	Tuned CPU Time (s)
Prakash & Parker 1 ⟨4⟩	7	28	N. A.	N. A.	7	3.3	0.2
Prakash & Parker 1 ⟨7⟩	5	37	5	0.2	5	2.1	0.1
Prakash & Parker 2 ⟨8⟩	7	4,511	N. A.	N. A.	7	2.1	0.2
Prakash & Parker 2 ⟨15⟩	5	385,012	5	1.5	5	2.3	0.1

Table 3: Yen's large random examples

Example	Yen		MOGAC		
	Price	CPU Time (s)	Price	CPU Time (s)	Tuned CPU Time (s)
Yen's Random 1	281	10,252	75	6.4	0.2
Yen's Random 2	637	21,979	81	7.8	0.2

Table 4: Power consumption examples

Example	MOGAC Ignoring Power			MOGAC Optimizing Power		
	Price	Power	CPU Time (s)	Price	Power	CPU Time (s)
Hou 1 & 2 (unclustered)	170	66.4	8.3	170	53.3	39.4
Hou 3 & 4 (unclustered)	170	69.0	8.3	170	64.4	47.2
Hou 1 & 2 (clustered)	170	71.2	6.5	170	56.1	
				190	55.1	18.4
				290	51.4	
Hou 3 & 4 (clustered)	170	47.1	2.2	170	43.3	
				200	36.6	23.9
				270	34.9	
Prakash & Parker 1 ⟨4⟩	7	75.4	3.4	7	75.4	10.3
Prakash & Parker 1 ⟨7⟩	5	44.4	2.2	5	44.4	5.9
Prakash & Parker 2 ⟨8⟩	7	70.6	2.2	7	49.8	7.2
Prakash & Parker 2 ⟨15⟩	5	48.0	1.5	5	48.0	
				7	26.8	16.6
				12	22.0	
Yen's Random 1	75	26.3	6.8	75	17.4	
				173	6.4	
				293	5.8	228.4
				299	5.4	
				323	3.4	
				339	2.9	
Yen's Random 2	68	48.5	14.4	68	38.5	
				81	34.1	
				119	24.9	
				158	15.8	571.7
				200	13.9	
				214	9.9	
				338	7.0	
				530	5.7	

Table 2 compares MOGAC's performance with that of Prakash and Parker's optimal mixed integer linear programming approach and COSYN when they are applied to Prakash and Parker's task graphs. The performance number shown by each task graph is the worst-case finish time for the task graph. For instance, "Prakash & Parker 1 ⟨4⟩," refers to Prakash and Parker's first task graph with a worst-case finish time of 4 time units. In these graphs, an unconventional model for communication is used [4]. A task may begin executing before all of its input data have arrived. We converted their specifications into graphs which conform to the conventional communication model, *i.e.*, a task can only begin execution when all of its input data have arrived. Their model implies that part of each task is independent of the task's input data. This is expressed by splitting each task into a portion which depends on input data and a portion which is independent of its input data. We assure that each task's subtasks are assigned to the same PE. For Prakash & Parker 2, a point-to-point communication model is used. For each of these examples, we can see that MOGAC also obtains optimal results.

Table 3 compares MOGAC's performance with that of Yen's system when each system is applied to Yen's large random task graphs [2]. Random 1 consists of 6 task graphs, each of which contains approximately 20 tasks. There are 8 PE types available in this example. Random 2 consists of 8 task graphs, each of which contains approximately 20 tasks. There are 12 PE types available in this example. Neither of these examples contains communication links; all communication costs are 0.

The task graph periods in these systems are co-prime. Therefore, the hyperperiod contraction heuristic presented in Section 3.3 significantly reduces the number of task graph copies that MOGAC is required to schedule. The heuristic was prevented from specifying task graph periods to be less than the corresponding deadlines, or greater than the periods specified in [2].

4.2 Multi-Objective Power and Price Optimization

Table 4 displays the results of simultaneously optimizing the price and power consumption of system architectures based on examples presented in past work. The database for the example called Yen's Random 2 contains two IC types and two grouped PE types in addition to the independent PEs specified by Yen, for a total of 14 PEs. The values shown in the "Ignoring Power" column indicate the results of running MOGAC, in single objective price optimization mode, on the same embedded system specifications. MOGAC was given the same parameters when doing multiobjective optimization for all of the examples in this subsection, although the general parameter set used for multiobjective price and power optimization differs from that used for price optimization. The database files used for these examples are available via anonymous FTP at ftp://ftp.ee.princeton.edu/pub/dickrp/

The advantage of multiobjective optimization, over the use of a linear weighted sum, can clearly be seen in Table 4. When MOGAC simultaneously optimizes power and price, it provides a designer with its entire set of non-inferior solutions. For each system specification, only a single co-synthesis run was necessary to produce all of the corresponding architectures whose costs are listed in Table 4.

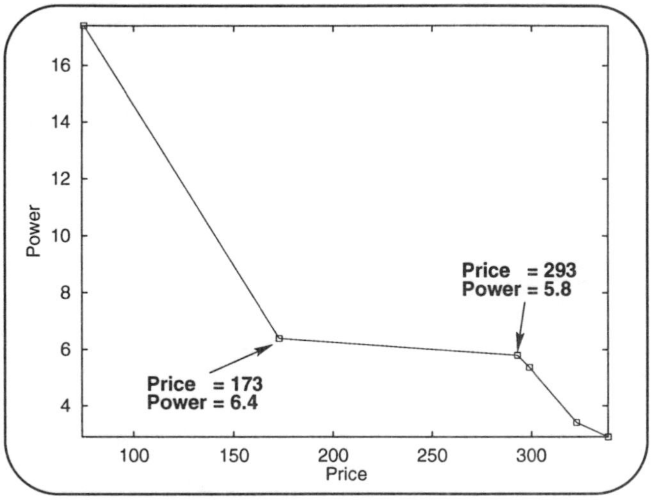

Figure 3: Non-inferior solutions for Yen's Random 1 Example

MOGAC provides information about the shape of a problem's Pareto-optimal solution set instead of merely producing a single solution. This approach allows a designer to see the relationship between the costs of different architectures which satisfy the same system specification. Figure 3 illustrates the danger of selecting a solution without knowing the shape of a system's non-inferior solution curve. Although all of MOGAC's solutions for Yen's Random 1 example are non-inferior, a designer would rarely select the solution with a price of 293 and a power consumption of 5.8 when, for a power penalty of only 0.6, a solution with a price of 173 can be obtained. Exploration of the problem instance's Pareto-optimal curve gives the designer information about the trade-offs available between different implementations of an embedded system.

5 Conclusions

In this paper, we have presented a method for the co-synthesis of low-power real-time multi-rate heterogeneous hardware-software distributed embedded systems. A novel multiobjective genetic algorithm, which allows exploration of the Pareto-optimal set of architectures instead of providing a designer with a single solution, has been practically applied to a number of examples found in the literature. MOGAC has been shown to rapidly synthesize architectures with costs that are lower than or equal to those presented in previous work. When applied to large system specifications, MOGAC produces significantly lower-cost solutions than previous co-synthesis systems, despite requiring orders of magnitude less run-time. It has been demonstrated that adaptive multiobjective genetic algorithms are well suited to solving the co-synthesis problem.

References

[1] W. H. Wolf, "Hardware-software co-design of embedded systems," *Proc. IEEE*, vol. 82, pp. 967–989, July 1994.

[2] T.-Y. Yen, *Hardware-Software Co-Synthesis of Distributed Embedded Systems*. PhD thesis, Dept. of Electrical Engg., Princeton University, June 1996.

[3] M. R. Garey and D. S. Johnson, *Computers and Intractability: A Guide to the Theory of NP-Completeness*. W. H. Freeman and Company, NY, 1979.

[4] S. Prakash and A. Parker, "SOS: Synthesis of application-specific heterogeneous multiprocessor systems," *J. Parallel & Distributed Computers*, vol. 16, pp. 338–351, Dec. 1992.

[5] J. D'Ambrosio and X. Hu, "Configuration-level hardware/software partitioning for real-time systems," in *Proc. Int. Workshop Hardware/Software Codesign*, vol. 14, pp. 34–41, Aug. 1994.

[6] B. Dave, G. Lakshminarayana, and N. K. Jha, "COSYN: Hardware-software co-synthesis of embedded systems," in *Proc. Design Automation Conf.*, pp. 703–708, June 1997.

[7] J. Hou and W. Wolf, "Process partitioning for distributed embedded systems," in *Proc. Int. Workshop Hardware/Software Codesign*, pp. 70–76, Mar. 1996.

[8] D. Saha, R. Mitra, and A. Basu, "Hardware software partitioning using genetic algorithm approach," in *Proc. Int. Conf. VLSI Design*, Jan. 1997.

[9] E. L. Lawler and C. U. Martel, "Scheduling periodically occurring tasks on multiple processors," *Information Processing Letters*, vol. 7, pp. 9–12, Feb. 1981.

[10] D. E. Goldberg, *Genetic Algorithms in Search, Optimization, and Machine Learning*. Addison-Wesley, Reading, MA, 1989.

[11] S. Kim and J. Browne, "A general approach to mapping of parallel computations upon multiprocessor architectures," in *Proc. Int. Conf. Parallel Processing*, vol. 2, pp. 1–8, Aug. 1988.

SESSION 9C

PLACEMENT

Moderators:

Dwight D. Hill, Synopsys, Inc.,

Mountain View, CA

Malgorzata Marek-Sadowska, University of California,

Santa Barbara, CA

NRG: Global and Detailed Placement

Majid Sarrafzadeh Maogang Wang
Department of Electrical and Computer Engineering, Northwestern University
majid@ece.nwu.edu

Abstract

We present a new approach to the placement problem. The proposed approach consists of analyzing the input circuit and deciding on a two-dimensional global grid *for that particular input.*

After determination of the grid size, the placement is carried out in three steps: global placement, detailed placement, *and* final optimization. *We will show that the output of the global placement can also serve as a fast and accurate predictor. Current implementation is based on simulated annealing.*

We have put all algorithms together in a placement package called NRG (pronounced N-er-G). In addition to area minimization, NRG can perform timing-driven placement. Experimental results are strong. We improve TimberWolf's results (version 1.2, the commercial version which is suppose to be better than all university versions including version 7) by about 5 %. Our predictor can estimate the wirelength within 10-20 % accuracy offering 2-20x speedup compared with the actual placement algorithm.

1 Introduction

Performance-driven, issues related to deep submicron, reliability and many more factors make the placement problem a real challenge. In this paper we show that even the classical (area minimization) placement problem is yet unsolved. We demonstrate some general issues that need to be considered in designing a placement algorithm. We will make use of them in designing a new placement package called NRG.

In addition to good placement algorithms, we need good predictors that can quickly estimate the placement cost function.

Numerous approaches to the placement problem has been proposed. For example, force directed [2, 7, 16] simulated annealing [11, 13], and partitioning-based placement [4, 3, 6]. A constructive placement method that employs resistive networks as a working domain was proposed in [5]. In [15], there is a comparison between linear and quadratic cost functions. The linear cost function used in Gordian**L** placement tool achieves results with up to 20% less area than the quadratic cost function of the original Gordian procedure. Therefore, in this paper, we will use the half-perimeter cost function for area minimization.

Timing-driven placement problem has also been studied. The notion of zero-slack was introduced in [9]. In [8] criticality was used as a guide to select cells from a cell library. For a history of the timing-driven placement problem see [1, 14, 10].

In an attempt to simplify and possibly speed up the placement process, this paper presents a new formulation that splits the domain of the placement problem. We define two new problems known as the global placement and detailed placement problems. The intuition behind our strategy is that we should be able to quickly determine a good global placement of gates for a circuit without devoting too much attention to details. After performing the global placement, detailed placement can concentrate further on the exact position and timing of a gate given that its final general vicinity is favorable and known.

One of the main issues in performing global placement is determination of the global grid size. We will show an arbitrary grid in the global placement problem is not necessarily good. Indeed, we show examples where a wrong choice of the grid produces very bad placement results. We propose an input (circuit) analysis scheme, based on breadth-first search of the circuit, followed by a correlation analysis to decide on the size of the global grid.

Once the grid size has bee determined global placement phase starts. by performing iterative improvement. Finally, a detailed placement followed by local optimization is performed.

This paper is organized as follows: In Section 2 we introduce some terminology and modeling of the problem. In Section 3 a motivating example is provided followed by a summary of the proposed NRG placement tool in Section 4. In Section 5, details of the proposed placement tool is discussed followed by experiments in Section 6. We conclude the paper in Section 7.

2 Terminology

In this paper we assume that we are given a synchronous circuit denoted $\mathcal{C}(\mathcal{M},\mathcal{N})$, which consists of a set of modules $\mathcal{M} = \{M_i | i = 1, \ldots, |\mathcal{M}|\}$, and a set of nets $\mathcal{N} = \{N_i | i = 1, \ldots, |\mathcal{N}|\}$. The set of modules consists of four subsets: primary inputs $\mathcal{I}$, primary outputs $\mathcal{O}$, storage elements $\mathcal{R}$, and combinational elements $\mathcal{A}$, i.e., $\mathcal{M} = \mathcal{I} \cup \mathcal{O} \cup \mathcal{R} \cup \mathcal{A}$. A sample circuit is given in Figure 1.

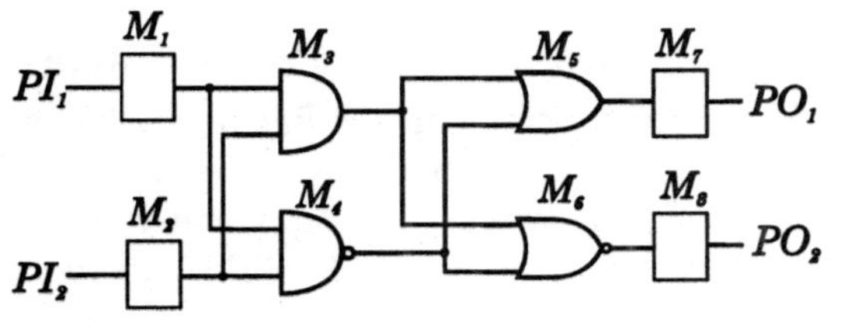

Figure 1: Sample circuit.

For this work, we use a row-based placement model, which cover standard cell and sea of gates layout styles. The concepts developed here can be applied to other styles, however, we have not explored them yet.

3 A Motivating Example: Linear Placement

Consider the linear placement problem as shown in Figure 2a. Consider a circuit C_{lin} containing n modules. For simplicity, assume all modules have the same width. Size of the solution space is $n!$, for there are $n!$ permutations of the modules.

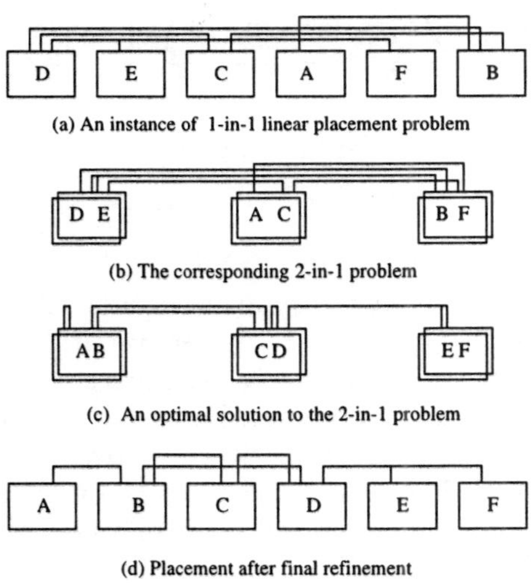

Figure 2: Example of the linear placement problem.

Now, let's conduct an experiment. Suppose that instead of n positions for the modules, we can use only $n/2$ positions, with exactly two modules to each position, as shown in Figure 2b. We will call the new problem the 2-in-1 problem (meaning 2 modules in one position) and the original problem 1-in-1. The objective is to solve the 2-in-1 problem optimally as shown in Figure 2c. Then refine it, that is, to "locally" move the modules to their final position, as shown in Figure 2d. The hope is that the two step approach can find a good solution to the original problem. Thus, we need to investigate the size of the reduced solution space and its quality.

Fact 1 *The search space in the 2-in-1 problem is reduced by a factor of $2^{n/2}$ with respect to the original 1-in-1 problem.*

Proof: There are a total of n modules. In the 2-in-1 problem $\binom{n}{2}$ of them can be placed in the leftmost position. Once that is decided, we are left with $n-2$ modules. Thus, $\binom{n-2}{2}$ modules can be placed in the second position and so on. Thus, the total number of solutions is:

$$\binom{n}{2} \times \binom{n-2}{2} \times \binom{n-4}{2} \times \ldots \times \binom{2}{2}$$
$$= \frac{n \times (n-1)}{2} \times \frac{(n-2) \times (n-3)}{2} \times \ldots \frac{2 \times 1}{2}$$
$$= \frac{n!}{2^{n/2}}$$

□

Given that the solution space is reduced by a "large" factor, there is a hope to obtain an optimal solution to the 2-in-1 problem very quickly and then refine it to obtain a good solution to the original problem. We call the 2-in-1 problem the *global placement problem* (GP) and the subsequent refinement, the *detailed placement problem* (DP) and the combined step the global-detailed placement (or GDP) problem. The main question that remains is the quality of GDP. To answer this question, we have done experiments on a number of benchmarks. Lets look at the MCNC benchmark *highway2*. Results are summarized in Table 1. For quick prototyping, all methods used in the table are simulated annealing (SA) based. In summary, Table 1 shows that in 4.1 seconds (1.4 plus 2.7) we can obtain results that are of comparable quality to the best solution. Therefore, **we can reduce the search space without sacrificing the quality.** Certainly, this is just one small example. We will show in later sections that that same behavior can be observed in all benchmarks.

Method	WireLength	RunTime (sec)
1-in-1	14712	18
2-in-1 GP	15065	1.4
DP	14790	2.7

Table 1: Experiments with highway2 (62 cells).

Note that we can generalize the idea to 3-in-1 GP, 4-in-1, etc. Results of quality versus GP size is summarized in Table 2. As can be observed, not every GP size is suitable. Indeed, some produce very poor results. We will make use of this observation in the NRG placement algorithm.

	2-in-1	4-in-1	8-in-1	16-in-1
GP	15065	15887	19535	19385
Time	1.4	1.3	1.3	1.1
DP	14790	15556	20180	17940
Time	2.7	2.8	3.1	3.3

Table 2: Various GP grids in highway2.

4 Summary of NRG

The main objective of global and detailed placement (GDP) is to reduce the search space and thus obtain better results faster. Two major advantages are:

- It will be much faster to get a similar (or better) placement results.
- It can be used as a very good placement predictor. This feature will be very useful when used in a logic-synthesis or high-level synthesis environment.

We divide the circuit placement problem into five phases: input analysis, grid determination, GP, DP and final optimization. In the next section, we will elaborate on each step.

5 Details of NRG

In this section, we will discuss each phase of NRG.

5.1 Input Analysis

Consider a circuit $\mathcal{C}$. It can be modeled as a hypergraph $G_{\mathcal{C}}$: Vertices associated with primary inputs of $\mathcal{C}$ are called *PI vertices. PO vertices* are symmetrically defined. We perform a breadth-first search (BFS) of $G_{\mathcal{C}}$: PI vertices will be placeed in level 1, all vertices connected to vertices in level i will be placed in level $i+1$. *Level number* of a circuit $\mathcal{C}$ is the number of levels in BFS of the corresponding graph $G_{\mathcal{C}}$. Intuitively, given two circuits with the same number of modules, the one with a higher level number is less tightly connected and thus easier to place. To account the number of vertices, we define the *BFS number* of $G_{\mathcal{C}}$ as n divided by the level-number, where n is the total number of modules. BFS number of a circuit will be used in determination of the GP grid.

5.2 Determination of the GP Grid

As observed before (in the linear placement experiment), size of the global grid makes a big difference in the result. Lets look at a similar experiment done with Primary1. As shown in Table 3 different GP grids produce very different placement results. Note that we have run the algorithm very fast to obtain these results. Thus, the final results is not as good as the best we have obtained. The point is, even in this case, we can get a sense of which grid size can potentially produce good solutions. As can be seen, GP grids of size 16×6 and 16×8 produces good placement results.

	2×2	4×4	8×8	16×2
GP	838800	919700	968700	870800
DP	1373500	1091600	1062600	1143800
	16×4	16×6	16×8	16×10
GP	925400	963700	970900	991600
DP	1032100	982700	982500	1004200
	16×12	16×14	16×16	16×18
GP	1022300	1022200	1033400	1037200
DP	1025700	1029000	1011000	992600

Table 3: Grid sizes in GP for Primary 1.

BFS number suggests whether a larger GP grid is most suitable for the problem or a smaller GP grid. To find the exact grid to choose, we perform a *correlation analysis.* It basically determines the how well is the cost function obtained during GP is correlated to DP. The difference of wirelength between GP and DP is shown is Figure 3. As can be seen the Δ function is convex. Therefore we can perform a binary search to find the right grid size. To find Δ for a given grid size, we perform a very fast GP followed by a very fast DP. Since simulated annealing is our current implementation, so a "fast" GP or DP can be easily obtained by reducing the number of random moves at each tempture.

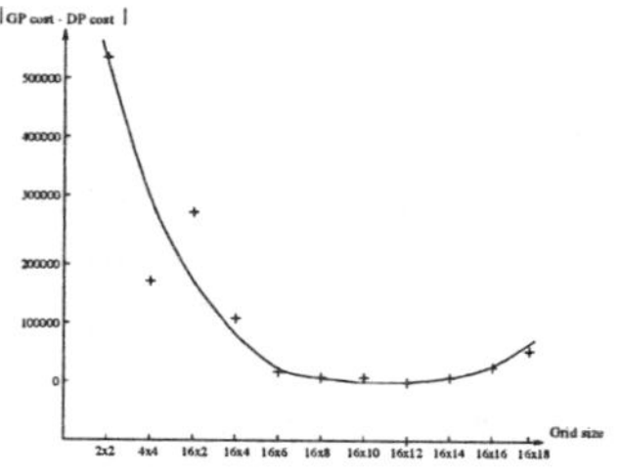

Figure 3: Correlation between GP and DP in Primary1

5.3 The Global Placement Problem

Consider an $a \times b$ GP grid imposed on the chip area. A total of ab disjoint *bins* is obtained,

A good solution to the Global Placement Problem will manage to keep a fairly even distribution while minimizing the given cost function.

In this paper we propose the following **Global Placement Problem:**

> *Given a standard cell circuit and a GP grid, assign the modules to GP regions so as to minimize a cost function based on the wirelength Furthermore, assure that the modules are distributed evenly among GP regions.*

These two factors can be combined and expressed as a singular objective cost function:

$$f(x) = P_{WIRELENGTH} + \lambda P_{GBCD} \tag{1}$$

where x is a certain placement needs to be evaluated, $P_{WIRELENGTH}$ is the sum of the bounding box of all nets and and P_{GBCD} is the GP region distribution penalty. λ is a simple scaling factor.

We chose to use a simulated annealing approach in iteratively improving the GP results. We defined our move set as follows: pick two cells in two different bins and evaluate the cost of swapping them with each other. We set all parameters using trial-and-error and making use of published results, e.g., [12].

5.4 The Detailed Placement Problem

Given a "good" global placement, we must then create a "good" final placement. This step is called the detailed placement stage. Its goal is to take the global bin assignments and produce a legal placement while trying to minimize its objective function. We implement DP using a low tempreture annealer. The objective function is a combination of wirelength, overlap penalty and row penalty. Contact the anthor for more details.

5.5 Final Optimization

Althouth we put the overlapping penalty in the cost function of DP, there still might be some overlapping exist in the final placement of DP. So the first thing we need to do is to perform a "clean up" operation to shift cells to eliminate overlapping. After this is done, we flip the cells. We chose to implement the same algorithm reported in [11]. For details of this phase, see [11].

5.6 Comparison of NRG with Other Placement Algorithms

TimberWolf's commercial placement tool has a hierarchical methodology which shows more or less the similiar idea as NRG. The similarity between NRG and TimberWolf's hierarchical placement is: *Both algorithms try to simplify the placement problem by trying to determine an approximate location for each module first.*

Although they have the same goal in general, they take different approaches. First of all, the major difference lies between the idea of *global* vs. the idea of *clustering*. Hierarchical placement is based on the idea of clustering, i.e., by combining a certain number of cells to form a bigger cell(cluster) to reduce the problem size. The main problem is once a cluster is formed in an iteration it cannot be broken during an iteration. Thus, modules do not have the required moving flexibility. So the problem arises that a move might be good for only some modules in that moving cluster but In NRG, we do not cluster the modules. So, potentially, a move takes place only if it is good for all modules.

6 Experimental Results

NRG placement tool were implemented in C++ and the experiments were run on a Sun Spark-20 workstation. Five MCNC benchmark standcell circuits are used for experiments. Table 4 lists the characteristics of all 5 test circuits.

TestCase	# Cells	# IO	# Nets	# Rows
highway2	62	11	87	4
fract	125	24	163	6
struct	1888	64	1920	16
Primary1	833	107	1266	16
Primary2	3014	132	3817	32

Table 4: Testing benchmark circuits.

The first experiments we did was to compare NRG with TimberWolfSC1.2.6 (the commercial version) using the half-perimeter cost function. We ran TimberWolf three times on each benchmark and have reported the best result of the three runs in Table 5. NRG results have been obtained also by running the algorithm three times. Since, NRG also use simulated annealing in parts of it, different outputs is obtained in different runs. However, NRG's output is more deterministic than that of TimberWolf. Results are summarized in Table 5. As can be seen, NRG produces results better than that of TimberWolf in most cases. This is a surprising result, given that TimberWolf is a "mature" tools and has many details not yet implemented in NRG. It shows that better algorithms can improve the placement quality.

Test Case	TW	NRG	% improvement
highway2	9221	8646	6.2%
fract	26773	25602	4.4%
struct	314762	287631	8.6%
Primayr1	900745	894545	0.7%
Primary2	3401378	3412195	-0.3%

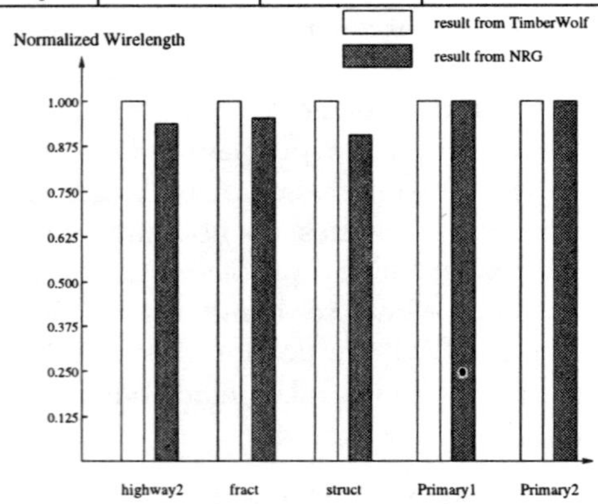

Table 5: Wirelength result: NRG vs. TimberWolf 1.2.6

Table 6 shows how well GP can predict the cost function. As can be seen the prediction error is within 3-20%. Therefore, in addition to providing a good input to DP, GP can be used as a good predictor (e.g, in a high-level synthesis system).

Table 7 shows the speed-up offered by GDP versus the flat approach and the quality tradeoff. In summary, by sacrificing 1-3 % in quality a speed-up of 2x is obtained.

7 Conclusions

We proposed a two-step (GP followed by DP) approach to the classical placement problem. It is very important how the the placement problem is divided between these two step. Algorithms, based on input analysis, for determination of this division along with techniques for performing GP and DP have been proposed.

Test Case	NRG	GP predict.	% accur.	spdup
highway2	8646	9009	4.2%	19
fract	25602	28494	11.3%	4.9
struct	287631	349399	21.4%	2.3
Primayr1	894545	918435	2.7%	7.3
Primary2	3412195	3941040	15.4%	5.1

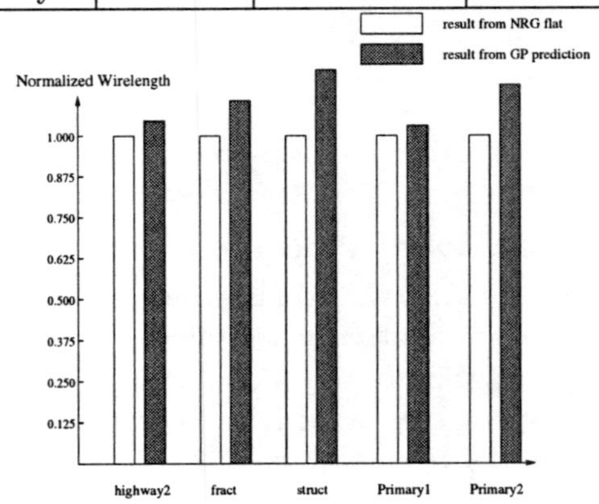

Table 6: Wirelength result: NRG vs. GP prediction

The two step approach allows for fast exploration of the search space. It results in good quality solution with about 3x speed-up. The notion of global and detailed placement will be more important as design problems get harder. We also showed that GP alone can serve as a good predictor if the corresponding grid has been carefully determined.

The notion of GDP can be coupled with most existing algorithms to speed them up and possibly produce better quality solutions. Future work include theoretical study of the quality of GP as a function of the corresponding GP grid and inclusion of non-uniform grids in GP.

Acknowledgments

This work was supported in part by the National Science Foundation under Grant MIP-9527389.

References

[1] "Issues in Timing Driven Layout". pages 1–24, 1993. M. Sarrafzadeh and D. T. Lee, editors.

[2] H. Anway, G. Farnham, and R. Reid. "Plint Layout System for VLSI Chip Design". In

Test Case	HQ NRG	Fast NRG	% deg.	spdup
highway2	8646	8877	2.7%	2.1
fract	25602	26075	1.8%	2.0
struct	287631	291078	1.2%	1.3
Primayr1	894545	904520	1.1%	2.0
Primary2	3412195	3512926	3.0%	1.3

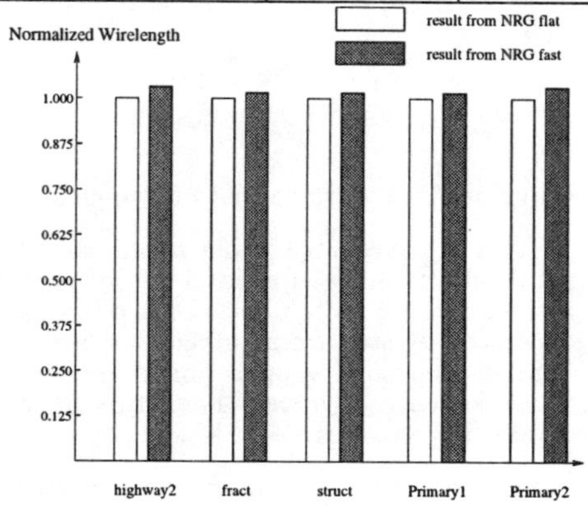

Table 7: Wirelength result: Fast NRG vs. high-quality

Design Automation Conference, pages 449–452. IEEE/ACM, 1985.

[3] M. A. Breuer. "A Class of Min-cut Placement Algorithms". In *Design Automation Conference*, pages 284–290. IEEE/ACM, 1977.

[4] M. A. Breuer. "Min-cut Placement". *J. Design Automation and Fault-Tolerant Computing*, 1(4):343–382, 1977.

[5] C. K. Cheng and E. S. Kuh. "Module Placement Based on Resistive Network Optimization". *IEEE Transactions on Computer Aided Design*, 3(3):218–225, 1984.

[6] A. E. Dunlop and B. W. Kernighan. "A Procedure for Placement of Standard Cell VLSI Circuits". *IEEE Transactions on Computer Aided Design*, 4(1):92–98, January 1985.

[7] C. P. Hsu et al. "APLS2: A Standard Cell Layout System for Double-layer Metal Technology". In *Design Automation Conference*, pages 443–448. IEEE/ACM, 1985.

[8] S.P. Lin, M. Marek-Sadowska, and E.S. Kuh. "Delay and Area Optimization in Standard Cell Design". In *Design Automation Conference*, pages 349–352. IEEE/ACM, 1990.

[9] R. Nair, C. L. Berman, P. S. Hauge, and E. J. Yoffa. "Generation of Performance Constraints for Layout". *IEEE Transactions on Computer Aided Design*, CAD-8(8):860–874, August 1989.

[10] M. Sarrafzadeh and C. K. Wong. *An Introduction to VLSI Physical Design*. McGrwa Hill, 1996.

[11] C. Sechen. *VLSI Placement and Global Routing Using Simulated Annealing*. Kluwer, B. V., Deventer, The Netherlands, 1988.

[12] C. Sechen and K. W. Lee. "An Improved Simulated Annealing Algorithm for Row–Based Placement". In *Design Automation Conference*, pages 180–183. IEEE/ACM, 1988.

[13] C. Sechen and A. Sangiovanni-Vincentelli. "TimberWolf3.2: A New Standard Cell Placement and Global Routing Package". In *Design Automation Conference*, pages 432–439. IEEE/ACM, 1986.

[14] N. A. Sherwani. *Algorithms For VLSI Physical Design Automation*. Kluwer Academic Publishers, 1993.

[15] G. Sigl, K. Doll, and F. M. Johannes. "Analytical Placement: A Linear or a Quadratic Objective Function". In *Design Automation Conference*, pages 427–431. IEEE/ACM, 1991.

[16] T. Ohtsuki T. Sudo and S. Goto. "CAD Systems for VLSI in Japan". In *Information and Control*, volume 59, 1983.

Simulated Quenching: a New Placement Method for Module Generation

Shinji Sato
Fujitsu Laboratories Ltd.
Kamiodanaka 4-1-1, Nakahara-ku, Kawasaki, Kanagawa, 211-88 Japan

Abstract

This paper addresses a placement method good for module generation. Conventional partitioning based method can not guarantee the best quality in consecutive partitioning. Also, when size of cells varies very much, it is sometimes too strong constraint for them to get the minimum partitioning under "partitioning into two similar size of subcircuits". On the other hand, although conventional Simulated Annealing (SA) based method gives a better result, it requires extremely long computation time. It is the purpose of this paper to propose an algorithm which is based on SA method and employs the divide and conquer technique so that it gives better quality than partitioning based method and also it gives drastically faster computation time than SA method. As the first step, we applied this idea to the linear placement. It is found that the total wiring length is improved about 10% compared to that of spectral method which was recognized to be the best [7]. Also, computation time was dramatically reduced over the SA method.

1 Introduction

Currently circuit partitiong is playing an important role in design automation of VLSI chips. In the case of Gate Array design, partitioning based placement method is a good approach to design random circuit. But increasing requirement of predesigned functional module preparation may change such domination on VLSI design automation. Partitioning based placement approach inherently assumes following ideas:

1. Top down slicing of layout area is a reasonable design scheme.
2. Partitioning into two similar sized circuits (about 45 ~ 55 % of original circuit) doesn't mess up connective structure of circuit.

If the partitioning of circuit provides the exactly the best solution every time, believing two ideas above may not matter on the quality of placement result. But actually each partitioning result is little far from the best one, and two ideas above bring following drawbacks:

1. Previous partitioning hinders the quality of consequent partitioning.
2. Circuit doesn't always consist of two clusters.

Our algorithm is based on sorting inside subgroups, and generation of subgroups is done by cut-lines placed with a constant pitch (p). This pitch value p is decreased step by step from sufficiently large value to small value. This sorting operation should be done enough time for each p value. Then this algorithm provides following features:

1. Placement procedure is flat and former operation can be improved at all time.
2. Changing pitch value ($= p$) of cut-lines can adapt to diverse granularity of circuit clusters.

Experiments on MCNC benchmarks show that our algorithm can achieve about 10% shorter total wire length compared to the best result of spectral method [7]. Comparing to SA Method, our algorithm has achieved dramatic reduction of computing time.

2 Simulated Quenching

2.1 Preliminaries

A circuit is modeled by a hypergraph $G_H = (V_H, E_H)$, where the vertex set V_H is the components, and the hyperedge set E_H is the nets connecting the components. The linear placement problem of a circuit is defined that each component should have placed in equally spaced slots without duplication such that the total wire length over all net is minimal. The wire length of a net is calculated by the span of its component set. Let $e = |E_H|$ be the number of edges in G_H. And $E_H = \{E_1, E_2, ...\}$. The weight of the edge E_i is w_i. Then we can formulate the linear placement problem as below:

$$min \sum_{i=1}^{e} w_i(max\{d(v_j)|v_j \in E_i\} - min\{d(v_k)|v_k \in E_i\})$$

where $d(v_j)$ is the coordinate of the slot in which vertex v_j is put in the linear placement.

2.2 Subgroup Generation

Subgroup generation is done by placing cut-lines with a constant pitch ($= p$) on the current linear placement, where all components are placed from the lowest order to the highest order in a line. Consecutive p components which are between two cut-lines become a subgroup. Both subgroups at the lowest order and at the highest order may have components less than p. The lowest order subgroup may have components from 1 to p (if the total component number is large enough comparing to the value p), and these are the variation of applying cut-lines with the same pitch value p. Each time we need to generate subgroups with pitch value p we randomly choose the number of components in the lowest order subgroup (we call it offset value o). Figure 1 shows a linear placement with eleven components. The pitch of subgroup generation is three, and the offset is one. That is to say, the lowest order subgroup, subgroup1, contains one component. The remaining ten components are divided into three-component-groups as far as they can. The final subgroup, subgroup5, only has one component.

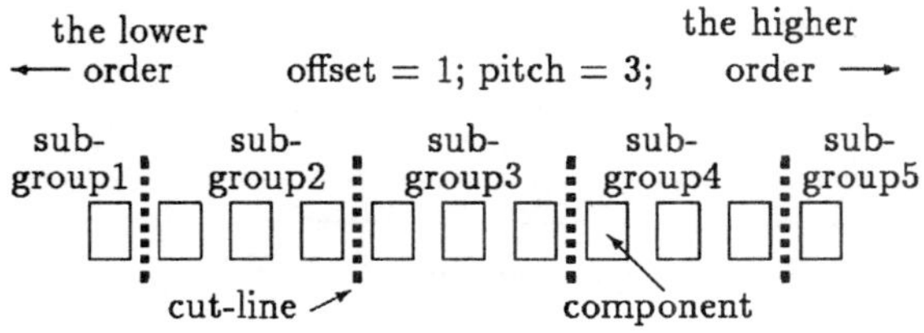

Figure1: Subgroup Generation

2.3 Accumulate force value for each component

We accumulate the force value for each component in order to make use for sorting of components in each subgroup. Force value can be either plus or minus value and represents the direction in which this component can decrease the net length by movement. We only take nets which exist over more than two different subgroups into consideration in this process. This is similar to that Min-Cut algorithm mainly talks about nets which are cut by the cul-line. But unlike Min-Cut algorithm, we only apply force value only at the components which are either at the lowest order or the highest order among components connected to the net. If a component has such a net, and if this component is located at the lowest order among components connected to the net, this component will add the net weight to its total force value. On the other hand, if a component has such a net, and if this component is located at the highest order among components connected to the net, this component will subtract the net weight from its total force value. After checking up all nets we can decide total force value for each component. Figure2 shows that eleven components have five connecting wires, and only three of them are connections between different subgroups. These three connections which have solid lines are considered, and two connections which have dotted lines are inside each subgroup and ignored. Each solid line has only two components at both the lowest and the highest terminal position, then total of six forces are calculated. If the wire weight value are all one, the accumulated force value are shown just below each component.

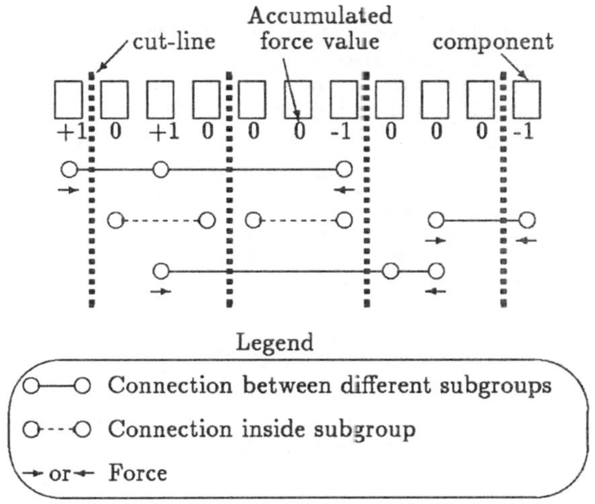

Figure2: Force Value Accumulation

2.4 Sorting inside Subgroups

According to the force value of components, we sort components within each subgroup. If a component has a large plus force value, this component is likely to move to the higher order within the subgroup. Otherwise, it will goes down to the lower order within the subgroup. Sorting algorithms are well surveyed, and we can make use of up to $\sim O(n)$ order sorting algorithm which is probably the fastest operation imagined for $O(n)$ components. If we adopt more accurate ordering algorithm on each subgroup rearrangement, our placement method will lose the ability of hill-climb, and final result will be much worse.

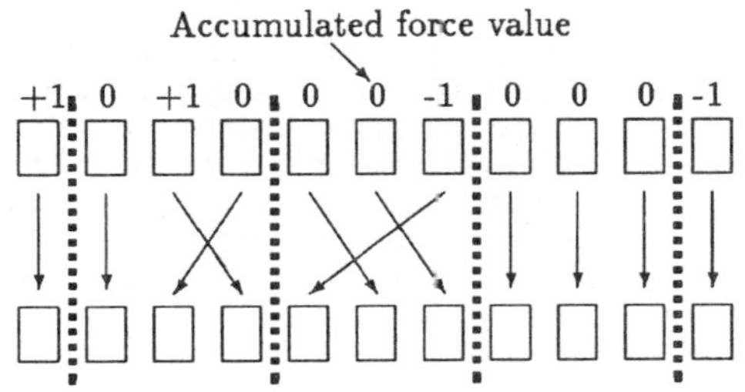

Figure3: Sorting inside Subgroups

2.5 Scheduling of subgroup pitch value p

We gradually decrease subgroup pitch value p from sufficiently large value to small value. And for each p value we repeatedly sort within subgroups enough time. Of course, these sorting use randomly different offset value ($= o$) each time. Therefore, for a pitch value p we submit following procedure with iteration of s time.

1. Subgroup Generation (randomly choose offset o)

2. Accumulate force value for each component

3. Sorting within Subgroups

After s iteration, we decrease p to the next value. It is difficult to analogize our algorithm into Thermodynamics Equilibrium, but we can calculate entropy of information. If the component number W is large enough, the number of subgroup is $\sim \frac{W}{p}$, and for each subgroup, possible arrangement inside is $p!$. And there is p variation of offset. Then total possible arrangement is $p(p!)^{\frac{W}{p}}$. We call this N_p. Information Theory says that if there are possibile $1 \sim j$ states, and their possibilities are $P_1 \sim P_j$, the current entropy of information is

$$S = \sum_{i=1}^{j} P_i log_2 P_i$$

Therefore if we assume that every possible state has the same possibility value for the pitch value p:

$$S_p = \sum_{i=1}^{N_p} \frac{1}{N_p} log_2 \frac{1}{N_p} = log_2 \frac{1}{N_p} = -log_2 N_p$$

If we change pitch value p to $\acute{p}$, the abstract difference of entropy is

$$S_p - S_{\acute{p}} = log_2 N_{\acute{p}} - log_2 N_p = log_2 \frac{N_{\acute{p}}}{N_p}$$

$$= log_2 \frac{\acute{p}(\acute{p}!)^{\frac{W}{\acute{p}}}}{p(p!)^{\frac{W}{p}}}$$

When we think about the case where $\frac{\acute{p}}{p} \sim 1$ and $\acute{p} = p - 1$ and W is sufficiently large:

$$dS_p \sim \frac{W}{p} log_2 \frac{(\acute{p}!)}{(p!)} \sim -\frac{W}{p} log_2 p$$

If we change subgroup pitch value p according to the schedule above, we can keep entropy difference constant. Actually, we might have overcounted the number of total possible arrangement above, but we can find some improvement by using this scheduling scheme comparing to the simple scheduling such as successive multiplication of constant ratio like "0.9".

2.6 Algorithm

```
 W: Number of components
Set the initial subgroup pitch value p = W;
Do{
  i = 1;
  Do{
    Subgroup Generation (randomly choose offset o)
    Accumulate force value for each component
    Sorting within Subgroups
    i = i + 1;
  } while ( i ≤ s )
  p -= 0.03 × p/log2p
} while ( p ≥ 2.0)
```

3 Experiments

We implemented our linear placement algorithm, which we call Simulated Quenching (SQ) and tested it with a set of benchmarks from MCNC. We have improved the total wire length by about 10% compared to the best result of spectral method called SLPC2 [7]. As reported in [3], s1423 has a discrepancy of its node count and net count. Since we have s1423 with 753 nodes and 748 nets, this may be an another version of s1423. If we get rid of s1423 wire length comparison, improvemnt over SLPC2 will be larger. Our algorithm spent about 8 hours for s38417 to get a stable result by Hypersparc with 166 MHz clock.

Circuits	Node	Wire Length		Improve
		SLPC2	SQ	over(%)
s1423	753	9254	10000	-8.0
s9234	5866	248999	220374	11.5
s13207	8772	465214	380908	18.2
s15850	10470	591372	432277	27.0
s35932	18148	871937	774414	11.2
s38417	23949	1325547	1254195	5.4
s38584	20995	1487277	1275551	14.3
Average				11.3

Table1: Comparison with SLPC2

We also compared our algorithm with SA method. In order to know the average performance of both SA and SQ method, we adopted following steps:

- Initial solution is the same both for SA and SQ method.
- More than twenty different random number sequences are used, and we get the average final total wire length from these program runs.
- Iteration for each temperature (SA method) and for each pitch (SQ method) is varied.

Accordingly, we got the graphs which decrease the average final total wire length (y-axis) with the increase of iteration for each temperature or pitch (x-axis). By using these graphs we checked the run-time when both SA and SQ method achieved the similar final total wire length.

Circuits	Node		SA	SQ
s27	18	Wire Length	37	37
		Run Time	0.5s	0.3s
s298	142	Wire Length	1244	1237
		Run Time	38.3s	0.4s
s832	329	Wire Length	7475	7454
		Run Time	3m28.8s	0.6s

Table2: Comparison with SA method

In the case of s27 (18 nodes, 17 nets), both run-times are similar. But in the case of s298 (142 nodes, 136 nets), SA method required a much longer run-time. Finally in the case of s832 (329 nodes, 310 nets), SA method run-time is greatly larger than that of SQ method. We can say that SQ method is much faster than SA method, and this difference of speed becomes larger with the increase of circuit size. We took a sequence of total wire length data during our algorithm was performed. Graph1 shows a case of s1423 with 20 iteration for each pitch value p. The schedule of the pitch value p is the same as section 2.7 above. This graph tells us that there is a sort of convergence phenomenon in the sequence of our algorithm like SA method. We can say that divide and conquer technique was introduced into SA method by using subgroup generation and sorting inside subgroups. Since our sorting operation has some inaccuracy inherently, our algorithm doesn't reach the exactly the best solution. Then our algorithm has a faster operation and little worse final solution than SA Method. Therefore we call our algorithm "Simulated Quenching".

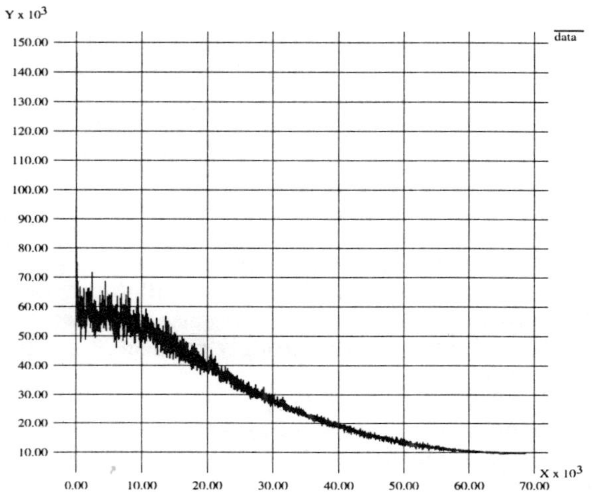

Graph1: Sequence of Total Wire Length

4 Conclusion

We have developed a new placement algorithm with generality and simplicity similar to SA method while computing time is dramatically reduced by divide and conquer technique. And our algorithm has achieved about 10% improvement over SLPC2 algorithm which is currently the best known algorithm for linear placement. Unlike common partitioning based placement method, our algorithm doesn't ignore structure of circuit and definitely good for module generation. Our algorithm consists of iteration: (1) Subgroup Generation (2) Force Value Accumulation. (3) Sorting within Subgroups. Subgroup generation pitch p is decreased like the temperature of SA method. It is difficult to analogize our algorithm to Thermodynamics Equilibrium directly, but entropy of Information Theory gives us a good schedule how to decrease the pitch value p. Since enhancement of our algorithm to the 2-dimensional placement was easy and started to give us some good result, this algorithm may have opened a new theory for placement like SA method.

References

[1] Kirkpatrick, S., C. D. Gelatt, and M. P. Vecchi, "Optimization by Simulated Annealing," *Science*, Vol. 220, (1983), pp671-680.

[2] C. K. Cheng, and E. S. Kuh, "Module Placement Based on Resistive Network Optimization," *IEEE Trans. on Computer-Aided Design* Vol. CAD-3(3), Jul. 1984, pp218-25.

[3] J. Li, J. Lillis and C. K. Cheng, "Linear Decomposition Algorithm for VLSI Design Applications," *Proc. IEEE Int. Conf. on Computer-Aided Design* 1995, pp223-8.

[4] L. Hagen, and A. B. Kahng, "Fast Spectral Methods for Ratio Cut Partitioning and Clustering," *Proc. IEEE Int. Conf. on Computer-Aided Design*, 1991, pp10-3.

[5] B. M. Riess, K. Doll, and F. M. Johannes, "Partitioning Very Large Circuits Using Analytical Placement Techniques," *Proc. 31th ACM/IEEE Design Automation Conference*, 1994, pp646-51.

[6] G. Sigl, K. Doll, and F. M. Johanness, "Analytical Placement: A Linear or a Quadratic Objective Function?" *Proc. 28th ACM/IEEE Design Automation Conference*, 1991, pp427-32.

[7] J. Li., J. Lillis, L. T. Liu, and C. K. Cheng. "New Spectral Linear Placement and Clustering Approach," *Proc. 33rd ACM/IEEE Design Automation Conference*, 1996.

[8] R. S. Tsay, E. S. Kuh, and C. P. Hsu, "PROUD: A Fast Sea-of-Gates Placement Algorithm", *Proc. 25th ACM/IEEE Design Automation Conference*, 1988, pp318-23.

[9] R. S. Tsay, and E. S. Kuh, "A unified approach to partitioning and placement (VLSI layout)," *IEEE Trans. on Circuits and Systems*, Vol.38(5), May 1991, pp521-33.

[10] J.M. Kleinhans, G. Sigl, F. M. Johannes, and K. J. Antreich, "GORDIAN: VLSI Placement by Quadratic Programming and Slicing Optimization," *IEEE Trans. on Computer-Aided Design*, Vol.10(3), Mar. 1991, pp356-65.

[11] N.R.Quinn, "The Placement Problem as Viewed from the Physics of Classical Mechanics," *Proceedings of the 12th Design Automation Conference*, pp. 173-178, 1975

[12] D.F.Wong, H.W.Leong, and C.L.Liu, *Simulated Annealing for VLSI Design*, Kluwer Academic Publishers, 1988

A Signature Based Approach to Regularity Extraction

Srinivasa R. Arikati*
Mathematical Sciences Department
University of Memphis
Memphis, TN 38152
arikati@cadence.com

Ravi Varadarajan
Cadence Design Systems
555 River Oaks Prkwy
San Jose, CA 95134
rrv@cadence.com

Abstract

Regularity extraction is an important step in the design flow of datapath-dominated circuits. This paper outlines a new method that automatically extracts regular structures from the netlist. The method is general enough to handle two types of designs: designs with structured cluster information for a portion of the datapath components that are identified at the HDL level; and designs with no such structured cluster information. The method analyzes the circuit connectivity and uses signature based approaches to recognize regularity.

1 Introduction

In a traditional design flow the circuit regularity may not be fully extracted. As a result certain gates that are strongly connected to the datapath by busses might be outside the datapath and hence viewed by the floorplanning tool as random logic. This results in inferior place and route results as these busses will have to peel out of the datapath region, connect to the gates in the random logic, and reenter the datapath region. Moreover, the structured placement information of these gates is not captured. In a typical top-down timing-driven HDL design flow for datapath-dominated designs, the datapath components are generated before the rest of the circuit is synthesized and optimized. Logic synthesis then operates on the datapath netlist along with the rest of the design, and synthesizes the control logic. During logic optimization new buffer gates may be introduced to meet timing requirements. Many of these buffer gates are between the datapath functions and should actually belong to the datapath. Moreover in some design flows, through behavioral and RTL synthesis, certain datapath components are not inferred correctly and hence are synthesized as random logic.

The methodology of Odawara, Hiraide, and Nishina [5] was one of the first approaches to regularity extraction. The method is based on the concept of a location macro, which is a group of gates of the same kind that share nets connected to the common input terminal. The location macros are extracted using the design information such as gate type, terminals, and logical hierarchy. Using these macros as placement initializers, the placement is refined by the subsequent standard cell placement. The papers [3, 4, 6] present improvements and modifications to the above method. Hirsch and Siewiorek [3] use flexible data structures and more structural characteristics (such as storage cells) to extract regularity. Nijssen and Jess [4] extend the work of [5] to extract 2-dimensional datapath regularity. Their work expands a search wave through the circuit, stage by stage; the stages are refined location macros. It uses local regularity metric to guide the search wave. Tsay and Lin [6] use different characteristics to extract regularity; they use primary outputs instead of gates to find strongly connected subcircuits called cones.

Compared to general placement, all the above methods lead to some improvements in area, wirelength and run-time. A major drawback of the approaches in [5, 3, 4] is that they all use only local information to extract regularity; they extract one location macro (or stage) at a time. The approach of [6] is not flexible in the sense that it uses only primary outputs to guide the extraction. Also, in all these approaches, the regularity may not be fully extracted. In our experiments, we have found that in most cases, extracting partial regularity produces poorer place and route results than extracting no regularity at all.

This paper outlines a new algorithm that automatically extracts regular structures. The algorithm is very flexible and is based on a generalization of the above-mentioned approaches. The algorithm analyzes the circuit connectivity and uses signature-based approaches to recognize regularity. The algorithm has been integrated into a *Cadence* HDL-based design flow. Experimental results demonstrate that our approach results in better designs (in terms of area and total wirelength), as compared to the designs obtained without regularity extraction.

Our method is general enough to handle the following types of designs:
(1) Designs in which a portion of the datapath components is identified at the HDL level, and the structured cluster information for these components exists in the netlist.
(2) Designs with no such structured cluster information. In this case, our approach automatically creates such information for datapath components. This is achieved by using hints from bus names and datapath features such as high-fanout control nets.

*This work is fully funded by a research grant from Cadence Design Systems, San Jose, CA.

1092-3152/97 $10.00 © 1997 IEEE

The rest of the paper is organized as follows. Section 2 presents definitions and other preliminaries. Section 3 presents an algorithm for regularity extraction and a detailed explanation of the algorithm with an example. Some improvements to the algorithm are the topic of Section 4. Section 5 provides experimental results. Section 6 presents the concluding remarks.

2 Preliminaries

We work with the netlist representation of the input circuits. The netlist consists of **cell instances** of masters from a cell library, and **nets**. A net is connected to **terminals** of instances. Figure 2 shows a netlist, as explained in Section 3.2.

Relative placement information captures the structured cluster information of the datapth portion of the input circuit and is stored in **tile files**. In our flow, the tile files are automatically generated by the datapath generators during datapath synthesis. Each tile file is a group of cell instances that perform a datapath operation, like addition or multiplication. The tile file may be viewed as a column or as a matrix of cells. Each instance in a tile file has a **bit number** which indicates its relative placement (row number) in the group. In addition, instances in matrix tile files (say, a multiplier) have **bit orders** which indicate the column numbers.

A **datapath function** is an instance of a tile file[1]. The **size** of a datapath function is the number of bits (i.e., rows) it spans. A cell instance is a **datapath instance** if it belongs to a datapath function; otherwise it is a **random instance**.

A **regular function** is a set of random instances of the same master cell, along with bit numbers for the instances[2]. The major distinction between datapath functions and regular functions is that the datapath functions are part of the input, while regular functions are part of the output[3].

Given a circuit and possibly its datapath functions, the problem of **regularity extraction** is to group random instances into regular functions such that the given objective function (area, wirelength,...) is optimized. When no input datapath functions are given, our approach automatically creates the initial datapath functions.

We use a signature-based approach to solve the regularity extraction problem. Our definition of signatures is inspired by the work of Ebeling and Zajicek on validating circuit layouts [2]. The **signature** of a random instance is dictated by its master cell and its connectivity to datapath instances. For example, consider the random instance A shown in Figure 1. It is connected to datapath instance P at terminal x and to datapath instance Q at terminal y. The signature of instance A is given by

$$\mathsf{Sign}(A) = f(M(A), h(M(P), x), h(M(Q), y)),$$

where f and h are properly chosen hash functions, and the function M maps cell instances to their master cells.

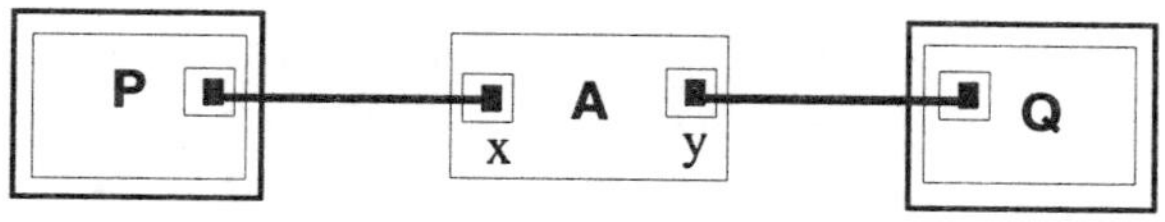

Figure 1: Signature definition.

In general, suppose a random instance A is connected to datapath instances $P_1, P_2, \ldots$ at terminals $x_1, x_2, \ldots$ The signature of instance A is

$$f(M(A), h(M(P_1), x_1), h(M(P_2), x_2), \ldots).$$

3 Regularity Extraction

As the input to the regularity extraction problem, we are given a circuit's netlist and its datapath functions. Let MaxSize denote the maximum of the sizes of the datapath functions. The data structure for a random instance A consists of:

- the signature $\mathsf{Sign}(A)$, and
- array $\mathsf{CostArray}(A, i)$, $0 \leq i \leq \mathsf{MaxSize} - 1$.

The element $\mathsf{CostArray}(A, i)$ indicates the connectivity cost of assigning the random instance A to bit position i.

Let random instances $A_0, A_1, \ldots, A_{k-1}$ form a regular function. Suppose that the bit numbers of the random instances are, respectively, $b_0, b_1, \ldots, b_{k-1}$. The **cost** of the regular function is $\sum_{i=0}^{k-1} \mathsf{CostArray}(A_i, b_i)$.

3.1 The Algorithm

Algorithm 1 presents a solution for the regularity extraction problem. The algorithm takes as input a parameter MinSize that indicates the acceptable minimum regular function size. An example is given below after the explanation of the algorithm.

If no datapath functions are provided as part of the input, the algorithm creates them by using hints from bus names and control nets. Step 1 of the algorithm initializes MaxSize by iterating through the given datapath functions. The computation of Sign(.) and CostArray(.,.) in Step 2 is explained below.

Computing Signatures: A collision of signatures occurs if two random instances with different connectivity patterns get the same signatures. Proper choice of hash functions can almost always prevent collisions (one in one billion for 32-bit signatures). In practice, the Sign(.) is an integer. All the arithmetic is done modulo a large prime number. The modulo arithmetic avoids over-flow, and the selection of a large prime number prevents collisions. Our choice for hash functions f and h, which has not resulted in collisions in all our experiments, is:

$$f(a, b) = a + b, \text{ and } \; h(a, b) = a * 2^b.$$

Computing Connectivity Costs: The computation of CostArray(.,.) is flexible in the sense that the connectivity costs can vary depending on our objective. For example, suppose a net connects a random instance A to an instance P in a datapath function. Let the bit number of P be b. The contribution of this net to $\mathsf{CostArray}(A, i)$ reflects the "vertical distance"

[1] In general, there is a many-to-one correspondence from the set of datapath functions to the set of tile files.

[2] Our approach handles user-specified equivalence classes of the master cells as well.

[3] In an iterative approach, regular functions generated in one iteration become datapath functions in the next iteration.

Input: A circuit's netlist and its datapath functions. Parameter MinSize.
Output: A collection of regular functions.

1. Compute MaxSize; RegularFunctionList := $\emptyset$.
2. Compute Sign(.) and CostArray(.,.) of each random instance.
3. Partition all random instances into blocks of instances with same Sign(.).
4. For each block $\mathcal{A}$ do
   While $\mathcal{A} \neq \emptyset$ do
   (a) Compute a minimum cost regular function $\mathcal{F}$ of the maximum size.
   (b) If the size of $\mathcal{F} \geq$ MinSize, add $\mathcal{F}$ to RegularFunctionList.
   (c) Delete the instances of $\mathcal{F}$ from block $\mathcal{A}$.

Algorithm 1: An algorithm for regularity extraction.

of bit position i from position b, i.e., the contribution is $|i - b|$. Thus, the contribution to CostArray(A, b) is 0, and the contribution to every other CostArray(A, i) is positive and reflects a penalty to place instance A at bit position i.

Step 3 sorts the random instances based on their signatures, and partitions them into blocks with same signature.

Step 4 generates regular functions from the blocks, taking CostArray(.,.) into consideration. To explain this step, we need to review some results from network-flows [1].

Let $H = (X, Y; F)$ be a bipartite graph with vertex bipartition (X, Y) and the edge set $F \subseteq X \times Y$. Each edge has a cost. A **matching** in the graph H is a set of edges such that no two edges are incident at the same vertex. The **size** of a matching is the number of edges in the matching, and the **cost** is the sum of the costs of the edges. A **maximum matching** is a matching that has the largest size. The **minimum cost maximum matching** is a maximum matching with the minimum cost.

The generation of a minimum cost regular function of the maximum size from a block $\mathcal{A}$ can easily be modeled as a minimum cost maximum matching problem. The vertex set $X = \{0, 1, \ldots, \text{MaxSize} - 1\}$, and the set Y is all the instances in the block $\mathcal{A}$. The bipartite graph is complete, i.e., $F = X \times Y$, and the edge costs are given by CostArray(.,.).

The problem of finding a minimum cost maximum matching in a bipartite graph is a special case of the minimum cost maximum flow problem. The latter problem can be solved using a successive shortest path algorithm; see Chapter 9 of [1] for full details.

3.2 An Example

We now apply the algorithm to the netlist shown in Figure 2. The parameter MinSize= 2.

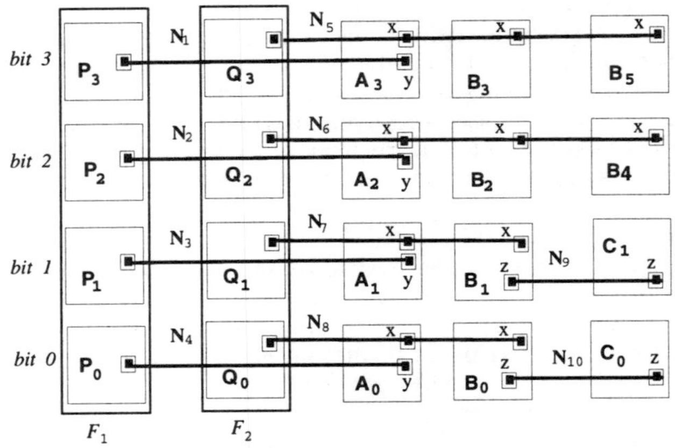

Figure 2: A netlist and datapath functions.

The netlist of Figure 2 has the following components.
Instances: A generic instance X_i is a cell instance of a library cell X. So, P_0, P_1, P_2, and P_3 are all instances of a library cell P, and C_0 and C_1 are instances of a cell C. The important terminals are shown as small rectangles inside the instances, i.e., instance A_3 has terminals x and y.
Nets: There are 10 nets, namely, $N_1, N_2, \ldots, N_{10}$.
Datapath Functions: Instances P_0, P_1, P_2, and P_3 form a datapath function $\mathcal{F}_1$. The bit numbers of these instances are, respectively, 0,1,2,3. Similarly, instances Q_0, Q_1, Q_2, and Q_3 form a datapath function $\mathcal{F}_2$. These eight instances are datapath instances, and the remaining instances are random instances. $\mathcal{F}_1$ and $\mathcal{F}_2$ might be given as part of the input, or they might be generated by the previous iteration of the algorithm.

During the signature computation, all the instances A_0, A_1, A_2, and A_3 get the same signature, because they have similar connectivity to datapath instances. Also, all the instances B_0–B_5 get the same signature, which is different from A_0's signature. Instances C_0 and C_1 don't get any signature, since they are not connected to datapath instances. So, there are two signature blocks, namely block $\mathcal{A}$ consisting of all A_i's, and block $\mathcal{B}$ containing all B_i's.

In CostArray(.,.) computation, MaxSize= 4. Since A_3 is connected only to bit 3, the element CostArray$(A_3, 3)$ is 0, and the array CostArray$(A_3, .)$ = (3,2,1,0). Similarly, CostArray$(B_2, .)$ = (2,1,0,1), as B_2 is connected only to bit 2.

Consider now the generation of regular functions from the block $\mathcal{A}$. The minimum cost maximum matching algorithm applied to this block finds one matching: instances A_0, A_1, A_2, and A_3 are matched to bit positions 0,1,2,3 respectively. So, a new regular function $\mathcal{F}_3 = \{A_0, A_1, A_2, A_3\}$ is generated, and the bit number of A_i is i. The matching algorithm applied to the block $\mathcal{B}$ generates two regular functions, namely, $\mathcal{F}_4 = \{B_0, B_1, B_2, B_3\}$ and $\mathcal{F}_5 = \{B_4, B_5\}$[4]. In $\mathcal{F}_4$, the bit number of B_i is i. In $\mathcal{F}_5$, the bit numbers

[4] Or, $\mathcal{F}_4 = \{B_0, B_1, B_4, B_5\}$ and $\mathcal{F}_5 = \{B_2, B_3\}$.

of B_4 and B_5 are 2 and 3, respectively. This completes the first iteration.

In the second iteration, there are five datapath functions, namely, $\mathcal{F}_1$–$\mathcal{F}_5$, and two random instances C_0 and C_1. These random instances are extracted as a regular function $\mathcal{F}_6$, and the bit number of C_i is i.

The final circuit is shown in Figure 3.

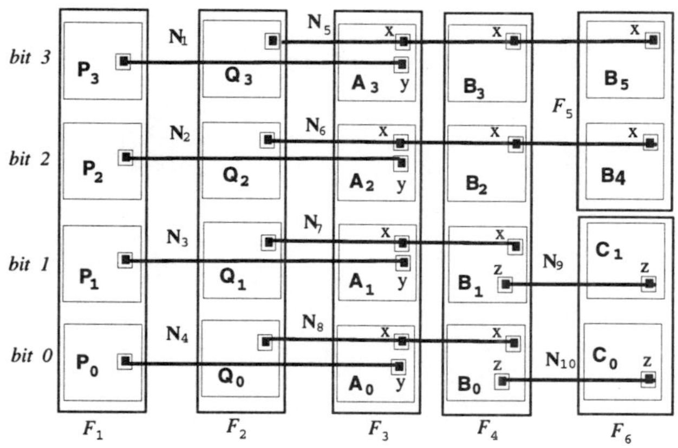

Figure 3: Extracted regular functions from the circuit of Figure 2.

4 Relaxed Signatures

For some circuits, the signature definition given in section 2 may be very restrictive: two random instances, whose connectivities to datapath instances differ only slightly, will get distinct signatures. Consequently, during the generation of regular functions, these two instances will belong to different functions. To overcome this problem, we relax the signature definition.

We may view the previous signature as an *instance-based* signature. We propose a *function-based* signature below.

Suppose a random instance A is connected to instances in datapath functions $\mathcal{F}_1, \mathcal{F}_2, \ldots$ The function-based signature of the instance A is given by: $\mathsf{Sign}(A) = f(M(A), \mathcal{F}_1, \mathcal{F}_2, \ldots)$.

The improved algorithm is shown in Algorithm 2.

1. Apply Algorithm 1 with instance-based signatures.
2. Use function-based signatures and apply Algorithm 1 to all random instances that don't belong to the regular functions generated in the previous step.

Algorithm 2: Improved algorithm for regularity extraction.

5 Experimental Results

Table 1 shows the area and total wire length results on final (after routing) designs. Tst1, Tst2, and Tst3 are designs without regularity extraction; Tst1Ext, Tst2Ext, and Tst3Ext are obtained from these designs using extraction. Tst1Ext has 21 % less wirelength than Tst1. Tst2Ext has 15 % less wirelength than Tst2. Tst3Ext has 43 % less area and 50 % less wirelength than Tst3.

design	cells	nets	area	wirelength
Tst1	1318	1126	1190x443	242218
Tst1Ext	1318	1126	1192x 443	189570
Tst2	883	977	414x707	99953
Tst2Ext	883	977	437x691	84883
Tst3	3724	4279	18204x17868	38300000
Tst3Ext	3724	4279	7512x24804	19200000

Table 1: Experimental Results.

6 Conclusion

We presented a general and flexible approach to extract regularity from datapath-oriented circuits. The approach is signature based and analyzes the circuit connectivity. The experimental results demonstrate that the approach results in better designs, as compared to the designs obtained without regularity extraction.

Acknowledgement: We thank Raymond Nijssen for his valuable suggestions on this paper; he suggested to us to use high-fanout control nets to generate initial datapath functions.

References

[1] R. Ahuja, T. Magnanti, and J. Orlin. *Network Flows.* Prentice Hall, New Jersey, 1993.

[2] C. Ebeling and O. Zajicek. Validating vlsi circuit layout by wirelist comparison. *Proceedings of the International Conference on Computer Aided Design (ICCAD)*, pages 172–173, 1983.

[3] M. Hirsch and D. Siewiorek. Automatically extracting structures from a logical design. *Proceedings of the International Conference on Computer Aided Design (ICCAD)*, pages 456–459, 1988.

[4] R.X.T. Nijssen and J.A.G. Jess. Two-dimensional datapath regularity extraction. *Proceedings of the 5th ACM/IEEE Physical Design Workshop*, Reston, Virginia, 1996.

[5] G. Odawara, T. Hiraide, and O. Nishina. Partitioning and placement technique for cmos gate arrays. *IEEE Transactions on Computer Aided Design*, CAD-6(3):355–363, 1987.

[6] Y.-W. Tsay and Y.-L. Lin. A row-based cell placement method that utilizes circuit structural properties. *IEEE Transactions on Computer Aided Design*, CAD-14(3):393–397, 1995.

SESSION 9D

FAULT SIMULATION AND DIAGNOSIS

Moderators:

Robert Aitken, Hewlett-Packard Co., Palo Alto, CA

Kwang-Ting Cheng, University of California,

Santa Barbara, CA

Fault Simulation of Interconnect Opens in Digital CMOS Circuits

Haluk Konuk
haluk_konuk@hp.com
California Design Center-ICBD, Hewlett-Packard Company

Abstract

We describe a highly accurate but efficient fault simulator for interconnect opens, based on characterizing the standard cell library with SPICE; using transistor charge equations for the site of the open; using logic simulation for the rest of the circuit; taking four different factors, that can affect the voltage of an open, into account; and considering the oscillation and sequential behavior potential of opens. A novel test technique based on controlling the die surface voltage is also described. We present simulation results of ISCAS85 layouts using stuck-at and IDDQ test sets.

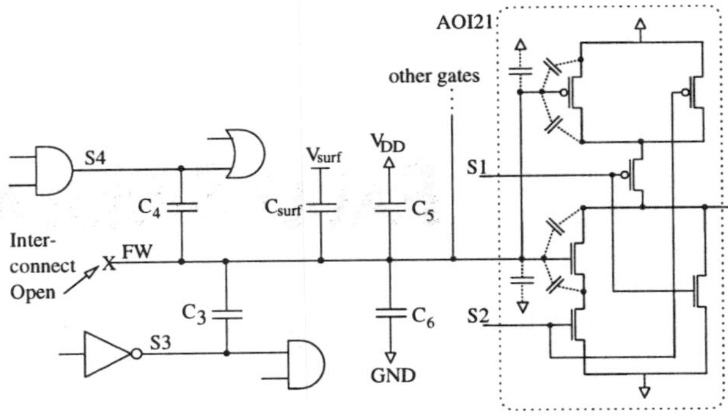

Figure 1: An example for an interconnect open.

1 Introduction

Breaks are one of the common types of defects that occur during an IC manufacturing process [1]. Breaks fall into different categories depending on their location in a digital CMOS circuit. A break can occur inside a CMOS cell affecting transistor drain and source connections [2, 3, 4, 5]. A break can disconnect a single transistor gate from its driver [6, 7]. Yet another break can disconnect a set of logic-gate inputs from their drivers; thus causing the voltage of these inputs to float. In order for this to happen a break needs to occur in the interconnect wiring. In today's CMOS ICs with five or more metal layers, interconnect wiring seems to be the most likely place for a break to occur. This is well supported by the critical area analysis by Xue, *et al.* [8]. Also, vias are especially susceptible to breaks [9], and the number of vias is exceeding the number of transistors in some microprocessor designs [10].

We call the fault created by a break in the interconnect wiring an **interconnect open**. In this paper, we describe a fault simulation algorithm for interconnect opens, that take into account all known factors affecting the voltage of a floating wire created by an interconnect open. We also make use of a novel test technique based on controlling the surface voltage of a die. To the best of our knowledge, this is the first fault simulator reported for interconnect opens; therefore, comparison to prior work is not applicable. In the following section, we discuss the factors affecting the voltage of a floating wire. Then, we describe our fault simulation algorithm, followed by the description of our novel test technique for interconnect opens. Finally, we present the results of our experiments with ISCAS85 circuits.

2 Floating Wire Voltage

Knowing the factors that determine the voltage of a floating wire is essential in building a fault simulator for interconnect opens. The following subsections describe four such factors. Due to lack of space, we do not cover here how the effect of charge collector diodes can be handled, which is described in Chapter 4 in [11].

2.1 Wiring Capacitances

Figure 1 shows an example interconnect open. C_5 is the total wiring capacitance from floating wire FW to the n-wells and to the V_{DD} supply wires. C_6 is the total wiring capacitance from FW to the substrate and to the GND supply wires. The sizes of C_3, C_4, C_5, and C_6 together with the voltages on signal lines $S3$ and $S4$ contribute to the value of FW voltage. What V_{surf} and C_{surf} mean is discussed later.

One needs to know the exact location of an open in

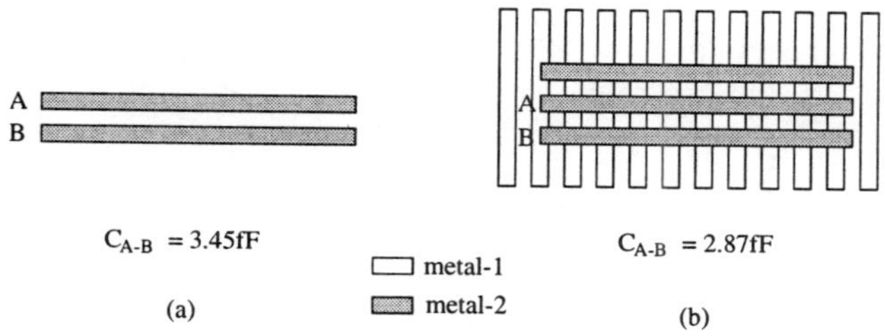

Figure 2: Wire-to-wire capacitance variation.

the interconnect in order to obtain the list and sizes of wiring capacitances to the corresponding floating wire. If an open is going to occur on a piece of straight metal track, we are not aware of any way of predicting where the open defect will land on this metal track. Besides, contacts are much more susceptible to opens than metal tracks are, according to the defect distribution statistics by Feltham and Maly [9]. Also, the increasing number of metal layers in IC processes tends to increase the number of vias per metal layer. In this work, each via, that produces a floating wire when broken, is considered to be a potential interconnect open defect site. The fault list for our simulator is produced by considering each such via.

Accuracy in wiring capacitance extraction is another important issue. Several layout tools that are capable of two-dimensional capacitance extraction exist in both industry and academia (e.g. *Magic*). The problem with two-dimensional capacitance extraction, which is based on the area and the perimeter of the overlap between two conducting surfaces, is its poor accuracy due to the fact that the same area and perimeter can result in different capacitances depending on the surrounding layout topology.

For example; consider the capacitance between two parallel metal-2 wires A and B in Figure 2. Both wires are 0.9μ by 60.0μ separated by 0.9μ. Using a three-dimensional capacitance extraction program, called SPACE3D [12], and wire height and silicon-dioxide thickness parameters for an HP 0.6μ process, we obtained 3.45fF when there are no other wires in the surroundings, as shown in part (a) of Figure 2. However, when there are other metal-1 and metal-2 wires in the surroundings as shown in part (b), the capacitance goes down to 2.87fF. *Magic* extracts 2.88fF for both cases, while the actual capacitance in part (a) is about 20% larger than the one in part (b).

Three-dimensional capacitance extraction is sufficiently accurate, but not feasible for the entire chip in terms of CPU time. One way to deal with this problem is to use two-dimensional capacitance extraction, and to assume that the actual capacitance is within +/- x% of the computed capacitance. This way, our fault simulator uses a range for each wiring capacitance to compute a voltage range for a given open.

2.2 Transistor Capacitances

These capacitances are in the cells driven by FW in Figure 1. They are gate-drain, gate-source, and gate-bulk capacitances, which are connected to transistor terminals with dotted lines to emphasize that they are not additionally inserted, but they are part of any CMOS transistor. Values of transistor capacitances significantly vary depending on the transistor terminal voltages. For this reason, we use transistor gate charge equations expressed as functions of transistor terminal voltages [13, 2] and transistor geometry, rather than using fixed worst case capacitance values. Transistor geometries can be tightly controlled in today's CMOS processes, and transistor capacitances are much less affected by surrounding structures than wiring capacitances are. Therefore, we do not use a value range for a transistor capacitance as we do for a wiring capacitance.

2.3 Trapped Charge

Experiments by Johnson [14] and Konuk and Ferguson [15] showed that the trapped charge deposited during fabrication can build up a voltage from -4.0V to 2.3V on floating gates with poly extensions, and -1.0V to 1.0V on floating gates connected to metal wires. We are not aware of any technique to predict the amount of trapped charge on a particular interconnect open. Therefore, our fault simulator makes no assumptions for the amount of the trapped charge.

2.4 The Die Surface

Konuk and Ferguson [15] reported an experimental observation that the die surface acted as an RC interconnect, capacitively coupling the floating wire to almost all other signals in a chip. The die surface resistance for this phenomenon to occur is in the tera-Ohms range. When coupled with wiring capacitances in the femto-Farads range, a time constant of one second or less is produced. If the die surface has a sufficiently large resistivity, then the capacitance to the die surface can be ignored. Otherwise, C_{surf} in Figure 1 needs to be taken into account.

3 Processing the Cell Library

We assume that each cell in the library is either a basic cell or is composed of basic cells, where we define a **basic cell** as a network of p-channel transistors and a complementary network of n-channel transistors, where each cell input drives the gates of one p- and one n-channel transistor, such as the AOI21 cell in Figure 1. All the MCNC cells used in the ISCAS85 circuit layouts satisfy this condition.

We first determine the **$L0\_th$** and **$L1\_th$** values, which denote the maximum voltage that is still logic-0 and the minimum voltage that is still logic-1 for the cell library, respectively [2], which we computed as 1.05V and 1.90V for the MCNC library using HP 0.6μ HSPICE level-13 parameters from MOSIS.

We define a **composite input** or a **c-input** for a cell as either a single cell input or multiple input ports of the same cell tied together. $\boldsymbol{V_{L0,g,ci}}$ denotes the logic-0 threshold voltage for c-input ci of cell g, that is, the voltage on the c-input ci of g such that the output of g is at L1_th and is sensitized to ci. $\boldsymbol{Q_{L0,g,ci}}$ denotes the total electrical charge on the transistor gates that are driven by ci, when the voltage on ci is $V_{L0,g,ci}$ with g's output sensitized to ci. $\boldsymbol{V_{L1,g,ci}}$ and $\boldsymbol{Q_{L1,g,ci}}$ are similarly defined.

For IDDQ testing [16], a threshold current $\boldsymbol{I_{ddq,th}}$ needs to be determined such that a quiescent power supply current larger than $I_{ddq,th}$ indicates a defective chip. $\boldsymbol{V_{iddq0,g,ci}}$ denotes the logic-0 voltage on c-input ci such that $I_{ddq,th}$ flows through cell g. $\boldsymbol{Q_{iddq0,g,ci}}$ denotes the total electrical charge on the transistor gates that are driven by ci, when the voltage on ci is $V_{iddq0,g,ci}$, and $I_{ddq,th}$ flows through g. $\boldsymbol{V_{iddq1,g,ci}}$ and $\boldsymbol{Q_{iddq1,g,ci}}$ are similarly defined. For every cell g and c-input ci in the library, $V_{L0,g,ci}$, $V_{L1,g,ci}$, $V_{iddq0,g,ci}$, $V_{iddq1,g,ci}$, $Q_{L0,g,ci}$, $Q_{L1,g,ci}$, $Q_{iddq0,g,ci}$, and $Q_{iddq1,g,ci}$ are computed and recorded using HSPICE. In addition, the slope and the y-intercept values for the straight line defined by points $(V_{iddq0,g,ci}, Q_{iddq0,g,ci})$ and $(V_{L0,g,ci}, Q_{L0,g,ci})$ are recorded to be used for charge interpolation in our fault simulation algorithm. Similarly, the slope and the y-intercept for the straight line defined by points $(V_{L1,g,ci}, Q_{L1,g,ci})$ and $(V_{iddq1,g,ci}, Q_{iddq1,g,ci})$ are recorded. For example; consider the HSPICE charge-voltage plot in Figure 3 for the a input of the 2-input NAND gate in the MCNC library using HP 0.6μ process parameters. The V_{iddq0}, V_{L0}, V_{L1}, and V_{iddq1} points are marked using $I_{ddq,th} = 50\mu A$.

4 Fault Simulation Algorithm

The top level structure of our algorithm is as follows:

```
FOREACH 32-vector DO
  FOREACH interconnect open DO
    Perform parallel pattern single fault
    propagation [17] after flipping the
    fault-free logic value on the floating wire.
    FOR vector 1 THROUGH 32 DO
      IF vector can detect the open THEN
        Compute the range of trapped charge
        for this vector to detect the open, and
        add this range to the detection ranges
        computed from previous vectors.
ENDFOR; ENDFOR; ENDFOR
```

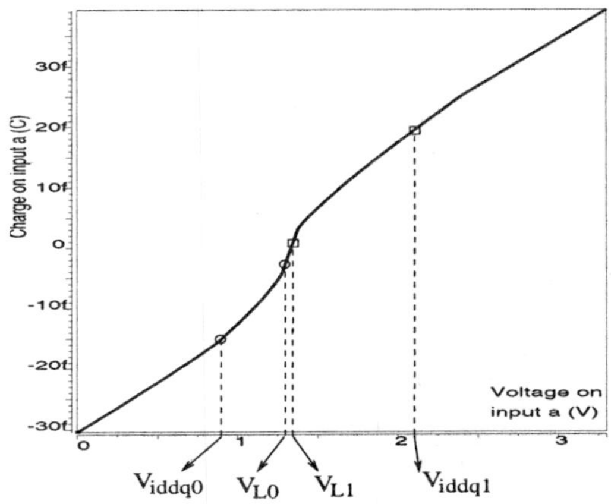

Figure 3: Charge on the a input of a NAND gate.

After all the vectors and opens are processed, an interconnect open is marked detected if the detection range for the trapped charge spans from $-\infty$ to $+\infty$. Alternatively, our program lets the user specify a voltage range, such that the voltage created by the trapped charge on any interconnect open is guaranteed to fall within this range. If specified, then this range is used to decide whether an open is detected or not. Detection of a defect can be accomplished by either voltage sensing (stuck-at testing) or current sensing (IDDQ testing) or both.

4.1 Stuck-at Detection

For a given vector and a given logic value on floating wire FW, let's first describe how we split a c-input of a cell driven by FW into sensitized and unsensitized parts. A **sensitized c-input** is formed by those input ports of a c-input, that drive those transistors through which an IDDQ current flows if the c-input voltage turns both p- and n-channel transistors on, while all other inputs of the cell are kept at V_{DD} or GND. The remaining part of the c-input is called an **unsensitized c-input**.

If an applied vector detects a stuck-at-0 or a stuck-at-1 fault on FW, then the first step to determine the trapped charge range for this vector to detect the open is to find the maximum FW voltage that is still logic-0 in case of stuck-at-0, or the minimum FW

voltage that is still logic-1 in case of stuck-at-1. We assume the stuck-at-0 case for the rest of this subsection without loss of generality. We determine the maximum logic-0 voltage on FW for the applied vector vec, $\boldsymbol{V_{L0,FW,vec}}$, as the minimum logic-0 threshold voltage (minimum $V_{L0,g,ci}$) over all the sensitized c-inputs driven by FW.

Then, we compute the trapped charge on FW, that corresponds to $V_{L0,FW,vec}$. Section 4.3 describes the computation of the trapped charge in detail. Let's call this computed charge $\boldsymbol{Q_0}$. Intuitively, if the actual trapped charge is smaller than Q_0, then the FW voltage will be smaller than $V_{L0,FW,vec}$, that is, the interconnect open will be detected as a stuck-at-0 fault by vec. However, this is not always true due to the potential sequential behavior of interconnect opens, due to feedback capacitive coupling, as described by Konuk and Ferguson[18]. For this reason, we re-compute the trapped charge by using $V_{L0,FW,vec}$ with still vec applied to the circuit, but this time with logic-1 on FW propagated to all circuit nodes that are sensitized to FW. We call this computed charge $\boldsymbol{Q_1}$.

Then, the maximum actual trapped charge with which vec is guaranteed to detect the open as a stuck-at-0 fault is $Q_{trapped,max,sa0} = min(Q_0, Q_1)$. In other words, the detection range for vector vec is $(-\infty, Q_{trapped,max,sa0})$. In addition to sequential behavior, an interconnect open can also oscillate under certain conditions [18]. The way we compute $Q_{trapped,max,sa0}$ guarantees that neither sequential behavior nor oscillation can invalidate our results.

4.2 Current sensing (IDDQ detection)

For IDDQ detection, we first check whether the given vector vec and a logic-0 on FW create any sensitized c-input driven by FW. If so, we determine the minimum voltage on FW, $\boldsymbol{V_{iddq0,FW,vec}}$, such that an IDDQ that is larger than or equal to $I_{ddq,th}$ still flows through a cell driven by FW. Note that V_{iddq0} is less than V_{L0}, and V_{iddq1} is greater than V_{L1} for a basic cell, as illustrated in Figure 3. So, we determine $V_{iddq0,FW,vec}$ as the minimum logic-0 IDDQ threshold voltage (minimum $V_{iddq0,g,ci}$) over all the sensitized c-inputs driven by FW.

Then, we compute the trapped charge on FW, that corresponds to a voltage of $V_{iddq0,FW,vec}$, as explained in Section 4.3. Note that the FW voltage needs to be larger than $V_{iddq0,FW,vec}$ for IDDQ detection. Let's call this computed charge $\boldsymbol{Q_{trapped,min,iddq0}}$.

Similarly, we compute $\boldsymbol{Q_{trapped,max,iddq1}}$, that corresponds to the maximum actual trapped charge with which vec can detect the open as an IDDQ fault. Note that if a sensitized c-input exists when FW is logic-0, a sensitized c-input must also exist when FW is logic-1, because there will be at least one cell driven by FW, whose other inputs do not have any combinational path to them starting from FW. Then, the IDDQ detection range for vec is $(Q_{trapped,min,iddq0}, Q_{trapped,max,iddq1})$. Oscillation [18] is possible within this detection range; however, we assume that if oscillation occurs, it will draw sufficient IDDQ current so that the open will still be detected.

If voltage and current are both measured for a given vector, then the open might be detected as a stuck-at and/or an IDDQ fault. Due to lack of space, we defer the discussion of this case to a future paper.

4.3 Trapped Charge Computation

This subsection describes how we compute $Q_{trapped}$ for a given voltage V_{FW} and a given test vector vec. It is important to emphasize that what we compute here is not the actual trapped charge on a floating wire, since we are not aware of any method to compute that. The trapped charge computed here is a consequence of the V_{FW} and the vec applied, and it is used as a boundary value for the actual trapped charge in order for the open to be detected.

The total charge on FW has two components: (i) the charge on the transistor gates driven by FW, denoted by $\boldsymbol{Q_{gate}}$, and (ii) the charge on FW due to the wiring capacitances between FW and other nodes (including the substrate and the die surface), denoted by $\boldsymbol{Q_{wire}}$. From the law of charge conservation, the trapped charge on FW is $Q_{trapped} = Q_{gate} + Q_{wire}$.

The equation for Q_{gate} is as follows, where $\boldsymbol{SCI}$ and $\boldsymbol{UCI}$ denote the sets of sensitized and unsensitized c-inputs driven by FW, respectively.

$$Q_{gate} = \sum_{ci \in SCI} (a_{ci} + b_{ci} \cdot V_{FW}) + \sum_{ci \in UCI} Q_{eqn}(ci, V_{FW}, vec) \qquad (1)$$

where a_{ci} and b_{ci} are the y-intercept and the slope values recorded for c-input ci during our library processing step in Section 3. Recall that two sets of y-intercept and slope values are computed per ci; one for the line passing through the IDDQ threshold and the logic threshold points on the Q-V curve as shown in Figure 3 when the c-input voltage is logic-0, and the other for the line when the c-input voltage is logic-1. This interpolation-based computation in Equation 1 is an efficient way of approximating the charge on a sensitized c-input with reasonable accuracy.

For an unsensitized c-input ci, the charge on the gate of each transistor driven by ci is computed by using Equations 3 and 5 in [2]. These gate charges are added up to find $Q_{eqn}(ci, V_{FW}, vec)$ in Equation 1. We could not use interpolation to compute $Q_{eqn}(ci, V_{FW}, vec)$; because, unlike a sensitized c-input, V_{FW} alone is not sufficient to determine the drain/source voltages of the transistors driven by an unsensitized c-input. Transistor drain/source voltages are determined, when needed, using the algorithm described in [2].

With regard to computing Q_{wire}, recall from Section 2.1 that our algorithm uses a range for each wiring capacitance due to the accuracy limitations of extraction tools. Let $\boldsymbol{C_{w0}(C_{w1})}$ denote a wiring capacitance from FW to a neighboring node that is at logic-0 (logic-1) value. Then, the following equation shows how to pick the worst case values for C_{w0} and C_{w1} in order to guarantee detection. The detection of the open might occur below V_{FW}, for instance, when V_{FW} is the maximum logic-0 voltage for the floating wire, and the vector applied is a test for FW stuck-at-0. In this case, $C_{w1,max}$ will be used for C_{w1} as the worst case.

$$C_{w0}(C_{w1}) = \begin{cases} C_{w0,min}(C_{w1,max}) \text{ if } FW \text{ voltage} \\ \quad \text{needs to be} < V_{FW} \text{ for detection} \\ C_{w0,max}(C_{w1,min}) \text{ if } FW \text{ voltage} \\ \quad \text{needs to be} > V_{FW} \text{ for detection} \end{cases}$$

If the die surface does not have a big enough resistivity, then the min and max values for the capacitance between FW and the surface needs to be considered, also, together with a voltage range $V_{surf,min}$ and $V_{surf,max}$ the die surface can acquire.

5 A Novel Test Technique

The passivation layer deposited on top of the last metal layer in a fabrication process usually has a similar thickness with the inter-metal dielectric. Therefore, if a conducting plate is placed on the die surface during wafer probing as illustrated by Figure 4, there will be capacitances to this plate from almost all the wires in the chip. If there is an interconnect open in the chip, then there will also be a capacitance from the floating wire to this plate, as denoted by C_{surf} in Figure 1. Playing with the voltage of this plate, V_{surf}, provides a handle to control the voltage of the floating wire; thus changing the amount of IDDQ current flowing in the cells driven by the floating wire. Note that if a chip is defect-free, a change in the die surface voltage will not cause any change in its IDDQ current, which must be below $I_{ddq,th}$, anyway.

An extension of this technique is to use a set of conducting plates forming tiles on the die surface, whose voltages can be individually controlled. This way, a floating wire can be localized to a chip area depending on the size of each tile used on the die surface. This technique has been filed for a patent.

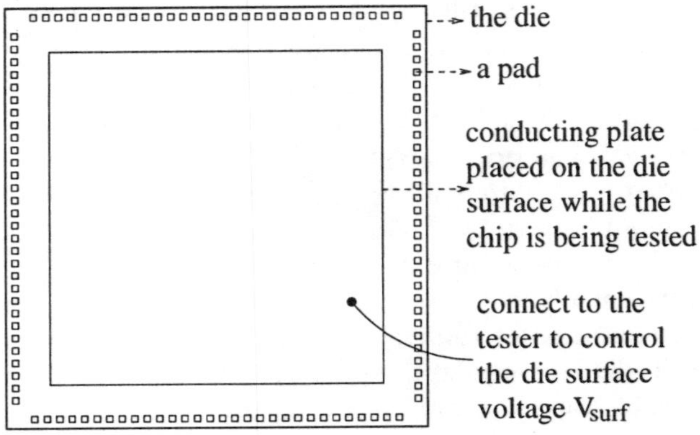

Figure 4: Controlling the die surface voltage.

6 Experiments and Results

We used the two metal layer channel routed layouts of the ISCAS85 circuits for our experiments. Due to lack of space, we are reporting our results only for the largest five ISCAS85 circuits in this paper. Since we consider each via (the contact between metal 1 and 2) as an interconnect open site, we process each layout with a program that is an extended version of *Carafe* [19] to analyze each via to find out whether a floating wire is created if the via is broken. The program removes each via, that can create a floating wire, from the layout, and labels the wire pieces in a systematic fashion. Then, we run *Magic* using the HP 0.6μ parameters in the technology file 8.2.8 from MOSIS to extract the capacitances from the layout.

There is a metal-2 wire across the height of each MCNC cell layout for every input port of the cell. A via connects this metal-2 wire to a small piece of metal-1, which is connected to poly that drives transistor gates. When this via is broken, the floating poly together with a small piece of metal-1 form a very short floating wire (s-FW), which has very small capacitances to neighboring nodes and to the die surface. The numbers of breaks corresponding to these vias are listed in the first column of Table 1. The remaining via-breaks are considered to create "long" floating wires (l-FW), and are listed in the second column. The IDDQ and stuck-at vectors are generated by *Nemesis* [20]. The pseudo-stuck-at fault model is used for IDDQ ATPG.

For a given chip, the wiring capacitances are fixed, even though their values may not be accurately

Circuit	# of *s-FW* via-breaks	# of *l-FW* via-breaks	# of IDDQ vecs	IDDQ cov.	# of stuck-at vecs	stuck-at cov.
c2670	3141	1286	42	97.78 %	117	96.33 %
c3540	4420	1854	67	97.71 %	175	96.58 %
c5315	7652	2938	60	99.62 %	137	98.79 %
c6288	8260	4232	34	99.40 %	33	99.42 %
c7552	9054	3464	86	99.62 %	221	98.89 %

Table 1: Via-break and test vector statistics

known due to limitations of extraction tools. So, we decided to use the extracted capacitance values as the real values, and assume that it is theoretically possible to modify the given circuit layout to exactly match these capacitance values, and the actual design is this modified layout. We also assumed that the die surface effect of Section 2.4 does not apply.

Table 2 shows our simulation results. Columns 2 to 5 show the % of *s-FW* and *l-FW* opens guaranteed to be detected no matter what the actual trapped charge is[1], when stuck-at (SA) vectors are used alone or in combination with IDDQ vectors. SA vectors are good at detecting interconnect opens when the magnitude of the actual trapped charge is large, forcing the floating wire to behave as stuck at 0 or 1. In contrast, IDDQ vectors tend to detect opens when the trapped charge magnitude is small, resulting in floating wire voltages being pulled to the vicinity of $V_{DD}/2$ by wiring and transistor capacitances. This is why SA and IDDQ vectors together produce much better guaranteed coverages in columns 4 and 5.

If the initial voltage on a floating wire due to the trapped charge can be bounded, then the detection ranges our algorithm computes, as explained in Section 4, can be compared to the size of the total possible range to give a probabilistic range coverage number. This is what we did for the rest of Table 2. Assuming that the actual trapped charge voltages are bounded by the [-1.0V, 1.0V] range, and assuming a homogeneous distribution of actual trapped charge voltages in this range, we obtained the range coverage numbers in columns 6 and 7. Using the [-0.5V, 0.5V] range decreased the coverage numbers, as we expected, because we used only the SA vectors, and SA vectors get worse in detection when the trapped charge magnitude gets smaller. Still, these range coverage numbers are much better than the guaranteed coverage numbers in columns 2 and 3.

In order to be certain of the coverage of a set of test vectors for a particular given design, even when the trapped charge voltage is bounded, one needs to take into account the inaccuracy of the capacitance extraction tools. Assuming that the actual value for a wiring capacitance is within the range from $0.7 * C_{extracted}$ to $1.3 * C_{extracted}$, and assuming that trapped charge voltage is bounded by [-0.5V, 0.5V], we obtained the range coverage numbers in Table 3. We also assumed that the die surface voltage can vary, and the "no surf cntrl" columns are for the case where we used either V_{DD} or GND for the die surface voltage depending on which one being the worst case. V_{DD} is 3.3V for all our experiments.

Note that the coverage numbers in column 3 for *l-FW* opens is particularly low, because long floating wires are affected by the die surface more than the short floating wires are. Applying the SA vectors twice, once with $V_{surf} = V_{DD}$ and once with $V_{surf} =$ GND using the setup in Figure 4, helps long floating wires behave more like stuck-at faults, thus significantly increasing the range coverage numbers as listed in column 5. However, *s-FW* opens still have fairly low range coverages as listed in column 4, because the die surface voltage does not have as much effect on the short floating wire defects.

Using IDDQ vectors in addition to SA vectors boosts the coverage numbers as listed in columns 6 and 7, compared to the columns 2 and 3. However, the *l-FW* opens still do not reach the coverage numbers obtained by the two-pass SA testing of column 5. Finally, controlling the surface voltage at $V_{surf} = V_{DD}/2$, and using both SA and IDDQ vectors produce very high range coverage values for both *s-FW* and *l-FW* opens as listed in the last two columns of Table 3.

We used an HP-735 99MHz workstation with 180MB memory for our fault simulations. The maximum wall clock time was 4 minutes 24 seconds for circuit c7552, which shows us promise for the feasibility of a fault simulator for real chips.

In conclusion, we presented an accurate but efficient fault simulator for interconnect opens, which take many factors that can affect the voltage of an open into account. We also presented a novel test technique based on controlling the die surface voltage. Our results from ISCAS85 circuit layouts show that

[1] Note that excessive trapped charge may create a dangerous voltage level such that a gate-oxide punch through may occur, creating a gate-oxide short coupled with an interconnect open. We do not consider this case and leave it to future research.

Circuit	% opens guaranteed to be detected				Trapped charge range cov. (%)			
	SA only		SA and IDDQ		SA only, -1.0V to 1.0V trapped Q volt.		SA only, -0.5V to 0.5V trapped Q volt.	
	s-FW	l-FW	s-FW	l-FW	s-FW	l-FW	s-FW	l-FW
c2670	0.00	5.19	93.86	97.33	86.52	89.89	77.46	83.61
c3540	0.00	16.99	93.91	97.22	86.85	91.04	79.26	85.27
c5315	0.00	11.43	98.03	97.28	88.78	92.06	80.06	86.76
c6288	0.00	18.67	99.13	99.84	88.35	91.51	77.71	84.44
c7552	0.00	6.57	97.89	99.14	88.89	90.80	80.32	85.57

Table 2: Via-break coverages assuming no surface effect and using extracted capacitance values.

Circuit	SA only				SA and IDDQ			
	no surf cntrl		two pass: $V_{surf} = V_{DD}$ and GND		no surf cntrl		$V_{surf} = V_{DD} / 2$	
	s-FW	l-FW	s-FW	l-FW	s-FW	l-FW	s-FW	l-FW
c2670	64.21	17.74	72.85	94.31	99.63	66.28	99.65	99.76
c3540	67.06	19.47	74.74	94.83	99.63	70.48	99.66	99.73
c5315	67.08	18.99	75.44	96.01	99.97	64.89	99.97	99.93
c6288	64.02	22.24	72.98	94.63	99.62	75.85	99.62	99.85
c7552	66.97	17.35	75.35	95.32	99.99	61.57	100.00	99.95

Table 3: Trapped charge range cov.'s with cap. variation and trapped charge volt. bounded to [-0.5V, 0.5V]

combination of high coverage stuck-at and IDDQ test sets can result in high coverage of interconnect opens, especially when the die surface voltage is controlled, while stuck-at tests alone may not always guarantee such high coverage.

ACKNOWLEDGMENT: Prof. F. Joel Ferguson of UC Santa Cruz is gratefully acknowledged for his guidance and valuable technical discussions.

References

[1] C.F. Hawkins, J.M. Soden, A.W. Righter, and F.J. Ferguson. Defect classes - an overdue paradigm for CMOS IC testing. In *Proceedings of ITC*, Oct. 1994.

[2] H. Konuk, F.J. Ferguson, and T. Larrabee. Charge-based fault simulation for CMOS network breaks. *IEEE Transactions on Computer-Aided Design*, Dec. 1996.

[3] C. Di and J.A.G. Jess. On accurate modeling and efficient simulation of CMOS opens. In *Proceedings of ITC*, 1993.

[4] M. Favalli, M. Dalpasso, P. Olivo, and B. Ricco. Modeling of broken connections faults in CMOS ICs. In *Proceedings of European Design and Test Conference*, 1994.

[5] W.M. Maly, P.K. Nag, and P. Nigh. Testing oriented analysis of CMOS ICs with opens. In *Proceedings of ICCAD*, 1988.

[6] V.H. Champac, A. Rubio, and J. Figueras. Electrical model of the floating gate defect in CMOS IC's: Implications on IDDQ testing. *IEEE Transactions on Computer-Aided Design*, March 1994.

[7] M. Renovell and G. Cambon. Electrical analysis and modeling of floating-gate fault. *IEEE Transactions on Computer-Aided Design*, pages 1450–58, Nov. 1992.

[8] H. Xue, C. Di, and J.A.G. Jess. Probability analysis for CMOS floating gate faults. In *Proceedings of European Design and Test Conference*, 1994.

[9] D.B.I. Feltham and W. Maly. Physically realistic fault models for analog CMOS neural networks. *IEEE Journal of Solid-State Circuits*, Sep. 1991.

[10] K.M. Thompson. Intel and the myths of test. In *The Keynote Address of ITC*, 1995.

[11] H. Konuk. Testing for opens in digital CMOS circuits. *Ph.D. Thesis, Computer Eng. Dept., UC Santa Cruz*, Dec. 96.

[12] A.J. van Genderen and N.P. van der Meijs. *Space3d Capacitance Extraction User's Manual.* Delft University of Technology, 1997.

[13] B.J. Sheu, W.-J. Hsu, and P.K. Ko. An MOS transistor charge model for VLSI design. *IEEE Transactions on Computer-Aided Design*, pages 520–527, April 1988.

[14] S. Johnson. Residual charge on the faulty floating gate MOS transistors. In *Proceedings of ITC*, October 1994.

[15] H. Konuk and F.J. Ferguson. An unexpected factor in testing for CMOS opens: The die surface. In *IEEE VLSI Test Symposium*, 1996.

[16] A.D. Singh, H. Rasheed, and W.W. Weber. IDDQ testing of CMOS opens: An experimental study. In *Proceedings of ITC*, 1995.

[17] J.A. Waicukauski, E.B. Eichelberger, D.O. Forlenza, E. Lindbloom, and Th. McCarthy. Fault simulation for structured VLSI. In *VLSI Systems Design*, Dec. 1985.

[18] H. Konuk and F.J. Ferguson. Oscillation and sequential behavior caused by interconnect opens in digital CMOS circuits. In *Proceedings of ITC*, 1997.

[19] A. Jee and F.J. Ferguson. Carafe: An inductive fault analysis tool for CMOS VLSI circuits. In *Proceedings of the IEEE VLSI Test Symposium*, 1993.

[20] T. Larrabee. Test pattern generation using Boolean satisfiability. *IEEE Transactions on Computer-Aided Design*, January 1992.

GOLDENGATE: A Fast and Accurate Bridging Fault Simulator Under A Hybrid Logic/I_{DDQ} Testing Environment*

Tzuhao Chen and Ibrahim N. Hajj
Department of Electrical and Computer Engineering and
Coordinated Science Laboratory
University of Illinois, Urbana, IL, USA

Abstract

In this paper we describe GOLDENGATE - a bridging fault simulator for cell-based digital VLSI circuits with the following features: 1. It targets both combinational and sequential circuits. 2. It simulates general (routing, adjacency, and intra-cell) realistic bridging faults efficiently through a table-based scheme. The pre-computed table contains accurate cell output voltage and I_{DDQ} values obtained through electrical-level simulations. 3. It simulates both feedback and non-feedback bridging faults (BFs) efficiently through a cycling event-driven technique. 4. It allows mixed voltage and I_{DDQ} simulation to support a fully hybrid test scheme where mixed logic and I_{DDQ} sensings are allowed. The experimental results show that GOLDENGATE is both accurate and fast.

1 Introduction

Due to the high integration density of VLSI circuits, bridging faults (a physical defect that form a faulty resistive short between two conducting nets in the layout), have become one of the most frequently occurring physical faults.

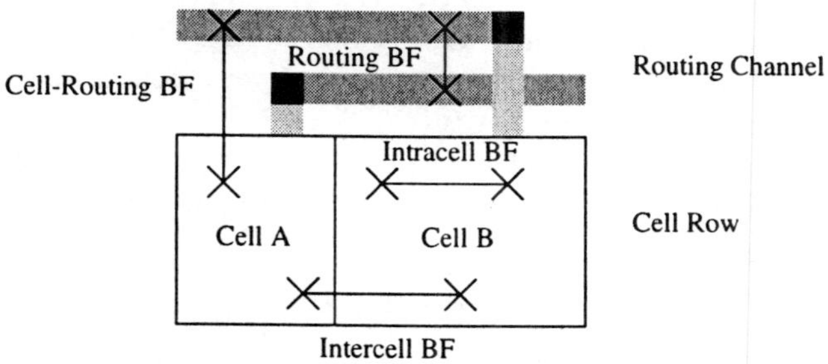

Figure 1: Realistic bridging fault types.

When the layout of a circuit is not available, an all-pair bridging fault set of size $\binom{N}{2}$ (N is the number of nodes in the circuit) need to be targeted for test generation, which is computationally expensive for large circuits. However, [1] showed that by simulating the effects of spot defects on circuit layouts using the inductive fault analysis(IFA), $O(N)$ realistic bridging faults can be extracted. For cell-based circuits, realistic bridging faults can be grouped into three classes according to their physical connectivities[2] as shown in Figure 1. A routing-channel BF involves two conducting nets external to cells. A cell-routing BF involves one external and one internal net; an inter-cell BF involves two internal nets that belong to two separate cells. The cell-routing and inter-cell BFs are jointly named adjacency BFs. An intra-cell BF involves two internal nets within the same cell.

Existing work on bridging fault simulation can be divided into the following five types: gate-level, switch-level, electrical-level, mixed-level, and table-based. Gate-level simulators ([3, 4], to mention a few) employ either wired-and or wired-or logic to represent a BF so that the fault simulation can be done at the gate level speed. However, it was pointed out in [5, 6] that the circuit behavior under a BF could not be well modeled by permanent wired-logic. Therefore a better BF modeling using the Primitive Bridge Functions (PBFs) was suggested. In general, the gate-level methods have the following problems: 1. The circuit need to be structurally altered for each BF which can be expensive for large circuits with a large number of BFs. 2. An intermediate cell output voltage can be interpreted differently (as logic 1 or 0) by different fanout cells[7, 8], and this "Byzantine General's Problem" cannot be handled by gate-level approaches. 3. Only routing(external) BFs can be handled since the gate internal information is opaque to the gate-level simulators.

Switch-level simulators[9, 10, 11] model a BF as a permanent conducting transistor. They are applicable if the BFs can be modeled as transistors with allowable strength levels. The switch-level approach, however, may be pessimistic since a conducting path from V_{DD} to GND may create an unknown state. Furthermore,

*This research was supported by the Semiconductor Research Corporation under Contract SRC 96-DP-109

the switch-level approach may be slow since a circuit represented in transistor-level is more complex.

Electrical-level simulators such as SPICE[12] are accurate, but expensive. It calculates the voltage and current of every electrical node. Practically, electrical-level fault simulation is only applicable to small circuits because of the extremely long computation time. The following two reasons illustrate the inefficiency of simulating bridging faults using electrical-level simulators: 1. It is not necessary to calculate the detailed voltage and current values in fault simulation since only the logic state of each primary output pin is needed for the logic testing and only the I_{DDQ} value is needed for the I_{DDQ} testing. 2. Even with the existence of BFs, most nodes in a circuit assume voltage values good enough to be interpreted as logic 1 or 0. Therefore logic simulation is accurate enough at those nodes.

Due to the above reasons, mixed-mode bridging fault simulation methods [13, 14] were proposed for accurate results at higher speed. In [13, 14], switch- or gate-level simulation is first performed starting with the primary inputs, then electrical-level simulation is performed at the bridged cells and their fanout cones for a few levels before the simulation switches back to switch- or gate-level. In [13], ALVL, a constant number of levels for electrical-level simulation is used; all unresolved intermediate voltage values are then mapped to logic values. In [14], electrical-level simulation remains as long as the cell outputs cannot be interpreted as definite logic 1 or 0. Although more accurate than switch-level simulators and faster than electrical-level simulators, the mixed-mode approaches have the following limitations: 1. Electrical-level convergence problems may cause pessimistic results. 2. Repeated electrical-level DC analysis are often done on the same circuit cluster unnecessarily. 3. Feedback bridging faults are not handled. 4. Speed is only practical for medium-sized circuits.

Since mixed-mode simulators may still be too slow for large circuits, table-based simulators[8, 15] were proposed as a time-accuracy trade-off to the mixed-level simulators. In a mixed-level simulator EPROOFS described in the last paragraph, larger ALVL values lead to more accurate results while smaller ALVL values make simulation faster. However, [13] shows that when setting ALVL to 3, it requires 35% longer simulation time to merely detect a few more BFs as compared with when setting ALVL to 1, which has comparable accuracy as the table-based simulators. Therefore table-based methods have the advantage of faster speed with only minimum inaccuracies introduced. In the table-based simulators, output voltage values of the bridged cells for each possible BF in a cell library are pre-computed with electrical-level simulators. Therefore simulation can be done at gate-level everywhere except at the bridged cells, where a table look-up is performed with the input logic values for the bridged cells to obtain the analog cell output voltage values. These analog voltage values are then compared to the pre-computed switching threshold voltage values for each fanout pin to determine their logic interpretations, therefore the "Byzantine General's Problem" is properly handled. These simulators are faster than the mixed-mode ones since gate-level simulation and table look-up are both fast. However, existing table-based simulators have the following limitations: 1. Only routing BFs are handled; adjacency and intra-cell BFs are not handled. 2. Feedback bridging faults are not considered. 3. Only logic testing scheme is supported. In [15] a gate-level hard short ($R_b = 0$) BF model is used. This model is only applicable to routing BFs with zero resistance. Whereas in reality most of the BFs have finite non-zero resistance.

GOLDENGATE, our BF simulator, is designed for both combinational and sequential circuits using a table-based simulation scheme for best efficiency. The advantages of GOLDENGATE compared to existing table-based bridging fault simulators[13, 15] are as follows:

1. It handles general (routing, adjacency, and intra-cell) realistic BFs extracted by our hierarchical bridging fault extractor[16]. Existing work target only routing BFs. However, we found out by extracting some typical circuit layouts that the adjacency and intra-cell BFs constitute 5% to 25% of all the realistic BFs.

2. It simulates both feedback and non-feedback BFs using a cycling event-driven technique. Existing work target only non-feedback BFs. However, from the fault extraction results we found that feedback BFs constitute 30% to 75% of all the the realistic BFs. Therefore the feedback BFs should not be ignored in order to achieve high defect coverage.

3. It supports a hybrid (logic+I_{DDQ}) testing scheme where mixed logic and I_{DDQ} sensings are allowed by a mixed voltage and I_{DDQ} simulation scheme.

This paper is organized as follows, Section 2 describes the pre-computed voltage/I_{DDQ} table used for fast bridging fault simulation. Section 3 describes the fault simulation techniques. Section 4 presents the experimental data. Section 5 concludes this paper.

2 The Pre-computed Table

The fast speed of GOLDENGATE is partly achieved by the use of a pre-computed faulty voltage/I_{DDQ} table based on a given cell library. This table contains, for each possible BF that is inside an individual cell or in between a cell-pair and for each input pattern, the output voltage values for the bridged cells and the I_{DDQ} value; it is of size $O(C^2)$ with C being the size of the cell library. The table entries are obtained using an electrical-level circuit simulator PSPICE[18] with a BF resistance R_b which is user specified. For a real on-chip BF with a larger(smaller) resistance than the specified R_b, the simulation result can be optimistic(pessimistic) since such a BF can cause less(more) serious faulty behavior in the circuit than the specified R_b does. Since our goal in fault simulation is to find BFs that can be detected by the given test set, choosing a large enough R_b ensures that for all BFs with resistance less than or equal to R_b, the simulation result may be conservative, but not wrong.

Since a typical low-resistive R_b ranges from 0 to a few tens of ohms, we chose $R_b = 100\Omega$. For a different R_b, a different table needs to be constructed. Although the table building is of complexity $O(C^2)$, it needs to be done only once during the cell library characterization stage, and can be used throughout the life of the cell library. To control the table building cost, the table can be built for only the most frequently used library cells. For circuits with less frequently used cells or custom-designed cells, only $O(C)$ time is required in table augmentation for each new cell.

For all but a flip-flop cell in our 14-component CMOS standard-cell library that we used, a total number of 1,062 possible BFs exist (91 routing, 913 adjacency, and 58 intra-cell), the table construction required 110,676 DC simulations in approximately 23 hours on a SPARCstation5. For a large cell library, the table construction process can be parallelized and the table size can be reduced by various compression techniques such as discretizing every floating-point voltage and I_{DDQ} value to be represented as an 8-bit integer or by the technique presented in [15] where repetitive values for different input patterns are represented by a logic minterm.

3 Bridging Fault Simulation Scheme

GOLDENGATE is a table-based, fast and memory efficient bridging fault simulator for both combinational and sequential circuits targeting general (routing/adjacency/intra-cell, feedback/non-feedback) realistic bridging faults. Figure 2 shows its flowchart.

Upon initialization, the pre-computed cell output voltage and I_{DDQ} values for each BF for each input pattern are loaded. The logic switching threshold voltage (V_{th}) value for each input pin of each library cell is also loaded for determining the logic interpretation of a signal line, given an intermediate voltage value. The initial state of a sequential circuit can be assigned or left unknown. For fast simulation, event-driven simulation style is used with an event queue that keeps the cells in the order of increased levels; therefore the events are processed level by level. A flag is maintained for each cell instance in the circuit to ensure that a cell with two or more updated input signals is only evaluated once. For each time frame, one fault-free gate-level simulation is done. Then for each BF in the fault list, the event queue is initialized with the events induced by the flip-flops. These flip-flop events are the ones created by the very same BF from the last time frame; these events represent a corrupted state. In the evaluation step, cells are classified as either "bridged" or "not bridged". An event for a "not bridged" cell is processed by a logic evaluation followed by the creation of new events for the fanout cells; an event for a "bridged" cell is processed by a table look-up followed by comparisons to the threshold voltage values for all its fanout cells and then by the creation of new events. A table look-up for a BF takes the logic input values for the cell(s) involved and gets the cell output voltage values and I_{DDQ} value as returns.

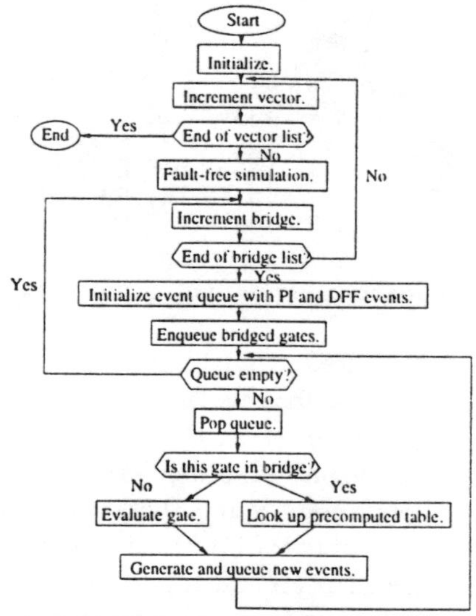

Figure 2: GOLDENGATE simulation flowchart.

A cycling event-driven technique is developed to facilitate the simulation of both feedback and non-feedback bridging faults. It is explained by the following example. In Figure 3, cells G1 and G6 are bridged together and the state of G6 depends on the state of

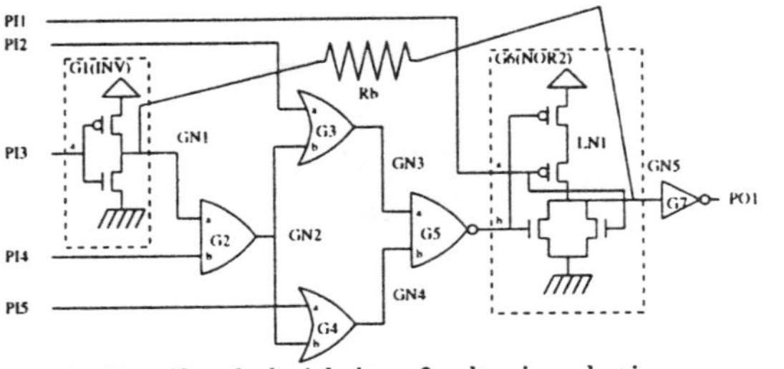

Figure 3: Feedback bridging fault simulation example.

G1, thus forming a feedback BF. Shortly after the start of the simulation pass for this BF, both cells are in the event queue with the event of G1 ahead of that of G6. When G1 is first dequeued, a new event G2 is queued if it has an altered input value. Later when G6 is dequeued, the new events for both bridged cells (G2 and G7) will be queued if altered input values are found. The event for G2 may in turn induce a new event for G6, which in turn may induce new events for G2 and G7, thus becoming a cycle of events. If after G1 has been visited CYCLE_LIMIT (the maximum number of allowable cycles) times and a stable condition has not been reached, an oscillation occurs as shown in Figure 4.

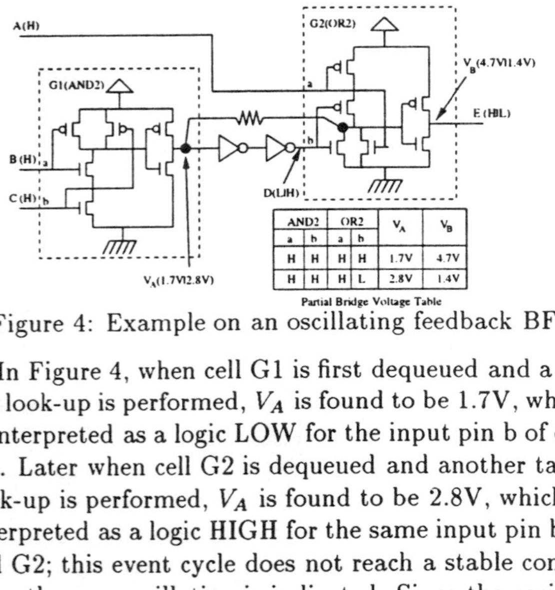

Figure 4: Example on an oscillating feedback BF.

In Figure 4, when cell G1 is first dequeued and a table look-up is performed, V_A is found to be 1.7V, which is interpreted as a logic LOW for the input pin b of cell G2. Later when cell G2 is dequeued and another table look-up is performed, V_A is found to be 2.8V, which is interpreted as a logic HIGH for the same input pin b of cell G2; this event cycle does not reach a stable condition, thus an oscillation is indicated. Since the oscillations are inevitable while simulating the feedback BFs, it is important to handle oscillations properly to avoid pessimistic results. GOLDENGATE keeps a record of the minimum and maximum V_A and V_B throughout the event cycles, when the number of cycles exceeds CYCLE_LIMIT, the event cycle is broken and the minimum and maximum V_A and V_B obtained thus far are used as a voltage range to determine the fanout logic states. The logic state of a fanout pin can be determined as the following:

$$\begin{cases} \text{HIGH} & \text{iff } V_{MIN} > V_{th,c} + V_m, \\ \text{LOW} & \text{iff } V_{MAX} < V_{th,c} - V_m, \\ \text{UNKNOWN} & \text{others,} \end{cases} \quad (1)$$

where $V_{th,c}$ is the switching threshold voltage for pin "c" of a fanout cell, V_m is the switching voltage margin. [15] pointed out that using the pin threshold voltage to determine the cell output logic value is only accurate when no other input pin has an intermediate value. The use of a properly selected V_m helps in reducing the inaccuracies caused by the intermediate voltage values at the price of slightly increased UNKNOWN counts.

After each simulation pass for a BF in the fault list, four states are possible: 1. Excess I_{DDQ} occured; BF detected by I_{DDQ} testing. 2. Faulty effect propagated to one or more primary outputs; BF detected by logic testing. 3. Faulty effect propagated to one or more flip-flops; record faulty flip-flops and keep this BF. 4. No faulty effect found, keep this BF. Unknown logic values are common in sequential circuit fault simulation. Each unknown input value is enumerated to both HIGH and LOW and multiple table look-up are conducted to obtain an analog voltage range (V_{MAX}, V_{MIN}), Equation 3 is then used in cell evaluation.

4 Experimental Results

GOLDENGATE was implemented in C++. All experiments were done on a SUN SPARCstation5 with a 66MHz CPU and 32MB of RAM. All realistic BFs were extracted from layouts generated by Mentor Design Tools using a bridging fault extractor[16]. In the experiments, the initial state for all circuits are assumed known, although they can be left unknown. In the following, we discuss in sequence the three experiments: 1. Accuracy verification with comparison to PSPICE. 2. Simulations on realistic bridging fault sets for ISCAS89 sequential circuits. 3. A demo for mixed voltage/I_{DDQ} simulation.

To verify the accuracy of GOLDENGATE, we designed a comparison experiment with PSPICE. In order to have sufficient data samples to achieve high confidence considering the long computational time of PSPICE, we chose circuit s298 with 133 cells, 3 primary input pins, and 6 flip-flop pins as the subject circuit along with a single stuck-at (SSA) test set of 259 vectors and a realistic bridging fault set of 596 BFs (264 feedback and 332 non-feedback). In this accuracy test, a PSPICE static(DC) run was executed based on the primary input and flip-flop values for each BF at each time frame. Then one of two comparisons (voltage or I_{DDQ}) between the GOLDENGATE and PSPICE results was performed, depending on the simulation mode. In the voltage simulation mode, logic voltage comparisons were done for each primary output and flip-flop cell. In Table 1, a pin is defined as either a primary output or the input of a flip-flop cell; a correct(incorrect) pin is a pin with the same(opposite) logic values in GOLDENGATE and PSPICE results. An incorrect pass is a simulation pass with at least one incorrect pin; a correct pass is a pass with no incorrect pin. In this performance verification, BFs which induced incorrect results in GOLDENGATE were recorded and dropped from the fault list. For the I_{DDQ} simulation mode, the I_{DDQ} from PSPICE run was compared against the preset threshold of $200\mu A$ to determine the detection state and then compared with the detection state of the GOLDENGATE pass. A comparison in I_{DDQ} simulation mode is correct(incorrect) if the I_{DDQ} detection states of GOLDENGATE and PSPICE agree(disagree). Table 1 shows the GOLDENGATE performance verification results for circuit s298. Sub-columns "F" and "NF" contain results for feedback and non-feedback BFs, respectively. For the voltage simulation mode, GOLDENGATE has a pin error rate of around 1 per 10,000 and a pass error rate of around 1 per 1,000. The CPU time for the PSPICE run and for GOLDENGATE run are listed in column T_s and T_g, respectively; a speed ratio between GOLDENGATE and PSPICE of around 3,000 is observed in the voltage simulation mode. The simulation accuracies for the feedback and non-feedback BFs are comparable in the voltage simulation mode. For the I_{DDQ} simulation mode, GOLDENGATE achieves perfect accuracy as compared with the PSPICE simulation. A comparable speed ratio between GOLDENGATE and PSPICE is observed in the I_{DDQ} simulation mode. The same non-feedback BF set is targeted using a mixed-mode BF simulator EPROOFS with ALVL=1, a pin error count of 10 and pass error count of 7 were observed in comparison with PSPICE. Therefore GOLDENGATE presents very similar accuracy to that of EPROOFS. The speed ratio of GOLDENGATE to EPROOFS is 86 in this experiment.

Table 1: GOLDENGATE accuracy verification with PSPICE using circuit s298.

Mode		Correct		Incorrect	
		F	NF	F	NF
Voltage	Pin	62,341	138,715	9	12
	Pass	3,127	6,953	5	8
I_{DDQ}		554	1,468	0	0

To understand which BFs may cause incorrect results, we classify the BFs as shown in Table 2 and Figure 5. It can be seen that most of the simulation problems were created by BFs between two cells close together in the circuit schematics as shown in Figure 5. Also a majority of the BFs that induce simulation errors are type C faults where simultaneous input switchings in gate Z are caused by the switching of outputs of gate X and Y. The simultaneous switching of input signals compromises the accuracy of the logic interpretation using threshold voltage, therefore can lead to simulation errors.

Table 2: Distribution for the bridges that cause incorrect results.

Mode	Feedback			Non-Feedback	
	Type A	Type B	Others	Type C	Others
Voltage	3	1	1	8	0
I_{DDQ}	0	0	0	0	0

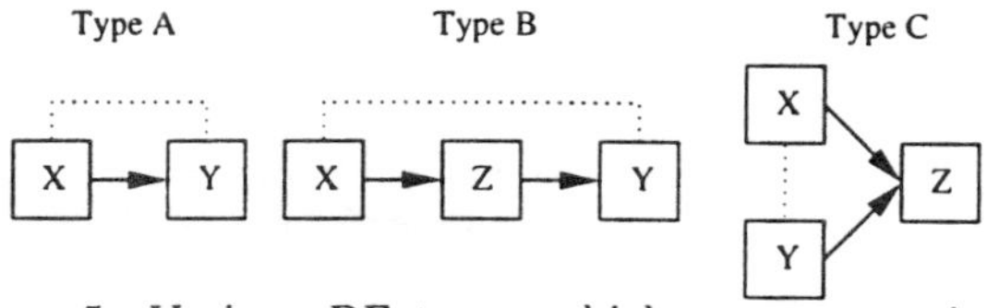

Figure 5: Various BF types which may cause simulation inaccuracies.

Having verified the accuracy of GOLDENGATE, simulations on ISCAS89 benchmark circuits were done using SSA test sets generated by HITEC[19] with results in Table 3. For circuits s5378, s9234.1, and s35932, the BF sets were generated randomly since we were not able to generate the layouts for these circuits. The only appreciable difference between a realistic BF set and a randomly generated BF set is that there are much less feedback BFs in a randomly generated BF set. In this experiment, two simulations were done for each circuit using the voltage mode and I_{DDQ} mode. BFs that involve the V_{DD}, GND, primary input, or flip-flop cell were not considered. For a proper comparison between the voltage and I_{DDQ} simulations modes, only those BFs that were detectable by logic testing were considered. In Table 3, the bridging faults and detection rates are divided into five subgroups with the totals in the "TTL" column. The five BF subgroups are: feedback routing (G1), feedback adjacency (G2), non-feedback routing (G3), non-feedback adjacency (G4) and non-feedback intra-cell (G5). In general, the detection rates for feedback BFs are slightly lower than that of the non-feedback ones because of oscillations caused by the feedback loop. Also, the detection rates for logic testing are, in some cases, low. However the detection rates for I_{DDQ} testing are usually high. This difference is caused by the high sensitivity associated with the I_{DDQ} testing and the difficulties of propagating the faulty effects to the primary output pins for the logic testing. The simulation CPU time are in the "T" columns. The memory requirement is dominated by the size of the BF list for large circuits and is approximately 20MB for the s35932 case with 230 thousand BFs.

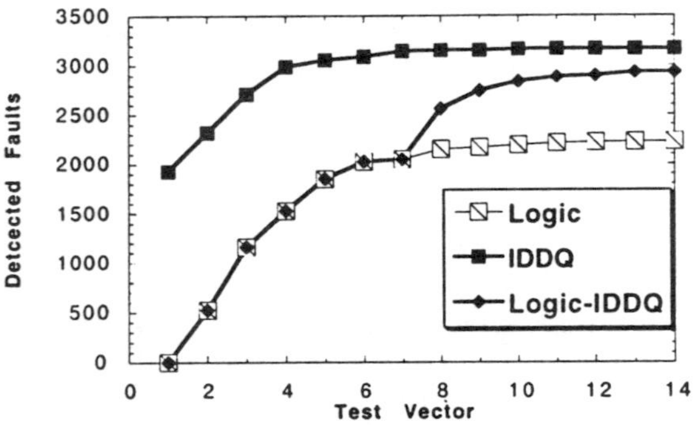

Figure 6: Fault detection pattern for various test schemes.

In [17], a hybrid (logic+I_{DDQ}) testing scheme was proposed for efficient detection of the bridging faults. In this hybrid testing scheme, a SSA test set was first used to filter out the BFs that could be detected by the logic testing and then the remaining undetected BFs were targeted by an I_{DDQ} test generator. This approach achieved high defect coverage with short I_{DDQ} test sets. A fully hybrid testing scheme allows mixed voltage and I_{DDQ} sensings. To support such a hybrid scheme, GOLDENGATE allows mixed voltage/I_{DDQ} simulation. Figure 6 shows the fault detection curves for three different testing schemes, namely "pure logic", "pure I_{DDQ}", and "hybrid (Logic+I_{DDQ})" for circuit s953 using 14 test vectors. For the pure logic(I_{DDQ}) scheme, all test vectors were simulated under the voltage(I_{DDQ}) mode; for the hybrid scheme, first 7 test vectors were simulated under voltage mode and the remaining 7 vectors were simulated under I_{DDQ} mode. As can be seen in Figure 6, the pure I_{DDQ} scheme produces the best overall detection rate, the pure logic scheme is more economical with fast test speed. The hybrid scheme has the benefit of a higher detection rate than that of the logic testing and shorter testing time than that of the I_{DDQ} testing.

5 Conclusion

In this paper, we described GOLDENGATE, a bridging fault simulator for cell-based digital VLSI circuits with the following features: 1. It targets both combinational and sequential circuits. 2. It handles general (routing, adjacency, and intra-cell) realistic bridging faults through an efficient table-based scheme. 3. It simulates both feedback and non-feedback BFs through a cycling event-driven simulation technique. 4. It allows mixed voltage and I_{DDQ} simulation thus enables fault simulation under a fully hybrid test environment where mixed logic and I_{DDQ} sensings are allowed. Experimental results showed GOLDENGATE to be both accurate and fast.

References

[1] F. J. Ferguson, J. P. Shen, W. Maly, "Inductive fault analysis of nMOS and CMOS integrated circuits," Deptartment of Electrical and Computer Engineering, Carnegie Mellon University, Pittsburg, August, 1985.

[2] M. Calha, M. Santos, F. Gonçalves, J. P. Teixeira, "Back annotation of physical defects into gate-level, realistic faults in digital ICs," *IEEE International Test Conference (ITC)*, pp. 720–728, 1994.

[3] K. C. Y. Mei, "Bridging and stuck-at faults," *IEEE Transactions on Computers*, pp. 720–727, 1974.

[4] M. Abramovici and P. Menon, "A practical approach to fault simulation and test generation for bridging faults," *IEEE Transactions on Computes*, pp. 658–663, 1985.

[5] J. M. Acken and S. D. Millman, "Accurate modeling and simulation of bridging faults," *IEEE Custom Integrated Circuit Conference (CICC)*, pp. 17.4.1-17.4.4, 1991.

[6] B. Chess and T. Larrabee, "Bridging fault simulation strategies for CMOS integrated circuits," *ACM/IEEE Design Automation Conference (DAC)*, pp. 458-462, 1993.

[7] J. M. Acken and S. D. Millman, "Fault model evolution for diagnosis: accuracy vs. precision," *IEEE Custom Integrated Circuit Conference (CICC)*, pp. 13.4.1-13.4.4, 1992.

[8] J. Rearick, and J. H. Patel, "Fast and accurate CMOS bridging fault simulation," *IEEE International Test Conference (ITC)*, pp. 54-62, 1993.

[9] R. E. Bryant, "COSMOS: A compiled simulator for CMOS circuits," *ACM/IEEE Design Automation Conference (DAC)*, pp. 9–16, 1987.

[10] D. G. Saab, R. B. Mueller-Thuns, D. Blaauw, J. A. Abraham, and J. T. Rahmeh, "Champ: Concurrent hierarchical and multilevel program for simulation of VLSI circuits," *IEEE International Conference on Computer-Aided Design (ICCAD)*, pp. 246–249, 1988.

[11] T. Lee and I. Hajj, "A switch-level matrix approach to transistor-level fault simulation," *IEEE International Conference on Computer-Aided Design (ICCAD)*, pp. 554–557, 1991.

[12] W. Nagle, "SPICE2: A computer program to simulate semiconductor circuits," Ph.D. Dissertation, University of California at Berkeley, 1975.

[13] G. S. Greenstein and J. H. Patel, "EPROOFS: A CMOS bridging fault simulator," *IEEE International Conference on Computer-Aided Design (ICCAD)*, pp. 268–271, 1992.

[14] W. Chuang and I. Hajj, "Fast mixed-mode simulation for accurate MOS bridging fault detection," *IEEE International Symposium on Circuits and Systems*, pp. 1503–1506, 1993.

[15] C. Di and A. G. Jess, "An efficient CMOS bridging fault simulator: with SPICE accuracy," *IEEE Transactions on Computer-Aided Design of Integrated Circuits and Syste ms*, Vol. 15, No. 9, pp. 1072–1080, 1996.

[16] T. Chen and I. Hajj, "A hierarchical fault extraction approach for VLSI circuit layouts," *International Symposium on VLSI Technology, Systems, and Applications*, June, 1997

[17] T. Chen, I. N. Hajj, E. M. Rudnick, J. H. Patel, "An efficient I_{DDQ} test generation scheme for bridging faults in CMOS digital circuits," *IEEE International Workshop on I_{DDQ} Testing*, pp. 74–78, 1996.

[18] "MicroSim PSpice A/D reference manual version 6.3a," MicroSim Corporation, 1996.

[19] T. M. Niermann and J. H. Patel, "HITEC: A test generation package for sequential circuits," *European Conference on Design Automation (EDAC)*, pp. 214–218, Feb. 1991.

Ckt	Vtr	Realistic Bridging Faults						Voltage Sim. Mode for Logic Test							I_{DDQ} Sim. Mode for I_{DDQ} Test						
		Feedback		Nonfeedback			TTL	Detection Rate (%)						T	Detection Rate (%)						T
								Feedback		Nonfeedback			TTL		Feedback		Nonfeedback			TTL	
		G1	G2	G3	G4	G5		G1	G2	G3	G4	G5			G1	G2	G3	G4	G5		
s298	259	116	88	65	30	51	350	90.5	85.2	98.5	96.7	100	92.6	4s	98.3	100	100	96.7	100	99.1	1s
s344	108	198	133	126	32	53	542	83.8	94.7	98.4	96.9	100	92.3	4s	88.4	99.2	100	96.9	100	95.4	1s
s349	117	209	120	149	36	54	568	85.6	93.3	98.7	100	100	92.6	4s	89.0	97.5	100	100	100	95.4	2s
s953	14	947	166	2,362	80	89	3,644	60.2	39.8	62.7	51.3	77.5	61.1	9s	83.9	93.4	87.3	83.8	98.9	86.9	3s
s1196	460	855	479	1,964	144	223	3,665	93.8	98.3	99.9	97.2	100	98.2	29s	98.9	99.6	100	100	100	99.7	7s
s1238	478	910	511	1,953	175	254	3,803	93.2	97.3	99.7	98.3	100	97.8	35s	99.6	100	100	100	100	99.9	9s
s5378	900	45	11	1,685	516	540	2,797	82.2	90.9	85.5	62.2	70.2	78.2	109s	100	100	97.6	95.9	88.7	95.6	31s
s9234.1	21	288	183	10,620	6,931	4,984	23,006	28.5	8.7	17.3	9.7	9.3	13.3	153s	83.3	80.3	91.7	88.0	78.7	87.6	38s
s35932	381	337	99	155,009	52,542	22,572	230,559	62.3	73.7	90.4	92.2	88.8	90.6	335m	95.3	99.0	99.9	99.9	98.6	99.8	36m

Table 3: GOLDENGATE simulation results for ISCAS89 benchmark circuits.

A Deductive Technique for Diagnosis of Bridging Faults

Srikanth Venkataraman
Coordinated Science Laboratory
University of Illinois, Urbana, IL 61801

W. Kent Fuchs
School of Electrical and Computer Engineering
Purdue University, West Lafayette, IN 47907-1285

Abstract

A deductive technique is presented that uses voltage testing for the diagnosis of single bridging faults between two gate input or output lines and is applicable to combinational or full-scan sequential circuits. For defects in this class of faults the method is accurate by construction while making no assumptions about the logic-level wired-AND/OR behavior. A path-trace procedure starting from failing outputs deduces potential lines associated with the bridge. The information obtained from the path-trace from failing outputs is combined using an intersection graph to make further deductions. All candidate faults are implicitly represented, thereby obviating the need to enumerate faults and hence allowing the exploration of the space of all faults. Results are provided for all large ISCAS89 benchmark circuits.

1 Introduction

A *bridging fault* [1] between two lines A and B in a circuit occurs when the two lines are unintentionally shorted. When the lines A and B have different logic values, the gates driving the lines will be engaged in a drive fight (logic contention). Depending on the gates driving the lines A and B, their input values, and the resistance of the bridge, the bridged lines can have intermediate voltage values V_A and V_B (not well defined logic values of 1 or 0). This is interpreted by the logic that fans out from the bridge as shown in the shaded region in Figure 1 (a).

The logic gates downstream from the bridged nodes can have variable input logic thresholds. Thus the intermediate voltage at a bridged node may be interpreted differently by different gates. This is known as the *Byzantine Generals Problem* [2, 3] and is illustrated in Figure 1 (b). The voltage at the node A (V_A) is interpreted as a faulty value (0) by gate d and a good value (1) by gate c. Thus, different branches from a single fanout stem can have different logic values.

The feasibility of any diagnosis scheme can be evaluated using the parameters: *accuracy, precision, storage requirements* and *computational complexity*. Accurate simulation of bridging faults [4, 3] is computationally expensive. Thus, it may not be feasible to perform bridging fault simulation during diagnosis. Further, the space of all bridging faults is extremely large. For example, for the large ISCAS89 benchmark circuits, it is of the order of 10^9 faults.

Several techniques have been proposed for the diagnosis of bridging faults in combinational circuits using voltage testing. Millman, McCluskey and Acken [5] presented an approach to diagnose bridging faults using stuck-at dictionaries. Chess et al. [6], and Lavo et al. [7] improved on this technique. These techniques enumerate bridging faults and are hence constrained to using a reduced set of bridging faults extracted from the layout. Further, the construction and *storage requirements* of fault dictionaries may be prohibitive. Chakravarty and Gong [8] describe a voltage-based algorithm that uses the wired-AND (wired-OR) model and stuck-at fault dictionaries. The wired-AND and wired-OR models work only for technologies for which one logic value is always more strongly driven than the other.

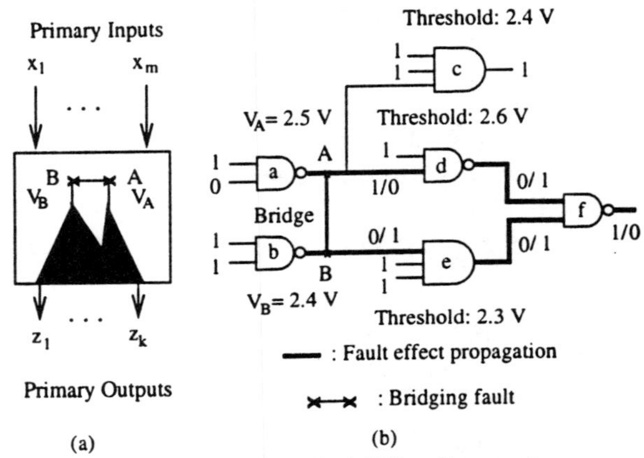

Figure 1: Bridging Fault Effect Propagation

In this paper we present a deductive technique that does not require fault dictionaries and does not explicitly simulate faults, either stuck-at or bridging. Further, no model such as wired-AND or wired-OR is assumed at the logic-level. The class of bridging faults considered are all single bridging faults between two lines in the circuit. The lines could be gate outputs, gate inputs, or primary inputs. For defects in this class of faults, the method is accurate in that the defect is guaranteed to be in the candidate list. In the following, a *failing vector* and a *failing output* refer to a vector and a primary output that fail the test on a tester (not during simulation). The deductive technique consists of two deductive procedures. The first is a path-trace procedure that starts from failing outputs and uses the logic values obtained by the logic simulation of the good circuit for each failing vector. This is used to deduce lines potentially associated with the bridging faults. The second procedure is an intersection graph constructed from the information obtained through path-tracing from failing outputs. The path-trace and the intersection graph are constructed and processed dynamically during diagnosis. The intersection graph implicitly represents all candidate bridging faults under consideration, thereby allowing pro-

This research was supported in part by Defense Advanced Research Projects Agency (DARPA) under contract DABT 63-96-C-0069, by the Semiconductor Research Corporation (SRC) under grant 95-DP-109, by the Office of Naval Research (ONR) under grant N00014-95-1-1049, and by an equipment grant from Hewlett-Packard.

1092-3152/97 $10.00 © 1997 IEEE

cessing of the entire space of all bridging faults in an implicit manner. During diagnosis, a reduced version of the graph is maintained that retains all diagnostic information. This reduces memory usage and simulation time. Since the technique uses only logic simulation and does not explicitly simulate faults, it is fast. The technique outputs a list of candidate faults. If the resolution (the size of the candidate list) is adequate, the diagnosis is complete. Otherwise, either the candidate list can be simulated with a bridging fault simulator or other techniques [5, 6, 7, 8] can be used to improve the resolution.

2 The Path-Trace Procedure

The path-trace procedure deduces lines in the circuit that are potentially associated with a bridging fault. A *potential source of error* with respect to a failing output is defined as follows.

Definition 1 *A* **potential source of error**, *with respect to a failing output, is a line in the circuit from which there exists a sensitized path to that failing output on the application of the corresponding failing vector.*

Note that there is a distinction between potential sources of error and the actual source(s) of error associated with the defect. In the following, the actual source(s) of error are simply referred to as the source(s) of error. The path-trace procedure is similar to *critical path tracing* [9], and *star algorithm* [10]. However, there are some important differences. The above procedures were developed for single stuck-at faults. Hence, only one line in the circuit is assumed to be faulty. However, for bridging faults, due to the Byzantine Generals Problem, both lines could be sources of fault effects. Further, these effects may reconverge, leading to effects such as multiple-path sensitization as shown in Figure 1 (b). The voltages at lines A (V_A) and B (V_B) are both interpreted as faulty by gates d and e, and the fault effect reconverges at gate f. However, the assumption of a single bridging fault between two lines ensures that at most two lines in the circuit can be sources of error.

The logic-value of a gate input is said to be *controlling* if it determines the gate's output value regardless of other input values [11]. The path-trace procedure proceeds as follows. Start from a failing output and process the lines of the circuit in a reverse topological order up to the inputs. When a gate output is reached, observe the input values. If all inputs have noncontrolling values, continue the trace from all inputs. If one or more inputs have controlling values, continue the trace from any one controlling input. When a fanout branch is reached, continue tracing from the stem. The choice in selecting the controlling value can be exploited, as will be explained later.

We first consider the case of a single line being the source of error for a failing output, and then consider the case where both lines of a bridging fault are sources of error for a failing output. Consider a single line being the source of errors on a failing vector. When reconvergent fanout exists, the following situations could occur. In Figure 2 (a), the effects of an error from the stem c propagate to the output. However, if the paths have different parities, they will cancel each other when they reconverge. This is referred to as *self-masking* [9]. Figure 2 (b) shows an example of *multiple path sensitization* [9]. The bold lines indicate error propagation. The error from line c propagates through two paths before reconverging and propagating to an output.

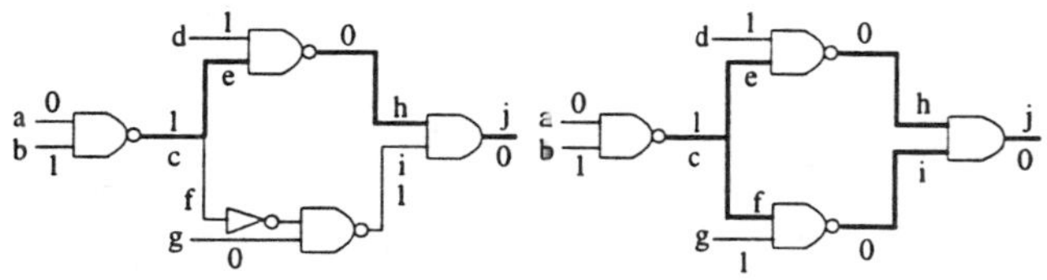

Figure 2: Reconvergent Fanout with Single Source of Error

Lemma 1 *On any failing vector, the path-trace procedure includes all potential sources of error with respect to the failing outputs, assuming there is a single source of error.*

Proof: When the path-trace reaches a fanout branch, it continues from the stem. Hence, if the stem were a source of error, it would be included. If a gate has multiple controlling values on its inputs, then fault effects can propagate through this gate only if there exists a stem from which errors reconverge at this gate to collectively change all the controlling values. When the path-trace reaches this gate, it will continue along one of the lines having controlling values. Hence it will include the stem. □

Lemma 1 can be interpreted as follows. If the defect causes a single line to be faulty on some failing vector and this fault effect propagates to some failing output, then the path-trace includes all lines that are sensitized to that failing output. The path-trace procedure is conservative with respect to single sources of error. Not all lines in the path-trace may be potential sources of error. For example, line h in Figure 2 (b) is not a potential source of error but would be included in the path-trace. However, this conservative approach is necessary when both lines of a bridging fault could be sources of error with respect to some failing output. Note that for a single source of error, the potential sources of error are the same as critical lines [9] in the circuit. Next, we consider the case where both lines of a bridging fault are sources of error on some failing vector. If there exists at least one path between the lines of a bridging fault, then the bridging fault creates one or more feedback loops. Such a fault is referred to as a *feedback bridging fault* [11]. If no paths exist between the lines of a bridging fault, then it is called a *nonfeedback bridging fault*. A feedback bridging fault may cause *oscillations* to occur if the input vector creates a sensitized path from one line of the bridging fault to the other and this path has odd inversion parity. If such oscillations are detectable by the tester, then they can be used as additional failing outputs for the path-trace procedure. The following Lemma, Theorem and Corollary are applicable to both feedback and nonfeedback bridging faults. The symbol $A@B$ is used to represent a bridging fault.

Lemma 2 *If a bridging fault $A@B$ causes fault effect propagation to an output due to reconvergence of bridging fault effects from both lines of the bridging fault, then the path-trace procedure starting from that failing output will include at least one of the lines of the bridging fault.*

Proof: At the reconvergent gate, there exist one or more controlling input values. The path-trace continues from one of the lines with controlling input value. Thus, one of the lines of the bridging fault is covered by the path-trace. □

A case of Lemma 2 is illustrated in Figure 3. The output of gate e fails. Path-trace starts from this output and proceeds to the inputs. Since gate e has two controlling inputs, the trace continues from one of them. Node B, which is part of the bridging fault $A@B$, is covered by the path-trace.

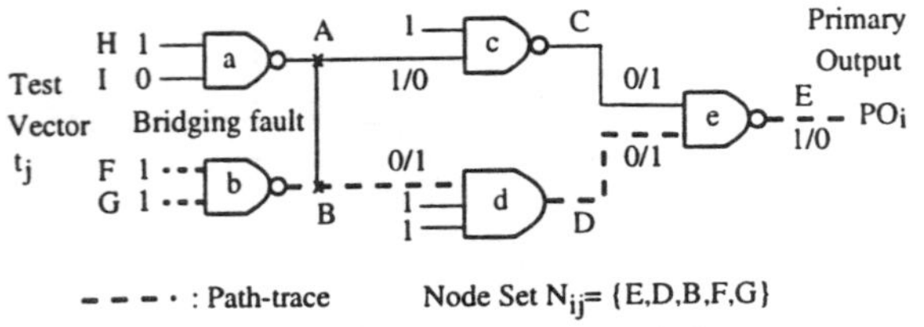

Figure 3: Path-Trace and Node Set

Definition 2 *The* **node set** N_{ij} *is defined as the set of lines that lie on the path-trace starting from failing output* PO_i *under the application of test-vector* t_j.

Theorem 1 *If neither line A nor line B of a bridging fault A@B is in a node set* N_{ij}, *then the fault A@B could not have caused output* PO_i *to fail under test vector* t_j.

Proof: [By contradiction] Assume that the bridging fault $A@B$ caused an output PO_i to fail on some test-vector t_j. This implies that there exists a sensitized path from A, or B, or the interaction of fault effects from both A and B, to the primary output PO_i under the application of test-vector t_j. If neither line A nor line B is in N_{ij}, then due to Lemmas 1 and 2, there exists no sensitized path to PO_i. This leads to a contradiction. □

Corollary 1 *If the defect is a single bridging fault A@B, then a node set* N_{ij} *must contain at least one of the lines A and B.*

Proof: Follows directly from Theorem 1. □

Note that Theorem 1 and Corollary 1 are conservative in that they make no assumptions about the resistance of the bridging fault, the gates feeding the bridging fault and their input values, and the logic input thresholds of the gates downstream from the bridging fault. The only assumption made is the presence of a single bridging fault. The information from a group of node sets can be used to make further deductions. This is performed using the concept of an *intersection graph.*

3 The Intersection Graph and Its Processing

Given a group of node sets $\{N_{ij}\}$ the intersection graph is defined as follows.

Definition 3 *The* intersection graph *is a simple undirected graph (no loops or multiple edges)* $G_I = (V_I, E_I)$ *with a vertex set* $V_I = \{N_{ij} \mid N_{ij} \text{ is a node set}\}$ *and edge* $(N_{ij}, N_{kl}) \in E$ *if* $(((i \neq k)$ *or* $(j \neq l))$ *and* $(N_{ij} \cap N_{kl} \neq \phi))$.

Figure 4 shows an intersection graph with 7 vertices. The corresponding node sets are shown within the curly brackets. The intersection graph has similar structure to the initialization graph proposed by Chakravarty and Gong [8]. However, there are important differences. The initialization graph is constructed using only structural information while the intersection graph is constructed using logic information exploited by the path-trace procedure. The initialization graph is created statically once before diagnosis and processed. However, the intersection graph is updated and processed dynamically during diagnosis. A reduction procedure maintains a reduced version of the graph without losing diagnostic information. The intersection graph has interesting structural properties that are useful for performing deduction and for maintaining reduced graphs to help reduce memory requirements and simulation time.

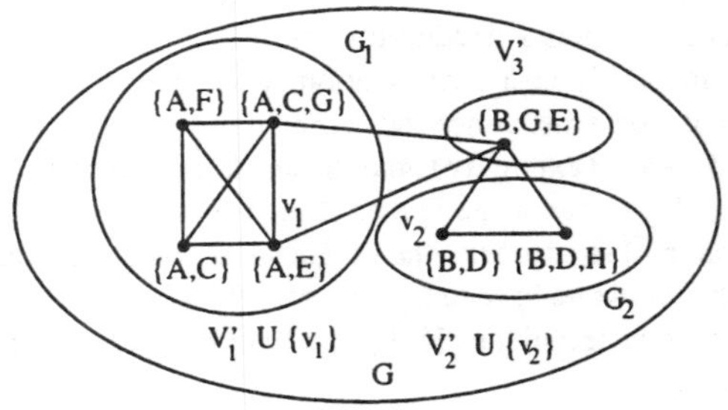

Figure 4: Intersection Graph and Its Properties

3.1 Structural Properties

Property 1 *If* G_I *has two vertices such that* $(v_1, v_2) \notin E_I$. *The set of vertices* $V_I' = V_I - \{v_1, v_2\}$ *can be partitioned into three sets* V_1', V_2' *and* V_3' *such that* $\forall v_1' \in V_1'$, $(v_1', v_1) \in E_I$ *and* $(v_1', v_2) \notin E_I$; $\forall v_2' \in V_2'$, $(v_2', v_1) \notin E_I$ *and* $(v_2', v_2) \in E_I$; $\forall v_3' \in V_3'$, $(v_3', v_1) \in E_I$ *and* $(v_3', v_2) \in E_I$.

Proof: Let N_{ij}^1 and N_{ij}^2 be the node sets corresponding to v_1 and v_2. From Corollary 1, N_{ij}^1 and N_{ij}^2 contain at least one of the lines of the bridging fault $A@B$. Since $(v_1, v_2) \notin E_I$, N_{ij}^1 contains only one of the lines A and B (say A). This implies that N_{ij}^2 contains the other line (B). Consider any arbitrary vertex $v_3 \in V_I' = V_I - \{v_1, v_2\}$. From Corollary 1 it follows that the node set corresponding to v_3 contains at least one of the lines A and B. Thus v_3 is adjacent to at least one of v_1 and v_2. This implies that one of the following three conditions holds: v_3 is adjacent to v_1 and not adjacent to v_2; v_3 is adjacent to v_2 and not adjacent to v_1; v_3 is adjacent to both v_1 and v_2. □

Property 2 *If* V_1', V_2', *and* V_3' *are the three sets obtained by Property 1 when* $(v_1, v_2) \notin E_I$, *then* $V_1' \cup \{v_1\}$ *and* $V_2' \cup \{v_2\}$ *are cliques.*

Proof: From Corollary 1 and Property 1 it follows that the node sets corresponding to every $v_i \in V_1' \cup \{v_1\}$ contain one and only one of A and B (say A), while the node sets corresponding to every $v_j \in V_2' \cup \{v_2\}$ contain the other line (B). Thus $V_1' \cup \{v_1\}$ and $V_2' \cup \{v_2\}$ are cliques. □

Figure 4 illustrates these properties. The intersection graphs can be reduced while maintaining their properties. This reduces the number of vertices and edges. Further, this also reduces the number of node sets that need to be maintained and their sizes. Thus the reduction process, which is done dynamically during diagnosis, can help reduce memory and simulation time. The following Corollary, which follows from Property 2, is used in the reduction process.

Corollary 2 *If the intersection graph is not a clique, and* $G_1 = (V_1, E_1)$ *and* $G_2 = (V_2, E_2)$ *are the subgraphs induced by* $V_1' \cup \{v_1\}$ *and* $V_2' \cup \{v_2\}$ *respectively using Property 1, then all node sets in* V_1 *contain only one of the lines A or B of the bridge, while all the node sets in* V_2 *contain the other line.*

3.2 Intersection Graph Processing

Corollary 2 is used by the procedure shown in Figure 5 to reduce the intersection graph. An irreducible intersection graph is either a complete graph or has the following characteristic. For each $(v_i, v_j) \notin E_I$, the V_1' and V_2' sets are empty. An example of the reduction procedure is shown in Figure 6. The initial intersection

$G_I = (V_I, E_I)$: The intersection graph
$V(N_{ij})$: Vertex corresponding to node set N_{ij}
Procedure Reduce_Intersection_Graph(G_I)
while (!irreducible)
  if (!$clique(G_I)$)
    Let $(v_1, v_2) \notin E_I$
    // Possible to find v_1, v_2 since G_I is not a clique
    $V_1' = \{v_i \mid (v_i, v_1) \in E_I$ and $(v_i, v_2) \notin E_I\}$
    $V_2' = \{v_j \mid (v_j, v_2) \in E_I$ and $(v_j, v_1) \notin E_I\}$
    // By Property 2 and Corollary 2
    if $(V_1' \neq \phi)$
      $N^1_{reduced} = \cap N_{ij}\ \forall V(N_{ij}) \in V_1' \cup \{v_1\}$
    if $(V_2' \neq \phi)$
      $N^2_{reduced} = \cap N_{ij}\ \forall V(N_{ij}) \in V_2' \cup \{v_2\}$
    Replace $v_i \in V_1' \cup \{v_1\}$ with $V(N^1_{reduced}) = v_1'$
    Replace $v_j \in V_2' \cup \{v_2\}$ with $V(N^2_{reduced}) = v_2'$
    Recompute edges incident on v_1' and v_2'

Figure 5: Procedure for Reducing the Intersection Graph

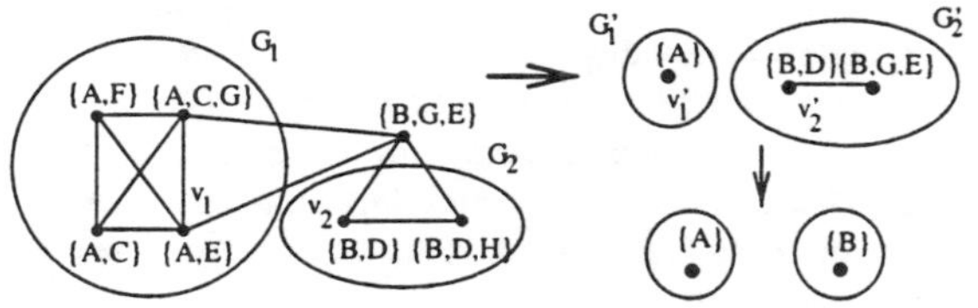

(a) Initial intersection graph (b) Reduced intersection graph

Figure 6: An Example of the Intersection Graph Reduction

graph is reduced two times to obtain an irreducible graph with two disjoint vertices. The dynamic processing of G_I proceeds as follows. After each node set N_{ij} is obtained, update G_I. Reduce the intersection graph until an irreducible graph is obtained. After all node sets are processed, the irreducible intersection graph obtained contains the candidate bridging faults. The candidate list (C) is obtained from the irreducible graph (G_{IR}) using the following rules.

1. If G_{IR} has two disconnected components, each of which has one vertex, then let N^1_{ij} and N^2_{ij} be the node sets associated with the two vertices. $C = \{A@B \mid A \in N^1_{ij}$ and $B \in N^2_{ij}\}$.
2. If G_{IR} has one component that is not a complete graph, then for each $(v_1, v_2) \notin E$ let N^1_{ij} and N^2_{ij} be the node sets associated with v_1 and v_2. $C_k = \{A@B \mid A \in N^1_{ij}$ and $B \in N^2_{ij}\}$. $C = \cap_{\forall k} C_k$.
3. If G_{IR} is a complete graph, then let $|N_{ij}| \leq |N_{kl}| \forall N_{ij}, N_{kl} \in V$. $C = \{A@B \mid A \in N_{ij}\}$.

The reduced intersection graph is a compact way to implicitly represent the space of candidate bridging faults. Further, the reduction procedure prunes the space of candidate bridging faults without losing diagnostic information. The defect is guaranteed to be in the candidate list by construction. The candidate list will include other faults which are logically equivalent or diagnostically equivalent with respect to the test set. A better test set may distinguish between some of these faults, thereby increasing the diagnostic resolution. When G_{IR} is a complete graph, only one of the lines of the bridge can be determined with certainty. This results in a *partial diagnosis*. The experimental results indicate that partial diagnosis does not occur often.

3.3 Implementation Issues and Complexity

The major operation performed during G_I processing is its reduction. The basic operation needed by the reduction procedure is set intersection. Further, the node sets need to be stored for each vertex of G_I. The node sets are represented as bit-vectors with a value of 1 indicating the presence of a node and a 0 indicating the absence of one. If there are n lines in the circuit, the size of a node set is $\lceil n/8 \rceil$ bytes. The bit vector representation allows for efficient set intersection using the bitwise AND operator. As a result of the dynamic processing of G_I, its size grows and shrinks. Hence, the data structure chosen to represent G_I is a two-dimensional linked list. G_I has $|V_I|$ vertices. Assuming 4 bytes each for pointers and vertex indices, the worst-case memory requirement for G_I and its associated node sets is $(|V_I| \times \lceil n/8 \rceil + 8|V_I| + 8|V_I|^2)$ bytes. Since $|V_I|$ is typically much smaller than n, the worst-case space complexity is $O(|V_I| \times n)$. The worst-case size of $|V_I|$ is n_{fail}, where n_{fail} is the total number of failing outputs on all failing vectors. The reduction procedure results in $|V_I|$ being much smaller than n_{fail}, thereby reducing the memory requirements.

The reduction procedure computes the V_1' and V_2' sets based on Corollary 2 by exploring the edges of $\overline{E_I}$. Typically, $|\overline{E_I}|$ is small. For each edge in $\overline{E_I}$ the reduction procedure computes V_1' and V_2'. Each intersection operation between the node sets of two vertices of G_I reduces the number of vertices of G_I by 1. Thus the maximum number of intersections possible in the procedure $reduce\_intersection\_graph()$ is $|V_I| - 2$. Thus the worst-case time complexity for the procedure $reduce\_intersection\_graph()$ is $O(|V_I|)$ intersections. Here again, the reduction procedure results in small $|V_I|$ values, thereby reducing the simulation time.

4 Heuristics to Improve Resolution

When the path-tracing procedure reaches a gate with multiple controlling inputs, one of them is chosen. The choice of input impacts the size of the resultant node set, its elements, and hence, impacts the diagnostic resolution. The smaller the size of the node set, the smaller is the intersection with other node sets, and the greater is the likelihood of reducing the intersection graph. Two conditions are checked to select the controlling input in such a manner that the size of the resultant node set is reduced. The first is based on *fanout*. When the path-trace reaches a stem, it continues from the stem unconditionally. When a controlling input is the branch of a stem, one of whose other branches has been chosen, then this input should be selected, since the stem has to be selected anyway [10]. The second condition involves checking the *controllability* of the line. SCOAP controllability measures are used. The most easily controllable input (check for 0-controllability if the logic value of the line is 0 and vice-versa) is likely to give the smallest node set. If the same gate is reached in two different applications of the path-trace and the same choice of controlling inputs exists, then selecting different inputs for the two runs can potentially result in a smaller intersection between the two resultant node sets. A *dirty bit* is set when the path-trace chooses a controlling input. This input is avoided in future invocations of the path-trace procedure.

Based on the above conditions, three heuristics are defined below. *Heuristic 1* chooses controlling input randomly. *Heuristic 2* chooses controlling input by checking for fanout followed by controllability. *Heuristic 3* chooses controlling input by checking for dirty bit followed by fanout and then controllability. The overall diagnosis procedure is shown in Figure 7.

---

for each test vector t_i
    if faulty outputs
        Perform good circuit simulation with t_i
        for each failing output PO_j
            $N_{ij} \leftarrow$ path-trace from failing output PO_j
            $update\_intersection\_graph(G_I, N_{ij})$
            $reduce\_intersection\_graph(G_I)$
$output\_candidate\_list(G_I)$

Figure 7: The Diagnosis Procedure

5 Experimental Results

The diagnosis procedure was implemented in C++. All experiments were performed on a SUN SPARCStation 20 with 64MB of memory for the full-scan versions of the ISCAS89 sequential benchmark circuits [12]. In practice, the failing responses used as input for the diagnosis procedure would be obtained by testing the failing circuit on a tester. For our diagnosis experiments, the failing responses were generated using the accurate bridging fault simulator E-PROOFS [4] to ensure that the diagnostic experiments were as realistic as possible. The cell libraries for the circuits were generated manually [4]. The test vectors used were compact tests generated to target stuck-at faults [13]. Ideally, diagnostic test sets for bridging faults would be the best choice. All large ISCAS89 benchmark circuits were considered.

For each of the benchmark circuits, a random sample of 500 single two-line bridging faults were injected one at a time. For each one of these faults, the failing responses were obtained by performing bridging fault simulation on the given test set using E-PROOFS. Faults that do not produce any failing outputs were dropped. For the rest of the faults, the failing responses were used to perform diagnosis. The diagnosis results are summarized in Tables 1 and 2. The average, minimum and maximum sizes of the candidate lists are shown in Table 1 for the three different heuristics. The average size of the candidate list is a few hundred faults, which is a significant reduction from the space of all faults. Further, as expected, heuristics 2 and 3 improve the diagnostic resolution over heuristic 1. The reduction can be significant. For example, for s38584, the average size of the candidate list is reduced by a factor of 4. Note that in some cases, the method uniquely identifies the fault (resolution of 1). The best resolutions are indicated in bold.

The average sizes of the node sets and the intersection graph are shown in Figure 2. As expected, heuristic 2 does the best in terms of node set sizes. Both heuristic 2 and heuristic 3 do better than heuristic 1 in terms of the average size of the intersection graph. The average values of the execution time, number of failing outputs and percentage of faults that were partially diagnosed is given for heuristic 2. Other interesting observations can be made from Table 2. Note that the average size of the sets is very small and appears to be independent of the circuit size. Further, it is about 2–3 orders of magnitude smaller than the total number of lines in the circuit, thereby suggesting that the path-trace procedure is efficient. The average size of the intersection graph ($|V_I|$) is about a quarter of the total number of failing outputs, indicating that the graph reduction procedure is useful. As expected heuristic 2 does the best in terms of the average size of the node set and heuristic 3 does the best in terms of the average size of the intersection graph ($|V_I|$).

Note that the procedure is accurate by construction; that is, the defect is guaranteed to be in the candidate list. The distribution of the sizes of the candidate lists is shown in Figure 8 for s13207 and s38417. This trend is observed for the other circuits as well. For about 10% of the faults, the resolution is adequate (less than 20 candidates) to consider the diagnosis complete. For about 80% of the faults, the resolution is such (between 20 – 500 faults) that the candidate list is small enough to be accurately simulated using a bridging fault simulator as a post-processing step. In about 25% of the cases, the diagnosis is partial; that is, only one of the lines of the bridge can be determined with certainty. In such cases, and if the resolution is so large that bridging fault simulation cannot be performed, then the diagnosis procedure can be followed with other techniques [5, 6, 7, 8] using the candidate list to improve the resolution. Note that these resolutions were obtained using a compacted stuck-at test set. We expect that there would be better resolution with better test sets.

Table 1: Diagnostic Resolution

Circuit	Candidate List Size								
	Heuristic 1			Heuristic 2			Heuristic 3		
	Ave.	Min.	Max.	Ave.	Min.	Max.	Ave.	Min.	Max.
s1196f	125.2	1	1656	**60.7**	1	828	76.7	1	765
s1238f	123.0	1	1080	**62.7**	1	722	76.3	1	1092
s1423f	98.2	1	2303	**80.9**	1	3526	83.9	1	3526
s1488f	70.7	8	165	**65.7**	2	280	68.9	2	375
s1494f	74.5	4	120	**68.9**	2	140	71.8	2	140
s5378f	284.2	2	3243	203.2	1	1659	**194.2**	2	1386
s9234f	866.9	18	7848	**771.4**	12	7020	809.4	12	7020
s13207f	240.3	1	4199	167.8	1	3809	**160.5**	1	1328
s15850f	694.4	1	10206	679.4	1	9100	**557.3**	1	9178
s35932f	128.6	4	690	125.6	4	630	**115.4**	4	630
s38417f	280.4	1	2793	240.1	1	2842	**219.3**	1	2475
s38584f	743.5	48	2130	**191.6**	1	2288	204.2	1	2600

The diagnosis procedure requires very small execution times, as seen in column 8 of Table 2. The procedure requires only the logic simulation of failing vectors and the path-trace procedure from failing outputs. Both of these procedures are linear in the size of the circuit. Further, the graph reduction procedure is linear in the size of its vertex set ($|V_I|$). Techniques such as those used in [5, 6, 7, 8] require either the storage of stuck-at fault dictionaries or the simulation of stuck-at faults during diagnosis. As seen in columns 12 and 13 of Table 2, the storage requirements for dictionaries can be very large, and the simulation time is about an order of magnitude larger than that required for the diagnosis procedure. This is expected since fault simulation has greater than linear complexity in the size of the circuit. Further, fault simulation without fault dropping needs to be performed. Techniques such as those used in [5, 6, 7] also need to enumerate bridging faults and are hence constrained to use a small set of realistic faults. This trade-off between resolution and complexity suggests that our diagnosis procedure, which is both space- and time-efficient, could be attempted first, and then be complemented by other procedures if greater resolution is required.

Table 2: Diagnosis Results and Comparison with Techniques Using Stuck-at Fault Information

Circuit	Average Size of Node Set			Average $\|V_I\|$			Average Values (Heuristic 2)			Stuck-at fault Information		
	Heu.1	Heu.2	Heu.3	Heu.1	Heu.2	Heu.3	Exec. Time (s)	# Fail POs	Partial Diag. (%)	# of Faults	Storage † (Bytes)	Exec. Time ‡ Fault Sim. (s)
s1196f	32.3	**22.7**	25.3	23.6	20.5	**19.9**	0.28	71.8	0.24	1242	0.57 M	4.25
s1238f	30.6	**22.7**	24.9	27.5	25.2	**23.6**	0.35	77.3	0.25	1355	0.67 M	4.63
s1423f	28.8	25.1	**24.9**	7.8	**6.9**	7.1	0.11	26.1	0.12	1515	0.38 M	1.51
s1488f	35.6	**29.2**	30.6	20.6	20.6	**19.5**	0.23	42.8	0.28	1486	0.47 M	4.13
s1494f	29.5	**20.9**	25.2	14.9	11.4	**10.7**	0.20	27.5	0.24	1506	0.47 M	4.08
s5378f	52.9	**48.7**	49.5	13.9	13.4	**13.2**	1.32	66.5	0.22	4603	24.6 M	16.01
s9234f	40.2	**36.3**	37.0	18.7	19.3	**19.3**	2.32	65.4	0.35	6927	47.1 M	34.61
s13207f	29.6	28.2	**27.4**	62.5	58.2	**27.4**	31.1	298.3	0.16	12311	0.51 G	131.55
s15850f	68.8	**62.5**	66.3	21.6	**22.0**	24.6	7.43	92.3	0.28	11725	0.17 G	62.70
s35932f	20.1	18.4	**17.6**	3.7	3.6	**3.6**	6.4	8.5	0.34	46006	0.24 G	35.71
s38417f	46.4	**38.2**	38.9	11.6	11.5	**11.5**	25.0	61.6	0.14	31180	1.13 G	151.30
s38584f	38.9	**28.7**	29.4	31.3	**28.7**	29.4	30.4	64.9	0.38	36303	1.56 G	214.51

† Full fault dictionary in matrix format
‡ w/o fault dropping

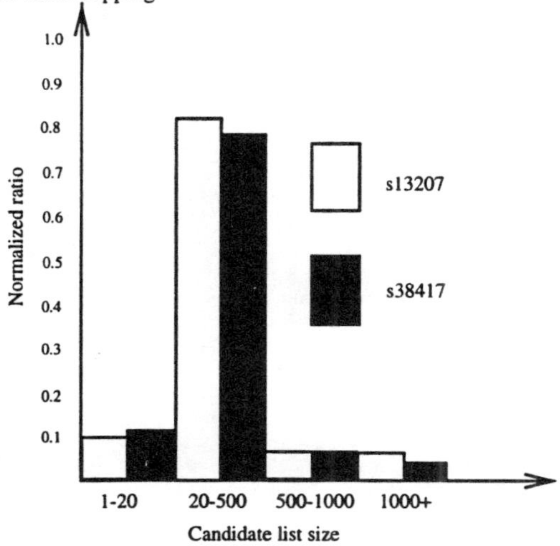

Figure 8: Distribution of Candidate List Size

6 Conclusions and Future Work

A deductive procedure for the diagnosis of bridging faults, which is accurate and experimentally shown to be both space- and time-efficient, has been described. The information obtained from a path-trace procedure from failing outputs is combined using an intersection graph, which is constructed and processed dynamically, to make the deduction. The intersection graph provides an implicit means of representing and processing the space of candidate bridging faults without using dictionaries or explicit fault simulation. The procedure assumes a single bridging fault between two lines. If the defect involves multiple faults or shorts between multiple lines, then the properties of G_I may be violated. Extensions to multiple faults or shorts between multiple lines require looking for larger sized cliques (K_n, $n \geq 3$) in the graph $\overline{G_I}$. An interesting application of this work is in the area of design error location. For design errors of multiplicity 2, the diagnosis procedure can be used without any modification. Higher multiplicity errors require extensions.

References

[1] K. C. Y. Mei, "Bridging and Stuck-at Faults," *IEEE Tran. on Computers*, vol. C-23(7), pp. 720–727, July 1974.

[2] J. M. Acken and S. D. Millman, "Fault Model Evolution for Diagnosis: Accuracy vs. Precision," in *Proc. of the Custom Integrated Circuits Conf.*, pp. 13.4.1–13.4.4, 1992.

[3] P. C. Maxwell and R. C. Aitken, "Biased Voting: A Method for Simulating CMOS Bridging Faults in the Presence of Variable Gate Logic Thresholds," in *Proc. of the IEEE Intl. Test Conf.*, pp. 63–72, Oct. 1993.

[4] G. S. Greenstein and J. H. Patel, "E-PROOFS: A CMOS Bridging Fault Simulator," in *Proc. of the IEEE/ACM Intl. Conf. on Computer-Aided Design*, pp. 268–271, Nov. 1992.

[5] S. D. Millman, E. J. McCluskey, and J. M. Acken, "Diagnosing CMOS Bridging Faults with Stuck-at Fault Dictionaries," in *Proc. of the IEEE Intl. Test Conf.*, pp. 860–870, Oct. 1990.

[6] B. Chess, D. B. Lavo, F. J. Ferguson, and T. Larrabee, "Diagnosing of Realistic Bridging Faults with Stuck-at Information," in *Proc. of the IEEE/ACM Intl. Conf. on Computer-Aided Design*, pp. 185–192, Nov. 1995.

[7] D. B. Lavo, T. Larrabee, and B. Chess, "Beyond the Byzantine Generals: Unexpected Behavior and Bridging Faults Diagnosis," in *Proc. of the IEEE Intl. Test Conf.*, pp. 611–619, Oct. 1996.

[8] S. Chakravarty and Y. Gong, "An Algorithm for Diagnosing Two-Line Bridging Faults in CMOS Combinational Circuits," in *Proc. of the Design Automation Conf.*, pp. 520–524, June 1993.

[9] P. R. Menon, Y. Levendel, and M. Abramovici, "SCRIPT: A Critical Path Tracing Algorithm for Synchronous Sequential Circuits," *IEEE Tran. on Computer Aided Design*, vol. 10, pp. 738–747, June 1991.

[10] S. B. Akers, B. Krishnamurthy, S. Park, and A. Swaminathan, "Why is Less Information From Logic Simulation More Useful in Fault Simulation?," in *Proc. of the IEEE Intl. Test Conf.*, pp. 786–800, Sept. 1990.

[11] M. Abramovici, M. A. Breuer, and A. D. Friedman, *Digital System Testing and Testable Design*. AT&T Bell Laboratories and W. H. Freeman and Company, 1990.

[12] F. Brglez, D. Bryan, and K. Kozminski, "Combinational Profiles of Sequential Benchmark Circuits," *IEEE Intl. Symp. on Circuits and Systems*, pp. 1929–1934, May 1989.

[13] S. Kajihara, I. Pomeranz, K. Kinoshita, and S. M. Reddy, "Cost-Effective Generation of Minimal Test Sets for Stuck-at Faults in Combinational Logic Circuits," *IEEE Tran. on Computer Aided Design*, vol. 14, pp. 1496–1504, December 1995.

Session 10A

Logic Synthesis for Low Power

Moderators:

Jordi Cortadella, University Politecnica de Catalunya, Barcelona, Spain

Luciano Lavagno, Politecnico di Torino, Torino, Italy

Low Power Logic Synthesis for XOR Based Circuits *

Unni Narayanan C. L. Liu

Department of Computer Science
University of Illinois at Urbana-Champaign
Urbana, Illinois 61801

Abstract

An abundance of research efforts in low power logic synthesis have so far been focused on AND/OR or NAND/NOR based logic. A typical approach is to first generate an initial multi-level AND/OR or NAND/NOR representation of a boolean function. Next, the representation is optimized in terms of power. However, there are major classes of circuits such as arithmetic functions which have sizable AND/OR representations but have very compact AND/XOR representations. For these functions AND/OR based optimization approach often yields poor results. In this paper, we put forth a paradigm for low power logic synthesis based on AND/XOR representations of boolean functions. Specifically, we propose transforming a boolean function into a Fixed Polarity Reed Muller form that allows us to efficiently synthesize XOR trees and AND trees with provably minimum switching activity. Preliminary experimental results show that we attain good power savings with negligible area overhead and often area reduction when compared to conventional AND/XOR based synthesis methods and the Berkeley SIS system.

1 Introduction

The advent of portable digital devices such as laptop personal computers has made low power circuit design an increasingly important research area. For example, laptop computers have limited battery life, and so the circuitry in the computer must be designed to dissipate as little power as possible without sacrificing performance in terms of speed. Additionally, high power consumption increases the cost of handling heat dissipation and diminishes the reliability of today's increasingly complex circuits with higher transistor counts and faster clock rates. It is well known that in CMOS technology a large portion of power dissipation on chip is due to dynamic power consumption at the gates which is computed according to the formula:

$$\sum_{i=1}^{N} \frac{1}{2} C_i V_{dd}^2 f_i$$

where C_i is the output capacitance of the ith gate, V_{dd} is the supply voltage, f_i is the frequency of transitions at the output of the ith gate, and N is the total number of gates on the chip. Clearly, a reduction in f_i will lead to a corresponding reduction in the total power consumption of the circuit. We can compute f_i as $2P_i(1-P_i)$ where P_i is the probability that the output of the ith gate is high.

Till now most efforts in power reduction have focused on reducing the power consumption in AND/OR or NAND/NOR based circuits. The typical approach is to first generate an initial AND/OR or NAND/NOR representation of a boolean function. Next, the representation is optimized in terms of switching activity through a variety of well known techniques [5]. For example, past research has encompassed low power technology decomposition of AND and OR gates [4, 12, 3] as well as low power technology mapping of combinational circuits implemented in terms of AND and OR gates [9]. However, there are major classes of circuits which have sizable AND/OR representations, but have very compact AND/XOR representations [11, 8]. Arithmetic functions such as adders, multipliers, and error correcting codes are some standard examples [7, 11]. For these functions AND/OR based optimizations often yield poor results. Recently, there has been some success in achieving area reduction by employing optimization techniques specifically targeted towards initial AND/XOR representations in the well known Fixed Polarity Reed Muller (FPRM) form [11]. In this paper, we propose techniques for low power logic synthesis of AND/XOR based circuits. We are able to efficiently synthesize a power optimal multi-level representation of a circuit in the sense that each XOR tree, AND tree, and OR tree in the circuit consumes prov-

*This research was supported in part by the National Science Foundation (NSF) under grant MIP-96-12184 and a research grant from IBM.

1092-3152/97 $10.00 © 1997 IEEE

ably minimum power under the zero-delay model with the temporal and spatial independence assumptions. We believe that this approach will become increasingly important in the synthesis of a large class of boolean functions because the area cost of XOR gates implemented in CMOS technology is decreasing [13].

An FPRM form for a boolean function f is simply a representation of f in which each variable of the function has been expanded with either the positive Davio expansion or the negative Davio expansion [1, 11]. An FPRM representation of f is an XOR of products representation in which each variable is either complemented or uncomplemented throughout the whole expression. For example, consider the function:

$$f = \overline{x_1}\, x_2 \oplus \overline{x_1}\, x_3 \oplus \overline{x_1}\, x_9 \oplus x_4\, x_5\, x_6 \oplus x_7 \oplus x_8 \quad (1)$$

Observe that x_1 appears only in complemented form and x_2 appears only in uncomplemented form. The same is true for the remaining variables in the expression. We can associate with f an nine bit polarity vector $(0,1,1,1,1,1,1,1,1)$ which describes whether a particular variable is complemented or not. The ith entry in the polarity vector is 0 if x_i appears in complemented form and is 1 if x_i appears in uncomplemented form. An alternative representation of the function f in (1) is :

$$f = \overline{x_1}\,\overline{x_2} \oplus \overline{x_1}\,\overline{x_3} \oplus \overline{x_1}\, x_9 \oplus x_4\, x_5\, x_6 \oplus \overline{x_7} \oplus \overline{x_8} \quad (2)$$

In this case the corresponding polarity vector is $(0,0,0,1,1,1,0,0,1)$. It should be noted that given any boolean function and any polarity vector we can *always* efficiently retrieve the corresponding FPRM form from Ordered Function Decision Diagrams (OFDD) which are based upon the Davio expansions [11, 10, 2]. However, the size of the FPRM representations for the same function may be different. Figure 1 shows the respective multi-level implementations, A and B, corresponding to the FPRM forms in (1) and (2). When we take into consideration power consumption, the two FPRM representations differ greatly. For example, suppose that the on probabilities for the primary inputs are: $P_{x_1} = .90, P_{x_2} = .99, P_{x_3} = .99, P_{x_4} = .40, P_{x_5} = .10, P_{x_6} = .20, P_{x_7} = .90, P_{x_8} = .50$, and $P_{x_9} = .50$. If we realistically assume that we have both the primary inputs and complements of the primary inputs available to us and we account for internal correlations then the expected number of transitions or power consumption for Synthesis A is 2.6. The expected number of transitions for Synthesis B is 1.3. Hence, there is a 50% difference in the power consumption between the two multi-level realizations.

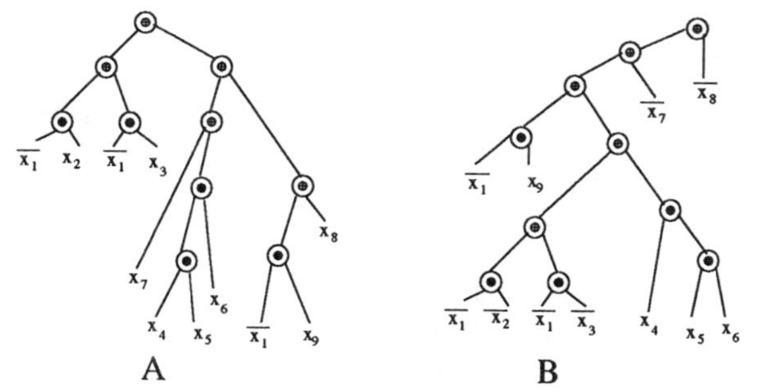

Figure 1: Respective multi-level implementations of Expression 1 and Expression 2

In this paper we study the relationship between the polarity vector, structure, and power consumption of XOR based logic and put forth a paradigm for low power synthesis of such circuits. In Section 2 we present our main theoretical results on low power logic synthesis based upon FPRM forms. In Section 3 we illustrate how the effects of the low power synthesis are preserved after factorization and reduction rules are applied to reduce the area of the circuit. In Section 4 we present experimental results. In Section 5 we summarize our results and present future directions for this research.

2 Theoretical Results

In this section we demonstrate how to choose a polarity vector (and hence the corresponding FPRM form) such that we can efficiently synthesize every XOR tree, AND tree, and OR tree in the circuit with provably minimum power dissipation. Suppose we have an XOR gate g with inputs a and b. Then the on probability at the output of the gate denoted by P_g is $P_a+P_b-2P_aP_b$ where P_a and P_b are the on probabilities of a and b. The power consumed by g is $2P_g(1-P_g)$. If we assume that both the primary inputs and their complements are available then there are some interesting consequences:

Theorem 2.1 *Suppose we have an XOR tree T consisting of n inputs. If we replace any subset of the n inputs by their complement the power dissipation in the tree remains unchanged under the zero delay model.*

Observe that if we complement an even number of inputs to an XOR tree then the functionality of the tree is preserved. We define the notion of a power vector as follows:

Definition 2.1 *Given a set S of n data signals $s_1, \ldots, s_n$ we define the power vector $V_s = V_{s_1}, \ldots, V_{s_n}$ to be an n-bit vector such that $V_{s_i} = 0$ if $P_{s_i} \leq 1/2$ and $V_{s_i} = 1$ if $P_{s_i} > 1/2$.*

Definition 2.2 *A power vector $V_s = (V_{s_1}, \ldots, V_{s_n})$ is said to be low signal biased (LSB) if at most one V_{s_i} is equal to 1. Similarly, V_s is said to be high signal based (HSB) if at most one V_{s_i} is equal to 0. We call an XOR tree whose primary inputs have an LSB power vector an LSB XOR tree. Similarly, we call an XOR tree whose primary inputs have an HSB power vector an HSB XOR tree.*

XOR trees have the following interesting property:

Theorem 2.2 *Suppose we have an XOR tree T that implements a boolean function f and consumes power P with respect to an arbitrary power vector V. Then, we can always transform T into a tree T' that realizes f with power vector V' such that $P' \leq P$ and V' is LSB or HSB.*

Theorem 2.2 means that we never increase the power dissipation in a tree by transforming it into a new tree whose inputs have an LSB power vector. The result is significant because of the following theorem:

Theorem 2.3 (LSB/HSB Optimality Theorem) *If we have n data signals which have an LSB power vector then the Huffman algorithm synthesizes an XOR tree that consumes the minimum power under the zero delay model. Furthermore, if the n data signals have an HSB power vector then the Anti-Huffman algorithm synthesizes an XOR tree that consumes the minimum power under the zero delay model.*

Theorem 2.2 together with Theorem 2.3 suggest an efficient polynomial time algorithm for synthesizing a power minimum XOR tree given arbitrary input on probabilities. The algorithm is as follows: Let k be the number of primary inputs to the XOR tree with probabilities greater than half. If k is even replace all k inputs by their respective complements. If k is odd then replace any $k-1$ inputs by their respective complements. Then simply use the Huffman algorithm to build the optimal tree. For AND and OR trees we have the following theorems that are analogous to Theorem 2.3 for XOR trees:

Theorem 2.4 *If the on probabilities of the primary inputs to an AND tree are less than half then the Huffman algorithm synthesizes the minimum power tree. Similarly if the off probabilities of the primary inputs to an OR tree are less than half then the Huffman algorithm synthesizes the minimum power tree.*

Theorem 2.5 *If the product of the on probabilities of the primary inputs to an AND tree are greater than half then the Anti-Huffman algorithm synthesizes the minimum power tree. Similarly if the product of the off probabilities of the primary inputs to an OR tree are greater than half then the Anti-Huffman algorithm synthesizes the minimum power tree.*

Hence, if we choose a polarity vector such that all the primary inputs have on probabilities less than 1/2, then we can directly apply Theorems 2.3-2.5 to efficiently synthesize every XOR tree, AND tree, and OR tree in the circuit with provably minimum power dissipation.

3 Factorization and Reduction Rules

In practice we want to reduce the size of a circuit to satisfy area constraints. Area reduction can be achieved through the application of factorization rules such as: (1) $ab \oplus ac \oplus ad \ldots = a(b \oplus c \oplus d \oplus \ldots)$ (2) $ab+ac+ad\ldots = a(b+c+d+\ldots)$, and reduction rules such as: (1) $ab \oplus a = a\bar{b}$, (2) $ab \oplus ac \oplus abc = a(b+c)$, (3) $ab \oplus \bar{b} = a + \bar{b}$.

We observe that factorization does not change the polarities of the primary inputs, and so we can still directly apply Theorems 2.3-2.5 to efficiently synthesize power optimal trees. For example, Figure 3 contains the factored realizations of Expressions 1 and 2. Synthesis B, the power optimal realization, consumes 40% less power than Synthesis A. The reduction rules, however, may change the polarity of some of the primary inputs. In this case, we employ an efficient branch and bound algorithm that makes use of Theorems 2.3-2.5 to prune the search space in order to synthesize power optimal trees.

4 Experimental Results

Our algorithms have been implemented in C++ and executed on a Sparc 1 workstation. We used the PUMA OKFDD package from the University of Freiburg to generate the initial FPRM forms. In the tables the parameter α is the percentage of on probabilities of inputs that lie between $[0, .5-\beta]$ and $[.5+\beta, 1]$. The power measurements were conducted using the power estimation tool in SIS 1.2 assuming a 20MHZ clock. The circuits that we used came from the MCNC benchmark suite. Finally, all of the power measurements were of *mapped* circuits using the well-known MCNC generic library (mcnc.genlib).

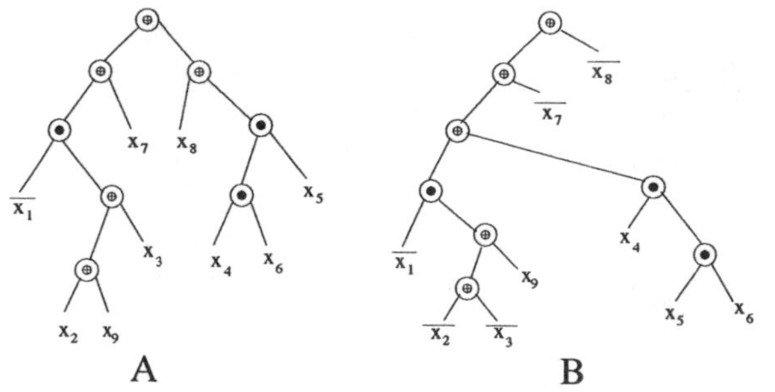

Figure 2: Respective factored multi-level implementations of Expression 1 and Expression 2

In Table 1, we compare the results of the balanced tree synthesis algorithm (denoted with a "B") from [11] using the the area minimization heuristic described in [10] to generate the initial FPRM form against the results of our algorithm which is referred to as the non-balanced synthesis (denoted with an "N"). First we see that our algorithm produced results that differ negligibly in area from the best known area minimization heuristic. In fact, overall, our realizations have a slightly smaller area. Second, we achieve an average 18% power reduction from the best known XOR based synthesis technique. Additionally, circuits such as `f51m` and `pcle` highlight the fact that the power savings is due to the optimal synthesis of the trees and the polarity of the variables and not a fortuitous initial FPRM form that has fewer literals.

For the sake of completeness, in Table 2 we compare the performance of SIS (by using the AND/OR based commands: `collapse` and `resub` and denoted with an "S".) against that of our algorithm. We selected four circuits which realize arithmetic functions as our benchmark circuits. On the average we have a 37% area savings and a 53% power savings. In fact, the best known SIS scripts (*boolean, rugged,* and *algebraic*) perform very poorly against XOR based techniques in terms of area and power for arithmetic circuits. The reader is referred to [11] for a detailed comparison between arithmetic circuits synthesized from the SIS scripts and arithmetic circuits synthesisized from FPRM forms.

5 Conclusion

In this paper we have presented a low power synthesis paradigm for XOR based logic. We have taken advantage of special properties of the FPRM form and XOR gates to develop an efficient optimal low power synthesis algorithm for XOR trees, AND trees, and OR trees. There are two natural extensions of this work. The first would be to modify the mapping phase to preserve the effects of the low power synthesis. The special properties of XOR gates and FPRM forms might yield additional opportunities for power savings beyond those presented in [9]. Second, the reduction and factorization rules have to be studied further in terms of their effect on power consumption of XOR based logic.

Acknowledgement

The authors would like to thank Chien-Chung Tsai of Mentor Graphics for his valuable suggestions.

References

[1] M. Davio, J. P. Deschamps, and A. Thayse. *Discrete and Switching Functions.* McGraw-Hill, Inc., 1978.

[2] R. Dreschsler, A. Sarabi, M. Theobald, B. Becker, and M. A. Perkowski. Efficient representation and manipulation of switching functions based on ordered kronecker functional decision diagrams. In *Design Automation Conference,* 1994.

[3] Unni Narayanan, Hon Wai Leong, Ki-Seok Chung, and C. L. Liu. Low power multiplexer decomposition. In *International Symposium on Lower Power Electronics and Design,* 1997.

[4] R. Panda and F. Najm. Technology decomposition for low-power synthesis. In *IEEE Custom Integrated Circutis Conference,* pages 627–630, 1995.

[5] R. Panda and F. Najm. Technology-dependent transformations for low-power synthesis. In *Design Automation Conference,* pages 650–655, 1997.

[6] D. S. Parker. Conditions for optimality of the huffman algorithm. *SIAM Journal of Computing,* 9(3):470–489, August 1980.

[7] I. S. Reed. A class of multiple-error-correcting codes and the decoding scheme. *IRE Transactions on Information Theory,* PGIT-4:38–49, 1954.

[8] Tsutomu Sasao, editor. *Logic Synthesis and Optimization.* Kluwer Academic Publishers, 1983.

[9] V. Tiwari, P. Ashar, and S. Malik. Technology mapping for low power. In *Design Automation Conference,* pages 74–79, June 1993.

[10] Chien-Chung Tsai and Malgorzata Marek-Sadowska. Minimization of fixed-polarity and/xor canonical networks. In *IEE Proceedings of Comput. Digital Technology,* volume 141, 1994.

[11] Chien-Chung Tsai and Malgorzata Marek-Sadowska. Multilevel logic synthesis for arithmetic functions. In *Design Automation Conference,* 1996.

[12] Chi-Ying Tsui, Massoud Pedram, and Alvin M. Despain. Technology decomposition and mapping targeting low power dissipation. In *Desgin Automation Conference,* pages 68–73, 1993.

[13] Neil H. E. Weste and Kamran Eshraghian. *Principles of CMOS VLSI Design: A Systems Perspective.* Addison-Wesley, 1993.

Circuit	PI	PO	α	β	Area			Power		
					Lit-B	Lit-N	% L Imp	Power-B	Power-N	% Pow. Imp
9symml	9	1	0.00	0.00	430	470	-9.30	1213.0	1206.2	-0.57
			0.50	0.25	430	534	-24.10	1103.2	1189.7	-7.84
			1.00	0.25	430	418	2.80	916.5	621.5	32.19
b1	3	4	0.00	0.00	25	20	20.00	61.9	68.4	-10.50
			0.50	0.25	25	20	20.00	39.7	35.3	11.08
			1.00	0.25	25	20	20.00	34.6	28.5	17.63
CM150	21	1	0.00	0.00	379	274	27.70	606.0	370.5	38.60
			0.50	0.25	379	321	15.30	612.6	407.9	33.41
			1.00	0.25	379	360	5.00	323.4	156.5	51.60
CM42	4	10	0.00	0.00	139	147	-5.70	308.0	311.8	-1.23
			0.50	0.25	139	118	15.10	263.2	190.5	27.69
			1.00	0.25	139	126	9.30	81.9	81.3	0.73
CM85	11	3	0.00	0.00	840	892	-0.60	2248.6	2257.9	-0.41
			0.50	0.25	840	503	40.10	2076.2	929.7	55.22
			1.00	0.25	840	531	36.80	1072.0	426.0	60.26
f51m	8	8	0.00	0.00	300	300	0.00	813.2	798.2	1.84
			0.50	0.25	300	290	3.33	703.3	534.8	23.96
			1.00	0.25	300	317	-5.60	497.8	347.2	30.25
pcle	19	9	0.00	0.00	250	266	-6.40	622.2	561.2	9.80
			0.50	0.25	250	495	-98.00	668.6	828.3	-23.90
			1.00	0.25	250	415	-66.00	365.2	310.0	15.12
t481	16	1	0.00	0.00	140	123	12.10	360.4	315.3	12.51
			0.50	0.25	140	135	3.60	268.0	262.3	2.10
			1.00	0.25	140	116	17.14	193.3	102.8	46.81
Average			0.00	0.00			4.72			6.30
			0.50	0.25			-3.08			15.20
			1.00	0.25			2.43			31.80
Overall Average							1.36			17.77

Table 1: Comparison between balanced and nonbalanced approaches where the minimum cubes heuristic was used for the balanced approach and the LSB power vector was used for the nonbalanced approach.

Circuit	PI	PO	α	β	Area			Power		
					Lit-S	Lit-N	% L Imp	Power-S	Power-N	% Pow. Imp
9symml	9	1	0.00	0.00	739	470	36.40	2647.0	1206.2	54.30
			0.50	0.25	739	534	27.70	1746.4	1103.2	36.83
			1.00	0.25	739	418	43.40	1228.4	621.5	49.40
f51m	8	8	0.00	0.00	445	300	32.50	1731.4	798.2	53.90
			0.50	0.25	445	290	34.80	1118.4	534.8	52.18
			1.00	0.25	445	317	28.80	743.2	347.2	53.30
pcle	19	9	0.00	0.00	335	266	20.60	1131.4	561.2	50.40
			0.50	0.25	335	495	-47.80	764.4	828.3	-8.35
			1.00	0.25	335	415	-23.90	323.4	310.0	4.10
t481	16	1	0.00	0.00	6847	123	98.20	19322.7	315.3	98.40
			0.50	0.25	6847	135	98.00	13441.7	262.3	98.00
			1.00	0.25	6847	116	98.21	7588.0	7588.0	98.60
Average			0.00	0.00			46.93			64.25
			0.50	0.25			28.18			44.67
			1.00	0.25			33.63			51.35
Overall Average							37.24			53.42

Table 2: Comparison between SIS and the nonbalanced approach using the LSB power vector.

An Exact Gate Decomposition Algorithm for Low-Power Technology Mapping

Hai Zhou and D.F. Wong
Department of Computer Sciences
University of Texas at Austin
Austin, TX 78712-1188

Abstract

With the remarkable growth of portable application and the increasing frequency and integration density, power is being given comparable weight to speed and area in IC designs. In technology mapping, how decomposition is done can have a significant impact on the power dissipation of the final implementation. In the literature, only heuristic algorithms are given for the low-power gate decomposition *problem. In this paper, we prove many properties an optimal decomposition tree must have. Based on these optimality properties, we design an efficient exact algorithm to solve the low-power gate decomposition problem. Moreover, the exact algorithm can be easily modified to a heuristic algorithm which performs much better than the known heuristics.*

1 Introduction

With the remarkable growth of portable application and the increasing frequency and integration density, power is being given comparable weight to speed and area in IC designs. Power dissipation in digital CMOS circuits is dominated by the *dynamic dissipation*, which is mainly the charging and discharging of the node capacitances [5]. It can be modeled as

$$P = 0.5V_{dd}^2 f_{clk} C_L E_{sw}$$

where V_{dd} is the supply voltage, f_{clk} is the clock frequency, C_L is the physical capacitance at the output of the node, and E_{sw} (referred to as the *switching activity*) is the average number of output transitions per clock cycle. As we can see, V_{dd} and f_{clk} are fixed by the technology, but C_L and E_{sw} can be controlled in design process.

In technology mapping, the subject netlist is usually first decomposed into a netlist composed of only inverters and two-input NAND gates. How the decomposition is done can have a significant impact on the power dissipation of the final implementation [4, 6, 7]. We deal with the *low-power gate decomposition* problem in this paper.

The problem appears in a few recent papers. Tiwari *et al.* [6] mentioned the importance of a good decomposition on the final result of technology mapping, but did not give any solution. At the same time, Tsui *et al.* [7] analyzed the problem and found that Huffman's algorithm [3] can only be used in domino dynamic logic. For static logic which is more important in low-power applications, only a greedy heuristic called the *modified Huffman algorithm* is given. Murgai *et al.* [4] also considered the decomposition problem, but their minimization objective was the power consumptions due to glitches.

Since the problem for dynamic logics can be easily solved, we only consider static logics. In our approach, we first study the structure of an optimal decomposition tree. This is given by a set of properties an optimal tree must have. Then, based on these properties, we designed an exact algorithm for the construction of an optimal decomposition tree. The time complexity of the algorithm is $O(n2^n)$, which, though still exponential, should be regarded as efficient considering the total of more than $(2n-1)^{n-1}$ trees in the solution space.

As a by-product, a heuristic algorithm can be easily derived from the exact algorithm. Its running time is $O(n \log n)$, which is much faster than the $O(n^2 \log n)$ running time of the modified Huffman algorithm [7]. Since the heuristic is strongly based on the optimality properties, it also performs much better than the modified Huffman algorithm. In fact our experimental results show that our heuristic gives optimal results in most cases.

The rest of the paper is organized as follows. In section 2, we define the low-power gate decomposition problem. In section 3, we describe Huffman's algorithm for tree construction and identify two special cases of the problem which can be solved. Section 4 studies the properties of an optimal decomposition tree. Based on these properties, section 5 presents two algorithms: one exact algorithm and one heuristic. Section 6 gives the experimental results and some concluding remarks. Due to space limit, most of the proofs are omitted. All of them can be found in [9].

2 Problem formulation

In technology decomposition, we need to decompose a multi-input gate into a tree of two-input gates. Since an OR gate can be treated as a NAND gate with negations of the inputs, what we need to solve is how to decompose an n-input AND gate into a tree of 2-input AND gates. We call this *gate decomposition*.

We will treat the signals in a circuit as random variables and define the *signal probability* of a signal x as the probability of x being 1, denoted by $p(x)$. We use the same model as in [6, 7], that is, we assume the *zero delay model* where gate delays are assumed to be zero and thus signal transitions due to glitching are ignored; primary inputs are assumed to be uncorrelated (*spatial independent*); and the present input signal value is independent of those in the past (*temporal independent*). Under these assumptions, given the input signal probabilities and a decomposition tree, the probabilities of internal signals can be computed as follows. Start from the primary inputs, for each $z = x$ AND y, let $p(z) = p(x)p(y)$. Thus, the signal probability of any node v is equal to the product of all leaf probabilities in the subtree rooted at v. For example, Figure 1 shows one gate decomposition and all signal probabilities of the nodes.

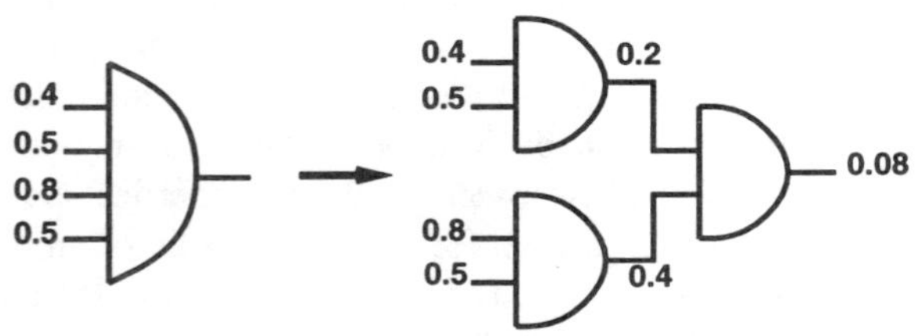

Figure 1: Gate decomposition

The switching activity E_{sw} depends on the implementation logic style. In p-domino logic designs, the gate outputs are pre-discharged to 0, thus the switching activity of a node is equal to the probability of being 1. Let $T = (V, E)$ represent the decomposition tree, and $p(v)$, for any $v \in V$, denote the output signal probability of node v. The objective function we want to minimize in domino logic is $\sum_{v \in V} p(v)$. Because of this simple objective function, it can be shown that Huffman's algorithm can be used to give an optimal decomposition tree in domino logic designs [7].

Because of the pre-discharges or pre-charges, domino logic designs dissipate more power than static logic designs, which never do extra charges or discharges. In static logic, under the temporal independence assumption, the switching activity E_{sw} of signal x can be written as

$$\begin{aligned} E_{sw}(x) &= Pr[x : 0 \to 1] + Pr[x : 1 \to 0] \\ &= Pr[x = 0]Pr[x = 1] + Pr[x = 1]Pr[x = 0] \\ &= 2Pr[x = 1]Pr[x = 0] \\ &= 2p(x)(1 - p(x)) \end{aligned}$$

However, in their recent work [8], Wu *et al.* showed that, even in the absence of temporal independence, $2p(x)(1 - p(x))$ also gives the expected value of the switching activities among all sequences that satisfy the given signal probability.

The problem we will solve in this paper can be defined as follows.

Low-power gate decomposition problem: Given an n-input AND gate with inputs $s_1, s_2, \ldots, s_n$ and their signal probabilities $p(s_1), p(s_2), \ldots, p(s_n)$, construct a tree $T = (V, E)$ of 2-input AND gates with $s_1, s_2, \ldots, s_n$ as its leaves such that

$$E_{sw}(T) = \sum_{v \in V} p(v)(1 - p(v))$$

is minimized.

According to Knuth [2], the number of different *labeled oriented* binary trees with n leaves is $\binom{2n-1}{n-1}(2n-2)!/2^{n-1}$. In a decomposition tree, only leaves are labeled, the internal nodes are indistinguishable. Therefore, the number of different decomposition trees is

$$\frac{\binom{2n-1}{n-1}(2n-2)!}{2^{n-1}(n-1)!} > (2n-1)^{n-1}.$$

Thus, an exhaustive enumeration method is prohibitively expensive. Tsui *et al.* [7] found Huffman's algorithm can not solve this problem. Instead, they gave a heuristic which was called modified Huffman algorithm. It starts with a forest composed of all the inputs, and incrementally combines two trees into one until there is only one tree. It is a greedy algorithm, and each time tries all pairs and chooses the combination which gives the minimum increase on the objective function. The time complexity of the algorithm is $O(n^2 \log n)$ [7].

This algorithm is by far not optimal. This can be shown by a simple example. Here we have six input signals with the following probabilities: 0.4, 0.4, 0.4, 0.94, 0.94, 0.95. The decomposition tree constructed by the modified Huffman algorithm is shown in Figure 2(a), where the summation of switching activities is 1.3337. Nevertheless, a decomposition tree shown in Figure 2(b) has 1.22748 as its total switching activities.

3 Huffman's algorithm

Given n leaves $v_1, v_2, \ldots, v_n$ with their weights $w(v_1), w(v_2), \ldots, w(v_n)$, Huffman [3] gave an algorithm to construct a binary tree with minimum weighted path length $\sum_{i=1}^{n} w(v_i)l_i$, where l_i is the path length from the root to v_i. The algorithm can be described as follows. Starting from a forest composed of all the leaves, it combines two trees with the minimum weights, use the summation of the weights as the weight of the combined tree and substitute the two trees by the combined one; this process is continued until there is only one tree.

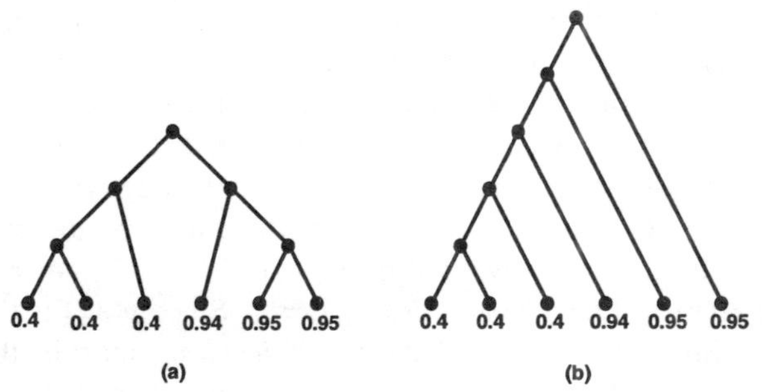

Figure 2: (a) Decomposition tree by modified Huffman has switching activities 1.3337; (b) A decomposition tree with switching activities 1.22748

If, for each internal node r with two children u and v, we define the weight $w(r) = w(u) + w(v)$, then

$$\sum_{i=1}^{n} w(v_i)l_i = \sum_{u \in V} w(u),$$

where V represents the set of internal nodes. This formulation leads us to consider Huffman's algorithm for the low-power gate decomposition problem. Unfortunately, it can not solve the problem in general case [7]. However, we find that under some conditions Huffman's algorithm can give optimal solutions. Before we give these conditions, we will describe two variations of Huffman's algorithm, which are a little different with the original one.

> *Min-Huffman algorithm*: Start with all the input signals; combine the two signals of minimum probabilities and substitute the two signals with the new signal; continue the process until there remains only one signal.

> *Max-Huffman algorithm*: Start with all the input signals; combine the two signals of maximum probabilities and substitute the two signals with the new signal; continue the process until there remains only one signal.

As stated by the following theorem, two special cases can be solved efficiently.

Theorem 1 *If all input signal probabilities are not greater than 0.5, the low-power gate decomposition problem can be solved by the Min-Huffman algorithm; If the product of all input signal probabilities is not less than 0.5, it can be solved by the Max-Huffman algorithm.*

4 Optimality properties

In previous section, we identified two special cases of the low-power gate decomposition problem which can be solved efficiently. In order to solve the general case, in this section, we will study the properties of an optimal decomposition tree.

First, we have the following simple observations.

Lemma 1 *On any path from a leaf to the root in a decomposition tree, the signal probabilities are decreasing. Each subtree in an optimal decomposition tree is also optimal.*

Further analysis gives us the following result.

Lemma 2 *In an optimal decomposition tree, all inputs whose probabilities are not greater than 0.5 must form a separate subtree.*

Lemma 2 tells us, in order to construct an optimal decomposition tree, we can always combine the signals whose probabilities are not greater than 0.5 into a subtree. By Lemma 1, this subtree needs to be an optimal one. According to Theorem 1, it can be constructed by the Min-Huffman algorithm. In fact, since the product of two smallest probabilities is still the smallest, in the Min-Huffman algorithm, signals are combined sequentially from low probability to high probability.

Similar analysis gives the following lemma.

Lemma 3 *In an optimal decomposition tree, the internal nodes whose probabilities are not greater than 0.5 form a path.*

In order to present the next optimality property, we need to define two labels for each node in an optimal decomposition tree. For each v, let *level*(v) be the distance of v from the root. That is, the root has level 0, its children have level 1, etc. For each v, if v is an internal node and $p(v) \leq 0.5$, then let *rank*(v) $= 0$. Otherwise, let *rank*(v) be the minimum distance of v from any node in rank 0. The property can be stated as follows.

Theorem 2 *Let u and v be any two nodes in an optimal decomposition tree. If rank(u) $=$ rank(v) $\neq 0$ and level(u) $<$ level(v), then $p(u) \geq p(v)$.*

This theorem states that, in an optimal decomposition tree, for the nodes in the same rank other than 0, the probabilities are non-increasing with respect to their levels. According to the definition, the probability of each internal node in rank 1 is greater than 0.5. By Theorem 1, each subtree rooted at rank 1 node can be constructed by the Max-Huffman algorithm. Therefore, it is possible to arrange each subtree in such a way that, in each rank, the probabilities is non-decreasing from left to right. Under these arrangements, an optimal decomposition tree can be visualized in Figure 3, where the nodes in rank 0 form a path, and the probabilities in other ranks are non-decreasing along the arrows.

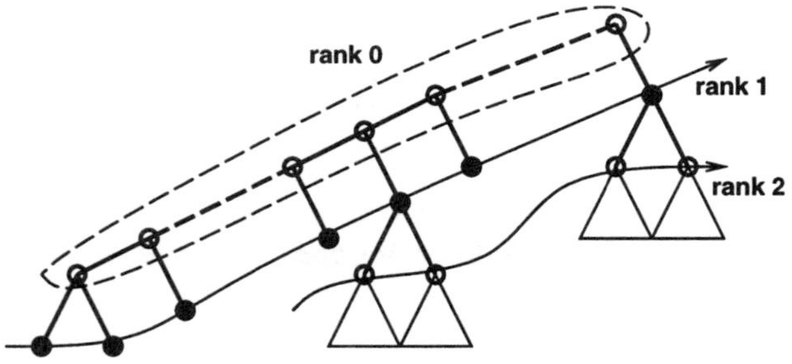

Figure 3: Probabilities are non-decreasing along the arrows in an optimal tree

The following theorem gives another important property of an optimal decomposition tree.

Theorem 3 *Let u and v be any siblings in an optimal decomposition tree such that $0.5 < p(u) < p(v)$, there can not exist node y in the tree such that $p(u) < p(y) < p(v)$.*

5 Decomposition algorithms

In the previous section, we have derived some properties an optimal decomposition tree must have. Since these properties are necessary conditions of an optimal tree, other trees which do not observe them need not to be considered during the optimization process. This can reduce the search space and help us to design an efficient algorithm for the low-power gate decomposition problem.

The following theorem combines all optimality properties given in previous section and is the basis of our exact algorithm.

Theorem 4 *Given n input signals $s_1, s_2, \ldots, s_n$ such that $p(s_1) \leq p(s_2) \ldots \leq p(s_n)$, there is an optimal decomposition tree where s_n either is combined with s_{n-1} or is a direct child of the root.*

Proof: We have two cases based on $p(s_{n-1})$.

Case 1. $p(s_{n-1}) \leq 0.5$. We claim s_n must be a direct child of the root in an optimal tree. Here we have $p(s_i) \leq 0.5$ for all $1 \leq i \leq n-1$. If $p(s_n) \leq 0.5$, according to Theorem 1, the optimal tree can be constructed by the Min-Huffman algorithm and s_n will be a direct child of the root. On the other hand, if $p(s_n) > 0.5$, according to Lemma 2, signals $s_1, s_2, \ldots, s_{n-1}$ must form a separate subtree, which will finally be combined with s_n. This also means s_n is a direct child of the root.

Case 2. $p(s_{n-1}) > 0.5$. We show there is an optimal tree where s_n either is combined with s_{n-1} or is a direct child of the root. Denote the sibling of s_n in an optimal tree by s. According to Lemma 1, we have $p(s) \leq p(s_{n-1})$. If $p(s) > 0.5$ then it must be that $p(s) = p(s_{n-1})$. Otherwise, we will have $0.5 < p(s) < p(s_{n-1}) < p(s_n)$, which contradicts with Theorem 3. But if $p(s) = p(s_{n-1})$, we can always exchange the subtree rooted at s with s_{n-1} and get an optimal tree where s_n is combined with s_{n-1}. On the other hand, if $p(s) \leq 0.5$, then, let v be the parent of s and s_{n-1}, we will have $p(v) \leq 0.5$. This means *rank*$(v) = 0$ and hence *rank*$(s_n) = 1$. Since $p(s_n)$ is the maximum, according to Theorem 2, *level*(s_n) must be the minimum. Therefore, *level*$(s_n) = 1$, which means s_n is a direct child of the root. □

In other words, the theorem says that there is always an optimal tree between the two configurations shown in Figure 4. More specifically, if $p(s_{n-1}) \leq 0.5$ it must be configuration I; otherwise, it can be either configuration I or configuration II.

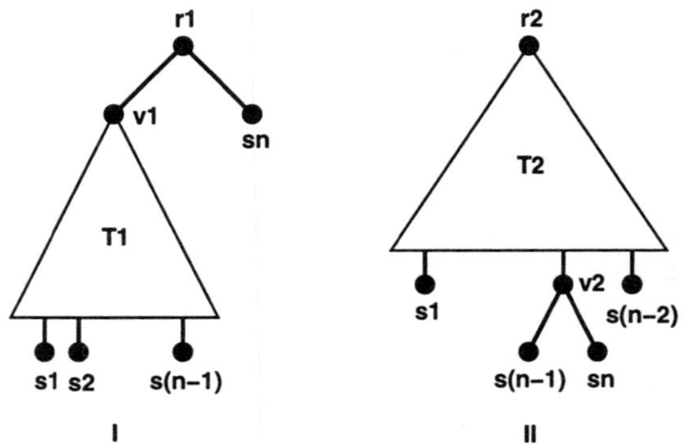

Figure 4: Two configurations of an optimal decomposition tree

Based on Theorem 4, we can design an exact algorithm for the low-power gate decomposition problem as follows. Given n input signals, we first sort them according to their probabilities such that $p(s_1) \leq p(s_2) \ldots \leq p(s_n)$. If $p(s_{n-1}) \leq 0.5$, we construct configuration I; otherwise, we construct both configurations I and II and output the one with the minimum switching activities. According to Lemma 1, the subgraphs T_1 and T_2 in Figure 4 must also be optimal. Since their input sizes are both only $n-1$, we can construct them recursively. This algorithm is called **ExDecomp** and its pseudo-code is given in Figure 5.

The correctness of the algorithm comes directly from Theorem 4 and can be stated as the following corollary.

Corollary 4.1 *The* **ExDecomp** *algorithm exactly solves the low-power gate decomposition problem.*

At each recursion in **ExDecomp**, we need to store the current configuration, which is upper bounded by n. Since the recursion depth is at most n, the space usage in the worst case is n^2. Let $T(n)$ represent the running time of

```
Input: a set of signals S = {s_1, ..., s_n}
       such that p(s_1) ≤ ... ≤ p(s_n)
Output: a decomposition tree T
ExDecomp(S)
{
  if |S| = 1
    return s_n;
  T_1 = ExDecomp(S − {s_n});
  if (p(s_{n-1}) ≤ 0.5)
    return combine(T_1, s_n);
  s = combine(s_{n-1}, s_n);
  T_2 = ExDecomp(S + {s} − {s_{n-1}, s_n});
  if (E_sw(combine(T_1, s_n)) < E_sw(T_2))
    return combine(T_1, s_n);
  else return T_2;
}
```

Figure 5: Pseudo-code of **ExDecomp**

```
Input: a set of signals S = {s_1, ..., s_n}
       such that p(s_1) ≤ ... ≤ p(s_n)
Output: a decomposition tree T
HeuDecomp(S)
{
  if (p(s_{n-1}) ≤ 0.5 or choose configuration I) {
    T_1 = HeuDecomp(S − {s_n});
    return combine(T_1, s_n);
  }
  else {
    s = combine(s_{n-1}, s_n);
    T_2 = HeuDecomp(S + {s} − {s_{n-1}, s_n});
    return T_2;
  }
}
```

Figure 6: Pseudo-code of **HeuDecomp**

ExDecomp on an instance of size n. It is easy to see that

$$T(n) = 2T(n-1) + n.$$

This gives us $T(n) = O(n2^n)$. Although in the worst case it is still need exponential time, compared with the total of more than $(2n-1)^{n-1}$ decomposition trees, it is efficient.

Besides the exact algorithm, the optimality properties can also be used to derive a set of efficient heuristic algorithms. As we can see, the complexity of **ExDecomp** comes from the fact that it is not known beforehand which configuration in Figure 4 will give the minimum switching activities. Trade accuracy for speed, we can use heuristics to choose only one configuration at each recursion. This gives us the algorithm scheme shown in Figure 6 which can be tuned into different heuristic algorithms based on different decision criteria.

The heuristic we used in our implementation can be described as follows. Since the structures of T_1 and T_2 in Figure 4 are not known until we recursively construct them, we can not compare their switching activities beforehand. But we can find that, for the two trees, except one leaf, all other $n-2$ leaves are the same. Therefore, we can assume the difference between the internal switching activities of T_1 and T_2 is not too much. We also know $p(r_1) = p(r_2)$. So the only concern comes from the difference between v_1 and v_2. Our decision criteria then is: if $E_{sw}(v_1) < E_{sw}(v_2)$, choose configuration I, otherwise choose configuration II.

Since only one configuration is chosen at each recursion in **HeuDecomp**, we need only keep one copy of the tree structure, hence the space usage is only n. Implemented by the priority queue data structure [1], the running time can also be upper bounded by $O(n \log n)$, which is much faster than the modified Huffman algorithm. Furthermore, since **HeuDecomp** is strongly based on the optimality properties, its performance should be better than that of the modified Huffman algorithm. This is supported by our experimental results.

6 Experimental results

We implement both the exact algorithm **ExDecomp** and the heuristic algorithm **HeuDecomp** in C++ on a Sun Sparc 5 workstation. Our experiments focus on two aspects: the running time of the exact algorithm and the performance of the heuristic. In order to compare the performance of the heuristic, we also implement the modified Huffman algorithm [7].

According to Lemma 2 and Theorem 1, the input signals whose probabilities are not greater than 0.5 can be easily combined into a subtree by the Min-Huffman algorithm. Therefore, the complexity only depends on the number of signals whose probabilities are greater than 0.5. In our experiments, the input signal probabilities are randomly generate, and based on the above reason, all signal probabilities are generated to be greater than 0.5.

On each different input size ranging from 5 to 20, we randomly generated 100 instances. We run **ExDecomp**, **HeuDecomp** and the modified Huffman algorithm on each of them. We compute the average running time of **ExDecomp** on each input size. To measure the performance

Table 1: Experimental results

#input	ExDecomp	Modified Huffman			HeuDecomp		
	time(sec.)	#bad	MaxRatio	AvgRatio	#bad	MaxRatio	AvgRatio
5	0.0009	43	5.51%	0.76%	6	0.430%	0.010%
6	0.0014	66	5.59%	1.29%	6	0.187%	0.006%
7	0.0028	83	7.33%	2.30%	9	0.288%	0.008%
8	0.0057	89	11.31%	4.05%	9	0.268%	0.007%
9	0.0105	93	9.95%	5.02%	8	0.254%	0.008%
10	0.0187	93	14.87%	5.97%	5	0.265%	0.005%
11	0.0424	96	14.61%	7.55%	1	0.108%	0.001%
12	0.0752	97	16.17%	8.45%	2	0.111%	0.002%
13	0.1377	100	19.41%	9.78%	0	0.000%	0.000%
14	0.3050	97	19.97%	9.83%	0	0.000%	0.000%
15	0.5465	100	20.44%	11.32%	0	0.000%	0.000%
16	1.1539	98	20.82%	11.09%	0	0.000%	0.000%
18	3.9232	99	25.23%	12.25%	0	0.000%	0.000%
20	14.2497	100	29.55%	12.32%	0	0.000%	0.000%

of **HeuDecomp** and the modified Huffman algorithm, we compare their solutions with the optimal solution given by **ExDecomp**. The number of non-optimal solutions is counted. For each instance I, let $Opt(I)$ represent the optimal solution, we use the ratio

$$R = \frac{S(I) - Opt(I)}{Opt(I)}$$

to measure the performance of solution $S(I)$. For each algorithm, the maximum and average ratios are computed.

Based on the results reported in Table 1, we have the following conclusions. First, **ExDecomp** is efficient in practice. For 20 input probabilities which are greater than 0.5, the average running time is less than 15 seconds. In reality, usually only half of the input probabilities are greater than 0.5. This means a problem with 40 inputs can be solved in less than 15 seconds. Second, the performance of **HeuDecomp** is very good. Among all the 1400 solutions reported in Table 1, only 46 of them are not optimal. Among these non-optimal solutions, the largest deviation from the optimal solution is only 0.43%. Finally, an interesting phenomenon is that, with the increasing of the input size, **HeuDecomp** performs better and better. Starting from 13 inputs, all solutions given by **HeuDecomp** are optimal. Based on this phenomenon and the fact that **ExDecomp** runs very fast when the input size is not too large, we can use the following strategy for the low-power gate decomposition problem: if the input size is not too large, use **ExDecomp**; otherwise, use **HeuDecomp**.

References

[1] T.H. Cormen, C.E. Leiserson, and R.L. Rivest, *Introduction to Algorithms*. MIT Press, 1990.

[2] D.E. Knuth, *Fundamental Algorithms*, Volume 1 of *The Art of Computer Programming*. Addison-Wesley, 1968. Second edition, 1973.

[3] D.A. Huffman, A Method for the Construction of Minimum Redundancy Codes. In *Proceedings of the IRE*, volume 40, pages 1098-1101, Sept. 1952.

[4] R. Murgai, R.K. Brayton, and A. Sangiovanni-Vincentelli, Decomposition of Logic Functions for Minimum Transition Activity. *Proceeding of the International Workshop on Low Power Design*, 1994.

[5] M. Pedram, Power Minimization in IC Design: Principles and Applications. *ACM Trans. on Design Automation of Electronic Systems*, Jan., 1996.

[6] V. Tiwari, P. Ashar, and S. Malik, Technology Mapping for Low Power. *ACM/IEEE Design Automation Conference*, 1993.

[7] C.-Y. Tsui, M. Pedram, and A.M. Despain, Technology Decomposition and Mapping Targeting Low Power Dissipation. *ACM/IEEE Design Automation Conference*, 1993.

[8] Q. Wu, M. Pedram, and X. Wu, A Note on the Relationship Between Signal Probability and Switching Activity. *Asian and South Pacific Design Automation Conference*, 1997.

[9] H. Zhou and D.F. Wong, An Exact Gate Decomposition Algorithm for Low-Power Technology Mapping. Technical Report TR97-21, Department of Computer Sciences, University of Texas at Austin, 1997.

Trace Driven Logic Synthesis - Application to Power Minimization

Luca P. Carloni† Patrick C. McGeer‡ Alexander Saldanha‡
Alberto L. Sangiovanni-Vincentelli†

† University of California at Berkeley
Berkeley, CA 94720
{lcarloni,alberto}@ic.eecs.berkeley.edu

‡ Cadence Berkeley Laboratories
Berkeley, CA 94704-1103
{mcgeer,saldanha}@cadence.com

Abstract

A trace driven methodology for logic synthesis and optimization is proposed. Given a logic description of a digital circuit $\mathcal{C}$ and an expected trace of input vectors $\mathcal{T}$, an implementation of $\mathcal{C}$ that optimizes a cost function under application of $\mathcal{T}$ is derived. This approach is effective in capturing and utilizing the correlations that exist between input signals on an application specific design. The idea is novel since it propose synthesis and optimization at the logic level where the goal is to optimize the **average case** *rather than the* **worst case** *for a chosen cost metric. This paper focuses on the development of algorithms for trace driven optimization to minimize the switching power in multi-level networks. The average net power reduction (internal plus I/O power) obtained on a set of benchmark FSMs is 14%, while the average reduction in internal power is 25%. We also demonstrate that the I/O transition activity provides an upper bound on the power reduction that can be achieved by combinational logic synthesis.*

1 Introduction

Logic synthesis tools have traditionally been applied to problems where the cost function used in optimization depends only on the Boolean function representing the circuit to be implemented. This approach, of course, is appropriate for minimizing the area or longest path delay of a circuit. However, there are certain cost criteria which cannot be measured just by analysis of the Boolean function denoting the circuit. This is typically the case when the **average case** rather than the **worst case** cost is of interest. One such example is switching power minimization where it is well known that the correlations between signals have a profound impact on the switching activity of a circuit. Another example is event driven logic simulation where the speed of simulation is directly proportional to the event activity within the circuit which is determined by the correlations in the input stimulus. An even more compelling example is the approach used by computer architects in designing a modern microprocessor. Given the goal of improving the SPECmark performance of a processor, all architectures are tuned to perform optimally for the given instruction traces generated from the benchmark suites. All three examples correspond to optimization of an average case cost function.

Trace $\mathcal{T}_1$ $x_1x_2x_3$	Values g_1	g_2	Trace $\mathcal{T}_2$ $x_1x_2x_3$	Values g_1	g_2
1 1 1	1	0	1 1 0	0	0
1 0 0	0	0	1 0 1	0	0
1 1 1	1	0	1 1 0	0	0
0 0 0	0	0	0 0 1	0	0
1 1 1	1	0	1 1 0	0	0
0 0 0	0	0	0 0 1	0	0
1 1 1	1	0	1 1 0	0	0
1 0 0	0	0	1 0 1	0	0
1 1 1	1	0	1 1 0	0	0
0 0 0	0	0	0 0 1	0	0
0 1 1	1	1	0 1 0	0	0

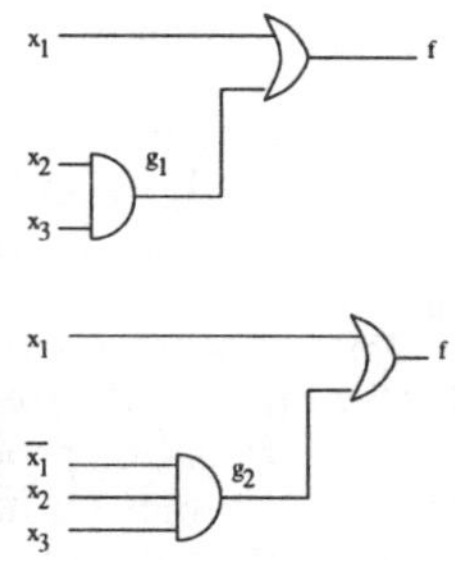

Figure 1: The two implementations of $f = x_1 + x_2 \cdot x_3$.

In this paper we propose a trace driven methodology for logic synthesis and optimization of Boolean circuits. Given an initial logic description of a digital circuit $\mathcal{C}$ and an expected trace of input vectors $\mathcal{T}$, an implementation of $\mathcal{C}$ that optimizes a cost function with respect to $\mathcal{T}$ is derived. This approach is effective in capturing and utilizing the correlations that exist between input signals and minimizes an average (or amortized) cost function rather than a worst case cost function. This paper is devoted to the case where the cost function is to minimize the average switching activity of the circuit under the sequence. The approach is mainly applicable to the combinational logic of finite state networks, where capturing the correlations between the state variables can play a significant role in power minimization.

Consider the simple example of a Boolean function f with *on-set*:

$$\mathcal{ON}(f) = \{x_1\overline{x_2}\,\overline{x_3}, x_1\overline{x_2}x_3, x_1x_2\overline{x_3}, x_1x_2x_3, \overline{x_1}x_2x_3\}$$

The minimum area implementation is $f = x_1 + g_1$ with $g_1 = x_2 \cdot x_3$. A second implementation of f is $f = x_1 + g_2$ with $g_2 = \overline{x_1} \cdot x_2 \cdot x_3$.

Consider the two traces $\mathcal{T}_1$ and $\mathcal{T}_2$ shown in Figure 1. Assume momentarily that only the number of gate switches is of concern, and the absolute power due to capacitance loading are being ignored. The first implementation generates 41 switches while the second yields 37 switches under

1092-3152/97 $10.00 © 1997 IEEE

trace $\mathcal{T}_1$. On the trace $\mathcal{T}_2$ the first circuit generates 30 switches while the second yields 35.

Now, assuming the input signals are uncorrelated, the transition probabilities [10] for both traces are identical, *i.e.*, $p(x_1) = 0.5$, $p(x_2) = 1.0$, $p(x_3) = 1.0$. Thus, previous approaches described by Najm [10] or Iman and Pedram [6] using signal and/or transition probabilities cannot distinguish between the two traces. Hence, the same implementation is selected for both traces. Our approach, in contrast, differentiates between the two traces and always selects the desirable implementation.

It is a widely accepted that the only effective approach to accurate power estimation is to perform logic simulation to obtain the switching activity from which the switching power can be estimated. The main reason behind this conclusion is the inaccuracy of the estimated power using probabilistic or statistical techniques. Specifically the correlations between the values on input signals within a vector as well as across vectors cannot be captured by existing probabilistic and statistical methods [9, 7]. Our approach extends the use of the actual vectors employed in power estimation to logic synthesis and optimization as well, thus narrowing the discrepancy in estimated power between analysis and synthesis tools while providing room for reduction in the power dissipation due to trace driven optimization.

Past approaches have suggested techniques to account for the effects of correlated inputs. One approach to approximating transition probabilities in the presence of correlated inputs is suggested in [15]. Another approach relevant to FSMs is the derivation of the steady state probabilities (*e.g.* using the Chapman-Kolmogorov equations [16]). However, capturing accurate transition probabilities on the inputs of a combinational network (even augmented with correlation values between pairs of inputs) still does not easily allow the derivation of accurate transition probabilities (and correlations between signals) on internal nodes of the network. This is the major drawback we seek to remedy using the trace-driven approach. All forms of signal correlations are captured by this method. Of course, the assumption required for successful application is that the trace set be representative of the input values during actual operation.

There is no *a priori* restriction on the length of the trace set that is used in the proposed methodology. Although it is conceivable that the trace sets generated using a naive simulation based procedure may be represented by a smaller trace set without much impact on the information essential for logic optimization, our approach is only marginally impacted by large trace sets for two reasons: (1) a trace set is compactly represented as a set of vector pairs - each vector pair has an associated frequency count of its occurrence in the trace set, (2) the size of the trace set only impacts the time for simulations needed during the logic optimization algorithms. Most of these simulations are performed in a pre-processing step and the running time can be improved by employing state-of-the-art logic simulation techniques. Nonetheless, trace driven synthesis can be performed with traces which are produced by vector compaction tools: for example, Tsui *et al.* [14] propose a technique with a compaction ratio of 100X while preserving most correlations.

2 Trace driven logic optimization problem

The problem of trace driven logic optimization for minimum switching activity is: Given a logic circuit represented as a set of Boolean functions and a sequence of input vectors, synthesize a circuit which dissipates minimum power due to switching activity under the application of the given sequence.

The focus of our work is on reduction of the switching power. We assume that the application of proper physical design techniques will minimize the power dissipated due to short-circuit and leakage currents. The switching power is estimated using a zero-delay model during logic optimization. While the principal reasons guiding this decision are the speed of the zero delay logic simulation versus timing simulation and the lack of availability of good delay models at the technology independent stage of logic synthesis, any other model that accounts for glitch occurrence may be utilized. At the technology independent level we account for the fanout of each gate as well as the size of the gate by using a decomposition into two-input gates. The accuracy of the model is verified by reporting results for the power dissipation obtained by running timing simulation using delays and capacitance loads obtained after technology mapping of the synthesize circuits.

B^n is the set of all vertices (or vectors) in the n-dimensional Boolean space. A **trace** $\mathcal{T} = \{v_1, v_2, ..., v_L\}$ of dimension n is an ordered sequence of vectors in B^n. Every input either has value 0 or 1 in each vector in a trace. A switch occurs when the value of f changes from 0 to 1 or 1 to 0. The switching activity of f under $\mathcal{T}$ is deduced by considering pairs of vectors. Let $\mathcal{P}_\mathcal{T}$ denote the set of pairs of adjacent vectors of $\mathcal{T}$, *i.e.*,

$$\mathcal{P}_\mathcal{T} = \{(v_i, v_j) \mid v_i \in \mathcal{T}, v_j \in \mathcal{T}, i = 1, ..., L-1, j = i+1\}$$

Associated with each element $(v_i, v_j) \in \mathcal{P}_\mathcal{T}$ is the frequency of occurrence of v_i and v_j as successive vectors in $\mathcal{T}$, denoted $\mathcal{F}_\mathcal{T}(v_i, v_j)$.

	$\mathcal{T}_1$	$\mathcal{T}_2$	$\mathcal{T}_3$
vector	$x_1x_2x_3x_4$	$x_1x_2x_3x_4$	$x_1x_2x_3x_4$
v_1	0 0 0 0	0 1 1 1	1 1 1 1
v_2	0 0 0 1	1 0 0 1	0 0 0 0
v_3	0 0 1 0	0 1 1 1	1 1 1 1
v_4	0 0 1 1	1 0 0 1	0 0 0 0
v_5	0 1 0 0	0 1 1 1	1 1 1 1
v_6	0 1 0 1	1 0 0 1	0 0 0 0
v_7	0 1 1 0	0 1 1 1	1 1 1 1
v_8	0 1 1 1	1 0 0 1	0 0 0 0
v_9	1 0 0 0	0 1 1 1	1 1 1 1
v_{10}	1 0 0 1	1 0 0 1	0 0 0 0

Table 1: Example traces

As an example, consider the three traces shown in Table 1. We have:

$$\begin{aligned}\mathcal{P}_{\mathcal{T}_1} &= \{(0000,0001),(0001,0010),(0010,0011),\\ &\quad (0011,0100),(0100,0101),(0101,0110),\\ &\quad (0110,0111),(0111,1000),(1000,1010)\}\\ \mathcal{P}_{\mathcal{T}_2} &= \{(0111,1001),(1001,0111)\}\\ \mathcal{P}_{\mathcal{T}_3} &= \{(0000,1111),(1111,0000)\}\end{aligned}$$

Suppose we wish to calculate the switching activity of a gate $g = x_2 \cdot x_3$ on each of the traces. Define

$$\mathcal{P}_\mathcal{T}(g) = \{(v_i, v_j) \mid (v_i, v_j) \in \mathcal{P}_\mathcal{T} \wedge g(v_i) \neq g(v_j)\}$$

and

$$\mathcal{F}^g_\mathcal{T} = \Sigma_{(v_i,v_j)\in\mathcal{P}_\mathcal{T}(g)}\ \mathcal{F}_\mathcal{T}(v_i, v_j)$$

For the example, we have $\mathcal{F}^g_{\mathcal{T}_1} = 2$, $\mathcal{F}^g_{\mathcal{T}_2} = 9$, and $\mathcal{F}^g_{\mathcal{T}_3} = 9$, each of which denotes exactly the switching activity of g under the respective trace set. The switching activity of an input variable x is obtained by setting $g = x$ in the above formulae.

The key transformation performed by the formulae above is the representation of all the information of a trace needed for calculating the switching power by a set of vectors pairs, each associated with a count of the frequency of occurrence of the vector pair in the trace. This representation of a trace by a set of vector pairs is critical in the formulation and implementation of the algorithms for exact and heuristic two-level logic minimization and heuristics for multi-level logic optimization algorithms for decomposition and factorization.

3 Trace driven two-level minimization

In this section we address the problem of synthesis of a two-level logic circuit for a Boolean function with minimum power dissipation for a given trace. We first provide an exact formulation of the two-level covering problem for minimum power dissipation and then describe a heuristic procedure to allow the solution of larger problems. As already indicated by the example of Figure 1, the minimum power cover may contain non-prime implicants. The cost of an implicant is computed according to the following definition:

Definition 3.1 *Given trace $\mathcal{T} = \{v_1, v_2, \ldots, v_L\}$ and an implicant $q = x_1 \cdot x_2 \cdot \ldots \cdot x_K$ of f, the* **power cost** *of q under $\mathcal{T}$, denoted $W_\mathcal{T}(q)$, is*

$$W_\mathcal{T}(q) = \mathcal{ISA}_\mathcal{T}(q) + \mathcal{OSA}_\mathcal{T}(q) \qquad (1)$$

with:

$$\mathcal{OSA}_\mathcal{T}(q) = 0.5 \cdot C_{load} \cdot V^2_{dd} \cdot \mathcal{F}^q_{\mathcal{T}_1} \qquad (2)$$

$$\mathcal{ISA}_\mathcal{T}(q) = \Sigma_{x_k \in q} 0.5 \cdot C_{x_k} \cdot V^2_{dd} \cdot \mathcal{F}^{x_k}_{\mathcal{T}_1} \qquad (3)$$

The term $\mathcal{OSA}_\mathcal{T}(q)$ represent the power dissipation due to the output switching activity of a gate g_q implementing q. C_{load} is the output load capacitance of g_q and V_{dd} is the supply voltage. Since there is an output transition only if $g_q(v_i) \neq g_q(v_{i+1})$, $\mathcal{OSA}_\mathcal{T}(q)$ sums the output power dissipation due to the entire trace $\mathcal{T}$. Similarly, the term $\mathcal{ISA}_\mathcal{T}(q)$ is the sum of the contributions to the total power dissipation due to the switching activity on each gate input x_k with capacitance C_{x_k}. Notice that $\mathcal{ISA}_\mathcal{T}(q)$ can be computed by simply observing the input trace and using the inputs that appear in q regardless of the specific function f.

Given the trace $\mathcal{T}$, the power cost of a cover $\mathcal{Q}$ of f, is given by

$$W_\mathcal{T}(\mathcal{Q}) = \sum_{q\in\mathcal{Q}} W_\mathcal{T}(q)$$

Thus we have the typical logic minimization problem: Given a Boolean function f and a trace $\mathcal{T}$, find the cover $\mathcal{Q}_\mathcal{T}$ of f which has the minimum power cost $W_\mathcal{T}(\mathcal{Q})$. A **minimum cover** is denoted $\mathcal{Q}^\star_\mathcal{T}$.

Following [1, 13], a minimum-weight unate covering problem (UCP) is solved using $W_\mathcal{T}(q)$ as the cost of each implicant q. In the case of trace driven two-level power minimization a minimum cover may contain an implicant which is not a prime. Since it is practically infeasible to solve the problem considering the set $\mathcal{I}$ of all the implicants [1], one wishes to identify a set $\mathcal{I}^\star_\mathcal{T} \subseteq \mathcal{I}$ of implicants sufficient to find a minimum cover. $\mathcal{I}^\star_\mathcal{T}$ is termed the set of candidate implicants.

The following definitions identify which implicants are elements of $\mathcal{I}^\star_\mathcal{T}$. An implicant q is **dominated** by an implicant $\tilde{q}$ if for every minimum cover which contains q there is another minimum cover which contains $\tilde{q}$. From Definition 3.1 it follows that an implicant q is dominated by another implicant $\tilde{q}$ if $q \subseteq \tilde{q}$ and $W_\mathcal{T}(q) \geq W_\mathcal{T}(\tilde{q})$ Given a function f and an input trace $\mathcal{T}$, a **candidate implicant** is an implicant of f that is not dominated by another implicant.

3.1 Generation of candidate implicants

An exact algorithm to generate $\mathcal{I}^\star_\mathcal{T}$ is presented in this section. The algorithm proceeds by generating implicants by *reduction* of larger candidate implicants thus eliminating implicants that are not candidate implicants as soon as possible.

Given $f : B^N \to B$, an implicant $q = x_1 \cdot x_2 \cdot \ldots \cdot x_K$ of f that is not a minterm is said to be **reducible**. The set $\mathcal{Y}$ of literals of the $N - K$ variables on which q does not depend is called the **external variable set** of q. A **reduced implicant** of q is an implicant $q \cdot y_1 \cdot y_2 \cdot \ldots \cdot y_H$ obtained by lowering q using one or more literals in $\mathcal{Y}$.

If q is a reducible implicant and qy is the reduced implicant obtained by lowering q using literal y, the following result holds for each possible trace $\mathcal{T}$:

$$\mathcal{ISA}_\mathcal{T}(qy) = \mathcal{ISA}_\mathcal{T}(q) + \mathcal{ISA}_\mathcal{T}(y)$$

Theorem 3.1 *Let q be a reducible candidate implicant and let qy be a reduced implicant of q obtained by lowering q using the literal y. qy is dominated by q if*

$$\Phi_\mathcal{T}(q, y) \geq 0 \qquad (4)$$

where

$$\Phi_\mathcal{T}(q, y) = \mathcal{OSA}_\mathcal{T}(qy) - \mathcal{OSA}_\mathcal{T}(q) + \mathcal{ISA}_\mathcal{T}(y) \quad (5)$$

Theorem 3.1 provides a basic rule for the generation of the set of candidate implicants $\mathcal{I}^\star$. Starting from the set of primes of f, which are considered *a priori* candidate implicants, equation (4) is applied to decide if a reduced implicant obtained by lowering a prime with a single literal is a candidate implicant. The same equation is applied recursively to each new candidate implicant. However, Theorem 3.1 does not apply to implicants that can be generated by reduction from implicants not inserted in $\mathcal{I}^\star_\mathcal{T}$. Note that qy could still be part of $\mathcal{I}^\star_\mathcal{T}$ even if q is not. The following theorem applies to this case.

[1] For an n-input Boolean function f, $\mid \mathcal{I} \mid = O(2^{2^n})$.

Theorem 3.2 *Let q be a reducible candidate implicant and let $q_h = qy_h$ be a reduced implicant of q such that $\Phi_{\mathcal{T}}(q, y_h) > 0$. Consider $q_{h+1} = q_h y_{h+1}$, which is another reduced implicant of q obtained by lowering q_h with a literal y_{h+1} different from y_h. q_{h+1} is dominated by q if*

$$\Phi_{\mathcal{T}}(q, y_h) + \Phi_{\mathcal{T}}(q_h, y_{h+1}) \geq 0 \quad (6)$$

Recursive application of Theorems 3.1 and 3.2 yields all the implicants in $\mathcal{I}^{\star}_{\mathcal{T}}$. Note that memorizing dominated implicants ensures that a dominated implicant is not inserted later into $\mathcal{I}^{\star}_{\mathcal{T}}$. We conclude this sub-section presenting a simple example of trace driven two level minimization.

Consider the Boolean function f and trace $\mathcal{T}$ in Figure 2. The table shows the correspondences between the input vectors and the vertices of the Boolean space B^5. Table 2 reports the power cost of the implicants of f obtained using equation (1). The column labeled with $\mathcal{I}^{\star}$ is obtained using Theorem 3.1 and 3.2 (a $\star$ is indicated if the implicant is a candidate implicant, otherwise a dominating implicant is indicated). The minimum power cost cover $\mathcal{Q}^{\star} = \{c_2, p_2, p_4, p_5\}$ has $W_{\mathcal{T}}(\mathcal{Q}^{\star}) = 122$, while the area minimum cover is $\mathcal{Q} = \{p_1, p_2, p_3, p_4\}$ has power cost $W_{\mathcal{T}}(\mathcal{Q}) = 135$.

Although the approach of enumerating only candidate implicants and early discarding of dominated implicants performs efficiently in practice, the final step of finding a minimum cost unate covering problem is often a bottleneck. Even extending the classical branch-and-bound based covering algorithm with *lower-bound* computation techniques recently presented in [2] do not provide much improvement. As an alternative, we have adapted the two-level heuristic minimization program *espresso* [1] to perform trace driven two-level minimization. This new heuristic program, called *elp*, is described briefly in the next sub-section.

3.2 Trace driven two-level heuristic minimization

elp inherits two basic principles from *espresso*: the use of the *unate recursive paradigm* and the presence, at the core of the algorithm, of an optimization loop which is performed until no improvement in cost function is seen. The main difference, naturally, is the introduction of trace based weights for the implicants of f. This implies an important difference from *espresso*: essential primes and prime implicants are not necessarily the target of the minimization procedure. Instead, the goal of *elp* is to determine those primes which are "essential" from a power minimization point of view and then determine sub-covers for the remaining minterms which produce low switching activity.

Let p be an essential prime of f and let $\mathcal{EM}(p)$ be the set of minterms of f which are covered only by p. Consider all possible covers of $\mathcal{EM}(p)$ composed of reduced implicants of p : let $\mathcal{C}^{\mathcal{EM}}$ be the cover which has the minimum power cost $W_{\mathcal{T}}(\mathcal{C}^{\mathcal{EM}})$. If $W_{\mathcal{T}}(\mathcal{C}^{\mathcal{EM}}) \geq W_{\mathcal{T}}(p)$ then p is in the minimum cover $\mathcal{Q}^{\star}$ of f. To make this decision it is necessary to solve a *local* and *usually small* unate covering problem. Once the essential primes from a power standpoint have been extracted, *elp* enters the typical *espresso* loop.

The first step is *reduce* which attempts to move the current solution out of a local minimum. This routine is unchanged in *elp*. *elp* differs significantly from *espresso* in the *expand* step. While *espresso* examines each cube q of the current cover and replaces it with a prime implicant d such that $q \subseteq d$, *elp* looks for the largest cube d' (not necessarily prime) which contains q and that has smaller power cost. This step is still characterized by the fact that the cardinality of the cover does not increase. The final step derives an *irredundant* cover using a greedy covering problem. *elp* follows the same strategy as *espresso* using the power costs of the implicants as the weights in the covering problem.

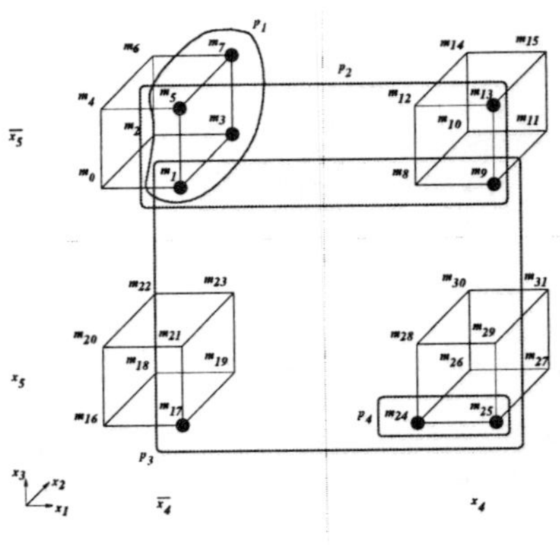

Input Trace $\mathcal{T}$

$x_1x_2x_3x_4x_5$	vertex
1 0 1 0 0	m_5
0 1 1 0 0	m_6
0 0 1 0 0	m_4
1 1 1 0 0	m_7
1 1 0 0 0	m_3
1 0 0 1 0	m_9
1 0 0 0 0	m_1
0 0 0 0 0	m_0
1 0 0 0 0	m_1
0 1 1 1 0	m_{14}
1 1 1 0 0	m_7
0 1 1 0 0	m_6
1 0 0 0 0	m_1
0 0 0 0 0	m_0
0 0 1 0 0	m_4
1 0 0 0 0	m_1
0 0 0 0 0	m_0
1 1 0 1 0	m_{11}
0 1 1 1 0	m_{14}
1 0 0 0 0	m_1
1 0 0 1 0	m_9
0 0 0 0 0	m_0

Figure 2: The function f and input trace $\mathcal{T}$.

implicant q	$\mathcal{ISA}_{\mathcal{T}}(q)$	$\mathcal{OSA}_{\mathcal{T}}(q)$	$W_{\mathcal{T}}(q)$	$\mathcal{I}^{\star}$
$p_1 = x_1\overline{x_4x_5}$	15	23	38	$\star$
$p_2 = x_1\overline{x_2x_5}$	11	23	34	$\star$
$p_3 = x_1\overline{x_2x_3}$	10	30	40	$\star$
$p_4 = \overline{x_2x_3}x_4x_5$	0	23	23	$\star$
$p_5 = x_1\overline{x_2x_3}x_5$	0	30	30	$\star$
$c_1 = x_1\overline{x_2x_4x_5}$	11	31	44	p_2
$c_2 = x_1x_2\overline{x_4x_5}$	4	31	35	$\star$
$c_3 = x_1\overline{x_3x_4x_5}$	12	30	42	p_1
$c_4 = x_1x_3\overline{x_4x_5}$	5	30	35	$\star$
$c_5 = x_1\overline{x_2x_3x_5}$	10	30	40	p_2
$c_6 = x_1\overline{x_2}x_3\overline{x_5}$	1	30	31	$\star$
$c_7 = x_1\overline{x_2}x_4\overline{x_5}$	4	31	35	p_2
$c_8 = x_1\overline{x_2x_3x_4}$	10	38	48	p_3
$c_9 = x_1\overline{x_2x_3}x_4$	4	38	42	p_3
$m_1 = x_1\overline{x_2x_3x_4x_5}$	10	38	48	p_1
$m_3 = x_1x_2\overline{x_3x_4x_5}$	2	38	40	p_1
$m_5 = x_1\overline{x_2}x_3\overline{x_4x_5}$	1	38	39	p_1
$m_7 = x_1x_2x_3\overline{x_4x_5}$	4	38	42	p_1
$m_9 = x_1\overline{x_2x_3}x_4\overline{x_5}$	4	38	44	p_2
$m_{13} = x_1\overline{x_2}x_3x_4\overline{x_5}$	0	38	38	p_2
$m_{17} = x_1\overline{x_2x_3x_4}x_5$	0	38	38	p_5
$m_{24} = \overline{x_1x_2x_3}x_4x_5$	0	38	38	p_4
$m_{25} = x_1\overline{x_2x_3}x_4x_5$	0	38	38	p_4

Table 2: Implicant Power Costs.

4 Trace driven multi-level minimization

In this section we describe the algorithms developed for the four main technology independent logic optimization procedures to achieve minimum power dissipation for a given trace.

4.1 Trace driven simplification and elimination

The node simplification strategy adopted for multi-level logic optimization is based on performing a two-level logic minimization at each node. Although this is an effective strategy for area minimization, since a local optimization at each node yields a local minimization of the area, it is less clear how simplification should be used for power reduction. A two-level minimization is effective only in reducing the output switching activity ($\mathcal{OSA}$) of the implicants of the function. This may change the fanout of the input variables and has to be carefully managed to avoid reaching a negative result. We simply adopt the logic simplification strategy already existing for area minimization, modified to use the procedure described for heuristic power minimization; alternatives to this naive approach remain an interesting problem for future work. To attempt to climb out of a local minimum, a trace-driven elimination command [17] has been developed using as the figure of merit the change in switching activity under the given trace. Due to the compact representation of traces by a set of vector pairs it is efficient to compute the local trace for the fanin of node n as well as to evaluate its output transition activity.

4.2 Trace driven decomposition

In multi-level logic optimization it is typical to decompose a gate with large fanin into a tree of gates with bounded fanin; this is performed for example during delay optimization or as a pre-process step of technology mapping. For our purposes the decomposition of a complex gate is also used to guide the estimation of the internal switching activity during the logic extraction step (Section 4.3).

Murgai, *et al.* [8] analyze the problem of decomposing a large-fanin gate for minimum switching activity using input transition probabilities (assuming independence between the input signals) and demonstrate that it is equivalent to the problem of finding a minimum weighted binary tree, where the weight of each node is its 1-controllability. An elegant solution to this problem was given by Huffman and can be exactly applied in the zero-delay case for general circuits. A Huffman style algorithm is not exact for a trace-driven decomposition. In fact, the trace driven setting allows us to achieve better decompositions than that obtained by a vanilla implementation of Huffman's algorithm.

We describe the decomposition for an AND gate, and the procedure can be easily dualized for the case of an OR gate. We build a **decomposition matrix** having K rows and columns corresponding to the K input variables of gate g. We use the rows to guarantee that all the variables x_k are "covered" and the columns to choose the next gate in the decomposition. Each column j, $1 \leq j \leq K$ is associated with a variable x_j. For each pair of distinct variables x_i, x_j the entry a_{ij} is a pair of numbers $(\mathcal{F}_\mathcal{T}, \mathcal{Z}_\mathcal{T})$ for the gate $g_{ij} = x_i \cdot x_j$. The first number is the output switching activity of g_{ij} under the trace $\mathcal{T}$. The second counts the number of pairs of successive zero values on the output of g_{ij} under application of $\mathcal{T}$. On each step of the algorithm the minimum entry a_{ij} is selected. An AND gate with inputs corresponding to i and j is created and the rows i and j are deleted from the matrix while a new column for the AND gate is added and the values of its entries are obtained via a local simulation of $\mathcal{T}$.

Let $f = x_1 \cdot x_2 \cdot x_3 \cdot x_4 \cdot x_5$ be the Boolean function for which we must find the best decomposition with respect to the trace $\mathcal{T}$ listed in Table 3. The initial decomposition matrix is as follows:

Input Trace $\mathcal{T}$	Output Traces of relevant gates						
$x_1x_2x_3x_4x_5$	g_1	g_1x_3	g_1x_4	g_1x_5	g_2	g_2x_4	g_2x_5
1 1 1 1 1	1	1	1	1	1	1	1
0 1 0 0 0	0	0	0	0	0	0	0
1 1 1 0 1	1	1	0	1	1	0	1
1 1 0 1 1	1	0	1	1	0	0	0
0 0 1 1 0	0	0	0	0	0	0	0
0 1 1 1 1	0	0	0	0	0	0	0
1 0 1 0 1	0	0	0	0	0	0	0
1 0 1 1 0	0	0	0	0	0	0	0
1 1 0 0 0	1	0	0	0	0	0	0

Table 3: The input trace $\mathcal{T}$ for decomposition example

$$\begin{array}{c} \\ x_1 \\ x_2 \\ x_3 \\ x_4 \\ x_5 \end{array} \begin{array}{c} \begin{array}{ccccc} x_1 & x_2 & x_3 & x_4 & x_5 \end{array} \\ \left[\begin{array}{ccccc} (\infty,0) & (4,3) & (5,2) & (5,3) & (5,2) \\ (4,3) & (\infty,0) & (5,3) & (5,3) & (5,2) \\ (5,2) & (5,3) & (\infty,0) & (5,2) & (5,2) \\ (5,3) & (5,3) & (5,2) & (\infty,0) & (5,3) \\ (5,2) & (5,3) & (5,2) & (5,3) & (\infty,0) \end{array}\right] \end{array}$$

Since the entry $(4,3)$ has the minimum value, we create the gate $g_1 = (x_1, x_2)$; the new matrix is shown in Table 3,

$$\begin{array}{c} \\ x_3 \\ x_4 \\ x_5 \\ g_1 \end{array} \begin{array}{c} \begin{array}{cccc} x_3 & x_4 & x_5 & g_1 \end{array} \\ \left[\begin{array}{cccc} (\infty,0) & (5,2) & (5,2) & (3,5) \\ (5,2) & (\infty,0) & (5,3) & (3,5) \\ (5,2) & (5,3) & (\infty,0) & (3,4) \\ (3,5) & (3,5) & (3,4) & (\infty,0) \end{array}\right] \end{array}$$

Three entries, namely (x_3, g_1), (x_4, g_1), and (x_5, g_1), have minimum value of $\mathcal{F}_\mathcal{T}$. A vanilla implementation of Huffman using only the first field would consider all three choices equal. However, in our procedure ties on the first field of an entry are broken by choosing the entry with the largest value of $\mathcal{Z}_\mathcal{T}$. The intuition behind this is that for an AND gate a larger value on the second field implies that the gate output is 0 more often than with a smaller value. This heuristic provides a better upper bound on the total number of switches that may occur for the remainder of the decomposition.

For the example, assume we select $g_2 = (g_1, x_3)$. After updating the decomposition matrix, the last two choices are trivial and produce a final decomposition which has 9 switches under $\mathcal{T}$. The unmodified Huffman algorithm yields a decomposition with 11 switches.

4.3 Trace driven extraction

The problem of logic extraction for low power has been previously addressed in two ways. Roy and Prasad [12] present a kernel extraction algorithm to reduce power dissipation by common sub-expression extraction guided by power values for nodes computed on the given factored form expressions for the nodes. A potential weakness of this approach is that the initial factored forms are not altered, leading to sub-optimum extractions. In [5] an alternate approach is proposed to solve this problem: the power values of the common sub-expressions are computed using the power cost of a node represented using a sum-of-products representation. Since this conforms to the underlying assumptions for traditional algebraic extraction and decomposition algorithms [13, 17], the authors can rely on these algorithms to extract the set of all single cube intersections and kernel intersections among the network nodes in order to choose the sub-expression having the maximum power reduction. The shortcoming of this approach is that after each extraction the switching activity of all the affected internal nodes must be re-estimated by computing the global BDD and the signal probabilities of each function. This operation is generally time consuming and is sped-up by using an approximation for the signal probabilities on the immediate fanin of a node [5].

Our technique is similar to the previous approaches in that a value is associated with each sub-expression to denote the power saving obtained if the logic extraction is performed. On the other hand, it differs from the previous approaches in three aspects. First, since the methodology is trace driven, signal probabilities are not employed. Instead, exact switching activity for any node is computed for the given trace by performing a local logic simulation. Since the global function of any node does not change during extraction a complete simulation of all the nodes on the trace is performed once. All subsequent simulations on sub-expressions are obtained by evaluating the function of the sub-expression on the known fanin values. Second, neither a factored form nor a sum-of-products representation is used to estimate the switching activity inside a node. Instead, each node is decomposed on the fly into gates with fanin two, by using the procedure outlined in Section 4.2. This represents a structure that is better correlated to the final network after technology mapping. Finally, our algorithm derives directly from the algorithm of Rajski and Vasudevamurthy [11] which is widely considered the most efficient method for Boolean extraction.

The basic objects used in extraction are single-cube divisors having exactly two literals, double cube divisors and their complements. The motivation for using objects of size two is that they ensure that the operations have polynomial running times, while they can be used to find single-cube divisors of arbitrary size and multiple-cube divisors. The complete definitions of double-cube divisor, set and subset of double-cube divisors, base of a double-cube divisor, single-cube divisor and its coincidence are found in [11]. We illustrate some of the terms for the benefit of the reader. Given four cubes $q_1 = x_1x_2, q_2 = x_1x_3, q_3 = x_1x_2x_3$ and $q_4 = x_1x_3x_4$, the set of two-literal single-cube divisors contains x_1x_2 which has coincidence 2 and x_1x_3 which has coincidence 3. (Coincidence K means that if d is extracted to create a new node n_d in the network then the fanout of this node will be K). Given a Boolean expression $f = x_1x_4x_5 + x_1x_6 + x_2x_3x_4x_5 + x_2x_3x_6$ the set of all its double cube divisors is $D(f) = \{x_6 + x_4x_5, x_1 + x_2x_3, x_1x_4x_5 + x_2x_3x_6, x_1x_6 + x_2x_3x_4x_5\}$. This set can be partitioned in subsets denoted by the symbol $D_{K,H,K+H}$ where K is the number of literals in the first cube and H the number of literals in the second cube. Hence, $x_6 + x_4x_5 \in D_{1,2,3}, x_1 + x_2x_3 \in D_{1,2,3}, x_1x_4x_5 + x_2x_3x_6 \in D_{3,3,6}$ and $x_1x_6 + x_2x_3x_4x_5 \in D_{2,4,6}$. Finally $x_6 + x_4x_5$ has two bases, namely x_1 and x_2x_3; $x_1 + x_2x_3$ has two bases, namely x_6 and x_4x_5 and the remaining two double-cube divisors have empty base. The greedy algorithm we propose is an extension of the Rajski and Vasudevamurthy extraction algorithm [11], modified to use cost values denoting the power dissipation due to single-cube and double-cube divisors.

The **power value** of a two literal single cube divisor $d = x_1x_2$ with coincidence equal to $K(d)$ is given by:

$$PV_{\mathcal{T}}(d) = (K(d) - 1) \cdot [\mathcal{F}_{\mathcal{T}}^{x_1} + \mathcal{F}_{\mathcal{T}}^{x_2}] - K(d) \cdot \mathcal{F}_{\mathcal{T}}^{d} + \mathcal{FISAD}$$

To understand this equation, suppose that extraction of d has been performed creating a new node n_d. The first term of the equation accounts for the power saving related to the variables x_1, x_2 which now feeds only node n_d instead of $K(d)$ nodes. The second term represents the switching activity of the output variable of n_d multiplied by its fanout. The third term ("fanout internal switching activity difference") denotes the change in power dissipation for each fanout n_j of n_d due to extraction.

Consider a double cube divisor $d \in D_{K,H,K+H}$ having the following characteristics:

- $d = x_1 \cdot x_2 \cdot \ldots \cdot x_K + y_1 \cdot y_2 \cdot \ldots \cdot y_H$;
- The node n_d which can be extracted has fanout $\mathcal{FO}$ in $\mathcal{N}$; e.g. d divides $\mathcal{FO}$ expressions associated two the nodes $n_1, n_2 \ldots n_{\mathcal{FO}}$;
- d has B bases $b_1 = z_1 \cdot z_2 \cdot \ldots \cdot z_{M_{b_1}}, \ldots b_B = z_1 \cdot z_2 \cdot \ldots \cdot z_{M_{b_2}}$.

Input Trace $\mathcal{T}$									Div. Output Traces		
x_1	x_2	x_3	x_4	x_5	x_6	x_7	x_8	x_9	$\mathcal{F}_{\mathcal{T}}^{d_1}$	$\mathcal{F}_{\mathcal{T}}^{d_2}$	$\mathcal{F}_{\mathcal{T}}^{d_3}$
0	1	0	0	1	0	0	0	1	0	0	0
1	1	0	0	1	0	0	0	1	1	0	0
0	1	0	0	1	0	0	0	1	0	0	0
1	1	0	0	1	0	0	0	1	1	0	0
0	1	0	0	1	0	0	0	1	0	0	0
1	1	0	1	0	0	1	1	0	1	0	0
0	1	0	0	1	0	0	0	0	0	0	0
1	1	1	1	0	0	1	1	0	1	0	0
0	1	0	0	1	0	0	0	0	0	0	0
1	1	1	1	0	0	1	0	1	1	0	0
0	1	0	0	1	0	0	1	1	0	0	0
1	1	1	1	0	0	1	1	1	1	0	0
0	1	0	0	1	0	0	0	1	0	0	0
1	1	0	1	0	0	1	1	1	1	0	0
0	1	0	0	1	0	0	1	1	0	0	0
1	1	0	0	1	0	0	0	1	1	0	0
0	1	0	0	1	0	0	0	1	0	0	0
1	1	0	0	1	0	0	0	1	1	0	0
0	1	0	0	1	0	0	0	1	0	0	0
1	1	0	0	1	0	0	0	1	1	0	0

Table 4: Traces for extraction example

The **power value** of d under the trace $\mathcal{T}$ is given by:

$$\begin{aligned} PV_{\mathcal{T}}(d) &= (\mathcal{FO}(d) - 1) \cdot \left[\sum_{k=1}^{K} (\mathcal{F}_{\mathcal{T}}^{x_k}) + \sum_{k=1}^{H} (\mathcal{F}_{\mathcal{T}}^{y_k}) \right] + \\ &- \mathcal{FO}(d) \cdot \mathcal{F}_{\mathcal{T}}^{d} + \sum_{i=1}^{B} \left[\sum_{j=1}^{M_{b_i}} (\mathcal{F}_{\mathcal{T}}^{z_j}) \right] + \mathcal{FISAD} + \mathcal{CG} \end{aligned}$$

As before, to understand this equation, suppose that the extraction of d has been performed creating a new node n_d. The first term accounts for the power saving related to the input variables $x_1, \ldots, x_K$ and $y_1, \ldots, y_H$ which now feed just the node n_d instead of $\mathcal{FO}$ nodes. The second term represents the switching activity of the output variable of n_d multiplied by its fanout. The third term is the power

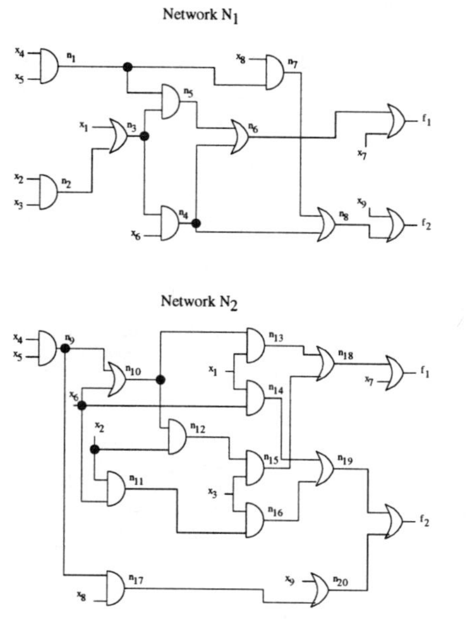

Figure 3: Two alternative extraction results

saving due to the occurrence of each variable z_i in a base of d. Consider a fanout node n_g before the extraction of d and suppose that two cubes of its function g are respectively $(x_1 \cdot x_2 \cdot \ldots \cdot x_K) \cdot b_1$ and $(y_1 \cdot y_2 \cdot \ldots \cdot y_H) \cdot b_1$, with $b_1 = z_1 z_2$. Obviously b_1 is a base of d and, if d is chosen to be extracted, the previous function will be replaced by $d \cdot b_1$. As a consequence, the node n_g will see the input switching activity decreased by a quantity equal to $\mathcal{F}_{\mathcal{T}}^{z_1} + \mathcal{F}_{\mathcal{T}}^{z_2}$. The last term ("complementary gain")is non-zero only if $d \in D_{1,1,2}$, *e.g.* if $d = x_1 + y_1$, where x_1 and y_1 are two distinct literals. In this case, the complement of d is a single cube divisor and the power value of $\overline{d}$ is added to $PV_{\mathcal{T}}(d)$. The term $\mathcal{FISAD}$ is the sum of $P^{n_j}_{orig} - P^{n_j}_{new}$ for each fanout n_j of d. $P^{n_j}_{orig}$ is the power dissipation before extraction, $P^{n_j}_{new}$ the power dissipation after extraction. The representation of traces by a set of vector pairs permits this computation to be performed very efficiently since only a local evaluation of the node functions is involved. Hence it is very feasible to estimate $P^{n_j}_{new}$ for each fanout n_j each time a divisor is evaluated.

Consider the Boolean Network which has 9 inputs, 2 outputs and 2 internal nodes f_1 and f_2.

$$
\begin{aligned}
f_1 &= x_1x_4x_5 + x_1x_6 + x_2x_3x_4x_5 + x_2x_3x_6 + x_7 \\
f_2 &= x_1x_6 + x_2x_3x_6 + x_4x_5x_8 + x_9
\end{aligned}
$$

Performing extraction using the area minimal option described in the algorithm of Rajski and Vasudevamurthy [11], followed by decomposition into 2-input AND and OR gates yields $\mathcal{N}_1$ in Figure 3. Now, suppose that we want to perform the best extraction for low power on $\mathcal{N}$ with respect to the input trace $\mathcal{T}$ specified in the same Figure. First, the power values of all the two-literal single-cube divisors and two-cubes divisors are computed. For the example, there are just two double-cube divisors $d_1 = x_1 + x_2 \cdot x_3$ and $d_2 = x_6 + x_4 \cdot x_5$, and one single divisor $d_3 = x_4 \cdot x_5$ which have positive power value. Using the equations presented in this section,

$$
\begin{aligned}
PV_{\mathcal{T}}(d_1) &= (3-1)\cdot[19+0+6] - 3\cdot 19 + [10+10] + 0 = 13 \\
PV_{\mathcal{T}}(d_2) &= (2-1)\cdot[0+10+10] - 2\cdot 0 + [19+0+6] + 0 = 45 \\
PV_{\mathcal{T}}(d_3) &= (2-1)\cdot[10+10] - 2\cdot 0 = 20
\end{aligned}
$$

d_2 is extracted (preferred over d_1) to obtain:

$$
\begin{aligned}
d_2 &= x_6 + x_4x_5 \\
f_1 &= d_2x_1 + d_2x_2x_3 + x_7 \\
f_2 &= x_1x_6 + x_2x_3x_6 + x_4x_5x_8 + x_9
\end{aligned}
$$

Trace-driven decomposition algorithm yields $\mathcal{N}_2$ in Figure 3. While $\mathcal{N}_2$ has 14 gates, $\mathcal{N}_1$ has 11, but there is a 14% reduction in power since:

$$
\begin{aligned}
\mathcal{F}_{\mathcal{T}}^{\mathcal{N}_1} &= 65 + 10 + 19\cdot 2 + 6 = 119 \\
\mathcal{F}_{\mathcal{T}}^{\mathcal{N}_2} &= 65 + 10 + 19 + 6 + 2 = 102
\end{aligned}
$$

5 Experimental Results

The first set of experiments (data not reported in this paper for lack of space) compared the trace-driven two-level heuristic and exact minimization algorithm against *espresso*. The traces for these examples were artificially generated as follows: Given a function f with p primes two successive vectors were created for each pair of primes such that the first vector is contained in the first prime and the second is contained in the second prime. The trace was intentionally biased towards obtaining poor results with *espresso* to determine what reductions may be achieved by this step alone. For the two-level case we assume that the output capacitance load on each implicant is equal to one unit, while the input capacitance is one unit for each literal. A more realistic model is not used here since this model is used for multi-level logic simplification where the inputs of a node are the outputs of other nodes. The following conclusions were inferred:

1. Reductions of up to 95% can be achieved for the quantity $\mathcal{OSA}_{\mathcal{T}}$ (*c.f.* Section 3) by selection of the appropriate implicants for minimal switching power compared to *espresso*.
2. The overall power reduction $W_{\mathcal{T}}(Q)$ is limited by the input switching activity $\mathcal{ISA}_{\mathcal{T}}$ which is a function only of the given trace. Two-level minimization cannot impact this significantly, since the number of literals varies little between *espresso* and *elp*. Thus, **two-level minimization can provide only a net incremental reduction in power once the trace has been determined**.

The next experiment was performed on 20 FSMs from the *ISCAS89 benchmark suite*. For these FSMs, given a reset state, 10000 random primary input vectors were applied. The trace of the primary input $\mathcal{T}^{PI}$ and the corresponding trace $\mathcal{T}^{L}$ of the latch values, obtained by sequential logic simulation, were combined together to serve as the trace for power minimization. The average power reduction is 16% before technology mapping, and 14% after technology mapping (Table 5).

We also report the fraction of power dissipation due to the transition activity related to primary inputs and latches (column marked "I/O Power Fraction"). These values were obtained by simulating the circuit after technology independent optimization with *script.rugged*. These results prove an important point on logic synthesis for low power: **the I/O power provides an upper bound on the power reduction that can be achieved**, because combinational logic synthesis only reduces power consumed in the internal nodes of the circuit. For example, consider the data reported for FSM *s298* in Table 5. A final power reduction of 25% has been obtained with the *low power* script, even though in the initial circuit 40% of the total power P was due just to primary input and latch switching activity. We have:

$$P \cdot (0.40 + x \cdot 0.60) = P \cdot (1 - 0.25) \quad \Rightarrow x = 0.35/0.60 = 0.58$$

Hence, for this example, trace driven logic synthesis provided a reduction of the power due to internal transition activity of 42%. From Table 5, the average reduction of internal power is 25%.

FSM	I/O/L	Gate #	I/O Power Fract.	tech. independent ratio: LP/rugg. Area	Power	mapp. networks ratio: LP/rugg. Area	Power
s27	4/1/3	9	0.46	0.88	0.95	0.97	0.95
s208	10/1/8	70	0.41	0.96	0.61	1.09	0.89
s298	3/6/14	111	0.40	1.00	0.72	0.99	0.75
s344	9/11/15	123	0.23	0.97	0.83	1.06	0.91
s349	9/11/15	122	0.22	1.03	0.84	1.07	0.89
s382	3/6/21	142	0.37	1.13	0.78	1.07	0.76
s386	7/7/6	108	0.26	1.08	0.76	1.04	0.78
s400	3/6/21	137	0.36	1.37	0.86	1.20	0.84
s420	18/1/16	143	0.42	1.04	1.00	1.12	0.84
s444	3/6/21	136	0.35	1.21	0.77	1.12	0.78
s510	19/7/6	255	0.24	0.99	0.87	1.04	0.91
s526	3/6/21	171	0.46	1.36	0.98	1.23	1.07
s526n	3/6/21	191	0.40	1.20	0.92	1.15	0.96
s641	35/23/17	156	0.33	0.90	0.76	0.93	0.83
s713	35/23/17	157	0.33	0.81	0.73	0.91	0.78
s820	18/19/5	298	0.39	1.05	0.90	1.08	0.93
s832	18/19/5	288	0.38	1.11	0.92	1.13	0.99
s838	34/1/32	355	0.43	1.27	0.84	1.11	0.66
s1488	8/19/6	641	0.20	0.99	0.82	1.00	0.81
s1494	8/19/6	641	0.20	1.00	0.84	1.01	0.85

Table 5: Results on *ISCAS89* FSMs

6 Conclusions and Future Work

This paper has proposed a new trace drive methodology for logic synthesis which captures and exploits the correlations that exist between signal values in an application specific design. The idea has been applied to the minimization of the switching activity in the combinational logic portion of finite state machines. In this paper we have focussed on technology independent optimizations. The extension to technology mapping, based on applying trace driven optimization to the methods proposed in [3] remains for the future. Our results have also indicated that additional gains can only be realized by changing the sequential behavior of the FSMs to impact the I/O switching activity. The application of encoding and re-encoding techniques [4] to reduce I/O activity is a promising avenue for exploration.

Acknowledgments

The authors would like to thank Alberto Ferrari and Tiziano Villa for their support and useful discussions.

References

[1] R. K. Brayton, G. D. Hachtel, C. T. McMullen, and A. L. Sangiovanni-Vincentelli. *Logic Minimization Algorithms for VLSI Synthesis*. Kluwer Academic Publishers, 1984.

[2] O. Coudert. On Solving Covering Problems. In *Proc. of the Design Automation Conf.*, pages 197–202, June 1996.

[3] O. Coudert and R. Haddad. Integrated Resynthesis for Low Power. In *ISLPED Digest of Technical Papers*, pages 169–174, August 1996.

[4] G. D. Hachel, M. Hermida, A. Pardo, M. Poncino, and F. Somenzi. Re-Encoding Sequential Circuits to Reduce Power Dissipation. In *Proceedings of the Design Automation Conference*, pages 70–73, June 1994.

[5] S. Iman and M. Pedram. Logic Extraction and Factorization for Low Power. In *Proceedings of the Design Automation Conference*, pages 248–253, June 1995.

[6] S. Iman and M. Pedram. Two-Level Logic Minimization for Low Power. In *Proceedings of the International Conference on Computer-Aided Design*, pages 433–438, November 1995.

[7] R. Marculescu, D. Marculescu, and M. Pedram. Efficient Power Estimation for Higly Correlated Input Streams. In *Proceedings of the Design Automation Conference*, pages 628–634, June 1994.

[8] R. Murgai, R. K. Brayton, and A. L. Sangiovanni-Vincentelli. Decomposition for Minimum Transition Activity. In *Proceedings of the Low Power Workshop - Napa Valley*, April 1994.

[9] F. N. Najm. A Survey of Power Estimation Techniques in VLSI Circuits. *IEEE Transactions on VLSI Systems*, 2:446–455, 1994.

[10] F. N. Najm. Feedback, Correlation, and Delay Concerns in the Power Estimation of VLSI Circuits. In *Proceedings of the* 32th *Design Automation Conference*, pages 612–617, June 1995.

[11] J. Rajski and J. Vasudevamurthy. The Testability-Preserving Concurrent Decomposition and Factorization of Boolean Espression. *IEEE Transactions on Computer-Aided Design*, 11:778–793, 1992.

[12] K. Roy and S.C. Prasad. Circuit Activity Based Logic Synthesis for Low Power Reliable Operations. *IEEE Transactions on VLSI Systems*, 1:503–513, 1993.

[13] Richard L. Rudell. *Logic Synthesis for VLSI Design*. PhD thesis, University of California Berkeley, Electronics Research Laboratory, College of Engineering, University of California, Berkeley, CA 94720, April 1989. Memorandum No. UCB/ERL M89/49.

[14] C-Y. Tsui, R. Marculescu, D. Marculescu, and M. Pedram. Improving the Efficiency of Power Simulators by Input Vector Compaction. In *Proceedings of the Design Automation Conference*, pages 165–168, June 1996.

[15] C-Y. Tsui, M. Pedram, and A. M. Despain. Efficient Estimation of Dynamic Power Consumption under a Real Delay Model. In *Proceedings of the International Conference on Computer-Aided Design*, pages 224–228, Nov 1993.

[16] C-Y. Tsui, M. Pedram, and A. M. Despain. Exact and Approximate Methods for Calculating Signal and Transition Probabilities in FSMs. In *Proceedings of the* 29th *Design Automation Conference*, pages 18–23, June 1994.

[17] A. Wang. *Algorithms for Multi-Level Logic Optimization*. PhD thesis, University of California Berkeley, Electronics Research Laboratory, College of Engineering, University of California, Berkeley, CA 94720, April 1989.

SESSION 10B

ANALYSIS OF REAL TIME SYSTEMS

Moderators:

Wayne Wolf, Princeton University, Princeton, NJ

Ahmed A. Jerraya, TIMA-CMP Lab., Grenoble, France

Performance Analysis of a System of Communicating Processes

Sujit Dey and Surendra Bommu
C&C Research Laboratories, NEC USA, Inc.
Princeton, NJ 08540

Abstract

Efficient exploration of the system design space necessitates fast and accurate performance estimation as opposed to the computationally prohibitive alternative of exhaustive simulation. This paper addresses the issue of worst-case performance analysis of a system described as a set of concurrent communicating processes. We show that the synchronization overhead associated with inter-process communication can contribute significantly to the overall system performance. Application of existing performance analysis techniques, which target single process descriptions, lead to inaccurate performance estimates as the synchronization overhead is not accounted for. We present PERC, a fast and accurate worst-case performance analysis technique which analyzes inter-process communication, and accounts for synchronization overhead while computing the worst-case performance estimate of a given system implementation. Application of PERC to example systems described as multiple communicating processes shows the ability of the proposed method to accurately estimate the worst-case performance of the system implementation.

I. Introduction

Increasing complexity, aggressive design requirements, and shorter product cycles are necessitating fast and efficient exploration of the system design space, requiring the capability of analyzing the system performance, power, and other design metrics for several system implementations at high levels of abstraction. This paper introduces a technique to estimate the worst-case performance of a system described as a set of concurrent communicating processes. The performance of a system is determined by both the number of clock cycles required by the system implementation, as well as the clock period of the implementation. A possible way of evaluating the worst case system performance is by exhaustive simulation of the system implementation. However, the approach can be computationally inhibitive, especially in an iterative design framework, where at every iteration, multiple implementation alternatives need to be evaluated. Hence the need for fast static performance analysis and estimation tools.

Several performance analysis and delay estimation techniques have been developed recently. In [1, 2], analysis techniques were developed to compute the average number of clock cycles required by a scheduled implementation of a behavioral description. Markov chain model based metrics for evaluating the performance of schedules was suggested in [3]. Several clock period estimation techniques have also been developed [4, 5, 6, 7, 8] for ASIC implementations. Static performance analysis techniques for software implementation on processors have been proposed in [9, 10].

Many real-life systems, including telecommunication and networking applications, embedded control applications, and multimedia applications among others are described as a set of concurrent communicating processes. The clock period estimation of an implementation is not affected whether the system is described and implemented as a single process or as a set of multiple communicating processes; hence, the clock period estimation techniques described above [4, 5, 6, 7, 8] are applicable to such multi-process systems. However, applying existing performance analysis techniques to estimate number of clock cycles [1, 2, 9] of systems described as concurrent communicating processes will lead to inaccurate results. This is because the above performance analysis techniques target single-process descriptions, and the synchronization overhead associated with inter-process communication, which can contribute significantly to the overall performance, is ignored. Synthesis of a system of communicating processes has been considered in [11] but performance analysis has not been addressed. Optimization of a behavioral description of multiple communicating processes specified in VHDL is suggested in [12]. In [13] the analysis of multi-process systems is addressed using a petri-net model, but the associated data structure could become exponentially large. Consequently, there is a need for a fast and efficient analysis technique which estimates the performance (number of clock cycles) of a system of communicating processes.

This paper introduces PERC, a technique to analyze the communication structure of a set of concurrent communicating processes. Given the system implementation, like the schedule of each process, PERC estimates the worst-case performance of the system. The performance analysis technique relies on computing the time taken per iteration of each loop of the system. Loops which communicate with each other are clustered into sets called communication layers, so that the time taken per iteration of each communicating loop in the layer can be computed including the synchronization overhead. The proposed technique is hierarchical in nature, computing the time taken by the loops in the next level of communication layer using the time taken by loops in the current layer, along with the information on loop bounds. The overall system performance is computed when the top level of communication layer is analyzed. Our analysis approach is also able to identify the critical paths in the system description, which can be used to improve the system performance by guiding the synthesis tools.

In the next section, we motivate the need for a performance analysis technique which takes into account the synchronization overhead due to the communication of multiple concurrent processes. Section III describes the terminology and definitions used in the subsequent sections, and introduces the synchronization graph used to capture the underlying com-

1092-3152/97 $10.00

munication structure of a system. Section IV introduces the concept of communication layers, while Section V discusses the procedure of identifying the communication layers. Section VI gives a method of analyzing all the loops of a single communication layer and computing the time taken by each loop in the layer. Section VII describes the technique to estimate the overall system performance. Results of application of the proposed performance analysis tool PERC to example systems of concurrently communicating processes are provided in Section VIII.

II. MOTIVATION

In this section, we illustrate an example system of concurrent communicating processes. Using the example system, we motivate the need for a global performance analysis technique which analyzes and includes the synchronization overhead while computing the system performance.

Figure 1 shows parts of the control-flow graph (CFG) of an ethernet controller description. The ethernet protocol involves sending data packets over the network. If a particular transmission of a packet is not successful (a collision detected over the network), the packet has to be re-transmitted after a specified amount of time. The protocol also ensures that a minimum amount of time has elapsed between successive transmissions of the packet. The overall communication pattern of the ethernet controller is shown in Figure 1.

Communication between processes can be achieved using various protocols, depending upon the language used to describe the system. Depending on the semantics allowed by a particular language the communication between concurrently executing entities could be of several types, but the underlying concept involves one entity sending an event to another concurrent entity which would be waiting for the event. The systems considered in this paper are assumed to be communicating using event and wait statements as shown in the *ethernet controller* example in Figure 1. An assignment to a global signal generates an event which is received by a process waiting on the event. The global signals are divided into *synchronizing signals* and *data transfer signals*. The synchronizing signals are used to generate events and synchronize among the processes, while the data transfer signals are used to exchange information between processes. In the example, shown in Figure-1, the signal *XmitBegin* is a synchronizing signal, whereas the signal *NewCollision* represents a data transfer signal as this signal does not play a role in the synchronization between processes.

To investigate the issue of performance analysis of a system described as a set of concurrent communicating processes, we generated a scheduled implementation of the ethernet controller using a scheduling tool [1]. We then considered the problem of computing the worst-case number of clock cycles needed by the scheduled implementation. The result obtained by simulating the scheduled description using some test cases is shown in Table 2, which is 767 clock cycles. Next, we used an existing performance analysis technique [1] to compute the number of clock cycles taken by each process. Note that since the existing technique(s) can be applied only to a single process at a time, the communication between the processes, and hence the time spent in synchronization (wait statements), is ignored. The result is shown in Table 2. Processes 1, 2, and 3 are estimated to take 175, 48, and 291 respectively. Hence, the worst case performance of the system, which is the maximum of the number of clock cycles needed to execute each process, is 291 clock cycles. The large percentage difference with the simulation result, -62%, represents a significant under-estimate of the worst-case performance of the system. The large error can be attributed to ignoring the synchronization overhead among the processes.

On the other hand, if the performance estimation technique can perform a global analysis of all the processes and their communication, and the time taken in process synchronization is accounted for while estimating the performance of each process, the system performance estimate is much more accurate. The result of applying the performance estimation technique PERC discussed in this paper is also shown in Table 2. The performance of processes 1, 2, and 3 is now estimated to be 902, 334, and 334 clock cycles respectively, with a total system performance to be 902 clock cycles. The PERC estimate has a significantly smaller difference (18%) with the result obtained by simulation. Also, as expected, the PERC estimate is more conservative than that obtained by simulation, which is not exhaustive and cannot always identify the worst-case behavior of a system.

Note the significant difference in clock cycle estimates between PERC and the technique which analyzes each process individually. For example, PERC estimates process 1 to take 902 clock cycles, as opposed to the estimate of 175 clock cycles obtained when time spent in wait statements is ignored. The difference in the estimates is due to the significant time the processes spend in waiting for synchronizing events, and demonstrates the critical need for considering synchronization overhead during performance analysis.

In the next few sections, we describe the proposed performance analysis technique which estimates the worst-case performance taking into account the synchronization overhead.

III. CHARACTERISTICS OF SYNCHRONIZING PROCESSES

In this section, we introduce some terminology and definitions used in the paper. We also discuss the assumptions made regarding the allowed communication between processes.

An event or wait statement is termed as a synchronizing statement. A loop l_i is said to contain a synchronizing statement if the statement is present in the loop and is not present in any loop nested by l_i. A loop containing a synchronizing statement will be referred to as a *synchronizing loop*. Since individual processes could iterate more than once, each process itself is considered to be a loop. Consider the description of the ethernet controller shown in Figure 1. The loop representing the process *BitTransmitter* is a synchronizing loop as it contains synchronizing statements like $XmitEnd \leftarrow 1$.

We next introduce the *Synchronization Graph* which captures the communication/synchronization among the system processes. The synchronization graph is a directed graph with vertex set V and edge set E. The set of vertices V consists of the the following types of node: *Loop Nodes* corresponding to the beginning and the end of each loop l in the system description, where loop l is either a synchronizing loop or nests a synchronizing loop; *Event nodes* corresponding to an event statement in the behavioral specification, and *Wait nodes* corresponding to a wait statement in the behavioral specification.

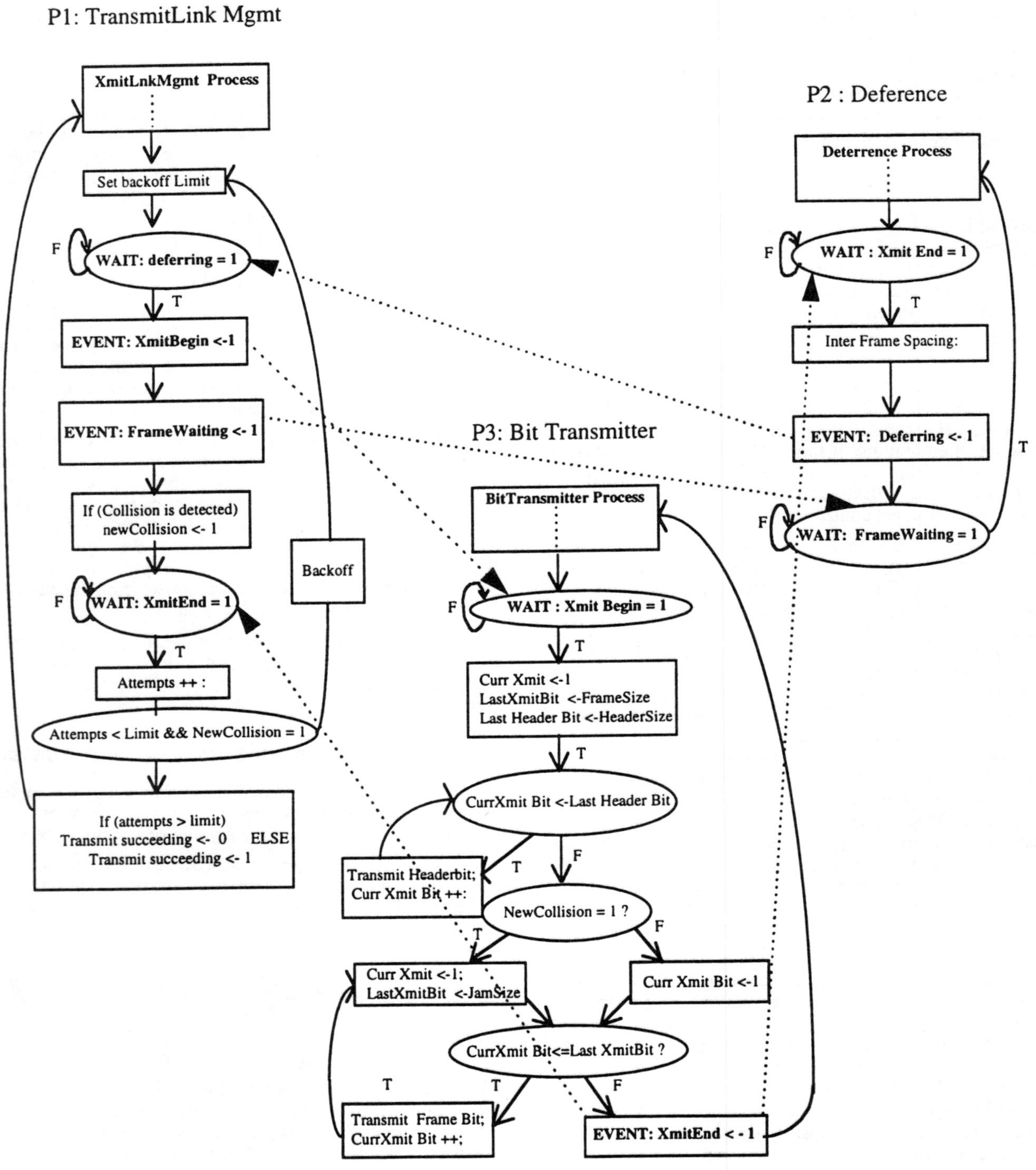

Figure 1: Partial description of an Ethernet Controller, showing inter-process communication

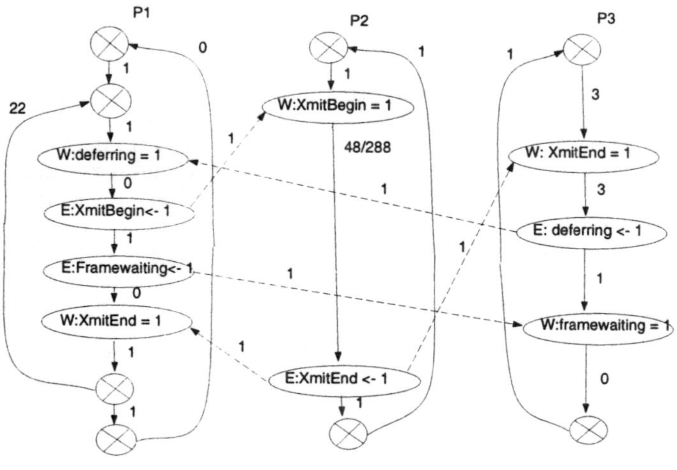

Figure 2: Synchronization Graph of the Ethernet Controller

There exists a process edge between two nodes if they belong to the same process and there is a direct path connecting the corresponding behavioral statements in the system specification, not containing any statement that can be represented as a node in the synchronization graph. The weight of a process edge represents the worst case time needed by the system implementation (in this paper, the schedule) to execute the statements in the corresponding path. There exists a synchronizing edge between an event node (v_1) and wait node (v_2), if v_1 and v_2 do not belong to the same process, and the event generated by v_1 is meant to be received by wait node v_2. The weight associated with a synchronizing edge represents the communication overhead involved in sending the event, and depends on the system implementation.

Figure 2 shows the synchronization graph corresponding to the ethernet controller description partially shown in Figure 1. For example, in the *Deference* process of Figure 1, there is a wait node in the synchronization graph corresponding to the statement *WAIT: XmitEnd = 1*, and an event node in the synchronization graph corresponding to the statement *Event:Deferring* $\leftarrow$ 1. A process edge exists between the above two nodes, representing the block of code *InterFrameSpacing* shown in Figure 1. The weight of the process edge is 3, since it takes 3 clock cycles in the worst case to execute the statements corresponding to the process edge. A synchronizing edge exists between the node representing *Event: Deferring* $\leftarrow$ 1 (process Deference) and the wait statement *WAIT: Deferring* $\leftarrow$ 1 of process *TransmitLinkMgmt*. In this example, communication between the processes is assumed to go through registers, requiring a single clock cycle; hence, each synchronizing edge has been assigned a weight of 1. In general, the weight assigned to each synchronizing edge will depend upon the mode of communication implemented.

Each synchronizing loop, l_i, is associated with a quadruple $(N(l_i), W(l_i), E(l_i), P(l_i))$, where *N($l_i$)* represents the set of synchronizing loops nested by the synchronizing loops l_i, *E(l_i)* represents the set of synchronizing loops which wait on an event generated inside l_i, *W(l_i)* represents the set of synchronizing loops which generate an event that l_i could be waiting on, and P(l_i) represents the process containing the loop l_i.

We shall now discuss some of the assumptions made regarding the communication between concurrent processes. As mentioned before, the system communicates using event and wait statments. An event is generated by setting a synchronizing variable to one, and the synchronizing variable is reset by the receiving process immediately after receiving the event and coming out of the wait statement. The following assumptions are made regarding the generation/consumption of events: (1) The rate of generation of an event is less than or equal to the rate of consumption of the corresponding event. Relaxing this assumption would mean that buffers will be needed to store the outstanding events. In this paper we will not consider system implementations which use buffers to store the events which have not yet been consumed, and (2) A synchronizing signal cannot be assigned to or waited on more than once in a loop. This assumption can be enforced as a semantic restriction; while not being too restrictive on the designer, this constraint facilitates the analysis of the system.

In the next section, we propose a method to analyze and take into account the effect of synchronization overhead in system performance.

IV. Considering Synchronization Overhead in Performance Analysis

To compute the performance of a system, the time taken by the loops of the system description have to be computed. In a system of communicating processes, the time taken by a synchronizing loop containing a wait statement depends not only on the time to execute the statements in the loop, but also on the *synchronization overhead*, which is the time taken by the wait statements in waiting for events generated by other communicating loops. To enable our performance analysis to include the synchronization overhead, we introduce the concept of a *communication layer*, which is a set of synchronizing loops communicating with each other simultaneously. Considering all the loops in a communication layer together during performance analysis is sufficient to account for the synchronization overhead. Next, we describe the notion of communication layers.

A loop l_i is said to *communicate* with another loop l_j if either l_i has a wait node waiting for an event generated in l_j, or vice versa. That is, $l_i \subset (E(l_j) \cup W(l_j))$. A loop is said to be *alive* in a given clock cycle, if any node (statement) in the loop is executed in that cycle. If two loops are simultaneously alive in a given clock cycle, they are said to be executing *concurrently*. A **communication layer** is defined as a maximal set of synchronizing loops such that

C1 each loop of the set communicates with at least one other loop of the set, and

C2 all the loops of the set should execute concurrently.

Consider the synchronization graph shown in Figure 3, which corresponds to the description of a blackjack game controller, containing three communicating processes. Consider the set of loops $L = \{l_1, l_2, l_3, l_6, l_7\}$ in Figure 3. Each loop of the set communicates with at least one other loop of the set. For instance, l_7 communicates with l_6, and each of l_1, l_2, l_3 communicates with l_6. Consequently, the set L satisfies condition C1 of the definition of a communication layer. Loops l_1, l_2, l_3 do not execute concurrently (violates condition C2), and hence do not belong to the same layer. The set of loops which are concurrent are $L_1 = \{l_1, l_6, l_7\}$,

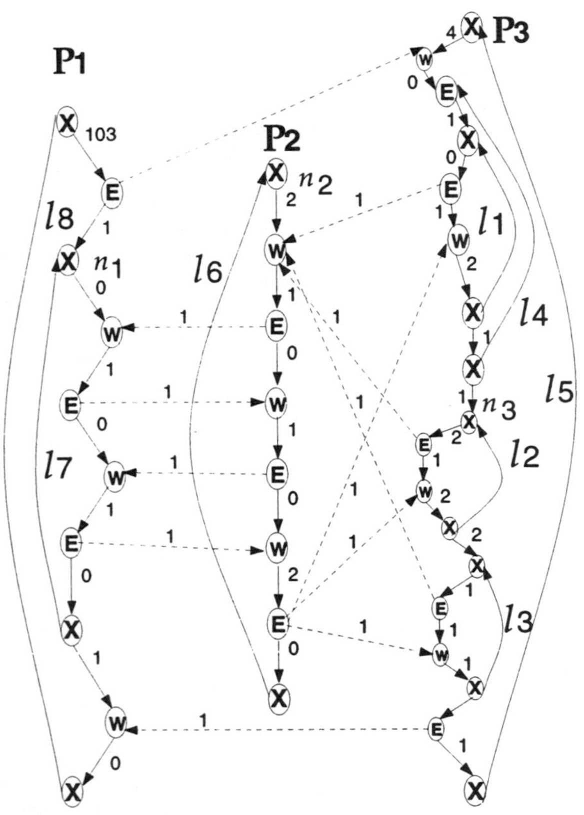

Figure 3: Synchronization Graph of Blackjack Game Controller

$L_2 = \{l_2, l_6, l_7\}$ and $L_3 = \{l_3, l_6, l_7\}$. Since the loops in the above sets also satisfy condition C1, they form three communication layers. The set $L_4 = \{l_8, l_5\}$ forms a fourth communication layer.

A layer L_1 is said to nest a layer L_2 if a loop in L_1 nests a loop belonging to L_2. That is, $\exists$ a loop $l \in L_1$ such that $N(l) \cap L_2 \neq nil$. Let $N(L)$ be the set of layers nested by L. The *nesting level* of a layer L, *Level*(L), is defined as:

$$Level(L) = \begin{cases} 1 & \text{if } N(L) = nil \\ \max_{L_i \in N(L)} Level(L_i) + 1 & \text{otherwise} \end{cases}$$

Consider the layers formed above for the synchronization graph of Figure 3. None of the loops in L_1, l_2 and L_3 nest other loops and hence the nesting level of L_1, L_2 and L_3 is 1. In the layer $L_4 = \{l_8, l_5\}$, loop l_5 nests the loops l_1, l_2, and l_3. Since $l_1 \in L_1, l_2 \in L_2$, and $l_3 \in L_3$, we have the nesting level of L_4 = 1 + Max(nesting levels(L_1, L_2, L_3)) = 2.

Our performance analysis method analyzes each communication layer in an increasing order of their nesting level. For each layer, the time taken by each loop belonging to the layer is computed as explained in Section VI. After a communication layer L is analyzed, the loops in L are collapsed, and the layer nesting L is analyzed using the time taken by the collapsed loops. This process is continued till all the layers have been analyzed; the analysis of the final layer gives the system performance. The overall system analysis method is explained in Section VII. In the next section, the procedure for identifying communication layers along with their nesting levels is presented.

V. Identifying Communication Layers

The formation of communication layers needs information about the concurrent execution of two synchronizing loops, which depends on the pattern of communication and the characteristics of the implementation of the system. In the synchronization graph shown in Figure 3, loops l_6 and l_7 execute concurrently, but loops l_1, l_2, l_3 do not. In the subsequent discussions, the concurrency information for communicating loops is assumed to be available.

A. Creating Layers

In this section we shall describe a procedure for identifying the layers from a set of loops S. First, the set of loops s is partitioned into classes. A class is a maximal subset of communicating loops, A, of S satisfying the following conditions: (1) all the loops of subset A should communicate with at least one other loop of A, and (2) the loops of A do not communicate with any loops outside A.

The members of a class, clearly, satisfy condition C1 of a communication layer. In Figure 3, the set $\{l_1, l_2, l_3, l_6, l_7\}$ forms a class. The concurrency information between synchronizing loops is then used to further divide each class into layers. The algorithm given below partitions a class into communication layers and returns a list of communication layers formed.

Algorithm 1 $ClassToLayers(Class\ C)$

```
    /* C represents set of loops belonging to the same class */
    /* If class is already a layer return*/
        if(∀l_i, l_j ∈ C, l_i and l_j are concurrent)
            return C;
    /* If class is not a layer do the following */
        if(∃l_i, l_j ∈ C|l_i l_j are not concurrent){
            C° = C − {l_i, l_j};
            C_1 = C° ∪ {l_i}; C_2 = C° ∪ {l_j};
            return ClassToLayers(C_1)
                   ∪ ClassToLayers(C_2);
        }
```

The above recursive algorithm returns a list of layers formed from the class C, given as input to the algorithm. We shall illustrate the execution of Algorithm 1 using the set $C = \{l_1, l_2, l_3, l_6, l_7\}$ of the synchronization graph in Figure 3. In the first iteration of Algorithm 1, the set C is divided into the sets $C_1 = \{l_6, l_7, l_2, l_3\}$ and $C_2 = \{l_6, l_7, l_1, l_3\}$, since l_1 and l_2 do not execute concurrently. A recursive call is made on each of the sets C_1 and C_2. The loops l_2, l_3 of C_1 and l_1, l_3 of C_2 do not execute concurrently, hence the classes C_1 and C_2 are further divided into the following: $C_{11} = C_{21} = \{l_6, l_7, l_3\}$, $C_{12} = \{l_6, l_7, l_1\}$ and $C_{22} = \{l_6, l_7, l_2\}$; each of the above classes are layers since all the loops in the class run concurrently. Hence the layers formed are: $L_1 = C_{12} = \{l_1, l_6, l_7\}$, $L_2 = C_{22} = \{l_2, l_6, l_7\}$ and $L_3 = C_{11} = C_{22} = \{l_3, l_6, l_7\}$.

B. Identifying Layers and their nesting levels

In this section, the overall procedure used to identify all the communication layers is given, first the pseudo-code, followed by a brief description.

Algorithm 2 $Identify\_Layers(U)$

```
level = 1;
While(U ≠ nil){
    S = {l | l does not nest any loop in U};
    Layer[level] = Create_Layers(S);
    /*Each element of the array Layer represents */
    /*all the layers of the same level */
    U = U − {l | l ∈ Layer[level]};
    level++;
}
```

The input to the above algorithm is the set of all synchronizing loops of the system. The function *Create_Layers* identifies layers from a set of loops S by first dividing S into classes, and then using the function *ClasstoLayers* (section IV) to compute the layers of each class. At each iteration i of the *while* loop, layers of level i are formed. All the loops which are partitioned into layers are removed from consideration for partitioning in the remaining iterations; the procedure is continued till all the loops are partitioned. Consider the blackjack example shown in Figure 3. The set U is initialized to all the loops of the system. In the first iteration the set S contains $\{l_1, l_2, l_3, l_6, l_7\}$, and the corresponding layers formed are given by the sets L_1, L_2, L_3 as described in section A. Hence the nesting level of layers L_1, L_2, L_3 is 1. In the second and final iteration, set $S = \{l_8, l_9\}$, yielding the fourth layer $L_4 = \{l_8, l_9\}$, with a nesting level of 2.

VI. Analyzing a Single Layer of Communication

In this section, we discuss a technique to analyze a given communication layer. We first show that the time taken per iteration of all the loops in a layer will be the same. Subsequently, we describe a technique to analyze the layer, and compute the time taken by the loops in the layer.

Lemma 1: The time taken per iteration of all loops in a communication layer are equal.

Proof: Consider loop l_i communicating with another loop l_j. Say $l_j \subset E(l_i)$, that is, l_i generates an event to be received by a wait node in l_j. Also, say the time taken per iteration of loop l_i is T_{l_i}, and that of loop l_j is T_{l_j}. Since l_j has to wait on every iteration for the generation of the event by l_i, we have: (1) $T_{l_j} \geq T_{l_i}$. Since the rate of generation of events is assumed to be less than their consumption, and with the restriction that each event is generated or received only once in every iteration of a loop (this is one of the constraints enforced on the communication pattern of the system, as described in Section III), we have: (2) $\frac{1}{T_{l_i}} \leq \frac{1}{T_{l_j}}$. From equation (2), we have: (3) $T_{l_i} \geq T_{l_j}$.

From equations (1) and (3), we get $T_{l_i} = T_{l_j}$. By definition, all the loops in a layer communicate with each other, hence the time taken per iteration for all the loops in a layer is the same. □

Next, we describe a method to compute the time taken by each loop in a layer. Associated with each layer is a *layer graph,* which is a cyclic subgraph of the synchronization graph consisting of the nodes and edges of the loops belonging to the layer. There is a start node and end node for each loop in the layer graph. For example, in the synchronization graph of Figure 3, n_1, n_2 and n_3 represent the start nodes of loops l_6, l_7 and l_2 respectively of the layer graph of layer L_2.

Our method involves computing the arrival times of the nodes in the layer graph. The arrival time of a node v, a(v), is computed in terms of the arrival times of its fanin nodes as:

$$a(v) = \max_{v_i \in Fanin(v)} a(v_i) + Edge\_Weight(v_1 \rightarrow v). \quad (1)$$

Clearly, the arrival times of fanin nodes need to be known before the arrival time of a node can be determined, which is a problem in a cyclic graph like the layer graph. We account for the cyclic nature of the layer graph as follows. Initially, the arrival times of the start nodes are set to 0. Also, the synchronizing variables corresponding to some event nodes may be initialized in the behavioral description. The arrival times of such event nodes will be set to 0 in the layer graph.

Beginning with the loop start nodes, a breadth first traversal of the layer graph produces the arrival times of all the loop end nodes. The time taken by a loop is given by the difference between the arrival times of the end and start nodes of the loop. At the end of the first iteration, the time taken by the various loops in the layer may be different. Hence, the timing analysis procedure is iterated, recomputing the arrival times of the nodes from the start nodes to the end nodes, till the time taken by all the loops are equal. Note that from the second iteration, the arrival times of each start node is computed using the arrival times of the end nodes in the previous iteration, and the weight of the back edges.

VII. Analysis of Multi-Layer Communication Systems

In this section, we shall discuss the overall strategy for the worst case performance analysis of a system of concurrent communicating processes. At first, the synchronization graph is partitioned into communication layers, and their nesting levels identified. The time taken per iteration of loops in a layer L_j depends on the time taken by the loops in layers nested by L_j. Hence, the layers are analyzed in an increasing order of their nesting levels, so that all the layers nested by layer L_j are analyzed before layer L_j is analyzed. Consider the layers of the synchronization graph of Figure 3 which are derived in section V. The layers L_1, L_2, L_3 are of level 1, and hence analyzed first. Subsequently, the layer L_4, of level 2, is analyzed.

Before analyzing a communication layer of level i, $i > 1$, all the layers of level $i - 1$ are analyzed and collapsed. Collapsing a layer effectively removes the corresponding loops from the synchronization graph, updating the graph accordingly to reflect the time taken by the collapsed layer. The time taken by a layer is the time taken by the loops in the layer, plus the time taken to execute other statements in the layer not included in the loops. The time taken by each loop in a layer is the product of the time taken per iteration of the loop and the corresponding loop bound. As discussed in Section VI, the time taken per iteration of all the loops in a layer are identical, and are simultaneously computed. We next briefly discuss the issue of loop bounds. Since all the synchronizing loops of a layer run concurrently and communicate with each other, the loop bounds for each of the loops in the layer are assumed to be equal. The loops which belong to more than one layer can have more than one loop bound, depending on the particular layer under consideration. The loop bounds of each layer is extracted from the behavioral description with some feedback from the user.

Collapsing a layer removes all the nodes and edges of the

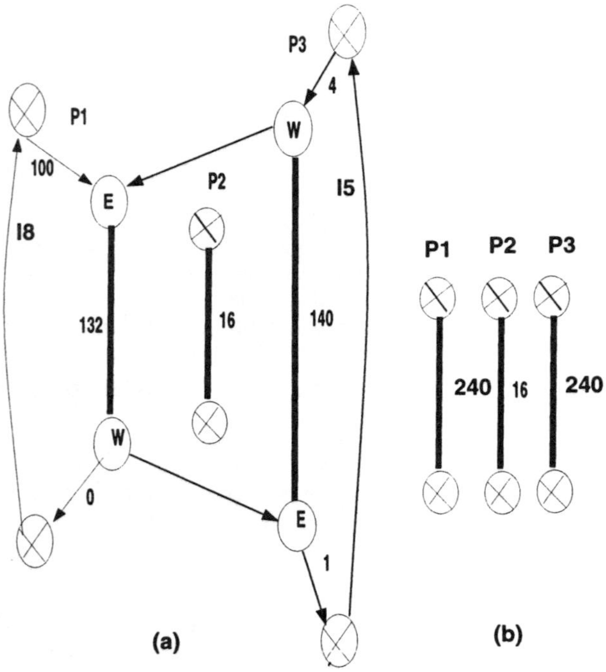

Figure 4: (a) Synchronization graph after collapsing loops in level one layers, (b) Final Synchronization graph after collapsing loops in level two layer

loops of the layer being collapsed, replacing each loop with an edge representing the time taken by the loop. If a loop belongs to more than one layer, it is removed from the synchronization graph only after all the corresponding layers are collapsed and the edge weight of the added edge is equal to: (1) The sum of the delays associated with each of the layers, if the loop is not a process loop. This is to reflect the fact that the time taken per iteration of a process depends on the overall time taken by each of the loops nested by the process loop. (2) The maximum of the delays, if the loop corresponds to a process loop. This is because we just need in the worst case the time taken per iteration of each process to determine the system performance. Consider the blackjack example shown in Figure 3. Loop l_7 is present in three layers, L_1, L_2, L_3 (section V), and it does not correspond to a process loop. Hence, l_7 is replaced by an edge of weight equal to the sum of the delays of layers L_1, L_2, and L_3. On the other hand, loop l_6 belongs to more than one layer (L_1, L_2, L_3) but represents a process loop; hence, l_6 is replaced by an edge with weight equal to the maximum among the layers L_1, L_2, L_3. The synchronization graph for the *blackjack* example after collapsing layers L_1, L_2 and L_3 is given in Figure 4(a), with the new edge weights shown.

Since the collapsing of a layer involves the removal of the associated synchronizing edges, after all the layers of communication are analyzed and collapsed, the synchronization graph will not contain any synchronizing edges. The final graph would be a collection of independent components, each component being an edge representing a process of the system. Figure 4(b) shows the final synchronization graph after layer L_4 is analyzed and collapsed. The component with maximum edge weight represents the process which requires the maximum number of clock cycles to complete, and hence is the system performance. In the *blackjack* example, the worst case system performance is 240 clock cycles.

The overall performance analysis procedure can be summarized as follows: (1) Create synchronization graph. (2) Identify communication layers and their nesting levels. (3) For each layer in increasing nesting level: (a) Compute time taken by the layer, (b) Collapse layer and update synchronization graph. (4) System performance = weight of maximum weighted edge/component of the final synchronization graph.

VIII. Experimental Results

A prototype of the proposed performance analysis technique, PERC, has been developed. In this section, we shall present the results of applying PERC to three systems, an ethernet controller, a blackjack game controller, and a DMA controller, the first two examples having been discussed in this paper. Each system has been described as a set of concurrent communicating processes. Table 1 reports some characteristics of the behavioral description and the corresponding synchronization graph of the three systems. The number of processes and the lines of behavioral code of the systems are given under the system description column. The number of synchronizing nodes, synchronizing edges, and communication layers of the corresponding synchronization graph are given in the next few columns. For example, the description of the ethernet controller consists of 3 processes and 323 lines of code, while the corresponding synchronization graph contains 9 synchronizing nodes, 5 synchronizing edges, and one communication layer.

Table 1: Characteristics of the systems

	System Description		Synch. Graph		
	Process	Lines of code	Synch. nodes	Synch. edges	Comm. Layers
Ethernet	3	323	9	5	1
Blackjack	3	399	18	12	4
DMA	3	241	20	10	2

For each system description, we generated a scheduled implementation using a scheduling tool [1]. Next, we obtained the worst-case performance (number of clock cycles) taken by the scheduled implementation using (1) simulation with functional test cases, (2) static performance analysis without considering the inter-process communication (considering each process separately), and (3) static performance analysis using PERC, which includes synchronization overhead. For the analysis part, the edge weights of the synchronization graph are computed using the scheduled implementations of the individual processes. Table 2 reports the worst-case system performance as computed by the three above mentioned approaches, in columns `Simulation` (S), `Performance Estimate without synchronization overhead` (E_1), and `Performance Estimate using PERC` (E_2), respectively. While the performance of the complete system is reported in the column `System`, the performance estimates of individual processes are reported in the columns `P1`, `P2`, and `P3` respectively. Finally, for the results obtained using the analysis methods, the percentage difference between the performance numbers obtained by the analysis method and simulation, $(E_1 - S)/S * 100$, and $(E_2 - S)/S * 100$, are shown in the two columns Δ_1 and Δ_2

Table 2: Performance analysis results

	Simulation (S)	Performance Estimate without synch overhead (E_1)					Performance Estimate by PERC (E_2)				
		P_1	P_2	P_3	System	Δ_1%	P_1	P_2	P_3	System	Δ_2%
Ethernet	767	175	48	291	291	-62	902	334	334	902	+18
Blackjack	205	121	7	41	121	-40	240	16	240	240	+17
DMA	67	29	42	13	42	-37	74	50	23	74	+10

$\Delta_1 = (E_1 - S)/S * 100$; $\Delta_2 = (E_2 - S)/S * 100$

respectively. Note that the performance estimates obtained by the analysis method which does not consider inter-process communication grossly under-estimates the worst-case performance, as is reflected by the percentage difference with simulation Δ_1. Such under-estimation of performance may not be acceptable for certain systems, like real-time systems. On the other hand, the performance estimates obtained by PERC have significantly smaller percentage difference with the simulation results, as shown by the column Δ_2. Also, the estimates obtained by PERC are always more conservative than the simulation results; this is expected since simulation, unless exhaustive, can only produce a lower bound of the worst case performance.

For example, for the ethernet controller, simulation produced a worst-case performance of 767 clock cycles. Using existing performance analysis techniques without considering the synchronization overhead, the performance estimates of the individual processes P1, P2, and P3 are 175, 48, and 291 clock cycles respectively, giving a total system performance of 291 clock cycles. The large percentage difference with the simulation result, -62%, represents a significant under-estimate of the worst-case performance of the system. The large error can be attributed to ignoring the synchronization overhead of inter-process communication. Using PERC, the performance estimates obtained for processes P1, P2, and P3 are 902, 334, and 334 clock cycles respectively, with a total system performance of 902 clock cycles. The PERC estimate has a significantly smaller difference (18%) with the result obtained by simulation. Also, as expected, the PERC estimate is more conservative than that obtained by simulation, which is not exhaustive and cannot always identify the worst-case behavior of a system.

The difference in the estimates is due to the significant time the processes spend in waiting for synchronizing events, and demonstrate the critical need for considering synchronization overhead during performance analysis. The results show that the proposed technique, by considering synchronizing overhead, can obtain fairly accurate performance estimates, unlike existing performance analysis techniques, which do not consider inter-process communication.

IX. Conclusion

This paper introduced a static performance analysis technique for estimating the worst-case performance of a system of concurrently communicating processes. The need for analyzing and estimating the synchronization overhead incurred by the communicating processes, to obtain accurate estimate of the system performance, has been demonstrated. The proposed technique has been applied to analyze systems implemented in hardware. However, as long as the worst case time taken between any two synchronization points of a system can be computed, the analysis technique can be used independent of the actual implementation of individual processes. We are currently studying the possibility of extending *PERC* to analyze systems implemented as mixed software and hardware. Also, we are exploring ways of using the information regarding the critical parts of the system in a synthesis framework to improve the system performance.

Acknowledgement The authors would like to thank S. Biswas and A. Raghunathan for helpful discussions, and T. Misawa for help with the designs.

References

[1] S. Bhattacharya, S. Dey, and F. Brglez, "Performance Analysis and Optimization of Schedules for Conditional and Loop-Intensive Specifications," in *Proc. Design Automation Conference*, pp. 491–496, June 1994.

[2] M. Rahmouni and A. Jerraya, "Formulation and Evaluation Of Scheduling Techniques For Control Flow Graphs," in *Proc. of the European Design Automation Conference*, Sept. 1995.

[3] F. Brewer and D. Gajski, " Chippe: A System for Constraint Driven Behavioral Synthesis ," *IEEE Transactions on Computer Aided Design*, vol. Vol. 9, pp. 681–695, July 1990.

[4] A. Kuehlmann and R. A. Bergamaschi, " Timing Analysis in High-Level Synthesis," in *Proceedings of the IEEE International Conference on Computer-Aided Design*, August 1992.

[5] S. Narayan and D. D. Gajski, "System Clock Estimation based on Clock Slack Minimization," in *Proc. of the European Design Automation Conference*, 1992.

[6] C. Ramachandran and F. J. Kurdahi, "Combined Topological and Functionality Based Delay Estimation Using a Layout-Driven Approach for High Level Applications," *IEEE Transactions on Computer-Aided Design*, vol. 13, pp. 1450 – 1460, Dec. 1994.

[7] S. Bhattacharya, S. Dey, and F. Brglez, "Fast True Delay Estimation During High Level Synthesis," *IEEE Trans. on Computer-Aided Design*, vol. 15, pp. 1088 – 1105, Sept 1996.

[8] C. Safinia, R. Leveugle, and G. Saucier, "Taking Advantage of High Level Functional Information to Refine Timing Analysis and Timing Modeling," in *Proceedings of the European Design Automation Conference*, 1994.

[9] Y.-T. S. Li, S. Malik, and A. Wolfe, "Performance estimation of embedded software with instruction cache modeling," in *IEEE/ACM International Conference on Computer Aided Design.*, pp. 380–7, November 1995.

[10] K. Suzuki and A. Sangiovanni-Vincentelli, "Efficient software performance estimation methods for hardware/software codesign," in *33rd Design Automation Conf.*, pp. 605–610, 1996.

[11] W. Wolfe, A. Takach, C.-Y. Huang, and R. Manno, "The princeton university behavioral synthesis system," in *Proc. 29th Design Automation Conference*, pp. 182–7, 1992.

[12] F. Martinolle, "Fusion of vhdl processes," tech. rep., Center For Reliable Computing, Computer Systems Laboratory, Department of Electrical and Computer Engineering, Stanford University, 1991.

[13] J. Miller and H. Kramer, "Analysis of multi-process specifications with a petri-net model," in *Proceedings EURO-DAC'93. European Design Automation Conference with EURO-VHDL'93*, pp. 474–9, 1993.

Embedded program timing analysis based on path clustering and architecture classification

R. Ernst, W. Ye
Technische Universität Braunschweig, Institut für Datenverarbeitungsanlagen
Hans-Sommer-Str. 66
38106 Braunschweig
ernst@ida.ing.tu-bs.de, ye@ida.ing.tu-bs.de

Abstract

Formal Program running time verification is an important issue in system design required for performance optimization under "first-time-right" design constraints and for real-time system verification. Simulation based approaches or simple instruction counting are not appropriate and risky for more complex architectures in particular with data dependent execution paths. Formal analysis techniques have suffered from loose timing bounds leading to significant performance penalties when strictly adhered to. We present an approach which combines simulation and formal techniques in a safe way to improve analysis precision and tighten the timing bounds. Using a set of processor parameters, it is adaptable to arbitrary processor architectures. The results show an unprecedented analysis precision allowing to reduce performance overhead for provably correct system or interface timing.

1 Introduction

Program running time determination is an important issue in embedded system design required for performance optimization. In hard real time systems, program timing is part of the system functionality and incorrect timing assumptions can have disastrous consequences. Formal running time analysis is, therefore, highly desirable. Rather than a single value, formal analysis techniques provide upper and/or lower running time bounds. One reason is that program timing is data dependent, other reasons are imperfect program path analysis (in principle a known undecidable problem) and computer architecture impacts which are very computation expensive to analyze. While data dependent program timing is real and leads to unavoidable differences in lower and upper timing bounds, inaccuracies in path analysis and architectural modeling are artifacts leading to wider bounds than can occur in reality. To assure correct minimum and maximum timing of the design, bounds must always be conservative, i.e. maximum bounds must be higher and minimum bounds must be lower than the real timing bounds. Therefore, inaccurate bounds are expensive because they require to design systems with higher performance to meet the maximum time or rate constraints. As an example, if an analysis has 50% inaccuracy, the designer must provide 50% more performance than needed in reality to be able to verify correct timing using timing analysis. The problem is that 50% inaccuracy of the analysis is already pretty good in practice if all effects are taken into account and if more complex architectures are considered.

We developed a classification of orthogonal architecture and program properties which covers all practical processor designs. These properties are used to assign on individual analysis technique to each class which is highly accurate for the respective class. While these individual analysis techniques themselves are taken from practice or from literature, this paper shows for which classes they can be applied in a safe way.

In previous work on timing analysis a single general technique has been applied to the problem. Specific program or architecture properties have hardly been exploited, except for few instances such as cache properties. A detailed discussion of program path characteristics and target architectures reveals that bounds can be much closer if the analysis approach uses architectural knowledge. We also show that program path analysis must consider certain characteristics, such as pipelining, to be reliable.

In this paper, we consider program path characteristics as well as architecture properties to maximize the accuracy of timing bounds thereby minimizing analysis cost. The paper is organized as follows. Section 2 focuses on program path analysis. It starts with a problem definition and a summary of previous work. Then, a path classification is introduced which isolates input data dependent from independent path segments. In section 3 the hardware architectural impacts on timing analysis are described and an architecture classification that fits the program path classification is introduced. In section 4 and 5 we present our SYMTA approach which is based on these classifications and its implementation. Finally, in section 6 we summarize the experimental results for the SYMTA approach.

2 Program Path analysis

2.1 Problems and previous work

For path analysis techniques [10] [7], a program is divided in **basic blocks**.

Definition 1 *A* **basic block** *is a program segment which is only entered at the first statement and only left at the last statement [1].*

Function calls are considered as single statements. Any program can be partitioned into disjoint basic blocks. The program structure is represented on a directed program flow graph with basic blocks as nodes. Fig. 1 shows an example.

For each basic block the worst or best case execution time for each basic block is determined. Then, a longest or

1092-3152/97 $10.00 © 1997 IEEE

shortest path analysis on the program flow graph is used to identify lower and upper running time bounds.

This procedure does not yet provide sufficient accuracy. For acceptable program timing analysis one must identify **feasible paths** through a program.

Definition 2 *A* **feasible program path** *(or trace) is a path in this flow graph corresponding to a possible sequence of basic blocks when the program is executed, i.e. leading from the first to the last basic block of a program.*

Definition 3 *A* **program path segment** *is a segment of a program flow graph.*

This definition implies a *hierarchy* of program path segments. However, not all paths in the program flow graph represent feasible program paths.

Definition 4 *A* **false program path** *is a path in the program flow graph which cannot be executed under any input condition.*

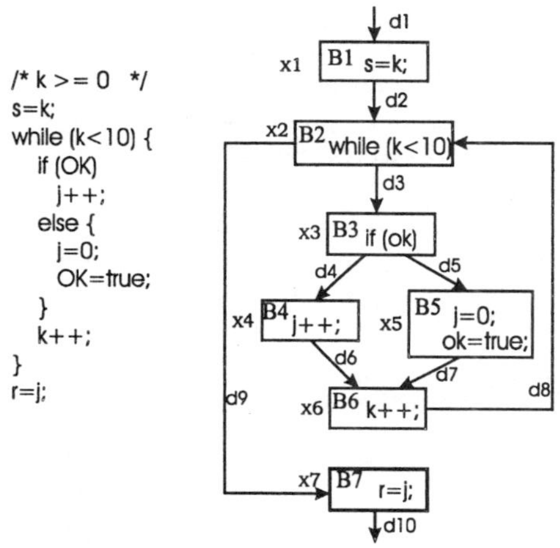

Figure 1: An example program flow graph

False path identification is mandatory for programs with loops since loops correspond to cycles in the flow graph which lead to an infinite number of potential paths. The approaches by Mok [9], Puschner and Koza [12], Park and Shaw [11] require iteration bounds for all loops in the program which the user must provide by loop annotation. The approach by Gong and Gajski [4] can identify more *false paths* by specifying the branching probabilities.

While making formal analysis feasible, loop bounding alone is not sufficient for accurate timing analysis. Nested loops are often interdependent, function timing is invocation dependent and conditions depend on each other. These dependencies can be rather complex as shown in the example in fig. 1, taken from [7]. Here, block $x5$ is executed at most once which would not be detected by program flow graph analysis alone. Therefore, as a second step, the user is asked to annotate false paths. The number of *false paths* can be very large. Instead of enumerating false paths (or, conversely, feasible paths), a language for user annotation with regular expressions is introduced in [11]. Still, the number of required path annotations can be extremely large in practice, as demonstrated with even small examples in [7].

A major step forward was the introduction of implicit path enumeration [5], [7]. Here, the user provides linear (in)equations to define false paths. For fig. 1, a simple equation would be "$x5 \leq x1$" meaning that node $x5$ is at most executed as often as node $x1$. To evaluate these (in)equations, Malik et al. map the upper and lower bound timing identification to two **ILP (integer linear programming)** optimization problems, the one optimizing for the shortest program running time, the other one for the longest running time.

2.2 Execution time model

The standard execution time model is the **sum–of–basic–blocks** model. Let a program consist of N basic blocks with c_i execution count of basic block bb_i and t_i execution time of basic block bb_i, $i = 1, 2, ..., N$. Then, the **sum–of–basic–blocks** model assumes for the total program execution time T [7]:

$$T = \sum_{i=0}^{N} c_i \times t_i$$

This model assumes that all executions of a basic block take identical time. However, data dependent instruction execution times and superscalar or superpipelined architectures with overlapped basic block execution have widely varying basic block execution times, with a substantial effect the overall execution time, as demonstrated in [13]. For these common architectures, the **sum–of–basic–blocks** model cannot provide close bounds, but must be pessimistic to be correct.

For higher accuracy, basic block sequences and data flow must be considered. This shall be called the **sequence–of–basic–blocks** model.

2.3 Path classification and analysis

Complete **sequence–of–basic–blocks** analysis requires exhaustive path analysis in the worst case and therefore, must be considered infeasible. It is, however possible to exploit program properties to simplify path analysis. The first observation is that many embedded system programs or at least parts of such programs have a single feasible program path. An FIR filter is a simple example and an FFT is a more complex one. In other words, there is only one path executed for any input pattern, even though this path may wrap around many loops, conditional statements and even function calls which are used for program structuring and compacting. This shall be called **single feasible path (SFP)** property. The current analysis approaches give different lower and upper timing bounds for SFP programs because they do not distinguish between input data dependent control flow and program structuring aids. In the best case, they may be accurate but require much user interaction for SFP programs. In contrast, simulation would choose the one correct path for any input pattern without further user interaction. Fig. 2, a part of an FFT algorithm, shows that the *if/else* and the inner *while* loop are very difficult to annotate, although the program is SFP. Obviously, most practical systems contain non-SFP parts. These parts shall have the **MFP property (multiple feasible paths)**. Interestingly, a look at

```
n = nn << 1;
j = 1;
for (i=1; i<n; i+=2) {
  if (j > i) {
    swap(data[i],data[j]);
    swap(data[i+1],data[j+1]);
  }
  m = n >> 1;
  while ((m >= 2)&&(j > m)) {
          j -= m;
          m >>= 1;
  }
  j += m;
}
```

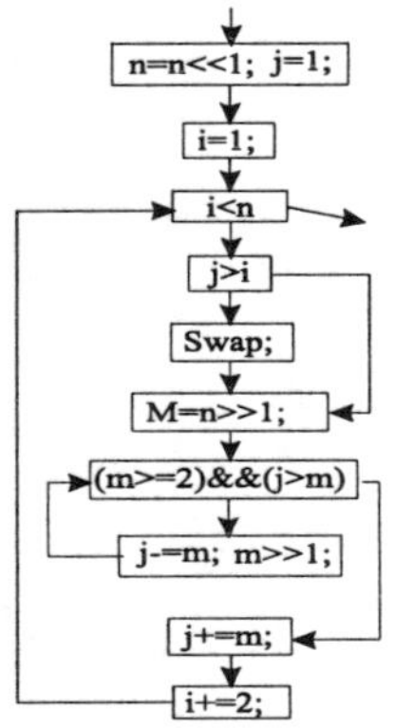

Figure 2: An example of the SFP property

embedded system algorithms reveals that at least for data dominated applications or applications with a signal processing component or complex computation, we find long program path segments with SFP property. So, it seems worth while to have a closer look at SFP exploitation. If we would be able to isolate SFP and MFP parts then we could try to exploit the SFP property in all programs.

To apply different techniques to MFP and SFP parts, we need some disjoint program partitioning. This is the first difficulty since the set of program paths is not disjoint. The solution is a program partitioning which will be explained later. For the moment, let us assume that SFP and MFP program segments are not overlapping.

So, the first parameter for classification refers to the application program and distinguishes MFP and SFP program segments.

2.4 Data flow analysis

Data flow analysis is relevant to program timing when the data access timing is address dependent. One example are architectures with data caches, the other important case are interleaved memory banks. The SFP property does not cover this case. However, if for a given (non false) program path segment,

- all instructions or statements always access the same data variables and array indices under whatever input conditions
- and the program path segment is SFP

then the data access sequence is unique for this part of the program. This shall be the **single data access sequence (SDS)** property. Examples for programs with SDS are filter or FFT algorithms. For all other cases we use the term **multiple data access sequences (MDS)**[1]. So, data access is the second classification parameter.

2.5 Multitasking and context switch impact

Static scheduling and context switch as in many smaller or high-performance signal processing systems can be treated with the same path analysis techniques.

Static priority scheduling (e.g. RMS) or dynamic scheduling (e.g. EDF) are hard to analyze if the process executions are interdependent. This is the case for cache architectures. There are, however, efficient approaches to improve cache performance and predictability, e.g. [8] and [6], which can directly be applied to our case. Then, the program path segments must be analyzed to identify potential remaining cache misses due to context switch. This is not a major limitation but has not been investigated in this project.

3 Architecture classification and analysis

Architecture properties are important for basic block timing as well as path timing. We are interested in architecture properties from the analysis perspective. Two techniques to determine the timing of basic block and path segments are used.

1. **Instruction timing addition (ITA)**
   The instruction or statement execution times in a basic block or along a path segment are added. These execution times are taken from a table. This is a very computation time efficient approach. It is somewhat similar to circuit timing analysis. As in circuit timing analysis, minimum and maximum instruction execution times can be considered.
2. **Path segment simulation (PSS)**
   The basic block or path segment is simulated using a cycle true processor model which can be exactly modeled hardware timing and architectures [2].

We distinguish several orthogonal architecture properties relevant this context:

- *data dependent instruction execution times*
  This is typical for some microcoded CISC architectures. Examples are multiplication instructions implemented with *shift − and − add* or *blockmove* instructions. It can also occur in processor families where some of the processors have not implemented all instructions but trigger an exception on not implemented instructions to emulate them by software functions with possibly data dependent execution times. Data dependent instruction execution times lead to data dependent basic block execution times. PSS cannot generally guarantee accurate timing results, here, even for segments with SFP property. ITA would be appropriate.
- *pipelined architectures*
  Pipelining makes ITA imprecise. Pipelining is used in RISC processors. If pipelining is deep enough to allow overlapping execution of several basic blocks, which is the case for most of the larger RISC processors, then even basic block simulation would not help. More precisely, ITA must neglect most of the performance gain due to pipelining because it cannot anticipate pipeline hazards. In other words, if a user would design a system based on ITA data, RISC processor performance gain through pipelining would be of no or very little use. PSS precision depends on the length of the simulated path since, to be conservative, worst and best case behavior must be assumed at the beginning and at the end of a path segment. This causes imprecision

[1] Note that SDS could be defined such that it would not require SFP as a necessary condition, but an exploitation of SDS without SFP would require intricate architecture analysis which shall be omitted here.

which depends on the pipeline length. So, the longer the paths, the more precise is PSS.

- *superscalar architectures*
  Superscalar architectures can execute several basic blocks at a time. They apply dynamic instruction scheduling leading to out-of-order execution and out-of-order completion and even speculative computation [3] . Here, ITA is completely inappropriate. PSS is the correct choice and it's precision, again, depends on the path segment length.
- *program caches*
  Program cache behavior depends on the sequence of instruction fetches. Therefore, PSS is exact for SFP program path segments (supposed the cache is modeled in simulation). ITA alone does not cover caches, unless one would count a potential cache miss for every access to another memory page. There are, however, efficient extensions to ITA to regard at least direct mapped caches [7].
- *data caches*
  Data cache behavior depends on the sequence of data accesses. Therefore, PSS is precise for path segments with SDS. ITA has the same problems as for program caches.

A typical processor can combine several of the properties.

The comparison shows that ITA alone is only suitable for very simple architectures. On the other hand, PSS is a problem for data dependent architecture behavior. The comparison shows that there is not a single technique which is best for all cases.

4 The SYMTA approach

SYMTA (Symbolic hybrid timing analysis) is a hybrid approach combining simulation and formal analysis adaptable to different architecture and program properties.

4.1 Hierarchical flow graph clustering

As a first step, the input program is mapped to a hierarchical control flow graph. In this graph, every control construct, such as $if, case, loop$, corresponds to a hierarchical node and the leaf cells are the basic blocks of the program. Each of the control constructs has an associated condition that decides which of the paths of the construct is executed. Functions are mapped to extra graphs, but can be copied to the calling statement for higher analysis accuracy. This way, an MFP function with an invocation dependent control flow can become an SFP function. Like in [7], we assume structured programs without goto's between hierarchical nodes, because this simplifies flow analysis.

4.2 SFP identification

The second step in the approach is the identification of SFP program parts. More precisely, we want to partition the flow graph nodes into SFP and MFP nodes.

(1) Since MFP requires that at least one control construct depends on input data, we can immediately conclude that every path segment which does not contain an input data dependent control construct must be SFP.

(2) Now we can apply a simple induction over the levels of hierarchy:

- Leaf nodes (basic blocks) are SFP by definition
- (1) ⇒ A hierarchical node is SFP, if
  - it only contains SFP nodes
  - and its associated condition is independent of input data.

This defines a simple recursive clustering approach to flow graph partitioning. It automatically cuts the program into SFP and MFP path segments. The FFT in fig. 2 would completely be clustered in one SFP.

SFP clustering is not sufficient when MFP path segments are embedded. Fig. 3(a) shows an example. The example implements a bubble sort algorithm. In this program, the two loops are input data independent such that they always have the same iteration count while the if condition is dependent on the input data a[ ].

We extend the clustering algorithm to merge adjacent SFP blocks:

(3) If the associated condition of a hierarchical node depends on input data, this node is MFP. Set cut points at the beginning and the end of the MFP nodes.

(4) Repeat clustering according to (2) ignoring the MFP nodes but regarding the cut points.

The new clusters found in (4) shall also be defined as SFP, since, except for the path fork and join in the embedded MFP blocks, there is only one path outside these blocks. To be conservative for correct timing analysis, it is, therefore, sufficient to analyze the MFP node separately and assume worst case behavior at the remaining cut points[2]. This is guaranteed by leaving the cut points in (4) inside the SFP clusters. Then no false SFP paths leading to incorrect bounds can be introduced in the next steps. So, the result is still correct, but (4) maximizes SFP path length. Since for most higher performance architectures as well as for architectures with caches, analysis precision increases with path length, this appears to be a good compromise for high precision without path explosion. The results will show the high efficiency.

Fig. 3(b) shows the result for the example in fig. 3(a). Only blocks b5, the condition basic block, and b6, are in MFP path segments. Fig. 3(c) shows how the remaining program path segments are clustered to SFP nodes.

What we need for this clustering approach is an algorithm to determine condition (see above), i.e. input data dependency of conditions. This requires a global data flow analysis [1] with a transitive closure over all data dependencies of variables in control statements. A global data flow analysis, however, does typically not cover dependencies over array elements and operation on data. Therefore, the global data flow analysis is complemented with symbolic simulation of basic blocks [14][3].

In the same step using the same technique, basic block symbolic simulation also determines the SDS property for basic blocks in SFP paths. This is a very useful side effect.

[2]Worst case behavior here means the maximally extended upper and lower timing bounds for that architecture

[3]We also tried complete symbolic program analysis but this was only feasible for very small examples and with unacceptable memory resources and computation time. Also, in the examples which we tried it did not provide much additional information useful to SFP determination.

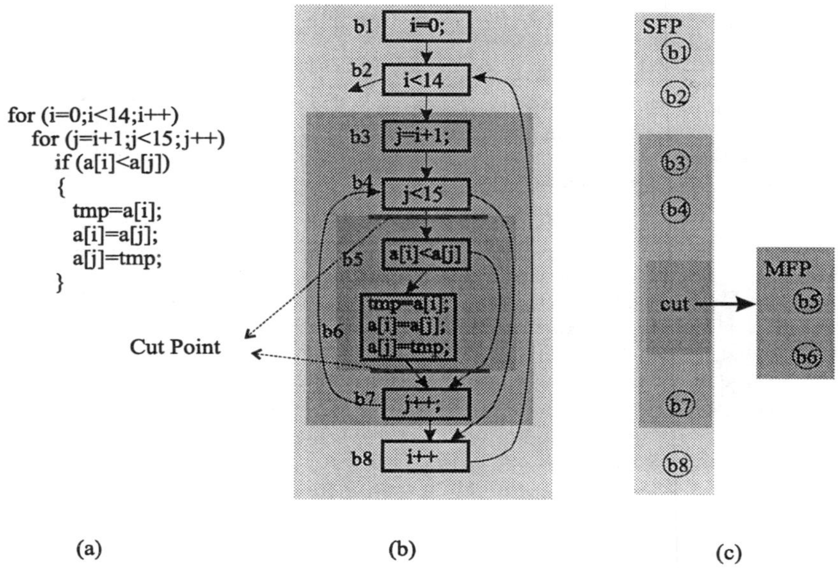

Figure 3: An example program for the SFP identification

4.3 Path segment timing - adaptation to processor architectures

Next problem is the running time determination of the remaining complex SFP nodes. As seen before this is strongly architecture dependent. So far, we have presented PSS and ITA for basic block timing analysis. While PSS can be directly applied to any SFP segment if a cycle true simulator is available, this is not the case for ITA which is only applicable to basic blocks. On the other hand, ITA can be useful for simple architectures without pipelining in particular with data dependent instruction timing.

Again, the solution resorts to the SFP property. The ITA approach obtains the same timing result on whatever path a basic block is executed. So, all we need to know is the number of times it_i a basic block b_i is executed. Then we can multiply this iteration count by the basic block running time $t(b_i)$. Note that it_i is unique because of the SFP property and can therefore be obtained by source code profiling which does not need a simulator but can run on a workstation[4].

Given the hierarchical SFP node p which appears in the reduced flow graph, we can simply use the **sum–of–basic–blocks** model.

$$t(p) = \sum it_i \times t(b_i)$$

So, whenever ITA is accurate it is a good choice, since it is faster than PSS which must use a cycle true simulator. A famous example for such an architecture is the 8051.

In case of data dependent instruction timing, ITA provides a lower and an upper bound for each basic block, $t_{min}(b_i)$ and $t_{max}(b_i)$ and, therefore a lower and an upper bound $t_{min}(p)$ and $t_{max}(p)$ which is then used for MFP analysis.

Pipelined and superscalar architectures can accurately be treated with PSS, as already shown. At the transition point between SFP nodes, worst case behavior must be assumed, i.e. no stalling for the lower bound and maximum time stalling for the upper bound. This overhead time can be added to SFP blocks or can be collected in extra nodes as e.g. proposed in [13].

Program cache miss timing can be treated with PSS. At the transition point between SFP nodes, one can either assume a default cache miss when accessing another memory page or use a more precise cache model and analyze potential misses with higher precision. The difference in precision between PSS and ITA depends on the number of page transitions and real cache misses in the SFP nodes, but generally PSS seems to be the much better choice when applicable (see above).

Similar arguments hold for data caches if one replaces the role of SFP nodes by SFP nodes with SDS property.

A major problem are high performance architectures with data dependent instruction execution times since neither ITA nor PSS are directly applicable with acceptable precision. As an example, many RISC processors, such as the PowerPC (used in embedded systems, e.g., as Motorola RCPU) implement integer divisions with data dependent timing. One approach is to analyze basic blocks with data dependent instructions using ITA hoping that there are few such instructions (which is usually true), another one is to extend the timing bounds by the difference between minimum and maximum instruction execution timing. Both approaches are conservative. One could choose whatever gives the narrower bounds. This extension would be sufficient, but we currently cannot present results for this specific feature since it is not yet implemented in the timing

[4] In reality the problem is a bit more complicated since we have to take care of source code and assembly code basic block correspondence.

analysis tool.

All other combinations of properties lead to subproblems of the architecture in the previous paragraph. So, the approach is complete over processor architecture and program properties, now.

4.4 Global timing analysis using nodes with bounded timing property

For global timing analysis, each hierarchical SFP node is merged to a single SFP node with a single running time. All remaining hierarchical nodes are MFP nodes and all leaf nodes are SFP with accurate running time. When leaf node timing has been determined, we apply the ILP approach presented in [7] which seems to be the most powerful MFP analysis approach known today.

In fig. 3 we let the program simulate on a SPARC simulator. Thereby we obtain the execution time of the SFP cluster $T_{sim}(SFP) = 2113$ cycles. By ILP solution, for one iteration of the MFP cluster (block 5 and 6) we get $T_{ilp}(5,6) = 43$ cycles in the worst case and 22 cycles in the best case. The MFP part is embedded in the SFP cluster and will be still executed 105 times for both worst and best case. Therefore, $T_{ilp}^{worst}(MFP) = 105 \cdot T_{ilp}^{worst}(5,6) = 105 \times 43 = 6825$ cycles in the worst case and $T_{ilp}^{best}(MFP) = 105 \cdot T_{ilp}^{best}(5,6) = 105 \times 22 = 2310$ cycles in the best case. The total number of cycles of the program is given as:

worst case: $T = T_{sim}(SFP) + T_{ilp}^{worst}(MFP) = 2113 + 6825 = 8938$ cycles.

best case: $T = T_{sim}(SFP) + T_{ilp}^{best}(MFP) = 2113 + 2310 = 4423$ cycles.

The execution time for the program in fig. 2 will be simulated entirely without ILP solution because it is completely SFP.

5 A SYMTA timing analysis tool

We have developed a tool using the SYMTA approach. Figure 4 shows the flow graph. First step is symbolic program execution and data flow analysis. The analysis results are used for clustering. Next step is either a PSS of the whole program or program profiling with subsequent ITA analysis.

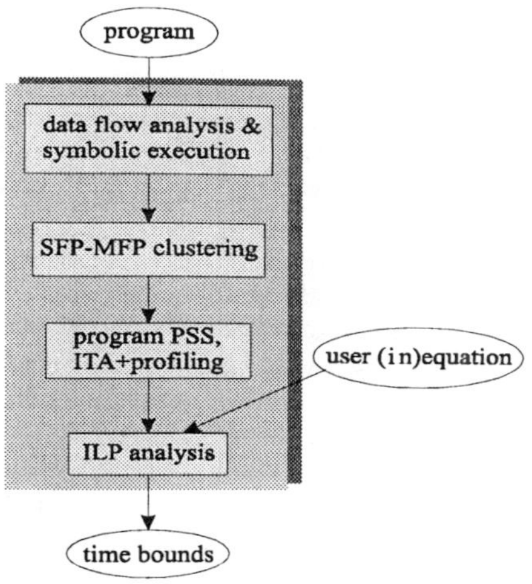

Figure 4: The flow graph of SYMTA timing analysis tool

PSS takes user provided input data for simulation which must be complete to cover all paths in the program. If not, ITA must be executed for the remaining basic blocks. The tool is able to identify basic blocks which are not covered and, then, switches to ITA for these blocks. This can only occur for basic blocks embedded in hierarchical MFP nodes.

We have selected two processors for our experiments: a complex 32-bit superscalar SPARC RISC processor with 4-stage pipeline and floating point operations; and a simple 8-bit processor Intel 8051 with no pipelining and no data dependent operations which is widely used in microcontrol systems. PSS is used as primary analysis technique for the SPARC while the 8051 is analyzed using ITA with profiling. For the SPARC processor, we use the GNU C compiler and for the 8051 we use a commercial compiler. Debug information is used to identify the source level basic blocks in the assembly code.

Now, the following timing information is produced by the PSS:

- the execution time of the SFP nodes including the SFP clusters.
- the worst case and best case execution times for data dependent operations and the execution counts of basic blocks of the program. They are later used for the ILP solver.

Final step is the ILP solution on the reduced program flow graph. The system accepts user provided (in)equations to improve accuracy for MFP parts.

In the next section we will give some experimental results using SYMTA.

6 Experimental results

The first table demonstrates the cluster results for a variety of algorithms taken from different sources. We have evaluated the SFP analysis which is shown in table 1. The first column provides the total number of nodes in the program flow graph. The second column contains the nodes which are located in SFP parts. The third column contains the number of nodes in MFP parts. The experimental results have revealed that many parts of the programs have SFP property which can be precisely analyzed using simulation.

Programs	Total nodes	Nodes in SFP		Nodes in MFP		Source lines
3D-image	94	85	90%	9	10%	164
diesel	65	65	100%	0	0%	160
fft	78	78	100%	0	0%	145
bsort	14	8	57%	6	43%	25
smooth	48	39	81%	9	19%	86
blue	80	53	66%	27	34%	127
check-data	18	0	0%	18	100%	44
whetstone	122	122	100%	0	0%	251
line	101	19	19%	82	81%	250
key3	100	100	100%	0	0%	151

Table 1: Experimental results for the Clustering

Programs	Measured bounds(cycles)		Analyzed bounds(cycles)		Analysis time* (sec)
	BCET**	WCET**	BCET	WCET	
SPARC					
3D-image	34908	37848	33874	38037	0.79
diesel	62944	62994	61445	63333	0.84
fft	1498817	1499176	1494650	1499290	135.69
bsort	4423	8938	4423	8938	0.34
smooth	3635651	4846511	3570227	4881135	304.90
blue	3564938	316865761	3345041	346541760	4325.23
check-data	80	431	65	435	0.23
whetstone	2928459	3369459	2880230	3378098	298.19
line	514	1619	381	2035	0.39
8051					
fft	26421460	26421460	26419338	26488288	0.23
bsort	9347	15045	7804	18167	0.12
smooth	9737378	9737516	9737469	9737522	0.23
key3	1218229	1223314	1164883	1265227	0.39
check-data	68	559	63	588	0.17

** The example programs have been analyzed on the SPARC 10 workstation.*
*** WCET: The worst case execution time; BCET: The best case execution time.*

Table 2: Experimental results of the example programs in SYMTA

Table 2 shows the timing results and compare them with the results of an extensive simulation. In order to evaluate the results of our approach, we have to know the real bounds of the programs. Therefore, we selected such programs, where worst case input data can be clearly identified with some effort. The measured bounds in the first column are obtained by simulating the program using these data. The second contains the analyzed bounds of the example programs running on both processors using our approach.

7 Conclusion

We have presented an approach to formal timing analysis and verification with tight timing bounds. The approach combines several analysis and simulation techniques to best exploit different program and architecture properties. Data flow analysis and symbolic execution are used to safely select the analysis technique with the tightest bounds for each program segment. The approach was applied to two very different processor architectures and a variety of programs showing a very high precision. Other potential applications of the approach are software test generation and timing analysis in the high-level synthesis.

References

[1] A.V. Aho, R. Sethi, J.D. Ullman, *Compiler principles, Techniques and Tools,* Bell Telephone Laboratories, Inc. 1987.

[2] T.M. Conte, Ch.E. Gimarc, *Fast simulation of computer architectures,* Kluwer Academic Publishers, 1995.

[3] M. Johnson, *Superscalar Microprocessor Design,* Prentice Hall, Englewood Cliffs, NJ, 1991.

[4] J. Gong, D. D. Gajski, S. Narayan *Software execution from executable specification,* The Journal of Computer & Software Engineering, 2(3), 239–258(1994).

[5] Y-T.S Li, S. Malik, A. Wolfe, *Performance Analysis of Embedded Software with Instruction Cache Modelling,* Proc. of ICCAD 1995. IEEE Society Press, pp. 380-387, 1993.

[6] D.B. Kirk, *Predictable Cache Design for Real-Time Systems.* PhD Thesis Department of Electrical and Computer Engineering Carnegie-Mellon Uni versity, Nov. 1990.

[7] S. Malik, W. Wolf, A. Wolfe, Y. S. Li, T. Yen, *Performance Analysis of Embedded Systems,* NATO ASI, Workshop on Hardware–Software Co-Design, Tremezzo, Italy, 1995.

[8] F. Mueller, R. Arnold, D. Whalley, *Bounding Worst-Case Instruction Cache Performance,* in Real-Time Systems Symposium. 1994 . Krithi, A., Editor. Puerto-Rico: IEEE P ress. p. 172-181.

[9] A. Mok et al. *Evaluating Tight Execution Time Bounds of Programs by Annotations,* Proc. IEEE WS Real-Time Operating Systems and Software, May 89, pp. 74-80.

[10] C. Y. Park, *Predicting Deterministic Execution Times of Real–Time Programs,* PhD Thesis, University of Washington, Seattle 98195, Aug. 1992.

[11] C.Y. Park, A.C. Shaw, *Experiments with a program timing tool based on source-level timing schema.* Proc 11th IEEE Real-Time system Symp., pp. 72-81,1990

[12] P. Puschner Ch. Koza, *Calculating the maximum execution time of real–time programs,* The Journal of Real–Time Systems, 1(2), 160–176, Sept. 1989.

[13] W. Ye, R. Ernst, Th. Benner, J. Henkel, *Fast Timing Analysis for Harware–Software Cosynthesis,* Proc. of ICCD 1993. IEEE Society Press, pp. 452-457, 1993

[14] W. Ye, R. Ernst, *Worst Case Timing Estimation based on Symbolic Execution,* COBRA report, Institute of Computer Engineering, Technical University Braunschweig, Oct. 1995.

Real Time Analysis and Priority Scheduler Generation for Hardware-Software Systems with a Synthesized Run-Time System

Vincent J. Mooney III & Giovanni De Micheli
Computer Systems Laboratory, Stanford University
Gates Computer Science Building
Stanford, CA 94305
mooney@pampulha.stanford.edu, nanni@galileo.stanford.edu

Abstract

We present a tool that performs real-time analysis and priority assignment for software tasks in a mixed hardware-software system with a custom run-time scheduler. The tasks in hardware and software have precedence constraints, resource constraints, relative timing constraints, and a rate constraint. A dynamic programming formulation assigns the static priorities such that a hard real-time rate constraint can be predictably met.

We describe the task control/data-flow extraction, run-time scheduler implementation, real-time analysis and priority scheduler template. We show how our approach fits into an overall tool flow and target architecture. Finally, we conclude with a sample application of the system to a design example.

1 Introduction

Designers of real-time embedded systems often have timing constraints that they must meet for the design to be successful. To support soft and hard real-time constraints, system designers need tight bounds on execution delays. In hardware-software codesign, scheduling resources to meet these tight bounds is a critical problem because there may be parallel threads of execution in the application with the same resource required by different threads. In this paper, we consider the following formulation of the real-time analysis problem : we represent the system with a single graph where the nodes represent software or hardware, the graph edges represent dependencies (precedence constraints), and the graph is invoked at a fixed rate (a rate constraint). We assume that to coordinate the system we use the *run-time scheduler* of [19].

Previous approaches to real time analysis have focused on software [1] since the performance analysis of ASICs is considered a well studied problem already. Rate Monotonic Analysis (RMA) [3] and Generalized Rate Monotonic Analysis (GRMA) [4] both assume that tasks are independent and that each task has its own period and deadline. RMA has been extended to account for release jitter and resource contention [5, 6]. RMA has also been extended to allow precedence among tasks by formulating the problem as a big task with the length of the least common multiple (LCM) of all the periods [7]. Unfortunately, this approach is usually impractical for hardware-software codesign[10].

Our formulation is similar to [7, 10, 15]. However, in our case we synthesize a custom run-time scheduler in hardware and software for the application [19]. As a result, we have more information about the scheduling of hardware and software tasks. Given this more exact level of control, we can perform tight real-time analysis with very high CPU utilization. In performance- or safety-critical systems (e.g. a mobile robot control system for capture of a satellite in space) our approach can provide precise real-time bounds.

In our approach, if a solution is found, we output the task priorities and guarantee that the system meets its relative timing constraints and its rate constraint, assuming the system uses a custom run-time scheduler. While the approach of [8, 9] is more general for verification purposes after the priority for each task is assigned, it does not address the issue of finding optimal priorities.

The rest of the paper is organized as follows. Section 2 explains our design approach and corresponding requirements. Section 3 talks about how we extract a graph of the system corresponding to control flow at the task level as opposed to the operation level. Section 4 describes our implementation of the run-time scheduler, including the priority scheduler template. Section 5 presents the real-time analysis and priority generation for software tasks. Section 6 describes the tool flow and target architecture. Section 7 gives some experimental results and presents an example from robotics. Finally, Section 8 concludes the paper.

2 Motivation

System-level design requires a division of the system application into tasks which coordinate with each other. We call a task implemented in hardware a *hardware-task*; a task implemented in software is called a *software-task*. A *coarse-grained* partition specifies these tasks and their overall flow. We consider the system application after a designer or a partitioning tool has split the application into hardware-tasks and software-tasks.

We assume that the system requires some static scheduling, especially in the coordination of hardware-tasks, as well as dynamic scheduling, given the inexact delay of software and the randomness of the stimuli coming from the envi-

1092-3152/97 $10.00 © 1997 IEEE

ronment. The run-time scheduler synthesis of [19] supports the execution of software-tasks through an interrupt triggering mechanism where the hardware communicates to a software scheduler which software-tasks are ready to execute. However, the software scheduler was implemented by hand; in this paper, we implement the software portion of the run-time scheduler with a preemptive fixed priority scheduler. Our tool, called CLARA, automates the generation of priorities for the software-tasks, as well as *worst case execution time (wcet)* calculation for subsets of hardware- and software-tasks under a hard real-time rate constraint.

A typical application domain for such a design style is embedded systems. We assume the existence of mature high-level synthesis tools and software compilers, as well as the availability of processor cores. A typical task size is 50 to 200 lines of Verilog or C; the only limit on task size, however, comes from the high-level synthesis tool or compiler chosen. We assume that tasks are custom written for a target architecture. This approach matches design practice, where designers often describe their systems in a heterogeneous way, using description languages appropriate to the subsystem being implemented.

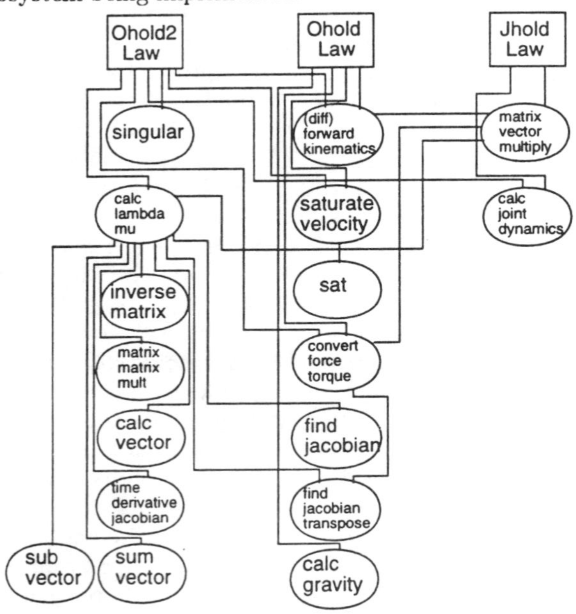

Figure 1: Robotics Example: Concurrent Control Laws

3 TaskSIF Extraction

The input specification is a collection of tasks written in Verilog or C, with one of the tasks designated as the *main task*. The main task begins execution and calls the other tasks. The main task specifies the overall sequence of tasks in the application (an example of a main task can be seen in Figure 2). From each task we extract a Control/Data-Flow Graph (CDFG) of the tasks it invokes, where each node in the CDFG corresponds to a call to another task. If a task does not call any other task, then it has no such CDFG. We call this kind of task a *leaf task*. A task which is not the main task nor a leaf task is an *intermediate task*. An intermediate task must trace back its invocation to the main task, and the intermediate task must itself invoke at least one leaf task. We assume that an intermediate task has all computation specified in leaf tasks. If an intermediate task does contain some computations, a new leaf task can be generated containing these computations. This allows us to flatten the hierarchical description and generate a CDFG of the system where all nodes are leaf tasks. We represent the flattened CDFG in ASCII in the Task Sequencing Intermediate Format (TaskSIF). We assume that we have a rate constraint specified for the TaskSIF graph of the system. In other words, we assume that the main task is invoked at a fixed rate.

We support the specification of tasks that cannot execute concurrently through the use of $NEVER$ sets. In general, $NEVER$ sets can model mutual exclusion; here, we use $NEVER$ sets to model resource constraints. For example, $NEVER = \{a, b, c\}$ indicates that tasks a, b, and c can never be active at that same time. We make use of this feature to specify resource constraints such as **(i)** multiple calls to the same piece of physical hardware (which implements a hardware-task), or **(ii)** software-tasks executed on the same microprocessor. In general, you can have multiple $NEVER$ sets. In this paper, however, we consider the case in which we have a single $NEVER$ set which we use to serialize the software-tasks executed on the same CPU. Similarly, tasks that must begin execution at the same time are specified through the use of $ALWAYS$ sets; e.g. $ALWAYS = \{a, b, c\}$ indicates that tasks a, b, and c must each begin execution at the same time. Note that this is the same as having bilateral relative timing constraints of zero weight, which our run-time scheduler also supports[19]. Thus, we do not consider $ALWAYS$ sets explicitly in the formulation of our problem.

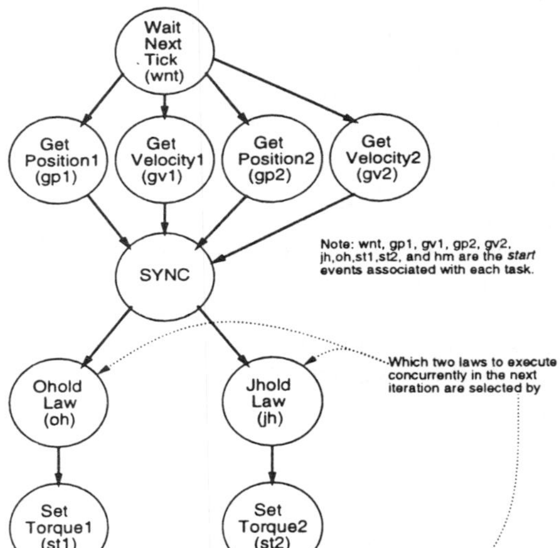

Figure 2: Robotics Example: Main Task

Example 1 As a motivational example, consider a set of control algorithms (laws) used to calculate appropriate torques for a robot arm. We assume that the controller manages two arms at the same time. Thus, any two of the laws (algorithms) may be selected in each execution. An execution of the arm controller must complete once every millisecond. Figure 1 shows three of the ten different laws used with a PUMA arm; `Ohold2 Law`, `Ohold Law`, and `Jhold Law` are intermediate tasks which call other intermediate tasks and leaf tasks in a particular sequence.

Figure 2 shows the overall flow of execution of the robot controller in the form of a CDFG of the main task for the system. The original specification of the main task was in Verilog. The other tasks are specified in C and Verilog.

Note that Figure 2 must complete once every millisecond. Thus, we have a rate constraint on the graph. □

We wrote a new backend for CINDERELLA[1] for MIPS assembly run on a MIPS R4K processor; we call the new tool CINDERELLA-M. The leaf software-tasks are compiled and input to CINDERELLA-M, which outputs a *worst-case execution time (wcet)* for each task. Similarly, the Synopsys Behavioral Compiler^{TM} (BC^{TM})[11] generates an exact execution time for each hardware-task, which we take as a *wcet* for the hardware-tasks. These values are used to annotate the leaf nodes in the final TaskSIF graph of the system specification. Figure 3 will show a sample TaskSIF graph and a corresponding table with the *wcet* annotations.

4 Run-Time Scheduler Implementation

We implement our run-time scheduler as follows. Starting from the hierarchical CDFG specified by the main task, intermediate task(s), and leaf tasks, we flatten the description until we have a single TaskSIF graph. Since we assume that the main task in invoked at a fixed rate, the TaskSIF graph we obtain is also invoked at a fixed rate. The TaskSIF graph has an equivalent Control-Flow Expression[23] which is used to synthesize a hardware FSM[19]. This FSM implements the overall system control and can predictably meet the relative timing constraints, if satisfiable, specified in exact numbers of cycles between the start times of tasks, which we hypothesize cannot be satisfied by software.

4.1 Task Execution

Task execution is described in [19]. Briefly, we associate a *start* and a *done* event with each task. In hardware the two events are simply signals on an input port and an output port, respectively. For software, we have a *start* vector and a *done* vector which encapsulate the *start* and *done* events for each software-task. If there are less than 32 distinct software-tasks, each vector can be contained in a single word with a simple one-hot encoding (otherwise more words can be used).

The run-time scheduler hardware FSM, synthesized to implement the control-flow of the TaskSIF graph, updates the *start* vector in software as follows. First, it updates a local register containing the *start* vector. Then it triggers an interrupt on the CPU. The CPU Interrupt Service Routine (ISR) reads the register using a memory-mapped I/O read and places it into the software copy of the *start* vector. When a software-task is finished executing, it updates the *done* vector by writing the value out with memory mapped I/O. Thus, the the *done* vector in the run-time scheduler in hardware is updated.

The *start* vector may specify that several software tasks are ready. Thus, we generate a preemptive static priority scheduler which executes the highest priority software-task among the tasks indicated by the hardware FSM as ready to execute. The priority based scheduler is always called by the ISR after fetching the new *start* vector into memory.

Therefore we split the run-time scheduler into two parts:

- An executive manager in hardware with cycle-based semantics that can satisfy hard real-time constraints.
- A preemptive static priority scheduler that executes different threads based on eligible software-tasks as indicated by the *start* vector.

We have described the synthesis of the hardware executive manager in [19, 23]. In this paper we focus on the generation of a priority scheduler for the software-tasks.

4.2 Priority Scheduler Template for Software

A task can be in one of four distinct states: *ready*, *running*, *suspended*, or *terminated*. We accomplish this with a single *ready* list, implemented as a linked list. The *running* task is at the top of the *ready* list. *Ready* tasks are below the *running* task in the order of their priorities. A *suspended* task is pushed down the *ready* list according to its priority, with the higher priority task which caused its suspension on top. A *terminated* task does no appear on the list. (Note that we eliminate the *delay* list traditionally used in priority schedulers, e.g. as described in [18].) The register file that contains the process state information is saved only when a task is suspended (i.e. we eliminate context switching when one task ends and another begins, in which case there is no need to save the register file). In operating systems terms, the run-time scheduler software portion implements priority-based job scheduling (multiprogramming). Strictly speaking, this is not multitasking since there is no time-shared access to CPU compute cycles.

Clearly, for this implementation to work, we need a priority for each software-task. We obtain the priorities from the real time analysis.

5 Real Time Analysis

We aim to predictably satisfy real-time constraints in the form of control-flow (precedence) constraints, resource constraints, relative timing constraints, and a rate constraint. We assume that we have as input a TaskSIF, a rate constraint on the graph, and a $NEVER$ set specifying a resource constraint on software-tasks. The formulation shown here does not include $NEVER$ sets of hardware-tasks (hardware resource constraints) for the sake of simplicity.

To predictably satisfy the rate constraint, we need a *worst case execution time (wcet)* for each task and a *wcet* for the control-flow of the set of tasks under the rate constraint. We obtain the *wcet* times for the individual tasks from CINDERELLA-M and BC^{TM}[11]. We need some assumptions to compute the *wcet* for the set of tasks.

Assumption 5.1 *We have a directed acyclic graph (TaskSIF) representing the set of tasks under the rate constraint, a wcet for each task, and a NEVER set specifying tasks that must be executed in a mutually exclusive manner.*

The use of *NEVER* sets to provide mutual exclusion for hardware-tasks is covered in [23]. We consider here only a single *NEVER* set of software-tasks executed on the same CPU.

Assumption 5.2 *Each task, once started, runs to completion.*

We will relax this assumption later when calculating *wcet* involving software-tasks which can be partially executed before being interrupted.

Assumption 5.3 *Hardware-software communication time is included in the wcet of each task and/or is included as a distinct task.*

We have several communication primitives, such as shared memory and FIFOs, with interface generation along the lines of [16, 17].

Assumption 5.4 *Interrupts that switch context come only from the hardware run-time scheduler as described in Section 4.1.*

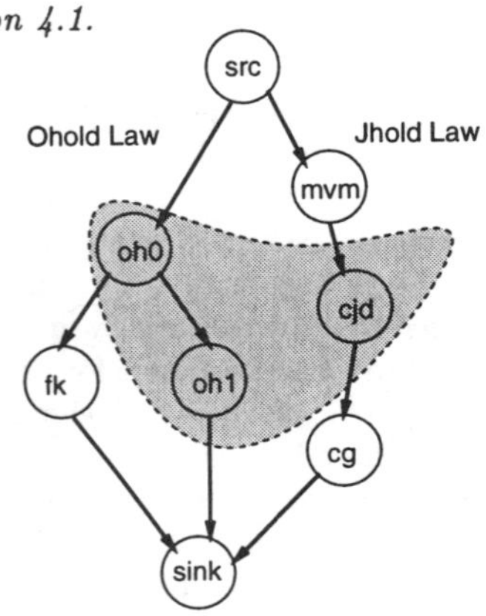

NEVER = {oh0,oh1,cjd}

task	wcet (cycles)
mvm	4,400
oh0	2,554
oh1	20,581
fk	4,500
cjd	14,878
cg	11,000
src	0
sink	0

Figure 3: Dynamic Programming Example

Example 2 As an example, consider Figure 3. This represents a subset of the tasks in our robot control algorithm. The *wcet* times for the individual tasks have already been calculated by CINDERELLA-M and BC^{TM}. Three tasks are specified in Verilog: `mvm`, `fk`, and `cg`, corresponding to `matrix vector multiply`, `(diff) forward kinematics`, and `calc gravity`, respectively, in Figure 1. Similarly, three tasks are specified in C: `oh0`, `oh1`, and `cjd`, where `cjd` corresponds to `calc joint dynamics` in Figure 1 and both `oh0` and `oh1` are coarser-grained groupings of tasks called by `Ohold Law` in Figure 1. Since our target architecture for this example contains only one microprocessor, all three software-tasks are put into a single *NEVER* set which states that their execution times cannot overlap at all. Thus, the tasks must be serialized.

Consider the *NEVER* set shaded in Figure 3. A first-come-first-serve scheduling algorithm would schedule `oh0` first, then `oh1` (since `mvm` is still executing when `oh0` finishes), and `cjd` last, resulting in a *wcet* of 49,013 cycles for the graph. However, if `oh1` were executed **after** `cjd`, the *wcet* would be 39,859 for the graph. □

Example 2 shows a difficult problem in that a *NEVER* set of software-tasks may cross parallel paths. We cannot use one execution of a longest path algorithm to solve this problem because the execution time of each node in a *NEVER* set depends upon the scheduling of the other nodes in the *NEVER* set [2]. We could enumerate all the possible orderings and then execute a longest path algorithm for each permutation. However, we would then perform many redundant calculations. This problem can be shown to be NP-Complete using the Resource Constrained Scheduling NP-Complete problem of [20].

5.1 Dynamic Programming

We want to find an exact scheduling of the tasks, with a *NEVER* set containing all the software-tasks, where the other tasks are all hardware-tasks. So we design an algorithm to suit this specific problem.

We find an optimal ordering of the software-tasks with a dynamic programming formulation of the problem. Dynamic programming is an exact solution method that in our application is above polynomial in the worst case. However, due to the coarse granularity of the model, the number of tasks is usually not large and dynamic programming can be executed quickly. Dynamic programming allows us to take into account the control-flow constraints and store subcalculations, thus reducing the number of computations. A good overview of dynamic programming is contained in [22].

5.1.1 Dynamic Programming Formulation

We take as input both the TaskSIF graph annotated with *wcets* for each leaf task and a *NEVER* set specifying the mutually exclusive tasks. We divide the problem into stages according to the number of elements in the *NEVER* set. We use the following definitions:

Definition 5.1 *Let there be n stages, where in each stage we decide which among n tasks to schedule.*

The number of stages n is set equal to the number of nodes in the *NEVER* set plus two (for the source and the sink).

Definition 5.2 *Let state s in stage i denote the current task ready to start execution and the subsequent tasks executed in stages $\{i+1,\ldots,n\}$.*

We name state s with the name of the current task ready to start execution. Note that given an ordering of software-tasks, the rest of the graph is scheduled with an ASAP schedule. Since dynamic programming stores all optimal states, i.e. sets of task schedules for stages $\{i, i+1,\ldots,n\}$, the Markov property necessary for dynamic programming to produce an optimal solution holds [22].

Definition 5.3 *Let the decision variables x_i, $i \in \{1,2,\ldots,n-1\}$ denote the task scheduled to occur next, i.e. after stage i.*

Note that the decision variable in Operations Research literature is not restricted to binary values. In this case, x_i takes on symbolic values, i.e. task names.

Example 3 For Figure 3 we have $n = 5$: tasks under consideration are `src`, `oh0`, `oh1`, `cjd`, and `sink`. Since the `sink` is always executed last, $x_{n-1} = x_4 =$ `sink`. The possible tasks executed before the `sink`, and thus in stage 4, are $s =$ `oh1` and $s =$ `cjd`. □

Definition 5.4 *Let $f_i(s, x_i)$, $i \in \{1,2,\ldots,n-1\}$, be the worst case execution time for stages $\{i, i+1,\ldots,n\}$, given that the first task in s is executed in stage i and task x_i is*

executed in stage $i+1$. $f_n(s)$ is defined to be zero since there is no task to execute after the last stage, and the last task executed is always the **sink**, *which takes zero cycles.*
Recall that tasks not in the $NEVER$ set are all hardware-tasks and are scheduled ASAP.

Definition 5.5 *Let $f_i^*(s)$, $i \in \{1,2,\ldots,n-1\}$, be the corresponding minimum value of $f_i(s,x_i)$ over all possible x_i.*

Definition 5.6 *Given state s and stage i, let x_i^* denote the value of x_i that minimizes $f_i(s,x_i)$.*

Example 4 Continuing with Figure 3, $f_5(s)$ is defined to be zero, and, as in Example 3, $x_4 = \mathtt{sink}$. Then $f_4(oh1,x_4) = 20,581$ and $f_4(\mathtt{cjd},x_4) = 25,878$. Since there is only one possibility for x_4, $f_4^*(\mathtt{oh1}) = 20,581$ and $f_4^*(\mathtt{cjd}) = 25,878$. Figure 4 shows the two sets of nodes scheduled and their *wcet* paths. □

Definition 5.7 *Given state s, task x_i to execute next, and $wcet_{succ}$ = wcet of the successors of task s, let*

$$wcet_{extra} = \begin{cases} wcet_{succ} - wcet_{x_i} & \text{if } wcet_{succ} > wcet_{x_i} \\ 0 & \text{otherwise} \end{cases}$$

and let $wcet_{sx_i} = wcet_s + wcet_{extra}$.
In calculating $wcet_{succ}$, we schedule the subgraph covered by the successors of task s using an ASAP schedule (a worst-case polynomial time computation). If we find a successor that is in the $NEVER$ set, then we use $wcet_{x_j}$, where x_j is the decision variable, already scheduled, corresponding to the successor (if no such x_j exists, then we disallow this order of tasks).

Thus we have the following:

$$f_i^*(s) = \min_{x_i} f_i(s,x_i) = f_i(s,x_i^*), i \in \{1,2,\ldots,n-1\}$$

where $f_i(s,x_i) = wcet_{sx_i} + f_{i+1}^*(x_i)$.

5.1.2 Dynamic Programming Solution

The number of stages n is set equal to the number of nodes in the $NEVER$ set(s) plus two (for the source and the sink). Our approach starts with the last stage, stage n, and progressively works its way back to the first stage. We set the last stage to be the sink and the first stage to be the source (we always have a source and a sink according to Assumption 5.1).

In order to begin with the last stage, we schedule the sink, yielding $f_n^*(s) = 0$.

For stage $n-1$, the *wcet* is determined entirely by the current state (whichever task is chosen to execute). Therefore, our dynamic programming table need only include s, $f_{n-1}^*(s)$, and x_{n-1}^*.

s	$f_4^*(s)$	x_4^*
oh0	-	sink
oh1	20,581	sink
cjd	25,878	sink

Table 1: Dynamic Programming Example Stage $n-1$

Example 5 Consider Figure 3. We have $n = 5$ stages. For stage 5 we found that $f_n^*(s) = f_5^*(s) = 0$. Table 1 shows the calculations for stage 4. Note one optimization already: oh0 is not schedulable in this stage due to control-flow (precedence) constraints.

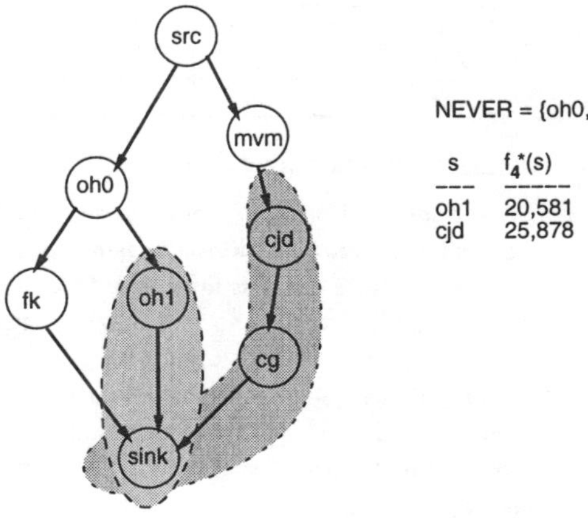

Figure 4: Dynamic Programming Example Stage $n-1$

Figure 4 shows the two sets of nodes scheduled and their *wcet* paths in this pass of the algorithm. □

For stages $n-2$ through 2, we calculate a table of values containing each possible task that can be scheduled in that stage and each possible task than can be scheduled in the next stage. In the worst case, the table has $(n-2)^2 - n$ entries. Note that for each entry, in the worst case $|V|$ operations have to be performed in calculating $wcet_{sx_i}$, where V denotes the vertices in the task-CDFG graph.

x_3	$f_3(s,x_3) = wcet_{sx_3} + f_4^*(x_3)$			
s	oh1	cjd	$f_3^*(s)$	x_3^*
oh0	23,135	-	23,135	oh1
oh1	-	46,459	46,459	cjd
cjd	35,459	-	35,459	oh1

Table 2: Dynamic Programming Example Stage $n-2$

Example 6 Continuing our attempt to optimally schedule Figure 3, we pass now to stage 3. Table 2 shows the calculations for this stage. The first entry contains the it wcet if oh0 is scheduled in stage 3 and oh1 in stage 4 (and the sink in stage 5). Note that it is not possible to schedule oh0 in stage 3 and cjd in stage 4 due to control-flow constraints, so the entry is empty. Note also that there is no column for oh0 since it was not possible to schedule it in stage 4.

To calculate the additional *wcet*, $wcet_{sx_3}$, given that we execute task s in this stage (3) and task x_3 in the next stage (4), requires scheduling the subgraph covered by task s, task x_3 and their successors. We use an ASAP schedule. □

x_2	$f_2(s,x_2) = wcet_{sx_2} + f_3^*(x_2)$				
s	oh0	oh1	cjd	$f_2^*(s)$	x_2^*
oh0	-	49,013	38,013	38,013	cjd
oh1	-	-	-	-	-
cjd	38,013	-	-	38,013	oh0

Table 3: Dynamic Programming Example Stage 2

Example 7 Next consider stage 2. Table 3 shows the calculations for this stage. Note that for state $s = \mathtt{oh1}$, it does not make sense to consider $x_2 = \mathtt{cjd}$ since we cannot have $x_1 = \mathtt{oh0}$ (oh0 must execute *before* oh1, not after). Since the other entries are similarly not possible, the entire row is empty. □

For our last computation, namely stage 1, there is only one starting state: the source. So the table has only one row.

Example 8 Now for the last set of computations, stage 1. Ta-

x_1	$f_1(s,x_1) = wcet_{sx_1} + f_2^*(x_1)$				
s	oh0	oh1	cjd	$f_1^*(s)$	x_1^*
src	39,859	-	42,413	39,859	oh0

Table 4: Dynamic Programming Example Stage 1

ble 4 shows the calculations for this stage. Note that the algorithm finally takes into account the *wcet* for task `mvm`, making the option of selecting `cjd` to execute before `oh1` less favorable. □

The final optimal ordering of tasks can be found by tracing back the x_i^* vectors, starting with x_1^*.

Example 9 The optimal order for our example starts with x_1^* = `oh0`. The entry for `oh0` in x_2^* is `cjd`. Finally, the entry for `cjd` in x_1^* is `oh1`. So the optimal order of execution is `oh0` first, `cjd` second, and `oh1` last. □

Thus we have the optimal order (given our assumptions) of execution of tasks in the *NEVER* set. We use this order to statically set the priorites for the software-tasks.

5.2 Calculation of *wcet*

To calculate the *wcet* of the entire graph, we use the following costs, obtained by analyzing our run-time scheduler software code executed on a MIPS R4K model: context switch = 126 cycles, interrupt overhead = 20 cycles, and priority scheduler task selection = 44 cycles.

For the interrupt, we use pin **Int(0)** on the MIPS R4K model and do not save the register set before passing control to the priority scheduler software. Otherwise our interrupt overhead would be much larger. The priority scheduler software executes a context switch only if necessary to save/restore the state of a suspended process. Note that the context switch time includes time for storing the floating point registers.

With these costs, we calculate the *wcet* of the entire graph. We use the priority scheduler with the priorities found via dynamic programming. This increases our CPU utilization by starting execution of a low priority task that is ready when no higher priority task is yet ready. In other words, we relax Assumption 5.2 and support multiprogramming. However, without Assumption 5.2, our static priorities are no longer optimal – in fact, priorities may have to by dynamic to guarantee optimality with tasks allowed to interrupt each other. However, relaxing Assumption 5.2 can allow us to reduce *wcet* for the graph, thus improving our solution.

Note that we assume no semaphores are used, and that precedence constraints are enforced by the run-time scheduler. We could support the use of semaphores in two ways. One simple way is to reinstate Assumption 5.2 and execute software-tasks only in order of priority (e.g. the task with priority 3 cannot execute until the task with priority 2 has completed, and the priority 2 task can only execute after the priority 1 task has completed). Another way is to increase the time for priority scheduler task selection to allow enough time for any task to exit a critical section; in other words, calculate a *wcet* for any task's critical section, and add that amount to the priority scheduler task selection time (the scheduler would know, of course, if a task is in a critical section and when the task has exited).

Example 10 Consider Figure 3. We use the priorities found in Example 9. We find that the run-time scheduler causes three interrupts. After the second interrupt, `oh1` executes until it is suspended when task `cjd` is ready. After `cjd` finishes, the priority scheduler switches back to `oh1`.

A straightforward ASAP schedule is used. Several of the software tasks have loops, but none of the tasks use semaphores. In this example, the critical path is in the execution of software.

sw-task	# cycles	hw-task	# cycles
int-ser-routine	20	mvm	4,400
priority-sch-sw	44		
oh0	2,554		
int-ser-routine	20		
priority-sch-sw	44		
oh1	1,718		
int-ser-routine	20	fk	4,500
context-switch	126		
priority-sch-sw	44		
cjd	14,878		
priority-sch-sw	44	cg	11,000
context-switch	126		
oh1	18,863		

Table 5: *WCET* Calculation Example

The overall *wcet* is 38,501 cycles. □

This final output is an upper bound on the *wcet* of the graph given the priorities assigned to software-tasks in the same *NEVER* set.

So we now can analyze satisfiability of a rate constraint in a dynamically changing, concurrent execution of hardware-tasks and software-tasks, given our run-time scheduler implementation.

6 Tool Flow and Target Architecture

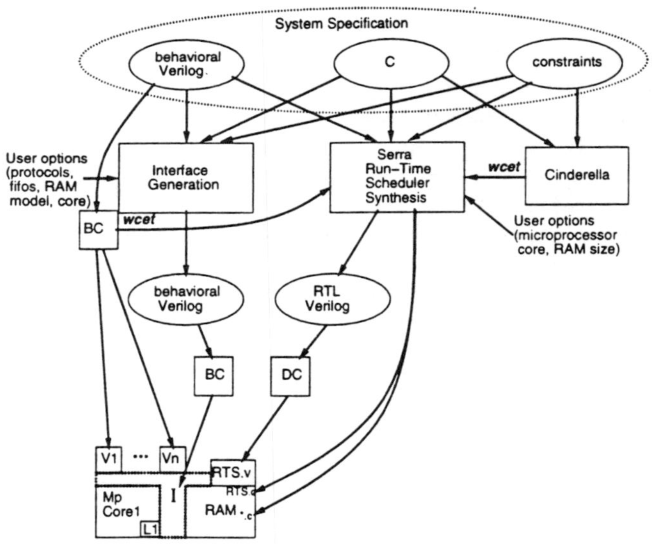

Figure 5: Tool Flow and Target Architecture

Figure 5 shows our tool flow, where `BC` labels the Synopsys Behavioral Compiler^{TM}[11] and `DC` labels the Synopsys Design Compiler^{TM}. Hardware-tasks are specified in Verilog and software-tasks are written in C. Microprocessor cores, memories (DRAM, SRAM), FIFO models, and other custom blocks are assumed as available inputs to the system. The implementation of a synthesized system can vary from a system on a chip to a board or set of interconnected components.

Constraints include rate constraints, relative timing constraints (minimum and maximum separation), and software resource constraints. Precedence constraints are implicit in the task specification.

The system-level tasks in Verilog and C, as well as constraints, are input to SERRA and to a tool that generates the interface. One of the tasks is specified as the main task. CINDERELLA-M, which we have ported to the MIPS R4K, takes input in C and outputs a *worst-case execution time (wcet)* for each software-task (note that bounds on loops must be provided by the user)[1]. Similarly, BC^{TM} generates an exact execution time for each hardware-task, which we take as a *wcet* (loop bounds must be provided here in some cases as well). When comparing BC^{TM}-generated *wcets* with software *wcet*, we convert all delays to the number of microprocessor clock cycles (since the hardware clock speed is typically slower.)

Figure 6: Block diagram of SERRA

6.1 SERRA Run-Time Scheduler Synthesis

The flow of the SERRA Run-Time Scheduler Synthesis tool is shown in Figure 6. SERRA synthesizes the control-unit of the scheduler into a hardware FSM and generates the static priorities for the software-tasks. SERRA does not generate the run-time C code but instead uses templates of the priority scheduler in C, the Interrupt Service Routine (ISR) in MIPS assembly and context switch code in MIPS assembly.

For the software that runs on the microprocessor core (CPU), the individual software-tasks are compiled together with the priority scheduler, ISR, and context switch code using standard C compilers and linkers. Memory-mapped I/O is called with C pointers set explicitly to the appropriate addresses.

Data and program memory are statically allocated. The ISR, which is the interrupt handling portion of the run-time scheduler, reads in a *start* vector that specifies which tasks are ready to be executed in software.

We end up with a set of software-tasks and their start addresses in the program code. Thus, we have a table of software-tasks and their entry points as seen in Table 6.

Entry	Value
0	Pointer to sw-task 0
1	Pointer to sw-task 1
.	...
n	Pointer to sw-task n

Table 6: Entry Table for Software-Tasks

Therefore, given a particular value of the *start* vector, the appropriate software-task(s) can be executed by the priority scheduler.

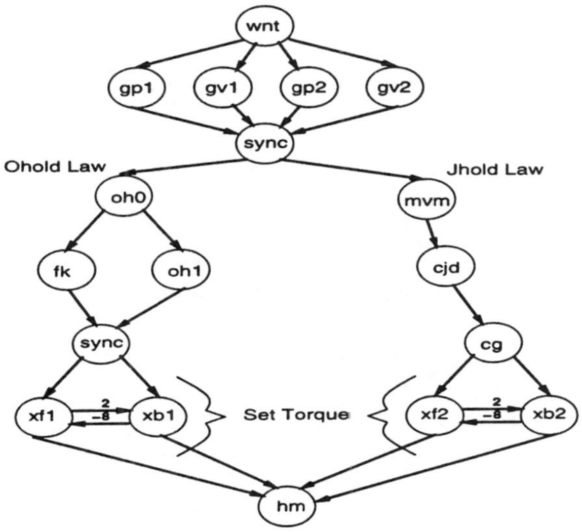

Figure 7: TaskSIF graph of Robot Arm Controller

7 Example and Experimental Results

For our example, we consider the code of Figure 2. `Jhold Law` and `Ohold Law` of Figure 2 are implemented with the subtasks shown in Figure 3. The TaskSIF graph, including the leaf tasks that implement `Set Torque`, are shown in Figure 7. Note that `Xmit Frame1` (*xf1*) and `Xmit Bit1` (*xb1*) of `Set Torque1` have a strict relative timing constraint of *xb1* starting no less than 2 cycles after *xf1* and no more than 8 cycles after. The exact same constraint holds for `Set Torque2`. This constraint could not always be satisfied with control signals generated by a run-time scheduler in software (note in Figure 5 we have an L1 cache).

We perform real-time analysis using the CLARA tool which has been implemented in 14,000 lines of C. The optimal order of execution for the software-tasks is passed to the priority scheduler. This provides for the upper bound on execution speed for the code under worst-case conditions.

The system begins each iteration once a millisecond. After obtaining the positions and velocities of the two robot arms, the run-time scheduler starts the execution of *mvm* in hardware for `Jhold Law` and *oh0* in software for `Ohold Law`. It continues with interleaved hardware-software execution as shown in Table 5. Finally, it tightly schedules accesses to `Xmit Frame` and `Xmit Bit` to set the torques for the robot.

The scheduling of tasks shown in Figure 7 but not in Figure 3 – *wnt*, *gp1*, *xf1*, *hm*, etc. – together take 61,200 cycles in the worst case. Since our MIPS R4K core runs at 100 MHz, the rate constraint allows us to use 100,000 cycles. Thus, we have 38,800 cycles left for the remaining tasks – *oh0*, *oh1*, *fk*, *mvm*, *cjd* and *cg*. The *wcet* found in Example 10 fits our rate constraint (note that the two schedules considered in Example 2 would violate the constraint). Thus, our schedule guarantees that we meet our hard real-time rate constraint.

Software-Task	Lines C	Lines Assem.	*bcet*	*wcet*
cjd	286	1177	9,989	14,878
oh0	90	237	1,598	2,554
oh1	693	3263	12,424	20,581
int-ser-routine	N/A	26	11	20
context-switch	N/A	42	34	126
priority-sch-sw	107	141	26	44

Table 7: Code space, *bcet* and *wcet* for sw-tasks.

Hardware-Task	Lines Verilog	Area	*bcet*	*wcet*
mvm	629	33,645	4,400	4,400
fk	2362	42,168	4,500	4,500
cg	2897	59,587	11,000	11,000
run-time-sch-hw	484	413	N/A	99,701

Table 8: Results for the synthesis of hw-tasks.

Table 7 presents the results for the compilation of the software and best- and worst-case execution time estimation with CINDERELLA-M. Unfortunately, due to the presence of interrupts and context switches, we had to turn CINDERELLA-M's instruction cache analysis capabilities off. In Table 8, we see the results for the synthesis of the hardware tasks of Figure 3 using the Behavioral Compiler^{TM}, except for the run-time scheduler hardware part which was synthesized with the Design Compiler^{TM}. The third column in Table 8 shows the number of gate equivalents the hardware required using the LSI 10K Logic library. We clock the hardware at 10 MHz. Using a MIPS R4K model in Verilog, we simulated the Robot Arm Controller in Verilog using Chronologic's VCS^{TM}.

8 Conclusion

We have addressed the important problem of real-time analysis in hardware-software codesign with a custom run-time system. The CLARA Real-Time Analysis tool, in conjunction with the SERRA Run-Time Scheduler tool, helps designers perform system-level design with hardware and software at a coarse level of granularity. We can predictably meet hard real-time constraints with our approach, based on static priority assignment, a custom priority scheduler, and a synthesized run-time scheduler, which allows a more detailed analysis of the system. The final result is tighter execution bounds thus squeezing more performance out of the same components than with a traditional RTOS and associated real-time analysis.

For our future work we plan to address more fully the issues of semaphores and hardware-software partitioning of the run-time scheduler.

Acknowledgements

ARPA sponsored this research under grant No. DABT63-95-C-0049. We also acknowledge the contributions of Sera Linardi, who ported CINDERELLA to MIPS, and Toshiyuki Sakamoto, who wrote the Verilog hardware-tasks and implemented interrupts in the MIPS R4K model.

References

[1] S. Malik, W. Wolf, A. Wolf, Y. Li, and T. Yen, "Performance Analysis of Embedded Systems," in G. De Micheli and M. Sami, editors, *Hardware/Software Co-Design*, pp. 45-74, Kluwer Academic Publishers, Norwell, MA, 1996.

[2] This is the same observation made in Malik et. al., ibid., pg. 69.

[3] C. Liu and J. Layland, "Scheduling algorithms for multiprogramming in a hard-real time environment," *Journal of the ACM*, 20(1):46-61, January 1973.

[4] L. Sha, R. Rajkumar and S. Sathaye, "Generalized rate monotonic scheduling theory: a framework for developing real-time systems," *Proceedings of the IEEE*, 82(1):68-82, January 1994.

[5] N. Audsley, A. Burns, M. Richardson, K. Tindell and A. J. Wellings, "Applying new scheduling theory to static priority pre-emptive scheduling," *Software Engineering Journal*, pp. 284-292, September 1993.

[6] N. Audsley, A. Burns, R. Davis, K. Tindell and A. J. Wellings, "Fixed Priority Pre-emptive scheduling: A Historical Perspective," *Real-Time Systems*, (8):173-198, 1995.

[7] K. Ramamritham, "Allocation and Scheduling of Precedence-Related Periodic Tasks," *IEEE Proceedings on Parallel and Distributed Systems*, 6(4):412-420, April 1995.

[8] F. Balarin, K. Petty, A. Sangiovanni-Vincentelli and Pravin Varaiya, "Formal Verification of the PATHO Real-Time Operating System," *Proceedings of the 33rd Conference on Decision and Control, CDC '94*, December 1994.

[9] F. Balarin, H. Hsieh, A. Jurecska, L. Lavagno and A. Sangiovanni-Vincentelli, "Formal Verification of Embedded Systems based on CFSM Networks," *Proceedings of the 33nd Design Automation Conference*, June 1996.

[10] T. Yen and W. Wolf, "Performance Estimation for Real-Time Distributed Embedded Systems," *Proceedings of International Conference on Computer Design*, pp. 64-69, 1995.

[11] D. Knapp, *Behavioral Synthesis: Digital System Design Using the Synopsys Behavioral Compiler*, Prentice Hall, Upper Saddle River, NJ, 1996.

[12] G. De Micheli and M. Sami, editors, *Hardware/Software Co-Design*, Kluwer Academic Publishers, Norwell, MA, 1996.

[13] R. Ernst, J. Henkel, Th. Benner, W. Ye, U. Holtmann, D. Herrmann and M. Trawny, "The COSYMA environment for hardware/software cosynthesis of small embedded systems," *Microprocessors and Microsystems*, 20 (1996) pp. 159-166.

[14] R. K. Gupta, *Co-Synthesis of Hardware and Software for Digital Embedded Systems*, Kluwer Academic Publishers, Boston, MA, 1995.

[15] Pai H. Chou and Gaetano Borriello, "Software Scheduling in the Co-Synthesis of Reactive Real-Time Systems," *Proceedings of the 31st Design Automation Conference*, pp. 1-4, June 1994.

[16] Pai H. Chou, Ross B. Ortega, and Gaetano Borriello, "The Chinook Hardware/Software Co-Synthesis System," *International Symposium on System Synthesis*, pp. 22-27, September 1995.

[17] D. Verkest, K. Van Rompaey, I. Bolsens & H. De Man, "CoWare-A Design Environment for Heterogeneous Hardware/Software Systems," *Design Automation for Embedded Systems*, Vol. 1, No. 4, pp. 357-386, October 1996.

[18] A. W. Leigh, *Real Time Software For Small Systems* , Sigma Press, Wilmslow, U.K., 1988.

[19] V. Mooney, T. Sakamoto, G. De Micheli, "Run-Time Scheduler Synthesis For Hardware-Software Systems and Application to Robot Control Design," *5th. Int'l Workshop on Hardware/Software Codesign,*, pp. 95-99, Braunschweig, Germany, March 1997.

[20] M. Garey and D. Johnson, *Computers and Intractability A Guide to the Theory of NP-Completenes*, W. H. Freeman and Company, N.Y., 1979, pg. 239.

[21] T. Cormen, C. Leiserson and R. Rivest, *Introduction to Algorithms*, The MIT Press, Cambridge, 1990, pg. 35.

[22] F. Hillier and G. Lieberman, *Introduction to Operations Research*, 6th edition, McGraw-Hill, Inc., New York, 1995, pp. 424 - 469.

[23] C. N. Coelho Jr. and G. De Micheli, "Analysis and Synthesis of Concurrent Digital Circuits Using Control-Flow Expressions," *IEEE Transactions on CAD/ICAS*, Vol. 15, No. 8, August 1996 .

SESSION 10C

INTERCONNECT OPTIMIZATION

Moderators:

Wayne W.-M. Dai, University of California, Santa Cruz, CA

John M. Cohn, IBM Corp., Richmond, VT

A New Approach to Simultaneous Buffer Insertion and Wire Sizing

Chris C. N. Chu and D. F. Wong
cnchu@cs.utexas.edu and wong@cs.utexas.edu
Department of Computer Sciences, University of Texas at Austin, Austin, TX 78712.

Abstract

In this paper, we present a completely new approach to the problem of delay minimization by simultaneous buffer insertion and wire sizing for a wire. We show that the problem can be formulated as a convex quadratic program, which is known to be solvable in polynomial time. Nevertheless, we explore some special properties of our problem and derive an optimal and very efficient algorithm to solve the resulting program. Given m buffers and a set of n discrete choices of wire width, the running time of our algorithm is $O(mn^2)$ and is independent of the wire length in practice. For example, an instance of 100 buffers and 100 choices of wire width can be solved in 3 seconds. Besides, our formulation is so versatile that it is easy to consider other objectives like wire area or power dissipation, or to add constraints to the solution. Also, wire capacitance lookup tables, or very general wire capacitance models which can capture area capacitance, fringing capacitance, coupling capacitance, etc. can be used.

1 Introduction

In the past, gate delay is the dominating factor in circuit design. However, as the feature size of VLSI devices continues to decrease, interconnect delay becomes increasingly important. Nowadays, feature size has been down to $0.25\mu m$ in advance technology. Interconnect delay has become the dominating factor in determining system performance. In many systems designed today, as much as 50% to 70% of clock cycle are consumed by interconnect delay [9]. It is predicted in [12] that the feature size will be reduced to $0.18\mu m$ by 1999 and $0.13\mu m$ by 2002. So we expect the significance of interconnect delay will further increase in near future.

In this paper, we will mainly consider the simultaneous buffer insertion and wire sizing problem as stated in Problem 1. (Elmore delay model [13] is used for delay calculation.) Both buffer insertion and wire sizing have been shown to be effective techniques to reduce interconnect delay and many work has been done during the past few years. See below for a brief overview or see [9] for a comprehensive survey.

For wire sizing alone, almost all the previous work gives an approximate solution by the approach of dividing the wire into small fixed-length segments and optimizing the width of each segment iteratively (e.g. [1, 3, 7, 8, 10, 11, 20, 21, 23]). In order to obtain accurate results, the wire usually needs to be divided into a large number of (much more than n) segments. [2, 4, 14, 15] consider a variant such that the set H of choices of wire width is a continuous interval. Therefore, the resulting wire width function $f(x)$ is continuous. However, a continuous shape is expensive to fabricate.

PROBLEM 1: The Simultaneous Buffer Insertion and Wire Sizing Problem

Given: wire length L, driver resistance R_D, load capacitance C_L, a set $H = \{h_1, \ldots, h_n\}$ of choices of wire width such that $h_1 > \cdots > h_n$, and m buffers $B_1, \ldots, B_m$.

Determine: the positions $x_1, \ldots, x_m$ at which the buffers are inserted and the wire width $f(x)$ at each point x along the wire such that the delay from source to sink is minimized.

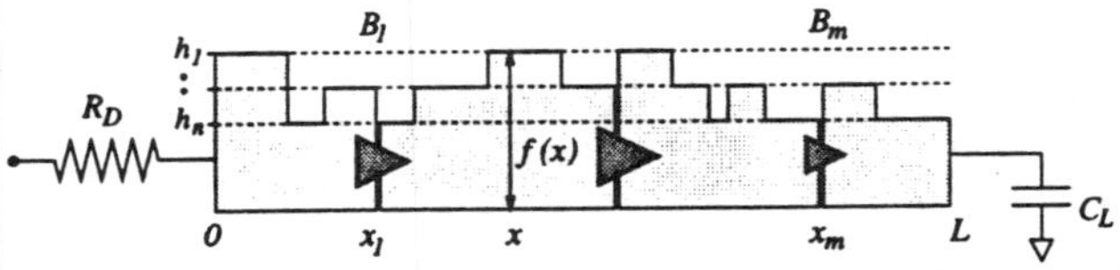

Not much work has been done on simultaneous buffer insertion and wire sizing. Recently, [18] generalizes the dynamic programming algorithm in [22] to handle buffer insertion and wire sizing simultaneously. Their algorithm also allows choices of buffers of different size and includes power consideration. However, their algorithm runs in pseudo-polynomial time and requires a substantial amount of memory. [6] also considers buffer insertion, buffer sizing and wire sizing simultaneously and a closed form optimal solution is obtained. However, in that paper, only wire area capacitance is considered (terms like wire fringing capacitance are ignored).

We present a completely new approach in this paper. Instead of solving Problem 1 directly, we will solve an equivalent problem which will be introduced later (see Problem 1′ in Section 3). Our new approach has many advantages over the previous approaches:

1. The problem of our approach has much less vari-

1092-3152/97 $10.00 © 1997 IEEE

ables than the problem of the traditional approach of dividing a wire into small fixed-length segments. If m buffers are to be inserted and a set of n choices of wire width is given, the problem we formulated will have $(m+1)n$ variables no matter how long the wire is. As in practice, usually only a few buffers and a few choices for the wire width are allowed, $(m+1)n$ is a small number. Moreover, the problem of our approach is completely equivalent to Problem 1 (not an approximation).

2. The problem of our approach can be solved optimally and very efficiently even for large m and n. We will show that our problem is a convex quadratic program. Convex quadratic programming has been well studied and can be solved efficiently by many public domain or commercial software systems. Nevertheless, we explore some special properties of our problem and derive an even more efficient iterative algorithm such that each iteration needs only linear time. In practice, the algorithm runs in about n iterations only. For example, an instance of 100 buffers and 100 choices of wire width (i.e. 10100 variables) can be solved in 3 seconds by our algorithm.

3. Buffer insertion is generally considered a hard problem and usually some heuristics or dynamic programming are needed to handle it. However, it is interesting to note how naturally and easily buffer insertion is handled in our approach. We will see that it is no more difficult than wire sizing alone.

4. Besides delay, our formulation can be easily extended to consider other objectives like wire area or power dissipation. For example, we can optimally solve the problems of minimizing a weighted sum of delay and wire area, minimizing delay with bounded area, minimizing area with bounded delay, etc. Our formulation also allows adding constraints to the solution. Moreover, our efficient algorithm can still be applied to get optimal results.

5. We can use very general wire capacitance models which can capture area capacitance, fringing capacitance, coupling capacitance (the capacitance due to an adjacent parallel wire), etc. A wire segment is modeled as a π-type RC circuit as shown in Figure 1. The capacitance of a wire segment of width h and length l is given by $c(h)l$, where $c(h)$ is the unit length wire capacitance for a segment of width h. The only restriction on c is that it has to be an increasing function from $\mathcal{R}^+$ to $\mathcal{R}^+$. For example, to model wire area capacitance, wire fringing capacitance and coupling capacitance at the same time, suppose the distance to an adjacent parallel wire is $d-h$ when the wire width is h. Then we can set $c(h) = c_0 h + c_f + c_c/(d-h)$, where c_0 is the unit wire area capacitance, c_f is the unit wire fringing capacitance and c_c is the unit wire coupling capacitance. The values of $c(h)$ for each h in H can also be obtained from a lookup table.

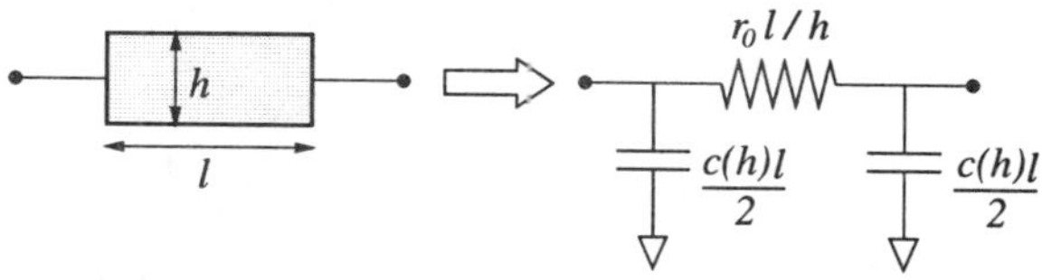

Figure 1: *The model of a wire segment of length l and width h by a π-type RC circuit. r_0 is the unit wire resistance. $c(h)$ is the wire capacitance per unit length for a segment of width h. We assume $c(h)$ is an increasing function in this paper.*

The paper is organized as follows. In Section 2, we will first consider the problem of wire sizing without buffer insertion. Once the formulation and the algorithm for wire sizing is understood, the extension to simultaneous buffer insertion and wire sizing will be easy and will be discussed in Section 3. In Section 4, we will further extend our results to consider other objectives like wire area or power, and to handle additional constraints to the solution. In Section 5, some experimental results to show the efficiency of our algorithm will be presented. In Section 6, we discuss some directions for future research.

2 Wire Sizing

For the rest of the paper, we will use uppercase boldface letters to denote matrices and lowercase boldface letters to denote vectors. We will use the convention that indices of matrices and vectors start from one. To simplify the presentation, if we refer to an element of a matrix or a vector such that the index is out of range, we assume that the value is zero.

2.1 Our New Approach

We want to solve the wire sizing problem as stated in Problem 2, where the optimal wire width is represented by a step function $f : [0, L] \to H$. Instead of solving Problem 2 directly, we approach the problem by looking at an equivalent problem. Before we introduce the new problem, we will first prove that f must be a decreasing function. A similar monotone property for simpler wire capacitance model and fixed-length segments has been proved in [11].

Lemma 1 *The optimal wire sizing function f is a decreasing function.*

Proof outline: Suppose f changes from a smaller value h to a larger value h' at a point of a distance l from the source. Therefore, $f(x) = h$ for $l - \delta \le x \le l$ and $f(x) = h'$ for $l < x \le l + \delta$ for some $\delta > 0$. Let g

PROBLEM 2: The Wire Sizing Problem

Given: wire length L, driver resistance R_D, load capacitance C_L, a set $H = \{h_1, \ldots, h_n\}$ of choices of wire width such that $h_1 > \cdots > h_n$.

Determine: the wire width $f(x)$ at each point x along the wire such that the delay from source to sink is minimized.

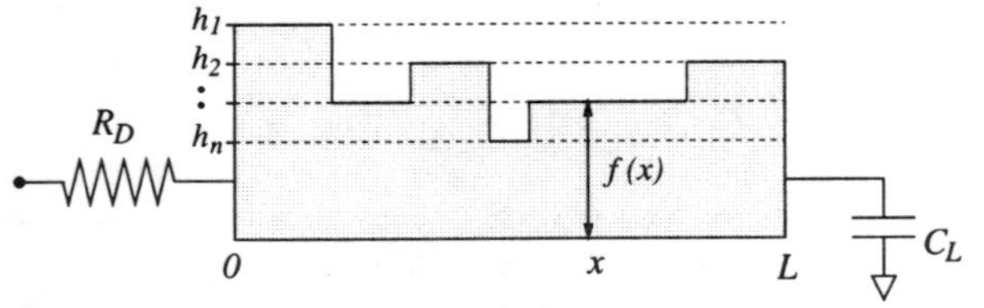

be another wire sizing function defined as $g(x) = h'$ for $l - \delta \le x \le l$, $g(x) = h$ for $l < x \le l + \delta$ and $g(x) = f(x)$ otherwise. We can show that g is better than f, which contradicts to the fact that f is optimal. □

Instead of solving Problem 2 directly, we will solve Problem 2′ below. In Problem 2′, the wire is divided into n segments such that the width of the ith segment is h_i, and the length of each segment is to be determined. By Lemma 1, it is clear that Problem 2′ is equivalent to Problem 2. Note that our new approach divides the wire into only n segments and gives an optimal solution to the original problem. If we approach Problem 2 by dividing the wire into small fixed-length segments, the solution will not be exact. In order to obtain a good approximation, the wire needs to be divided into much more than n segments.

PROBLEM 2′: The Wire Sizing Problem of Our Approach (equivalent to Problem 2)

Given: wire length L, driver resistance R_D, load capacitance C_L, a set $H = \{h_1, \ldots, h_n\}$ of choices of wire width such that $h_1 > \cdots > h_n$.

Determine: the segment lengths $l_i \ge 0$ for $1 \le i \le n$ such that the delay from source to sink is minimized.

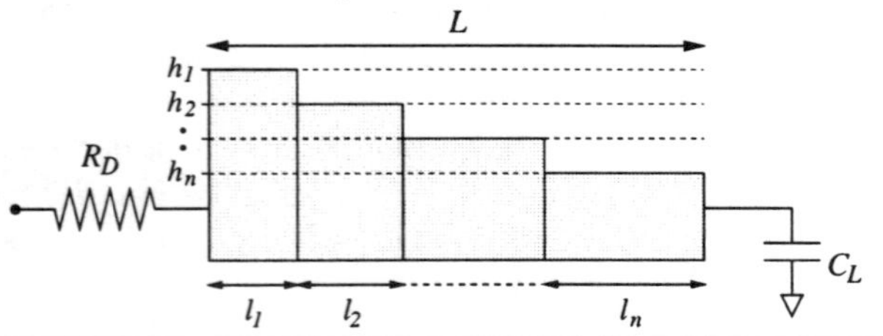

2.2 Problem formulation

We will show in this subsection that Problem 2′ can be formulated as a convex quadratic program.

Let $c_i = c(h_i)$ for $1 \le i \le n$. Then for Problem 2′, the delay from source to sink is

$$\begin{aligned} D &= R_D(c_1 l_1 + c_2 l_2 + \cdots + c_n l_n + C_L) \\ &+ \frac{r_0 l_1}{h_1}\left(\frac{c_1 l_1}{2} + c_2 l_2 + \cdots + c_n l_n + C_L\right) \\ &+ \frac{r_0 l_2}{h_2}\left(\frac{c_2 l_2}{2} + c_3 l_3 + \cdots + c_n l_n + C_L\right) \\ &\vdots \\ &+ \frac{r_0 l_n}{h_n}\left(\frac{c_n l_n}{2} + C_L\right) \\ &= \frac{1}{2}\boldsymbol{l}^T \boldsymbol{\Phi} \boldsymbol{l} + \boldsymbol{\rho}^T \boldsymbol{l} + R_D C_L \end{aligned}$$

where

$$\boldsymbol{\Phi} = \begin{pmatrix} c_1 r_0/h_1 & c_2 r_0/h_1 & c_3 r_0/h_1 & \cdots & c_n r_0/h_1 \\ c_2 r_0/h_1 & c_2 r_0/h_2 & c_3 r_0/h_2 & \cdots & c_n r_0/h_2 \\ c_3 r_0/h_1 & c_3 r_0/h_2 & c_3 r_0/h_3 & \cdots & c_n r_0/h_3 \\ \vdots & \vdots & \vdots & \ddots & \vdots \\ c_n r_0/h_1 & c_n r_0/h_2 & c_n r_0/h_3 & \cdots & c_n r_0/h_n \end{pmatrix},$$

$$\boldsymbol{\rho} = \begin{pmatrix} R_D c_1 + C_L r_0/h_1 \\ R_D c_2 + C_L r_0/h_2 \\ R_D c_3 + C_L r_0/h_3 \\ \vdots \\ R_D c_n + C_L r_0/h_n \end{pmatrix} \text{ and } \boldsymbol{l} = \begin{pmatrix} l_1 \\ l_2 \\ l_3 \\ \vdots \\ l_n \end{pmatrix}.$$

So Problem 2′ can be formulated as follows:

$$\begin{array}{ll} \text{minimize} & \frac{1}{2}\boldsymbol{l}^T \boldsymbol{\Phi} \boldsymbol{l} + \boldsymbol{\rho}^T \boldsymbol{l} \\ \text{subject to} & l_1 + \cdots + l_n = L \\ & l_i \ge 0 \text{ for } 1 \le i \le n \end{array} \qquad (1)$$

This is a quadratic program. In general, quadratic program is a mathematical program with a quadratic objective function subject to linear equality and inequality constraints. If the matrix $\boldsymbol{\Phi}$ is positive definite, it is called a convex quadratic program. Note that quadratic programming is NP-hard [16] but convex quadratic programming can be solved in polynomial time [17]. In the following, we will prove that the quadratic program (1) is convex. First, we make the following two definitions.

Definition 1 *(Symmetric Decomposable Matrix)* *Let $\boldsymbol{Q} = (q_{ij})$ be an $n \times n$ symmetric matrix. If for some $\boldsymbol{\alpha} = (\alpha_1, \ldots, \alpha_n)^T$ and $\boldsymbol{v} = (v_1, \ldots, v_n)^T$ such that $0 < \alpha_1 < \cdots < \alpha_n$, $q_{ij} = q_{ji} = \alpha_i v_i v_j$ for $i \le j$, then $\boldsymbol{Q}$ is called a symmetric decomposable matrix. We denote $\boldsymbol{Q} = SDM(\boldsymbol{\alpha}, \boldsymbol{v})$.*

Definition 2 *(Upper Triangular Decomposable Matrix)* *Let $\boldsymbol{U} = (u_{ij})$ be an $n \times n$ upper triangular matrix. If for some $\boldsymbol{\beta} = (\beta_1, \ldots, \beta_n)^T$ and $\boldsymbol{v} = (v_1, \ldots, v_n)^T$ such that $\beta_i > 0$ for all i, $u_{ij} = \beta_i v_j$ for $i \le j$ and $u_{ij} = 0$ for $i > j$, then $\boldsymbol{U}$ is called an upper triangular decomposable matrix. We denote $\boldsymbol{U} = UTDM(\boldsymbol{\alpha}, \boldsymbol{v})$.*

Lemma 2 *Φ in (1) is symmetric decomposable.*

Proof:
Let $\alpha = (\frac{r_0}{c_1 h_1}, \ldots, \frac{r_0}{c_n h_n})^T$ and $v = (c_1, \ldots, c_n)^T$. Note that $0 < \frac{r_0}{c_1 h_1} < \cdots < \frac{r_0}{c_n h_n}$. Then $\Phi = SDM(\alpha, v)$. □

Lemma 3 *If Q is symmetric decomposable, then $Q = U^T U$ where U is upper triangular decomposable. In particular, if $Q = SDM(\alpha, v)$, then $Q = U^T U$ where $U = UTDM(\beta, v)$, $\beta_i = \sqrt{\alpha_i - \alpha_{i-1}}$ for $1 \le i \le n$.*

Proof outline:
Can be verified by multiplying U^T and U. □

Lemma 4 *If Q is symmetric decomposable, then Q is positive definite.*

Proof: Let $Q = SDM(\alpha, v)$. By Lemma 3, $Q = U^T U$ where $U = UTDM(\beta, v)$ for some β. For any $x \neq 0$, let $y = Ux$. Note that $y \neq 0$ as U is nonsingular and $x \neq 0$. So $x^T Q x = x^T U^T U x = y^T y > 0$. In other words, Q is positive definite. □

By Lemma 2, Lemma 4 and [17], we have Theorem 1.

Theorem 1 *The quadratic program (1) is convex, and hence can be solved in polynomial time.*

2.3 Algorithm

In the following, we will make some interesting observations on the convex quadratic program (1) and then derive a very efficient algorithm to solve it based on the idea of active set method. Active set method is a classical technique for constrained optimization problems. It is also one of the most popular methods to solve quadratic programming. It has been shown to be efficient in practice. We will first give a brief outline on how to solve convex quadratic programming by active set method. See [19] for details.

If a convex quadratic program consists of equality constraints only, it is particularly easy to solve. Consider the following program:

$$\begin{array}{ll} \text{minimize} & \frac{1}{2} l^T \Phi l + \rho^T l \\ \text{subject to} & \Gamma l = b \end{array} \tag{2}$$

where Φ is positive definite and Γ is of full rank. Consider the associated Lagrangian:

$$\ell(l, \lambda) = \frac{1}{2} l^T \Phi l + \rho^T l + \lambda^T (\Gamma l - b)$$

The Lagrange necessary conditions of optimality are $\partial \ell(l, \lambda)/\partial l_i = 0$ and $\partial \ell(l, \lambda)/\partial \lambda_i = 0$ for all i. The conditions can be written in matrix form as follows:

$$\begin{array}{lcl} \Phi l + \Gamma^T \lambda + \rho & = & 0 \\ \Gamma l - b & = & 0 \end{array}$$

Since Φ is positive definite and Γ is of full rank, it can be shown that the conditions can be uniquely solved:

$$\begin{array}{lcl} \lambda & = & -(\Gamma \Phi^{-1} \Gamma^T)^{-1} (\Gamma \Phi^{-1} \rho + b) \\ l & = & -\Phi^{-1} \Gamma^T \lambda - \Phi^{-1} \rho \end{array} \tag{3}$$

Now consider a general convex quadratic program, which can have both equality and inequality constraints. If we solve the program by ignoring all the inequality constraints and the solution obtained is feasible with respect to all constraints, then it should be the optimal solution of the original program. If it is non-feasible, the optimal solution should be on the boundary of the set of feasible solutions. Active set method is a systematic way to search for the optimal solution on the boundary.

The idea underlying active set method is to partition the inequality constraints into two groups: active and inactive. In each iteration, those active constraints are treated as equality constraints and those inactive constraints are essentially ignored (i.e. the feasible space is restricted to some boundary). The resulting equality constrained program is solved. If the solution is infeasible with respect to the original program, some inactive constraints will be added to the set of active constraints. If the solution is feasible but not optimal (i.e. some Lagrange multipliers are negative), some constraints will be removed from the current active set. The process is repeated until the optimal solution is found (in that case, the active set will define the boundary the optimal solution is on).

Therefore if we apply active set method to (1), we need to solve an equality constrained problem in the form of (2) (i.e. compute (3)) in each iteration. Each iteration can be done in cubic time in general. However, we will show below that (3) can be solved in linear time in our case.

First, note that all the inequality constraints in (1) are of the form $l_i \ge 0$. If we set $l_i = 0$ and substitute it into (1), the resulting program is of exactly the same form as (1) but of smaller size. In fact, if for some iteration, all constraints except $l_{j_1} \ge 0, \ldots, l_{j_r} \ge 0$ are in the active set $\mathcal{A}$, then the equality constrained program corresponding to that iteration will be equivalent to the following reduced program:

$$\begin{array}{ll} \text{minimize} & \frac{1}{2} l_{\mathcal{A}}^T \Phi_{\mathcal{A}} l_{\mathcal{A}} + \rho_{\mathcal{A}}^T l_{\mathcal{A}} \\ \text{subject to} & \Gamma_{\mathcal{A}} l_{\mathcal{A}} = L \end{array} \tag{4}$$

where $l_{\mathcal{A}} = (l_{j_1}, \ldots, l_{j_r})^T$, $\Gamma_{\mathcal{A}} = (1 \ 1 \ \cdots \ 1)$, $\rho_{\mathcal{A}} = (R_D c_{j_1} + C_L r_0/h_{j_1}, \ldots, R_D c_{j_r} + C_L r_0/h_{j_r})^T$, and $\Phi_{\mathcal{A}}$ is the symmetric decomposable matrix corresponding to $\mathcal{A}$ (i.e. $\Phi_{\mathcal{A}} = SDM(\alpha_{\mathcal{A}}, v_{\mathcal{A}})$ with $\alpha_{\mathcal{A}} = (\frac{r_0}{c_{j_1} h_{j_1}}, \ldots, \frac{r_0}{c_{j_r} h_{j_r}})^T$ and $v_{\mathcal{A}} = (c_{j_1}, \ldots, c_{j_r})^T$).

As before, the Lagrange necessary conditions of optimality for (4) are

$$\begin{aligned}\lambda_{\mathcal{A}} &= -(\Gamma_{\mathcal{A}}\Phi_{\mathcal{A}}^{-1}\Gamma_{\mathcal{A}}^T)^{-1}(\Gamma_{\mathcal{A}}\Phi_{\mathcal{A}}^{-1}\rho_{\mathcal{A}} + L)\\ l_{\mathcal{A}} &= -\Phi_{\mathcal{A}}^{-1}\Gamma_{\mathcal{A}}^T\lambda_{\mathcal{A}} - \Phi_{\mathcal{A}}^{-1}\rho_{\mathcal{A}}\end{aligned}$$

The crucial observation is that $\Phi_{\mathcal{A}}^{-1}$ is tridiagonal, as proved in the following lemma.

Lemma 5 *If Q is symmetric decomposable, then Q^{-1} is tridiagonal. In particular, if $Q = SDM(\alpha, v)$, then $Q^{-1} = (\theta_{ij})$ where $\theta_{ii} = 1/((\alpha_i - \alpha_{i-1})v_i^2) + 1/((\alpha_{i+1} - \alpha_i)v_i^2)$, $\theta_{i,i+1} = \theta_{i+1,i} = -1/((\alpha_{i+1} - \alpha_i)v_i v_{i+1})$ for $1 \le i \le n-1$, $\theta_{nn} = 1/((\alpha_n - \alpha_{n-1})v_n^2)$, and $\theta_{ij} = 0$ otherwise.*

Proof outline: Can be verified by multiplying the matrices $Q = SDM(\alpha, v)$ and (θ_{ij}) defined above. □

By Lemma 2 and Lemma 5, we have the Theorem 2.

Theorem 2 *$\Phi_{\mathcal{A}}^{-1}$ in (4) is tridiagonal.*

Let $\Phi_{\mathcal{A}}^{-1} = (\theta_{ij})$ where θ_{ij} is given by Lemma 5 and let $\rho_{\mathcal{A}} = (\rho_1, \ldots, \rho_r)^T$. Then the Lagrange optimality conditions for (4) can be written in closed form as follows:

$$\begin{aligned}\lambda_{\mathcal{A}} &= -\frac{L + \sum_{i=1}^{r}(\theta_{i-1,i} + \theta_{ii} + \theta_{i+1,i})\rho_i}{\sum_{i=1}^{r}(\theta_{i-1,i} + \theta_{ii} + \theta_{i+1,i})}\\ l_{j_i} &= -(\theta_{i-1,i}\rho_{i-1} + \theta_{ii}\rho_i + \theta_{i+1,i}\rho_{i+1})\\ &\quad - (\theta_{i-1,i} + \theta_{ii} + \theta_{i+1,i})\lambda_{\mathcal{A}} \quad \text{for } 1 \le i \le r\end{aligned}$$

Obviously, $l_j = 0$ for all $j \notin \{j_1, \ldots, j_r\}$. Once l is found, it is not difficult to see that λ in (3) can also be found in linear time. Hence (3) can be computed in linear time. The algorithm can be summarized as below.

Algorithm MASM (Modified Active Set Method)
1. Set the active set $\mathcal{A} = \emptyset$.
2. **repeat**
3. Solve for λ and l with respect to $\mathcal{A}$
4. by our special technique.
5. **if** ($l \not\ge 0$) **then** /* check for feasibility */
6. Add some inactive constraints to $\mathcal{A}$.
7. **else if** ($\lambda \not\ge 0$) **then** /* check for optimality */
8. Remove some active constraints from $\mathcal{A}$.
9. **until** ($l \ge 0$ and $\lambda \ge 0$)

Theorem 3 *The wire sizing problem (Problem 2, or equivalently, Problem 2′) can be solved by algorithm MASM such that each iteration takes $O(n)$ time.*

The number of iterations of the algorithm depends on how constraints are added to and remove from $\mathcal{A}$. For step 6, we add all the inactive constraints corresponding to negative segment lengths. For step 8, we remove the one corresponding to the most negative λ_j. In Section 5, we will see for this implementation, the number of iterations of our algorithm MASM is less than n in practice.

3 Simultaneous Buffer Insertion and Wire Sizing

In this section, simultaneous buffer insertion and wire sizing will be discussed. m buffers $B_1, \ldots, B_m$ are given and they will be inserted into a wire in this order (with B_1 nearest to the source). A buffer is modeled as a switch-level RC circuit as shown in Figure 2. For convenience, we treat the source and the sink as buffers and we call the source B_0 and the sink B_{m+1}.

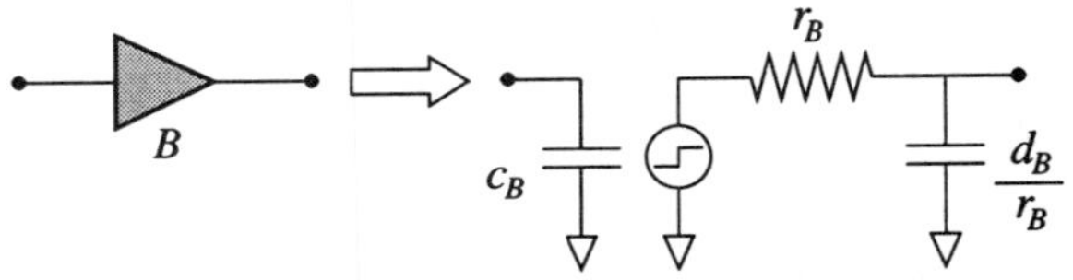

Figure 2: *The model of a buffer B by a switch-level RC circuit. c_B, r_B and d_B are the input capacitance, output resistance and the intrinsic delay of buffer B respectively.*

We want to solve Problem 1 introduced in Section 1. Note that the wire width is not necessary to be decreasing across a buffer. However, the sizing problem of the piece of wire between B_k and B_{k+1} for any k is basically the same as Problem 2 discussed in Section 2 (except that the length of that piece of wire is not fixed). So by Lemma 1, the optimal wire sizing function between two buffers will still be a decreasing step function. Hence, we can approach the problem as before by dividing the piece of wire between every pair of consecutive buffers into n segments of decreasing width, and determining the length of each segment. Instead of having a total length constraint for each piece of wire between buffers, we will have a single constraint specifying that the sum of all segment lengths equals L. See Problem 1′ below.

Let Φ' be the matrix corresponding to the coefficients of the quadratic terms and ρ_k be the vector corresponding to the coefficients of the linear terms for the delay from B_k to B_{k+1}. Let

$$\Phi = \begin{pmatrix} \Phi' & & & 0 \\ & \Phi' & & \\ & & \ddots & \\ 0 & & & \Phi' \end{pmatrix} \text{ and } \rho = \begin{pmatrix} \rho_0 \\ \rho_1 \\ \vdots \\ \rho_m \end{pmatrix}.$$

PROBLEM 1′: The Simultaneous Buffer Insertion and Wire Sizing Problem of Our Approach (equivalent to Problem 1)

Given: wire length L, driver resistance R_D, load capacitance C_L, a set $H = \{h_1, \ldots, h_n\}$ of choices of wire width such that $h_1 > \cdots > h_n$, and m buffers $B_1, \ldots, B_m$.

Determine: the segment lengths $l_i \geq 0$ for $1 \leq i \leq (m+1)n$ such that the delay from source to sink is minimized.

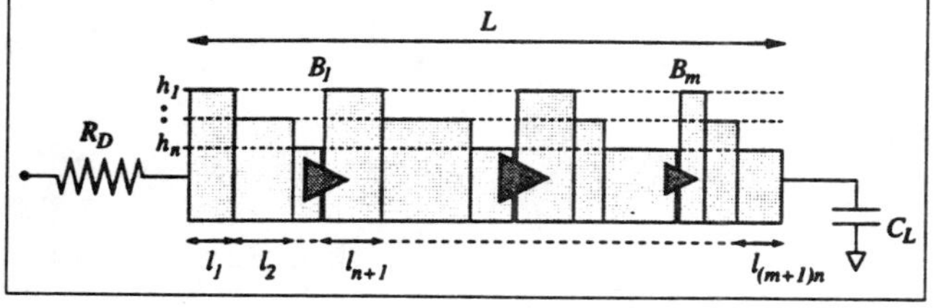

Then the delay from source to sink is

$$D = \frac{1}{2}\boldsymbol{l}^T \boldsymbol{\Phi} \boldsymbol{l} + \boldsymbol{\rho}^T \boldsymbol{l} + \sum_{k=0}^{m} r_{B_k} c_{B_{k+1}} + \sum_{k=1}^{m} d_{B_k}$$

So Problem 1′ can be formulated as follows:

$$\begin{array}{ll} \text{minimize} & \frac{1}{2}\boldsymbol{l}^T \boldsymbol{\Phi} \boldsymbol{l} + \boldsymbol{\rho}^T \boldsymbol{l} \\ \text{subject to} & l_1 + \cdots + l_{(m+1)n} = L \\ & l_i \geq 0 \text{ for } 1 \leq i \leq (m+1)n \end{array}$$

which is of the same form as (1). $\boldsymbol{\Phi}$ is clearly positive definite as $\boldsymbol{\Phi}'$ is positive definite. Hence the quadratic program is again convex. In addition, for each iteration, we can find $\boldsymbol{l}$ and $\boldsymbol{\lambda}$ as before by reducing the equality constrained program as in (2) to one as in (4). The matrix $\boldsymbol{\Phi}_{\mathcal{A}}$ will be:

$$\boldsymbol{\Phi}_{\mathcal{A}} = \begin{pmatrix} \boldsymbol{\Phi}_{\mathcal{A}_0} & & & 0 \\ & \boldsymbol{\Phi}_{\mathcal{A}_1} & & \\ & & \ddots & \\ 0 & & & \boldsymbol{\Phi}_{\mathcal{A}_m} \end{pmatrix}$$

where $\boldsymbol{\Phi}_{\mathcal{A}_k}$ is the symmetric decomposable matrix corresponding to the set of active constraints for segments between B_k and B_{k+1}. So

$$\boldsymbol{\Phi}_{\mathcal{A}}^{-1} = \begin{pmatrix} \boldsymbol{\Phi}_{\mathcal{A}_0}^{-1} & & & 0 \\ & \boldsymbol{\Phi}_{\mathcal{A}_1}^{-1} & & \\ & & \ddots & \\ 0 & & & \boldsymbol{\Phi}_{\mathcal{A}_m}^{-1} \end{pmatrix}$$

Therefore $\boldsymbol{\Phi}_{\mathcal{A}}^{-1}$ is also tridiagonal as $\boldsymbol{\Phi}_{\mathcal{A}_0}^{-1}, \boldsymbol{\Phi}_{\mathcal{A}_1}^{-1}, \ldots, \boldsymbol{\Phi}_{\mathcal{A}_m}^{-1}$ are all tridiagonal. Hence, Problem 1′ can be solved as before.

Theorem 4 *The simultaneous buffer insertion and wire sizing problem (Problem 1, or equivalently, Problem 1′) can be solved by algorithm MASM such that each iteration takes $O(mn)$ time.*

We will see in Section 5 that the number of iterations of our algorithm MASM is about n in practice.

4 Extensions

In the following two subsections, we will extend our result for simultaneous buffer insertion and wire sizing to consider wire area (and hence power dissipation), and to handle additional constraints to the solution respectively. We will show that for both extensions, the resulting problem can still be solved by MASM such that each iteration can be done in linear time. Besides, it is easy to see that we can also handle a combination of the two extensions and the resulting program can again be solved by MASM such that each iteration takes linear time.

4.1 Wire Area Consideration

Besides delay, we sometimes want to consider some other objectives as well. In this subsection, we will use wire area as an example and we will consider three cases:

1. *Minimization of a weighted sum of delay and area:* First, note that

$$\text{wire area} = \sum_{k=0}^{m} h_1 l_{kn+1} + \cdots + h_n l_{(k+1)n} = \boldsymbol{h}^T \boldsymbol{l}$$

where $\boldsymbol{h} = (h_1, \ldots, h_n, \ldots\ldots, h_1, \ldots, h_n)^T$. Then the objective will be $\mu(\boldsymbol{l}^T \boldsymbol{\Phi} \boldsymbol{l}/2 + \boldsymbol{\rho}^T \boldsymbol{l}) + (1-\mu)\boldsymbol{h}^T \boldsymbol{l} = (\mu/2)\boldsymbol{l}^T \boldsymbol{\Phi} \boldsymbol{l} + (\mu \boldsymbol{\rho}^T + (1-\mu)\boldsymbol{h}^T)\boldsymbol{l}$ for some weight μ. So the problem can be formulated as follows:

$$\begin{array}{ll} \text{minimize} & (\mu/2)\boldsymbol{l}^T \boldsymbol{\Phi} \boldsymbol{l} + (\mu \boldsymbol{\rho}^T + (1-\mu)\boldsymbol{h}^T)\boldsymbol{l} \\ \text{subject to} & l_1 + \cdots + l_{(m+1)n} = L \\ & l_i \geq 0 \text{ for } 1 \leq i \leq (m+1)n \end{array}$$

Note that this program is of the same form as (1) and hence can be solved by MASM as in Section 2.3.

2. *Delay minimization with bounded area:* The problem can be formulated as follows:

$$\begin{array}{ll} \text{minimize} & \frac{1}{2}\boldsymbol{l}^T \boldsymbol{\Phi} \boldsymbol{l} + \boldsymbol{\rho}^T \boldsymbol{l} \\ \text{subject to} & l_1 + \cdots + l_{(m+1)n} = L \\ & \boldsymbol{h}^T \boldsymbol{l} \leq b_{area} \\ & l_i \geq 0 \text{ for } 1 \leq i \leq (m+1)n \end{array}$$

where b_{area} is the area bound. We can solve the program by active set method. If the area constraint is inactive, that iteration can be solved in closed form as before. If the area constraint is active, the matrix $\boldsymbol{\Gamma}_{\mathcal{A}}$ in (4) for that iteration will contain two rows. However, it is clear that it can still be solved in linear time. In fact, it is not difficult to see that if $\mathbf{\Gamma}_{\mathcal{A}}$ has $O(1)$ rows (i.e. we have $O(1)$ nontrivial equalities), the iteration still takes linear time.

3. *Area minimization with bounded delay:*
This case is not as simple since the resulting mathematical program is no longer a quadratic program:

$$\begin{array}{ll} \text{minimize} & \boldsymbol{h}^T\boldsymbol{l} \\ \text{subject to} & \frac{1}{2}\boldsymbol{l}^T\boldsymbol{\Phi}\boldsymbol{l} + \boldsymbol{\rho}^T\boldsymbol{l} \leq b_{delay} \\ & l_1 + \cdots + l_{(m+1)n} = L \\ & l_i \geq 0 \text{ for } 1 \leq i \leq (m+1)n \end{array}$$

where b_{delay} is the delay bound. We can solve this problem by the Lagrangian relaxation technique as in [1]. The relaxed program will be as follows:

$$\begin{array}{ll} \text{minimize} & \boldsymbol{h}^T\boldsymbol{l} + \lambda(\frac{1}{2}\boldsymbol{l}^T\boldsymbol{\Phi}\boldsymbol{l} + \boldsymbol{\rho}^T\boldsymbol{l} - b_{delay}) \\ \text{subject to} & l_1 + \cdots + l_{(m+1)n} = L \\ & l_i \geq 0 \text{ for } 1 \leq i \leq (m+1)n \end{array}$$

where λ is the Lagrange multiplier. It is again of the form as (1) and hence can be solved by MASM.

4.2 Additional Constraints

Sometimes, we may want to have some constraints on the solution. We can do this by adding constraints to the convex quadratic program. For example, we may require that the section of the wire within a distance l' from the sink cannot be wider than h'. If t is the index such that $h_t > h' \geq h_{t+1}$, then the corresponding program will be:

$$\begin{array}{ll} \text{minimize} & \frac{1}{2}\boldsymbol{l}^T\boldsymbol{\Phi}\boldsymbol{l} + \boldsymbol{\rho}^T\boldsymbol{l} \\ \text{subject to} & l_1 + \cdots + l_{mn+t} \leq L - l' \\ & l_1 + \cdots + l_{(m+1)n} = L \\ & l_i \geq 0 \text{ for } 1 \leq i \leq (m+1)n \end{array}$$

As we mentioned above, as long as $O(1)$ constraints are added, the resulting program can be handled by MASM such that each iteration can be done in linear time.

5 Experimental Results

In this section, we will show that the algorithm MASM is efficient in practice. We have implemented the version for delay minimization by simultaneous buffer insertion and wire sizing in C. We run it on an IBM PowerPC 25 using several different values for the number of choices of wire width n and for the number of buffers m. For each pair of values of n and m, we run our algorithm on 100 instances with $R_D, C_L, B_1, \ldots, B_m, H$, and L being randomly generated. The average number of iterations and CPU time over the 100 instances are reported in Table 1.

Nowadays, the values of n and m that actually used are usually less than 10. So the running time is negligible. Even for an instance of 100 choices of wire width and 100 buffers, the algorithm still takes only 3 seconds. An interesting observation is that the number of iterations is about n (except when $m = 0$) and is basically independent of m. So for Problem 1′, algorithm MASM runs in $O(mn^2)$ time in practice.

# width choices	# buffers	# variables	Algorithm MASM	
n	m	$(m+1)n$	# iter.	CPU(s)
10	0	10	3.93	0.00
10	10	110	11.34	0.00
10	40	410	12.74	0.01
10	70	710	13.18	0.03
10	100	1010	13.31	0.04
40	0	40	15.79	0.00
40	10	440	40.19	0.05
40	40	1640	41.89	0.20
40	70	2840	42.36	0.35
40	100	4040	42.64	0.49
70	0	70	31.22	0.01
70	10	770	68.39	0.15
70	40	2870	71.01	0.60
70	70	4970	71.65	1.05
70	100	7070	72.24	1.53
100	0	100	42.61	0.01
100	10	1100	96.37	0.31
100	40	4100	100.16	1.24
100	70	7100	101.21	2.14
100	100	10100	101.69	3.06

Table 1: *The average number of iterations and CPU time of the algorithm MASM for simultaneous buffer insertion and wire sizing.*

There are also many public domain or commercial software systems that can solve convex quadratic programs (e.g. LOQO, CPlex, OSL, MINO). LOQO is one of the fastest system available. So we compare the running time of LOQO with our algorithm MASM. We notice that MASM, being based on the observations in Section 2.3, is much faster than LOQO. For small problems ($n = 10$ and $m = 10$), our algorithm is about 15 times faster. For larger problems ($n = 100$ and $m = 100$), our algorithm is more than 30 times faster.

6 Discussion

Tree topology: For weighted delay objective, our algorithm can be applied to handle nets with tree topology by a similar technique as in [5]. That is we use an iterative algorithm to optimize the tree edges one at a time. At each time we manipulate an edge, we keep all the other edges fixed and apply our algorithm to that edge. For other objectives like minimizing maximum delay or minimizing area with delay bounds, we can apply the Lagrangian relaxation technique as in [5] to reduce the problems to a problem of minimizing weighted delay. For these cases, we need to fix the number of buffers used on each wire beforehand. If only the total number of buffers to be used is given, a possible approach would be to combine dynamic programming with our algorithm to distribute the buffers among the edges.

Simultaneous buffer insertion, buffer sizing and wire sizing: If choices of buffers of several different sizes are allowed, we can find the optimal solution by trying all possible combinations of buffer sizes. For each combination, we can use our algorithm to handle buffer insertion and wire sizing. As our algorithm is really fast, the total running time will still be very short. For example, if we have 10 choices of wire width, 6 choices of buffer size and 4 buffers to be inserted ($6^4 = 1296$ combinations), the total running time to find the optimal solution is only 2.05 seconds. So our algorithm can even be used for simultaneous buffer insertion, buffer sizing and wire sizing in practice.

Note that the number of segments by our approach is independent of the wire length. For the example above, our problem has only $(4 + 1) \times 10 = 50$ segments. For the traditional approach, in order to obtain comparable accuracy, a longer wire needs to be divided into more segments. For a wire of $3000\mu m$ long, if we divide it into $1\mu m$ segments, we will have 3000 segments. The running time will be long if we use dynamic programming to solve this problem.

Of course, it would be nice if we can have better technique to handle buffer sizing than trying all possibilities.

References

[1] Chung-Ping Chen, Yao-Wen Chang, and D. F. Wong. Fast performance-driven optimization for buffered clock trees based on Lagrangian relaxation. In *Proc. IEEE ICCAD*, pages 405–408, 1996.

[2] Chung-Ping Chen, Yao-Ping Chen, and D. F. Wong. Optimal wire-sizing formula under the Elmore delay model. In *Proc. ACM/IEEE DAC*, pages 487–490, 1996.

[3] Chung-Ping Chen and D. F. Wong. A fast algorithm for optimal wire-sizing under Elmore delay model. In *Proc. IEEE ISCAS*, volume 4, pages 412–415, 1996.

[4] Chung-Ping Chen and D. F. Wong. Optimal wire-sizing function with fringing capacitance consideration. In *Proc. ACM/IEEE DAC*, 1997.

[5] Chung-Ping Chen, Hai Zhou, and D. F. Wong. Optimal non-uniform wire-sizing under the Elmore delay model. In *Proc. IEEE ICCAD*, pages 38–43, 1996.

[6] Chris C. N. Chu and D. F. Wong. Closed form solution to simultaneous buffer insertion/sizing and wire sizing. In *Proc. Intl. Symp. on Physical Design*, pages 192–197, 1997.

[7] Jason Cong and Lei He. An efficient approach to simultaneous transistor and interconnect sizing. In *Proc. IEEE ICCAD*, pages 181–186, 1996.

[8] Jason Cong and Lei He. Optimal wiresizing for interconnects with multiple sources. *ACM Trans. Design Automation of Electronic Systems*, 1(4), October 1996.

[9] Jason Cong, Lei He, Cheng-Kok Koh, and Patrick H. Madden. Performance optimization of VLSI interconnect layout. *INTEGRATION, the VLSI Journal*, 21:1–94, 1996.

[10] Jason Cong and Cheng-Kok Koh. Simultaneous buffer and wire sizing for performance and power optimization. In *Proc. Intl. Symp. on Low Power Electronics and Design*, pages 271–276, August 1996.

[11] Jason Cong and Kwok Shing Leung. Optimal wiresizing under the distributed Elmore delay model. *IEEE Trans. on CAD*, 14(3):321–336, March 1995.

[12] Jim DeTar. Advances outpace SIA roadmap (Semiconductor Industry Association alters projections) (Industry Trend or Event). *Electronic News*, 42(2147):1, December 16 1996.

[13] W. C. Elmore. The transient response of damped linear network with particular regard to wideband amplifiers. *J. Applied Physics*, 19:55–63, 1948.

[14] J. P. Fishburn. Shaping a VLSI wire to minimize Elmore delay. In *Proc. European Design and Test Conference*, 1997.

[15] J. P. Fishburn and C. A. Schevon. Shaping a distributed-RC line to minimize Elmore delay. *IEEE Transactions on Circuits and Systems-I: Fundamental Theory and Applications*, 42(12):1020–1022, December 1995.

[16] M. R. Garey and D. S. Johnson. *Computers and Intractability: A Guide to the Theory of NP-Completeness.* Freeman, NY, 1979.

[17] M. K. Kozlov, S. P. Tarasov, and L. G. Khachiyan. Polynomial solvability of convex quadratic programming. *Soviet Mathematics Doklady*, 20:1108–1111, 1979.

[18] John Lillis, Chung-Kuan Cheng, and Ting-Ting Y. Lin. Optimal wire sizing and buffer insertion for low power and a generalized delay model. *IEEE Journal of Solid State Circuits*, 31(3):437–447, March 1996.

[19] D. G. Luenberger. *Linear and Nonlinear Programming.* Addison Wesley, second edition, 1984.

[20] N. Menezes, R. Baldick, and L. T. Pileggi. A sequential quadratic programming approach to concurrent gate and wire sizing. In *Proc. IEEE ICCAD*, pages 144–151, 1995.

[21] Sachin S. Sapatnekar. RC interconnect optimization under the Elmore delay model. In *Proc. ACM/IEEE DAC*, pages 387–391, 1994.

[22] L. P. P. P. van Ginneken. Buffer placement in distributed RC-tree networks for minimal Elmore delay. In *Proc. Intl. Symp. on Circuits and Systems*, pages 865–868, 1990.

[23] Qing Zhu, Wayne W.-M. Dai, and Joe G. Xi. Optimal sizing of high-speed clock networks based on distributed RC and lossy transmission line models. In *Proc. IEEE ICCAD*, pages 628–633, 1993.

Optimal Shape Function for a Bi-directional Wire under Elmore Delay Model

Youxin Gao and D.F. Wong
Department of Computer Science
University of Texas at Austin
Austin, Texas 78712

Abstract

In this paper, we determine the optimal shape function for a bi-directional wire under the Elmore delay model. Given a bi-directional wire of length L, let $f(x)$ be the width of the wire at position x, $0 \leq x \leq L$. Let T_{DR} be the right-to-left delay. Let T_{DL} be the left-to-right delay. Let $T_{BD} = \alpha T_{DR} + \beta T_{DL}$ be the total weighted delay where $\alpha \geq 0$ and $\beta \geq 0$ are given weights such that $\alpha + \beta = 1$. We determine $f(x)$ so that T_{BD} is minimized. Our study shows that, if $\alpha = \beta$, the optimal shape function is $f(x) = c$, for some constant c; if $\alpha \neq \beta$, the optimal shape function can be expressed in terms of the Lambert's W function as $f(x) = -\frac{c_f}{2c_0}(\frac{1}{W(-ae^{-bx})} + 1)$, where c_f is the unit length fringing capacitance, c_0 is the unit area capacitance, a and b are constants in terms of the given circuit parameters. If $\alpha = 0$ or $\beta = 0$, our result gives the optimal shape function for a uni-directional wire.

1 Introduction

In today's sub-micron design, interconnect delay becomes an important factor in determining total delay of a system. Roughly speaking, interconnect delay is determined by driver resistance, load capacitance, as well as interconnect wire resistance and capacitance. As the feature size of VLSI device decreases, interconnect wire resistance becomes comparable to or sometimes even bigger than the driver resistance, therefore interconnect wire delay can no longer be neglected. Several attempts have been made to minimize the interconnect delay by optimizing the shape of an interconnect wire ([1]-[4], see [11] for a good survey). In [1] and [3], it was found that the optimal shape under Elmore delay model is an exponential function. Unfortunately, the fringing capacitance (which is comparable to the area capacitance as the feature size decreases [7, 8]) was not taken into consideration in [1, 3]. More recently, with fringing capacitance consideration, it was shown in [2] that the optimal wire shape function can be expressed in terms of the *Lambert's W* function [1] in a closed form. At the same time, by using calculus of variations, Fishburn in [4] independently presented a power series solution to the optimal shape function.

All previous work ([1]-[4]) on finding optimal shape functions are for uni-directional wires. In practice, some wires are bi-directional (e.g. wires in a signal net with multiple sources [10]). In this paper, we determine the optimal shape function for a bi-directional wire under the Elmore delay model. Given a bi-directional wire of length L, let $f(x)$ be the width of the wire at position x, $0 \leq x \leq L$. Let T_{DR} be the right-to-left delay. Let T_{DL} be the left-to-right delay. Let $T_{BD} = \alpha T_{DR} + \beta T_{DL}$ be the total weighted delay where $\alpha \geq 0$ and $\beta \geq 0$ are given weights such that $\alpha + \beta = 1$. We determine $f(x)$ so that T_{BD} is minimized. Our study shows that, if $\alpha = \beta$, the optimal shape function is $f(x) = c$, for some constant c; if $\alpha \neq \beta$, the optimal shape function can be expressed in terms of the *Lambert's W* function as $f(x) = -\frac{c_f}{2c_0}(\frac{1}{W(-ae^{-bx})} + 1)$, where c_f is the unit length fringing capacitance, c_0 is the unit area capacitance, a and b are constants in terms of the given circuit parameters. If $\alpha = 0$ or $\beta = 0$, our result gives the optimal shape function for a uni-directional wire.

2 Elmore Delay Model

Given a nonuniformly sized wire whose width is given by a function $f(x)$ as shown in Fig.1 (a), we partition it into n equal-length wire segments, each of length $\Delta x = \frac{L}{n}$, and approximate it as a distributed RC network shown in Fig.1 (b). Let $x_i = i\Delta x$, $1 \leq x \leq n$. The capacitance and resistance of segment i can be approximated by $C_i = (c_0 f(x_i) + c_f)\Delta x$ and $R_i = r_0 \Delta x / f(x_i)$, respectively, where c_0 is unit area capacitance, c_f is unit length fringing capacitance, r_0

[1] The *Lambert's W* function [12] was first introduced by Euler in 1779 when he studied Lambert's transcendental equation. $W(x)$ function is defined as the value of w that satisfies $we^w = x$.

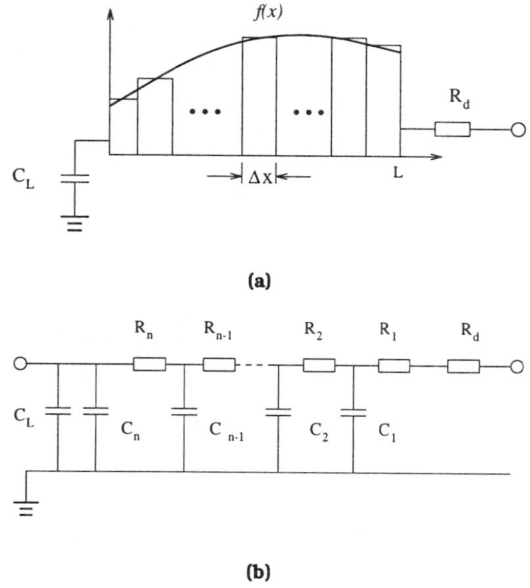

Figure 1: Distributed circuit model for calculating Elmore delay.

is unit length resistance. The Elmore delay [5] of the distributed RC network [6] is given by

$$T_D = \sum_{i=1}^{n} \frac{r_0 \Delta x}{f(x)} \sum_{j=i}^{n} ((c_0 f(x_j) + c_f)\Delta x + C_l)$$

$$+R_d(C_l + \sum_{i=1}^{n} (c_0 f(x_i) + c_f)\Delta x)$$

where T_D is equivalent to the sum over all segment resistance (R_i) multiplied by its down stream capacitance ([5, 6]). As $n \to \infty$, T_D thus becomes

$$T_D = \int_0^L \frac{r_0}{f(x)} (\int_0^x c_0 f(t) dt + \int_0^x c_f dt + C_l) dx$$

$$+ R_d(C_l + \int_0^L (c_0 f(x) + c_f) dx) \qquad (1)$$

Moreover, T_D can be written in a slightly different way, which is given by the following lemma.

Lemma 1

$$T_D = \int_0^L (c_0 f(x) + c_f)(R_d + \int_x^L \frac{r_0 dt}{f(t)}) dx$$

$$+ C_l(R_d + \int_0^L \frac{r_0 dx}{f(x)}) \qquad (2)$$

Lemma 1 can be proved by changing the order of integration in (1). It follows from Lemma 1 that T_D is also equivalent to the sum over all segment capacitance multiplied by its upstream resistance. In the next section, we will start from the delay expression in (2) and give a closed form solution for the optimal shape function. The reason of not using the delay expression in (1) will be explained later.

3 Optimal Wire Shape Function

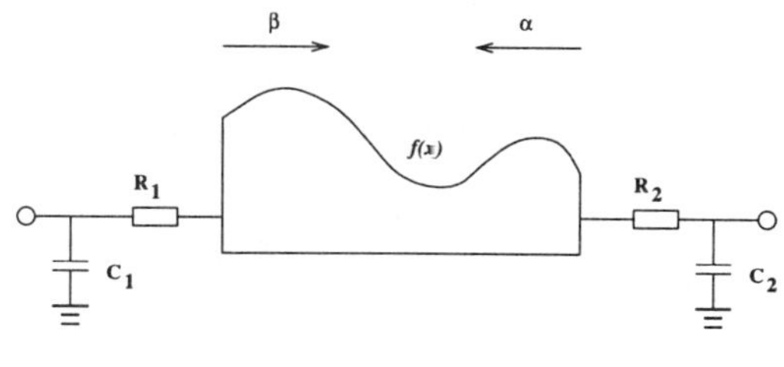

Figure 2: A bi-directional wire.

For a bi-directional wire shown in Fig.2, R_1 and R_2 are the driver resistances, and C_1 and C_2 are the load capacitances. Let T_{DR} be the delay when the signal is transmitted from right to left. Let T_{DL} be the delay when the signal is transmitted from left to right. According to Lemma 1, we have

$$T_{DR} = \int_0^L (c_f + c_0 f(x))(\int_x^L \frac{r_0 dt}{f(t)} + R_2) dx$$

$$+C_1(R_2 + r_0 \int_0^L \frac{dx}{f(x)})$$

$$T_{DL} = \int_0^L (c_f + c_0 f(x))(\int_0^x \frac{r_0 dt}{f(t)} + R_1) dx$$

$$+C_2(R_1 + r_0 \int_0^L \frac{dx}{f(x)})$$

We define the total weighted delay T_{BD} as

$$T_{BD} = \alpha T_{DR} + \beta T_{DL} \qquad (3)$$

where $\alpha \geq 0$ and $\beta \geq 0$ are given weights such that $\alpha + \beta = 1$.

In the rest of this section, we will derive the optimal wire shape function so that the weighted delay T_{BD} is minimized.

Lemma 2 *For a bi-directional wire, if $\alpha = \beta$, the optimal shape function is the constant function*

$$f(x) = \sqrt{\frac{r_0 c_f L + r_0(C_1 + C_2)}{c_0(R_1 + R_2)}} \qquad (4)$$

Proof: We introduce $u(x) = \int_x^L \frac{dx}{f(x)}$, so that $f(x) = -\frac{1}{u'(x)}$, $u(L) = 0$, and $\int_0^x \frac{dx}{f(x)} = u(0) - u(x)$. T_{BD} in (3) can be rewritten as an integration over $x, u(x), u'(x)$ as

$$T_{BD} = \alpha R_2(C_1 + c_f L) + \beta R_1(C_2 + c_f L) + \int_0^L F(u(x), u'(x))dx$$

where

$$\begin{aligned} F(u(x), u'(x)) &= -r_0(\alpha C_1 + \beta C_2)u'(x) - \frac{c_0}{u'(x)} \\ &\times (\alpha R_2 + \beta R_1) + r_0(c_f - \frac{c_0}{u'(x)}) \\ &\times (\beta u(0) + (\alpha - \beta)u(x)) \end{aligned}$$

Based on calculus of variations [9], the necessary condition to minimize T_{BD} is that $u(x)$ must satisfy Euler's differential equation:

$$F - u'F_{u'} = c$$

i.e.

$$-\frac{2c_0}{u'(x)}R_{12} + r_0(c_f - \frac{2c_0}{u'(x)})(\beta u(0) + \eta u(x)) = c \quad (5)$$

where c is a constant to be determined, $R_{12} = \alpha R_2 + \beta R_1$, and $\eta = \alpha - \beta$. By defining

$$c^* = c - r_0 c_f \beta u(0) \quad (6)$$

$$R_{12}^* = R_{12} + r_0 \beta u(0) \quad (7)$$

where $u(0)$ is a constant, equation (5) can be simplified as

$$\frac{c^* - r_0 c_f \eta u(x)}{-2c_0(R_{12}^* + r_0 \eta u(x))} u'(x) = 1 \quad (8)$$

Since $\alpha = \beta$, i.e. $\eta = 0$, equation (8) thus becomes

$$\frac{c^*}{-2c_0 R_{12}^*} u'(x) = 1$$

Obviously, the solution is $f(x) = -\frac{1}{u'(x)} = \frac{c^*}{2c_0 R_{12}^*}$. This means the optimal shape function is a uniform width function. In fact, the constant can be determined directly from the expression of T_{BD}. If we let $f(x) = f$, where f is a constant, then the delay can be written as,

$$\begin{aligned} T_{BD} &= \alpha R_2(C_1 + c_f L) + \beta R_1(C_2 + c_f L) \\ &+ \frac{r_0 L}{f}(\alpha C_1 + \beta C_2) + c_0 f L(\alpha R_2 + \beta R_1) \\ &+ \frac{L^2 r_0}{2f}(c_f + c_0 f) \end{aligned}$$

Thus $\frac{dT_{BD}}{df} = 0$ gives

$$f = \sqrt{\frac{r_0 c_f L + r_0(C_1 + C_2)}{c_0(R_1 + R_2)}}$$

□

Lemma 3 *Given a bi-directional wire, if $\alpha \neq \beta$, the optimal shape function is*

$$f(x) = -\frac{c_f}{2c_0}\left(\frac{1}{W(-ae^{-bx})} + 1\right) \quad (9)$$

where $W(x)$ is the Lambert's W function, and

$$a = \frac{R_{12}^* c_f}{R_{12}^* c_f + c^*} \cdot exp\left(\frac{2r_0 c_0 \eta L - R_{12}^* c_f}{R_{12}^* c_f + c^*}\right) \quad (10)$$

$$b = \frac{2\eta r_0 c_0}{R_{12}^* c_f + c^*} \quad (11)$$

Proof: Under the condition $u(L) = 0$, the solution to equation (8) is

$$u(x) = \frac{R_{12}^*}{\eta r_0}\left[exp\left(\frac{\eta r_0(c_f u - 2c_0(x - L))}{R_{12}^* c_f + c^*}\right) - 1\right] \quad (12)$$

The wire shape function $f(x)$ is thus

$$f(x) = -\frac{1}{u'(x)} = \frac{R_{12}^* c_f + c^*}{R_{12}^* + r_0 u(x)} \frac{1}{2c_0} - \frac{c_f}{2c_0} \quad (13)$$

Rearranging the terms in equation (12), we get

$$\begin{aligned} & exp\left[-\frac{2c_0 r_0(x - L) + R_{12}^* c_f}{R_{12}^* c_f + c^*}\right] \cdot exp\left[\frac{r_0 c_f u + R_{12}^* c_f}{R_{12}^* c_f + c^*}\right] \\ &= \frac{R_{12}^* c_f + c^*}{R_{12}^* c_f} \frac{r_0 c_f u + R_{12}^* c_f}{R_{12}^* c_f + c^*} \end{aligned} \quad (14)$$

If we let

$$y = \frac{r_0 c_f u + R_{12}^* c_f}{R_{12}^* c_f + c^*}$$

$$A = \frac{R_{12}^* c_f}{R_{12}^* c_f + c^*} \cdot exp\left[-\frac{2c_0 r_0(x - L) + R_{12}^* c_f}{R_{12}^* c_f + c^*}\right]$$

we can rewrite equation (14) as

$$Ae^y = y, \text{ i.e. } (-y)e^{-y} = -A \quad (15)$$

From the definition of the *Lambert's W* function, $W(x)$ is defined by $We^W = x$. In terms of W function, equation (15) becomes $y = -W(-A)$. Expanding y in terms of u, we have

$$u(x) = -\left(\frac{R_{12}^*}{r_0} + \frac{c^*}{r_0 c_f}\right)W(-A) - \frac{R_{12}^*}{r_0} \quad (16)$$

Substitute (16) into (13) and observe that $A = ae^{-bx}$, we get

$$f(x) = -\frac{c_f}{2c_0}\left(\frac{1}{W(-ae^{-bx})} + 1\right)$$

□

Remark 1 $f(x)$ depends on two parameters a and b. As it can be found from the definitions in (6), (7), (10) and (11), in order to get the values of a and b, we should know the values of the other two constants c and $u(0)$ first. In Lemma 5, we will derive the corresponding nonlinear equations for solving c and $u(0)$.

Remark 2 It is well known that $W(x)$ is monotonically increasing in the interval $[-e^{-1}, \infty]$. Because $a > 0$ and when $\alpha > \beta$, $b > 0$, $W(-ae^{-bx})$ increases as x increases. Therefore, $f(x)$ is monotonically increasing in the interval $[0, L]$. Similarly, when $\alpha < \beta$, $f(x)$ is a monotonically decreasing function in the interval $[0, L]$. Based on the above analysis and Lemma 2, a schematic solution of $f(x)$ can be sketched out as shown in Fig. 3.

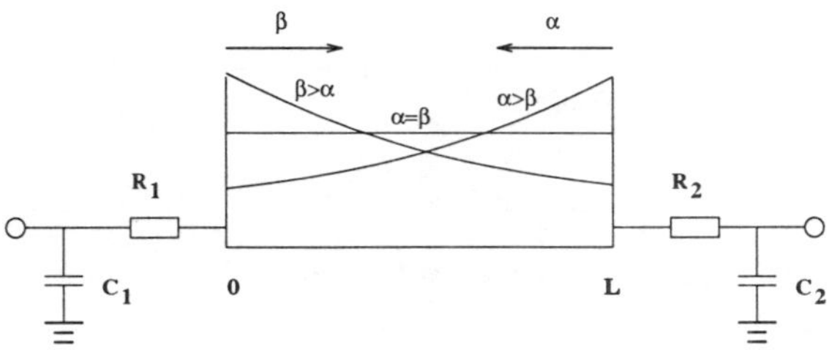

Figure 3: Optimal shape function for a bi-directional wire.

Without loss of generality, we assume $\alpha > \beta$ in the rest of the paper. Before we derive Lemma 5, first we give the following relations which will be used in deriving Lemma 5.

Lemma 4 *Given the optimal wire shape function* $f(x) = -\frac{c_f}{2c_0}(\frac{1}{W(-ae^{-bx})} + 1)$, *we have*

$$\int_0^L \frac{dx}{f(x)} = \frac{2c_0}{bc_f}(w_1 - w_0) \quad (17)$$

$$\int_0^L \left(\int_x^L \frac{dt}{f(t)}\right)dx = \frac{2c_0}{bc_f}w_1 L + \frac{c_0}{b^2 c_f}(w_1^2 - w_0^2) + \frac{2c_0}{b^2 c_f}(w_1 - w_0) \quad (18)$$

where

$$w_0 = W(-a) \quad (19)$$

$$w_1 = W(-ae^{-bL}) = -\frac{R_{12}^* c_f}{R_{12}^* c_f + c^*} \quad (20)$$

Proof sketch: Let $Y = W(-ae^{-bx})$. It can be shown that

$$\frac{dY}{dx} = -\frac{bY}{1+Y}$$

By changing the variable from x to Y, the left hand side of equation (17) becomes

$$\int_x^L \frac{dx}{f(x)} = \frac{2c_0}{bc_f}\int_{Y(x)}^{Y(L)} dY = \frac{2c_0}{bc_f}(w_1 - w_0)$$

Similarly, we can prove (18).

□

To solve the two unknown parameters c and $u(0)$, we have the following lemma.

Lemma 5 *The two constants* $u(0)$ *and* c *are the roots of the following two nonlinear equations*

$$-\left(\frac{2C_{21}}{c_f} + \alpha L + \frac{\eta w_1}{b} + \frac{\eta}{b}\right)\frac{\beta c_f}{c_0 \eta}\frac{du(0)}{dz} + L + \frac{1}{\eta}\left(\frac{2C_{21}}{c_f} + \beta L + \frac{\eta w_0}{b} + \frac{\eta}{b}\right)\left\{\left[\frac{ab}{2\eta}(2\eta L + c') - \frac{c^* a\beta}{c_0 R_{12}^*}\frac{du(0)}{dz}\right]\frac{dw_0}{da} - w_0\right\} + \frac{1}{b}(w_1 - w_0) = 0 \quad (21)$$

$$u(0) = \frac{R_{12}^*}{r_0 \eta}\left[exp\left(\frac{\eta r_0}{R_{12}c_f + c}(c_f u(0) + 2c_0 L)\right) - 1\right] \quad (22)$$

where

$$c' = c^*/(r_0 c_0) \quad (23)$$

$$R'_c = R_{12}^* c_f/(r_0 c_0) \quad (24)$$

$$C_{21} = \alpha C_1 + \beta C_2 \quad (25)$$

$$\frac{dw_0}{da} = \frac{w_0}{a(1 + w_0)} \quad (26)$$

$$\frac{du(0)}{dz} = -\frac{R_{12} + r_0 \alpha u(0)}{R'_c + c'} \times \frac{R'_c u(0) + 2LR_{12}^*/r_0}{R_{12}c' - R'_c r_0 \alpha u(0)} \quad (27)$$

Proof sketch: Equation (22) is derived directly from (12) by setting $x = 0$, where we make use of the relation $R_{12}^* c_f + c^* = R_{12}c_f + c$. Equation (21) comes from $\frac{dT_{BD}}{dc} = 0$. First, we substitute $f(x)$ back into the delay expression in (3). Let $T'_{BD} = T_{BD}/(r_0 c_0)$, $z = c/(r_0 c_0)$, and make use of (5), Lemma 4 and (23-25), then the delay expression can be simplified as

$$T'_{BD} = R_{12}\frac{(C_1 + c_f L)}{r_0 c_0} + \frac{\beta R_1(C_2 - C_1)}{r_0 c_0} + \frac{1}{2}Lz + \frac{2C_{21}}{bc_f}(w_1 - w_0) + \frac{L}{b}(\alpha w_1 - \beta w_0) + \frac{\eta}{2b^2}(w_1^2 - w_0^2) + \frac{\eta}{b^2}(w_1 - w_0) \quad (28)$$

$\frac{dT'_{BD}}{dz} = \frac{dT_{BD}}{dc} = 0$ gives equation (21).

□

In practice, we employ bisection method to solve these two nonlinear equations in Lemma 5, because we found it to be more efficient than Newton Raphson method in our experiments. Algorithms for calculating the W function can be found in [12]. The efficiency of bisection method depends on the initial root range, which can be estimated from the following lemma.

Lemma 6 *If c' is the root of nonlinear equation (21), it must satisfy*

$$c' \geq \frac{2\eta L - R'_c}{W^*} - R'_c \tag{29}$$

In terms of z, where $z = c/(r_0 c_0)$, this relation is

$$z \geq \frac{2\eta L - R_{12}c_f/(r_0 c_0)}{W^*} - \frac{\beta u(0) c_f}{W^* c_0} - \frac{R_{12} c_f}{r_0 c_0} \tag{30}$$

where $W^* = W(e^{-1}\frac{2\eta L - R'_c}{R'_c})$ and R'_c is as defined in (24).

Proof: This idea originates from the definition of the W function. For the function $W(x)$, the range of x is not from $-\infty$ to $+\infty$, but from $-e^{-1}$ to $+\infty$ instead. There are two different W function values in (21) need to be calculated, namely w_0 and w_1, i.e. $W(-a)$ and $W(-ae^{-bL})$. Therefore, the constraint on x in W function gives a limit on the values of a and b, which depend on the root c' that we are finding. Obviously, $-a < -ae^{-bL}$, thus we need only consider the constraint on w_0, i.e. we need to know what kind of constraint on c' can satisfy $-a \geq -e^{-1}$. In terms of c', it is

$$\frac{R'_c}{R'_c + c'} \cdot exp(\frac{2\eta L - R'_c}{R'_c + c'}) \leq e^{-1}$$

If we let $y = \frac{2\eta L - R'_c}{R'_c + c'}$, then the above inequality is simplified as

$$ye^y \leq e^{-1}\frac{2\eta L - R'_c}{R'_c}$$

i.e.

$$y \leq W(e^{-1}\frac{2\eta L - R'_c}{R'_c}) \tag{31}$$

There is no problem in calculating the W function in (31), since L is always positive and thus the term inside this W function is always larger than $-e^{-1}$. Substituting c' back into (31), then we find the constraint on root c',

$$c' \geq \frac{2\eta L - R'_c}{W^*} - R'_c \tag{32}$$

To get (30), we substitute (23) and (6) into (32). In the above, we have implicitly assumed that $2\eta L - R'_c > 0$. In fact, the same inequality can be proved if $2\eta L - R'_c < 0$.

□

So far, we have determined the optimal shape function for a bi-directional wire. Unidirectional wire optimization, which has been studied in [2, 4], can be thought of as a special case of bi-directional wire with either $\alpha = 0$ or $\beta = 0$. The authors in [2] give a closed form optimal wire shape function, and the author in [4] gives a power series solution. Based on Lemmas 3 and 5, it is easy to get the following results for uni-directional wire by setting $\alpha = 1$, $\beta = 0$.

Lemma 7 *Given a uni-directional wire with driver resistance R_d and load capacitance C_l, the optimal shape function is*

$$f(x) = -\frac{c_f}{2c_0}(\frac{1}{W(-ae^{-bx})} + 1) \tag{33}$$

where

$$a = \frac{R_d c_f}{R_d c_f + c} \cdot exp(\frac{2r_0 c_0 L - R_d c_f}{R_d c_f + c})$$
$$b = \frac{2r_0 c_0}{R_d c_f + c}$$

The constant c is the root of the following nonlinear equation

$$-(\frac{2C_l}{c_f} + \frac{w_0}{b} + \frac{1}{b})(w_0 - \frac{1}{2}ab(2L + \frac{c}{r_0 c_0})\frac{dw_0}{da})$$
$$+ L + \frac{1}{b}(w_1 - w_0) = 0 \tag{34}$$

where

$$w_0 = W(-a) \tag{35}$$
$$w_1 = W(-ae^{-bL}) = -\frac{R_d c_f}{R_d c_f + c} \tag{36}$$

Remark 3 The wire shape function in (33) is equivalent to but looks different from the one in [2]. This is because, the derivation in [2] was based on the assumption that the driver is on the left end of the wire, whereas here we assume it is on the right end.

Remark 4 Comparing with the shape function of bi-directional wire in Lemma 3, the uni-directional wire shape function has the same form of solution. But the uni-directional wire shape function only depends on one constant c, whereas the bi-directional wire shape function depends on two constants a and b.

Remark 5 Fishburn in [4] also used calculus of variations to determine the optimal function for a uni-directional wire. But his result is based on the delay expression in (1). The Euler's differential equation in [4] is

$$c_0 u(x) + \frac{1}{2} c_f x + C_l = c u'(x) \tag{37}$$

where $u(x)$ is defined as $u(x) = \int_0^x f(t)dt$, which is different from our definition. However, it is difficult to get a closed form solution for equation (37), and hence [4] had to rely on series expansion instead. However, if we start from the delay expression (2), and define $u(x)$ in the same way as what we did in Lemma 2, the Euler's equation will be

$$-2c_0(R_d + r_0 u(x)) + r_0 c_f u(x) u'(x) = c u'(x) \tag{38}$$

which is equivalent to (8). This can be solved analytically, and the solution has been shown in (33).

4 Experimental Results

In this section, we will show some experimental results. The parameters in our experiment are as follows: $L = 30,000\mu m$, $r_0 = 0.03\Omega/\mu m$, $c_0 = 0.2fF/\mu m^2$, $c_f = 20fF/\mu m$, $R_1 = 100\Omega$, $C_2 = 200pF$, $R_2 = 10\Omega$, $C_1 = 20pF$. We choose several values for α ranging from 0.5 to 1.0. The calculated weighted delays T_{BD} are summarized in Table 1.

α	β	Weighted delay (ns)
0.9	0.1	27.27
0.8	0.2	37.94
0.7	0.3	48.20
0.6	0.4	58.15

Table 1: Calculated weighted delays for bi-directional wires.

The calculated optimal wire shape functions are shown Fig. 4. When $\alpha = 1$ and $\beta = 0$, bi-directional wire reduces to uni-directional wire.

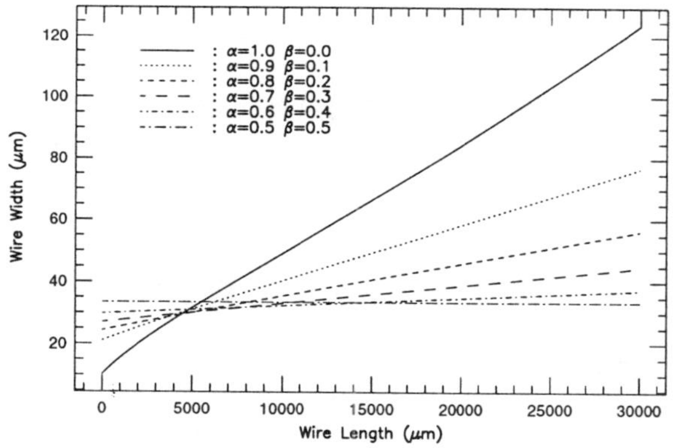

Figure 4: Optimal bi-directional wire shape functions for different values of α.

References

[1] C.-P. Chen, Y.P. Chen, and D.F. Wong, Optimal wire-sizing formula under the Elmore delay model, *Proc. ACM/IEEE DAC*, pp.487-490, 1996.

[2] C.-P. Chen and D.F. Wong, Optimal wire-sizing function with fringing capacitance consideration, *Proc. ACM/IEEE DAC*, pp.604-607, 1997.

[3] J.P. Fishburn and C.A. Schevon, Shaping a distributed RC line to minimize Elmore delay, *IEEE Transactions on CAS-I*, vol.42, pp.1020-1022, 1995.

[4] J.P. Fishburn, Shaping a VLSI wire to minimize Elmore delay, *Proc. ED&TC*, 1997.

[5] W.C. Elmore, The transient response of damped linear network with particular regard to wide-band amplifier, *Journal of Applied Physics*, vol.19, pp.55-63, 1948.

[6] J. Rubinstein, P. Penfield, and M.A. Horowitz, Signal delay in RC tree network, *IEEE Transaction on CAD*, vol.CAD-2, pp.202-211, 1983.

[7] T. Sakurai and K. Tamaru, Simple formulas for two- and three-dimensional capacitance, *IEEE Transactions on ED*, vol.ED-30, No.2, pp.183-185, 1983.

[8] T. Sakurai, Closed-form expressions for interconnection delay, coupling, and crosstalk in VLSI's, *IEEE Transactions on ED*, vol.ED-40, No.1, pp.118-124, 1993.

[9] L.E. Elsgolc, *Calculus of Variations*, Pergamon Press Ltd., 1962.

[10] J. Cong and L. He, Optimal wire-sizing for interconnects with multiple sources, *Proc. IEEE Int'l. Conf. on Computer Aided Design*, Nov. 1995, pp.568-574.

[11] J. Cong, L. He, C.K. Koh and P.H. Madden, Performance optimization of VLSI interconnect layout, *Integration, the VLSI Journal*, V.21, Nos. 1&2, Nov. 1996, pp.1-94.

[12] R.M. Corless, G.M. Gonnet, D.E.G. Hare, D.J. Jeffrey and D.E. Knuth, On the Lambert W function, *Tech. Report CS-93-03*, Department of Computer Science, University of Waterloo, Canada. It is also available for anonymous ftp from daisy.uwaterloo.ca at /cs-archive/CS-93-03/W.ps.Z.

GLOBAL INTERCONNECT SIZING AND SPACING WITH CONSIDERATION OF COUPLING CAPACITANCE

Jason Cong, Lei He, Cheng-Kok Koh, and Zhigang Pan
Department of Computer Science
University of California, Los Angeles, CA 90095 *

ABSTRACT

This paper presents an efficient approach to perform *global interconnect sizing and spacing* (GISS) for multiple nets to minimize interconnect delays with consideration of coupling capacitance, in addition to area and fringing capacitances. We introduce the formulation of *symmetric* and *asymmetric* wire sizing and spacing. We prove two important results on the *symmetric* and *asymmetric effective-fringing properties* which lead to a very effective bound computation algorithm to compute the upper and lower bounds of the optimal wire sizing and spacing solution for *all* nets under consideration. Our experiments show that in most cases the upper and lower bounds meet quickly after a few iterations and we actually obtain the optimal solution. To our knowledge, this is the first in-depth study of global wire sizing and spacing for *multiple nets* with consideration of coupling capacitance. Experimental results show that our GISS solutions lead to substantial delay reduction than existing single net wire-sizing solutions without consideration of coupling capacitance.

1. INTRODUCTION

Since the formulation of the optimal wire-sizing problem [1], there have been extensive studies in recent years on optimal wire-sizing algorithm. Most early works used Elmore delay model [2] for interconnects and study the discrete wire sizing [1, 3, 4] and continuous wire shaping or sizing [5, 6]. The wire-sizing problem is also studied under high-order delay model in [7, 8]. A comprehensive survey of these optimization techniques can be found in [9]. These works showed that significant delay reduction can be achieved by optimal wire-sizing in submicron designs. However, none of them explicitly considered the coupling capacitance.

As VLSI technology continues to push toward deep submicron, the coupling capacitance between adjacent wires has become the dominating component in the total interconnect capacitance, due to the decreasing spacing between adjacent wires and the increasing wire aspect ratio for deep submicron processes. Therefore, it is unlikely that an optimal wire-sizing solution which considers only the area and fringing capacitances would remain optimal when the coupling capacitance is considered.

High coupling capacitance in deep submicron design results in both noise (capacitive crosstalk) and additional delay. In this paper, we study the *global interconnect sizing and spacing* (GISS) problem for delay minimization with consideration of the coupling capacitance, in addition to the area and fringing capacitances. In Section 2, we introduce the problem formulation for *symmetric* and *asymmetric* wire sizing and spacing for both single and multiple nets. In Section 3, we present a dynamic programming based algorithm for single net optimization. Then in Section 4, we reveal two *effective-fringing properties* for both symmetric and asymmetric wire-sizing, and propose a very efficient bound computation algorithm to compute the upper and lower bounds of the optimal wire sizing and spacing solution for *all* nets, not just *one* net, under consideration. Experimental results in Section 5 show that the algorithm often leads to identical lower and upper bounds, and therefore achieves optimal solutions. It gives substantial improvement over the single net wire-sizing algorithm without coupling capacitance consideration. Discussion and Future work will be given in Section 6.

2. PROBLEM FORMULATION

2.1. Symmetric and Asymmetric Wire Sizing

Given a layout of n nets, denoted $\mathcal{N}_i$ for $i = 1...n$. Net $\mathcal{N}_i$ consists of $n_i + 1$ terminals $\{s_0^i, \cdots, s_{n_i}^i\}$ connected by a routing tree, denoted T_i. s_0^i is the source of $\mathcal{N}_i$, and the driver D_i at the source has an effective output resistance of R_i. The rest of the terminals are sinks. The terminals (source and sinks) of T_i are at fixed locations, and T_i consists of m_i wire segments denoted by $\{E_1^i, \cdots, E_{m_i}^i\}$. The *center-line* of a wire segment divides the original wire segment evenly. In Figure 1(a), for example, two horizontal wire segments E_1 and E_2 are shown with their center-lines. We assume that the center-line for each wire segment is fixed during wire sizing and spacing.

Each wire segment has a set of discrete choices of wire widths $\{W_1 = W_{min}, W_2, \cdots, W_r\}$. We use w_E to denote the width of the wire segment E. All previous works implicitly assumed *symmetric wire-sizing*, which widens or narrows each wire segment in a symmetric way above and below the center-line of the original wire segment. An example of symmetric wire-sizing of the two wire segments E_1 and E_2 with a neighboring net is shown in Figure 1(b).

However, symmetric wire-sizing may be too restrictive for interconnect sizing and spacing, especially when coupling capacitance is considered. In this paper, we propose an *asymmetric wire-sizing* scheme where we may widen or narrow above and below the center-line of the original wire segment asymmetrically. Using the same example as in Figure 1(b), we would like E_1 to be farther away from its neighboring wire. As a result, we grow only the bottom half of the wire segment, keeping the top half intact, as shown in Figure 1(c). Let $w_E^{\downarrow}$ ($w_E^{\uparrow}$) represent the width of the wire

*This work is partially supported by the NSF Young Investigator Award MIP-9357582 and a grant from Intel under the California MICRO Program.

1092-3152/97 $10.00 © 1997 IEEE

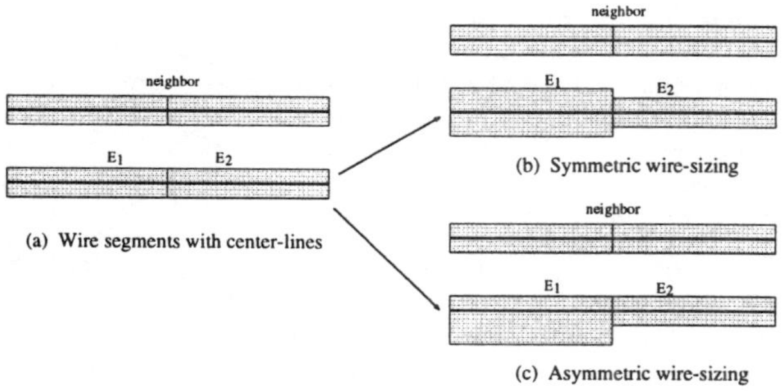

Figure 1. (a) Wire segments with center-lines. (b) Symmetric wire-sizing. (c) Asymmetric wire-sizing.

below (above) a horizontal line segment. The new wire width is defined as $w_E = w_E^{\downarrow} + w_E^{\uparrow}$. An asymmetric wire-sizing solution is valid if $w_E^{\downarrow} \geq W_{min}/2$ and $w_E^{\uparrow} \geq W_{min}/2$. Note that for symmetric wire-sizing, $w_E^{\downarrow} = w_E^{\uparrow} = w_E/2$. To avoid introducing additional notation, we also use $w_E^{\downarrow}$ and $w_E^{\uparrow}$ to denote the asymmetric wire widths for the left and right parts of a vertical wire segment, respectively.

2.2. Interconnect Sizing and Spacing for Single Net

Given a layout of n routing trees T_i's, the interconnect sizing and spacing problem for a single net is to find a symmetric wire assignment $\mathcal{W} = \{w_{E_1^j}, \cdots, w_{E_{m_j}^j}\}$ or an asymmetric wire assignment $\mathcal{W} = \{w_{E_1^j} = (w^{\downarrow}_{E_1^j}, w^{\uparrow}_{E_1^j}), \cdots, w_{E_{m_j}^j} = (w^{\downarrow}_{E_{m_j}^j}, w^{\uparrow}_{E_{m_j}^j})\}$ for a routing tree of interest, say T_j, in order to optimize the following weighted delay objective (as used in [1]) with consideration of *the area, fringing* and *coupling* capacitances:

$$t_{T_j}(\mathcal{W}) = \sum_{k=1}^{m_j} \lambda_k^j \cdot t_{T_j}(s_k^j, \mathcal{W}), \qquad (1)$$

where λ_k^j is the criticality of sink s_k^j in net $\mathcal{N}_j$, and $t_{T_j}(s_k^j, \mathcal{W})$ is the sink delay with wire-sizing solution $\mathcal{W}$.

We model the routing tree of each net by an RC tree and use the distributed Elmore delay model [2] to measure the interconnect delays. The formulations used in this section are similar to those in [1]. For clarity of presentation, we assume that a uniform grid structure is superimposed on the routing plane, and each wire segment in the routing plane is divided into a sequence of wires of unit length. Nonetheless, the results presented in this paper can be extended easily to the case where the wire segments are of non-uniform lengths in the same way as in [1].

Assume that the sheet resistance is r, the unit wire area capacitance coefficient c_a, the unit wire fringing capacitance coefficient c_f, and the unit wire lateral capacitance c_{xl}, then the wire resistance r_E and wire capacitance c_E for any grid edge E can be written as follows:

$$r_E = \frac{r}{w_E} \quad \text{and} \quad c_E = c_a \cdot w_E + c_f + c_{xl}(w_E, s_E^{\downarrow}, s_E^{\uparrow})$$

Note that $c_{xl}(w_E, s_E^{\downarrow}, s_E^{\uparrow})$ depends on the spacings $s_E^{\downarrow}$ and $s_E^{\uparrow}$ between E and its lower and upper (or left and right) neighboring wire segments, respectively, whereas c_a and c_f are assumed constants depending only the technology [1].

Note that we focus on the objective of minimizing the weighted sum of sink delays as in [1]. A previous work [10] showed that by assigning appropriate criticality/weight of each sink based on Lagrangian relaxation, the weighted-sum formulation can be used iteratively to meet the required arrival times.

2.3. Global Interconnect Sizing and Spacing for Multiple Nets

In the global interconnect sizing and spacing problem for multiple nets, again, we assume that an initial layout of n routing trees T_i's is given. With consideration of the area, fringing and coupling capacitances, the GISS problem for multiple nets is to find a symmetric wire assignment $\mathcal{W} = \{w_{E_1^1}, \cdots, w_{E_{m_1}^1}, \cdots, w_{E_1^n}, \cdots, w_{E_{m_n}^n}\}$ or an asymmetric wire assignment $\mathcal{W} = \{w_{E_1^1} = (w^{\downarrow}_{E_1^1}, w^{\uparrow}_{E_1^1}), \cdots, w_{E_{m_1}^1} = (w^{\downarrow}_{E_{m_1}^1}, w^{\uparrow}_{E_{m_1}^1}), \cdots w_{E_1^n} = (w^{\downarrow}_{E_1^n}, w^{\uparrow}_{E_1^n}), \cdots, w_{E_{m_n}^n} = (w^{\downarrow}_{E_{m_n}^n}, w^{\uparrow}_{E_{m_n}^n})\}$ for all T_i's such that, the summation of the weighted performance measure of all nets, i.e.,

$$t(\mathcal{W}) = \sum_{j=1}^{n} \delta_j t_{T_j}(\mathcal{W}) \qquad (2)$$

is minimized, where δ_j indicates the criticality of net j.

2.4. 2D Capacitance Model

A table-based 2.5D capacitance model suitable for layout optimization was presented in [11] recently, where the lumped capacitance for a wire contains the following components: area and fringing capacitances, lateral coupling capacitance, and cross-over and cross-under capacitances. Based on this model, we consider only area, fringing and lateral coupling capacitances in this paper, since they are the major part of the lumped capacitance. That is, we use a 2D capacitance model simplified from the original 2.5D model. We first use 3D field solver to build tables for area, fringing and lateral coupling capacitances under different width and spacing combinations. During layout optimization, we generate area, fringing and lateral coupling capacitances from pre-built tables. Details and justification of this method can be found in [11].

3. OPTIMAL SIZING AND SPACING FOR SINGLE NET

The optimal wire sizing and spacing problem for a single net with fixed surrounding wire segments can be solved by adapting the bottom-up dynamic programming(DP)-based buffer insertion and wire-sizing algorithm proposed by [3]. Note that in [3], the objective function is to minimize the maximum delay or to meet arrival time requirements, while

[1] In fact, in deep sub-micron designs, c_a and c_f are no longer constants. Their values depend on the width and spacings. A more general notation should be $c_a(w_E, s_E^{\downarrow}, s_E^{\uparrow})$ and $c_f(w_E, s_E^{\downarrow}, s_E^{\uparrow})$. Our GISS algorithm for single-net optimization (Section 3) is able to handle this general capacitance model. The optimality of our bound computation algorithm for multiple nets (Section 4), however, assumes that both c_a and c_f are constants. Its extension for more general 2D capacitance model is discussed in Section 4.3.

our objective is to minimize the weighted sum of all sink delays, which is similar to that in [12]. The major differences of the bottom-up dynamic programming part between this paper and [12] are: (1) we include lateral coupling capacitance between neighboring wires for delay calculation; (2) for the more general asymmetric wire sizing and spacing formulation, we keep two-piece ($w_E^{\downarrow}$ and $w_E^{\uparrow}$) information for each grid edge while performing bottom-up accumulation and top-down pruning. Other details about the DP-based algorithm can be found in [3] and [12].

The single net wire-sizing and spacing can be used for the post-layout optimization for a single critical net (e.g., the clock net). However, this optimization will largely depend on the previous layout of other neighboring nets. And also since many critical nets may share the limited routing resource, just optimizing one net may indeed sacrifice the performance of other critical nets. In the next section, we will look into the global layout optimization for multiple nets.

4. GLOBAL INTERCONNECT SIZING AND SPACING FOR MULTIPLE NETS

The difficulty of the GISS problem for multiple nets arises from the fact that the lateral coupling capacitance coefficient for each wire segment changes with the width and spacings. Moreover, there is no closed form representation for lateral coupling capacitance. The key to solving the multiple-net wire sizing and spacing problem is the *effective-fringing property* of wire-sizing solutions under different spacing conditions. The beauty of this property is that we are able to reduce the GISS problem with variable lateral coupling capacitance to an optimal wire-sizing problem with consideration of only constant area capacitance coefficient and different effective-fringing capacitance coefficients for different wire segments. Such a reduction allows us to compute *global* upper and lower bounds of the optimal wire sizing and spacing solution for *all* nets. In the following, we first state the symmetric and asymmetric effective-fringing properties and discuss their implications. Then, we will describe the bound computation algorithm, followed by a refinement algorithm to obtain the final global interconnect sizing and spacing solution when the lower and upper bounds computed as above do not meet. Extensions to more general 2D capacitance models will then be discussed.

4.1. Effective-Fringing Property: Theorems and Implications

First, we consider the case of symmetric GISS. We define the dominance relation between symmetric wire-sizing solutions of a routing tree in the same way as in [1]:

Definition 1 Symmetric Dominance Relation: *Given two wire width assignments $\mathcal{W}$ and $\mathcal{W}'$, let w_E be the width assignment of edge E in $\mathcal{W}$ and w'_E be the wire width of E in $\mathcal{W}'$. Then, $\mathcal{W}$* dominates *$\mathcal{W}'$ ($\mathcal{W} \geq \mathcal{W}'$) if for any segment E, $w_E \geq w'_E$.*

In the following, we consider an optimization problem called *optimal wire-sizing under variable effective-fringing coefficients (OWS-EF)*. While we still assume a constant area capacitance coefficient c_a, we now define for each wire segment E the *effective-fringing capacitance coefficient* $c_{ef}(E) = c_f + c_{xl}(w_E, s_E^{\downarrow}, s_E^{\uparrow})$ which incorporates the lateral coupling capacitance. It shall be clear later on that this set of effective-fringing capacitance coefficients for all edges allows us to capture the lateral coupling capacitance effectively. The performance measure that we aim at optimizing for OWS-EF problem is the same as in Eqn. (1) except that c_f is replaced by $c_{ef}(E)$ and c_{xl} disappears. Let $\mathcal{C}_{ef}$ denote the set of effective-fringing capacitance coefficients $c_{ef}(E)$'s for all edges in T. We define $\mathcal{C}_{ef} \geq \mathcal{C}'_{ef}$ if $c_{ef}(E) \geq c'_{ef}(E)$ for every E in T. Then the symmetric effective-fringing property can be stated as follows:

Theorem 1 Symmetric Effective-Fringing Property: *For the same routing tree T and a constant c_a, let $\hat{\mathcal{W}}(c_a, \mathcal{C}_{ef})$ be an optimal wire-sizing solution to the OWS-EF problem under a set of variable effective-fringing capacitance coefficients $\mathcal{C}_{ef} = \{c_{ef}(E) \mid E \in T\}$, and $\hat{\mathcal{W}}(c_a, \mathcal{C}'_{ef})$ be an optimal sizing solution under a different set of $\mathcal{C}'_{ef} = \{c'_{ef}(E) \mid E \in T\}$. Then $\mathcal{C}_{ef} \geq \mathcal{C}'_{ef}$ implies that $\hat{\mathcal{W}}(c_a, \mathcal{C}_{ef})$ dominates $\hat{\mathcal{W}}(c_a, \mathcal{C}'_{ef})$.*

The proof of this theorem can be found at [13]. The theorem can be used very effectively to determine the upper and lower bounds of the original optimal GISS problem. Suppose $\mathcal{W}^*$ denotes the global optimal wire-sizing solution optimizing t_T. Let $\mathcal{S}^{\downarrow *}$ and $\mathcal{S}^{\uparrow *}$ denote the spacing obtained based on $\mathcal{W}^*$, and $c_{xl}(w_E^*, s_E^{\downarrow *}, s_E^{\uparrow *})$ be the lateral coupling capacitance coefficient for each edge E based on $\mathcal{W}^*$, $\mathcal{S}^{\downarrow *}$, and $\mathcal{S}^{\uparrow *}$. Let $\mathcal{W}^{\downarrow U}$ and $\mathcal{W}^{\uparrow U}$ be upper bounds of $\mathcal{W}^{\downarrow *}$ and $\mathcal{W}^{\uparrow *}$, and $\mathcal{S}^{\downarrow L}$ and $\mathcal{S}^{\uparrow L}$ be lower bounds of $\mathcal{S}^{\downarrow *}$ and $\mathcal{S}^{\uparrow *}$, respectively. Then $c_{xl}(w_E^U, s_E^{\downarrow L}, s_E^{\uparrow L}) \geq c_{xl}(w_E^*, s_E^{\downarrow *}, s_E^{\uparrow *})$, as the lateral coupling capacitance coefficient decreases when the width of E decreases and the spacings between E and its neighbors increases.

Now consider two instances of the OWS-EF problem. In the first instance, the effective-fringing capacitance coefficient of edge E is $c_{ef}(E) = c_f + c_{xl}(w_E^U, s_E^{\downarrow L}, s_E^{\uparrow L})$. In the second instance, the effective-fringing capacitance coefficient of edge E is $c'_{ef}(E) = c_f + c_{xl}(w_E^*, s_E^{\downarrow *}, s_E^{\uparrow *})$. Clearly, $\mathcal{C}_{ef} \geq \mathcal{C}'_{ef}$. From the symmetric effective-fringing property, the optimal solution $\hat{\mathcal{W}}(c_a, \mathcal{C}_{ef})$ dominates the optimal solution $\hat{\mathcal{W}}(c_a, \mathcal{C}'_{ef})$. Note that $\hat{\mathcal{W}}(c_a, \mathcal{C}'_{ef}) = \mathcal{W}^*$. Therefore, $\hat{\mathcal{W}}(c_a, \mathcal{C}_{ef})$ is also an upper bound of the optimal solution $\mathcal{W}^*$. This procedure can be applied to compute wire width upper bounds (equivalently, lower bounds of spacings) for *all* nets.

Similarly, suppose we are given a lower bound of the optimal wire-sizing solution, denoted $\mathcal{W}^L$. From $\mathcal{W}^L$, we can calculate a spacing upper bound $\mathcal{S}^U$. Now, applying the optimization process for the OWS-EF problem as in the above discussion, $\hat{\mathcal{W}}(c_a, \mathcal{C}_{ef})$ will be dominated by $\hat{\mathcal{W}}(c_a, \mathcal{C}'_{ef}) = \mathcal{W}^*$, since $\mathcal{C}_{ef} \leq \mathcal{C}'_{ef}$. In other words, we have computed a lower bound of the optimal solution.

For asymmetric GISS, we can define

Definition 2 Asymmetric Dominance Relation: *Given two wire width assignments $\mathcal{W} = (\mathcal{W}^{\downarrow}, \mathcal{W}^{\uparrow})$ and $\mathcal{W}' = (\mathcal{W}^{\downarrow\prime}, \mathcal{W}^{\uparrow\prime})$, let $w_E = (w_E^{\downarrow}, w_E^{\uparrow})$ be the width assignment of edge E in $\mathcal{W}$ and $w'_E = (w_E^{\downarrow\prime}, w_E^{\uparrow\prime})$ be the wire width of E in $\mathcal{W}'$. Then, $\mathcal{W}$* dominates *$\mathcal{W}'$ if for any segment E, $w_E^{\downarrow} \geq w_E^{\downarrow\prime}$ and $w_E^{\uparrow} \geq w_E^{\uparrow\prime}$ for any edge E, respectively.*

Then, the asymmetric effective-fringing property can be stated as follows:

Theorem 2 Asymmetric Effective-Fringing Property: *For the same routing tree and a constant c_a, let*

$\hat{\mathcal{W}}^{\uparrow}(c_a, \mathcal{C}_{ef}, \mathcal{W}^{\downarrow})$ *be an optimal asymmetric wire-sizing solution to the OWS-EF problem with a fixed* $\mathcal{W}^{\downarrow}$ *and a set of effective-fringing capacitance coefficients* $\mathcal{C}_{ef}$, *and* $\hat{\mathcal{W}}^{\uparrow}(c_a, \mathcal{C}'_{ef}, \mathcal{W}^{\downarrow\prime})$ *be an optimal sizing solution under another fixed* $\mathcal{W}^{\downarrow\prime}$ *and a different set of* $\mathcal{C}'_{ef}$. *Then,* $\mathcal{W}^{\downarrow} \geq \mathcal{W}^{\downarrow\prime}$ *and* $\mathcal{C}_{ef} \geq \mathcal{C}'_{ef}$ *imply* $\hat{\mathcal{W}}^{\uparrow}(c_a, \mathcal{C}_{ef}, \mathcal{W}^{\downarrow})$ *dominates* $\hat{\mathcal{W}}^{\uparrow}(c_a, \mathcal{C}'_{ef}, \mathcal{W}^{\downarrow\prime})$.

Again, the proof of this theorem can be found at [13]. We can also apply the asymmetric effective-fringing property to compute global upper and lower bounds of the optimal wire sizing and spacing solution by solving asymmetric OWS-EF problem. From an upper bound $(\mathcal{W}^{\downarrow U}, \mathcal{W}^{\uparrow U})$, we can again compute lower bound spacings $\mathcal{S}^{\downarrow L}$ and $\mathcal{S}^{\uparrow L}$, and set of lateral coupling capacitance coefficients $c_{xl}((w_E^{\downarrow U}, w_E^{\uparrow U}), s_E^{\downarrow L}, s_E^{\uparrow L})$'s. Similarly, we can compute another set of lateral coupling capacitance coefficients, $c_{xl}((w_E^{\downarrow *}, w_E^{\uparrow *}), s_E^{\downarrow *}, s_E^{\uparrow *})$'s from an optimal wire-sizing solution $\mathcal{W}^* = (\mathcal{W}^{\downarrow *}, \mathcal{W}^{\uparrow *})$.

We denote $c_{ef}(E) = c_f + c_{xl}((w_E^{\downarrow U}, w_E^{\uparrow U}), s_E^{\downarrow L}, s_E^{\uparrow L})$ and $c'_{ef}(E) = c_f + c_{xl}((w_E^{\downarrow *}, w_E^{\uparrow *}), s_E^{\downarrow *}, s_E^{\uparrow *})$ as before. By the asymmetric effective-fringing property, $\hat{\mathcal{W}}^{\uparrow}(c_a, \mathcal{C}_{ef}, \mathcal{W}^{\downarrow U})$ dominates $\hat{\mathcal{W}}^{\uparrow}(c_a, \mathcal{C}'_{ef}, \mathcal{W}^{\downarrow *}) = \mathcal{W}^{\uparrow *}$, and therefore, it is still an upper bound of $\mathcal{W}^{\uparrow *}$, the optimal wire-sizing for the top or right portion of each edge. Similar argument applies for the lower bounds and for the bottom (or left) portion of each edge.

4.2. Algorithm for Upper and Lower Bound Computation

The effective-fringing properties (both symmetric and asymmetric) lead to a very effective algorithm to compute the upper and lower bounds of the optimal wire sizing and spacing solution for all nets under consideration. The following presentation considers asymmetric wire sizing and spacing in general. Symmetric wire sizing and spacing can be achieved by simply enforcing $w_E^{\downarrow} = w_E^{\uparrow}$ for all edges.

Upper Bound Computation

$i \leftarrow 0$
$(\mathcal{W}_U^{\downarrow}(i), \mathcal{W}_U^{\uparrow}(i)) \leftarrow$ `Initialize Wire Width Upper Bound`
do
  $\mathcal{C}_{xl}^U(i) \leftarrow$ `Compute Lateral Coefficient(`$\mathcal{W}_U^{\downarrow}(i), \mathcal{W}_U^{\uparrow}(i)$`)`
  $\mathcal{C}_{ef}^U(i) \leftarrow$ `Compute Effective-Fringing Coefficient(`$\mathcal{C}_{xl}^U(i)$`)`
  $\mathcal{W}_U^{\downarrow}(i+1) \leftarrow$ `DPW(`$\mathcal{W}_U^{\uparrow}(i), \mathcal{C}_{ef}^U(i)$`) /* for all nets */`
  $\mathcal{C}_{xl}^{U\prime}(i) \leftarrow$ `Compute Lateral Coefficient(`$\mathcal{W}_U^{\downarrow}(i+1), \mathcal{W}_U^{\uparrow}(i)$`)`
  $\mathcal{C}_{ef}^{U\prime}(i) \leftarrow$ `Compute Effective-Fringing Coefficient(`$\mathcal{C}_{xl}^{U\prime}(i)$`)`
  $\mathcal{W}_U^{\uparrow}(i+1) \leftarrow$ `DPW(`$\mathcal{W}_U^{\downarrow}(i+1), \mathcal{C}_{ef}^{U\prime}(i)$`) /* for all nets */`
  $i \leftarrow i + 1$
while $(\mathcal{W}_U^{\downarrow}(i), \mathcal{W}_U^{\uparrow}(i)) \neq (\mathcal{W}_U^{\downarrow}(i-1), \mathcal{W}_U^{\uparrow}(i-1))$

Figure 2. Algorithm to compute an upper bound of the global optimal wire-sizing.

The algorithm to compute an upper bound of the optimal solution is illustrated in Figure 2. The algorithm starts at the iteration $i = 0$. First we initialize upper bounds of all wire widths specified by the layout constraints. A sample initialization is shown in Figure 3. Let E_l and E_u be two parallel horizontal edges, with E_l below E_u. Let W_{min} be

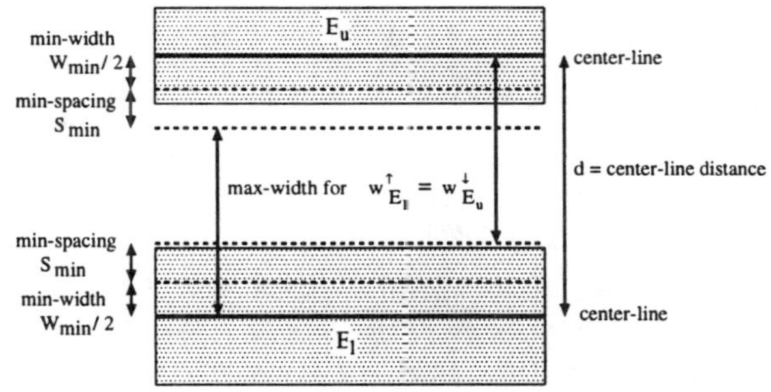

Figure 3. Initialization of upper-bound wire widths.

the minimum wire width, and S_{min} be the minimum spacing between two parallel wires from the layout constraints. If the distance between the center-lines of E_l and E_u is d, then the maximum width (i.e., the initial upper bound) for $w_{E_l}^{\uparrow}$ (the side closer to E_u) and $w_{E_u}^{\downarrow}$ (the side closer to E_l) is $d - W_{min}/2 - S_{min}$.

From the upper bound $(\mathcal{W}_U^{\downarrow}, \mathcal{W}_U^{\uparrow})$, we compute the upper bound effective-fringing capacitance coefficients. Again, consider E_l and E_u which are of distance d. Let $w_{E_l}^{\uparrow U}$ be the width of E_l in $\mathcal{W}_U^{\uparrow}$, and $w_{E_u}^{\downarrow U}$ the width of E_u in $\mathcal{W}_U^{\downarrow}$. If $d - w_{E_l}^{\uparrow U} - w_{E_u}^{\downarrow U} < S_{min}$, then, the upper bound wire widths overlap and we assign the lower bound spacing between E_l and E_u to be S_{min}, i.e., $s_{E_l}^{\uparrow L} = s_{E_u}^{\downarrow L} = S_{min}$. Otherwise, the lower bound spacings $s_{E_l}^{\uparrow L}$ and $s_{E_u}^{\downarrow L}$ are $d - w_{E_l}^{\uparrow U} - w_{E_u}^{\downarrow U}$. Similarly, for E_l and its lower neighbor we compute $s_{E_l}^{\downarrow L}$. From $s_{E_l}^{\uparrow L}$ and $s_{E_l}^{\downarrow L}$, we can compute $c_{xl}((w_{E_l}^{\downarrow U}, w_{E_l}^{\uparrow U}), s_{E_l}^{\downarrow L}, s_{E_l}^{\uparrow L})$. Let $\mathcal{C}_{xl}^U$ denote such set of lateral coupling capacitance coefficients obtained from $(\mathcal{W}_U^{\downarrow}, \mathcal{W}_U^{\uparrow})$. We then compute the effective-fringing coefficient $c_{ef}(E_l) = c_f + c_{xl}((w_{E_l}^{\downarrow U}, w_{E_l}^{\uparrow U}), s_{E_l}^{\downarrow L}, s_{E_l}^{\uparrow L})$. Similarly we can calculate the upper bound $c_{ef}(E_u)$. We refer to the set of upper bound $c_{ef}(E)$ for all edges based on $\mathcal{C}_{xl}^U$ as $\mathcal{C}_{ef}^U$.

We then perform the following iterative process to update the wire width upper bounds. To compute $\mathcal{W}_U^{\downarrow}(i+1)$, we apply the bottom-up dynamic programming-based wire-sizing (DPW) algorithm outlined in Section 3 to each net with fixed $\mathcal{W}_U^{\uparrow}(i)$ and $\mathcal{C}_{ef}^U(i)$, without explicitly dealing with lateral coupling capacitance. Then, we can similarly compute $\mathcal{W}_U^{\uparrow}(i+1)$ for each net using $\mathcal{W}_U^{\downarrow}(i)$, and updated $\mathcal{W}_U^{\downarrow}(i+1)$ and $\mathcal{C}_{ef}^{U\prime}(i)$. The process is iterated until $(\mathcal{W}_U^{\downarrow}(i), \mathcal{W}_U^{\uparrow}(i))$ is identical to $(\mathcal{W}_U^{\downarrow}(i+1), \mathcal{W}_U^{\uparrow}(i+1))$.

For the lower bound computation, we start with the minimum allowable width for each wire $(\mathcal{W}_L^{\downarrow}(0), \mathcal{W}_L^{\uparrow}(0))$, and compute $\mathcal{C}_{xl}^L(0)$, a set of lateral capacitance coefficients obtained under lower bound wire widths. Subsequently $\mathcal{C}_{ef}^L(0)$ is computed from $\mathcal{C}_{xl}^L(0)$. Then, we apply the iterative process as in the upper bound computation.

Our experiments show that in most cases, the lower and upper bounds computed as above will meet after a few iterations and we actually obtain the optimal solution from the bound computations. When the upper and lower bounds do not meet, we will use the following refinement algorithm to obtain the final wire sizing and spacing solution for each net: We first take the lower bound of each side for each wire segment as our initial layout. Then we will iteratively perform single net wire sizing and spacing optimization method presented in Section 3 to obtain the final GISS solution following the order of each net's priority. We call the overall bound computations and final refinement algorithm GISS/FAF, where FAF denotes the fixed area and fringing capacitance coefficients.

4.3. Extension to Variable Area and Fringing Capacitance Coefficients

The optimality of bound computation in the above GISS/FAF algorithm is based on the effective-fringing properties which assume the area capacitance coefficient c_a and the fringing capacitance coefficient c_f are constants independent of wire widths and spacings. However, in deep submicron designs, c_a and c_f are dependent on wire widths and spacings (e.g., there are about 30% variations on c_a and c_f values in our 2D capacitance tables). Nevertheless, the GISS algorithm can still be used in this case simply by computing the area and fringing capacitances from the general 2D model directly during the bottom up dynamic programming optimization. However, the effective-fringing properties cannot be used to guarantee that the optimal solution is always within the upper and lower bounds computed by the GISS algorithm. We call the algorithm using variable c_a and c_f's as GISS/VAF. Experimental results in Section 5.2 show that GISS/VAF often achieves better results when compared with GISS/FAF.

5. EXPERIMENTAL RESULTS

We have implemented GISS using C++ under the Sun SPARC station environment. In this section, we present the experimental results. The parameters used in our experiments are based on the $0.18\mu m$ technology specified in the SIA roadmap [14]. The sheet resistance is $0.0638\ \Omega/\Box$. The minimum wire sizing W_{min} is $0.22\mu m$ and minimum spacing S_{min} between neighboring wires is $0.33\mu m$. Then, *pitch* spacing, defined as the sum of minimum spacing and minimum wire size, is equal to $0.55\mu m$. The allowable wire widths for each side along the center line are from 0.11 to 1.1 μm, with the incremental step to be 0.11 μm. The area, fringing and lateral coupling capacitances are obtained by a look-up table obtained through the 2D capacitance extraction model [11]. The driver effective resistance is 119 Ω. The input capacitance for each sink is set to be 12.0fF.

5.1. Optimal Sizing and Spacing for a Single Net

We perform experiments for the optimal single-net sizing and spacing algorithm on 5 nets provided by Intel. The routing trees are the same as used in [4]. These trees originally have multiple sources and we randomly assign one as the unique single source. We assign equal criticality for each sink so the weighted delay becomes the average delay. Given the initial layout of these five nets, we randomly assign some surrounding wire segments with spacing from the net being 1 to 5 × *pitch*.

In Table 1, we summarize the average and maximum HSPICE delays from different algorithms: minimum wire sizing (MIN); symmetric optimal wire-sizing (OWS-S) algorithm without considering the coupling capacitance (but coupling capacitance through the 2D model is included in its final HSPICE simulation); symmetric GISS algorithm (GISS-S) and asymmetric GISS algorithm (GISS-A). In the parentheses under OWS-S, GISS-S and GISS-A, we list the percentage of improvement over MIN. From the table, we can see that GISS-A consistently outperforms all other algorithms. In terms of its average delay, which is our objective function, the reduction is up to 52.4% compared with the MIN solution (Net4), and 29.4% with OWS-S (Net5) and 29.4% with GISS-S (Net5).

Although the average delay is our objective, experimental results show that this formulation reduces the maximum delays as well. From the table, we can see that GISS-A outperform MIN, OWS-S and GISS-S by up to 45.2% (Net2), 21.2% and 22.0% (Net5) compared with MIN, OWS-S and GISS-S respectively.

5.2. Optimal Sizing and Spacing for Multiple Nets

To demonstrate the effectiveness of GISS algorithm, we perform experiments for global optimal wire sizing and spacing for multiple nets on a 16-bit parallel bus structure of 10 *mm* long with the center distance between adjacent bus line set to be {2, 3, 4, 5, 6}×*pitch* respectively.

In Table 2, we give the average delays (maximum delays are the same due to the symmetry of the bus structure) from HSPICE simulations and normalized wire widths (ratio of average wire size to W_{min}). We still list in the parentheses the percentage of delay reduction over MIN. In the table, column GISS/FAF uses the GISS algorithm with fixed c_a and c_f (obtained through the 2D table-look-up with $3 \cdot W_{min}$ width and $5 \cdot S_{min}$ spacing) to guide the layout optimization, whereas GISS/VAF directly uses the 2D model with variable area and fringing capacitance coefficients during the layout optimization. All these algorithms use the 2D model for final HSPICE simulations.

We observe that the upper and lower bounds often meet quickly after just a few iterations for both GISS/FAF and GISS/VAF. For GISS/FAF, from the effective fringing property, we indeed obtain the optimal solution under the given constant c_a and c_f.

From the table, we can see that the average delays of GISS/FAF outperform those of MIN by up to 56.6%, and outperform those of OWS by up to 43.4% respectively. Although GISS/VAF cannot guarantee optimality, our experiments do show that it outperforms GISS/FAF by up to 26.9%. This is due to that: (i) c_a and c_f are no longer constants for deep submicron design, (ii) we use the 2D model with variable c_a and c_f's for both HSPICE simulations, which GISS/VAF also uses during GISS optimization. It actually suggests that our GISS algorithm may indeed have the capability to handle more general capacitance models.

The normalized width from GISS is larger than that from OWS since the effective fringing capacitance coefficients for GISS are larger than those for OWS, which confirms our effective-fringing properties.

6. DISCUSSIONS AND FUTURE WORK

Our study has shown convincingly that it is very important to consider coupling capacitance into VLSI interconnect optimization for deep submicron designs. We have proposed two general formulations, symmetric and asymmetric, for the global interconnect sizing and spacing problem and revealed the effective-fringing properties for both symmetric and asymmetric scenarios. We develop an effective algorithm to compute the lower and upper bounds for the global optimal sizing and spacing solution. Our experiments show that in most cases, the upper and lower bounds meet in a few iterations so we will get the optimal GISS solution for fixed area and fringing capacitance coefficients.

We prove the effective-fringing properties and derive the GISS algorithm under the assumption of fixed c_a and c_f.

	length	Average Delay (ns)				Maximum Delay (ns)			
	(mm)	MIN	OWS-S	GISS-S	GISS-A	MIN	OWS-S	GISS-S	GISS-A
Net1	3.6	0.08	0.08 (-0.00%)	0.08 (-0.00%)	0.08 (-0.00%)	0.13	0.13 (-0.00%)	0.13 (-0.00%)	0.13 (-0.00%)
Net2	6.6	0.29	0.17 (-41.4%)	0.16 (-44.8%)	0.14 (-51.7%)	0.31	0.19 (-38.7%)	0.19 (-38.7%)	0.17 (-45.2%)
Net3	10.07	0.62	0.49 (-21.0%)	0.49 (-21.0%)	0.47 (-24.2%)	0.81	0.66 (-18.5%)	0.66 (-18.5%)	0.64 (-21.0%)
Net4	10.57	0.42	0.22 (-47.6%)	0.21 (-50.0%)	0.20 (-52.4%)	0.56	0.37 (-33.9%)	0.33 (-41.1%)	0.31 (-44.6%)
Net5	31.98	2.17	1.80 (-17.1%)	1.80 (-17.1%)	1.27 (-41.5%)	3.52	3.11 (-11.6%)	3.14 (-10.8%)	2.45 (-30.4%)

Table 1. Comparison of the average and maximum delays using different algorithms.

	Average Delay (ns)				Normalized wire width			
center spacing	MIN	OWS	GISS/FAF	GISS/VAF	MIN	OWS	GISS/FAF	GISS/VAF
$2 \times pitch$	1.75	1.45 (-17.1%)	0.82 (-53.1%)	0.82 (-53.1%)	1.00	1.75	2.60	2.99
$3 \times pitch$	1.51	0.83 (-45.0%)	0.63 (-58.3%)	0.56 (-62.9%)	1.00	2.40	2.64	3.56
$4 \times pitch$	1.29	0.66 (-48.8%)	0.56 (-56.6%)	0.45 (-65.1%)	1.00	2.50	2.64	3.70
$5 \times pitch$	1.21	0.60 (-50.4%)	0.53 (-56.2%)	0.42 (-65.3%)	1.00	2.50	2.64	3.75
$6 \times pitch$	1.16	0.56 (-51.7%)	0.52 (-55.2%)	0.38 (-67.2%)	1.00	2.50	2.59	4.06

Table 2. Comparison of average delays and normalized wire widths for a 16-bit parallel bus structure under 5 different pitch spacings using different algorithms.

Our experiments indeed show that it is also very effective under variable c_a and c_f's. It suggests that the GISS algorithm actually have the capability to handle more general capacitance models. Further validation is planned as a future work.

An alternative for computing lower and upper bounds is to use the local refinement method based on dominance property similar to those used in [1, 12, 15]. In particular, the GISS problem under variable c_a and c_f's may be formulated as a general CH-posynomial program [15]. Therefore, a local refinement based algorithm similar to that used in [15] may be used to compute the lower and upper bounds of the global optimal solution under variable c_a and c_f's. According to our experience, the local refinement based algorithm can be much faster than the dynamic-programming based algorithm used in this paper. We plan to implement it in the future. Also, we plan to develop efficient noise models and extend our GISS algorithm for noise control and minimization.

ACKNOWLEDGMENTS

The authors would like to thank Mosur K. Mohan, Krishnamurthy Soumyanath, Ganapati Srinivasa from Intel for their input and support of this project, and Kei-Yong Khoo, Patrick Madden at UCLA for their helpful discussions.

REFERENCES

[1] J. Cong and K. S. Leung, "Optimal wiresizing under the distributed Elmore delay model," *IEEE Trans. on Computer-Aided Design*, vol. 14, no. 3, pp. 321–336, Mar. 1995.

[2] W. C. Elmore, "The transient response of damped linear networks with particular regard to wide-band amplifiers," *Journal of Applied Physics*, vol. 19, no. 1, pp. 55–63, Jan. 1948.

[3] J. Lillis, C. K. Cheng, and T. T. Y. Lin, "Simultaneous routing and buffer insertion for high performance interconnect," in *Proc. the Sixth Great Lakes Symp. on VLSI*, 1996.

[4] J. Cong and L. He, "Optimal wiresizing for interconnects with multiple sources," *ACM Trans. on Design Automation of Electronic Systems*, vol. 1, pp. 478–511, Oct. 1996.

[5] J. P. Fishburn and C. A. Schevon, "Shaping a distributed-RC line to minimize elmore delay," *IEEE Trans. on Circuits and Systems-I: Fundamental Theory and Applications*, vol. 42, pp. 1020–1022, Dec., 1995.

[6] C. P. Chen, Y. P. Chen, and D. F. Wong, "Optimal wire-sizing formula under the Elmore delay model," in *Proc. Design Automation Conf.*, pp. 487–490, 1996.

[7] N. Menezes, S. Pullela, F. Dartu, and L. Pillage, "RC interconnect synthesis – a moment fitting appraoch," in *Proc. Int. Conf. Computer Aided Design*, pp. 418–425, 1994.

[8] T. Xue, E. Kuh, and Q. Yu, "A sensitivity-based wiresizing approach to interconnect optimization of lossy transmission line topologies," in *Proc. IEEE Multi-Chip Module Conf.*, pp. 117–121, 1996.

[9] J. Cong, L. He, C.-K. Koh, and P. H. Madden, "Performance optimization of VLSI interconnect layout," *Integration, the VLSI Journal*, vol. 21, pp. 1–94, 1996.

[10] C. P. Chen, Y. W. Chang, and D. F. Wong, "Fast performance-driven optimization for buffered clock trees based on Lagrangian relaxation," in *Proc. Design Automation Conf.*, pp. 405–408, 1996.

[11] J. Cong, L. He, A. B. Kahng, D. Noice, N. Shirali, and S. H.-C. Yen, "Analysis and justification of a simple, practical 2 1/2-d capacitance extraction methodology," in *Proc. ACM/IEEE Design Automation Conf.*, pp. 40.1.1–40.1.6, June, 1997.

[12] J. Cong, C.-K. Koh, and K.-S. Leung, "Simultaneous buffer and wire sizing for performance and power optimization," in *Proc. Int. Symp. on Low Power Electronics and Design*, pp. 271–276, Aug. 1996.

[13] J. Cong, L. He, C.-K. Koh and Z. Pan, "Global interconnect sizing and spacing with coupling capacitance," Tech. Rep. 970031, UCLA CS Dept, 1997.

[14] Semiconductor Industry Association, *National Technology Roadmap for Semiconductors*. 1994.

[15] J. Cong and L. He, "An efficient approach to simultaneous transistor and interconnect sizing," in *Proc. Int. Conf. on Computer Aided Design*, pp. 181–186, Nov. 1996.

SESSION 10D

IMPLICATION AND TEST GENERATION TECHNIQUES

Moderators:

Pranav Ashar, C&C Research Labs., NEC USA, Inc., Princeton, NJ

Jawahar Jain, Fujitsu Labs. of America, Inc., Santa Clara, CA

Test Generation for Primitive Path Delay Faults in Combinational Circuits*

Ramesh C. Tekumalla Prem R. Menon
Department of Electrical and Computer Engineering
University of Massachusetts
Amherst, MA 01003 USA

Abstract

This paper presents a method of identifying primitive path-delay faults in combinational circuits, and deriving robust tests for all robustly testable primitive faults. It uses the concept of sensitizing cubes to reduce the search space. This approach helps identify faults that cannot be part of any primitive fault, and avoids attempting test generation for them. Sensitization conditions determined for primitive fault identification are also used in test generation, reducing test generation effort. Experimental results on some of the ISCAS'85 and MCNC'91 benchmark circuits indicate that they contain a fair number of primitive multiple path delay faults which must be tested.

1 Introduction

Delay fault testing is the phase that succeeds the functional and logic testing phases. In this phase, the circuit is assumed to be functionally correct and free from logic faults. The propagation delays along leads and gates in a circuit determine its timing behavior. The accuracy of timing behavior of a circuit is determined by delay fault testing. There are two kinds of fault models used for this purpose. One is the gate delay fault model and other is the path delay fault model[1]. Since the clock period is determined by the delay of the longest sensitizable path, the path delay fault model has been widely used. In this model, the delay of the path is assumed to increase. Testing path delay faults makes testing gate delay faults unnecessary because path delays include gate delays also.

There has been considerable amount of work in delay testing [2, 3, 4, 5, 6, 7, 8, 9, 10, 11, 12] of combinational circuits. The focus of the work has been on obtaining robust tests for single path delay faults. (A robust test detects a fault independent of the delays in the rest of the circuit.) It has been observed that a large fraction of faults in most circuits do not have robust tests. Some of these may be redundant and need not be tested because they do not affect circuit timing. Thus, an important problem in delay testing is "What are the faults that may affect circuit timing and must be tested ?"

A necessary and sufficient set of faults, called primitive faults, that must be tested to guarantee timing correctness of the circuit was identified in [7]. A method for identifying primitive faults in two-level circuits was also proposed in [7]. Its extension to multi-level circuits using the Equivalent Normal Form (ENF) [13], is not practical for large circuits. More recently, a method of identifying primitive faults in combinational circuits and generating tests for them was reported in [15]. Results were presented only for identifying primitive faults of size 2. Another method of identifying faults based on signal stabilization times has been published in [14], but test generation was not discussed.

The goal of this paper is to develop a method for identifying all primitive faults in combinational circuits, and deriving tests for all robustly testable primitive faults. If a primitive fault is not robustly testable, non-robust tests for such faults are obtained. A distinguishing feature of our method is the use of sensitizing cubes for achieving both the above goals. The sensitizing cubes of a path specify all mandatory assignments for testing it, and reduce the search space for test generation.

The rest of the paper is organized as follows. The concept of sensitizing cubes of paths in multi-level combinational circuits, and a method of deriving them are discussed in Section 2. Section 3 shows how this concept can be used in deriving tests for single and multiple faults. Experimental results are presented in Section 4, followed by the summary and conclusions in Section 5.

2 Sensitizability of paths

In this section, we introduce the concept of sensitizing cubes of a combinational circuit, and discuss some of their properties. A method of deriving sensitizing cubes is also presented.

*This research was supported in part by the NSF grant MIP-9320886.

1092-3152/97 $10.00 © 1997 IEEE

We consider the circuit feeding each output of the circuit separately. A rising (falling) transition delay fault on a path π will be represented by $\uparrow$ $(\downarrow)\pi$, where the arrow denotes the direction of signal transition at the destination.

Definition 1: A value assignment to a subset of inputs of a circuit that produces a 0 or 1 at the output is called a *cube*. A cube that produces 0(1) is referred to as a 0(1)-cube. A cube may also be represented as a set (or product) of input literals. A value assignment to all inputs corresponds to a vertex, also called an *input vector* or simply a *vector*.

Definition 2: A *multipath* π consists of a set of single paths $\{\pi_1, \pi_2, ...\pi_n\}$ to the same destination. Every on-path input of every gate G on $\pi_i \in \pi$ is an on-path input of π. Every other input of G is a side-input of π. A multiple path delay fault $\uparrow(\downarrow)\pi$ is a situation in which every single path in π has a rising(falling) transition delay fault.

Definition 3: A multipath π is *static sensitized* to 1(0) by a vector v if it sets the destination to 1(0) and sets all side inputs to their respective non-controlling values.

Definition 4: A fault $\uparrow(\downarrow)\pi$ is *primitive* if 1) π is static sensitizable for a 1(0) at its destination and 2) there exists no multipath $\psi \subset \pi$ that is static sensitizable for a 1(0) at its destination [7].

Definition 5: A cube q is a *sensitizing* cube of a multipath π if (1) it sets every side-input to the non-controlling value when the on-path input is non-controlling, (2) no-side input has a controlling value when the on-path input is controlling and (3) there exists no $q' \subset q$ that satisfies these conditions. A sensitizing cube that produces 1(0) at the output is called a sensitizing 1(0)-cube.

The set of sensitizing cubes of a multipath π that produce 1(0) at its destination will be denoted $S_{1(0)}(\pi)$. We shall now discuss some properties of sensitizing cubes, explicitly considering only cubes in $S_1(\pi)$. Similar results hold for the sensitizing cubes in $S_0(\pi)$.

Lemma 1: If a cube $q \in S_1(\pi)$ contains a literal l_i, then there exists a multipath π that contains a single path from x_i, where x_i is the input corresponding to the literal l_i.

The proofs of all lemmas and theorems can be found in [16].

Lemma 2: No vector in $q \in S_1(\pi)$ will static sensitize $\lambda \subset \pi$.

Lemma 3: Any vector in $q \in S_1(\pi)$ will static sensitize a multipath $\psi \supseteq \pi$.

Lemmas 2 and 3 show a method of limiting the search for identifying static sensitizable multipaths. For the fault on a multipath to be primitive, it should not contain any static sensitizable subset of multipaths.

Lemma 4: Consider a pair of sensitizing cubes $q_1 \in S_1(\pi)$ and and $q_2 \in S_1(\psi)$. If $q_1 \subseteq q_2$, then $\pi \supseteq \psi$.

Lemma 4 shows that the sensitizability conditions of π can be derived from the sensitizing cubes in $S_1(\psi)$. Thus, sensitizing cubes in $S_1(\pi)$ do not provide any useful information for identifying multipaths that may contribute to primitive faults.

Lemma 5: If $S_1(\pi)$ is empty, then π is not static sensitizable for a 1 at its destination.

Before discussing the proposed method for obtaining sensitizing cubes, we shall discuss the ENF [13] of multi-level circuits. The ENF is a two-level expression obtained from the multi-level circuit by writing the expression for each gate output in a two-level form. Boolean simplification rules are not used to reduce the expression. The output of a gate is a set of cubes with the gate number tagged to literals in the cubes. Literals corresponding to the same primary input but with different tags are treated as different primary inputs as we proceed from the primary inputs to the ouput. The expression at the output of a gate is obtained by manipulating the expression on its inputs depending on the function realized by the gate. The final ENF expression contains product terms that may have a literal and its complement but with different tags. Example 1 shows the ENF of the circuit in Fig. 1.

Each literal in the ENF corresponds to a path from a primary input to output. A literal is complemented (uncomplemented) if the corresponding path in the original multi-level circuit has an odd (even) inversion parity. Also, an input combination that makes all the terms containing a literal l_π equal to 1 and all other terms equal to 0 is a static sensitizing condition for the path π [8]. Similarly, it can be shown that a necessary assignment of inputs that makes a product term containing l_{π_i} equal to 1 is a sensitizing cube of a multipath π, where $\pi_i \in \pi$.

No efficient algorithm has been suggested for obtaining the ENF of a given circuit. The major factor that prohibits such a task is the space requirement for storing the cubes as we go along from the input to the output. The other deterring factor is the number of variables that have to be kept track of. The final ENF expression may contain as many distinct literals (with different tags) as the number of single paths in the circuit. We shall see in Lemma 6 that some of the cubes in the ENF do not correspond to any sensitizing cubes and hence do not identify any primitive faults. We use the following approach for obtaining all the necessary sensitizing cubes for the circuit.

We obtain the sensitizing 1-cubes of a multi-level circuit from a two-level sum-of-products expression, called the collapsed form of the circuit. The collapsed form is obtained by expanding the (usually) factored expression representing the circuit on a gate by gate basis. All the rules of boolean algebra (including $a + ab = a$) are used to reduce the expression. The inputs to a gate before collapsing the gate are sets of cubes and the output of the gate after collapse is a set of cubes obtained by using the logic implemented by the gate. For example, if there is a two input NAND gate with the sets of cubes f_1 and f_2 on its inputs, the output of the gate after collapse is $\overline{f_1} + \overline{f_2}$. The sensitizing 0-cubes of the circuit are obtained from the collapsed version of the complemented (the destination gate of the original multi-level circuit is replaced by a complementary gate, e.g NAND by AND, OR by NOR etc.) circuit. Let us call the set of cubes in the collapsed form of original (complemented) circuit as C^1 (C^0).

The following lemmas show the relationship between the collapsed form and the ENF.

Lemma 6: Consider a cube q in the ENF that has a literal and its complement but with different tags. Then, q is not a sensitizing cube for any multipath.

Lemma 7: Every cube in C^1 contains at least one cube in the ENF and the cubes in the ENF that are not contained in any cube in C^1 contain only false vertices.

Lemmas 6 and 7 show that the cubes of the collapsed form expression are sufficient for identifying all primitive faults in the circuit.

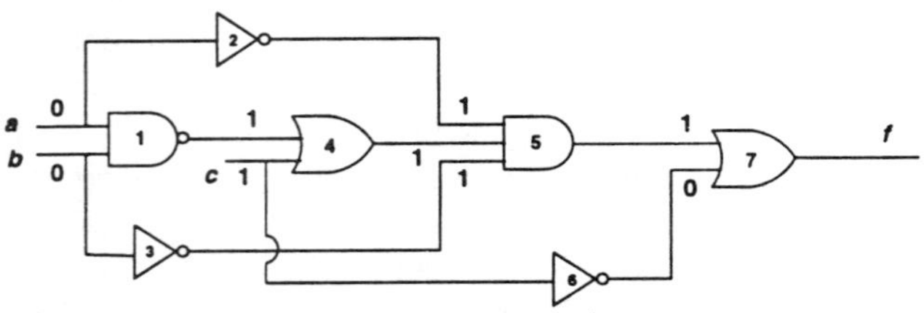

Figure 1: Sensitizing cubes for multi-level circuits

Example 1: Consider the circuit in Fig. 1. The ENF expression for the circuit is $\overline{a_{1457}}\,\overline{a_{257}}\,\overline{b_{357}} + \overline{a_{257}}\,\overline{b_{1457}}\,\overline{b_{357}} + \overline{a_{257}}\,\overline{b_{357}}\,c_{457} + \overline{c_{67}}$. The sensitizing cubes $C^1 = \overline{a}\,\overline{b} + \overline{c}$. It can be seen that all in information in the ENF is contained in the sensitizing cubes and the terms in the collapsed are lost only because of the simplifications $f_1 \cdot f_1 = f_1$ and the cube containment $f_1 + f_1 \cdot f_2 = f_1$. □

The sensitizing cubes of a multipath are similar to functional sensitizing cubes [4]. However, the sensitizing cubes differ from functional sensitizing cubes in that the latter have no restrictions on side inputs when the on-path inputs are controlling. Therefore, a sensitizing cube for a multipath is also a functional sensitizing cube of every single path in the multipath. It follows from Lemmas 6 and 7 that the cubes of the collapsed form constitute all the sensitizing cubes in the on-set of the multi-level circuit. Similarly, the sensitizing cubes in the off-set are C^0.

Example 2: Consider the circuit in Fig. 1. The $S_1(\pi)$ for $\pi = [\{a, 1, 4, 5, 7f\}, \{b, 1, 4, 5, 7f\}]$ is *00x*, i.e. $\overline{a} \cdot \overline{b}$. It can be seen that no proper subset of π in the above multipath has a sensitizing 1-cube. The cube *00x* is a functional sensitizing cube for a 1 at the destination of every single path in π. □

3 Primitive fault identification and test generation in combinational circuits

We shall now use the sensitizing cubes discussed in the preceding section for primitive fault identification and test generation. The process of primitive fault identification can be made simpler if we can identify static sensitizable multipaths such that no proper subset of such multipaths are static sensitizable. Lemma 4 shows conditions under which some static sensitizable multipaths can be discarded. The following theorems identify primitive faults for rising and falling transitions using cubes in C^1 and C^0.

Theorem 1: Consider a set of sensitizing cubes $S = \{q_1, q_2, \ldots q_n\}$. The appropriate fault on a multipath π with a static sensitizing vector v, is *primitive* iff (1) v is a common vertex for each of the cubes in S (2) no cube $q_i \in S$ has an essential vertex and (3) there exists no vertex that is common to only a subset of cubes in S.

Theorem 2: An essential vertex v in a sensitizing cube q is a static sensitizing vector for a multipath π and the appropriate path delay fault on it is *primitive*.

Theorems 1 and 2 show that only essential vertices and common vertices in sensitizing cubes that do not have essential vertices need be considered for identifying primitive faults.

The primitive fault identification algorithm is shown in Fig. 2. After identifying the sets of sensitizing cubes C^1 and C^0, it uses Theorems 1 and 2 to identify vectors and the corresponding static sensitizable multipaths. The static sensitizable multipaths are identified by tracing paths in the multilevel circuit, after applying the vectors identified by Theorems 1 and 2. The appropriate faults on the multipaths thus identified are primitive.

Cubes containing essential vertices are identified and processed first. Cubes without essential vertices are processed in a separate phase. An essential vertex in a cube is identified by assigning values to the inputs so that only the product representing that cube evaluates to 1. Starting with the values specified in the cube, additional input values are assigned so that all other terms evaluate to 0. The paths sensitized by this vector are determined by tracing the paths going backwards towards primary inputs. All the primitive single faults are identified during this phase.

Theorem 1 is applied to cubes without essential vertices to identify primitive multiple path faults. Let S be the set of sensitizing cubes without essential vertices. The vertices common to proper subsets of S are determined. A common vertex of a set of cubes is determined by making input assignments consistent with all cubes in the set. Let v_i be the common vertex of a set of cubes $S_i \subset S$. The multiple fault static sensitized by v_i is primitive if no $S_j \supset S_i$ has a common vertex.

Example 3: Consider the circuit in Fig. 3. The set

Procedure_Identify_Primitive_faults()
{
enumerate the paths in the circuit;
obtain the sensitizing cubes for each output logic;
for each sensitizing cube q_i{
obtain an essential vertex in q_i;
if such a vertex exists, identify the multipath π *for which it is a static sensitizing vector;*
the appropriate transition on π *is primitive;*
else retain the sensitizing cube for processing at a later stage;
}
if there exist sensitizing cubes $S = \{q_1, \ldots q_n\}$ *without essential vertices*
for $i = 1, 2 \ldots n${
$q_{v1} = q_i$;
for $j = 2, \ldots n${
for $k = j, \ldots n${
obtain the non-null intersection, $q_{v1} = q_{v1} \cap q_k$;}
identify a vertex in q_{v1} *that is not contained in any sensitizing cube that is not in S;*
identify a multipath π *static sensitizable by* q_{v1};
the appropriate fault on π *is primitive;*
$q_{v1} = q_i$;
}
}
}

Figure 2: Primitive Fault Identification

of sensitizing cubes C^1 for the circuit are *10x*, *1x0*, *x10* and *01x*. In the first phase, the essential vertices 101 in *10x* and 011 in *01x* are obtained. These two vertices static sensitize the multipaths $\{(b, 1, 3, 5, f)\}$ and $\{(a, 2, 4, 5, f)\}$ respectively. The cubes *1x0* and *x10* are left for processing in phase two because they do not have essential vertices. In phase two, the intersection of the above two cubes 110 is obtained, which is a static sensitizing vector for the multipath $\{(c, 1, 3, 5\, f), (c, 2, 4, 5\, f)\}$. It can be verified that all static sensitizable multipaths that contribute to primitive faults, are identified by the above three vertices. The primitive faults identified are $\uparrow\{b, 1, 3, 5, f\}$, $\uparrow\{a, 2, 4, 5, f\}$ and $\uparrow\{(c, 1, 3, 5\, f), (c, 2, 4, 5\, f)\}$. The primitive faults for the falling transitions can be identified using the cubes in C^0. □

The test generation procedure is given in Fig. 4. The static sensitizing vectors obtained during primitive fault identification are used as final vectors in tests for primitive faults. The initial vector is obtained by complementing the values at the start of the target multipath. If all remaining inputs are kept constant in the vector pair, all side inputs to

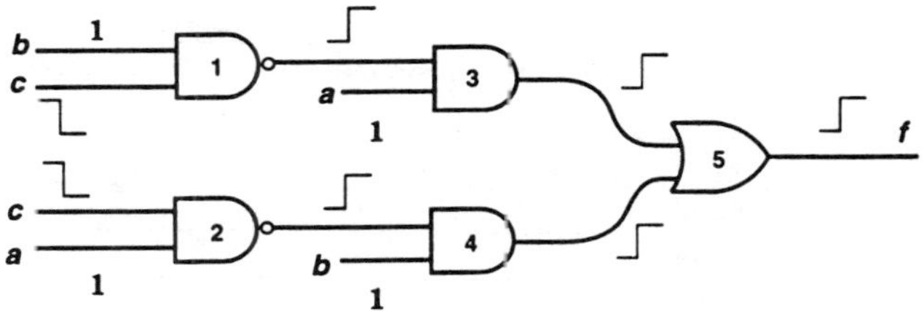

Figure 3: Circuit with a primitive multiple fault

Procedure_Test_Generation()
{
Procedure_Identify_Primitive_Faults();
for each primitive fault $\uparrow(\downarrow)\pi${
obtain a vector pair $<V_1, V_2>$ *such that* V_2 *is a static sensitizing vector that produces 1(0) at the destination of* π *and* V_1 *differs from* V_2 *only on the values on literals at the start of* π;
apply the vector pair and check for robustness conditions;
if robustness conditions are not satisfied, the vector pair is a non-robust test;
}
}

Figure 4: Test generation for primitive faults

the multipath will have a stable non-controlling value or a final non-controlling value. The vector pair is a robust test if all gates with a final controlling value on on-path inputs have stable controlling values on side inputs. Since the final vector in the test is a static sensitizing vector, the vector pair is a non-robust test for the target fault if robustness conditions are not satisfied.

Example 4: Consider the circuit in Fig. 3. The vector 110 static sensitizes the multipath $\{(c, 1, 3, 5, f), (c, 2, 4, 5, f)\}$ to 1. Since the variable at the start of the multipath is c, the initial vector can be obtained by complementing the value on c in the final vector. It can be seen that $<111, 110>$ is a robust test for the multiple fault $\uparrow\{(c, 1, 3, 5, f), (c, 2, 4, 5, f)\}$. □

4 Experimental Results

A test generator for primitive path delay faults using the methods discused in the preceding sections has been implemented in the C language. Primitive fault identification and test generation were performed on combinational versions of several of the ISCAS'89 and MCNC'91 benchmark circuits, using the following procedure: First, the single paths in the circuit were enumerated by a depth-first traversal of the circuit starting from each circuit output. SIS [17]

Circuit	# Gates	# Faults	# Single Primitive Faults		# Multiple Primitive Faults		Test Time
			Total	Robust	Total	Robust	*Sec*
s208	104	284	257	256	6	1	11.31
s298	119	502	343	312	32	5	16.04
s344	160	710	632	613	130	3	86.81
s349	161	730	633	613	133	4	82.01
s382	158	800	666	636	22	9	48.66
s386	159	414	400	394	34	1	35.61
s400	162	896	685	638	33	14	34.23
s420	218	948	826	826	14	1	140.16
s444	181	1070	718	656	39	14	94.42
s510	211	738	706	658	64	2	123.31
s526	193	820	686	663	81	7	89.46
s641	379	3444	2048	1872	274	54	412.61
s713	393	43624	4291	2693	305	0	1050.74
s820	289	984	936	887	103	6	438.16
s832	287	1012	928	828	205	10	534.77
s838	446	3428	2932	2931	30	1	492.28
s1488	590	2762	1973	1759	291	54	1521.19
s1494	472	2064	1773	1681	223	25	1562.80
s1196	529	6194	3010	2783	1347	58	1572.98
bbsse	101	358	330	321	35	2	14.59
cse	146	914	725	696	112	18	64.49
dk16	244	898	623	559	106	19	144.39
keyb	2238	1192	874	783	164	16	187.82
planet	646	3924	2773	2267	688	61	921.67
sse	117	410	350	311	33	0	22.06
scf	916	7036	5076	3074	410	27	1683.13
s1	446	2556	1824	1491	735	44	682.52
styr	477	1964	1373	1238	432	32	1701.68
tma	140	506	476	444	63	4	34.54

Table 1: Primitive Fault Coverages for ISCAS'89 and MCNC'91 benchmark circuits

was then used to obtain the collapsed form expressions for each output and its complement. The product terms of these expression are the sensitizing cubes used for primitive fault identification and test generation. The robust tests for multipaths are obtained as explained in the procedure. A multipath can have many sensitizing cubes. As explained in the procedure and since all the cubes are considered, a robust test will be found if one exists.

Experimental results for combinational versions of the benchmarks are shown in Table 1. The circuit and the number of gates are shown in columns 1 and 2 respectively. Column 3 gives the total number of single faults in the circuit. Columns 4 and 5 show the number of primitive single faults and the number of robustly testable single faults, respectively. Columns 6 and 7 show the number of primitive multiple faults and the number of robustly testable primitive multiple faults, respectively. Non-robust tests are derived for all the robustly untestable primitive faults. Total run times on a SUN SPARC 20 workstation for primitive fault identification and test generation, are shown in Column 8.

5 Conclusions

This paper has presented a test generation algorithm for primitive path-delay faults in combinational circuits. Experimental results obtained with an implementation of the algorithm show good delay-fault coverage and reasonable run times. One of the main features of the algorithm is the use of sensitizing cubes to determine mandatory assignments for path-delay tests. This helps reduce the search space for primitive fault identification and test generation.

The set of tests derived by our method detect not only all robustly testable single faults but also robustly testable multiple faults which can affect circuit timing. This set of tests would therefore be more effective in detecting timing problems in comparison with a test set for singly robust testable faults alone. The experimental results presented indicate that the number of primitive multiple faults is less than the number of single faults in all the circuits considered. Thus, the number of multiple faults to be tested is much less than the total number of multiple faults (the latter usually being much greater than the number of single faults). Still, the number of primitive multiple faults is not negligible in most cases. A measure of the effectiveness of a delay test set should include coverage of both single and multiple primitive faults.

The algorithm presented here derives robust and non-robust tests (if a robust test does not exist) for primitive faults. It is possible to modify it to obtain validatable robust tests for some of the robustly untestable faults. Further work is needed to develop a general algorithm that does not involve collapsing the circuit, to derive robust or VNR tests for all testable primitive faults. The algorithm presented here is also being extended to sequential circuits.

References

[1] G.L. Smith, "Model for delay faults based upon paths", *Proc. Intl. Test Conf., 1985*, pp.342-349.

[2] C.J. Lin and S.M. Reddy, "On delay fault testing in logic circuits", *IEEE Trans. on CAD*, pp.694-703, Sept. 1987.

[3] A. Saldanha, R.K. Brayton and A.L. Sangiovanni-Vincentelli, "Equivalence of robust delay-fault and single stuck-fault test generation", *Proc. Design Automation Conf.*, 1992, pp.173-176.

[4] K.-T. Cheng and H.C. Chen, "Delay testing for non-robust untestable circuits", *Proc. Intl. Test Conf.*, 1993, pp.954-961.

[5] W.K. Lam, A. Saldanha, R.K. Brayton and A.L. Sangiovanni-Vincentelli, "Delay fault coverage and performance tradeoffs" *Proc. Design Automation Conf.*, 1993, pp.446-452.

[6] C. Lin, S.M. Reddy and S. Patil, "An automatic test pattern generator for the detection of path delay faults", *Proc. ICCAD*, 1987, pp.284-287.

[7] W. Ke and P.R. Menon, "Synthesis of delay-verifiable combinational circuits", *IEEE Trans. on Computers.*, vol. 44, pp. 213-222, February 1995.

[8] S. Devadas and K. Keutzer, "Synthesis of robust delay-fault-testable circuits:practice", *IEEE Trans. on CAD*, vol.11, no.3, pp.277-300, March 1992.

[9] S. Devadas and K. Keutzer, "Validatable nonrobust delay-fault-testable circuits via logic synthesis", *IEEE Trans. on CAD*, vol.11, pp.1559-1573, December 1992.

[10] K. Roy, K. De, J.A. Abraham and S. Lusky, "Synthesis of delay fault testable combinational logic", *Proc. ICCAD*, 1989, pp.418-421.

[11] A. K. Pramanick and S.M. Reddy, "On the design of path delay fault testable combinational circuits", *Proc. Intl. Symposium on Fault Tolerant Computing*, 1990, pp.374-381.

[12] I. Pomeranz and S.M. Reddy, "Design-for-Testability for path delay faults in large combinational circuits using test-points", *Proc. Design Automation Conf.*, 1994, pp.358-364.

[13] D.B. Armstrong, "On finding a nearly minimal set of fault detection tests for combinational logic nets", *IEEE Trans. Electron. Computers*, vol. EC-15, pp.66-73, February 1966.

[14] M. Sivaraman and A. J. Strojwas, "Primitive path delay fault identification", *Proc.* 10th *Intl. Conf. on VLSI Design*, January 1997, pp.95-100.

[15] A. Krstic, K.-T. Cheng and S.T. Chakradhar, "Identification and test generation for primitive faults", *Proc. Intl. Test Conf.*, 1996, pp.423-432.

[16] R. Tekumalla and P.R. Menon, "On test generation for primitive path delay faults in combinational circuits", *Tech. Report, TR-CSE-97-5, Dept. of ECE*, Univ. of Massachusetts, Amherst.

[17] E.M. Sentovich, K.J. Singh et al., "SIS : A system for sequential circuit synthesis", Memo. No. UCB/ERL M92/41, Univ. of California, Berkeley, 1992.

[18] Chih-Ang Chen and Sandip Gupta, "A satisfiability based test generator for path delay faults in combinational circuits", *Proc. Design Automation Conf.*, 1996, pp.209-214.

Fast Identification of Untestable Delay Faults Using Implications*

Keerthi Heragu
Janak H. Patel
Center for Reliable and High-Performance Computing
University of Illinois at Urbana-Champaign, Urbana, IL 61801
heragu@crhc.uiuc.edu, patel@crhc.uiuc.edu

Vishwani D. Agrawal
Bell Labs, Lucent Technologies
700 Mountain Avenue
Murray Hill, NJ 07974
va@research.bell-labs.com

Abstract

We propose a novel algorithm to rapidly identify untestable delay faults using pre-computed static logic implications. Our fault-independent analysis identifies large sets of untestable faults, if any, without enumerating them. The cardinalities of these sets are obtained by using a counting algorithm that has quadratic complexity in the number of lines. Since our method is based on an incomplete set of logic implications, it gives only a lower bound on the number of untestable faults. A post-processing step can list the untestable faults, if desired. Targeting untestable delay faults for test generation by an automatic test pattern generation (ATPG) tool can be avoided. The method works for the segment delay fault model and its special case, the path delay fault model, and identifies robustly untestable, non-robustly untestable, and functionally unsensitizable delay faults. Results on benchmark circuits show that many delay faults are identified as untestable in a very short time. For the benchmark circuit c6288, our algorithm identified 1.978×10^{20} functionally unsensitizable path faults in 3 CPU seconds.

1 Introduction

Physical defects that cause timing violations are modeled by delay faults at the logic level. *Path delay faults* [1, 2] model defects that cause cumulative propagation delays along paths to exceed specified limits. Segment delay faults [3, 4] model defects on segments, whose length L can be as small as 1 or as large as the maximum logic depth.

It is known that ATPG algorithms spend most of their time in generating tests for hard-to-detect faults or in trying to prove that a fault is untestable. This makes it very attractive to explore techniques that identify untestable faults quickly so that they need not be targeted by an ATPG tool. An estimate of the number of untestable faults can be used during the design phase to obtain a quick and approximate idea of the testability of a circuit. A lot of research has been done in the area of identifying untestable stuck-at-faults. While most of the algorithms are ATPG-based [5, 6], some use fault-independent techniques [7, 8], based on logic implications [9, 10], to identify untestable faults. Previous algorithms for identifying untestable path delay faults are ATPG-based and they involve identifying unsensitizable segments [11, 12]. Explicit enumeration of all path faults that pass through arbitrary unsensitizable segments is prohibitively complex for circuits with a large number of delay faults [11]. The runtime becomes lower when specific segments are used [12].

We propose a novel algorithm to identify untestable delay faults using pre-computed static logic implications. Using logic implications of both value assignments (0 and 1), at each line g, we perform a fault-independent analysis to identify a set of lines S, such that every fault passing through g and $\{m : m \in S\}$ is untestable with respect to some combination of signal values. Information about stuck-fault redundancies and constant logic values, generated from static logic implications, can also be used in our analysis. We propose a non-enumerative counting technique, based on previously published algorithms [13, 3], that uses information gathered from our implication analysis and computes a lower bound on the number of untestable delay faults. The counting procedure has a quadratic complexity in the number of lines.

Our algorithm is applicable to the segment delay fault model and its special case, the path delay fault model. In this paper, we only illustrate our algorithm for identifying untestable path delay faults. Results are presented for both models and they include robustly untestable [1, 2], non-robustly untestable [14] and functionally unsensitizable [11] delay faults.

2 Notation and Definitions

The following discussion is limited to combinational circuits composed of simple gates (AND, OR, NOT,

*This research was supported in part by Semiconductor Research Corporation under contract SRC 96-DP-109, in part by ARPA under contract DABT63-96-C-0069, and in part by Hewlett-Packard under an equipment grant.

1092-3152/97 $10.00 © 1997 IEEE

NAND, and NOR). Let *line* denote an interconnection between two gates, $gt(l)$ denote the gate for which line l is an input, and $in(g)$ denote the set of inputs of gate g. Let $n(V)$ represent the stable signal value of n under a vector V, where n is either a gate or a line.

A physical path P is a sequence $(g_0, l_0, ..., l_{n-1}, g_n)$, where $(g_1, ..., g_{n-1})$ are gates, $(l_0, ..., l_{n-1})$ are lines, g_0 is a primary input (PI), and g_n is a primary output (PO). Lines $(l_0, ..., l_{n-1})$ are called *on-path inputs* of P. An input $\{i : i \in in(g_k), i \neq l_{k-1}, 1 < k < n\}$ is called a *side-input* of P. There are two *logical paths*, P^1 and P^0, associated with P, corresponding to a rising and a falling transition respectively on g_0. Logical paths are also called *path delay faults*. In this paper, we use the terms *path delay faults* and *path faults* interchangeably to denote logical paths. A test for a path delay fault consists of a vector pair $<V_1, V_2>$.

Definition 2.1 ([11]) *A vector pair $<V_1, V_2>$ is said to functionally sensitize a path fault $P^\psi = (g_0, l_0, ..., g_n)$, where $\psi \in \{0,1\}$, iff:*
(1) $g_0(V_1) = \overline{\psi}$, $g_0(V_2) = \psi$, and
(2) if an on-path input of P^ψ has a non-controlling value under V_2, the corresponding side-inputs have non-controlling values under V_2.

Definition 2.2 ([14]) *A vector pair $<V_1, V_2>$ is said to be a non-robust test for a path delay fault $P^\psi = (g_0, l_0, ..., g_n)$, where $\psi \in \{0,1\}$, iff:*
(1) $g_0(V_1) = \overline{\psi}$, $g_0(V_2) = \psi$, and
(2) all side-inputs of P^ψ have non-controlling values under V_2.

Definition 2.3 ([1, 2]) *A vector pair $< V_1, V_2 >$ is said to be a robust test for a path delay fault $P^\psi = (g_0, l_0, ..., g_n)$, where $\psi \in \{0,1\}$, if it guarantees detection of the fault irrespective of the delays of all other signals in the circuit. This condition is satisfied iff:*
(1) $<V_1, V_2>$ is a non-robust test for P^ψ, and
(2) if an on-path input of P^ψ has a controlling value under V_2, the corresponding side-inputs have steady non-controlling values on both vectors.

Remark 2.1 *The existence of a vector V_1, that satisfies the requirement on it given by Definitions 2.1 and 2.2, can be guaranteed for a circuit without any restrictions on its input values.*

Remark 2.2 *The set of functionally sensitizable path faults is a superset of the set of non-robustly testable path faults, which in turn is a superset of the set of robustly testable path faults.*

Remark 2.3 *Only the robustness criterion imposes the requirement $\forall_{1<k<n}\{g_k(V_1) \neq g_k(V_2)\}$ which in turn implies $\forall_{1<k<n-1}\{l_k(V_1) \neq l_k(V_2)\}$*

We say that a path fault P^ψ is *sensitized* on a vector pair $<V_1, V_2>$ iff P^ψ is either functionally sensitized, robustly tested, or non-robustly tested by $<V_1, V_2>$.

Lemma 2.1 *If a path fault $P^\psi = (g_0, l_0, ..., g_n)$, where $\psi \in \{0,1\}$, is sensitized on a vector pair $<V_1, V_2>$, $\forall_{0<k<n}\{g_k(V_2) = \psi$ if the number of inversions between g_0 and the output of g_k is even; $g_k(V_2) = \overline{\psi}$ otherwise$\}$.*

Proof: We will prove the lemma by induction.
Induction Basis: Since P^ψ is sensitized by $<V_1, V_2>$, from the above definitions, we know that $g_0(V_2) = \psi$.
Induction Hypothesis: Suppose the claim is true for $\{g_m : 0 < m < n\}$.
Induction Step: Let $g_m(V_2) = \xi$ and g_{m+1} be non-inverting. Since g_{m+1} is non-inverting, the number of inversions between g_0 and the output of g_m is equal to the number of inversions between g_0 and the output of g_{m+1}. If ξ is the controlling value of g_{m+1}, $g_{m+1}(V_2) = \xi$. If ξ is the non-controlling value of g_{m+1}, by the above definitions, the side-inputs corresponding to g_{m+1} *have to be non-controlling* for P^ψ to be sensitized and hence, $g_{m+1}(V_2) = \xi$. Since $g_m(V_2) = g_{m+1}(V_2)$ and the number of inversions remains unchanged, by the induction hypothesis, the claim holds for g_{m+1}. A similar argument can be made for the case when g_{m+1} is inverting. □

3 Implication-based Analysis

We assume that logic implications of both value assignments (0 and 1) for every line in the circuit are available. We present lemmas that use logic implications on a line g to help identify a set of lines S, such that every path fault passing through g and $\{m : m \in S\}$ is untestable with respect to some combination of signal values. Let $S_P(x^\alpha, y^\beta)$, where $\alpha, \beta \in \{0,1\}$, denote the set of path faults passing through lines x and y such that for every path fault $\{P^\psi : P^\psi \in S_P(x^\alpha, y^\beta)\}$, $[x(V_2) = \alpha]$ and $[y(V_2) = \beta]$ are necessary conditions for P^ψ to be sensitized on a vector pair $<V_1, V_2>$ (refer to Lemma 2.1).

3.1 Robust Untestability Analysis

We say that $[S_P(x^\alpha, y^\beta) = RU]$ if all path faults in the set $S_P(x^\alpha, y^\beta)$ are robustly untestable.

Lemma 3.1 *For lines x and y, if $(x = \alpha) \Rightarrow (y = \beta)$, where $\alpha, \beta \in \{0,1\}$ and β is the controlling value of $g = gt(y)$, then $\forall_{z \in in(g), z \neq y} \forall_{\xi \in \{0,1\}}[S_P(x^\alpha, z^\xi) = RU]$.*

Proof: Consider a path fault $\{P^\psi : P^\psi \in S_P(x^\alpha, z^\xi)\}$, where $\psi \in \{0,1\}$. Line y is a side-input of P^ψ. For a vector pair $<V_1, V_2>$ to be a robust test for P^ψ, the following conditions are necessary: (1) $x(V_2) = \alpha$ since $P^\psi \in S_P(x^\alpha, z^\xi)$, and (2) $y(V_2) = \overline{\beta}$, the non-controlling value of g (by Definition 2.3). However, since $(x = \alpha) \Rightarrow (y = \beta)$, a vector V_2 that satisfies conditions (1) and (2) cannot exist and hence, P^ψ is robustly untestable. □

Lemma 3.2 *For lines x and y, if $(x=\alpha) \Rightarrow (y=\beta)$, where α is the non-controlling value of $f = gt(x)$, and β is the controlling value of $g = gt(y)$, then* $\forall_{a \in in(f), a \neq x} \forall_{b \in in(g), b \neq y} \forall_{\varsigma \in \{0,1\}} \forall_{\xi \in \{0,1\}} [S_P(a^{\varsigma}, b^{\xi}) = RU]$

Proof: Consider a path fault $\{P^{\psi} : P^{\psi} \in P\}$, where $\psi \in \{0,1\}$ and P is the set of all path faults that pass though $\{a : a \in in(f), a \neq x\}$ and $\{b : b \in in(g), b \neq y\}$. Lines x and y are side-inputs of P^{ψ}. By Definition 2.3, for a vector pair $<V_1, V_2>$ to be a robust test for P^{ψ}, the following conditions are necessary: (1) $x(V_2) = \alpha$, the non-controlling value of f, and (2) $y(V_2) = \overline{\beta}$, the non-controlling value of g. However, since $(x=\alpha) \Rightarrow (y=\beta)$, a vector V_2 that satisfies conditions (1) and (2) cannot exist and hence, P^{ψ} is robustly untestable. □

Lemma 3.3 *For lines x and y, if $(x=\alpha) \Rightarrow (y=\beta)$, where $\alpha, \beta \in \{0,1\}$ and β is the controlling value of $g = gt(y)$, then* $\forall_{z \in in(g), z \neq y} [S_P(x^{\overline{\alpha}}, z^{\beta}) = RU]$.

Proof: Consider a path fault $\{P^{\psi} : P^{\psi} \in S_P(x^{\overline{\alpha}}, z^{\beta})\}$, where $\psi \in \{0,1\}$. Line y is a side-input of P^{ψ}. For a vector pair $<V_1, V_2>$ to be a robust test for P^{ψ}, the following conditions are necessary: (1) $x(V_2) = \overline{\alpha}$ since $P^{\psi} \in S_P(x^{\overline{\alpha}}, z^{\beta})$ and hence $x(V_1) = \alpha$ (by Remark 2.3), and (2) $y(V_1) = \overline{\beta}$, the non-controlling value of g (by Definition 2.3(2)). However, since $(x=\alpha) \Rightarrow (y=\beta)$, a vector V_1 that satisfies conditions (1) and (2) cannot exist and hence, P^{ψ} is robustly untestable. □

Lemma 3.4 *For lines x and y, if $(x=\alpha) \Rightarrow (y=\beta)$, where $\alpha, \beta \in \{0,1\}$, then $[S_P(x^{\overline{\alpha}}, y^{\beta}) = RU]$ and $[S_P(x^{\alpha}, y^{\overline{\beta}}) = RU]$.*

Proof: By definition, to sensitize a path fault $\{P^{\psi} : P^{\psi} \in S_P(x^{\overline{\alpha}}, y^{\beta})\}$ on a vector pair $<V_1, V_2>$, $[x(V_2) = \overline{\alpha}]$ and $[y(V_2) = \beta]$ are necessary conditions. Hence, by Remark 2.3, for $<V_1, V_2>$ to be a robust test for P^{ψ}, the following conditions are necessary: (1) $[x(V_1) = \alpha]$, and (2) $[y(V_1) = \overline{\beta}]$. However, since $(x=\alpha) \Rightarrow (y=\beta)$, a vector V_1 that satisfies conditions (1) and (2) cannot exist and hence, P^{ψ} is robustly untestable. Similarly, to robustly test a path fault $\{P^{\psi} : P^{\psi} \in S_P(x^{\alpha}, y^{\overline{\beta}})\}$, (1) $[x(V_2) = \alpha]$, and (2) $[y(V_2) = \overline{\beta}]$ are necessary conditions. Since a vector V_2 that satisfies conditions (1) and (2) cannot exist, P^{ψ} is robustly untestable. □

Lemma 3.5 *If a line x is identified as having a constant value assignment $\{\alpha : \alpha \in \{0,1\}\}$, then* $\forall_{\varsigma \in \{0,1\}} [S_P(x^{\varsigma}, x^{\varsigma}) = RU]$.

Proof: Since a vector pair $< V_1, V_2 >$ that satisfies $\{x(V_1) \neq x(V_2)\}$ cannot exist, by Remark 2.3, all path faults that pass through x are robustly untestable. □

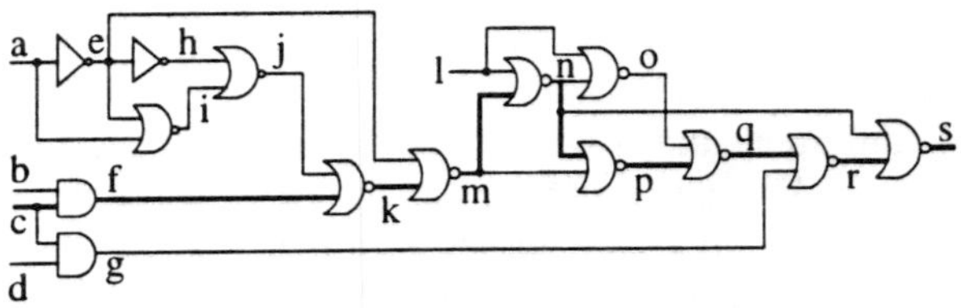

Figure 1: Portion of ISCAS-85 benchmark *c*6288

3.2 Functional Unsensitizability Analysis

Functionally unsensitizable path faults can be ignored during delay fault testing and timing analysis [11]. We say that $[S_P(x^{\alpha}, y^{\beta}) = FU]$ if all path faults in the set $S_P(x^{\alpha}, y^{\beta})$ are functionally unsensitizable.

Lemma 3.6 *For lines x and y, if $(x=\alpha) \Rightarrow (y=\beta)$, where $\alpha, \beta \in \{0,1\}$, then $[S_P(x^{\alpha}, y^{\overline{\beta}}) = FU]$.*

Proof: Similar to the proof of Lemma 3.4. □

Lemma 3.7 *If a line x is identified as having a constant value assignment $\{\alpha : \alpha \in \{0,1\}$, then $[S_P(x^{\overline{\alpha}}, x^{\overline{\alpha}}) = FU]$.*

Proof: Similar to the proof of Lemma 3.5. □

Other lemmas similar to those presented in Section 3.1 can be derived for identifying functionally unsensitizable path faults. However, in our experiments, we found that they do not help identify any additional functionally unsensitizable path faults.

Figure 1 illustrates an example of identifying a functionally unsensitizable path fault using Lemma 3.6. Consider the path fault $P^0 = (c, f, k, m, n, p, q, r, s)$. We make two observations:

- For a vector pair $<V_1, V_2>$ to functionally sensitize P^0, the following conditions are necessary: (1) $[c(V_2) = 0]$ (from Definition 2.1), and (2) $[s(V_2) = 1]$ since the number of inversions between c and s is seven (from Lemma 2.1). Hence $[P^0 \in S_P(c^0, s^1)]$.
- $(c=0) \Rightarrow (s=0)$ from static implication learning [10].

From Lemma 3.6, we can conclude that P^0 is functionally unsensitizable. Similarly $Q^0 = (c, f, k, m, n, o, q, r, s)$ is functionally unsensitizable. We explicitly enumerate untestable path faults in this example only for illustration. Our algorithm obtains the number of untestable path faults without enumerating them.

3.3 Non-robust Untestability Analysis

We say that $[S_P(x^{\alpha}, y^{\beta}) = NU]$ if all path faults in the set $S_P(x^{\alpha}, y^{\beta})$ are non-robustly untestable. To identify non-robustly untestable path faults, Lemmas 3.1 and 3.2 can be used by replacing *RU* by *NU* in them and Lemmas 3.6 and 3.7 can be used by replacing *FU* by *NU* in them.

4 Using Pre-computed Implications

We assume that some set of implications of both value assignments for every line in the circuit are available.

4.1 Maintaining Untestability Information

Using our fault-independent implication analysis at each line g, we construct four sets of lines associated with g: $O^1E^1(g)$, $O^1E^0(g)$, $O^0E^1(g)$, and $O^0E^0(g)$.

Definition 4.1 *A set $O^\alpha E^\beta(g)$ associated with a line g, where $\alpha, \beta \in \{0,1\}$, consists of lines $\{x : [S_P(g^\alpha, x^\beta) = Untestable]\}$*

Depending on the specific testability criterion used, rules that help construct the OE sets can be derived from the lemmas presented in Section 3. For conciseness, we only present an example involving the functional sensitization criterion. If we know that $(x=\alpha) \Rightarrow (y=\beta)$, where $\alpha, \beta \in \{0,1\}$, and y is in the fanout cone of x, from Lemma 3.6, y is added to $O^\alpha E^{\overline{\beta}}(x)$.

4.2 Counting Untestable Path Faults

Pomeranz and Reddy propose a linear-time counting algorithm [13] that can compute the number of paths in a single pass from POs to PIs. Based on their idea, we propose a counting algorithm that uses the OE sets on every line to compute a lower bound on the number of untestable path faults.

A *partial path fault* is a path fault without the restriction that its origin should be a PI. In this section, we use the terms *path faults* and *partial path faults* interchangeably. Consider a circuit with T lines. Let $B(x)$ denote the set of all branches of a fanout stem x. For a line y that is not a stem, let S^y denote the output of $gt(y)$. We associate a few variables with each line m:

- N_1^m (N_0^m) : number of testable path faults, as determined by our procedure, that originate at m and require a value of 1 (0) on m to be *sensitized*
- T_α^m : temporary values of N_α^m on a specific iteration
- $eval^m$: indicates whether T_1^m and T_0^m have been computed on a specific iteration
- $P(m)$: set of all immediate predecessor lines of m
- red_α^m : indicates if $\{S_P(m^\alpha, m^\alpha) = Untestable\}$, where $\alpha \in \{0,1\}$, on a specific iteration

To avoid reseting flags such as $eval^m$ and red_α^m, we use unique identifiers on each iteration. With no implications available, all path faults originating at a line $\{m : m \in \text{fanout cone of line } a\}$ contribute towards the computation of N^a. Suppose $O^0E^1(a) = \{m\}$. By definition, N_1^m can now be ignored when computing N_0^a. However, it is possible that N_1^m may contribute towards the computation of N values for other lines in the fanin cone of m. Assuming that the OE sets associated with every line are available, Algorithm 4.1 processes lines in a reverse topological order (POs to PIs) to compute a lower bound on the number of untestable path faults.

Algorithm 4.1
testable-path-count() {
  $\forall_{1<m<T}$ $\{eval^m = red_1^m = red_0^m = 0\}$
  $\forall_{1<m<T}$ $\{N_0^m = N_1^m = \infty\}$
  for $x = T$ **to** 1 // reverse topological order
    foreach($a \in O^1E^1(x)$) {
      insert(a); $red_1^a = x$ }
    foreach($a \in O^1E^0(x)$) {
      insert(a); $red_0^a = x$ }
    label(x, x)
    $N_1^x = T_1^x$
    foreach($a \in O^0E^1(x)$) {
      insert(a); $red_1^a = x+T$ }
    foreach($a \in O^0E^0(x)$) {
      insert(a); $red_0^a = x+T$ }
    label(x, $x+T$)
    $N_0^x = T_0^x$
  # of testable faults (T_P) = $\sum_{i \text{ is a } PI}\{N_1^i + N_0^i\}$
  # of untestable faults = Total # of path faults - T_P
}
label(x, id) {
  insert(x)
  while(n = dequeue())
    $eval^n = id$; $T_0^n = T_1^n = 0$
    if($red_1^n \neq id$)
      if(n is connected to a PO)$\{T_1^n = 1\}$ **else**
      if(n is a stem)$T_1^n = \sum_{b \in B(n)}$choose$(N_1^b, T_1^b, b, id)$
      else $\{T_1^n =$ choose$(N_\alpha^{S^n}, T_\alpha^{S^n}, S^n, id)$
        // $\alpha = 1$ if $gt(n)$ is non-inverting; 0 otherwise
    T_1^n =lesser(T_1^n, N_1^n) // lesser of the two values
    if($red_0^n \neq id$)
      if(n is connected to a PO)$\{T_0^n = 1\}$ **else**
      if(n is a stem)$T_0^n = \sum_{b \in B(n)}$choose$(N_0^b, T_0^b, b, id)$
      else $\{T_0^n =$ choose$(N_\alpha^{S^n}, T_\alpha^{S^n}, S^n, id)$
        // $\alpha = 0$ if $gt(n)$ is non-inverting; 1 otherwise
    T_0^n =lesser(T_0^n, N_0^n)
    if($T_1^n \neq N_1^n$) **or if**($T_0^n \neq N_0^n$)
      $\forall_{a \in P(n)}$ {(if a is closer to a PO than x) insert(a)}
}
choose(x, y, n, id) {
  if($eval^n \neq id$){**return**(x)} **else** {**return**(y)} }
insert(x) {insert x into an event list EL}
dequeue() {
  if EL is non-empty, dequeue and return element of EL that is closest to a PO; return 0 otherwise }

4.3 Counting Untestable Segment Faults

The discussion in Sections 3 and 4.1 is also applicable to the segment delay fault model. We modify the segment counting algorithm presented in the literature [3] to use implications to determine a lower bound on the number of untestable segment faults.

Table 1: A lower bound on the number of untestable delay faults

Ckt. Name	Segment faults: Robustly untestable, L=3 #	L=3 %	L=5 #	L=5 %	Path faults: Robustly untestable #	%	cpu(s)	Non-robustly untestable #	%	Functionally unsensitizable #	%	cpu(s)
c880	0	0.0	0	0.0	326	1.9	0	163	0.9	163	0.9	0
c1355	576	8.8	7,840	33.9	8,005,696	95.9	2	7,150,240	85.7	6,745,120	80.8	1
c1908	8	0.1	1,260	6.0	1,070,307	73.4	4	1,067,159	73.2	442,048	30.3	1
c2670	253	2.6	1,307	6.7	1,321,906	97.2	2	1,317,795	96.9	1,314,962	96.7	1
c3540	673	4.7	4,129	12.7	53,610,698	93.5	18	52,488,315	91.5	34,300,319	59.8	6
c5315	238	1.1	1,486	3.6	2,013,498	75.1	14	1,865,548	69.5	1,129,995	42.1	4
c6288	2,442	8.1	23,577	26.1	1.978×10^{20}	99.9	3	1.978×10^{20}	99.9	1.978×10^{20}	99.9	3
c7552	563	1.5	3,709	4.1	981,720	67.6	24	910,926	62.7	555,050	38.2	7
s5378	284	1.8	815	3.0	6,396	23.6	9	4,869	18.0	3,718	13.7	4
s9234	1,225	4.3	4,275	8.7	442,526	90.4	58	413,785	84.5	282,149	57.6	21
s13207	1,817	5.0	5,091	8.8	2,300,812	85.5	50	1,870,582	69.5	1,722,492	64.0	24
s15850	3,349	7.1	12,321	15.3	322,581,591	97.9	101	303,523,949	92.1	274,843,560	83.4	40
s35932	11,866	12.5	35,372	27.4	354,324	89.9	519	265,863	67.4	248,567	63.0	241
s38417	3,229	2.9	15,149	7.6	1,675,008	60.2	86	1,377,425	49.5	796,701	28.6	42
s38584	1,608	1.3	6,938	3.6	1,623,570	75.1	26	1,169,090	54.1	1,123,814	52.0	15

†Only a subset of direct implications was available for s38584

5 Results

We implemented our algorithm in C++ and ran experiments using a HP 9000/735 workstation with 256MB of memory. We use the implications generated by Zhao et. al. [10] for our work. Direct implications, determined by forward and backward propagation starting at the node under consideration, and indirect implications, found by applying the contrapositive law [9], transitive law and backward implications [10] were available for most circuits. Only a subset of direct implications was available for *s*38584. Information on constant value assignments that is generated as a by-product of their implication procedure is also used. For all the ISCAS-85 circuits, their program took less than 150 seconds to generate the relevant information [10]. Times taken by their program for the ISCAS-89 circuits were not available.

Table 1 shows results of the algorithm for a subset of all values that segment length L, an input parameter to the program, can take. For path delay faults, we consider the robust, non-robust and functional sensitization criteria. For segment faults with $(L = 3)$ and $(L = 5)$, we only consider the robust testability criteria. Columns with the heading # show the number of untestable faults determined by our procedure. Columns with the heading % indicate the percentage of untestable faults with respect to the total number of faults. The runtimes in CPU seconds are shown only for identifying robustly untestable and functionally unsensitizable path faults. Runtimes for identifying robustly untestable segment faults and non-robustly untestable path faults were similar to those for identifying robustly untestable path faults. However, there is a marginal increase in the runtimes as L is increased. In all cases, the runtime of our method is very small and is independent of the number of faults. While our method identifies more untestable path faults in some circuits, previously published methods [11, 12] do better for some circuits.

Since we identify only a subset of all untestable faults, firm conclusions cannot be drawn. However, for circuits such as *c*1908, it appears that many non-robustly untestable path faults do not belong to the set of functionally unsensitizable faults. Such path faults are testable only as a multiple fault [16]. Dealing with multiple path faults may be computationally intractable for large circuits. In such cases, using the segment delay fault model, with a small value of L, may be a feasible alternative. For circuits like *c*2670, most of the path faults are functionally unsensitizable. These path faults can be ignored for the purposes of delay testing and the

Table 2: Our results versus ATPG results

Ckt. Name	Non-robustly untestable path faults: Exact [15]	Our procedure
s5378	19.0%	18.0%
s9234	87.8%	84.5%
s13207	82.3%	69.5%
s15850	96.7%	92.1%
s35932	85.2%	67.4%
s38417	59.1%	49.5%
s38584	84.5%	54.1%

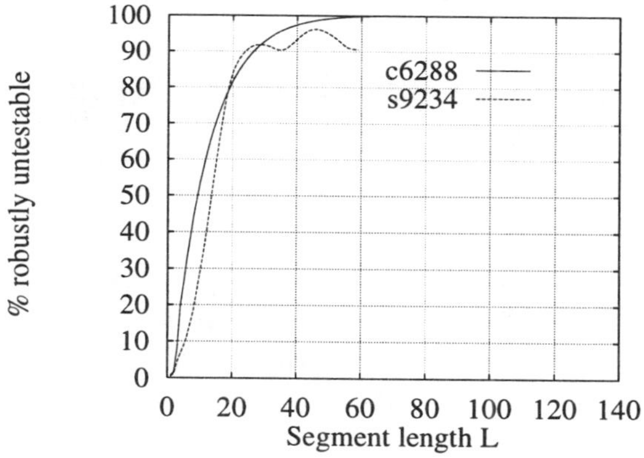

Figure 2: % of untestable faults versus segment length

path fault model may be practical in such cases.

Table 2 compares our results with the exact results obtained from a test generator [15] for the ISCAS-89 circuits. The exact number of untestable faults is unknown for many of the ISCAS-85 circuits. Our method gives only a lower bound on the number of untestable faults since it is based on an incomplete set of implications. During an ATPG run, a lower bound on the number of untestable faults may be useful as a stopping criterion if the required fault efficiency is reached.

In our experiments, the percentage of untestable faults increases monotonically with L and then decreases as L approaches the maximum logic depth. Figure 2 shows this trend for robustly untestable faults in *c*6288 (maximum logic depth: 125) and *s*9234 (maximum logic depth: 59). For *c*6288, we identified 1.9788271×10^{20} robustly untestable path faults, of which 1.9778345×10^{20} were also functionally unsensitizable.

6 Concluding Remarks

Our algorithm uses static logic implications and rapidly computes a lower bound on the number of robustly untestable, non-robustly untestable, and functionally unsensitizable delay faults by using a non-enumerative counting procedure. Untestable faults can also be listed if desired and targeting them for test generation by an ATPG tool can be avoided. One of the main features of the algorithm is that its complexity of computation does not grow with the number of delay faults. This is especially important when considering the path delay fault model since circuits typically have a large number of path faults. The implication analysis presented in this paper considers one implication at a time. It may be possible to obtain better results by considering multiple implications simultaneously.

References

[1] G. L. Smith, "Model for Delay Faults Based Upon Paths," in *Proc. International Test Conf.*, pp. 342–349, Nov. 1985.

[2] C. J. Lin and S. M. Reddy, "On Delay Fault Testing in Logic Circuits," *IEEE Trans. on CAD*, vol. 6, pp. 694–703, Sept. 1987.

[3] K. Heragu, J. H. Patel, and V. D. Agrawal, "Segment Delay Faults: A New Fault Model," in *Proc. VLSI Test Symp.*, pp. 32–39, Apr. 1996.

[4] K. Heragu, J. H. Patel, and V. D. Agrawal, "SIGMA: A Simulator for Segment Delay Faults," in *Proc. International Conf. CAD*, pp. 502–508, Nov. 1996.

[5] I. Pomeranz and S. M. Reddy, "On Achieving Complete Testability of Synchronous Sequential Circuits with Synchronizing Sequences," in *Proc. International Test Conf.*, pp. 1007–1016, Oct. 1994.

[6] V. D. Agrawal and S. T. Chakradhar, "Combinational ATPG Theorems for Identifying Untestable Faults in Sequential Circuits," *IEEE Trans. on CAD*, vol. 14, pp. 1155–1160, Sep. 1995.

[7] M. A. Iyer and M. Abramovici, "FIRE: A Fault-Independent Combinational Redundancy Identification Algorithm," *IEEE Trans. on VLSI Systems*, vol. 4, pp. 295–301, Jun. 1996.

[8] M. A. Iyer, D. E. Long, and M. Abramovici, "Identifying Sequential Redundancies Without Search," in *Proc. 33rd Design Automation Conf.*, Jun. 1996.

[9] W. Kunz and D. K. Pradhan, "Accelerated Dynamic Learning for Test Pattern Generation in Combinational Circuits," *IEEE Trans. on CAD*, vol. 12, pp. 684–694, May 1993.

[10] J. Zhao, E. M. Rudnick, and J. H. Patel, "Static Logic Implication with Application to Redundancy Identification," in *Proc. VLSI Test Symp.*, pp. 288–293, Apr. 1997.

[11] K. T. Cheng and H. C. Chen, "Delay Testing for Non-Robust Untestable Circuits," in *Proc. International Test Conf.*, pp. 954–961, Oct. 1993.

[12] S. Kajihara, K. Kinoshita, I. Pomeranz, and S. Reddy, "A Method for Identifying Robust Dependent and Functionally Unsensitizable Paths," in *Proc. 10th International Conf. on VLSI Design*, pp. 82–87, Jan. 1996.

[13] I. Pomeranz and S. M. Reddy, "An Efficient Non-Enumerative Method to Estimate the Path Delay Fault Coverage in Combinational Circuits," *IEEE Trans. CAD*, vol. 13, pp. 240–250, Feb. 1994.

[14] E. S. Park and M. R. Mercer, "Robust and Nonrobust Tests for Path Delay Faults in a Combinational Circuit," in *Proc. International Test Conf.*, pp. 1027–1034, Sept. 1987.

[15] K. Fuchs, M. Pabst, and T. Rossel, "RESIST: A Recursive Test Pattern Generation Algorithm for Path Delay Faults Considering Various Test Classes," *IEEE Trans. on CAD*, vol. 13, pp. 1550–1561, Dec. 1994.

[16] W. Ke and P. R. Menon, "Synthesis of Delay-verifiable Combinational Circuits," *IEEE Trans. on CAD*, vol. 44, pp. 213–222, Feb. 1995.

A SAT-Based Implication Engine for Efficient ATPG, Equivalence Checking, and Optimization of Netlists

Paul Tafertshofer Andreas Ganz

Institute of Electronic Design Automation
Technical University of Munich
80290 Munich,Germany
{tafertshofer,ganz}@regent.e-technik.tu-muenchen.de

Manfred Henftling

Siemens AG, HL IT PE 5
P.O.-Box 801709
81617 Munich, Germany
mah@earl.hl.siemens.de

Abstract

This paper presents a flexible and efficient approach to evaluating implications as well as deriving indirect implications in logic circuits. Evaluation and derivation of implications are essential in ATPG, equivalence checking, and netlist optimization. Contrary to other methods, our approach is based on a graph model of a circuit's clause description called implication graph. It combines both the flexibility of SAT-based techniques and high efficiency of structure based methods. As the proposed algorithms operate only on the implication graph, they are independent of the chosen logic. Evaluation of implications and computation of indirect implications are performed by simple and efficient graph algorithms. Experimental results for various applications relying on implication demonstrate the effectiveness of our approach.

1 Introduction

Recently, substantial progress has been achieved in the fields of Boolean equivalence checking and optimization of netlists. Techniques for deriving indirect implications, which were originally developed for ATPG tools, play a key role in this development.

Indirect implications have been successfully applied in algorithms for optimizing netlists. For this task, either a set of permissible transformations is derived [1, 2, 3] or promising transformations are applied and their permissibility is later verified by an ATPG tool [4, 5, 6]. Furthermore, they are of great importance in ATPG-based approaches to Boolean equivalence checking of both combinational and sequential circuits [7, 8, 9, 10, 11] as they help identify equivalent internal signals in the circuits to be compared.

In the late 1980s, Schulz et al. incorporated computation of indirect implications into the ATPG tool SOCRATES[12]. Indirect implications are indispensable when dealing with redundant faults as they help to efficiently prune the search space of the branch-and-bound search. In order to derive more indirect implications, the originally static technique of SOCRATES, which the authors refer to as (static) learning, has been extended to dynamic learning [13, 14].

Recursive learning [7], proposed by Kunz et al. in 1992, was the first complete algorithm for determining indirect implications. As the problem of finding all indirect implications is NP-complete, only small depths of recursion are feasible. Recently, it has been shown that recursive learning can be adequately modelled by AND-OR reasoning graphs [3]. Another complete method for deriving indirect implications based on BDDs was suggested by Mukherjee et al. [15]. Very recently, Zhao et al. presented an approach that combines iterated static learning with recursive learning constrained to recursion level one [16]. It is based on set algebra and is similar to single pass deductive fault simulation.

Contrary to the above methods, which work on the structural description of a circuit, other approaches use a Boolean satisfiability (SAT) based model. The SAT-model allows an elegant problem formulation which can easily be adapted to various logics. This abstraction, however, often impedes development of efficient algorithms as structural information is lost. Larrabee included a clause based formulation of Schulz's algorithm into NEMESIS[17]. Her approach has been improved by the iterated method of TEGUS [18]. The transitive closure algorithms suggested by Chakradhar et al. rely on a relational model of binary clauses [19]. Silva et al. proposed another form of dynamic learning in GRASP [20] where indirect implications are determined by a conflict analysis during the backtracking phase of a SAT-solver.

In many areas of logic synthesis and formal verification Binary Decision Diagrams (BDD) have become the most widely used data structure as they provide many advantageous properties, e.g. canonicity and high flexibility. Besides their exponential memory complexity, when used for ATPG, equivalence checking, and optimization of large netlists, BDDs suffer from the drawback that implications cannot be derived efficiently on this data structure. For a given signal assignment it can only be decided if another signal assignment is implied or not. So, finding all possible implications from a given signal assignment is expensive because theoretically all possible combinations of signal pairs have to be checked. Therefore, BDD-based approaches such as functional learning [15] restrict their search to potential learning areas, which are identified by non BDD-based implication. Consequently, structural or hybrid approaches, i.e. BDDs combined with other methods, are predominant in ATPG, equivalence checking and optimization of netlists. Even though most of these approaches make heavy use of implications, the data structures that are used for deriving and evaluating implications are often suboptimal and inflexible. That is why we propose a flexible data structure which is specifically optimized with respect to implication.

In this paper, we introduce a framework for implication based algorithms which inherits the advantages of structural as well as SAT-based approaches. Our approach combines both the flexibility and elegance of a SAT-based algorithm and the efficiency of a structural method by working on a graph model of the clause

1092-3152/97 $10.00 © 1997 IEEE

system, called *implication graph*. Its memory complexity is only linear in the number of modules in the circuit. Due to structural information available in the graph, fundamental problems such as justification, propagation and particularly implication are carried out efficiently on the graph. The search for indirect implications reduces to graph algorithms that can be executed very fast and are easily extended to exploit bit-parallelism. As the implication graph can automatically be generated for any arbitrary logic, all presented algorithms remain valid independent of the chosen logic. This allows rapid prototyping of implication based tools for new multi-valued logics.

The remainder of this paper is organized as follows. In Sec. 2, we show how to derive the implication graph. Next, we discuss how implications are evaluated and how indirect implications can be computed in Sec. 3 and 4, respectively. In order to demonstrate the high efficiency of our approach, experimental results for various applications using the proposed implication engine are presented in Sec. 5. Sec. 6 concludes the paper.

2 Implication graph

As performing implications is one of the most prominent and time consuming tasks in ATPG, equivalence checking, and optimization of netlists, it is of utmost importance to use a data structure that is best suited. Unlike other graphical representations of clause systems, our data structure represents all information contained in both the structural netlist and the clause database. The implication graphs used in NEMESIS[17] and TRAN[19] model only binary clauses, clauses of a higher order are solely included in the clause database.

Since our approach is generic in nature, any combinational circuit can automatically be compiled into its implication graph representation. Only information about a logic and its encoding as well as the truth table descriptions of supported module types have to be provided. The basic steps of compilation are given in Fig. 1. First, all supported module types are individually compiled into

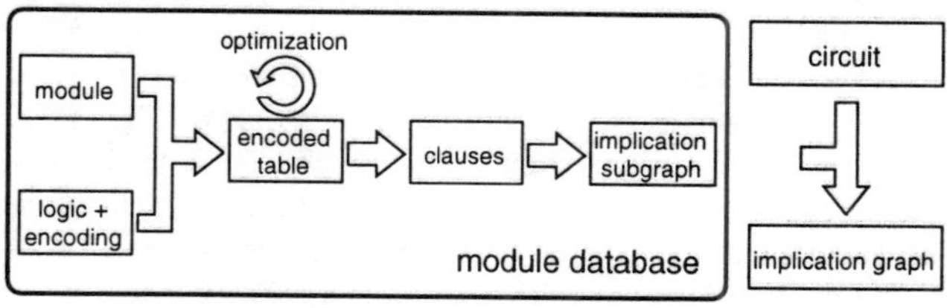

Figure 1: Deriving the implication graph

encoded truth tables. Then, these tables are optimized by a two-level logic optimizer, e.g. ESPRESSO. This step is explained in Sec. 2.1. Next, a set of clauses is extracted from the optimized table, which is shown in Sec. 2.2. As shown in Sec. 2.3, the set of clauses is transformed into an implication subgraph that is stored in the module database. Then, for every module in the circuit the appropriate generic subgraph is taken from the module database and personalized with the input and output signals of the given module. Finally, all identical nodes are merged into a single node resulting in the complete implication graph.

The following sections only consider the 3-valued logic $\mathcal{L}_3 = \{0,1,X\}$ in order to present the basic ideas of our approach. Generation of an implication graph for an arbitrary multi-valued logic, e.g. the 10-valued logic $\mathcal{L}_{10}$ known from robust path delay ATPG, is discussed in [21].

2.1 Encoding

A signal variable $x \in \mathcal{L}_3$ requires two encoding bits c_x and c_x^* for its internal representation. The complete scheme of encoding for $\mathcal{L}_3$ is shown in Table 1. In order to easily detect inconsistencies,

$x \in \mathcal{L}_3$	encoding		interpretation
	c_x	c_x^*	
0	0	1	signal x is 0
1	1	0	signal x is 1
X	0	0	signal x is unknown
	1	1	conflict at signal x

Table 1: 3-valued logic and its encoding

conflicting signal assignments are denoted by $c_x = 1 \wedge c_x^* = 1$. This property is expressed in the following definition:

DEFINITION 1 *An assignment is called non-conflicting iff $c_x \wedge c_x^* \Leftrightarrow 0$ holds for all signal variables x.*

Based on this encoding, the truth tables of all supported module types are converted into encoded tables. For example, the truth table of a 2-input AND-gate ($c = AND(a,b)$) found in Table 2 is converted into the encoded table of Table 2. This encoded table can

truth table

a	b	c
0	0	0
0	1	0
1	0	0
1	1	1
0	X	0
1	X	X
X	0	0
X	1	X
X	X	X

encoded table

c_a	c_a^*	c_b	c_b^*	c_c	c_c^*
0	1	0	1	0	1
0	1	1	0	0	1
1	0	0	1	0	1
1	0	1	0	1	0
0	1	0	0	0	1
1	0	0	0	0	0
0	0	0	1	0	1
0	0	1	0	0	0
0	0	0	0	0	0
1	1	-	-	-	-
-	-	1	1	-	-

optimized table

c_a	c_a^*	c_b	c_b^*	c_c	c_c^*
-	1	-	-	-	1
-	-	-	1	-	1
1	-	1	-	1	-

Table 2: AND-gate: truth table — encoded table — optimized table

be interpreted as specifying the on-set as well as the off-set of two Boolean functions c_c and c_c^*. Conflicting assignments belong to the don't-care-set, as they are explicitly checked for by the implication engine. Exploiting these don't-cares, functions c_c and c_c^* in the encoded table are optimized by ESPRESSO.

2.2 Clause description

The characteristic function describing the AND-gate with respect to the given encoding can easily be given in its *Conjunctive Normal Form (CNF)* by analyzing the individual rows of the optimized table of Table 2. Every row in this table corresponds to a clause contained in the *CNF*. Here, the *CNF* comprises the three clauses $\neg c_a^* \vee c_c^*$, $\neg c_b^* \vee c_c^*$, and $\neg c_a \vee \neg c_b \vee c_c$. That is, all valid value assignments to the inputs and outputs of the AND-gate are implicitly given by the non-conflicting satisfying assignments to the characteristic equation:

$$CNF \Leftrightarrow (\neg c_a^* \vee c_c^*) \wedge (\neg c_b^* \vee c_c^*) \wedge (\neg c_a \vee \neg c_b \vee c_c) \Leftrightarrow 1 \quad (1)$$

2.3 Building the implication graph

By exploiting the following equivalencies the clause description of Eq. (1) is converted into the corresponding implication graph.

$$x \vee y \quad \Leftrightarrow \quad (\neg x \rightarrow y) \wedge (\neg y \rightarrow x) \qquad (2)$$

$$x \vee y \vee z \quad \Leftrightarrow \quad (\neg x \wedge \neg y \rightarrow z) \wedge (\neg x \wedge \neg z \rightarrow y) \wedge (\neg y \wedge \neg z \rightarrow x) \qquad (3)$$

It is sufficient to provide equivalencies for binary and ternary clauses only, as any clause system of a higher order can be decomposed into a system of binary and ternary clauses [21]. Having transformed all clauses into binary and ternary clauses, the subgraphs shown in Fig. 2 are used for representation of these clauses. These graphs contain two types of nodes. While the first type rep-

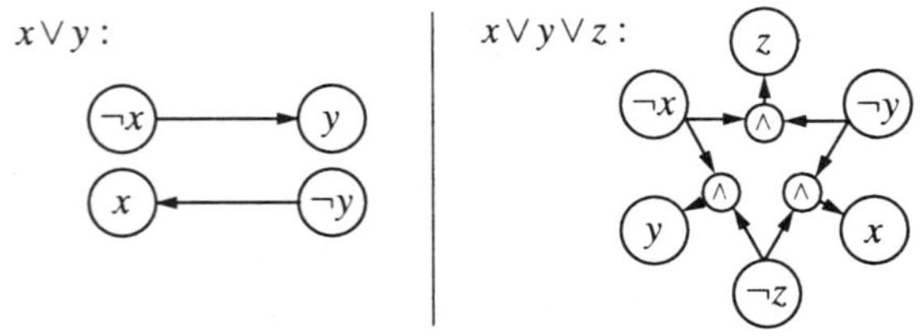

Figure 2: Implication subgraph for a binary and a ternary clause

resents the encoded signal values, the second one symbolizes the conjunction operation. The latter type is depicted by $\wedge$ or a shaded triangle. Every ternary clause has three associated $\wedge$-nodes that uniquely represent the ternary clause in the implication graph.

Coming back to the 2-input AND-gate, its *CNF*-description is transformed into the implication graph shown in Fig. 3. Every bit of the encoding for a signal x is represented by a corresponding node in the implication graph, e.g. node $c_a(c_a^*)$ in Fig. 3 gives bit $c_a(c_a^*)$ of signal a. As we require non-conflicting assignments, literals $\neg c_x$ $(\neg c_x^*)$ can be replaced by c_x^* (c_x) such that only nodes corresponding to non-negated encoding bits are contained in Fig. 3.

So far, the implication graph only captures the logic functionality of a circuit. Since structural information is indispensable for some tasks, such as justification and propagation, we provide this information within the implication graph by marking its edges with three different tags f, b, and o. Edges that denote an implication from an input to an output signal of a module are marked with f (forward edge). Relations from output to input signals are tagged with b (backward edge). All other edges, e.g. input to input relations and indirect implications, are given tag o (other edge)[1]. The tags for the 2-input AND-gate are found in Fig. 3. By means of these tags, a directed acyclic graph (DAG) can be extracted from the implication graph. If all edges but the forward edges are removed, we obtain a DAG that forms the base of an efficient algorithm for backtracing and justification.

For a simple circuit, the three different circuit descriptions introduced above are presented in Ex. 2.1. Please observe that most clause based approaches work on a *CNF* in $\mathcal{L}_2$. Our approach operates on a *CNF* of variables encoded with respect to a given logic, here $\mathcal{L}_3$.

[1]Tags denoting other edges have been omitted in later examples.

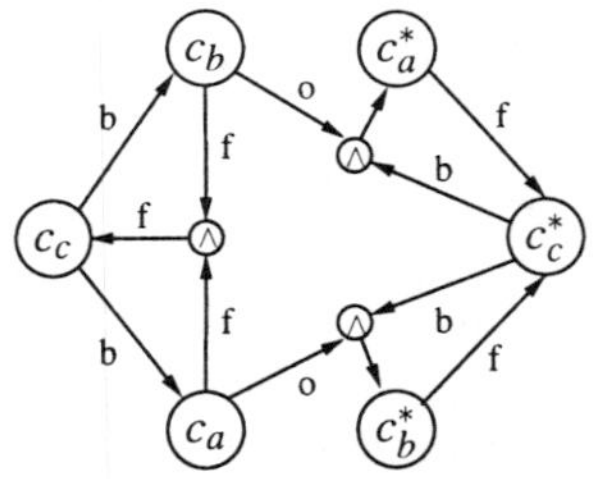

Figure 3: Implication graph for 2-input AND-gate

2.4 Advantages

Using the proposed implication graph as a core data structure in CAD algorithms has many advantages.

(1) Important tasks such as implication and justification can be carried out on the implication graph in the same manner for any arbitrary logic. The peculiarities of the chosen logic are included in the graph. Implication and derivation of indirect implications reduce to efficient graph algorithms as will be shown in Sec. 3.3 and 4.4.

(2) Most SAT-based algorithms use a static order for variable assignments during their search for a satisfying assignment [17, 19]. Furthermore, these algorithms assign values to internal signals during justification. Since PODEM, it has been well known that assigning values only to primary input signals helps to reduce the search space. Obviously, primary inputs are a special property of the given instance of SAT which is not exploited by algorithms for solving arbitrary SAT problems. The algorithm of TEGUS tries to mimic PODEM by ordering the clauses in a special manner [18]. Our approach does not need such techniques, as structural information is provided by edge tags.

(3) Algorithms working on the implication graph can easily exploit bit-parallelism as the status of every node can be represented by one bit only. For example, on a 64-bit machine 64 value assignments can be processed in parallel, making bit-parallel implication very efficient.

(4) Sequential circuits are often modelled as an iterative logic array (ILA). In this model the time domain is unfolded into multiple copies of the combinational logic block. These logic blocks can be compiled into the corresponding implication graphs. Using bit-parallel techniques, a 64-bit machine allows to keep 64 time-frames without increasing the size of the implication graph.

3 How to perform implications

3.1 Structure based

Structure based implication is a special form of event-driven simulation. Contrary to ordinary simulation, which starts at the primary inputs, implication is started at an arbitrary signal in the circuit. Therefore, it has to proceed towards the primary outputs as well as the primary inputs such that implications are often categorized into forward and backward implications. Obviously, this technique requires many table lookups for evaluating the module functions. This becomes particularly costly for multi-valued logics, e.g. the ones used in path delay ATPG.

3.2 Clause based

Clause based implication relies on *Boolean Constraint Propagation (BCP)*. BCP corresponds to an iterative application of the

Example 2.1 Circuit descriptions: structural — clauses — implication graph

- Structural:

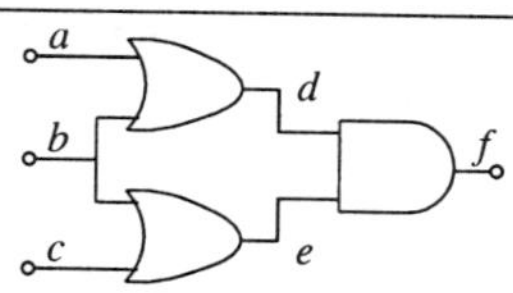

- *CNF* for $\mathcal{L}_3$:

$$
\begin{array}{ll|l}
CNF_3 & \Leftrightarrow & \\
(\neg c_d^* \vee c_f^*) \wedge (\neg c_e^* \vee c_f^*) \wedge (\neg c_d \vee \neg c_e \vee c_f) & \wedge & f = AND(d,e) \\
(\neg c_a \vee c_d) \wedge (\neg c_b \vee c_d) \wedge (\neg c_a^* \vee \neg c_b^* \vee c_d^*) & \wedge & d = OR(a,b) \\
(\neg c_b \vee c_e) \wedge (\neg c_c \vee c_e) \wedge (\neg c_b^* \vee \neg c_c^* \vee c_e^*) & \wedge & e = OR(b,c) \\
 & \Leftrightarrow 1 &
\end{array}
$$

- Implication graph for $\mathcal{L}_3$:

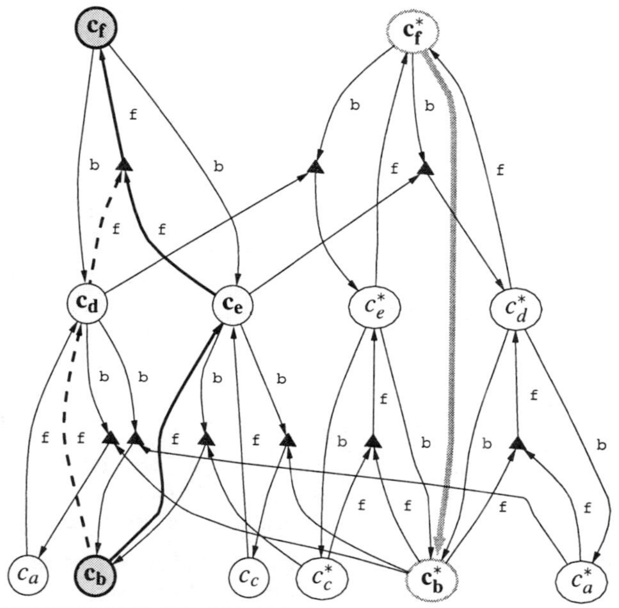

unit clause rule proposed by Davis et al. in 1960 [22]. In BCP, unary clauses are used to simplify other clauses until no further simplification is possible or some clause becomes unsatisfied. Implication is started by adding a unary clause, which represents the initial signal assignment, to the *CNF*. All unary clauses computed by BCP correspond to implications from the initial assignment as they force the corresponding signals to a certain logic value. The most time consuming task in BCP is the search for clauses that can be simplified by the unit clause rule. This search is not necessary when working on the implication graph since clauses that share common variables are connected in the graph.

3.3 Implication graph based

Implication graph based implication is simple and efficient, as it only requires a partial traversal of the implication graph. Implying from a signal assignment means that first the corresponding nodes are marked in the implication graph. Then, the implication procedure traverses the implication graph obeying the following rule:

RULE 1 *Starting from an initial set S_I of marked nodes, all successor nodes s_j are marked*

- *if node s_j is a $\wedge$-node and **all** its predecessors are marked.*
- *if node s_j represents an encoding bit and **at least one** predecessor is marked .*

This rule is applied until no further propagation of marks is possible.

All nodes that have been marked represent signal values that can be implied from the initial assignment given by S_I. Conflicting signal assignments are easily detected during implication, since they cause both nodes c_x and c_x^* to be marked.

Let us use the circuit of Ex. 2.1 for the sake of explanation. Assigning logical value 0 to signal e corresponds to marking node c_e^* in the implication graph. After running the implication procedure, the following nodes are marked: c_b^*, c_c^* and c_f^*. To finally obtain the implied signal values with respect to the given logic, the marked nodes are decoded according to the given encoding, i.e. we determine $b = 0$, $c = 0$, $f = 0$.

4 Deriving indirect implications

Contrary to direct implications, detection of indirect implications requires a special analysis of the logic function of a circuit as they represent information on the circuit that is not obvious from its description. Most methods for computation of indirect implications are subject to order dependency. That is, some indirect implications can only be found if certain other indirect implications have already been discovered. In order to avoid this problem, it has been suggested to iterate their computation [18].

4.1 Structure based

The SOCRATES algorithm [12] was the first to introduce computation of indirect implications using the following tautologies:

$$(a \rightarrow b) \quad \Leftrightarrow \quad (\neg b \rightarrow \neg a) \qquad (4)$$

$$(a \rightarrow b) \wedge (a \rightarrow \neg b) \quad \Rightarrow \quad \neg a \qquad (5)$$

While Eq. (4) (*law of contraposition*) may generate a candidate for an indirect implication, Eq. (5) identifies a fix value.

Indirect implications are primarily computed in a pre-processing phase. The idea is to temporarily set a given signal to a certain logic value. Then, all possible direct implications from this signal assignment are computed. For all implied signal values, it is checked if the contrapositive cannot be deduced by direct implications (learning criterion). In this case, the contrapositive is an indirect implication. As indirect implications cannot be represented within the data structure used to describe the circuit, structural algorithms have to store them in an external data structure. This adds additional complexity to structure based algorithms.

4.2 Clause based

Clause based computation [17, 18] is similar to the structural algorithm of Sec. 4.1. Each free literal a contained in the *CNF* is temporarily set to 1. Then BCP is used to derive all possible direct implications, i.e. unary clauses. For all generated unary clauses b, it is checked if the contrapositive $\neg b \rightarrow \neg a$ is an indirect implication. In this case, the corresponding clause $b \vee \neg a$ is added to the clause database. Thereby, indirect implications enrich the data structure used for representing the circuit functionality. Once an indirect implication has been added to the clause database, it does no longer require any special attention. This is one important advantage of clause based algorithms over structure based approaches [18].

4.3 AND-OR enumeration

A different approach, known as recursive learning, has been taken by Kunz et al. [3, 7]. Indirect implications are deduced by an AND-OR search [23] for all possible implications resulting from a signal assignment. This search is performed by recursively injecting and reversing signal assignments, which correspond to the different possibilities for justifying a gate, followed by deriving all direct implications. Signal values that are common to all justifications of a gate yield indirect implications. Only a simple structural algorithm for executing implications is applied.

Let us illustrate the principles of the AND-OR enumeration with the circuit of Ex. 2.1 and the AND-OR tree found in Fig. 4. The

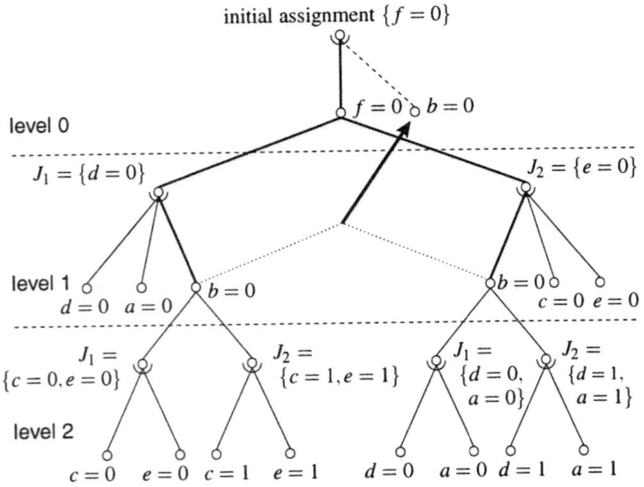

Figure 4: AND-OR enumeration

root node of the AND-OR tree reflects the initial assignment, it is of the AND-type[2]. In our example, a logical 0 is assigned to signal f. As no further signal values can be implied, OR-node $f = 0$ is the only successor of the root node. The justifications for $f = 0$ are $J_1 = \{d = 0\}$ and $J_2 = \{e = 0\}$. In order to derive an indirect implication, we have to search for implied signal values that are common to both justifications. Here, $b = 0$ is implied for both justifications. This is represented by a new OR-node $b = 0$ in level 0 of the AND-OR tree. In general, new OR-nodes in level 0 correspond to indirect implications. Further examination of gates in level 2, which have become unjustified because of setting b to 0, does not yield additional indirect implications.

4.4 Implication graph based

An implication graph based method for computing indirect implications inherits all advantages of clause based techniques but eliminates the costly search process required during BCP-based implication. Moreover, our approach integrates computation of indirect implications based on the law of contraposition and AND-OR enumeration into the same framework.

[2]In general, an AND-node (marked by an arc) represents a signal assignment due to justification of an unjustified gate, whereas an OR-node denotes a signal value that can be implied from a chosen justification. Justified gates correspond to OR-leaves and unjustified gates to internal OR-nodes in the AND-OR graph [3].

4.4.1 Reconvergence analysis

The basic idea of determining indirect implications by a search for reconvergencies is shown in Fig. 5. While implication $c_a \rightarrow c_b$

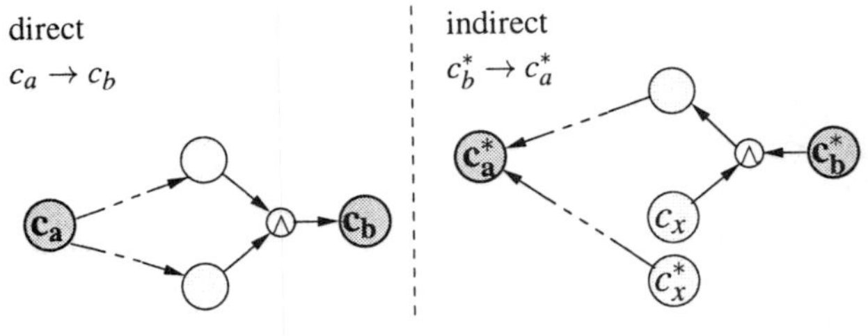

Figure 5: Learning by contraposition on the implication graph

is deduced by direct implication, $c_b^* \rightarrow c_a^*$ forms an indirect implication. The $\wedge$-node can only be passed if both of its predecessors are marked, i.e. it forms a reconvergent $\wedge$-node during implication. If we start implication at node c_b^*, however, we cannot pass the $\wedge$-node, as its other predecessor c_x is not marked. Applying the law of contraposition to $c_a \rightarrow c_b$, we deduce $c_b^* \rightarrow c_a^*$ such that c_a^* is implied from c_b^*.

This observation is expressed in the following lemma:

LEMMA 1 *Let c_x represent the initial assignment. A reconvergent structure (c_x, c_y) in the implication graph yields an indirect implication $c_y^* \rightarrow c_x^*$ only if*

- *c_x is a fanout node in the implication graph.*
- *a node c_y is marked via a $\wedge$-node and both predecessors of the $\wedge$-node have been marked by implying along disjoint paths in the implication graph.* (Proof: [21])

Using Lemma 1 it can be shown that the search for reconvergencies in the implication graph detects all indirect implications, which are found by clause and structural based approaches.

THEOREM 1 *All indirect implications found by BCP on the (encoded) clause description can be identified by a search for the reconvergent structures defined in Lemma 1.* (Proof: [21])

We explain the reconvergence analysis with the implication graph of Ex. 2.1. Let's assume that fanout node c_b is marked. Then, the implication procedure of Sec. 3.3 is invoked. As both c_d and c_e have been marked, the succeeding $\wedge$-node and c_f are marked, too. The $\wedge$-node has been reached via two disjoint paths in the graph (indicated by the dashed and solid line, respectively) such that the contrapositive $c_f^* \rightarrow c_b^*$ forms an indirect implication. This indirect implication is included into the graph in form of the grey edge leading from node c_f^* to node c_b^*.

Applying our graph analysis offers the following advantages:

(1) The search for reconvergence regions in the implication graph reduces the set of candidate signals that may yield an indirect implication. Clause based methods have to temporarily assign a value to all literals contained in the *CNF*.

(2) Reconvergence analysis is carried out very fast by an adapted version of the algorithm presented in [24].

(3) Our method does not require a learning criterion such as the approach of [12].

4.4.2 Extended reconvergence analysis

Contrary to the reconvergence analysis of Sec. 4.4.1, the extended reconvergence analysis detects conditional reconvergencies at signal nodes. As it corresponds to an AND-OR search in the implication graph, we need the following definitions:

DEFINITION 2 *A clause $C = c_1 \vee c_2 \vee \ldots \vee c_n$ is called unjustified iff all literals $c_1, c_2, \ldots, c_n$ do not evaluate to 1 and at least one complement $\neg c_i$ of a literal c_i is 1.*

Unjustified ternary clauses are found in the implication graph without effort. They are represented by $\wedge$-nodes that have exactly one of their two predecessors marked.

DEFINITION 3 *Let $c_1, c_2, \ldots, c_m$ be some unspecified literals in a clause $C = c_1 \vee c_2 \vee \ldots \vee c_n$ that is unjustified, and let $V_1, V_2, \ldots, V_m$ denote the assigned values. Then, the set of non-conflicting assignments $J = \{c_1 = V_1, c_2 = V_2, \ldots, c_m = V_m\}$ is called a justification of clause C, if the value assignments in J make C evaluate to 1.*

In a clause based framework a complete set of justifications J_c for an unjustified clause C is easily given by $J_c = \{\{c_1 = 1\}, \{c_2 = 1\}, \ldots, \{c_m = 1\}\}$. For our approach, set J_c is even simpler, as only ternary clauses can be unjustified.[3] Therefore, J_c always consists of exactly two justifications.

We will now explain how these two justifications can be derived in the implication graph with Fig. 6. The given ternary clause

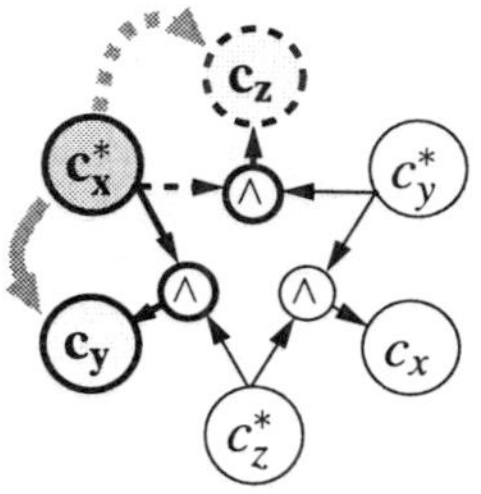

Figure 6: Unjustified ternary clause $c_x \vee c_y \vee c_z$ due to assignment $c_x^* = 1$

$c_x \vee c_y \vee c_z$ is unjustified due to an assignment of $c_x^* = 1$. This is indicated by the two $\wedge$-nodes that have exactly one predecessor (c_x^*) marked. Here, the ternary clause can be justified by setting c_z or c_y to 1. If we consider that the subgraph denoting the ternary clause $c_x \vee c_y \vee c_z$ is a straightforward graphical representation of the following formulae

$$c_x^* \wedge c_y^* \rightarrow c_z \Leftrightarrow c_x^* \wedge c_z^* \rightarrow c_y \Leftrightarrow c_y^* \wedge c_z^* \rightarrow c_x$$

it becomes apparent that both possible justifications in J_c are found in the consequents of those implications which have the literal making the clause unjustified, i.e. c_x^*, in their antecedent. These consequents correspond to the successors of the two $\wedge$-nodes.

Let us now explain how the extended reconvergence analysis corresponds to an efficient AND-OR search on the implication graph with help of Fig. 7 showing the implication graph of Ex. 2.1. An initial assignment of $c_f^* = 1$ makes clause $C_\alpha = c_d^* \vee c_e^* \vee c_f$ unjustified. Next, the possible justifications $J_{\alpha_1} = \{c_e^* = 1\}$, $J_{\alpha_2} = \{c_d^* = 1\}$ for C_α are determined as the successors of the two $\wedge$-nodes α_1 and α_2 belonging to clause C_α. These $\wedge$-nodes correspond to AND-nodes J_{α_1} and J_{α_2} in the AND-OR tree, respectively. So as to distinguish between the consequences of the two justifications, each one is assigned a different color. Thus, node $c_e^* = 1$ is given a green marker (represented by dashed lines in Fig. 7) and all signals that can be implied from $c_e^* = 1$ are marked green. The same is done for $c_d^* = 1$ using a red marker (dotted lines in Fig. 7). Nodes that are assigned both colors, i.e. nodes where the markers reconverge, can be implied independent of the chosen justification. These nodes can therefore be elevated to the previous level in the AND-OR tree. In our example, only node c_b^* is marked by both colors and we derive the indirect implication $c_f^* \rightarrow c_b^*$. Further analysis of unjustified clauses C_β and C_γ in level 2 of the AND-OR tree does not yield additional indirect implications.

This example indicates that the trace of the extended reconvergence analysis is identical to the AND-OR tree generated by AND-OR enumeration if marked $\wedge$-nodes are converted to AND-nodes and marked signal nodes to OR-nodes. Obviously the extended reconvergence analysis is capable of determining all indirect implications given enough colors, i.e. it is complete.

An efficient procedure implementing this extended reconvergence analysis is given in [21]. It takes advantage of the implication graph by encoding the colors locally at the nodes using only bit slices of a full machine word. Thus, subtrees of the AND-OR tree are stored in parallel in different bit-levels. Additionally, a bit-parallel version of the implication algorithm introduced in Sec. 3.3 is used. Our algorithm supports a depth of r levels in the AND-OR tree on a 2^r-bit architecture. On a DECAlphaStation, for example, a maximal depth of 6 levels is available.

Let us briefly summarize the advantages of our approach:

(1) The implication graph model allows the full word size to be exploited by means of bit-parallel techniques. The search for indirect implications, requires efficient set operations as an OR-node may only be elevated if it is a successor of both AND-nodes belonging to an unjustified clause. These set operations are carried out effectively on the implication graph by performing local bit-operations at signal nodes such that no separate data structure is needed. Please note, that the advantage of efficient set operations remains, if we extend our algorithm to handle arbitrary depths of AND-OR enumeration, which has already been done.

(2) The notion of unjustified gates necessary in [3, 7] reduces to the simple concept of unjustified ternary clauses. Due to this concept and the uniformity of our description, AND-OR enumeration can easily be performed for arbitrary logics applying the same procedure. This has already been done for logic $\mathcal{L}_{10}$. On the contrary, higher valued logics are complicated to deal with in the structural approach of [7, 3].

(3) Detected indirect implications can be included into the graph immediately, which often facilitates the computation of other indirect implications.

(4) Some indirect implications are easily computed by the law of contraposition while requiring a high depth of AND-OR search. As our approach integrates both methods into one framework, indirect implications can be identified by the best suited technique.

5 Experimental results

The implication engine, presented in this paper, has been implemented in a C language library of functions that has been applied successfully to several CAD problems. Please note, that some of

[3] If a binary clause is unjustified according to Definition 2, it reduces to a unary clause. Unary clauses represent necessary assignments (implied signal values) for the given signal assignment.

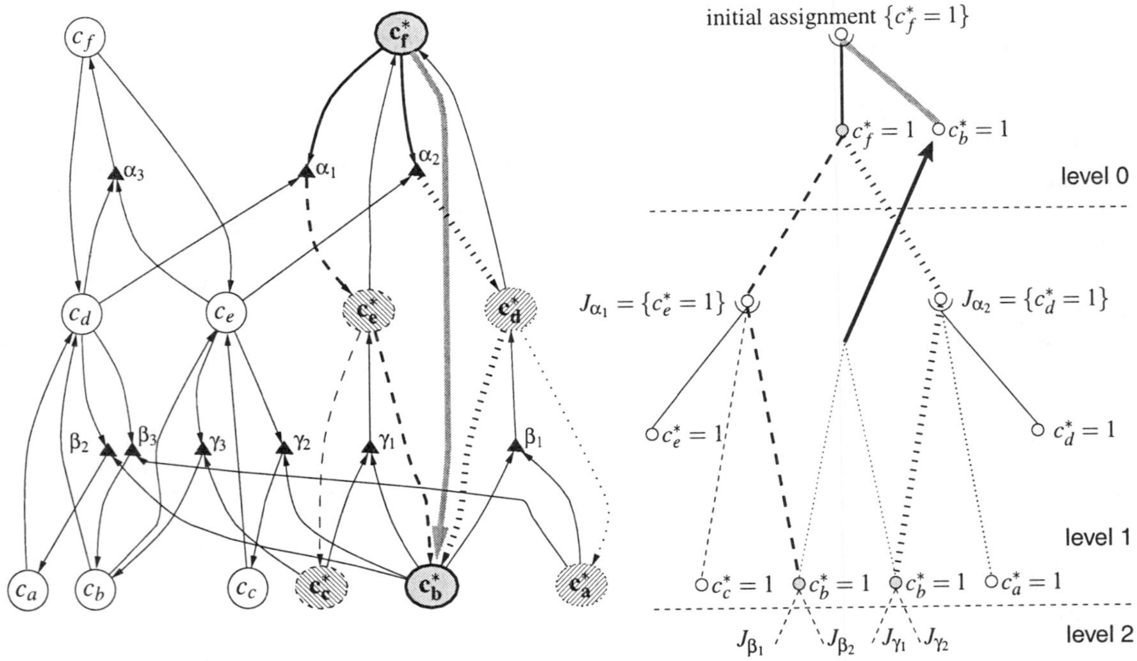

Figure 7: Extended reconvergence analysis on the implication graph

the presented results have already been published in papers dealing with application specific issues. The underlying implication engine was not discussed. We have included these results in order to show the efficiency of our flexible approach. While the experiments for ATPG and netlist optimization were carried out on a DECStation3000/600, the experiments for equivalence checking were performed on a DECAlphaStation250$^{4/266}$. ATPG and netlist optimization rely on an earlier version of our implication engine, that does not support the techniques of Sec. 4.4.2. So far, these advanced techniques have only been used for equivalence checking.

Table 3 presents results for ATPG considering various fault models [25, 26, 27]. Due to the flexibility of the implication graph

circuit	non–robust		robust		stuck–at	
	# tested	time [s]	# tested	time [s]	# tested	time [s]
c432	15855	9.6	3730	31.9	520	0.2
c499	367744	112.5	133557	17242.4	750	0.1
c2670	130626	53.9	15370	60.3	2630	1.0
c3540	1202580	6032.3	88354	10595.7	3291	2.4
c5315	342117	643.4	81435	5251.8	5291	1.2
s5378	21928	11.2	18656	43.6	4397	1.3
c6288	30688133	61832.2	26254	31225.4	7710	0.6
c7552	277244	1499.4	86252	5746.0	7419	5.2
s9234	59854	50.6	21389	153.4	6475	18.2
s13207	476145	1364.4	27603	848.5	9608	15.6
s15850	10782994	21320.7	182673	2221.8	11330	9.0
s38417	1138194	2385.6	598062	13001.5	30859	68.6
s38584	334927	2004.1	92239	2071.5	34493	88.7

Table 3: Result of test pattern generation

the various logics ($\mathcal{L}_3, \mathcal{L}_9, \mathcal{L}_{10}, \mathcal{L}_{20}$) required for the different fault models could easily be handled. Table 3 gives the number of tested faults and CPU time required for performing ATPG for non-robust and robust path delay faults as well as stuck-at faults in combinational circuits (or sequential circuits with enhanced scan design). The excellent quality of the achieved results can be seen from further tables in [25, 26, 27] where an extensive comparison to other state-of-the-art tools is made.

circuit	# gates		# literals		delay		time
	before	after	before	after	before	after	[s]
c432	150	140	318	302	29.9	26.4	238
c499	370	352	920	772	23.4	19.0	2416
c1355	370	352	920	772	23.4	19.0	2400
c880	337	289	722	650	50.6	41.0	658
c1908	488	402	933	803	41.2	33.9	1364
c5315	1576	1374	3249	2790	37.3	31.0	16288
c6288	3148	3009	5357	5923	117.7	92.3	60083
Σ:	6439	5918	12419	12012	323.5	262.6	-
red.:		8.1%		3.2%		18.8%	-

Table 4: Results of delay optimization

Results for optimization of mapped netlists with respect to delay are provided in Table 4. The basic idea and the approach, that applies our implication engine to verify the permissibility of circuit transformations, is described in [6]. The number of gates, literals, and the circuit delay before and after optimization, as well as the required CPU time are given.

Results for equivalence checking of netlists are presented in Table 5. It lists the total time required for equivalence checking, i.e.

circuit	time[s]		level_{max}
	total	indirect implications	
c432	1.3	1.2	1
c499	1.4	1.4	1
c1355	7.0	6.6	1
c1908	19.5	18.9	1
c2670	24.1	20.7	2
c3540	791.0	742.1	2
c5315	33.4	24.8	2
c6288	8.9s	4.4s	1
c7552	570.1	525.0	3

Table 5: Results for verifying against redundancy free circuits

ATPG plus computation of indirect implications, and the time consumed by the latter in columns 2 and 3, respectively. The maximal depth of AND-OR search necessary for successful verification is also given in column 4. We provide these early results in order to show that our implication engine forms a suitable data structure for building an efficient equivalence checker. Our straightforward approach adopts the basic idea of the well-known equivalence checker HANNIBAL [28] but does not include its advanced heuristics, e.g. observability implications and heuristics for candidate selection. Nevertheless, the results shown in Table 5 are comparable to the ones reported in [28]. This indicates that our implication engine is well suited for equivalence checking. Please note, that it is easily incorporated into state-of-the-art implication based or hybrid, i.e. BDDs combined with implications, equivalence checkers such that these approaches can benefit, too.

6 Conclusion

In this paper we have proposed an efficient implication engine working on a flexible data structure called implication graph. It has been shown that indirect implications can be effectively computed by analysis of the graph. Experimental results confirm the efficiency and flexibility of our approach.

In the future, our preliminary equivalence checker will be extended by deriving observability implications directly on the implication graph. Furthermore, we will investigate how a hybrid technique using BDDs and the implication graph can be advantageous for equivalence checking.

Acknowledgements

The authors are very grateful to Prof. Kurt J. Antreich for many valuable discussions and his advice. They like to thank Bernhard Rohfleisch and Hannes Wittmann for using the implication engine in the netlist optimization tool and developing the path delay ATPG tool, respectively.

References

[1] W. Kunz and P. R. Menon, "Multi-level logic optimization by implication analysis," in *IEEE/ACM International Conference on Computer-Aided Design (ICCAD)*, pp. 6–13, November 1994.

[2] M. Chatterjee, D. K. Pradhan, and W. Kunz, "LOT: Logic optimization with testability - new transformations using recursive learning," in *IEEE/ACM International Conference on Computer-Aided Design (ICCAD)*, pp. 318–325, November 1995.

[3] D. Stoffel, W. Kunz, and S. Gerber, "And/or reasoning graphs for determining prime implicants in multi-level combinational networks," in *Asia and South Pacific Design Automation Conference*, pp. 529–538, January 1997.

[4] L. A. Entrena and K.-T. Cheng, "Combinational and sequential logic optimization by redundancy addition and removal," *IEEE Transactions on Computer-Aided Design of Integrated Circuits and Systems CAD*, vol. 14, pp. 909–916, July 1995.

[5] S.-C. Chang and M. Marek-Sadowska, "Perturb and simplify: Multi-level boolean network optimizer," in *IEEE/ACM International Conference on Computer-Aided Design (ICCAD)*, pp. 2–5, November 1994.

[6] B. Rohfleisch, B. Wurth, and K. Antreich, "Logic clause analysis for delay optimization," in *ACM/IEEE Design Automation Conference (DAC)*, pp. 668–672, June 1995.

[7] W. Kunz and D. K. Pradhan, "Recursive learning; a new implication technique for efficient solutions to cad problems — test, verification, and optimization," *IEEE Transactions on Computer-Aided Design of Integrated Circuits and Systems CAD*, vol. 13, pp. 1143–1158, September 1994.

[8] J. Jain, R. Mukherjee, and M. Fujita, "Advanced verification techniques based on learning," in *ACM/IEEE Design Automation Conference (DAC)*, pp. 420–426, June 1995.

[9] W. Kunz, D. K. Pradhan, and S. M. Reddy, "A novel framework for logic verification in a synthesis environment," *IEEE Transactions on Computer-Aided Design of Integrated Circuits and Systems CAD*, vol. 15, pp. 20–32, January 1996.

[10] D. K. Pradhan, D. Paul, and M. Chatterjee, "Verilat: Verification using logic augmentation and transformations," in *IEEE/ACM International Conference on Computer-Aided Design (ICCAD)*, pp. 88–95, November 1996.

[11] S.-Y. Huang, K.-T. Cheng, and K -C. Chen, "Aquila: An equivalence verifier for large sequential circuits," in *Asia and South Pacific Design Automation Conference*, pp. 455–460, January 1997.

[12] M. H. Schulz, E. Trischler, and T. M. Sarfert, "Socrates: A highly efficient automatic test pattern generation system," *IEEE Transactions on Computer-Aided Design of Integrated Circuits and Systems CAD*, vol. 7, pp. 126–137, January 1988.

[13] M. H. Schulz and E. Auth, "Improved deterministic test pattern generation with applications to redundancy identification," *IEEE Transactions on Computer-Aided Design of Integrated Circuits and Systems CAD*, vol. 8, pp. 811–816, July 1989.

[14] W. Kunz and D. K. Pradhan, "Accelerated dynamic learning for test pattern generation in combinational circuits," *IEEE Transactions on Computer-Aided Design of Integrated Circuits and Systems CAD*, vol. 12, pp. 684–694, May 1993.

[15] R. Mukherjee, J. Jain, and D. Pradhan, "Functional learning: A new approach to learning in digital circuits," in *IEEE VLSI Test Symposium*, pp. 122–127, April 1994.

[16] J.-K. Zhao, E. M. Rudnick, and J. H. Patel, "Static logic implication with application to redundancy identification," in *IEEE VLSI Test Symposium*, pp. 288–293, 4 1997.

[17] T. Larrabee, "Test pattern generation using boolean satisfiability," *IEEE Transactions on Computer-Aided Design of Integrated Circuits and Systems CAD*, vol. 11, pp. 4–15, January 1992.

[18] P. Stephan, R. K. Brayton, and A. L. Sangiovanni-Vincentelli, "Combinational test generation using satisfiability," *IEEE Transactions on Computer-Aided Design of Integrated Circuits and Systems CAD*, vol. 15, pp. 1167–1176, September 1996.

[19] S. T. Chakradhar, V. D. Agrawal, and S. G. Rothweiler, "A transitive closure algorithm for test generation," *IEEE Transactions on Computer-Aided Design of Integrated Circuits and Systems CAD*, vol. 12, pp. 1015–1028, July 1993.

[20] J. P. M. Silva and K. A. Sakallah, "Grasp — a new search algorithm for satisfiability," in *IEEE/ACM International Conference on Computer-Aided Design (ICCAD)*, pp. 220–227, November 1996.

[21] P. Tafertshofer, A. Ganz, and M. Henftling, "A sat-based implication engine," Tech. Rep. TUM-LRE-97-2, Technical University of Munich, April 1997.

[22] M. Davis and H. Putnam, "A computing procedure for quantification theory," *Journal of the ACM*, vol. 7, pp. 201–215, 1960.

[23] E. Rich, *Artificial Intelligence*. McGraw-Hill, 1983.

[24] F. Maamari and J. Rajski, "A method of fault simulation based on stem regions," *IEEE Transactions on Computer-Aided Design of Integrated Circuits and Systems CAD*, pp. 212–220, February 1990.

[25] M. Henftling, H. Wittmann, and K. J. Antreich, "A formal non–heuristic atpg approach," in *European Design Automation Conference with EURO-VHDL (EURO-DAC)*, pp. 248–253, September 1995.

[26] M. Henftling and H. Wittmann, "Bit parallel test pattern generation for path delay faults," in *European Design and Test Conference (ED&TC)*, pp. 521–525, March 1995.

[27] H. Wittmann and M. Henftling, "Path delay atpg for standard scan designs," in *European Design Automation Conference with EURO-VHDL (EURO-DAC)*, pp. 202–207, September 1995.

[28] W. Kunz, "Hannibal: An efficent tool for logic verification based on recursive learning," in *IEEE/ACM International Conference on Computer-Aided Design (ICCAD)*, pp. 538–543, 1993.

SESSION 11A

TECHNOLOGY DRIVEN SYNTHESIS

Moderators:

K.-C. Chen, Verplex Systems, Inc., Fremont, CA

Shih-Chieh Chang, National Chung-Cheng University, Chaiayi, Taiwan

Library–Less Synthesis for Static CMOS Combinational Logic Circuits

S. Gavrilov, A. Glebov
Research Institute for VLSI CAD Systems, Russian Academy of Sciences, Moscow Russia.
S. Pullela, S. C. Moore, A. Dharchoudhury, R. Panda, G. Vijayan, D. T. Blaauw
Unified Design Systems Laboratory, Motorola, Austin.

Abstract

Traditional synthesis techniques optimize CMOS circuits in two phases i) logic minimization and ii) library mapping phase. Typically, the structures and the sizes of the gates in the library are chosen to yield a good synthesis results over many blocks or even for an entire chip. Consequently, this approach precludes an optimal design of individual blocks which may need custom structures. In this paper we present a new transistor level technique that optimizes CMOS circuits both structurally and size-wise. Our technique is independent of a library and hence can explore a design space much larger than that possible due to gate level optimization. Results demonstrate a significant improvement in circuit performance of our resynthesized circuits.

1. Introduction

CMOS circuit optimization can be performed at various levels of design description [1]. At the lower end of the design process, synthesis tools typically perform optimization at the gate level and operate in two phases. The technology-independent phase performs manipulation of boolean functions, which can be represented by logic equations or BDD networks of simple logic gates [2-5]. The technology-dependent phase subsequently maps the boolean functions into a target library—typically consisting of a few hundred logic gates [4, 6] designed and fixed apriori, to yield desirable area-performance tradeoffs across multiple blocks and sometimes across multiple chips. Consequently, the circuit structures are forced to stay within the predetermined library precluding an optimal solution that effectively utilizes the total design space of transistor structures. Custom design circuits to some extent alleviate this problem, however, there are no known techniques for automatic synthesis of custom logic.

It is apparent that the finer the granularity of the logic structures available for optimization, the greater is the quality of solution obtained in terms of area, power, and performance. In this regard, optimization of logic circuits at the transistor level, as opposed to gate level yields a better solution, since a much larger design space is explored. In addition, a transistor level approach would permit the use of significantly more accurate models for power, area, and delay, thereby increasing the scope of agreement with simulation results. However, state-of-the-art transistor level optimization techniques are limited to simple reordering of the transistor chains [6] and to transistor sizing.

In this paper, we propose a new approach which operates on a synthesized circuit and performs a transistor level logic optimization by transistor level restructuring. Consequently, we extend the design space beyond the traditional limits set by cell libraries. In addition, we also consider sizing of the individual transistors during structural optimization This ensures that the performance of a given structure is optimal at the given area of interest. We refer to our technique as transistor level resynthesis or simply resynthesis. The output of resynthesis is an area-delay trade-off curve shown in Figure 1. Each point on this curve represents a solution which is structurally as well size-wise optimized for circuit delay. While the smooth continuous parts represent transistor level circuit sizing with a fixed topology, the discontinuities result due to the timing improvements from restructuring.

2. Overview of Resynthesis

As one can observe, the number of transistors is extremely large if the whole circuit must be considered for sizing and restructuring simultaneously. Therefore, resynthesis breaks the circuit into smaller segments of logic which we refer to as *windows*. Typically, each window contains up to 50 transistors or approximately 10-20 gates. For each window, a large number of functionally equivalent, transistor level structures are generated using a simulated annealing method. These windows differ both in how the overall logic is implemented in terms of individual gates as well as the structure of the gate. Each window is also sized with a fast approximate sizing algorithm to match the size of the original window. We refer to this process as local resynthesis and it is described in more detail in section 4.2. Internally, local resynthesis evaluates all new windows relative to the original timing constraints of the window. The best window is inserted back in the circuit at minimum size. The overall circuit is then evaluated for relative merit after sizing the circuit back to the original area. (the dotted curves in Figure 1 show the resizing with new window). The best window in terms of timing is preserved after every iteration while

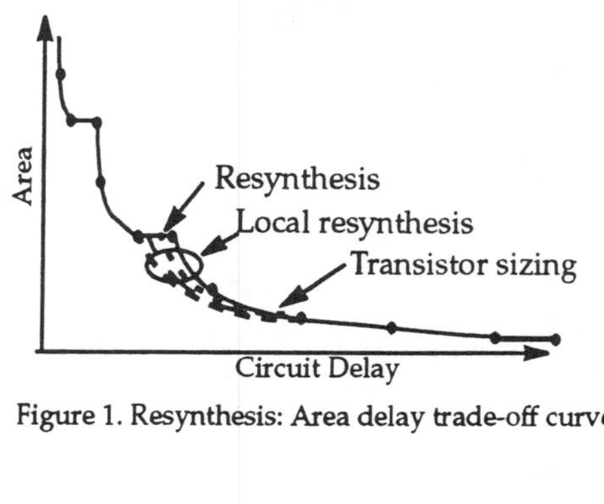

Figure 1. Resynthesis: Area delay trade-off curve.

1092-3152/97 $10.00 © 1997 IEEE

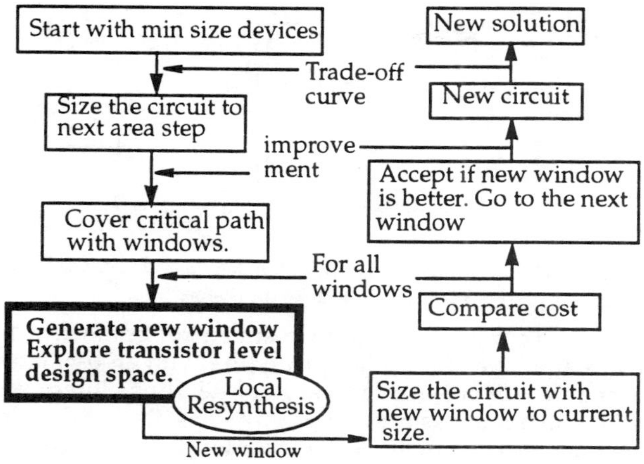

Figure 2. Resynthesis Flow.

the rest are discarded. For efficiency only the critical path in the circuit is covered with windows and each window is evaluated for improvement in timing. This step is repeated till no further improvement is possible at this size. Subsequently the whole circuit is sized to a predetermined percentage, and the above procedure is repeated. Figure 2 shows the basic steps involved in resynthesis.

As one can observe, to operate on an equivalent design space, a library based synthesis approach will need an enormously large number of cells in the library, in order to cover the functionality, power, and delay characteristics provided by the transistor level design space. The layout for the resynthesized windows is generated using a proprietary layout tool [12].

The local resynthesis step indicated in Figure 2 forms the core of the structural optimization technique and is discussed in Section 4. Section 3 briefly describes circuit and logic models used in the remainder of the paper. In section 5 we analyze the design space covered by local resynthesis and demonstrate that this is much larger compared to a typical cell-based synthesis. Section 6 shows some experimental results.

3. CMOS Logic and Circuit Models

3.1 Logic Representation

The SP-BDD [8] representation is an efficient means of capturing the logic functionality and the structure of static CMOS gates whose pull-up and pull-down structures are complementary series-parallel networks. In the remainder of this paper, we limit our focus to series-parallel CMOS structures. Figure 3 shows an example of CMOS gate and its gate-BDD. Each vertex of the gate-BDD corresponds to a gate input and a pair of transistors (one in pull-up and one in pull-down). A combinational circuit composed of CMOS gates may be represented as an ordered network of gate-BDDs.

3.2 Power and delay model

Since the SP-BDD captures the structural information of the gate, the delay and the power can be calculated directly from the SP-BDD representation. The SP-BDD representation allows the use of accurate transistor level models at gate level efficiency. The transistor level power model used in resynthesis is described in [9]. The delay of the gate is estimated using a proprietary semi-analytical piece-wise quadratic approximation of the MOS characteristics [11] for circuit timing during global resynthesis. During the local resynthesis however, since we need to evaluate only the relative merit of the windows, we use the well known Elmore delay model to evaluate the gate delay.

4. Resynthesis

4.1 Global Resynthesis

The overall global resynthesis flow is shown in Figure 2. As described inSection 2, global resynthesis is based on covering the entire circuit with a sequence of windows and performing detailed local resynthesis on each window. When comparing the costs of different structures for the same window, we consider timing, area and power appropriately depending upon the optimization objective. Timing is performed using static timing analysis techniques.Windows are sequentially selected to minimize timing recalculations. The circuit is covered in topological order from primary inputs to primary outputs. Consequently, to calculate old and new time slack correctly, we need to recalculate arrival/required times before and after every local resynthesis only for those gates that fall in the cone of influence of the window.

4.2 Local Resynthesis

Local resynthesis is an optimization procedure that minimizes the cost which is a function of area, delay, power, or any convex combination of these variables for a given window. In addition, user specified constraints such as a limit on the maximum stack depth, maximum number of transistors per stage or maximum fan out can all be considered during local resynthesis by assigning appropriate penalties when a violation of these constraints occurs. Local resynthesis is a sequence of the following basic steps:

- A. DeMorgan transform changes a gate to a complementary one and adds or deletes inverters on its inputs and output.
- B. Reordering changes places of two SP-networks connected in series in either pull-up or pull-down network of a gate.
- C. Decomposition step decomposes a complex gate into two subsequent gates with an inverter between them.

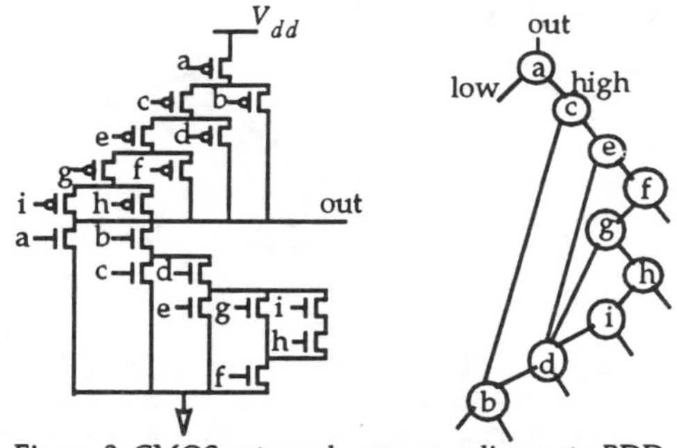

Figure 3. CMOS gate and corresponding gate-BDD.

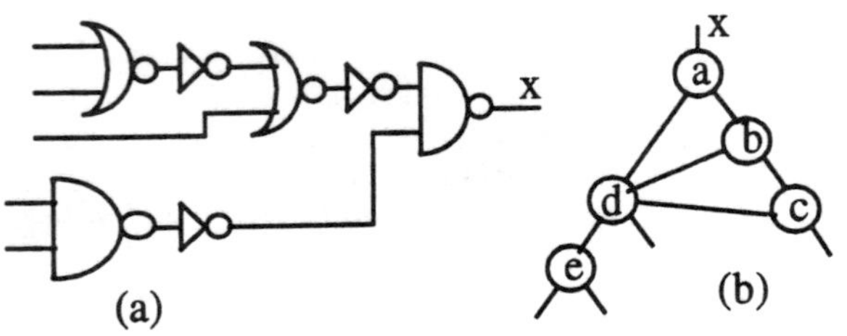

Figure 5. (a) Window state and (b). merged gate-BDD.

- D. Merging converts two subsequent gates with an inverter between them into one complex gate. If there is no inverter, then preliminary DeMorgan transform may be done for one of the two gates. The result of merging may be a gate with redundant structure. Therefore merging is followed by gate-BDD minimization.

Step A allows us to explore every possible structure of a window that can be reached by DeMorgan transforms on the given structure. This set of window structures obtained by closure under DeMorgan is referred to as a *superstate.* In addition, there are also some auxiliary steps:

- deleting double gates: deletes one of two identical gates with pairwise common inputs, this step is performed whenever possible;
- splitting a gate: inverse of deleting double gate, this step precedes merging when necessary;
- deleting buffers: deletes two subsequent inverters, this step is performed every time when possible for reducing power;
- inserting buffer: inverse of deleting buffer, this step is performed when it is necessary to reduce delay.

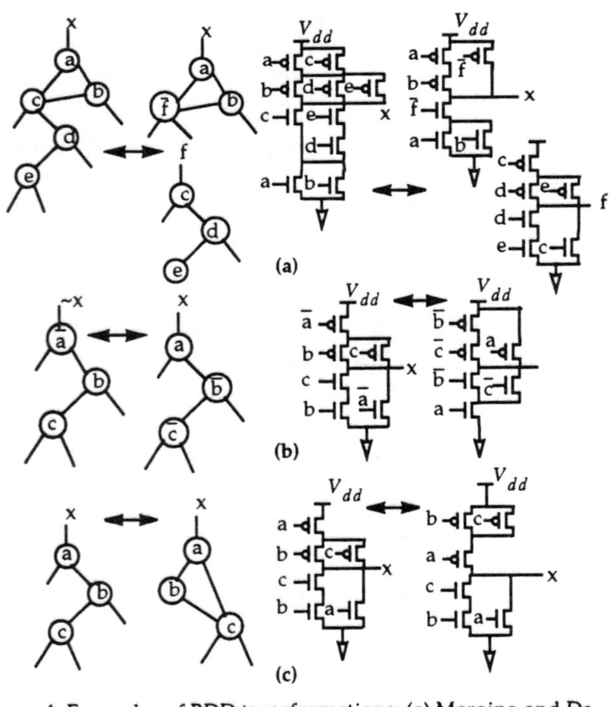

Figure 4. Examples of BDD transformations: (a) Merging and Decomposition–forward arrow indicates decomposition and the reverse arrow indicates merging. (b) DeMorgan transforms. (c) Re-ordering. Note that the re-ordering shown in (c) cannot be achieved by simple input swapping.

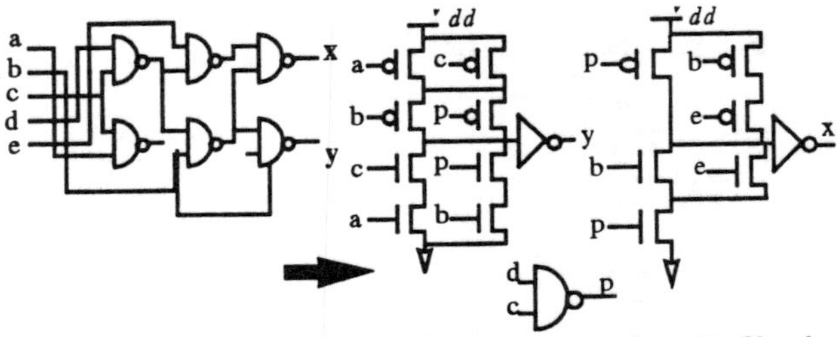

Figure 6. Initial circuit (c17) with 24 transistors and result of local resynthesis with 22 transistors.

To investigate each superstate for optimality, we use a simulated annealing procedure with an oscillating schedule [10] consisting of several iterations interposed with fully random steps and greedy steps. Every annealing step contains randomly (with proper weights) selected basic resynthesis steps (reordering, decomposition or merging) followed by a full superstate investigation and a fast sizing of the optimal structure. The best visited state during resynthesis is taken as the result of local resynthesis. The local resynthesis algorithm can be described by the following pseudo-code. The variables Dim, N_INF, and N_ZERO are calculated specifically for each window as explained in Section 5.

```
calculate Dim;
estimate N_INF and N_ZERO;
for (iter=0; iter<MAX_ITER; iter++) {
    for (i=0; i<N_INF+N_ZERO; i++) {
        select basic step type;
        select basic step object;
        make basic step;
        investigate superstate;
        fast sizing;
        if (i>=N_INF) {
            calculate cost;
            if (cost is increased)
                decline step result;
        }
    }
}
    take best solution;
```

An example of the result of local resynthesis is shown in Figure 6.

5. Design space for local resynthesis

In this section, we provide an overview of the design space explored during local resynthesis. The design space is much larger than that obtainable using library based synthesis. First we define several useful notions.

Definition 1. *A window is a connected subcircuit under local resynthesis, that is cut out from some larger circuit.*

Definition 2. *A **Superstate** is the set of window states that can be obtained from a single state by all possible DeMorgan transforms* (combined with inserting/deleting buffers).

Definition 3. *A **Merged gate-BDD** is a gate-BDD resulting from merging all structures in a window.* (For an arbitrary window we have a merged gate-BDD for every window output.) Figure 5 shows an example of a window state and the merged gate-BDD for this window. The gate-BDD is a single SP-BDD that represents the function performed by the entire window and can represent all possible circuits that are obtainable from this circuit using DeMorgan transforms.

Definition 4. *An **SP-fragment** is either a single gate-BDD vertex, or a maximal series connection of two or more SP-fragments, or a maximal parallel connection of two or more SP-fragments.*For example in Figure 5b, the single vertices (a), (b), (c) are SP-fragments and the entire gate-BDD is also an SP-fragment. The series connection of vertices (a,b) is not an SP-fragment because this series structure is not maximal.

Definition 5. *A **SP-chain** is a series or parallel connection of two or more SP-fragments.* A gate-BDD with more than one vertex consists of a hierarchy of SP-chains. For example, the gate-BDD in Figure 5 contains two SP-chains–((a,b,c),(d),(e)) - 1st (top) level of hierarchy, and ((a),(b),(c)) - 2nd level of hierarchy.

Statement 1. The number of SP-chains in a gate-BDD is equal to the number of SP-fragments with length more than one, where the length of an SP-chain is the number of vertices on the chain.

Definition 6. An *SP-interval of a SP-chain* is one or more neighboring SP-fragments of the same SP-chain (but not the whole chain). For example in Figure 5b, (a), (a,b), (a,b,c,d), (d,e) are SP-intervals, while (c,d) is not a SP-interval.

Definition 7. *A **Marking of a SP-chain** is an assignment of a mark to each SP-interval (containing at least one vertex), satisfying the condition*:

- if A, B are SP-intervals with the same mark, then either A contains B, or B contains A, or A and B are non-intersecting.

Definition 8. A *Marking on gate-BDD* is a set of markings of all its SP-chains.

Statement 2. There is a bi-jection between all possible markings on a merged gate-BDD and all possible window superstates that can be obtained from the merged gate-BDD by decomposition steps.

The decomposition step of a gate-BDD discussed in section 4.2 is performed by replacing any SP-interval of the gate-BDD by a single new vertex. This removed SP-interval is a separate gate-BDD and connects the two gate-BDD's through an inverter. Thus the original gate-BDD is decomposed into three gate-BDD's (an inverter and two other gate-BDD's). This decomposition process can be repeated to obtain other structures from the original gate-BDD. For example, the circuit in the window state shown in Figure 5a can be obtained by first decomposing the SP-intervals (a,b,c) and (d,e) from the gate-BDD, and then further decomposing the sub SP-interval (a,b) from (a,b,c).

Statement 2 above indicates that the number of structures reachable from a window state structure is equal to the number of ways of marking a merged gate-BDD. Clearly, the number of markings is exponential resulting in an exponential solution space.

Again, we can shown that the reordering step in section 4.2 yields an exponential solution space. For a merged gate-BDD, for every SP-chain we can take all possible permutations of its SP-fragments. It is easy to show that permutations in any two SP-chains commute. It is also easy to show that for arbitrary window superstate there is an injection from the set of possible reordering to the set of reordering on a merged gate-BDD. Thus, a large number of new structures are also explored through reordering.

The design space for local resynthesis in terms of superstates can be represented by a Cartesian product of ***Dim=m+n*** one-dimensional subspaces, where ***m*** is the number of reordering subspaces and ***n*** is the number of merging/decomposition subspaces. For the example of Figure 5 we have ***Dim=2+2=4***. Finally, it should be noted that we use the following simple motivation for the simulated annealing procedure under use. Supposing that the design space consists of identical ***Dim***-dimensional cubes with local minimum of cost function inside each cube. By maximizing the expected number of cubes of finite length visited during annealing, we get the oscillating schedule as the optimal temperature schedule, with the following parameters for the local resynthesis algorithm:

*N_INF = Kinf * sqrt(Dim), N_ZERO = Kzero * Dim,* where

Kinf, Kzero are empirical constants (nearly equal to 1–2).

6. Results

A prototype version of the resynthesis algorithm described above was implemented on a UNIX workstation. In this version the timing control and also some additional constraints (maximal gate size, maximal pull-up/pull-down path length, maximal fanout, etc.) can be switched on/off.

Figure 7 shows the area delay trade-off curve generated by resynthesis on a logic circuit consisting of about 120 gates (~ 500 transistors). The graph shows the point that corresponds to a solution generated by a commercial synthesis tool with settings to yield the maximum performance using a well designed fine grain library. The library consisted of a total of 150 cells with 4-5 strengths for each type of logic gate. Curve 1 in the graph is the area vs. delay trade-off of the same circuit generated using an optimal sensitivity based sizing algorithm with very accurate delay models. Typically on a critical path our delay model incurs no more 5% error on a gate-by-gate basis. Note that this sizing method produced solutions with about 15% improvement in timing for the same area or a 25% improvement in area for the same timing over the cell-based solution. This is not surprising since the sensitivity based method has the freedom to vary the sizes of every transistor in the circuit.

In the same graph, curve 2 demonstrates the gains due to resynthesis. Resynthesis is run on the same cell-based solution as before. Note that there is a significant improve-

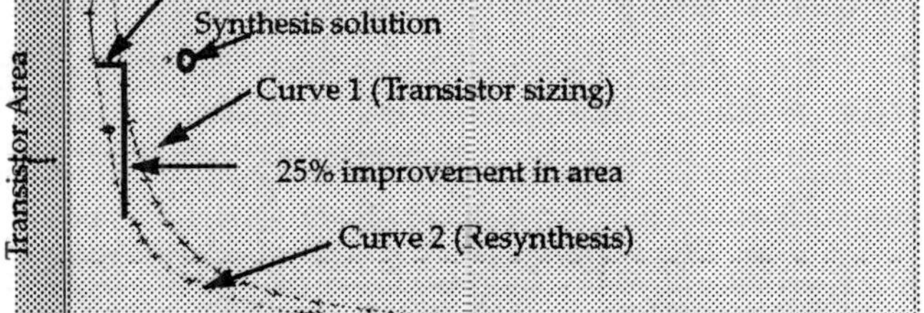

Figure 7. Results of resynthesis on a proprietary high performance circuit.

ment in area/performance of the resynthesized solutions even over the custom sized circuit. A 15% improvement is observed in timing at the same area while a 25% improvement is achieved in area at the same timing over transistor level sizing. Overall our technique improved the timing by 20% at the same transistor area and the area by about 37% for the same timing. We must also mention that there was about 20% reduction in the total number of transistors at the minimum area point. As we would expect once the circuit was sized up the original area point, total gain in transistor count fell to 5% due to addition of buffers for drive strength and implementation using smaller gates. The run time for this example was approximately 1hr for generating the entire curve on a Sparc-station 20 with 64 Mb of RAM.

Figure 8 shows the same results for a decoder circuit. This circuit has about 600 gates (2500 transistors) original synthesis was performed with a 400 cell library of which include a combination of nand gates, nor gates, and an extensive set of aoi's (and-or-invert) and oai's. Resynthesis yielded about 20% improvement in timing at the same area point and a 35% improvement in area at the same time point for this example over a cell-based design.This example took about 8hrs for the complete curve on the same machine.

Table 1 demonstrates the trade-off of performance and power obtained on 6 circuits. In this experiment we compare the inherent power-delay trade-off between a circuit obtained by library based synthesis and the corresponding circuit resynthesized for power. We select one solution from the area-delay trade-off space, and resize it to obtain the power-delay trade-off information for several delay constraints. Each of the sub columns show the different delay and power trade-offs for that circuit. In addition the rows 5 and 6 show the reduction in the number of transistors for each circuit. Observe that for the same delay, the resynthesized circuit consumes much less power than the original circuit from logic synthesis. Runtimes shown in the last column for generating the local curves were also reasonable as shown in the last row.

Figure 8. Resynthesis: Second example.

7. Conclusion

We have presented a new method to synthesize custom logic circuits. This technique could successfully improve the area-delay characteristics of the synthesized circuits. An analysis of the structural design space explored by this method is presented. Results show that transistor level resynthesis can yield performance improvements up to 20% with smaller transistor count and better power characteristics. In addition, results indicate that the overall delay-area characteristics of the circuits synthesized at transistor level are superior compared to circuits synthesized at gate level.

References

[1] S.Devadas, S.Malik. "A Survey of Optimization Techniques Targeting Low Power VLSI Circuits," DAC-95, p.242.

[2] S.Iman, M.Pedram. "Logic Extraction and Factorization for Low Power," DAC-95, p.248.

[3] R.E.Bryant. "Graph-Based Algorithms for Boolean Function Manipulation," IEEE Trans on Computers, 1986, v.35, n.8, p.677.

[4] C.Y.Tsui, M.Pedram, A.M.Despain. "Technology Decomposition and Mapping Targeting Low Power Dissipation," DAC-93, p.68.

[5] J.P.Fishburn. "A Depth-Decreasing Heuristic for Combinational Logic; or How to Convert a Ripple-Carry Adder into a Carry-Look ahead Adder or Anything In-Between," DAC-90, p.361.

[6] V.Tiwari, P.Ashar, S.Malik. "Technology Mapping for Low Power," DAC-93, p.74.

[7] B.S.Carlson, S.J.Lee. "Delay Optimization of Digital CMOS VLSI Circuits by Transistor Reordering," IEEE Trans. on CAD, 1995, v.14, n.10, p.1183.

[8] A.L.Glebov, D.Blaauw, L.G.Jones. "Transistor Reordering for Low Power CMOS Gates Using SP-BDD Representation," Intern. Symp. on Low Power Design, 1995, p.161.

[9] S.Gavrilov, A.Glebov, S.Rusakov, D.Blaauw, L.Jones, G.Vijayan. "Fast Power Loss Calculation for Digital Static CMOS Circuits," European Design & Test Conf., 1997, p.411.

[10] K.D.Boese, A.B.Kahng, C.W.A.Tsao. "Best-So-Far vs. Where-You-Are: New Perspectives on Simulated Annealing for CAD," Euro-DAC'93, p.78.

[11] A. Dharchoudhury, S. M. Kang, K. H. Kim, and S. H. Lee, "Fast and Accurate Timing Simulation with Regionwise Quadratic Models for MOS," Int'l Conf on Computer Aided Design, Nov 1994, p. 190.

[12] Mohan Guruswamy, Robert L. Maziasz, Daniel Dulitz, Srilata Raman, Venkat Chiluvuri, Andrea Fernandez, and Larry G. Jones, "CELLERITY: A Fully Automatic Layout Synthesis System for Standard Cell Libraries," Design Automation Conf, Jun 1997, p. 327.

Table 1: Results of Resynthesis

Ckt	c1355			c1908			cla			cla1			cnt_0			cnt_1		
Constraint(ns)	27.46	21.99	17.77	32.34	24.86	23.13	22.97	14.70	10.21	24.57	15.73	10.7	24.01	15.37	11.86	23.76	15.15	11.49
P(nW) Before	592	629	698	640	654	717	367	378	471	358	370	494	85	93	138	81	88	137
P(nW) After	438	463	502	437	455	526	349	362	446	343	355	486	80	88	125	73	83	117
# trans (before)	2308			3482			1008			956			352			372		
# trans (after)	1904			1690			820			838			298			294		
Run Time (s)	500			639			181			198			95			71		

Logic Synthesis for Large Pass Transistor Circuits

Premal Buch Amit Narayan A. Richard Newton A. Sangiovanni-Vincentelli

Department of Electrical Engineering & Computer Sciences
University of California, Berkeley, CA 94720

Abstract

Pass transistor logic (PTL) can be a promising alternative to static CMOS for deep sub-micron design. In this work, we motivate the need for CAD algorithms for PTL circuit design and propose decomposed BDDs as a suitable logic level representation for synthesis of PTL networks. Decomposed BDDs can represent large, arbitrary functions as a multi-stage circuit and can exploit the natural, efficient mapping of a BDD to PTL.

A comprehensive synthesis flow based on decomposed BDDs is outlined for PTL design. We show that the proposed approach allows us to make logic-level optimizations similar to the traditional multi-level network based synthesis flow for static CMOS, and also makes possible optimizations with a direct impact on area, delay and power of the final circuit implementation which do not have any equivalent in the traditional approach. We also present a set of heuristical algorithms to synthesize PTL circuits optimized for area, delay and power which are key to the proposed synthesis flow.

Experimental results on ISCAS benchmark circuits show that our technique yields PTL circuits with substantial improvements over static CMOS designs. In addition, to the best of our knowledge this is the first time PTL circuits have been synthesized for the entire ISCAS benchmark set.

1 Introduction

Static CMOS has long been the design style of choice for IC designers due to the ease of designing safe, scalable circuits. However, switching capacitances in a static CMOS circuit can be fairly large. With the shrinking feature sizes and increasing transistor counts on chips, the push for higher speed and lower power makes it necessary to look for alternative design styles which can offer better performance characteristics to static CMOS. These include pass-transistor-based logic families, domino-like dynamic logic styles etc.

Among these, pass transistor logic (PTL) circuits offer great promise. Compared to domino circuits, they are less susceptible to crosstalk problems, which is a major issue in deep sub-micron technology. Several case studies ([4][21]) have shown that PTL can implement most functions with fewer transistors than static CMOS. This reduces the overall capacitance, resulting in faster switching times and lower power. It was reported in [21] that a complementary PTL multiplier was twice as fast as conventional CMOS due to lower input capacitance and higher logic functionality. At a supply voltage of 4V, PTL designs typically consume 30% less power than static CMOS designs ([5]). To illustrate this point, we take a function F = A'+BC'. Fig. 1(a) shows our implementation of this function in PTL and Fig. 1(b) shows the corresponding static CMOS implementation. Clearly, the PTL design style can yield a circuit which can be much more compact than static CMOS. It was reported in [22] that the PTL yielded a 32% improvement in area, 29% improvement in delay and a 47% improvement in power over a static CMOS OR/NAND-based implementation of this function.

This work was supported in part by SRC contract 97-DC324 abd by DEC

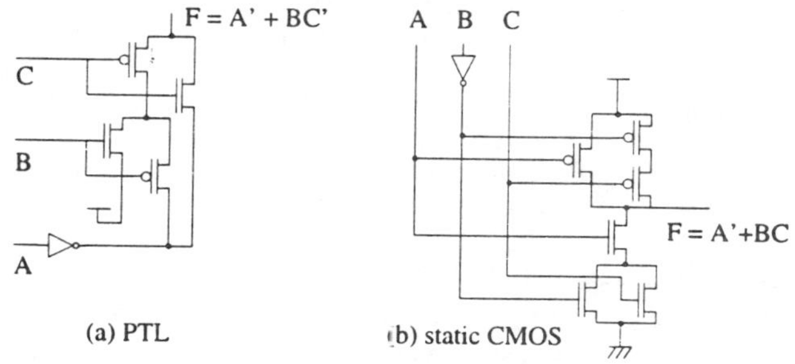

Figure 1: Comparing pass transistor and static CMOS implementations of an example function F = A'+BC'

The circuit in Fig. 1(b) can in fact, also be interpreted as a PTL circuit. The only difference between PTL and static CMOS is that in static CMOS, unlike PTL, all paths from V_{dd} to the output are connected via pMOS (the pull-up network) and paths from output to ground are connected via nMOS (pull-down network). Thus, static CMOS can be viewed as restricted case of PTL. These restrictions make the task of synthesizing safe, large static CMOS circuits easier, but reduce the potential of circuit optimization. Thus, given a methodology to synthesize safe, large circuits, PTL can be more attractive then static CMOS.

The lack of such a methodology is why the use of pass transistors in industry circuits has been very limited. While there have been several attempts in this area ([3][7][10][13][15][16][17][18][22]), limitations of some of which are discussed later in the paper, there are no algorithms which can be used to design safe, large PTL circuits. Thus, while designers can manually design very efficient small PTL circuits as in Fig. 1, a satisfactory solution to automatic synthesis of circuits realizing the expected benefits of PTL does not exist.

In this work we address this void by proposing a decomposed BDD-based approach which exploits some of the strengths of PTL logic and is scalable in that it can be used to obtain compact, multi-stage transistor-level circuits for large, arbitrary designs.

The main contribution of this work is as follows: a comprehensive synthesis flow is outlined for PTL design starting from an unoptimized logic level netlist, all the way up to generating a spice netlist. For this, a suitable logic level abstraction based on decomposed BDDs is proposed which allows us to make logic level optimizations similar to the traditional multi-level network based synthesis flow for static CMOS. This representation takes advantage of the correspondence between PTL circuits and BDDs without suffering from the drawbacks imposed by properties of monolithic BDDs. A straightforward mapping exists from this logic level abstraction to a transistor-level PTL netlist which preserves all the interconnection information. This makes possible optimizations with a direct impact on area, delay and power of the final circuit implementation. We present a set of heuristical algo-

1092-3152/97 $10.00

rithms to synthesize PTL circuits optimized for area, delay and power which are key to the proposed synthesis flow. Initial experimental results on ISCAS benchmark circuits show that our technique yields PTL circuits with substantial improvements over conventional static CMOS designs. To the best of our knowledge this is the first time PTL circuits have been synthesized for the entire ISCAS benchmark sets.

This paper is structured as follows: in Section 2, we argue why a BDD-based approach is suitable for PTL circuit synthesis and review the shortcomings of monolithic BDD-based approaches. In Section 3 we motivate decomposed BDDs as a suitable logic level abstraction for PTL synthesis. Section 4 compares the proposed decomposed BDD-based synthesis flow and the traditional approach for static CMOS. Section 5 presents decomposition techniques to obtain PTL circuits optimized for area, delay and power. Section 6 presents the experimental results. Section 7 outlines issues for future research and Section 8 concludes with a summary of this work.

2 PTL Networks and BDDs

One of the main strengths of static CMOS designs is that they are guaranteed to not have a steady-state sneak path connecting a node to both power supply and ground at the same time under some input combination. From Section 1, PTL admits more general circuit structures than static CMOS. However, it suffers from the drawback that there is no guarantee on the absence of sneak paths in the circuit. Hence, special care needs to be taken to ensure that the circuit is sneak path-free. For example, the PTL circuit in Fig. 2 requires only three transistors to implement the example function from Fig. 1. However, this circuit has a sneak path as shown, forcing the output to be connected to both ground and power supply at the same time when A=1, B=0, C=0. We therefore need a methodology to synthesize PTL circuits which ensure the absence of such sneak paths.

The basic unit in PTL is a MOS transistor which is used as a switch. When the control signal at the MOS gate is enabled, the input (drain/source) is connected to the output (source/drain). The output is in a high impedance state when the control signal is disabled. This switching characteristic of the MOS makes it very easy to implement a multiplexer in PTL as a wired OR of transistors.

A 2-input multiplexer implements the same functionality as a BDD node, with the BDD node variable corresponding to the control signal of the multiplexer and the outgoing and incoming branches of the BDD node corresponding to the inputs and output of the multiplexer respectively. Fig. 3 shows two different ways of implementing a BDD node using two MOS transistors.

Thus, the BDD representation of the target function can be very easily mapped to a multiplexer network, which in turn can be implemented compactly using pass transistors. This provides a way to construct efficient PTL circuits [15]. In fact, the PTL implementation in Fig. 1(a) corresponds to the BDD of F, as shown in Fig. 4.

The main advantage of such a BDD-based approach is that it always gives correct, sneak-path-free circuits, since at a time, only one path connecting the ground/power supply to the output is active. Using the two different implementations of a BDD node from Fig. 3 yields the two circuits shown in Fig. 5(a)and 5(b), both smaller than the static CMOS implementation in Fig. 5(c). Note that the nMOS-only implementation in Fig. 5(b) uses more transistors than the implementation in Fig. 5(a) because it needs

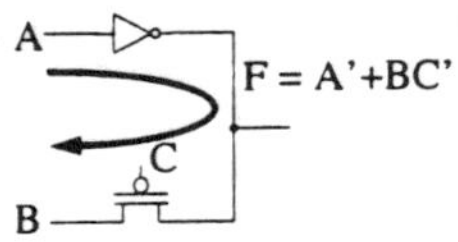

Figure 2: A PTL circuit with a sneak path

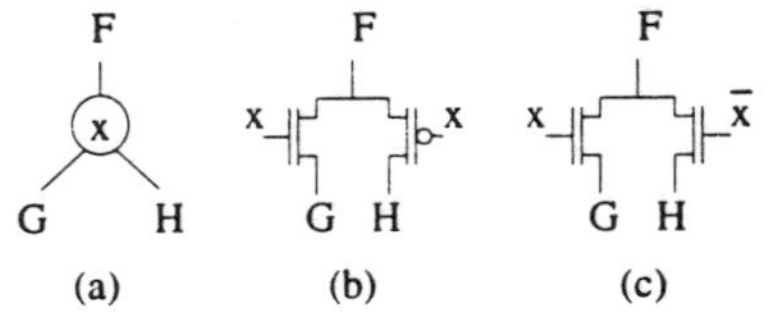

Figure 3: Implementing a BDD node in PTL

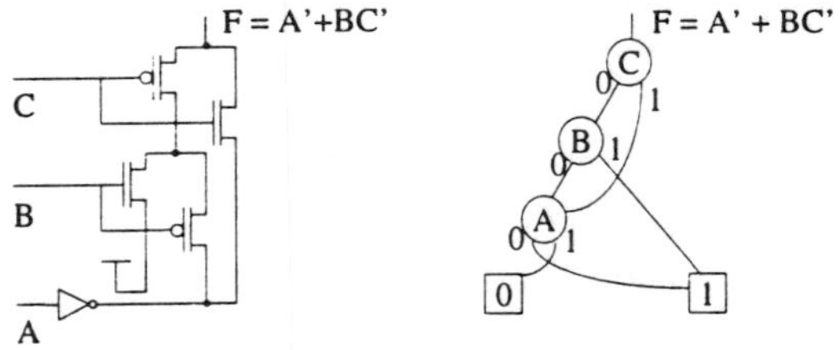

Figure 4: Comparing pass transistor implementations of the example function of Fig. 1 with its BDD

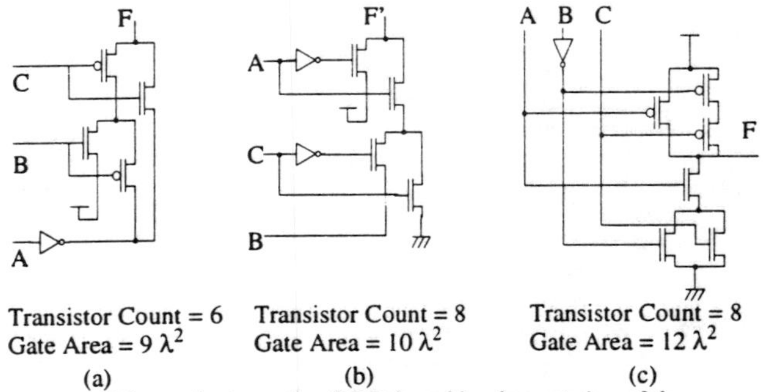

Figure 5: alternative BDD-based implementation of the example function from Fig. 1 (F = A'+BC')

signal and $\overline{\text{signal}}$ for each BDD node. However, it is quite competitive in terms of gate area. This is due to the fact that to obtain a similar current drive, pMOS has to be twice as big as nMOS in terms of the gate size (a minimum size pMOS has dimensions $3\lambda \times \lambda$ while a minimum size nMOS is $1.5\lambda \times \lambda$). This results in higher active gate area per transistor in the case of static CMOS and a pMOS/nMOS PTL. Also, in a pMOS/nMOS PTL, a pMOS can be in a path propagating a "1" and an nMOS can be in a path propagating "0", resulting in output levels of V_t and V_{dd}-V_t for "0" and "1" respectively. In comparison, in the nMOS-only case, the voltage is V_{dd}-V_t for output "1", and 0V for output "0" since nMOS are good conductors of "0".

This has three advantages:

- Each nMOS is at a better operating point when propagating "0" and has a higher drive, resulting in a faster circuit.
- The output has a better noise margin, which can be particularly important if it is driving MOS gates (of buffers or subsequent stages).
- Apart from the savings in active gate area, the smaller size of nMOS also means a lower gate capacitance. This results in a lower switching capacitance for the circuit making it faster and also reducing its power dissipation.

In fact, for large circuits, we found that the overhead of generating $\overline{\text{signal}}$ was quite small (in most cases, particularly in case of large circuits, $\overline{\text{signal}}$ was required in the circuit anyway as $\overline{A}$ is in Fig. 5(a)), and the gate area savings and performance gains more than offset this. For this reason, we have used the nMOS-only implementation of Fig. 3(c) in synthesizing transistor-level circuits.

While a BDD-based PTL network can be quite compact, a naive BDD-based methodology for implementing PTL circuits suffers from the drawback that for many functions of practical interest, the size of a BDD representing the function can be exponential in the number of inputs. Also, a circuit generated from a monolithic BDD can have long chains of transistors corresponding to long paths from the root to the 0/1 terminals for the BDD. This is equivalent to implementing a single-stage static CMOS circuit and can make the circuit very slow.

A technique for generating PTL circuits in which buffers are inserted in the monolithic BDD to solve the speed problem is given in [22]. However, this approach still suffers from the BDD size problem. A multi-level pass transistor logic is introduced in [17], which tries to maximize the logic shared between different parts of the circuit by looking at the structure of a monolithic BDD. Using a monolithic BDD as the starting point and modifying its structure has two disadvantages: first, the approach will not be viable for large circuits with exponentially sized BDDs. Secondly, even when a monolithic BDD can be built, the resulting circuit is highly unoptimal in area because the optimizations are based on the topology of the BDD and not the logic implemented in it, thereby restricting the sharing to sub-graphs found in the starting monolithic BDD.

3 PTL Networks and Decomposed BDDs

We propose a synthesis approach which does not construct monolithic BDDs for the circuit at all. The common problem of the previous works outlined in Section 2 is that they try to improve a monolithic BDD-based solution. Our approach is truly multi-stage in that we always work with a multi-level representation of the PTL circuit which is similar to the traditional multi-level network for static CMOS. For such a flow, we propose decomposed BDDs as a suitable logic level abstraction of the circuit which exploits the correspondence between PTL circuits and BDDs without suffering from the drawbacks imposed by properties of monolithic BDDs which may be useful for logic level data representation but are unnecessary for circuit generation (e.g. canonicity).

The growth in the BDD size can be controlled by introducing new, intermediate variables during the construction of the BDD itself. These intermediate variables are called decomposition points and the resulting set of BDDs (BDDs of the decomposition points, and the BDD of the target function in terms of the primary inputs and decomposition points) is called a decomposed BDD [8]. An example of a decomposed BDD is shown in Fig. 6[1]. Note that the output of a decomposition point BDD can be a node variable for the BDDs of subsequently introduced decomposition points or the target function. From Section 2, this corresponds to the output of a decomposition point driving MOS gates in the circuits of subsequent decomposition points or the target function. The resulting circuit is then a multi-stage circuit with cells in any given stage being driven by the primary inputs and the outputs of preceding stages.

The intuition behind the savings in BDD size due to decomposition is as follows: in general, when constructing the graph of a function $F = G_1$ <op> G_2, the size of F, $|F|$, is $O(|G_1||G_2|)$, where $|G_1|$ and $|G_2|$ are the sizes of the input graphs. By introducing decomposition points for G_1 and G_2, the size of the decomposed BDD is reduced to $O(|G_1|+|G_2|)$. Thus, decomposition can be very useful when there is a memory explosion due to a difficult BDD manipulation during BDD construction. The trade-off here is that while monolithic ROBDDs are canonical for a given ordering, a decomposed BDD is not, since a BDD for a given function can be decomposed in many ways. This however does not pose a problem in our case, since we are interested in generating PTL circuits and not in manipulating BDD as a data structure.

1. Although a more efficient ordering for this monolithic BDD exists [4], for the given ordering this case serves to illustrate the potential BDD size reduction due to decomposition.

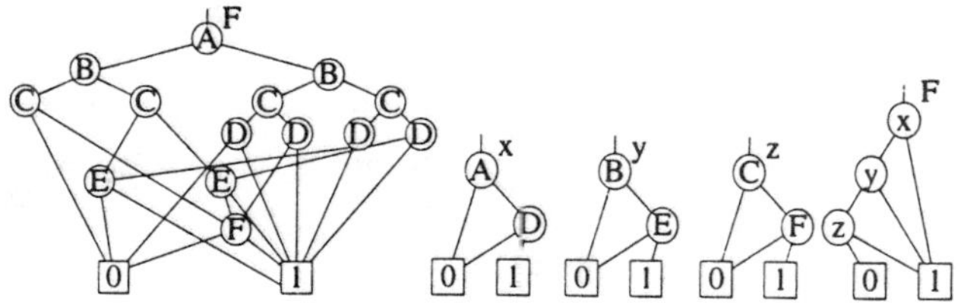

F = AD + BE + CF   x = AD, y = BE, z = CF

Figure 6: Comparing monolithic and decomposed ROBDDs

Note that our approach is orthogonal to the approach of [22] in that, decomposed BDDs can be used to obtain a compact, BDD representation of the circuit. Each individual BDD can then be optimized by the techniques presented in this work and then mapped to a transistor-level circuit with appropriate buffering using [22]. Similarly, optimization algorithms for area, delay and power presented here can be applied to BDDs generated using [17] as well. In Section 5.2, we provide some more arguments on why, from a delay perspective for large circuits, a decomposed BDD approach is better than a monolithic BDD-based approach combined with buffer insertion.

Finally, we would like to mention that the idea of introducing intermediate variables to control the size of BDDs has previously been used in [8][9] for unrelated problems. In these papers decomposition was used in a different context - In [8] decomposition was used to reduce the intermediate memory requirements during BDD construction and in [9] it was used for cycle-based simulation. In this work, we apply decomposition to construct a compact, decomposed BDD representation of the target logic function which can be directly mapped to a PTL network. The objective then is to develop decomposition techniques such that the PTL network corresponding to the resulting BDD is optimized for the desired objectives (e.g. area, speed, power).

4 A Synthesis Flow for PTL Design

Apart from proposing a decomposed BDD-based representation for PTL synthesis, a major contribution of this work is a comprehensive synthesis flow for PTL design.

Fig. 7 outlines the key steps of the traditional multi-level network based synthesis flow for static CMOS. We propose an analogous synthesis flow where a decomposed BDD is used to represent a circuit similar to the multi-level network in the traditional flow and each decomposition point BDD is manipulated similar to a complex node in the multi-level network.

A big advantage of the BDD-based PTL network design is that the one-to-one mapping between the BDD and the PTL network makes the technology mapping problem very straightforward. As a result, we can perform circuit level optimizations by manipulating the BDD. The fact that mapping preserves the circuit structure allows us to make high-level changes which can have significant impact on area, power and performance, but for which gains made at the high level hold at the circuit level as well. This addresses a big problem with the existing multi-level network based synthesis flow where technology independent

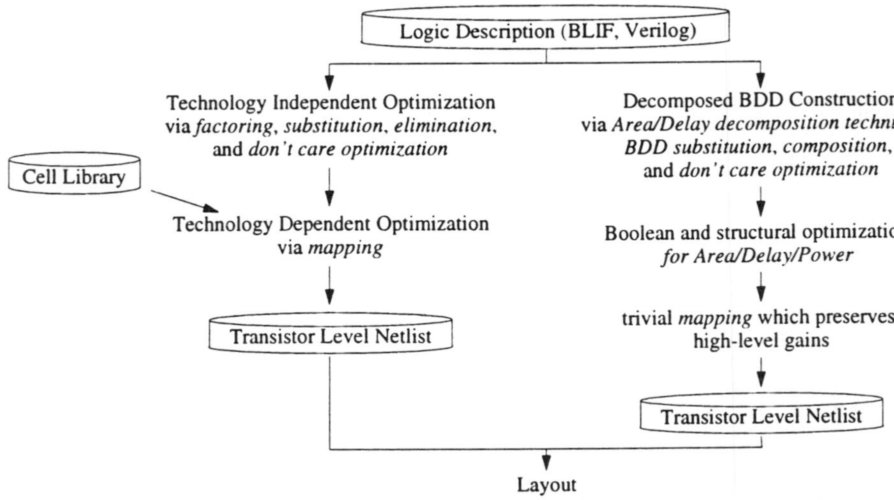

Figure 7: The traditional static CMOS synthesis flow vs. the proposed decomposed BDD synthesis flow

optimizations are becoming increasingly irrelevant with respect to the final performance of the transistor-level design because the technology mapping does not preserve the structure. This is particularly important in the context of deep sub-micron designs, where logic level optimizations need to be driven by physical issues which depend on the circuit structure and topology.

The *factoring* operation of the conventional flow aims at extracting common sub-expressions out of a function description. This is similar to selecting good decomposition points in the proposed flow. *Substitution* is similar to using a decomposition point as a BDD variable in the construction of the BDDs of subsequent decomposition points and the target function. *Elimination* is similar to composition operation on decomposition point BDDs, where a decomposition point BDD is composed into the BDDs of the rest of the circuit and the BDD node variable corresponding to the decomposition point eliminated if there is an overall saving in BDD nodes. Design optimization using don't cares can be employed in the proposed flow in a fashion very similar to the conventional flow. This is discussed in more detail in Section 7.1.

Apart from above operations which are analogous to optimization steps in the conventional synthesis flow, the decomposed BDD-based approach allows us to optimize circuits in several ways which have no equivalent in the conventional multi-level network based synthesis flow. These are outlined in Section 5.

5 Decomposition Techniques for BDD-based PTL Networks

5.1 Area Minimization

Since each node of a BDD corresponds to a PTL multiplexer cell, minimizing the area of the final circuit implementation is the same as minimizing the size of the decomposed BDD representation.

We employ a simple, greedy heuristic to control the size of the decomposed BDD by monitoring the BDD size while it is constructed. This is similar to [8]. When building the BDD depth-first from inputs to outputs, a decomposition point is introduced whenever the BDD size increases by a disproportionate amount. This attempts to avoid difficult BDD manipulations. A decomposition point is also introduced when an individual BDD grows beyond a threshold value. This ensures that none of the individual BDDs in the decomposed representation exceeds the threshold. This is particularly important in the PTL context since both resistance and capacitance increase linearly with the number of transistor in series. Thus, a very deep BDD can result in a slow circuit.

Due to the local, greedy nature of our heuristic, it is possible that the introduction of a decomposition point prevents Boolean simplification in the target function BDD. To discover some of these simplifications the decomposition points are composed back into the target function BDD as long as the overall BDD size reduces. An example of BDD size reduction by composition due to Boolean simplification is shown in Fig. 8. Since the amount of reduction is dependent on the order of composition, we experiment with several different orderings to determine a good choice.

Complementary edges can be used to reduce the size of the BDDs even further. A complementary edge introduces an inverter in the circuit, saves at least one BDD node and in the best case reduces the BDD size by half [1]. Thus, the net transistor count can only decrease. Also, these inverters provide the added benefit of restoring the signal to the rail values, thus offsetting any signal degradation due to its passage through a long pass transistor chain. Additionally, the output of decomposition points are buffered if they are connected to MOS gates of a subsequent stage.

Further, when synthesizing PTL networks from a decomposed BDD, a global variable ordering for all BDDs is not required. This provides an additional flexibility for reducing the size of each BDD by reordering them independently.

5.2 Performance

In a monolithic BDD implementation, the critical path cannot be longer than the number of input variables n and can be as low as $\log n$. Decomposition introduces extra control variables whose critical paths can be in series with the critical path of the primary outputs' BDD. Note that the critical path length of the decomposition point BDD is bounded by the number of its variables, which can be more then n if the decomposition point is expressed

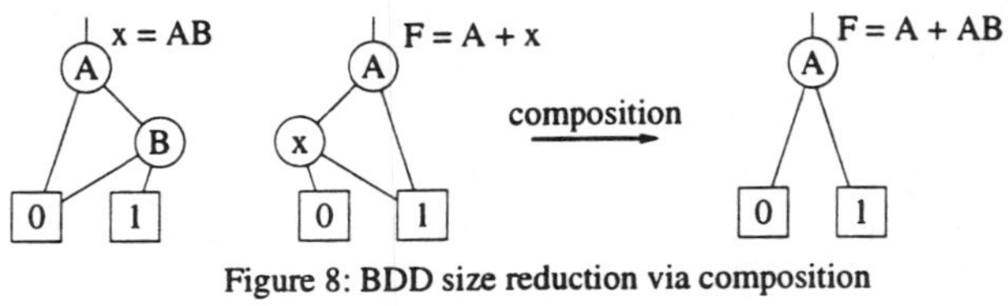

Figure 8: BDD size reduction via composition

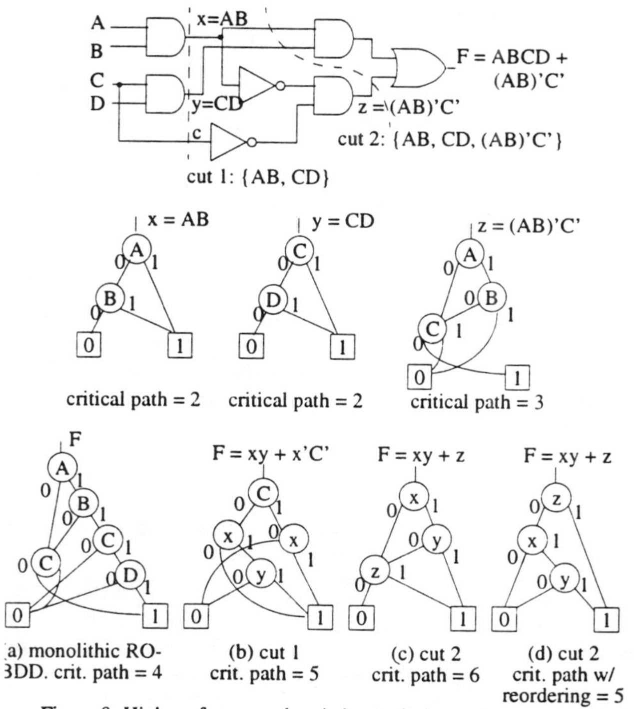

Figure 9: High performance heuristics (ordering: A,B,C,D,x,y,z)

in terms of other decomposition points. The critical path of the decomposed BDD is then bounded by *max* {critical paths of decomposition point BDDs, length of the longest path in the primary output BDDs}. Thus, the critical path length of the decomposed BDD is bounded by the critical path of the corresponding monolithic BDD. However, when circuit level issues are considered, the quadratic dependence of delay on the transistor chain length more than offsets the advantages of a shorter critical path. For today's static CMOS it is known that transistor chains longer than 3-4 transistors in series can be unacceptably slow [12]. A monolithic BDD-based circuit would require buffer insertion as in [22] for all but the smallest circuits. In comparison, a decomposed BDD-based circuit where outputs of decomposition points are buffered allows us to exploit area gains (and the associated reduction in switching capacitance) while controlling the length of unbuffered chains. Selecting decomposition points with appropriate thresholds on the depth of decomposition point BDDs is thus a more powerful strategy than selecting buffer insertion points in a monolithic BDD.

Apart from controlling the depth of decomposition point BDDs, the choice of decomposition points can be targeted at delay minimization when speed is the main concern. If a cutset[1] of the circuit is selected as the set of decomposition points, then the critical path in the BDDs of the primary outputs is bounded by the cutset cardinality (because BDDs of the primary outputs can be constructed in terms of the cutset variables only). Using the minimum cardinality cutset of the circuit as the decomposition set is then a good heuristic to reduce the critical path length. An example to illustrate this heuristic is shown in Fig. 9. Fig. 9(b) and 9(c) compare the critical path length when two different cutsets are chosen as decomposition points. The critical path is lower when the mincut is selected as the decomposition set (Fig. 9(b)) but longer than the monolithic ROBDD (Fig. 9(a)).

1. set of nodes such that all paths from primary inputs to primary outputs pass through some node in the set

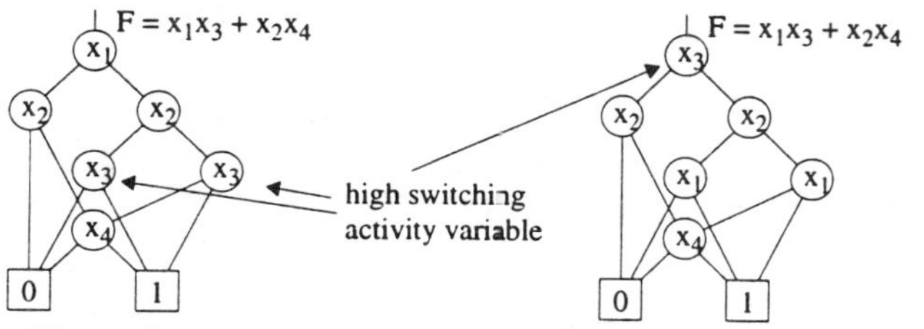

Figure 10: Reducing occurrences of high switching activity node

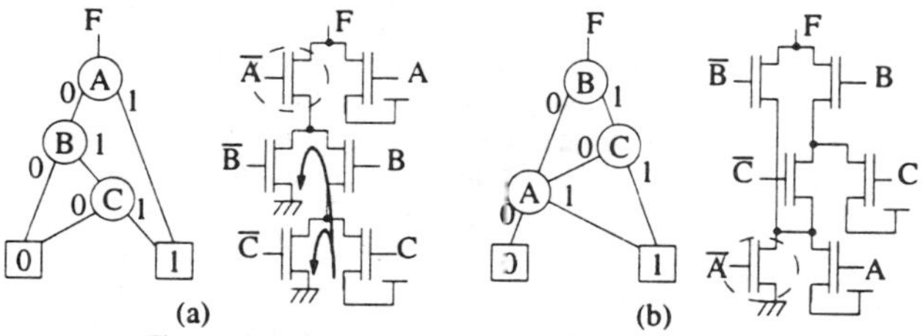

Figure 11: Low Power heuristic to minimize glitching: $F = A + BC$, $p(A=1) \approx 1 \Rightarrow p(F=1) \approx 1$

BDD variable ordering has a great impact on the BDD size and consequently the circuit area. This ordering can also influence the circuit power and speed. Placing late arriving signals closer to the outputs can speed-up the circuit by minimizing the number of transistors that need to be charged after the late signal arrives. Signal flow in a BDD-based PTL network corresponds to traversing the BDD from leaf nodes up. Thus it is advantageous to place late arriving control variables close to the top of the BDD. Variables in a BDD can be swapped pairwise as long as the resulting variable order does not cause the BDD size to increase significantly. In the example of Fig. 9, placing the late arriving signal z at the top (Fig. 9(d)) reduces the critical path by 1 unit over Fig. 9(c). The best known dynamic reordering algorithms for BDD size ([14][11]) move each variable or a block of variables throughout the order to find an optimal position for the variable. A similar reordering can be performed for delay, where the optimal position is the one resulting in the smallest depth BDD instead of the smallest sized BDD. As in Section 5.1, each decomposition point BDD can be reordered independently to optimize for total delay.

5.3 Low Power

Power dissipation in a circuit is a function of switching capacitance and switching activity. It is thus desirable that the capacitance connected to nodes with high switching activity is minimized. Since the gate capacitance of a transistor is substantially higher than the drain/source capacitances, this translates into ensuring that the high switching activity nodes are not connected to the gates of too many transistors. Note that neglecting drain-source capacitance switching is analogous to ignoring the internal node switching in a static CMOS gate.

In the case of PTL networks, only control variables are connected to the gate terminals of transistors. In our decomposed BDD-based approach, the control variables consist of primary inputs and decomposition points. Note that every node in the BDD is implemented as a multiplexer in the corresponding circuit and the node variable in the BDD is connected to the gates of two transistors of the multiplexer. Minimizing the occurrences of high switching activity node then translates into minimizing the occurrences of the corresponding variable in the BDD. Re-ordering BDD variables can be used to achieve this. Fig. 10 illustrates a case where re-ordering reduces the occurrences of the high switching activity variable at the expense of more occurrences of a lower switching activity variable.

A node in the PTL network is charged high when there is a path connecting it to the power supply and discharged when there is a path connecting it to ground. Even when the output does not change, glitching (charging and discharging of internal nodes) can consume a significant amount of power. Glitching can be minimized by placing variables which have a low switching probability close to the bottom of the BDD. This implies that the transistors controlled by these variables are close to the power supply and ground in the PTL network. Depending upon their state, this will cut-off the rest of the PTL network from the power supply or ground, resulting in a lower switching power dissipation. In the example in Fig. 11, since the probability of A being high is almost 1, the nMOS connected to $\overline{A}$ is almost always cut-off, and F is almost always 1. The ordering in Fig. 11(a) can however result in a significant power dissipation due to the internal nodes being charged through the nMOS connected to C and discharged through the nMOS connected to $\overline{B}$ and $\overline{C}$. Compared to this, the ordering in Fig. 11(b) has no internal power dissipation as the nMOS connected to $\overline{A}$ cuts-off the rest of the circuit from ground.

Note that these heuristics are similar to re-ordering transistors for low power at the circuit level in static CMOS ([6]). However, in our approach, technology mapping is straightforward and there is a one-to-one correspondence between BDDs and PTL circuits. This allows us to perform Boolean manipulations at a high level in which we can trade-off circuit area for power, rather then making restricted structural changes at the circuit level.

6 Results

The techniques described in this paper have been tested on ISCAS benchmarks circuits, which include circuits which are *hard* for monolithic BDD-based approaches (e.g. C6288). In the following we present results comparing our PTL synthesis algorithm with different static CMOS synthesis algorithms to demonstrate the area and delay gains achieved by our approach, and HSPICE simulations to verify the validity of the logic level gains.

The PTL synthesis algorithm was implemented in the SIS framework. It is compared against four synthesis scripts for static CMOS: area and delay optimization scripts which do not use don't cares, and *script.rugged* and *script.delay* of SIS. Technology mapping was performed using three different libraries: msu.genlib, 33-4.genlib, and 44-3.genlib. All experiments were carried out on a 400 MHz DEC Alpha with a SPECint_92 rating of 341, DEC 21164 CPU, 4Mb cache and 2Gb total memory.

PTL circuits were synthesized with four different threshold parameters. This threshold parameter from Section 5.1 controls the depth of decomposition point BDDs. For a given logic circuit, the best of the four PTL transistor-level circuits was selected and data for this circuit is presented in all tables. Compared to this, static CMOS circuit in each table is the best of several test runs with different parameters. Moreover, not the same circuit is used in all tables. That is, the same PTL circuit data is compared with the area optimized static CMOS circuit in the area columns of the tables and against the delay optimized static CMOS circuit in the delay columns. The gains achieved by PTL are thus very conservative, since the area-optimal static CMOS circuit is far from delay-optimal and vice versa.

Table 1 compares the PTL results against results from area and delay optimization scripts for static CMOS which do not use don't cares (mapped for area and delay respectively using msu.genlib). Since our PTL implementation does not perform don't care optimization yet, this table gives the best picture of the efficiency of our PTL algorithm. Column 1 contains the names of the ISCAS benchmark circuits. Column 2 and 3 compare the active gate area (measured in λ^2) of circuits synthesized by the PTL and minimum area static CMOS algorithm. Column 4 contains the relative gain in area achieved by our PTL algorithm over the static CMOS algorithm. Columns 5 and 6 compare the critical path length of the circuits generated by PTL and minimum delay static CMOS. Column 7 contains the relative gains of PTL over the static CMOS algorithm.

Table 2 presents results in the same format, this time comparing the PTL data of Table 1 with static CMOS results optimized using local optimizations and full don't cares. The static CMOS results in Column 2 are optimized using *script.rugged* and the results in Column 5 are optimized using *script.delay*. Note that the current PTL implementation does not perform local optimizations or don't care optimizations. This is not an algorithmic limitation and will be implemented in the near future (techniques for this have already been outlined in Section 7). In spite of this handicap, the current PTL implementation yields impressive gains over the *script.rugged* and *script.delay*.

Table 3 compares the runtimes of the PTL synthesis algorithm (Column 6) with the area and delay optimization scripts without don't cares, and *script.rugged* and *script.delay* (Columns 2, 3, 4 and 5 respectively). Note that the output of static CMOS algorithms is a mapped logic network while the output of the PTL algorithm is an HSPICE netlist. The results clearly indicate that PTL synthesis is substantially faster than all static CMOS techniques.

When using the critical path length as the metric to compare delays of two circuits, it is important to ensure that the amount of logic implemented in a cell is similar for each case, because a circuit with large individual cells can have a small critical path but be slow due to high cell propagation delay. Table 4 compares the cell count of the PTL circuit with the area and delay optimized static CMOS circuits of Table 1 in Columns 2, 3 and 4 respectively, and the average cell size in Columns 5, 6, and 7 respectively. The data indicates that the PTL circuit indeed uses fewer cells with more logic in each individual cell. Thus, while the delay of each cell is not directly related to the cell size (since each cell in the PTL circuit implements a BDD structure, while the static CMOS cells implement a series-parallel pull-up and pull-down tree structure), we do need further analysis to ensure that the savings in the critical path length translate to delay reduction in the final transistor-level circuit. We analyze a full adder circuit and perform HSPICE analysis to examine the delay trade-off between a larger cell implementing a BDD structure vs. a smaller series-parallel logic cell. These results are presented in Fig. 12.

As an aside, we also synthesized static CMOS using larger libraries like 33-4.genlib (87 cells, average cell size: 27.4 λ^2) and 44-4.genlib (625 cells, average cell size 43.4 λ^2) to see if a greater choice of cells, including very large cells, improved the static CMOS results. However, we found that there was no major change in the results, and in fact, the synthesis runtimes for static CMOS increased by factors of 5-100 due to the library size.

Table 5 presents the logic synthesis and HSPICE analysis results for a full adder circuit implemented in PTL and static CMOS. Columns 2, 3, 4, and 5 provide logic level data (area, number of transistors, number of cells and average cell size respectively) for the two test cases. Columns 6 and 7 contain the slowest rise and fall times from an exhaustive HSPICE simulation. Fig. 12(a) and 12(b) show the rise and fall time waveform plot. The results indicate that PTL has a smaller fall time and the same rise time as static CMOS. This is to be expected since an nMOS-only PTL circuit is good at conducting "0". The critical path thus seems to be a good indicator of the fall times. In general, a lower area implies a smaller switching capacitance, which does indeed correlate with a faster circuits. Thus, the 20-50+% gains achieved at logic level should translate to gains at the transistor level, albeit in slightly smaller numbers. Columns 8 and 9 present the average and rms power dissipation results. The static CMOS circuit has a lower average power dissipation but a higher rms power dissipation. Fig. 12(c) indicates that the static CMOS has a higher peak power dissipation as well. While the lower average power dissipation of static CMOS is good from the battery life perspective, a higher peak and rms power dissipation is undesirable from the electromigration and IR drop point of view.

Circuit	Area			Delay		
	static CMOS	PTL	gain	static CMOS	PTL	gain
C17	54.0	58.5	-8 %	3	2	33 %
C432	1620.0	1468.5	9 %	18	23	-28 %
C499	3424.5	2920.5	15 %	12	9	25 %
C880	2673.0	2433.0	9 %	16	9	44 %
C1355	3424.5	2953.5	14 %	14	6	57 %
C1908	4851.0	3174.0	35 %	20	14	30 %
C2670	5787.0	4797.0	17 %	18	11	39 %
C3540	9279.0	7495.5	19 %	28	18	36 %
C5315	13266.0	12415.5	6 %	24	11	54 %
C6288	21321.0	16180.5	24 %	120	70	42 %
C7552	18310.5	19902.0	-9 %	21	14	33 %

Table 1 : Best area & best delay static CMOS vs. PTL

Circuit	Area			Delay		
	script. rugged	PTL (no DC)	gain	*script. delay*	PTL (no DC)	gain
C17	49.5	58.5	-16 %	3	2	33 %
C432	1233.0	1468.5	-19 %	18	23	-28 %
C499	3244.5	2920.5	10 %	11	9	18 %
C880	2596.5	2433.0	6 %	16	9	44 %
C1355	3244.5	2953.5	9 %	11	6	45 %
C1908	3226.5	3174.0	2 %	18	14	22 %
C2670	4491.0	4797.0	-9 %	-	11	-
C3540	8176.5	7495.5	8 %	26	18	31 %
C5315	9985.5	12415.5	-24 %	23	11	52 %
C6288	19885.5	16180.5	19 %	61	70	-15 %
C7552	-	19902.0	-	-	14	-

Table 2 : Best area & best delay static CMOS using DC vs. PTL (which does not use DC).

Circuit	static CMOS				PTL
	area	delay	*script.rugged*	*script.delay*	
C17	0.01	0.01	0.10	0.10	0.01
C432	0.6	0.6	113.2	91.4	0.2
C499	1.1	1.0	12.9	10.5	0.6
C880	0.9	0.9	4.3	11.0	0.4
C1355	1.4	1.4	13.3	24.4	0.6
C1908	1.7	1.7	15.9	47.7	1.1
C2670	3.0	2.6	100.4	-	1.8
C3540	4.3	3.5	30.0	371.4	2.8
C5315	7.2	5.9	22.9	664.9	5.1
C6288	5.5	6.1	65.0	287.2	10.4
C7552	10.1	8.6	-	-	14.3

Table 3 : Static CMOS vs. PTL: runtime (in seconds)

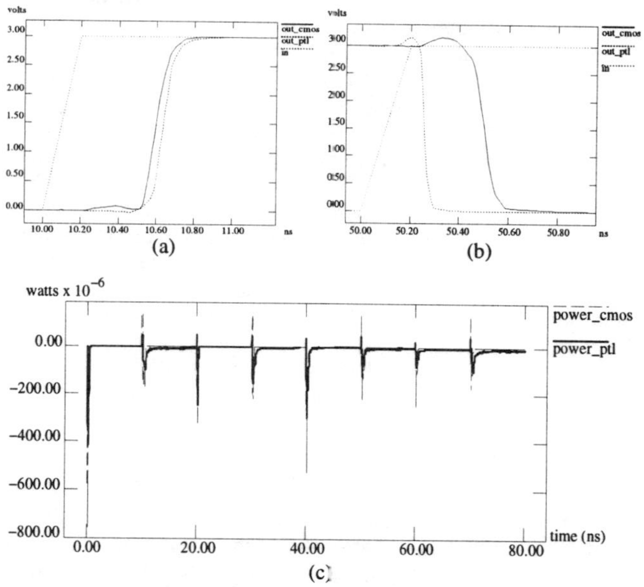

Figure 12: HSPICE results on timing and power dissipation of static CMOS and PTL circuits for a full adder

Circuit	Cell Count			Average Cell Size		
	static CMOS		PTL	static CMOS		PTL
	area opt	delay opt		area opt	delay opt	
C17	6	6	3	6.0	6.0	13.0
C432	141	144	58	7.7	7.7	16.9
C499	238	243	133	9.6	9.8	14.6
C880	223	215	94	8.0	8.8	17.2
C1355	238	235	41	9.6	10.8	48.0
C1908	356	345	189	9.1	10.1	11.2
C2670	425	514	227	9.1	8.8	14.1
C3540	778	789	382	8.0	8.5	13.1
C5315	1030	1238	316	8.6	8.7	26.2
C6288	2326	2340	929	6.1	6.1	11.6
C7552	1596	1512	989	7.6	8.3	13.4

Table 4 : Static CMOS vs. PTL: cell counts and average cell size

Logic	Area (λ^2)	# MOS	# Cell	Avg Cell Size (λ^2)	Delay			Power	
					Crit Path	HSPICE		Avg.	RMS
						t_{rise}	t_{fall}		
PTL	42	22	1	42.0	1	0.6ns	0.2ns	30μW	83μW
CMOS	81	36	8	10.1	4	0.6ns	0.5ns	17μW	122μW

Table 5 : Simulation data for a full adder circuit

7 Enhancing the Decomposed BDD-based Approach

7.1 Don't Care Optimization

The PTL synthesis tool benchmarked in Section 6 does not use don't cares for design optimization. Don't cares provide a significant amount of flexibility in minimizing a circuit as witnessed from the improvement of the static CMOS area and delay results between Table 1 and Table 2 in Section 6.

Extending the proposed approach to handle don't cares is relatively straightforward. Several heuristics to minimize BDD size using don't cares are presented in [20]. Since the area of a decomposed BDD-based PTL circuit is proportional to the BDD size, the results of [20] can be applied to PTL synthesis directly. The synthesis algorithm would then be modified as follows: after generating the decomposed BDD representation, we minimize the target function BDD and each decomposition point BDD travelling from the primary outputs of the circuit to primary inputs. In the context of the multi-stage circuit represented by the decomposed BDDs, travelling from the outputs to the inputs amounts to first minimizing the target function BDD and then each decomposed BDD in the reverse order of decomposition point introduction. For each BDD, we compute the compatible observability don't cares for the output function in terms of the primary inputs. This is mapped to a local don't care set via image computation. The don't care set construction is the same as in the case of the multi-level network minimization and we refer the reader to [18] for more details. The heuristics of [20] are then applied to minimize the BDD. Based on the results reported in [20], we expect this extension to yield significant reduction in the area of the PTL circuits.

7.2 Synthesis of Mixed static CMOS/PTL Circuits

This work has proposed the use of PTL for large deep sub-micron designs. PTL can provide substantial gains in area and delay over static CMOS, while the static CMOS has the advantage of a well-established design flow for synthesizing robust circuits. Static CMOS may be preferable over PTL in cases where a static CMOS implementation of a gate is particularly efficient, or where an nMOS conducting "1" is not allowed.

The PTL synthesis flow proposed in this work is very general in nature and allows synthesis of mixed static CMOS/PTL circuits which can leverage the strengths of static CMOS as well as PTL as appropriate. Each decomposition point BDD can be viewed as a complex node and can be implemented by static CMOS logic or PTL as desired.

Among other issues, currently we use ROBDDs as the underlying data structure for the decomposed BDDs. General BDDs ([2]), which allow input variables to appear multiple times along any path in the BDD, may be more appropriate from the PTL network design point of view since we are more interested in compactness than in canonicity. We plan to look into incorporating general BDDs in our synthesis algorithm.

8 Conclusions

PTL can be a promising alternative to static CMOS for deep submicron design. In this work, we have motivated the need for CAD algorithms for PTL circuit design and have proposed a methodology for synthesizing PTL circuits. The main contributions of this work are the following:

- A decomposed BDD-based representation is proposed to take advantage of the correspondence between PTL circuits and BDDs without suffering from the drawbacks imposed by properties of monolithic BDDs.
- A comprehensive synthesis flow is outlined for PTL design. We showed that the proposed approach allows us to make logic level optimizations similar to the traditional multi-level network based synthesis flow for static CMOS, and also makes possible optimizations with a direct impact on area, delay and power of the final circuit implementation which do not have any equivalent in the traditional approach. Using these techniques we were able to synthesize PTL circuits for the entire ISCAS benchmark set.
- A set of heuristical algorithms to synthesize PTL circuits optimized for area, delay and power which are key to the proposed synthesis flow, are presented. These algorithms are very intuitive and simple and have a great impact on the optimality of the resulting circuit.

Initial experimental results on ISCAS benchmark circuits show that our technique yields PTL circuits with substantial improvements in area and delay over conventional static CMOS designs. We believe that with more research in this area PTL can become a viable alternative to static CMOS, and that this work is the first step in that direction.

9 Acknowledgments

The authors would like to thank Prof. Takayasu Sakurai and Ravi Gunturi for useful discussions on this work.

References

[1] S. Akers, "Binary decision diagrams," *IEEE Trans. on Computers*, vol. C-27, no. 6, June 1978.

[2] P. Ashar. A. Ghosh, S. Devadas, "Boolean satisfiability and equivalence checking using general binary decision diagrams," *ICCD* 1991.

[3] W. Al-Assadi, A.P. Jayasumana, and Y.K. Malaiya, "Pass-transistor logic design," *Int'l J. Electronics*, vol. 70, no. 4, 1991.

[4] R.E. Bryant, "Graph-Based Algorithms for Boolean Function Manipulation," *IEEE Trans. on Computers*, vol. C-35, no. 8, Aug.1986.

[5] A. P. Chandrakasan, S. Sheng, and R.W. Brodersen, "Low Power CMOS Digital Design," *IEEE JSSC*, vol. SC-20, 1985.

[6] R. Hossain, M. Zheng, and A. Albicki, "Reducing power dissipation in CMOS circuits by signal probability based transistor reordering," *IEEE Trans. CAD*, vol.15, no. 3, March 1996.

[7] A. Jaekel, G.A. Jullien, and S. Bandyopadhyay, "A multilevel factorization technique for pass transistor logic," *9th Int'l Conf. on VLSI Design*, Jan. 1996.

[8] J. Jain, A. Narayan, C. Coelho, S.P. Khatri, A. Sangiovanni-Vincentelli, R.K. Brayton, and M. Fujita, "Decomposition techniques for efficient ROBDD construction,", *Int'l Conf. in FM-CAD*, 1996.

[9] P.C. McGeer, K.L. McMillan, A. Saldanha, A. Sangiovanni-Vincentelli, and P. Scaglia, "Fast discrete function evaluation using decision diagrams," *ICCAD*, Nov. 1995.

[10] J.L. Neves, and A. Albicki, "A pass transistor regular structure for implementing multi-level combinational circuits," *7th Int'l ASIC Conf. and Exhibit*, 1994.

[11] S. Panda, and F. Somenzi, "Who are the variables in your neighborhood," *ICCAD*, Nov. 1995.

[12] J. Rabaey, *Digital Integrated Circuits*, Prentice-Hall, Inc. 1996.

[13] D. Radhakrishnan, S.R. Whitaker, and G.K. Maki, "Formal design procedures for pass transistor switching circuits," *IEEE JSSC*, vol. SC-20, no. 2, April 1985.

[14] R. Rudell, "Dynamic variable ordering for ordered binary decision diagrams," *ICCAD*, Nov. 1993.

[15] T. Sakurai, B. Lin, and A.R. Newton, "Multiple-Output Shared Transistor Logic (MOSTL) Family Synthesized Using Binary Decision Diagram," *Tech. Report, Univ. of California, Berkeley*, M90/21, 1990.

[16] F. Salice, "Automatic synthesis of logic functions using transmission gates," *J. Microelectronic Systems Integration*, vol. 3, no.1, 1995.

[17] Y. Sasaki, K. Yano, S. Yamashita, H. Chikata, K. Rikino, K. Uchiyama, and K. Seki, "Multi-level pass-transistor logic for low-power ULSIs," *Int'l Symp. on Low Power Electronics*, Oct. 1995.

[18] H. Savoj, "Don't cares in multi-level network optimization," *Ph.D. Dissertation, Univ. of California, Berkeley*, M92/122, Oct. 1992.

[19] M. Shamanna, K. Cameron, S.R. Whitaker, "Multiple-input, multiple-output pass transistor logic," *Int'l J. Elect.*, vol.79, no.1, 1995.

[20] T. Shiple, R. Hojati, A. Sangiovanni-Vincentelli, R.K. Brayton, "Heuristic minimization of BDDs using don't cares," *DAC* 1994.

[21] K. Yano, T. Yamanaka, T. Nishida, M. Saito, K. Shimohigashi, and A. Shimizu, "A 3.8-ns CMOS 16x16-b multiplier using complementary pass-transistor logic," *IEEE JSSC*, vol. 25, no. 2, April 1990.

[22] K. Yano, Y. Sasaki, K. Rikino, and K. Seki, "Top-down pass-transistor logic design," *IEEE JSSC*, vol. 31, no. 6, June 1996.

An Exact Solution to Simultaneous Technology Mapping and Linear Placement Problem*

Jinan Lou, Amir H. Salek, Massoud Pedram
Department of Electrical Engineering – Systems
University of Southern California, Los Angeles, CA 90089

Abstract

In this paper, we present an optimal algorithm for solving the simultaneous technology mapping and linear placement problem for tree-structured circuits with the objective of minimizing the post-layout area. The proposed algorithm relies on generation of gate-area versus cut-width curves using a dynamic programming approach. A novel design flow, which extends this algorithm to minimize the circuit delay and handle general DAG structures, is also presented. Experimental results on MCNC benchmarks are reported.

I. Introduction

In a top-down design flow, optimizations at each step are made without considering their impacts on the subsequent design steps. For example, technology mapping algorithms minimize gate area or delay without considering the interconnect structure and routing overhead of the resulting circuit. This lack of information reduces the effectiveness of the optimization techniques. Existing enhancements to synthesis and physical design tools, such as better delay and wire load models, post-layout re-mapping, and gate resizing have not been able to solve this problem. This means that designers have to resort to costly design iterations. This problem is compounded as feature sizes shrink to quarter micron and below because interconnect delay and area become even more dominant, the number of gates in the circuit increases, and the number of nets that are at a performance risk rises rapidly. It is therefore necessary to develop new design methodologies and tools to cope with the problem.

This paper proposes a solution by introducing a new algorithm for simultaneous technology mapping and linear placement of tree-structured circuits. This algorithm combined with a novel floorplan-driven design flow leads to a highly effective approach for performing technology mapping and cell placement for general circuits, hence combing the two design steps.

This paper is organized as follows: In Section II, we give the background knowledge for technology mapping and linear placement algorithms. Section III presents details of our algorithm for combining technology mapping and linear placement for trees. We introduce a design flow which uses this algorithm to simultaneously map and place general circuits and minimize circuit delay in section IV. Experimental results and concluding remarks are given in Sections V and VI, respectively.

II. Background

The problem of technology mapping for general circuit structures is NP-hard [5]. In 1987 Keutzer [7] pointed out the similarity between the library binding problem and the optimal code generation in a compiler. In his algorithm the circuit is partitioned into tree sub-graphs and each tree sub-graph is mapped using a dynamic programming algorithm which finds the minimum gate area mapping of the tree in polynomial time. This work was later extended by Rudell [14] to minimum delay technology mapping and by Touati et al. [19] to minimize area mapping under delay constraints. In [1], Chaudhary and Pedram presented a dynamic programming algorithm to construct the set of all possible mappings of a tree with different area-delay trade-off.

Neither of the above-mentioned works considers wiring area or delay during technology mapping. This was the motivation for Pedram and Bhat's work in [11] to couple technology mapping and placement in order to consider the effect of wires during mapping. Their proposed algorithm assumes that the dynamic programming principle holds during the bottom-up process of concurrent mapping and placement. This is however only an approximation.

For the sake of completeness, we give the following (well-known) result:

Lemma 1: Keutzer's algorithm produces the best gate area mapping of a tree [7].

The linear placement problem of a graph has been extensively studied. The MINSUM problem is to find a linear placement that minimizes the total length of connecting wire segments. On the other hand, the MINCUT problem is to find a linear placement that minimizes the maximum cut-width. Both problems are NP-hard for the general graphs [21]. In 1979, Shiloach [18] gave an $O(n^{2.2})$ algorithm to solve the MINSUM problem for trees, and in 1984 Chung [2] improved it to $O(n^{1.58})$. For MINCUT problems, Lengauer [9] introduced a polynomial time algorithm for trees whose cost is within a factor of two of the optimal in 1982, and

* This work was supported in part by NFS under contract No. MIP-94/57392, and by grants from IBM Corp. and ViewLogic Inc.

1092-3152/97 $10.00 © 1997 IEEE

Yannakakis [23] gave an $O(n\log n)$ dynamic programming algorithm to find the optimal solution for trees in 1985. In this paper, we exploit Yannakakis' algorithm for the MINCUT problem.

Lemma 2: Yannakakis' algorithm produces the minimum cut width linear placement of a tree [21].

III. SiMPA

In this section, we introduce our Simultaneous Technology Mapping and Linear Placement Algorithm (SiMPA) which finds the minimum total area (gate plus routing) implementation of a tree.

III.1. Problem Formulation

PROBLEM: *Given a library L and a tree T, find a simultaneous technology mapping and linear placement solution for T which has the smallest total area (gate plus routing area).*

Keutzer's algorithm (KA) finds the minimum gate area technology mapping for a tree. KA cannot account for the wiring area since it has no knowledge about the gate positions. Yannakakis' algorithm (YA) finds the minimum cut-width linear placement of a tree. What remains for us to do is to combine the two algorithms.

Lemma 3: The following equation gives the exact total area for a one-dimensional standard-cell layout (cf. Figure 1):

$$A = a + \frac{\beta}{h}\cdot(a\cdot c)$$

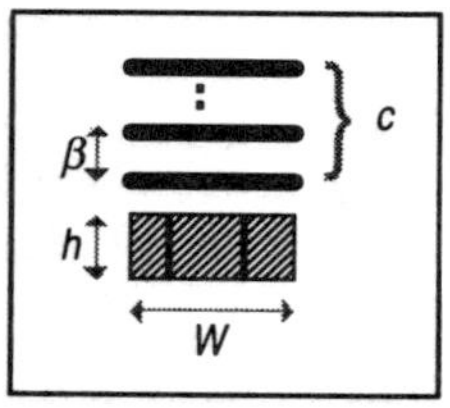

Figure 1. Total area calculation

where $a = W\cdot h$ is the total gate area, W is sum of the cell widths, h is the cell height (assumed to be a constant), β is the minimum distance between the centers of two adjacent wires, and c is the maximum cut width (also referred to as the cut-density) [†].

The above equation is exact since in one-dimensional routing, there are no vertical constraints and the channel height is set by the maximum clique size in the horizontal constraint graph [17]. Clearly, a is determined from the technology mapping whereas c is determined from the placement. To find the minimum total area A, technology mapping and placement must be done simultaneously.

III.2. Gate-area versus cut-width curve

During KA, mapping solutions which have larger area than the best solution (found up to that point) are dropped. However, this notation of inferiority does not hold for simultaneous technology mapping and linear placement. The following counter example shows how this can happen.

Example: Assume at one step of dynamic programming, when solving the problem of minimizing the total area of a tree, there are two sub-problems, T_1 and T_2. For T_1 one design S_1, and for T_2 two designs $S_{2.1}$ and $S_{2.2}$, have been found (Figure 2), and $totalArea(S_{2.1}) < totalArea(S_{2.2})$, that is, $S_{2.2}$ appears to be inferior to $S_{2.1}$. However, figure 3 shows that the combination of S_1 and $S_{2.1}$ is inferior to the combination of S_1 and $S_{2.2}$. Therefore, we cannot simply throw away $S_{2.2}$. That is, we cannot drop a solution simply because it has a larger total area than that of the best solution found so far.

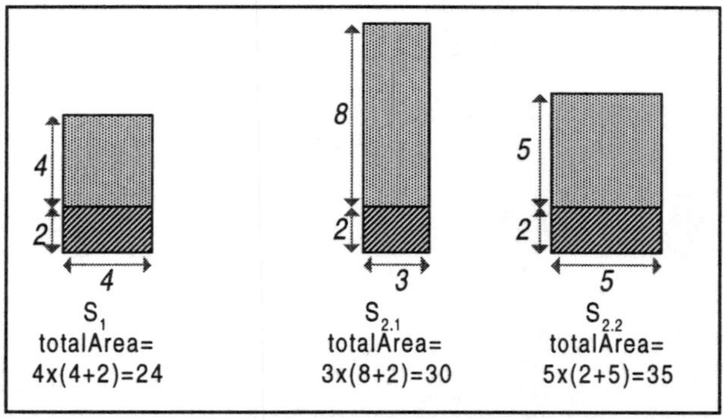

Figure 2. Example before combining sub-solutions

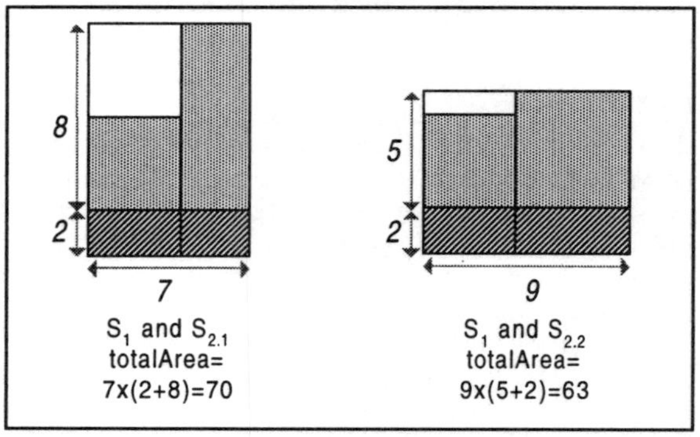

Figure 3. Example after combining sub-solutions

Definition: S_1 is inferior to S_2 if and only if the following conditions hold:

$gateArea(S_1) >= gateArea(S_2)$ **and**
$cutWidth(S_1) >= cutWidth(S_2)$

Our algorithm is to maintain all non-inferior <gateArea, cutWidth> points for each node in the tree. SiMPA thus combines KA and YA; its pseudo code is given next:

```
1. Technology decompose circuit N
2. Perform a Depth-First-Search (DFS) on N
3. For each node n in the reverse-DFS order do
4.    For every match m of n do
5.        gateArea = sum of gateAreas of all inputs of this
              match + gate area of this match
6.        cutWidth = the cut width from linear placement of
              the mapped tree rooted at m
7.     Store the solution <gateArea, cutWidth> in n
8.   Prune inferior solutions from the curve of n
9. Select the best solution by starting from the primary
   output, and recursively finding the solutions for all
   inputs of this best solution
```

† Proofs can be found in [10].

For each gate from the library that matches a set of nodes rooted at n, we calculate the gate area and the cut width of this match. The current match and the inputs to this match are stored with the gate area and cut width, so that later (i.e. during step 9) we can construct the best solutions for the inputs. Note that step 6 is performed using YA which itself uses dynamic programming. That is, we build the optimal linear placement of the problem at hand from optimal placement of its constituent sub-problems. After all matches are enumerated and all solutions are generated, we prune out the inferior solutions and only keep the non-inferior solutions in node n. After reaching the tree root, the best solution is selected from the curve of the root. Since we stored the match and inputs of n, we can then construct the best solutions for all of its inputs recursively.

In the example discussed in section III.1, since $gateArea(S_{2,1}) < gateArea(S_{2,2})$ but $cutWidth(S_{2,1}) > cutWidth(S_{2,2})$, we must keep both solutions as non-inferior solutions. In effect, we are generating a gate-area versus cut-width curve (Figure 4) at every node. The lower left corner points on the curve are non-inferior points with respect to each other. We will then generate the curve on the next higher level of the tree by combining the curves from the lower level curves and by pruning the inferior points.

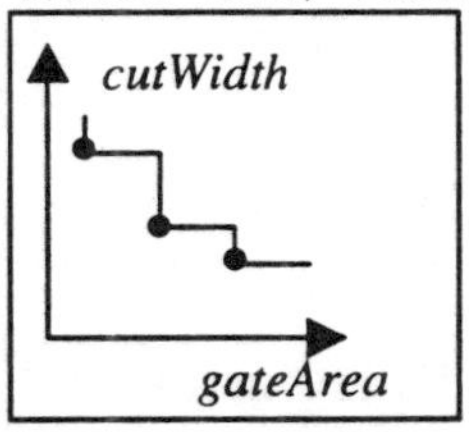

Figure 4. A gateArea versus cutWidth curve

Consider tree T with root n. Let S represent the mapping solution for T with match m at the root. Let a_i denote the gate area of the mapping solution S_i of child i of m. Let c denote the cut-width of the S obtained by YA.

Lemma 4: $$totalArea(S) = \sum_i a_i + \frac{\beta}{h}\left(c \cdot \sum_i a_i\right)$$

Consider two solutions S_1 and S_2. For tree T, these solutions are the same except that S_1 contains sub-solution $S_{i,1}$ and S_2 contains sub-solution $S_{i,2}$.

Lemma 5: If $S_{i,1}$ is inferior to $S_{i,2}$, then S_1 is inferior to S_2.

Theorem 1: The final curve generated by SiMPA at the root of tree T includes all non-inferior gate area versus cut width solutions for the simultaneous technology mapping and linear placement problem of T.

Corollary 1: Given an upper bound on the number of tracks, *maxCut*, the points in the gate-area versus cut-width curve with the cut width less than *maxCut* constitute all the non-inferior implementations of the circuit satisfying that constraint.

Corollary 2: Given an upper bound on the area, *maxArea*, the points in the gate-area versus cut-width curve with the gate area less than *maxArea* constitute all the non-inferior implementations of the circuit satisfying that constraint.

Corollaries 1 and 2 show how SiMPA can be used in applications such as layout-driven logic synthesis and post-layout re-synthesis. Given a cut width constraint, we can find the best gate area implementation which satisfies this constraint. Similarly, given a gate area constraint, we can find the best cut width implementation which meets this constraint.

Theorem 2: The solution SiMPA chooses in the last step (step 9), is the solution with the minimum total area.

IV. FPD-SiMPA

In this section, we present our floorplan driven design flow (FPD-SiMPA) which extends SiMPA to minimize the circuit delay and to handle general DAG structures. This new flow partitions the DAG into a set of trees, floorplans them, uses the floorplanning and global routing results to generate delay budgets for trees, and finally uses a timing-driven version of SiMPA to pick a timing correct solution for each tree.

IV.1 Extension to Delay Minimization

There are many different models for the gate delay calculation. In SIS [16], the gate delay is calculated using this equation for both rise and fall delays:

$$GateDelay = K_1 + K_2 \cdot load$$

where K_1 and K_2 are the intrinsic gate delay and the fanout-dependent load delay, respectively. This delay equation is pin-dependent, uses a linear model, and assumes step input signals. It is simple but rather inaccurate (especially in 0.5μ design and below).

We extend the SIS delay model to a four-parameter delay model where we add the effect of the input slew rate:

$$GateDelay = (K_1 + K_2 \cdot load) + slew \cdot (K_3 + K_4 \cdot load)$$

where K_1 to K_4 are constants. We use the same equation form but obviously with different coefficients to calculate the rise and fall delays, as well as the rise and fall slew rates for gate outputs. Our delay equation is also pin-dependent. We get these constants by doing curve fittings for every library cell based on the results from extensive circuit-level simulation using HSpice.

For wire delay calculation, the lumped RC model is widely used, but the Elmore delay model gives higher accuracy [4]. The latter model calculates the delay of each wire segment using the equation shown in Figure 5:

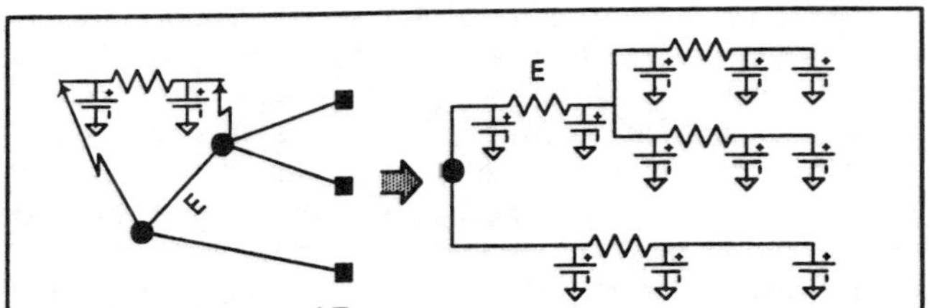

r_E: *wire resistance of E*
c_E: *wire capacitance of E*
C_E: *total capacitance rooted at E*

$$Delay(E) = r_E \times (\frac{c_E}{2} + C_E)$$

Figure 5. Elmore delay model

The delay minimization cannot be done exactly due to the following problems. During each step of dynamic programming, the mapping and placement information for the fanouts of the current node are not known. Therefore, the load of the current node cannot be accurately determined. Moreover, the delay of the wire cannot be calculated exactly since the sub-trees may be broken up and separated during placement of an ancestor node in the tree by YA. To solve the first problem, we use a heuristic similar to that in [14,19] to do delay calculation. During each step of the dynamic programming procedure, we assume a constant load ahead (that, is the input capacitance of a 2-input NAND gate and the capacitance of a wire segment whose length is statistically estimated based on the fanout count of the node [20]). After a match is found, we update the delay of all fanins of this match to use the correct load information since the match is henceforth known and the fanins are already placed and mapped. This is similar to the timing recalculation step of [19]. The second problem mentioned above introduces some errors in the delay calculation which cannot be helped.

As pointed out in section III.2, we maintain a gate area versus cut-width curve at each node. Adding delay to SiMPA means we must generate and store a three-dimensional curve (Figure 6) in each node during dynamic programming. The three dimensions are gate area, cut width and delay. Pruning is again performed to ensure the polynomial running time of the algorithm. However, note that the delay values in this curve are not exact as explained before.

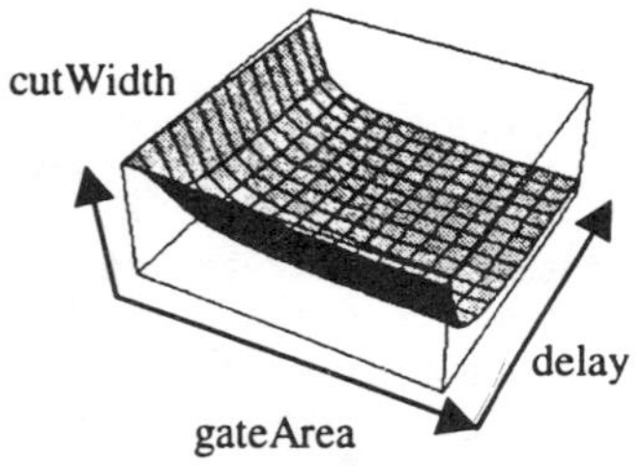

Figure 6 A three-dimensional curve

IV.2 Extension to DAGs

Similar to KA, SiMPA can be used as a basic routine for mapping and placement of general DAG-structured circuits as follows.

As a first step, we partition the original circuit into a set of trees. Restriction to tree partitioning may sacrifice the overall quality of the technology mapping, but we benefit from the exactness of SiMPA. Therefore, the overall chip area/delay can still be improved (see Section V). We treat each tree as a block (macro-cell). Because we target standard cell layout, the height of each block is the same as the height of the cells in the standard cell library. Next, a minimum gate-area mapping of each tree is performed to get an estimation of the width of the block. With the dimensions of the blocks known, we floorplan these blocks and route the global wires that are connecting them. The delay of each block is estimated from the number of logic levels in each block (which is obtained from the initial mapping solution), and the load of the block. We calculate the global wire delays using the Elmore delay model. Since the physical location of each block is known, the global wire delays are fairly accurate. Next, the delay budget for each block (tree) is obtained using a technique similar to that of [6]. We use the budget as the constraint to pick up a timing feasible solution from the set of non-inferior solutions generated by SiMPA for each tree. Finally, we refine the floorplan solution to eliminate overlaps, and generate the final chip layout. The pseudo code is given blow.

1. *Cluster the original circuit into a set of trees*
2. *Estimate the area of each tree*
3. *Treat each tree as a macro-cell and do floorplanning*
4. *Perform global routing on wires that connect trees*
5. *Do delay calculation and budgeting for each tree*
6. *Call SiMPA on each tree*
7. *Use the delay budget generated in step 5 to pick the feasible solution from the set of all non-inferior solutions generated by SiMPA*
8. *Eliminate block overlaps and complete detailed routing*

V. Experimental Results

We present our experimental results in two tables. The area and delay in both tables refer to the total chip area and the total chip delay after detailed routing. In all cases, we use the four-parameter delay equation (see Section IV.1) to calculate the gate delays and the Elmore delay model to calculate the wire delays. We use a CASCADE generated standard cell library (0.5μ HP 14B CMOS process) to produce these results.

In Table I we present the results of SiMPA on trees and compare them with the results obtained by the conventional flow of performing technology mapping and linear placement separately. It is important to mention here that in order to keep the comparison fair, we also use Yannakakis' MINCUT placement algorithm to do the linear placement in the conventional flow. Otherwise, we would have obtained larger improvements because other placement tools, such as Gordian [8] or TimberWolf [15] do not generate the minimum cut width placement. The suffix of the tree name represents the number of inputs. Our results show an average improvement of 20% in the total post-layout area.

In Table II we present the results using a conventional flow and FPD-SiMPA. In the conventional flow, we use SIS to do a minimum delay technology mapping, followed by Gordian and Domino [3] for placement, TimberWolf for global routing and YACR [13] for detailed routing. In FPD-SiMPA, we use tree clustering and initial mapping of each tree for block width estimation, followed by Bear-FP [12] which does floorplanning and global routing. Then we call SiMPA for each tree subject to the delay budgets generated in the floorplanning stage. Domino is used to eliminate overlaps while TimberWolf is used to improve the global routing solution. Finally YACR is called to do the detailed routing. Our results show an average 21% improvement of the delay without any area penalty.

	Conventional			SiMPA			
	Gate Area	*	Total Area	Gate Area	*	Total Area	Ratio
tree8	64438	5	369054	62986	4	288590	0.78
tree10	94604	5	541823	94916	4	434888	0.80
tree20	30536	4	139910	30536	3	104933	0.75
tree24	97468	5	558226	100437	4	460184	0.82
tree64	74701	6	513400	77616	5	444528	0.87
							0.80

Table I Tree results (* column is the number of tracks)

	Conventional		FPD-SiMPA			
	Area	Delay	Area	Delay	Area Ratio	Delay Ratio
apex6	4212505	12.94	3753360	9.40	0.89	0.73
b12	422831	4.34	412191	3.40	0.97	0.78
b9	563030	4.00	667318	3.18	1.19	0.80
C17	40050	0.74	40762	0.38	1.02	0.51
C1908	4031118	16.99	3487815	12.86	0.87	0.76
C3540	9803363	28.86	7897600	22.49	0.81	0.78
C432	1747635	12.80	1362132	15.25	0.78	1.19
C7552	12631941	24.53	15747725	22.67	1.25	0.92
C880	2352900	10.00	2378453	9.46	1.01	0.95
cm150a	216952	4.10	207928	1.65	0.96	0.40
cm151a	117725	2.28	116477	1.44	0.99	0.63
cm162a	246800	2.13	201912	2.03	0.82	0.95
con1	74690	1.58	100441	0.88	1.34	0.56
cordic	398763	2.42	311535	2.04	0.78	0.84
dalu	9818750	25.90	8593920	25.30	0.88	0.98
frg1	689931	3.71	689142	3.18	1.00	0.86
lal	553268	4.79	613118	4.50	1.11	0.94
med	166453	3.48	142105	2.72	0.85	0.78
misex3c	2670030	20.67	2747928	19.07	1.03	0.92
pcle	365859	3.87	391327	3.92	1.07	1.01
pcler8	536095	5.43	518830	4.25	0.97	0.78
rd53	224296	3.90	222800	2.20	0.99	0.56
rd73	387907	5.59	348119	5.21	0.90	0.93
rd84	888122	8.75	771825	6.92	0.87	0.79
ritex1	91133	1.16	90025	0.84	0.99	0.72
squar5	327627	6.84	278800	5.40	0.85	0.79
vg2	546742	3.90	501599	3.35	0.92	0.86
xor5	121009	2.64	106945	1.37	0.88	0.52
z4ml	203600	3.97	202032	2.89	0.99	0.73
					0.96	0.79

Table II Benchmark results

VI. Conclusion

In this paper we proposed an algorithm for performing technology mapping and linear placement simultaneously in order to capture the information related to the wiring area during the mapping. This technique uses dynamic programming and has polynomial time complexity. We also presented a new design flow which uses SiMPA and a partitioning / floorplanning step to handle general circuit structures. Furthermore, we extended SiMPA to generate three-dimensional trade-off curves for minimum delay mapping, although delay calculation is not exact. Our future work will focus on developing an improved timing driven SiMPA.

VII. Reference

[1] K. Chaudhary, and M. Pedram, "A near-optimal algorithm for technology mapping minimizing area under delay constraints," in *Proceeding 29th Design Automation Conference*, June 1992.

[2] F. R. K. Chung, "On optimal linear arrangements of trees," in *Comput. Math. Applic.* 10, pages 43-60, 1984.

[3] K. Doll, F. M. Johannes, and G. Sigl, "DOMINO: Deterministic placement improvement with hill-climbing capabilities," in *IFIP International Conference VLSI*, 1991.

[4] R. Gupta, B. Krauter, B. Tutuianu, and T. Pileggi, "The Elmore Delay as a Bound for RC Trees with Generalized Input Signals," in *Proceedings of 32nd Design Automation Conference*, pages 364-369, 1995.

[5] G. D. Hachtel, and F. Somenzi, "Logic synthesis and verification algorithm," *Kluwer Academic Publishers*, Norwell, MA, 1996.

[6] P.S. Hauge, R. Nair, and E. J. Yoffa, "Circuit placement for predictable performance," in *Proceedings of IEEE Inter. Conference of Computer-Aided Design*, Nov. 1987, pp.88-91.

[7] K. Keutzer, "DAGON: Technology mapping and local optimization," *In Proceedings of Design Automation Conference*, pages 341-347, June 1987.

[8] J. M. Kleinhans, G. Sigl, F. M. Johannes, and K. J. Antreich, "GRODIAN: VLSI Placement by Quadratic Programming and Slicing Optimization," in *IEEE Transactions on Computer-Aided Design*, Vol. 10, No. 3, March, 1991.

[9] T. Lengauer, "Upper and lower bounds on the complexity of the min-cut linear arrangement problem on trees," in *SIAM J. Alg. Disc. Meth.*, vol. 3, no. 1, pages 99-113, March 1982.

[10] J. Lou and A. H. Salek, "Optimal Algorithm for Simultaneous Technology Mapping and Linear Placement," *CENG Technical Report*, Electrical Engineering-Systems, University of Southern California, July 1997.

[11] M. Pedram, and N. Bhat, "Layout driven technology mapping," *In Proceedings of the 28th Design Automation Conference*, pages 99-105, June 1991.

[12] M. Pedram, and E. Kuh, "BEAR-FP: A Robust Framework for Floorplanning," in *International Journal of High Speed Electronics*, Vol. 3, No.1, pages 137-170, 1992.

[13] J. Reed, A. Sangiovanni-Vincentelli, and M. Santamauro, "A new symbolic channel router: YACR2," in *IEEE Trans. on CAD*, Vol. CAD-4, pages 203-219, March 1985.

[14] R. Rudell, "Logic synthesis for VLSI design," *Memorandum UCB/ERL M89/49*, Ph.D. Dissertation, University of California at Berkeley, April 1989.

[15] C. Sechen, and A. Sangiovanni-Vincentelli, "TimberWolf3.2: A new standard cell placement and global routing package," in *Proc. of 23rd Design Automation Conf.*, pages 432-439, 1986.

[16] E. M. Sentovich, K. J. Singh, L. Lavagno, C. Moon, R. Murgai, A. Saldanha, H. Savoj, P. R. Stephan, R. K. Brayton and A. Sangiovanni-Vincentelli, "SIS: A System for Sequential Circuit Synthesis", *Memorandum No. UCB/ERL M92/41*, Electronics Research Laboratory, College of Engineering, University of California, Berkeley, CA 94720, May 1992.

[17] N. Sherwani, "Algorithms for VLSI Physical Design Automation," *Kluwer Academic Publishers*, 1993.

[18] Y. Shiloach, "A minimum linear arrangement algorithm for undirected trees," in *SIAM J. Comput.* 8, pages 15-32, 1979.

[19] H. J. Touati, C. W. Moon, R. K. Brayton, and A. Wang, "Performance oriented technology mapping," in *Proc. of Sixth MIT Conference Advanced Res. VLSI*, pages 79-97, April 1990.

[20] H. Vaishnav, and M. Pedram, "Logic extraction based on normalized netlengths," in *Proceedings of the International Conference on Computer Design*, October 1995.

[21] M. Yannakakis, "A polynomial algorithm for the min-cut linear arrangement of trees," *in Journal of the Association for Computing Machinery*, vol. 32, no. 4, pages 950-988, October 1985.

SESSION 11B

SYSTEM SPECIFICATION AND PRODUCT ENGINEERING

Moderators:

Bernard Courtois, TIMA Lab., Grenoble, France

Jerry R. Burch, Cadence Berkeley Labs., Berkeley, CA

An Efficient Statistical Analysis Methodology and Its Application to High-Density DRAMs

Sang-Hoon Lee, Chang-Hoon Choi, Jeong-Taek Kong, Won-Seong Lee, and Jei-Hwan Yoo

Semiconductor R & D Center, Samsung Electronics Co., Ltd.
San #24 Nongseo-Ri, Kiheung-Eup, Yongin-Si, Kyungki-Do, Korea
e-mail : tcad@semigw.semi.samsung.co.kr

Abstract

In this work, a new approach for the statistical worst case of full-chip circuit performance and parametric yield prediction, using both the Modified-Principal Component Analysis (MPCA) and the Gradient Method (GM), is proposed and verified. This method enables designers not only to predict the standard deviations of circuit performances but also track the circuit performances associated with the process shift using wafer test structure measurements. This new method is validated experimentally during the development and production of high density DRAMs.

1 Introduction

As the device feature size of VLSI shrinks with new technologies, the relative variability of the process makes the circuit performances more sensitive to the fluctuations in process steps. Accordingly, the statistical circuit design methodology becomes extremely crucial for designers to meet the circuit performances to the tight specification across the entire range of process fluctuations. However, the applications of true statistical techniques are limited to the research stage or a few special purpose circuits [1] and most designers still rely on the conventional method. The previous works for statistical design can be categorized as follows:

· the statistical modeling of SPICE parameters

· the simulation techniques for yield prediction

An important task in developing a statistical SPICE model is the identification of the critical model parameters and the translations of the physical process variations into the SPICE model. For examples, Bolt et al. [2] and Cox et al. [3] attempted to describe the total MOSFET variances in terms of the inter-die variances of four physically meaningful parameters: channel length, channel width, flat-band voltage, and gate oxide thickness. Since these parameters are determined by different steps in the manufacturing process, they can be assumed to be statistically independent. The rest model parameters can be expressed as functions of these four parameters to account for model parameter correlations. However, each SPICE model parameter for empirical models such as BSIM or HSPICE level 28 cannot be represented as a function of these physically meaningful parameters. Therefore, an incomplete work on treating statistical SPICE model parameters could lead to erroneous conclusions in statistical analysis and optimization. Furthermore, it cannot trace the parametrized SPICE model associated with the process shift which frequently occurs in the development of products.

Statistical simulation techniques are essential for estimating yields, designing manufacturable and robust systems, deriving worst-case models, and testing. The most widely used technique for performing the statistical characterization is the Monte Carlo analysis [4]. Unfortunately, the accuracy of the result produced using the Monte Carlo analysis is only proportional to the square root of the number of design variables and statistical parameters. Moreover, the number of Monte Carlo simulations required to produce a relatively accurate result increases exponentially with the number of statistical variables. Therefore, the Monte Carlo analysis is too expensive to apply to the real VLSI designs at the full-chip level.

One promising approach to deal with these shortcomings is proposed in this paper. In this design methodology, two statistical methods, the Modified-Principal Component Analysis (MPCA) and the Gradient Method (GM), are used and verified throughout various experiments. First, we have used a technique incorporating the Principal Component Analysis [5], which takes the distributions of SPICE parameters and electrical test measurements (E-tests) as inputs. Thus, each SPICE model parameter can be expressed as a function of independent E-tests. Then, the Gradient Method [2, 6] is used to predict the standard deviations of circuit performance with a few independent E-tests.

We present our statistical characterization system for prediction of yield distribution in Section 2. In Section 3, the Principal Component Analysis and the Gradient Method for our methodology are introduced at the point of the mathematical formula. In Section 4, an experimental qualification of the method is discussed based on the development and VLSI products such as the full density test vehicle of 256 Mbit DRAMs. Finally, we summarize this work in Section 5.

1092-3152/97 $10.00 © 1997 IEEE

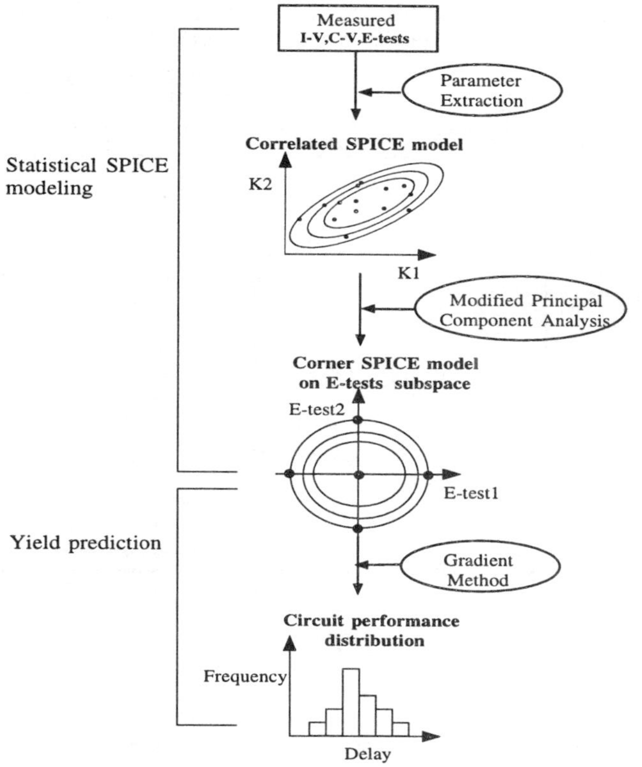

Figure 1: A global view of the statistical characterization system

2 The Statistical Characterization System for Worst Case Corners

A global view of the product design and characterization process is shown in Fig. 1. The proposed procedure constists of two parts: statistical SPICE modeling with parameter extraction and yield prediction.

First, APEX [7], which uses a nonlinear optimization method [8], automatically extracts SPICE model parameters from the database for I-V, C-V and E-tests together with the device geometries and layout design rules. After parameter extraction with mapping the process variations to SPICE model parameters, pdPCA [9, 10], a commercial tool exploiting correlations between parameters, interprets the covariance of correlated SPICE model parameters. Using pdPCA, we can derive a few independent E-tests which account for the total variance in SPICE model parameters. The SPICE model parameters can be expressed as functions of the critical independent E-tests.

After this, we can treat circuit performances as functions of reduced orthogonal spaces of E-tests, instead of fully correlated spaces of SPICE model parameters and deduce the relationship between the E-tests and circuit performances, geometrically and effectively. This result can be directly applied to the Gradient Method (GM), which lead to a more efficient prediction of circuit performances.

3 The Statistical Modeling Approach

3.1 Modified Principal Component Analysis

The Principal Component Analysis is a technique of transforming the correlated variables into uncorrelated variables, called principal components. Using this, each variable is a linear or nonlinear combination of the principal components. Thus, if $p_1, ...p_n$ are the principal components for n normalized response variables $x_1, x_2...x_n$, then the following formula for principal components (p_j) can be determined using the principal components analysis:

$$x_i = u_{i1}p_1 + u_{i2}p_2 + ... + u_{ij}p_j + ...u_{in}p_n \quad (1)$$
$$i, j = 1, 2, ...n$$

where
x_i is the ith SPICE model parameter,
p_j is the jth principal component and
u_{ij} is the loading value of x_i on p_j
(i.e., the correlation between x_i and p_j).
The coefficient u_{ij} is chosen to satisfy 2 requirements:

$$Var(p_i) > Var(p_j) \ where \ i > j \ and \quad (2)$$

$$p_i \cdot p_j = 0 \ (i \neq j). \quad (3)$$

Eq. (2) implies that the principal components are arranged in the order of decreasing variances and the most informative principal component is the first, and the least informative is the last. On the other hand, the variance of p_1 is as large as possible. Eq. (3) is important to deal with statistical simulation techniques because we want to express the circuit performance in terms of statistically uncorrelated, independent parameters [2, 3]. Therefore, based on the principal components, the original covariance of correlated SPICE model parameters can be explained by a few independent principal components (or pseudo parameters). However, these pseudo parameters represented in Eq. (1) from the traditional PCA are of no use because we cannot understand a physical meaning of them. Knowing the physical interpretation would enable us to track how changes in the process impacts circuit performance. It should be noticed that the principal components result statistically from the existence of a set of low level, independently varying physical quantities, called the process disturbances [11], that affect each process step in terms of the statistical variations of an IC process. However, since process disturbances are nonmeasurable quantities in general, a matching algorithm [12, 13], which looks for similarities between the principal components and E-tests, was incorporated in this work in order to replace the principal components with E-tests having the largest correlation value.

3.2 The Gradient Method

Despite of potential benefits of statistical design, it is difficult to apply it to statistical prediction of full-chip circuit performance because all statistical design tools and algorithms are too expensive in computational and engineering efforts. Therefore, a worst case design method to predict the standard deviations of circuit performances is more effective in terms of simulation time. The Gradient Method [2, 6] can be used to predict the standard deviation of the circuit performance. It amounts to the following problems:

$$z = f(x_1, x_2 ...) \tag{4}$$

where z is the simulated circuit performance (response) and x_i is an input parameter (design variable or SPICE model parameter). The standard deviation of circuit performance z can be predicted as:

$$\sigma_z = \sqrt{(\frac{\partial z}{\partial x_1})^2 \sigma_{x1}{}^2 + (\frac{\partial z}{\partial x_2})^2 \sigma_{x2}{}^2 + \cdots} \quad . \tag{5}$$

The expression of Eq. (5) is valid, if the input parameters are independent each other and the circuit performance z is a linear function in 3 σ window of component-space x_i (this assumption will be verified throughout experiments). In this simple equation, the standard deviation σ_{x_i} of x_i is measured and the gradient $\frac{\partial P}{\partial x_i}$ is calculated using circuit simulation. Therefore, the statistical distribution of the circuit performance can be estimated using GM with the minimum number of statistically uncorrelated independent factors that represent the variability in SPICE model parameters using MPCA.

4 Experimental Results

To demonstrate the use of statistical analysis on equivalent full-chip circuits of DRAMs, the circuit performances t_{RAC}, which is defined as the time-interval between RAS (Row Address Strobe) and DOUT (Data Out), was analyzed in the page mode operation. The primary interest for this example is the variation in the time delay t_{RAC} as a function of the statistical device parameters.

4.1 Worst Case Design

The measurements for this work consist of I-V/C-V curve collections and E-tests with temperature of 357 K. Table 1 lists the number of the devices and the SPICE model parameters for the parameter extraction and the statistical SPICE modeling. All sixteen devices (i.e, eight nMOSFETs and pMOSFETs) were included in this experiment. To determine the repeatability of the parameter extractor, many sets of 31 and 38 model parameters for nMOSFETs and pMOSFETs were extracted for the same device size. The simulation results using extracted SPICE model parameters agree well with the actual curves for both nMOSFETs and pMOSFETs, as shown in Fig. 2. The average RMS (Root of Mean Square) errors for sixteen devices is less than 5%. The total 69 × 69 correlation matrix for SPICE model parameters was obtained in order to preserve dependencies between nNMOSFET and pMOSFET. As described in the previous section,

Table 1: The number of transistors and HSPICE level 28 parameters used for parameter extraction

	NMOS	PMOS
The number of MOSFETs	8	8
The number of SPICE parameters	31	38

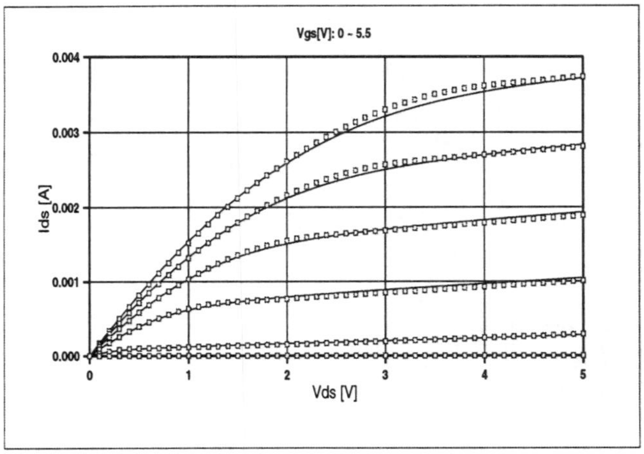

Figure 2: I-V characteristics of measured (line) and calculated (symbol) data of L = 0.35 μm nMOSFET

we apply pdPCA to determine the minimum number of statistically uncorrelated independent factors that represent the variability in SPICE model parameters.

As shown in Fig. 3 [10], total 12 principal components account for 100% of total variances in SPICE model parameters and each SPICE model parameter can be represented as a function of those, as in Eq. (1). Using the matching algorithm [13], the first 4-components can be replaced with Gmmax of L = 0.40 μm pMOSFET (G_{mmax}), the junction capacitance of n^+p type (C_j), the sheet resistance of plate poly (R_{spp}), and the threshold voltage of L = 25 μm pMOSFET (V_{th}), as shown in Fig. 4. The first factor accounts for 34% of the variance of the key I-V points and device physicals (E-tests and SPICE model parameters). The first factor mainly accounts for the variance of gate oxide thickness (TOXM), linear Vds threshold coefficient (ETA0), weak inversion factor (WFAC), back bias correction (X2M), and mobility reduction related sensitivity parameters (LU0 and LU1). Similarly, factors 2, 3, and 4 account for 15%, 12%, and 11%, respectively.

In Eq. (5), the GM is modeled assuming that the circuit performance is a linear function of principal components. This assumption has been verified using measurements for t_{RAC} versus the first component variation, as shown in Fig. 5. In this plot, we have observed that t_{RAC} can be approximated as a linear function of the first component (Gmmax). In [14], the algorithms are investigated in the case that the data points look like they could be better fit with a

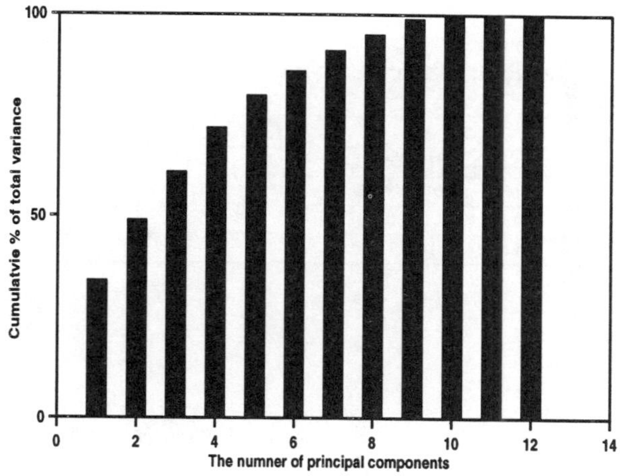

Figure 3: Cumulative percentage of total variances in SPICE model versus the selected number of principal components

	FACTOR1	FACTOR2	FACTOR3	FACTOR4	
Tracking E-tests	Gmmax	Cj	Rspp	Vth	SUM[%]
Ave.	34.0	15.0	12.0	11.0	72.0
toxm	90.8	1.3	2.2	0.0	94.3
eta0	78.6	4.8	1.8	0.0	85.2
k1	43.5	0.1	9.6	0.2	53.4
k2	1.6	3.3	26.2	10.1	41.1
muz	12.6	15.1	4.5	45.4	77.6
phi0	14.3	30.8	0.7	13.7	59.4
u00	1.9	15.1	12.3	7.6	36.9
u1	0.0	5.3	20.4	25.9	51.7
vfb0	45.7	33.7	0.1	0.3	79.9
wfac	76.8	1.1	1.4	7.4	86.6
x2m	82.6	0.6	0.1	1.2	84.5
leta	19.5	1.9	40.6	1.8	63.9
lk1	28.8	11.9	15.7	26.5	82.9
lk2	7.2	2.6	22.9	44.5	77.2
lmuz	5.9	1.2	25.0	51.7	83.8
lu0	72.0	1.1	12.6	1.0	86.7
lu1	80.4	0.7	4.5	0.7	86.3
lvfb	17.0	30.4	0.4	0.1	47.8
wk1	13.9	20.1	15.1	13.0	62.2
wk2	5.3	10.2	7.5	39.1	62.1
wmuz	51.1	4.9	20.8	7.3	84.1
wu0	26.3	8.1	0.2	9.1	43.7
wu1	0.2	25.7	23.8	6.2	55.9
wvfb	37.6	12.5	14.4	17.6	82.1
cj	2.3	88.0	5.9	0.1	96.3
cjsw	87.2	1.9	5.7	4.2	99.0
pb	4.3	22.2	31.5	8.6	66.6
mj	12.8	44.1	15.6	6.0	78.5
php	86.1	3.0	2.8	4.4	96.3
njsw	88.5	1.7	3.5	4.5	98.0
CGSO	35.5	0.2	6.1	12.1	54.0

Figure 4: Percentages of the HSPICE level 28 parameter variances which can be monitored by E-tests for nMOSFETs

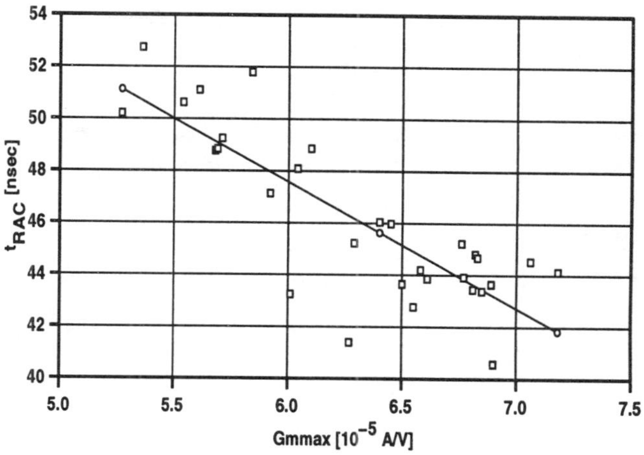

Figure 5: Experimental (box symbol) read access time, t_{RAC}, versus Gmmax of L = 0.40 μm pMOSFET (The solid line is a linear interpolation of data.)

piecewise-linear function.

As an example of the proposed approach, we compared the variations of t_{RAC} of 256 Mbit DRAMs with the predicted performances. The typical set of SPICE model parameters for the nominal design was determined by setting a mean value of G_{mmax}, C_j, R_{spp}, and V_{th} from measured data in Eq. (1). Then, best/worst values of t_{RAC} for statistical design can be obtained using GM. It is shown that the predicted performance variations agree well with the measured variations, as shown in Fig. 6.

Table 2 shows the comparison of the old method [2, 3, 15] and the new method. The old method uses the physically measurable model parameters and the key parameters in order to predict the actual circuit response to the extreme conditions of a manufacturing process. These physically measurable model parameters are called skew parameters [15] or principal factors [3]. The skew parameters are generally chosen to be independent of each other so that the combinations of skew parameters can be used to represent the worst case. The typical skew parameters for a CMOS technology include:

- XL - poly silicon variations
- XW - active width variations
- TOX - gate oxide thickness variations
- RSH - active layer resistivity variations
- DELVTO - threshold voltage variations

The worst case is simulated by taking all variables to their 2-σ or 3-σ worst case value (3-σ in this work). From Table 2, the new method models the real distribution of t_{RAC} more accurately than the old method.

4.2 The Estimation of the Process Shift Effects

The proposed method is also applied to 64 Mbit DRAMs. In this case, we have found that the first 4 components account for 75% of the total variance in

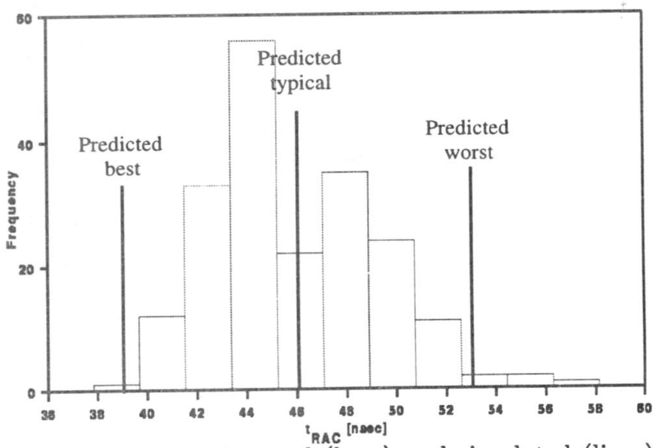

Figure 6: Experimental (bars) and simulated (lines) read access time, t_{RAC}, from 256 Mbit DRAM

Table 2: The comparison of thw new method and the old method

t_{RAC} [ns]	measured	new method	old method
best	39	39	41
typical	46	46	46
worst	57	53	52

the process variations and these components can be replaced with *Tox*, *Vth* and so on using the matching algorithm. From this result, we can resolve the problems related to the process shift. Actually, under development of the CMOS DRAM, gate oxide thickness (*Tox*), the channel implant for nMOSFETs, and heat annealing conditions were changed in order to obtain the margin of electrical characteristics on the dynamic condition of some critical circuits. The changed process conditions are shown in Table 3. From a parameterized SPICE model associated with some E-tests, a unified approach to SPICE model parameter monitoring can be maintained as the process shifts. Thus, the model parameter set corresponding to the process shift can be determined. In order to verify the shift model parameters, the threshold voltage and saturation current of L = 0.40 μm nMOSFET and L = 0.45 μm pMOSFET are shown in Table 4. The predicted values of V_{th} and I_{dsat} agree well with the measured values. In Table 5, the experiments and simulation results are compared. We can see that the calculated value of t_{RAC} agrees well with experimental data while the traditional method does not provide this result.

Yield estimation has been performed on the same product with an inexpensive Monte Carlo analysis [1, 16, 17]. As mentioned previously, since only a few statistical variables are responsible for the most of the process-induced variations on circuit performances, the parametric yield can be estimated efficiently using the RSM [18] model and the Monte Carlo analysis. Circuit simulations are performed by sampling from the normal distributions of the principal

Table 3: The conditions of process shifts

Process	Changed rate [%]
Channel dose	-10
Field-stop dose	12.5
Gate oxide thickness	11
Heat cycle time	100

Table 4: Calculated and measured *Vth* [V] and *Idsat* [mA] of NMOS and PMOS

	NMOS		PMOS	
	Vth	*Idsat*	*Vth*	*Idsat*
Measured	0.58	2.27	0.80	1.07
Calculated	0.60	2.28	0.80	1.15

Table 5: The comparison of measured and calculated typical t_{RAC}[ns]

Measured	Calculated	Error rate[%]
43	42.4	1.5

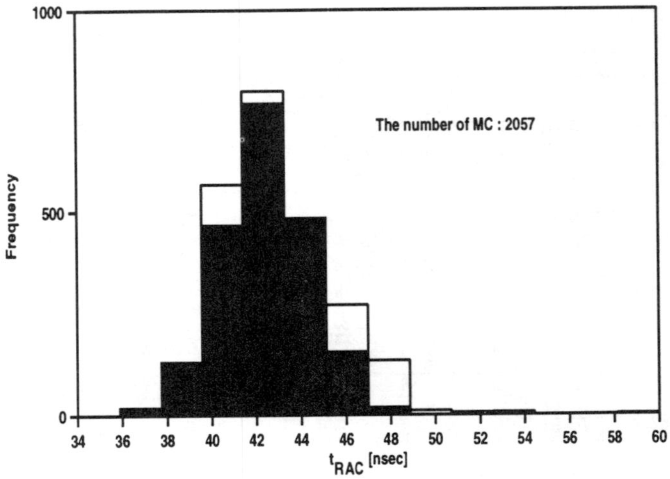

Figure 7: The comparison of measured (white bars) and predicted (black bars) distribution of t_{RAC}

components which are the results of PCA. Because it is sufficient to fit the linear model to the relationship between circuit performances and E-tests, we apply an Orthogonal Array (OA) design [19] which does not consider interactions of two variables. In the examples, the corresponding yield was estimated to be approximately 90% with 2057 Monte Carlo runs, as shown in Fig. 7. The measurement estimation gives us the yield of 80%.

5 Conclusions

An efficient methodology for yield prediction of full-chip circuit performance has been described in this paper. These algorithms are based on the Modified-Principal Component Analysis the and the Gradient Method. There are several distinct features in this work: 1) the Gradient Method allows a great simplification in obtaining the statistical worst case of full-chip circuit performance, 2) this methodology enables designers to track the circuit performance according to the process shift using measured E-tests, and 3) the parametric yield can be estimated effectively with an inexpensive Monte Carlo analysis without any need for the usual multitude of circuit simulations. Throughout the application to the full-chip circuits of high density DRAMs, it is proved that the new method provides designers with the accurate distributions of circuit performance and yield prediction.

Acknowledgments

The authors would like to thank Soon-Cheol Hong, Won-Woo Lee, and Jin-Kyu Park for valuable discussions and measurements. We would also like to thank Dr. Kyung-Ho Kim and Dr. Soo-In Cho who originally initiated and inspired this project.

References

[1] S. G. Duvall, "A practical methodology for the statistical design of complex logic products for performance," *IEEE Trans. VLSI Systems*, vol. 3, pp. 112–123, Jan. 1995.

[2] M. Bolt, M. Rocchi, and J. Engel, "Realistic statistical worst-case simulation of VLSI circuits," *IEEE Trans. Semiconductor Manufacturing*, vol. 4, pp. 193–198, Aug. 1991.

[3] P. Cox, P. Yang, S. S. Mahant-Shetti, and P. Chatterjee, "Statistical modeling for efficient parametric yield estimation of MOS VLSI circuits," *IEEE Trans. Electron Devices*, vol. ED-32, pp. 471–478, Feb. 1985.

[4] S. W. Director and G. D. Hachtel, "The simplicial approximation approach to design centering," *IEEE Trans. Circuits Syst.*, vol. CAS-24, pp. 363–372, July 1977.

[5] D. F. Morrison, *Multivariate Statistical Methods*, New York:McGraw-Hill, 1976.

[6] S. H. Lee, K. H. Kim, J. K. Park, C. H. Choi, J. T. Kong, W. W. Lee, W. S. Lee, J. H. Yoo, and S. I. Cho, "A realistic methodology for the worst case analysis of VLSI circuit performances," in *Int. Conf. on Simulation of Semiconductor Process and Devices*, pp. 155–156, 1996.

[7] C. H. Choi, J. K. Park, Y. G. Kim, K. H. Kim, and S. H. Lee, "New model parameter extraction environment for the submicron circuit models," *IEEE International Symposium on Circuit and Systems*, pp. 1535–1538, 1993.

[8] K. Doganis and D. L. Scharfetter, "General optimization and extraction of IC device model parameters," *IEEE Trans. Electron Devices*, ED-30, pp. 1219–1228, 1983.

[9] *pdPCA User's Manual*, PDF Solutions, 1996.

[10] D. A. Hanson and R. J.G. Goossens, "Analysis of Mixed-Signal Manufacturability with statistical TCAD," in *Int. Symp. on Semiconductor Manufacturing*, pp. 271–276, 1995.

[11] C. J. B. Spanos and S. W. Director, "Parameter extraction for statistical IC process characterization," *IEEE Trans. Computer-Aided Design*, vol. CAD-5, pp. 66–78, Jan. 1986.

[12] C. R. Shyamsundar, P. K. Mozumder, and A. J. Strojwas, "Statistical control of VLSI fabrication processes: a software system," *IEEE Trans. Semiconductor Manufacturing*, vol. 1, pp. 72–82, May 1988.

[13] J. Kibarian, "Statistical diagnosis of IC process faults," Ph. D. dissertation, CMUCAD 90-52, December 1990.

[14] Mien Li and Linda Milor, "Computing Parametric Yield Adaptively Using Local Linear Models," in *Proc. of the 33rd Design Automation Conference*, pp. 831–836, 1996.

[15] *HSPICE User's Manual*, Meta Software, 1996.

[16] T. K. Yu, S. M. Kang, I. N. Hajj, and T. N. Trick, "iEDISON: An interactive statistical design tool for MOS VLSI circuits," in *Proc. IEEE Int. Conf. Computer-Aided Design*, pp. 20–23, Nov. 1988.

[17] L. Milnor and A. Sangiovanni-Vincentelli, "Computing parametric yield accurately and efficiently," in *Proc. IEEE Int. Conf. Computer-Aided Design*, pp. 116–119, 1990.

[18] R. H. Myers and D. C. Montgomery, *Response Surface Methodology: Process and Product Optimization Using Designed Experiments*, John Wiley and Sons, New York, 1995.

[19] A. Dey, *Orthogonal Fractional Factorial*, New York: Halsted Press, 1985.

Fast field solver programs for thermal and electrostatic analysis of microsystem elements

Vladimir Székely
szekely@eet.bme.hu

Márta Rencz
rencz@eet.bme.hu

Technical University of Budapest, H-1521 Budapest, Hungary

Abstract

To solve the problem of fast thermal and electrostatic simulation of microsystem elements two different field solver tools have been developed at TUB. The μS-THERMANAL program is capable for the fast steady state and dynamic simulation of suspended multi-layered microsystem structures, while the 2D-SUNRED program is the first version of a general field solver program, based on an original method, the Successive Network Reduction. This program offers a very fast and accurate substitute of FEM programs for the solution of the Poisson equation, e.g. solving a 32000 grid problem in about 6 minutes on a 586 PC. Application examples show the usability of the tools.

1. Introduction

Thermal effects play fundamental role in the operation of many microsystem elements, as infrared sensors, rms meters, etc. Even if the thermal effect is not the base of the operation like in the previous examples, exact calculation of the always present thermal effects is required in many cases during the design of microsystem elements. Electrostatic fields have to be calculated during microsystem design e.g. in the case of capacitive displacement sensors and during the analysis of actuators based on the electrostatic force. All these problems require fast and reliable field solver programs capable to solve the Laplace or Poisson equations.

FEM methods can always be used for this purpose, but the drawbacks are well known, the huge amount of time required to define the problem and for the calculation, and the difficulty of modifying the once already analyzed structure.

There exist well established methods and tools for the thermal simulation of integrated circuits and other layer-structured systems, but the integrated microsystems raise new problems in the thermal simulation, since the frequently used suspended structures, such as cantilevers, membranes, bridges etc. have different boundary conditions from those of the simple silicon cubes of conventional integrated circuits. The μS-THERMANAL program has been developed for the thermal simulation of suspended microsystem elements, based on the THERMANAL program, which has been used for the steady state and frequency domain thermal simulation of multi-layered semiconductor structures for more than 18 years. In this paper after a short presentation of the THERMANAL program we present those features of the μS-THERMANAL program that were developed especially for the simulation of dedicated microsystem elements.

During our work in the thermal simulation of 3D SOI structures we encountered the problem, that the accuracy of the applied FEM simulation tool had to be limited down to an unacceptable value if we wanted to have the simulation results in a reasonable time (in days, in this case). To overcome this problem we have developed a new dedicated field solver program, which works currently in two dimensions, but it is expandable to 3D, it is very fast, accurate and very easy to use. The applied method is a finite difference method, the algorithm is successive node reduction, leading finally to the thermal impedance matrix of the boundary nodes. The temporary name of the program is 2D-SUNRED, coming from SUccessive Node REDuction. In the second part of our paper we present this program with application examples.

2. The μS-THERMANAL program

Overview of the features

The ancestor of this program, the THERMANAL program was an early realization of the well known algorithm of Kokkas [1], with the extension for unlimited number of layers [2]. In the model of Kokkas the structure consists of equally shaped rectangular layers stacked on an ideal heat sink. The dissipating elements are on the surface of the uppermost layer only, and the heat is removed via the bottom surface, the side walls are adiabatic. Heat transfer is assumed only by conduction. The differential equation of the heat flow (the Laplace equation) is written up for each layer, and the solutions are matched on the layer interfaces.

In the algorithm of [1] the solution of the differential equation is constructed in the form of two-dimensional Fourier-cosine series. In our program this series is calculated by Fast Fourier Transformation (FFT) method – resulting in a quick solution method in most cases.

1092-3152/97 $10.00 © 1997 IEEE

We have extended this model by the consideration of free convection cooling, the detailed description can be found in [4]. This extension is very important in the case of microsystems, where the presence and cooling effect of the surrounding air can not be neglected in most of the cases.

The assumption that the dissipation occurs only on the surface is rather rough, even in the case of ICs. This is why we modified the original algorithm also towards considering dissipators in several different layers. The mathematical description of the algorithm can be found in [5].

Simulation of membranes

The above discussed algorithm relatively easily can be extended to calculate the temperature distribution on multi-layer structured membranes as well, where the dissipation pattern and the structure of the membrane are given. In this case the boundary conditions are different from the usual IC structure: the top and the bottom surface of a membrane are adiabatic, while the side walls are isothermal, considering the bulk silicon nearly ideal heat sink.

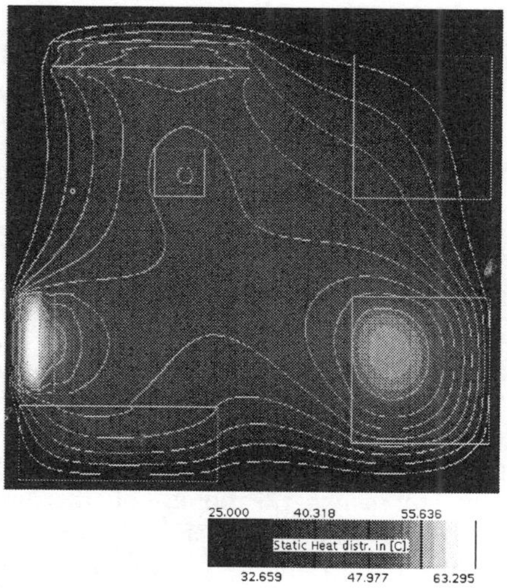

Fig.1. Steady-state temperature distribution on a membrane surface. The rectangular shapes are the dissipating elements.

These boundary conditions are fulfilled by using Fourier-sine expansion instead of Fourier-cosine [4]. Simulation results of a membrane structure are presented in Fig.1.

Simulation of bridge structures

On the top and bottom surface of the bridges the boundary condition for the temperature is adiabatic, like in the case of membranes. The side wall conditions are different now for the neighbor sides, the two isothermal sides (the fixings of the bridge) are between the two adiabatic sides. These boundary conditions are fulfilled using Fourier-sine expansion in x_1 direction and Fourier-cosine expansion in x_2 direction [4]. μS-THERMANAL simulation results of a multi-layer bridge structure are presented in Fig.2. Fulfilling of the side wall conditions are easily observable, the effect of the presence of air under the surface is considered appropriately. The structure and the dissipation pattern is the same as in Fig.1, but the difference in the temperature distribution because of the different side wall conditions is considerable.

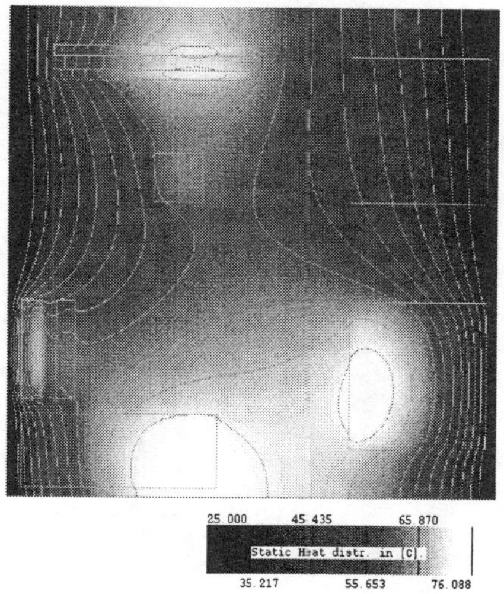

Fig.2. Steady-state temperature distribution on the surface of a multi-layer bridge structure. The left and right sides are the fixings of the bridge.

Simulation of cantilevers

A cantilever is fixed only by one side wall, consequently it can be always considered as a half bridge with special symmetry conditions. This is how cantilever problems are solved in the μS-THERMANAL. The cantilever is mirrored to form a symmetric bridge, and the bridge problem is solved with the previously discussed boundary conditions. This way the symmetry axis of the bridge, which is the free end of the cantilever, automatically fulfills also the adiabatic boundary condition.

Extension for heat transfer via beam leads

From heat transfer point of view a special class of microsystem elements are the parts suspended on thin and narrow strips. H shaped membranes and cantilevers with a narrow neck belong to this class, just like the ball grid array attachment of conventional IC chips. In these structures the leads act as heat sinking elements. In the μS-THERMANAL program we consider them as dissipating elements with negative dissipation. [3].

The analysis of a membrane structure suspended at two opposite sides by two narrow necks is shown in Fig.3. This example is also appropriate for the comparison of the μS-THERMANAL simulations with FEM simulations. The good agreement in the simulation results of the two programs is clearly visible in Fig.3, but the μS-THERMANAL program needed 500 times less CPU time for the calculation than the SYSTHERM [6] program. About 9 minute was required to prepare the μS-THERMANAL task in contrast with the 1 hour preparation time required for the SYSTHERM task preparation for someone who uses SYSTHERM every day.

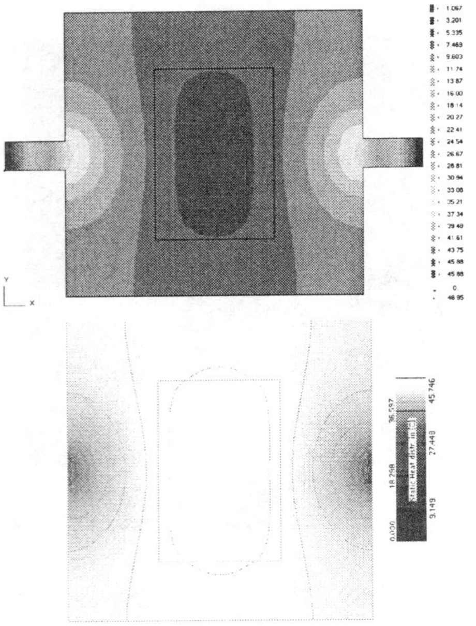

Fig.3. Comparison of narrow-neck suspended membrane simulations. Top: SYSTHERM simulation, bottom: μS-THERMANAL simulation

3. SUNRED: a 2D thermal and electrostatic simulator

This tool is designed especially for the fast calculation of the thermal behavior of arbitrary shape integrated microstructures. A special requirement was to calculate on a grid that is fine enough to obtain not only the temperature distribution but the accurate streamlines of the heat-flow as well.

An interesting feature of this simulator is that characteristic methods of three disjunct disciplines are combined in it. These fields are

- the electromagnetic field theory,
- the linear network theory and
- image processing.

Combination of these methods resulted in a very useful tool.

The model

The current 2D version of the program treats the linear heat conduction problems in two dimensions. Anisotropy can be taken into account. The equation being solved is

$$\partial_i \lambda_{ij} \partial_j T(x_i) = p(x_i) \qquad {}_{i,j=1...2} \qquad (1)$$

where λ_{ij} is the heat conductivity, $T(x_i)$ is the thermal field and $p(x_i)$ is the incoming heat flux density. This is the well-known Poisson equation, the mathematical description of many physical phenomenon. Electrical current-stream fields and electrostatic potential fields can be described by the same equation, which means that the program is capable to solve such problems as well.

The investigated area is a rectangle. A dense equidistant grid is spawned to this area defining a cell matrix. The suggested grid size is either 128×128 or 256×256 (for a PC, higher resolution can be used on workstations). A material type is assigned to each cell. This assignment is performed by constructing an image – in the sense of the digital image handling methods. Each pixel of this digital image corresponds to a grid-cell whereas the material type constituting the cell is coded by the color of the pixel. Thus, in order to enter a problem two files have to prepared:

- the "problem-image" which can be in any usual image format (the suggested format is the BMP),
- the "material-table" assigning different material parameters to each color.

This method of problem definition provides a very easy and fast input of arbitrary shaped complex geometrical arrangements (using any general picture editing tools). Limitation is coming only from the finite resolution of the digital image. Real images, e.g. a microscopic image of some IC structure may also be used as geometry input.

On the edges of the investigated area either forced temperature or zero heat-flow can be prescribed – individually, for any grid points of the boundary. Excitations can be defined inside the area as well, forcing a given temperature or a given heat-flux to any cell, only a new "color" should be introduced for each excitation value in the problem image.

The solution of Eq.(1) is accomplished using the method of *finite differences* . The cells of the field are squares (or rectangles) described by an electrical model, with a node in their center (Fig.4a.). Heat flux can be forced into them – this corresponds to the current flowing into this node. Forced temperature means the forced voltage value of the cell node.

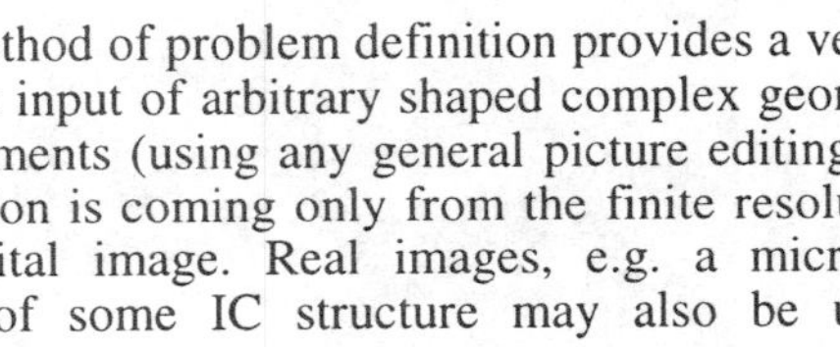

Fig.4. Cell, center node and terminal nodes

The boundary between different materials is lying always on the cell edges. In other words: each cell is "filled" by a single material. Each cell has four terminals in the direction of its four neighbors (Fig.4b.). On the terminals each cell can be described by a 4×4 matrix. This way the center node is hidden, but knowing the terminal temperatures the temperature of the center node can be back-calculated. Fig.4c. presents that the cell shows four terminals to the outside and the inner node is hidden.

The model of the cell is shown in Fig.5. In the present steady state version it contains four thermal conductances. The value of these depend on the thermal conductivity of the material filling the cell and on the geometry. This basic cell can be described by an admittance matrix of 4×4 size.

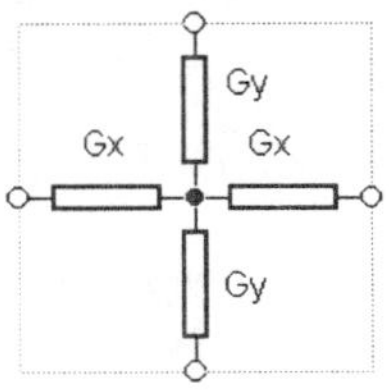

Fig.5. Circuit model of a single cell

The solution algorithm

The solution of the problem is done by the electrical solution of the whole model network. This raises serious problems because of the size of this network. Using a grid of 128×128 lines the model network consists of 32768 nodes. For a 256×256 grid arrangement this number is 131072. Although the corresponding circuit matrix is extremely sparse the solution of such a big network is a hard problem.

We have not considered iterative solutions – only direct methods have been investigated. A successive procedure has been developed for the network reduction – the essential features of which are briefly presented in the following.

Four basic cells can be assembled to form a block or macrocell as shown in Fig.6a. In other words: a *1st order cell* has been built from four *zero-order cells*. The four inner connecting terminals of the cells can be eliminated; they should not appear in the outside-directed description (Fig.6b.). The size of the Y matrix of the 1st level cell is 8x8 containing 64 values (which is equal to the 4x16 elements of the four zero-level cells).

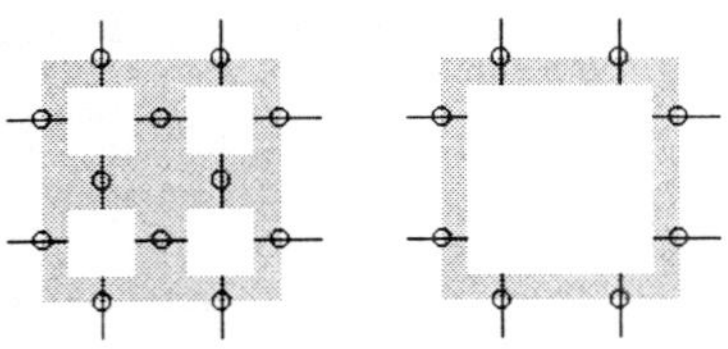

Fig.6. Four basic cells will constitute a 1st level cell

Using four 1st level cells we can assemble a 2nd level cell as shown in Fig.7. The inner terminals can be eliminated again.

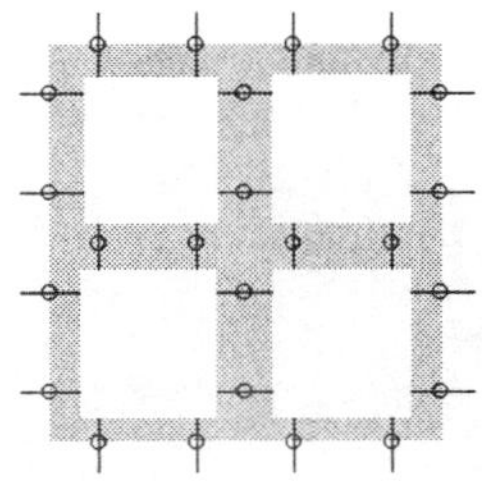

Fig.7. Building a 2nd level cell

Continuing this successive building of higher and higher level cells we obtain finally the matrix of a single cell – the terminals of which are lying on the four edges of the investigated rectangular field. Matching with the boundary conditions means the solution of this matrix for the U or I constraints, given individually for the terminals lying on the boundaries of the investigated field. The voltages of all the inside nodes can then be calculated by a successive back-substitution.

The advantage of the presented solution algorithm lies in the fact that most of the grid nodes are eliminated before the final solution of the system equation. Supposing e.g. a problem field of 128×128 grid points we have 32768 inner nodes but we should solve an equation of only 4×128=512 unknowns.

The hierarchical network reduction requires $\log_2(128)=7$ successive steps for the 128×128 grid, 8 steps for the grid-size of 256 and so on. The detailed analysis of the T total computing time gives

$$T = 63.5\ N^{3/2}\ (T_{*+}) \qquad (2)$$

where N is the node number for the whole model network and (T_{*+}) is the time of one multiplication and one addition. This time should be compared to the Ordo(N^3) time requirement of a "brutal force" Gauss elimination. For a 32768 node problem the solution time is only 6 minutes on a 586 PC, thanks to the efficiency of the successive network reduction algorithm.

It should be emphasized that the network reduction step has to be executed only once for a structure. Changes in the excitations or in the boundary conditions require to repeat the back-substitution only – which requires much less time than the reduction itself.

In the present phase of the development the algorithm handles the steady-state case only. The implementation of the frequency and time-domain solutions does not hold any difficulties however, we are currently working on these extensions.

Presentation of the results

The results of the simulation are treated as images again. The temperature (or potential) fields which are essentially 2D scalar functions can be considered as black-and-white images. The brightness of the image points is proportional to the temperature (or potential) of each point. The program provides the results in form of digital images, in the standard BMP image format. Such a potential image is shown in Fig.8.

Fig.8. Grayscale image of a potential field (a horizontal electrode in a conducting corner)

Although this image gives a good qualitative view of the potential field, the potential values can not be read from this picture. A basic procedure of image processing can help to overcome this problem. This procedure is the intensity transformation: an arbitrary $b_{tr}=f(b)$ function is used to map the original b pixel intensities into the b_{tr} brightness values. A set of appropriately chosen functions offer a rich variety of presentations for the same temperature (potential) field, and provides the good quantitative evaluation at the same time. Fig.9a. is an example for the intensity mapping functions, the corresponding image is shown

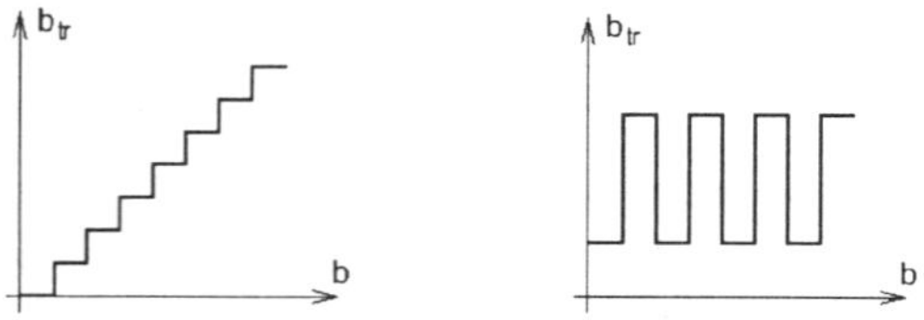

a.) *b.)*

Fig.9. Brightness mapping functions

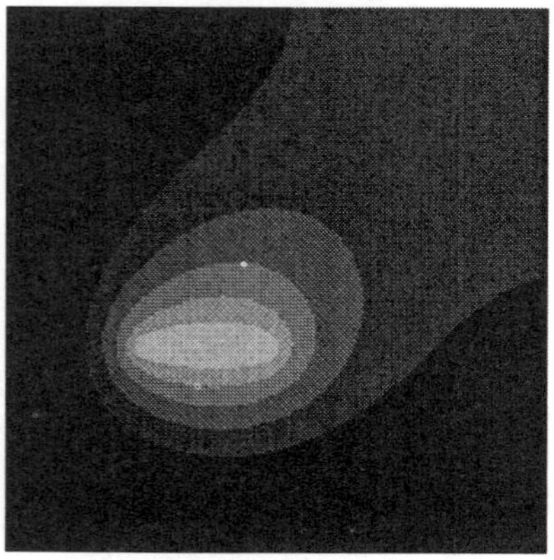

Fig.10. The stepped brightness mapping function and the resulting image

in Fig.10. The stepped character of the *f(b)* function results in abrupt intensity changes in the image, and the boundary between the different intensities traces an equipotential line. The telegraph-signal-like intensity mapping of Fig.9b. produces an even more explicit drawing of the equipotential lines (see Fig.11.) Using color displays intensity-color mappings are possible as well providing striking, rainbow-like pictures.

Fig.11. Potential or temperature field using the telegraph signal like intensity mapping.

The temperature field or potential image is usually not enough to visualize thermal, electrostatic or streaming fields. Tracing of the heat-stream lines (or electrical field lines) is an often encountered requirement. Especially in the case of temperature fields the streamlines provide an easy way to "discover" how and where the heat flux is streaming.

To obtain streamline pictures further image processing steps are required. The simulator provides the J_x, J_y components of the $\boldsymbol{J}$ current density vector in form of two intensity images. These vectors have to be turned by 90°. This can be made simply by interchanging the two images and negating one of them:

$$G_x = J_y \qquad (3)$$
$$G_y = -J_x$$

It can be easily proven that the *P(x,y)* potential function of this $\boldsymbol{G}$ field is suitable to trace the streamlines. The equipotential lines of this *P pseudo potential* are the streamlines of the original field. Visualization of these lines can be proceeded in the same way as in case of the real potential field.

For the sake of the mathematical correctness it should be mentioned that this pseudo potential can be constructed if and only if there is no divergence in the ***J****(x,y)* vector-field. This means that the procedure can be applied only on the divergence-free regions of the field.

Examples

In the first example the thermal field of a micromachined bridge is calculated. In order to demonstrate the capability of the program an irregularly shaped bridge has been analyzed. A single dissipating shape is defined on the bridge. The calculated temperature distribution of the structure is shown in Fig.12. It is not so easy to see from this plot where the most important part of the heat stream is flowing. The streamline calculation helps us to have an image. In Fig.13. the streamlines are plotted. These streamlines are suitable to examine the division of the heat flux between the two possible paths.

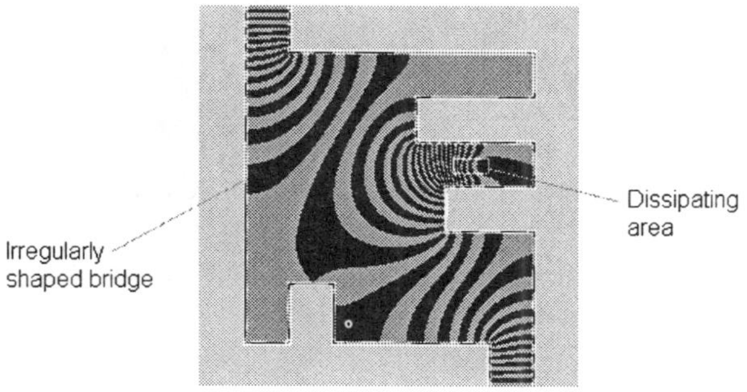

Fig.12. Isothermal lines on the bridge

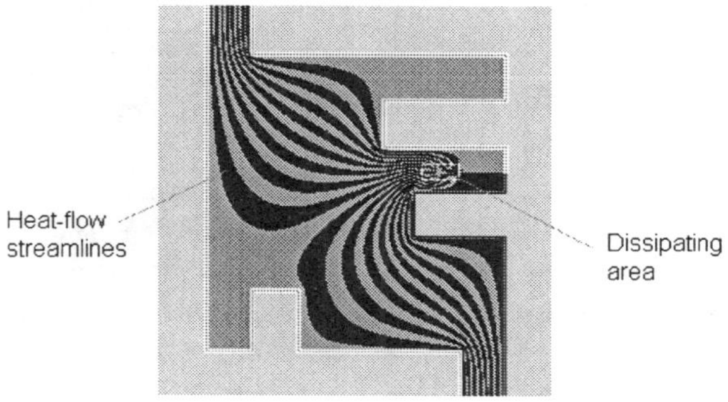

Fig. 13. Streamlines of the heat-flow

In the second example a 3D stacked submicron CMOS SOI structure [8] is investigated. The heat is generated in the upper transistor. The results of the simulation are shown in Fig.14. The highly different thermal conductivity of the silicon and the SiO_2 leads to the surprising fact that the heat stream makes a detour (see the white arrows) around the SiO_2 region.

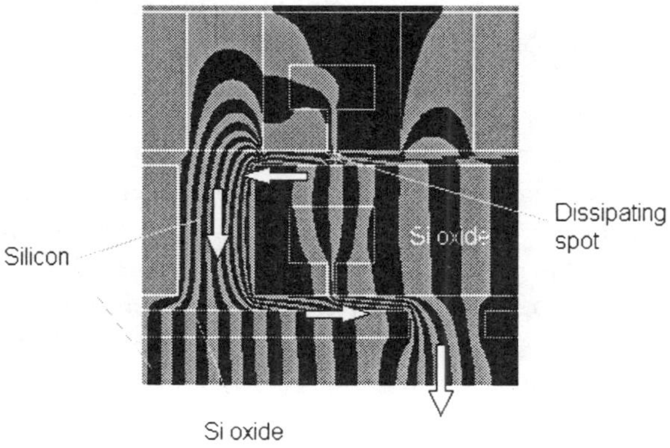

Fig.14. Heat-flow in a stacked SOI structure

4. Conclusions

Two new, fast and easy-to-use simulation tools have been developed for the accurate thermal and electrostatic simulation of dedicated microsystem elements and special 3D structures.

With the help of the novel 2D-SUNRED program arbitrarily shaped structures can be analyzed with very high accuracy in minutes in a PC – enabling also the visualization of the accurate heat flow paths in the material, that we could not obtain with usual FEM programs. The program calculates currently in two dimensions. The development of the dynamic and the 3D version of the program is in progress, they can be hopefully presented already at the conference.

Using the μS-THERMANAL simulator as the field solver of electro-thermal simulators, like the SISSI program [7], even the accurate dynamic electro-thermal simulation of electronic circuits realized on microsystem elements becomes possible.

Acknowledgments

We wish to acknowledge the financial support of the BARMINT EU ESPRIT-III basic research project, the HIPERLOGIC EU ESPRIT-IV long term research project, and the financial support of the OMFB Hungarian Research and Development Fund.

References

[1] **A.G. Kokkas:** Thermal analysis of multiple-layer structures, IEEE Trans. on El. Dev., V. ED-21, No. 11, pp. 674-681 (1974)

[2] **V. Székely, P. Baji, M. Rencz:** Graphical computer methods in the design of integrated circuits, Periodica Polytechnica, V. 23, No. 3-4, pp. 331-338 (1979)

[3] **V. Székely, A. Poppe:** Novel trools for thermal and electrical analysis of circuits, Electrosoft, V. 1. No. 4. pp. 234-252 (1990)

[4] **V. Székely, A. Csendes, M. Rencz:** μS-THERMANAL: An efficient thermal simulation tool for microsystem elements and MCM's. *SPIE'96 Symposium on Micromachining and Microfabrication, 14-15 October 1996, Austin, Texas, USA, SPIE Proc. Vol. 2880, pp. 64-75.*

[5] **A. Csendes, V. Székely, M. Rencz:** An efficient thermal simulation tool for IC's, microsystem elements and MCM's: the μS-THERMANAL, *Accepted for publication, Microelectronics Journal, 1997*

[6] SYSTUS: User's manual, Rev. A and SYSTHERM: Advanced thermics manual, Rev A, Framasoft, Sept. 1992

[7] **V. Székely, A. Páhi, A. Poppe, M. Rencz, A. Csendes:** SISSSI – a tool for dynamic electro-thermal simulation of analog VLSI cells, EDAC-ETC-ASIC European Design and Test Conference, 17-20 March 1997, Paris, France, pp. 617

[8] **V. Dudek, V.O. Keck, G. Mayer, B. Höfflinger:** Design considerations for high performance low-power Silicon-on-insulator gate arrays, Custom Integrated Circuits Conference 1995, Santa Clara, CA, May 1995

Java as a Specification Language for Hardware-Software Systems

Rachid Helaihel and Kunle Olukotun
Computer Systems Laboratory
Stanford University, Stanford, CA 94305
{rashhel, kunle}@ogun.stanford.edu

Abstract

The specification language is a critical component of the hardware-software co-design process since it is used for functional validation and as a starting point for hardware-software partitioning and co-synthesis. This paper proposes the Java programming language as a specification language for hardware-software systems. Java has several characteristics that make it suitable for system specification. However, static control and dataflow analysis of Java programs is problematic because Java classes are dynamically linked. This paper provides a general solution to the problem of statically analyzing Java programs using a technique that pre-allocates most class instances and aggressively resolves memory aliasing using global analysis. The output of our analysis is a control dataflow graph for the input specification. Our results for sample designs show that the analysis can extract fine to coarse-grained concurrency for subsequent hardware-software partitioning and co-synthesis steps of the hardware-software co-design process to exploit.

1 Introduction

Hardware-software system solutions have increased in popularity in a variety of design domains [1] because these systems provide both high performance and flexibility. Mixed hardware-software implementations have a number of benefits. Hardware components provide higher performance than can be achieved by software for certain time-critical subsystems. Hardware also provides interfaces to sensors and actuators that interact with the physical environment. On the other hand, software allows the designer to specify the system at high levels of abstraction in a flexible environment where errors - even at late stages in the design - can be rapidly corrected [2]. Software therefore contributes to decreased time-to-market and decreased system cost.

Hardware-software system design can be broken down into the following main steps: system specification, partitioning, and co-synthesis. The first step in an automatic hardware-software co-design process is to establish a complete system specification. This specification is used to validate the desired behavior without considering implementation details. Functional validation of the system specification is critical to keep the system development time short because functional errors are easier to fix and less costly to handle earlier in the development process. Given a validated system specification, the hardware-software partitioner step divides the system into hardware, software subsystems, and necessary interfaces by analyzing the concurrency available in the specification. The partitioner maps concurrent blocks into communicating hardware and software components in order to satisfy performance and cost constraints of the design. The final co-synthesis step generates implementations of the different subsystems by generating machine code for the software subsytems and hardware configuration data for the hardware subsystems.

The system specification is a critical step in the co-design methodology because it drives the functional validation step and the hardware-software partitioning process. Thus, the choice of a specification language is important. Functional validation entails exploration of the design space using simulation; hence, the specification must allow efficient execution. This requires a compile and run-time environment that efficiently maps the specification onto general-purpose processor platforms. On the other hand, the partitioning process requires a precise input specification whose concurrency can be clearly identified. Generating a precise specification requires language constructs and abstractions that directly correspond to characteristics of hardware or software. Traditionally, designers have not been able to reconcile these two objectives in one specification language, but have instead been forced to maintain multiple specifications. Obviously, maintaining multiple specifications of the design is at best tedious due to the need to keep all specifications synchronized. It is also error-prone because different specification languages tend to have different programming models and semantics. This need for multiple specifications is due to shortcomings of

1092-3152/97 $10.00

current specification languages used in hardware-software co-design.

Hardware-software specification languages currently used by system designers can be divided into software programming languages and hardware description languages. Software languages such as C or C++ generate high-performance executable specifications of system behavior for functional validation. Software languages are traditionally based on a sequential execution model derived from the execution semantics of general purpose processors. However, software languages generally do not have support for modeling concurrency or dealing with hardware issues such as timing or events. These deficiencies can be overcome by providing the designer with library packages that emulate the missing features [15]. A more serious problem is that software languages allow the use of indirect memory referencing which is very difficult to analyze statically. This makes it difficult for static analysis to extract implicit concurrency within the specification. Hardware description languages such as Verilog [5] and VHDL [6] are optimized for specifying hardware with support for a variety of hardware characteristics such as hierarchy, fine-grained concurrency, and elaborate timing constructs. Esterel is another specification language similar to Verilog with more constructs for handling exceptions [7]. SpecCharts builds on a graphical structural hierarchy while using VHDL to specify the implementations of the various structures in the hierarchy [4]. These languages do not have high-level programming constructs, and this limits their expressiveness and makes it difficult to specify software. Furthermore, these languages are based on execution models that require a great deal of run-time interpretation such as event-driven semantics. This results in low-performance execution compared to software languages.

This paper advocates the use of Java as a single specification language for hardware-software systems by identifying key language characteristics that enable both efficient functional validation and concurrency exploration by the hardware-software partitioner. Java is a general-purpose, concurrent, object-oriented, platform-independent programming language [10]. Java is implementation-independent because its run-time environment is an abstract machine called the Java virtual machine (JVM) with its own instruction set called bytecodes [11]. The virtual machine uses a stack-based architecture; therefore, Java bytecodes use an operand stack to store temporary results to be used by later bytecodes. Java programs are set in an object-oriented framework and consist of multiple classes, each of which is compiled into a binary representation called the classfile format. This representation lays out all the class information including the class's data fields and methods whose code segments are compiled into bytecodes. These fields and methods can be optionally declared as static. Static fields or methods of a class are shared by all instances of that class while non-static fields or methods are duplicated for each new instance. Data types in Java are either *primitive types* such as integers, floats, and characters or *references* (pointers) to class instances and arrays [10]. Since Java classes are predominantly linked at run-time, references to class instances cannot be resolved at compile-time. This presents a challenge to static analyzers in determining data flow through data field accesses and control flow through method calls.

This paper also outlines a control/dataflow analysis technique that can be used as a framework for detecting concurrency in the design. Our analysis technique provides a general solution for the problem of dynamic class allocation by aggressively pre-allocating most class instances at compile-time and performing global reference analysis.

The rest of the paper is organized as follows. In Section 2 we explain why Java is well-suited for hardware-software system specification. In Section 3 we identify the problems that arise when analyzing Java programs and present a general solution for building control flow and dataflow dependence information. We apply our technique to three sample designs and analyze both explicit and implicit concurrency in these designs in Section 4. We conclude and briefly discuss future directions in Section 5.

2 Hardware-Software Specification with Java

It is desirable for the hardware-software co-design process to use a single specification language for design entry because specifications using different languages for software and hardware combine different execution models. This makes these specifications difficult to simulate and to analyze. Some researchers begin with a software programming language usually C++ and extend this language with constructs to support concurrency, timing, and events by providing library packages or by adding new language constructs. Examples of these approach are Scenic [15] and V++ [17]. We take a slightly different approach. Instead of requiring the designer to specify the hardware implementation details in the specification, in our approach the designer models the complete system in an algorithmic or behavioral fashion. Software languages are well-suited for this type of modeling. Once the specification is complete, an automatic compilation process is used to analyze the specification to identify the coarse-grained concurrency described by the designer and uncover the finer-grained concurrency implicit in the specification. The partitioning and synthesis steps of the hardware-software co-design process use the concurrency uncovered by this analysis to create an optimized hardware-software system. The specification language used with this approach must have the ability to specify explicit concurrency and make it easy to uncover the implicit concurrency.

Coarse-grained concurrency is intuitive for the designer to specify because hardware-software systems are often conceptualized as sets of concurrent behaviors [2]. Java is a multi-threaded language and can readily express this sort of concurrency. Such concurrent behaviors can be modeled by sub-classing the *Thread* class and overriding its *run* method to encode the thread behavior as shown in Figure 1.

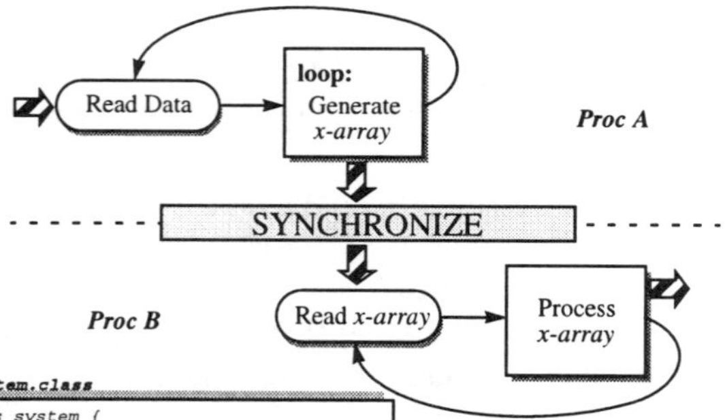

system.class

```
class system {
  static Thread procA, procB;
  public static void main(String argv[])
  {
    procA = new procAClass();
    procB = new procBClass(procA);
    // Launch threads
    procA.start();
    procB.start();
    ...
  }
}
```

procAClass.class

```
class procAClass extends Thread {
  boolean xready = false;
  synchronized void setXArray(...)
  {
    xready = true;
    ... // Write x-array data
  }
  synchronized arr_t getXArray(...)
  {
    xready = false;
    ... // Return x-array data
  }
  public void run()
  {
    while (...not done...) {
      while (this.xready == true)
        yield();
      for (int i = 0; i < 100; i++)
        x[i] = compute_xarray(...);
      setXArray(...);
    }
  }
}
```

procBClass.class

```
class procBClass extends Thread {
  procAClass procA;
  procBClass(Thread procA_in)
  {
    procA = (procAClass) procA_in;
  }
  public void run()
  {
    while (...not done...) {
      while (this.xready == false)
        yield();
      getXArray(...);
      ... // Process data
    }
  }
}
```

Figure 1. Concurrency in Java

The *Thread* class provides methods such as *suspend* and *resume*, *yield*, and *sleep* that manipulate the thread. Synchronization, however, is supported at a lower level using monitors implemented in two bytecode operations that provide an entry and an exit to the monitor. The sample design shown in Figure 1 maintains synchronization when reading and writing the *x-array* in methods *getXArray* and *setXArray* which are tagged as *synchronized.*

Fine-grained concurrency is usually either non-intuitive or cumbersome for the designer to express in the specification. This implies that an automated co-design tool must be able to uncover fine-grained concurrency by analyzing the specification. The primary form of concurrency to look for is loop-level concurrency where multiple iterations of the same loop can be executed simultaneously. This form of concurrency is important to detect because algorithms generally spend most of their time within core loops. Identifying and exploiting parallel core loops can thus provide significant performance enhancements. Determining whether loop iterations are parallel requires analysis to statically determine if data dependencies exist across these loop iterations. In the *run* method of *procAClass* shown in Figure 1, if the *compute_xarray* call does not depend on values generated in previous iterations of the for-loop, then all the iterations of the loop may be executed simultaneously. The major hurdle that the data dependence analysis must overcome is dealing with memory references because these references introduce a level of indirection in reading and writing physical memory locations. Compile-time analysis has to be conservative in handling such references. This conservatism is necessary to guarantee correct system behavior across transformations introduced by the partitioning step based on the results of the analysis. However, this conservatism causes the analysis to generate false data dependences which are nonexistent at the system level. These dependences reduce the data parallelism that the analysis detects. In the simple design shown in Figure 1, without the ability to analyze dependences within the for-loop and across the associated method call, conservative analysis would determine that the loop iterations are interdependent and hence can only be performed sequentially reducing the degree of data parallelism in that section of the specification by 100-fold. The advantage that Java has over a language like C++ is that Java restricts the programmer's use of memory references. In Java, memory references are strongly typed. Also, references are strictly treated as object handles and not as memory addresses. Consequently, pointer arithmetic is disallowed. This restrictive use of references enables more aggressive analysis to reduce false data dependences.

A co-design specification language should provide high-performance execution to enable rapid functional validation. Java's execution environment uses a virtual machine. The JVM provides platform-independence; however, this independence requires Java code to be executed by an interpreter which reduces execution performance compared to an identical specification modeled in C++. Although this performance degradation is at least an order of magnitude for Sun's JDK 1.0 run-time environment, techniques such as just-in-time compilation are closing the performance gap to less than two-times that of C++[12][16]. This evolution in Java tools and technology has been and will be driven by Java's success in other domains, especially network-based applications. Moreover, the Java run-time environment makes it easy to instrument and gather profiling information which can be used to guide hardware-software partitioning.

3 Analyzing Java Programs

Control and dataflow analysis of the Java specification is required for partitioning and co-synthesis steps of the codesign process. This analysis examines the bytecodes of invoked methods to determine their relative ordering and data dependencies. These bytecodes have operand and result types that are either primitive types, or classes and arrays. While primitive types are always handled *by value*, class and array variables are handled *by reference*. These object (class instance) references are pointers; however, they are well-behaved compared to their C/C++ counterparts because these references are strongly typed and cannot be manipulated.

Object references point to class instances that are linked dynamically during run-time. So, prior to executing the Java program, we can only allocate the static fields and methods of the program's classes. This makes it difficult to statically analyze Java programs because if object references cannot be resolved, calls to methods of these dynamically linked objects cannot be resolved either. This makes it impossible to determine control flow. The only way to deal with this problem is to conservatively assign the method invocation to software so that the software run-time system can handle the dynamic resolution. However, this reduces the opportunities for extracting parallelism in hardware and thus leads to inferior hardware-software design.

In order to avoid the problem with dynamically linked objects, the specification could be restricted to use only static fields and methods or be forced to allocate all necessary objects linearly at the beginning of the program. However, this would significantly restrict the use of the language. Our solution is to attempt to *pre-allocate* objects during static analysis. It should be noted that this approach does not handle class instantiations within loops or recursive method invocations.

Pre-allocation only partially solves the problem with dynamically allocated class instances. A class reference can point to any instance of compatible class type; therefore, two references of compatible class types can *alias*. Conservative handling of reference aliasing reduces the apparent concurrency in the specification. More aggressive reference aliasing analysis requires global dataflow analysis to determine a class instance or set of instances that a reference may point to.

```
ProcessMethod (current_method) {
    Perform local analysis on current_method to build local control
        flow information and resolve local dependencies.
    Pre-allocate new instantiations if not inside loops or recursion.
    For each method invoked {
        ProcessMethod (invoked_method)
        Resolve reference global analysis impacted by invoked_method
    }
    Resolve global dependencies given complete reference analysis
}

ProcessMethod (main)
```

Figure 2. Analysis technique outline

An outline of our analysis technique is shown in Figure 2. The analysis starts with the static *main* method. For each method processed, local analysis is performed to determine local control and dataflow. Next, all methods invoked by the current method are recursively analyzed. Finally, reference point-to values are resolved in order to determine global data dependence information. Before elaborating on the techniques used to perform the local and global analyses, we describe the target representation of the CDFG.

The CDFG representation shown in Figure 3 involves two main structures. The first structure is a table of static and pre-allocated class instances. Aside from object accounting information, this table maintains a list of entries per object; each entry represents either a method or a non-

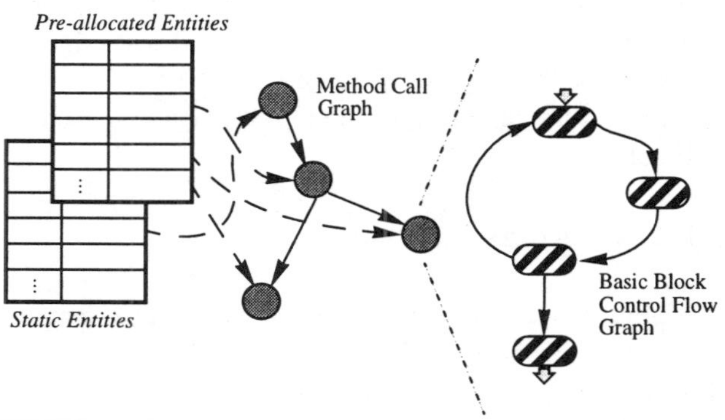

Figure 3. Target representation

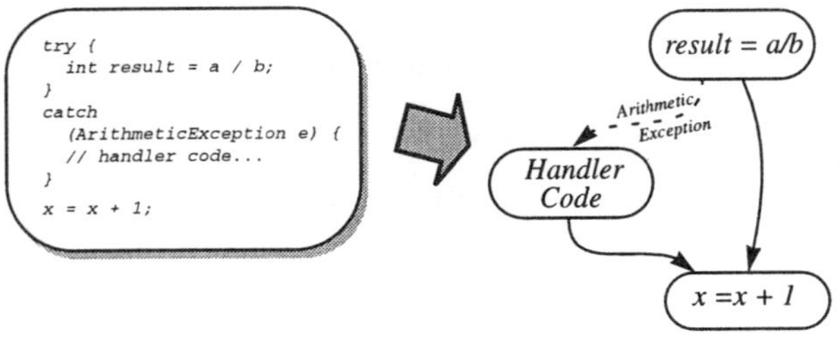

Figure 4. Exception edges in CDFG

primitive type data field. The data field entry is necessary for global analysis because data fields have a global scope during the life of their instances. Arrays are treated exactly as class instances. In fact, arrays are modeled as classes with no methods. The method entries point to portions of the second main structure in the representation. The second structure is the control dataflow information. Its nodes are bytecode basic blocks. The edges represent local control flow between basic blocks within a methods as well as global control flow across method invocations and returns.

The CDFG representation models multi-threading and exceptions using special control flow edges that annotate information about the thread operation performed or the exception trapped. Thread operations in Java are implemented in methods of the *Thread* class. The CDFG abstracts invocations of these methods by encoding the associated operation in the control flow edge corresponding to the method call. For example, Java threads are initiated by invoking *Thread* class *start* method. When the CDFG encounters an invocation of the start method, a new control flow edge is inserted between the invocation and the start of the thread's *run* method. This edge also indicates that a new thread is being forked. On the other hand, Exceptions in Java use *try-catch* blocks where the code which may cause an exception is placed inside the *try* clause followed by one or more subsequent *catch* clauses. Catch blocks trap on a specified *thrown* exception and execute the corresponding handler code. The CDFG inserts special control flow edges between the block that may cause the exception and the handler block. These edges are annotated with the type of exception the handler is trapping. An example of how exceptions are handled in shown in Figure 4.

3.1 Local Analysis

This step targets a particular method, identifying and sequencing its basic blocks to capture the local control flow. It also resolves local dependencies at two distinct levels. First, since Java bytecodes rely on an operand stack for the intermediate results, the extra level of dependency indirection through the stack needs to be factored out. This is achieved using *bytecode numbering*. Second, dependencies through local method variables are identified using reaching definition dataflow analysis.

Local Control Flow. Local control flow is represented by the method's basic blocks and the corresponding sequencing. Basic blocks are sequences of bytecodes such that only the first bytecode can be directly reached from outside the block and if the first bytecode is executed, then all the bytecodes are sequentially executed. The control flow edges simply represent the predecessor-successor ordering of all the basic blocks.

Local Dataflow Analysis. Dependencies exist between bytecodes through an extra level of indirection - the operand stack. We resolve this indirection by using "bytecode numbering." Bytecode numbering simply denotes the replacement of the stack semantics of each bytecode analyzed with physical operands that point to the bytecode that generated the required result. This is simply achieved by traversing the method's bytecodes in program order. Instead of executing the bytecode, its stack behavior is simulated using a compile-time operand stack, *OpStack.* If the bytecode reads data off the stack, entries are popped off OpStack, and new operands are created with the values retrieved from the stack. If the bytecode writes a result to the stack, a pointer to it is pushed onto OpStack. This process has to account for data that requires more than one stack entry such as double precision floating point and long integer results. Also, stack-manipulating bytecodes such as *dup* (duplicate top entry) or *swap* (swap top two entries) are interpreted by manipulating OpStack accordingly. Then, these bytecodes are discarded since they are no longer needed for the purposes of code functionality. An outline and an example of bytecode numbering are shown in Figure 5.

Data dependencies across local variables are resolved by computing the reaching definitions for the particular method. A definition of a variable is a bytecode that may assign a value to that variable. A definition d reaches some point p if there exists a path from the position of d to p such that no other definition that overwrites d is encountered. Once all the reaching definitions are computed, it would be clear that there exists a data dependency between bytecode m and bytecode n if m defines a local variable used by n and m's definition reaches the point immediately following n.

Computing the reaching definitions uses the iterative dataflow Worklist algorithm [8]. This algorithm iterates over all the basic blocks. A particular basic block propa-

Initialize symbolic operand stack, ***OpStack****, to empty.*
Traverse basic blocks in reverse postorder.
If current bytecode ***reads*** *data from the stack,*
pop OpStack *into the appropriate bytecode operand slot.*
If current bytecode ***writes*** *data to the stack,*
push *the bytecode's PC unto* ***OpStack****.*

0	*iload_1*	*push local variable onto operand stack*
1	*ldc_w #4*	*push constant onto operand stack*
4	*if_icmplt 9*	*pop two entries, if first < second -> jump to PC= 9*
7	*iconst_1*	*push constant = 1*
8	*ireturn*	*pop entry and return from method with entry as return value*
9	*iconst_m1*	*push constant = -1*
10	*ireturn*	*pop entry and return from method with entry as return value*

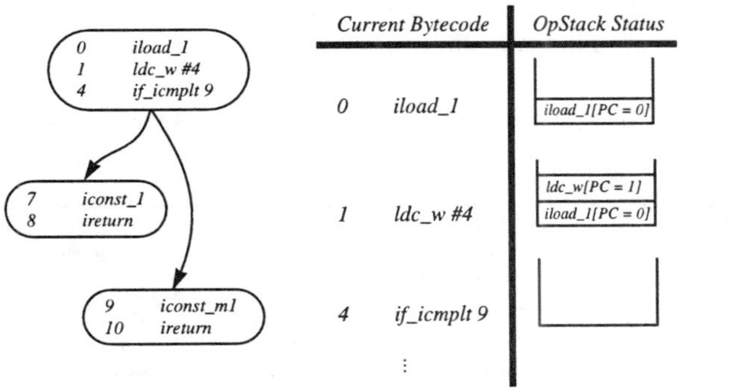

Figure 5. Bytecode numbering example

gates definitions it does not overwrite. At a join point of multiple control branches, the set of reaching definitions is the union of the individual sets. The algorithm iterates over the set of successors of all basic blocks whose output set of reaching definitions changes and converges when no more changes in these sets of reaching definitions materialize.

3.2 Global Analysis

To handle data dependencies between references, global analysis generates for each reference the set of object instances to which it may point out of the set of pre-allocated instances. Once this points-to relation is determined, simple dataflow analysis techniques such as global reaching definition can compute dataflow dependencies between these references.

A straightforward solution is to examine the entire control flow graph while treating method invocations as regular control flow edges. Then, iterative dataflow analysis can generate the points-to information for every reference. However, this approach suffers from the problem of unrealizable paths which cause global aliasing information to propagate from one invocation site to a non-corresponding return site [9].

A more context-sensitive solution motivated by [9] is to generate a transfer function for each method to summarize the impact of invoking that method on globally accessible data and references. The variables that this transfer function maps are the formal method parameters that are references. In addition, this set of variables is extended to include global references used inside the method through (1) creating new instances, (2) invoking other methods that return object references, or (3) accessing class instance fields that are references. Input to this transfer function is the initial points-to values of the extended parameters set. Output generated by this transfer function is the final points-to values of the extended parameters due to the method invocation.

This transfer function is a summary of the accesses (reads and writes) of the method's extended parameters generated using interval analysis [8]. These accesses are ordered according to the method's local control flow information. Accesses can be one of the following five primitive operations: *read, assign, new, meet* and *invoke*. The *read* primitive requires one operand which is a reference; the result is the set of potential class instances to which the reference points. The *assign* primitive is used to summarize an assignment whose left-hand side is an extended parameter. It requires two operands the first of which is the target reference. The second is a set of potential point-to instances. The *new* primitive indicates the creation of a new class instance. This primitive returns a set composed of a single instance, if pre-allocation is possible (not within loop or recursion). Otherwise, it conservatively points-to the set of compatible class instances. The *meet* primitive is necessary to handle joining branches in the control flow. At a meet point, the alias set of some reference assigned in one or more of the meeting branches is the union of the alias sets for that reference from each of the meeting control flow edges. Finally, the *invoke* primitive is used to resolve change in reference alias sets due to invoking some method. Effectively, this primitive causes the transfer function of the invoked method to be executed.

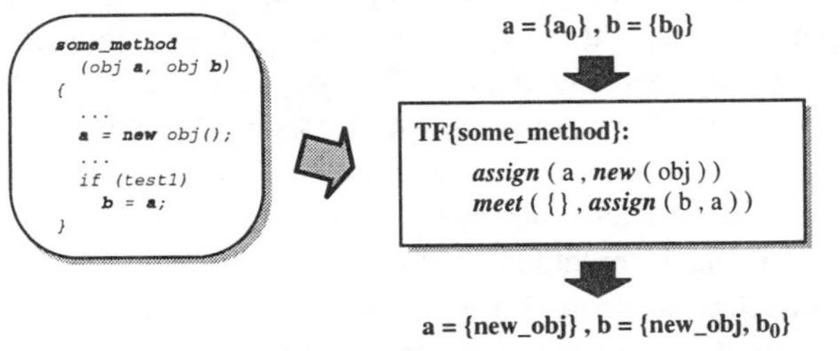

Figure 6. Transfer functions for global reference analysis

4 Experimental Results

Hardware-software systems are multi-process systems, so partitioning and co-synthesis tools which map behavioral specifications to these systems need to make hardware-software trade-offs [13]. To make these trade-offs with the objective of maximizing the cost-performance of the mixed implementation, it is necessary to be able to identify the concurrency in the input specification. We have implemented our Java front-end analysis step as a stand-alone compilation pass that reads the design's class files and generates a corresponding CDFG representation. We tested our technique using the designs listed in Table 1.

	Lines of Java	Classes	Instances	Basic Blocks
raytracer	698	6	37	358
robotarm	1325	10	53	583
decoder	3177	23	136	2342

Table 1: Design characteristics

The first design, *raytracer*, is a simple graphical application. It renders two spheres on top of a plane with shadows and reflections due to a single, specular light source. The second application, *robotarm*, is a robot arm controller. The third design, *decoder*, is a digital signal processing application featuring a video decoder for H.263-encoded bitstreams [14].

The resulting control-dataflow graphs were analyzed to identify concurrency in the specification. The analysis examined concurrency at three levels: thread-level, loop-level, and bytecode-level. Thread-level concurrency is exhibited as communicating, concurrent processes which can span the control flow of several methods. Loop-level concurrency is exhibited by core loops usually confined to a single method. Bytecode-level concurrency is exhibited by bytecode operations that can proceed provided their data dependencies are satisfied irrespective of a control flow ordering. This form of concurrency exists within basic blocks.

Thread-level concurrency is explicitly expressed by the designer through Java threads. Since threads are uniquely identified in the CDFG, no work is required to uncover this form of parallelism. Loop-level concurrency requires analysis of control and dataflow information associated with inner loops to identify data dependencies spanning different loop iterations and determine if these are true dependencies, that is, dependencies between a write in some iteration of the loop and a read in a subsequent iteration. So, loops with independent iterations can execute these iterations concurrently as mini-threads. The coarse-grained concurrency expressed at the thread or loop level can be exploited by allocating these threads to different subsystems in our target architecture.

On the other hand, bytecode-level concurrency in the CDFG does not span multiple basic blocks; it exists at the bytecode level within each basic block. Its degree depends on the basic block's "inter-bytecode" data dependencies. This fine-grained concurrency impacts the performance improvement of a hardware implementation of the basic block. Hardware is inherently parallel; therefore, parallelism in the design is implemented without any cost overhead given enough structural resources to support the parallelism. The only limitation on the degree of parallelism is synchronization due to data dependencies. Hence the execution time of some block in hardware decreases with increased data parallelism.

Table 2 presents the results of analyzing the three different forms of parallelism in our sample designs . The first column indicates the number of designer-specified threads. The second column shows the number of parallelizable loops while the third column indicates the average number of bytecodes per loop. The fourth column shows the average number of bytecodes per basic block while the fifth column assesses the average data parallelism in these basic blocks. This bytecode-level concurrency is measured as the average number of bytecodes that can execute simultaneously during a cycle of the JVM. These results show that it is possible to extract parallelism at various levels of granularity for Java programs.

	Thread-level Concurrency	Loop-level Concurrency		Bytecode-level Concurrency	
	Number of threads	Number of loops	Avg. bytecodes per loop	Avg. bytecodes/ basic block	Avg. bytecode parallelism
raytracer	2	10	20	6.6	2.0
robotarm	3	9	31	6.9	2.1
decoder	3	28	27	7.1	2.5

Table 2: Parallelism assessment results

5 Conclusions and Future Work

The specification language is the starting point of the hardware-software co-design process. We have described key requirements of such a language. A specification language should be expressive so that design concepts can be easily modeled but should provide a representation that is relatively easy to analyze and optimize for performance. The language should also provide high-performance execution. We have shown that the Java programming language satisfies these requirements.

To be able to partition and eventually co-synthesize input Java specifications, we must be able to analyze the specification. However, a major problem facing this analysis step in Java are dynamic links to class instances. To make static analysis possible, we proposed a technique that relies on aggressive reference analysis to resolve ambiguity in global control and dataflow. This technique generates a control dataflow graph representation for the specification. Our results show that using this technique it is possible to extract concurrency which can be exploited from the Java specification.

In the future, our analysis technique will serve as a front-end to a co-design tool which maps the Java system specification to a target architecture composed of one or more microprocessors tightly coupled to programmable hardware resources.

Acknowledgments

This work was sponsored by ARPA under grant no. MIP DABT 63-95-C-0049.

References

[1] J. Henkel, F. Vahid, and L. Ramachandran. *Hardware/Software Codesign of Embedded Systems Tutorial.* ICCAD 1995.

[2] M. Horowitz and K. Keutzer. "Hardware-Software Co-Design," in the *Proceedings of the Synthesis and Simulation Meeting and International Interchange* (SASIMI), 1993.

[3] D. Gajski and F. Vahid. "Specification and Design of Embedded Hardware-Software Systems," in *IEEE Design & Test of Computers*, pp. 53-67, Spring 1995.

[4] D. Gajski, F. Vahid, S. Narayan, and J, Gong. *Specification and Design of Embedded Systems.* Prentice Hall, 1994.

[5] D. Thomas and P. Moorby. *The Verilog Hardware Description Language.* Kluwer Academic Publishers, 1991.

[6] IEEE Inc., NY. *IEEE Standard VHDL Language Reference Manual*, 1988.

[7] G. Berry and G. Gonthier. "The Esterel Synchronous Programming Language: Design, Semantics, Implementation," *Science of Computer Programming* vol. 19, n°2, pp 87-152, 1992.

[8] A. Aho, R. Sethi, and J. Ullman. *Compilers Principles, Techniques and Tools.* Addison-Wesley, 1986.

[9] R. Wilson and M. Lam. "Efficient Context-Sensitive Pointer Analysis for C Programs," in the *Proceedings of the Conference on Programming Language Design and Implementation*, June 1995.

[10] J. Gosling, B. Joy, and G. Steele. *The Java Language Specification.* Addison-Wesley, 1996.

[11] T. Lindholm and F. Yellin. *The Java Virtual Machine Specification.* Addison-Wesley, 1996.

[12] B. Case. "Java Performance Advancing Rapidly," in *Microprocessor Report*, pp. 17-19, vol. 10, issue 7, May 27, 1996.

[13] J. Adams and D. Thomas. "Multiple-Process Behavioral Synthesis for Mixed Hardware-Software Systems," in the *Proceedings of the International Symposium on System Synthesis*, 1995.

[14] Telenor, Norway. *Enhanced H.263.* at http://www.fou.telenor.no/brukere/DVC/mpeg4/H.263+.html.

[15] S. Liao, S. Tjiang, and R. Gupta. "An Efficient Implementation of Reactivity for Modeling Hardware in Scenic Design Environment," in the *Proceedings of the 34th Design Automation Conference*, June 1997.

[16] T. Cramer, et al. "Compiling Java Just in Time," in *IEEE Micro*, pp. 36-43, Vol. 17, No. 2, May-June 1997.

[17] R. McGeer. "The V++ Systems Design Language," a talk sponsored by the Stanford CAD group, May 1997.

SESSION 11C

PERFORMANCE-DRIVEN ROUTING

Moderators:

D.F. Wong, University of Texas, Austin, TX

Rajeev Jayaraman, Xilinx, Inc., San Jose, CA

Post-Route Optimization for Improved Yield Using a Rubber-Band Wiring Model

Jeffrey Z. Su and Wayne W. Dai
Dept. of Computer Engineering, University of California, Santa Cruz, CA 95064

Abstract

This paper presents a unique approach to improve yield given a routed layout. Currently after routing has been completed and compacted, it generally proceeds to verification without further modifications. However, to improve manufacturability, we introduce a concept called even wire distribution, a key element of the SURF physical design tool. To alleviate congestion, we first move vias and wires towards less dense areas in a manner which preserves the existing wiring paths. Depending on the locally available area, we then increase wire spacing to reduce defect sensitivity, without changing the area of the design. Carafe, an inductive fault analysis tool is used to evaluate the new layout.

1.0 Introduction

Design for manufacturability (DFM) is becoming increasingly more important as feature sizes have shrunk to the submicron level and die sizes have increased dramatically for high performance microprocessor designs. Although progress has been made in improving manufacturing process capabilities, this alone cannot provide acceptable yield levels for cost sensitive products. As a result, DFM plays an increasing role in the physical design process as solutions require routing and layout changes to optimize for yield. This paper presents a strategy to improve yield by reducing a class of faults commonly known as bridging faults. Bridging faults are shorts between conductors and represent a significant amount of defects responsible for chip failure.

We propose a new strategy called *even wire distribution* (EWD), which reduces defect sensitivity of a routed design by adjusting movable objects and increasing interwire spacing without changing the chip size. Areas of the design with high wiring density are particularly vulnerable to faults. To alleviate congestion in this area, we adjust locations of movable elements, such as vias, to free up area before attempting to increase the spacing. Initial via placement during the routing phase may be sub-optimal from a yield perspective since the router is generally aiming to generate a minimal length route at minimum design rules. EWD is implemented within SURF, an area based router. The EWD optimization takes place after a design rule correct layout has been generated by SURF. Results are then streamed out in GDSII. We then use Carafe, an inductive fault analysis tool, to read the GDSII layout and generate critical area measurements[1]. This critical area measurement determines the defect sensitivity of the layout.

1.1 SURF

EWD is unique in that it operates on a canonical form of topological wiring, called a *rubber-band sketch* (RBS), which is generated by the SURF router[6]. The RBS, is gridless with a more compact data representation of a routed layout, than a typical geometric representation. A RBS represents a single layer of interconnect as flexible rubber-bands which have elastic properties. These rubber-band wires are initially considered to have zero width and zero spacing requirements with other objects in the design. Therefore the rubber-band geometry of a wire path can be envisioned as having minimum length for a specified planar path (Fig. 1a). A set of RBS represents a multilayer area based layout, called a *rubber-band layout* (RBL).

From an RBS, we enforce width and spacing constraints in a process called *spoke creation*, which will be covered in more detail later in this paper. Basically the spoke creation process pushes wires away from nearby objects creating an *extended rubber-band sketch* ERBS (Fig. 1b)[12]. The ERBS naturally represents all-angle wiring and can be constrained to a 45° (octilinear) or a

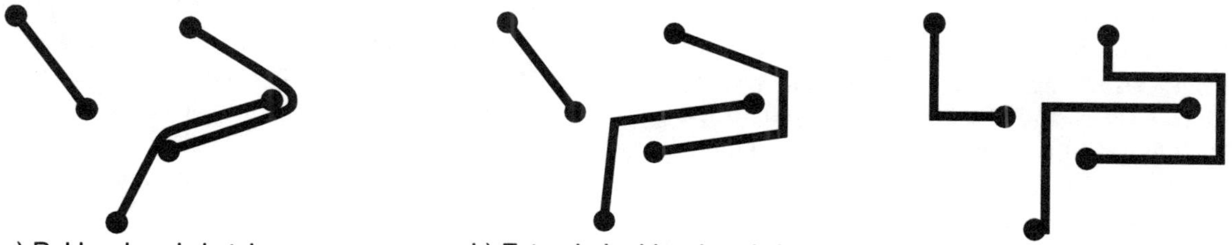

a) Rubber-band sketch b) Extended rubber-band sketch c) Geometric transformation

Figure 1: RBS and geometric transformation

Manhattan (rectilinear) wiring pattern (Fig. 1c). A set of multiple ERBS, which compose a layout, is called an *extended rubber-band layout* (ERBL).

The flexibility of the RBS is provided by a key operation called *rubber-band updating* (RBU). RBU is a continuous operation which models the rubber-band behavior by allowing objects within the layout to move while always maintaining wire connectivity. This operation alone provides the mechanism to adjust object locations and manipulate wiring[2].

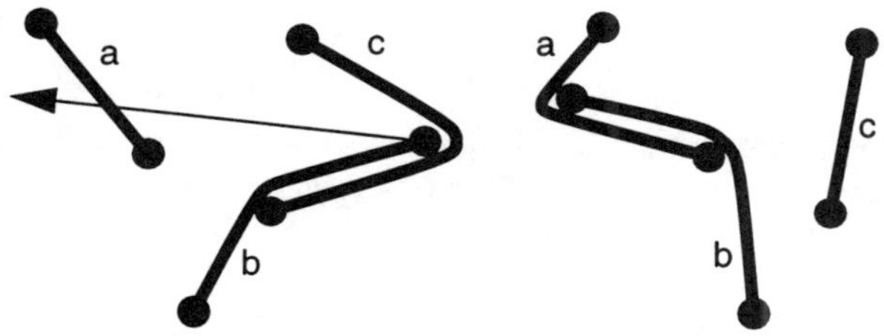

a) proposed RBU operation b) RBU result

Figure 2: Rubber-Band Updating Operation

A RBS is composed of *terminals* and *branches*. Terminals generally represent pins, via contacts, junction points, or pads. Branches represent the rubber-band wire which connects two terminals. In turn each branch is composed of a polyline where each linear segment of the branch is called a *wire segment*. In Fig. 2a we depict a proposed move of a terminal. Fig. 2b illustrates the result of the move with the branches automatically updated as if they were rubber-bands. Branch *a* which was obstructing the terminal's path, automatically flexes to accommodate the move. Meanwhile branch *c*, originally stretched by the move, snaps to a single wire segment as the terminal moves away.

Since RBU is a layer based operation, we can extend RBU to handle objects which span multiple layers. A *stack* is a set of one or more terminals which exist on different signal layers, share the same x-y coordinates, and must be moved as an entity. However not all stacks, such as I/O pads or pins, can be moved. We define a *movable stack* as any stack whose position is subject to optimization. For the most part, the movable stack is generally a via or a junction point.

The rubber-band sketch concept was originally proposed by Maley and was used to determine if a topological embedding of wiring paths was design rule correct while generating a legal layout (similar to the ERBS) in the process[7]. Chen and Lee implemented a batch mode design rule check which is asymptotically faster than Maley's work[8]. Other works used a topological based layout representation for compaction strategies[9][10][11].

1.2 Previous Work

There are several works which improve yield by spacing or compacting the layout. Chiluvuri and Koren introduced a compaction strategy which took a compacted channel and incrementally shifted wire locations to reduce layout defect sensitivity[3]. A strategy was also presented in this work which increased wire width to reduce the possibility of breaks. Another post-route optimization strategy is called the LocDes spacer[4]. This work introduced local design rules which were used to adjust elements in an IC layout wherever possible to improve yield. The Yield Optimizing Router (YOR), a channel router, introduced the concept of net burying and net floating[5]. Although this approach is primarily focused on routing, the post route optimization aspect includes a via shifting strategy (sliding vias in a horizontal or vertical direction) and net bumping, which shifted wires to unused wiring tracks.

In general, the previous works take a geometric layout and improve yield by manipulating wire and feature geometry. The shortcoming of this approach is that the optimization only considers the nearest geometry to improve the layout without considering the congestion of the surrounding area. Layout geometry is also complex to manipulate for pushing or plowing operations especially if design rules and connectivity are maintained. The amount of memory resources required to edit the layout geometry is also becoming a factor with larger designs.

Current trends in today's IC designs indicate a shift towards high density area-based layouts with a higher number of signal layers. Two works are based on a channel based layout [3][5] which is becoming less popular. Area based layouts are not exclusive to IC design but also applicable to various packaging technologies such as MCMs, and board layouts such as PCMCIA. Also, octilinear wiring is also becoming more popular as designers attempt to reduce wire length. In addition to this, some packaging technologies can even accommodate all-angle wiring patterns. However the previous works are only applicable to rectilinear layouts.

SURF is a versatile area based physical design tool which has been used to route IC and various packaging technologies[6]. One key advantage of using rubber-band wiring, is that for any layout, a topologically equivalent RBS has minimum wire length. Since the RBS naturally represents all-angle wiring, it can make the most efficient use of the layout for all-angle processes with a simple optional conversion to either a rectilinear or octilinear geometry.

Two works have demonstrated the ability to relocate vias[3][5]. However neither has the ability to incrementally move a via and propogate the results to the surrounding geometry. Only the RBU operation within SURF can move objects while preserving the connectivity of all wires affected by the move and maintain the RBS minimum wiring length property.

2.0 Background

In this paper, we propose a strategy to minimize bridging faults caused by spot defects. Spot defects occur during the manufacturing process, resulting in spots of extra or missing material on the wafer. The size of spot defects are comparable to the feature sizes of the layout such that their presence can alter the intended functionality or performance of the circuit. Another type of defect is a pinhole defect, which are generally much smaller than a micrometer. Dielectric pinholes often occur in chip insulators resulting in missing dielectric material. This defect has the potential to cause a short between overlapping wires on different metal layers. Both spot defects and pinholes have the capability of causing a *bridge fault*. Bridging faults occur when the defect shorts nearby wires. Bridging faults caused by pinholes will not be covered by this paper.

Spot defects are characterized by a circle having a given radius χ. Yet not all spot defects will cause faults. The presence of faults depends on the area where the defect appears, called the *critical area*. The size of the critical area depends on the size of the defect and the spacing between the wires, therefore the larger the defect, the larger the critical area. Since the probability of having a fault depends on the size of the critical area, the goal of EWD is to minimize the critical area for all defect sizes.

We first present some commonly known formulae for critical area calculation based on previous work. We then present an overview of the spoke creation process which will introduce some terminology used in the cost computation before defining a global cost function of an ERBL, based on the estimated critical area.

2.1 Critical Area Definitions

The critical area is defined as a function of the defect size. Stapper's work characterized the critical area for short circuits of two conductors parallel for length *L*, separated by spacing *s*, and a defect diameter of χ [13].

$$A(\chi) = \begin{cases} 0 & \text{for } 0 \le \chi \le s \\ L(\chi - s) & \text{for } s \le \chi \le \infty \end{cases} \quad (1)$$

Stapper described a defect density function which is characterized by two parts. The first part describes a positively sloping linear function from $0 \le \chi \le \chi_0$, where χ_0 is the resolution of the photolithography process. Defects $\chi \ge \chi_0$ are characterized by the second part of the function which falls off by a factor of $1/\chi^n$. Experimentation at IBM found that $n = 3$ produces a reasonably accurate fit of the observed defects. With this value the distributions are

$$D(\chi) = \begin{cases} (\chi\bar{D})/\chi_0^2 & \text{for } 0 \le \chi \le \chi_0 \\ (\chi_0^2\bar{D})/\chi^3 & \text{for } \chi_0 \le \chi \le \infty \end{cases} \quad (2)$$

where $\bar{D}$ is the average defect density. We can use these functions to calculate λ, the average number of faults .

$$\lambda = \int_0^\infty A(\chi)D(\chi)d\chi \quad (3)$$

Since design rules are set at some value $s > \chi_0$ defects with a diameter $\chi \le \chi_0$ are not expected to create intralayer shorts. Substituting functions 1 and 2 and evaluating yields the following equation.

$$\lambda = (L\chi_0^2\bar{D})/(2s) \quad (4)$$

From this we can define the average critical area for intralayer shorts between two conductors.

$$\bar{A} = (L\chi_0^2)/(2s) \quad (5)$$

2.2 Design Rule Enforcement in an RBS

The quality of a layout can be determined by calculating the critical area for the design. With an

ERBL, initial wire geometry is known, which is used to provide a estimate of critical area. We use the estimated critical area of the ERBL as a global cost to guide the EWD. However, to understand how the EWD determines wiring density and increases interwire spacing, we first describe the spoke creation process. The spoke creation process checks the minimum design rules and creates a design rule correct embedding using RBU.

The spoke creation is an incremental layer based operation, where each RBS of the layout will be converted to a corresponding ERBS[12]. Each terminal of the layer is processed in a sequential order. For each terminal we first need to perform a design rule check before enforcing the spacing constraints. Design rules of an RBS are checked between pairs of terminals (Fig. 3). A *cut* is a line segment $c = (a, b)$ between two terminals, which has two attributes, *flow* and *capacity*. The flow captures the minimum amount of spacing and routing resources required by branches crossing the cut. The capacity indicates the total amount of available spacing resources between the terminals.

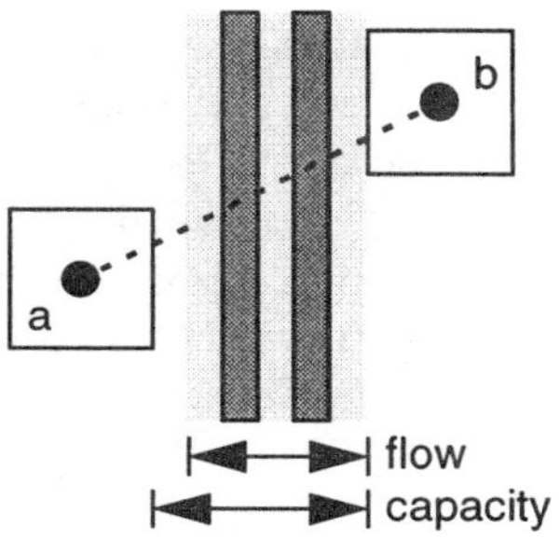

Figure 3: Properties of a cut

A cut (a,b) is routable if $flow(a, b) \leq capacity(a, b)$ and is unroutable otherwise. An unroutable cut indicates the presence of a design rule violation (DRV). For a given terminal of an RBS, we check the cuts with respect to other nearby terminals. If no DRVs are found, we then enforce the spacing constraints.

The minimum separation between objects are enforced at the terminals by line segments called *spokes*. Spokes radiate out from a terminal pushing away and separating nearby wires. The spokes take into account the terminal geometry, spacing rules, and branch width. Depending on the final wiring pattern, either four spoke directions are used for rectilinear wiring or eight directions are used for octilinear and all-angle wiring. Once the required spokes have been created for each terminal, we have an ERBS. The ERBS was proven to be routable (design rule correct) by Maley and guarantees a legal geometric transformation[7].

a) Rectilinear spoke pattern b) Octilinear spoke pattern

Figure 4: Spoke creation

2.3 Critical area estimation

The critical area estimation is used as the global cost of the ERBL during the EWD optimization process. For any stack move the EWD considers, the critical area estimation can determine the impact on critical area without having to actually move. However to generate critical area estimation for an ERBL, we need to identify parallel wire segments as well as the parallel length L and the spacing s (Eq. 5)

In order to determine relative positioning of objects within an ERBS, we construct an adjacency graph $G_{adj}(V, E)$ by applying a Delaunay Triangulation of the terminals. In a Delaunay Triangulation, the layout area is partitioned into triangular regions where each terminal has edges with the closest neighboring terminals. The edges of this triangulation also represent cuts which will be used in the EWD.

For a given cut, we define the *cut order* $(w_1, ..., w_n)$ as the order in which the wire segments cross the cut Wire segments w_i, w_j of the cut are defined to be *adjacent* if they are a consecutive pair in the cut order. Each wire segment in turn intersects a *sequence* of ordered cuts $S = (c_1, ..., c_m)$. Wire segments w_1, w_2 which are adjacent for one or more consecutive cuts, form a *common sequence* $C_{12} = (c_i, ..., c_{i+k})$ (Fig. 5). We use this common sequence to determine an *interval* during which both w_1 and w_2 are roughly parallel. For each wire segment, this interval is bounded by the cut immediately preceding and immediately following the common sequence $(c_{i-1}, ..., c_{i+k+1})$ (see arrows for w_1). Note that if c_{i-1} or c_{i+k+1} does not exist for a wire segment, the endpoint of the wire segment is used as the interval endpoint (see arrows for w_2). We average the length of both intervals to estimate L for w_1 and w_2.

The spacing of parallel wire segments is defined by available space from each cut of the common sequence. We assume the EWD will evenly distribute wires across the cut and enforce some maximal spacing s between each pair of wire segments and the terminals. The spacing of a cut (p,a) is calculated from the flow and capacity. The flow is composed of two components, one

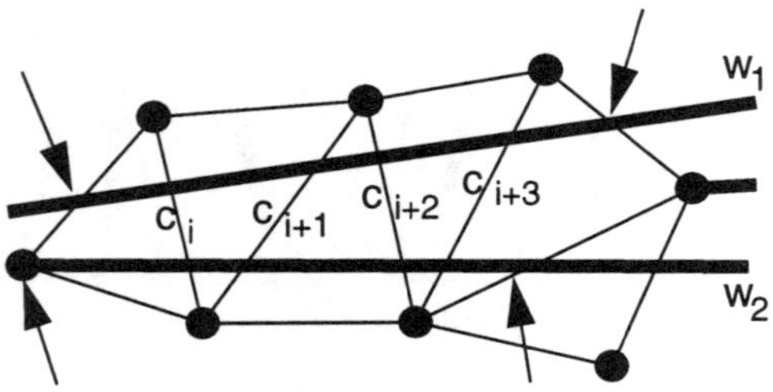

Figure 5: Parallel length approximation

contributed by the sum of the wire widths f_b, and another contributed by the minimum spacing requirements f_s, $f_{ttl}(p, a) = f_b + f_s$. The capacity however, can be expressed as a Euclidean distance function

$$capacity(p, a) = ((x_p - x_a)^2 + (y_p - y_a)^2)^{1/2} - (r_p + r_a) \quad (6)$$

where r represents the respective radii of r and a. From here we can compute the maximal spacing s for this cut with $|W|$ indicating the number of wire segments crossing the cut.

$$s = \frac{((x_p - x_a)^2 + (y_p - y_a)^2)^{1/2} - (r_p + r_a + f_b)}{|W| + 1} \quad (7)$$

The estimated critical area cost, ω_w, for two wire segments is Eq. 5 without the constants

$$\omega_w(w_i, w_j) = \begin{cases} 0 & \text{if not adjacent} \\ L/s & \text{otherwise} \end{cases} \quad (8)$$

The global cost of an ERBL is defined as the sum of the estimated critical area for every pair of wire segments

$$\Omega_g = \sum_i \sum_j \omega_w(w_i, w_j) \quad (9)$$

3.0 Problem Formulation

We divide the EWD procedure into two stages. The first stage is *stack optimization* stage, which starts from the adjacency graph, and iteratively optimizes each movable stack location in multiple passes based on a local cost function $\Omega_l(p, A_T)$ determined from critical area estimated from neighboring wires. The second stage is *wire spacing* phase. For each terminal, we calculate the amount of increased separation for nearby wire segments based on the surrounding area. We then enforce this larger spacing value by increasing spoke lengths which has the effect of spreading parallel wire segments apart.

3.1 Stack Optimization

Given a set of all possible locations for a movable stack T and a set of neighbors A_T, we assign a cost of moving T to p. We will then use this cost function to evaluate a number of prospective locations prior to moving the stack. The *neighbors* of a terminal t, are the set of terminals $A_t = (a_1, a_2, \ldots, a_n)$ where there exists an edge $(t, a_i) \in E$. The *star region* of t, R_t is the area defined as the union of all triangular areas formed by t and its neighbors Fig. 6.

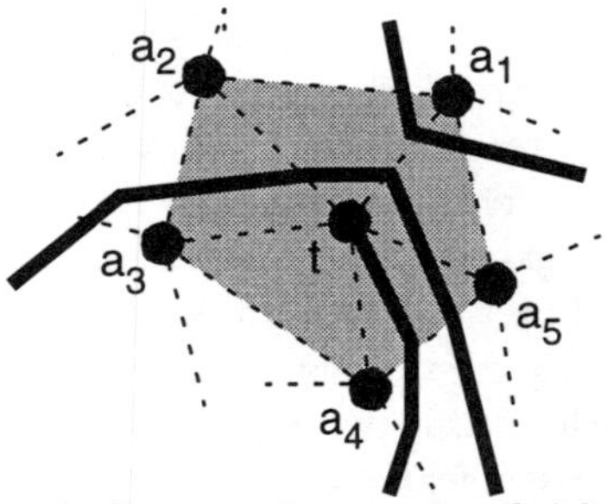

Figure 6: Star region and neighbors

The neighbors of stack T are defined as $\bigcup A_t, \forall (t \in T)$. The *local area* of T is defined as $\bigcap R_t, \forall (t \in T)$ (Fig. 7) for convex star regions (concave star regions need to be trimmed such that they are convex). We will use this local area to restrict the possible locations of the movable stack. Finally we will refer to p as an x-y coordinate located within the local area of which represents a prospective location for the movable stack. By restricting the move to the local area, the triangulation is kept planar. Non-planar triangulation will introduce inaccuracy in the local cost.

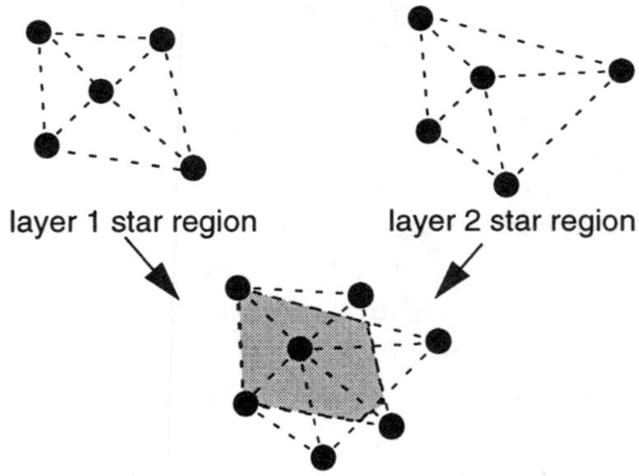

Figure 7: Local area of *T*

A local cost function Ω_l captures the critical area of the star regions for all $t \in T$. This cost, Ω_l will be used to estimate the critical area if T were to move to p. The cost Ω_l is defined as the sum of the cut costs $\omega_c(p, a_j)$ with respect to each neighbor in A_t.

$$\Omega_l(p, A_t) = \sum_{t \in T} \sum_{j=1}^{|A_t|} \omega_c(p, a_j) \quad (10)$$

Each pair of adjacent wires (w_i, w_{i+1}) of the cut

contributes some fraction of ω_w to the overall cut cost ω_c. By considering a move to p, we need recalculate each ω_w contributing to cut (p, a_j). In this case we assume the spacing s will be dictated by (p, a_j) rather than the average spacing specified in Eq. 8. s for each ω_w is recomputed using Eq. 7. Since ω_w includes the cost of span multiple cuts, we divide ω_w by $|C|$ the number of cuts in the common sequence to determine the fraction which contributes to (p, a_j). By summing these fractions for each adjacent wire segment pair (w_i, w_{i+1}), we compute ω_c. In Fig. 5 there are 4 common cuts between w_1 and w_2, therefore $|C| = 4$

$$\omega_c(p, a_j) = \sum_{\forall(w_i, w_{i+1})} \frac{\omega_w(w_i, w_{i+1})}{|C_{w_j, w_{j+1}}|} \tag{11}$$

The overall strategy is to apply the stack positioning optimization for all movable stacks. The optimization will only move the stack if the cost decreases. After each pass, the global cost is recalculated to measure the rate of improvement. This process of processing all stacks and evaluating the cost continues until the global cost converges. Since the local cost is a fraction of global cost, for a given localized area, the algorithm will terminate.

4.0 Implementation

To minimize Ω_g, we minimize the local cost for each stack. The most challenging aspect of this problem is choosing p. The ideal solution is to choose p an infinite distance from A_t where the cost will reach zero. To prevent this, we constrain the domain of p to the local area. There are several problems which may occur if p is allow to be any legal location within the sketch. First if p is located sufficiently far from A_t, there may be other terminals $u \notin A_t$ closer to t, violating key assumptions since these terminals were not factored into the original cost equation. Second, a long distance via move has a higher probability of creating large increases in wire length. Finally p must not cause a design rule violation. In Eq. 7, a sufficiently small distance would create a negative spacing value. To prevent undesired behavior, we constrain the domain of p to locations within the local area where

$$((x_p - x_a)^2 + (y_p - y_a)^2)^{1/2} > r_p + r_a + f_{ttl} \tag{12}$$

with r_p representing the radius of t, r_a the radius of neighbor terminal a, and f_{ttl} which is the total flow between p and a.

In Fig. 8 we used MATLAB to graph a topographical map based on cost for the star region. The polygon indicates the boundary of the combined area of all star regions of t, with the corners indicating the neighboring terminals for all layers. Curves in the figure indicate places of equal cost. The blank areas near the corner of the polygon indicate areas where p would cause a design rule violation.

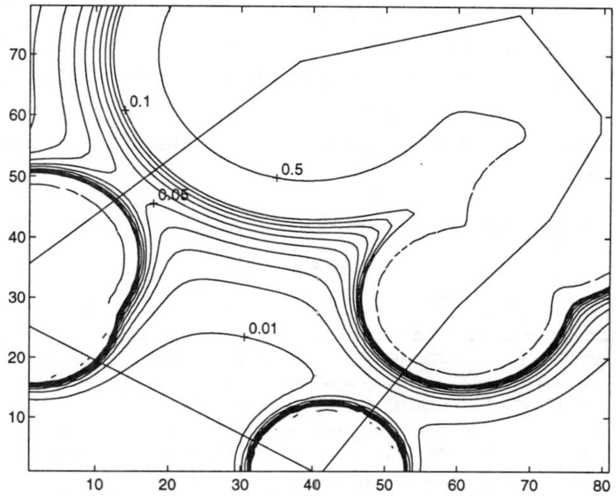

Figure 8: Cost curves of a star region

The EWD algorithm iterates through multiple passes of each movable stack in the design. For each stack, it first calculates an optimal location before moving. Once the global cost converges, the new spacing rules are calculated and enforced by the spoke creation process.

To solve stack optimization problem, we formulate it as a nonlinear constrained optimization. Equation 10 is used as the objective function. The constraints are the line equations which define the local region and Equation 12, to prevent DRVs. We use the Optimal Steepest Descent, using the gradient to find the initial search direction. From the search direction we use a Golden Section Search, a popular 1-D search technique, to find a new point with minimum cost. From this new minimum we calculate a new search direction. This process continues for some predetermined number of iterations or unless the distance between successive iterations reaches some minimum threshold η.

The wire spacing algorithm iterates through the set of neighbors on the appropriate layer for the terminals t of each via. For the given pair of corresponding terminals, the algorithm will calculate the amount of space the cut can support using (Eq. 10). The algorithm chooses and enforces the smallest space s from among the terminal pairs checked. The minimum spacing is set by the design rules while the ideal wire spacing rule is a value set by the user. However, enforcing arbitrarily large spacing values will not have a significant impact on yield while resulting in increased wire length.

5.0 Experiments

The experiments were run on a Sun Sparc 20 running SunOS 4.1.3. The designs represent sections of MCM-D substrates. For the purposes of the experiment we set the maximum enforced spacing to 2X the minimum wire-to-wire design rule. Each design, was written out to GDSII from SURF both before and after the optimization process. The results were then streamed into CARAFE, which evaluated the critical area of each layout. We also compared the change in wire length resulting from EWD (Table 1).

	Nets	Crit. area before	Crit. area after	Pct. reduction	Change in Wire length
ex1	20	1.42e+08	6.12e+07	57%	+7%
ex2	25	2.61e+08	1.69e+08	35%	+8%
ap1	43	1.26e+09	8.14e+08	35%	+6%
ap2	70	2.18e+09	6.60e+08	69%	+10%
ap3	68	1.75e+09	5.32e+08	69%	+9%
ap4	61	6.53e+08	5.29e+08	9%	+3%

Table 1: Carafe critical area measurements

In each of the designs, we assume a high quality of routing. That is each trace is routed with minimal wire length and a minimal number of vias. We believe that this will allow EWD to make the most significant reductions in critical area. However the largest reduction in critical area also results in the largest increase in wire length although layout area is unaffected by our approach. In future work, we plan to take a closer look at the relationship between the critical area and the wire length

6.0 Conclusion

This work demonstrates the potential of EWD based on a rubber-band wiring model. The ERBL, a data efficient layout representation, has enough information about the routing to provide a critical area estimation. This estimation is used as cost function to determine an ideal location for a movable stack. The RBU operation provides EWD with the ability to manipulate the layout in a unique manner, allowing the optimization to find a local solution which minimizes critical area. Overall, much effort has been put into making RBU a robust operation and because of its versatility, it is an essential asset in improving the quality of the design.

7.0 Acknowledgments

Special thanks to Eric Thorne and F. Joel Ferguson for providing Carafe and much appreciated help.

8.0 References

[1] Alvin Jee and F. Joel Ferguson, "Carafe: An inductive fault analysis tool for CMOS VLSI circuits," *IEEE VLSI Test Symposium*, pp. 92-98, 1993.

[2] W. Dai, R. Kong, J. Jue, and M. Sato. "Rubber band routing and dynamic data representation," *ICCAD*, Santa Clara, CA, Nov. 1990, pp. 45-48.

[3] V. Chiluvuri, and I. Koren, "Layout-Synthesis Techniques for Yield Enhancement," *IEEE Trans. on Semiconductor Manufacturing*, vol. 8, no. 2, pp. 178-187, May 1995.

[4] G. Allan, A. Walton, and R. Holwill, "An Yield Improvement Technique for IC Layout Using Local Design Rules," *IEEE Trans. on CAD*, vol. 11, no. 11, pp. 1355-1362, Nov. 1992.

[5] Sy-Yen Kuo, "YOR: A Yield-Optimizing Routing Algorithm by Minimizing Critical Areas and Vias," *IEEE Trans. on CAD*, vol. 12, no. 9, pp. 1303-1311, Sep.r 1993.

[6] D. Staepelaere, J. Jue, T. Dayan, and W. Dai, "Surf: a rubber-band routing system for multichip modules," IEEE Design & Test, pp. 18-26, Dec. 1993.

[7] F. Miller Maley, "Single-layer wire routing and compaction," Cambridge, Massachusetts, The MIT Press, 1990.

[8] H. Chen and D. T. Lee, "A faster algorithm for rubber-band equivalent transformation for planar VLSI layouts," *IEEE Trans. on CAD*, 15(2):217-227, Feb. 1996.

[9] Kurt Mehlhorn and Sefan Näher, "A faster compaction algorithm with automatic jog insertion," *IEEE Trans. on CAD*, 9(2):158-166, Feb. 1990.

[10] P.l deDood, J. Wawrzynek, E. Liu, and R. Suaya, "A two-dimensional topological compactor with octagonal geometry," *28th DAC*, June 1991, pp. 727-731.

[11] Hiroshi Murata and Yoji Kajitani, "Interactive terminal sliding algorithm for hybrid IC layout," Trans. on Information Processing Society of Japan, Dec. 1994, vol. 35, no. 12, pp. 2806-15 (in Japanese).

[12] W. Dai, R. Kong, and M. Sato, "Routability of a rubber-band sketch," *28th DAC*, June 1991, pp. 45-48.

[13] C. H. Stapper, "Modeling of defect in integrated circuit photolithographic patterns," IBM Journal of Research and Development, vol. 28, no. 4, pp. 461-475, July 1984.

Delay Bounded Buffered Tree Construction for Timing Driven Floorplanning

Maggie Kang Wayne W.-M. Dai
Computer Engineering Department
University of California, Santa Cruz, CA 95064

Tom Dillinger
Rockwell Semiconductor
San Diego, CA 92121

David LaPotin
IBM Austin Research Lab.
Austin, Texas 78758

Abstract

As devices and lines shrink into the deep submicron range, the propagation delay of signals can be effectively improved by repowering the signals using intermediate buffers placed within the routing trees. Almost no existing timing driven floorplanning and placement approaches consider the option of buffer insertion. As such, they may exclude solutions, particularly early in the design process, with smaller overall area and better routability. In this paper, we propose a new methodology in which buffered trees are used to estimate wire delay during floorplanning. Instead of treating delay as one of the objectives, as done by the majority of previous work, we formulate the problem in terms of Delay Bounded Buffered Trees (DBB-tree) and propose an efficient algorithm to construct a DBB spanning tree for use during floorplanning. Experimental results show that the algorithm is very effective. Using buffer insertion at the floorplanning stage yields significantly better solutions in terms of both chip area and total wire length.

1 Introduction

In high speed design, long on-chip interconnects can be modeled as distributed delay lines, where the delay of the lines can often be reduced by buffer insertion. Intermediate buffers can effectively decouple a large load off of a critical path or divide a long wire into smaller segments, each of which has less line resistance and makes the path delay more linear with overall length. It is commonplace for production chips to contain tens of thousands of buffers.

Floorplanning has a significant impact on critical path delay, however almost no existing timing driven floorplanning technique considers the option of buffer insertion. Typically, only wire length or Elmore delay is used for delay calculation. This practice is too restrictive as evidenced by the reliance industry has placed on intermediate buffering as a means for achieving aggressive cycle times.

This paper attempts to leverage the additional freedom gained by incorporating buffer insertion into floorplanning stage. We propose a new methodology of floorplanning using buffered trees to estimate the wiring delay. We formulate the Delay Bounded Buffered Tree (DBB-tree) problem which optimizes the total wire length subject to given timing constraints. Based on the Elmore delay model, we present an efficient algorithm to construct DBB spanning trees for use in floorplanning. The experimental results show that using buffer insertion at the floorplanning stage provides an additional degree of freedom not present in past approaches and typically leads to solutions with significantly smaller area and increased routability.

2 Overview of Related Works

2.1 Elmore Delay Model

The *Elmore delay model* provides a simple closed-form expression with greatly improved accuracy for delay compared to the lumped RC model. For each wire segment modeled as a π−type circuit, given the interconnect tree T, the Elmore delay from the source s_0 to sink s_i can be expressed as follows:

$$\tau(0,i) = R_0 C_0 + \sum_{e(u,v)\in Path(0,i)} rl_{u,v}\left(\frac{cl_{u,v}}{2} + C_v\right)$$

where R_0 is the driver resistance at the source and C_0 is the total capacitance charged by the driver. Given a uniform wire width, r and c are the unit resistance and capacitance, respectively. Let $e(u,v)$ denotes the wire connecting s_v to its parent s_u, both wire resistance $rl_{u,v}$ and wire capacitance $cl_{u,v}$ are proportional to the wire length $l_{u,v}$. C_v denotes the total capacitance of a subtree rooted at s_v, which is charged through wire $e(u,v)$. The first term of $\tau(0,i)$ is linear with the total wire length of T, while the second term has quadratic dependence on the length of the path from the source to s_i, denoted by $Path(0,i)$.

2.2 Interconnect Optimization

From the discussion of Elmore delay, we can conclude that total tree length and the path length from the driver to the critical sinks are two major concerns for interconnect topology optimization. The early works [1, 2] observed the existence of conflicting min-cost and min-radius (the longest source-to-sink path length of the tree) objectives. A number of algorithms [3, 2, 4, 5, 6]have been proposed to make the trade-offs between them. On the other hand, for deep submicron design, path length is no longer an accurate estimate of path delay. Several attempts [7, 8, 9, 10] have been made to directly optimize Elmore delay rather than using geometric objectives.

Intermediate buffer insertion creates another degree of freedom for interconnect optimization. Early works on fanout optimization problem focused on the construction of buffered trees during logic synthesis [11, 12, 13] without taking into account the wiring effect. Recently, layout driven fanout optimization have been proposed [14, 15]. For a given Steiner tree, a polynomial time dynamic programming algorithm was proposed for the delay-optimal buffer insertion problem [16]. Using dynamic programming, [17] integrated wire sizing and power minimization with the tree construction under a more accurate delay model taking signal slew into account. Inspired by the same dynamic programming algorithm, Okamoto and Cong [18] proposed a simultaneous Steiner tree construction and buffer insertion algorithm. Later the work was extended to include wire sizing [19]. In the formulation of the problem [18, 19], the main objective is to maximize the required arrival time at the root of the tree, which is defined as the minimum among the differences between the arrival time of the sinks and the delay from the root to the sinks.

To achieve optimal delay, multiple buffers may be necessary for a single edge. An early work [20] developed the optimal solution for the size, number and position of buffers driving a uniform line that minimizes the delay of the line. Given single sized buffer, recent work [21] presented the optimal buffer insertion on a uniform wire based on Elmore delay.

2.3 Delay Minimized vs. Delay Bounded

Since floorplanning and placement are usually iterated with static timing analysis tools, the critical path information is often available and the timing requirement for critical sinks converges as the design and layout progresses. It is sufficient to have bounded delay rather than minimized delay. On the other hand, the minimization of total wire length is of interest since total wire length not only contributes to circuit area and routing congestion, but also contributes a significant factor to the switching power. In this paper, instead of minimizing the source to sink delays, we define the delay bounded buffered tree (DBB-tree) problem to minimize the total wire length while satisfying timing constraints. Without considering buffer insertion, [22] proposed a "Delay Bounded Minimum Steiner Tree" (DBMST) to construct a low cost tree subject to bounded delays.

2.4 DBB-tree Problem

In this paper, we define the new Delay Bounded Buffered tree (DBB-tree) problem as follows: Given a signal net and delay bounds associated with critical sinks, construct a routing tree with intermediate buffers inserted to minimize the total wiring length and the number of buffers while satisfying the delay bounds. Based on Elmore delay, we develop an efficient algorithm for constructing DBB spanning tree, which consists of three phases:

1. Calculate the minimum Elmore delay for each critical sink and exclude the floorplanning solution which is timing infeasible.
2. Construct a buffered spanning tree which has minimized total wire length and bounded delays at critical sinks.
3. Revisit the topology obtained in 2 and delete unnecessary buffers subject to delay bounds.

Our DBB-tree algorithm makes the following three major contributions:

- Treating delays as constraints rather than formulating it into the optimized objectives.
- Constructing the topology and inserting buffers simultaneously, the algorithm is very effective to minimize both wire length and the number of buffers.
- Allowing multiple buffers to be inserted on each single edge and calculating the precise buffer positions for the optimal solution. In contrast, most previous work assumes at most one buffer is inserted at the fixed location for each single edge.

3 Description of DBB-tree Algorithm

For floorplanning purpose, we assume uniform wire width and consider only non-inverting buffers. Given a signal net $S = \{s_0, s_1, \cdots, s_n\}$, s_0 is the source and $s_1, \cdots, s_n$ the sinks. The geometric location for each terminal of S is determined by floorplanning. Let $\vec{B} = (t_b, r_b, c_b)$ describes the internal delay, resistance and capacitance of the non-inverting buffer, respectively. Before presenting the detailed DBB-tree algorithm, we first state some theoretical results developed by [21] which calculate the number and position of identical buffers placed on a single edge to minimize the edge delay.

Theorem 1 *Given a uniform line $e(0, i)$ connecting sink s_i to source s_0, and identical buffers $\vec{B}$, the*

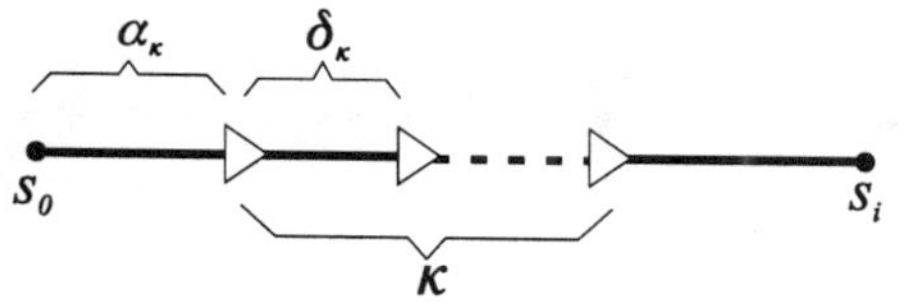

Figure 1: Given a uniform line $e(0,i)$ and identical buffer $\vec{B}$, the Elmore delay through $e(0,i)$ is minimized if $\kappa(0,i)$ buffers are placed on the wire in such way that the first buffer is α_κ away from source s_0, each pair of adjacent buffers are equally spaced each other by δ_κ.

Elmore delay through $e(0,i)$ is minimized if $\kappa(0,i)$ buffers are inserted on the edge such that the first buffer is $\alpha_\kappa(0,i)$ away from the source s_0, and each pair of adjacent buffers are $\delta_\kappa(0,i)$ away from each other :

$$\kappa(0,i) = \max(0, \lfloor -\frac{1}{2} + \sqrt{1 + \frac{2(r(cl_{0,i} + c_b - c_i) - c(r_b - R_0))^2}{rc(r_b c_b + t_b)}} \rfloor),$$

$$\alpha_\kappa(0,i) = \frac{1}{\kappa+1}(l_{0,i} + \frac{t_b(r_b - R_0)}{r} + \frac{c_i - c_b}{c}),$$

$$\delta_\kappa(0,i) = \frac{1}{\kappa+1}(l_{0,i} - \frac{r_b - R_0}{r} + \frac{c_i - c_b}{c}).$$

where R_0 is the driver resistance at source s_0 and c_i the loading capacitance at sink s_i.

By replacing R_0 with 0, the results can be applied to any wire which connects two sinks in routing tree T. Based on the discussion above, we will present the detailed DBB-tree algorithm in the following section.

3.1 Lower Bound of Elmore Delay

The first phase of DBB-tree algorithm calculates the lower bound of Elmore delay for each critical sink s_i. It may not be possible to achieve this delay simultaneously for all critical sinks, but no achievable delay will be less than it. Formally, the lower bound of Elmore delay for s_i can be given by:

$$\tau^*(0,i) = \tau_\kappa(0,i)$$

where $\tau_\kappa(0,i)$ is the minimized Elmore delay through edge $e(0,i)$ as shown in Figure 1. That is, the lower bound of sink s_i is the minimized delay through the direct connection between source s_0 and s_i without considering other terminals' effect. The floorplanning is timing infeasible if there exists a critical sink s_i such that its lower bound $\tau^*(0,i)$ is greater than the given delay bound D_i : $\tau^*(0,i) > D_i$. The infeasible solution will be excluded, otherwise the algorithm continues to phase 2 and 3.

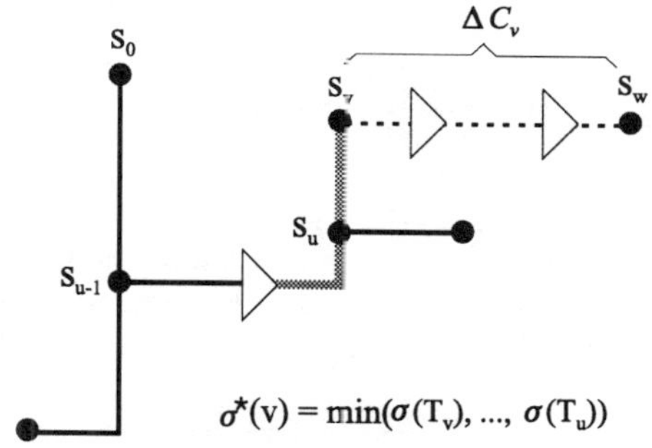

Figure 2: For particular sink $s_v \in T$, the last buffer on edge $e(u-1,u)$ drives T_v, the subtree rooted at s_v, if $e(u-1,u)$ is the last buffered edge on the path between the source and s_v.

3.2 DBB Spanning Tree Construction

The second phase constructs a buffered spanning tree such that the total wire length is minimized and bounded delays are satisfied. Similar with Prim's MST algorithm, it starts with the trivial tree: $T = \{s_0\}$, iteratively edge $e(v,w)$ with $\kappa(v,w)$ buffers is added into T, where $s_v \in T$ and $s_w \in S - T$ are chosen such that the length of $e(v,w)$ is minimized and the timing constraints in T are still satisfied. T grows up incrementally until it spans all terminals, or there is no edge that can be added without exceeding the delay bounds. In the latter case, the floorplanning is considered timing infeasible and the solution is excluded.

For the incremental construction of the DBB-tree, the key issue is how to quickly evaluate the timing constraints each time a new edge is added, i.e. whether or not the delay bound at each critical sink is satisfied. Recall for edge $e(v,w)$, the number of buffers, $\kappa(v,w)$, and the position of buffers $\alpha_\kappa(v,w)$ and $\delta_\kappa(v,w)$, inserted on the edge which minimize the edge delay can be calculated in constant time. Let T_v denote the subtree rooted at s_v, after adding edge $e(v,w)$ in which $s_v \in T$ and $s_w \in S - T$, the loading capacitance of T_v will be increased by ΔC_v:

$$\Delta C_v = \begin{cases} cl_{v,w} + c_w & \text{if } \kappa(v,w) = 0, \\ c\alpha_\kappa(v,w) + c_b & \text{otherwise.} \end{cases}$$

where $l_{v,w}$ is the length of edge $e(v,w)$ and c_w the loading capacitance at sink s_w. Let $e(u-1,u)$ denote the last buffered edge on the path from the source to s_v as shown in Fig. 2, the last buffer on edge $e(u-1,u)$ drives T_v. If there is no buffer from the source to s_v, the source drives T_v directly. According to Elmore delay, T_v is driven through the resistance between the driver and s_v, defined as *driving resistance* of T_v, denoted by $R(T_v)$. Given s_{v-1} is the parent of s_v, and κ, α_κ and δ_κ are abbreviations of $\kappa(v-1,v)$, $\alpha_\kappa(v-1,v)$ and $\delta_\kappa(v-1,v)$, respectively, $R(T_v)$ can be calculated as follows:

$$R(T_v) = \begin{cases} R(T_{v-1}) + rl_{v-1,v} & \text{if } \kappa = 0, \\ r_b + r(l_{v-1,v} - \alpha_\kappa - (\kappa-1)\delta_\kappa) & \text{otherwise.} \end{cases}$$

Let $T_i - T_{i+1}$ denote the set of sinks in subtree T_i but not in T_{i+1} and $s_{u+1}, \cdots, s_{v-1}$ denote the intermediate terminals from s_u to s_v. The Elmore delay of sinks in $T_i - T_{i+1}$ for $i = u, u+1, \cdots, v$, is given by:

$$\Delta\tau(0,s) = R(T_i)\Delta C_v$$

On the other hand, due to the isolation of buffers on edge $e(u-1,u)$, the increased loading capacitance of T_v will not affect on the delay of sinks which are not in T_u. We define the *delay slack* of each sink $s \in T$ as:

$$\lambda(s) = D_s - \tau(0,s),$$

and the delay slack of each subtree T_i as:

$$\lambda(T_i) = \min_{s \in T_i} \lambda(s) \tag{1}$$

The timing constraints will be satisfied for the sinks in $T_u - \{s_w\}$ if and only if for $i = u, u+1, \cdots v$, the following condition holds:

$$\lambda(T_i) \geq R(T_i)\Delta C_v \tag{2}$$

By introducing the *loading capacitance slack* of each subtree T_i :

$$\sigma(T_i) = \frac{\lambda(T_i)}{R(T_i)}, \tag{3}$$

and the minimum loading capacitance slack among subtrees T_i for $i = u, u+1, \cdots v$:

$$\sigma^*(v) = \min_{i=u,u+1,\cdots,v} \sigma(T_i),$$

the condition in Eq. 2 can be simply rewritten as:

$$\sigma^*(v) \geq \Delta C_v.$$

By keeping track of $\sigma^*(v)$, this condition can be checked in constant time. The Elmore delay of s_w can also be calculated from the Elmore delay of s_v:

$$\tau(0,w) = \tau(0,v) + R(T_v)\Delta C_v + \tau_\kappa(v,w).$$

From above analysis, we can conclude:

Theorem 2 *Given a routing tree T with bounded delays at critical sinks, after a new edge $e(v,w)$ is added, the necessary and sufficient condition for satisfying the bounded delays in T is:*

$$\sigma^*(v) \geq \Delta C_v \quad \textit{and} \quad D_w \geq \tau(0,w), \tag{4}$$

By keeping track of $\sigma^*(v)$, this condition can be checked in constant time.

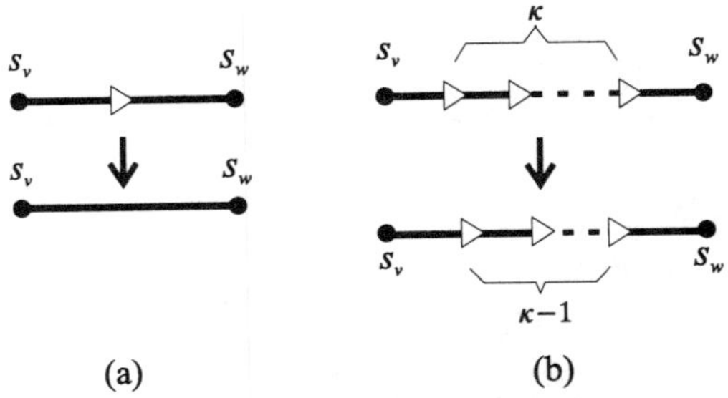

Figure 3: In case of (a), edge $e(v,w)$ becomes unbuffered after deleting the buffer, otherwise $\kappa(v,w)-1>0$ buffers are re-inserted on $e(v,w)$, as shown in (b).

At each iterative step, $s_v \in T$ and $s_w \in S-T$ can be selected in linear time such that $l_{v,w}$ is minimum and the timing constraints are satisfied. After adding the new edge $e(v,w)$, a two-pass traversal of T is sufficient to update the delay slack and loading capacitance slack of each subtree in T: (1) traverse T bottom up and calculate the delay slack and loading capacitance slack of each subtree T_i according to Equations 1 and 3; (2) traverse T top down and calculate $\sigma^*(i)$ from $\sigma^*(i-1)$, given s_{i-1} is the parent of s_i:

$$\sigma^*(i) = \begin{cases} \sigma(i) & \text{if } \kappa(i-1,i) > 0, \\ \min(\sigma^*(i-1),\ \sigma(i)) & \text{otherwise.} \end{cases}$$

Since each new edge can be added into T in linear time, the overall DBB spanning tree can be constructed in $O(n^2)$ time for net S with n terminals.

3.3 Buffer Deletion

In phase 2, buffers are inserted on each edge to minimize the edge delay in order to maximize the choice of tree topology. Some buffers may not be necessary for meeting the delay bounds. The third phase deletes unnecessary buffers from the spanning tree obtained in phase 2. In general, the buffers closest to the source can unload the critical path the most. The algorithm traverses T bottom up and deletes one buffer at a time without violating timing constraints. The deletion continues until all buffers left in T are necessary, that is, the delays would not be bounded if any of the remaining buffers is deleted.

For particular edge $e(v,w)$ with $\kappa(v,w) > 0$ buffers, if one buffer is deleted from $e(v,w)$, the wire delay will be increased by $\Delta\tau_\kappa(v,w)$:

$$\Delta\tau_\kappa(v,w) = \frac{(rcl_{v,w} + r(c_w - c_b) - cr_b)^2}{2\kappa(v,w)(\kappa(v,w)+1)rc} - t_b - r_b c_b.$$

In case of $\kappa(v,w) = 1$ as shown in Fig. 3 (a), $e(v,w)$ becomes unbuffered edge after deletion, the load capacitance of subtree T_v is increased by:

$$\Delta C_v = cl_{v,w} + C_w - c\alpha_\kappa(v,w) - c_b.$$

Otherwise $\kappa(v,w)-1$ buffers are re-inserted on edge $e(v,w)$, as shown in Fig. 3 (b): $\alpha_\kappa \rightarrow \alpha_{\kappa-1}$ and $\delta_\kappa \rightarrow \delta_{\kappa-1}$. The load capacitance of T_v is increased by :

$$\Delta C_v = c(\alpha_{\kappa-1} - \alpha_\kappa).$$

Similar to phase 2, let $e(u-1,u)$ denote the last buffered edge from the source to s_v. The delay of the sinks in subtree T_u will be increased due to the increased loading capacitance of T_v. In addition, the delay of sinks in subtree T_w will be further increased due to the increased edge delay of $e(v,w)$. Based on the analysis in phase 2, we can conclude that:

Theorem 3 *Given a buffered routing tree T with bounded delays at critical sinks, one buffer can be deleted from edge $e(v,w)$ without causing timing violation if and only if the following condition holds:*

$$\sigma^*(v) \geq \Delta C_v \quad and \quad \lambda(T_w) \geq R(T_v)\Delta C_v + \Delta\tau_\kappa(v,w) \quad (5)$$

Therefore the timing constraints of T can be evaluated in constant time for deleting a buffer from edge $e(v,w)$. The buffer can be found by searching at most $n-1$ edges. After deleting a buffer, the delay slack and loading capacitance slack of subtrees in T are incrementally updated in $O(n)$ time as in phase 2. So one buffer will be deleted in linear time. There are at most kn buffers in T where k is the maximum number of buffers on single edge, The timing complexity of buffer deletion is $O(kn^2)$ which dominates the overall DBB-tree algorithm. Following experimental results show that the buffer deletion effectively minimizes the total number of buffers and it can delete up to 93% of the buffers inserted in the previous phase.

4 Experimental Results

In the first part of the experiments, we implemented the DBB spanning tree algorithm on a Sun SPARC 20 workstation under the C/UNIX environment. The algorithm was tested on signal nets with 2, 5, 10, 25, 50 and 100 pins. For each net size, 100 nets are randomly generated on a $10mm \times 10mm$ routing region, and the delay bounds of critical sinks are randomly chosen from $[1.0ns, 5.0ns]$. The parameters used in the experiments are based on [18], which are summarized in Table 1.

The average results are reported in Table 2, the CPU time consumed per net shows that the algorithm is fast enough that can be applied during the stochastic optimization. The average number of buffers inserted in DBB-tree is very reasonable considering the number of terminals of the net. In addition, the number of buffers before the third phase of DBB-tree algorithm is also listed, the percentage of buffers reduced is as high as 93%. Therefore the buffer deletion is quite effective at removing unnecessary buffers.

Table 1: Experimental Parameters for Signal Nets

Output Resistance of Driver	R_0	500Ω – 1000Ω
Unit Wire Resistance	c	$0.12\Omega/\mu m$
Unit Wire Capacitance	r	$0.15fF/\mu m$
Output Resistance of Buffer	r_b	500Ω
Loading Capacitance of Buffer	c_b	$0.05pF$
Intrinsic Delay of Buffer	t_b	$0.1ns$
Loading Capacitance of Sink	c_i	$0.05pF$ – $0.15pF$

Table 2: Average Results of DBB-trees

Pins	CPU	Number of Buffers		
(#)	(*sec.*)	Before Del.	After Del.	Reduction (%)
2	0.0004	3.24	0.23	92.90
5	0.0019	7.09	1.43	79.83
10	0.0049	13.99	2.82	79.84
25	0.0816	36.34	4.57	87.42
50	0.6259	79.61	7.15	91.02
100	4.9228	171.24	10.53	93.85

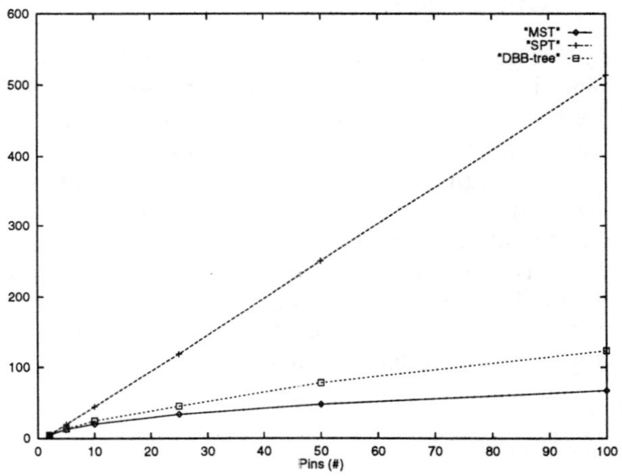

Figure 4: Average length of MST, SPT and DBB-trees.

Furthermore, we compared the average results with the minimum spanning tree (MST) and shortest path tree (SPT) on the same examples. Figure 4 shows the average length achieved by three different trees, DBB-tree is much closer to MST than to SPT.

To compare with the traditional approaches which do not consider buffer insertion during the floorplanning, in the second part of the experiments, we apply DBB-tree, MST and SPT to evaluate the timing performance during the floorplanning, respectively. Four examples are generated, in which blocks, netlists and timing bounds are randomly generated within some nominal ranges. Table 3 reports the consistant improvement of chip area and total wire length by using DBB-tree. The area can be improved up to 31% over MST and 22% over SPT, on the other hand, the total

Table 3: Improvement of Floorplanning Using DBB-tree.

Blocks (#)	Nets (#)	Area(%) MST	Area(%) SPT	Wire Length(%) MST	Wire Length(%) SPT
10	50	31.10	21.01	14.71	47.04
25	75	27.74	14.28	13.42	43.85
50	150	24.24	9.48	19.23	46.02
100	250	22.27	22.06	14.17	63.04

wire length can be improved up to 19% over MST and 63% over SPT. This substantial improvement demonstrates that using buffer insertion at the floorplanning stage yields significantly better solutions in terms of both chip area and total wire length. It should be noted that future research is needed to extend the approach to distribute buffers into the empty space between macros subject to timing constraints. However, the area of such buffers is typically a small fraction of a given macro area and can be accommodated.

5 Conclusion

In this paper, we propose a new methodology of floorplanning where intermediate buffer insertion is used as another degree of freedom in the delay calculation. A more realistic model for the path based timing driven layout design is defined: Delay Bounded Buffered tree (DBB-tree), in which we treat the delay bounds as constraints rather than formulating the delay into the objectives as is done in most of the previous work. The efficient DBB spanning tree algorithm made our buffered tree based floorplanning very effective and applicable to industrial problems.

References

[1] J. P. Cohoon and L. J. Randall, "Critical net routing," in *Proc. IEEE Intl. Conf. on Computer Design*, pp. 174–177, 1991.

[2] J. Cong, A. B. Kahng, G. Robins, M. Sarrafzadeh, and C. K. Wong, "Performance-Driven global routing for cell based IC's," in *Proc. IEEE Intl. Conf. Computer Design*, (Cambridege, MA), pp. 170–173, October 1991.

[3] J. M. Ho, D. J. Lee, C. H. Chang, and C. K. Wong, "Bounded-diameter spanning tree and related problems," in *Proc. ACM Symp. on Computational Geometry*, pp. 276–282, 1989.

[4] A. Lim and S. Wing Cheng, "Performance oriented rectilinear steiner trees," in *Proc. of 30th Design Automation Conf.*, pp. 171–176, June 1992.

[5] C. J. Alpert, T. C. Hu, J. H. Huang, and A. B. Kahng, "A direct combination of the prim and dijkstra constructions for improved performance-driven global routing," in *Proc. of IEEE Intl. Symp. on Circuits and Systems*, pp. 1869–1872, 1993.

[6] J. Cong, K. Shing Leung, and D. Zhou, "Performance-Driven interconnect design based on distributed RC delay model," in *Proc. 30th ACM/IEEE Design Automation Conf.*, pp. 606–611, June 1993.

[7] K. D. Boese, A. B. Kahng, and G. Robins, "High-Performance routing trees with identified critical sinks," in *Proc. 30th ACM/IEEE Design Automation Conf.*, pp. 182–187, June 1993.

[8] K. D. Boese, A. B. Kahng, B. A. McCoy, and G. Robins, "Rectilinear steiner trees with minimum elmore delay," in *Proc. 31st ACM/IEEE Design Automation Conf.*, pp. 381–387, June 1994.

[9] X. Hong, T. Xue, E. S. Kuh, C. K. Cheng, and J. Huang, "Performance-Driven steiner tree algorithms for global routing," in *Proc. 30th ACM/IEEE Design Automation Conf.*, (Baltimore, MD), pp. 177–181, June 1993.

[10] S. Prasitjutrakul and W. J. Kubitz, "A timing-Driven global router for custom chip design," in *IEEE Intl. Conf. on Computer Aided Design*, pp. 48–51, 1990.

[11] K. J. Singh and A. Sangiovanni-Vincentelli, "A heuristic algorithm for the fanout problem," in *Proc. ACM/IEEE Design Automation Conf.*, pp. 357–360, 1990.

[12] H. J. Touati, C. W. Moon, R. K. Brayton, and A. Wang, "Performance oriented technology mapping," in *Proc. 6th MIT VLSI Conf.*, pp. 79–97, 1990.

[13] C. L. Berman, J. L. Carter, and K. F. Day, "The fanout problem: From theory to practice," in *Proc. 1989 Decennial Caltech Conf.*, pp. 69–99, 1989.

[14] L. N. Kannan, P. R. Suaris, and H. G. Fang, "A methodology and algorithms for post-Placement delay optimization," in *Proc. ACM/IEEE Design Automation Conf.*, pp. 327–332, 1994.

[15] H. Vaishnav and M. Pedram, "Routability-Driven fanout optimization," in *Proc. ACM/IEEE Design Automation Conf.*, pp. 230–235, 1993.

[16] L. P. P. P. van Ginneken, "Buffer placement in distributed RC-tree networks for minimal elmore delay," in *Proc. International Symposium on Circuits and Systems*, pp. 865–868, 1990.

[17] J. Lillis, C. Kuan Cheng, and T. Ting Y. Lin, "Optimal and efficient buffer insertion and wire sizing," in *Proc. IEEE 1995 Custom Integrated Circuits Conf.*, pp. 259–262, 1995.

[18] T. Okamoto and J. Cong, "Interconnect layout optimization by simultaneous steiner tree construction and buffer insertion," in *Proc. 5th ACM/SIGDA Physical Design Workshop*, (Reston, Virginia), pp. 1–6, April 1996.

[19] T. Okamoto and J. Cong, "Buffered steiner tree construction with wire sizing for interconnect layout optimization," in *Proc. 1996 IEEE/ACM International Conf. on Computer Aided Design*, (San Jose, CA), pp. 44–49, Nov. 1996.

[20] S. Dhar and M. A. Franklin, "Optimum buffer circuits for driving long uniform lines," *IEEE Journal of Solid-State Circuits*, vol. 26, pp. 32–40, January 1991.

[21] C. Alpert and A. Devgan, "Wire segmenting for improved buffer insertion," in *to appear in Proc. of 34th Design Automation Conf.*, June 1997.

[22] Q. Zhu, *Chip and Package Co-Synthesis of Clock Networks*. PhD thesis, Univ. of California, Santa Cruz, Santa Cruz, CA, June 1995.

Interconnect Layout Optimization Under Higher-Order RLC Model*

Jason Cong and Cheng-Kok Koh
UCLA Computer Science Dept., Los Angeles, CA 90095-1596

Abstract

In this paper, we study the interconnect layout optimization problem under a higher-order RLC model to optimize not just *delay*, but also *waveform* for RLC circuits with non-monotone signal response. We propose a unified approach that considers topology optimization, wiresizing optimization, and waveform optimization simultaneously. Our algorithm considers a large class of routing topologies, ranging from shortest-path Steiner trees to bounded-radius Steiner trees and Steiner routings. We construct a set of *required-arrival-time Steiner trees* or RATS-trees, providing a smooth trade-off among signal delay, waveform, and routing area. Using a new *incremental* moment computation algorithm, we interleave topology construction with moment computation to facilitate accurate delay calculation and evaluation of waveform quality. Experimental results show that our algorithm is able to construct a set of topologies providing a smooth trade-off among signal delay, signal settling time, voltage overshoot, and routing cost.

1 Introduction

As VLSI circuitry reaches deep submicron device dimension, operates at giga-Hertz clock frequencies, and is packaged in highly integrated multichip modules, the performance of interconnect structures has become the dominating factor in determining system performance. Recent studies show that interconnect delay can be reduced by interconnect topology optimization, wiresizing optimization, and/or buffer optimization. A comprehensive survey of these optimization techniques can be found in [1]. In this paper, we study the interconnect layout optimization problem under a higher-order RLC model. Our objective is to perform topology and wiresizing optimization for performance and signal integrity under a higher-order moment-based interconnect model. It has the following advantages:

(1) Most of the previous works on interconnect optimization were achieved under RC interconnect models only, including recent studies on topology optimization [2, 3], wiresizing optimization [4, 5, 6, 7], as well as the most recent works that combined topology construction with buffer insertion and/or wiresizing [8, 9, 10]. They did not consider the inductance effect, which may be an important factor in high-speed MCM/PCB designs and high frequency deep sub-micron designs. In this study, we overcome this shortcoming by considering a higher-order moment-based RLC interconnect model in the optimization process. We also present a new algorithm to *incrementally* compute moments of sinks in an RLC tree in a bottom-up manner.

(2) A few approaches have proposed to use higher-order RLC models for topology optimization [11, 12], wiresizing optimization [13], and termination optimization [14, 15, 16]. But none of them can consider all three optimization simultaneously for both delay and signal integrity optimization. Our optimization algorithm takes a more global approach; it considers wiresizing during routing topology construction, optimizes for both signal delays and response waveforms, and returns a set of routing topologies with appropriate wire width assignments.

(3) Our method is capable of constructing a large class of routing topologies, ranging from shortest-path Steiner trees to bounded-radius Steiner trees and Steiner routings. All of the previous topology construction algorithms are limited to a single class of routing topology. For example, the A-tree algorithm considered shortest-path Steiner trees only [2], and the set of topologies generated by the P-tree algorithm [9] is restricted to a permutation-induced abstract topology pre-determined by a Traveling Salesman heuristic. By considering a large class of routing topologies, our algorithm is able to produce a set of topologies with a smooth trade-off among signal delay, waveform, and routing area.

In order to optimize signal delay, waveform, and wiring area, we construct a set of *required-arrival-time Steiner trees* (RATS-trees) by recursively merging subtrees in a bottom-up fashion. Using this bottom-up tree construction, we can easily compute sink moments in an incremental manner. For each subset of sinks, we maintain a set of topologies which correspond to a trade-off among routing costs, time domain waveforms, and signal delays. Moreover, we also consider interconnect sizing (and possibly, buffer insertion) in the subtree merging process. At the end of the bottom-up process, the designer would have a set of solutions to choose from. In this paper, we also introduce a space-efficient *reduced tree representation* to capture all wiresized topologies constructed during the execution of our algorithm.

The rest of the paper is organized as follows: Section 2 formulates the interconnect layout optimization problem that we aim to solve. In Section 3, we present the RATS-tree algorithm in detail, including the reduced tree representation and the incremental bottom-up moment computation algorithm. We present the experimental results in Section 4 and conclude the paper in Section 5.

2 Problem Formulation

Given a net of pins or terminals $\{s_0, s_1, s_2, \cdots, s_n\}$ to be electrically connected, we assume that s_0 denotes the source (or driver) of the net and the rest of the pins are sinks (or receivers). In this paper, we are interested in interconnect trees We use $P_T(u,v)$ to denote the unique path from u to v in an interconnect tree T, $d_T(u,v)$ the pathlength of $P_T(u,v)$, and $d(u,v)$ the Manhattan distance between u and v. We denote the signal delay from u to v by $t_T(u,v)$. The source node s_0 will generally be referred to as the root of an interconnect tree, and each node v in the tree is connected to its parent by edge e_v. We use T_v to denote the subtree that is rooted at v. Given an edge e, we use T_e to denote the subtree with e being its root edge. $l(e)$ denotes the length of e.

Let q_i be the required arrival time of sink s_i. A minimal *required-arrival-time Steiner tree* (RATS-tree) is a minimum-cost Steiner tree such that $q_i \geq t_T(s_0, s_i)$ for all sinks. RATS-trees include several commonly used topologies when we use the pathlength delay formulation with $t_T(u,v) = d_T(u,v)$. For example, by setting $q_i = d(s_0, s_i)$ for all sinks, an optimal RATS-tree is an optimal Steiner arborescence [17]. If we relax the requirement such that all sinks have the same required arrival time, then an optimal RATS-tree is an optimal bounded-radius Steiner tree [18]. Lastly, an optimal RATS-tree with unbounded q_i's is an optimal Steiner tree [19].

The pathlength formulation captures the delay for unloaded lossless transmission lines in MCM/PCB designs perfectly. In this case, the output response is a replica of the input signal delayed by the time-of-flight (or propagation delay) $t_f = \sqrt{LC}l$ where L and C are the unit-length interconnect inductance and capacitance, respectively, and l is the length of the interconnect. In general, it is assumed that $\sqrt{LC}$ is a constant unchanged by wiresizing. Therefore, the time-of-flight (or propagation delay) on the path from the source to sink s_i is $t_f(s_0, s_i) =$

*This work is partially supported by DARPA/ETO under Contract DAAL01-96-K-3600 and a grant from Intel Corporation under the California MICRO Program.

1092-3152/97 $10.00 © 1997 IEEE

$\sum_{e_v \in P_T(s_0,s_i)} \sqrt{LC} l(e_v)$, which is proportional to the pathlength $d_T(s_0, s_i)$.

A more general formulation is to model MCM/PCB and IC interconnect structures as lossy transmission lines. Under this formulation, the delay at each sink is the sum of the propagation delay and the rising/falling (or transition) delay of the signal response waveform [13]. The transition delay can be estimated by a higher-order moment-based delay model as follows: Let $h_i(t)$ be the impulse response at a node of interest, say sink s_i, in an interconnect. Let $v_{in}(t)$ be the input voltage of the linear circuit, $v_i(t)$ be the output voltage of sink s_i in the circuit, $V_{in}(s)$ and $V_i(s)$ be the Laplace transform of $v_{in}(t)$ and $v_i(t)$, respectively. Then, $H_i(s) = V_i(s)/V_{in}(s)$ is the transfer function, which can be written as:

$$\begin{aligned} H_i(s) &= \int_0^\infty h_i(t)e^{-st}dt = \sum_{j=0}^{\infty} \frac{(-1)^j}{j!} s^j \int_0^\infty t^j h_i(t)dt \\ &= \sum_{j=0}^{\infty} (-1)^j \cdot m_i^j \cdot s^j. \end{aligned} \quad (1)$$

where m_i^j is the j-th *moment* of the transfer function.

Moments of an RLC interconnect can be computed by the methods proposed in [20, 21]. From the first $2q-1$ moments, one can construct a q-pole transfer function $\hat{H}_i(s)$ to approximate the actual transfer function $H_i(s)$ as follows:

$$\hat{H}_i(s) = \sum_{j=1}^{q} \frac{k_j}{s - p_j}, \quad (2)$$

where p_j's are poles and k_j's are residues, all of which can be determined uniquely by matching the initial boundary conditions, denoted m_i^{-1}, and the first $2q-1$ moments m_i^j of $H_i(s)$ to those of $\hat{H}_i(s)$ [22]. The choice of order q depends on the accuracy required but is always much less than the order of the circuit. In practice, $q \leq 5$ is commonly used. When q is chosen to be two, it is known as the *two-pole model* [23, 11, 24]. From $\hat{H}_i(s)$, one can derive the approximated output voltage $\hat{v}_i(t)$ and solve for the transition delay $t_x(i)$ of the output signal at s_i to reach x% of V_{DD} (assuming a rising output) for the first time. In this paper, we use the two-pole delay model proposed in [24] to approximate the rise/fall delays of a signal as follows:

$$t_{90}(i) = \begin{cases} 2.36 \cdot \frac{m_i^1 + \sqrt{4m_i^2 - 3(m_i^1)^2}}{2} & \text{if } 4m_i^2 - 3(m_i^1)^2 > 0 \\ 1.66 \cdot \frac{2((m_i^1)^2 - m_i^2)}{\sqrt{3(m_i^1)^2 - 4m_i^2}} & \text{if } 4m_i^2 - 3(m_i^1)^2 < 0 \\ 3.90 \cdot \frac{m_i^1}{2} & \text{if } 4m_i^2 - 3(m_i^1)^2 = 0 \end{cases} \quad (3)$$

Signal response waveform is another important factor in interconnect design. Under the ideal situation, one would prefer the transmission of the input signal to the output not to be distorted. However, due to impedance mismatch and reflection, ringing may occur at the output node, resulting in excessive settling time and voltage overshoot or undershoot, and adversely affecting the circuit performance. Similar to [14, 15, 16], we propose to use moments as an indirect metric to measure signal quality.

For example, if we use the two-pole model to model the interconnect, then ringing can be attributed to the existence of complex poles in $\hat{H}_i(t)$. The condition for the poles to be complex (i.e., for the output response to be non-monotonic, or *underdamped*) is for $\lambda_i = 4m_i^2 - 3(m_i^1)^2$ to be negative. When λ_i is strictly positive, we have a *overdamped* and monotone response. When λ_i is exactly zero, the signal is said to be *critically damped*. On the other hand, an underdamped signal generally has a faster rise delay when compared to a damped signal. Other metrics that involved even higher order moments include the third *central moment* proposed in [15]. With other attributes (such as the signal delay and the wiring length) being the same, we would prefer a RATS-tree with λ_i's as close to zero as possible.

To summarize, we propose to solve the following problem:

Required-Arrival-Time Steiner Tree Routing: Given a set of terminals s_i's and required arrival times q_i's, construct a required-arrival-time Steiner tree T such that $q_i \geq t_T(s_0, s_i)$, critical damping is achieved for good signal quality (i.e., λ_i's are as close to zero as possible), and the total wirelength or wiring area is minimized.

3 RATS-Tree Algorithm

We construct required-arrival-time Steiner trees (RATS-trees) by recursively merging subtrees in a bottom-up fashion. Using this bottom-up tree construction, we can compute moments of sinks and consider interconnect sizing and possibly buffer insertion in the subtree merging process easily.

3.1 Overview of RATS-Tree Algorithm

In the following discussion, we assume that the source is at the origin and the sinks are in the first quadrant. We generalize the algorithm to handle the case where the terminals are at arbitrary locations in Section 3.7. Given a set of terminals, the RATS-Tree algorithm operates on a Hanan grid [25] induced by the terminals. All Hanan grid points are ordered according to their distance from the source, with arbitrary tie breaking.

Let (x_m, y_m) denote the coordinates of grid point m, and $|m| = x_m + y_m$. Given two distinct points p and q, we define the Steiner merging point for p and q, denoted $\langle p, q \rangle$, as the point with coordinates We say that q is dominated by p, or $q \preceq p$ if and only if $x_q \leq x_p$, $y_q \leq y_p$, and $p \neq q$.

In general, the RATS-Tree algorithm follows a branch-and-bound paradigm, by considering *merging* and *skipping* (of merging) of subtrees at a Steiner merging point as introduced in [17], as well as *re-rooting* of a subtree, a concept introduced in [26], at Hanan grid points. Each node in the branch-and-bound (B&B) search tree is associated with a *peer topology set* $\mathcal{T}$ which contains a forest of subtrees constructed so far and a scan level $K = |m|$ where m is the Steiner merging point last considered in the subtree merging process. Not to be confused with a node in a constructed topology, we refer to a node in the B&B search tree as a B&B node.

Starting with a B&B node where the peer topology set contains all single-terminal trees and the scan level $K = \infty$, we expand a B&B node characterized by $(\mathcal{T}, K)$ by considering a new Steiner merging point m with the highest order among all Steiner merging points of tree roots in $\mathcal{T}$ such that $|m| < K$. If the new Steiner merging point is a terminal, then such a merging is called a *terminal merging*. Otherwise, it is called a *Steiner merging*. These operations are similar to those in [17].

Let $P_{\succeq}(m) = \{p | m \preceq p, T_p \in \mathcal{T}\}$ denote the set of tree roots in $\mathcal{T}$ that dominates m. Both terminal and Steiner merging connect from m to each node p in $P_{\succeq}(m)$ and eliminate T_p from $\mathcal{T}$. We make a shortest path connection between m and p by *growing* T_p along the Hanan grid points from p to m in a bottom-up fashion. A new subtree T_m is added to $\mathcal{T}$ and K is updated to $|m|$. Note that when $x_m \neq x_p$ and $y_m \neq y_p$, there are several shortest Manhattan paths from m to p. We consider only the two shortest Manhattan paths that correspond to the boundary of the smallest bounding box containing m and p.

As in the branch-and-bound-based minimum rectilinear Steiner arborescence (MRSA) algorithms in [17], we also consider *skipping* a Steiner merging. In this case, while K is updated to $|m|$, we keep $\mathcal{T}$ unchanged. Therefore, skipping a Steiner merging operation generates an additional child B&B node in the B&B search tree.

Both terminal merging and Steiner merging consider merging at the roots of sub-trees only, thereby producing shortest path trees only. In order to consider a large class of routing solutions, we allow merging at non-root nodes of the sub-trees. We achieve non-root merging by *re-rooting*. After each terminal merging or Steiner merging, the resultant topology T is re-rooted at various Hanan grid points in T, creating several topologies that consist of the same nodes and edges in T,

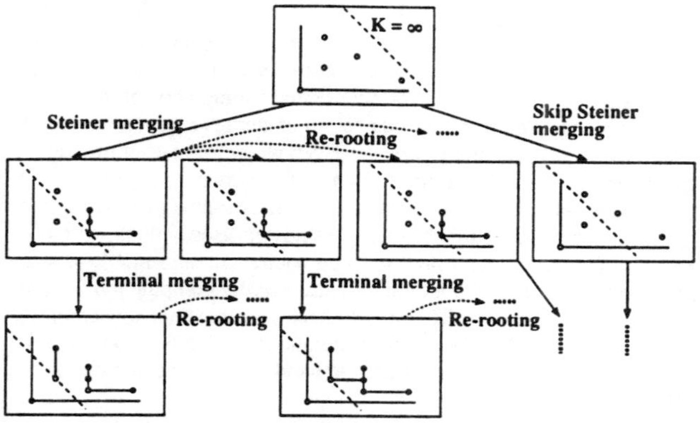

Figure 1: A snapshot of the B&B search tree illustrating the RATS-algorithm applied to a 5-terminal net.

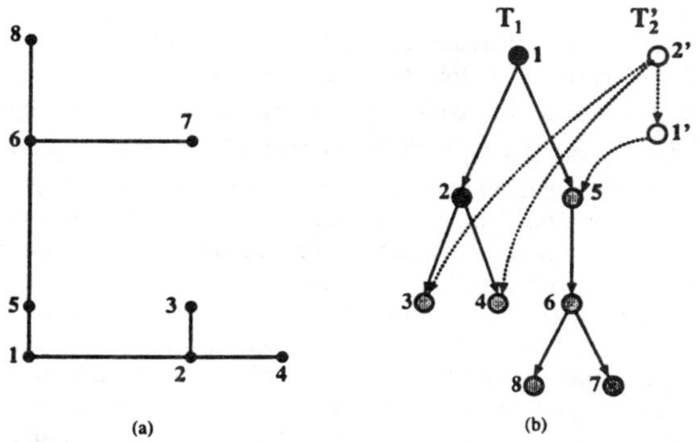

Figure 2: (a) An interconnect with 8 nodes. (b) Reduced tree representations for topologies T_1 and T_2' rooted at node 1 (filled circle) and 2 (empty circle) of the same interconnect in (a), respectively. The shared nodes are shaded.

but rooted at different nodes. These re-rooted topologies have identical routing structure, but different sink delays and signal waveforms. Therefore, re-rooting creates several sibling B&B nodes for the newly generated child B&B node.

Figure 1 shows a partial B&B search tree corresponding to the application of the RATS-tree algorithm applied to a 5-terminal net. In the B&B search tree, root nodes of the peer topology set are depicted by empty circles, and non-root nodes by filled circles. For illustrative purpose, the scan level K is shown as a dash line. Note that after the first Steiner merging, the newly created subtree and its re-rooted topologies include a new Hanan grid point.

From the above discussion, it is obvious that growing of a subtree and its subsequent merger with sibling subtrees are bottom-up in nature. As we shall see in Section 3.3, topologies are also re-rooted in a bottom-up manner. It is therefore natural to incorporate bottom-up wiresizing (and buffer insertion for IC designs) optimization as in [9, 8] during the subtree merging and re-rooting process (see Section 3.4). For an effective evaluation of different wiresizing solutions, as well as topologies, we present in Section 3.5 an efficient incremental bottom-up moment computation method to compute higher-order sink moments for a more accurate delay computation and signal waveform evaluation.

We explore the B&B search tree in a breadth-first traversal order. In other words, nodes at the same level of the B&B search tree are expanded first before any of their children are expanded. The reason for the breadth-first expansion order is to facilitate as much pruning as possible (see Section 3.4). A breadth-first traversal essentially trades space for time. We would like to point out that our algorithm can potentially generate an exponential number of topologies and wiresizing solutions. However, for interconnect optimization problems in practice, most nets have no more than 10 sinks, So the run-time and space requirement of our algorithm are not a problem. For very large nets, our algorithm can selectively store a subset of topologies and their wiresizing solutions for runtime and memory efficiency. Moreover, since these topologies share many sub-topologies, we develop a space efficient *reduced tree representation* which supports sub-tree sharing in different routing topologies. The reduced tree representation will be presented in Section 3.2.

Although the RATS-tree algorithm follows the branch-and-bound paradigm, we would like to point out that in general, it does not guarantee optimal RATS-tree construction even under the pathlength formulation for two reasons. First, an optimal RATS-tree may not lie on the Hanan grid. An example of such a RATS-tree can be found in [27]. Second, our algorithm may miss the optimal solutions due to the greedy nature of terminal merging. Nonetheless, if it is required that all the sinks have a shortest path to the source, then our RATS-tree algorithm will always return an optimal rectilinear Steiner arborescence.

3.2 Reduced Tree Representation

To achieve an efficient implementation, we introduce the notion of a *reduced tree representation* to allow topologies to share common sub-topologies. This is analogous to the concept of *reduced ordered binary decision diagram* (ROBDD) [28] that is commonly used in logic synthesis.

We illustrate the idea of a reduced tree representation in Figure 2. Consider two topologies T_1 and T_2' that correspond to the same interconnect structure with 8 nodes in Figure 2(a). T_1 is rooted at node 1 and T_2' is rooted at node 2. Suppose we already have a reduced tree representation of T_1 as shown by the filled and shaded circles and solid line edges in Figure 2(b). To avoid confusion, any new node created for T_2' to represent node i of the interconnect structure in Figure 2(a) is labeled i'. Since T_2' shares the subtree T_5, and leaf nodes 3 and 4 in T_1, to create a reduced tree representation of the topology T_2', we only need to create two additional nodes $2'$ and $1'$ (empty circles in Figure 2(b)) to represent T_2' completely.

Sharing is allowed not just among re-rooted topologies which cover the same set of nodes, as depicted in the above example. It is also possible to share sub-topologies in topologies that cover different sets of nodes. This, again, is analogous to multi-root ROBDD's for multiple-output functions where instead of keeping one distinct ROBDD for each output function, different outputs share common structures (co-factors) in the ROBDDs. Note that a topology can be uniquely identified by the root node and the child topologies of the root note. In our implementation, we keep each topology in a hash table so that each topology will be created only once.

3.3 Re-rooting of Topology

Now, we present a linear time algorithm to re-root a topology T_r rooted at node r. Let T_w denote the sub-tree rooted at node w in T_r. Let the k children of r be u_i for $i = 1 \cdots k$. Suppose we want to re-root T_r at one of the child nodes, say u_j where $1 \leq j \leq k$. Let T'_{u_j} denote the new topology. Let T'_w be the sub-tree rooted at node w in T'_{u_j}. Re-rooting of T_r at node u_j effectively swaps the parent-child relationship of r and u_j. The parent-child relationships of other nodes are not affected. For example, in Figure 2 where T_1 is being re-rooted at node 2, only two changes are required to reflect the re-rooting operation. First, node 1 becomes a child node of node 2 in T_2', and nodes 3 and 4 which are child nodes of 2 in T_1 remain as children of node 2 after the re-rooting operation. Moreover, while the child nodes of 1 in T_1 are nodes 5 and 2, node 5 is the only child node of node 1 in T_2' after re-rooting.

We note that the original topology can be re-rooted at all nodes in the topology by a simple depth-first traversal. Using the tree T_r in the preceding discussion as an example, where u_j is the next node in the traversal order, we first create T'_r, which takes time linear to the degree of T_r. T'_r differs from T_r in that it does not contain T_{u_j} as its child topology. Next, we create T'_{u_j}, which again takes time linear to the degree of T_{u_j}. T'_{u_j} differs from T_{u_j} in that it contains T'_r. Only two additional nodes and $O(k)$ edges are created where k is the maximum degree of a node in the topology. This process is repeated for all child nodes of T_r in the depth-first traversal. Therefore, the total time complexity to re-root an topology with g grid points in it is $O(g \cdot k)$. Since we are dealing with planar single-layer Manhattan routing, the degree of each node is bounded by 4. We can conclude that it takes linear time to re-root a topology. Moreover, instead of requiring $O(g^2)$ nodes and edges to represent all possible re-rooted topologies under an explicit representation, a reduced tree representation can represent all re-rooted topologies using only $O(g)$ nodes and edges.

3.4 Wiresizing Optimization

From the above description of the re-rooting operation, the basic operations to create re-rooted topologies are still growing and merging of subtrees in a bottom-up manner (albeit a top-down depth-first traversal). Therefore, it is natural to incorporate bottom-up wiresizing optimization into the algorithm as in [9, 8]. Note that it is easy to extend it to consider buffer insertion as well for IC designs.

Basically, given a subtree with a set of I wiresizing configurations. When we grow a subtree, we consider a given set of $|W|$ candidate wire widths for the new root edge e, resulting in $I \times |W|$ combinations of wire width assignments for T_e, the new subtree tree rooted at e. Similarly, merging of two subtrees with I and J wiresizing configurations, respectively, produces a total of $I \times J$ possible wire width assignments for the new subtree.

Clearly, such an approach generates an exponential number of wiresizing configuration. Similar to the previous bottom-up wiresizing algorithms [6, 8], we perform pruning of wiresizing solutions of a topology T. Each wiresizing solution $\mathcal{W}$ of T is associated with a triple $(Cap(T,\mathcal{W}), Slack(T,\mathcal{W}), SQ(T,\mathcal{W}))$, where $Cap(T,\mathcal{W})$ is the total capacitance, $Slack(T,\mathcal{W}) = \min_{s_i \in T}(q_i - t_{T,\mathcal{W}}(s_i))$ with $t_{T,\mathcal{W}}(s_i)$ being the two-pole sink delay of s_i in T (Section 2), and $SQ(T,\mathcal{W})$ is the signal quality of the topology and wiresizing solution defined as follows: Recall that $\lambda_i = 4m_i^2 - 3(m_i^1)^2$ is a measure of the degree of damping for sink s_i. If $\lambda_i > 0$, s_i is overdamped. If $\lambda_i < 0$, s_i is underdamped. Otherwise, s_i is critically damped. We propose to measure the signal quality of a tree T with wiresizing solution $\mathcal{W}$ by $SQ(T,\mathcal{W}) = \min_{s_i \in T} \lambda_i$. In other words, the signal quality is measured by the worst signal response waveform among all sinks.

Given two wiresizing solutions $\mathcal{W}$ and $\mathcal{W}'$ for T, we say that $\mathcal{W}'$ is redundant if $Cap(T,\mathcal{W}) \leq Cap(T,\mathcal{W}')$, $Slack(T,\mathcal{W}) \geq Slack(T,\mathcal{W}')$, $SQ(T,\mathcal{W}) \geq SQ(T,\mathcal{W}')$, *and* at least one of the three inequalities is a strict inequality. Note that the pruning criterion is similar to that in [6, 8] if we do not consider $SQ(T,\mathcal{W})$. The basic idea of our pruning criterion is as follows: with other attributes such as the Cap's and SQ's being identical, we would prefer a solution with a larger $Slack$ in order to reduce the possibility of constructing an infeasible topology (with negative $Slack$). Similarly, with Cap's and $Slack$'s being identical, we would always pick the solution with a better signal quality, i.e., larger SQ. Finally, we would always choose a solution with a smaller Cap if other attributes of the two solutions are identical. Essentially, we are trading-off total capacitance for timing slack or signal quality and vice versa.

We prune all redundant wiresizing solutions from the solution space. To perform such a pruning, we have to compute the higher order moments and evaluate the sink delays and signal quality for each wiresizing solution. We present an incremental bottom-up moment computation algorithm in the following.

3.5 Incremental Bottom-Up Moment Computation

Moments can be computed by the polynomial-time algorithms in [20, 21]. However, these works compute moments by traversing the entire tree iteratively, and do not allow incremental computation of moments. As the topology changes, another round of iterative tree traversals is needed to re-compute the moments. Even when we restrict the topology change to a simple addition of an RLC segment to the root of the original tree, which is the basis of our bottom-up topology construction algorithm, moments cannot be incrementally updated with the previous methods. Therefore, these previous approaches are not suitable for our RATS-tree algorithm. A method to incrementally compute moment in a bottom-up fashion for RC interconnects was recently presented in [10]. However, it did not consider the inductance effect. In the following, we generalize the algorithm to handle moment computation of a RLC tree.

Consider an RLC tree T_v rooted by node v. For any node w in T_v, let m_w^p be the p-th moment of node w and $C_{T_w}^p = \sum_{j \in T_w} m_j^p \cdot C_j$ be the total p-th order moment weighted capacitance of T_w [20] where C_j is the capacitance connected to node j. Now, we add a new edge uv at the root of T_v to obtain a new tree T_u rooted at u. Let $\overline{C}_{T_w}^p$ be the new total p-th order moment weighted capacitances of T_w for w in T_u. Similarly, let $\overline{m}_w^p$ be the new p-th moment of node w in T_u. Let R_v, L_v, and C_v be the total resistance, inductance, and capacitance of the edge uv, respectively. The following theorem illustrates how we can express $\overline{m}_w^p$ for $p \geq 0$ in terms of $\overline{m}_v^q$ and m_w^q for $q = 0 \cdots p$.

Theorem 1 *For root node u,*

$$\overline{m}_u^p = \begin{cases} 0 & \text{if } p = -1 \text{ or } p > 0 \\ 1 & \text{if } p = 0. \end{cases} \tag{4}$$

For $p \geq 0$,

$$\overline{C}_{T_v}^{p-1} = \overline{m}_v^{p-1} C_v + \sum_{q=0}^{p-1} \overline{m}_v^{p-1-q} C_{T_v}^q \tag{5}$$

$$\overline{m}_v^p = R_v \overline{C}_{T_v}^{p-1} - L_v \overline{C}_{T_v}^{p-2} \tag{6}$$

$$\overline{m}_w^p = \sum_{q=0}^{p} \overline{m}_v^{p-q} m_w^q \ \forall\, w \in T_v \tag{7}$$

The proof of the theorem is left out due to space limitation. The reader may refer to [27] for details. The theorem implies that if we keep $C_{T_v}^i$ for $i = 0 \cdots p-1$, we can compute up to the p-th order the new moments for v by computing $\overline{C}_{T_v}^{i-1}$ followed by $\overline{m}_v^i$ for $i = 0 \cdots p$ by Eqns. (5) and (6). Then, we can update the moments of all the sinks in the topology by Eqn. (7). From the above theorem, we can state the following corollary which allows us to incrementally update sink moments during the merging operation and compute the total p-th order moment weighted capacitance at the new root u:

Corollary 1 *Consider k topologies, denoted* T_{v_i} *for* $i = 1 \cdots k$. *If the k topologies are merged at a new node u, then for* $p \geq 0$ *and* $i = 1 \cdots k$, *then* $\overline{C}_{T_{v_i}}^{p-1}$, $\overline{m}_{v_i}^p$ *and* $\overline{m}_w^p$ $\forall\, w \in T_{v_i}$ *can be computed by Eqns. (5–7), respectively. Let* c_u^s *be the sink capacitance at the root node u, i.e.,* $c_u^s = 0$ *if u is not a sink. For* $p \geq 0$,

$$\overline{C}_{T_u}^{p-1} = \overline{m}_u^{p-1} c_u^s + \sum_{i=0}^{k} \overline{C}_{T_{v_i}}^{p-1} \tag{8}$$

From Theorem 1 and Corollary 1, the time complexity to update the moments of n sinks in a tree is $O(n \cdot p^2)$. The auxiliary space requirement is $O(p)$. On the other hand, the time complexity of the method proposed by [20] is $O(g \cdot p)$ where g is the total number of grid nodes in the tree and the auxiliary space requirement is $O(g)$. Since our RATS-tree algorithm is based on the Hanan-grid, g could be in the order of $O(n^2)$.

We can integrate the incremental bottom-up moment computation algorithm with our RATS-tree algorithm easily. For each topology constructed by our algorithm, we keep a set of irredundant wiresizing solutions and their corresponding sink moments (up to a pre-specified p-th order) for the topology. Note that all these are stored in the reduced tree representation. As we grow a topology along the path of Hanan grid points towards the new root in the merge operation, we compute the length of each new edge and for each candidate wire width of the new edge, derive the interconnect resistance, inductance and capacitance. These RLC parasitics are used to update the moments of the sinks using Theorem 1. We then use Corollary 1 to compute the weighted capacitances at the new root. The RATS-tree algorithm then prunes the wiresizing solutions of the newly created topology.

3.6 Further Pruning of Solution Space

Removal of redundant wiresizing solutions from a topology is not the only pruning technique employed by the RATS-tree algorithm. We apply several other techniques to prune the B&B search tree. For example, with a clever arrangement of the tree roots in $\mathcal{T}$, it is possible to find the new Steiner merging point m and $P_{\succeq}(m)$ in $O(n)$ time and partially avoid generation of non-planar routings during the merging operation (see [17] for details.)

Due to the re-rooting operation, however, it is possible that we may create many sibling B&B nodes which will generate non-planar routings in subsequent merging operations. While we can prune away B&B nodes that contain non-planar routings, a better approach is to avoid creating them as much as possible. We introduce the ***visible set*** of a RATS-tree, which is a subset of the Hanan grid points in the RATS-tree defined as follows:

A node p dominates q, denoted $q \preceq p$ if and only if $\langle p,q \rangle = q$ and $p \neq q$. Node p x-dominates q, denoted $q \preceq_x p$, if $q \preceq p$ and $p_y = q_y$. Given a RATS-tree T, $p \in T$ is x-visible if it does not x-dominates any node in T. We define the y-dominance relation and y-visibility similarly. A node p is visible if it is either x-visible or y-visible. In Figure 2(a), for example, except for nodes 3 and 7, the rest of the nodes are visible. We can show that if we order the x-visible nodes by their y-coordinates, then the merging operations can generate the x-visible nodes of the new topology from the x-visible nodes of its child topologies in linear time. Similarly, the y-visible nodes can be computed in linear time. We do not re-root at all Hanan grid points in the tree but only at the visible nodes, i.e., grid points in the visible set.

Another pruning technique that we employ is to prune wiresizing solutions among ***different*** topologies. We say that two RATS-trees T and T' share the same ***alias*** if they are rooted at the same node and cover the same set of sinks. Consider wiresizing solutions $\mathcal{W}$ of T and $\mathcal{W}'$ of T' where T and T' share the same alias, we say that $\mathcal{W}'$ is redundant if $Cap(T,\mathcal{W}) \leq Cap(T',\mathcal{W}')$, $Slack(T,\mathcal{W}) \geq Slack(T',\mathcal{W}')$, $SQ(T',\mathcal{W}) \geq SQ(T',\mathcal{W}')$, *and* at least one of the three inequalities is a strict inequality. A RATS-tree is redundant if all of its wiresizing solutions are redundant with respect to the wiresizing solutions of topologies with the same alias.

We use a hash table to store aliases. For each alias in the table, we maintain a set of irredundant wiresized RATS-trees. For each RATS-tree generated (whether by merging or re-rooting operation), our algorithm updates the set of irredundant wiresized RATS-trees that share the same alias as the newly generated RATS-tree. All B&B nodes that are associated with redundant RATS-trees are pruned.

3.7 Summary

The RATS-tree can be generalized by the following re-definitions to handle the case where the sinks are not restricted to the first quadrant, and the source is not located at the origin. Given two distinct points p and q, we define the Steiner merging point $\langle p,q \rangle$ to be $(\text{med}(x_{s_0},x_p,x_q), \text{med}(y_{s_0},y_p,y_q))$ where med() returns the median of three numbers. We say that $q \preceq p$ if and only if $\langle p,q \rangle = q$ and $p \neq q$. $|m| = d(s_0,m)$ is the Manhattan distance between s_0 and m. Lastly, the visible nodes of a topology are ordered and kept in their respective quadrants with respect to the source to facilitate computation of the visible nodes of parent topologies.

RATS-tree Algorithm

```
B&B-Queue ← {(({{s0},{s1},{s2},···,{sn}},∞)}
while B&B-Queue not empty do
  (T,K) ← Remove-Head-of-Queue(B&B-Queue)
  if all RATS-trees in T irredundant then
    (m, mN, mE, Merger-Type) ← Find-Merging-Point((T,K))
    if Merger-Type = TERMINAL-MERGING then
      (T',K') ←(Terminal-Merge(m, T),|m|)
    else
      /* STEINER-MERGING */
      (T',K') ←(Steiner-Merge(m, mN, mE, T),|m|)
      /* SKIP STEINER-MERGING */
      K ← |m|
      Append (T,K) to B&B-Queue
    end if
    New-B&B-Set ← Re-root((T',K')) + (T',K')
    Append all B&B nodes in New-B&B-Set to B&B-Queue
  end if
end while
```

Figure 3: Outline of the RATS-tree algorithm.

To summarize, we use a queue to implement breadth-first traversal of the B&B search tree. At the beginning of the algorithm, the queue contains a B&B node with a peer topology set $\mathcal{T}$ containing all single-terminal subtrees and a scan level $K = \infty$. We use the pair $(\mathcal{T},K)$ to denote a B&B node. Until the queue is empty, the algorithm iterates the expansion of a B&B node removed from the head of the queue by either performing a terminal/Steiner merging operation, or skipping a Steiner merging operation. In the case of subtree merging, the resultant topology is re-rooted to generate sibling B&B nodes. All newly generated B&B nodes are appended to the end of the queue. A brief outline of our RATS-tree algorithm is given in Figure 3.

The above summary assumes no pruning of the B&B search tree. To consider such pruning, two simple modifications are made to the algorithm. A B&B node with $(\mathcal{T},K)$ is only expanded if all partial RATS-trees in $\mathcal{T}$ are irredundant. After each partial RATS-tree is constructed (by either merging or re-rooting operation), the irredundant list of RATS-trees with the same alias as the newly created topology is updated.

4 Experimental results

We have implemented the RATS-tree algorithm in C++ language and evaluated the algorithm for MCM designs. We use randomly generated netlists with 6 to 12 terminals on a $10cm \times 10cm$ MCM substrate. In the first set of experiments, we run the RATS-tree algorithm under the pathlength formulation to investigate the trade-off between the pathlength and the routing cost of the topologies generated. Ten random n-pin nets are generated for each n ranging from 6 to 12. For each routing instance, we consider four different arrival time (or pathlength) requirements, namely $q_i = k \times d(s_0,s_i)$, where $k = \{1, 1.2, 1.5, 2\}$ for sinks s_i's. Note that when $k = 1$, it is known as the shortest path Steiner routing.

Table 1 shows the trade-off between the pathlength requirement and routing cost. We normalize the length of each resultant topology with respect to that of the shortest path routing. Therefore, we do not show the routing length when $k = 1$. The columns labeled "CPU" give the worst-case CPU seconds incurred among the ten nets for each n and

	$k=1$	$k=1.2$		$k=1.5$		$k=2$	
n	CPU	Length	CPU	Length	CPU	Length	CPU
6	0.3	0.996	0.3	0.987	0.3	0.984	0.3
7	0.9	1.000	0.9	0.996	0.9	0.982	0.9
8	0.8	0.989	0.9	0.973	0.9	0.963	0.9
9	4.3	0.991	4.7	0.976	4.2	0.973	4.3
10	8.7	0.972	8.8	0.956	9.3	0.948	8.6
11	37.4	0.988	47.7	0.971	40.4	0.951	36.3
12	96	0.978	152.2	0.958	145.0	0.942	125.0

Table 1: Pathlength requirement and routing cost trade-off.

Topology	Max-delay (ns)	Settling Time (ns)	Overshoot	Wire Cap. (pF)
*RATS*1	2.15	0.83	0.10	33.4
*RATS*2	2.28	0.76	0.07	38.3
*RATS*3	2.26	0.00	0.04	37.7
*RATS*4	2.24	0.71	0.06	35.7
*RATS*5	2.18	0.82	0.10	31.9

Table 2: Trade-off among maximum sink delay, signal settling time, voltage overshoot, and routing cost for a small $k=2$.

k. In general, the average CPU time is much lower. For example, the average CPU time for 12-pin net is only 22 seconds whereas the worst-case CPU time is 152 seconds. While the average gain in terms of total routing length is a modest 5% when we relaxed k from 1 to 2, in some instances, the gain could be as high as 15%. Such high gains in general occur more frequently in larger nets than in smaller nets. Moreover, the shortest path routings generated by our algorithm is optimal in terms of wirelength, and therefore, it is more difficult to achieve much reduction in wirelength.

In the second set of experiments, we apply the RATS-tree algorithm without consideration of wiresizing under the two-pole model. The purpose of this experiment is to investigate the impact of routing topology on signal delay and integrity. The interconnect parameters that are used by our algorithms for moment, delay, and signal quality computations are obtained from the Micro Module System (MMS) D500 process on Aluminum offered through MIDAS. Assuming a nominal width of $19\mu m$, the interconnect resistance, inductance, and capacitance are $236.84\Omega/m$, $301.49nH/m$, and $128.99pF/m$, respectively. The load capacitance of each sink is assumed to be $1pF$, and the driver resistance ranges from 10Ω to 30Ω, depending on the size of the net and the proximity of the terminals.

For each net, we set the required arrival time of sink s_i to be $k \times \sqrt{LC}d(s_0, s_i)$ where $k > 1$. Note that k is larger than 1 in order to account for the rise/fall delay. For each net, our algorithm constructs a large class of topologies satisfying the delay requirements. We then run SPICE simulations using the transmission line model to evaluate the sink delay and measure signal integrity in terms of the signal settling time and voltage overshoot of these constructed topologies. We measure the signal delay at the 90% V_{dd} (assuming a rising signal) and the signal settling time is the time taken for the signal to settle above the 90% V_{dd}. In general, the large class of topologies generated by our algorithm is able to provide a trade-off among maximum sink delay, signal settling time, voltage overshoot, and routing cost.

For example, Table 2 shows the maximum delays, signal settling times, voltage overshoots, and routing costs for the topologies generated by our RATS-tree algorithm for one of the randomly generated 9-pin nets. Both the delay and settling time of each topology are in ns, and the total wire capacitance is in pF. The voltage overshoot is normalized with respect to V_{dd}. In this example, due to a small k of 2, most of the RATS-trees generated are shortest-path Steiner tree. As we can see from Figure 4, except for *RATS*5, the topologies *RATS*1–4 are all shortest-path Steiner tree. In fact, *RATS*1 is an optimal Steiner arborescence. While it is the best in terms of maximum delay, its total wire

Topology	Max-delay (ns)	Settling Time (ns)	Overshoot	Wire Cap. (pF)
*RATS*6	2.65	0.00	0.09	29.9
*RATS*7	2.39	0.58	0.15	30.5

(a) $k=3$

Topology	Max-delay (ns)	Settling Time (ns)	Overshoot	Wire Cap. (pF)
*RATS*8	2.84	0.00	0.12	26.7
*RATS*9	2.81	0.00	0.11	27.4

(b) $k=6$

Table 3: Trade-off among maximum sink delay, signal integrity, and routing cost for the case where (a) $k=3$ and (b) $k=6$.

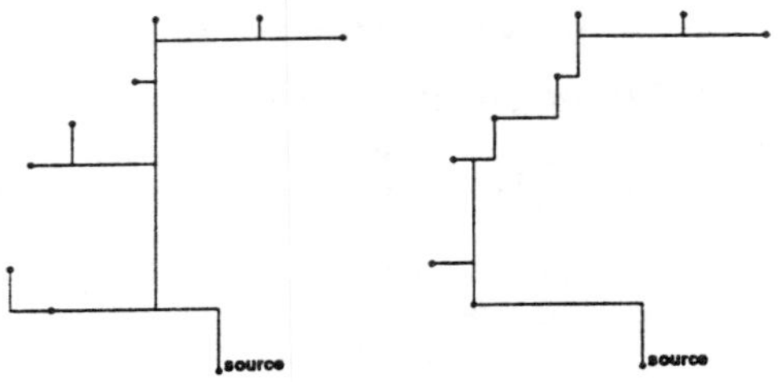

(a) *RATS*6 (b) *RATS*8

Figure 5: An example of the topologies generated by the RATS-tree algorithm for a 9-pin net for (a) $k=3$ and (b) $k=6$.

capacitance, settling time, and voltage overshoot are not necessary the smallest.

Table 3(a) and (b) show the routing solutions (for the same net as in Table 2) for the case where we relax k to 3 and 6, respectively. Figure 5 shows an example of the topologies generated for each k. Note that the total wire capacitance of *RATS*10 is 20% smaller than that of *RATS*1. Due to space constraints in the paper, we only show the simulation results of a subset of the topologies generated by our algorithm in Table 3. In total, 16, and 20 topologies are generated for the two different k's, respectively. Note that if we do not consider pruning, the numbers could be much larger. There are also overlaps between the three sets of topologies.

In the final set of experiments, we apply the RATS-tree algorithm with wiresizing under the two-pole model to investigate the impact of wiresizing on signal delay and signal integrity. In addition to the nominal width of $19\mu m$, we allow four other different wire widths $\{39\mu m, 59\mu m, 79\mu m, 99\mu m\}$ for the interconnect. The interconnect parameters for the four additional wire widths are given in Table 4. In this experiment, the RATS-tree algorithm produces a much larger number of solutions when compared to the previous two experiments. For instance, there are a total of 123 wiresized solutions generated for the above 9-pin sample net. The run-times also increase significantly due to the wiresizing optimization. For example, if we keep *all* the irredundant wiresizing solutions for each irredundant topologies generated in the algorithm, the average run-times for 6-pin, 9-pin, and 12-pin nets are 5 seconds, 341 seconds, and 12,702 seconds, respectively.

However, we observe that a majority of the irredundant wiresizing solutions of a topology are very similar to each other in terms of $Cap(T,\mathcal{W})$, $Slack(T,\mathcal{W})$, and $SQ(T,\mathcal{W})$. Therefore, we adopt a more aggressive pruning approach where we keep only a user-specified number, say l, of irredundant wiresizing solutions for each topology. In this approach, we first apply the pruning technique outlined in Section 3.4. If the number of irredundant wiresizing solutions is greater than l, then we always keep the wiresizing solutions that correspond to the smallest $Cap(T,\mathcal{W})$, largest $Slack(T,\mathcal{W})$, and largest $SQ(T,\mathcal{W})$. We select the rest of the solutions uniformly by their ordering based on $Cap(T,\mathcal{W})$'s.

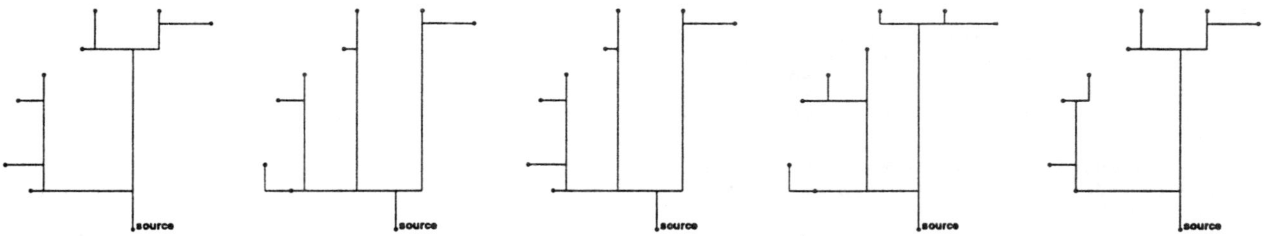

(a) *RATS*1 (b) *RATS*2 (c) *RATS*3 (d) *RATS*4 (e) *RATS*5

Figure 4: Topologies generated by the RATS-tree algorithm for a 9-pin net for a small $k = 2$.

	39μm	59μm	79μm	99μm
R (Ω/m)	115.38	76.27	59.96	45.45
L (nH/m)	205.88	157.82	128.50	108.62
C (pF/m)	188.89	246.42	302.64	358.03

Table 4: MMS interconnect parameters.

Topology	Max-delay (ns)	Settling Time (ns)	Overshoot	Wire Cap. (pF)
*RATS*1.*a*	1.82	0.77	0.08	37.6
*RATS*1.*b*	2.18	0.85	0.04	44.8
*RATS*2.*a*	2.64	0.92	0.04	57.9
*RATS*3.*a*	2.19	0.69	0.03	44.2
*RATS*3.*b*	2.64	0.00	0.01	56.0
*RATS*10.*a*	2.71	0.00	0.00	64.3

Table 5: Impact of wiresizing on signal delay and integrity.

Using this approach, we are able to cut down the run-time significantly while maintaining high solution quality. For example, the average run-times for 6-pin, 9-pin, and 12-pin nets are reduced to 4 seconds, 72 seconds, and 604 seconds, respectively when we set I to 15. Note that the run-times for the RATS-tree algorithm in the first two experiments are similar. While the run-times of the RATS-tree algorithm may compare unfavorably with those of algorithms in [9, 8] which also consider wiresizing with topology construction, the higher computational complexity is due to its ability to handle a large class of topologies.

Again, we use the same 9-pin net in the above discussion to illustrate the impact of wiresizing. In general, we observe that most of the topologies that resemble shortest-path Steiner tree more have more wiresizing solutions. For example, topologies such as *RATS*1–5 have more wiresizing solutions than *RATS*6–9. We also observe that most of the wiresizing solutions are monotone, i.e., the widths decrease from source to sinks. Note that these solutions are obtained by the RATS-tree algorithm with aggressive pruning of wiresizing solutions. Table 4 shows the impact of wiresizing on *RATS*1-3 and a new shortest-path Steiner tree, denoted *RATS*10. We use *RATSj.a* and *RATSj.b* to refer to two different wiresizing solutions of *RATSj*. From the table, we see that it is possible to improve both max-delay and voltage overshoot simultaneously by wiresizing (*RATS*1.*a* and *RATS*3.*a*). On the other hand, we can also use wiresizing to minimize voltage overshoot at the expense of signal delay. In all cases, the total wire capacitance increases.

5 Concluding Remarks

To summarize, this paper describes a RATS-tree construction algorithm under a higher-order RLC interconnect model. Our algorithm considers the impact of routing on signal delays and response waveforms, and returns not one, but a set of appropriately wiresized routing topologies. Our algorithm optimizes signal waveform, not just delay, and due to its capability to handle a large class of topologies, provides a trade-off among routing cost, signal delay, and signal integrity. In the algorithm, we introduce a space-efficient reduced tree representation to capture all topologies and wiresizing solutions constructed during the execution of our algorithm. We also present a new algorithm to incrementally compute moments of sinks in a bottom-up manner.

Currently, we are working towards improving the run-time of the algorithm. Besides the simple yet effective pruning technique that we outlined in Section 4, we are investigating the effectiveness of other pruning techniques to reduce run-time while maintaining high solution quality. For example, we can perform pruning using bin sorting based on $Cap(T, \mathcal{W})$, and keep only a representative wiresizing solution from each bin. Furthermore, we observe that the re-rooting operation generates many child B&B nodes. By limiting the number of re-rooting allowed along any branch of the B&B search tree, it is possible to reduce the run-time without any solution quality degradation. We are also focusing our efforts on generalizing the RATS-tree algorithm for general graph routing, which would enable us to handle multi-layer routing more effectively.

Acknowledgment

The authors would like to thank Dr. Dian Zhou of University of North Carolina, and Yean-Yow Hwang, Kei-Yong Khoo, Hardy Leung, and Patrick Madden at UCLA for their helpful discussions and critical comments.

REFERENCES

[1] J. Cong, L. He, C.-K. Koh, and P. H. Madden, "Performance optimization of VLSI interconnect layout," *Integration, the VLSI Journal*, vol. 21, pp. 1–94, 1996.

[2] J. Cong, K. S. Leung, and D. Zhou, "Performance-driven interconnect design based on distributed RC delay model," in *Proc. Design Automation Conf*, pp. 606–611, 1993.

[3] K. D. Boese, A. B. Kahng, B. A. McCoy, and G. Robins, "Near-optimal critical sink routing tree constructions," *IEEE Trans. on Computer-Aided Design of Integrated Circuits and Systems*, vol. 14, pp. 1417–1436, Dec. 1995.

[4] J. Cong and K. S. Leung, "Optimal wiresizing under the distributed Elmore delay model," *IEEE Trans. on Computer-Aided Design of Integrated Circuits and Systems*, vol. 14, pp. 321–336, Mar. 1995.

[5] N. Menezes, S. Pullela, F. Dartu, and L. T. Pillage, "RC interconnect synthesis — a moment fitting appraoch," in *Proc. Int. Conf. on Computer Aided Design*, pp. 418–425, 1994.

[6] J. Lillis, C. K. Cheng, and T. T. Y. Lin, "Optimal wire sizing and buffer insertion for low power and a generalized delay model," in *Proc. Int. Conf. on Computer Aided Design*, pp. 138–143, Nov. 1995.

[7] C. P. Chen, Y. P. Chen, and D. F. Wong, "Optimal wire-sizing formula under the Elmore delay model," in *Proc. Design Automation Conf*, pp. 487–490, 1996.

[8] T. Okamoto and J. Cong, "Buffered Steiner tree construction with wire sizing for interconnect layout optimization," in *Proc. Int. Conf. on Computer Aided Design*, pp. 44–49, Nov. 1996.

[9] J. Lillis, C. K. Cheng, T. T. Y. Lin, and C. Y. Ho, "New performance driven routing techniques with explicit area/delay tradeoff and simultaneous wire sizing," in *Proc. Design Automation Conf*, pp. 395–400, June 1996.

[10] F.-J. Liu, J. Lillis, and C.-K. Cheng, "A new layout-driven timing model for incremental layout optimization," in *Proc. Asia South Pacific Design Automation Conf.*, 1997.

[11] D. Zhou, F. Tsui, and D. S. Gao, "High performance multichip interconnection design," in *Proc. 4th ACM/SIGDA Physical Design Workshop*, pp. 32–43, Apr. 1993.

[12] M. Sriram and S. M. Kang, "Performance driven MCM routing using a second order RLC tree delay model," in *Proc. Int. Conf. on Wafer Scale Integration*, pp. 262–267, 1993.

[13] T. Xue, E. S. Kuh, and Q. Yu, "A sensitivity-based wiresizing approach to interconnect optimization of lossy transmission line topologies," in *Proc. IEEE Multi-Chip Module Conf.*, pp. 117–121, 1996.

[14] R. Gupta and L. T. Pillage, "OTTER: Optimal termination of transmission lines excluding radiation," in *Proc. Design Automation Conf*, pp. 640–645, 1994.

[15] B. Krauter, R. Gupta, J. Willis, and L. T. Pileggi, "Transmission line synthesis," in *Proc. Design Automation Conf*, pp. 358–363, 1995.

[16] R. Gupta and L. T. Pileggi, "Constrained multivariable optimization of transmission lines with general topologies," in *Proc. Int. Conf. on Computer Aided Design*, pp. 130–137, 1995.

[17] K.-S. Leung and J. Cong, "Fast optimal algorithms for the minimum rectilinear Steiner arborescence problem," in *Proc. IEEE Int. Symp. on Circuits and Systems*, 1997.

[18] J. Cong, A. B. Kahng, G. Robins, M. Sarrafzadeh, and C. K. Wong, "Provably good performance-driven global routing," *IEEE Trans. on Computer-Aided Design of Integrated Circuits and Systems*, vol. 11, pp. 739–752, June 1992.

[19] A. B. Kahng and G. Robins, "A new class of iterative Steiner tree heuristics with good performance," *IEEE Trans. on Computer-Aided Design of Integrated Circuits and Systems*, vol. 11, pp. 893–902, July 1992.

[20] Q. Yu and E. S. Kuh, "Exact moment matching model of transmission lines and application to interconnect delay estimation," *IEEE Trans. on Very Large Scale Integration (VLSI) Systems*, vol. 3, pp. 311–322, June 1995.

[21] A. B. Kahng and S. Muddu, "Two-pole analysis of interconnection trees," in *Proc. IEEE Multi-Chip Module Conf.*, pp. 105–110, Jan. 1995.

[22] L. T. Pillage and R. A. Rohrer, "Asymptotic waveform evaluation for timing analysis," *IEEE Trans. on Computer-Aided Design of Integrated Circuits and Systems*, vol. 9, pp. 352–366, Apr. 1990.

[23] M. A. Horowitz, *Timing Models for MOS Circuits*. PhD thesis, Stanford University, 1984.

[24] A. B. Kahng and S. Muddu, "An analytical delay model for RLC interconnects," in *Proc. IEEE Int. Symp. on Circuits and Systems*, pp. 4.237–4.240, May 1996.

[25] M. Hanan, "On Steiner's problem with rectilinear distance," *SIAM Journal of Applied Mathematics*, vol. 14, pp. 255–265, 1966.

[26] J. H. Huang, A. B. Kahng, and C.-W. A. Tsao, "On the bounded-skew routing tree problem," in *Proc. Design Automation Conf*, pp. 508–513, June 1995.

[27] J. Cong and C.-K. Koh, "Interconnect layout optimization under higher-order RLC model," Tech. Rep. 970033, UCLA CS Dept, Aug. 1997.

[28] R. Bryant, "Graph-based algorithms for boolean function manipulation," *IEEE Trans. on Computers*, vol. C-35, no. 8, pp. 677–691, Aug. 1986.

SESSION 11D

TEST THEORY AND APPLICATIONS

Moderators:

Fadi Maamari, LogicVision, Inc.,

San Jose, CA

Sandeep K. Gupta, University of Southern California,

Los Angeles, CA

Test and Diagnosis of Faulty Logic Blocks in FPGAs

Sying-Jyan Wang and Tsi-Ming Tsai
Institute of Computer Science
National Chung-Hsing University
Taichung 402, Taiwan, R.O.C.
E-mail: sjwang@cs.nchu.edu.tw

Abstract

Since Field programmable gate arrays (FPGAs) are reprogrammable, faults in them can be easily tolerated once fault sites are located. In this paper we present a method for the testing and diagnosis of faults in FPGAs. The proposed method imposes no hardware overhead, and requires minimal support from external test equipments. Test time depends only on the number of faults, and is independent of the chip size. With the help of this technique, chips with faults can still be used. As a result, the chip yield can be improved and chip cost is reduced. Experimental results are given to show the feasibility of this method.

1. Introduction

Field programmable gate arrays (FPGAs) can be programmed in the field to implement any logic circuits. They are widely used in rapid system prototyping because of their reprogrammability, and they have also been used in many practical circuits. An FPGA usually consists of configurable logic blocks (CLBs), programmable I/O blocks (IOBs), and programmable interconnects.

Testing faults in general FPGAs has been studied by many researchers [1]-[4]. In these methods the FPGA under test is not mapped to a specific logic function. As a result, usually multiple test sessions are required, with each session dealing with one configuration. Stroud *et al* propose a Built-In Self-Test (BIST) method for FPGAs [5]. This approach is attractive for two reasons. First of all, it requires no extra hardware. Since FPGAs are programmable, the BIST structure is implemented only once during test time. Secondly, the requirement for automatic test equipment (ATE) is much simplified. The ATE only needs to download the configurations that are used during test time, while the actual testing process is conducted by the circuit itself.

Traditional chip-level testing usually deals with fault detection only, while fault diagnosis is often conducted in the system-level. This is because components in chip can hardly be repaired. However, faults in FPGAs can be easily tolerated by not including faulty elements in the final circuit. Therefore, FPGA chips with faults can still be used if we can identify the fault sites. In this paper we propose a chip-level diagnosis methodology for faults in CLBs. Our method is also based on BIST technique, which means the requirement for external ATE support is limited. The amount of testing time is affected by the number of faults on chip only and is independent of the chip size. Since the die yield of larger chips is lower than smaller ones with the same defect density, our method is especially attractive for larger chips.

2. Preliminaries

A well-studied model for system-level diagnosis is known as the PMC model [6]. This model is based on the following assumptions. (1) A system is divided into many units, and each unit can test another one. (2) The test outcome is either "pass" or "fail". (3) If the testing unit is fault-free, the test outcome is always correct. The test outcome obtained by a faulty testing unit is not reliable.

Based on these assumptions, we may model a diagnostic system with a diagnostic graph. A diagnostic graph $G = <V, E, W>$ is a directed graph, where V is the set of vertices, E is the set of edges, and W is the set of weights associated with all edges. A vertex v in V represents a unit in the system. An edge from v_i to v_j in E (denoted as e_{ij}) corresponds to the existence of a test in which unit v_i evaluates v_j. The test outcome a_{ij} associated with e_{ij} may assume the following values:

$a_{ij} =$ 0 if both v_i and v_j are fault-free;
$a_{ij} =$ 1 if v_i is fault-free and v_j is faulty;
$a_{ij} =$ $\times$ if v_i is faulty, no matter what is the status of v_j (i.e., $\times$ is either 0 or 1).

1092-3152/97 $10.00 © 1997 IEEE

For example, consider the diagnostic graph shown in Fig. 1. Some possible syndromes are shown in Fig. 1. If all units are fault-free, the syndrome would be all 0's. It can be seen that any single fault can be correctly diagnosed since two different faults will not produce the same syndrome. On the other hand, proper diagnosis is not possible if two or more faults are present. For example, the syndrome for fault $\{v_0\}$ and $\{v_0, v_1\}$ may be identical. This system is thus called 1-fault diagnosable since any single fault is guaranteed to be located.

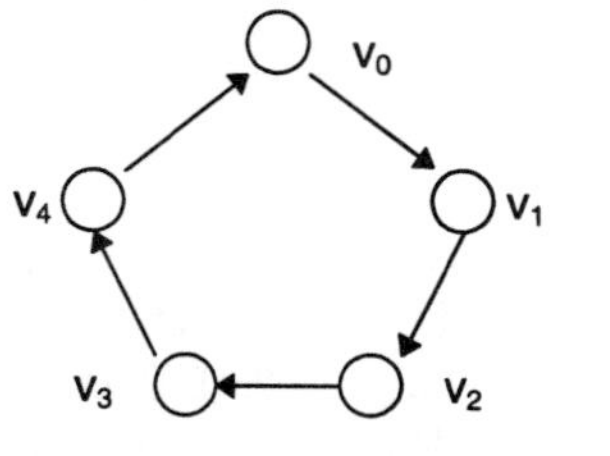

faulty units	a_{01}	a_{12}	a_{23}	a_{34}	a_{40}
None	0	0	0	0	0
v_0	x	0	0	0	1
v_1	1	x	0	0	0
v_0, v_1	x	x	0	0	1
v_0, v_2	x	1	x	0	1

Fig. 1. A diagnostic system

A system of n units is *one-step t-fault diagnosable* if faulty units can be identified without replacement, given that the number of faulty units is at most t [6]. The next theorem provides necessary conditions for such systems.

Theorem 1 [6]: In a one-step t-fault diagnosable system S

1) There must be at least $2t+1$ units.
2) Each unit must be diagnosed by at least t other units.

Many sufficient and necessary conditions have been provided for one-step t-fault diagnosable systems.

Theorem 2 [7]: Let S be a system with the property that no two units test each other. Then S is one-step t-fault diagnosable if and only if each unit is tested by at least t other units.

The above results deal with the diagnosability of a system. Another issue is how to identify the faulty units for a given syndrome. Many diagnosing algorithms have been proposed. An $O(n^{2.5})$ algorithm was given for any diagnosable system [8], and the complexity can be even lower for systems with regular test structure.

3. Test architecture

In order to diagnose faults, first there must be a way to test modules in FPGAs. A candidate for this purpose is BIST [9]. The BIST structure reconfigures part of the functional circuit to be a test pattern generator (TPG) and some other to be an output response analyzer (ORA). The rest circuit consists of the circuit under test (CUT). The TPG is either a linear feedback shift register (LFSR) or a counter. The test inputs are fed to the CUT, while the output responses are collected and analyzed by the ORA. The ORA can be either a signature analyzer or a comparator-based analyzer.

3.1. Basic Architecture

Our test architecture works as follows. An FPGA is divided into disjoint sets of CLBs, where each set can be configured into a TPG and an ORA. Such a set acts as a unit in the PMC model since it is able to test another unit. In Fig. 2 we illustrate the testing method. All the CLBs under test are programmed in the same way; therefore, they perform the same logic function and could be applied with the same test patterns. Thus outputs of the TPG are fed to all CLBs in the set under test, and the results are analyzed by the ORA.

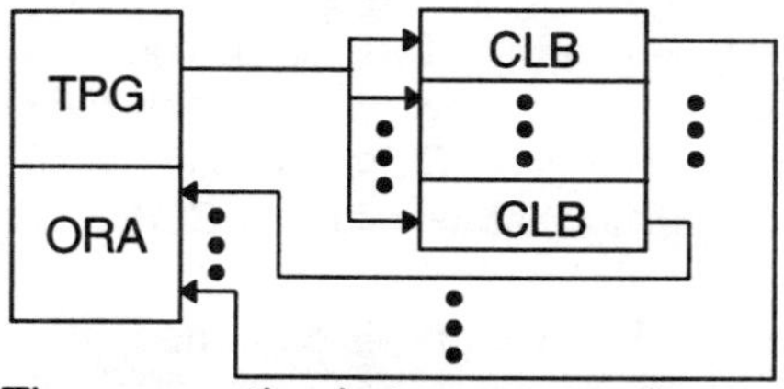

Fig. 2. The connection between a testing unit and a set of CLBs under test

Since each CLB can be programmed in many ways, it is not possible to test any CLB in a single test run. A complete test for a CLB requires several steps, and in each step a CLB is programmed in a particular way.

Definition 1: A *test phase* is the procedure of testing faults in a CLB that is programmed in a particular way.

Definition 2: A *test session* consists of many test phases that completely test CLBs for all modeled faults.

Each test session corresponds to an edge in a diagnostic graph.

Definition 3: A *node* is a set of CLBs that can be reconfigured to a TPG and an ORA when it acts as a testing unit. A node is said to be in *T-mode* when it contains a TPG and an ORA. When the node is corresponding to a tested unit in the PMC model, all CLBs in it are configured in the same way, and the configuration changes from phase to phase. At this moment the node is said to be in *C-mode*.

A node corresponds to a vertex in a diagnostic graph. The only requirement for a node is that it must be large enough to accommodate a TPG and an ORA; and any two nodes are not required to be equal in size. However, if we use homogeneous nodes, the testing and diagnosis procedures can be greatly simplified. Therefore we will assume that all nodes are equal in size throughout the remaining part of this paper.

Definition 4: A *test group* is a set of nodes in which the target number of faulty nodes can be correctly diagnosed.

Our test and diagnosis strategy works as follows. The CLBs on a chip are grouped into nodes, where each node must be able to accommodate at least a TPG and an ORA. Let the maximum number of faulty CLBs allowed on a chip be t. The nodes are again assembled into test groups, where each group must contain at least $2t+1$ nodes. Let the number of nodes in a group be n. We will label these nodes as $v_0, v_1, \ldots, v_{n-1}$. Such a group is t-fault diagnosable according to Theorem 2. A node v_i tests v_j, if $j - i = m \pmod{n}$, where $1 \le m \le t$. For example, the system in Fig. 1 is a 1-fault diagnosable test group.

After the above procedure having been finished, all faulty nodes can be identified. However, faulty CLBs are not known at this stage since a node contains multiple CLBs. If we need to exactly identify all faulty CLBs, a second step is required. This can be done since we have more than half good nodes and we know the locations of good nodes. The good CLBs are again configured into TPGs and ORAs to locate the faulty CLBs.

3.2. An Efficient Diagnosis Scheme

If an n-unit system is t-fault diagnosable, at least $n \cdot t$ test sessions are required. If the number of faults is smaller than t, then many test sessions are redundant. When the time required to conduct all test sessions is much larger than the time required to carry out the diagnosing algorithm, it is worthwhile to execute the diagnosing algorithm several times so that the required number of test sessions can be reduced.

Consider the test group discussed in Sec. 3.1. This group can be represented by an n-vertex directed graph where an edge (v_i, v_j) exists if $(j-i) \bmod n$ is a member of $\{1, 2, \ldots, t\}$. We divide the $n \cdot t$ test sessions into t sets, each containing n test sessions. These sets are called $T_1, T_2, \ldots, T_t$, where $T_j = \{(v_i, v_{(i+j \bmod n)}) \mid 0 \le i \le n-1\}$ for all $1 \le j \le t$. An adaptive one-step t-fault diagnosing scheme is possible with the above test sets.

Procedure 1: Adaptive One-Step *t*-Fault Diagnosis

```
PreviousFaults = ∅;
AccumulatedOutCome = ∅
for (i = 1; i <= t; i++) {
    Outcome = Apply_Test_Session(Ti);
    AccumulatedOutcome = AccumulatedOutcome ∪ Outcome;
    Faults = Fault_Diagnosis(AccumulatedOutcome, i);
            /* Diagnosis for i-fault */
    if (Faults == PreviousFaults) break;
    else PreviousFaults = Faults;
}
return faults;
```

Fault_Diagnosis() can be any diagnosis algorithm. In the i-th iteration of the loop, Fault_Diagnosis() tries to solve the given syndrome by assuming that at most i faults exist. We may not be able to reach a consistent result in iteration i since the actual number of faults could be larger than i. If a consistent diagnosis result is not possible at iteration i, the comparison with the previous result is false. The above algorithm says that, if we have the same valid diagnosis results in two successive iterations of the loop, then the remaining test sessions can be omitted since the number of faults in the test group is i.

Theorem 3: Procedure 1 is t-fault diagnosable.

A proof of the correctness of the procedure can be found in [10].

3.3. Analysis

3.3.1. Capability of the Test Architecture. Let a node contain B CLBs, and the number of CLBs on a chip be N. Then the number of nodes on a chip is $\lfloor N/B \rfloor$. If B does not divide N evenly, there will be less than B remaining CLBs that cannot form a complete node. We may ignore these CLBs first. When all correct nodes are identified, these remaining CLBs can be tested separately.

Under the PMC model, at most $t = \lfloor n/2 \rfloor$ faulty nodes can be diagnosed if sufficient tests are applied. Since the interconnects between nodes can be reconfigured in an FPGA, the required tests can always be arranged. Since a chip has $n = \lfloor N/B \rfloor$ nodes, we have $t = \lfloor N/2B \rfloor$. Therefore, a chip with $\lfloor N/2B \rfloor$ or less faulty CLBs is guaranteed to be correctly diagnosed, and in the optimal condition up to $\lfloor N/2 \rfloor \times B$ faulty CLBs can be diagnosed.

3.3.2. Structure of a Test Block. The constraint for a node is that it must be able to accommodate a TPG and an ORA. The proposed model does not impose an upper bound on the number of CLBs in a node. However, we want to make a node as small as possible. As shown in Fig. 2, the output of a TPG drives all CLBs in a C-mode node (i.e., the fanout of a TPG output line is B). Therefore, a large B means a large load for the TPG. If B is larger than the driving capability of a TPG, output buffers must be provided to the TPG. The second reason for a smaller B is the diagnostic capability. Since the maximum number of faulty CLBs that are guaranteed to be diagnosed is $\lfloor N/2B \rfloor$, smaller nodes imply more faulty CLBs are diagnosable. For these reasons, we assume that a node can accommodate exactly a TPG and an ORA.

Let the sizes of a TPG and an ORA be B_{TPG} and B_{ORA}, respectively. By the above arguments,

$$B = B_{TPG} + B_{ORA} \qquad (1)$$

Define the following parameters of a CLB:

O: Number of outputs of a CLB

I: Number of inputs of a CLB

F: Number of flip-flops in a CLB

In an exhaustive test of a CLB for a given

configuration, all 2^I input vectors are required. This means that the TPG must have I independent output signals, which implies I flip-flops are required:

$$B_{TPG} \geq \lceil I/F \rceil \quad (2)$$

In practice, if two input lines do not affect the same output, they may be applied with the same signal to achieve pseudoexhaustive testing [9]. In this case, p ($< I$) signals may be enough, and some of the p lines may be connected to two or more inputs of a CLB:

$$B_{TPG} \geq \lceil p/F \rceil \quad (2a)$$

Since the outputs of all CLBs in a node under test are analyzed by the same ORA, we have:

$$B \times O \leq B_{ORA} \times I \quad (3)$$

3.3.3. A Test Group. If we want to achieve maximum diagnosability, only one test group is allowed on chip. In this case $\lfloor N/2B \rfloor$ faulty nodes can be identified. On the other hand, if it is known that the number of faulty nodes on a chip, t, is much less than $\lfloor N/2B \rfloor$, it is possible to have smaller test groups. The only requirement for a test group is that it must contain at least $2t+1$ nodes.

Employing multiple test groups does not improve diagnosability. The advantage of smaller test groups is the reduced diagnosing time. Since all test groups conduct their test sessions simultaneously and the time required for diagnosis is $O(n^{2.5})$, the diagnosing time is greatly reduced for smaller test groups.

4. Case Study: XC4000 FPGA FAMILY

We implemented the above test architecture with Xilinx XC400 FPGAs, and the details are discussed here.

4.1. Testing a CLB

A simplified diagram of a CLB in Xilinx XC4000 Family is shown in Fig. 3. This CLB has 13 inputs (I = 13), in which one is clock input (K), nine signals are input to the combinational part (F1 to F4, G1 to G4, and H1), and the other three are for the sequential part (DIN, S/R, and EC). There are four outputs in a CLB (O = 4). The combinational part consists of 3 Look-Up Tables (LUTs) and three multiplexers (MUXs) whose outputs are H1, X, and Y, respectively. The sequential part contains the remaining components: two D flip-flops (F = 2), the S/R control, and the remaining MUXs.

The LUTs are made of SRAM. To test the LUTs, each bit in them has to be set to both 0 and 1. Therefore, at least two phases are required to exercise all possible faults in the LUTs. There are 4-to-1 MUXs in a CLB. As a result, we need at least four test phases so that each input-to-output connection of these MUXs can be exercised. We found that four test phases are enough to exercise all possible configurations in the CLB.

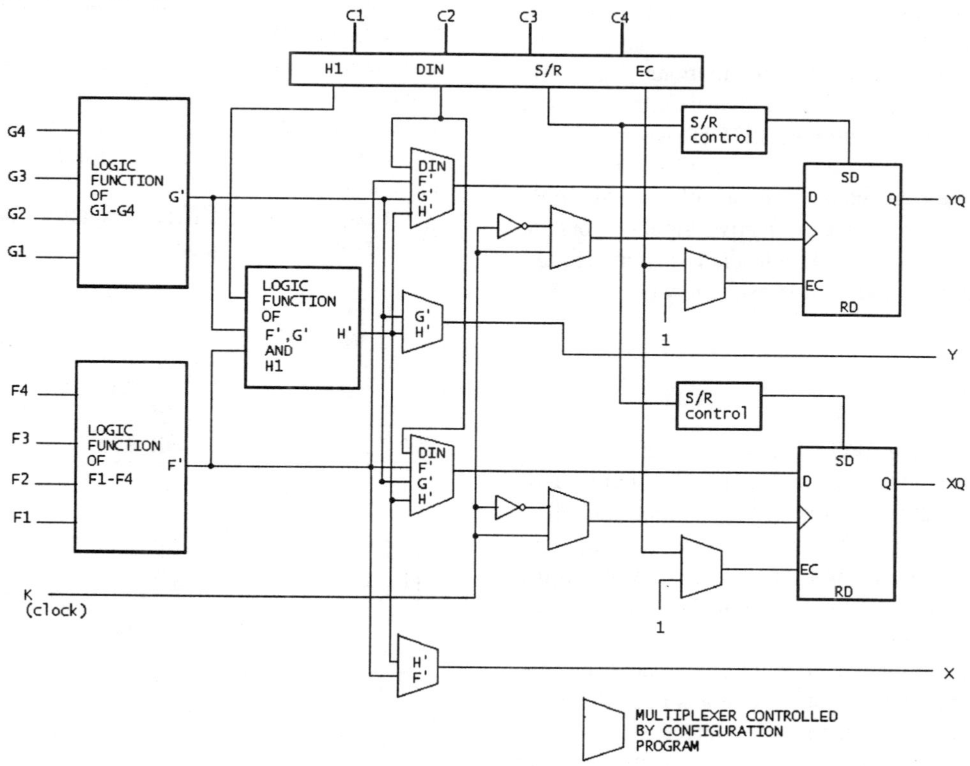

Fig. 3. A simplified diagram of a CLB in XC4000

- **Phase 1:** The LUTs are configured as Exclusive-OR of the nine inputs. F′ is connected to both flip-flops, G′ is connected to Y, and H′ is connected to X.
- **Phase 2:** The LUTs are configured as Exclusive-NOR of the nine inputs. G′ is connected to both flip-flops, F′ is connected to X, and H′s is connected to Y.
- **Phase 3:** The LUTs implement XOR, and DIN is connected to both flip-flops.
- **Phase 4:** The LUTs implement XNOR, and H′ is connected to both flip-flops.

The combinational part is tested in the first two phases. Flip-flops are tested in all four phases. In order to fully test the upper MUXs, in Phase 1 the connections are (C1, C2, C3, C4) ⇒ (H1, DIN, S/R, EC) (i.e., H1 is connected to C1, etc.). In Phase 2 the connection is (C2, C3, C4, C1) ⇒ (H1, DIN, S/R, EC), etc. As a result, all connections are exercised in four phases.

In each phase, we apply pseudo-exhaustive test vectors to test all faults in a CLB. The question is how many independent signals are required to carry out the test. In the 13 inputs to the CLB, the clock (K) is fed by the system clock and thus is not considered. The three input signals (DIN, S/R, and EC) for the sequential part are independent of the combinational inputs (that is, they do not affect the same output), so these three signals can be connected to any 3 of the nine combinational inputs. Therefore, we need no more than 9 test signals. A further reduction can be made. If we fed all 2^8 vectors to inputs F1 to F4 and G1 to G4, both LUTs F′ and G′ are exhaustively tested, and all four combinations (00, 01, 10, 11) will appear on F′ and G′ since they are either XOR or XNOR. Now in order to fully test LUT H′, we need $2^3 = 8$ independent inputs for each configuration. The third input (H1) can be connected to any one of the other eight combinational inputs to get exhaustive input vectors for H′. Therefore, we need only 8 independent signals to test each configuration of the CLB exhaustively (i.e., $p = 8$ in Eq. 2a).

4.2. Test Blocks

In our design, the TPG is made of a type I LFSR [9] which implements the polynomial $x^8+x^6+x^5+x+1$. This LFSR generates 255 patterns (2^8-1) except the all 0 vector. In order to get all 256 exhaustive vectors, we reset all FFs in the first cycle, and then set the first bit in the second cycle. The rest vectors will be automatically generated. This TPG consists of 4 CLBs ($B_{TPG} = 4$).

We use the comparator-based ORAs because they are easier to be implemented and do not suffer the alias problem. An ORA compares the outputs of all tested CLBs; whenever there are inconsistent results, an error bit is set to record the fault. The ORA design also consists of 4 CLBs ($B_{ORA} = 4$). Therefore, a test node contains 8 CLBs ($B = 8$). It is easy to verify that this design satisfies conditions in Sec. 3.3.2.

4.3. Experimental Results

We experiment our method on an XC40003A PC84 FPGA chip. An XC4003A chip has 100 CLBs arranged in a 10×10 array. Since $B = 8$, this chip may have up to $\lfloor 100/8 \rfloor = 12$ nodes. However, it is difficult to construct nodes from CLBs locating at the chip boundary. Therefore, we construct only 10 nodes in this case. The remaining 20 CLBs are considered after we have identified faulty nodes. Fig. 4 shows the structure of our design on an XC3003A chip. All nodes locate at center part of the chip, while the top and bottom rows of CLBs are not configured.

Since CLBs are configurable, we can "inject" faults into CLBs by simulating the effects of logic faults. We consider two types of faults: stuck-at faults and open faults. We simulate the effect of a stuck-at fault by connecting the faulty line to logic "0" or "1". To simulate the effect of an open fault, all we have to do is to disconnect the faulty line from its driving source. Unfortunately, we are unable to simulate the bridging fault. The reason is that, if we try to short two lines that are driven by different sources, a DRC error occurs and the design is not realizable. In our experiment we inject 48 faults into the chip, in which there are 25 stuck-at faults and 23 open faults. These faults appear in 17 different CLBs. Eleven faulty CLBs locate in four test nodes, and the remaining 6 faulty CLBs are in the top and bottom rows. Fig. 4 shows the locations of faulty CLBs and faulty nodes.

It requires three different stages to identify all faulty CLBs, and the three stages are described as follows.

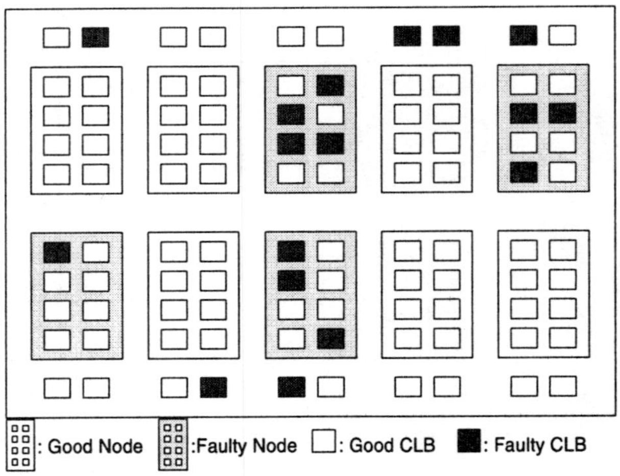

Fig. 4. Experimental environment

Stage 1: Identify faulty nodes. Since there are 10 nodes on the chip, we are able to identify all four faulty nodes. We apply test sets T_1, T_2, T_3, and T_4 in sequence. Each test set consists of 10 test sessions. These test sessions, however, cannot be completed in one step for several reasons. First of all, each node is in C-mode in one session while it is in T-mode in another session. Since a node cannot be in both C-mode and T-mode, it requires at least two steps to execute a test set. Secondly, due to the limited routing resource, it may not be possible to have maximum test sessions running concurrently.

Stage 2: Identify faulty CLBs in faulty nodes. The locations of faulty CLBs are known at this stage. One good node is configured as a TPG. Output of the TPG drives two nodes: one is faulty and the other is faulty-free. The two nodes are programmed in the same way during test time. A comparator compares the output responses of the two tested nodes. The TPG design is the same as before, while the comparator is somewhat different here.

Stage 3: Identify faulty CLBs in the remaining part. The remaining CLBs are divided into three nodes. We repeat the process in stage 2 to identify faulty CLBs. It requires 3 test sessions for the remaining CLBs.

The time used to apply all test sessions in Stage 1 is:

$$\text{Time}_{\text{Stage\_1}} = \sum_{i=1}^{t}(D + C \times 2^{v}) \times S_i \times P \quad (4)$$

in which D is the time for download, C is the clock cycle time, v the number of outputs of a TPG, S_i is the number of steps required to apply test sessions in set T_i, and P is the number of phases in a session. Among them, D, C, v, and P are constant for a given FPGA technology.

The test time of our method depends on the number of diagnosable faults t and the number of steps to arrange all the test sessions (form Eq. 4). It is independent of the chip size. Therefore, we need to reduce the summation of all S_i if we want to reduce the test time. Procedure 1 in Sec 3.2 is developed for this purpose.

The time required to complete Stage 2 is:

$$\text{Time}_{\text{Stage\_2}} = (D + C \times 2^{v}) \times P \times t_F \quad (5)$$

where t_F is number of actual faulty nodes. The time required to complete Stage 3 is:

$$\text{Time}_{\text{Stage\_3}} = (D + C \times 2^{v}) \times P \times R \quad (6)$$

where R is the number of remaining nodes.

The following parameters are valid for the XC4000 family CLBs. A test session requires four phases ($P = 4$). In each phase we need to download the configuration once and apply 2^8 test vectors ($v = 8$). Our experimental results show that downloading a bitstream needs about 7.8 seconds. We use a 8MHz clock, that is, C=1.25×10^{-7} sec. The time required to apply all test vectors in a test phase is thus 2^8×1.25×10^{-7} = 32μs. Since the test application time is negligent compared with the time for downloading, we can ignore this term.

We need 15 steps in the first stage. For the second and third stage, we have $t_F = 4$ and $R = 3$. Put everything together, we need 7.8×4×(15+4+3) = 686.4 seconds.

In terms of diagnosability, all 17 faulty CLBs in the experiment are properly located, as we expect.

5. Concluding Remarks

In this paper we present a method to diagnose faulty CLBs in FPGAs. The advantages of this method include: (1) no hardware overhead, (2) all tests and responses are processed on chip, (3) test time depends on the number of faults only, and is independent of the chip size. With this method, FPGAs with faulty CLBs can still be used.

A significant part of the FPGA die area is dedicated to the interconnections. Faults on interconnections are not considered in this paper; we will explore this issue in the future.

REFERENCES

[1] T. Liu, W.K. Huang, and F. Lombardi, "Testing of uncustomized segmented channel FPGAs," in *Proc. ACM Intl. Symp. on FPGAs*, pp. 125-131, 1995.

[2] T. Inoue, H. Fujiwara, H. Michinishi, T. Yokohira, and T. Okamoto, "Universal test complexity of field-programmable gate arrays," in *Proc. 4th Asian Test Symp.*, pp. 259-265, 1995.

[3] W.K. Huang and F. Lombardi, "An approach for testing programmable/configurable FPGAs," in *Proc. IEEE 14th VLSI Test Symp.*, pp. 125-131, 1995.

[4] H. Michinishi, T. Yokohira, T. Okamoto, T. Inoue, and H. Fujiwara, "A test methodology for interconnect structures of LUT-based FPGAs," in *Proc. 5th Asian Test Symp.*, pp. 68-74, 1996.

[5] C. Stroud, S. Konala, P. Chen, M. Abramovici, "Built-in self-test of logic blocks in FPGAs," in *Proc. IEEE 14th VLSI Test Symp.*, pp. 387-392, 1996.

[6] F.P. Preparata, G. Metze, and R.T. Chien, "On the connection assignment problem of diagnosable systems," *IEEE Trans. Electronic Comput.*, EC-16, pp. 848-854, Dec. 1967.

[7] S.L. Hakimi and A.T. Amin, "Characterization of the connection assignment of diagnosable systems," *IEEE Trans. Comput.*, C-23, pp. 86-88, 1974.

[8] A.T. Dahbura and G.M. Masson, "An O($n^{2.5}$) fault identification algorithm for diagnosable systems," *IEEE Trans. Comput.*, C-33, pp. 486-492, June 1984.

[9] M. Abramovici, M.A. Breuer, and A.D. Friedman, *Digital Systems Testing and Testable Design*, W. H. Freeman and Company, 1990.

[10] S.-J. Wang, "Adaptive system-level diagnosis and its application," in *Proc. 1997 Pacific Rim Intl. Symp. On Fault-Tolerant Systems.*

Partial Scan Delay Fault Testing of Asynchronous Circuits *

Michael Kishinevsky
The University of Aizu
Aizu-Wakamatsu, 965-80 Japan

Alex Kondratyev
The University of Aizu
Aizu-Wakamatsu, 965-80 Japan

Luciano Lavagno
Politecnico di Torino
10129 Torino, Italy

Alexander Saldanha
Cadence Berkeley Laboratories
Berkeley - CA 94704

Alexander Taubin
The University of Aizu
Aizu-Wakamatsu, 965-80 Japan

Abstract

Asynchronous circuits operate correctly only under timing assumptions. Hence testing those circuits for delay faults is crucial. This paper describes a three-step method to detect possible delay faults in a sequential *asynchronous circuit. The delays that are to be tested must be provided by the synthesis system. By using this information a set of paths in the circuit that must be tested is identified (step 1). For these paths the circuit is made acyclic by inserting at least one scan latch in every cycle (step 2). Then test patterns are generated for these paths (step 3). These test patterns consist of setup and initialization vectors and the final test vector. We provide effective procedures to solve both the initialization and the test pattern generation problem. The latter problem is solved by reduction to a classical problem of* stuck-at *test pattern generation for a related* combinational *circuit. Finally, a heuristic is proposed to determine which state variables must become part of a scan chain, or for which input variables the positive and negative phase must be driven independently in test mode. Experimental results shows that a high level of path delay fault testability can be achieved with partial scan.*

1 Introduction

Correct operation of asynchronous circuits depends on timing assumptions that are much more complex than those in the synchronous case. In particular, an asynchronous circuit is by construction insensitive to most *delay faults*, because they often affect only its *performance*, not its *functionality*. Some delay faults, though, may have an effect on the correctness as well, and hence it is necessary to be able to test them ([23]). Unfortunately, testing asynchronous circuits is a difficult problem, due to the following main reasons:

- All known asynchronous design methodologies ensure correct *operation* (hazard-freedom) by using some level of *redundancy*, i.e., by sacrificing testability.
- Asynchronous control circuits tend to have more feedback and more registers than their synchronous counterparts. This means that full-scan testing may be unacceptably expensive.

This paper deals with the problem of generating test sequences for a given set of paths in an asynchronous circuit. We assume that the information about which delays in the manufactured circuit must be tested to ensure correct operation is available (e.g., from the synthesis tools). Previous work in the area of asynchronous circuit testing either used greedy heuristic techniques ([4]) to justify and propagate stuck-at faults, or used exhaustive synchronous mode testing for stuck-at faults ([3, 19]) or used manual transformations to ensure that a simple functional testing approach could test all stuck-at faults ([20]), or used a full-scan approach to robustly test all delay faults ([8, 12, 17]).

We consider two versions of the path delay fault testing problem: *robust* path delay fault testing (**RPDFT**) and *hazard-free robust* path delay fault testing (**HFRPDFT**). The former test may allow better coverage and is simpler to generate. It guarantees that hazards in a circuit under test cannot produce false positives, but false negatives can occur. The latter guarantees that during the test, hazards cannot propagate along the paths under test, and does not admit false negatives. For sequential circuits it also guarantees that meta-stability cannot occur in the latches on the paths under test. (See [23] for an in-depth discussion of different versions of the path delay fault testing problems.)

We solve the problem of path delay fault testing for asynchronous sequential circuits as follows.

Step 1: identification of a set of paths that cover all potentially dangerous faults[1] (Section 2.2). This is obtained by finding a set of linear inequalities that bound every relevant delay constraint (e.g., determining that the difference between two delays in a fanout stem is less than a given amount). All known synthesis procedures for asynchronous circuits provide this information either in the form of path delay bounds (e.g. [13]) or in the form of constraints on the relative delays of the branches of a fanout stem (e.g. [10]).

Step 2: reduction to asynchronous circuits with acyclic behavior (Section 2.1). The problem of testing an asynchronous circuit is reduced, by using a *partial scan* approach, to that of testing an object called an *asynchronous net*, in which feedbacks are allowed only inside asynchronous latches (e.g., Muller C elements, with inputs a and b and next state equation $c' = ab + ac + bc$). An asynchronous net is still a sequential object with internal memory, but it can exhibit only *acyclic behavior*.

Step 3: test sequence generation. For a combinational circuit, a delay fault test consists of *pairs* of vectors

*This work has been partially supported by by the Esprit project 21949 - ACID WG (M. Kishinevsky, L. Lavagno and A. Taubin) and EPSRC Visiting Fellowship GR/L24038 (A. Kondratyev and L. Lavagno).

[1] A delay fault is "dangerous" if it violates some assumption made during synthesis, e.g. a fundamental mode constraint, an isochronic fork and so on [13].

1092-3152/97 $10.00 © 1997 IEEE

$< v_0, v_1 >$ applied to the primary inputs of a circuit. Vector v_0 sets the outputs and the side inputs of the gates along the path under test to values which allow the propagation of the desired transition when v_1 is applied. For sequential circuits, testing a delay fault requires in general the application of a *sequence* of vectors. The first part of this sequence performs correct *initialization* of latches along the path. The second part of the sequence is a *testing pair* $< v_0, v_1 >$, where the *setup vector*, v_0, sets the outputs and the side inputs of the gates along the path under the condition that all latches are already initialized as required. The *test vector*, v_1 propagates the transition along the path.

We decompose the problem of testing asynchronous nets into that of initializing memory elements, followed by path delay fault testing.

Step 3a: generating testing pairs $< v_0, v_1 >$ (Section 3). This problem is solved by reduction to stuck-at test pattern generation for a *combinational circuit* that can be directly derived from an asynchronous net. This approach was proposed in [21] for RPDFT of combinational circuits. Additional conditions on the generated stuck-at test patterns for reduction of HFRPDFT are given. The method is further generalized for *sequential* nets, by modeling each latch with a combinational model (similar to modeling of latches in time-frame unrolling [1]). We derive conditions on the value of the state inputs under which the test for the combinational circuit is valid also for the asynchronous net, without resorting to time-frame unrolling.

Step 3a: Step 3b: generating initialization sequences (Section 4). Vector v_0 obtained at step 3a is the target of the initialization procedure. We present a heuristic algorithm for monotonous initialization that (if successful) generates initialization sequences bounded by $n^2/2$, where n is the latch count. Otherwise, we resort to classical time-frame unrolling [1] (that has an upper bound on the test sequence length of 4^n).

We improve with respect to previous work because our approach:

- Is complete, because it finds a test sequence for a given fault if one exists (while [4] heuristically maximized the number of tested paths, by using a greedy search algorithm). Note that previous work ([12]) has shown that asynchronous circuits generated with every known synthesis technique can be tested for delay faults by using a full-scan approach, so we can claim that every delay fault can be tested using the proposed method.

- Is automated (while [20] requires the designer to manually insert special circuitry, acting only in functional test mode, under guidance from a testability analysis tool).

- Requires only partial scan (while [8] required full scan and required additional test inputs and [17] is based on full scan and uses transformations of combinational logic increasing the level of testability).

- Requires only the output of a memory element to be scanned (while [12] required both inputs to each element to be independently scanned, that in general can be quite expensive).

The paper is organized as follows. Section 2 reviews the basic notions of delay fault testing and adapts them to asynchronous sequential circuits. Section 3 describes the reduction of HFRPDFT of sequential nets to that of combinational nets. Section 4 presents a procedure for initialization of asynchronous nets. Section 5 provides experimental results.

2 Preliminaries

2.1 Asynchronous circuits and nets

An *asynchronous circuit* is an arbitrary interconnection of logic gates and input nodes, with each gate input connected to strictly one gate output or one input node, and with no two gate outputs tied together. Feedback can be either *local* inside gates (like SR latches or C-elements) or *global* outside gates.

Our strategy for testing asynchronous circuits is based on breaking all *global* feedback loops, by selecting a Minimum Feedback Vertex Set of the circuit graph, and converting all its gates into scan memory elements (like [5, 14] in the synchronous case). Such transformation is obviously easier and cheaper if the selected gates are memory elements (see [12] for a scan SR latch circuit). Outputs of such gates then become simultaneously new primary inputs and primary outputs of the circuit.

We call the resulting circuit, in which feedback can only be local, an *asynchronous net*. In this paper we will consider a particular class of asynchronous nets, which are composed from *simple gates* (AND, OR, NAND, NOR, and NOT) and C-elements. Using the macro-expansion operator [16], any complex gate can be converted to an equivalent connection of simple gates preserving testability properties. Handling asynchronous memory elements other than C-elements is a possible area of future work.

2.2 Identifying the paths to be tested

An asynchronous circuit operates correctly without hazards only if some delay constraints, which differ according to the design style used, are satisfied. All such constraints can be formulated in terms of comparisons among event propagation times along some circuit paths. For example, speed-independent circuits ([10]) operate correctly if and only if all the branches of a multiple fanout point have similar delays (generally, the maximum admissible spread is comparable with one gate delay).

Let us model the delay of each wire i in a circuit by using a variable d_i. In that case, the set of delay constraints that ensure the correct operation of the circuit can be modeled by a set $\mathcal{A}$ of linear inequalities over those variables. The problem, then, is to find a set of paths that allow us to prove that $\mathcal{A}$ is indeed satisfied, by bounding the delay along them. In other words, we would like to be able to find a set $\mathcal{D}$ of linear inequalities, each involving a measurable delay along an I/O path of the corresponding asynchronous net, such that the set of feasible solutions (assignments to the d_is) of $\mathcal{A} \cup \mathcal{D}$ is *the same* as that of $\mathcal{D}$.

The simplest solution to this problem is to greedily add testable path after testable path, until the inequalities in $\mathcal{A}$ all become *redundant* (i.e., the *assumed* delay bounds are *implied* by the *measured* delay bounds). A better solution, that is left to future work, would require to minimize the cardinality of the set of tested paths.

Note that in this case the trade-off between test sequence length and speed at which the circuit can operate ([11]) is possible only if the objective of the test is the determination of the actual performance of the circuit, because no compromise about its correctness is generally possible.

2.3 Path delay faults

In this paper we will use delay fault testing models originally developed for combinational circuits, and extend them to asynchronous nets. Testing for delay faults in that case requires the application of a *pair* of vectors $< v_0, v_1 >$ to the primary inputs to force a signal transition propagation along the path under test $\pi = \{g_0, g_1, g_2, \ldots, g_k\}$. Vector v_0 is called the *setup vector*, vector v_1 is called the *test vector*. The testability conditions are based on considering side-inputs and side-paths.

Definition 2.1 *Let $\pi = \{g_0, g_1, \ldots, g_k\}$ be a path. The inputs of g_i other than g_{i-1} are called* **side-inputs** *of g_i along π and denoted as $S(g_i, \pi)$.*

A path that starts at a primary input and ends at a side-input of $g_i \in \pi$ is a **side-path** *of π. If a side-path starts at the same primary input g_0 as path π, then it is called a* **reconvergent side-path** *of π.*

Definition 2.2 *A* **controlling value** *for a gate g (denoted as $C(g)$) is a value of* one *of its inputs that determines the value at the output independent of the other inputs. Otherwise a value of the input is called* **non-controlling** *and denoted $NC(g)$.*

Note that a C-element has no controlling values, since the next value at the output always depends either on the value at *both* inputs, or on the previous value at the output. We then extend the definition to asynchronous nets as follows.

Definition 2.3 *A* **controlling set** *for a gate g (denoted as $CS(g)$) is a set of values at* some *of its inputs that determines the value at the output independent of the other inputs or the previous state of the gate. Otherwise a set of values at some inputs is called* **non-controlling** *and denoted $NCS(g)$.*

For example, $\{1,1\}$ and $\{0,0\}$ are two controlling sets for a two-input C-element and $\{1,0\}$ and $\{0,1\}$ are two non-controlling sets.

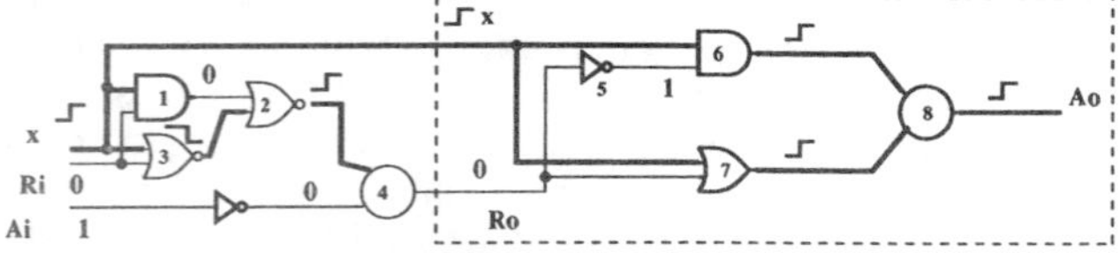

Figure 1: Path delay fault testing in asynchronous nets

A setup vector v_0 for a combinational path has two functions: (1) it sets the outputs of all the gates along the path, and (2) it sets the side inputs of the same gates to values which allow the propagation of the desired transition. The first function is called *initialization*, the second is called *setting*. This may also work for a sequential path, as shown in Figure 1. Assume that path $\pi_1 = \{x, 6, 8\}$ is under test for the rising input transition. It is easy to see that vector $v_0 =< x = 0, Ri = 0, Ai = 1 >$ will initialize the C-elements 4 and 8 into state 0 and also will set the side-input for gate 6 on the path $\pi_1 = \{x, 6, 8\}$ and the side-input for gate 7 on the path $\pi_2 = \{x, 7, 8\}$ at non-controlling values. Then, by applying vector $v_1 =< x = 1, Ri = 0, Ai = 1 >$ a rising transition will propagate from input x to output Ao along two paths π_1 and π_2. If there is a delay fault in at least one of the paths, it will be observed at the output.

Multiple paths can be tested with the same pair of vectors (see Figure 1). In that case, more than one constraint is obviously added to the set $\mathcal{D}$ that is used to bound the timing assumptions.

However, as will be shown in Section 4, testing for delay fault in a sequential path requires in general the application of a *sequence* of vectors. The first part of this sequence is called an *initialization sequence* and is concerned only with correct initialization of C-elements (latches) along the path. Such initialization sequence (which would not invalidate the test) may not exist or may require applying multiple vectors. The second part of the sequence is called a *testing pair* since it always consists of a setup and a test vector. If no such sequence exists for a given fault, we can always introduce new scan registers. In the limit, when all sequential elements are scanned, the circuit becomes testable under very weak assumptions (absence of single-cube-contained implicants [12]).

2.4 Path Delay Fault Testing

In this paper we consider two possible approaches to path delay fault testing ([21, 7, 23, 18, 22]):

RPDFT: A path is *robust delay fault testable* if there is a test pair for the path delay fault that is valid under arbitrary delays along other paths. In other words, hazards cannot invalidate a robust test. However some hazards may propagate to the output node of the path.

HFRPDFT: A path is *hazard-free robust delay fault testable* if there is a robust test vector pair for which hazards may not occur along the path under test.

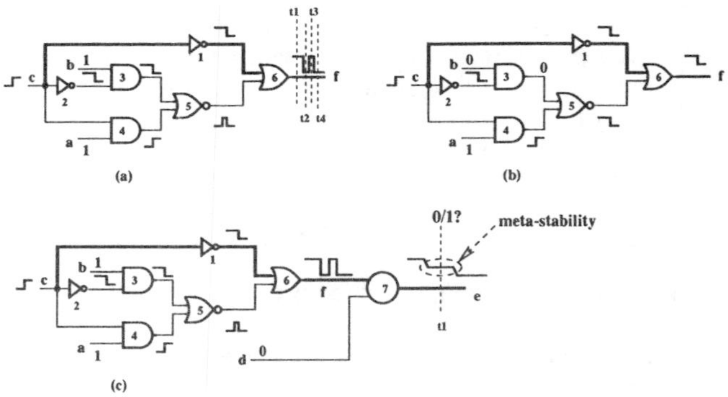

Figure 2: Robust and hazard-free robust delay fault testing for combinational (a,b) and sequential (c) nets.

The difference between these two models for combinational nets is illustrated by checking the testability of path $\pi = \{c, 1, 6\}$ in Figure 2. As shown in Figure 2,a test pair $< v_0, v_1 >=< 110, 111 >$ (the variable order is $< a, b, c >$) may cause a dynamic 1-to-0 hazard at the output of gate 6. However, if π has a longer delay than expected, then a falling transition at the output of gate 6 is delayed. In this case hazards cannot invalidate the test and $< 110, 111 >$ is a robust test. If the output of gate 6 is observed at t_1, when it has value 1, then we correctly conclude that there is a delay fault along π. If the output is observed at t_2 or t_4, when the output is at 0, we correctly conclude that there is no delay fault along π. However, if the output is observed at t_3, when the output is at 1 due to hazards at the output of gate 5, then a false negative occurs. We incorrectly report a delay fault along π. Therefore, the robust test is conservative and can produce false negatives. As shown in Figure 2,b test pair $< v_0, v_1 >=< 100, 101 >$, propagating transition along two paths $\pi = \{c, 1, 6\}$ and $\{c, 4, 5, 6\}$, is HFRPDFT since no hazards may occur along π.

One may consider that hazard propagation is particularly dangerous for asynchronous circuits, because hazards may lead memory elements into a meta-stable state. Figure 2,c shows an example of such behavior: a C-element (gate 7) with output e at 1 and input d at 0 sees a 1-0-1-0 dynamic hazard on input f. The second vector of a test pair, whose application may cause internal hazards under the RPDFT model, always forces a *controlling set* for all the gates (including C-elements) on the path under test. This means that any C-element that may enter a meta-stable state due to a hazard is also forced to leave the meta-stable state by the time v_1 finishes propagating. Nevertheless, if (due to a delay fault) the output of the C-element is observed at $t1$, when it is in meta-stable state, then it may cause uncertainty in the test machine. A meta-stable output either keeps a value between the logical "0" and logical "1" or oscillates. Hence the effect of meta-stable values on the primary outputs is similar to that of hazards. Both can cause false negative results.

We will then discuss both hazard-free and non-hazard-free testing, because the latter may allow better coverage at the expense of more false negative results.

Definition 2.4 *Let $\pi = \{g_0, g_1, \ldots, g_k\}$ be a path in an asynchronous net. We say that gate $g_i, 0 \leq i \leq k$, has an* **even input parity** *if there is an even number of inverters along the path π from g_0 to the output of g_i. Otherwise, g_i has an* **odd input parity**. *Similarly, we define* **output parity** *as the number of inverters on a path from g_i to g_k. The input parity is denoted as $IP(g_i, \pi)$ and the output parity as $OP(g_i, \pi)$. $IP(g_i, \pi), OP(g_i, \pi) \in \{even, odd\}$.*

Definition 2.5 (RPDFT [21])
A path $\pi = \{g_0, g_1, \ldots, g_k\}$ in an asynchronous net is said to be **robustly path delay fault testable** *for the rising input transition by the vector pair $< v_0, v_1 >$ if for each $g_i \in \pi$ and for each side-input $f_j \in S(g_i, \pi)$ the following conditions hold:*

(1) $g_i(v_0) \neq g_i(v_1)$; (2) if $IP(g_i) = even$, then $g_i(v_1) = 1$ otherwise $g_i(v_1) = 0$; (3) $f_j(v_1) \in NC(g_i)$; (4) if $g_{i-1}(v_1) \in C(g_i)$, then there is no transition on f_j.

This definition also applies to C-elements. In particular, condition 1 requires that the input values of every C-element on π is a controlling set under the vector v_1, and the C-element output has the opposite value under v_0. Conditions 3 and 4 do not apply to C-elements, since they refer to controlling and non-controlling values. Note that there is no constraint on the transitions on side-inputs for C-elements, other than that specified by condition 1.

Definition 2.5 does not restrict transitions at the side-inputs if $g_{i-1}(v_1)$ has a non-controlling value. Therefore hazards may occur.

Testability for the falling input or rising and falling output transitions is defined similarly and differs only in condition 2 (e.g., for the falling output transition condition 2 is as follows: if $OP(g_i) = even$, then $g_i(v_1) = 0$ otherwise $g_i(v_1) = 1$).

For the **HFRPDFT** one more condition must be added to prevent hazards along the path under test:

(5) if $g_{i-1}(v_1) \in NC(g_i)$ or g_i is a C-element, then either there is no transition on f_j or there is one monotonous transition on f_j such that $f_j(v_1) = g_{i-1}(v_1)$.

In the next section we develop the theory for HFRPDFT, since it is the most complex case. A simplified version of the theory, that applies to RPDFT, can be easily derived as well.

3 Reduction of HFRPDFT to stuck-at

The problem of HFRPDF test generation for asynchronous nets is solved by reducing it to classical stuck-at test pattern generation for a combinational circuit which can be directly derived from the asynchronous net. Since asynchronous nets contain latches they exhibit sequential behavior. Hence, in general, a stuck at test for an asynchronous net is not a single vector but may require applying a sequence of vectors. For this reason the reduction is done in two steps:

- Relating sequential HFRPDFT to combinational HFRPDFT (Section 3.1)
- Relating HFRPDFT for a combinational circuit to stuck-at test generation for a slightly modified combinational circuit. This approach was proposed in [21] for RPDFT of combinational circuits. Additional conditions on the generated stuck-at test patterns for reduction of HFRPDFT can be found in [9].

Note that, in practice, the first step is performed *relative to a particular test vector pair* (Section 4 describes one such approach), so the order in the algorithmic implementation is reversed. Moreover, potentially there is a need to backtrack and select another test pair if it does not satisfy the initializability conditions.

3.1 Relating sequential HFRPDFT to combinational HFRPDFT

Given an asynchronous net, C, let us substitute each C-element $c_j = a_j b_j + a_j c_j + b_j c_j$ with its combinational model, that is a majority gate (M-gate) M_j. An M-gate implements the following boolean function: $c_j = a_j b_j + a_j m_j + b_j m_j$, where m_j is an additional primary input (called M-input). Since the majority function is unate and each M-input fans out only to one M-gate M_j, there is no need to decompose M_j into simple gates. In the following we will always consider M_j as an atomic gate. The conversion of C-elements to combinational M-gates is purely logical and is done for the algorithm of test generation for the original sequential circuit, no actual physical transformation of the original sequential circuit is required.

Definition 3.1 *The combinational circuit obtained from an asynchronous net C by replacing each C-element with an M-gate, is called an* **M-net** *and is denoted $M(C)$.*

If an asynchronous net has primary inputs $I = \{i_1, \ldots, i_k\}$ and C-elements $L = \{c_1, \ldots, c_l\}$, then the corresponding M-net has $k + l$ primary inputs $\{i_1, \ldots, i_k, m_1, \ldots, m_l\}$. The following conditions determine the value of the M-input that implies a stable behavior of the M-gate if its output is connected to its input (thus forming a C-element again). Figure 3 shows an example of M-net, corresponding to the asynchronous net from Figure 1.

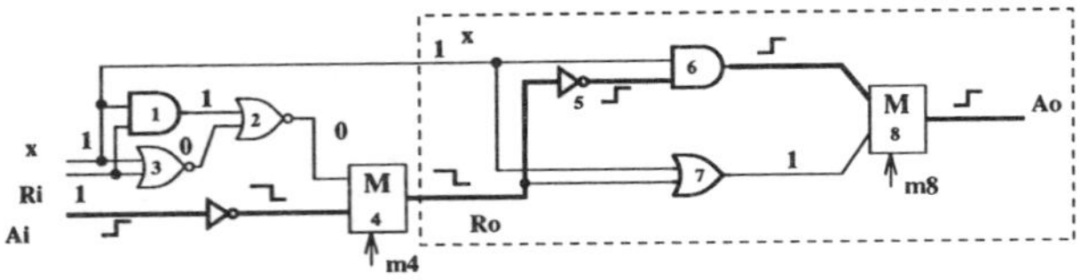

Figure 3: M-net

Definition 3.2 *A vector v of inputs to the M-net is called* **consistent with initialization** *if for each M-gate, M_j, the following condition is satisfied: $c_j(v) = m_j(v)$.*

In other words, the final value c_j at the output of each M-gate after applying v is the same as that of the M-input m_j.

Let $v = < v_0, \ldots, v_k >$ be a binary or ternary vector ($v_i \in \{0, 1, -\}$) for variables from set X and let $Z \subseteq X$. Then $v \downarrow Z$ denotes the sub-vector of v corresponding only to variables from Z. The following theorem states the conditions under which a *combinational* logic test derived for an M-net is valid also for the corresponding *sequential* asynchronous net.

Theorem 3.3 *Let C be an asynchronous net with set of primary inputs I and set of C-elements L. Let $\pi = \{i, g_0, \ldots, g_k\}$ be a path in C and $\pi' = \{i', g_0', \ldots, g_k'\}$ be the path corresponding to π in the M-net $M(C)$. If $< v_0, v_1 >$ is a HFRPDFT for π' in the M-net and v_0 is consistent with initialization, then $< v_0 \downarrow I, v_1 \downarrow I >$ is a HFRPDFT for C under the following initialization condition: each C-element $c_j \in L$ has the same value $c_j(v_0)$ as $m_j(v_0)$ in the M-net.*

The proof of the theorem can be found in [9]. Note that there is no need to check a similar condition for v_1, because v_1 must impose a *forcing set* on every C-element along the path, and hence the output of the M-gates is independent of the M-input values.

If the condition for v_0 to be consistent with initialization is violated, then the behavior of an asynchronous net and of the corresponding M-net is different and, in general, the test for the latter is not valid for the former. Assume that the order of the primary inputs for the M-net in Figure 3 is as follows: $< x, Ri, Ai, m_4, m_8 >$. A vector pair $< v_0, v_1 >=< 00011, 00111 >$ is a HFRPDFT for the falling output transition at the path $\pi' = \{Ai, 4, 7, 8\}$ in the M-net. Since v_0 is consistent with initialization ($m_4(v_0) = Ro(v_0) = 1$ and $m_8(v_0) = Ao(v_0) = 1$, a vector pair $< v_0 \downarrow I, v_1 \downarrow I >=< 000, 001 >$ is a HFRPDFT for the falling output transition at the path $\pi = \{Ai, 4, 7, 8\}$ in the asynchronous net. The same path can be tested in the M-net with a vector pair $< v1_0, v1_1 >=< 01001, 01101 >$. However, $v1_0$ is not consistent with initialization because $m_4(v1_0) = 0$, while the output of this M-gate $Ro(v1_0) = 1$. It is easy to check that $< v_0 \downarrow I, v_1 \downarrow I >=< 010, 011 >$ is not a HFRPDFT for the falling output transition along the path $\pi = \{Ai, 4, 7, 8\}$ in the asynchronous net.

4 Initialization conditions

Let $< v_0, v_1 >$ be a HFRPDFT for the path π in the M-net and let v_0 be consistent with initialization. Vector v_0 defines the values of the primary inputs and of the M-inputs. By Theorem 3.3 $< v_0 \downarrow I, v_1 \downarrow I >$ will be a HFRPDFT for the asynchronous net only if the values on the outputs of C-elements $L = \{c_1, \ldots, c_l\}$ coincide with those of the majority gates. These values are given by a ternary vector $\alpha = v_0 \downarrow L$. The aim of the initialization procedure is to set all C-elements according to α.

The proposed monotonous initialization procedure begins from those C-elements that are closer to the primary outputs (in backward topological order). The polynomial bound on the (possibly non-existing) monotonous initialization sequence length is due to the fact that a C-element is not disturbed after having been set.

We can associate four Boolean functions (defined over the space of primary inputs and C-element outputs) with each element g (gate or C-element) of an asynchronous net.

- $S1(g)$ and $S0(g)$ – setting g to 1 or 0 respectively and
- $H1(g)$ and $H0(g)$ – holding g to 1 or 0 respectively.

If g is a basic combinational gate with output function f then $S1(g) = H1(g) = f$ while $S0(g) = H0(g) = \overline{f}$. In case of a C-element, the holding and setting functions are different. For C-element c_j with inputs $i_1, \ldots, i_k$ they are: $S1(c_j) = H1(i_1) * \ldots * H1(i_k)$ and $H1(c_j) = c_j * (H1(i_1) + \ldots + H1(i_k))$ (similarly for $S0(c_j)$ and $H0(c_j)$).

To set a C-element c_j we must apply an input vector under which the corresponding setting function evaluates to 1. However only for C-elements of the first level the value of a setting function is completely determined by primary inputs. For c_j in level i the setting function depends also on the outputs of C-elements from the lower levels. Therefore the process of setting c_j may require the recursive setting of "preceding" C-elements.

Let us consider in more detail the process of setting c_j to 1 by using an input vector v (resetting it to 0 can be done similarly). Let C_s denote the C-elements from levels higher than i. If v sets c_j then two conditions must be satisfied:

1. there exists cube $\beta \in S1(c_j)$ such that $\beta \downarrow I$ covers v.
2. C-elements C_β whose outputs have a value of 0 or 1 in β (these are the C-elements on which c_j depends) have already been set by previous input vectors $w_1, \ldots, w_n$.

Application of vector v after w_n can lead to the following difficulties:

- $c_m \in C_\beta$ can change its value inside the transition cube between w_n and v. In such case the value of β in v does not evaluate to 1 and c_j is not set.

- $c_m \in C_s$ can change its value inside the transition cube between w_n and v. In such case the requirement of monotonicity of the initialization procedure is violated.

These two conditions restrict the set of valid vectors v that can be applied after w_n, leading towards v_0, that is the objective of initialization. If we denote by $Hold$ the product of the holding functions of C-elements in $C_s \cup C_\beta$, then a valid transition path between w_n and v must belong to $Hold$. The task of finding a valid path can be reduced to a search in a graph with: (1) vertices corresponding to cubes of $Hold$ and (2) edges between every pair of intersecting cubes from $Hold$.

If no valid path exists, then c_j cannot be set by the cube β and another cube from the setting function of c_j is tried. If we fail to find such a path for all cubes c_j, then we need to backtrack. The procedure converges, because full scan testing is always possible.

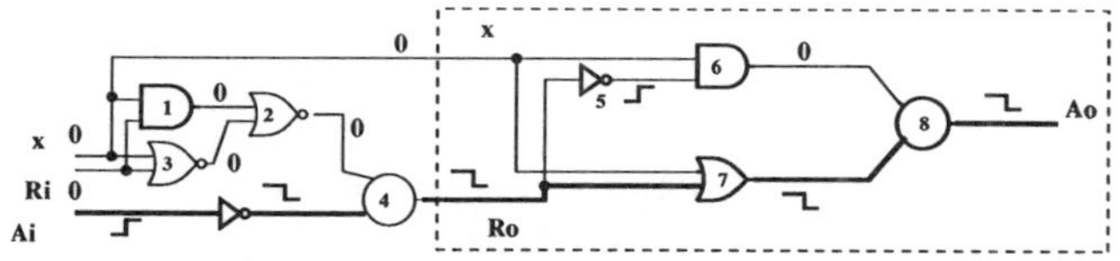

Figure 4: Initialization of asynchronous nets

Return to our example and consider (Figure 4) path $\pi\{Ai, 4, 7, 8, Ao\}$ under the rising transition on Ai. The vector pair $< v_0 = \{x = 0, R_i = 0, A_i = 0\}, v_1 = \{x = 0, R_i = 0, A_i = 1\} >$ will be a HFRPDFT for the falling output transition for π under the condition that Ro and Ao are initialized to 1. Let us find a corresponding initialization sequence. The holding and setting functions for C-elements Ro and Ao are:

$S1(Ro) = \overline{Ai} * (\overline{x}Ri + x\overline{Ri})$

$H1(Ro) = Ro * (\overline{Ai} + \overline{x}Ri + x\overline{Ri})$

$S0(Ro) = Ai * (xRi + \overline{x}\overline{Ri})$

$H0(Ro) = \overline{Ro} * (Ai + xRi + \overline{x}\overline{Ri})$

$S1(Ao) = x * H0(Ro) * (x + H1(Ro))$

$H1(Ao) = Ao * (x * H0(Ro) + x + H1(Ro))^2$

After substituting of $H1(Ro)$ and $H0(Ro)$ into the functions for Ao we get: $S1(Ao) = x\overline{Ro}Ai + x\overline{Ro}Ri$ and

$H1(Ao) = xAo + AoRo\overline{Ai} + AoRo\overline{x}Ri$

From $S1(Ao)$ it follows that to set Ao at level 2 we first need to reset Ro at level 1. The latter can be done by the vector $w_1 =< Ai = 1, x = 1, Ri = 1 >$. Note that after Ro is reset, the same vector w_1 sets Ao to 1.

The next initialization step is to set Ro. To do this we can try cube $\overline{Ai}\overline{x}Ri$ of function $S1(Ro)$. However, if we apply vector $w_2 =< Ai = 0, x = 0, Ri = 1 >$ after w_1 we cannot keep the value 1 on the output of Ao because $H1(Ao)$ is equal to 0 under w_2 (remember that after w_1, Ro is reset to 0). Therefore no valid path from w_1 to w_2 exists and we need to try the next cube in $S1(Ro)$, that is $\overline{Ai}x\overline{Ri}$. This cube defines vector $w_3 =< Ai = 0, x = 1, Ri = 0 >$ and in any minterm of the transient cube between w_1 and w_3, Ao keeps the value 1 (due to cube xAo of $H1(Ao)$). Therefore, any path inside the transient cube is valid and w_3 can be applied immediately after w_1.

The last task is to check that in the transition from w_3 to v_0 no C-element changes the output. This condition is satisfied, because w_3 and v_1 are adjacent and both belong to $H1(Ao)$ and $H1(Ro)$. Hence, w_1, w_3, v_0 is a valid initialization sequence.

[2] $S0(Ao)$ and $H0(Ao)$ functions are not considered here because in this case Ao is not set to 0.

5 Experimental results

This section presents experimental results which illustrate the RPDFT properties of two classes of asynchronous logic circuits: (1) speed-independent random control logic synthesized from Signal Transition Graph specifications using the so-called Monotonous Cover technique [10]; (2) regular logic from delay-insensitive data-paths [24, 6, 15]. Similar experiments could also be performed with the HFR-PDFT model, with obviously lower coverage figures.

The experimental procedure has three main steps:

1. Selecting a set of C-elements to scan.
2. Translating the asynchronous net into an M-net by replacing each C-element with a majority gate. A robust test for each path in the M-net is obtained by test generation of a single stuck-fault in a modified net obtained from the M-net, as described in [9].
3. Generating a sequence of initialization vectors to set the output value of each C-element along the path being tested to the desired value.

As already mentioned, if initialization does not succeed for a chosen test vector pair, additional vector pairs are selected until initialization succeeds for at least one or fails for all.

Circuits from the first class are characterized by a very high density of signal interconnections. We checked four techniques for achieving high-testability: full input scan, full output scan, partial output scan and partial output scan with splitting of primary inputs. Splitting of input connections (that was defined in [12] for true and complemented phases only) is a powerful technique to increase the testability of asynchronous circuits, because it reduces the redundancy level.

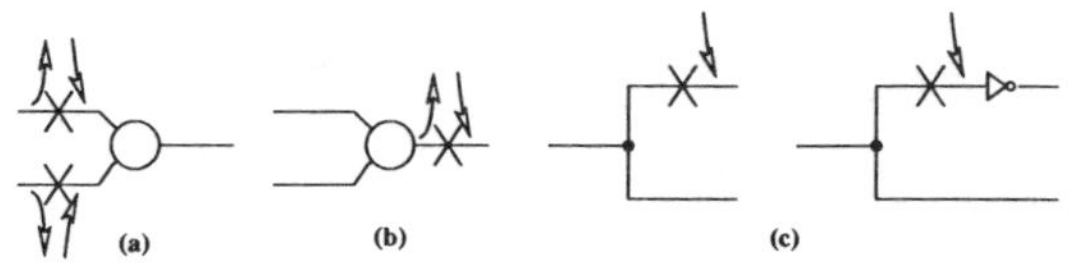

Figure 5: Techniques for testability: input scan (a), output scan (b), fork and phase splitting (c).

As illustrated by Figure 5, input scan requires scan-in and scan-out operations for both inputs of a latch, output scan requires scan-in and scan-out only for the output of the latch. Fork and phase splitting requires scan-in in addition to scan out. Fork splitting means the possibility to scan independently the fanout branches of a fork. Phase splitting means the possibility to drive independently the true and complemented phase of each primary input and sequential element.

Circuit	paths	signals	approach of [12]		partial scan		partial scan with splitting		
			input	output	scan	%	scan	split	%
converta	30	3	100	80	2	64	2	1	71
chu150	22	3	100	91	1	91	1	1	91
chu172	12	3	100	100	0	100	0	0	100
rpdft.map2	36	6	100	97	0	83	0	1	94
alloc-outbound.map2	34	6	100	86	2	86	2	1	97
c3.map2	42	6	100	93	2	71	2	1	83
rcv-setup.map2	20	5	100	100	1	83	1	1	89
master-read-csc.map2	80	16	100	91	5	62	5	2	84
pe-send-ifc-csc	146	5	100	84	4	54	4	2	72
full	16	2	100	50	1	50	1	1	75
dc	36	4	100	89	3	88	3	1	90
qr42	28	3	100	79	1	38	1	1	51
chu133	24	4	100	96	3	89	3	1	96

Table 1: Experimental results for speed-independent control

Table 1 presents the results for speed-independent control logic. The first two columns describe circuit complexity: the number of paths and the number of *non-input* (i.e., feedback) signals of the circuit. There is no column on runtime because for our small circuits test generation always took less then 10 msec. The "approach of [12]" columns show the percent level of testability for input scan and for output scan of all non-input signals respectively, using the technique of [12]. The "partial scan" columns show the level of testability for a selected number of scanned signals for the output scan technique. The last group of columns shows how the level of testability can be increased if the splitting technique is used in addition to partial scan. The column labeled "split" gives the number of split signals. For example, the best level of testability that can be achieved by partial output scan for circuit "converta" (two out of three signals are scanned) is 64%. If one additional signal is split, then testability reaches 71%.

The sets of signals for partial scan and for splitting are selected to achieve the required testability level. In Table 1 we attempt to reach a testability level of 70%, and limit the number of signals which are allowed to be scanned and split as explained in the algorithm Figure 6. For example, we do not allow more than one signal to split for circuit "converta" and to scan more than five signals for circuit "master-read-csc.map2". The requested level of testability cannot be achieved by scanning only five signals in "master-read-csc.map2", but can be achieved by splitting two additional signals.

Our algorithm for selecting a set of signals for partial scan and for signal splitting operates on the directed graph of signal interconnections. It is sketched in Figure 6.

Circuits from the second class are known to have high stuck-at testability. We expected that a high level of path delay fault testability could be achieved with a low scan ratio. Table 2 presents the results for a DIMS-adder [24], for a delay-insensitive adder with a status detector for dual-rail input wires [6] and for a reduced direct logic adder [15]. The numbers are obtained for one bit adders. Since the circuits have no global loops, no scan is required. The last line of the table shows the result for a bit-slice of a serial-parallel carry-save multiplier with pipeline latches

begin
  Select a Minimum Feedback Vertex Set, $Scan$,
  with a maximal sum of vertex degrees among all MFVSs;
  repeat /* Updating scan set */
    Add a vertex with a maximal degree to $Scan$;
    If testability is less than requested **then**
      repeat /* Updating split set */
        Split a signal $g \in Scan$ with a max. out-degree;
        Choose bi-partition of g's fan-out set
        to minimize the number of reconvergent paths;
      until The requested level of testability is achieved
        or the splitting limit is exceeded;
  until The requested level of testability is achieved or
    the scan limit is exceeded;
end

Figure 6: Algorithm

for the two operands, the sum-in and the carry-in, and output latches for the sum-out and the carry-out. To obtain full testability, four feedback wires between the result latches and the operand latches must be scanned. The pipelined adder example is a DIMS-adder incorporated into the pipelined ring.

A few interesting observations can be made:

- Although dependency graphs are very dense for speed-independent random control logic, partial scan augmented with splitting techniques can provide a high level of testability.
- Full *output* scan (which can be achieved by inserting transparent latches after each C-element) provides a relatively good testability level around 80%-90%. This gives, to the best of our knowledge, the first experimental evidence that speed-independent circuits are easily testable even when more accurate fault models than pure output stuck-at are used ([2] first proved their self-checking properties with respect to this kind of fault).
- Experiments with delay-insensitive adders show that the optimization technique used for area efficiency reduces the level of testability from 100% in the DIMS adder to 74% in Martin's adder (which is competitive in

Circuit	Paths	Signals	Testability (%)	Scan (latches)	Scan (% of latches)
DIMS	96	12	100	0	0
DGY	92	18	79	0	0
Martin	84	24	74	0	0
pipelined adder	420	30	100	1	5%
pipelined multiplier	1062	48	100	4	13%

Table 2: Experimental results for delay-insensitive data path

area and faster than a synchronous ripple-carry adder). We may conclude that the optimization transformations which correspond to quasi-delay-insensitive substitution do not retain testability.

6 Conclusions

In this paper we have described a complete path-delay fault testing algorithm for asynchronous *sequential* circuits. We have shown that it is possible to perform such tests by partial scan on a sequential object called an *asynchronous net*. We defined the set of paths that must be tested to check all the timing assumptions. We decomposed the testing problem for sequential circuits into:

1. insertion of enough scan elements to make the asynchronous circuit *functionally acyclic*,
2. initialization (using a heuristic technique, with a fall-back strategy for the sake of completeness).
3. test pattern generation, by reduction to combinational ATPG.

Experimental results show that the technique is effective in providing a substantial savings in the number of scan memory elements, versus a small reduction in the testability figures. This is true of control-dominated dense circuits, and even more of regular data path objects.

References

[1] M. Abramovici, M. A. Breuer, and A. D. Friedman. *Digital Systems Testing and Testable Design*. IEEE Press, 1990. Revised printing.

[2] D. B. Armstrong, A. D. Friedman, and P. R. Menon. Design of asynchronous circuits assuming unbounded gate delays. *IEEE Transactions on Computers*, C-18(12):1110–1120, December 1969.

[3] S. Banerjee, S.T. Chakradhar, and R.K. Roy. Synchronous test generation model for asynchronous circuits. In *Proceedings of the Int. Conf. on VLSI Design*, pages 178–185, January 1995.

[4] K.-T. Cheng, V. Agrawal, and E. Kuh. A simulation-based method for generating tests for sequential circuits. *IEEE Transactions on Computers*, 39(12):1456–1463, December 1990.

[5] K.-T. Cheng and V. D. Agrawal. A partial scan method for sequential circuits with feedback. *IEEE Transactions on Computers*, C-39(4):544–548, April 1990.

[6] I. David, R. Ginosar, and M. Yoeli. An efficient implementation of boolean functions as self-timed circuits. *IEEE Transactions on Computers*, 41(1):2–11, January 1992.

[7] S. Devadas and K. Keutzer. Synthesis of robust delay-fault testable circuits: Theory. *IEEE Transactions on Computer-Aided Design of Integrated Circuits and Systems*, 11(1):87–101, January 1992.

[8] K. Keutzer, L. Lavagno, and A. Sangiovanni-Vincentelli. Synthesis for testability techniques for asynchronous circuits. *IEEE Transactions on Computer-Aided Design*, 14(12):1569–1577, December 1995.

[9] M. Kishinevsky, A. Kondratyev, L. Lavagno, A. Saldanha, and A. Taubin. Hazard free robust path delay fault testing of asynchronous nets. Technical Report TR: 96-2-001, The University of Aizu, Japan, March 1996.

[10] A. Kondratyev, M. Kishinevsky, B. Lin, P. Vanbekbergen, and A. Yakovlev. Basic gate implementation of speed-independent circuits. In *Proceedings of the Design Automation Conference*, pages 56–62, June 1994.

[11] W. Lam, A. Saldanha, R. Brayton, and A. Sangiovanni-Vincentelli. Delay fault coverage and performance tradeoffs. In *Proc. ACM/IEEE Design Automation Conference*, pages 446–452, June 1993.

[12] L. Lavagno, M. Kishinevsky, and A. Lioy. Testing redundant asynchronous circuits by variable phase splitting. In *Proceedings of the EURO-DAC'94*, pages 328–333, Grenoble, France, September 1994.

[13] L. Lavagno and A. Sangiovanni-Vincentelli. *Algorithms for Synthesis and Testing of Asynchronous Circuits*. Kluwer Academic Publishers, 1993.

[14] D.H. Lee and S.M. Reddy. On determining scan flip-flops in partial-scan designs. In *Proc. International Conf. Computer-Aided Design (ICCAD)*, pages 322–325, November 1990.

[15] A.J. Martin. Asynchronous datapaths and the design of an asynchronous adder. *Formal Methods in System Design*, 1:117–137, 1992.

[16] P. McGeer and R. Brayton. Provably correct critical paths. In *The Proceedings of the Decennial Caltech VLSI Conference*, 1989.

[17] S. Nowick, N. Jha, and F-C. Cheng. Synthesis of asynchronous circuits for stuck-at and robust path delay fault testability. In *Proceedings of the Int. Conf. on VLSI Design*, January 1995.

[18] A. Pramanick and S. Reddy. On the design of path delay fault testable combinational circuits. In *Proceedings of the* 20th *Fault Tolerant Computing Symposium*, pages 374–381, June 1990.

[19] O. Roig, J. Cortadella, M.A. Pe na, and E. Pastor. Automatic generation of synchronous test patterns for asynchronous circuits. In *Proceedings of the 34th Design Automation Conference*, June 1997.

[20] M. Roncken and R. Saeijs. Linear test times for delay-insensitive circuits: a compilation strategy. In S. Furber and M. Edwards, editors, *Proceedings of IFIP Working Conference on Asynchronous Design Methodologies*, pages 13–27, Manchester, UK, 31 March – 2 April 1993, 1993.

[21] A. Saldanha, R. Brayton, and A. Sangiovanni-Vincentelli. Equivalence of robust delay-fault and single stuck-fault test generation. In *Proc. ACM/IEEE Design Automation Conference*, pages 173–176, June 1992.

[22] J. Savir and W.H. Anney. Random pattern testability of delay faults. In *Proceedings of the International Test Conference*, pages 263–273, October 1986.

[23] G. L. Smith. A Model for Delay Faults Based on Paths. In *Proceedings of the Int'l Test Conference*, pages 342–349, September 1985.

[24] Jens Sparsø and Jørgen Staunstrup. Delay-insensitive multi-ring structures. *INTEGRATION, the VLSI Journal*, 15(3):313–340, 1993.

Maximum Independent Sets on Transitive Graphs and their Applications in Testing and CAD *

Dimitrios Kagaris
Electrical Engineering Dept.
Southern Illinois University
Carbondale, IL 62901

Spyros Tragoudas
Computer Science Dept.
Southern Illinois University
Carbondale, IL 62901

Abstract We present a polynomial–time algorithm that finds the maximum weighted independent set of a transitive graph. The studied problem finds applications in a variety of VLSI contexts, including path delay fault testing, scheduling in high level synthesis and channel routing in physical design automation. The algorithm has been implemented and incorporated in a CAD tool for path delay fault testing. We experimentally verify its impact in the latter context.

1 Introduction

A directed graph $G = (V, E)$ is called *transitive* if the existence of any two directed edges (a, b) and (b, c), $a, b, c \in V$, implies that edge $(a, c) \in E$ [4]. The goal in the independent set problem on a graph is to find a set of nodes that are independent, i.e., not pairwise connected by an edge, and such that the sum of their weights is maximum. The maximum independent set problem is well–known to be NP–complete on general graphs even when all nodes have uniform weights [3]. However, this paper introduces a polynomial–time algorithm for locating a maximum weighted independent set on a transitive graph with integer weights on its nodes.

Transitive graphs arise in a variety of contexts in CAD for VLSI. Applications of the studied problem may be found in Testing, High level Synthesis and Physical Design Automation. They are discussed in Section 2. There is no efficient polynomial–time algorithm for selecting a maximum weighted independent set of a transitive graph. The problem is polynomially solvable since it has been shown to be polynomially solvable for perfect graphs, which include transitive graphs [6]. However, this is based on the ellipsoid method, uses a polynomial–time algorithm for a convex nonpolyhedral set, and is rather a theoretical contribution [6]. Section 3 describes our low order polynomial time complexity algorithm. Section 4 discusses its implementation and its incorporation in a CAD tool for fault coverage estimation in path delay fault testing. The significance of selecting optimally a maximum independent set is analyzed in the latter context. Section 5 concludes.

*Partially supported by NSF grant MIP-9409905

2 Testing, CAD applications

We discuss first an application in path delay fault coverage. Given a test set, consisting of a sequence of pairs of test patterns, the goal is to compute the number of path delay faults that can be detected by the input test set. A path delay fault is any path along which a $0 \rightarrow 1$ or $1 \rightarrow 0$ transition occurs along every edge in the path [1, 10, 9, 13]. The total number of such faults is at most twice the number of paths in the circuit. A simple approach can be used to *estimate* the number of faults detected by a given test set without requiring their explicit enumeration [13, 9, 7, 8]. For each applied pair of patterns a lower bound on the number of path delay faults is computed by only considering delay faults containing at least one new line. (A line is a new line, if the current pair of test patterns associates to it either a $0 \rightarrow 1$ or a $1 \rightarrow 0$ transition provided that has not been already associated to it.)

In [13, 9] an approach was proposed which guarantees an improved lower bound. Let $\mathcal{C}$ be a collection of lines whose removal disconnects the primary inputs from the primary outputs, i.e. a cut. It was proposed to consider *strong cuts* $\mathcal{C}$ with the property that no two lines $e_i, e_j \in \mathcal{C}$ are on the same path. Any path delay fault contains exactly one line in a strong cut $\mathcal{C}$. We can search for new lines in each subcircuit $\mathcal{C}(e)$ consisting of all the path containing e, $e \in \mathcal{C}$. The objective in [13, 9] was to find a strong cut $\mathcal{C}$ with maximum cardinality, and in [9] was proven to be equivalent to computing a maximum independent set in a transi-

1092-3152/97 $10.00 © 1997 IEEE

tive graph, the line dependency graph (LDG). In the LDG every node corresponds to a line, and edge (a, b) indicates that line a is a predecessor of line b.

Our algorithm can be used to enhance this approach by selecting a strong cut $\mathcal{C}$ so that the sum of the lines on all subcircuits $\mathcal{C}(e)$, $e \in \mathcal{C}$ is maximized. This is a natural way for forming subcircuits as the performance of the estimation scheme depends on the number of new lines on the path delay faults for each applied pair of patterns. Let us associate a weight $w(e)$ for each line e which is equal to the number of lines in $\mathcal{C}(e)$. It is easy to see that the proposed approach amounts to the problem of computing a strong cut $\mathcal{C}$ so that $\sum_{e \in \mathcal{C}} w(e)$ is maximum. This in turn amounts to computing a maximum weighted independent set on the respective LDG graph.

Another improvement, which is also based on the computation of a maximum weighted independent set on the respective LDG graph, aims at generating more subcircuits than the approach in [9]. For every line e we compute the maximum number of all paths that start from line e, contain at most k edges (k is an input parameter) and such that their end lines form a maximum independent set in the line dependency graph. We then assign a weight $w(e)$ on line e which equal to the latter quantity. Observe that weights $w(e)$ are not necessarily polynomial in size. For each selected line we generate $|w(e)|$ subcircuits. Each subcircuit contains exactly one of the $|w(e)|$ paths of depth k starting from line e. Observe that the above approach does not double-count path delay faults.

In the remaining, we discuss applications in CAD for VLSI Design. Scheduling problems arise in High Level Synthesis [12]. In this context, transitive graphs represent interrelations between tasks in a given schedule where each node corresponds to a task and the directed edge (a, b) implies that task a must be executed before task b. Finding a maximum independent set in an unweighted transitive graph amounts to determining an upper bound on the number of processors needed for parallel execution. The maximum weighted independent set arises on instances where each node is a complex parallelizable task, and the weight of each node indicates the number of processors needed for its execution.

Algorithms for the channel routing problem in physical design automation also utilize transitive graphs. All existing routers manipulate the nets based on their horizontal and vertical constraints which are depicted by two graphs, the Horizontal Constraints Graph (HCG) and the Vertical Constraints Graph (VCG) where every node corresponds to a net [14]. A common approach for k–layer routing for Printed Circuit Boards and Multi–Chip Modules is to iteratively apply net merging [14]. Assume that all but one layers are available in the horizontal direction. Any $k-1$ nets that do not have pairwise on a path of the VCG may be placed on the same track but on different layers. Thus, existing routers iteratively select nets based on an independency property of a transitive graph constructed from the VCG. The nodes of the latter transitive graph may be assigned weights that reflect priorities on their selection.

3 The proposed algorithm

A preprocessing step of the proposed algorithm requires that we compute the value of the of the maximum weighted independent set, i.e., the sum of the weights on its nodes. In a directed transitive graph, every path from an input to an output of G constitutes a set of nodes that form a clique in G, if the direction of the edges is ignored. Such a path will be referred to as a *clique path*. A clique path is said to *cover* the set of nodes from which it passes. Transitive graphs are perfect graphs [4]. The *minimum number* of clique paths in a transitive graph that cover all the nodes of the graph, is equal to the size of the maximum independent set in the graph [4]. A polynomial–time algorithm for finding a minimum number of clique paths is based on a minimum flow algorithm [4]. The value of the minimum flow equals the number of the clique paths or, equivalently, the cardinality of the maximum independent set. A minimum set of clique paths consists of all paths that have a positive flow on all their edges and differ in at least one node.

We extend the above idea to compute the weight of a maximum weighted independent set. We have used the Duplication Lemma [11] to show that the value of the maximum independent set in G is equal to the value of the minimum flow in a copy of G where all inputs are joined to a source, all outputs to a sink, each edge is assigned an infinite capacity, but now each node u is required to tranship at least $w(u)$ units of flow. (Details are omitted here.) Let n, e denote the number of nodes and the number of edges of the given transitive graph. We note that the minimum flow problem is polynomially solvable in $O(n \cdot e \cdot \log(n^2/e))$ time using the preflow–push technique in [5].

A brute force enumeration of the clique paths may result to an exponential quantity. However, we present an algorithm F_PATHS() which given the flow routing found by the minimum flow algorithm, identifies at most e flow paths which deliver to the outpus the same amount of flow. F_PATHS() visits the nodes in a topological order starting from the inputs and for each node u applies a procedure F_ROUTE(u), described below.

Let $f(e)$ denote the amount of flow that has been assigned to edge e under a flow f. We define as a *flow path*, a (simple) path $(u_0, u_1, u_2, ..., u_k)$ that starts from an input node u_0, ends in an output node u_k and carries at least a flow amount $x > 0$ in each edge, i.e., $f(u_{i-1}, u_i) \geq x, \forall i, 1 \leq i \leq k$.

For each node u, procedure F_ROUTE(u) considers the outgoing edges of u as well as all the (already constructed) flow paths that terminate at u. As shown below the number of these paths, denoted by m_u, is a small polynomial quantity. Each such "incoming" flow path will be considered by F_ROUTE(u) as being an incoming edge to u. If u is an input (output) node, it is considered to have a single fictitious incoming (outgoing) edge which consists of only one flow path equal to the weight of u. The goal of F_ROUTE(u) is to partition the flow on each outgoing edge from u into flow paths, so that the total number of the generated flow paths on all its outgoing edges is not more than $m_u + n_u$, where n_u is the the number of outgoing edges from u.

F_ROUTE(u) maps flow paths form the incoming edges of u (actually corresponding to flow paths) to u to the outgoing edges from u in a conservative manner which preserves the abovementioned upper bound on the total number of formed flow paths on the outgoing edges from u. Let $x_1, x_2, ..., x_{u_m}$ be the (fictitious) head nodes of the u_m incoming edges (flow paths) to u and $y_1, y_2, ..., y_{u_n}$ be the tail nodes of the u_n outgoing edges (actual edges) of u. The ordering in each set of these nodes is arbitrary, but fixed. Let $f(e)$ be the original flow on an edge e, $a(x_i, u)$ be the current amount of flow assigned from (x_i, u) to some outgoing edge(s) of u, and $b(u, y_j)$ be the current amount of flow assigned to (u, y_j) from some incoming edge(s) of u. Procedure F_ROUTE(u) works as follows:

PROCEDURE F_ROUTE(u)
1. Initialize $i := 1$, $j := 1$;
2. IF $i \leq m_u$ THEN pivot := 'in'; $\varepsilon := (x_i, u)$;
3. ELSE IF $j \leq n_u$ THEN pivot := 'out'; $\varepsilon := (u, x_j)$;
4. ELSE Terminate;
5. IF pivot = 'in' THEN
6. $\quad r := \max(f(\varepsilon), f(u, y_j))$;
7. $\quad a(\varepsilon) := a(\varepsilon) + r$; $b(u, y_j) := b(u, y_j) + r$;
8. $\quad$ Generate flow path $(\varepsilon, (u, y_j))$ with flow r;
9. $\quad$ IF $f(\varepsilon) > a(\varepsilon)$ THEN $j := j + 1$; GOTO 5;
10. $\quad$ ELSE
11. $\qquad$ IF $f(u, y_j) > b(u, y_j)$ THEN $i := i + 1$;

¿ $\quad$ pivot := 'out'; $\varepsilon := (u, x_j)$; GOTO 5;
12. $\qquad$ ELSE $i := i + 1$; $j := j + 1$; GOTO 2;
13. ELSE
14. $\quad r := \max(f(\varepsilon), f(x_i, u))$;
15. $\quad b(\varepsilon) := b(\varepsilon) + r$; $a(x_i, u) := a(x_i, u) + r$;
16. $\quad$ Generate flow path $((x_i, u), \varepsilon)$ with flow r;
17. $\quad$ IF $f(\varepsilon) > b(\varepsilon)$ THEN $i := i + 1$; GOTO 5;
18. $\quad$ ELSE
19. $\qquad$ IF $f(x_i, u) > a(x_i, u)$ THEN $j := j + 1$;
$\qquad\quad$ pivot := 'in'; $\varepsilon := (x_i, u)$; GOTO 5;
20. $\qquad$ ELSE $i := i + 1$; $j := j + 1$; GOTO 2;
21. END F_ROUTE

Procedure F_ROUTE() works around a "pivot" edge denoted by ε. Initially the pivot edge is the first incoming or outgoing edge (in the given order). The maximum amount of flow that can be assigned to the (next in order) outgoing edge (u, x_j) from the pivot edge is denoted by r (Line 6). If not all the flow on the pivot edge can be assigned to (u, x_j), then the next outgoing edge (j+1) is considered (Line 9) since (u, x_j) is "flooded" in this case. We also observe at this point that edge (u, x_{j+1}) is bound to exist, since the original flow is a valid flow. Otherwise, if all the flow on the pivot edge can be assigned to (u, x_j), then a check is done to see whether edge (u, x_j) has been flooded. If it is not, it is this that becomes the pivot edge and the next in order incoming edge (i+1) is considered (Line 11). Otherwise, both the next incoming and outgoing edges are considered (Line 12) from which a new pivot element will be chosen (Line 2). (In Lines 2, 3, if index $i > m_u$ or index $j > n_u$, they are considered for the remaining to be equal to m_u or n_u, respectively.) Symmetric action is taken in case the pivot element is an outgoing edge (Lines 13–20).

Figure 1 illustrates F_ROUTE(u) and shows which flow path is generated in each iteration. The number of flow paths that pass through each edge is equal to the number of integers that label the edge. The pivot edge before each iteration (together with its latest $a()$ or $b()$ value) is indicated by *. We note again that each incoming edge is not an actual edge, but represents a previously generated single flow path. Each integer value corresponds to the amount of flow on the flow path.

When F_ROUTE(u) terminates, all the flow paths on each (actual) outgoing edge (u, y_j) are considered as different parallel incoming edges to node y_j. These will be treated as different incoming edges to y_j when the call of F_ROUTE(y_j) by F_PATHS() occurs during the topological traversal of the graph. We have shown that F_ROUTE(u) guarantees that the number of flow paths that pass through node u is no more than $m_u + n_u$, and its time complexity is $O(m_u + n_u)$. Furthermore, the total number of flow paths generated by F_PATHS() is no more than $|E|$, the number of the edges of the given transitive graph $G = (V, E)$, and its time complexity is $O(|E|)$.

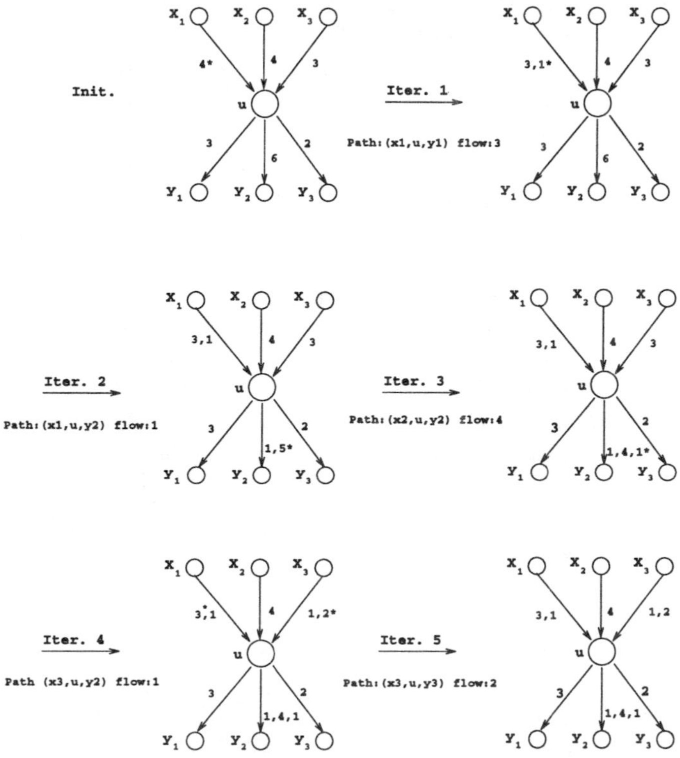

Fig. 1: An application of F_ROUTE() on a node u. At the end of each iteration, the flow path generated and the pivot edge for the next iteration (marked with *) are shown.

F_PATHS() identifies a set of flow paths { P_1, P_2, ..., P_k}, $k \leq e$, the number of edges in the transitive graph. *The goal is now to select a representative node from each of these paths (some paths may share the same representative) such that no representative points to any other and the sum of the weights of the distinct representatives equals the amount of the minimum flow. Under these conditions the set of the selected representatives constitutes a valid independent set of maximum weight.*

In the following we show how the latter can be done in $O(e)$ time. Let $f(P_i)$ denote the amount of flow delivered by selected path P_i. Consider a node u and let SP(u) be the subset of paths from $\{P_1, P_2, ..., P_k\}$ that pass through u. Node u can serve as a representative of all paths in SP(u) only when $w(u) = \sum_{P_x \in \mathrm{SP}(u)} f(P_x)$. Based therefore on the set of paths $\{P_1, P_2, ..., P_k\}$ returned by F_PATHS and the above, we apply the algorithm Weighted_MIS below that returns the Weighted Maximum Independent Set on a Transitive graph.

PROCEDURE Weighted_MIS($\mathcal{G}$)
1. Apply the minimum–flow algorithm and F_PATHS() to find $\{P_1, ..., P_k\}$, $k \leq e$, clique paths.
2. FOR each path P_i DO
3. Mark each node for which $w(u) = \sum_{P_x \in \mathrm{SP}(u)} f(P_x)$.
4. Set m_i to the marked node of P_i closest to its end.
5. MIS $\leftarrow \{m_i : 1 \leq i \leq k\}$.
6. WHILE some node in MIS points to another in MIS DO
7. FOR each i, $1 \leq i \leq k$, DO
8. FOR each node m_j that m_i points to DO
9. set m_j to the closest previous marked node on P_j.
10 ENDFOR
11. ENDFOR
12. ENDWHILE
13. Output MIS as a maximum independent set.
14. END Weighted_MIS

We have shown the following theorem.

Theorem 3.1 *Weighted_MIS() finds a maximum weighted independent set on a transitive graph in $O(n \cdot e \cdot \log(n^2/e))$ time. The time complexity is determined by the time required to solve the minimum flow in the first step.*

4 Experimental results

We implemented the proposed algorithm in C and on a Sun SPARC 5 workstation. Subsequently, we generated two path delay fault coverage estimation tools that use the algorithm of Section 3.

Table 1 below lists the fault coverage estimation obtained by the first of the two proposed delay fault coverage proposed schemes of Section 2, which we call WIS (Weighted Independent Set). We compare its performance to the scheme in [13], denoted by PR, and the one in [9], denoted by KT. Comparisons were made on the ISCAS'85 combinational circuits. We use the same test matrices that were used in [9]. We have computed functionally sensitizable path delay faults [10].

The experiments show that the performance of WIS is consistently better than the previous approaches. The time responses were similar to those in [9]. All circuits besides the last three executed in less than one hour. The worst execution times where observed for c6288 (approximately 20 hours) but the delays were due to memory paging problems. (We used large arrays for storing the LDGs on which the min flow algorithm was executed.) Improvements over the approaches in [9, 13] were also obtained by the alternative application of the maximum weighted independent set in path delay fault estimation described in Section 2.

Circuit	$\|S\|$	KT	PR	WIS
c432	100	595	515	642
c432	1000	2097	849	2111
c499	100	133	113	141
c499	1000	563	392	612
c880	100	735	662	862
c880	1000	1733	966	1733
c1355	100	128	128	142
c1908	100	308	271	353
c2670	50	831	805	901
c2670	100	1105	895	1105
c3540	50	1638	1365	1805
c5315	50	1915	1602	2221
c6288	50	1426	1349	1600
c7552	50	1996	1759	2033

Table 1 Average fault coverage on functionally sensitizable paths for 20 random test sets of size $|S|$

5 Conclusions

We presented a polynomial time algorithm for the maximum weighted independent set problem on transitive graphs. Applications are shown in the contexts of path delay fault testing, scheduling in high-level synthesis, and channel routing in physical design automation. The algorithm improves existing nonenumerative path delay fault estimation approaches and we suspect that it will also be successfully applied in the remaining contexts. We also suspect that it may apply to other areas in VLSI Design and Test.

References

[1] M. Abramovici, M. A. Breuer, A. D. Friedman, *Digital Systems Testing and Testable Design*, Computer Science Press, New York, 1990.

[2] F. Gavril, "Algorithms for maximum k-coloring and minimum k-covering of transitive graphs," *Networks*, vol. 17, pp. 465–470, 1987.

[3] M. R. Garey, D. S. Johnson, *Computers and Intractability – A Guide to The Theory of NP-Completeness*, W. H. Freeman and Co., New York, 1979.

[4] M.C. Golumbic, *Algorithmic Graph Theory and Perfect Graphs*, Academic Press, 1980.

[5] A.V. Goldberg, R.E. Tarjan, "A new approach to the maximum flow problem," *Proc. 18th Symposium on Theory of Computing*, 1986, pp. 136–146.

[6] M.L. Grotschel, L. Lovasz, A. Schrijver, "Polynomial algorithms for perfect graphs," *Ann. Discrete Math.*, v. 21, pp. 325–357, 1985.

[7] K. Heragu, M.L. Bushnell, V.D. Agrawal, "An efficient path delay fault coverage estimator," *Proc. DAC, pp. 516–521, June 1994.*

[8] K. Heragu, J.H. Patel, V.D. Agrawal, "Improving accuracy in path delay fault coverage estimation," *Proc. 9th International Conference on VLSI Design*, pp. 422–425, Jan. 1996.

[9] D. Kagaris, S. Tragoudas, D. Karayiannis, "Improved Nonenumerative Path Delay Fault Coverage Estimation," *IEEE Transactions on CAD/ICAS*, vol. 16, no. 3, pp.309–315.

[10] A. Krstic, K.-T. Cheng, "Generation of High Quality Tests for Functional Sensitizable Paths," *Proc. IEEE VLSI Test Symposium*, 1995, pp. 374–379.

[11] L. Lovasz, "Normal hypergraphs and the perfect graph conjecture," *Discrete Math.*, vol. 2, pp. 253–267, 1972.

[12] G. De Micheli, *Synthesis and Optimization of Digital Circuits*, McGraw-Hill Inc., 1994.

[13] I. Pomeranz, S.M. Reddy, "An Efficient Nonenumerative Method to Estimate the Path Delay Fault Coverage in Combinational Circuits," *IEEE Transactions on CAD/ICAS*, vol. 13, no. 2, pp. 240–250, 1994.

[14] N.A. Sherwani, *Algorithms for VLSI physical design automation*, Kluwer Academic Publishers, 1993.

SESSION 12A

EMBEDDED TUTORIAL: VERIFYING HARDWARE IN ITS SOFTWARE CONTEXT

Moderator:

Ellen M. Sentovich, Cadence Berkeley Labs., Berkeley, CA

Verifying Hardware in its Software Context

R. Kurshan V. Levin M. Minea D. Peled H. Yenigün

Bell Laboratories
Lucent Technologies
Murray Hill, NJ 07974

Abstract

We describe a method for verifying hardware whose correct behavior depends upon its software interface. It is presumed that the hardware is presented as a synchronous RTL model whereas the software is presented as an asynchronous abstraction. Our methodology incorporates partial order reduction on the software side, and localization reduction, to deal with the computational complexity of the verification. The partial order reduction is implemented as a constraint on the transition relation of a synchronous transformation of the software model. The reduced transformed model then may be verified using a verification algorithm whose scope is purely synchronous models, without modification. Thus, independent of the interface verification problem, this gives a general method for combining partial order reduction with symbolic model-checking.

1 Introduction

One facet of hardware/software co-design is dealing with verification at the hardware/software interface. In the typical case that the hardware and software are designed separately, a common problem is that the expectations of each design group do not match the implementation of the other. This can lead to logical failures and costly delays in production. The familiar presumption that the hardware and the software each can be designed successfully with only a sketchy understanding of the other side may be unwarranted. Each design team often needs a precise description of its "environment" as defined by the other design. If formal models of the hardware design and the software design are used in support of this need, the problem of interface mismatch is moved to a problem of how to develop a design in the context of a formal environment description.

Conceptually, formal verification could offer a solution to this new problem. Direct application of model-checking in this context is mostly infeasible, however, since each side individually is often near the limit of feasible verification. Moreover, there is an intrinsic difficulty in applying finite-state verification to software, which often is viewed as an infinite-state system on account of its dependence on memory.

We describe a methodology which seeks to overcome these obstacles. An environment description need not capture the entire design, but should be precise for those functions on which the other side depends for its correct operation. For the software model, we use an asynchronous abstraction which captures the level at which the software and hardware interact. In our case, this software model is written in the international standard protocol specification language SDL [12]. The SDL model can be formally refined into an implementation whose consistency with the SDL model can be verified. The hardware is expressed in a synthesizable subset of VHDL or Verilog. Both the software and hardware models are compiled together into S/R, the input language of the verification tool COSPAN [4]. The two models coordinate through interfaces each of which looks like an SDL process to the software side, and an HDL module to the hardware side.

To deal with the computational complexity of the interface verification, a partial order reduction [11] is applied to the software model. The combined hardware/software model is localized [7] relative to each respective property to be checked. In order to have the partial order reduction of the asynchronous software model be compatible with the synchronous hardware model, we transform the asynchronous model to an equivalent synchronous model [9] and implement the partial order reduction in terms of constraints defined by automata. These automata are defined at compile time. The synchronous transformation uses nondeterminism to simulate asynchrony and the constraints remove transitions which are redundant with respect to the partial order reduction. Thus, an implicit form of the entire partial order reduction is cre-

1092-3152/97 $10.00

ated statically by the compiler, without any need to modify the COSPAN verification tool. The reduced model is checked by COSPAN in the same manner as any synchronous model. Independent of the interface verification problem, this gives a general method for combining partial order reduction with symbolic model-checking.

1.1 Previous Work

While hardware/software co-design has been treated extensively in terms of methodology, little has been published on formal co-verification. The co-verification problem is treated mainly as a testing problem, and a number of commercial tools have appeared for testing software in the context of hardware, and vice versa.

Partial order reduction and symbolic state space search have been applied widely to cope with the intrinsic computational complexity of model-checking. Typically, these techniques are applied separately – only one or the other – since they appear to be incompatible. Partial order reduction algorithms in the literature [3, 6, 11, 13] are based intrinsically upon explicit state enumeration in the context of a depth-first search. The partial order reduction is derived dynamically in the course of enumerating the states. Symbolic verification deals only with sets of states defined by respective Boolean functions. State reachability is expressed in terms of the convergence of a monotone state set operator which implements a breadth-first search of the state space. What makes partial order reduction problematic in this context has to do with guaranteeing that certain transitions which may be deferred in the course of the state space search (thus giving rise to the desired reduction), are not deferred indefinitely (resulting in an incomplete search). The usual way this is implemented in the context of explicit-state enumeration, is to explore all such deferred transitions in the course of closing any cycle during a depth-first search.

Nonetheless, there is no intrinsic reason that partial order reduction and symbolic verification cannot be combined. Perhaps the first published proposal for such a combination is [1]. In that paper, the cycle-closing condition is replaced by some additional steps in the course of the symbolic breadth-first search, requiring the normal model-checking algorithm to be altered.

In contrast, the algorithm presented here constructs an automaton which implements the partial order reduction implicitly. The reduction is completely isolated from the model-checking algorithm and it therefore does not depend on a specific search technique.

2 Hardware/Software Co-verification

One could envision a design methodology which starts from an abstract behavioral design model. This model may not distinguish hardware from software. If it does, it need not be reflected syntactically and need not be evident architecturally either, appearing perhaps only as an annotation. Such a unified abstract behavioral model could be formally verified and then formally refined (in a verifiable manner) to separate hardware and software components. The verification of the refinement would guarantee that the properties verified in the abstract design model are inherited by the coordinated behavior of the hardware and software implementation models [7], relieving the need to further check these properties in the refinement.

An advantage of this approach is that functional verification which today is conducted at the synthesizable (RTL) level, instead could be conducted at an abstract behavioral level, where the design model is simpler. This not only aids the verification process, but also simplifies and accelerates the functional debugging itself, as there are fewer constructs that need to be altered to fix a design error. At this earlier stage of design development, the verification can be used to support architectural design evolution by spotting logical weaknesses in a preliminary architecture. Moreover, supporting debugging at an earlier stage in the design cycle is a well-known accelerant of the entire design development. In contrast, conventional design methodologies normally support testing and functional debugging only at a much later stage, once the synthesizable model is complete. Thus, the successive refinements design development methodology both accelerates the design process and produces more reliable designs.

Although the benefits of design though formal stepwise refinement have been corroborated in pilot projects and reported for some time [5], there has been no evident surge in the CAD industry to embrace this apparently promising methodology. Reasons for this may lie with the significant methodological changes it would entail and perhaps even more, with a lack of commercial technology available to support this methodology. Nonetheless, now that formal verification is a commercial reality [8], users are beginning to awaken to the benefits of abstraction and refinement. In the case of the Lucent Technologies verification tool FormalCheck^{TM}, this is the single most sought-after advanced enhancement requested by users.

There are a number of ways such a feature could be introduced and supported. One good way is as a solution to a well-known important problem such as dealing with design complexity.

In this article, we suppose that the technology for abstraction and refinement already has been introduced into a verification tool such as FormalCheck, and we explore how this technology could be extended to solve the titled problem. At some future further in the distance, we may imagine a unified representation of hardware and software. Pragmatically, we believe such a unified representation will need to be approached incrementally, and only after proving the over-all methodology using contemporary frameworks. Thus, we have developed a system for co-verification based on existing programming environments developed for VHDL, Verilog and SDL as we will describe presently. However, the methodology described here is not strongly tied to a particular representation of hardware or software, except with regard to the granularity of time as a mediating design factor. For hardware, it is assumed that the design is (clock) cycle dependent and thus we use a synchronous model of coordination. By contrast, software is presumed to operate under synchronization conditions guaranteed by its host, and thus coordination among software design components is modelled as asynchronous, and in fact as interleaving. (There may be occasion to model asynchronous hardware. For this, interleaving semantics may not be an appropriate model, if the possibility of two simultaneous asynchronous events needs to be considered.)

At least for the present, since hardware and software are viewed at different levels of abstraction and embrace conceptually different aspects of a design, it is not unnatural to represent them with different languages tailored to their respective applications. The choice of a hardware description language within this context is strongly dictated by current use: it must be VHDL or Verilog. While these languages are closer in their use to low-level programming languages than to formal description techniques, the strong semantics which adheres to them from synthesis, as well as the perceived support for more structural constructs, make them suitable formal description languages. Our platform supports both. Unlike with hardware, there is no widely accepted formal description language for software. As the size of the software projects makes their management increasingly difficult, the value of using formal languages and formal verification in the software development has been better understood. Some companies have designed their own formal languages and tools, and other languages have been promoted by international standardization. The Specification and Description Language (SDL), a standard language of ITU-T (formerly CCITT), is one of the most promising of these languages. It is regularly updated by ITU-T and has already found some applications in software projects. Likewise, we have focused on the use of SDL for software description, in order to advance software programming to a more abstract level, as it has been achieved to a certain extent with hardware level through the use of the hardware description languages VHDL and Verilog. Once it has been verified, an SDL description of a system can serve as a formal documentation and be used in the development phase. With the support of formal verification, a refinement may be checked against an abstract SDL model, and then synthesized automatically by generated C code as is supported through COSPAN.

Our approach takes advantage of an existing compiler [2] from SDL to S/R (the native language of COSPAN), which has been implemented in order to verify software systems written in SDL using COSPAN. A modified version of this compiler, together with COSPAN, form the tool basis for our co-verification method. We assume that the hardware part of the co-design is described either in VHDL or Verilog, for which a translator to S/R is supported by the commercial tool FormalCheck, and the software part is described in SDL. The interface between hardware and software is also described in SDL, but with a slight modification in semantics, described in [10]. In essence, it allows an interface process to read and write (combinational) signals from the hardware part. The coordination of an interface process with software processes and with other interface processes is handled completely by the SDL communication mechanism, namely the signal exchange through buffers. Therefore an interface process looks like another software process from the view point of the software part. An interface process interacts with the hardware using shared variables called *interface variables* in the synchronous fashion of the hardware. Therefore, it appears like another hardware module to the hardware part of the system. The hardware, software and the interface parts of a co-design system are translated into S/R. This enables us to treat the entire co-design system having different parts with different natures, as a single synchronous system.

We distinguish between two types of global transitions in a co-design system. The transition of a single SDL process is called a *software transition*. The other kind of global transition is a *hardware transition*. Since hardware has a synchronous nature, a hardware transition corresponds to simultaneous transitions of all the hardware modules in a synchronous hardware component. An interface process can have both kinds of transitions. A transition of an interface process in which an interface variable is referenced counts as a hardware transition. Otherwise, it counts as a software transition. Since different abstraction levels can be used for hardware and software, we do not make an assumption about the relative speeds of the software and hardware.

Conventional verification of purely hardware or purely software systems already faces great problems in dealing with complexity. In order to be able to deal with the far greater complexity when both a hardware and a software system are considered together, we use two different approaches to co-verification, assuming that the properties to be verified refer mainly either to the hardware part or to the software part.

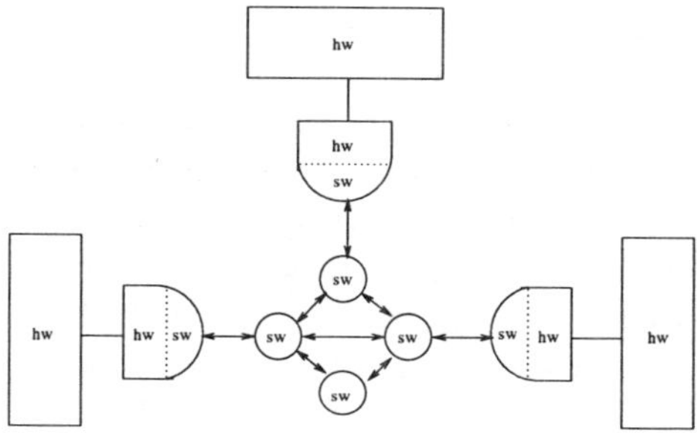

Figure 1: Software-centric view

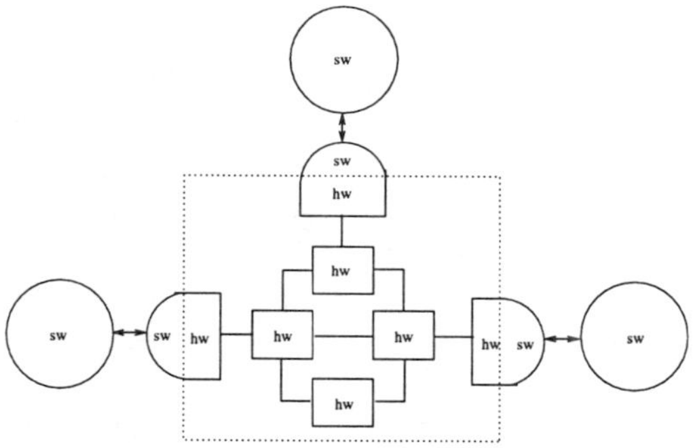

Figure 2: Hardware-centric view

2.1 Software-Centric Verification

To verify software properties of a co-design, we use a software-centric approach. While verifying the software part may not at first appear to be a fundamental part of the hardware verification, in fact it is. The reason is that it is not useful to verify the hardware in the context of a faulty software model. The software model must also be debugged. Of course the same argument applies to verifying the software model in the context of a buggy hardware model. Thus, a few software-hardware-software iterations of verification centricity may be necessary before the co-design stabilizes, and both sides verify.

In the software-centric view of a co-design system, each interface process encapsulates a set of hardware modules, which may be common for two or more interface processes. In other words, several interface processes may coordinate with one hardware subsystem which forms their shared resource.

Figure 1 illustrates the structure of the software-centric view of a system. The software system represented by the circles form a pure SDL system, with all processes coordinating asynchronously. The interface processes together with the hardware components form an environment for this SDL system. Therefore, the concept of environment, which is considered to be completely non-deterministic in [12], becomes a structured world which enforces constraints on the behavior of the SDL system. Since the aim of the software-centric approach is to verify software properties, the hardware part typically can be reduced automatically to a high level of abstraction through localization reduction (see below). The role of the hardware part is to adequately constrain the software part, in support of its verification.

In order to further cope with the complexity of the software-centric verification, we incorporate partial order reduction to reduce complexity of the SDL model. Unlike other applications of this reduction technique which implement the reduction dynamically in the course of the state reachability, we needed an algorithm which would be compatible with the synchronous nature of the companion hardware parts. Moreover, on account of the large state space contributed by the hardware, we needed to be able to apply the reachability analysis symbolically. These needs led us to search for a way to implement the partial order reduction statically (during compile time) in a fashion that would be compatible with symbolic search. We started with the idea that a partial order reduction can be viewed as a constraint on the transition relation of the unreduced system, and that such a constraint could be represented synchronously as an automaton, compatible with COSPAN's underlying automata-theoretic basis. Furthermore, COSPAN efficiently implements safety constraints in a fashion that prevents the exploration of unaccepted traces. Although we originally envisioned that we would need to augment COSPAN's core algorithms to implement the cycle-closing condition discussed above, it clearly is of great advantage that we have discovered a way to avoid this. Instead, the cycle-closing condition is implemented into the statically defined constraint automaton as well. No change to COSPAN was necessary – the partial order reduction is encoded completely into the input program by the SDL compiler.

The SDL model is transformed to an equivalent synchronous model using nondeterminism to simulate asynchrony, as described in [9]. The statically derived automaton which implements the partial order reduction is then composed with this synchronous transformation of the SDL model, and the (unreduced) synchronous hardware model. Localization reduction [7] is then applied to this combined synchronous model, in order to reduce it relative to the property being checked. When the property is implemented mainly through control structures in the SDL model, it can be anticipated that much of the hardware will be abstracted by this automatic procedure.

2.2 Hardware-Centric Verification

Hardware-centric verification is used to check properties relating mainly to the hardware side of the co-design. Figure 2 shows an example of a a hardware-centric view of a co-design system. The software modules in Figure 2 correspond to distinct SDL systems which can coordinate only through the hardware. Each SDL system has only one interface process. Unlike the dual software-centric view, in the hardware-centric view, only hardware modules which are part of the same subsystem are considered at any one time. Thus, within the dashed box of Figure 2, all the modules coordinate synchronously. If there are other hardware components in the greater system, they must be treated in a separate hardware-centric model. The interface processes together with the pure SDL systems form an environment for the hardware part and establish constraints on the primary inputs of the hardware.

Just as with the software-centric system, partial order reduction followed by localization reduct may be applied. However, if little of the software side gets entailed in the hardware-centric verification, localization reduction may suffice, and be faster than running both algorithms in succession.

3 Partial Order Reduction

There is an extensive literature on partial order reduction techniques (see, for example, [3, 11, 13]). Here, we use the ample set method of Peled [11]. Partial order reduction in general exploits the observation that in models of coordination with the semantics of interleaved events, concurrent events are modelled by executing the events in all possible orders. The reduction exploits the fact that properties for such systems cannot distinguish among the different orders, producing a representation of the checked system which contains only a subset of the states and transitions of the original system. This representation is a quotient of the unreduced model, being equivalent to the unreduced model with respect to the property. The subset of the behaviors in the quotient, which are the paths in a *reduced state graph*, need only preserve the checked property. Namely, when the model-checking algorithm is applied to the reduced state graph, it would result in a positive answer when the property holds, and a counter example when it does not hold.

3.1 The Ample Sets Method

For each state s of the modelled system, there is a set of (atomic) transitions that can be executed next, or are *enabled*. These will be denoted by $enabled(s)$. The simple model-checking algorithm constructs the state graph of the program by performing a search, typically, a depth or breadth first search. The search starts with an initial state and progresses to explore its immediate successors, generated by applying the enabled transitions, then their successors, and so on. Different search strategies vary from each other by the order in which the successors are searched.

From a given state s, the partial order reduction explores only a subset of the enabled transitions: the set $ample(s)$. Such an *ample set* is chosen to enforce some conditions that guarantee the preservation of the checked property in the resulting quotient.

We assume that every state is labeled by some subset of the atomic propositions that appear in the formulation of the checked property. We denote by $L(s)$ the set of propositions that hold in s. Before presenting the conditions we use for choosing $ample(s)$, we define two more concepts. A pair of transitions is said to be *independent*, if executing one and then the other starting at any state s results in the same subsequent state s', regardless of the order of execution. We require moreover that if one of them is enabled, then after executing the other, the first remains enabled. The second concept is that of *invisible transitions*. A transition is invisible if when executed, it does not change the state labeling. That is, for each pair of states s and s', if executing the transition from s results in s', then $L(s) = L(s')$.

We now give sufficient conditions on the sets $ample(s)$ for the resulting partial order reduction to preserve the given property. The explanation of these conditions and a proof that they guarantee a reduced state graph that preserves the given property appears in [11]. A state s is said to be *fully expanded* when $ample(s) = enabled(s)$, *i.e.*, all the transitions are selected.

C0 [Non-emptiness condition] *ample*(s) is empty if and only if *enabled*(s) is empty.

C1 [Ample decomposition] For every behavior of the system, starting from the state s, a transition that is dependent on some transition in *ample*(s) never appears (in the unreduced model) before a transition from *ample*(s).

C2 [Non-visibility condition] If s is not fully expanded then none of the transitions in it is visible.

C3 [Cycle closing condition] At least one state along each cycle of the reduced state graph is fully expanded.[1]

The first model-checking system to implement these conditions was SPIN [6]. In order to guarantee these conditions, the search mechanism of SPIN was changed and specialized for the reduction. Conditions **C0** and **C2** are trivial to check. **C0** is a local syntactic check and **C2** is guaranteed through scoping rules imposed syntactically on the design. Condition **C1** was translated into a set of checks on the transitions enabled at the current state s. For example, if some process can execute from its current program counter only local transitions that do not involve global variables or exchanging messages, then its set of transitions are guaranteed to satisfy Condition **C1**. Condition **C3** was handled by checking whether a selected ample set closed a cycle (in depth-first search this happens when a state that is already on the search stack is reached). If so, the currently selected ample set was discarded in favor of an alternative selection.

In translating SDL to COSPAN, we wanted to use a partial order reduction. As already discussed, several goals dictated a solution different than the one used in [6]. Most particularly, in order to be able to use a symbolic state space search, we wanted a reduction algorithm which was not dependent on the use of depth-first search. The reduction described next has the added benefit that it can be used with any model-checking algorithm for synchronous models, without any modification of the model-checking algorithm whatsoever. Moreover, this new partial order reduction algorithm is very general, being insensitive to the mode of state space search employed.

[1] There are other stronger and weaker conditions that can be used instead of Condition **C3**. This particular version fits well with our framework.

3.2 A Generic Partial Order Reduction

The main obstacle to implementing the reduction in the context of a breadth-first search is that we need to avoid the possibility of a cycle which does not contain any state which is fully expanded. At first sight, Condition **C3** suggests a substantial change to the model-checking algorithm would be required to achieve this in the context of a breadth-first search (*cf.* [1]). We show how this may be accomplished in fact very simply and generally, without modification to the model-checking algorithm. In principle, it should be capable of producing at least as good a reduction (measured in terms of reached states) as [6] or [1], although with symbolic analysis, the number of reached states is a poor complexity measure. Moreover, there are trade-offs between the size of the reduction and the cost of producing the reduction, which are hard to compare across algorithms, in general.

For our purposes we strengthen Condition **C3** as follows:

C3' There is a set of transitions T such that each cycle in the reduced state space includes at least one transition from T. If *ample*(s) includes a transition from T, then s is fully expanded.

We call the set of transitions T *sticky transitions*, since intuitively, they stick to all other enabled transitions.

An easy way to find such a set T to look at the static control flow graph of each process of the checked system. Any cycle in the global state space projects to a cycle (or possibly a self-loop) in each component process. By breaking each local cycle, we are guaranteed to break each global cycle. This suggests the following further strengthening, which guarantees the above Condition **C3'**:

C3" Each cycle in the static control flow of a process of the modelled system contains at least one sticky transition, and if *ample*(s) includes a sticky transition, then s is fully expanded.

Condition **C3"** can be satisfied by using a static analysis algorithm on the (small) component processes, to find a set of sticky transitions T, lifted to the global state space from each respective component process. While finding a minimal sticky set is NP hard, (it is the same as removing transitions - the sticky ones - until there are no cycles left in the static control flow graph), it is NP hard in the size of the local control flow graph (*i.e.*, each process) which is small, not the much bigger global state graph. Moreover, one need not find a minimal T. One way to find a set of sticky transitions in a local control graph is to choose all the back-edges in the course of a depth-first search, *i.e.*, an edge from the currently searched state to a state currently in the search stack. The resulting T is the lifting of each local back-edge. Since the local control graphs are small, they can be searched at compile time, at no perceptible cost. (Any syntactic transition is assumed to be an edge in the local control graph – while this heuristic could be foiled by a process with many unsatisfiable transitions, this is not commonly the case, and we envision a process as not only small, but as having a sparse set of transitions).

Note that priority is given to transitions that are not sticky. Sticky transitions may be deferred, although no cycle can be closed without having passed through at least one sticky transition. It is possible that a global cycle may include more than one fully expanded state, due to sticky transitions lifted from different processes. However, since sticky transitions have low priority, and the reduction algorithm tries to select the other transitions first, it may be worthwhile to defer several of them to a point where they all can be taken from the same state. This is possible because the expansion for sticky transitions may occur anywhere along a cycle.

3.3 The COSPAN Implementation

In practice, one may weaken **C3"**, as follows. A cycle in the reduced state graph cannot consist of only receiving messages, since all message queues would then become eventually empty, and some sends would be required to close the cycle. Thus, local control flow cycles with only message receives do not have to include a sticky transition; it must be part of another cycle projected from a cycle in the global state graph. (While that this is true also for sending messages, – the queues will eventually get filled – if the same relaxation is allowed at the same time to both sending and receiving messages, they can cancel the effect of one another and be part of a global state graph cycle.) This observation can be used to design an algorithm that is linear in the size of the control graphs of each process. After removing the receiving transitions from the control graph of a process, a linear time search can be performed on the remaining transitions to identify any back-edges and mark them as the sticky transitions.

There are many ways to further relax **C3"**. One is to involve the user to some extent in further marking sticky transitions. This would reduce the more arbitrary assignment which would result from choosing all back-edges as above. Another way is to perform the back-edge analysis after combining a few processes – only the cycles of the larger structure need be broken.

In order to achieve in COSPAN a partial order reduction that is independent of the search control, we exploit the selection mechanism of S/R. This mechanism consists of using *selection variables*. These variables are combinational, not part of the state, and thus do not incur any memory overhead. When deciding on the successor state, each process chooses non-deterministically among some possible values of its selection variables. The choice of any process can be dependent on the choice of the selections of the other processes (as long as this relationship is acyclic). In particular, we heuristically optimize the size of $ample(s)$ by selecting the process with $|ample(s)|$ as samll as possible, *i.e.*, with the fewest number of enabled transitions.

At each local state of a process, we calculate whether the currently enabled transitions satisfy Condition **C1**. If so, we say that the process is *ample* at this state. In the current version of our compiler, a process is considered to be ample at a state if it does not have an enabled sticky transition and all its enabled transitions either are receiving or internal transitions. If the process has only internal transitions (the transitions in which only the local variables are referred), then it is clear that the enabled transitions of the process satisfy **C1** since no other process can refer to those variables. Similarly, when the process has only receiving transitions, the enabled transitions of the process again satisfies **C1**. Although the send transition of another process can change the same message queue from which the receiving transition reads, their execution orders do not matter. The problem is that several processes may have enabled transitions that are potentially ample sets. Selecting all of these sets would be counter to our goal to minimize the selected transitions. We can use the selection mechanism to resolve this. When a process is ample, it can use global selection variables to inform the other processes about this fact. If several processes are ample at the same time, they choose one of them through a static (index number) priority. The other ample processes are informed via the selection variables that they are not the chosen candidate for providing an ample set, and do not contribute transitions to this set.

4 Summary and Conclusions

We have described a methodology for hardware/software co-verification which confronts the computational complexity issues directly. Our current implementation supports VHDL or Verilog for hardware and SDL for software. However, the methodology is general and could be applied to any finite-state modelling paradigm in which the hardware is represented synchronously and the software is represented in terms of interleaving semantics. The general approach to complexity reduction lies with a combination of partial order reduction and localization reduction. The partial order reduction is introduced as a constraint on a transformation of the software model, and as such supports symbolic model-checking without need to alter the model-checking algorithm. In particular, this gives a method for combining partial order reduction with symbolic search.

By introducing the methodology in terms of currently accepted paradigms, it may be easier to introduce this technology into the commercial CAD arena. If this turns out to show signs of success, one may wish to consider supporting a larger subset of SDL, other languages in place of SDL, and eventually, a unified formalism which embraces both hardware and software.

References

[1] R. Alur, R.K. Brayton, T.A. Henzinger, S. Qadeer, S.K. Rajamani, Partial order reduction in symbolic state space exploration, *Conference on Computer Aided Verification (CAV 97)*, LNCS **1254**, Springer-Verlag, (1997) pp 340 - 351.

[2] O. Başbuğoğlu, K. İnan, Compiling SDL into the finite state specification language COSPAN. *Proceedings of the Tenth International Symposium on Computer and Information Sciences(ISCIS X)*, Kuşadası, Turkey, 1995.

[3] P. Godefroid, P. Wolper, A Partial Approach to Model Checking, *6th Annual IEEE Symposium on Logic in Computer Science*, 1991, Amsterdam, pp 406–415.

[4] R. H. Hardin, Z. Har'El, R. P. Kurshan, COSPAN, *Conference on Computer Aided Verification (CAV 96)*, LNCS **1102**, Springer-Verlag, (1996) pp 423 - 427.

[5] Z. Har'El, R. P. Kurshan, Software for Analytical Development of Communication Protocols, AT&T Tech. J. **69** (1) (1990), pp 45 - 59.

[6] G.J. Holzmann, D. Peled, An Improvement in Formal Verification, *7th International Conference on Formal Description Techniques*, Berne, Switzerland, 1994, pp 177–194.

[7] R. P. Kurshan, *Computer-Aided Verification of Coordinating Processes: The Automata-Theoretic Approach*, Princeton Univ. Press, 1994.

[8] R. P. Kurshan, Formal Verification in a Commercial Setting, *Proc. 34th Design Automation Conf. (DAC'97)*, ACM, 1997, pp 258 - 262.

[9] R. P. Kurshan, M. Merritt, A. Orda, S. Sachs, Modelling Asynchrony with a Synchronous Model, *Conference on Computer Aided Verification (CAV 95)*, LNCS **939**, Springer-Verlag, (1995) pp 339 - 352.

[10] V. Levin, E. Bounimova, O. Başbuğoğlu and K. İnan, A Verifiable Software/Hardware Codesign Using SDL and COSPAN, *Proceedings of the COST 247 International Workshop on Applied Formal Methods In System Design*, Maribor, Slovenia, 1996, pp 6–16.

[11] D. Peled. Combining partial order reductions with on-the-fly model-checking. *Formal Methods in System Design* **8** (1996), pp 39–64.

[12] Functional Specification and Description Language (SDL), CCITT Blue Book, Recommendation Z.100, Geneva, 1992.

[13] A. Valmari, Stubborn sets for reduced state space generation, *10th International Conference on Application and Theory of Petri Nets*, Bonn, Germany, LNCS **483**, Springer-Verlag, (1989) pp 491–515.

SESSION 12B

EMBEDDED TUTORIAL: SIMULATION METHODS FOR RF INTEGRATED CIRCUITS

Moderator:

Ralph H.J.M. Otten, Delft University of Technology,

Delft, The Netherlands

Simulation Methods for RF Integrated Circuits

Ken Kundert

Cadence Design Systems, San Jose, California, USA

Abstract — **The principles employed in the development of modern RF simulators are introduced and the various techniques currently in use, or expected to be in use in the next few years, are surveyed. Frequency- and time-domain techniques are presented and contrasted, as are steady-state and envelope techniques and large- and small-signal techniques.**

I. RF Circuits

The increasing demand for low-cost mobile communication systems has greatly expanded the need for simulation algorithms that are both efficient and accurate when applied to RF communication circuits.

RF circuits have several unique characteristics that are barriers to the application of traditional circuit simulation techniques. Over the last decade, researchers have developed many special purpose algorithms that overcome these barriers to provide practical simulation for RF circuits, often by exploiting the very characteristic that represented the barrier to traditional methods.

Despite dramatic progress, the average design cycle of an RFIC is still twice the length of that for other ICs found in a communication system, such as a cellular phone. This represents a significant practical barrier to integration of the RF and baseband sections of a transceiver onto a single chip. Clearly, more progress is necessary.

This paper is a overview of RF simulation methods that seeks to provide an understanding of how the various methods address the RF simulation problem, and how they relate to each other.

It begins by describing the unique characteristics of RF circuits. The basic solution methods of transient analysis, harmonic balance, and shooting methods are presented and contrasted. Small-signal analysis versions of both harmonic balance and shooting methods are covered. Composite methods are next. These methods apply the base methods in layers to provide dramatic new capabilities. The composite methods are divided into two groups. The first is based on a multidimensional representation of time. The second is based on sampling the RF signal and finding its envelope. The paper concludes with comparisons of the methods.

Published in the *Proceedings of ICCAD'97*, November 9-13, 1997 in San Jose, California. Manuscript received August 11, 1997.

This work was supported by the Defense Advanced Research Projects Agency under the MAFET program.

K. Kundert can be reached via e-mail at kundert@cadence.com.

A. Narrowband Signals

RF circuits process narrowband signals in the form of modulated carriers. Modulated carriers are characterized as having a periodic high-frequency carrier signal and a low-frequency modulation signal that acts on either the amplitude, phase, or frequency of the carrier. For example, a typical cellular telephone transmission has a 10-30 kHz modulation bandwidth riding on a 1-2 GHz carrier. In general, the modulation is arbitrary, though it is common to use simple periodic or quasiperiodic modulations constructed from a small number of sinusoids for test signals.

The ratio between lowest frequency present in the modulation and the frequency of the carrier is a measure of the relative frequency resolution required of the simulation. General purpose circuit simulators, such as SPICE, use transient analysis to predict the nonlinear behavior of a circuit. Transient analysis is inefficient when it is necessary to resolve low modulation frequencies in the presence of a high carrier frequency because the high-frequency carrier forces a small time step while a low-frequency modulation forces a long simulation interval.

Passing a narrowband signal though a nonlinear circuit results in a broadband signal whose spectrum is relatively sparse, as shown in Figure 1. In general, this spectrum

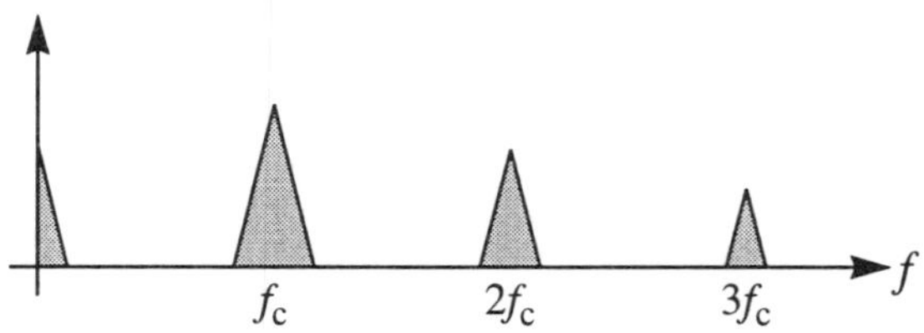

Fig. 1. Spectrum of a narrowband signal centered at a carrier frequency f_c after passing though a nonlinear circuit.

consists of clusters of frequencies near the harmonics of the carrier. These clusters take the form of a discrete set of

1092-3152/97 $10.00 © 1997 IEEE

frequencies if the modulation is periodic or quasiperiodic, and a continuous distribution of frequencies otherwise.

RF simulators exploit the "sparse" nature of this spectrum in various ways and with varying degrees of success. Steady-state methods are used when the spectrum is discrete, and transient methods are used when the spectrum is continuous.

B. Time-Varying Linear Nature of the RF Signal Path

Another important but less appreciated aspect of RF circuits is that they are generally designed to be as linear as possible from input to output to prevent distortion of the *modulation* or *information signal*. Some circuits, such as mixers, are designed to translate signals from one frequency to another. To do so, they are driven by an additional signal, the LO, a large periodic signal the frequency of which equals the amount of frequency translation desired. For best performance, mixers are designed to respond in a strongly nonlinear fashion to the LO. Thus, mixers behave both near-linearly (to the input) and strongly nonlinearly (to the LO).

Since *timing* or *synchronization signals*, such as the LO or the clock, are not part of the path of the information signal, they may be considered to be part of the circuit rather than an input to the circuit. This simple change of perspective allows the mixer to be treated as having a single input and a near-linear, though periodically time-varying, transfer function. As an example, consider a mixer made from an ideal multiplier and followed by a low-pass filter. A multiplier is nonlinear and has two inputs. Applying an LO signal of $\cos(\omega_{LO}t)$ consumes one input and results in a transfer function of

$$v_{out}(t) = \mathrm{LPF}\{\cos(\omega_{LO}t)v_{in}(t)\}, \qquad (1)$$

which is clearly time-varying and is easily shown to be linear with respect to v_{in}. If the input signal is

$$v_{in}(t) = m(t)\cos(\omega_c t), \qquad (2)$$

then

$$v_{out}(t) = \mathrm{LPF}\{m(t)\cos(\omega_c t)\cos(\omega_{LO}t)\} \qquad (3)$$

and

$$v_{out}(t) = m(t)\cos((\omega_c - \omega_{LO})t). \qquad (4)$$

This demonstrates that a linear periodically-varying transfer function implements frequency translation.

Often we can assume that the information signal is small enough to allow the use of a linear approximation of the circuit from its input to its output. Thus, a small-signal analysis can be performed, as long as it accounts for the periodically varying nature of the signal path, which is done by linearizing about the periodic operating point. This is the idea behind the small-signal analyses of Section III. Traditional simulators such as SPICE provide several small-signal analyses, such as the AC and noise analyses, that are considered essential when analyzing amplifiers and filters. However, they start by linearizing a nonlinear time-invariant circuit about a constant operating point, and so generate a linear time-invariant representation, which cannot exhibit frequency translation. By linearizing a nonlinear circuit about a periodically varying operating point, we extend small-signal analysis to circuits that must have a periodic timing signal present to operate properly, such as mixers, switched filters, samplers, and oscillators (for oscillators the timing signal is the desired output of the oscillator, while the information signal is generally an undesired signal, such as the noise). In doing so, a periodically varying linear representation results, which does exhibit frequency translation.

All of the traditional small-signal analyses can be extended in this manner, enabling a wide variety of applications (some of which are described in [36,42]). In particular, a noise analysis that accounts for noise folding and cyclostationary noise sources can be implemented [23,29], which fills a critically important need for RF circuits. When applied to oscillators, it also accounts for phase noise.

The linearity of the RF signal path can also be exploited to improve the convergence of the methods, as will be presented later.

C. Linear Passive Components

At the high frequencies present in RF circuits, the passive components, such as transmission lines, spiral inductors, packages (including bond wires) and substrates, often play a significant role in the behavior of the circuit. The nature of such components often make them difficult to include in the simulation.

Generally the passive components are linear and are modeled with phasors in the frequency-domain. This greatly simplifies the modeling of distributed components such as transmission lines, using either analytical expressions or tables of S-parameters. Large distributed structures, such as packages, spirals, and substrates, often interface with the rest of the circuit through a small number of ports. Thus, they can be easily replaced by a N-port macromodel that consists of the N^2 transfer functions. These transfer functions are found by reducing the large systems of equations that describe these structures, leaving only the equations that relate the signals at their ports. The relatively expensive reduction step is done once for each frequency as a preprocessing step. The resulting model is one that is efficient to evaluate if N is small. This is usually true for transmission lines and spirals, and less often true for packages and substrates.

Time-domain simulators are formulated to solve sets of first-order ordinary-differential equations (ODE). However, distributed components, such as transmission lines, are described with partial-differential equations (PDE) and so are problematic for time-domain simulators. Generally, the PDEs are converted to a set of ODE using some form of discretization [20]. Such approaches suffer from bandwidth limits. A more general approach is to compute the impulse response for a distributed component from a frequency domain description and use convolution to determine the response of the component in the circuit [11,31]. Evaluating lossy or dispersive transmission line models or tables of S-parameters with this approach is generally expensive and error-prone [33]. Packages, substrates and spirals can be modeled with large lumped networks, but such systems are too large to be efficiently incorporated into a time domain simulation, and so some form of reduction is necessary [6,25].

II. Numerical Solution of DAEs

If we ignore distributed components for the moment, the basic idea behind circuit simulation is to solve a nonlinear set of differential-algebraic equations (DAEs). We start by proposing the form of the solution as a linear combination of basis functions. A primary requirement of the basis functions is that we must know their derivatives. This allows us to analytically evaluate the derivatives in the DAE, thereby converting the DAE to a system of nonlinear algebraic equations that can be solved with Newton's method. Examples of possible basis functions are polynomials and sinusoids. The efficiency and accuracy of the simulation is dependent on the choice of basis functions. A careful choice of basis functions can result in tremendous performance advantages.

The choice of basis functions defines the solution space for the method. Note that this space may not contain good approximations to all of the solutions to the original DAE, in which case the method based on that choice of basis functions will not be able to find those solutions. This is used to advantage to avoid particular solutions that are either uninteresting or undesirable. For example, if the basis functions are chosen to be sinusoids, then only steady-state behavior is representable and so the initial transient behavior is avoided. Furthermore, the circuit can be simulated even if it is unstable.

The other way to avoid undesired solutions is to apply constraints on the solution in the form of initial or boundary conditions. In general, DAEs have an infinite continuum of solutions, and so constraints must be applied before they can be solved for a particular solution unless the solution space of the method contains only isolated solutions of the DAE.

A. *Transient Analysis*

Transient analysis breaks the time continuum into a series of adjacent short intervals and uses low-order polynomials as the basis functions over each interval (the time step) with the constraint that the solution must be continuous across interval boundaries (the time points). For example, consider the nonlinear DAE

$$f(v(t), t) = i(v(t)) + \frac{dq(v(t))}{dt} + u(t) = 0. \qquad (5)$$

While this equation is capable of modeling any lumped time-invariant nonlinear system, it is convenient to think it as being generated from nodal analysis, and so representing a statement of Kirchhoff's Current Law for a circuit containing nonlinear conductors, nonlinear capacitors, and current sources. In this case, $v(t) \in \mathcal{R}^N$ is the node voltage, $i(v(t)) \in \mathcal{R}^N$ represents the current out of the node from the conductors, $q(v(t))$ represents the charge out of the node from the capacitors, and $u(t)$ represents the current out of the node from the sources.

Consider trapezoidal rule. This is a second-order method that assumes that the solution and its first derivative are continuous at the interval boundaries. As such, they would be known at the start of the interval from the solution of the previous interval. With a small amount of algebra, one can show that if t_{s-1} is the initial point in the interval, t_s is the final point, and $h_s = t_s - t_{s-1}$, then for a second-order polynomial,

$$\frac{dq(v(t_s))}{dt} = \frac{2}{h_s}(q(v(t_s)) - q(v(t_{s-1}))) - \frac{dq(v(t_{s-1}))}{dt}. \qquad (6)$$

Substituting (6) into (5) converts it into a sequence of nonlinear algebraic systems of equations that can be solved with Newton's method to build up a pointwise approximation to the solution from some initial state.

Under certain mild conditions, it is possible to show that Newton's method will converge at every time point of a transient analysis. Newton's method is an iterative procedure that converges to the solution of a nonlinear system of equations, *if* the initial starting point is close to the final solution. As long as the solution trajectory for the DAE is continuous, which it must be except at a set of distinct points (usually small in number and often zero), and if the starting point used for the Newton iteration is an extrapolation from the values at previous time points, then one can always take a time step small enough for Newton's method to converge.

B. Harmonic Balance

Harmonic balance [15,21,26] uses harmonically related sinusoids for basis functions. As noted earlier, such basis functions cannot represent the initial transient, so harmonic balance directly computes the steady-state behavior of the circuit.

For simplicity, we will use phasors (complex exponentials) as basis functions rather than sines and cosines. We will also treat the time-domain signals as being complex valued and simply ignore the imaginary parts. While this is not as efficient as if we assumed real-valued signals, it results in a simpler presentation. For more efficient implementations, see [15,18,27].

With phasors as basis functions, harmonic balance has a natural ability to incorporate the frequency-domain descriptions of distributed components. Thus, we formulate a new test problem that is similar to (5), except that the signals are complex valued and another term is added to model distributed components. In addition, we assume that the circuit is driven (i.e. that $u(t)$ is not constant).

$$i(v(t)) + \frac{dq(v(t))}{dt} + \int_{-\infty}^{t} y(t-\tau)v(\tau)d\tau + u(t) = 0 \quad (7)$$

or

$$f(v,t) = 0, \quad (8)$$

where $v(t)$, $u(t)$, $y(t)$, $i(v(t))$, $q(v(t))$, and $f(v,t) \in C^N$, $v(t)$ and $u(t)$ are assumed to be T-periodic, $y(t)$ is the impulse response of the linear components, while i and q now represent only the nonlinear components.

Harmonic balance assumes that both v and f of (8) are formulated as Fourier series,

$$x(t) = \sum_{k=-\infty}^{\infty} X(k)e^{j\omega_k t}, \quad (9)$$

where $\omega_k = k\lambda$ and $\lambda = 2\pi/T$ is the fundamental frequency. Now (8) is rewritten as

$$\sum_{k=-\infty}^{\infty} F(V,k)e^{j\omega_k t} = 0, \quad (10)$$

where

$$F(V,k) = j\omega_k Q(V,k) + I(V,k) + Y(k)V(k) + U(k) \quad (11)$$

Since $e^{j\omega_{k_1}}$ and $e^{j\omega_{k_2}}$ are linearly independent if $k_1 \neq k_2$, $F(V, k) = 0$ for each k individually. In vector form,

$$F(V) = I(V) + \Omega Q(V) + YV + U = 0, \quad (12)$$

where $F(V)$, $I(V)$, $Q(V)$, V, $U \in C^{(2K+1)N}$ are vectors of vectors. Each is composed of N vectors that represent the spectrum at each node. Ω, Y are block matrices. Ω is block diagonal and

$$\Omega_{nn} = \operatorname{diag}\{-j\omega_K, \ldots, 0, \ldots, j\omega_K\} \quad (13)$$

is the frequency-domain differentiation operator and $j = \sqrt{-1}$. Y_{mn} is the Laplace transform of y_{mn} evaluated at $j\omega_k$ for each k. It is diagonal because the components modeled by y are time-invariant.

While it is possible to model some types of nonlinearities directly in the frequency domain [34], this is not practical or desirable in all cases. Instead, a procedure is employed where V is first converted into the time domain at evenly spaced sample points using the Inverse Discrete Fourier Transform (IDFT),

$$x(s) = \frac{1}{K}\sum_{k=-K}^{K} X(k)e^{j2\pi ks/S}. \quad (14)$$

where $s = 0, 1, \ldots, S-1$ and $S \geq S_{\min} = 2K+1$. While S may be set equal to $S_{\min}$, typically it is chosen in the range $2S_{\min} < S < 10S_{\min}$ to reduce aliasing. For each time point, both $i(v(s))$ and $q(v(s))$ are evaluated, and the result converted back into the frequency domain using the forward Discrete Fourier Transform (DFT),

$$X(k) = \sum_{s=0}^{S-1} x(s)e^{-j2\pi ks/S}. \quad (15)$$

Both the DFT and the IDFT can be written a matrix operations [15]:

$$X = \mathcal{F}x, \quad (16)$$

$$x = \mathcal{F}^{-1}X, \quad (17)$$

where $\mathcal{F}$ represents the DFT and $\mathcal{F}^{-1}$ of represents the IDFT. (16) is a restatement of (15) and (17) is a restatement of (14). If $S > S_{\min}$, these matrices are not square. Now

$$v = [v_n] = [\mathcal{F}^{-1}V_n], \quad (18)$$

$$I_m(V) = \mathcal{F}i_m(v), \quad (19)$$

$$Q_m(V) = \mathcal{F}q_m(v). \quad (20)$$

Applying Newton-Raphson to solve (12) results in the iteration

$$J(V^{(r)})(V^{(r+1)} - V^{(r)}) = -F(V^{(r)}), \quad (21)$$

where r is the iteration number and

$$J(V) = \frac{\partial F(V)}{\partial V} = \frac{\partial I(V)}{\partial V} + \Omega\frac{\partial Q(V)}{\partial V} + Y \quad (22)$$

is the *harmonic Jacobian*.

$$J(V) = [J_{mn}(V)] = \left[\frac{\partial F_m(V)}{\partial V_n}\right], \quad (23)$$

where

$$\frac{\partial F_m(V)}{\partial V_n} = \frac{\partial I_m(V)}{\partial V_n} + \Omega_{mm}\frac{\partial Q_m(V)}{\partial V_n} + Y_{mn} \quad (24)$$

is a *conversion matrix*. The derivation of $\partial I_m(V)/\partial V_n$ follows from the chain rule.

$$I_m(V) = \mathcal{F} i_m(v) \quad (25)$$

$$\frac{\partial I_m(V)}{\partial V_n} = \mathcal{F}\frac{\partial i_m(v)}{\partial v_n}\frac{\partial v_n}{\partial V_n} \quad (26)$$

Since $i(v)$ is algebraic, $\partial i_m/\partial v_n$ is diagonal.

$$\frac{\partial i_m(v)}{\partial v_n} = \text{diag}\{g_{mn}(v(t_s))\}, \quad (27)$$

where $g_{mn}(v(t)) = \partial i_m(v(t))/\partial v_n(t)$ is the conductance waveform for the nonlinear resistors.

From $v_n = \mathcal{F}^{-1}V_n$,

$$\frac{\partial I_m(V)}{\partial V_n} = \mathcal{F}\frac{\partial i_m(v)}{\partial v_n}\mathcal{F}^{-1}. \quad (28)$$

$\partial Q_m/\partial V_n$ is derived and constructed from c_{mn} in a similar manner, where $c_{mn}(v(t)) = \partial q_m(v(t))/\partial v_n(t)$ is the capacitance waveform for the nonlinear capacitors.

Efficiency: $J(V)$ is big and relatively dense, and so expensive to store and factor. To reduce the cost of solving (21), matrix-implicit methods are used. In these methods, only the component pieces of the Jacobian (g, c, and Y) are stored and iterative linear equation solvers such as the Krylov-subspace methods [30] are employed. These methods solve this linear system of equations by evaluating a sequence of matrix-vector products (MVP) that involve the Jacobian. The MVPs can be evaluated with nearly linear time and storage by exploiting the structure of (28) and by using fast algorithms such as the FFT to implement $\mathcal{F}$ and $\mathcal{F}^{-1}$ [19]. Unfortunately, these iterative linear solvers are not guaranteed to converge and require the use of a preconditioner to improve their convergence. The original linear system of equations

$$Ax = b \quad (29)$$

is preconditioned by multiplying both sides by $\hat{A}^{-1}$. One then applies the iterative solver to the preconditioned system

$$\hat{A}^{-1}Ax = \hat{A}^{-1}b. \quad (30)$$

Generally, the preconditioner $\hat{A}$ is chosen to be a close approximation to A that is also easy to invert. For mildly nonlinear problems, constructing $\hat{A} = J(V_{DC})$ by linearizing about the DC operating point and performing a simple AC analysis at each ω_k is an effective and efficient choice [9,19,37]. In this case, $\hat{A}$ is the Jacobian generated by the Gauss-Jacobi-Newton harmonic relaxation algorithm [15]. This preconditioner is not sufficient for strongly nonlinear problems. To handle these problems, it is necessary to adaptively prune the full harmonic Jacobian as in the harmonic-relaxation Newton algorithm [15,18].

When using the matrix-implicit methods, harmonic balance requires roughly $O(NK)$ operations, where N is the number of circuit equations and K is the number of frequencies required to accurately represent both v and f. This does not include the operations required to precondition the system of equations, which on strongly nonlinear problem may be far from negligible.

Extensions: An extremely important application of harmonic balance is determining the steady-state behavior of oscillators. However, as presented, harmonic balance is not suitable for autonomous circuits such as oscillators. The method was derived assuming the circuit was driven, which made it possible to know the operating frequency in advance. Instead, it is necessary to modify harmonic balance to directly compute the operating frequency [15].

Applications: Harmonic balance is generally used to predict the distortion of RF circuits. It is also used to compute the operating point about which small-signal analyses are performed (presented later). When applied to oscillators, it is used to predict the operating frequency and power, and can also be used to determine how changes in the load affect these characteristics (load pull).

Its space of application is similar to that of shooting methods (presented next). It is preferred over shooting methods when the circuit includes distributed components.

C. Shooting Methods

Transient analysis solves initial-value problems. A shooting method is an iterative procedure layered on top of transient analysis that is designed to solve boundary-value problems. Boundary-value problems play an important role in RF simulation. For example, assume that (5) is driven with a non-constant T-periodic stimulus. The T-periodic steady state solution is the one that also satisfies the two-point boundary constraint,

$$v(T) - v(0) = 0. \quad (31)$$

If the initial state $v(t_0)$ is known, then transient analysis can solve (5) and compute the state as some later time t_1. In general, one writes

$$v(t_1) = v(t_0) + \phi(v(t_0), t_0, t_1) \quad (32)$$

where ϕ is the state transition function for the differential equation. Shooting methods reformulate (5) and (31) as

$$\phi_T(v(0), 0) = 0, \quad (33)$$

where $\phi_T(v(t_0), t_0) = \phi(v(t_0), t_0, T + t_0)$, which is a nonlinear algebraic problem and so standard Newton methods can be used to solve for $v(0)$. We refer to the combination of the Newton and shooting methods as the shooting-Newton algorithm.

When applying Newton's method directly to (33), it is necessary to compute both the response of the circuit over one period and the sensitivity of the final state $v(T)$ with respect to changes in the initial state $v(0)$. The sensitivity is used to determine how to correct the initial state to reduce the difference between the initial and final state.

Applying Newton's method to (33) results in the iteration

$$v_0^{(r)} = v_0^{(r-1)} - [J_\phi(v_0^{(r-1)}) - 1]^{-1}[\phi_T(v_0^{(r-1)}, 0) - v_0^{(r-1)}] \tag{34}$$

where r is the iteration number, $v_0 = v(0)$, 1 is the identity matrix, and

$$J_\phi(v_0) = \frac{d\phi_T(v_0, 0)}{dv_0} = \frac{dv(T)}{dv_0}. \tag{35}$$

There are two important pieces to the computation of the Newton iteration given in (34): evaluating the state-transition function $\phi_T(v_0, 0)$, and forming and factoring the matrix $J_\phi(v_0)$, which is a dense matrix in general.

The state-transition function is computed by integrating (5) numerically over the shooting interval. The derivative of the state-transition function, referred to as the sensitivity matrix, is computed simultaneously because there are several quantities that are common to both computations [1,15,35,37].

Efficiency: Forming J_ϕ requires $O(N^2S)$ operations where S is the number of time points used to evaluate ϕ_T. Factoring $J_\phi - 1$ requires $O(N^3)$ operations. As a result, forming and factoring $J_\phi - 1$ becomes intractable when N exceeds several hundred. As with harmonic balance, matrix-implicit Krylov-subspace methods are used to avoid forming and factoring $J_\phi - 1$ [35]. Again, the component pieces of $J_\phi - 1$ are saved and the matrix-vector products are performed on the fly. The component pieces are

$$J_f(v(t_s)) = G(v(t_s)) + \frac{C(v(t_s))}{h_s} \tag{36}$$

and $C(v(t_s))$ at each time point s, where

$$G(v(t)) = \frac{di(v(t))}{dv(t)}, \tag{37}$$

$$C(v(t)) = \frac{dq(v(t))}{dv(t)}, \tag{38}$$

and $h_s = t_s - t_{s-1}$. A natural preconditioner is applied simply by saving and applying J_f in LU factored form [37]. This preconditioner has proven itself to be extremely robust.

Convergence: Newton's method is applied both in the outer loop to solve (33) and in the inner loop to solve (5) at each time point, making this a multi-level Newton method. As described before, the ability to adjust the time step during transient analysis results in Newton's method being extremely reliable in the inner loop. The outer loop is also quite reliable because ϕ_T is generally near linear as a direct result of RF circuits having near linear signal paths. Thus, shooting-Newton represents a well-designed multi-level Newton method where the inner loop is robust and shields the outer loop from the nonlinearity inherent in the problem.

Extensions: As with harmonic balance, it is extremely important to be able to determine the steady-state behavior of oscillators. To do so it is necessary to modify shooting methods to directly compute the period of the oscillator [15].

Applications: Shooting methods are applied in the same situations as harmonic balance. It is generally preferred if the circuit is driven with strongly discontinuous signals (pulses as opposed to sinusoids). As such, shooting methods are well suited for simulating switching mixers, switched filters, samplers, frequency dividers, and relaxation oscillators as long as the circuits do not contain distributed components.

III. Small-Signal Analysis

Consider a circuit whose input is the sum of two periodic signals, $u(t) = u_L(t) + u_s(t)$, where $u_L(t)$ is an arbitrary periodic waveform with period T_L and $u_s(t)$ is a sinusoidal waveform of radial frequency ω_s whose amplitude is small.

Let $v_L(t)$ be the steady-state solution waveform when $u_s(t)$ is zero. Then allow $u_s(t)$ to be small, but nonzero. We can consider the new solution $v(t)$ to be a perturbation $v_s(t)$ on $v_L(t)$, as in $v(t) = v_L(t) + v_s(t)$. The small-signal solution $v_s(t)$ is computed by linearizing the circuit about $v_L(t)$ and applying one of the methods for finding the steady-state solution already described. From the theory of periodically time-varying systems [5,40], it is known that for

$$u_s(t) = U_s e^{j\omega_s t} \tag{39}$$

the steady-state response is given by

$$v_s(t) = \sum_{k=-\infty}^{\infty} V_s(k) e^{j(\omega_s + k\lambda)t}. \tag{40}$$

where $\lambda = 2\pi/T_L$ is the large signal fundamental frequency. $V_s(k)$ represents the sideband for the kth harmonic of V_L. In this situation, there is only one sideband per harmonic because U_s is a single frequency complex exponential and the circuit is linear. This representation has terms at negative frequencies. If these terms are mapped to positive frequencies, then the sidebands with $k < 0$ become lower sidebands of the harmonics of v_L and those with $k > 0$ become upper sidebands.

$V_s(k)/U_s$ is the transfer function for the input at ω_s to the output at $\omega_s + k\lambda$. Notice that with periodically-varying linear systems there are an infinite number of transfer functions between any particular input and output. Each represents a different frequency translation.

Extensions: In the next few sections, the basic techniques are introduced that are used to compute the small-signal steady state response of a circuit linearized about a time varying operating point. This is sufficient for performing a time-varying AC analysis and can be extended to other types of small-signal analyses, such as computing the S-parameters of the circuit. These small-signal analyses are also extendable to cyclostationary noise analysis [3,7], which is an extremely important capability for RF designers [36].

These methods can also be extended so as to allow a small-signal analysis about a quasiperiodic operating point or small-signal analysis of autonomous circuits.

Applications: Small-signal analyses are tremendously useful for computing transfer functions (such as conversion gain and supply rejection) and predicting noise performance. In this way, they are similar to the AC and noise analyses in SPICE, but they can be applied to all kinds of circuits that the traditional small-signal analyses cannot, such as mixers, switched-filters, and samplers. Because they compute transfer functions in the presence of large signals, they can be used to determine the degradation of gain and noise when there is a large interfering signal on an adjacent channel. They can also be used to estimate intermodulation distortion [36].

When performing noise analysis, they accurately capture noise folding present in all circuits that have time-varying operating points, but which is especially important in mixers, samplers, and oscillators. In addition, they can be used to predict the phase noise of oscillators.

A. Transient Small-Signal Analysis

Though beyond the scope of this paper, there has been recent progress on performing small-signal noise analysis about a transient operating point [3]. However, in most cases, it is the small-signal behavior when the circuit is in steady state that is of interest. Using these methods generally requires integrating through any initial transient.

B. Harmonic Balance Small-Signal Analysis

Consider (12) where $U = U_L + U_s$ and $V = V_L + V_s$. Initially set $U_s = 0$ and solve (12) for V_L such that

$$F(V_L) = I(V_L) + \Omega Q(V_L) + YV_L + U_L = 0. \quad (41)$$

Since U_s is expected to be small, we can expand about V_L using a Taylor series truncated to first order.

$$\frac{\partial I(V_L)}{\partial V} V_s + \Omega_s \frac{\partial Q(V)}{\partial V} V_s + YV_s + U_s \approx 0 \quad (42)$$

or

$$J(V_L)V_s \approx -U_s \quad (43)$$

where $J(V_L)$ is computed as in (22) and Ω_s is as in (13) except with $\omega_k = \omega_s + k\lambda$.

Solving (43) for V_s gives the sidebands generated by U_s.

These ideas are extended to cyclostationary noise analysis in [10,12,29].

C. Shooting Method Small-Signal Analysis

Consider the circuit described by (5). Assume $u_s(t) = 0$ and let $v_L(t)$ be the resulting solution that also satisfies the two-point constraint (31). Linearizing (5) about $v_L(t)$ yields a time-varying linear system

$$\frac{dC(v_L(t))}{dt} v_s(t) + G(v_L(t))v_s(t) + u_s(t) = 0 \quad (44)$$

that can be solved for $v_s(t)$ if $u_s(t)$ is small.

From (40) it follows that

$$v_s(t + T_L) = v_s(t)e^{j\omega_s T_L}. \quad (45)$$

Equation (45) in the periodically time-varying linear steady-state problem is analogous to (31) in the standard steady-state problem. It is solved using a modified shooting method [22,38]. Note that (45) implies that the entire small-signal steady-state response of the periodic time-varying system is determined by the behavior of $v_s(t)$ on any interval of length T_L.

Since the solution is computed by performing a time-domain simulation, there is an upper bound on the analysis frequency that is imposed by the largest time step used. The period of analysis frequency must be much larger than the largest time step. Typically, the time steps are the same ones used when computing the large signal operating point.

Standard shooting methods can be used if we form $x_s(t) = v_s(t)e^{-j\omega_s t}$. Then, (45) becomes

$$x_s(t + T_L) = x_s(t), \quad (46)$$

which is the same form as (31) if $t = 0$. Now conventional shooting methods are applied to find x_s. Once known, Fourier analysis [16] is applied to find X_k, from which V_k is trivially computed. This is a different, but equivalent, way of deriving the method given in [22,38].

This procedure is applied to cyclostationary noise analysis in [23,38].

IV. Multi-Variate Methods

An interesting approach to solving narrowband problems uses a *multi-variate* representation of the signals and reformulates (5) as a partial-differential equation. Consider a simple two-tone quasiperiodic signal

$$x(t) = \cos(\omega_1 t)\cos(\omega_2 t), \tag{47}$$

where ω_1 is much smaller than ω_2. A large number of time points would be needed to accurately approximate such a signal. For example, if 15 points per period were needed to accurately represent the highest frequency, and if $\omega_2 = 1000\ \omega_1$, then 15,000 points are needed to accurately represent $x(t)$. Now consider a bi-variate representation obtained by replacing t with t_1 in the slowly varying parts of the expression, and t with t_2 in the rapidly varying parts. Then

$$\hat{x}(t_1, t_2) = \cos(\omega_1 t_1)\cos(\omega_2 t_2). \tag{48}$$

$x(t)$ is easily recovered from $\hat{x}(t_1, t_2)$ simply by setting $t = t_1 = t_2$. In this case, a grid of $15 \times 15 = 225$ points are needed to accurately represent $\hat{x}(t_1, t_2)$.

Using these ideas, we can replace (5) with

$$\frac{\partial q(\hat{v}(t_1, t_2))}{\partial t_1} + \frac{\partial q(\hat{v}(t_1, t_2))}{\partial t_2} + i(\hat{v}(t_1, t_2)) + \hat{u}(t_1, t_2) = 0 \tag{49}$$

or

$$f(\hat{v}(t_1, t_2), t_1, t_2) = 0. \tag{50}$$

A wide variety of methods are formulated from this equation by proposing different forms of the solution and different boundary conditions along each time axis. One can apply transient, harmonic balance, and shooting methods in layers and customize methods to particular classes of problems [2,28].

A. Quasiperiodic Harmonic Balance

If a circuit is driven with two signals at unrelated fundamental frequencies, it generally responds in steady state by generating quasiperiodic (also known as polyperiodic) signals. Quasiperiodic signals have the form of a Fourier series that is generalized in that the frequencies of the sinusoids are not just integer multiples of a single fundamental frequency. Instead, they are the linear combination of integer multiples of several fundamentals. For example, if there are two fundamentals, then

$$x(t) = \sum_{k_1=-\infty}^{\infty} \sum_{k_2=-\infty}^{\infty} X(k_1, k_2) e^{j(k_1\lambda_1 + k_2\lambda_2)t}, \tag{51}$$

where λ_1 and λ_2 are the fundamental frequencies.

The response contains components at multiples of each fundamental frequency as well as at the sums and differences of these frequencies. Rearranging (51) allows us to see this as being equivalent to constructing the waveform as a conventional Fourier series where the sinusoidal frequencies are at integer multiples of λ_1, except that the Fourier coefficients themselves are time-varying. In particular, the coefficient $\tilde{X}(t, k_1)$ is periodic with period $T_2 = 2\pi/\lambda_2$ and can itself be represented as a Fourier series in t_2.

$$x(t) = \sum_{k_1=-\infty}^{\infty} \underbrace{\sum_{k_2=-\infty}^{\infty} X(k_1, k_2) e^{jk_2\lambda_2 t}}_{\tilde{X}(t, k_1)} e^{jk_1\lambda_1 t} \tag{52}$$

Convert to a bi-variate representation by associating t_1 with λ_1 and t_2 with λ_2.

$$\hat{x}(t_1, t_2) = \sum_{k_1=-\infty}^{\infty} \sum_{k_2=-\infty}^{\infty} X(k_1, k_2) e^{jk_2\lambda_2 t_2} e^{jk_1\lambda_1 t_1} \tag{53}$$

This is a two-dimensional Fourier series, and so $\hat{x}$ and X are related by a two-dimensional Fourier transform.

Assuming v and f of (50) take the form of (53) (a linear combination of periodically AM modulated sinusoids) results in

$$\sum_{k_1=-\infty}^{\infty} \sum_{k_2=-\infty}^{\infty} F(V, k_1, k_2) e^{jk_1\lambda_1 t_1 + jk_2\lambda_2 t_2} = 0, \tag{54}$$

where

$$F(V, k_1, k_2) = j(k_1\lambda_1 + k_2\lambda_2)Q(V, k_1, k_2) + I(V, k_1, k_2) + U(k_1, k_2) \tag{55}$$

As with periodic harmonic balance, the terms in (54) are linearly independent, so $F(V, k_1, k_2) = 0$ for each k_1, k_2. In vector form,

$$F(V) = I(V) + \Omega Q(V) + U = 0, \tag{56}$$

where Ω is generalized such that $\omega_k = k_1\lambda_1 + k_2\lambda_2$. This becomes finite-dimensional by bounding $|k_j| \le K_j$. This is similar to (12), except the term for the distributed linear components (YV) is missing. This term can be included in (56) without difficulty because the spectrum of V is discrete. When evaluating I, and Q the multidimensional discrete Fourier transform is used.

Using a multidimensional Fourier transform is just one way of formulating harmonic balance for quasiperiodic problems. It is used here because of its simple derivation and because it represents an early application of multivariate methods [27,43]. An alternate approach that is generally preferred in practice is the false frequency method, which is based on a one-dimensional Fourier transform [8,15].

Parametric Harmonic Balance: Harmonic balance as described above exploits the sparse spectrum of modulated carrier signals and the linear nature of the passive components. However, it only incidentally exploits the nature of RF circuits to respond in a near-linear manner to the input signal (more effective preconditioner, fewer Newton iterations). Parametric harmonic balance [39] is a variation that retains the advantages of standard harmonic balance, but also exploits the near-linear nature of quasiperiodic RF circuits in a more deliberate manner. It splits harmonic balance into two phases, one to compute the response to the large periodic drive signal alone (ex., the LO in a mixer), and a second phase computes the response from the input as a perturbation of the solution computed in the first phase. The advantage of this method is that it solves for many fewer frequencies in the first phase when convergence is a struggle. In addition, information generated in the first phase can be used to accelerate the second phase. In this regard, parametric harmonic balance is similar to several of the methods presented later. Unfortunately, further description of this method is beyond the scope of this article.

Extensions: One obvious extension is to allow more than two fundamentals, though the method becomes expensive fast as the number of fundamentals increases, so in practice only two or three fundamentals are used. Another important extension would be to support autonomous or semi-autonomous circuits [43]. An example of an autonomous quasiperiodic circuit is one that consists of two coupled oscillators. An example of an semi-autonomous circuit is a free-running oscillator connected to a mixer with a driven input.

Applications: Quasiperiodic harmonic balance is used predict intermodulation distortion of narrowband circuits and both harmonic and intermodulation distortion of mixers. Both it and the mixed frequency-time method are used in similar situations. Quasiperiodic harmonic balance is preferred when the circuit includes distributed components.

B. Circuit Envelope Method

In the last section, the concept of harmonic balance with time-varying Fourier coefficients was introduced. In that case, the Fourier coefficients were assumed to be periodic, with the result that signals themselves were quasiperiodic. With circuit envelope [32], the Fourier coefficients are again time varying, but are not necessarily periodic. Instead, the Fourier coefficients $\tilde{X}(t, k)$ are taken to be transient waveforms. Thus, signals take the form

$$x(t) = \sum_{k=-\infty}^{\infty} \tilde{X}(t_1, k) e^{j\omega_k t_2}, \qquad (57)$$

where $\omega_k = k\lambda$ and λ is the fundamental frequency of the base Fourier series. $\tilde{X}(t_1, k)$ represents the complex modulation of the kth harmonic.

Now, (50) can be rewritten in the form of (57),

$$\sum_{k=-\infty}^{\infty} \tilde{F}(\tilde{V}(t_1), t_1, k) e^{j\omega_k t_2} = 0, \qquad (58)$$

where

$$\tilde{F}(\tilde{V}(t_1), t_1, k) = \frac{d\tilde{Q}(\tilde{V}(t_1), k)}{dt} + j\omega_k \tilde{Q}(\tilde{V}(t_1), k) + \tilde{I}(\tilde{V}(t_1), k) + \tilde{U}(t_1, k) \qquad (59)$$

Because $e^{j\omega_{k_1} t_2}$ is linearly independent of $e^{j\omega_{k_2} t_2}$ if $k_1 \neq k_2$, and because $\tilde{F}(\tilde{V}(t_1), t_1, k)$ is independent of t_2, each term in (58) is zero independently of the others. In other words, $\tilde{F}(\tilde{V}(t), t, k) = 0$ for each k, or in vector form

$$\tilde{F}(\tilde{V}(t), t) = \frac{d\tilde{Q}(\tilde{V}(t))}{dt} + \Omega\tilde{Q}(\tilde{V}(t)) + \tilde{I}(\tilde{V}(t)) + \tilde{U}(t) = 0 \qquad (60)$$

As with transient analysis, discretization methods such as trapezoidal rule or the backward difference formulae replace *dQ/dt* with a finite-difference approximation, converting (60) to a system of nonlinear algebraic equations that is solved with Newton's method. For example, applying backward Euler converts (60) to

$$\frac{\tilde{Q}(\tilde{V}(t_s)) - \tilde{Q}(\tilde{V}(t_{s-1}))}{t_s - t_{s-1}} + \Omega\tilde{Q}(\tilde{V}(t_s)) + \tilde{I}(\tilde{V}(t_s)) + \tilde{U}(t_s) = 0 \qquad (61)$$

One of the important strengths of harmonic balance is its ability to easily incorporate frequency-domain models for the linear components such as lossy or dispersive transmission lines. Unfortunately, this is not true with the circuit envelope method. The transient nature of the modulations $\tilde{V}(t, k)$ introduces the same difficulties that are present with distributed components in transient analysis, which are addressed using similar techniques. In particular, one can use convolution [11,31], or the model for the distributed component can be separated into delay and dispersion, with the dispersion being replaced by a lumped approximation [33].

As the distributed components are linear, the sidebands for each harmonic k can be treated individually. Thus, a separate model is generated for each harmonic k, which greatly reduces the bandwidth requirements on the models. The model for each harmonic must only be valid over the bandwidth of the sidebands associated with that harmonic. In RF circuits, the bandwidths of the sidebands are usually small relative to the carrier frequency, and so generating models of distributed components for use in the circuit envelope method is much easier than for conventional transient analysis. In fact, it is not uncommon for the bandwidth of an RF circuit to be so small that the transfer function of a distributed component does not change appreciably over the bandwidth of the sidebands. In this case, the transfer function is taken to be constant. In other words, $Y_{mn}(\omega, k)$ is simply replaced with $Y_{mn}(\omega_k, k)$ where $\omega = \omega_k + \delta\omega$.

Extensions: One can build circuit envelope on top of a quasiperiodic harmonic balance rather than on top of periodic harmonic balance as has been done here. One can also build it on top of autonomous harmonic balance.

One can also wrap shooting around circuit envelope to find a periodic or quasiperiodic modulation waveform, which results the multi-variate mixed frequency-time method [28].

Applications: Circuit envelope has two primary applications. The first is predicting the response of a circuit when it is driven with a complex digital modulation. An important problem is to determine the interchannel interference that results from intermodulation distortion. Simple intermodulation tests involving a small number of sinusoids as can be performed with quasiperiodic harmonic balance is not a good indicator of how the nonlinearity of the circuit couples digitally modulated signals between adjacent channels. Instead, one must apply the digital modulation, simulate with circuit envelope, and then determine how the modulation spectrum spreads into adjacent channels.

Another important application of circuit envelope is to predict the long term transient behavior of certain RF circuits. Examples include the turn-on behavior of oscillators, power supply droop or thermal transients in power amplifiers, and the capture and lock behavior of phase-locked loops. Another important example is determining the turn-on and turn-off behavior of TDMA transmitters. In TDMA (time-division multiple access), transmitters broadcast during a narrow slice of time. During that interval the transmitter must power up, stabilize, send the message, and then power down. If it powers up and down too slowly, the transmitter does not work properly. If it powers up and down too quickly, the resulting spectrum will be too wide to fit in the allotted channel. Simulating with traditional transient analysis would be prohibitively expensive because the time slice lasts on the order of 100 ms and the carrier frequency is typically at 1 GHz or greater.

The capabilities of circuit envelope are similar to envelope following (presented next). Circuit envelope is preferred when the circuit contains distributed components.

V. Sampling Methods

RF circuits are generally influenced by one periodic timing signal, often referred to as the LO or the clock, and one or more information signals. For oscillators, the timing signal is the oscillation signal itself and the information signal is generally noise. With sampling methods, we designate the one timing signal as the *clock*. If there is more than one timing signal, then usually the largest and fastest is chosen to be the clock. The discrete sample-envelope for a signal x is defined as signal x_{env} that results when x is sampled with a period equal to that of the clock, as shown in Figure 2. The continuous sample-envelope is the trajectory that is traced out if the phase of both the clock and the sampling is allowed to drift relative to the other signals present. The sampling is assumed to always occur at the same phase of the clock.

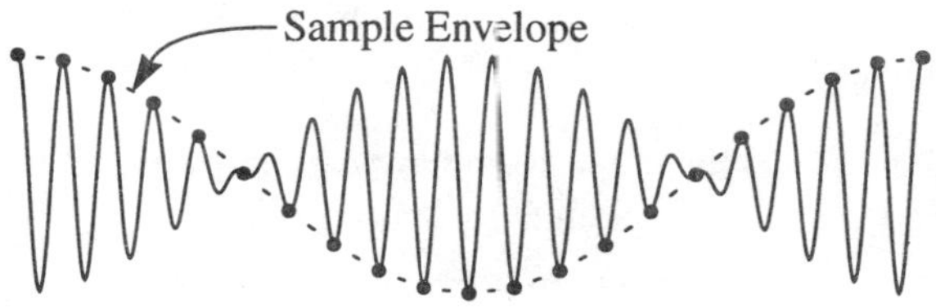

Fig. 2. Sample envelope is the waveform traced out when signal is sampled with a period equal to that of the clock.

The sample-envelope methods apply shooting methods over one or more clock cycles using boundary conditions that are formulated based on assumptions about the sample envelope. One can apply a wide variety of constraints on the sampled envelope, which results in a plethora of methods. For example, assuming the sampled envelope is constant results in simple shooting with a periodic boundary constraint. Assuming the circuit is linear and the sample envelope is sinusoidal results in periodic small-signal analysis. However, more interesting methods result when we make different assumptions about the sample envelope.

A. Envelope Following

Envelope Following approximates the sample envelope as a piecewise polynomial [13,24] in a manner that is analogous to conventional transient analysis. This approach is efficient if the sequence formed by sampling the state at the beginning of each clock cycle, $v(0)$, $v(T)$, $v(2T)$, ..., $v(mT)$, changes slowly as a function of m. A "differential-like" equation is formed from (32)

$$\Delta v(mT) = \phi_T(v(mT), mT), \tag{62}$$

where $\Delta v(mT) = v((m+1)T) - v(mT)$ is a measure of the time-derivative of the sample envelope at mT. We can apply traditional integration methods to compute an approximation to the solution using a procedure that involves solving (62) at isolated time points. If the sample envelope is accurately approximated by a low-order polynomial, then this procedure should allow us to skip many cycles, and so find the solution over a vast number of cycles in an efficient manner. For RF circuits, (62) is stiff and so requires implicit integration methods such as trapezoidal rule, which can be written as

$$\Delta v(mT) \approx \frac{2}{l}(v(mT) - v((m-l)T)) - \Delta v((m-l)T), \tag{63}$$

where l is the time step, which is measured in terms of cycles. This equation represents a 2-point boundary constraint on (62), and so together they can be solved with shooting-Newton methods to find $v(mT)$. As with transient analysis, once $v(mT)$ is computed, it is necessary to check that the trajectory is following the low-order polynomial as assumed. If not, the point should be discarded and the step l should be reduced. If desired, other integration methods can be used, such as the backward-difference formulae.

Extensions: Envelope following can be extended to support autonomous circuits such as oscillators.

One can wrap shooting around envelope following to find a periodic or quasiperiodic envelope, which results the hierarchical shooting method [28].

Applications: The applications of envelope following are the same as circuit envelope. Envelope following is preferred when the carrier signal is strongly discontinuous (consists of pulses rather than sinusoids). As such, envelope following is suitable for simulating switched filters and switching power supplies in addition to the traditional RF circuits.

B. Mixed Frequency-Time Method

The Mixed Frequency-Time (or MFT) Method [14,15] makes the assumption that the sample envelope can be accurately approximated by a Fourier series with K terms (excluding DC), where K is presumed to be small. If true, then once the value of $S = 2K+1$ distinct points along the sample envelope are known, then all points can be found. Specifically, once the S points are known, then the $2K+1$ Fourier coefficients can be determined using the DFT, and then the resulting Fourier series can be evaluated to determine the value of any point. In particular, let

$$\mathcal{V}_0 = [v(t_1), v(t_2), \ldots, v(t_S)] \tag{64}$$

be the value of S points, then we can find the value of the S points that follow them by one cycle,

$$\mathcal{V}_T = [v(t_1 + T), v((t_2) + T), \ldots, v(t_S + T)] \quad . \tag{65}$$

Since the DFT is a linear operator $\mathcal{F}$, there exists a linear operator $D_T = \mathcal{F}^{-1} e^{j\omega_k T} \mathcal{F}$ that maps $\mathcal{V}_0$ to $\mathcal{V}_T$.

$$\mathcal{V}_T = D_T \mathcal{V}_0 \tag{66}$$

This is SN equations with $2SN$ unknowns. They were formulated purely from the constraints on the sample envelope. It represents a boundary condition on solution to (5) in a way analogous to (31) and (45). Designate Φ_T as the collection of S state transition functions from t_s to t_s+T. Then

$$\mathcal{V}_T = \Phi_T(\mathcal{V}_0) \tag{67}$$

Applying (66) to (67) gives

$$D_T \mathcal{V}_0 - \Phi_T(\mathcal{V}_0) = 0, \tag{68}$$

which can be solved using Newton's method for $\mathcal{V}_0$. As pointed out earlier, from $\mathcal{V}_0$ one can calculate any point on the sample envelope. Any point $v(t)$ on the original waveform is found by integrating (5) from the appropriate point on the sample envelope.

Extensions: As with quasiperiodic harmonic balance, the mixed frequency-time method can be extended to an arbitrary number of fundamentals, though in practice is limited to two or three. It can also be extended to handle autonomous and semi-autonomous circuits.

Applications: The applications of the mixed frequency-time method are the same as quasiperiodic harmonic balance. The mixed frequency-time method is preferred when the carrier signal is strongly discontinuous (consists of pulses rather than sinusoids).

VI. Comparisons

The methods presented can be grouped into two broad families, those methods based on harmonic balance, and those based on shooting methods. Table I shows how the various methods are related. to baseband methods, and to each other.

Most of the differences between the methods emanate from the attributes of the base methods (harmonic balance and shooting methods). So only the base methods will be compared.

Progress on developing RF simulation methods has been rapid over the last decade and is continuing. As a result,

TABLE I
RELATING THE RF SIMULATION METHODS

Baseband (SPICE)	*HB Family*	*SM Family*
DC	HB	SM
AC, Noise	Sm Sig HB	Sm Sig SM
Transient	Ckt Env	Env Follow
HB, SM	QPHB	MFT

any comparisons based on currently implemented versions of the methods will quickly become dated. So instead, I will try to extrapolate from current trends and compare what is likely to be the eventual attributes of the methods.

A. *Strengths of Harmonic Balance*

The main strength of harmonic balance is its natural support for frequency-domain models — both linear and nonlinear. Distributed components such as lossy and dispersive transmission lines and interpolated tables of S-parameters from either measurements or electromagnetic simulators are examples of linear models that are handled easily and efficiently with harmonic balance. Nonlinear frequency domain models are based on Volterra series and are derived either from simulation or from measurement [41]. In addition, it is becoming more common for abstract behavioral models to be written directly in the frequency domain. There is, however, one caveat. It is relatively easy to generate nonphysical models in the frequency domain.

Harmonic balance is extremely efficient and accurate if both v and f in (8) are nearly sinusoidal. However this is not a feature that finds much application in practice. It is generally only significant when trying to determine the distortion of very low distortion amplifiers and filters. It does not help analyzing mixers, amplifiers, and samplers because they contain signals that are far from sinusoidal.

B. *Strengths of Shooting Methods*

The strengths of shooting methods stem from the properties of its underlying transient analysis. In particular, it chooses nonuniform timesteps in order to control error, and it has excellent convergence properties.

The ability of transient analysis, and so shooting methods, to place time points in a nonuniform manner allows it to accurately and efficiently follow abruptly discontinuous waveforms. Small time steps can be used to accurately resolve rapid transitions without taking small steps everywhere. This is very important for circuits such as mixers, relaxation oscillators, switched-capacitor and switched-current filters, samplers, sample-and-holds, and chopper stabilized amplifiers. In addition, the timestep is automatically chosen to control error. Though not an inherent issue, it is a failing of existing harmonic balance simulators that they do not automatically control error.

The strong convergence properties of shooting methods result from its implementation as a multilevel Newton method, and not from the fact it is a time-domain method. Indeed, it is possible to formulate harmonic balance as a time-domain method [15,37], yet its convergence properties do not fundamentally change.

Harmonic balance can be made as robust as shooting methods by incorporating them in a carefully designed continuation or homotopy method [15]. However, because continuation methods end up calling harmonic balance tens, or perhaps hundreds, of times, they can be slow. The ability of shooting methods to converge on a large class of strongly nonlinear circuits without the need for continuation methods represents a significant advantage in efficiency over harmonic balance.

With shooting methods, it is natural to perform transient analysis for a while before starting the shooting iteration in order to generate a good starting point. This is usually sufficient to get convergence even on troublesome circuits except when the time constants in the circuit are much larger than the period of the signal. If this is not sufficient, one can also use continuation methods with shooting methods.

Finally, the preconditioner available in shooting methods seems to be more robust and less burdensome than the preconditioners available with harmonic balance. The preconditioner is used to implement the matrix-implicit linear solvers that allow both shooting methods and harmonic balance to handle large problems. This is currently an area of innovation, and so this situation may change.

A significant disadvantage of shooting methods is that they do not support distributed components. While it is conceivable that shooting methods can be extended to handle distributed components, doing so will likely compromise their strong convergence properties and their preconditioner.

The fundamental strengths of shooting methods and harmonic balance are compared in Table II.

TABLE II
STRENGTHS OF SHOOTING METHODS AND HARMONIC BALANCE

Shooting Methods	*Harmonic Balance*
• Convergence • Nonuniform timesteps • Robust preconditioner	• Frequency domain models • No frequency limit on "small" signals

VII. Conclusion

There has been a tremendous amount of innovation and progress in RF simulation methods in the past decade, with the result being the wide variety of methods available today. Each method carries with it limiting assumptions that it exploits to perform efficiently when those assumptions are satisfied. However, the assumptions also prevent each method from being used in a general setting. There is no universal method, and it is unlikely there will ever be one. This is mainly a problem in that it prevents the whole RF section of a transceiver from being simulated together. While it is starting to be possible to simulate the whole signal path of a receiver or a transmitter, incorporating the frequency synthesizer and any digital signal processing is still beyond reach.

While the existing methods and their obvious extensions do not solve all RF simulation problems for individual blocks, their coverage is pretty good. As such, work in developing new methods is expected to gradually decline. A new area of effort is expected to be in using the existing methods to generate high level models of individual blocks that will allow more general methods to simulate the whole system. Examples of this new trend include using Volterra series to model the nonlinear behavior of RF blocks [41] and using the small-signal time-varying noise analyses on the individual blocks in a phase-locked loop to generate behavioral models that include jitter [3,17], which allows accurate and efficient noise prediction for frequency synthesizers.

Acknowledgments

I would like to thank Dave Sharrit of HP and Jacob White of MIT for their direct and significant contributions to this paper.

References

[1] T. Aprille and T. Trick. Steady-state analysis of nonlinear circuits with periodic inputs. *Proceedings of the IEEE*, vol. 60, no. 1, pp. 108-114, January 1972.

[2] H. Brachtendorf, G. Welsch, R. Laur and A. Bunse-Gerstner. Numerical steady state analysis of electronic circuits driven by multi-tone signals. *Electrical Engineering*, Springer-Verlag, vol. 79, pp. 103-112, 1996.

[3] A. Demir. *Analysis and Simulation of Noise in Nonlinear Electronic Circuits and Systems*. To be published by Kluwer Academic Publishers in 1997.

[4] C. Dragone. Analysis of thermal and shot noise in pumped resistive diodes. *The Bell System Technical Journal*, vol. 47, no. 9, pp. 1883-1902, November 1968.

[5] S. Egami. Nonlinear, linear analysis and computer-aided design of resistive mixers. *IEEE Transactions on Microwave Theory and Techniques*, vol. MTT-22, no. 3, pp. 270-275, March 1974.

[6] P. Feldmann and R. Freund. Efficient linear circuit analysis by Padé Approximation via the Lanczos Process. *IEEE Transactions on Computer-Aided Design of Integrated Circuits and Systems*, vol. 14, no. 5, pp. 639-649, May 1995.

[7] W. Gardner. *Introduction to Random Processes: With Applications to Signals and Systems*. McGraw-Hill, 1989.

[8] D. Hente and R. Jansen. Frequency-domain continuation method for the analysis and stability investigation of nonlinear microwave circuits. *IEE Proceedings*, part H, vol. 133, no. 5, pp. 351–362, October 1986.

[9] P. Heikkilä. *Object-Oriented Approach to Numerical Circuit Analysis*. Ph. D. dissertation. Helsinki University of Technology, January 1992.

[10] D. Held and A. Kerr. Conversion loss and noise of microwave and millimeter-wave mixers: part 1 — theory. *IEEE Transactions on Microwave Theory and Techniques*, vol. MTT-26, no. 2, pp. 49-55, February 1978.

[11] S. Kapur, D. Long and J. Roychowdhury. Efficient time-domain simulation of frequency-dependent elements. *IEEE/ACM International Conference on Computer-Aided Design: Digest of Technical Papers*, November 1996.

[12] A. Kerr. Noise and loss in balanced and subharmonically pumped mixers: part 1 — theory. *IEEE Transactions on Microwave Theory and Techniques*, vol. MTT-27, no. 12, pp. 938-950, December 1979.

[13] K. Kundert, J. White and A. Sangiovanni-Vincentelli. An envelope-following method for the efficient transient simulation of switching power and filter circuits. *IEEE International Conference on Computer-Aided Design: Digest of Technical Papers*, November 1988.

[14] K. Kundert, J. White and A. Sangiovanni-Vincentelli. A mixed frequency-time approach for distortion analysis of switching filter circuits. *IEEE Journal of Solid-State Circuits*, April 1989, vol. 24, no. 2, pp. 443-451.

[15] K. Kundert, J. White and A. Sangiovanni-Vincentelli. *Steady-State Methods for Simulating Analog and Microwave Circuits*. Kluwer Academic Publishers, 1990.

[16] K. Kundert. Accurate Fourier analysis for circuit simulators. *Proceedings of the IEEE Custom Integrated Circuits Conference*, May 1994.

[17] K. Kundert. Modeling and simulation of jitter in phase-locked loops. To appear in *Analog Circuit Design* by Sansen, Huijsing, and van de Plassche (editors), Kluwer Academic Publishers, 1997.

[18] D. Long, R. Melville, K. Ashby and B. Horton. Full-chip harmonic balance. *Proceedings of the IEEE Custom Integrated Circuits Conference*, May 1997.

[19] R. Melville, P. Feldmann and J. Roychowdhury. Efficient multi-tone distortion analysis of analog integrated circuits. *Proceedings of the IEEE Custom Integrated Circuits Conference*, May 1995.

[20] K. Nabors, T. Fang, H. Chang, K. Kundert, and J. White. Lumped Interconnect Models Via Gaussian Quadrature.

Proceedings of the 34th Design Automation Conference, June 1997.

[21] M. Nakhla and J. Vlach. A piecewise harmonic balance technique for determination of periodic response of nonlinear systems. *IEEE Transactions of Circuits and Systems*. vol. CAS-23, no. 2, pp. 85-91, February 1976.

[22] M. Okumura, T. Sugawara and H. Tanimoto. An efficient small signal frequency analysis method for nonlinear circuits with two frequency excitations. *IEEE Transactions of Computer-Aided Design of Integrated Circuits and Systems*, vol. 9, no. 3, pp. 225-235, March 1990.

[23] M. Okumura, H. Tanimoto, T, Itakura and T. Sugawara. Numerical noise analysis for nonlinear circuits with a periodic large signal excitation including cyclostationary noise sources. *IEEE Transactions on Circuits and Systems — I. Fundamental Theory and Applications*, vol. 40, no. 9, pp. 581-590, September 1993.

[24] L. Petzold. An efficient numerical method for highly oscillatory ordinary differential equations. *SIAM Journal of Numerical Analysis*, vol. 18, no. 3, June 1981.

[25] J. Phillips, E. Chiprout and D. Ling. Efficient full-wave electromagnetic analysis via model-order reduction of fast integral transforms. *Proceedings of the 33nd Design Automation Conference*, June 1996.

[26] V. Rizzoli and A. Neri. State of the art and present trends in nonlinear microwave CAD techniques. *IEEE Transactions on Microwave Theory and Techniques*, vol. 36, no. 2, pp. 343-365, February 1988.

[27] V. Rizzoli, C. Cechetti, A. Lipparini and F. Mastri. General-purpose harmonic balance analysis of nonlinear microwave circuits under multitone excitation. *IEEE Transactions on Microwave Theory and Techniques*, vol. 36, no. 12, pp. 1650–1660, December 1988.

[28] J. Roychowdhury. Efficient methods for simulating highly nonlinear multi-rate circuits. *Proceedings of the 34th Design Automation Conference*, June 1997.

[29] J. Roychowdhury, D. Long and P. Feldmann. Cyclostationary noise analysis of large RF circuits with multi-tone excitations. *Proceedings of the IEEE Custom Integrated Circuits Conference*, May 1997.

[30] Y. Saad. Iterative *Methods for Sparse Linear Systems*. PWS Publishing, 1996.

[31] J. Schutt-Aine and R. Mittra. Scattering parameter transient analysis of transmission lines loaded with nonlinear terminations. *IEEE Transactions on Microwave Theory and Techniques*, vol. MTT-36, no. 3, pp. 529-536, March 1988.

[32] D. Sharrit. New method of analysis of communication systems. *MTTS'96 WMFA: Nonlinear CAD Workshop, June 1996.*

[33] M. Silveira, I. El-Fadel, J. White, M. Chilukuri, and K. Kundert. Efficient frequency-domain modeling and circuit simulation of transmission lines. *IEEE Transactions on Components, Packaging, and Manufacturing Technology — Part B: Advanced Packaging*, November 1994.

[34] G. Rhyne, M. Steer and B. Bates. Frequency-domain nonlinear circuit analysis using generalized power series. *IEEE Transactions on Microwave Theory and Techniques*, vol. 36, no. 2, pp. 717-720, February 1988.

[35] R. Telichevesky, K. Kundert and J. White. Efficient steady-state analysis based on matrix-free Krylov-subspace methods. *Proceedings of the 32nd Design Automation Conference*, June 1995.

[36] R. Telichevesky, K. Kundert and J. White. Receiver characterization using periodic small-signal analysis. *Proceedings of the IEEE Custom Integrated Circuits Conference*, May 1996.

[37] R. Telichevesky, K. Kundert, I. El-Fadel and J. White. Fast simulation algorithms for RF circuits. *Proceedings of the 1996 IEEE Custom Integrated Circuits Conference*, May 1996.

[38] R. Telichevesky, K. Kundert and J. White. Efficient AC and noise analysis of two-tone RF circuits. *Proceedings of the 33rd Design Automation Conference*, June 1996.

[39] Y. Thodesen and K. Kundert. Parametric harmonic balance. *IEEE MTT-S International Microwave Symposium Digest*, June 1996.

[40] H. Torrey and C. Whitmer. *Crystal Rectifiers*. McGraw-Hill, 1948.

[41] F. Verbeyst and M. Vanden Bossche. VIOMAP, the S-parameter equivalent for weakly nonlinear RF and microwave devices. *IEEE Transactions on Microwave Theory and Techniques*, vol. 42, no. 12, pp. 2531-2535, December 1994.

[42] N. Verghese and D. Allstot. Verification of RF and mixed-signal integrated circuits for substrate coupling effects. *Proceedings of the IEEE Custom Integrated Circuits Conference*, May 1997.

[43] A. Usihda, L. Chua and T. Sugawara. A substitution algorithm for solving nonlinear circuits with multi-frequency components. *International Journal on Circuit Theory and Application*, vol. 15, pp. 327–355, 1987.

Author Index

Notes

Notes

Notes

Notes